MASTER ATLAS OF GREATER LONDON

CONTENTS

REFERENCE

Motorway	M1
Motorway under construction	
Dual Carriageway	
'A' Road	A21
'A' Road under construction	
'B' Road	B3047
One Way Street One-way traffic flow is indicated on 'A' roads by a heavy line on the drivers left.	➡
British Rail Station	Station Level Crossing
Docklands Light Railway Station	DLR
Underground Station	●
County Boundary	— ·· — ·· —
District & Borough Boundaries	— · — · —
Posttown & London Postal District Boundaries By arrangement with the Post Office.	EC1
Postcode Boundary (within Posttowns)	BR1
Disabled Toilet National Key Scheme	♿
Fire Station	■
Hospital	Ⓗ
House Numbers 'A' & 'B' Roads only	22 35
Information Centre	𝒊
Map Continuation	▲ 130
National Grid Reference	578
Place of Worship	✛
Police Station	▲
Post Office	★

© Edition 7 1995

Edition 7A (Part Revision) 1995

The representation on the maps of a road, track or footpath is no evidence of the existence of a Right of Way.

Every possible care has been taken to ensure that the information given in this Atlas is accurate and whilst the publishers would be grateful to learn of any errors, they regret they can accept no responsibility for any expense or loss thereby caused.

The maps in this Atlas are based upon the Ordnance Survey 1:10,560 and 1:10,000 Maps with the sanction of The Controller of Her Majesty's Stationery Office. Crown Copyright

No reproduction by any method whatsoever of any part of this publication is permitted without the prior consent of the copyright owners.

The grid on this map is the National Grid taken from the Ordnance Survey map with the permission of the Controller of Her Majesty's Stationery Office.

An A to Z publication

ISBN 0 85039 002 8

SCALE

1:19,000 (Sectional Maps at approx. 3⅓ or 3.3347 inches to 1 mile)

0 ¼ ½ ¾ 1 mile

0 250 500 750 1 kilometre

Geographers' A-Z Map Company Ltd.

Head Office : Fairfield Road, Borough Green, Sevenoaks, Kent. TN15 8PP Telephone 01732-781000

Showrooms: 44 Gray's Inn Road, London, WC1X 8HX   Telephone 0171-242-9246

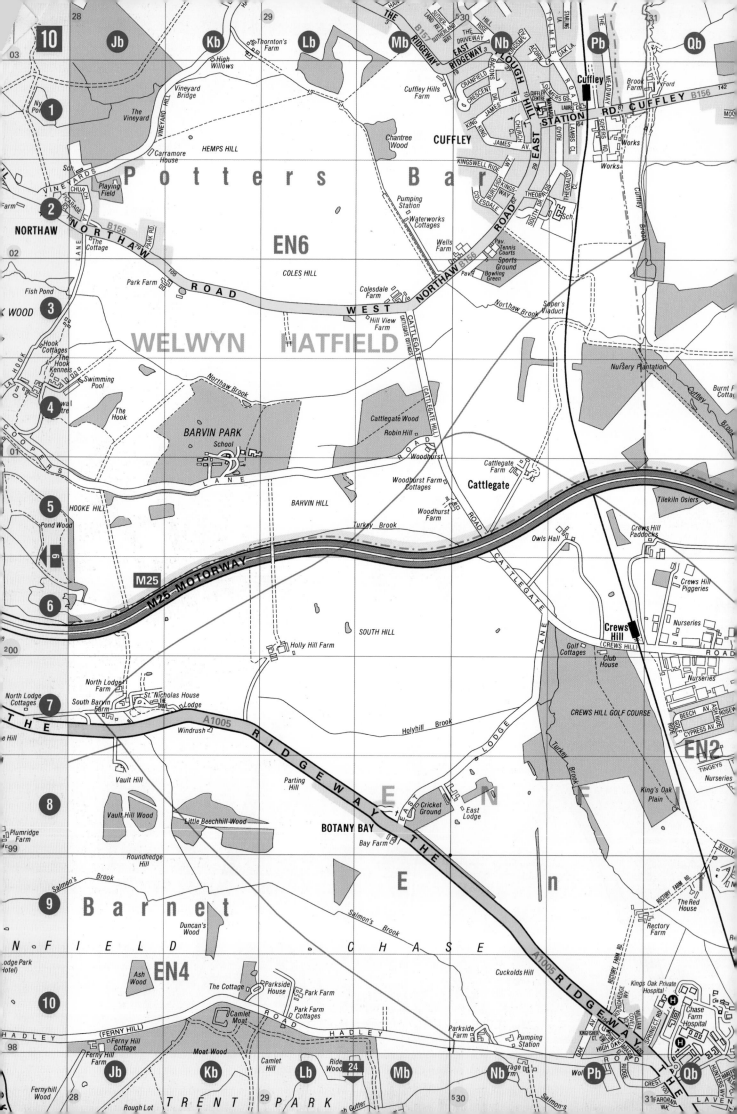

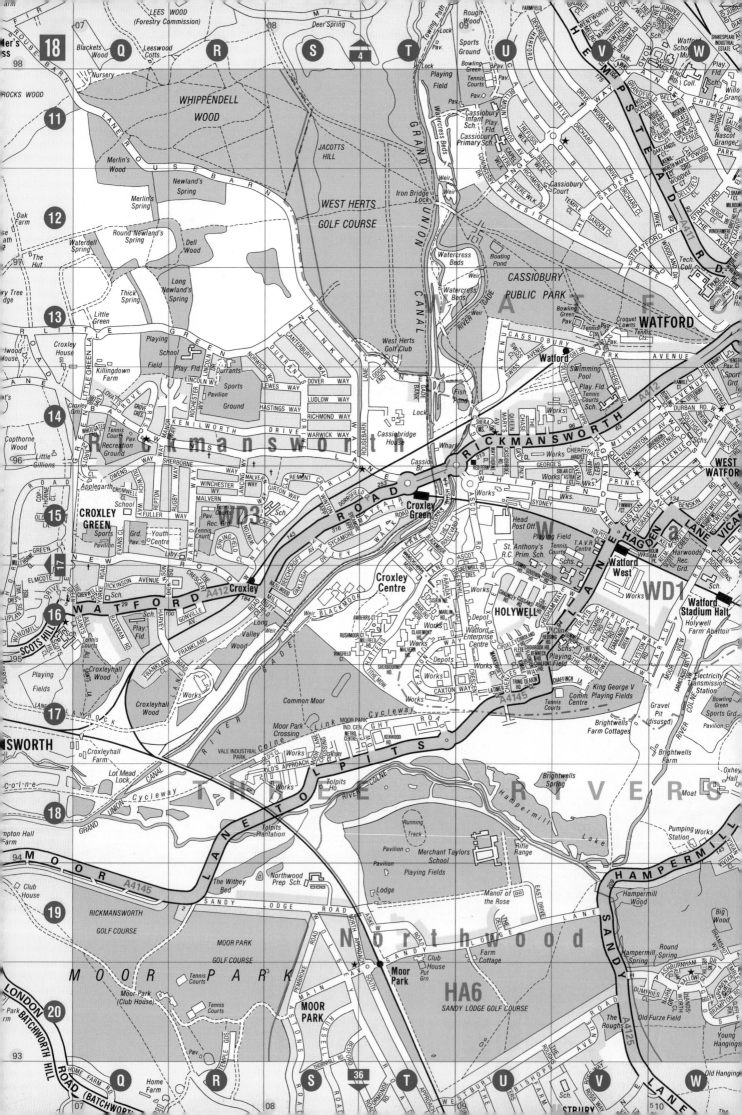

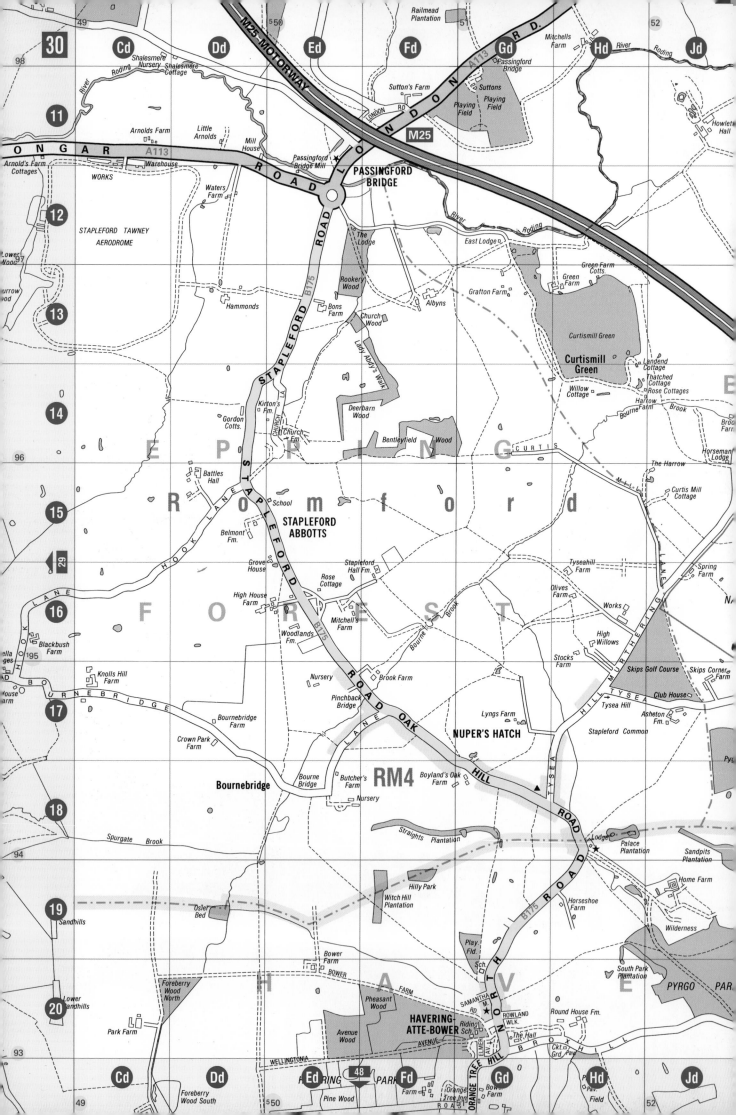

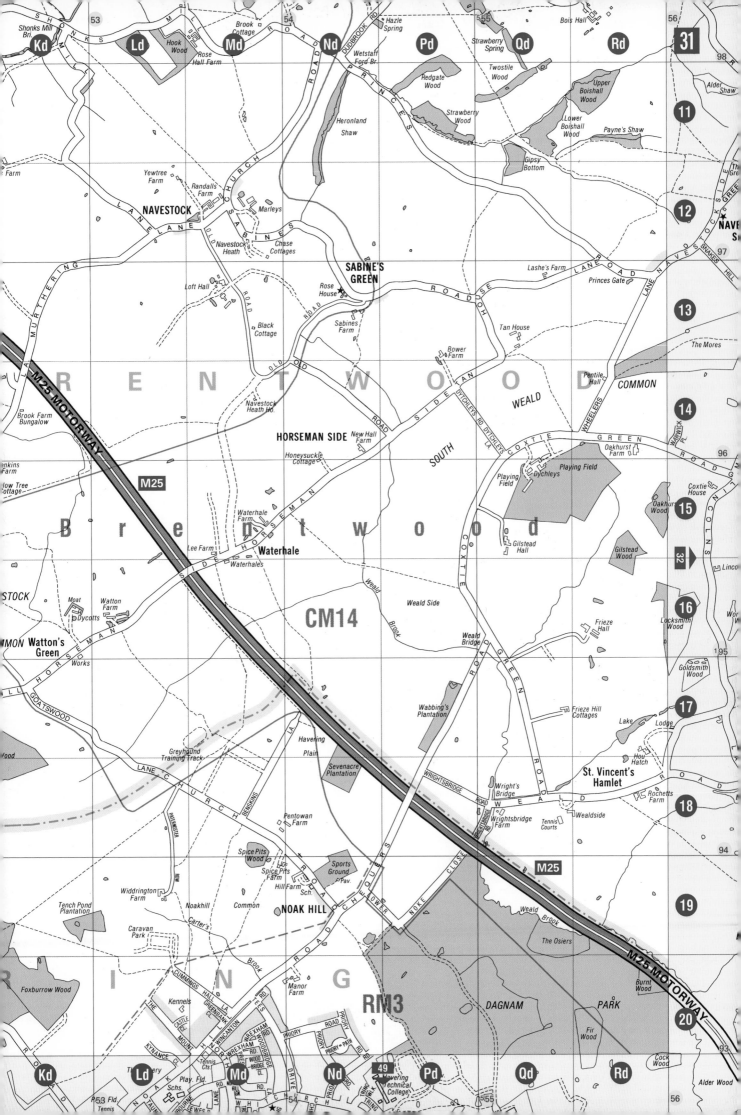

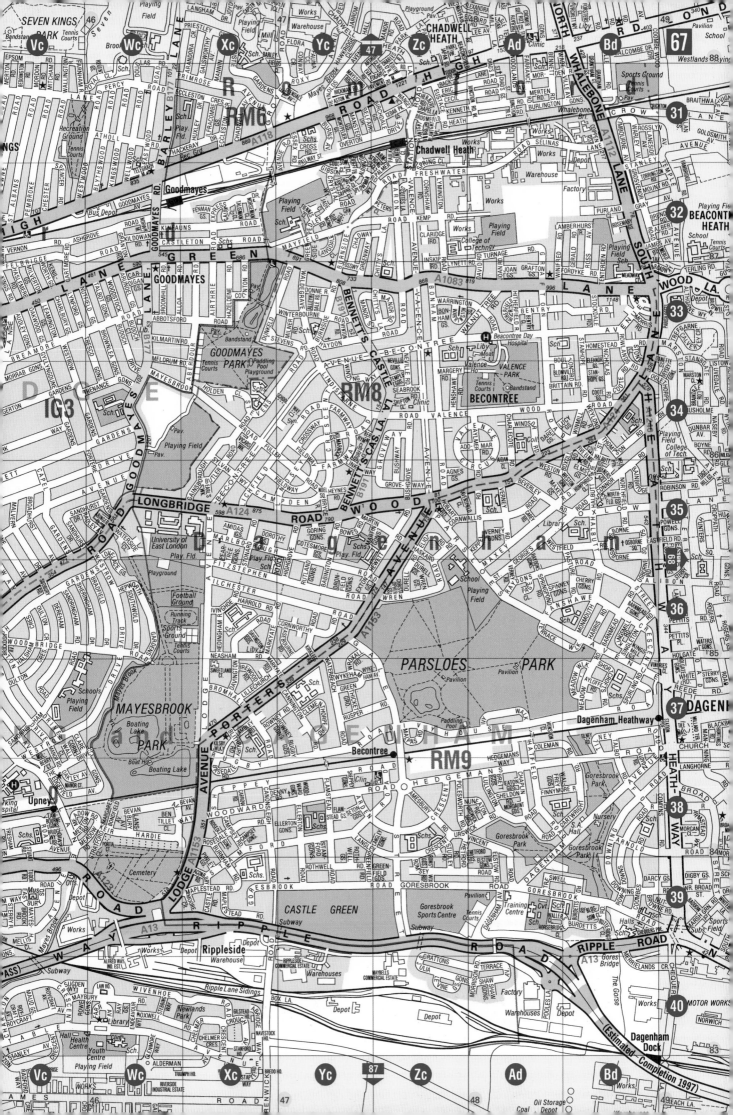

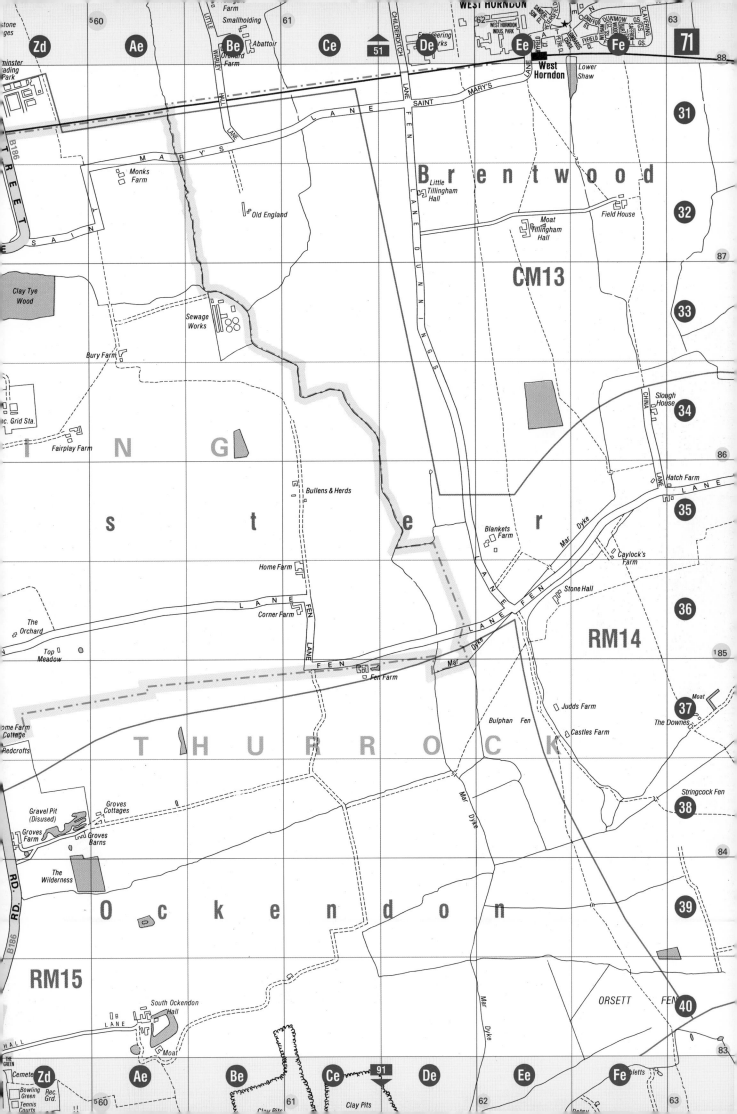

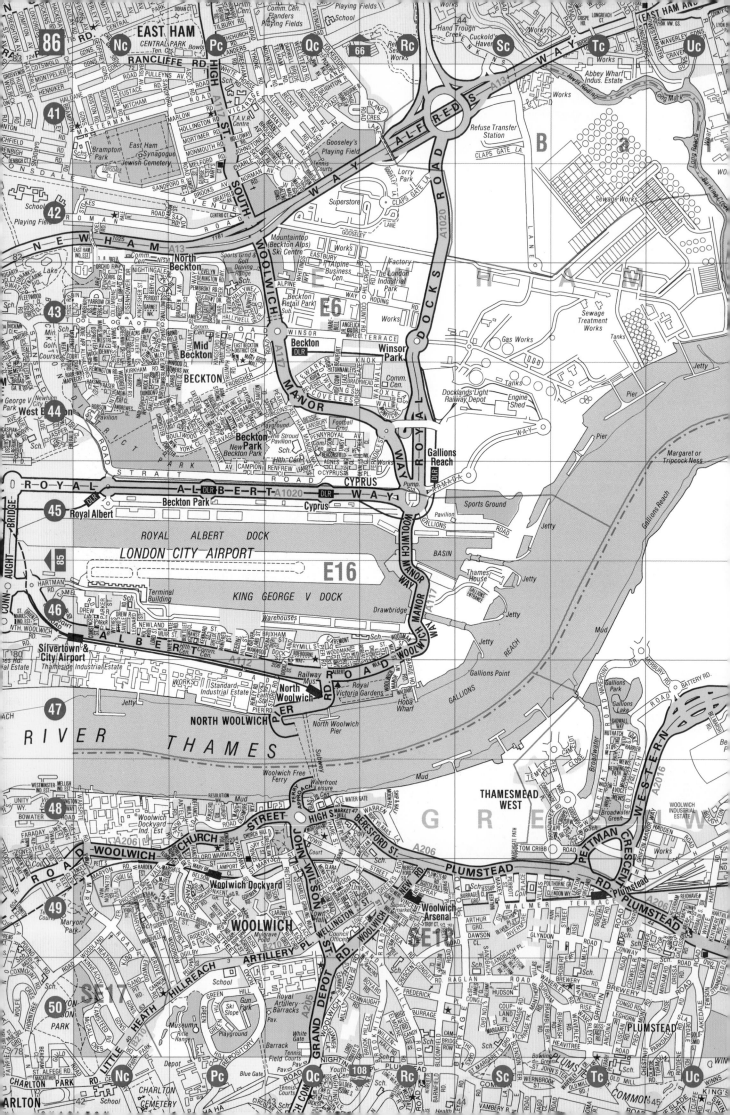

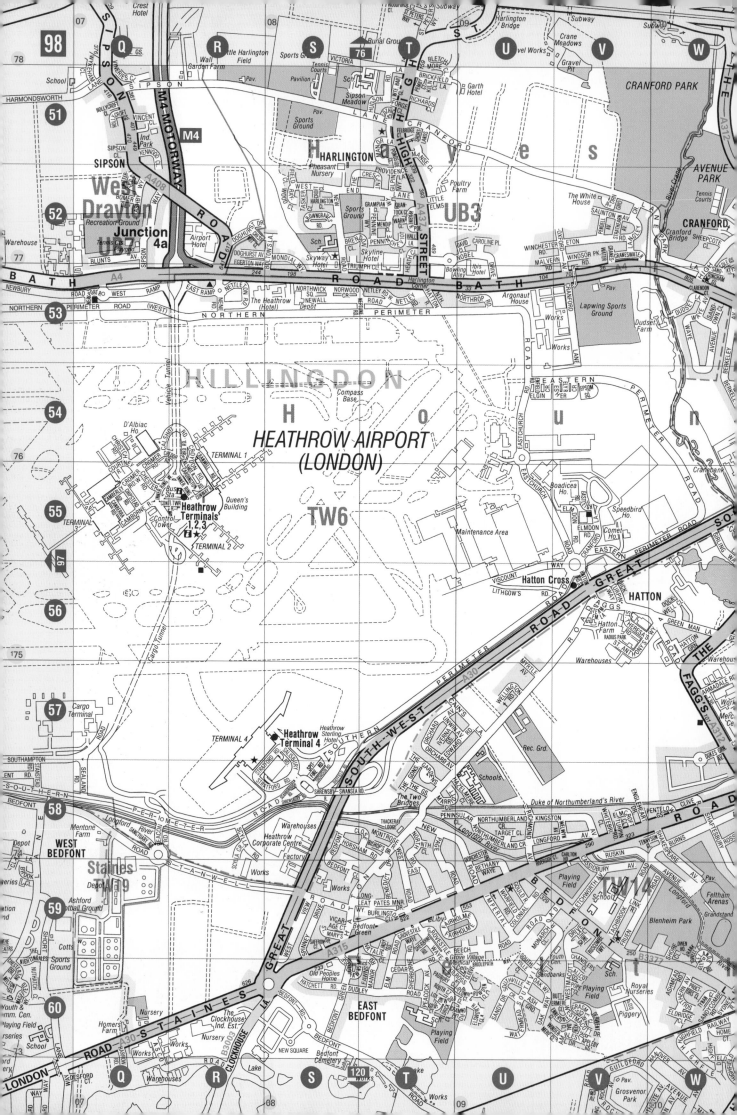

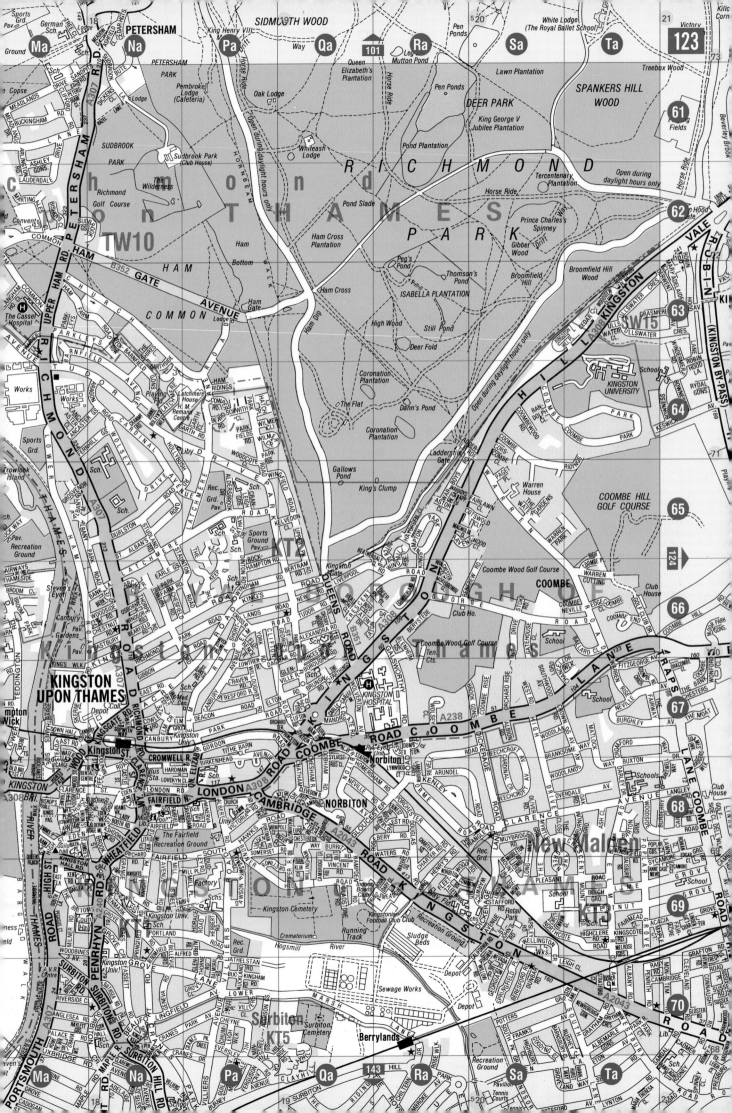

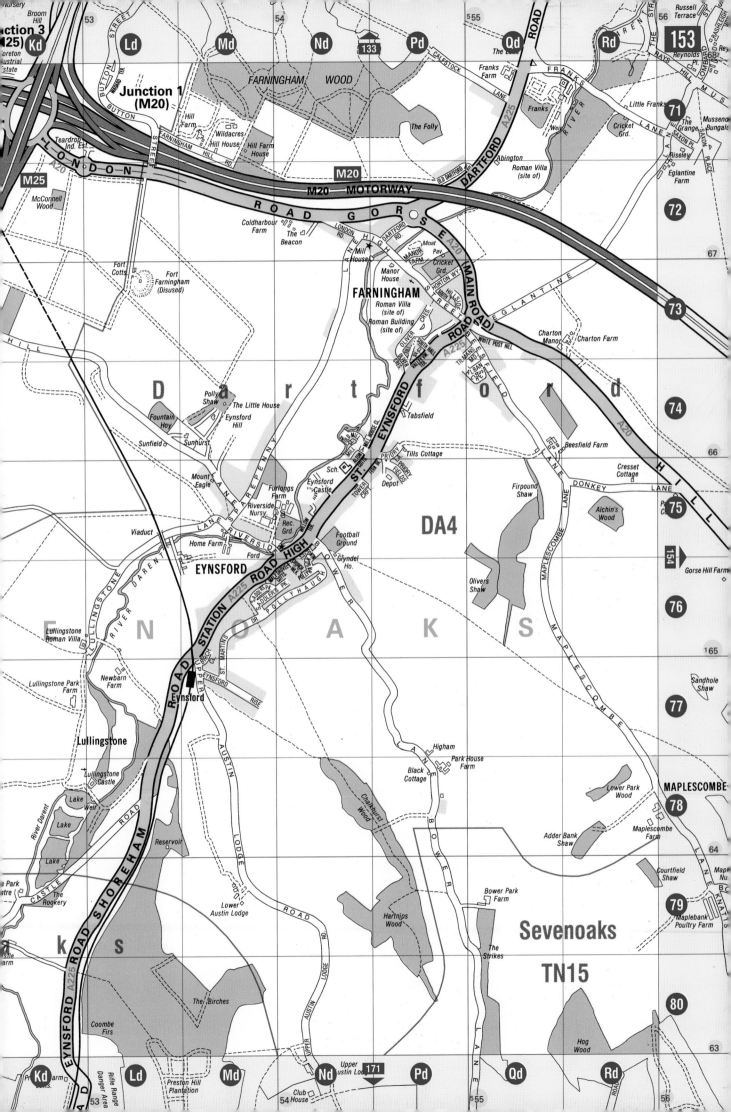

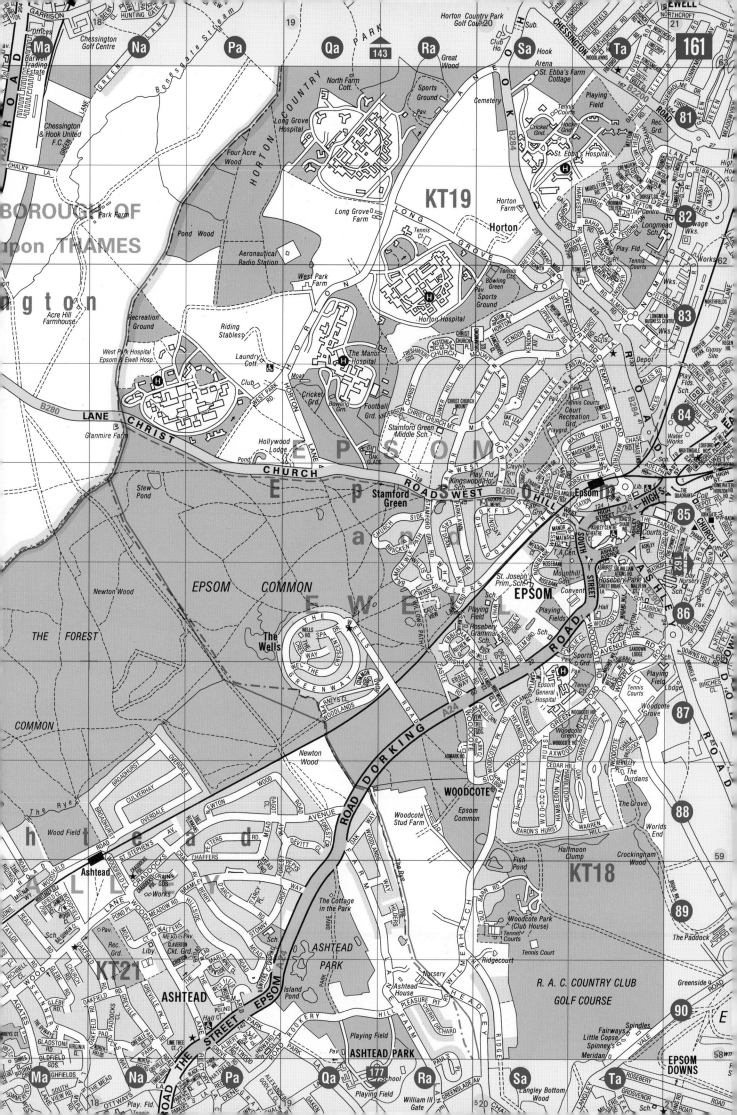

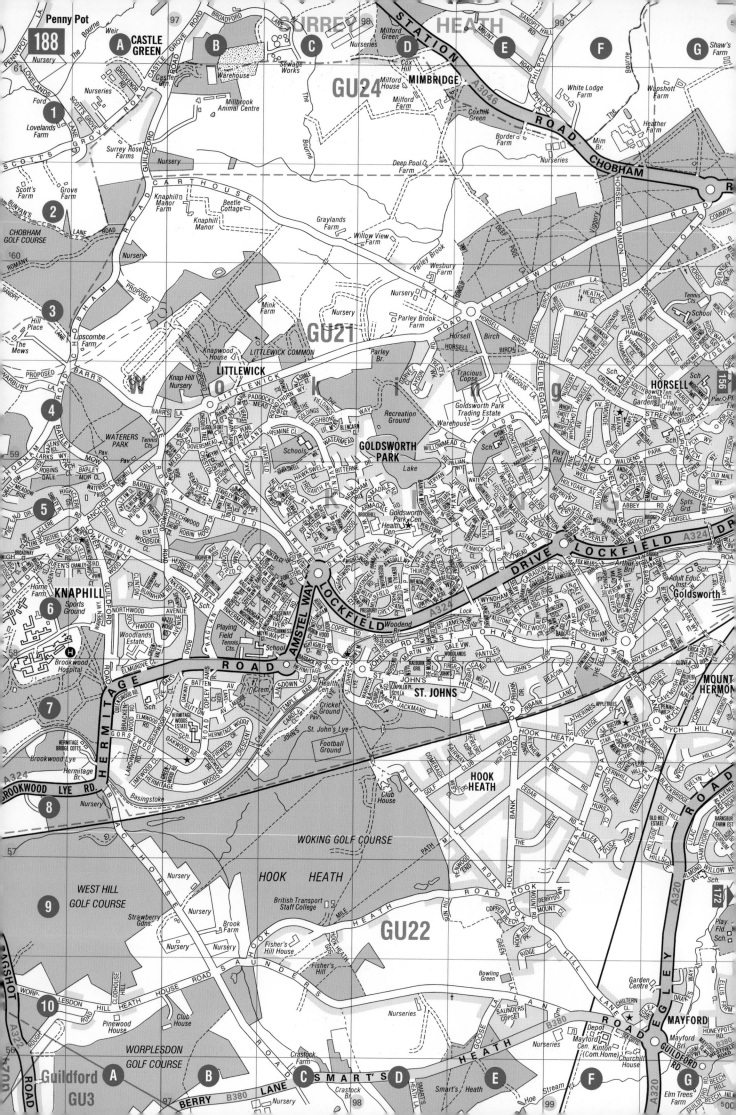

Large Scale Section

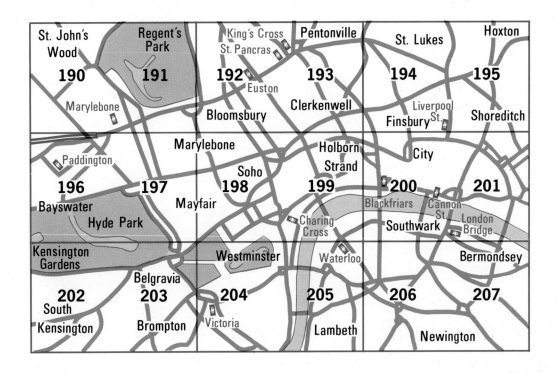

REFERENCE

Motorway	
'A' Road	A240
'B' Road	B463
Dual Carriageway	
House Numbers 'A' & 'B' Roads only	2 89
One Way Streets	
Buildings open to the Public	
District & Borough Boundary	
Fire Station	■
Hospital	
Information Centre	𝑖
Map Continuation	130
National Grid Reference	578
Places of Interest	
Police Station	▲
Postal Boundary	EC1
Post Office	★
Railway Station Entrance	Dockland Light Railway DLR British Rail ⇄ Underground ⊖
Toilet Disabled Toilet- National Key Scheme	▽ ⬇

Scale: 9 inches to 1 mile 1:7040

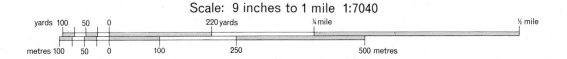

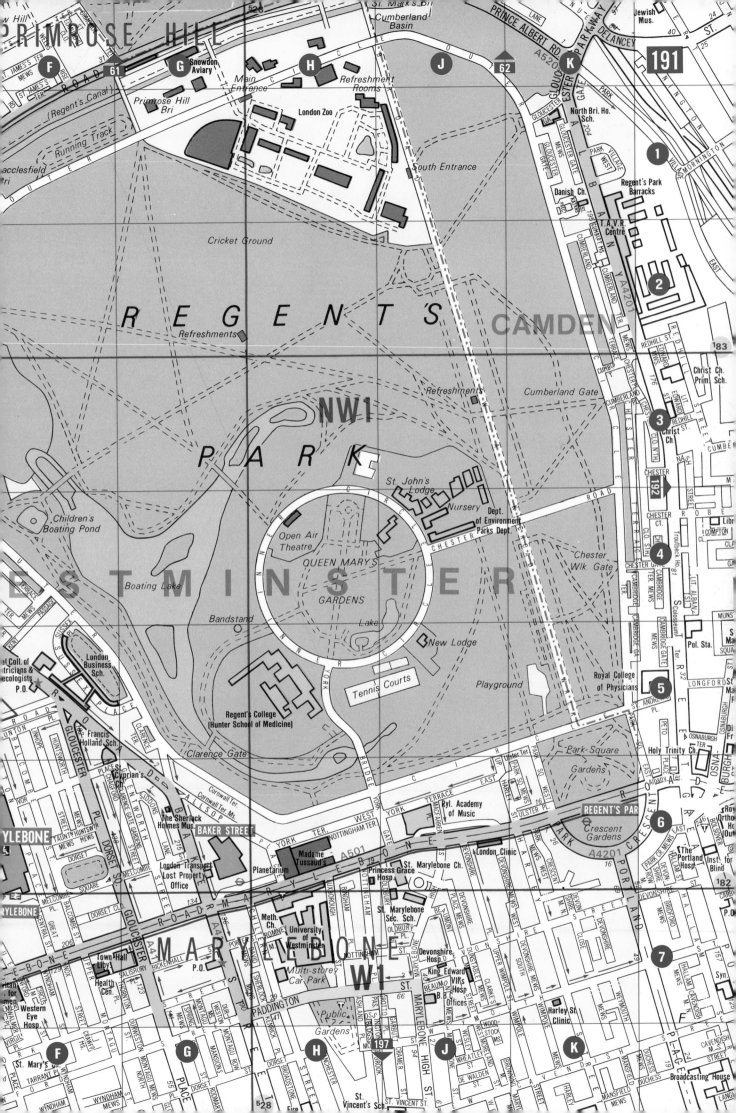

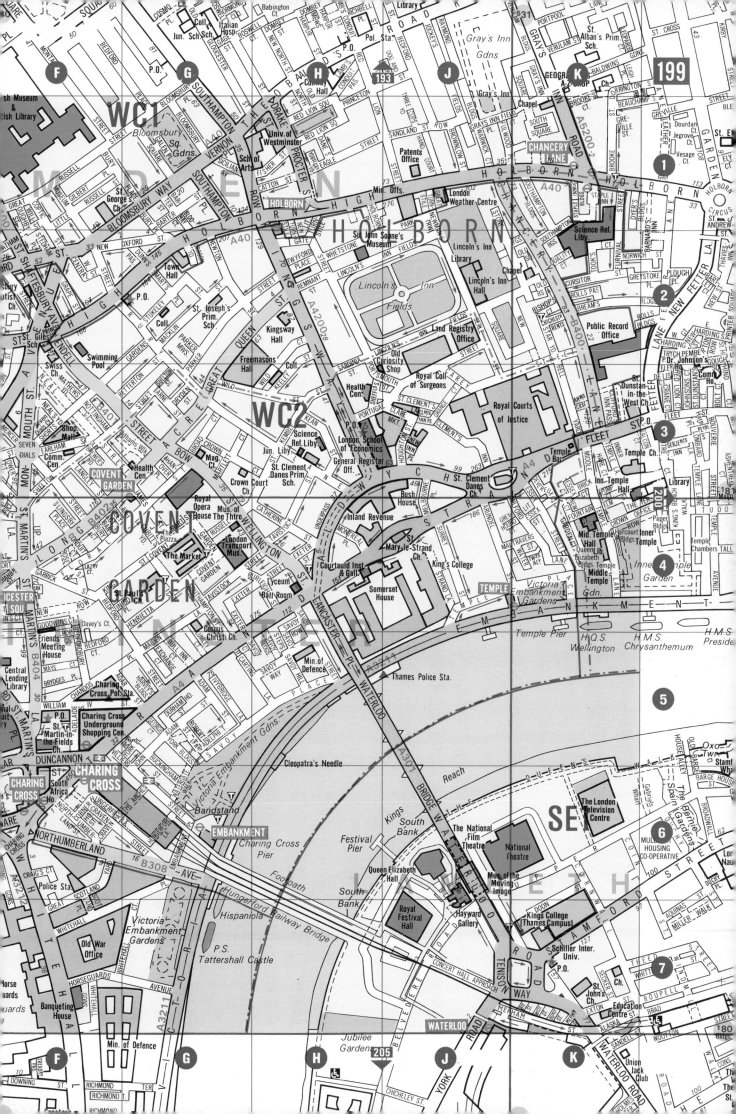

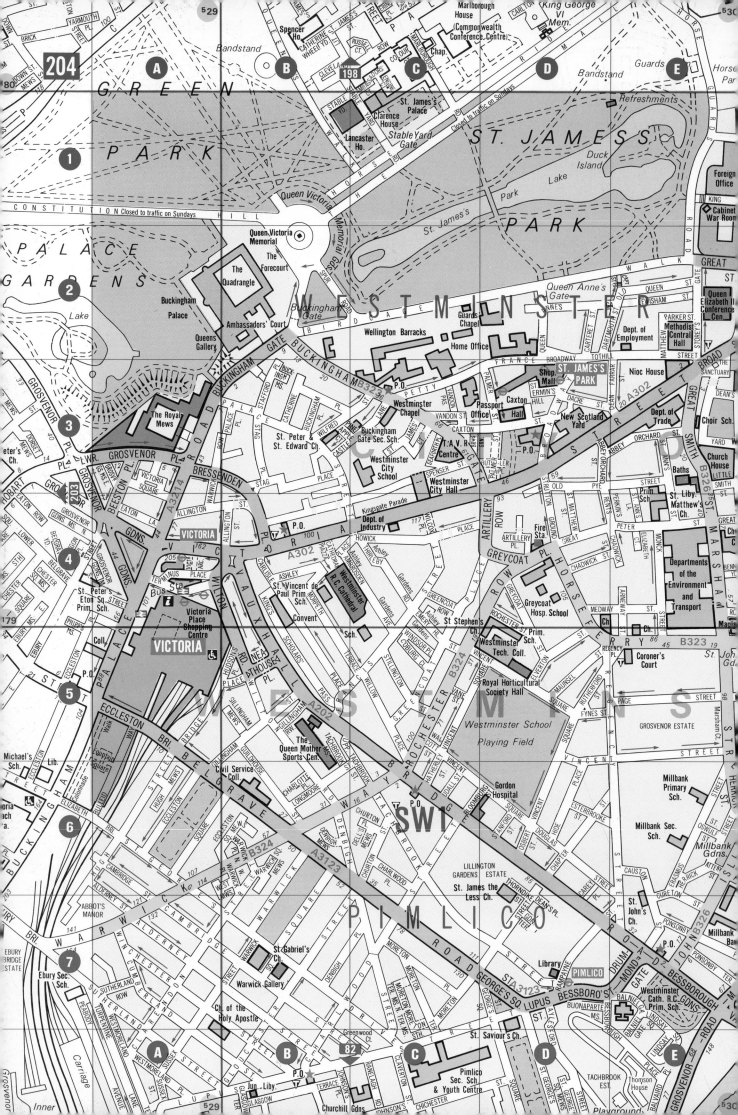

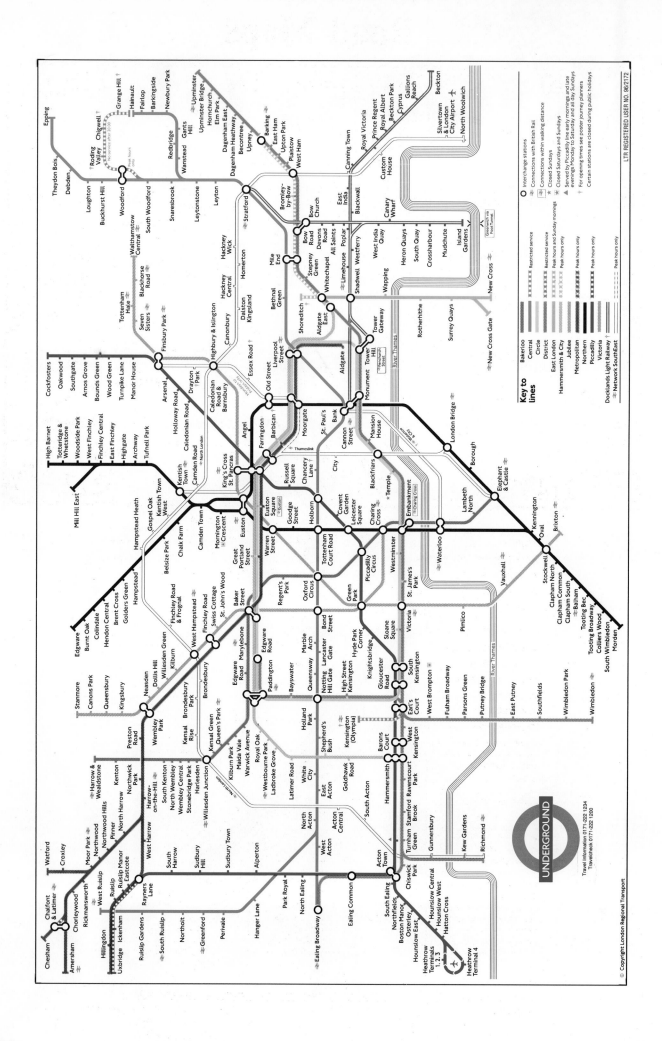

Road Maps

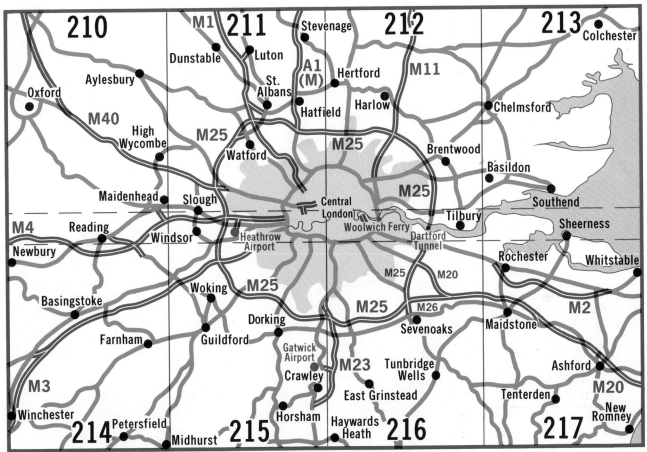

Reference and Tourist Information

MOTORWAY	**M1**
MOTORWAY UNDER CONSTRUCTION	
MOTORWAY PROPOSED	
MOTORWAY JUNCTION WITH NUMBER	
Unlimited interchange	**22**
Limited interchange	**21**
MOTORWAY SERVICE OR REST AREA........	HESTON Ⓢ
PRIMARY ROUTE	**A41**
PRIMARY ROUTE DESTINATION	**DOVER**
DUAL CARRIAGEWAY (A & B Roads)..........	
CLASS 'A' ROAD	**A129**
CLASS 'B' ROAD	**B177**
MAJOR ROAD UNDER CONSTRUCTION........	
MAJOR ROAD PROPOSED	

GRADIENT 1:5(20%) & STEEPER	
ascent in direction of arrow	
TOLL	*TOLL*
MILEAGE BETWEEN MARKERS	8
RAILWAY AND STATION	
LEVEL CROSSING	
CANAL	
BOUNDARY, COUNTY................................	
BUILT UP AREA	
VILLAGE OR HAMLET	O
WOODED AREA	
SPOT HEIGHT IN FEET.............................	.1581
HEIGHT ABOVE SEA LEVEL	400´ – 1,000´
	1,000´ – 1,400´
	1,400´ – 2,000´
	2,000´ +
NATIONAL GRID REFERENCE (Kilometres)...	30

AIRPORT, INTERNATIONAL	⊕
AIRFIELD	
HELIPORT	
BATTLE SITE & DATE...........................	
CASTLE..	
CASTLE WITH GARDEN (Open to Public)	
CATHEDRAL, ABBEY, PRIORY etc.................	✝
COUNTRY PARK	
FERRY (VEHICULAR)	
(FOOT ONLY)	
GARDEN (Open to Public)	
GOLF COURSE 9. 18........................	
HISTORIC BUILDING (Open to Public)	
HISTORIC BUILDING WITH GARDEN(Open to Public) .	
HORSE RACECOURSE	
INFORMATION CENTRE	**i**

LIGHTHOUSE	
MOTOR RACING CIRCUIT	
MUSEUM	
NATIONAL & FOREST PARK	
NATIONAL TRUST PROPERTY (Open)	*NT*
(Restricted Opening)	*NT*
NATURE RESERVE & BIRD SANCTUARY	
NATURE TRAIL & FOREST WALK	
PLACE OF INTEREST	.
PICNIC SITE	
RAILWAY, STEAM or NARROW GAUGE	
TELEPHONE, PUBLIC (Selection) ... AA or RAC	
VIEW POINT	
WILDLIFE PARK.............................	
WINDMILL	
ZOO or SAFARI PARK........................	

Scale:
3.156 miles to 1 inch
1:200,000

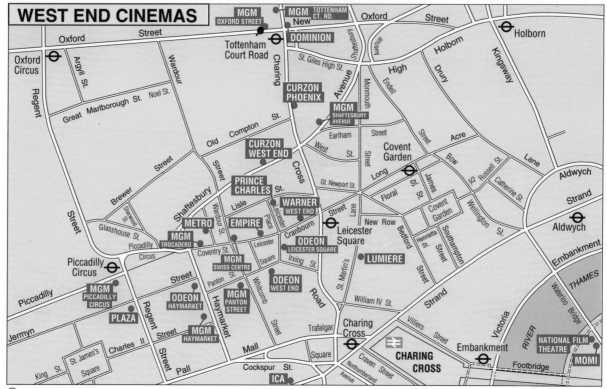

WEST END CINEMAS

Oxford Circus
Oxford Street
Regent Street
Argyll St.
Great Marlborough St.
Noel St.
Wardour Street
MGM OXFORD STREET
MGM New
MGM TOTTENHAM CT. RD.
Tottenham Court Road
Oxford Street
Holborn
St. Giles High St.
High
Holborn
Drury
Kingsway
DOMINION
Charing
Avenue
Endell
CURZON PHOENIX
Old Compton St.
Earlham Street
MGM SHAFTESBURY AVENUE
Covent Garden
Acre
Aldwych
Brewer Street
Shaftesbury Street
CURZON WEST END
West St.
Long
James St.
Bow
Russell St.
Lane
Strand
Glasshouse St.
Sherwood Sq.
PRINCE CHARLES
Lisle St.
WARNER WEST END
Gt. Newport St.
Floral St.
Covent Garden
Wellington
Catherine St.
Aldwych
Embankment
THAMES
METRO
EMPIRE
Leicester Place
Cranbourn
Leicester Square
New Row
Bedford Street
Henrietta St.
Southampton Street
MGM TROCADERO
Coventry St.
MGM SWISS CENTRE
ODEON LEICESTER SQUARE
Irving St.
LUMIERE
Piccadilly Circus
Piccadilly
Circus
Leicester Square
Panton St.
ODEON WEST END
St. Martin's
Strand
Waterloo Bridge
Piccadilly
MGM PICCADILLY CIRCUS
ODEON HAYMARKET
Whitcomb
MGM PANTON STREET
William IV St.
Charing Cross
Villiers Street
Victoria
RIVER
THAMES
PLAZA
Regent Street
Haymarket
Road
Trafalgar
Charing Cross
Embankment
NATIONAL FILM THEATRE
Jermyn
Charles II
MGM HAYMARKET
Mall
Square
CHARING CROSS
Footbridge
MOMI
King St.
St. James's Square
Pall
Cockspur St.
Northumberland Avenue
Craven Street
ICA

© *Copyright:* Geographers' A-Z Map Company Ltd.

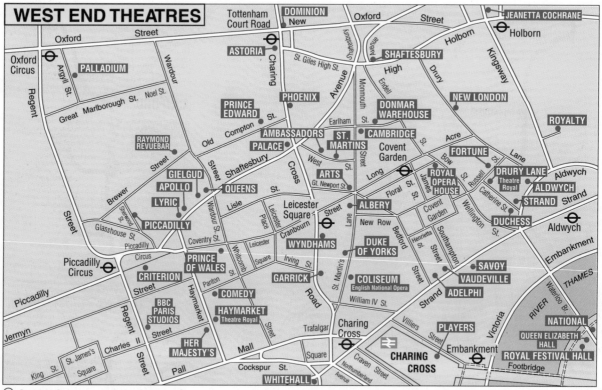

WEST END THEATRES

Tottenham Court Road
DOMINION New
Oxford Street
JEANETTA COCHRANE
Holborn
Oxford Circus
Oxford Street
ASTORIA
Charing
St. Giles High St.
SHAFTESBURY
High
Holborn
Kingsway
Regent
Argyll St.
PALLADIUM
Great Marlborough St.
Noel St.
Wardour
PHOENIX
Avenue
Monmouth
Endell
Drury
NEW LONDON
ROYALTY
PRINCE EDWARD
Old Compton St.
Earlham St.
DONMAR WAREHOUSE
Covent Garden
Acre
RAYMOND REVUEBAR
AMBASSADORS
ST. MARTINS
CAMBRIDGE
FORTUNE
Lane
PALACE
West St.
Long
Bow
Russell St.
DRURY LANE Theatre Royal
Aldwych
Brewer Street
GIELGUD
Shaftesbury
ARTS
Gt. Newport St.
ROYAL OPERA HOUSE
Floral St.
Covent Garden
Wellington
Catherine St.
ALDWYCH
Strand
APOLLO
QUEENS St.
Lisle
Leicester Place
STRAND
Aldwych
LYRIC
Glasshouse St.
Sherwood Sq.
Leicester Square
Cranbourn
ALBERY
New Row
Bedford
Henrietta St.
Southampton Street
DUCHESS
Aldwych
PICCADILLY
Piccadilly
Coventry St.
WYNDHAMS
DUKE OF YORKS
Embankment
Piccadilly Circus
Circus
PRINCE OF WALES
Panton St.
Whitcomb
Irving St.
SAVOY
THAMES
RIVER
CRITERION
GARRICK
St. Martin's
COLISEUM English National Opera
VAUDEVILLE
Jermyn
Regent
COMEDY
Road
William IV St.
Strand
ADELPHI
Victoria
NATIONAL
BBC PARIS STUDIOS
Haymarket
HAYMARKET Theatre Royal
Trafalgar
Charing Cross
PLAYERS
Embankment
QUEEN ELIZABETH HALL
Charles II
Street
HER MAJESTY'S
Mall
Square
Villiers Street
ROYAL FESTIVAL HALL
King St.
St. James's Square
Pall
Cockspur St.
Craven Street
CHARING CROSS
Northumberland Avenue
Footbridge
WHITEHALL
Waterloo Br.

© *Copyright:* Geographers' A-Z Map Company Ltd.

INDEX TO STREETS

HOW TO USE THIS INDEX

1. Each street name is followed by its Postal District (or, if outside the London Postal District, by its Posttown or Postal Locality), and then by its map reference; e.g. Abberley M. SW4 —55Kb **104** is in the South West 4 Postal District and is to be found in square 55Kb on page **104**. The page number being shown in bold type.
   A strict alphabetical order is followed in which Av., Rd., St., etc. (though abbreviated) are read in full and as part of the street name; e.g. Abbeydale Rd. appears after Abbey Cres. but before Abbey Dri.

2. Streets and a selection of Subsidiary names not shown on the Maps, appear in the index in *Italics* with the thoroughfare to which it is connected shown in brackets; e.g. *Aberdeen Pde. N18 —22Xb* **43** *(off Angel Rd.)*

3. Map references shown in brackets; e.g. Abbey Gdns. NW8 —40Eb **61** (2A **190**) and *Abchurch Yd. EC4 —45Tb* **83** *(4F 201) (off Abchurch La.)* refer to streets shown on the Large Scale Maps of Inner London, pages 190-207. In the first example Abbey Gdns. is shown as appearing in the Large Scale Map section as well as the standard Master Atlas section, whereas in the second example, *Abchurch Yd.* is shown as appearing in the Large Scale Map section only.

4. With the now general usage of Postcodes for addressing mail, it is not recommended that this index is used for such a purpose.

GENERAL ABBREVIATIONS

All: Alley	Cen: Centre	Dri: Drive	Ind: Industrial	N: North	St: Street
App: Approach	Chu: Church	E: East	Junct: Junction	Pal: Palace	Ter: Terrace
Arc: Arcade	Chyd: Churchyard	Embkmt: Embankment	La: Lane	Pde: Parade	Up: Upper
Av: Avenue	Circ: Circle	Est: Estate	Lit: Little	Pk: Park	Vs: Villas
Bk: Back	Cir: Circus	Gdns: Gardens	Lwr: Lower	Pas: Passage	Wlk: Walk
Boulevd: Boulevard	Clo: Close	Ga: Gate	Mnr: Manor	Pl: Place	W: West
Bri: Bridge	Comn: Common	Gt: Great	Mans: Mansions	Rd: Road	Yd: Yard
B'way: Broadway	Cotts: Cottages	Grn: Green	Mkt: Market	S: South	
Bldgs: Buildings	Ct: Court	Gro: Grove	M: Mews	Sq: Square	
Bus: Business	Cres: Crescent	Ho: House	Mt: Mount	Sta: Station	

POSTTOWN AND POSTAL LOCALITY ABBREVIATIONS

Abb L: Abbots Langley	Chst: Chislehurst	Ger X: Gerrards Cross	Kenl: Kenley	Pet W: Petts Wood	Sut G: Sutton Green
Abr: Abridge	Chob: Chobham	Gid P: Gidea Park	Kent: Kenton	Pil H: Pilgrims Hatch	Swan: Swanley
Add: Addlestone	Chor: Chorleywood	God G: Godden Green	Kes: Keston	Pinn: Pinner	Swans: Swanscombe
Ald: Aldenham	Cipp: Cippenham	God: Godstone	Kew: Kew	Platt: Platt	Tad: Tadworth
Amer: Amersham	Clar P: Claremont Park	Grav: Gravesend	Kingf: Kingfield	Pot B: Potters Bar	Tap: Taplow
Ark: Arkley	Clay: Claygate	Grays: Grays	K Lan: Kings Langley	Prat B: Pratts Bottom	Tats: Tatsfield
Asc: Ascot	Cob: Cobham (Surrey)	Gt War: Great Warley	King T: Kingston Upon Thames	Purf: Purfleet	Tedd: Teddington
Ash: Ash	Cobh: Cobham (Kent)	Gnfd: Greenford	Knap: Knaphill	Purl: Purley	Th Dit: Thames Ditton
Ashf: Ashford	Cockf: Cockfosters	Grnh: Greenhithe	Knat: Knatts Valley	Pyr: Pyrford	They B: Theydon Bois
Asht: Ashtead	Col R: Collier Row	Grn St: Green Street Green	Knock: Knockholt	Rad: Radlett	They G: Theydon Garnon
Badg M: Badgers Mount	Coln: Colnbrook	Guild: Guildford	Lale: Laleham	Rain: Rainham	They M: Theydon Mount
Bans: Banstead	Col S: Colney Street	Hack: Hackbridge	Langl: Langley	Red: Redhill	T Hth: Thornton Heath
Bark: Barking	Coop: Coopersale	Hals: Halstead	Lat: Latimer	Reig: Reigate	Thorpe: Thorpe
B'side: Barkingside	Corr: Corringham	Ham: Ham	Lea: Leatherhead	Rich: Richmond	Til: Tilbury
B'hurst: Barnehurst	Coul: Coulsdon	Hamp: Hampton	Leav: Leavesden	Rick: Rickmansworth	T'sey: Titsey
Barn: Barnet	Coul N: Coulsdon North	Hamp H: Hampton Hill	Let H: Letchmore Heath	Ridge: Ridge	Twic: Twickenham
B Hth: Batchworth Heath	Cow: Cowley	Hamp W: Hampton Wick	Limp: Limpsfield	Rip: Ripley	Under: Underriver
Beac: Beaconsfield	Cran: Cranford	Hanw: Hanworth	Linf: Linford	Riv: Riverhead	Upm: Upminster
Bean: Bean	Cray: Crayford	Hare: Harefield	L Chal: Little Chalfont	Romf: Romford	Uxb: Uxbridge
Beck: Beckenham	Crock: Crockenhill	Harm: Harmondsworth	L Hth: Little Heath	Ruis: Ruislip	Vir W: Virginia Water
Bedd: Beddington	Crou: Crouch	H Hill: Harold Hill	L War: Little Warley	Rush: Rush Green	Wall: Wallington
Bedf: Bedfont	Crox: Croxley Green	H Wood: Harold Wood	Lon C: London Colney	St Alb: St Albans	Wal A: Waltham Abbey
Belm: Belmont	Croy: Croydon	Harr: Harrow	Longc: Longcross	St G: St Georges Hill	Wal X: Waltham Cross
Belv: Belvedere	Cud: Cudham	Har W: Harrow Weald	Long: Longfield	St J: St Johns	W on T: Walton-on-Thames
Berr G: Berrys Green	Cuff: Cuffley	Hart: Hartley	Loud: Loudwater	St M: St Mary Cray	War: Warley
Bex: Bexley	Dag: Dagenham	H End: Hatch End	Lou: Loughton	St P: St Pauls Cray	Warl: Warlingham
Bexh: Bexleyheath	Dart: Dartford	Hat: Hatfield	Ludd: Luddesdown	Sarr: Sarratt	Wat: Watford
Big H: Biggin Hill	Dat: Datchet	Hav: Havering Atte Bower	Lyne: Lyne	Seal: Seal	W'stone: Wealdstone
Bisl: Bisley	Den: Denham	Hawl: Hawley	Mawn: Mawneys	Send: Send	Well E: Well End
B'more: Blackmore	Dit H: Ditton Hill	Hay: Hayes (Middlesex)	Mayf: Mayford	Sev: Sevenoaks	Well: Welling
Blet: Bletchingley	Dodd: Doddinghurst	Hayes: Hayes (Kent)	Meop: Meopham	Sheer: Sheerwater	Wemb: Wembley
Bookh: Bookham	Dor: Dorney	Head: Headley	Mers: Merstham	Shenf: Shenfield	W Byf: West Byfleet
Borwd: Borehamwood	Dow: Downe	H'row: Heathrow	Mid: Middlegreen	Shenl: Shenley	W Cla: West Clandon
Bor G: Borough Green	D'side: Downside	H'row A: Heathrow Airport (London)	Mill: Mill End	Shep: Shepperton	W Dray: West Drayton
Bov: Bovingdon	Dun G: Dunton Green	Hedg: Hedgerley	Mitc: Mitcham	Shor: Shoreham	West: Westerham
Bras: Brasted	Eastc: Eastcote	Heron: Herongate	Mit J: Mitcham Junction	Shorne: Shorne	W Ewe: West Ewell
Bren: Brentford	E Hor: East Horsley	Herons: Heronsgate	Moor P: Moor Park	Short: Shortlands	W Horn: West Horndon
Brtwd: Brentwood	E Mol: East Molesey	Hex: Hextable	Mord: Morden	Sidc: Sidcup	W Hor: West Horsley
Brick: Bricket Wood	E Til: East Tilbury	H Bar: High Barnet	Mount: Mountnessing	Slou: Slough	W Hyd: West Hyde
Brom: Bromley	Edgw: Edgware	H Bee: High Beech	Nave: Navestock	Sole S: Sole Street	W King: West Kingsdown
Brook P: Brookmans Park	Eff: Effingham	High W: High Wycombe	N'side: Navestockside	S'hall: Southall	W Mol: West Molesey
Brkwd: Brookwood	Eff J: Effingham Junction	Hill: Hillingdon	New Ad: New Addington	S Croy: South Croydon	W Thur: West Thurrock
Buck H: Buckhurst Hill	Egh: Egham	Hin W: Hinchley Wood	New Ash: New Ash Green	S Dar: South Darenth	W Til: West Tilbury
Bulp: Bulphan	Elm P: Elm Park	Hods: Hodsoll Street	New Bar: New Barnet	S'fleet: Southfleet	W Wick: West Wickham
Bur H: Burgh Heath	Els: Elstree	Holyp: Holyport	New Haw: New Haw	S Harr: South Harrow	Wex: Wexham
Burn: Burnham	Enf: Enfield	Hook: Hook End	N Mald: New Malden	S Mim: South Mimms	Wey: Weybridge
Bush: Bushey	Epp: Epping	Hool: Hooley	Noak H: Noak Hill	S Ock: South Ockendon	W Vill: Whiteley Village
Byfl: Byfleet	Eps: Epsom	Horn: Hornchurch	N'thaw: Northaw	S Ruis: South Ruislip	Whit: Whitton
Cars: Carshalton	Eri: Erith	Horn H: Horndon-on-the-hill	N'fleet: Northfleet	S Stif: South Stifford	Whyt: Whyteleafe
Cat: Caterham	Esh: Esher	Hors: Horsell	N Har: North Harrow	S Wea: South Weald	Wilm: Wilmington
Chad: Chadwell Heath	Eton: Eton	Hort: Horton	N Mym: North Mymms	Stai: Staines	Wind: Windsor
Chaf H: Chafford Hundred	Eton C: Eton College	Hort K: Horton Kirby	N Ock: North Ockendon	Stanf: Stanford-le-Hope	Wind C: Windsor Castle
Chal G: Chalfont St Giles	Eton W: Eton Wick	Houn: Hounslow	N'holt: Northolt	Stan: Stanmore	Wink: Winkfield
Chal P: Chalfont St Peter	Ewe: Ewell	Hut: Hutton	N Stif: North Stifford	Stans: Stansted	Wis: Wisley
Chalv: Chalvey	Eyns: Eynsford	Ick: Ickenham	N Nth: Northumberland Heath	Stanw: Stanwell	Wok: Woking
Chan X: Chandlers Cross	Fair: Fairseat	Ide: Ide Hill	N'wd: Northwood	Stap A: Stapleford Abbotts	Wold: Woldingham
Cheam: Cheam	Farn: Farnborough	Igh: Ightham	Oak G: Oakley Green	Stap T: Stapleford Tawney	Wbrn G: Wooburn Green
Chels: Chelsfield	Farn C: Farnham Common	Ilf: Ilford	Ock: Ockham	Stoke D: Stoke D'abernon	Wfd G: Woodford Green
Chen: Chenies	Farn R: Farnham Royal	Ing: Ingatestone	Old Win: Old Windsor	Stoke P: Stoke Poges	Wdhm: Woodham
Cher: Chertsey	F'ham: Farningham	Ingve: Ingrave	Old Wok: Old Woking	Ston M: Stondon Massey	Wor Pk: Worcester Park
Che: Chesham	Fawk: Fawkham	Iswth: Isleworth	Ong: Ongar	S'leigh: Stoneleigh	Wray: Wraysbury
Chesh: Cheshunt	Felt: Feltham	Iver: Iver	Orp: Orpington	Sun: Sunbury-on-Thames	Wro: Wrotham
Chess: Chessington	Fet: Fetcham	Iver H: Iver Heath	Ors: Orsett	Sund: Sundridge	Wro H: Wrotham Heath
Chev: Chevening	Fid H: Fiddlers Hamlet	Ivy H: Ivy Hatch	Ott: Ottershaw	S'dale: Sunningdale	Wy G: Wyatts Green
Chig: Chigwell	Flau: Flaunden	Jac: Jacob's Well	Oxs: Oxshott	S'hill: Sunninghill	Yiew: Yiewsley
Chfd: Chipperfield	Frog: Frogmore	Kel C: Kelvedon Common	Oxt: Oxted	Surb: Surbiton	
Chip: Chipstead (Kent)	Ful: Fulmer	Kel H: Kelvedon Hatch	Park: Park Street	Sutt: Sutton	
Chips: Chipstead (Surrey)	G Grn: George Green	Kems: Kemsing		S at H: Sutton at Hone	

INDEX TO STREETS

Abbott's Tilt—Albert Rd.

Abbott's Tilt. W on T —76Aa 141
Abbott's Wlk. Bexh —52Zc 109
Abbotts Wlk. Cat —94Xb 181
Abbotts Way. Slou —6B 72
Abbs Cross. Horn —32Ld 69
Abbs Cross Gdns. Horn —32Ld 69
Abbs Cross La. Horn —34Ld 69
Abchurch La. EC4 —45Tb 83 (4G 201)
Abchurch Yd. EC4 —45Tb 83 (4F 201)
(off Abchurch La.)
Abdale Rd. W12 —46Xa 80
Abel Ho. SE11 —51Qb 104
Abenburg Way. Hut —19De 33
Abenglen Ind. Est. Hay —47T 76
Aberavon Rd. E3 —41Ac 84
Abercairn Rd. SW16 —66Lb 126
Aberconway Rd. Mord —70Db 125
Abercorn Clo. NW7 —24Ab 40
Abercorn Clo. NW8 —41Eb 81 (2A 190)
Abercorn Clo. S Croy —85Zb 166
Abercorn Commercial Cen. Wemb —39Ma 59
Abercorn Cres. Harr —32Da 57
Abercorn Gdns. Harr —31Ma 59
Abercorn Gdns. Romf —30Xc 47
Abercorn Gro. Ruis —28T 36
Abercorn Pl. NW8 —41Eb 81
Abercorn Rd. NW7 —24Ab 40
Abercorn Rd. Stan —24La 38
Abercorn Way. SE1 —50Wb 83
Abercorn Way. Wok —6D 188
Abercrombie St. SW11 —54Gb 103
Aberdale Gdns. Pot B —4Bb 9
Aberdare Clo. W Wick —75Ec 148
Aberdare Gdns. NW6 —38Db 61
Aberdare Gdns. NW7 —24Za 40
Aberdare Rd. Enf —14Yb 26
Aberdeen Av. Slou —5E 72
Aberdeen La. N5 —36Sb 63
Aberdeen Pde. N18 —22Xb 43
(off Angel Rd.)
Aberdeen Pk. N5 —36Sb 63
Aberdeen Pl. NW8 —42Fb 81 (6B 190)
Aberdeen Rd. N5 —35Sb 63
Aberdeen Rd. N18 —22Xb 43
Aberdeen Rd. NW10 —36Va 60
Aberdeen Rd. Croy —77Tb 147
Aberdeen Rd. Harr —26Ha 38
Aberdeen Ter. SE3 —54Fc 107
Aberdour Rd. Ilf —34Xc 67
Aberdour St. SE1 —49Ub 83 (4H 207)
Aberfeldy Ho. SE5 —52Rb 105
Aberfeldy St. E14 —44Ec 84
(in two parts)
Aberford Gdns. SE18 —53Nc 108
Aberford Rd. Borwd —12Qa 21
Aberfoyle Rd. SW16 —66Mb 126
Abergeldie Rd. SE12 —58Kc 107
Abernethy Rd. SE13 —56Gc 107
Abersham Rd. E8 —36Vb 63
Abery St. SE18 —49Uc 86
Abingdon Clo. NW1 —37Mb 62
Abingdon Clo. SE1 —50Vb 83 (7K 207)
(off Bushwood Dri.)
Abingdon Clo. SW19 —65Eb 125
Abingdon Clo. Uxb —39P 55
Abingdon Clo. Wok —6F 188
Abingdon Ct. W8 —48Cb 81
(off Abingdon Vs.)
Abingdon Gdns. W8 —48Cb 81
Abingdon Lodge. W8 —48Cb 81
Abingdon Pl. Pot B —4Db 9
Abingdon Rd. N3 —26Eb 41
Abingdon Rd. SW16 —68Nb 126
Abingdon Rd. W8 —48Cb 81
Abingdon St. SW1 —48Nb 82 (3F 205)
Abingdon Vs. W8 —48Cb 81
Abingdon Way. Orp —77Xc 151
Abinger Av. Sutt —81Ya 162
Abinger Clo. Bark —35Wc 67
Abinger Clo. Brom —69Nc 130
Abinger Clo. Wall —78Nb 146
Abinger Ct. Wall —78Nb 146
Abinger Gdns. Iswth —55Ga 100
Abinger Gro. SE8 —51Bc 106
Abinger M. W9 —42Cb 81
Abinger Rd. W4 —48Ua 80
Abington Ct. Upm —32Sd 70
Ablett St. SE16 —50Yb 84
Abney Gdns. N16 —33Vb 63
Aboyne Dri. SW20 —68Wa 124
Aboyne Rd. NW10 —34Ua 60
Aboyne Rd. SW17 —62Fb 125
Abridge Clo. Wal X —7Zb 12
Abridge Gdns. Romf —23Cd 48
Abridge Pk. Caravan Pk. Abr —14Wc 29
Abridge Rd. Chig —17Tc 28
Abridge Rd. They B & Abr —9Uc 14
Abridge Way. Bark —40Xc 67
Abyssinia Clo. SW11 —56Gb 103
Acacia Av. N17 —24Tb 43
Acacia Av. Bren —52Ka 100
Acacia Av. Hay —44V 76
Acacia Av. Horn —33Hd 68
Acacia Av. Rich —54Pa 101
Acacia Av. Ruis —32W 56
Acacia Av. Shep —71Q 140
Acacia Av. Wemb —36Na 59
Acacia Av. W Dray —45P 75
Acacia Av. Wok —8G 188
Acacia Av. Wray —56A 96
Acacia Bus. Cen. E11 —34Gc 65
(off Howard Rd.)
Acacia Clo. SE20 —68Wb 127
Acacia Clo. Orp —71Tc 150
Acacia Clo. Stan —23Ga 38
Acacia Clo. Wdhm —82H 157
Acacia Ct. Grav —9C 114
Acacia Ct. Harr —29Da 37
Acacia Dri. Bans —86Za 162
Acacia Dri. Sutt —74Cb 145
Acacia Dri. Upm —35Qd 69
Acacia Dri. Wdhm —82H 157
Acacia Gdns. NW8 —40Fb 61 (1C 190)
Acacia Gdns. Upm —31Vd 70
Acacia Gdns. W Wick —75Ec 148
Acacia Gro. SE21 —61Tb 127
Acacia Gro. N Mald —69Ta 123
Acacia Ho. N22 —25Qb 42
(off Douglas Rd.)
Acacia Ho. Ger X —25A 34
Acacia Ho. Slou —6K 73
Acacia M. W Dray —51M 97
Acacia Pl. NW8 —40Fb 61 (1C 190)
Acacia Rd. E11 —33Gc 65
Acacia Rd. E17 —30Ac 44
Acacia Rd. N22 —25Qb 42
Acacia Rd. NW8 —40Fb 61 (1C 190)
Acacia Rd. SW16 —67Pb 126
Acacia Rd. W3 —45Sa 79
Acacia Rd. Beck —69Bc 128
Acacia Rd. Dart —60Md 111
Acacia Rd. Enf —11Tb 25
Acacia Rd. Grnh —58Ud 112
Acacia Rd. Hamp —65Ca 121
Acacia Rd. Mitc —68Jb 126
Acacia Rd. Stai —64K 119
Acacias, The. Barn —15Fb 23
Acacia Wlk. Swan —68Fd 132
Acacia Way. Sidc —60Vc 109
Academy Bldgs. N1 —41Ub 83 (3H 195)
(off Fanshaw St.)
Academy Gdns. Croy —74Vb 147
Academy Gdns. N'holt —40Z 57
Academy Pl. SE18 —53Pc 108
Academy Rd. SE18 —53Pc 108
Acanthus Dri. SE1 —50Wb 83
Acanthus Rd. SW11 —55Jb 104
Accommodation La. W Dray —53J 97
Accommodation Rd. NW11 —32Bb 61
Accommodation Rd. Longc —76A 138
Accommodation Rd. Wor Pk —78Wa 144
A.C. Court. Th Dit —72Ja 142
Acer Av. Rain —41Md 89
Acer Rd. Big H —88Mc 167
Acers. St Alb —1Ea 6
Acfold Rd. SW6 —53Db 103
Achilles Clo. SE1 —50Wb 83
Achilles Pl. Wok —5F 188
Achilles Rd. NW6 —36Cb 61
Achilles St. SE14 —52Bc 106
Achilles Way. W1 —46Jb 82 (7J 197)
Acklam Rd. W10 —43Ab 80
Acklington Dri. NW9 —25Ua 40
Ackmar Rd. SW6 —53Cb 103
Ackroyd Dri. E3 —43Bc 84
Ackroyd Rd. SE23 —59Zb 106
Acland Clo. SE18 —52Tc 108
Acland Cres. SE5 —55Tb 105
Acland Ho. SW9 —54Pb 104
Acland Rd. NW2 —37Xa 60
Acme Rd. Wat —10W 4
Acol Cres. Ruis —36X 57
Acol Rd. NW6 —38Cb 61
Aconbury Rd. Dag —39Xc 67
Acorn Cen., The. Ilf —23Xc 47
Acorn Clo. E4 —22Dc 44
Acorn Clo. Chst —64Sc 130
Acorn Clo. Enf —11Rb 25
Acorn Clo. Hamp —65Da 121
Acorn Clo. Stan —24Ka 38
Acorn Ct. E6 —38Nc 66
Acorn Ct. Ilf —30Uc 46
Acorn Gdns. SE19 —67Vb 127
Acorn Gdns. W3 —43Ta 79
Acorn Gro. Hay —52V 98
Acorn Gro. Ruis —35V 56
Acorn Gro. Tad —96Ab 178
Acorn Gro. Wok —93A 172
Acorn Ind. Pk. Dart —57Hd 110
Acorn La. Cuff —1Nb 10
Acorn Pde. SE15 —52Xb 105
Acorn Pl. Wat —9W 4
Acorn Rd. Dart —57Hd 110
Acorns, The. Chig —21Uc 46
Acorns, The. Sev —95Jd 186
Acorns Way. Esh —78Ea 142
Acorn Trading Est. S Stif —51Zd 113
Acorn Wlk. SE16 —46Ac 84
Acorn Way. SE23 —62Zb 128
Acorn Way. Orp —77Rc 150
Acrefield Ho. NW4 —28Za 40
(off Belle Vue Est.)
Acrefield Rd. Ger X —27A 34
Acre La. SW2 —56Nb 104
Acre La. Cars & Wall —77Jb 146
Acre Pas. Wind —3H 95
Acre Path. N'holt —37Aa 57
(off Arnold Rd.)
Acre Rd. SW19 —65Fb 125
Acre Rd. Dag —38Dd 68
Acre Rd. King T —67Na 123
Acres Gdns. Tad —91Za 178
Acres, The. Stanf —1P 93
Acre View. Horn —28Nd 49
Acre Way. N'wd —25V 36
Acris St. SW18 —57Eb 103
Acton Clo. N9 —19Wb 25
Acton Clo. Chesh —3Ac 12
Acton La. NW10 —41Sa 79
Acton La. W3 —47Sa 79
Acton La. W4 & W3 —49Sa 79
(in three parts)
Acton M. E8 —39Vb 63
Acton Pk. Ind. Est. W3 —47Ta 79
Acton St. WC1 —41Pb 82 (4H 193)
Acuba Rd. SW18 —61Db 125
Acworth Clo. N9 —17Yb 26
Acworth Pl. Dart —58Ld 111
Ada Gdns. E14 —44Fc 85
Ada Gdns. E15 —39Hc 65
Adair Clo. SE25 —69Xb 127
Adair Rd. W10 —42Ab 80
Adam and Eve Ct. W1 —44Lb 82 (2C 198)
(off Oxford St.)
Adam and Eve M. W8 —48Cb 81
Adam Clo. Slou —6E 72
Adam Ct. SW7 —49Eb 81 (5A 202)
(off Gloucester Rd.)
Adams Clo. N3 —24Cb 41
Adams Clo. NW9 —33Ra 59
Adams Clo. Surb —72Pa 143
Adams Ct. E17 —30Ac 44
Adams Ct. EC2 —44Ub 83 (2G 201)
Adams Ct. Wemb —37Ra 59
Adams Cres. Romf —29Hd 48
Adams Gdns. Est. SE16 —47Yb 84
Adamson Ct. N2 —27Gb 41
Adamson Rd. E16 —44Jc 85
Adamson Rd. NW3 —38Fb 61
Adams Pl. E14 —46Dc 84
(off N. Colonnade)
Adams Pl. N7 —36Pb 62
Adamsrill Clo. Enf —16Tb 25
Adamsrill Rd. SE26 —63Zb 128
Adams Rd. N17 —26Tb 43
Adams Rd. Beck —71Ac 148
Adams Rd. Stanf —2N 93
Adam's Row. W1 —45Jb 82 (5J 197)
Adams Sq. Bexh —55Ad 109
Adam St. WC2 —45Nb 82 (5G 199)
Adams Wlk. King T —68Na 123
Adams Way. SE25 —72Vb 147
Adams Way. Croy —72Vb 147
Adam Wlk. SW6 —52Ya 102
(off Crabtree La.)
Ada Pl. E2 —39Xb 63
Adare Wlk. SW16 —62Pb 126
Ada Rd. SE5 —52Ub 105
Ada Rd. Wemb —34Ma 59
Ada St. E8 —39Xb 63
Ada Workshops. E8 —39Xb 63
Adcock Wlk. Orp —77Vc 151
Adderley Gdns. SE9 —63Qc 130
Adderley Gro. SW11 —57Jb 104
Adderley Rd. Harr —25Ha 38
Adderley St. E14 —44Ec 84
Addington Clo. Wind —5E 94
Addington Ct. SW14 —55Ta 101
Addington Dri. N12 —23Fb 41
Addington Gro. SE26 —63Ac 128
Addington Heights. New Ad —83Ec 166
Addington Ho. SW9 —54Pb 104
(off Stockwell Rd.)
Addington Rd. E3 —41Cc 84
Addington Rd. E16 —42Gc 85
Addington Rd. N4 —30Qb 42
Addington Rd. Croy —74Qb 146
Addington Rd. S Croy —84Wb 165
Addington Rd. W Wick —77Ec 148
Addington Sq. SE5 —51Tb 105
Addington St. SE1 —47Pb 82 (2J 205)
Addington Village Rd. Croy
(in two parts) —79Bc 148
Addis Clo. Enf —11Zb 26
Addiscombe Av. Croy —74Wb 147
Addiscombe Clo. Harr —29La 38
Addiscombe Ct. Rd. Croy —74Ub 147
Addiscombe Gro. Croy —75Ub 147
Addiscombe Rd. Croy —75Ub 147
Addiscombe Rd. Wat —14X 19
Addison Av. N14 —16Kb 24
Addison Av. W11 —46Ab 80
Addison Av. Houn —53Ea 100
Addison Bri. Pl. W14 —49Bb 81
Addison Clo. Cat —94Tb 181
Addison Clo. Iver —45G 74
Addison Clo. N'wd —25W 36
Addison Clo. Orp —72Sc 150
Addison Ct. E2 —40Wb 63
(off Pritchard's Rd.)
Addison Cres. W14 —48Ab 80
Addison Dri. SE12 —57Kc 107
Addison Gdns. W14 —48Za 80
Addison Gdns. Grays —49Ee 91
Addison Gdns. Surb —70Pa 123
Addison Gro. W4 —48Ua 80
Addison Pl. SE25 —70Wb 127
Addison Pl. W11 —46Ab 80
Addison Pl. S'hall —45Ca 77
Addison Rd. E11 —30Jc 45
Addison Rd. E17 —29Dc 44
Addison Rd. SE25 —70Wb 127
Addison Rd. W14 —47Ab 80
Addison Rd. Brom —71Mc 149
Addison Rd. Cat —93Tb 181
Addison Rd. Enf —11Yb 26
Addison Rd. Ilf —25Sc 46
Addison Rd. Tedd —65Ka 122
Addison Rd. Wok —89B 156
Addisons Clo. Croy —75Bc 148
Addison Ter. W4 —49Sa 79
(off Chiswick Rd.)
Addison Way. NW11 —28Bb 41
Addison Way. Hay —44W 76
Addison Way. N'wd —25V 36
Addle Hill. EC4 —44Rb 83 (3C 200)
Addlestone Moor. Add —75L 139
Addlestone Pk. Add —78K 139
Addlestone Rd. Add & Wey —77N 139
Addle St. EC2 —44Sb 83 (2E 200)
Addmar Rd. Dag —34Ad 67
Adecroft Way. W Mol —69Ea 122
Adela Av. N Mald —71Xa 144
Adelaide Av. SE4 —56Bc 106
Adelaide Clo. Enf —10Ub 11
Adelaide Clo. Slou —7E 72
Adelaide Clo. Stan —21Ja 38
Adelaide Cotts. W7 —47Ha 78
Adelaide Ct. Beck —66Bc 128
Adelaide Gdns. Romf —29Ad 47
Adelaide Gro. W12 —46Wa 80
Adelaide Ho. E15 —40Hc 65
Adelaide Ho. SE5 —54Ub 105
Adelaide Pl. Wey —77T 140
Adelaide Rd. E10 —34Ec 64
Adelaide Rd. NW3 —38Fb 61
Adelaide Rd. SW18 —57Cb 103
Adelaide Rd. W13 —46Ja 78
Adelaide Rd. Ashf —64M 119
Adelaide Rd. Chst —64Rc 130
Adelaide Rd. Houn —53Aa 99
Adelaide Rd. Ilf —33Rc 66
Adelaide Rd. Rich —56Pa 101
Adelaide Rd. S'hall —49Aa 77
Adelaide Rd. Surb —71Na 143
Adelaide Rd. Tedd —65Ha 122
Adelaide Rd. Til —3B 114
Adelaide Rd. W on T —76W 140
Adelaide Sq. Wind —4H 95
Adelaide St. WC2 —45Nb 82 (5F 199)
Adelaide Ter. Bren —50Ma 79
Adelaide Wlk. SW9 —56Qb 104
Adela St. W10 —42Ab 80
Adelina Gro. E1 —43Yb 84
Adelina M. SW12 —60Mb 104
Adeline Pl. WC1 —43Mb 82 (1E 198)
Adelphi Ct. W4 —51Ta 101
Adelphi Cres. Hay —41U 76
Adelphi Cres. Horn —33Jd 68
Adelphi Gdns. Slou —7J 73
Adelphi Rd. Eps —85Ta 161
Adelphi Ter. WC2 —45Nb 82 (5G 199)
Adelphi Way. Hay —41V 76
Adeney Clo. W6 —51Za 102
Aden Gro. N16 —35Tb 63
Adenmore Rd. SE6 —59Cc 106
Aden Rd. Enf —14Ac 26
Aden Rd. Ilf —31Rc 66
Aden Ter. N16 —35Tb 63
Adeyfield Ho. EC1 —41Tb 83 (4G 195)
(off Cranwood St.)
Adhara Rd. N'wd —22V 36
Adia Ho. Borwd —12Sa 21
Adie Rd. W6 —48Ya 80
Adine Rd. E13 —42Kc 85
Adler Ind. Est. Hay —47T 76
Adler St. E1 —44Wb 83
Adley St. E5 —36Ac 64
Adlington Clo. N18 —22Tb 43
Admail Ho. Eps —87Ra 161
Admaston Rd. SE18 —52Sc 108
Admiral Ct. SW10 —53Eb 103
(off Thames Av.)
Admiral Ct. Cars —74Gb 145
Admiral Hood Ho. Ger X —21A 34
Admiral Hyson Ind. Est. SE16 —50Xb 83
Admiral M. W10 —42Za 80
Admiral Pl. SE16 —46Ac 84
Admirals Clo. E18 —28Kc 45
Admiral Seymour Rd. SE9 —56Pc 108
Admirals Lodge. Romf —29Hd 48
Admiral Sq. SW10 —53Eb 103
Admirals Rd. Bookh & Lea —100Ea 176
Admiral St. SE8 —53Cc 106
Admirals Wlk. NW3 —34Eb 61
Admirals Wlk. Coul —92Pb 180
Admirals Wlk. Grnh —57Xd 112
Admirals Way. E14 —47Cc 84
Admiralty Clo. SE8 —52Cc 106
Admiralty Rd. Tedd —65Ha 122
Admiral Wlk. W9 —43Cb 81
Adnams Wlk. Rain —37Jd 68
Adolf St. SE6 —63Dc 128
Adolphus Rd. N4 —33Rb 63
Adolphus St. SE8 —52Bc 106
Adpar St. W2 —43Fb 81 (7B 190)
Adrian Av. NW2 —32Xa 60
Adrian Clo. Harr —25M 35
Adrian Ho. N1 —39Pb 62 (1J 193)
(off Barnsbury Est.)
Adrian M. SW10 —51Db 103
Adrian Rd. Abb L —3U 4
Adrienne Av. S'hall —42Ba 77
Adstock Way. Grays —49Be 91
Advance Rd. SE27 —63Sb 127
Advice Av. Grays —47Ce 91
Adys Lawn. NW2 —37Xa 60
Ady's Rd. SE15 —55Vb 105
Aerodrome Rd. NW9 & NW4 —27Va 40
Aerodrome Way. Houn —51Y 99
Aeroville. NW9 —26Ua 40
Affleck St. N1 —40Pb 62 (2J 193)
Afghan Rd. SW11 —54Gb 103
Afton Dri. S Ock —44Xd 90
Agamemnon Rd. NW6 —36Bb 61
Agar Clo. Surb —75Pa 143
Agar Gro. NW1 —38Lb 62
Agar Gro. Est. NW1 —38Mb 62
Agar Pl. NW1 —38Lb 62
Agars Pl. Dat —1L 95
Agar St. WC2 —45Nb 82 (5F 199)
Agate Clo. E16 —44Mc 85
Agate Rd. W6 —48Ya 80
Agates La. Asht —90Ma 161
Agatha Clo. E1 —46Xb 83
Agaton Rd. SE9 —61Sc 130
Agave Rd. NW2 —35Ya 60
Agdon St. EC1 —42Rb 83 (5B 194)
Agincourt Rd. NW3 —35Hb 61
Agister Rd. Chig —22Wc 47
Agnes Av. Ilf —35Qc 66
Agnes Clo. E6 —45Qc 86
Agnes Gdns. Dag —35Zc 67
Agnes Rd. W3 —46Va 80
Agnes St. E14 —44Bc 84
Agnew Rd. SE23 —59Zb 106
Agricola Pl. Enf —15Vb 25
Aidan Clo. Dag —34Ad 67
Aigburth Mans. SW9 —52Qb 104
(off Mowll St.)
Aileen Wlk. E15 —38Hc 65
Ailsa Av. Twic —57Ja 100
Ailsa Rd. Twic —57Ka 100
Ailsa St. E14 —43Ec 84
Ainger M. NW3 —38Hb 61
(off Ainger Rd.)
Ainger Rd. NW3 —38Hb 61
Ainsdale Clo. Orp —74Tc 150
Ainsdale Cres. Pinn —27Ca 37
Ainsdale Rd. W5 —42Ma 79
Ainsdale Rd. Wat —20Y 19
Ainsdale Way. Wok —6D 188
Ainsley Av. Romf —30Dd 48
Ainsley Clo. N9 —18Ub 25
Ainsley St. E2 —41Xb 83
Ainslie Ct. Wemb —40Na 59
Ainslie Wlk. SW12 —59Kb 104
Ainslie Wood Cres. E4 —22Dc 44
Ainslie Wood Gdns. E4 —21Dc 44
Ainslie Wood Rd. E4 —22Cc 44
Ainsty Est. SE16 —47Zb 84
Ainsty St. SE16 —47Yb 84
Ainsworth Clo. NW2 —34Wa 60
Ainsworth Rd. E9 —38Yb 64
Ainsworth Rd. Croy —75Rb 147
Ainsworth Way. NW8 —39Db 61
Aintree Av. E6 —39Nc 66
Aintree Clo. Coln —53G 96
Aintree Clo. Grav —2D 136
Aintree Clo. Uxb —44R 76
Aintree Cres. Ilf —26Sc 46
Aintree Est. SW6 —52Ab 102
(off Aintree St.)
Aintree Gro. Upm —34Pd 69
Aintree Rd. Gnfd —40Ka 58
Aintree St. SW6 —52Ab 102
Airbourne Ho. Wall —77Lb 146
(off Maldon Rd.)
Airdrie Clo. N1 —38Pb 62
Airdrie Clo. Hay —43Aa 77
Airedale Av. W4 —49Va 80
Airedale Av. S. W4 —50Va 80
Airedale Clo. Dart —60Sd 112
Airedale Rd. SW12 —59Hb 103
Airedale Rd. W5 —48La 78
Aire Dri. S Ock —42Xd 90
Airey Neave Ct. Grays —47Ce 91
Airfield Pathway. Horn —38Ld 69
Airfield Way. Horn —38Kd 69
Airlie Gdns. W8 —46Cb 81
Airlie Gdns. Ilf —32Rc 66
Airlinks Ind. Est. Houn —50Y 77
Airport Ind. Est. Big H —87Mc 167
Airport Way. Stai —56J 97
Air St. W1 —45Lb 82 (5C 198)
Airthrie Rd. Ilf —33Xc 67
Aisgill Av. W14 —50Bb 81
Aisher Rd. SE28 —45Yc 87
Aislibie Rd. SE12 —56Gc 107
Aitken Clo. E8 —39Wb 63
Aitken Rd. SE6 —61Dc 128
Aitken Rd. Barn —15Ya 22
Ajax Av. NW9 —27Ua 40
Ajax Av. Slou —5F 72
Ajax Rd. NW6 —36Bb 61
Akehurst La. Sev —97Ld 187
Akehurst St. SW15 —58Wa 102
Akenside Rd. NW3 —36Fb 61
Akerman Rd. SW9 —54Rb 105
Akerman Rd. Surb —72La 142
Akers La. Chor —16F 16
Alabama St. SE18 —52Tc 108
Alacross Rd. W5 —47La 78
Alamein Gdns. Dart —59Td 112
Alamein Rd. Swans —58Zd 113
Alan Barclay Clo. N15 —30Vb 43
Alanbrooke. Grav —9E 114
Alan Clo. Dart —56Ld 111
Alandale Dri. Pinn —25X 37
Aland Ct. SE16 —48Ac 84
Alan Dri. Barn —16Ab 22
Alan Gdns. Romf —31Cd 68
Alan Hilton Ct. Ott —79F 138
(off Cheshire Clo.)
Alan Hocken Way. E15 —40Gc 65
Alan Rd. SW19 —64Ab 124
Alanthus Clo. SE12 —58Jc 107
Alan Way. G Grn —44A 74
Alaska St. SE1 —46Qb 82 (7K 199)
Alba Clo. Hay —42Z 77
Albacore Cres. SE13 —58Dc 106
Alba Gdns. NW11 —30Ab 40
Albain Cres. Ashf —61N 119
Alban Cres. Borwd —11Qa 21
Alban Cres. F'ham —74Qd 153
Alban Highwalk. EC2
(in two parts) —43Sb 83 (1E 200)
Alban Ho. Borwd —11Ra 21
Albans View. Wat —5X 5
Albany. N12 —23Db 41
Albany. W1 —45Lb 82 (5B 198)
Albany Clo. N15 —28Rb 43
Albany Clo. SW14 —56Ra 101
Albany Clo. Bex —59Yc 109
Albany Clo. Bush —17Fa 20
Albany Clo. Esh —81Ca 159
Albany Clo. Uxb —36Q 56
Albany Ct. E4 —22Bc 44
Albany Ct. E10 —31Cc 64
Albany Ct. NW9 —25Ta 39
Albany Ct. Epp —2Vc 15
Albany Ct. Yd. W1 —45Lb 82 (5C 198)
(off Piccadilly)
Albany Cres. Clay —79Ga 142
Albany Cres. Edgw —24Qa 39
Albany M. N1 —38Qb 62
Albany M. SE5 —51Sb 105
Albany M. Brom —65Jc 129
Albany M. King T —65Ma 123
Albany M. Sutt —78Db 145
Albany Pde. Bren —51Na 101
Albany Pk. Coln —52F 96
Albany Pk. Av. Enf —11Yb 26
Albany Pk. Rd. King T —65Ma 123
Albany Pk. Rd. Lea —91Ja 176
Albany Pas. Rich —57Na 101
Albany Pl. N7 —35Qb 62
Albany Pl. Bren —51Ma 101
Albany Pl. Egh —63D 118
Albany Rd. E10 —31Cc 64
Albany Rd. E12 —35Mc 65
Albany Rd. E17 —30Ac 44
Albany Rd. N4 —30Qb 42
Albany Rd. N18 —22Xb 43
Albany Rd. SE5 —51Sb 105
Albany Rd. SW19 —64Db 125
Albany Rd. W13 —45Ka 78
Albany Rd. Belv —51Bd 109
Albany Rd. Bex —59Yc 109
Albany Rd. Bren —51Ma 101
Albany Rd. Chst —64Rc 130
Albany Rd. Enf —9Zb 12
Albany Rd. Horn —32Jd 68
Albany Rd. N Mald —70Ta 123
Albany Rd. Old Win —7L 95
Albany Rd. Pil H —16Xd 32
Albany Rd. Rich —57Pa 101
Albany Rd. Romf —30Bd 47
Albany Rd. Til —3C 114
Albany Rd. W on T —77Z 141
Albany Rd. Wind —4H 95
Albany St. NW1 —40Kb 62 (1K 191)
Albany Ter. NW1 —42Kb 82 (6A 192)
(off Marylebone Rd.)
Albany, The. Wfd G —21Hc 45
Albany View. Buck H —18Jc 27
Alba Pl. W11 —44Bb 81
Albatross. NW9 —26Va 40
Albatross Gdns. S Croy —83Zb 166
Albatross St. SE18 —52Uc 108
Albatross Way. SE16 —47Zb 84
Albemarle. SW19 —61Za 124
Albemarle Av. Chesh —1Yb 12
Albemarle Av. Pot B —4Db 9
Albemarle Clo. Grays —47Ce 91
Albemarle Gdns. N Mald —70Ta 123
Albemarle Pk. Stan —22La 38
Albemarle Rd. Barn —17Gb 23
Albemarle Rd. Beck —67Dc 128
Albemarle St. W1 —45Kb 82 (5A 198)
Albemarle Way. EC1 —42Rb 83 (6B 194)
Albermarle App. Ilf —30Rc 46
Albermarle Av. Twic —60Ba 99
Albermarle Gdns. Ilf —30Rc 46
Albermarle Ho. SW9 —55Qb 104
Alberon Gdns. NW11 —28Bb 41
Alberta Av. Sutt —77Ab 144
Alberta Est. SE17 —50Rb 83 (7C 206)
Alberta Rd. Enf —16Vb 25
Alberta Rd. Eri —53Ed 110
Alberta St. SE17 —50Rb 83 (7B 206)
Albert Av. E4 —21Cc 44
Albert Av. SW8 —52Pb 104
Albert Av. Cher —69J 119
Albert Bigg Point. E15 —39Ec 64
(off Godfrey St.)
Albert Bri. SW3 & SW11 —51Gb 103
Albert Bri. Rd. SW11 —52Gb 103
Albert Carr Gdns. SW16 —64Nb 126
Albert Clo. E9 —39Xb 63
Albert Clo. N22 —25Mb 42
Albert Clo. Grays —48Ee 91
Albert Clo. Slou —8K 73
Albert Ct. E7 —35Jc 65
Albert Ct. SW7 —47Fb 81 (2B 202)
Albert Cres. E4 —21Cc 44
Albert Dane Cen. S'hall —48Aa 77
Albert Dri. SW19 —61Ab 124
Albert Dri. Wok —87E 156
Albert Embkmt. SE1 —50Nb 82
Albert Gdns. E1 —44Zb 84
Albert Ga. SW1 —47Hb 81 (1G 203)
Albert Gro. SW20 —67Za 124
Albert Hall Mans. SW7 —47Fb 81 (2B 202)
Albert Ho. E18 —27Kc 45
(off Albert Rd.)
Albert M. N4 —32Pb 62
Albert M. W8 —48Eb 81
Albert Pl. N3 —25Cb 41
Albert Pl. N17 —27Vb 43
Albert Pl. W8 —47Db 81
Albert Pl. Eton W —10E 72
Albert Rd. E10 —33Ec 64
Albert Rd. E16 —46Nc 86
Albert Rd. E17 —29Cc 44
Albert Rd. E18 —27Kc 45
Albert Rd. N4 —32Pb 62
Albert Rd. N15 —30Ub 43
Albert Rd. N22 —25Lb 42
Albert Rd. NW4 —28Za 40
Albert Rd. NW6 —40Bb 61
Albert Rd. NW7 —22Va 40
Albert Rd. SE9 —62Nc 130
Albert Rd. SE20 —65Zb 128
Albert Rd. SE25 —70Wb 127
Albert Rd. W5 —42Ka 78
Albert Rd. Add —77M 139
Albert Rd. Ashf —64P 119
Albert Rd. Asht —90Pa 161
Albert Rd. Barn —14Eb 23
Albert Rd. Belv —50Bd 87
Albert Rd. Bex —58Cd 110
Albert Rd. Brom —71Mc 149
Albert Rd. Buck H —19Mc 27
Albert Rd. Chels —78Wc 151

Albert Rd.—Alpine Rd.

Albert Rd. Dag —32Cd 68
Albert Rd. Dart —62Ld 133
Albert Rd. Egh —5P 117
Albert Rd. Eps —85Va 162
Albert Rd. Hamp —64Ea 122
Albert Rd. Harr —27Ea 38
Albert Rd. Hay —48U 76
Albert Rd. Houn —56Ca 99
Albert Rd. Ilf —34Rc 66
Albert Rd. King T —68Pa 123
Albert Rd. Mitc —69Hb 125
Albert Rd. N Mald —70Va 124
Albert Rd. Old Win —5H 95
Albert Rd. Red —100Lb 180
Albert Rd. Rich —57Na 101
Albert Rd. Romf —29Hd 48
Albert Rd. S'hall —48Z 77
Albert Rd. St M —72Xc 151
Albert Rd. Sutt —78Fb 145
Albert Rd. Swans —58Be 113
Albert Rd. Tedd —65Ha 122
Albert Rd. Twic —60Ha 100
Albert Rd. Warl —90Bc 166
Albert Rd. W Dray —46N 75
Albert Rd. Est. Belv —50Bd 87
Albert Rd. N. Wat —13X 19
Albert Rd. S. Wat —13X 19
Albert Sq. E15 —36Gc 65
Albert Sq. SW8 —52Pb 104
Albert Starr Ho. SE8 —49Zb 84
(off Haddonfield)
Albert St. N12 —22Eb 41
Albert St. NW1 —39Kb 62 (1A 192)
Albert St. Slou —8K 73
Albert St. War —22Yd 50
Albert St. Wind —3F 94
Albert Studios. SW11 —53Hb 103
Albert Ter. NW1 —39Jb 62
Albert Ter. NW10 —39Sa 59
Albert Ter. Buck H —19Nc 28
Albert Ter. M. NW1 —39Jb 62
Albert Victoria Ho. N22 —25Qb 42
(off Pellatt Gro.)
Albert Wlk. E16 —47Qc 86
Albert Westcott Ho. SE17
—50Rb 83 (7C 206)
Albert Whicker Ho. E17 —28Ec 44
Albert Yd. SE19 —65Vb 127
Albion Av. N10 —25Jb 42
Albion Av. SW8 —54Mb 104
Albion Clo. W2 —45Gb 81 (4E 196)
Albion Clo. Romf —30Fd 48
Albion Clo. Slou —6L 73
Albion Dri. E8 —38Vb 63
Albion Est. SE16 —47Zb 84
Albion Gdns. W6 —49Xa 80
Albion Gro. N16 —35Ub 63
Albion Hill. Lou —15Lc 27
Albion Ho. E16 —46Rc 86
(off Church St.)
Albion Ho. Langl —50D 74
Albion M. N1 —39Qb 62
Albion M. NW6 —38Bb 61
Albion M. W2 —45Gb 81 (4E 196)
Albion M. W6 —49Xa 80
Albion Pde. Grav —8F 114
Albion Pk. Lou —15Mc 27
Albion Pl. EC1 —43Rb 83 (7B 194)
Albion Pl. EC2 —43Tb 83 (1G 201)
Albion Pl. SE25 —69Wb 127
Albion Pl. W6 —49Xa 80
Albion Rd. E17 —27Ec 44
Albion Rd. N16 —35Tb 63
Albion Rd. N17 —26Vb 43
Albion Rd. Bexh —56Bd 109
Albion Rd. Grav —9E 114
Albion Rd. Hay —44U 76
Albion Rd. Houn —56Ca 99
Albion Rd. King T —67Sa 123
Albion Rd. Sutt —79Fb 145
Albion Rd. Twic —60Ga 100
Albion Sq. E8 —38Vb 63
Albion St. SE16 —47Yb 84
Albion St. W2 —44Gb 81 (3E 196)
Albion St. Croy —74Rb 147
Albion Ter. E8 —38Vb 63
Albion Ter. Grav —8E 114
Albion Vs. Rd. SE26 —62Yb 128
Albion Way. EC1 —43Sb 83 (1D 200)
Albion Way. SE13 —56Ec 106
Albion Way. Wemb —34Qa 59
Albion Yd. N1 —40Nb 62 (2G 193)
Albrighton Rd. SE22 —55Ub 105
Albuhera Clo. Enf —11Qb 24
Albury Av. Bexh —54Ad 109
Albury Av. Iswth —52Ha 100
Albury Av. Sutt —81Ya 162
Albury Clo. Hamp —65Da 121
Albury Ct. Sutt —77Eb 145
Albury Dri. Pinn —25Y 37
Albury Gro. Rd. Chesh —2Zb 12
Albury Pl. Mers —100Lb 180
Albury Ride. Chesh —3Zb 12
Albury Rd. Chess —78Na 143
Albury Rd. Red —100Lb 180
Albury Rd. W on T —79U 140
Albury St. SE8 —51Cc 106
Albury Wlk. Chesh —2Yb 12
(in two parts)
Albyfield. Brom —70Pc 130
Albyn Rd. SE8 —53Cc 106
Albyns Clo. Rain —38Jd 68
Alcester Cres. E5 —33Xb 63
Alcester Rd. Wall —77Kb 146
Alcock Clo. Wall —80Mb 146
Alcock Rd. Houn —52Z 99
Alcocks Clo. Tad —92Ab 178
Alcocks La. Tad —93Ab 178
Alconbury. Bexh —57Dd 110
Alconbury Rd. E5 —33Wb 63
Alcorn Clo. Sutt —75Cb 145
Alcott Clo. W7 —43Ha 78
Alcuin Ct. Stan —24La 38
Aldam Pl. N16 —33Vb 63
Aldborough Rd. Dag —37Ed 68
Aldborough Rd. Upm —33Pd 69
Aldborough Rd. N. Ilf —29Vc 47
Aldborough Rd. S. Ilf —32Uc 66
Aldborough Spur. Slou —4J 73
Aldbourne Rd. W12 —46Va 80
Aldbourne Rd. Burn —3A 72
Aldbridge St. SE17
—50Ub 83 (7J 207)
Aldburgh M. W1 —44Jb 82 (2J 197)
(in two parts)
Aldbury Av. Wemb —38Ra 59
Aldbury Clo. Wat —8Z 5
Aldbury M. N9 —17Tb 25
Aldbury Rd. Rick —17H 17
Aldebert Ter. SW8 —52Nb 104
Aldeburgh Clo. E5 —33Xb 63
Aldeburgh Pl. Wfd G —21Jc 45
Alden Av. E15 —42Hc 85
Alden Ct. Croy —76Ub 147
Aldenham Av. Rad —8Ja 6
Aldenham Dri. Uxb —42R 76
Aldenham Gro. Rad —6Ka 6
Aldenham Rd. Els —13Ja 20
Aldenham Rd. Let H & Borwd
—11Ga 20
Aldenham Rd. Rad —7Ja 6
Aldenham Rd. Wat & Bush
—16Aa 19
Aldenham St. NW1
—40Lb 62 (2C 192)
Aldenholme. Wey —79U 140
Aldensley Rd. W6 —48Xa 80
Alden View. Wind —3B 94
Alder Av. Upm —35Pd 69
Alderbourne La. Ful & Iver —35A 54
Alderbrook Rd. SW12 —58Kb 104
Alderburgh St. SE10 —50Jc 85
Alderbury Rd. SW13 —51Wa 102
Alderbury Rd. Slou —47B 74
Alderbury Rd. W. Slou —47B 74
Alder Clo. SE15 —51Vb 105
Alder Clo. Egh —64A 118
Alder Clo. Park —1Ea 6
Alder Clo. Slou —6D 72
Aldercombe La. Cat —99Ub 181
Aldercroft. Coul —88Pb 164
Alder Gro. NW2 —33Wa 60
Aldergrove Gdns. Houn —54Aa 99
Aldergrove Wlk. Horn —37Ld 69
Alderholt Way. SE15 —52Ub 105
Alder Lodge. SW6 —53Za 102
Alderman Av. Bark —41Wc 87
Aldermanbury. EC2
—44Sb 83 (2E 200)
Aldermanbury Sq. EC2
—43Sb 83 (1E 200)
Alderman Judge Mall. King T
—68Na 123
Aldermans Hill. N13 —21Nb 42
Aldermans Wlk. EC2
—43Ub 83 (1H 201)
Aldermary Rd. Brom —67Jc 129
Alder M. N19 —33Lb 62
Alderminster Rd. SE1 —50Wb 83
Aldermoor Rd. SE6 —62Bc 128
Alderney Av. Houn —52Da 99
Alderney Gdns. N'holt —38Ba 57
Alderney Ho. Enf —10Zb 12
Alderney Rd. E1 —42Zb 84
Alderney Rd. Eri —52Jd 110
Alderney St. SW1
—49Kb 82 (6A 204)
Alder Rd. SW14 —55Ta 101
Alder Rd. Den —37L 55
Alder Rd. Iver —40F 54
Alder Rd. Sidc —62Vc 131
Alders Av. Wfd G —23Gc 45
Aldersbrook Av. Enf —12Ub 25
Aldersbrook Dri. King T —65Pa 123
Aldersbrook La. E12 —34Pc 66
Aldersbrook Rd. E11 & E12
—33Kc 65
Alders Clo. E11 —33Kc 65
Alders Clo. W5 —48Ma 79
Alders Clo. Edgw —22Sa 39
Aldersey Gdns. Bark —37Tc 66
Aldersford Clo. SE4 —57Zb 106
Aldersgate St. EC1
—43Sb 83 (7D 194)
Alders Gro. E Mol —71Fa 142
Aldersgrove. Wal A —6Gc 13
Aldersgrove Av. SE9 —62Mc 129
Aldershot Rd. NW6 —39Bb 61
Alderside Wlk. Egh —64A 118
Aldersmead Av. Croy —72Zb 148
Aldersmead Rd. Beck —66Ac 128
Alderson Pl. S'hall —46Ea 78
Alderson St. W10 —42Ab 80
Alders Rd. Edgw —22Sa 39
Alderstead La. Red —97Mb 180
Alders, The. N21 —16Rb 25
Alders, The. SW16 —63Lb 126
Alders, The. Felt —63Aa 121
Alders, The. Houn —51Ba 99
Alders, The. W Wick —75Dc 148
Alderton Clo. NW10 —34Ta 59
Alderton Clo. Lou —14Qc 28
Alderton Clo. Pil H —15Xd 32
Alderton Cres. NW4 —29Xa 40
Alderton Hall La. Lou —14Qc 28
Alderton Hill. Lou —15Nc 28
Alderton Rise. Lou —14Qc 28
Alderton Rd. SE24 —55Sb 105
Alderton Rd. Croy —73Vb 147
Alderton Rd. Ors —5F 92
Alderton Way. NW4 —29Xa 40
Alderton Way. Lou —15Pc 28
Alderville Rd. SW6 —54Bb 103
Alder Wlk. Wat —7X 5
Alder Way. Swan —68Fd 132
Alderwick Dri. Houn —55Fa 100
Alderwood Clo. Abr —13Xc 29
Alderwood Clo. Cat —97Ub 181
Alderwood Dri. Abr —13Xc 29
Alderwood Rd. SE9 —58Tc 108
Aldford St. W1 —46Jb 82 (6H 197)
Aldgate. EC3 —44Ub 83 (3K 201)
Aldgate Av. E1 —44Vb 83 (2K 201)
Aldgate Barrs. E1
—44Vb 83 (2K 201)
Aldgate High St. EC3
—44Vb 83 (3K 201)
Aldin Av. N. Slou —7L 73
Aldin Av. S. Slou —7L 73
Aldine Ct. W12 —47Ya 80
(off Aldine St.)
Aldine Pl. W12 —47Ya 80
Aldine St. W12 —47Ya 80
Aldingham Ct. Horn —36Kd 69
(off Easedale Dri.)
Aldingham Gdns. Horn —36Jd 68
Aldington Clo. Dag —32Yc 67
Aldington Ct. E8 —38Wb 63
Aldington Rd. SE18 —48Mc 85
Aldis M. SW17 —64Gb 125
Aldis St. SW17 —64Gb 125
Aldred Rd. NW6 —36Cb 61
Aldren Rd. SW17 —62Eb 125
Aldrich Cres. New Ad —81Ec 166
Aldriche Way. E4 —23Ec 44
Aldrich Ter. SW18 —61Eb 125
Aldridge Av. Edgw —20Ra 21
Aldridge Av. Enf —10Cc 12
Aldridge Av. Ruis —33Y 57
Aldridge Av. Stan —25Na 39
Aldridge Rise. N Mald —73Ua 144
Aldridge Rd. Slou —2E 72
Aldridge Rd. Vs. W11 —43Bb 81
Aldridge Wlk. N14 —17Nb 24
Aldrin Clo. Stanf —1N 93
Aldrington Rd. SW16 —64Lb 126
Aldsworth Clo. W9 —42Db 81
Aldwick Clo. SE9 —62Tc 130
Aldwick Rd. Croy —76Pb 146
Aldworth Gro. SE13 —58Ec 106
Aldworth Rd. E15 —38Gc 65
Aldwych. WC2 —44Pb 82 (4H 199)
Aldwych Av. Ilf —28Sc 46
Aldwych Clo. Horn —33Jd 68
Alers Rd. Bexh —57Zc 109
Alestan Beck Rd. E16 —44Mc 85
Alexa Ct. W8 —49Db 81
Alexa Ct. Sutt —79Cb 145
Alexander Av. NW10 —38Xa 60
Alexander Clo. Barn —14Fb 23
Alexander Clo. Brom —74Jc 149
Alexander Clo. Sidc —58Uc 108
Alexander Clo. S'hall —46Ea 78
Alexander Clo. Twic —61Ha 122
Alexander Ct. SE16 —46Bc 84
Alexander Ct. Beck —67Fc 129
Alexander Ct. Chesh —2Zb 12
(off Turner's Hill)
Alexander Ct. Stan —27Pa 39
Alexander Evans M. SE23
—61Zb 128
Alexander Godley Clo. Asht
—91Pa 177
Alexander La. Hut & Shenf
—16De 33
Alexander M. W2 —44Db 81
Alexander Pl. SW7
—49Gb 81 (5D 202)
Alexander Rd. N19 —34Nb 62
Alexander Rd. Bexh —54Zc 109
Alexander Rd. Chst —65Rc 130
Alexander Rd. Coul —87Kb 164
Alexander Rd. Egh —64E 118
Alexander Rd. Grnh —57Yd 112
Alexander Sq. SW3 —49Gb 81
Alexander St. W2 —44Cb 81
Alexanders Wlk. Cat —98Vb 181
Alexandra Av. N22 —25Mb 42
Alexandra Av. SW11 —53Jb 104
Alexandra Av. W4 —52Ta 101
Alexandra Av. Harr —32Ba 57
Alexandra Av. S'hall —45Ba 77
Alexandra Av. Sutt —76Cb 145
Alexandra Av. Warl —89Bc 166
Alexandra Clo. Ashf —66T 120
Alexandra Clo. Grays —7D 92
Alexandra Clo. Harr —34Ca 57
Alexandra Clo. Stai —65M 119
Alexandra Clo. Swan —68Gd 132
Alexandra Clo. W on T —75W 140
Alexandra Cotts. SE14 —53Bc 106
Alexandra Ct. N14 —15Lb 24
Alexandra Ct. Ashf —65T 120
Alexandra Ct. Houn —54Da 99
Alexandra Cres. Brom —65Hc 129
Alexandra Dri. SE19 —64Ub 127
Alexandra Dri. Surb —73Qa 143
Alexandra Gdns. N10 —28Kb 42
Alexandra Gdns. W4 —52Ua 102
Alexandra Gdns. Cars —80Jb 146
Alexandra Gdns. Houn —54Da 99
Alexandra Gro. N4 —32Rb 63
Alexandra Gro. N12 —22Db 41
Alexandra M. N2 —27Hb 41
Alexandra M. SW19 —65Bb 125
Alexandra Pal. Way. N22 —28Lb 42
Alexandra Pk. Rd. N10 —26Kb 42
Alexandra Pk. Rd. N22 —25Lb 42
Alexandra Pl. NW8 —39Eb 61
Alexandra Pl. SE25 —71Tb 147
Alexandra Pl. Croy —74Ub 147
Alexandra Rd. E6 —41Qc 86
Alexandra Rd. E10 —34Ec 64
Alexandra Rd. E17 —30Bc 44
Alexandra Rd. E18 —27Kc 45
Alexandra Rd. N8 —27Qb 42
Alexandra Rd. N9 —17Xb 25
Alexandra Rd. N10 —25Kb 42
Alexandra Rd. N15 —29Tb 43
Alexandra Rd. NW4 —28Za 40
Alexandra Rd. NW8 —39Eb 61
Alexandra Rd. SE26 —65Zb 128
Alexandra Rd. SW14 —55Ta 101
Alexandra Rd. SW19 —65Bb 125
Alexandra Rd. W4 —47Ta 79
Alexandra Rd. Add —77M 139
Alexandra Rd. Ashf —66T 120
Alexandra Rd. Big H —91Kc 183
Alexandra Rd. Borwd —10Ta 7
Alexandra Rd. Bren —51Ma 101
Alexandra Rd. Brtwd —20Yd 32
Alexandra Rd. Chad —30Ad 47
Alexandra Rd. Chfd —2J 3
Alexandra Rd. Croy —74Ub 147
Alexandra Rd. Egh —5N 117
Alexandra Rd. Enf —14Zb 26
Alexandra Rd. Eps —85Va 162
Alexandra Rd. Eri —51Hd 110
Alexandra Rd. Grav —9G 114
Alexandra Rd. Houn —54Da 99
Alexandra Rd. K Lan —1Q 4
Alexandra Rd. King T —66Qa 123
Alexandra Rd. Mitc —66Gb 125
Alexandra Rd. Rain —39Hd 68
Alexandra Rd. Rich —54Pa 101
Alexandra Rd. Romf —30Hd 48
Alexandra Rd. Sarr —8J 3
Alexandra Rd. Slou —8H 73
Alexandra Rd. Th Dit —71Ha 142
Alexandra Rd. Til —4B 114
Alexandra Rd. Twic —58La 100
Alexandra Rd. Uxb —40M 55
Alexandra Rd. Warl —89Bc 166
Alexandra Rd. Wat —12W 18
Alexandra Rd. Wind —4H 95
Alexandra Rd. / Alma Rd. Ind. Est. Enf
—14Zb 26
Alexandra Sq. SW3
—49Gb 81 (5D 202)
Alexandra Sq. Mord —71Cb 145
Alexandra St. E16 —43Jc 85
Alexandra St. SE14 —52Ac 106
Alexandra Wlk. SE19 —64Ub 127
Alexandra Way. Til —9K 93
Alexandra Way. Wal X —6Bc 12
Alexandra Yd. E9 —39Zb 64
Alexandria Rd. W13 —45Ja 78
Alexis St. SE16 —49Wb 83
Alfan La. Dart —64Fd 132
Alfearn Rd. E5 —35Yb 64
Alford Grn. New Ad —79Fc 149
Alford Ho. N6 —30Lb 42
Alford Pl. N1 —40Sb 63 (2E 194)
Alford Rd. Eri —50Ed 88
Alfoxton Av. N15 —28Rb 43
Alfreda St. SW11 —53Kb 104
Alfred Finlay Ho. N22 —26Rb 43
Alfred Gdns. S'hall —45Aa 77
Alfred Ho. E9 —36Ac 64
(off Homerton Rd.)
Alfred Ho. Grav —10B 114
Alfred La. Felt —61Y 121
Alfred M. W1 —43Mb 82 (7D 192)
Alfred Pl. WC1 —43Mb 82 (7D 192)
Alfred Pl. Grav —10B 114
Alfred Prior Ho. E12 —35Qc 66
Alfred Rd. E15 —36Hc 65
Alfred Rd. SE25 —71Wb 147
Alfred Rd. SW8 —53Mb 104
Alfred Rd. W2 —43Cb 81
Alfred Rd. W3 —46Sa 79
Alfred Rd. Belv —50Bd 87
Alfred Rd. Brtwd —19Zd 33
Alfred Rd. Buck H —19Mc 27
Alfred Rd. Dart —63Nd 133
(in two parts)
Alfred Rd. Grav —1D 136
Alfred Rd. King T —69Na 123
Alfred Rd. S Ock —46Sd 90
Alfred Rd. Sutt —78Eb 145
Alfred's Gdns. Bark —40Uc 66
Alfred St. E3 —41Bc 84
Alfred St. Grays —51Ee 113
Alfreds Way. Bark —41Rc 86
Alfred's Way Ind. Est. Bark
—40Wc 67
Alfreton Clo. SW19 —62Za 124
Alfriston. Surb —72Pa 143
Alfriston Av. Croy —73Nb 146
Alfriston Av. Harr —30Ca 37
Alfriston Clo. Surb —71Pa 143
Alfriston Rd. SW11 —57Hb 103
Algar Clo. Iswth —55Ja 100
Algar Clo. Stan —22Ha 38
Algar Ho. SE1 —47Rb 83 (2B 206)
(off Webber Row)
Algar Rd. Iswth —55Ja 100
Algarve Rd. SW18 —60Db 103
Algernon Rd. NW4 —30Wa 40
Algernon Rd. NW6 —39Cb 61
Algernon Rd. SE13 —56Dc 106
Algers Clo. Lou —15Mc 27
Algers Mead. Lou —15Mc 27
Algers Rd. Lou —15Mc 27
Algiers Rd. SE13 —56Cc 106
Alibon Gdns. Dag —36Cd 68
Alibon Rd. Dag —36Bd 67
Alice Burrell Cen. E10 —33Ec 64
(off Sidmouth Rd.)
Alice Ct. SW15 —56Bb 103
Alice Gilliatt Ct. W14 —51Bb 103
(off Star Rd.)
Alice La. E3 —39Bc 64
Alice M. Tedd —64Ha 122
Alice Ruston Pl. Wok —7F 188
Alice St. SE1 —48Ub 83 (3H 207)
Alice Thompson Clo. SE12
—61Lc 129
Alice Walker Clo. SE24 —56Rb 105
Alice Way. Houn —56Da 99
Alicia Av. Harr —28Ka 38
Alicia Clo. Harr —29La 38
Alicia Gdns. Harr —28Ka 38
Alicia Rd. Ilf —33Wc 67
Alie St. E1 —44Vb 83 (3K 201)
Alington Cres. NW9 —31Sa 59
Alington Gro. Wall —81Lb 164
Alison Clo. E6 —44Qc 86
Alison Clo. Croy —74Zb 148
Alison Clo. Wok —87A 156
Aliwal Rd. SW11 —56Gb 103
Alkerden La. Grnh & Swans
—58Yd 112
Alkerden Rd. W4 —50Ua 80
Alkham Rd. N16 —33Vb 63
Allan Clo. N Mald —71Ta 143
Allandale Av. N3 —27Ab 40
Allandale Cres. Pot B —4Ab 8
Allandale Pl. Orp —76Zc 151
Allandale Rd. Enf —8Zb 12
Allandale Rd. Horn —31Hd 68
Allan Way. W3 —43Sa 79
Allard Clo. Orp —73Yc 151
Allard Cres. Bush —18Ea 20
Allard Gdns. SW4 —57Mb 104
Allardyce St. SW4 —56Pb 104
Allbrook Clo. Tedd —64Ga 122
Allcot Clo. Felt —60V 98
Allcroft Rd. NW5 —36Jb 62
Allenby Av. S Croy —81Sb 165
Allenby Clo. Gnfd —41Ca 77
Allenby Cres. Grays —50De 91
Allenby Dri. Horn —32Nd 69
Allenby Rd. SE23 —62Ac 128
Allenby Rd. Big H —89Nc 168
Allenby Rd. S'hall —44Ca 77
Allen Clo. Sun —67X 121
Allen Ct. E17 —30Cc 44
(off Yunus Khan Clo.)
Allen Ct. Gnfd —36Ha 58
Allendale Av. S'hall —44Ca 77
Allendale Clo. SE5 —54Tb 105
Allendale Clo. SE26 —64Zb 128
Allendale Clo. Dart —60Td 112
Allendale Rd. Gnfd —37Ka 58
Allen Edwards Dri. SW8 —53Nb 104
Allen Ho. Pk. Wok —8F 188
Allen Rd. E3 —39Bc 64
Allen Rd. N16 —35Ub 63
Allen Rd. Beck —68Zb 128
Allen Rd. Bookh —98Da 175
Allen Rd. Croy —74Qb 146
Allen Rd. Rain —41Ld 89
Allen Rd. Sun —67X 121
Allensbury Pl. NW1 —38Mb 62
Allens Rd. Enf —15Yb 26
Allen St. W8 —48Cb 81
Allensway. Stanf —1P 93
Allenswood Rd. SE9 —55Nc 108
Allerds Rd. Farn R —9D 52
Allerford Ct. Harr —29Ea 38
Allerford Rd. SE6 —62Dc 128
Allerton Clo. Borwd —10Pa 7
Allerton Ho. N1 —40Tb 63 (2F 195)
(off Provost Est.)
Allerton Rd. N16 —33Sb 63
Allerton Rd. Borwd —10Na 7
Allerton Wlk. N7 —33Pb 62
Allestree Rd. SW6 —52Ab 102
Alleyn Cres. SE21 —61Tb 127
Alleyndale Rd. Dag —33Yc 67
Alleyn Pk. SE21 —61Tb 127
Alleyn Pk. S'hall —50Ca 77
Alleyn Rd. SE21 —62Tb 127
Allfarthing La. SW18 —58Db 103
Allgood Clo. Mord —72Za 144
Allgood St. E2 —40Vb 63
Allhallows La. EC4
—45Tb 83 (5F 201)
Allhallows Rd. E6 —43Nc 86
All Hallows Rd. N17 —25Ub 43
Allhusen Gdns. Ful —35A 54
Alliance Clo. Wemb —35Ma 59
Alliance Rd. E13 —43Lc 85
Alliance Rd. SE18 —51Wc 109
Alliance Rd. W3 —42Ra 79
Allied Ind. Est. W3 —47Ua 80
Allied Way. W3 —47Ua 80
Allingham Clo. W7 —45Ha 78
Allingham St. N1
—40Sb 63 (1D 194)
Allington Av. N17 —23Ub 43
Allington Clo. SW19 —64Za 124
Allington Clo. Grav —10H 115
Allington Clo. Gnfd —38Ea 58
Allington Ct. Enf —15Zb 26
Allington Ct. Slou —4K 73
Allington Rd. NW4 —29Xa 40
Allington Rd. W10 —41Ab 80
Allington Rd. Harr —29Ea 38
Allington Rd. Orp —75Tc 150
Allington St. SW1
—48Kb 82 (4A 204)
Allison Clo. SE10 —53Ec 106
Allison Clo. Wal A —4Jc 13
Allison Gro. SE21 —60Ub 105
Allison Rd. N8 —29Qb 42
Allison Rd. W3 —44Sa 79
Alliston Way. Stanf —1P 93
Allitsen Rd. NW8
—40Gb 61 (2D 190)
Allnuts Rd. Epp —4Wc 15
Allnutt Way. SW4 —57Mb 104
Alloa Rd. SE8 —50Zb 84
Alloa Rd. Ilf —33Wc 67
Allonby Dri. Ruis —31R 56
Allonby Gdns. Wemb —32La 58
Allotment La. Sev —94Ld 187
Alloway Clo. Wok —6E 188
Alloway Rd. E3 —41Ac 84
All Saints Clo. N9 —19Vb 25
All Saints Clo. Chig —20Xc 29
All Saints Clo. Swans —57Be 113
All Saints Ct. Houn —53Z 99
(off Springwell Rd.)
All Saints Cres. Wat —5Z 5
All Saints Dri. SE3 —54Gc 107
All Saints Dri. S Croy —84Vb 165
All Saints La. Crox —16Q 18
All Saints M. Harr —23Ga 38
All Saints Pas. SW18 —57Cb 103
All Saints Rd. SW19 —66Eb 125
All Saints Rd. W3 —48Sa 79
All Saints Rd. W11 —43Bb 81
All Saints Rd. Grav —10B 114
All Saints Rd. Sutt —76Db 145
All Saints St. N1
—40Pb 62 (1H 193)
All Saints Tower. E10 —31Dc 64
All Seasons Ct. E1 —46Wb 83
(off Aragon M.)
Allsop Pl. NW1 —42Hb 81 (6G 191)
All Souls Av. NW10 —40Xa 60
All Souls' Pl. W1 —43Kb 82 (1A 198)
Allum Clo. Els —14Na 21
Allum Gro. Tad —93Xa 178
Allum La. Els —15Na 21
Allum Way. N20 —18Eb 23
Allwood Clo. SE26 —63Zb 128
Allyn Clo. Stai —65H 119
Alma Av. E4 —24Ec 44
Alma Av. Horn —35Nd 69
Almack Rd. E5 —35Yb 64
Alma Clo. N10 —25Kb 42
(off Alma Rd.)
Alma Clo. Knap —5B 188
Alma Ct. Borwd —10Pa 7
Alma Ct. Burn —1A 72
Alma Ct. Cat —93Sb 181
(off Coulsdon Rd.)
Alma Cres. Sutt —78Ab 144
Alma Gro. SE1 —49Vb 83
Alma Ho. Bren —51Na 101
Alma Pl. NW10 —41Xa 80
Alma Pl. SE19 —66Vb 127
Alma Pl. T Hth —71Qb 146
Alma Rd. N10 —24Kb 42
Alma Rd. SW18 —56Eb 103
Alma Rd. Cars —78Gb 145
Alma Rd. Enf —15Ac 26
Alma Rd. Esh —74Ga 142
Alma Rd. Eton W —9D 72
Alma Rd. Orp —75Zc 151
Alma Rd. Sidc —62Wc 131
Alma Rd. S'hall —45Aa 77
Alma Rd. Swans —57Be 113
Alma Rd. Wind —4G 94
Alma Row. Harr —25Fa 38
Alma Sq. NW8 —40Eb 61 (3A 190)
Alma St. E15 —37Fc 65
Alma St. NW5 —37Kb 62
Alma Ter. SW18 —59Fb 103
Alma Ter. W8 —48Cb 81
Alma, The. Grav —3H 137
Almeida St. N1 —39Rb 63
Almeric Rd. SW11 —56Hb 103
Almer Rd. SW20 —66Wa 124
Almington St. N4 —32Pb 62
Almners Rd. Lyne —74C 138
Almond Av. W5 —48Ma 79
Almond Av. Cars —75Hb 145
Almond Av. Uxb —34R 56
Almond Av. W Dray —48Q 76
Almond Av. Wok —9G 188
Almond Clo. SE15 —54Wb 105
Almond Clo. Brom —73Qc 150
Almond Clo. Egh —5M 117
Almond Clo. Grays —8C 92
Almond Clo. Hay —45U 76
Almond Clo. Ruis —34V 56
Almond Clo. Shep —68S 120
Almond Clo. Wind —4F 94
Almond Dri. Swan —68Fd 132
Almond Gro. Bren —52Ka 100
Almond Rd. N17 —24Wb 43
Almond Rd. SE16 —49Xb 83
Almond Rd. Burn —10A 52
Almond Rd. Dart —59Sd 112
Almond Rd. Eps —83Ta 161
Almonds Av. Buck H —19Jc 27
Almondsbury Ct. SE15 —52Ub 105
(off Lynbrook Clo.)
Almond Ville. Burn —1A 72
Almond Way. Borwd —14Ra 21
Almond Way. Brom —73Qc 150
Almond Way. Harr —26Da 37
Almond Way. Mitc —71Mb 146
Almons Way. Slou —3M 73
Almorah Rd. N1 —38Tb 63
Almorah Rd. Houn —53Z 99
Alms Heath. Ock —93R 174
Almshouse La. Chess —81Ma 161
Almshouse La. Enf —9Xb 11
Alms Row. Bras —96Xc 185
Alnwick. N17 —24Xb 43
Alnwick Gro. Mord —70Db 125
Alnwick Rd. E16 —44Lc 85
Alnwick Rd. SE12 —59Kc 107
Alperton La. Gnfd & Wemb
—41La 78
Alperton St. W10 —42Bb 81
Alphabet Gdns. Cars —72Fb 145
Alphabet Sq. E3 —43Cc 84
Alpha Bus. Cen. E17 —29Bc 44
Alpha Clo. NW1 —42Gb 81 (4E 190)
Alpha Est. Hay —47U 76
Alpha Gro. E14 —47Cc 84
Alpha Pl. NW6 —40Cb 61
Alpha Pl. SW3 —51Gb 103
Alpha Rd. E4 —20Cc 26
Alpha Rd. N18 —23Wb 43
Alpha Rd. SE14 —53Bc 106
Alpha Rd. Croy —74Ub 147
Alpha Rd. Enf —14Ac 26
Alpha Rd. Hut —16Fe 33
Alpha Rd. Surb —72Pa 143
Alpha Rd. Tedd —64Fa 122
Alpha Rd. Uxb —42R 76
Alpha Rd. Wok —88D 156
Alpha St. SE15 —54Wb 105
Alpha St. N. Slou —7L 73
Alpha St. S. Slou —8K 73
Alpha Way. Egh —67E 118
Alphea Clo. SW19 —66Gb 125
Alpine Av. Surb —75Sa 143
Alpine Bus. Cen. E6 —43Qc 86
Alpine Clo. Croy —76Ub 147
Alpine Copse. Brom —68Qc 130
Alpine Rd. SE16 —49Zb 84
(in two parts)

Alpine Rd.—Archibald M.

Alpine Rd. W on T —73W 140
Alpine View. Sutt —78Gb 145
Alpine Wlk. Stan —19Ga 20
Alpine Way. E6 —43Qc 86
Alric Av. NW10 —38Ta 59
Alric Av. N Mald —69Ua 124
Alroy Rd. N4 —31Qb 62
Alsace Rd. SE17 —50Ub 83 (7H 207)
Alscot Rd. SE1 —49Vb 83 (5K 207) (in three parts)
Alscot Way. SE1 —49Vb 83 (5K 207)
Alsike Rd. Eri —48Zc 87
Alsom Av. Wor Pk —77Wa 144
Alston Clo. Surb —73Ka 142
Alston Rd. N18 —22Xb 43
Alston Rd. SW17 —63Fb 125
Alston Rd. Barn —13Ab 22
Altair Clo. N17 —23Vb 43
Altair Way. N'wd —21V 36
Altash Way. SE9 —61Pc 130
Altenburg Av. W13 —48Ka 78
Altenburg Gdns. SW11 —56Hb 103
Alterton Clo. Wok —5D 188
Alt Gro. SW19 —66Bb 125
Altham Rd. Pinn —24Aa 37
Althea St. SW6 —54Db 103
Althorne Gdns. E18 —28Hc 45
Althorne Way. Dag —33Cd 68
Althorpe M. SW11 —53Fb 103 (in two parts)
Althorpe Rd. Harr —29Ea 38
Althorp Rd. SW17 —60Hb 103
Altior Ct. N6 —30Lb 42
Altmore Av. E6 —38Pc 66
Alton Av. Stan —24Ha 38
Altona Way. Slou —4F 72
Alton Clo. Bex —60Ad 109
Alton Clo. Iswth —54Ha 100
Alton Cotts. F'ham —74Nd 153
Alton Ct. Stai —67G 118
Alton Gdns. Beck —66Cc 128
Alton Gdns. Twic —59Fa 100
Alton Rd. N17 —27Tb 43
Alton Rd. SW15 —60Wa 102
Alton Rd. Croy —76Qb 146
Alton Rd. Rich —56Na 101
Alton St. E14 —44Dc 84
Altwood Clo. Slou —3C 72
Altyre Clo. Beck —71Bc 148
Altyre Rd. Croy —75Tb 147
Altyre Way. Beck —71Bc 148
Alvanley Gdns. NW6 —36Db 61
Alva Way. Wat —19Z 19
Alverstoke Rd. Romf —24Nd 49
Alverstone Av. SW19 —61Cb 125
Alverstone Av. Barn —17Gb 23
Alverstone Gdns. SE9 —60Sc 108
Alverstone Ho. SE11 —51Qb 104
Alverstone Rd. E12 —35Qc 66
Alverstone Rd. NW2 —38Ya 60
Alverstone Rd. N Mald —70Va 124
Alverstone Rd. Wemb —32Pa 59
Alverston Gdns. SE25 —71Ub 147
Alverton Rd. N16 —33Sb 63
Alverton St. SE8 —50Bc 84 (in two parts)
Alveston Av. Harr —27Ka 38
Alvey St. SE17 —50Ub 83 (7H 207)
Alvia Gdns. Sutt —77Eb 145
Alvington Cres. E8 —36Vb 63
Alvista Av. Tap —4A 72
Alway Av. Eps —78Ta 143
Alwen Gro. S Ock —44Xd 90
Alwold Cres. SE12 —58Kc 107
Alwyn Av. W4 —50Ta 79
Alwyn Clo. Els —16Pa 21
Alwyn Clo. New Ad —80Dc 148
Alwyne Av. Shenf —16Ce 33
Alwyne Ct. Wok —88A 156
Alwyne La. N1 —38Rb 63
Alwyne Pl. N1 —37Sb 63
Alwyne Rd. N1 —38Sb 63
Alwyne Rd. SW19 —65Bb 125
Alwyne Rd. W7 —45Ga 78
Alwyne Sq. N1 —37Sb 63
Alwyne Vs. N1 —38Rb 63
Alwyn Gdns. NW4 —28Wa 40
Alwyn Gdns. W3 —44Ra 79
Alwyns Clo. Cher —72J 139
Alwyns La. Cher —72H 139
Alyth Gdns. NW11 —30Cb 41
Amalgamated Dri. Bren —51Ja 100
Amanda Clo. Chig —23Tc 46
Amanda Ct. Slou —8P 73
Amar Ct. SE18 —49Vc 87
Amar Deep Ct. SE18 —50Vc 87
Amazon St. E1 —44Wb 83
Ambassador Clo. Houn —54Aa 99
Ambassador Gdns. E6 —43Pc 86
Ambassadors' Ct. SW1 —46Lb 82 (7C 198)
(off St James' Pal.)
Ambassador Sq. E14 —49Dc 84
Amber Av. E17 —25Ac 44
Ambercroft Way. Coul —91Rb 181
Amberden Av. N3 —27Cb 41
Ambergate St. SE17 —50Rb 83 (7B 206)
Amberley Clo. Orp —78Vc 151
Amberley Clo. Pinn —27Ba 37
Amberley Clo. Send —97H 173
Amberley Ct. Beck —66Bc 128
Amberley Ct. Sidc —64Yc 131
Amberley Dri. Wdhm —83H 157 (in two parts)
Amberley Gdns. Enf —17Ub 25
Amberley Gdns. Eps —77Va 144
Amberley Gro. SE26 —64Xb 127
Amberley Gro. Croy —73Vb 147
Amberley Rd. E10 —31Cc 64
Amberley Rd. N13 —19Pb 24
Amberley Rd. SE2 —51Zc 109
Amberley Rd. W9 —43Cb 81
Amberley Rd. Buck H —18Lc 27
Amberley Rd. Enf —17Vb 25
Amberley Rd. Slou —3C 72
Amberley Way. Houn —57Y 99
Amberley Way. Mord —73Bb 145
Amberley Way. Romf —28Dd 48
Amberley Way. Uxb —40N 55
Amber St. E15 —38Fc 65
Amberwood Rise. N Mald —72Ua 144
Amblecote. Cob —84Z 159
Amblecote Clo. SE12 —62Kc 129
Amblecote Meadows. SE12 —62Kc 129
Amblecote Rd. SE12 —62Kc 129
Ambler Rd. N4 —34Rb 63
Ambleside. Brom —65Fc 129
Ambleside. Epp —3Wc 15
Ambleside Av. SW16 —63Mb 126
Ambleside Av. Beck —71Ac 148
Ambleside Av. Horn —36Kd 69
Ambleside Av. W on T —74Y 141
Ambleside Clo. E9 —36Yb 64
Ambleside Clo. E10 —31Dc 64
Ambleside Cres. Enf —13Zb 26
Ambleside Dri. Felt —60W 98
Ambleside Gdns. SW16 —64Mb 126
Ambleside Gdns. Ilf —28Nc 46
Ambleside Gdns. S Croy —82Zb 166
Ambleside Gdns. Sutt —79Eb 145
Ambleside Gdns. Wemb —32Ma 59
Ambleside Point. SE15 —52Yb 106
(off Tustin Est.)
Ambleside Rd. NW10 —38Va 60
Ambleside Rd. Bexh —54Cd 110
Ambleside Wlk. Uxb —39M 55
(off Cumbrian Way)
Ambleside Way. Egh —66D 118
Ambrey Way. Wall —81Mb 164
Ambrooke Rd. Belv —48Cd 88
Ambrosden Av. SW1 —48Lb 82 (4C 204)
Ambrose Av. NW11 —31Ab 60
Ambrose Clo. E6 —43Pc 86
Ambrose Clo. Orp —76Vc 151
Ambrose M. SW11 —54Hb 103
Ambrose St. SE16 —49Xb 83
Ambrose Wlk. E3 —40Cc 64
AMC Bus. Cen. NW10 —41Ra 79
Amelia St. SE17 —50Rb 83 (7C 206)
Amen Corner. EC4 —44Rb 83 (3C 200)
Amen Corner. SW17 —65Jb 126
Amen Ct. EC4 —44Rb 83 (3C 200)
Amerden Way. Slou —7E 72
America Sq. EC3 —45Vb 83 (4K 201)
America St. SE1 —46Sb 83 (7D 200)
Ameriand Rd. SW18 —57Bb 103
Amersham Av. N18 —23Tb 43
Amersham Clo. Romf —23Pd 49
Amersham Dri. Romf —23Nd 49
Amersham Gro. SE14 —52Bc 106
Amersham Ho. Wat —17U 18
(off Chenies Way)
Amersham Rd. SE14 —53Bc 106
Amersham Rd. Chal P —21A 34
Amersham Rd. Croy —72Sb 147
Amersham Rd. Ger X & Uxb —30C 34
Amersham Rd. L Chal & Chor —11A 16
Amersham Rd. Romf —23Nd 49
Amersham Vale. SE14 —52Bc 106
Amersham Wlk. Romf —23Pd 49
Amersham Way. Amer —11A 16
Amery Gdns. NW10 —39Xa 60
Amery Gdns. Romf —27Md 49
Amery Rd. Harr —33Ja 58
Amesbury. Wal A —4Jc 13
Amesbury Av. SW2 —61Nb 126
Amesbury Clo. Epp —3Vc 15
Amesbury Clo. Wor Pk —74Ya 144
Amesbury Ct. Enf —12Qb 24
Amesbury Dri. E4 —16Dc 26
Amesbury Rd. Brom —69Mc 129
Amesbury Rd. Dag —38Zc 67
Amesbury Rd. Epp —3Vc 15
Amesbury Rd. Felt —61Z 121
Amesbury Tower. SW8 —54Lb 104
Ames Rd. Swans —58Ae 113
Amethyst Rd. E15 —35Fc 65
Amey Dri. Bookh —96Ea 176
Amherst Av. W13 —44La 78
Amherst Clo. Orp —70Xc 131
Amherst Dri. Orp —70Vc 131
Amherst Hill. Sev —95Hd 186
Amherst Rd. W13 —44La 78
Amherst Rd. Sev —94Kd 187
Amhurst Gdns. Iswth —54Ha 100
Amhurst Pk. N16 —31Tb 63
Amhurst Pas. E8 —36Wb 63
Amhurst Rd. E8 —36Xb 63
Amhurst Rd. N16 & E8 —35Vb 63
Amhurst Ter. E8 —35Wb 63
Amhurst Wlk. SE28 —46Wc 87
Amidas Gdns. Dag —35Xc 67
Amiel St. E1 —42Yb 84
Amies St. SW11 —55Hb 103
Amina Way. SE16 —48Wb 83
Amis Av. Eps —79Ra 143
Amis Av. New Haw —82J 157
Amis Rd. Wok —7B 188
Amity Gro. SW20 —67Xa 124
Amity Rd. E15 —39Hc 65
Ammanford Grn. NW9 —30Ua 40
Amner Rd. SW11 —58Jb 104
Amor Rd. W6 —48Ya 80
Amos Est. SE16 —46Zb 84
Amott Rd. SE15 —55Wb 105
Amoy Pl. E14 —45Cc 84
Ampere Way. Bedd —74Pb 146
Ampleforth Rd. SE2 —47Xc 87
Ampthill Est. NW1 —40Lb 62 (2C 192)
Ampthill Ho. H Hill —22Md 49
(off Montgomery Cres.)
Ampton Pl. WC1 —41Pb 82 (4H 193)
Ampton St. WC1 —41Pb 82 (4H 193)
Amroth Clo. SE23 —60Xb 105
Amroth Grn. NW9 —30Ua 40
Amstel Way. Knap —6C 188
Amsterdam Rd. E14 —48Ec 84
Amunsden Ho. NW10 —38Ta 59
(off Stonebridge Pk.)
Amwell Clo. Enf —15Tb 25
Amwell Ct. Wal A —5Hc 13
Amwell Ct. Est. N4 —33Sb 63
Amwell St. EC1 —41Qb 82 (3K 193)
Amwell View. Ilf —22Xc 47
Amyand Cotts. Twic —58Ka 100
Amyand La. Twic —59Ka 100
Amyand Pk. Gdns. Twic —59Ka 100
Amyand Pk. Rd. Twic —59Ja 100
Amy Johnson. Edgw —26Ra 39
Amy Rd. Oxt —100Gc 183
Amyruth Rd. SE4 —57Cc 106
Anatola Rd. N19 —33Lb 62
Ancaster Cres. N Mald —72Wa 144
Ancaster M. Beck —69Zb 128
Ancaster Rd. Beck —69Zb 128
Ancaster St. SE18 —52Uc 108
Anchorage Clo. SW19 —64Cb 125
Anchor Bay Ind. Est. Eri —51Jd 110
Anchor Boulevd. Dart —56Sd 112
Anchor Brewhouse. SE1 —46Vb 83 (7K 201)
Anchor Ct. Enf —15Ub 25
Anchor Ct. Eri —52Hd 110
Anchor Cres. Knap —5A 188
Anchor Dri. Rain —41Kd 89
Anchor Hill. Knap —5A 188
Anchor & Hope La. SE7 —48Kc 85
Anchor M. SW12 —58Kb 104
Anchor St. SE16 —49Xb 83
Anchor Yd. EC1 —42Sb 83 (5E 194)
Ancient Almshouses. Wal X —2Zb 12
(off Turner's Hill)
Ancill Clo. W6 —51Za 102
Ancona Rd. NW10 —40Wa 60
Ancona Rd. SE18 —50Tc 86
Andace Pk. Gdns. Brom —68Lc 129
Andalus Rd. SW9 —55Nb 104
Ander Clo. Wemb —35Ma 59
Andermans. Wind —3B 94
Anderson Clo. W3 —44Ta 79
Anderson Clo. Eps —84Ra 161
Anderson Clo. Hare —25J 35
Anderson Ct. NW2 —32Ya 60
Anderson Dri. Ashf —63S 120
Anderson Ho. Bark —40Tc 66
Anderson Pl. Houn —56Da 99
Anderson Rd. E9 —37Zb 64
Anderson Rd. Shenl —5Qa 7
Anderson Rd. Wey —76T 140
Anderson Rd. Wfd G —27Mc 45
Andersons. Stanf —1P 93
Anderson St. SW3 —50Hb 81 (7F 203)
Anderson Way. Belv —47Dd 88
Anderton Clo. SE5 —55Tb 105
Anderton Ct. N22 —26Mb 42
Andorra Ct. Brom —67Lc 129
Andover Av. E16 —44Mc 85
Andover Clo. Eps —83Ta 161
Andover Clo. Gnfd —42Da 77
Andover Clo. Uxb —40K 55
Andover Pl. NW6 —40Db 61
Andover Rd. N7 —33Pb 62
Andover Rd. Orp —75Uc 150
Andover Rd. Twic —60Fa 100
Andoversford Ct. SE15 —51Ub 105
(off Bibury Clo.)
Andreck Ct. Beck —68Dc 128
Andre St. E8 —36Wb 63
Andrew Borde St. WC1 —44Mb 82
Andrew Borde St. WC2 —44Mb 82 (2E 198)
Andrew Clo. Dart —57Fd 110
Andrew Clo. Ilf —23Tc 46
Andrew Ct. SE23 —61Zb 128
Andrewes Clo. E6 —44Nc 86
Andrewes Highwalk. EC2
(off Barbican) —43Sb 83 (1E 200)
Andrewes Ho. EC2
(off Barbican) —43Sb 83 (1E 200)
Andrewes Ho. Sutt —77Cb 145
Andrew Hill La. Hedg —3G 52
Andrew Pl. SW8 —53Mb 104
Andrews Clo. Buck H —19Lc 27
Andrew's Clo. Eps —86Va 162
Andrew's Clo. Harr —31Fa 58
Andrew's Clo. Orp —68Zc 131
Andrews Clo. Wor Pk —75Za 144
Andrews Crosse. WC2 —44Qb 82 (3K 199)
(off Chancery La.)
Andrew's La. Chesh —1Ub 11
Andrews Pl. SE9 —58Rc 108
Andrew's Rd. E8 —39Xb 63
Andrew St. E14 —44Ec 84
Andrews Wlk. SE17 —51Rb 105
Andromeda Ct. H Hill —24Ld 49
Andwell Clo. SE2 —47Xc 87
Anerley Gro. SE19 —66Vb 127
Anerley Hill. SE19 —65Vb 127
Anerley Pk. SE20 —66Wb 127
Anerley Pk. Rd. SE20 —66Xb 127
Anerley Rd. SE19 & SE20 —66Wb 127
Anerley Sta. Rd. SE20 —67Xb 127
Anerley St. SW11 —54Hb 103
Anerley Vale. SE19 —66Vb 127
Aneurin Bevan Ct. NW2 —33Xa 60
Aneurin Bevan Ho. N11 —24Mb 42
Anfield Clo. SW12 —59Lb 104
Angas Ct. Wey —78S 140
Angela Davies Ind. Est. SW9 —56Rb 105
Angel All. E1 —44Vb 83
Angel Clo. N18 —21Vb 43
Angel Corner Pde. N18 —22Wb 43
Angel Ct. EC2 —44Tb 83 (2G 201)
Angel Ct. SW1 —46Lb 82 (7C 198)
Angelfield. Houn —57Da 99
Angel Ga. EC1 —41Rb 83 (3C 194)
Angel Hill. Sutt —76Db 145
Angel Hill Dri. Sutt —76Db 145
Angelica Dri. E6 —43Qc 86
Angelica Gdns. Croy —74Zb 148
Angel La. E15 —37Fc 65
Angel La. Hay —43T 76
Angell Pk. Gdns. SW9 —55Qb 104
Angell Rd. SW9 —54Qb 104
Angel M. N1 —40Qb 62 (2A 194)
Angel Pas. EC4 —45Tb 83 (5F 201)
Angel Pl. N18 —22Wb 43
Angel Pl. SE1 —47Tb 83 (1F 207)
Angel Pl. SW1 —47Tb 83
Angel Rd. N18 —22Wb 43
Angel Rd. Harr —30Ga 38
Angel Rd. Th Dit —73Ja 142
Angel Sq. N1 —40Qb 62 (2A 194)
Angel St. EC1 —44Sb 83 (2D 200)
Angel Wlk. W6 —49Ya 80
Angel Way. Romf —29Gd 48
Angel Yd. N6 —32Jb 62
Angerstein La. SE3 —53Hc 107
Angle Clo. Uxb —39Q 56
Angle Grn. Dag —32Yc 67
Angle Rd. Grays —51Zd 113
Anglers Clo. Rich —63La 122
Angler's La. NW5 —37Kb 62
Anglesea Av. SE18 —49Rc 86
Anglesea Cen. Grav —8D 114
Anglesea Rd. SE18 —49Rc 86
Anglesea Rd. King T —70Ma 123
Anglesea Rd. Orp —72Yc 151
Anglesey Clo. Ashf —62Q 120
Anglesey Ct. Rd. Cars —79Jb 146
Anglesey Dri. Rain —42Jd 88
Anglesey Gdns. Cars —79Jb 146
Anglesey Rd. Enf —14Xb 25
Anglesey Rd. Wat —22Y 37
Anglesmede Cres. Pinn —27Ca 37
Anglesmede Way. Pinn —27Ca 37
Angles Rd. SW16 —63Nb 126
Anglia Wlk. E6 —39Qc 66
(off Napier Rd.)
Anglo Rd. E3 —40Bc 64
Angmering Ho. H Hill —22Md 49
(off Barnstaple Rd.)
Angrave Ct. E8 —39Vb 63
Angrave Pas. E8 —39Vb 63
Angus Clo. Chess —78Qa 143
Angus Dri. Ruis —35Y 57
Angus Gdns. NW9 —25Ta 39
Angus Ho. SW2 —59Mb 104
Angus Rd. E13 —41Lc 85
Angus St. SE14 —52Ac 106
Anhalt Rd. SW11 —52Gb 103
Ankerdine Cres. SE18 —52Rc 108
Anlaby Rd. Tedd —64Ga 122
Anley Rd. W14 —47Za 80
Anmersh Gro. Stan —25Ma 39
Annabel Av. Ors —4F 92
Annabel Clo. E14 —44Dc 84
Anna Clo. E8 —39Vb 63
Annalee Gdns. S Ock —43Xd 90
Annalee Rd. S Ock —43Xd 90
Annandale Gro. Uxb —34S 56
Annandale Rd. SE10 —51Hc 107
Annandale Rd. W4 —50Ua 80
Annandale Rd. Croy —75Wb 147
Annandale Rd. Sidc —60Uc 108
Anna Neagle Clo. E7 —35Jc 65
Annan Way. Romf —25Gd 48
Anne Boleyn's Wlk. King T —64Na 123
Anne Boleyn's Wlk. Sutt —80Za 144
Anne Case M. N Mald —69Ua 124
Anne Nastri Ct. Romf —29Kd 49
(off Heath Pk. Rd.)
Anne of Cleves Rd. Dart —57Md 111
Annerley Rd. SE19 & SE20 —66Wb 127
Anners Clo. Egh —69E 118
Annesley Av. NW9 —27Ta 39
Annesley Clo. NW10 —34Ua 60
Annesley Dri. Croy —76Bc 148
Annesley Ho. SW9 —52Qb 104
Annesley Rd. SE3 —53Kc 107
Annesley Wlk. N19 —33Lb 62
Anne St. E13 —42Jc 85
Anne Sutherland Ho. Beck —66Ac 128
Anne's Wlk. Cat —92Ub 181
Annett Clo. Shep —70U 120
Annette Clo. Harr —26Ga 38
Annette Rd. N7 —34Pb 62
Annett Rd. W on T —73W 140
Annetts Cres. N1 —38Sb 63
Anne Way. Ilf —23Sc 46
Anne Way. W Mol —70Da 121
Annie Besant Clo. E3 —39Bc 64
Annie Taylor Ho. E12 —35Qc 66
(off Walton Rd.)
Annifer Way. S Ock —43Xd 90
Anning St. EC2 —42Ub 83 (5J 195)
Annington Rd. N2 —27Hb 41
Annis Rd. E9 —37Ac 64
Ann La. SW10 —51Fb 103
Ann Moss Way. SE16 —48Yb 84
Ann's Clo. SW1 —47Hb 81 (2G 203)
(off Kinnerton St.)
Ann's Pl. E1 —43Vb 83 (1K 201)
(off Wentworth St.)
Ann St. SE18 —50Sc 86 (in two parts)
Annsworthy Av. T Hth —69Tb 127
Annsworthy Cres. SE25 —68Tb 127
Ansculf Rd. Slou —1E 72
Ansdell Rd. SE15 —54Yb 106
Ansdell St. W8 —48Db 81
Ansdell Ter. W8 —48Db 81
Ansell Gro. Cars —74Jb 146
Ansell Rd. SW17 —62Gb 125
Anselm Clo. Croy —76Vb 147
Anselm Rd. SW6 —51Cb 103
Anselm Rd. Pinn —24Ba 37
Ansford Rd. Brom —64Ec 128
Ansleigh Pl. W11 —45Za 80
Ansley Clo. S Croy —86Xb 165
Anslow Gdns. Iver —40F 54
Anslow Pl. Slou —3A 72
Anson Clo. Kenl —92Tb 181
Anson Clo. Romf —26Dd 48
Anson Rd. N7 —35Lb 62
Anson Rd. NW2 —35Xa 60
Anson Ter. N'holt —37Da 57
Anson Wlk. N'wd —21S 36
Anstead Dri. Rain —40Jd 68
Anstey Ct. W3 —47Ra 79
Anstey Rd. SE15 —55Wb 105
Anstey Wlk. N15 —28Rb 43
Anstice Clo. W4 —52Ua 102
Anstridge Path. SE9 —58Tc 108
Anstridge Rd. SE9 —58Tc 108
Antelope Av. Grays —48Ce 91
Antelope Rd. SE18 —48Pc 86
Anthony Clo. Dun G —92Gd 186
Anthony Clo. Wat —18Y 19
Anthony Cope Ct. N1
(off Chart St.) —41Tb 83 (3G 195)
Anthony La. Swan —67Jd 132
Anthony Rd. SE25 —72Wb 147
Anthony Rd. Borwd —12Pa 21
Anthony Rd. Gnfd —41Ga 78
Anthony Rd. Well —53Wc 109
Anthony St. E1 —44Xb 83
Anthony Way. Slou —5B 72
Anthorne Clo. Pot B —3Db 9
Anthus M. N'wd —24U 36
Antigua Wlk. SE19 —64Tb 127
Antill Rd. E3 —41Ac 84
Antill Rd. N15 —28Wb 43
Antill Ter. E1 —44Zb 84
Antlers Hill. E4 —15Dc 26
Antoinette Ct. Abb L —1V 4
Anton Cres. Sutt —76Cb 145
Antoneys Clo. Pinn —26Z 37
Anton Rd. S Ock —43Xd 90
Anton St. E8 —36Wb 63
Antrim Gro. NW3 —37Hb 61
Antrim Rd. NW3 —37Hb 61
Antrobus Clo. Sutt —78Bb 145
Antrobus Rd. W4 —49Sa 79
Anvil Ct. Langl —49C 74
Anvil La. Cob —86W 158
Anvil Rd. Sun —69W 120
Anworth Clo. Wfd G —23Kc 45
Anyards Rd. Cob —85X 159
Apeldoorn Dri. Wall —81Nb 164
Aperdele Rd. Lea —90Ja 160
Aperfield Rd. Big H —89Nc 168
Aperfield Rd. Eri —51Hd 110
Apperfields. W'ham —89Nc 168
Apers Av. Wok —93B 172
Apex Clo. Beck —67Dc 128
Apex Clo. Wey —76T 140
Apex Corner. NW7 —21Ua 40
Apex Ct. W13 —45Ja 78
Aplin Way. Iswth —53Ga 100
Apollo Av. Brom —67Kc 129
Apollo Av. N'wd —22W 36
Apollo Bus. Cen. SE14 —50Zb 84
Apollo Clo. Horn —33Kd 69
Apollo Ho. N6 —31Hb 61
Apollo Pl. SW10 —52Fb 103
Apollo Pl. St J —7D 188
Apollo Way. SE28 —48Tc 86
Apothecary St. EC4 —44Rb 83 (3B 200)
Appach Rd. SW2 —58Qb 104
Appleby Clo. E4 —23Ec 44
Appleby Clo. N15 —29Tb 43
Appleby Clo. Twic —61Fa 122
Appleby Dri. Romf —22Ld 49
Appleby Gdns. Felt —60Y 98
Appleby Grn. Romf —22Ld 49
Appleby Rd. E8 —38Wb 63
Appleby Rd. E16 —44Hc 85
Appleby St. E2 —40Vb 63 (1K 195)
Applecroft. Park —1Da 5
Appledore Av. Bexh —53Ed 110
Appledore Av. Ruis —34X 57
Appledore Clo. Brom —71Jc 149
Appledore Clo. Edgw —25Qa 39
Appledore Clo. Romf —25Ld 49
Appledore Cres. Sidc —62Uc 130
Appledown Rise. Coul —87Lb 164
Appleford Rd. W10 —42Ab 80
Apple Garth. Bren —49Ma 79
Applegarth. Clay —78Ha 142
Applegarth. New Ad —80Dc 148 (in two parts)
Applegarth Dri. Ilf —28Vc 47
Applegarth Ho. Eri —54Hd 110
Applegarth Rd. SE28 —46Xc 87
Applegarth Rd. W14 —48Za 80
Apple Gro. Chess —77Na 143
Apple Gro. Enf —13Ub 25
Apple Mkt. King T —68Ma 123
Appleshaw Clo. Grav —4C 136
Appleton Gdns. N Mald —72Wa 144
Appleton Rd. SE9 —55Nc 108
Appleton Rd. Lou —13Rc 28
Appleton Sq. Mitc —67Gb 125
Appleton Way. Horn —32Md 69
Apple Tree Av. Uxb & W Dray —43P 75
Apple Tree Clo. Dodd —11Zd 33
Appletree Gdns. Barn —14Gb 23
Appletree La. Slou —8N 73
Appletrees Pl. Wok —7F 188
Appletree Wlk. Wat —6X 5
Apple Tree Yd. SW1 —46Lb 82 (6C 198)
Applewood Clo. N20 —18Gb 23
Applewood Clo. NW2 —34Xa 60
Appleyard Ter. Enf —9Yb 12
Appold St. EC2 —43Ub 83 (7H 195)
Appold St. Eri —51Hd 110
Apprentice Way. E5 —35Xb 63
Approach Clo. N16 —35Ub 63
Approach Rd. E2 —40Yb 64
Approach Rd. SW20 —68Ya 124
Approach Rd. Ashf —65S 120
Approach Rd. Barn —14Fb 23
Approach Rd. Purl —84Qb 164
Approach Rd. Tats —95Kc 183
Approach Rd. W Mol —71Ca 141
Approach, The. NW4 —29Za 40
Approach, The. W3 —44Ta 79
Approach, The. Bookh —95Ba 175
Approach, The. Enf —12Xb 25
Approach, The. Orp —75Vc 151
Approach, The. Pot B —4Bb 9
Approach, The. Upm —34Rd 69
Aprey Gdns. NW4 —28Ya 40
April Clo. W7 —45Ga 78
April Clo. Asht —90Pa 161
April Clo. Felt —62W 120
April Clo. Orp —78Vc 151
April Glen. SE23 —62Zb 128
April St. E8 —35Vb 63
Aprilwood Clo. Wdhm —83H 157
Apsledene. Grav —5F 136
Apsley Clo. Harr —29Ea 38
Apsley Rd. SE25 —70Xb 127
Apsley Rd. N Mald —69Sa 123
Apsley Way. NW2 —33Wa 60
Apsley Way. W1 —47Jb 82 (1J 203)
Aquarius Way. N'wd —22W 36
Aquila Clo. Lea —93Na 177
Aquila Clo. N'wd —21W 36
Aquila St. NW8 —40Fb 61 (1C 190)
Aquinas St. SE1 —46Qb 82 (7A 200)
Arabella Dri. SW15 —56Ua 102
Arabia Clo. E4 —17Fc 27
Arabin Rd. SE4 —56Ac 106
Araglen Av. S Ock —43Xd 90
Aragon Av. Eps —82Xa 162
Aragon Av. Th Dit —71Ha 142
Aragon Clo. Brom —74Pc 150
Aragon Clo. Enf —10Pb 10
Aragon Clo. New Ad —82Gc 167
Aragon Clo. Romf —23Dd 48
Aragon Clo. Sun —65V 120
Aragon Dri. Ilf —24Sc 46
Aragon Dri. Ruis —32Z 57
Aragon M. E1 —46Wb 83
Aragon Rd. King T —64Na 123
Aragon Rd. Mord —72Za 144
Aragon Rd. Twic —59Ja 100
Aragon Tower. SE8 —49Bc 84
Aran Ct. Wey —75T 140
Arandora Cres. Romf —31Xc 67
Aran Dri. Stan —21La 38
Arbery Rd. E3 —41Ac 84
Arbinger Ct. W5 —45La 78
Arbor Clo. Beck —68Dc 128
Arbor Ct. N16 —33Tb 63
Arborfield Clo. Slou —8J 73
Arbor Rd. E4 —20Fc 27
Arbour Clo. Felt —95Ha 176
Arbour Clo. War —22Yd 50
Arbour Rd. Enf —13Zb 26
Arbour Sq. E1 —44Zb 84
Arbour Way. Horn —36Kd 69
Arbroath Grn. Wat —20W 18
Arbroath Rd. SE9 —55Nc 108
Arbrook Clo. Orp —69Wc 131
Arbrook La. Esh —79Ea 142
Arbuthnot La. Bex —58Ad 109
Arbuthnot Rd. SE14 —54Zb 106
Arbutus St. E8 —39Vb 63
Arcade Pl. Romf —29Gd 48
Arcade, The. E14 —44Dc 84
Arcade, The. E17 —28Cc 44
Arcade, The. EC2 —43Ub 83 (1H 201)
(off Liverpool St.)
Arcade, The. Bark —38Sc 66
Arcade, The. Romf —22Md 49
(off Farnham Rd.)
Arcadia Av. N3 —25Cb 41
Arcadian Av. Bex —58Ad 109
Arcadian Clo. Bex —58Ad 109
Arcadian Gdns. N22 —24Pb 42
Arcadian Rd. Bex —58Ad 109
Arcadia Rd. Grav —7B 136
Arcadia St. E14 —44Cc 84
Arcany Rd. S Ock —42Xd 90
Archangel St. SE16 —47Zb 84
Archates Av. Grays —48Ce 91
Archbishop's Pl. SW2 —59Pb 104
Archdale Rd. SE22 —57Vb 105
Archel Rd. W14 —51Bb 103
Archer Clo. K Lan —1P 3
Archer Clo. King T —66Na 123
Archer M. Hamp —65Ea 122
Archer Rd. SE25 —70Xb 127
Archer Rd. Orp —71Wc 151
Archers Ct. Brom —70Kc 129
Archers Ct. S Ock —43Xd 90
Archers Dri. Enf —12Yb 26
Archer St. W1 —45Mb 82 (4D 198)
Archers Wlk. SE15 —53Vb 105
(off Exeter Rd.)
Archer Ter. W Dray —45N 75
Archer Tower. SE14 —51Ac 106
Archer Way. Swan —68Hd 132
Archery Clo. W2 —44Gb 81 (3E 196)
Archery Clo. Harr —27Ha 38
Archery Rd. SE9 —57Pc 108
Arches, The. WC2 —46Nb 82 (6G 199)
(off Villiers St.)
Arches, The. Harr —33Da 57
Archibald M. W1 —45Jb 82 (5K 197)

Archibald Pl.—Ashmere Av.

Archibald Pl. NW3 —38Hb 61
Archibald Rd. N7 —35Mb 62
Archibald Rd. Romf —25Qd 49
Archibald St. E3 —41Cc 84
Arch Rd. W on T —76Z 141
Arch St. SE1 —48Sb 83 (4D 206)
Arch Way. Romf —23Kd 49
Archway Bus. Cen. N19 —34Mb 62
Archway Clo. N19 —33Lb 62
Archway Clo. SW19 —62Db 125
Archway Clo. W10 —43Za 80
Archway Clo. Wall —76Nb 146
Archway Mall. N19 —33Lb 62
Archway Rd. N6 & N19 —30Jb 42
Archway St. SW13 —55Ua 102
Arcola St. E8 —36Vb 63
Arcon Ter. N9 —17Wb 25
Arctic St. NW5 —36Jb 62
Arcus Rd. Brom —65Gc 129
Ardbeg Rd. SE24 —57Tb 105
Arden Clo. Bov —1C 2
Arden Clo. Bush —17Ha 20
Arden Clo. Harr —34Fa 58
Arden Ct. Gdns. N2 —30Fb 41
Arden Cres. E14 —49Cc 84
Arden Cres. Dag —38Yc 67
Arden Est. N1 —40Ub 63 (2H 195)
Arden Grange. N12 —21Eb 41
Arden Gro. Orp —77Rc 150
Arden Ho. SW9 —54Nb 104
(off Grantham Rd.)
Arden M. E17 —29Dc 44
Arden Mhor. Pinn —28X 37
Arden Rd. N3 —27Bb 41
Arden Rd. W13 —45La 78
Ardent Clo. SE25 —69Ub 127
Ardesley Wood. Wey —77U 140
Ardfern Av. SW16 —69Qb 126
Ardfillan Rd. SE6 —60Fc 107
Ardgowan Rd. SE6 —59Gc 107
(in two parts)
Ardilaun Rd. N5 —35Sb 63
Ardleigh Clo. Horn —27Md 49
Ardleigh Ct. Shenf —17Be 33
Ardleigh Gdns. Hut —16Fe 33
Ardleigh Gdns. Sutt —73Cb 145
Ardleigh Grn. Rd. Horn —29Md 49
Ardleigh Ho. Bark —39Sc 66
Ardleigh M. Ilf —34Rc 66
Ardleigh Rd. E17 —25Bc 44
Ardleigh Rd. N1 —37Ub 63
Ardleigh Ter. E17 —25Bc 44
Ardley Clo. NW10 —34Ua 60
Ardley Clo. SE6 —62Ac 128
Ardley Clo. Ruis —31S 56
Ardlui Rd. SE27 —61Sb 127
Ardmay Gdns. Surb —71Na 143
Ardmere Rd. SE13 —58Fc 107
Ardmore La. Buck H —17Kc 27
Ardmore Rd. S Ock —42Xd 90
Ardoch Rd. SE6 —61Fc 129
Ardra Rd. N9 —20Zb 26
Ardrossan Gdns. Wor Pk
—76Wa 144
Ardross Av. N'wd —22U 36
Ardshiel Clo. SW15 —55Za 102
Ardwell Av. Ilf —29Sc 46
Ardwell Rd. SW2 —61Nb 126
Ardwick Rd. NW2 —35Cb 61
Arena Bus. Cen. N4 —30Sb 43
Argali Ho. Eri —48Ad 87
(off Kale Rd.)
Argall Av. E10 —31Zb 64
Argent Cen., The. Hay —47W 76
Argent St. Grays —51Ae 113
Argles Clo. Grnh —57Wd 112
Argon M. SW6 —52Cb 103
Argosy Gdns. Stai —65H 119
Argosy Ho. SE8 —49Ac 84
Argosy La. Stai —59M 97
Argus Clo. Romf —25Dd 48
Argus Way. W3 —48Ra 79
Argus Way. N'holt —41Aa 77
Argyle Av. Houn —58Ca 99
Argyle Av. S'hall —46Da 77
Argyle Clo. W13 —42Ja 78
Argyle Ct. Wat —14V 18
Argyle Gdns. Upm —33Td 70
Argyle Pl. W6 —49Xa 80
Argyle Rd. E1 —42Zb 84
Argyle Rd. E15 —35Gc 65
Argyle Rd. E16 —44Kc 85
Argyle Rd. N12 —22Db 41
Argyle Rd. N17 —25Wb 43
Argyle Rd. N18 —21Wb 43
Argyle Rd. Barn —14Ya 22
Argyle Rd. Gnfd & W13 —41Ha 78
Argyle Rd. Harr —30Da 37
Argyle Rd. Houn —57Da 99
Argyle Rd. Ilf —33Qc 66
Argyle Rd. Sev —97Kd 187
Argyle Sq. WC1 —41Nb 82 (3G 193)
Argyle St. WC1 —41Nb 82 (3F 193)
Argyle Wlk. WC1
—41Nb 82 (4F 193)
Argyll Av. Slou —5E 72
Argyll Clo. SW9 —55Pb 104
Argyll Gdns. Edgw —26Ra 39
Argyll Mans. SW3 —51Fb 103
Argyll Rd. W8 —47Cb 81
Argyll Rd. Grays —50Ce 91
Argyll St. W1 —44Lb 82 (3B 198)
Arica Rd. SE4 —56Ac 106
Aricola Pl. Enf —15Vb 25
Ariel Clo. Grav —3H 137
Ariel Rd. NW6 —37Cb 61
Ariel Way. W12 —46Ya 80
Ariel Way. Houn —55X 99
Arisdale Av. S Ock —43Xd 90
Aristotle Rd. SW4 —55Mb 104
Ark Av. Grays —48Ce 91
Arkell Gro. SE19 —66Rb 127
Arkindale Rd. SE6 —62Ec 128
Arkley Cres. E17 —29Bc 44
Arkley Dri. Barn —14Wa 22
Arkley La. Barn —10Va 8
Arkley Rd. E17 —29Bc 44
Arkley View. Barn —14Xa 22
Arklow M. Surb —75Na 143
Arklow Rd. SE14 —51Bc 106
Arkwright Ho. SW2 —59Nb 104
(off Streatham Pl.)
Arkwright Rd. NW3 —36Eb 61
Arkwright Rd. Coln —54G 96
Arkwright Rd. S Croy —82Vb 165
Arkwright Rd. Til —4C 114
Arlesey Clo. SW15 —57Ab 102
Arlesford Rd. SW9 —55Nb 104
Arlingford Rd. SW2 —57Qb 104
Arlington. N12 —20Cb 23
Arlington Av. N1
—39Sb 63 (1E 194)
Arlington Clo. Sidc —59Uc 108
Arlington Clo. Sutt —75Cb 145
Arlington Clo. Twic —58La 100
Arlington Ct. Hay —50U 76
Arlington Cres. Wal X —6Ac 12
Arlington Dri. Cars —75Hb 145
Arlington Dri. Ruis —30T 36
Arlington Gdns. W4 —50Sa 79
Arlington Gdns. Ilf —32Qc 66
Arlington Gdns. Romf —25Nd 49
Arlington Lodge. SW2 —56Pb 104
Arlington Lodge. Wey —77R 140
Arlington M. Twic —58Ka 100
Arlington Pk. Mans. W4 —50Sa 79
(off Sutton La. N.)
Arlington Pas. Tedd —63Ha 122
Arlington Pl. SE10 —52Ec 106
Arlington Rd. N14 —19Kb 24
Arlington Rd. NW1 —39Kb 62
Arlington Rd. W13 —44Ka 78
Arlington Rd. Ashf —64P 119
Arlington Rd. Rich —61Ma 123
Arlington Rd. Surb —72Ma 143
Arlington Rd. Tedd —63Ha 122
Arlington Rd. Twic —58La 100
Arlington Rd. Wfd G —24Jc 45
Arlington Sq. N1
—39Sb 63 (1E 194)
Arlington St. SW1
—46Lb 82 (6B 198)
Arlington Way. EC1
—41Qb 82 (3A 194)
Arliss Way. N'holt —39Y 57
Arlow Rd. N21 —18Qb 24
Armada Ct. SE8 —51Cc 106
Armada Ct. Grays —49Ce 91
Armadale Clo. N17 —28Xb 43
Armadale Rd. SW6 —51Cb 103
Armadale Rd. Felt —57W 98
Armadale Rd. Wok —5D 188
Armada Way. E6 —45Rc 86
Armagh Rd. E3 —39Bc 64
Armand Clo. Wat —10V 4
Armfield Clo. W Mol —71Ba 141
Armfield Cres. Mitc —68Hb 125
Armfield Rd. Enf —11Tb 25
Arminger Rd. W12 —46Xa 80
Armitage Clo. Loud —14M 17
Armitage Rd. NW11 —32Ab 60
Armitage Rd. SE10 —50Hc 85
Armitage Rd. Houn —52Z 99
Armor Rd. Purf —49Td 90
Armour Clo. N7 —37Pb 62
Armoury Dri. Grav —9E 114
Armoury Rd. SE8 —54Dc 106
Armoury Way. SW18 —57Cb 103
Armstead Wlk. Dag —38Cd 68
Armstrong Av. Wfd G —23Gc 45
Armstrong Clo. E6 —44Pc 86
Armstrong Clo. Dag —31Zc 67
Armstrong Clo. Hals —87Dd 170
Armstrong Clo. Pinn —30W 36
Armstrong Clo. Stanf —1N 93
Armstrong Clo. W on T —72W 140
Armstrong Cres. Barn —13Fb 23
Armstrong Gdns. Shenl —4Na 7
Armstrong Rd. SW7
—48Fb 81 (4B 202)
Armstrong Rd. W3 —46Va 80
Armstrong Rd. Egh —5N 117
Armstrong Rd. Felt —64Aa 121
Armstrong Way. S'hall —47Da 77
Arnal Cres. SW18 —59Ab 102
Arndale Cen., The. SW18
—58Db 103
Arndale Wlk. SW18 —57Db 103
Arndale Way. Egh —64C 118
Arne Clo. Stanf —1M 93
Arne Gro. Orp —76Vc 151
Arne Ho. SE11 —50Pb 82 (7H 205)
(off Tyers St.)
Arne St. WC2 —44Nb 82 (3G 199)
Arnett Clo. Rick —16J 17
Arnett Way. Rick —16J 17
Arne Wlk. SE3 —56Hc 107
Arneways Av. Romf —27Zc 47
Arneway St. SW1
—48Mb 82 (4E 204)
Arnewood Clo. SW15 —60Wa 102
Arnewood Clo. Oxs —86Da 159
Arneys La. Mitc —72Jb 146
Arngask Rd. SE6 —59Fc 107
Arnhem Av. S Ock —46Sd 90
Arnhem Dri. New Ad —83Fc 167
Arnhem Way. SE22 —57Ub 105
Arnison Rd. E Mol —70Fa 122
Arnold Av. E. Enf —10Cc 12
Arnold Av. W. Enf —10Bc 12
Arnold Cir. E2 —41Vb 83 (4K 195)
Arnold Clo. Harr —31Pa 59
Arnold Ct. N22 —24Nb 42
Arnold Cres. Iswth —57Fa 100
Arnold Est. SE1 —47Vb 83 (2K 207)
Arnold Gdns. N13 —22Rb 43
Arnold Ho. SE17 —50Rb 83
Arnold Pl. Til —3E 114
Arnold Rd. E3 —41Cc 84
Arnold Rd. N15 —27Vb 43
Arnold Rd. SW17 —66Hb 125
Arnold Rd. Dag —38Bd 67
Arnold Rd. Grav —1F 136
Arnold Rd. N'holt —37Aa 57
Arnold Rd. Stai —66L 119
Arnold Rd. Wok —87D 156
Arnolds Av. Hut —15Ee 33
Arnolds Clo. Hut —15Ee 33
Arnolds Farm La. Mount —13Fe 33
Arnold's La. S at H —65Pd 133
Arnos Gro. N14 —21Mb 42
Arnos Gro. Ct. N11 —22Lb 42
(off Palmer's Rd.)
Arnos Rd. N11 —21Lb 42
Arnot Ho. SE5 —52Sb 105
(off Comber Gro.)
Arnott Clo. SE28 —46Yc 87
Arnott Clo. W4 —49Ta 79
Arnould Av. SE5 —56Tb 105
Arnsberg Way. Bexh —56Cd 110
Arnside Gdns. Wemb —32Ma 59
Arnside Rd. Bexh —53Cd 110
Arnside St. SE17 —51Tb 105
Arnulf St. SE6 —63Dc 128
Arnulls Rd. SW16 —65Rb 127
Arodene Rd. SW2 —58Pb 104
Arragon Gdns. SW16 —66Nb 126
Arragon Gdns. W Wick —76Dc 148
Arragon Rd. E6 —39Mc 65
Arragon Rd. SW18 —60Cb 103
Arran Clo. Eri —51Fd 110
Arran Clo. Wall —77Kb 146
Arran Ct. NW9 —26Va 40
Arran Ct. NW10 —34Ta 59
Arran Dri. E12 —32Mc 65
Arran M. W5 —46Pa 79
Arranmore Ct. Bush —14Aa 19
Arran Rd. SE6 —61Dc 128
Arran Wlk. N1 —38Sb 63
Arran Way. Esh —75Da 141
Arras Av. Mord —71Eb 145
Arrel Ho. SE1 —48Sb 83 (4E 206)
Arrol Rd. Beck —69Yb 128
Arrowhead Ct. E11 —30Fc 45
Arrow Rd. E3 —41Dc 84
Arrowscout Wlk. N'holt —41Aa 77
Arrowsmith Clo. Chig —22Vc 47
Arrowsmith Ho. SE11
(off Tyers St.) —50Pb 82 (7H 205)
Arrowsmith Path. Chig —22Vc 47
Arrowsmith Rd. Chig —22Uc 46
Arsenal Rd. SE9 —54Pc 108
Artemis Clo. Grav —9G 114
Arterberry Rd. SW20 —66Ya 124
Arterial Av. Rain —42Kd 89
Arterial Rd. Stanf —1L 93
Arterial Rd. W Horn —29Ce 51
Arterial Rd. N. Stifford. N Stif
—47Zd 91
Arterial Rd. Purfleet. Purf —48Qd 89
Arterial Rd. W. Thurrock. W Thur
—48Vd 90
Arteris Rd. Wfd G —24Kc 45
Artesian Clo. NW10 —38Ta 59
Artesian Clo. Horn —30Hd 48
Artesian Rd. W2 —44Cb 81
Arthingworth St. E15 —39Gc 65
Arthur Barnes Ct. Grays —8E 92
Arthur Ct. W10 —44Za 80
(off Silchester Rd.)
Arthurdon Rd. SE4 —57Cc 106
Arthur Gro. SE18 —49Sc 86
Arthur Rd. E6 —40Pc 66
Arthur Rd. N7 —35Pb 62
Arthur Rd. N9 —19Vb 25
Arthur Rd. SW19 —63Cb 125
Arthur Rd. Big H —87Lc 167
Arthur Rd. King T —66Qa 123
Arthur Rd. N Mald —71Xa 144
Arthur Rd. Romf —30Yc 47
Arthur Rd. Slou —7H 73
Arthur Rd. Wind —3G 94
Arthur's Bri. Rd. Wok —5G 188
Arthur St. EC4 —45Tb 83 (5G 201)
Arthur St. Bush —13Z 19
Arthur St. Eri —52Hd 110
Arthur St. Grav —9C 114
Arthur St. Grays —51Ee 113
Arthur St. W. Grav —9C 114
Arthur Toft Ho. Grays —51De 113
(off New Rd.)
Artichoke Hill. E1 —45Xb 83
Artichoke M. SE5 —53Tb 105
(off Artichoke Pl.)
Artichoke Pl. SE5 —53Tb 105
Artillery Clo. Ilf —30Sc 46
Artillery Ho. E15 —37Gc 65
Artillery La. E1 —43Ub 83 (1J 201)
Artillery Pas. E1 —43Ub 83 (1J 201)
(off Artillery La.)
Artillery Pl. SE18 —49Qc 86
Artillery Pl. SW1 —48Mb 82 (4D 204)
Artillery Pl. Harr —24Ea 38
Artillery Rd. W12 —44Wa 80
Artillery Row. SW1
—48Mb 82 (4D 204)
Artillery Row. Grav —10E 114
Artington Clo. Orp —77Sc 150
Artizan St. E1 —44Ub 83 (2J 201)
(off Harrow Pl.)
Arun. E Til —9L 93
Arun Ct. SE25 —71Wb 147
Arundel Av. Eps —82Xa 162
Arundel Av. Mord —70Bb 125
Arundel Av. S Croy —82Wb 165
Arundel Bldgs. SE1
—48Ub 83 (4J 207)
(off Swan Mead)
Arundel Clo. E15 —35Gc 65
Arundel Clo. SW11 —57Gb 103
Arundel Clo. Bex —58Dd 109
Arundel Clo. Chesh —1Xb 11
Arundel Clo. Croy —76Rb 147
Arundel Clo. Hamp —64Da 121
Arundel Ct. N12 —23Gb 41
Arundel Ct. N17 —25Wb 43
Arundel Ct. Short —68Gc 129
Arundel Ct. Slou —9P 73
Arundel Ct. S Harr —35Ca 57
Arundel Dri. Borwd —15Sa 21
Arundel Dri. Harr —35Ba 57
Arundel Dri. Orp —78Xc 151
Arundel Dri. Wfd G —24Jc 45
Arundel Gdns. N21 —18Qb 24
Arundel Gdns. W11 —45Bb 81
Arundel Gdns. Edgw —24Ta 39
Arundel Gdns. Ilf —33Wc 67
Arundel Gro. N16 —36Ub 63
Arundel Ho. Borwd —14Sa 21
Arundel Ho. Uxb —42L 75
Arundel Mans. SW6 —53Bb 103
(off Kelvedon Rd.)
Arundel Pl. N1 —37Qb 62
Arundel Rd. Barn —13Gb 23
Arundel Rd. Croy —72Tb 147
Arundel Rd. Dart —56Ld 111
Arundel Rd. Houn —55Y 99
Arundel Rd. King T —68Ra 123
Arundel Rd. Romf —24Pd 49
Arundel Rd. Sutt —80Bb 145
Arundel Rd. Uxb —40K 55
Arundel Sq. N7 —37Qb 62
Arundel St. WC2
—45Pb 82 (4J 199)
Arundel Ter. SW13 —51Xa 102
Arvon Rd. N5 —36Qb 62
Asa Ct. Hay —48V 76
Asburnham Gdns. Upm —32Rd 69
Ascalon St. SW8 —52Lb 104
Ascension Rd. Romf —23Ed 48
Ascham Dri. E4 —24Dc 44
Ascham End. E17 —25Ac 44
Ascham St. NW5 —36Lb 62
Aschurch Rd. Croy —73Vb 147
Ascot Clo. Els —15Qa 21
Ascot Clo. Ilf —23Uc 46
Ascot Clo. N'holt —36Ca 57
Ascot Ct. Bex —59Bd 109
Ascot Gdns. Enf —9Yb 12
Ascot Gdns. Horn —35Nd 69
Ascot Gdns. S'hall —43Ba 77
Ascot M. Wall —81Lb 164
Ascot Pl. Stan —22La 38
Ascot Rd. E6 —41Pc 86
Ascot Rd. N15 —29Tb 43
Ascot Rd. N18 —21Wb 43
Ascot Rd. SW17 —65Jb 126
Ascot Rd. Felt —60Q 98
Ascot Rd. Grav —2D 136
Ascot Rd. Orp —70Vc 131
Ascot Rd. Wat —15U 18
Ascott Av. W5 —47Na 79
Ascott Clo. Pinn —28W 36
Ashalnds Ct. Til —9L 93
Ashbeam Clo. Gt War —23Yd 50
Ashbourne Av. E18 —28Kc 45
Ashbourne Av. N20 —19Hb 23
Ashbourne Av. NW11 —29Bb 41
Ashbourne Av. Bexh —52Ad 109
Ashbourne Av. Harr —33Fa 58
Ashbourne Clo. N12 —21Db 41
Ashbourne Clo. W5 —43Qa 79
Ashbourne Clo. Coul —90Lb 164
Ashbourne Ct. E5 —35Ac 64
Ashbourne Ct. N12 —21Db 41
(off Ashbourne Clo.)
Ashbourne Gro. NW7 —22Ta 39
Ashbourne Gro. SE22 —56Vb 105
Ashbourne Gro. W4 —50Ua 80
Ashbourne Ho. Chalv —7J 73
Ashbourne Pde. W5 —42Pa 79
Ashbourne Rise. Orp —77Uc 150
Ashbourne Rd. W5 —42Pa 79
Ashbourne Rd. Mitc —66Jb 126
Ashbourne Rd. Romf —21Ld 49
Ashbourne Sq. N'wd —23U 36
Ashbourne Ter. SW19 —66Cb 125
Ashbourne Way. NW11 —28Bb 41
Ashbridge Rd. E11 —31Gc 65
Ashbridge St. NW8
—42Gb 81 (6D 190)
Ashbrook Rd. N19 —32Mb 62
Ashbrook Rd. Dag —34Dd 68
Ashbrook Rd. Old Win —9M 95
Ashburn Gdns. SW7 —49Eb 81
Ashburnham Av. Harr —30Ha 38
Ashburnham Clo. N2 —27Fb 41
Ashburnham Clo. Sev —99Ld 187
Ashburnham Clo. Wat —20W 18
Ashburnham Ct. Beck —68Ec 128
Ashburnham Ct. Pinn —27Z 37
Ashburnham Dri. Wat —20W 18
Ashburnham Gdns. Harr —30Ha 38
Ashburnham Gdns. Upm —32Rd 69
Ashburnham Gro. SE10 —52Dc 106
Ashburnham Pk. Esh —77Ea 142
Ashburnham Pl. SE10 —52Dc 106
Ashburnham Retreat. SE10
—52Dc 106
Ashburnham Rd. NW10 —41Ya 80
Ashburnham Rd. SW10 —52Eb 103
Ashburnham Rd. Belv —49Ed 88
Ashburnham Rd. Rich —62Ka 122
Ashburnham Tower. SW10
(off Worlds End Est.) —52Fb 103
Ashburn M. SW7
—49Eb 81 (5A 202)
Ashburn Pl. SW7 —49Eb 81
Ashburton Av. Croy —74Xb 147
Ashburton Av. Ilf —36Uc 66
Ashburton Clo. Croy —74Wb 147
Ashburton Enterprise Cen. SW15
—58Ya 102
Ashburton Gdns. Croy —75Wb 147
Ashburton Gro. N7 —35Qb 62
Ashburton Memorial Homes. Croy
—73Xb 147
Ashburton Rd. E16 —44Jc 85
Ashburton Rd. Croy —75Wb 147
Ashburton Rd. Ruis —33W 56
Ashburton Ter. E13 —40Jc 65
Ashbury Dri. Uxb —34R 56
Ashbury Gdns. Romf —29Zc 47
Ashbury Rd. SW11 —55Hb 103
Ashby Av. Chess —79Qa 143
Ashby Clo. Horn —32Qd 69
Ashby Clo. Ors —4F 92
Ashby Gro. N1 —38Sb 63
Ashby Ho. SW9 —54Rb 105
Ashby M. SE4 —54Bc 106
Ashby Rd. N15 —29Wb 43
Ashby Rd. SE4 —54Bc 106
Ashby Rd. Wat —10W 4
Ashby St. EC1 —41Rb 83 (4C 194)
Ashby Wlk. Croy —72Sb 147
Ashby Way. W Dray —52Q 98
Ashchurch Gro. W12 —48Wa 80
Ashchurch Pk. Vs. W12 —48Wa 80
Ashchurch Ter. W12 —48Wa 80
Ash Clo. SE20 —68Yb 128
Ash Clo. Abb L —4T 4
Ash Clo. Cars —75Hb 145
Ash Clo. Edgw —21Sa 39
Ash Clo. Hare —25M 35
Ash Clo. N Mald —68Ta 123
Ash Clo. Orp —71Tc 150
Ash Clo. Pil H —15Vd 32
Ash Clo. Pyr —87J 157
Ash Clo. Romf —24Dd 48
Ash Clo. Sidc —62Xc 131
Ash Clo. Slou —48D 74
Ash Clo. Stan —23Ja 38
Ash Clo. Swan —68Ed 132
Ash Clo. Wat —7X 5
Ash Clo. Wok —92A 172
Ashcombe Av. Surb —73Ma 143
Ashcombe Gdns. Edgw —21Qa 39
Ashcombe Pk. NW2 —34Ua 60
Ashcombe Rd. SW19 —64Cb 125
Ashcombe Rd. Cars —79Jb 146
Ashcombe Rd. Red —99Lb 180
Ashcombe Sq. N Mald —69Sa 123
Ashcombe St. SW6 —54Db 103
Ashcombe Ter. Tad —92Xa 178
Ash Copse. Brick —3Ba 5
Ash Ct. SW19 —66Ab 124
Ash Ct. Add —78K 139
Ash Ct. Eps —77Sa 143
Ashcroft. N14 —19Mb 24
Ash Croft. Pinn —23Ca 37
Ashcroft Av. Sidc —58Wc 109
Ashcroft Ct. N20 —19Fb 23
Ashcroft Ct. Burn —10A 52
Ashcroft Cres. Sidc —58Wc 109
Ashcroft Dri. Den —30H 35
Ashcroft Pk. Cob —84Aa 159
Ashcroft Rise. Coul —88Nb 164
Ashcroft Rd. E3 —41Ac 84
Ashcroft Rd. Chess —76Pa 143
Ashcroft Sq. W6 —49Ya 80
Ashdale. Bookh —98Ea 176
Ashdale Clo. Stai —61N 119
Ashdale Clo. Twic —59Ea 100
Ashdale Gro. Stan —23Ha 38
Ashdale Ho. N4 —31Tb 63
Ashdale Rd. SE12 —60Kc 107
Ashdale Way. Twic —59Da 99
Ashdene. SE15 —53Xb 105
Ashdene. Pinn —27Y 37
Ashdene Clo. Ashf —66S 120
Ashdon Clo. Hut —16Ee 33
Ashdon Clo. Wfd G —23Kc 45
Ashdon Rd. NW10 —39Va 60
Ashdown. W13 —43Ka 78
(off Clivedon Ct.)
Ashdown Clo. Beck —68Dc 128
Ashdown Cres. NW5 —36Jb 62
Ashdown Cres. Chesh —1Ac 12
Ashdown Dri. Borwd —12Na 21
Ashdowne Ct. N17 —25Wb 43
Ashdown Est. E11 —35Fc 65
Ashdown Gdns. S Croy —87Xb 165
Ashdown Rd. Enf —12Yb 26
Ashdown Rd. Eps —85Va 162
Ashdown Rd. King T —68Na 123
Ashdown Rd. Uxb —40Q 56
Ashdown Rd. Wat —13Z 19
Ashdown Wlk. E14 —49Cc 84
(off Copeland Dri.)
Ashdown Wlk. Romf —25Dd 48
Ashdown Way. SW17 —61Jb 126
Ashenden Rd. E5 —36Ac 64
Ashenden Wlk. Farn C —5H 53
Ashen Dri. Dart —59Jd 110
Ashen Gro. SW19 —62Cb 125
Ashen Gro. Rd. Knat —82Rd 171
Ashentree Ct. EC4
—44Qb 82 (3A 200)
(off Whitefriars St.)
Ashen Vale. S Croy —81Zb 166
Asher Way. E1 —45Wb 83
Ashfield Av. Bush —16Da 19
Ashfield Av. Felt —60X 99
Ashfield Clo. Beck —66Cc 128
Ashfield Clo. Rich —60Na 101
Ashfield La. Chst —65Rc 130
(in three parts)
Ashfield Pde. N14 —18Mb 24
Ashfield Rd. N4 —30Sb 43
Ashfield Rd. N14 —20Lb 24
Ashfield Rd. W3 —46Va 80
Ashfields. Lou —12Pc 28
Ashfields. Wat —7V 4
Ashfield St. E1 —43Xb 83
Ashford Av. N8 —28Nb 42
Ashford Av. Ashf —65R 120
Ashford Av. Brtwd —20Xd 32
Ashford Av. Hay —44Z 77
Ashford Clo. E17 —30Bc 44
Ashford Clo. Ashf —63N 119
Ashford Ct. Edgw —20Ra 21
Ashford Cres. Ashf —62N 119
Ashford Cres. Enf —12Yb 26
Ashford Gdns. Cob —88Z 159
Ashford Grn. Wat —22Z 37
Ashford Ind. Est. Ashf —63S 120
Ashford La. Dor —7A 72
Ashford Pas. NW2 —35Za 60
Ashford Rd. E6 —38Qc 66
Ashford Rd. E18 —26Kc 45
Ashford Rd. NW2 —35Za 60
Ashford Rd. Ashf —66S 120
Ashford Rd. Felt —63T 120
Ashford Rd. Iver —38E 54
Ashford Rd. Stai —68L 119
Ashford St. N1 —41Ub 83 (3H 195)
Ash Grn. Den —37K 55
Ash Gro. E8 —39Xb 63
Ash Gro. N13 —20Sb 25
Ash Gro. NW2 —35Za 60
Ash Gro. SE20 —68Yb 128
Ash Gro. W5 —47Na 79
Ash Gro. Enf —17Ub 25
Ash Gro. Felt —60U 98
Ash Gro. Hare —25M 35
Ash Gro. Hay —45T 76
Ash Gro. Houn —53Z 99
Ash Gro. S'hall —43Ca 77
Ash Gro. Stai —65L 119
Ash Gro. Stoke P —8K 53
Ash Gro. Wemb —35Ja 58
Ash Gro. W Dray —45P 75
Ash Gro. W Wick —75Ec 148
Ashgrove Rd. Ashf —64S 120
Ashgrove Rd. Brom —65Fc 129
Ashgrove Rd. Ilf —32Vc 67
Ashgrove Rd. Sev —99Jd 186
Ash Hill Clo. Bush —18Da 19
Ash Hill Dri. Pinn —27Y 37
Ash Ho. New Ash —75Ae 155
Ashingdon Clo. E4 —20Ec 26
Ashington Rd. SW6 —54Bb 103
Ashlake Rd. SW16 —63Nb 126
Ashland Pl. W1 —43Jb 82 (7H 191)
Ash La. Horn —28Qd 49
Ash La. Romf —23Jd 48
Ash La. Wind —4B 94
Ashlea Rd. Ger X —26A 34
Ashleigh Av. Egh —66E 118
Ashleigh Commercial Est. SE7
—48Lc 85
Ashleigh Ct. N14 —17Lb 24
Ashleigh Gdns. Sutt —75Db 145
Ashleigh Gdns. Upm —34Td 70
Ashleigh Rd. SE20 —69Xb 127
Ashleigh Rd. SW14 —55Ua 102
Ashley Av. Eps —85Ta 161
Ashley Av. Ilf —26Rc 46
Ashley Av. Mord —71Cb 145
Ashley Cen. Eps —85Ta 161
Ashley Clo. NW4 —26Ya 40
Ashley Clo. Bookh —97Ba 175
Ashley Clo. Pinn —26X 37
Ashley Clo. Sev —96Kd 187
Ashley Clo. W on T —74V 140
Ashley Ct. NW4 —26Ya 40
Ashley Ct. SW18 —59Db 103
Ashley Ct. Barn —15Eb 23
Ashley Ct. Eps —85Ta 161
Ashley Ct. Wok —6C 188
Ashley Cres. N22 —26Qb 42
Ashley Cres. SW11 —55Jb 104
Ashley Dri. Bans —86Cb 163
Ashley Dri. Borwd —15Sa 21
Ashley Dri. Iswth —51Ga 100
Ashley Dri. Twic —59Da 99
Ashley Dri. W on T —76W 140
Ashley Gdns. N13 —21Sb 43
Ashley Gdns. SW1
—48Lb 82 (4C 204)
Ashley Gdns. Grays —46Ee 91
Ashley Gdns. Orp —78Uc 150
Ashley Gdns. Rich —61Ma 123
Ashley Gdns. Wemb —33Na 59
Ashley La. NW4 —26Ya 40
Ashley La. Croy —77Rb 147
Ashley Pk. Av. W on T —75V 140
Ashley Pk. Cres. W on T —74W 140
Ashley Pk. Rd. W on T —75W 140
Ashley Pl. SW1 —48Lb 82 (4B 204)
Ashley Rise. W on T —77V 140
Ashley Rd. E4 —23Cc 44
Ashley Rd. E7 —38Lc 65
Ashley Rd. N17 —27Wb 43
Ashley Rd. N19 —32Nb 62
Ashley Rd. SW19 —65Db 125
Ashley Rd. Enf —12Yb 26
Ashley Rd. Eps —85Ta 161
Ashley Rd. Hamp —67Ca 121
Ashley Rd. Rich —55Na 101
Ashley Rd. Sev —96Kd 187
Ashley Rd. Th Dit —72Ha 142
Ashley Rd. T Hth —70Pb 126
Ashley Rd. Uxb —40K 55
Ashley Rd. W on T —77V 140
Ashley Rd. Wok —6C 188
Ashleys. Rick —17H 17
Ashley Sq. Eps —85Ta 161
(off Ashley Cen.)
Ashley Wlk. NW7 —24Ya 40
Ashling Rd. Croy —74Wb 147
Ashlin Rd. E15 —35Fc 65
Ashlone Rd. SW15 —55Za 102
Ashlyn Clo. Bush —14Aa 19
Ashlyn Ct. Wat —14Aa 19
Ashlyn Gro. Horn —27Md 49
Ashlyns Pk. Cob —85Aa 159
Ashlyns Rd. Epp —2Vc 15
Ashlyns Way. Chess —79Ma 143
Ashmead. N14 —15Lb 24
Ashmead Bus. Cen. E16 —42Fc 85
Ashmead Dri. Den —33J 55
Ashmead Ga. Brom —67Lc 129
Ashmead Ho. E9 —36Ac 64
(off Homerton Rd.)
Ashmead La. Den —33J 55
Ashmead Rd. SE8 —54Cc 106
Ashmead Rd. Felt —60W 98
Ashmeads. Lou —13Pc 28
Ashmere Av. Beck —68Fc 129

Ashmere Clo.—Aylesbury Ct.

Ashmere Clo. Sutt —78Za 144
Ashmere Gro. SW2 —56Nb 104
Ash M. Eps —85Ua 162
Ashmill St. NW1 —43Gb 81 (7D 190)
Ashmole Pl. SW8 —51Pb 104
Ashmole St. SW8 —51Pb 104
Ashmore Ct. N11 —23Hb 41
Ashmore Ct. Houn —51Ca 99
Ashmore Gro. Well —55Tc 108
Ashmore La. Kes —83Lc 167
Ashmore Rd. W9 —41Bb 81
Ashmount Est. N19 —31Mb 62
Ashmount Rd. N15 —29Vb 43
Ashmount Rd. N19 —31Lb 62
Ashmount Ter. W5 —49Ma 79
Ashmour Gdns. Romf —26Fd 48
Ashneal Gdns. Harr —34Fa 58
Ashness Gdns. Gnfd —37Ka 58
Ashness Rd. SW11 —57Hb 103
Ash Platt Rd. Seal —93Nd 187
Ash Platt, The. Seal —92Nd 187
Ash Ride. Enf —7Qb 10
Ashridge Clo. Harr —30La 38
Ashridge Ct. N14 —15Lb 24
Ashridge Cres. SE18 —52Sc 108
Ashridge Dri. Brick —2Aa 5
Ashridge Dri. Wat —22Y 37
Ashridge Gdns. N13 —22Mb 42
Ashridge Gdns. Pinn —28Aa 37
Ashridge Ho. Wat —17U 18
(off Chenies Way)
Ashridge Way. Mord —70Bb 125
Ashridge Way. Sun —65W 120
Ash Rd. E15 —36Gc 65
Ash Rd. Ash & New Ash —77Zd 155
Ash Rd. Croy —75Cc 148
Ash Rd. Dart —60Md 111
Ash Rd. Grav —3E 136
Ash Rd. Hart —69Ae 135
Ash Rd. Hawl —63Pd 133
Ash Rd. Orp —80Vc 151
Ash Rd. Shep —70Q 120
Ash Rd. Sutt —73Ab 144
Ash Rd. W'ham —97Tc 184
Ash Rd. Wok —8G 188
Ash Row. Brom —73Qc 150
Ashstead Rd. N16 —31Wb 63
Ashtead Gap. Lea —88Ka 160
Ashtead Rd. E5 —31Wb 63
Ashtead Woods Rd. Asht —89La 160
Ashton Clo. Sutt —77Cb 145
Ashton Clo. W on T —79X 141
Ashton Ct. Harr —34Ha 58
Ashton Gdns. Houn —56Ba 99
Ashton Gdns. Romf —30Ad 47
Ashton Heights. SE23 —60Yb 106
Ashton Ho. SW9 —52Qb 104
Ashton Rd. E15 —36Fc 65
Ashton Rd. Enf —8Ac 12
Ashton Rd. H Hill —24Md 49
Ashton Rd. Wok —5C 188
Ashton St. E14 —45Ec 84
Ashtree Av. Mitc —68Fb 125
Ash Tree Clo. Croy —72Ac 148
Ashtree Clo. Orp —77Rc 150
Ash Tree Clo. Surb —75Na 143
Ash Tree Clo. W King —80Vd 154
Ashtree Ct. Wal A —6Jc 13
(off Horseshoe Clo.)
Ashtree Dell. NW9 —29Ta 39
Ash Tree Dri. W King —80Vd 154
Ash Tree Rd. Wat —8X 5
Ash Tree Way. Croy —71Zb 148
Ashurst. Eps —86Ta 161
Ashurst Clo. SE20 —67Xb 127
Ashurst Clo. Dart —55Hd 110
Ashurst Clo. Kenl —87Tb 165
Ashurst Clo. N'wd —24U 36
Ashurst Dri. Ilf —30Rc 46
Ashurst Dri. Shep —71N 139
Ashurst Gdns. SW2 —60Qb 104
Ashurst Rd. N12 —22Gb 41
Ashurst Rd. Barn —15Hb 23
Ashurst Rd. Tad —93Xa 178
Ashurst Wlk. Croy —75Xb 147
Ash Vale. Rick —22F 34
Ashvale Dri. Upm —33Ud 70
Ashvale Gdns. Romf —22Fd 48
Ashvale Gdns. Upm —33Ud 70
Ashvale Rd. SW17 —64Hb 125
Ash View Clo. Ashf —65N 119
Ash View Gdns. Ashf —64N 119
Ashville Rd. E11 —33Fc 65
Ash Wlk. Wemb —34La 58
Ashwater Clo. NW9 —29Ta 39
Ashwater Rd. SE12 —60Jc 107
Ashwell Clo. E6 —44Nc 86
Ashwells Rd. Pil H —13Td 32
Ashwindham Ct. Wok —6C 188
Ashwin St. E8 —37Vb 63
Ashwood. Warl —92Yb 182
Ashwood Av. Rain —42Kd 89
Ashwood Av. Uxb —44Q 76
Ashwood Gdns. Hay —49V 76
Ashwood Gdns. New Ad —79Dc 148
Ashwood Pk. Fet —96Ea 176
Ashwood Pk. Wok —90C 156
Ashwood Pl. Bean —62Xd 134
Ashwood Rd. E4 —20Fc 27
Ashwood Rd. Egh —5M 117
Ashwood Rd. Pot B —5Db 9
Ashwood Rd. Wok —90B 156
Ashworth Clo. SE5 —54Tb 105
Ashworth Ind. Est. Bedd —74Nb 146
Ashworth Rd. W9 —41Db 81
Asilone Rd. SW15 —55Ya 102
Asker Ho. N7 —35Nb 62
Askern Clo. Bexh —56Zc 109
Aske St. N1 —41Ub 83 (3H 195)
Askew Cres. W12 —47Va 80
Askew Est. W12 —46Va 80
(off Uxbridge Rd.)
Askew Rd. W12 —46Va 80
Askew Rd. N'wd —19T 18
Askews Farm La. Grays —50Ae 91
Askham Ct. W12 —46Wa 80
Askham Rd. W12 —46Wa 80
Askill Dri. SW15 —57Ab 102
Askwith Rd. Rain —41Fd 88
Asland Rd. E15 —39Gc 65
Aslett St. SW18 —59Db 103
Asmara Rd. NW2 —36Ab 60
Asmar Clo. Coul —87Nb 164
Asmuns Hill. NW11 —29Cb 41
Asmuns Pl. NW11 —29Bb 41
Aspdin Rd. Grav —62Fe 135
Aspen Clo. N19 —33Lb 62
Aspen Clo. W5 —47Pa 79
Aspen Clo. Brick —2Aa 5
Aspen Clo. Orp —78Wc 151
Aspen Clo. Slou —3F 72
Aspen Clo. Stai —62H 119
Aspen Clo. Stoke D —88Aa 159
Aspen Clo. Swan —67Fd 132
Aspen Clo. W Dray —46P 75
Aspen Copse. Brom —68Pc 130
Aspen Ct. E8 —37Vb 63
Aspen Dri. Wemb —34Ja 58
Aspen Gdns. W6 —50Xa 80
Aspen Gdns. Mitc —71Jb 146
Aspen Grn. Eri —48Bd 87
Aspen Gro. Upm —35Qd 69
Aspen Ho. Sidc —62Wc 131
Aspen La. N'holt —41Aa 77
Aspenlea Rd. W6 —51Za 102
Aspen Pk. Dri. Wat —7X 5
Aspen Sq. Wey —76T 140
Aspen Way. E14 —45Cc 84
Aspen Way. Bans —86Za 162
Aspen Way. Enf —7Zb 12
Aspen Way. Felt —62X 121
Aspern Gro. NW3 —36Gb 61
Aspinall Rd. SE4 —55Zb 106
Aspinden Rd. SE16 —49Xb 83
Aspley Rd. E17 —29Bc 44
Aspley Rd. SW18 —57Db 103
Asplins Rd. N17 —25Wb 43
Asquith Clo. Dag —32Yc 67
Assam St. E1 —44Wb 83
Assata M. N1 —37Rb 63
Assembly Pas. E1 —43Yb 84
Assembly Wlk. Cars —73Gb 145
Assher Rd. W on T —76Aa 141
Ass Ho. La. Har W —21Da 37
Astall Clo. Harr —25Ga 38
Astbury Rd. SE15 —53Yb 106
Astell St. SW3 —50Gb 81 (7E 202)
Aste St. E14 —47Ec 84
Astey's Row. N1 —38Sb 63
Asthall Gdns. Ilf —28Sc 46
Astins Ho. E17 —28Dc 44
Astleham Rd. Shep —69N 119
Astle St. SW11 —54Jb 104
Astley. Grays —51Be 113
Astley Av. NW2 —36Ya 60
Astley Ho. SE1 —50Vb 83 (7K 207)
Aston Av. Harr —31La 58
Aston Clo. Asht —90La 160
Aston Clo. Sidc —62Wc 131
Aston Ct. Wfd G —23Jc 45
Aston Grn. Houn —54Y 99
Aston Ho. SW8 —53Mb 104
Aston Mead. Wind —2C 94
Aston M. Romf —31Yc 67
Aston Rd. SW20 —68Ya 124
Aston Rd. W5 —44Ma 79
Aston Rd. Clay —78Ga 142
Astons Rd. N'wd —20S 18
Aston St. E14 —43Ac 84
Astonville St. SW18 —60Cb 103
Aston Way. Eps —87Va 162
Aston Way. Pot B —4Fb 9
Astor Av. Romf —30Ed 48
Astor Clo. Add —77M 139
Astor Clo. King T —65Ra 123
Astoria Mans. SW16 —62Nb 126
Astoria Wlk. SW9 —55Qb 104
Astor Rd. W King —79Ud 154
Astra Clo. Horn —37Kd 69
Astra Ct. Wat —15V 18
Astra Dri. Grav —4G 136
Astrop M. W6 —48Ya 80
Astrop Ter. W6 —47Ya 80
Astwood M. SW7 —49Eb 81
Asylum Rd. SE15 —52Xb 105
Atalanta Clo. Purl —82Qb 164
Atalanta St. SW6 —52Za 102
Atbara Rd. Tedd —65Ka 122
Atcham Rd. Houn —56Ea 100
Atcost Rd. Bark —43Wc 87
Atcraft Cen. Wemb —39Na 59
Atheldene Rd. SW18 —60Db 103
Athelney St. SE6 —62Cc 128
Athelstan Clo. Romf —26Pd 49
Athelstane Gro. E3 —40Bc 64
Athelstane M. N4 —32Qb 62
Athelstan Gdns. NW6 —38Ab 60
Athelstan Rd. King T —70Pa 123
Athelstan Rd. Romf —25Pd 49
Athelstone Rd. Harr —26Fa 38
Athena Clo. Harr —33Fa 58
Athenaeum Ct. N5 —35Sb 63
Athenaeum Pl. N10 —27Kb 42
Athenaeum Rd. N20 —18Eb 23
Athena Pl. N'wd —25V 36
Athenlay Rd. SE15 —57Zb 106
Athens Gdns. W9 —42Cb 81
Atherden Rd. E5 —35Yb 64
Atherfold Rd. SW9 —55Nb 104
Atherley Way. Houn —59Ba 99
Atherstone M. SW7 —49Eb 81 (5A 202)
Atherton Clo. Stai —58M 97
Atherton Ct. Wind —2H 95
Atherton Dri. SW19 —63Za 124
Atherton Gdns. Grays —9E 92
Atherton Heights. Wemb —37La 58
Atherton Ho. H Hill —24Nd 49
(off Leyburn Cres.)
Atherton M. E7 —37Hc 65
Atherton Pl. Harr —27Fa 38
Atherton Pl. S'hall —45Ca 77
Atherton Rd. E7 —37Hc 65
Atherton Rd. SW13 —52Wa 102
Atherton Rd. Ilf —26Nc 46
Atherton St. SW11 —54Gb 103
Athill Ct. Sev —94Ld 187
Athlone. Clay —79Ga 142
Athlone Clo. E5 —36Xb 63
Athlone Clo. Rad —8Ja 6
Athlone Ct. E17 —27Fc 45
Athlone Rd. SW2 —59Pb 104
Athlone Sq. Wind —3G 94
Athlone St. NW5 —37Jb 62
Athlon Ind. Est. Wemb —40Ma 59
Athlon Rd. Wemb —40Ma 59
Athol Clo. Pinn —25X 37
Athole Gdns. Enf —15Ub 25
Athol Gdns. Pinn —25X 37
Atholl Rd. Ilf —31Wc 67
Athol Rd. Eri —50Ed 88
Athol Sq. E14 —44Ec 84
Athol Way. Uxb —41Q 76
Atkins Clo. Wok —6D 188
Atkins Dri. W Wick —75Fc 149
Atkinson Clo. Orp —78Wc 151
Atkinson Ct. E10 —31Dc 64
(off Kings Clo.)
Atkinson Rd. E16 —43Lc 85
Atkins Rd. E10 —30Dc 44
Atkins Rd. SW12 —59Lb 104
Atlanta Boulevd. Romf —30Gd 48
Atlantic Rd. SW9 —56Qb 104
Atlas Bus. Cen. NW2 —33Xa 60
Atlas Gdns. SE7 —49Lc 85
Atlas M. N7 —37Pb 62
Atlas Rd. E13 —40Jc 65
Atlas Rd. NW10 —41Ua 80
Atlas Rd. Wemb —35Sa 59
Atlas Wharf. E9 —37Cc 64
Atley Rd. E3 —39Cc 64
Atlip Rd. Wemb —39Na 59
Atney Rd. SW15 —56Ab 102
Atria Rd. N'wd —22W 36
Atterbury Clo. W'ham —98Tc 184
Atterbury Rd. N4 —30Rb 43
Atterbury St. SW1 —49Nb 82 (6E 204)
Attewood Av. NW10 —34Ua 60
Attewood Rd. N'holt —37Aa 57
Attfield Clo. N20 —19Fb 23
Attleborough Ct. SE23 —61Xb 127
Attle Clo. Uxb —40Q 56
Attlee Ct. Grays —48Ce 91
Attlee Dri. Dart —57Qd 111
Attlee Rd. SE28 —45Xc 87
Attlee Rd. Hay —41W 76
Attlee Ter. E17 —28Dc 44
Attneave St. WC1 —41Qb 82 (5K 193)
Attwood Clo. S Croy —86Xb 165
Atwater Clo. SW2 —60Qb 104
Atwell Clo. E10 —30Dc 44
Atwell Rd. SE15 —54Wb 105
Atwood. Bookh —96Aa 175
Atwood Av. Rich —54Qa 101
Atwood Rd. W6 —49Xa 80
Atwoods All. Rich —53Qa 101
Aubert Ct. N5 —35Rb 63
Aubert Pk. N5 —35Rb 63
Aubert Rd. N5 —35Rb 63
Aubretia Clo. H Wood —25Nd 49
Aubrey Gdns. NW8 —40Eb 61 (2A 190)
(off Abbey Rd.)
Aubrey Moore Point. E15 —40Ec 64
(off Abbey La.)
Aubrey Pl. NW8 —40Eb 61 (2A 190)
Aubrey Rd. E17 —27Cc 44
Aubrey Rd. N8 —29Nb 42
Aubrey Rd. W8 —46Bb 81
Aubrey Wlk. W8 —46Bb 81
Aubyn Hill. SE27 —63Sb 127
Aubyn Sq. SW15 —57Wa 102
Auckland Av. Rain —41Hd 88
Auckland Clo. SE19 —67Vb 127
Auckland Clo. Enf —9Xb 11
Auckland Clo. Til —4C 114
Auckland Gdns. SE19 —67Ub 127
Auckland Hill. SE27 —63Sb 127
Auckland Ho. W12 —45Xa 80
(off White City Est.)
Auckland Rise. SE19 —67Ub 127
Auckland Rd. E10 —34Dc 64
Auckland Rd. SE19 —67Vb 127
Auckland Rd. SW11 —56Gb 103
Auckland Rd. Cat —94Ub 181
Auckland Rd. Ilf —32Rc 66
Auckland Rd. King T —70Pa 123
Auckland Rd. Pot B —4Za 8
Auckland St. SE11 —50Pb 82
Auden Pl. NW1 —39Jb 62
Auden Pl. Cheam —77Ya 144
Audleigh Pl. Chig —23Qc 46
Audley Clo. SW11 —55Jb 104
Audley Clo. Add —78K 139
Audley Clo. Borwd —13Qa 21
Audley Ct. E18 —28Hc 45
Audley Ct. Pinn —26Y 37
Audley Ct. Twic —62Fa 122
Audley Dri. Warl —87Yb 166
Audley Firs. W on T —77Y 141
Audley Gdns. Ilf —33Vc 67
Audley Gdns. Lou —12Sc 28
(in two parts)
Audley Gdns. Wal A —6Ec 12
Audley Ho. Add —78K 139
Audley Pl. Sutt —80Db 145
Audley Rd. NW4 —29Wa 40
Audley Rd. W5 —43Pa 79
Audley Rd. Enf —12Rb 25
Audley Rd. Rich —57Pa 101
Audley Sq. W1 —46Jb 82 (6J 197)
Audley Wlk. Orp —72Yc 151
Audrey Clo. Beck —72Dc 148
Audrey Gdns. Wemb —33Ka 58
Audrey Rd. Ilf —34Rc 66
Audrey St. E2 —40Wb 63
Audric Clo. King T —67Qa 123
Audwick Clo. Chesh —1Ac 12
Augur Clo. Stai —64H 119
Augusta Clo. W Mol —70Ba 121
Augusta Rd. Twic —61Ea 122
Augusta St. E14 —44Dc 84
August End. G Grn —44A 74
Augustine Clo. Coln —55G 96
Augustine Rd. W14 —48Za 80
Augustine Rd. Grav —9E 114
Augustine Rd. Harr —25Da 37
Augustine Rd. Orp —69Zc 131
Augustus Clo. Bren —52La 100
Augustus Ct. SW16 —61Mb 126
Augustus Ct. Felt —63Ba 121
Augustus La. Orp —75Wc 151
Augustus Rd. SW19 —60Za 102
Augustus St. NW1 —40Kb 62 (2A 192)
Aultone Way. Cars —76Hb 145
Aultone Way. Sutt —75Db 145
Aulton Pl. SE11 —50Qb 82
Aurelia Gdns. Croy —71Pb 146
Aurelia Rd. Croy —72Nb 146
Auric Clo. Grays —9D 92
Auriel Av. Dag —37Fd 68
Auriga M. N1 —36Ub 63
Auriol Clo. Wor Pk —76Ua 144
Auriol Dri. Gnfd —38Fa 58
Auriol Dri. Uxb —37Q 56
Auriol Pk. Rd. Wor Pk —76Ua 144
Auriol Rd. W14 —49Ab 80
Austell Gdns. NW7 —20Ua 22
Austen Clo. SE28 —46Xc 87
Austen Clo. Grnh —58Yd 112
Austen Clo. Lou —13Tc 28
Austen Clo. Til —4E 114
Austen Gdns. Dart —56Pd 111
Austen Rd. Harr —33Da 57
Austenway. Ger X —27A 34
Austenwood La. Ger X —26A 34
Austin Av. Brom —71Nc 150
Austin Clo. SE23 —59Bc 106
Austin Clo. Coul —90Rb 165
Austin Clo. Twic —57La 100
Austin Ct. E6 —39Lc 65
Austin Ct. Enf —15Ub 25
Austin Friars. EC2 —44Tb 83 (2G 201)
Austin Friars Pas. EC2 —44Tb 83 (2G 201)
(off Austin Friars)
Austin Friars Sq. EC2 —44Tb 83 (2G 201)
(off Austin Friars)
Austin Rd. SW11 —53Jb 104
Austin Rd. Grav —10B 114
Austin Rd. Hay —47V 76
Austin Rd. Orp —72Wc 151
Austin's La. Uxb —34S 56
Austins Mead. Bov —1D 2
Austin St. E2 —41Vb 83 (4K 195)
Austin Waye. Uxb —39L 55
Austral Clo. Sidc —62Vc 131
Austral Dri. Horn —31Md 69
Australia Rd. W12 —45Xa 80
Australia Rd. Slou —7M 73
Austral St. SE11 —49Rb 83 (5B 206)
Austyn Gdns. Surb —74Ra 143
Autumn Clo. Enf —11Wb 25
Autumn Clo. Slou —6D 72
Autumn St. E3 —39Cc 64
Auxiliares Way. Den —29H 35
Avalon Clo. SW20 —68Ab 124
Avalon Clo. W13 —43Ja 78
Avalon Clo. Enf —12Qb 24
Avalon Clo. Orp —76Zc 151
Avalon Clo. Wat —4Aa 5
Avalon Rd. SW6 —53Db 103
Avalon Rd. W13 —42Ja 78
Avalon Rd. Orp —75Yc 151
Avard Gdns. Orp —77Sc 150
Avarn Rd. SW17 —65Hb 125
Avebury. Slou —5E 72
Avebury Ct. N1 —39Tb 63 (1F 195)
(off Colville Est.)
Avebury Pk. Surb —73Ma 143
Avebury Rd. E11 —32Ec 65
Avebury Rd. SW19 —67Bb 125
Avebury Rd. Orp —76Tc 150
Avebury St. N1 —39Tb 63 (1F 195)
Aveley By-Pass. S Ock —45Sd 90
Aveley Clo. S Ock —46Td 90
Aveley Mans. Bark —38Rc 66
(off Whiting Av.)
Aveley Rd. Romf —28Fd 48
Aveley Rd. Upm —37Rd 69
Aveline St. SE11 —50Qb 82 (7J 205)
Aveling Clo. Purl —85Pb 164
Aveling Pk. Rd. E17 —25Cc 44
Avelon Rd. Rain —39Jd 68
Avelon Rd. Romf —23Fd 48
Ave Maria La. EC4 —44Rb 83 (3C 200)
Avenell Rd. N5 —34Rb 63
Avening Rd. SW18 —59Cb 103
Avening Ter. SW18 —59Cb 103
Avenons Rd. E13 —42Jc 85
Avenue App. K Lan —2Q 4
Avenue Clo. N14 —16Lb 24
Avenue Clo. NW8 —39Gb 61 (1E 190)
Avenue Clo. Add —76N 139
Avenue Clo. Houn —53X 99
Avenue Clo. Romf —24Pd 49
Avenue Clo. Tad —94Xa 178
Avenue Clo. W Dray —48M 75
Avenue Ct. N14 —16Lb 24
Avenue Ct. NW2 —34Bb 61
Avenue Ct. Tad —95Xa 178
Avenue Cres. W3 —47Ra 79
Avenue Cres. Houn —53X 99
Avenue Elmers. Surb —71Na 143
Avenue Gdns. SE25 —68Wb 127
Avenue Gdns. SW14 —55Ua 102
Avenue Gdns. W3 —47Ra 79
Avenue Gdns. Houn —52X 99
Avenue Gdns. Tedd —66Ha 122
Avenue Ind. Est. E4 —23Bc 44
Avenue Ind. Est. Romf —26Md 49
Avenue Mans. NW3 —36Db 61
(off Finchley Rd.)
Avenue M. N10 —27Kb 42
Avenue One. Add —77N 139
Avenue Pk. Rd. SE27 —61Rb 127
Avenue Rise. Bush —15Ca 19
Avenue Rd. E7 —35Kc 65
Avenue Rd. N6 —31Lb 62
Avenue Rd. N12 —21Eb 41
Avenue Rd. N14 —17Lb 24
Avenue Rd. N15 —29Tb 43
Avenue Rd. NW3 & NW8 —38Fb 61 (1E 190)
Avenue Rd. NW10 —40Va 60
Avenue Rd. SE20 & Beck —67Yb 128
Avenue Rd. SE25 —68Vb 127
Avenue Rd. SW16 —68Mb 126
Avenue Rd. SW20 —68Xa 124
Avenue Rd. W3 —47Ra 79
Avenue Rd. Bans —87Db 163
Avenue Rd. Belv —49Dd 88
Avenue Rd. Bexh —55Ad 109
Avenue Rd. Bren —50La 78
Avenue Rd. Cat —94Tb 181
Avenue Rd. Chad —31Yc 67
Avenue Rd. Cob —88Z 159
Avenue Rd. Eps —86Ta 161
Avenue Rd. Eri —52Ed 110
(in three parts)
Avenue Rd. Felt —62V 120
Avenue Rd. Hamp —67Da 121
Avenue Rd. H Wood —24Pd 49
Avenue Rd. Iswth —53Ha 100
Avenue Rd. King T —69Na 123
Avenue Rd. N Mald —70Ua 124
Avenue Rd. Pinn —27Aa 37
Avenue Rd. Sev —96Ld 187
Avenue Rd. S'hall —46Ba 77
Avenue Rd. Stai —64F 118
Avenue Rd. Sutt —82Cb 163
Avenue Rd. Tats —92Nc 184
Avenue Rd. Tedd —66Ja 122
Avenue Rd. They B —8Tc 14
Avenue Rd. Wall —80Lb 146
Avenue Rd. War —21Yd 50
Avenue Rd. Wfd G —23Lc 45
Avenue S. Surb —73Qa 143
Avenue Ter. N Mald —69Sa 123
Avenue Ter. Wat —16Aa 19
Avenue, The. E4 —21Gc 45
Avenue, The. E11 —29Kc 45
Avenue, The. N3 —26Cb 41
Avenue, The. N8 —27Qb 42
Avenue, The. N10 —26Lb 42
Avenue, The. N11 —22Kb 42
Avenue, The. N17 —26Ub 43
Avenue, The. NW6 —39Ab 60
Avenue, The. SE7 —52Lc 107
Avenue, The. SE9 —58Pc 108
Avenue, The. SE10 —52Fc 107
Avenue, The. SW4 —57Kb 104
Avenue, The. SW18 —59Gb 103
Avenue, The. W4 —48Ua 80
Avenue, The. W13 —44Ka 78
Avenue, The. Barn —13Ab 22
Avenue, The. Beck —67Dc 128
Avenue, The. Bex —59Zc 109
Avenue, The. Brtwd —22Ae 51
Avenue, The. Brom —69Mc 129
Avenue, The. Bush —15Ba 19
Avenue, The. Cars —80Jb 146
Avenue, The. Clay —78Ga 142
Avenue, The. Cobh —9L 137
Avenue, The. Coul —87Mb 164
Avenue, The. Cow —42M 75
Avenue, The. Cran —53W 98
Avenue, The. Croy —76Ub 147
Avenue, The. Dat —3M 95
Avenue, The. Egh —63D 118
Avenue, The. Eps & Sut —80Xa 144
Avenue, The. Farn C —6F 52
Avenue, The. Grav —9C 114
Avenue, The. Grnh —57Xd 112
Avenue, The. Hamp —65Ba 121
Avenue, The. Harr —25Ha 38
Avenue, The. H End —23Ba 37
Avenue, The. Horn —33Ld 69
Avenue, The. Houn —57Da 99
Avenue, The. Ick —35Q 56
Avenue, The. Kel H —11Ud 32
Avenue, The. Kes —76Mc 149
Avenue, The. Lou —16Nc 28
Avenue, The. New Haw —82J 157
Avenue, The. N'wd —23S 36
Avenue, The. Old Win —7M 95
Avenue, The. Orp —75Vc 151
Avenue, The. Oxs —84Ha 160
Avenue, The. Pinn —31Ba 57
Avenue, The. Pot B —3Cb 9
Avenue, The. Rad —6Ka 6
Avenue, The. Rich —54Pa 101
Avenue, The. Romf —28Fd 48
Avenue, The. Stai —67K 119
Avenue, The. St P —67Xc 131
Avenue, The. Sun —68X 121
Avenue, The. Surb —73Qa 143
Avenue, The. Sutt —82Bb 163
Avenue, The. Tad —94Xa 178
Avenue, The. Twic —57Ka 100
Avenue, The. Wat —12W 18
Avenue, The. Wemb —33Pa 59
Avenue, The. W'ham —95Qc 184
Avenue, The. W Wick —73Gc 149
Avenue, The. Whyt —91Wb 181
Avenue, The. Wor Pk —75Va 144
Avenue, The. Wray —56A 96
Avenue Three. Add —76N 139
Avenue Two. Add —76N 139
Averil Ct. Tap —4A 72
Averil Gro. SW16 —65Rb 127
Averill St. W6 —51Za 102
Avern Gdns. W Mol —70Da 121
Avern Rd. W Mol —70Da 121
Avery Farm Row. SW1 —49Kb 82 (6K 203)
Avery Gdns. Ilf —29Pc 46
Avery Hill Rd. SE9 —58Tc 108
Avery Row. W1 —45Kb 82 (4K 197)
Avey La. Wal A & Lou —8Fc 13
Aviary Clo. E16 —43Hc 85
Aviary Rd. Wok —88J 157
Aviemore Clo. Beck —71Bc 148
Aviemore Way. Beck —71Ac 148
Avignon Rd. SE4 —55Zb 106
Avington Gro. SE20 —66Yb 128
Avington Way. SE15 —52Vb 105
Avior Dri. N'wd —21V 36
Avis Sq. E1 —44Zb 84
Avoca Rd. SW17 —63Jb 126
Avocet M. SE28 —48Tc 86
Avon Clo. Add —79J 139
Avon Clo. Grav —1F 136
Avon Clo. Hay —42Y 77
Avon Clo. Slou —5C 72
Avon Clo. Sutt —77Eb 145
Avon Clo. Wat —6Y 5
Avon Clo. Wor Pk —75Wa 144
Avon Ct. N12 —22Db 41
Avon Ct. Buck H —18Kc 27
Avon Ct. Gnfd —42Da 77
Avondale Av. N12 —22Db 41
Avondale Av. NW2 —34Ua 60
Avondale Av. Barn —18Hb 23
Avondale Av. Esh —76Ja 142
Avondale Av. Stai —66H 119
Avondale Av. Wor Pk —74Va 144
Avondale Clo. Lou —17Pc 28
Avondale Clo. W on T —78Y 141
Avondale Ct. E11 —32Gc 65
Avondale Ct. E16 —43Gc 85
Avondale Ct. E18 —25Kc 45
Avondale Cres. Enf —13Ac 26
Avondale Cres. Ilf —29Mc 45
Avondale Dri. Hay —46W 76
Avondale Dri. Lou —17Pc 28
Avondale Gdns. Houn —57Ba 99
Avondale Ho. SE1 —50Wb 83
(off Avondale Sq.)
Avondale Pk. Gdns. W11 —45Ab 80
Avondale Pk. Rd. W11 —45Ab 80
Avondale Rise. SE15 —55Vb 105
Avondale Rd. E16 —43Gc 85
Avondale Rd. E17 —31Cc 64
Avondale Rd. N3 —25Eb 41
Avondale Rd. N13 —19Qb 24
Avondale Rd. N15 —29Rb 43
Avondale Rd. SE9 —61Nc 130
Avondale Rd. SW14 —55Ua 102
Avondale Rd. SW19 —64Db 125
Avondale Rd. Ashf —62M 119
Avondale Rd. Brom —65Hc 129
Avondale Rd. Harr —27Ha 38
Avondale Rd. S Croy —79Sb 147
Avondale Rd. Well —54Yc 109
Avondale Sq. SE1 —50Wb 83
Avonfield Ct. E17 —27Fc 45
Avon Grn. S Ock —44Xd 90
Avon Ho. W8 —48Cb 81
(off Allen St.)
Avonley Rd. SE14 —52Yb 106
Avonmead. Wok —6F 188
Avon M. Pinn —24Ba 37
Avonmore Gdns. W14 —49Bb 81
Avonmore Rd. W14 —49Bb 80
Avonmouth Rd. Dart —57Md 111
Avonmouth St. SE1 —48Sb 83 (3D 206)
Avon Path. S Croy —79Sb 147
Avon Pl. SE1 —47Sb 83 (2E 206)
Avon Rd. E17 —27Fc 45
Avon Rd. SE4 —55Cc 106
Avon Rd. Gnfd —42Ca 77
Avon Rd. Sun —66V 120
Avon Rd. Upm —30Td 50
Avontar Rd. S Ock —42Xd 90
Avon Way. E18 —27Jc 45
Avonwick Rd. Houn —54Da 99
Avril Way. E4 —22Ec 44
Avro Way. Wall —80Nb 146
Avro Way. Wey —82N 157
Awberry Ct. Wat —16S 18
Awlfield Av. N17 —25Tb 43
Awliscombe Rd. Well —54Vc 109
Axe Ct. E2 —41Vb 83 (3K 195)
(off Long St.)
Axe St. Bark —39Sc 66
Axholme Av. Edgw —25Qa 39
Axis Bus. Cen. W4 —51Ua 102
Axminster Cres. Well —53Yc 109
Axminster Rd. N7 —34Nb 62
Axtaine Rd. Orp —73Zc 151
Axtane. S'fleet —66Be 135
Axtane Clo. S at H —67Sd 134
Axwood. Eps —87Sa 161
Aybrook St. W1 —43Jb 82 (1H 197)
Aycliffe Clo. Brom —70Pc 130
Aycliffe Rd. W12 —46Wa 80
Aycliffe Rd. Borwd —11Na 21
Ayebridges Av. Egh —66E 118
Ayelands. New Ash —75Ae 155
Ayelands La. New Ash —76Ae 155
Ayerst Ct. E10 —31Ec 64
Aylands Clo. Wemb —33Na 59
Aylands Rd. Enf —8Zb 12
Aylesbury Clo. E7 —37Hc 65
Aylesbury Ct. Sutt —76Eb 145

Aylesbury Cres.—Barncroft Clo.

Aylesbury Cres. Slou —4H **73**
Aylesbury Rd. SE17 —50Tb **83** (7G **207**)
Aylesbury Rd. Brom —69Jc **129**
Aylesbury St. EC1 —42Rb **83** (6B **194**)
Aylesbury St. NW10 —34Ta **59**
Aylesford Av. Beck —71Ac **148**
Aylesford St. SW1 —50Mb **82** (7D **204**)
Aylesham Cen., The. SE15 —53Wb **105**
Aylesham Rd. Orp —73Vc **151**
Ayles Rd. Hay & N'holt —41X **77**
Aylestone Av. NW6 —38Za **60**
Aylesworth Av. Slou —1F **72**
Aylesworth Spur. Old Win —9M **95**
Aylett Rd. SE25 —70Xb **127**
Aylett Rd. Iswth —54Ga **100**
Aylett Rd. Upm —33Sd **70**
Ayley Croft. Enf —15Wb **25**
Ayliffe Clo. King T —68Qa **123**
Aylmer Clo. Stan —21Ja **38**
Aylmer Ct. N2 —29Hb **41**
Aylmer Dri. Stan —21Ja **38**
Aylmer Pde. N2 —29Hb **41**
Aylmer Rd. E11 —32Hc **65**
Aylmer Rd. N2 —29Gb **41**
Aylmer Rd. W12 —47Va **80**
Aylmer Rd. Dag —34Ad **67**
Ayloffe Rd. Dag —37Bd **67**
Ayloffs Clo. Horn —28Md **49**
Ayloffs Wlk. Horn —29Md **49**
Aylsham Dri. Uxb —33S **56**
Aylsham La. Romf —21Ld **49**
Aylton Est. SE16 —48Yb **84**
Aylward Rd. SE23 —61Zb **128**
Aylward Rd. SW20 —68Bb **125**
Aylwards Rise. Stan —21Ja **38**
Aylward St. E1 —44Yb **84**
Aylwin Est. SE1 —48Ub **83** (3J **207**)
Aymer Clo. Stai —67G **118**
Aymer Dri. Stai —67G **118**
*Aynhoe Mans. W14 —49Za **80***
(off Aynhoe Rd.)
Aynhoe Rd. W14 —49Za **80**
Aynho St. Wat —15X **19**
Aynscombe Angle. Orp —73Wc **151**
Aynscombe Path. SW14 —54Sa **101**
Ayot Path. Borwd —9Qa **7**
Ayr Ct. W3 —43Qa **79**
Ayres Clo. E13 —41Jc **85**
Ayres Cres. NW10 —38Ta **59**
Ayres St. SE1 —47Sb **83** (1E **206**)
Ayr Grn. Romf —25Gd **48**
Ayron Rd. S Ock —42Xd **90**
Ayrsome Rd. N16 —34Ub **63**
Ayrton Rd. SW7 —48Fb **81** (3B **202**)
Ayr Way. Romf —25Gd **48**
Aysgarth Ct. Sutt —76Db **145**
Aysgarth Rd. SE21 —59Ub **105**
Aytoun Pl. SW9 —54Pb **104**
Aytoun Rd. SW9 —54Pb **104**
Azalea Clo. W7 —46Ha **78**
Azalea Clo. Ilf —36Rc **66**
Azalea Ct. W7 —46Ha **78**
Azalea Ct. Wok —7G **188**
Azalea Dri. Swan —70Fd **132**
Azalea Wlk. Pinn —29X **37**
Azalea Way. G Grn —44A **74**
Azenby Rd. SE15 —54Vb **105**
Azof St. SE10 —49Gc **85**

Baalbec Rd. N5 —36Rb **63**
Babbacombe Clo. Chess —78Ma **143**
Babbacombe Gdns. Ilf —28Nc **46**
Babbacombe Rd. Brom —67Jc **129**
Baber Dri. Felt —58Y **99**
*Babington Ct. WC1 —43Pb **82** (7H **193**)*
(off Orde Hall St.)
Babington Rise. Wemb —37Qa **59**
Babington Rd. NW4 —28Xa **40**
Babington Rd. SW16 —64Mb **126**
Babington Rd. Dag —36Yc **67**
Babington Rd. Horn —32Kd **69**
Babmaes St. SW1 —45Mb **82** (5D **198**)
Babylon La. Tad —99Cb **179**
*Bacchus Wlk. N1 —40Ub **63** (2H **195**)*
(off Hoxton St.)
Bachelors Acre. Wind —3H **95**
Bachelors La. Ock —96P **173**
Bache's St. N1 —41Tb **83** (4G **195**)
Bk. Church La. E1 —44Wb **83**
Back Grn. W on T —79Y **141**
Back Hill. EC1 —42Qb **82** (6A **194**)
*Backhouse Pl. SE17 —49Ub **83** (6J **207**)*
(off Surrey Sq.)
Back La. E15 —40Fc **65**
Back La. N8 —29Nb **42**
Back La. NW3 —35Eb **61**
Back La. Bark —39Sc **66**
Back La. Bex —59Cd **110**
Back La. Bren —51Ma **101**
Back La. Chen —10D **2**
Back La. Edgw —25Sa **39**
Back La. God G —96Qd **187**
Back La. Grays —48Ud **90**
Back La. Ide & Sev —100Dd **186**
Back La. Let H —11Ga **20**
Back La. N Stif —46Yd **90**
Back La. Rich —61La **122**
(in two parts)
Back La. Romf —31Zc **67**
Back La. Sev —96Fd **186**
Back La. Wind —3H **95**
Back Rd. Sidc —63Wc **131**
Bacon Gro. SE1 —48Vb **83** (4K **207**)
Bacon La. NW9 —28Ra **39**
Bacon La. Edgw —25Qa **39**
Bacon Link. Romf —23Dd **48**
Bacons Dri. Cuff —1Nb **10**
Bacons La. N6 —32Jb **62**
Bacons Mead. Den —33J **55**
Bacon St. E1 & E2 —42Vb **83** (5K **195**)
Bacton St. E2 —41Yb **84**
Badburgham Ct. Wal A —5Hc **13**
*Baddesley Ho. SE11 —50Pb **82** (7J **205**)*
(off Jonathan St.)
Baddow Clo. Dag —39Cd **68**
Baddow Clo. Wfd G —23Mc **45**
Baden. Belv —48Cd **88**
Baden Clo. Stai —66J **119**
Baden Pl. SE1 —47Tb **83** (1F **207**)
Baden Pl. SW1 —47Tb **83**
Baden-Powell Clo. Surb —75Pa **143**
*Baden-Powell Ho. SW7 —49Eb **81** (5A **202**)*
(off Queens Ga.)
Baden Powell Rd. Sev —94Gd **186**
Baden Rd. N8 —28Mb **42**
Baden Rd. Ilf —36Rc **66**
Bader Clo. Kenl —87Tb **165**
Bader Gdns. Slou —7E **72**
Bader Wlk. Grav —2B **136**
Bader Way. Rain —37Jd **68**
Badger Clo. Felt —62X **121**
Badger Clo. Houn —55Y **99**
Badgersbridge Ride. Wind —9A **94**
Badgers Clo. Ashf —64P **119**
Badgers Clo. Borwd —12Pa **21**
Badgers Clo. Enf —12Rb **25**
Badgers Clo. Harr —30Fa **38**
Badgers Clo. Hay —45U **76**
Badgers Clo. Wok —6F **188**
Badgers Copse. Orp —75Vc **151**
Badgers Copse. Wor Pk —75Va **144**
Badger's Ct. Eps —85Ua **162**
Badgers Croft. N20 —17Ab **22**
Badgers Croft. SE9 —62Qc **130**
Badgers Hill. Vir W —10N **117**
Badgers Hole. Croy —77Zb **148**
Badgers La. Warl —92Yb **182**
Badgers Mt. Ors —7B **92**
Badger's Rise. Badg M —82Cd **170**
Badgers Rd. Badg M —82Dd **170**
Badgers Wlk. N Mald —68Ua **124**
Badgers Wlk. Purl —83Lb **164**
Badgers Wlk. Whyt —90Vb **165**
Badgers Wood. Cat —97Tb **181**
Badgers Wood. Farn C —6G **52**
Badgers Wood. Ott —79F **138**
Badingham Dri. Fet —95Ga **176**
Badlis Rd. E17 —27Cc **44**
Badlow Clo. Eri —52Gd **110**
Badminton Clo. Borwd —12Qa **21**
Badminton Clo. Harr —28Ga **38**
Badminton Clo. N'holt —37Ca **57**
Badminton Rd. SW12 —58Jb **104**
Badsworth Rd. SE5 —53Sb **105**
*Baffins Pl. SE1 —48Tb **83** (3G **207**)*
(off Long La.)
Bagford St. N1 —39Tb **63**
Bagley Clo. W Dray —47N **75**
Bagley's La. SW6 —53Db **103**
Bagleys Spring. Romf —28Ad **47**
Bagot Clo. Asht —88Pa **161**
Bagshot Ct. SE18 —53Qc **108**
Bagshot Rd. Egh —6N **117**
Bagshot Rd. Enf —17Vb **25**
Bagshot Rd. Wok & Guild —9A **188**
Bagshot St. SE17 —50Ub **83** (7J **207**)
Bahram Rd. Eps —82Ta **161**
Baildon St. SE8 —52Bc **106**
Bailey Clo. E4 —21Ec **44**
Bailey Clo. Purf —49Td **90**
Bailey Clo. Wind —4E **94**
Bailey Pl. SE26 —65Zb **128**
Baillie Clo. Rain —42Kd **89**
Baillies Wlk. W5 —47Ma **79**
Bainbridge Rd. Dag —35Bd **67**
Bainbridge St. WC1 —44Mb **82** (2E **198**)
Bainton Mead. Wok —5D **188**
Baird Av. S'hall —45Da **77**
Baird Clo. NW9 —30Sa **39**
Baird Clo. Bush —16Da **19**
Baird Clo. Slou —7F **72**
Baird Gdns. SE19 —63Ub **127**
*Baird Ho. W12 —45Xa **80***
(off White City Est.)
Baird Rd. Enf —14Xb **25**
Baird St. EC1 —42Sb **83**
Bairstow Clo. Borwd —11Na **21**
Baizdon Rd. SE3 —54Gc **107**
Bakeham La. Egh —6P **117**
Baker Beal Ct. Bexh —55Dd **110**
Baker Boy La. New Ad —85Ac **166**
Baker Ct. Borwd —12Ra **21**
Bakerhill Clo. Grav —3B **136**
Baker La. Mitc —68Jb **126**
Baker M. N16 —33Vb **63**
Baker Rd. NW10 —39Ua **60**
Baker Rd. SE18 —52Nc **108**
Bakers Av. E17 —30Dc **44**
Bakers Av. W King —80Ud **154**
Bakers Ct. SE25 —69Ub **127**
Bakers End. SW20 —68Ab **124**
Baker's Field. N7 —35Nb **62**
Bakers Hall Ct. EC3 —45Ub **83** (5H **201**)
Bakers Hill. E5 —32Yb **64**
Bakers Hill. Barn —12Db **23**
Bakers La. N6 —30Hb **41**
Bakers La. Epp —2Vc **15**
Baker's M. W1 —44Jb **82** (2H **197**)
Bakers M. Grn St —79Vc **151**
*Bakers Pas. NW3 —35Eb **61***
(off Heath St.)
Baker's Rents. E2 —41Vb **83** (4K **195**)
Bakers Rd. Chesh —2Xb **11**
Bakers Rd. Uxb —38M **55**
Baker's Row. E15 —40Gc **65**
Baker's Row. EC1 —42Qb **82** (6K **193**)
Baker St. NW1 & W1 —42Hb **81** (6G **191**)
Baker St. Enf —13Tb **25**
Baker St. Ors —4A **92**
Baker St. Pot B —7Ab **8**
Baker St. Wey —77Q **140**
Bakers Vs., The. Epp —2Vc **15**
Bakers Wood. Den —33F **54**
*Baker's Yd. EC1 —42Qb **82** (6K **193**)*
(off Bakers Rd.)
Bakers Yd. Uxb —38M **55**
Bakery Pl. SW11 —56Hb **103**
Bakewell Ct. E5 —34Ac **64**
Bakewell Way. N Mald —68Ua **124**
Balaam Ho. Sutt —77Cb **145**
Balaams La. N14 —19Mb **24**
Balaam St. E13 —42Jc **85**
Balaclava Rd. SE1 —49Vb **83** (6K **207**)
Balaclava Rd. Surb —73La **142**
Balben Path. E9 —38Yb **64**
Balcaskie Rd. SE9 —57Pc **108**
Balchen Rd. SE3 —54Mc **107**
Balchier Rd. SE22 —58Xb **105**
Balcombe Clo. Bexh —56Zc **109**
Balcombe St. NW1 —42Hb **81** (5F **191**)
Balcon Ct. W5 —44Pa **79**
Balcon Way. Borwd —11Sa **21**
Balcorne St. E9 —38Yb **64**
Balder Rise. SE12 —61Kc **129**
Balderton St. W1 —44Jb **82** (3J **197**)
Baldewyne Ct. N17 —25Wb **43**
Baldocks Rd. They B —7Uc **14**
Baldock St. E3 —40Dc **64**
Baldock Way. Borwd —11Pa **21**
Baldry Gdns. SW16 —65Nb **126**
Baldwin Cres. SE5 —53Sb **105**
Baldwin Ho. SW2 —60Qb **104**
Baldwin Rd. Burn —1A **72**
Baldwins Gdns. EC1 —43Qb **82** (7K **193**)
Baldwins Hill. Lou —12Pc **28**
Baldwins La. Crox —14Q **18**
Baldwins Shore. Eton —1H **95**
Baldwin St. EC1 —41Tb **83** (4F **195**)
Baldwin Ter. N1 —40Sb **63** (1D **194**)
Baldwyn Gdns. W3 —45Ta **79**
Baldwyn's Pk. Bex —61Fd **132**
Baldwyn's Rd. Bex —61Fd **132**
Bales Ter. N9 —20Vb **25**
Balfern Gro. W4 —50Ua **80**
Balfern St. SW11 —54Gb **103**
Balfe St. N1 —40Nb **62** (1G **193**)
Balfont Clo. S Croy —85Wb **165**
Balfron Tower. E14 —44Ec **84**
Balfour Av. W7 —46Ha **78**
Balfour Av. Wok —94A **172**
Balfour Bus. Cen. S'hall —48Y **77**
Balfour Gro. N20 —20Hb **23**
Balfour M. N9 —20Wb **25**
Balfour M. W1 —46Jb **82** (6J **197**)
Balfour Pl. SW15 —56Xa **102**
Balfour Pl. W1 —45Jb **82** (5J **197**)
Balfour Rd. N5 —35Sb **63**
Balfour Rd. SE25 —70Wb **127**
Balfour Rd. SW19 —66Db **125**
Balfour Rd. W3 —43Sa **79**
Balfour Rd. W13 —47Ja **78**
Balfour Rd. Brom —71Mc **149**
Balfour Rd. Cars —80Hb **145**
Balfour Rd. Grays —49Ee **91**
Balfour Rd. Harr —29Fa **38**
Balfour Rd. Houn —55Da **99**
Balfour Rd. Ilf —33Rc **66**
Balfour Rd. S'hall —48Z **77**
Balfour Rd. Wey —77Q **140**
Balfour St. SE17 —49Tb **83** (5F **207**)
Balfour Ter. N3 —26Db **41**
Balgonie Rd. E4 —18Fc **27**
Balgores Cres. Romf —27Kd **49**
Balgores La. Romf —27Kd **49**
Balgores Sq. Romf —28Kd **49**
Balgowan Clo. N Mald —71Ua **144**
Balgowan Rd. Beck —68Ac **128**
Balgowan St. SE18 —49Vc **87**
*Balham Continental Mkt. SW12 —60Kb **104***
(off Shipka Rd.)
Balham Gro. SW12 —59Jb **104**
Balham High Rd. SW17 & SW12 —62Jb **126**
Balham Hill. SW12 —59Kb **104**
Balham New Rd. SW12 —59Kb **104**
Balham Pk. Rd. SW12 —60Hb **103**
Balham Rd. N9 —19Wb **25**
Balham Sta. Rd. SW12 —60Kb **104**
Balkan Wlk. E1 —45Xb **83**
Ballamore Rd. Brom —62Jc **129**
Ballance Rd. E9 —37Zb **64**
Ballands N., The. Fet —94Ga **176**
Ballands S., The. Fet —95Ga **176**
Ballantrae Ho. NW2 —35Bb **61**
Ballantyne Dri. Tad —93Bb **179**
Ballard Clo. King T —66Ta **123**
Ballard Grn. Wind —2C **94**
Ballards Clo. Dag —39Dd **68**
Ballards Farm Rd. S Croy & Croy —79Wb **147**
Ballards Grn. Tad —91Ab **178**
Ballards La. N3 & N12 —25Cb **41**
Ballards La. Oxt —100Lc **183**
Ballards Rise. S Croy —79Wb **147**
Ballards Rd. NW2 —33Wa **60**
Ballards Rd. Dag —40Dd **68**
Ballards Way. S Croy & Croy —79Wb **147**
Ballards Yd. Edgw —23Qa **39**
Ballast Quay. SE10 —50Fc **85**
Ballater Clo. Wat —21Y **37**
Ballater Rd. SW2 —56Nb **104**
Ballater Rd. S Croy —78Vb **147**
Ballantine St. SW18 —56Eb **103**
*Ball Ct. EC3 —44Tb **83** (3G **201**)*
(off Cornhill)
Ballenger Ct. Wat —13X **19**
Ballina St. SE23 —59Zb **106**
Ballingdon Rd. SW11 —58Jb **104**
Balliol Av. E4 —21Gc **45**
Balliol Rd. N17 —25Ub **43**
Balliol Rd. W10 —44Ya **80**
Balliol Rd. Well —54Xc **109**
Balloch Rd. SE6 —60Fc **107**
Ballogie Av. NW10 —35Ua **60**
Ballow Clo. SE5 —52Ub **105**
Ball's Pond Pl. N1 —37Tb **63**
Balls Pond Rd. N1 —37Tb **63**
Balmain Clo. W5 —46Ma **79**
Balmain Ct. Houn —53Da **99**
Balmer Rd. E3 —40Bc **64**
Balmes Rd. N1 —39Tb **63**
Balmoral Av. Beck —70Ac **128**
Balmoral Clo. SW15 —58Za **102**
Balmoral Clo. Park —1Ea **6**
Balmoral Clo. Slou —4C **72**
Balmoral Ct. SE12 —63Kc **129**
Balmoral Ct. SE27 —63Sb **127**
Balmoral Ct. Sutt —80Cb **145**
Balmoral Ct. Wemb —34Pa **59**
Balmoral Cres. W Mol —69Ca **121**
Balmoral Dri. Borwd —15Ta **21**
Balmoral Dri. Hay —42U **76**
Balmoral Dri. S'hall —42Ba **77**
Balmoral Dri. Wok —88E **156**
Balmoral Gdns. W13 —48Ja **78**
Balmoral Gdns. Bex —59Bd **109**
Balmoral Gdns. Ilf —32Vc **67**
Balmoral Gdns. Wind —5H **95**
Balmoral Gro. N7 —37Pb **62**
Balmoral M. W12 —48Va **80**
Balmoral Rd. E7 —35Lc **65**
Balmoral Rd. E10 —33Dc **64**
Balmoral Rd. NW2 —37Xa **60**
Balmoral Rd. Enf —8Zb **12**
Balmoral Rd. Harr —35Ca **57**
Balmoral Rd. Horn —34Md **69**
Balmoral Rd. King T —70Pa **123**
Balmoral Rd. Pil H —16Xd **32**
Balmoral Rd. Romf —29Kd **49**
Balmoral Rd. S at H —66Rd **133**
Balmoral Rd. Wat —10Y **5**
Balmoral Rd. Wor Pk —76Xa **144**
Balmoral Way. Sutt —82Cb **163**
Balmore Cres. Barn —15Jb **24**
Balmore St. N19 —33Kb **62**
Balmuir Gdns. SW15 —56Ya **102**
Balnacraig Av. NW10 —35Ua **60**
Balniel Ga. SW1 —50Mb **82** (7E **204**)
Balquhain Clo. Asht —89Ma **161**
Baltic Cen. Bren —50Ma **79**
Baltic Clo. SW19 —66Fb **125**
Baltic Ct. SE16 —47Zb **84**
Baltic Ho. SE5 —54Sb **105**
Baltic St. EC1 —42Sb **83** (6D **194**)
*Baltimore Ho. SE11 —50Qb **82** (7K **205**)*
(off Hotspur St.)
Baltimore Pl. Well —54Vc **109**
Balvaird Pl. SW1 —50Mb **82** (7E **204**)
Balvernie Gro. SW18 —59Bb **103**
Bamber Ho. Bark —39Sc **66**
Bamborough Gdns. W12 —47Ya **80**
Bamburgh. N17 —24Xb **43**
Bamford Av. Wemb —39Pa **59**
Bamford Rd. Bark —37Sc **66**
Bamford Rd. Brom —64Ec **128**
Bamford Way. Romf —22Ed **48**
Bampfylde Clo. Wall —76Lb **146**
Bampton Rd. SE23 —62Zb **128**
Bampton Rd. Romf —25Nd **49**
Bampton Way. St J —6D **188**
Banavie Gdns. Beck —67Ec **128**
Banbury Av. Slou —3D **72**
Banbury Clo. Enf —11Rb **25**
*Banbury Ct. WC2 —45Nb **82** (4F **199**)*
(off Long Acre)
Banbury Ct. Sutt —80Cb **145**
Banbury Ho. E9 —38Zb **64**
Banbury Rd. E9 —38Zb **64**
Banbury Rd. E17 —24Zb **44**
Banbury St. SW11 —54Gb **103**
Banbury St. Wat —15W **18**
Banbury Vs. S'fleet —65Be **135**
*Banbury Wlk. N'holt —40Ca **57***
(off Brabazon Rd.)
Banchory Rd. SE3 —52Kc **107**
Banckside. Hart —70Ae **135**
Bancroft Av. N2 —29Gb **41**
Bancroft Av. Buck H —19Jc **27**
Bancroft Clo. Ashf —64Q **120**
Bancroft Clo. N'holt —39Y **57**
*Bancroft Ct. SW8 —52Nb **104***
(off Allen Edwards Dri.)
Bancroft Gdns. Harr —25Ea **38**
Bancroft Gdns. Orp —74Vc **151**
Bancroft Rd. E1 —41Zb **84**
Bancroft Rd. Harr —26Ea **38**
Band La. Egh —64B **118**
Bandon Clo. Uxb —40P **55**
Bandon Rise. Wall —78Mb **146**
Bangalore St. SW15 —55Ya **102**
Bangor Clo. N'holt —36Da **57**
Bangors Clo. Iver —44G **74**
Bangors Rd. N. Iver —39F **54**
Bangors Rd. S. Iver —41G **74**
Banim St. W6 —49Xa **80**
Banister Ho. E9 —36Zb **64**
Banister Rd. W10 —41Za **80**
Bank Av. Mitc —68Fb **125**
Bank Ct. Dart —58Nd **111**
Bank End. SE1 —46Sb **83** (6E **200**)
Bankfoot. Grays —50Be **91**
Bankfoot Rd. Brom —63Gc **129**
Bankhurst Rd. SE6 —59Bc **106**
Bank La. SW15 —57Ua **102**
Bank La. King T —66Na **123**
Bank M. Sutt —79Eb **145**
Bank Pl. Brtwd —19Yd **32**
Banksian Wlk. Iswth —53Ga **100**
Banksia Rd. N18 —22Yb **44**
Bankside. SE1 —45Sb **83** (5D **200**)
Bankside. Enf —11Rb **25**
Bankside. N'fleet —58Ee **113**
Bankside. S'hall —46Z **77**
Bankside. S Croy —79Vb **147**
Bankside. Wok —6E **188**
Bankside Av. N'holt —40W **56**
Bankside Clo. Bex —63Fd **132**
Bankside Clo. Big H —90Lc **167**
Bankside Clo. Cars —79Gb **145**
Bankside Dri. Th Dit —74Ka **142**
Bankside Way. SE19 —65Ub **127**
Banks La. Bexh —56Bd **109**
Banks La. Eff J —95W **174**
Banks La. They G —5Ad **15**
Banks Rd. Borwd —12Sa **21**
Banks Spur. Chalv —7F **72**
Bank St. Grav —8D **114**
Bank St. Sev —97Kd **187**
Bank, The. N6 —32Kb **62**
Bankton Rd. SW2 —56Qb **104**
Bankwell Rd. SE13 —56Gc **107**
Bann Clo. S Ock —45Xd **90**
Banner Clo. Purf —49Td **90**
Bannerman Ho. SW8 —51Pb **104**
Banner St. EC1 —42Sb **83** (6E **194**)
Banning St. SE10 —50Gc **85**
Bannister Clo. SW2 —60Qb **104**
Bannister Clo. Gnfd —36Fa **58**
Bannister Clo. Slou —47A **74**
Bannister Dri. Hut —16Ee **33**
Bannister Gdns. Orp —69Yc **131**
Bannockburn Rd. SE18 —49Uc **86**
Banstead Gdns. N9 —20Ub **25**
Banstead Rd. Cars —81Fb **163**
Banstead Rd. Cat —93Tb **181**
Banstead Rd. Eps & Bans —82Xa **162**
Banstead Rd. Purl —83Qb **164**
Banstead Rd. S. Sutt —83Eb **163**
Banstead St. SE15 —55Yb **106**
Banstead Way. Wall —78Nb **146**
Banstock Rd. Edgw —23Ra **39**
Banting Ho. NW2 —34Wa **60**
Banton Clo. Enf —12Xb **25**
Bantry St. SE5 —52Tb **105**
Banwell Rd. Bex —58Zc **109**
Banyard Rd. SE16 —48Xb **83**
Banyards. Horn —28Nd **49**
Bapchild Pl. Orp —70Yc **131**
Baptist Gdns. NW5 —37Jb **62**
Barandon Wlk. W11 —45Za **80**
Barataria Caravan Site. Rip —93H **173**
Barbara Brosnan Ct. NW8 —40Fb **61** (2B **190**)
Barbara Clo. Shep —71R **140**
Barbara Hucklesby Clo. N22 —26Rb **43**
Barbauld Rd. N16 —34Ub **63**
Barbel Clo. Wal X —6Cc **12**
Barber Clo. N21 —17Qb **24**
Barberry Clo. Romf —24Ld **49**
Barbers All. E13 —41Kc **85**
Barbers Rd. E15 —40Dc **64**
Barbican. EC2 —43Sb **83** (1E **200**)
Barbican Rd. Gnfd —44Da **77**
Barb M. W6 —48Ya **80**
Barbon Clo. WC1 —43Pb **82** (7G **193**)
Barbot Clo. N9 —20Wb **25**
Barchard St. SW18 —57Db **103**
Barchester Clo. W7 —46Ha **78**
Barchester Clo. Uxb —41L **75**
Barchester Rd. Harr —26Fa **38**
Barchester Rd. Slou —47B **74**
Barchester St. E14 —43Dc **84**
Barclay Clo. SW6 —52Cb **103**
Barclay Clo. Fet —95Da **175**
Barclay Oval. Wfd G —21Jc **45**
Barclay Path. E17 —29Ec **44**
Barclay Rd. E11 —32Hc **65**
Barclay Rd. E13 —42Lc **85**
Barclay Rd. E17 —29Ec **44**
Barclay Rd. N18 —23Tb **43**
Barclay Rd. SW6 —52Cb **103**
Barclay Rd. Croy —76Tb **147**
Barclay Way. SE22 —60Wb **105**
Barclay Way. W Thur —50Vd **90**
Barcombe Av. SW2 —61Nb **126**
Barcombe Clo. Orp —69Wc **131**
Barden Clo. Hare —24L **35**
Barden St. SE18 —52Uc **108**
Bardeswell Clo. Brtwd —19Yd **32**
Bardfield Av. Romf —27Zc **47**
Bardney Rd. Mord —70Db **125**
Bardolph Av. Croy —81Ac **166**
Bardolph Rd. N7 —35Nb **62**
Bardolph Rd. Rich —55Pa **101**
Bardon Wlk. Wok —5E **188**
Bard Rd. W10 —45Za **80**
Bardsey Wlk. N1 —37Sb **63**
Bardsley Clo. Croy —76Vb **147**
Bardsley La. SE10 —51Ec **106**
Barfett St. W10 —42Bb **81**
Barfield. S at H —67Rd **133**
Barfield Av. N20 —19Hb **23**
Barfield Rd. E11 —32Hc **65**
Barfield Rd. Brom —69Qc **130**
Barfields. Lou —14Qc **28**
Barfields Gdns. Lou —14Qc **28**
Barfields Path. Lou —14Qc **28**
Barfleur Ho. SE8 —50Bc **84**
Barford Clo. NW4 —26Wa **40**
Barford St. N1 —39Qb **62** (1A **194**)
Barforth Rd. SE15 —55Xb **105**
Barfreston Way. SE20 —67Xb **127**
Bargate Clo. SE18 —50Vc **87**
Bargate Clo. N Mald —73Wa **144**
Barge Ho. Rd. E16 —47Rc **86**
Barge Ho. St. SE1 —46Qb **82** (6A **200**)
Bargery Rd. SE6 —60Dc **106**
Barge Wlk. E Mol —69Fa **122**
Barge Wlk. King T —67Ma **123**
Bargrove Clo. SE20 —66Wb **127**
Bargrove Cres. SE6 —61Bc **128**
Barham Av. Els —13Pa **21**
Barham Clo. Brom —74Nc **150**
Barham Clo. Chst —64Rc **130**
Barham Clo. Romf —26Dd **48**
Barham Clo. Wemb —37Ka **58**
Barham Clo. Wey —77S **140**
Barham Rd. SW20 —66Wa **124**
Barham Rd. Chst —64Rc **130**
Barham Rd. Dart —59Qd **111**
Barham Rd. S Croy —78Sb **147**
Baring Clo. SE12 —61Jc **129**
Baring Rd. SE12 —59Jc **107**
Baring Rd. Barn —14Fb **23**
Baring Rd. Croy —74Wb **147**
Baring St. N1 —39Tb **63** (1F **195**)
Bark Burr Rd. Grays —47Be **91**
Barker Dri. NW1 —38Lb **62**
Barker Rd. Cher —73G **138**
Barkers Arc. W8 —47Db **81**
Barker's Row. EC1 —42Qb **82**
Barker St. SW10 —51Eb **103**
Barker Wlk. SW16 —62Mb **126**
Barker Way. SE22 —59Wb **105**
Barkham Rd. N17 —24Tb **43**
Bark Hart Rd. Orp —74Xc **151**
Barking Northern Relief Rd. Bark —38Rc **66**
Barking Rd. E16, E13 & E6 —43Hc **85**
Barkis Way. SE16 —50Xb **83**
Bark Pl. W2 —45Db **81**
Barkston Gdns. SW5 —49Db **81**
Barkston Path. Borwd —10Qa **7**
Barkway Ct. N4 —33Sb **63**
Barkwood Clo. Romf —29Ed **48**
Barkworth Rd. SE16 —50Xb **83**
Barlborough St. SE14 —52Zb **106**
Barlby Gdns. W10 —42Za **80**
Barlby Rd. W10 —43Ya **80**
Barlee Cres. Uxb —43L **75**
Barle Gdns. S Ock —44Xd **90**
Barley Clo. Bush —15Da **19**
Barleycorn Way. E14 —45Bc **84**
Barleycorn Way. Horn —30Pd **49**
Barleyfields Clo. Romf —30Xc **47**
Barley La. Ilf & Romf —31Wc **67**
Barley Mow Clo. Knap —5A **188**
Barley Mow La. Knap —4A **188**
*Barleymow Pas. EC1 —43Rb **83** (1C **200**)*
(off Long La.)
Barley Mow Pas. W4 —50Ta **79**
Barley Mow Rd. Egh —4N **117**
Barleymow Way. Shep —70Q **120**
Barley Clo. Wall —79Nb **146**
*Barlow Ho. N1 —41Tb **83** (3F **195**)*
(off Provost Est.)
Barlow Pl. W1 —45Kb **82**
Barlow Rd. NW6 —37Bb **61**
Barlow Rd. W3 —46Ra **79**
Barlow Rd. Hamp —66Ca **121**
Barlow St. SE17 —49Tb **83**
Barlow Way. Rain —43Fd **88**
Barmeston Rd. SE6 —61Dc **128**
Barmor Clo. Harr —26Da **37**
Barmouth Av. Gnfd —40Ha **58**
Barmouth Rd. SW18 —58Eb **103**
Barmouth Rd. Croy —75Zb **148**
Barnabas Ct. N21 —15Rb **25**
Barnabas Rd. E9 —36Zb **64**
Barnaby Clo. Harr —33Ea **58**
Barnaby Clo. NW9 —27Ua **40**
*Barnaby Pl. SW7 —49Fb **81** (6B **202**)*
(off Brompton Rd.)
Barnaby Way. Chig —20Rc **28**
Barnacre Clo. Uxb —44M **75**
Barnard Clo. SE18 —48Qc **86**
Barnard Clo. Chst —67Tc **130**
Barnard Clo. Sun —66X **121**
Barnard Clo. Wall —80Mb **146**
*Barnard Ct. Dart —58Rd **111***
(off Clifton Wlk.)
*Barnard Ct. Dart —58Rd **111***
(off Osborne Rd.)
Barnard Ct. Wok —6B **188**
Barnard Gdns. Hay —42X **77**
Barnard Gdns. N Mald —70Wa **124**
Barnard Gro. E15 —38Hc **65**
Barnard Hill. N10 —25Kb **42**
Barnard Lodge. New Bar —14Eb **23**
Barnard M. SW11 —56Gb **103**
Barnardo Dri. Ilf —28Sc **46**
Barnardo Gdns. E1 —45Zb **84**
Barnardo St. E1 —44Zb **84**
Barnardos Village. B'side —27Sc **46**
Barnard Rd. SW11 —56Gb **103**
Barnard Rd. Enf —12Xb **25**
Barnard Rd. Mitc —69Jb **126**
Barnard Rd. Warl —91Dc **182**
*Barnard's Inn. EC1 —44Qb **82** (2A **200**)*
(off Fetter La.)
Barnards Pl. S Croy —81Rb **165**
Barnato Clo. W Byf —84N **157**
Barnby Rd. St J —5A **188**
Barnby Sq. E15 —39Gc **65**
Barnby St. E15 —39Gc **65**
Barnby St. NW1 —40Lb **62** (2C **192**)
Barn Clo. Ashf —64R **120**
Barn Clo. Bans —87Nb **163**
Barn Clo. Eps —87Sa **161**
Barn Clo. Farn C —5F **52**
Barn Clo. N'holt —40Y **57**
Barn Clo. Rad —7Ja **6**
Barn Cres. Purl —85Tb **165**
Barn Cres. Stan —23La **38**
Barncroft Clo. Lou —15Qc **28**
Barncroft Clo. Uxb —43R **76**

Barncroft Grn.—Beatson Wlk.

Barncroft Grn. Lou —15Qc 28
Barncroft Rd. Lou —15Qc 28
Barnehurst Av. Eri & Bexh —53Ed 110
Barnehurst Clo. Eri —53Ed 110
Barnehurst Rd. Bexh —54Ed 110
Barn Elms Pk. SW15 —55Ya 102
Barn End Dri. Dart —63Ld 133
Barn End La. Dart —64Ld 133
Barnes All. Hamp —68Ea 122
Barnes Av. SW13 —52Wa 102
Barnes Av. S'hall —49Ba 77
Barnes Clo. E12 —35Mc 65
Barnes Ct. E16 —43Lc 85
Barnes Ct. Wfd G —22Mc 45
Barnes Cray Rd. Dart —56Jd 110
Barnesdale Cres. Orp —72Wc 151
Barnes End. N Mald —71Wa 144
Barnes High St. SW13 —54Va 102
Barnes Ho. Bark —39Tc 66
Barnes La. K Lan —1N 3
Barnes Pikle. W5 —45Ma 79
Barnes Rd. N18 —21Yb 44
Barnes Rd. Ilf —36Sc 66
Barnes St. E14 —44Ac 84
Barnes Wallis Ct. Wemb —34Sa 59
Barnes Wallis Dri. Wey —83N 157
Barnes Way. Iver —45H 75
Barnet By-Pass Rd. Borwd & Barn —16Ta 21
Barnet Dri. Brom —75Nc 150
Barnet Ga. La. Barn —16Va 22
Barnet Gro. E2 —41Wb 83
Barnet Hill. Barn —14Bb 23
Barnet Ho. N20 —19Eb 23
Barnet La. N20 & Barn —18Bb 23
Barnet La. Els —16Na 21
Barnet Rd. Barn —16Ta 21
Barnet Rd. Pot B —8Cb 9
Barnett Clo. Eri —54Hd 110
Barnett Clo. Lea —91Ka 176
Barnet Trading Est. H Bar —13Bb 23
Barnett Row. Jac —100A 172
Barnetts Ct. Harr —34Da 57
Barnett's Shaw. Oxt —99Fc 183
Barnett St. E1 —44Xb 83
Barnett Wood La. Lea & Asht —92Ka 176
Barnet Way. NW7 —20Ta 21
Barnet Wood Rd. Brom —75Lc 149
Barney Clo. SE7 —50Lc 85
Barn Field. NW3 —36Hb 61
Barnfield. Bans —86Db 163
Barnfield. Epp —1Wc 15
Barnfield. Iver —44G 74
Barnfield. N Mald —72Ua 144
Barnfield. Slou —6B 72
Barnfield Av. Croy —75Yb 148
Barnfield Av. King T —63Ma 123
Barnfield Av. Mitc —69Kb 126
Barnfield Clo. N4 —31Nb 62
Barnfield Clo. SW17 —62Fb 125
Barnfield Clo. Coul —91Sb 181
Barnfield Clo. Long —69Fe 135
Barnfield Clo. Swan —73Ed 152
Barnfield Cres. Kems —89Nd 171
Barnfield Gdns. King T —63Na 123
Barnfield Pl. E14 —49Cc 84
Barnfield Rd. SE18 —51Rc 108
(in two parts)
Barnfield Rd. W4 —42La 78
Barnfield Rd. Belv —51Bd 109
Barnfield Rd. Edgw —25Sa 39
Barnfield Rd. Orp —69Zc 131
Barnfield Rd. Sev —95Gd 186
Barnfield Rd. S Croy —81Ub 165
Barnfield Rd. Tats —92Mc 183
Barnfield Wood Clo. Beck —72Fc 149
Barnfield Wood Rd. Beck —72Fc 149
Barnham Clo. Grav —10H 115
Barnham Rd. Gnfd —41Ea 78
Barnham St. SE1 —47Ub 83 (1J 207)
Barnhill. Pinn —29Y 37
Barn Hill. Wemb —32Qa 59
Barnhill Av. Brom —71Hc 149
Barnhill La. Hay —41X 77
Barnhill Rd. Hay —41X 77
Barnhill Rd. Wemb —34Sa 59
Barnhurst Path. Wat —22Y 37
Barningham Way. NW9 —30Ta 39
Barn Lea. Rick —18J 17
Barnlea Clo. Felt —61Aa 121
Barn Mead. They B —8Uc 14
Barnmead Gdns. Dag —36Bd 67
Barn Meadow La. Bookh —96Ba 175
Barnmead Rd. Beck —67Zb 128
Barnmead Rd. Dag —36Bd 67
Barn M. S Harr —34Ca 57
Barn Rise. Wemb —32Qa 59
Barnsbury Clo. N Mald —70Sa 123
Barnsbury Cres. Surb —74Sa 143
Barnsbury Est. N1 —39Qb 62 (1K 193)
Barnsbury Farm Est. Wok —8G 188
Barnsbury Gro. N7 —38Pb 62
Barnsbury La. Surb —75Ra 143
Barnsbury M. N1 —38Qb 62
Barnsbury Pk. N1 —38Qb 62
Barnsbury Rd. N1 —40Qb 62 (1K 193)
Barnsbury Sq. N1 —38Qb 62
Barnsbury St. N1 —38Qb 62
Barnsbury Ter. N1 —38Pb 62
Barnscroft. SW20 —69Xa 124
Barnsdale Av. E14 —49Dc 84
Barnsdale Clo. Borwd —11Pa 21
Barnsdale Rd. W9 —42Bb 81
Barnsfield Pl. Uxb —38L 55
Barnsley Rd. Romf —24Pd 49
Barnsley St. E1 —42Xb 83
Barnstaple Path. Romf —22Md 49
Barnstaple Rd. Romf —22Ld 49
Barnstaple Rd. Ruis —34Y 57
Barnston Way. Hut —15Ee 33
Barn St. N16 —33Ub 63
Barnsway. K Lan —1N 3
Barn, The. Grays —49De 91
Barnway. Egh —4N 117
Barn Way. Wemb —32Qa 59
Barnwell Rd. SW2 —57Qb 104
Barnwood Clo. W9 —42Db 81
Barnwood Clo. Ruis —33T 56
Barnwood Ct. E16 —46Kc 85
Barnyard, The. Tad —96Wa 178
Baron Clo. N1 —40Qb 62 (1K 193)
Baroness Rd. E2 —41Vb 83 (3K 195)
Baronet Gro. N17 —25Wb 43
Baronet Rd. N17 —25Wb 43
Baron Gdns. Ilf —27Sc 46
Baron Gro. Mitc —70Gb 125
Baron Rd. Dag —32Zc 67
Baronsclere Ct. N6 —31Lb 62
Barons Ct. Ilf —33Tc 66
Barons Ct. Wall —76Mb 146
Baron's Ct. Rd. W14 —50Ab 80
Baronsfield Rd. Twic —58Ka 100
Barons Ga. Barn —16Gb 23
Baron's Hurst. Eps —88Sa 161
Barons Keep. W14 —50Ab 80
Barons Mead. Harr —28Ga 38
Baronsmead Rd. SW13 —53Wa 102
Baronsmede. W5 —47Pa 79
Baronsmere Ct. Barn —14Ab 22
Baronsmere Rd. N2 —28Gb 41
Baron's Pl. SE1 —47Qb 82 (2A 206)
Barons, The. Twic —58Ka 100
Baron St. N1 —40Qb 62 (1K 193)
Baron's Wlk. Croy —72Ac 148
Barons Way. Egh —65F 118
Baron Wlk. E16 —43Hc 85
Baron Wlk. Mitc —70Gb 125
Barque M. SE8 —51Cc 106
Barrack Path. Wok —6C 188
Barrack Rd. Houn —56Z 99
Barrack Row. Grav —8D 114
Barracks, The. Add —76K 139
Barrack Yd. SW1 —47Jb 82
Barra Hall Cir. Hay —45U 76
Barra Hall Rd. Hay —45U 76
Barratt Av. N22 —26Pb 42
Barratt Ind. Pk. E3 —42Ec 84
Barratt Ind. Pk. S'hall —47Ca 77
Barratt Way. Harr —26Fa 38
Barr Bank Ter. Wilm —63Ld 133
Barrenger Rd. N10 —25Hb 41
Barrens Brae. Wok —90C 156
Barrens Clo. Wok —90C 156
Barrens Pk. Wok —90C 156
Barrets Grn. Rd. NW10 —41Sa 79
Barrett Clo. Romf —24Kd 49
Barrett Ho. SE17 —50Sb 83 (7E 206)
(off Browning St.)
Barrett Ho. SW9 —55Pb 104
(off Benedict Rd.)
Barrett Rd. E17 —28Ec 44
Barrett Rd. Fet —96Fa 176
Barrett's Gro. N16 —36Ub 63
Barretts Rd. Dun G —92Fd 186
Barrett St. W1 —44Jb 82 (3J 197)
Barrhill Rd. SW2 —61Nb 126
Barricane. Wok —7E 188
Barrie Clo. Coul —88Lb 164
Barrie Ct. New Bar —15Eb 23
(off Lyonsdown Rd.)
Barriedale. SE14 —54Ac 106
Barrie Est. W2 —45Fb 81 (4B 196)
Barrie Ho. Add —80J 139
Barrier App. SE7 —48Mc 85
Barringers Ct. Ruis —31T 56
Barringer Sq. SW17 —63Jb 126
Barrington Clo. NW5 —36Jb 62
Barrington Clo. Ilf —25Pc 46
Barrington Clo. Lou —13Sc 28
Barrington Ct. NW5 —36Jb 62
Barrington Ct. Hut —16Ee 33
Barrington Grn. Lou —14Sc 28
Barrington Lodge. Wey —78S 140
Barrington Pk. Gdns. Chal G —18A 16
Barrington Rd. E12 —37Qc 66
Barrington Rd. N8 —29Mb 42
Barrington Rd. SW9 —55Rb 105
Barrington Rd. Bexh —54Zc 109
Barrington Rd. Lou —14Sc 28
Barrington Rd. Purl —84Lb 164
Barrington Rd. Sutt —75Cb 145
Barrington Vs. SE18 —53Qc 108
Barrosa Dri. Hamp —67Ca 121
Barrow Av. Cars —80Hb 145
Barrow Clo. N21 —20Rb 25
Barrowdene Clo. Pinn —26Aa 37
Barrowell Grn. N21 —19Rb 25
Barrowfield Clo. N9 —20Xb 25
Barrowgate Rd. W4 —50Sa 79
Barrow Grn. Rd. Oxt —100Dc 182
Barrow Hedges Clo. Cars —80Gb 145
Barrow Hedges Way. Cars —80Gb 145
Barrowhill. Wor Pk —75Ua 144
Barrowhill Clo. Wor Pk —75Ua 144
Barrow Hill Est. NW8 —40Gb 61 (2D 190)
(off Barrow Hill Rd.)
Barrow Hill Rd. NW8 —40Gb 61 (2D 190)
Barrow La. Chesh —3Vb 11
Barrow Lodge. Slou —2G 72
Barrow Point Av. Pinn —26Aa 37
Barrow Point La. Pinn —26Aa 37
Barrow Rd. SW16 —65Mb 126
Barrow Rd. Croy —78Qb 146
Barrowsfield. S Croy —84Vb 165
Barrow Wlk. Bren —51La 100
Barr Rd. Grav —1H 137
Barr Rd. Pot B —5Eb 9
Barr's La. Knap —4A 188
Barrs Rd. NW10 —38Ta 59
Barr's Rd. Tap —4A 72
Barry Av. N15 —30Vb 43
Barry Av. Bexh —52Ad 109
Barry Av. Wind —2G 94
Barry Clo. Grays —8C 92
Barry Clo. Orp —76Uc 150
Barry Ct. Romf —22Fd 48
Barrydene. N20 —18Fb 23
Barry Rd. E6 —44Nc 86
Barry Rd. NW10 —38Sa 59
Barry Rd. SE22 —58Wb 105
Barset Rd. SE15 —55Yb 106
(in three parts)
Barson Clo. SE20 —66Yb 128
Barstable Rd. Stanf —1M 93
Barston Rd. SE27 —62Sb 127
Barstow Cres. SW2 —60Pb 104
Bartelotts Rd. Slou —2B 72
Barter St. WC1 —43Nb 82 (1G 199)
Barters Wlk. Pinn —27Aa 37
Bartholomew Clo. EC1 —43Sb 83 (1C 200)
(in two parts)
Bartholomew Clo. SW18 —56Eb 103
Bartholomew Ct. EC1 —42Sb 83 (5E 194)
(off Old St.)
Bartholomew Ct. Enf —9Ac 12
Bartholomew Ct. Shopping Cen. Chesh —5Ac 12
Bartholomew Dri. H Wood —26Md 49
Bartholomew La. EC2 —44Tb 83 (3G 201)
Bartholomew Pl. EC1 —43Sb 83 (1D 200)
(off Bartholomew Clo.)
Bartholomew Rd. NW5 —37Lb 62
Bartholomew Sq. E1 —42Xb 83
Bartholomew Sq. EC1 —42Sb 83 (5E 194)
Bartholomew St. SE1 —48Tb 83 (4G 207)
Bartholomew Vs. NW5 —37Lb 62
Bartholomew Way. Swan —69Gd 132
Barth Rd. SE18 —49Uc 86
Bartle Av. E6 —40Nc 66
Bartle Rd. W11 —44Ab 80
Bartlett Clo. E14 —44Cc 84
Bartlett Ct. EC4 —44Qb 82 (2A 200)
Bartlett Houses. Dag —38Dd 68
(off Vicarage Rd.)
Bartlett Rd. Grav —10C 114
Bartlett Rd. W'ham —98Sc 184
Bartlett St. S Croy —78Tb 147
Bartlow Gdns. Romf —25Fd 48
Barton Av. Romf —32Dd 68
Barton Clo. E6 —44Pc 86
Barton Clo. E9 —36Yb 64
Barton Clo. SE15 —55Xb 105
Baryta Clo. Add —79J 139
Barton Clo. Bexh —57Ad 109
Barton Clo. Chig —19Sc 28
Barton Clo. Shep —72R 140
Barton Grn. N Mald —68Ta 123
Barton Ho. SW6 —55Db 103
(off Wandsworth Bri. Rd.)
Barton Meadows. Ilf —28Rc 46
Barton Rd. W14 —50Ab 80
Barton Rd. Horn —32Jd 68
Barton Rd. Sidc —65Ad 131
Barton Rd. Slou —47B 74
Barton Rd. S at H —67Rd 133
Bartons, The. Els —16Ma 21
Barton St. SW1 —48Nb 82 (3F 205)
Barton, The. Cob —84Z 159
Barton Way. Borwd —12Qa 21
Barton Way. Crox —15R 18
Bartram Clo. Uxb —42R 76
Bartram Rd. SE4 —57Ac 106
Bartrams La. Barn —10Eb 9
Barville Clo. SE4 —56Ac 106
Barwell Trading Est. Chess —81Ma 161
Barwick Rd. E7 —35Kc 65
Barwood Av. W Wick —74Dc 148
Baryta Clo. Stanf —2L 93
Basden Gro. Felt —61Ca 121
Basden Ho. Felt —61Ca 121
Basedale Rd. Dag —38Xc 67
Baseing Clo. E6 —45Qc 86
Basford Way. Wind —5B 94
Bashley Rd. NW10 —42Ta 79
Basil Av. E6 —41Nc 86
Basildene Rd. Houn —55Z 99
Basildon Av. Ilf —25Qc 46
Basildon Clo. Sutt —81Db 163
Basildon Rd. SE2 —50Wc 87
Basil Gdns. Croy —74Zb 148
Basilon Rd. Bexh —54Ad 109
Basil Spence Ho. N22 —25Pb 42
Basil St. SW3 —48Hb 81 (3F 203)
Basing Clo. Th Dit —73Ha 142
Basing Ct. SE15 —53Vb 105
Basingdon Way. SE5 —56Tb 105
Basing Dri. Bex —58Bd 109
Basingfield Rd. Th Dit —73Ha 142
Basinghall Av. EC2 —44Tb 83 (2F 201)
Basinghall Gdns. Sutt —81Db 163
Basinghall St. EC2 —44Tb 83 (2E 200)
Basing Hill. NW11 —32Bb 61
Basing Hill. Wemb —33Pa 59
Basing Ho. Bark —39Tc 66
(off St Margarets)
Basing Ho. Yd. E2 —41Ub 83 (3J 195)
Basing Pl. E2 —41Ub 83 (3J 195)
Basing Rd. Bans —86Bb 163
Basing Rd. Rick —18H 17
Basing St. W11 —44Bb 81
Basing Way. N3 —27Cb 41
Basing Way. Th Dit —73Ha 142
Basire St. N1 —39Sb 63
Baskerville Rd. SW18 —59Gb 103
Basket Gdns. SE9 —57Nc 108
Baslow Clo. Harr —25Fa 38
Baslow Wlk. E5 —35Zb 64
Basnett Rd. SW11 —55Jb 104
Bassano St. SE22 —57Vb 105
Bassant Rd. SE18 —51Vc 109
Bassein Pk. Rd. W12 —47Va 80
Basset Clo. Wdhm —82L 157
Bassett Clo. Sutt —81Db 163
Bassett Gdns. Iswth —52Ea 100
Bassett Rd. E7 —35Mc 65
Bassett Rd. W10 —44Za 80
Bassett Rd. Uxb —38L 55
Bassett Rd. Wok —88E 156
Bassett's Clo. Orp —77Rc 150
Bassett St. NW5 —37Jb 62
Bassett's Way. Orp —77Rc 150
Bassett Way. Gnfd —44Da 77
Bassett Way. Slou —2D 72
Bassingham Rd. SW18 —59Eb 103
Bassingham Rd. Wemb —37Ma 59
Bassishaw Highwalk. EC2 —43Tb 83 (1F 201)
(off London Wall)
Basswood Clo. SE15 —55Xb 105
Bastable Av. Bark —40Uc 66
Basterfield Ho. EC1 —42Sb 83 (6D 194)
(off Golden La. Est.)
Bastion Highwalk. EC2 —43Sb 83 (1D 200)
(off London Wall)
Bastion Ho. EC2 —43Sb 83 (1E 200)
(off London Wall)
Bastion Rd. SE2 —50Wc 87
Baston Mnr. Rd. Brom —76Kc 149
Baston Rd. Brom —75Kc 149
Bastwick St. EC1 —42Sb 83 (5D 194)
Basuto Rd. SW6 —53Cb 103
Bata Av. E Til —10K 93
Batavia Clo. Sun —67X 121
Batavia M. SE14 —52Ac 106
Batavia Rd. SE14 —52Ac 106
Batavia Rd. Sun —67X 121
Bat & Ball Rd. Sev —93Ld 187
Batchelor St. N1 —39Qb 62 (1A 194)
Batchwood Grn. Orp —69Wc 131
Batchworth Heath Hill. Moor P —21Q 36
Batchworth Hill. Rick —19N 17
(in two parts)
Batchworth La. N'wd —22S 36
Bateman Clo. Bark —37Sc 66
Bateman Rd. E4 —23Cc 44
Bateman Rd. Crox —16Q 18
Bateman's Bldgs. W1 —44Mb 82 (3D 198)
(off Bateman St.)
Bateman's Row. EC2 —42Ub 83 (5J 195)
Bateman St. W1 —44Mb 82 (3D 198)
Bates Clo. G Grn —44A 74
Bates Cres. SW16 —66Lb 126
Bates Cres. Croy —78Qb 146
Bateson St. SE18 —49Uc 86
Bateson Way. Wok —86E 156
Bates Point. E13 —39Jc 65
(off Pelly Rd.)
Bates Rd. Romf —24Qd 49
Bate St. E14 —45Bc 84
Bates Wlk. Add —79L 139
Bath Clo. SE15 —53Yb 106
Bath Ct. EC1 —42Qb 82 (6K 193)
(off St Lukes Est.)
Bath Ct. Clo. EC1 —41Ub 83 (4H 195)
(off Bath Pl.)
Bathgate Rd. SW19 —62Za 124
Bath Ho. Rd. Bedd —74Nb 146
Bath Pas. King T —68Ma 123
Bath Pl. EC2 —41Ub 83 (4H 195)
Bath Pl. W6 —50Ya 80
(off Square, The)
Bath Pl. Barn —13Bb 23
Bath Rd. E7 —37Mc 65
Bath Rd. N9 —19Xb 25
Bath Rd. W4 —49Ua 80
Bath Rd. Coln —51D 96
(Brands Hill)
Bath Rd. Coln —53G 96
(Poyle)
Bath Rd. Dart —59Kd 111
Bath Rd. Houn —53Y 99
Bath Rd. Mitc —69Fb 125
Bath Rd. Romf —30Ad 47
Bath Rd. Slou —4A 72
Bath Rd. W Dray & Hay —53K 97
Baths Rd. Brom —70Mc 129
Bath St. EC1 —41Sb 83 (4E 194)
Bath St. Grav —8D 114
Bath Ter. SE1 —48Sb 83 (4D 206)
Bathurst Av. SW19 —67Db 125
Bathurst Clo. Iver —47H 75
Bathurst Gdns. NW10 —40Xa 60
Bathurst M. W2 —45Fb 81 (4C 196)
Bathurst Rd. Ilf —32Rc 66
Bathurst St. W2 —45Fb 81 (4C 196)
Bathurst Wlk. Iver —47G 74
Bathway. SE18 —49Qc 86
Batley Pl. N16 —34Vb 63
Batley Rd. N16 —34Vb 63
Batley Rd. Enf —11Sb 25
Batman Clo. W12 —46Xa 80
Batoum Gdns. W6 —48Ya 80
Batson St. W12 —47Wa 80
Batsworth Rd. Mitc —69Fb 125
Batten Av. Wok —7B 188
Battenberg Wlk. SE19 —65Ub 127
Batten Clo. E6 —44Pc 86
Batten Ho. SW4 —57Lb 104
Batten St. SW11 —55Gb 103
Battersby Rd. SE6 —61Fc 129
Battersea Bri. SW3 & SW11 —52Fb 103
Battersea Bri. Rd. SW11 —52Gb 103
Battersea Chu. Rd. SW11 —53Fb 103
Battersea High St. SW11 —53Fb 103
Battersea Pk. Rd. SW11 & SW8 —54Gb 103
Battersea Rise. SW11 —57Gb 103
Battersea Sq. SW11 —53Fb 103
Battery Rd. SE28 —47Uc 86
Battleson St. SE18 —49Uc 86
Battishill St. N1 —38Rb 63
Battis, The. Romf —30Gd 48
Battlebridge Ct. N1 —40Nb 62 (1G 193)
(off Wharfdale Rd.)
Battle Bri. La. SE1 —46Ub 83 (7H 201)
Battle Bri. Rd. NW1 —40Nb 62 (2F 193)
Battle Clo. SW19 —65Eb 125
Battledean Rd. N5 —36Rb 63
Battle Rd. Belv & Eri —49Ed 88
Battlers Grn. Dri. Rad —8Ga 6
Battle St. Cobh —9H 137
Batt's Cotts. Shorne —10H 137
Batt's Rd. Ludd —10J 137
Batty St. E1 —44Wb 83
Baudwin Rd. SE6 —61Gc 129
Baugh Rd. Sidc —64Yc 131
Baulk, The. SW18 —59Cb 103
Bavant Rd. SW16 —68Nb 126
Bavaria Rd. N19 —33Nb 62
Bavent Rd. SE5 —54Sb 105
Bawdale Rd. SE22 —57Vb 105
Bawdsey Av. Ilf —28Vc 47
Bawtree Clo. Sutt —82Eb 163
Bawtree Rd. SE14 —52Ac 106
Bawtree Rd. Uxb —37M 55
Bawtry Rd. N20 —20Hb 23
Baxendale. N20 —19Eb 23
Baxendale St. E2 —41Wb 83
Baxter Clo. Uxb —41R 76
Baxter Rd. E16 —44Lc 85
Baxter Rd. N1 —37Tb 63
Baxter Rd. N18 —21Xb 43
Baxter Rd. Ilf —36Rc 66
Bayard Ct. Bexh —56Dd 110
Bayards. Warl —90Yb 166
Bay Ct. W5 —48Na 79
Baydon Ct. Short —69Hc 129
Bayer Ho. EC1 —42Sb 83 (6D 194)
(off Golden La. Est.)
Bayes Clo. SE26 —64Yb 128
Bayeux. Tad —94Za 178
Bayfield Rd. SE9 —56Mc 107
Bayford Rd. NW10 —41Za 80
Bayford St. E8 —38Xb 63
Bayham Pl. NW1 —39Lb 62 (1B 192)
Bayham Rd. W4 —48Ta 79
Bayham Rd. W13 —45Ka 78
Bayham Rd. Mord —70Db 125
Bayham Rd. Sev —95Ld 187
Bayham St. NW1 —39Lb 62
Bayhurst Dri. N'wd —23V 36
Bayleys Mead. Hut —19Ee 33
Bayley St. WC1 —43Mb 82 (1D 198)
Bayley Wlk. SE2 —50Ad 87
Baylin Rd. SW18 —58Db 103
Baylis Pde. Slou —4J 73
Baylis Rd. SE1 —47Qb 82 (2K 205)
Baylis Rd. Slou —5H 73
Bayliss Av. SE28 —45Zc 87
Bayly Rd. Dart —58Qd 111
Bay Mnr. La. Grays —51Vd 112
Baymans Wood. Shenf —19Be 33
Bayne Clo. E6 —44Pc 86
Baynes Clo. Enf —11Wb 25
Baynes M. NW3 —37Fb 61
Baynes Pl. NW1 —38Lb 62
Baynes St. NW1 —38Lb 62
Baynham Clo. Bex —58Bd 109
Bayonne Rd. W6 —51Ab 102
Bays Ct. Edgw —22Ra 39
Baysfarm Ct. W Dray —53L 97
Bayston Rd. N16 —34Vb 63
Bayswater Rd. W2 —45Db 81
Bay Tree Clo. Brom —67Mc 129
Baytree Clo. Sidc —60Vc 109
Baytree Ct. SW2 —56Pb 104
Baytree Ct. Burn —1A 72
Baytree Ho. E4 —17Dc 26
Baytree Rd. SW2 —56Pb 104
Bay Tree Wlk. Wat —10V 4
Baywood Sq. Chig —21Xc 47
Bazalgette Clo. N Mald —71Ta 143
Bazalgette Gdns. N Mald —71Ta 143
Bazely St. E14 —45Ec 84
Bazes Shaw. New Ash —75Be 155
(in two parts)
Bazile Rd. N21 —16Qb 24
Beacham Clo. SE7 —50Mc 85
Beachborough Rd. Brom —63Ec 128
Beachcroft Rd. E11 —34Gc 65
Beachcroft Way. N19 —32Mb 62
Beach Gro. Felt —61Ca 121
Beach Ho. Felt —61Ca 121
Beachy Rd. E3 —38Cc 64
Beacon Clo. Bans —88Za 162
Beacon Clo. Ger X —24A 34
Beacon Clo. Uxb —36M 55
Beacon Dri. Bean —62Xd 134
Beaconfield Av. Epp —1Vc 15
Beaconfield Rd. Epp —1Vc 15
Beaconfields. Sev —98Hd 186
Beaconfield Way. Epp —1Vc 15
Beacon Gro. Cars —77Jb 146
Beacon Hill. N7 —36Nb 62
Beacon Hill. Purf —50Rd 89
Beacon Hill. Wok —7F 188
Beacon Rise. Sev —98Jd 186
Beacon Rd. SE13 —58Fc 107
Beacon Rd. Eri —52Kd 111
Beacon Rd. H'row A —58Q 98
Beacons Clo. E6 —43Nc 86
Beaconsfield Clo. N11 —22Jb 42
Beaconsfield Clo. SE3 —51Jc 107
Beaconsfield Clo. W4 —50Sa 79
Beaconsfield Comn. La. Beac —1G 52
Beaconsfield Ct. Leav —4X 5
Beaconsfield Pde. SE9 —63Nc 130
Beaconsfield Pl. Eps —84Ua 162
Beaconsfield Rd. E10 —34Ec 64
Beaconsfield Rd. E16 —42Hc 85
Beaconsfield Rd. E17 —30Bc 44
Beaconsfield Rd. N9 —20Wb 25
Beaconsfield Rd. N11 —20Jb 24
Beaconsfield Rd. N15 —28Ub 43
Beaconsfield Rd. NW10 —37Va 60
Beaconsfield Rd. SE3 —52Hc 107
Beaconsfield Rd. SE9 —61Nc 130
Beaconsfield Rd. SE17 —50Tb 83
Beaconsfield Rd. W4 —48Ta 79
Beaconsfield Rd. W5 —47La 78
Beaconsfield Rd. Bex —61Gd 132
Beaconsfield Rd. Brom —69Mc 129
Beaconsfield Rd. Clay —80Ga 142
Beaconsfield Rd. Croy —72Tb 147
Beaconsfield Rd. Enf —9Zb 12
Beaconsfield Rd. Eps —91Ta 177
Beaconsfield Rd. Farn R —10G 52
Beaconsfield Rd. Hay —46Y 77
Beaconsfield Rd. N Mald —68Ta 123
Beaconsfield Rd. S'hall —46Z 77
Beaconsfield Rd. Surb —73Pa 143
Beaconsfield Rd. Twic —58Ka 100
Beaconsfield Rd. Wok —92B 172
Beaconsfield Ter. Romf —30Zc 47
Beaconsfield Ter. Rd. W14 —48Ab 80
Beaconsfield Wlk. E6 —44Qc 86
Beaconsfield Wlk. SW6 —53Bb 103
Beacons, The. Lou —10Qc 14
Beacontree Av. E17 —25Fc 45
Beacontree Rd. E11 —31Hc 65
Beacon Way. Bans —88Za 162
Beacon Way. Rick —17J 17
Beadle's Pde. Dag —37Ed 68
Beadlow Clo. Cars —72Fb 145
Beadman Pl. SE27 —63Rb 127
Beadman St. SE27 —63Rb 127
Beadnell Rd. SE23 —60Zb 106
Beadon Rd. W6 —49Ya 80
Beadon Rd. Brom —70Jc 129
Beads Hall La. Pil H —14Xd 32
Beaford Gro. SW20 —69Ab 124
Beagle Clo. Felt —63X 121
Beagle Clo. Rad —9Ha 6
Beagles Clo. Orp —75Zc 151
Beak St. W1 —45Lb 82 (4C 198)
Beal Clo. Well —53Wc 109
Beale Clo. N13 —22Rb 43
Beale Pl. E3 —40Bc 64
Beale Rd. E3 —39Bc 64
Beales La. Wey —76R 140
Beales Rd. Bookh —99Da 175
Beal Rd. Ilf —33Qc 66
Beam Av. Dag —39Dd 68
Beaminster Gdns. Ilf —26Rc 46
Beaminster Ho. SW8 —52Pb 104
(off Dorset Rd.)
Beamish Dri. Bush —18Ea 20
Beamish Ga. NW1 —38Mb 62
Beamish Rd. N9 —18Wb 25
Beamish Rd. Orp —73Yc 151
Beam Vs. Dag —40Fd 68
Beamway. Dag —38Fd 68
Beanacre Clo. E9 —37Bc 64
Bean Hill Cotts. Grn St —63Yd 134
(in two parts)
Bean La. Bean —61Xd 134
Bean Rd. Bexh —56Zc 109
Bean Rd. Grnh —60Wd 112
Beanshaw. SE9 —63Qc 130
Beansland Gro. Romf —27Ad 47
Bear All. EC4 —44Rb 83 (2B 200)
Bear Clo. Romf —30Dd 48
Beardell St. SE19 —65Vb 127
Beardow Gro. N14 —16Lb 24
Beard Rd. King T —64Pa 123
Beardsfield. E13 —40Jc 65
Beard's Hill. Hamp —67Ca 121
Beard's Hill Clo. Hamp —67Ca 121
Beardsley Way. W3 —47Ta 79
Beard's Rd. Ashf —65U 120
Bearfield Rd. King T —66Na 123
Bear Gdns. SE1 —46Sb 83 (6D 200)
Bearing Clo. Chig —21Wc 47
Bearing Way. Chig —21Wc 47
Bear La. SE1 —46Rb 83 (6C 200)
Bear Rd. Felt —63Z 121
Bears Den. Tad —94Bb 179
Bearsted Rise. SE4 —57Bc 106
Bearsted Ter. Beck —67Cc 128
Bear St. WC2 —45Mb 82 (4E 198)
Bearwood Clo. Add —79J 139
Bearwood Clo. Pot B —3Fb 9
Beasley's Ait. Sun —72V 140
Beasley's Ait La. Sun —72V 140
Beatrice Av. SW16 —69Pb 126
Beatrice Av. Wemb —36Na 59
Beatrice Clo. E13 —42Jc 85
Beatrice Clo. Pinn —28W 36
Beatrice Gdns. Grav —1A 136
Beatrice Pl. W8 —48Db 81
Beatrice Rd. E17 —29Cc 44
Beatrice Rd. N4 —31Qb 62
Beatrice Rd. N9 —17Yb 26
Beatrice Rd. SE1 —49Wb 83
Beatrice Rd. Oxt —100Gc 183
Beatrice Rd. Rich —57Pa 101
Beatrice Rd. S'hall —46Ba 77
Beatrice Wilson Flats. Sev —97Kd 187
(off Rockdale Rd.)
Beatson Wlk. SE16 —46Ac 84

Beattie Clo.—Bellmount Wood Av.

Beattie Clo. Bookh —96Ba 175
Beattock Rise. N10 —28Kb 42
Beatty Ho. E14 —47Cc 84 (off Admirals Way)
Beatty Rd. N16 —35Ub 63
Beatty Rd. Stan —23La 38
Beatty St. NW1 —40Lb 62 (1B 192)
Beattyville Gdns. Ilf —28Qc 46
Beauchamp Clo. W4 —48Sa 79
Beauchamp Ct. Stan —22La 38
Beauchamp Gdns. Rick —18J 17
Beauchamp Pl. SW3 —48Gb 81 (3E 202)
Beauchamp Rd. E7 —38Kc 65
Beauchamp Rd. SE19 —67Tb 127
Beauchamp Rd. SW11 —56Gb 103
Beauchamp Rd. Sutt —77Cb 145
Beauchamp Rd. Twic —59Ja 100
Beauchamp Rd. W Mol —71Da 141
Beauchamp St. EC1 —43Qb 82 (1K 199)
Beauchamp Ter. SW15 —55Xa 102
Beauclare Clo. Lea —93Ma 177
Beauclerc Ct. Sun —68Y 121
Beauclerc Rd. W6 —48Xa 80
Beauclerk Clo. Felt —60X 99
Beaudesert Rd. W Dray —47N 75
Beaufort. E6 —44Sc 86
Beaufort Av. Harr —28Ja 38
Beaufort Clo. E4 —23Dc 44
Beaufort Clo. SW15 —59Xa 102
Beaufort Clo. W5 —43Pa 79
Beaufort Clo. Romf —28Ed 48
Beaufort Clo. Wok —88E 156
Beaufort Ct. N11 —22Kb 42 (off Limes Av, The.)
Beaufort Ct. New Bar —15Eb 23
Beaufort Ct. Rich —63La 122
Beaufort Dri. NW11 —28Cb 41
Beaufort Gdns. NW4 —30Ya 40
Beaufort Gdns. SW3 —48Gb 81 (3E 202)
Beaufort Gdns. SW16 —66Pb 126
Beaufort Gdns. Houn —53Aa 99
Beaufort Gdns. Ilf —32Qc 66
Beaufort M. SW6 —51Bb 103
Beaufort Pk. NW11 —28Cb 41
Beaufort Rd. W5 —43Pa 79
Beaufort Rd. King T —70Na 123
Beaufort Rd. Rich —63La 122
Beaufort Rd. Ruis —33T 56
Beaufort Rd. Twic —59La 100
Beaufort Rd. Wok —88E 156
Beauforts. Egh —4N 117
Beaufort St. SW3 —51Fb 103
Beaufort Way. Eps —80Wa 144
Beaufoy Ho. SE27 —62Rb 127
Beaufoy Rd. N17 —24Ub 43
Beaufoy Wlk. SE11 —49Pb 82 (6J 205)
Beaulieu Gdns. N21 —17Sb 25
Beaulieu Av. SE26 —63Xb 127
Beaulieu Clo. NW9 —28Ua 40
Beaulieu Clo. SE5 —55Tb 105
Beaulieu Clo. Dat —3M 95
Beaulieu Clo. Houn —57Ba 99
Beaulieu Clo. Mitc —67Jb 126
Beaulieu Clo. Twic —58Ma 101
Beaulieu Clo. Wat —18Y 19
Beaulieu Dri. Pinn —30Z 37
Beaulieu Pl. W4 —48Sa 79
Beauly Way. Romf —25Gd 48
Beaumanor Gdns. SE9 —63Qc 130
Beaumaris Ct. Slou —3F 72
Beaumaris Dri. Wfd G —24Mc 45
Beaumaris Grn. NW9 —30Ua 40 (off Pendragon Wlk.)
Beaumont Av. W14 —50Bb 81
Beaumont Av. Harr —30Da 37
Beaumont Av. Rich —55Pa 101
Beaumont Av. Wemb —36La 58
Beaumont Clo. King T —66Qa 123
Beaumont Clo. Romf —26Ld 49
Beaumont Ct. E5 —34Xb 63
Beaumont Ct. W4 —50Sa 79
Beaumont Cres. W14 —50Bb 81
Beaumont Cres. Rain —37Jd 68
Beaumont Dri. Ashf —64T 120
Beaumont Dri. Grav —9A 114
Beaumont Gdns. NW3 —34Cb 61
Beaumont Gdns. Hut —16Ee 33
Beaumont Ga. Rad —7Ka 6
Beaumont Gro. E1 —42Zb 84
Beaumont Ho. E10 —31Dc 64
Beaumont Ho. E15 —39Hc 65 (off John St.)
Beaumont M. W1 —43Jb 82 (7J 191)
Beaumont Pl. W1 —42Lb 82 (5C 192)
Beaumont Pl. Barn —11Bb 23
Beaumont Pl. Iswth —57Ha 100
Beaumont Rise. N19 —32Mb 62
Beaumont Rd. E10 —31Dc 64
Beaumont Rd. E13 —41Kc 85
Beaumont Rd. SE19 —65Sb 127
Beaumont Rd. SW19 —59Ab 102
Beaumont Rd. W4 —48Sa 79
Beaumont Rd. Orp —72Tc 150
Beaumont Rd. Purl —85Qb 164
Beaumont Rd. Slou —2H 73
Beaumont Rd. Wind —4G 94
Beaumont Sq. E1 —43Zb 84
Beaumont St. W1 —43Jb 82 (7J 191)
Beaumont Wlk. NW3 —38Hb 61
Beauvais Ter. N'holt —41Z 77
Beauval Rd. SE22 —58Vb 105
Beav Callender Clo. SW8 —55Kb 104
Beaverbank Rd. SE9 —60Tc 108
Beaverbrook Roundabout. Lea —95Ma 177
Beaver Clo. SE20 —66Wb 127
Beaver Clo. Hamp —67Da 121
Beavercote Wlk. Belv —50Bd 87
Beaver Ct. Beck —66Dc 128
Beaver Gro. N'holt —41Aa 77
Beaver Rd. Ilf —22Yc 47
Beavers Cres. Houn —56Y 99
Beavers La. Houn —54Y 99
Beavers Lodge. Sidc —63Vc 131
Beaverwood Rd. Chst —64Uc 130
Beavor Gro. W6 —50Wa 80 (off Beavor La.)
Beavor La. W6 —49Wa 80
Bebbington Rd. SE18 —49Uc 86
Beblets Clo. Orp —78Vc 151
Beccles Dri. Bark —37Uc 66
Beccles St. E14 —45Bc 84
Bec Clo. Ruis —34Z 57
Beck Clo. SE13 —53Dc 106
Beckenham Bus. Cen. Beck —65Ac 128
Beckenham Gdns. N9 —20Ub 25
Beckenham Gro. Brom —68Fc 129
Beckenham Hill Est. Beck —64Dc 128
Beckenham Hill Rd. Beck & SE6 —65Dc 128
Beckenham La. Brom —68Gc 129
Beckenham Pl. Pk. Beck —66Dc 128
Beckenham Rd. Beck —67Zb 128
Beckenham Rd. W Wick —73Ec 148
Beckenshaw Gdns. Bans —87Gb 163
Beckers, The. N16 —34Wb 63
Becket Av. E6 —41Qc 86
Becket Clo. SE25 —72Wb 147
Becket Clo. SW19 —67Db 125 (off High Path)
Becket Clo. Gt War —23Yd 50
Becket Fold. Harr —29Ha 38
Becket Ho. SE1 —47Tb 83 (2F 207) (off Tabard St.)
Becket Rd. N18 —21Yb 44
Becket St. SE1 —48Tb 83 (3F 207)
Beckett Av. Kenl —87Rb 165
Beckett Clo. NW10 —37Ua 60
Beckett Clo. SW16 —61Mb 126
Beckett Clo. Belv —48Bd 87
Beckett Ho. SW9 —54Nb 104
Becketts Clo. Felt —58X 99
Becketts Clo. Orp —76Vc 151
Becketts Ho. Ilf —34Qc 66
Becketts Pl. Hamp W —67Ma 123
Beckett Wlk. Beck —65Ac 128
Beckford Dri. Orp —73Tc 150
Beckford Ho. N16 —36Ub 63
Beckford Pl. SE17 —50Sb 83 (7E 206)
Beckford Rd. Croy —72Vb 147
Beck La. Beck —69Zb 128
Beckley Clo. Grav —1K 137
Becklow Gdns. W12 —46Wa 80 (off Becklow Rd.)
Becklow Rd. W12 —47Va 80
Beckman Clo. Hals —87Ed 170
Beck River Pk. Beck —67Cc 128
Beck Rd. E8 —39Xb 63
Becks Rd. Sidc —62Wc 131
Beckton Retail Pk. E6 —43Qc 86
Beckton Rd. E16 —43Hc 85
Beck Way. Beck —69Bc 128
Beckway Rd. SW16 —68Mb 126
Beckway St. SE17 (in two parts) —49Ub 83 (6G 207)
Beckwith Rd. SE24 —57Tb 105
Beclands Rd. SW17 —65Jb 126
Becmead Av. SW16 —63Mb 126
Becmead Av. Harr —29Ka 38
Becondale Rd. SE19 —64Ub 127
Becontree Av. Dag —35Xc 67
Bective Pl. SW15 —56Bb 103
Bective Rd. E7 —35Jc 65
Bective Rd. SW15 —56Bb 103
Becton Pl. Eri —52Dd 110
Bedale Rd. Enf —10Sb 11
Bedale Rd. Romf —22Qd 49
Bedale St. SE1 —46Tb 83 (7F 201)
Bedale Wlk. Dart —60Rd 111
Beddalls Farm Ct. E6 —43Nc 86
Beddington Farm Rd. Bedd —73Nb 146
Beddington Farm Rd. Croy —73Nb 146
Beddington Gdns. Cars & Wall (in two parts) —79Jb 146
Beddington Grn. Orp —67Vc 131
Beddington Gro. Wall —78Mb 146
Beddington La. Croy —71Lb 146
Beddington Pk. Cotts. Wall —76Mb 146
Beddington Path. St P —67Vc 131
Beddington Rd. Ilf —31Vc 67
Beddington Rd. Orp —67Uc 130
Beddington Ter. Croy —73Pb 146
Beddlestead La. Warl —89Hc 167
Bede Clo. Pinn —25Z 37
Bedefield. WC1 —41Nb 82 (4G 193)
Bedens Rd. Sidc —65Ad 131
Bede Rd. Romf —30Yc 47
Bedfont Clo. Felt —58S 98
Bedfont Clo. Mitc —68Jb 126
Bedfont Ct. Stai —55J 97
Bedfont Grn. Clo. Felt —60S 98
Bedfont La. Felt —59U 98
Bedfont Rd. Felt —60S 98
Bedfont Rd. Stai —58N 97
Bedford Av. WC1 —43Mb 82 (1E 198)
Bedford Av. Amer —11A 16
Bedford Av. Barn —15Bb 23
Bedford Av. Hay —44X 77
Bedford Av. Slou —4D 72
Bedfordbury. WC2 —45Nb 82 (5F 199)
Bedford Clo. N10 —24Jb 42
Bedford Clo. Chen —10D 2
Bedford Corner. W4 —49Ua 80 (off South Pde.)
Bedford Ct. WC2 —45Nb 82 (5F 199)
Bedford Cres. Enf —7Ac 12
Bedford Dri. Farn C —7F 52
Bedford Gdns. W8 —46Cb 81
Bedford Gdns. Horn —33Ld 69
Bedford Hill. SW12 & SW16 —60Kb 104
Bedford Ho. SW4 —56Nb 104 (off Solon New Rd. Est.)
Bedford Pk. W4 —48Ua 80
Bedford Pk. Croy —74Sb 147
Bedford Pk. Corner. W4 —49Ua 80
Bedford Pk. Mans. W4 —49Ta 79
Bedford Pas. SW6 —52Ab 102 (off Dawes Rd.)
Bedford Pas. W1 —43Lb 82 (7C 192)
Bedford Pl. W1 —43Lb 82
Bedford Pl. WC1 —43Nb 82 (7F 193)
Bedford Pl. Croy —74Tb 147
Bedford Rd. E6 —39Qc 66
Bedford Rd. E17 —26Cc 44
Bedford Rd. E18 —26Jc 45
Bedford Rd. N2 —27Gb 41
Bedford Rd. N8 —30Mb 42
Bedford Rd. N9 —17Xb 25
Bedford Rd. N15 —28Ub 43
Bedford Rd. N22 —25Nb 42
Bedford Rd. NW7 —19Ua 22
Bedford Rd. SW4 —56Nb 104
Bedford Rd. W4 —48Ta 79
Bedford Rd. W13 —45Ka 78
Bedford Rd. Dart —59Qd 111
Bedford Rd. Grav —1B 136
Bedford Rd. Grays —50De 91
Bedford Rd. Harr —30Ea 38
Bedford Rd. Ilf —34Rc 66
Bedford Rd. N'wd —20S 18
Bedford Rd. Orp —75Xc 151
Bedford Rd. Ruis —35V 56
Bedford Rd. Sidc —62Uc 130
Bedford Rd. Twic —62Fa 122
Bedford Rd. Wor Pk —75Ya 144
Bedford Row. WC1 —43Pb 82 (7J 193)
Bedford Sq. WC1 —43Mb 82 (1E 198)
Bedford Sq. Long —69Ae 135
Bedford St. WC2 —45Nb 82 (4F 199)
Bedford St. Wat —11X 19
Bedford Way. WC1 —42Mb 82 (6E 192)
Bedgebury Gdns. SW19 —61Ab 124
Bedgebury Rd. SE9 —56Mc 107
Bedivere Rd. Brom —62Jc 129
Bedlow Way. Croy —77Pb 146
Bedmond Rd. Abb L —1V 4
Bedonwell Rd. Bexh & Belv —53Bd 109
Bedser Clo. T Hth —69Sb 127
Bedser Dri. Gnfd —36Fa 58
Bedster Gdns. W Mol —68Da 121
Bedwardine Rd. SE19 —66Ub 127
Bedwell Ct. Romf —31Zc 67 (off Broomfield Rd.)
Bedwell Gdns. Hay —50U 76 (in two parts)
Bedwell Ho. SW9 —54Qb 104
Bedwell Rd. N17 —25Ub 43
Bedwell Rd. Belv —50Cd 88
Bedwin Way. SE16 —50Xb 83
Beeby Rd. E16 —43Kc 85
Beecham M. Chesh —1Ac 12 (off Lawrence Gdns.)
Beech Av. N20 —18Gb 23
Beech Av. W3 —46Ua 80
Beech Av. Bren —52Ka 100
Beech Av. Brtwd —20Be 33
Beech Av. Buck H —19Kc 27
Beech Av. Eff —100Z 175
Beech Av. Enf —7Qb 10
Beech Av. Rad —5Ja 6
Beech Av. Ruis —32X 57
Beech Av. Sidc —59Wc 109
Beech Av. S Croy —83Tb 165
Beech Av. Swan —70Hd 132
Beech Av. Tats —91Mc 183
Beech Av. Upm —34Rd 69
Beech Clo. N9 —16Wb 25
Beech Clo. SE8 —51Cc 106
Beech Clo. SW15 —59Wa 102
Beech Clo. SW19 —65Ya 124
Beech Clo. Ashf —64T 120
Beech Clo. Byfl —84N 157
Beech Clo. Cars —75Hb 145
Beech Clo. Cob —83Ca 159
Beech Clo. Eff —100Z 175
Beech Clo. Horn —34Kd 69
Beech Clo. Sun —68Z 121
Beech Clo. W on T —77Y 141
Beech Clo. W Dray —48Q 76
Beech Clo. Ct. Cob —83Ba 159
Beech Copse. Brom —68Pc 130
Beech Copse. S Croy —78Ub 147
Beech Ct. E17 —27Fc 45
Beech Ct. Beck —66Dc 128
Beech Ct. N'wd —24U 36
Beech Ct. Surb —73Ma 143
Beech Cres. Ct. N5 —35Rb 63
Beechcroft. Asht —91Pa 177
Beechcroft. Chst —66Qc 130
Beechcroft Av. NW11 —31Bb 61
Beechcroft Av. Bexh —53Fd 110
Beechcroft Av. Crox —16S 18
Beechcroft Av. Harr —31Ca 57
Beechcroft Av. Kenl —87Tb 165
Beechcroft Av. Linf —9J 93
Beechcroft Av. N Mald —67Sa 123
Beechcroft Av. S'hall —46Ba 77
Beechcroft Clo. SW16 —64Pb 126
Beechcroft Clo. Asc —10B 116
Beechcroft Clo. Houn —52Aa 99
Beechcroft Clo. Orp —77Tc 150
Beechcroft Ct. NW11 —31Bb 61 (off Beechcroft Av.)
Beechcroft Gdns. Wemb —34Pa 59
Beechcroft Mnr. Wey —76T 140
Beechcroft Rd. E18 —26Kc 45
Beechcroft Rd. SW14 —55Sa 101
Beechcroft Rd. SW17 —61Gb 125
Beechcroft Rd. Bush —15Aa 19
Beechcroft Rd. Chess —76Pa 143
Beechcroft Rd. Orp —77Tc 150
Beechdale. N21 —19Pb 24
Beechdale Rd. SW2 —58Pb 104
Beech Dell. Kes —77Pc 150
Beechdene. Tad —94Xa 178
Beech Dri. N2 —26Hb 41
Beech Dri. Borwd —12Pa 21
Beech Dri. Rip —96J 173
Beech Dri. Tad —94Bb 179
Beechen Cliff Way. Iswth —54Ha 100
Beechen Gro. Pinn —27Ba 37
Beechen Gro. Wat —13X 19
Beechen La. Tad —97Bb 179
Beechenlea La. Swan —70Jd 132
Beechen Pl. SE23 —61Zb 128
Beeches Av. Cars —80Gb 145
Beeches Clo. SE20 —67Yb 128
Beeches Clo. Tad —95Cb 179
Beeches Dri. Farn C —6F 52
Beeches Rd. SW17 —62Gb 125
Beeches Rd. Farn C —6F 52
Beeches Rd. Sutt —74Ab 144
Beeches, The. E12 —38Pc 66
Beeches, The. Bans —88Db 163
Beeches, The. Brtwd —20Xd 32
Beeches, The. Fet —96Ga 176
Beeches, The. Houn —53Da 99
Beeches, The. Sole S —10F 136
Beeches, The. S Croy —78Tb 147
Beeches, The. Til —4D 114
Beeches Wlk. Cars —81Fb 163
Beeches Wood. Tad —94Cb 179
Beech Farm Rd. Warl —92Ec 182
Beechfield. Bans —85Db 163
Beechfield. K Lan —2P 3
Beechfield Cotts. Brom —68Lc 129
Beechfield Gdns. Romf —31Ed 68
Beechfield Rd. N4 —30Sb 43
Beechfield Rd. SE6 —60Bc 106
Beechfield Rd. Brom —68Lc 129
Beechfield Rd. Eri —52Gd 110
Beechfield Wlk. Wal A —7Fc 13
Beech Gdns. EC2 —43Sb 83 (7D 194) (off Beech St.)
Beech Gdns. W5 —47Na 79
Beech Gdns. Dag —38Ed 68
Beech Gdns. Wok —87A 156
Beech Gro. Add —77K 139
Beech Gro. Cat —98Ub 181
Beech Gro. Eps —89Xa 162
Beech Gro. Ilf —23Uc 46
Beech Gro. Mitc —71Mb 146
Beech Gro. N Mald —69Ta 123
Beech Gro. S Ock —47Sd 90
Beech Hale Cres. E4 —24Fc 45
Beech Hall. Ott —80E 138
Beech Hall Rd. E4 —24Ec 44
Beech Haven Ct. Dart —57Fd 110 (off London Rd.)
Beech Hill. Barn —10Fb 9
Beech Hill. Wok —95A 172
Beech Hill Av. Barn —11Eb 23
Beech Hill Gdns. Wal A —9Kc 13
Beech Holt. Lea —94La 176
Beech Ho. Hut —16Ee 33
Beech Ho. Rd. Croy —76Tb 147
Beechhill Rd. SE9 —57Qc 108
Beechlands Clo. Hart —71Ce 155
Beech La. Buck H —19Kc 27
Beech Lawns. N12 —22Fb 41
Beechlee. Wall —82Lb 164
Beech Lodge. Stai —64G 118
Beechmont Av. Vir W —71A 138
Beechmont Clo. Brom —64Gc 129
Beechmore Gdns. Sutt —75Za 144
Beechmore Rd. SW11 —53Hb 103
Beechmount Av. W7 —43Fa 78
Beecholme. N12 —21Db 41
Beecholme. Bans —86Ab 162
Beecholme Av. Mitc —67Kb 126
Beecholme Est. E5 —34Xb 63
Beechpark Way. Wat —9U 4
Beech Pl. Epp —3Vc 15
Beech Rd. N11 —23Nb 42
Beech Rd. SW16 —68Pb 126
Beech Rd. Big H —91Kc 183
Beech Rd. Dart —60Md 111
Beech Rd. Eps —87Va 162
Beech Rd. Felt —59U 98
Beech Rd. Orp —80Wc 151
Beech Rd. Red —98Lb 180
Beech Rd. Sev —97Kd 187
Beech Rd. Slou —47A 74
Beech Rd. Wat —9W 4
Beech Rd. Wey —77T 140
Beech Row. Ham —63Na 123
Beech St. EC2 —43Sb 83 (7D 194)
Beech St. Romf —28Ed 48
Beechtree Av. Egh —5M 117
Beech Tree Clo. Stan —22La 38
Beech Tree Glade. E4 —18Hc 27
Beech Tree La. Stai —68K 119
Beech Tree Pl. Sutt —78Cb 145
Beechvale. Wok —90B 156 (off Fairview Av.)
Beechvale Clo. N12 —22Gb 41
Beech Wlk. NW7 —23Ua 40
Beech Wlk. Dart —56Jd 110
Beech Wlk. Eps —83Wa 162
Beech Way. NW10 —38Ta 59
Beechway. Bex —58Zc 109
Beech Way. Eps —87Va 162
Beech Way. S Croy —85Zb 166
Beech Way. Twic —62Ca 121
Beech Waye. Ger X —31B 54
Beechwood Av. N3 —27Bb 41
Beechwood Av. Chor —14E 16
Beechwood Av. Coul —87Kb 164
Beechwood Av. Gnfd —41Da 77
Beechwood Av. Harr —34Da 57
Beechwood Av. Hay —45T 76
Beechwood Av. Orp —79Uc 150
Beechwood Av. Pot B —5Db 9
Beechwood Av. Rich —53Qa 101
Beechwood Av. Ruis —33V 56
Beechwood Av. Stai —65K 119
Beechwood Av. Sun —65W 120
Beechwood Av. Tad —93Cb 179
Beechwood Av. T Hth —70Rb 127
Beechwood Av. Uxb —44Q 76
Beechwood Av. Wey —77U 140
Beechwood Circ. Harr —34Da 57
Beechwood Clo. N2 —28Hb 41 (off Western Rd.)
Beechwood Clo. NW7 —22Ua 40
Beechwood Clo. Knap —5B 188
Beechwood Clo. Surb —73La 142
Beechwood Clo. Wey —77U 140
Beechwood Ct. SE19 —64Vb 127
Beechwood Ct. W4 —51Ta 101
Beechwood Ct. Cars —77Hb 145
Beechwood Ct. Sun —65W 120
Beechwood Cres. Bexh —55Zc 109
Beechwood Dri. Cob —83Ca 159
Beechwood Dri. Kes —77Mc 149
Beechwood Dri. Wfd G —22Hc 45
Beechwood Gdns. NW10 —41Pa 79
Beechwood Gdns. Cat —94Wb 181
Beechwood Gdns. Harr —34Da 57
Beechwood Gdns. Ilf —29Pc 46
Beechwood Gdns. Rain —43Kd 89
Beechwood Gro. W3 —45Ua 80
Beechwood Gro. Surb —73La 142
Beechwood Hall. N3 —27Bb 41
Beechwood La. Warl —91Zb 182
Beechwood Mnr. Wey —77U 140
Beechwood M. N9 —19Wb 25
Beechwood Pk. E18 —27Jc 45
Beechwood Pk. Lea —94La 176
Beechwood Rise. Chst —63Rc 130
Beechwood Rise. Wat —8X 5
Beechwood Rd. E8 —37Vb 63
Beechwood Rd. N8 —28Mb 42
Beechwood Rd. Cat —94Wb 181
Beechwood Rd. Knap —5B 188
Beechwood Rd. Slou —3H 73
Beechwood Rd. S Croy —82Ub 165
Beechwood Rd. Wfd G —22Hc 45
Beechwoods Ct. SE19 —64Vb 127
Beechworth Clo. NW3 —33Cb 61
Beechy Lees Rd. Otf —89Md 171
Beecot La. W on T —75Y 141
Beecroft Rd. SE4 —57Ac 106
Beehive Clo. Els —16Ma 21
Beehive Clo. Uxb —38P 55
Beehive La. Ilf —29Pc 46
Beehive Pl. SW9 —55Qb 104
Beehive Rd. Chesh —1Rb 11
Beehive Rd. Stai —64H 119
Beeken Dene. Orp —77Sc 150
Beeleigh Rd. Mord —70Db 125
Beesfield La. F'ham —73Qd 153
Beeston Clo. E8 —36Wb 63
Beeston Clo. Wat —21Z 37
Beeston Ct. Dart —58Rd 111 (off Hardwick Cres.)
Beeston Pl. SW1 —48Kb 82 (4A 204)
Beeston Rd. Barn —16Fb 23
Beeston Way. Felt —58Y 99
Beethoven Rd. Els —16La 20
Beethoven St. W10 —41Ab 80
Beeton Clo. Grnh —57Xd 112
Beeton Clo. Pinn —24Ca 37
Begbie Rd. SE3 —53Lc 107
Beggars Bush La. Wat —15T 18
Beggar's Hill. Eps —80Va 144
Beggars Hollow. Enf —9Tb 11
Beggars La. W'ham —97Tc 184
Beggars Roost La. Sutt —79Cb 145
Begonia Pl. Hamp —65Ca 121
Begonia Wlk. W12 —44Va 80
Beira St. SW12 —59Kb 104
Beken Ct. Wat —7Y 5
Bekesbourne St. E14 —44Ac 84
Belcombe Av. Wor Pk —74Ya 144
Belcroft Clo. Brom —66Hc 129
Beldam Haw. Hals —84Cd 170
Beldanes Lodge. NW10 —38Wa 60
Beldham Gdns. W Mol —68Da 121
Belfairs Dri. Romf —31Yc 67
Belfast Av. Slou —4G 72
Belfast Gdns. SE3 —51Hc 107
Belfast Rd. N16 —33Vb 63
Belfast Rd. SE25 —70Xb 127
Belfield Rd. Eps —81Ta 161
Belfont Wlk. N7 —35Nb 62
Belford Gro. SE18 —49Qc 86
Belford Ho. E8 —39Vb 63
Belford Rd. Borwd —10Pa 7
Belfort Rd. SE15 —54Yb 106
Belfry Av. Hare —25J 35
Belfry La. Rick —18L 17
Belgrade Rd. N16 —35Ub 63
Belgrade Rd. Hamp —67Da 121
Belgrave Av. Romf —27Ld 49
Belgrave Av. Wat —15V 18
Belgrave Clo. N14 —15Lb 24
Belgrave Clo. W3 —47Ra 79
Belgrave Clo. Orp —70Yc 131
Belgrave Clo. W on T —77X 141
Belgrave Ct. E13 —42Lc 85
Belgrave Ct. W4 —50Sa 79
Belgrave Cres. Sun —67X 121
Belgrave Dri. K Lan —1S 4
Belgrave Gdns. N14 —14Mb 24
Belgrave Gdns. NW8 —39Db 61
Belgrave Gdns. Stan —22La 38
Belgrave Mnr. Wok —91A 172
Belgrave M. Uxb —42M 75
Belgrave M. N. SW1 —47Jb 82 (2H 203)
Belgrave M. S. SW1 —48Jb 82 (3J 203)
Belgrave M. W. SW1 —48Jb 82 (3H 203)
Belgrave Pl. SW1 —48Jb 82 (3J 203)
Belgrave Pl. Slou —7L 73
Belgrave Rd. E10 —32Ec 64
Belgrave Rd. E11 —33Jc 65
Belgrave Rd. E13 —42Lc 85
Belgrave Rd. E17 —29Cc 44
Belgrave Rd. SE25 —70Vb 127
Belgrave Rd. SW1 —49Kb 82 (5A 204)
Belgrave Rd. SW13 —52Va 102
Belgrave Rd. Houn —55Ba 99
Belgrave Rd. Ilf —32Pc 66
Belgrave Rd. Mitc —69Fb 125
Belgrave Rd. Slou —5J 73
Belgrave Rd. Sun —67X 121
Belgrave Sq. SW1 —48Jb 82 (3H 203)
Belgrave St. E1 —44Zb 84
Belgrave Ter. Wfd G —20Jc 27
Belgrave Wlk. Mitc —69Fb 125
Belgrave Yd. SW1 —48Kb 82 (4K 203) (off Lwr. Belgrave St.)
Belgravia Gdns. Brom —65Gc 129
Belgravia Ho. SW4 —58Mb 104
Belgravia M. King T —70Ma 123
Belgrove St. WC1 —41Nb 82 (3G 193)
Belham Rd. K Lan —1Q 4
Belhaven Ct. Borwd —11Pa 21
Belinda Rd. SW9 —55Rb 105
Belitha Vs. N1 —38Pb 62
Bellamy Clo. W14 —50Bb 81
Bellamy Clo. Uxb —34Q 56
Bellamy Clo. Wat —11W 18
Bellamy Ct. Stan —25Ka 38
Bellamy Dri. Stan —25Ka 38
Bellamy Ho. Houn —51Ca 99
Bellamy Rd. E4 —23Dc 44
Bellamy Rd. Chesh —1Ac 12
Bellamy Rd. Enf —12Tb 25
Bellamy St. SW12 —59Kb 104
Bellasis Av. SW2 —61Nb 126
Bell Av. Romf —25Kd 49
Bell Av. W Dray —49P 75
Bell Clo. Grnh —57Vd 112
Bell Clo. Pinn —26Y 37
Bell Clo. Ruis —34V 56
Bell Clo. Slou —3M 73
Bellclose Rd. W Dray —47N 75
Bell Comn. Epp —4Uc 14
Bell Corner. Upm —33Sd 70
Bell Ct. NW4 —28Ya 40
Bell Cres. Coul —93Kb 180
Bell Dri. SW18 —59Ab 102
Bellefield Rd. Orp —71Xc 151
Bellefields Rd. SW9 —55Pb 104
Bellegrove Clo. Well —54Vc 109
Bellegrove Pde. Well —55Vc 109
Bellegrove Rd. Well —54Uc 108
Bellenden Rd. SE15 —55Vb 105
Bellestaines Pleasaunce. E4 —19Cc 26
Belleville Rd. SW11 —57Gb 103
Belle Vue. Gnfd —39Fa 58
Belle Vue Clo. Stai —67J 119
Bellevue La. Bush —18Fa 20
Bellevue M. N11 —22Jb 42
Bellevue Pk. T Hth —69Sb 127
Bellevue Pl. E1 —42Yb 84
Belle Vue Rd. E17 —26Fc 45
Bellevue Rd. N11 —21Jb 42
Bellevue Rd. SW13 —54Wa 102
Bellevue Rd. SW17 —60Gb 103
Bellevue Rd. W13 —42Ka 78
Bellevue Rd. Bexh —57Bd 109
Bellevue Rd. Horn —32Pd 69
Bellevue Rd. King T —69Na 123
Belle Vue Rd. Orp —82Qc 168
Bellevue Rd. Romf —23Ed 48
Bellevue Ter. Hare —24J 35
Bellew St. SW17 —62Eb 125
Bell Farm Av. Dag —34Ed 68
Bell Farm Cotts. Epp —4Uc 14
Bellfield. Croy —81Ac 166
Bellfield Av. Harr —23Fa 38
Bellflower Clo. E6 —43Nc 86
Bellflower Path. Romf —24Ld 49
Bell Gdns. Orp —71Yc 151
Bellgate M. NW5 —35Kb 62
Bell Grn. SE26 —63Bc 128
Bell Grn. La. SE26 —64Bc 128
Bell Hill. Croy —75Sb 147
Bellhouse Cotts. Hay —45U 76
Bellhouse La. Pil H —15Ud 32
Bell Ho. Rd. Romf —32Ed 68
Bellingham. N17 —24Xb 43
Bellingham Grn. SE6 —62Cc 128
Bellingham Rd. SE6 —62Dc 128
Bell Inn Yd. EC3 —44Tb 83 (3G 201)
Bell Junct. Houn —55Da 99
Bell La. E1 —43Vb 83 (1K 201)
Bell La. E16 —46Jc 85
Bell La. NW4 & NW11 —28Ya 40
Bell La. Enf —10Zb 12
Bell La. Eton W —9D 72
Bell La. Fet —95Fa 176
Bell La. Lon C —1Na 7
Bell La. Twic —60Ja 100
Bell La. Wemb —34Ma 59
Bell La. Clo. Fet —95Fa 176
Bellman Av. Grav —10G 114
Bellmarsh Rd. Add —77K 139
Bell Meadow. SE19 —64Ub 127
Bell Moor. NW3 —34Eb 61 (off E. Heath Rd.)
Bellmount Wood Av. Wat —11U 18

Bello Clo.—Bevington Rd.

Bello Clo. SE24 —60Rb 105
Bellot St. SE10 —50Gc 85
Bell Pde. Wind —4D 94
Bellring Clo. Belv —51Cd 110
Bell Rd. E Mol —71Fa 142
Bell Rd. Enf —11Tb 25
Bell Rd. Houn —56Da 99
Bells All. SW6 —54Cb 103
Bells Hill. Barn —15Za 22
Bells Hill. Stoke P —9L 53
Bells Hill Grn. Stoke P —8L 53
Bells La. Hort —55D 96
Bell St. NW1 —43Gb 81 (7D 190)
Bellswood La. Iver —43D 74
Belltrees Gro. SW16 —64Pb 126
Bell View. Wind —5D 94
Bell View Clo. Wind —4D 94
Bell View Mnr. Ruis —31U 56
Bellvue Pl. Slou —8K 73
Bell Water Ga. SE18 —48Qc 86
Bellway Ho. Mers —100Lb 180
Bellweir Clo. Stai —61D 118
Bell Wharf La. EC4
—45Sb 83 (5E 200)
Bellwood Rd. SE15 —56Zb 106
Bell Yd. WC2 —44Qb 82 (3K 199)
Belmarsh Rd. SE28 —47Uc 86
Belmont. Slou —3E 72
Belmont Av. N9 —18Wb 25
Belmont Av. N13 —22Pb 42
Belmont Av. N17 —27Sb 43
Belmont Av. Barn —15Hb 23
Belmont Av. N Mald —71Wa 144
Belmont Av. S'hall —48Aa 77
Belmont Av. Upm —33Pd 69
Belmont Av. Well —55Uc 108
Belmont Av. Wemb —39Pa 59
Belmont Circ. Harr —25Ka 38
Belmont Clo. E4 —22Fc 45
Belmont Clo. N20 —18Db 23
Belmont Clo. SW4 —55Lb 104
Belmont Clo. Barn —14Hb 23
Belmont Clo. Uxb —37M 55
Belmont Clo. Wfd G —21Kc 45
Belmont Ct. NW11 —29Bb 41
Belmont Gro. SE13 —55Fc 107
Belmont Gro. W4 —49Ta 79
Belmont Hill. SE13 —55Ec 106
Belmont La. Chst —64Sc 130
(in two parts)
Belmont La. Stan —24La 38
Belmont Lodge. Har W —24Fa 38
Belmont Pde. Chst —64Sc 130
Belmont Pde. S Harr —34Da 57
Belmont Pk. SE13 —56Fc 107
Belmont Pk. Clo. SE13 —56Gc 107
Belmont Pk. Rd. E10 —30Dc 44
Belmont Rise. Sutt —79Bb 145
Belmont Rd. N15 & N17 —28Sb 43
Belmont Rd. SE25 —71Xb 147
Belmont Rd. SW4 —55Lb 104
Belmont Rd. W4 —49Ta 79
Belmont Rd. Beck —68Bc 128
Belmont Rd. Bush —15Aa 19
Belmont Rd. Chst —64Rc 130
Belmont Rd. Eri —52Cd 110
Belmont Rd. Grays —51Ee 113
Belmont Rd. Harr —27Ha 38
Belmont Rd. Horn —34Md 69
Belmont Rd. Ilf —34Sc 66
Belmont Rd. Lea —94Ja 176
Belmont Rd. Sutt —82Cb 163
Belmont Rd. Twic —61Fa 122
Belmont Rd. Uxb —38M 55
Belmont Rd. Wall —78Kb 146
Belmont St. NW1 —38Jb 62
Belmont Ter. W4 —49Ta 79
Belmor. Els —16Qa 21
Belmore Av. Hay —44W 76
Belmore Av. Wok —88F 156
Belmore La. N7 —36Mb 62
Belmore St. SW8 —53Mb 104
Beloe Clo. SW15 —56Wa 102
Belsham St. E9 —37Yb 64
Belsize Av. N13 —23Pb 42
Belsize Av. NW3 —37Fb 61
Belsize Av. W13 —48Ka 78
Belsize Ct. NW3 —36Fb 61
Belsize Cres. NW3 —36Fb 61
Belsize Gdns. Sutt —77Db 145
Belsize Gro. NW3 —37Gb 61
Belsize La. NW3 —37Fb 61
Belsize M. NW3 —37Fb 61
Belsize Pk. NW3 —37Fb 61
Belsize Pk. Gdns. NW3 —37Fb 61
Belsize Pk. M. NW3 —37Fb 61
Belsize Pl. NW3 —36Fb 61
Belsize Rd. NW6 —39Cb 61
Belsize Rd. Harr —24Fa 38
Belsize Sq. NW3 —37Fb 61
Belsize Ter. NW3 —37Fb 61
Belson Rd. SE18 —49Pc 86
Beltana Dri. Grav —3G 136
Beltane Dri. SW19 —62Za 124
Beltham Wlk. SE5 —53Tb 105
Belthorn Cres. SW12 —59Lb 104
Beltinge Rd. Romf —27Pd 49
Belton Rd. E7 —38Kc 65
Belton Rd. E11 —35Gc 65
Belton Rd. N17 —27Ub 43
Belton Rd. NW2 —37Wa 60
Belton Rd. Sidc —63Wc 131
Belton Way. E3 —43Cc 84
Beltran Rd. SW6 —54Db 103
Beltwood Rd. Belv —49Ed 88
Belvedere Av. SW19 —64Ab 124
Belvedere Av. Ilf —26Rc 46
Belvedere Bldgs. SE1
—47Rb 83 (2C 206)
Belvedere Clo. Esh —78Da 141
Belvedere Clo. Grav —10E 114
Belvedere Clo. Tedd —64Ga 122
Belvedere Clo. Wey —78Q 140
Belvedere Dri. SW19 —64Ab 124
Belvedere Gdns. W Mol —71Ba 141
Belvedere Gro. SW19 —64Ab 124
Belvedere Link Bus. Pk. Eri
—48Fd 88
Belvedere Mans. Chalv —7H 73
Belvedere M. SE15 —55Yb 106
Belvedere Pl. SE1
—47Rb 83 (2C 206)
Belvedere Rd. E10 —32Ac 64
Belvedere Rd. SE1
—47Pb 82 (1J 205)
Belvedere Rd. SE2 —46Yc 87
Belvedere Rd. SE19 —66Vb 127
Belvedere Rd. W7 —48Ha 78
Belvedere Rd. Bexh —55Bd 109
Belvedere Rd. Big H —90Pc 168
Belvedere Rd. Brtwd —20Vd 32
Belvedere Sq. SW19 —64Ab 124
Belvedere Strand. NW9 —26Va 40
Belvedere, The. SW10 —53Eb 103
(off Chelsea Harbour)
Belvedere Way. Harr —30Na 39
Belvoir Clo. SE9 —62Nc 130
Belvoir Rd. SE22 —59Wb 105
Belvue Bus. Cen. N'holt —38Da 57
Belvue Clo. N'holt —38Ca 57
Belvue Rd. N'holt —38Ca 57
Bembridge Clo. NW6 —38Ab 60
Bembridge Ct. Slou —8K 73
Bembridge Gdns. Ruis —33T 56
Bembridge Ho. SE8 —49Bc 84
(off Longshore)
Bembridge Pl. Wat —5W 4
Bemersyde Point. E13 —41Kc 85
(off Dongola Rd. W.)
Bemerton Est. N1 —38Nb 62
Bemerton St. N1 —39Pb 62
Bemish Rd. SW15 —55Za 102
Bempton Dri. Ruis —33X 57
Bemsted Rd. E17 —27Bc 44
Benares Rd. SE18 —49Vc 87
Benbow Rd. W6 —48Xa 80
Benbow St. SE8 —51Cc 106
Benbow Way. Uxb —43L 75
Benbury Clo. Brom —64Ec 128
Bence Ho. SE8 —50Ac 84
Bence, The. Egh —69D 118
Bench Field. S Croy —78Vb 147
Bench, The. Rich —62La 122
Bencombe Rd. Purl —86Qb 164
Bencroft Rd. SW16 —66Lb 126
Bencurtis Pk. W Wick —76Fc 149
Bendall M. NW1 —43Gb 81 (7E 190)
(off Bell St.)
Bendemeer Rd. SW15 —55Za 102
Bendish Rd. E6 —38Nc 66
Bendmore Av. SE2 —50Wc 87
Bendon Valley. SW18 —59Db 103
Bendysh Rd. Bush —13Aa 19
Benedict Clo. Belv —48Ad 87
Benedict Clo. Orp —76Uc 150
Benedict Dri. Felt —59T 98
Benedict Rd. SW9 —55Pb 104
Benedict Rd. Mitc —69Fb 125
Benedict Way. N2 —27Eb 41
Benenden Grn. Brom —71Jc 149
Benen-Stock Rd. Stai —57J 97
Benets Rd. Horn —32Qd 69
Benett Gdns. SW16 —68Nb 126
Benfleet Clo. Cob —84Aa 159
Benfleet Clo. Sutt —76Eb 145
Benfleet Ct. E8 —39Vb 63
Bengal Ct. EC3 —44Tb 83 (3G 201)
(off Birchin La.)
Bengal Rd. Ilf —34Rc 66
Bengarth Dri. Harr —26Fa 38
Bengarth Rd. N'holt —39Aa 57
Bengeworth Rd. SE5 —55Sb 105
Bengeworth Rd. Harr —33Ja 58
Ben Hale Clo. Stan —22Ka 38
Benham Clo. SW11 —55Fb 103
Benham Clo. Coul —90Rb 165
Benham Gdns. Houn —57Ba 99
Benham Rd. W7 —43Ga 78
Benham's Pl. NW3 —35Eb 61
Benhill Av. Sutt —77Db 145
Benhill Rd. SE5 —52Tb 105
Benhill Rd. Sutt —76Eb 145
Benhill Wood Rd. Sutt —76Eb 145
Benhilton Gdns. Sutt —76Db 145
Benhurst Av. Horn —35Kd 69
Benhurst Clo. S Croy —82Zb 166
Benhurst Ct. SW16 —64Qb 126
Benhurst Gdns. S Croy —83Yb 166
Benhurst La. SW16 —64Qb 126
Benin St. SE13 —59Fc 107
Benjafield Clo. N18 —21Xb 43
Benjamin Clo. E8 —39Wb 63
Benjamin Clo. Horn —30Jd 48
Benjamin Ct. Belv —51Bd 109
Benjamin St. EC1
—43Rb 83 (7B 194)
Ben Jonson Ct. N1
—40Ub 63 (1J 195)
Ben Jonson Ho. EC2
(off Barbican) —43Sb 83 (7E 194)
Ben Jonson Pl. EC2
(off Beech St.) —43Sb 83 (7E 194)
Ben Jonson Rd. E1 —43Zb 84
Benledi St. E14 —44Fc 85
Benneck Ho. Wat —16U 18
Bennerley Rd. SW11 —57Gb 103
Bennets Field Rd. Uxb —46R 76
Bennet's Hill. EC4
—45Sb 83 (4C 200)
Bennet St. SW1 —46Lb 82 (6B 198)
Bennett Clo. Cob —85W 158
Bennett Clo. Hamp W —67La 122
Bennett Clo. N'wd —24V 36
Bennett Clo. Well —55Wc 109
Bennett Ct. N7 —34Pb 62
Bennett Gro. SE13 —53Dc 106
Bennett Ho. Grav —2B 136
Bennett Pk. SE3 —55Hc 107
Bennett Rd. E13 —42Lc 85
Bennett Rd. Romf —30Ad 47
Bennetts Av. Croy —75Ac 148
Bennetts Av. Gnfd —39Ga 58
Bennett's Castle La. Dag —33Yc 67
Bennetts Clo. N17 —24Vb 43
Bennetts Clo. Mitc —67Kb 126
Bennetts Clo. Slou —6E 72
Bennetts Copse. Chst —65Nc 130
Bennett's Rd. N16 —35Ub 63
Bennett St. W4 —51Ua 102
Bennetts Way. Croy —75Ac 148
Bennet's Yd. SW1
—48Nb 82 (4E 204)
Bennett's Yd. Uxb —38L 55
Bennett Way. Dart —63Td 134
Bennett Way. W Cla —100J 173
Benning Clo. Wind —5B 94
Benningholme Rd. Edgw —23Ua 40
Bennington Rd. E4 —24Gc 45
Bennington Rd. N17 —25Ub 43
Bennions Clo. Horn —37Md 69
Bennison Dri. H Wood —26Md 49
Benn's All. Hamp —68Da 121
Benn St. E9 —37Ac 64
Benns Wlk. Rich —56Na 101
Benrek Clo. Ilf —24Sc 46
Bensbury Clo. SW15 —59Xa 102
Bensham Clo. T Hth —70Sb 127
Bensham Gro. T Hth —68Sb 127
Bensham La. T Hth & Croy
—71Rb 147
Bensham Mnr. Rd. T Hth
—70Sb 127
Benskin Rd. Wat —15W 18
Benskins La. Noak H —18Md 31
Bensley Clo. N11 —22Hb 41
Ben Smith Way. SE16 —48Wb 83
Benson Av. E6 —40Lc 65
Benson Clo. Houn —56Ca 99
Benson Clo. Slou —6L 73
Benson Clo. Uxb —43N 75
Benson Quay. E1 —45Yb 84
Benson Rd. SE23 —60Yb 106
Benson Rd. Croy —76Qb 146
Benson Rd. Grays —51Ee 113
Bentall Cen., The. King T
—67Ma 123
Bentfield Gdns. SE9 —62Mc 129
Benthall Gdns. Kenl —89Sb 165
Benthal Rd. N16 —34Wb 63
Bentham Av. Wok —87E 156
Bentham Rd. E9 —37Zb 64
Bentham Rd. SE28 —45Xc 87
Bentham Wlk. NW10 —36Sa 59
Ben Tillet Clo. E16 —46Pc 86
Ben Tillet Clo. Bark —38Wc 67
Ben Tillet Ho. N15 —27Rb 43
Bentinck M. W1 —44Jb 82 (2J 197)
Bentinck Rd. W Dray —46M 75
Bentinck St. W1 —44Jb 82 (2J 197)
Bentley Clo. Long —69Ee 135
Bentley Dri. Ilf —30Sc 46
Bentley Dri. Wey —81Q 158
Bentley Heath La. Barn —6Ab 8
Bentley Ho. SE5 —53Ub 105
(off Peckham Rd.)
Bentley Pk. Burn —10B 52
Bentley Rd. N1 —37Ub 63
Bentley Rd. Slou —6E 72
Bentley's Meadow. Seal —92Pd 187
Bentley St. Grav —8E 114
Bentley St. Ind. Est. Grav —8F 114
Bentley Way. Stan —22Ja 38
Bentley Way. Wfd G —20Jc 27
Benton Rd. Ilf —32Tc 66
Benton Rd. Wat —22Z 37
Bentons La. SE27 —63Sb 127
Bentons Rise. SE27 —64Tb 127
Bentry Clo. Dag —33Ad 67
Bentry Rd. Dag —33Ad 67
Bentworth Rd. W12 —44Xa 80
Benville Ho. SW8 —52Pb 104
(off Oval Pl.)
Benwell Ct. Sun —67W 120
Benwell Rd. N7 —36Qb 62
Benwick Clo. SE16 —49Xb 83
Benwood Ct. Sutt —76Eb 145
Benworth St. E3 —41Bc 84
Benyon Path. S Ock —40Yd 70
Beomonds Row. Cher —73J 139
Berberis Wlk. W Dray —49N 75
Berber Rd. SW11 —57Hb 103
Berceau Wlk. Wat —11U 18
Bercta Rd. SE9 —61Sc 130
Beredens La. Gt War —27Vd 50
Berenger Tower. SW10 —52Fb 103
(off Worlds End Est.)
Berens Rd. NW10 —41Za 80
Berens Rd. Orp —71Zc 151
Berens Way. Chst —69Vc 131
Beresford Av. N20 —19Hb 23
Beresford Av. W7 —43Fa 78
Beresford Av. Slou —5N 73
Beresford Av. Surb —74Ra 143
Beresford Av. Twic —58La 100
Beresford Av. Wemb —39Pa 59
Beresford Dri. Brom —69Nc 130
Beresford Dri. Wfd G —21Lc 45
Beresford Gdns. Enf —14Ub 25
Beresford Gdns. Houn —57Ba 99
Beresford Gdns. Romf —29Ad 47
Beresford Rd. E4 —18Gc 27
Beresford Rd. E17 —25Dc 44
Beresford Rd. N2 —27Gb 41
Beresford Rd. N5 —36Tb 63
Beresford Rd. N8 —29Qb 42
Beresford Rd. Grav —9A 114
Beresford Rd. Harr —29Fa 38
Beresford Rd. King T —67Pa 123
Beresford Rd. N Mald —70Sa 123
Beresford Rd. Rick —18H 17
Beresford Rd. S'hall —46Z 77
Beresford Rd. Sutt —80Bb 145
Beresford Sq. SE18 —49Rc 86
Beresford St. SE18 —48Rc 86
Beresford Ter. N5 —36Sb 63
Berestede Rd. W6 —50Va 80
Bere St. E1 —45Zb 84
Bergen Sq. SE16 —48Ac 84
Berger Clo. Orp —72Tc 150
Berger Rd. E9 —37Zb 64
Berghem M. W14 —48Za 80
Bergholt Av. Ilf —29Nc 46
Bergholt Cres. N16 —31Ub 63
Bergholt M. NW1 —38Lb 62
Bering Wlk. E16 —44Mc 85
Berkeley Av. Bexh —53Zc 109
Berkeley Av. Gnfd —37Ga 58
Berkeley Av. Houn —54W 98
Berkeley Av. Ilf —26Qc 46
Berkeley Av. Romf —24Ed 48
Berkeley Clo. Abb L —4V 4
Berkeley Clo. Bren —51Ja 100
Berkeley Clo. Els —15Qa 21
Berkeley Clo. Horn —33Rd 69
Berkeley Clo. King T —66Na 123
Berkeley Clo. Orp —73Uc 150
Berkeley Clo. Pot B —4Ab 8
Berkeley Clo. Ruis —34W 56
Berkeley Ct. N3 —25Db 41
Berkeley Ct. NW11 —31Bb 61
(off Ravenscroft Av.)
Berkeley Ct. Surb —73Ma 143
Berkeley Ct. Swan —70Gd 132
Berkeley Ct. Wall —76Lb 146
Berkeley Ct. Wey —75T 140
Berkeley Cres. Barn —15Fb 23
Berkeley Cres. Dart —60Pd 111
Berkeley Dri. Horn —32Qd 69
Berkeley Dri. W Mol —69Ba 121
Berkeley Dri. Wink —10A 94
Berkeley Gdns. N21 —17Tb 25
Berkeley Gdns. W8 —46Cb 81
Berkeley Gdns. Clay —79Ja 142
Berkeley Gdns. W on T —73V 140
Berkeley Ho. Bren —51Ma 101
(off Albany Rd.)
Berkeley M. W1 —44Hb 81 (3G 197)
Berkeley M. Burn —4B 72
Berkeley Pl. SW19 —65Za 124
Berkeley Pl. Eps —88Ta 161
Berkeley Rd. E12 —36Nc 66
Berkeley Rd. N8 —29Mb 42
Berkeley Rd. N15 —30Tb 43
Berkeley Rd. NW9 —28Qa 39
Berkeley Rd. SW13 —53Wa 102
Berkeley Rd. Uxb —38S 56
Berkeley Sq. W1
—45Kb 82 (5A 198)
Berkeleys, The. Fet —96Ga 176
Berkeley St. W1 —45Kb 82 (5A 198)
Berkeley Wlk. N7 —33Pb 62
(off Durham Rd.)
Berkeley Waye. Houn —51Z 99
Berkhampstead Rd. Belv —50Cd 88
Berkhamsted By-Pass. K Lan —1M 3
Berkhemsted Av. Wemb —37Pa 59
Berkley Av. Wal X —6Zb 12
Berkley Clo. Stai —61F 118
Berkley Cres. Grav —8E 114
Berkley Gdns. W Byf —86H 157
Berkley Gro. NW1 —38Hb 61
Berkley Pl. Wal X —6Zb 12
Berkley Rd. NW1 —38Hb 61
Berkley Rd. Grav —8D 114
Berks Hill. Chor —15E 16
Berkshire Av. Slou —4F 72
Berkshire Clo. Cat —94Tb 181
Berkshire Gdns. N13 —23Qb 42
Berkshire Gdns. N18 —22Xb 43
Berkshire Rd. E9 —37Bc 64
Berkshire Sq. Mitc —70Nb 126
Berkshire Way. Horn —29Qd 49
Berkshire Way. Mitc —70Nb 126
Berman's Clo. Hut —19De 33
Bermans Way. NW10 —35Ua 60
Bermondsey Sq. SE1
—48Ub 83 (3J 207)
Bermondsey St. SE1
—46Ub 83 (7H 201)
Bermondsey Trading Est. SE16
—50Yb 84
Bermondsey Wall E. SE16
—47Wb 83
Bermondsey Wall W. SE16
—47Wb 83
Bermuda Rd. Til —4C 114
Bernal Clo. SE28 —45Zc 87
Bernard Ashley Dri. SE7 —50Kc 85
Bernard Av. W13 —48Ka 78
Bernard Cassidy St. E16 —43Hc 85
Bernard Gdns. SW19 —64Bb 125
Bernard Rd. N15 —29Vb 43
Bernard Rd. Romf —31Ed 68
Bernard Rd. Wall —77Kb 146
Bernards Clo. Ilf —24Tc 46
Bernard St. WC1
—42Nb 82 (6F 193)
Bernard St. Grav —8D 114
Bernays Clo. Stan —23La 38
Bernay's Gro. SW9 —56Pb 104
Bernel Dri. Croy —76Bc 148
Berne Rd. T Hth —71Sb 147
Berners Clo. Slou —5C 72
Berners Dri. W13 —45Ja 78
Berners M. W1 —43Lb 82 (1C 198)
Berners Pl. W1 —44Lb 82 (2C 198)
Berners Rd. N1 —39Rb 63 (1B 194)
Berners Rd. N22 —25Qb 42
Berners St. W1 —43Lb 82 (1C 198)
Berney Ho. Beck —71Ac 148
Berney Rd. Croy —73Tb 147
Bernice Clo. Rain —42Ld 89
Bernville Way. Harr —29Pa 39
Bernwell Rd. E4 —20Gc 27
Berridge Grn. Edgw —24Qa 39
Berridge M. NW6 —36Cb 61
(off Hillfield Rd.)
Berridge Rd. SE19 —64Tb 127
Berriman Rd. N7 —34Pb 62
Berrington Dri. Eff J —96V 174
Berriton Rd. Harr —32Ba 57
Berry Av. Wat —8X 5
Berrybank Clo. E4 —19Ec 26
Berry Clo. N21 —18Rb 25
Berry Clo. NW10 —38Ua 60
Berry Clo. Horn —36Ld 69
Berry Clo. Rick —17K 17
Berry Ct. Houn —57Ba 99
Berrydale Rd. Hay —42Aa 77
Berryfield. Slou —4N 73
Berryfield Clo. E17 —28Dc 44
Berryfield Clo. Brom —67Nc 130
Berryfield Rd. SE17
—50Rb 83 (7C 206)
Berry Gro. La. Wat —10Aa 5
(in two parts)
Berryhill. SE9 —56Rc 108
Berry Hill. Stan —21Ma 39
Berryhill Gdns. SE9 —56Rc 108
Berrylands. SW20 —70Ya 124
Berrylands. Hart —72Ce 155
Berrylands. Orp —76Yc 151
Berrylands. Surb —72Pa 143
Berrylands Rd. Surb —72Pa 143
Berry La. SE21 —63Tb 127
Berry La. Chor —16F 16
Berryman Clo. Dag —34Yc 67
Berryman's La. SE26 —63Zb 128
Berry Meade. Asht —89Pa 161
Berrymead Gdns. W3 —47Sa 79
Berrymede Rd. W4 —48Ta 79
Berry Pl. EC1 —41Rb 83 (4C 194)
Berryscroft Ct. Stai —66L 119
Berryscroft Rd. Stai —66L 119
Berry's Grn. Rd. Berr G —88Rc 168
Berry's Hill. Berr G —87Rc 168
Berry's La. Byfl —83M 157
Berry St. EC1 —42Rb 83 (5C 194)
Berry Wlk. Asht —91Pa 177
Berry Way. W5 —48Na 79
Berry Way. Rick —17K 17
Bersham La. Grays —49Be 91
Bertal Rd. SW17 —63Fb 125
Berther Rd. Horn —31Md 69
Berthon St. SE8 —52Cc 106
Bertie Rd. NW10 —37Wa 60
Bertie Rd. SE26 —65Zb 128
Bertram Cotts. SW19 —66Cb 125
Bertram Rd. NW4 —30Wa 40
Bertram Rd. Enf —14Wb 25
Bertram Rd. King T —66Qa 123
Bertram St. N19 —34Kb 62
Bertrand St. SE13 —55Dc 106
Bertrand Way. SE28 —45Xc 87
Bert Rd. T Hth —71Sb 147
Bert Way. Enf —14Vb 25
Berwick Av. Hay —44Z 77
Berwick Av. Slou —4F 72
Berwick Clo. Stan —23Ha 38
Berwick Clo. Wal X —6Cc 12
Berwick Cres. Sidc —58Uc 108
Berwick Ho. N2 —26Fb 41
Berwick Pond Clo. Rain —40Md 69
Berwick Pond Rd. Rain & Upm
—40Nd 69
Berwick Rd. E16 —44Kc 85
Berwick Rd. N22 —25Rb 43
Berwick Rd. Borwd —10Pa 7
Berwick Rd. Rain —40Md 69
Berwick Rd. Well —53Xc 109
Berwick St. W1 —44Lb 82 (2C 198)
Berwick Tower. SE14 —51Ac 106
Berwick Way. Orp —74Wc 151
Berwick Way. Sev —92Kd 187
Berwyn Av. Houn —53Da 99
Berwyn Rd. SE24 —60Rb 105
Berwyn Rd. Rich —56Ra 101
Beryl Av. E6 —43Nc 86
Beryl Rd. W6 —50Za 80
Berystede. King T —66Ra 123
Besant Ct. N1 —36Tb 63
Besant Ho. Wat —12Z 19
Besant Rd. NW2 —35Ab 60
Besant Wlk. N7 —33Pb 62
Besant Way. NW10 —36Sa 59
Besley St. SW16 —65Lb 126
Bessborough Gdns. SW1
—50Mb 82 (7E 204)
Bessborough Pl. SW1
—50Mb 82 (7E 204)
Bessborough Rd. SW15
—60Wa 102
Bessborough Rd. Harr —32Fa 58
Bessborough St. SW1
—50Mb 82 (7D 204)
Bessels Grn. Rd. Sev —95Fd 186
Bessels Meadow. Sev —96Fd 186
Bessels Way. Sev —96Ed 186
Bessemer Rd. SE5 —54Sb 105
Bessie Lansbury Clo. E6 —44Qc 86
Bessingby Rd. Ruis —33X 57
Besson St. SE14 —53Yb 106
Bessy St. E2 —41Yb 84
Bestobell Rd. Slou —4G 72
Best Ter. Swan —71Ed 152
Bestwood St. SE8 —49Zb 84
Beswick M. NW6 —37Db 61
Betam Rd. Hay —47T 76
Beta Rd. Wok —88D 156
Beta Way. Egh —67E 118
Betchworth Clo. Sutt —78Fb 145
Betchworth Rd. Ilf —33Uc 66
Betchworth Way. New Ad —81Ec 166
Bethal Est. SE1 —46Ub 83 (7J 201)
(off Tooley St.)
Betham Rd. Gnfd —42Fa 78
Bethany Pl. Wok —6G 188
Bethany Waye. Felt —59U 98
Bethecar Rd. Harr —29Ga 38
Bethell Av. E16 —42Hc 85
Bethell Av. Ilf —31Qc 66
Bethel Rd. Sev —95Ld 187
Bethel Rd. Well —55Yc 109
Bethersden Clo. Beck —66Bc 128
Bethnal Grn. Rd. E1 & E2
—42Vb 83 (5K 195)
Bethune Av. N11 —21Hb 41
Bethune Clo. N16 —32Ub 63
Bethune Rd. N16 —31Tb 63
Bethune Rd. NW10 —42Ta 79
Bethwin Rd. SE5 —52Rb 105
Betjeman Clo. Chesh —1Wb 11
Betjeman Clo. Pinn —28Ca 37
Betjeman Ct. W Dray —46M 75
Betjemen Clo. Coul —89Pb 164
Betley Ct. W on T —76X 141
Betony Clo. Croy —74Zb 148
Betony Rd. Romf —23Ld 49
Betoyne Av. E4 —21Gc 45
Betsham Rd. Eri —52Hd 110
Betsham Rd. S'fleet —64Zd 135
Betsham Rd. Swans —59Ae 113
Betstyle Cir. N11 —21Kb 42
Betstyle Ho. N10 —24Jb 42
Betstyle Rd. N11 —21Kb 42
Betterton Dri. Sidc —61Ad 131
Betterton Rd. Rain —41Gd 88
Betterton St. WC2
—44Nb 82 (3G 199)
Bettles Clo. Uxb —40L 55
Bettons Pk. E15 —39Gc 65
Bettridge Rd. SW6 —54Bb 103
Betts Clo. Beck —68Ac 128
Betts M. E17 —30Bc 44
Betts Rd. E16 —45Kc 85
Betts St. E1 —45Xb 83
Betts Way. SE20 —67Xb 127
Betts Way. Surb —74Ka 142
Betula Clo. Kenl —87Tb 165
Betula Way. Rain —41Md 89
Between Streets. Cob —86W 158
Beulah Av. T Hth —68Sb 127
Beulah Clo. Edgw —20Ra 21
Beulah Cres. T Hth —68Sb 127
Beulah Gro. Croy —72Sb 147
Beulah Hill. SE19 —65Rb 127
Beulah Path. E17 —29Ec 44
Beulah Rd. E17 —29Dc 44
Beulah Rd. SW19 —66Bb 125
Beulah Rd. Epp —1Wc 15
Beulah Rd. Horn —34Ld 69
Beulah Rd. Sutt —77Cb 145
Beulah Rd. T Hth —69Sb 127
Beulah Wlk. Wold —92Ac 182
Beult Rd. Dart —56Jd 110
Bevan Av. Bark —38Wc 67
Bevan Ct. Croy —78Qb 146
Bevan Ho. Grays —47Fe 91
Bevan Ho. Wat —12Z 19
Bevan Pl. Swan —70Hd 132
Bevan Rd. SE2 —50Xc 87
Bevan Rd. Barn —14Hb 23
Bevans Clo. Grnh —58Yd 112
Bevan St. N1 —39Sb 63 (1E 194)
Bevan Way. Horn —35Pd 69
Bev Callender Clo. SW8 —55Kb 104
Bevenden St. N1
—41Tb 83 (3G 195)
Beveridge Rd. NW10 —38Ua 60
Beverley Av. SW20 —67Va 124
Beverley Av. Houn —56Ba 99
Beverley Av. Sidc —59Vc 109
Beverley Clo. N21 —18Sb 25
Beverley Clo. SW11 —56Fb 103
Beverley Clo. SW13 —54Wa 102
Beverley Clo. Add —78M 139
Beverley Clo. Chess —77La 142
Beverley Clo. Enf —14Ub 25
Beverley Clo. Eps —83Ya 162
Beverley Clo. Horn —31Pd 69
Beverley Clo. Ors —4F 92
Beverley Clo. Wey —75U 140
Beverley Ct. N2 —28Hb 41
(off Western Rd.)
Beverley Ct. N14 —17Lb 24
Beverley Ct. SE4 —55Bc 106
Beverley Ct. W4 —50Sa 79
Beverley Ct. Harr —27Fa 38
Beverley Ct. Houn —56Ba 99
Beverley Ct. Kent —28La 38
Beverley Ct. Slou —7M 73
Beverley Cres. Wfd G —25Kc 45
Beverley Dri. Edgw —27Qa 39
Beverley Gdns. NW11 —31Ab 60
Beverley Gdns. SW13 —55Va 102
Beverley Gdns. Chesh —2Vb 11
Beverley Gdns. Horn —31Pd 69
Beverley Gdns. Stan —25Ja 38
Beverley Gdns. Wemb —32Pa 59
Beverley Gdns. Wor Pk —74Wa 144
Beverley La. SW15 —62Va 124
Beverley La. King T —66Ua 124
Beverley M. E4 —23Fc 45
Beverley Path. SW13 —54Va 102
Beverley Rd. E4 —23Fc 45
Beverley Rd. E6 —41Mc 85
Beverley Rd. SE20 —68Xb 127
Beverley Rd. SW13 —55Va 102
Beverley Rd. W4 —50Va 80
Beverley Rd. Bexh —54Ed 110
Beverley Rd. Brom —75Nc 150
Beverley Rd. Dag —35Ad 67
Beverley Rd. King T —67La 122
Beverley Rd. Mitc —70Mb 126
Beverley Rd. N Mald —70Wa 124
Beverley Rd. Ruis —33W 56
Beverley Rd. S'hall —49Aa 77
Beverley Rd. Sun —67V 120
Beverley Rd. Whyt —89Ub 165
Beverley Rd. Wor Pk —75Ya 144
Beverley Way. N Mald & SW20
—67Va 124
Beversbrook Rd. N19 —34Mb 62
Beverstone Rd. SW2 —57Pb 104
Beverstone Rd. T Hth —70Qb 126
Bevile Ho. Grays —52De 113
Bevill Allen Clo. SW17 —64Hb 125
Bevin Clo. SE16 —46Ac 84
Bevington Rd. W10 —43Ab 80

Bevington Rd.—Blandford Sq.

Bevington Rd. Beck —68Dc 128
Bevington St. SE16 —47Wb 83
Bevin Rd. Hay —41W 76
Bevin Wlk. Stanf —1M 93
Bevin Way. WC1
—40Qb 62 (3K 193)
Bevis Clo. Dart —59Sd 112
Bevis Marks. EC3
—44Ub 83 (2J 201)
Bewcastle Gdns. Enf —14Nb 24
Bew Ct. SE22 —59Wb 105
Bewdley St. N1 —38Qb 62
Bewick St. SW8 —54Kb 104
Bewley Clo. Chesh —3Zb 12
Bewley St. E1 —45Yb 84
Bewlys Rd. SE27 —64Rb 127
Bexhill Clo. Felt —61Aa 121
Bexhill Rd. N11 —22Mb 42
Bexhill Rd. SE4 —58Bc 106
Bexhill Rd. SW14 —55Sa 101
Bexhill Wlk. E15 —39Gc 65
Bexley Clo. Dart —57Gd 110
Bexley Cotts. Hort K —70Sd 134
Bexley Gdns. N9 —20Tb 25
Bexley High St. Bex —59Cd 110
Bexley La. Dart —57Gd 110
Bexley La. Sidc —63Yc 131
Bexley Rd. SE9 —57Rc 108
Bexley Rd. Eri —52Ed 110
(in two parts)
Bexley St. Wind —3G 94
Beynon Rd. Cars —78Hb 145
Bianca Rd. SE15 —51Wb 105
Bibsworth Rd. N3 —26Bb 41
Bibury Clo. SE15 —51Ub 105
Bicester Rd. Rich —55Qa 101
Bickenhall St. W1
—43Hb 81 (7G 191)
Bickersteth Rd. SW17 —65Hb 125
Bickerton Rd. N19 —33Lb 62
Bickley Cres. Brom —70Nc 130
Bickley Pk. Rd. Brom —69Nc 130
Bickley Rd. E10 —31Dc 64
Bickley Rd. Brom —68Mc 129
Bickley St. SW17 —64Gb 125
Bicknell Rd. SE5 —55Sb 105
Bickney Way. Fet —94Ea 176
Bicknoller Clo. Sutt —82Db 163
Bicknoller Rd. Enf —11Ub 25
Bicknor Rd. Orp —73Uc 150
Bidborough Clo. Brom —71Hc 149
Bidborough St. WC1
—41Nb 82 (4F 193)
Biddenden Way. SE9 —63Qc 130
Biddenden Way. Grav —6A 136
Biddenham Turn. Wat —7V 5
Bidder St. E16 —43Gc 85
(in two parts)
Biddestone Rd. N7 —35Pb 62
Biddulph Ho. SE18 —49Pc 86
Biddulph Mans. W9 —41Db 81
(off Elgin Av.)
Biddulph Rd. W9 —41Db 81
Biddulph Rd. S Croy —82Sb 165
Bideford Av. Gnfd —40Ka 58
Bideford Clo. Edgw —25Qa 39
Bideford Clo. Felt —62Ba 121
Bideford Clo. Romf —25Ld 49
Bideford Gdns. Enf —17Ub 25
Bideford Rd. Brom —62Hc 129
Bideford Rd. Enf —10Bc 12
Bideford Rd. Ruis —34X 57
Bideford Rd. Well —52Xc 109
Bideford Spur. Slou —1F 72
Bidhams Cres. Tad —93Ya 178
Bidwell Gdns. N11 —24Lb 42
Bidwell St. SE15 —53Xb 105
Bigbury Clo. N17 —24Tb 43
Biggerstaff Rd. E15 —39Ec 64
Biggerstaff St. N4 —33Qb 62
Biggin Av. Mitc —67Hb 125
Biggin Hill. SE19 —66Rb 127
Biggin Hill Bus. Pk. Big H
—87Mc 167
Biggin Hill Civil Airport. Big H
—85Mc 167
Biggin La. Grays —1D 114
Biggin Way. SE19 —66Rb 127
Bigginwood Rd. SW16 —66Rb 127
Biggs Row. SW15 —55Za 102
Big Hill. E5 —32Xb 63
Bigland St. E1 —44Xb 83
Bignell Rd. SE18 —50Rc 86
Bignells Corner. S Mim —6Xa 8
Bignold Rd. E7 —35Jc 65
Bigwood Ct. NW11 —29Db 41
Bigwood Rd. NW11 —29Db 41
Biko Clo. Uxb —43L 75
Billericay Rd. Heron —24Fe 51
Billet Clo. Romf —27Zc 47
Billet Hill. Ash —77Yd 154
Billet La. Horn —32Md 69
Billet La. Iver & Slou —41D 74
Billet La. Stanf —2M 93
Billet Rd. E17 —25Zb 44
Billet Rd. Romf —27Xc 47
Billet Rd. Stai —62J 119
Bill Hamling Clo. SE9 —61Pc 130
Billingford Clo. SE4 —56Zb 106
Billing Pl. SW10 —52Db 103
Billing Rd. SW10 —52Db 103
Billingsgate Rd. E14 —45Cc 84
Billings Hill Shaw. Hart —72Be 155
Billing St. SW10 —52Db 103
Billington Rd. SE14 —52Zb 106
Billiter Sq. EC3 —44Ub 83 (3J 201)
(off Fenchurch Av.)
Billiter St. EC3 —44Ub 83 (3J 201)
Billockby Clo. Chess —79Pa 143
Billson St. E14 —49Ec 84
Billy Lows La. Pot B —3Cb 9
Bilsby Gro. SE9 —63Mc 129
Bilsby Lodge. Wemb —34Sa 59
(off Chalklands)
Bilton Clo. Coln —54G 96
Bilton Rd. Eri —52Jd 110
Bilton Rd. Gnfd —39Ja 58
Bilton Way. Enf —11Ac 26
Bilton Way. Hay —47X 77
Bina Gdns. SW5
—49Eb 81 (6A 202)
Bincote Rd. Enf —13Pb 24
Binden Rd. W12 —48Va 80
Bindon Grn. Mord —70Db 125
Binfield Rd. SW4 —53Nb 104
Binfield Rd. Byfl —84N 157
Binfield Rd. S Croy —78Vb 147
Bingfield St. N1 —39Nb 62
(in two parts)
Bingham Clo. S Ock —44Yd 90
Bingham Dri. Stai —66M 119
Bingham Dri. Wok —6C 188
Bingham Pl. W1 —43Jb 82 (7H 191)
Bingham Rd. Croy —74Wb 147
Bingham St. N1 —37Tb 63
Bingley Rd. E16 —44Lc 85
Bingley Rd. Gnfd —42Ea 78
Bingley Rd. Sun —66W 120
Binney St. W1 —44Jb 82 (3J 197)
Binns Rd. W4 —50Ua 80
Binsey Wlk. SE2 —47Yc 87
Binyon Cres. Stan —22Ha 38
Birbetts Rd. SE9 —61Pc 130
Birchanger Rd. SE25 —71Wb 147
Birch Av. N13 —20Sb 25
Birch Av. Cat —96Tb 181
Birch Av. W Dray —44P 75
Birch Clo. E16 —43Gc 85
Birch Clo. N19 —33Lb 62
Birch Clo. SE15 —54Wb 105
Birch Clo. Bren —52Ka 100
Birch Clo. Buck H —20Mc 27
Birch Clo. Eyns —77Md 153
Birch Clo. Iver —40F 54
Birch Clo. Long —68Ee 135
Birch Clo. New Haw —81M 157
Birch Clo. Romf —27Dd 48
Birch Clo. Send —97H 173
Birch Clo. Sev —95Kd 187
Birch Clo. Shep —68U 120
Birch Clo. Tedd —64Ja 122
Birch Clo. Wok —7F 188
Birch Copse. Brick —2Aa 5
Birch Ct. N'wd —23S 36
Birch Ct. Wall —77Kb 146
Birch Cres. Horn —28Nd 49
Birch Cres. Uxb —39P 55
Birchcroft Clo. Cat —97Sb 181
Birchdale. Ger X —2P 53
Birchdale Clo. W Byf —83L 157
Birchdale Gdns. Romf —31Zc 67
Birchdale Rd. E7 —36Lc 65
Birchdene Dri. SE28 —46Wc 87
Birch Dri. Rick —22F 34
Birchen Clo. NW9 —33Ta 59
Birchend Clo. S Croy —79Tb 147
Birchen Gro. NW9 —33Ta 59
Birches Clo. Eps —87Ua 162
Birches Clo. Mitc —69Hb 125
Birches Clo. Pinn —29Aa 37
Birches, The. N21 —16Pb 24
Birches, The. SE7 —51Kc 107
Birches, The. Brtwd —20Ae 33
Birches, The. Bush —15Ea 20
Birches, The. E Hor —98U 174
Birches, The. Houn —59Ba 99
Birches, The. Orp —77Qc 150
Birches, The. Swan —68Gd 132
Birches, The. Wok —90B 156
Birchfield Clo. Add —77K 139
Birchfield Clo. Coul —88Pb 164
Birchfield Gro. Eps —82Ya 162
Birchfield Rd. Chesh —1Xb 11
Birchfield St. E14 —45Cc 84
Birch Gdns. Dag —34Ed 68
Birch Grn. NW9 —24Ua 40
Birch Grn. Stai —63J 119
Birch Gro. SE12 —59Hc 107
Birch Gro. W3 —46Qa 79
Birch Gro. Cob —86Y 159
Birch Gro. Pot B —4Cb 9
Birch Gro. Shep —68U 120
Birch Gro. Slou —3F 72
Birch Gro. Tad —96Ab 178
Birch Gro. Well —56Wc 109
Birch Gro. Wind —3B 94
Birch Gro. Wok —87F 156
Birch Hill. Croy —78Zb 148
Birch Ho. SW2 —58Qb 104
(off Tulse Hill)
Birchin Cross Rd. Knat —87Nd 171
Birchington Clo. Bexh —53Dd 110
Birchington Clo. Orp —74Yc 151
Birchington Ho. E5 —36Xb 63
Birchington Rd. N8 —30Mb 42
Birchington Rd. NW6 —39Cb 61
Birchington Rd. Surb —73Pa 143
Birchington Rd. Wind —4E 94
Birchin La. EC3 —44Tb 83 (3G 201)
Birchlands Av. SW12 —59Hb 103
Birch La. Flau —5D 2
Birch La. Purl —83Nb 164
Birchmead. Orp —75Qc 150
Birchmead. Wat —10V 4
Birchmead Av. Pinn —28Y 37
Birchmere Row. SE3 —54Hc 107
Birchmore Wlk. N5 —34Sb 63
Birch Pk. Harr —24Ea 38
Birch Pl. Grnh —58Ud 112
Birch Rd. Felt —64Z 121
Birch Rd. Romf —27Dd 48
Birch Row. Brom —73Qc 150
Birch Tree Av. W Wick —78Hc 149
Birch Tree Wlk. Wat —9V 4
Birch Tree Way. Croy —75Xb 147
Birch Vale. Cob —85Ca 159
Birchview. Epp —1Xc 15
Birch Wlk. Borwd —11Qa 21
Birch Wlk. Eri —51Ed 110
Birch Wlk. Mitc —67Kb 126
Birch Wlk. W Byf —84J 157
Birchway. Hay —46W 78
Birch Way. Warl —90Ac 166
Birchway. W King —80Vd 154
Birchwood. Shenl —6Qa 7
Birchwood. Wal A —6Gc 13
Birchwood Av. N10 —27Jb 42
Birchwood Av. Beck —70Bc 128
Birchwood Av. Sidc —62Xc 131
Birchwood Av. Wall —76Jb 146
Birchwood Clo. Gt War —23Yd 50
Birchwood Clo. Mord —70Db 125
Birchwood Ct. N13 —22Rb 43
Birchwood Ct. Edgw —26Sa 39
Birchwood Dri. NW3 —34Db 61
Birchwood Dri. Dart —63Gd 132
Birchwood Dri. W Byf —84J 157
Birchwood Gro. Hamp —65Ca 121
Birchwood La. Cat —97Rb 181
Birchwood La. Esh & Oxs
—81Fa 160
Birchwood Pde. Wilm —63Gd 132
Birchwood Pk. Av. Swan
—69Gd 132
Birchwood Rd. SW17 —64Kb 126
Birchwood Rd. Orp —70Tc 130
Birchwood Rd. Swan & Dart
—67Ed 132
Birchwood Rd. W Byf —84J 157
Birchwood Way. Park —1Da 5
Birdbrook Clo. Dag —38Ed 68
Birdbrook Clo. Hut —16De 33
Birdbrook Rd. SE3 —55Lc 107
Birdcage Wlk. SW1
—47Lb 82 (2B 204)
Birdham Clo. Brom —71Nc 150
Birdhouse La. Orp —87Pc 168
Birdhurst Av. S Croy —77Tb 147
Birdhurst Gdns. S Croy —77Tb 147
Birdhurst Rise. S Croy —78Ub 147
Birdhurst Rd. SW18 —57Eb 103
Birdhurst Rd. SW19 —65Gb 125
Birdhurst Rd. S Croy —78Ub 147
Bird in Bush Rd. SE15 —52Wb 105
Bird in Hand La. Brom —68Mc 129
Bird-in-Hand Pas. SE23 —61Yb 128
Bird in Hand Yd. NW3 —35Eb 61
(off Hampstead High St.)
Bird La. Gt War —27Zd 51
Bird La. Hare —26L 35
Bird La. Upm —29Td 50
Birdlington Rd. N9 —17Xb 25
Birdlip Clo. SE15 —51Ub 105
Birdport Rd. Gnfd —39Da 57
Birds Farm Av. Romf —25Dd 48
Birdsfield La. E3 —39Bc 64
Birds Hill Dri. Oxs —85Fa 160
Birds Hill Rise. Oxs —85Fa 160
Birds Hill Rd. Oxs —84Fa 160
Bird St. W1 —44Jb 82 (3J 197)
Birdswood Dri. Wok —7B 188
Bird Wlk. Twic —60Ba 99
Birdwood Clo. S Croy —83Yb 166
Birdwood Clo. Tedd —63Ga 122
Birkbeck Av. W3 —45Sa 79
Birkbeck Av. Gnfd —39Ea 58
Birkbeck Gdns. Wfd G —19Jc 27
Birkbeck Gro. W3 —47Ta 79
Birkbeck Hill. SE21 —60Rb 105
Birkbeck M. E8 —36Vb 63
Birkbeck Pl. SE21 —61Sb 127
Birkbeck Rd. E8 —36Vb 63
Birkbeck Rd. N8 —28Nb 42
Birkbeck Rd. N12 —22Eb 41
Birkbeck Rd. N17 —25Vb 43
Birkbeck Rd. NW7 —22Va 40
Birkbeck Rd. SW19 —64Db 125
Birkbeck Rd. W3 —46Ta 79
Birkbeck Rd. W5 —49La 78
Birkbeck Rd. Beck —68Yb 128
Birkbeck Rd. Enf —11Tb 25
Birkbeck Rd. Hut —16Fe 33
Birkbeck Rd. Ilf —29Tc 46
Birkbeck Rd. Romf —32Fd 68
Birkbeck Rd. Sidc —62Wc 131
Birkbeck St. E2 —41Xb 83
Birkbeck Way. Gnfd —39Fa 58
Birkdale Av. Pinn —27Ca 37
Birkdale Av. Romf —24Qd 49
Birkdale Clo. Orp —73Tc 150
Birkdale Gdns. Croy —77Zb 148
Birkdale Gdns. Wat —20Z 19
Birkdale Rd. SE2 —49Wc 87
Birkdale Rd. W5 —42Na 79
Birkenhead Av. King T —68Pa 123
Birkenhead St. WC1
—41Nb 82 (3G 193)
Birken M. N'wd —22R 36
Birkett Way. Chal G —13A 16
Birkhall Rd. SE6 —60Fc 107
Birkwood Clo. SW12 —59Mb 104
Birley Rd. N20 —19Eb 23
Birley Rd. Slou —4H 73
Birley St. SW11 —54Jb 104
Birling Rd. Eri —52Fd 110
Birnam Rd. N4 —33Pb 62
Birnbeck Ct. NW11 —29Bb 41
Birnbeck Ct. Barn —14Za 22
Birnham Clo. Rip —96J 173
Birrell Ho. SW9 —54Pb 104
(off Stockwell Rd.)
Birse Cres. NW10 —34Ua 60
Birstall Grn. Wat —21Z 37
Birstall Rd. N15 —29Ub 43
Birtrick Dri. Meop —10B 136
Biscay Rd. W6 —50Za 80
Biscoe Clo. Houn —51Ca 99
Biscoe Way. SE13 —55Fc 107
Bisenden Rd. Croy —75Ub 147
Bisham Clo. Cars —74Hb 145
Bisham Ct. Slou —7K 73
Bisham Gdns. N6 —32Jb 62
Bishop Butt Clo. Orp —76Vc 151
Bishop Clo. W4 —50Sa 79
Bishop Ct. N12 —21Db 41
Bishop Duppas Pk. Shep —73U 140
Bishop Fox Way. W Mol —70Ba 121
Bishop Ken Rd. Harr —26Ha 38
Bishop King's Rd. W14 —49Ab 80
Bishop Rd. N14 —17Kb 24
Bishop's Av. E13 —39Kc 65
Bishops Av. SW6 —54Za 102
Bishops Av. Brom —68Lc 129
Bishops Av. Els —15Pa 21
Bishops Av. N'wd —21U 36
Bishop's Av. Romf —30Yc 47
Bishops Av., The. N2 —30Fb 41
Bishop's Bri. Rd. W2 —44Db 81
Bishops Clo. E17 —28Dc 44
Bishop's Clo. N19 —34Lb 62
Bishop's Clo. SE9 —61Sc 130
Bishops Clo. Barn —16Za 22
Bishop's Clo. Coul —90Qb 164
Bishops Clo. Enf —12Xb 25
Bishops Clo. Rich —62Ma 123
Bishop's Clo. Sutt —76Cb 145
Bishops Clo. Uxb —40Q 56
Bishop's Ct. EC4 —44Rb 83 (2B 200)
(off Old Bailey)
Bishop's Ct. WC2
—44Qb 82 (2K 199)
(off Star Yd.)
Bishops Ct. Grnh —57Vd 112
Bishops Ct. Rich —55Na 101
Bishop's Dri. Felt —58T 98
Bishops Dri. N'holt —39Aa 57
Bishops Farm Clo. Oak G —4A 94
Bishopsford Rd. Mord —73Eb 145
Bishopsgate. EC2
—44Ub 83 (3H 201)
Bishopsgate Arc. EC2
—43Ub 83 (1J 201)
(off Bishopsgate)
Bishopsgate Chu. Yd. EC2
—43Ub 83 (2H 201)
Bishopsgate Rd. Egh —2L 117
Bishops Grn. Brom —67Lc 129
(off Up. Park Rd.)
Bishops Gro. N2 —30Gb 41
Bishop's Gro. Hamp —63Ba 121
Bishop's Hall. King T —68Ma 123
Bishops Hall Rd. Pil H —16Xd 32
Bishops Hill. W on T —73W 140
Bishop's Mans. SW6 —53Ab 102
(in two parts)
Bishopsmead Clo. E Hor —100U 174
Bishopsmead Dri. E Hor —100V 174
Bishopsmead Pde. E Hor
—100V 174
Bishops Orchard. Farn R —1F 72
Bishop's Pk. Rd. SW6 —54Za 102
Bishops Pk. Rd. SW16 —67Nb 126
Bishops Rd. N6 —30Jb 42
Bishop's Rd. SW6 —53Ab 102
Bishops Rd. SW11 —52Gb 103
Bishops Rd. W7 —47Ga 78
Bishop's Rd. Croy —73Rb 147
Bishop's Rd. Hay —44S 76
Bishops Rd. Slou —7L 73
Bishops Rd. Stanf —1P 93
Bishop's Ter. SE11
—49Qb 82 (5A 206)
Bishopsthorpe Rd. SE26 —63Zb 128
Bishop St. N1 —39Sb 63
Bishops Wlk. Chst —67Sc 130
Bishops Wlk. Croy —78Zb 148
Bishops Wlk. Pinn —27Aa 37
Bishop's Way. E2 —40Xb 63
Bishops Way. Egh —65F 118
Bishops Wood. Wok —5C 188
Bishopswood Rd. N6 —31Hb 61
Bishop Way. NW10 —38Ua 60
Bishop Wilfred Wood Clo. SE15
—54Xb 105
Biskra Flats. Wat —11W 18
Bisley Clo. Wal X —5Zb 12
Bisley Clo. Wor Pk —74Ya 144
Bison Ct. Felt —59X 99
Bispham Rd. NW10 —41Pa 79
Bisson Rd. E15 —40Ec 64
Bisterne Av. E17 —27Fc 45
Bittacy Clo. NW7 —23Za 40
Bittacy Ct. NW7 —24Ab 40
Bittacy Hill. NW7 —23Za 40
Bittacy Pk. Av. NW7 —22Za 40
Bittacy Rise. NW7 —23Ya 40
Bittacy Rd. NW7 —23Za 40
Bittams La. Cher —77F 138
Bittern Clo. Hay —43Z 77
Bittern Ct. NW9 —26Ua 40
Bittern Ct. SE8 —51Cc 106
Bitterne Dri. Wok —5C 188
Bittern Pl. N22 —26Pb 42
Bittern St. SE1 —47Sb 83 (2D 206)
Bittoms, The. King T —69Ma 123
Bixley Clo. S'hall —49Ba 77
Blackacre Rd. They B —9Uc 14
Blackall St. EC2 —42Ub 83 (5H 195)
Blackberry Clo. Shep —70U 120
Blackberry Farm Clo. Houn
—52Aa 99
Blackbird Ct. NW9 —33Ta 59
Blackbird Hill. NW9 —33Sa 59
Blackbirds La. Ald —6Ea 6
Blackbird Yd. E2 —41Vb 83
Blackborne Rd. Dag —37Cd 68
Black Boy La. N15 —29Sb 43
Black Boy Wood. Brick —2Ca 5
Blackbridge Rd. Wok —8G 188
Blackbrook La. Brom —71Qc 150
Blackburn. NW6 —26Va 40
Blackburne's M. W1
—45Jb 82 (4H 197)
Blackburn Rd. NW6 —37Db 61
Blackburn, The. Bookh —96Ba 175
Blackbury Clo. Pot B —3Eb 9
Blackbush Av. Romf —29Zc 47
Blackbush Clo. Sutt —80Db 145
Black Bush La. Horn H —1F 92
Black Ditch Rd. Wal A —8Ec 12
Blackdown Av. Wok —87G 156
Blackdown Clo. Wok —88F 156
Black Eagle Clo. W'ham —99Sc 184
Blackett Clo. Stai —68G 118
Blackett St. SW15 —55Za 102
Blacketts Wood Dri. Chor —15D 16
Black Fan Clo. Enf —11Sb 25
Blackfen Pde. Sidc —58Wc 109
Blackfen Rd. Sidc —57Uc 108
Blackford Clo. S Croy —81Rb 165
Blackford Rd. Wat —22Z 37
Blackford's Path. SW15 —59Wa 102
Blackfriars Bri. SE1 & EC4
—45Rb 83 (5B 200)
Blackfriars Ct. EC4
—45Rb 83 (4B 200)
(off New Bridge St.)
Black Friars La. EC4
—45Rb 83 (4B 200)
Blackfriars Pas. EC4
—45Rb 83 (4B 200)
Blackfriars Rd. SE1
—47Rb 83 (2B 206)
Blackfriars Underpass. EC4
—45Rb 83 (4B 200)
Black Gates. Pinn —27Ba 37
Blackhall La. Sev —95Md 187
Blackheath Av. SE10 —52Fc 107
Blackheath Gro. SE3 —54Hc 107
Blackheath Hill. SE10 —53Ec 106
Blackheath Pk. SE3 —55Hc 107
Blackheath Rise. SE13 —54Ec 106
Blackheath Rd. SE10 —53Dc 106
Blackheath Vale. SE3 —54Gc 107
Blackheath Village. SE3 —54Hc 107
Blackhills. Esh —81Ba 159
Black Horse Clo. Wind —4B 94
Black Horse Ct. SE1
—48Tb 83 (4G 207)
(off Gt. Dover St.)
Blackhorse La. E17 —28Zb 44
Black Horse La. Croy —73Wb 147
Blackhorse La. Pot B —2Ua 8
Blackhorse La. Reig —100Db 179
Blackhorse La. S Mim —4Wa 8
Blackhorse La. Tad —100Db 179
Blackhorse M. E17 —27Zb 44
Black Horse Pde. Eastc —29X 37
Blackhorse Rd. E17 —28Zb 44
Blackhorse Rd. SE8 —51Ac 106
Blackhorse Rd. Sidc —63Wc 131
Blackhorse Rd. Wok —8A 188
Black Lake Clo. Egh —67C 118
Blacklands Dri. Hay —42S 76
Blacklands Rd. SE6 —63Ec 128
Blacklands Ter. SW3
—49Hb 81 (6G 203)
Blackley Clo. Wat —9V 4
Black Lion Hill. Shenl —4Na 7
Black Lion La. W6 —49Wa 80
Black Lion M. W6 —49Wa 80
Blackmans Clo. Dart —60Ld 111
Blackman's La. Warl —86Gc 167
Blackmoor La. Wat —16S 18
Blackmore Av. S'hall —46Fa 78
Blackmore Clo. Grays —50Ee 91
Blackmore Ct. Wal A —5Jc 13
Blackmore Cres. Wok —87E 156
Blackmore Ho. N1
—39Pb 62 (1J 193)
(off Barnsbury Est.)
Blackmore Rd. Buck H —17Nc 28
Blackmore Rd. Kel H & Ing
—11Ud 32
Blackmore's Gro. Tedd —65Ja 122
Blackmore Way. Uxb —37M 55
Blackness La. Kes —80Mc 149
Blackness La. Wok —91A 172
Blacknest Ga. Rd. Asc —9F 116
Blacknest Rd. S'dale & Vir W
—9H 117
Black Pk. Rd. Wex —40A 54
Black Path. E10 —31Zb 64
Blackpond La. Farn C —7F 52
Blackpool Gdns. Hay —42U 76
Blackpool Rd. SE15 —54Xb 105
Black Prince Clo. Byfl —86P 157
Black Prince Rd. SE1 & SE11
—49Pb 82 (6H 205)
Black Rod Clo. Hay —48V 76
Blackshaw Pl. N1 —38Ub 63
Blackshaw Rd. SW17 —63Eb 125
Blackshots La. Grays —45Ee 91
Blacksmith Clo. Asht —91Pa 177
Blacksmith Row. Slou —6Ac 74
Blacksmiths Clo. Romf —30Yc 47
Blacksmiths Hill. S Croy
—85Wb 165
Blacksmiths La. Cher —73J 139
Blacksmiths La. Den —33E 54
Blacksmith's La. Orp —71Yc 151
Blacksmith's La. Rain —39Hd 68
Blacksmiths La. Stai —69L 119
Blacks Rd. W6 —50Ya 80
Blackstock M. N4 —33Rb 63
Blackstock Rd. N4 & N5 —33Rb 63
Blackstone Est. E8 —38Xb 63
Blackstone Rd. NW2 —36Ya 60
Black Swan Yd. SE1
—47Ub 83 (1H 207)
Blackthorn Av. W Dray —49Q 76
Blackthorn Clo. Wat —4X 5
Blackthorn Clo. W King —80Vd 154
Blackthorn Ct. Houn —52Aa 99
Blackthorn Dell. Slou —8N 73
Blackthorne Av. Croy —74Yb 148
Blackthorne Ct. SE1 —52Vb 105
(off Cator St.)
Blackthorne Cres. Coln —54G 96
Blackthorne Dri. E4 —21Fc 45
Blackthorne Rd. Bookh —98Ea 176
Blackthorne Rd. Coln —55G 96
Blackthorn Gro. Bexh —55Ad 109
Blackthorn Rd. Big H —88Mc 167
Blackthorn Rd. Grays —46De 91
Blackthorn St. E3 —42Cc 84
Blackthorn Way. War —22Zd 51
Blackthorne M. SW9 —55Qb 104
Blackwall La. SE10 —50Gc 85
(in two parts)
Blackwall Trading Est. E14
—43Fc 85
Blackwall Tunnel. E14 & SE10
—46Fc 85
Blackwall Tunnel App. E14
—45Ec 84
Blackwall Tunnel Northern App. E3 & E14 —40Dc 64
Blackwall Tunnel Southern App. SE10
—48Gc 85
Blackwall Way. E14 —46Ec 84
(in two parts)
Blackwater. Brtwd —18Xd 32
Blackwater Clo. E7 —36Hc 65
Blackwater Clo. Rain —43Fd 88
Blackwater St. SE22 —57Vb 105
Blackwell Clo. E5 —35Zb 64
Blackwell Clo. Harr —24Fa 38
Blackwell Dri. Wat —16Y 19
Blackwell Gdns. Edgw —20Qa 21
Blackwell Rd. K Lan —1Q 4
Blackwood Clo. W Byf —84L 157
Blackwood St. SE17
—50Tb 83 (7F 207)
Blade M. SW15 —56Bb 103
Bladen Clo. Wey —79U 140
Blades Clo. Lea —92Ma 177
Blades Ct. SW15 —56Bb 103
Blades Ho. SE11 —51Qb 104
(off Kennington Oval)
Bladindon Dri. Bex —59Yc 109
Bladon Ct. SW16 —65Nb 126
Bladon Gdns. Harr —30Da 37
Blagdens Clo. N14 —19Mb 24
Blagdens La. N14 —19Mb 24
Blagdon Rd. SE13 —58Dc 106
Blagdon Rd. N Mald —70Va 124
Blagdon Wlk. Tedd —65La 122
Blagrove Rd. W10 —43Ab 80
Blair Av. NW9 —31Ua 60
Blair Av. Esh —75Ea 142
Blair Clo. N1 —37Sb 63
Blair Clo. Sidc —57Uc 108
Blair Ct. Beck —67Dc 128
Blairderry Rd. SW2 —61Nb 126
Blair Dri. Sev —95Kd 187
Blairhead Dri. Wat —20X 19
Blair Ho. SW9 —54Pb 104
Blair Rd. Slou —6J 73
Blair St. E14 —44Ec 84
Blake Av. Bark —39Uc 66
Blakeborough Dri. H Wood
—26Nd 49
Blake Clo. W10 —43Ya 80
Blake Clo. Cars —74Gb 145
Blake Clo. Rain —39Hd 68
Blake Clo. Well —53Uc 108
Blakeden Dri. Clay —79Ha 142
Blake Gdns. SW6 —53Db 103
Blake Gdns. Dart —56Pd 111
Blake Hall Cres. E11 —32Jc 65
Blake Hall Rd. E11 —31Jc 65
Blakehall Rd. Cars —79Hb 145
Blake Ho. E14 —47Dc 84
(off Admirals Way)
Blakeney Cotts. SE10 —47Fc 85
Blakemore Rd. SW16 —62Nb 126
Blakemore Rd. T Hth —71Pb 146
Blakemore Way. Belv —48Ad 87
Blakeney Av. Beck —67Bc 128
Blakeney Clo. E8 —36Wb 63
Blakeney Clo. N20 —18Eb 23
Blakeney Clo. NW1 —38Mb 62
Blakeney Clo. Eps —83Ta 161
Blakeney Rd. Beck —66Bc 128
Blakenham Rd. SW17 —63Hb 125
Blake Rd. E16 —42Hc 85
Blake Rd. N11 —24Lb 42
Blake Rd. Croy —75Ub 147
Blake Rd. Mitc —69Gb 125
Blaker Rd. E15 —39Ec 64
Blakes Av. N Mald —71Va 144
Blake's Grn. W Wick —74Ec 148
Blakes La. N Mald —71Va 144
Blakesley Av. W5 —44La 78
Blakesley Wlk. SW20 —68Bb 125
Blake's Rd. SE15 —52Ub 105
Blakes Ter. N Mald —71Wa 144
Blakesware Gdns. N9 —17Tb 25
Blake Way. Til —4E 114
Blakewood Clo. Felt —63Y 121
Blanchard Clo. SE9 —62Nc 130
Blanchards Hill. Jac —100A 172
Blanchard Way. E8 —37Wb 63
Blanch Clo. SE15 —52Yb 106
Blanchedowne. SE5 —56Tb 105
Blanche La. Pot B —5Va 8
Blanche St. E16 —42Hc 85
Blanchland Rd. Mord —71Db 145
Blanchman's Rd. Warl —90Ac 166
Blandfield Rd. SW12 —59Jb 104
Blandford Av. Beck —68Ac 128
Blandford Av. Twic —60Da 99
Blandford Clo. N2 —28Eb 41
Blandford Clo. Croy —76Nb 146
Blandford Clo. Romf —28Cd 48
Blandford Clo. Slou —8P 73
Blandford Clo. Wok —89D 156
Blandford Ct. NW6 —38Ab 60
Blandford Ct. Slou —8P 73
Blandford Cres. E4 —17Ec 26
Blandford Rd. W4 —48Ua 80
Blandford Rd. W5 —47Ma 79
Blandford Rd. Beck —68Yb 128
Blandford Rd. S'hall —49Ca 77
Blandford Rd. Tedd —64Fa 122
Blandford Rd. N. Slou —8P 73
Blandford Rd. S. Slou —8P 73
Blandford Sq. NW1
—42Gb 81 (6E 190)

Blandford St.—Bourne Rd.

Blandford St. W1 —44Hb 81 (2G 197)
Blandford Waye. Hay —44Y 77
Bland Ho. SE11 —50Pb 82 (7J 205)
(off Vauxhall St.)
Bland St. SE9 —56Mc 107
Blaney Cres. E6 —41Rc 86
Blanmerle Rd. SE9 —60Rc 108
Blann Clo. SE9 —58Mc 107
Blantyre St. SW10 —52Fb 103
Blantyre Wlk. SW10 —52Fb 103
(off Worlds End Est.)
Blashford St. SE13 —59Fc 107
Blasker Wlk. E14 —50Dc 84
Blawith Rd. Harr —28Ga 38
Blaxland Ho. W12 —45Xa 80
(off White City Est.)
Blaydon Clo. N17 —24Xb 43
Blaydon Clo. Ruis —31U 56
Blay's Clo. Egh —5N 117
Blay's La. Egh —6M 117
Bleak Hill La. SE18 —51Vc 109
Blean Gro. SE20 —66Yb 128
Blear Ho. Eps —83Va 162
Bleasdale Av. Gnfd —40Ja 58
Blechynden St. W10 —45Za 80
Bleddyn Clo. Sidc —58Yc 109
Bledlow Clo. SE28 —45Yc 87
Bledlow Rise. Gnfd —40Ea 58
Bleeding Heart Yd. EC1 —43Qb 82 (1A 200)
(off Greville St.)
Blegborough Rd. SW16 —65Lb 126
Blencarn Clo. Wok —4C 188
Blendon Dri. Bex —58Zc 109
Blendon Path. Brom —66Hc 129
Blendon Rd. Bex —58Zc 109
Blendon Ter. SE18 —50Sc 86
Blendworth Way. SE15 —52Ub 105
Blenheim Av. Ilf —30Qc 46
Blenheim Clo. N21 —18Sb 25
Blenheim Clo. SW20 —69Ya 124
Blenheim Clo. Dart —58Ld 111
Blenheim Clo. Gnfd —40Fa 58
Blenheim Clo. Romf —28Ed 48
Blenheim Clo. Upm —32Ud 70
Blenheim Clo. Wall —80Lb 146
Blenheim Clo. Wat —17Y 19
Blenheim Clo. W Byf —85H 157
Blenheim Ct. N19 —33Nb 62
Blenheim Ct. Horn —36Ld 69
Blenheim Ct. Kent —30Ja 38
Blenheim Ct. Sidc —62Tc 130
Blenheim Ct. Sutt —79Eb 145
Blenheim Cres. W11 —45Ab 80
Blenheim Cres. Ruis —33T 56
Blenheim Cres. S Croy —80Sb 147
Blenheim Dri. Well —53Vc 109
Blenheim Gdns. NW2 —37Ya 60
Blenheim Gdns. SW2 —58Pb 104
Blenheim Gdns. King T —66Ra 123
Blenheim Gdns. S Croy —84Wb 165
Blenheim Gdns. S Ock —46Rd 89
Blenheim Gdns. Wall —79Lb 146
Blenheim Gdns. Wemb —34Na 59
Blenheim Gdns. Wok —7E 188
Blenheim Gro. SE15 —54Wb 105
Blenheim Gro. Grav —9E 114
Blenheim Ho. Houn —55Ca 99
Blenheim Pk. Rd. S Croy —81Sb 165
Blenheim Pas. NW8 —40Eb 61
(off Carlton Hill)
Blenheim Pl. NW8 —40Eb 61
Blenheim Rise. N15 —28Vb 43
Blenheim Rd. E6 —41Mc 85
Blenheim Rd. E15 —35Gc 65
Blenheim Rd. E17 —27Zb 44
Blenheim Rd. NW8 —40Eb 61 (1A 190)
Blenheim Rd. SE20 —66Yb 128
Blenheim Rd. SW20 —69Ya 124
Blenheim Rd. W4 —48Ua 80
Blenheim Rd. Barn —13Za 22
Blenheim Rd. Brom —70Nc 130
Blenheim Rd. Dart —58Ld 111
Blenheim Rd. Eps —83Ta 161
Blenheim Rd. Harr —30Da 37
Blenheim Rd. N'holt —37Da 57
Blenheim Rd. Orp —75Yc 151
Blenheim Rd. Pil H —16Wd 32
Blenheim Rd. Sidc —60Yc 109
Blenheim Rd. Slou —9P 73
Blenheim Rd. Sutt —76Cb 145
Blenheim Shopping Cen. SE20 —66Yb 128
Blenheim St. W1 —44Kb 82 (3K 197)
Blenheim Ter. NW8 —40Eb 61
Blenkarne Rd. SW11 —58Hb 103
Bleriot. NW9 —26Va 40
(off Belvedere Strand)
Bleriot Rd. Houn —52Y 99
Blessbury Rd. Edgw —25Sa 39
Blessington Clo. SE13 —55Fc 107
Blessington Rd. SE13 —56Fc 107
Bletchingley Clo. Red —100Lb 180
Bletchingley Clo. T Hth —70Rb 127
Bletchingley Rd. Mers —100Lb 180
Bletchley St. N1 —40Sb 63 (2E 194)
Bletchmore Clo. Hay —50T 76
Bletsoe Wlk. N1 —40Sb 63 (1E 194)
Blewbury Ho. SE2 —47Zc 87
Blewitts Cotts. Rain —41Hd 88
(off Dunedin Rd.)
Bligh Rd. Grav —8C 114
Bligh's Rd. Sev —97Ld 187
Blincoe Clo. SW19 —61Za 124
Blinco La. G Grn —44A 74
Blind La. Bans —87Gb 163
Blind La. Wal A —5Lc 13
Blindman's La. Chesh —2Zb 12
Bliss Cres. SE13 —54Dc 106
Blissett St. SE10 —53Ec 106
Blisworth Clo. Hay —42Aa 77
Blithbury Rd. Dag —37Xc 67
Blithdale Rd. SE2 —49Wc 87
Blithfield St. W8 —48Db 81
Blockhouse Rd. Grays —51Ee 113
Blockley Rd. Wemb —33Ka 58
Bloemfontein Av. W12 —46Xa 80
Bloemfontein Rd. W12 —45Xa 80
Blomfield Rd. W9 —43Db 81
Blomfield St. EC2 —43Tb 83 (1G 201)
Blomfield Vs. W2 —43Db 81
Blomville Rd. Dag —34Ad 67
Blondell Clo. W Dray —51M 97
Blondel St. SW11 —54Jb 104
Blondin Av. W5 —49La 78
Blondin St. E3 —40Cc 64
Bloomburg St. SW1 —49Mb 82 (6C 204)
Bloomfield Clo. Knap —5C 188
Bloomfield Ct. N6 —30Jb 42
Bloomfield Cres. Ilf —30Rc 46
Bloomfield Pl. W1 —45Kb 82 (4A 198)
(off Grosvenor Hill)
Bloomfield Rd. N6 —30Jb 42
Bloomfield Rd. SE18 —50Rc 86
Bloomfield Rd. Brom —71Mc 149
Bloomfield Rd. King T —69Na 123
Bloomfields, The. Bark —37Sc 66
Bloomfield Ter. SW1 —50Jb 82 (7J 203)
Bloomfield Ter. W'ham —97Uc 184
Bloom Gro. SE27 —62Rb 127
Bloomhall Rd. SE19 —64Tb 127
Bloom Pk. Rd. SW6 —52Bb 103
Bloomsbury Clo. W5 —45Pa 79
Bloomsbury Clo. Eps —82Ta 161
Bloomsbury Ct. WC1 —43Nb 82 (1G 199)
(off Barter St.)
Bloomsbury Ct. Houn —53X 99
Bloomsbury Ct. Pinn —27Ba 37
Bloomsbury Ho. SW4 —58Mb 104
Bloomsbury Pl. SW18 —57Eb 103
Bloomsbury Pl. WC1 —43Nb 82 (1G 199)
Bloomsbury Sq. WC1 —43Nb 82 (1G 199)
Bloomsbury St. WC1 —43Mb 82 (1E 198)
Bloomsbury Way. WC1 —43Nb 82 (1F 199)
Blore Clo. SW8 —53Mb 104
Blore Ct. SW8 —53Mb 104
Blore Ct. W1 —45Mb 82 (4D 198)
(off Berwick St.)
Blossom Clo. W5 —47Na 79
Blossom Clo. Dag —39Bd 67
Blossom Clo. S Croy —78Vb 147
Blossom La. Enf —11Sb 25
Blossom St. E1 —42Ub 83 (7J 195)
Blossom Way. Uxb —38P 55
Blossom Way. W Dray —49Q 76
Blossom Waye. Houn —51Aa 99
Blount St. E14 —44Ac 84
Bloxhall Rd. E10 —32Bc 64
Bloxham Cres. Hamp —66Ba 121
Bloxham Gdns. SE9 —57Nc 108
Bloxworth Clo. Wall —76Lb 146
Bloxworth Gro. N1 —39Pb 62
Blucher Rd. SE5 —52Sb 105
Blue Anchor All. Rich —56Na 101
Blue Anchor La. SE16 —49Wb 83
Blue Anchor La. W Til —9G 92
Blue Anchor Yd. E1 —45Wb 83
Blue Ball La. Egh —64B 118
Blue Ball Yd. SW1 —46Lb 82 (7B 198)
Blue Barn La. Wey —83Q 158
Bluebell Av. E12 —36Mc 65
Bluebell Clo. SE26 —63Vb 127
Bluebell Clo. Orp —75Sc 150
Bluebell Clo. Wall —74Kb 146
Bluebell Ct. Wok —7G 188
Bluebell Way. Ilf —37Rc 66
Blueberry Gdns. Coul —88Pb 164
Blueberry La. Knock —88Yc 169
Bluebird Wlk. Wemb —34Ra 59
Bluebridge Rd. Brook P —1Bb 9
Blue Cedars. Bans —86Za 162
Blue Chalet Ind. Pk. W King —79Td 154
Bluefield Clo. Hamp —64Ca 121
Bluegates. Ewe —80Wa 144
Bluehouse Gdns. Oxt —100Jc 183
Bluehouse La. Oxt —100Gc 183
Bluehouse Rd. E4 —20Gc 27
Blue Riband Ind. Est. Croy —75Rb 147
Blumfield Ct. Slou —2B 72
Blumfield Cres. Slou —3B 72
Blundel La. Stoke D —88Ba 159
Blundell Ho. SE14 —52Ac 106
Blundell Rd. Edgw —25Ta 39
Blundell St. N7 —38Nb 62
Blunden Clo. Dag —32Yc 67
Blunesfield. Pot B —3Fb 9
Blunt Rd. S Croy —78Tb 147
Blunts Av. W Dray —52Q 98
Blunts Rd. SE9 —57Qc 108
Blurton Rd. E5 —35Yb 64
Blydon Ho. N21 —15Pb 24
(off Chaseville Pk. Rd.)
Blyth Clo. E14 —49Fc 85
Blyth Clo. Borwd —11Pa 21
Blyth Clo. Twic —58Ha 100
Blythe Clo. SE6 —59Bc 106
Blythe Clo. Iver —44H 75
Blythe Hill. SE6 —59Bc 106
Blythe Hill. Orp —67Vc 131
Blythe Hill La. SE6 —59Bc 106
Blythe Ho. SE11 —51Qb 104
Blythe M. W14 —48Za 80
Blythe Rd. W14 —48Za 80
Blythe St. E2 —41Xb 83
Blythe Vale. SE6 —60Bc 106
Blyth Rd. E17 —31Bc 64
Blyth Rd. SE28 —45Yc 87
Blyth Rd. Brom —67Hc 129
Blyth Rd. Hay —47U 76
Blythswood Rd. Ilf —32Wc 67
Blyth Wlk. Upm —30Ud 50
Blythwood. Pinn —25Z 37
Blyth Wood Pk. Brom —67Hc 129
Blythwood Rd. N4 —31Nb 62
Blythwood Rd. Pinn —25Z 37
Boades M. NW3 —35Fb 61
Boadicea St. N1 —39Pb 62 (1H 193)
Boakes Clo. NW9 —28Sa 39
Boakes Meadow. Shor —83Hd 170
Boar Clo. Chig —22Wc 47
Boardman Av. E4 —15Dc 26
Board School Rd. Wok —88B 156
Boarhound. NW9 —26Va 40
(off Further Acre)
Boarlands Clo. Slou —5D 72
Boarlands Path. Cipp —5D 72
Boars Head Yd. Bren —52Ma 101
Boathouse Wlk. SE15 —52Wb 105
Boat Lifter Way. SE16 —48Ac 84
Bob Anker Clo. E13 —41Jc 85
Bobbin Clo. SW4 —55Lb 104
Bob Marley Way. SE24 —56Qb 104
Bobs La. Romf —25Jd 48
Bocketts La. Fet —96Ha 176
Bockhampton Rd. King T —66Pa 123
Bocking St. E8 —39Xb 63
Boddicott Clo. SW19 —61Ab 124
Bodell Clo. Grays —48De 91
Bodeney Ho. SE5 —53Ub 105
(off Peckham Rd.)
Bodiam Clo. Enf —12Ub 25
Bodiam Rd. SW16 —66Mb 126
Bodle Av. Swans —59Ae 113
Bodley Clo. N Mald —71Ua 144
Bodley Mnr. Way. SW2 —59Qb 104
Bodley Rd. N Mald —72Ta 143
Bodmin. NW9 —26Va 40
(off Further Acre)
Bodmin Av. Slou —3E 72
Bodmin Gro. Mord —71Db 145
Bodmin St. SW18 —60Cb 103
Bodnant Gdns. SW20 —69Wa 124
Bodney Rd. E8 —36Xb 63
Boeing Way. S'hall —48X 77
Boevey Path. Belv —50Bd 87
Bogey La. Orp —80Qc 150
Bognor Gdns. Wat —22Y 37
Bognor Rd. Well —53Zc 109
Bohemia Pl. E8 —37Yb 64
Bohun Gro. Barn —16Gb 23
Boileau Pde. W5 —44Pa 79
(off Boileau Rd.)
Boileau Rd. SW13 —52Wa 102
Boileau Rd. W5 —44Pa 79
Bois Hall Rd. Add —78M 139
Bolden St. SE8 —54Dc 106
Bolderwood Way. W Wick —75Dc 148
Boldmere Rd. Pinn —31Y 57
Boleyn Av. Enf —11Xb 25
Boleyn Av. Eps —82Wa 162
Boleyn Clo. E17 —28Cc 44
Boleyn Clo. Stai —64G 118
Boleyn Ct. Buck H —18Jc 27
Boleyn Dri. Ruis —33Z 57
Boleyn Dri. W Mol —69Ba 121
Boleyn Gdns. Brtwd —20Ce 33
Boleyn Gdns. Dag —38Ed 68
Boleyn Gdns. W Wick —75Dc 148
Boleyn Gro. W Wick —75Ec 148
Boleyn Rd. E6 —40Mc 65
Boleyn Rd. E7 —38Jc 65
Boleyn Rd. N16 —36Ub 63
Boleyn Rd. Kems —89Nd 171
Boleyn Way. Barn —13Eb 23
Boleyn Wlk. Lea —92Ha 176
Boleyn Way. Ilf —23Sc 46
Boleyn Way. Swans —59Ae 113
Bolina Rd. SE16 —50Yb 84
Bolingbroke Gro. SW11 —56Gb 103
Bolingbroke Rd. W14 —48Za 80
Bolingbroke Wlk. SW11 —53Fb 103
Bolingbroke Way. Hay —46T 76
Bollo Bri. Rd. W3 —48Ra 79
Bollo La. W3 & W4 —47Ra 79
Bolney Ga. SW7 —47Gb 81 (2D 202)
Bolney St. SW8 —52Pb 104
Bolney Way. Felt —62Aa 121
Bolsover Gro. Red —100Nb 180
Bolsover St. W1 —42Kb 82 (6A 192)
Bolstead Rd. Mitc —67Kb 126
Bolster Gro. N22 —25Mb 42
Bolt Cellar La. Epp —2Uc 14
Bolt Ct. EC4 —44Qb 82 (3A 200)
Bolters La. Bans —86Bb 163
Boltmore Clo. NW4 —27Za 40
Bolton Av. Wind —5H 95
Bolton Clo. SE20 —68Wb 127
Bolton Clo. Chess —79Ma 143
Bolton Cres. SE5 —52Rb 105
Bolton Cres. Wind —5G 94
Bolton Gdns. NW10 —40Za 60
Bolton Gdns. SW5 —50Db 81
Bolton Gdns. Brom —65Hc 129
Bolton Gdns. Tedd —65Ja 122
Bolton Gdns. M. SW10 —50Eb 81
Bolton Ho. SE10 —50Gc 85
(off Trafalgar Rd.)
Bolton Rd. E15 —37Hc 65
Bolton Rd. N18 —22Vb 43
Bolton Rd. NW8 —39Db 61
Bolton Rd. NW10 —39Ua 60
Bolton Rd. W4 —52Sa 101
Bolton Rd. Chess —79Ma 143
Bolton Rd. Harr —28Ea 38
Bolton Rd. Wind —5G 94
Boltons Clo. Wok —88J 157
Bolton's La. Hay —52S 98
Boltons La. Wok —88J 157
Boltons, The. SW10 —50Eb 81
Boltons, The. Wemb —35Ha 58
Bolton St. W1 —46Kb 82 (6A 198)
Bolton Wlk. N7 —33Pb 62
(off Durham Rd.)
Bombay St. SE16 —49Xb 83
Bombers La. W'ham —91Tc 184
Bomer Clo. W Dray —52Q 98
Bomore Rd. W11 —45Ab 80
Bonar Pl. Chst —66Nc 130
Bonar Rd. SE15 —52Wb 105
Bonaventure Ct. Grav —3H 137
Bonchester Clo. Chst —66Qc 130
Bonchurch Clo. Sutt —80Db 145
Bonchurch Ct. Purf —50Sd 90
Bonchurch Rd. W10 —43Ab 80
Bonchurch Rd. W13 —46Ka 78
Bond Clo. Knock —87Zc 169
Bond Clo. W Dray —44P 75
Bondfield Av. Hay —41W 76
Bondfield Clo. E6 —43Pc 86
Bondfield Wlk. Dart —55Pd 111
Bond Gdns. Wall —77Lb 146
Bonding Yd. Wlk. SE16 —48Ac 84
Bond Rd. E15 —39Dc 64
Bond Rd. Mitc —68Gb 125
Bond Rd. Surb —75Pa 143
Bond Rd. Warl —90Zb 166
Bond St. E15 —36Gc 65
Bond St. W4 —49Ta 79
Bond St. W5 —45Ma 79
Bond St. Egh —4M 117
Bond St. Grays —51Ee 113
Bond St. Knock —87Ad 169
Bondway. SW8 —51Nb 104
Boneta Rd. SE18 —48Pc 86
Bonfield Rd. SE13 —56Ec 106
Bonham Gdns. Dag —33Zc 67
Bonham Rd. SW2 —57Pb 104
Bonham Rd. Dag —33Zc 67
Bonheur Rd. W4 —47Ta 79
Bonhill St. EC2 —42Tb 83 (6G 195)
Boniface Gdns. Harr —24Da 37
Boniface Rd. Uxb —34R 56
Boniface Wlk. Harr —24Da 37
Bon Marche Ter. SE27 —63Ub 127
Bonner Ct. Chesh —1Zb 12
(off Coopers Wlk.)
Bonner Hill Rd. King T —68Pa 123
Bonner Rd. E2 —40Yb 64
Bonners Clo. Wok —94B 172
Bonnersfield Clo. Harr —30Ha 38
Bonnersfield La. Harr —30Ha 38
Bonner St. E2 —40Zb 64
Bonner Wlk. Grays —48Be 91
Bonneville Gdns. SW4 —58Lb 104
Bonney Gro. Chesh —2Wb 11
Bonney Way. Swan —68Gd 132
Bonnington Rd. Horn —36Md 69
Bonningtons. Brtwd —20De 33
Bonnington Sq. SW8 —51Pb 104
Bonny St. NW1 —38Lb 62
Bonser Rd. Twic —61Ha 122
Bonsey Clo. Wok —93A 172
Bonsey La. Wok —93A 172
Bonseys La. Chob —81B 156
Bonsey's Yd. Uxb —38M 55
Bonsor Dri. Tad —94Ab 178
Bonsor St. SE5 —52Ub 105
Bonville Gdns. NW4 —28Xa 40
Bonville Rd. Brom —64Hc 129
Bookbinders Cottage Homes. N20 —20Hb 23
Booker Clo. E14 —43Bc 84
Booker Rd. N18 —22Wb 43
Bookham Comn. Rd. Bookh —93Aa 175
Bookham Ct. Bookh —95Ba 175
Bookham Gro. Bookh —98Da 175
Bookham Ind. Est. Bookh —95Ba 175
Bookham Rd. D'side —91Y 175
Book M. WC2 —44Mb 82 (3E 198)
Boone Ct. N9 —20Yb 26
Boones Rd. SE13 —56Gc 107
Boone St. SE13 —56Gc 107
Boord St. SE10 —48Gc 85
Boothby Ct. E4 —20Ec 26
Boothby Rd. N19 —33Mb 62
Booth Clo. SE28 —46Xc 87
Booth Dri. Stai —65M 119
Booth La. EC4 —45Sb 83 (4D 200)
(off Baynard St.)
Boothman Ho. Kent —27Ma 39
Booth Rd. NW9 —26Ta 39
Booth Rd. Croy —75Rb 147
Booth's Ct. Hut —16Ee 33
Booth's Pl. W1 —43Lb 82 (1C 198)
Boot Pde. Edgw —23Qa 39
(off High St. Edgware)
Boot St. N1 —41Ub 83 (4H 195)
Bordars Rd. W7 —43Ga 78
Bordars Wlk. W7 —43Ga 78
Borden Av. Enf —16Tb 25
Border Cres. SE26 —64Xb 127
Border Gdns. Croy —77Dc 148
Bordergate. Mitc —67Hb 125
Border Rd. SE26 —64Xb 127
Borderside. Slou —4L 73
Border's La. Lou —14Qc 28
Bordesley Rd. Mord —70Db 125
Bordon Wlk. SW15 —59Wa 102
Boreas Wlk. N1 —40Rb 63 (2C 194)
(off Nelson Pl.)
Boreham Av. E16 —44Jc 85
Boreham Clo. E11 —32Ec 64
Boreham Holt. Els —14Pa 21
Boreham Rd. N22 —26Sb 43
Borehamwood Ind. Pk. Borwd —12Ta 21
Borgard Rd. SE18 —49Pc 86
Borkwood Pk. Orp —77Vc 151
Borkwood Way. Orp —77Uc 150
Borland Clo. Grnh —57Wd 112
Borland Rd. SE15 —56Yb 106
Borland Rd. Tedd —66Ka 122
Borley Ct. Rd. Ors —4F 92
Bornedene. Pot B —3Ab 8
Borneo St. SW15 —55Ya 102
Borough High St. SE1 —47Sb 83 (2E 206)
Borough Hill. Croy —76Rb 147
Borough Rd. SE1 —48Rb 83 (3B 206)
Borough Rd. Iswth —53Ga 100
Borough Rd. King T —67Qa 123
Borough Rd. Mitc —68Gb 125
Borough Rd. Tats —93Mc 183
Borough Sq. SE1 —47Sb 83 (2D 206)
(off MacCoid Way)
Borough Way. Pot B —4Ab 8
Borrett Clo. SE17 —50Sb 83 (7D 206)
Borrodaile Rd. SW18 —58Db 103
Borrowdale Av. Harr —26Ja 38
Borrowdale Clo. Egh —66C 118
Borrowdale Clo. Ilf —28Nc 46
Borrowdale Clo. S Croy —85Vb 165
Borrowdale Dri. S Croy —84Vb 165
Borthwick M. E15 —35Gc 65
Borthwick Rd. E15 —35Gc 65
Borthwick Rd. NW9 —30Va 40
Borthwick St. SE8 —50Cc 84
Borwick Av. E17 —27Bc 44
Bosanquet Clo. Uxb —42M 75
Bosbury Rd. SE6 —62Ec 128
Boscastle Rd. NW5 —34Kb 62
Boscobel Pl. SW1 —49Jb 82 (5J 203)
Boscobel St. NW8 —42Fb 81 (6C 190)
Bosco Clo. Orp —77Vc 151
Boscombe Av. E10 —31Fc 65
Boscombe Av. Grays —49Fe 91
Boscombe Av. Horn —31Md 69
Boscombe Clo. E5 —36Ac 64
Boscombe Clo. Egh —67E 118
Boscombe Gdns. SW16 —65Nb 126
Boscombe Rd. SW17 —65Jb 126
Boscombe Rd. SW19 —67Cb 125
Boscombe Rd. W12 —46Wa 80
Boscombe Rd. Wor Pk —74Ya 144
Bosgrove. E4 —19Ec 26
Boss St. SE1 —47Vb 83 (1K 207)
Bostal Hill Rd. SE2 —51Yc 109
Bostall Hill. SE2 —50Wc 87
Bostall La. SE2 —50Xc 87
Bostall Mnr. SE2 —49Xc 87
Bostall Pk. Av. Bexh —52Ad 109
Bostall Rd. Orp —66Xc 131
Bostal Row. Bexh —55Bd 109
Bostock Ho. Houn —51Ca 99
Boston Gdns. W4 —51Ua 102
Boston Gdns. W7 —49Ja 78
Boston Gdns. Bren —49Ja 78
Boston Gro. Ruis —30S 36
Boston Gro. Slou —4G 72
Boston Mnr. Rd. Bren —49Ja 78
Boston Pde. W7 —49Ja 78
Boston Pk. Rd. Bren —50La 78
Boston Pl. NW1 —42Hb 81 (5F 191)
Boston Rd. E6 —41Nc 86
Boston Rd. E17 —30Cc 44
Boston Rd. W7 —46Ga 78
Boston Rd. Croy —72Pb 146
Boston Rd. Edgw —24Sa 39
Bostonthorpe Rd. W7 —47Ga 78
Boston Vale. W7 —49Ja 78
Bosville Av. Sev —95Jd 186
Bosville Dri. Sev —95Jd 186
Bosville Rd. Sev —95Jd 186
Boswell Clo. Orp —72Yc 151
Boswell Ct. WC1 —43Nb 82 (7G 193)
Boswell Path. Hay —49V 76
Boswell Rd. T Hth —70Sb 127
Boswell St. WC1 —43Nb 82 (7G 193)
Bosworth Clo. E17 —25Bc 44
Bosworth Cres. Romf —23Ld 49
Bosworth Ho. Eri —50Gd 88
(off Saltford Clo.)
Bosworth Rd. N11 —23Mb 42
Bosworth Rd. W10 —42Ab 80
Bosworth Rd. Barn —13Cb 23
Bosworth Rd. Dag —34Cd 68
Botany Bay La. Chst —68Sc 130
Botany Clo. New Bar —14Gb 23
Botany Rd. Grav —56Ce 113
Botany Way. Purf —50Rd 89
Boteley Clo. E4 —19Fc 27
Botham Clo. Edgw —24Sa 39
Botha Rd. E13 —43Kc 85
Bothwell Clo. E16 —43Hc 85
Bothwell Rd. New Ad —82Ec 166
Bothwell St. W6 —51Za 102
Bothwick St. SE8 —50Cc 84
Botolph All. EC3 —45Ub 83 (4H 201)
(off Botolph La.)
Botolph La. EC3 —45Ub 83 (5H 201)
Botsford Rd. SW20 —68Ab 124
Botsom La. W King —79Td 154
Bottle Cotts. Sev —94Jd 186
Bottom La. K Lan —7K 3
Bott Rd. Dart —63Pd 133
Botts M. W2 —44Cb 81
Botwell Comn. Rd. Hay —45T 76
Botwell Cres. Hay —44U 76
Botwell La. Hay —45U 76
Boucher Clo. Tedd —64Ha 122
Boucher Dri. Grav —2B 136
Bouchier Wlk. Rain —37Jd 68
Bough Beech Ct. Enf —9Zb 12
Boughton Av. Brom —73Hc 149
Boughton Hall Av. Send —96H 173
Boughton Rd. SE28 —48Uc 86
Boulcott St. E1 —44Zb 84
Boulevard 25 Shopping Cen. Borwd —13Qa 21
Boulevard, The. SW17 —61Jb 126
Boulevard, The. Pinn —28Ca 37
(in two parts)
Boulevard, The. Wat —15T 18
Boulmer Rd. Uxb —41L 75
Boulogne Rd. Croy —72Sb 147
Boulter Gdns. Rain —37Jd 68
Boulters Clo. Slou —7E 72
Boulton Ho. Bren —50Na 79
Boulton Rd. Dag —33Ad 67
Boultwood Rd. E6 —44Pc 86
Bounaparte M. SW1 —50Mb 82
Bounces La. N9 —19Xb 25
Bounces Rd. N9 —19Xb 25
Boundaries Rd. SW12 —61Hb 125
Boundaries Rd. Felt —60Y 99
Boundary Av. E17 —31Bc 64
Boundary Clo. SE20 —68Wb 127
Boundary Clo. Ilf —35Uc 66
Boundary Clo. King T —69Ra 123
Boundary Clo. S'hall —50Ca 77
Boundary Ct. N18 —23Vb 43
(off Snells Pk.)
Boundary Dri. Hut —17Fe 33
Boundary Ho. SE5 —52Sb 105
Boundary Houses. Grav —10B 114
(off Victoria Rd.)
Boundary La. E13 —42Mc 85
Boundary La. SE5 & SE17 —51Sb 105
Boundary La. SE17 —51Sb 105
(in two parts)
Boundary Pas. E2 —42Vb 83 (5K 195)
Boundary Rd. E13 —40Lc 65
Boundary Rd. E17 —31Bc 64
Boundary Rd. N2 —25Fb 41
Boundary Rd. N9 —16Yb 26
Boundary Rd. N22 —27Rb 43
Boundary Rd. NW8 —39Db 61
Boundary Rd. SW19 —65Fb 125
Boundary Rd. Ashf —64L 119
Boundary Rd. Bark —40Sc 66
(in two parts)
Boundary Rd. Cars —79Kb 146
Boundary Rd. Pinn —31Z 57
Boundary Rd. Romf —30Jd 48
Boundary Rd. Sidc —57Uc 108
Boundary Rd. Upm —34Qd 69
Boundary Rd. Wemb —34Ma 59
Boundary Rd. Wok —88C 156
Boundary Row. SE1 —47Rb 83 (1B 206)
Boundary St. E2 —41Vb 83 (4K 195)
(in two parts)
Boundary St. Eri —52Hd 110
Boundary Way. Croy —78Cc 148
Boundary Way. Leav —4X 5
Boundfield Rd. SE6 —62Gc 129
Bounds Grn. Ct. N11 —23Mb 42
(off Bounds Grn. Rd.)
Bounds Grn. Ind. Est. N11 —23Lb 42
Bounds Grn. Rd. N11 & N22 —23Lb 42
Bourbon Ho. SE6 —64Ec 128
Bourcher Clo. Sev —98Kd 187
Bourchier St. W1 —45Mb 82 (4D 198)
Bourdon Pl. W1 —45Kb 82 (4A 198)
(off Bourdon St.)
Bourdon Rd. SE20 —68Yb 128
Bourdon St. W1 —45Kb 82 (5K 197)
Bourke Clo. NW10 —37Ua 60
Bourke Clo. SW4 —58Nb 104
Bourke Hill. Coul —90Hb 163
Bourlet Clo. W1 —43Lb 82 (1B 198)
Bourn Av. N15 —28Tb 43
Bourn Av. Uxb —42Q 76
Bournbrook Rd. SE3 —55Mc 107
Bourne Av. N14 —19Nb 24
Bourne Av. Barn —15Fb 23
Bourne Av. Hay —48S 76
Bourne Av. Ruis —36Y 57
Bourne Av. Sun —69J 119
Bourne Av. Wind —5G 94
Bournebridge Clo. Hut —17Fe 33
Bournebridge La. Stap A —17Bd 29
Bourne Cir. Hay —48S 76
Bourne Clo. W Byf —85K 157
Bourne Ct. W4 —51Sa 101
Bourne Ct. S Ruis —36X 57
Bourne Dri. Mitc —68Fb 125
Bourne End. Horn —31Qd 69
Bourne End Rd. N'wd —21U 36
Bourne Est. EC1 —43Qb 82 (7K 193)
Bournefield Rd. Whyt —90Wb 165
Bourne Gdns. E4 —21Dc 44
Bourne Gro. Asht —91Ma 177
Bournehall Av. Bush —15Ca 19
Bournehall La. Bush —16Ca 19
Bournehall Rd. Bush —16Ca 19
Bourne Hill. N13 —19Pb 24
Bourne Hill Clo. N13 —19Pb 24
Bourne Ind. Pk., The. Dart —57Gd 110
Bourne La. Cat —93Tb 181
Bourne Mead. Bex —57Fd 110
Bournemead Av. N'holt —40W 56
Bournemead Clo. N'holt —41W 76
Bourne Meadow. Egh —70D 118
Bournemead Way. N'holt —40X 57
Bournemouth Rd. SE15 —54Wb 105
Bournemouth Rd. SW19 —67Cb 125
Bourne Pde. Bex —59Dd 110
Bourne Pk. Clo. Kenl —88Ub 165
Bourne Pl. W4 —50Ta 79
Bourne Rd. E7 —34Hc 65
Bourne Rd. N8 —30Nb 42
Bourne Rd. Bex & Dart —59Dd 110
Bourne Rd. Brom —70Mc 129

Bourne Rd.—Bream St.

Bourne Rd. Bush —15Ca 19
Bourne Rd. Grav —1H 137
Bourne Rd. Slou —7H 73
Bourne Rd. Vir W —10P 117
Bournes Ho. N15 —30Ub 43
(off Chisley Rd.)
Bourneside Cres. N14 —18Mb 24
Bourneside Gdns. SE6 —64Ec 128
Bourneside Rd. Add —77M 139
Bourne St. SW1 —49Jb 82
Bourne St. Croy —75Rb 147
Bourne Ter. W2 —43Db 81
Bourne, The. N14 —19Nb 24
Bourne Vale. Brom —74Hc 149
Bournevale Rd. SW16 —63Nb 126
Bourne View. Gnfd —37Ha 58
Bourne View. Kenl —87Tb 165
Bourneville Rd. SE6 —59Cc 106
Bourne Way. Add —78L 139
Bourne Way. Brom —75Hc 149
Bourne Way. Eps —77Sa 143
Bourne Way. Sutt —78Bb 145
Bourne Way. Swan —69Ed 132
Bourne Way. Wok —10G 188
Bournewood Rd. SE18 —52Wc 109
Bournewood Rd. Orp —73Yc 151
Bournwell Clo. Barn —13Hb 23
Bourton Clo. Hay —46W 76
Bousefield Rd. SE14 —54Zb 106
Bousley Rise. Ott —79F 138
Boutflower Rd. SW11 —56Gb 103
Bouverie Gdns. Harr —30Ma 39
Bouverie M. N16 —33Ub 63
Bouverie Pl. W2 —44Fb 81 (2C 196)
Bouverie Rd. N16 —33Ub 63
Bouverie Rd. Coul —90Jb 164
Bouverie Rd. Harr —30Ea 38
Bouverie St. EC4
—44Qb 82 (3A 200)
Bouverie Way. Slou —50A 74
Bouvier Rd. Enf —10Yb 12
Boveney Clo. Slou —7E 72
Boveney New Rd. Eton W —9C 72
Boveney Rd. SE23 —59Zb 106
Boveney Rd. Dor —10A 72
Boveney Wood La. Burn —4B 52
Bovey Way. S Ock —43Xd 90
Bovill Rd. SE23 —59Zb 106
Bovingdon Av. Wemb —37Qa 59
Bovingdon Clo. N19 —33Lb 62
Bovingdon Cres. Wat —6Z 5
Bovingdon La. NW9 —25Ua 40
Bovingdon Rd. SW6 —53Db 103
Bovingdon Sq. Mitc —70Nb 126
Bow Arrow La. Dart —58Qd 111
Bowater Clo. NW9 —29Ta 39
Bowater Clo. SW2 —58Nb 104
Bowater Ho. EC1
—42Sb 83 (6D 194)
(off Golden La. Est.)
Bowater Pl. SE3 —52Kc 107
Bowater Rd. SE18 —48Mc 85
Bow Bri. Est. E3 —41Dc 84
Bow Chyd. EC4 —44Sb 83 (3E 200)
(off Cheapside)
Bow Comn. La. E3 —42Ac 84
Bowden Clo. Felt —60U 98
Bowden Dri. Horn —32Nd 69
Bowden Rd. Asc —10A 116
Bowden St. SE11
—50Qb 82 (7A 206)
Bowditch. SE8 —49Bc 84
Bowdon Rd. E17 —31Cc 64
Bowen Dri. SE21 —62Ub 127
Bowen Rd. Harr —31Ea 58
Bowen St. E14 —44Dc 84
Bowens Wood. Croy —81Bc 166
Bower Av. SE10 —53Gc 107
Bower Clo. N'holt —40Y 57
Bower Clo. Romf —24Fd 48
Bower Ct. Epp —3Wc 15
Bower Ct. Wok —88D 156
Bowerdean St. SW6 —53Db 103
Bower Farm Rd. Hav —20Ed 30
Bower Hill. Epp —3Wc 15
Bower La. Eyns & Knat —76Nd 153
Bowerman Av. SE14 —51Ac 106
Bowerman Ct. N19 —33Mb 62
(off St Johns Way)
Bowerman Rd. Grays —9C 92
Bower Rd. Swan —66Jd 132
Bowers Av. Grav —3B 136
Bowers La. Jac —100C 172
Bowers Rd. Shor —83Hd 170
Bower St. E1 —44Zb 84
Bowers Wlk. E6 —44Pc 86
Bower Ter. Epp —4Wc 15
Bower Vale. Epp —4Wc 15
Bower Way. Slou —5C 72
Bowes Clo. Sidc —58Xc 109
Bowes Ct. Dart —58Rd 111
(off Osborne Rd.)
Bowesden La. Shorne —6N 137
Bowesdon La. Cobh & Roch
—6P 137
Bowe's Ho. Bark —38Rc 66
Bowes-Lyon Clo. Wind —3G 94
(off Alma Rd.)
Bowes Rd. N11 & N13 —22Lb 42
Bowes Rd. W3 —45Ua 80
Bowes Rd. Dag —35Yc 67
Bowes Rd. Stai —65G 118
Bowes Rd. W on T —75X 141
Bowes Wood. New Ash —76Ce 155
Bowfell Rd. W6 —51Ya 102
Bowford Av. Bexh —53Ad 109
Bowhay. Hut —19Ce 33
Bowhill Clo. SW9 —52Qb 104
Bowie Clo. SW4 —59Mb 104
Bow Ind. Pk. E15 —38Cc 64
Bowland Rd. SW4 —56Mb 104
Bowland Rd. Wfd G —22Lc 45
Bowland Yd. SW1
—47Hb 81 (2G 203)
(off Kinnerton St.)
Bow La. EC4 —44Sb 83 (3E 200)
Bow La. N12 —24Eb 41
Bow La. Mord —72Ab 144
Bowl Ct. EC2 —42Ub 83 (6J 195)
Bowles Grn. Enf —8Xb 11
Bowles Rd. SE1 —51Wb 105
Bowley Clo. SE19 —65Vb 127
Bowley Ho. SE16 —48Wb 83
Bowley La. SE19 —64Vb 127
Bowling Clo. Uxb —39P 55
Bowling Ct. Wat —14W 18
Bowling Grn. Clo. SW15 —59Xa 102
Bowling Grn. Ct. Wemb —33Pa 59
Bowling Grn. La. EC1
—42Qb 82 (6A 194)
Bowling Grn. Pl. SE1
—47Tb 83 (1F 207)
Bowling Grn. Pl. SW1 —47Tb 83
Bowling Grn. Row. SE18 —48Pc 86
Bowling Grn. St. SE11 —51Qb 104
Bowling Grn. Wlk. N1
—41Ub 83 (3H 195)
Bowls Clo. Stan —22Ka 38
Bowls, The. Chig —20Uc 28
Bowman Av. E16 —45Hc 85
Bowman M. SW18 —60Bb 103
Bowmans Clo. W13 —46Ka 78
Bowmans Clo. Burn —10A 52
Bowmans Clo. Pot B —4Fb 9
Bowmans Grn. Wat —8Aa 5
Bowmans Lea. SE23 —59Yb 106
Bowmans Meadow. Wall
—76Kb 146
Bowmans M. E1 —45Wb 83
Bowman's M. N7 —34Nb 62
Bowman's Pl. N7 —34Nb 62
Bowman's Rd. Dart —59Hd 110
Bowmead. SE9 —61Pc 130
Bowmont Clo. Hut —16De 33
Bowmore Wlk. NW1 —38Mb 62
Bown Clo. Til —4D 114
Bowness Clo. E8 —37Xb 63
(off Beechwood Rd.)
Bowness Cres. SW15 —64Ua 124
Bowness Dri. Houn —56Aa 99
Bowness Ho. SE15 —52Yb 106
(off Hillbeck Clo.)
Bowness Rd. SE6 —59Dc 106
Bowness Rd. Bexh —54Dd 110
Bowness Way. Horn —36Jd 68
Bownles Grn. Enf —8Xb 11
Bowood Rd. SW11 —57Jb 104
Bowood Rd. Enf —12Zb 26
Bowring Grn. Wat —22Y 37
Bow Rd. E3 —41Bc 84
Bowrons Av. Wemb —38Ma 59
Bowry Dri. Wray —58B 96
Bowsprit, The. Cob —87Y 159
Bow St. E15 —36Gc 65
Bow St. WC2 —44Nb 82 (3G 199)
Bow Triangle Bus. Cen. E3
—42Cc 84
Bowyer Clo. E6 —43Pc 86
Bowyer Ct. E4 —18Ec 26
(off Ridgeway, The.)
Bowyer Cres. Den —30H 35
Bowyer Dri. Slou —6C 72
Bowyer Ho. N1 —39Ub 63 (1J 195)
(off Whitmore Est.)
Bowyer Pl. SE5 —52Sb 105
Bowyers Clo. Asht —90Pa 161
Bowyer St. SE5 —52Sb 105
Boxall Rd. SE21 —58Ub 105
Boxford Clo. S Croy —84Zb 166
Boxgrove Rd. SE2 —48Yc 87
Boxhill Rd. Tad —100Ta 177
Box La. Bark —40Xc 67
Boxley Rd. Mord —70Eb 125
Boxley St. E16 —46Kc 85
Boxmoor Ho. W11 —46Za 80
(off Queensdale Cres.)
Boxmoor Rd. Harr —28Ka 38
Boxmoor Rd. Romf —22Ed 48
Boxoll Rd. Dag —35Bd 67
Box Ridge Av. Purl —84Pb 164
Boxted Clo. Buck H —18Nc 28
Boxtree La. Harr —25Ea 38
Boxtree Rd. Harr —24Fa 38
Box Tree Wlk. Orp —74Zc 151
Boxwood Clo. W Dray —47P 75
Boxwood Way. Warl —89Zb 166
Boxworth Gro. N1 —39Pb 62
Boyard Rd. SE18 —50Rc 86
Boyce Clo. Borwd —11Na 21
Boyce Rd. Stanf —1L 93
Boyce St. SE1 —46Qb 82 (7K 199)
(off Mepham St.)
Boyce Way. E13 —42Jc 85
Boycroft Av. NW9 —30Sa 39
Boyd Av. S'hall —46Ba 77
Boyd Clo. King T —66Qa 123
Boydel Ct. NW8 —39Fb 61
Boyden Ho. E17 —27Ec 44
Boyd Rd. SW19 —65Fb 125
Boyd St. E1 —44Wb 83
Boyfield St. SE1 —47Rb 83 (2C 206)
Boyland Rd. Brom —64Hc 129
Boyle Av. Stan —23Ja 38
Boyle Clo. Uxb —40P 56
Boyle Farm Rd. Th Dit —72Ja 142
Boyle St. W1 —45Lb 82 (4B 198)
Boyne Av. NW4 —28Za 40
Boyne Rd. SE13 —55Ec 106
Boyne Rd. Dag —34Cd 68
Boyne Ter. M. W11 —46Bb 81
Boyseland Ct. Edgw —19Sa 21
Boyson Rd. SE17 —51Tb 105
Boyson Wlk. SE17 —51Tb 105
Boythorn Rd. SE16 —50Xb 83
Boythorn Way. SE16 —50Xb 83
Boyton Clo. E1 —42Yb 84
Boyton Clo. N8 —27Nb 42
Boyton Rd. N8 —27Nb 42
Brabant Ct. EC3 —45Ub 83 (4H 201)
(off Philpot La.)
Brabant Rd. N22 —26Pb 42
Brabazon Av. Wall —80Nb 146
Brabazon Rd. Houn —52Y 99
Brabazon Rd. N'holt —40Ca 57
Brabazon St. E14 —44Dc 84
Brabourne Clo. SE19 —64Ub 127
Brabourne Cres. Bexh —51Bd 109
Brabourne Heights. NW7 —20Ua 22
Brabourne Rise. Beck —71Ec 148
Brabourn Gro. SE15 —54Yb 106
Brabrook Ct. Wall —77Kb 146
Bracer Ho. N1 —40Ub 63 (1J 195)
(off Whitmore Est.)
Bracewell Av. Gnfd —36Ha 58
Bracewell Rd. W10 —43Ya 80
Bracewood Gdns. Croy —76Vb 147
Bracey St. N4 —33Nb 62
Bracken Av. SW12 —58Jb 104
Bracken Av. Croy —76Dc 148
Brackenbridge Dri. Ruis —34Z 57
Brackenbury. N4 —32Qb 62
(off Osborne Rd.)
Brackenbury Gdns. W6 —48Xa 80
Brackenbury Rd. N2 —27Eb 41
Brackenbury Rd. W6 —48Xa 80
Bracken Clo. E6 —43Pc 86
Bracken Clo. Bookh —96Ba 175
Bracken Clo. Farn C —5H 53
Bracken Clo. Twic —59Ca 99
Bracken Clo. Wok —90B 156
Brackendale. N21 —19Pb 24
Brackendale. Pot B —5Cb 9
Brackendale Clo. Houn —53Da 99
Brackendale Gdns. Upm —35Sd 70
Bracken Dene. Brick —2Ba 5
Brackendene. Dart —63Gd 132
Brackendene Clo. Wok —87C 156
Bracken Dri. Chig —23Rc 46
Bracken Dri. War —22Yd 50
Bracken End. Iswth —57Fa 100
Brackenfield Clo. E5 —34Xb 63
Brackenforde. Slou —7N 73
Bracken Gdns. SW13 —54Wa 102
Brackenhill. Cob —84Da 159
Bracken Hill Clo. Brom —67Hc 129
Bracken Hill La. Brom —67Hc 129
Bracken Ind. Est. Ilf —24Vc 47
Bracken M. E4 —18Ec 26
Bracken M. Romf —30Dd 48
Bracken Path. Eps —85Ra 161
Brackens. Beck —66Cc 128
Brackens, The. Enf —17Ub 25
Brackens, The. Orp —78Wc 151
Bracken, The. E4 —19Ec 26
Brackenwood. Sun —67W 120
Brackenwood Rd. Wok —7A 188
Brackley. Wey —78T 140
Brackley Clo. Wall —80Nb 146
Brackley Rd. W4 —50Ua 80
Brackley Rd. Beck —66Bc 128
Brackley Sq. Wfd G —24Mc 45
Brackley St. EC1
—42Sb 83 (7E 194)
Brackley Ter. W4 —50Ua 80
Bracklyn Ct. N1 —40Tb 63 (1F 195)
Bracklyn St. N1 —40Tb 63 (1F 195)
Bracknell Clo. N22 —25Qb 42
Bracknell Gdns. NW3 —35Db 61
Bracknell Ga. NW3 —36Db 61
Bracknell Way. NW3 —35Db 61
Bracondale. Esh —78Ea 142
Bracondale Av. Grav —7B 136
Bracondale Rd. SE2 —49Wc 87
Bradbery. Rick —22F 34
Bradbourne Ct. Sev —93Kd 187
Bradbourne Pk. Rd. Sev —95Jd 186
Bradbourne Rd. Bex —59Cd 110
Bradbourne Rd. Grays —51De 113
Bradbourne Rd. Sev —94Kd 187
Bradbourne St. SW6 —54Cb 103
Bradbourne Vale Rd. Sev
—94Hd 186
Bradbury Clo. Borwd —11Ra 21
Bradbury Clo. S'hall —49Ba 77
Bradbury Ct. Grav —10B 114
Bradbury Gdns. Ful —5P 53
Bradbury St. N16 —36Ub 63
Braddon Rd. Rich —55Pa 101
Braddyll St. SE10 —50Gc 85
Bradenham Av. Well —56Wc 109
Bradenham Rd. Harr —28Ka 38
Bradenham Rd. Hay —41U 76
Bradenhurst Clo. Cat —98Vb 181
Braden St. W9 —42Db 81
Bradfield Clo. Wok —90A 156
Bradfield Dri. Bark —36Wc 67
Bradfield Rd. E16 —47Jc 85
Bradfield Rd. Ruis —36Aa 57
Bradford Clo. SE26 —63Xb 127
Bradford Clo. Brom —74Pc 150
Bradford Dri. Eps —79Va 144
Bradford Rd. W3 —47Ua 80
Bradford Rd. Herons —17E 16
Bradford Rd. Ilf —32Tc 66
Bradford Rd. Slou —4E 72
Bradgate Rd. SE6 —58Dc 106
Brading Cres. E11 —33Kc 65
Brading Rd. SW2 —59Pb 104
Brading Rd. Croy —72Pb 146
Bradiston Rd. W9 —41Bb 81
Bradleigh Av. Grays —50Ee 91
Bradley Clo. N7 —37Nb 62
Bradley Ct. Enf —10Ac 12
(off Bradley Rd.)
Bradley Gdns. W13 —44Ka 78
Bradley Ho. SE16 —49Yb 84
(off Raymouth Rd.)
Bradley M. SW17 —60Hb 103
Bradley Rd. N22 —26Pb 42
Bradley Rd. SE19 —65Sb 127
Bradley Rd. Enf —10Ac 12
Bradley Rd. Slou —5H 73
Bradley's Clo. N1
—40Qb 62 (1A 194)
Bradman Row. Edgw —24Sa 39
Bradmead. SW8 —52Kb 104
Bradmore Pk. Rd. W6 —49Xa 80
Bradmore Way. Coul —89Nb 164
Bradshaw Clo. Wind —3C 94
Bradshawe Rd. Grays —46Ce 91
Bradshawe Waye. Uxb —43P 75
Bradshaw Rd. Wat —11Y 19
Bradshaws Clo. SE25 —69Wb 127
Bradstock Ho. E9 —38Ac 64
Bradstock Rd. E9 —37Zb 64
Bradstock Rd. Eps —78Wa 144
Bradstone Rd. Rich —53Pa 101
Brad St. SE1 —46Qb 82 (7A 200)
Bradwell Av. Dag —33Cd 68
Bradwell Clo. E18 —28Hc 45
Bradwell Clo. Horn —37Kd 69
Bradwell Ct. Hut —16Ee 33
(off Bradwell Grn.)
Bradwell Grn. Hut —16Ee 33
Bradwell M. N18 —21Wb 43
Bradwell Rd. Buck H —18Nc 28
Brady Av. Lou —12Sc 28
Bradymead. E6 —44Qc 86
Brady St. E1 —42Xb 83
Braeburn Ct. Barn —14Gb 23
Braefield Rd. Eps —23Ac 42
Braemar Av. N22 —25Nb 42
Braemar Av. NW10 —34Ta 59
Braemar Av. SW19 —61Cb 125
Braemar Av. Bexh —56Ed 110
Braemar Av. S Croy —82Sb 165
Braemar Av. T Hth —69Rb 127
Braemar Av. Wemb —38Ma 59
Braemar Gdns. NW9 —25Ta 39
Braemar Gdns. Horn —30Qd 49
Braemar Gdns. Sidc —62Tc 130
Braemar Gdns. Slou —7E 72
Braemar Gdns. W Wick —74Ec 148
Braemar Rd. E13 —42Hc 85
Braemar Rd. N15 —29Ub 43
Braemar Rd. Bren —51Ma 101
Braemar Rd. Wor Pk —76Xa 144
Braeside. Beck —64Cc 128
Braeside. New Haw —83K 157
Braeside Av. SW19 —67Ab 124
Braeside Av. Sev —96Hd 186
Braeside Clo. Pinn —24Ca 37
Braeside Clo. Sev —95Hd 186
Braeside Cres. Bexh —56Ed 110
Braeside Rd. SW16 —66Lb 126
Braes St. N1 —38Rb 63
Braesyde Clo. Belv —49Bd 87
Brafferton Rd. Croy —77Sb 147
Braganza St. SE17
—50Rb 83 (7B 206)
Bragmans La. Sarr —6E 2
Braham Ho. SE11
—50Pb 82 (7J 205)
Braham St. E1 —44Vb 83 (3K 201)
Braid Av. W3 —44Ua 80
Braid Clo. Felt —61Ba 121
Braidwood Pas. EC1
—43Sb 83 (1D 200)
(off Aldersgate St.)
Braidwood Rd. SE6 —60Fc 107
Braidwood St. SE1
—46Ub 83 (7H 201)
Brailsford Clo. Mitc —66Gb 125
Brailsford Rd. SW2 —57Qb 104
Brainton Av. Felt —59X 99
Braintree Av. Ilf —28Nc 46
Braintree Rd. Dag —34Cd 68
Braintree Rd. Ruis —35X 57
Braintree St. E2 —41Yb 84
Braithwaite Av. Romf —31Cd 68
Braithwaite Gdns. Stan —25La 38
Braithwaite Ho. E14 —44Fc 85
Braithwaite Rd. Enf —13Bc 26
Brakefield Rd. S'fleet —65De 135
Bramah Grn. SW9 —53Qb 104
Bramalea Clo. N6 —30Jb 42
Bramall Clo. E15 —36Hc 65
Bramall Ct. N7 —37Pb 62
(off Georges Rd.)
Bramber. WC1 —41Nb 82 (4F 193)
(off Cromer St.)
Bramber Ct. W5 —49Na 79
Bramber Ct. Bren —49Na 79
Bramber Ct. Dart —58Rd 111
(off Bow Arrow La.)
Bramber Ct. Dart —58Rd 111
(off Osborne Rd.)
Bramber Ct. Slou —6E 72
Bramber Rd. N12 —22Gb 41
Bramber Rd. W14 —51Bb 103
Brambleacres. Sutt —80Cb 145
(off Overton Rd.)
Bramble Av. Bean —62Yd 134
Bramble Banks. Cars —81Jb 164
Bramblebury Rd. SE18 —50Sc 86
Bramble Clo. N15 —28Wb 43
Bramble Clo. Croy —77Cc 148
Bramble Clo. Shep —69T 120
Bramble Clo. Stan —24Ma 39
Bramble Clo. Uxb —44P 75
Bramble Clo. Wat —6W 4
Bramble Croft. Eri —49Ed 88
Brambledene Clo. Wok —6F 188
Brambledown. Hart —70Be 135
Bramble Down. Stai —67K 119
Brambledown Clo. W Wick
—71Gc 149
Brambledown Rd. Cars & Wall
—80Jb 146
Brambledown Rd. S Croy
—80Ub 147
Bramblefield Clo. Long —69Ae 135
Bramble Gdns. W12 —45Va 80
Bramble La. Hamp —65Ba 121
Bramble La. Sev —100Kd 187
Bramble La. Upm —39Sd 70
Bramble Rise. Cob —87Y 159
Brambles Clo. Cat —94Ub 181
Brambles Clo. Iswth —52Ka 100
Brambles Farm Dri. Uxb —41Q 76
Brambles, The. Chesh —3Zb 12
Brambles, The. Chig —22Sc 46
Brambles, The. W Dray —49N 75
Bramble Wlk. Eps —86Ra 161
Bramble Way. Rip —96H 173
Bramblewood. Red —100Kb 180
Bramblewood Clo. Cars —74Gb 145
Brambling Clo. Bush —14Aa 19
Bramblings, The. E4 —21Fc 45
Bramcote Av. Mitc —70Hb 125
Bramcote Gro. SE16 —50Yb 84
Bramcote Rd. SW15 —56Xa 102
Bramdean Cres. SE12 —60Jc 107
Bramdean Gdns. SE12 —60Jc 107
Bramerton Rd. Beck —69Bc 128
Bramerton St. SW3 —51Gb 103
Bramfield. Wat —6Aa 5
Bramfield Ct. N4 —34Sb 63
(off Queens Dri.)
Bramfield Rd. SW11 —58Gb 103
Bramford Rd. SW18 —56Eb 103
Bramham Ct. N'wd —22U 36
Bramham Gdns. SW5 —50Db 81
Bramham Gdns. Chess —77Ma 143
Bramham Ho. SE22 —56Ub 105
Bramhope La. SE7 —51Lc 107
Bramlands Clo. SW11 —55Gb 103
Bramleas. Wat —15V 18
Bramley Av. Coul —87Lb 164
Bramley Clo. E17 —26Ac 44
Bramley Clo. N14 —15Kb 24
Bramley Clo. Cher —74K 139
Bramley Clo. Grav —6B 136
Bramley Clo. Hay —45W 76
Bramley Clo. Orp —74Rc 150
Bramley Clo. S Croy —78Sb 147
Bramley Clo. Stai —65L 119
Bramley Clo. Swan —70Gd 132
Bramley Clo. Twic —58Ea 100
Bramley Ct. Barn —14Gb 23
Bramley Ct. Well —53Xc 109
Bramley Cres. SW8 —52Mb 104
Bramley Cres. Ilf —30Qc 46
Bramley Gdns. Wat —22Y 37
Bramley Hill. S Croy —78Rb 147
Bramley Ho. W10 —44Za 80
Bramley Pde. N14 —14Lb 24
Bramley Pl. Dart —56Jd 110
Bramley Rd. N14 —15Kb 24
Bramley Rd. W5 —48La 78
Bramley Rd. W10 —45Za 80
Bramley Rd. Cheam —81Za 162
Bramley Rd. Sutt —78Fb 145
Bramleys. Stanf —1M 93
Bramley Shaw. Wal A —5Hc 13
Bramley St. W10 —44Za 80
Bramley Way. Asht —89Pa 161
Bramley Way. Houn —57Ba 99
Bramley Way. W Wick —75Dc 148
Brammas Clo. Slou —8G 72
Brampton Clo. E5 —33Xb 63
Brampton Clo. Chesh —1Wb 11
Brampton Gdns. N15 —29Sb 43
Brampton Gdns. W on T —78Y 141
Brampton Gro. NW4 —28Xa 40
Brampton Gro. Harr —28Ja 38
Brampton Gro. Wemb —32Pa 59
Brampton La. NW4 —28Ya 40
Brampton Pk. Rd. N22 —27Qb 42
Brampton Rd. E6 —41Mc 85
Brampton Rd. N15 —29Sb 43
Brampton Rd. NW9 —28Qa 39
Brampton Rd. Bexh & SE2
—55Zc 109
Brampton Rd. Croy —72Vb 147
Brampton Rd. Uxb —40R 56
Brampton Rd. Wat —20W 18
Brampton Ter. Borwd —10Qa 7
(off Stapleton Rd.)
Bramshaw Rd. Wat —22Z 37
Bramshaw Rise. N Mald —72Ua 144
Bramshaw Rd. E9 —37Zb 64
Bramshill Clo. Chig —22Uc 46
Bramshill Gdns. NW5 —34Kb 62
Bramshill Rd. NW10 —40Ua 60
Bramshot Av. SE7 —51Jc 107
Bramshot Way. Wat —19W 18
Bramston Clo. Ilf —23Vc 47
Bramston Rd. NW10 —40Wa 60
Bramston Rd. SW17 —62Eb 125
Bramwell Clo. Sun —68Z 121
Bramwell Ho. SE1
—48Sb 83 (4E 206)
Brancaster La. Purl —83Sb 165
Brancaster Rd. E12 —35Pc 66
Brancaster Rd. SW16 —62Nb 126
Brancaster Rd. Ilf —30Uc 46
Brancepeth Gdns. Buck H —19Jc 27
Branch Hill. NW3 —34Eb 61
Branch Hill Ho. NW3 —34Db 61
Branch Pl. N1 —39Tb 63
Branch Rd. E14 —45Ac 84
Branch Rd. Ilf —22Xc 47
Brancker Clo. Wall —80Nb 146
Brancker Rd. Harr —27Ma 39
Brancroft Way. Enf —11Ac 26
Brandlehow Rd. SW15 —56Bb 103
Brandon. NW9 —26Va 40
(off Further Acre)
Brandon Clo. Chaf H —47Be 91
Brandon Est. SE17 —51Rb 105
Brandon M. EC2 —43Tb 83 (1F 201)
(off Barbican)
Brandon Rd. E17 —28Ec 44
Brandon Rd. N7 —38Nb 62
Brandon Rd. Dart —59Qd 111
Brandon Rd. S'hall —50Ba 77
Brandon Rd. Sutt —77Db 145
Brandon St. SE17
(in three parts) —49Sb 83 (6E 206)
Brandon St. Grav —9D 114
Brandram Rd. SE13 —55Gc 107
Brandreth Ct. Harr —30Ha 38
Brandreth Rd. E6 —44Pc 86
Brandreth Rd. SW17 —61Kb 126
Brandries, The. Wall —76Mb 146
Brands Hatch Rd. Fawk —77Wd 154
Brands Rd. Slou —51D 96
Brand St. SE10 —52Ec 106
Brandt Ct. Borwd —12Ta 21
Brandville Gdns. Ilf —28Rc 46
Brandville Rd. W Dray —47N 75
Brandy Way. Sutt —80Cb 145
Branfill Rd. Upm —33Rd 69
Brangbourne Rd. Brom —64Ec 128
Brangton Rd. SE11 —50Qb 82
Brangwyn Cres. SW19 —67Eb 125
Branksea St. SW6 —52Ab 102
Branksome Av. N18 —23Vb 43
Branksome Clo. W on T —75Z 141
Branksome Rd. SW2 —57Nb 104
Branksome Rd. SW19 —67Cb 125
Branksome Way. Harr —30Pa 39
Branksome Way. N Mald
—67Sa 123
Branksone Ct. N2 —27Eb 41
Bransby Rd. Chess —79Na 143
Branscombe Ct. Brom —71Hc 149
Branscombe Gdns. N21 —17Qb 24
Branscombe St. SE13 —55Dc 106
Bransdale Clo. NW6 —39Cb 61
Bransell Clo. Swan —72Ed 152
Bransgrove Rd. Edgw —25Pa 39
Branston Cres. Orp —74Tc 150
Branstone Ct. Purf —50Sd 90
Branstone Rd. Rich —53Pa 101
Branton Rd. Grnh —58Vd 112
Brants Wlk. W7 —42Ga 78
Brantwood Av. Eri —52Ed 110
Brantwood Av. Iswth —56Ja 100
Brantwood Clo. E17 —27Ec 44
Brantwood Clo. W Byf —85J 157
Brantwood Ct. W Byf —85H 157
(off Brantwood Dri.)
Brantwood Dri. W Byf —85H 157
Brantwood Gdns. Enf —14Nb 24
Brantwood Gdns. Ilf —28Nc 46
Brantwood Gdns. W Byf —85H 157
Brantwood Rd. N17 —23Wb 43
Brantwood Rd. SE24 —57Sb 105
Brantwood Rd. Bexh —54Dd 110
Brantwood Rd. S Croy —81Sb 165
Brantwood Way. Orp —69Yc 131
Brasher Clo. Gnfd —36Fa 58
Brassett Point. E15 —39Gc 65
(off Abbey Rd.)
Brassey Rd. NW6 —37Bb 61
Brassey Sq. SW11 —55Jb 104
Brassie Av. W3 —44Ua 80
Brass Tally All. SE16 —47Zb 84
Brasted Clo. SE26 —63Yb 128
Brasted Clo. Bexh —57Zc 109
Brasted Clo. Orp —75Wc 151
Brasted Clo. Sutt —82Cb 163
Brasted Hill. Knock —92Wc 185
Brasted Hill Rd. Bras —93Xc 185
Brasted La. Knock —91Wc 185
Brasted Lodge. SE20 —66Cc 128
Brasted Rd. Eri —52Gd 110
Brasted Rd. W'ham —98Uc 184
Brathway Rd. SW18 —59Db 103
Bratley St. E1 —42Wb 83
Bratten Ct. Croy —72Tb 147
Brattle Wood. Sev —100Kd 187
Braund Av. Gnfd —42Da 77
Braundton Av. Sidc —60Vc 109
Braunston Dri. Hay —42Aa 77
Bravington Clo. Shep —71P 139
Bravington Pl. W9 —42Bb 81
Bravington Rd. W9 —41Bb 81
Brawlings La. Ger X —21C 34
Braxfield Rd. SE4 —56Ac 106
Braxted Pk. SW16 —65Pb 126
Brayards Rd. SE15 —54Xb 105
Brayards Rd. Est. SE15 —54Yb 106
(off Brayards Rd.)
Braybourne Clo. Uxb —37L 55
Braybourne Dri. Iswth —52Ha 100
Braybrooke Gdns. SE19 —66Vb 127
Braybrook St. W12 —43Va 80
Brayburne Av. SW4 —54Lb 104
Bray Clo. Borwd —11Sa 21
Bray Ct. SW16 —64Nb 126
Braycourt Av. W on T —73X 141
Bray Cres. SE16 —47Zb 84
Braydon Rd. N16 —32Wb 63
Bray Dri. E16 —45Hc 85
Brayfield Ter. N1 —38Qb 62
Brayford Sq. E1 —44Yb 84
Bray Gdns. Wok —88G 156
Bray Pas. E16 —45Jc 85
Bray Pl. SW3 —49Hb 81 (7F 203)
Bray Rd. NW7 —23Za 40
Bray Rd. Stoke D —88Aa 159
Brayton Gdns. Enf —14Mb 24
Braywood Av. Egh —65B 118
Braywood Rd. SE9 —56Tc 108
Brazil Clo. Bedd —73Nb 146
Breach La. Dag —41Cd 88
Breach Rd. Grays —51Vd 112
Bread St. EC4 —44Sb 83 (4E 200)
Breakfield. Coul —88Nb 164
Breakneck Hill. Grnh —57Xd 112
Breakspeare Clo. Wat —10X 5
Breakspear Ho. Ruis —29S 36
Breakspear Path. Hare —27M 35
Breakspear Rd. Ruis —31R 56
Breakspear Rd. N. Hare —25L 35
Breakspear Rd. S. Ick & Hare
—34P 55
Breakspears Dri. Orp —67Wc 131
Breakspears M. SE4 —54Bc 106
Breakspears Rd. SE4 —56Bc 106
Breakspere Rd. Abb L —3U 4
Bream Clo. N17 —28Xb 43
Bream Gdns. E6 —41Qc 86
Breamore Clo. SW15 —60Wa 102
Breamore Rd. Ilf —33Vc 67
Bream's Bldgs. EC4
—44Qb 82 (2K 199)
Bream St. E3 —38Cc 64

Bream St. E9 —38Cc 64
Breamwater Gdns. Rich —62Ka 122
Brearley Clo. Edgw —24Sa 39
Brearley Clo. Uxb —37N 55
Breasley Clo. SW15 —56Ya 102
Brechin Pl. SW7 —49Eb 81 (7A 202)
Brecknock M. N7 —36Mb 62
Brecknock Rd. N19 & N7 —35Lb 62
Brecknock Rd. Est. N19 —35Lb 62
Breckonmead. Brom —68Lc 129
Brecon Clo. Mitc —69Nb 126
Brecon Clo. Wor Pk —75Ya 144
Brecon Ct. Chalv —7G 72
Brecon Grn. NW9 —30Ua 40
Brecon Rd. W6 —51Ab 102
Brecon Rd. Enf —14Yb 26
Brede Clo. E6 —41Qc 86
Bredgar Rd. N19 —33Lb 62
Bredhurst Clo. SE20 —65Yb 128
Bredo Ho. Bark —41Xc 87
Bredon Rd. Croy —73Vb 147
Bredune. Kenl —87Tb 165
Bredward Clo. Burn —1A 72
Breech La. Tad —96Wa 178
Breer St. SW6 —55Db 103
Breezer's Hill. E1 —45Wb 83
Breeze Ter. Chesh —1Zb 12
Brember Rd. Harr —33Ea 58
Bremer Rd. Stai —62J 119
Bremner Clo. Swan —70Jd 132
Bremner Rd. SW7 —48Eb 81 (3A 202)
Brenchley Av. Grav —4D 136
Brenchley Clo. Brom —72Hc 149
Brenchley Clo. Chst —67Qc 130
Brenchley Gdns. SE23 —58Yb 106
Brenchley Rd. Orp —68Vc 131
Brendans Clo. Horn —32Nd 69
Brenda Rd. SW17 —61Hb 125
Brenda Ter. Swans —59Ae 113
Brende Gdns. W Mol —70Da 121
Brendon Av. NW10 —36Ua 60
Brendon Clo. Eri —53Gd 110
Brendon Clo. Esh —79Ea 142
Brendon Clo. Hay —52S 98
Brendon Ct. Rad —7Ka 6
Brendon Dri. Esh —79Ea 142
Brendon Gdns. Harr —35Da 57
Brendon Gdns. Ilf —29Uc 46
Brendon Rd. SE9 —61Tc 130
Brendon Rd. Dag —32Bd 67
Brendon St. W1 —44Gb 81 (2E 196)
Brendon Vs. N21 —18Sb 25
Brendon Way. Enf —17Ub 25
Brenley Clo. Mitc —69Jb 126
Brenley Gdns. SE9 —56Mc 107
Brennand Ct. N19 —34Lb 62
Brennan Rd. Til —4D 114
Brent Clo. Bex —60Ad 109
Brent Clo. Dart —58Rd 111
Brentcot Clo. W13 —42Ka 78
Brent Ct. NW11 —31Za 60
Brent Ct. W7 —45Fa 78
Brent Cres. NW10 —40Pa 59
Brent Cross Fly-Over. NW2 —31Za 60
Brent Cross Shopping Cen. NW4 —31Ya 60
Brentfield. NW10 —38Ra 59
Brentfield Clo. NW10 —37Ta 59
Brentfield Gdns. NW2 —31Za 60
Brentfield Ho. NW10 —38Ta 59
Brentfield Rd. NW10 —37Ta 59
Brentfield Rd. Dart —58Qd 111
Brentford Bus. Cen. Bren —52La 100
Brentford Clo. Hay —42Z 77
Brentford Ho. Twic —59Ka 100
Brent Grn. NW4 —29Ya 40
Brent Grn. Wlk. Wemb —34Sa 59
Brentham Way. W5 —42Ma 79
Brenthouse Rd. E9 —37Yb 64
Brenthurst Rd. NW10 —37Va 60
Brentlands Dri. Dart —60Qd 111
Brent La. Dart —59Pd 111
Brent Lea. Bren —52La 100
Brentleigh Ct. Brtwd —20Wd 32
Brentmead Clo. W7 —45Ga 78
Brentmead Gdns. NW10 —40Pa 59
Brentmead Pl. NW11 —30Za 40
Brent New Enterprise Cen. NW10 —37Va 60
Brenton St. E14 —44Ac 84
Brent Pk. Ind. Est. W7 —48X 77
Brent Pk. Rd. NW9 & NW4 —31Wa 60
(in two parts)
Brent Pl. Barn —15Bb 23
Brent Rd. E16 —44Jc 85
Brent Rd. SE18 —52Rc 108
Brent Rd. Bren —51La 100
Brent Rd. S'hall —48Y 77
Brent Rd. S Croy —81Xb 165
Brent Side. Bren —51La 100
Brentside Clo. W13 —42Ja 78
Brentside Executive Pk. Bren —51La 100
Brent St. NW4 —28Ya 40
Brent Ter. NW2 —32Ya 60
Brent, The. Dart —59Qd 111
Brent Trading Cen. NW10 —36Ua 60
Brentvale Av. S'hall —46Fa 78
Brentvale Av. Wemb —39Pa 59
Brent View Rd. NW9 —30Wa 40
Brentwater Bus. Pk. Bren —52La 100
Brent Way. N3 —23Cb 41
Brent Way. Bren —52Ma 101
Brent Way. Dart —58Rd 111
Brent Way. Wemb —37Ra 59
Brentwick Gdns. Bren —49Na 79
Brentwood By-Pass. Brtwd —21Td 50
Brentwood Clo. SE9 —60Sc 108
Brentwood Ct. Add —77K 139
Brentwood Lodge. NW4 —29Za 40
(off Holmdale Gdns.)
Brentwood Pl. Brtwd —18Zd 33
Brentwood Rd. Grays —9D 92
Brentwood Rd. Ingve —21Ce 51
Brentwood Rd. Romf —30Hd 48
Brereton Rd. N17 —24Vb 43
Bressenden Pl. SW1 —48Kb 82 (3A 204)
Bressey Gro. E18 —26Hc 45
Bretlands Rd. Cher —75G 138
Breton Highwalk. EC2 —43Sb 83 (7E 194)
(off Golden La.)
Breton Ho. EC2 —43Sb 83 (7E 194)
(off Barbican)
Brett Clo. N16 —33Ub 63
Brett Clo. N'holt —41Z 77
Brett Ct. N9 —19Yb 26
Brett Cres. NW10 —39Ta 59
Brettell St. SE17 —50Tb 83 (7G 207)
Brettenham Av. E17 —25Cc 44
Brettenham Rd. E17 —26Cc 44
Brettenham Rd. N18 —21Wb 43
Brett Gdns. Dag —38Ad 67
Brettgrave. Eps —82Sa 161
Brett Ho. Chesh —1Zb 12
(off Coopers Wlk.)
Brett Ho. Clo. SW15 —59Za 102
Brett Pas. E8 —36Xb 63
Brett Pl. Wat —9W 4
Brett Rd. E8 —36Xb 63
Brett Rd. Barn —15Ya 22
Brevet Clo. Purf —49Td 90
Brewer's Field. Dart —63Ld 133
Brewers Grn. SW1 —48Lb 82 (3C 204)
(off Buckingham Ga.)
Brewer's Hall Garden. EC2 —43Sb 83 (1E 200)
(off London Wall)
Brewers La. Rich —57Ma 101
Brewers Rd. Shorne —7L 137
Brewer St. W1 —45Lb 82 (5C 198)
Brewery Clo. Wemb —36Ja 58
Brewery La. Byfl —85N 157
Brewery La. Sev —97Kd 187
Brewery La. Twic —59Ha 100
Brewery M. Bus. Cen. Iswth —55Ha 100
Brewery Rd. N7 —38Nb 62
Brewery Rd. SE18 —50Tc 86
Brewery Rd. Brom —74Nc 150
Brewery Rd. Wok —5G 188
Brewery Sq. SE1 —46Vb 83 (7K 201)
(off Horselydown La.)
Brewhouse La. E1 —46Xb 83
Brewhouse Rd. SE18 —49Pc 86
Brewhouse St. SW15 —55Ab 102
Brewhouse Wlk. SE16 —46Ac 84
Brewhouse Yd. EC1 —42Rb 83 (5B 194)
Brewhouse Yd. Grav —8D 114
Brewood Rd. Dag —37Xc 67
Brewster Gdns. W10 —43Ya 80
Brewster Rd. E10 —32Dc 64
Brian Av. S Croy —84Ub 165
Brian Clo. Horn —35Kd 69
Briane Rd. Eps —82Sa 161
Brian Rd. Romf —29Yc 47
Briant Ho. SE1 —48Pb 82 (4J 205)
(off Hercules Rd.)
Briants Clo. Pinn —26Ba 37
Briant St. SE14 —53Zb 106
Briar Av. SW16 —66Pb 126
Briarbank Rd. W13 —44Ja 78
Briar Banks. Cars —81Jb 164
Briar Clo. N2 —27Db 41
Briar Clo. N13 —20Sb 25
Briar Clo. Buck H —19Mc 27
Briar Clo. Chesh —1Yb 12
Briar Clo. Hamp —64Ba 121
Briar Clo. Iswth —57Ha 100
Briar Clo. Tap —4A 72
Briar Clo. W Byf —83L 157
Briar Ct. E8 —38Vb 63
Briar Ct. Sutt —77Ya 144
Briar Cres. N'holt —37Da 57
Briardale Gdns. NW3 —34Cb 61
Briarfield Av. N3 —26Db 41
Briar Gdns. Brom —74Hc 149
Briar Gro. S Croy —85Wb 165
Briar Hill. Purl —83Nb 164
Briar La. Cars —81Jb 164
Briar La. Croy —77Dc 148
Briarleas Gdns. Upm —31Ud 70
Briar Rd. NW2 —35Ya 60
Briar Rd. SW16 —69Nb 126
Briar Rd. Bex —62Fd 132
Briar Rd. Harr —29La 38
Briar Rd. Romf —24Ld 49
Briar Rd. Send —95D 172
Briar Rd. Shep —71P 139
Briar Rd. Twic —60Ga 100
Briar Rd. Wat —6W 4
Briars Clo. N17 —24Xb 43
Briars Ct. Oxs —86Fa 160
Briars, The. Bush —17Ga 20
Briars, The. Chesh —3Ac 12
Briars, The. Kel H —11Ud 32
Briars, The. Sarr —8K 3
Briars, The. Slou —50B 74
Briars, The. Stai —58J 97
Briars, The. W King —79Td 154
Briars Wlk. Romf —26Nd 49
Briars Way. Hart —71Ce 155
Briarswood Way. Orp —78Vc 151
Briar Wlk. SW15 —56Xa 102
Briar Wlk. W10 —42Ab 80
Briar Wlk. Edgw —24Sa 39
Briar Wlk. W Byf —84J 157
Briar Way. Slou —3F 72
Briar Way. W Dray —47Q 76
Briarwood Clo. NW9 —30Sa 39
Briarwood Clo. Felt —62U 120
Briarwood Dri. N'wd —26W 36
Briarwood Rd. SW4 —57Mb 104
Briarwood Rd. Eps —79Wa 144
Briarwood Rd. Wok —7A 188
Briary Clo. NW3 —38Gb 61
Briary Ct. Sidc —64Xc 131
Briary Gdns. Brom —64Kc 129
Briary Gro. Edgw —26Ra 39
Briary La. N9 —20Vb 25
Briary Lodge. Beck —67Ec 128
Briavels Ct. Eps —87Ua 162
Brickbat All. Lea —94Ka 176
Brick Ct. EC4 —44Qb 82 (3K 199)
Brick Ct. Grays —51Ce 113
(off Jetty Wlk.)
Brickenden Ct. Wal A —5Hc 13
Brickett Clo. Ruis —29S 36
Brick Farm Clo. Rich —53Ra 101
Brickfield Clo. Bren —52La 100
Brickfield Cotts. SE18 —51Vc 109
Brickfield Farm Gdns. Orp —77Sc 150
Brickfield La. Ark —16Va 22
Brickfield La. Hay —51T 98
Brickfield Rd. SW19 —63Db 125
Brickfield Rd. Coop —1Zc 15
Brickfield Rd. T Hth —67Rb 127
Brickfields. Harr —33Fa 58
(in two parts)
Brickfields Cotts. Borwd —13Pa 21
Brick La. E1 —42Vb 83
Brick La. E2 —41Vb 83 (4K 195)
Brick La. Enf —12Xb 25
Brick La. Stan —24Ma 39
Brick St. W1 —46Kb 82 (7K 197)
Brickwall La. Ruis —32U 56
Brickwood Clo. SE26 —62Xb 127
Brickwood Rd. Croy —75Ub 147
Brickworks Cotts. Sev —92Md 187
Bride Ct. EC4 —44Rb 83 (3B 200)
(off Bride La.)
Bride La. EC4 —44Rb 83 (3B 200)
Bride St. N7 —37Pb 62
Bridewell Pl. E1 —46Xb 83
Bridewell Pl. EC4 —44Rb 83 (3B 200)
Bridford M. W1 —43Kb 82 (7A 192)
Bridge App. NW1 —38Jb 62
Bridge Av. W6 —49Ya 80
Bridge Av. W7 —43Fa 78
Bridge Av. Upm —34Qd 69
Bridge Barn La. Wok —6G 188
Bridge Clo. Brtwd —21Be 51
Bridge Clo. Byfl —84P 157
Bridge Clo. Enf —12Xb 25
Bridge Clo. Slou —5D 72
Bridge Clo. Stai —63G 118
Bridge Clo. Tedd —63Ha 122
Bridge Clo. W on T —73V 140
Bridge Clo. Wok —5F 188
Bridge Ct. E10 —32Bc 64
Bridge Ct. Grays —51De 113
(off Bridge Rd.)
Bridge Ct. Rad —7Ka 6
Bridge Ct. Wey —77R 140
Bridge Ct. Wok —5G 188
Bridge Dri. N13 —21Pb 42
Bridge End. E17 —25Ec 44
Bridgefield Clo. Bans —87Ya 162
Bridgefield Rd. Sutt —79Cb 145
Bridgefoot. SE1 —50Nb 82
Bridgefoot. Sun —67V 120
Bridgefoot La. Pot B —5Ya 8
Bridgeford Ho. Wat —13X 19
Bridge Gdns. Ashf —66S 120
Bridge Gdns. E Mol —70Fa 122
Bridge Ga. N21 —17Sb 25
Bridgeham Clo. Wey —78Q 140
Bridge Hill. Epp —5Vc 15
Bridge Ho. E9 —37Zb 64
(off Homerton High St.)
Bridge Ho. Dart —59Nd 111
Bridge Ho. Sutt —79Db 145
(off Bridge Rd.)
Bridge Ho. Quay. E14 —46Ec 84
Bridgeland Rd. E16 —45Jc 85
Bridge La. NW11 —29Ab 40
Bridge La. SW11 —53Gb 103
Bridge La. Vir W —71A 138
Bridgeman Dri. Wind —4E 94
Bridgeman Rd. N1 —38Pb 62
Bridgeman Rd. Tedd —65Ja 122
Bridgeman St. NW8 —40Gb 61 (2D 190)
Bridge Meadows. SE14 —51Zb 106
Bridge M. St J —5G 188
Bridgend Rd. SW18 —56Eb 103
Bridgend Rd. Enf —7Yb 12
Bridgenhall Rd. Enf —11Vb 25
Bridgen Rd. Bex —59Ad 109
Bridgepark. SW18 —57Cb 103
Bridge Pl. SW1 —49Kb 82 (5A 204)
Bridge Pl. Croy —74Tb 147
Bridge Pl. Wat —15Z 19
Bridgeport Pl. E1 —46Wb 83
Bridger Clo. Wat —5Z 5
Bridge Rd. E6 —38Pc 66
Bridge Rd. E15 —38Fc 65
Bridge Rd. E17 —31Bc 64
Bridge Rd. N9 —20Wb 25
Bridge Rd. N22 —25Nb 42
Bridge Rd. NW10 —37Ua 60
Bridge Rd. Asc —10B 116
Bridge Rd. Beck —66Bc 128
Bridge Rd. Bexh —54Ad 109
Bridge Rd. Cher —73K 139
Bridge Rd. Chess —78Na 143
Bridge Rd. E Mol —70Fa 122
Bridge Rd. Eps —84Va 162
Bridge Rd. Eri —54Hd 110
Bridge Rd. Grays —51De 113
Bridge Rd. Houn & Iswth —55Fa 100
Bridge Rd. K Lan —5S 4
Bridge Rd. Orp —72Xc 151
Bridge Rd. Rain —42Jd 88
Bridge Rd. Romf —30Gd 48
Bridge Rd. S'hall —47Ba 77
Bridge Rd. Sutt —79Db 145
Bridge Rd. Twic —58Ka 100
Bridge Rd. Uxb —40L 55
Bridge Rd. Wall —78Lb 146
Bridge Rd. Wemb —34Qa 59
Bridge Rd. Wey —77P 139
Bridge Row. Croy —74Tb 147
Bridges Ct. SW11 —54Fb 103
(in two parts)
Bridges Dri. Dart —57Rd 111
Bridges La. Croy —77Nb 146
Bridges Pl. SW6 —53Bb 103
Bridges Rd. SW19 —65Db 125
Bridges Rd. Stan —22Ha 38
Bridges Rd. M. SW19 —65Db 125
Bridge St. SW1 —47Nb 82 (2F 205)
Bridge St. W4 —49Ta 79
Bridge St. Coln —52F 96
Bridge St. Lea —94Ja 176
Bridge St. Pinn —27Aa 37
Bridge St. Rich —57Ma 101
Bridge St. Stai —63G 118
Bridge St. W on T —74U 140
Bridge Ter. E15 —38Fc 65
(in two parts)
Bridge, The. Harr —28Ha 38
Bridgetown Clo. SE19 —64Ub 127
Bridge View. W6 —50Ya 80
Bridgeview Ct. Ilf —23Uc 46
Bridgewater. Bush —16Da 19
Bridgewater Clo. Chst —69Uc 130
Bridgewater Clo. Romf —22Md 49
Bridgewater Ct. Slou —49C 74
Bridgewater Gdns. Edgw —26Pa 39
Bridgewater Rd. E15 —39Ec 64
Bridgewater Rd. Romf —22Ld 49
Bridgewater Rd. Ruis —35W 56
Bridgewater Rd. Wemb —37La 58
Bridgewater Rd. Wey —79T 140
Bridgewater Sq. EC2 —43Sb 83 (7D 194)
Bridgewater St. EC2 —43Sb 83 (7D 194)
Bridgewater Ter. Wind —3H 95
Bridgewater Wlk. Romf —22Md 49
Bridge Way. N11 —20Lb 24
Bridge Way. NW11 —29Bb 41
Bridgeway. Bark —38Vc 67
Bridge Way. Cob —85V 158
Bridge Way. Coul —91Gb 179
Bridge Way. Twic —59Ea 100
Bridge Way. Uxb —36R 56
Bridge Way. Wemb —38Na 59
Bridgeway St. NW1 —40Lb 62 (2C 192)
Bridge Wharf. E3 —40Zb 64
Bridge Wharf. Cher —73L 139
Bridge Wharfe Rd. Iswth —55Ka 100
Bridge Wharf Rd. Iswth —55Ka 100
Bridgewood Clo. SE20 —66Xb 127
Bridgewood Rd. SW16 —66Mb 126
Bridgewood Rd. Wor Pk —77Wa 144
Bridge Yd. SE1 —46Tb 83 (6G 201)
Bridgford St. SW18 —62Eb 125
Bridgman Rd. W4 —48Sa 79
Bridle Clo. Enf —9Bc 12
Bridle Clo. Eps —78Ta 143
Bridle Clo. King T —70Ma 123
Bridle Clo. Sun —69W 120
Bridle End. Eps —86Va 162
Bridle La. W1 —45Lb 82 (4C 198)
Bridle La. Loud —13L 17
Bridle La. Stoke D & Oxs —87Da 159
Bridle Path. Croy —76Nb 146
Bridle Path. Wat —12X 19
Bridle Path, The. E4 —24Gc 45
Bridlepath Way. Felt —60U 98
Bridle Rd. Clay —79Ka 142
Bridle Rd. Croy —76Cc 148
(in two parts)
Bridle Rd. Eps —85Va 162
Bridle Rd. Pinn —30X 37
Bridle Rd. S Croy —81Wb 165
Bridle Rd., The. Purl —82Nb 164
Bridle Way. Croy —77Cc 148
Bridle Way. Orp —77Sc 150
Bridleway Clo. Eps —82Ya 162
Bridle Way, The. Croy —82Ac 166
Bridleway, The. Wall —78Lb 146
Bridlington Clo. Big H —91Kc 183
Bridlington Rd. N9 —17Xb 25
Bridlington Rd. Wat —20Z 19
Bridlington Spur. Slou —8F 72
Bridport Av. Romf —30Dd 48
Bridport Ho. N1 —39Tb 63
(off Colville Est.)
Bridport Pl. N1 —39Tb 63
(in three parts)
Bridport Rd. N18 —22Ub 43
Bridport Rd. T Hth —69Qb 126
Bridport Ter. SW8 —53Mb 104
Bridport Way. Slou —2F 72
Bridstow Pl. W2 —44Cb 81
Brief St. SE5 —53Rb 105
Brier Lea. Tad —98Bb 179
Brierley. New Ad —79Dc 148
(in two parts)
Brierley Av. N9 —18Yb 26
Brierley Clo. SE25 —70Wb 127
Brierley Clo. Horn —30Ld 49
Brierley Rd. E11 —35Fc 65
Brierley Rd. SW12 —61Lb 126
Brierly Gdns. E2 —40Yb 64
Briery Field. Chor —14J 17
Brigade Clo. Harr —33Fa 58
Brigade St. SE3 —54Hc 107
Brigadier Av. Enf —10Sb 11
Brigadier Hill. Enf —10Sb 11
Briggeford Clo. E5 —33Wb 63
Brighstone Ct. Purf —50Rd 89
Bright Clo. Belv —49Zc 87
Brightfield Rd. SE12 —57Gc 107
Brightlands. Grav —3A 136
Brightling Rd. SE4 —58Bc 106
Brightlingsea Pl. E14 —45Bc 84
Brightman Rd. SW18 —60Fb 103
Brighton Av. E17 —29Bc 44
Brighton Bldgs. SE1 —48Ub 83 (4H 207)
(off Tower Bri. Rd.)
Brighton Clo. Add —78L 139
Brighton Clo. Uxb —38R 56
Brighton Dri. N'holt —37Ca 57
Brighton Gro. SE14 —53Ac 106
Brighton Rd. E6 —41Qc 86
Brighton Rd. N2 —26Eb 41
Brighton Rd. N16 —35Ub 63
Brighton Rd. Add —78L 139
Brighton Rd. Coul & Purl —87Mb 164
Brighton Rd. Hool & Coul —95Kb 180
Brighton Rd. S Croy —78Sb 147
Brighton Rd. Surb —72La 142
Brighton Rd. Sutt —83Cb 163
Brighton Rd. Tad & Bans —94Ab 178
Brighton Rd. Wat —10W 4
Brighton Spur. Slou —2F 72
Brighton Ter. SW9 —56Pb 104
Brights Av. Rain —42Kd 89
Brightside Av. Stai —66L 119
Brightside Rd. SE13 —58Fc 107
Brightside, The. Enf —11Ac 26
Bright St. E14 —44Dc 84
Brightview Clo. Brick —1Aa 5
Brightwell Cres. SW17 —64Hb 125
Brightwell Rd. Wat —15W 18
Brig M. SE8 —51Cc 106
Brigstock Ho. SE5 —54Sb 105
Brigstock Rd. Belv —49Dd 88
Brigstock Rd. Coul —87Kb 164
Brigstock Rd. T Hth —71Qb 146
Brill Pl. NW1 —40Mb 62 (2E 192)
Brimfield Rd. Purf —49Td 90
Brim Hill. N2 —28Eb 41
Brimpsfield Clo. SE2 —48Xc 87
Brimsdon Ind. Est. Enf —12Bc 26
Brimsdown Av. Enf —12Ac 26
Brimsdown Ind. Est. Enf —11Bc 26
Brimstone Clo. Orp —80Yc 151
Brindle Ga. Sidc —60Uc 108
Brindles. Horn —28Nd 49
Brindles Clo. Hut —19Ee 33
Brindles Clo. Linf —9J 93
Brindles, The. Bans —89Bb 163
Brindley Clo. Bexh —55Dd 110
Brindley St. SE14 —53Bc 106
Brindley Way. Brom —64Jc 129
Brindley Way. S'hall —45Da 77
Brindwood Rd. E4 —20Bc 26
Brinkburn Clo. SE2 —49Wc 87
Brinkburn Clo. Edgw —27Ra 39
Brinkburn Gdns. Edgw —27Qa 39
Brinkley Rd. Wor Pk —75Xa 144
Brinklow Cres. SE18 —52Rc 108
Brinkworth Rd. Ilf —27Nc 46
Brinkworth Way. E9 —37Bc 64
Brinley Clo. Chesh —3Zb 12
Brinsdale Rd. NW4 —27Za 40
Brinsley Rd. Harr —26Fa 38
Brinsley St. E1 —44Xb 83
Brinsmead Rd. Romf —26Qd 49
Brinsworth Clo. Twic —61Fa 122
Brinsworth Ho. Twic —61Fa 122
Brinton Wlk. SE1 —46Rb 83 (7B 200)
(off Chancel St.)
Brion Pl. E14 —43Ec 84
Brisbane Av. SW19 —67Db 125
Brisbane Ho. Til —3C 114
Brisbane Rd. E10 —33Dc 64
Brisbane Rd. W13 —47Ja 78
Brisbane Rd. Ilf —31Rc 66
Brisbane St. SE5 —52Tb 105
Briscoe Clo. E11 —34Hc 65
Briscoe Rd. SW19 —65Fb 125
Briscoe Rd. Rain —40Ld 69
Briset Rd. SE9 —55Mc 107
Briset St. EC1 —43Rb 83 (7B 194)
Briset Way. N7 —33Pb 62
Brisson Clo. Esh —78Ba 141
Bristol Clo. Stai —58N 97
Bristol Ct. Stanw —58N 97
Bristol Gdns. SW15 —59Ya 102
Bristol Gdns. W9 —42Db 81
Bristol Ho. Bark —38Wc 67
(off Margaret Bondfield Av.)
Bristol Ho. Borwd —12Qa 21
Bristol M. W9 —42Db 81
Bristol Pk. Rd. E17 —28Ac 44
Bristol Rd. E7 —37Lc 65
Bristol Rd. Grav —2F 136
Bristol Rd. Gnfd —39Da 57
Bristol Rd. Mord —71Eb 145
Bristol Way. Slou —6K 73
Briston Gro. N8 —30Nb 42
Bristow Rd. SE19 —64Ub 127
Bristow Rd. Bexh —53Ad 109
Bristow Rd. Croy —77Nb 146
Bristow Rd. Houn —55Ea 100
Britannia Clo. SW4 —56Mb 104
Britannia Clo. N'holt —41Z 77
Britannia Ct. W Dray —48M 75
(off Green, The)
Britannia Dri. Grav —4H 137
Britannia Ind. Est. Coln —54G 96
Britannia La. Twic —59Ea 100
Britannia Rd. E14 —49Cc 84
Britannia Rd. N12 —20Eb 23
Britannia Rd. SW6 —52Db 103
Britannia Rd. Ilf —34Rc 66
Britannia Rd. Surb —73Pa 143
Britannia Rd. Wal X —6Bc 12
Britannia Rd. War —22Yd 50
Britannia Row. N1 —39Rb 63
Britannia St. WC1 —41Pb 82 (3H 193)
Britannia Wlk. N1 —40Tb 63 (2F 195)
(in two parts)
Britannia Way. NW10 —42Ra 79
Britannia Way. SW6 —52Db 103
Britannia Way. Stai —59M 97
Britannic Highwalk. EC2 —43Tb 83 (1F 201)
(off Moor La.)
Britannic Ho. EC2 —43Tb 83 (7F 195)
(off Finsbury Cir.)
British Gro. W4 —50Va 80
British Gro. W6 —50Va 80
British Gro. S. W6 —50Wa 80
British Legion Rd. E4 —19Hc 27
British St. E3 —41Bc 84
Briton Clo. S Croy —83Ub 165
Briton Cres. S Croy —83Ub 165
Briton Hill Rd. S Croy —82Ub 165
Brittain Ho. SE9 —60Nc 108
Brittain Rd. Dag —34Ad 67
Brittain Rd. W on T —78Z 141
Brittains La. Sev —96Hd 186
Brittany Point. SE11 —49Qb 82 (6K 205)
Britten Clo. NW11 —32Db 61
Britten Clo. Els —16Ma 21
Britten Ct. E15 —40Fc 65
Brittenden Clo. Orp —79Vc 151
Brittenden Pde. Grn St —79Vc 151
Britten Dri. S'hall —44Ca 77
Britten St. SW3 —50Gb 81 (7D 202)
Britton St. EC1 —42Rb 83 (6B 194)
Britwell Rd. Burn —1A 72
Brixham Cres. Ruis —32W 56
Brixham Gdns. Ilf —36Uc 66
Brixham Rd. Well —53Zc 109
Brixham St. E16 —46Qc 86
Brixton Est. Edgw —26Ra 39
Brixton Hill. SW2 —59Nb 104
Brixton Hill Ct. SW2 —57Pb 104
Brixton Hill Pl. SW2 —59Nb 104
Brixton Oval. SW2 —56Qb 104
Brixton Rd. SW9 & SE11 —56Qb 104
Brixton Rd. Wat —11X 19
Brixton Sta. Rd. SW9 —55Qb 104
Brixton Water La. SW2 —57Pb 104
Broad Acre. Brick —2Aa 5
Broadacre. Stai —64J 119
Broadacre Clo. Uxb —34R 56
Broadbent Clo. N6 —32Kb 62
Broadbent St. W1 —45Kb 82 (4K 197)
Broadbridge Clo. SE3 —52Jc 107
Broadbury Ct. N18 —23Xb 43
Broad Clo. W on T —76Aa 141
Broad Comn. Est. N16 —32Wb 63
(off Osbaldeston Rd.)
Broadcoombe. S Croy —80Zb 148
Broad Ct. WC2 —44Nb 82 (3G 199)
Broadcroft Av. Stan —26Ma 39
Broadcroft Rd. Orp —73Tc 150
Broad Ditch Rd. S'fleet —66Ee 135
Broadfield Clo. NW2 —34Ya 60
Broadfield Clo. Croy —75Nb 146
Broadfield Clo. Romf —29Hd 48
Broadfield Clo. Tad —92Ya 178
Broadfield Ct. Bush —19Ga 20
Broadfield Ct. N Har —25Da 37
(off Broadfields)
Broadfield Heights. NW7 —21Ra 39
Broadfield La. NW1 —38Mb 62
Broadfield Rd. SE6 —59Gc 107
Broadfields. Chesh —1Rb 11
Broadfields. E Mol —72Ga 142
Broadfields. Harr —26Da 37
Broadfields Av. N21 —17Qb 24
Broadfields Av. Edgw —21Ra 39
Broadfields Cen. Edgw —18Ra 21
Broadfields La. Wat —18X 19
Broadfield Sq. Enf —12Xb 25
Broadfields Way. NW10 —36Va 60
Broadfield Way. Buck H —20Lc 27
Broadford La. Chob —1B 188
Broadgate. EC2 —42Ub 83 (7H 195)
Broadgate. Wal A —5Hc 13
Broadgate Circ. EC2 —43Ub 83 (1H 201)
(off Broadgate)
Broadgate Cir. EC2 —43Ub 83
Broadgate Ct. EC2 —43Ub 83 (7H 195)
Broadgate Rd. E16 —44Mc 85
Broadgates Av. Barn —11Db 23
Broadgates Ct. SE11 —50Qb 82 (7A 206)
(off Cleaves St.)
Broadgates Rd. SW18 —60Fb 103
Broad Grn. Av. Croy —73Rb 147
Broadhead Strand. NW9 —25Va 40
Broadheath Dri. Chst —64Pc 130
Broad Highway. Cob —87Z 159
Broadhinton Rd. SW4 —55Kb 104
Broadhope Av. Stanf —3L 93
Broadhurst. Asht —88Na 161
Broadhurst Av. Edgw —21Ra 39
Broadhurst Av. Ilf —35Vc 67
Broadhurst Clo. NW6 —37Eb 61
Broadhurst Clo. Rich —57Pa 101
Broadhurst Gdns. NW6 —37Db 61
Broadhurst Gdns. Chig —21Sc 46
(in two parts)
Broadhurst Gdns. Ruis —33Y 57
Broadhurst Wlk. Rain —37Jd 68
Broadlands. E17 —27Ac 44
Broadlands. Grays —50Be 91
Broadlands Av. SW16 —61Nb 126
Broadlands Av. Enf —13Xb 25
Broadlands Av. Shep —72S 140
Broadlands Clo. N6 —31Jb 62
Broadlands Clo. SW16 —61Nb 126

Broadlands Clo.—Browning St.

Broadlands Clo. Enf —13Yb 26
Broadlands Clo. Wal X —6Yb 12
Broadlands Ct. Rich —52Qa 101 (off Kew Gdns. Rd.)
Broadlands Dri. Warl —91Yb 182
Broadlands Lodge. N6 —31Hb 61
Broadlands Rd. N6 —31Hb 61
Broadlands Rd. Brom —63Kc 129
Broadlands, The. Felt —62Ca 121
Broadlands Way. N Mald —72Va 144
Broad La. N8 —29Pb 42
Broad La. N15 —28Vb 43
Broad La. Dart —63Jd 132
Broad La. Hamp —66Ba 121
Broad Lawn. SE9 —61Qc 130
Broadlawns Ct. Harr —25Ha 38
Broadley St. NW8 —43Fb 81 (7C 190)
Broadley Ter. NW1 —42Gb 81 (6E 190)
Broadmark Rd. Slou —5M 73
Broadmead. SE6 —62Cc 128
Broad Mead. Asht —90Pa 161
Broadmead. Mers —100Lb 180 (off Station Rd.)
Broadmead Av. Wor Pk —73Wa 144
Broadmead Clo. Hamp —65Ca 121
Broadmead Clo. Pinn —24Aa 37
Broadmead Ct. Wfd G —23Jc 45
Broadmead Rd. Hay & N'holt —42Aa 77
Broadmead Rd. Send & Old Wok —94D 172
Broadmead Rd. Wfd G —23Jc 45
Broadmeads. Wok —94D 172
Broad Oak. Slou —2G 72
Broad Oak. Wfd G —22Kc 45
Broadoak Av. Enf —7Zb 12
Broad Oak Clo. E4 —22Cc 44
Broad Oak Clo. Orp —68Wc 131
Broadoak Ct. Slou —2G 72
Broadoak Rd. Eri —52Fd 110
Broadoaks. Epp —3Vc 15
Broadoaks. Surb —75Ra 143
Broadoaks Cres. W Byf —85K 157
Broadoaks Way. Brom —71Hc 149
Broad Platts. Slou —8P 73
Broad Rd. Swans —58Ae 113
Broad Sanctuary. SW1 —47Mb 82 (2E 204)
Broadstone Pl. W1 —43Jb 82 (1H 197)
Broadstone Rd. Horn —33Jd 68
Broad St. Dag —38Cd 68
Broad St. Tedd —65Ha 122
Broad St. Av. EC2 —43Ub 83 (1H 201)
Broad St. Mkt. Dag —38Dd 68
Broad St. Pl. EC2 —43Tb 83 (1G 201) (off Blomfield St.)
Broadstrood. Lou —10Qc 14
Broad View. NW9 —30Qa 39
Broadview Av. Grays —47Fe 91
Broadview Rd. SW16 —66Mb 126
Broadwalk. E18 —27Hc 45
Broad Wlk. N21 —19Pb 24
Broad Wlk. NW1 —39Jb 62 (1J 191)
Broad Wlk. SE3 —54Lc 107
Broad Wlk. W2 & W1 —45Hb 81 (5G 197)
Broad Wlk. Cat —94Vb 181
Broad Wlk. Coul —95Jb 180
Broad Wlk. Eps —89Ua 162 (Epsom Downs)
Broad Wlk. Eps —91Za 178 (Tattenham Corner)
Broad Wlk. Houn —53Z 99
Broadwalk. N Har —29Ca 37
Broad Wlk. Orp —76Zc 151
Broad Wlk. Rich —52Pa 101
Broad Wlk. Sev —100Nd 187
Broad Wlk. La. NW11 —31Bb 61
Broad Wlk. N., The. Brtwd —20Ce 33
Broadwalk Shopping Cen. Edgw —23Ra 39
Broad Wlk. S., The. Brtwd —21Ce 51
Broad Wlk., The. W8 —46Db 81
Broad Wlk., The. E Mol —70Ha 122
Broadwalk, The. N'wd —26S 36
Broadwall. SE1 —46Qb 82 (6A 200)
Broadwater. Pot B —2Db 9
Broadwater Clo. W on T —78W 140
Broadwater Clo. Wok —84F 156
Broadwater Clo. Wray —59A 96
Broadwater Farm Est. N17 —26Tb 43
Broadwater Gdns. Hare —28L 35
Broadwater Gdns. Orp —77Rc 150
Broadwater La. Hare —28L 35
Broadwater Pk. Ind. Est. Den —29J 35
Broadwater Rd. N17 —25Ub 43
Broadwater Rd. SE28 —48Tc 86
Broadwater Rd. SW17 —63Gb 125
Broadwater Rd. N. W on T —78V 140
Broadwater Rd. S. W on T —78V 140
Broadway. E13 —40Kc 65
Broadway. E15 —38Fc 65 (in two parts)
Broadway. NW9 —31Wa 60
Broadway. SW1 —48Mb 82 (3D 204)
Broadway. Bark —39Sc 66
Broadway. Bexh —56Ad 109
Broadway. Grays —51Ee 113
Broadway. Knap —6A 188
Broadway. Rain —42Jd 88
Broadway. Romf —26Jd 48
Broadway. Surb —74Ra 143
Broadway. Swan —72Fd 152
Broadway. Til —4B 114
Broadway. Wink —10A 94
Broadway Arc. W6 —49Ya 80 (off Hammersmith B'way.)
Broadway Av. Croy —71Tb 147
Broadway Av. Twic —58Ka 100
Broadway Clo. S Croy —86Xb 165
Broadway Clo. Wfd G —23Kc 45
Broadway Ct. SW19 —65Cb 125
Broadway Ct. Beck —69Ec 128
Broadway Ct. Knap —5A 188
Broadway Gdns. Mitc —70Gb 125
Broadway Ho. Knap —6A 188
Broadway Mkt. E8 —39Xb 63
Broadway M. E5 —31Vb 63
Broadway M. N13 —22Pb 42
Broadway M. N21 —18Rb 25
Broadway Pde. N8 —30Nb 42
Broadway Pde. Harr —29Da 37
Broadway Pde. Horn —35Kd 69 (off Broadway)
Broadway Pl. SW19 —65Bb 125
Broadway Rd. Hay & N'holt —42Aa 77
Broadway Shopping Cen. Bexh —56Cd 110
Broadway Shopping Mall. SW1 —48Mb 82 (3D 204)
Broadway, The. E4 —23Fc 45
Broadway, The. N8 —30Nb 42
Broadway, The. N9 —20Wb 25
Broadway, The. N22 —26Qb 42
Broadway, The. NW7 —22Ua 40
Broadway, The. SW13 —54Ua 102
Broadway, The. SW19 —65Cb 125
Broadway, The. W3 —47Qa 79
Broadway, The. W5 —45Ma 79
Broadway, The. W7 & W13 (in two parts) —46Ga 78
Broadway, The. Cheam —79Ab 144
Broadway, The. Croy —77Nb 146
Broadway, The. Dag —33Bd 67
Broadway, The. Gnfd —42Ea 78
Broadway, The. Horn —35Kd 69
Broadway, The. Lou —14Sc 28
Broadway, The. New Haw —82J 157
Broadway, The. Pot B —4Bb 9
Broadway, The. S'hall —46Aa 77
Broadway, The. Stai —69L 119
Broadway, The. Stan —22La 38
Broadway, The. Sutt —78Eb 145
Broadway, The. Th Dit —74Ga 142
Broadway, The. Wat —13Y 19
Broadway, The. W'stone —26Ga 38
Broadway, The. Wemb —34Na 59
Broadway, The. Wok —89B 156
Broadway, The. Wfd G —23Kc 45
Broadwell. SE1 —46Qb 82
Broadwell Ct. Houn —53Z 99 (off Springwell Rd.)
Broadwick St. W1 —45Lb 82 (4C 198)
Broadwood. Grav —4D 136
Broadwood Av. Ruis —30U 36
Broad Yd. EC1 —42Rb 83 (6B 194)
Brocas Clo. NW3 —38Gb 61
Brocas St. Eton —2H 95
Brockdish Av. Bark —36Vc 67
Brockenhurst. W Mol —72Ba 141
Brockenhurst Av. Wor Pk —74Ua 144
Brockenhurst Clo. Wok —86B 156
Brockenhurst Dri. Stanf —3L 93
Brockenhurst Gdns. NW7 —22Ua 40
Brockenhurst Gdns. Ilf —36Sc 66
Brockenhurst Rd. Croy —73Xb 147
Brockenhurst Way. SW16 —68Mb 126
Brocket Clo. Chig —21Vc 47
Brocket Ho. SW8 —54Mb 104
Brockett Rd. Grays —8C 92
Brocket Way. Chig —22Uc 46
Brock Grn. S Ock —44Xd 90
Brockham Clo. SW19 —64Bb 125
Brockham Cres. New Ad —80Fc 149
Brockham Dri. SW2 —59Pb 104
Brockham Dri. Ilf —30Rc 46
Brockham Ho. SW2 —59Pb 104 (off Brockham Dri.)
Brockham St. SE1 —48Sb 83 (3E 206)
Brockhill. Wok —5D 188
Brockhurst Clo. Stan —23Ha 38
Brockill Cres. SE4 —56Ac 106
Brocklebank Ct. Whyt —90Wb 165
Brocklebank Ho. E16 —46Qc 86 (off Glenister St.)
Brocklebank Rd. SE7 —49Kc 85
Brocklebank Rd. SW18 —59Eb 103
Brocklebank Rd. Ind. Est. SE7 —49Jc 85
Brocklehurst St. SE14 —52Zb 106
Brocklesbury Clo. Wat —13Y 19
Brocklesby Rd. SE25 —70Xb 127
Brockley Av. N. Stan —20Na 21
Brockley Av. S. Stan —20Na 21
Brockley Clo. Stan —21Na 39
Brockley Combe. Wey —77T 140
Brockley Cres. Romf —24Ed 48
Brockley Cross. SE4 —55Ac 106
Brockley Cross Bus. Cen. SE4 —55Ac 106
Brockley Footpath. SE4 —57Ac 106
Brockley Footpath. SE15 —56Yb 106
Brockley Gdns. SE4 —54Bc 106
Brockley Gro. SE4 —57Bc 106
Brockley Gro. Hut —18Ce 33
Brockley Hall Rd. SE4 —57Ac 106
Brockley Hill. Stan —18La 20
Brockley Pk. SE23 —59Ac 106
Brockley Rise. SE23 —60Ac 106
Brockley Rd. SE4 —55Bc 106
Brockley Side. Stan —21Na 39
Brockley View. SE23 —59Ac 106
Brockley Way. SE4 —57Zb 106
Brockman Rise. Brom —63Fc 129
Brock Pl. E3 —42Dc 84
Brock Rd. E13 —43Kc 85
Brocks Dri. Sutt —76Ab 144
Brockshot Clo. Bren —50Ma 79
Brocksparkwood. Brtwd —20De 33
Brock St. SE15 —55Yb 106
Brockton Clo. Romf —27Hd 48
Brock Way. Vir W —10N 117
Brockway Clo. E11 —33Gc 65
Brockway Ho. Langl —50D 74
Brockwell Clo. Orp —71Vc 151
Brockwell Ct. SW2 —57Qb 104
Brockwell Pk. Gdns. SE24 —59Rb 105
Brockworth Clo. SE15 —51Ub 105
Broderick Gro. SE2 —49Xc 87
Broderick Gro. Bookh —98Ca 175
Brodewater Rd. Borwd —12Ra 21
Brodia Rd. N16 —34Ub 63
Brodie Rd. E4 —18Ec 26
Brodie Rd. Enf —10Sb 11
Brodie St. SE1 —50Vb 83 (7K 207)
Brodlove La. E1 —45Zb 84
Brodrick Rd. SW17 —61Gb 125
Brograve Gdns. Beck —68Dc 128
Broke Farm Dri. Orp —81Yc 169
Broken Furlong. Eton —10F 72
Brokengate La. Den —32E 54
Broken Wharf. EC4 —45Sb 83 (4D 200)
Brokesley St. E3 —41Bc 84
Broke Wlk. E8 —39Wb 63
Bromar Rd. SE5 —55Ub 105
Bromborough Grn. Wat —22Y 37
Bromefield. Stan —25La 38
Bromefield Ct. Wal A —5Jc 13
Brome Rd. SE9 —55Pc 108
Bromet Clo. Wat —10V 4
Bromfelde Rd. SW4 —55Mb 104
Bromfelde Wlk. SW4 —54Mb 104
Bromfield St. N1 —40Qb 62 (1A 194)
Bromhall Rd. Dag —37Xc 67
Bromhedge. SE9 —62Pc 130
Bromholm Rd. SE2 —48Xc 87
Bromleigh Clo. Chesh —1Ac 12
Bromleigh Ct. SE23 —61Xb 127
Bromley. Grays —51Be 113
Bromley Av. Brom —66Gc 129
Bromley Comn. Brom —70Lc 129
Bromley Cres. Brom —69Hc 129
Bromley Cres. Ruis —35V 56
Bromley Gdns. Brom —69Hc 129
Bromley Gro. Brom —68Fc 129
Bromley Hall Rd. E14 —43Ec 84
Bromley High St. E3 —41Dc 84
Bromley Hill. Brom —65Gc 129
Bromley La. Chst —66Sc 130
Bromley Pk. Brom —67Hc 129
Bromley Pl. W1 —43Lb 82 (7B 192)
Bromley Rd. E10 —30Dc 44
Bromley Rd. E17 —27Cc 44
Bromley Rd. N17 —25Vb 43
Bromley Rd. N18 —20Tb 25
Bromley Rd. SE6 & Brom —60Dc 106
Bromley Rd. Beck & Brom —67Dc 128
Bromley Rd. Chst —67Rc 130
Bromley St. E1 —43Zb 84
Brompton Arc. SW3 —47Hb 81 (2G 203) (off Brompton Rd.)
Brompton Clo. SE20 —68Wb 127
Brompton Clo. Houn —57Ba 99
Brompton Dri. Eri —52Kd 111
Brompton Gro. N2 —28Gb 41
Brompton Pk. Cres. SW6 —51Db 103
Brompton Pl. SW3 —48Gb 81 (3E 202)
Brompton Rd. SW3, SW7 & SW1 —49Gb 81 (5D 202)
Brompton Sq. SW3 —48Gb 81 (3D 202)
Brompton Ter. SE18 —53Pc 108
Bromwells Rd. SW4 —56Lb 104
Bromwich Av. N6 —33Jb 62
Bromyard Av. W3 —45Ua 80
Bromycroft Rd. Slou —1E 72
Brondesbury M. NW6 —38Cb 61
Brondesbury Pk. NW2 & NW6 —37Xa 60
Brondesbury Rd. NW6 —40Bb 61
Brondesbury Vs. NW6 —40Bb 61
Bronsart Rd. SW6 —52Ab 102
Bronsdon Way. Den —33H 55
Bronson Rd. SW20 —68Za 124
Bronte Clo. E7 —35Jc 65
Bronte Clo. Ilf —28Qc 46
Bronte Clo. Til —4E 114
Bronte Gro. Dart —56Pd 111
Bronte Ho. N16 —36Ub 63
Bronte Ho. SW4 —59Lb 104
Bronte View. Grav —10E 114
Bronti Clo. SE17 —50Sb 83 (7E 206)
Bronze St. SE8 —52Cc 106
Brook Av. Dag —38Dd 68
Brook Av. Edgw —22Ra 39
Brook Av. Wemb —34Pa 59
Brook Bank. Enf —9Xb 11
Brookbank Av. W7 —42Fa 78
Brookbank Rd. SE13 —55Cc 106
Brook Bus. Cen. Cow —40K 55
Brook Clo. NW7 —24Ab 40
Brook Clo. SW20 —69Xa 124
Brook Clo. W3 —46Qa 79
Brook Clo. Borwd —12Ra 21
Brook Clo. Romf —25Hd 48
Brook Clo. Ruis —31U 56
Brook Clo. Stai —59P 97
Brook Ct. E11 —34Gc 65
Brook Ct. E15 —36Dc 64 (off Clays La.)
Brook Ct. E17 —27Ac 44
Brook Ct. Edgw —22Ra 39
Brook Cres. E4 —21Cc 44
Brook Cres. N9 —21Xb 43
Brook Cres. Slou —4C 72
Brookdale. N11 —21Lb 42
Brookdale Av. Upm —34Qd 69
Brookdale Clo. Upm —34Rd 69
Brookdale Rd. E17 —27Cc 44
Brookdale Rd. SE6 —59Dc 106
Brookdale Rd. Bex —58Ad 109
Brookdene Av. Wat —17X 19
Brookdene Dri. N'wd —24V 36
Brookdene Rd. SE18 —49Vc 87
Brook Dri. SE11 —48Qb 82 (4A 206)
Brook Dri. Harr —28Ea 38
Brook Dri. Rad —5Ha 6
Brook Dri. Ruis —31U 56
Brook Dri. Sun —65U 120
Brooke Av. Harr —34Ea 58
Brooke Clo. Bush —17Ea 20
Brooke Dri. Grav —10K 115
Brookehowse Rd. SE6 —61Cc 128
Brookend Rd. Sidc —60Uc 108
Brooke Rd. E5 —34Wb 63
Brooke Rd. E17 —28Ec 44
Brooke Rd. N16 —34Vb 63
Brooke Rd. Grays —50Ce 91
Brooker Rd. Wal A —6Ec 12
Brookers Clo. Asht —89Ma 161
Brooke's Ct. EC1 —43Qb 82 (1K 199)
Brooke's Mkt. EC1 —43Qb 82 (7A 194) (off Dorrington St.)
Brooke St. EC1 —43Qb 82 (1K 199)
Brooke Way. Bush —17Ea 20
Brook Farm Rd. Cob —87Z 159
Brookfield. N6 —34Jb 62
Brookfield. Kems —89Nd 171
Brookfield. Wok —4E 188
Brookfield Av. E17 —28Ec 44
Brookfield Av. NW7 —23Xa 40
Brookfield Av. W5 —42Ma 79
Brookfield Av. Sutt —77Gb 145
Brookfield Clo. NW7 —23Xa 40
Brookfield Clo. Hut —16Ee 33
Brookfield Clo. Ott —79F 138
Brookfield Ct. Chesh —1Zb 12 (off Brookfield La. E.)
Brookfield Ct. Gnfd —41Ea 78
Brookfield Cres. NW7 —23Xa 40
Brookfield Cres. Harr —29Na 39
Brookfield Gdns. Clay —79Ha 142
Brookfield La. W. Chesh —1Xb 11 (in two parts)
Brookfield Pk. NW5 —34Kb 62
Brookfield Path. E4 —23Gc 45
Brookfield Rd. E9 —37Ac 64
Brookfield Rd. N9 —20Wb 25
Brookfield Rd. W4 —47Ta 79
Brookfields. Enf —14Zb 26
Brookfields Av. Mitc —71Gb 145
Brook Gdns. E4 —21Dc 44
Brook Gdns. SW13 —55Va 102
Brook Gdns. King T —67Sa 123
Brook Ga. W1 —45Hb 81 (5G 197)
Brook Grn. W6 —48Za 80
Brook Hill Clo. SE18 —50Rc 86
Brookhill Clo. Barn —15Gb 23
Brookhill Rd. SE18 —50Rc 86
Brookhill Rd. Barn —15Gb 23
Brookhouse Gdns. E4 —21Gc 45
Brookhurst Rd. Add —79K 139
Brooking Rd. E7 —36Jc 65
Brookland Clo. NW11 —28Cb 41
Brookland Garth. NW11 —28Cb 41
Brookland Hill. NW11 —28Db 41
Brookland Rise. NW11 —28Cb 41
Brooklands. Dart —60Nd 111
Brooklands. Wey —82P 157
Brooklands App. Romf —28Fd 48
Brooklands Av. SW19 —61Db 125
Brooklands Av. Sidc —61Tc 130
Brooklands Clo. Cob —87Aa 159
Brooklands Clo. Romf —28Fd 48
Brooklands Clo. Sun —67U 120
Brooklands Ct. N21 —15Tb 25
Brooklands Ct. Mitc —68Fb 125
Brooklands Ct. New Haw —82M 157
Brooklands Dri. Gnfd —39Ma 59
Brooklands Gdns. Horn —30Ld 49
Brooklands Gdns. Pot B —4Ab 8
Brooklands La. Romf —28Fd 48
Brooklands La. Wey —79P 139
Brooklands Pk. SE3 —55Jc 107
Brooklands Rd. Romf —28Fd 48
Brooklands Rd. Th Dit —74Ha 142
Brooklands Rd. Wey —83Q 158
Brooklands St. SW8 —53Mb 104
Brooklands, The. Iswth —53Fa 100
Brook La. SE3 —54Kc 107
Brook La. Bex —58Zc 109
Brook La. Brom —65Jc 129
Brook La. Send —94G 172
Brook La. N. Bren —50Ma 79 (in two parts)
Brook La. Trading Cen. Bren —50Ma 79
Brooklea Clo. NW9 —25Ua 40
Brook Lodge. Romf —28Fd 48 (off Brooklands Rd.)
Brooklyn Av. SE25 —70Xb 127
Brooklyn Av. Lou —14Nc 28
Brooklyn Clo. Cars —75Gb 145
Brooklyn Clo. Wok —91A 172
Brooklyn Ct. Wok —91A 172
Brooklyn Gro. SE25 —70Xb 127
Brooklyn Rd. SE25 —70Xb 127
Brooklyn Rd. Brom —71Mc 149
Brooklyn Rd. Wok —90A 156
Brooklyn Way. W Dray —48M 75
Brookman's Av. Grays —46Fe 91
Brookmans Clo. Upm —31Ud 70
Brook Mead. Eps —79Ua 144
Brookmead Av. Brom —71Pc 150
Brookmead Clo. Orp —72Xc 151
Brookmead Ind. Est. Croy —72Lb 146
Brook Meadow. N12 —20Db 23
Brook Meadow Clo. E4 —23Gc 45
Brookmead Rd. Croy —72Lb 146
Brookmead Way. Orp —72Xc 151
Brook M. N. W2 —45Eb 81 (4A 196)
Brookmill Rd. SE8 —53Cc 106
Brook Pde. Chig —20Rc 28
Brook Pk. Clo. N21 —16Rb 25
Brook Pas. SW6 —52Cb 103
Brook Path. Lou —14Nc 28
Brook Path. Slou —5D 72 (in two parts)
Brook Pl. Barn —15Cb 23
Brook Rise. Chig —20Qc 28
Brook Rd. N2 —24Gb 41
Brook Rd. N8 —28Nb 42
Brook Rd. N22 —27Pb 42
Brook Rd. NW2 —33Va 60
Brook Rd. Borwd —11Qa 21
Brook Rd. Brtwd —20Vd 32
Brook Rd. Buck H —19Jc 27
Brook Rd. Epp —5Wc 15
Brook Rd. Grav —10A 114
Brook Rd. Ilf —30Uc 46
Brook Rd. Lou —14Nc 28
Brook Rd. Mers —100Lb 180
Brook Rd. Romf —26Hd 48
Brook Rd. Surb —75Na 143
Brook Rd. Swan —69Fd 132
Brook Rd. T Hth —70Sb 127
Brook Rd. Twic —58Ja 100
Brook Rd. Wal X —6Bc 12
Brook Rd. S. Bren —51Ma 101
Brooks Av. E6 —42Pc 86
Brooksbank St. E9 —37Zb 64
Brooksby M. N1 —38Qb 62
Brooksby St. N1 —38Qb 62
Brooksby's Wlk. E9 —36Zb 64
Brooks Clo. SE9 —61Qc 130
Brooks Clo. Wey —82Q 158
Brookscroft. Croy —82Bc 166
Brookscroft Rd. E17 —25Dc 44 (in two parts)
Brookshill. Harr —22Fa 38
Brookshill Av. Harr —22Fa 38
Brookshill Dri. Harr —22Fa 38
Brooks Ho. Brtwd —18Yd 32
Brookside. N21 —16Pb 24
Brookside. Barn —16Gb 23
Brookside. Cars —78Jb 146
Brookside. Cher —73G 138
Brookside. Coln —52E 96
Brookside. Guild —100A 172
Brookside. Horn —29Nd 49
Brookside. Ilf —23Sc 46
Brookside. Orp —73Vc 151
Brookside. Pot B —4Wa 8
Brookside. Uxb —38P 55
Brookside. Wal A —4Gc 13
Brookside. Wat —9Z 5 (North Watford)
Brookside. Wat —17X 19 (Watford)
Brookside Av. Ashf —64L 119
Brookside Av. Wray —55A 96
Brookside Clo. Barn —16Ab 22
Brookside Clo. Felt —62W 120
Brookside Clo. Kent —29Ma 39
Brookside Clo. S Harr —35Aa 57
Brookside Cres. Wor Pk —74Wa 144
Brookside Gdns. Enf —9Yb 12
Brookside Rd. N9 —21Xb 43
Brookside Rd. N19 —33Lb 62
Brookside Rd. NW11 —30Ab 40
Brookside Rd. Grav —6B 136
Brookside Rd. Hay —45Y 77
Brookside S. Barn —17Jb 24
Brookside Wlk. N12 —23Cb 41
Brookside Way. Croy —72Zb 148
Brooks La. W4 —51Qa 101
Brooks M. W1 —45Kb 82 (4K 197)
Brooks Rd. E13 —39Jc 65
Brooks Rd. W4 —50Qa 79
Brookstone Ct. SE15 —56Xb 105
Brook St. N17 —26Vb 43
Brook St. W1 —45Kb 82 (4J 197)
Brook St. W2 —45Fb 81 (4C 196)
Brook St. Belv & Eri —50Dd 88
Brook St. Brtwd —22Td 50
Brook St. King T —68Na 123
Brook St. Wind —4H 95
Brooksville Av. NW6 —39Ab 60
Brooks Wlk. N3 —27Ab 40
Brooks Way. St P —68Yc 131
Brook Vale. Eri —53Dd 110
Brookview Ct. Enf —15Ub 25
Brookview Rd. SW16 —64Lb 126
Brookville Rd. SW6 —52Bb 103
Brook Wlk. N2 —25Fb 41
Brook Wlk. Edgw —23Ta 39
Brookway. SE3 —55Jc 107
Brook Way. Chig —20Qc 28
Brook Way. Lea —90Ja 160
Brook Way. Rain —43Kd 89
Brookwood Av. SW13 —54Va 102
Brookwood Clo. Brom —70Hc 129
Brookwood Lye Rd. Brkwd & Wok —8A 188
Brookwood Rd. SW18 —60Bb 103
Brookwood Rd. Houn —54Da 99
Broom Av. Orp —68Xc 131
Broom Clo. Brom —72Nc 150
Broom Clo. Esh —78Da 141
Broom Clo. Tedd —66Ma 123
Broomcroft Av. N'holt —41Y 77
Broomcroft Clo. Wok —88F 156
Broomcroft Dri. Wok —87F 156
Broome Clo. H'ley —98Sa 177
Broome Ct. Tad —91Ab 178
Broome Pl. S Ock —46Td 90
Broome Rd. Hamp —66Ba 121
Broome Way. SE5 —52Tb 105
Broomfield. E17 —31Bc 65
Broomfield. Stai —65J 119
Broomfield. Sun —67W 120
Broomfield Av. N13 —22Pb 42
Broomfield Av. Lou —16Pc 28
Broomfield Clo. Romf —24Fd 48
Broomfield Ct. SE16 —48Wb 83 (off John Roll Way)
Broomfield Ct. Wey —79R 140
Broomfield Ho. Stan —20Ja 20 (off Stanmore Hill)
Broomfield La. N13 —21Nb 42
Broomfield Pl. W13 —46Ka 78
Broomfield Ride. Oxs —84Fa 160
Broomfield Rise. Abb L —4T 4
Broomfield Rd. N13 —22Nb 42
Broomfield Rd. W13 —46Ka 78
Broomfield Rd. Beck —69Bc 128
Broomfield Rd. Bexh —57Cd 110
Broomfield Rd. New Haw —83K 157
Broomfield Rd. Rich —53Pa 101
Broomfield Rd. Romf —31Zc 67
Broomfield Rd. Sev —94Hd 186
Broomfield Rd. Surb —74Pa 143
Broomfield Rd. Swans —57Ae 113
Broomfield Rd. Tedd —65La 122
Broomfields. Esh —78Ea 142
Broomfields. Hart —71Ae 155
Broomfield St. E14 —43Cc 84
Broom Gdns. Croy —76Cc 148
Broom Gro. Wat —10W 4
Broomgrove Gdns. Edgw —25Qa 39
Broomgrove Rd. SW9 —54Pb 104
Broom Hall. Oxs —86Fa 160
Broomhall End. Wok —88A 156
Broomhall La. Wok —88A 156
Broomhall Rd. SW18 —57Cb 103
Broomhall Rd. S Croy —81Tb 165
Broomhall Rd. Wok —88A 156
Broom Hill. Stoke P —8L 53
Broomhill Ct. Wfd G —23Jc 45
Broom Hill Rise. Bexh —57Cd 110
Broomhill Rd. Dart —58Kd 111
Broomhill Rd. Ilf —33Wc 67
Broomhill Rd. Orp —73Wc 151
Broomhill Rd. Wfd G —23Jc 45 (in two parts)
Broomhills. S'fleet —63Ae 135
Broomhill Wlk. Wfd G —24Hc 45
Broom Ho. Langl —49B 74
Broomhouse La. SW6 —54Cb 103
Broomhouse Rd. SW6 —54Cb 103
Broomlands La. Oxt —98Mc 183
Broomloan La. Sutt —75Cb 145
Broom Lock. Tedd —65La 122
Broom Mead. Bexh —57Cd 110
Broom Pk. Tedd —66Ma 123
Broom Rd. Croy —76Cc 148
Broom Rd. Tedd —64Ka 122
Broomsleigh Bus. Pk. SE26 —64Bc 128 (off Worsley Bri. Rd.)
Broomsleigh St. NW6 —36Bb 61
Broomstick Hall Rd. Wal A —5Gc 13
Broom Water. Tedd —65La 122
Broom Water W. Tedd —64La 122
Broom Way. Wey —77U 140
Broomwood Gdns. Pil H —16Wd 32
Broomwood Rd. SW11 —58Hb 103
Broomwood Rd. Orp —68Xc 131
Broseley Gdns. Romf —21Nd 49
Broseley Gro. SE26 —64Ac 128
Broseley Rd. Romf —21Nd 49
Broster Gdns. SE25 —69Vb 127
Brougham Ct. Dart —58Rd 111 (off Hardwick Cres.)
Brougham Rd. E8 —39Wb 63
Brougham Rd. W3 —44Sa 79
Brougham St. SW11 —54Hb 103
Brough Clo. SW8 —52Nb 104
Broughinge Rd. Borwd —12Ra 21
Brough St. SW8 —52Nb 104
Broughton Av. N3 —27Ab 40
Broughton Av. Rich —62Ka 122
Broughton Ct. W13 —45Ka 78
Broughton Dri. SW9 —56Rb 105
Broughton Gdns. N6 —30Lb 42
Broughton Rd. SW6 —54Db 103
Broughton Rd. W13 —45Ka 78
Broughton Rd. Orp —75Tc 150
Broughton Rd. Otf —88Jd 170
Broughton Rd. T Hth —72Qb 146
Broughton St. SW8 —54Jb 104
Brouncker Rd. W3 —47Sa 79
Brow Clo. Orp —73Zc 151
Brow Cres. Orp —74Yc 151
Browells La. Felt —61X 121
Brown Bear Ct. Felt —63Z 121
Brown Clo. Wall —80Nb 146
Browne Clo. Romf —22Dd 48
Brownfield St. E14 —44Dc 84
Browngraves Rd. Hay —52S 98
Brown Hart Gdns. W1 —45Jb 82 (4J 197)
Brownhill Rd. SE6 —59Dc 106
Browning Av. W7 —44Ha 78
Browning Av. Sutt —77Gb 145
Browning Av. Wor Pk —74Xa 144
Browning Clo. W9 —42Eb 81 (6A 190)
Browning Clo. Col R —24Bd 47
Browning Clo. Hamp —63Ba 121
Browning Clo. Well —53Uc 108
Browning M. W1 —43Kb 82 (1J 197)
Browning Rd. E11 —31Hc 65
Browning Rd. E12 —36Pc 66
Browning Rd. Dart —56Pd 111
Browning Rd. Enf —9Tb 11
Browning Rd. Fet —97Fa 176
Browning St. SE17 —50Sb 83 (7E 206)

Browning Wlk.—Burnley Clo.

Browning Wlk. Til —4E 114
Browning Way. Houn —53Z 99
Brownlea Gdns. Ilf —33Wc 67
Brownlow Ct. N2 —29Fb 41
Brownlow Ct. N11 —23Nb 42
(off Brownlow Rd.)
Brownlow Ho. SE16 —47Wb 83
(off George Row)
Brownlow M. WC1 —42Pb 82 (6J 193)
Brownlow Rd. E7 —35Jc 65
Brownlow Rd. E8 —39Wb 63
Brownlow Rd. N3 —24Db 41
Brownlow Rd. N11 —23Nb 42
Brownlow Rd. NW10 —38Ua 60
Brownlow Rd. W13 —46Ja 78
Brownlow Rd. Borwd —14Qa 21
Brownlow Rd. Croy —77Ub 147
Brownlow St. WC1 —43Pb 82 (1J 199)
Brownrigg Rd. Ashf —63Q 120
Brown Rd. Grav —10G 114
Browns Arc. W1 —45Lb 82 (5C 198)
(off Regent St.)
Brown's Bldgs. EC3 —44Ub 83 (3J 201)
Browns La. NW5 —36Kb 62
Browns La. Eff —99Z 175
Brownspring Dri. SE9 —63Rc 130
Browns Rd. E17 —27Cc 44
Brown's Rd. Surb —73Pa 143
Brown St. W1 —44Hb 81 (2F 197)
Brownswell Rd. N2 —26Fb 41
Brownswood Rd. N4 —34Rb 63
Brow, The. Chal G —20A 16
Brow, The. Wat —5X 5
Broxash Rd. SW11 —58Jb 104
Broxbourne Av. E18 —28Kc 45
Broxbourne Rd. E7 —34Jc 65
Broxbourne Rd. Orp —74Vc 151
Broxburn Dri. S Ock —45Wd 90
Broxburn Pde. S Ock —45Xd 90
Broxhill Rd. Hav —20Gd 30
Broxholme Ho. SW6 —53Db 103
(off Harwood Rd.)
Broxholm Rd. SE27 —62Qb 126
Brox La. Ott —80E 138
Brox Rd. Ott —79E 138
Broxted M. Brtwd —16Ee 33
Broxted Rd. SE6 —61Bc 128
Broxwood Way. NW8 —39Gb 61 (1E 190)
Bruce Av. Horn —33Ld 69
Bruce Av. Shep —72S 140
Bruce Castle Ct. N17 —25Vb 43
(off Lordship La.)
Bruce Castle Rd. N17 —25Vb 43
Bruce Clo. W10 —43Za 80
Bruce Clo. Byfl —85N 157
Bruce Clo. Slou —6E 72
Bruce Clo. Well —53Xc 109
Bruce Ct. Sidc —63Vc 131
Bruce Dri. S Croy —81Zb 166
Bruce Gdns. N20 —20Hb 23
Bruce Gro. N17 —25Ub 43
Bruce Gro. Orp —74Wc 151
Bruce Gro. Wat —10Y 5
Bruce Hall M. SW17 —63Jb 126
Bruce Rd. E3 —41Dc 64
Bruce Rd. NW10 —38Ta 59
Bruce Rd. SE25 —70Tb 127
Bruce Rd. Barn —13Ab 22
Bruce Rd. Harr —26Ga 38
Bruce Rd. Mitc —66Jb 126
Bruces Wharf Rd. Grays —51Ce 113
Bruce Wlk. Wind —4B 94
Bruce Way. Wal X —5Zb 12
Brudenell. Wind —5D 94
Brudenell Rd. SW17 —62Hb 125
Bruffs Meadow. N'holt —37Aa 57
Bruges Pl. NW1 —38Lb 62
Brumana Clo. Wey —79R 140
Brumfield Rd. Eps —78Sa 143
Brummel Clo. Bexh —55Ed 110
Brumwill Rd. W5 —40Na 59
Brunel Clo. SE19 —65Vb 127
Brunel Clo. Houn —52X 99
Brunel Clo. N'holt —41Ba 77
Brunel Clo. Til —5D 114
Brunel Est. W2 —43Cb 81
Brunel Pl. S'hall —45Da 77
Brunel Rd. SE16 —47Yb 84
Brunel Rd. W3 —43Ua 80
Brunel Rd. Wfd G —22Pc 46
Brunel St. E16 —44Hc 85
Brunel Wlk. N15 —28Ub 43
Brunel Wlk. Twic —59Ca 99
Brunel Way. Slou —6K 73
Bruner Rd. W5 —42Ma 79
Brune St. E1 —43Vb 83 (1K 201)
Brunner Clo. NW11 —29Db 41
Brunner Ct. Ott —78E 138
Brunner Ho. SE6 —63Ec 128
Brunner Rd. E17 —29Ac 44
Bruno Pl. NW9 —33Sa 59
Brunswick Av. N11 —20Jb 24
(in two parts)
Brunswick Av. Upm —31Ud 70
Brunswick Cen. WC1 —42Nb 82 (5F 193)
Brunswick Clo. Bexh —56Zc 109
Brunswick Clo. Pinn —30Aa 37
Brunswick Clo. Th Dit —74Ha 142
Brunswick Clo. Twic —62Fa 122
Brunswick Clo. W on T —75Y 141
Brunswick Clo. Est. EC1 —41Rb 83 (4B 194)
(off Wyclif St.)
Brunswick Ct. SE1 —47Ub 83 (2J 207)
Brunswick Ct. Barn —15Fb 23
Brunswick Ct. Sutt —77Db 145
Brunswick Ct. Upm —31Ud 70
Brunswick Cres. N11 —20Jb 24
Brunswick Gdns. W5 —42Na 79
Brunswick Gdns. W8 —46Cb 81
Brunswick Gdns. Ilf —24Sc 46
Brunswick Gro. N11 —20Jb 24
Brunswick Gro. Cob —85Y 159
Brunswick Ho. N3 —25Bb 41
Brunswick Ind. Pk. N11 —21Kb 42
Brunswick M. SW16 —65Mb 126
Brunswick M. W1 —44Hb 81 (2G 197)
Brunswick Pk. SE5 —53Ub 105
Brunswick Pk. Gdns. N11 —19Jb 24
Brunswick Pk. Rd. N11 —19Jb 24
Brunswick Pl. N1 —41Tb 83 (4G 195)
Brunswick Pl. SE19 —66Wb 127
Brunswick Quay. SE16 —48Zb 84
Brunswick Rd. E10 —32Ec 64
Brunswick Rd. E14 —44Ec 84
Brunswick Rd. N15 —28Ub 43
(in two parts)
Brunswick Rd. W5 —42Ma 79
Brunswick Rd. Bexh —56Zc 109
Brunswick Rd. King T —67Qa 123
Brunswick Rd. Sutt —77Db 145
Brunswick Sq. N17 —23Vb 43
Brunswick Sq. WC1 —42Nb 82 (5G 193)
Brunswick St. E17 —29Ec 44
Brunswick Vs. SE5 —53Ub 105
Brunswick Wlk. Grav —9F 114
Brunswick Way. N11 —21Kb 42
Brunton Pl. E14 —44Ac 84
Brushfield St. E1 —43Ub 83 (1J 201)
Brushwood Dri. Chor —14E 16
Brussels Rd. SW11 —56Fb 103
Bruton Clo. Chst —66Pc 130
Bruton La. W1 —45Kb 82 (5A 198)
Bruton Pl. W1 —45Kb 82 (5A 198)
Bruton Rd. Mord —70Eb 125
Bruton St. W1 —45Kb 82 (5A 198)
Bruton Way. W13 —43Ja 78
Bryan Av. NW10 —38Xa 60
Bryan Clo. Sun —66W 120
Bryan Ho. SE16 —48Bc 84
Bryan Rd. SE16 —47Bc 84
Bryanston Av. Twic —60Da 99
Bryanstone Clo. S'hall —49Ba 77
Bryanstone Ct. Sutt —77Eb 145
Bryanstone Rd. N8 —30Mb 42
Bryanstone Rd. Wal X —6Bc 12
Bryanston M. E. W1 —43Hb 81 (1F 197)
Bryanston M. W. W1 —43Hb 81 (1F 197)
Bryanston Pl. W1 —43Hb 81 (1F 197)
Bryanston Rd. Til —4E 114
Bryanston Sq. W1 —44Hb 81 (1F 197)
Bryanston St. W1 —44Hb 81 (3F 197)
Bryant Av. Romf —25Md 49
Bryant Av. Slou —3H 73
Bryant Clo. Barn —15Bb 23
Bryant Ct. E2 —40Vb 63 (1K 195)
(off Whiston Rd.)
Bryant Rd. N'holt —41Y 77
Bryant St. E15 —38Fc 65
Bryantwood Rd. N7 —36Qb 62
Brycedale Cres. N14 —21Mb 42
Bryce Rd. Dag —35Yc 67
Bryden Clo. SE26 —64Ac 128
Brydges Pl. WC2 —45Nb 82 (5F 199)
Brydges Rd. E15 —36Fc 65
Brydon Wlk. N1 —39Nb 62
Bryer Ct. EC2 —43Sb 83 (7D 194)
(off Barbican)
Bryer Pl. Wind —5B 94
Bryet Rd. N7 —34Nb 62
Brymay Clo. E3 —40Cc 64
Brynford Clo. Wok —87A 156
Brynmaer Rd. SW11 —53Hb 103
Brynmawr Rd. Enf —14Vb 25
Bryony Clo. Uxb —43P 75
Bryony Rd. W12 —45Wa 80
Bryony Way. Sun —65W 120
Bubblestone Rd. Otf —88Kd 171
Buccleuch Rd. Dat —2L 95
Buccleugh Ho. E5 —31Wb 63
Buchanan Clo. Borwd —12Sa 21
Buchanan Clo. S Ock —46Sd 90
Buchanan Gdns. NW10 —40Xa 60
Buchan Clo. Uxb —41L 75
Buchan Rd. SE15 —55Yb 106
Bucharest Rd. SW18 —59Eb 103
Buckbean Path. Romf —24Ld 49
Buckden Clo. N2 —28Hb 41
Buckden Clo. SE12 —58Hc 107
Buckettsland La. Borwd —10Ta 7
Buckfast Rd. Mord —70Db 125
Buckfast St. E2 —41Wb 83
Buckham Thorns Rd. W'ham —98Sc 184
Buck Hill Wlk. W2 —45Fb 81 (5C 196)
Buckhold Rd. SW18 —58Cb 103
Buckhurst Av. Cars —74Gb 145
Buckhurst Av. Sev —97Ld 187
Buckhurst Ho. N7 —36Mb 62
Buckhurst La. Asc —9D 116
Buckhurst La. Sev —97Ld 187
Buckhurst Rd. Asc —8D 116
Buckhurst Rd. W'ham —93Qc 184
Buckhurst St. E1 —42Xb 83
Buckhurst Way. Buck H —21Mc 45
Buckingham Arc. WC2 —45Nb 82 (5G 199)
(off Strand)
Buckingham Av. N20 —17Eb 23
Buckingham Av. Felt —58X 99
Buckingham Av. Gnfd —39Ja 58
Buckingham Av. Slou —4C 72
Buckingham Av. T Hth —67Qb 126
Buckingham Av. Well —56Uc 108
Buckingham Av. W Mol —68Da 121
Buckingham Av. E. Slou —4G 72
Buckingham Clo. Enf —12Ub 25
Buckingham Clo. Gnfd —43La 78
Buckingham Clo. Hamp —64Ba 121
Buckingham Clo. Horn —30Md 49
Buckingham Clo. Orp —73Uc 150
Buckingham Ct. NW4 —27Wa 40
Buckingham Ct. N'holt —40Aa 57
Buckingham Ct. Sutt —81Cb 163
Buckingham Dri. Chst —64Sc 130
Buckingham Gdns. Edgw —24Pa 39
Buckingham Gdns. Slou —7K 73
Buckingham Gdns. T Hth —68Qb 126
Buckingham Gdns. W Mol —68Da 121
Buckingham Ga. SW1 —48Lb 82 (3B 204)
Buckingham Gro. Borwd —14Ta 21
Buckingham Gro. Uxb —40Q 56
Buckingham Hill Rd. Stanf —3J 93
Buckingham La. SE23 —59Ac 106
Buckingham Mans. NW6 —36Db 61
(off W. End La.)
Buckingham M. NW10 —40Va 60
Buckingham M. SW1 —48Lb 82 (3B 204)
(off Stafford Pl.)
Buckingham Pal. Rd. SW1 —49Kb 82 (6K 203)
Buckingham Pde. Stan —22La 38
Buckingham Pl. SW1 —48Lb 82 (3B 204)
Buckingham Rd. E10 —34Dc 64
Buckingham Rd. E11 —29Lc 45
Buckingham Rd. E15 —36Hc 65
Buckingham Rd. E18 —25Hc 45
Buckingham Rd. N1 —37Ub 63
Buckingham Rd. N22 —25Nb 42
Buckingham Rd. NW10 —40Va 60
Buckingham Rd. Borwd —14Ta 21
Buckingham Rd. Edgw —24Pa 39
Buckingham Rd. Grav —59Fe 113
Buckingham Rd. Hamp —63Ba 121
Buckingham Rd. Harr —29Fa 38
Buckingham Rd. Ilf —33Tc 66
Buckingham Rd. King T —70Pa 123
Buckingham Rd. Mitc —71Nb 146
Buckingham Rd. Rich —61Ma 123
Buckingham Rd. Wat —9Y 5
Buckingham St. WC2 —46Nb 82 (5G 199)
Buckingham Way. Wall —81Lb 164
Buckinham Hill Rd. Stanf —5H 93
Buckland Av. Slou —9M 73
Buckland Ct. N1 —40Ub 63 (1H 195)
(off St Johns Est.)
Buckland Ct. Ick —33S 56
Buckland Cres. NW3 —38Fb 61
Buckland Cres. Wind —3D 94
Buckland La. Tad —100Wa 178
Buckland Rise. Pinn —25Y 37
Buckland Rd. E10 —33Ec 64
Buckland Rd. Chess —78Pa 143
Buckland Rd. Orp —77Uc 150
Buckland Rd. Sutt —82Ya 162
Buckland Rd. Tad —100Bb 179
Bucklands Rd. Tedd —65La 122
Bucklands, The. Rick —17J 17
Buckland St. N1 —40Tb 63 (2G 195)
Buckland's Wharf. King T —68Ma 123
Buckland Wlk. W3 —47Sa 79
Buckland Wlk. Mord —70Eb 125
Buckland Way. Wor Pk —74Ya 144
Buck La. NW9 —29Ta 39
Buckleigh Av. SW20 —69Ab 124
Buckleigh Rd. SW16 —65Mb 126
Buckleigh Way. SE19 —66Vb 127
Buckler Gdns. SE9 —62Pc 130
Bucklers All. SW6 —51Bb 103
Bucklersbury. EC4 —44Tb 83 (3F 201)
(in two parts)
Bucklers Ct. War —22Yd 50
Buckler's Way. Cars —76Hb 145
Buckles Ct. Belv —49Zc 87
Buckles La. S Ock —43Yd 90
Buckle St. E1 —44Vb 83
Buckles Way. Bans —88Ab 162
Buckley Clo. Dart —54Hd 110
Buckley Rd. NW6 —38Bb 61
Buckley St. SE1 —46Qb 82 (7K 199)
(off Mepham St.)
Buckmaster Ho. N7 —35Pb 62
Buckmaster Rd. SW11 —56Gb 103
Bucknalls Clo. Wat —4Aa 5
Bucknalls Dri. Brick —3Ba 5
Bucknalls La. Wat —4Z 5
Bucknall St. WC2 —44Nb 82 (2E 198)
Bucknell Clo. SW2 —56Pb 104
Buckner Rd. SW2 —56Pb 104
Buckner St. W10 —41Ab 80
Bucknills Clo. Eps —86Sa 161
Buckrell Rd. E4 —19Fc 27
Buck's Av. Wat —17Aa 19
Bucks Clo. W Byf —86K 157
Bucks Cross Rd. Grav —2B 136
Bucks Cross Rd. Orp —78Ad 151
Bucks Hill. K Lan —5L 3
Buckstone Clo. SE23 —58Yb 106
Buckstone Rd. N18 —22Wb 43
Buck St. NW1 —38Kb 62
Buckters Rents. SE16 —46Ac 84
Buckthorne Rd. SE4 —57Ac 106
Buckton Rd. Borwd —10Pa 7
Buck Wlk. E17 —28Fc 45
Buckwheat Ct. Eri —48Zc 87
Budd Clo. N12 —21Db 41
Buddings Circ. Wemb —34Sa 59
Budd's All. Twic —57La 100
Budebury Rd. Stai —64J 119
Budge Row. EC4 —45Tb 83 (4F 201)
Budge's Wlk. W2 —46Eb 81 (7A 196)
(off North Wlk.)
Budgin's Hill. Prat B —84Yc 169
Budleigh Cres. Well —53Yc 109
Budoch Ct. Ilf —33Wc 67
Budoch Dri. Ilf —33Wc 67
Buer Rd. SW6 —54Ab 102
Buff Av. Bans —86Db 163
Bug Hill. Wold —92Zb 182
Bugsby's Way. SE10 & SE7 —49Hc 85
Bulganak Rd. T Hth —70Sb 127
Bulinga St. SW1 —49Nb 82 (6F 205)
Bulkeley Av. Wind —5F 94
Bulkeley Clo. Egh —4N 117
Bullace La. Dart —58Nd 111
Bullace Row. SE5 —53Tb 105
Bull All. SE1 —45Qb 82 (5A 200)
Bull All. Well —55Xc 109
Bullard's Pl. E2 —41Zb 84
Bullbanks Rd. Belv —49Ed 88
Bullbeggars La. Wok —4E 188
Bull Clo. Grays —47Be 91
Bulleid Way. SW1 —49Kb 82 (6A 204)
Bullen St. SW11 —54Gb 103
Buller Clo. SE15 —52Wb 105
Buller Rd. N17 —26Wb 43
Buller Rd. N22 —26Qb 42
Buller Rd. NW10 —41Za 80
Buller Rd. Bark —38Uc 66
Buller Rd. T Hth —68Tb 127
Bullers Clo. Sidc —64Ad 131
Bullers Wood Dri. Chst —66Pc 130
Bullescroft Rd. Edgw —20Qa 21
Bullfinch Clo. Sev —94Fd 186
Bullfinch Dene. Sev —94Fd 186
Bullfinch La. Sev —94Fd 186
Bullfinch Rd. S Croy —82Zb 166
Bullhead Rd. Borwd —13Sa 21
Bull Hill. Lea —93Ja 176
Bullingham Mans. W8 —47Cb 81
Bull Inn Ct. WC2 —45Nb 82 (5G 199)
(off Strand)
Bullivant St. E14 —44Ec 84
Bull La. N18 —22Ub 43
Bull La. Chst —66Tc 130
Bull La. Dag —34Dd 68
Bull La. Ger X —27A 34
Bull Rd. E15 —40Hc 65
Bullrush Gro. Uxb —42L 75
Bull's All. SW14 —54Ta 101
Bull's Bri. Ind. Est. S'hall —49X 77
Bullsbridge Rd. S'hall —49Y 77
Bullsbrook Rd. Hay —46Y 77
Bull's Cross. Enf —7Wb 11
Bulls Cross Ride. Wal X —7Wb 11
Bulls Gdns. SW3 —49Gb 81 (5E 202)
Bulls Head Pas. EC3 —44Ub 83 (3H 201)
(off Gracechurch St.)
Bullsland Gdns. Chor —16D 16
Bullsland La. Ger X & Chor —18D 16
Bullsmoor Clo. Wal X —7Yb 12
Bullsmoor Gdns. Wal X —7Xb 11
Bullsmoor La. Enf —7Wb 11
Bullsmoor Ride. Wal X —7Yb 12
Bullsmoor Way. Wal X —7Yb 12
Bullwell Cres. Chesh —1Ac 12
Bull Yd. SE15 —53Wb 105
Bulmer Gdns. Harr —31Ma 59
Bulmer M. W11 —45Cb 81
Bulmer Pl. W11 —46Cb 81
Bulmer Wlk. Rain —40Ld 69
Bulow Est. SW6 —53Db 103
(off Pearscroft Rd.)
Bulstrode Ct. Ger X —30A 34
Bulstrode Av. Houn —54Ba 99
Bulstrode Gdns. Houn —55Ca 99
Bulstrode La. Chfd —1G 2
Bulstrode Pl. W1 —43Jb 82 (1J 197)
Bulstrode Rd. Houn —55Ca 99
Bulstrode St. W1 —44Jb 82 (2J 197)
Bulstrode Way. Ger X —29A 34
Bulwer Ct. E11 —32Fc 65
Bulwer Ct. Rd. E11 —32Fc 65
Bulwer Gdns. Barn —14Eb 23
Bulwer Rd. E11 —31Fc 65
Bulwer Rd. N18 —21Ub 43
Bulwer Rd. Barn —14Db 23
Bulwer St. W12 —46Ya 80
Bunbury Way. Eps —88Xa 162
Bunby Rd. Stoke P —8K 53
Bunce's Clo. Eton W —10F 72
Bunce's La. Wfd G —24Hc 45
Bundy's Way. Stai —65H 119
Bungalow Rd. SE25 —70Ub 127
Bungalow Rd. Ock —96S 174
Bungalows, The. E10 —30Ec 44
Bungalows, The. SW16 —66Kb 126
Bungalows, The. Ilf —25Uc 46
Bunhill Row. EC1 —42Tb 83 (5F 195)
Bunhouse Pl. SW1 —50Jb 82 (7J 203)
Bunkers Hill. NW11 —31Eb 61
Bunkers Hill. Belv —49Cd 88
Bunker's Hill. Hods —79De 155
Bunkers Hill. Sidc —62Bd 131
Bunning Way. N7 —38Nb 62
Bunns La. NW7 —23Ua 40
(in two parts)
Bunsen St. E3 —40Ac 64
Bunten Meade. Slou —6F 72
Buntingbridge Rd. Ilf —29Tc 46
Bunting Clo. N9 —18Zb 26
Bunting Clo. Mitc —71Hb 145
Bunting Ct. NW9 —26Ua 40
Bunton St. SE18 —48Qc 86
Bunyan Ct. EC2 —43Sb 83 (7D 194)
(off Barbican)
Bunyan Rd. E17 —27Ac 44
Bunyan's La. Knap —2A 188
Bunyard Dri. Wok —86E 156
Buonaparte M. SW1 —50Mb 82 (7D 204)
Burbage Clo. SE1 —48Tb 83 (4F 207)
Burbage Clo. Chesh —3Bc 12
Burbage Ho. N1 —39Tb 63
(off Poole St.)
Burbage Rd. SE24 & SE21 —58Sb 105
Burberry Clo. N Mald —68Ua 124
Burbidge Rd. Shep —70Q 120
Burbridge Way. N17 —26Wb 43
Burcham St. E14 —44Dc 84
Burcharbro Rd. SE2 —51Zc 109
Burchell Ct. Bush —17Ea 20
Burchell Ho. SE11 —50Pb 82 (7J 205)
(off Jonathan St.)
Burchell Rd. E10 —32Dc 64
Burchell Rd. SE15 —53Xb 105
Burchetts Way. Shep —72R 140
Burchett Way. Romf —30Bd 47
Burch Rd. Grav —8B 114
Burchwall Clo. Romf —24Ed 48
Burcote. Wey —79T 140
Burcote Rd. SW18 —59Fb 103
Burcott Gdns. Add —79L 139
Burcott Rd. Purl —86Qb 164
Burden Clo. Bren —50La 78
Burdenshott Av. Rich —56Ra 101
Burden Way. E11 —33Kc 65
Burder Clo. N1 —37Ub 63
Burder Rd. N1 —37Ub 63
Burdet M. W2 —44Db 81
Burdett Av. SW20 —67Wa 124
Burdett Av. Shorne —3N 137
Burdett Clo. W7 —46Ha 78
(off Silverdale Clo.)
Burdett Clo. Sidc —64Ad 131
Burdett M. NW3 —37Fb 61
Burdett M. W2 —44Db 81
Burdett Rd. E3 & E14 —42Ac 84
Burdett Rd. Croy —72Tb 147
Burdett Rd. Rich —54Pa 101
Burdetts Rd. Dag —39Bd 67
Burdett St. SE1 —48Qb 82 (3K 205)
Burdock Clo. Croy —74Zb 148
Burdock Rd. N17 —27Wb 43
Burdon La. Sutt —80Ab 144
Bure. E Til —8L 93
Bure Ct. New Bar —15Db 23
Burfield Clo. SW17 —63Fb 125
Burfield Dri. Warl —91Yb 182
Burfield Rd. Chor —15D 16
Burfield Rd. Old Win —8L 95
Burford Clo. Dag —34Yc 67
Burford Clo. Ilf —28Sc 46
Burford Clo. Uxb —35N 55
Burford Gdns. N13 —20Pb 24
Burford Gdns. Slou —3A 72
Burford Ho. Bren —50Na 79
Burford Ho. Eps —83Ya 162
Burford La. Eps —83Ya 162
Burford Rd. E6 —41Nc 86
Burford Rd. E15 —39Fc 65
Burford Rd. SE6 —61Bc 128
Burford Rd. Bren —50Na 79
Burford Rd. Brom —70Nc 130
Burford Rd. Sutt —75Cb 145
Burford Rd. Wor Pk —73Va 144
Burford Wlk. SW6 —52Eb 103
Burford Way. New Ad —79Ec 148
Burgate Clo. Dart —55Hd 110
Burge Rd. E7 —35Mc 65
Burges Clo. Horn —30Pd 49
Burges Rd. E6 —38Nc 66
Burgess Av. NW9 —30Ta 39
Burgess Av. Stanf —2N 93
Burgess Clo. Felt —63Aa 121
Burgess Ct. E6 —38Qc 66
Burgess Ct. Brtwd —18Zd 33
Burgess Hill. NW2 —35Cb 61
Burgess Ind. Pk. SE5 —52Tb 105
Burgess Pk. Ind. Est. SE5 —52Tb 105
Burgess Rd. E15 —35Gc 65
Burgess Rd. Sutt —77Db 145
Burgess St. E14 —43Cc 84
Burge St. SE1 —48Tb 83 (4G 207)
Burges Way. Stai —65J 119
Burgett Rd. Slou —8F 72
Burgh Croft. Eps —87Va 162
Burghfield. Eps —87Va 162
Burghfield Rd. Grav —6B 136
Burgh Heath Rd. Eps —86Va 162
Burghill Rd. SE26 —63Ac 128
Burghley Av. Borwd —15Sa 21
Burghley Av. N Mald —67Ta 123
Burghley Pl. Mitc —71Hb 145
Burghley Rd. E11 —32Gc 65
Burghley Rd. N8 —27Qb 42
Burghley Rd. NW5 —35Kb 62
Burghley Rd. SW19 —63Za 124
Burghley Rd. Chaf H —48Yd 90
Burgh Mt. Bans —87Bb 163
Burgh St. N1 —40Rb 63 (1C 194)
Burgh Wood. Bans —87Ab 162
Burgon St. EC4 —44Rb 83 (3C 200)
Burgos Gro. SE10 —53Dc 106
Burgoyne Rd. N4 —30Rb 43
Burgoyne Rd. SE25 —70Vb 127
Burgoyne Rd. SW9 —55Pb 104
Burgoyne Rd. Sun —65V 120
Burham Clo. SE20 —66Yb 128
Burhill Gro. Pinn —26Aa 37
Burhill Rd. W on T —81X 159
Burke Clo. SW15 —56Ua 102
Burke Lodge. E13 —41Kc 85
Burke St. E16 —43Hc 85
Burland Rd. SW11 —57Hb 103
Burland Rd. Brtwd —18Zd 33
Burland Rd. Romf —23Ed 48
Burlea Clo. W on T —78X 141
Burleigh Av. Sidc —57Vc 109
Burleigh Av. Wall —76Jb 146
Burleigh Clo. Add —78K 139
Burleigh Gdns. N14 —18Lb 24
Burleigh Gdns. Ashf —64S 120
Burleigh Pde. N14 —18Mb 24
Burleigh Pk. Cob —84Aa 159
Burleigh Pl. SW15 —57Za 102
Burleigh Rd. Add —78K 139
Burleigh Rd. Chesh —4Ac 12
Burleigh Rd. Enf —14Ub 25
Burleigh Rd. Sutt —74Ab 144
Burleigh Rd. Uxb —39R 56
Burleigh St. WC2 —45Pb 82 (4H 199)
Burleigh Wlk. SE6 —60Ec 106
Burleigh Way. Cuff —2Nb 10
Burleigh Way. Enf —13Tb 25
Burley Clo. E4 —22Cc 44
Burley Clo. SW16 —68Mb 126
Burley Orchard. Cher —72J 139
Burley Rd. E16 —44Lc 85
Burlings La. Knock —89Vc 169
Burlington Arc. W1 —45Lb 82 (5B 198)
Burlington Av. Rich —53Qa 101
Burlington Av. Romf —30Dd 48
Burlington Av. Slou —7J 73
Burlington Clo. E6 —44Nc 86
Burlington Clo. W9 —42Bb 81
Burlington Clo. Felt —59T 98
Burlington Clo. Orp —75Rc 150
Burlington Clo. Slou —7J 73
Burlington Gdns. W1 —45Lb 82 (5A 198)
Burlington Gdns. W3 —46Sa 79
Burlington Gdns. W4 —50Sa 79
Burlington Gdns. Romf —31Ad 67
Burlington La. W4 —52Sa 101
Burlington M. W3 —46Sa 79
Burlington Pl. SW6 —54Ab 102
Burlington Pl. Wfd G —20Kc 27
Burlington Rise. Barn —17Gb 23
Burlington Rd. N10 —27Jb 42
Burlington Rd. N17 —25Wb 43
Burlington Rd. SW6 —54Ab 102
Burlington Rd. W4 —50Sa 79
Burlington Rd. Burn —2A 72
Burlington Rd. Enf —11Tb 25
Burlington Rd. Iswth —53Fa 100
Burlington Rd. N Mald —70Va 124
Burlington Rd. Slou —7J 73
Burlington Rd. T Hth —68Sb 127
Burma M. N16 —35Tb 63
Burman Clo. Dart —59Sd 112
Burma Rd. N16 —35Tb 63
Burmarsh Ct. SE20 —67Yb 128
Burma Ter. SE19 —64Ub 127
Burmester Rd. SW17 —62Eb 125
Burnaby Cres. W4 —51Sa 101
Burnaby Gdns. W4 —51Ra 101
Burnaby Rd. Grav —9A 114
Burnaby St. SW10 —52Eb 103
Burnage Ct. SE26 —63Xb 127
Burnard Pl. N7 —36Pb 62
Burnaston Ho. E5 —34Wb 63
Burnbrae Clo. N12 —23Db 41
Burnbury Rd. SW12 —60Lb 104
Burn Clo. Add —77M 139
Burn Clo. Bush —13Fa 20
Burncroft Av. Enf —12Yb 26
Burne Jones Ho. W14 —49Ab 80
(off N. End Rd.)
Burnell Av. Rich —64La 122
Burnell Av. Well —54Wc 109
Burnell Gdns. Stan —26Ma 39
Burnell Rd. Sutt —77Db 145
Burnell Wlk. SE1 —50Vb 83 (7K 207)
(off Abingdon Clo.)
Burnell Wlk. Gt War —23Yd 50
Burnels Av. E6 —41Qc 86
Burness Clo. N7 —37Pb 62
Burness Clo. Uxb —40M 55
Burne St. NW1 —43Gb 81 (7D 190)
Burnet Gro. Eps —85Sa 161
Burnett Clo. E9 —36Yb 64
Burnett Rd. Eri —51Md 111
Burnetts Rd. Wind —3C 94
Burney Av. Surb —71Pa 143
Burney Clo. Fet —97Ea 176
Burney Dri. Lou —12Rc 28
(in two parts)
Burney St. SE10 —52Ec 106
Burnfoot Av. SW6 —53Ab 102
Burnham Av. Uxb —35S 56
Burnham Clo. SE1 —50Vb 83 (7K 207)
Burnham Clo. Enf —10Ub 11
Burnham Clo. Knap —6A 188
Burnham Clo. W'stone —28Ja 38
Burnham Clo. Wind —4B 94
Burnham Cres. E11 —28Lc 45
Burnham Cres. Dart —56Ld 111
Burnham Dri. Wor Pk —75Za 144
Burnham Gdns. Croy —73Vb 147
Burnham Gdns. Hay —48T 76
Burnham Gdns. Houn —53X 99
Burnham La. Slou —3B 72
Burnham Rd. E4 —22Bc 44
Burnham Rd. Dag —38Xc 67
Burnham Rd. Dart —56Ld 111
Burnham Rd. Knap —6A 188
Burnham Rd. Mord —70Db 125
Burnham Rd. Romf —27Fd 48
Burnham Rd. Sidc —61Ad 131
Burnhams Rd. Bookh —96Aa 175
Burnham St. E2 —41Yb 84
Burnham St. King T —67Qa 123
Burnham Ter. Dart —57Md 111
Burnham Trading Est. Dart —56Md 111
Burnham Way. SE26 —64Bc 128
Burnham Way. W13 —49Ka 78
Burnhill Rd. Beck —68Cc 128
Burnings La. Knock —89Vc 169
Burnley Clo. Wat —22Y 37

Burnley Rd.—Cambria Clo.

Burnley Rd. NW10 —36Va **60**
Burnley Rd. SW9 —54Pb **104**
Burnley Rd. Grays —52Vd **112**
Burnsall St. SW3 —50Gb **81** (7E **202**)
Burns Av. Chad —31Yc **67**
Burns Av. Felt —58W **98**
Burns Av. Sidc —58Xc **109**
Burns Av. S'hall —45Ca **77**
Burnsbury Ho. SW4 —58Mb **104**
Burns Clo. SW19 —65Fb **125**
Burns Clo. Eri —53Hd **110**
Burns Clo. Hay —43V **76**
Burns Clo. Oxs —87Fa **160**
Burns Clo. Well —53Vc **109**
Burns Dri. Bans —86Ab **162**
Burns Ho. SE17 —50Rb ***83***
(off Doddington Gro.)
Burn Side. N9 —20Yb **26**
Burnside. Asht —90Pa **161**
Burnside Clo. SE16 —46Zb **84**
Burnside Clo. Barn —13Cb **23**
Burnside Clo. Twic —58Ja **100**
Burnside Cres. Wemb —39Ma **59**
Burnside Rd. Dag —33Yc **67**
Burns Pl. Til —3D **114**
Burns Rd. NW10 —39Va **60**
Burns Rd. SW11 —54Hb **103**
Burns Rd. W13 —47Ka **78**
Burns Rd. Wemb —40Na **59**
Burns Way. Houn —54Z **99**
Burns Way. Hut —17Fe **33**
Burnt Ash Hill. SE12 —58Hc **107**
(in two parts)
Burnt Ash La. Brom —66Jc **129**
Burnt Ash Rd. SE12 —57Hc **107**
Burntcommon Clo. Rip —97H **173**
Burntcommon La. Rip —97J **173**
Burntfarm Ride. Enf & Wal X —6Rb **11**
Burnt Ho. La. Dart —63Nd **133**
(in two parts)
Burnthwaite Rd. SW6 —52Bb **103**
Burnt Oak B'way. Edgw —24Ra **39**
Burnt Oak Fields. Edgw —25Sa **39**
Burnt Oak La. Sidc —58Wc **109**
Burntwood. Brtwd —20Yd **32**
Burntwood Av. Horn —30Md **49**
Burntwood Clo. SW18 —60Gb **103**
Burntwood Clo. Cat —93Wb **181**
Burntwood Clo. W Horn —30Fe **51**
Burntwood Grange Rd. SW18 —60Fb **103**
Burntwood Gro. Sev —99Kd **187**
Burntwood La. SW17 —62Eb **125**
Burntwood La. Cat —94Ub **181**
Burntwood Rd. Sev —100Kd **187**
Burntwood View. SE19 —64Vb **127**
Burn Wlk. Burn —1A **72**
Burnway. Horn —31Nd **69**
Buross St. E1 —44Xb **83**
Burrage Gro. SE18 —49Sc **86**
Burrage Pl. SE18 —50Rc **86**
Burrage Rd. SE18 —50Sc **86**
Burrard Rd. E16 —44Kc **85**
Burrard Rd. NW6 —36Cb **61**
Burr Bank Ter. Wilm —63Ld **133**
Burr Clo. E1 —46Wb **83**
Burr Clo. Bexh —55Bd **109**
Burrel Clo. Edgw —19Ra **21**
Burrell Clo. Croy —72Ac **148**
Burrell Row. Beck —68Cc **128**
Burrell St. SE1 —46Rb **83** (6B **200**)
Burrell's Wharf Sq. E14 —50Dc **84**
Burrfield Dri. Orp —71Zc **151**
Burritt Rd. King T —66Qa **123**
Burroughs Gdns. NW4 —28Xa **40**
Burroughs Pde. NW4 —28Xa **40**
Burroughs, The. NW4 —28Xa **40**
Burroway Rd. Slou —48D **74**
Burrow Clo. Chig —22Vc **47**
Burrow Grn. Chig —22Vc **47**
Burrow Ho. SW9 —54Pb ***104***
(off Stockwell Pk. Rd.)
Burrow Rd. Chig —22Vc **47**
Burrows Clo. Bookh —96Ba **175**
Burrows Hill Clo. Houn —55L **97**
Burrows Hill La. Houn —56K **97**
Burrows M. SE1 —47Rb **83** (1B **206**)
Burrows Rd. NW10 —41Ya **80**
Burrow Wlk. SE21 —59Sb **105**
Burr Rd. SW18 —60Cb **103**
Bursar St. SE1 —46Ub ***83*** *(7H* ***201****)*
(off Tooley St.)
Bursdon Clo. Sidc —61Vc **131**
Burses Way. Hut —17De **33**
Bursland Rd. Enf —14Zb **26**
Burslem Av. Ilf —23Wc **47**
Burslem St. E1 —44Wb **83**
Burstead Clo. Cob —84Z **159**
Burstock Rd. SW15 —56Ab **102**
Burston Dri. Park —1Ea **6**
Burston Rd. SW15 —57Za **102**
Burstow Rd. SW20 —67Ab **124**
Burtenshaw Rd. Th Dit —73Ja **142**
Burtley Clo. N4 —32Sb **63**
Burton Av. Wat —14W **18**
Burton Clo. Chess —80Ma **143**
Burton Ct. Beck —68Yb **128**
Burton Gdns. Houn —53Ba **99**
Burton Gro. SE17 —50Tb **83** (7F **207**)
Burtonhole Clo. NW7 —21Za **40**
Burtonhole La. NW7 —22Ya **40**
Burton La. SW9 —54Qb **104**
(in two parts)
Burton La. Chesh —1Ub **11**
Burton M. SW1 —49Jb **82** (6J **203**)
Burton Pl. WC1 —42Mb **82** (5E **192**)
Burton Rd. E18 —27Kc **45**
Burton Rd. NW6 —38Bb **61**
Burton Rd. SW9 —54Qb **104**
(in two parts)
Burton Rd. King T —66Na **123**
Burton Rd. Lou —14Sc **28**
Burtons Ct. E15 —38Fc **65**
Burton's La. Chal G & Chor —13A **16**
Burton's Rd. Hamp —63Da **121**
Burton St. WC1 —41Mb **82** (4E **192**)
Burton Way. Wind —5C **94**
Burtonwood Ho. N4 —31Tb **63**
Burt Rd. E16 —46Lc **85**
Burtwell La. SE27 —63Tb **127**
Burvale Ct. Wat —13X **19**
Burwash Ct. St M —71Yc **151**
Burwash Rd. SE18 —50Tc **86**
Burway Cres. Cher —70J **119**
Burwell Av. Gnfd —37Ga **58**
Burwell Clo. E1 —44Xb **83**
Burwell Rd. E10 —32Ac **64**
Burwell Wlk. E3 —42Cc **84**
Burwood Av. Brom —75Kc **149**
Burwood Av. Kenl —86Rb **165**
Burwood Av. Pinn —29X **37**
Burwood Clo. Surb —74Qa **143**
Burwood Clo. W on T —79Y **141**
Burwood Gdns. Rain —41Hd **88**
Burwood Pk. Rd. W on T —77X **141**
Burwood Pl. W2 —44Gb **81** (2E **196**)
Burwood Rd. W on T —80U **140**
Bury Av. Hay —40U **56**
Bury Av. Ruis —30S **36**
Bury Clo. SE16 —46Zb **84**
Bury Clo. Wok —4G **188**
Bury Ct. EC3 —44Ub **83** (2J **201**)
Bury Grn. Rd. Chesh —4Wb **11**
(in two parts)
Bury Gro. Mord —71Db **145**
Bury Hall Vs. N9 —18Vb **25**
Bury La. Epp —1Tc **14**
Bury La. Rick —18M **17**
Bury La. Wok —4F **188**
Bury Meadows. Rick —18M **17**
Bury Pl. WC1 —43Nb **82** (1F **199**)
Bury Rd. E4 —14Fc **27**
Bury Rd. N22 —26Qb **42**
Bury Rd. Dag —36Dd **68**
Bury Rd. Epp —3Uc **14**
Bury St. EC3 —44Ub **83** (3J **201**)
Bury St. N9 —17Vb **25**
Bury St. SW1 —46Lb **82** (6C **198**)
Bury St. Ruis —29S **36**
Bury St. W. N9 —17Tb **25**
Bury Wlk. SW3 —49Gb **81** (6D **202**)
Busby M. NW5 —37Mb **62**
Busby Pl. NW5 —37Mb **62**
Busby St. E2 —42Vb **83**
Bushbarns. Chesh —1Wb **11**
Bushberry Rd. E9 —37Ac **64**
Bush Clo. Add —78L **139**
Bush Clo. Ilf —29Tc **46**
Bush Cotts. SW18 —57Cb **103**
Bush Ct. N14 —18Mb **24**
Bush Ct. W12 —47Za ***80***
(off Shepherd's Bush Grn.)
Bushell Clo. SW2 —61Pb **126**
Bushell Grn. Bush —19Fa **20**
Bushell St. E1 —46Wb **83**
Bushell Way. Chst —64Qc **130**
Bush Elms Rd. Horn —31Jd **68**
Bushetts Gro. Red —100Kb **180**
Bushey Av. E18 —27Hc **45**
Bushey Av. Orp —73Tc **150**
Bushey Clo. E4 —20Ec **26**
Bushey Clo. Kenl —88Vb **165**
Bushey Clo. Uxb —33Q **56**
Bushey Ct. SW20 —68Xa **124**
Bushey Down. SW12 —61Kb **126**
Bushey Gro. Rd. Bush —14Z **19**
Bushey Hall Dri. Bush —14Aa **19**
Bushey Hall Rd. Bush —14Z **19**
Bushey Hill Rd. SE5 —53Ub **105**
Bushey La. Sutt —77Cb **145**
Bushey Mill Cres. Wat —9Y **5**
Bushey Mill La. Wat —9Y **5**
Bushey Rd. E13 —40Lc **65**
Bushey Rd. N15 —30Ub **43**
Bushey Rd. SW20 —69Xa **124**
Bushey Rd. Croy —75Cc **148**
Bushey Rd. Sutt —77Cb **145**
Bushey Rd. Uxb —33Q **56**
Bushey Shaw. Asht —89La **160**
Bushey View Wlk. Wat —12Z **19**
Bushey Way. Beck —72Fc **149**
Bush Fair Ct. N14 —16Kb **24**
Bushfield Clo. Edgw —19Ra **21**
Bushfield Cres. Edgw —19Ra **21**
Bushfields. Lou —15Qc **28**
Bushfield Wlk. Swans —58Ae **113**
Bush Gro. NW9 —31Sa **59**
Bush Gro. Stan —24Ma **39**
Bushgrove Rd. Dag —35Zc **67**
Bush Hill. N21 —17Sb **25**
Bush Hill Rd. N21 —16Tb **25**
Bush Hill Rd. Harr —30Pa **39**
Bush Ind. Est. NW10 —42Ta **79**
Bush La. EC4 —45Tb **83** (4F **201**)
Bush La. Send —96F **172**
Bushmead Clo. N15 —28Vb **43**
Bushmoor Cres. SE18 —52Rc **108**
Bushnell Rd. SW17 —61Kb **126**
Bushrise. Wat —8X **5**
Bush Rd. E8 —39Xb **63**
Bush Rd. E11 —31Hc **65**
Bush Rd. SE8 —49Zb **84**
Bush Rd. Buck H —21Mc **45**
Bush Rd. Rich —51Pa **101**
Bush Rd. Shep —71P **139**
Bushway. Dag —35Zc **67**
Bushwood. E11 —31Hc **65**
Bushwood Dri. SE1 —49Vb **83** (6K **207**)
Bushwood Rd. Rich —51Qa **101**
Bushy Ct. King T —67La ***122***
(off Up. Teddington Rd.)
Bushy Lees. Sidc —58Vc **109**
Bushy Pk. Gdns. Tedd —64Fa **122**
Bushy Pk. Rd. Tedd —66Ka **122**
(in two parts)
Bushy Rd. Fet —94Da **175**
Bushy Rd. Hay —49U **76**
Bushy Rd. Tedd —65Ha **122**
Business Cen., The. Romf —24Md **49**
Business Village, The. Slou —6M **73**
Butcher Row. E14 & E1 —45Zb **84**
Butchers Hill. Shorne —4N **137**
Butcher's La. New Ash —75Zd **155**
Butchers Rd. E16 —44Jc **85**
Butcher Wlk. Swans —59Ae **113**
Bute Av. Rich —61Na **123**
Bute Ct. Wall —78Lb **146**
Bute Gdns. W6 —49Za **80**
Bute Gdns. Wall —78Lb **146**
Bute Gdns. W. Wall —78Lb **146**
Bute Rd. Croy —74Qb **146**
Bute Rd. Ilf —29Rc **46**
Bute Rd. Wall —77Lb **146**
Bute St. SW7 —49Fb **81** (5B **202**)
Bute Wlk. N1 —37Tb **63**
Butler Av. Harr —31Fa **58**
Butler Ct. Wemb —35Ja **58**
Butler Pl. SW1 —48Mb ***82*** *(3D* ***204****)*
(off Palmer St.)
Butler Rd. NW10 —38Ua **60**
Butler Rd. Dag —35Xc **67**
Butler Rd. Harr —31Ea **58**
Butlers Clo. Wind —3B **94**
Butlers Dene Rd. Wold —92Bc **182**
Butlers Dri. E4 —10Ec **12**
Butler's Pl. Ash —76Ae **155**
Butler St. E2 —41Yb **84**
Butler St. Uxb —42R **76**
Butlers Wharf. SE1 —47Vb ***83*** *(1K* ***207****)*
(off Shad Thames)
Butler Wlk. Grays —49Fe **91**
Buttercross La. Epp —2Wc **15**
Buttercup Sq. Stai —60M **97**
Butterfield Clo. SE16 —47Xb **83**
Butterfield Clo. Twic —58Ha **100**
Butterfields. E17 —29Ec **44**
Butterfield Sq. E6 —44Pc **86**
Butterfly La. SE9 —58Rc **108**
Butterfly La. Els —13Ga **20**
Butterfly Wlk. SE5 —54Tb **105**
Butterfly Wlk. Warl —92Yb **182**
Butter Hill. Wall —76Jb **146**
Butteridges Clo. Dag —39Bd **67**
Buttermere Av. Slou —3A **72**
Buttermere Clo. SE1 —49Vb **83** (6K **207**)
Buttermere Clo. Felt —60V **98**
Buttermere Clo. Mord —72Za **144**
Buttermere Dri. SW15 —57Ab **102**
Buttermere Gdns. Purl —85Tb **165**
Buttermere Pl. Wat —5W **4**
Buttermere Rd. Orp —70Zc **131**
Buttermere Wlk. E8 —37Vb **63**
Buttermere Way. Egh —66D **118**
Butterwick. W6 —49Ya **80**
Butterwick. Wat —8Aa **5**
Butterworth Gdns. Wfd G —22Jc **45**
Buttesland St. N1 —41Tb **83** (3G **195**)
Buttfield Clo. Dag —37Dd **68**
Buttlehide. Rick —22F **34**
Buttmarsh Clo. SE18 —50Rc **86**
Button St. Swan —68Ld **133**
Buttsbury Rd. Ilf —36Sc **66**
(in two parts)
Butts Cotts. Felt —62Aa **121**
Butts Cres. Felt —62Ba **121**
Butts Grn. Rd. Horn —30Md **49**
Butts La. L War —26Be **51**
Butts La. Stanf —2K **93**
Buttsmead. N'wd —24S **36**
Butts Rd. Brom —64Gc **129**
Butts Rd. Stanf —2L **93**
Butts Rd. Wok —89A **156**
Butts, The. Bren —51Ma **101**
Butts, The. Otf —89Kd **171**
Butts, The. Sun —69Y **121**
Buxted Clo. E8 —38Vb **63**
Buxted Rd. N12 —22Gb **41**
Buxton Av. Cat —93Ub **181**
Buxton Clo. Wfd G —23Mc **45**
Buxton Ct. N1 —41Sb ***83*** *(3E* ***194****)*
(off Thoresby St.)
Buxton Cres. Sutt —77Ab **144**
Buxton Dri. E11 —28Gc **45**
Buxton Dri. N Mald —68Ta **123**
Buxton Gdns. W3 —45Ra **79**
Buxton Ho. E11 —28Gc **45**
Buxton La. Cat —92Ub **181**
Buxton Path. Wat —20Y **19**
Buxton Rd. E4 —17Fc **27**
Buxton Rd. E6 —41Nc **86**
Buxton Rd. E15 —36Gc **65**
Buxton Rd. E17 —28Ac **44**
Buxton Rd. N19 —32Mb **62**
Buxton Rd. NW2 —37Xa **60**
Buxton Rd. SW14 —55Ua **102**
Buxton Rd. Ashf —64M **119**
Buxton Rd. Eri —52Fd **110**
Buxton Rd. Grays —7A **92**
Buxton Rd. Ilf —30Uc **46**
Buxton Rd. They B —8Uc **14**
Buxton Rd. T Hth —71Rb **147**
Buxton Rd. Wal A —4Jc **13**
Buxton St. E1 —42Vb **83**
Buzzard Creek Ind. Est. Bark —43Wc **87**
Byam St. SW6 —54Eb **103**
Byards Croft. SW16 —67Mb **126**
Byatt Wlk. Hamp —65Aa **121**
Bybend Clo. Farn R —9F **52**
Bychurch End. Tedd —64Ha **122**
Bycliffe Ter. Grav —9B **114**
Bycroft Rd. S'hall —42Ca **77**
Bycroft St. SE20 —66Zb **128**
Bycullah Av. Enf —13Rb **25**
Bycullah Rd. Enf —12Rb **25**
Byegrove Rd. SW19 —65Fb **125**
Byelands Clo. SE16 —46Zb **84**
Byers Clo. Pot B —6Eb **9**
Bye, The. W3 —44Ua **80**
Byeways. Twic —62Da **121**
Byeways, The. Surb —71Qa **143**
Byeway, The. SW14 —55Sa **101**
Bye Way, The. Harr —25Ha **38**
Byeway, The. Rick —19N **17**
Byfeld Gdns. SW13 —53Wa **102**
Byfield Ct. W Horn —30Ee **51**
Byfield Pas. Iswth —55Ja **100**
Byfield Rd. Iswth —55Ja **100**
Byfleet Ind. Est. Byfl —83M **157**
Byfleet Rd. Byfl & Cob —84Q **158**
Byfleet Rd. New Haw —80M **139**
Byford Clo. E15 —38Gc **65**
Byford Ho. Barn —14Za **22**
Bygrove. New Ad —79Cc **148**
Bygrove St. E14 —44Dc **84**
Byland Clo. N21 —17Pb **24**
Bylands. Wok —90C **156**
Bylands Clo. SE2 —48Xc **87**
Byne Rd. SE26 —65Yb **128**
Byne Rd. Cars —75Gb **145**
Bynes Rd. S Croy —80Tb **147**
Byng Dri. Pot B —3Cb **9**
Byng Pl. WC1 —42Mb **82** (6E **192**)
Byng Rd. Barn —12Za **22**
Byng St. E14 —47Cc **84**
Bynon Av. Bexh —55Bd **109**
By-Pass Rd. Horn H —1J **93**
Byrd Way. Stanf —1L **93**
Byre Rd. N14 —16Kb **24**
Byre Rd., The. N14 —16Kb **24**
Byrne Rd. SW12 —60Kb **104**
Byron Av. E12 —37Nc **66**
Byron Av. E18 —27Hc **45**
Byron Av. NW9 —28Ra **39**
Byron Av. Borwd —15Qa **21**
Byron Av. Coul —87Nb **164**
Byron Av. Houn —54W **98**
Byron Av. N Mald —71Wa **144**
Byron Av. Sutt —77Fb **145**
Byron Av. Wat —11Z **19**
Byron Av. E. Sutt —77Fb **145**
Byron Clo. E8 —39Wb **63**
Byron Clo. SE20 —69Xb **127**
Byron Clo. SE26 —64Ac **128**
Byron Clo. SE28 —46Yc **87**
Byron Clo. Hamp —63Ba **121**
Byron Clo. Knap —5B **188**
Byron Clo. W on T —74Aa **141**
Byron Ct. Chesh —1Xb **11**
Byron Ct. Harr —30Ha **38**
Byron Dri. N2 —30Fb **41**
Byron Gdns. Sutt —77Fb **145**
Byron Gdns. Til —3E **114**
Byron Hill Rd. Harr —32Fa **58**
Byron Ho. Dart —57Gd **110**
Byron Ho. Langl —50D **74**
Byron Mans. Upm —34Sd **70**
Byron Pl. Lea —94Ka **176**
Byron Rd. E10 —32Dc **64**
Byron Rd. E17 —27Cc **44**
Byron Rd. NW2 —33Xa **60**
Byron Rd. NW7 —22Wa **40**
Byron Rd. W5 —46Pa **79**
Byron Rd. Add —77N **139**
Byron Rd. Dart —56Rd **111**
Byron Rd. Harr —30Ga **38**
Byron Rd. Hut —17Fe **33**
Byron Rd. S Croy —82Xb **165**
Byron Rd. W'stone —26Ha **38**
Byron Rd. Wemb —33La **58**
Byrons Ct. Wind —5E **94**
Byron St. E14 —44Ec **84**
Byron Ter. N9 —16Yb **26**
Byron Way. Hay —41V **76**
Byron Way. N'holt —41Aa **77**
Byron Way. Romf —25Ld **49**
Byron Way. W Dray —49P **75**
Bysouth Clo. Ilf —25Rc **46**
By the Wood. Wat —19Z **19**
Bythorn St. SW9 —55Pb **104**
Byton Rd. SW17 —65Hb **125**
Bytom Hill. Mick —98La **176**
Byward Av. Felt —58Y **99**
Byward St. EC3 —45Ub **83** (5J **201**)
Bywater Pl. SE16 —46Ac **84**
Bywater St. SW3 —50Hb **81** (7F **203**)
Byway. E11 —29Lc **45**
Byways, The. Asht —90Ma **161**
Byway, The. Eps —77Va **144**
Byway, The. Pot B —5Cb **9**
Byway, The. Sutt —81Fb **163**
Bywell Pl. W1 —43Lb ***82*** *(1B* ***198****)*
(off Wells St.)
Bywood Av. Croy —72Yb **148**
Bywood Clo. Kenl —87Rb **165**
By-Wood End. Ger X —22B **34**
Byworth Wlk. N19 —32Nb **62**

Cabbell Pl. Add —77L **139**
Cabbell St. NW1 —43Gb **81** (1D **196**)
Cabborns Cres. Stanf —3M **93**
Cabinet Way. E4 —22Bc **44**
Cable Pl. SE10 —53Ec **106**
Cable St. E1 —45Wb **83**
Cabot Sq. E14 —46Cc **84**
Cabot Way. E6 —39Mc **65**
Cabrera Av. Vir W —71A **138**
Cabul Rd. SW11 —54Gb **103**
Cacket's La. Cud —87Tc **168**
Cacketts Cotts. Bras —98Yc **185**
Cactus Wlk. W12 —44Va **80**
Cadbury Clo. Iswth —53Ja **100**
Cadbury Clo. Sun —66U **120**
Cadbury Rd. Sun —66U **120**
Cadbury Way. SE16 —49Vb **83** (5K **207**)
Caddington Clo. Barn —15Gb **23**
Caddington Rd. NW2 —34Ab **60**
Caddis Clo. Stan —24Ha **38**
Caddy Clo. Egh —65C **118**
Cade La. Sev —100Ld **187**
Cadell Clo. E2 —40Vb **63**
Cade Rd. SE10 —53Fc **107**
Cader Rd. SW18 —58Eb **103**
Cadet Dri. SE1 —50Vb **83**
Cadet Pl. SE10 —50Gc **85**
Cadiz Rd. Dag —38Ed **68**
Cadiz St. SE17 —50Sb **83** (7E **206**)
Cadley Ter. SE23 —61Yb **128**
Cadlocks Hill. Hals —82Bd **169**
Cadman Ct. W4 —50Ra ***79***
(off Chaseley Dri.)
Cadmer Clo. N Mald —70Ua **124**
Cadmore Ct. Chesh —1Zb **12**
Cadmore La. Chesh —1Zb **12**
Cadmus Clo. SW4 —55Mb **104**
Cadogan Av. Dart —59Td **112**
Cadogan Av. W Horn —30Fe **51**
Cadogan Clo. Beck —67Fc **129**
Cadogan Clo. Harr —35Da **57**
Cadogan Clo. Tedd —64Ga **122**
Cadogan Ct. Sutt —79Db **145**
Cadogan Gdns. E18 —27Kc **45**
Cadogan Gdns. N3 —25Db **41**
Cadogan Gdns. N21 —15Qb **24**
Cadogan Gdns. SW3 —49Hb **81** (5G **203**)
Cadogan Ga. E9 —38Bc **64**
Cadogan Ga. SW1 —49Hb **81** (5G **203**)
Cadogan La. SW1 —48Jb **82** (4H **203**)
Cadogan Pl. SW1 —48Hb **81** (3G **203**)
Cadogan Rd. Surb —71Ma **143**
Cadogan Sq. SW1 —48Hb **81** (4F **203**)
Cadogan St. SW3 —49Hb **81** (6F **203**)
Cadogan Ter. E9 —37Bc **64**
Cadoxton Av. N15 —30Vb **43**
Cadwallon Rd. SE9 —61Rc **130**
Caedmon Rd. N7 —35Pb **62**
Caenshill Rd. Wey —80Q **140**
Caenswood Hill. Wey —82Q **158**
Caenwood Clo. Wey —79Q **140**
Caen Wood Rd. Asht —90La **160**
Caerleon Clo. Sidc —64Yc **131**
Caerlon Ter. SE2 —49Xc **87**
Caernarvon Clo. Horn —32Qd **69**
Caernarvon Clo. Mitc —69Nb **126**
Caernarvon Dri. Ilf —25Qc **46**
Caesars Wlk. Mitc —71Hb **145**
Caesars Way. Shep —72T **140**
Cage Pond Rd. Shenl —5Pa **7**
Cages Wood Dri. Farn C —5F **52**
Cahill St. EC1 —42Sb **83** (6F **195**)
Cahir St. E14 —49Dc **84**
Caillard Rd. Byfl —83N **157**
Cain's La. Felt —57U **98**
Caird St. W10 —41Ab **80**
Cairn Av. W5 —46Ma **79**
Cairn Ct. Eps —82Va **162**
Cairndale Clo. Brom —66Hc **129**
Cairnfield Av. NW2 —34Ua **60**
Cairngorm Clo. Tedd —64Ja **122**
Cairngorm Pl. Slou —2H **73**
Cairns Av. Wfd G —23Nc **46**
Cairns Clo. Dart —57Md **111**
Cairns Rd. SW11 —57Gb **103**
Cairn Way. Stan —23Ha **38**
Cairo New Rd. Croy —75Rb **147**
Cairo Rd. E17 —28Cc **44**
Caishowe Rd. Borwd —11Ra **21**
Caister Ho. N7 —37Pb **62**
Caistor M. SW12 —59Kb **104**
Caistor Pk. Rd. E15 —39Hc **65**
Caistor Rd. SW12 —59Kb **104**
Caithness Gdns. Sidc —58Vc **109**
Caithness Ho. N1 —39Pb ***62***
(off Bemerton Est.)
Caithness Rd. W14 —48Za **80**
Caithness Rd. Mitc —66Kb **126**
Calabria Rd. N5 —37Rb **63**
Calais Cotts. Fawk —75Wd **154**
Calais Ga. SE5 —53Rb **105**
Calais St. SE5 —53Rb **105**
Calbourne Av. Horn —36Kd **69**
Calbourne Rd. SW12 —59Hb **103**
Calbroke Rd. Slou —2D **72**
Calbrooke Rd. Slou —1D **72**
Calcott Clo. Brtwd —18Xd **32**
Calcott Wlk. SE9 —63Nc **130**
Calcutta Rd. Til —4B **114**
Caldbeck. Wal A —6Fc **13**
Caldbeck Av. Wor Pk —75Xa **144**
Caldecote Gdns. Bush —17Ga **20**
Caldecote La. Bush —16Ha **20**
Caldecote Towers. Bush —17Ga **20**
Caldecot Rd. SE5 —54Sb **105**
Caldecott Way. E5 —34Zb **64**
Calder. E Til —9L **93**
Calder Av. Gnfd —40Ha **58**
Calder Clo. Enf —13Ub **25**
Calder Ct. Langl —50B **74**
Calder Gdns. Edgw —27Qa **39**
Calderon Pl. W10 —43Ya **80**
Calderon Rd. E11 —35Ec **64**
Calder Rd. Mord —71Eb **145**
Caldervale Rd. SW4 —57Mb **104**
Calder Way. Coln —55G **96**
Calderwood St. SE18 —49Qc **86**
Caldew St. SE5 —52Tb **105**
Caldicot Grn. NW9 —30Ua **40**
Caldwell Rd. Stanf —2K **93**
Caldwell Rd. Wat —21Z **37**
Caldwell St. SW9 —52Pb **104**
Caldy Rd. Belv —48Dd **88**
Caldy Wlk. N1 —37Sb **63**
Caleb St. SE1 —47Sb **83** (1D **206**)
Caledonian Clo. Ilf —32Xc **67**
Caledonian Ct. Wat —12X **19**
Caledonian Rd. N1 & N7 —40Nb **62** (2G **193**)
Caledonian Wharf. E14 —49Fc **85**
Caledonia Rd. Stai —60N **97**
Caledonia St. N1 —40Nb **62** (2G **193**)
Caledon Rd. E6 —39Pc **66**
Caledon Rd. Wall —77Jb **146**
Cale St. SW3 —50Gb **81** (7D **202**)
Caletock Way. SE10 —50Hc **85**
Calfstock La. F'ham —70Pd **133**
Caliban Tower. N1 —40Ub ***63*** *(2H* ***195****)*
(off Purcell St.)
Calico Row. SW11 —55Eb **103**
Calidore Clo. SW2 —58Pb **104**
California Ct. Bush —18Fa ***20***
(off High Rd.)
California La. Bush —18Fa **20**
California Rd. N Mald —69Sa **123**
Caling Croft. New Ash —74Be **155**
Caliph Clo. Grav —2H **137**
Callaghan Clo. SE13 —56Gc **107**
Callanby Ter. N1 —37Tb **63**
Callander Rd. SE6 —61Dc **128**
Callanders, The. Bush —18Ga **20**
Callan Gro. S Ock —45Xd **90**
Callard Av. N13 —21Rb **43**
Callcott Rd. NW6 —38Bb **61**
Callcott St. W8 —46Cb **81**
Callendar Rd. SW7 —48Fb **81** (3B **202**)
Callenders Cotts. Belv —47Fd **88**
Calley Down Cres. New Ad —82Fc **167**
Callingham Clo. E14 —43Bc **84**
Callis Farm Clo. Stai —58N **97**
Callis Rd. E17 —30Bc **44**
Callonfield. E17 —28Ac **44**
Callow Field. Purl —85Qb **164**
Callow Hill. Vir W —9N **117**
Callowland Clo. Wat —10X **5**
Callow St. SW3 —51Fb **103**
Calluna Ct. Wok —90B **156**
Calmington Rd. SE5 —51Ub **105**
Calmont Rd. Brom —65Fc **129**
Calmore Clo. Horn —36Ld **69**
Calne Av. Ilf —25Rc **46**
Calonne Rd. SW19 —63Za **124**
Calshot Av. Chaf H —47Be **91**
Calshot Ct. Dart —58Rd ***111***
(off Osborne Rd.)
Calshot Rd. Houn —54Q **98**
Calshot St. N1 —40Pb **62** (1H **193**)
Calshot Way. Enf —13Rb **25**
Calstock Ho. SE11 —50Qb ***82*** *(7A* ***206****)*
(off Kennings Way)
Calthorpe Gdns. Edgw —22Na **39**
Calthorpe Gdns. Sutt —76Eb **145**
Calthorpe St. WC1 —42Pb **82** (5J **193**)
Calton Av. SE21 —58Ub **105**
Calton Rd. Barn —16Eb **23**
Calvary Gdns. SW15 —57Bb **103**
Calverley Clo. Beck —65Dc **128**
Calverley Cres. Dag —33Cd **68**
Calverley Gdns. Harr —31Ma **59**
Calverley Gro. N19 —32Mb **62**
Calverley Rd. Eps —79Wa **144**
Calvert Av. E2 —41Vb **83** (4J **195**)
Calvert Clo. Belv —49Cd **88**
Calvert Clo. Sidc —65Ad **131**
Calverton. SE17 —51Ub ***105***
(off Albany Rd.)
Calverton Rd. E6 —39Qc **66**
Calvert Rd. SE10 —50Hc **85**
Calvert Rd. Barn —12Za **22**
Calvert Rd. Eff —100X **175**
Calvert's Bldgs. SE1 —46Tb ***83*** *(7F* ***201****)*
(off Southwark St.)
Calvert St. NW1 —39Jb **62**
Calvin Clo. Orp —69Zc **131**
Calvin St. E1 —42Vb **83** (6K **195**)
Calydon Rd. SE7 —50Kc **85**
Calypso Way. SE16 —48Bc **84**
Camac Rd. Twic —60Fa **100**
Cambalt Rd. SW15 —57Za **102**
Camber Ho. SE15 —51Yb **106**
Camberley Av. SW20 —68Xa **124**
Camberley Av. Enf —14Ub **25**
Camberley Clo. Sutt —76Za **144**
Camberley Rd. Houn —55Q **98**
Cambert Way. SE3 —56Kc **107**
Camberwell Chu. St. SE5 —53Tb **105**
Camberwell Glebe. SE5 —53Ub **105**
Camberwell Grn. SE5 —53Tb **105**
Camberwell Gro. SE5 —53Tb **105**
Camberwell New Rd. SE5 —51Qb **104**
Camberwell Pl. SE5 —53Sb **105**
Camberwell Rd. SE17 & SE5 —51Sb **105**
Camberwell Sta. Rd. SE5 —53Sb **105**
Camberwell Trading Est. SE5 —53Sb **105**
Cambeys Rd. Dag —36Dd **68**
Camborne Av. W13 —47Ka **78**
Camborne Av. Romf —24Nd **49**
Camborne M. W11 —44Ab **80**
Camborne Rd. SW18 —59Cb **103**
Camborne Rd. Croy —73Wb **147**
Camborne Rd. Mord —71Za **144**
Camborne Rd. Sidc —62Yc **131**
Camborne Rd. Sutt —80Cb **145**
Camborne Rd. Well —54Vc **109**
Camborne Way. Houn —53Ca **99**
Camborne Way. Romf —24Nd **49**
Cambourne Av. N9 —17Zb **26**
Cambourne Rd. Houn —55Q **98**
Cambourne Wlk. Rich —58Ma **101**
Cambrai Ct. N13 —20Nb **24**
Cambray Rd. SW12 —60Lb **104**
Cambray Rd. Orp —73Vc **151**
Cambria Clo. Houn —56Ca **99**
Cambria Clo. Sidc —60Tc **108**

Cambria Ct.—Carlton Ho. Ter.

Cambria Ct. Felt —59X 99
Cambria Ct. Slou —7N 73
Cambria Ct. Stai —63G 118
Cambria Cres. Grav —3G 136
Cambria Gdns. Stai —59N 97
Cambria Ho. Eri —52Gd 110
(off Larner Rd.)
Cambrian Av. Ilf —29Uc 46
Cambrian Grn. NW9 —29Ua 40
(off Snowden Dri.)
Cambrian Gro. Grav —9C 114
Cambrian Rd. E10 —31Cc 64
Cambrian Rd. Rich —58Pa 101
Cambria Rd. SE5 —55Sb 105
Cambria St. SW6 —52Db 103
Cambridge Av. NW6 —40Cb 61
Cambridge Av. Burn —10A 52
Cambridge Av. Gnfd —36Ha 58
Cambridge Av. N Mald —69Ua 124
(in two parts)
Cambridge Av. Romf —27Ld 49
Cambridge Av. Slou —4E 72
Cambridge Av. Well —56Vc 109
Cambridge Barracks Rd. SE18 —49Pc 86
Cambridge Cir. WC2 —44Mb 82 (3E 198)
Cambridge Clo. N22 —25Qb 42
Cambridge Clo. NW10 —34Ta 59
Cambridge Clo. SW20 —67Xa 124
Cambridge Clo. Chesh —1Yb 12
Cambridge Clo. Houn —56Aa 99
Cambridge Clo. W Dray —51M 97
Cambridge Clo. Wok —6C 188
Cambridge Cotts. Rich —51Qa 101
Cambridge Ct. N16 —31Ub 63
(off Amhurst Pk.)
Cambridge Cres. E2 —40Xb 63
Cambridge Cres. Tedd —64Ja 122
Cambridge Dri. SE12 —57Jc 107
Cambridge Dri. Pot B —3Za 8
Cambridge Dri. Ruis —33Y 57
Cambridge Gdns. N10 —25Jb 42
Cambridge Gdns. N17 —24Tb 43
Cambridge Gdns. N21 —17Tb 25
Cambridge Gdns. NW6 —40Cb 61
Cambridge Gdns. W10 —44Za 80
Cambridge Gdns. Enf —12Wb 25
Cambridge Gdns. Grays —9C 92
Cambridge Gdns. King T —68Qa 123
Cambridge Ga. NW1 —42Kb 82 (5K 191)
Cambridge Ga. M. NW1 —42Kb 82 (5A 192)
Cambridge Grn. SE9 —60Rc 108
Cambridge Gro. SE20 —67Xb 127
Cambridge Gro. W6 —49Xa 80
Cambridge Gro. Rd. King T —69Qa 123
Cambridge Heath Rd. E1 & E2 —42Xb 83
Cambridge Ho. Wind —3G 94
Cambridge Lodge Vs. E8 —39Xb 63
Cambridge Pde. Enf —11Wb 25
Cambridge Pk. E11 —31Jc 65
Cambridge Pk. Twic —58La 100
Cambridge Pk. Ct. Twic —59Ma 101
Cambridge Pk. Rd. E11 —31Hc 65
Cambridge Pl. NW6 —41Cb 81
Cambridge Pl. W8 —47Db 81
Cambridge Rd. E4 —18Fc 27
Cambridge Rd. E11 —30Hc 45
Cambridge Rd. NW6 —40Cb 61
(in two parts)
Cambridge Rd. SE20 —69Xb 127
Cambridge Rd. SW11 —53Hb 103
Cambridge Rd. SW13 —54Va 102
Cambridge Rd. SW20 —67Wa 124
Cambridge Rd. W7 —47Ha 78
Cambridge Rd. Ashf —66S 120
Cambridge Rd. Bark —38Sc 66
Cambridge Rd. Brom —66Jc 129
Cambridge Rd. Cars —79Gb 145
Cambridge Rd. Hamp —66Ba 121
Cambridge Rd. Harr —29Ca 37
Cambridge Rd. Houn —56Aa 99
Cambridge Rd. Ilf —32Uc 66
Cambridge Rd. King T —68Pa 123
Cambridge Rd. Mitc —69Lb 126
Cambridge Rd. N Mald —70Ua 124
Cambridge Rd. Rich —52Qa 101
Cambridge Rd. Sidc —63Uc 130
Cambridge Rd. S'hall —46Ba 77
Cambridge Rd. Tedd —63Ha 122
Cambridge Rd. Twic —58Ma 101
Cambridge Rd. Uxb —37M 55
Cambridge Rd. W on T —72X 141
Cambridge Rd. Wat —14Y 19
Cambridge Rd. W Mol —70Ba 121
Cambridge Rd. N. W4 —50Ra 79
Cambridge Rd. S. W4 —50Ra 79
Cambridge Row. SE18 —50Rc 86
Cambridge Sq. W2 —44Gb 81 (2D 196)
Cambridge St. SW1 —49Kb 82 (6A 204)
Cambridge Ter. N9 —17Vb 25
Cambridge Ter. NW1 —41Kb 82 (4K 191)
Cambridge Ter. M. NW1 —41Kb 82 (4A 192)
Cambus Clo. Hay —43Aa 77
Cambus Rd. E16 —43Jc 85
Cam Ct. SE15 —51Vb 105
(off Bibury Clo.)
Camdale Rd. SE18 —52Vc 109
Camden Av. Felt —60Y 99
Camden Av. Hay —45Z 77
Camden Clo. Chst —67Sc 130
Camden Clo. Grays —9D 92
Camden Ct. Belv —50Cd 88
Camden Est. SE15 —53Vb 105
Camden Gdns. NW1 —38Kb 62
Camden Gdns. Sutt —78Db 145
Camden Gdns. T Hth —69Rb 127
Camden Gro. Chst —65Rc 130
Camden High St. NW1 —38Kb 62
Camden Hill Rd. SE19 —65Ub 127
Camden Ho. SE8 —50Bc 84
Camdenhurst St. E14 —44Ac 84
Camden La. N7 —36Mb 62
Camden Lock Pl. NW1 —38Kb 62
Camden M. NW1 —38Lb 62
Camden Pk. Rd. NW1 —37Mb 62
Camden Pk. Rd. Chst —66Pc 130
Camden Pas. N1 —39Rb 63 (1B 194)
Camden Rd. E11 —30Kc 45
Camden Rd. E17 —30Bc 44
Camden Rd. NW1 & N7 —38Lb 62
Camden Rd. Bex —60Bd 109
Camden Rd. Cars —77Hb 145
Camden Rd. Grays —48Ae 91
Camden Rd. Sev —94Kd 187
Camden Rd. Sutt —78Db 145
Camden Row. SE3 —54Gc 107
Camden Row. Pinn —27Y 37
Camden Sq. NW1 —37Mb 62
Camden Sq. SE15 —53Vb 105
Camden St. NW1 —38Lb 62
Camden Ter. NW1 —37Mb 62
Camden Ter. Seal —93Pd 187
Camden Wlk. N1 —39Rb 63 (1B 194)
Camden Way. Chst —66Pc 130
Camden Way. T Hth —69Rb 127
Cameford Ct. SW12 —59Nb 104
Camelford Ct. W11 —44Ab 80
Camelford Ho. SE1 —50Nb 82 (7G 205)
(off Albert Embkmt.)
Camelford Wlk. W11 —44Ab 80
Camellia Clo. Romf —25Nd 49
Camellia Pl. Twic —59Da 99
Camellia St. SW8 —52Nb 104
Camelot Clo. SE28 —47Tc 86
Camelot Clo. SW19 —63Cb 125
Camelot Clo. Big H —88Lc 167
Camel Rd. E16 —46Mc 85
Camera Pl. SW10 —51Fb 103
Cameron Clo. N18 —21Xb 43
Cameron Clo. N20 —19Fb 23
Cameron Clo. Bex —62Gd 132
Cameron Clo. War —21Zd 51
Cameron Dri. Wal X —6Zb 12
Cameron Ho. SE5 —52Sb 105
Cameron Pl. E1 —44Xb 83
Cameron Rd. SE6 —61Bc 128
Cameron Rd. Brom —71Jc 149
Cameron Rd. Croy —72Rb 147
Cameron Rd. Ilf —32Uc 66
Cameron Sq. Mitc —67Gb 125
Cameron Ter. SE12 —62Kc 129
Camerton Clo. E8 —37Vb 63
Cam Grn. S Ock —44Xd 90
Camilla Clo. Bookh —97Da 175
Camilla Clo. Sun —65V 120
Camilla Rd. SE16 —49Xb 83
Camille Clo. SE25 —69Wb 127
Camlan Rd. Brom —63Hc 129
Camlet St. E2 —42Vb 83 (5K 195)
Camlet Way. Barn —12Cb 23
Camley St. NW1 —38Mb 62
Camm Av. Wind —5C 94
Camm Gdns. King T —68Pa 123
Camm Gdns. Th Dit —73Ha 142
Camomile Av. Mitc —67Hb 125
Camomile St. EC3 —44Ub 83 (2H 201)
Campana Rd. SW6 —53Cb 103
Campbell Av. Ilf —28Rc 46
Campbell Av. Wok —93B 172
Campbell Clo. SE18 —53Qc 108
Campbell Clo. SW16 —63Mb 126
Campbell Clo. Romf —23Gd 48
Campbell Clo. Ruis —30W 36
Campbell Clo. Twic —60Fa 100
Campbell Ct. N17 —25Vb 43
Campbell Ct. SE22 —60Wb 105
Campbell Croft. Edgw —22Qa 39
Campbell Ho. W12 —45Xa 80
(off White City Est.)
Campbell Rd. E3 —41Cc 84
Campbell Rd. E6 —39Nc 66
Campbell Rd. E15 —35Hc 65
Campbell Rd. E17 —28Bc 44
Campbell Rd. N17 —25Wb 43
Campbell Rd. W7 —45Ga 78
Campbell Rd. Cat —93Tb 181
Campbell Rd. Croy —73Rb 147
Campbell Rd. E Mol —69Ga 122
Campbell Rd. Grav —10B 114
Campbell Rd. Twic —61Fa 122
Campbell Rd. Wey —80Q 140
Campbell Wlk. N1 —39Nb 62 (1G 193)
(off Outram Pl.)
Campdale Rd. N7 —34Mb 62
Campden Clo. SW19 —61Ab 124
Campden Cres. Dag —35Xc 67
Campden Cres. Wemb —34Ka 58
Campden Gro. W8 —47Cb 81
Campden Hill. W8 —47Cb 81
Campden Hill Gdns. W8 —46Cb 81
Campden Hill Ga. W8 —47Cb 81
Campden Hill Pl. W11 —46Bb 81
Campden Hill Rd. W8 —46Cb 81
Campden Hill Sq. W8 —46Bb 81
Campden Ho. Clo. W8 —47Cb 81
Campden Rd. S Croy —78Ub 147
Campden Rd. Uxb —34P 55
Campden St. W8 —46Cb 81
Campe Ho. N10 —24Jb 42
Camp End Rd. Wey —84S 158
Camperdown St. E1 —44Vb 83
Campfield Rd. SE9 —59Mc 107
Camphill Ct. W Byf —84J 157
Camphill Ind. Est. W Byf —83K 157
Camphill Rd. W Byf —84J 157
Campion Clo. E6 —45Pc 86
Campion Clo. Croy —77Ub 147
Campion Clo. Den —34J 55
Campion Clo. Grav —3A 136
Campion Clo. Harr —30Pa 39
Campion Clo. Uxb —43P 75
Campion Clo. Wat —5W 4
Campion Ct. Grays —51Fe 113
Campion Ct. Wemb —40Na 59
Campion Pl. SE28 —46Wc 87
Campion Rd. SW15 —56Ya 102
Campion Rd. Isw th —53Ha 100
Campions. Lou —10Qc 14
Campions Clo. Borwd —9Ra 7
Campions, The. Borwd —10Pa 7
Campion Ter. NW2 —34Za 60
Cample La. S Ock —45Wd 90
Camplin Rd. Harr —29Na 39
Camplin St. SE14 —52Zb 106
Camp Rd. SW19 —64Xa 124
Camp Rd. Ger X —1N 53
Camp Rd. Wold —93Ac 182
Campsbourne Rd. N8 —27Nb 42
(in two parts)
Campsbourne, The. N8 —28Nb 42
Campsey Gdns. Dag —38Xc 67
Campsey Rd. Dag —38Xc 67
Campsfield Rd. N8 —27Nb 42
Campshill Pl. SE13 —57Ec 106
Campshill Rd. SE13 —57Ec 106
Campus Rd. E17 —30Bc 44
Camp View. SW19 —64Xa 124
Cam Rd. E15 —39Fc 65
Camrose Av. Edgw —26Pa 39
Camrose Av. Eri —51Dd 110
Camrose Av. Felt —63Y 121
Camrose Clo. Croy —73Ac 148
Camrose Clo. Mord —70Cb 125
Camrose St. SE2 —50Wc 87
Canada Av. N18 —23Sb 43
Canada Cres. W3 —42Sa 79
Canada Est. SE16 —48Yb 84
Canada Farm Rd. S Dar —70Wd 134
Canada Gdns. SE13 —57Ec 106
Canada Rd. W3 —43Sa 79
Canada Rd. Byfl —83M 157
Canada Rd. Cob —85Y 159
Canada Rd. Slou —7M 73
Canada Sq. E14 —46Dc 84
Canada St. SE16 —47Zb 84
Canada Way. W12 —45Xa 80
Canadian Av. SE6 —59Dc 106
Canadian Memorial Av. Asc —8K 117
Canal App. SE8 —51Ac 106
Canal Basin. Grav —8F 114
Canal Clo. E1 —42Ac 84
Canal Gro. SE15 —51Wb 105
Canal Head. SE15 —53Wb 105
Canal Ind. Est. Langl —47C 74
Canal Ind. Pk. Grav —8F 114
Canal Rd. E3 —42Ac 84
Canal Rd. Grav —8E 114
Canalside. SE28 —45Zc 87
Canal St. SE5 —51Tb 105
Canal Wlk. N1 —39Tb 63
Canal Wlk. SE26 —64Yb 128
Canal Wlk. Croy —72Vb 147
Canal Way. W10 —42Za 80
Canal Wharf. Langl —47C 74
Canberra Clo. NW4 —27Wa 40
Canberra Clo. Dag —39Fd 68
Canberra Clo. Horn —36Ld 69
Canberra Cres. Dag —38Fd 68
Canberra Dri. N'holt —41Y 77
Canberra Rd. E6 —39Pc 66
Canberra Rd. SE7 —52Lc 107
Canberra Rd. W13 —46Ja 78
Canberra Rd. Bexh —51Zc 109
Canberra Rd. Houn —55Q 98
Canberra Sq. Til —4C 114
Canbury Av. King T —67Pa 123
Canbury M. SE26 —62Wb 127
Canbury Pk. Rd. King T —67Na 123
Canbury Pas. King T —67Ma 123
Canbury Path. Orp —70Wc 131
Canbury Pl. King T —67Na 123
Cancell Rd. SW9 —53Qb 104
Candahar Rd. SW11 —54Gb 103
Cander Way. S Ock —45Xd 90
Candler St. N15 —30Tb 43
Candover Clo. W Dray —52M 97
Candover Rd. Horn —32Kd 69
Candover St. W1 —43Lb 82 (1B 198)
Candy Croft. Bookh —98Da 175
Candy St. E3 —39Bc 64
Cane Clo. Wall —80Nb 146
Cane Hill. H Wood —26Nd 49
Caneland Ct. Wal A —6Hc 13
Canewden Clo. Wok —91A 172
Caney M. NW2 —33Za 60
Canfield Dri. Ruis —36X 57
Canfield Gdns. NW6 —38Db 61
Canfield Ho. N15 —30Ub 43
(off Albert Rd.)
Canfield Pl. NW6 —37Eb 61
Canfield Rd. Rain —39Hd 68
Canfield Rd. Wfd G —24Nc 46
Canford Av. N'holt —39Ba 57
Canford Clo. Enf —12Qb 24
Canford Dri. Add —75K 139
Canford Gdns. N Mald —72Ua 144
Canford Rd. SW11 —57Jb 104
Canham Rd. SE25 —69Ub 127
Canham Rd. W3 —47Ua 80
Can Hatch. Tad —90Ab 162
Canmore Gdns. SW16 —66Lb 126
Cann Hall Rd. E11 —35Gc 65
Canning Cres. N22 —25Pb 42
Canning Cross. SE5 —54Ub 105
Canning Ho. W12 —45Xa 80
(off White City Est.)
Canning Pas. W8 —48Eb 81
Canning Pl. W8 —48Eb 81
Canning Pl. M. W8 —48Eb 81 (3A 202)
(off Canning Pl.)
Canning Rd. E15 —40Fc 65
Canning Rd. E17 —28Ac 44
Canning Rd. N5 —34Rb 63
Canning Rd. Croy —75Vb 147
Canning Rd. Harr —27Ga 38
Cannington Rd. Dag —37Yc 67
Cannizaro Rd. SW19 —65Ya 124
Cannock Ho. N4 —31Sb 63
Cannonbury Av. Pinn —30Z 37
Cannon Clo. SW20 —70Ya 124
Cannon Clo. Hamp —65Da 121
Cannon Clo. Stanf —1P 93
Cannon Dri. E14 —45Cc 84
Cannon Gro. Fet —94Ga 176
Cannon Hill. N14 —20Nb 24
Cannon Hill. NW6 —36Cb 61
Cannon Hill La. SW20 —71Za 144
Cannon Hill M. N14 —20Nb 24
Cannon La. NW3 —34Fb 61
Cannon La. Pinn —29Aa 37
Cannon Pl. NW3 —34Fb 61
Cannon Pl. SE7 —50Nc 86
Cannon Rd. N14 —20Nb 24
Cannon Rd. Bexh —53Ad 109
Cannon Rd. Wat —15Y 19
Cannonside. Fet —94Ga 176
Cannon St. EC4 —44Sb 83 (3D 200)
Cannon St. Rd. E1 —44Xb 83
Cannon Trading Est. Wemb —35Ra 59
Cannon Wlk. Grav —9E 114
Cannon Way. Fet —93Ga 176
Cannon Way. W Mol —70Ca 121
Cannon Wharf Bus. Pk. SE8 —49Ac 84
Canon Av. Romf —29Yc 47
Canon Beck Rd. SE16 —47Yb 84
Canonbie Rd. SE23 —59Yb 106
Canonbury Cres. N1 —38Sb 63
Canonbury Gro. N1 —38Sb 63
Canonbury La. N1 —38Rb 63
Canonbury Pk. N. N1 —37Sb 63
Canonbury Pk. S. N1 —37Sb 63
Canonbury Pl. N1 —37Rb 63
Canonbury Rd. N1 —37Rb 63
Canonbury Rd. Enf —11Ub 25
Canonbury Sq. N1 —38Rb 63
Canonbury St. N1 —38Sb 63
Canonbury Vs. N1 —38Rb 63
Canon Mohan Clo. N14 —16Jb 24
Canon Mohon Clo. N14 —16Kb 24
Canon Murnane Rd. SE1 —48Vb 83 (4K 207)
(off Grange Rd.)
Canon Rd. Brom —69Lc 129
Canon Row. SW1 —47Nb 82 (1F 205)
Canon's Clo. N2 —31Fb 61
Canons Clo. Edgw —23Pa 39
Canons Clo. Rad —7Ka 6
Canons Corner. Edgw —21Na 39
Canons Ct. Edgw —23Pa 39
Canons Dri. Edgw —23Na 39
Canons Hill. Coul —90Qb 164
Canons La. Tad —90Ab 162
Canonsleigh Rd. Dag —38Xc 67
Canons Pk. Stan —23Ma 39
Canon St. N1 —39Sb 63 (1D 194)
Canon's Wlk. Croy —76Zb 148
Canopus Way. N'wd —21W 36
Canopus Way. Stai —59N 97
Canrobert St. E2 —40Xb 63
Cantelowes Rd. NW1 —37Mb 62
Canterbury Av. Ilf —31Nc 66
Canterbury Av. Sidc —61Xc 131
Canterbury Av. Slou —2G 72
Canterbury Av. Upm —32Vd 70
Canterbury Clo. E6 —44Pc 86
Canterbury Clo. Beck —67Dc 128
Canterbury Clo. Chig —20Vc 29
Canterbury Clo. Dart —59Qd 111
Canterbury Clo. Gnfd —43Da 77
Canterbury Clo. N'wd —23V 36
Canterbury Ct. NW9 —26Ua 40
Canterbury Ct. SE12 —62Kc 129
Canterbury Cres. SW9 —55Qb 104
Canterbury Gro. SE27 —63Qb 126
Canterbury Ho. SE1 —48Pb 82 (3J 205)
Canterbury Ho. SW9 —52Qb 104
Canterbury Ho. Bark —38Wc 67
(off Margaret Bondfield Av.)
Canterbury Ho. Borwd —12Qa 21
(off Stratfield Rd.)
Canterbury Ho. Eri —52Hd 110
Canterbury Ind. Pk. SE15 —51Yb 106
Canterbury Pde. S Ock —41Yd 90
Canterbury Pl. SE17 —49Rb 83 (6C 206)
Canterbury Pl. Grays —50Fe 91
Canterbury Rd. E10 —31Ec 64
Canterbury Rd. NW6 —40Cb 61
Canterbury Rd. Borwd —12Qa 21
Canterbury Rd. Croy —73Pb 146
Canterbury Rd. Felt —61Aa 121
Canterbury Rd. Grav —1E 136
Canterbury Rd. Harr —29Da 37
Canterbury Rd. Mord —73Db 145
Canterbury Rd. Wat —12X 19
Canterbury Ter. NW6 —40Cb 61
Canterbury Way. Crox —13S 18
Canterbury Way. Gt War —23Yd 50
Canterbury Way. W Thur —52Ud 112
Cantley Gdns. SE19 —67Vb 127
Cantley Gdns. Ilf —30Sc 46
Cantley Rd. W7 —48Ja 78
Canton St. E14 —44Cc 84
Cantrel Lodge. Enf —8Zb 12
Cantrell Rd. E3 —42Bc 84
Cantwell Rd. SE18 —52Rc 108
Canvey St. SE1 —46Sb 83 (6D 200)
Cape Clo. Bark —38Rc 66
Capelands. New Ash —75Ce 155
Capel Av. Wall —78Pb 146
Capel Clo. N20 —20Eb 23
Capel Clo. Brom —74Nc 150
Capel Clo. Stanf —1N 93
Capel Ct. SE20 —67Yb 128
Capel Gdns. Ilf —35Vc 67
Capel Gdns. Pinn —28Ba 37
Capella Rd. N'wd —21V 36
Capell Av. Chor —15E 16
Capell Rd. Chor —15F 16
Capell Way. Chor —15F 16
Capel Pl. Dart —63Ld 133
Capel Rd. E7 & E12 —35Kc 65
Capel Rd. Barn —16Gb 23
Capel Rd. Enf —8Xb 11
Capel Rd. Wat —16Aa 19
Capelvere Wlk. Wat —11U 18
Capener's Clo. SW1 —47Jb 82 (2H 203)
(off Kinnerton St.)
Capern Rd. SW18 —60Eb 103
Cape Rd. N17 —27Wb 43
Cape Yd. E1 —45Wb 83
Capital Bus. Cen. W3 —43Ra 79
Capital Bus. Cen. Wat —8Z 5
Capital Bus. Cen. Wemb —40Ma 59
Capital Interchange Way. Bren —50Qa 79
Capital Pk. Wok —93D 172
Capital Pl. Croy —78Pb 146
Capitol Ind. Pk. NW9 —27Sa 39
Capitol Way. NW9 —27Sa 39
Capland St. NW8 —42Fb 81 (5C 190)
Caple Rd. NW10 —40Va 60
Capon Clo. Brtwd —18Xd 32
Capper St. WC1 —42Lb 82 (6C 192)
Capri Rd. Croy —74Vb 147
Capstan Cen. Ind. Est. Til —52Fe 113
Capstan Clo. Romf —30Xc 47
Capstan Ct. Dart —56Sd 112
Capstan Ride. Enf —12Qb 24
Capstan Rd. SE8 —49Bc 84
Capstan Sq. E14 —47Ec 84
Capstan Way. SE16 —46Ac 84
Capstone Rd. Brom —63Hc 129
Capthorne Av. Harr —32Aa 57
Capuchin Clo. Stan —23Ka 38
Capworth St. E10 —32Cc 64
Caractacus Cottage View. Wat —17W 18
Caractacus Grn. Wat —16V 18
Caradoc Clo. W2 —44Cb 81
Caradoc Evans Clo. N11 —22Kb 42
(off Springfield Rd.)
Caradoc St. SE10 —50Gc 85
Caradon Clo. E11 —32Gc 65
Caradon Clo. Wok —6E 188
Caradon Way. N15 —28Tb 43
Carage Clo. Eri —51Ed 110
Caravan La. Rick —17N 17
Caravel Clo. Grays —48Ge 91
Caravel M. SE8 —51Cc 106
Caraway Clo. E13 —43Kc 85
Carberry Rd. SE19 —65Ub 127
Carbery Av. W3 —47Pa 79
Carbery La. Asc —9A 116
Carbis Clo. E4 —18Fc 27
Carbis Rd. E14 —44Bc 84
Carbuncle Pas. Way. N17 —26Wb 43
Carburton St. W1 —43Kb 82 (7A 192)
Carbury Clo. Horn —37Ld 69
Cardale St. E14 —47Ec 84
Carden Rd. SE15 —55Xb 105
Cardiff Rd. W7 —48Ja 78
Cardiff Rd. Enf —14Xb 25
Cardiff Rd. Wat —16X 19
Cardiff St. SE18 —52Uc 108
Cardigan Clo. Wok —6B 188
Cardigan Gdns. Ilf —33Wc 67
Cardigan Rd. E3 —40Bc 64
Cardigan Rd. SW13 —54Wa 102
Cardigan Rd. SW19 —65Eb 125
Cardigan Rd. Rich —58Na 101
Cardigan St. SE11 —50Qb 82 (7K 205)
Cardigan Wlk. N1 —38Sb 63
(off Ashby Gro.)
Cardinal Av. Borwd —13Ra 21
Cardinal Av. King T —64Na 123
Cardinal Av. Mord —72Ab 144
Cardinal Bourne St. SE1 —48Tb 83 (4G 207)
(off Burge St.)
Cardinal Cap All. SE1 —46Sb 83 (6D 200)
Cardinal Clo. Chst —67Uc 130
Cardinal Clo. Mord —72Ab 144
Cardinal Clo. Wor Pk —77Wa 144
Cardinal Cres. N Mald —68Sa 123
Cardinal Dri. Ilf —23Sc 46
Cardinal Dri. W on T —74Z 141
Cardinal Pl. SW15 —56Za 102
Cardinal Rd. Felt —60X 99
Cardinal Rd. Ruis —32Z 57
Cardinals Wlk. Hamp —66Ea 122
Cardinals Wlk. Sun —65U 120
Cardinals Wlk. Tap —4A 72
Cardinals Way. N19 —32Mb 62
Cardinal Way. Harr —27Ga 38
Cardinal Way. Rain —40Md 69
Cardine M. SE15 —52Xb 105
Cardingham. Wok —5D 188
Cardington Rd. Houn —55R 98
Cardington Sq. Houn —56Z 99
Cardington St. NW1 —41Lb 82 (3C 192)
Cardozo Rd. N7 —36Nb 62
Cardrew Av. N12 —22Fb 41
Cardrew Clo. N12 —22Gb 41
Cardrew Ct. N12 —22Fb 41
Cardross St. W6 —48Xa 80
Cardwell Cres. Asc —10A 116
Cardwell Rd. N7 —35Nb 62
Cardwell Rd. SE18 —49Qc 86
Carew Clo. N7 —33Pb 62
Carew Clo. Coul —91Rb 181
Carew Ct. Sutt —81Db 163
Carew Mnr. Cotts. Wall —76Mb 146
Carew Rd. N17 —26Wb 43
Carew Rd. W13 —47La 78
Carew Rd. Ashf —65S 120
Carew Rd. Mitc —68Jb 126
Carew Rd. N'wd —23U 36
Carew Rd. T Hth —70Rb 127
Carew Rd. Wall —79Lb 146
Carew St. SE5 —54Sb 105
Carey Clo. Wind —5F 94
Carey Ct. Bexh —57Dd 110
Carey Gdns. SW8 —53Lb 104
Carey La. EC2 —44Sb 83 (2D 200)
Carey Pl. SW1 —49Mb 82 (6D 204)
Carey Rd. Dag —35Ad 67
Carey St. WC2 —44Pb 82 (3J 199)
Carey Way. Wemb —35Ra 59
Carfax Pl. SW4 —56Mb 104
Carfax Rd. Hay —50V 76
Carfax Rd. Horn —35Hd 68
Carfree Clo. N1 —38Qb 62
Cargill Rd. SW18 —60Db 103
Cargreen Pl. SE25 —70Vb 127
Cargreen Rd. SE25 —70Vb 127
Cargrey Ho. Stan —22La 38
Carholme Rd. SE23 —60Bc 106
Carillon Ct. W5 —45Ma 79
Carina M. SE27 —63Sb 127
Carisbrook Clo. Epp —3Wc 15
Carisbrook Clo. Stan —26Ma 39
Carisbrooke Av. Bex —60Zc 109
Carisbrooke Av. Wat —11Z 19
Carisbrooke Clo. Enf —11Vb 25
Carisbrooke Clo. Horn —32Qd 69
Carisbrooke Ct. Dart —58Rd 111
(off Clifton Wlk.)
Carisbrooke Ct. Dart —58Rd 111
(off Osborne Rd.)
Carisbrooke Ct. N'holt —39Ba 57
(off Eskdale Av.)
Carisbrooke Ct. Slou —5K 73
Carisbrooke Gdns. SE15 —52Vb 105
Carisbrooke Rd. E17 —28Ac 44
Carisbrooke Rd. Brom —70Lc 129
Carisbrooke Rd. Mitc —70Mb 126
Carisbrooke Rd. Pil H —16Xd 32
Carker's La. NW5 —36Kb 62
Carl Ekman Ho. Grav —59Fe 113
Carleton Av. Wall —81Mb 164
Carleton Clo. Esh —74Fa 142
Carleton Gdns. N19 —36Lb 62
Carleton Pl. Hort K —70Sd 134
Carleton Rd. N7 —36Mb 62
Carleton Rd. Dart —59Qd 111
Carleton Vs. NW5 —36Lb 62
Carlile Clo. E3 —40Bc 64
Carlingford Gdns. Mitc —66Jb 126
Carlingford Rd. N15 —27Rb 43
Carlingford Rd. NW3 —35Fb 61
Carlingford Rd. Mord —72Za 144
Carlisle Av. EC3 —44Vb 83 (3K 201)
Carlisle Av. W3 —44Ua 80
Carlisle Clo. King T —67Qa 123
Carlisle Gdns. Harr —31Ma 59
Carlisle Gdns. Ilf —30Nc 46
Carlisle Ho. Borwd —12Qa 21
Carlisle La. SE1 —48Pb 82 (4J 205)
Carlisle M. NW8 —43Fb 81 (7C 190)
Carlisle M. King T —67Qa 123
Carlisle Pl. N11 —21Kb 42
Carlisle Pl. SW1 —48Lb 82 (4B 204)
Carlisle Rd. E10 —32Cc 64
Carlisle Rd. N4 —31Qb 62
Carlisle Rd. NW6 —39Ab 60
Carlisle Rd. NW9 —27Sa 39
Carlisle Rd. Dart —58Qd 111
Carlisle Rd. Hamp —66Da 121
Carlisle Rd. Romf —29Jd 48
Carlisle Rd. Slou —5H 73
Carlisle Rd. Sutt —79Bb 145
Carlisle St. W1 —44Mb 82 (3D 198)
Carlisle Wlk. E8 —37Vb 63
Carlisle Way. SW17 —64Jb 126
Carlos Pl. W1 —45Jb 82 (5J 197)
Carlow St. NW1 —40Lb 62 (1B 192)
Carlton Av. N14 —15Mb 24
Carlton Av. Felt —58Y 99
Carlton Av. Grnh —58Ud 112
Carlton Av. Harr —29Ka 38
Carlton Av. Hay —49U 76
Carlton Av. S Croy —80Ub 147
Carlton Av. E. Wemb —33Ma 59
Carlton Av. W. Wemb —33Ka 58
Carlton Clo. NW3 —33Cb 61
Carlton Clo. Borwd —14Ta 21
Carlton Clo. Chess —79Ma 143
Carlton Clo. Edgw —22Qa 39
Carlton Clo. N'holt —36Ea 58
Carlton Clo. Upm —33Rd 69
Carlton Clo. Wok —86B 156
Carlton Ct. SE20 —67Xb 127
Carlton Ct. SW9 —53Rb 105
Carlton Ct. Ilf —27Tc 46
Carlton Ct. Stai —64J 119
Carlton Ct. Uxb —43M 75
Carlton Cres. Sutt —77Ab 144
Carlton Dri. SW15 —57Za 102
Carlton Dri. Ilf —27Tc 46
Carlton Gdns. SW1 —46Mb 82 (7D 198)
Carlton Gdns. W5 —44La 78
Carlton Gro. SE15 —53Xb 105
Carlton Hill. NW8 —40Db 61
Carlton Ho. Felt —58V 98
Carlton Ho. Ter. SW1 —46Mb 82 (7D 198)

Carlton Lodge—Cedar Gdns.

*Carlton Lodge. N4 —31Qb **62***
(off Carlton Rd.)
Carlton Pde. Orp —73Xc **151**
Carlton Pde. Sev —94Ld **187**
Carlton Pk. Av. SW20 —68Za **124**
Carlton Pl. N'wd —22R **36**
Carlton Rd. E11 —32Hc **65**
Carlton Rd. E12 —35Mc **65**
Carlton Rd. E17 —25Ac **44**
Carlton Rd. N4 —31Qb **62**
Carlton Rd. N11 —22Jb **42**
Carlton Rd. SW14 —55Sa **101**
Carlton Rd. W4 —47Ta **79**
Carlton Rd. W5 —45La **78**
Carlton Rd. Eri —51Dd **110**
Carlton Rd. Grays —7B **92**
Carlton Rd. N Mald —68Ua **124**
Carlton Rd. Romf —29Hd **48**
Carlton Rd. Sidc —64Vc **131**
Carlton Rd. Slou —5M **73**
Carlton Rd. S Croy —79Tb **147**
Carlton Rd. Sun —66V **120**
Carlton Rd. W on T —73X **141**
Carlton Rd. Well —55Xc **109**
Carlton Rd. Wok —86C **156**
Carlton Sq. E1 —42Zb **84**
(in two parts)
Carlton St. SW1 —45Mb **82** (5D **198**)
Carlton Ter. E7 —38Lc **65**
Carlton Ter. E11 —29Kc **45**
Carlton Ter. N18 —20Tb **25**
Carlton Ter. SE26 —62Yb **128**
*Carlton Tower Pl. SW1 —49Hb **81** (5G **203**)*
(off Cadogan Pl.)
Carlton Vale. NW6 —40Bb **61**
Carlwell St. SW17 —64Gb **125**
Carlyle Av. Brom —69Mc **129**
Carlyle Av. S'hall —45Ba **77**
Carlyle Clo. N2 —30Eb **41**
Carlyle Clo. NW10 —39Ta **59**
Carlyle Clo. W Mol —68Da **121**
*Carlyle Ct. SW6 —53Db **103***
(off Maltings Pl.)
*Carlyle Ct. SW10 —53Eb **103***
(off Chelsea Harbour)
Carlyle Gdns. S'hall —45Ba **77**
Carlyle Pl. SW15 —56Za **102**
Carlyle Rd. E12 —35Nc **66**
Carlyle Rd. SE28 —45Xc **87**
Carlyle Rd. W5 —50La **78**
Carlyle Rd. Croy —75Wb **147**
Carlyle Rd. Stai —66H **119**
Carlyle Sq. SW3 —50Fb **81**
Carlyon Av. Harr —35Ba **57**
Carlyon Clo. Wemb —39Na **59**
Carlyon Rd. Hay —43Y **77**
(in two parts)
Carlyon Rd. Wemb —40Na **59**
Carmalt Gdns. SW15 —56Ya **102**
Carmalt Gdns. W on T —78Y **141**
*Carmarthen Grn. NW9 —29Ua **40***
(off Snowden Dri.)
Carmarthen Pl. SE1 —47Ub **83** (1H **207**)
Carmarthen Rd. Slou —5J **73**
Carmel Clo. Wok —90A **156**
*Carmel Ct. W8 —47Db **81***
(off Holland St.)
Carmelite Clo. Harr —25Ea **38**
Carmelite Rd. Harr —25Ea **38**
Carmelite St. EC4 —45Qb **82** (4A **200**)
Carmelite Wlk. Harr —25Ea **38**
Carmelite Way. Harr —26Ea **38**
Carmelite Way. Hart —71Be **155**
Carmen St. E14 —44Dc **84**
Carmichael Clo. SW11 —55Fb **103**
Carmichael Clo. Ruis —35W **56**
Carmichael M. SW18 —58Fb **103**
Carmichael Rd. SE25 —71Wb **147**
Carminia Rd. SW17 —61Kb **126**
Carnaby St. W1 —44Lb **82** (3B **198**)
Carnach Grn. S Ock —45Wd **90**
Carnac St. SE27 —63Tb **127**
Carnanton Rd. E17 —25Fc **45**
Carnarvon Av. Enf —13Vb **25**
Carnarvon Dri. Hay —48S **76**
Carnarvon Rd. E10 —29Ec **44**
Carnarvon Rd. E15 —37Hc **65**
Carnarvon Rd. E18 —25Hc **45**
Carnarvon Rd. Barn —13Ab **22**
Carnation St. SE2 —50Xc **87**
Carnbrook Rd. SE3 —55Mc **107**
Carnecke Gdns. SE9 —57Nc **108**
Carnegie Clo. Surb —75Pa **143**
Carnegie Pl. SW19 —62Za **124**
Carnegie Rd. Harr —31Ha **58**
Carnegie St. N1 —39Pb **62** (1H **193**)
Carnforth Clo. Eps —79Ra **143**
Carnforth Gdns. Horn —36Jd **68**
Carnforth Rd. SW16 —66Mb **126**
Carnie Hall. SW17 —62Kb **126**
Carnoustie Dri. N1 —38Nb **62**
(in two parts)
Carnwath Rd. SW6 —55Cb **103**
Carolina Clo. E15 —36Gc **65**
Carolina Rd. T Hth —68Rb **127**
Caroline Clo. N10 —26Kb **42**
Caroline Clo. SW16 —62Pb **126**
*Caroline Clo. W2 —45Db **81***
(off Bayswater Rd.)
Caroline Clo. Croy —77Ub **147**
Caroline Clo. Iswth —52Fa **100**
Caroline Clo. W Dray —47M **75**
Caroline Ct. Ashf —65R **120**
Caroline Ct. Stan —23Ja **38**
Caroline Gdns. E2 —41Ub **83** (3J **195**)
Caroline Gdns. SE15 —52Wb **105**
Caroline Pl. SW11 —54Jb **104**
Caroline Pl. W2 —45Db **81**
Caroline Pl. Hay —52U **98**
Caroline Pl. Wat —16Aa **19**
Caroline Pl. M. W2 —45Db **81**
Caroline Rd. SW19 —66Bb **125**
Caroline St. E1 —44Zb **84**
Caroline Ter. SW1 —49Jb **82** (6H **203**)
Caroline Wlk. W6 —51Ab **102**
Carol St. NW1 —39Lb **62**
Carolyn Clo. Wok —7C **188**
Carolyn Dri. Orp —76Wc **151**
Caroon Dri. Sarr —8K **3**
Carpenders Av. Wat —20Aa **19**
Carpenter Clo. Eps —81Va **162**
Carpenter Gdns. N21 —19Rb **25**
Carpenter Ho. NW11 —30Eb **41**
Carpenters Ct. Twic —61Ga **122**
Carpenters M. N7 —36Nb **62**
Carpenters Path. Hut —15Fe **33**
Carpenters Pl. SW4 —56Mb **104**
Carpenter's Rd. E15 —37Cc **64**
Carpenters Rd. Enf —8Yb **12**
Carpenter St. W1 —45Kb **82** (5K **197**)
Carpenters Wood Dri. Chor —14D **16**
Carpenter Way. Pot B —5Eb **9**
*Carrack Ho. Eri —50Gd **88***
(off Saltford Clo.)
Carrara Wlk. SW9 —56Qb **104**
Carr Gro. SE18 —49Nc **86**
Carr Ho. Dart —57Gd **110**
Carriage Dri. E. SW11 —52Jb **104**
Carriage Dri. N. SW11 —52Hb **103**
Carriage Dri. S. SW11 —53Hb **103**
Carriage Dri. W. SW11 —52Hb **103**
Carriage Way, The. Bras —96Zc **185**
Carrick Clo. Iswth —55Ja **100**
Carrick Dri. Ilf —25Sc **46**
Carrick Dri. Sev —95Kd **187**
Carrick Gdns. N17 —24Ub **43**
Carrick Ga. Esh —76Ea **142**
*Carrick Ho. N7 —37Pb **62***
(off Caledonian Rd.)
Carrick Ho. SE11 —50Rb **83** (7B **206**)
Carrick M. SE8 —51Cc **106**
Carrill Way. Belv —48Zc **87**
Carrington Av. Borwd —15Ra **21**
Carrington Av. Houn —57Da **99**
Carrington Clo. Ark —15Wa **22**
Carrington Clo. Borwd —15Sa **21**
Carrington Clo. Croy —73Ac **148**
Carrington Gdns. E7 —35Jc **65**
Carrington Pl. W1 —46Kb **82**
Carrington Rd. Dart —58Pd **111**
Carrington Rd. Rich —56Qa **101**
Carrington Rd. Slou —5J **73**
Carrington Sq. Harr —23Ea **38**
Carrington St. W1 —46Kb **82** (7K **197**)
Carrol Clo. NW5 —35Kb **62**
Carroll Clo. E15 —36Hc **65**
Carroll Hill. Lou —13Pc **28**
Carron Clo. E14 —44Dc **84**
Carroun Rd. SW8 —52Pb **104**
Carroway La. Gnfd —41Fa **78**
Carrow Rd. Dag —38Xc **67**
Carrow Rd. W on T —76Z **141**
Carr Rd. E17 —26Bc **44**
Carr Rd. N'holt —37Ca **57**
Carrs La. N21 —15Sb **25**
Carr St. E14 —43Ac **84**
(in two parts)
Carshalton Gro. Sutt —77Fb **145**
Carshalton Pk. Rd. Cars —78Hb **145**
Carshalton Pl. Cars —78Jb **146**
Carshalton Rd. Bans —86Hb **163**
Carshalton Rd. Mitc —70Jb **126**
Carshalton Rd. Sutt & Cars —78Eb **145**
Carsington Gdns. Dart —61Md **133**
Carslake Rd. SW15 —58Ya **102**
Carson Rd. E16 —42Jc **85**
Carson Rd. SE21 —61Tb **127**
Carson Rd. Barn —14Hb **23**
Carstairs Rd. SE6 —62Ec **128**
Carston Clo. SE12 —57Hc **107**
Carswell Clo. Hut —16Fe **33**
Carswell Clo. Ilf —28Mc **45**
Carswell Rd. SE6 —59Ec **106**
Cartaret St. SW1 —47Mb **82**
Cartbridge Clo. Send —95D **172**
Cartel Clo. Purf —49Td **90**
Carter Clo. Romf —24Cd **48**
Carter Clo. Wall —80Mb **146**
Carter Clo. Wind —4E **94**
*Carter Ct. EC4 —44Rb **83** (3C **200**)*
(off Carter La.)
Carter Dri. Romf —24Dd **48**
Carteret St. SW1 —47Mb **82** (2D **204**)
Carteret Way. SE8 —49Ac **84**
Carterhatch La. Enf —10Vb **11**
Carterhatch Rd. Enf —12Yb **26**
Carter La. EC4 —44Rb **83** (3C **200**)
Carter Pl. SE17 —50Sb **83** (7E **206**)
Carter Rd. E13 —39Kc **65**
Carter Rd. SW19 —65Fb **125**
Carters Clo. Wor Pk —74Za **144**
Cartersfield Rd. Wal A —6Ec **12**
Carters Hill. Under —100Rd **187**
Carters Hill Clo. SE9 —60Lc **107**
Carters La. SE23 —61Ac **128**
Carters La. Wok —92E **172**
Carters Rd. Eps —87Va **162**
Carters Row. Grav —10B **114**
Carter St. SE17 —51Sb **105**
Carter's Yd. SW18 —57Cb **103**
Carthew Rd. W6 —48Xa **80**
Carthew Vs. W6 —48Xa **80**
Carthouse La. Wok —2B **188**
Carthusian St. EC1 —43Sb **83** (7D **194**)
Cartier Circ. E14 —46Dc **84**
Carting La. WC2 —45Nb **82** (5G **199**)
Cart La. E4 —18Gc **27**
Cartmel Clo. N17 —24Xb **43**
Cartmell Gdns. Mord —71Eb **145**
Cartmel Rd. Bexh —53Cd **110**
*Carton Ho. SE16 —48Wb **83***
(off Marine St.)
Cart Path. Wat —5Y **5**
Cartwright Gdns. WC1 —41Nb **82** (4F **193**)
Cartwright Rd. Dag —38Bd **67**
Cartwright St. E1 —45Vb **83**
Carvelle Gdns. N'holt —41Z **77**
Carver Rd. SE24 —58Sb **105**
Carville Cres. Bren —49Na **79**
Cary Rd. E11 —35Gc **65**
Carysfort Rd. N8 —29Mb **42**
Carysfort Rd. N16 —34Tb **63**
Cary Wlk. Rad —6Ka **6**
Cascade Av. N10 —28Lb **42**
Cascade Clo. Buck H —19Mc **27**
Cascade Clo. Orp —69Yc **131**
Cascade Rd. Buck H —19Mc **27**
Cascades. Croy —82Bc **166**
Cascades Tower. E14 —46Bc **84**
Caselden Clo. Add —78L **139**
Casella Rd. SE14 —52Zb **106**
Casewick Rd. SE27 —64Qb **126**
Casimir Rd. E5 —33Yb **64**
Casino Av. SE24 —57Sb **105**
Caspian St. SE5 —52Tb **105**
Caspian Wlk. E16 —44Mc **85**
Cassandra Clo. N'holt —35Fa **58**
Casselden Rd. NW10 —38Ta **59**
*Cassell Ho. SW9 —54Pb **104***
(off Stockwell Gdns. Est.)
Cassidy Rd. SW6 —52Cb **103**
Cassilda Rd. SE2 —49Wc **87**
Cassilis Rd. Twic —57Ka **100**
Cassiobridge Rd. Wat —14U **18**
Cassiobury Av. Felt —59V **98**
Cassiobury Dri. Wat —10U **4**
Cassiobury Pk. Av. Wat —13U **18**
Cassiobury Rd. E17 —29Ac **44**
Cassio Rd. Wat —13X **19**
Cassis Ct. Lou —14Sc **28**
Cassland Rd. E9 —38Zb **64**
Cassland Rd. T Hth —70Tb **127**
Casslee Rd. SE6 —59Bc **106**
Cassocks Sq. Shep —73T **140**
Casson St. E1 —43Wb **83**
Casstine Clo. Swan —66Hd **132**
Castalia Sq. E14 —47Ec **84**
Castano Ct. Abb L —3U **4**
*Castellain Mans. W9 —42Db **81***
(off Castellain Rd.)
Castellain Rd. W9 —42Db **81**
Castellan Av. Romf —27Kd **49**
Castellane Clo. Stan —24Ha **38**
Castello Av. SW15 —57Ya **102**
Castell Rd. Lou —11Sc **28**
Castelnau. SW13 —53Wa **102**
Castelnau Gdns. SW13 —51Xa **102**
Castelnau Pl. SW13 —51Xa **102**
Castelnau Row. SW13 —51Xa **102**
Casterbridge Rd. SE3 —55Jc **107**
Casterton St. E8 —37Xb **63**
Castile Rd. SE18 —49Qc **86**
Castillon Rd. SE6 —61Gc **129**
Castlands Rd. SE6 —61Bc **128**
Castle Av. E4 —22Fc **45**
Castle Av. Dat —1L **95**
Castle Av. Eps —81Wa **162**
Castle Av. Rain —38Gd **68**
Castle Av. W Dray —45N **75**
Castlebar Ct. Gnfd —43La **78**
Castlebar Hill. W5 —43La **78**
Castlebar M. W5 —43La **78**
Castlebar Pk. Gnfd —42Ka **78**
Castlebar Rd. W5 —43La **78**
Castle Baynard St. EC4 —45Rb **83** (4C **200**)
Castle Clo. E9 —36Ac **64**
Castle Clo. SW19 —62Za **124**
Castle Clo. W3 —47Ra **79**
Castle Clo. Brom —69Gc **129**
Castle Clo. Bush —16Da **19**
Castle Clo. Romf —20Ld **31**
Castle Clo. Sun —66U **120**
Castlecombe Dri. SW19 —59Za **102**
Castlecombe Rd. SE9 —63Nc **130**
*Castle Ct. EC3 —44Tb **83** (3G **201**)*
(off Birchin La.)
Castle Ct. SE26 —63Ac **128**
Castledine Rd. SE20 —66Xb **127**
Castle Dri. Ilf —30Nc **46**
Castle Dri. Kems —89Nd **171**
Castle Farm Caravan Site. Wind —4B **94**
(off White Horse Rd.)
Castle Farm Rd. Shor —81Hd **170**
Castlefield Rd. Enf —9Ac **12**
Castlefields. Grav —7B **136**
Castleford Av. SE9 —60Rc **108**
Castlegate. Rich —55Pa **101**
Castle Grn. Wey —76U **140**
Castle Gro. Rd. Chob —1A **188**
Castlehaven Rd. NW1 —38Kb **62**
Castle Hill. Hart —71Zd **155**
Castle Hill. Wind —3H **95**
Castle Hill Av. New Ad —81Dc **166**
Castle Hill Rd. Egh —2M **117**
Castle Ind. Est. SE17 —49Sb **83** (5D **206**)
Castle La. SW1 —48Lb **82** (3B **204**)
Castle La. Grav —1K **137**
Castleleigh Ct. Enf —15Tb **25**
Castlemaine Av. Eps —81Xa **162**
Castlemaine Av. S Croy —78Vb **147**
Castle Mead. SE17 —52Sb **105**
Castle M. N12 —22Eb **41**
Castle M. NW1 —37Kb **62**
Castle Pde. Eps —80Wa **144**
Castle Pl. NW1 —37Kb **62**
Castle Pl. W4 —49Ua **80**
*Castle Point. E13 —40Lc **65***
(off Boundary Rd.)
Castlereagh St. W1 —44Gb **81** (2F **197**)
Castle Rd. N12 —22Eb **41**
Castle Rd. NW1 —37Kb **62**
Castle Rd. Coul —92Gb **179**
Castle Rd. Dag —39Xc **67**
Castle Rd. Enf —11Ac **26**
Castle Rd. Eps —87Ra **161**
Castle Rd. Eyns —79Kd **153**
Castle Rd. Grays —51Be **113**
Castle Rd. Iswth —54Ha **100**
Castle Rd. N'holt —37Da **57**
Castle Rd. S'hall —48Ba **77**
Castle Rd. Swans —58Be **113**
Castle Rd. Wey —76U **140**
Castle Rd. Wok —86B **156**
Castle Row. W4 —50Ta **79**
Castle St. E6 —40Lc **65**
Castle St. Grnh —57Wd **112**
Castle St. King T —68Na **123**
Castle St. Slou —8K **73**
Castle St. Swans —58Be **113**
Castleton. Cars —83Fb **163**
Castleton Av. Bexh —53Fd **110**
Castleton Av. Wemb —35Na **59**
Castleton Clo. Bans —87Cb **163**
Castleton Dri. Bans —86Cb **163**
Castleton Gdns. Wemb —34Na **59**
Castleton Rd. E17 —26Fc **45**
Castleton Rd. SE9 —63Mc **129**
Castleton Rd. Ilf —32Wc **67**
Castleton Rd. Mitc —70Mb **126**
Castleton Rd. Ruis —32Z **57**
Castletown Rd. W14 —50Ab **80**
Castle View. Eps —82Ra **161**
Castleview Gdns. Ilf —30Nc **46**
Castleview Pde. Slou —9P **73**
Castleview Rd. Slou —9N **73**
Castle View Rd. Wey —77R **140**
Castle Wlk. Sun —69Y **121**
Castle Way. SW19 —62Za **124**
Castle Way. Eps —82Wa **162**
Castle Way. Felt —63Y **121**
Castlewood Dri. SE9 —54Pc **108**
Castlewood Rd. N15 & N16 —30Wb **43**
Castlewood Rd. Barn —13Fb **23**
Castle Yd. N6 —31Jb **62**
Castle Yd. SE1 —46Rb **83** (6C **200**)
Castle Yd. Rich —57Ma **101**
Castor La. E14 —45Dc **84**
Caterham Av. Ilf —26Pc **46**
Caterham By-Pass. Cat —93Xb **181**
Caterham Clo. Cat —92Ub **181**
Caterham Ct. Wal A —6Hc **13**
Caterham Dri. Coul —90Rb **165**
Caterham Rd. SE13 —55Ec **106**
Catesby St. SE17 —49Tb **83** (6G **207**)
Catford B'way. SE6 —59Dc **106**
Catford Hill. SE6 —61Bc **128**
Catford M. SE6 —59Dc **106**
Catford Rd. SE6 —59Cc **106**
Cathall Rd. E11 —33Fc **65**
Cathay Ho. SE16 —47Xb **83**
Cathay St. SE16 —47Xb **83**
*Cathay Wlk. N'holt —40Ca **57***
(off Brabazon Rd.)
Cathcart Dri. Orp —75Uc **150**
Cathcart Hill. N19 —34Lb **62**
Cathcart Rd. SW10 —51Db **103**
Cathcart St. NW5 —37Kb **62**
*Cathedral Pl. EC4 —44Sb **83** (3D **200**)*
(off Paternoster Row)
Cathedral Piazza. SW1 —48Lb **82** (4B **204**)
Cathedral St. SE1 —46Tb **83** (6F **201**)
Catherall Rd. N5 —34Sb **63**
Catherine Clo. Byfl —86N **157**
Catherine Clo. Chaf H —47Be **91**
Catherine Clo. Pil H —15Wd **32**
Catherine Ct. N14 —15Lb **24**
Catherine Ct. SW19 —64Bb **125**
Catherine Ct. Ilf —30Sc **46**
Catherine Dri. Sun —65V **120**
Catherine Gdns. Houn —56Fa **100**
Catherine Gro. SE10 —53Dc **106**
*Catherine Ho. N1 —39Ub **63** (1J **195**)*
(off Whitmore Est.)
Catherine Pl. SW1 —48Lb **82** (3B **204**)
Catherine Rd. Enf —9Ac **12**
Catherine Rd. Romf —29Kd **49**
Catherine Rd. Surb —71Ma **143**
Catherines Clo. W Dray —47M **75**
Catherine St. WC2 —45Pb **82** (4H **199**)
Catherine Wheel All. E1 —43Ub **83** (1J **201**)
Catherine Wheel Rd. Bren —52Ma **101**
*Catherine Wheel Yd. SW1 —46Lb **82** (7B **198**)*
(off Lit. St James's St.)
*Catherwood Ct. N1 —41Tb **83** (3F **195**)*
(off Murray Gro.)
Cat Hill. Barn —16Gb **23**
Cathles Rd. SW12 —58Kb **104**
Cathnor Hall Ct. W12 —47Xa **80**
Cathnor Rd. W12 —47Xa **80**
Catlin Cres. Shep —71T **140**
Catling Clo. SE23 —62Yb **128**
Catlin's La. Pinn —27X **37**
Catlin St. SE16 —50Wb **83**
Cator Clo. New Ad —83Gc **167**
Cator Cres. New Ad —83Gc **167**
Cator La. Beck —67Bc **128**
Cato Rd. SW4 —55Mb **104**
Cator Rd. SE26 —65Zb **128**
Cator Rd. Cars —78Hb **145**
Cator St. SE15 —51Vb **105**
(in two parts)
Cato's Hill. Esh —77Da **141**
Cato St. W1 —44Gb **81** (1E **196**)
Catsey La. Bush —17Ea **20**
Catsey Wood. Bush —17Ea **20**
Catterick Way. Borwd —11Pa **21**
Cattistock Rd. SE9 —64Pc **130**
Cattistock Rd. SE12 —64Nc **130**
Cattlegate Hill. Cuff —4Mb **10**
Cattlegate Rd. N'thaw & Enf —3Mb **10**
Catton St. WC1 —43Pb **82** (1H **199**)
Caulfield Rd. E6 —39Nc **66**
Caulfield Rd. SE15 —54Xb **105**
Causeway Cen. Houn —55X **99**
Causeway Clo. Pot B —3Fb **9**
Causeway Ct. Wok —6C **188**
Causeway Est. Stai —63D **118**
Causeway, The. N2 —28Gb **41**
Causeway, The. SW18 —56Db **103**
Causeway, The. SW19 —64Ya **124**
Causeway, The. Cars —75Jb **146**
Causeway, The. Chess —77Na **143**
Causeway, The. Clay —80Ha **142**
Causeway, The. Felt & Houn —55X **99**
Causeway, The. Pot B —3Fb **9**
Causeway, The. Stai —63F **118**
Causeway, The. Sutt —81Eb **163**
Causeway, The. Tedd —65Ha **122**
Causeyware Rd. N9 —17Yb **26**
Causton Rd. N6 —31Kb **62**
Causton St. SW1 —49Mb **82** (6E **204**)
Cautley Av. SW4 —57Lb **104**
Cavalier Clo. Romf —28Zc **47**
Cavalier Ct. Surb —72Pa **143**
Cavalier Gdns. Hay —44T **76**
Cavalry Cres. Houn —56Z **99**
Cavalry Cres. Wind —5G **94**
Cavaye Pl. SW10 —50Eb **81**
Cavell Cres. Dart —56Qd **111**
Cavell Cres. H Wood —26Nd **49**
Cavell Dri. Enf —12Qb **24**
Cavell Ho. Ott —79F **138**
Cavell Rd. N17 —24Tb **43**
Cavell St. E1 —43Xb **83**
Cavendish Av. N3 —26Cb **41**
Cavendish Av. NW8 —40Fb **61** (2C **190**)
Cavendish Av. W13 —43Ja **78**
Cavendish Av. Eri —51Ed **110**
Cavendish Av. Harr —35Fa **58**
Cavendish Av. Horn —37Kd **69**
Cavendish Av. N Mald —71Xa **144**
Cavendish Av. Ruis —36X **57**
Cavendish Av. Sev —94Jd **186**
Cavendish Av. Sidc —59Wc **109**
Cavendish Av. Well —55Vc **109**
Cavendish Av. Wfd G —25Kc **45**
Cavendish Clo. N18 —22Xb **43**
Cavendish Clo. NW6 —37Bb **61**
Cavendish Clo. NW8 —41Fb **81** (3C **190**)
Cavendish Clo. Hay —43U **76**
Cavendish Clo. Sun —65V **120**
*Cavendish Ct. EC3 —44Ub **83** (2J **201**)*
(off Devonshire Row)
*Cavendish Ct. Cher —74J **139***
(off Victory Rd.)
Cavendish Ct. Coln —53G **96**
Cavendish Ct. Sun —65V **120**
Cavendish Cres. Els —14Qa **21**
Cavendish Cres. Horn —37Kd **69**
Cavendish Dri. E11 —32Fc **65**
Cavendish Dri. Clay —78Ga **142**
Cavendish Dri. Edgw —23Pa **39**
Cavendish Gdns. SW4 —58Lb **104**
Cavendish Gdns. Bark —36Uc **66**
Cavendish Gdns. Ilf —32Qc **66**
Cavendish Gdns. Romf —29Ad **47**
Cavendish Mans. NW6 —36Cb **61**
Cavendish M. N. W1 —43Kb **82** (7A **192**)
Cavendish M. S. W1 —43Kb **82**
Cavendish Pl. W1 —44Kb **82** (2A **198**)
Cavendish Rd. E4 —23Ec **44**
Cavendish Rd. N4 —30Rb **43**
Cavendish Rd. N18 —22Xb **43**
Cavendish Rd. NW6 —38Ab **60**
Cavendish Rd. SW12 —58Kb **104**
Cavendish Rd. SW19 —66Fb **125**
Cavendish Rd. W4 —53Sa **101**
Cavendish Rd. Barn —13Ya **22**
Cavendish Rd. Croy —74Rb **147**
Cavendish Rd. N Mald —70Va **124**
Cavendish Rd. Sun —65V **120**
Cavendish Rd. Sutt —80Eb **145**
Cavendish Rd. Wey —81R **158**
Cavendish Rd. Wok —7G **188**
Cavendish Sq. W1 —44Kb **82** (2A **198**)
Cavendish Sq. Long —69Ae **135**
Cavendish St. N1 —40Tb **63** (2F **195**)
Cavendish Ter. Felt —61W **120**
Cavendish Way. W Wick —74Dc **148**
Cavenham Clo. Wok —91A **172**
Cavenham Gdns. Horn —29Ld **49**
Cavenham Gdns. Ilf —34Tc **66**
Caverleigh Way. Wor Pk —74Wa **144**
Cave Rd. E13 —41Kc **85**
Cave Rd. Rich —63La **122**
Caversham Av. N13 —20Qb **24**
Caversham Av. Sutt —75Ab **144**
Caversham Ct. N11 —19Jb **24**
*Caversham Ho. N15 —28Sb **43***
(off Caversham Rd.)
Caversham M. SW3 —51Hb **103**
Caversham Rd. N15 —28Sb **43**
Caversham Rd. NW5 —37Lb **62**
Caversham Rd. King T —68Pa **123**
Caversham St. SW3 —51Hb **103**
Caverswall St. W12 —44Ya **80**
Caveside Clo. Chst —67Qc **130**
Cawcott Dri. Wind —3C **94**
Cawdor Av. S Ock —45Xd **90**
Cawdor Cres. W7 —49Ja **78**
Cawdor Ho. Brtwd —21Zd **51**
Cawnpore St. SE19 —64Ub **127**
Cawsey Way. Wok —89A **156**
Caxton Av. Add —79J **139**
Caxton Clo. Hart —70Be **135**
Caxton Dri. Uxb —40M **55**
Caxton Gro. E3 —41Cc **84**
Caxton M. Bren —51Ma **101**
Caxton Pl. Ilf —34Qc **66**
Caxton Rd. N22 —26Pb **42**
Caxton Rd. SW19 —64Eb **125**
Caxton Rd. W12 —47Za **80**
Caxton Rd. S'hall —48Z **77**
Caxton St. SW1 —48Mb **82** (3C **204**)
Caxton St. N. E16 —44Hc **85**
Caxton St. S. E16 —45Jc **85**
Caxton Trading Est. Hay —47U **76**
Caxton Wlk. WC2 —44Mb **82** (3E **198**)
Caxton Way. Wat —17T **18**
*Cayenne Ct. SE1 —47Vb **83** (1K **207**)*
(off Lafone St.)
Caygill Clo. Brom —70Hc **129**
Cayley Clo. Wall —80Nb **146**
*Cayton Pl. EC1 —41Tb **83** (4F **195**)*
(off Cayton St.)
Cayton Rd. Gnfd —40Ga **58**
Cayton St. EC1 —41Tb **83** (4F **195**)
Cazenove Rd. E17 —25Cc **44**
Cazenove Rd. N16 —33Vb **63**
Cearns Ho. E6 —39Mc **65**
Cearn Way. Coul —87Pb **164**
Cecil Av. Bark —38Tc **66**
Cecil Av. Enf —14Vb **25**
Cecil Av. Grays —47Be **91**
Cecil Av. Horn —27Nd **49**
Cecil Av. Wemb —36Pa **59**
Cecil Clo. W5 —43Ma **79**
Cecil Clo. Ashf —66S **120**
Cecil Clo. Chess —77Ma **143**
Cecil Ct. WC2 —45Nb **82** (5F **199**)
Cecil Ct. Barn —13Za **22**
Cecile Pk. N8 —30Nb **42**
Cecil Ho. E17 —25Cc **44**
Cecilia Clo. N2 —27Eb **41**
Cecilia Rd. E8 —36Vb **63**
Cecil Pk. Pinn —28Aa **37**
Cecil Pl. Mitc —71Hb **145**
Cecil Rd. E11 —34Hc **65**
Cecil Rd. E13 —39Jc **65**
Cecil Rd. E17 —25Cc **44**
Cecil Rd. N10 —26Kb **42**
Cecil Rd. N14 —18Lb **24**
Cecil Rd. NW9 —27Ua **40**
Cecil Rd. NW10 —39Ua **60**
Cecil Rd. SW19 —66Db **125**
Cecil Rd. W3 —43Sa **79**
Cecil Rd. Ashf —66S **120**
Cecil Rd. Chesh —4Ac **12**
Cecil Rd. Croy —72Pb **146**
Cecil Rd. Enf —14Sb **25**
Cecil Rd. Grav —10B **114**
Cecil Rd. Harr —27Ha **38**
Cecil Rd. Houn —54Ea **100**
Cecil Rd. Ilf —35Rc **66**
Cecil Rd. Iver —44G **74**
Cecil Rd. Romf —31Zc **67**
Cecil Rd. S Mim —4Wa **8**
Cecil Rd. Sutt —79Bb **145**
Cecil Rosen Ct. Wemb —34Ka **58**
Cecil St. Wat —10X **5**
Cecil Way. Brom —74Jc **149**
Cecil Way. Slou —2D **72**
Cedar Av. Barn —17Gb **23**
Cedar Av. Cob —87Y **159**
Cedar Av. Enf —12Yb **26**
Cedar Av. Grav —3E **136**
Cedar Av. Hay —44W **76**
Cedar Av. Romf —29Ad **47**
Cedar Av. Ruis —36Y **57**
Cedar Av. Sidc —59Wc **109**
Cedar Av. Twic —58Da **99**
Cedar Av. Upm —35Qd **69**
Cedar Av. Wal X —5Zb **12**
Cedar Av. W Dray —45P **75**
Cedar Clo. SE21 —60Sb **105**
Cedar Clo. SW15 —63Ta **123**
Cedar Clo. Brom —76Nc **150**
Cedar Clo. Buck H —19Mc **27**
Cedar Clo. Burn —2B **72**
Cedar Clo. Cars —79Hb **145**
Cedar Clo. E Mol —70Ga **122**
Cedar Clo. Eps —86Va **162**
Cedar Clo. Esh —79Ba **141**
Cedar Clo. Hut —17Fe **33**
Cedar Clo. Pot B —2Cb **9**
Cedar Clo. Romf —28Ed **48**
Cedar Clo. Stai —69L **119**
Cedar Clo. Swan —68Ed **132**
Cedar Clo. Warl —91Ac **182**
Cedar Copse. Brom —68Pc **130**
Cedar Ct. E8 —38Vb **63**
Cedar Ct. E18 —25Jc **45**
Cedar Ct. N1 —38Sb **63**
Cedar Ct. N10 —26Jb **42**
Cedar Ct. N11 —22Lb **42**
Cedar Ct. N20 —18Fb **23**
Cedar Ct. SW19 —62Za **124**
*Cedar Ct. Bren —51Ma **101***
(off Boston Mnr. Rd.)
Cedar Ct. Egh —63C **118**
Cedar Ct. Epp —3Wc **15**
Cedar Ct. Wind —4E **94**
Cedar Cres. Kes —76Nc **150**
Cedarcroft Rd. Chess —77Pa **143**
Cedar Dri. N2 —28Gb **41**
Cedar Dri. Fet —95Ga **176**
Cedar Dri. Pinn —24Ca **37**
Cedar Dri. S'hill —10H **117**
Cedar Dri. S at H —68Rd **133**
Cedar Gdns. Sutt —79Eb **145**

Cedar Gdns.—Charlton Dene

Cedar Gdns. Upm —34Sd 70
Cedar Gdns. Wok —6E 188
Cedar Grange. Enf —15Ub 25
Cedar Gro. W5 —48Na 79
Cedar Gro. Bex —58Zc 129
Cedar Gro. S'hall —43Ca 77
Cedar Gro. Wey —77S 140
Cedar Heights. Rich —60Na 101
Cedar Hill. Eps —88Sa 161
Cedar Ho. N22 —25Qb 42
(off Acacia Rd.)
Cedar Ho. W8 —48Db 81
(off Marloes Rd.)
Cedar Ho. Hay —42Y 77
Cedarhurst. Brom —66Gc 129
Cedarhurst Cotts. Bex —60Cd 110
Cedarhurst Dri. SE9 —57Lc 107
Cedarland Ter. SW20 —66Xa 124
Cedar Lawn Av. Barn —15Ab 22
Cedar Mt. SE9 —60Mc 107
Cedarne Rd. SW6 —52Db 103
Cedar Pk. Gdns. Romf —31Zc 67
Cedar Pk. Rd. Enf —10Sb 11
Cedar Pl. SE7 —50Lc 85
Cedar Pl. N'wd —23S 36
Cedar Rise. N14 —17Jb 24
Cedar Rd. N17 —25Vb 43
Cedar Rd. NW2 —35Ya 60
Cedar Rd. Brom —68Lc 129
Cedar Rd. Cob —86X 159
Cedar Rd. Croy —75Ub 147
Cedar Rd. Dart —60Md 111
Cedar Rd. E Mol —70Ga 122
Cedar Rd. Enf —10Rb 11
Cedar Rd. Eri —53Jd 110
Cedar Rd. Felt —60T 98
Cedar Rd. Grays —8C 92
Cedar Rd. Horn —34Ld 69
Cedar Rd. Houn —54Y 99
Cedar Rd. Hut —16Fe 33
Cedar Rd. Romf —28Ed 48
Cedar Rd. Sutt —79Eb 145
Cedar Rd. Tedd —64Ja 122
Cedar Rd. Wat —16Y 19
Cedar Rd. Wey —77Q 140
Cedar Rd. Wok —8E 188
Cedars. Bans —86Hb 163
Cedars. Stanf —1N 93
Cedars Av. E17 —29Cc 44
Cedars Av. Mitc —70Jb 126
Cedars Av. Rick —18L 17
Cedars Clo. NW4 —27Za 40
Cedars Clo. Borwd —14Ra 21
Cedars Clo. Ger X —22A 34
Cedars Ct. N9 —19Ub 25
Cedars Dri. Uxb —40P 55
Cedars Ho. E17 —27Dc 44
Cedars M. SW4 —56Kb 104
Cedars Rd. E15 —37Gc 65
Cedars Rd. N9 —19Wb 25
Cedars Rd. N21 —19Rb 25
Cedars Rd. SW4 —55Kb 104
Cedars Rd. SW13 —54Wa 102
Cedars Rd. W4 —51Sa 101
Cedars Rd. Beck —68Ac 128
Cedars Rd. Croy —76Nb 146
Cedars Rd. King T —67La 122
Cedars Rd. Mord —70Cb 125
Cedars, The. W13 —44La 78
Cedars, The. Buck H —18Jc 27
Cedars, The. Byfl —84P 157
Cedars, The. Lea —93Ma 177
Cedars, The. Tedd —65Ha 122
Cedars, The. Wall —77Lb 146
Cedar Ter. Rich —56Na 101
Cedar Ter. Rd. Sev —95Ld 187
Cedar Tree Gro. SE27 —64Rb 127
Cedarville Gdns. SW16 —65Pb 126
Cedar Vista. Rich —54Na 101
Cedar Wlk. Kenl —88Sb 165
Cedar Wlk. Tad —92Ab 178
Cedar Wlk. Wal A —6Fc 13
Cedar Way. NW1 —38Mb 62
Cedar Way. Slou —50A 74
Cedar Way. Sun —66U 120
Cedar Wood Dri. Wat —7X 5
Cedra Ct. N16 —32Wb 63
Cedric Av. Romf —27Gd 48
Cedric Rd. SE9 —62Sc 130
Celadon Clo. Enf —13Ac 26
Celandine Clo. E3 —43Cc 84
Celandine Clo. S Ock —42Yd 90
Celandine Ct. E4 —20Dc 26
Celandine Dri. SE28 —46Xc 87
Celandine Rd. W on T —77Aa 141
Celandine Way. E15 —41Gc 85
Celbridge M. W2 —44Db 81
(off Porchester Rd.)
Celebridge M. W2 —43Db 81
Celedon Clo. Grays —48Ae 91
Celestial Gdns. SE13 —56Fc 107
Celia Cres. Ashf —65M 119
Celia Ho. N1 —40Ub 63 (2H 195)
(off Arden Est.)
Celia Johnston Ct. Borwd —11Sa 21
Celia Rd. N19 —35Lb 62
Cell Farm Av. Old Win —7M 95
Celtic Av. Brom —69Gc 129
Celtic Rd. Byfl —86N 157
Celtic St. E14 —43Dc 84
Cement Block Cotts. Grays
—51Ee 113
Cemetery La. SE7 —51Nc 108
Cemetery Rd. E7 —35Hc 65
Cemetery Rd. N17 —24Ub 43
Cemetery Rd. SE2 —52Xc 109
Cenacle Clo. NW3 —34Cb 61
Centaurs Bus. Cen. Iswth —51Ja 100
Centaur St. SE1 —48Pb 82 (3J 205)
Centenary Rd. Enf —14Bc 26
Centenary Trading Est. Enf
—14Bc 26
Central Av. E11 —33Fc 65
Central Av. N2 —26Fb 41
(East Finchley)
Central Av. N2 —28Db 41
(St Marylebone Cemetery)
Central Av. N9 —20Ub 25
Central Av. SW11 —52Hb 103
Central Av. Enf —12Xb 25
Central Av. Grav —1D 136
Central Av. Grays —50Vd 90
Central Av. Hay —46V 76
Central Av. Houn —56Ea 100
Central Av. Pinn —30Ba 37
Central Av. S Ock —47Sd 90
Central Av. Til —3C 114
Central Av. Wall —78Nb 146
Central Av. Wal X —5Ac 12
Central Av. Well —54Vc 109
Central Av. W Mol —70Ba 121
Central Bus. Cen. NW10 —36Ua 60
Central Cir. NW4 —29Xa 40
Central Dri. Horn —34Nd 69
Central Dri. Slou —5D 72
Central Hill. SE19 —65Tb 127
Central Ho. E15 —40Ec 64
Central La. Wink —10A 94
Central Mans. NW4 —30Xa 40
(off Watford Way)
Central Markets. EC1
—43Rb 83 (1B 200)
(off Charterhouse St.)
Central Pde. E17 —28Cc 44
Central Pde. SE20 —66Zb 128
(off High St. Penge)
Central Pde. W3 —47Ra 79
Central Pde. Felt —59Y 99
Central Pde. Gnfd —41Ja 78
Central Pde. Harr —29Ha 38
Central Pde. New Ad —82Ec 166
Central Pde. Uxb —41Q 76
Central Pk. Av. Dag —34Dd 68
Central Pk. Est. Houn —57Z 99
Central Pk. Rd. E6 —40Mc 65
Central Rd. Dart —57Nd 111
Central Rd. Mord —72Cb 145
Central Rd. Stanf —2M 93
Central Rd. Wemb —36Ka 58
Central Rd. Wor Pk —74Wa 144
Central School Path. SW14
—55Sa 101
Central Sq. NW11 —30Db 41
Central Sq. Wemb —36Na 59
Central St. EC1 —41Sb 83 (3D 194)
Central Ter. Beck —69Zb 128
Central Way. SE28 —46Wc 87
Central Way. Cars —80Gb 145
Central Way. Felt —57W 98
Central Way. N'wd —24U 36
Central Way. Oxt —99Fc 183
Central Way. Wink —10A 94
Centre Av. N2 —26Gb 41
Centre Av. W3 —46Ta 79
Centre Av. Epp —4Vc 15
Centre Clo. Epp —4Vc 15
Centre Comn. Rd. Chst —65Sc 130
Centre Ct. W2 —45Eb 81
(off Princes Sq.)
Centre Ct. Shopping Cen. SW19
—65Bb 125
Centre Dri. E7 —35Lc 65
Centre Dri. Epp —4Vc 15
Centre Grn. Epp —4Vc 15
Centre Rd. E11 & E7 —33Jc 65
Centre Rd. Dag —40Dd 88
Centre Rd. New Ash —76Ae 155
Centre St. E2 —40Xb 63
Centre, The. Felt —61W 120
Centre, The. W on T —74V 140
Centre Way. E17 —24Ec 44
Centre Way. N9 —19Yb 26
Centre Way. Ilf —33Sc 66
Centre Way. Wal A —7Ec 12
Centric Clo. NW1 —39Jb 62
Centro Ct. E6 —42Pc 86
Centurion Clo. N7 —38Pb 62
Centurion La. E3 —40Bc 64
Centurion Way. Eri —48Bd 87
Centurion Way. Purf —49Pd 89
Centuryan Pl. Dart —56Kd 111
Century Ct. Wat —17S 18
Century Ho. SW15 —56Za 102
Century Rd. E17 —27Ac 44
Century Rd. Stai —64E 118
Cephas Av. E1 —42Yb 84
Cephas St. E1 —42Yb 84
Ceres Rd. SE18 —49Vc 87
Cerise Rd. SE15 —53Wb 105
Cerne Clo. Hay —45Y 77
Cerne Rd. Grav —3G 136
Cerne Rd. Mord —72Eb 145
Cerotus Pl. Cher —73H 139
Cervantes Ct. W2 —44Db 81
Cervantes Ct. N'wd —24V 36
Cervia Way. Grav —2H 137
Cester St. E2 —39Wb 63
Ceylon Rd. W14 —48Za 80
Chace Av. Pot B —4Fb 9
Chadacre Av. Ilf —27Pc 46
Chadacre Ct. E13 —39Jc 65
(off Vicars Clo.)
Chadacre Rd. Eps —79Xa 144
Chadbourn St. E14 —43Dc 84
Chadbury Ct. NW7 —24Wa 40
Chadd Dri. Brom —69Nc 130
Chadfields. Til —2C 114
Chad Grn. E13 —39Jc 65
(in two parts)
Chadville Gdns. Romf —29Zc 47
Chadway. Dag —32Yc 67
Chadwell Av. Chesh —1Yb 12
Chadwell Av. Romf —31Xc 67
Chadwell By-Pass. Grays —10B 92
Chadwell Heath La. Chad —28Xc 47
Chadwell Hill. Grays —10D 92
Chadwell Rd. Grays —49Ee 91
Chadwell St. EC1
—41Qb 82 (3A 194)
Chadwick Av. E4 —21Fc 45
Chadwick Clo. W7 —44Ha 78
Chadwick Clo. Grav —2A 136
Chadwick Clo. Tedd —65Ja 122
Chadwick Dri. H Wood —26Md 49
Chadwick Rd. E11 —31Gc 65
Chadwick Rd. NW10 —39Va 60
Chadwick Rd. SE15 —54Vb 105
Chadwick Rd. Ilf —34Rc 66
Chadwick St. SW1
—48Mb 82 (4D 204)
Chadwick Way. SE28 —45Zc 87
Chadwin Rd. E13 —43Kc 85
Chadworth Ho. N4 —32Sb 63
Chadworth Way. Clay —78Fa 142
Chaffers Mead. Asht —88Pa 161
Chaffinch Av. Croy —72Zb 148
Chaffinch Clo. N9 —18Zb 26
Chaffinch Clo. Croy —71Zb 148
Chaffinch Clo. Surb —76Qa 143
Chaffinch La. Wat —17V 18
Chaffinch Rd. Beck —67Ac 128
Chafford. Brtwd —18Xd 32
Chafford Gdns. W Horn —30Fe 51
Chafford Wlk. Rain —40Ld 69
Chafford Way. Grays —46Ce 91
Chafford Way. Romf —28Yc 47
Chagford St. NW1
—42Hb 81 (6F 191)
Chailey Av. Enf —12Vb 25
Chailey Clo. Houn —53Z 99
Chailey Ind. Est. Hay —47W 76
Chailey Pl. W on T —77Aa 141
Chailey St. E5 —34Yb 64
Chairmans Av. Den —29H 35
Chalbury Wlk. N1
—40Qb 62 (1K 193)
Chalcombe Rd. SE2 —48Xc 87
Chalcot Clo. Sutt —80Cb 145
Chalcot Cres. NW1 —39Hb 61
Chalcot Gdns. NW3 —37Hb 61
Chalcot M. SW16 —62Nb 126
Chalcot Rd. NW1 —38Jb 62
Chalcot Sq. NW1 —38Jb 62
Chalcott. Chalv —8J 73
Chalcott Gdns. Surb —74La 142
Chalcroft Rd. SE13 —57Gc 107
Chaldon Comn. Rd. Cat —96Sb 181
Chaldon Ct. SE19 —67Tb 127
Chaldon Rd. SW6 —52Ab 102
Chaldon Rd. Cat —96Tb 181
Chaldon Way. Coul —89Nb 164
Chale Ct. Stanf —3L 93
(off St Margaret's Av.)
Chale Rd. SW2 —58Nb 104
Chalet Clo. Bex —63Fd 132
Chale Wlk. Sutt —81Db 163
Chalfont Av. Amer —11A 16
Chalfont Av. Wemb —37Ra 59
Chalfont Ct. NW9 —27Va 40
Chalfont Ct. Harr —30Ha 38
(off Northwick Pk. Rd.)
Chalfont Grn. N9 —20Ub 25
Chalfont Ho. Wat —16U 18
Chalfont La. Chor —15D 16
Chalfont La. Ger X & W Hyd
—24E 34
Chalfont Rd. N9 —20Ub 25
Chalfont Rd. SE25 —69Vb 127
Chalfont Rd. Ger X & Chor —19D 16
Chalfont Rd. Hay —47W 76
Chalfont St Peter By-Pass. Chal P &
Ger X —25A 34
Chalfont Wlk. Pinn —26Y 37
Chalfont Way. W13 —48Ka 78
Chalford Clo. W Mol —70Ca 121
Chalforde Gdns. Romf —28Kd 49
Chalford Rd. SE21 —63Tb 127
Chalford Wlk. Wfd G —25Mc 45
Chalgrove Av. Mord —71Cb 145
Chalgrove Cres. Ilf —26Nc 46
Chalgrove Gdns. N3 —27Ab 40
Chalgrove Rd. E9 —37Yb 64
Chalgrove Rd. N17 —25Xb 43
Chalgrove Rd. Sutt —80Fb 145
Chalice Clo. Wall —79Mb 146
Chalice Ct. N2 —28Gb 41
Chalice Way. Grnh —57Ud 112
Chalk Ct. Grays —51Ce 113
Chalkenden Clo. SE20 —66Xb 127
Chalk Farm Rd. NW1 —38Jb 62
Chalk Hill. Wat —16Z 19
Chalkhill Rd. W6 —49Za 80
Chalkhill Rd. Wemb —34Qa 59
Chalklands. Wemb —35Sa 59
Chalk La. Asht —91Pa 177
Chalk La. Barn —13Hb 23
Chalk La. Eps —87Ta 161
Chalkley Clo. Mitc —68Hb 125
Chalk Paddock. Eps —87Ta 161
Chalk Pit Av. Orp —69Yc 131
Chalk Pit Caravan Site. Sidc
—66Bd 131
Chalkpit La. Bookh —100Ba 175
Chalk Pit La. Burn —8A 52
Chalkpit La. Oxt —98Ec 182
Chalk Pit Rd. Bans —89Cb 163
Chalk Pit Rd. Eps —91Sa 177
Chalk Pit Way. Sutt —79Eb 145
Chalkpit Wood. Oxt —99Fc 183
Chalk Rd. E13 —43Kc 85
Chalk Rd. Grav —10J 115
Chalkstone Clo. Well —53Wc 109
Chalkwell Pk. Av. Enf —14Ub 25
Chalky Bank. Grav —3C 136
Chalky La. Chess —82Ma 161
Challacombe Clo. Hut —18De 33
Challenge Clo. Grav —3H 137
Challenge Ct. Lea —91Ka 176
Challenge Rd. Ashf —62T 120
Challice Way. SW2 —60Pb 104
Challin St. SE20 —67Yb 128
Challis Rd. Bren —50Ma 79
Challock Clo. Big H —88Lc 167
Challoner Clo. N2 —26Fb 41
Challoner Cres. W14 —50Bb 81
Challoners Clo. E Mol —70Fa 122
Challoner St. W14 —50Bb 81
Chalmers Ho. E17 —29Dc 44
Chalmers Rd. Ashf —64R 120
Chalmers Rd. Bans —87Fb 163
Chalmers Rd. E. Ashf —63R 120
Chalmer's Wlk. SE17 —51Rb 105
(off Hillingdon St.)
Chalmers Way. Felt —57X 99
Chalsey Rd. SE4 —56Bc 106
Chalton Dri. N2 —30Fb 41
Chalton St. NW1
—40Lb 62 (1C 192)
Chalvey Gdns. Slou —7J 73
Chalvey Gro. Slou —8F 72
Chalvey Pk. Slou —7J 73
Chalvey Rd. E. Slou —7J 73
Chalvey Rd. W. Slou —7H 73
Chamberlain Clo. SE28 —48Tc 86
Chamberlain Cotts. SE5 —53Tb 105
Chamberlain Cres. W Wick
—74Dc 148
Chamberlain La. Pinn —28W 36
Chamberlain Pl. E17 —27Ac 44
Chamberlain Rd. N2 —26Eb 41
Chamberlain Rd. N9 —20Wb 25
Chamberlain Rd. W13 —47Ja 78
Chamberlain St. NW1 —38Hb 61
Chamberlain Way. Felt —63Aa 121
Chamberlain Way. Pinn —27X 37
Chamberlain Way. Surb —73Na 143
Chamberlayne Rd. NW10 —38Ya 60
Chambers Gdns. N2 —25Fb 41
Chambers La. NW10 —38Xa 60
Chambers Rd. N7 —35Nb 62
Chambers St. SE16 —47Wb 83
Chamber St. E1 —45Vb 83
Chambers Wharf. SE16 —47Wb 83
Chambord St. E2
—41Vb 83 (4K 195)
Chamomile Ct. E17 —30Cc 44
(off Yunus Khan Clo.)
Champion Clo. Stanf —1N 93
Champion Cres. SE26 —63Ac 128
Champion Gro. SE5 —55Tb 105
Champion Hill. SE5 —55Tb 105
Champion Hill Est. SE5 —55Ub 105
Champion Pk. SE5 —54Tb 105
Champion Rd. SE26 —63Ac 128
Champion Rd. Upm —33Rd 69
Champlain Ho. W12 —45Xa 80
(off White City Est.)
Champness Clo. SE27 —63Tb 127
Champneys Clo. Sutt —80Bb 145
Chance Clo. Grays —48Be 91
Chancel Clo. W King —80Ud 154
Chancel Ind. Est. NW10 —37Va 60
Chancellor Gdns. S Croy
—81Rb 165
Chancellor Gro. SE21 —61Sb 127
Chancellor Pas. E14 —46Cc 84
Chancellors Ct. WC1
—43Pb 82 (7H 193)
(off Olde Hall St.)
Chancellor's Rd. W6 —50Ya 80
Chancellor's St. W6 —50Ya 80
Chancellors Wharf. W6 —50Ya 80
Chancellor Way. Sev —94Jd 186
Chancelot Rd. SE2 —49Xc 87
Chancel St. SE1 —46Rb 83 (7B 200)
Chancery Ct. Dart —59Qd 111
Chancery La. WC2
—44Qb 82 (1J 199)
Chancery La. Beck —68Dc 128
Chance St. E2 & E1
—42Vb 83 (5K 195)
Chanctonbury Clo. SE9 —62Rc 130
Chanctonbury Gdns. Sutt
—80Db 145
Chanctonbury Way. N12 —23Bb 41
Chandler Av. E16 —43Jc 85
Chandler Clo. Hamp —67Ca 121
Chandler Rd. Lou —11Rc 28
Chandlers Clo. Felt —59V 98
Chandlers Corner. Rain —41Ld 89
Chandler's La. Chan X —8N 3
Chandlers M. E14 —47Cc 84
Chandler St. E1 —46Xb 83
Chandlers Way. SW2 —59Qb 104
Chandlers Way. Romf —29Gd 48
Chandos Av. E17 —26Cc 44
Chandos Av. N14 —20Lb 24
Chandos Av. N20 —18Eb 23
Chandos Av. W5 —49La 78
Chandos Clo. Buck H —19Kc 27
Chandos Ct. N14 —19Mb 24
Chandos Ct. Edgw —24Pa 39
Chandos Cres. Edgw —24Pa 39
Chandos Mall. Chalv —7K 73
Chandos Pde. Edgw —24Pa 39
Chandos Pl. WC2
—45Nb 82 (5F 199)
Chandos Rd. E15 —36Fc 65
Chandos Rd. N2 —26Fb 41
Chandos Rd. N17 —26Ub 43
Chandos Rd. NW2 —36Ya 60
Chandos Rd. NW10 —42Ua 80
Chandos Rd. Borwd —12Pa 21
Chandos Rd. Harr —29Ea 38
Chandos Rd. Pinn —31Z 57
Chandos Rd. Stai —64F 118
Chandos St. W1 —43Kb 82 (1A 198)
Chandos Way. NW11 —32Db 61
Change All. EC3 —44Tb 83 (3G 201)
Chanlock Path. S Ock —45Xd 90
Channel Clo. Houn —53Ca 99
Channelsea Rd. E15 —39Fc 65
Channing Clo. Horn —31Pd 69
Chanton Dri. Eps —82Ya 162
Chantree Grn. W4 —49Sa 79
Chantrey Rd. SW9 —55Pb 104
Chantreywood. Brtwd —20Ce 33
Chantry Av. Hart —72Ae 155
Chantry Clo. Asht —91La 176
Chantry Clo. Enf —10Sb 11
Chantry Clo. Harr —29Pa 39
Chantry Clo. K Lan —1Q 4
Chantry Clo. Sidc —64Ad 131
Chantry Clo. W Dray —45M 75
Chantry Clo. Wind —3E 94
Chantry Ct. Grav —8E 114
Chantry Cres. Stanf —2L 93
Chantry Hurst. Eps —87Ta 161
Chantry La. Brom —71Mc 149
Chantry Pl. Harr —25Da 37
Chantry Rd. Cher —73L 139
Chantry Rd. Chess —78Pa 143
Chantry Rd. Harr —25Da 37
Chantry Sq. W8 —48Db 81
Chantry St. N1 —39Rb 63 (1C 194)
Chantry, The. E4 —18Ec 26
Chantry, The. Uxb —41P 75
Chantry Way. Rain —40Fd 68
Chant Sq. E15 —38Fc 65
Chant St. E15 —38Fc 65
Chanute Gdns. SE16 —49Zb 84
Chapel Av. Add —77K 139
Chapel Clo. Dart —57Gd 110
Chapel Clo. Grays —51Xd 112
Chapel Clo. Wat —6V 4
Chapel Ct. N2 —27Gb 41
Chapel Ct. SE1 —47Tb 83 (1F 207)
(off Borough High St.)
Chapel Ct. SW1 —47Tb 83
Chapel Croft. Chfd —3J 3
Chapel Farm Rd. SE9 —62Pc 130
Chapel Gro. Add —77K 139
Chapel Gro. Eps —91Ya 178
Chapel High. Brtwd —19Yd 32
(off High St. Brentwood)
Chapel High Shopping Cen. Brtwd
—19Yd 32
Chapel Hill. N2 —26Gb 41
Chapel Hill. Dart —57Gd 110
Chapel Hill. Eff —99Z 175
Chapel Ho. St. E14 —50Dc 84
Chapel La. Bookh —100Ea 176
Chapel La. Chig —20Vc 29
Chapel La. Pinn —27Z 37
Chapel La. Romf —31Zc 67
Chapel La. Stoke P —8M 53
Chapel La. Uxb —44Q 76
Chapel Mkt. N1 —40Qb 62 (1K 193)
Chapelmount Rd. Wfd G —23Pc 46
Chapel Pk. Rd. Add —77K 139
Chapel Path. E11 —30Jc 45
(off Woodbine Pl.)
Chapel Pl. EC2 —41Ub 83 (4H 195)
Chapel Pl. N1 —40Qb 62 (1A 194)
Chapel Pl. N17 —24Vb 43
Chapel Pl. W1 —44Kb 82 (3K 197)
Chapel Rd. SE27 —63Rb 127
Chapel Rd. W13 —46Ka 78
Chapel Rd. Bexh —56Cd 110
Chapel Rd. Epp —2Vc 15
Chapel Rd. Houn —55Da 99
Chapel Rd. Ilf —34Qc 66
Chapel Rd. Tad —95Ya 178
Chapel Rd. Twic —59Ka 100
Chapel Rd. Warl —90Zb 166
Chapel Row. Hare —25L 35
Chapel Side. W2 —45Db 81
Chapel Stones. N17 —25Vb 43
Chapel St. NW1 —43Gb 81 (1D 196)
Chapel St. SW1 —48Jb 82 (3J 203)
Chapel St. Enf —13Tb 25
Chapel St. Slou —7K 73
Chapel St. Uxb —39L 55
Chapel St. Wok —89B 156
Chapel Ter. Lou —14Nc 28
Chapel View. S Croy —79Yb 148
Chapel Wlk. NW4 —28Xa 40
(in two parts)
Chapel Wlk. Croy —75Sb 147
Chapel Way. N7 —34Pb 62
Chapel Way. Eps —91Ya 178
Chapel Wood. New Ash —74Ae 155
Chapel Wood Rd. Ash & Hart
—76Ae 155
Chaplaincy Gdns. Horn —32Nd 69
Chaplin Clo. SE1
—47Rb 83 (1A 206)
Chaplin Cres. Sun —65U 120
Chaplin Gro. Wemb —37Ma 59
Chaplin Rd. E15 —40Hc 65
Chaplin Rd. N17 —27Vb 43
Chaplin Rd. NW2 —37Wa 60
Chaplin Rd. Dag —38Ad 67
Chaplin Rd. Wemb —37La 58
Chapman Clo. W Dray —48P 75
Chapman Cres. Harr —30Na 39
Chapman Rd. E9 —37Bc 64
Chapman Rd. Belv —50Dd 88
Chapman Rd. Croy —74Qb 146
Chapman's Hill. Meop —79Fe 155
Chapman's La. SE2 & Belv —49Zc 87
Chapman's La. Orp —68Zc 131
Chapmans Rd. Sund —96Ad 185
Chapman St. E1 —45Xb 83
Chapmans Yd. Wat —14Z 19
Chapone Pl. W1
(off Dean St.) —44Mb 82 (3D 198)
Chapter Clo. W4 —48Sa 79
Chapter Clo. Uxb —38P 55
Chapter Ho. Ct. EC4
—44Sb 83 (3D 200)
(off St Paul's All.)
Chapter M. Wind —2H 95
Chapter Rd. NW2 —36Wa 60
Chapter Rd. SE17 —50Rb 83
Chapter St. SW1
—49Mb 82 (6D 204)
Chapter Ter. SE17 —51Rb 105
Chapter Way. Hamp —63Ca 121
Chara Pl. W4 —51Ta 101
Charcroft Ct. W14 —47Za 80
(off Minford Gdns.)
Charcroft Gdns. Enf —14Zb 26
Chardin Rd. W4 —49Ua 80
Chardmore Rd. N16 —32Wb 63
Chard Rd. Houn —54R 98
Chardwell Clo. E6 —44Pc 86
Charecroft Way. W12 —47Za 80
Charfield Ct. W9 —42Db 81
(off Shirland Rd.)
Charford Rd. E16 —43Jc 85
Chargate Clo. W on T —79V 140
Chargeable La. E13 —42Hc 85
Chargeable St. E16 —42Hc 85
Chargrove Clo. SE16 —47Zb 84
Charing Clo. Orp —77Vc 151
Charing Ct. Short —68Gc 129
Charing Cross. SW1
(off Whitehall) —46Nb 82 (6F 199)
Charing Cross Rd. WC2
—44Mb 82 (2E 198)
Charing Ho. SE1 —47Qb 82 (1A 206)
(off Windmill Wlk.)
Chariots Pl. Wind —3H 95
Charlbert St. NW8
—40Gb 61 (1D 190)
Charlbury Av. Stan —22Ma 39
Charlbury Clo. Romf —23Ld 49
Charlbury Cres. Romf —23Ld 49
Charlbury Gdns. Ilf —33Vc 67
Charlbury Gro. W5 —44La 78
Charlbury Rd. Uxb —34P 55
Charldane Rd. SE9 —62Rc 130
Charlecote Gro. SE26 —62Xb 127
Charlecote Rd. Dag —34Ad 67
Charlemont Rd. E6 —41Pc 86
Charles Barry Clo. SW4 —55Lb 104
Charles Bradlaugh Ho. N17
—24Xb 43
(off Haynes Clo.)
Charles Clo. Sidc —63Xc 131
Charles Ct. Eri —51Gd 110
Charles Cres. Harr —31Fa 58
Charles Curran Ho. Uxb —34R 56
Charle Sevright Dri. NW7 —22Za 40
Charlesfield. SE9 —62Lc 129
Charles Gdns. Slou —4M 73
Charles Gardner Ct. N1
—41Tb 83 (3G 195)
(off Haberdasher Est.)
Charles Grinling Wlk. SE18
—49Qc 86
Charles Ho. N15 —24Vb 43
(off Love La.)
Charles Ho. Wind —3G 94
Charles La. NW8
—40Gb 61 (2C 190)
Charles Pl. NW1 —41Lb 82 (4C 192)
Charles Rd. E7 —38Lc 65
Charles Rd. SW19 —67Cb 125
Charles Rd. W13 —44Ja 78
Charles Rd. Badg M —82Dd 170
Charles Rd. Dag —37Fd 68
Charles Rd. Romf —30Zc 47
Charles Rd. Stai —65M 119
Charles II Pl. SW3
—50Gb 81 (7E 202)
Charles II St. SW1
—46Mb 82 (6D 198)
Charles Sq. N1 —41Tb 83 (4G 195)
Charles Sq. Est. N1
—41Tb 83 (4G 195)
(off Charles Sq.)
Charles St. E16 —46Lc 85
Charles St. SW13 —54Ua 102
Charles St. W1 —46Kb 82 (6K 197)
Charles St. Cher —74H 139
Charles St. Croy —76Sb 147
Charles St. Enf —15Vb 25
Charles St. Epp —4Wc 15
Charles St. Grays —51De 113
Charles St. Grnh —57Vd 112
Charles St. Houn —54Ba 99
Charles St. Uxb —42R 76
Charles St. Wind —3G 94
Charles St. Trading Est. E16
—46Lc 85
Charleston Clo. Felt —62W 120
Charleston St. SE17
—49Sb 83 (6E 206)
Charles Uton Ct. E8 —35Wb 63
Charleville Cir. SE26 —64Wb 127
Charleville Mans. W14 —50Ab 80
(off Charleville Rd.)
Charleville Rd. W14 —50Ab 80
Charlieville Rd. Eri —52Ed 110
Charlmont Rd. SW17 —65Gb 125
Charlock Way. Wat —16V 18
Charlotte Clo. Bexh —57Ad 109
Charlotte Ct. N8 —30Mb 42
Charlotte Ct. Ilf —30Pc 46
Charlotte Despard Av. SW11
—53Jb 104
Charlotte Gdns. Romf —23Dd 48
Charlotte M. W1 —43Lb 82 (7C 192)
Charlotte M. W14 —49Ab 80
Charlotte Pl. NW9 —29Sa 39
Charlotte Pl. SW1
—49Lb 82 (6B 204)
Charlotte Pl. W1 —43Lb 82 (1C 198)
Charlotte Pl. Grays —51Xd 112
Charlotte Rd. EC2
—41Ub 83 (4H 195)
Charlotte Rd. SW13 —53Va 102
Charlotte Rd. Dag —37Dd 68
Charlotte Rd. Wall —79Lb 146
Charlotte Row. SW4 —55Lb 104
Charlotte Sq. Rich —58Pa 101
Charlotte St. W1
—43Lb 82 (7C 192)
Charlotte Ter. N1
—39Pb 62 (1J 193)
Charlow Clo. SW6 —54Eb 103
Charlton. Wind —4A 94
Charlton Av. W on T —77X 141
Charlton Chu. La. SE7 —50Lc 85
Charlton Clo. Slou —7F 72
Charlton Clo. Uxb —33R 56
Charlton Ct. E2 —39Vb 63 (1K 195)
Charlton Cres. Bark —40Vc 67
Charlton Dene. SE7 —52Lc 107

Charlton Dri.—Chesterfield Rd.

Charlton Dri. Big H —89Mc 167
Charlton Gdns. Coul —90Lb 164
Charlton Ho. Bren —51Na 101
Charlton Kings. Wey —76U 140
Charlton King's Rd. NW5 —36Mb 62
Charlton La. SE7 —49Mc 85
Charlton La. Shep —69S 120
Charlton Pk. La. SE7 —52Mc 107
Charlton Pk. Rd. SE7 —51Mc 107
Charlton Pl. N1 —40Rb 63 (1B 194)
Charlton Rd. N9 —18Zb 26
Charlton Rd. NW10 —39Ua 60
Charlton Rd. SE3 & SE7 —52Jc 107
Charlton Rd. Harr —28Ma 39
Charlton Rd. Shep —69S 120
Charlton Rd. Wemb —32Pa 59
Charlton Sq. Wind —4A 94
Charlton St. Grays —51Zd 113
Charlton Way. SE3 —53Gc 107
Charlwood. Croy —81Bc 166
Charlwood Clo. Harr —23Ga 38
Charlwood Dri. Oxs —87Fa 160
Charlwood Pl. SW1 —49Lb 82 (6C 204)
Charlwood Rd. SW15 —56Za 102
Charlwood St. SW1 —50Lb 82 (7B 204)
Charlwood Ter. SW15 —56Za 102
Charmian Av. Stan —27Ma 39
Charminster Av. SW19 —68Cb 125
Charminster Ct. Surb —73Ma 143
Charminster Rd. SE9 —63Mc 129
Charminster Rd. Wor Pk —74Za 144
Charmouth Ct. Rich —57Pa 101
Charmouth Ho. SW8 —52Pb 104
Charmouth Rd. Well —53Yc 109
Charmwood La. Orp —81Xc 169
Charne, The. Otf —89Jd 170
Charnock. Swan —70Gd 132
Charnock Rd. E5 —34Xb 63
Charnwood Av. SW19 —68Cb 125
Charnwood Clo. N Mald —70Ua 124
Charnwood Dri. E18 —27Kc 45
Charnwood Gdns. E14 —49Cc 84
Charnwood Pl. N20 —20Eb 23
Charnwood Rd. SE25 —71Tb 147
Charnwood Rd. Enf —8Xb 11
Charnwood Rd. Uxb —40Q 56
Charnwood St. E5 —33Xb 63
Charrington Rd. Croy —75Sb 147
Charrington St. NW1 —40Mb 62 (1D 192)
Charsley Rd. SE6 —61Dc 128
Charta Rd. Egh —65E 118
Chart Clo. Brom —67Gc 129
Chart Clo. Croy —72Yb 148
Charter Av. Ilf —32Tc 66
Charter Clo. Slou —8K 73
Charter Ct. N4 —32Qb 62
Charter Ct. N22 —25Mb 42
Charter Ct. N Mald —69Ua 124
Charter Ct. S'hall —46Ca 77
Charter Cres. Houn —56Aa 99
Charter Dri. Bex —59Ad 109
Charterhouse Av. Wemb —36La 58
Charterhouse Bldgs. EC1 —42Rb 83 (6D 194)
Charterhouse Dri. Sev —95Jd 186
Charterhouse M. EC1 —43Rb 83 (7C 194)
Charterhouse Rd. Orp —76Wc 151
Charterhouse Sq. EC1 —43Rb 83 (7C 194)
Charterhouse St. EC1 —43Qb 82 (1A 200)
Charteris Rd. N4 —32Qb 62
Charteris Rd. NW6 —39Bb 61
Charteris Rd. Wfd G —24Kc 45
Charter Pl. Uxb —38M 55
Charter Pl. Wat —13Y 19
Charter Rd. King T —69Ra 123
Charter Rd. Slou —5C 72
Charter Rd., The. Wfd G —23Gc 45
Charters Clo. SE19 —64Ub 127
Charter Sq. King T —68Ra 123
Charter Way. N3 —28Bb 41
Charter Way. N14 —16Lb 24
Chartfield Av. SW15 —57Xa 102
Chartfield Sq. SW15 —57Za 102
Chartham Ct. SW9 —55Qb 104
(off Canterbury Cres.)
Chartham Gro. SE27 —62Rb 127
Chartham Rd. SE25 —69Xb 127
Chart La. Bras —100Xc 185
Chartley Av. NW2 —34Ua 60
Chartley Av. Stan —23Ha 38
Charton Clo. Belv —51Cd 110
Chartridge Clo. Barn —15Wa 22
Chartridge Clo. Bush —16Ea 20
Chart St. N1 —41Tb 83 (3G 195)
Chart View. Kems —89Rd 171
Chartway. Sev —96Ld 187
Chartwell Clo. SE9 —61Tc 130
Chartwell Clo. Croy —74Tb 147
Chartwell Clo. Gnfd —39Da 57
Chartwell Clo. Wal A —5Gc 13
Chartwell Ct. Barn —14Ab 22
Chartwell Ct. Hay —45V 76
Chartwell Ct. Wfd G —24Hc 45
Chartwell Dri. Orp —78Tc 150
Chartwell Gdns. Sutt —77Ab 144
Chartwell Pl. Eps —86Ua 162
Chartwell Pl. Harr —33Fa 58
Chartwell Pl. Sutt —76Bb 145
Chartwell Rd. N'wd —23V 36
Chartwell Way. SE20 —67Xb 127
Charville Ct. Harr —30Ha 38
Charville La. Hay —41S 76
Charville La. W. Uxb —41R 76
Char Wood. SW16 —63Qb 126
Chase Bank Ct. N14 —16Lb 24
(off Avenue Rd.)
Chase Ct. Iswth —54Ja 100
Chase Ct. Gdns. Enf —13Sb 25
Chase Cross Rd. Romf —24Ed 48
Chase End. Eps —84Ta 161
Chasefield Rd. SW17 —63Hb 125
Chase Gdns. E4 —21Cc 44
Chase Gdns. Twic —59Fa 100
Chase Grn. Enf —13Sb 25
Chase Grn. Av. Enf —12Rb 25
Chase Hill. Enf —13Sb 25
Chase Ho. Gdns. Horn —29Pd 49
Chase La. Chig —20Vc 29
Chase La. Ilf —29Tc 46
(in two parts)
Chaseley Dri. W4 —50Ra 79
Chaseley St. E14 —44Ac 84
Chasemore Gdns. Croy —78Qb 146
Chase Ridings. Enf —12Qb 24
Chase Rd. N14 —15Lb 24
Chase Rd. NW10 —42Ta 79
Chase Rd. Brtwd —20Yd 32
Chase Rd. Corr —1P 93
Chase Rd. Eps —84Ta 161
Chase Rd. Trading Est. NW10 —42Ta 79
Chase Side. N14 —15Jb 24
Chase Side. Enf —12Sb 25
Chaseside Av. SW20 —68Ab 124
Chase Side Av. Enf —12Sb 25
Chaseside Clo. Romf —22Gd 48
Chase Side Cres. Enf —11Sb 25
Chaseside Gdns. Cher —73K 139
Chase Side Pl. Enf —13Sb 25
Chase Side Works Ind. Est. N14 —17Mb 24
Chase Sq. Grav —8D 114
Chase, The. E12 —35Mc 65
Chase, The. SW4 —56Kb 104
Chase, The. SW16 —66Pb 126
Chase, The. SW20 —67Ab 124
Chase, The. Asht —90La 160
Chase, The. Bexh —55Dd 110
Chase, The. Brtwd —20Zd 33
Chase, The. Brom —69Kc 129
Chase, The. Chad —30Ad 47
Chase, The. Chesh —1Rb 11
Chase, The. Chig —21Sc 46
Chase, The. Coul —86Mb 164
Chase, The. Eastc —30Y 37
Chase, The. E Hor —98V 174
Chase, The. Edgw —25Ra 39
Chase, The. Ingve —22Ee 51
Chase, The. Kems —88Nd 171
Chase, The. Oxs —87Ea 160
Chase, The. Pinn —28Ba 37
Chase, The. Rad —7Ha 6
Chase, The. Rain —39Ld 69
Chase, The. Romf —27Gd 48
Chase, The. Rush —34Gd 68
Chase, The. S Stif —51Zd 113
Chase, The. Stan —23Ja 38
Chase, The. Sun —67X 121
Chase, The. Tad —93Eb 179
Chase, The. Upm —34Ud 70
Chase, The. Uxb —36R 56
Chase, The. Wall —78Pb 146
Chase, The. War —21Xd 50
Chase, The. Wat —14U 18
Chaseville Pde. N21 —15Pb 24
Chaseville Pk. Rd. N21 —15Nb 24
Chase Way. N14 —19Kb 24
Chaseways Vs. Romf —25Bd 47
Chasewood Av. Enf —12Rb 25
Chasewood Ct. NW7 —22Ta 39
Chasewood Pk. Harr —34Ga 58
Chastilian Rd. Dart —59Hd 110
Chaston St. NW5 —36Jb 62
(off Grafton Ter.)
Chatfield. Slou —3E 72
Chatfield Ct. Cat —94Tb 181
Chatfield Rd. SW11 —55Eb 103
Chatfield Rd. Croy —74Rb 147
Chatham Av. Brom —73Hc 149
Chatham Clo. NW11 —29Cb 41
Chatham Clo. Sutt —73Bb 145
Chatham Hill Rd. Sev —93Ld 187
Chatham Pl. E9 —37Yb 64
Chatham Rd. E17 —27Ac 44
Chatham Rd. E18 —26Hc 45
Chatham Rd. SW11 —58Hb 103
Chatham Rd. King T —68Qa 123
Chatham Rd. Orp —78Sc 150
Chatham St. SE17 —49Tb 83 (5F 207)
Chatsfield. Eps —82Wa 162
Chatsfield Pl. W5 —44Na 79
Chatsworth Av. NW4 —26Ya 40
Chatsworth Av. SW20 —67Ab 124
Chatsworth Av. Brom —63Kc 129
Chatsworth Av. Sidc —60Wc 109
Chatsworth Av. Wemb —36Pa 59
Chatsworth Clo. NW4 —26Ya 40
Chatsworth Clo. W4 —51Sa 101
Chatsworth Clo. Borwd —13Qa 21
Chatsworth Clo. W Wick —74Hc 149
Chatsworth Ct. Stan —22La 38
Chatsworth Cres. Houn —56Fa 100
Chatsworth Dri. Enf —17Wb 25
Chatsworth Est. E5 —35Zb 64
Chatsworth Gdns. W3 —46Ra 79
Chatsworth Gdns. Harr —32Da 57
Chatsworth Gdns. N Mald —71Va 144
Chatsworth Pde. Orp —71Sc 150
Chatsworth Pl. Mitc —69Hb 125
Chatsworth Pl. Tedd —63Ja 122
Chatsworth Rise. W5 —42Pa 79
Chatsworth Rd. E5 —34Yb 64
Chatsworth Rd. E15 —36Hc 65
Chatsworth Rd. NW2 —37Ya 60
Chatsworth Rd. W4 —51Sa 101
Chatsworth Rd. W5 —42Pa 79
Chatsworth Rd. Croy —77Tb 147
Chatsworth Rd. Dart —57Ld 111
Chatsworth Rd. Hay —42X 77
Chatsworth Rd. Sutt —78Za 144
Chatsworth Way. SE27 —62Rb 127
Chatteris Av. Romf —23Ld 49
Chattern Hill. Ashf —63R 120
Chattern Rd. Ashf —63S 120
Chatterton Ct. Rich —54Pa 101
Chatterton Rd. N4 —34Rb 63
Chatterton Rd. Brom —70Mc 129
Chatto Rd. SW11 —57Hb 103
Chaucer Av. Hay —43W 76
Chaucer Av. Houn —54X 99
Chaucer Av. Rich —55Qa 101
Chaucer Av. Wey —80Q 140
Chaucer Clo. N11 —22Lb 42
Chaucer Clo. Bans —86Ab 162
Chaucer Clo. Til —4E 114
Chaucer Ct. New Bar —15Db 23
Chaucer Dri. SE1 —49Vb 83 (6K 207)
Chaucer Gdns. Sutt —76Cb 145
Chaucer Grn. Croy —73Xb 147
Chaucer Ho. Barn —14Za 22
Chaucer Ho. Sutt —76Cb 145
(off Chaucer Gdns.)
Chaucer Pk. Dart —59Pd 111
Chaucer Rd. E7 —37Jc 65
Chaucer Rd. E11 —30Jc 45
Chaucer Rd. E17 —26Ec 44
Chaucer Rd. SE24 —57Qb 104
Chaucer Rd. W3 —46Sa 79
Chaucer Rd. Ashf —63N 119
Chaucer Rd. Grav —62Fe 135
Chaucer Rd. Romf —24Kd 49
Chaucer Rd. Sidc —60Yc 109
Chaucer Rd. Sutt —77Cb 145
Chaucer Rd. Well —53Uc 108
Chaucer Way. SW19 —65Fb 125
Chaucer Way. Add —79J 139
Chaucer Way. Dart —56Qd 111
Chaulden Ho. EC1 —41Tb 83 (4G 195)
(off Cranwood St.)
Chauncey Clo. N9 —20Wb 25
Chauncey Ho. Wat —16U 18
Chauncy Av. Pot B —5Eb 9
Chaundrye Clo. SE9 —58Pc 108
Chave Croft. Eps —91Ya 178
Chave Croft Ter. Eps —91Ya 178
Chave Rd. Dart —62Nd 133
Chaville Ho. N11 —21Jb 42
Chaworth Rd. Ott —79E 138
Cheam Clo. Tad —93Xa 178
Cheam Comn. Rd. Wor Pk —75Xa 144
Cheam Mans. Sutt —80Ab 144
Cheam Pk. Way. Sutt —79Ab 144
Cheam Rd. Eps & Cheam —82Wa 162
Cheam Rd. Sutt —79Bb 145
Cheam St. SE15 —55Yb 106
Cheapside. EC2 —44Sb 83 (2D 200)
Cheapside. N13 —21Tb 43
Cheapside. Wok —2G 188
Cheapside La. Den —33H 55
Cheapside Rd. Asc —9A 116
Cheddar Rd. Houn —54R 98
Cheddar Waye. Hay —44X 77
Cheddington Rd. N18 —20Ub 25
Chedworth Clo. E16 —44Hc 85
Cheelson Rd. S Ock —40Yd 70
Cheena Ho. Ger X —24B 34
Cheeseman Clo. Hamp —65Aa 121
Cheesemans Ter. W14 —50Bb 81
Chelford Rd. Brom —64Fc 129
Chelmer Cres. Bark —40Xc 67
Chelmer Dri. Hut —16Fe 33
Chelmer Ho. Grays —10C 92
(off River View)
Chelmer Rd. E9 —36Zb 64
Chelmer Rd. Grays —10C 92
Chelmer Rd. Upm —30Td 50
Chelmsford Av. Romf —24Fd 48
Chelmsford Clo. E6 —44Pc 86
Chelmsford Clo. W6 —51Za 102
Chelmsford Ct. N14 —17Mb 24
(off Ivy Rd.)
Chelmsford Dri. Upm —34Pd 69
Chelmsford Gdns. Ilf —31Nc 66
Chelmsford Ho. N7 —45Pb 82
(off Holloway Rd.)
Chelmsford Rd. E11 —32Fc 65
Chelmsford Rd. E17 —30Cc 44
Chelmsford Rd. E18 —25Hc 45
Chelmsford Rd. N14 —17Lb 24
Chelmsford Rd. Shenf —16Be 33
Chelmsford Sq. NW10 —39Ya 60
Chelmsine Ct. Ruis —29S 36
Chelsea Bri. SW1 & SW8 —51Kb 104
Chelsea Bri. Bus. Cen. SW8 —52Kb 104
Chelsea Bri. Rd. SW1 —50Jb 82 (7H 203)
Chelsea Bri. Wharf. SW8 —51Kb 104
Chelsea Cloisters. SW3 —49Gb 81 (6E 202)
Chelsea Clo. NW10 —39Ta 59
Chelsea Clo. Edgw —26Qa 39
Chelsea Clo. Hamp —64Ea 122
Chelsea Clo. Wor Pk —73Wa 144
Chelsea Ct. Brom —70Nc 130
Chelsea Cres. SW10 —53Eb 103
Chelsea Embkmt. SW3 —51Gb 103
Chelsea Garden Mkt. SW10 —53Eb 103
Chelsea Gdns. Sutt —77Ab 144
Chelsea Harbour. SW10 —53Eb 103
Chelsea Harbour Dri. SW10 —53Eb 103
Chelsea Mnr. Ct. SW3 —51Gb 103
Chelsea Mnr. Gdns. SW3 —50Gb 81
Chelsea Mnr. St. SW3 —50Gb 81 (7D 202)
Chelsea Pk. Gdns. SW3 —51Fb 103
Chelsea Reach Tower. SW10
(off Worlds End Est.) —52Fb 103
Chelsea Sq. SW3 —50Fb 81 (7C 202)
Chelsea Towers. SW3 —51Gb 103
(off Chelsea Mnr. Gdns.)
Chelsfield Av. N9 —17Zb 26
Chelsfield Gdns. SE26 —62Yb 128
Chelsfield Grn. N9 —17Zb 26
Chelsfield Hill. Orp —81Yc 169
Chelsfield La. Badg M —80Cd 152
Chelsfield La. Orp —73Zc 151
Chelsfield Rd. Orp —72Yc 151
Chelsham Clo. Warl —90Ac 166
Chelsham Comn. Rd. Warl —89Cc 166
Chelsham Ct. Rd. Warl —90Fc 167
Chelsham Rd. SW4 —55Mb 104
Chelsham Rd. S Croy —80Tb 147
Chelsham Rd. Warl —90Bc 166
Chelsiter Ct. Sidc —63Vc 131
Chelston App. Ruis —33W 56
Chelston Rd. Ruis —32W 56
Chelsworth Clo. Romf —25Pd 49
Chelsworth Dri. SE18 —51Tc 108
Chelsworth Dri. Romf —25Nd 49
Cheltenham Av. Twic —59Ja 100
Cheltenham Clo. Grav —4E 136
Cheltenham Clo. N Mald —69Sa 123
Cheltenham Clo. N'holt —37Da 57
Cheltenham Ct. Stan —22La 38
(off Marsh La.)
Cheltenham Gdns. E6 —40Nc 66
Cheltenham Gdns. Lou —16Nc 28
Cheltenham Pl. W3 —46Ra 79
Cheltenham Pl. Harr —28Na 39
Cheltenham Rd. E10 —30Ec 44
Cheltenham Rd. SE15 —56Yb 106
Cheltenham Rd. Orp —76Wc 151
Cheltenham Ter. SW3 —50Hb 81 (7G 203)
Cheltenham Vs. Stai —58H 97
Chelverton Rd. SW15 —56Za 102
Chelwood. N20 —19Fb 23
Chelwood Clo. E4 —16Dc 26
Chelwood Clo. Eps —84Va 162
Chelwood Clo. N'wd —24S 36
Chelwood Gdns. Rich —54Qa 101
Chelwood Gdns. Pas. Rich —54Qa 101
Chelwood Wlk. SE4 —56Ac 106
Chenappa Clo. E13 —41Jc 85
Chenduit Way. Stan —22Ha 38
Cheney Ct. SE23 —60Zb 106
Cheney Rd. NW1 —40Nb 62 (2F 193)
Cheney Row. E17 —25Bc 44
Cheneys Rd. E11 —34Gc 65
Cheney St. Pinn —28Y 37
Chenies M. WC1 —42Mb 82 (6D 192)
Chenies Pl. NW1 —40Mb 62 (1E 192)
Chenies Rd. Chor —12F 16
Chenies St. WC1 —43Mb 82 (7D 192)
Chenies, The. Orp —72Uc 150
Chenies, The. Wilm —63Gd 132
Chenies Way. Wat —17U 18
Cheniston Clo. W Byf —85J 157
Cheniston Gdns. W8 —48Db 81
Chepstow Av. Horn —34Nd 69
Chepstow Clo. SW15 —57Ab 102
Chepstow Cres. W11 —45Cb 81
Chepstow Cres. Ilf —30Uc 46
Chepstow Gdns. S'hall —44Ba 77
Chepstow Pl. W2 —44Db 81
Chepstow Rise. Croy —76Ub 147
Chepstow Rd. W2 —44Cb 81
Chepstow Rd. W7 —48Ja 78
Chepstow Rd. Croy —76Ub 147
Chepstow Vs. W11 —45Bb 81
Chepstow Way. SE15 —53Vb 105
Chequers. Buck H —18Kc 27
Chequers Clo. Grav —8A 136
Chequers Clo. Orp —70Vc 131
Chequers Clo. Tad —97Wa 178
Chequers La. Dag —43Bd 87
Chequers La. Tad —97Wa 178
Chequers La. Wat —2X 5
Chequers Orchard. Iver —44H 75
Chequers Pde. N13 —22Sb 43
Chequers Pde. Dag —39Bd 67
Chequers Rd. Lou —15Qc 28
Chequers Rd. Romf & S Wea —19Nd 31
Chequers Sq. Uxb —38L 55
Chequers, The. Pinn —27Z 37
Chequer St. EC1 —42Sb 83 (6E 194)
(in two parts)
Chequers Wlk. Wal A —5Hc 13
Chequers Way. N13 —22Rb 43
Chequer Tree Clo. Knap —4B 188
Cherbury Clo. SE28 —44Zc 87
Cherbury Ct. N1 —40Tb 63 (2G 195)
(off St Johns Est.)
Cherbury St. N1 —40Tb 63 (2G 195)
Cherchefelle M. Stan —22Ka 38
Cherimoya Gdns. W Mol —69Da 121
Cherington Rd. W7 —46Ga 78
Cheriton Av. Brom —71Hc 149
Cheriton Av. Ilf —26Pc 46
Cheriton Clo. W5 —43La 78
Cheriton Ct. SE12 —59Jc 107
Cheriton Ct. W on T —74Y 141
Cheriton Dri. SE18 —52Tc 108
Cheriton Sq. SW17 —61Jb 126
Cherkley Hill. Lea —98La 176
Cherries, The. Slou —4M 73
Cherry Acre. Ger X —21A 34
Cherry Av. Brtwd —20Be 33
Cherry Av. Slou —7P 73
Cherry Av. S'hall —46Z 77
Cherry Av. Swan —70Fd 132
Cherry Clo. E17 —29Dc 44
Cherry Clo. SW2 —59Qb 104
Cherry Clo. W5 —48Ma 79
Cherry Clo. Bans —86Za 162
Cherry Clo. Cars —75Hb 145
Cherry Clo. Mord —70Ab 124
Cherry Clo. Ruis —34V 56
Cherrycot Hill. Orp —77Tc 150
Cherrycot Rise. Orp —77Sc 150
Cherry Cotts. Tad —96Xa 178
Cherry Ct. W3 —46Ua 80
Cherry Cres. Bren —52Ka 100
Cherrycroft Gdns. Pinn —24Ba 37
Cherrydale. Wat —14V 18
Cherrydown. Grays —46Fe 91
Cherrydown Av. E4 —20Bc 26
Cherrydown Clo. E4 —20Cc 26
Cherrydown Rd. Sidc —61Zc 131
Cherrydown Wlk. Romf —26Dd 48
Cherry Gdns. Dag —36Bd 67
Cherry Gdns. N'holt —38Da 57
Cherry Garden St. SE16 —47Xb 83
Cherry Garth. Bren —50Ma 79
Cherry Gro. Hay —46X 77
Cherry Gro. Uxb —43S 76
Cherry Hill. Barn —16Db 23
Cherry Hill. Harr —23Ha 38
Cherry Hill. Loud —13K 17
Cherry Hill Gdns. Croy —77Pb 146
Cherry Hollow. Abb L —3V 4
Cherrylands Clo. NW9 —33Sa 59
Cherry La. W Dray —49P 75
Cherry Laurel Wlk. SW2 —58Pb 104
Cherry Orchard. SE7 —51Lc 107
Cherry Orchard. Asht —90Ra 161
Cherry Orchard. Stai —64J 119
Cherry Orchard. Stoke P —8M 53
Cherry Orchard. W Dray —47N 75
Cherry Orchard Clo. Orp —71Yc 151
Cherry Orchard Gdns. Croy —74Ub 147
Cherry Orchard Gdns. W Mol —69Ba 121
Cherry Orchard Rd. Brom —75Nc 150
Cherry Orchard Rd. Croy —75Tb 147
Cherry Orchard Rd. W Mol —69Ca 121
Cherry Rise. Chal G —19A 16
Cherry Rd. Enf —10Yb 12
Cherry St. Romf —29Fd 48
Cherry St. Wok —90A 156
Cherry Tree Av. Stai —65K 119
Cherry Tree Av. W Dray —44P 75
Cherry Tree Clo. Grays —51Fe 113
Cherry Tree Clo. Rain —40Jd 68
Cherry Tree Clo. Wemb —35Ja 58
Cherry Tree Ct. NW9 —28Sa 39
Cherry Tree Ct. Coul —90Pb 164
Cherrytree Dri. SW16 —62Nb 126
Cherry Tree Grn. S Croy —86Xb 165
Cherry Tree Gro. Knat —82Rd 171
Cherry Tree Hill. N2 —29Gb 41
Cherry Tree La. Ful —37B 54
Cherrytree La. Ger X —26A 34
Cherry Tree La. Herons —18E 16
Cherrytree La. Iver —39J 55
Cherry Tree La. Pot B —6Db 9
Cherry Tree La. Rain —41Gd 88
Cherry Tree La. Wilm —62Hd 132
Cherry Tree Rise. Buck H —21Lc 45
Cherry Tree Rd. E15 —36Gc 65
Cherry Tree Rd. N2 —28Hb 41
Cherry Tree Rd. Farn R —8G 52
Cherry Tree Rd. Wat —8X 5
Cherry Trees. Hart —71Be 155
Cherry Tree Wlk. EC1 —42Sb 83 (6E 194)
Cherry Tree Wlk. Beck —70Bc 128
Cherry Tree Wlk. Big H —88Lc 167
Cherry Tree Wlk. W Wick —77Hc 149
Cherrytree Way. Stan —23Ka 38
Cherry Wlk. Brom —74Jc 149
Cherry Wlk. Grays —8C 92
Cherry Wlk. Loud —12L 17
Cherry Wlk. Rain —40Hd 68
Cherry Way. Eps —79Ta 143
Cherry Way. Hort —55E 96
Cherry Way. Shep —70T 120
Cherrywood Av. Egh —6M 117
Cherry Wood Clo. King T —66Qa 123
Cherrywood Ct. Tedd —64Ja 122
Cherrywood Dri. SW15 —57Za 102
Cherrywood Dri. Grav —3A 136
Cherrywood La. Mord —70Ab 124
Cherry Wood Way. W5 —43Qa 79
Cherston Gdns. Lou —14Qc 28
Cherston Path. Lou —14Qc 28
Cherston Rd. Lou —14Qc 28
Chertsey Bri. Rd. Cher —73M 139
Chertsey Clo. Kenl —87Rb 165
Chertsey Cres. New Ad —82Ec 166
Chertsey Dri. Sutt —75Ab 144
Chertsey La. Stai —64G 118
Chertsey Rd. E11 —33Fc 65
Chertsey Rd. Add —75K 139
Chertsey Rd. Ashf & Sun —66T 120
Chertsey Rd. Byfl —83M 157
Chertsey Rd. Chob & Cher —82A 156
Chertsey Rd. Ilf —35Tc 66
Chertsey Rd. Shep —73N 139
Chertsey Rd. Sun & Felt —64U 120
Chertsey Rd. Twic —61Da 121
Chertsey Rd. Wok —89B 156
Chertsey St. SW17 —64Jb 126
Chertsey Wlk. Cher —73J 139
Chervil Clo. Felt —62W 120
Chervil M. SE28 —46Xc 87
Cherwell Clo. Crox —16Q 18
Cherwell Clo. Slou —51D 96
Cherwell Ct. Eps —77Sa 143
Cherwell Gro. S Ock —45Xd 90
Cherwell Way. Ruis —30S 36
Cheryls Clo. SW6 —53Db 103
Cheseman St. SE26 —62Xb 127
Chesfield Rd. King T —66Na 123
Chesham Av. Orp —72Rc 150
Chesham Clo. SW1 —48Jb 82 (4H 203)
(off Lyall St.)
Chesham Clo. Romf —28Fd 48
Chesham Clo. Sutt —82Ab 162
Chesham Ct. N'wd —23V 36
Chesham Cres. SE20 —67Yb 128
Chesham Ho. H Hill —23Nd 49
(off Leyburn Cres.)
Chesham La. Ger X & Chal G —21A 34
Chesham M. SW1 —48Jb 82 (3H 203)
(off Belgrave M. W.)
Chesham Pl. SW1 (in two parts) —48Jb 82 (4H 203)
Chesham Rd. SE20 —68Yb 128
Chesham Rd. SW19 —64Fb 125
Chesham Rd. Bov —1B 2
Chesham Rd. King T —68Qa 123
Chesham St. NW10 —34Ta 59
Chesham St. SW1 —48Jb 82 (4H 203)
Chesham Ter. W13 —47Ka 78
Chesham Way. Wat —16U 18
Cheshire Clo. SE4 —54Bc 106
Cheshire Clo. Cher —79F 138
Cheshire Clo. Horn —29Qd 49
Cheshire Clo. Mitc —69Nb 126
Cheshire Ct. Slou —7M 73
Cheshire Gdns. Chess —79Ma 143
Cheshire Ho. Mord —73Db 145
Cheshire Ho. Ott —79F 138
(off Cheshire Clo.)
Cheshire Rd. N22 —24Pb 42
Cheshire St. E2 —42Vb 83
Cheshir Ho. NW4 —28Ya 40
Chesholm Rd. N16 —34Ub 63
Cheshunt Rd. E7 —37Kc 65
Chesil Ct. E2 —40Yb 64
Chesil Ct. SW3 —51Gb 103
Chesilton Rd. SW6 —53Bb 103
Chesil Way. Hay —41V 76
Chesley Gdns. E6 —40Mc 65
Chesney Cres. New Ad —80Ec 148
Chesney St. SW11 —53Jb 104
Chesnut Gro. N17 —27Vb 43
Chesnut Rd. N17 —27Vb 43
Chess Clo. Lat —8A 2
Chess Clo. Loud —14M 17
Chessfield Pk. Amer —11A 16
Chess Hill. Loud —14M 17
Chessholme Rd. Ashf —65S 120
Chessing Ct. N2 —27Hb 41
(off Fortis Grn.)
Chessington Av. N3 —27Ab 40
Chessington Av. Bexh —52Ad 109
Chessington Clo. Eps —79Sa 143
Chessington Ct. N3 —27Bb 41
(off Charter Way)
Chessington Ct. Pinn —28Ba 37
Chessington Hall Gdns. Chess —79Ma 143
Chessington Hill Pk. Chess —78Qa 143
Chessington Ho. SW8 —54Mb 104
Chessington Ho. Eps —81Va 162
(off Spring St.)
Chessington Lodge. N3 —27Bb 41
Chessington Mans. E10 —31Cc 64
Chessington Mans. E11 —31Gc 65
Chessington Pde. Chess —79Ma 143
Chessington Rd. Eps —79Qa 143
Chessington Way. W Wick —75Dc 148
Chess La. Loud —14M 17
Chesson Rd. W14 —51Bb 103
Chess Vale Rise. Crox —16P 17
Chess Way. Chor —13J 17
Chesswood Way. Pinn —26Z 37
Chestbrook Ct. Enf —15Ub 25
(off Forsyth Pl.)
Chester Av. Rich —58Pa 101
Chester Av. Twic —60Ba 99
Chester Av. Upm —33Ud 70
Chester Clo. SW1 —47Kb 82 (2K 203)
Chester Clo. SW15 —55Xa 102
Chester Clo. Ashf —64T 120
Chester Clo. Lou —11Sc 28
Chester Clo. Sutt —75Cb 145
Chester Clo. Uxb —44R 76
Chester Clo. N. NW1 —41Kb 82 (3A 192)
Chester Clo. S. NW1 —41Kb 82 (4A 192)
Chester Cotts. SW1 —49Jb 82 (6H 203)
(off Bourne St.)
Chester Ct. NW1 —41Kb 82 (3A 192)
Chester Cres. E8 —36Vb 63
Chester Dri. Harr —30Ba 38
Chesterfield Clo. SE13 —54Fc 107
Chesterfield Clo. Orp —70Ad 131
Chesterfield Dri. Dart —57Kd 111
Chesterfield Dri. Esh —75Ja 142
Chesterfield Dri. Sev —93Fd 186
Chesterfield Flats. Barn —15Za 22
(off Bells Hill)
Chesterfield Gdns. N4 —29Rb 43
Chesterfield Gdns. W1 —46Kb 82 (6K 197)
Chesterfield Gro. SE22 —57Vb 105
Chesterfield Hill. W1 —46Kb 82 (6K 197)
Chesterfield Lodge. N21 —17Pb 24
(off Church Hill)
Chesterfield Rd. E10 —30Ec 44
Chesterfield Rd. N3 —23Cb 41
Chesterfield Rd. W4 —51Sa 101
Chesterfield Rd. Ashf —63N 119
Chesterfield Rd. Barn —15Za 22
Chesterfield Rd. Enf —9Ac 12

Chesterfield Rd. Eps —80Ta 143
Chesterfield St. W1 —46Kb 82 (6K 197)
Chesterfield Wlk. SE10 —53Fc 107
Chesterfield Way. SE15 —52Yb 106
Chesterfield Way. Hay —47W 76
Chesterford Gdns. NW3 —35Db 61
Chesterford Rd. E12 —36Pc 66
Chester Gdns. W13 —44Ka 78
Chester Gdns. Enf —16Xb 25
Chester Gdns. Mord —72Eb 145
Chester Ga. NW1 —41Kb 82 (4K 191)
Chester Grn. Lou —11Sc 28
Chester Ho. Uxb —42L 75
Chester M. SW1 —48Kb 82 (3K 203)
Chester Path. Lou —11Sc 28
Chester Pl. NW1 —41Kb 82 (3K 191)
Chester Rd. E7 —38Mc 65
Chester Rd. E11 —30Kc 45
Chester Rd. E16 —42Gc 85
Chester Rd. E17 —29Zb 44
Chester Rd. N9 —18Xb 25
Chester Rd. N17 —27Tb 43
Chester Rd. N19 —33Kb 62
Chester Rd. NW1 —41Jb 82 (4J 191)
Chester Rd. SW19 —65Ya 124
Chester Rd. Borwd —13Sa 21
Chester Rd. Chig —20Qc 28
Chester Rd. Houn —55X 99
Chester Rd. Ilf —32Vc 67
Chester Rd. H'row A —55Q 98
Chester Rd. Lou —12Rc 28
Chester Rd. N'wd —24U 36
Chester Rd. Sidc —57Uc 108
Chester Rd. Slou —4H 73
Chester Rd. Wat —15W 18
Chester Row. SW1 —49Jb 82 (6H 203)
Chester Sq. SW1 —49Jb 82 (5J 203)
Chester Sq. M. SW1 —48Kb 82 (4K 203) (off Chester Sq.)
Chesters, The. N Mald —67Ua 124
Chester St. E2 —42Wb 83
Chester St. SW1 —48Jb 82 (3J 203)
Chester Ter. NW1 —41Kb 82 (3K 191)
Chester Ter. Bark —37Tc 66
Chesterton Clo. SW18 —57Cb 103
Chesterton Clo. Gnfd —40Da 57
Chesterton Ct. W3 —43Ma 79
Chesterton Dri. Red —100Nb 180
Chesterton Dri. Stai —60P 97
Chesterton Rd. E13 —41Jc 85
Chesterton Rd. W10 —43Za 80
Chesterton Sq. W8 —49Bb 81
Chesterton Ter. E13 —41Jc 85
Chesterton Ter. King T —68Qa 123
Chesterton Way. Til —4E 114
Chester Way. SE11 —49Qb 82 (6A 206)
Chesthunte Rd. N17 —25Sb 43
Chestnut All. SW6 —51Bb 103
Chestnut Av. E7 —35Kc 65
Chestnut Av. N8 —29Nb 42
Chestnut Av. SW14 —55Ta 101
Chestnut Av. Bren —49Ma 79
Chestnut Av. Brtwd —17Ud 32
Chestnut Av. Buck H —20Mc 27
Chestnut Av. E Mol & Tedd —69Ha 122
Chestnut Av. Edgw —23Na 39
Chestnut Av. Eps —77Ua 144
Chestnut Av. Esh —73Fa 142
Chestnut Av. Grays —47De 91
Chestnut Av. Hamp —66Ca 121
Chestnut Av. Horn —33Hd 68
Chestnut Av. N'wd —26V 36
Chestnut Av. Rick —15J 17
Chestnut Av. Slou —47A 74
Chestnut Av. Tats —94Mc 183
Chestnut Av. Vir W —10K 117
Chestnut Av. Wemb —36Ka 58
Chestnut Av. W Dray —45P 75
Chestnut Av. W Wick —78Gc 149
Chestnut Av. Wey —80S 140
Chestnut Av. N. E17 —28Fc 45
Chestnut Av. S. E17 —29Ec 44
Chestnut Clo. N14 —15Mb 24
Chestnut Clo. N16 —33Tb 63
Chestnut Clo. SE6 —64Ec 128
Chestnut Clo. SW16 —63Qb 126
Chestnut Clo. Add —78M 139
Chestnut Clo. Ashf —63R 120
Chestnut Clo. Buck H —20Mc 27
Chestnut Clo. Cars —74Hb 145
Chestnut Clo. Egh —5M 117
Chestnut Clo. Ger X —25B 34
Chestnut Clo. Grav —8B 114
Chestnut Clo. Hay —45U 76
Chestnut Clo. Horn —35Ld 69
Chestnut Clo. Orp —78Wc 151
Chestnut Clo. Rip —97H 173
Chestnut Clo. Sun —65V 120
Chestnut Clo. Tad —95Cb 179
Chestnut Clo. W Dray —52R 98
Chestnut Ct. N8 —29Nb 42
Chestnut Ct. SW6 —51Bb 103
Chestnut Ct. Felt —64Z 121
Chestnut Cres. W Vill —81U 158
Chestnut Dri. E11 —30Jc 45
Chestnut Dri. Bexh —55Zc 109
Chestnut Dri. Egh —5P 117
Chestnut Dri. Harr —24Ha 38
Chestnut Dri. Pinn —30Z 37
Chestnut Dri. Wind —6C 94
Chestnut Glen. Horn —33Hd 68
Chestnut Gro. SE20 —66Xb 127
Chestnut Gro. SW12 —59Jb 104
Chestnut Gro. W5 —48Ma 79
Chestnut Gro. Barn —15Hb 23
Chestnut Gro. Brtwd —19Yd 32
Chestnut Gro. Dart —64Fd 132
Chestnut Gro. Ilf —23Uc 46
Chestnut Gro. Iswth —56Ja 100
Chestnut Gro. Mitc —71Mb 146
Chestnut Gro. N Mald —69Ta 123
Chestnut Gro. S Croy —80Xb 147
Chestnut Gro. Stai —65L 119
Chestnut Gro. Wemb —36Ka 58
Chestnut Gro. Wok —92A 172
Chestnut La. N20 —18Ab 22
Chestnut La. Sev —96Kd 187
Chestnut La. Wey —78R 140
Chestnut Lodge. SE12 —62Kc 129
Chestnut Mnr. Clo. Stai —64K 119
Chestnut Rise. SE18 —51Tc 108
Chestnut Rise. Bush —17Da 19
Chestnut Rd. SE27 —62Rb 127
Chestnut Rd. SW20 —68Za 124
Chestnut Rd. Ashf —63R 120
Chestnut Rd. Belv —50Cd 88
Chestnut Rd. Dart —60Md 111
Chestnut Rd. Enf —8Ac 12
Chestnut Rd. King T —66Na 123
Chestnut Rd. Twic —61Ga 122
Chestnut Row. N3 —24Cb 41
Chestnuts. Hut —18De 33
Chestnuts, The. N5 —35Sb 63 (off Highbury Grange)
Chestnuts, The. Abr —13Xc 29
Chestnuts, The. Pinn —24Ba 37
Chestnuts, The. W on T —75W 140
Chestnut Ter. Sutt —77Db 145
Chestnut Wlk. Byfl —84N 157
Chestnut Wlk. Ger X —22A 34
Chestnut Wlk. Sev —100Pd 187
Chestnut Wlk. Shep —70U 120
Chestnut Wlk. Wat —9W 4
Chestnut Wlk. W Vill —81U 158
Chestnut Wlk. Wfd G —22Jc 45
Chestnut Way. Felt —62X 121
Cheston Av. Croy —75Ac 148
Chestwood Gro. Uxb —38P 55
Cheswick Clo. Dart —56Hd 110
Chesworth Clo. Eri —54Gd 110
Chettle Clo. SE1 —48Tb 83 (3F 207) (off Spurgeon St.)
Chettle Ct. N8 —30Qb 42
Chetwode Dri. Eps —90Za 162
Chetwode Rd. SW17 —62Hb 125
Chetwode Rd. Tad —91Ya 178
Chetwood Wlk. E6 —43Nc 86 (off Greenwich Cres.)
Chetwynd Av. Barn —18Hb 23
Chetwynd Dri. Uxb —40P 55
Chetwynd Rd. NW5 —35Kb 62
Cheval Pl. SW7 —48Gb 81 (3E 202)
Cheval St. E14 —48Cc 84
Chevely Clo. Coop —1Zc 15
Cheveney Wlk. Brom —69Jc 129
Chevening La. Knock —88Ad 169
Chevening Rd. NW6 —40Za 60
Chevening Rd. SE10 —50Hc 85
Chevening Rd. SE19 —65Tb 127
Chevening Rd. Chev & Chip —91Bd 185
Chevening Rd. Sund —95Ad 185
Chevenings, The. Sidc —62Yc 131
Cheverton Rd. N19 —32Mb 62
Chevet St. E9 —36Ac 64
Chevington Way. Horn —35Md 69
Cheviot. N17 —24Xb 43
Cheviot Clo. Bans —87Db 163
Cheviot Clo. Bexh —54Gd 110
Cheviot Clo. Bush —16Ea 20
Cheviot Clo. Enf —12Tb 25
Cheviot Clo. Hay —52T 98
Cheviot Clo. Sutt —81Fb 163
Cheviot Ct. S'hall —49Da 77
Cheviot Gdns. NW2 —33Za 60
Cheviot Gdns. SE27 —63Rb 127
Cheviot Ga. NW2 —33Ab 60
Cheviot Ho. Grav —58Fe 113 (off Laburnum Gro.)
Cheviot Rd. SE27 —64Qb 126
Cheviot Rd. Horn —31Jd 68
Cheviot Rd. Slou —50C 74
Cheviot Way. Ilf —29Uc 46
Chevley Gdns. Burn —10A 52
Chevron Clo. E16 —44Jc 85
Chevron Ho. Grays —52De 113
Chevy Rd. S'hall —46Ea 78
Chewton Rd. E17 —28Ac 44
Cheyham Gdns. Sutt —82Za 162
Cheyham Way. Sutt —82Ab 162
Cheyne Av. E18 —27Hc 45
Cheyne Av. Twic —60Ba 99
Cheyne Clo. NW4 —29Ya 40
Cheyne Clo. Brom —76Nc 150
Cheyne Clo. Ger X —32A 54
Cheyne Ct. SW3 —51Hb 103
Cheyne Ct. Bans —87Db 163
Cheyne Ct. Bush —14Aa 19
Cheyne Gdns. SW3 —51Gb 103
Cheyne Hill. Surb —70Pa 123
Cheyne M. SW3 —51Gb 103
Cheyne Path. W7 —44Ha 78
Cheyne Pl. SW3 —51Hb 103
Cheyne Rd. Ashf —66T 120
Cheyne Row. SW3 —51Gb 103
Cheyne, The. Ger X —29B 34
Cheyne Wlk. N21 —15Rb 25
Cheyne Wlk. NW4 —30Ya 40
Cheyne Wlk. SW10 & SW3 (in three parts) —52Fb 103
Cheyne Wlk. Croy —75Wb 147
Cheyne Wlk. Long —69Ae 135
Cheyneys Av. Edgw —23Ma 39
Chichele Gdns. Croy —77Ub 147
Chichele Rd. NW2 —36Za 60
Chichele Rd. Oxt —100Gc 183
Chicheley Gdns. Harr —24Ea 38 (in two parts)
Chicheley Rd. Harr —24Ea 38
Chicheley St. SE1 —47Pb 82 (1J 205)
Chichester Av. Ruis —33T 56
Chichester Bldgs. SE1 —48Ub 83 (4H 207) (off Swan Mead)
Chichester Clo. E6 —44Nc 86
Chichester Clo. SE3 —53Lc 107
Chichester Clo. Hamp —65Ba 121
Chichester Clo. S Ock —46Td 90
Chichester Ct. Edgw —23Qa 39 (off Whitchurch La.)
Chichester Ct. Eps —81Va 162
Chichester Ct. Slou —8M 73
Chichester Ct. Stan —27Na 39
Chichester Dri. Purl —84Pb 164
Chichester Dri. Sev —97Hd 186
Chichester Gdns. Ilf —31Nc 66
Chichester Ho. Brtwd —19Yd 32 (off Sir Francis Way)
Chichester M. SE27 —63Qb 126
Chichester Rents. WC2 —44Qb 82 (2K 199) (off Chancery La.)
Chichester Rise. Grav —3F 136
Chichester Rd. E11 —34Gc 65
Chichester Rd. N9 —18Wb 25
Chichester Rd. NW6 —40Cb 61
Chichester Rd. W2 —43Db 81
Chichester Rd. Croy —76Ub 147
Chichester Rd. Grnh —58Vd 112
Chichester St. SW1 —50Lb 82 (7C 204)
Chichester Way. E14 —49Fc 85
Chichester Way. Felt —59Y 99
Chichester Way. Wat —5Aa 5
Chicksand St. E1 —43Vb 83
Chidbrook Ho. Wat —16U 18
Chiddingfold. N12 —20Cb 23
Chiddingstone Av. Bexh —52Bd 109
Chiddingstone Clo. Sutt —82Cb 163
Chiddingstone St. SW6 —54Cb 103
Chieftan Dri. Purf —49Qd 89
Chieveley Pde. Bexh —56Dd 110
Chieveley Rd. Bexh —56Dd 110
Chiffinch Gdns. Grav —2A 136
Chignell Pl. W13 —46Ja 78
Chigwell Hill. E1 —45Xb 83
Chigwell Hurst Ct. Pinn —27Z 37
Chigwell La. Lou & Chig —15Sc 28
Chigwell Pk. Chig —21Rc 46
Chigwell Pk. Dri. Chig —21Qc 46
Chigwell Rise. Chig —19Qc 28
Chigwell Rd. E18 & Wfd G —27Kc 45
Chigwell View. Romf —23Cd 48
Chilbrook Rd. D'side —90W 158
Chilcot Clo. E14 —44Dc 84
Chilcott Rd. Wat —8U 4
Childebert Rd. SW17 —61Kb 126
Childerditch Hall Dri. L War —26Be 51
Childerditch Ind. Pk. L War —27Be 51
Childerditch La. L War —24Ae 51
Childerditch St. L War —26Ce 51
Childeric Rd. SE14 —52Ac 106
Childerley St. SW6 —53Ab 102
Childers St. SE8 —51Ac 106
Childers, The. Wfd G —22Pc 46
Childs Av. Hare —26L 35
Childsbridge La. Kems —90Nd 171
Childsbridge Way. Seal —92Pd 187
Childs Clo. Horn —30Ld 49
Childs Ct. Hay —45W 76
Childs Cres. Swans —58Zd 113
Childs Hall Clo. Bookh —97Ba 175
Childs Hall Dri. Bookh —97Ba 175
Childs Hall Rd. Bookh —97Ba 175
Childs Hill Wlk. NW2 —34Bb 61 (off Cricklewood La.)
Child's La. SE19 —65Ub 127
Child's Pl. SW5 —49Cb 81
Child's St. SW5 —49Cb 81
Child's Wlk. SW5 —49Cb 81
Childs Way. NW11 —29Bb 41
Chilham Clo. Bex —59Bd 109
Chilham Clo. Gnfd —40Ja 58
Chilham Ho. SE1 —48Tb 83 (3G 207)
Chilham Rd. SE9 —63Nc 130
Chilham Way. Brom —73Jc 149
Chillerton Rd. SW17 —64Jb 126
Chillingworth Gdns. Twic —62Ha 122
Chillingworth Rd. N7 —36Qb 62
Chilmans Dri. Bookh —97Da 175
Chilmark Gdns. N Mald —72Wa 144
Chilmark Gdns. Red —100Nb 180
Chilmark Rd. SW16 —68Mb 126
Chilsey Grn. Rd. Cher —72G 138
Chiltern Av. Bush —16Ea 20
Chiltern Av. Twic —60Ca 99
Chiltern Bus. Village. Uxb —40K 55
Chiltern Clo. Bexh —53Gd 110
Chiltern Clo. Borwd —12Pa 21
Chiltern Clo. Bush —16Da 19
Chiltern Clo. Croy —76Ub 147
Chiltern Clo. Uxb —33Q 56
Chiltern Clo. Wok —10F 188
Chiltern Clo. Wor Pk —75Ya 144
Chiltern Ct. N10 —26Jb 42
Chiltern Ct. Harr —29Fa 38
Chiltern Ct. New Bar —15Eb 23
Chiltern Ct. Uxb —42R 76
Chiltern Dene. Enf —14Pb 24
Chiltern Dri. Rick —17H 17
Chiltern Dri. Surb —72Qa 143
Chiltern Gdns. NW2 —34Za 60
Chiltern Gdns. Brom —70Hc 129
Chiltern Gdns. Horn —34Ld 69
Chiltern Hill. Ger X —25A 34
Chiltern Ho. W5 —43Na 79
Chiltern Rd. E3 —42Cc 84
Chiltern Rd. Burn —3A 72
Chiltern Rd. Grav —2A 136
Chiltern Rd. Ilf —29Uc 46
Chiltern Rd. Pinn —29Y 37
Chiltern Rd. Sutt —81Db 163
Chiltern St. W1 —43Jb 82 (7H 191)
Chiltern View Rd. Uxb —40L 55
Chiltern Way. Wfd G —20Jc 27
Chilthorne Clo. SE6 —59Bc 106
Chilton Av. W5 —49Ma 79
Chilton Ct. N22 —24Nb 42 (off Truro Rd.)
Chilton Ct. Tap —4A 72
Chilton Ct. W on T —77W 140
Chilton Gro. SE8 —49Zb 84
Chilton Rd. Edgw —23Qa 39
Chilton Rd. Grays —8C 92
Chilton Rd. Rich —55Qa 101
Chiltons Clo. Bans —87Db 163
Chiltons, The. E18 —26Jc 45
Chilton St. E2 —42Vb 83
Chilver St. SE10 —50Hc 85
Chilwell Gdns. Wat —21Y 37
Chilwick Rd. Slou —2D 72
Chilworth Ct. SW19 —60Za 102
Chilworth Gdns. Sutt —76Eb 145
Chilworth M. W2 —44Fb 81 (3B 196)
Chilworth St. W2 —44Eb 81 (3A 196)
Chimes Av. N13 —22Qb 42
China La. Bulp —34Fe 71
China Wharf. SE1 —47Wb 83 (off Mill St.)
Chinbrook Cres. SE12 —62Kc 129
Chinbrook Rd. SE12 —62Kc 129
Chinchilla Dri. Houn —54Y 99
Chindits La. War —22Yd 50
Chine, The. N10 —28Lb 42
Chine, The. N21 —16Rb 25
Chine, The. Wemb —36La 58
Chingdale Rd. E4 —20Gc 27
Chingford Av. E4 —20Cc 26
Chingford Hall Est. E4 —23Bc 44
Chingford La. Wfd G —21Gc 45
Chingford Mt. Rd. E4 —21Cc 44
Chingford Rd. E4 —23Cc 44
Chingford Rd. E17 —25Dc 44
Chingley Clo. Brom —65Gc 129
Chinnery Clo. Enf —11Vb 25
Chinnor Cres. Gnfd —40Da 57
Chipka St. E14 —47Ec 84
Chipley St. SE14 —51Ac 106
Chipmunk Gro. N'holt —41Aa 77
Chippendale All. Uxb —38M 55
Chippendale St. E5 —34Zb 64
Chippendale Way. Uxb —38M 55
Chippenham Av. Wemb —36Ra 59
Chippenham Clo. Pinn —28V 36
Chippenham Clo. Romf —22Md 49
Chippenham Gdns. NW6 —41Cb 81
Chippenham Gdns. Romf —22Md 49
Chippenham M. W9 —42Cb 81
Chippenham Rd. W9 —42Cb 81
Chippenham Rd. H Hill —23Md 49
Chippenham Wlk. Romf —23Md 49
Chipperfield Clo. Upm —32Ud 70
Chipperfield Rd. Abb L —2L 3
Chipperfield Rd. Bov —1E 2
Chipperfield Rd. Orp —67Wc 131
Chipping Clo. Barn —13Ab 22
Chipstead Av. T Hth —70Rb 127
Chipstead Clo. SE19 —66Vb 127
Chipstead Clo. Coul —88Jb 164
Chipstead Clo. Sutt —81Db 163
Chipstead Ct. Knap —5B 188
Chipstead Gdns. NW2 —33Xa 60
Chipstead La. Sev —94Fd 186
Chipstead La. Tad & Coul —97Bb 179
Chipstead Pk. Sev —94Fd 186
Chipstead Pk. Clo. Sev —94Ed 186
Chipstead Pl. Gdns. Sev —94Ed 186
Chipstead Rd. Bans —89Bb 163
Chipstead Rd. Eri —52Gd 110
Chipstead Rd. Houn —55Q 98
Chipstead Sq. Sev —94Ed 186
Chipstead St. SW6 —53Cb 103
Chipstead Valley Rd. Coul —88Jb 164
Chipstead Way. Bans —88Hb 163
Chip St. SW4 —55Mb 104
Chirdland Ho. Wat —16U 18
Chirk Clo. Hay —42Aa 77
Chirton Wlk. Wok —6D 188
Chisenhale Rd. E3 —40Ac 64
Chisholm Rd. Croy —75Ub 147
Chisholm Rd. Rich —58Pa 101
Chisledon Wlk. E9 —37Bc 64 (off Eastway)
Chislehurst Av. N12 —24Eb 41
Chislehurst Rd. Brom & Chst —68Mc 129
Chislehurst Rd. Orp —70Uc 130
Chislehurst Rd. Rich —57Na 101
Chislehurst Rd. Sidc —64Wc 131
Chislet Clo. Beck —66Cc 128
Chisley Rd. N15 —30Ub 43
Chiswell Ct. Wat —10Y 5
Chiswell Sq. SE3 —54Kc 107
Chiswell St. EC1 —43Tb 83 (7E 194)
Chiswick Bri. SW14 & W4 —54Sa 101
Chiswick Clo. Croy —76Pb 146
Chiswick Comn. Rd. W4 —49Ta 79
Chiswick Ct. Pinn —27Ba 37
Chiswick High Rd. Bren & W4 (in two parts) —50Qa 79
Chiswick La. N. W4 —50Ua 80
Chiswick La. S. W4 —51Va 102
Chiswick Mall. W4 & W6 —51Va 102
Chiswick Plaza. W4 —51Sa 101
Chiswick Quay. W4 —53Sa 101
Chiswick Rd. N9 —19Wb 25
Chiswick Rd. W4 —49Sa 79
Chiswick Sq. W4 —51Ua 102
Chiswick Staithe. W4 —52Ra 101
Chiswick Ter. W4 —49Sa 79
Chiswick Village. W4 —51Qa 101
Chiswick Wharf. W4 —51Va 102
Chittenden Cotts. Wis —88N 157
Chitterfield Ga. W Dray —52Q 98
Chitty's La. Dag —33Zc 67
Chitty St. W1 —43Lb 82 (7C 192)
Chivalry Rd. SW11 —57Gb 103
Chive Clo. Croy —74Zb 148
Chivers Rd. E4 —20Dc 26
Chiver St. SE10 —50Hc 85
Choats Mnr. Way. Dag —40Bd 67
Choats Rd. Dag —41Ad 87
Chobham Clo. Ott —79D 138
Chobham Gdns. SW19 —61Za 124
Chobham Rd. E15 —36Fc 65
Chobham Rd. Ott —80C 138
Chobham Rd. Wok —1F 188
Choir Grn. Knap —5B 188
Cholmeley Cres. N6 —31Kb 62
Cholmeley Lodge. N6 —32Kb 62
Cholmeley Pk. N6 —32Kb 62
Cholmley Gdns. NW6 —36Cb 61
Cholmley Rd. Th Dit —72Ka 142
Cholmondeley Av. NW10 —40Wa 60
Cholmondeley Wlk. Rich —57La 100
Choppin's Ct. E1 —46Xb 83
Chopwell Clo. E15 —38Gc 65
Chorleywood Bottom. Chor —15F 16
Chorleywood Clo. Rick —17M 17
Chorleywood Cres. Orp —68Vc 131
Chorleywood Ho. Chor —13G 16
Chorleywood Rd. Rick —14J 17
Choumert Gro. SE15 —54Wb 105
Choumert Rd. SE15 —55Vb 105
Choumert Sq. SE15 —54Wb 105
Chrislaine Clo. Stai —58M 97
Chrisp St. E14 —43Dc 84 (in two parts)
Christchurch Av. N12 —23Eb 41
Christchurch Av. NW6 —39Za 60
Christchurch Av. Eri —51Fd 110
Christchurch Av. Harr —28Ha 38
Christchurch Av. Rain —41Hd 88
Christchurch Av. Tedd —64Ja 122
Christchurch Av. Wemb —37Na 59
Christchurch Clo. N12 —24Fb 41
Christchurch Clo. SW19 —66Fb 125
Christchurch Ct. NW10 —39La 60
Christ Chu. Cres. Grav —9E 114
Christchurch Cres. Rad —8Ja 6
Christchurch Gdns. Eps —83Ra 161
Christchurch Gdns. Harr —28Ja 38
Christchurch Grn. Wemb —37Na 59
Christchurch Hill. NW3 —34Fb 61
Christchurch Ho. SW2 —60Pb 104 (off Christchurch Rd.)
Christchurch La. Barn —12Ab 22
Christ Chu. Mt. Eps —84Ra 161
Christchurch Pk. Sutt —80Eb 145
Christchurch Pas. NW3 —34Eb 61
Christchurch Pas. H Bar —12Ab 22
Christchurch Pl. SW8 —54Mb 104
Christchurch Pl. Eps —83Ra 161
Christchurch Rd. N8 —30Nb 42
Christchurch Rd. SW2 —60Pb 104
Christ Chu. Rd. SW14 —57Ra 101
Christchurch Rd. SW19 —66Fb 125
Christ Chu. Rd. Beck —68Cc 128
Christchurch Rd. Dart —59Ld 111
Christ Chu. Rd. Eps —84Na 161
Christchurch Rd. Grav —9E 114
Christchurch Rd. Houn —54Q 98
Christchurch Rd. Ilf —32Rc 66
Christchurch Rd. Purl —83Rb 165
Christchurch Rd. Sidc —63Vc 131
Christchurch Rd. Surb —72Pa 143
Christchurch Rd. Til —3C 114
Christchurch Rd. Vir W —9L 117
Christchurch Sq. E9 —39Yb 64
Christchurch St. SW3 —51Hb 103
Christchurch Ter. SW3 —51Hb 103 (off Christchurch St.)
Christchurch Way. SE10 —50Gc 85
Christchurch Way. Wok —89B 156
Christian Ct. SE16 —46Bc 84
Christian Fields. SW16 —66Qb 126
Christian Fields Av. Grav —3E 136
Christian Sq. Wind —3G 94
Christian St. E1 —44Wb 83
Christie Ct. N19 —33Nb 62
Christie Gdns. Chad —30Xc 47
Christie Rd. E9 —37Ac 64
Christies Av. Badg M —82Cd 170
Christina Sq. N4 —32Rb 63
Christina St. EC2 —42Ub 83 (5H 195)
Christine Ct. Rain —42Jd 88
Christmas La. Farn C —4G 52
Christopher Av. W7 —48Ja 78
Christopher Clo. SE16 —47Zb 84
Christopher Clo. Horn —35Md 69
Christopher Clo. Sidc —58Vc 109
Christopher Ct. Tad —95Ya 178
Christopher Gdns. Dag —36Zc 67
Christopher Ho. Sidc —61Wc 131 (off Longlands Rd.)
Christopher Pl. NW1 —41Mb 82 (3E 192)
Christopher Rd. S'hall —49X 77
Christopher St. EC2 —42Tb 83 (7G 195)
Christy Rd. Big H —87Lc 167
Chryssell Rd. SW9 —52Qb 104
Chrystie La. Bookh —98Da 175
Chubworthy St. SE14 —51Ac 106
Chucks La. Tad —96Xa 178
Chudleigh. Sidc —63Xc 131
Chudleigh Cres. Ilf —35Uc 66
Chudleigh Gdns. Sutt —76Eb 145
Chudleigh Rd. NW6 —38Za 60
Chudleigh Rd. SE4 —57Bc 106
Chudleigh Rd. Romf —21Nd 49
Chudleigh Rd. Twic —58Ga 100
Chudleigh St. E1 —44Zb 84
Chudleigh Way. Ruis —32W 56
Chulsa Rd. SE26 —64Xb 127
Chumleigh St. SE5 —51Ub 105
Chumleigh Wlk. Surb —70Pa 123
Church All. Ald —10Ea 6
Church All. Croy —74Qb 146
Church App. SE21 —62Tb 127
Church App. Cud —87Sc 168
Church App. Egh —69E 118
Church App. Stanw —58M 97
Church Av. E4 —23Fc 45
Church Av. N2 —26Fb 41
Church Av. NW1 —37Kb 62
Church Av. SW14 —55Ta 101
Church Av. Beck —67Cc 128
Church Av. N'holt —38Ba 57
Church Av. Pinn —30Aa 37
Church Av. Ruis —32T 56
Church Av. Sidc —64Wc 131
Church Av. S'hall —48Aa 77
Churchbank. E17 —28Cc 44 (off Teresa M.)
Churchbury Clo. Enf —12Ub 25
Churchbury La. Enf —13Tb 25
Churchbury Rd. SE9 —59Mc 107
Churchbury Rd. Enf —12Ub 25
Church Cloisters. EC3 (off Lovat La.) —45Ub 83 (5H 201)
Church Clo. N20 —20Gb 23
Church Clo. W8 —47Db 81
Church Clo. Add —77K 139
Church Clo. Cuff —1Nb 10
Church Clo. Edgw —22Sa 39
Church Clo. Eton —1H 95
Church Clo. Fet —96Fa 176
Church Clo. Hay —43T 76
Church Clo. Horn H —1H 93
Church Clo. Hors —4G 188
Church Clo. Lou —12Pc 28
Church Clo. Mount —11Fe 33
Church Clo. N'wd —24V 36
Church Clo. Rad —8Ja 6
Church Clo. Stai —69L 119
Church Clo. Tad —99Bb 179
Church Clo. Uxb —40K 55
Church Clo. W Dray —48N 75
Church Cotts. Add —76N 139
Church Ct. Rich —57Ma 101
Church Ct. Wfd G —23Lc 45
Church Cres. E9 —38Zb 64
Church Cres. N3 —25Bb 41
Church Cres. N10 —28Kb 42
Church Cres. N20 —20Gb 23
Church Cres. Mount —11Fe 33
Church Cres. S Ock —41Yd 90
Churchcroft Clo. SW12 —59Jb 104
Churchdown. Brom —63Gc 129
Church Dri. NW9 —32Ta 59
Church Dri. Harr —30Ca 37
Church Dri. W Wick —76Gc 149
Church Elm La. Dag —37Cd 68
Church End. E17 —28Dc 44
Church End. NW4 —27Xa 40
Church Entry. EC4 (off Carter La.) —44Rb 83 (3C 200)
Church Farm Clo. Swan —72Ed 152
Church Farm La. Sutt —79Ab 144
Church Field. Dart —61Md 133
Churchfield Av. N12 —23Fb 41
Churchfield Clo. Harr —28Ea 38
Churchfield Clo. Hay —45V 76
Churchfield Mans. SW6 —54Bb 103 (off New King's Rd.)
Churchfield M. Slou —4L 73
Churchfield Path. Chesh —1Yb 12 (in two parts)
Churchfield Rd. W3 —46Sa 79
Churchfield Rd. W7 —47Ga 78
Churchfield Rd. W13 —46Ka 78
Churchfield Rd. Ger X —25A 34
Churchfield Rd. W on T —74W 140
Churchfield Rd. Well —55Wc 109
Churchfield Rd. Wey —77Q 140
Churchfields. E18 —25Jc 45
Churchfields. SE10 —51Ec 106
Churchfields. Hors —88A 156
Churchfields. Lou —14Nc 28
Churchfields. Sev —94Hd 186
Churchfields. W Mol —69Ca 121
Churchfields Av. Felt —62Ba 121
Churchfields Av. Wey —77R 140
Churchfields Rd. Beck —68Zb 128
Churchfield Way. N12 —23Eb 41
Church Gdns. W5 —47Ma 79
Church Gdns. Lea —92Ka 176
Church Gdns. Wemb —35Ja 58
Church Ga. SW6 —55Ab 102
Churchgate. Chesh —1Xb 11
Churchgate Rd. Chesh —1Xb 11
Church Grn. Hay —44V 76
Church Grn. W on T —79Y 141
Church Gro. SE13 —57Dc 106
Church Gro. Amer —11A 16
Church Gro. King T —67La 122
Church Gro. Wex —3N 73
Church Hill. E17 —28Cc 44
Church Hill. N21 —17Pb 24
Church Hill. SE18 —48Pc 86
Church Hill. SW19 —64Bb 125
Church Hill. Cars —78Hb 145
Church Hill. Cat —96Vb 181
Church Hill. Cud —87Sc 168
Church Hill. Dart —56Gd 110
Church Hill. Epp —1Wc 15
Church Hill. Grnh —57Ud 112
Church Hill. Hare —27L 35
Church Hill. Harr —32Ga 58
Church Hill. Hors —4G 188
Church Hill. Lou —13Nc 28
Church Hill. Mers —98Kb 180
Church Hill. Orp —73Wc 151
Church Hill. Purl —82Nb 164

Church Hill—Claughton Rd.

Church Hill. Pyr —89H 157
Church Hill. Stanf —2L 93
Church Hill. Tats —94Mc 183
Church Hill. Wilm —61Md 133
Church Hill Rd. E17 —28Dc 44
Church Hill Rd. Barn —16Gb 23
Church Hill Rd. Surb —71Na 143
Church Hill Rd. Sutt —76Za 144
Church Hill Wood. Orp —71Vc 151
Church Hollow. Purf —50Qd 89
Church Hyde. SE18 —51Uc 108
Churchill Av. Harr —30Ka 38
Churchill Av. Uxb —41R 76
Churchill Clo. Dart —60Rd 111
Churchill Clo. Fet —95Ga 176
Churchill Clo. Uxb —41R 76
Churchill Clo. Warl —89Yb 166
Churchill Clo. W'ham —98Tc 184
Churchill Ct. N4 —31Qb 62
Churchill Ct. W5 —42Pa 79
Churchill Ct. N'holt —36Ca 57
Churchill Ct. N'wd —23T 36
Churchill Ct. S Harr —29Da 37
Churchill Ct. Stai —65K 119
Churchill Dri. Wey —77S 140
Churchill Gdns. SW1 —50Lb 82
Churchill Gdns. SW7
—48Fb 81 (4B 202)
Churchill Gdns. W3 —44Qa 79
Churchill Gdns. Rd. SW1 —50Kb 82
Churchill M. Wfd G —23Hc 45
Churchill Pl. E14 —46Dc 84
Churchill Pl. Harr —28Ga 38
Churchill Rd. E16 —44Lc 85
Churchill Rd. NW2 —37Xa 60
Churchill Rd. NW5 —35Kb 62
Churchill Rd. Edgw —23Pa 39
Churchill Rd. Grav —10B 114
Churchill Rd. Grays —51Fe 113
Churchill Rd. Hort K —70Sd 134
Churchill Rd. Slou —49B 74
Churchill Rd. S Croy —80Sb 147
Churchills M. Wfd G —23Jc 45
Churchill Ter. E4 —21Cc 44
Churchill Wlk. E9 —36Yb 64
Churchill Way. Brom —69Jc 129
Churchill Way. Sun —64W 120
Church La. E11 —32Gc 65
Church La. E17 —28Dc 44
Church La. N2 —27Fb 41
Church La. N8 —28Pb 42
Church La. N9 —19Wb 25
Church La. N17 —25Ub 43
Church La. NW9 —30Sa 39
Church La. SW17 —64Hb 125
Church La. SW19 —67Cb 125
Church La. W5 —47La 78
Church La. Abr —12Ad 29
Church La. Brom —74Nc 150
Church La. Cat —96Qb 180
Church La. Chal P —25A 34
Church La. Chesh —1Xb 11
Church La. Chess —79Pa 143
Church La. Chst —67Sc 130
Church La. Coul —94Jb 180
Church La. Dag —38Ed 68
Church La. Dodd —11Wd 32
Church La. Enf —13Tb 25
Church La. Eps —89Za 162
Church La. Grav —1L 137
Church La. Gt War —30Zd 51
Church La. Harr —25Ha 38
Church La. H'ley —96Sa 177
Church La. Kems —89Rd 171
Church La. K Lan —1Q 4
Church La. Lou —13Pc 28
Church La. Mill E —18J 17
Church La. N'thaw —2Jb 10
Church La. N Ock —36Xd 70
Church La. Oxt —100Gc 183
Church La. Pinn —27Aa 37
Church La. Purf —50Qd 89
Church La. Rain —44Md 89
Church La. Rich —60Na 101
Church La. Romf —28Gd 48
Church La. Sarr —10H 3
Church La. Send —98D 172
Church La. Stap A —14Ed 30
Church La. Stoke P —2K 73
Church La. S'dale —10F 116
Church La. S'hill —10B 116
Church La. Tats —94Mc 183
Church La. Tedd —64Ha 122
Church La. Th Dit —72Ha 142
Church La. Twic —60Ja 100
Church La. Uxb —40K 55
Church La. Wall —76Mb 146
Church La. Warl —88Dc 166
(Chelsham)
Church La. Warl —89Zb 166
(Warlingham)
Church La. Wex —2M 73
Church La. Wind —3H 95
Church La. Av. Coul —94Kb 180
Church La. Dri. Coul —94Kb 180
Churchley Rd. SE26 —63Xb 127
Church Manorway. SE2 —49Wc 87
Church Manorway. Eri —49Fd 88
Churchmead Clo. Barn —16Gb 23
Church Meadow. Surb —75La 142
Churchmead Rd. NW10 —37Wa 60
Churchmore Rd. SW16 —67Lb 126
Church Mt. N2 —29Fb 41
Church Pde. Ashf —63P 119
Church Pas. Surb —71Na 143
Church Pas. Twic —60Ka 100
Church Path. E11 —29Jc 45
Church Path. E17 —28Dc 44
Church Path. N5 —36Rb 63
(Highbury New Pk.)
Church Path. N5 —35Sb 63
(Highbury Pl.)
Church Path. N17 —25Ub 43
Church Path. N20 —21Eb 41
Church Path. NW10 —38Ua 60
Church Path. SW14 —55Ta 101
(in two parts)
Church Path. SW19 —68Bb 125
Church Path. W4 & W3 —48Sa 79
Church Path. W7 —46Ga 78
Church Path. Bark —39Sc 66
Church Path. Barn —14Ab 22
Church Path. Cob —86X 159
Church Path. Coul —90Qb 164
Church Path. Croy —75Sb 147
Church Path. Grav —58Ee 113
Church Path. Grays —51Be 113
Church Path. Grnh —57Vd 112
Church Path. Mers —99Kb 180
Church Path. Mitc —69Gb 125
Church Path. Romf —29Gd 48
Church Path. S'hall —48Ba 77
(Southall Green)
Church Path. S'hall —46Ca 77
(Southall)
Church Path. S'hill —9C 116
Church Path. Swan —67Kd 133
Church Path. Wok —89B 156
Church Pl. SW1 —45Lb 82 (5C 198)
Church Pl. W5 —47Ma 79
Church Pl. Ick —34S 56
Church Pl. Mitc —69Gb 125
Church Rise. SE23 —61Zb 128
Church Rise. Chess —79Pa 143
Church Rd. E10 —32Cc 64
Church Rd. E12 —36Nc 66
Church Rd. E17 —26Ac 44
Church Rd. N6 —30Jb 42
Church Rd. N17 —25Ub 43
Church Rd. NW4 —28Xa 40
Church Rd. NW10 —38Ua 60
Church Rd. SE19 —67Ub 127
Church Rd. SW13 —54Va 102
Church Rd. SW19 & Mitc
(Merton) —67Fb 125
Church Rd. SW19 —64Ab 124
(Wimbledon)
Church Rd. W3 —46Sa 79
Church Rd. W7 —45Fa 78
Church Rd. Add —78J 139
Church Rd. Ashf —62P 119
Church Rd. Asht —90Ma 161
Church Rd. Bark —37Sc 66
Church Rd. Bexh —54Bd 109
Church Rd. Big H —89Mc 167
Church Rd. Bookh —95Ba 175
Church Rd. Bras —96Xc 185
Church Rd. Brom —68Jc 129
Church Rd. Buck H —18Kc 27
Church Rd. Byfl —86N 157
Church Rd. Cat —95Vb 181
Church Rd. Chels —80Yc 151
Church Rd. Clay —79Ha 142
Church Rd. Cobh —8E 136
Church Rd. Cran —50X 77
Church Rd. Crock —73Fd 152
Church Rd. Croy —76Sb 147
(in two parts)
Church Rd. E Mol —70Fa 122
Church Rd. Egh —64B 118
Church Rd. Enf —16Yb 26
Church Rd. Eps —84Ua 162
Church Rd. Eri —50Fd 88
Church Rd. Ewe —80Ta 143
Church Rd. Farn R —1G 72
Church Rd. Felt —64Z 121
Church Rd. Grnh —57Vd 112
Church Rd. Hals —83Ad 169
Church Rd. Ham —63Ma 123
Church Rd. Hare —27L 35
Church Rd. H Wood —25Qd 49
Church Rd. Hart —71Be 155
Church Rd. Hay —46V 76
Church Rd. Hors —87A 156
Church Rd. Houn —52Ca 99
Church Rd. Ilf —30Uc 46
Church Rd. Iswth —53Fa 100
Church Rd. Iver —41E 74
Church Rd. Kenl —87Tb 165
Church Rd. Kes —80Mc 149
Church Rd. King T —68Pa 123
Church Rd. Lea —94Ka 176
Church Rd. Lou —13Jc 27
Church Rd. Nave —12Md 31
Church Rd. New Ash —75Be 155
Church Rd. Noak H —18Ld 31
Church Rd. N'holt —40Z 57
Church Rd. N'wd —24V 36
Church Rd. Old Win —7L 95
Church Rd. Pot B —2Cb 9
Church Rd. Purl —82Nb 164
Church Rd. Rich —56Na 101
Church Rd. Seal —93Pd 187
Church Rd. Shep —73R 140
Church Rd. Short —69Gc 129
Church Rd. Sidc —63Wc 131
Church Rd. Sole S —5E 136
Church Rd. Stan —22Ka 38
Church Rd. St J —7D 188
Church Rd. Sund —99Ad 185
Church Rd. Surb —74La 142
Church Rd. Sutt —79Ab 144
Church Rd. S at H —66Nd 133
Church Rd. Swan —67Md 133
Church Rd. Swans —58Be 113
Church Rd. Tedd —63Ga 122
Church Rd. Til —3B 114
Church Rd. Uxb —42M 75
Church Rd. Wall —76Mb 146
Church Rd. Warl —89Zb 166
Church Rd. Wat —11W 18
Church Rd. Well —54Xc 109
Church Rd. W Dray —48M 75
Church Rd. W King —80Ud 154
Church Rd. W Til —1G 114
Church Rd. Whyt —90Vb 165
Church Rd. Wold —94Ac 182
Church Rd. Wor Pk —74Ua 144
Church Rd. N. N2 —26Fb 41
Church Rd. S. N2 —26Fb 41
Church Row. NW3 —35Eb 61
Church Row. Chst —67Sc 130
Church Row. M. Chst —66Sc 130
Church Side. Eps —85Ra 161
Churchside Clo. Big H —89Lc 167
Church Sq. Shep —73R 140
Church St. E15 —39Gc 65
Church St. E16 —46Rc 86
Church St. N9 —17Tb 25
Church St. W2 & NW8
—43Fb 81 (7C 190)
Church St. W4 —51Va 102
Church St. Burn —2A 72
Church St. Chalv —7G 72
Church St. Cob —87X 159
Church St. Croy —75Rb 147
Church St. Dag —37Dd 68
Church St. Eff —99Z 175
Church St. Enf —13Sb 25
Church St. Eps —85Ua 162
Church St. Esh —77Da 141
Church St. Ewe —81Wa 162
Church St. Grav —8D 114
Church St. Grays —51Ee 113
Church St. Hamp —67Ea 122
Church St. Iswth —55Ka 100
Church St. King T —68Ma 123
Church St. Lea —94Ka 176
(in two parts)
Church St. Old Wok —93E 172
Church St. Rick —18N 17
Church St. Seal —93Pd 187
Church St. Shor —83Hd 170
Church St. Slou —7K 73
Church St. S'fleet —64Ce 135
Church St. Stai —63F 118
Church St. Sun —69X 121
Church St. Sutt —78Db 145
Church St. Twic —60Ja 100
Church St. Wal A —5Ec 12
Church St. W on T —74W 140
Church St. Wat —14Y 19
Church St. Wey —77Q 140
Church St. Wind —3H 95
Church St. E. Wok —89B 156
Church St. Est. NW8
—42Fb 81 (6C 190)
Church St. N. E15 —39Gc 65
Church St. Pas. E15 —39Gc 65
Church St. W. Wok —89A 156
Church Stretton Rd. Houn
—57Ea 100
Church Ter. NW4 —27Xa 40
Church Ter. SE13 —55Gc 107
Church Ter. Rich —57Ma 101
Church Ter. Wind —4C 94
Church Trading Est., The. Eri
—52Jd 110
Church Vale. N2 —27Hb 41
Church Vale. SE23 —61Zb 128
Church View. Rich —57Na 101
Church View. S Ock —47Sd 90
Church View. Swan —69Fd 132
Church View. Upm —33Rd 69
Churchview Rd. Twic —60Fa 100
Church Vs. Sev —94Gd 186
Church Wlk. N6 —34Jb 62
Church Wlk. N16 —34Tb 63
Church Wlk. NW2 —34Bb 61
Church Wlk. NW4 —27Ya 40
Church Wlk. NW9 —33Ta 59
Church Wlk. SW13 —53Wa 102
Church Wlk. SW15 —57Xa 102
Church Wlk. SW16 —68Lb 126
Church Wlk. SW20 —69Ya 124
Church Wlk. Bren —51La 100
(in two parts)
Church Wlk. Burn —2A 72
Church Wlk. Cat —96Wb 181
Church Wlk. Cher —72J 139
Church Wlk. Dart —62Md 133
Church Wlk. Eyns —76Nd 153
Church Wlk. Grav —10F 114
Church Wlk. Hay —44U 76
Church Wlk. Lea —94Ka 176
Church Wlk. Rich —57Ma 101
Church Wlk. Th Dit —72Ha 142
Church Wlk. W on T —74W 140
Church Wlk. Wey —76Q 140
Churchward Ho. W14 —50Bb 81
(off Ivatt Pl.)
Church Way. N20 —20Gb 23
Churchway. NW1
—41Mb 82 (3E 192)
Church Way. Barn —14Hb 23
Church Way. Edgw —23Qa 39
Church Way. S Croy —82Vb 165
Churchwell Path. E9 —36Yb 64
Churchwood Gdns. Wfd G —21Jc 45
Churchyard Pas. SE5 —53Tb 105
Churchyard Row. SE11
—49Rb 83 (5C 206)
Churnfield. N4 —33Qb 62
Churston Av. E13 —39Kc 65
Churston Clo. SW2 —60Qb 104
Churston Dri. Mord —71Za 144
Churston Gdns. N11 —23Lb 42
Churton Pl. SW1
—49Lb 82 (6C 204)
Churton St. SW1
—49Lb 82 (6C 204)
Chusan Pl. E14 —44Bc 84
Chute Ho. SW9 —54Qb 104
(off Stockwell Pk. Rd.)
Chuters Clo. Byfl —84N 157
Chuters Gro. Eps —84Va 162
Chyngton Clo. Sidc —62Vc 131
Cibber Rd. SE23 —61Zb 128
Cicada Rd. SW18 —58Eb 103
Cicely Rd. SE15 —53Wb 105
Cilfton Pl. W2 —45Fb 81 (4C 196)
Cimba Wood. Grav —3G 136
Cinderford Way. Brom —63Gc 129
Cinder Path. Wok —7F 188
Cinnamon Row. SW11 —55Eb 103
Cinnamon St. E1 —46Xb 83
Cintra Pk. SE19 —66Vb 127
Cippenham Clo. Slou —5D 72
Cippenham La. Slou —5D 72
Circle Gdns. SW19 —68Cb 125
Circle Gdns. Byfl —85P 157
Circle Rd. W Vill —81U 158
Circle, The. NW2 —34Ua 60
Circle, The. NW7 —23Ta 39
Circle, The. Til —3C 114
Circuits, The. Pinn —28Y 37
Circular Rd. N2 —26Fb 41
Circular Rd. N17 —27Vb 43
Circular Way. SE18 —51Pc 108
Circus M. W1 —43Hb 81 (7F 191)
(off Enford St.)
Circus Pl. EC2 —43Tb 83 (1G 201)
Circus Rd. NW8 —41Fb 81 (3B 190)
Circus St. SE10 —52Ec 106
Cirencester St. W2 —43Db 81
Cirrus Cres. Grav —4G 136
Cissbury Ho. SE26 —62Wb 127
Cissbury Ring N. N12 —22Bb 41
Cissbury Ring S. N12 —22Bb 41
Cissbury Rd. N15 —29Tb 43
Citadel Pl. SE11 —50Pb 82 (7H 205)
Citizen Rd. N7 —35Qb 62
City Garden Row. N1
—40Rb 63 (2C 194)
City Ho. Wall —74Jb 146
(off Corbet Clo.)
City Rd. EC1 —40Rb 63 (2B 194)
Civic Sq. Til —4C 114
Civic Way. Ilf —28Sc 46
Clabon M. SW1 —48Hb 81 (4F 203)
Clacket La. W'ham —96Nc 184
Clack La. Ruis —32S 56
Clack St. SE16 —47Yb 84
Clacton Rd. E6 —41Mc 85
Clacton Rd. E17 —30Ac 44
Clacton Rd. N17 —26Vb 43
Claigmar Gdns. N3 —25Db 41
Claire Ct. N12 —21Eb 41
Claire Ct. NW2 —37Ab 60
Claire Ct. Bush —18Fa 20
Claire Ct. Pinn —24Ba 37
Claire Gdns. Stan —22La 38
Claire Ho. Edgw —26Sa 39
(off Burnt Oak B'way.)
Claire Pl. E14 —48Cc 84
Clairvale. Horn —31Nd 69
Clairvale Rd. Houn —53Aa 99
Clairview Rd. SW16 —64Kb 126
Clairville Gdns. W7 —46Ga 78
Clammas Way. Uxb —43L 75
Clamp Hill. Stan —21Fa 38
Clancarty Rd. SW6 —54Cb 103
Clandeboyne Ho. E15 —39Hc 65
(off John St.)
Clandon Av. Egh —66E 118
Clandon Clo. W3 —47Ra 79
Clandon Clo. Eps —79Va 144
Clandon Gdns. N3 —27Cb 41
Clandon Rd. Ilf —33Uc 66
Clandon Rd. W Cla —97H 173
Clandon St. SE8 —54Cc 106
Clanfield Way. SE15 —52Vb 105
Clanricarde Gdns. W2 —45Cb 81
Clapgate Rd. Bush —16Da 19
Clapham Comn. N. Side. SW4
—56Hb 103
Clapham Comn. S. Side. SW4
—58Kb 104
Clapham Comn. W. Side. SW4
—56Hb 103
Clapham Cres. SW4 —56Mb 104
Clapham High St. SW4 —56Mb 104
Clapham Junc. App. SW11
—56Gb 103
Clapham Mnr. St. SW4 —55Lb 104
Clapham Pk. Est. SW4 —58Mb 104
Clapham Pk. Rd. SW4 —56Mb 104
Clapham Rd. SW9 —55Nb 104
Clapham Rd. Est. SW4 —55Nb 104
Clap La. Dag —33Dd 68
Claps Ga. La. E6 & Bark —42Rc 86
(in two parts)
Clapton Comn. E5 —31Vb 63
Clapton Pk. Est. E5 —35Zb 64
Clapton Pas. E5 —36Yb 64
Clapton Sq. E5 —36Yb 64
Clapton Ter. N16 —32Wb 63
Clapton Way. E5 —35Wb 63
Clara Nehab Ho. NW11 —29Bb 41
(off Leeside Cres.)
Clara Pl. SE18 —49Qc 86
Clare Clo. N2 —27Eb 41
Clare Clo. Els —16Pa 21
Clare Clo. W Byf —85J 157
Clare Corner. SE9 —59Rc 108
Clare Ct. Enf —7Ac 12
Clare Ct. Wold —95Cc 182
Clare Cres. Lea —90Ja 160
Claredale. Wok —91A 172
Claredale St. E2 —40Wb 63
Clare Dri. Farn C —5F 52
Clare Gdns. E7 —35Jc 65
Clare Gdns. W11 —44Ab 80
Clare Gdns. Bark —37Vc 67
Clare Gdns. Egh —64C 118
Clare Hill. Esh —78Da 141
Clare La. N1 —38Sb 63
Clare Lawn Av. SW14 —57Ta 101
Clare Mkt. WC2 —44Pb 82 (3J 199)
Clare M. SW6 —52Db 103
Claremont. Brick —3Ca 5
Claremont. Chesh —1Vb 11
Claremont. Shep —72R 140
Claremont Av. Esh —79Ba 141
Claremont Av. Harr —29Na 39
Claremont Av. N Mald —71Wa 144
Claremont Av. Sun —67X 121
Claremont Av. W on T —77Z 141
Claremont Av. Wok —91A 172
Claremont Clo. E16 —46Qc 86
Claremont Clo. N1
—40Qb 62 (2A 194)
Claremont Clo. SW2 —60Nb 104
Claremont Clo. Grays —48Ee 91
Claremont Clo. Orp —77Qc 150
Claremont Clo. S Croy —87Xb 165
Claremont Clo. W on T —78Y 141
Claremont Cres. Crox —15S 18
Claremont Cres. Dart —56Gd 110
Claremont Dri. Esh —79Da 141
Claremont Dri. Wok —91A 172
Claremont End. Esh —79Da 141
Claremont Gdns. Ilf —33Uc 66
Claremont Gdns. Surb —71Na 143
Claremont Gdns. Upm —32Td 70
Claremont Gro. W4 —52Ua 102
Claremont Gro. Wfd G —23Lc 45
Claremont Ho. Wat —16T 18
Claremont La. Esh —78Da 141
Claremont Pk. N3 —25Ab 40
Claremont Pk. Rd. Esh —79Da 141
Claremont Pl. Grav —9D 114
Claremont Rd. E7 —36Kc 65
Claremont Rd. E11 —34Fc 65
Claremont Rd. E17 —26Ac 44
Claremont Rd. N6 —31Lb 62
Claremont Rd. NW2 —31Za 60
Claremont Rd. W9 —40Ab 60
Claremont Rd. W13 —43Ja 78
Claremont Rd. Barn —10Hb 9
Claremont Rd. Brom —70Nc 130
Claremont Rd. Clay —80Ga 142
Claremont Rd. Croy —74Wb 147
Claremont Rd. Harr —26Ga 38
Claremont Rd. Horn —30Jd 48
Claremont Rd. Stai —64F 118
Claremont Rd. Surb —71Na 143
Claremont Rd. Swan —66Gd 132
Claremont Rd. Tedd —64Ha 122
Claremont Rd. Twic —59Ka 100
Claremont Rd. W Byf —84J 157
Claremont Rd. Wind —4G 94
Claremont Sq. N1
—40Qb 62 (2K 193)
Claremont St. E16 —47Qc 86
Claremont St. N18 —23Wb 43
Claremont St. SE10 —51Dc 106
Claremont Way. NW2 —32Ya 60
(in two parts)
Claremont Way Ind. Est. NW2
—32Ya 60
Claremount Clo. Eps —89Ya 162
Claremount Gdns. Eps —89Ya 162
Clarence Av. SW4 —59Mb 104
Clarence Av. Brom —70Nc 130
Clarence Av. Ilf —30Qc 46
Clarence Av. N Mald —68Sa 123
Clarence Av. Upm —33Qd 69
Clarence Clo. Bush —17Ha 20
Clarence Clo. W on T —77X 141
Clarence Ct. NW7 —22Va 40
Clarence Ct. Grays —51De 113
(off Clarence Rd.)
Clarence Cres. SW4 —58Mb 104
Clarence Cres. Sidc —62Xc 131
Clarence Cres. Wind —3G 94
Clarence Dri. Egh —3N 117
Clarence Gdns. NW1
—41Kb 82 (4A 192)
Clarence Ga. Gdns. NW1
—42Hb 81 (6G 191)
(off Chagford St.)
Clarence La. SW15 —58Ua 102
Clarence M. E5 —36Xb 63
Clarence Pas. NW1
—40Nb 62 (2F 193)
Clarence Pl. E5 —36Xb 63
Clarence Pl. Grav —9D 114
Clarence Rd. E5 —35Xb 63
Clarence Rd. E12 —36Mc 65
Clarence Rd. E16 —42Gc 85
Clarence Rd. E17 —26Zb 44
Clarence Rd. N15 —29Sb 43
Clarence Rd. N22 —24Nb 42
Clarence Rd. NW6 —38Bb 61
Clarence Rd. SE9 —61Nc 130
Clarence Rd. SW19 —65Db 125
Clarence Rd. W4 —50Qa 79
Clarence Rd. Bexh —56Ad 109
Clarence Rd. Big H —90Pc 168
Clarence Rd. Brom —69Mc 130
Clarence Rd. Croy —73Tb 147
Clarence Rd. Enf —15Yb 26
Clarence Rd. Grays —51Ce 113
Clarence Rd. Pil H —16Xd 32
Clarence Rd. Rich —53Pa 101
Clarence Rd. Sidc —62Xc 131
Clarence Rd. Sutt —78Db 145
Clarence Rd. Tedd —65Ha 122
Clarence Rd. Wall —78Kb 146
Clarence Rd. W on T —77X 141
Clarence Rd. Wind —3E 94
Clarence Row. Grav —9D 114
Clarence St. Egh —65B 118
Clarence St. King T —68Ma 123
Clarence St. Rich —56Na 101
Clarence St. S'hall —48Z 77
Clarence St. Stai —63G 118
Clarence Ter. NW1
—42Hb 81 (5G 191)
Clarence Ter. Houn —56Da 99
Clarence Wlk. SW4 —54Nb 104
Clarence Way. NW1 —38Kb 62
Clarence Yd. SE17
—50Sb 83 (7D 206)
(off Penton Pl.)
Clarendon Clo. W2
—45Gb 81 (4D 196)
Clarendon Clo. St P —69Wc 131
Clarendon Ct. NW11 —28Bb 41
Clarendon Ct. Beck —67Dc 128
(off Albemarle Rd.)
Clarendon Ct. Houn —53W 98
Clarendon Ct. Rich —53Pa 101
Clarendon Ct. Slou —5M 73
Clarendon Cres. W11 —45Ab 80
Clarendon Cres. Twic —62Fa 122
Clarendon Dri. SW15 —56Ya 102
Clarendon Gdns. NW4 —27Wa 40
Clarendon Gdns. W9
—42Eb 81 (6A 190)
Clarendon Gdns. Dart —59Td 112
Clarendon Gdns. Ilf —31Pc 66
Clarendon Gdns. Wemb —34Ma 59
Clarendon Grn. Orp —70Wc 131
Clarendon Gro. NW1
—41Mb 82 (3D 192)
Clarendon Gro. Mitc —69Hb 125
Clarendon Gro. St P —70Wc 131
Clarendon M. W2
—45Gb 81 (4D 196)
Clarendon M. Bex —60Dd 110
Clarendon M. Borwd —13Qa 21
Clarendon Pde. Chesh —1Zb 12
Clarendon Path. St P —70Wc 131
(in two parts)
Clarendon Pl. W2
—45Gb 81 (4D 196)
Clarendon Pl. Sev —97Jd 186
Clarendon Pl. Wilm —64Gd 132
Clarendon Rise. SE13 —56Ec 106
Clarendon Rd. E11 —32Fc 65
Clarendon Rd. E17 —30Dc 44
Clarendon Rd. E18 —27Jc 45
Clarendon Rd. N8 —27Pb 42
Clarendon Rd. N15 —28Sb 43
Clarendon Rd. N18 —23Wb 43
Clarendon Rd. N22 —26Pb 42
Clarendon Rd. SW19 —66Gb 125
Clarendon Rd. W5 —42Na 79
Clarendon Rd. W11 —45Ab 80
Clarendon Rd. Ashf —63P 119
Clarendon Rd. Borwd —13Qa 21
Clarendon Rd. Chesh —1Zb 12
Clarendon Rd. Croy —75Rb 147
Clarendon Rd. Grav —8E 114
Clarendon Rd. Harr —30Ga 38
Clarendon Rd. Hay —47V 76
Clarendon Rd. Sev —96Jd 186
Clarendon Rd. Wall —79Lb 146
Clarendon Rd. Wat —12X 19
Clarendon St. SW1
—50Kb 82 (7A 204)
Clarendon Ter. W9
—42Eb 81 (5A 190)
Clarendon Way. N21 —16Sb 25
Clarendon Way. Chst & St M
—69Vc 131
Clarens St. SE6 —61Bc 128
Clare Pl. SW15 —59Va 102
Clare Rd. E11 —30Fc 45
Clare Rd. NW10 —38Wa 60
Clare Rd. SE14 —54Bc 106
Clare Rd. Gnfd —37Fa 58
Clare Rd. Houn —55Ba 99
Clare Rd. Stai —60M 97
Clare Rd. Tap —4A 72
Clare St. E2 —40Xb 63
Claret Gdns. SE25 —69Ub 127
Clareville Gro. SW7
—49Eb 81 (6A 202)
Clareville Gro. M. SW7
—49Eb 81 (6A 202)
Clareville Rd. Cat —96Wb 181
Clareville Rd. Orp —75Sc 150
Clareville St. SW7
—49Eb 81 (6A 202)
Clare Way. Bexh —53Ad 109
Clare Way. Sev —100Ld 187
Clare Wood. Lea —90Ka 160
Clarewood Wlk. SW9 —56Qb 104
Clarges M. W1 —46Kb 82 (6K 197)
Clarges St. W1 —46Kb 82 (7A 198)
Claribel Rd. SW9 —54Rb 105
Clarice Way. Wall —81Nb 164
Claridge Rd. Dag —32Zc 67
Clarissa Rd. Romf —31Zc 67
Clarissa St. E8 —39Vb 63
Clark Clo. Eri —53Jd 110
Clarkebourne Dri. Grays —51Fe 113
Clarke Ct. NW10 —38Sa 59
Clarke Grn. Wat —7W 4
Clarke Mans. Bark —38Vc 67
(off Upney La.)
Clarke Path. N16 —32Wb 63
Clarkes Av. Wor Pk —74Za 144
Clarkes Dri. Uxb —43N 75
Clarke's Grn. Rd. Sev —86Qd 171
Clarke's M. W1 —43Jb 82 (7J 191)
(off Beaumont St.)
Clarke Way. Wat —7W 4
Clarkfield. Mill E —18K 17
Clark's La. WC2 —44Pb 82 (3H 199)
Clarks La. Epp —3Vc 15
Clarks La. Hals —84Bd 169
Clarks La. Warl & Tats —95Jc 183
Clarks Mead. Bush —17Ea 20
Clarkson Rd. E16 —44Hc 85
Clarkson Row. NW1
—40Lb 62 (1B 192)
(off Mornington Ter.)
Clarksons, The. Bark —40Sc 66
Clarkson St. E2 —41Xb 83
Clark's Pas. SW8 —51Nb 104
(off Bond Way)
Clark's Pl. EC2 —44Ub 83 (2H 201)
Clark's Rd. Ilf —33Tc 66
Clark St. E1 —43Yb 84
Clark Way. Houn —52Z 99
Classon Clo. W Dray —47N 75
Claston Clo. Dart —56Gd 110
Claude Rd. E10 —33Ec 64
Claude Rd. E13 —39Kc 65
Claude Rd. SE15 —54Xb 105
Claude St. E14 —49Cc 84
Claudia Jones Ho. N17 —25Sb 43
Claudia Jones Way. SW2 —58Nb 104
Claudian Way. Grays —8D 92
Claudia Pl. SW19 —60Ab 102
Claughton Rd. E13 —40Lc 65

Claughton Way—Cobill Clo.

Claughton Way. Hut —16Fe 33
Clauson Av. N'holt —36Da 57
Clavell St. SE10 —51Ec 106
Claverdale Rd. SW2 —59Pb 104
Claverhambury Rd. Wal A —1Jc 13
Clavering Av. SW13 —51Xa 102
Clavering Clo. Twic —63Ja 122
Clavering Gdns. W Horn —30Fe 51
Clavering Rd. E12 —32Mc 65
Clavering Way. Hut —16Ee 33
Claverley Gro. N3 —25Db 41
Claverley Vs. N3 —24Db 41
Claverton. Asht —89Na 161
Claverton Clo. Bov —1C 2
Claverton St. SW1
—50Lb 82 (7C 204)
Clave St. E1 —46Yb 84
Claxton Gro. W6 —50Za 80
Clay Av. Mitc —68Kb 126
Claybank Gro. SE13 —55Dc 106
Claybourne M. SE19 —66Ub 127
Claybridge Rd. SE12 —63Lc 129
Claybrook Clo. N2 —27Fb 41
Claybrook Rd. W6 —51Za 102
Clayburn Gdns. S Ock —45Xd 90
Claybury. Bush —17Da 19
Claybury B'way. Ilf —27Nc 46
Claybury Rd. Wfd G —24Nc 46
Clay Clo. Add —78K 139
(off Monks Cres.)
Clay Corner. Cher —74K 139
Clay Ct. E17 —27Fc 45
Claydon Dri. Croy —77Nb 146
Claydon End. Ger X —27A 34
Claydon Ho. NW4 —26Za 40
(off Holders Hill Rd.)
Claydon La. Ger X —27A 34
Claydon Rd. Wok —4D 188
Clay Farm Rd. SE9 —61Sc 130
Claygate Clo. Horn —35Jd 68
Claygate Cres. New Ad —79Ec 148
Claygate La. Esh —75Ja 142
Claygate La. Th Dit —74Ja 142
Claygate La. Wal A —2Gc 13
(in two parts)
Claygate Lodge Clo. Clay
—80Ga 142
Claygate Rd. W13 —48Ka 78
Clayhall Av. Ilf —27Nc 46
Clayhall La. Old Win —7K 95
Clay Hill. Enf —9Sb 11
Clayhill. Surb —71Qa 143
Clayhill Cres. SE9 —63Mc 129
Claylands Pl. SW8 —52Qb 104
Claylands Rd. SW8 —51Pb 104
Clay La. Bush —17Ga 20
Clay La. Edgw —19Qa 21
Clay La. Guild —100A 172
Clay La. H'ley —96Ra 177
Clay La. Stanw —59P 97
Claymore Clo. Mord —73Cb 145
Claypit Hill. Wal A —8Lc 13
Claypole Ct. E17 —30Cc 44
(off Yunus Khan Clo.)
Claypole Rd. E15 —40Ec 64
Clayponds Av. W5 & Bren
—49Na 79
Clayponds Gdns. W5 —49Ma 79
Clayponds La. Bren —50Na 79
Clay Ride. Lou —11Mc 27
Clayside. Chig —22Sc 46
Clays La. E15 —36Dc 64
Clay's La. Lou —11Qc 28
Clays La. Clo. E15 —36Dc 64
Clay St. W1 —43Hb 81 (1G 197)
Clayton Av. Upm —36Rd 69
Clayton Av. Wemb —38Na 59
Clayton Clo. E6 —44Pc 86
Clayton Ct. E17 —26Ac 44
Clayton Ct. Langl —48C 74
Clayton Cres. Bren —50Ma 79
Clayton Croft Rd. Dart —61Jd 132
Clayton Field. NW9 —24Ua 40
Clayton Rd. SE15 —53Wb 105
Clayton Rd. Chess —77La 142
Clayton Rd. Eps —84Ua 162
Clayton Rd. Hay —47U 76
Clayton Rd. Iswth —55Ga 100
Clayton Rd. Romf —32Ed 68
Clayton St. SE11 —51Qb 104
Clayton Ter. Hay —43Aa 77
Clayton Way. Uxb —42M 75
Clay Tye Rd. Upm —33Yd 70
Claywood Clo. Orp —73Uc 150
Claywood La. Bean —62Zd 135
Clayworth Clo. Sidc —58Xc 109
Cleadon Clo. Enf —13Ac 26
Cleall Av. Wal A —6Ec 12
Cleanthus Clo. SE18 —53Rc 108
Cleanthus Rd. SE18 —53Rc 108
Clearbrook Way. E1 —44Yb 84
Cleardown. Wok —90D 156
Clearway Caravan Pk. W King
—80Td 154
Clearways Bus. Est. W King
—80Ud 154
Clearwell Dri. W9 —42Db 81
Cleave Av. Hay —49U 76
Cleave Av. Orp —79Uc 150
Cleaveland Rd. Surb —71Ma 143
Cleave Prior. Coul —91Gb 179
Cleaverholme Clo. SE25 —72Xb 147
Cleaver Sq. SE11
—50Qb 82 (7A 206)
Cleaver St. SE11
—50Qb 82 (7A 206)
Cleeve Ct. Felt —60U 98
Cleeve Hill. SE23 —60Xb 105
Cleeve Pk. Gdns. Sidc —61Xc 131
Cleeve Rd. Lea —92Ha 176
Clegg St. E1 —46Xb 83
Clegg St. E13 —40Jc 65
Cleland Path. Lou —11Rc 28
Cleland Rd. Ger X —26A 34
Clemants Clo. Slou —7M 73
Clematis Clo. Romf —24Ld 49
Clematis St. W12 —45Wa 80
Clem Attlee Ct. SW6 —51Bb 103
Clem Attlee Est. SW6 —51Bb 103
Clemence St. E14 —43Bc 84
Clement Av. SW4 —56Mb 104
Clement Clo. NW6 —38Ya 60
Clement Clo. W4 —49Ta 79
Clement Clo. Purl —88Rb 165
Clement Gdns. Hay —49U 76
Clementhorpe Rd. Dag —37Yc 67
Clement Ho. SE8 —49Ac 84
Clementina Rd. E10 —32Bc 64
Clementine Clo. W13 —47Ka 78
Clement Rd. SW19 —64Ab 124
Clement Rd. Beck —68Zb 128
Clement's Av. E16 —45Jc 85
Clements Ct. Houn —56Z 99
Clements Ct. Ilf —34Rc 66
Clement's Inn. WC2
—44Pb 82 (3J 199)
Clement's Inn Pas. WC2
—44Pb 82 (3J 199)
(off Grange Ct.)
Clements La. EC4
—45Tb 83 (4G 201)
Clements La. Ilf —34Rc 66
Clements Mead. Lea —91Ja 176
Clements Pl. Bren —50Ma 79
Clements Rd. E6 —38Nc 66
Clement's Rd. SE16 —48Wb 83
Clement's Rd. Chor —15F 16
Clements Rd. Ilf —34Rc 66
Clements Rd. W on T —75X 141
Clement St. Swan —65Ld 133
Clement Way. Upm —34Pd 69
Clemson Ho. E8 —39Vb 63 (1K 195)
Clenches Farm La. Sev —98Jd 186
Clenches Farm Rd. Sev —98Jd 186
Clendon Way. SE18 —49Tc 86
Clennam St. SE1
—47Sb 83 (1E 206)
Clensham Ct. Sutt —75Cb 145
Clensham La. Sutt —75Cb 145
Clenston M. W1 —44Hb 81 (2F 197)
Clephane Rd. N1 —37Sb 63
Clere Pl. EC2 —42Tb 83 (5G 195)
Clere St. EC2 —42Tb 83 (5G 195)
Clerics Wlk. Shep —73T 140
Clerkenwell Clo. EC1
(in two parts) —42Qb 82 (5A 194)
Clerkenwell Grn. EC1
—42Rb 83 (6B 194)
Clerkenwell Rd. EC1
—42Qb 82 (7K 193)
Clerk's Piece. Lou —13Pc 28
Clermont Rd. E9 —39Yb 64
Clevedon. Wey —78T 140
Clevedon Clo. N16 —34Vb 63
Clevedon Gdns. Hay —48T 76
Clevedon Gdns. Houn —53X 99
Clevedon Pas. N16 —33Vb 63
Clevedon Rd. SE20 —67Zb 128
Clevedon Rd. King T —68Qa 123
Clevedon Rd. Twic —58Ma 101
Clevehurst Clo. Stoke P —7L 53
Cleveland Av. SW20 —68Bb 125
Cleveland Av. W4 —49Va 80
Cleveland Av. Hamp —66Ba 121
Cleveland Clo. W on T —76X 141
Cleveland Cres. Borwd —15Sa 21
Cleveland Dri. Stai —68K 119
Cleveland Gdns. N4 —29Sb 43
Cleveland Gdns. NW2 —33Za 60
Cleveland Gdns. SW13 —54Va 102
Cleveland Gdns. W2
—44Eb 81 (3A 196)
Cleveland Gdns. Wor Pk —75Ua 144
Cleveland Gro. E1 —42Yb 84
Cleveland Ho. N2 —26Fb 41
(off Grange, The)
Cleveland Ho. Grav —58Fe 113
Cleveland La. N9 —17Xb 25
Cleveland M. W1
—43Lb 82 (7B 192)
Cleveland Pk. Stai —58N 97
Cleveland Pk. Av. E17 —28Cc 44
Cleveland Pk. Cres. E17 —28Cc 44
Cleveland Pl. SW1
—46Lb 82 (6C 198)
Cleveland Rise. Mord —73Za 144
Cleveland Rd. E18 —27Jc 45
Cleveland Rd. N1 —38Tb 63
Cleveland Rd. SW13 —54Va 102
Cleveland Rd. W4 —48Sa 79
Cleveland Rd. W13 —43Ja 78
Cleveland Rd. Ilf —34Rc 66
Cleveland Rd. Iswth —56Ja 100
Cleveland Rd. N Mald —70Ua 124
Cleveland Rd. Uxb —42M 75
Cleveland Rd. Well —54Vc 109
Cleveland Rd. Wor Pk —75Ua 144
Cleveland Row. SW1
—46Lb 82 (7B 198)
Cleveland Sq. W2
—44Eb 81 (3A 196)
Cleveland St. W1
—42Kb 82 (6A 192)
Cleveland Ter. W2
—44Eb 81 (3A 196)
Cleveland Way. E1 —42Yb 84
Cleveley Clo. SE7 —49Mc 85
Cleveley Cres. W5 —40Na 59
Cleveleys Rd. E5 —34Xb 63
Cleverly Est. W12 —46Wa 80
Cleve Rd. NW6 —38Cb 61
Cleve Rd. Sidc —62Zc 131
Cleves Av. Eps —81Wa 162
Cleves Clo. Cob —86X 159
Cleves Ct. Dart —59Nd 111
Cleves Ct. Eps —84Va 162
Cleves Ct. Wind —5D 94
Cleves Cres. New Ad —83Ec 166
Cleves Rd. E6 —39Mc 65
Cleves Rd. Kems —89Nd 171
Cleves Rd. Rich —62La 122
Cleves Wlk. Ilf —24Sc 46
Cleves Way. Hamp —66Ba 121
Cleves Way. Ruis —32Z 57
Cleves Way. Sun —65V 120
Cleves Wood. Wey —71U 140
Clewer Av. Wind —4E 94
Clewer Ct. Rd. Wind —2F 94
Clewer Cres. Harr —25Fa 38
Clewer Fields. Wind —3G 94
Clewer Hill Rd. Wind —4C 94
Clewer Ho. SE2 —47Zc 87
(off Wolvercote Rd.)
Clewer New Town. Wind —4E 94
Clewer Pk. Wind —2E 94
Clichy Est. E1 —43Yb 84
Clifden Rd. E5 —36Yb 64
Clifden Rd. Bren —51Ma 101
Clifden Rd. Twic —60Ha 100
Cliff End. Purl —84Rb 165
Cliffe Rd. S Croy —78Tb 147
Clifford Av. SW14 —55Ra 101
Clifford Av. Chst —65Pc 130
Clifford Av. Ilf —25Rc 46
Clifford Av. Wall —77Lb 146
Clifford Clo. N'holt —39Aa 57
Clifford Dri. SW9 —56Rb 105
Clifford Gdns. NW10 —40Ya 60
Clifford Gro. Ashf —63Q 120
Clifford Rd. E16 —42Hc 85
Clifford Rd. E17 —26Ec 44
Clifford Rd. N9 —16Yb 26
Clifford Rd. SE25 —70Wb 127
Clifford Rd. Barn —13Db 23
Clifford Rd. Grays —48Be 91
Clifford Rd. Houn —55Z 99
Clifford Rd. Rich —61Ma 123
Clifford Rd. Wemb —38Ma 59
Clifford's Inn Pas. EC4
—44Qb 82 (3K 199)
Clifford's Inn Pas. WC2 —44Qb 82
Clifford St. W1 —45Lb 82 (5B 198)
Clifford Way. NW10 —35Va 60
Cliff Pl. S Ock —41Zd 91
Cliff Rd. NW1 —37Mb 62
Cliffsend Ho. SW9 —53Qb 104
(off Cowley Rd.)
Cliff Ter. SE8 —54Cc 106
Cliffview Rd. SE13 —55Cc 106
Cliff Vs. NW1 —37Mb 62
Cliff Wlk. E16 —43Hc 85
(in two parts)
Clifton Av. E17 —27Zb 44
Clifton Av. N3 —25Bb 41
Clifton Av. W12 —46Va 80
Clifton Av. Felt —62Y 121
Clifton Av. Stan —26Ka 38
Clifton Av. Sutt —83Db 163
Clifton Av. Wemb —37Pa 59
Clifton Clo. Add —75K 139
Clifton Clo. Cat —95Tb 181
Clifton Clo. Chesh —1Ac 12
Clifton Clo. Orp —78Sc 150
Clifton Copse. SE8 —50Bc 84
Clifton Ct. N4 —33Qb 62
(off Playford Rd.)
Clifton Ct. NW8 —42Fb 81 (5B 190)
(off Maida Vale)
Clifton Ct. SE15 —52Xb 105
Clifton Ct. Stanw —58N 97
Clifton Ct. Wfd G —23Jc 45
Clifton Cres. SE15 —52Xb 105
(in two parts)
Clifton Est. SE15 —53Xb 105
Clifton Gdns. N15 —30Vb 43
Clifton Gdns. NW11 —30Bb 41
Clifton Gdns. W4 —49Ta 79
Clifton Gdns. W9 —42Eb 81
Clifton Gdns. Enf —14Nb 24
Clifton Gdns. Uxb —40R 56
Clifton Gro. E8 —37Wb 63
Clifton Gro. Grav —9D 114
Clifton Hill. NW8 —40Db 61
Clifton Ho. E11 —33Gc 65
Clifton Marine Pde. Grav —8B 114
Clifton Pde. Felt —63Y 121
Clifton Pk. Av. SW20 —68Ya 124
Clifton Pl. SE16 —47Yb 84
Clifton Pl. W2 —44Fb 81
Clifton Pl. Bans —87Cb 163
Clifton Rise. SE14 —52Ac 106
Clifton Rise. Wind —3B 94
Clifton Rd. E7 —37Mc 65
Clifton Rd. E16 —43Gc 85
Clifton Rd. N3 —25Eb 41
Clifton Rd. N8 —30Mb 42
Clifton Rd. N22 —25Lb 42
Clifton Rd. NW10 —40Wa 60
Clifton Rd. SE25 —70Ub 127
Clifton Rd. SW19 —65Za 124
Clifton Rd. W9 —42Eb 81 (5A 190)
Clifton Rd. Coul —87Kb 164
Clifton Rd. Grav —8C 114
Clifton Rd. Gnfd —42Ea 78
Clifton Rd. Harr —28Pa 39
Clifton Rd. Horn —30Jd 48
Clifton Rd. Ilf —30Tc 46
Clifton Rd. Iswth —54Ga 100
Clifton Rd. King T —66Pa 123
Clifton Rd. Lou —14Nc 28
Clifton Rd. Sidc —63Uc 130
Clifton Rd. Slou —7M 73
Clifton Rd. S'hall —49Aa 77
Clifton Rd. Tedd —63Ga 122
Clifton Rd. Wall —78Kb 146
Clifton Rd. Wat —15X 19
Clifton Rd. Well —55Yc 109
Clifton St. EC2 —43Ub 83 (7H 195)
Clifton Ter. N4 —33Qb 62
Clifton Vs. W9 —43Eb 81
Cliftonville Ct. SE12 —60Jc 107
Clifton Wlk. W6 —49Xa 80
(off King St.)
Clifton Wlk. Dart —58Rd 111
Clifton Way. SE15 —52Yb 106
Clifton Way. Borwd —11Qa 21
Clifton Way. Hut —18Fe 33
Clifton Way. Knap —5C 188
Clifton Way. Wemb —39Na 59
Climb, The. Rick —16K 17
Clinch Ct. E16 —43Jc 85
(off Plymouth Rd.)
Cline Rd. N11 —23Lb 42
Clinger Ct. N1 —39Ub 63 (1H 195)
Clink St. SE1 —46Tb 83 (6E 200)
Clinton Av. E Mol —70Ea 122
Clinton Av. Well —56Wc 109
Clinton Clo. Knap —6A 188
Clinton Cres. Ilf —23Uc 46
Clinton Rd. E3 —41Ac 84
Clinton Rd. E7 —35Jc 65
Clinton Rd. N15 —28Tb 43
Clinton Rd. Lea —95La 176
Clipper Boulevd. Dart —56Ud 112
Clipper Clo. SE16 —47Zb 84
Clipper Cres. Grav —3H 137
Clipper Way. SE13 —56Ec 106
Clippesby Clo. Chess —79Pa 143
Clipstone M. W1
—43Lb 82 (7B 192)
Clipstone Rd. Houn —55Ca 99
Clipstone St. W1
—43Kb 82 (7A 192)
Clissold Clo. N2 —27Hb 41
Clissold Ct. N16 —33Sb 63
Clissold Cres. N16 —35Tb 63
Clissold Rd. N16 —34Tb 63
Clitheroe Av. Harr —32Ca 57
Clitheroe Gdns. Wat —20Z 19
Clitheroe Rd. SW9 —54Nb 104
Clitheroe Rd. Romf —22Ed 48
Clitherow Av. W7 —48Ja 78
Clitherow Ct. Bren —50La 78
Clitherow Pas. Bren —50La 78
Clitherow Rd. Bren —50Ka 78
Clitterhouse Cres. NW2 —32Ya 60
Clitterhouse Rd. NW2 —32Ya 60
Clive Av. N18 —23Wb 43
Clive Av. Dart —58Hd 110
Clive Clo. Pot B —3Bb 9
Clive Ct. W9 —42Eb 81 (5A 190)
(off Maida Vale)
Clive Ct. Slou —7H 73
Cliveden Clo. N12 —21Eb 41
Cliveden Clo. Shenf —17Be 33
Cliveden Pl. SW1
—49Jb 82 (5H 203)
Cliveden Pl. Shep —72S 140
Cliveden Rd. SW19 —67Bb 125
Clivedon Ct. W13 —43Ka 78
Clivedon Rd. E4 —22Gc 45
Clive Lloyd Ho. N15 —29Sb 43
(off Woodlands Pk. Rd.)
Clive Lodge. NW4 —30Za 40
Clive Pde. N'wd —24U 36
Clive Pas. SE21 —62Tb 127
Clive Rd. SE21 —62Tb 127
Clive Rd. SW19 —65Gb 125
Clive Rd. Belv —49Cd 88
Clive Rd. Enf —14Wb 25
Clive Rd. Esh —77Da 141
Clive Rd. Felt —58W 98
Clive Rd. Grav —8D 114
Clive Rd. Gt War —24Yd 50
Clive Rd. Romf —29Kd 49
Clive Rd. Twic —63Ja 122
Clivesdale Dri. Hay —46X 77
Clive Way. Enf —14Wb 25
Clive Way. Wat —11Y 19
Cloak La. EC4 —45Sb 83 (4E 200)
Clochar Ct. NW10 —39Va 60
Clock Ho. E17 —28Fc 45
(off Wood St.)
Clockhouse Av. Bark —39Sc 66
Clockhouse Clo. SW19 —61Ya 124
Clock Ho. Clo. Byfl —84P 157
Clockhouse Ct. Beck —68Ac 128
Clockhouse Ind. Est., The. Felt
—60R 98
Clockhouse La. Ashf & Felt
—63Q 120
Clockhouse La. N Stif —46Zd 91
Clockhouse La. Romf —24Dd 48
Clock Ho. La. Sev —95Jd 186
Clockhouse La. E. Egh —66D 118
Clockhouse La. W. Egh —66C 118
Clockhouse Mead. Oxs —86Da 159
Clockhouse Pde. N13 —22Qb 42
Clock Ho. Rd. Beck —69Ac 128
Clockouse La. E. Egh —66D 118
Clock Pde. Enf —15Tb 25
Clock Pl. SE1 —49Rb 83 (5C 206)
(off Newington Butts)
Clock Tower M. N1
—39Sb 63 (1E 194)
Clock Tower Pl. N7 —37Nb 62
Clock Tower Rd. Iswth —55Ha 100
Clodhouse Hill. Wok —10A 188
Cloister Clo. Rain —42Kd 89
Cloister Clo. Tedd —64Ka 122
Cloister Gdns. SE25 —72Xb 147
Cloister Gdns. Edgw —22Sa 39
Cloister Rd. NW2 —34Bb 61
Cloister Rd. W3 —43Sa 79
Cloisters. Stanf —1N 93
Cloisters Av. Brom —71Pc 150
Cloisters Bus. Cen. SW8 —52Kb 104
(off Battersea Pk. Rd.)
Cloisters Mall. King T —68Na 123
Cloisters, The. E1
—43Vb 83 (7K 195)
(off Commercial St.)
Cloisters, The. SW9 —53Qb 104
Cloisters, The. Bush —16Da 19
Cloisters, The. K Lan —1Q 4
Cloisters, The. Rick —17N 17
Cloisters, The. Wok —93D 172
Clonard Way. Pinn —23Ca 37
Clonbrock Rd. N16 —35Ub 63
Cloncurry St. SW6 —54Za 102
Clonmel Clo. Harr —33Fa 58
Clonmell Rd. N17 —27Tb 43
Clonmel Rd. SW6 —52Bb 103
Clonmel Rd. Tedd —63Fa 122
Clonmel Way. Burn —1A 72
Clonmore St. SW18 —60Bb 103
Cloonmore Av. Orp —77Vc 151
Clorane Gdns. NW3 —34Cb 61
Closemead Clo. N'wd —23S 36
Close, The. E4 —24Ec 44
Close, The. N10 —26Kb 42
Close, The. N14 —19Mb 24
Close, The. N20 —19Bb 23
Close, The. SE25 —72Wb 147
Close, The. Barn —16Hb 23
Close, The. Beck —70Ac 128
Close, The. Berr G —88Rc 168
Close, The. Bex —58Cd 110
Close, The. Brtwd —20Zd 33
Close, The. Bush —16Da 19
Close, The. Cars —81Gb 163
Close, The. Eastc —31Y 57
Close, The. Grays —47Ee 91
Close, The. Harr —26Ea 38
Close, The. Iswth —54Fa 100
Close, The. Iver —41E 74
Close, The. Long —68De 135
Close, The. Mitc —70Hb 125
Close, The. N Mald —68Sa 123
Close, The. Orp —72Uc 150
Close, The. Pinn —31Ba 57
Close, The. Pot B —4Cb 9
Close, The. Purl —82Rb 165
(Pampisford Rd.)
Close, The. Purl —82Pb 164
(Russell Hill)
Close, The. Rad —5Ha 6
Close, The. Rich —55Ra 101
Close, The. Rick —18K 17
Close, The. Romf —30Ad 47
Close, The. Sev —96Gd 186
Close, The. Sidc —63Xc 131
Close, The. Slou —5B 72
Close, The. Sutt —73Bb 145
Close, The. Uxb —39Q 56
(Court Dri.)
Close, The. Uxb —38N 55
(Honeycroft Hill)
Close, The. Vir W —10P 117
Close, The. Wemb —34Sa 59
(Wembley Park)
Close, The. Wemb —37Na 59
(Wembley)
Close, The. W Byf —85J 157
Close, The. Wilm —62Md 133
Cloth Ct. EC1 —43Rb 83 (1C 200)
(off Cloth Fair)
Cloth Fair. EC1 —43Rb 83 (1C 200)
Clothier St. E1 —44Ub 83 (2J 201)
Cloth St. EC1 —43Sb 83 (7D 194)
Clothworkers Rd. SE18 —52Tc 108
Cloudberry Rd. Romf —23Md 49
Cloudesdale Rd. SW17 —61Kb 126
Cloudesley Pl. N1
—39Qb 62 (1K 193)
Cloudesley Rd. N1 —39Qb 62
Cloudesley Rd. Bexh —53Bd 109
Cloudesley Rd. Eri —53Hd 110
Cloudesley Sq. N1 —39Qb 62
Cloudesley St. N1
—39Qb 62 (1A 194)
Clouston Clo. Wall —78Nb 146
Clova Rd. E7 —37Hc 65
Clove Cres. E14 —45Ec 84
Clove Hitch Quay. SW11 —55Eb 103
Clovelly Av. NW9 —28Va 40
Clovelly Av. Uxb —35S 56
Clovelly Av. Warl —91Xb 181
Clovelly Clo. Pinn —27Y 37
Clovelly Clo. Uxb —35S 56
Clovelly Ct. Horn —33Qd 69
Clovelly Gdns. SE19 —67Vb 127
Clovelly Gdns. Enf —17Ub 25
Clovelly Gdns. Romf —25Dd 48
Clovelly Rd. N8 —28Mb 42
Clovelly Rd. W4 —47Ta 79
Clovelly Rd. W5 —47La 78
Clovelly Rd. Bexh —51Ad 109
Clovelly Rd. Houn —54Ca 99
Clovelly Way. E1 —44Yb 84
Clovelly Way. Orp —72Vc 151
Clovelly Way. S Harr —33Ba 57
Clover Clo. E11 —33Fc 65
Clover Ct. Grays —51Fe 113
Clover Ct. Wok —7G 188
Cloverdale Gdns. Sidc —58Vc 109
Clover Hill. Coul —93Kb 180
Clover Leas. Epp —1Vc 15
Cloverleys. Lou —15Mc 27
Clover M. SW3 —51Hb 103
Clovers, The. Grav —3A 136
Clover Way. Wall —74Jb 146
Clove St. E13 —42Jc 85
Clowders Rd. SE6 —62Bc 128
Clowser Clo. Sutt —78Eb 145
Cloysters Grn. E1 —46Wb 83
Cloyster Wood. Edgw —24Ma 39
Club Gdns. Rd. Hayes —73Jc 149
Club Row. E2 & E1
—42Vb 83 (5K 195)
Cluff Ct. War —22Yd 50
Clumps, The. Ashf —63T 120
Clump, The. Rick —15K 17
Clunas Gdns. Romf —27Md 49
Clunbury Av. S'hall —50Ba 77
Clunbury St. N1 —40Tb 63 (2G 195)
Cluny Est. SE1 —48Ub 83 (3H 207)
Cluny M. SW5 —49Cb 81
Cluny Pl. SE1 —48Ub 83 (3H 207)
Clutton St. E14 —43Dc 84
Clydach Rd. Enf —14Vb 25
Clyde. E Til —9L 93
Clyde Av. S Croy —87Xb 165
Clyde Cir. N15 —28Ub 43
Clyde Cres. Upm —30Ud 50
Clyde Ho. SE15 —52Wb 105
(off Sumner Est.)
Clyde Pl. E10 —31Dc 64
Clyde Rd. N15 —28Ub 43
Clyde Rd. N22 —25Mb 42
Clyde Rd. Croy —75Vb 147
Clyde Rd. Stai —60M 97
Clyde Rd. Sutt —78Cb 145
Clyde Rd. Wall —79Lb 146
Clydesdale. Enf —14Zb 26
Clydesdale Av. Stan —27Ma 39
Clydesdale Clo. Borwd —15Ta 21
Clydesdale Ct. N20 —18Fb 23
Clydesdale Gdns. Rich —56Ra 101
Clydesdale Ho. Eri —47Ad 87
(off Kale Rd.)
Clydesdale Path. Borwd —15Ta 21
Clydesdale Rd. W11 —44Bb 81
Clydesdale Rd. Horn —31Hd 68
Clyde St. SE8 —51Bc 106
Clyde Ter. SE23 —61Yb 128
Clyde Vale. SE23 —61Yb 128
Clyde Way. Romf —24Gd 48
Clyde Wharf. E16 —46Jc 85
Clydon Clo. Eri —51Gd 110
Clyfford Rd. Ruis —35V 56
Clymping Dene. Felt —59X 99
Clynes Ho. Dag —34Cd 68
(off Uvedale Rd.)
Clyston Rd. Wat —16V 18
Clyston St. SW8 —54Lb 104
Clyve Way. Stai —67G 118
Cmabrian Clo. SE27 —62Rb 127
Coach & Horses Yd. W1
—45Lb 82 (4B 198)
Coach Ho. La. N5 —35Rb 63
Coach Ho. La. SW19 —63Za 124
Coach Ho. M. SE20 —66Xb 127
Coach Ho. M. SE23 —58Zb 106
Coach Ho. Yd. NW3 —35Eb 61
(off Hampstead High St.)
Coach Ho. Yd. SW18 —56Db 103
Coach Rd. Grav —8A 114
Coach Rd. Ott —79E 138
Coal Ct. Grays —52Ce 113
Coaldale Wlk. SE21 —59Sb 105
Coalecroft Rd. SW15 —56Ya 102
Coalport Ho. SE11
—49Qb 82 (5K 205)
(off Walnut Tree Wlk.)
Coal Rd. Til —9H 93
Coal Wharf Rd. W12 —46Za 80
Coates Dell. Wat —5Aa 5
Coates Hill Rd. Brom —68Qc 130
Coates Rd. Els —17Ma 21
Coate St. E2 —40Wb 63
Coates Wlk. Bren —50Na 79
Cobalt Way. Wat —5Z 5
Cobalt Sq. SW8 —51Pb 104
(off S. Lambeth Rd.)
Cobb Clo. Dat —3P 95
Cobbett Clo. Enf —8Yb 12
Cobbett Rd. SE9 —55Nc 108
Cobbett Rd. Twic —60Ca 99
Cobbetts Av. Ilf —29Mc 45
Cobbetts Clo. Wok —5E 188
Cobbetts Hill. Wey —79R 140
Cobbett St. SW8 —52Pb 104
Cob Grn. Wat —4X 5
Cobbinsbank. Wal A —5Fc 13
Cobbinsend Rd. Wal A —1Mc 13
Cobbins, The. Wal A —5Gc 13
Cobblers Clo. Farn R —10F 52
Cobblers Wlk. Hamp & Tedd
—67Ea 122
Cobbles, The. Brtwd —19Ae 33
Cobbles, The. Upm —31Vd 70
Cobblestone Pl. Croy —74Sb 147
Cobbold Est. NW10 —37Va 60
Cobbold M. W12 —47Va 80
Cobbold Rd. E11 —34Hc 65
Cobbold Rd. NW10 —37Va 60
Cobbold Rd. W12 —47Ua 80
Cobb's Ct. EC4 —44Rb 83 (3C 200)
(off Carter La.)
Cobb's Rd. Houn —56Ba 99
Cobb St. E1 —43Vb 83 (1K 201)
Cob Clo. Borwd —15Ta 21
Cobden Clo. Uxb —39L 55
Cobden Ct. Brom —70Lc 129
Cobden Hill. Rad —8Ka 6
Cobden Rd. E11 —34Gc 65
Cobden Rd. SE25 —71Wb 147
Cobden Rd. Orp —77Tc 150
Cobden Rd. Sev —95Ld 187
Cobden St. E14 —43Dc 84
Cob Dri. Shorne —4N 137
Cobham. Grays —47De 91
Cobham Av. N Mald —71Wa 144
Cobhambury Rd. Cobh —10J 137
Cobham Clo. SW11 —58Gb 103
Cobham Clo. Brom —73Nc 150
Cobham Clo. Sidc —58Xc 109
Cobham Clo. Wall —79Nb 146
Cobham Ct. Mitc —68Fb 125
Cobham Ga. Cob —86X 159
Cobham Ho. Bark —39Sc 66
(in two parts)
Cobham Ho. Eri —52Hd 110
Cobham M. NW1 —38Mb 62
Cobham Pk. Rd. Cob —89X 159
Cobham Pl. Bexh —56Ad 109
Cobham Rd. E17 —25Ec 44
Cobham Rd. N22 —27Rb 43
Cobham Rd. Houn —52Y 99
Cobham Rd. Ilf —33Uc 66
Cobham Rd. King T —68Qa 123
Cobham Rd. Stoke D & Fet
—90Ca 159
Cobham St. Grav —9C 114
Cobham Ter. Grav —10B 114
(off Southfleet Rd.)
Cobham Way. E Hor —98U 174
Cobill Clo. Horn —28Ld 49

Cobland Rd.—Condell Rd.

Cobland Rd. SE12 —63Lc **129**
Coborn Rd. E3 —41Bc **84**
Coborn St. E3 —41Bc **84**
Cobourg Rd. SE5 —51Vb **105**
Cobourg St. NW1
—41Lb **82** (4C **192**)
Cobsdene. Grav —5F **136**
Cobs Way. New Haw —82L **157**
Coburg Clo. SW1
*—49Lb **82** (5C **204**)*
(off Windsor Pl.)
Coburg Cres. SW2 —60Pb **104**
Coburg Gdns. Ilf —26Mc **45**
Coburg Rd. N22 —27Pb **42**
*Cochrane Ct. E14 —47Cc **84***
(off Admirals Way)
Cochrane Clo. NW8
*—40Fb **61** (2C **190**)*
(off Cochrane St.)
Cochrane M. NW8
—40Fb **61** (2C **190**)
Cochrane Rd. SW19 —66Bb **125**
Cochrane St. NW8
—40Fb **61** (2C **190**)
*Cockabourne Ct. H Wood —26Qd **49***
(off Archibald Rd.)
Cockayne Way. SE8 —49Ac **84**
Cockerhurst Rd. Shor —79Fd **152**
Cocker Rd. Enf —8Xb **11**
Cockett Rd. Slou —48A **74**
Cockfosters Pde. Barn —14Jb **24**
Cockfosters Rd. Pot B & Barn
—7Fb **9**
Cock Hill. E1 —43Ub **83** (1J **201**)
Cockhill Rd. SE2 —48Xc **87**
Cock La. EC1 —43Rb **83** (1B **200**)
Cock La. Fet —94Ea **176**
Cockmannings La. Orp —74Zc **151**
Cockmannings Rd. Orp —73Zc **151**
Cockpit Steps. SW1
*—47Mb **82** (2E **204**)*
(off Birdcage Wlk.)
Cockpit Yd. WC1
—43Pb **82** (7J **193**)
Cocks Cres. N Mald —70Va **124**
Cocksett Av. Orp —79Uc **150**
Cockspur Ct. SW1
—46Mb **82** (6E **198**)
Cockspur St. SW1
—46Mb **82** (6E **198**)
Cocksure La. Sidc —62Cd **132**
Code St. E1 —42Vb **83**
Codham Hall La. Gt War —28Xd **50**
Codicote Dri. Wat —6Z **5**
Codicote Ter. N4 —33Sb **63**
Codling Clo. E1 —46Wb **83**
Codling Way. Wemb —35Ma **59**
Codmore Wood Rd. Lat —5A **2**
Codrington Ct. Wok —6C **188**
Codrington Cres. Grav —4E **136**
Codrington Gdns. Grav —4F **136**
Codrington Hill. SE23 —59Ac **106**
Codrington M. W11 —44Ab **80**
Cody Clo. Harr —27Ma **39**
Cody Clo. Wall —80Mb **146**
Cody Rd. E16 —42Fc **85**
Coe Av. SE25 —72Wb **147**
Coe's All. Barn —14Ab **22**
Coe Spur. Slou —8F **72**
Cofers Circ. Wemb —34Ra **59**
Coftards. Slou —4N **73**
Cogan Av. E17 —25Ac **44**
Coin St. SE1 —46Qb **82** (6K **199**)
Coity Rd. NW5 —37Jb **62**
Cokers La. SE21 —60Tb **105**
Coke St. E1 —44Wb **83**
Colas M. NW6 —39Cb **61**
Colbeck M. SW7 —49Db **81**
Colbeck Rd. Harr —31Ea **58**
Colberg Pl. N16 —31Vb **63**
Colborne Ho. Wat —16U **18**
Colborne Way. Wor Pk —76Ya **144**
Colbourne Clo. Stanf —1P **93**
Colbrook Av. Hay —48T **76**
Colbrook Clo. Hay —48T **76**
Colburn Av. Cat —96Vb **181**
Colburn Av. Pinn —23Aa **37**
Colburn Way. Sutt —76Fb **145**
Colby M. SE19 —64Ub **127**
Colby Rd. SE19 —64Ub **127**
Colby Rd. W on T —74W **140**
Colchester Av. E12 —34Pc **66**
Colchester Dri. Pinn —29Z **37**
Colchester Rd. E10 —31Ec **64**
Colchester Rd. E17 —30Cc **44**
Colchester Rd. Edgw —24Sa **39**
Colchester Rd. N'wd —26W **36**
Colchester Rd. Romf & S Wea
—25Md **49**
Colchester St. E1 —44Vb **83**
Colcokes Rd. Bans —88Cb **163**
Cold Arbor Rd. Sev —96Fd **186**
Coldbath Sq. EC1
—42Qb **82** (5K **193**)
Coldbath St. SE13 —53Dc **106**
Cold Blow Cres. Bex —60Fd **110**
Cold Blow La. SE14 —51Zb **106**
Cold Blows. Mitc —69Hb **125**
Coldershaw Rd. W13 —46Ja **78**
Coldfall Av. N10 —26Jb **42**
Coldham Ct. N22 —25Rb **43**
Coldham Gro. Enf —9Ac **12**
Coldharbour. E14 —47Ec **84**
Coldharbour Clo. Egh —69E **118**
Coldharbour Ho. Wat —8Aa **5**
Coldharbour La. SW9 & SE5
—56Qb **104**
Coldharbour La. Bush —16Da **19**
Coldharbour La. Egh —69E **118**
Coldharbour La. Hay —46W **76**
Coldharbour La. Purl —82Qb **164**
Coldharbour La. Rain —44Gd **88**
Coldharbour La. Wok —87H **157**
Coldharbour Pl. SE5 —54Sb **105**
Coldharbour Rd. Croy —78Qb **146**
Coldharbour Rd. Grav —1A **136**
Coldharbour Rd. W Byf & Wok
—87H **157**
Coldharbour Way. Croy —78Qb **146**
Coldstream Gdns. SW18
—58Bb **103**
Colebeck M. N1 —37Rb **63**
Colebert Av. E1 —42Yb **84**
Colebrook. Ott —79F **138**
Colebrook Clo. SW15 —59Za **102**
Colebrooke Av. W13 —44Ka **78**
*Colebrooke Ct. Sidc —63Xc **131***
(off Granville Rd.)
Colebrooke Dri. E11 —31Kc **65**
Colebrooke Pl. N1
—39Rb **63** (1C **194**)
Colebrooke Rise. Brom —68Gc **129**
Colebrooke Row. N1
(in two parts) —40Rb **63** (2B **194**)
Colebrook Gdns. Lou —12Rc **28**
Colebrook La. Lou —12Rc **28**
Colebrook Path. Lou —12Rc **28**
Colebrook Rd. SW16 —67Nb **126**
Colebrook Way. N11 —22Kb **42**
Coleby Path. SE5 —52Tb **105**
Cole Clo. SE28 —46Xc **87**
Cole Ct. H Hill —22Nd **49**
Cole Ct. Twic —59Ja **100**
Coledale Dri. Stan —25La **38**
Coleford Rd. SW18 —57Eb **103**
Cole Gdns. Houn —52W **98**
Colegrave Rd. E15 —36Fc **65**
Colegrove Rd. SE15 —51Vb **105**
Coleherne Ct. SW5 —50Db **81**
Coleherne M. SW10 —50Db **81**
Coleherne Rd. SW10 —50Db **81**
Colehill Gdns. SW6 —53Ab **102**
Colehill La. SW6 —53Ab **102**
*Cole Ho. SE1 —47Qb **82** (2K **205**)*
(off Baylis Rd.)
Coleman Clo. SE25 —68Wb **127**
Coleman Fields. N1 —39Sb **63**
Coleman Mans. N8 —31Nb **62**
Coleman Rd. SE5 —52Ub **105**
Coleman Rd. Belv —49Cd **88**
Coleman Rd. Dag —37Ad **67**
Coleman's Bldgs. EC2
*—44Tb **83** (2F **201**)*
(off Colman St.)
Colemans Heath. SE9 —62Qc **130**
Coleman St. EC2
—44Tb **83** (2F **201**)
Colenorton Cres. Eton W —9C **72**
Colenso Rd. E5 —35Yb **64**
Colenso Rd. Ilf —32Uc **66**
Cole Pk. Gdns. Twic —58Ja **100**
Cole Pk. Rd. Twic —58Ja **100**
Cole Pk. View. Twic —58Ja **100**
Colepits Wood Rd. SE9 —57Tc **108**
Coleraine Rd. N8 —27Qb **42**
Coleraine Rd. SE3 —51Hc **107**
Coleridge Av. E12 —37Nc **66**
Coleridge Av. Sutt —77Gb **145**
Coleridge Clo. SW8 —54Kb **104**
*Coleridge Ct. New Bar —15Db **23***
(off Station Rd.)
Coleridge Cres. Coln —53G **96**
Coleridge Gdns. NW6 —38Eb **61**
Coleridge Ho. SE17
*—50Sb **83** (7E **206**)*
(off Browning St.)
Coleridge La. N8 —30Nb **42**
Coleridge Rd. E17 —28Bc **44**
Coleridge Rd. N4 —33Qb **62**
Coleridge Rd. N8 —30Mb **42**
Coleridge Rd. N12 —22Eb **41**
Coleridge Rd. Ashf —63N **119**
Coleridge Rd. Croy —73Yb **148**
Coleridge Rd. Dart —56Rd **111**
Coleridge Rd. Romf —24Kd **49**
Coleridge Rd. Til —4E **114**
Coleridge Sq. W13 —44Ja **78**
Coleridge Wlk. NW11 —28Cb **41**
Coleridge Wlk. Hut —17Ee **33**
Coleridge Way. Hay —44W **76**
Coleridge Way. Orp —72Wc **151**
Coleridge Way. W Dray —49N **75**
Cole Rd. Twic —58Ja **100**
Cole Rd. Wat —11X **19**
*Colesbourne Ct. SE15 —52Ub **105***
(off Birdlip Clo.)
Colesburg Rd. Beck —69Bc **128**
Coles Cres. Harr —33Da **57**
Colescroft Hill. Purl —87Qb **164**
Colesdale. Cuff —2Nb **10**
Coles Grn. Bush —18Ea **20**
Coles Grn. Lou —11Qc **28**
Coles Grn. Ct. NW2 —33Wa **60**
Coles Grn. Rd. NW2 —32Wa **60**
Coleshill Rd. Tedd —65Ga **122**
Coles La. Bras —95Yc **185**
Colestown St. SW11 —54Gb **103**
Cole St. SE1 —47Sb **83** (2E **206**)
*Colesworth Ho. Edgw —26Sa **39***
(off Burnt Oak B'way.)
Colet Clo. N13 —23Rb **43**
Colet Gdns. W14 —49Za **80**
*Colet Ho. SE17 —50Rb **83***
(off Doddington Gro.)
Colet Rd. Hut —15Ee **33**
Colets Orchard. Otf —88Kd **171**
Coley Av. Wok —90C **156**
Coley St. WC1 —42Pb **82** (6J **193**)
Colfe Rd. SE23 —60Ac **106**
Colham Av. W Dray —46N **75**
Colham Grn. Rd. Uxb —43Q **76**
Colham Mill Rd. W Dray —47M **75**
Colham Rd. Uxb —42P **75**
Colina M. N15 —28Rb **43**
Colina Rd. N15 —29Rb **43**
Colin Clo. NW9 —28Ua **40**
Colin Clo. Croy —76Bc **148**
Colin Clo. Dart —58Rd **111**
Colin Clo. W Wick —76Hc **149**
Colin Cres. NW9 —28Va **40**
Colindale Av. NW9 —27Ta **39**
Colindale Bus. Pk. NW9 —25Sa **39**
Colindeep Gdns. NW4 —28Wa **40**
Colindeep La. NW9 & NW4
—27Ua **40**
Colin Dri. NW9 —29Va **40**
Colinette Rd. SW15 —56Ya **102**
Colin Gdns. NW9 —28Va **40**
Colin Pde. NW9 —28Ua **40**
Colin Pk. Rd. NW9 —28Ua **40**
Colin Rd. NW10 —37Wa **60**
Colin Rd. Cat —95Wb **181**
Colinton Rd. Ilf —33Xc **67**
Colin Way. Slou —8F **72**
*Colin Winter Ho. E1 —42Yb **84***
(off Nicholas Rd.)
Coliston Pas. SW18 —59Cb **103**
Coliston Rd. SW18 —59Cb **103**
Collamore Av. SW18 —60Gb **103**
Collapit Clo. Harr —30Da **37**
Collard Av. Lou —12Sc **28**
Collard Grn. Lou —12Sc **28**
College App. SE10 —51Ec **106**
College Av. Egh —65D **118**
College Av. Eps —86Va **162**
College Av. Grays —49De **91**
College Av. Harr —25Ga **38**
College Av. Slou —8J **73**
College Clo. E9 —36Yb **64**
College Clo. N18 —22Vb **43**
College Clo. Add —76M **139**
College Clo. Grays —49Ee **91**
College Clo. Harr —24Ga **38**
College Clo. Twic —60Fa **100**
*College Ct. SW3 —50Hb **81***
(off West Rd.)
College Ct. W5 —45Na **79**
*College Ct. W6 —50Ya **80***
(off Queen Caroline St.)
College Ct. Chesh —2Yb **12**
College Ct. Enf —14Yb **26**
College Cres. NW3 —37Eb **61**
(in two parts)
College Cres. Wind —4F **94**
College Cross. N1 —38Qb **62**
College Dri. Ruis —31W **56**
College E. E1 —43Vb **83** (1K **201**)
College Fields Bus. Cen. SW19
—67Fb **125**
College Gdns. E4 —17Dc **26**
College Gdns. N18 —22Vb **43**
College Gdns. SE21 —60Ub **105**
College Gdns. SW17 —61Gb **125**
College Gdns. Ilf —29Nc **46**
College Gdns. N Mald —71Va **144**
College Gdns. Rd. Enf —11Tb **25**
College Grn. SE19 —66Ub **127**
College Gro. NW1 —39Lb **62**
College Hill. EC4
—45Sb **83** (4E **200**)
College Hill Rd. Harr —24Ga **38**
College La. NW5 —35Kb **62**
College La. Wok —7F **188**
*College M. SW1 —48Nb **82** (3F **205**)*
(off Gt. College St.)
College M. SW18 —57Db **103**
College Pk. Clo. SE13 —56Fc **107**
College Pk. Rd. N17 —23Vb **43**
College Pl. E17 —28Gc **45**
College Pl. NW1 —39Lb **62**
College Pl. SW10 —52Eb **103**
College Point. E15 —37Hc **65**
College Rd. E17 —29Ec **44**
College Rd. N17 —23Vb **43**
College Rd. N21 —19Qb **24**
College Rd. NW10 —40Ya **60**
College Rd. SE21 & SE19
—59Ub **105**
College Rd. SW19 —65Fb **125**
College Rd. W13 —44Ka **78**
College Rd. Abb L —3V **4**
College Rd. Brom —67Jc **129**
College Rd. Chesh —2Yb **12**
College Rd. Cipp —6D **72**
College Rd. Croy —75Tb **147**
College Rd. Eps —86Va **162**
College Rd. Grav —57De **113**
College Rd. Grays —49Ee **91**
College Rd. Harr —30Ga **38**
College Rd. Har W —25Ga **38**
College Rd. Iswth —53Ha **100**
College Rd. Swan —67Gd **132**
College Rd. Wemb —32Ma **59**
College Rd. Wok —88D **156**
College Roundabout. King T
—69Na **123**
College Row. E9 —36Zb **64**
College Slip. Brom —67Jc **129**
College St. EC4 —45Sb **83** (4E **200**)
College Ter. E3 —41Bc **84**
College Ter. N3 —26Bb **41**
College View. SE9 —60Mc **107**
College Wlk. King T —69Na **123**
College Way. Ashf —63P **119**
College Way. N'wd —23T **36**
Collent St. E9 —37Yb **64**
Colleraine Rd. SE3 —51Hc **107**
Coller Cres. Dart —64Ud **134**
Colless Rd. N15 —29Vb **43**
Collett Rd. Kems —89Nd **171**
Collett Clo. Chesh —1Zb **12**
Collett Gdns. Chesh —1Zb **12**
Collett Rd. SE16 —48Xb **83**
Collett Way. S'hall —47Da **77**
Colley Hill La. Hedg —4K **53**
Colleyland. Chor —14F **16**
Collier Clo. Eps —79Qa **143**
Collier Dri. Edgw —26Qa **39**
Collier Row La. Romf —24Dd **48**
Collier Row Rd. Romf —25Bd **47**
Colliers. Cat —97Wb **181**
Colliers Clo. Wok —5E **188**
Colliers Ct. Croy —77Tb **147**
Colliers Shaw. Kes —78Mc **149**
Collier St. N1 —40Pb **62** (2H **193**)
Colliers Water La. T Hth —71Qb **146**
Collindale Av. Eri —52Dd **110**
Collindale Av. Sidc —60Wc **109**
Collingbourne. Add —77L **139**
Collingbourne Rd. W12 —46Xa **80**
Collingham Gdns. SW5 —49Db **81**
Collingham Pl. SW5 —49Db **81**
Collingham Rd. SW5 —49Db **81**
Collings Clo. N13 —23Pb **42**
Collington Clo. Grav —9A **114**
Collington St. SE10 —50Fc **85**
Collingtree Rd. SE26 —63Yb **128**
Collingwood Av. N10 —27Jb **42**
Collingwood Av. Surb —74Sa **143**
Collingwood Clo. SE20 —67Xb **127**
Collingwood Clo. Twic —59Ca **99**
Collingwood Ct. New Bar —15Db **23**
Collingwood Ho. Grnh —57Yd **112**
Collingwood Pl. W on T —76W **140**
Collingwood Rd. E17 —30Cc **44**
Collingwood Rd. N15 —28Ub **43**
Collingwood Rd. Mitc —69Gb **125**
Collingwood Rd. Sutt —76Cb **145**
Collingwood Rd. Uxb —42R **76**
Collingwood St. E1 —42Xb **83**
Collins Av. Stan —26Na **39**
Collins Clo. Stanf —1N **93**
Collins Ct. E8 —37Wb **63**
Collins Dri. Ruis —33Y **57**
*Collins Ho. E15 —39Hc **65***
(off John St.)
Collinson St. SE1
—47Sb **83** (2D **206**)
Collinson Wlk. SE1
—47Sb **83** (2D **206**)
Collins Path. Hamp —65Ba **121**
Collins Rd. N5 —35Sb **63**
Collins St. SE3 —55Gc **107**
Collinswood Rd. Farn C —2E **52**
Collin's Yd. N1 —39Rb **63** (1B **194**)
Collinwood Av. Enf —13Yb **26**
Collinwood Gdns. Ilf —29Pc **46**
Collis All. Twic —60Ga **100**
Colls Rd. SE15 —53Yb **106**
Collum Grn. Rd. Hedg —4H **53**
Collyer Av. Croy —77Nb **146**
Collyer Pl. SE15 —53Wb **105**
Collyer Rd. Bedd —77Nb **146**
Colman Clo. Eps —89Ya **162**
Colman Clo. Stanf —1M **93**
Colman Ct. N12 —23Eb **41**
Colman Ct. Stan —23Ka **38**
Colman Rd. E16 —43Lc **85**
Colmar Clo. E1 —42Zb **84**
Colmer Pl. Harr —24Fa **38**
Colmer Rd. SW16 —67Nb **126**
Colmore M. SE15 —53Xb **105**
Colmore Rd. Enf —14Yb **26**
Colnbrook By-Pass. Coln & W Dray
—51E **96**
Colnbrook Ct. Coln —53H **97**
Colnbrook St. SE1
—48Rb **83** (4B **206**)
Colndale Rd. Coln —54G **96**
Colne. E Til —8L **93**
Colne Av. Rick —19J **17**
Colne Av. Wat —16X **19**
Colne Av. W Dray —47L **75**
Colnebridge Clo. Stai —63G **118**
Colne Ct. Eps —77Sa **143**
Colnedale Rd. Uxb —36M **55**
Colne Dri. Romf —23Pd **49**
Colne Dri. W on T —76Z **141**
Colne Mead. Rick —19J **17**
Colne Orchard. Iver —44H **75**
Colne Pk. Caravan Site. W Dray
—49L **75**
Colne Reach. Stai —57H **97**
Colne Rd. E5 —35Ac **64**
Colne Rd. N21 —17Tb **25**
Colne Rd. Twic —60Ga **100**
Colne St. E13 —41Jc **85**
Colne Valley. Upm —30Ud **50**
Colne Way. Stai —61D **118**
Colne Way. Wat —8Z **5**
(in two parts)
Colne Way Ind. Est. Wat —9Z **5**
Colney Hatch La. N11 & N10
—23Hb **41**
Colney Rd. Dart —58Pd **111**
Coln Trading Est. Coln —53H **97**
Cologne Rd. SW11 —56Fb **103**
Colombo Rd. Ilf —31Sc **66**
Colombo St. SE1
—46Rb **83** (7B **200**)
Colomb St. SE10 —50Gc **85**
Colonade, The. Chesh —1Zb **12**
Colonel's La. Cher —72J **139**
Colonel's Wlk. Enf —13Rb **25**
Colonial Av. Twic —57Ea **100**
Colonial Bus. Pk. Wat —11Y **19**
Colonial Dri. W4 —49Sa **79**
Colonial Rd. Felt —59U **98**
Colonial Rd. Slou —7L **73**
Colonial Way. Wat —11Y **19**
Colonnade. WC1
—42Nb **82** (6G **193**)
Colonnades, The. W2 —44Db **81**
Colonnade, The. SE8 —49Bc **84**
Colonnade Wlk. SW1
—49Kb **82** (6K **203**)
Colosseum Ter. NW1
*—41Kb **82** (4A **192**)*
(off Albany St.)
*Colour Ct. SW1 —46Lb **82** (7C **198**)*
(off St James' Pal.)
Colroy Ct. NW11 —29Ab **40**
Colson Gdns. Lou —14Rc **28**
Colson Path. Lou —14Qc **28**
Colson Rd. Croy —75Ub **147**
Colson Rd. Lou —14Rc **28**
Colson Way. SW16 —63Lb **126**
Colsterworth Rd. N15 —28Vb **43**
(in two parts)
Colston Av. Cars —77Gb **145**
*Colston Ct. Cars —77Hb **145***
(off West St.)
Colston Rd. E7 —37Mc **65**
Colston Rd. SW14 —56Sa **101**
Coltishall Rd. Horn —37Ld **69**
Coltness Cres. SE2 —50Xc **87**
Colton Gdns. N17 —27Sb **43**
Colton Rd. Harr —29Ga **38**
Coltsfoot Ct. Grays —51Fe **113**
Coltsfoot Dri. W Dray —44N **75**
Coltsfoot Path. Romf —24Ld **49**
(in three parts)
Coltstead. New Ash —75Ae **155**
Columbia Av. Edgw —25Ra **39**
Columbia Av. Ruis —32X **57**
Columbia Av. Wor Pk —73Va **144**
Columbia Rd. E2
—41Vb **83** (3K **195**)
Columbia Rd. E13 —42Hc **85**
Columbia Row. E2 —41Vb **83**
Columbia Sq. SW14 —56Sa **101**
Columbia Wharf. SE16 —46Bc **84**
Columbia Wharf Rd. Grays
—51Ce **113**
Columbine Av. E6 —43Nc **86**
Columbine Av. S Croy —80Rb **147**
Columbine Way. SE13 —54Ec **106**
Columbine Way. Romf —25Nd **49**
Columbus Ct. Eri —52Hd **110**
Columbus Courtyard. E14 —46Cc **84**
Columbus Gdns. N'wd —25W **36**
Columbus Sq. Eri —51Hd **110**
Colva Wlk. NW19 —33Kb **62**
Colvestone Cres. E8 —36Vb **63**
Colview Ct. SE9 —60Mc **107**
*Colville Est. N1 —39Ub **63** (1H **195**)*
(off Whitmore Rd.)
Colville Gdns. W11 —44Bb **81**
Colville Houses. W11 —44Bb **81**
Colville M. W11 —44Bb **81**
Colville Pl. W1 —43Lb **82** (1C **198**)
Colville Rd. E11 —34Ec **64**
Colville Rd. E17 —26Ac **44**
Colville Rd. N9 —18Xb **25**
Colville Rd. W3 —48Ra **79**
Colville Rd. W11 —44Bb **81**
Colville Sq. W11 —44Bb **81**
Colville Sq. M. W11 —44Bb **81**
Colville Ter. W11 —44Bb **81**
Colvin Clo. SE26 —64Yb **128**
Colvin Gdns. E4 —20Ec **26**
Colvin Gdns. E11 —28Kc **45**
Colvin Gdns. Ilf —25Sc **46**
Colvin Gdns. Wal X —7Zb **12**
Colvin Rd. E6 —38Nc **66**
Colvin Rd. T Hth —71Qb **146**
Colwell Rd. SE22 —57Vb **105**
Colwick Clo. N6 —31Mb **62**
Colwith Rd. W6 —51Ya **102**
Colwood Gdns. SW19 —66Fb **125**
Colworth Gro. SE17
—49Sb **83** (6E **206**)
Colworth Rd. E11 —30Gc **45**
Colworth Rd. Croy —74Wb **147**
Colwyn Av. Gnfd —40Ha **58**
Colwyn Clo. SW16 —64Lb **126**
Colwyn Cres. Houn —53Ea **100**
*Colwyn Grn. NW9 —30Ua **40***
(off Snowden Dri.)
Colwyn Rd. NW2 —34Xa **60**
Colwyn Way. N18 —22Wb **43**
Colyer Clo. N1 —40Pb **62** (1J **193**)
Colyer Clo. SE9 —61Rc **130**
Colyer Rd. Grav —61Ee **135**
Colyers Clo. Eri —53Fd **110**
Colyers La. Eri —53Ed **110**
Colyers Wlk. Eri —53Gd **110**
Colyton Clo. Well —53Zc **109**
Colyton Clo. Wemb —37La **58**
Colyton Clo. Wok —6F **188**
Colyton Rd. SE22 —57Xb **105**
Combe Av. SE3 —52Hc **107**
Combedale Rd. SE10 —50Jc **85**
Combe Ho. Wat —16U **18**
Combe Lodge. SE7 —51Lc **107**
Combemartin Rd. SW18 —59Ab **102**
Combe M. SE3 —52Hc **107**
Comber Clo. NW2 —34Xa **60**
Comber Gro. SE5 —52Sb **105**
Comber Ho. SE5 —52Sb **105**
Combermere Clo. Wind —4F **94**
Combermere Rd. SW9 —55Pb **104**
Combermere Rd. Mord —72Db **145**
Combe Rd. Wat —16V **18**
Comberton Rd. E5 —33Xb **63**
Combeside. SE18 —52Vc **109**
Combe, The. NW1
—41Lb **82** (4B **192**)
Combwell Cres. SE2 —48Wc **87**
Comely Bank Rd. E17 —29Ec **44**
Comeragh Clo. Wok —8D **188**
Comeragh M. W14 —50Ab **80**
Comeragh Rd. W14 —50Ab **80**
Comerell Pl. SE10 —50Hc **85**
Comerford Rd. SE4 —56Ac **106**
Comet Clo. Purf —49Qd **89**
Comet Clo. Wat —6V **4**
Comet Pl. SE8 —52Cc **106**
Comet Rd. Stai —59M **97**
Comet St. SE8 —52Cc **106**
Comfrey Ct. Grays —51Fe **113**
Commerce Rd. N22 —25Pb **42**
Commerce Rd. Bren —52La **100**
Commerce Way. Croy —75Pb **146**
Commercial Pl. Grav —8E **114**
Commercial Rd. E1 & E14
—44Wb **83**
Commercial Rd. N18 —23Ub **43**
Commercial Rd. Stai —65J **119**
Commercial Rd. Ind. Est. N18
—23Vb **43**
Commercial St. E1
—42Vb **83** (6K **195**)
Commercial Way. NW10 —40Ra **59**
Commercial Way. SE15 —52Vb **105**
Commercial Way. Wok —89A **156**
Commerell St. SE10 —50Gc **85**
Commodity Quay. E1 —45Vb **83**
Commodore Sq. SW10 —53Eb **103**
Commodore St. E1 —42Ac **84**
Common Clo. Wok —2G **188**
Commondale. SW15 —55Ya **102**
Commonfield La. SW17 —64Gb **125**
Commonfield Rd. Bans —86Cb **163**
Common Ga. Rd. Chor —15F **16**
Common La. Burn —4B **52**
Common La. Clay —80Ja **142**
Common La. Dart —61Jd **132**
Common La. Eton C —10G **72**
Common La. K Lan —1P **3**
Common La. Let H & Rad
—11Ga **20**
Common La. New Haw —81L **157**
Commonmeadow La. Wat —6Da **5**
Common Rd. SW13 —55Xa **102**
Common Rd. Chor —14F **16**
Common Rd. Clay —79Ja **142**
Common Rd. Dor —9A **72**
Common Rd. Eton W —9D **72**
Common Rd. Ingve —22Ee **51**
Common Rd. Slou —49C **74**
Common Rd. Stan —21Fa **38**
Commonside. Bookh —94Ca **175**
(in two parts)
Common Side. Eps —87Qa **161**
Commonside. Kes —77Lc **149**
Commonside Clo. Sutt —83Db **163**
Commonside E. Mitc —69Jb **126**
Commonside W. Mitc —69Hb **125**
Common, The. W5 —46Na **79**
Common, The. Chfd —4K **3**
Common, The. S'hall —49Z **77**
Common, The. Stan —20Ha **20**
Common, The. W Dray —49L **75**
Commonwealth Av. W12 —45Xa **80**
(in three parts)
Commonwealth Av. Hay —44T **76**
Commonwealth Rd. N17 —24Wb **43**
Commonwealth Rd. Cat —95Wb **181**
Commonwealth Way. SE2
—50Xc **87**
Common Wood. Farn C —5G **52**
Community Clo. Houn —53X **99**
Community Clo. Uxb —34S **56**
Community La. N7 —36Mb **62**
Community Rd. E15 —36Fc **65**
Community Rd. Gnfd —39Ea **58**
Como Rd. SE23 —61Ac **128**
Como St. Romf —29Fd **48**
Compass Hill. Rich —58Ma **101**
Compayne Gdns. NW6 —38Db **61**
Comport Grn. New Ad —86Kc **167**
Compton Av. E6 —40Mc **65**
Compton Av. N1 —37Rb **63**
Compton Av. N6 —31Gb **61**
Compton Av. Hut —18Ee **33**
Compton Av. Romf —27Ld **49**
Compton Clo. NW1
*—41Kb **82** (4A **192**)*
(off Robert St.)
Compton Clo. W13 —44Ja **78**
Compton Clo. Edgw —24Sa **39**
Compton Clo. Esh —79Fa **142**
Compton Ct. SE19 —65Ub **127**
Compton Ct. Burn —4C **72**
Compton Ct. Sutt —77Eb **145**
Compton Cres. N17 —24Sb **43**
Compton Cres. W4 —51Sa **101**
Compton Cres. Chess —78Na **143**
Compton Cres. N'holt —39Z **57**
*Compton Gdns. Add —78K **139***
(off Monks Cres.)
Compton Pas. EC1
*—42Rb **83** (5C **194**)*
(off Compton St.)
Compton Pl. EC1 —42Rb **83**
Compton Pl. WC1
—42Nb **82** (5F **193**)
Compton Pl. Eri —51Hd **110**
Compton Pl. Wat —20Aa **19**
Compton Rise. Pinn —29Aa **37**
Compton Rd. N1 —37Rb **63**
Compton Rd. N21 —18Qb **24**
Compton Rd. NW10 —41Za **80**
Compton Rd. SW19 —65Bb **125**
Compton Rd. Croy —74Xb **147**
Compton Rd. Hay —45U **76**
Compton St. EC1
—42Rb **83** (5B **194**)
Compton Ter. N1 —37Rb **63**
Compton Ter. N21 —18Qb **24**
Comreddy Clo. Enf —11Rb **25**
Comus Pl. SE17
—49Ub **83** (6H **207**)
Comyne Rd. Wat —8V **4**
Comyn Rd. SW11 —56Gb **103**
Comyns Clo. E16 —43Hc **85**
Comyns Rd. Dag —38Cd **68**
Comyns, The. Bush —18Ea **20**
Conant M. E1 —45Wb **83**
Conaways Clo. Eps —82Wa **162**
Concanon Rd. SW2 —56Pb **104**
Concert Hall App. SE1
—46Pb **82** (7J **199**)
Concord Bus. Cen. W3 —42Ra **79**
Concord Clo. N'holt —41Z **77**
Concorde Bus. Cen. Big H
—87Mc **167**
Concorde Clo. Houn —54Da **99**
Concorde Clo. Uxb —40N **55**
Concorde Dri. E6 —43Pc **86**
*Concorde Ho. Horn —37Kd **69***
(off Astra Clo.)
Concorde Way. Slou —7G **72**
*Concord Ho. N17 —24Vb **43***
(off Park La.)
Concord Rd. W3 —42Ra **79**
Concord Rd. Enf —15Xb **25**
Concourse, The. NW9 —25Va **40**
Condell Rd. SW8 —53Lb **104**

Conder St. E14 —44Ac 84
Condor Rd. Stai —69L 119
Condor Wlk. Horn —38Kd 69
Condover Cres. SE18 —52Rc 108
Condray Pl. SW11 —52Gb 103
Conduit Ct. WC2 —45Nb 82 (4F 199)
(off Floral St.)
Conduit La. Croy —78Wb 147
Conduit La. Dat —51A 96
Conduit La. Enf —17Ac 26
Conduit La. S Croy & Croy
—78Wb 147
Conduit M. W2 —44Fb 81 (3B 196)
Conduit Pas. W2 —44Fb 81 (3B 196)
(off Conduit Pl.)
Conduit Pl. W2 —44Fb 81 (3B 196)
Conduit Rd. SE18 —50Rc 86
Conduit St. W1 —45Kb 82 (4A 198)
Conduit, The. Blet —100Tb 181
Conduit Way. NW10 —38Sa 59
Conegar Ct. Slou —6J 73
Conewood St. N5 —34Rb 63
Coney Acre. SE21 —60Sb 105
Coney Burrows. E4 —19Gc 27
Coneybury Clo. Warl —91Xb 181
Coney Gro. Uxb —41Q 76
Coneygrove Path. N'holt —37Aa 57
(off Arnold Rd.)
Coney Hall Pde. W Wick —76Gc 149
Coney Hill Rd. W Wick —75Gc 149
Coney Way. SW8 —51Pb 104
Conference Clo. E4 —19Ec 26
Conference Rd. SE2 —49Yc 87
Congleton Gro. SE18 —50Sc 86
Congo Rd. SE18 —50Tc 86
Congreave Rd. Wal A —5Gc 13
Congress Rd. SE2 —49Yc 87
Congreve Ct. SE11
—49Qb 82 (6A 206)
Congreve Ho. N16 —36Ub 63
Congreve Rd. SE9 —55Pc 108
Congreve St. SE17
—49Ub 83 (5H 207)
Congreve Wlk. E16 —43Mc 85
(off Stansfield Rd.)
Conical Corner. Enf —12Sb 25
Conifer Av. Hart —72Ae 155
Conifer Av. Romf —22Dd 48
Conifer Clo. Orp —77Tc 150
Conifer Clo. Wal X —1Vb 11
Conifer Dri. War —22Zd 51
Conifer Gdns. SW16 —62Pb 126
Conifer Gdns. Enf —16Ub 25
Conifer Gdns. Sutt —75Db 145
Conifer La. Egh —64E 118
Conifer Pk. Eps —83Ua 162
Conifers. Wey —77U 140
Conifers Clo. Tedd —66Ka 122
Conifers, The. Wat —7Y 5
Conifer Way. Hay —45W 76
Conifer Way. Swan —67Ed 132
Conifer Way. Wemb —34La 58
Coniffe Ct. SE9 —57Rc 108
Coniger Rd. SW6 —54Cb 103
Coningesby Dri. Wat —11U 18
Coningham M. W12 —46Wa 80
Coningham Rd. W12 —47Xa 80
Coningsby Cotts. W5 —47Ma 79
Coningsby Gdns. E4 —23Dc 44
Coningsby Rd. N4 —31Rb 63
Coningsby Rd. W5 —47Ma 79
Coningsby Rd. S Croy —81Sb 165
Conington Rd. SE13 —54Dc 106
Conisbee Ct. N14 —15Lb 24
Conisborough Ct. Dart —58Rd 111
(off Osborne Rd.)
Conisborough Cres. SE6 —62Ec 128
Coniscliffe Clo. Chst —67Qc 130
Coniscliffe Rd. N13 —20Sb 25
Conista Ct. Wok —4C 188
Coniston Av. Bark —38Uc 66
Coniston Av. Gnfd —41Ka 78
Coniston Av. Upm —35Sd 70
Coniston Av. Well —55Uc 108
Coniston Clo. N20 —20Fb 23
Coniston Clo. SW13 —52Va 102
Coniston Clo. SW20 —72Za 144
Coniston Clo. W4 —52Sa 101
Coniston Clo. Bark —38Uc 66
Coniston Clo. Bexh —53Ed 110
Coniston Clo. Dart —60Kd 111
Coniston Clo. Eri —52Gd 110
Coniston Cres. Burn —3A 72
Coniston Way. N7 —38Nb 62
Coniston Gdns. N9 —18Yb 26
Coniston Gdns. NW9 —29Ta 39
Coniston Gdns. Ilf —28Nc 46
Coniston Gdns. Pinn —28W 36
Coniston Gdns. Sutt —79Fb 145
Coniston Gdns. Wemb —32La 58
Coniston Rd. N10 —26Kb 42
Coniston Rd. N17 —23Wb 43
Coniston Rd. Bexh —53Ed 110
Coniston Rd. Brom —65Gc 129
Coniston Rd. Coul —88Lb 164
Coniston Rd. Croy —73Wb 147
Coniston Rd. K Lan —1P 3
Coniston Rd. Twic —58Da 99
Coniston Rd. Wok —92D 172
Coniston Wlk. E9 —36Yb 64
Coniston Way. Chess —76Na 143
Coniston Way. Egh —66D 118
Coniston Way. Horn —36Jd 68
Conlan St. W10 —42Ab 80
Conley Rd. NW10 —37Ua 60
Conley St. SE10 —50Gc 85
Connaught Av. E4 —17Fc 27
Connaught Av. SW14 —55Sa 101
Connaught Av. Ashf —63N 119
Connaught Av. Barn —18Hb 23
Connaught Av. Enf —12Ub 25
Connaught Av. Grays —47De 91
Connaught Av. Houn —56Aa 99
Connaught Av. Lou —14Mc 27
Connaught Bri. E16 —46Mc 85
Connaught Bus. Cen. NW9
—29Va 40
Connaught Clo. E10 —33Ac 64
Connaught Clo. W2
—44Gb 81 (3E 196)
(off Connaught St.)
Connaught Clo. Enf —12Ub 25
Connaught Clo. Sutt —75Fb 145
Connaught Clo. Uxb —42S 76
Connaught Dri. NW11 —28Cb 41
Connaught Gdns. N10 —29Kb 42
Connaught Gdns. N13 —21Rb 43
Connaught Gdns. Mord —70Eb 125
Connaught Hill. Lou —14Mc 27
Connaught La. Ilf —33Sc 66
Connaught Lodge. N4 —31Qb 62
(off Connaught Rd.)
Connaught M. SE18 —50Qc 86
Connaught M. W2
—44Hb 81 (3F 197)
Connaught Pl. W2
—45Hb 81 (4F 197)
Connaught Rd. E4 —17Gc 27
Connaught Rd. E11 —32Fc 65
Connaught Rd. E16 —46Mc 85
Connaught Rd. E17 —29Cc 44
Connaught Rd. N4 —31Qb 62
Connaught Rd. NW10 —39Ua 60
Connaught Rd. SE18 —50Qc 86
Connaught Rd. W13 —45Ka 78
Connaught Rd. Barn —16Za 22
Connaught Rd. Harr —25Ha 38
Connaught Rd. Horn —34Md 69
Connaught Rd. Ilf —33Tc 66
Connaught Rd. N Mald —70Ua 124
Connaught Rd. Rich —57Pa 101
Connaught Rd. Slou —7M 73
Connaught Rd. Sutt —75Fb 145
Connaught Rd. Tedd —64Fa 122
Connaught Sq. W2
—44Hb 81 (3F 197)
Connaught St. W2
—44Gb 81 (3E 196)
Connaught Way. N13 —21Rb 43
Connections Bus. Pk. Sev
—91Ld 187
Connell Cres. W5 —42Pa 79
Connemara Clo. Borwd —16Ta 21
Connicut La. Bookh —100Da 175
Conningsby Ct. Rad —8Ha 6
Conningsby Dri. Pot B —5Fb 9
Connington Cres. E4 —20Fc 27
Connop Rd. Enf —10Zb 12
Connor Rd. Dag —35Bd 67
Connor St. E9 —39Zb 64
Conolly Rd. W7 —46Ga 78
Conqueror Ct. H Hill —24Md 49
Conquest Rd. Add —78J 139
Conrad Clo. Grays —47De 91
Conrad Dri. Wor Pk —74Ya 144
Conrad Gdns. Grays —47De 91
Conrad Ho. N16 —36Ub 63
(off Mayville Est.)
Conrad Rd. Stanf —1N 93
Consfield Av. N Mald —70Wa 124
Consort Clo. War —22Yd 50
Consort M. Iswth —57Fa 100
Consort Rd. SE15 —53Xb 105
Consort Way. Den —29H 35
Cons St. SE1 —47Qb 82 (1A 206)
Constable Clo. NW11 —30Db 41
Constable Clo. Hay —40S 56
Constable Ct. W4 —50Ra 79
(off Chaseley Dri.)
Constable Cres. N15 —29Wb 43
Constable Gdns. Edgw —25Qa 39
Constable Gdns. Iswth —57Fa 100
Constable Ho. E16 —44Mc 85
Constable Rd. Grav —2A 136
Constable Wlk. SE21 —62Ub 127
Constance Cres. Brom —73Hc 149
Constance Rd. Croy —73Rb 147
Constance Rd. Enf —16Ub 25
Constance Rd. Sutt —77Eb 145
Constance Rd. Twic —59Da 99
Constance St. E16 —46Nc 86
Constantine Rd. NW3 —35Gb 61
Constitution Cres. Grav —10E 114
(off Constitution Hill)
Constitution Hill. SW1
—47Kb 82 (1K 203)
Constitution Hill. Grav —10E 114
Constitution Hill. Wok —91A 172
Constitution Rise. SE18 —53Qc 108
Content St. SE17
—49Tb 83 (6F 207)
Contessa Clo. Orp —78Uc 150
Control Tower Rd. Houn —55Q 98
Convair Wlk. N'holt —41Z 77
Convent Gdns. W5 —49La 78
Convent Gdns. W11 —44Ab 80
Convent Hill. SE19 —65Sb 127
Convent La. Cob —83U 158
Convent Lodge. Ashf —64R 120
Convent Rd. Ashf —64Q 120
Convent Rd. Wind —4E 94
Convent Way. S'hall —49Y 77
Conway Clo. Rain —38Jd 68
Conway Clo. Stan —23Ja 38
Conway Cres. Gnfd —40Ga 58
Conway Cres. Romf —30Yc 47
Conway Dri. Ashf —66S 120
Conway Dri. Hay —48S 76
Conway Dri. Sutt —79Db 145
Conway Gdns. Enf —10Ub 11
Conway Gdns. Grays —52De 113
Conway Gdns. Mitc —70Nb 126
Conway Gdns. Wemb —31La 58
Conway Gro. W3 —43Ta 79
Conway Ho. E17 —29Ac 44
(off Mission Gro.)
Conway Ho. Borwd —14Sa 21
Conway M. W1 —42Lb 82 (6B 192)
(off Conway St.)
Conway Rd. N14 —20Nb 24
Conway Rd. N15 —29Rb 43
Conway Rd. NW2 —33Ya 60
Conway Rd. SE18 —49Tc 86
Conway Rd. SW20 —67Ya 124
Conway Rd. Felt —64Z 121
Conway Rd. Houn —59Ba 99
Conway Rd. H'row A —55R 98
Conway Rd. Tap —4A 72
Conways Rd. Ors —1C 92
Conway St. W1 —42Lb 82 (6B 192)
(in two parts)
Conway Wlk. Hamp —65Ba 121
Conybeare. NW3 —38Gb 61
Conybury Clo. Wal A —4Jc 13
Conyers Clo. W on T —78Z 141
Conyers Clo. Wfd G —23Gc 45
Conyer's Rd. SW16 —64Mb 126
Conyer St. E3 —40Ac 64
Conyers Way. Lou —13Rc 28
Cooden Clo. Brom —66Kc 129
Cook All. EC2 —44Sb 83 (2E 200)
Cook Ct. Eri —52Hd 110
Cookes Clo. E11 —33Hc 65
Cookes La. Sutt —79Ab 144
Cookham Cres. SE16 —47Zb 84
Cookham Dene Clo. Chst
—67Tc 130
Cookham Hill. Orp —76Cd 152
Cookham Rd. Swan —67Cd 132
Cookhill Rd. SE2 —47Xc 87
Cook's Clo. Romf —25Ed 48
Cooks Hole Rd. Enf —10Rb 11
Cooks Mead. Bush —16Da 19
Cook Sq. Eri —52Hd 110
Cook's Rd. E15 —40Dc 64
Cook's Rd. SE17 —51Rb 105
Coolfin Rd. E16 —44Jc 85
Coolgardie Av. E4 —22Fc 45
Coolgardie Av. Chig —20Qc 28
Coolgardie Rd. Ashf —64S 120
Coolhurst Rd. N8 —30Mb 42
Cool Oak La. NW9 —32Ua 60
Coomassie Rd. W9 —42Bb 81
Coombe Av. Croy —77Ub 147
Coombe Av. Sev —92Kd 187
Coombe Bank. King T —67Ua 124
Coombe Bank Dri. Sund —94Ad 185
Coombe Clo. Edgw —26Pa 39
Coombe Clo. Houn —56Ca 99
Coombe Corner. N21 —18Rb 25
Coombe Cres. Hamp —66Ba 121
Coombe Dri. Add —79H 139
Coombe Dri. Ruis —32X 57
Coombe End. King T —66Ta 123
Coombefield Clo. N Mald
—71Ua 144
Coombe Gdns. SW20 —68Wa 124
Coombe Gdns. N Mald —70Va 124
Coombe Hill Ct. Wind —6B 94
Coombe Hill Glade. King T
—66Ua 124
Coombe Hill Rd. King T —66Ua 124
Coombe Hill Rd. Rick —17J 17
Coombe Ho. E4 —23Bc 44
Coombe Ho. N7 —36Mb 62
Coombe Ho. Chase. N Mald
—67Ta 123
Coombehurst Clo. Barn —12Hb 23
Coombelands La. Add —79J 139
Coombe La. SW20 —67Va 124
Coombe La. Asc —10A 116
Coombe La. Croy —78Xb 147
Coombe La. King T —67Ra 123
Coombe La. W Vill —81V 158
Coombe La. Flyover. King T
—67Va 124
Coombe La. W. King T —67Ra 123
Coombe Lea. Brom —69Nc 130
Coombe Neville. King T —66Ta 123
Coombe Pk. King T —64Sa 123
Coomber Ho. SW6 —55Db 103
(off Wandsworth Bri. Rd.)
Coombe Ridings. King T —64Sa 123
Coombe Rise. King T —67Sa 123
Coombe Rise. Shenf —18Be 33
Coombe Rise. Stanf —1N 93
Coombe Rd. N22 —26Qb 42
Coombe Rd. NW10 —34Ta 59
Coombe Rd. SE26 —63Xb 127
Coombe Rd. W4 —50Ua 80
Coombe Rd. W13 —48Ka 78
Coombe Rd. Bush —17Ea 20
Coombe Rd. Croy —77Tb 147
Coombe Rd. Grav —1E 136
Coombe Rd. Hamp —65Ba 121
Coombe Rd. King T —67Qa 123
Coombe Rd. N Mald —68Ua 124
Coombe Rd. Otf —87Ld 171
Coombe Rd. Romf —27Pd 49
Coomber Way. Croy —73Mb 146
Coombes Rd. Dag —39Bd 67
Coombe Vale. Ger X —32A 54
Coombe Wlk. Sutt —76Db 145
Coombe Way. Byfl —84P 157
Coombe Wood Dri. Romf —30Bd 47
Coombe Wood Hill. Purl —85Sb 165
Coombewood Rd. King T —64Sa 123
Coombfield Dri. Dart —63Td 134
Coombs St. N1 —40Rb 63 (2C 194)
Coomer M. SW6 —51Bb 103
Coomer Pl. SW6 —51Bb 103
Coomer Rd. SW6 —51Bb 103
Cooms Wlk. Edgw —25Sa 39
Cooperage Clo. N17 —23Vb 43
Cooper Av. E17 —25Ac 44
Cooper Clo. Grnh —57Vd 112
Cooper Ct. E15 —36Dc 64
Cooper Cres. Cars —76Hb 145
Cooper Ho. Houn —55Ba 99
Cooper Rd. NW4 —30Za 40
Cooper Rd. NW10 —36Va 60
Cooper Rd. Croy —78Qb 146
Coopersale Clo. Wfd G —24Lc 45
Coopersale Comn. Coop —1Zc 15
Coopersale La. They B —9Wc 15
Coopersale Rd. E9 —36Zb 64
Coopers Clo. E1 —42Yb 84
Coopers Clo. Chig —19Xc 29
Coopers Clo. Dag —37Dd 68
Coopers Clo. S Dar —67Td 134
Coopers Clo. Stai —64G 118
Coopers Ct. Iswth —54Ha 100
(off Woodlands Rd.)
Coopers Cres. Borwd —11Sa 21
Coopers Hill La. Egh —2N 117
(in three parts)
Coopers La. E10 —32Dc 64
Coopers La. NW1
—40Mb 62 (1E 192)
Cooper's La. SE12 —61Kc 129
Cooper's La. Pot B —3Fb 9
Cooper's La. W Til —2F 114
Coopers La. Rd. Pot B —3Fb 9
Cooper's Rd. SE1
—50Vb 83 (7K 207)
Coopers Rd. Grav —10B 114
Coopers Rd. Pot B —2Eb 9
Cooper's Row. EC3
—45Vb 83 (4K 201)
Coopers Row. Iver —42E 74
Cooper St. E16 —43Hc 85
Coopers Wlk. E15 —36Gc 65
Coopers Wlk. Chesh —12b 12
Cooper's Yd. SE19 —65Ub 127
Cooper Way. Slou —8F 72
Coote Gdns. Dag —34Bd 67
Coote Rd. Bexh —53Bd 109
Coote Rd. Dag —34Bd 67
Copeland Dri. E14 —49Cc 84
Copeland Ho. SE11
—48Pb 82 (4J 205)
(off Lambeth Wlk.)
Copeland Rd. E17 —30Dc 44
Copeland Rd. SE15 —54Xb 105
Copeman Clo. SE26 —64Yb 128
Copeman Rd. Hut —17Fe 33
Copenhagen Gdns. W4 —47Ta 79
Copenhagen Ho. N1
—39Qb 62 (1K 193)
(off Barnsbury Est.)
Copenhagen Pl. E14 —44Bc 84
Copenhagen St. N1
—39Nb 62 (1G 193)
Copenhagen Way. W on T
—76X 141
Cope Pl. W8 —48Cb 81
Copers Cope Rd. Beck —66Bc 128
Cope St. SE16 —49Zb 84
Copford Clo. Wfd G —23Nc 46
Copford Wlk. N1 —39Sb 63
(off Popham St.)
Copinger Wlk. Edgw —25Ra 39
Copland Av. Wemb —36Ma 59
Copland Clo. Wemb —36La 58
Copland Rd. Stanf —2M 93
Copland Rd. Wemb —37Na 59
Copleigh Dri. Tad —92Ab 178
Copleston M. SE15 —54Vb 105
Copleston Pas. SE15 —54Vb 105
Copleston Rd. SE15 —55Vb 105
Copley Clo. SE17 —51Sb 105
Copley Clo. W7 —42Ha 78
Copley Clo. Wok —7B 188
Copley Dene. Brom —67Mc 129
Copley Pk. SW16 —65Pb 126
Copley Rd. Stan —22La 38
Copley St. E1 —43Zb 84
Copley Way. Tad —92Za 178
Copmans Wick. Chor —15F 16
Copner Way. SE15 —52Vb 105
Coppelia Rd. SE3 —56Hc 107
Coppen Rd. Dag —31Bd 67
Copperas St. SE8 —51Dc 106
Copperbeech Clo. NW3 —36Fb 61
Copper Beech Clo. Grav —9F 114
Copper Beech Clo. Ilf —25Pc 46
Copper Beech Clo. Orp —71Yc 151
Copper Beech Clo. Wind —3B 94
Copper Beech Clo. Wok —9E 188
Copper Beech Ct. Lou —11Qc 28
Copper Beeches Ct. Iswth
—53Fa 100
Copper Beech Rd. S Ock —41Yd 90
Copper Clo. SE19 —66Vb 127
Copperdale Rd. Hay —47W 76
Copperfield. Chig —22Tc 46
Copperfield App. Chig —23Tc 46
Copperfield Av. Uxb —43Q 76
Copperfield Clo. Grav —10J 115
Copperfield Clo. S Croy —83Sb 165
Copperfield Ct. Lea —93Ja 176
Copperfield Dri. N15 —28Vb 43
Copperfield Gdns. Brtwd —18Xd 32
Copperfield M. N18 —21Ub 43
Copperfield Rise. Add —78H 139
Copperfield Rd. E3 —42Ac 84
Copperfield Rd. SE28 —44Yc 87
Copperfields. Beck —67Ec 128
Copperfields. Fet —94Ea 176
Copperfields. Harr —31Ga 58
Copperfields. Kems —89Pd 171
Copperfields Clo. Kems —89Pd 171
Copperfields Ct. W3 —47Qa 79
Copperfields Orchard. Kems
—89Pd 171
Copperfield St. SE1
—47Rb 83 (1C 206)
Copperfields Wlk. Kems —89Pd 171
Copperfields Way. Romf —25Md 49
Copperfield Way. Chst —65Sc 130
Copperfield Way. Pinn —28Ba 37
Coppergate Clo. Brom —67Kc 129
Copperidge. Ger X —22B 34
Copper Mead Clo. NW2 —34Ya 60
Coppermill Ct. W Hyd —24H 35
Copper Mill Dri. Iswth —54Ha 100
Coppermill La. E17 —30Yb 44
Copper Mill La. SW17 —63Eb 125
Coppermill La. Rick & Hare
—24G 34
Coppermill Rd. Wray —58C 96
Copper Row. SE1
—46Vb 83 (7K 201)
(off Horselydown La.)
Coppetts Cen. N11 —24Hb 41
Coppetts Clo. N12 —24Gb 41
Coppetts Rd. N10 —24Hb 41
Coppice Clo. SW20 —69Ya 124
Coppice Clo. Ruis —30T 36
Coppice Clo. Stan —23Ha 38
Coppice Dri. SW15 —58Xa 102
Coppice Dri. Wray —9P 95
Coppice End. Wok —88G 156
Coppice Path. Chig —21Xc 47
Coppice Row. They B —8Sc 14
Coppice, The. Ashf —65R 120
Coppice, The. Enf —14Rb 25
Coppice, The. New Bar —16Db 23
(off Gt. North Rd.)
Coppice, The. Wat —16Y 19
Coppice, The. W Dray —44N 75
Coppice Wlk. N20 —20Cb 23
Coppice Way. E18 —28Hc 45
Coppies Gro. N11 —21Jb 42
Copping Clo. Croy —77Ub 147
Coppins Clo. Iver —43H 75
Coppins, The. Harr —23Ga 38
Coppins, The. New Ad —79Dc 148
Coppock Clo. SW11 —54Gb 103
Coppsfield. W Mol —69Ca 121
Copse Av. W Wick —76Dc 148
Copse Bank. Seal —92Pd 187
Copse Clo. SE7 —51Kc 107
Copse Clo. N'wd —26S 36
Copse Clo. W Dray —48M 75
Copse Edge Av. Eps —85Va 162
Copse Glade. Surb —73Ma 143
Copse Hill. SW20 —67Wa 124
Copse Hill. Purl —85Nb 164
Copse Hill. Sutt —80Db 145
Copsem Dri. Esh —79Da 141
Copsem La. Esh & Oxs —79Ea 142
Copsem Way. Esh —80Ea 142
Copse Rd. Cob —85X 159
Copse Rd. Wok —6C 188
Copse Side. Hart —69Ae 135
Copse, The. E4 —18Hc 27
Copse, The. N2 —27Hb 41
Copse, The. Cat —98Wb 181
Copse, The. Fet —95Da 175
Copse, The. Wat —4Aa 5
Copse View. S Croy —81Zb 166
Copse Wood. Iver —39F 54
Copsewood Rd. Wat —11X 19
Copse Wood Way. N'wd —25R 36
Coptefield Dri. Belv —48Zc 87
Coptfold Rd. Brtwd —19Yd 32
Copthall Av. EC2
—44Tb 83 (2G 201)
Copthall Bldgs. EC2
—44Tb 83 (2G 201)
(off Copthall Av.)
Copthall Clo. EC2
—44Tb 83 (2F 201)
Copthall Clo. Ger X —24B 34
Copthall Corner. Ger X —24A 34
Copthall Dri. NW7 —24Wa 40
Copthall Gdns. NW7 —24Wa 40
Copthall Gdns. Twic —60Ha 100
Copthall La. Ger X —24A 34
Copt Hall Rd. Cobh —10D 136
Copthall Rd. E. Uxb —33Q 56
Copthall Rd. W. Uxb —33Q 56
Copthall Way. New Haw —82H 157
Copt Hill La. Tad —92Ab 178
Copthorne Av. SW12 —59Mb 104
Copthorne Av. Brom —75Pc 150
Copthorne Av. Ilf —23Rc 46
Copthorne Chase. Ashf —63P 119
Copthorne Clo. Crox —15P 17
Copthorne Clo. Shep —72S 140
Copthorne Ct. Lea —94Ja 176
Copthorne Gdns. Horn —29Qd 49
Copthorne M. Hay —49U 76
Copthorne Rise. S Croy —85Tb 165
Copthorne Rd. Crox —16P 17
Copthorne Rd. Lea —92Ka 176
Coptic St. WC1 —43Nb 82 (1F 199)
Copwood Clo. N12 —21Fb 41
Coral Clo. Romf —28Yc 47
Coraline Clo. S'hall —41Ba 77
Coralline Wlk. SE2 —47Yc 87
Coral Row. SW11 —55Eb 103
Coral St. SE1 —47Qb 82 (2A 206)
Coram Grn. Hut —16Fe 33
Coram Ho. W4 —50Ua 80
(off Wood St.)
Coram St. WC1 —42Nb 82 (6F 193)
Coran Clo. N9 —17Zb 26
Corban Rd. Houn —55Ca 99
Corbar Clo. Barn —11Fb 23
Corbet Clo. Wall —74Jb 146
Corbet Ct. EC3 —44Tb 83 (3G 201)
Corbet Pl. E1 —43Vb 83 (7K 195)
Corbet Rd. Eps —82Ua 162
Corbets Av. Upm —36Rd 69
Corbets Tey Rd. Upm —35Rd 69
Corbett Clo. Croy —84Fc 167
Corbett Ct. SE26 —63Bc 128
Corbett Gro. N22 —24Nb 42
Corbett Rd. E11 —30Lc 45
Corbett Rd. E17 —27Ec 44
Corbetts La. SE16 —49Yb 84
(in two parts)
Corbett W. E11 —30Lc 45
Corbicum. E11 —31Gc 65
Corbiere Ct. SW19 —65Za 124
Corbins La. Harr —34Da 57
Corbridge. N17 —24Xb 43
Corbridge Cres. E2 —40Xb 63
Corby Cres. Enf —14Nb 24
Corby Dri. Egh —5N 117
Corbylands Rd. Sidc —60Uc 108
Corbyn St. N4 —32Nb 62
Corby Rd. NW10 —40Ta 59
Corby Way. E3 —42Cc 84
Corcorans. Pil H —16Yd 32
Cordelia Clo. SE24 —56Rb 105
Cordelia Gdns. Stai —59N 97
Cordelia Ho. N1 —40Ub 63 (1J 195)
(off Arden Est.)
Cordelia Rd. Stai —59N 97
Cordelia St. E14 —44Dc 84
Cordell Clo. Chesh —1Ac 12
Cordell Ho. N15 —29Vb 43
(off Newton Rd.)
Corderoy Pl. Cher —72H 139
Cordingley Rd. Ruis —33T 56
Cording St. E14 —43Dc 84
Cordons Clo. Ger X —25A 34
Cordova Rd. E3 —41Ac 84
Cordrey Gdns. Coul —87Nb 164
(in two parts)
Cordrey Ho. Add —75K 139
Cordwainers Wlk. E13 —40Jc 65
Cord Way. E14 —48Cc 84
Cordwell Rd. SE13 —57Gc 107
Corelli Rd. SE3 —54Nc 108
Corfe Av. Harr —35Ca 57
Corfe Clo. Asht —90La 160
Corfe Clo. Hay —44Y 77
Corfe Gdns. Slou —5E 72
Corfe Ho. SW8 —52Pb 104
(off Dorset Rd.)
Corfe Tower. W3 —47Sa 79
Corfield St. E2 —41Xb 83
Corfton Rd. W5 —44Na 79
Corhaven Ho. Eri —52Gd 110
Coriander Av. E14 —44Fc 85
Corinium Clo. Wemb —35Pa 59
Corinne Rd. N19 —35Lb 62
Corinthian Manorway. Eri —49Fd 88
Corinthian Rd. Eri —49Fd 88
Corinthian Way. Stanw —59M 97
Corkers Path. Ilf —33Sc 66
Corker Wlk. N7 —33Pb 62
Corkran Rd. Surb —73Ma 143
Corkscrew Hill. W Wick —75Ec 148
Cork Sq. E1 —46Xb 83
Cork St. W1 —45Lb 82 (5B 198)
Cork St. M. W1 —45Lb 82 (5B 198)
(off Cork St.)
Cork Tree Ho. SE27 —64Rb 127
(off Lakeview Rd.)
Cork Tree Way. E4 —22Ac 44
Corlett St. NW1 —43Gb 81 (7D 190)
Cormont Rd. SE5 —53Rb 105
Cormorant Clo. E17 —24Zb 44
Cormorant Rd. E7 —36Hc 65
Cormorant Wlk. Horn —37Kd 69
Cornbury Rd. Edgw —24Ma 39
Cornel Ho. Sidc —62Wc 131
Cornelia Pl. Eri —51Gd 110
Cornelia St. N7 —37Pb 62
Cornell Clo. Sidc —65Ad 131
Cornell Ho. S Harr —34Ba 57
Cornell Way. Romf —22Cd 48
Corner Fielde. SW2 —60Pb 104
Corner Grn. SE3 —54Jc 107
Corner Ho. St. WC2
—46Nb 82 (6F 199)
(off Lit. Britain)
Corner Mead. NW9 —24Va 40
Cornerside. Ashf —66S 120
Cornerstone Ho. Croy —73Sb 147
Corner, The. W Byf —85J 157
Cornerways. Dodd —11Zd 33
Corney Rd. W4 —51Ua 102
Cornfield Clo. Uxb —40M 55
Cornfield Rd. Bush —14Da 19
Cornflower La. Croy —74Zb 148
Cornflower Ter. SE22 —58Xb 105
Cornflower Way. Romf —25Nd 49
Cornford Clo. Brom —71Jc 149
Cornford Gro. SW12 —61Kb 126
Cornhill. EC3 —44Tb 83 (3G 201)
Cornhill Clo. Add —75K 139
Cornish Ct. N9 —17Xb 25
Cornish Gro. SE20 —67Xb 127
(in two parts)
Cornish Ho. Bren —50Pa 79
Cornmill. Wal A —5Dc 12
Corn Mill Dri. Orp —73Wc 151
Cornmill La. SE13 —55Ec 106
Cornmow Dri. NW10 —36Va 60
Cornshaw Rd. Dag —32Zc 67
Cornsland. Brtwd —20Zd 33
Cornsland Ct. Brtwd —20Zd 33
Cornthwaite Rd. E5 —34Yb 64
Cornwall Av. E2 —41Yb 84
Cornwall Av. N3 —24Cb 41
Cornwall Av. N22 —25Nb 42
Cornwall Av. Byfl —86P 157
Cornwall Av. Clay —80Ha 142
Cornwall Av. Grav —2E 136
Cornwall Av. Slou —2G 72
Cornwall Av. S'hall —43Ba 77
Cornwall Av. Well —55Uc 108
Cornwall Clo. Bark —37Vc 67
Cornwall Clo. Eton W —10C 72
Cornwall Clo. Horn —28Qd 49
Cornwall Clo. Wal X —5Ac 12
Cornwall Ct. Pinn —24Ba 37
Cornwall Cres. W11 —44Ab 80
Cornwall Dri. Orp —66Yc 131
Cornwall Gdns. NW10 —37Xa 60
Cornwall Gdns. SW7 —48Db 81
Cornwall Gdns. Wlk. SW7
—48Db 81
Cornwall Gdns. W. SW7 —48Db 81
Cornwall Ga. Purf —49Ed 88
Cornwall Gro. W4 —50Ua 80
Cornwallis Av. N9 —19Xb 25
Cornwallis Av. SE9 —61Tc 130
Cornwallis Clo. Eri —51Hd 110
Cornwallis Ct. SW8 —53Nb 104
(off Lansdowne Grn.)
Cornwallis Gro. N9 —19Xb 25
Cornwallis Ho. W12 —45Xa 80
(off White City Est.)

Cornwallis Rd.—Cranleigh Gdns.

Cornwallis Rd. E17 —28Zb 44
Cornwallis Rd. N9 —19Xb 25
Cornwallis Rd. N19 —33Nb 62
Cornwallis Rd. Dag —35Zc 67
Cornwallis Sq. N19 —33Nb 62
Cornwallis Wlk. SE9 —55Pc 108
Cornwall M. S. SW7 —48Eb 81
Cornwall M. W. SW7 —48Db 81
Cornwall Rd. N4 —31Qb 62
Cornwall Rd. N15 —29Tb 43
Cornwall Rd. N18 —22Wb 43
Cornwall Rd. SE1
—46Qb 82 (6K 199)
Cornwall Rd. Croy —75Rb 147
Cornwall Rd. Harr —30Ea 38
Cornwall Rd. Old Win —8L 95
Cornwall Rd. Pil H —15Xd 32
Cornwall Rd. Pinn —24Ba 37
Cornwall Rd. Ruis —34V 56
Cornwall Rd. Sutt —80Bb 145
Cornwall Rd. Twic —59Ja 100
Cornwall Rd. Uxb —37M 55
Cornwall St. E1 —45Xb 83
Cornwall Ter. NW1
—42Hb 81 (6G 191)
Cornwall Ter. M. NW1
—42Hb 81 (6G 191)
(off Allsop Pl.)
Cornwall Way. Stai —65G 118
Cornwell Cres. E7 —35Lc 65
Cornwell Cres. Stanf —1N 93
Cornwood Clo. N2 —29Fb 41
Cornwood Dri. E1 —44Yb 84
Cornworthy Rd. Dag —36Yc 67
Corona Rd. SE12 —59Jc 107
Coronation Av. N16 —35Vb 63
Coronation Av. E Til —9K 93
Coronation Av. G Grn —43A 74
Coronation Av. Wind —4L 95
Coronation Clo. Bex —58Zc 109
Coronation Clo. Ilf —28Sc 46
Coronation Ct. E15 —37Hc 65
Coronation Ct. E Til —9L 93
(off Coronation Av.)
Coronation Ct. Eri —52Fd 110
Coronation Dri. Horn —36Kd 69
Coronation Hill. Epp —2Vc 15
Coronation Rd. E13 —41Lc 85
Coronation Rd. NW10 —41Pa 79
Coronation Rd. Hay —49V 76
Coronation Wlk. Twic —60Ca 99
Coronet St. N1 —41Ub 83 (4H 195)
Corporate Dri. Felt —62X 121
Corporate Ho. Har W —25Ga 38
Corporation Av. Houn —56Aa 99
Corporation Row. EC1
—42Qb 82 (5A 194)
Corporation St. E15 —40Gc 65
Corporation St. N7 —36Nb 62
Corrance Rd. SW2 —56Nb 104
Corran Way. S Ock —45Xd 90
Corri Av. N14 —21Mb 42
Corrib Ct. N13 —20Pb 24
Corrib Dri. Sutt —78Gb 145
Corrie Rd. Add —77M 139
Corrie Rd. Wok —92D 172
Corrigan Av. Coul —87Jb 164
Corringham Clo. Corr —1P 93
Corringham Ct. NW11 —31Cb 61
Corringham Rd. NW11 —31Cb 61
Corringham Rd. Corr —2M 93
(in two parts)
Corringham Rd. Wemb —33Qa 59
Corringway. NW11 —31Db 61
Corringway. W5 —43Pa 79
Corris Grn. NW9 —30Ua 40
Corronade Pl. SE28 —48Sc 86
Corsair Clo. Stai —59M 97
Corsair Rd. Stai —59N 97
Corscombe Clo. King T —64Sa 123
Corsehill St. SW16 —65Lb 126
Corsham St. N1 —41Tb 83 (4G 195)
Corsica St. N5 —37Rb 63
Corsley Way. E9 —37Bc 64
Cortayne Ct. Twic —61Ga 122
Cortayne Rd. SW6 —54Bb 103
Cortis Rd. SW15 —58Xa 102
Cortis Ter. SW15 —58Xa 102
Corunna Rd. SW8 —53Lb 104
Corunna Ter. SW8 —53Lb 104
Corve La. S Ock —45Xd 90
Corvette Sq. SE10 —51Fc 107
Corwell Gdns. Uxb —44S 76
Corwell La. Uxb —44S 76
Cory Dri. Hut —17De 33
Coryton Path. W9 —42Bb 81
Cosbycote Av. SE24 —57Sb 105
Cosdach Av. Wall —80Mb 146
Cosedge Cres. Croy —78Qb 146
Cosgrove Clo. N21 —19Sb 25
Cosgrove Clo. Hay —42Aa 77
Cosmo Pl. WC1 —43Nb 82 (7G 193)
Cosmos Ho. Brom —70Lc 129
Cosmur Clo. W12 —48Va 80
Cossall Wlk. SE15 —54Xb 105
Cosser St. SE1 —48Qb 82 (3K 205)
Costa St. SE15 —54Wb 105
Costead Mnr. Rd. Brtwd —18Xd 32
Costells Meadow. W'ham
—98Tc 184
Costons Av. Gnfd —41Fa 78
Costons La. Gnfd —41Fa 78
Cosway St. NW1
—43Gb 81 (7E 190)
Cotall St. E14 —43Cc 84
Coteford Clo. Lou —12Rc 28
Coteford Clo. Pinn —29W 36
Coteford St. SW17 —63Hb 125
Cotelands. Croy —76Ub 147
Cotesbach Rd. E5 —34Yb 64
Cotesmore Gdns. Dag —35Yc 67
Cotford Rd. T Hth —70Sb 127
Cotham St. SE17
—49Sb 83 (6E 206)
Cotherstone. Eps —82Ta 161
Cotherstone Rd. SW2 —60Pb 104
Cotleigh Av. Bex —61Zc 131
Cotleigh Rd. NW6 —38Cb 61
Cotleigh Rd. Romf —30Fd 48
Cotman Clo. NW11 —30Eb 41
Cotman Clo. SW15 —58Za 102
Cotmandene Cres. Orp —68Xc 131
Cotman Gdns. Edgw —26Qa 39
Cotman's Ash La. Kems —86Rd 171
Cotmans Clo. Hay —46W 76
Coton Rd. Well —55Wc 109
Cotsford Av. N Mald —71Sa 143
Cotswold Av. Bush —16Ea 20
Cotswold Clo. N11 —21Jb 42
Cotswold Clo. Bexh —54Gd 110
Cotswold Clo. King T —65Sa 123
Cotswold Clo. Slou —8G 72
Cotswold Clo. Stai —64J 119
Cotswold Clo. Uxb —39L 55
Cotswold Gdns. E6 —41Mc 85
Cotswold Gdns. NW2 —33Za 60
Cotswold Gdns. Hut —17Fe 33
Cotswold Gdns. Ilf —31Tc 66
Cotswold Ga. NW2 —32Ab 60
Cotswold Grn. Enf —14Pb 24
Cotswold M. SW11 —53Fb 103
Cotswold Rise. Orp —72Vc 151
Cotswold Rd. Grav —2A 136
Cotswold Rd. Hamp —65Ca 121
Cotswold Rd. Romf —26Pd 49
Cotswold Rd. Sutt —82Db 163
Cotswold St. SE27 —63Rb 127
Cotswold Way. Enf —13Pb 24
Cotswold Way. Wor Pk —75Ya 144
Cottage Av. Brom —74Nc 150
Cottage Clo. Ott —79E 138
Cottage Clo. Ruis —32T 56
Cottage Farm Way. Egh —69E 118
Cottage Field Clo. Sidc —60Yc 109
Cottage Grn. SE5 —52Tb 105
Cottage Gro. SW9 —55Nb 104
Cottage Gro. Surb —72Ma 143
Cottage Pk. Rd. Hedg —3H 53
Cottage Pl. SW3
—48Gb 81 (3D 202)
Cottage Rd. Eps —80Ta 143
Cottage St. E14 —45Dc 84
Cottage Wlk. N16 —34Vb 63
Cottage Wlk. SE15 —53Vb 105
Cottage Wlk. SW1
—48Hb 81 (3G 203)
Cottenham Dri. SW20 —66Xa 124
Cottenham Pk. Rd. SW20
(in two parts) —67Wa 124
Cottenham Pl. SW20 —66Xa 124
Cottenham Rd. E17 —28Bc 44
Cotterill Rd. Surb —75Na 143
Cottesbrooke Clo. Coln —53F 96
Cottesbrooke St. SE14 —52Ac 106
Cottesmore Av. Ilf —26Qc 46
Cottesmore Ct. W8 —48Db 81
(off Stanford Rd.)
Cottesmore Gdns. W8 —48Db 81
Cottimore Av. W on T —74X 141
Cottimore Cres. W on T —73X 141
Cottimore La. W on T —73X 141
Cottimore Ter. W on T —73X 141
Cottingham Chase. Ruis —34W 56
Cottingham Rd. SE20 —66Zb 128
Cottingham Rd. SW8 —52Pb 104
Cottington Clo. SE11
—50Rb 83 (7B 206)
Cottington Rd. Felt —63Z 121
Cottington St. SE11
—50Rb 83 (7A 206)
Cotton Av. W3 —44Ta 79
Cottongrass Clo. Croy —74Zb 148
Cotton Hill. Brom —63Ec 128
Cotton Ho. SW12 —59Nb 104
Cotton La. Dart & Grnh —58Sd 112
Cotton Rd. Pot B —3Eb 9
Cotton Row. SW11 —55Fb 103
Cottons App. Romf —29Fd 48
Cottons Cen. SE1
—46Ub 83 (6H 201)
Cottons Ct. Romf —29Fd 48
Cotton's Gdns. E2
—41Ub 83 (3J 195)
Cottons La. SE1 —46Tb 83 (6G 201)
Cotton St. E14 —45Ec 84
Cotts Clo. W7 —43Ha 78
Cotts Wood Dri. Guild —100C 172
Couchmore Av. Esh —75Ga 142
Couchmore Av. Ilf —26Pc 46
Couldridge La. Eri —48Zc 87
Coulgate St. SE4 —55Ac 106
Coulsdon Ct. Rd. Coul —88Pb 164
Coulsdon La. Coul —91Jb 180
Coulsdon Pl. Cat —94Tb 181
Coulsdon Rise. Coul —89Nb 164
Coulsdon Rd. Coul & Cat
—87Pb 164
Coulson Clo. Dag —32Yc 67
Coulson St. SW3
—50Hb 81 (7F 203)
Coulson Way. Burn —3A 72
Coulter Clo. Hay —42Aa 77
Coulter Rd. W6 —48Xa 80
Coulton Av. Grav —9A 114
Council Av. Grav —58Ee 113
Council Cotts. Wis —87M 157
Councillor St. SE5 —52Sb 105
Counter Ct. SE1 —46Tb 83 (7F 201)
(off Borough High St.)
Counter St. SE1 —46Ub 83 (7H 201)
(off Hays La.)
Countess Clo. Hare —26L 35
Countess Rd. NW5 —36Lb 62
Countisbury Av. Enf —17Vb 25
Countisbury Gdns. Add —78K 139
Country Way. Felt —65X 121
County Gdns. Bark —40Uc 66
County Ga. SE9 —62Sc 130
County Ga. Barn —16Db 23
County Gro. SE5 —53Sb 105
County Pde. Bren —52Ma 101
County Rd. E6 —43Rc 86
County Rd. T Hth —68Rb 127
County St. SE1 —48Sb 83 (4E 206)
Coupland Pl. SE18 —50Sc 86
Courage Clo. Horn —30Ld 49
Courage Ct. Hut —16Ee 33
Courage Wlk. Hut —16Fe 33
Courcy Rd. N8 —27Qb 42
Courland Gro. SW8 —53Mb 104
Courland Rd. Add —76K 139
Courland St. SW8 —53Mb 104
(in two parts)
Course, The. SE9 —62Qc 130
Courtauld Clo. SE28 —46Wc 87
Courtauld Rd. N19 —32Nb 62
Court Av. Belv —50Bd 87
Court Av. Coul —90Qb 164
Court Av. Romf —24Qd 49
Court Bushes Rd. Whyt —91Wb 181
Court Clo. Harr —27Na 39
Court Clo. Twic —62Da 121
Court Clo. Wall —80Mb 146
Court Clo. Av. Twic —62Da 121
Court Cres. Chess —79Ma 143
Court Cres. Slou —4H 73
Court Cres. Swan —70Gd 132
Court Downs Rd. Beck —68Dc 128
Court Dri. Croy —77Pb 146
Court Dri. Stan —21Na 39
Court Dri. Sutt —77Gb 145
Court Dri. Uxb —39P 55
Courtenay Av. N6 —31Gb 61
Courtenay Av. Harr —24Ea 38
Courtenay Av. Sutt —81Cb 163
Courtenay Dri. Beck —68Fc 129
Courtenay Gdns. Harr —26Ea 38
Courtenay Gdns. Upm —32Sd 70
Courtenay M. E17 —29Ac 44
Courtenay M. Wok —88C 156
Courtenay Pl. E17 —29Ac 44
Courtenay Rd. E11 —34Hc 65
Courtenay Rd. E17 —28Zb 44
Courtenay Rd. SE20 —65Zb 128
Courtenay Rd. Wemb —34Ma 59
Courtenay Rd. Wok —88C 156
Courtenay Rd. Wor Pk —76Ya 144
Courtenay Sq. SE11
—50Qb 82 (7K 205)
Courtenay St. SE11
—50Qb 82 (7K 205)
Courtens M. Stan —24La 38
Court Farm Av. Eps —78Ta 143
Court Farm La. N'holt —38Ca 57
Court Farm Rd. SE9 —61Mc 129
Court Farm Rd. N'holt —38Ca 57
Court Farm Rd. Warl —90Wb 165
Courtfield. W5 —43La 78
Courtfield Av. Harr —29Ha 38
Courtfield Cres. Harr —29Ha 38
Courtfield Gdns. SW5 —49Db 81
Courtfield Gdns. W13 —44Ja 78
Courtfield Gdns. Den —34J 55
Courtfield Gdns. Ruis —33V 56
Courtfield M. SW5 —49Db 81
Courtfield M. SW7 —49Eb 81
Courtfield Rise. W Wick —76Fc 149
Courtfield Rd. SW7 —49Eb 81
Courtfield Rd. Ashf —65R 120
Court Gdns. N1 —37Rb 63
Court Gdns. Romf —23Qd 49
Court Grn. Heights. Wok —8F 188
Court Haw. Bans —87Gb 163
Court Hill. Coul —90Gb 163
Court Hill. S Croy —84Ub 165
Courthill Rd. SE13 —56Ec 106
Courthope Rd. NW3 —35Hb 61
Courthope Rd. SW19 —64Ab 124
Courthope Rd. Gnfd —40Fa 58
Courthope Vs. SW19 —66Ab 124
Court Ho. Gdns. N3 —23Cb 41
Courthouse Rd. N12 —23Db 41
Courtland Av. E4 —19Hc 27
Courtland Av. NW7 —19Ta 21
Courtland Av. SW16 —66Pb 126
Courtland Av. Ilf —33Pc 66
Courtland Dri. Chig —20Rc 28
Courtland Gro. SE28 —45Zc 87
Courtland Rd. E6 —39Nc 66
Courtlands. Rich —57Qa 101
Courtlands Av. SE12 —57Kc 107
Courtlands Av. Brom —74Gc 149
Courtlands Av. Esh —79Ba 141
Courtlands Av. Hamp —65Ba 121
Courtlands Av. Rich —53Ra 101
Courtlands Av. Slou —9P 73
Courtlands Clo. Ruis —31V 56
Courtlands Clo. S Croy —82Vb 165
Courtlands Clo. Wat —7U 4
Courtlands Cres. Bans —88Cb 163
Courtlands Dri. Eps —79Ua 144
Courtlands Dri. Wat —9U 4
Courtlands Rd. Surb —73Qa 143
Court La. SE21 —58Ub 105
Court La. Burn —1B 72
Court La. Dor —8A 72
Court La. Eps —85Sa 161
Court La. Iver —46J 75
(in two parts)
Court La. Gdns. SE21 —59Ub 105
Courtleas. Cob —85Ca 159
Courtleet Dri. Eri —53Dd 110
Courtleigh. NW11 —29Bb 41
Courtleigh Av. Barn —10Eb 9
Courtleigh Gdns. NW11 —28Ab 40
Court Lodge. Shorne —5N 137
Courtman Rd. N17 —24Sb 43
Court Mead. N'holt —41Ba 77
Courtmead Clo. SE24 —58Sb 105
Courtnell St. W2 —44Cb 81
Courtney Clo. SE19 —65Ub 127
Courtney Ct. N7 —36Qb 62
Courtney Cres. Cars —80Hb 145
Courtney Ho. NW4 —27Ya 40
(off Mulberry Clo.)
Courtney Pl. Croy —76Qb 146
Courtney Rd. N7 —36Qb 62
Courtney Rd. SW19 —66Gb 125
Courtney Rd. Croy —76Qb 146
Courtney Rd. Grays —7E 92
Courtney Rd. Houn —55Q 98
Courtrai Rd. SE23 —58Ac 106
Court Rd. SE9 —58Pc 108
Court Rd. SE25 —68Vb 127
Court Rd. Bans —88Cb 163
Court Rd. Cat —95Tb 181
Court Rd. Dart —64Ud 134
Court Rd. Orp —73Xc 151
Court Rd. S'hall —49Ba 77
Court Rd. Uxb —36R 56
Courtside. N8 —30Mb 42
Courtside. SE26 —62Xb 127
Court St. E1 —43Xb 83
Court St. Brom —68Jc 129
Court, The. Ruis —35Aa 57
Court, The. Warl —90Ac 166
Court Way. NW9 —28Ua 40
Court Way. W3 —43Sa 79
Court Way. Ilf —27Sc 46
Court Way. Romf —26Nd 49
Court Way. Twic —59Ha 100
Court Way. Wfd G —22Lc 45
Courtway, The. Wat —19Aa 19
Courtwood Dri. Sev —96Jd 186
Court Wood La. Croy —83Bc 166
Court Yd. SE9 —58Pc 108
Courtyards, The. Langl —47C 74
Courtyard, The. N1 —38Pb 62
Courtyard, The. NW1 —38Jb 62
Courtyard, The. W'ham —99Tc 184
Cousin La. EC4 —45Tb 83 (5F 201)
Cousins Clo. W Dray —45N 75
Couthurst Rd. SE3 —52Kc 107
Coutts Av. Chess —78Na 143
Coutts Av. Shorne —3N 137
Coutt's Cres. NW5 —34Jb 62
Coval Gdns. SW14 —56Ra 101
Coval La. SW14 —56Ra 101
Coval Pas. SW14 —56Sa 101
Coval Rd. SW14 —56Sa 101
Coveham Cres. Cob —85W 158
Covelees Wall. E6 —44Qc 86
Covell Ct. SE8 —52Cc 106
Covell Ct. Enf —10Pb 10
Covenbrook. Brtwd —20De 33
Coventery Rd. SE25 —70Wb 127
Covent Garden. WC2
—45Nb 82 (4G 199)
Coventry Clo. E6 —44Pc 86
Coventry Clo. NW6 —40Cb 61
Coventry Cross. E3 —42Ec 84
Coventry Rd. E1 & E2 —42Xb 83
Coventry Rd. SE25 —70Wb 127
Coventry Rd. Ilf —33Rc 66
Coventry St. W1
—45Mb 82 (5D 198)
Coverack Clo. N14 —16Lb 24
Coverack Clo. Croy —73Ac 148
Coverdale Clo. Stan —22Ka 38
Coverdale Ct. Enf —9Ac 12
Coverdale Gdns. Croy —76Vb 147
Coverdale Rd. NW2 —38Za 60
Coverdale Rd. W12 —47Xa 80
Coverdales, The. Bark —40Tc 66
Coverdale Way. Slou —2C 72
Coverley Clo. E1 —43Wb 83
Coverley Clo. Gt War —23Yd 50
Coverton Rd. SW17 —64Gb 125
Covert Rd. Ilf —22Vc 47
Coverts Rd. Clay —80Ha 142
Coverts, The. Hut —18Ce 33
Covert, The. N'wd —25S 36
Covert, The. Orp —72Uc 150
Covert Way. Barn —12Eb 23
Covet Wood Clo. Orp —72Vc 151
Covington Gdns. SW16 —66Rb 127
Covington Way. SW16 —65Pb 126
(in two parts)
Cowan Clo. E6 —43Nc 86
Cowbridge La. Bark —38Rc 66
Cowbridge Rd. Harr —28Pa 39
Cowcross St. EC1
—43Rb 83 (7B 194)
Cowdenbeath Path. N1 —39Pb 62
Cowden Rd. Orp —73Vc 151
Cowden St. SE6 —63Cc 128
Cowdray Rd. Uxb —39S 56
Cowdray Way. Horn —35Hd 68
Cowdrey Clo. Enf —12Ub 25
Cowdrey Ct. Dart —59Kd 111
Cowdrey Rd. SW19 —64Db 125
Cowdry Rd. E9 —37Ac 64
Cowen Av. Harr —33Fa 58
Cowgate Rd. Gnfd —41Fa 78
Cowick Rd. SW17 —63Hb 125
Cowings Mead. N'holt —37Aa 57
Cowland Av. Enf —14Yb 26
Cow La. Gnfd —40Fa 58
Cow La. Wat —8Y 5
Cow Leaze. E6 —44Qc 86
Cowleaze Rd. King T —67Na 123
Cowley Av. Cher —73H 139
Cowley Av. Grnh —57Vd 112
Cowley Bus. Pk. Cow —41L 75
Cowley Clo. S Croy —81Yb 166
Cowley Cres. Uxb —43L 75
Cowley Cres. W on T —77Y 141
Cowley Hill. Borwd —9Qa 7
Cowley La. E11 —34Gc 65
Cowley La. Cher —73H 139
Cowley Lodge. Ott —73H 139
Cowley Mill Rd. Uxb —40K 55
Cowley Mill Trading Est. Uxb
—40K 55
Cowley Pl. NW4 —29Ya 40
Cowley Rd. E11 —29Kc 45
Cowley Rd. SW9 —53Qb 104
Cowley Rd. SW14 —55Ua 102
Cowley Rd. W3 —46Va 80
Cowley Rd. Ilf —31Pc 66
Cowley Rd. Romf —24Kd 49
Cowley Rd. Uxb —40L 55
Cowley St. SW1 —48Nb 82 (4F 205)
Cowling Clo. W11 —45Ab 80
Coworth Pk. S'hill —10G 116
Coworth Rd. Asc —10E 116
Cowper Av. E6 —38Nc 66
Cowper Av. Sutt —77Fb 145
Cowper Av. Til —3D 114
Cowper Clo. Brom —70Mc 129
Cowper Clo. Cher —72H 139
Cowper Clo. Well —57Wc 109
Cowper Ct. Wat —9W 4
Cowper Gdns. N14 —16Kb 24
Cowper Gdns. Wall —79Lb 146
Cowper Ho. SE17
—50Sb 83 (7E 206)
(off Browning St.)
Cowper Rd. N14 —18Kb 24
Cowper Rd. N16 —36Ub 63
Cowper Rd. N18 —22Wb 43
Cowper Rd. SW19 —65Eb 125
Cowper Rd. W3 —46Ta 79
Cowper Rd. W7 —45Ha 78
Cowper Rd. Belv —49Cd 88
Cowper Rd. Brom —70Mc 129
Cowper Rd. King T —64Pa 123
Cowper Rd. Rain —42Jd 88
Cowper Rd. Slou —2E 72
Cowper's Ct. EC3
—44Tb 83 (3G 201)
(off Birchin La.)
Cowper St. EC2 —42Tb 83 (5G 195)
Cowper Ter. W10 —43Za 80
Cowslip Clo. Uxb —38N 55
Cowslip La. Hors —3E 188
Cowslip La. Mick —100Ja 176
Cowslip Rd. E18 —26Kc 45
Cowthorpe Rd. SW8 —53Mb 104
Cox Clo. Shenl —4Pa 7
Coxdean. Eps —91Ya 178
Coxes Clo. Stanf —1M 93
Cox Ho. W6 —51Ab 102
(off Field Rd.)
Cox La. Chess —77Pa 143
Cox La. Eps —78Ra 143
Coxley Rise. Purl —85Sb 165
Coxmount Rd. SE7 —50Mc 85
Coxon Way. SE1
—47Vb 83 (2K 207)
Cox's Ct. E1 —43Vb 83 (1K 201)
(off Bell La.)
Coxson Way. SE1
—47Vb 83 (2K 207)
Cox's Wlk. SE21 & SE26
—60Wb 105
Coxtie Grn. Rd. Brtwd —14Qd 31
Coxwell Rd. SE18 —50Tc 86
Coxwell Rd. SE19 —66Ub 127
Coxwold Path. Chess —80Na 143
Crabbs Croft Clo. Orp —78Sc 150
Crab Hill. Beck —66Fc 129
Crab La. Ald —7Da 5
Crabtree Av. Romf —28Zc 47
Crabtree Av. Wemb —40Na 59
Crabtree Clo. Bookh —98Ea 176
Crabtree Clo. Bush —15Da 19
Crabtree Ct. E15 —36Dc 64
Crabtree Ct. New Bar —14Db 23
Crabtree Dri. Lea —96La 176
Crabtree La. SW6 —52Ya 102
(in two parts)
Crabtree La. Bookh —98Ea 176
Crabtree Manorway N. Belv
—47Ed 88
Crabtree Manorway S. Belv
—48Ed 88
Crabtree Office Village. Egh
—68E 118
Crabtree Rd. Egh —68E 118
Crabtree Wlk. SE15 —53Vb 105
(off Exeter Rd.)
Crabtree Wlk. Croy —74Wb 147
Crabwood. Oxt —100Gc 183
Crace St. NW1 —41Mb 82 (3D 192)
Craddock Rd. Enf —13Vb 25
Craddocks Av. Asht —89Na 161
Craddocks Pde. Asht —89Na 161
(in two parts)
Craddock St. NW5 —37Jb 62
Cradley Rd. SE9 —60Tc 108
Cragg Av. Rad —8Ha 6
Craigdale Rd. Horn —30Hd 48
Craig Dri. Uxb —44R 76
Craigen Av. Croy —74Xb 147
Craigerne Rd. SE3 —52Kc 107
Craig Gdns. E18 —26Hc 45
Craigholm. SE18 —54Qc 108
Craigmore Ct. N'wd —24U 36
(off Murray Rd.)
Craig Mt. Rad —7Ka 6
Craigmuir Pk. Wemb —39Pa 59
Craignair Rd. SW2 —59Qb 104
Craignish Av. SW16 —68Pb 126
Craig Pk. Rd. N18 —22Xb 43
Craig Rd. Rich —63La 122
Craig's Ct. SW1 —46Nb 82 (6F 199)
Craigton Rd. SE9 —56Pc 108
Craigweil Clo. Stan —22Ma 39
Craigweil Dri. Stan —22Ma 39
Craigwell Av. Felt —62W 120
Craigwell Av. Rad —7Ka 6
Craigwell Clo. Stai —66G 118
Crailey Av. Enf —12Vb 25
Crail Row. SE17 —49Tb 83 (6G 207)
Crakers Mead. Wat —13X 19
Cramer St. W1 —43Jb 82 (1J 197)
Crammavill St. Grays —46Ce 91
Crammerville Wlk. Rain —42Kd 89
Crammond Clo. W6 —51Ab 102
Cramond Ct. Felt —60U 98
Cramonde Ct. Well —54Wc 109
Crampshaw La. Asht —91Pa 177
Crampton Rd. SE20 —65Yb 128
Cramptons Rd. Sev —92Kd 187
Crampton St. SE17
—49Sb 83 (6D 206)
Cranberry Clo. N'holt —40Z 57
Cranberry La. E16 —42Gc 85
Cranborne Av. S'hall —49Ca 77
Cranborne Av. Surb —76Qa 143
Cranborne Clo. Pot B —3Ab 8
Cranborne Ct. Enf —8Zb 12
Cranborne Cres. Pot B —3Ab 8
Cranborne Gdns. Upm —33Rd 69
Cranborne Ind. Est. Pot B —2Ab 8
Cranborne Pde. Pot B —3Za 8
Cranborne Rd. Bark —39Tc 66
Cranborne Rd. Chesh —4Zb 12
Cranborne Rd. Pot B —3Ab 8
Cranborne Waye. Hay —45Y 77
Cranbourn All. WC2
—45Mb 82 (4E 198)
(off Cranbourn St.)
Cranbourne Av. E11 —28Kc 45
Cranbourne Av. Wind —4D 94
Cranbourne Clo. SW16 —69Nb 126
Cranbourne Clo. Slou —6G 72
Cranbourne Cotts. Wind —2A 116
Cranbourne Dri. Pinn —29Z 37
Cranbourne Gdns. NW11 —29Ab 40
Cranbourne Gdns. Ilf —27Sc 46
Cranbourne Hall Cotts. Wind
—10A 94
Cranbourne Rd. E12 —36Nc 66
Cranbourne Rd. E15 —35Ec 64
Cranbourne Rd. N10 —26Kb 42
Cranbourne Rd. N'wd —27V 36
Cranbourne Rd. Slou —6G 72
Cranbourne Waye. Hay —44X 77
Cranbourn Pl. SE16 —47Xb 83
Cranbourn St. WC2
—45Mb 82 (4E 198)
Cranbrook Clo. Brom —72Jc 149
Cranbrook Ct. Bren —51Ma 101
(off Somerset Rd.)
Cranbrook Dri. Esh —74Ea 142
Cranbrook Dri. Romf —28Kd 49
Cranbrook Dri. Twic —60Da 99
Cranbrook Est. E2 —40Zb 64
Cranbrook Ho. Eri —52Hd 110
(off Boundary St.)
Cranbrook M. E17 —29Bc 44
Cranbrook Pk. N22 —25Qb 42
Cranbrook Point. E16 —46Jc 85
Cranbrook Rise. Ilf —30Pc 46
Cranbrook Rd. SE8 —53Cc 106
Cranbrook Rd. SW19 —66Ab 124
Cranbrook Rd. W4 —50Ua 80
Cranbrook Rd. Barn —16Fb 23
Cranbrook Rd. Bexh —53Bd 109
Cranbrook Rd. Houn —56Ba 99
Cranbrook Rd. Ilf —31Qc 66
Cranbrook Rd. T Hth —68Sb 127
Cranbrook St. E2 —40Zb 64
Cranbury Rd. SW6 —54Db 103
Crandley Ct. SE8 —49Ac 84
Crane Av. W3 —45Sa 79
Crane Av. Isleworth —57Ja 100
Cranebrook. Twic —61Ea 122
Crane Clo. Dag —37Cd 68
Crane Ct. EC4 —44Qb 82 (3A 200)
Crane Ct. Eps —77Sa 143
Cranefield Dri. Wat —4Aa 5
Craneford Clo. Twic —59Ha 100
Craneford Way. Twic —59Ga 100
Crane Gdns. Hay —49V 76
Crane Gro. N7 —37Qb 62
Crane Ho. Felt —62Ca 121
Cranell Grn. S Ock —46Xd 90
Crane Lodge Rd. Houn —51X 99
Cranemead. SE16 —49Zb 84
Crane Mead Ct. Twic —59Ha 100
Crane Pk. Rd. Twic —61Da 121
Crane Rd. Twic —60Ga 100
Cranes Dri. Surb —70Pa 123
Cranes Pk. Surb —70Na 123
Cranes Pk. Av. Surb —70Na 123
Cranes Pk. Cres. Surb —70Pa 123
Crane St. SE10 —50Fc 85
Craneswater. Hay —52V 98
Craneswater Pk. S'hall —50Ba 77
Cranes Way. Borwd —15Sa 21
Crane Way. Twic —59Ea 100
Cranfield Clo. SE27 —62Sb 127
Cranfield Ct. St J —6D 188
Cranfield Cres. Cuff —1Nb 10
Cranfield Dri. NW9 —24Ua 40
Cranfield Rd. SE4 —55Bc 106
Cranfield Rd. E. Cars —81Jb 164
Cranfield Rd. W. Cars —81Jb 164
Cranfield Row. SE1
—48Qb 82 (3A 206)
(off Gerridge St.)
Cranford Av. N13 —22Nb 42
Cranford Av. Stai —59N 97
Cranford Clo. SW20 —66Xa 124
Cranford Clo. Stai —59N 97
Cranford Dri. Hay —49V 76
Cranford La. Hay —51T 98
Cranford La. H'row —53V 98
(in two parts)
Cranford La. Houn —52X 99
Cranford Pk. Rd. Hay —49V 76
Cranford Rise. Esh —78Ea 142
Cranford Rd. Dart —60Nd 111
Cranford St. E1 —45Zb 84
Cranford Way. N8 —28Pb 42
Cranham Gdns. Upm —32Ud 70
Cranham Rd. Horn —30Kd 49
Cranhurst Rd. NW2 —36Ya 60
Cranleigh Clo. SE20 —67Xb 127
Cranleigh Clo. Bex —58Dd 110
Cranleigh Clo. Chesh —1Wb 11
Cranleigh Clo. Orp —76Wc 151
Cranleigh Clo. S Croy —84Wb 165
Cranleigh Dri. Swan —70Gd 132
Cranleigh Gdns. N21 —15Qb 24
Cranleigh Gdns. SE25 —69Ub 127
Cranleigh Gdns. Bark —38Tc 66

Cranleigh Gdns.—Cross Rd.

Cranleigh Gdns. Harr —29Na 39
Cranleigh Gdns. King T —65Pa 123
Cranleigh Gdns. Lou —16Pc 28
Cranleigh Gdns. S'hall —44Ba 77
Cranleigh Gdns. S Croy —84Wb 165
Cranleigh Gdns. Sutt —75Db 145
Cranleigh M. SW11 —54Gb 103
Cranleigh Rd. N15 —29Sb 43
Cranleigh Rd. SW19 —69Cb 125
Cranleigh Rd. Esh —74Ea 142
Cranleigh Rd. Felt —63V 120
Cranleigh St. NW1 —40Lb 62 (2C 192)
Cranley Dene Ct. N10 —28Kb 42
Cranley Dri. Ilf —31Sc 66
Cranley Dri. Ruis —33V 56
Cranley Gdns. N10 —28Kb 42
Cranley Gdns. N13 —20Pb 24
Cranley Gdns. SW7 —50Eb 81 (7A 202)
Cranley Gdns. Wall —80Lb 146
Cranley M. SW7 —50Eb 81 (7A 202)
Cranley Pde. SE9 —63Nc 130
Cranley Pl. SW7 —49Fb 81 (6B 202)
Cranley Pl. Knap —6A 188
Cranley Rd. E13 —43Kc 85
Cranley Rd. Ilf —30Sc 46
Cranley Rd. W on T —78V 140
Cranmer Av. W13 —48Ka 78
Cranmer Clo. Mord —72Za 144
Cranmer Clo. Pot B —2Eb 9
Cranmer Clo. Ruis —32Z 57
Cranmer Clo. Stan —24La 38
Cranmer Clo. Warl —89Ac 166
Cranmer Clo. Wey —80Q 140
Cranmer Ct. N3 —26Ab 40
Cranmer Ct. SW3 —49Gb 81 (6E 202)
Cranmer Ct. SW4 —55Mb 104
Cranmere Ct. Enf —12Qb 24
Cranmer Farm Clo. Mitc —70Hb 125
Cranmer Gdns. Dag —35Ed 68
Cranmer Gdns. Warl —89Ac 166
Cranmer Rd. E7 —35Kc 65
Cranmer Rd. SW9 —52Qb 104
Cranmer Rd. Croy —76Rb 147
Cranmer Rd. Edgw —20Ra 21
Cranmer Rd. Hamp —64Da 121
Cranmer Rd. Hay —44T 76
Cranmer Rd. King T —64Na 123
Cranmer Rd. Mitc —70Hb 125
Cranmer Rd. Sev —95Gd 186
Cranmer St. W1 —43Jb 82
Cranmer Ter. SW17 —64Fb 125
Cranmore Av. Iswth —52Ea 100
Cranmore Cotts. W Hor —100R 174
Cranmore La. W Hor —100R 174
(in two parts)
Cranmore Rd. Brom —62Hc 129
Cranmore Rd. Chst —64Pc 130
Cranmore Way. N10 —28Lb 42
Cranston Clo. Houn —54Aa 99
Cranston Clo. Uxb —33T 56
Cranston Est. N1 —40Tb 63 (2G 195)
Cranston Gdns. E4 —23Dc 44
Cranston Pk. Av. Upm —35Rd 69
Cranston Rd. SE23 —60Ac 106
Cranswick Rd. SE16 —50Xb 83
Crantock Rd. SE6 —61Dc 128
Cranwell Clo. E3 —42Dc 84
Cranwell Gro. Shep —70P 119
Cranwell Rd. Houn —54R 98
Cranwich Av. N21 —17Tb 25
Cranwich Rd. N16 —31Tb 63
Cranwood Ct. EC1
(off Vince St.) —41Tb 83 (4G 195)
Cranwood St. EC1 —41Tb 83 (4G 195)
Cranworth Cres. E4 —18Fc 27
Cranworth Gdns. SW9 —53Qb 104
Craster Rd. SW2 —59Pb 104
Crathie Rd. SE12 —58Kc 107
Cravan Av. Felt —61W 120
Craven Av. W5 —45La 78
Craven Clo. N16 —31Wb 63
Craven Clo. Hay —44W 76
Craven Ct. NW10 —39Ua 60
Craven Ct. Romf —30Ad 47
Craven Gdns. SW19 —64Cb 125
Craven Gdns. Bark —40Uc 66
Craven Gdns. Col R —22Cd 48
Craven Gdns. H Wood —23Sd 50
Craven Gdns. Ilf —26Tc 46
Craven Hill. W2 —45Eb 81 (4A 196)
Craven Hill Gdns. W2 —45Eb 81 (4A 196)
Craven Hill M. W2 —45Eb 81 (4A 196)
Craven M. SW11 —55Jb 104
Craven Pk. NW10 —39Ta 59
Craven Pk. M. NW10 —38Ua 60
Craven Pk. Rd. N15 —30Vb 43
Craven Pk. Rd. NW10 —39Ua 60
Craven Pas. WC2 —46Nb 82 (6F 199)
(off Craven St.)
Craven Rd. NW10 —39Ta 59
Craven Rd. W2 —45Eb 81 (4A 196)
Craven Rd. W5 —45La 78
Craven Rd. Croy —74Xb 147
Craven Rd. King T —67Pa 123
Craven Rd. Orp —76Zc 151
Craven St. WC2 —46Nb 82 (6F 199)
Craven Ter. W2 —45Eb 81 (4A 196)
Craven Wlk. N16 —31Wb 63
Crawford Av. Grays —46De 91
Crawford Av. Wemb —36Ma 59
Crawford Clo. Iswth —54Ga 100
Crawford Compton Clo. Horn —37Ld 69
Crawford Est. SE5 —54Sb 105
Crawford Gdns. N13 —20Rb 25
Crawford Gdns. N'holt —48Ba 77
Crawford M. W1 —43Hb 81 (1F 197)
Crawford Pas. EC1 —42Qb 82 (6A 194)
Crawford Pl. W1 —44Gb 81 (2E 196)
Crawford Point. E16 —44Hc 85
(off Wouldham Rd.)
Crawford Rd. SE5 —53Sb 105
Crawfords. Swan —66Gd 132
Crawford St. W1 —43Gb 81 (1E 196)
Crawley Ct. Grav —7D 114
Crawley Rd. E10 —32Dc 64
Crawley Rd. N22 —26Sb 43
Crawley Rd. Enf —17Ub 25
Crawshaw Rd. Ott —79F 138
Crawshay Clo. Sev —95Jd 186
Crawshay Ct. SW9 —53Qb 104
Crawthew Gro. SE22 —56Vb 105
Cray Av. Asht —88Na 161
Cray Av. Orp —72Xc 151
Craybrooke Rd. Sidc —63Xc 131
Crayburne. S'fleet —64Be 135
Craybury End. SE9 —61Sc 130
Cray Clo. Dart —56Jd 110
Craydene Rd. Eri —53Hd 110
Crayfield Ind. Pk. Orp —68Yc 131
Crayford Clo. E6 —44Nc 86
Crayford High St. Dart —57Gd 110
Crayford Ind. Est. Cray —57Hd 110
Crayford Rd. N7 —35Mb 62
Crayford Rd. Dart —57Hd 110
Crayford Way. Dart —57Hd 110
Crayke Hill. Chess —80Na 143
Craylands. Orp —69Yc 131
Craylands La. Swans —57Zd 113
Craylands Sq. Swans —57Zd 113
Crayle St. Slou —1E 72
Craymill Sq. Dart —54Hd 110
Crayonne Clo. Sun —67U 120
Cray Rd. Belv —51Cd 110
Cray Rd. Sidc —65Yc 131
Cray Rd. Swan —72Ed 153
Crayside Ind. Est. Dart —56Kd 111
Crays Pde., The. St P —68Yc 131
Cray Valley Rd. Orp —72Wc 151
Crealock Gro. Wfd G —22Hc 45
Crealock St. SW18 —58Db 103
Creasey Clo. Horn —33Kd 69
Creasy Clo. Abb L —3V 4
Creasy Est. SE1 —48Ub 83 (4H 207)
Creasy St. SE1 —48Ub 83 (4H 207)
Crebor St. SE22 —58Wb 105
Credenhall Dri. Brom —74Pc 150
Credenhill St. SW16 —65Lb 126
Crediton Hill. NW6 —36Db 61
Crediton Rd. E16 —44Jc 85
Crediton Rd. NW10 —39Za 60
Crediton Way. Clay —78Ja 142
Credon Rd. E13 —40Lc 65
Credon Rd. SE16 —50Xb 83
Credo Way. Grays —51Xd 112
Creechurch La. EC3 —44Ub 83 (3J 201)
Creechurch Pl. EC3 —44Ub 83 (3J 201)
(off Creechurch La.)
Creed Ct. EC4 —44Rb 83 (3C 200)
(off Ludgate Hill)
Creed La. EC4 —44Rb 83 (3C 200)
Creek Rd. SE8 & SE10 —51Cc 106
Creek Rd. Bark —41Vc 87
Creek Rd. E Mol —70Ga 122
Creekside. SE8 —52Dc 106
Creekside. Rain —42Gd 88
Creek, The. Grav —57De 113
Creek, The. Sun —71W 140
Creeland Gro. SE6 —60Bc 106
Cree Way. Romf —24Gd 48
Crefeld Clo. W6 —51Ab 102
Creffield Rd. W5 & W3 —45Pa 79
Creighton Av. E6 —40Mc 65
Creighton Av. N2 & N10 —27Gb 41
Creighton Clo. W12 —45Wa 80
Creighton Rd. N17 —24Ub 43
Creighton Rd. NW6 —40Za 60
Creighton Rd. W5 —48Ma 79
Cremer St. E2 —40Vb 63 (2K 195)
Cremorne Est. SW10 —51Fb 103
Cremorne Gdns. Eps —81Ta 161
Cremorne Rd. SW10 —52Eb 103
Cremorne Rd. Grav —9B 114
Crescent. EC3 —45Vb 83 (4K 201)
Crescent Av. Grays —50Fe 91
(in two parts)
Crescent Av. Horn —33Hd 68
Crescent Cotts. Sev —92Gd 186
Crescent Ct. Grays —50Fe 91
Crescent Ct. Surb —71Ma 143
Crescent Ct. Bus. Cen. E16 —42Fc 85
Crescent Dri. Orp —72Rc 150
Crescent Dri. Shenf —18Ae 33
Crescent E. Barn —10Eb 9
Crescent Gdns. SW19 —62Cb 125
Crescent Gdns. Ruis —31X 57
Crescent Gdns. Swan —68Ed 132
Crescent Gro. SW4 —56Lb 104
Crescent Gro. Mitc —71Gb 145
Crescent Ho. EC1 —42Sb 83 (6D 194)
(off Golden La. Est.)
Crescent La. SW4 —56Lb 104
Crescent M. N22 —25Nb 42
Crescent Pl. SW3 —49Gb 81 (5E 202)
Crescent Rise. N22 —25Mb 42
Crescent Rise. Barn —15Gb 23
Crescent Rd. E4 —17Gc 27
Crescent Rd. E6 —39Lc 65
Crescent Rd. E10 —33Dc 64
Crescent Rd. E13 —39Jc 65
Crescent Rd. E18 —25Lc 45
Crescent Rd. N3 —25Bb 41
Crescent Rd. N8 —30Mb 42
Crescent Rd. N9 —18Wb 25
Crescent Rd. N11 —21Hb 41
Crescent Rd. N15 —27Rb 43
Crescent Rd. N22 —25Mb 42
Crescent Rd. SE18 —50Rc 86
Crescent Rd. SW20 —67Za 124
Crescent Rd. Barn —14Fb 23
Crescent Rd. Beck —68Dc 128
Crescent Rd. Brom —66Jc 129
Crescent Rd. Cat —96Wb 181
Crescent Rd. Dag —34Dd 68
Crescent Rd. Enf —14Rb 25
Crescent Rd. Eri —51Hd 110
Crescent Rd. King T —66Qa 123
Crescent Rd. Sev —92Gd 186
Crescent Rd. Shep —71S 140
Crescent Rd. Sidc —62Vc 131
Crescent Rd. S Ock —47Sd 90
Crescent Rd. War —21Xd 50
Crescent Row. EC1 —42Sb 83 (6D 194)
Crescent Stables. SW15 —57Ab 102
Crescent St. N1 —38Pb 62
Crescent, The. E17 —29Ac 44
Crescent, The. N9 —19Xb 25
Crescent, The. N11 —21Jb 42
Crescent, The. NW2 —34Xa 60
Crescent, The. SW13 —54Wa 102
Crescent, The. SW19 —62Cb 125
Crescent, The. W3 —44Ua 80
Crescent, The. Abb L —2V 4
Crescent, The. Ald —10Da 5
Crescent, The. Ashf —64P 119
Crescent, The. Barn —12Db 23
Crescent, The. Beck —67Cc 128
Crescent, The. Belm —83Cb 163
Crescent, The. Bex —59Yc 109
Crescent, The. Brick —2Ca 5
Crescent, The. Cher —69J 119
Crescent, The. Crox —16R 18
Crescent, The. Croy —72Tb 147
Crescent, The. Egh —65B 118
Crescent, The. Epp —4Vc 15
Crescent, The. Eps —86Qa 161
(in two parts)
Crescent, The. Grav —1B 136
Crescent, The. Grnh —57Yd 112
Crescent, The. Harr —32Ea 58
Crescent, The. Hay —52T 98
Crescent, The. Ilf —30Qc 46
Crescent, The. Lea —94Ka 176
Crescent, The. Long —69Ae 135
Crescent, The. Lou —16Nc 28
Crescent, The. N Mald —68Ta 123
Crescent, The. Sev —93Md 187
Crescent, The. Shep —73V 140
Crescent, The. Sidc —63Vc 131
Crescent, The. Slou —7J 73
Crescent, The. S'hall —47Ba 77
Crescent, The. Surb —71Na 143
Crescent, The. Sutt —78Fb 145
Crescent, The. Upm —31Vd 70
Crescent, The. Wat —14Y 19
Crescent, The. Wemb —33Ka 58
Crescent, The. W Mol —70Ca 121
Crescent, The. W Wick —72Gc 149
Crescent, The. Wey —76Q 140
Crescent, The. Wold —95Cc 182
Crescent View. Lou —16Mc 27
Crescent Wlk. S Ock —45Sd 90
Crescent Way. N12 —23Gb 41
Crescent Way. SE4 —55Cc 106
Crescent Way. SW16 —65Pb 126
Crescent Way. Orp —78Uc 150
Crescent Way. S Ock —46Td 90
Crescent W. Barn —11Eb 23
Crescent Wharf. E16 —47Kc 85
Crescent Wood Rd. SE26 —62Wb 127
Cresford Rd. SW6 —53Db 103
Crespigny Rd. NW4 —30Xa 40
Cressage Clo. S'hall —42Ca 77
Cressage Ho. Bren —51Na 101
(off Ealing Rd.)
Cressal Clo. Lea —92Ka 176
Cressal Mead. Lea —92Ka 176
Cresset Rd. E9 —37Yb 64
Cresset St. SW4 —55Mb 104
Cressfel. Sidc —64Xc 131
Cressfield Clo. NW5 —36Jb 62
Cressida Rd. N19 —32Lb 62
Cressingham Gdns. Est. SW2 —59Qb 104
Cressingham Gro. Sutt —77Eb 145
Cressingham Rd. SE13 —55Ec 106
Cressingham Rd. Edgw —23Ta 39
Cressington Clo. N16 —36Ub 63
Cress Rd. Slou —7F 72
Cresswell. NW9 —26Va 40
Cresswell Gdns. SW5 —50Eb 81 (7A 202)
Cresswell Pk. SE3 —55Hc 107
Cresswell Pl. SW10 —50Eb 81 (7A 202)
Cresswell Rd. SE25 —70Wb 127
Cresswell Rd. Felt —62Aa 121
Cresswell Rd. Twic —58Ma 101
Cresswell Way. N21 —17Qb 24
Cressy Ct. E1 —43Yb 84
Cressy Ct. W6 —48Xa 80
Cressy Houses. E1 —43Yb 84
(off Hannibal Rd.)
Cressy Pl. E1 —43Yb 84
Cressy Rd. NW3 —36Hb 61
Cresta Dri. Wdhm —82H 157
Crest Av. Grays —52De 113
Crestbrook Av. N13 —20Rb 25
Crestbrook Pl. N13 —20Rb 25
(off Green Lanes)
Crest Clo. Badg M —83Dd 170
Crest Ct. NW4 —29Xa 40
Crest Dri. Enf —10Yb 12
Crestfield St. WC1 —41Nb 82 (3G 193)
Crest Gdns. Ruis —34Y 57
Cresthill Av. Grays —49Ee 91
Creston Av. Knap —4B 188
Creston Way. Wor Pk —74Za 144
Crest Rd. NW2 —33Wa 60
Crest Rd. Brom —73Hc 149
Crest Rd. S Croy —80Xb 147
Crest, The. N13 —21Qb 42
Crest, The. NW4 —29Za 40
Crest, The. Surb —71Qa 143
Crest View. Grnh —56Xd 112
Crest View. Pinn —28Z 37
Crest View Dri. Pet W —71Rc 150
Crestway. SW15 —58Wa 102
Crestwood Way. Houn —57Ba 99
Creswell Corner. Knap —5A 188
Creswick Rd. W3 —45Ra 79
Creswick Wlk. E3 —41Cc 84
Creswick Wlk. NW11 —28Bb 41
Crete Hall Rd. Grav —58Fe 113
Creton St. SE18 —48Qc 86
Crewdson Rd. SW9 —52Qb 104
Crewe Ct. Tad —94Ya 178
Crewe Pl. NW10 —41Va 80
Crewe's Av. Warl —88Yb 166
Crewe's Clo. Warl —89Yb 166
Crewe's Farm La. Warl —89Zb 166
Crewe's La. Warl —88Yb 166
Crews Hill. Enf —6Pb 10
Crews St. E14 —49Cc 84
Crewys Rd. NW2 —33Bb 61
Crewys Rd. SE15 —54Xb 105
Crichton Av. Wall —78Mb 146
Crichton Gdns. Romf —31Cd 68
Crichton Ho. Sidc —65Zc 131
Crichton Rd. Cars —80Hb 145
Cricketers Clo. N14 —17Lb 24
Cricketers Clo. Chess —77Ma 143
Cricketers Clo. Eri —50Gd 88
Cricketer's Ct. SE11 —49Rb 83 (6B 206)
Cricketers La. Heron —24Fe 51
Cricketers Rd. Enf —12Sb 25
Cricketers Row. Heron —24Fe 51
Cricketfield Rd. E5 —35Xb 63
Cricket Field Rd. Uxb —39M 55
Cricketfield Rd. W Dray —49L 75
Cricket Grn. Mitc —69Hb 125
Cricket Ground Rd. Chst —67Rc 130
Cricket La. Beck —64Ac 128
Cricket Way. Wey —75U 140
Cricklade Av. SW2 —61Nb 126
Cricklade Av. Romf —23Md 49
Cricklewood B'way. NW2 —34Ya 60
Cricklewood La. NW2 —35Za 60
Cricklewood Trading Est. NW2 —34Ab 60
Cridland St. E15 —39Hc 65
Crieff Ct. Tedd —66La 122
Crieff Rd. SW18 —58Eb 103
Criffel Av. SW2 —61Mb 126
Crimp Hill. Old Win & Egh —9K 95
Crimscott St. SE1 —48Ub 83 (4J 207)
Crimsworth Rd. SW8 —53Mb 104
Crinan St. N1 —40Nb 62 (1G 193)
Cringle St. SW8 —52Lb 104
Cripplegate St. EC2 —43Sb 83 (7E 194)
Cripps Grn. Hay —42X 77
Crispe Ho. N1 —39Pb 62 (1J 193)
(off Barnsbury Est.)
Crispe Ho. Bark —40Tc 66
Crispen Rd. Felt —63Aa 121
Crispian Clo. NW10 —35Ua 60
Crispin Clo. Asht —89Pa 161
Crispin Clo. Croy —75Nb 146
Crispin Cres. Croy —76Mb 146
Crispin Lodge. N11 —22Hb 41
Crispin Rd. Edgw —23Sa 39
Crispin St. E1 —43Vb 83 (1K 201)
Crispin Way. Farn C —5H 53
Crisp Rd. W6 —50Ya 80
Cristowe Rd. SW6 —54Bb 103
Criterion M. N19 —33Mb 62
Crockenhall Way. Grav —6A 136
Crockenhill La. Eyns —73Jd 152
Crockenhill Rd. Orp & Swan —71Zc 151
Crockenhill Rd. Swan —72Dd 152
Crockerton Rd. SW17 —61Hb 125
Crockery La. E Clan —100N 173
Crockford Clo. Add —77L 139
Crockford Pk. Rd. Add —78L 139
Crockham Way. SE9 —63Qc 130
Crocus Clo. Croy —74Zb 148
Crocus Field. Barn —16Bb 23
Croffets. Tad —93Za 178
Croft Av. W Wick —74Ec 148
Croft Clo. NW7 —20Ua 22
Croft Clo. Belv —50Bd 87
Croft Clo. Chfd —2J 3
Croft Clo. Chst —64Pc 130
Croft Clo. Hay —52S 98
Croft Clo. Uxb —38Q 56
Croft Ct. SE13 —58Ec 106
Croftdown Rd. NW5 —34Jb 62
Croft End Rd. Chfd —2J 3
Crofters Clo. Iswth —57Fa 100
Crofters Mead. Croy —81Bc 166
Crofters Rd. N'wd —21U 36
Crofters, The. Old Win —8L 95
Crofters Way. NW1 —39Mb 62
Croft Field. Chfd —2J 3
Croft Gdns. W7 —47Ja 78
Croft Gdns. Ruis —32U 56
Crofthill Rd. Slou —2F 72
Croft Ho. E17 —28Dc 44
Croft La. Chfd —2J 3
Croftleigh Av. Purl —88Rb 165
Croft Lodge Clo. Wfd G —23Kc 45
Croft Meadow. Chfd —2J 3
Crofton. Asht —90Na 161
Crofton Av. W4 —52Ta 101
Crofton Av. Bex —59Zc 109
Crofton Av. Orp —75Sc 150
Crofton Av. W on T —76Y 141
Crofton Clo. Ott —80E 138
Croftongate Way. SE4 —57Ac 106
Crofton La. Orp —74Tc 150
Crofton Pk. Rd. SE4 —58Bc 106
Crofton Rd. E13 —42Kc 85
Crofton Rd. SE5 —53Ub 105
Crofton Rd. Grays —7A 92
Crofton Rd. Orp —76Qc 150
Crofton Ter. E5 —36Ac 64
Crofton Ter. Rich —56Pa 101
Crofton Way. Barn —16Db 23
Crofton Way. Enf —12Qb 24
Croft Rd. SW16 —67Qb 126
Croft Rd. SW19 —66Eb 125
Croft Rd. Brom —65Jc 129
Croft Rd. Enf —11Ac 26
Croft Rd. Ger X —26A 34
Croft Rd. Sutt —78Gb 145
Croft Rd. W'ham —98Rc 184
Croft Rd. Wold —94Cc 182
Crofts Rd. Harr —30Ja 38
Crofts St. E1 —45Wb 83
Crofts, The. Shep —70U 120
Crofts Vs. Harr —30Ja 38
Croft St. SE8 —49Ac 84
Croft, The. NW10 —40Va 60
Croft, The. W5 —43Na 79
Croft, The. Barn —14Ab 22
Croft, The. Eps —86Va 162
Croft, The. Houn —52Aa 99
Croft, The. Lou —12Qc 28
Croft, The. Pinn —31Ba 57
Croft, The. Ruis —35Y 57
Croft, The. Swan —69Ed 132
Croft, The. Wemb —36La 58
Croftway. NW3 —35Cb 61
Croftway. Rich —62Ka 122
Croft Way. Sev —97Hd 186
Croft Way. Sidc —62Uc 130
Crogsland Rd. NW1 —38Jb 62
Croham Clo. S Croy —80Ub 147
Croham Mnr. Rd. S Croy —80Ub 147
Croham Mt. S Croy —80Ub 147
Croham Pk. Av. S Croy —78Vb 147
Croham Rd. S Croy —78Ub 147
Croham Valley Rd. S Croy —79Wb 147
Croindene Rd. SW16 —67Nb 126
Crokesley Ho. Edgw —26Sa 39
(off Burnt Oak B'way.)
Cromar Ct. Hors —4F 188
Cromartie Rd. N19 —31Mb 62
Cromarty Ct. SW2 —57Pb 104
Cromarty Ho. E1 —43Ac 84
Cromarty Rd. Edgw —19Ra 21
Cromberdale Ct. N17 —25Wb 43
(off Spencer Rd.)
Crombie Clo. Ilf —29Pc 46
Crombie M. SW11 —54Gb 103
Crombie Rd. Sidc —60Tc 108
Cromer Clo. Uxb —44S 76
Cromer Pl. Orp —74Tc 150
Cromer Rd. E10 —31Fc 65
Cromer Rd. N17 —26Wb 43
Cromer Rd. SE25 —69Xb 127
Cromer Rd. SW17 —65Jb 126
Cromer Rd. Barn —14Eb 23
Cromer Rd. Chad —30Ad 47
Cromer Rd. Horn —31Md 69
Cromer Rd. H'row A —54Q 98
Cromer Rd. Romf —30Ed 48
Cromer Rd. Wat —10Y 5
Cromer Rd. Wfd G —21Jc 45
Cromer Rd. W. Houn —55Q 98
Cromer St. WC1 —41Nb 82 (4F 193)
Cromer Ter. E8 —36Wb 63
Cromer Vs. Rd. SW18 —58Bb 103
Cromford Clo. Orp —76Uc 150
Cromford Path. E5 —35Zb 64
Cromford Rd. SW18 —57Cb 103
Cromford Way. N Mald —68Ta 123
Cromlix Clo. Chst —68Rc 130
Crompton Pl. Eri —51Hd 110
Crompton St. W2 —42Fb 81 (6B 190)
Cromwell Av. N6 —32Kb 62
Cromwell Av. W6 —50Xa 80
Cromwell Av. Brom —70Kc 129
Cromwell Av. Chesh —2Wb 11
Cromwell Av. N Mald —71Va 144
Cromwell Cen. NW10 —41Ta 79
Cromwell Clo. E1 —46Wb 83
Cromwell Clo. N2 —28Fb 41
Cromwell Clo. W3 —46Sa 79
Cromwell Clo. Brom —70Kc 129
Cromwell Clo. Crox —15Q 18
Cromwell Clo. W on T —74X 141
Cromwell Ct. Enf —15Zb 26
Cromwell Cres. SW5 —49Cb 81
Cromwell Dri. Slou —4J 73
Cromwell Gdns. SW7 —48Fb 81 (4C 202)
Cromwell Gro. W6 —48Ya 80
Cromwell Gro. Cat —93Sb 181
Cromwell Highwalk. EC2
(off Barbican) —43Sb 83 (7E 194)
Cromwell Ind. Est. E10 —32Ac 64
Cromwell Lodge. Bexh —57Ad 109
Cromwell M. SW7 —49Fb 81 (5C 202)
Cromwell Pl. EC2
(off Barbican) —43Sb 83 (7E 194)
Cromwell Pl. N6 —32Kb 62
Cromwell Pl. SW7 —49Fb 81 (5C 202)
Cromwell Pl. SW14 —55Sa 101
Cromwell Rd. E7 —38Lc 65
Cromwell Rd. E17 —29Ec 44
Cromwell Rd. N3 —25Eb 41
Cromwell Rd. N10 —24Jb 42
(in two parts)
Cromwell Rd. SW5 & SW7 —49Cb 81
Cromwell Rd. SW9 —53Rb 105
Cromwell Rd. SW19 —64Cb 125
Cromwell Rd. Asc —10A 116
Cromwell Rd. Beck —68Ac 128
Cromwell Rd. Borwd —11Na 21
Cromwell Rd. Cat —93Sb 181
Cromwell Rd. Croy —73Tb 147
Cromwell Rd. Felt —60X 99
Cromwell Rd. Grays —49Ce 91
Cromwell Rd. Hay —44T 76
Cromwell Rd. Houn —56Ca 99
Cromwell Rd. King T —67Na 123
Cromwell Rd. Tedd —65Ja 122
Cromwell Rd. W on T —74X 141
Cromwell Rd. War —21Xd 50
Cromwell Rd. Wemb —40Na 59
Cromwell Rd. Wor Pk —76Ta 143
Cromwells Mere. Romf —23Fd 48
Cromwell St. Houn —56Ca 99
Cromwell Tower. EC2
(off Barbican) —43Sb 83 (7E 194)
Crondace Rd. SW6 —53Cb 103
Crondall Ct. N1 —40Tb 63 (2G 195)
(off St Johns Est.)
Crondall St. N1 —40Tb 63 (2G 195)
Crooked Billet. SW19 —65Ya 124
Crooked Billet Yd. E2 —41Ub 83 (3J 195)
Crooked La. Grav —8D 114
Crooked Mile. Wal A —5Ec 12
Crooked Usage. N3 —27Ab 40
Crooke Rd. SE8 —50Ac 84
Crookham Rd. SW6 —53Bb 103
Crook Log. Bexh —55Zc 109
Crookston Rd. SE9 —55Qc 108
Croombs Rd. E16 —43Lc 85
Croom's Hill. SE10 —52Ec 106
Croom's Hill Gro. SE10 —52Ec 106
Cropley St. N1 —40Tb 63 (1F 195)
Croppath Rd. Dag —35Cd 68
Cropthorne Ct. W9 —41Eb 81 (4A 190)
(off Maida Vale)
Crosbie. NW9 —26Va 40
Crosbie Ho. E17 —27Ec 44
(off Prospect Hill.)
Crosby Clo. Felt —62Aa 121
Crosby Clo. Mount —11Fe 33
Crosby Ct. SE1 —47Tb 83 (1F 207)
(off Crosby Row)
Crosby Ct. Chig —20Wc 29
Crosby Ho. E7 —37Jc 65
Crosby Rd. E7 —37Jc 65
Crosby Rd. Dag —40Dd 68
Crosby Row. SE1 —47Tb 83 (2F 207)
Crosby Row. SW1 —47Tb 83
Crosby Sq. EC3 —44Ub 83 (3H 201)
Crosby Wlk. E8 —37Vb 63
Crosby Wlk. SW2 —59Qb 104
Crosier Rd. Uxb —35S 56
Crosier Way. Ruis —34U 56
Crosland Pl. SW11 —55Jb 104
Crossacres. Wok —87G 156
Cross Av. SE10 —51Fc 107
Crossbow Rd. Chig —22Vc 47
Crossbrook Rd. SE3 —55Nc 108
Crossbrook St. Wal X —3Zb 12
Cross Deep. Twic —61Ha 122
Cross Deep Gdns. Twic —61Ha 122
Crossfield Pl. Wey —80R 140
Crossfield Rd. N17 —27Sb 43
Crossfield Rd. NW3 —37Fb 61
Crossfields. Lou —15Rc 28
Crossfield St. SE8 —52Cc 106
Crossford St. SW9 —54Pb 104
Cross Ga. Edgw —20Qa 21
Crossgate. Gnfd —37Ka 58
Crossing Rd. Epp —4Wc 15
Cross Keys Clo. W1 —43Jb 82 (1J 197)
Cross Keys Clo. Sev —99Jd 186
Cross Keys Cotts. Sev —99Jd 186
Cross Keys Sq. EC1 —43Sb 83 (1D 200)
(off Lit. Britain)
Cross Lances Rd. Houn —56Da 99
Crossland Rd. T Hth —72Rb 147
Crosslands. Cher —77G 138
Crosslands Av. W5 —46Pa 79
Crosslands Av. S'hall —50Ba 77
Crosslands Rd. Eps —79Ta 143
Cross La. EC3 —45Ub 83 (5H 201)
Cross La. N8 —27Pb 42
(in two parts)
Cross La. Bex —59Bd 109
Cross La. Ott —79D 138
Cross La. E. Grav —1D 136
Cross Lanes. Ger X —22A 34
Cross Lanes Clo. Ger X —22B 34
Cross La. W. Grav —1D 136
Crosslet St. SE17 —49Tb 83 (5G 207)
Crosslet Vale. SE10 —53Dc 106
Crossley Clo. Big H —87Mc 167
Crossley St. N7 —37Qb 62
Crossmead. SE9 —60Pc 108
Crossmead. Wat —16X 19
Crossmead Av. Gnfd —41Ca 77
Crossness Footpath. Eri —46Bd 87
Crossness La. SE28 —45Zc 87
Crossness Rd. Bark —41Vc 87
Cross Oak. Wind —4E 94
Crossoaks La. Borwd & S Mim —7Ta 7
Crosspath. Rad —7Ja 6
Cross Rd. E4 —18Gc 27
Cross Rd. N11 —22Kb 42
Cross Rd. N22 —24Qb 42
Cross Rd. SW19 —66Cb 125
Cross Rd. Belm —82Cb 163
Cross Rd. Brom —75Nc 150
Cross Rd. Chad —31Yc 67
Cross Rd. Croy —74Tb 147
Cross Rd. Dart —58Ld 111

Dale End—De Frene Rd.

Dale End. Dart —58Hd 110
Dale Gdns. Wfd G —21Kc 45
Dalegarth Gdns. Purl —85Tb 165
Dale Grn. Rd. N11 —20Kb 24
Dale Gro. N12 —22Eb 41
Daleham Av. Egh —65C 118
Daleham Dri. Uxb —44R 76
Daleham Gdns. NW3 —36Fb 61
Daleham M. NW3 —37Fb 61
Dale Lodge. N6 —30Lb 42
Dale Lodge Rd. Asc —10E 116
Dale Pk. Av. Cars —75Hb 145
Dale Pk. Rd. SE19 —67Tb 127
Dale Rd. NW5 —36Jb 62
Dale Rd. SE17 —51Rb 105
Dale Rd. Dart —58Hd 110
Dale Rd. Gnfd —43Da 77
Dale Rd. Purl —84Qb 164
Dale Rd. S'fleet —63Ce 135
Dale Rd. Sun —66V 120
Dale Rd. Sutt —77Bb 145
Dale Rd. Swan —68Ed 132
Dale Rd. W on T —73V 140
Dale Row. W11 —44Ab 80
Dale Side. Ger X —32A 54
Daleside. Orp —78Wc 151
Daleside Clo. Orp —79Wc 151
Daleside Dri. Pot B —5Bb 9
Daleside Gdns. Chig —20Sc 28
Daleside Rd. SW16 —64Kb 126
Daleside Rd. Eps —79Ta 143
Dales Path. Borwd —15Ta 21
Dales Rd. Borwd —15Ta 21
Dale St. W4 —50Ua 80
Dale, The. Kes —77Mc 149
Dale, The. Wal A —6Gc 13
Dale View. Eri —54Hd 110
Dale View. H'ley —95Ra 177
Dale View. Wok —6E 188
Dale View Av. E4 —19Ec 26
Dale View Cres. E4 —19Ec 26
Dale View Gdns. E4 —20Fc 27
Daleview Rd. N15 —30Ub 43
Dale Wlk. Dart —60Sd 112
Dalewood Clo. Horn —31Pd 69
Dalewood Gdns. Wor Pk —75Xa 144
Dale Wood Rd. Orp —73Uc 150
Daley St. E9 —37Zb 64
Daley Thompson Way. SW8 —55Kb 104
Dalgarno Gdns. W10 —43Ya 80
Dalgarno Way. W10 —42Ya 80
Dalgleish St. E14 —44Ac 84
Daling Way. E3 —40Ac 64
Dalkeith Gro. Stan —22Ma 39
Dalkeith Rd. SE21 —60Sb 105
Dalkeith Rd. Ilf —34Sc 66
Dallas Rd. NW4 —31Wa 60
Dallas Rd. SE26 —62Xb 127
Dallas Rd. W5 —43Pa 79
Dallas Rd. Sutt —79Ab 144
Dallas Ter. Hay —48V 76
Dallega Clo. Hay —45T 76
Dallinger Rd. SE12 —58Hc 107
Dalling Rd. W6 —49Xa 80
Dallington Clo. W on T —79Y 141
Dallington St. EC1 —42Rb 83 (5C 194)
Dallin Rd. SE18 —52Rc 108
Dallin Rd. Bexh —56Zc 109
Dalmain Rd. SE23 —60Zb 106
Dalmally Rd. Croy —73Vb 147
Dalmeny Av. N7 —35Mb 62
Dalmeny Av. SW16 —68Qb 126
Dalmeny Clo. Wemb —37La 58
Dalmeny Cres. Houn —56Fa 100
Dalmeny Rd. N7 —34Mb 62
Dalmeny Rd. Barn —16Eb 23
Dalmeny Rd. Cars —80Jb 146
Dalmeny Rd. Eri —53Dd 110
Dalmeny Rd. Wor Pk —76Xa 144
Dalmeyer Rd. NW10 —37Va 60
Dalmore Av. Clay —79Ga 142
Dalmore Rd. SE21 —61Sb 127
Dalroy Clo. S Ock —44Wd 90
Dalrymple Clo. N14 —17Mb 24
Dalrymple Rd. SE4 —56Ac 106
Dalston Cross Shopping Cen. E8 —37Vb 63
Dalston Gdns. Stan —25Na 39
Dalston La. E8 —37Vb 63
Dalton Av. Mitc —68Gb 125
Dalton Clo. Hay —42T 76
Dalton Clo. Orp —76Uc 150
Dalton Clo. Purl —84Sb 165
Dalton Rd. W'stone —26Fa 38
Daltons Rd. Orp & Swan —76Dd 152
Daltons Rd. Swan —74Ed 152
Dalton St. SE27 —61Rb 127
Dalwood St. SE5 —53Ub 105
Daly Ct. E15 —36Dc 64
Dalyell Rd. SW9 —55Pb 104
Damascene Wlk. SE21 —60Wa 102
Damask Cres. E16 —42Gc 85
Damer Ter. SW10 —52Eb 103
Dames Rd. E7 —34Jc 65
Dame St. N1 —40Sb 63 (1D 194)
Damien St. E1 —44Xb 83
Damigos Rd. Grav —10H 115
Damon Clo. Sidc —62Xc 131
Damson Ct. Swan —70Fd 132
Damsonwood Rd. S'hall —48Ca 77
Danbrook Rd. SW16 —67Nb 126
Danbury Clo. Pil H —15Vd 32
Danbury Clo. Romf —27Zc 47
Danbury Mans. Bark —38Rc 66
(off Whiting Av.)
Danbury M. Wall —77Kb 146
Danbury Rd. Lou —17Nc 28
Danbury Rd. Rain —39Hd 68
Danbury St. N1 —40Rb 63 (1C 194)
Danbury Way. Wfd G —23Lc 45
Danby Ct. Enf —13Sb 25
(off Horshoe La.)
Danby St. SE15 —55Vb 105
Dancer Rd. SW6 —53Bb 103
Dancer Rd. Rich —55Qa 101
Dancers Hill Rd. Barn —8Ya 8
Dancers La. Barn —7Ya 8
Dando Cres. SE3 —55Kc 107
Dandridge Clo. SE10 —50Hc 85
Dandridge Clo. Slou —9P 73
Danebury. New Ad —79Dc 148
Danebury Av. SW15 —58Ua 102
(in two parts)
Daneby Rd. SE6 —62Dc 128
Dane Clo. Bex —59Cd 110
Dane Clo. Orp —78Tc 150
Dane Ct. Wok —87H 157
Danecourt Gdns. Croy —76Vb 147
Danecroft Rd. SE24 —57Sb 105
Danehill Wlk. Sidc —62Wc 131
Dane Ho. N14 —17Mb 24
Danehurst Ct. Eps —85Va 162
Danehurst Gdns. Ilf —29Nc 46
Danehurst St. SW6 —53Ab 102
Daneland. Barn —16Hb 23
Danemead Gro. N'holt —36Da 57
Danemere St. SW15 —55Ya 102
Dane Pl. E3 —40Bc 64
Dane Rd. N18 —21Yb 44
Dane Rd. SW19 —67Eb 125
Dane Rd. W13 —46La 78
Dane Rd. Ashf —65S 120
Dane Rd. Ilf —36Sc 66
Dane Rd. Otf —89Hd 170
Dane Rd. S'hall —45Aa 77
Dane Rd. Warl —89Zb 166
Danesbury Rd. Felt —60X 99
Danes Clo. Grav —62Ee 135
Danes Clo. Oxs —86Ea 160
Danescombe. SE12 —60Jc 107
Danes Ct. Wemb —34Ra 59
Danescourt Cres. Sutt —75Eb 145
Danescroft. NW4 —29Za 40
Danescroft Av. NW4 —29Za 40
Danescroft Gdns. NW4 —29Za 40
Danesdale Rd. E9 —37Ac 64
Danesfield. SE17 —51Ub 105
(off Albany Rd.)
Danes Ga. Harr —27Ga 38
Danes Hill. Wok —90D 156
Danes Rd. Romf —31Ed 68
Danes, The. Park —1Ea 6
Dane St. WC1 —43Pb 82 (1H 199)
Danes Way. Oxs —86Fa 160
Danes Way. Pil H —15Wd 32
Daneswood Av. SE6 —62Ec 128
Daneswood Clo. Wey —78R 140
Danethorpe Rd. Wemb —37Ma 59
Danetree Clo. Eps —80Sa 143
Danetree Rd. Eps —80Sa 143
Danette Gdns. Dag —33Cd 68
Daneville Rd. SE5 —53Tb 105
Dangan Rd. E11 —30Jc 45
Daniel Bolt Clo. E14 —43Dc 84
Daniel Clo. N18 —21Yb 44
Daniel Clo. SW17 —65Gb 125
Daniel Clo. Chaf H —47Ae 91
Daniel Clo. Grays —8D 92
Daniel Ct. NW9 —25Ua 40
Daniel Gdns. SE15 —52Vb 105
Daniel Ho. N1 —40Tb 63 (1G 195)
(off Cranston Est.)
Daniel Pl. NW4 —31Xa 60
Daniel Rd. W5 —45Pa 79
Daniels La. Warl —88Bc 166
Daniels Rd. SE15 —55Yb 106
Daniel Way. Bans —86Db 163
Danleigh Ct. N14 —17Mb 24
Dan Leno Wlk. SW6 —52Db 103
Dansey Pl. W1 —45Mb 82 (4D 198)
(off Wardour St.)
Dansington Rd. Well —56Wc 109
Danson Cres. Well —55Xc 109
Danson La. Well —56Xc 109
Danson Mead. Well —55Yc 109
Danson Rd. Bex & Bexh —57Zc 109
(in two parts)
Danson Underpass. Sidc —58Yc 109
Dante Pl. SE11 —49Rb 83 (6C 206)
(off Dante Rd.)
Dante Rd. SE11 —49Rb 83 (5B 206)
Danube St. SW3 —50Gb 81 (7E 202)
Danvers Rd. N8 —28Mb 42
Danvers St. SW3 —51Fb 103
Danyon Clo. Rain —40Ld 69
Danziger Way. Borwd —11Sa 21
Daphne Gdns. E4 —20Ec 26
Daphne Ho. N22 —25Qb 42
(off Acacia Rd.)
Daphne St. SW18 —58Eb 103
Daplyn St. E1 —43Wb 83
D'Arblay St. W1 —44Lb 82 (3C 198)
Darby Clo. Cat —94Sb 181
Darby Cres. Sun —68Y 121
Darby Dri. Wal A —5Ec 12
Darby Gdns. Sun —68Y 121
Darcy Av. Wall —77Lb 146
Darcy Clo. N20 —19Fb 23
Darcy Clo. Chesh —3Ac 12
Darcy Clo. Coul —91Rb 181
Darcy Clo. Hut —17De 33
D'Arcy Dri. Harr —28Ma 39
Darcy Gdns. Dag —39Bd 67
D'Arcy Gdns. Harr —28Ma 39
D'Arcy Pl. Asht —89Pa 161
Darcy Rd. SW16 —68Nb 126
D'Arcy Rd. Asht —89Pa 161
D'Arcy Rd. Sutt —77Za 144
Dare Ct. E10 —31Ec 64
Dare Gdns. Dag —34Ad 67
Darell Rd. Rich —55Qa 101
Darenth Clo. Chip —94Ed 186
Darenth Dri. Grav —10K 115
Darenth Gdns. W'ham —98Tc 184
Darenth Hill. Dart —64Rd 133
Darenth La. Dun G —93Gd 186
Darenth La. S Ock —44Wd 90
Darenth Rd. N16 —31Vb 63
Darenth Rd. Dart —59Pd 111
Darenth Rd. Hawl —63Rd 133
Darenth Rd. Well —53Wc 109
Darenth Way. Shor —83Jd 170
Darenth Wood Rd. Dart —63Ud 134
(in two parts)
Darent Ind. Est. Eri —51Ld 111
Darent Mead. S at H —67Rd 133
Darfield Rd. SE4 —57Bc 106
Darfield Way. W10 —44Za 80
Darfur St. SW15 —55Za 102
Dargate Clo. SE19 —66Vb 127
Darien Rd. SW11 —55Fb 103
Darkeys La. Pot B —4Bb 9
Dark Ho. Wharf. EC3 —45Tb 83 (5G 201)
Dark La. Chesh —2Wb 11
Dark La. Gt War —22Vd 50
Darlan Rd. SW6 —52Bb 103
Darlaston Rd. SW19 —66Za 124
Darley Clo. Add —78L 139
Darley Clo. Croy —72Ac 148
Darley Croft. Park —1Da 5
Darley Dene Ct. Add —77L 139
Darley Dri. N Mald —68Ta 123
Darley Gdns. Mord —72Eb 145
Darley Ho. SE11 —50Pb 82 (7H 205)
(off Laud St.)
Darley Rd. N9 —18Vb 25
Darley Rd. SW11 —58Hb 103
Darling Rd. SE4 —55Cc 106
Darling Row. E1 —42Xb 83
Darlington Gdns. Romf —22Md 49
Darlington Path. Romf —22Md 49
Darlington Rd. SE27 —64Rb 127
Darlton Clo. Dart —55Hd 110
Darlton Ct. Pil H —16Wd 32
Darmaine Clo. S Croy —80Sb 147
Darnay Ho. SE16 —48Wb 83
Darnets Field. Otf —89Hd 170
Darnley Ct. Grav —9C 114
(off Darnley Rd.)
Darnley Pk. Wey —76Q 140
Darnley Rd. E9 —37Yb 64
Darnley Rd. Grav —10C 114
(in two parts)
Darnley Rd. Grays —51De 113
Darnley Rd. Wfd G —25Jc 45
Darnley St. Grav —9C 114
Darnley Ter. W11 —46Za 80
Darrel Clo. Langl —49B 74
Darrell Rd. SE22 —57Wb 105
Darren Clo. N4 —31Pb 62
Darrick Wood Rd. Orp —75Tc 150
Darrington Rd. Borwd —11Na 21
Darris Clo. Hay —42Aa 77
Darsley Dri. SW8 —53Mb 104
Dart Clo. Slou —51D 96
Dart Clo. Upm —30Td 50
Dartfields. Romf —23Md 49
Dartford Av. N9 —16Yb 26
Dartford By-Pass. Bex & Dart —60Gd 110
Dartford Crossing. Dart & Grays —55Td 112
Dartford Rd. Bex —60Ed 110
Dartford Rd. Dart —58Jd 110
Dartford Rd. F'ham —72Pd 153
(in two parts)
Dartford Rd. Sev —96Ld 187
Dartford St. SE17 —51Sb 105
Dartford Trade Pk. Dart —61Nd 133
Dartford Tunnel. Dart & Grays —55Td 112
Dartford Tunnel App. Rd. Dart —59Rd 111
Dart Grn. S Ock —43Xd 90
Dartington Ho. SW8 —54Mb 104
(off Union Gro.)
Dartmoor Wlk. E14 —49Cc 84
(off Charnwood Gdns.)
Dartmouth Av. Sheer —86E 156
Dartmouth Clo. W11 —44Cb 81
Dartmouth Ct. SE10 —53Fc 107
Dartmouth Grn. Wok —86F 156
Dartmouth Gro. SE10 —53Ec 106
Dartmouth Hill. SE10 —53Ec 106
Dartmouth Pk. Av. NW5 —34Kb 62
Dartmouth Pk. Hill. N19 & NW5 —32Kb 62
Dartmouth Pk. Rd. NW5 —35Kb 62
Dartmouth Path. Wok —86F 156
Dartmouth Pl. SE23 —61Yb 128
Dartmouth Pl. W4 —51Ua 102
Dartmouth Rd. NW2 —37Za 60
Dartmouth Rd. NW4 —30Wa 40
Dartmouth Rd. SE26 & SE23 —62Xb 127
Dartmouth Rd. Brom —73Jc 149
Dartmouth Rd. Ruis —34W 56
Dartmouth Row. SE10 —53Ec 106
Dartmouth St. SW1 —47Mb 82 (2E 204)
Dartmouth Ter. SE10 —53Fc 107
Dartnell Av. W Byf —84K 157
Dartnell Clo. W Byf —84K 157
Dartnell Cres. W Byf —84K 157
Dartnell Pk. Rd. W Byf —84K 157
Dartnell Pl. W Byf —84K 157
Dartnell Rd. Croy —73Vb 147
Dartnon Ct. W3 —46Sa 79
Dartrey Tower. SW10 —52Eb 103
(off Worlds End Est.)
Dartrey Wlk. SW10 —52Fb 103
Dart St. W10 —41Ab 80
Dartview Clo. Grays —9A 92
Darvel Clo. Wok —4D 188
Darville Rd. N16 —34Vb 63
Darvill's La. Slou —7H 73
Darwell Clo. E6 —40Qc 66
Darwin Clo. N11 —20Kb 24
Darwin Clo. Orp —78Tc 150
Darwin Dri. S'hall —44Da 77
Darwin Gdns. Wat —22Y 37
Darwin Rd. N22 —25Rb 43
Darwin Rd. W5 —50La 78
Darwin Rd. Slou —47B 74
Darwin Rd. Til —3B 114
Darwin Rd. Well —55Vc 109
Darwin St. SE17 —49Tb 83 (5G 207)
(in two parts)
Darynngton Dri. Gnfd —40Ga 58
Dashwood Clo. Bexh —57Cd 110
Dashwood Clo. Slou —9N 73
Dashwood Clo. W Byf —84L 157
Dashwood Rd. N8 —30Pb 42
Dashwood Rd. Grav —10C 114
Dassett Rd. SE27 —64Rb 127
Datchelor Pl. SE5 —53Tb 105
Datchet Pl. Dat —3M 95
Datchet Rd. SE6 —61Bc 128
Datchet Rd. Hort —55B 96
Datchet Rd. Old Win —6L 95
Datchet Rd. Slou —9K 73
Datchet Rd. Wind —2H 95
Datchworth Ct. Enf —15Ub 25
Date St. SE17 —50Tb 83 (7E 206)
Daubeney Gdns. N17 —24Sb 43
Daubeney Rd. E5 —35Ac 64
Daubeney Rd. N17 —24Sb 43
Dault Rd. SW18 —58Eb 103
Dauncey Ho. SE1 —47Rb 83 (2B 206)
(off Webber Row)
Davema Clo. Chst —67Qc 130
Davenant Rd. N19 —33Mb 62
Davenant Rd. Croy —77Rb 147
Davenant St. E1 —43Wb 83
Davenham Av. N'wd —22V 36
Davenport Clo. Tedd —65Ja 122
Davenport Ho. SE11 —49Qb 82 (5K 205)
(off Walnut Tree Wlk.)
Davenport Lodge. Houn —52Aa 99
Davenport Rd. SE6 —58Dc 106
Davenport Rd. Sidc —61Ad 131
Daventer Dri. Stan —24Ha 38
Daventry Av. E17 —30Cc 44
Daventry Clo. Coln —53H 97
Daventry Gdns. Romf —22Ld 49
Daventry Grn. Romf —22Ld 49
Daventry Rd. Romf —22Ld 49
Daventry St. NW1 —43Gb 81 (7D 190)
Daver Ct. SW3 —50Gb 81 (7E 202)
Davern Clo. SE10 —49Hc 85
Davey Clo. N7 —37Pb 62
Davey Rd. E9 —38Cc 64
Davey's Ct. WC2 —45Nb 82 (4F 199)
(off Bedfordbury)
Davey St. SE15 —51Vb 105
David Av. Gnfd —41Ga 78
David Clo. Hay —52U 98
David Coffer Ct. Belv —49Dd 88
David Ct. N20 —20Eb 23
David Crompton Lodge, The. H Hill —22Nd 49
David Dri. Romf —23Qd 49
Davidge Ho. SE1 —47Qb 82 (2A 206)
(off Coral St.)
Davidge St. SE1 —47Rb 83 (2C 206)
David Ho. Sidc —62Wc 131
David Lee Point. E15 —39Gc 65
(off Leather Gdns.)
David M. W1 —43Hb 81 (7H 191)
David Rd. Dag —33Ad 67
Davidson Gdns. SW8 —52Nb 104
Davidson La. Harr —31Ha 58
Davidson Rd. Croy —73Ub 147
Davidson Ter. E7 —36Kc 65
(off Claremont Rd.)
Davidson Ter. E7 —36Kc 65
(off Windsor Rd.)
Davidson Way. Romf —30Gd 48
David's Rd. SE23 —60Yb 106
David St. E15 —37Fc 65
David's Way. Ilf —24Uc 46
David Ter. Romf —24Qd 49
Davies Clo. Croy —72Wb 147
Davies Clo. Rain —41Ld 89
Davies La. E11 —33Gc 65
Davies M. W1 —45Kb 82 (4K 197)
Davies St. W1 —44Kb 82 (3K 197)
Davington Gdns. Dag —36Xc 67
Davington Rd. Dag —37Xc 67
Davinia Clo. Wfd G —23Pc 46
Davis Av. Grav —10A 114
Davison Clo. Chesh —1Zb 12
Davison Dri. Chesh —1Zb 12
Davis Rd. W3 —46Va 80
Davis Rd. Chess —77Qa 143
Davis Rd. S Ock —46Td 90
Davis St. E13 —40Kc 65
Davisville Rd. W12 —47Wa 80
Davmor Ct. Bren —50La 78
Davos Clo. Wok —91A 172
Davy's Pl. Grav —5G 136
Dawell Dri. Big H —89Lc 167
Dawes Av. Horn —34Md 69
Dawes Av. Iswth —57Ja 100
Dawes Clo. Chesh —1Zb 12
Dawes Ct. Esh —78Da 141
Dawes E. Rd. Burn —2A 72
Dawes La. Sarr —9G 2
Dawes Moor Clo. Slou —4N 73
Dawes Rd. SW6 —52Ab 102
Dawe's Rd. Uxb —40N 55
Dawes St. SE17 —50Tb 83 (7G 207)
Dawley Av. Uxb —43S 76
Dawley Grn. S Ock —44Wd 90
Dawley Pde. Hay —45S 76
Dawley Ride. Coln —53G 96
Dawley Rd. Hay —47T 76
Dawlish Av. N13 —21Nb 42
Dawlish Av. SW18 —61Db 125
Dawlish Av. Gnfd —40Ja 58
Dawlish Dri. Ilf —35Uc 66
Dawlish Dri. Pinn —29Aa 37
Dawlish Dri. Ruis —33W 56
Dawlish Rd. E10 —32Ec 64
Dawlish Rd. N17 —27Wb 43
Dawlish Rd. NW2 —37Za 60
Dawlish Wlk. Romf —25Ld 49
Dawnay Gdns. SW18 —61Fb 125
Dawnay Rd. SW18 —61Eb 125
Dawnay Rd. Bookh —98Da 175
Dawn Clo. Houn —55Aa 99
Dawn Cres. E15 —39Fc 65
Dawn Redwood Clo. Hort —55C 96
Dawpool Rd. NW2 —33Va 60
Daws Hill. E4 —12Ec 26
Daws La. NW7 —22Va 40
Dawson Av. Bark —38Uc 66
Dawson Av. Orp —68Xc 131
Dawson Clo. SE18 —49Sc 86
Dawson Clo. Hay —43T 76
Dawson Clo. Wind —4E 94
Dawson Dri. Rain —38Kd 69
Dawson Dri. Swan —66Gd 132
Dawson Gdns. Bark —38Vc 67
Dawson Hts. SE22 —59Wb 105
Dawson Pl. W2 —45Cb 81
Dawson Rd. NW2 —36Ya 60
Dawson Rd. Byfl —83M 157
Dawson Rd. King T —69Pa 123
Dawson St. E2 —40Vb 63
Dawson Ter. N9 —17Yb 26
Daybrook Rd. SW19 —68Db 125
Daylesford Av. SW15 —56Wa 102
Daylop Dri. Chig —20Xc 29
Daymer Gdns. Pinn —28X 37
Daymerslea Ridge. Lea —93La 176
Days Acre. S Croy —82Vb 165
Daysbrook Rd. SW2 —60Pb 104
Days La. Pil H —14Wd 32
Days La. Sidc —59Uc 108
Dayton Dri. Eri —50Md 89
Dayton Gro. SE15 —53Yb 106
Deacon Clo. D'side —91X 175
Deacon Clo. Purl —81Nb 164
Deaconess Ct. N15 —28Vb 43
(off Tottenham Grn. E.)
Deacon Est., The. E4 —23Bc 44
Deacon Rd. NW2 —36Wa 60
Deacon Rd. King T —67Pa 123
Deacons Clo. Els —14Qa 21
Deacons Clo. Pinn —26X 37
Deacons Ct. Twic —61Ha 122
Deacons Heights. Els —16Qa 21
Deacons Hill. Borwd —16Qa 21
Deacons Hill. Wat —16Y 19
Deacon's Hill Rd. Els —14Pa 21
Deacons Leas. Orp —77Tc 150
Deacons Wlk. Hamp —63Ca 121
Deacon Way. SE17 —49Sb 83 (5D 206)
Deacon Way. Wfd G —23Pc 46
Deadhearn La. Chal G —18A 16
Deadman's Ash La. Sarr —8K 3
Deakin Clo. Wat —17U 18
Deal Av. Slou —4D 72
Deal Porters Way. SE16 —48Yb 84
Deal Rd. SW17 —65Jb 126
Deal's Gateway. SE10 —53Cc 106
Deal St. E1 —43Wb 83
Dealtry Rd. SW15 —56Ya 102
Deal Wlk. SW9 —52Qb 104
Deamer Ho. Ger X —22A 34
Deanacre Clo. Ger X —23A 34
Dean Bradley St. SW1 —48Nb 82 (4F 205)
Dean Clo. E9 —36Yb 64
Dean Clo. SE16 —46Zb 84
Dean Clo. Tad —95Xa 178
Dean Clo. Uxb —38P 55
Dean Clo. Wind —5B 94
Dean Clo. Wok —88G 156
Dean Ct. Edgw —23Ra 39
Dean Ct. Romf —29Fd 48
Dean Ct. Wat —5Z 5
Dean Ct. Wemb —34Ka 58
Deancroft Rd. Ger X —23A 34
Deancross St. E1 —44Yb 84
Dean Dri. Stan —26Na 39
Deane Av. Ruis —36Y 57
Deane Ct. N'wd —25U 36
Deane Croft Rd. Pinn —30X 37
Deanery Clo. N2 —28Gb 41
Deanery M. W1 —46Jb 82 (6J 197)
(off Deanery St.)
Deanery Rd. E15 —38Gc 65
Deanery St. W1 —46Jb 82 (6J 197)
Deane Way. Ruis —30X 37
Dean Farrar St. SW1 —48Mb 82 (3E 204)
Dean Gdns. E17 —28Fc 45
Deanhill Ct. SW14 —56Ra 101
Deanhill Rd. SW14 —56Ra 101
Dean La. Red —95Kb 180
Dean Rd. NW2 —37Ya 60
Dean Rd. Croy —77Tb 147
Dean Rd. Hamp —64Ca 121
Dean Rd. Houn —57Da 99
Dean Ryle St. SW1 —49Nb 82 (5F 205)
Deansbrook Clo. Edgw —24Sa 39
Deansbrook Rd. Edgw —24Ra 39
Dean's Bldgs. SE17 —49Tb 83 (6F 207)
Deans Clo. W4 —51Ra 101
Deans Clo. Abb L —4T 4
Deans Clo. Croy —76Vb 147
Deans Clo. Edgw —23Sa 39
Deans Clo. Stoke P —9M 53
Deans Clo. Tad —96Xa 178
Dean's Ct. EC4 —44Rb 83 (3C 200)
Deanscroft Av. NW9 —32Sa 59
Deans Dri. N13 —23Rb 43
Deans Dri. NW7 —22Ta 39
Deans Dri. Edgw —22Ta 39
Deansfield. Cat —97Vb 181
Deans Ga. Clo. SE23 —62Zb 128
Deans La. W4 —51Ra 101
(off Deans Clo.)
Deans La. Edgw —23Sa 39
Dean's La. Tad —96Xa 178
Dean's M. W1 —44Kb 82 (2A 198)
Dean's Pl. SW1 —50Mb 82 (7D 204)
Deans Rd. W7 —46Ha 78
Deans Rd. Sutt —76Db 145
Deans Rd. War —20Xd 32
Dean Stanley St. SW1 —48Nb 82 (4F 205)
Deanston Wharf. E16 —47Kc 85
Dean St. E7 —36Jc 65
Dean St. W1 —44Mb 82 (2D 198)
Dean's Wlk. Coul —90Qb 164
Deansway. N2 —28Fb 41
Deansway. N9 —20Ub 25
Deans Way. Edgw —22Sa 39
Deanswood. N11 —23Mb 42
Dean's Yd. SW1 —48Mb 82 (3E 204)
(off Sanctuary, The.)
Dean Trench St. SW1 —48Nb 82 (4F 205)
Dean Wlk. Bookh —98Da 175
Dean Wlk. Edgw —23Sa 39
Dean Way. S'hall —47Da 77
Dearne Clo. Stan —22Ja 38
Dearn Gdns. Mitc —69Gb 125
Deason St. E15 —39Ec 64
Deauville Ct. SW4 —58Lb 104
De Barowe M. N5 —35Rb 63
Debden. N7 —27Tb 43
(off Gloucester Rd.)
Debden Clo. Wfd G —24Lc 45
Debden Ho. Lou —10Rc 14
Debden La. Lou —10Sc 14
Debden Rd. Lou —10Rc 14
Debden Wlk. Horn —37Kd 69
De Beauvoir Cres. N1 —39Ub 63
De Beauvoir Est. N1 —39Ub 63
De Beauvoir Pl. N1 —37Ub 63
De Beauvoir Rd. N1 —39Ub 63
De Beauvoir Sq. N1 —38Ub 63
Deben. E Til —8L 93
Debenham Ct. Barn —15Ya 22
Debenham Ho. Ger X —21A 34
Debnams Rd. SE16 —49Yb 84
De Bohun Av. N14 —16Kb 24
Deborah Clo. Iswth —53Ga 100
Deborah Ct. E18 —27Kc 45
(off Victoria Rd.)
Deborah Cres. Ruis —31T 56
Deborah Lodge. Edgw —25Ra 39
Debrabant Clo. Eri —51Fd 110
De Bruin Ct. E14 —50Ec 84
De Burgh Pk. Bans —87Db 163
De Burgh Rd. SW19 —66Eb 125
Debussy. NW9 —26Va 40
Decies Way. Stoke P —9L 53
Decima St. SE1 —48Ub 83 (3H 207)
Deck Clo. SE16 —46Zb 84
Decoy Av. NW11 —29Ab 40
De Crespigny Pk. SE5 —54Tb 105
Dedswell Dri. W Cla —100J 173
Dedworth Dri. Wind —3D 94
Dedworth Rd. Wind —4A 94
Dee Clo. Upm —30Ud 50
Deeley Rd. SW8 —53Mb 104
Deena Clo. W3 —44Pa 79
Deena Clo. Slou —5C 72
Deepdale. SW19 —63Za 124
Deepdale Av. Brom —70Hc 129
Deepdene. W5 —42Pa 79
Deepdene. Pot B —3Za 8
Deepdene Av. Croy —76Vb 147
Deepdene Clo. E11 —28Jc 45
Deepdene Ct. N21 —16Rb 25
Deepdene Gdns. SW2 —59Pb 104
Deepdene Path. Lou —14Qc 28
(in two parts)
Deepdene Rd. SE5 —56Tb 105
Deepdene Rd. Lou —14Qc 28
Deepdene Rd. Well —55Wc 109
Deepfield. Dat —2M 95
Deepfield Way. Coul —88Nb 164
Deep Pool La. Hors —2E 188
Deepwell Clo. Iswth —53Ja 100
Deepwood La. Gnfd —41Fa 78
Deerbrook Rd. SE24 —60Rb 105
Deerdale Rd. SE24 —56Sb 105
Deere Av. Rain —37Jd 68
Deerfield Cotts. NW9 —29Va 40
Deerhurst Clo. Felt —63X 121
Deerhurst Clo. Long —69Ee 135
Deerhurst Rd. NW2 —37Za 60
Deerhurst Rd. SW16 —64Pb 126
Deerings Dri. Pinn —29W 36
Deerleap Gro. E4 —15Dc 26
Deerleap La. Hals —85Zc 169
Dee Rd. Rich —56Pa 101
Deer Pk. Clo. King T —66Ra 123
Deer Pk. Gdns. Mitc —70Fb 125
Deer Pk. Rd. SW19 —68Db 125
Deer Pk. Way. W Wick —75Hc 149
Deers Farm Clo. Wis —88N 157
Deeside Rd. SW17 —62Fb 125
Dee St. E14 —44Ec 84
Deeves Hall La. Ridge —5Ua 8
Dee Way. Eps —82Ua 162
Dee Way. Romf —24Gd 48
Defiance Wlk. SE18 —48Pc 86
Defiant. NW9 —26Va 40
(off Further Acre)
Defiant Way. Wall —80Nb 146
Defoe Av. Rich —52Qa 101
Defoe Clo. SE16 —47Bc 84
Defoe Clo. SW17 —65Gb 125
Defoe Clo. Eri —53Hd 110
Defoe Ho. EC2 —43Sb 83 (7D 194)
(off Barbican)
Defoe Pde. Grays —8D 92
Defoe Pl. EC2 —43Sb 83 (7E 194)
(off Beech St.)
Defoe Rd. N16 —34Ub 63
Defoe Way. Romf —23Cd 48
De Frene Rd. SE26 —63Zb 128

Degema Rd.—Digby St.

Degema Rd. Chst —64Rc 130
Dehar Cres. NW9 —31Va 60
Dehavilland Clo. N'holt —41Z 77
De Havilland Ct. Shenl —4Na 7
De Havilland Dri. Wey —83N 157
De Havilland Rd. Edgw —26Ra 39
De Havilland Rd. Houn —52Y 99
De Havilland Rd. Wall —80Nb 146
De Havilland Way. Abb L —4V 4
De Havilland Way. Stai —58N 97
Dekker Rd. SE21 —58Ub 105
Delabole Rd. Red —100Nb 180
Delacourt Rd. SE3 —52Kc 107
Delafield Rd. SE7 —50Kc 85
Delafield Rd. Grays —50Fe 91
Delaford Clo. Iver —44J 75
Delaford Rd. SE16 —50Xb 83
Delaford St. SW6 —52Ab 102
Delagarde Rd. W'ham —98Sc 184
Delamare Rd. Chesh —2Ac 12
Delamere Cres. Croy —72Yb 148
Delamere Gdns. NW7 —23Ta 39
Delamere Rd. SW20 —67Za 124
Delamere Rd. W5 —47Na 79
Delamere Rd. Borwd —11Ra 21
Delamere Rd. Hay —45Z 77
Delamere Ter. W2 —43Db 81
Delancey Pas. NW1
—39Kb 62 (1A 192)
(off Dalancey St.)
Delancey St. NW1
—39Kb 62 (1K 191)
Delaporte Clo. Eps —84Ua 162
De Lapre Clo. Orp —73Zc 151
De Lara Way. Wok —66 188
Delargy Clo. Grays —8D 92
De Laune St. SE17 —50Rb 83
Delaware Mans. W9 —42Db 81
(off Delaware Rd.)
Delaware Rd. W9 —42Db 81
Delawyk Cres. SE24 —58Sb 105
Delcombe Av. Wor Pk —74Ya 144
Delderfield. Lea —93Ma 177
Delderfield Ho. Romf —26Fd 48
(off Portnoi Clo.)
Delft Way. SE22 —57Ub 105
Delhi Rd. Enf —17Vb 25
Delhi St. N1 —39Nb 62 (1G 193)
Delia St. SW18 —59Db 103
Delius Clo. Els —16La 20
Delius Way. Stanf —1L 93
Della Path. E5 —34Wb 63
Dellbow Rd. Felt —57X 99
Dell Clo. E15 —39Fc 65
Dell Clo. Farn C —6G 52
Dell Clo. Fet —95Ga 176
Dell Clo. Mick —99La 176
Dell Clo. Wall —77Mb 146
Dell Clo. Wfd G —20Kc 27
Dell Ct. Horn —33Nd 69
Dell Ct. N'wd —24T 36
Dell Farm Rd. Ruis —29S 36
Dellfield Clo. Beck —67Ec 128
Dellfield Clo. Rad —7Ha 6
Dellfield Clo. Wat —12W 18
Dellfield Cres. Uxb —42M 75
Dell La. Eps —78Wa 144
Dellmeadow. Abb L —2U 4
Dellors Clo. Barn —15Za 22
Dellow Clo. Ilf —31Tc 66
Dellow St. E1 —45Xb 83
Dell Rd. Enf —10Yb 12
Dell Rd. Eps —79Wa 144
Dell Rd. Grays —49De 91
Dell Rd. Wat —9W 4
Dell Rd. W Dray —49P 75
Dells Clo. E4 —17Dc 26
Dellside. Hare —29L 35
Dellside. Wat —9W 4
Dell's M. SW1 —49Lb 82 (6C 204)
(off Churton Pl.)
Dell, The. SE2 —50Wc 87
Dell, The. SE19 —67Vb 127
Dell, The. Bex —60Gd 110
Dell, The. Bren —51La 100
Dell, The. Felt —59X 99
Dell, The. Ger X —23A 34
Dell, The. Gt War —23Xd 50
Dell, The. N'wd —19U 18
Dell, The. Pinn —26Z 37
Dell, The. Rad —8Ja 6
Dell, The. Tad —93Ya 178
Dell, The. Wemb —36Ka 58
Dell, The. Wok —7F 188
Dell, The. Wfd G —20Kc 27
Dell Wlk. N Mald —68Ua 124
Dell Way. W13 —44La 78
Dellwood Clo. Rick —18K 17
Dellwood Gdns. Ilf —27Qc 46
Delmare Clo. SW9 —56Pb 104
Delme Cres. SE3 —54Kc 107
Delmey Clo. Croy —76Vb 147
Delorme St. W6 —51Za 102
Delroy Ct. N20 —17Eb 23
Delta Bus. Pk. SW18 —56Db 103
Delta Cen. Wemb —39Pa 59
Delta Clo. Wor Pk —76Va 144
Delta Ct. NW2 —33Wa 60
Delta Gain. Wat —19Z 19
Delta Gro. N'holt —41Z 77
Delta Rd. Hut —16Fe 33
Delta Rd. Wok —88C 156
Delta Rd. Wor Pk —76Ua 144
Delta St. E2 —41Wb 83
Delta Way. Egh —67E 118
De Luci Rd. Eri —50Ed 88
De Lucy St. SE2 —49Xc 87
Delvan Clo. SE18 —52Qc 108
Delvers Mead. Dag —35Ed 68
Delverton Rd. SE17
—50Rb 83 (7C 206)
Delves. Tad —93Za 178
Delvino Rd. SW6 —53Cb 103
Demead Way. SE15 —52Vb 105
(off Pentridge St.)
Demesne Rd. Wall —77Mb 146
Demeta Clo. Wemb —34Sa 59
De Montfort Rd. SW16 —61Nb 126
De Morgan Rd. SW6 —55Db 103
Dempster Clo. Surb —74La 142
Dempster Rd. SW18 —57Eb 103
Denbar Pde. Romf —28Ed 48
Denberry Dri. Sidc —62Xc 131
Denbigh Clo. NW10 —38Ua 60
Denbigh Clo. W11 —45Bb 81
Denbigh Clo. Chst —65Pc 130
Denbigh Clo. Horn —28Qd 49
Denbigh Clo. Ruis —33V 56
Denbigh Clo. S'hall —44Ba 77
Denbigh Clo. Sutt —78Bb 145
Denbigh Ct. E6 —41Mc 85
Denbigh Dri. Hay —47S 76
Denbigh Gdns. Rich —57Pa 101
Denbigh M. SW1
—49Lb 82 (6B 204)
(off Denbigh St.)
Denbigh Pl. SW1
—50Lb 82 (7B 204)
Denbigh Rd. E6 —41Mc 85
Denbigh Rd. W11 —45Bb 81
Denbigh Rd. W13 —45Ka 78
Denbigh Rd. Houn —54Da 99
Denbigh Rd. S'hall —44Ba 77
Denbigh St. SW1
—49Lb 82 (6B 204)
Denbigh Ter. W11 —45Bb 81
Denbridge Ind. Est. Uxb —38L 55
Denbridge Rd. Brom —68Pc 130
Denby Ct. SE11 —49Pb 82 (5J 205)
(off Lambeth Wlk.)
Denby Rd. Cob —84Y 159
Denchworth Ho. SW9 —54Qb 104
Den Clo. Beck —69Fc 129
Dendridge Clo. Enf —9Xb 11
Dene Av. Houn —55Ba 99
Dene Av. Sidc —59Xc 109
Dene Clo. SE4 —55Ac 106
Dene Clo. Brom —74Hc 149
Dene Clo. Dart —63Gd 132
Dene Clo. Wor Pk —75Va 144
Dene Ct. W5 —43La 78
Denecroft Cres. Uxb —39R 56
Denecroft Gdns. Grays —48Fe 91
Dene Dri. Long —68De 135
Dene Dri. Orp —76Xc 151
Denefield Dri. Kenl —87Tb 165
Dene Gdns. Stan —22La 38
Dene Gdns. Th Dit —75Ja 142
Dene Holm Rd. Grav —62Fe 135
Denehurst Gdns. NW4 —30Ya 40
Denehurst Gdns. W3 —46Ra 79
Denehurst Gdns. Rich —56Qa 101
Denehurst Gdns. Twic —59Fa 100
Denehurst Gdns. Wfd G —21Kc 45
Dene Path. S Ock —44Wd 90
Dene Pl. Wok —6F 188
Dene Rd. N11 —18Hb 23
Dene Rd. Asht —91Pa 177
Dene Rd. Buck H —18Mc 27
Dene Rd. Dart —59Pd 111
Dene Rd. N'wd —23S 36
Denesfield Ct. Sev —95Ed 186
Denesmead. SE24 —57Sb 105
Dene, The. W13 —43Ka 78
Dene, The. Croy —77Zb 148
Dene, The. Sev —98Kd 187
Dene, The. Sutt —83Bb 163
Dene, The. Wemb —35Na 59
Dene, The. W Mol —71Ba 141
Dene Wlk. Long —69Ae 135
Denewood. Barn —15Eb 23
Denewood Clo. Wat —9V 4
Denewood Rd. N6 —30Hb 41
Denford St. SE10 —50Hc 85
Dengie Wlk. N1 —39Sb 63
(off Basire St.)
Denham Av. Den —33H 55
Denham Clo. Den —34J 55
Denham Clo. Well —55Yc 109
Denham Cres. Mitc —70Hb 125
Denham Dri. Ilf —30Sc 66
Denham Grn. Clo. Den —31J 55
Denham Grn. La. Den —29G 34
Denham Ho. W12 —45Xa 80
(off White City Est.)
Denham La. Ger X —23B 34
Denham Rd. N20 —20Hb 23
Denham Rd. Egh —63C 118
Denham Rd. Eps —84Va 162
Denham Rd. Felt —59Y 99
Denham Rd. Iver —39F 54
Denham Rd. Uxb —37H 55
Denham St. SE10 —50Jc 85
Denham Wlk. Ger X —23B 34
Denham Way. Bark —39Uc 66
Denham Way. Borwd —11Ta 21
Denham Way. Den —34J 55
Denham Way. Rick & Den
—23G 34
Denholme Rd. W9 —41Bb 81
Denholm Wlk. Rain —37Hd 68
Denison Clo. N2 —27Eb 41
Denison Rd. SW19 —65Fb 125
Denison Rd. W5 —42La 78
Denison Rd. Felt —63V 120
Deniston Av. Bex —60Ad 109
Denis Way. SW4 —55Mb 104
Denleigh Gdns. N21 —18Qb 24
Denleigh Gdns. Th Dit —72Ga 142
Denley Sq. Uxb —38L 55
Denman Dri. NW11 —29Cb 41
Denman Dri. Ashf —65R 120
Denman Dri. Clay —78Ja 142
Denman Dri. N. NW11 —29Cb 41
Denman Dri. S. NW11 —29Cb 41
Denman Rd. SE15 —53Vb 105
Denman St. W1 —45Mb 82
Denmark Av. SW19 —66Ab 124
Denmark Ct. Mord —72Cb 145
Denmark Gdns. Cars —76Hb 145
Denmark Gro. N1
—40Qb 62 (1K 193)
Denmark Hill. SE5 —53Tb 105
Denmark Hill Dri. NW9 —28Wa 40
Denmark Hill Est. SE5 —56Tb 105
Denmark Path. SE25 —71Xb 147
Denmark Pl. WC2
—44Mb 82 (2E 198)
Denmark Rd. N8 —28Qb 42
Denmark Rd. NW6 —40Bb 61
(in two parts)
Denmark Rd. SE5 —53Sb 105
Denmark Rd. SE25 —71Wb 147
Denmark Rd. SW19 —65Za 124
Denmark Rd. W13 —45Ka 78
Denmark Rd. Brom —67Kc 129
Denmark Rd. Cars —76Hb 145
Denmark Rd. King T —69Na 123
Denmark Rd. Twic —62Fa 122
Denmark St. E11 —34Gc 65
Denmark St. E13 —43Kc 85
Denmark St. N17 —25Xb 43
Denmark St. WC2
—44Mb 82 (3E 198)
Denmark St. Wat —12X 19
Denmark Ter. N2 —27Hb 41
Denmark Wlk. SE27 —63Sb 127
Denmead Clo. Ger X —31A 54
Denmead Rd. Croy —74Rb 147
Dennan Rd. Surb —74Pa 143
Denner Rd. E4 —19Cc 26
Denne Ter. E8 —39Vb 63
Dennett Rd. Croy —74Qb 146
Dennetts Gro. SE14 —53Yb 106
Dennett's Rd. SE14 —54Zb 106
Denning Av. Croy —77Qb 146
Denning Clo. NW8
—41Eb 81 (4A 190)
Denning Clo. Hamp —64Ba 121
Denning Rd. NW3 —35Fb 61
Dennington Clo. E5 —33Yb 64
Dennington Pk. Rd. NW6 —37Cb 61
Denningtons, The. Wor Pk
—75Ua 144
Dennis Av. Wemb —36Pa 59
Dennis Clo. Ashf —66T 120
Dennises La. Upm —39Ud 70
Dennis Gdns. Stan —22La 38
Dennis Ho. Sutt —77Db 145
Dennis La. Stan —20Ka 20
Dennison Gro. SW14 —55Ta 101
Dennison Point. E15 —38Ec 64
Dennis Pde. N14 —18Mb 24
Dennis Pk. Cres. SW20 —67Ab 124
Dennis Reeve Clo. Mitc —67Hb 125
Dennis Rd. E Mol —70Ea 122
Dennis Rd. Grav —2C 136
Dennis Rd. S Ock —38Wd 70
Dennis Way. Slou —5B 72
Denny Av. Wal A —6Fc 13
Denny Clo. E6 —43Nc 86
Denny Ct. Dart —58Rd 111
(off Bow Arrow La.)
Denny Ct. Dart —58Rd 111
(off Hardwick Cres.)
Denny Cres. SE11
—50Qb 82 (7A 206)
Denny Gdns. Dag —38Yc 67
Denny Rd. N9 —18Xb 25
Denny Rd. Slou —49B 74
Denny St. SE11 —50Qb 82 (7A 206)
Den Rd. Brom —69Fc 129
Densham Rd. E15 —39Gc 65
Densole Clo. Beck —67Ac 128
Densworth Gro. N9 —19Yb 26
Dent Clo. S Ock —44Wd 90
Denton Caravan Site. Grav
—10H 115
Denton Clo. Barn —15Ya 22
Denton Ct. Rd. Grav —9G 114
Denton Gro. W on T —75Aa 141
Denton Rd. N8 —29Pb 42
Denton Rd. N18 —21Ub 43
Denton Rd. NW10 —38Sa 59
Denton Rd. Bex —60Gd 110
Denton Rd. Dart —59Gd 110
Denton Rd. Twic —58Ma 101
Denton Rd. Well —52Yc 109
Denton St. SW18 —58Db 103
Denton St. Grav —9G 114
Denton Ter. Bex —61Gd 132
Denton Way. E5 —34Zb 64
Denton Way. St J —6C 188
Dents Gro. Tad —100Bb 179
Dents Rd. SW11 —58Hb 103
Denvale Wlk. Wok —6D 188
Denver Clo. Orp —72Uc 150
Denver Rd. N16 —31Ub 63
Denver Rd. Dart —59Jd 110
Denyer St. SW3 —49Gb 81 (6E 202)
Denziloe Av. Uxb —41R 76
Denzil Rd. NW10 —36Va 60
Deodara Clo. N20 —20Gb 23
Deodar Rd. SW15 —56Ab 102
Depot App. N3 —25Db 41
Depot App. NW2 —35Za 60
Depot App. NW10 —38Ra 59
Depot Rd. Eps —85Ua 162
Depot Rd. Houn —55Fa 100
Depot St. SE5 —51Tb 105
Deptford Bri. SE8 —53Cc 106
Deptford B'way. SE8 —53Cc 106
Deptford Chu. St. SE8 —51Cc 106
Deptford Ferry Rd. E14 —49Cc 84
Deptford Grn. SE8 —51Cc 106
Deptford High St. SE8 —51Cc 106
Deptford Pk. Bus. Cen. SE8
—50Ac 84
Deptford Strand. SE8 —49Bc 84
Deptford Wharfe. SE8 —49Bc 84
De Quincey Rd. N17 —25Tb 43
Derby Arms Rd. Eps —89Va 162
Derby Av. N12 —22Eb 41
Derby Av. Harr —25Fa 38
Derby Av. Romf —30Ed 48
Derby Av. Upm —34Pd 69
Derby Clo. Eps —91Xa 178
Derby Est. Houn —56Da 99
Derby Ga. SW1 —47Nb 82 (1F 205)
Derby Hill. SE23 —61Yb 128
Derby Hill Cres. SE23 —61Yb 128
Derby Ho. SE11 —49Qb 82 (5K 205)
(off Walnut Tree Wlk.)
Derby Ho. Pinn —26Z 37
Derby Rd. E7 —38Mc 65
Derby Rd. E9 —39Zb 64
Derby Rd. E18 —25Hc 45
Derby Rd. N18 —22Yb 44
Derby Rd. SW14 —56Ra 101
Derby Rd. SW19 —66Cb 125
Derby Rd. Croy —74Rb 147
Derby Rd. Enf —15Xb 25
Derby Rd. Grays —50De 91
Derby Rd. Gnfd —39Da 57
Derby Rd. Houn —56Da 99
Derby Rd. Surb —74Qa 143
Derby Rd. Sutt —79Bb 145
Derby Rd. Uxb —40L 55
Derby Rd. Wat —14Y 19
Derby Rd. Bri. Grays —51De 113
Derbyshire St. E2 —41Wb 83
Derby Stables Rd. Eps —89Ua 162
Derby St. W1 —46Jb 82 (7J 197)
Dereham Pl. EC2
—41Ub 83 (4J 195)
Dereham Rd. Bark —36Vc 67
Derek Av. Eps —79Qa 143
Derek Av. Wall —77Kb 146
Derek Av. Wemb —38Ra 59
Derek Clo. Ewe —78Ra 143
Derek Walcott Clo. SE24
—57Rb 105
Derham Gdns. Upm —34Sd 70
Deri Av. Rain —42Kd 89
Dericote St. E8 —39Xb 63
Deridene Clo. Stai —58N 97
Derifall Clo. E6 —43Pc 86
Dering Pl. Croy —77Sb 147
Dering Rd. Croy —77Sb 147
Dering St. W1 —44Kb 82 (3K 197)
Dering Way. Grav —10H 115
Dering Yd. W1 —44Kb 82 (3A 198)
Derinton Rd. SW17 —63Hb 125
Derley Rd. S'hall —48Y 77
Dermody Gdns. SE13 —57Fc 107
Dermody Rd. SE13 —57Fc 107
Deronda Est. SW2 —60Rb 105
Deronda Rd. SE24 —60Rb 105
De Ros Pl. Egh —65C 118
Deroy Clo. Cars —79Hb 145
Derrick Av. S Croy —82Sb 165
Derrick Gdns. SE7 —49Lc 85
Derrick Rd. Beck —69Bc 128
Derry Av. S Ock —44Wd 90
Derrydown. Wok —9F 188
Derry Downs. Orp —72Yc 151
Derry Rd. Croy —76Nb 146
Derry St. W8 —47Db 81
Dersingham Av. E12 —35Pc 66
Dersingham Rd. NW2 —34Ab 60
Derwent Av. N18 —22Tb 43
Derwent Av. NW7 —23Ta 39
Derwent Av. NW9 —29Ua 40
Derwent Av. SW15 —63Ua 124
Derwent Av. Barn —18Hb 23
Derwent Av. Pinn —23Aa 37
Derwent Av. Uxb —33Q 56
Derwent Clo. Add —78M 139
Derwent Clo. Clay —79Ga 142
Derwent Clo. Dart —60Kd 111
Derwent Clo. Felt —60V 98
Derwent Cres. N20 —20Eb 23
Derwent Cres. Bexh —54Cd 110
Derwent Cres. Stan —26La 38
Derwent Dri. Hay —43U 76
Derwent Dri. Orp —73Tc 150
Derwent Dri. Purl —85Tb 165
Derwent Dri. Slou —3A 72
Derwent Gdns. Ilf —28Nc 46
Derwent Gdns. Wemb —31La 58
Derwent Gro. SE22 —56Vb 105
Derwent Ho. SE20 —68Xb 127
(off Derwent Rd.)
Derwent Lodge. Isw —54Fa 100
Derwent Lodge. Wor Pk —75Xa 144
Derwent Pde. S Ock —44Wd 90
Derwent Rise. NW9 —30Ua 40
Derwent Rd. N13 —21Pb 42
Derwent Rd. SE20 —68Wb 127
Derwent Rd. SW20 —71Za 144
Derwent Rd. W5 —48La 78
Derwent Rd. Egh —66C 118
Derwent Rd. S'hall —44Ca 77
Derwent Rd. Twic —58Da 99
Derwent St. SE10 —50Gc 85
Derwent Wlk. Wall —80Kb 146
Derwentwater Rd. W3 —46Sa 79
Derwent Way. Horn —36Kd 69
Derwent Yd. W5 —48La 78
(off Derwent Rd.)
De Salis Rd. Uxb —42S 76
Desborough Clo. Shep —74Q 140
Desborough Ho. W14 —51Bb 103
(off N. End Rd.)
Desenfans Rd. SE21 —58Ub 105
Desford Ct. Ashf —61Q 120
Desford Rd. E16 —42Gc 85
Desford Way. Ashf —61P 119
Desmond Ho. Barn —16Gb 23
Desmond Rd. Wat —8V 4
Desmond St. SE14 —52Ac 106
Desmond Tutu Ho. Wemb
—31Pa 59
Despard Rd. N19 —32Lb 62
Detillens La. Oxt —100Jc 183
Detling Clo. Horn —36Ld 69
Detling Rd. Brom —64Jc 129
Detling Rd. Eri —52Fd 110
Detling Rd. Grav —60Fe 113
Detmold Rd. E5 —33Yb 64
Devalls Clo. E6 —45Rc 86
Devana End. Cars —76Hb 145
Devas Rd. SW20 —67Ya 124
Devas St. E3 —42Dc 84
Devenay Rd. E15 —38Hc 65
Devenish Rd. SE2 —47Wc 87
Deventer Cres. SE22 —57Ub 105
De Vere Gdns. W8 —47Eb 81
De Vere Gdns. Ilf —33Pc 66
Deverell St. SE1 —48Tb 83 (4F 207)
De Vere M. W8 —48Eb 81
(off De Vere Gdns.)
Devereux Ct. WC2
(off Essex St.) —44Qb 82 (3K 199)
Devereux Dri. Wat —10U 4
Devereux Rd. SW11 —58Hb 103
Devereux Rd. Grays —48Be 91
Devereux Rd. Wind —4H 95
De Vere Wlk. Wat —12U 18
Deveron Gdns. S Ock —44Wd 90
Deveron Way. Romf —25Gd 48
Devil's La. Egh & Stai —65E 118
Devitt Clo. Asht —88Qa 161
Devizes Ho. H Hill —22Md 49
(off Montgomery Cres.)
Devoke Way. W on T —75Z 141
Devon Av. Slou —4G 72
Devon Av. Twic —60Ea 100
Devon Clo. N17 —27Vb 43
Devon Clo. Buck H —19Kc 27
Devon Clo. Gnfd —39La 58
Devon Clo. Kenl —88Ub 165
Devon Ct. Hamp —66Ca 121
Devon Ct. S at H —67Kd 133
Devoncroft Gdns. Twic —59Ja 100
Devon Gdns. N4 —30Rb 43
Devon Ho. Cat —96Vb 181
Devonhurst Pl. W4 —50Ta 79
Devonia Gdns. N18 —23Sb 43
Devonia Rd. N1 —40Rb 63 (1C 194)
Devonport Gdns. Ilf —30Pc 46
Devonport M. W12 —47Xa 80
Devonport Rd. W12 —46Xa 80
Devonport St. E1 —44Zb 84
Devon Rise. N2 —28Fb 41
Devon Rd. Bark —39Uc 66
Devon Rd. S Dar —67Rd 133
Devon Rd. Sutt —81Ab 162
Devon Rd. W on T —77Y 141
Devon Rd. Wat —11Z 19
Devons Est. E3 —41Dc 84
Devonshire Av. Dart —58Kd 111
Devonshire Av. Sutt —80Eb 145
Devonshire Av. Wok —86E 156
Devonshire Clo. E15 —35Gc 65
Devonshire Clo. N13 —20Qb 24
Devonshire Clo. W1
—43Kb 82 (7K 191)
Devonshire Clo. Farn R —10F 52
Devonshire Ct. Pinn —25Ba 37
(off Devonshire Rd.)
Devonshire Cres. NW7 —24Za 40
Devonshire Dri. SE10 —52Dc 106
Devonshire Dri. Surb —74Ma 143
Devonshire Gdns. N17 —23Sb 43
Devonshire Gdns. N21 —17Sb 25
Devonshire Gdns. W4 —52Sa 101
Devonshire Gdns. Linf —8J 93
Devonshire Grn. Farn R —10F 52
Devonshire Gro. SE15 —51Xb 105
Devonshire Hill La. N17 —23Sb 43
Devonshire Ho. Sutt —80Eb 145
Devonshire M. N13 —21Qb 42
Devonshire M. W4 —50Ua 80
Devonshire M. N. W1
—43Kb 82 (7K 191)
Devonshire M. S. W1
—43Kb 82 (7K 191)
Devonshire M. W. W1
—42Jb 82 (6J 191)
Devonshire Pas. W4 —50Ua 80
Devonshire Pl. NW2 —34Cb 61
Devonshire Pl. W1
—42Jb 82 (6J 191)
Devonshire Pl. W4 —50Ua 80
Devonshire Pl. W8 —48Db 81
Devonshire Pl. M. W1
—43Jb 82 (7J 191)
Devonshire Rd. E15 —35Gc 65
Devonshire Rd. E16 —44Kc 85
Devonshire Rd. E17 —30Cc 44
Devonshire Rd. N9 —18Yb 26
Devonshire Rd. N13 —21Pb 42
Devonshire Rd. N17 —23Sb 43
Devonshire Rd. NW7 —24Za 40
Devonshire Rd. SE9 —61Nc 130
Devonshire Rd. SE23 —60Yb 106
Devonshire Rd. SW19 —66Gb 125
Devonshire Rd. W4 —50Ua 80
Devonshire Rd. W5 —48La 78
Devonshire Rd. Bexh —56Ad 109
Devonshire Rd. Cars —77Jb 146
Devonshire Rd. Chaf H —49Ae 91
Devonshire Rd. Croy —73Tb 147
Devonshire Rd. Eastc —30Y 37
Devonshire Rd. Felt —62Aa 121
Devonshire Rd. Grav —10D 114
Devonshire Rd. Harr —30Fa 38
Devonshire Rd. Horn —33Ld 69
Devonshire Rd. Ilf —31Uc 66
Devonshire Rd. Orp —73Wc 151
Devonshire Rd. Pinn —25Ba 37
Devonshire Rd. S'hall —43Ca 77
Devonshire Rd. Sutt —80Eb 145
Devonshire Rd. Wey —77Q 140
Devonshire Row. EC2
—43Ub 83 (1J 201)
Devonshire Row M. W1 —42Kb 82 (6A 192)
(off Devonshire St.)
Devonshire Sq. E1
—44Ub 83 (2J 201)
Devonshire Sq. EC2
—44Ub 83 (2J 201)
Devonshire Sq. Brom —70Kc 129
Devonshire St. W1
—43Jb 82 (7J 191)
Devonshire St. W4 —50Ua 80
Devonshire Ter. W2
—44Eb 81 (3A 196)
Devonshire Way. Croy —75Ac 148
Devonshire Way. Hay —45X 77
Devons Rd. E3 —43Cc 84
Devon St. SE15 —51Xb 105
Devon Way. Chess —78La 142
Devon Way. Eps —78Ra 143
Devon Way. Uxb —40P 55
Devon Waye. Houn —52Ba 99
De Walden St. W1
—43Jb 82 (1J 197)
Dewar St. SE15 —55Wb 105
Dewberry Gdns. E6 —43Nc 86
Dewberry St. E14 —43Ec 84
Dewey Path. Horn —37Ld 69
Dewey Rd. N1 —40Qb 62 (1K 193)
Dewey Rd. Dag —37Dd 68
Dewey St. SW17 —64Hb 125
Dewgrass Gro. Wal X —7Zb 12
Dewhurst Rd. W14 —48Za 80
Dewhurst Rd. Chesh —1Xb 11
Dewlands Av. Dart —59Rd 111
Dewsbury Clo. Pinn —30Aa 37
Dewsbury Clo. Romf —23Md 49
Dewsbury Ct. W4 —49Sa 79
Dewsbury Gdns. Romf —23Md 49
Dewsbury Gdns. Wor Pk
—76Wa 144
Dewsbury Rd. NW10 —36Wa 60
Dewsbury Rd. Romf —23Md 49
Dewsbury Ter. NW1 —39Kb 62
Dexter Clo. Grays —48Ce 91
Dexter Ho. Eri —48Ad 87
(off Kale Rd.)
Dexter Rd. Barn —16Za 22
Dexter Rd. Hare —26L 35
Deyncourt Gdns. Upm —33Sd 70
Deyncourt Rd. N17 —25Sb 43
Deynecourt Gdns. E11 —28Lc 45
D'Eynsford Rd. SE5 —53Tb 105
Diadem Ct. W1 —44Mb 82 (3D 198)
(off Dean St.)
Dial Clo. Grnh —57Zd 113
Dial Wlk., The. W8 —47Db 81
(off Broad Wlk., The)
Diamedes Av. Stai —59M 97
Diameter Rd. Orp —72Sc 150
Diamond Clo. Dag —32Yc 67
Diamond Clo. Grays —48Be 91
Diamond Est. SW17 —62Gb 125
Diamond Rd. Ruis —35Z 57
Diamond Rd. Slou —7L 73
Diamond Rd. Wat —10W 4
Diamond St. SE15 —52Ub 105
Diamond Ter. SE10 —53Ec 106
Diana Clo. E18 —25Kc 45
Diana Clo. G Grn —4A 74
Diana Clo. Grays —48Be 91
Diana Ct. Eri —51Gd 110
Diana Gdns. Surb —75Pa 143
Diana Ho. SW13 —53Va 102
Diana Pl. NW1 —42Kb 82 (5A 192)
Diana Rd. E17 —27Bc 44
Dianne Way. Barn —14Gb 23
Dianthus Clo. SE2 —50Xc 87
Dianthus Clo. Cher —73G 138
Dianthus Ct. Wok —6G 188
Diban Av. Horn —35Kd 69
Diban Ct. Horn —35Kd 69
(off Broadway)
Dibden Ho. SE5 —52Ub 105
Dibden La. Ide & Sev —98Gd 186
Dibden St. N1 —39Sb 63
Dibdin Clo. Sutt —76Cb 145
Dibdin Rd. Sutt —76Cb 145
Dibdin Row. SE1
—48Qb 82 (3A 206)
Diceland Rd. Bans —88Bb 163
Dicey Av. NW2 —35Ya 60
Dickens Av. N3 —25Eb 41
Dickens Av. Dart —56Qd 111
Dickens Av. Til —3D 114
Dickens Av. Uxb —44R 76
Dickens Clo. Hart —71Be 155
Dickens Clo. Hay —49U 76
Dickens Clo. Rich —61Na 123
Dickens Dri. Add —79H 139
Dickens Dri. Chst —65Sc 130
Dickens Est. SE1 —47Wb 83
Dickens Est. SE16 —48Wb 83
Dickens Ho. SE17 —50Rb 83
(off Doddington Gro.)
Dickens La. N18 —22Ub 43
Dickenson Ho. N8 —30Pb 42
Dickenson Rd. N8 —31Nb 62
Dickenson Rd. Felt —64Z 121
Dickensons La. SE25 —71Wb 147
Dickensons Pl. SE25 —72Wb 147
Dickenson St. NW5 —37Jb 62
Dickens Rise. Chig —20Rc 28
Dickens Rd. E6 —40Mc 65
Dickens Rd. Grav —10G 114
Dickens Sq. SE1
—48Sb 83 (3E 206)
Dickens St. SW8 —54Kb 104
Dickerage La. N Mald —69Sa 123
Dickerage Rd. King T —67Sa 123
Dickinson Av. Crox —16Q 18
Dickinson Sq. Crox —16Q 18
Dickson Fold. Pinn —28Z 37
Dickson Rd. SE9 —55Nc 108
Dick Turpin Way. Felt —56V 98
Didsbury Clo. E6 —39Pc 66
Digby Cres. N4 —33Sb 63
Digby Gdns. Dag —39Cd 68
Digby Mans. W6 —50Xa 80
(off Hammersmith Bri. Rd.)
Digby Pl. Croy —76Vb 147
Digby Rd. E9 —37Zb 64
Digby Rd. Bark —38Vc 67
Digby St. E2 —41Yb 84

Digby Wlk. Horn —37Ld 69
Digby Way. Byfl —84P 157
Digdens Rise. Eps —87Sa 161
Diggens Ct. Lou —13Nc 28
Diggon St. E1 —43Zb 84
Dighton Ct. SE5 —51Sb 105
(off John Ruskin St.)
Dighton Rd. SW18 —57Eb 103
Dignum St. N1 —40Qb 62 (1K 193)
Digswell Clo. Borwd —10Qa 7
Digswell St. N7 —37Qb 62
Dilhorne Clo. SE12 —62Kc 129
Dilke St. SW3 —51Hb 103
Dilloway La. S'hall —47Aa 77
Dilston Clo. N'holt —41Y 77
Dilston Gro. SE16 —49Yb 84
Dilston Rd. Lea —91Ja 176
Dilton Gdns. SW15 —60Wa 102
Dilwyn Ct. E17 —26Ac 44
Dimes Pl. W6 —49Xa 80
Dimmock Dri. Gnfd —36Fa 58
Dimmocks La. Sarr —8K 3
Dimond Clo. E7 —35Jc 65
Dimsdale Dri. NW9 —32Sa 59
Dimsdale Dri. Enf —16Wb 25
Dimsdale Dri. Farn C —6B 52
Dimsdale Wlk. E13 —40Jc 65
Dingle Clo. Barn —16Va 22
Dingle Gdns. E14 —45Cc 84
Dingle Rd. Ashf —64R 120
Dingles Ct. Pinn —25Z 37
Dingle, The. Uxb —41R 76
Dingley. Sidc —64Xc 131
Dingley La. SW16 —61Mb 126
Dingley Pl. EC1 —41Sb 83 (4E 194)
Dingley Rd. EC1
 —41Sb 83 (4D 194)
Dingwall Av. Croy —75Sb 147
Dingwall Gdns. NW11 —30Cb 41
Dingwall Rd. SW18 —59Eb 103
Dingwall Rd. Cars —81Hb 163
Dingwall Rd. Croy —74Tb 147
Dinmont Est. E2 —40Wb 63
Dinmont St. E2 —40Xb 63
Dinsdale Clo. Wok —90C 156
Dinsdale Gdns. SE25 —71Ub 147
Dinsdale Barn —15Db 23
Dinsdale Rd. SE3 —51Hc 107
Dinsmore Rd. SW12 —59Kb 104
Dinton Rd. SW19 —65Fb 125
Dinton Rd. King T —66Pa 123
Diploma Av. N2 —28Gb 41
Diploma Ct. N2 —28Gb 41
Dippers Clo. Kems —89Pd 171
Dirdene Gdns. Eps —84Va 162
Dirdene Gro. Eps —84Ua 162
Dirleton Rd. E15 —39Hc 65
Dirtham La. Eff —100X 175
Disbrowe Rd. W6 —51Ab 102
Discovery Wlk. E1 —45Xb 83
Dishforth La. NW9 —24Ua 40
Disney Pl. SE1 —47Sb 83 (1E 206)
Disney St. SE1 —47Sb 83 (1E 206)
Dison Clo. Enf —11Zb 26
Dison Clo. Horn —32Gd 68
Disraeli Clo. SE28 —46Yc 87
Disraeli Clo. W4 —48Ta 79
Disraeli Ct. Coln —51D 96
Disraeli Gdns. SW15 —56Bb 103
Disraeli Rd. E7 —37Jc 65
Disraeli Rd. NW10 —40Ta 59
Disraeli Rd. SW15 —56Ab 102
Disraeli Rd. W5 —46Ma 79
Diss St. E2 —41Vb 83 (3K 195)
Distaff La. EC4 —45Sb 83 (4D 200)
Distillery La. W6 —50Ya 80
Distillery Rd. W6 —50Ya 80
Distillery Wlk. Bren —51Na 101
Distin St. SE11 —49Qb 82 (6K 205)
District Rd. Wemb —36Ka 58
Ditchburn St. E14 —45Ec 84
Ditches La. Coul & Cat —92Nb 180
Ditches Ride, The. Lou & Epp
 —9Qc 14
Ditchfield Rd. Hay —42Aa 77
Dittisham Rd. SE9 —63Nc 130
Ditton Clo. Th Dit —73Ja 142
Ditton Grange Clo. Surb —74Ma 143
Ditton Grange Dri. Surb —74Ma 143
Ditton Hill. Surb —74La 142
Ditton Hill Rd. Surb —74La 142
Ditton Lawn. Th Dit —74Ja 142
Ditton Pk. Rd. Slou —51Va 96
Ditton Pl. SE20 —67Xb 127
Ditton Reach. Th Dit —72Ka 142
Ditton Rd. Bexh —57Zc 109
Ditton Rd. Dat —3P 95
Ditton Rd. Langl —50Ab 74
Ditton Rd. S'hall —50Ba 77
Ditton Rd. Surb —75Na 143
Divis Way. SW15 —58Xa 102
Dixon Clark Ct. N1 —37Rb 63
Dixon Clo. E6 —44Pc 86
Dixon Pl. W Wick —74Dc 148
Dixon Rd. SE14 —53Ac 106
Dixon Rd. SE25 —69Ub 127
Dixon's All. SE16 —47Xb 83
Dobbin Clo. Harr —26Ja 38
Dobell Rd. SE9 —57Pc 108
Doble Ct. S Croy —84Wb 165
Dobree Av. NW10 —38Xa 60
Dobson Clo. NW6 —38Fb 61
Dobson Rd. Grav —4G 136
Digby Ct. EC4 —45Sb 83 (4E 200)
(off Skinners La.)
Dockers Tanner Rd. E14 —49Cc 84
Dockett Eddy. Cher —74N 139
Dockett Eddy La. Shep —74P 139
Dockhead. SE1 —47Wb 83 (2K 207)
Dock Hill Av. SE16 —46Zb 84
Dockland St. E16 —46Qc 86
(in two parts)
Dockley Rd. SE16 —48Wb 83

Dock Rd. E16 —45Hc 85
Dock Rd. Bren —52Ma 101
Dock Rd. Grays —51Fe 113
Dock Rd. Til —3A 114
Dock St. E1 —45Wb 83
Dockwell Clo. Felt —56W 98
Doctor Johnson Av. SW17
 —62Kb 126
Doctors Clo. SE26 —64Yb 128
Doctors La. Cat —95Qb 180
Docwra's Bldgs. N1 —37Ub 63
Dodbrooke Rd. SE27 —62Qb 126
Doddinghurst Rd. Brtwd —16Yd 32
Doddington Gro. SE17 —51Rb 105
Doddington Pl. SE17 —51Rb 105
Dodds Cres. W Byf —86K 157
Doddsfield Rd. Slou —1E 72
Dodd's La. Wok —86J 157
Dodsley Pl. N9 —20Yb 26
Dodson St. SE1 —47Qb 82 (2A 206)
Dod St. E14 —44Cc 84
Doebury Wlk. SE18 —52Wc 109
(off Prestwood Clo.)
Doel Clo. SW19 —66Eb 125
Dog and Duck Yd. WC1
 —43Pb 82 (7J 193)
(off Princeton St.)
Doggett Rd. SE6 —59Cc 106
Doggett's Corner. Horn —33Pd 69
Doggetts Courts. Barn —15Gb 23
Doggetts Farm Rd. Den —31E 54
Doghurst Av. Hay —52R 98
Doghurst Dri. W Dray —52R 98
Doghurst La. Coul —92Hb 179
Dog Kennel Hill. SE22 —55Ub 105
Dog Kennel Hill Est. SE22
 —55Ub 105
Dog Kennel La. Chor —14H 17
Dog La. NW10 —35Ua 60
Dogwood Clo. Grav —3B 136
Doherty Rd. E13 —42Jc 85
Dokal Ind. Est. S'hall —48Aa 77
Dolben Ct. SE8 —49Bc 84
Dolben St. SE1 —46Rb 83 (7B 200)
(in two parts)
Dolby Rd. SW6 —54Bb 103
Dolland Ho. SE11
 —50Pb 82 (7J 205)
(off Newburn St.)
Dolland St. SE11
 —50Pb 82 (7J 205)
Dollis Av. N3 —25Bb 41
Dollis Brook Wlk. Barn —16Ab 22
Dollis Cres. Ruis —32Y 57
Dolliscroft. NW7 —24Ab 40
Dollis Hill Av. NW2 —34Xa 60
Dollis Hill Est. NW2 —34Wa 60
Dollis Hill La. NW2 —35Va 60
Dollis Pk. N3 —25Bb 41
Dollis Rd. NW7 & N3 —24Ab 40
Dollis Valley Way. Barn —16Bb 23
Dolman Rd. W4 —49Ta 79
Dolman St. SW4 —56Pb 104
Dolphin App. Romf —28Hd 48
Dolphin Clo. SE16 —47Zb 84
Dolphin Clo. SE28 —44Zc 87
Dolphin Clo. Surb —71Ma 143
Dolphin Clo. NW11 —30Ab 40
Dolphin Ct. Chig —20Rc 28
Dolphin Ct. Slou —7M 73
Dolphin Ct. Stai —62J 119
Dolphin Ct. N. Stai —62J 119
Dolphin La. E14 —45Dc 84
Dolphin Rd. N'holt —40Ba 57
Dolphin Rd. Slou —7M 73
Dolphin Rd. Sun —67U 120
Dolphin Rd. N. Sun —67U 120
Dolphin Rd. S. Sun —67U 120
Dolphin Rd. W. Sun —67U 120
Dolphin Sq. SW1 —50Lb 82
Dolphin Sq. W4 —52Ua 102
Dolphin St. King T —68Na 123
Dombey St. WC1
 —43Pb 82 (7H 193)
Dome Hill. Cat —99Ub 181
Dome Hill Pk. SE26 —63Vb 127
Dome Hill Peak. Cat —98Ub 181
Domett Clo. SE5 —56Tb 105
Domfe Pl. E5 —35Yb 64
Domingo St. EC1
 —42Sb 83 (6D 194)
Dominion Bus. Pk. N9 —19Zb 26
Dominion Cen., The. S'hall
 —47Aa 77
Dominion Dri. Romf —23Dd 48
Dominion Pde. Harr —29Ha 38
Dominion Rd. Croy —73Vb 147
Dominion Rd. S'hall —47Aa 77
Dominion St. EC2
 —43Tb 83 (7G 195)
Dominion Way. Rain —41Jd 88
Domitian Pl. Enf —15Vb 25
Domonic Dri. SE9 —63Rc 130
Domville Clo. N20 —19Fb 23
Domville Gro. SE5
 —50Vb 83 (7K 207)
Donald Dri. Romf —29Yc 47
Donald Rd. E13 —39Kc 65
Donald Rd. Croy —73Pb 146
Donaldson Rd. NW6 —39Bb 61
Donaldson Rd. SE18 —53Qc 108
Doncaster Dri. N'holt —36Ba 57
Doncaster Gdns. N4 —30Sb 43
Doncaster Gdns. N'holt —36Ba 57
Doncaster Grn. Wat —22Y 37
Doncaster Rd. N9 —17Yb 26
Doncaster Way. Upm —34Pd 69
Doncel Ct. E4 —17Fc 27
Donegal St. N1 —40Pb 62 (2J 193)
Doneraile St. SW6 —54Za 102
Dongola Rd. E13 —41Kc 85
Dongola Rd. N17 —27Ub 43
Dongola Rd. W. E13 —41Kc 85
Donington Av. Ilf —29Sc 46
Donkey La. Enf —12Wb 25

Donkey La. F'ham —75Rd 153
Donkey La. W Dray —49L 75
Donnay Clo. Ger X —30A 34
Donne Ct. SE24 —58Sb 105
Donnefield Av. Edgw —24Na 39
Donne Gdns. Wok —87G 156
Donne Pl. SW3 —49Gb 81 (5E 202)
Donne Pl. Mitc —70Kb 126
Donne Rd. Dag —33Yc 67
Donnington Ct. Dart —58Rd 111
(off Bow Arrow La.)
Donnington Rd. NW10 —38Xa 60
Donnington Rd. Dun G —92Fd 186
Donnington Rd. Harr —29Ma 39
Donnington Rd. Wor Pk
 —75Wa 144
Donnybrook Rd. SW16 —66Lb 126
Donovan Av. N10 —26Kb 42
Donovan Clo. Eps —82Ta 161
Donovan Ct. NW10 —38Sa 59
Donovan's Garden. Heron —24Fe 51
Don Phelan Clo. SE5 —53Tb 105
Don Way. Romf —24Gd 48
Doone Clo. Tedd —65Ja 122
Doran Ct. E6 —40Pc 66
Doran Gro. SE18 —52Uc 108
Doran Mnr. N2 —29Hb 41
(off Gt. North Rd.)
Doran Wlk. E15 —38Ec 64
Dora Rd. SW19 —64Cb 125
Dora St. E14 —44Bc 84
Dorchester Av. N13 —21Sb 43
Dorchester Av. Bex —60Zc 109
Dorchester Av. Harr —30Ea 38
Dorchester Clo. Dart —59Pd 111
Dorchester Clo. N'holt —36Da 57
Dorchester Clo. Orp —66Xc 131
Dorchester Ct. N10 —27Kb 42
Dorchester Ct. N14 —17Kb 24
Dorchester Ct. NW2 —34Za 60
Dorchester Ct. SE24 —56Sb 105
Dorchester Ct. Stai —63J 119
Dorchester Ct. Wok —86E 156
Dorchester Dri. SE24 —57Sb 105
Dorchester Dri. Felt —58U 98
Dorchester Gdns. E4 —21Cc 44
Dorchester Gdns. NW11 —28Cb 41
Dorchester Gro. W4 —50Ua 80
Dorchester M. N Mald —70Ta 123
Dorchester Rd. Grav —2F 136
Dorchester Rd. Mord —73Db 145
Dorchester Rd. N'holt —36Da 57
Dorchester Rd. Wey —76R 140
Dorchester Rd. Wor Pk —74Ya 144
Dorchester Way. Harr —30Pa 39
Dorchester Waye. Hay —44X 77
(in two parts)
Dorcis Av. Bexh —54Ad 109
Dordrecht Rd. W3 —46Ua 80
Dore Av. E12 —36Qc 66
Doreen Av. NW9 —32Ta 59
Dore Gdns. Mord —73Db 145
Dorell Clo. S'hall —43Ba 77
Doria Dri. Grav —2G 136
Dorian Dri. Asc —7C 116
Dorian Rd. Horn —32Jd 68
Doria Rd. SW6 —54Bb 103
Doric Dri. Tad —92Bb 179
Doric Way. NW1
 —41Mb 82 (3D 192)
Dorien Rd. SW20 —68Za 124
Dorin Ct. Warl —92Xb 181
Dorincourt. Wok —87G 156
Dorinda St. N7 —37Qb 62
Doris Av. Eri —53Ed 110
Doris Emmerton Ct. SW11
 —56Eb 103
Doris Rd. E7 —38Jc 65
Doris Rd. Ashf —65T 120
Doritt M. N18 —22Ub 43
Dorking Clo. SE8 —51Bc 106
Dorking Clo. Wor Pk —75Za 144
Dorking Ct. N17 —25Wb 43
(off Hampden La.)
Dorking Glen. H Hill —21Md 49
Dorking Ho. SE1
 —48Tb 83 (3G 207)
Dorking Rise. Romf —21Md 49
Dorking Rd. Bookh —98Da 175
Dorking Rd. Eps —88Qa 161
Dorking Rd. Lea —94Ka 176
Dorking Rd. Romf —22Md 49
Dorking Rd. Tad —100Ua 178
Dorking Vs. Knap —5A 188
Dorking Wlk. Romf —21Md 49
Dorkins Way. Upm —31Ud 70
Dorlcote Rd. SW18 —59Gb 103
Dorling Dri. Eps —84Va 162
Dorly Clo. Shep —71U 140
Dorman Pl. N9 —19Wb 25
Dormans Clo. N'wd —24T 36
Dorman Wlk. NW10 —36Ta 59
Dorman Way. NW8 —39Fb 61
Dorma Trading Pk. E10 —32Zb 64
Dormay St. SW18 —57Db 103
Dormer Clo. E15 —37Hc 65
Dormer Clo. Barn —15Za 22
Dormers Av. S'hall —44Ca 77
Dormer's Rise. S'hall —44Da 77
Dormer's Wells La. S'hall —44Ca 77
Dormywood. Ruis —29V 36
Dornberg Clo. SE3 —52Jc 107
Dornberg Rd. SE3 —52Kc 107
Dorncliffe Rd. SW6 —54Ab 102
Dornels. Slou —4N 73
Dorney Gro. Wey —75R 140
Dorney Hill S. High W & Slou
 —1E 52
Dorney Rise. Orp —70Vc 131
Dorney Way. Houn —57Aa 99
Dorney Wood Rd. Burn —9A 52

Dornfell St. NW6 —36Bb 61
Dornford Gdns. Coul —91Sb 181
Dornton Rd. SW12 —61Kb 126
Dornton Rd. S Croy —79Tb 147
Dorothy Av. Wemb —38Na 59
Dorothy Evans Clo. Bexh
 —56Dd 110
Dorothy Gdns. Dag —35Xc 67
Dorothy Pettingell Ho. Sutt
 —76Db 145
(off Angel Hill)
Dorrell Pl. SW9 —56Qb 104
Dorrien Wlk. SW16 —61Mb 126
Dorrington Ct. SE19 —68Ub 127
Dorrington Gdns. Horn —32Md 69
Dorrington St. EC1
 —43Qb 82 (7K 193)
Dorrit Way. Chst —65Sc 130
Dorrofield Clo. Crox —15S 18
Dorryn Ct. SE26 —64Zb 128
Dors Clo. NW9 —32Ta 59
Dorset Av. Hay —41U 76
Dorset Av. Romf —27Fd 48
Dorset Av. S'hall —49Ca 77
Dorset Av. Well —56Vc 109
Dorset Bldgs. EC4
 —44Rb 83 (3B 200)
Dorset Clo. NW1
 —43Hb 81 (7F 191)
Dorset Ct. Eps —84Va 162
Dorset Cres. Grav —3G 136
Dorset Dri. Edgw —23Pa 39
Dorset Dri. Wok —89D 156
Dorset Gdns. Linf —7J 93
Dorset Gdns. Mitc —70Pb 126
Dorset M. SW1 —48Kb 82 (3K 203)
Dorset Pl. E15 —37Fc 65
Dorset Rise. EC4
 —44Rb 83 (3B 200)
Dorset Rd. E7 —38Lc 65
Dorset Rd. N15 —28Tb 43
Dorset Rd. N22 —25Nb 42
Dorset Rd. SE9 —61Nc 130
Dorset Rd. SW8 —52Nb 104
Dorset Rd. SW19 —67Cb 125
Dorset Rd. W5 —48La 78
Dorset Rd. Ashf —62M 119
Dorset Rd. Beck —69Zb 128
Dorset Rd. Harr —30Ea 38
Dorset Rd. Mitc —68Gb 125
Dorset Rd. Sutt —82Cb 163
Dorset Rd. Wind —3G 94
Dorset Sq. NW1 —42Hb 81 (6F 191)
Dorset Sq. Eps —82Ta 161
Dorset St. W1 —43Hb 81 (1G 197)
Dorset St. Sev —97Ld 187
Dorset Way. Byfl —82M 157
Dorset Way. Twic —60Fa 100
Dorset Way. Uxb —40P 55
Dorset Waye. Houn —52Ba 99
Dorton Dri. Sev —94Pd 187
Dorville Cres. W6 —48Xa 80
Dorville Rd. SE12 —57Hc 107
Dothill Rd. SE18 —52Sc 108
Douai Gro. Hamp —67Ea 122
Doubleday Rd. Lou —13Sc 28
Doughty Ho. SW10 —51Eb 103
Doughty M. WC1
 —42Pb 82 (6H 193)
Doughty St. WC1
 —42Pb 82 (5H 193)
Douglas Av. E17 —25Bc 44
Douglas Av. N Mald —70Xa 124
Douglas Av. Romf —26Nd 49
Douglas Av. Wat —9Z 5
Douglas Av. Wemb —38Na 59
Douglas Clo. Guild —100A 172
Douglas Clo. Stan —22Ja 38
Douglas Clo. Wall —79Nb 146
Douglas Cres. Hay —42Y 77
Douglas Dri. Croy —76Cc 148
Douglas Est. N1 —37Sb 63
Douglas Ho. Surb —74Pa 143
Douglas Houses. Bookh —96Ca 175
Douglas La. Wray —57B 96
Douglas Mans. Houn —55Da 99
(off Douglas Rd.)
Douglas Pl. E14 —49Ec 84
Douglas Rd. Bookh —98Da 175
Douglas Rd. E4 —17Gc 27
Douglas Rd. E16 —43Jc 85
Douglas Rd. N1 —38Sb 63
Douglas Rd. N22 —25Qb 42
Douglas Rd. NW6 —39Bb 61
Douglas Rd. Add —76K 139
Douglas Rd. Esh —75Da 141
Douglas Rd. Horn —30Hd 48
Douglas Rd. Houn —55Da 99
Douglas Rd. Ilf —31Wc 67
Douglas Rd. King T —68Ra 123
Douglas Rd. Slou —3H 73
Douglas Rd. Stai —58M 97
Douglas Rd. Surb —75Pa 143
Douglas Rd. N. N1 —37Sb 63
Douglas Rd. S. N1 —37Sb 63
Douglas Sq. Mord —72Cb 145
Douglas St. SW1
 —49Mb 82 (6D 204)
Douglas Ter. E17 —25Bc 44
Douglas Way. SE8 —52Bc 106
(in two parts)
Doulton M. NW6 —37Db 61
Doultons, The. Stai —65J 119
Dounesforth Gdns. SW18
 —60Db 103
Dounsell Ct. Pil H —16Wd 32
Dourdan Ct. EC1
 —43Qb 82 (1A 200)
(off Greville St.)
Douro Pl. W8 —48Db 81
Douro St. E3 —40Cc 64
Douthwaite Sq. E1 —46Wb 83

Dove App. E6 —43Nc 86
Dove Clo. N'holt —42Z 77
Dove Clo. S Croy —83Zb 166
Dove Commercial Cen. NW5
 —36Lb 62
Dovecot Clo. Pinn —29Y 37
Dovecote Av. N22 —27Qb 42
Dove Cote Clo. Wey —76R 140
Dovecote Gdns. SW14 —55Ta 101
Dove Ct. EC2 —44Tb 83 (3F 201)
(off Old Jewry)
Dovedale Av. Harr —30La 38
Dovedale Av. Ilf —26Qc 46
Dovedale Clo. Hare —26L 35
Dovedale Clo. Well —54Wc 109
Dovedale Rise. Mitc —66Hb 125
Dovedale Rd. SE22 —57Xb 105
Dovedale Rd. Dart —60Sd 112
Dovedon Clo. N14 —19Nb 24
Dove Ho. Cres. Slou —1C 72
Dove Ho. Gdns. E4 —19Cc 26
Dovehouse Grn. Wey —77T 140
Dovehouse Mead. Bark —40Tc 66
Dovehouse St. SW3
 —50Fb 81 (7C 202)
Dove La. Pot B —6Db 9
Dove M. SW5 —49Eb 81 (6A 202)
Doveney Clo. Orp —69Yc 131
Dove Pk. Chor —16D 16
Dove Pk. Pinn —24Ca 37
Dover Clo. NW2 —33Za 60
Dover Clo. Romf —26Ed 48
Dovercourt Av. T Hth —71Qb 146
Dovercourt Est. N1 —37Tb 63
Dovercourt Gdns. Stan —22Na 39
Dovercourt La. Sutt —76Eb 145
Dovercourt Rd. SE22 —58Ub 105
Doverfield. Chesh —5Is 11
Doverfield Rd. SW2 —59Nb 104
Dover Flats. SE1
 —49Ub 83 (6J 207)
Dover Ho. SE15 —51Yb 106
Dover Ho. Rd. SW15 —56Wa 102
Doveridge Gdns. N13 —21Rb 43
Dove Rd. N1 —37Tb 63
Dove Row. E2 —39Wb 63
Dover Pk. Dri. SW15 —58Xa 102
Dover Rd. E12 —33Lc 65
Dover Rd. N9 —19Yb 26
Dover Rd. SE19 —65Tb 127
Dover Rd. Grav —59Fe 113
Dover Rd. Romf —30Ad 47
Dover Rd. Slou —4D 72
Dover Rd. E. Grav —9A 114
Dover St. W1 —45Kb 82 (5A 198)
Dover Way. Crox —14S 18
Dover Yd. W1 —46Lb 82 (6B 198)
(off Berkeley St.)
Doves Clo. Brom —75Nc 150
Doves Cotts. Ching —20Wc 29
Dovet Ct. SW8 —53Pb 104
Doveton Rd. S Croy —78Tb 147
Doveton St. E1 —42Yb 84
Dove Wlk. SW1 —50Jb 82 (7H 203)
Dove Wlk. Horn —37Kd 69
Dowanhill Rd. SE6 —60Fc 107
Dowdeswell Clo. SW15 —56Ua 102
Dowding Ho. N6 —31Jb 62
(off Hillcrest)
Dowding Pl. Stan —23Ja 38
Dowding Rd. Big H —87Mc 167
Dowding Rd. Uxb —38P 55
Dowding Way. Horn —38Kd 69
Dowend Ct. SE15 —51Ub 105
(off Longhope Clo.)
Dower Av. Wall —81Kb 164
Dower Pk. Wind —6C 94
Dowgate Hill. EC4
 —45Tb 83 (4F 201)
Dowland Clo. Stanf —1L 93
Dowland St. W10 —41Ab 80
Dowlans Clo. Bookh —99Ca 175
Dowlans Rd. Bookh —99Da 175
Dowlas St. SE5 —52Ub 105
Dowlerville Rd. Orp —79Vc 151
Dowman Clo. SW19 —67Db 125
Downage. NW4 —27Ya 40
Downage, The. Grav —1C 136
Downalong. Bush —18Fa 20
Downbank Av. Bexh —53Fd 110
Down Barns Rd. Ruis —34Z 57
Downbury M. SW18 —57Cb 103
Down Clo. N'holt —40X 57
Downderry Rd. Brom —62Fc 129
Downe Av. Cud —84Sc 168
Downe Clo. Well —52Yc 109
Down End. SE18 —52Rc 108
Downe Dri. Sarr —8J 3
Downe Rd. Cud —85Nc 168
Downe Rd. Kes —81Mc 167
Downe Rd. Mitc —68Hb 125
Downers Cotts. SW4 —56Lb 104
Downes Clo. Twic —58Ka 100
Downes Ct. N21 —18Qb 24
Downes Pl. SE15 —51Wb 105
Downe Ter. Rich —58Na 101
Downfield. Wor Pk —74Va 144
Downfield Clo. W9 —42Db 81
Downfield Rd. Chesh —3Ac 12
Down Hall Rd. King T —67Ma 123
Downham Clo. Romf —24Cd 48
Downham La. Brom —64Fc 129
Downham Rd. N1 —38Tb 63
Downham Way. Brom —64Fc 129
Downhills Av. N17 —27Tb 43
Downhills Pk. Rd. N17 —27Sb 43
Downhills Way. N17 —27Sb 43
Downhurst Av. NW7 —22Ta 39
Downhurst Rd. NW4 —27Ya 40
Downing Clo. Harr —27Ea 38
Downing Dri. Gnfd —39Fa 58
Downing Path. Slou —2C 72

Downings. E6 —44Qc 86
Downing St. SW1
 —47Nb 82 (1F 205)
Downings Wood. Rick —22F 34
Downland Clo. N20 —18Eb 23
Downland Clo. Coul —86Kb 164
Downland Clo. Eps —90Xa 162
Downland Gdns. Eps —90Xa 162
Downlands. Wal A —6Gc 13
Downlands Rd. Purl —85Nb 164
Downland Way. Eps —90Xa 162
Downleys Clo. SE9 —61Nc 130
Downman Rd. SE9 —55Nc 108
Down Pl. W6 —49Xa 80
Down Rd. Tedd —65Ka 122
Downs Av. Chst —64Pc 130
Downs Av. Dart —59Qd 111
Downs Av. Eps —86Ua 162
Downs Av. Pinn —30Aa 37
Downsbridge Rd. Beck —67Fc 129
Downs Ct. Rd. Purl —84Rb 165
Downsell Rd. E15 —35Ec 64
Downsfield Rd. E17 —30Ac 44
Downshall Av. Ilf —30Uc 46
Downs Hill. Beck —66Fc 129
Downs Hill. S'fleet —66Ee 135
Downs Hill Rd. Eps —86Ua 162
Downshire Hill. NW3 —35Fb 61
Downs Ho. Sev —94Ld 187
Downs Ho. Rd. Eps —90Ua 162
Downside. Eps —86Ua 162
Downside. Sun —67W 120
Downside. Twic —62Ha 122
Downside Bri. Rd. Cob —86X 159
Downside Clo. SW19 —65Eb 125
Downside Comn. Rd. D'side
 —90X 159
Downside Ct. Mers —100Lb 180
Downside Cres. NW3 —36Gb 61
Downside Cres. W13 —42Ja 78
Downside Ind. Est. Cher —74H 139
Downside Orchard. Wok —89C 156
Downside Rd. Sutt —79Fb 145
Downside Wlk. N'holt —41Ba 77
Downsland Dri. Brtwd —20Yd 32
Downs La. E5 —35Xb 63
Downs La. Lea —95Ka 176
Downs Lodge Ct. Eps —86Ua 162
Downs Pk. Rd. E8 & E5 —36Vb 63
Downs Rd. E5 —35Wb 63
Downs Rd. Beck —68Dc 128
Downs Rd. Coul —90Mb 164
Downs Rd. Enf —14Ub 25
Downs Rd. Eps —86Ua 162
Downs Rd. Grav —63Fe 135
Downs Rd. Mick —100La 176
Downs Rd. Purl —83Rb 165
Downs Rd. Slou —7P 73
Downs Rd. Sutt —82Db 163
Downs Rd. T Hth —67Sb 127
Downs Side. Sutt —83Bb 163
Downs, The. SW20 —66Za 124
Downs, The. Lea —97Ka 176
Down St. W1 —46Kb 82 (7K 197)
Down St. W Mol —71Ca 141
Down St. M. W1
 —46Kb 82 (7K 197)
Downs Valley. Hart —70Ae 135
Downs View. Iswth —53Ha 100
Downs View. Tad —93Xa 178
Downsview Av. Wok —93B 172
Downs View Clo. Orp —82Yc 169
Downsview Clo. Swan —69Hd 132
Downsview Gdns. SE19 —66Rb 127
Downsview Rd. SE19 —66Sb 127
Downsview Rd. Sev —97Hd 186
Downs Way. Bookh —98Ea 176
Downs Way. Eps —88Va 162
Downsway. Orp —78Uc 150
Downs Way. Oxt —99Gc 183
Downsway. S Croy —83Ub 165
Downs Way. Tad —93Xa 178
Downsway, The. Sutt —81Eb 163
Downs Way Clo. Tad —93Wa 178
Downsway, The. Sutt —81Eb 163
Downs Wood. Eps —89Xa 162
Downton Av. SW2 —61Nb 126
Downtown Rd. SE16 —47Ac 84
Downview Clo. D'side —91X 175
Downway. N12 —24Gb 41
Down Way. N'holt —41X 77
Dowrey St. N1 —39Qb 62
Dowry Wlk. Wat —9V 4
Dowsett Rd. N17 —26Vb 43
Dowson Clo. SE5 —56Tb 105
Doyce St. SE1 —47Sb 83 (1D 206)
Doyle Clo. Eri —53Gd 110
Doyle Gdns. NW10 —39Wa 60
Doyle Rd. SE25 —70Wb 127
Doyle Way. Til —4E 114
D'Oyley St. SW1
 —49Jb 82 (5H 203)
Doynton St. N19 —33Kb 62
Draco St. SE17 —51Sb 105
Dragmire La. Mitc —70Fb 125
Dragonfly Clo. E13 —41Kc 85
Dragon La. Wey —83Q 158
Dragon Yd. WC1
 —44Nb 82 (2G 199)
(off High Holborn)
Dragoon Rd. SE8 —50Bc 84
Dragor Rd. NW10 —42Sa 79
Drake Av. Cat —94Sb 181
Drake Av. Slou —9P 73
Drake Av. Stai —64H 119
Drake Clo. SE16 —47Zb 84
Drake Clo. War —22Ae 51
Drake Ct. Eri —52Hd 110
(off Frobisher Rd.)
Drake Cres. SE28 —44Yc 87
Drakefell Rd. SE14 & SE4
 —54Zb 106

Drakefield Rd.—Duxford Clo.

Drakefield Rd. SW17 —62Jb 126
Drakeley Ct. N5 —35Rb 63
Drake Rd. SE4 —55Cc 106
Drake Rd. Chess —78Qa 143
Drake Rd. Croy —73Pb 146
Drake Rd. Grays —47Ae 91
Drake Rd. Harr —33Ba 57
Drake Rd. Mitc —72Jb 146
Drake's Clo. Esh —77Ca 141
Drakes Courtyard. NW6 —38Bb 61
Drakes Dri. N'wd —25R 36
Drake St. WC1 —43Pb 82 (1H 199)
Drake St. Enf —11Tb 25
Drakes Wlk. E6 —39Pc 66
(in two parts)
Drakes Way. Wok —10G 188
Drakewood Rd. SW16 —66Mb 126
Draper Clo. Belv —49Bd 87
Draper Ct. Brom —70Nc 130
Draper Ho. SE1 —49Sb 83 (5D 206)
(off Elephant & Castle)
Drapers Gdns. EC2
—44Tb 83 (2G 201)
Drapers Rd. E15 —35Fc 65
Drapers Rd. N17 —27Vb 43
Drapers Rd. Enf —12Rb 25
Drappers Way. SE16 —49Wb 83
Drawdock Rd. SE10 —47Fc 85
Drawell Clo. SE18 —50Uc 86
Drax Av. SW20 —66Wa 124
Draxmont App. SW19 —65Ab 124
Draycot Rd. E11 —30Kc 45
Draycot Rd. Surb —74Qa 143
Draycott Av. SW3
—49Gb 81 (5E 202)
Draycott Av. Harr —30Ka 38
Draycott Clo. Harr —30Ka 38
Draycott Pl. SW3
—49Hb 81 (6F 203)
Draycott Ter. SW3
—49Hb 81 (6G 203)
Dray Ct. Wor Pk —75Wa 144
Drayford Clo. W9 —42Bb 81
Dray Gdns. SW2 —57Pb 104
Drayson Clo. Wal A —4Gc 13
Drayson M. W8 —47Cb 81
Drayton Av. W13 —45Ja 78
Drayton Av. Lou —17Pc 28
Drayton Av. Orp —74Rc 150
Drayton Av. Pot B —4Ab 8
Drayton Bri. Rd. W7 & W13
—45Ha 78
Drayton Clo. Fet —96Ga 176
Drayton Clo. Houn —57Ba 99
Drayton Clo. Ilf —32Tc 66
Drayton Ford. Rick —19J 17
Drayton Gdns. N21 —17Rb 25
Drayton Gdns. SW10
—50Eb 81 (7A 202)
Drayton Gdns. W13 —45Ja 78
Drayton Gdns. W Dray —47N 75
Drayton Grn. W13 —45Ja 78
Drayton Grn. Rd. W13 —45Ka 78
Drayton Gro. W13 —45Ja 78
Drayton Ho. E11 —32Fc 65
Drayton Pk. N5 —35Qb 62
Drayton Pk. M. N5 —36Qb 62
Drayton Rd. E11 —32Fc 65
Drayton Rd. N17 —26Ub 43
Drayton Rd. NW10 —39Va 60
Drayton Rd. W13 —45Ja 78
Drayton Rd. Borwd —14Qa 21
Drayton Rd. Croy —75Rb 147
Drayton Waye. Harr —30Ka 38
Dreadnought St. SE10 —48Gc 85
Drenon Sq. Hay —45V 76
Dresden Clo. NW6 —37Db 61
Dresden Rd. N19 —32Lb 62
Dresden Way. Wey —78S 140
Dressington Av. SE4 —58Cc 106
Drew Av. NW7 —23Ab 40
Drew Gdns. Gnfd —37Ha 58
Drewitts Ct. W on T —74V 140
Drew Meadow. Farn C —5G 52
Drew Rd. E16 —46Mc 85
(in three parts)
Drewstead Rd. SW16 —61Mb 126
Drey, The. Ger X —22A 34
Driffield Ct. NW9 —25Ua 40
(off Pageant Av.)
Driffield Rd. E3 —40Ac 64
Drift La. Stoke D —89Ba 159
Drift Rd. E Hor —96U 174
Drift, The. Brom —76Mc 149
Drift Way. Coln —53E 96
Driftway, The. Bans —87Ya 162
Driftway, The. Lea —95Ka 176
(in two parts)
Driftway, The. Mitc —67Jb 126
Driftwood Dri. Kenl —89Sb 165
Drill Hall Rd. Cher —73J 139
Drinkwater Rd. Harr —33Da 57
Drive Mans. SW6 —54Ab 102
(off Fulham Rd.)
Drive Mead. Coul —86Nb 164
Drive Rd. Coul —92Mb 180
Drive Spur. Tad —93Db 179
Drive, The. E4 —17Gc 27
Drive, The. E17 —28Dc 44
Drive, The. E18 —27Jc 45
Drive, The. N3 —24Cb 41
Drive, The. N6 —29Hb 41
Drive, The. N7 —37Pb 62
Drive, The. N11 —23Mb 42
Drive, The. NW10 —39Va 60
Drive, The. NW11 —31Ab 60
Drive, The. SW16 —69Pb 126
Drive, The. SW20 —66Ya 124
Drive, The. W3 —44Sa 79
Drive, The. Ashf —66T 120
Drive, The. Bans —88Bb 163
Drive, The. Bark —38Vc 67
Drive, The. Beck —67Cc 128
Drive, The. Bex —59Zc 109
Drive, The. Buck H —17Lc 27
Drive, The. Chesh —1Sb 11
Drive, The. Chst —69Vc 131
Drive, The. Cob —86Aa 159
Drive, The. Col R —24Fd 48
Drive, The. Coul —86Nb 164
Drive, The. Dat —3M 95
Drive, The. Edgw —22Ra 39
Drive, The. Enf —11Tb 25
Drive, The. Eps —79Va 144
Drive, The. Eri —52Dd 110
Drive, The. Esh —74Ea 142
Drive, The. Felt —59Y 99
Drive, The. Fet —94Ga 176
Drive, The. Ger X —24A 34
Drive, The. Grav —3G 136
Drive, The. Gt War —23Yd 50
Drive, The. H Wood —25Pd 49
Drive, The. Harr —31Ca 57
Drive, The. H Bar —13Ab 22
Drive, The. Houn & Iswth
—54Fa 100
Drive, The. Ilf —31Pc 66
Drive, The. King T —66Sa 123
Drive, The. Lea —95Pa 177
Drive, The. Long —69De 135
Drive, The. Lou —13Nc 28
(in two parts)
Drive, The. Mord —71Fb 145
Drive, The. New Bar —16Eb 23
Drive, The. N'wd —25U 36
Drive, The. Orp —75Vc 151
Drive, The. Pot B —4Bb 9
Drive, The. Purf —51Rd 111
Drive, The. Rad —6Ka 6
Drive, The. Rick —15K 17
Drive, The. Sev —96Kd 187
Drive, The. Sidc —63Xc 131
Drive, The. Slou —47A 74
Drive, The. Surb —73Na 143
Drive, The. Sutt —83Cb 163
Drive, The. T Hth —70Tb 127
Drive, The. Uxb —34N 55
Drive, The. Vir W —71B 138
Drive, The. Wall —81Mb 164
Drive, The. Wat —9U 4
Drive, The. Wemb —33Sa 59
Drive, The. W Wick —73Fc 149
Drive, The. Wok —8E 188
Drive, The. Wray —7P 95
Driveway, The. Cuff —1Nb 10
Droitwich Clo. SE26 —62Wb 127
Dromey Gdns. Harr —24Ha 38
Dromore Rd. SW15 —58Ab 102
Dronfield Gdns. Dag —36Yc 67
Droop St. W10 —41Za 80
Drop La. Brick —3Da 5
Dropmore Rd. Burn —9A 52
Drovers Pl. SE15 —52Yb 106
Drovers Rd. S Croy —78Tb 147
Droveway. Lou —12Rc 28
Drove Way., The. Grav —6A 136
Druce Rd. SE21 —58Ub 105
Drudgeon Way. Bean —62Xd 134
Druids Clo. Asht —92Pa 177
Druid St. SE1 —47Ub 83 (1J 207)
Druids Way. Brom —70Fc 129
Druid Tower. SE14 —51Ac 106
Drumaline Ridge. Wor Pk
—75Ua 144
Drummond Av. Romf —28Fd 48
Drummond Cen. Croy —75Sb 147
Drummond Clo. Eri —53Gd 110
Drummond Ct. Brtwd —17Yd 32
Drummond Cres. NW1
—41Mb 82 (3D 192)
Drummond Dri. Stan —24Ha 38
Drummond Gdns. Eps —83Sa 161
Drummond Ga. SW1
—50Mb 82 (7E 204)
Drummond Pl. Croy —75Sb 147
Drummond Pl. Twic —58Ka 100
Drummond Rd. E11 —30Lc 45
Drummond Rd. SE16 —48Xb 83
Drummond Rd. Croy —75Sb 147
Drummond Rd. Romf —28Fd 48
Drummonds, The. Buck H
—19Kc 27
Drummonds, The. Epp —2Wc 15
Drummond St. NW1
—42Lb 82 (5B 192)
Drum St. E1 —44Vb 83
Drury Cres. Croy —75Qb 146
Drury Ind. Est. NW10 —36Sa 59
Drury La. WC2 —44Nb 82 (2G 199)
Drury Rd. Harr —31Ea 58
Drury Way. NW10 —36Ta 59
Dryad St. SW15 —55Za 102
Dryburgh Gdns. NW9 —27Qa 39
Dryburgh Rd. SW15 —55Xa 102
Dryden Av. W7 —44Ha 78
Dryden Clo. Ilf —23Vc 47
Dryden Ct. SE11 —49Rb 83
Dryden Pl. Til —3D 114
Dryden Rd. SW19 —65Eb 125
Dryden Rd. Enf —16Ub 25
Dryden Rd. Harr —25Ha 38
Dryden Rd. Well —53Vc 109
Dryden St. WC2
—44Nb 82 (3G 199)
Dryden Way. Orp —74Wc 151
Dryfield Clo. NW10 —37Sa 59
Dryfield Rd. Edgw —23Sa 39
Dryfield Wlk. SE8 —51Cc 106
Dryhill La. Sund —95Dd 186
Dryhill Rd. Belv —51Bd 109
Dryland Av. Orp —77Vc 151
Drylands Rd. N8 —30Nb 42
Drynham Pk. Wey —76U 140
Drysdale Av. E4 —17Dc 26
Drysdale Clo. N'wd —24U 36
Drysdale Ho. N1 —41Ub 83 (3J 195)
(off Drysdale St.)
Drysdale Pl. N1 —41Ub 83 (3J 195)
Drysdale St. N1 —41Ub 83 (4J 195)
Duarte Pl. Grays —48Be 91
Dublin Av. E8 —39Wb 63
Dublin Ct. S Harr —33Fa 58
Du Burstow Ter. W7 —47Ga 78
Ducal St. E2 —41Vb 83 (4K 195)
Du Cane Clo. W12 —44Ya 80
(off Wood La.)
Du Cane Ct. SW12 —60Jb 104
Du Cane Rd. W12 —44Va 80
Ducavel Ho. SW2 —60Pb 104
Duchess M. W1 —43Kb 82 (1A 198)
Duchess of Bedford's Wlk. W8
—47Cb 81
Duchess St. W1 —43Kb 82 (1A 198)
Duchess Wlk. Sev —97Nd 187
Duchy Pl. SE1 —46Qb 82 (6A 200)
Duchy Rd. Barn —10Fb 9
Duchy St. SE1 —46Qb 82 (6A 200)
Ducie St. SW4 —56Pb 104
Duckett Rd. N4 —30Qb 42
Ducketts Rd. Dart —57Hd 110
Duckett St. E1 —42Zb 84
Ducking Stool Ct. Romf —28Gd 48
Duck La. W1 —44Mb 82 (3D 198)
(off Broadwick St.)
Duck Lees La. Enf —14Ac 26
Duck's Hill Rd. N'wd & Ruis
—25R 36
Ducks Wlk. Twic —57La 100
Du Cros Dri. Stan —23Ma 39
Du Cros Rd. W3 —46Ua 80
Dudbrook Rd. Kel C —11Nd 31
Dudden Hill La. NW10 —35Va 60
Dudden Hill Pde. NW10 —35Va 60
Duddington Clo. SE9 —63Mc 129
Dudley Av. Harr —27La 38
Dudley Av. Wal X —4Zb 12
Dudley Clo. Add —76L 139
Dudley Clo. Grays —47Ae 91
Dudley Cotts. Add —77K 139
Dudley Ct. NW11 —28Bb 41
Dudley Ct. Slou —8L 73
Dudley Dri. Mord —74Ab 144
Dudley Dri. Ruis —36X 57
Dudley Gdns. W13 —47Ka 78
Dudley Gdns. Harr —32Fa 58
Dudley Gdns. Romf —23Md 49
Dudley Gro. Eps —86Sa 161
Dudley Rd. E17 —26Cc 44
Dudley Rd. N3 —26Db 41
Dudley Rd. NW6 —40Ab 60
Dudley Rd. SW19 —65Cb 125
Dudley Rd. Ashf —63P 119
Dudley Rd. Felt —60S 98
Dudley Rd. Grav —9A 114
Dudley Rd. Harr —33Ea 58
Dudley Rd. Ilf —35Rc 66
Dudley Rd. King T —69Pa 123
Dudley Rd. Rich —54Pa 101
Dudley Rd. Romf —23Md 49
Dudley Rd. S'hall —47Z 77
Dudley Rd. W on T —72W 140
Dudley St. W2 —43Fb 81 (1B 196)
Dudlington Rd. E5 —33Yb 64
Dudmaston M. SW3
—50Fb 81 (7C 202)
(off Fulham Rd.)
Dudsbury Rd. Dart —58Kd 111
Dudsbury Rd. Sidc —65Xc 131
Dudset La. Houn —53W 98
Duffell Ho. SE11 —50Pb 82 (7J 205)
(off Loughborough St.)
Dufferin Av. EC1 —42Tb 83 (6F 195)
(off Loughborough St.)
Dufferin St. EC1 —42Sb 83 (6E 194)
Duffield Clo. Harr —29Ha 38
Duffield Dri. N15 —28Vb 43
Duffield La. Stoke P —7K 53
Duffield Pk. Stoke P —1L 73
Duffield Rd. Tad —96Xa 178
Duffins Orchard. Ott —80E 138
Duff St. E14 —44Dc 84
Dufour's Pl. W1 —44Lb 82 (3C 198)
Dugdale Hill La. Pot B —5Ab 8
Dugdale Ho. Egh —64E 118
(off Pooley Grn. Rd.)
Dugdales. Crox —14Q 18
Duke Gdns. Ilf —28Tc 46
Duke Humphrey Rd. SE3 —53Gc 107
(in two parts)
Duke of Cambridge Clo. Twic
—58Fa 100
Duke of Edinburgh Rd. Sutt
—75Fb 145
Duke of Wellington Pl. SW1
—47Jb 82 (2J 203)
Duke of York St. SW1
—46Lb 82 (6C 198)
Duke Rd. W4 —50Ta 79
Duke Rd. Ilf —28Tc 46
Dukes Av. N3 —25Db 41
Duke's Av. N10 —27Kb 42
Duke's Av. W4 —50Ta 79
Duke's Av. Edgw —23Pa 39
Dukes Av. Grays —48Ce 91
Dukes Av. Harr —28Ga 38
Dukes Av. Houn —56Aa 99
Dukes Av. N Mald —69Va 124
Dukes Av. N Har —30Ba 37
Dukes Av. N'holt —38Aa 57
Dukes Av. Rich & King T
—63La 122
Dukes Av. They B —7Uc 14
Dukes Clo. Ashf —63S 120
Dukes Clo. Ger X —2P 53
Dukes Clo. Hamp —64Ba 121
Dukes Ct. E6 —39Qc 66
Dukes Ct. SE13 —54Ec 106
Dukes Ct. Wok —89B 156
Dukes Dri. Farn C —6D 52
Dukes Grn. Av. Felt —57W 98
Dukes Head Pas. Hamp —66Ea 122
Dukes Hill. Wold —92Ac 182
Duke Shore Pl. E14 —45Bc 84
Dukes Kiln Dri. Ger X —2N 53
Duke's La. W8 —47Db 81
Dukes La. Asc —6E 116
Dukes La. Ger X —31A 54
Dukes M. N10 —27Kb 42
Duke's M. W1 —44Jb 82 (2J 197)
(off Duke St.)
Dukes Orchard. Bex —60Ed 110
Duke's Pas. E17 —28Ec 44
Duke's Pl. EC3 —44Ub 83 (3J 201)
Duke's Pl. Brtwd —18Yd 32
Dukes Ride. Ger X —32A 54
Dukes Ride. Uxb —35N 55
Dukes Rd. E6 —39Qc 66
Dukes Rd. W3 —42Qa 79
Duke's Rd. WC1
—41Mb 82 (4E 192)
Dukes Rd. W on T —78Z 141
Dukesthorpe Rd. SE26 —63Zb 128
Duke St. SW1 —46Lb 82
Duke St. W1 —44Jb 82 (2J 197)
Duke St. Rich —56Ma 101
Duke St. Sutt —77Fb 145
Duke St. Wat —13Y 19
Duke St. Wind —2G 94
Duke St. Wok —89B 156
Duke St. Hill. SE1
—46Tb 83 (6G 201)
Duke St. St James's. SW1
—46Lb 82 (6C 198)
Dukes Valley. Ger X —3M 53
Dukes Way. W Wick —76Gc 149
Dukes Wood Av. Ger X —31A 54
Dukes Wood Dri. Ger X —2N 53
Duke's Yd. W1 —45Jb 82 (4J 197)
Dulas St. N4 —32Qb 62
Dulford St. W11 —45Ab 80
Dulka Rd. SW11 —57Hb 103
Dulverton Mans. WC1
—42Pb 82 (6J 193)
(off Grays Inn Rd.)
Dulverton Rd. SE9 —61Sc 130
Dulverton Rd. Romf —23Md 49
Dulverton Rd. Ruis —32W 56
Dulverton Rd. S Croy —82Yb 166
Dulwich Comn. SE21 & SE22
—60Ub 105
Dulwich Lawn Clo. SE22
—57Vb 105
Dulwich Oaks Pl. SE21 —62Vb 127
Dulwich Rise Gdns. SE22
—57Vb 105
Dulwich Rd. SE24 —57Qb 104
Dulwich Village. SE21 —58Ub 105
Dulwich Way. Crox —15Q 18
Dulwich Wood Av. SE19
—63Ub 127
Dulwich Wood Pk. SE19
—63Ub 127
Dumbarton Av. Wal X —6Zb 12
Dumbarton Ct. SW2 —59Nb 104
Dumbarton Rd. SW2 —58Nb 104
Dumbleton Clo. King T —67Ra 123
Dumbreck Rd. SE9 —56Pc 108
Dumfries Clo. Wat —20V 18
Dumont Rd. N16 —34Ub 63
Dumpton Pl. NW1 —38Jb 62
Dumsey Eyot. Cher —73N 139
Dunally Pk. Shep —73T 140
Dunbar Av. SW16 —68Qb 126
Dunbar Av. Beck —70Ac 128
Dunbar Av. Dag —34Cd 68
Dunbar Clo. Hay —43X 77
Dunbar Clo. Slou —4L 73
Dunbar Ct. W on T —74Y 141
Dunbar Gdns. Dag —36Cd 68
Dunbar Rd. E7 —37Jc 65
Dunbar Rd. N22 —25Qb 42
Dunbar Rd. N Mald —70Sa 123
Dunbar St. SE27 —62Sb 127
Dunblane Clo. Edgw —19Ra 21
Dunblane Rd. SE9 —55Nc 108
Dunboe Pl. Shep —73S 140
Dunboyne Rd. NW3 —36Hb 61
Dunbridge St. E2 —42Wb 83
Duncan Clo. Barn —14Eb 23
Duncan Gro. W3 —44Ua 80
Duncannon St. WC2
—45Nb 82 (5F 199)
Duncan Rd. E8 —39Xb 63
Duncan Rd. Rich —56Na 101
Duncan Rd. Tad —91Ab 178
Duncan St. N1 —40Rb 63 (1B 194)
Duncans Yd. W'ham —98Tc 184
Duncan Ter. N1 —40Rb 63 (2B 194)
Duncan Way. Bush —12Ba 19
Duncombe Hill. SE23 —59Ac 106
Duncombe Rd. N19 —32Mb 62
Duncrievie Rd. SE13 —58Fc 107
Duncroft. SE18 —52Uc 108
Duncroft. Wind —5D 94
Dundalk Rd. SE4 —55Ac 106
Dundas Gdns. W Mol —69Da 121
Dundas Rd. SE15 —54Yb 106
Dundee Rd. E13 —40Kc 65
Dundee Rd. SE25 —71Xb 147
Dundee Rd. Slou —4D 72
Dundee St. E1 —46Xb 83
Dundela Gdns. Wor Pk —77Xa 144
Dundonald Clo. E6 —44Nc 86
Dundonald Rd. NW10 —39Za 60
Dundonald Rd. SW19 —66Ab 124
Dundrey Cres. Red —100Nb 180
Dundry Ho. SE26 —62Wb 127
Dunedin Dri. Cat —97Ub 181
Dunedin Rd. E10 —34Dc 64
Dunedin Rd. Ilf —32Sc 66
Dunedin Rd. Rain —41Hd 88
Dunedin Way. Hay —42Y 77
Dunelm Gro. SE27 —62Sb 127
Dunelm St. E1 —44Zb 84
Dunfee Way. W Byf —84N 157
Dunfield Gdns. SE6 —64Dc 128
Dunfield Rd. SE6 —64Dc 128
(in two parts)
Dunford Ct. Pinn —24Ba 37
Dunford Rd. N7 —35Pb 62
Dungarvan Av. SW15 —56Wa 102
Dunheved Clo. T Hth —72Qb 146
Dunheved Rd. N. T Hth —72Qb 146
Dunheved Rd. S. T Hth —72Qb 146
Dunheved Rd. W. T Hth —72Qb 146
Dunholme Grn. N9 —20Vb 25
Dunholme La. N9 —20Vb 25
Dunholme Rd. N9 —20Vb 25
Dunkeld Rd. SE25 —70Tb 127
Dunkeld Rd. Dag —33Xc 67
Dunkellin Gro. S Ock —44Wd 90
Dunkellin Way. S Ock —44Wd 90
Dunkery Rd. SE9 —63Mc 129
Dunkin Rd. Dart —56Qd 111
Dunkirk Clo. Grav —4E 136
Dunkirk St. SE27 —63Sb 127
Dunlace Rd. E5 —35Yb 64
Dunleary Clo. Houn —59Ba 99
Dunley Dri. New Ad —80Dc 148
Dunloe Av. N17 —27Tb 43
Dunloe Ct. E2 —40Vb 63 (2K 195)
Dunloe St. E2 —40Vb 63 (2K 195)
Dunlop Pl. SE16 —48Vb 83
Dunlop Point. E16 —46Kc 85
Dunlop Rd. Til —3B 114
Dunmail Dri. Purl —86Ub 165
Dunmore Rd. NW6 —39Ab 60
Dunmore Rd. SW20 —67Ya 124
Dunmow Clo. Felt —62Aa 121
Dunmow Clo. Lou —16Nc 28
Dunmow Clo. Romf —29Xc 47
Dunmow Dri. Rain —39Hd 68
Dunmow Gdns. W Horn —30Fe 51
Dunmow Ho. SE11
—50Pb 82 (7J 205)
(off Newburn St.)
Dunmow Rd. E15 —35Fc 65
Dunmow Wlk. N1 —39Sb 63
(off Popham St.)
Dunnets. Knap —5B 188
Dunnimans Rd. Bans —87Bb 163
Dunning Clo. S Ock —44Wd 90
Dunningford Clo. Horn —36Hd 68
Dunnings La. W Horn & Bulp
—33De 71
Dunn Mead. NW9 —24Va 40
Dunnock Clo. N9 —18Zb 26
Dunnock Clo. Borwd —14Qa 21
Dunnock Rd. E6 —44Nc 86
Dunn's Pas. WC1
—44Nb 82 (2G 199)
(off High Holborn)
Dunn St. E8 —36Vb 63
Dunny La. Chfd —4G 2
Dunnymans Rd. Bans —87Bb 163
Dunollie Pl. NW5 —36Lb 62
Dunollie Rd. NW5 —36Lb 62
Dunoon Ho. N1 —39Pb 62
(off Bemerton Est.)
Dunoon Rd. SE23 —59Yb 106
Dunraven Dri. Enf —12Qb 24
Dunraven Rd. W12 —46Wa 80
Dunraven St. W1
—45Hb 81 (4G 197)
Dunsany Rd. W14 —48Za 80
Dunsbury Clo. Sutt —81Db 163
Dunsdale Rd. SE3 —51Hc 107
Dunsfold Rise. Coul —85Mb 164
Dunsfold Way. New Ad —81Dc 166
Dunsmore Clo. Bush —16Fa 20
Dunsmore Clo. Hay —42Aa 77
Dunsmore Rd. W on T —72X 141
Dunsmore Way. Bush —16Fa 20
Dunsmure Rd. N16 —32Ub 63
Dunspring La. Ilf —26Rc 46
Dunstable Clo. Romf —23Md 49
Dunstable M. W1
—43Jb 82 (7J 191)
Dunstable Rd. Rich —56Na 101
Dunstable Rd. Romf —23Md 49
Dunstable Rd. Stanf —1M 93
Dunstable Rd. W Mol —70Ba 121
Dunstall Rd. SW20 —65Xa 124
Dunstall Way. W Mol —69Da 121
Dunstall Welling Est. Well
—54Xc 109
Dunstan Clo. N2 —27Eb 41
Dunstan Glade. Orp —72Tc 150
Dunstan Houses. E1 —43Yb 84
(off Stepney Grn.)
Dunstan Rd. E8 —39Vb 63
Dunstan Rd. NW11 —32Bb 61
Dunstan Rd. Coul —89Mb 164
Dunstan's Gro. SE22 —58Xb 105
Dunstan's Rd. SE22 —59Wb 105
Dunster Av. Mord —74Za 144
Dunster Clo. Barn —14Za 22
Dunster Clo. Hare —25K 35
Dunster Clo. Romf —26Ed 48
Dunster Ct. EC3 —45Ub 83 (4J 201)
Dunster Cres. Horn —33Qd 69
Dunster Dri. NW9 —32Sa 59
Dunster Gdns. NW6 —38Bb 61
Dunster Gdns. Slou —5E 72
Dunster Ho. SE6 —62Ec 128
Dunsterville Way. SE1
—47Tb 83 (2G 207)
Dunsterville Way. SW1 —47Tb 83
Dunster Way. Harr —34Aa 57
Dunston Rd. E8 —39Vb 63
Dunston Rd. SW11 —54Jb 104
Dunston St. E8 —39Vb 63
Dunton Clo. Surb —74Na 143
Dunton Ct. SE23 —61Xb 127
Dunton Rd. E10 —31Dc 64
Dunton Rd. SE1
—50Vb 83 (7K 207)
Dunton Rd. Romf —28Gd 48
Duntshill Rd. SW18 —60Db 103
Dunvegan Clo. W Mol —70Da 121
Dunvegan Rd. SE9 —56Pc 108
Dunwich Rd. Bexh —53Bd 109
Dunworth M. W11 —44Bb 81
Duplex Ride. SW1
—47Hb 81 (2G 203)
Duplex Rd. SW1 —47Hb 81
Dupont Rd. SW20 —68Za 124
Dupont St. E14 —44Ac 84
Duppas Av. Croy —77Rb 147
Duppas Clo. Shep —71T 140
Duppas Hill La. Croy —77Rb 147
Duppas Hill Rd. Croy —77Qb 146
Duppas Hill Ter. Croy —76Rb 147
Duppas Rd. Croy —76Qb 146
Dupree Rd. SE7 —50Kc 85
Duraden Clo. Beck —66Dc 128
Durand Clo. Cars —74Hb 145
Durand Gdns. SW9 —53Pb 104
Durands Wlk. SE16 —47Bc 84
Durand Way. NW10 —38Sa 59
Durant Rd. Swan —65Jd 132
Durants Pk. Av. Enf —14Zb 26
Durants Rd. Enf —14Yb 26
Durant St. E2 —40Wb 63
Durban Ct. E7 —38Mc 65
Durban Gdns. Dag —38Ed 68
Durban Rd. E15 —41Gc 85
Durban Rd. E17 —25Bc 44
Durban Rd. N17 —23Ub 43
Durban Rd. SE27 —63Sb 127
Durban Rd. Beck —68Bc 128
Durban Rd. Ilf —32Uc 66
Durban Rd. E. Wat —14W 18
Durban Rd. W. Wat —14W 18
Durbin Rd. Chess —77Na 143
Durdans Rd. S'hall —44Ba 77
Durell Gdns. Dag —36Zc 67
Durell Rd. Dag —36Zc 67
Durford Cres. SW15 —60Xa 102
Durham Av. Brom —70Hc 129
Durham Av. Houn —50Ba 77
Durham Av. Romf —28Ld 49
Durham Av. Slou —4E 72
Durham Av. Wfd G —22Mc 45
Durham Clo. SW20 —68Xa 124
Durham Ct. Tedd —63Fa 122
Durham Hill. Brom —63Hc 129
Durham Ho. WC2
—45Nb 82 (5G 199)
(off John Adam St.)
Durham Ho. Bark —38Wc 67
(off Margaret Bondfield Av.)
Durham Ho. Borwd —12Qa 21
(off Canterbury Rd.)
Durham Ho. Dag —36Ed 68
Durham Pl. SW3
—50Hb 81 (7F 203)
Durham Pl. Ilf —35Sc 66
Durham Rise. SE18 —50Sc 86
Durham Rd. E12 —35Mc 65
Durham Rd. E16 —42Gc 85
Durham Rd. N2 —27Gb 41
Durham Rd. N7 —33Pb 62
Durham Rd. N9 —19Wb 25
Durham Rd. SW20 —67Xa 124
Durham Rd. W5 —48Ma 79
Durham Rd. Borwd —13Sa 21
Durham Rd. Brom —69Hc 129
Durham Rd. Dag —36Ed 68
Durham Rd. Felt —59Y 99
Durham Rd. Harr —29Da 37
Durham Rd. Sidc —64Xc 131
Durham Row. E1 —43Zb 84
Durham St. SE11 —50Pb 82
Durham Ter. W2 —44Db 81
Durham Wharf. Bren —52La 100
Durham Yd. E2 —41Xb 83
Durleston Pk. Dri. Bookh
—97Ea 176
Durley Av. Pinn —31Aa 57
Durley Gdns. Orp —76Xc 151
Durley Rd. N16 —31Ub 63
Durlston Rd. E5 —33Wb 63
Durlston Rd. King T —65Na 123
Durndale La. Grav —3A 136
Durnell Way. Lou —14Qc 28
Durnford Ho. SE6 —62Ec 128
Durnford St. N15 —29Ub 43
Durnford St. SE10 —51Ec 106
Durninge Wlk. Grays —45De 91
Durning Rd. SE19 —64Tb 127
Durnsford Av. SW19 —61Cb 125
Durnsford Rd. N11 —25Mb 42
Durnsford Rd. SW19 —61Cb 125
Durrant Ct. Har W —26Ga 38
Durrants Clo. Rain —40Ld 69
Durrants Dri. Crox —13S 18
Durrant Way. Orp —78Tc 150
Durrant Way. Swans —59Ae 113
Durrell Rd. SW6 —54Bb 103
Durrell Way. Shep —72T 140
Durrington Av. SW20 —66Ya 124
Durrington Pk. Rd. SW20
—67Ya 124
Durrington Rd. E5 —35Ac 64
Durrington Tower. SW8 —54Lb 104
Durrisdeer Ho. NW2 —35Bb 61
(off Lyndale)
Dursley Clo. SE3 —54Lc 107
Dursley Ct. SE15 —51Ub 105
(off Lydney Clo.)
Dursley Gdns. SE3 —53Mc 107
Dursley Rd. SE3 —54Lc 107
Durward St. E1 —43Xb 83
Durweston M. W1
—43Hb 81 (7G 191)
(off Crawford St.)
Durweston St. W1
—43Hb 81 (1G 197)
Dury Falls Clo. Horn —32Qd 69
Dury Falls Ct. Romf —26Ed 48
Dury Rd. Barn —11Bb 23
Dutch Barn Clo. Stai —58M 97
Dutch Elm Av. Wind —2K 95
Dutch Gdns. King T —65Ra 123
Dutch Yd. SW18 —57Cb 103
Duthie St. E14 —45Ec 84
Dutton St. SE10 —53Ec 106
Dutton Way. Iver —44G 74
Duxberry Clo. Brom —71Nc 150
Duxford Clo. Horn —37Ld 69

Duxford Ho.—Edmunds Clo.

Duxford Ho. SE2 —47Zc 87
(off Wolvercote Rd.)
Dwight Rd. Wat —17U 18
Dye Ho. La. E3 —39Cc 64
Dyer Ho. Hamp —67Da 121
Dyer's Bldgs. EC1
—43Qb 82 (1K 199)
Dyers Hall Rd. E11 —33Gc 65
Dyers La. SW15 —56Xa 102
Dyers Way. Romf —24Kd 49
Dyke Ct. E17 —29Bc 44
Dyke Dri. Orp —73Yc 151
Dykes Path. Wok —87E 156
Dykes Way. Brom —69Hc 129
Dykewood Clo. Bex —62Fd 132
Dylan Clo. Els —17Ma 21
Dylan Rd. SE24 —56Rb 105
Dylan Rd. Belv —48Cd 88
Dylan Thomas Ho. N8 —28Pb 42
Dylways. SE5 —56Tb 105
Dymchurch Clo. Ilf —26Qc 46
Dymchurch Clo. Orp —77Uc 150
Dymes Path. SW19 —61Za 124
Dymock Ct. SE15 —51Ub 105
(off Lydney Clo.)
Dymock St. SW6 —55Db 103
Dymoke Rd. Horn —31Hd 68
Dyneley Rd. SE12 —62Lc 129
Dyne Rd. NW6 —38Ab 60
Dynes Rd. Kems —89Md 171
Dynes, The. Kems —89Md 171
Dynevor Rd. N16 —34Ub 63
Dynevor Rd. Rich —57Na 101
Dynham Rd. NW6 —38Cb 61
Dyott St. WC1 —44Mb 82 (2E 198)
Dyrham La. Barn —8Wa 8
Dysart Av. King T —64La 122
Dysart St. EC2 —42Tb 83 (6H 195)
Dyson Clo. Wind —5F 94
Dyson Ct. NW2 —31Ya 60
Dyson Ct. Wat —15Y 19
Dyson Ct. Wemb —33Ja 58
Dyson Ho. SE10 —50Hc 85
(off Blackwall La.)
Dyson Rd. E11 —30Gc 45
Dyson Rd. E15 —37Hc 65
Dysons Clo. Wal X —5Zb 12
Dysons Rd. N18 —22Xb 43
Dytchleys La. N'side —14Qd 31
Dytchleys Rd. Brtwd —14Pd 31

Eade Rd. N4 —31Sb 63
Eagans Clo. N2 —27Fb 41
Eagle Av. Romf —30Ad 47
Eagle Clo. Enf —14Yb 26
Eagle Clo. Horn —37Kd 69
Eagle Clo. Wal A —6Jc 13
Eagle Ct. EC1 —43Rb 83 (7B 194)
Eagle Ct. N1 —37Ub 63
Eagle Dri. NW9 —26Ua 40
Eagle Hill. SE19 —65Tb 127
Eagle La. E11 —28Jc 45
Eagle Lodge. NW11 —31Bb 61
Eagle Pl. SW1 —45Lb 82 (5C 198)
(off Piccadilly)
Eagle Pl. SW7 —50Eb 81 (7A 202)
(off Rolandway)
Eagle Rd. Wemb —38Ma 59
Eagles Dri. Tats —90Mc 167
Eaglesfield Rd. SE18 —53Rc 108
Eagles Rd. Grnh —56Xd 112
Eagle St. WC1 —43Pb 82 (1H 199)
Eagle Ter. Wfd G —24Kc 45
Eagle Way. Grav —57Ce 113
Eagle Way. Gt War —23Xd 50
Eagle Wharf E. E14 —45Ac 84
(off Narrow St.)
Eagle Wharf Rd. N1
—40Sb 63 (1E 194)
Eagle Wharf W. E14 —45Ac 84
(off Narrow St.)
Ealdham Sq. SE9 —56Lc 107
Ealing B'way. Cen. W5 —45Ma 79
Ealing Clo. Borwd —11Ta 21
Ealing Downs Ct. Gnfd —41Ja 78
Ealing Grn. W5 —46Ma 79
Ealing Pk. Gdns. W5 —49La 78
Ealing Rd. Bren —49Ma 79
Ealing Rd. N'holt —39Ca 57
Ealing Rd. Wemb —37Na 59
Ealing Village. W5 —44Na 79
Eamont Clo. Ruis —31R 56
Eamont St. NW8
—40Gb 61 (1D 190)
Eardemont Clo. Dart —56Hd 110
Eardley Cres. SW5 —50Cb 81
Eardley Rd. SW16 —64Lb 126
Eardley Rd. Belv —50Cd 88
Eardley Rd. Sev —96Kd 187
Earldom Rd. SW15 —56Ya 102
Earle Gdns. King T —66Na 123
Earlham Gro. E7 —36Hc 65
Earlham Gro. N22 —24Pb 42
Earlham St. WC2
—44Nb 82 (3E 198)
Earl Rise. SE18 —49Tc 86
Earl Rd. SE1 —50Vb 83 (7K 207)
Earl Rd. SW14 —56Sa 101
Earl Rd. Grav —1A 136
Earls Ct. Gdns. SW5 —49Db 81
Earl's Ct. Rd. W8 & SW5 —48Cb 81
Earls Ct. Sq. SW5 —50Db 81
Earlsdown Ho. Bark —40Tc 66
Earlsferry Way. N1 —38Pb 62
Earlsfield Rd. SW18 —60Eb 103
Earlshall Rd. SE9 —56Pc 108
Earls La. Pot B —4Ua 8
Earlsmead. Harr —35Ba 57
Earlsmead Rd. N15 —29Vb 43
Earlsmead Rd. NW10 —41Ya 80
Earl's Path. Lou —12Lc 27
Earls Ter. W8 —48Bb 81
Earlsthorpe M. SW12 —58Jb 104
Earlsthorpe Rd. SE26 —63Zb 128
Earlstoke St. EC1
—41Rb 83 (3B 194)
Earlston Gro. E9 —39Xb 63
Earl St. EC2 —43Tb 83 (7H 195)
Earl St. Wat —13Y 19
Earls Wlk. W8 —48Cb 81
Earl's Wlk. Dag —35Xc 67
Earlswood. Cob —84Aa 159
Earlswood Av. T Hth —71Qb 146
Earlswood Clo. SE10 —51Gc 107
Earlswood Gdns. Ilf —27Qc 46
Earlswood St. SE10 —50Gc 85
Early M. NW1 —39Kb 62
Earne Rd. W4 —51Qa 101
Earnshaw St. WC2
—44Mb 82 (2E 198)
Earsby St. W14 —49Ab 80
Easby Cres. Mord —72Db 145
Easebourne Rd. Dag —36Yc 67
Easedale Dri. Horn —36Jd 68
Easington Way. S Ock —43Wd 90
Easley's M. W1 —44Jb 82 (2J 197)
(off Wigmore St.)
E. Acton La. W3 —46Ua 80
E. Arbour St. E1 —44Zb 84
East Av. E12 —38Nc 66
East Av. E17 —28Dc 44
East Av. N2 —28Db 41
East Av. Hay —47V 76
East Av. S'hall —45Ba 77
East Av. Wall —78Pb 146
East Av. W Vill —82V 158
E. Bank. N16 —31Ub 63
Eastbank Rd. Hamp —64Ea 122
E. Barnet Rd. Barn —14Fb 23
E. Beckton District Cen. E6
—43Pc 86
E. Boundary Rd. E12 —34Pc 66
Eastbourne Av. W3 —44Ta 79
Eastbourne Bldgs. SE1
—48Ub 83 (4H 207)
(off Swan Mead)
Eastbourne Gdns. SW14 —55Sa 101
Eastbourne M. W2
—44Eb 81 (2A 196)
Eastbourne Rd. E6 —41Qc 86
Eastbourne Rd. E15 —39Gc 65
Eastbourne Rd. N15 —30Ub 43
Eastbourne Rd. SW17 —65Jb 126
Eastbourne Rd. W4 —51Sa 101
Eastbourne Rd. Bren —50La 78
Eastbourne Rd. Felt —61Z 121
Eastbourne Rd. Slou —4D 72
Eastbourne Ter. W2
—44Eb 81 (2A 196)
Eastbournia Av. N9 —20Xb 25
East Bri. Slou —6N 73
Eastbrook Av. N9 —17Yb 26
Eastbrook Av. Dag —35Ed 68
Eastbrook Clo. Wok —88C 156
Eastbrook Dri. Romf —33Gd 68
Eastbrook Rd. SE3 —53Kc 107
Eastbrook Rd. Wal A —5Gc 13
E. Burnham La. Farn R —9E 52
Eastbury Av. Bark —39Uc 66
Eastbury Av. Enf —11Vb 25
Eastbury Av. N'wd —22V 36
Eastbury Ct. Bark —39Uc 66
Eastbury Ct. New Bar —15Eb 23
(off Lyonsdown Rd.)
Eastbury Gro. W4 —50Ua 80
Eastbury Pl. N'wd —22V 36
Eastbury Rd. E6 —42Qc 86
Eastbury Rd. King T —66Na 123
Eastbury Rd. N'wd —23U 36
Eastbury Rd. Orp —72Tc 150
Eastbury Rd. Romf —30Fd 48
Eastbury Rd. Wat —17X 19
Eastbury Sq. Bark —39Vc 67
Eastbury Ter. E1 —42Zb 84
Eastcastle St. W1
—44Lb 82 (2B 198)
Eastcheap. EC3 —45Tb 83 (4G 201)
E. Churchfield Rd. W3 —46Ta 79
Eastchurch Rd. Houn —54U 98
East Clo. W5 —42Qa 79
East Clo. Barn —14Jb 24
East Clo. Gnfd —40Ea 58
East Clo. Rain —42Kd 89
Eastcombe Av. SE7 —51Kc 107
East Comn. Ger X —30A 34
Eastcote. Orp —74Vc 151
Eastcote Av. Gnfd —36Ja 58
Eastcote Av. Harr —33Da 57
Eastcote Av. W Mol —71Ba 141
Eastcote High Rd. Pinn —30W 36
Eastcote Ind. Est. Ruis —31Y 57
Eastcote La. Harr —35Aa 57
Eastcote La. N'holt —36Ba 57
Eastcote La. N. N'holt —37Ba 57
Eastcote Rd. Harr —34Ea 58
Eastcote Rd. Pinn —29Z 37
Eastcote Rd. Ruis —31U 56
Eastcote Rd. Well —54Tc 108
Eastcote St. SW9 —54Pb 104
Eastcote View. Pinn —28Y 37
East Ct. Wemb —33La 58
East Cres. N11 —21Hb 41
East Cres. Enf —15Vb 25
East Cres. Wind —3D 94
E. Crescent Rd. Grav —8E 114
Eastcroft. Slou —2F 72
Eastcroft Rd. Eps —80Ua 144
E. Cross Route. E9 & E3 —38Bc 64
Eastdean Av. Eps —85Ra 161
E. Dene Dri. H Hill —22Md 49
Eastdown Ct. SE13 —56Fc 107
Eastdown Ho. E8 —35Wb 63
Eastdown Pk. SE13 —56Fc 107
East Dri. Cars —81Gb 163
East Dri. N'wd —19U 18
East Dri. Orp —72Xc 151
East Dri. Stoke P —1J 73
East Dri. Wat —8X 5
E. Dulwich Gro. SE22 —58Ub 105
E. Dulwich Rd. SE22 & SE15
—56Vb 105
E. End Farm. Pinn —27Ba 37
East End Rd. N3 & N2 —26Cb 41
E. End Way. Pinn —27Aa 37
E. Entrance. Dag —40Dd 68
Eastern Av. E11 —30Kc 45
Eastern Av. Cher —69J 119
Eastern Av. Ilf & Romf —30Mc 45
Eastern Av. Pinn —31Z 57
Eastern Av. S Ock —47Sd 90
Eastern Av. Wal X —5Ac 12
Eastern Av. W Thur —50Vd 90
Eastern Av. E. Romf —27Fd 48
Eastern Av. W. Romf —28Ad 47
(in two parts)
Eastern Ind. Est. Eri —47Cd 88
Eastern Path. Horn —39Ld 69
Eastern Perimeter Rd. Houn
—54V 98
Eastern Rd. E13 —40Kc 65
Eastern Rd. E17 —29Ec 44
Eastern Rd. N2 —27Hb 41
Eastern Rd. N22 —25Nb 42
Eastern Rd. SE4 —56Cc 106
Eastern Rd. Grays —49Fe 91
Eastern Rd. Romf —29Gd 48
Eastern View. Big H —89Lc 167
Easternville Gdns. Ilf —30Sc 46
Eastern Way. SE28 —47Wc 87
Eastern Way. Grays —51Ce 113
E. Ferry Rd. E14 —49Dc 84
Eastfield Av. Wat —11Z 19
Eastfield Clo. Slou —8L 73
Eastfield Ct. W3 —46Ua 80
Eastfield Gdns. Dag —35Cd 68
Eastfield Pde. Pot B —4Fb 9
Eastfield Rd. E17 —28Cc 44
Eastfield Rd. N8 —27Nb 42
Eastfield Rd. Brtwd —19Zd 33
Eastfield Rd. Dag —35Cd 68
Eastfield Rd. Enf —10Zb 12
Eastfield Rd. Wal X —3Bc 12
Eastfields. Pinn —29Y 37
Eastfields Rd. W3 —43Sa 79
Eastfields Rd. Mitc —68Jb 126
East Gdns. SW17 —65Gb 125
East Gdns. Wok —89E 156
Eastgate. Bans —86Bb 163
Eastgate Clo. SE28 —44Zc 87
Eastglade. N'wd —22V 36
Eastglade. Pinn —27Ba 37
E. Hall La. Rain —44Md 89
E. Hall Rd. Orp —73Ad 151
E. Ham and Barking By-Pass. Bark
—40Uc 66
Eastham Clo. Barn —15Bb 23
Eastham Cres. Brtwd —21Ce 51
E. Ham Ind. Est. E6 —42Nc 86
E. Ham Mnr. Way. E6 —44Qc 86
E. Harding St. EC4
—44Qb 82 (2A 200)
E. Heath Rd. NW3 —34Eb 61
East Hill. SW18 —57Db 103
East Hill. Big H —90Kc 167
East Hill. Dart —59Pd 111
East Hill. S Croy —82Ub 165
East Hill. S Dar —68Sd 134
East Hill. Wemb —33Qa 59
East Hill. Wok —88E 156
E. Hill Dri. Dart —59Pd 111
E. Hill Rd. Knat —84Rd 171
E. Hill Rd. Oxt —100Gc 183
Eastholm. NW11 —28Db 41
East Holme. Eri —53Fd 110
East Holme. Hay —46W 76
E. India Dock Ho. E14 —44Ec 84
E. India Dock Rd. E14 —44Cc 84
E. India Dock Wall Rd. E14
—45Fc 85
E. Kent Av. Grav —58Ee 113
Eastlake Rd. SE5 —54Sb 105
Eastlands Clo. Oxt —99Fc 183
Eastlands Cres. SE21 —58Vb 105
Eastlands Way. Oxt —99Fc 183
East La. SE16 —47Wb 83
East La. Abb L —1W 4
East La. King T —69Ma 123
East La. Wemb —34La 58
East La. W Hor —98S 174
Eastlea Av. Wat —9Aa 5
Eastleigh Av. Harr —33Da 57
Eastleigh Clo. NW2 —34Ua 60
Eastleigh Clo. Sutt —80Db 145
Eastleigh Rd. Bexh —55Ed 110
Eastleigh Rd. H'row A —55V 98
Eastleigh Wlk. SW15 —59Wa 102
E. Lodge La. Enf —8Mb 10
East Mall. Stai —63H 119
Eastman Ho. SW4 —58Lb 104
Eastman Rd. W3 —47Ta 79
East Mead. Ruis —34Z 57
Eastmead. Wok —5E 188
Eastmead Av. Gnfd —41Da 77
Eastmead Clo. Brom —68Nc 130
Eastmearn Rd. SE21 —61Sb 127
E. Milton Rd. Grav —9F 114
Eastmont Rd. Esh —75Ha 142
Eastmoor St. SE7 —48Mc 85
E. Mount St. E1 —43Xb 83
Eastney Rd. Croy —74Rb 147
Eastney St. SE10 —50Fc 85
Eastnor Rd. SE9 —60Sc 108
Easton Gdns. Borwd —14Ua 22
Easton St. WC1 —42Qb 82 (5K 193)
East Pk. Clo. Romf —29Zc 47
East Pas. EC1 —43Sb 83 (7D 194)
(off Cloth St.)
East Pier. E1 —46Xb 83
East Pl. SE27 —63Sb 127
E. Poultry Av. EC1
—43Rb 83 (1B 200)
East Ramp. Houn —53R 98
E. Ridgeway. Cuff —1Nb 10
East Rd. E15 —39Jc 65
East Rd. N1 —41Tb 83 (4F 195)
East Rd. N2 —25Gb 41
East Rd. SW19 —65Eb 125
East Rd. Barn —18Jb 24
East Rd. Chad —29Ad 47
East Rd. Edgw —25Ra 39
East Rd. Enf —10Yb 12
East Rd. Felt —59T 98
East Rd. King T —67Na 123
East Rd. Purf —51Rd 111
East Rd. Rush —31Fd 68
East Rd. Well —54Xc 109
East Rd. W Dray —49P 75
East Rd. Wey —80T 140
E. Rochester Way. Well —56Uc 108
East Row. E11 —30Jc 45
East Row. W10 —42Ab 80
Eastry Av. Brom —72Hc 149
Eastry Rd. Eri —52Cd 110
E. Sheen Av. SW14 —57Ta 101
Eastside Rd. NW11 —28Bb 41
E. Smithfield. E1
—45Vb 83 (5K 201)
East St. SE17 —50Sb 83 (7E 206)
East St. Bark —39Sc 66
East St. Bexh —56Cd 110
East St. Bookh —97Da 175
East St. Bren —52La 100
East St. Brom —68Jc 129
East St. Cher —73J 139
East St. Eps —85Ua 162
East St. Grays —51Ee 113
East St. S Stif —51Ae 113
E. Surrey Gro. SE15 —52Vb 105
E. Tenter St. E1 —44Vb 83
East Ter. Grav —8E 114
East Ter. Sidc —60Uc 108
E. Thurrock Rd. Grays —51Ee 113
E. Tilbury Rd. Linf —7J 93
East Towers. Pinn —29Z 37
E. Vale. W3 —46Va 80
East View. E4 —22Ec 44
East View. Barn —12Bb 23
Eastview Av. SE18 —52Uc 108
Eastville Av. NW11 —30Bb 41
East Wlk. Barn —17Jb 24
East Wlk. Hay —46W 76
Eastway. E9 —37Bc 64
East Way. E11 —29Kc 45
East Way. Brom —73Jc 149
East Way. Croy —75Ac 148
Eastway. Eps —83Ta 161
East Way. Hay —46W 76
Eastway. Mord —71Za 144
East Way. Ruis —32W 56
Eastway. Wall —77Lb 146
Eastway Commercial Cen. E9
—36Cc 64
Eastwell Clo. Beck —66Ac 128
Eastwick Cres. Rick —19H 17
Eastwick Dri. Bookh —95Ca 175
Eastwick Pk. Av. Bookh —96Da 175
Eastwick Rd. Bookh —97Da 175
Eastwick Rd. W on T —79X 141
Eastwood Clo. E18 —26Jc 45
Eastwood Dri. Rain —44Kd 89
Eastwood Rd. E18 —26Jc 45
Eastwood Rd. N10 —26Jb 42
Eastwood Rd. Ilf —31Wc 67
E. Woodside. Bex —60Ad 109
Eastwood St. SW16 —65Lb 126
Eastworth Rd. Cher —74J 139
Eatington Rd. E10 —29Fc 45
Eaton Clo. SW1 —49Jb 82 (6H 203)
Eaton Clo. Stan —21Ka 38
Eaton Dri. SW9 —56Rb 105
Eaton Dri. King T —66Qa 123
Eaton Dri. Romf —24Dd 48
Eaton Gdns. Dag —38Ad 67
Eaton Ga. SW1 —49Jb 82 (5H 203)
Eaton Ga. N'wd —23S 36
Eaton La. SW1 —48Kb 82 (4A 204)
Eaton M. N. SW1
—49Jb 82 (5H 203)
Eaton M. S. SW1
—49Jb 82 (5J 203)
Eaton M. W. SW1
—49Jb 82 (5J 203)
Eaton Pk. Cob —86Aa 159
Eaton Pk. Rd. N13 —19Qb 24
Eaton Pk. Rd. Cob —86Aa 159
Eaton Pl. SW1 —49Jb 82 (4H 203)
Eaton Rise. E11 —29Lc 45
Eaton Rise. W5 —43Ma 79
Eaton Rd. NW4 —29Ya 40
Eaton Rd. Enf —14Ub 25
Eaton Rd. Houn —56Fa 100
Eaton Rd. Sidc —61Zc 131
Eaton Rd. Sutt —79Eb 145
Eaton Row. SW1
—48Kb 82 (4K 203)
Eatons Mead. E4 —19Cc 26
Eaton Sq. SW1 —49Jb 82 (5H 203)
Eaton Sq. Long —69Ae 135
Eaton Ter. E3 —41Ac 84
Eaton Ter. SW1 —49Jb 82 (5H 203)
Eaton Ter. M. SW1
—49Jb 82 (5H 203)
(off Eaton Ter.)
Eatonville Rd. SW17 —61Hb 125
Eatonville Vs. SW17 —61Hb 125
Eaton Wlk. SE15 —52Vb 105
(off Commercial Way)
Ebbas Way. Eps —87Ra 161
Ebbisham Dri. SW8 —51Pb 104
Ebbisham La. Tad —93Va 178
Ebbisham Rd. Eps —86Ra 161
Ebbisham Rd. Wor Pk —75Ya 144
Ebbsfleet Ind. Est. Grav —57Ce 113
Ebbsfleet Rd. NW2 —36Ab 60
Ebbsfleet Wlk. Grav —58De 113
Ebdon Way. SE3 —55Kc 107
Ebenezer St. N1 —41Tb 83 (3F 195)
Ebenezer Wlk. SW16 —67Lb 126
Ebley Clo. SE15 —51Vb 105
Ebner St. SW18 —57Db 103
Ebon Way. SE3 —55Kc 107
Ebor Cotts. SW15 —62Ua 124
Ebor St. E1 —42Vb 83
Ebrington Rd. Harr —30Ma 39
Ebsworth St. SE23 —59Zb 106
Eburne Rd. N7 —34Nb 62
Ebury App. Rick —18M 17
Ebury Bri. SW1 —50Kb 82 (7K 203)
Ebury Bri. Est. SW1
—50Kb 82 (7K 203)
(off Ebury Bri. Rd.)
Ebury Bri. Rd. SW1 —50Jb 82
Ebury Clo. Kes —76Nc 150
Ebury Clo. N'wd —22S 36
Ebury M. SE27 —62Rb 127
Ebury M. SW1 —49Kb 82 (5J 203)
Ebury M. E. SW1
—48Kb 82 (5K 203)
Ebury Rd. Rick —18M 17
Ebury Rd. Wat —13Y 19
Ebury Sq. SW1 —49Jb 82 (6J 203)
Ebury St. SW1 —49Jb 82 (7J 203)
Ecclesbourne Clo. N13 —22Qb 42
Ecclesbourne Gdns. N13 —22Qb 42
Ecclesbourne Rd. N1 —38Sb 63
Ecclesbourne Rd. T Hth —71Sb 147
Eccles Rd. SW11 —56Hb 103
Eccleston Bri. SW1
—49Kb 82 (5A 204)
Eccleston Clo. Barn —14Hb 23
Eccleston Clo. Orp —74Tc 150
Eccleston Cres. Romf —31Xc 67
Ecclestone Ct. Wemb —36Na 59
Ecclestone M. Wemb —36Na 59
Ecclestone Pl. Wemb —36Pa 59
Eccleston Ho. SW2 —58Qb 104
Eccleston M. SW1
—48Jb 82 (4J 203)
Eccleston Pl. SW1
—49Kb 82 (6K 203)
Eccleston Rd. W13 —45Ja 78
Eccleston Sq. SW1
—49Kb 82 (6A 204)
Eccleston Sq. M. SW1
—49Lb 82 (6B 204)
Eccleston St. SW1
—48Kb 82 (4J 203)
Echelforde Dri. Ashf —63Q 120
Echo Heights. E4 —18Dc 26
Echo Sq. Grav —1E 136
Eckersley St. E1 —42Wb 83
Eckford St. N1 —40Qb 62 (1K 193)
Eckington Ho. N15 —30Tb 43
(off Fladbury Rd.)
Eckstein Rd. SW11 —56Gb 103
Eclipse Rd. E13 —43Kc 85
Ecton Rd. Add —77K 139
Ector Rd. SE6 —61Gc 129
Edam Ct. Sidc —62Wc 131
Edans Ct. W12 —47Va 80
Edbrooke Rd. W9 —42Cb 81
Eddington St. N4 —32Qb 62
Eddisbury Ho. SE26 —62Wb 127
Eddiscombe Rd. SW6 —54Bb 103
Eddy Clo. Romf —30Dd 48
Eddystone. Cars —83Fb 163
Eddystone Rd. SE4 —57Ac 106
Eddystone Tower. SE8 —50Ac 84
Eddystone Wlk. Stai —59N 97
Ede Clo. Houn —55Ba 99
Edenbridge Clo. Orp —70Zc 131
Edenbridge Rd. E9 —38Zb 64
Edenbridge Rd. Enf —16Ub 25
Eden Clo. W8 —48Cb 81
Eden Clo. Bex —63Fd 132
Eden Clo. New Haw —82K 157
Eden Clo. Slou —50C 74
Eden Clo. Wemb —39Ma 59
Edencourt Rd. SW16 —65Kb 126
Edendale Rd. Bexh —53Fd 110
Edenfield Gdns. Wor Pk —76Va 144
Eden Grn. S Ock —43Xd 90
Eden Gro. E17 —29Dc 44
Eden Gro. N7 —36Pb 62
Eden Gro. Rd. Byfl —85N 157
Edenhall Clo. Romf —22Ld 49
Edenhall Glen. Romf —22Ld 49
Edenhall Rd. Romf —22Ld 49
Edenham Way. W10 —42Bb 81
Edenhurst. Sev —97Jd 186
Edenhurst Av. SW6 —55Bb 103
Eden M. SW17 —62Eb 125
Eden Pk. Av. Beck —70Ac 128
Eden Pl. Grav —9D 114
Eden Rd. E17 —29Dc 44
Eden Rd. SE27 —63Rb 127
Eden Rd. Beck —70Ac 128
Eden Rd. Bex —63Ed 132
Eden Rd. Croy —77Tb 147
Edenside Rd. Bookh —96Ba 175
Edensor Gdns. W4 —52Ua 102
Edensor Rd. W4 —52Ua 102
Eden St. King T —68Ma 123
Edenvale Rd. Mitc —66Jb 126
Edenvale St. SW6 —54Db 103
Eden Wlk. King T —68Na 123
Eden Way. Beck —71Bc 148
Eden Way. Warl —90Ac 166
Ederline Av. SW16 —69Pb 126
Edgar Clo. Swan —69Hd 132
Edgar Ct. N Mald —69Ua 124
Edgar Ho. E9 —36Ac 64
(off Homerton Rd.)
Edgar Ho. E11 —31Jc 65
Edgarley Ter. SW6 —53Ab 102
Edgar Rd. E3 —41Dc 84
Edgar Rd. Houn —59Ba 99
Edgar Rd. Kems —89Nd 171
Edgar Rd. Romf —31Zc 67
Edgar Rd. S Croy —81Tb 165
Edgar Rd. Tats —93Mc 183
Edgar Rd. W Dray —45N 75
Edgbaston Dri. Shenl —4Na 7
Edgbaston Rd. Wat —20X 19
Edgcombe Rd. E11 —32Hc 65
Edgeborough Way. Brom
—66Mc 129
Edgebury. Chst —63Rc 130
Edgebury Wlk. Chst —63Sc 130
Edge Bus. Cen., The. NW2
—33Xa 60
Edge Clo. Wey —80Q 140
Edgecombe Ho. SE5 —54Ub 105
Edgecoombe. S Croy —80Yb 148
Edgecoombe Clo. King T —66Ta 123
Edgecote Clo. W3 —46Sa 79
Edgecot Gro. N15 —29Ub 43
Edgefield Av. Bark —38Vc 67
Edgefield Clo. Dart —60Rd 111
Edgefield Ct. Bark —38Vc 67
(off Edgefield Av.)
Edgefoot Gro. N15 —29Ub 43
Edge Hill. SE18 —51Rc 108
Edge Hill. SW19 —66Za 124
Edgehill Av. N3 —28Cb 41
Edge Hill Ct. SW19 —66Za 124
Edge Hill Ct. Sidc —63Vc 131
Edgehill Ct. W on T —74Y 141
Edgehill Gdns. Dag —35Cd 68
Edgehill Gdns. Grav —7B 136
Edgehill Ho. SW9 —54Rb 105
Edgehill Rd. W13 —43La 78
Edgehill Rd. Chst —62Sc 130
Edgehill Rd. Mitc —67Kb 126
Edgehill Rd. Purl —82Rb 165
Edgeley. Bookh —96Aa 175
Edgeley La. SW4 —55Mb 104
Edgeley Rd. SW4 —55Mb 104
Edgell Clo. Vir W —69B 118
Edgell Rd. Stai —64H 119
Edgel St. SW18 —56Db 103
Edgepoint Clo. SE27 —64Rb 127
Edge St. W8 —46Cb 81
Edgewood Dri. Orp —78Wc 151
Edgewood Grn. Croy —74Zb 148
Edgeworth Av. NW4 —29Wa 40
Edgeworth Clo. NW4 —29Wa 40
Edgeworth Clo. Whyt —90Wb 165
Edgeworth Cres. NW4 —29Wa 40
Edgeworth Rd. SE9 —56Lc 107
Edgeworth Rd. Barn —14Gb 23
Edgington Rd. SW16 —65Mb 126
Edgington Way. Sidc —66Yc 131
Edgwarebury Gdns. Edgw
—22Qa 39
Edgwarebury La. Els & Edgw
(in three parts) —17Na 21
Edgware Ct. Edgw —23Qa 39
Edgware Rd. NW2 —32Xa 60
Edgware Rd. NW9 —26Sa 39
Edgware Rd. W2
—42Fb 81 (6B 190)
Edgware Way. Edgw —18Ma 21
Edinburgh Av. Rick —16J 17
Edinburgh Av. Slou —3E 72
Edinburgh Clo. Uxb —35R 56
Edinburgh Ct. SW20 —71Za 144
Edinburgh Ct. Eri —52Fd 110
Edinburgh Cres. Wal X —5Ac 12
Edinburgh Dri. Den —30H 35
Edinburgh Dri. Romf —28Ed 48
Edinburgh Dri. Stai —65M 119
Edinburgh Dri. Uxb —35R 56
Edinburgh Gdns. Wind —4H 95
Edinburgh Ga. SW1
—47Hb 81 (2F 203)
Edinburgh Ho. NW4 —27Ya 40
Edinburgh M. Til —4D 114
Edinburgh Rd. E13 —40Kc 65
Edinburgh Rd. E17 —29Bc 44
Edinburgh Rd. N18 —22Wb 43
Edinburgh Rd. W7 —47Ha 78
Edinburgh Rd. Sutt —75Eb 145
Edington Rd. SE2 —48Xc 87
Edington Rd. Enf —12Yb 26
Edison Av. Horn —32Hd 68
Edison Clo. Horn —32Hd 68
Edison Dri. S'hall —44Da 77
Edison Gro. SE18 —52Vc 109
Edison Ho. Wemb —34Sa 59
(off Barnhill Rd.)
Edison Rd. N8 —30Mb 42
Edison Rd. Brom —68Jc 129
Edison Rd. Enf —12Bc 26
Edison Rd. Well —53Vc 109
Edis St. NW1 —39Jb 62
Edith Bell Ho. Ger X —23A 34
Edith Cavell Clo. N19 —31Nb 62
Edith Gdns. Surb —73Ra 143
Edith Gro. SW10 —51Eb 103
Edith Ho. W6 —50Ya 80
(off Queen Caroline St.)
Edithna St. SW9 —55Nb 104
Edith Rd. E6 —38Mc 65
Edith Rd. E15 —36Fc 65
Edith Rd. N11 —24Mb 42
Edith Rd. SE25 —71Tb 147
Edith Rd. SW19 —65Db 125
Edith Rd. W14 —49Ab 80
Edith Rd. Orp —78Wc 151
Edith Rd. Romf —31Zc 67
Edith Row. SW6 —53Db 103
Edith St. E2 —40Wb 63
Edith Ter. SW10 —52Eb 103
Edith Vs. W14 —49Bb 81
Edith Yd. SW10 —52Eb 103
Ediva Rd. Meop —10C 136
Edmansons Clo. N17 —25Vb 43
Edmeston Clo. E9 —37Ac 64
Edmond Ct. SE14 —53Yb 106
Edmund Clo. Meop —10C 136
Edmund Ho. SE17 —50Rb 83
Edmund Rd. Mitc —69Gb 125
Edmund Rd. Orp —72Yc 151
Edmund Rd. Rain —40Gd 68
Edmund Rd. Well —55Wc 109
Edmunds Av. Orp —69Zc 131
Edmunds Clo. Hay —43Y 77

Edmund St.—Elm Rd.

Edmund St. SE5 —52Tb 105
Edmunds Wlk. N2 —28Gb 41
Edmunds Way. Slou —3M 73
Edna Rd. SW20 —68Za 124
Edna St. SW11 —53Gb 103
Edred Ho. E9 —35Ac 64
(off King's Mead Way)
Edrich Ho. SW4 —53Nb 104
Edrick Rd. Edgw —23Sa 39
Edrick Wlk. Edgw —23Sa 39
Edric Rd. SE14 —52Zb 106
Edridge Clo. Bush —15Ea 20
Edridge Clo. Horn —36Md 69
Edridge Rd. Croy —76Sb 147
Edulf Rd. Borwd —11Ra 21
Edward Amey Clo. Wat —8Y 5
Edward Av. E4 —23Dc 44
Edward Av. Mord —71Fb 145
Edward Clo. N9 —17Vb 25
Edward Clo. Abb L —4V 4
Edward Clo. Hamp —64Ea 122
Edward Clo. N'holt —40Y 57
Edward Clo. Romf —27Ld 49
Edward Ct. E16 —43Jc 85
Edward Ct. Stai —64L 119
Edward Ct. Wal A —5Hc 13
Edward Dodd Ct. N1
(off Chart St.) —41Tb 83 (3G 195)
Edward Edward's Ho. SE1
—46Rb 83 (7B 200)
(off Nicholson St.)
Edwardes Pl. W8 —48Bb 81
Edwardes Sq. W8 —48Bb 81
Edward Gro. Barn —15Fb 23
Edward Ho. SE11 —50Pb 82 (7J 205)
(off Newburn St.)
Edward M. NW1 —41Kb 82 (3A 192)
Edward M. W1 —44Jb 82
Edward Pl. SE8 —51Bc 106
Edward Rd. E17 —28Zb 44
Edward Rd. SE20 —65Zb 128
Edward Rd. Barn —15Fb 23
Edward Rd. Big H —90Nc 168
Edward Rd. Brom —66Kc 129
Edward Rd. Chst —64Rc 130
Edward Rd. Coul —87Mb 164
Edward Rd. Croy —73Ub 147
Edward Rd. Felt —57T 98
Edward Rd. Hamp —64Ea 122
Edward Rd. Harr —27Ea 38
Edward Rd. N'holt —40Y 57
Edward Rd. Romf —30Ad 47
Edward's Av. Ruis —37X 57
Edwards Clo. Hut —16Fe 33
Edwards Clo. Wor Pk —75Za 144
Edwards Cotts. N1 —37Rb 63
Edwards Ct. Slou —7J 73
Edwards Dri. N11 —24Mb 42
Edward II Av. Byfl —86P 157
Edwards Gdns. Swan —70Fd 132
Edwards La. N16 —33Ub 63
Edwards Mans. Bark —38Vc 67
(off Upney La.)
Edwards M. W1 —44Jb 82 (3H 197)
Edward Sq. N1 —39Pb 62 (1H 193)
Edwards Rd. Belv —49Cd 88
Edward St. E16 —42Jc 85
Edward St. SE8 —51Bc 106
Edward St. SE14 —52Ac 106
Edwards Way. Hut —16Fe 33
Edward Temme Av. E15 —38Hc 65
Edward Way. Ashf —61P 119
Edwick Ct. Chesh —1Zb 12
Edwina Gdns. Ilf —29Nc 46
Edwin Arnold Ct. Sidc —63Vc 131
Edwin Av. E6 —40Qc 66
(in two parts)
Edwin Clo. Bexh —51Bd 109
Edwin Clo. Rain —41Hd 88
Edwin Clo. W Hor —97T 174
Edwin Pl. Croy —74Ub 147
Edwin Rd. Dart —62Kd 133
Edwin Rd. Edgw —23Ta 39
Edwin Rd. Twic —60Ga 100
Edwin Rd. W Hor —97S 174
Edwin's Mead. E9 —35Ac 64
Edwinstray Ho. Felt —62Ca 121
Edwin St. E1 —42Yb 84
Edwin St. E16 —43Jc 85
Edwin St. Grav —9D 114
Edwin Ware Ct. Pinn —26Y 37
Edwis Ho. SE15 —52Wb 105
Edwyn Clo. Barn —16Ya 22
Eel Pie Island. Twic —60Ja 100
Effie Pl. SW6 —52Cb 103
Effie Rd. SW6 —52Cb 103
Effingham Clo. Sutt —80Db 145
Effingham Comn. Rd. Eff —95W 174
Effingham Ct. Wok —91A 172
Effingham Rd. N8 —29Qb 42
Effingham Rd. SE12 —57Gc 107
Effingham Rd. Croy —73Pb 146
Effingham Rd. Surb —73Ka 142
Effort St. SW17 —64Gb 125
Effra Ct. SW2 —57Pb 104
(off Brixton Hill)
Effra Pde. SW2 —57Qb 104
Effra Rd. SW2 —56Qb 104
Effra Rd. SW19 —65Db 125
Egan Way. SE16 —50Xb 83
Egan Way. Hay —45U 76
Egbert St. NW1 —39Jb 62
Egbwerts Way. E4 —18Ec 26
Egdean Wlk. Sev —95Ld 187
Egerton Av. Swan —66Hd 132
Egerton Clo. Dart —60Kd 111
Egerton Clo. Pinn —28W 36
Egerton Ct. E11 —31Fc 65
Egerton Cres. SW3
—49Gb 81 (5E 202)
Egerton Dri. SE10 —53Dc 106
Egerton Gdns. NW4 —28Xa 40
Egerton Gdns. NW10 —39Ya 60
Egerton Gdns. SW3
—48Gb 81 (4D 202)
Egerton Gdns. W13 —44Ka 78
Egerton Gdns. Ilf —34Vc 67
Egerton Gdns. M. SW3
—48Gb 81 (4E 202)
Egerton M. SW3 —48Gb 81
Egerton Pl. SW3 —48Gb 81 (4E 202)
Egerton Pl. Wey —79S 140
Egerton Rd. N16 —31Vb 63
Egerton Rd. SE25 —69Ub 127
Egerton Rd. N Mald —70Va 124
Egerton Rd. Slou —2C 72
Egerton Rd. Twic —59Ga 100
Egerton Rd. Wemb —38Pa 59
Egerton Rd. Wey —79S 140
Egerton Ter. SW3
—48Gb 81 (4E 202)
Egerton Way. Hay —52R 98
Eggardon Ct. N'holt —37Ea 58
Eggerton Rd. W9 —42Bb 81
Egg Hall. Epp —1Wc 15
Egham By-Pass. Egh —64B 118
Egham Clo. SW19 —61Ab 124
Egham Clo. Sutt —75Ab 144
Egham Cres. Sutt —76Za 144
Egham Hill. Egh —5P 117
Egham Rd. E13 —43Kc 85
Eglantine La. F'ham —73Qd 153
Eglantine Rd. SW18 —57Eb 103
Egleston Rd. Mord —72Db 145
Egley Dri. Wok —10G 188
Egley Rd. Wok —10G 188
Eglington Ct. SE17 —51Sb 105
Eglington Rd. E4 —17Fc 27
Eglinton Hill. SE18 —51Rc 108
Eglinton Rd. SE18 —51Qc 108
Eglinton Rd. Swans —58Ae 113
Eglise Rd. Warl —89Ac 166
Egliston M. SW15 —55Ya 102
Egliston Rd. SW15 —55Ya 102
Eglon M. NW1 —38Hb 61
Egmont Av. Surb —74Pa 143
Egmont Pk. Rd. Tad —97Wa 178
Egmont Rd. N Mald —70Va 124
Egmont Rd. Surb —74Pa 143
Egmont Rd. Sutt —80Eb 145
Egmont Rd. W on T —73X 141
Egmont St. SE14 —52Zb 106
Egmont Way. Tad —91Ab 178
Egremont Gdns. Slou —6E 72
Egremont Rd. SE27 —62Qb 126
Egret Way. Hay —44Z 77
Egypt La. Farn C —3F 52
Eider Clo. E7 —36Hc 65
Eider Clo. Hay —43Z 77
Eight Acres. Burn —2A 72
Eighteenth Rd. Mitc —70Nb 126
Eighth Av. E12 —35Pc 66
Eighth Av. Hay —46W 76
Eileen Rd. SE25 —71Tb 147
Einstein Ho. Wemb —34Sa 59
Eisenhower Dri. E6 —43Nc 86
Elaine Gro. NW5 —36Jb 62
Elam Clo. SE5 —54Rb 105
Elam St. SE5 —54Rb 105
Eland Pl. Croy —76Rb 147
Eland Rd. SW11 —55Hb 103
Eland Rd. Croy —76Rb 147
Elba Pl. SE17 —49Sb 83 (5E 206)
Elberon Av. Croy —72Lb 146
Elbe St. SW6 —54Eb 103
Elborough Rd. SE25 —71Wb 147
Elborough St. SW18 —60Cb 103
Elbow Meadow. Coln —53H 97
Elbury Dri. E16 —44Jc 85
Elcho St. SW11 —52Gb 103
Elcot Av. SE15 —52Xb 105
Elder Av. N8 —29Nb 42
Elderbeck Clo. Chesh —1Wb 11
Elderberry Gro. SE27 —63Sb 127
Elderberry Rd. W5 —47Na 79
Elderberry Way. Wat —7X 5
Elder Clo. W Dray —45N 75
Elder Ct. Bush —19Ga 20
Elderfield Rd. E5 —35Yb 64
Elderfield Rd. Stoke P —7K 53
Elderfield Wlk. E11 —29Kc 45
Elder Oak Clo. SE20 —67Xb 127
Elder Oak Ct. SE20 —67Wb 127
Elder Rd. SE27 —63Sb 127
Elderslie Clo. Beck —72Dc 148
Elderslie Rd. SE9 —57Qc 108
Elder St. E1 —42Vb 83 (7K 195)
Elderton Rd. SE26 —63Ac 128
Eldertree Pl. Mitc —67Lb 126
Eldertree Way. Mitc —67Lb 126
Elder Way. Langl —47B 74
Elder Way. Rain —41Md 89
Elderwood Pl. SE27 —64Sb 127
Eldon Av. Borwd —12Qa 21
Eldon Av. Croy —75Yb 148
Eldon Av. Houn —52Ca 99
Eldon Gro. NW3 —36Fb 61
Eldon Pk. SE25 —70Xb 127
Eldon Rd. E17 —28Bc 44
Eldon Rd. N9 —18Yb 26
Eldon Rd. N22 —25Rb 43
Eldon Rd. W8 —48Db 81
Eldon Rd. Cat —93Tb 181
Eldon St. EC2 —43Tb 83 (1G 201)
Eldon Way. NW10 —41Ra 79
Eldred Dri. Orp —75Yc 151
Eldred Gdns. Upm —31Ud 70
Eldred Rd. Bark —39Uc 66
Eldrick Ct. Felt —60T 98
Eldridge Clo. Felt —60W 98
Eldridge Ct. SE16 —48Wb 83
Eleanor Av. Eps —82Ta 161
Eleanor Clo. N15 —27Vb 43
Eleanor Clo. SE16 —47Zb 84
Eleanor Cres. NW7 —22Za 40
Eleanor Cross Rd. Wal X —6Ac 12
(in two parts)
Eleanor Gdns. Barn —15Za 22
Eleanor Gdns. Dag —33Bd 67
Eleanor Gro. SW13 —55Ua 102
Eleanor Gro. Uxb —3R 56
Eleanor Rd. E8 —37Xb 63
Eleanor Rd. E15 —37Hc 65
Eleanor Rd. N11 —23Nb 42
Eleanor Rd. Wal X —5Ac 12
Eleanor St. E3 —41Cc 84
Eleanor Wlk. SE18 —49Nc 86
Eleanor Way. Wal X —6Bc 12
Eleanor Way. War —22Zd 51
Electric Av. SW9 —56Qb 104
Electric La. SW9 & SW2 —56Qb 104
(in two parts)
Electric Pde. Surb —72Ma 143
Elephant & Castle. SE1
—49Rb 83 (5C 206)
Elephant La. SE16 —47Yb 84
Elephant Rd. SE17
—49Sb 83 (5D 206)
Elers Rd. W13 —47La 78
Elers Rd. Hay —49T 76
Eleven Acre Rise. Lou —13Pc 28
Eley Ind. Est. N18 —21Zb 44
(in two parts)
Eley Rd. N18 —21Yb 44
Elfindale Rd. SE24 —57Sb 105
Elfin Gro. Tedd —64Ha 122
Elford Clo. SE3 —56Kc 107
Elford M. SW4 —57Lb 104
Elfort Rd. N5 —35Qb 62
Elfrida Cres. SE6 —63Cc 128
Elfrida Rd. Wat —15Y 19
Elf Row. E1 —45Yb 84
Elfwine Rd. W7 —43Ga 78
Elgal Clo. Orp —78Rc 150
Elgar. N8 —27Nb 42
(off Boyton Clo.)
Elgar Av. NW10 —37Ta 59
(in two parts)
Elgar Av. SW16 —69Nb 126
Elgar Av. W5 —47Na 79
Elgar Av. Surb —74Qa 143
Elgar Clo. E13 —40Lc 65
Elgar Clo. SE8 —52Cc 106
Elgar Clo. Buck H —19Mc 27
Elgar Clo. Els —17La 20
Elgar Clo. Uxb —33Q 56
Elgar Gdns. Til —3C 114
Elgar St. SE16 —48Ac 84
Elgin Av. W9 —42Bb 81
Elgin Av. Ashf —65S 120
Elgin Av. Harr —26Ka 38
Elgin Av. Romf —24Rd 49
Elgin Ct. W9 —42Db 81
Elgin Cres. W11 —45Ab 80
Elgin Cres. Cat —94Wb 181
Elgin Cres. Houn —54U 98
Elgin Dri. N'wd —24U 36
Elgin Ho. War —21Zd 51
Elgin M. W11 —44Ab 80
Elgin M. N. W9 —41Db 81
Elgin M. S. W9 —41Db 81
Elgin Rd. N22 —26Lb 42
Elgin Rd. Chesh —2Yb 12
Elgin Rd. Croy —75Vb 147
Elgin Rd. Ilf —32Uc 66
Elgin Rd. Sutt —76Eb 145
Elgin Rd. Wall —79Lb 146
Elgin Rd. Wey —78Q 140
Elgood Av. N'wd —23W 36
Elgood Clo. W11 —45Ab 80
Elham Clo. Brom —66Mc 129
Elham Ho. E5 —36Xb 63
Elia M. N1 —40Rb 63 (2B 194)
Elias Pl. SW8 —51Qb 104
Elia St. N1 —40Rb 63 (2B 194)
Elibank Rd. SE9 —56Pc 108
Elim Est. SE1 —48Ub 83 (3G 207)
Elim St. SE1 —48Tb 83 (3G 207)
(in two parts)
Elim Way. E13 —41Hc 85
Eliot Bank. SE23 —61Xb 127
Eliot Cotts. SE3 —54Gc 107
Eliot Dri. Harr —33Da 57
Eliot Hill. SE13 —54Ec 106
Eliot Pk. SE13 —54Ec 106
Eliot Pl. SE3 —54Gc 107
Eliot Rd. Dag —35Zc 67
Eliot Rd. Dart —57Rd 111
Eliot Vale. SE3 —54Fc 107
Elizabethan Clo. Stai —60M 97
Elizabethan Way. Stai —60M 97
Elizabeth Av. N1 —39Sb 63
Elizabeth Av. Amer —11A 16
Elizabeth Av. Enf —13Rb 25
Elizabeth Av. Ilf —33Tc 66
Elizabeth Av. Stai —65L 119
Elizabeth Blackwell Ho. N22
(off Progress Way) —25Qb 42
Elizabeth Bri. SW1
—49Kb 82 (6K 203)
Elizabeth Clo. E14 —44Dc 84
Elizabeth Clo. W9
—42Eb 81 (6A 190)
Elizabeth Clo. Barn —13Za 22
Elizabeth Clo. Romf —25Dd 48
Elizabeth Clo. Til —4D 114
Elizabeth Clyde Clo. N15 —28Ub 43
Elizabeth Cotts. Rich —53Pa 101
Elizabeth Ct. E4 —22Bc 44
Elizabeth Ct. SW1
—48Mb 82 (4E 204)
(off Milmans Ct.)
Elizabeth Ct. Eri —52Fd 110
(off Valence Rd.)
Elizabeth Ct. Grav —8C 114
Elizabeth Ct. Slou —7L 73
Elizabeth Ct. Tedd —64Ga 122
Elizabeth Ct. Wat —10V 4
Elizabeth Ct. Whyt —90Vb 165
Elizabeth Dri. They B —8Uc 14
Elizabeth Fry Ho. Hay —49V 76
Elizabeth Fry Ho. Ott —79F 138
(off Vernon Clo.)
Elizabeth Fry Rd. E8 —38Xb 63
Elizabeth Gdns. W3 —46Va 80
Elizabeth Gdns. Asc —10A 116
Elizabeth Gdns. Stan —23La 38
Elizabeth Gdns. Sun —69Y 121
Elizabeth Garrett Anderson Ho. Belv
—48Cd 88
Elizabeth Ho. SE11
—49Qb 82 (6A 206)
(off Reedworth St.)
Elizabeth Ho. Grays —46De 91
Elizabeth Huggins Cotts. Grav
—1D 136
Elizabeth M. NW3 —37Gb 61
Elizabeth M. Harr —30Ga 38
Elizabeth Newcomen Ho. SE1
—47Tb 83 (1F 207)
(off Newcomen St.)
Elizabeth Pl. N15 —28Tb 43
Elizabeth Ride. N9 —17Xb 25
Elizabeth Rd. E6 —39Mc 65
Elizabeth Rd. N15 —29Ub 43
Elizabeth Rd. Grays —47Be 91
Elizabeth Rd. Pil H —16Xd 32
Elizabeth Rd. Rain —43Kd 89
Elizabeth St. SE1 —47Vb 83
Elizabeth St. SW1
—49Jb 82 (5J 203)
Elizabeth St. Grnh —57Ud 112
Elizabeth Ter. SE9 —58Pc 108
Elizabeth Way. SE19 —66Tb 127
Elizabeth Way. Felt —63Y 121
Elizabeth Way. Orp —71Yc 151
Elizabeth Way. Stoke P —9K 53
Elkington Rd. E13 —42Kc 85
Elkins Rd. Hedg —3J 53
Elkins, The. Romf —26Gd 48
Elkstone Ct. SE15 —51Ub 105
(off Birdlip Clo.)
Elkstone Rd. W10 —43Bb 81
Ellaline Rd. W6 —51Za 102
Ellanby Cres. N18 —21Xb 43
Elland Rd. SE15 —56Yb 106
Elland Rd. W on T —75Z 141
Ella Rd. N8 —31Nb 62
Ellement Clo. Pinn —29Z 37
Ellena Ct. N14 —20Nb 24
(off Conway Rd.)
Ellenborough Ho. W12 —45Xa 80
(off White City Est.)
Ellenborough Pl. SW15 —56Wa 102
Ellenborough Rd. N22 —25Sb 43
Ellenborough Rd. Sidc —64Zc 131
Ellenbridge Way. S Croy —81Ub 165
Ellen Clo. Brom —69Mc 129
Ellen Ct. E4 —18Ec 26
(off Ridgeway, The.)
Ellen Ct. N9 —19Yb 26
Ellen St. E1 —44Wb 83
Ellen Wilkinson Ho. Dag —34Cd 68
Elleray Rd. Tedd —65Ha 122
Ellerby St. SW6 —53Za 102
Ellerdale Clo. NW3 —35Eb 61
Ellerdale Rd. NW3 —36Eb 61
Ellerdale St. SE13 —56Dc 106
Ellerdine Rd. Houn —56Ea 100
Ellerker Gdns. Rich —58Na 101
Ellerman Av. Twic —60Ba 99
Ellerman Rd. Til —4B 114
Ellerslie. Grav —9F 114
Ellerslie Gdns. NW10 —39Wa 60
Ellerslie Rd. W12 —46Xa 80
Ellerslie Sq. Ind. Est. SW2
—57Nb 104
Ellerton Gdns. Dag —38Yc 67
Ellerton Rd. SW13 —53Wa 102
Ellerton Rd. SW18 —60Fb 103
Ellerton Rd. SW20 —66Wa 124
Ellerton Rd. Dag —38Yc 67
Ellerton Rd. Surb —75Pa 143
Ellery Ho. SE17 —49Tb 83 (6G 207)
Ellery Rd. SE19 —66Tb 127
Ellery St. SE15 —54Xb 105
Ellesborough Clo. Wat —22Y 37
Ellesmere Av. NW7 —20Ta 21
Ellesmere Av. Beck —68Ec 128
Ellesmere Clo. E11 —29Hc 45
Ellesmere Clo. Ruis —31S 56
Ellesmere Ct. W4 —51Ta 101
Ellesmere Dri. S Croy —86Xb 165
Ellesmere Gdns. Ilf —29Nc 46
Ellesmere Gro. Barn —15Bb 23
Ellesmere Rd. E3 —40Ac 64
Ellesmere Rd. NW10 —36Wa 60
Ellesmere Rd. W4 —51Sa 101
Ellesmere Rd. Gnfd —42Ea 78
Ellesmere Rd. Twic —58La 100
Ellesmere Rd. Wey —80U 140
Ellesmere St. E14 —44Dc 84
Elleswood Ct. Surb —73Ma 143
Ellice Rd. Oxt —100Hc 183
Elliman Av. Slou —5J 73
Elliman Sq. Slou —7K 73
Ellingfort Rd. E8 —38Xb 63
Ellingham. Wok —91A 172
Ellingham Rd. E15 —35Fc 65
Ellingham Rd. W12 —47Wa 80
Ellingham Rd. Chess —79Ma 143
Ellington Ct. N14 —19Mb 24
Ellington Ho. SE1
—48Sb 83 (4E 206)
Ellington Rd. N10 —28Kb 42
Ellington Rd. Felt —63V 120
Ellington Rd. Houn —54Da 99
Ellington St. N7 —37Qb 62
Elliot Clo. E15 —38Gc 65
Elliot Gdns. SW15 —56Wa 102
Elliot Rd. NW4 —30Xa 40
Elliott Av. Ruis —33X 57
Elliott Clo. Wemb —34Qa 59
Elliott Gdns. Romf —25Kd 49
Elliott Gdns. Shep —70Q 120
Elliott Rd. SW9 —52Rb 105
Elliott Rd. W4 —49Ua 80
Elliott Rd. Brom —70Mc 129
Elliott Rd. Stan —23Ja 38
Elliott Rd. T Hth —70Rb 127
Elliotts La. Bras —96Yc 185
Elliott's Pl. N1 —39Rb 63 (1C 194)
Elliott Sq. NW3 —38Gb 61
Elliotts Row. SE11
—49Rb 83 (5C 206)
Elliott St. Grav —9F 114
Ellis Av. Ger X —25B 34
Ellis Av. Rain —43Jd 88
Ellis Av. Slou —7J 73
Ellis Clo. SE9 —61Sc 130
Ellis Clo. Coul —92Pb 180
Elliscombe Rd. SE7 —51Lc 107
Ellis Ct. W7 —43Ha 78
Ellis Farm Clo. Wok —10G 188
Ellisfield Dri. SW15 —59Wa 102
Ellis Ho. SE17 —50Tb 83 (7F 207)
Ellis M. SE7 —51Lc 107
Ellison Clo. Wind —5D 94
Ellison Gdns. S'hall —49Ba 77
Ellison Ho. SE13 —54Ec 106
Ellison Rd. SW13 —54Va 102
Ellison Rd. SW16 —66Mb 126
Ellison Rd. Sidc —60Tc 108
Ellis Rd. Coul —92Pb 180
Ellis Rd. Mitc —72Hb 145
Ellis Rd. S'hall —46Ea 78
Ellis St. SW1 —49Jb 82 (5G 203)
Ellmore Clo. Romf —25Kd 49
Ellora Rd. SW16 —64Mb 126
Ellsworth St. E2 —41Xb 83
Ellwood Ct. W9 —42Db 81
(off Clearwell Dri.)
Ellwood Ct. Wat —6X 5
Ellwood Gdns. Wat —6Y 5
Elmar Grn. Slou —1E 72
Elmar Rd. N15 —28Tb 43
Elm Av. W5 —46Na 79
Elm Av. Ruis —32W 56
Elm Av. Upm —34Rd 69
Elm Av. Wat —17Aa 19
Elm Bank. N14 —17Nb 24
Elmbank Av. Barn —14Ya 22
Elmbank Av. Egh —5M 117
Elm Bank Dri. Brom —68Lc 129
Elm Bank Gdns. SW13 —54Ua 102
Elmbank Way. W7 —43Fa 78
Elmbourne Dri. Belv —49Dd 88
Elmbourne Rd. SW17 —62Kb 126
Elmbridge Av. Surb —71Ra 143
Elmbridge Clo. Ruis —30W 36
Elmbridge Dri. Ruis —29V 36
Elm Bri. Est. Wok —91B 172
Elmbridge La. Wok —91B 172
Elmbridge Rd. Ilf —23Wc 47
Elmbridge Wlk. E8 —38Wb 63
Elmbrook Clo. Sun —67W 120
Elmbrook Gdns. SE9 —56Nc 108
Elmbrook Rd. Sutt —77Bb 145
Elm Clo. E11 —30Kc 45
Elm Clo. N19 —33Lb 62
Elm Clo. NW4 —29Za 40
Elm Clo. SW20 —70Ya 124
Elm Clo. Buck H —19Mc 27
Elm Clo. Cars —74Hb 145
Elm Clo. Dart —60Ld 111
Elm Clo. Farn C —7G 52
Elm Clo. Harr —30Da 37
Elm Clo. Hay —44W 76
Elm Clo. Lea —94Ka 176
Elm Clo. Rip —96J 173
Elm Clo. Romf —25Dd 48
Elm Clo. S Croy —79Ub 147
Elm Clo. Stai —60M 97
Elm Clo. Surb —73Sa 143
Elm Clo. Twic —61Da 121
Elm Clo. Wal A —6Fc 13
Elm Clo. Warl —89Zb 166
Elm Clo. Wok —3G 188
Elmcote. Pinn —26Z 37
Elmcote Way. Crox —16P 17
Elm Ct. EC4 —45Qb 82 (4K 199)
(off Terrace, The)
Elm Ct. Knap —5A 188
Elm Ct. Wat —13X 19
Elm Ct. W Mol —70Da 121
Elmcourt Rd. SE27 —61Rb 127
Elm Cres. W5 —47Na 79
Elm Cres. King T —67Na 123
Elmcroft. N6 —31Lb 62
Elmcroft. Bookh —96Ca 175
Elm Croft. Dat —3N 95
Elmcroft Av. E11 —29Kc 45
Elmcroft Av. N9 —16Xb 25
Elmcroft Av. NW11 —31Bb 61
Elmcroft Av. Sidc —59Vc 109
Elmcroft Clo. E11 —28Kc 45
Elmcroft Clo. W5 —44Ma 79
Elmcroft Clo. Chess —76Na 143
Elmcroft Clo. Felt —58V 98
Elmcroft Cres. NW11 —31Ab 60
Elmcroft Cres. Harr —27Ca 37
Elmcroft Dri. Ashf —64Q 120
Elmcroft Dri. Chess —76Na 143
Elmcroft Gdns. NW9 —28Qa 39
Elmcroft Ho. N8 —29Pb 42
Elmcroft Rd. Orp —73Wc 151
Elmcroft St. E5 —35Yb 64
Elmdale Rd. N13 —22Pb 42
Elmdene. Surb —74Sa 143
Elmdene Av. Horn —29Pd 49
Elmdene Clo. Beck —72Bc 148
Elmdene Rd. SE18 —50Rc 86
Elmdon Rd. Houn —54Aa 99
Elmdon Rd. H'row A —55Y 98
Elmdon Rd. S Ock —43Wd 90
Elm Dri. Chesh —1Ac 12
Elm Dri. Harr —30Da 37
Elm Dri. Lea —95Ka 176
Elm Dri. Sun —68Y 121
Elm Dri. Swan —68Fd 132
Elm Dri. Wink —10A 94
Elmer Av. Hav —20Gd 30
Elmer Clo. Enf —13Pb 24
Elmer Clo. Rain —38Jd 68
Elmer Cotts. Fet —95Ja 176
Elmer Gdns. Edgw —24Ra 39
Elmer Gdns. Iswth —55Fa 100
Elmer Gdns. Rain —38Jd 68
Elmer M. Fet —94Ja 176
Elmer Rd. SE6 —59Ec 106
Elmers Dri. Tedd —65Ka 122
Elmers End Rd. SE20 & Beck
—68Yb 128
Elmerside Rd. Beck —70Ac 128
Elmers Rd. SE25 —73Wb 147
Elmfield. Bookh —95Ca 175
Elmfield Av. N8 —29Nb 42
Elmfield Av. Mitc —67Jb 126
Elmfield Av. Tedd —64Ha 122
Elmfield Clo. Grav —10D 114
Elmfield Clo. Harr —33Ga 58
Elmfield Clo. Pot B —5Ab 8
Elmfield Ct. Well —53Xc 109
Elmfield Ho. N2 —26Fb 41
(off Grange, The)
Elmfield Pk. Brom —69Jc 129
Elmfield Rd. E4 —19Ec 26
Elmfield Rd. E17 —30Zb 44
Elmfield Rd. N2 —27Fb 41
Elmfield Rd. SW17 —61Jb 126
Elmfield Rd. Brom —68Jc 129
Elmfield Rd. Pot B —4Ab 8
Elmfield Rd. S'hall —48Aa 77
Elmfield Way. S Croy —81Vb 165
Elm Friars Wlk. NW1 —38Mb 62
Elm Gdns. N2 —27Eb 41
Elm Gdns. Clay —79Ha 142
Elm Gdns. Enf —10Tb 11
Elm Gdns. Eps —91Ya 178
Elm Gdns. Mitc —70Mb 126
Elmgate Av. Felt —62Y 121
Elmgate Gdns. Edgw —22Sa 39
Elm Grn. W3 —44Ua 80
Elm Grn. Clo. E15 —39Gc 65
Elm Gro. N8 —30Nb 42
Elm Gro. NW2 —35Za 60
Elm Gro. SE15 —54Vb 105
Elm Gro. SW19 —66Ab 124
Elm Gro. Cat —94Ub 181
Elm Gro. Eps —86Sa 161
Elm Gro. Eri —52Fd 110
Elm Gro. Harr —31Ca 57
Elm Gro. Horn —30Nd 49
Elm Gro. King T —67Na 123
Elm Gro. Orp —74Vc 151
Elm Gro. Sutt —77Db 145
Elm Gro. Wat —9W 4
Elm Gro. W Dray —45P 75
Elm Gro. Wfd G —22Hc 45
Elmgrove Clo. Wok —7A 188
Elmgrove Cres. Harr —29Ha 38
Elmgrove Gdns. Harr —29Ja 38
Elm Gro. Pde. Wall —76Jb 146
Elm Gro. Rd. SW13 —53Wa 102
Elm Gro. Rd. W5 —47Na 79
Elm Gro. Rd. Cob —88Z 159
Elmgrove Rd. Croy —73Xb 147
Elmgrove Rd. Harr —29Ha 38
Elmgrove Rd. Kent —29Ja 38
Elmgrove Rd. Wey —76Q 140
Elm Hall Gdns. E11 —30Kc 45
(in two parts)
Elm Hatch. Pinn —24Ba 37
(off Westfield Pk.)
Elmhurst. Belv —51Ad 109
Elmhurst Av. N2 —27Fb 41
Elmhurst Av. Mitc —66Kb 126
Elmhurst Dri. E18 —26Jc 45
Elmhurst Dri. Horn —32Ld 69
Elmhurst Lodge. Sutt —80Eb 145
Elmhurst Mans. SW4 —55Mb 104
Elmhurst Rd. E7 —38Kc 65
Elmhurst Rd. N17 —26Vb 43
Elmhurst Rd. SE9 —61Nc 130
Elmhurst Rd. Enf —9Yb 12
Elmhurst Rd. Slou —48C 74
Elmhurst St. SW4 —55Mb 104
Elmhurst Way. Lou —17Pc 28
Elmington Clo. Bex —58Dd 110
Elmington Est. SE5 —52Tb 105
Elmington Rd. SE5 —52Tb 105
Elmira St. SE13 —55Dc 106
Elm La. SE6 —61Bc 128
Elm La. Ock —91Q 174
Elm Lawn Clo. Uxb —38N 55
Elmlea Dri. Hay —43U 76
Elmlee Clo. Chst —65Pc 130
Elmley Clo. E6 —43Nc 86
Elmley St. SE18 —50Tc 86
Elm Lodge. SW6 —53Za 102
Elm M. Rich —58Pa 101
Elmore Clo. Wemb —40Na 59
Elmore Ho. SW9 —54Rb 105
Elmore Rd. E11 —34Ec 64
Elmore Rd. Coul —93Hb 179
Elmore Rd. Enf —10Zb 12
Elmores. Lou —14Qc 28
Elmore St. N1 —38Sb 63
Elm Pde. Sidc —63Wc 131
Elm Pk. SW2 —58Pb 104
Elm Pk. Stan —22Ka 38
Elm Pk. Av. N15 —29Vb 43
Elm Pk. Av. Horn —35Jd 68
Elm Pk. Ct. Pinn —27Y 37
Elm Pk. Gdns. NW4 —29Za 40
Elm Pk. Gdns. SW10 —50Fb 81
Elm Pk. Gdns. S Croy —82Yb 166
Elm Pk. La. SW3 —50Fb 81
Elm Pk. Mans. SW10 —51Eb 103
(off Park Wlk.)
Elm Pk. Rd. E10 —32Ac 64
Elm Pk. Rd. N3 —24Bb 41
Elm Pk. Rd. N21 —17Sb 25
Elm Pk. Rd. SE25 —69Vb 127
Elm Pk. Rd. SW3 —51Fb 103
Elm Pk. Rd. Pinn —26Y 37
Elm Pas. Barn —14Bb 23
Elm Pl. SW7 —50Fb 81 (7B 202)
Elm Quay Ct. SW8 —51Mb 104
Elm Rd. E7 —37Hc 65

Elm Rd.—Etheridge Rd.

Elm Rd. E11 —33Fc 65
Elm Rd. E17 —29Ec 44
Elm Rd. N22 —25Rb 43
Elm Rd. SW14 —55Sa 101
Elm Rd. Barn —14Bb 23
Elm Rd. Beck —68Bc 128
Elm Rd. Chess —77Na 143
Elm Rd. Clay —79Ha 142
Elm Rd. Dart —60Md 111
Elm Rd. Eps —79Va 144
Elm Rd. Eri —53Jd 110
Elm Rd. Felt —60T 98
Elm Rd. Grav —2E 136
Elm Rd. Grays —51Ee 113
Elm Rd. Grnh —58Ud 112
Elm Rd. Hors —87B 156
Elm Rd. King T —67Pa 123
Elm Rd. Lea —94Ka 176
Elm Rd. N Mald —68Ta 123
Elm Rd. Orp —80Wc 151
Elm Rd. Purl —85Rb 165
Elm Rd. Romf —26Dd 48
Elm Rd. Sidc —63Wc 131
Elm Rd. S Ock —46Td 90
Elm Rd. St J —6G 188
Elm Rd. T Hth —70Tb 127
Elm Rd. Wall —74Jb 146
Elm Rd. Warl —89Zb 166
Elm Rd. Wemb —36Na 59
Elm Rd. W'ham —97Uc 184
Elm Rd. Wind —5F 94
Elm Rd. Wok —7A 188
Elm Rd. W. Sutt —73Bb 145
Elm Row. NW3 —34Eb 61
Elmroyd Av. Pot B —5Bb 9
Elmroyd Clo. Pot B —5Bb 9
Elms Av. N10 —27Kb 42
Elms Av. NW4 —29Za 40
Elmscott Gdns. N21 —16Sb 25
Elmscott Rd. Brom —64Gc 129
Elms Ct. Wemb —35Ja 58
Elms Cres. SW4 —58Lb 104
Elmscroft Gdns. Pot B —4Bb 9
Elmsdale Rd. E17 —28Bc 44
Elms Farm Rd. Horn —36Ld 69
Elms Gdns. Dag —35Bd 67
Elms Gdns. Wemb —35Ja 58
Elmshaw Rd. SW15 —57Wa 102
Elmshorn. Eps —88Ya 162
Elmshott La. Slou —5C 72
Elmshurst Cres. N2 —28Fb 41
Elmside. New Ad —79Dc 148
Elmside Rd. Wemb —34Qa 59
Elms Ind. Est. H Wood —24Rd 49
Elms La. Wemb —35Ja 58
Elmsleigh Av. Harr —28Ka 38
Elmsleigh Cen., The. Stai —63H 119
Elmsleigh Ct. Sutt —76Db 145
Elmsleigh Ho. Twic —61Fa 122
(off Staines Rd.)
Elmsleigh Rd. Stai —64H 119
Elmsleigh Rd. Twic —61Fa 122
Elmslie Clo. Eps —86Sa 161
Elmslie Clo. Wfd G —23Pc 46
Elms M. W2 —45Fb 81 (4B 196)
Elms Pk. Av. Wemb —35Ja 58
Elms Rd. SW4 —57Lb 104
Elms Rd. Ger X —24A 34
Elms Rd. Harr —24Ga 38
Elmstead Av. Chst —64Pc 130
Elmstead Av. Wemb —32Na 59
Elmstead Clo. N20 —19Cb 23
Elmstead Clo. Eps —78Ua 144
Elmstead Clo. Sev —94Gd 186
Elmstead Gdns. Wor Pk —76Wa 144
Elmstead Glade. Chst —65Pc 130
Elmstead La. Chst —66Nc 130
Elmstead Rd. Eri —53Gd 110
Elmstead Rd. Ilf —33Uc 66
Elmstead Rd. W Byf —85J 157
Elmsted Cres. Well —51Yc 109
Elms, The. SW13 —55Va 102
Elmstone Rd. SW6 —53Cb 103
Elm St. WC1 —42Pb 82 (6J 193)
Elmsway. Ashf —64Q 120
Elmswood. Bookh —96Ba 175
Elmsworth Av. Houn —54Da 99
Elm Ter. NW2 —34Cb 61
Elm Ter. NW3 —35Gb 61
Elm Ter. SE9 —58Qc 108
Elm Ter. Grays —51Xd 112
Elm Ter. Harr —25Fa 38
Elm Ter. Stan —22La 38
Elmton Way. E5 —34Wb 63
Elm Tree Av. Esh —73Fa 142
Elm Tree Clo. NW8
—41Fb 81 (3B 190)
Elm Tree Clo. Ashf —62R 120
Elm Tree Clo. Byfl —85N 157
Elm Tree Clo. Cher —75G 138
Elm Tree Clo. N'holt —40Ba 57
Elm Tree Rd. NW8
—41Fb 81 (3B 190)
Elmtree Rd. Tedd —63Ga 122
Elm View Ho. Hay —50U 76
Elm Wlk. NW3 —33Cb 61
Elm Wlk. SW20 —70Ya 124
Elm Wlk. Orp —76Pc 150
Elm Wlk. Rad —8Ha 6
Elm Wlk. Romf —27Jd 48
Elm Way. N11 —23Jb 42
Elm Way. NW10 —35Ua 60
Elm Way. Brtwd —21Wd 50
Elm Way. Eps —78Ta 143
Elmway. Grays —45Ee 91
Elm Way. Rick —18K 17
Elm Way. Wor Pk —76Ya 144
Elmwood Av. N13 —22Nb 42
Elmwood Av. Borwd —14Ra 21
Elmwood Av. Felt —61W 120
Elmwood Av. Harr —29Ja 38
Elmwood Clo. Asht —89Ma 161
Elmwood Clo. Eps —80Wa 144
Elmwood Clo. Wall —75Kb 146
Elmwood Ct. E10 —32Cc 64
(off Goldsmith Rd.)
Elmwood Ct. Wemb —34Ja 58
Elmwood Cres. NW9 —28Sa 39
Elmwood Dri. Bex —59Ad 109
Elmwood Dri. Eps —79Wa 144
Elmwood Gdns. W7 —44Ga 78
Elmwood Pk. Ger X —32A 54
Elmwood Rd. SE24 —57Tb 105
Elmwood Rd. W4 —51Sa 101
Elmwood Rd. Croy —73Rb 147
Elmwood Rd. Mitc —69Hb 125
Elmwood Rd. Slou —5M 73
Elmwood Rd. Wok —7A 188
Elmworth Gro. SE21 —61Tb 127
Elnathan M. W9 —42Db 81
Elphinstone Ct. SW16 —65Nb 126
Elphinstone Rd. E17 —26Bc 44
Elphinstone St. N5 —35Rb 63
Elrick Clo. Eri —51Gd 110
Elrington Rd. E8 —37Wb 63
Elruge Clo. W Dray —48M 75
Elsa Ct. Beck —67Bc 128
Elsa Rd. Well —54Xc 109
Elsa St. E1 —43Ac 84
Elsdale St. E9 —37Yb 64
Elsden M. E2 —40Yb 64
Elsden Rd. N17 —25Vb 43
Elsdon Rd. Wok —6D 188
Elsenham Rd. E12 —36Qc 66
Elsenham St. SW18 —60Bb 103
Elsham Rd. E11 —34Gc 65
Elsham Rd. W14 —47Ab 80
Elsham Ter. W14 —48Ab 80
(off Elsham Rd.)
Elsiedene Rd. N21 —17Sb 25
Elsiemaud Rd. SE4 —57Bc 106
Elsie Rd. SE22 —56Vb 105
Elsinge Rd. Enf —8Xb 11
Elsinore Av. Stai —60N 97
Elsinore Gdns. NW2 —34Ab 60
Elsinore Rd. SE23 —60Ac 106
Elsinore Way. Rich —55Ra 101
Elsley Rd. SW11 —55Hb 103
Elspeth Rd. SW11 —56Hb 103
Elspeth Rd. Wemb —36Na 59
Elsrick Av. Mord —71Cb 145
Elstan Way. Croy —73Ac 148
Elstead Ct. Sutt —74Ab 144
Elstead Ho. SW2 —59Pb 104
(off Redlands Way)
Elsted St. SE17 —49Tb 83 (6G 207)
Elstow Clo. SE9 —57Qc 108
(in two parts)
Elstow Clo. Ruis —31Z 57
Elstow Gdns. Dag —39Ad 67
Elstow Rd. Dag —39Ad 67
Elstree Gdns. N9 —18Xb 25
Elstree Gdns. Belv —49Ad 87
Elstree Gdns. Ilf —36Sc 66
Elstree Hill. Brom —66Gc 129
Elstree Hill N. Els —15Ma 21
Elstree Hill S. Els —17Ma 21
Elstree Ho. Borwd —12Ta 21
Elstree Rd. Bush & Borwd
—17Fa 20
Elstree Tower. Borwd —12Ta 21
Elstree Way. Borwd —13Ra 21
Elswick Rd. SE13 —54Dc 106
Elswick St. SW6 —54Eb 103
Elsworth Clo. Felt —60U 98
Elsworthy. Th Dit —72Ga 142
Elsworthy Rise. NW3 —38Gb 61
Elsworthy Rd. NW3 —39Gb 61
Elsworthy Ter. NW3 —38Gb 61
Elsynge Rd. SW18 —57Fb 103
Eltham Grn. SE9 —57Mc 107
Eltham Grn. Rd. SE9 —56Lc 107
Eltham High St. SE9 —58Pc 108
Eltham Hill. SE9 —57Mc 107
Eltham Pal. Rd. SE9 —58Lc 107
Eltham Pk. Gdns. SE9 —56Qc 108
Eltham Rd. SE12 & SE9 —57Jc 107
Elthiron Rd. SW6 —53Cb 103
Elthorne Av. W7 —47Ha 78
Elthorne Ct. Felt —60Y 99
Elthorne Pk. Rd. W7 —47Ha 78
Elthorne Rd. N19 —33Mb 62
Elthorne Rd. NW9 —31Ta 59
Elthorne Rd. Uxb —40M 55
Elthorne Way. NW9 —30Ta 39
Elthruda Rd. SE13 —58Fc 107
Eltisley Rd. Ilf —35Rc 66
Elton Av. Barn —15Bb 23
Elton Av. Gnfd —37Ga 58
Elton Av. Wemb —36Ka 58
Elton Clo. King T —66La 122
Elton Pk. Wat —12W 18
Elton Pl. N16 —36Ub 63
Elton Rd. King T —67Pa 123
Elton Rd. Purl —84Lb 164
Elton Way. Wat —12Da 19
Eltringham St. SW18 —56Eb 103
Elvaston M. SW7
—48Eb 81 (3A 202)
Elvaston Pl. SW7
—48Eb 81 (4A 202)
Elveden Clo. Wok —89K 157
Elveden Ho. SE24 —57Rb 105
Elveden Pl. NW10 —40Qa 59
Elveden Rd. NW10 —40Qa 59
Elvedon Rd. Cob —83X 159
Elvendon Rd. N13 —23Nb 42
Elver Gdns. E2 —41Wb 83
Elverson Rd. SE8 —54Dc 106
Elverton St. SW1
—49Mb 82 (5D 204)
Elvet Av. Romf —28Ld 49
Elvington Grn. Brom —71Hc 149
Elvington La. NW9 —25Ua 40
Elvino Rd. SE26 —64Ac 128
Elvis Rd. NW2 —37Ya 60
Elwell Clo. Egh —65C 118
Elwick Ct. Dart —61Nd 133
Elwick Rd. S Ock —44Yd 90
Elwill Way. Beck —70Ec 128
Elwill Way. Grav —7B 136
Elwin St. E2 —41Wb 83
Elwood St. N5 —34Rb 63
Elwyn Gdns. SE12 —59Jc 107
Ely Av. Slou —3G 72
Ely Clo. SW20 —68Wa 124
Ely Clo. Eri —54Hd 110
Ely Cotts. SW8 —52Pb 104
Ely Ct. EC1 —43Qb 82 (1A 200)
(off Ely Pl.)
Ely Gdns. Borwd —15Ta 21
Ely Gdns. Dag —34Ed 68
Ely Gdns. Ilf —31Nc 66
Elyne Rd. N4 —30Qb 42
Ely Pl. EC1 —43Qb 82 (1A 200)
Ely Pl. Wfd G —23Qc 46
Ely Rd. E10 —30Ec 44
Ely Rd. Croy —71Tb 147
Ely Rd. Houn —55Y 99
Ely Rd. H'row A —54V 98
Elysian Av. Orp —72Vc 151
Elysium Pl. SW6 —54Bb 103
(off Elysium St.)
Elysium St. SW6 —54Bb 103
Elystan Bus. Cen. Hay —45Y 77
Elystan Clo. Wall —80Lb 146
Elystan Pl. SW3 —50Gb 81 (7E 202)
Elystan St. SW3
—49Gb 81 (6D 202)
Elystan Wlk. N1 —39Qb 62 (1K 193)
Emanuel Av. W3 —44Sa 79
Embankment. SW15 —54Za 102
Embankment Gdns. SW3
—51Hb 103
Embankment Pl. WC2
—46Nb 82 (6G 199)
Embankment, The. Twic —60Ja 100
Embankment, The. Wray —10N 95
Embassy Ct. N11 —23Mb 42
(off Bounds Grn. Rd.)
Embassy Ct. NW8
—40Fb 61 (2C 190)
(off Wellington Rd.)
Embassy Ct. Sidc —62Xc 131
Embassy Ct. Well —55Xc 109
Embassy Gdns. Beck —67Bc 128
Emba St. SE16 —47Wb 83
Ember Clo. Add —78N 139
Ember Clo. Orp —73Sc 150
Embercourt Rd. Th Dit —72Ga 142
Ember Ct. NW9 —26Va 40
Ember Ct. Rd. Th Dit —72Ga 142
Ember Farm Av. E Mol —72Fa 142
Ember Farm Way. E Mol —72Fa 142
Ember Gdns. Th Dit —73Ga 142
Ember La. Esh & E Mol —73Fa 142
Ember Rd. Slou —48D 74
Emberton. SE17 —51Ub 105
(off Albany Rd.)
Embleton Rd. SE13 —56Dc 106
Embleton Rd. Wat —20W 18
Embleton Wlk. Hamp —64Ba 121
Embley Point. E5 —35Xb 63
(off Tiger Way)
Embry Clo. Stan —21Ja 38
Embry Dri. Stan —23Ja 38
Embry Way. Stan —22Ja 38
Emden St. SW6 —53Db 103
Emerald Clo. E16 —44Mc 85
Emerald Ct. Coul —87Mb 164
Emerald Ct. Slou —7J 73
Emerald Gdns. Dag —32Cd 68
Emerald St. WC1
—43Pb 82 (7H 193)
Emerson Dri. Horn —31Md 69
Emerson Gdns. Harr —30Pa 39
Emerson Rd. Ilf —31Qc 66
Emersons Av. Swan —66Hd 132
Emerson St. SE1
—46Sb 83 (6D 200)
Emerton Clo. Bexh —56Ad 109
Emerton Rd. Fet —93Ea 176
Emery Hill St. SW1
—48Lb 82 (4C 204)
Emery St. SE1 —48Qb 82 (3A 206)
Emes Rd. Eri —52Ed 110
Emily Pl. N7 —35Qb 62
Emily St. E16 —44Hc 85
(off Jude St.)
Emley Rd. Add —76J 139
Emlyn Gdns. W12 —47Ua 80
Emlyn La. Lea —94Ja 176
Emlyn Rd. W12 —47Ua 80
Emmanuel Ct. E10 —31Dc 64
Emmanuel Lodge. Chesh —2Yb 12
Emmanuel Rd. SW12 —60Lb 104
Emmanuel Rd. N'wd —24V 36
Emma Rd. E13 —40Hc 65
Emma St. E2 —40Xb 63
Emmaus Way. Chig —22Qc 46
Emmetts Clo. Wok —5G 188
Emmott Av. Ilf —29Sc 46
Emmott Clo. E1 —42Ac 84
Emmott Clo. NW11 —30Eb 41
Emms Pl. King T —68Ma 123
Emperor's Ga. SW7 —48Db 81
Empire Av. N18 —22Sb 43
Empire Cen. Wat —11Y 19
Empire Ct. Wemb —34Ra 59
Empire Pde. N18 —23Tb 43
Empire Pde. Wemb —34Qa 59
Empire Rd. Gnfd —39La 58
Empire Way. Wemb —35Pa 59
Empire Wharf Rd. E14 —49Fc 85
Empire Yd. N7 —34Nb 62
Empress Av. E4 —24Dc 44
Empress Av. E12 —33Lc 65
Empress Av. Ilf —33Pc 66
Empress Av. Wfd G —24Hc 45
Empress Dri. Chst —65Rc 130
Empress Pde. E4 —24Dc 44
(off Empress Rd.)
Empress Pl. SW6 —50Cb 81
Empress Rd. Grav —9G 114
Empress St. SE17 —51Sb 105
Empson St. E3 —42Dc 84
Emsworth Clo. N9 —18Yb 26
Emsworth Ct. SW16 —62Nb 126
Emsworth Rd. Ilf —26Rc 46
Emsworth St. SW2 —61Pb 126
Emu Rd. SW8 —54Kb 104
Ena Rd. SW16 —69Nb 126
Enborne Grn. S Ock —43Wd 90
Enbrook St. W10 —41Ab 80
Endale Clo. Cars —75Hb 145
Endeavour Way. SW19 —63Db 125
Endeavour Way. Bark —40Wc 67
Endeavour Way. Croy —73Nb 146
Endell St. WC2 —44Nb 82 (2F 199)
Enderby St. SE10 —50Gc 85
Enderley Clo. Harr —26Ga 38
Enderley Rd. Harr —25Ga 38
Endersby Rd. Barn —15Ya 22
Endersleigh Gdns. NW4 —28Wa 40
Endlebury Rd. E4 —19Ec 26
Endlesham Rd. SW12 —59Jb 104
Endsleigh Clo. S Croy —82Yb 166
Endsleigh Gdns. WC1
—42Mb 82 (5D 192)
Endsleigh Gdns. Ilf —33Pc 66
Endsleigh Gdns. Surb —72La 142
Endsleigh Gdns. W on T —78Y 141
Endsleigh Pl. WC1
—42Mb 82 (5E 192)
Endsleigh Rd. W13 —45Ja 78
Endsleigh Rd. Red —100Lb 180
Endsleigh Rd. S'hall —49Aa 77
Endsleigh St. WC1
—42Mb 82 (5D 192)
End Way. Surb —73Qa 143
Endwell Rd. SE4 —54Ac 106
Endymion Rd. N4 —31Qb 62
Endymion Rd. SW2 —58Pb 104
Enfield Clo. Uxb —40M 55
Enfield Ho. SW9 —54Nb 104
(off Stockwell Rd.)
Enfield Ho. H Hill —24Nd 49
(off Leyburn Cres.)
Enfield Rd. N1 —38Ub 63
Enfield Rd. W3 —47Ra 79
Enfield Rd. Bren —50Ma 79
Enfield Rd. Enf —14Mb 24
Enfield Rd. Houn —54U 98
Enfield Wlk. Bren —50Ma 79
Enford St. W1 —43Hb 81 (7F 191)
Engadine Clo. Croy —76Vb 147
Engadine St. SW18 —60Cb 103
Engate St. SE13 —56Ec 106
Engayne Gdns. Upm —32Rd 69
Engel Pk. NW7 —23Ya 40
Engine Ct. SW1 —46Lb 82 (7C 198)
(off St James' Palace)
Engineer Clo. SE18 —51Qc 108
Engineers Dri. Bush —14Ca 19
Engineers Way. Wemb —35Qa 59
England's La. NW3 —37Hb 61
Englands La. Lou —12Qc 28
Englefield Clo. Croy —72Sb 147
Englefield Clo. Egh —5N 117
Englefield Clo. Enf —12Qb 24
Englefield Clo. Orp —70Vc 131
Englefield Cres. Orp —70Vc 131
Englefield Path. Orp —70Wc 131
Englefield Rd. N1 —38Tb 63
Englefield Rd. Knap —5A 188
Engleheart Dri. Felt —58V 98
Engleheart Rd. SE6 —59Dc 106
Englehurst. Egh —5N 117
Englewood Rd. SW12 —58Kb 104
Engliff La. Wok —88J 157
English Gdns. Wray —7P 95
English Grounds. SE1
—46Ub 83 (7H 201)
English St. E3 —42Bc 84
Enid Clo. Brick —3Ba 5
Enid St. SE16 —48Vb 83 (3K 207)
Enmore Av. SE25 —71Wb 147
Enmore Gdns. SW14 —57Ta 101
Enmore Rd. SE25 —71Wb 147
Enmore Rd. SW15 —56Ya 102
Enmore Rd. S'hall —42Ca 77
Ennerdale Av. Horn —36Jd 68
Ennerdale Av. Stan —27La 38
Ennerdale Clo. Felt —60V 98
Ennerdale Clo. Sutt —77Bb 145
Ennerdale Cres. Slou —3A 72
Ennerdale Dri. NW9 —29Ua 40
Ennerdale Gdns. Wemb —32La 58
Ennerdale Rd. Bexh —53Cd 110
Ennerdale Rd. Rich —54Pa 101
Ennersdale Rd. SE13 —57Fc 107
Ennismore Av. W4 —49Va 80
Ennismore Av. Gnfd —37Ga 58
Ennismore Gdns. SW7
—47Gb 81 (2D 202)
Ennismore Gdns. Th Dit —72Ga 142
Ennismore Gdns. M. SW7
—48Gb 81 (3D 202)
Ennismore M. SW7
—48Gb 81 (3D 202)
Ennismore St. SW7
—48Gb 81 (3D 202)
Ennis Rd. N4 —32Qb 62
Ennis Rd. SE18 —51Sc 108
Ennor Ct. Sutt —79Za 144
Ensign Clo. Purl —82Qb 164
Ensign Clo. Stai —60M 97
Ensign Dri. N13 —20Sb 25
Ensign Ind. Cen. E1 —45Wb 83
(off Ensign St.)
Ensign St. E1 —45Wb 83
Ensign Way. Stai —60M 97
Enslin Rd. SE9 —59Qc 108
Ensor M. SW7 —50Fb 81 (7B 202)
Enstone Rd. Enf —13Ac 26
Enstone Rd. Uxb —34P 55
Enterprise Bus. Pk. E14 —47Cc 84
Enterprise Clo. Croy —74Qb 146
Enterprise Ho. Bark —41Vc 87
Enterprise Ind. Est. SE16 —50Yb 84
Enterprise Way. NW10 —41Va 80
Enterprise Way. SW18 —56Cb 103
Enterprise Way. Tedd —65Ha 122
Enterprize Way. SE8 —49Bc 84
Epcot M. NW10 —41Za 80
Epirus M. SW6 —52Cb 103
Epirus Rd. SW6 —52Bb 103
Epping Clo. E14 —49Cc 84
Epping Clo. Romf —27Dd 48
Epping Glade. E4 —16Ec 26
Epping New Rd. Buck H & Lou
—19Kc 27
Epping Pl. N1 —37Qb 62
Epping Rd. Epp —8Pc 14
(Epping Forest)
Epping Rd. Epp —1Yc 15
(Epping)
Epping Way. E4 —16Dc 26
Epple Rd. SW6 —53Bb 103
Epsom Clo. Bexh —55Dd 110
Epsom Clo. N'holt —36Ba 57
Epsom Downs Metro Cen. Tad
—92Xa 178
Epsom Gap. Lea —87Ka 160
Epsom La. N. Eps & Tad
—90Xa 162
Epsom La. S. Tad —93Ya 178
Epsom Rd. E10 —30Ec 44
Epsom Rd. Asht —90Pa 161
Epsom Rd. Croy —77Qb 146
Epsom Rd. Eps —83Va 162
Epsom Rd. Ilf —30Vc 47
Epsom Rd. Lea —93Ka 176
Epsom Rd. Sutt & Mord —73Bb 145
Epsom Sq. H'row A —54V 98
Epsom Way. Horn —35Pd 69
Epstein Rd. SE28 —46Wc 87
Epworth Rd. Iswth —52Ka 100
Epworth St. EC2
—42Tb 83 (6G 195)
Erasmus St. SW1
—49Mb 82 (6E 204)
Erconwald St. W12 —44Va 80
Eresby Dri. Beck —74Cc 148
Eresby Pl. NW6 —38Cb 61
Erica Clo. Slou —5C 72
Erica Ct. Swan —70Gd 132
Erica Ct. Wok —6G 188
Erica Gdns. Croy —76Dc 148
Erica Ho. N22 —25Qb 42
(off Acacia Rd.)
Erica St. W12 —45Wa 80
Eric Clo. E7 —35Jc 65
Ericcson Clo. SW18 —57Cb 103
Eric Rd. E7 —35Jc 65
Eric Rd. NW10 —37Va 60
Eric Rd. Romf —31Zc 67
Eric St. E3 —42Bc 84
Eridge Grn. Clo. Orp —74Yc 151
Eridge Rd. W4 —48Ta 79
Erin Clo. Brom —66Gc 129
Erindale. SE18 —51Tc 108
Erindale Ter. SE18 —51Tc 108
Eriswell Cres. W on T —79U 140
Eriswell Rd. W on T —78V 140
Erith Ct. Purf —49Qd 89
Erith Cres. Romf —25Ed 48
Erith High St. Eri —50Gd 88
Erith Rd. Belv & Eri —50Cd 88
Erith Rd. Bexh & N Hth —50Cd 88
Erkenwald Clo. Cher —72Gd 138
Erlanger Rd. SE14 —53Zb 106
Erlesmere Gdns. W13 —48Ja 78
Ermine Clo. Chesh —3Xb 11
Ermine Clo. Houn —54Y 99
Ermine Rd. N15 —30Vb 43
Ermine Rd. SE13 —56Dc 106
Ermine Side. Enf —15Wb 25
Ermington Rd. SE9 —61Sc 130
Ermyn Clo. Lea —93Ma 177
Ermyn Way. Lea —93Ma 177
Ernald Av. E6 —40Nc 66
Ernan Clo. S Ock —43Wd 90
Ernan Rd. S Ock —43Wd 90
Erncroft Way. Twic —58Ha 100
Ernest Av. SE27 —63Rb 127
Ernest Clo. Beck —71Cc 148
Ernest Gdns. W4 —51Ra 101
Ernest Gro. Beck —71Bc 148
Ernest Rd. Horn —30Nd 49
Ernest Rd. King T —68Ra 123
Ernest Sq. King T —68Ra 123
Ernest St. E1 —42Zb 84
Ernle Rd. SW20 —66Xa 124
Ernshaw Pl. SW15 —57Ab 102
Erpingham Rd. SW15 —55Ya 102
Erridge Rd. SW19 —68Cb 125
Erriff Dri. S Ock —43Wd 90
Errington Clo. Grays —8D 92
Errington Dri. Wind —3E 94
Errington Rd. W9 —42Bb 81
Errol Gdns. Hay —42X 77
Errol Gdns. N Mald —70Wa 124
Erroll Rd. Romf —28Hd 48
Errol St. EC1 —42Sb 83 (6E 194)
Erskine Clo. Sutt —76Gb 145
Erskine Cres. N17 —28Xb 43
Erskine Hill. NW11 —28Cb 41
Erskine Ho. Sev —97Jd 186
Erskine M. NW3 —38Hb 61
(off Erskine Rd.)
Erskine Rd. E17 —28Bc 44
Erskine Rd. NW3 —38Hb 61
Erskine Rd. Sutt —77Fb 145
Erwood Rd. SE7 —50Nc 86
Esam Way. SW16 —64Qb 126
Eschle Ct. Slou —4J 73
Escott Gdns. SE9 —63Nc 130
Escott Pl. Ott —79E 138
Escot Way. Barn —15Ya 22
Escreet Gro. SE18 —49Qc 86
Esdaile Gdns. Upm —31Td 70
Esher Av. Romf —30Ed 48
Esher Av. Sutt —76Za 144
Esher Av. W on T —73W 140
Esher By-Pass. Cob & Esh
—85V 158
Esher Clo. Bex —60Ad 109
Esher Clo. Esh —78Da 141
Esher Cres. H'row A —54V 98
Esher Gdns. SW19 —61Za 124
Esher Grn. Esh —77Da 141
Esher Grn. Dri. Esh —77Da 141
Esher M. Mitc —69Jb 126
Esher Pk. Av. Esh —77Da 141
Esher Pl. Av. Esh —77Da 141
Esher Rd. E Mol —72Fa 142
Esher Rd. Ilf —34Uc 66
Esher Rd. W on T —78Z 141
Eskdale Av. N'holt —39Ba 57
Eskdale Clo. Dart —60Sd 112
Eskdale Clo. Wemb —33Ma 59
Eskdale Gdns. Purl —86Tb 165
Eskdale Rd. Bexh —54Cd 110
Eskdale Rd. Uxb —40K 55
Eskley Gdns. S Ock —43Xd 90
Eskmont Ridge. SE19 —66Ub 127
Esk Rd. E13 —42Jc 85
Esk Way. Romf —24Fd 48
Esmar Cres. NW9 —31Wa 60
Esmeralda Rd. SE1 —49Wb 83
Esmond Clo. Rain —38Kd 69
Esmond Gdns. W4 —49Ta 79
Esmond Rd. NW6 —39Bb 61
Esmond Rd. W4 —49Ta 79
Esmond St. SW15 —56Ab 102
Esparto St. SW18 —59Db 103
Essendene Clo. Cat —95Ub 181
Essendene Rd. Cat —95Ub 181
Essenden Rd. Belv —50Cd 88
Essenden Rd. S Croy —80Ub 147
Essendine Rd. W9 —42Cb 81
Essex Av. Iswth —55Ga 100
Essex Av. Slou —3G 72
Essex Clo. E17 —28Ac 44
Essex Clo. Add —77L 139
Essex Clo. Mord —73Za 144
Essex Clo. Romf —28Dd 48
Essex Clo. Ruis —32Z 57
Essex Ct. EC4 —44Qb 82 (3K 199)
(off Temple)
Essex Ct. SW13 —54Va 102
Essex Ct. Romf —24Md 49
Essex Gdns. N4 —30Rb 43
Essex Gdns. Horn —29Qd 49
Essex Gdns. Linf —7J 93
Essex Gro. SE19 —65Tb 127
Essex Hall. E17 —25Zb 44
Essex La. K Lan —5T 4
Essex Mans. E11 —31Fc 65
Essex Pk. N3 —23Db 41
Essex Pk. M. W3 —46Ua 80
Essex Pl. W4 —49Sa 79
Essex Pl. Sq. W4 —49Ta 79
Essex Rd. E4 —18Gc 27
Essex Rd. E10 —30Ec 44
Essex Rd. E12 —36Nc 66
Essex Rd. E17 —30Ac 44
Essex Rd. E18 —26Kc 45
Essex Rd. N1 —39Rb 63 (1B 194)
Essex Rd. NW10 —38Ua 60
Essex Rd. W3 —45Sa 79
Essex Rd. W4 —49Ta 79
Essex Rd. Bark —38Tc 66
Essex Rd. Borwd —13Qa 21
Essex Rd. Chad —31Yc 67
Essex Rd. Dag —36Ed 68
Essex Rd. Dart —58Md 111
(in two parts)
Essex Rd. Enf —14Tb 25
Essex Rd. Grav —10C 114
Essex Rd. Grays —51Wd 112
Essex Rd. Long —68Zd 135
Essex Rd. Romf —28Dd 48
Essex Rd. Wat —12W 18
Essex Rd. S. E11 —31Fc 65
Essex St. E7 —36Jc 65
Essex St. WC2 —45Qb 82 (3K 199)
Essex Vs. W8 —47Cb 81
Essex Way. Gt War —23Yd 50
Essex Wharf. E5 —33Zb 64
Essian St. E1 —43Ac 84
Essoldo Way. Edgw —27Pa 39
Estate Cotts. Mick —99Ma 177
Estate Way. E10 —32Bc 64
Estcourt Rd. SE25 —72Xb 147
Estcourt Rd. SW6 —52Bb 103
Estcourt Rd. Wat —13Y 19
Estella Av. N Mald —70Xa 124
Estelle Rd. NW3 —35Hb 61
Esterbrooke St. SW1
—49Mb 82 (6D 204)
Este Rd. SW11 —55Gb 103
Esther Clo. N21 —17Qb 24
Esther Rd. E11 —31Gc 65
Estreham Rd. SW16 —65Mb 126
Estridge Clo. Houn —56Ca 99
Eswyn Rd. SW17 —63Hb 125
Etchingham Ct. N3 —24Eb 41
Etchingham Pk. Rd. N3 —24Db 41
Etchingham Rd. E15 —35Ec 64
Etchworth Av. Felt —59V 98
Eternit Wlk. SW6 —53Za 102
Etfield Gro. Sidc —64Xc 131
Ethelbert Clo. Brom —68Jc 129
Ethelbert Gdns. Ilf —29Pc 46
Ethelbert Rd. SW20 —67Za 124
Ethelbert Rd. Brom —69Jc 129
Ethelbert Rd. Dart —63Nd 133
Ethelbert Rd. Eri —52Ed 110
Ethelbert Rd. Orp —69Zc 131
Ethelbert St. SW12 —60Kb 104
Ethelburga Rd. Romf —25Pd 49
Ethelburga St. SW11 —53Gb 103
Etheldene Av. N10 —28Lb 42
Ethelden Rd. W12 —46Xa 80
Ethel Rd. E16 —44Kc 85
Ethel Rd. Ashf —64N 119
Ethel St. SE17 —49Sb 83 (6E 206)
Ethel Ter. Orp —81Yc 169
Etheridge Grn. Lou —13Sc 28
Etheridge Rd. NW4 —31Ya 60

Etheridge Rd.—Falcon Gro.

Etheridge Rd. Lou —12Rc 28
Etherley Rd. N15 —29Sb 43
Etherow St. SE22 —59Wb 105
Etherstone Grn. SW16 —63Qb 126
Etherstone Rd. SW16 —63Qb 126
Ethnard Rd. SE15 —51Xb 105
Ethorpe Clo. Ger X —29A 34
Ethronvi Rd. Bexh —55Ad 109
Etloe Rd. E10 —33Cc 64
Eton Av. N12 —24Eb 41
Eton Av. NW3 —38Fb 61
Eton Av. Barn —16Gb 23
Eton Av. Houn —51Ba 99
Eton Av. N Mald —71Ta 143
Eton Av. Wemb —35Ka 58
Eton Clo. SW18 —59Db 103
Eton Clo. Dat —1L 95
Eton College Rd. NW3 —37Hb 61
Eton Ct. Eton —2H 95
Eton Ct. Stai —64H 119
Eton Ct. Wemb —35La 58
Eton Garages. NW3 —37Gb 61
Eton Gro. NW9 —27Qa 39
Eton Gro. SE13 —55Gc 107
Eton Ho. N5 —35Rb 63
(off Leigh Rd.)
Eton Pl. NW3 —38Jb 62
Eton Rise. NW3 —37Hb 61
Eton Rd. NW3 —38Hb 61
Eton Rd. Dat —10K 73
Eton Rd. Hay —52V 98
Eton Rd. Ilf —35Sc 66
Eton Rd. Orp —77Xc 151
Eton Sq. Eton —2H 95
Eton St. Rich —57Na 101
Eton Vs. NW3 —37Hb 61
Eton Way. Dart —56Ld 111
Eton Wick Rd. Eton W —9C 72
Etta St. SE8 —51Ac 106
Etton Clo. Horn —33Nd 69
Ettrick St. E14 —44Ec 84
(in two parts)
Etwell Pl. Surb —72Pa 143
Euclid Way. W Thur —50Vd 90
Eugene Clo. Romf —28Ld 49
Eugenia Rd. SE16 —49Yb 84
Eureka Rd. King T —68Qa 123
Eurolink Bus. Cen. SW2 —57Qb 104
Europa Pl. EC1 —41Sb 83 (4D 194)
Europa Trading Cen. Grays —50Yd 90
Europa Trading Est. Eri —50Fd 88
Europe Rd. SE18 —48Pc 86
Eustace Pl. SE18 —49Pc 86
Eustace Rd. E6 —41Nc 86
Eustace Rd. SW6 —52Cb 103
Eustace Rd. Romf —31Zc 67
Euston Av. Wat —15V 18
Euston Gro. NW1 —41Mb 82 (4D 192)
(off Euston Sq.)
Euston Rd. NW1 —42Kb 82 (6A 192)
Euston Rd. Croy —74Qb 146
Euston Sq. NW1 —41Mb 82 (4D 192)
Euston Sta. Colonnade. NW1 —41Mb 82 (4D 192)
Euston St. NW1 —41Lb 82 (5C 192)
Evandale Rd. SW9 —54Qb 104
Evangelist Rd. NW5 —35Kb 62
Evans Av. Wat —7V 4
Evans Clo. E8 —37Vb 63
Evans Clo. Crox —15Q 18
Evans Clo. Grnh —57Wd 112
Evansdale. Rain —41Hd 88
Evans Gro. Felt —61Ca 121
Evans Ho. W12 —45Xa 80
(off White City Est.)
Evans Ho. Felt —61Ca 121
Evans Rd. SE6 —61Gc 129
Evanston Av. E4 —24Ec 44
Evanston Gdns. Ilf —30Nc 46
Eva Rd. Romf —31Yc 67
Evelina Mans. SE5 —52Tb 105
Evelina Rd. SE15 —55Xb 105
Evelina Rd. SE20 —66Yb 128
Eveline Rd. Mitc —67Hb 125
Evelyn Av. NW9 —28Ta 39
Evelyn Av. Ruis —31U 56
Evelyn Av. T'sey —96Lc 183
Evelyn Clo. Twic —59Da 99
Evelyn Clo. Wok —8G 188
Evelyn Ct. E8 —35Wb 63
Evelyn Cres. Sun —67V 120
Evelyn Denington Rd. E6 —43Pc 86
Evelyn Dri. Pinn —24Z 37
Evelyn Fox Ct. W10 —43Ya 80
Evelyn Gdns. SW7 —50Eb 81 (7A 202)
Evelyn Gdns. Rich —56Na 101
Evelyn Gro. W5 —46Pa 79
Evelyn Gro. S'hall —44Ba 77
Evelyn Ho. W12 —47Va 80
(off Cobbold Rd.)
Evelyn Lowe Est. SE16 —48Wb 83
Evelyn Rd. E16 —46Kc 85
Evelyn Rd. E17 —28Ec 44
Evelyn Rd. SW19 —64Db 125
Evelyn Rd. W4 —48Ta 79
Evelyn Rd. Barn —14Hb 23
Evelyn Rd. Ham —62Ka 122
Evelyn Rd. Otf —88Ld 171
Evelyn Rd. Rich —55Na 101
Evelyns Clo. Uxb —44Q 76
Evelyn Sharp Clo. Romf —27Md 49
Evelyn Sharp Ho. Romf —27Md 49
Evelyn St. SE8 —49Ac 84
Evelyn Ter. Rich —55Na 101
Evelyn Wlk. N1 —40Tb 83 (2F 195)
Evelyn Wlk. Gt War —23Yd 50
Evelyn Way. Stoke D —88Ba 159
Evelyn Way. Sun —67V 120
Evelyn Way. Wall —77Mb 146
Evelyn Yd. W1 —44Mb 82 (2D 198)
Evening Hill. Beck —66Ec 128
Evenwood Clo. SW15 —57Ab 102
Everall Av. SW6 —54Db 103
Everall Clo. Chor —15G 16
Everard Av. Brom —74Jc 149
Everard Av. Slou —7J 73
Everard Ct. N13 —20Pb 24
(off Crothall Clo.)
Everard La. Cat —94Xb 181
Everard Way. Wemb —34Na 59
Everatt Clo. SW18 —58Bb 103
Everdon Rd. SW13 —51Wa 102
Everest Clo. Grav —2A 136
Everest Ct. Wok —4B 188
Everest Pl. E14 —43Ec 84
Everest Pl. Swan —70Fd 132
Everest Rd. SE9 —57Pc 108
Everest Rd. Stai —59M 97
Everett Clo. Pinn —27V 36
Everett Wlk. Belv —50Bd 87
Everglade. Big H —90Mc 167
Everglade Clo. Hart —70Be 135
Everglade Strand. NW9 —25Va 40
Evergreen Ct. Stai —59M 97
Evergreen Oak Av. Wind —5L 95
Evergreen Way. Hay —45U 76
Evergreen Way. Stai —59M 97
Everilda St. N1 —39Pb 62
Evering Rd. N16 & E5 —34Vb 63
Everington Rd. N10 —26Hb 41
Everington St. W6 —51Za 102
Everitt Rd. NW10 —41Ta 79
Everitts Corner. Slou —5C 72
Everlands Clo. Wok —90A 156
Everleigh St. N4 —32Pb 62
Eve Rd. E11 —35Gc 65
Eve Rd. E15 —40Gc 65
Eve Rd. N17 —27Ub 43
Eve Rd. Iswth —56Ja 100
Eve Rd. Wok —87D 156
Eversfield Gdns. NW7 —23Ua 40
Eversfield Rd. Rich —54Pa 101
Eversholt St. NW1 —40Lb 62 (1B 192)
Evershot Rd. N4 —32Pb 62
Eversleigh Gdns. Upm —32Td 70
Eversleigh Rd. E6 —39Mc 65
Eversleigh Rd. N3 —24Bb 41
Eversleigh Rd. SW11 —55Hb 103
Eversleigh Rd. Barn —15Eb 23
Eversley Av. Bexh —54Fd 110
Eversley Av. Wemb —33Qa 59
Eversley Clo. N21 —16Pb 24
Eversley Cres. N21 —16Qb 24
Eversley Cres. Iswth —53Fa 100
Eversley Cres. Ruis —33U 56
Eversley Cross. Bexh —54Gd 110
Eversley Mt. N21 —16Pb 24
Eversley Pk. SW19 —65Xa 124
Eversley Pk. Rd. N21 —16Pb 24
Eversley Rd. SE7 —51Kc 107
Eversley Rd. SE19 —66Tb 127
Eversley Rd. Surb —70Pa 123
Eversley Way. Croy —76Cc 148
Eversley Way. Egh —68E 118
Everthorpe Rd. SE15 —55Vb 105
Everton Bldgs. NW1 —41Lb 82 (4B 192)
Everton Dri. Stan —27Na 39
Everton Rd. Croy —74Wb 147
Evesham Av. E17 —26Cc 44
Evesham Clo. Gnfd —40Da 57
Evesham Clo. Sutt —80Cb 145
Evesham Grn. Mord —72Db 145
Evesham Rd. E15 —38Hc 65
Evesham Rd. N11 —22Lb 42
Evesham Rd. Grav —1F 136
Evesham Rd. Mord —72Db 145
Evesham St. W11 —45Za 80
Evesham Wlk. SE5 —54Tb 105
Evesham Wlk. SW9 —54Qb 104
Evesham Way. SW11 —55Jb 104
Evesham Way. Ilf —27Qc 46
Evreham Rd. Iver —44G 74
Evry Rd. Sidc —65Yc 131
Ewald Rd. SW6 —54Bb 103
Ewanrigg Ter. Wfd G —22Lc 45
Ewan Rd. H Wood —26Md 49
Ewart Gro. N22 —25Qb 42
Ewart Pl. E3 —40Bc 64
Ewart Rd. SE23 —59Zb 106
Ewe Clo. N7 —37Nb 62
Ewell By-Pass. Eps —80Wa 144
Ewell Ct. Av. Ewe —78Ua 144
Ewell Downs Rd. Eps —83Wa 162
Ewell Ho. Gro. Eps —82Va 162
Ewellhurst Rd. Ilf —26Nc 46
Ewell Pk. Way. Eps —79Wa 144
Ewell Rd. Dit H —73Ka 142
Ewell Rd. Surb —72Na 143
Ewell Rd. Sutt —80Za 144
Ewelme Rd. SE23 —60Yb 106
Ewen Cres. SW2 —60Qb 104
Ewen Ho. N1 —39Pb 62 (1J 193)
(off Barnsbury Est.)
Ewer St. SE1 —46Sb 83 (7D 200)
Ewhurst Av. S Croy —81Vb 165
Ewhurst Clo. Sutt —81Ya 162
Ewhurst Rd. SE4 —58Bc 106
Exbury Ho. E9 —37Yb 64
Exbury Rd. SE6 —61Cc 128
Excel Ct. WC2 —45Mb 82 (5E 198)
(off Whitcomb St.)
Excelsior Clo. King T —68Qa 123
Excelsior Gdns. SE13 —54Ec 106
Exchange Arc. EC2 —43Ub 83 (7J 195)
Exchange Ct. WC2 —45Nb 82 (5G 199)
Exchange Mans. NW11 —31Bb 61
Exchange Pl. EC2 —43Ub 83 (7H 195)
Exchange Rd. Asc —10A 116
Exchange Rd. Wat —13X 19
Exchange Sq. EC2 —43Ub 83 (7J 195)
Exchange St. Romf —29Gd 48
Exchange, The. Ilf —33Rc 66
Exeford Av. Ashf —63Q 120
Exeter Clo. E6 —44Pc 86
Exeter Gdns. Ilf —32Nc 66
Exeter Ho. Bark —38Wc 67
(off Margaret Bondfield Av.)
Exeter Ho. Borwd —12Qa 21
Exeter Ho. Felt —61Aa 121
(off Watermill Way)
Exeter M. NW6 —37Db 61
Exeter Rd. E16 —43Jc 85
Exeter Rd. E17 —29Cc 44
Exeter Rd. N9 —19Yb 26
Exeter Rd. N14 —18Kb 24
Exeter Rd. NW2 —36Ab 60
Exeter Rd. SE15 —52Vb 105
Exeter Rd. Croy —73Ub 147
Exeter Rd. Dag —37Dd 68
Exeter Rd. Enf —13Zb 26
Exeter Rd. Felt —62Ba 121
Exeter Rd. Grav —2F 136
Exeter Rd. Harr —33Aa 57
Exeter Rd. Well —54Vc 109
Exeter St. WC2 —45Nb 82 (4G 199)
Exeter Way. SE14 —52Bc 106
Exford Gdns. SE12 —60Kc 107
Exford Rd. SE12 —61Kc 129
Exhibition Clo. W12 —45Ya 80
Exhibition Rd. SW7 —47Fb 81 (2C 202)
Exmoor Clo. Ilf —25Rc 46
Exmoor St. W10 —43Za 80
Exmouth Mkt. EC1 —42Qb 82 (5K 193)
Exmouth M. NW1 —41Lb 82 (4C 192)
Exmouth Pl. E8 —38Xb 63
Exmouth Rd. E17 —29Bc 44
Exmouth Rd. Brom —69Kc 129
Exmouth Rd. Grays —51De 113
Exmouth Rd. Hay —41U 76
Exmouth Rd. Ruis —34Y 57
Exmouth Rd. Well —53Yc 109
Exmouth St. E1 —44Yb 84
Exning Rd. E16 —42Hc 85
Exon St. SE17 —50Ub 83 (7H 207)
Explorer Av. Stai —60M 97
Express Dri. Ilf —32Xc 67
Exton Cres. NW10 —38Sa 59
Exton Gdns. Dag —36Yc 67
Exton St. SE1 —46Qb 82 (7K 199)
Eyebright Clo. Croy —74Zb 148
Eyhurst Av. Horn —34Jd 68
Eyhurst Clo. NW2 —33Wa 60
Eyhurst Clo. Tad —95Bb 179
Eyhurst Spur. Tad —96Bb 179
Eylewood Rd. SE27 —64Sb 127
Eynella Rd. SE22 —59Vb 105
Eynham Rd. W12 —44Ya 80
Eynsford Clo. Orp —73Sc 150
Eynsford Cres. Bex —60Yc 109
Eynsford Rise. Eyns —77Md 153
Eynsford Rd. F'ham —74Pd 153
Eynsford Rd. Grnh —57Yd 112
Eynsford Rd. Ilf —33Uc 66
Eynsford Rd. Shor & Eyns —80Kd 153
Eynsford Rd. Swan —72Fd 152
Eynsford Ter. W Dray —44P 75
Eynsham Dri. SE2 —49Wc 87
Eynswood Dri. Sidc —64Xc 131
Eyot Gdns. W6 —50Va 80
Eyot Grn. W4 —50Va 80
Eyre Clo. Romf —28Kd 49
Eyre Ct. NW8 —40Fb 61 (1B 190)
Eyre Grn. Slou —1E 72
Eyre St. Hill. EC1 —42Qb 82 (6K 193)
Eysdown Rd. SE9 —61Nc 130
Eysham Ct. New Bar —15Db 23
Eyston Dri. Wey —82Q 158
Eythorne Rd. SW9 —53Qb 104
Ezra St. E2 —41Vb 83

Faber Gdns. NW4 —29Wa 40
Fabian Rd. SW6 —52Bb 103
Fabian St. E6 —42Nc 86
Fackenden La. Shor —85Kd 171
Factory La. N17 —26Vb 43
Factory La. Croy —74Qb 146
Factory Path. Stai —63G 118
Factory Pl. E14 —50Dc 84
Factory Rd. E16 —46Mc 85
Factory Rd. Grav —58Ee 113
Factory Sq. SW16 —65Nb 126
Factory Yd. W7 —46Ga 78
Faesten Way. Bex —62Gd 132
Faggots Clo. Rad —7La 6
Faggs Rd. Felt —56V 98
Fagus Av. Rain —41Md 89
Fairacre. N Mald —69Ua 124
Fairacre Ct. N'wd —24U 36
Fairacre Pl. Hart —69Ae 135
Fairacres. SW15 —56Wa 102
Fair Acres. Brom —71Jc 149
Fairacres. Cob —84Z 159
Fair Acres. Croy —81Bc 166
Fairacres. Ruis —31V 56
Fairacres. Tad —93Ya 178
Fairacres Clo. Pot B —5Bb 9
Fairacres Ind. Est. Wind —4B 94
Fairbairn Clo. Purl —85Qb 164
Fairbairn Grn. SW9 —53Rb 105
Fairbank Av. Orp —75Rc 150
Fairbank Est. N1 —41Tb 83 (3G 195)
Fairbanks Rd. N17 —27Vb 43
Fairbourne. Cob —85Z 159
Fairbourne Clo. Wok —5D 188
Fairbourne Ho. Hay —48S 76
Fairbourne La. Cat —94Sb 181
Fairbourne Rd. N17 —27Ub 43
Fairbridge Rd. N19 —33Mb 62
Fairbrook Clo. N13 —22Qb 42
Fairbrook Rd. N13 —23Qb 42
Fairburn Clo. Borwd —11Qa 21
Fairburn Ct. SW15 —57Ab 102
Fairburn Ho. W14 —50Bb 81
(off Ivatt Pl.)
Fairby Grange. Hart —71Ae 155
Fairby La. Hart —72Ae 155
Fairby Rd. SE12 —57Kc 107
Faircharm Trading Est. SE8 —52Dc 106
Fairchild Clo. SW11 —54Fb 103
Fairchildes Av. New Ad —84Fc 167
Fairchildes Rd. Warl —86Fc 167
Fairchild Ho. N3 —25Cb 41
Fairchild Pl. EC2 —42Ub 83 (6J 195)
(off Gt. Eastern St.)
Fairchild St. EC2 —42Ub 83 (6J 195)
Fair Clo. Bush —17Da 19
Fairclough St. E1 —44Wb 83
Faircroft. Slou —2F 72
Faircroft Ct. Tedd —65Ja 122
Faircross Av. Bark —37Sc 66
Faircross Av. Romf —24Fd 48
Faircross Pde. Bark —37Uc 66
Fairdale Gdns. SW15 —56Xa 102
Fairdale Gdns. Hay —47W 76
Fairdene Rd. Coul —90Mb 164
Fairey Av. Hay —49V 76
Fairfax Av. Eps —82Xa 162
Fairfax Clo. W on T —74X 141
Fairfax Gdns. SE3 —53Lc 107
Fairfax Pl. NW6 —38Eb 61
Fairfax Rd. N8 —28Qb 42
Fairfax Rd. NW6 —38Eb 61
Fairfax Rd. W4 —48Ua 80
Fairfax Rd. Grays —50De 91
Fairfax Rd. Tedd —65Ja 122
Fairfax Rd. Til —3B 114
Fairfax Rd. Wok —92D 172
Fairfield. N20 —17Fb 23
Fairfield App. Wray —8P 95
Fairfield Av. NW4 —30Xa 40
Fairfield Av. Dat —2N 95
Fairfield Av. Edgw —23Ra 39
Fairfield Av. Grays —45Ee 91
Fairfield Av. Ruis —31S 56
Fairfield Av. Stai —63H 119
Fairfield Av. Twic —60Da 99
Fairfield Av. Upm —34Sd 70
Fairfield Av. Wat —20Y 19
Fairfield Clo. N12 —21Eb 41
Fairfield Clo. Dat —2P 95
Fairfield Clo. Enf —14Zb 26
Fairfield Clo. Ewe —78Ua 144
Fairfield Clo. Horn —32Jd 68
Fairfield Clo. Kems —90Qd 171
Fairfield Clo. Mitc —66Gb 125
Fairfield Clo. N'wd —23R 36
Fairfield Clo. Rad —9Ga 6
Fairfield Clo. Sidc —58Vc 109
Fairfield Cotts. Bookh —97Da 175
Fairfield Ct. NW10 —39Wa 60
Fairfield Ct. N'wd —26W 36
Fairfield Ct. Ruis —32T 56
Fairfield Cres. Edgw —23Ra 39
Fairfield Dri. SW18 —57Db 103
Fairfield Dri. Gnfd —39La 58
Fairfield Dri. Harr —27Ea 38
Fairfield E. King T —68Na 123
Fairfield Gdns. N8 —29Nb 42
Fairfield Gro. SE7 —51Mc 107
Fairfield La. Farn R —10F 52
Fairfield N. King T —68Na 123
Fairfield Pk. Cob —86Z 159
Fairfield Path. Croy —76Tb 147
Fairfield Pl. King T —69Na 123
Fairfield Rd. E3 —40Cc 64
Fairfield Rd. E17 —26Ac 44
Fairfield Rd. N8 —29Nb 42
Fairfield Rd. N18 —21Wb 43
Fairfield Rd. Beck —68Cc 128
Fairfield Rd. Bexh —54Bd 109
Fairfield Rd. Brtwd —20Yd 32
Fairfield Rd. Brom —66Jc 129
Fairfield Rd. Burn —1A 72
Fairfield Rd. Croy —76Tb 147
Fairfield Rd. Epp —1Xc 15
Fairfield Rd. Ilf —37Rc 66
Fairfield Rd. King T —68Na 123
Fairfield Rd. Lea —93Ka 176
Fairfield Rd. Orp —72Tc 150
Fairfield Rd. S'hall —44Ba 77
Fairfield Rd. Uxb —37M 55
Fairfield Rd. W Dray —45N 75
Fairfield Rd. Wfd G —23Jc 45
Fairfield Rd. Wray —8P 95
Fairfields Clo. NW9 —29Sa 39
Fairfields Cres. NW9 —29Sa 39
Fairfield S. King T —69Na 123
Fairfields Rd. Houn —55Ea 100
Fairfield St. SW18 —57Db 103
Fairfield Wlk. Lea —93Ka 176
(off Fairfield Rd.)
Fairfield Way. Barn —15Cb 23
Fairfield Way. Coul —86Mb 164
Fairfield Way. Eps —78Ua 144
Fairfield W. King T —68Na 123
Fairfolds. Wat —8Aa 5
Fairfoot Rd. E3 —42Cc 84
Fairford Av. Bexh —53Fd 110
Fairford Av. Croy —71Zb 148
Fairford Clo. Croy —71Ac 148
Fairford Clo. Romf —23Rd 49
Fairford Clo. W Byf —86H 157
Fairford Ct. Sutt —80Db 145
Fairford Gdns. Wor Pk —76Va 144
Fairford Ho. SE11 —49Qb 82 (6A 206)
Fairford Way. Romf —23Rd 49
Fairgreen. Barn —13Hb 23
Fairgreen Ct. Barn —15Jb 24
Fairgreen E. Barn —13Hb 23
Fairgreen Rd. T Hth —71Rb 147
Fairham Av. S Ock —45Wd 90
Fairhaven. Egh —64B 118
Fairhaven Av. Croy —72Zb 148
Fairhaven Ct. Egh —64B 118
Fairhaven Cres. Wat —20W 18
Fairhazel Gdns. NW6 —37Db 61
Fairholme. Felt —59T 98
Fairholme Av. Romf —29Jd 48
Fairholme Clo. N3 —28Ab 40
Fairholme Ct. H End —23Ba 37
Fairholme Cres. Asht —89La 160
Fairholme Cres. Hay —42V 76
Fairholme Gdns. N3 —27Ab 40
Fairholme Gdns. Upm —31Vd 70
Fairholme Rd. W14 —50Ab 80
Fairholme Rd. Ashf —64N 119
Fairholme Rd. Croy —73Qb 146
Fairholme Rd. Harr —29Ha 38
Fairholme Rd. Ilf —31Pc 66
Fairholme Rd. Sutt —79Bb 145
Fairholt Clo. N16 —32Ub 63
Fairholt Rd. N16 —32Tb 63
Fairholt St. SW7 —48Gb 81 (3E 202)
Fairkytes Av. Horn —32Md 69
Fairland Rd. E15 —37Hc 65
Fairlands Av. Buck H —19Jc 27
Fairlands Av. Sutt —75Cb 145
Fairlands Av. T Hth —70Pb 126
Fairlands Ct. SE9 —58Qc 108
Fair La. Coul —97Eb 179
Fairlawn. SE7 —51Lc 107
Fairlawn. Bookh —96Ba 175
Fairlawn. Wey —78U 140
Fairlawn Av. N2 —28Gb 41
Fairlawn Av. W4 —49Sa 79
Fairlawn Av. Bexh —54Zc 109
Fairlawn Clo. N14 —16Lb 24
Fair Lawn Clo. Clay —79Ha 142
Fairlawn Clo. King T —65Sa 123
Fairlawn Ct. W4 —49Sa 79
Fairlawn Ct. Felt —63Ba 121
Fairlawn Dri. Wfd G —24Jc 45
Fairlawn Gdns. S'hall —45Ba 77
Fairlawn Gro. W4 —49Sa 79
Fairlawn Gro. Bans —85Fb 163
Fairlawn Mans. SE14 —53Zb 106
Fairlawn Pk. SE26 —64Ac 128
Fairlawn Pk. Wind —6C 94
Fairlawn Pk. Wok —86A 156
Fairlawn Rd. SW19 —66Bb 125
Fairlawn Rd. Bans —83Eb 163
(in three parts)
Fairlawns. Add —78K 139
Fairlawns. Brtwd —20Wd 32
Fairlawns. Epp —1Xc 15
Fairlawns. Pinn —26Z 37
Fairlawns. Sun —69V 120
Fairlawns. Twic —58La 100
Fairlawns. Wall —78Kb 146
Fairlawns. Wat —10V 4
Fairlawns. Wdhm —83H 157
Fairlawns Clo. Horn —31Pd 69
Fairlawns Clo. Stai —65K 119
Fairlea Pl. W5 —42Ma 79
Fairley Way. Chesh —1Xb 11
Fairlie Gdns. SE23 —59Yb 106
Fairlie Rd. Slou —4E 72
Fairlight Av. E4 —19Fc 27
Fairlight Av. NW10 —40Ua 60
Fairlight Av. Wind —4H 95
Fairlight Av. Wfd G —23Jc 45
Fairlight Clo. E4 —19Fc 27
Fairlight Clo. Wor Pk —77Ya 144
Fairlight Ct. NW10 —40Ua 60
Fairlight Cross. Long —69De 135
Fairlight Dri. Uxb —37M 55
Fairlight Rd. SW17 —63Fb 125
Fairline Ct. Beck —68Ec 128
Fairlop Clo. Horn —37Kd 69
Fairlop Ct. E11 —32Fc 65
Fairlop Gdns. Ilf —23Sc 46
Fairlop Pl. NW8 —41Fb 81 (4C 190)
Fairlop Rd. E11 —31Fc 65
Fairlop Rd. Ilf —26Sc 46
Fairman Ter. Kent —28Ma 39
Fairmark Dri. Uxb —37Q 55
Fairmead. Brom —70Pc 130
Fairmead. Surb —74Ra 143
Fairmead. Wok —6F 188
Fairmead Clo. Brom —70Pc 130
Fairmead Clo. Houn —52Z 99
Fairmead Clo. N Mald —69Ta 123
Fairmead Ct. Rich —54Ra 101
Fairmead Cres. Edgw —20Sa 21
Fairmead Gdns. Ilf —29Nc 46
Fairmead Ho. E9 —35Ac 64
Fairmead Rd. N19 —34Mb 62
Fairmead Rd. Croy —73Pb 146
Fairmead Rd. Lou —15Kc 27
Fairmeads. Cob —85Ba 159
Fairmeads. Lou —15Lc 27
Fairmeadside. Lou —15Lc 27
Fairmile Av. SW16 —64Mb 126
Fairmile Av. Cob —85Aa 159
Fairmile La. Cob —84Z 159
Fairmile Pk. Copse. Cob —85Ba 159
Fairmile Pk. Rd. Cob —85Ba 159
Fairmont Clo. Belv —50Bd 87
Fairmount Rd. SW2 —58Pb 104
Fairoak Clo. Kenl —87Rb 165
Fairoak Clo. Orp —73Rc 150
Fairoak Clo. Oxs —84Fa 160
Fairoak Dri. SE9 —57Tc 108
Fairoak Gdns. Romf —26Gd 48
Fairoak La. Oxs & Chess —84Ea 160
Fairoaks Airport. Chob —82A 156
Fairoaks Ct. Add —78K 139
(off Lane Clo.)
Fairoaks Gro. Enf —9Zb 12
Fairseat Clo. Bush —19Ga 20
Fairseat La. Fair —80Ce 155
Fairs Rd. Lea —91Ja 176
Fairstead Wlk. N1 —39Sb 63
(off Popham St.)
Fair St. SE1 —47Ub 83 (1J 207)
Fair St. Houn —55Ea 100
Fairthorn Rd. SE7 —50Jc 85
Fairtrough Rd. Orp —84Xc 169
Fairview. Dart —76Xd 154
Fairview. Eps —83Ya 162
Fairview. Eri —51Hd 110
Fair View. Pot B —1Db 9
Fairview Av. Hut —17Fe 33
Fairview Av. Rain —40Md 69
Fairview Av. Stanf —2L 93
Fairview Av. Wemb —37Ma 59
Fairview Av. Wok —90A 156
Fairview Chase. Stanf —3L 93
Fairview Clo. E17 —25Ac 44
Fairview Clo. Chig —21Uc 46
Fairview Clo. Wok —90B 156
Fairview Ct. NW4 —26Za 40
Fairview Ct. Ashf —64Q 120
Fairview Cres. Harr —32Ca 57
Fairview Dri. Chig —22Uc 46
Fairview Dri. Orp —77Tc 150
Fairview Dri. Shep —71P 139
Fairview Dri. Wat —8U 4
Fairview Gdns. Meop —10C 136
Fairview Gdns. Wfd G —25Kc 45
Fairview Ho. SW2 —59Pb 104
Fairview Ind. Pk. Rain —43Fd 88
Fairview Pl. SW2 —59Pb 104
Fairview Rd. N15 —29Vb 43
Fairview Rd. SW16 —67Pb 126
Fairview Rd. Chig —21Uc 46
Fairview Rd. Enf —11Qb 24
Fairview Rd. Eps —83Va 162
Fairview Rd. Grav —66Fe 135
Fairview Rd. Slou —2D 72
Fairview Rd. Sutt —78Gb 145
Fairview Way. Edgw —21Qa 39
Fairwall Ho. SE5 —53Ub 105
Fairwater Av. Well —56Wc 109
Fairwater Clo. N15 —28Ub 43
Fairwater Dri. New Haw —81M 157
Fairway. SW20 —69Ya 124
Fairway. Bexh —57Ad 109
Fairway. Cars —83Eb 163
Fairway. Cher —74K 139
Fairway. Grays —46De 91
Fairway. Orp —71Tc 150
Fair Way. Wfd G —22Lc 45
Fairway Av. NW9 —27Ra 39
Fairway Av. Borwd —12Ra 21
Fairway Av. W Dray —46L 75
Fairway Clo. NW11 —31Eb 61
Fairway Clo. Croy —71Ac 148
Fairway Clo. Eps —77Sa 143
Fairway Clo. Houn —57Y 99
Fairway Clo. W Dray —46M 75
Fairway Clo. Wok —7E 188
Fairway Ct. NW7 —20Ta 21
Fairway Ct. New Bar —16Db 23
Fairway Dri. Dart —59Rd 111
Fairway Dri. Gnfd —38Da 57
Fairway Gdns. Beck —72Fc 149
Fairway Gdns. Ilf —36Sc 66
Fairway Ho. Borwd —13Ra 21
Fairways. Ashf —65R 120
Fairways. Kenl —89Sb 165
Fairways. Stan —26Na 39
Fairways. Tedd —66Ma 123
Fairways. Wal A —6Gc 13
Fairways Bus. Pk. E10 —33Bc 64
Fairway, The. N13 —20Tb 25
Fairway, The. N14 —16Lb 24
Fairway, The. NW7 —20Ta 21
Fairway, The. W3 —44Ua 80
Fairway, The. W7 —45Fa 78
Fairway, The. Abb L —4T 4
Fairway, The. Barn —16Db 23
Fairway, The. Brom —71Pc 150
Fairway, The. Burn —10A 52
Fairway, The. Grav —1D 136
Fairway, The. Lea —90Ja 160
Fairway, The. N Mald —67Ta 123
Fairway, The. N'holt —37Ea 58
Fairway, The. N'wd —21U 36
Fairway, The. Ruis —35Y 57
Fairway, The. Upm —31Td 70
Fairway, The. Uxb —40P 55
Fairway, The. Wemb —33Ka 58
Fairway, The. W Mol —69Da 121
Fairway, The. Wey —83Q 158
Fairweather Clo. N15 —28Ub 43
Fairweather Rd. N16 —30Wb 43
Fairwell La. W Hor —100R 174
Fairwyn Rd. SE26 —63Ac 128
Fakenham Clo. N'holt —37Ba 57
Fakruddin St. E1 —42Wb 83
Falaise. Egh —64A 118
Falcon Av. Brom —70Nc 130
Falcon Av. Grays —52De 113
Falconberg Ct. W1 —44Mb 82 (2E 198)
Falconberg M. W1 —44Mb 82 (2D 198)
Falcon Clo. SE1 —46Rb 83 (6C 200)
Falcon Clo. W4 —51Sa 101
Falcon Clo. Dart —57Pd 111
Falcon Clo. N'wd —24U 36
Falcon Clo. Wal A —6Jc 13
Falcon Ct. E18 —27Kc 45
(off Albert Rd.)
Falcon Ct. EC4 —44Qb 82 (3A 200)
Falcon Ct. N1 —40Rb 63 (2C 194)
(off City Garden Row)
Falcon Ct. SE1 —46Rb 83
Falcon Ct. New Bar —14Eb 23
Falcon Ct. Ruis —33V 56
Falcon Ct. Wok —85E 156
Falcon Cres. Enf —15Zb 26
Falcon Dri. Stai —58M 97
Falconer Ct. N17 —24Sb 43
Falconer Rd. Bush —16Ba 19
Falconer Rd. Ilf —22Xc 47
Falconer Wlk. N7 —33Pb 62
Falcon Gro. SW11 —55Gb 103

Falconhurst—Fetherstone Clo.

Falconhurst. Oxs —87Fa 160
Falcon La. SW11 —55Hb 103
Falcon M. Grav —10A 114
Falcon Point. SE1
—46Rb 83 (6C 200)
Falcon Rd. SW11 —54Gb 103
Falcon Rd. Enf —15Zb 26
Falcon Rd. Hamp —66Ba 121
Falcons Clo. Big H —89Mc 167
Falcon St. E13 —42Hc 85
Falcon Ter. SW11 —55Gb 103
Falcon Way. E11 —28Jc 45
Falcon Way. E14 —49Dc 84
Falcon Way. NW9 —26Ua 40
Falcon Way. Felt —57X 99
Falcon Way. Harr —29Na 39
Falcon Way. Horn —38Jd 68
Falcon Way. Sun —68U 120
Falcon Way. Wat —6Aa 5
Falconwood. E Hor —96V 174
Falconwood. Egh —66A 118
Falconwood Av. Well —54Tc 108
Falconwood Ct. SE3 —54Hc 107
Falconwood Pde. Well —56Vc 109
Falconwood Rd. Croy —81Bc 166
Falcourt Clo. Sutt —78Db 145
Falkirk Clo. Horn —32Qd 69
Falkirk Gdns. Wat —22Z 37
Falkirk St. N1 —40Ub 63 (2J 195)
Falkland Av. N3 —24Cb 41
Falkland Av. N11 —21Kb 42
Falkland Ho. W8 —48Db 81
Falkland Pk. Av. SE25 —69Ub 127
Falkland Pl. NW5 —36Lb 62
Falkland Rd. N8 —28Qb 42
Falkland Rd. NW5 —36Lb 62
Falkland Rd. Barn —12Ab 22
Fallaize Av. Ilf —35Rc 66
Falling La. W Dray & Uxb —45N 75
Falloden Way. NW11 —28Cb 41
Fallow Clo. Chig —22Vc 47
Fallow Ct. Av. N12 —24Eb 41
Fallowfield. Stan —21Ja 38
Fallowfield Clo. Hare —25L 35
Fallowfield Ct. Stan —20Ja 20
Fallowhurst Path. N3 —24Eb 41
Fallsbrook Rd. SW16 —65Kb 126
Falmer Rd. E17 —27Dc 44
Falmer Rd. N15 —29Sb 43
Falmer Rd. Enf —14Ub 25
Falmouth Av. E4 —22Fc 45
Falmouth Clo. N22 —24Pb 42
Falmouth Clo. SE12 —57Hc 107
Falmouth Gdns. Ilf —28Mc 45
Falmouth Ho. SE11
(off Tavy Clo.) —50Qb 82 (7A 206)
Falmouth Ho. Pinn —24Ba 37
Falmouth Rd. SE1
—48Sb 83 (4E 206)
Falmouth Rd. Slou —4E 72
Falmouth Rd. W on T —77Y 141
Falmouth St. E15 —36Fc 65
Falstaff Ho. N1 —40Ub 63 (2H 195)
(off Arden Est.)
Falstaff M. Hamp —67Ea 122
Falstone. Wok —6E 188
Fambridge Clo. SE26 —63Bc 128
Fambridge Ct. Romf —29Fd 48
(off Marks Rd.)
Fambridge Rd. Dag —32Cd 68
Famet Av. Purl —85Sb 165
Famet Clo. Purl —85Sb 165
Famet Gdns. Kenl —85Sb 165
Famet Wlk. Purl —85Sb 165
Fancett Ho. SE5 —56Tb 105
Fane St. W14 —51Bb 103
Fanns Rise. Purf —49Qd 89
Fann St. EC1 & EC2
—42Sb 83 (6D 194)
Fann St. EC2 & EC1 —42Sb 83
Fanshawe Av. Bark —37Sc 66
Fanshawe Cres. Dag —36Ad 67
Fanshawe Cres. Horn —30Md 49
Fanshawe Rd. Grays —8C 92
Fanshawe Rd. Rich —63La 122
Fanshaw St. N1 —41Ub 83 (3H 195)
Fanthorpe St. SW15 —55Ya 102
Faraday Av. Sidc —61Wc 131
Faraday Clo. N7 —37Pb 62
Faraday Clo. Slou —3F 72
Faraday Clo. Wat —16T 18
Faraday Ho. Wemb —34Sa 59
Faraday Rd. E15 —37Hc 65
Faraday Rd. SW19 —65Cb 125
Faraday Rd. W3 —45Sa 79
Faraday Rd. W10 —43Ab 80
Faraday Rd. Slou —3F 72
Faraday Rd. S'hall —45Da 77
Faraday Rd. Well —55Wc 109
Faraday Rd. W Mol —70Ca 121
Faraday Way. SE18 —48Mc 85
Faraday Way. Croy —74Pb 146
Faraday Way. Orp —70Xc 131
Fareham Rd. Felt —59Y 99
Fareham St. W1
—44Mb 82 (2D 198)
Farewell Pl. Mitc —67Gb 125
Faringdon Av. Brom —73Qc 150
Faringdon Av. H Hill —25Ld 49
Faringford Clo. Pot B —3Fb 9
Faringford Rd. E15 —38Gc 65
Farington Acres. Wey —76T 140
Faris Barn Dri. Wdhm —84H 157
Faris La. Wdhm —83H 157
Farjeon Rd. SE3 —53Mc 107
Farleigh Av. Brom —73Hc 149
Farleigh Ct. Rd. Warl —86Bc 166
Farleigh Dean Cres. New Ad
—83Dc 166
Farleigh Pl. N16 —35Vb 63
Farleigh Rd. N16 —35Vb 63
Farleigh Rd. New Haw —83J 157
Farleigh Rd. Warl —90Zb 166
Farleton Clo. Wey —79T 140
Farleycroft. W'ham —98Sc 184
Farley Dri. Ilf —32Uc 66
Farley Ho. SE26 —62Xb 127
Farley La. W'ham —98Rc 184
Farley Nursery. W'ham —99Sc 184
Farley Pl. SE25 —70Wb 127
Farley Rd. SE6 —59Dc 106
Farley Rd. Grav —10H 115
Farley Rd. S Croy —80Wb 147
Farleys Clo. W Hor —98S 174
Farlington Pl. SW15 —59Xa 102
Farlow Clo. Grav —2B 136
Farlow Rd. SW15 —55Za 102
Farlton Rd. SW18 —59Db 103
Farman Gro. N'holt —41Z 77
Farm Av. NW2 —34Ab 60
Farm Av. SW16 —63Nb 126
Farm Av. Harr —31Ba 57
Farm Av. Swan —69Ed 132
Farm Av. Wemb —37La 58
Farmborough Clo. Harr —31Fa 58
Farm Clo. N14 —16Kb 24
Farm Clo. SW6 —52Cb 103
(off Farm La.)
Farm Clo. Asc —10A 116
Farm Clo. Barn —15Ya 22
Farm Clo. Borwd —10Ma 7
Farm Clo. Buck H —20Lc 27
Farm Clo. Byfl —84N 157
Farm Clo. Cher —72C 138
Farm Clo. Chesh —2Yb 12
Farm Clo. Coul —92Hb 179
Farm Clo. Dag —38Ed 68
Farm Clo. E Hor —100V 174
Farm Clo. Fet —96Fa 176
Farm Clo. Hut —17Ee 33
Farm Clo. Shep —73Q 140
Farm Clo. S'hall —45Da 77
Farm Clo. Stai —64G 118
Farm Clo. Sutt —80Fb 145
Farm Clo. Uxb —33R 56
Farm Clo. Wall —82Lb 164
Farm Clo. W Wick —76Hc 149
Farmcote Rd. SE12 —60Jc 107
Farm Ct. NW4 —27Wa 40
Farm Cres. Slou —3M 73
Farmcroft. Grav —1C 136
Farmdale Rd. SE10 —50Jc 85
Farmdale Rd. Cars —80Gb 145
Farm Dri. Croy —75Bc 148
Farm Dri. Grays —45Ee 91
Farm Dri. Purl —83Mb 164
Farm End. E4 —15Gc 27
Farm End. N'wd —25R 36
Farmer Rd. E10 —32Dc 64
Farmers Clo. Wat —5X 5
Farmers Ct. Wal A —5Jc 13
Farmer's Rd. SE5 —52Rb 105
Farmers Rd. Stai —64G 118
Farmer St. W8 —46Cb 81
Farmfield. Wat —10U 4
Farmfield Rd. Brom —64Gc 129
Farm Fields. S Croy —83Ub 165
Farm Hill Rd. Wal A —5Fc 13
Farm Holt. New Ash —74Be 155
Farm Ho. Clo. Wok —87F 156
Farm Ho. Ct. NW7 —24Wa 40
Farmhouse Rd. SW16 —66Lb 126
Farmilo Rd. E17 —31Bc 64
Farmington Av. Sutt —76Fb 145
Farmlands. Enf —11Qb 24
Farmlands. Pinn —28W 36
Farmlands, The. N'holt —37Ca 57
Farmland Wlk. Chst —64Rc 130
Farm La. N14 —16Jb 24
Farm La. SW6 —51Cb 103
Farm La. Add —80J 139
Farm La. Asht & Eps —89Qa 161
Farm La. Cipp —5H 73
Farm La. Croy —75Bc 148
Farm La. E Hor —100V 174
Farm La. Loud —13L 17
Farm La. Purl —82Lb 164
Farm La. Send —96E 172
Farmleigh. N14 —17Lb 24
Farmleigh Gro. W on T —78V 140
Farmleigh Ho. SE24 —57Rb 105
Farm M. Mitc —68Kb 126
Farm Pl. W8 —46Cb 81
Farm Pl. Dart —56Jd 110
Farm Rd. N21 —18Sb 25
Farm Rd. Chor —14C 16
Farm Rd. E Til —9L 93
Farm Rd. Edgw —23Ra 39
Farm Rd. Esh —74Da 141
Farm Rd. Houn —60Aa 99
Farm Rd. Mord —71Db 145
Farm Rd. N'wd —22R 36
Farm Rd. Ors —7B 92
Farm Rd. Rain —41Ld 89
Farm Rd. Sev —92Ld 187
Farm Rd. Stai —65K 119
Farm Rd. Sutt —80Fb 145
Farm Rd. Warl —91Ac 182
Farm Rd. Wok —92D 172
Farmstead Rd. SE6 —63Dc 128
Farmstead Rd. Harr —25Fa 38
Farm St. W1 —45Kb 82 (5K 197)
Farm Vale. Bex —58Dd 110
Farmview. Cob —88Z 159
Farm Wlk. NW11 —29Bb 41
Farm Way. Buck H —21Lc 45
Farm Way. Bush —14Da 19
Farmway. Dag —34Yc 67
Farm Way. Horn —35Ld 69
Farm Way. N'wd —21U 36
Farm Way. Stai —58H 97
Farm Way. Wor Pk —76Ya 144
Farm Yd. Wind —2H 95
Farnaby Dri. Sev —98Hd 186
Farnaby Rd. SE9 —56Lc 107
Farnaby Rd. Brom —66Fc 129
Farnaby Way. Stanf —1L 93
Farnan Av. E17 —26Cc 44
Farnan Rd. SW16 —64Nb 126
Farnborough Av. E17 —27Ac 44
Farnborough Av. S Croy —81Zb 166
Farnborough Clo. Wemb —33Ra 59
Farnborough Comn. Orp —76Pc 150
Farnborough Cres. Brom
—74Hc 149
Farnborough Cres. S Croy
—81Ac 166
Farnborough Hill. Orp —78Tc 150
Farnborough Way. SE15 —52Vb 105
Farnborough Way. Orp —77Sc 150
Farnburn Av. Slou —3F 72
Farncombe St. SE16 —47Wb 83
Farndale Av. N13 —20Rb 25
Farndale Cres. Gnfd —41Ea 78
Farnell M. SW5 —50Db 81
Farnell Point. E5 —35Wb 63
Farnell Rd. Iswth —55Fa 100
Farnell Rd. Stai —62J 119
Farnes Dri. Romf —26Ld 49
Farnham Clo. N20 —17Eb 23
Farnham Clo. Bov —1C 2
Farnham Ct. Sutt —79Ab 144
Farnham Gdns. SW20 —68Xa 124
Farnham La. Slou —1C 72
Farnham Pk. La. Farn R —8G 52
Farnham Pl. SE1
—46Rb 83 (7C 200)
Farnham Rd. Ilf —31Vc 67
Farnham Rd. Romf —22Md 49
Farnham Rd. Slou —1F 72
Farnham Rd. Well —54Yc 109
Farnham Royal. SE11 —50Pb 82
Farningham Cres. Cat —95Wb 181
Farningham Hill Rd. F'ham
—71Ld 153
Farningham Ho. N4 —31Tb 63
Farningham Rd. N17 —24Wb 43
Farningham Rd. Cat —95Wb 181
Farnley. Wok —5C 188
Farnley Ho. SW8 —54Mb 104
Farnley Rd. E4 —17Gc 27
Farnley Rd. SE25 —70Tb 127
Farnol Rd. Dart —57Qd 111
Faro Clo. Brom —68Qc 130
Faroe Rd. W14 —48Za 80
Farorna Wlk. Enf —11Qb 24
Farquhar Rd. SE19 —64Vb 127
Farquhar Rd. SW19 —62Cb 125
Farquharson Rd. Croy —74Sb 147
Farraline Rd. Wat —14X 19
Farrance Rd. Romf —31Ad 67
Farrance St. E14 —44Cc 84
Farrans Ct. Harr —31Ka 58
Farrant Av. N22 —26Qb 42
Farrant Clo. Orp —80Wc 151
Farrant Way. Borwd —11Na 21
Farr Av. Bark —40Wc 67
Farren Rd. SE23 —61Ac 128
Farrer Ct. Twic —59Ma 101
Farrer M. N8 —28Mb 42
Farrer Rd. N8 —28Mb 42
Farrer Rd. Harr —29Na 39
Farrer's Pl. Croy —77Zb 148
Farrier Clo. Sun —69W 120
Farrier Rd. N'holt —40Ca 57
Farriers Clo. Eps —84Ua 162
Farriers Clo. Grav —10H 115
Farriers Ct. Leav —4X 5
Farriers Rd. Eps —83Ua 162
Farrier St. NW1 —38Kb 62
Farriers Way. Borwd —15Ta 21
Farringdon La. EC1
—42Qb 82 (6A 194)
Farringdon Rd. EC1
—42Qb 82 (5K 193)
Farringdon St. EC4
—43Rb 83 (1B 200)
Farrington Av. Orp —69Xc 131
Farrington Pl. Chst —66Tc 130
Farrins Rents. SE16 —46Ac 84
Farrow Gdns. Grays —46De 91
Farrow La. SE14 —52Yb 106
Farrow Pl. SE16 —48Ac 84
Farr Rd. Enf —11Tb 25
Farthingale Ct. Wal A —6Jc 13
Farthingale La. Wal A —6Jc 13
(in two parts)
Farthingale Wlk. E15 —38Fc 65
Farthing All. SE1 —47Wb 83
Farthing Barn La. Orp —81Qc 168
Farthing Clo. Dart —56Pd 111
Farthing Fields. E1 —46Xb 83
Farthing Grn. La. Stoke P —10L 53
Farthings. Chal G —13A 16
Farthings. Knap —4B 188
Farthings Clo. E4 —20Gc 27
Farthings Clo. Pinn —30X 37
Farthings, The. King T —67Qa 123
Farthing St. Orp —80Pc 150
Farwell Rd. Sidc —63Xc 131
Farwig La. Brom —67Hc 129
Fashion St. E1 —43Vb 83 (1K 201)
Fashoda Rd. Brom —70Mc 129
Fassett Rd. E8 —37Wb 63
Fassett Rd. King T —70Na 123
Fassett Sq. E8 —37Wb 63
Fassnidge View. Uxb —38L 55
Fauconberg Ct. W4 —51Sa 101
(off Fauconberg Rd.)
Fauconberg Rd. W4 —51Sa 101
Faulkner Clo. Dag —31Zc 67
Faulkners All. EC1
—43Rb 83 (7B 194)
Faulkners Rd. W on T —78Y 141
Faulkner St. SE14 —53Yb 106
Fauna Clo. Romf —30Yc 47
Faunce St. SE17 —50Rb 83
Favart Rd. SW6 —53Cb 103
Faversham Av. E4 —18Gc 27
Faversham Av. Enf —16Tb 25
Faversham Clo. Chig —19Xc 29
Faversham Rd. SE6 —59Bc 106
Faversham Rd. Beck —68Bc 128
Faversham Rd. Mord —72Db 145
Fawcett Clo. SW11 —54Fb 103
Fawcett Est. E5 —32Wb 63
Fawcett Rd. NW10 —39Va 60
Fawcett Rd. Croy —76Sb 147
Fawcett Rd. Wind —3F 94
Fawcett St. SW10 —51Eb 103
Fawcus Clo. Clay —79Ga 142
Fawe Pk. Rd. SW15 —56Bb 103
Fawe St. E14 —43Dc 84
Fawkham Av. Long —69Ee 135
Fawkham Grn. Rd. Fawk —76Xd 154
Fawkham Rd. Fawk & W King
—77Vd 154
Fawkham Rd. Long —70Zd 135
Fawley Rd. NW6 —36Db 61
Fawnbrake Av. SE24 —57Rb 105
Fawn Rd. E13 —40Lc 65
Fawn Rd. Chig —22Vc 47
Fawns Mnr. Clo. Felt —60S 98
Fawns Mnr. Rd. Felt —60T 98
Fawood Av. NW10 —38Ta 59
Fawsley Clo. Coln —52G 96
Fawters Clo. Hut —16Fe 33
Fayerfield. Pot B —3Fb 9
Faygate Cres. Bexh —57Cd 110
Faygate Rd. SW2 —61Pb 126
Fay Grn. Abb L —5T 4
Fayland Av. SW16 —64Lb 126
Faymore Gdns. S Ock —44Wd 90
Fearn Clo. E Hor —100U 174
Fearney Mead. Rick —18L 17
Fearnley Cres. Hamp —64Aa 121
Fearnley Ho. SE5 —54Ub 105
Fearnley St. Wat —14X 19
Fearns Mead. War —22Yd 50
Fearon St. SE10 —50Jc 85
Featherbed La. Croy & Warl
—80Bc 148
Featherbed La. Romf —17Ad 29
Feathers La. Wray —61C 118
Feathers Pl. SE10 —51Fc 107
Featherstone Av. SE23 —61Yb 128
Featherstone Gdns. Borwd —14Ta 21
Featherstone Ho. Hay —43Y 77
Featherstone Rd. NW7 —23Xa 40
Featherstone Rd. S'hall —48Aa 77
Featherstone St. EC1
—42Tb 83 (5F 195)
Featherstone Ter. S'hall —48Aa 77
Featley Rd. SW9 —55Rb 105
Federal Rd. Gnfd —39La 58
Federal Way. Wat —11Y 19
Federation Rd. SE2 —49Xc 87
Fee Farm Rd. Clay —80Ha 142
Feenan Highway. Til —4D 114
Felbridge Av. Stan —25Ja 38
Felbridge Clo. SW16 —63Qb 126
Felbridge Clo. Sutt —81Db 163
Felbridge Ct. Hay —51T 98
Felbrigge Rd. Ilf —33Vc 67
Felcott Clo. W on T —76Y 141
Felcott Rd. W on T —76Y 141
Felday Rd. SE13 —58Dc 106
Felden Clo. Pinn —24Aa 37
Felden Clo. Wat —6Z 5
Felden St. SW6 —53Bb 103
Feldman Clo. N16 —32Wb 63
Felgate M. W6 —49Xa 80
Felhampton Rd. SE9 —62Rc 130
Felhurst Cres. Dag —35Dd 68
Felicia Way. Grays —9D 92
Felix Av. N8 —30Nb 42
Felix Ct. E17 —29Dc 44
Felix Dri. W Cla —100J 173
Felix La. Shep —72U 140
Felix Mnr. Chst —65Uc 130
Felix Rd. W13 —45Ja 78
Felix Rd. W on T —72W 140
Felixstowe Rd. N9 —21Wb 43
Felixstowe Rd. N17 —27Vb 43
Felixstowe Rd. NW10 —41Xa 80
Felixstowe Rd. SE2 —48Xc 87
Felix St. E2 —40Xb 63
Fellbrigg Rd. SE22 —57Vb 105
Fellbrigg St. E1 —42Xb 83
Fellbrook. Rich —62Ka 122
Fellowes Clo. Hay —42Z 77
Fellowes Rd. Cars —76Gb 145
Fellows Ct. E2 —40Vb 63 (2K 195)
Fellows Rd. NW3 —38Fb 61
Fell Path. Borwd —15Ta 21
Fell Rd. Croy —76Sb 147
Felltram Way. SE7 —50Jc 85
Fell Wlk. Edgw —25Sa 39
Felmersham Clo. SW4 —56Nb 104
Felmingham Rd. SE20 —68Yb 128
Felnex Trading Est. NW10 —40Ta 59
Felsberg Rd. SW2 —59Nb 104
Fels Clo. Dag —34Dd 68
Fels Farm Av. Dag —34Ed 68
Felsham Rd. SW15 —55Ya 102
Felspar Clo. SE18 —50Vc 87
Felstead Av. Ilf —25Qc 46
Felstead Clo. Hut —16Ee 33
Felstead Gdns. E14 —50Ec 84
Felstead Rd. E11 —31Jc 65
Felstead Rd. Eps —83Ta 161
Felstead Rd. Lou —17Nc 28
Felstead Rd. Orp —75Wc 151
Felstead Rd. Romf —24Ed 48
Felstead Rd. Wal X —4Ac 12
Felstead St. E9 —37Bc 64
Felsted Wharf. E14 —50Ec 84
Felsted Rd. E16 —44Mc 85
Feltham Av. E Mol —70Ga 122
Felthambrook Way. Felt —62X 121
Feltham Hill Rd. Ashf —64Q 120
Felthamhill Rd. Felt —63W 120
Feltham Rd. Ashf —64Q 120
Feltham Rd. Mitc —68Jb 126
Felton Clo. Borwd —10Na 7
Felton Clo. Orp —72Rc 150
Felton Ct. N1 —39Tb 63
Felton Gdns. Bark —39Uc 66
Felton Ho. N1 —39Tb 63
(off Colville Est.)
Felton Lea. Sidc —64Vc 131
Felton Rd. W13 —47La 78
Felton Rd. Bark —40Uc 66
Fencepiece Rd. Chig —22Sc 46
Fenchurch Av. EC3
—44Ub 83 (3H 201)
Fenchurch Bldgs. EC3
—44Ub 83 (3J 201)
Fenchurch Pl. EC3
—45Ub 83 (4J 201)
Fenchurch St. EC3
—45Ub 83 (4H 201)
Fen Clo. Shenf —14De 33
Fen Ct. EC3 —44Ub 83 (3H 201)
Fendall Rd. Eps —78Sa 143
Fendall St. SE1 —48Ub 83 (4J 207)
Fendt Clo. E16 —44Hc 85
Fendyke Rd. Belv —49Zc 87
Fenelon Pl. W14 —49Bb 81
Fen Gro. Sidc —57Vc 109
Fenham Rd. SE15 —52Wb 105
Fenhurst Gdns. Edgw —23Qa 39
Fen La. N Ock —36Yd 70
Fen La. Ors —2A 92
Fen La. W Horn —31De 71
Fenman Ct. N17 —25Xb 43
Fenman Gdns. Ilf —32Xc 67
Fenn Clo. Brom —65Jc 129
Fennel Clo. E16 —42Gc 85
Fennel Clo. Croy —74Zb 148
Fennells Mead. Eps —81Va 162
Fennell St. SE18 —51Qc 108
Fenner Clo. SE16 —49Xb 83
Fenner Sq. SW11 —55Fb 103
Fenn Ho. Iswth —53Ka 100
Fenning St. SE1
—47Ub 83 (1H 207)
Fenn St. E9 —36Yb 64
Fenns Way. Wok —87A 156
Fenstanton Av. N12 —22Fb 41
Fen St. E16 —45Hc 85
Fens Way. Swan —65Jd 132
Fenswood Clo. Bex —58Cd 110
Fentiman Rd. SW8 —51Nb 104
Fentiman Way. Horn —32Nd 69
Fenton Av. Stai —65L 119
Fenton Clo. E8 —37Vb 63
Fenton Clo. SW9 —54Pb 104
Fenton Clo. Chst —64Pc 130
Fenton Ho. Houn —51Ca 99
Fenton Rd. N17 —24Sb 43
Fentons Av. E13 —41Kc 85
Fenwick Clo. SE18 —51Qc 108
Fenwick Clo. Wok —5E 188
Fenwick Gro. SE15 —55Wb 105
Fenwick Path. Borwd —10Pa 7
Fenwick Pl. SW9 —55Nb 104
Fenwick Rd. SE15 —55Wb 105
Ferby Ct. Sidc —63Vc 131
(off Main Rd.)
Ferdinand Pl. NW1 —38Jb 62
Ferdinand St. NW1 —38Jb 62
Ferguson Av. Grav —3E 136
Ferguson Av. Romf —26Ld 49
Ferguson Av. Surb —71Pa 143
Ferguson Clo. Brom —69Fc 129
Ferguson Ct. Romf —26Md 49
Ferguson Dri. W3 —44Ta 79
Ferguson Ho. E17 —30Ac 44
Ferguson Ho. SE10 —53Ec 106
Fergus Rd. N5 —36Rb 63
Fermain Ct. N1 —39Ub 63
(off De Beauvoir Est.)
Ferme Pk. Rd. N8 & N4 —29Nb 42
Fermony Rd. Gnfd —42Da 77
Fermor Rd. SE23 —60Ac 106
Fermoy Rd. W9 —42Bb 81
Fern Av. Mitc —70Mb 126
Fernbank. Buck H —18Kc 27
Fern Bank. Eyns —75Pd 153
Fernbank Av. Horn —35Ld 69
Fernbank Av. W on T —73Aa 141
Fernbank Av. Wemb —35Ha 58
Fernbank Rd. Add —78J 139
Fernbrook Av. Sidc —57Uc 108
Fernbrook Dri. Harr —31Da 57
Fernbrook Rd. SE13 —58Gc 107
Ferncliff Rd. E8 —36Wb 63
Fern Clo. Warl —90Ac 166
Fern Ct. Stanf —1M 93
Ferncroft Av. N12 —23Hb 41
Ferncroft Av. NW3 —34Cb 61
Ferncroft Av. Ruis —33Y 57
Ferndale. Brom —68Lc 129
Ferndale. Sev —94Ld 187
Ferndale Av. E17 —29Fc 45
Ferndale Av. Cher —76G 138
Ferndale Av. Houn —55Aa 99
Ferndale Cres. Uxb —41L 75
Ferndale Rd. E7 —38Kc 65
Ferndale Rd. E11 —33Gc 65
Ferndale Rd. N15 —30Vb 43
Ferndale Rd. SE25 —71Xb 147
Ferndale Rd. SW4 & SW9
—56Nb 104
Ferndale Rd. Ashf —64M 119
Ferndale Rd. Bans —88Bb 163
Ferndale Rd. Enf —9Ac 12
Ferndale Rd. Grav —1D 136
Ferndale Rd. Romf —26Ed 48
Ferndale Rd. Wok —88B 156
Ferndale St. E6 —45Rc 86
Ferndale Ter. Harr —28Ha 38
Ferndale Way. Orp —78Tc 150
Ferndell Av. Bex —62Fd 132
Ferndene. Brick —3Ba 5
Ferndene. Long —69Fe 135
Ferndene Rd. SE24 —56Sb 105
Fernden Way. Romf —30Dd 48
Ferndown. Horn —30Pd 49
Ferndown. N'wd —26W 36
Ferndown Av. Orp —74Tc 150
Ferndown Clo. Pinn —24Aa 37
Ferndown Clo. Sutt —79Fb 145
Ferndown Gdns. Cob —85Y 159
Ferndown Rd. SE9 —59Mc 107
Ferndown Rd. Wat —21Y 37
Fern Dri. Tap —4A 72
Fernery, The. Stai —64G 118
Fernes Clo. Uxb —44L 75
Ferney Ct. Byfl —83M 157
Ferney Rd. Barn —17Jb 24
Ferney Rd. Byfl —84M 157
Fern Gro. Felt —59X 99
Fernhall Dri. Ilf —29Mc 45
Fernhall La. Wal A —3Mc 13
Fernham Rd. T Hth —69Sb 127
Fernhead Rd. W9 —41Bb 81
Fernheath Way. Dart —64Fd 132
Fern Hill. Oxs —86Fa 160
Fernhill Clo. Wok —8F 188
Fernhill Ct. E17 —26Fc 45
Fernhill Gdns. King T —64Ma 123
Fernhill La. Wok —8F 188
Fernhill Pk. Wok —8F 188
Fern Hill Pl. F'boro —78Sc 150
Fernhills. K Lan —6T 4
Fernhill St. E16 —46Pc 86
Fernholme Rd. SE15 —57Zb 106
Fernhurst Gdns. Edgw —23Qa 39
Fernhurst Rd. SW6 —53Ab 102
Fernhurst Rd. Ashf —63S 120
Fernhurst Rd. Croy —74Xb 147
Fernie Clo. Chig —22Wc 47
Fernie Way. Chig —22Wc 47
Fernihough Clo. Wey —82Q 158
Fernlands Clo. Cher —76G 138
Fern La. Houn —50Ba 77
Fernlea. Bookh —96Da 175
Fernlea Rd. SW12 —60Kb 104
Fernlea Rd. Mitc —68Jb 126
Fernleigh Clo. Croy —77Qb 146
Fernleigh Ct. Harr —26Da 37
Fernleigh Ct. Romf —29Ed 48
Fernleigh Ct. Wemb —33Na 59
Fernleigh Rd. N21 —19Qb 24
Fernsbury St. WC1
—41Qb 82 (4K 193)
Ferns Clo. Enf —8Ac 12
Ferns Clo. S Croy —82Xb 165
Fernshaw Rd. SW10 —51Eb 103
Fernside. NW11 —33Cb 61
Fernside. Buck H —18Kc 27
Fernside Av. NW7 —20Ta 21
Fernside Av. Felt —63X 121
Fernside Ct. NW4 —26Za 40
Fernside Rd. SW12 —60Hb 103
Fernsleigh Clo. Ger X —23A 34
Ferns Rd. E15 —37Hc 65
Fern St. E3 —42Cc 84
Fernthorpe Rd. SW16 —65Lb 126
Ferntower Rd. N5 —36Tb 63
Fern Towers. Cat —97Wb 181
Fern Way. Wat —7X 5
Fernways. Ilf —35Rc 66
Fernwood. Croy —81Ac 166
Fernwood Av. SW16 —63Mb 126
Fernwood Av. Wemb —37La 58
Fernwood Clo. Brom —68Lc 129
Fernwood Cres. N20 —20Hb 23
Ferny Hill. Barn —10Jb 10
Ferranti Clo. SE18 —49Mc 85
Ferrard Clo. Houn —51Ca 99
Ferrers Av. Wall —77Mb 146
Ferrers Av. W Dray —47M 75
Ferrers Rd. SW16 —64Mb 126
Ferrestone Rd. N8 —28Pb 42
Ferriby Clo. N1 —38Qb 62
Ferrier Point. E16 —43Jc 85
(off Forty Acre La.)
Ferrier St. SW18 —56Db 103
Ferriers Way. Eps —90Ya 162
Ferring Clo. Harr —32Ea 58
Ferrings. SE21 —62Ub 127
Ferris Av. Croy —76Bc 148
Ferris Rd. SE22 —56Wb 105
Ferron Rd. E5 —34Xb 63
Ferro Rd. Rain —42Jd 88
Ferry App. SE18 —48Qc 86
Ferry Av. Stai —66G 118
Ferrybridge Ho. SE11
—48Pb 82 (4J 205)
(off Lambeth Wlk.)
Ferrydale Lodge. NW4 —28Ya 40
(off Church Rd.)
Ferryhills Clo. Wat —20Y 19
Ferry Ho. E5 —32Xb 63
(off Harrington Hill)
Ferry La. N17 —28Wb 43
Ferry La. SW13 —51Va 102
Ferry La. Bren —51Na 101
Ferry La. Cher —71J 139
Ferry La. Lale —69L 119
Ferry La. Rain —44Gd 88
Ferry La. Rich —51Pa 101
Ferry La. Shep —74Q 140
Ferry La. Stai —61D 118
Ferrymead Av. Gnfd —41Ca 77
Ferrymead Dri. Gnfd —40Ca 57
Ferrymoor. Rich —62Ka 122
Ferry Pl. SE18 —48Qc 86
Ferry Rd. SW13 —52Wa 102
Ferry Rd. Tedd —64Ka 122
Ferry Rd. Th Dit —72Ka 142
Ferry Rd. Til —5C 114
Ferry Rd. Twic —60Ka 100
Ferry Rd. W Mol —69Ca 121
Ferry Sq. Bren —52Na 101
Ferry Sq. Shep —73R 140
Ferry St. E14 —50Ec 84
Feryby Rd. Grays —8D 92
Festing Rd. SW15 —55Za 102
Festival Av. Long —69Fe 135
Festival Clo. Bex —60Zc 109
Festival Clo. Eri —52Hd 110
Festival Clo. Uxb —39R 56
Festival Wlk. Cars —78Hb 145
Fetcham Comn. La. Fet —93Da 175
Fetcham Pk. Dri. Fet —95Ga 176
Fetherstone Clo. Pot B —4Fb 9

Fetherston Rd.—Fordhook Av.

Fetherston Rd. Stanf —1M 93
Fetter La. EC4 —44Qb 82 (3A 200) (in two parts)
Ffinch St. SE8 —52Cc 106
Fiddicroft Av. Bans —86Db 163
Fiddlers Clo. Grnh —56Xd 112
Fidler Pl. Bush —16Da 19
Field Clo. E4 —23Dc 44
Field Clo. Abr —13Xc 29
Field Clo. Brom —68Lc 129
Field Clo. Buck H —20Lc 27
Field Clo. Chess —78La 142
Field Clo. Hay —52S 98
Field Clo. Houn —54X 99
Field Clo. Ruis —32S 56
Field Clo. S Croy —86Xb 165
Field Clo. Uxb —33R 56
Field Clo. W Mol —71Da 141
Fieldcommon La. W on T —74Aa 141
Field Ct. SW19 —62Cb 125
Field Ct. WC1 —43Pb 82 (1J 199)
Field Ct. Oxt —99Gc 183
Field End. Barn —14Xa 22
Field End. Coul —86Mb 164
Field End. N'holt —37Aa 57
Field End. Ruis —37Y 57
Field End. Twic —63Ha 122
Field End Clo. Wat —17Aa 19
Fieldend Rd. SW16 —67Lb 126
Field End Rd. Eastc & Ruis —29X 37
Fielders Clo. Enf —14Ub 25
Fielders Clo. Harr —32Ea 58
Fieldfare Rd. SE28 —45Yc 87
Fieldgate La. Mitc —68Gb 125
Fieldgate St. E1 —43Wb 83
Fieldhouse Rd. SW12 —60Lb 104
Fieldhouse Vs. Bans —87Gb 163
Fieldhurst. Slou —50B 74
Fieldhurst Clo. Add —78K 139
Fielding Av. Til —3D 114
Fielding Av. Twic —62Ea 122
Fielding Ho. W4 —51Ua 102 (off Devonshire Rd.)
Fielding Rd. W4 —48Ta 79
Fielding Rd. W14 —48Za 80
Fieldings Rd. Chesh —1Bc 12
Fieldings, The. SE23 —60Yb 106
Fieldings, The. Wok —4C 188
Fielding St. SE17 —51Sb 105
Fielding Ter. W5 —45Pa 79
Fieldings Way. Hut —16Ee 33
Field La. Bren —52La 100
Field La. Tedd —64Ja 122
Field Mead. NW9 & NW7 —24Ua 40
Field Pl. N Mald —72Va 144
Field Point. E7 —35Jc 65
Field Rd. E7 —35Jc 65
Field Rd. N17 —27Tb 43
Field Rd. W6 —50Ab 80
Field Rd. Den —35G 54
Field Rd. Felt —58X 99
Field Rd. S Ock —46Sd 90
Field Rd. Wat —16Aa 19
Fields Ct. Pot B —5Fb 9
Fieldsend Rd. Sutt —78Ab 144
Fields Est. E8 —38Wb 63
Fieldside Clo. Orp —77Sc 150
Fieldside Rd. Brom —64Fc 129
Fields Pk. Cres. Romf —29Zc 47
Fields, The. Slou —7H 73
Field St. WC1 —41Pb 82 (3H 193)
Fieldsway Ho. N5 —36Qb 62
Fieldview. SW18 —60Fb 103
Field View. Egh —64E 118
Field View. Felt —63T 120
Field View Rise. Brick —1Aa 5
Field View Rd. Pot B —5Cb 9
Field Way. NW10 —38Sa 59
Fieldway. Dag —34Yc 67
Field Way. Ger X —24A 34
Fieldway. Grays —46Ce 91
Field Way. Gnfd —39Da 57
Field Way. New Ad —80Dc 148
Fieldway. Orp —72Tc 150
Field Way. Rick —18K 17
Field Way. Rip —97H 173
Field Way. Ruis —32S 56
Field Way. Uxb —42M 75
Fieldway Cres. N5 —36Qb 62
Fiennes Clo. Dag —32Yc 67
Fiennes Way. Sev —99Ld 187
Fifehead Clo. Ashf —65N 119
Fife Rd. E16 —43Jc 85
Fife Rd. N22 —24Rb 43
Fife Rd. SW14 —57Sa 101
Fife Rd. King T —68Na 123
Fife Ter. N1 —40Pb 62 (1J 193)
Fife Way. Bookh —97Ca 175
Fifield Path. SE23 —62Zb 128
Fifth Av. E12 —35Pc 66
Fifth Av. W10 —41Ab 80
Fifth Av. Grays —51Wd 112
Fifth Av. Hay —46V 76
Fifth Av. Wat —7Z 5
Fifth Cross Rd. Twic —61Fa 122
Fifth Way. Wemb —35Ra 59
Figges Rd. Mitc —66Jb 126
Fig St. Sev —100Hd 186
Fig Tree Clo. NW10 —39Ua 60
Filborough Way. Grav —1K 137
Filby Rd. Chess —79Pa 143
Filey Av. N16 —32Wb 63
Filey Clo. Big H —91Kc 183
Filey Clo. Sutt —80Eb 145
Filey Spur. Slou —8F 72
Filey Waye. Ruis —33W 56
Fillebrook Av. Enf —12Ub 25
Fillebrook Rd. E11 —32Gc 65
Filmer La. Sev —93Nd 187
Filmer Rd. SW6 —53Ab 102
Filmer Rd. Wind —4B 94
Filston La. Sev —88Fd 170
Filston Rd. Eri —50Ed 88
Filton Ct. SE15 —51Ub 105 (off Brockworth Clo.)
Finborough Rd. SW10 —50Db 81
Finborough Rd. SW17 —65Hb 125
Finchale Rd. SE2 —48Wc 87
Fincham Clo. Uxb —34S 56
Finch Av. SE27 —63Tb 127
Finch Clo. NW10 —37Ta 59
Finch Clo. Barn —15Cb 23
Finch Clo. Knap —5A 188
Finch Ct. Sidc —62Xc 131
Finchdean Way. SE15 —52Vb 105
Finch Dri. Felt —59Z 99
Finchingfield Av. Wfd G —24Lc 45
Finch La. EC3 —44Tb 83 (3G 201)
Finch La. Bush —13Ba 19
Finchley Clo. Dart —58Qd 111
Finchley Ct. N3 —23Db 41
Finchley Ind. Est. N12 —21Eb 41
Finchley La. NW4 —28Ya 40
Finchley Pk. N12 —21Eb 41
Finchley Pl. NW8 —40Fb 61 (1B 190)
Finchley Rd. NW3 —35Cb 61
Finchley Rd. NW8 —39Fb 61
Finchley Rd. NW11 & NW2 —28Bb 41
Finchley Rd. Grays —51De 113
Finchley Way. N3 —24Cb 41
Finch's Ct. E14 —45Dc 84
Finck St. SE1 —47Pb 82 (2J 205)
Finden Rd. E7 —36Lc 65
Findhorn Av. Hay —43X 77
Findhorn St. E14 —44Ec 84
Findon Clo. SW18 —58Cb 103
Findon Clo. Harr —34Da 57
Findon Ct. Add —78H 139
Findon Gdns. Rain —43Jd 88
Findon Rd. N9 —18Xb 25
Findon Rd. W12 —47Wa 80
Fine Bush La. Hare —30R 36
Fineleigh Ct. Slou —6J 73
Fingal St. SE10 —50Hc 85
Fingleham Clo. Orp —74Zc 151
Finians Clo. Uxb —38P 55
Finland Rd. SE4 —55Ac 106
Finland St. SE16 —48Ac 84
Finlay Gdns. Add —77L 139
Finlays Clo. Chess —78Qa 143
Finlay St. SW6 —53Za 102
Finmere Ho. N4 —31Sb 63
Finnart Clo. Wey —77S 140
Finnart Ho. Dri. Wey —77S 140
Finnemore Rd. Ilf —24Wc 47
Finnis St. E2 —41Xb 83
Finnymore Rd. Dag —38Ad 67
Finsbury Av. EC2 —43Tb 83 (1G 201)
Finsbury Av. Sq. EC2 —43Ub 83 (7H 195) (off Finsbury Av.)
Finsbury Cir. EC2 —43Tb 83 (1G 201)
Finsbury Cotts. N22 —24Nb 42
Finsbury Ct. Wal X —6Ac 12
Finsbury Est. EC1 —41Qb 82 (4A 194)
Finsbury Ho. N22 —25Nb 42
Finsbury Mkt. EC2 (in two parts) —42Ub 83 (6H 195)
Finsbury Pk. Av. N4 —30Sb 43
Finsbury Pk. Rd. N4 —33Rb 63
Finsbury Pavement. EC2 —43Tb 83 (7G 195)
Finsbury Rd. N22 —24Pb 42
Finsbury Sq. EC2 —42Tb 83 (7G 195)
Finsbury St. EC2 —43Tb 83 (7F 195)
Finsbury Way. Bex —58Bd 109
Finsen Rd. SE5 —56Sb 105
Finstock Rd. W10 —44Za 80
Finucane Dri. Orp —73Yc 151
Finucane Gdns. Rain —37Jd 68
Finucane Rise. Bush —19Ea 20
Finway Ct. Wat —15V 18
Fiona Clo. Bookh —96Ca 175
Firbank Clo. E16 —43Mc 85
Firbank Clo. Enf —14Sb 25
Firbank Dri. Wat —17Aa 19
Firbank Dri. Wok —7E 188
Firbank La. Wok —7E 188
Firbank Pl. Egh —5M 117
Firbank Rd. SE15 —54Xb 105
Firbank Rd. Romf —22Dd 48
Fir Clo. W on T —73W 140
Fircroft Clo. Stoke P —7L 53
Fircroft Clo. Wok —90B 156
Fircroft Ct. Wok —90B 156
Fircroft Gdns. Harr —34Ga 58
Fircroft Rd. SW17 —61Hb 125
Fircroft Rd. Chess —77Pa 143
Fir Dene. Orp —76Qc 150
Firdene. Surb —74Sa 143
Fire Bell La. Surb —72Na 143
Firecrest Clo. Long —69De 135
Firecrest Dri. NW3 —34Db 61
Firefly Clo. Wall —80Nb 146
Fire Sta. All. H Bar —13Ab 22
Fire Sta. M. Beck —67Dc 128
Firfield Rd. Add —77J 139
Firfields. Wey —79R 140
Fir Grange Av. Wey —78R 140
Fir Gro. N Mald —72Va 144
Firgrove. Wok —7D 188
Firham Pk. Av. Romf —24Qd 49
Firhill Rd. SE6 —63Cc 128
Firlands. Wey —79U 140
Firle Ct. Eps —84Va 162
Firmingers Rd. Orp —78Dd 152
Firmin Rd. Dart —57Ld 111
Fir Rd. Felt —64Z 121
Fir Rd. Sutt —74Bb 145
Firs Av. N10 —27Jb 42
Firs Av. N11 —23Hb 41
Firs Av. SW14 —56Sa 101
Firs Av. Wind —5D 94
Firsby Av. Croy —74Zb 148
Firsby Rd. N16 —32Wb 63
Firs Clo. N10 —28Jb 42
Firs Clo. SE23 —59Ac 106
Firs Clo. Clay —79Ga 142
Firs Clo. Mitc —67Kb 126
Firs Croft. N13 —20Sb 25
Firs Dene Clo. Ott —79F 138
Firs Dri. Houn —52X 99
Firs Dri. Lou —11Qc 28
Firs End. Ger X —27A 34
Firsgrove Cres. War —21Xd 50
Firsgrove Rd. War —21Xd 50
Firs Ho. N22 —25Qb 42 (off Acacia Rd.)
Firside Gro. Sidc —60Vc 109
Firs La. N13 & N21 —20Sb 25
Firs La. N21 —17Sb 25
Firs La. Pot B —5Db 9
Firs Pk. Av. N21 —18Tb 25
Firs Pk. Gdns. N21 —18Tb 25
Firs Rd. Kenl —87Rb 165
First Av. E12 —35Nc 66
First Av. E13 —41Jc 85 (in two parts)
First Av. E17 —29Cc 44
First Av. N18 —21Yb 44
First Av. N21 —16Vb 25
First Av. NW4 —28Ya 40
First Av. SW14 —55Ua 102
First Av. W3 —46Va 80
First Av. W10 —42Bb 81
First Av. Bexh —52Yc 109
First Av. Dag —40Dd 68
First Av. Enf —15Vb 25
First Av. Eps —81Ua 162
First Av. Grav —10A 114
First Av. Grays —51Wd 112
First Av. Hay —46V 76
First Av. Romf —29Yc 47
First Av. Stanf —1M 93
First Av. W on T —72X 141
First Av. Wat —7Y 5
First Av. Wemb —33Ma 59
First Av. W Mol —70Ba 121
First Clo. W Mol —69Ea 122
First Cres. Slou —3G 72
First Cross Rd. Twic —61Ga 122
Firs, The. E6 —38Nc 66
Firs, The. N20 —18Fb 23
Firs, The. W5 —43Ma 79
Firs, The. Bex —60Fd 110
Firs, The. Cat —94Tb 181 (off Chatfield Ct.)
Firs, The. Grays —46Ee 91
Firs, The. Pil H —16Wd 32
Firs, The. Sidc —62Vc 131
First Slip. Lea —90Ja 160
First St. SW3 —49Gb 81 (5E 202)
Firstway. SW20 —68Ya 124
First Way. Wemb —35Ra 59
Firs Wlk. N'wd —23T 36
Firs Wlk. Wfd G —22Jc 45
Firswood Av. Eps —78Va 144
Firth Gdns. SW6 —53Ab 102
Firtree Av. Mitc —68Jb 126
Fir Tree Av. Stoke P —2K 73
Fir Tree Av. W Dray —48Q 76
Firtree Clo. SW16 —64Lb 126
Fir Tree Clo. W5 —44Na 79
Fir Tree Clo. Eps —87Ya 162
Fir Tree Clo. Esh —78Ea 142
Firtree Clo. Ewe —77Va 144
Fir Tree Clo. Grays —51Fe 113
Fir Tree Clo. Lea —95La 176
Fir Tree Clo. Orp —78Vc 151
Fir Tree Clo. Romf —27Fd 48
Firtree Ct. Borwd —14Pa 21
Firtree Gdns. Croy —77Cc 148
Fir Tree Gro. Cars —80Hb 145
Fir Tree Hill. Chan X —10P 3
Fir Tree Pl. Ashf —64Q 120
Fir Tree Rd. Bans —86Ya 162
Fir Tree Rd. Eps —88Xa 162
Fir Tree Rd. Houn —56Aa 99
Fir Tree Rd. Lea —95La 176
Fir Trees. Epp —1Xc 15
Fir Trees Clo. SE16 —46Ac 84
Fir Tree Wlk. Dag —34Ed 68
Fir Tree Wlk. Enf —13Tb 25
Fir Wlk. Sutt —79Za 144
Firwood Clo. Wok —7B 188
Fisher Clo. Croy —74Vb 147
Fisher Clo. Gnfd —41Ca 77
Fisher Clo. K Lan —1Q 4
Fisher Clo. W on T —77X 141
Fisher Ho. N1 —39Qb 62 (1K 193) (off Barnsbury Est.)
Fisherman Clo. Rich —63La 122
Fishermans Dri. SE16 —47Zb 84
Fisherman's Pl. W4 —51Va 102
Fisherman's Wlk. E14 —46Cc 84
Fishermens Hill. Grav —57De 113
Fisher Rd. Harr —26Ha 38
Fishers Clo. Wal X —6Cc 12
Fishers Ct. SE14 —53Zb 106
Fishers Dene. Clay —80Ja 142
Fisher's La. W4 —49Ta 79
Fishers Oak. Sev —93Ld 187
Fisher St. E16 —43Jc 85
Fisher St. WC1 —43Pb 82 (1H 199)
Fishers Way. Belv —46Ed 88
Fisherton St. NW8 —42Fb 81 (6B 190)
Fishguard Spur. Slou —7M 73
Fishmongers Hall Wharf. EC4 (off Swan La.) —45Tb 83 (5G 201)
Fishponds Rd. SW17 —63Gb 125
Fishponds Rd. Kes —78Mc 149
Fish St. Hill. EC3 —45Tb 83 (5G 201)
Fish Wharf. EC3 —45Tb 83 (5G 201) (off Lwr. Thames St.)
Fiske Ct. N17 —25Wb 43
Fiske Ct. Bark —40Tc 66
Fisons Rd. E16 —46Jc 85
Fitzalan Rd. N3 —27Ab 40
Fitzalan Rd. Clay —80Ga 142
Fitzalan St. SE11 —49Qb 82 (5J 205)
Fitzgeorge Av. W14 —49Ab 80
Fitzgeorge Av. N Mald —67Ta 123
Fitzgerald Av. SW14 —55Ua 102
Fitzgerald Ho. SW9 —54Qb 104
Fitzgerald Rd. E11 —29Jc 45
Fitzgerald Rd. SW14 —55Ta 101
Fitzgerald Rd. Th Dit —72Ja 142
Fitzhardinge St. W1 —44Jb 82 (2H 197)
Fitzhugh Gro. SW18 —58Fb 103
Fitzilian Av. Romf —25Pd 49
Fitzjames Av. W14 —49Ab 80
Fitzjames Av. Croy —75Wb 147
Fitzjohn Av. Barn —15Ab 22
Fitzjohn's Av. NW3 —35Eb 61
Fitzmaurice Pl. W1 —46Kb 82 (6A 198)
Fitzneal St. W12 —44Va 80
Fitzrobert Pl. Egh —65C 118
Fitzroy Clo. N6 —32Hb 61
Fitzroy Ct. N6 —30Lb 42
Fitzroy Ct. W1 —42Lb 82 (6C 192) (off Tottenham Ct. Rd.)
Fitzroy Cres. W4 —52Ta 101
Fitzroy Gdns. SE19 —66Ub 127
Fitzroy M. W1 —42Lb 82 (6B 192) (off Cleveland St.)
Fitzroy Pk. N6 —32Hb 61
Fitzroy Rd. NW1 —39Jb 62
Fitzroy Sq. W1 —42Lb 82 (6B 192)
Fitzroy St. W1 —42Lb 82 (6B 192) (in two parts)
Fitzstephen Rd. Dag —36Xc 67
Fitzwarren Gdns. N19 —32Lb 62
Fitzwilliam Av. Rich —54Pa 101
Fitzwilliam Heights. SE23 —61Yb 128
Fitzwilliam Ho. Rich —56Ma 101
Fitzwilliam Rd. SW4 —55Lb 104
Fitzwygram Clo. Hamp —64Ea 122
Five Acre. NW9 —26Va 40
Fiveacre Clo. T Hth —72Qb 146
Five Acres. K Lan —1P 3
Five Acres Av. Brick —1Ba 5
Fiveash Rd. Grav —9B 114
Five Elms Rd. Brom —75Kc 149
Five Elms Rd. Dag —34Bd 67
Five Oaks. Add —79H 139
Five Oaks Clo. Wok —7A 188
Five Oaks La. Chig —23Ad 47
Fiveways Rd. SW9 —54Qb 104
Five Wents. Swan —68Jd 132
Flack Ct. E10 —31Dc 64
Fladbury Rd. N15 —30Tb 43
Fladgate Rd. E11 —30Gc 45
Flag Clo. Croy —74Zb 148
Flagstaff Rd. Wal A —5Dc 12
Flag Wlk. Pinn —30W 36
Flambard Rd. Harr —30Ja 38
Flamborough Clo. Big H —91Kc 183
Flamborough Ho. SE15 —53Wb 105 (off Oliver Goldsmith Est.)
Flamborough Rd. Ruis —34W 56
Flamborough Spur. Slou —7E 72
Flamborough St. E14 —44Ac 84
Flamingo Gdns. N'holt —41Aa 77
Flamingo Wlk. Horn —37Jd 68
Flamstead End Relief Rd. Chesh —3Vb 11
Flamstead End Relief Rd. Wal X —4Wb 11
Flamstead End Rd. Chesh —1Xb 11
Flamstead Gdns. Dag —38Yc 67
Flamstead Rd. Dag —38Yc 67
Flamsted Av. Wemb —37Qa 59
Flamsteed Rd. SE7 —50Nc 86
Flanchford Rd. W12 —48Va 80
Flanders Ct. E17 —30Ac 44
Flanders Ct. Egh —64E 118
Flanders Cres. SW17 —66Hb 125
Flanders Mans. W4 —49Va 80
Flanders Rd. E6 —40Pc 66
Flanders Rd. W4 —49Ua 80
Flanders Way. E9 —37Zb 64
Flank St. E1 —45Wb 83
Flash La. Enf —9Rb 11
Flask Wlk. NW3 —35Eb 61
Flats, The. Chal G —15A 16
Flats, The. Grnh —57Yd 112
Flaunden Bottom. Lat —9A 2
Flaunden Hill. Flau —5B 2
Flaunden Ho. Wat —17U 18
Flaunden La. Bov —4D 2
Flaunden La. Sarr —5E 2
Flaunden Pk. Caravan Site. Bov —3C 2
Flaxen Clo. E4 —20Dc 26
Flaxen Rd. E4 —20Dc 26
Flaxley Rd. Mord —73Db 145
Flaxman Ct. W1 —44Mb 82 (3D 198) (off Flaxman Ct.)
Flaxman Ct. Belv —50Cd 88 (off Hoddesdon Rd.)
Flaxman Ho. W4 —50Ua 80 (off Devonshire St.)
Flaxman Rd. SE5 —55Rb 105
Flaxman Ter. WC1 —41Mb 82 (4E 192)
Flaxmore Pl. Beck —72Fc 149
Flaxton Rd. SE18 —52Uc 108
Flecker Clo. Stan —22Ha 38
Fleece Rd. Surb —74La 142
Fleece Wlk. N7 —37Nb 62
Fleeming Clo. E17 —26Bc 44
Fleeming Rd. E17 —26Bc 44
Fleet Av. Dart —60Sd 112
Fleet Av. Upm —30Td 50
Fleet Bldgs. EC4 —44Rb 83 (2B 200) (off Shoe Pl.)
Fleet Clo. Ruis —30S 36
Fleet Clo. Upm —30Td 50
Fleet Clo. W Mol —71Ba 141
Fleetdale Pde. Dart —60Sd 112
Fleethall Gro. Grays —46Ce 91
Fleet Houses. S'fleet —65De 135
Fleet La. W Mol —72Ba 141
Fleet Pl. EC4 —44Rb 83 (2B 200) (off Old Fleet La.)
Fleet Rd. NW3 —36Gb 61
Fleet Rd. Dart —60Sd 112
Fleet Rd. Grav —62Ee 135
Fleetside. W Mol —71Ba 141
Fleet Sq. WC1 —41Pb 82 (4J 193)
Fleet St. EC4 —44Qb 82 (3K 199)
Fleet St. Hill. E1 —42Wb 83
Fleetway. Egh —69E 118
Fleetway Bus. Cen. NW2 —32Va 60
Fleetway Bus. Pk. Gnfd —40Ka 58
Fleetwood Clo. E16 —43Mc 85
Fleetwood Clo. Chess —80Ma 143
Fleetwood Clo. Croy —76Vb 147
Fleetwood Clo. Tad —92Za 178
Fleetwood Ct. E6 —43Pc 86 (off Evelyn Dennington Rd.)
Fleetwood Ct. Stanw —58N 97
Fleetwood Ct. W Byf —85J 157
Fleetwood Rd. NW10 —36Wa 60
Fleetwood Rd. King T —69Ra 123
Fleetwood Rd. Slou —6K 73
Fleetwood Sq. King T —69Ra 123
Fleetwood St. N16 —33Ub 63
Fleetwood Way. Wat —21Y 37
Fleming Ct. W2 —43Fb 81 (7B 190) (off St Marys Sq.)
Fleming Ct. Croy —78Qb 146
Fleming Gdns. H Wood —26Md 49
Fleming Gdns. Til —3E 114
Fleming Ho. N4 —32Sb 63
Fleming Ho. SE16 —47Wb 83 (off George Row)
Fleming Ho. Wemb —34Sa 59 (off Barnhill Rd.)
Fleming Mead. Mitc —66Hb 125
Fleming Rd. SE17 —51Rb 105
Fleming Rd. S'hall —44Da 77
Flemings. Gt War —23Yd 50
Fleming Way. SE28 —45Zc 87
Fleming Way. Iswth —56Ha 100
Flemish Fields. Cher —73J 139 (in two parts)
Flemming Av. Ruis —32X 57
Flempton Rd. E10 —32Ac 64
Fletcher Clo. Ott —79G 138
Fletcher La. E10 —31Ec 64
Fletcher Path. SE8 —52Cc 106
Fletcher Rd. W4 —48Sa 79
Fletcher Rd. Chig —22Vc 47
Fletcher Rd. Ott —79F 138
Fletchers Clo. Brom —70Kc 129
Fletcher St. E1 —45Wb 83
Fletching Rd. E5 —34Yb 64
Fletching Rd. SE7 —51Mc 107
Flete Ho. Wat —16U 18
Fletton Rd. N11 —24Nb 42
Fleur-de-Lis Ct. EC4 (off Fetter La.) —44Qb 82 (3A 200)
Fleur-de-Lis St. E1 —42Vb 83 (6J 195)
Fleur Gates. SW19 —59Za 102
Flexmere Rd. N17 —25Tb 43
Flight App. NW9 —26Va 40
Flimwell Clo. Brom —64Gc 129
Flint Clo. Bookh —98Ea 176
Flintlock Clo. Stai —56J 97
Flintmill Cres. SE3 —54Nc 108
Flinton St. SE17 —50Ub 83 (7J 207)
Flint St. SE17 —49Tb 83 (6G 207)
Flint St. Grays —51Xd 112
Flitcroft St. WC2 —44Mb 82 (3E 198)
Flockton St. SE16 —47Wb 83
Flodden Rd. SE5 —53Sb 105
Flood La. Twic —60Ja 100
Flood Pas. SE18 —47Pc 86
Flood St. SW3 —50Gb 81 (7E 202)
Flood Wlk. SW3 —51Gb 103
Flora Clo. E14 —44Dc 84
Flora Gdns. W6 —49Xa 80 (off Albion Gdns.)
Flora Gdns. New Ad —83Ec 166
Flora Gdns. Romf —30Yc 47
Floral Ct. Asht —90La 160
Floral Ho. Cher —74H 139 (off Fox La. S.)
Floral Pl. N1 —36Tb 63
Floral St. WC2 —45Nb 82 (4F 199)
Flora St. Belv —50Bd 87
Florence Av. Enf —13Sb 25
Florence Av. Mord —71Eb 145
Florence Av. New Haw —83J 157
Florence Clo. Grays —51Ae 113
Florence Clo. Horn —33Nd 69
Florence Clo. W on T —73X 141
Florence Clo. Wat —7W 4
Florence Ct. E5 —34Wb 63
Florence Ct. E11 —28Lc 45
Florence Ct. N1 —38Rb 63
Florence Ct. W9 —41Eb 81 (4A 190) (off Maida Vale)
Florence Dri. Enf —13Sb 25
Florence Farm Mobile Home Pk. W King —79Td 154
Florence Gdns. W4 —51Sa 101
Florence Gdns. Stai —66K 119
Florence Mans. NW4 —29Xa 40 (off Vivian Av.)
Florence Rd. E6 —39Lc 65
Florence Rd. E13 —40Hc 65
Florence Rd. N4 —31Pb 62 (in two parts)
Florence Rd. SE2 —49Zc 87
Florence Rd. SE14 —53Bc 106
Florence Rd. SW19 —65Db 125
Florence Rd. W4 —48Ta 79
Florence Rd. W5 —45Na 79
Florence Rd. Beck —68Ac 128
Florence Rd. Brom —67Jc 129
Florence Rd. Felt —60X 99
Florence Rd. King T —66Pa 123
Florence Rd. S'hall —49Z 77
Florence Rd. S Croy —81Tb 165
Florence Rd. W on T —73X 141
Florence St. E16 —42Hc 85
Florence St. N1 —38Rb 63
Florence St. NW4 —28Ya 40
Florence Ter. SE14 —53Bc 106
Florence Ter. SW15 —62Ua 124
Florfield Pas. E8 —37Xb 63 (off Florfield Rd.)
Florfield Rd. E8 —37Xb 63
Florian. SE5 —53Ub 105
Florian Av. Sutt —77Fb 145
Florian Rd. SW15 —56Ab 102
Florida Clo. Bush —19Fa 20
Florida Ct. Stai —63J 119
Florida Rd. T Hth —67Rb 127
Florida St. E2 —41Wb 83
Florin Ct. N18 —22Ub 43
Floriston Av. Uxb —38S 56
Floriston Clo. Stan —25Ka 38
Floriston Gdns. Stan —25Ka 38
Floss St. SW15 —54Ya 102
Flower Cres. Ott —79D 138
Flower & Dean Wlk. E1 —43Vb 83
Flowerfield. Otf —89Hd 170
Flowerhill Way. Grav —6A 136
Flower La. NW7 —22Va 40
Flower La. Gods —100Ac 182
Flowersmead. SW17 —61Jb 126
Flowers M. N19 —33Lb 62 (off Sandridge St.)
Flower Wlk., The. SW7 —47Eb 81 (2A 202)
Floyd Rd. SE7 —50Lc 85
Floyd's La. Wok —88J 157
Fludyer St. SE13 —56Gc 107
Flux's La. Epp —5Wc 15
Flyers Way, The. W'ham —98Tc 184
Folair Way. SE16 —50Xb 83
Foley M. Clay —79Ga 142
Foley Rd. Big H —90Mc 167
Foley Rd. Clay —80Ga 142
Foley St. W1 —43Lb 82 (1B 198)
Folgate St. E1 —43Ub 83 (7J 195)
Foliot St. W12 —44Va 80
Folkes La. Upm —29Vd 50
Folkestone Ct. Slou —50C 74
Folkestone Rd. E6 —40Qc 66
Folkestone Rd. E17 —28Dc 44
Folkestone Rd. N18 —21Wb 43
Folkington Corner. N12 —22Bb 41
Folland. NW9 —26Va 40 (off Hundred Acre)
Follet Dri. Abb L —3V 4
Follett Clo. Old Win —8M 95
Follett St. E14 —44Ec 84
Follingham Ct. N1 —41Ub 83 (3J 195) (off Drysdale Pl.)
Folly Clo. Rad —8Ha 6
Follyfield Rd. Bans —86Cb 163
Folly La. E4 —21Bc 44
Folly La. E17 —24Bc 44
Folly M. W11 —44Bb 81
Folly Pathway. Rad —7Ha 6
Folly Wall. E14 —47Ec 84
Fontaine Rd. SW16 —66Pb 126
Fontarabia Rd. SW11 —56Jb 104
Fontayne Av. Chig —21Sc 46
Fontayne Av. Rain —38Gd 68
Fontayne Av. Romf —26Gd 48
Fontenelle. SE5 —53Ub 105
Fontenoy Pas. SE11 —49Rb 83 (6B 206) (off Cottington Clo.)
Fontenoy Rd. SW12 —61Kb 126
Fonteyne Gdns. Wfd G —26Mc 45
Fonthill Clo. SE20 —68Wb 127
Fonthill M. N4 —33Qb 62
Fonthill Rd. N4 —32Pb 62
Font Hills. N2 —26Eb 41
Fontley Way. SW15 —59Wa 102
Fontmell Clo. Ashf —64Q 120
Fontmell Pk. Ashf —64P 119
Fontwell Clo. Harr —24Ga 38
Fontwell Dri. Brom —71Qc 150
Fontwell Pk. Gdns. Horn —35Nd 69
Football La. Harr —32Ha 58
Footbury Hill Rd. Orp —72Wc 151
Footpath, The. SW15 —57Wa 102
Foots Cray High St. Sidc —65Yc 131
Foots Cray La. Sidc —60Yc 109
Footscray Rd. SE9 —58Qc 108
Forbes Av. Pot B —5Fb 9
Forbes Clo. NW2 —33Wa 60
Forbes Clo. Horn —32Kd 69
Forbes St. E1 —44Wb 83
Forbes Way. Ruis —32X 57
Forburg Rd. N16 —32Wb 63
Force Grn. La. W'ham —96Tc 184
Fordbridge Clo. Cher —74K 139
Fordbridge Rd. Ashf —65N 119
Fordbridge Rd. Sun —72U 140
Ford Clo. Ashf —65N 119
Ford Clo. Bush —14Ea 20
Ford Clo. Harr —31Fa 58
Ford Clo. Rain —38Hd 68
Ford Clo. Shep —70Q 120
Ford Clo. T Hth —71Rb 147
Fordcroft Rd. Orp —71Xc 151
Forde Av. Brom —69Lc 129
Fordel Rd. SE6 —60Fc 107
Ford End. Den —33H 55
Ford End. Wfd G —23Kc 45
Fordham Clo. Barn —13Gb 23
Fordham Clo. Horn —31Qd 69
Fordham Rd. Barn —13Fb 23
Fordhams Row. Ors —3D 92
Fordham St. E1 —44Wb 83
Fordhook Av. W5 —46Pa 79

Ford Ho.—Friars Orchard

Ford Ho. Barn —15Db 23
Fordingley Rd. W9 —41Bb 81
Fordington Ho. SE26 —62Wb 127
Fordington Rd. N6 —29Hb 41
Ford La. Iver —44J 75
Ford La. Rain —38Hd 68
Fordmill Rd. SE6 —61Cc 128
Ford Rd. E3 —40Bc 64
Ford Rd. Ashf —63P 119
Ford Rd. Cher —74K 139
Ford Rd. Dag —38Bd 67
Ford Rd. Grav —57De 113
Ford Rd. Wok —92D 172
Fords Gro. N21 —18Sb 25
Fords Pk. Rd. E16 —44Jc 85
Ford Sq. E1 —43Xb 83
Ford St. E3 —39Ac 64
Ford St. E16 —44Hc 85
Fordwater Rd. Cher —74K 139
Fordwater Trading Est. Cher —74L 139
Fordwich Clo. Orp —73Vc 151
Fordwych Rd. NW2 —35Ab 60
Fordyce Clo. Horn —31Pd 69
Fordyce Rd. SE13 —58Ec 106
Fordyke Rd. Dag —33Bd 67
Foreign St. SE5 —54Rb 105
Foreland Ct. NW4 —25Za 40
Foreland St. SE18 —49Tc 86
Foreman Ct. W6 —49Ya 80
Foreman Ct. Twic —60Ha 100
Foremark Clo. Ilf —23Vc 47
Foreshore. SE8 —49Bc 84
Forest App. E4 —17Gc 27
Forest App. Wfd G —24Hc 45
Forest Av. E4 —17Gc 27
Forest Av. Chig —22Qc 46
Forest Bus. Pk. E17 —31Ac 64
Forest Clo. E11 —29Jc 45
Forest Clo. Chst —67Qc 130
Forest Clo. E Hor —97V 174
Forest Clo. Wal A —9Kc 13
Forest Clo. Wok —87F 156
Forest Clo. Wfd G —20Kc 27
Forest Ct. E4 —18Hc 27
Forest Ct. E11 —28Gc 45
Forest Ct. N12 —21Db 41
Forest Cres. Asht —88Qa 161
Forest Croft. SE23 —61Xb 127
Forestdale. N14 —21Mb 42
Forestdale Cen., The. Croy —80Bc 148
Forest Dene Ct. Sutt —79Eb 145
Forest Dri. E12 —34Mc 65
Forest Dri. Kes —77Nc 150
Forest Dri. Sun —66V 120
Forest Dri. Tad —93Cb 179
Forest Dri. They B —9Uc 14
Forest Dri. Wfd G —24Fc 45
Forest Dri. E. E11 —31Fc 65
Forest Dri. W. E11 —31Ec 64
Forest Edge. Buck H —21Lc 45
Forester Rd. SE15 —55Xb 105
Foresters Clo. Wall —80Mb 146
Foresters Clo. Wok —6C 188
Foresters Cres. Bexh —56Dd 110
Foresters Dri. E17 —28Fc 45
Foresters Dri. Wall —80Mb 146
Forest Gdns. N17 —26Vb 43
Forest Ga. NW9 —28Ua 40
Forest Glade. E4 —21Gc 45
Forest Glade. E11 —30Gc 45
Forest Gro. E8 —37Vb 63
Forest Hill Ind. Est. SE23 —61Yb 128
Forest Hill Rd. SE22 & SE23 —57Xb 105
Forestholme Clo. SE23 —61Yb 128
Forest Ind. Pk. Ilf —25Uc 46
Forest La. E15 & E7 —37Gc 65
Forest La. Chig —22Qc 46
Forest La. E Hor —96V 174
Forest Mt. Rd. E4 —24Fc 45
Forest Point. E7 —36Kc 65
(off Windsor Rd.)
Fore St. EC2 —43Sb 83 (1E 200)
Fore St. N18 & N9 —23Vb 43
Fore St. Pinn —27V 36
Fore St. Av. EC2 —43Tb 83 (1F 201)
Forest Ridge. Beck —69Cc 128
Forest Ridge. Kes —77Nc 150
Forest Rise. E17 —29Fc 45
Forest Rd. E7 —35Jc 65
Forest Rd. E8 —37Vb 63
Forest Rd. E11 —31Fc 65
Forest Rd. N9 —18Xb 25
Forest Rd. N17 & E17 —28Yb 44
Forest Rd. Chesh —1Zb 12
Forest Rd. E Hor —98V 174
Forest Rd. Eff J —96V 174
Forest Rd. Enf —8Ac 12
Forest Rd. Eri —53Jd 110
Forest Rd. Felt —61Y 121
Forest Rd. Ilf —26Tc 46
Forest Rd. Lou —13Mc 27
Forest Rd. Rich —52Qa 101
Forest Rd. Romf —27Dd 48
Forest Rd. Sutt —74Cb 145
Forest Rd. Wat —5X 5
Forest Rd. Wind —10B 94
(Cranbourne)
Forest Rd. Wind —4B 94
(Windsor)
Forest Rd. Wok —87F 156
Forest Rd. Wfd G —20Jc 27
Forest Side. E4 —17Hc 27
Forest Side. E7 —35Kc 65
Forest Side. Buck H —18Lc 27
Forest Side. Epp —5Tc 14
Forest Side. Wal A —8Lc 13
Forest Side. Wor Pk —74Va 144
Forest St. E7 —36Jc 65
Forest, The. E11 —28Gc 45
Forest Trading Est. E17 —27Zb 44
Forest View. E4 —17Fc 27
Forest View. E11 —31Hc 65
Forest View Av. E10 —29Fc 45
Forest View Rd. E12 —35Nc 66
Forest View Rd. E17 —25Ec 44
Forest View Rd. Lou —14Mc 27
Forest Wlk. Bush —11Ba 19
Forest Way. E11 —31Hc 65
Forest Way. N19 —33Lb 62
Forest Way. Asht —89Qa 161
Forest Way. Lou —13Nc 28
Forest Way. Orp —71Vc 151
Forest Way. Sidc —59Tc 108
Forest Way. Wfd G —21Kc 45
Forfar Rd. N22 —25Rb 43
Forfar Rd. SW11 —53Jb 104
Forge Av. Coul —92Qb 180
Forge Clo. Brom —74Jc 149
Forge Clo. Chfd —3J 3
Forge Clo. Hay —51T 98
Forge Dri. Clay —80Ja 142
Forge Dri. Farn C —7G 52
Forge End. Wok —89A 156
Forge Field. Big H —88Mc 167
Forge La. Felt —64Aa 121
Forge La. Grav —1H 137
Forge La. Hort K —70Sd 134
Forge La. N'wd —24U 36
Forge La. Shorne —4N 137
Forge La. Sun —69W 120
Forge La. Sutt —80Ab 144
Forge Pl. NW1 —37Jb 62
Forge Steading. Bans —87Db 163
Forge Way. Shor —83Hd 170
Forlong Path. N'holt —37Aa 57
(off Arnold Rd.)
Forman Pl. N16 —35Vb 63
Formby Av. Stan —27La 38
Formby Ct. N7 —36Qb 62
(off Morgan Rd.)
Formosa St. W9 —42Db 81
Formunt Clo. E16 —43Hc 85
Forres Gdns. NW11 —30Cb 41
Forres Ho. War —22Yd 50
Forrester Path. SE26 —63Yb 128
Forrest Gdns. SW16 —69Pb 126
Forris Av. Hay —46V 76
Forset St. W1 —44Gb 81 (2E 196)
Forstal Clo. Brom —69Jc 129
Forster Ho. Brom —62Fc 129
Forster Rd. E17 —30Ac 44
Forster Rd. N17 —27Vb 43
Forster Rd. SW2 —59Nb 104
Forster Rd. Beck —69Ac 128
Forsters Clo. Romf —30Bd 47
Forsters Way. Hay —44X 77
Forston St. N1 —40Sb 63 (1E 194)
Forsyte Cres. SE19 —67Ub 127
Forsythe Shades Ct. Beck —67Ec 128
Forsyth Gdns. SE17 —51Rb 105
Forsythia Clo. Ilf —36Rc 66
Forsythia Gdns. Slou —48A 74
Forsyth Path. Wok —85F 156
Forsyth Pl. Enf —15Ub 25
Forsyth Rd. Wok —86E 156
Forterie Gdns. Ilf —34Wc 67
Fortescue Av. E8 —38Xb 63
Fortescue Av. Twic —62Ea 122
Fortescue Rd. SW19 —66Fb 125
Fortescue Rd. Edgw —25Ta 39
Fortescue Rd. Wey —77P 139
Fortess Gro. NW5 —36Lb 62
Fortess Rd. NW5 —36Kb 62
Fortess Wlk. NW5 —36Kb 62
Forthbridge Rd. SW11 —56Jb 104
Forth Dri. Coul —88Mb 164
Forth Rd. Upm —30Td 50
Fortin Clo. S Ock —45Wd 90
Fortin Path. S Ock —45Wd 90
Fortin Way. S Ock —45Wd 90
Fortis Clo. E16 —44Lc 85
Fortis Ct. N10 —27Jb 42
Fortis Grn. N2 & N10 —28Gb 41
Fortis Grn. Av. N2 —27Hb 41
Fortis Grn. Rd. N10 —27Jb 42
Fortismere Av. N10 —27Jb 42
Fortnam Rd. N19 —33Mb 62
Fortnum's Acre. Stan —23Ha 38
Fort Rd. SE1 —49Vb 83 (6K 207)
Fort Rd. Hals —82Ed 170
Fort Rd. N'holt —38Ca 57
Fort Rd. Til —6D 114
Fort Rd. W Til —3E 114
Fortrose Gdns. SW2 —60Nb 104
Fortrye Clo. Grav —1A 136
Fort St. E1 —43Ub 83 (1J 201)
Fort St. E16 —46Kc 85
Fortuna Clo. N7 —37Pb 62
Fortuna Clo. Hart —70Be 135
Fortunegate Rd. NW10 —39Ua 60
Fortune Grn. Rd. NW6 —35Cb 61
Fortune Ho. SE11 —49Qb 82 (6K 205)
(off Marylee Way)
Fortune La. Els —16Ma 21
Fortunes Mead. N'holt —37Aa 57
Fortune St. EC1 —42Sb 83 (6E 194)
Fortune Wlk. SE28 —48Tc 86
(off Broadwater Rd.)
Fortune Way. NW10 —41Wa 80
Forty Acre La. E16 —43Jc 85
Forty Av. Wemb —34Pa 59
Forty Clo. Wemb —34Pa 59
Forty Footpath. SW14 —55Sa 101
Forty Foot Rd. Lea —93La 176
(in two parts)
Forty Hill. Enf —10Ub 11
Forty La. Wemb —33Ra 59
Forumside. Edgw —23Qa 39
Forum, The. W Mol —70Da 121
Forum Way. Edgw —23Qa 39
Forval Clo. Mitc —71Hb 145
Forward Bus. Cen. E16 —42Fc 85
Forward Dri. Harr —28Ha 38
Fosbury M. W2 —45Db 81
Foscote M. W9 —42Cb 81
Foscote Rd. NW4 —30Xa 40
Foskett Rd. SW6 —54Bb 103
Foss Av. Croy —78Qb 146
Fossdene Rd. SE7 —50Kc 85
Fossdyke Clo. Hay —43Aa 77
Fosset Lodge. Bexh —53Ed 110
Fosse Way. W13 —43Ja 78
Fosse Way. W Byf —85H 157
Fossil Rd. SE13 —55Cc 106
Fossington Rd. Belv —49Zc 87
Foss Rd. SW17 —63Fb 125
Fossway. Dag —33Zc 67
Foster Av. Wind —5C 94
Foster Ct. NW4 —28Ya 40
Foster La. EC2 —44Sb 83 (2D 200)
Foster Rd. E13 —42Jc 85
Foster Rd. W3 —45Ua 80
Foster Rd. W4 —50Ta 79
Fosters Clo. E18 —25Kc 45
Fosters Clo. Chst —64Pc 130
Fosters La. Knap —5A 188
Fosters Path. Slou —2D 72
Foster St. NW4 —28Ya 40
Foster Wlk. NW4 —28Ya 40
Fothergill Clo. E13 —40Jc 65
Fotheringay Gdns. Slou —5E 72
Fotheringham Rd. Enf —14Vb 25
Fotherley Rd. Rick —19H 17
Foubert's Pl. W1 —44Lb 82 (3B 198)
Foulden Rd. N16 —35Vb 63
Foulden Ter. N16 —35Vb 63
Foulis Ter. SW7 —50Fb 81 (7C 202)
Foulser Rd. SW17 —62Hb 125
Foulsham Rd. T Hth —69Tb 127
Founders Ct. EC2 —44Tb 83 (2F 201)
(off Lothbury)
Founders Dri. Den —30H 35
Founders Gdns. SE19 —66Sb 127
Foundry Clo. SE16 —46Ac 84
Foundry La. Hort —55D 96
Foundry M. NW1 —42Lb 82 (5C 192)
(off Drummond St.)
Fountain Clo. Uxb —42S 76
Fountain Ct. EC4 —45Qb 82 (4K 199)
Fountain Ct. SE23 —61Zb 128
Fountain Ct. Eyns —75Nd 153
Fountain Ct. Sidc —58Xc 109
Fountain Dri. SE19 —63Vb 127
Fountain Gdns. Wind —5H 95
Fountain M. N5 —35Sb 63
(off Highbury Grange)
Fountain Pl. SW9 —53Qb 104
Fountain Pl. Wal A —5Ec 12
Fountain Rd. SW17 —64Fb 125
Fountain Rd. T Hth —68Sb 127
Fountains Av. Felt —62Ba 121
Fountains Clo. Felt —61Ba 121
Fountains Cres. N14 —17Nb 24
Fountain Sq. SW1 —49Kb 82 (5A 204)
Fountains, The. N3 —24Db 41
(off Ballards La.)
Fountain Wlk. Grav —8A 114
Fountayne Bus. Cen. N15 —28Wb 43
Fountayne Rd. N15 —28Wb 43
Fountayne Rd. N16 —33Wb 63
Fount St. SW8 —52Mb 104
Four Acres. Cob —85Aa 159
Fouracres. Enf —11Ac 26
Fourfield Clo. Eps —94Sa 177
Fourland Wlk. Edgw —23Sa 39
Fournier St. E1 —43Vb 83 (7K 195)
Four Seasons Cres. Sutt —75Bb 145
Four Sq. Ct. Houn —58Ca 99
Fourth Av. E12 —35Pc 66
Fourth Av. W10 —41Ab 80
Fourth Av. Grays —51Wd 112
Fourth Av. Hay —46V 76
Fourth Av. Romf —32Fd 68
Fourth Av. Wat —7Z 5
Fourth Cross Rd. Twic —61Fa 122
Fourth Dri. Coul —88Mb 164
Fourth Way. Wemb —35Sa 59
Four Tubs, The. Bush —17Fa 20
Four Wents. Cob —86Y 159
Four Wents, The. E4 —18Fc 27
Fowey Av. Ilf —29Mc 45
Fowey Clo. E1 —42Xb 83
Fowey Ho. SE11 —50Qb 82 (7A 206)
(off Kennings Way)
Fowler Clo. SW11 —55Fb 103
Fowler Rd. E7 —35Jc 65
Fowler Rd. N1 —39Rb 63
Fowler Rd. Ilf —23Xc 47
Fowler Rd. Mitc —68Jb 126
Fowlers Clo. Sidc —64Ad 131
Fowler's Wlk. W5 —42Ma 79
Fownes St. SW11 —55Gb 103
Foxacre. Cat —94Ub 181
Fox All. Wat —15U 18
Foxberry Rd. SE4 —55Ac 106
Foxborough Clo. Slou —50C 74
Foxborough Gdns. SE4 —57Cc 106
Foxbourne Rd. SW17 —61Jb 126
Fox Burrow Rd. Chig —21Zc 47
Foxbury. New Ash —76Ae 155
Foxbury Av. Chst —65Tc 130
Foxbury Clo. Brom —65Kc 129
Foxbury Clo. Orp —78Wc 151
Foxbury Dri. Orp —79Wc 151
Foxbury Rd. Brom —65Jc 129
Fox Clo. E1 —42Yb 84
Fox Clo. E16 —43Jc 85
Fox Clo. Bush —15Da 19
Fox Clo. Els —16Ma 21
Fox Clo. Orp —78Wc 151
Fox Clo. Romf —22Dd 48
Fox Clo. Wey —78T 140
Fox Clo. Wok —87F 156
Foxcombe. New Ad —79Dc 148
(in two parts)
Foxcombe Clo. E6 —40Mc 65
Foxcombe Rd. SW15 —60Wa 102
Foxcote. SE5 —50Ub 83
Foxcote. SE17 —50Ub 83
(off Albany Rd.)
Fox Covert. Fet —96Fa 176
Foxcroft Rd. SE18 —53Rc 108
Foxdell. N'wd —23T 36
Foxdell Way. Ger X —22A 34
Foxearth Clo. Big H —90Nc 168
Foxearth Rd. S Croy —82Xb 165
Foxearth Spur. S Croy —81Yb 166
Foxes Dale. SE3 —55Jc 107
Foxes Dale. Brom —69Fc 129
Foxes Dri. Wal X —1Wb 11
Foxes Grn. Grays —7C 92
Foxes Path. Sut G —98B 172
Foxfield Clo. N'wd —23V 36
Foxfield Rd. Orp —75Tc 150
Foxglove Clo. Stai —60M 97
Foxglove Ct. Wemb —40Na 59
Foxglove Cres. Ilf —37Rc 66
Foxglove Gdns. E11 —28Lc 45
Foxglove Gdns. Purl —83Nb 164
Foxglove La. Chess —77Qa 143
Foxglove Rd. S Ock —44Yd 90
Foxglove St. W12 —45Va 80
Foxglove Way. Wall —74Kb 146
Foxgrove. N14 —20Nb 24
Foxgrove Av. Beck —66Dc 128
Foxgrove Dri. Wok —87C 156
Foxgrove Path. Wat —22Z 37
Foxgrove Rd. Beck —66Dc 128
Foxhall Rd. Upm —36Td 70
Foxham Rd. N19 —34Mb 62
Foxhanger Gdns. Wok —88C 156
Foxherne. Slou —7N 73
Fox Hill. SE19 —66Vb 127
Fox Hill. Kes —78Lc 149
Foxhill. Wat —8W 4
Fox Hill Gdns. SE19 —66Vb 127
Fox Hills. Wok —5F 188
Foxhills Clo. Ott —79D 138
Fox Hills Rd. Grays —46Fe 91
Foxhills Rd. Ott —77C 138
Foxhole Rd. SE9 —57Nc 108
Foxholes. Wey —78T 140
Fox Hollow Dri. Bexh —55Zc 109
Foxholt Gdns. NW10 —38Sa 59
Foxhome Clo. Chst —65Qc 130
Foxhounds La. S'fleet —62Be 135
Fox Ho. Rd. Belv —49Dd 88
(in two parts)
Fox & Knot St. EC1 —43Rb 83 (7C 194)
(off Charterhouse Sq.)
Foxlake Rd. Byfl —84P 157
Foxlands Clo. Leav —6W 4
Foxlands Cres. Dag —36Ed 68
Foxlands La. Dag —36Ed 68
Foxlands Rd. Dag —36Ed 68
Fox La. N13 —19Pb 24
Fox La. W5 —42Na 79
Fox La. Bookh —96Aa 175
Fox La. Cat —93Rb 181
Fox La. Kes —78Kc 149
Fox La. N. Cher —74H 139
Fox La. S. Cher —74H 139
Foxleas Ct. Brom —66Gc 129
Foxlees. Wemb —35Ja 58
Foxley Clo. E8 —36Wb 63
Foxley Clo. Lou —12Rc 28
Foxley Ct. Sutt —80Eb 145
Foxley Gdns. Purl —85Rb 165
Foxley Hall. Purl —85Qb 164
Foxley Hill Rd. Purl —84Qb 164
Foxley La. Purl —83Lb 164
Foxley Rd. SW9 —52Qb 104
Foxley Rd. Kenl —86Rb 165
Foxley Rd. T Hth —70Rb 127
Foxleys. Wat —20Aa 19
Foxley Sq. SW9 —53Rb 105
Fox Mnr. Way. Grays —51Xd 112
Foxmead Clo. Enf —13Pb 24
Foxmore St. SW11 —53Hb 103
Foxon Clo. Cat —93Ub 181
Foxon La. Cat —93Tb 181
Foxon La. Gdns. Cat —93Ub 181
Fox Rd. E16 —43Hc 85
Fox Rd. Slou —9P 73
Fox's Path. Mitc —68Gb 125
Foxton Ho. E16 —47Qc 86
(off Albert Rd.)
Foxton Rd. Grays —51Zd 113
Foxtree Ho. Wat —8Aa 5
Foxwarren. Clay —81Ha 160
Foxwell St. SE4 —55Ac 106
Foxwood Clo. Felt —62X 121
Foxwood Rd. SE3 —56Hc 107
Foxwood Rd. Bean —62Xd 134
Foxwood Way. Long —68Fe 135
Foyle Dri. S Ock —43Wd 90
Foyle Rd. N17 —25Wb 43
Foyle Rd. SE3 —51Hc 107
Frailey Clo. Wok —88D 156
Frailey Hill. Wok —88D 156
Framborough Clo. Harr —31Fa 58
Framewood Rd. Wex & Ful —8N 53
Framfield Clo. N12 —20Cb 23
Framfield Ct. Enf —16Ub 25
(off Queen Annes Gdns.)
Framfield Rd. N5 —36Rb 63
Framfield Rd. W7 —44Ga 78
Framfield Rd. Mitc —66Jb 126
Framlingham Clo. E5 —33Yb 64
Framlingham Cres. SE9 —63Nc 130
Frampton Clo. Sutt —80Cb 145
Frampton Pk. Est. E9 —38Yb 64
Frampton Pk. Rd. E9 —37Yb 64
Frampton Rd. Epp —1Wc 15
Frampton Rd. Pot B —2Eb 9
Frampton St. NW8 —42Fb 81 (6B 190)
Francemary Rd. SE4 —57Cc 106
Frances Ct. E17 —30Cc 44
Frances Gdns. S Ock —44Vd 90
Frances Rd. E4 —23Cc 44
Frances Rd. Wind —5G 94
Frances St. SE18 —49Pc 86
Franche Ct. Rd. SW17 —62Eb 125
Francis Av. Bexh —54Cd 110
Francis Av. Felt —62W 120
Francis Av. Ilf —33Tc 66
Francis Barber Clo. SW16 —64Pb 126
Franciscan Rd. SW17 —64Hb 125
Francis Chichester Clo. Asc —10A 116
Francis Chichester Way. SW11 —53Jb 104
Francis Clo. E14 —49Fc 85
Francis Clo. Eps —77Ta 143
Francis Clo. Horn H —1H 93
Francis Clo. Shep —70Q 120
Francis Ct. EC1 —43Rb 83 (7B 194)
(off Briset St.)
Francis Gro. SW19 —65Bb 125
Francis Ho. E10 —32Bc 64
Francis Rd. E10 —32Ec 64
Francis Rd. N2 —28Hb 41
Francis Rd. Cat —94Tb 181
Francis Rd. Croy —73Rb 147
Francis Rd. Dart —57Md 111
Francis Rd. Gnfd —40Ka 58
Francis Rd. Harr —29Ja 38
Francis Rd. Houn —54Z 99
Francis Rd. Ilf —33Tc 66
Francis Rd. Orp —69Zc 131
Francis Rd. Pinn —29Y 37
Francis Rd. Wall —79Lb 146
Francis Rd. Wat —14X 19
Francis St. E15 —36Gc 65
Francis St. SW1 —49Lb 82 (5B 204)
Francis St. Ilf —33Tc 66
Francis Ter. N19 —34Lb 62
Francis Wlk. N1 —39Pb 62
Francis Way. Slou —5B 72
Francklyn Gdns. Edgw —20Qa 21
Francombe Gdns. Romf —29Jd 48
Franconia Rd. SW4 —57Mb 104
Frank Bailey Wlk. E12 —37Qc 66
Frank Burton Clo. SE7 —50Kc 85
Frank Dixon Clo. SE21 —59Ub 105
Frank Dixon Way. SE21 —60Ub 105
Frankel Mt. SE9 —57Mc 107
Frank Foster Ho. They B —9Uc 14
Frankfurt Rd. SE24 —57Sb 105
Frankham St. SE8 —52Cc 106
Frankland Clo. SE16 —49Xb 83
Frankland Clo. Crox —17Q 18
Frankland Clo. Wfd G —22Lc 45
Frankland Rd. E4 —22Cc 44
Frankland Rd. SW7 —48Fb 81 (4B 202)
Frankland Rd. Crox —16R 18
Franklands Dri. Add —80H 139
Franklin Av. Chesh —2Wb 11
Franklin Av. Slou —3F 72
Franklin Clo. N20 —17Eb 23
Franklin Clo. SE13 —53Dc 106
Franklin Clo. SE27 —62Rb 127
Franklin Clo. King T —69Qa 123
Franklin Cotts. Stan —21Ka 38
Franklin Cres. Mitc —70Lb 126
Franklin Pas. SE9 —55Nc 108
Franklin Rd. SE20 —66Yb 128
Franklin Rd. Bexh —53Ad 109
Franklin Rd. Grav —4F 136
Franklin Rd. Horn —37Ld 69
Franklin Rd. Wat —12X 19
Franklins M. Harr —33Ea 58
Franklin Sq. W14 —50Bb 81
Franklin's Row. SW3 —50Hb 81 (7G 203)
Franklin St. E3 —41Dc 84
Franklin St. N15 —30Ub 43
Franklin Way. Croy —73Nb 146
Franklyn Cres. Wind —5B 94
Franklyn Gdns. Ilf —23Tc 46
Franklyn Rd. NW10 —37Va 60
Franklyn Rd. W on T —72X 141
Frank Martin Ct. Chesh —2Wb 11
Franks Av. N Mald —70Sa 123
Franks La. Hort K —71Rd 153
Frank St. E13 —42Jc 85
Franks Wood Av. Orp —71Rc 150
Frankswood Av. W Dray —44P 75
Frank Towell Ct. Felt —59W 98
Frank Welsh Ct. Pinn —28Y 37
Franlaw Cres. N13 —21Sb 43
Franmil Rd. Horn —32Jd 68
Fransfield Gro. SE26 —62Xb 127
Frans Hals Ct. E14 —48Fc 85
Frant Clo. SE20 —66Yb 128
Franthorne Way. SE6 —61Dc 128
Frant Rd. T Hth —71Rb 147
Fraser Clo. E6 —44Nc 86
Fraser Clo. Bex —60Ed 110
Fraser Ho. Bren —50Pa 79
Fraser Rd. E17 —29Dc 44
Fraser Rd. N9 —20Xb 25
Fraser Rd. Eri —50Fd 88
Fraser Rd. Gnfd —39Ka 58
Fraser St. W4 —50Ua 80
Frating Cres. Wfd G —23Kc 45
Frays Av. W Dray —47M 75
Frayslea. Uxb —40L 55
Frays Waye. Uxb —39L 55
Frazer Av. Ruis —36Y 57
Frazer Clo. Romf —31Hd 68
Frazier St. SE1 —47Qb 82 (2K 205)
Frean St. SE16 —48Wb 83
Freda Corbett Clo. SE15 —52Wb 105
Frederica Rd. E4 —17Fc 27
Frederica St. N7 —38Pb 62
Frederick Andrews Ct. Grays —51Fe 113
Frederick Clo. W2 —45Gb 81 (4F 197)
Frederick Clo. Sutt —77Bb 145
Frederick Cres. SW9 —52Rb 105
Frederick Cres. Enf —12Yb 26
Frederick Gdns. Sutt —78Bb 145
Frederick Pl. SE18 —50Rc 86
Frederick Rd. SE17 —51Rb 105
Frederick Rd. Rain —40Fd 68
Frederick Rd. Sutt —78Bb 145
Frederick's Pl. EC2 —44Tb 83 (3F 201)
Fredericks Pl. N12 —21Eb 41
Frederick's Row. EC1 —41Rb 83 (3B 194)
Frederick St. WC1 —41Pb 82 (4H 193)
Frederick Ter. E8 —38Vb 63
Frederic M. SW1 —47Hb 81 (2G 203)
(off Kinnerton St.)
Frederic St. E17 —29Ac 44
Fredora Av. Hay —42V 76
Freeborne Gdns. Rain —37Jd 68
Freedom Clo. E17 —36Zb 64
Freedom Rd. N17 —26Tb 43
Freedom St. SW11 —54Hb 103
Freedown La. Sutt —85Db 163
Freegrove Rd. N7 —36Nb 62
Freehold Ind. Cen. Houn —57Y 99
Freeland Ct. Sidc —62Wc 131
Freeland Pk. NW4 —26Ab 40
Freeland Rd. W5 —45Pa 79
Freelands Av. S Croy —81Zb 166
Freelands Gro. Brom —67Kc 129
Freelands Rd. Brom —67Kc 129
Freelands Rd. Cob —86X 159
Freeland Way. Eri —53Jd 110
Freeling St. N1 —38Nb 62
(in two parts)
Freeman Clo. N'holt —38Aa 57
Freeman Clo. Shep —70U 120
Freeman Dri. W Mol —69Ba 121
Freeman Rd. Grav —2G 136
Freeman Rd. Mord —71Fb 145
Freemans Clo. Stoke P —7K 53
Freemans La. Hay —45U 76
Freemantle Av. Enf —15Zb 26
Freeman Way. Horn —30Pd 49
Freemasons Rd. E16 —43Kc 85
Freemasons Rd. Croy —74Ub 147
Free Prae Rd. Cher —74J 139
Freesia Clo. Orp —78Vc 151
Freethorpe Clo. SE19 —67Ub 127
Free Trade Wharf. E1 —45Zb 84
Freightliner Depot Rd. NW10 —41Ua 80
Freke Rd. SW11 —55Jb 104
Fremantle Ho. Til —3B 114
Fremantle Rd. Belv —49Cd 88
Fremantle Rd. Ilf —26Rc 46
Fremantle St. SE17 —50Ub 83 (7H 207)
Fremont St. E9 —39Yb 64
French Apartments, The. Purl —84Qb 164
Frenchaye. Add —78L 139
French Gdns. Cob —86Y 159
Frenchlands Hatch. E Hor —99U 174
French Ordinary Ct. EC3 —45Ub 83 (4J 201)
(off Crutched Friars)
French Pl. E1 —42Ub 83 (5J 195)
French St. Sun —68Y 121
French St. W'ham —100Uc 184
French's Wells. Wok —5E 188
Frenchum Gdns. Slou —5C 72
Frendsbury Rd. SE4 —56Ac 106
Frensham Clo. S'hall —42Ba 77
Frensham Ct. Mitc —70Fb 125
Frensham Dri. SW15 —62Va 124
Frensham Dri. New Ad —80Ec 148
Frensham Rd. SE9 —61Tc 130
Frensham Rd. Kenl —86Rb 165
Frensham St. SE15 —51Wb 105
Frensham Wlk. Farn C —6G 52
Frensham Way. Eps —88Ya 162
Frere St. SW11 —54Gb 103
Freshfield Clo. SE13 —56Fc 107
(in two parts)
Freshfield Dri. N14 —17Kb 24
Freshfields. Croy —74Bc 148
Freshfields Av. Upm —36Rd 69
Freshford St. SW18 —62Eb 125
Freshmount Gdns. Eps —83Ra 161
Freshwater Clo. SW17 —65Jb 126
Freshwater Ct. S'hall —41Ca 77
Freshwater Rd. SW17 —65Jb 126
Freshwater Rd. Dag —32Zc 67
Freshwell Av. Romf —28Yc 47
Freshwell Gdns. W Horn —30Fe 51
Fresh Wharf Rd. Bark —39Rc 66
Freshwood Clo. Beck —67Dc 128
Freshwood Way. Wall —81Kb 164
Freston Gdns. Barn —15Jb 24
Freston Pk. N3 —26Bb 41
Freston Rd. W10 & W11 —45Za 80
Freta Rd. Bexh —57Bd 109
Frewin Rd. SW18 —60Fb 103
Friar M. SE27 —62Rb 127
Friar Rd. Hay —42Z 77
Friar Rd. Orp —71Wc 151
Friars Av. N20 —20Gb 23
Friars Av. SW15 —62Va 124
Friars Av. Shenf —18Ce 33
Friars Clo. E4 —20Ec 26
Friars Clo. N'holt —41Z 77
Friar's Clo. Shenf —17Ce 33
Friars Ct. E17 —25Bc 44
Friars Ct. SE1 —46Rb 83 (7C 200)
(off Bear La.)
Friars Gdns. W3 —44Ta 79
Friars Ga. Clo. Wfd G —21Jc 45
Friars Head. K Lan —2Q 4
Friars La. Rich —57Ma 101
Friars Mead. E14 —48Ec 84
Friars M. SE9 —57Qc 108
Friars Orchard. Fet —93Fa 176

Friars Pl. La. W3 —45Ta 79
Friars Rise. Wok —90C 156
Friars Rd. E6 —39Mc 65
Friars Rd. Vir W —10P 117
Friars Stile Pl. Rich —58Na 101
Friars Stile Rd. Rich —58Na 101
Friars, The. Chig —21Uc 46
Friar St. EC4 —44Rb 83 (3C 200)
Friars Wlk. N14 —17Kb 24
Friars Wlk. SE2 —50Zc 87
Friars Way. W3 —44Ta 79
Friars Way. Bush —11Ba 19
Friars Way. Cher —72H 139
Friars Way. K Lan —2Q 4
Friarswood. Croy —81Ac 166
Friary Clo. N12 —22Gb 41
Friary Clo. SW1 —46Lb 82 (7C 198)
(off St James Pal.)
Friary Ct. W3 —44Sa 79
Friary Ct. Wok —6C 188
Friary Est. SE15 —51Wb 105
Friary Island. Wray —8N 95
Friary La. Wfd G —21Jc 45
Friary Rd. N12 —21Fb 41
Friary Rd. SE15 —51Wb 105
Friary Rd. W3 —44Sa 79
Friary Rd. Wray —9N 95
Friary, The. Old Win —8N 95
Friary Way. N12 —21Gb 41
Friday Hill. E4 —19Gc 27
Friday Hill E. E4 —20Gc 27
Friday Hill W. E4 —19Gc 27
Friday Rd. Eri —50Fd 88
Friday Rd. Mitc —66Hb 125
Friday St. EC4 —45Sb 83 (4D 200)
Frideswide Pl. NW5 —36Lb 62
Friendly Pl. SE10 —53Dc 106
Friendly St. SE8 —54Cc 106
Friendly St. M. SE8 —54Cc 106
Friendship Wlk. N'holt —41Z 77
Friends Rd. Croy —76Tb 147
Friends Rd. Purl —84Rb 165
Friend St. EC1 —41Rb 83 (3B 194)
Friends Wlk. Stai —64H 119
Friends Wlk. Uxb —38M 55
Friern Barnet La. N20 & N11
—19Fb 23
Friern Barnet Rd. N11 —22Hb 41
Friern Ct. N20 —20Fb 23
Friern Mt. Dri. N20 —17Eb 23
Friern Pk. N12 —22Eb 41
Friern Rd. SE22 —59Wb 105
Friern Watch Av. N12 —21Eb 41
Frigate M. SE8 —51Cc 106
Frimley Av. Horn —32Qd 69
Frimley Av. Wall —78Pb 146
Frimley Clo. SW19 —61Ab 124
Frimley Clo. New Ad —80Ec 148
Frimley Ct. Sidc —64Yc 131
Frimley Cres. New Ad —80Ec 148
Frimley Gdns. Mitc —69Gb 125
Frimley Rd. Chess —78Ma 143
Frimley Rd. Ilf —34Uc 66
Frimley Way. E1 —42Zb 84
Fringewood Clo. N'wd —25R 36
Frinsted Clo. Orp —70Zc 131
Frinsted Rd. Eri —52Fd 110
Frinton Clo. Wat —19X 19
Frinton Dri. Wfd G —24Fc 45
Frinton M. Ilf —30Qc 46
Frinton Rd. E6 —41Mc 85
Frinton Rd. N15 —30Ub 43
Frinton Rd. SW17 —65Jb 126
Frinton Rd. Romf —24Bd 47
Frinton Rd. Sidc —61Ad 131
Friston Path. Chig —22Uc 46
Friston St. SW6 —54Db 103
Friswell Pl. Bexh —56Cd 110
Fritham Rd. N Mald —72Ua 144
Frith Ct. NW7 —24Ab 40
Frithe, The. Slou —5N 73
Frith Knowle. W on T —79X 141
Frith La. NW7 —24Ab 40
Frith Rd. E11 —35Ec 64
Frith Rd. Croy —75Sb 147
Frith St. W1 —44Mb 82 (3D 198)
Frithville Gdns. W12 —46Ya 80
Frithwald Rd. Cher —73H 139
Frithwood Av. N'wd —23U 36
Frizlands La. Dag —33Dd 68
Frobisher Clo. Kenl —89Sb 165
Frobisher Clo. Pinn —31Z 57
Frobisher Ct. NW9 —26Ua 40
Frobisher Ct. W12 —47Ya 80
(off Lime Gro.)
Frobisher Cres. EC2
(off Barbican) —43Sb 83 (7E 194)
Frobisher Cres. Stai —59N 97
Frobisher Gdns. Stai —59N 97
Frobisher Pas. E14 —46Cc 84
Frobisher Rd. E6 —44Pc 86
Frobisher Rd. N8 —28Qb 42
Frobisher Rd. Eri —52Hd 110
Frobisher Rd. St. SE10 —51Gc 107
Frobisher Way. Grav —4G 136
Froggy La. Uxb —34F 54
Froghall La. Chig —21Tc 46
Frog La. Rain —42Fd 88
Frog La. Sut G —97A 172
Frogley Rd. SE22 —56Vb 105
Frogmore. SW18 —57Cb 103
Frogmore. St Alb —1Ga 6
Frogmore Av. Hay —42U 76
Frogmore Border. Wind —5J 95
Frogmore Clo. Slou —7F 72
Frogmore Cotts. Wat —15Z 19
Frogmore Ct. B Hth —19M 17
Frogmore Ct. S'hall —49Ba 77
Frogmore Dri. Wind —3J 95
Frogmore Gdns. Hay —42U 76
Frogmore Gdns. Sutt —77Ab 144
Frogmore Ind. Est. NW10 —41Sa 79
Frogmore Ind. Pk. W Thur
—50Wd 90

Frogmore La. Rick —19M 17
Frognal. NW3 —35Eb 61
Frognal Av. Harr —28Ha 38
Frognal Av. Sidc —65Wc 131
Frognal Clo. NW3 —36Eb 61
Frognal Ct. NW3 —37Eb 61
Frognal Gdns. NW3 —35Eb 61
Frognal La. NW3 —36Db 61
Frognal Pde. NW3 —37Eb 61
Frognal Pl. Sidc —65Wc 131
Frognal Rise. NW3 —34Eb 61
Frognal Way. NW3 —35Eb 61
Frog St. Kel H —11Ud 32
Froissart Rd. SE9 —57Mc 107
Frome. E Til —9L 93
Frome Rd. N22 —27Rb 43
Frome Ho. SE15 —56Xb 105
Frome St. N1 —40Sb 63 (1D 194)
Fromondes Rd. Sutt —78Ab 144
Front La. Upm —33Ud 70
Frostic Wlk. E1 —43Wb 83
Froude St. SW8 —54Kb 104
Frowyke Cres. Pot B —4Wa 8
Fruen Rd. Felt —59V 98
Fryatt Rd. N17 —24Tb 43
(in two parts)
Fryatt St. E14 —44Gc 85
Fry Clo. Romf —22Cd 48
Fryent Clo. NW9 —30Qa 39
Fryent Cres. NW9 —30Ua 40
Fryent Fields. NW9 —30Ua 40
Fryent Gro. NW9 —30Ua 40
Fryent Way. NW9 —29Qa 39
Fryern Wood. Cat —96Sb 181
Frye's Bldgs. N1
—40Qb 62 (1A 194)
Frying Pan All. E1 —43Vb 83 (1K 201)
(off Bell La.)
Frylands Ct. New Ad —83Ec 166
Frymley View. Wind —3B 94
Fry Rd. E6 —38Mc 65
Fry Rd. NW10 —39Va 60
Fry Rd. Ashf —63M 119
Fryston Av. Coul —86Kb 164
Fryston Av. Croy —75Wb 147
Fuchsia St. SE2 —50Xc 87
Fulbeck Dri. NW9 —25Ua 40
Fulbeck M. N19 —35Lb 62
Fulbeck Rd. N19 —35Lb 62
Fulbeck Way. Harr —26Ea 38
Fulbourne Rd. E17 —25Ec 44
Fulbourne St. E1 —43Xb 83
Fulbrook Av. New Haw —83J 157
Fulbrook La. S Ock —45Vd 90
Fulbrook M. N19 —35Lb 62
Fulford Gro. Wat —19X 19
Fulford Ho. Eps —80Ta 143
Fulford Rd. Cat —93Tb 181
Fulford Rd. Eps —80Ta 143
Fulford St. SE16 —47Xb 83
Fulham B'way. SW6 —52Cb 103
Fulham Ct. Uxb —42S 76
Fulham High St. SW6 —54Ab 102
Fulham Pal. Rd. W6 & SW6
—50Ya 80
Fulham Pk. Gdns. SW6 —54Bb 103
Fulham Pk. Rd. SW6 —54Bb 103
Fulham Rd. SW6 —54Ab 102
Fulham Rd. SW10 & SW3
—51Eb 103
Fullarton Cres. S Ock —44Vd 90
Fullbrooks Av. Wor Pk —74Va 144
Fuller Clo. Orp —78Vc 151
Fuller Gdns. Wat —9X 5
Fuller Rd. Dag —34Xc 67
Fuller Rd. Wat —9X 5
Fullers Av. Surb —75Pa 143
Fullers Av. Wfd G —24Hc 45
Fullers Clo. Romf —24Ed 48
Fullers Clo. Wal A —5Jc 13
Fullers Hill. W'ham —98Tc 184
Fullers La. Romf —24Ed 48
Fullers Rd. E18 —25Hc 45
Fuller St. NW4 —28Ya 40
Fuller St. Sev —92Rd 187
Fullers Way N. Surb —76Pa 143
Fullers Way S. Chess —77Na 143
Fuller's Wood. Croy —77Cc 148
Fullerton Clo. Byfl —86P 157
Fullerton Dri. Byfl —86N 157
Fullerton Rd. SW18 —57Eb 103
Fullerton Rd. Byfl —86N 157
Fullerton Rd. Cars —81Gb 163
Fullerton Rd. Croy —73Vb 147
Fullerton Way. Byfl —86N 157
Fuller Way. Crox —15Q 18
Fuller Way. Hay —50V 76
Fullmer Way. Wdhm —82H 157
Fullwell Av. Ilf —25Pc 46
Fullwood's M. N1
—41Tb 83 (3G 195)
Fulmar Ct. Surb —72Pa 143
Fulmar Rd. Horn —38Jd 68
Fulmead St. SW6 —53Db 103
Fulmer Clo. Hamp —64Aa 121
Fulmer Comn. Rd. Ful & Iver
—6P 53
Fulmer Dri. Ger X —3P 53
Fulmer La. Ful & Ger X —34B 54
Fulmer Rd. E16 —43Mc 85
Fulmer Rd. Ger X & Ful —32A 54
Fulmer Way. W13 —48Ka 78
Fulmer Way. Ger X —29A 34
Fulready Rd. E10 —29Fc 45
Fulstone Clo. Houn —56Ba 99
Fulthorp Rd. SE3 —54Hc 107
Fulton M. W2 —45Eb 81
(off Porchester Ter.)
Fulton Rd. Wemb —34Qa 59
Fulwell Cross. Ilf —26Tc 46
Fulwell Pk. Av. Twic —61Da 121
Fulwell Rd. Tedd —63Fa 122
Fulwich Rd. Dart —58Pd 111

Fulwood Av. Wemb —39Pa 59
Fulwood Clo. Hay —44V 76
Fulwood Ct. Kent —30Ja 38
Fulwood Gdns. Twic —58Ha 100
Fulwood Pl. WC1
—43Pb 82 (1J 199)
Fulwood Wlk. SW19 —60Ab 102
Furber St. W6 —48Xa 80
Furham Field. Pinn —24Ca 37
Furley Rd. SE15 —52Wb 105
Furlong Clo. Wall —74Kb 146
Furlong Rd. N7 —37Qb 62
Furlough, The. Wok —89C 156
Furmage St. SW18 —59Db 103
Furneaux Av. SE27 —64Rb 127
Furner Clo. Dart —55Hd 110
Furness. Wind —4A 94
Furness Clo. Grays —10D 92
(in two parts)
Furness Rd. NW10 —40Wa 60
Furness Rd. SW6 —54Db 103
Furness Rd. Harr —31Da 57
Furness Rd. Mord —72Db 145
Furness Sq. Wind —4A 94
Furness Way. Horn —36Jd 68
Furnival Av. Slou —3F 72
Furnival Clo. Vir W —72A 138
Furnival St. EC4 —44Qb 82 (2K 199)
Furrow La. E9 —36Yb 64
Furrows Pl. Cat —95Vb 181
Furrows, The. Hare —29L 35
Furrows, The. W on T —75Y 141
Fursby Av. N3 —23Db 41
Further Acre. NW9 —26Va 40
Furtherfield. Abb L —4U 4
Furtherfield Clo. Croy —72Qb 146
Furtherfield Rd. SE6 —59Gc 107
Furzebank. Asc —10B 116
Furzedown Dri. SW17 —64Kb 126
Furzedown Rd. SW17 —64Kb 126
Furzedown Rd. Sutt —83Eb 163
Furze Farm Clo. Romf —26Ad 47
Furzefield. Chesh —1Xb 11
Furze Field. Oxs —85Fa 160
Furzefield Clo. Chst —65Rc 130
Furzefield Rd. SE3 —52Kc 107
Furzeground Way. Uxb —46S 76
Furze Gro. Tad —93Bb 179
Furzeham Rd. W Dray —47N 75
Furze Hill. Purl —83Nb 164
Furze Hill. Tad —92Bb 179
Furzehill Pde. Borwd —13Qa 21
Furzehill Rd. Borwd —14Qa 21
Furze La. Purl —83Nb 164
Furzen Clo. Slou —1E 72
Furzen Clo. Wat —22Y 37
Furze Rd. Add —79H 139
Furze Rd. T Hth —69Sb 127
Furze St. E3 —43Cc 84
Furze View. Chor —16E 16
Furzewood. Sun —67W 120
Fusedale Way. S Ock —45Vd 90
Fuzzens Wlk. Wind —4C 94
Fydler's Clo. Wink —5A 116
Fye Foot La. EC4
—45Sb 83 (4D 200)
Fyfe Way. Brom —68Jc 129
Fyfield. N4 —33Qb 62
(off Six Acres Est.)
Fyfield Clo. Brom —70Fc 129
Fyfield Clo. W Horn —30Fe 51
Fyfield Ct. E7 —37Jc 65
Fyfield Rd. E17 —27Fc 45
Fyfield Rd. SW9 —55Qb 104
Fyfield Rd. Enf —13Ub 25
Fyfield Rd. Rain —39Hd 68
Fyfield Rd. Wfd G —24Lc 45
Fynes St. SW1 —49Mb 82 (5D 204)

Gabion Av. Purf —49Td 90
Gable Clo. Abb L —4U 4
Gable Clo. Dart —57Jd 110
Gable Clo. Pinn —24Ca 37
Gable Ct. SE26 —63Xb 127
Gables Av. Ashf —64P 119
Gables Av. Borwd —13Pa 21
Gables Clo. SE5 —53Ub 105
Gables Clo. SE12 —60Jc 107
Gables Clo. Dart —1L 95
Gables Clo. Ger X —21A 34
Gables Clo. Kingf —92B 172
(in two parts)
Gables Ct. Kingf —92B 172
Gables Lodge. Barn —10Eb 9
Gables, The. N10 —27Jb 42
(off Fortis Grn.)
Gables, The. Bans —89Bb 163
Gables, The. Bark —37Sc 66
Gables, The. Brom —66Kc 129
Gables, The. Grays —49Be 91
Gables, The. Long —68Ee 135
Gables, The. Oxs —84Ea 160
Gabriel Clo. Felt —63Aa 121
Gabriel Gdns. Grav —4G 136
Gabrielle Clo. Wemb —34Pa 59
Gabrielle Ct. NW3 —37Fb 61
Gabrielspring Rd. Fawk —75Td 154
Gabrielspring Rd. E. Fawk
—75Ud 154
Gabriel St. SE23 —59Zb 106
Gabriel's Wharf. SE1
—46Qb 82 (6A 200)
Gaddesden Av. Wemb —37Pa 59
Gaddesden Cres. Wat —6Z 5
Gaddesden Ho. EC1
—41Tb 83 (4G 195)
(off Cranwood St.)
Gade Av. Wat —14U 18
Gade Bank. Wat —14T 18
Gade Clo. Hay —46X 77
Gade Clo. Wat —14U 18

Gadesden Rd. Eps —79Sa 143
(in two parts)
Gade Valley Clo. K Lan —1Q 4
Gade View Gdns. K Lan —4S 4
Gadsbury Clo. NW9 —30Va 40
Gadsden Clo. Upm —30Ud 50
Gadswell Clo. Wat —8Z 5
Gadwall Clo. E16 —44Kc 85
Gadwall Way. SE28 —47Tc 86
Gage Rd. E16 —43Gc 85
Gage St. WC1 —43Nb 82 (7G 193)
Gainford St. N1 —39Qb 62
Gainsborough Av. E12 —36Qc 66
Gainsborough Av. Dart —57Ld 111
Gainsborough Av. Til —3C 114
Gainsborough Clo. Beck —66Cc 128
Gainsborough Clo. Esh —74Ga 142
Gainsborough Ct. N12 —22Db 41
Gainsborough Ct. SE21 —61Ub 127
Gainsborough Ct. W4 —50Ra 79
(off Chaseley Dri.)
Gainsborough Ct. Brtwd —21Yd 50
(off Gt. Eastern Rd.)
Gainsborough Ct. W on T
—77W 140
Gainsborough Dri. Grav —62Fe 135
Gainsborough Dri. S Croy
—85Wb 165
Gainsborough Gdns. NW3 —34Fb 61
Gainsborough Gdns. NW11
—31Bb 61
Gainsborough Gdns. Edgw
—26Pa 39
Gainsborough Gdns. Gnfd
—36Ga 58
Gainsborough Gdns. Iswth
—57Fa 100
Gainsborough Ho. Dag —35Xc 67
(off Gainsborough Rd.)
Gainsborough Lodge. Harr —29Ha 38
(off Hindes Rd.)
Gainsborough Rd. E11 —31Gc 65
Gainsborough Rd. E15 —41Gc 85
Gainsborough Rd. N12 —22Db 41
Gainsborough Rd. W4 —49Va 80
Gainsborough Rd. Dag —35Xc 67
Gainsborough Rd. Eps —82Sa 161
Gainsborough Rd. Hay —40S 56
Gainsborough Rd. N Mald
—73Ta 143
Gainsborough Rd. Rain —39Jd 68
Gainsborough Rd. Rich —54Pa 101
Gainsborough Rd. Wfd G —24Nc 46
Gainsborough Sq. Bexh —55Zc 109
Gainsford Rd. E17 —28Bc 44
Gainsford St. SE1
—47Vb 83 (1K 207)
Gairloch Rd. SE5 —54Ub 105
Gaisford St. NW5 —37Lb 62
Gaist Av. Cat —94Yb 181
Gaitskell Ho. E6 —39Mc 65
Gaitskell Rd. E17 —27Dc 44
Gaitskell Rd. SE9 —58Sc 108
Gaitskell Ho. Grays —46De 91
(off Crammavill St.)
Galahad Clo. Slou —7E 72
Galahad Rd. Brom —63Jc 129
Galata Rd. SW13 —52Wa 102
Galatea Sq. SE15 —55Xb 105
Galba Ct. Bren —52Ma 101
Galbraith St. E14 —48Ec 84
Galdana Av. Barn —13Eb 23
Galeborough Av. Wfd G —24Fc 45
Gale Clo. Hamp —65Aa 121
Gale Clo. Mitc —69Fb 125
Gale Cres. Bans —89Cb 163
Galena Rd. W6 —49Xa 80
Galen Pl. WC1 —43Nb 82 (1G 199)
Galesbury Rd. SW18 —58Eb 103
Gales Gdns. E2 —41Xb 83
Gale St. E3 —43Cc 84
Gale St. Dag —36Yc 67
Gales Way. Wfd G —24Nc 46
Galey Grn. S Ock —44Xd 90
Galgate Clo. SW19 —60Ab 102
Galimont App. Wat —13X 19
Gallants Farm Rd. Barn —17Gb 23
Galleon Boulevd. Dart —56Td 112
Galleon Clo. SE16 —47Zb 84
Galleon Clo. Eri —49Fd 88
Galleons La. Wex —2N 73
Gallery Gdns. N'holt —40Z 57
Gallery Rd. SE21 —60Tb 105
Galley Hill Rd. Grav —57Be 113
Galleyhill Rd. Wal A —4Gc 13
Galley Hill Trading Est. Swans
—57Ae 113
Galley La. Barn —10Va 8
Galleymead Rd. Coln —53H 97
Galleywall Rd. SE16 —49Xb 83
Galleywood Cres. Romf —23Fd 48
Galliard Clo. N9 —16Yb 26
Galliard Rd. N9 —17Wb 25
Gallia Rd. N5 —36Rb 63
Gallions Clo. Bark —41Wc 87
Gallions Entrance. E16 —46Sc 86
Gallions Rd. E16 —45Rc 86
Gallions Rd. SE7 —49Kc 85
Galliver Pl. E5 —35Xb 63
Gallon Clo. SE7 —49Lc 85
Gallop, The. S Croy —80Xb 147
Gallop, The. Sutt —81Fb 163
Gallop, The. Wind —9G 94
Gallosson Rd. SE18 —49Uc 86
Galloway Rd. W12 —46Wa 80
Gallows Hill. K Lan —4S 4
Gallows Hill La. Abb L —4S 4
Gallows Wood. Fawk —77Wd 154
Gard St. EC1 —41Rb 83 (3C 194)
Garden Av. Bexh —55Bd 109
Garden Av. Mitc —66Kb 126

Galsworthy Av. Romf —31Xc 67
Galsworthy Clo. SE28 —46Xc 87
Galsworthy Cres. SE3 —53Lc 107
Galsworthy Rd. NW2 —35Ab 60
Galsworthy Rd. Cher —73J 139
Galsworthy Rd. King T —67Ra 123
Galsworthy Rd. Til —3E 114
Galsworthy Ter. N16 —34Ub 63
Galton St. W10 —41Ab 80
Galva Clo. Barn —14Jb 24
Galvani Way. Croy —74Pb 146
Galveston Rd. SW15 —57Bb 103
Galway Clo. SE16 —50Xb 83
Galway Ho. EC1 —41Sb 83 (4E 194)
Galway St. EC1 —41Sb 83 (4E 194)
Gambetta St. SW8 —54Kb 104
Gambia St. SE1 —46Rb 83 (7C 200)
Gambles La. Rip —96L 173
Gamble Rd. SW17 —63Gb 125
Games Rd. Barn —13Hb 23
Gamlen Rd. SW15 —56Za 102
Gammons Farm Clo. Wat —8V 4
Gammons La. Wat —8U 4
(in two parts)
Gander Grn. La. Sutt —75Ab 144
Ganders Ash. Wat —5W 4
Gandhi Clo. E17 —30Cc 44
Gandhi Ct. Wat —12Z 19
Gangers Hill. God & Wold
—100Ac 182
Gant Ct. Wal A —6Hc 13
Ganton St. W1 —45Lb 82 (4B 198)
Ganton Wlk. Wat —21Z 37
Gantshill Cres. Ilf —29Qc 46
Gap Rd. SW19 —64Cb 125
Garage Rd. W3 —44Ra 79
Garbrand Wlk. Eps —81Va 162
Garbutt Pl. W1 —43Jb 82 (1J 197)
Garden City. Edgw —23Qa 39
Garden Clo. E4 —22Cc 44
Garden Clo. SE12 —62Kc 129
Garden Clo. SW15 —59Ya 102
Garden Clo. Add —77M 139
Garden Clo. Ark —14Ya 22
Garden Clo. Ashf —65S 120
Garden Clo. Bans —87Cb 163
Garden Clo. Hamp —64Ba 121
Garden Clo. Lea —97La 176
Garden Clo. N'holt —39Aa 57
Garden Clo. Ruis —33U 56
Garden Clo. Wall —78Nb 146
Garden Clo. Wat —12V 18
Garden Cotts. St P —68Yc 131
Garden Ct. EC4 —45Qb 82 (4K 199)
(off Temple)
Garden Ct. W4 —48Sa 79
Garden Ct. Hamp —64Ba 121
Garden Ct. Rich —53Pa 101
Garden Ct. Stan —22La 38
Gardener Gro. Felt —61Ba 121
Gardeners Rd. Croy —74Rb 147
Gardener's Wlk. Bookh —98Da 175
Gardenfields. Tad —91Ab 178
Garden Ho. N2 —26Fb 41
(off Grange, The)
Gardenia Rd. Enf —16Ub 25
Gardenia Way. Wfd G —22Jc 45
Garden La. SW2 —60Pb 104
Garden La. Brom —66Kc 129
Garden M. W2 —45Cb 81
Garden M. Slou —6K 73
Garden Pl. Dart —62Md 133
Garden Reach. Chal G —13A 16
Garden Rd. NW8
—41Eb 81 (3A 190)
Garden Rd. SE20 —67Yb 128
Garden Rd. Abb L —3U 4
Garden Rd. Brom —66Kc 129
Garden Rd. Rich —55Qa 101
Garden Rd. Sev —94Md 187
Garden Rd. W on T —72X 141
Garden Row. SE1
—48Rb 83 (4B 206)
Garden Row. Grav —2B 136
Gardens, The. SE22 —56Wb 105
Gardens, The. Beck —68Fc 129
Gardens, The. Cob —91S 174
Gardens, The. Esh —77Ca 141
Gardens, The. Felt —58T 98
Gardens, The. Harr —30Ea 38
Gardens, The. Pinn —30Ba 37
Gardens, The. Uxb —33N 55
Gardens, The. Wat —12V 18
Garden Ter. SW1
—50Mb 82 (7D 204)
Garden Ter. SW7
(off Trevor Pl.) —47Gb 81 (2E 202)
Garden Ter. Seal —93Qd 187
Garden View. E7 —35Lc 65
Garden Wlk. EC2
—41Ub 83 (4H 195)
Garden Wlk. Beck —67Bc 128
Garden Wlk. Coul —95Kb 180
Garden Way. NW10 —37Sa 59
Garden Way. Lou —10Qc 14
Gardiner Av. NW2 —36Ya 60
Gardiner Clo. Dag —35Zc 67
Gardiner Clo. Enf —16Yb 26
Gardiner Clo. Orp —68Yc 131
Gardiner Ct. S Croy —79Sb 147
Gardner Clo. E11 —30Kc 45
Gardner Ho. Felt —61Ba 121
Gardner Rd. E13 —42Kc 85
Gardners La. EC4 —45Sb 83 (4D 200)
Gardner Rd. NW3 —35Fb 61

Gareth Gro. Brom —63Jc 129
Garfield. Enf —15Tb 25
(off Private Rd.)
Garfield M. SW11 —55Kb 104
Garfield Pl. Wind —4H 95
Garfield Rd. E4 —18Fc 27
Garfield Rd. E13 —42Hc 85
Garfield Rd. SW11 —55Jb 104
Garfield Rd. SW19 —64Eb 125
Garfield Rd. Add —78L 139
Garfield Rd. Enf —14Yb 26
Garfield Rd. Twic —60Ja 100
Garfield St. Wat —10X 5
Garford St. E14 —45Cc 84
Garganey Ct. NW10 —37Ta 59
(off Elgar Av.)
Garganey Wlk. SE28 —45Yc 87
Garibaldi St. SE18 —49Uc 86
Garland Rd. SE18 —52Tc 108
Garland Rd. Stan —25Na 39
Garlands Rd. Lea —93Ka 176
Garland Way. Cat —94Tb 181
Garland Way. Horn —28Nd 49
Garlichill Rd. Eps —89Xa 162
Garlick Hill. EC4 —45Sb 83 (4E 200)
Garlies Rd. SE23 —62Ac 128
Garlinge Rd. NW2 —37Bb 61
Garman Clo. N18 —22Ub 43
Garman Rd. N17 —24Yb 44
Garnault M. EC1 —41Qb 82 (4A 194)
(off Rosebery Av.)
Garnault Pl. EC1 —41Qb 82 (4A 194)
Garner Rd. E17 —25Ec 44
Garners Clo. Ger X —23B 34
Garners End. Ger X —23A 34
Garners Rd. Ger X —23A 34
Garner St. E2 —40Wb 63
Garnet Clo. Brick —1Ba 5
Garnet Clo. Slou —7E 72
Garnet Clo. Wat —9Z 5
Garnet Rd. NW10 —37Ua 60
Garnet Rd. T Hth —70Sb 127
Garnet St. E1 —45Yb 84
Garnett Clo. SE9 —55Pc 108
Garnett Rd. NW3 —36Hb 61
Garnet Wlk. E6 —43Nc 86
Garnet Way. E17 —25Ac 44
Garnham Clo. N16 —33Vb 63
Garnham St. N16 —33Vb 63
Garnies Clo. SE15 —52Vb 105
Garnon Mead. Coop —1Zc 15
Garrad's Rd. SW16 —62Mb 126
Garrard Clo. Bexh —55Cd 110
Garrard Clo. Chst —64Rc 130
Garrard Rd. Bans —88Cb 163
Garrard Rd. Slou —6C 72
Garrard Wlk. NW10 —37Ua 60
Garratt Rd. Edgw —24Qa 39
Garratt Clo. Croy —77Nb 146
Garratt La. SW18 —59Db 103
Garratt La. SW18 & SW17
—58Db 103
Garratts La. Bans —88Bb 163
Garratts Rd. Bush —17Ea 20
Garratt Ter. SW17 —63Gb 125
Garratt Wlk. W3 —43Ta 79
Garrett St. EC1 —42Sb 83 (5E 194)
Garrick Av. NW11 —30Ab 40
Garrick Clo. SW18 —56Eb 103
Garrick Clo. W5 —42Na 79
Garrick Clo. Rich —57Ma 101
Garrick Clo. Stai —66J 119
Garrick Cres. Croy —75Ub 147
Garrick Dri. NW4 —26Ya 40
Garrick Dri. SE28 —48Tc 86
Garrick Gdns. W Mol —69Ca 121
Garrick Ho. W4 —51Ua 102
Garrick Pk. NW4 —26Za 40
Garrick Rd. NW9 —30Va 40
Garrick Rd. Gnfd —42Da 77
Garrick Rd. Rich —54Qa 101
Garrick Rd. WC2 —45Nb 82 (4F 199)
Garrick St. Grav —8D 114
Garrick Way. NW4 —28Za 40
Garrick Yd. WC2 —45Nb 82 (4F 199)
(off St Martin's La.)
Garrison Clo. SE18 —52Qc 108
Garrison La. Chess —80Ma 143
Garrison Pde. Purf —49Qd 89
Garron La. S Ock —45Vd 90
Garrow. Long —69De 135
Garrowsfield. Barn —16Bb 23
Garry Clo. Romf —24Gd 48
Garry Way. Romf —24Gd 48
Garside Clo. SE28 —48Tc 86
Garside Clo. Hamp —65Da 121
Garside Dri. Stan —27Pa 39
Garside Grn. Se? —75Pc 108
Garsington M. SE4 —55Bc 106
Garsmouth Way. Wat —8Z 5
Garson Clo. Esh —78Ba 141
Garson La. Wray —9P 95
Garson Rd. Esh —79Ba 141
Garston Cres. Wat —6Y 5
Garston Dri. Wat —6Y 5
Garston Gdns. Kenl —87Tb 165
Garston La. Kenl —86Tb 165
Garston La. Wat —6Z 5
Garston Pk. Pde. Wat —6Z 5
Garstons, The. Bookh —97Ca 175
Garter Way. SE16 —47Zb 84
Garth Clo. W4 —50Ta 79
Garth Clo. King T —64Pa 123
Garth Clo. Mord —73Za 144
Garth Clo. Ruis —32Z 57
Garth Ct. W4 —51Ta 101
Garth Ct. Harr —30Ha 38
(off Northwick Pk. Rd.)
Garthland Dri. Barn —15Xa 22
Garth M. W5 —22Na 39
Garthorne Rd. SE23 —59Zb 106
Garth Rd. NW2 —33Bb 61

Garth Rd.—Glebe, The

Garth Rd. W4 —50Ta 79
Garth Rd. King T —64Pa 123
Garth Rd. Mord —73Ya 144
Garth Rd. Sev —100Ld 187
Garth Rd. S Ock —42Yd 90
Garthside. Ham —64Na 123
Garth, The. Abb L —5T 4
Garth, The. Cob —85Aa 159
Garth, The. Hamp —65Da 121
Garth, The. Harr —30Pa 39
Garthway. N12 —23Gb 41
Gartlet Rd. Wat —13Y 19
Gartmoor Gdns. SW19 —60Bb 103
Gartmore Rd. Ilf —33Vc 67
Garton La. S Ock —44Vd 90
Garton Pl. SW18 —58Eb 103
Gartons Clo. Enf —14Yb 26
Garvary Rd. E16 —44Kc 85
Garvock Dri. Sev —98Jd 186
Garway Rd. W2 —44Db 81
Gascoigne Gdns. Wfd G —24Gc 45
Gascoigne Pl. E2 —41Vb 83 (4K 195)
Gascoigne Rd. Bark —39Sc 66
Gascoigne Rd. New Ad —82Ec 166
Gascoigne Rd. Wey —76R 140
Gascon's Gro. Slou —2E 72
Gascony Av. NW6 —38Cb 61
Gascoyne Clo. Pot B —4Wa 8
Gascoyne Clo. Romf —24Md 49
Gascoyne Dri. Dart —55Hd 110
Gascoyne Ho. E9 —38Ac 64
Gascoyne Rd. E9 —38Zb 64
Gaselee St. E14 —45Ec 84
Gasholder Pl. SE11 —50Pb 82
Gaskarth Rd. SW12 —58Kb 104
Gaskarth Rd. Edgw —25Sa 39
Gaskell La. Ger X —22B 34
Gaskell Rd. N6 —30Hb 41
Gaskell St. SW4 —54Nb 104
Gaskin St. N1 —39Rb 63
Gaspar Clo. SW5 —49Db 81
(off Courtfield Gdns.)
Gaspar M. SW5 —49Db 81
Gassiot Rd. SW17 —63Hb 125
Gassiot Way. Sutt —76Fb 145
Gasson Rd. Swans —58Ae 113
Gastein Rd. W6 —51Za 102
Gaston Bell Clo. Rich —55Pa 101
Gaston Bri. Rd. Shep —72T 140
Gaston Rd. Mitc —69Jb 126
Gaston Way. Shep —71T 140
Gatcombe Ct. Beck —66Cc 128
Gatcombe Rd. N19 —34Mb 62
Gateacre Ct. Sidc —63Xc 131
Gate Cen., The. Bren —52Ja 100
Gate Clo. Borwd —11Sa 21
Gate End. N'wd —24W 36
Gateforth St. NW8 —42Gb 81 (6D 190)
Gatehill Rd. N'wd —24V 36
Gatehope Dri. S Ock —44Vd 90
Gatehouse Clo. King T —66Sa 123
Gatehouse Sq. SE1
(off Porter St.) —46Sb 83 (6E 200)
Gateley Rd. SW9 —55Pb 104
Gate M. SW7 —47Gb 81 (2E 202)
(off Rutland Ga.)
Gates. NW9 —26Va 40
Gatesborough St. EC2 —42Ub 83 (5H 195)
Gates Ct. SE17 —50Sb 83 (7D 206)
Gatesden. WC1 —41Nb 82 (4G 193)
Gatesden Rd. Fet —95Ea 176
Gates Grn. Rd. W Wick —76Hc 149
Gateshead Rd. Borwd —12Pa 21
Gateside Rd. SW17 —62Hb 125
Gatestone Rd. SE19 —65Ub 127
Gate St. WC2 —44Pb 82 (2H 199)
Gateway. SE17 —51Sb 105
Gateway. Wey —76R 140
Gateway Clo. N'wd —23S 36
Gateway Ho. Bark —39Sc 66
Gateway M. E8 —36Vb 63
Gateway Pde. Grav —3H 137
Gateways Ct. Wall —78Kb 146
Gateways, The. SW3 —50Gb 81 (7E 202)
(off Sprimont Pl.)
Gateway, The. Wok —86E 156
Gateway Trading Est. NW10 —41Va 80
Gatewick Clo. Slou —6J 73
Gatfield Gro. Felt —61Ca 121
Gatfield Ho. Felt —61Ca 121
Gathorne Rd. N22 —25Qb 42
Gathorne St. E2 —40Zb 64
Gatley Av. Eps —78Ra 143
Gatliff Rd. SW1 —50Kb 82 (7K 203)
Gatling Rd. SE2 —50Wc 87
Gatling Clo. Edgw —24Sa 39
Gatting Way. Uxb —37N 55
Gattis Wharf. N1 —40Nb 62 (1G 193)
(off New Wharf Rd.)
Gatton Bottom. Reig —100Eb 179
Gatton Clo. Sutt —81Db 163
Gatton Rd. SW17 —63Gb 125
Gattons Way. Sidc —63Bd 131
Gatward Clo. N21 —16Rb 25
Gatward Grn. N9 —19Vb 25
Gatwick Rd. SW18 —59Bb 103
Gatwick Rd. Grav —2D 136
Gatwick Way. Horn —35Pd 69
Gauden Clo. SW4 —55Mb 104
Gauden Rd. SW4 —54Mb 104
Gauntlet. NW9 —26Va 40
(off Five Acre)
Gauntlet Cres. Kenl —92Tb 181
Gauntlett Clo. N'holt —38Aa 57
Gauntlett Ct. Wemb —36Ka 58
Gauntlett Rd. Sutt —78Fb 145
Gaunt St. SE1 —48Sb 83 (3D 206)
Gautrey Rd. SE15 —54Yb 106
Gautrey Sq. E6 —44Pc 86
Gavell Rd. Cob —85W 158
Gavel St. SE17 —49Tb 83 (5G 207)
Gavenney Path. S Ock —44Vd 90
Gaveston Clo. Byfl —85P 157
Gavestone Cres. SE12 —59Kc 107
Gavestone Rd. SE12 —59Kc 107
Gaveston Rd. Lea —92Ja 176
Gaveston Rd. Slou —1D 72
Gaviller Pl. E5 —35Xb 63
Gavina Clo. Mord —71Gb 145
Gaviots Clo. Ger X —32B 54
Gaviots Grn. Ger X —31A 54
Gaviots Way. Ger X —31A 54
Gawber St. E2 —41Yb 84
Gawsworth Clo. E15 —36Hc 65
Gawthorne Av. NW7 —22Ab 40
Gay Clo. NW2 —36Xa 60
Gaydon La. NW9 —25Ua 40
Gayfere Rd. Eps —78Wa 144
Gayfere Rd. Ilf —27Pc 46
Gayfere St. SW1 —48Nb 82 (4F 205)
Gayford Rd. W12 —47Va 80
Gay Gdns. Dag —35Ed 68
Gay Ho. N16 —36Ub 63
Gayhurst Rd. E8 —38Wb 63
Gaylor Rd. N'holt —36Ba 57
Gaylor Rd. Til —3B 114
Gaynes Ct. Upm —35Rd 69
Gaynesford Rd. SE23 —61Zb 128
Gaynesford Rd. Cars —80Hb 145
Gaynes Hill Rd. Wfd G —23Nc 46
Gaynes Pk. Rd. Upm —35Qd 69
Gaynes Rd. Upm —33Rd 69
Gay Rd. E15 —40Fc 65
Gaysham Av. Ilf —29Qc 46
Gaysham Hall. Ilf —27Rc 46
Gaysley Ho. SE11 —49Qb 82 (6K 205)
(off Hotspur St.)
Gay St. SW15 —55Za 102
Gayton Ct. Harr —30Ha 38
Gayton Cres. NW3 —35Fb 61
Gayton Rd. NW3 —35Fb 61
Gayton Rd. SE2 —48Yc 87
Gayton Rd. Harr —30Ha 38
Gayville Rd. SW11 —58Hb 103
Gaywood Av. Chesh —2Zb 12
Gaywood Clo. SW2 —60Pb 104
Gaywood Rd. E17 —27Cc 44
Gaywood Rd. Asht —90Pa 161
Gaywood St. SE1 —48Rb 83 (4C 206)
Gaza St. SE17 —50Rb 83 (7B 206)
Gazelle Glade. Grav —4H 137
Geariesville Gdns. Ilf —28Rc 46
Geary Ct. Brtwd —18Yd 32
Geary Dri. Brtwd —18Yd 32
Geary Rd. NW10 —36Wa 60
Geary St. N7 —36Pb 62
Geddes Pl. Bexh —56Cd 110
Geddes Rd. Bush —14Ea 20
Geddy Ct. Romf —28Kd 49
Gedeney Rd. N17 —25Sb 43
Gedling Pl. SE1 —48Vb 83 (3K 207)
Geere Rd. E15 —39Hc 65
Geerings. The. Corr —1P 93
Gees Ct. W1 —44Jb 82 (3J 197)
Gee St. EC1 —42Sb 83 (5D 194)
Geffery's Ct. SE9 —62Nc 130
Geffrye Ct. N1 —40Ub 63 (2J 195)
Geffrye Est. N1 —40Ub 63 (2J 195)
Geffrye St. E2 —40Vb 63 (1K 195)
Geisthorp Ct. Wal A —5Jc 13
Geldart Rd. SE15 —52Xb 105
Geldeston Rd. E5 —33Wb 63
Gellatly Rd. SE14 —54Yb 106
Gell Clo. Uxb —34P 55
Gelsthorpe Rd. Romf —24Dd 48
Gemini Bus. Cen. E16 —42Fc 85
Gemini Gro. N'holt —41Aa 77
General Gordon Pl. SE18 —49Rc 86
General's Wlk., The. Enf —9Ac 12
General Wolfe Rd. SE10 —53Fc 107
Genesta Glade. Grav —4J 137
Genesta Rd. SE18 —51Rc 108
Geneva Clo. Shep —60U 120
Geneva Dri. SW9 —56Qb 104
Geneva Gdns. Romf —29Ad 47
Geneva Rd. King T —70Na 123
Geneva Rd. T Hth —71Sb 147
Genever Clo. E4 —22Cc 44
Genista Rd. N18 —22Xb 43
Genoa Av. SW15 —57Xa 102
Genoa Rd. SE20 —67Yb 128
Genotin Rd. Enf —13Tb 25
Genotin Ter. Enf —14Tb 25
Gentian Row. SE13 —53Ec 106
Gentlemans Row. Enf —13Sb 25
Gentry Clo. Stanf —1L 93
Gentry Gdns. E13 —41Jc 85
Geoffrey Av. Romf —23Qd 49
Geoffrey Clo. SE5 —54Sb 105
Geoffrey Ct. SE4 —55Bc 106
Geoffrey Gdns. E6 —40Nc 66
Geoffrey Jones Ct. NW10 —39Wa 60
Geoffrey Rd. SE4 —55Bc 106
George Beard Rd. SE8 —49Bc 84
George & Catherine Wheel All. EC2 —43Ub 83 (7J 195)
George Comberton Wlk. E12 —36Qc 66
George Ct. WC2 —45Nb 82 (5G 199)
(off John Adam St.)
George Cres. N10 —24Jb 42
George Crooks Ho. Grays
(off New Rd.) —51De 113
George Downing Est. N16 —33Vb 63
George V Av. Pinn —26Ba 37
George V Clo. Pinn —27Ca 37
George V Way. Gnfd —39Ka 58
George V Way. Sarr —8K 3
George Grn. Dri. G Grn —44A 74
George Grn. Rd. G Grn —4P 73
George Gro. Rd. SE20 —67Wb 127
George Inn Yd. SE1 —46Tb 83 (7F 201)
Georgelands. Rip —93K 173
George La. E18 —26Jc 45
George La. SE13 —58Dc 106
George La. Brom —74Kc 149
George Lansbury Ho. N22 —25Qb 42
(off Progress Way)
George M. NW1 —41Lb 82 (4C 192)
(off N. Gower St.)
George Pl. N17 —27Ub 43
George Rd. E4 —23Cc 44
George Rd. King T —66Ra 123
George Rd. N Mald —70Va 124
George Row. SE16 —47Wb 83
Georges Clo. Orp —69Yc 131
Georges Dri. Pil H —15Vd 32
Georges Mead. Els —16Na 21
George Sq. SW19 —69Cb 125
George's Rd. N7 —36Pb 62
George's Rd. Tats —92Mc 183
George's Sq. SW6 —51Bb 103
(off N. End Rd.)
Georges Ter. Cat —94Tb 181
George St. E16 —44Hc 85
George St. W1 —44Hb 81 (2F 197)
George St. W7 —46Ga 78
George St. Bark —38Sc 66
George St. Croy —75Sb 147
George St. Grays —51Ce 113
George St. Houn —54Ba 99
George St. Rich —57Ma 101
George St. Romf —30Hd 48
George St. S'hall —49Aa 77
George St. Stai —63H 119
George St. Uxb —38M 55
George St. Wat —14Y 19
George Tilbury Ho. Grays —7D 92
Georgetown Clo. SE19 —64Ub 127
Georgette Pl. SE10 —52Ec 106
Georgeville Gdns. Ilf —28Rc 46
George Wyver Clo. SW19 —59Ab 102
George Yd. EC3 —44Tb 83 (3G 201)
George Yd. W1 —45Jb 82 (4J 197)
Georgiana St. NW1 —39Lb 62
Georgian Clo. Brom —74Kc 149
Georgian Clo. Stai —63K 119
Georgian Clo. Stan —24Ja 38
Georgian Clo. Uxb —35N 55
Georgian Ct. N3 —25Bb 41
Georgian Ct. NW4 —29Xa 40
Georgian Ct. SW16 —63Nb 126
Georgian Ct. New Bar —14Eb 23
Georgian Ct. Wemb —37Qa 59
Georgian Way. Harr —33Fa 58
Georgia Rd. N Mald —70Sa 123
Georgia Rd. T Hth —67Rb 127
Georgina Gdns. E2 —41Vb 83 (3K 195)
Geraint Rd. Brom —63Jc 129
Geraldine Rd. SW18 —57Eb 103
Geraldine Rd. W4 —51Qa 101
Geraldine St. SE11 —48Rb 83 (4B 206)
Gerald M. SW1 —49Jb 82 (5J 203)
(off Gerald Rd.)
Gerald Rd. E16 —42Hc 85
Gerald Rd. SW1 —49Jb 82 (5J 203)
Gerald Rd. Dag —32Bd 67
Gerald Rd. Grav —9G 114
Geralds Gro. Bans —86Za 162
Gerard Av. Houn —59Ca 99
Gerard Gdns. Rain —40Gd 68
Gerard Rd. SW13 —53Va 102
Gerard Rd. Harr —30Ja 38
Gerda Rd. SE9 —61Sc 130
Gerdview Dri. Dart —63Ld 133
Germander Way. E15 —41Gc 85
Gernon Clo. Rain —40Md 69
Gernon Rd. E3 —40Ac 64
Geron Way. NW2 —33Xa 60
Gerpins La. Upm —40Pd 69
Gerrard Cres. Brtwd —20Yd 32
Gerrard Gdns. Pinn —29W 36
Gerrard Pl. W1 —45Mb 82 (4E 198)
Gerrard Rd. N1 —40Rb 63 (1B 194)
Gerrards Clo. N14 —15Lb 24
Gerrards Ct. W5 —48Ma 79
Gerrards Cross Rd. Stoke P —7L 53
Gerrards Mead. Bans —88Bb 163
Gerrard St. W1 —45Mb 82 (4D 198)
Gerridge St. SE1 —48Qb 82 (3A 206)
Gerry Raffles Sq. E15 —38Fc 65
Gertrude Rd. Belv —49Cd 88
Gertrude St. SW10 —51Eb 103
Gervase Clo. Wemb —34Sa 59
Gervase Rd. Edgw —25Sa 39
Gervase St. SE15 —52Xb 105
Gews Corner. Chesh —1Zb 12
Ghent St. SE6 —61Cc 128
Ghent Way. E8 —37Vb 63
Giant Arches Rd. SE24 —59Sb 105
Giant Tree Hill. Bush —18Fa 20
Gibbins Rd. E15 —38Ec 64
(in three parts)
Gibbon Rd. SE15 —54Yb 106
Gibbon Rd. W3 —45Ua 80
Gibbon Rd. King T —67Na 123
Gibbons Clo. Borwd —11Na 21
Gibbon's Rents. SE1 —46Ub 83 (7H 201)
(off Magdalen St.)
Gibbons Rd. NW10 —37Ua 60
Gibbon Wlk. SW15 —56Wa 102
Gibbs Av. SE19 —64Tb 127
Gibbs Clo. SE19 —64Tb 127
Gibbs Clo. Chesh —1Zb 12
Gibbs Couch. Wat —20Ba 19
Gibbs Grn. W14 —50Bb 81
Gibbs Grn. Edgw —22Sa 39
Gibb's Rd. N18 —21Yb 44
Gibbs Sq. SE19 —64Tb 127
Gibraltar Clo. Gt War —23Yd 50
Gibraltar Cres. Eps —82Ua 162
Gibraltar Wlk. E2 —41Vb 83
Gibson Clo. E1 —42Yb 84
Gibson Clo. Chess —78La 142
Gibson Clo. Grav —2B 136
Gibson Clo. Iswth —55Ga 100
Gibson Ct. Dat —50B 74
Gibson Ct. Hin W —76Ha 142
Gibson Gdns. N16 —33Vb 63
Gibson Ho. Sutt —77Cb 145
Gibson Pl. Stai —58L 97
Gibson Rd. SE11 —49Pb 82 (6J 205)
Gibson Rd. Dag —32Yc 67
Gibson Rd. Sutt —78Db 145
Gibson Rd. Uxb —35P 55
Gibsons Hill. SW16 —66Qb 126
Gibson Sq. N1 —39Qb 62
Gibson St. SE10 —50Gc 85
Gidd Hill. Coul —88Jb 164
Gidea Av. Romf —27Jd 48
Gidea Clo. Romf —27Jd 48
Gidea Clo. S Ock —40Yd 70
Gideon Clo. Belv —49Dd 88
Gideon Rd. SW11 —55Jb 104
Gideons Way. Stanf —1M 93
Giesbach Rd. N19 —33Mb 62
Giffard Rd. N18 —23Ub 43
Giffin St. SE8 —52Cc 106
Gifford Gdns. W7 —43Fa 78
Gifford Pl. War —22Zd 51
Giffords Cross Rd. Corr —1P 93
Giffordside. Grays —10D 92
Gifford St. N1 —38Nb 62
Gift La. E15 —39Hc 65
Giggs Hill. Orp —68Wc 131
Giggshill Gdns. Th Dit —74Ja 142
Giggshill Rd. Th Dit —73Ja 142
Gilbert Bri. EC2 —43Sb 83 (1E 200)
(off Barbican)
Gilbert Clo. SE3 —53Pc 108
Gilbert Clo. SW19 —67Db 125
(off High Path)
Gilbert Clo. Swans —58Zd 113
Gilbert Gro. Edgw —25Ta 39
Gilbert Ho. E17 —27Ec 44
Gilbert Ho. EC2 —43Sb 83 (7E 194)
(off Barbican)
Gilbert Pl. WC1 —43Nb 82 (1F 199)
Gilbert Rd. SE11 —49Qb 82 (6A 206)
Gilbert Rd. SW19 —66Eb 125
Gilbert Rd. Belv —48Cd 88
Gilbert Rd. Brom —66Jc 129
Gilbert Rd. Hare —26M 35
Gilbert Rd. Pinn —28Z 37
Gilbert Rd. Romf —28Hd 48
Gilbert St. E15 —35Gc 65
Gilbert St. W1 —44Jb 82 (3J 197)
Gilbert St. Enf —9Yb 12
Gilbert St. Houn —55Ea 100
Gilbey Clo. Uxb —35R 56
Gilbey Rd. SW17 —63Gb 125
Gilbourne Rd. SE18 —51Vc 109
Gilda Av. Enf —15Ac 26
Gilda Cres. N16 —32Wb 63
Gildea St. W1 —43Kb 82 (1A 198)
Gilden Cres. NW5 —36Jb 62
Gildenhill Rd. Swan —66Ld 133
Gilders Rd. Chess —80Pa 143
Giles Clo. Rain —40Md 69
Giles Coppice. SE19 —63Vb 127
Giles Hollow. Rad —8Ha 6
Giles Ho. SE16 —48Wb 83
(off Jamaica Rd.)
Gilesmead. SE5 —53Tb 105
Giles Travers Clo. Egh —69E 118
Gilfrid Clo. Uxb —44R 76
Gilhams Av. Bans —84Za 162
Gilkes Cres. SE21 —58Ub 105
Gilkes Pl. SE21 —58Ub 105
Gillam Way. Rain —37Jd 68
Gillan Grn. Bush —19Ea 20
Gill Av. E16 —44Jc 85
Gill Cres. Grav —2B 136
Gillender St. E3 & E14 —42Ec 84
Gillespie Rd. N5 —34Qb 62
Gillett Av. E6 —40Nc 66
Gillett Pl. N16 —36Ub 63
Gillett Rd. T Hth —70Tb 127
Gillett St. N16 —36Ub 63
Gillham Ter. N17 —23Wb 43
Gilliam Gro. Purl —82Qb 164
Gillian Cres. Romf —26Ld 49
Gillian Ho. Har W —23Ga 38
Gillian Pk. Rd. Sutt —74Bb 145
Gillian St. SE13 —57Dc 106
Gilliat Rd. Slou —5J 73
Gillies Rd. W King —78Ud 154
Gillies St. NW5 —36Jb 62
Gilling Ct. NW3 —37Gb 61
Gillingham M. SW1 —49Lb 82 (5B 204)
Gillingham Rd. NW2 —34Ab 60
Gillingham Rd. SW1 —49Lb 82
Gillingham Row. SW1 —49Lb 82 (5B 204)
Gillingham St. SW1 —49Lb 82 (5B 204)
Gillison Wlk. SE16 —48Xb 83
Gillman Dri. E15 —39Hc 65
Gillmans Rd. Orp —74Xc 151
Gills Hill. Rad —7Ha 6
Gills Hill La. Rad —8Ha 6
Gills Rd. S Dar —67Ud 134
Gill St. E14 —44Bc 84
Gillum Way. Barn —18Hb 23
Gilmais. Bookh —97Ea 176
Gilman Cres. Wind —5B 94
Gilmore Clo. Slou —7N 73
Gilmore Clo. Uxb —34Q 56
Gilmore Ct. N11 —22Hb 41
Gilmore Cres. Ashf —64Q 120
Gilmore Rd. SE13 —56Fc 107
Gilmour Clo. Enf —7Wb 11
Gilpin Av. SW14 —56Ta 101
Gilpin Clo. Mitc —68Gb 125
Gilpin Cres. N18 —22Vb 43
Gilpin Cres. Twic —59Da 99
Gilpin Rd. E5 —35Ac 64
Gilpin Way. Hay —52T 98
Gilroy Clo. Rain —37Hd 68
Gilroy Way. Orp —73Xc 151
Gilsland. Wal A —7Gc 13
Gilsland Rd. T Hth —70Tb 127
Gilstead Ho. Bark —40Xc 67
Gilstead Rd. SW6 —54Db 103
Gilston Rd. SW10 —50Eb 81
Gilton Rd. SE6 —62Gc 129
Giltspur St. EC1 —44Rb 83 (2C 200)
Gilwell Clo. E4 —14Dc 26
Gilwell La. E4 —14Ec 26
Gippeswyck Clo. Pinn —25Z 37
Gipsy Corner. W3 —43Ta 79
Gipsy Hill. SE19 —63Ub 127
Gipsy La. SW15 —55Xa 102
Gipsy La. Grays —51Ee 113
Gipsy La. Wey —75R 140
Gipsy Rd. SE27 —63Sb 127
Gipsy Rd. Well —54Zc 109
Gipsy Rd. Gdns. SE27 —63Sb 127
Giralda Clo. E16 —43Mc 85
Giraud St. E14 —44Dc 84
Girdler's Rd. W14 —49Za 80
Girdlestone Wlk. N19 —33Lb 62
Girdwood Rd. SW18 —59Ab 102
Girling Way. Felt —55W 98
Gironde Rd. SW6 —52Bb 103
Girtin Rd. Bush —15Da 19
Girton Av. NW9 —27Qa 39
Girton Clo. N'holt —37Ea 58
Girton Ct. Chesh —2Ac 12
Girton Gdns. Croy —76Cc 148
Girton Rd. SE26 —64Zb 128
Girton Rd. N'holt —37Ea 58
Girton Vs. W10 —44Za 80
Girton Way. Crox —15S 18
Gisborne Gdns. Rain —41Hd 88
Gisburn Rd. N8 —28Pb 42
Gissing Wlk. N1 —38Qb 62
Given Wilson Wlk. E13 —40Hc 65
Givons Gro. Roundabout. Lea —96Ka 176
Glacier Way. Wemb —40Ma 59
Gladbeck Way. Enf —14Rb 25
Gladding Rd. E12 —35Mc 65
Glade Bus. Cen., The. W Thur —50Vd 90
Glade Clo. Surb —75Ma 143
Glade Ct. Ilf —26Pc 46
Glade Gdns. Croy —73Ac 148
Glade La. S'hall —47Da 77
Glade Rd. E12 —34Pc 66
Gladeside. N21 —16Pb 24
Gladeside. Croy —72Zb 148
Gladeside Clo. Chess —80Ma 143
Gladeside Ct. Warl —92Xb 181
Gladesmore Rd. N15 —30Vb 43
Glades Pl. Brom —68Jc 129
Glade Spur. Tad —93Db 179
Glades Shopping Cen., The. Brom —68Jc 129
Glades, The. Grav —5F 136
Gladeswood Rd. Belv —49Dd 88
Glade, The. N21 —17Pb 24
Glade, The. SE7 —52Lc 107
Glade, The. Brom —68Mc 129
Glade, The. Coul —90Rb 165
Glade, The. Croy —73Ac 148
Glade, The. Enf —12Qb 24
Glade, The. Eps —79Wa 144
Glade, The. Fet —94Da 175
Glade, The. Ger X —3P 53
Glade, The. Hut —18Ce 33
Glade, The. Ilf —25Pc 46
Glade, The. Sev —95Kd 187
Glade, The. Stai —66K 119
Glade, The. Sutt —81Ab 162
Glade, The. Tad —93Db 179
Glade, The. Upm —36Sd 70
Glade, The. W Byf —85K 157
Glade, The. W Wick —76Dc 148
Glade, The. Wfd G —20Kc 27
Gladeway, The. Wal A —5Fc 13
Gladiator St. SE23 —59Ac 106
Glading Ter. N16 —34Vb 63
Gladioli Clo. Hamp —65Ca 121
Gladsdale Dri. Pinn —28X 37
Gladsmuir Clo. W on T —75Y 141
Gladsmuir Rd. N19 —32Lb 62
Gladsmuir Rd. Barn —12Ab 22
Gladstone Av. E12 —38Nc 66
Gladstone Av. N22 —26Qb 42
Gladstone Av. Felt —58W 98
Gladstone Av. Twic —59Fa 100
Gladstone M. NW6 —38Bb 61
Gladstone M. SE20 —66Yb 128
Gladstone Pk. Gdns. NW2 —34Xa 60
Gladstone Pl. E3 —40Bc 64
Gladstone Pl. Barn —14Za 22
Gladstone Pl. E Mol —71Ga 142
Gladstone Rd. SW19 —66Cb 125
Gladstone Rd. W4 —48Ta 79
Gladstone Rd. Asht —90Ma 161
Gladstone Rd. Buck H —18Lc 27
Gladstone Rd. Croy —73Tb 147
Gladstone Rd. Dart —58Pd 111
Gladstone Rd. King T —69Qa 123
Gladstone Rd. Orp —78Sc 150
Gladstone Rd. S'hall —47Aa 77
Gladstone Rd. Surb —75Ma 143
Gladstone Rd. Wat —13Y 19
Gladstone St. SE1 —48Rb 83 (4B 206)
Gladstone Ter. SW8 —53Kb 104
Gladstone Way. Slou —6E 72
Gladstone Way. W'stone —27Ga 38
Gladwell Rd. N8 —30Pb 42
Gladwell Rd. Brom —65Jc 129
Gladwyn Rd. SW15 —55Za 102
Gladys Rd. NW6 —38Cb 61
Glaigmar Gdns. N3 —25Db 41
Glaisher St. SE10 —52Ec 106
Glaisyer Way. Iver —40F 54
Glamis Clo. Chesh —1Wb 11
Glamis Cres. Hay —48S 76
Glamis Dri. Horn —32Nd 69
Glamis Pl. E1 —45Zb 84
Glamis Rd. E1 —45Yb 84
Glamis Way. N'holt —37Ea 58
Glamorgan Clo. Mitc —69Nb 126
Glamorgan Rd. King T —66La 122
Glams Ct. W3 —47Ra 79
Glanfield Rd. Beck —70Bc 128
Glanleam Rd. Stan —21Ma 39
Glanmead. Shenf —18Ae 33
Glanmor Rd. Slou —5M 73
Glanthams Clo. Shenf —19Be 33
Glanthams Rd. Shenf —19Be 33
Glanty, The. Egh —63E 118
Glanville Dri. Horn —32Pd 69
Glanville Rd. SW2 —57Nb 104
Glanville Rd. Brom —69Kc 129
Glasbrook Av. Twic —60Ba 99
Glasbrook Rd. SE9 —59Mc 107
Glaserton Rd. N16 —31Ub 63
Glasford St. SW17 —65Hb 125
Glasfryn Ho. S Harr —33Fa 58
Glasgow Ho. W9 —40Db 61
(off Maida Vale)
Glasgow Rd. E13 —40Kc 65
Glasgow Rd. N18 —22Xb 43
Glasgow Rd. Slou —4E 72
Glasgow Ter. SW1 —50Lb 82 (7B 204)
Glasse Clo. W13 —45Ja 78
Glasshill St. SE1 —47Rb 83 (1C 206)
Glasshouse Fields. E1 —45Zb 84
Glasshouse St. W1 —45Lb 82 (5C 198)
Glasshouse Wlk. SE11 —50Pb 82 (7G 205)
Glasshouse Yd. EC1 —42Sb 83 (6D 194)
Glasslyn Rd. N8 —29Mb 42
Glassmill La. Brom —68Hc 129
(in two parts)
Glass St. E2 —42Xb 83
Glass Yd. SE18 —48Qc 86
Glastonbury Av. Wfd G —24Mc 45
Glastonbury Rd. N9 —18Wb 25
Glastonbury Rd. Mord —73Cb 145
Glastonbury St. NW6 —36Bb 61
Glaucus St. E3 —43Dc 84
Glazbury Rd. W14 —49Ab 80
Glazebrook Clo. SE21 —61Tb 127
Glazebrook Rd. Tedd —66Ha 122
Glebe Av. Enf —13Rb 25
Glebe Av. Harr —28Na 39
Glebe Av. Mitc —68Gb 125
Glebe Av. Ruis —37X 57
Glebe Av. Uxb —34S 56
Glebe Av. Wfd G —23Jc 45
Glebe Clo. W4 —50Ua 80
Glebe Clo. Bookh —98Ca 175
Glebe Clo. S Croy —83Vb 165
Glebe Clo. Uxb —35S 56
Glebe Cotts. Felt —62Ca 121
Glebe Ct. N13 —20Qb 24
Glebe Ct. W7 —45Fa 78
Glebe Ct. Mitc —69Hb 125
Glebe Ct. Sev —98Kd 187
Glebe Ct. Stan —22La 38
Glebe Cres. NW4 —27Ya 40
Glebe Cres. Harr —27Na 39
Glebefield, The. Sev —95Hd 186
Glebe Gdns. Byfl —86N 157
Glebe Gdns. Heron —24Fe 51
Glebe Gdns. N Mald —73Ua 144
Glebe Ho. Dri. Brom —74Kc 149
Glebe Hyrst. SE19 —63Ub 127
Glebe Hyrst. S Croy —84Vb 165
Glebelands. Chig —20Xc 29
Glebelands. Clay —81Ha 160
Glebelands. Dart —56Hd 110
Glebelands. W Mol —71Da 141
Glebelands Av. E18 —26Jc 45
Glebelands Av. Ilf —31Tc 66
Glebelands Clo. SE5 —55Ub 105
Glebelands Gdns. Shep —72S 140
Glebelands Rd. Felt —60W 98
Glebe La. Barn —15Wa 22
Glebe La. Harr —28Na 39
Glebe La. Sev —99Kd 187
Glebe Path. Mitc —69Hb 125
Glebe Pl. SW3 —51Gb 103
Glebe Pl. Hort K —70Sd 134
Glebe Rd. E8 —38Vb 63
Glebe Rd. N3 —25Eb 41
Glebe Rd. N8 —28Pb 42
Glebe Rd. NW10 —37Va 60
Glebe Rd. SW13 —54Wa 102
Glebe Rd. Asht —90Ma 161
Glebe Rd. Brom —67Jc 129
Glebe Rd. Cars —79Hb 145
Glebe Rd. Dag —37Dd 68
Glebe Rd. Egh —65E 118
Glebe Rd. Grav —10B 114
Glebe Rd. Hay —46V 76
Glebe Rd. Old Win —7M 95
Glebe Rd. Rain —41Ld 89
Glebe Rd. Stai —64K 119
Glebe Rd. Stan —22La 38
Glebe Rd. Sutt —81Ab 162
Glebe Rd. Uxb —40L 55
Glebe Rd. Warl —89Zb 166
Glebe Side. Twic —58Ha 100
Glebe Sq. Mitc —69Hb 125
Glebe St. W4 —50Ua 80
Glebe, The. SE3 —55Gc 107
Glebe, The. SW16 —63Nb 126
Glebe, The. Chst —67Sc 130

Glebe, The—Gordon St.

Glebe, The. K Lan —1Q 4
Glebe, The. Wat —5Z 5
Glebe, The. W Dray —49P 75
Glebe, The. Wor Pk —74Va 144
Glebe Way. Eri —51Gd 110
Glebe Way. Felt —62Ca 121
Glebe Way. Horn —31Nd 69
Glebe Way. S Croy —84Vb 165
Glebe Way. W Wick —75Ec 148
Glebe Way. Wfd G —22Lc 45
Gledhow Gdns. SW5 —49Eb 81 (6A 202)
Gledhow Wood. Tad —93Db 179
Gledstanes Rd. W14 —50Ab 80
Gledwood Av. Hay —43V 76
Gledwood Cres. Hay —43V 76
Gledwood Dri. Hay —43V 76
Gledwood Gdns. Hay —43V 76
Gleed Av. Bush —19Fa 20
Gleeson Dri. Orp —77Vc 151
Glegg Pl. SW15 —56Za 102
Glenaffric Av. E14 —49Ec 84
Glen Albyn Rd. SW19 —61Za 124
Glenalla Rd. Ruis —31V 56
Glenalmond Rd. Harr —28Na 39
Glenalvon Way. SE18 —49Nc 86
Glena Mt. Sutt —77Eb 145
Glenarm Rd. E5 —35Yb 64
Glen Av. Ashf —63Q 120
Glenavon Clo. Clay —79Ja 142
Glenavon Ct. Wor Pk —75Xa 144
Glenavon Gdns. Slou —9N 73
Glenavon Lodge. Beck —66Cc 128
Glenavon Rd. E15 —38Gc 65
Glenbarr Clo. SE9 —55Rc 108
Glenbow Rd. Brom —65Gc 129
Glenbrook N. Enf —14Pb 24
Glenbrook Rd. NW6 —36Cb 61
Glenbrook S. Enf —14Pb 24
Glenbuck Rd. Surb —72Ma 143
Glenburnie Rd. SW17 —62Hb 125
Glencairn Dri. W5 —42La 78
Glencairne Clo. E16 —43Mc 85
Glencairn Rd. SW16 —67Nb 126
Glen Clo. Shep —70Q 120
Glen Clo. Tad —95Ab 178
Glencoe Av. Ilf —31Tc 66
Glencoe Dri. Dag —35Cd 68
Glencoe Rd. Bush —16Ca 19
Glencoe Rd. Hay —42Z 77
Glencoe Rd. Wey —76Q 140
Glencourse Grn. Wat —21Z 37
Glen Ct. Add —78H 139
Glen Ct. Sidc —63Wc 131
Glen Ct. St J —7D 188
Glen Cres. Wfd G —23Kc 45
Glendale. Swan —71Hd 152
Glendale Av. N22 —24Qb 42
Glendale Av. Edgw —21Pa 39
Glendale Av. Romf —31Yc 67
Glendale Clo. SE9 —55Qc 108
Glendale Clo. Shenf —18Ae 33
Glendale Clo. Wok —6F 188
Glendale Dri. SW19 —64Bb 125
Glendale Gdns. Wemb —32Ma 59
Glendale M. Beck —67Dc 128
Glendale Rise. Kenl —87Rb 165
Glendale Rd. Eri —49Ed 88
Glendale Rd. Grav —3A 136
Glendale Wlk. Chesh —2Ac 12
Glendale Way. SE28 —45Yc 87
Glendall St. SW9 —56Pb 104
Glendarvon St. SW15 —55Za 102
Glendean Ct. Enf —8Bc 12
Glendene Av. E Hor —98U 174
Glendevon Clo. Edgw —20Ra 21
Glendish Rd. N17 —25Xb 43
Glendor Gdns. NW7 —21Ta 39
Glendower Cres. Orp —72Wc 151
Glendower Gdns. SW14 —55Ta 101
Glendower Pl. SW7 —49Fb 81 (5B 202)
Glendower Rd. E4 —18Fc 27
Glendower Rd. SW14 —55Ta 101
Glendown Ho. E8 —36Wb 63
Glendown Rd. SE2 —50Wc 87
Glen Dunlop Ho., The. Sev —94Ld 187
Glendun Rd. W3 —45Ua 80
Gleneagle M. SW16 —64Mb 126
Gleneagle Rd. SW16 —64Mb 126
Gleneagles. Stan —24Ka 38
Gleneagles Clo. Orp —74Tc 150
Gleneagles Clo. Romf —24Pd 49
Gleneagles Clo. Stai —58M 97
Gleneagles Clo. Wat —21Z 37
Gleneagles Grn. Orp —74Tc 150
Gleneldon M. SW16 —63Nb 126
Gleneldon Rd. SW16 —63Nb 126
Glenelg Rd. SW2 —57Nb 104
Glenesk Rd. SE9 —55Qc 108
Glenfarg Rd. SE6 —60Ec 106
Glenfield Cres. Ruis —31T 56
Glenfield Rd. SW12 —60Lb 104
Glenfield Rd. W13 —47Ka 78
Glenfield Rd. Ashf —65R 120
Glenfield Rd. Bans —87Db 163
Glenfield Ter. W13 —47Ka 78
Glenfinlas Way. SE5 —52Rb 105
Glenforth St. SE10 —50Hc 85
Glengall Gro. E14 —48Dc 84
Glengall Rd. NW6 —39Bb 61
Glengall Rd. SE15 —50Vb 83
Glengall Rd. Bexh —55Ad 109
Glengall Rd. Edgw —20Ra 21
Glengall Rd. Wfd G —23Jc 45
Glengall Ter. SE15 —51Vb 105
Glen Gdns. Croy —76Qb 146
Glengarnock Av. E14 —49Ec 84
Glengarry Rd. SE22 —57Ub 105
Glenham Dri. Ilf —29Rc 46
Glenhaven Av. Borwd —13Qa 21
Glenhead Clo. SE9 —55Rc 108
Glenheadon Clo. Lea —95Ma 177
Glenheadon Rise. Lea —95Ma 177
Glenhill Clo. N3 —26Cb 41
Glen Ho. E16 —46Qc 86
(off Storey St.)
Glenhouse Rd. SE9 —57Qc 108
Glenhurst. Beck —67Ec 128
Glenhurst Av. NW5 —35Jb 62
Glenhurst Av. Bex —60Bd 109
Glenhurst Av. Ruis —31S 56
Glenhurst Rise. SE19 —66Sb 127
Glenhurst Rd. N12 —22Fb 41
Glenhurst Rd. Bren —51La 100
Glenilla Rd. NW3 —37Gb 61
Glenister Pk. Rd. SW16 —66Mb 126
Glenister Rd. SE10 —50Hc 85
Glenister St. E16 —46Qc 86
Glenlea Rd. SE9 —57Pc 108
Glenloch Rd. NW3 —37Gb 61
Glenloch Rd. Enf —12Yb 26
Glenluce Rd. SE3 —51Jc 107
Glenlyon Rd. SE9 —57Qc 108
Glenmead. Buck H —18Lc 27
Glenmere Av. NW7 —23Wa 40
Glenmill. Hamp —64Ba 121
Glenmore Clo. Add —76K 139
Glenmore Lodge. Beck —67Dc 128
Glenmore Pde. Wemb —39Na 59
Glenmore Rd. NW3 —37Gb 61
Glenmore Rd. Well —52Vc 109
Glenmore Way. Bark —40Wc 67
Glenmount Path. SE18 —50Sc 86
Glenn Av. Purl —83Rb 165
Glennie Rd. SE27 —62Qb 126
Glenny Rd. Bark —37Sc 66
Glenorchy Clo. Hay —43Aa 77
Glenparke Rd. E7 —37Kc 65
Glen Rise. Wfd G —23Kc 45
Glen Rd. E13 —42Lc 85
Glen Rd. E17 —29Bc 44
Glen Rd. Chess —77Pa 143
Glen Rd. End. Wall —81Kb 164
Glenrosa Gdns. Grav —4J 137
Glenrosa St. SW6 —54Eb 103
Glenrose Ct. Sidc —64Xc 131
Glenroy St. W12 —44Ya 80
Glensdale Rd. SE4 —55Bc 106
Glenshaw Mans. SW9 —52Qb 104
(off Brixton Rd.)
Glenshee Clo. N'wd —23S 36
Glenshiel Rd. SE9 —57Qc 108
Glenside. Chig —23Rc 46
Glentanner Way. SW17 —62Fb 125
Glentham Gdns. SW13 —51Xa 102
Glentham Rd. SW13 —51Wa 102
Glen, The. Add —78H 139
Glen, The. Brom —68Gc 129
Glen, The. Croy —76Zb 148
Glen, The. Eastc —29X 37
Glen, The. Enf —14Rb 25
Glen, The. N'wd —24T 36
Glen, The. Orp —76Qc 150
Glen, The. Pinn —31Aa 57
Glen, The. Rain —42Ld 89
Glen, The. Slou —9N 73
Glen, The. S'hall —50Ba 77
Glen, The. Stanf —1P 93
Glen, The. Wemb —35Ma 59
Glenthorne Av. Croy —74Yb 148
Glenthorne Clo. Sutt —74Cb 145
Glenthorne Clo. Uxb —41Q 76
Glenthorne Gdns. Ilf —27Rc 46
Glenthorne Gdns. Sutt —74Cb 145
Glenthorne M. W6 —49Xa 80
Glenthorne Rd. E17 —29Ac 44
Glenthorne Rd. N11 —22Hb 41
Glenthorne Rd. W6 —49Xa 80
Glenthorne Rd. King T —70Pa 123
Glenthorpe Rd. Mord —71Za 144
Glenton Clo. Romf —24Gd 48
Glenton Rd. SE13 —56Gc 107
Glenton Way. Romf —24Gd 48
Glentrammon Av. Orp —79Vc 151
Glentrammon Clo. Orp —78Vc 151
Glentrammon Gdns. Orp —79Vc 151
Glentrammon Rd. Orp —79Vc 151
Glentworth St. NW1 —42Hb 81 (6G 191)
Glenure Rd. SE9 —57Qc 108
Glenview. SE2 —51Zc 109
Glen View. Grav —10E 114
Glenview Rd. Brom —68Mc 129
Glenville Av. Enf —10Sb 11
Glenville Gro. SE8 —52Bc 106
Glenville M. SW18 —59Db 103
Glenville Rd. King T —67Qa 123
Glen Wlk. Iswth —57Fa 100
Glen Way. Wat —10U 4
Glenwood Av. NW9 —32Ua 60
Glenwood Av. Rain —42Jd 88
Glenwood Clo. Harr —29Ha 38
Glenwood Ct. E18 —27Jc 45
Glenwood Ct. Sidc —63Wc 131
Glenwood Dri. Romf —29Jd 48
Glenwood Gdns. Ilf —29Qc 46
Glenwood Gro. NW9 —32Sa 59
Glenwood Rd. N15 —29Rb 43
Glenwood Rd. NW7 —20Ua 22
Glenwood Rd. SE6 —60Cc 106
Glenwood Rd. Eps —79Wa 144
Glenwood Rd. Houn —55Fa 100
Glenwood Way. Croy —72Zb 148
Glenworth Av. E14 —49Fc 85
Glenworth Pl. Slou —6G 72
Gliddon Rd. W14 —49Ab 80
Glimpsing Grn. Eri —48Ad 87
Glisson Rd. Uxb —40Q 56
Gload Cres. Orp —75Zc 151
Global App. E3 —40Ec 64
Globe Pond Rd. SE16 —46Ac 84
Globe Rd. E2 & E1 —41Yb 84
(in two parts)
Globe Rd. E15 —36Hc 65
Globe Rd. Horn —30Jd 48
Globe Rd. Wfd G —23Lc 45
Globe Stairs. SE16 —46Zb 84
Globe St. SE1 —48Tb 83 (3F 207)
Globe Ter. E2 —41Yb 84
Globe Town Mkt. E2 —41Zb 84
Globe Yd. W1 —44Kb 82 (3K 197)
(off S. Molton St.)
Glossop Rd. S Croy —81Tb 165
Gloster Rd. N Mald —70Ua 124
Gloster Rd. Wok —92C 172
Gloucester Av. NW1 —38Jb 62
Gloucester Av. E Til —10L 93
Gloucester Av. Grays —47Ee 91
Gloucester Av. Horn —28Qd 49
Gloucester Av. Sidc —61Uc 130
Gloucester Av. Slou —3G 72
Gloucester Av. Wal X —5Ac 12
Gloucester Av. Well —56Vc 109
Gloucester Cir. SE10 —52Ec 106
Gloucester Clo. NW10 —38Ta 59
Gloucester Clo. S Ock —41Yd 90
Gloucester Clo. Th Dit —74Ja 142
Gloucester Ct. EC3 —45Ub 83 (5J 201)
Gloucester Ct. NW11 —31Bb 61
(off Golders Grn. Rd.)
Gloucester Ct. Harr —27Ga 38
Gloucester Ct. Mitc —71Nb 146
Gloucester Ct. Rich —52Qa 101
Gloucester Ct. Til —4B 114
Gloucester Cres. NW1 —39Kb 62
Gloucester Cres. Stai —65M 119
Gloucester Dri. N4 —33Rb 63
Gloucester Dri. NW11 —28Cb 41
Gloucester Dri. Stai —62E 118
Gloucester Gdns. W2 —44Eb 81
Gloucester Gdns. Barn —14Jb 24
Gloucester Gdns. Ilf —31Nc 66
Gloucester Gdns. Sutt —75Db 145
Gloucester Ga. NW1 —40Kb 62 (1K 191)
Gloucester Ga. M. NW1 —40Kb 62 (1K 191)
Gloucester Gro. Edgw —25Ta 39
Gloucester Ho. SW9 —52Qb 104
Gloucester Ho. Borwd —12Qa 21
Gloucester Ho. Rich —57Qa 101
Gloucester M. E10 —31Cc 64
Gloucester M. W2 —44Eb 81 (3A 196)
Gloucester M. W. W2 —44Eb 81 (3A 196)
Gloucester Pde. Sidc —57Wc 109
Gloucester Pl. NW1 & W1 —42Hb 81 (5F 191)
Gloucester Pl. Wind —4H 95
Gloucester Pl. M. W1 —43Hb 81 (1G 197)
Gloucester Rd. E10 —31Cc 64
Gloucester Rd. E11 —29Kc 45
Gloucester Rd. E12 —34Pc 66
Gloucester Rd. E17 —26Zb 44
Gloucester Rd. N17 —26Tb 43
Gloucester Rd. N18 —22Vb 43
Gloucester Rd. SW7 —48Eb 81 (3A 202)
Gloucester Rd. W3 —47Sa 79
Gloucester Rd. W5 —47La 78
Gloucester Rd. Barn —15Db 23
Gloucester Rd. Belv —50Bd 87
Gloucester Rd. Croy —73Tb 147
Gloucester Rd. Dart —59Kd 111
Gloucester Rd. Enf —10Sb 11
Gloucester Rd. Felt —60Y 99
Gloucester Rd. Grav —3E 136
Gloucester Rd. Hamp —66Da 121
Gloucester Rd. Harr —29Da 37
Gloucester Rd. Houn —56Aa 99
Gloucester Rd. King T —68Qa 123
Gloucester Rd. Pil H —15Xd 32
Gloucester Rd. Rich —52Qa 101
Gloucester Rd. Romf —30Gd 48
Gloucester Rd. Tedd —64Ga 122
Gloucester Rd. Twic —60Ea 100
Gloucester Sq. E2 —39Wb 63
Gloucester Sq. W2 —44Fb 81 (3C 196)
Gloucester Sq. Wok —89A 156
Gloucester St. SW1 —50Lb 82 (7B 204)
Gloucester Ter. W2 —44Db 81
Gloucester Ter. Gdns. NW11 —31Bb 61
Gloucester Wlk. W8 —47Cb 81
Gloucester Wlk. Wok —89A 156
Gloucester Way. EC1 —41Qb 82 (4A 194)
Glover Dri. N18 —23Yb 44
Glover Ho. SE15 —56Xb 105
Glover Rd. Pinn —30Z 37
Glovers Gro. Ruis —31R 56
Gloxinia Rd. S'fleet —65De 135
Gloxinia Wlk. Hamp —65Ca 121
Glycena Rd. SW11 —55Hb 103
Glyn Av. Barn —14Fb 23
Glyn Clo. SE25 —68Ub 127
Glyn Clo. Eps —81Wa 162
Glyn Ct. SE27 —62Qb 126
Glyndale Grange. Sutt —79Db 145
Glyndebourne Pk. Orp —75Rc 150
Glynde M. SW3 —48Gb 81 (4E 202)
(off Walton St.)
Glynde Reach. WC1 —41Nb 82 (4G 193)
(off Harrison St.)
Glynde Rd. Bexh —55Zc 109
Glynde St. SE4 —58Bc 106
Glyndon Rd. SE18 —49Sc 86
Glyn Dri. Sidc —63Xc 131
Glynfield Rd. NW10 —38Ua 60
Glynne Rd. N22 —26Qb 42
Glyn Rd. E5 —34Zb 64
Glyn Rd. Enf —14Yb 26
Glyn Rd. Wor Pk —75Za 144
Glyn St. SE11 —50Pb 82
Glynswood. Ger X —24B 34
Glynwood Ct. SE23 —61Yb 128
Goater's All. SW6 —52Bb 103
(off Dawes Rd.)
Goat La. Enf —10Vb 11
Goat Rd. Mitc —73Jb 146
Goatsfield Rd. Tats —92Lc 183
Goat St. SE1 —47Vb 83 (1K 207)
(off Boss St.)
Goatswood La. Brtwd —17Kd 31
Goat Wharf. Bren —51Na 101
Gobions Av. Romf —24Fd 48
Gobions Way. Pot B —1Db 9
Godalming Av. Wall —78Nb 146
Godalming Rd. E14 —43Dc 84
Godbold Rd. E15 —42Gc 85
Goddard Clo. Shep —69P 119
Goddard Ct. W'stone —26Ja 38
Goddard Rd. Beck —70Zb 128
Goddard Rd. Grays —46Ce 91
Goddards Way. Ilf —32Tc 66
Goddarts Ho. E17 —27Cc 44
Goddington Chase. Orp —77Xc 151
Goddington La. Orp —76Yc 151
Godfrey Av. N'holt —39Aa 57
Godfrey Av. Twic —59Fa 100
Godfrey Hill. SE18 —49Nc 86
Godfrey Rd. SE18 —49Pc 86
Godfrey St. E15 —40Ec 64
Godfrey St. SW3 —50Gb 81 (7E 202)
Godfrey Way. Houn —59Ba 99
Goding St. SE11 —50Pb 82 (7G 205)
Godley Rd. SW18 —60Fb 103
Godley Rd. Byfl —86P 157
Godliman St. EC4 —44Rb 83 (3D 200)
Godman Rd. SE15 —54Xb 105
Godman Rd. Grays —8C 92
Godolphin Clo. N13 —23Rb 43
Godolphin Clo. Sutt —83Bb 163
Godolphin Pl. W3 —45Ta 79
Godolphin Rd. W12 —46Xa 80
Godolphin Rd. Slou —5H 73
Godolphin Rd. Wey —79T 140
Godric Cres. New Ad —82Fc 167
Godson Rd. Croy —76Qb 146
Godson St. N1 —40Qb 62 (1K 193)
Godstone By-Pass. God —100Yb 182
Godstone Hill. Cat & God —99Xb 181
Godstone Mt. Purl —84Rb 165
Godstone Rd. Cat —96Wb 181
Godstone Rd. Purl & Whyt —84Rb 165
Godstone Rd. Sutt —77Eb 145
Godstone Rd. Twic —58Ka 100
Godstow Rd. SE2 —47Yc 87
Godwin Clo. E4 —11Ec 26
Godwin Clo. N1 —40Sb 63 (1E 194)
Godwin Clo. Eps —79Sa 143
Godwin Rd. E7 —35Kc 65
Godwin Rd. Brom —69Lc 129
Goffers Rd. SE3 —53Gc 107
Goffs Cres. Chesh —1Sb 11
Goff's La. Chesh —1Sb 11
Goffs Oak Av. Chesh —1Rb 11
Goffs Rd. Ashf —65T 120
Gogmore Farm Clo. Cher —73H 139
Gogmore La. Cher —73J 139
Goidel Clo. Wall —77Mb 146
Golborne Gdns. W10 —42Ab 80
Golborne M. W10 —43Ab 80
Golborne Rd. W10 —43Ab 80
Goldace. Grays —51Be 113
Golda Clo. Barn —16Za 22
Goldbath St. SE13 —53Dc 106
Goldbeaters Gro. Edgw —23Ua 40
Goldbeaters Wlk. Wemb —34Sa 59
Goldcliffe Clo. Mord —73Cb 145
Goldcrest Clo. E16 —43Mc 85
Goldcrest Clo. SE28 —45Yc 87
Goldcrest M. W5 —43Ma 79
Goldcrest Way. Bush —18Ea 20
Goldcrest Way. New Ad —81Fc 167
Goldcrest Way. Purl —82Mb 164
Golden Ct. Barn —14Gb 23
Golden Ct. Rich —57Ma 101
Golden Cres. Hay —46V 76
Golden La. EC1 —42Sb 83 (5D 194)
Golden La. Est. EC1 —42Sb 83 (6D 194)
Golden Mnr. W7 —45Ga 78
Golden M. SE20 —67Yb 128
Golden Oak Clo. Farn C —7G 52
Golden Plover Clo. E16 —44Jc 85
Golden Sq. W1 —45Lb 82 (4C 198)
Golders Clo. Edgw —22Ra 39
Golders Ct. NW11 —31Bb 61
Golders Gdns. NW11 —31Ab 60
Golders Grn. Cres. NW11 —31Bb 61
Golders Grn. Rd. NW11 —30Ab 40
Golders Mnr. Dri. NW11 —30Za 40
Golders Pk. Clo. NW11 —32Cb 61
Golders Rise. NW4 —29Za 40
Golders Way. NW11 —31Bb 61
Golderton. NW4 —28Ya 40
(off Prince Of Wales Clo.)
Goldeslea. NW11 —32Cb 61
Goldfinch Clo. Orp —78Wc 151
Goldfinch Rd. SE28 —48Tc 86
Goldfinch Rd. S Croy —82Zb 166
Goldfinch Way. Borwd —14Qa 21
Goldfort Wlk. Wok —4B 188
Goldhawk Ind. Est., The. W6 —48Xa 80
Goldhawk M. W12 —47Xa 80
Goldhawk Rd. W6 & W12 —49Va 80
Goldhaze Clo. Wfd G —24Mc 45
Gold Hill. Edgw —23Ta 39
Gold Hill E. Ger X —25A 34
Goldhurst Ter. NW6 —38Db 61
Goldie Ho. N19 —31Mb 62
Golding Ct. Ilf —34Qc 66
Golding Cres. Stanf —1N 93
Goldingham Av. Lou —12Sc 28
Golding Rd. Sev —94Ld 187
Goldings Hill. Lou —8Pc 14
Goldings Rise. Lou —11Qc 28
Goldings Rd. Lou —11Qc 28
Goldings, The. Wok —4C 188
Golding St. E1 —44Wb 83
Goldington Cres. NW1 —40Mb 62 (1D 192)
Goldington St. NW1 —40Mb 62 (1D 192)
Gold La. Edgw —23Ta 39
Goldman Clo. E2 —42Wb 83
Goldney Rd. W9 —42Cb 81
Goldrings Rd. Oxs —85Ea 160
Goldsborough Cres. E4 —19Dc 26
Goldsborough Rd. SW8 —53Mb 104
Goldsdown Clo. Enf —12Ac 26
Goldsdown Rd. Enf —12Zb 26
Goldsel Rd. Swan —71Fd 152
Goldsmid St. SE18 —50Uc 86
Goldsmith Av. E12 —37Nc 66
Goldsmith Av. NW9 —29Ua 40
Goldsmith Av. W3 —45Ta 79
Goldsmith Av. Romf —31Cd 68
Goldsmith Clo. W3 —46Ta 79
Goldsmith Clo. Harr —32Da 57
Goldsmith La. NW9 —28Ra 39
Goldsmith Rd. E10 —32Cc 64
Goldsmith Rd. E17 —26Zb 44
Goldsmith Rd. N11 —22Hb 41
Goldsmith Rd. SE15 —53Wb 105
Goldsmith Rd. W3 —46Ta 79
Goldsmiths. Grays —51Be 113
Goldsmiths Av. Corr —1P 93
Goldsmith's Bldgs. W3 —46Ta 79
Goldsmiths Clo. Wok —6F 188
Goldsmith's Pl. NW6 —39Db 61
(off Springfield La.)
Goldsmith's Row. E2 —40Wb 63
Goldsmith's Sq. E2 —40Wb 63
Goldsmith St. EC2 —44Sb 83 (2E 200)
Gold St. Sole S & Ludd —10F 136
Goldsworth Orchard. Wok —6D 188
Goldsworth Pk. Trading Est. Wok —4E 188
Goldsworth Rd. Wok —6F 188
Goldsworthy Gdns. SE16 —50Yb 84
Goldsworthy Way. Slou —4A 72
Goldwell Ho. SE22 —55Ub 105
Goldwell Rd. T Hth —70Pb 126
Goldwin Clo. SE14 —53Yb 106
Goldwing Clo. E16 —44Jc 85
Golf Clo. Bush —13Z 19
Golf Clo. Stan —24La 38
Golf Clo. Wok —86G 156
Golf Club Dri. King T —66Ta 123
Golf Club Rd. Wey —81R 158
Golf Club Rd. Wok —8D 188
Golfe Rd. Ilf —34Tc 66
Golf Links Av. Grav —4D 136
Golf Ride. Enf —7Qb 10
Golf Rd. W5 —44Pa 79
Golf Rd. Brom —69Qc 130
Golf Rd. Kenl —90Tb 165
Golf Side. Sutt —83Ab 162
Golf Side. Twic —62Fa 122
Golfside Clo. N20 —20Gb 23
Golfside Clo. N Mald —68Ua 124
Goliath Clo. Wall —80Nb 146
Gollogly Ter. SE7 —50Lc 85
Gomer Gdns. Tedd —65Ja 122
Gomer Pl. Tedd —65Ja 122
Gomm Rd. SE16 —48Yb 84
Gomshall Av. Wall —78Nb 146
Gomshall Gdns. Kenl —87Ub 165
Gomshall Rd. Sutt —82Ya 162
Gondar Gdns. NW6 —36Bb 61
Gonson St. SE8 —51Dc 106
Gonston Clo. SW19 —61Ab 124
Gonville Av. Crox —16R 18
Gonville Cres. N'holt —37Da 57
Gonville Rd. T Hth —71Pb 146
Gonville St. SW6 —55Ab 102
Gooch Ho. E5 —34Xb 63
Goodall Rd. E11 —34Ec 64
Goodbury Rd. Knat —85Qd 171
Gooden Ct. Harr —34Ga 58
Goodenough Clo. Coul —92Qb 180
Goodenough Rd. SW19 —66Bb 125
Goodenough Way. Coul —92Pb 180
Gooderham Ho. Grays —7D 92
Goodfellow Gdns. W'ham —5Ac 123
Goodge Pl. W1 —43Lb 82 (1C 198)
Goodge St. W1 —43Lb 82 (1C 198)
Goodhall St. NW10 —41Va 80
(in two parts)
Goodhart Pl. E14 —45Ac 84
Goodhart Way. W Wick —73Gc 149
Goodhew Rd. Croy —72Wb 147
Gooding Clo. N Mald —70Sa 123
Goodinge Clo. N7 —37Nb 62
Goodlake Ct. Den —31H 55
Goodley Stock. West —100Rc 184
Goodman Cres. SW2 —61Nb 126
Goodman Pk. Slou —6N 73
Goodman Pl. Stai —63H 119
Goodman Rd. E10 —31Ec 64
Goodman's Ct. E1 —45Vb 83 (4K 201)
Goodmans Ct. Wemb —35Ma 59
Goodman's Stile. E1 —44Wb 83
Goodmans Yd. E1 —45Vb 83 (4K 201)
Goodmayes Av. Ilf —32Wc 67
Goodmayes La. Ilf —35Wc 67
Goodmayes Rd. Ilf —32Wc 67
Goodmead Rd. Orp —73Wc 151
Goodrich Clo. Wat —7W 4
Goodrich Ct. W10 —44Za 80
Goodrich Rd. SE22 —58Vb 105
Goodson Rd. NW10 —38Ua 60
Goods Way. NW1 —39Mb 62 (1E 192)
Goodway Gdns. E14 —44Fc 85
Goodwin Clo. SE16 —48Wb 83
Goodwin Clo. Mitc —69Fb 125
Goodwin Ct. N8 —27Nb 42
(off Campsbourne Rd.)
Goodwin Ct. NW1 —40Lb 62 (1C 192)
(off Chalton St.)
Goodwin Ct. Barn —16Gb 23
Goodwin Ct. Chesh —1Ac 12
Goodwin Ct. Mitc —66Gb 125
Goodwin Dri. Sidc —62Zc 131
Goodwin Gdns. Croy —79Rb 147
Goodwin Ho. N9 —18Wb 25
Goodwin Ho. Wat —16U 18
Goodwin Rd. N9 —18Zb 26
Goodwin Rd. W12 —47Wa 80
Goodwin Rd. Croy —78Rb 147
Goodwin Rd. Slou —1D 72
Goodwins Ct. WC2 —45Nb 82 (4F 199)
Goodwin St. N4 —33Qb 62
Goodwood Av. Enf —9Yb 12
Goodwood Av. Horn —35Nd 69
Goodwood Av. Wat —7U 4
Goodwood Clo. Mord —70Cb 125
Goodwood Clo. Stan —22La 38
Goodwood Cres. Grav —5E 136
Goodwood Pde. Beck —70Ac 128
Goodwood Pde. Wat —8U 4
Goodwood Path. Borwd —12Qa 21
Goodwood Rd. SE14 —52Ac 106
Goodwyn Av. NW7 —22Ua 40
Goodwyns Vale. N10 —25Jb 42
Goodyear Pl. SE5 —51Sb 105
Goodyers Av. Rad —5Ha 6
Goodyers Gdns. NW4 —29Za 40
Goosander Way. SE28 —48Tc 86
Gooseacre La. Harr —29Ma 39
Goose Grn. D'side —91X 175
Goose Grn. Farn R —10F 52
Goose Grn. Clo. St P —68Wc 131
Goose La. Wok —11Qc 86
Gooseley La. E6 —41Qc 86
Goosepool. Cher —73H 139
Goose Sq. E6 —44Pc 86
Gooshays Dri. Romf —22Nd 49
Gooshays Gdns. Romf —23Nd 49
Goossens Clo. Sutt —78Eb 145
Gophir La. EC4 —45Tb 83 (4F 201)
Gopsall St. N1 —39Tb 63 (1G 195)
Goral Mead. Rick —18M 17
Gordon Av. E4 —23Gc 45
Gordon Av. SW14 —56Ua 102
Gordon Av. Horn —33Hd 68
Gordon Av. S Croy —82Sb 165
Gordon Av. Stan —24Ha 38
Gordon Av. Twic —57Ja 100
Gordonbrock Rd. SE4 —57Cc 106
Gordon Clo. E17 —30Cc 44
Gordon Clo. N19 —33Lb 62
Gordon Clo. Cher —76G 138
Gordon Clo. Stai —65K 119
Gordon Ct. W12 —44Ya 80
Gordon Ct. Edgw —22Pa 39
Gordon Cres. Croy —74Ub 147
Gordon Cres. Hay —48W 76
Gordondale Rd. SW19 —61Cb 125
Gordon Dri. Cher —76G 138
Gordon Dri. Shep —73T 140
Gordon Gdns. Edgw —26Ra 39
Gordon Gro. SE5 —54Rb 105
Gordon Hill. Enf —11Sb 25
Gordon Ho. E1 —45Yb 84
(off Glamis Rd.)
Gordon Ho. E1 —45Yb 84
(off Highway, The)
Gordon Ho. W5 —41Na 79
Gordon Ho. Rd. NW5 —35Jb 62
Gordon Pl. W8 —47Cb 81
Gordon Pl. Grav —8E 114
Gordon Promenade. Grav —8E 114
Gordon Promenade E. Grav —8F 114
Gordon Rd. E4 —17Gc 27
Gordon Rd. E11 —30Jc 45
Gordon Rd. E15 —35Ec 64
Gordon Rd. E18 —25Kc 45
Gordon Rd. N3 —24Bb 41
Gordon Rd. N9 —19Xb 25
Gordon Rd. N11 —24Mb 42
Gordon Rd. SE15 —54Xb 105
Gordon Rd. W4 —51Ra 101
Gordon Rd. W13 & W5 —45Ka 78
Gordon Rd. Ashf —62N 119
Gordon Rd. Bark —39Uc 66
Gordon Rd. Beck —69Bc 128
Gordon Rd. Belv —49Ed 88
Gordon Rd. Cars —79Hb 145
Gordon Rd. Cat —93Tb 181
Gordon Rd. Clay —80Ga 142
Gordon Rd. Dart —59Md 111
Gordon Rd. Enf —11Sb 25
Gordon Rd. Grav —9A 114
Gordon Rd. Grays —7A 92
Gordon Rd. Harr —27Ga 38
Gordon Rd. Horn H —1H 93
Gordon Rd. Houn —56Ea 100
Gordon Rd. Ilf —34Tc 66
Gordon Rd. King T —67Pa 123
Gordon Rd. Rich —54Pa 101
Gordon Rd. Romf —30Bd 47
Gordon Rd. Sev —97Kd 187
Gordon Rd. Shenf —18Ce 33
Gordon Rd. Shep —72T 140
Gordon Rd. Sidc —57Uc 108
Gordon Rd. S'hall —49Aa 77
Gordon Rd. Stai —63E 118
Gordon Rd. Surb —73Pa 143
Gordon Rd. Wal A —6Cc 12
Gordon Rd. W Dray —45N 75
Gordon Rd. Wind —4D 94
Gordon Sq. WC1 —42Mb 82 (5D 192)
Gordon St. E13 —41Jc 85

Gordon St.—Gt. Peter St.

Gordon St. WC1 —42Mb 82 (5D 192)
Gordons Way. Oxt —100Fc 183
Gordon Way. Barn —14Bb 23
Gordon Way. Brom —67Jc 129
Gore Cotts. Grn St —62Sd 134
Gore Ct. NW9 —29Qa 39
Gorefield Pl. NW6 —40Cb 61
Gorelands La. Chal G & Ger X —18A 16
Gore Rd. E9 —39Yb 64
Gore Rd. SW20 —68Ya 124
Gore Rd. Burn —1A 72
Gore Rd. Dart —61Sd 134
Goresbrook Rd. Dag —39Xc 67
Gore St. SW7 —48Eb 81 (3A 202)
Gorham Pl. W11 —45Ab 80
Goring Clo. Romf —25Ed 48
Goring Gdns. Dag —35Yc 67
Goring Rd. N11 —23Nb 42
Goring Rd. Dag —37Fd 68
Goring Rd. Stai —64F 118
Goring Sq. Stai —63G 118
Goring St. EC3 —44Ub 83 (2J 201)
(off Houndsditch)
Goring Way. Gnfd —40Ea 58
Gorle Clo. Wat —7W 4
Gorleston Rd. N15 —29Tb 43
Gorleston St. W14 —49Ab 80
Gorman Rd. SE18 —49Pc 86
Gorringe Av. S Dar —68Td 134
Gorringe Pk. Av. Mitc —66Hb 125
Gorse Clo. E16 —44Jc 85
Gorse Grn. Cob —91W 174
Gorse Hill. F'ham —72Nd 153
Gorse Hill La. Vir W —10P 117
Gorse Hill Rd. Vir W —10P 117
Gorselands Clo. W Byf —83L 157
Gorse Meade. Slou —6F 72
Gorse Rise. SW17 —64Jb 126
Gorse Rd. Croy —77Cc 148
Gorse Rd. Orp —75Cd 152
Gorse Wlk. W Dray —44N 75
Gorse Way. Hart —71Be 155
Gorseway. Romf —32Gd 68
Gorsewood Rd. Hart —71Be 155
(in two parts)
Gorsewood Rd. Wok —7A 188
Gorst Rd. NW10 —42Sa 79
Gorst Rd. SW11 —58Hb 103
Gorsuch Pl. E2 —41Vb 83 (3K 195)
Gorsuch St. E2 —41Vb 83 (3K 195)
Gosberton Rd. SW12 —60Hb 103
Gosbury Hill. Chess —77Na 143
Gosfield Rd. Dag —33Cd 68
Gosfield Rd. Eps —84Ta 161
Gosfield St. W1 —43Lb 82 (7B 192)
Gosford Gdns. Ilf —29Pc 46
Gosford Ho. Wat —16U 18
Gosforth La. Wat —20W 18
Gosforth Path. Wat —20W 18
Goshawk Gdns. Hay —41U 76
Goslar Way. Wind —4F 94
Goslett Yd. WC2 —44Mb 82 (3E 198)
Goslet Yd. WC2 —44Mb 82
Gosling Clo. Gnfd —41Ca 77
Gosling Grn. Slou —48A 74
Gosling Rd. Slou —48A 74
Gosling Way. SW9 —53Qb 104
Gospatrick Rd. N17 —24Sb 43
Gospel Oak Est. NW5 —36Hb 61
Gosport Dri. Horn —37Ld 69
Gosport Rd. E17 —29Bc 44
Gosport Wlk. N17 —28Xb 43
Gosport Way. SE15 —52Vb 105
Gossage Rd. SE18 —50Tc 86
Gossage Rd. Uxb —38P 55
Gossamers, The. Wat —8Aa 5
Gosset St. E2 —41Vb 83
Goss Hill. Swan —65Ld 133
Gosshill Rd. Chst —68Qc 130
Gossington Clo. Chst —63Rc 130
Gosterwood St. SE8 —51Ac 106
Gostling Rd. Twic —60Ca 99
Goston Gdns. T Hth —69Qb 126
Goswell Hill. Wind —3H 95
Goswell Pl. EC1 —41Rb 83 (4C 194)
(off Goswell Rd.)
Goswell Rd. EC1 —40Rb 63 (2B 194)
Goswell Rd. Wind —3H 95
Gothic Clo. Dart —62Md 133
Gothic Ct. Hay —51T 98
Gothic Rd. Twic —61Fa 122
Goudhurst Rd. Brom —64Gc 129
Gouge Av. Grav —10A 114
Gough Rd. E15 —35Hc 65
Gough Rd. Enf —12Xb 25
Gough Sq. EC4 —44Qb 82 (2A 200)
Gough St. WC1 —42Pb 82 (5J 193)
Gough Wlk. E14 —44Cc 84
Gould Rd. Felt —59U 98
Gould Rd. Twic —60Ga 100
Gould's Grn. Uxb —45R 76
Gould Ter. E8 —36Xb 63
Goulston St. E1 —44Vb 83 (2K 201)
Goulton Rd. E5 —35Xb 63
Gourley Pl. N15 —29Ub 43
Gourley St. N15 —29Ub 43
Gourney Gro. Grays —45De 91
Gourock Rd. SE9 —57Qc 108
Govan St. E2 —39Wb 63
Gover Ct. SW4 —54Nb 104
Government Row. Enf —10Cc 12
Governors Av. Den —29H 35
Govett Av. Shep —71S 140
Govier Clo. E15 —38Gc 65
Gowan Av. SW6 —53Ab 102
Gowan Rd. NW10 —37Xa 60
Gowar Field. Pot B —4Wa 8
Gower Clo. SW4 —58Lb 104
Gower Ct. WC1 —42Mb 82 (5D 192)
Gower Ho. E17 —27Cc 44
Gower M. WC1 —43Mb 82 (1E 198)
Gower Pl. WC1 —42Lb 82 (5C 192)
Gower Rd. E7 —37Jc 65
Gower Rd. Iswth —51Ha 100
Gower Rd. Wey —79T 140
Gowers La. Ors —7B 92
Gower St. WC1 —42Lb 82 (5C 192)
Gower's Wlk. E1 —44Wb 83
Gower, The. Egh —69D 118
Gowland Pl. Beck —68Bc 128
Gowlett Rd. SE15 —55Wb 105
Gowrie Rd. SW11 —55Jb 104
Goy Mnr. Rd. SW19 —65Za 124
Graburn Way. E Mol —69Fa 122
Grace Av. Bexh —54Bd 109
Gracechurch Ct. EC3 —45Tb 83 (4G 201)
(off Gracechurch St.)
Gracechurch St. EC3 —45Tb 83 (4G 201)
Grace Clo. SE9 —62Mc 129
Grace Clo. Borwd —11Ta 21
Grace Clo. Edgw —24Sa 39
Grace Clo. Ilf —23Vc 47
Grace Ct. Slou —6G 72
Gracedale Rd. SW16 —64Kb 126
Gracefield Gdns. SW16 —62Nb 126
Grace Ho. SE11 —51Pb 104
(off Vauxhall Rd.)
Grace Jones Clo. E8 —37Wb 63
Grace Path. SE26 —63Yb 128
Grace Pl. E3 —41Dc 84
Grace Rd. Croy —72Sb 147
Grace's All. E1 —45Wb 83
Graces M. NW8 —40Eb 61 (2A 190)
Grace's M. SE5 —54Ub 105
Grace's Rd. SE5 —54Ub 105
Grace St. E3 —41Dc 84
Gracious La. Bri. Sev —100Jd 186
Gradient, The. SE26 —63Wb 127
Graeme Rd. Enf —12Tb 25
Graemesdyke Av. SW14 —55Ra 101
Grafton Clo. W13 —44Ja 78
Grafton Clo. G Grn —44A 74
Grafton Clo. Houn —60Aa 99
Grafton Clo. W Byf —85H 157
Grafton Clo. Wor Pk —76Ua 144
Grafton Ct. Felt —60T 98
Grafton Cres. NW1 —37Kb 62
Grafton Gdns. N4 —30Sb 43
Grafton Gdns. Dag —33Ad 67
Grafton M. N1 —40Sb 63 (1D 194)
(off Frome St.)
Grafton M. W1 —42Lb 82 (6B 192)
Grafton Pk. Rd. Wor Pk —75Ua 144
Grafton Pl. NW1 —41Mb 82 (4E 192)
Grafton Rd. NW5 —36Jb 62
Grafton Rd. W3 —45Sa 79
Grafton Rd. Croy —74Qb 146
Grafton Rd. Dag —33Ad 67
Grafton Rd. Enf —13Pb 24
Grafton Rd. Harr —29Ea 38
Grafton Rd. N Mald —69Ua 124
Grafton Rd. Wor Pk —76Ta 143
Grafton Sq. SW4 —55Lb 104
Graftons, The. NW2 —34Cb 61
Grafton St. W1 —45Kb 82 (5A 198)
Grafton Ter. NW5 —36Hb 61
Grafton Way. W1 & WC1 —42Lb 82 (6B 192)
Grafton Way. W Mol —70Ba 121
Graham Av. W13 —47Ka 78
Graham Av. Mitc —67Jb 126
Graham Clo. Croy —75Cc 148
Graham Clo. Hut —15Ee 33
Graham Ct. N'holt —36Ba 57
Grahame Pk. Est. NW9 —25Ua 40
Grahame Pk. Way. NW7 & NW9 —24Va 40
Grahame White Ho. Kent —27Ma 39
Graham Gdns. Surb —74Na 143
Graham Ho. N9 —18Yb 26
(off Cumberland Rd.)
Graham Lodge. NW4 —30Xa 40
Graham Mans. Bark —38Wc 67
(off Lansbury Av.)
Graham Rd. E8 —37Wb 63
Graham Rd. E13 —42Jc 85
Graham Rd. N15 —27Rb 43
Graham Rd. NW4 —30Xa 40
Graham Rd. SW19 —66Bb 125
Graham Rd. W4 —48Ta 79
Graham Rd. Bexh —56Bd 109
Graham Rd. Hamp —63Ca 121
Graham Rd. Harr —27Ga 38
Graham Rd. Mitc —67Jb 126
Graham Rd. Purl —85Qb 164
Graham St. N1 —40Rb 63 (2C 194)
Graham Ter. SW1 —49Jb 82 (6H 203)
Grainger Clo. N'holt —37Ea 58
Grainger Ct. SE5 —52Sb 105
Grainger Rd. N22 —25Sb 43
Grainger Rd. Iswth —54Ha 100
Grainges Yd. Uxb —38L 55
Gramer Clo. E11 —33Fc 65
Gramophone La. Hay —47U 76
Grampian Clo. Hay —52T 98
Grampian Clo. Orp —72Vc 151
Grampian Gdns. NW2 —32Ab 60
Grampians, The. W6 —47Za 80
(off Shepherd's Bush Rd.)
Grampian Way. Slou —50C 74
Granada St. SW17 —64Gb 125
Granard Av. SW15 —57Xa 102
Granard Bus. Cen. NW7 —23Ua 40
Granard Ho. E9 —37Zb 64
Granard Rd. SW12 —59Hb 103
Granary Clo. N9 —17Yb 26
Granary Rd. E1 —42Xb 83
Granary St. NW1 —39Mb 62 (1D 192)
Granault Rd. Enf —10Vb 11
Granby Bldgs. SE11 —49Pb 82 (6H 205)
(off Black Prince Rd.)
Granby Pk. Rd. Chesh —1Vb 11
Granby Rd. SE9 —54Pc 108
Granby Rd. Grav —58Ee 113
Granby St. E2 —42Vb 83
Granby Ter. NW1 —40Lb 62 (2B 192)
Grand Arc. N12 —22Eb 41
Grand Av. EC1 —43Rb 83 (7C 194)
Grand Av. N10 —28Jb 42
Grand Av. Surb —71Ra 143
Grand Av. Wemb —36Qa 59
Grand Av. E. Wemb —36Ra 59
Grand Depot Rd. SE18 —50Qc 86
Grand Dri. SW20 —68Ya 124
Granden Rd. SW16 —68Nb 126
Grandfield Av. Wat —11V 18
Grandfield Ct. W4 —51Ta 101
Grandis Cotts. Rip —94K 173
Grandison Rd. SW11 —57Hb 103
Grandison Rd. Wor Pk —75Ya 144
Grand Pde. N4 —29Rb 43
Grand Pde. Wemb —33Qa 59
Grand Pde. M. SW15 —57Ab 102
Grandstand Rd. Eps —89Va 162
Grand Union Cres. E8 —38Wb 63
Grand Union Ind. Est. NW10 —40Ra 59
Grand Union Office Pk., The. Uxb —44L 75
Grand View Av. Big H —89Lc 167
Grand Wlk. E1 —42Ac 84
Granfield St. SW11 —53Fb 103
Grange Av. N12 —22Eb 41
Grange Av. N20 —17Ab 22
Grange Av. SE25 —68Ub 127
Grange Av. Barn —18Gb 23
Grange Av. Stan —26Ka 38
Grange Av. Twic —61Ga 122
Grange Av. Wfd G —23Jc 45
Grangecliffe Gdns. SE25 —68Ub 127
Grange Clo. Edgw —22Sa 39
Grange Clo. Ger X —25A 34
Grange Clo. Hay —43U 76
Grange Clo. Houn —51Ba 99
Grange Clo. Ingve —22Ee 51
Grange Clo. Lea —92Ma 177
Grange Clo. Mers —100Kb 180
Grange Clo. Sidc —62Wc 131
Grange Clo. Stai —64J 119
Grange Clo. W'ham —98Sc 184
Grange Clo. W Mol —70Da 121
Grange Clo. Wfd G —24Jc 45
Grange Clo. Wray —58A 96
Grange Ct. E8 —38Vb 63
Grange Ct. WC2 —44Pb 82 (3J 199)
Grange Ct. Egh —64B 118
Grange Ct. Harr —34Ha 58
Grange Ct. Lou —15Mc 27
Grange Ct. Mers —100Kb 180
Grange Ct. N'holt —40Y 57
Grange Ct. Pinn —27Aa 37
Grange Ct. Shep —70Q 120
Grange Ct. Stai —64J 119
Grange Ct. Wal A —6Ec 12
Grange Ct. W on T —75W 140
Grangecourt Rd. N16 —32Ub 63
Grange Cres. SE28 —44Yc 87
Grange Cres. Chig —22Tc 46
Grange Cres. Dart —58Rd 111
Grangedale Clo. N'wd —24U 36
Grange Dri. Chst —65Nc 130
Grange Dri. Mers —100Kb 180
Grange Dri. Orp —81Yc 169
Grange Dri. Wok —87A 156
Grange Farm Clo. Harr —33Ea 58
Grange Field. Ger X —25A 34
Grangefields Rd. Guild —100A 172
Grange Gdns. N14 —18Mb 24
Grange Gdns. NW3 —34Db 61
Grange Gdns. SE25 —68Ub 127
Grange Gdns. Bans —85Db 163
Grange Gdns. Farn C —6H 53
Grange Gdns. Pinn —27Aa 37
Grange Gro. N1 —37Sb 63
Grange Hill. SE25 —68Ub 127
Grange Hill. Edgw —22Sa 39
Grangehill Pl. SE9 —55Pc 108
Grangehill Rd. SE9 —56Pc 108
Grange Ho. SE1 —48Vb 83 (4K 207)
Grange Ho. Grav —9C 114
Grange La. SE21 —61Vb 127
Grange La. Hart —73Ce 155
Grange La. Let H —11Fa 20
Grange Lodge. Wind —2B 94
Grange Mans. Eps —80Va 144
Grange Meadow. Bans —85Db 163
Grangemill Rd. SE6 —62Cc 128
Grangemill Way. SE6 —61Cc 128
Grange Mt. Lea —92Ma 177
Grange Pk. E10 —33Dc 64
Grange Pk. W5 —46Na 79
Grange Pk. Wok —87A 156
Grange Pk. Av. N21 —16Sb 25
Grange Pk. Pl. SW20 —66Xa 124
Grange Pk. Rd. E10 —32Dc 64
Grange Pk. Rd. T Hth —70Tb 127
Grange Pl. NW6 —38Cb 61
Grange Pl. Stai —68L 119
Granger Gro. SE1 —47Tb 83 (1G 207)
Grange Rd. E10 —32Cc 64
Grange Rd. E13 —41Hc 85
Grange Rd. E17 —29Ac 44
Grange Rd. N6 —30Jb 42
Grange Rd. N17 & N18 —23Wb 43
Grange Rd. NW10 —37Xa 60
Grange Rd. SE1 —48Ub 83 (4J 207)
Grange Rd. SE25 & SE19 —69Tb 127
Grange Rd. SW13 —53Wa 102
Grange Rd. W4 —50Ra 79
Grange Rd. W5 —46Ma 79
Grange Rd. Bush —15Aa 19
Grange Rd. Cat —97Wb 181
Grange Rd. Chess —77Na 143
Grange Rd. Edgw —23Ta 39
Grange Rd. Egh —64B 118
(in two parts)
Grange Rd. Els —15Pa 21
Grange Rd. Ger X —25A 34
Grange Rd. Grav —9C 114
Grange Rd. Grays —51De 113
Grange Rd. Harr —29Ja 38
Grange Rd. Hay —44U 76
Grange Rd. Ilf —35Rc 66
Grange Rd. King T —69Na 123
Grange Rd. Lea —92Ma 177
Grange Rd. New Haw —82J 157
Grange Rd. Orp —76Tc 150
Grange Rd. Romf —23Kd 49
Grange Rd. Sev —99Jd 186
Grange Rd. S'hall —47Aa 77
Grange Rd. S Croy —82Sb 165
Grange Rd. S Harr —33Fa 58
Grange Rd. S Ock —46Sd 90
Grange Rd. Sutt —80Cb 145
Grange Rd. T Hth —70Tb 127
Grange Rd. W on T —77Aa 141
Grange Rd. W Mol —70Da 121
Grange Rd. Wok —86A 156
Granger Way. Romf —30Jd 48
Grange St. N1 —39Tb 63 (1G 195)
Grange, The. E17 —29Bc 44
(off Lynmouth Rd.)
Grange, The. N2 —26Fb 41
Grange, The. N20 —18Eb 23
Grange, The. SE1 —48Vb 83 (4K 207)
Grange, The. SW19 —65Za 124
Grange, The. Burn —1A 72
(off Green La.)
Grange, The. Croy —75Bc 148
Grange, The. S Dar —67Td 134
Grange, The. W on T —75X 141
Grange, The. Wemb —38Qa 59
Grange, The. W King —80Vd 154
Grange, The. Wor Pk —77Ta 143
Grange Vale. Sutt —80Db 145
Grangeview Rd. N20 —18Eb 23
Grange Wlk. SE1 —48Ub 83 (3J 207)
Grange Wlk. M. SE1 —48Ub 83 (4J 207)
(off Grange Wlk.)
Grange Way. N12 —21Db 41
Grange Way. NW6 —38Cb 61
Grange Way. Eri —52Kd 111
Grange Way. Hart —72Be 155
Grange Way. Iver —44H 75
Grange Way. Wfd G —21Lc 45
Grangeway Gdns. Ilf —29Nc 46
Grangeways Clo. Grav —3B 136
Grangeway, The. N21 —16Rb 25
Grangewood. Bex —60Bd 109
Grangewood. Pot B —2Db 9
Grangewood. Wex —3N 73
Grangewood Av. Grays —8A 92
Grangewood Av. Rain —42Ld 89
Grangewood Clo. Brtwd —20Be 33
Grangewood Clo. Pinn —29W 36
Grangewood Dri. Sun —66V 120
Grangewood La. Beck —65Bc 128
Grangewood St. E6 —39Mc 65
Grangewood Ter. SE25 —67Tb 127
Grange Yd. SE1 —48Vb 83 (4K 207)
Granham Gdns. N9 —19Vb 25
Granite St. SE18 —50Vc 87
Granleigh Rd. E11 —33Gc 65
Gransden Av. E8 —38Xb 63
Gransden Rd. W12 —47Va 80
Grant Av. Slou —4J 73
Grantbridge St. N1 —40Rb 63 (1C 194)
Grantchester Clo. Harr —34Ha 58
Grant Clo. N14 —17Lb 24
Grant Clo. Shep —72R 140
Grantham Clo. Edgw —20Na 21
Grantham Ct. Romf —31Bd 67
Grantham Gdns. Romf —30Bd 47
Grantham Grn. Borwd —15Sa 21
Grantham Pl. W1 —46Kb 82 (7K 197)
Grantham Rd. E12 —35Qc 66
Grantham Rd. SW9 —54Nb 104
Grantham Rd. W4 —52Ua 102
Grantham Way. Grays —46Ce 91
Grantley Rd. Houn —54Y 99
Grantley St. E1 —41Zb 84
Grantock Rd. E17 —25Fc 45
Granton Av. Upm —34Pd 69
Granton Rd. SW16 —67Lb 126
Granton Rd. Ilf —32Wc 67
Granton Rd. Sidc —65Yc 131
Grant Pl. Croy —74Vb 147
Grant Rd. SW11 —56Fb 103
Grant Rd. Croy —74Vb 147
Grant Rd. Harr —27Ha 38
Grants Clo. NW7 —24Ya 40
Grant St. E13 —41Jc 85
Grant St. N1 —40Qb 62 (1K 193)
Grantully Rd. W9 —41Db 81
Grant Way. Iswth —51Ja 100
Granville Arc. SW9 —56Qb 104
Granville Av. N9 —20Yb 26
Granville Av. Felt —61W 120
Granville Av. Houn —57Ca 99
Granville Av. Slou —3H 73
Granville Clo. Byfl —85P 157
Granville Clo. Croy —75Ub 147
Granville Clo. Wey —79S 140
Granville Ct. N1 —39Ub 63
Granville Gdns. SW16 —66Pb 126
Granville Gdns. W5 —46Pa 79
Granville Gro. SE13 —55Ec 106
Granville M. Sidc —63Wc 131
Granville Pk. SE13 —55Ec 106
Granville Pl. N12 —24Eb 41
Granville Pl. W1 —44Jb 82 (3H 197)
Granville Pl. Pinn —27Z 37
Granville Point. NW2 —33Bb 61
Granville Rd. E17 —30Dc 44
Granville Rd. E18 —26Kc 45
Granville Rd. N4 —30Pb 42
Granville Rd. N12 —24Db 41
Granville Rd. N13 —23Pb 42
Granville Rd. N22 —25Rb 43
Granville Rd. NW2 —33Bb 61
Granville Rd. NW6 —40Cb 61
(in two parts)
Granville Rd. SW18 —59Bb 103
Granville Rd. SW19 —66Cb 125
Granville Rd. Barn —14Ya 22
Granville Rd. Epp —1Xc 15
Granville Rd. Grav —9B 114
Granville Rd. Hay —49V 76
Granville Rd. Ilf —32Rc 66
Granville Rd. Oxt —100Hc 183
Granville Rd. Sev —96Jd 186
Granville Rd. Sidc —63Wc 131
Granville Rd. Uxb —37R 56
Granville Rd. Wat —14Y 19
Granville Rd. Well —55Yc 109
Granville Rd. W'ham —98Sc 184
Granville Rd. Wey —80S 140
Granville Rd. Wok —92B 172
Granville Sq. SE15 —52Ub 105
Granville Sq. WC1 —41Pb 82 (4J 193)
Granville St. WC1 —41Pb 82 (4J 193)
Granwood Ct. Iswth —53Ga 100
Grape St. WC2 —44Nb 82 (2F 199)
Graphite Sq. SE11 —50Pb 82 (7H 205)
Grasdene Rd. SE18 —52Wc 109
Grasmere Av. SW15 —63Ta 123
Grasmere Av. SW19 —69Cb 125
Grasmere Av. W3 —45Ta 79
Grasmere Av. Houn —58Da 99
Grasmere Av. Orp —76Rc 150
Grasmere Av. Ruis —31S 56
Grasmere Av. Slou —5L 73
Grasmere Av. Wemb —31La 58
Grasmere Clo. Felt —60V 98
Grasmere Clo. Leav —4X 5
Grasmere Clo. Lou —12Pc 28
Grasmere Ct. N22 —23Pb 42
Grasmere Ct. SE26 —64Wb 127
Grasmere Ct. SW13 —51Wa 102
Grasmere Gdns. Harr —26Ja 38
Grasmere Gdns. Ilf —29Nc 46
Grasmere Gdns. Orp —76Rc 150
Grasmere Pde. Slou —5M 73
Grasmere Point. SE15 —52Yb 106
(off Old Kent Rd.)
Grasmere Rd. E13 —40Jc 65
Grasmere Rd. N10 —25Kb 42
Grasmere Rd. N17 —23Wb 43
Grasmere Rd. SE25 —71Xb 147
Grasmere Rd. SW16 —64Pb 126
Grasmere Rd. Bexh —54Ed 110
Grasmere Rd. Brom —67Hc 129
Grasmere Rd. Horn —28Pd 49
Grasmere Rd. Orp —75Rc 150
Grasmere Rd. Purl —83Rb 165
Grasmere Way. Byfl —84P 157
Grassfield Clo. Coul —91Kb 180
Grassingham End. Ger X —24A 34
Grassingham Rd. Ger X —24A 34
Grassington Clo. Brick —2Ca 5
Grassington Rd. Sidc —63Wc 131
Grassmere Clo. Egh —66D 118
Grassmount. SE23 —61Xb 127
Grassmount. Purl —82Lb 164
Grass Pk. N3 —25Bb 41
Grass Rd. Hay —41W 76
(in two parts)
Grass Rd. Long —71Ee 155
Grass Rd. Til —1K 115
Grassy Way. Wall —77Lb 146
Grassy La. Sev —98Kd 187
Grasvenor Av. Barn —15Cb 23
Grately Way. SE15 —52Vb 105
Gratton Dri. Wind —6C 94
Gratton Rd. W14 —48Ab 80
Gratton Ter. NW2 —34Za 60
Gravel Clo. Chig —19Wc 29
Graveley Av. Borwd —15Sa 21
Gravel Hill. N3 —26Bb 41
Gravel Hill. Bexh —57Dd 110
Gravel Hill. Croy —79Zb 148
Gravel Hill. Ger X —23A 34
Gravel Hill. Lea —93Ka 176
Gravel Hill. Lou —10Jc 13
Gravel Hill. Uxb —36M 55
Gravel Hill Clo. Bexh —57Dd 110
Gravel La. E1 —44Vb 83 (2K 201)
Gravel La. Chig —19Wc 29
Gravelly Hill. Cat —100Vb 181
Gravel Pit La. SE9 —57Rc 108
Gravel Pit Way. Orp —75Wc 151
Gravel Rd. Brom —76Nc 150
Gravel Rd. S at H —66Rd 133
Gravel Rd. Twic —60Ga 100
Gravelwood Clo. Chst —62Sc 130
Gravenel Gdns. SW17 —64Gb 125
(off Nutwell St.)
Graveney Gro. SE20 —66Yb 128
Graveney Rd. SW17 —63Gb 125
Gravesend Rd. W12 —45Wa 80
Gravesend Rd. Shorne —2M 137
Gravesham Ct. Grav —9D 114
Gray Av. Dag —32Bd 67
Gray Clo. Add —78K 139
Gray Gdns. Rain —37Jd 68
Grayham Cres. N Mald —70Ta 123
Grayham Rd. N Mald —70Ta 123
Grayland Clo. Brom —67Mc 129
Graylands. They B —9Tc 14
Graylands. Wok —88A 156
Graylands Clo. Wok —88A 156
Grayling Clo. E16 —42Gc 85
Grayling Rd. N16 —33Tb 63
Grayling Sq. E2 —41Wb 83
(off Nelson Gdns.)
Graylings, The. Abb L —5T 4
Grays Ct. Dag —38Dd 68
Grayscroft Rd. SW16 —66Mb 126
Gray's End Clo. Grays —48Ce 91
Grays Farm Rd. Orp —67Xc 131
Grayshott Rd. SW11 —54Jb 104
Gray's Inn Pl. WC1 —43Pb 82 (1J 199)
Gray's Inn Rd. WC1 —41Nb 82 (3G 193)
Gray's Inn Sq. WC1 —43Pb 82 (7K 193)
Grays La. Ashf —63R 120
Gray's La. Asht —91Pa 177
Grays Pk. Rd. Stoke P —10L 53
Grays Pl. Slou —6K 73
Gray's Rd. Slou —6K 73
Grays Rd. Uxb —40N 55
Grays Rd. W'ham —93Rc 184
Gray St. SE1 —47Qb 82 (2A 206)
Grays Wlk. Hut —17Fe 33
Grayswood Gdns. SW20 —68Xa 124
Gray's Yd. W1 —44Jb 82 (2J 197)
(off James St.)
Graywood Ct. N12 —24Eb 41
Grazebrook Rd. N16 —33Tb 63
Grazeley Clo. Bexh —57Ed 110
Grazeley Ct. SE19 —64Ub 127
Gt. Acre Ct. SW4 —56Mb 104
Gt. Arthur Ho. EC1 —42Sb 83 (6D 194)
(off Golden La. Est.)
Gt. Bell All. EC2 —44Tb 83 (2F 201)
Gt. Benty. W Dray —49N 75
Gt. Brownings. SE21 —63Vb 127
Gt. Bushey Dri. N20 —18Db 23
Gt. Cambridge Rd. N9 & Enf —20Tb 25
Gt. Cambridge Rd. N17 & N18 —24Tb 43
Gt. Cambridge Rd. Wal X & Ches —6Yb 12
Gt. Cambridge Trading Est. Enf —15Wb 25
Gt. Castle St. W1 —44Kb 82 (2A 198)
Gt. Central Av. Ruis —36Y 57
Gt. Central St. NW1 —43Hb 81 (7F 191)
Gt. Central Way. Wemb & NW10 —35Sa 59
Gt. Chapel St. W1 —44Mb 82 (2D 198)
Gt. Chertsey Rd. W4 —54Sa 101
Gt. Chertsey Rd. Felt —62Ba 121
Gt. Church La. W6 —49Za 80
Gt. College St. SW1 —48Nb 82 (3F 205)
Gt. Cross Av. SE10 —52Gc 107
Gt. Cullings. Romf —33Gd 68
Gt. Cumberland M. W1 —44Hb 81 (3F 197)
Gt. Cumberland Pl. W1 —44Hb 81 (2F 197)
Gt. Dover St. SE1 —47Sb 83 (2E 206)
Greatdown Rd. W7 —42Ha 78
Gt. Eastern Enterprise Cen. E14 —47Dc 84
Gt. Eastern Rd. E15 —38Fc 65
Gt. Eastern Rd. Brtwd —21Yd 50
Gt. Eastern St. EC2 —41Ub 83 (4H 195)
Gt. Eastern Wlk. EC2 —43Ub 83 (1J 201)
Gt. Ellshams. Bans —88Cb 163
Gt. Elms Rd. Brom —70Lc 129
Gt. Field. NW9 —25Ua 40
Greatfield Av. E6 —42Pc 86
Greatfield Clo. N19 —35Lb 62
Greatfield Clo. SE13 —56Cc 106
Greatfields Dri. Uxb —43Q 76
Greatfields Rd. Bark —39Tc 66
Gt. Fox Meadow. Kel H —11Vd 32
Gt. Gardens Rd. Horn —30Kd 49
Gt. George St. SW1 —47Mb 82 (2E 204)
Gt. Gregories La. Epp —5Uc 14
Great Gro. Bush —14Da 19
Gt. Guildford St. SE1 —46Sb 83 (6D 200)
Greatham Rd. Bush —13Z 19
Greatham Wlk. SW15 —60Wa 102
Gt. Harry Dri. SE9 —62Qc 130
Greathurst End. Bookh —96Ba 175
Gt. James St. WC1 —43Pb 82 (7H 193)
Gt. Marlborough St. W1 —44Lb 82 (3B 198)
Gt. Maze Pond. SE1 —46Tb 83 (7G 201)
Gt. Maze Pond. SW1 —47Tb 83
Gt. Nelmes Chase. Horn —29Pd 49
Greatness La. Sev —93Ld 187
Greatness Rd. Sev —93Ld 187
Gt. Newport St. WC2 —45Nb 82 (4F 199)
Gt. New St. EC4 —44Qb 82 (2A 200)
Gt. North Rd. N2 & N6 —29Gb 41
Gt. North Rd. H Bar —12Bb 23
Gt. North Rd. New Bar —15Cb 23
Gt. North Rd. Pot B —1Eb 9
Gt. North Way. NW4 —26Xa 40
Gt. Oaks. Chig —21Sc 46
Gt. Oaks. Hut —16De 33
Greatorex St. E1 —43Wb 83
Gt. Ormond St. WC1 —43Nb 82 (7G 193)
Gt. Owl Rd. Chig —20Qc 28
Great Pk. K Lan —2P 3
Gt. Percy St. WC1 —41Pb 82 (3J 193)
Gt. Peter St. SW1 —48Mb 82 (4D 204)

Gt. Portland St.—Greystoke Dri.

Gt. Portland St. W1 —42Kb 82 (6A 192)
Gt. Pulteney St. W1 —45Lb 82 (4C 198)
Gt. Queen St. WC2 —44Nb 82 (3G 199)
Gt. Queen St. Dart —58Pd 111
Gt. Ropers La. War —23Wd 50
Gt. Russell St. WC1 —44Mb 82 (2E 198)
Gt. St Helen's. EC3 —44Ub 83 (2H 201)
Gt. St Thomas Apostle. EC4 —45Sb 83 (4E 200)
Gt. Scotland Yd. SW1 —46Nb 82 (7F 199)
Gt. Slades. Pot B —5Bb 9
Gt. Smith St. SW1 —48Mb 82 (3E 204)
Gt. South West Rd. Felt & Houn —59S 98
Gt. Spilmans. SE22 —57Ub 105
Gt. Strand. NW9 —25Va 40
Gt. Suffolk St. SE1 —46Rb 83 (7C 200)
Gt. Sutton St. EC1 —42Rb 83 (6C 194)
Gt. Swan All. EC2 —44Tb 83 (2F 201)
Gt. Tattenhams. Eps —90Xa 162
Gt. Thrift. Orp —70Sc 130
Gt. Titchfield St. W1 —43Kb 82 (6A 192)
Gt. Tower St. EC3 —45Ub 83 (4H 201)
Gt. Trinity La. EC4 —45Sb 83 (4E 200)
Gt. Turnstile. WC1 —43Pb 82 (1J 199)
Gt. Warley St. Gt War —25Wd 50
Gt. Western Ind. Pk. S'hall —47Da 77
Gt. Western Rd. W9 & W11 —43Bb 81
Gt. West Rd. W4 & W6 —50Va 80
Gt. West Rd. Bren —52Ja 100
Gt. West Rd. Houn & Iswth —54Z 99
Gt. West Rd. Trading Est. Bren —51Ka 100
Gt. Winchester St. EC2 —44Tb 83 (2G 201)
Gt. Windmill St. W1 —45Mb 82
Greatwood. Chst —66Qc 130
Greatwood Clo. Ott —81E 156
Gt. Woodcote Dri. Purl —82Mb 164
Gt. Woodcote Pk. Purl —82Mb 164
Great Yd. SE1 —47Ub 83 (1J 207) (off Crucifix La.)
Greaves Clo. Bark —38Tc 66
Greaves Pl. SW17 —63Gb 125
Greaves Tower. SW10 —52Eb 103 (off Worlds End Est.)
Grebe Av. Hay —44Z 77
Grebe Clo. E7 —36Hc 65
Grebe Clo. E17 —24Ac 44
Grebe Crest. W Thur —49Wd 90
Grecian Cres. SE19 —65Rb 127
Greding Wlk. Hut —19De 33
Greek Ct. W1 —44Mb 82 (3E 198)
Greek St. W1 —44Mb 82 (3E 198)
Greenacre. Dart —61Md 133
Green Acre. Knap —4B 188
Green Acre. Wind —4C 94
Greenacre Clo. Barn —10Bb 9
Greenacre Clo. N'holt —36Ba 57
Greenacre Clo. Swan —70Gd 132
Greenacre Ct. Egh —5N 117
Greenacre Gdns. E17 —28Ec 44
Greenacres. N3 —26Bb 41
Greenacres. SE9 —58Qc 108
Greenacres. Bookh —96Da 175
Greenacres. Bush —19Fa 20
Green Acres. Croy —76Vb 147
Greenacres. Epp —1Vc 15
Greenacres. Oxt —99Gc 183
Greenacres. Sidc —63Wc 131
Greenacres Av. Uxb —34P 55
Greenacres Clo. Orp —77Sc 150
Greenacres Clo. Rain —41Nd 89
Greenacres Dri. Stan —24Ka 38
Greenacre Sq. SE16 —47Zb 84
Greenacre Wlk. N14 —20Mb 24
Greenall Clo. Chesh —2Ac 12
Green Arbour Ct. EC1 —44Rb 83 (2B 200) (off Old Bailey)
Green Av. NW7 —21Ta 39
Green Av. W13 —48Ka 78
Greenaway Gdns. NW3 —35Db 61
Green Bank. E1 —46Xb 83
Greenbank. N12 —21Db 41
Greenbank Av. Wemb —36Ja 58
Green Bank Clo. E4 —19Ec 26
Greenbank Clo. Romf —20Md 31
Greenbank Cres. NW4 —28Ab 40
Greenbank Rd. Wat —8T 4
Greenbanks. Dart —61Nd 133
Greenbanks. Harr —35Ga 58
Greenbanks. Upm —30Ud 70
Greenbay Rd. SE7 —52Mc 107
Greenberry St. NW8 —40Gb 61 (2D 190)
Greenbrook Av. Barn —11Eb 23
Greenbury Clo. Chor —14E 16
Green Bus. Cen., The. Stai —63E 118
Green Clo. NW9 —30Sa 39
Green Clo. NW11 —31Eb 61
Green Clo. Brom —69Gc 129
Green Clo. Cars —75Hb 145
Green Clo. Chesh —4Ac 12
Green Clo. Felt —64Aa 121
Greencoat Pl. SW1 —49Lb 82 (5C 204)
Greencoat Row. SW1 —48Lb 82 (4C 204)
Green Comn. La. Wbrn G —1A 52
Greencourt Av. Croy —75Xb 147
Greencourt Av. Edgw —25Ra 39
Greencourt Gdns. Croy —75Xb 147
Greencourt Rd. Orp —71Tc 150
Green Ct. Rd. Swan —72Fd 152
Greencrest Pl. NW2 —34Wa 60
Greencroft. Edgw —22Sa 39
Greencroft Av. Ruis —33Y 57
Greencroft Clo. E6 —43Mc 85
Greencroft Gdns. NW6 —38Db 61
Greencroft Gdns. Enf —13Ub 25
Greencroft Rd. Houn —53Ba 99
Green Curve. Bans —86Bb 163
Green Dale. SE5 —56Tb 105
Green Dale. SE22 —57Ub 105
Greendale. Edgw —21Ua 40
Green Dale Clo. SE22 —57Ub 105
Greendale M. Slou —5L 73
Greendale Wlk. Grav —3A 136
Green Dragon Ct. SE1 (off Bedale St.) —46Tb 83 (7F 201)
Green Dragon La. N21 —16Qb 24
Green Dragon La. Bren —50Na 79
Green Dragon Yd. E1 —43Wb 83
Green Dri. Rip —95H 173
Green Dri. Slou —49A 74 (in two parts)
Green Dri. S'hall —46Ca 77
Green Edge. Wat —7W 4
Greene Fielde End. Stai —66M 119
Green End. N21 —19Rb 25
Green End. Chess —77Na 143
Greenend Rd. W4 —47Ua 80
Green Farm Clo. Orp —78Vc 151
Green Farm La. Shorne —1N 137
Greenfell St. SE10 —48Gc 85
Greenfern Av. Slou —4A 72
Greenfield Av. Surb —73Ra 143
Greenfield Av. Wat —19Z 19
Greenfield End. Ger X —23B 34
Greenfield Gdns. NW2 —33Ab 60
Greenfield Gdns. Dag —39Zc 67
Greenfield Gdns. Orp —73Tc 150
Greenfield Link. Coul —87Nb 164
Greenfield Rd. E1 —43Wb 83
Greenfield Rd. N15 —29Ub 43
Greenfield Rd. Dag —39Yc 67
Greenfield Rd. Dart —64Fd 132
Greenfield Rd. Sutt —77Db 145
Greenfields. Lou —14Qc 28
Greenfields. S'hall —44Ca 77
Greenfields Clo. Gt War —23Yd 50
Greenfields Clo. Lou —14Qc 28
Greenfield St. Wal A —6Ec 12
Greenfield Way. Harr —27Da 37
Greenfinches. Long —69De 135
Greenford Av. W7 —42Ga 78
Greenford Av. S'hall —45Ba 77
Greenford Gdns. Gnfd —41Da 77
Greenford Grn. Gnfd —37Ga 58
Greenford Ind. Est. N'holt —38Da 57
Greenford Rd. Harr —35Ga 58
Greenford Rd. S'hall & Gnfd —46Ea 78
Green Gdns. Orp —78Sc 150
Greengate. Gnfd —37Ka 58
Greengate Lodge. E13 —40Kc 65 (off Hollybush St.)
Greengate St. E13 —40Kc 65
Green Glade. They B —9Uc 14
Green Glades. Horn —30Pd 49
Greenhalgh Wlk. N2 —28Eb 41
Greenham Clo. SE1 —47Qb 82 (2K 205)
Greenham Ho. Houn —55Fa 100
Greenham Rd. N10 —26Jb 42
Greenham Wlk. Wok —6F 188
Greenhayes Av. Bans —86Cb 163
Greenhayes Gdns. Bans —87Cb 163
Green Hedge. Twic —58La 100
Greenheys Clo. N'wd —25U 36
Greenheys Dri. E18 —27Hc 45
Greenheys Pl. Wok —90B 156
Greenhill. NW3 —35Fb 61
Green Hill. SE18 —50Pc 86
Greenhill. Buck H —18Lc 27
Green Hill. Orp —84Pc 168
Greenhill. Sutt —75Eb 145
Greenhill. Wemb —33Ra 59
Greenhill Av. Cat —93Xb 181
Greenhill Cres. Wat —16U 18
Greenhill Gdns. N'holt —40Ba 57
Greenhill Gro. E12 —35Nc 66
Green Hill La. Warl —89Ac 166
Greenhill Pde. Barn —15Db 23
Greenhill Pk. NW10 —39Ua 60
Greenhill Pk. Barn —15Db 23
Greenhill Rd. NW10 —39Ua 60
Greenhill Rd. Grav —1B 136
Greenhill Rd. Harr —30Ga 38
Greenhill Rd. Otf —87Ld 171
Greenhills Clo. Rick —15K 17
Greenhill's Rents. EC1 —43Rb 83 (7B 194)
Greenhills Ter. N1 —37Tb 63
Greenhill Ter. N'holt —40Ba 57
Greenhill Way. Harr —30Ga 38
Greenhill Way. Wemb —33Ra 59
Greenhithe Clo. Sidc —59Uc 108
Greenholm Rd. SE9 —57Rc 108
Green Ho. Ger X —21A 34
Green Hundred Rd. SE15 —51Wb 105
Greenhurst Rd. SE27 —64Qb 126
Greening St. SE2 —49Yc 87
Greenlake Ter. Stai —66J 119
Greenland Cres. S'hall —48Y 77
Greenland M. SE8 —50Zb 84
Greenland Pl. NW1 —39Kb 62
Greenland Quay. SE16 —49Ac 84
Greenland Rd. NW1 —39Kb 62
Greenland Rd. Barn —16Ya 22
Greenlands. Sole S —10F 136
Greenlands Rd. Kems —91Rd 187
Greenlands Rd. Stai —63J 119
Greenlands Rd. Wey —76R 140
Greenland St. NW1 —39Kb 62
Green La. E4 —11Gc 27
Green La. NW4 —28Za 40
Green La. SE9 & Chst —60Rc 108
Green La. SE20 —66Zb 128
Green La. SW16 & T Hth —66Pb 126
Green La. W7 —47Ga 78
Green La. Asc —7C 116
Green La. Asht —89La 160
Green La. Blet —100Ub 181
Green La. Bov —1B 2
Green La. Brtwd —18Wd 32
Green La. Burn —1A 72
Green La. Byfl —84P 157
Green La. Cat —94Sb 181
Green La. Cher & Add —75G 138
Green La. Chess —81Ma 161
Green La. Chig —18Sc 28
Green La. Cob —84Aa 159
Green La. Crox —15P 17
Green La. Dat —3M 95
Green La. Edgw —21Pa 39
Green La. Egh —64D 118 (in two parts)
Green La. Farn C —7F 52
Green La. Felt —64Aa 121
Green La. Gt War —24Wd 50
Green La. Harr —34Ga 58
Green La. Houn —55X 99
Green La. Ilf & Dag —33Tc 66
Green La. Lea —93Ma 177 (in two parts)
Green La. Mord —73Ya 144 (Battersea Cemetery)
Green La. Mord —72Cb 145 (Morden)
Green La. N'side —12Sd 32
Green La. N Mald —71Sa 143
Green La. N'wd —24T 36
Green La. Ock —96R 174
Green La. Ors —43De 91
Green La. Pil H —15Yd 32
Green La. Purl —83Lb 164
Green La. Shep —72S 140
Green La. Shorne —5M 137
Green La. Stan —21Ka 38
Green La. Sun —66V 120
Green La. Tad & Coul —98Bb 179
Green La. Thorpe & Stai —68E 118
Green La. Upm —39Td 70
Green La. Uxb —43S 76
Green La. Wal A —6Lc 13
Green La. W on T —79X 141
Green La. Warl —88Ac 166
Green La. Wat —17Y 19
Green La. W Cla —99J 173
Green La. W Mol —71Da 141
Green La. Wind —4E 94
Green La. Wok —9E 188
Green La. Wor Pk —74Wa 144
Green La. Av. W on T —78Y 141
Green La. Clo. Byfl —84P 157
Green La. Clo. Cher —75G 138
Green La. Cotts. Stan —21Ka 38
Green La. Ct. Burn —1A 72
Green La. Gdns. T Hth —68Sb 127
Green Lanes. N8, N4 & N16 —27Rb 43
Green Lanes. N13 & N21 —20Qb 24
Green Lanes. Eps —81Ua 162 (in two parts)
Green La. W. W Hor —97Q 174
Greenlaw Ct. W5 —44Ma 79 (off Mount Pk. Rd.)
Greenlaw Gdns. N Mald —73Va 144
Greenlawns. N3 —23Db 41
Green Lawns. Ruis —32Y 57
Greenlaw St. SE18 —48Qc 86
Greenleaf Clo. SW2 —59Qb 104
Greenleafe Dri. Ilf —27Rc 46
Greenleaf Rd. E6 —39Lc 65
Greenleaf Rd. E17 —27Bc 44
Green Leas. Sun —65V 120
Greenleas. Wal A —6Gc 13
Greenlea Trading Pk. SW19 —67Fb 125
Greenleaves Ct. Ashf —65R 120
Greenleigh Av. St P —70Xc 131
Green Man Gdns. W13 —45Ja 78
Green Man La. W13 —45Ja 78
Green Man La. Felt —56W 98
Green Mnr. Way. Grav —56Be 113
Green Man Pas. W13 —45Ja 78 (in two parts)
Greenman St. N1 —38Sb 63
Greenmead. Eri —48Ad 87
Green Mead. Esh —79Ba 141
Green Meadow. Pot B —2Cb 9
Greenmeads. Wok —94A 172
Green Moor Link. N21 —17Rb 25
Greenmoor Rd. Enf —12Yb 26
Greenoak Rise. Big H —90Lc 167
Greenoak Way. SW19 —63Za 124
Greenock Rd. SW16 —67Mb 126
Greenock Rd. W3 —48Ra 79
Greenock Rd. Slou —4E 72
Greenock Way. Romf —24Gd 48
Greeno Cres. Shep —71Q 140
Green Pk. Stai —62G 118
Greenpark Ct. Wemb —38La 58
Green Pl. Dart —57Gd 110
Green Point. E15 —37Gc 65
Green Pond Clo. E17 —27Ac 44
Green Pond Rd. E17 —27Ac 44
Green Ride. Epp —7Rc 14
Green Ride. Lou —14Lc 27
Greenrigg Wlk. Wemb —34Ra 59
Green Rd. N14 —16Kb 24
Green Rd. N20 —20Eb 23
Green Rd. Egh —71B 138
Greens Clo., The. Lou —12Qc 28
Green's Ct. W1 —45Mb 82 (4D 198) (off Brewer St.)
Green's End. SE18 —49Rc 86
Greenshank Clo. E17 —24Ac 44
Green Shaw. Brtwd —18Wd 32
Greenshields Ind. Est. E16 —47Jc 85
Greenside. Bex —60Ad 109
Greenside. Borwd —10Qa 7
Green Side. Dag —32Yc 67
Greenside. Slou —3E 72
Greenside. Swan —68Fd 132
Greenside Clo. N20 —19Fb 23
Greenside Clo. Chst —65Rc 130
Greenside Cotts. Rip —93L 173
Greenside Rd. W12 —48Wa 80
Greenside Rd. Croy —73Qb 146
Greenside Wlk. Big H —90Kc 167
Greenslade Av. Asht —91Ra 177
Greenstead Av. Wfd G —24Lc 45
Greenstead Clo. Wfd G —23Lc 45
Greenstead Gdns. SW15 —57Xa 102
Greenstead Gdns. Wfd G —23Lc 45
Greensted Rd. Lou —17Nc 28
Greenstone M. E11 —30Jc 45
Green St. E7 & E13 —37Kc 65
Green St. W1 —45Jb 82 (4G 197)
Green St. Chor —11E 16
Green St. Enf —12Yb 26
Green St. Shenl & Borwd —7Qa 7
Green St. Sun —67W 120
Green St. Grn. Rd. Dart —60Rd 111
Green St. Grn. Rd. Long —68Zd 135
Greensward. Bush —16Da 19
Green, The. E4 —18Fc 27
Green, The. E11 —30Kc 45
Green, The. E15 —37Hc 65
Green, The. N9 —19Wb 25
Green, The. N14 —20Mb 24
Green, The. N21 —18Qb 24
Green, The. SW19 —64Za 124
Green, The. W3 —44Ua 80
Green, The. W5 —46Ma 79
Green, The. Bexh —53Cd 110
Green, The. Brom —62Jc 129
Green, The. Bur H —91Ab 178
Green, The. Burn —3A 72
Green, The. Cars —77Jb 146
Green, The. Chesh —1Yb 12
Green, The. Clay —79Ha 142
Green, The. Crox —14Q 18
Green, The. Croy —81Bc 166
Green, The. Dat —2M 95
Green, The. Eps —84Wa 162
Green, The. F'boro —78Rc 150
Green, The. Felt —61X 121
Green, The. Fet —96Fa 176
Green, The. Hare —25L 35
Green, The. Hayes —73Jc 149
Green, The. Houn —51Ca 99
Green, The. Ick —33S 56
Green, The. Mord —70Ab 124
Green, The. N Mald —69Sa 123
Green, The. Ors —3C 92
Green, The. Otf —88Kd 171
Green, The. Rain —45Nd 89
Green, The. Rich —57Ma 101
Green, The. Rip —93L 173
Green, The. Sarr —8J 3 (in two parts)
Green, The. Seal —93Pd 187 (off Church Rd.)
Green, The. Sev —94Md 187
Green, The. Shep —70U 120
Green, The. Sidc —63Wc 131
Green, The. Slou —8H 73
Green, The. S'hall —47Ba 77
Green, The. S Ock —43Zd 91
Green, The. Stanf —2L 93
Green, The. St P —66Xc 131
Green, The. Sutt —76Db 145
Green, The. They B —8Tc 14
Green, The. Twic —60Ga 100
Green, The. Wal A —6Ec 12
Green, The. Warl —90Zb 166
Green, The. Well —56Uc 108
Green, The. Wemb —33Ja 58
Green, The. W Dray —48M 75
Green, The. W'ham —98Tc 184
Green, The. W Vill —82U 158
Green, The. Wold —95Cc 182
Green, The. Wfd G —22Jc 45
Green, The. Wray —58A 96
Green Tiles La. Den —30H 35
Green Vale. W5 —44Pa 79
Green Vale. Bexh —57Zc 109
Greenvale Rd. SE9 —56Pc 108
Greenvale Rd. Knap —6A 188
Green Verges. Stan —24Ma 39
Green View. Chess —80Pa 143
Greenview Av. Beck —72Ac 148
Greenview Av. Croy —72Ac 148
Green View Clo. Bov —1C 2
Greenview Ct. Ashf —63P 119
Green Wlk. NW4 —29Za 40
Green Wlk. SE1 —48Ub 83 (4H 207)
Green Wlk. Dart —57Hd 110
Green Wlk. Hamp —65Ba 121
Green Wlk. Lou —17Nc 28
Green Wlk. Ruis —32V 56
Green Wlk. S'hall —50Ca 77
Green Wlk. Wfd G —23Nc 46
Green Wlk., The. E4 —18Fc 27
Greenway. N14 —19Nb 24
Greenway. N20 —19Cb 23
Green Way. SE9 —57Mc 107
Greenway. SW20 —70Ya 124
Greenway. Bookh —95Da 175
Green Way. Brom —72Nc 150
Greenway. Burn —1A 72
Greenway. Chst —64Qc 130
Greenway. Dag —33Yc 67
Green Way. Hart —71Ae 155
Greenway. Hay —41W 76
Greenway. Hut —17Ce 33
Greenway. Kent —29Na 39
Greenway. Pinn —26X 37
Greenway. Romf —23Rd 49
Green Way. Sun —70W 120
Greenway. Tats —92Lc 183
Green Way. Wall —77Lb 146
Green Way. Wfd G —22Lc 45
Greenway Av. E17 —28Fc 45
Greenway Clo. N4 —33Sb 63
Greenway Clo. N11 —23Kb 42
Greenway Clo. N15 —28Vb 43
Greenway Clo. N20 —19Cb 23
Greenway Clo. NW9 —26Ta 39
Greenway Clo. W Byf —85J 157
Greenway Dri. Stai —67M 119
Greenway Gdns. NW9 —26Ta 39
Greenway Gdns. Croy —76Bc 148
Greenway Gdns. Gnfd —41Ca 77
Greenway Gdns. Harr —26Ga 38
Greenways. Abb L —4U 4
Greenways. Beck —69Cc 128
Greenways. Chesh —1Rb 11
Greenways. Egh —64A 118
Greenways. Esh —77Ga 142
Greenways. Long —69Fe 135
Greenways. Tad —97Xa 178
Greenways Ct. Horn —30Md 49
Greenways, The. Twic —58Ja 100
Greenway, The. NW9 —26Ta 39
Greenway, The. Enf —7Zb 12
Greenway, The. Eps —87Qa 161
Greenway, The. Ger X —27A 34
Greenway, The. Houn —56Ba 99
Greenway, The. Ick —33S 56
Greenway, The. Orp —72Xc 151
Green Way, The. Pinn —30Ba 37
Greenway, The. Pot B —5Cb 9
Greenway, The. Rick —17J 17
Greenway, The. Slou —6B 72
Greenway, The. Uxb —40M 55
Green Way, The. W'stone —25Ga 38
Greenwell St. W1 —42Kb 82 (6A 192)
Greenwich Chu. St. SE10 —51Ec 106
Greenwich Cres. E6 —43Nc 86
Greenwich High Rd. SE10 —53Dc 106
Greenwich Pk. SE10 —51Fc 107
Greenwich S. St. SE10 —53Dc 106
Greenwich View Pl. E14 —48Dc 84
Greenwood Av. Chesh —3Xb 11
Greenwood Av. Dag —35Dd 68
Greenwood Av. Enf —12Ac 26
Greenwood Clo. Bush —17Ga 20
Greenwood Clo. Chesh —3Xb 11
Greenwood Clo. Mord —70Ab 124
Greenwood Clo. Orp —72Uc 150
Greenwood Clo. Sidc —61Wc 131
Greenwood Clo. Th Dit —74Ja 142
Greenwood Clo. Wdhm —83H 157
Greenwood Ct. SW1 —50Lb 82 (7C 204) (off Cambridge St.)
Greenwood Dri. E4 —22Fc 45
Greenwood Dri. Wat —6X 5
Greenwood Gdns. N13 —20Rb 25
Greenwood Gdns. Cat —97Wb 181
Greenwood Gdns. Ilf —24Sc 46
Greenwood Ho. N22 —25Qb 42
Greenwood La. Hamp —64Da 121
Greenwood Mans. Bark —38Wc 67 (off Lansbury Av.)
Greenwood Pk. King T —66Ua 124
Greenwood Pl. NW5 —36Kb 62
Greenwood Rd. E8 —37Wb 63
Greenwood Rd. E13 —40Jc 65
Greenwood Rd. Bex —63Fd 132
Greenwood Rd. Chig —21Xc 47
Greenwood Rd. Croy —73Rb 147
Greenwood Rd. Iswth —55Ha 100
Greenwood Rd. Mitc —69Mb 126
Greenwood Rd. Th Dit —74Ja 142
Greenwood Rd. Wok —8B 188
Greenwoods, The. S Harr —33Ea 58
Greenwood Ter. NW10 —39Ta 59
Greenwood Way. Sev —97Hd 186
Green Wrythe Cres. Cars —74Gb 145
Green Wrythe La. Cars —72Fb 145
Greenyard. Wal A —5Ec 12
Green Yd., The. EC3 —44Ub 83 (3H 201) (off Leadenhall St.)
Greer Rd. Harr —25Ea 38
Greet Ho. SE1 —47Qb 82 (2A 206) (off Frazier St.)
Greet St. SE1 —46Qb 82 (7A 200)
Gregories La. They B —7Tc 14
Gregory Av. Pot B —5Ya 8
Gregory Cres. SE9 —59Mc 107
Gregory Dri. Old Win —8M 95
Gregory M. SE3 —52Jc 107
Gregory Pl. W8 —47Db 81
Gregory Rd. Hedg —3H 53
Gregory Rd. Romf —28Zc 47
Gregory Rd. S'hall —48Ca 77
Gregson Clo. Borwd —11Sa 21
Gregson's Ride. Lou —10Qc 14
Greig Clo. N8 —29Nb 42
Greig Ter. SE17 —51Rb 105
Grenaby Av. Croy —73Tb 147
Grenaby Rd. Croy —73Tb 147
Grenada Rd. SE7 —52Lc 107
Grenade St. E14 —45Bc 84
Grenadier St. E16 —46Qc 86
Grena Gdns. Rich —56Pa 101
Grena Rd. Rich —56Pa 101
Grendon Gdns. Wemb —33Qa 59
Grendon Lodge. Edgw —19Sa 21
Grendon St. NW8 —42Gb 81 (5D 190)
Grenfell Av. Horn —32Hd 68
Grenfell Ct. NW7 —23Xa 40
Grenfell Gdns. Harr —31Na 59
Grenfell Gdns. Ilf —29Vc 47
Grenfell Ho. SE5 —52Sb 105
Grenfell Rd. W11 —45Za 80
Grenfell Rd. Mitc —65Hb 125
Grenfell Tower. W11 —45Za 80
Grenfell Wlk. W11 —45Za 80
Grennell Clo. Sutt —75Fb 145
Grennell Rd. Sutt —75Eb 145
Grenoble Gdns. N13 —23Qb 42
Grenside Rd. Wey —76R 140
Grenville Clo. N3 —25Ab 40
Grenville Clo. Burn —10A 52
Grenville Clo. Cob —85Z 159
Grenville Clo. Surb —74Sa 143
Grenville Clo. Wal X —4Zb 12
Grenville Gdns. Wfd G —25Lc 45
Grenville M. SW7 —49Eb 81 (6A 202) (off Harrington Gdns.)
Grenville M. Hamp —64Da 121
Grenville Pl. NW7 —22Ta 39
Grenville Pl. SW7 —48Eb 81
Grenville Rd. N19 —32Nb 62
Grenville Rd. New Ad —81Ec 166
Grenville St. WC1 —42Nb 82 (6G 193)
Gresham Av. N20 —21Hb 41
Gresham Av. Hart —71Be 155
Gresham Av. Warl —90Ac 166
Gresham Clo. Bex —58Bd 109
Gresham Clo. Enf —13Sb 25
Gresham Ct. Brtwd —20Yd 32
Gresham Dri. Romf —29Xc 47
Gresham Gdns. NW11 —32Ab 60
Gresham Lodge. E17 —29Dc 44
Gresham M. W4 —48Sa 79
Gresham Rd. E6 —40Pc 66
Gresham Rd. E16 —44Kc 85
Gresham Rd. NW10 —36Ta 59
Gresham Rd. SE25 —70Wb 127
Gresham Rd. SW9 —55Qb 104
Gresham Rd. Beck —68Ac 128
Gresham Rd. Brtwd —20Yd 32
Gresham Rd. Edgw —23Pa 39
Gresham Rd. Hamp —65Ca 121
Gresham Rd. Houn —53Ea 100
Gresham Rd. Oxt —100Hc 183
Gresham Rd. Slou —4E 72
Gresham Rd. Stai —64H 119
Gresham Rd. Uxb —40Q 56
Gresham St. EC2 —44Sb 83 (2D 200)
Gresham Way. SW19 —62Db 125
Gresley Clo. N15 —28Tb 43
Gresley Ct. Enf —7Yb 12
Gresley Ct. Pot B —1Db 9
Gresley Rd. N19 —32Lb 62
Gressenhall Rd. SW18 —58Bb 103
Gresse St. W1 —44Mb 82 (1D 198)
Gresswell Clo. Sidc —62Wc 131
Greswell St. SW6 —53Za 102
Greta Bank. W Hor —98S 174
Gretton Rd. N17 —24Vb 43
Greville Av. S Croy —82Zb 166
Greville Clo. Asht —91Na 177
Greville Clo. Twic —59Ka 100
Greville Ct. Asht —90Na 161
Greville Ct. Bookh —97Da 175
Greville Ct. Harr —35Ga 58
Greville Lodge. E13 —39Kc 65
Greville Lodge. N12 —21Db 41
Greville Lodge. Edgw —21Ra 39 (off Broadhurst Av.)
Greville M. NW6 —39Db 61 (off Greville Rd.)
Greville Pk. Av. Asht —90Na 161
Greville Pk. Rd. Asht —90Na 161
Greville Pl. NW6 —40Db 61
Greville Rd. E17 —28Ec 44
Greville Rd. NW6 —40Db 61
Greville Rd. Rich —58Pa 101
Greville St. EC1 —43Qb 82 (1K 199) (in two parts)
Grey Alders. Bans —86Ya 162
Greycaine Rd. Wat —9Z 5
Greycaine Trading Est. Wat —9Z 5
Grey Clo. NW11 —30Eb 41
Greycoat Pl. SW1 —48Mb 82 (4D 204)
Greycoat St. SW1 —48Mb 82 (4D 204)
Greycot Rd. Beck —64Cc 128
Grey Eagle St. E1 —42Vb 83 (6K 195)
Greyfell Clo. Stan —22La 38
Greyfields Clo. Purl —85Rb 165
Greyfriars. Hut —17De 33
Greyfriars Dri. Asc —10A 116
Greyfriars Pas. EC1 —44Rb 83 (2C 200)
Greyfriars Rd. Rip —96J 173
Greyhound Ct. WC2 —45Pb 82 (4J 199)
Greyhound Hill. NW4 —27Wa 40
Greyhound La. SW16 —65Mb 126
Greyhound La. Ors —7C 92
Greyhound La. Pot B —5Wa 8
Greyhound Rd. N17 —27Ub 43
Greyhound Rd. NW10 —41Xa 80
Greyhound Rd. W6 & W14 —51Za 102
Greyhound Rd. Sutt —78Eb 145
Greyhound Rd. Mans. W14 (off Greyhound Rd.) —51Ab 102
Greyhound Ter. SW16 —67Lb 126
Greyhound Way. Dart —57Gd 110
Grey Ho. W12 —45Xa 80 (off White City Est.)
Grey Ho., The. Wat —12W 18
Greys Pk. Clo. Kes —78Mc 149
Greystead Rd. SE23 —59Yb 106
Greystoke Av. Pinn —27Ca 37
Greystoke Ct. W5 —42Pa 79
Greystoke Dri. Ruis —30R 36

Greystoke Gdns.—Haines Wlk.

Greystoke Gdns. W5 —42Na 79
Greystoke Gdns. Enf —14Mb 24
Greystoke Pk. Ter. W5 —41Ma 79
Greystoke Pk. Ter. Gnfd —40Ea 58
Greystoke Pl. EC4 —44Qb 82 (2K 199)
Greystoke Rd. Slou —3C 72
Greystone Clo. S Croy —83Yb 166
Greystone Gdns. Harr —30La 38
Greystone Gdns. Ilf —26Sc 46
Greystone Pk. Sund —97Ad 185
Greystones Clo. Kems —89Nd 171
Greyswood St. SW16 —65Kb 126
Greythorne Rd. Wok —6D 188
Grey Towers. Horn —31Ld 69
Grey Towers Av. Horn —32Md 69
Grey Towers Gdns. Horn —31Ld 69
Grey Turner Ho. W12 —44Wa 80
Grice Av. Big H —85Kc 167
Gridiron Pl. Upm —33Rd 69
Grierson Rd. SE23 —59Zb 106
Grieves Rd. Grav —2B 136
Griffin Av. Upm —30Ud 50
Griffin Clo. NW10 —36Xa 60
Griffin Clo. Slou —7G 72
Griffin Ct. W4 —50Va 80
Griffin Ct. Asht —91Na 177
Griffin Ct. Bookh —98Da 175
Griffin Ct. Bren —51Na 101
Griffin Mnr. Way. SE28 —48Tc 86
Griffin Rd. N17 —26Ub 43
Griffin Rd. SE18 —50Tc 86
Griffins, The. Grays —47De 91
Griffin Wlk. Grnh —57Vd 112
Griffin Way. Bookh —98Ca 175
Griffin Way. Sun —68W 120
Griffith Clo. Dag —32Yc 67
Griffiths Clo. Wor Pk —75Xa 144
Griffiths Rd. SW19 —66Cb 125
Griggs App. Ilf —33Sc 66
Grigg's Pl. SE1 —48Ub 83 (4J 207) (off Grange Rd.)
Griggs Rd. E10 —30Ec 44
Grilse Clo. N9 —21Xb 43
Grimsby St. E2 —42Vb 83
Grimsdyke Cres. Barn —13Ya 22
Grimsdyke Rd. Pinn —24Aa 37
Grimsell Path. SE5 —52Rb 105
Grimshaw Clo. N6 —31Jb 62
Grimshaw Way. Romf —29Hd 48
Grimstone Clo. Romf —23Dd 48
Grimston Rd. SW6 —54Bb 103
Grimwade Av. Croy —76Wb 147
Grimwood Rd. Twic —59Ha 100
Grindall Clo. Croy —77Rb 147
Grindal St. SE1 —47Qb 82 (2K 205)
Grinling Pl. SE8 —51Cc 106
Grinstead Rd. SE8 —50Ac 84
Grisedale Clo. Purl —86Ub 165
Grisedale Gdns. Purl —86Ub 165
Grittleton Av. Wemb —37Ra 59
Grittleton Rd. W9 —42Cb 81
Grizedale Ter. SE23 —61Xb 127
Grobars Av. Wok —3F 188
Grocer's Hall Ct. EC2 —44Tb 83 (3F 201)
Grocer's Hall Gdns. EC2 —44Tb 83 (3F 201)
Grogan Clo. Hamp —65Ba 121
Groombridge Clo. W on T —78X 141
Groombridge Clo. Well —57Wc 109
Groombridge Rd. E9 —38Zb 64
Groom Cres. SW18 —59Fb 103
Groomfield Clo. SW17 —63Jb 126
Groom Pl. SW1 —48Jb 82 (3J 203)
Grooms Dri. Pinn —29W 36
Grosmont Rd. SE18 —51Vc 109
Grosse Way. SW15 —58Xa 102
Grosvenor Av. N5 —36Sb 63
Grosvenor Av. SW14 —55Ua 102
Grosvenor Av. Cars —79Hb 145
Grosvenor Av. Harr —30Da 37
Grosvenor Av. Hay —40V 56
Grosvenor Av. K Lan —1S 4
Grosvenor Av. Rich —57Na 101
Grosvenor Clo. Iver —41F 74
Grosvenor Clo. Lou —11Rc 28
Grosvenor Cotts. SW1 —49Jb 82 (5H 203)
Grosvenor Ct. E10 —32Dc 64
Grosvenor Ct. N14 —17Lb 24
Grosvenor Ct. NW6 —39Za 60
Grosvenor Ct. NW7 —22Ta 39 (off Hale La.)
Grosvenor Ct. W3 —46Qa 79
Grosvenor Ct. Barn —17Lb 24
Grosvenor Ct. Slou —4J 73
Grosvenor Cres. NW9 —28Qa 39
Grosvenor Cres. SW1 —47Jb 82 (2J 203)
Grosvenor Cres. Dart —57Md 111
Grosvenor Cres. Uxb —38R 56
Grosvenor Cres. M. SW1 —47Jb 82 (2H 203)
Grosvenor Dri. Horn —32Ld 69
Grosvenor Dri. Lou —12Rc 28
Grosvenor Est. SW1 —49Mb 82 (5E 204)
Grosvenor Gdns. E6 —41Mc 85
Grosvenor Gdns. N10 —27Lb 42
Grosvenor Gdns. N14 —15Mb 24
Grosvenor Gdns. NW2 —36Ya 60
Grosvenor Gdns. NW11 —30Bb 41
Grosvenor Gdns. SW1 —48Kb 82 (3K 203)
Grosvenor Gdns. SW14 —55Ua 102
Grosvenor Gdns. King T —65Ma 123
Grosvenor Gdns. Upm —32Td 70
Grosvenor Gdns. Wall —80Lb 146
Grosvenor Gdns. Wfd G —23Jc 45
Grosvenor Gdns. M. E. SW1 —48Kb 82 (3A 204) (off Beeston Pl.)
Grosvenor Gdns. M. N. SW1 (off Ebury St.) —48Kb 82 (4K 203)
Grosvenor Gdns. M. S. SW1 (off Ebury St.) —48Kb 82 (4A 204)
Grosvenor Ga. W1 —45Jb 82 (5H 197)
Grosvenor Hill. SW19 —65Ab 124
Grosvenor Hill. W1 —45Kb 82 (4K 197)
Grosvenor Pk. SE5 —52Sb 105
Grosvenor Pk. Rd. E17 —29Cc 44
Grosvenor Path. Lou —11Rc 28
Grosvenor Pl. SW1 —47Jb 82 (1J 203)
Grosvenor Pl. Wey —76T 140
Grosvenor Rise. E. E17 —29Dc 44
Grosvenor Rd. E6 —39Mc 65
Grosvenor Rd. E7 —37Kc 65
Grosvenor Rd. E10 —32Ec 64
Grosvenor Rd. E11 —29Kc 45
Grosvenor Rd. N3 —24Bb 41
Grosvenor Rd. N9 —18Xb 25
Grosvenor Rd. N10 —25Kb 42
Grosvenor Rd. SE25 —70Wb 127
Grosvenor Rd. SW1 —51Kb 104
Grosvenor Rd. W4 —50Ra 79
Grosvenor Rd. W7 —46Ja 78
Grosvenor Rd. Belv —51Cd 110
Grosvenor Rd. Bexh —57Zc 109
Grosvenor Rd. Borwd —13Qa 21
Grosvenor Rd. Bren —51Ma 101
Grosvenor Rd. Chob —1A 188
Grosvenor Rd. Dag —32Bd 67
Grosvenor Rd. Eps —91Ta 177
Grosvenor Rd. Houn —55Ba 99
Grosvenor Rd. Ilf —34Sc 66
Grosvenor Rd. N'wd —22V 36
Grosvenor Rd. Orp —72Uc 150
Grosvenor Rd. Ors —4F 92
Grosvenor Rd. Rich —57Na 101
Grosvenor Rd. Romf —31Fd 68
Grosvenor Rd. S'hall —48Ba 77
Grosvenor Rd. Stai —66J 119
Grosvenor Rd. Twic —60Ja 100
Grosvenor Rd. Wall —79Kb 146
Grosvenor Rd. Wat —13Y 19
Grosvenor Rd. W Wick —74Dc 148
Grosvenor Sq. W1 —45Jb 82 (4J 197)
Grosvenor Sq. Long —69Ae 135
Grosvenor St. W1 —45Kb 82 (4K 197)
Grosvenor Ter. SE5 —52Sb 105
Grosvenor Vale. Ruis —33V 56
Grosvenor Way. E5 —33Yb 64
Grosvenor Wharf Rd. E14 —49Fc 85
Grotes Bldgs. SE3 —54Gc 107
Grote's Pl. SE3 —54Gc 107
Groton Rd. SW18 —61Db 125
Grotto Ct. SE1 —47Sb 83 (1D 206)
Grotto Pas. W1 —43Jb 82 (7J 191)
Grotto Rd. Twic —61Ha 122
Grotto Rd. Wey —76R 140
Grove Av. N3 —24Cb 41
Grove Av. N10 —26Lb 42
Grove Av. W7 —44Ga 78
Grove Av. Eps —85Ua 162
Grove Av. Pinn —28Aa 37
Grove Av. Sutt —79Cb 145
Grove Av. Twic —60Ha 100
Grove Bank. Wat —18Z 19
Grovebury Clo. Eri —51Fd 110
Grovebury Ct. Bexh —57Dd 110
Grovebury Rd. SE2 —47Xc 87
Grove Clo. N14 —17Lb 24
Grove Clo. SE23 —60Ac 106
Grove Clo. Brom —75Jc 149
Grove Clo. Felt —63Aa 121
Grove Clo. King T —70Pa 123
Grove Clo. Old Win —9M 95
Grove Clo. Slou —8K 73
Grove Clo. Uxb —36Q 56
Grove Corner. Bookh —98Da 175
Grove Cotts. W4 —51Ua 102
Grove Ct. E Mol —71Fa 142
Grove Ct. Egh —64C 118
Grove Ct. Houn —56Ca 99
Grove Ct. Wal A —5Dc 12
Grove Cres. E18 —26Hc 45
Grove Cres. NW9 —28Sa 39
Grove Cres. SE5 —54Ub 105
Grove Cres. Crox —14Q 18
Grove Cres. Felt —63Aa 121
Grove Cres. King T —69Na 123
Grove Cres. W on T —73X 141
Grove Cres. Rd. E15 —37Fc 65
Grovedale Clo. Chesh —2Wb 11
Grovedale Rd. N19 —33Mb 62
Grove Dwellings. E1 —43Yb 84
Grove End. E18 —26Hc 45
Grove End. NW5 —35Kb 62
Grove End La. Esh —74Fa 142
Grove End Rd. NW8 —40Fb 61 (2B 190)
Grove Farm Ind. Est. Mitc —71Hb 145
Grove Farm Pk. N'wd —22T 36
Grovefield. N11 —21Kb 42 (off Coppies Gro.)
Grove Footpath. Surb —70Na 123
Grove Gdns. E15 —37Gc 65
Grove Gdns. NW4 —29Wa 40
Grove Gdns. NW8 —41Gb 81 (4E 190)
Grove Gdns. Dag —34Ed 68
Grove Gdns. Enf —10Zb 12
Grove Gdns. Rich —58Na 101
Grove Gdns. Tedd —63Ja 122
Grove Grn. N'wd —22T 36
Grove Grn. Rd. E11 —34Ec 64
Grove Hall Ct. NW8 —41Eb 81 (3A 190)
Grove Hall Rd. Bush —14Aa 19
Grove Heath Ct. Rip —96L 173
Grove Heath N. Rip —94K 173
Grove Heath Rd. Rip —95K 173
Grove Hill. E18 —26Hc 45
Grove Hill. Harr —32Ga 58
Grovehill Ct. Brom —65Hc 129
Grove Hill Rd. SE5 —55Ub 105
Grove Hill Rd. Harr —31Ha 58
Grove Ho. W5 —46La 78
Grove Ho. Bush —16Ba 19
Grove Ho. Chesh —2Xb 11
Grove Ho. War —21Xd 50
Grove Ho. Rd. N8 —28Nb 42
Groveland Av. SW16 —66Pb 126
Groveland Ct. EC4 (off Bow La.) —44Sb 83 (3E 200)
Groveland Rd. Beck —69Bc 128
Grovelands. W Mol —70Ca 121
Grovelands Clo. SE5 —54Ub 105
Grovelands Clo. Harr —34Da 57
Grovelands Ct. N14 —17Mb 24
Grovelands Rd. N13 —21Pb 42
Grovelands Rd. N15 —30Wb 43
Grovelands Rd. Orp —66Wc 131
Grovelands Rd. Purl —84Nb 164
Grovelands Way. Grays —50Be 91
Groveland Way. N Mald —71Sa 143
Grove La. SE5 —53Tb 105
Grove La. SE15 —52Xb 105
Grove La. Chig —20Vc 29
Grove La. Coul —85Jb 164
Grove La. Epp —2Wc 15
Grove La. King T —70Na 123
Grove La. Uxb —42P 75
Grove La.Ter. SE5 —54Tb 105
Groveley Rd. Sun —64V 120
Grove Mkt. Pl. SE9 —58Pc 108
Grove M. W6 —48Ya 80
Grove M. W11 —44Bb 81
Grove Mill La. Rick & Wat —9R 4
Grove Pde. Slou —7L 73
Grove Pk. E11 —30Kc 45
Grove Pk. NW9 —28Sa 39
Grove Pk. SE5 —54Ub 105
Grove Pk. Av. E4 —24Dc 44
Grove Pk. Bri. W4 —52Sa 101
Grove Pk. Gdns. W4 —52Ra 101
Grove Pk. Ind. Est. NW9 —28Ta 39
Grove Pk. M. W4 —52Sa 101
Grove Pk. Rd. N15 —28Ub 43
Grove Pk. Rd. SE9 —62Lc 129
Grove Pk. Rd. W4 —52Ra 101
Grove Pk. Rd. Rain —39Jd 68
Grove Pk. Ter. W4 —52Ra 101
Grove Pas. E2 —40Xb 63
Grove Path. Chesh —3Wb 11
Grove Pl. NW3 —34Fb 61
Grove Pl. W3 —46Sa 79
Grove Pl. Bark —39Sc 66
Grove Pl. Wey —78S 140
Grover Ct. SE13 —54Dc 106
Grover Ho. SE11 —50Pb 82 (7J 205)
Grove Rd. E3 —39Zb 64
Grove Rd. E4 —21Ec 44
Grove Rd. E11 —31Hc 65
Grove Rd. E17 —30Dc 44
Grove Rd. E18 —26Hc 45
Grove Rd. N11 —22Kb 42
Grove Rd. N12 —22Fb 41
Grove Rd. N15 —29Ub 43
Grove Rd. NW2 —37Ya 60
Grove Rd. SW13 —54Va 102
Grove Rd. SW19 —66Eb 125
Grove Rd. W3 —46Sa 79
Grove Rd. W5 —45Ma 79
Grove Rd. Asht —90Pa 161
Grove Rd. Barn —13Gb 23
Grove Rd. Belv —51Bd 109
Grove Rd. Bexh —56Ed 110
Grove Rd. Borwd —11Qa 21
Grove Rd. Bren —50La 78
Grove Rd. Burn —1B 72
Grove Rd. Cher —72H 139
Grove Rd. E Mol —70Fa 122
Grove Rd. Edgw —23Qa 39
Grove Rd. Eps —85Ua 162
Grove Rd. Grav —57De 113
Grove Rd. Grays —51De 113
Grove Rd. Houn —56Ca 99
Grove Rd. Iswth —53Ga 100
Grove Rd. L Hth —31Xc 67
Grove Rd. Mitc —69Jb 126
Grove Rd. N'wd —22T 36
Grove Rd. Pinn —29Ba 37
Grove Rd. Rich —58Pa 101
Grove Rd. Rick —19J 17
Grove Rd. Seal —94Qd 187
Grove Rd. Sev —93Ld 187
Grove Rd. Shep —72S 140
Grove Rd. Stanf —3M 93
Grove Rd. Surb —71Ma 143
Grove Rd. Sutt —79Cb 145
Grove Rd. Tats —92Lc 183
Grove Rd. T Hth —70Qb 126
Grove Rd. Twic —62Fa 122
Grove Rd. Uxb —38M 55
Grove Rd. Wind —4G 94
Grove Rd. Wok —88B 156
Grove Rd. W. Enf —9Yb 12
Grover Rd. Wat —17Z 19
Grovers Farm Cotts. Wdhm —83G 156
Grovesby Ct. N14 —17Mb 24
Grove Shaw. Tad —96Ab 178
Groveside. Bookh —99Ca 175
Groveside Clo. W3 —43Qa 79
Groveside Clo. Bookh —99Ca 175
Groveside Clo. Cars —75Gb 145
Groveside Rd. E4 —19Gc 27
Grovestile Waye. Felt —59T 98
Grove St. N18 —22Vb 43
Grove St. SE8 —49Bc 84
Grove Ter. NW5 —34Jb 62
Grove Ter. S'hall —45Ca 77
Grove Ter. Tedd —63Ja 122
Grove Ter. M. NW5 —34Kb 62
Grove, The. E15 —37Gc 65
Grove, The. N3 —24Cb 41
Grove, The. N4 —31Pb 62
Grove, The. N6 —32Jb 62
Grove, The. N8 —29Mb 42
Grove, The. N13 —21Qb 42 (in two parts)
Grove, The. N14 —15Lb 24
Grove, The. NW9 —29Ta 39
Grove, The. NW11 —31Ab 60
Grove, The. W5 —45Na 79
Grove, The. Add —78K 139
Grove, The. Bexh —56Zc 109
Grove, The. Big H —90Nc 168
Grove, The. Brtwd —21Vd 50
Grove, The. Cat —93Sb 181
Grove, The. Coul —86Mb 164
Grove, The. Edgw —21Ra 39
Grove, The. Egh —64C 118
Grove, The. Enf —12Qb 24
Grove, The. Eps —85Ua 162
Grove, The. Ewe —82Va 162
Grove, The. Grav —9D 114
Grove, The. Gnfd —44Ea 78
Grove, The. Iswth —53Ga 100
Grove, The. Lat —8A 2
Grove, The. Pot B —4Eb 9
Grove, The. Rad —6Ja 6
Grove, The. Sidc —63Ad 131
Grove, The. Slou —7L 73
Grove, The. Swan —69Hd 132
Grove, The. Swans —57Be 113
Grove, The. Tedd —63Ja 122
Grove, The. Twic —58Ka 100
Grove, The. Upm —36Rd 69
Grove, The. Uxb —36Q 56
Grove, The. W on T —73X 141
Grove, The. W Wick —75Ec 148
Grove, The. Wok —88B 156
Grove Vale. SE22 —56Vb 105
Grove Vale. Chst —65Qc 130
Grove Vs. E14 —45Dc 84
Groveway. SW9 —53Pb 104
Grove Way. Chor —15D 16
Groveway. Dag —34Zc 67
Grove Way. Esh —73Ea 142
Grove Way. Uxb —38M 55
Grove Way. Wemb —36Ra 59
Grovewood. Rich —53Qa 101
Grovewood Clo. Chor —15D 16
Grove Wood Hill. Coul —86Lb 164
Grub St. Oxt —100Lc 183
Grummant Rd. SE15 —53Vb 105
Grundy St. E14 —44Dc 84
Gruneisen Rd. N3 —24Db 41
Guardian Bus. Cen. H Hill —24Md 49
Guardian Clo. Horn —32Kd 69
Guardian Ct. SE12 —57Gc 107
Guardsman Clo. War —22Zd 51
Guards Rd. Wind —4A 94
Gubbins La. Romf —24Pd 49
Gubyon Av. SE24 —57Rb 105
Guerin Sq. E3 —41Bc 84
Guernsey Clo. Houn —52Ca 99
Guernsey Farm Dri. Wok —3G 188
Guernsey Gro. SE24 —59Sb 105
Guernsey Ho. N1 —37Sb 63
Guernsey Ho. Enf —10Zb 12 (off Eastfield Rd.)
Guernsey Rd. E11 —32Fc 65
Guest St. EC1 —42Sb 83 (6E 194) (off Chequer St.)
Guibal Rd. SE12 —59Kc 107
Guildersfield Rd. SW16 —66Nb 126
Guildersome St. SE18 —51Qc 108
Guildford Av. Felt —61V 120
Guildford Gdns. Romf —23Nd 49
Guildford Gro. SE10 —53Dc 106
Guildford La. Wok —91A 172
Guildford Lodge Dri. E Hor —100V 174
Guildford Pl. WC1 —42Pb 82 (6H 193)
Guildford Rd. E6 —44Pc 86
Guildford Rd. E17 —25Ec 44
Guildford Rd. SW8 —53Nb 104
Guildford Rd. Chob —1A 188
Guildford Rd. Croy —72Tb 147
Guildford Rd. E Hor & Bookh —100V 174
Guildford Rd. Fet —97Fa 176
Guildford Rd. Ilf —33Uc 66
Guildford Rd. Mayf —10G 188
Guildford Rd. Romf —23Nd 49
Guildford Rd. Sheer & Cher —83D 156
Guildford Rd. Wok —91A 172
Guildford St. WC1 —42Nb 82 (6F 193)
Guildford St. Cher —74H 139
Guildford St. Stai —65J 119
Guildford Way. Wall —78Nb 146
Guildhall Bldgs. EC2 —44Tb 83 (2F 201) (off Basinghall St.)
Guildhall Yd. EC2 —44Sb 83 (2E 200)
Guildhouse St. SW1 —49Lb 82 (5B 204)
Guildown Av. N12 —21Db 41
Guild Rd. SE7 —50Mc 85
Guild Rd. Eri —52Hd 110
Guildsway. E17 —25Bc 44
Guileshill La. Ock —95N 173
Guilford Av. Surb —71Pa 143
Guilford Pl. WC1 —42Pb 82
Guilford St. WC1 —42Nb 82
Guilfoyle. NW9 —26Va 40
Guillemot Ct. SE8 —51Bc 106
Guillemot Pl. N22 —26Pb 42
Guilsborough Clo. NW10 —38Ua 60
Guinevere Gdns. Wal X —3Ac 12
Guinness Clo. E9 —38Ac 64
Guinness Clo. Hay —48T 76
Guinness Ct. NW8 —39Gb 61 (1E 190)
Guinness Ct. SE1 —47Ub 83 (1H 207) (off Snowsfields)
Guinness Ct. Wok —6C 188
Guinness Sq. SE1 —49Ub 83 (5H 207)
Guinness Trust Bldgs. SE11 —50Rb 83 (7B 206)
Guinness Trust Bldgs. SE17 —50Rb 83
Guinness Trust Bldgs. W6 —50Za 80 (off Fulham Pal. Rd.)
Guinness Trust Est. N16 —32Ub 63
Guion Rd. SW6 —54Bb 103
Gulland Clo. Bush —15Ea 20
Gulland Wlk. N1 —37Sb 63 (off Oronsay Wlk.)
Gull Clo. Wall —80Nb 146
Gullet Wood Rd. Wat —7W 4
Gulliver Clo. N'holt —39Ba 57
Gulliver Rd. Sidc —61Tc 130
Gulliver's Ho. EC1 —42Sb 83 (6D 194) (off Goswell Rd.)
Gulliver St. SE16 —48Ac 84
Gull Wlk. Horn —38Kd 69
Gulston Wlk. SW3 —49Hb 81 (6G 203) (off Blackland Ter.)
Gumleigh Rd. W5 —49La 78
Gumley Gdns. Iswth —55Ja 100
Gumley Rd. Grays —51Zd 113
Gumping Rd. Orp —75Sc 150
Gunderson Corner. Mitc —69Hb 125
Gundulph Rd. Brom —69Lc 129
Gunfleet Clo. Grav —9G 114
Gun Hill. W Til —1F 114
Gunmaker's La. E3 —39Ac 64
Gunnell Clo. SE26 —63Wb 127
Gunner La. SE18 —50Qc 86
Gunnersbury Av. W5, W3 & W4 —46Pa 79
Gunnersbury Clo. W4 —50Ra 79
Gunnersbury Ct. W3 —47Ra 79
Gunnersbury Cres. W3 —47Qa 79
Gunnersbury Dri. W5 —47Pa 79
Gunnersbury Gdns. W3 —47Qa 79
Gunnersbury La. W3 —48Qa 79
Gunnersbury M. W4 —50Ra 79
Gunners Gro. E4 —20Ec 26
Gunners Rd. SW18 —61Fb 125
Gunning St. SE18 —49Uc 86
Gunn Rd. Swans —58Ae 113
Gunpowder Sq. EC4 —44Qb 82 (2A 200) (off Gough Sq.)
Gunsite La. Cob —85Y 159
Gunstor Rd. N16 —35Ub 63
Gun St. E1 —43Vb 83 (1K 201)
Gunter Gro. SW10 —51Eb 103
Gunter Gro. Edgw —25Ta 39
Gunterstone Rd. W14 —49Ab 80
Gunthorpe St. E1 —43Vb 83
Gunton Rd. E5 —34Xb 63
Gunton Rd. SW17 —65Jb 126
Gunwhale Clo. SE16 —46Zb 84
Gurdon Rd. SE7 —50Jc 85
Gurenne Ct. E4 —18Ec 26
Gurnard Clo. W Dray —45M 75
Gurnell Gro. W13 —42Ha 78
Gurney Clo. E15 —36Gc 65
Gurney Clo. E17 —25Zb 44
Gurney Clo. Bark —37Rc 66
Gurney Cres. Croy —74Pb 146
Gurney Dri. N2 —28Eb 41
Gurney Ho. Hay —49U 76
Gurney Rd. E15 —36Gc 65
Gurney Rd. Cars —77Jb 146
Gurney Rd. N'holt —41X 77
Guthrie Ct. SE1 —47Qb 82 (2A 206) (off Morley St.)
Guthrie St. SW3 —50Fb 81 (7D 202)
Gutter La. EC2 —44Sb 83 (2E 200)
Guyatt Gdns. Mitc —68Jb 126
Guy Barnett Gro. SE3 —55Jc 107
Guybon Av. SE24 —57Rb 105
Guy Rd. Wall —76Mb 146
Guyscliff Rd. SE13 —57Ec 106
Guysfield Clo. Rain —39Jd 68
Guysfield Dri. Rain —39Jd 68
Guys Retreat. Buck H —17Lc 27
Guy St. SE1 —47Tb 83 (1G 207)
Guy St. SW1 —47Tb 83
Gwalior Rd. SW15 —55Za 102
Gwendolen Av. SW15 —56Za 102
Gwendolen Clo. SW15 —57Za 102
Gwendoline Av. E13 —39Kc 65
Gwendwr Rd. W14 —50Ab 80
Gweneth Cotts. Edgw —23Qa 39
Gwent Clo. Wat —6Z 5
Gwillim Clo. Sidc —57Wc 109
Gwydor Rd. Beck —69Zb 128
Gwydyr Rd. Brom —69Hc 129
Gwyn Clo. SW6 —52Eb 103
Gwynne Av. Croy —73Zb 148
Gwynne Clo. Wind —3C 94
Gwynne Pk. Av. Wfd G —23Pc 46
Gwynne Pl. WC1 —41Pb 82 (4J 193)
Gwynne Rd. SW11 —54Fb 103
Gwynn Rd. Grav —61Ee 135
Gyfford Wlk. Chesh —3Xb 11
Gylcote Clo. SE5 —56Tb 105
Gyles Pk. Stan —25La 38
Gyllyngdune Gdns. Ilf —33Vc 67
Gypsy La. K Lan —7T 4
Gypsy La. Stoke P —5J 53

Haarlem Rd. W14 —48Za 80
Haberdasher Est. N1 —41Tb 83 (3G 195)
Haberdasher Pl. N1 —41Tb 83 (3H 195)
Haberdasher St. N1 —41Tb 83 (3G 195)
Habgood Rd. Lou —13Nc 28
Haccombe Rd. SW19 —65Eb 125
Hackbridge Grn. Wall —75Jb 146
Hackbridge Pk. Cars —75Hb 145
Hackbridge Pk. Gdns. Cars —75Hb 145
Hackbridge Rd. Wall —75Jb 146
Hacketts La. Wok —86H 157
Hackford Rd. SW9 —53Pb 104
Hackford Wlk. SW9 —53Pb 104
Hackforth Clo. Barn —15Xa 22
Hackington Cres. Beck —65Cc 128
Hacklington Ct. New Bar —15Db 23
Hackney Clo. Borwd —15Ta 21
Hackney Gro. E8 —37Xb 63
Hackney Rd. E2 —41Vb 83 (4J 195)
Hacton Dri. Horn —35Md 69
Hacton La. Horn & Upm —33Pd 69
Hadden Rd. SE28 —48Uc 86
Hadden Way. Gnfd —37Fa 58
Haddington Rd. Brom —62Fc 129
Haddon Clo. Borwd —12Qa 21
Haddon Clo. Enf —16Wb 25
Haddon Clo. N Mald —71Va 144
Haddon Clo. Wey —76U 140
Haddonfield. SE8 —49Zb 84
Haddon Gro. Sidc —59Vc 109
Haddon Rd. Chor —15E 16
Haddon Rd. Orp —71Yc 151
Haddon Rd. Sutt —77Db 145
Haddo St. SE10 —51Ec 106
Haden Ct. N4 —33Qb 62
Hadfield Rd. Stai —58M 97
Hadfield Rd. Stanf —2M 93
Hadleigh Clo. E1 —42Yb 84
Hadleigh Ct. E4 —17Gc 27
Hadleigh Ct. Brtwd —20Wd 32
Hadleigh Rd. N9 —17Xb 25
Hadleigh St. E2 —41Yb 84
Hadleigh Wlk. E6 —44Nc 86
Hadley Clo. N21 —16Qb 24
Hadley Clo. Els —16Pa 21
Hadley Comn. Barn —12Cb 23
Hadley Ct. N16 —32Wb 63
Hadley Ct. New Bar —13Db 23
Hadley Gdns. W4 —50Ta 79
Hadley Gdns. S'hall —50Ba 77
Hadley Grn. Rd. Barn —12Bb 23
Hadley Grn. W. Barn —12Bb 23
Hadley Gro. Barn —12Ab 22
Hadley Highstone. Barn —11Bb 23
Hadley Mnr. Trading Est. Barn —13Bb 23
Hadley Ridge. Barn —13Bb 23
Hadley Rd. Barn —12Db 23 (Barnet)
Hadley Rd. Barn & Enf —10Hb 9 (Hadley Wood)
Hadley Rd. Belv —49Bd 87
Hadley Rd. Mitc —70Mb 126
Hadley St. NW1 —37Kb 62
Hadley Way. N21 —16Qb 24
Hadley Wood Rise. Kenl —87Rb 165
Hadley Wood Rd. Barn —12Eb 23
Hadlow Ct. Slou —6G 72
Hadlow Pl. SE19 —66Wb 127
Hadlow Rd. Sidc —63Wc 131
Hadlow Rd. Well —52Yc 109
Hadlow Way. Grav —6A 136
Hadrian Clo. Stai —60N 97
Hadrian Clo. Wall —80Nb 146
Hadrian Ct. Sutt —80Db 145
Hadrian Est. E2 —40Wb 63
Hadrians Ride. Enf —15Vb 25
Hadrian St. SE10 —50Gc 85
Hadrian Way. Stai —59M 97
Hadyn Pk. Ct. W12 —47Wa 80 (off Curwen Rd.)
Hadyn Pk. Rd. W12 —47Wa 80
Hafer Rd. SW11 —56Hb 103
Hafton Rd. SE6 —60Gc 107
Hagden La. Wat —14V 18
Haggard Rd. Twic —59Ka 100
Hagger Ct. E17 —27Fc 45
Haggerston Rd. E8 —38Vb 63
Haggerston Rd. Borwd —10Na 7
Hague St. E2 —41Wb 83
Ha Ha Rd. SE18 —51Pc 108
Haig Dri. Slou —7F 72
Haig Gdns. Grav —9E 114
Haig Rd. Big H —89Nc 168
Haig Rd. Grays —8C 92
Haig Rd. Stan —22La 38
Haig Rd. Uxb —43R 76
Haig Rd. E. E13 —41Lc 85
Haig Rd. W. E13 —41Lc 85
Haigville Gdns. Ilf —28Rc 46
Hailes Clo. SW19 —65Eb 125
Haileybury Av. Enf —16Vb 25
Haileybury Rd. Orp —77Wc 151
Hailey Rd. Eri —47Cd 88
Hailsham Av. SW2 —61Pb 126
Hailsham Clo. Romf —22Ld 49
Hailsham Clo. Surb —73Ma 143
Hailsham Cres. Bark —36Vc 67
Hailsham Dri. Harr —27Fa 38
Hailsham Gdns. Romf —22Ld 49
Hailsham Rd. SW17 —65Jb 126
Hailsham Rd. Romf —22Ld 49
Hailsham Ter. N18 —22Tb 43
Haimo Rd. SE9 —57Mc 107
Hainault Ct. E17 —28Fc 45
Hainault Gore. Romf —29Ad 47
Hainault Gro. Chig —21Sc 46
Hainault Ind. Est. Ilf —23Yc 47
Hainault Rd. E11 —32Ec 64
Hainault Rd. Chad —30Bd 47
Hainault Rd. Chig —20Rc 28
Hainault Rd. Col R —26Ed 48
Hainault Rd. L Hth —24Xc 47
Hainault St. SE9 —60Rc 108
Hainault St. Ilf —33Sc 66
Haines Ct. Wey —78T 140
Haines St. SW8 —52Lb 104
Haines Wlk. Mord —73Db 145

Haines Way—Hardings Row

Haines Way. Wat —6W **4**
Hainford Clo. SE4 —56Zb **106**
Haining Clo. W4 —50Qa **79**
Hainthorpe Rd. SE27 —62Rb **127**
Hainton Pl. E1 —44Xb **83**
Halberd M. E5 —33Xb **63**
Halbutt Gdns. Dag —34Bd **67**
Halbutt St. Dag —35Bd **67**
Halcomb St. N1 —39Ub **63**
Halcot Av. Bexh —57Dd **110**
Halcrow St. E1 —43Xb **83**
*Halcyon. Enf —15Ub **25***
(off Private Rd.)
Halcyon Ct. Wemb —34Ra **59**
Halcyon Way. Horn —32Pd **69**
Haldane Clo. N10 —24Kb **42**
Haldane Pl. SW18 —60Db **103**
Haldane Rd. E6 —41Mc **85**
Haldane Rd. SE28 —45Zc **87**
Haldane Rd. SW6 —52Bb **103**
Haldane Rd. S'hall —45Ea **78**
Haldan Rd. E4 —23Ec **44**
Haldon Clo. Chig —22Uc **46**
Haldon Rd. SW18 —58Bb **103**
Hale Clo. E4 —20Ec **26**
Hale Clo. Edgw —22Sa **39**
Hale Clo. Orp —77Sc **150**
Hale Ct. Edgw —22Sa **39**
Hale Dri. NW7 —23Sa **39**
Hale End. Romf —23Kd **49**
Hale End Clo. Ruis —30W **36**
Hale End Rd. E17 —25Fc **45**
Hale End Rd. Wfd G & E4 —24Fc **45**
Halefield Rd. N17 —25Xb **43**
Hale Gdns. N17 —28Wb **43**
Hale Gdns. W3 —46Qa **79**
Hale Gro. Gdns. NW7 —22Ua **40**
*Hale Ho. Horn —30Jd **48***
(off Benjamin Clo.)
Hale La. NW7 —22Ta **39**
Hale La. Edgw —22Ra **39**
Hale La. Otf —89Hd **170**
Hale Path. SE27 —63Rb **127**
Hale Pit Rd. Bookh —98Ea **176**
Hale Rd. E6 —42Nc **86**
Hale Rd. N17 —27Wb **43**
Hales Oak. Bookh —98Ea **176**
Halesowen Rd. Mord —73Db **145**
Hales St. SE8 —52Cc **106**
Hale St. E14 —45Dc **84**
Hale St. Stai —63G **118**
Haleswood. Cob —86X **159**
Halesworth Clo. E5 —33Yb **64**
Halesworth Clo. Romf —24Nd **49**
Halesworth Rd. SE13 —55Dc **106**
Halesworth Rd. Romf —23Nd **49**
Hale, The. E4 —24Fc **45**
Hale, The. N17 —27Wb **43**
Hale Wlk. W7 —43Ga **78**
Haley Rd. NW4 —30Ya **40**
Half Acre. Bren —51Ma **101**
Half Acre. Stan —23La **38**
Half Acre Hill. Ger X —25B **34**
Half Acre Rd. W7 —46Ga **78**
Halfhides. Wal A —5Fc **13**
Half Moon Cotts. Rip —93L **173**
Half Moon Ct. EC1
*—43Sb **83** (1D **200**)*
(off Bartholomew Clo.)
Half Moon Cres. N1
—40Pb **62** (1J **193**)
Half Moon La. SE24 —58Sb **105**
Half Moon La. Epp —3Vc **15**
Half Moon Pas. E1 —44Vb **83**
Half Moon St. W1
—46Kb **82** (6A **198**)
Halford Rd. E10 —29Fc **45**
Halford Rd. SW6 —51Cb **103**
Halford Rd. Rich —57Na **101**
Halford Rd. Uxb —35Q **56**
Halfpence La. Cobh —9K **137**
Halfway Ct. Purf —49Qd **89**
Halfway Grn. W on T —76X **141**
Halfway St. Sidc —59Tc **108**
Haliburton Rd. Twic —57Ja **100**
*Haliday Ho. N1 —37Tb **63***
(off Newington Grn. Rd.)
Haliday Wlk. N1 —37Tb **63**
Halidon Clo. E9 —36Yb **64**
Halidon Rise. Romf —23Rd **49**
Halifax. NW9 —26Ua **40**
Halifax Rd. Enf —12Sb **25**
Halifax Rd. Gnfd —39Da **57**
Halifax Rd. Herons —17E **16**
Halifax St. SE26 —62Xb **127**
Halifield Dri. Belv —48Ad **87**
Haling Down Pas. Purl —82Rb **165**
Haling Gro. S Croy —80Sb **147**
Haling Pk. Gdns. S Croy —79Rb **147**
Haling Pk. Rd. S Croy —78Rb **147**
Haling Rd. S Croy —79Tb **147**
Halings La. Den —28F **34**
Halkin Arc. SW1 —48Hb **81** (3G **203**)
Halkingcroft. Slou —7N **73**
Halkin M. SW1 —48Jb **82** (3H **203**)
Halkin Pl. SW1 —48Jb **82** (3H **203**)
Halkin St. SW1 —47Jb **82** (2J **203**)
Hallam Clo. Chst —64Pc **130**
Hallam Gdns. Pinn —24Aa **37**
Hallam M. W1 —43Kb **82** (7A **192**)
Hallam Rd. N15 —28Rb **43**
Hallam Rd. SW13 —55Xa **102**
Hallam St. W1 —43Kb **82** (6A **192**)
Halland Way. N'wd —23T **36**
Hall Av. S Ock —46Sd **90**
Hall Clo. W5 —43Na **79**
Hall Clo. Rick —18J **17**
Hall Ct. Dat —2M **95**
Hall Ct. Tedd —64Ha **122**
Hall Cres. S Ock —47Sd **90**
Hall Dri. SE26 —64Yb **128**
Hall Dri. W7 —44Ga **78**
Hall Dri. Hare —25L **35**
Halley Gdns. SE13 —56Fc **107**
Halley Pl. E14 —43Ac **84**
Halley Rd. E7 & E12 —37Lc **65**
Halley's App. Wok —6D **188**
Halley's Ct. Wok —6D **188**
Halley St. E14 —43Ac **84**
Halley's Wlk. Add —80L **139**
Hall Farm Clo. Stan —21Ka **38**
Hall Farm Dri. Twic —59Fa **100**
Hallfield Est. W2 —44Eb **81**
Hallford Way. Dart —58Ld **111**
Hall Gdns. E4 —21Bc **44**
Hall Ga. NW8 —41Fb **81** (3B **190**)
Hall Grn. La. Hut —17Ee **33**
Hall Hill. Sev —95Rd **187**
Halliards. The. W on T —72W **140**
Halliday Sq. S'hall —46Fa **78**
Halliford Clo. Shep —70T **120**
Halliford Rd. Shep & Sun —71U **140**
Halliford St. N1 —38Sb **63**
Hallingbury Ct. E17 —27Dc **44**
Hallington Clo. Wok —5E **188**
Halliwell Ct. SE22 —57Wb **105**
Halliwell Rd. SW2 —58Pb **104**
*Halliwick Ct. Pde. N12 —23Hb **41***
(off Woodhouse Rd.)
Halliwick Rd. N10 —25Jb **42**
Hall La. E4 —22Ac **44**
Hall La. NW4 —25Wa **40**
Hall La. Hay —52T **98**
Hall La. Shenf —17Be **33**
Hall La. S Ock —40Zd **71**
Hall La. Upm —26Sd **50**
Hallmark Trading Cen. Wemb
—35Sa **59**
Hall Meadow. Burn —10A **52**
Hallmead Rd. Sutt —76Db **145**
Hall Oak Wlk. NW6 —37Bb **61**
Hallowell Av. Croy —77Nb **146**
Hallowell Clo. Mitc —69Jb **126**
Hallowell Rd. N'wd —24U **36**
Hallowes Cres. Wat —20W **18**
Hall Pk. Rd. Upm —36Sd **70**
Hall Pl. W2 —42Fb **81** (6B **190**)
Hall Pl. Wok —88C **156**
Hall Pl. Cres. Bex —57Ed **110**
Hall Pl. Dri. Wey —78U **140**
Hall Rd. E6 —39Pc **66**
Hall Rd. E15 —35Fc **65**
Hall Rd. NW8 —41Eb **81** (4A **190**)
Hall Rd. Chad —30Yc **47**
Hall Rd. Dart —56Pd **111**
Hall Rd. Gid P —27Kd **49**
Hall Rd. Grav —62Ee **135**
Hall Rd. Iswth —57Fa **100**
Hall Rd. S Ock —47Sd **90**
Hall Rd. Wall —81Kb **164**
Halls Farm Clo. Knap —5A **188**
Hallside Rd. Enf —10Vb **11**
Hall St. EC1 —41Rb **83** (3C **194**)
Hall St. N12 —22Eb **41**
Hallsville Rd. E16 —44Hc **85**
Hallswelle Pde. NW11 —29Bb **41**
Hallswelle Rd. NW11 —29Bb **41**
Hall Ter. Romf —24Qd **49**
Hall Ter. S Ock —47Td **90**
Hall, The. SE3 —55Jc **107**
Hall View. SE9 —61Mc **129**
Hall Way. Purl —85Rb **165**
Hallwood Cres. Shenf —17Ae **33**
Hallywell Cres. E6 —43Pc **86**
Halons Rd. SE9 —59Qc **108**
Halpin Pl. SE17 —49Tb **83** (6G **207**)
Halsbrook Rd. SE3 —55Mc **107**
Halsbury Clo. Stan —21Ka **38**
Halsbury Ct. Stan —21Ka **38**
Halsbury Rd. W12 —46Xa **80**
Halsbury Rd. E. N'holt —35Ea **58**
Halsbury Rd. W. N'holt —36Da **57**
Halse Dri. Farn C —5C **52**
Halsey M. SW3 —49Hb **81** (5F **203**)
Halsey Pl. Wat —10X **5**
Halsey Rd. Wat —13X **19**
Halsey St. SW3 —49Hb **81** (5F **203**)
Halsmere Rd. SE5 —53Rb **105**
*Halstead Ct. N1 —40Tb **63** (2G **195**)*
(off Fairbank Est.)
Halstead Gdns. N21 —18Tb **25**
Halstead Hill. Chesh —1Ub **11**
Halstead La. Knock —87Ad **169**
Halstead Rd. E11 —29Jc **45**
Halstead Rd. N21 —18Tb **25**
Halstead Rd. Enf —14Ub **25**
Halstead Rd. Eri —53Gd **110**
Halstead Way. Hut —16Ee **33**
Halston Clo. SW11 —58Hb **103**
Halstow Rd. NW10 —41Za **80**
Halstow Rd. SE10 —50Jc **85**
Halsway. Hay —46W **76**
Halt Dri. Linf —9J **93**
Halter Clo. Borwd —15Ta **21**
Halton Cross St. N1 —39Rb **63**
Halton Mans. N1 —38Rb **63**
Halton Rd. N1 —38Rb **63**
Halton Rd. Grays —8E **92**
Halt Robin La. Belv —49Dd **88**
Halt Robin Rd. Belv —49Cd **88**
(in two parts)
Hambalt Rd. SW4 —57Lb **104**
Hamble Clo. Ruis —33U **56**
Hamble Clo. Wok —5D **188**
Hamble Ct. Wat —14W **18**
Hambleden Pl. SE21 —60Ub **105**
Hambledon Clo. Uxb —42R **76**
Hambledon Gdns. SE25 —69Vb **127**
Hambledon Hill. Eps —88Sa **161**
Hambledon Rd. SW18 —59Bb **103**
Hambledon Vale. Eps —88Sa **161**
Hambledown Rd. Sidc —59Tc **108**
Hamble La. S Ock —43Vd **90**
Hamble St. SW6 —55Db **103**
Hambleton Clo. Wor Pk —75Ya **144**
*Hamble Wlk. N'holt —40Ca **57***
(off Brabazon Rd.)
Hamble Wlk. Wok —6D **188**
Hambridge Way. SW2 —59Qb **104**
Hambro Av. Brom —74Jc **149**
*Hambro Ho. Shenf —16De **33***
(off Rayleigh Rd.)
Hambrook Rd. SE25 —69Xb **127**
Hambro Rd. SW16 —65Mb **126**
Hambro Rd. Brtwd —19Zd **33**
Hambrough Ho. Hay —43Y **77**
Hambrough Rd. S'hall —46Aa **77**
*Hambury Ho. SW8 —52Nb **104***
(off Rite Rd.)
Ham Clo. Rich —62La **122**
(in two parts)
Ham Comn. Rich —62Ma **123**
Hamden Cres. Dag —34Dd **68**
Hamel Clo. Harr —28Ma **39**
Hamerton Rd. Grav —57De **113**
Hame Way. E6 —42Qc **86**
Ham Farm Rd. Rich —63Ma **123**
Hamfield Clo. Oxt —99Ec **182**
Hamfrith Rd. E15 —37Hc **65**
Ham Ga. Av. Rich —62Ma **123**
Hamhaugh Island. Shep —75Q **140**
Hamilton Av. N9 —17Wb **25**
Hamilton Av. Cob —85W **158**
Hamilton Av. Ilf —28Rc **46**
Hamilton Av. Romf —26Fd **48**
Hamilton Av. Surb —75Qa **143**
Hamilton Av. Sutt —75Ab **144**
Hamilton Av. Wok —87G **156**
Hamilton Bldgs. EC2
*—42Ub **83** (6J **195**)*
(off Gt. Eastern St.)
Hamilton Clo. N17 —27Vb **43**
Hamilton Clo. NW6 —41Cb **81**
Hamilton Clo. NW8
—41Fb **81** (4B **190**)
Hamilton Clo. SE16 —47Ac **84**
Hamilton Clo. Barn —14Gb **23**
Hamilton Clo. Brick —3Ca **5**
Hamilton Clo. Cher —74H **139**
Hamilton Clo. Eps —84Sa **161**
Hamilton Clo. Felt —64V **120**
Hamilton Clo. Pot B —5Wa **8**
Hamilton Clo. Purl —84Rb **165**
Hamilton Clo. Stan —19Ga **20**
Hamilton Ct. W5 —45Pa **79**
*Hamilton Ct. W9 —41Eb **81***
(off Maida Vale)
Hamilton Ct. Bookh —97Da **175**
*Hamilton Ct. Eri —52Hd **110***
(off Frobisher Rd.)
Hamilton Cres. N13 —21Qb **42**
Hamilton Cres. Harr —34Ba **57**
Hamilton Cres. Houn —57Da **99**
Hamilton Cres. War —21Yd **50**
Hamilton Dri. Romf —26Nd **49**
Hamilton Gdns. NW8
—41Eb **81** (3A **190**)
Hamilton Ho. W4 —51Ua **102**
Hamilton La. N5 —35Rb **63**
Hamilton M. W1
—47Kb **82** (7K **197**)
Hamilton Pde. Felt —63W **120**
Hamilton Pk. N5 —35Rb **63**
Hamilton Pk. W. N5 —35Rb **63**
Hamilton Pl. W1 —46Jb **82** (7J **197**)
Hamilton Pl. Sun —66X **121**
Hamilton Rd. E15 —41Gc **85**
Hamilton Rd. E17 —26Ac **44**
Hamilton Rd. N2 —27Eb **41**
Hamilton Rd. N9 —17Wb **25**
Hamilton Rd. NW10 —36Wa **60**
Hamilton Rd. NW11 —31Za **60**
Hamilton Rd. SE27 —63Tb **127**
Hamilton Rd. SW19 —66Db **125**
Hamilton Rd. W4 —47Ua **80**
Hamilton Rd. W5 —45Na **79**
Hamilton Rd. Barn —14Gb **23**
Hamilton Rd. Bexh —54Ad **109**
Hamilton Rd. Bren —51Ma **101**
Hamilton Rd. Felt —63V **120**
Hamilton Rd. Harr —29Ga **38**
Hamilton Rd. Hay —45X **77**
Hamilton Rd. Ilf —35Rc **66**
Hamilton Rd. K Lan —5S **4**
Hamilton Rd. Romf —29Kd **49**
Hamilton Rd. Sidc —63Wc **131**
Hamilton Rd. Slou —4E **72**
Hamilton Rd. S'hall —46Ba **77**
Hamilton Rd. T Hth —69Tb **127**
Hamilton Rd. Twic —60Ga **100**
Hamilton Rd. Uxb —42M **75**
Hamilton Rd. Wat —20X **19**
Hamilton Rd. Ind. Est. SE27
—63Tb **127**
Hamilton Rd. M. SW19 —66Db **125**
Hamilton Sq. N12 —23Fb **41**
Hamilton Sq. SE1
*—47Tb **83** (1G **207**)*
(off Kipling St.)
Hamilton St. SE8 —51Cc **106**
Hamilton St. Wat —15Y **19**
Hamilton Ter. NW8 —40Db **61**
Hamilton Wlk. Eri —52Hd **110**
Hamilton Way. N3 —23Cb **41**
Hamilton Way. N13 —21Rb **43**
Hamilton Way. Wall —81Mb **164**
Ham La. Egh —3M **117**
Ham La. Old Win —7N **95**
Hamlea Clo. SE12 —57Jc **107**
Hamlet Clo. SE13 —56Gc **107**
Hamlet Clo. Romf —24Cd **48**
*Hamlet Ct. SE11 —50Rb **83** (7B **206**)*
(off Opal St.)
Hamlet Ct. W6 —49Wa **80**
Hamlet Ct. Enf —15Ub **25**
Hamlet Gdns. W6 —49Wa **80**
Hamlet Ho. Eri —52Gd **110**
Hamlet Ind. Est. E9 —38Cc **64**
Hamlet Rd. SE19 —66Vb **127**
Hamlet Rd. Romf —24Cd **48**
Hamlet Sq. NW2 —34Ab **60**
Hamlets Way. E3 —42Bc **84**
Hamlet, The. SE5 —55Tb **105**
Hamlet Way. SE1
—47Tb **83** (1G **207**)
Hamlin Cres. Pinn —29Y **37**
Hamlin Rd. Sev —93Gd **186**
Hamlyn Clo. Edgw —20Na **21**
Hamlyn Ct. Sev —93Gd **186**
Hamlyn Gdns. SE19 —66Ub **127**
Hamm Ct. Wey —75P **139**
Hammelton Grn. SW9 —53Rb **105**
Hammelton Rd. Brom —67Hc **129**
Hammers La. NW7 —22Wa **40**
Hammersmith Bri. SW13 & W6
—51Xa **102**
Hammersmith Bri. Rd. W6
(in two parts) —50Xa **80**
Hammersmith B'way. W6 —49Ya **80**
Hammersmith Flyover. W6
—50Ya **80**
Hammersmith Gro. W6 —47Ya **80**
Hammersmith Ind. Est. W6
—51Ya **102**
Hammersmith Rd. W6 & W14
—49Za **80**
Hammersmith Ter. W6 —50Wa **80**
Hammet Clo. Hay —43Z **77**
Hammett St. EC3
—45Vb **83** (4K **201**)
Hamm Moor La. Add —78N **139**
Hammond Av. Mitc —68Kb **126**
Hammond Clo. Barn —15Ab **22**
Hammond Clo. Gnfd —36Fa **58**
Hammond Clo. Hamp —67Ca **121**
Hammond Clo. Wok —3F **188**
*Hammond Ct. E17 —29Ac **44***
(off Maude Rd.)
Hammond End. Farn C —5F **52**
Hammond Rd. Enf —12Xb **25**
Hammond Rd. S'hall —48Aa **77**
Hammond Rd. Wok —3F **188**
Hammonds La. Gt War —23Xd **50**
Hammond St. NW5 —37Lb **62**
Hamonde Clo. Edgw —19Ra **21**
*Hamond Sq. N1 —40Ub **63** (1H **195**)*
(off Hoxton St.)
Ham Pk. Rd. E15 & E7 —38Hc **65**
Hampden Av. Beck —68Ac **128**
Hampden Clo. NW1
—40Mb **62** (2E **192**)
Hampden Clo. Stoke P —1L **73**
Hampden Ct. N10 —24Jb **42**
Hampden Cres. Chesh —3Xb **11**
Hampden Cres. War —21Yd **50**
Hampden Gurney St. W1
—44Hb **81** (3F **197**)
Hampden Ho. SW9 —54Qb **104**
Hampden La. N17 —25Vb **43**
Hampden Pl. Frog —1Ga **6**
Hampden Rd. N8 —28Qb **42**
Hampden Rd. N10 —24Jb **42**
Hampden Rd. N17 —25Wb **43**
Hampden Rd. N19 —33Mb **62**
Hampden Rd. Beck —68Ac **128**
Hampden Rd. Ger X —25A **34**
Hampden Rd. Grays —50De **91**
Hampden Rd. Harr —25Ea **38**
Hampden Rd. King T —69Qa **123**
Hampden Rd. Romf —24Dd **48**
Hampden Rd. Slou —48B **74**
Hampden Sq. N14 —18Kb **24**
Hampden Way. N14 —18Kb **24**
Hampden Way. Wat —8U **4**
Hampermill La. Wat —19V **18**
Hampshire Av. Slou —3G **72**
Hampshire Clo. N18 —22Xb **43**
Hampshire Ct. Add —78L **139**
Hampshire Gdns. Linf —7J **93**
Hampshire Hog La. W6 —49Xa **80**
Hampshire Ho. Ger X —22A **34**
Hampshire Rd. N22 —24Pb **42**
Hampshire Rd. Horn —28Qd **49**
Hampshire St. NW5 —37Mb **62**
Hampson Way. SW8 —53Pb **104**
Hampstead Clo. SE28 —46Xc **87**
Hampstead Gdns. NW11 —30Cb **41**
Hampstead Grn. NW3 —36Gb **61**
Hampstead Gro. NW3 —34Eb **61**
Hampstead Heights. N2 —27Eb **41**
Hampstead High St. NW3 —35Fb **61**
Hampstead Hill Gdns. NW3
—35Fb **61**
Hampstead La. NW3 & N6
—32Fb **61**
Hampstead Rd. NW1
—40Lb **62** (1B **192**)
Hampstead Sq. NW3 —34Eb **61**
Hampstead Way. NW11 —29Bb **41**
Hampton Clo. SW20 —66Ya **124**
Hampton Ct. N1 —37Rb **63**
Hampton Ct. N22 —25Lb **42**
Hampton Ct. Av. E Mol —71Fa **142**
Hampton Ct. Bri. E Mol —70Ga **122**
Hampton Ct. Pde. E Mol —70Ga **122**
Hampton Ct. Rd. E Mol & King T
—68Fa **122**
Hampton Ct. Rd. Hamp —68Ea **122**
Hampton Ct. Way. Th Dit & E Mol
—75Ga **142**
Hampton Cres. Grav —1G **136**
Hampton Farm Ind. Est. Felt
—62Aa **121**
Hampton Gro. Eps —83Va **162**
*Hampton Ho. Bexh —54Dd **110***
(off Erith Rd.)
Hampton La. Felt —63Aa **121**
Hampton Mead. Lou —13Rc **28**
Hampton Rise. Harr —30Na **39**
Hampton Rd. E4 —22Bc **44**
Hampton Rd. E7 —36Kc **65**
Hampton Rd. E11 —32Fc **65**
Hampton Rd. Croy —72Sb **147**
Hampton Rd. Hamp & Tedd
—64Fa **122**
Hampton Rd. Ilf —35Rc **66**
Hampton Rd. Twic —62Ea **122**
Hampton Rd. Wor Pk —75Xa **144**
Hampton Rd. E. Felt —63Ba **121**
Hampton Rd. W. Felt —62Aa **121**
Hampton St. SE17 & SE1
—49Rb **83** (6C **206**)
Ham Ridings. Rich —64Pa **123**
Hamsey Grn. Gdns. Warl
—88Xb **165**
Hamsey Way. S Croy —87Xb **165**
Hamshades Clo. Sidc —62Vc **131**
Ham Sq. Rich —61La **122**
Ham St. Rich —60Ka **100**
Ham, The. Bren —52La **100**
Ham View. Croy —72Ac **148**
Ham Yd. W1 —45Mb **82** (4D **198**)
Hanah Ct. SW19 —66Za **124**
Hanameel St. E16 —46Kc **85**
Hanaway Pl. W1
—44Mb **82** (2D **198**)
Hanaway St. W1
—44Mb **82** (2D **198**)
Hanbury Clo. Chesh —1Ac **12**
Hanbury Ct. Harr —30Ha **38**
Hanbury Dri. Big H —85Kc **167**
Hanbury M. N1 —39Sb **63** (1E **194**)
Hanbury Path. Wok —86F **156**
Hanbury Rd. N17 —26Xb **43**
Hanbury Rd. W3 —47Ra **79**
Hanbury St. E1 —43Vb **83** (7K **195**)
Hanbury Wlk. Bex —62Gd **132**
Hancock Ct. Borwd —11Sa **21**
Hancock Rd. E3 —41Ec **84**
Hancock Rd. SE19 —65Tb **127**
Handa Wlk. N1 —37Tb **63**
Hand Ct. WC1 —43Pb **82** (1J **199**)
Handcroft Rd. Croy —73Rb **147**
Handel Clo. Edgw —23Pa **39**
Handel Cres. Til —2C **114**
*Handel Pde. Edgw —24Qa **39***
(off Whitchurch La.)
Handel Pl. NW10 —37Ta **59**
Handel St. WC1 —42Nb **82** (5F **193**)
Handel Way. Edgw —24Qa **39**
Handen Rd. SE12 —57Gc **107**
Handforth Rd. SW9 —52Qb **104**
Handforth Rd. Ilf —34Rc **66**
Handley Rd. E9 —39Yb **64**
Handowe Clo. NW4 —28Wa **40**
Handpost Hill. N'thaw —1Kb **10**
Handside Clo. Wor Pk —74Za **144**
Hands Wlk. E16 —44Jc **85**
Handsworth Av. E4 —23Fc **45**
Handsworth Clo. Wat —20W **18**
Handsworth Rd. N17 —27Tb **43**
Handtrough Way. Bark —40Rc **66**
Hanford Clo. SW18 —60Cb **103**
Hanford Rd. S Ock —46Sd **90**
Hanford Row. SW19 —65Ya **124**
Hangar Ruding. Wat —20Ba **19**
Hangboy Slade. Lou —9Pc **14**
Hanger Grn. W5 —42Qa **79**
Hanger Hill. Wey —79R **140**
Hanger La. W5 —40Na **59**
Hanger Vale La. W5 —44Pa **79**
Hanger View Way. W3 —44Qa **79**
Hanging Hill La. Ingve —20De **33**
Hanging Sword All. EC4
*(off Hood Ct.) —44Qb **82** (3A **200**)*
Hangrove Hill. Orp —85Rc **168**
Hankey Pl. SE1 —47Tb **83** (2G **207**)
Hankins La. NW7 —19Ua **22**
Hanley Clo. Wind —3B **94**
Hanley Pl. Beck —66Cc **128**
Hanley Rd. N4 —32Nb **62**
Hanmer Wlk. N7 —33Pb **62**
Hannah Clo. NW10 —35Sa **59**
Hannah Clo. Beck —69Ec **128**
Hannah Mary Way. SE1 —49Wb **83**
Hannah M. Wall —80Lb **146**
Hannards Way. Ilf —22Xc **47**
Hannay La. N8 —31Mb **62**
Hannay Wlk. SW16 —61Mb **126**
Hannell Rd. SW6 —52Ab **102**
Hannen Rd. SE27 —62Rb **127**
Hannibal Rd. E1 —43Yb **84**
Hannibal Rd. Stai —59M **97**
Hannibal Way. Croy —78Pb **146**
*Hannington Point. E9 —37Bc **64***
(off Eastway)
Hannington Rd. SW4 —55Kb **104**
Hanover Av. Felt —60W **98**
Hanover Circ. Hay —44S **76**
Hanover Clo. Egh —5M **117**
Hanover Clo. Red —100Lb **180**
Hanover Clo. Rich —52Qa **101**
Hanover Clo. Slou —8L **73**
Hanover Clo. Sutt —77Ab **144**
Hanover Clo. Wind —3D **94**
Hanover Ct. NW9 —27Ua **40**
Hanover Ct. SW15 —56Va **102**
*Hanover Ct. W12 —46Wa **80***
(off Uxbridge Rd.)
Hanover Ct. Ruis —34W **56**
*Hanover Ct. Wal A —5Ec **12***
(off Quaker La.)
Hanover Ct. Wok —7G **188**
Hanover Dri. Chst —63Sc **130**
Hanover Est. N22 —27Pb **42**
Hanover Gdns. SE11 —51Qb **104**
Hanover Gdns. Ilf —24Sc **46**
Hanover Ga. NW1
—41Gb **81** (4E **190**)
Hanover Ho. SW9 —55Qb **104**
Hanover Mead. NW11 —29Ab **40**
Hanover Pk. SE15 —53Wb **105**
Hanover Pl. WC2
—44Nb **82** (3G **199**)
Hanover Pl. New Ash —75Be **155**
Hanover Rd. N15 —28Vb **43**
Hanover Rd. NW10 —38Ya **60**
Hanover Rd. SW19 —66Eb **125**
Hanover Sq. W1
—44Kb **82** (3A **198**)
Hanover St. W1 —44Kb **82** (3A **198**)
Hanover St. Croy —76Rb **147**
Hanover Ter. NW1
—41Gb **81** (4F **191**)
Hanover Ter. Iswth —53Ja **100**
Hanover Ter. M. NW1
—41Gb **81** (4E **190**)
Hanover Trading Est. N7 —36Nb **62**
Hanover Wlk. Wey —76U **140**
Hanover Way. Bexh —55Zc **109**
Hanover Way. Wind —4D **94**
Hanover W. Ind. Est. NW10
—41Ta **79**
*Hanover Yd. N1 —40Sb **63** (1D **194**)*
(off Noel Rd.)
Hansard M. W14 —47Za **80**
Hansart Way. Enf —11Qb **24**
Hans Cres. SW1 —48Hb **81** (3F **203**)
Hanselin Clo. Stan —22Ha **38**
Hanshaw Dri. Edgw —25Ta **39**
Hansler Gro. E Mol —70Fa **122**
Hansler Rd. SE22 —57Vb **105**
Hansol Rd. Bexh —57Ad **109**
Hanson Clo. SW12 —59Kb **104**
Hanson Clo. SW14 —55Sa **101**
Hanson Clo. Beck —65Dc **128**
Hanson Clo. Lou —12Sc **28**
Hanson Ct. E17 —30Dc **44**
Hanson Dri. Lou —12Sc **28**
Hanson Gdns. S'hall —47Aa **77**
Hanson Gro. Lou —12Sc **28**
Hanson St. W1 —43Lb **82** (7B **192**)
Hans Pl. SW1 —48Hb **81** (3G **203**)
Hans Rd. SW3 —48Hb **81** (3F **203**)
Hans St. SW1 —48Hb **81** (4G **203**)
Hanway Pl. W1 —44Mb **82**
Hanway Rd. W7 —44Fa **78**
Hanway St. W1 —44Mb **82**
Hanworth Ho. SE5 —52Rb **105**
Hanworth La. Cher —74H **139**
Hanworth Rd. Felt —60X **99**
Hanworth Rd. Hamp —63Ba **121**
Hanworth Rd. Houn —60Aa **99**
Hanworth Rd. Sun —66W **120**
Hanworth Ter. Houn —56Da **99**
Hanworth Trading Est. Cher
—74H **139**
Hanworth Trading Est. Felt
—62Aa **121**
Hanyards La. Cuff —1Mb **10**
Hapgood Clo. Gnfd —36Fa **58**
Harad's Pl. E1 —45Wb **83**
Harben Rd. NW6 —38Eb **61**
Harberson Rd. E15 —39Hc **65**
Harberson Rd. SW12 —60Kb **104**
Harberton Rd. N19 —32Lb **62**
Harbet Rd. N18 —22Zb **44**
Harbet Rd. W2 —43Fb **81** (1C **196**)
Harbex Clo. Bex —59Dd **110**
Harbinger Rd. E14 —49Dc **84**
Harbledown Pl. St M —70Yc **131**
Harbledown Rd. SW6 —53Cb **103**
Harbledown Rd. S Croy —83Wb **165**
Harbord Clo. SE5 —54Tb **105**
Harbord St. SW6 —53Za **102**
Harborne Clo. Wat —22Y **37**
Harborough Av. Sidc —59Vc **109**
Harborough Clo. Slou —6B **72**
Harborough Rd. SW16 —63Pb **126**
Harbour Av. SW10 —53Eb **103**
Harbourer Clo. Ilf —22Xc **47**
Harbourer Rd. Ilf —22Xc **47**
Harbour Exchange Sq. E14
—47Dc **84**
Harbourfield Rd. Bans —87Db **163**
Harbour Quay. E14 —46Ec **84**
Harbour Rd. SE5 —55Sb **105**
Harbour Yd. SW10 —53Eb **103**
Harbridge Av. SW15 —59Va **102**
Harbury Rd. Cars —81Gb **163**
Harbut Rd. SW11 —56Fb **103**
Harcombe Rd. N16 —34Ub **63**
Harcourt Av. E12 —35Pc **66**
Harcourt Av. Edgw —20Sa **21**
Harcourt Av. Sidc —58Yc **109**
Harcourt Av. Wall —77Kb **146**
Harcourt Bldgs. EC4
*(off Temple) —45Qb **82** (4K **199**)*
Harcourt Clo. Egh —65E **118**
Harcourt Clo. Iswth —55Ja **100**
Harcourt Field. Wall —77Kb **146**
Harcourt Lodge. Wall —77Kb **146**
Harcourt Rd. E15 —40Hc **65**
Harcourt Rd. N22 —25Mb **42**
Harcourt Rd. SE4 —55Bc **106**
Harcourt Rd. SW19 —66Cb **125**
Harcourt Rd. Bexh —56Ad **109**
Harcourt Rd. Bush —15Ea **20**
Harcourt Rd. T Hth —71Pb **146**
Harcourt Rd. Wall —77Kb **146**
Harcourt Rd. Wind —3C **94**
Harcourt St. W1 —43Gb **81** (1E **196**)
Harcourt Ter. SW10 —50Db **81**
Hardcastle Clo. Croy —72Wb **147**
Hardcastle Clo. W Wick —76Dc **148**
Hardell Clo. Egh —64C **118**
Hardel Rise. SW2 —60Rb **105**
Hardel Wlk. SW2 —59Qb **104**
Harden Ho. SE5 —54Ub **105**
Harden Rd. Grav —2B **136**
Harden's Mnr. Way. SE7 —49Mc **85**
Harden St. SE18 —49Nc **86**
Harders Rd. SE15 —54Xb **105**
Hardess St. SE24 —55Sb **105**
Hardie Clo. NW10 —36Ta **59**
Hardie Rd. Dag —34Ed **68**
Hardie Rd. Stanf —1M **93**
Harding Clo. SE17 —51Sb **105**
Harding Clo. Wat —5Y **5**
Hardinge Clo. Uxb —43R **76**
Hardinge Rd. N18 —23Ub **43**
Hardinge Rd. NW10 —39Xa **60**
Hardinge St. E1 —44Yb **84**
Harding Ho. Hay —44X **77**
Harding Rd. Bexh —54Bd **109**
Harding Rd. Eps —91Ua **178**
Harding Rd. Grays —8C **92**
Hardings Clo. Iver —41E **74**
Hardings La. SE20 —65Zb **128**
Hardings Row. Iver —41E **74**

Hardingstone Ct.—Havant Way

Hardingstone Ct. Wal X —6Bc 12
Hardley Cres. Horn —28Md 49
Hardman Rd. SE7 —50Kc 85
Hardman Rd. King T —68Na 123
Hardwick Clo. Oxs —87Ea 160
Hardwick Clo. Stan —22La 38
Hardwick Ct. Eri —51Fd 110
Hardwick Cres. Dart —58Rd 111
Hardwicke Av. Houn —53Ca 99
Hardwicke Rd. N13 —23Nb 42
Hardwicke Rd. W4 —49Ta 79
Hardwicke Rd. Rich —63La 122
Hardwicke St. Bark —39Sc 66
Hardwick Grn. W13 —43Ka 78
Hardwick La. Lyne —73E 138
Hardwick St. EC1
—41Qb 82 (4A 194)
Hardwicks Way. SW18 —57Cb 103
Hardwidge St. SE1
—47Ub 83 (1H 207)
Hardy Av. Grav —1A 136
Hardy Av. Ruis —36X 57
Hardy Clo. SE16 —47Zb 84
Hardy Clo. Barn —16Ab 22
Hardy Clo. Pinn —31Z 57
Hardy Clo. Slou —6E 72
Hardy Ct. Eri —52Hd 110
Hardy Gro. Dart —56Qd 111
Hardy Ho. SW4 —59Lb 104
Hardying Ho. E17 —28Ac 44
Hardy Rd. SE3 —51Hc 107
Hardy Rd. SW19 —66Db 125
Hardys Clo. E Mol —70Ga 122
Hardy Way. Enf —11Qb 24
Harebell Dri. E6 —43Qc 86
Harebell Hill. Cob —86Z 159
Harebell Way. Romf —24Md 49
Hare & Billet Rd. SE3 —53Fc 107
Harebreaks, The. Wat —9W 4
Harecastle Clo. Hay —42Aa 77
Hare Ct. EC4 —44Qb 82 (3K 199)
Harecourt Rd. N1 —37Sb 63
Hare Cres. Wat —4W 4
Harecroft. Fet —96Da 175
Haredale Rd. SE24 —56Sb 105
Haredon Clo. SE23 —59Zb 106
Harefield. Esh —76Ga 142
Harefield Av. Sutt —81Ab 162
Harefield Clo. Enf —11Qb 24
Harefield Grn. NW7 —23Ya 40
Harefield M. SE4 —55Bc 106
Harefield Rd. N8 —29Mb 42
Harefield Rd. SE4 —55Bc 106
Harefield Rd. SW16 —66Pb 126
Harefield Rd. Rick —20M 17
Harefield Rd. Sidc —62Zc 131
Harefield Rd. Uxb —38L 55
Hare Hall La. Romf —28Kd 49
Harehatch La. Farn C —2C 52
Hare Hill. Add —79G 138
Harehill Clo. Wok —87J 157
Harelands Clo. Wok —5F 188
Harelands La. Wok —5F 188
Hare La. Clay —79Fa 142
Hare Marsh. E2 —42Wb 83
Harendon. Tad —93Ya 178
Hare Pl. EC4 —44Qb 82 (3A 200)
(off Pleydell St.)
Hare Row. E2 —40Xb 63
Hares Bank. New Ad —82Fc 167
Haresfield Rd. Dag —37Cd 68
Harestone Dri. Cat —96Vb 181
Harestone Hill. Cat —98Vb 181
Harestone La. Cat —97Ub 181
Harestone Valley Rd. Cat
—98Ub 181
Hare St. SE18 —48Qc 86
Hare Wlk. N1 —40Ub 63 (2J 195)
Harewood. Rick —14K 17
(in two parts)
Harewood Av. NW1
—42Gb 81 (6E 190)
Harewood Av. N'holt —38Ba 57
Harewood Clo. N'holt —38Ba 57
Harewood Dri. Ilf —26Pc 46
Harewood Gdns. S Croy —87Xb 165
Harewood Hill. They B —7Uc 14
Harewood Pl. W1
—44Kb 82 (3A 198)
Harewood Pl. Slou —8L 73
Harewood Rd. NW1 —43Gb 81
Harewood Rd. SW19 —65Gb 125
Harewood Rd. Iswth —52Ha 100
Harewood Rd. Pil H —16Xd 32
Harewood Rd. S Croy —79Ub 147
Harewood Rd. Wat —20X 19
Harewood Row. NW1
—43Gb 81 (7E 190)
Harewood Ter. S'hall —49Ba 77
Harfield Gdns. SE5 —55Ub 105
Harfield Rd. Sun —68Z 121
Harford Clo. E4 —17Dc 26
Harford Dri. Wat —10U 4
Harford Rd. E4 —17Dc 26
Harford St. E1 —42Ac 84
Harford Wlk. N2 —28Fb 41
Hargood Clo. Harr —30Na 39
Hargood Rd. SE3 —53Lc 107
Hargrave Mans. N19 —33Mb 62
Hargrave Pk. N19 —33Lb 62
Hargrave Pl. N7 —36Mb 62
Hargrave Rd. N19 —33Lb 62
Hargraves Ho. W12 —45Xa 80
(off White City Est.)
Hargreaves Av. Chesh —3Xb 11
Hargreaves Clo. Chesh —3Xb 11
Hargwyne St. SW9 —55Pb 104
Haringey Pk. N8 —30Nb 42
Haringey Rd. N8 —28Nb 42
Haringey Technopark. N17
—27Wb 43
Harington Ter. N9 —20Tb 25
Harkett Clo. Harr —26Ha 38
Harkett Ct. W'stone —26Ha 38
Harkness. Chesh —1Xb 11
Harkness Clo. Eps —88Ya 162
Harkness Clo. Romf —22Pd 49
Harland Av. Croy —76Wb 147
Harland Av. Sidc —62Tc 130
Harland Rd. SE12 —60Jc 107
Harlands Gro. Orp —77Rc 150
Harlech Gdns. Houn —51Y 99
Harlech Rd. N14 —20Nb 24
Harlech Tower. W3 —47Sa 79
Harlequin Av. Bren —51Ja 100
Harlequin Clo. Hay —43Z 77
Harlequin Clo. Iswth —57Ga 100
Harlequin Ct. NW10 —37Ta 59
(off Mitchellbrook Way)
Harlequin Ho. Eri —48Ad 87
(off Kale Rd.)
Harlequin Rd. Tedd —66Ka 122
Harlequin, The. Wat —14Y 19
Harlescott Rd. SE15 —56Zb 106
Harlesden Clo. Romf —24Pd 49
Harlesden Gdns. NW10 —39Va 60
Harlesden La. NW10 —39Wa 60
Harlesden Rd. NW10 —39Wa 60
Harlesden Rd. Romf —23Pd 49
Harlesden Wlk. Romf —24Pd 49
Harleston Clo. E5 —33Yb 64
Harley Clo. Wemb —37Ma 59
Harley Ct. E11 —31Jc 65
Harley Ct. N20 —20Eb 23
Harley Ct. Harr —28Fa 38
Harley Cres. Harr —28Fa 38
Harleyford. Brom —67Lc 129
Harleyford Ct. SE11 —51Pb 104
(off Harleyford Rd.)
Harleyford Rd. SE11 —51Pb 104
Harleyford St. SE11 —51Qb 104
Harley Gdns. SW10
—50Eb 81 (7A 202)
Harley Gdns. Orp —77Uc 150
Harley Gro. E3 —41Bc 84
Harley Ho. E11 —31Fc 65
Harley Ho. Borwd —12Ra 21
Harley Pl. W1 —43Kb 82 (1K 197)
Harley Rd. NW3 —38Fb 61
Harley Rd. NW10 —40Ua 60
Harley Rd. Harr —28Fa 38
Harley St. W1 —42Kb 82 (6K 191)
Harlington Clo. Hay —52S 98
Harlington Rd. Bexh —55Ad 109
Harlington Rd. Uxb —41Q 76
Harlington Rd. E. Felt —59X 99
Harlington Rd. W. Felt —58X 99
Harlowe Clo. E8 —39Wb 63
Harlow Gdns. Romf —23Ed 48
Harlow Mans. Bark —38Rc 66
(off Whiting Av.)
Harlow Rd. N13 —20Tb 25
Harlow Rd. Rain —39Hd 68
Harlton Ct. Wal A —6Hc 13
Harlyn Dri. Pinn —27X 37
Harman Av. Grav —4D 136
Harman Av. Wfd G —23Hc 45
Harman Clo. E4 —21Fc 45
Harman Clo. NW2 —34Ab 60
Harman Dri. NW2 —34Ab 60
Harman Dri. Sidc —58Vc 109
Harman Pl. S Croy —83Rb 165
Harman Rd. Enf —15Vb 25
Harmer Rd. Swans —58Be 113
Harmer St. Grav —8E 114
Harmond Ho. SE8 —49Bc 84
Harmondsworth La. W Dray
—51N 97
Harmondsworth Rd. W Dray
—50N 75
Harmony Clo. NW11 —29Ab 40
Harmony Clo. Wall —81Nb 164
Harmony Lodge. S'hall —48Ca 77
Harmood Gro. NW1 —38Kb 62
Harmood Pl. NW1 —38Kb 62
Harmood St. NW1 —37Kb 62
Harmsworth St. SE17 —51Rb 105
Harmsworth Way. N20 —18Bb 23
Harness Rd. SE28 —47Wc 87
Harold Av. Belv —50Bd 87
Harold Av. Hay —48V 76
Harold Ct. H Wood —24Rd 49
Harold Ct. Rd. Romf —23Rd 49
Harold Cres. Wal A —4Ec 12
Harold Est. SE1 —48Ub 83 (4J 207)
Harold Hill Ind. Est. H Hill
—24Md 49
Harold Pl. SE11 —50Qb 82
Harold Rd. E4 —21Ec 44
Harold Rd. E11 —32Gc 65
Harold Rd. E13 —39Kc 65
Harold Rd. N8 —29Pb 42
Harold Rd. N15 —29Vb 43
Harold Rd. NW10 —41Ta 79
Harold Rd. SE19 —66Tb 127
Harold Rd. Dart —63Pd 133
Harold Rd. Sutt —77Fb 145
Harold Rd. Wfd G —25Jc 45
Haroldstone Rd. E17 —29Zb 44
Harold View. Romf —26Pd 49
Harold Wilson Ho. SE28 —46Xc 87
Harold Wood Hall. H Hill —25Md 49
(off Widecombe Clo.)
Harp All. EC4 —44Rb 83 (2B 200)
Harp Bus. Cen. NW2 —33Wa 60
(off Apsley Way)
Harpenden Rd. E12 —33Lc 65
Harpenden Rd. SE27 —62Rb 127
Harpenmead Point. NW2 —33Bb 61
Harper Ho. SW9 —55Rb 105
Harper La. Rad —4Ha 6
Harper Rd. E6 —44Pc 86
Harper Rd. SE1 —48Sb 83 (3D 206)
Harper's Yd. N17 —25Vb 43
Harp Island Clo. NW10 —33Ta 59
Harp La. EC3 —45Ub 83 (5H 201)
Harpley Sq. E1 —42Zb 84
Harpour Rd. Bark —37Sc 66
Harp Rd. W7 —42Ha 78
Harpsden St. SW11 —53Jb 104
Harps Oak La. Red —97Hb 179
Harpur M. WC1 —43Pb 82 (7H 193)
Harpurs. Tad —94Za 178
Harpur St. WC1 —43Pb 82 (7H 193)
Harraden Rd. SE3 —53Lc 107
Harrap Chase. Grays —50Be 91
Harrier Clo. Horn —37Kd 69
Harrier M. SE28 —47Tc 86
Harrier Rd. NW9 —26Ua 40
Harriers Clo. W5 —45Na 79
Harrier Way. E6 —43Pc 86
Harriescourt. Wal A —4Jc 13
Harries Rd. Hay —42Y 77
Harriet Clo. E8 —39Wb 63
Harriet Gdns. Croy —75Wb 147
Harriet St. SW1 —47Hb 81 (2G 203)
Harriet Wlk. SW1
—47Hb 81 (2G 203)
Harriet Way. Bush —17Fa 20
Harringay Gdns. N8 —28Rb 43
Harringay Rd. N15 —29Rb 43
Harrington Clo. NW10 —34Ta 59
Harrington Clo. Croy —75Nb 146
Harrington Clo. Wind —6D 94
Harrington Gdns. SW7 —49Db 81
Harrington Hill. E5 —32Xb 63
Harrington Rd. E11 —32Gc 65
Harrington Rd. SE25 —70Xb 127
Harrington Rd. SW7
—49Fb 81 (5B 202)
Harrington Sq. NW1
—40Lb 62 (1B 192)
Harrington St. NW1
—40Lb 62 (2B 192)
Harrington Way. SE18 —48Mc 85
Harriott Clo. SE10 —49Hc 85
Harriott's Clo. Asht —92La 176
Harriott's La. Asht —91La 176
Harris Clo. Enf —11Rb 25
Harris Clo. Grav —2B 136
Harris Clo. Houn —53Ca 99
Harris Cotts. E15 —39Hc 65
(off Gift La.)
Harris Ct. Wemb —34Pa 59
Harris Ho. SW9 —55Qb 104
(off St James's Cres.)
Harris La. Shenl —6Qa 7
Harrison Clo. Hut —15Fe 33
Harrison Clo. N'wd —23S 36
Harrison Ct. Shep —71R 140
Harrison Rd. Dag —37Dd 68
Harrisons Rise. Croy —76Rb 147
Harrison St. WC1
—41Nb 82 (4G 193)
Harrison Wlk. Chesh —2Zb 12
Harrison Way. Sev —94Jd 186
Harrison Way. Slou —6B 72
Harris Rd. Bexh —53Ad 109
Harris Rd. Dag —36Bd 67
Harris Rd. Wat —7W 4
Harris St. E17 —31Bc 64
Harris St. SE5 —52Tb 105
Harris Way. Sun —67U 120
Harrogate Ct. SE12 —59Jc 107
Harrogate Ct. Slou —50C 74
Harrogate Rd. Wat —20Y 19
Harrold Rd. Dag —36Xc 67
Harrovian Bus. Village. Harr
—31Ga 58
Harrow Av. Enf —16Vb 25
Harroway Rd. SW11 —54Fb 103
Harrow Bottom Rd. Vir W —72B 138
Harrow Bri. Rd. W2 —43Eb 81
Harrowby Gdns. Grav —1A 136
Harrowby St. W1
—44Gb 81 (2E 196)
Harrow Clo. Add —75K 139
Harrow Clo. Chess —80Ma 143
Harrow Cres. Romf —24Kd 49
Harrowdene Clo. Wemb —35Ma 59
Harrowdene Gdns. Tedd —66Ja 122
Harrowdene Rd. Wemb —34Ma 59
Harrow Dri. N9 —18Vb 25
Harrow Dri. Horn —30Kd 49
Harrowes Meade. Edgw —20Qa 21
Harrow Fields Gdns. Harr —34Ga 58
Harrow Gdns. Orp —77Xc 151
Harrow Gdns. Warl —87Bc 166
Harrowgate Ho. E9 —37Zb 64
Harrowgate Rd. E9 —37Ac 64
Harrow Grn. E11 —34Gc 65
Harrow La. E14 —45Ec 84
Harrow Mnr. Way. SE2 —47Yc 87
Harrow Pk. Harr —33Ga 58
Harrow Pas. King T —68Ma 123
Harrow Pl. E1 —44Ub 83 (2J 201)
Harrow Rd. E6 —39Nc 66
Harrow Rd. E11 —34Gc 65
Harrow Rd. NW10 —41Wa 80
Harrow Rd. W2 —43Db 81
Harrow Rd. W10 & W9 —42Za 80
Harrow Rd. Bark —39Uc 66
Harrow Rd. Cars —79Gb 145
Harrow Rd. Felt —60Q 98
Harrow Rd. Ilf —35Sc 66
Harrow Rd. Knock —87Ad 169
Harrow Rd. Slou —48B 74
Harrow Rd. Warl —87Bc 166
Harrow Rd. Wemb —35Ha 58
(Sudbury)
Harrow Rd. Wemb —36Qa 59
(Wembley)
Harrow View. Harr —26Ea 38
Harrow View. Hay —44W 76
Harrow View. Uxb —41S 76
Harrow View Rd. W4 —42Ka 78
Harrow Way. Shep —68S 120
Harrow Way. Wat —20Aa 19
Harrow Weald Pk. Harr —23Fa 38
Harry Lambourn Ho. SE15
(off Gervase St.) —52Xb 105
Hart Ct. E6 —38Qc 66
Hart Cres. Chig —22Vc 47
Hart Dyke Cres. Swan —69Fd 132
Hart Dyke Rd. Orp —75Zc 151
Hart Dyke Rd. Swan —69Fd 132
Harte Rd. Houn —54Ba 99
Hartfield Av. Els —14Qa 21
Hartfield Av. N'holt —40X 57
Hartfield Clo. Els —15Qa 21
Hartfield Cres. SW19 —66Bb 125
Hartfield Cres. W Wick —76Jc 149
Hartfield Gro. SE20 —67Xb 127
Hartfield Pl. Grav —59Fe 113
Hartfield Rd. SW19 —66Bb 125
Hartfield Rd. Chess —78Ma 143
Hartfield Rd. W Wick —77Jc 149
Hartfield Ter. E3 —40Cc 64
Hartford Av. Harr —27Ja 38
Hartforde Rd. Borwd —12Qa 21
Hartford Rd. Bex —58Cd 110
Hartford Rd. Eps —79Ra 143
Hart Gro. W5 —46Qa 79
Hart Gro. S'hall —43Ca 77
Hart Gro. Ct. W5 —46Qa 79
Hartham Clo. N7 —36Nb 62
Hartham Clo. Iswth —53Ja 100
Hartham Rd. N7 —36Nb 62
Hartham Rd. N17 —26Vb 43
Hartham Rd. Iswth —53Ha 100
Hartin Clo. Uxb —40N 55
Harting Rd. SE9 —62Nc 130
Hartington Clo. Harr —35Ga 58
Hartington Ct. SW8 —53Nb 104
Hartington Ct. W4 —52Ra 101
Hartington Rd. E16 —44Kc 85
Hartington Rd. E17 —30Ac 44
Hartington Rd. SW8 —53Nb 104
Hartington Rd. W4 —52Ra 101
Hartington Rd. W13 —45Ka 78
Hartington Rd. S'hall —48Aa 77
Hartington Rd. Twic —59Ka 100
Hartismere Rd. SW6 —52Bb 103
Hartlake Rd. E9 —37Zb 64
Hartland Clo. Edgw —19Qa 21
Hartland Clo. New Haw —82L 157
Hartland Clo. Slou —6H 73
Hartland Dri. Edgw —19Qa 21
Hartland Dri. Ruis —34X 57
Hartland Rd. E15 —38Hc 65
Hartland Rd. N11 —22Hb 41
Hartland Rd. NW1 —38Kb 62
Hartland Rd. NW6 —40Bb 61
Hartland Rd. Add —80J 139
Hartland Rd. Chesh —2Zb 12
Hartland Rd. Epp —3Wc 15
Hartland Rd. Hamp —63Da 121
Hartland Rd. Horn —33Jd 68
Hartland Rd. Iswth —55Ja 100
Hartland Rd. Mord —73Cb 145
Hartlands Clo. Bex —58Bd 109
Hartlands, The. Houn —51X 99
Hartland Way. Croy —76Ac 148
Hartland Way. Mord —73Bb 145
Hartley Av. E6 —39Nc 66
Hartley Av. NW7 —22Va 40
Hartley Bottom Rd. Sev & Hart
—79Ce 155
Hartley Clo. NW7 —22Va 40
Hartley Clo. Brom —68Pc 130
Hartley Clo. Stoke P —9N 53
Hartley Copse. Old Win —8L 95
Hartley Down. Purl —87Pb 164
Hartley Farm Est. Purl —87Pb 164
Hartley Hill. Hart —74Ce 155
Hartley Hill. Purl —87Pb 164
Hartley Old Rd. Purl —87Pb 164
Hartley Rd. E11 —32Hc 65
Hartley Rd. Croy —73Sb 147
Hartley Rd. Long —68Ae 135
Hartley Rd. Well —52Yc 109
Hartley Rd. W'ham —97Tc 184
Hartley St. E2 —41Yb 84
(in two parts)
Hartley Way. Purl —87Pb 164
Hart Lodge. H Bar —13Ab 22
Hartman Rd. E16 —46Mc 85
Hartmoor M. Enf —9Zb 12
Hartnoll St. N7 —36Pb 62
Harton Clo. Brom —67Mc 129
Harton Rd. N9 —19Xb 25
Harton St. SE8 —53Cc 106
Hartop Point. SW6 —52Ab 102
(off Pellant Rd.)
Hart Rd. Byfl —85N 157
Hartsbourne Av. Bush —19Ea 20
Hartsbourne Clo. Bush —19Fa 20
Hartsbourne Rd. Bush —19Fa 20
Harts Clo. Bush —12Ca 19
Harts Croft. Croy —81Ac 166
Harts Gro. Wfd G —22Jc 45
Hart Shaw. Long —68De 135
Hartshill Clo. Uxb —37R 56
Hartshill Rd. Grav —1B 136
Hartshill Wlk. Wok —4E 188
Hartshorn All. EC3
—44Ub 83 (3J 201)
(off Leadenhall St.)
Hartshorn Gdns. E6 —42Qc 86
Hartslands Rd. Sev —95Ld 187
Hart's La. SE14 —53Ac 106
Harts La. Bark —38Rc 66
Hartslock Dri. SE2 —47Zc 87
Hartsmead Rd. SE9 —61Pc 130
Hartspring Ind. Est. Wat —12Ca 19
Hartspring La. Wat —12Ca 19
Hart St. EC3 —45Ub 83 (4J 201)
Hart St. Brtwd —19Yd 32
Hartsway. Enf —14Yb 26
Hartswood Clo. War —21Ae 51
Hartswood Gdns. W12 —48Va 80
Hartswood Rd. W12 —47Va 80
Hartswood Rd. War & L War
—21Ae 51
Hartsworth Clo. E13 —40Hc 65
Hartville Rd. SE18 —49Uc 86
Hartwell Dri. E4 —23Ec 44
Hartwell St. E8 —37Vb 63
Hartwood Grn. Bush —19Fa 20
Harty Clo. Grays —46De 91
Harvard Ct. NW6 —36Db 61
Harvard Hill. W4 —51Ra 101
Harvard La. W4 —50Sa 79
Harvard Rd. SE13 —57Ec 106
Harvard Rd. W4 —50Ra 79
Harvard Rd. Iswth —53Ga 100
Harvard Way. Horn —35Jd 68
Harvel Clo. Orp —69Wc 131
Harvel Cres. SE2 —50Zc 87
Harvest Bank Rd. W Wick
—76Hc 149
Harvest Ct. Shep —70Q 120
Harvest End. Wat —8Z 5
Harvester Rd. Eps —82Ta 161
Harvesters Clo. Iswth —57Fa 100
Harvest La. Th Dit —72Ja 142
Harvest Rd. Bush —14Da 19
Harvest Rd. Egh —4P 117
Harvest Rd. Felt —63W 120
Harvest Way. Swan —73Fd 152
Harvey. Grays —47De 91
Harvey Ct. E17 —29Cc 44
Harveyfields. Wal A —6Ec 12
Harvey Gdns. E11 —32Hc 65
Harvey Gdns. SE7 —49Mc 85
Harvey Gdns. Lou —13Nc 28
Harvey Ho. N1 —39Tb 63 (1G 195)
(off Colville Est.)
Harvey Ho. Bren —50Na 79
Harvey Ho. Romf —28Zc 47
Harvey Point. E16 —43Jc 85
(off Fife Rd.)
Harvey Rd. E11 —32Gc 65
Harvey Rd. N8 —29Pb 42
Harvey Rd. SE5 —53Tb 105
(in two parts)
Harvey Rd. Crox —16Q 18
Harvey Rd. Houn —59Ba 99
Harvey Rd. Ilf —36Rc 66
Harvey Rd. N'holt —38Y 57
Harvey Rd. Slou —48D 74
Harvey Rd. Uxb —40Q 56
Harvey Rd. W on T —73W 140
Harvey's Bldgs. WC2
—45Nb 82 (5G 199)
Harveys La. Romf —33Fd 68
Harvey St. N1 —39Tb 63 (1G 195)
Harvill Rd. Sidc —64Ad 131
Harvil Rd. Hare & Ick —28L 35
Harvington Wlk. E8 —38Wb 63
Harvist Est. N7 —35Qb 62
Harvist Rd. NW6 —40Za 60
Harvst Way. Swan —67Ed 132
Harwater Dri. Lou —12Pc 28
Harwell Clo. Ruis —32T 56
Harwell Pas. N2 —28Hb 41
Harwich La. EC2 —43Ub 83 (7J 195)
Harwich Rd. Slou —4E 72
Harwood Av. Brom —68Kc 129
Harwood Av. Horn —27Nd 49
Harwood Av. Mitc —69Gb 125
Harwood Clo. Wemb —35Ma 59
Harwood Ct. N1 —39Tb 63 (1G 195)
(off Colville Est.)
Harwood Dri. Uxb —39P 55
Harwood Gdns. Old Win —9N 95
Harwood Hall La. Upm —37Rd 69
Harwood Rd. SW6 —52Cb 103
Harwoods Rd. Wat —14W 18
Harwoods Yd. N21 —17Qb 24
Harwood Ter. SW6 —53Db 103
Haselbury Rd. N18 & N9 —21Ub 43
Haseley End. SE23 —59Yb 106
Haselrigge Rd. SW4 —56Mb 104
Haseltine Rd. SE26 —63Bc 128
Haselwood Dri. Enf —14Rb 25
Haskard Rd. Dag —35Zc 67
Hasker St. SW3 —49Gb 81 (5E 202)
Haskins. Stanf —1P 93
Haslam Av. Sutt —74Ab 144
Haslam Clo. N1 —38Qb 62
Haslam Clo. Uxb —33S 56
Haslam Ct. N11 —21Kb 42
Haslemere Av. NW4 —30Za 40
Haslemere Av. SW18 —61Db 125
Haslemere Av. W7 & W13
—48Ja 78
Haslemere Av. Barn —18Hb 23
Haslemere Av. Houn —54Y 99
Haslemere Av. Mitc —68Fb 125
Haslemere Clo. Hamp —64Ba 121
Haslemere Clo. Wall —78Nb 146
Haslemere Gdns. N3 —27Bb 41
Haslemere Rd. N8 —31Mb 62
Haslemere Rd. N21 —19Rb 25
Haslemere Rd. Bexh —54Bd 109
Haslemere Rd. Ilf —33Vc 67
Haslemere Rd. T Hth —71Rb 147
Haslemere Rd. Wind —3E 94
Hasler Clo. SE28 —45Xc 87
Haslethorn Ind. Est. Enf —14Xb 25
Haslett Rd. Shep —68U 120
Hasluck Gdns. Barn —16Eb 23
Hassard St. E2 —40Vb 63 (2K 195)
Hassenbrook Rd. Stanf —1M 93
Hassendean Rd. SE3 —51Kc 107
Hassett Rd. E9 —37Zb 64
Hassocks Clo. SE26 —62Xb 127
Hassocks Rd. SW16 —67Mb 126
Hassock Wood. Kes —77Mc 149
Hassop Rd. NW2 —35Za 60
Hassop Wlk. SE9 —63Nc 130
Hasted Clo. Grnh —58Yd 112
Hasted Rd. SE7 —50Mc 85
Hastings Av. Ilf —28Sc 46
Hastings Bldgs. SE1
—48Ub 83 (4H 207)
(off Swan Mead)
Hastings Clo. SE15 —52Wb 105
Hastings Clo. Barn —14Eb 23
Hastings Ct. Tedd —64Fa 122
Hastings Ho. W12 —45Xa 80
(off White City Est.)
Hastings Ho. W13 —45Ka 78
Hastings Rd. N11 —22Mb 42
Hastings Rd. N17 —27Tb 43
Hastings Rd. W13 —45Ka 78
Hastings Rd. Brom —74Nc 150
Hastings Rd. Croy —74Vb 147
Hastings Rd. Romf —29Kd 49
Hastings St. WC1
—41Nb 82 (4F 193)
Hastings Way. Bush —14Aa 19
Hastings Way. Crox —14S 18
Hastingwood Ct. E17 —29Dc 44
Hastingwood Trading Est. N18
—23Zb 44
Hastoe Clo. Hay —42Aa 77
Hat and Mitre Ct. EC1
—42Rb 83 (6C 194)
(off St John St.)
Hatcham Pk. M. SE14 —53Zb 106
Hatcham Pk. Rd. SE14 —53Zb 106
Hatcham Rd. SE15 —51Yb 106
Hatchard Rd. N19 —33Mb 62
Hatchcliffe St. SE10 —50Hc 85
Hatch Clo. Add —76K 139
Hatchcroft. NW4 —27Xa 40
Hatchet La. Wink —2A 116
Hatchett Rd. Felt —60S 98
Hatchfield Ho. N15 —30Ub 43
(off Albert Rd.)
Hatch Gdns. Tad —92Za 178
Hatchgate Gdns. Burn —1B 72
Hatch Gro. Romf —28Ad 47
Hatch La. E4 —21Fc 45
(in two parts)
Hatch La. Coul —87Jb 164
Hatch La. Ock —92R 174
(in two parts)
Hatch La. W Dray —52M 97
Hatch La. Wind —5E 94
Hatch Pl. King T —64Pa 123
Hatch Rd. SW16 —68Nb 126
Hatch Rd. Pil H —15Wd 32
Hatch Side. Chig —22Qc 46
Hatch, The. Enf —11Zb 26
Hatch, The. Wind —2A 94
Hatchwood Clo. Wfd G —21Hc 45
Hatcliffe Clo. SE3 —55Hc 107
Hatfield Clo. SE14 —52Zb 106
Hatfield Clo. Horn —36Md 69
Hatfield Clo. Hut —17Fe 33
Hatfield Clo. Ilf —27Rc 46
Hatfield Clo. Mitc —70Fb 125
Hatfield Mead. Mord —71Cb 145
Hatfield Rd. E15 —36Gc 65
Hatfield Rd. W4 —47Ta 79
Hatfield Rd. W13 —46Ja 78
Hatfield Rd. Asht —91Pa 177
Hatfield Rd. Dag —37Ad 67
Hatfield Rd. Pot B —2Eb 9
Hatfield Rd. Slou —7L 73
Hatfield Rd. Wat —11X 19
Hatfields. SE1 —46Qb 82 (6A 200)
Hatfields. Lou —13Rc 28
Hathaway Clo. Brom —74Pc 150
Hathaway Clo. Ruis —35V 56
Hathaway Clo. Stan —22Ja 38
Hathaway Cres. E12 —37Pc 66
Hathaway Gdns. W13 —43Ja 78
Hathaway Gdns. Grays —48Ce 91
Hathaway Gdns. Romf —29Zc 47
Hathaway Ho. N1
—40Ub 63 (2H 195)
Hathaway Rd. Croy —73Rb 147
Hathaway Rd. Grays —48De 91
Hatherleigh Clo. Chess —78Ma 143
Hatherleigh Clo. Mord —70Cb 125
Hatherleigh Gdns. Pot B —4Fb 9
Hatherleigh Rd. Ruis —33W 56
Hatherleigh Way. Romf —25Md 49
Hatherley Cres. Sidc —61Wc 131
Hatherley Gdns. E6 —41Mc 85
Hatherley Gdns. N8 —30Nb 42
Hatherley Gro. W2 —44Db 81
Hatherley Ho. E17 —28Cc 44
Hatherley M. E17 —28Cc 44
Hatherley Rd. E17 —28Bc 44
Hatherley Rd. Rich —54Pa 101
Hatherley Rd. Sidc —63Wc 131
Hatherley St. SW1
—49Lb 82 (6C 204)
Hathern Gdns. SE9 —63Qc 130
Hatherop Rd. Hamp —66Ba 121
Hathersage Ct. N1 —36Tb 63
Hatherwood. Lea —93Ma 177
Hathway St. SE15 —54Zb 106
Hatley Av. Ilf —28Sc 46
Hatley Clo. N11 —22Hb 41
Hatley Rd. N4 —33Pb 62
Hatteraick St. SE16 —47Yb 84
Hattersfield Clo. Belv —49Bd 87
Hatters La. Wat —16T 18
Hatton Av. Slou —2H 73
Hatton Clo. SE18 —52Tc 108
Hatton Clo. Grav —2A 136
Hatton Garden. EC1
—43Qb 82 (7A 194)
Hatton Gdns. Mitc —71Hb 145
Hatton Grn. Felt —56W 98
Hatton Gro. W Dray —47M 75
Hatton Pl. EC1 —43Qb 82 (7A 194)
Hatton Rd. Chesh —1Zb 12
Hatton Rd. Croy —74Qb 146
Hatton Rd. S. Felt —56V 98
Hatton Row. NW8
(off Hatton St.) —42Fb 81 (6C 190)
Hatton St. NW8 —42Fb 81 (6C 190)
Hatton Wall. EC1
—43Qb 82 (7A 194)
Haughmond. N12 —21Db 41
Haughton Clo. E8 —37Vb 63
Haunch of Venison Yd. W1
—44Kb 82 (3K 197)
Havana Clo. Romf —29Gd 48
Havana Rd. SW19 —61Cb 125
Havannah St. E14 —47Cc 84
Havant Rd. E17 —27Ec 44
Havant Way. SE15 —52Vb 105

Havelock Clo.—Heath Rd.

Havelock Clo. W12 —45Xa 80
(off White City Est.)
Havelock Pl. Harr —30Ga 38
Havelock Rd. N17 —26Wb 43
Havelock Rd. SW19 —64Eb 125
Havelock Rd. Belv —49Bd 87
Havelock Rd. Brom —70Lc 129
Havelock Rd. Croy —75Vb 147
Havelock Rd. Dart —59Kd 111
Havelock Rd. Grav —9B 114
Havelock Rd. Harr —27Ga 38
Havelock Rd. K Lan —1P 3
Havelock Rd. S'hall —48Aa 77
Havelock St. N1 —39Nb 62
Havelock St. Ilf —33Rc 66
Havelock Ter. SW8 —52Kb 104
Havelock Wlk. SE23 —60Yb 106
Haven Clo. SE9 —62Pc 130
Haven Clo. SW19 —62Za 124
Haven Clo. Grav —7B 136
Haven Clo. Hay —42U 76
Haven Clo. Sidc —65Yc 131
Haven Clo. Swan —68Hd 132
Haven Ct. Beck —68Ec 128
Havengore Av. Grav —9G 114
Haven Grn. W5 —44Ma 79
Haven Grn. Ct. W5 —44Ma 79
Haven Hill. Hods —79Ce 155
Havenhurst Rise. Enf —12Qb 24
Haven La. W5 —44Na 79
Haven Lodge. Enf —15Ub 25
(off Village Rd.)
Haven M. E3 —43Bc 84
Haven Pl. W5 —45Ma 79
Haven Pl. Grays —47Ee 91
Haven Rd. Ashf —63R 120
Havensfield. Chfd —3K 3
Haven St. NW1 —38Kb 62
Haven, The. Grays —10C 92
Haven, The. Rich —55Qa 101
Haven Wood. Wemb —34Ra 59
Havenwood Clo. Gt War —23Yd 50
Haverfield Gdns. Rich —52Qa 101
Haverfield Rd. E3 —41Ac 84
Haverford Way. Edgw —25Pa 39
Haverhill Rd. E4 —18Ec 26
Haverhill Rd. SW12 —60Lb 104
Havering Dri. Romf —28Gd 48
Havering Gdns. Romf —29Yc 47
Havering Rd. Romf —27Fd 48
Havering St. E1 —42Zb 84
Havering Way. Bark —41Xc 87
Havers Av. W on T —78Z 141
Haversham Clo. Twic —58Ma 101
Haversham Ho. SE16 —47Wb 83
Haverstock Ct. Orp —68Xc 131
(off Cotmandene Cres.)
Haverstock Hill. NW3 —36Gb 61
Haverstock Rd. NW5 —36Jb 62
Haverstock St. N1
—40Rb 63 (2C 194)
Haverthwaite Rd. Orp —75Tc 150
Havil St. SE5 —52Ub 105
Havisham Pl. SW16 & SE19
—65Rb 127
Havisham Rd. Grav —10J 115
Hawarden Gro. SE24 —59Sb 105
Hawarden Hill. NW2 —34Wa 60
Hawarden Rd. E17 —28Zb 44
Hawarden Rd. Cat —93Sb 181
Hawbridge Rd. E11 —32Fc 65
Hawes Clo. N'wd —24V 36
Hawes Ho. E17 —28Zb 44
Hawes La. E4 —10Ec 12
Hawes La. W Wick —74Ec 148
Hawes Rd. N18 —23Xb 43
Hawes Rd. Brom —67Kc 129
(in two parts)
Hawes Rd. Tad —92Za 178
Hawes St. N1 —38Rb 63
Hawfield Bank. Orp —76Zc 151
Hawgood St. E3 —43Cc 84
Hawk Clo. Wal A —6Jc 13
Hawkdene. E4 —16Dc 26
Hawke Pk. Rd. N22 —27Rb 43
Hawke Pl. SE16 —47Zb 84
Hawker. NW9 —25Va 40
Hawker Clo. Wall —80Nb 146
Hawker Ct. Langl —48C 74
Hawke Rd. SE19 —65Tb 127
Hawkesbury Rd. SW15 —57Xa 102
Hawkes Clo. Grays —51De 113
Hawkesfield Rd. SE23 —61Ac 128
Hawkesley Clo. Twic —63Ja 122
Hawkes Rd. Mitc —67Gb 125
Hawkesworth Clo. N'wd —24U 36
Hawke Tower. SE14 —51Ac 106
Hawkewood Rd. Sun —69W 120
Hawkfield Ct. Iswth —54Ga 100
Hawkhirst Rd. Kenl —87Tb 165
Hawkhurst. Cob —86Ca 159
Hawkhurst Gdns. Chess —77Na 143
Hawkhurst Gdns. Romf —22Fd 48
Hawkhurst Rd. SW16 —67Mb 126
Hawkhurst Rd. Kenl —89Ub 165
Hawkhurst Way. N Mald —71Ta 143
Hawkhurst Way. W Wick
—75Dc 148
Hawkinge. N17 —26Tb 43
(off Gloucester Rd.)
Hawkinge Wlk. Orp —69Xc 131
Hawkinge Way. Horn —37Ld 69
Hawkins Av. Grav —3E 136
Hawkins Clo. NW7 —22Ta 39
Hawkins Clo. Harr —31Fa 58
Hawkins Ct. SE18 —49Nc 86
Hawkins Rd. Tedd —65Ka 122
Hawkley Gdns. SE27 —61Rb 127
Hawkridge Clo. Romf —30Yc 47
Hawksbrook La. Beck —72Dc 148
Hawkshaw Clo. SW2 —60Nb 104
Hawkshead Clo. Brom —66Gc 129
Hawkshead La. N Mym —1Ya 8
Hawkshead Rd. NW10 —38Va 60
Hawkshead Rd. W4 —47Ua 80
Hawkshead Rd. Pot B —1Bb 9
Hawkshill Clo. Esh —79Ca 141
Hawks Hill Clo. Fet —95Ha 176
Hawkshill Rd. Slou —1E 72
Hawkshill Way. Esh —79Ba 141
Hawkslade Rd. SE15 —57Zb 106
Hawksley Rd. N16 —34Ub 63
Hawksmead Clo. Enf —8Zb 12
Hawks M. SE10 —52Ec 106
Hawksmoor. Shenl —5Qa 7
Hawksmoor Clo. E6 —44Nc 86
Hawksmoor Grn. Hut —15Fe 33
(in two parts)
Hawksmoor M. E1 —45Xb 83
Hawksmoor St. W6 —51Za 102
Hawksmouth. E4 —17Ec 26
Hawks Rd. King T —68Pa 123
Hawkstone Rd. SE16 —49Yb 84
Hawksview. Cob —85Ba 159
Hawks Way. Stai —62H 119
Hawkswell Clo. Wok —5C 188
Hawkswell Wlk. Wok —5C 188
Hawkswood Gro. Ful —37B 54
Hawkswood La. Ful & Ger X
—36B 54
Hawk Ter. S Stif —50Zd 91
Hawkwell Ct. E4 —20Ec 26
Hawkwell Wlk. N1 —39Sb 63
(off Basire St.)
Hawkwood Cres. E4 —16Dc 26
Hawkwood Dell. Bookh —98Ca 175
Hawkwood La. Chst —67Sc 130
Hawkwood Mt. E5 —32Xb 63
Hawkwood Rise. Bookh —98Ca 175
Hawlands Dri. Pinn —31Aa 57
Hawley Clo. Hamp —65Ba 121
Hawley Cres. NW1 —38Kb 62
Hawley M. NW1 —38Kb 62
Hawley Rd. N18 —22Zb 44
Hawley Rd. NW1 —38Kb 62
Hawley Rd. Dart —61Nd 133
Hawley St. NW1 —38Kb 62
Hawley Ter. Dart —64Qd 133
Hawley Way. Ashf —64Q 120
Haws La. Stai —58J 97
Hawstead La. Orp —78Bd 151
Hawstead Rd. SE6 —58Dc 106
Hawsted. Buck H —17Kc 27
Hawthordene Rd. Beck —75Hc 149
Hawthorn Av. Big H —87Mc 167
Hawthorn Av. Brtwd —20Be 33
Hawthorn Av. Rain —42Kd 89
Hawthorn Av. Rich —54Na 101
Hawthorn Cen. Harr —28Ha 38
Hawthorn Clo. Grav —3E 136
Hawthorn Clo. Hamp —64Ca 121
Hawthorn Clo. Houn —52X 99
Hawthorn Clo. Orp —72Tc 150
Hawthorn Clo. Wat —10V 4
Hawthorn Clo. Wok —92A 172
Hawthorn Ct. Pinn —26Y 37
(off Rickmansworth Rd.)
Hawthorn Cres. SW17 —64Jb 126
Hawthorn Cres. S Croy —83Yb 166
Hawthorndene Clo. Brom
—75Hc 149
Hawthorndene Rd. Brom
—75Hc 149
Hawthorn Dri. Den —37L 55
Hawthorn Dri. Harr —30Ca 37
Hawthorn Dri. W Wick —77Gc 149
Hawthorne Av. Cars —80Jb 146
Hawthorne Av. Chesh —3Xb 11
Hawthorne Av. Harr —30Ja 38
Hawthorne Av. Mitc —67Rb 127
Hawthorne Av. Ruis —30X 37
Hawthorne Av. T Hth —68Fb 125
Hawthorne Clo. N1 —37Ub 63
Hawthorne Clo. SE15 —54Xb 105
Hawthorne Clo. Brom —69Pc 130
Hawthorne Clo. Chesh —3Xb 11
Hawthorne Clo. Sutt —75Eb 145
Hawthorne Ct. N'wd —26W 36
Hawthorne Ct. Stai —59M 97
(off Hawthorne Way)
Hawthorne Cres. Slou —4J 73
Hawthorne Cres. W Dray —47P 75
Hawthorne Farm Av. N'holt
—39Aa 57
Hawthorne Gro. NW9 —31Sa 59
Hawthorne M. Gnfd —44Ea 78
Hawthorne Pl. Eps —84Ua 162
Hawthorne Pl. Hay —45V 76
Hawthorne Rd. E17 —27Cc 44
Hawthorne Rd. Brom —69Pc 130
Hawthorne Rd. Rad —6Ja 6
Hawthorne Rd. Stai —63E 118
Hawthorne Way. Wink —10A 94
Hawthorn Gdns. W5 —48Ma 79
Hawthorn Gro. SE20 —67Xb 127
Hawthorn Gro. Barn —16Va 22
Hawthorn Gro. Enf —10Tb 11
Hawthorn Hatch. Bren —52Ka 100
Hawthorn La. Farn C —8D 52
Hawthorn La. Sev —94Hd 186
Hawthorn M. NW7 —25Ab 40
Hawthorn Pl. Eri —50Ed 88
Hawthorn Rd. N8 —27Mb 42
Hawthorn Rd. N18 —23Vb 43
Hawthorn Rd. NW10 —38Wa 60
Hawthorn Rd. Bexh —56Bd 109
Hawthorn Rd. Bren —52Ka 100
Hawthorn Rd. Buck H —21Mc 45
Hawthorn Rd. Dart —61Md 133
Hawthorn Rd. Rip —96J 173
Hawthorn Rd. Sutt —79Gb 145
Hawthorn Rd. Wall —80Kb 146
Hawthorn Rd. Wok —8G 188
Hawthorns. Hart —70Be 135
Hawthorns. Wfd G —20Jc 27
Hawthorns, The. Coln —53H 97
Hawthorns, The. Eps —80Ua 144
Hawthorns, The. Lou —14Qc 28
Hawthorns, The. Rick —22F 34
Hawthorn Wlk. W10 —42Ab 80
Hawthorn Way. N9 —19Vb 25
Hawthorn Way. New Haw —82L 157
Hawthorn Way. Shep —70T 120
Hawtrees. Rad —7Ha 6
Hawtrey Av. N'holt —40Z 57
Hawtrey Clo. Slou —7M 73
Hawtrey Dri. Ruis —31W 56
Hawtrey Rd. NW3 —38Gb 61
Hawtrey Rd. Wind —4G 94
Haxted Rd. Brom —67Kc 129
Hayburn Way. Horn —32Hd 68
Hay Clo. E15 —38Gc 65
Hay Clo. Borwd —12Sa 21
Haycroft Clo. Coul —90Rb 165
Haycroft Gdns. NW10 —39Wa 60
Haycroft Rd. SW2 —57Nb 104
Haycroft Rd. Surb —75Ma 143
Hay Currie St. E14 —44Dc 84
Hayday Rd. E16 —43Jc 85
Hayden Ct. New Haw —83K 157
Haydens Clo. Orp —72Yc 151
Haydens M. W3 —44Sa 79
Hayden's Pl. W11 —44Bb 81
Hayden Way. Romf —26Ed 48
Haydn Av. Purl —86Qb 164
Haydock Av. N'holt —37Ca 57
Haydock Clo. Horn —35Pd 69
Haydock Grn. N'holt —37Ca 57
Haydon Clo. NW9 —28Sa 39
Haydon Clo. Enf —16Ub 25
Haydon Dri. Pinn —28W 36
Haydon Pk. Rd. SW19 —64Cb 125
Haydon Rd. Dag —33Yc 67
Haydon Rd. Wat —16Aa 19
Haydons Rd. SW19 —67Db 125
Haydon St. EC3 —44Vb 83 (4K 201)
Haydon Wlk. E1 —44Vb 83 (4K 201)
Hayes Barton. Wok —88F 156
Hayes Chase. W Wick —72Fc 149
Hayes Clo. Brom —75Jc 149
Hayes Clo. Grays —51Yd 112
Hayes Ct. SW2 —60Nb 104
Hayes Cres. NW11 —29Bb 41
Hayes Cres. Sutt —77Za 144
Hayes Dri. Rain —38Kd 69
Hayes End Clo. Hay —43T 76
Hayes End Dri. Hay —42T 76
Hayes End Rd. Hay —42T 76
Hayesford Pk. Dri. Brom —71Hc 149
Hayes Garden. Brom —74Jc 149
Hayes Hill. Brom —74Gc 149
Hayes Hill Rd. Brom —74Hc 149
Hayes La. Beck —69Ec 128
Hayes La. Brom —71Jc 149
Hayes La. Kenl —88Rb 165
Hayes Mead Rd. Brom —74Gc 149
Hayes Metro Cen. Hay —45Y 77
Hayes Pl. NW1 —42Gb 81 (6E 190)
Hayes Rd. Brom —70Jc 129
Hayes Rd. Grnh —59Ud 112
Hayes Rd. S'hall —49X 77
Hayes St. Brom —74Kc 149
Hayes Ter. Shorne —4N 137
Hayes, The. Eps —91Ua 178
Hayes Wlk. Pot B —5Db 9
Hayes Way. Beck —70Ec 128
Hayes Wood Av. Brom —74Kc 149
Hayfield Clo. Bush —14Da 19
Hayfield Pas. E1 —42Yb 84
Hayfield Rd. Orp —71Wc 151
Hayfield Yd. E1 —42Zb 84
Haygarth Pl. SW19 —64Za 124
Haygreen Clo. King T —65Ra 123
Hay Hill. W1 —45Kb 82 (5A 198)
Hayland Clo. NW9 —28Ta 39
Hay La. NW9 —28Sa 39
Hay La. Ful —5P 53
Hayle. E Til —8L 93
Hayles St. SE11 —49Rb 83 (5B 206)
Haylett Gdns. King T —70Ma 123
Hayling Av. Felt —62W 120
Hayling Clo. N16 —36Ub 63
Hayling Ct. Sutt —77Ya 144
Hayling Rd. Wat —20W 18
Haymaker Clo. Uxb —38P 55
Hayman Cres. Hay —40T 56
Hayman St. N1 —38Rb 63
Haymarket. SW1
—45Mb 82 (5D 198)
Haymarket Arc. SW1
—45Mb 82 (5D 198)
(off Haymarket)
Haymeads Dri. Esh —79Ea 142
Haymer Gdns. Wor Pk —76Wa 144
Haymerle Rd. SE15 —51Wb 105
Haymill Clo. Gnfd —41Ha 78
Haymill Rd. Slou —2B 72
Hayne Rd. Beck —68Bc 128
Haynes Clo. N11 —20Jb 24
Haynes Clo. N17 —24Xb 43
Haynes Clo. SE3 —55Gc 107
Haynes Clo. Slou —50B 74
Haynes La. SE19 —65Ub 127
Haynes Rd. Grav —2B 136
Haynes Rd. Horn —28Md 49
Haynes Rd. Wemb —38Na 59
Hayne St. EC1 —43Rb 83 (7C 194)
Haynt Wlk. SW20 —69Ab 124
Hayse Hill. Wind —3B 94
Hay's Galleria. SE1
—46Ub 83 (6H 201)
Hay's La. SE1 —46Ub 83 (7H 201)
Haysleigh Gdns. SE20 —68Wb 127
Hay's M. W1 —46Kb 82 (5K 197)
Haysoms Clo. Romf —28Gd 48
Haystall Clo. Hay —40U 56
Hay St. E2 —39Wb 63
Hays Wlk. Sutt —82Za 162
Hayter Ct. E11 —33Kc 65
Hayter Rd. SW2 —57Nb 104
Hayward Clo. SW19 —66Db 125
Hayward Clo. Dart —57Fd 110
Hayward Ct. SW9 —54Nb 104
(off Clapham Rd.)
Hayward Gdns. SW15 —58Ya 102
Hayward Rd. N20 —19Eb 23
Haywards Mead. Eton W —10D 72
Hayward's Pl. EC1
—42Rb 83 (6B 194)
Haywood Clo. Pinn —26Z 37
Haywood Ct. Wal A —6Hc 13
Haywood Lodge. N11 —23Nb 42
(off Oak La.)
Haywood Pk. Chor —15H 17
Haywood Rise. Orp —78Uc 150
Haywood Rd. Brom —70Mc 129
Hayworth Clo. Enf —12Ac 26
Hazel Av. W Dray —48Q 76
Hazel Bank. SE25 —68Ub 127
Hazel Bank. Surb —74Sa 143
Hazelbank Ct. Cher —74L 139
Hazelbank Rd. SE6 —61Fc 129
Hazelbank Rd. Cher —74L 139
Hazelbourne Rd. SW12 —58Kb 104
Hazelbrouck Gdns. Ilf —24Tc 46
Hazelbury Av. Abb L —4S 4
Hazelbury Clo. SW19 —68Cb 125
Hazelbury Grn. N9 —20Ub 25
Hazelbury La. N9 —20Ub 25
Hazel Clo. N13 —20Tb 25
Hazel Clo. N19 —33Lb 62
Hazel Clo. SE15 —54Wb 105
Hazel Clo. Bren —52Ka 100
Hazel Clo. Croy —73Zb 148
Hazel Clo. Egh —5M 117
Hazel Clo. Horn —34Kd 69
Hazel Clo. Mitc —70Mb 126
Hazel Clo. Twic —59Ea 100
Hazel Ct. W5 —45Na 79
Hazel Ct. Lou —13Pc 28
Hazel Croft. Pinn —23Da 37
Hazelcroft Clo. Uxb —38P 55
Hazeldean Rd. NW10 —38Ta 59
Hazel Dene. Add —78L 139
Hazeldene. Wal X —4Ac 12
Hazeldene Ct. Kenl —87Tb 165
Hazeldene Dri. Pinn —27Y 37
Hazeldene Gdns. Uxb —39S 56
Hazeldene Rd. Ilf —33Xc 67
Hazeldene Rd. Well —54Yc 109
Hazeldon Rd. SE4 —57Ac 106
Hazel Dri. Eri —53Kd 111
Hazel Dri. Rip —97H 173
Hazeleigh Gdns. Wfd G —22Nc 46
Hazel End. Swan —71Gd 152
Hazel Gdns. Edgw —21Ra 39
Hazel Gdns. Grays —8A 92
Hazelgreen Clo. N21 —18Rb 25
Hazel Gro. SE26 —63Zb 128
Hazel Gro. Orp —75Rc 150
Hazel Gro. Romf —27Ad 47
Hazel Gro. Stai —65K 119
Hazel Gro. Wat —7X 5
Hazel Gro. Wemb —39Na 59
Hazelhurst. Beck —67Fc 129
Hazelhurst Clo. Guild —100D 172
Hazelhurst Rd. SW17 —63Eb 125
Hazelhurst Rd. Burn —10A 52
Hazel La. Rich —61Na 123
Hazell Cres. Romf —25Dd 48
Hazellville Rd. N19 —31Mb 62
Hazell Way. Stoke P —8K 53
Hazel Mead. Barn —15Xa 22
Hazel Mead. Eps —82Wa 162
Hazelmere Clo. Felt —58U 98
Hazelmere Clo. Lea —91Ka 176
Hazelmere Clo. N'holt —40Ba 57
Hazelmere Dri. N'holt —40Ba 57
Hazelmere Gdns. Horn —29Ld 49
Hazelmere Rd. NW6 —39Bb 61
Hazelmere Rd. N'holt —40Ba 57
Hazelmere Rd. Orp —70Sc 130
Hazelmere Wlk. N'holt —40Ba 57
Hazelmere Way. Brom —72Jc 149
Hazel Pde. Fet —94Ea 176
Hazel Rise. Horn —30Ld 49
Hazel Rd. E15 —36Gc 65
Hazel Rd. NW10 —41Xa 80
(in two parts)
Hazel Rd. Dart —61Md 133
Hazel Rd. Eri —53Jd 110
Hazel Rd. Park —1Da 5
Hazel Rd. W Byf —86J 157
Hazeltree La. N'holt —41Aa 77
Hazel Tree Rd. Wat —9X 5
Hazel Wlk. Brom —72Qc 150
Hazel Way. E4 —23Bc 44
Hazel Way. SE1 —49Vb 83 (5K 207)
Hazel Way. Coul —91Hb 179
Hazel Way. Fet —94Ea 176
Hazelwood. Crox —16S 18
Hazelwood. Linf —9J 93
Hazelwood Av. Mord —70Db 125
Hazelwood Clo. W5 —47Na 79
Hazelwood Clo. Harr —28Da 37
Hazelwood Ct. N13 —21Qb 42
(off Hazelwood La.)
Hazelwood Ct. NW10 —34Ua 60
Hazelwood Ct. Surb —72Na 143
Hazelwood Cres. N13 —21Qb 42
Hazelwood Dri. Pinn —26X 37
Hazelwood Gdns. Pil H —16Wd 32
Hazelwood Gro. S Croy —85Xb 165
Hazelwood Ho. SE8 —49Ac 84
Hazelwood Houses. Short
—69Gc 129
Hazelwood La. N13 —21Qb 42
Hazelwood La. Abb L —4S 4
Hazelwood La. Coul —90Gb 163
Hazelwood Pk. Clo. Chig —22Uc 46
Hazelwood Rd. E17 —29Ac 44
Hazelwood Rd. Cud —84Tc 168
Hazelwood Rd. Enf —16Vb 25
Hazelwood Rd. Knap —6B 188
Hazlebury Rd. SW6 —54Db 103
Hazledean Rd. Croy —75Tb 147
Hazledene Rd. W4 —51Sa 101
Hazlemere Ct. SW2 —60Pb 104
Hazlemere Gdns. Wor Pk
—74Wa 144
Hazlemere Rd. Slou —6M 73
Hazlewell Rd. SW15 —57Ya 102
Hazlewood. Lou —15Mc 27
Hazlewood Cres. W10 —42Ab 80
Hazlitt Clo. Felt —63Aa 121
Hazlitt M. W14 —48Ab 80
Hazlitt Rd. W14 —48Ab 80
Hazon Way. Eps —84Sa 161
Heacham Av. Uxb —34S 56
Headbourne Ho. SE1
—48Tb 83 (3G 207)
Headcorn Pl. T Hth —70Pb 126
Headcorn Rd. N17 —24Vb 43
Headcorn Rd. Brom —64Hc 129
Headcorn Rd. T Hth —70Pb 126
Headfort Pl. SW1
—47Jb 82 (2J 203)
Headingley Clo. Ilf —23Vc 47
Headingley Clo. Shenl —4Na 7
Headington Rd. SW18 —61Eb 125
Headlam Rd. SW4 —58Mb 104
Headlam St. E1 —42Xb 83
Headley App. Ilf —29Rc 46
Headley Av. Wall —78Pb 146
Headley Chase. War —21Yd 50
Headley Clo. Eps —79Qa 143
Headley Comn. Rd. H'ley
—98Ta 177
Headley Ct. SE26 —64Yb 128
Headley Ct. H'ley —7Rc 46
Headley Dri. Eps —91Ya 178
Headley Dri. Ilf —30Rc 46
Headley Dri. New Ad —80Dc 148
Headley Gro. Tad —92Xa 178
Headley Rd. Eps —90Ra 161
Headley Rd. Lea & Eps —94La 176
Headley Rd. Mick —100La 176
Head's M. W11 —44Cb 81
Headstone Dri. Harr —27Fa 38
Headstone Gdns. Harr —28Ea 38
Headstone La. Harr —28Ca 37
Headstone Pde. Harr —28Fa 38
Headstone Rd. Harr —29Ga 38
Head St. E1 —44Zb 84
(in two parts)
Headway Clo. Rich —63La 122
Headway, The. Eps —81Va 162
Heald St. SE14 —53Cc 106
Healey Ho. SW9 —52Qb 104
Healey Rd. Wat —16V 18
Healey St. NW1 —37Kb 62
Healy Dri. Orp —76Vc 151
Heards La. Shenf —13Be 33
Hearn Bldgs. Wat —14Y 19
Hearne Rd. W4 —51Qa 101
Hearn Rise. N'holt —39Z 57
Hearn Rd. Romf —30Hd 48
Hearn's Bldgs. SE17
—49Tb 83 (6G 207)
Hearn's Clo. Orp —70Yc 131
Hearn's Rise. Orp —70Zc 131
Hearn's Rd. Orp —70Yc 131
Hearn St. EC2 —42Ub 83 (6J 195)
Hearnville Rd. SW12 —60Jb 104
Hearsall Av. Stanf —1N 93
Heathacre. Coln —53F 96
Heatham Pk. Twic —59Ha 100
Heath Av. Bexh —51Zc 109
Heathbourne Rd. Bush & Stan
—18Ga 20
Heathbridge. Wey —79Q 140
Heath Brow. NW3 —34Eb 61
Heath Bus. Cen. Houn —56Ea 100
Heath Clo. NW11 —31Db 61
Heath Clo. W5 —42Pa 79
Heath Clo. Bans —86Db 163
Heath Clo. Hay —52T 98
Heath Clo. Orp —73Yc 151
Heath Clo. Pot B —2Db 9
Heath Clo. Romf —27Jd 48
Heath Clo. Stai —58L 97
Heathclose. Swan —68Gd 132
Heath Clo. Vir W —10P 117
Heathclose Av. Dart —59Kd 111
Heathclose Rd. Dart —60Jd 110
Heathcote. Tad —93Za 178
Heathcote Av. Ilf —26Pc 46
Heathcote Ct. Ilf —26Pc 46
Heathcote Gro. E4 —20Ec 26
Heathcote Rd. Eps —86Ta 161
Heathcote Rd. Twic —58Ka 100
Heathcote St. WC1
—42Pb 82 (5H 193)
Heathcote Way. W Dray —46M 75
Heath Ct. Houn —56Ba 99
Heathcroft. NW11 —32Db 61
Heathcroft. W5 —42Pa 79
Heathcroft Av. Sun —66V 120
Heathdale Av. Houn —55Aa 99
Heathdene Dri. Belv —49Dd 88
Heathdene Rd. SW16 —66Pb 126
Heathdene Rd. Wall —80Kb 146
Heathdown Rd. Wok —87F 156
Heath Dri. NW3 —35Db 61
Heath Dri. SW20 —70Ya 124
Heath Dri. Pot B —2Cb 9
Heath Dri. Romf —25Jd 48
Heath Dri. Send —94D 172
Heath Dri. Sutt —81Eb 163
Heath Dri. Tad —97Wa 178
Heath Dri. They B —8Uc 14
Heathedge. SE26 —61Xb 127
Heath End Rd. Bex —60Gd 110
Heather Av. Romf —26Fd 48
Heatherbank. SE9 —54Pc 108
Heatherbank. Chst —68Qc 130
Heatherbank Clo. Dart —58Gd 110
Heather Clo. E6 —44Qc 86
Heather Clo. SW8 —55Kb 104
Heather Clo. Hamp —67Ba 121
Heather Clo. Iswth —57Fa 100
Heather Clo. New Haw —82K 157
Heather Clo. Pil H —15Xd 32
Heather Clo. Romf —25Fd 48
Heather Clo. Tad —94Ab 178
Heather Clo. Uxb —43P 75
Heather Clo. Wok —3F 188
Heatherdale Clo. King T —66Qa 123
Heatherdene. W Hor —97T 174
Heatherdene Clo. N12 —25Eb 41
Heatherdene Clo. Mitc —70Fb 125
Heatherden Grn. Iver —39E 54
Heather Dri. Dart —59Jd 110
Heather Dri. Enf —12Rb 25
Heather Dri. Romf —26Fd 48
Heather End. Swan —70Fd 132
Heatherfields. New Haw —82K 157
Heather Gdns. NW11 —30Ab 40
Heather Gdns. Romf —26Fd 48
Heather Gdns. Sutt —79Cb 145
Heather Glen. Romf —26Fd 48
Heatherlands. Sun —65W 120
Heather La. Wat —8W 4
Heather La. W Dray —44N 75
Heatherley Ct. N16 —34Wb 63
Heatherley Dri. Ilf —27Nc 46
Heather Pk. Dri. Wemb —38Qa 59
Heather Pl. Esh —77Da 141
Heather Rise. Bush —12Ba 19
Heather Rd. NW2 —33Va 60
Heather Rd. SE12 —60Jc 107
Heatherset Gdns. SW16 —66Pb 126
Heatherside Gdns. Farn C —4H 53
Heatherside Rd. Eps —80Ta 143
Heatherside Rd. Sidc —62Zc 131
Heathers, The. Stai —59P 97
Heatherton Ter. N3 —26Db 41
Heathervale Caravan Pk. New Haw
—82L 157
Heathervale Rd. New Haw
—82K 157
Heather Wlk. W10 —42Ab 80
Heather Wlk. Edgw —22Ra 39
Heather Wlk. Twic —59Ca 99
(off Stephenson Rd.)
Heather Wlk. W Vill —82U 158
Heather Way. Pot B —4Bb 9
Heather Way. Romf —26Fd 48
Heather Way. S Croy —81Zb 166
Heather Way. Stan —23Ha 38
Heatherwood Clo. E12 —33Lc 65
Heatherwood Dri. Hay —40T 56
Heath Farm Ct. Wat —9T 4
Heathfield. E4 —20Ec 26
Heathfield. Chst —65Sc 130
Heathfield. Cob —86Ca 159
Heathfield Av. SW18 —59Fb 103
Heathfield Av. Asc —10C 116
Heathfield Clo. E16 —43Mc 85
Heathfield Clo. Kes —78Lc 149
Heathfield Clo. Pot B —2Db 9
Heathfield Clo. Wok —90C 156
Heathfield Cotts. Swan —68Fd 132
(off London Rd.)
Heathfield Ct. SE20 —66Yb 128
Heathfield Ct. W4 —50Ta 79
Heathfield Dri. Mitc —67Gb 125
Heathfield Gdns. NW11 —30Za 40
Heathfield Gdns. SW18 —58Fb 103
Heathfield Gdns. W4 —50Sa 79
Heathfield Gdns. Croy —77Tb 147
Heathfield La. Chst —65Rc 130
Heathfield N. Twic —59Ga 100
Heathfield Pde. Swan —68Ed 132
Heathfield Pk. NW2 —37Ya 60
Heathfield Rise. Ruis —31S 56
Heathfield Rd. SW18 —58Eb 103
Heathfield Rd. W3 —47Ra 79
Heathfield Rd. Bexh —56Bd 109
Heathfield Rd. Brom —66Hc 129
Heathfield Rd. Burn —3A 52
Heathfield Rd. Bush —14Aa 19
Heathfield Rd. Croy —77Tb 147
Heathfield Rd. Kes —78Lc 149
Heathfield Rd. Sev —94Hd 186
Heathfield Rd. W on T —77Aa 141
Heathfield Rd. Wok —90C 156
Heathfields Ct. Houn —57Aa 99
Heathfield S. Twic —59Ha 100
Heathfield Sq. SW18 —59Fb 103
Heathfield Ter. SE18 —51Uc 108
Heathfield Ter. W4 —50Sa 79
Heathfield Vale. S Croy —81Zb 166
Heath Gdns. Dart —60Ld 111
Heath Gdns. Twic —60Ha 100
Heathgate. NW11 —30Db 41
Heathgate Pl. NW3 —36Hb 61
Heath Gro. SE20 —66Yb 128
Heath Gro. Sun —66V 120
Heath Ho. Sidc —63Vc 131
Heath Ho. Rd. Wok —10A 188
Heath Hurst Rd. NW3 —35Gb 61
Heathland Rd. N16 —32Ub 63
Heathlands. Tad —94Za 178
Heathlands Clo. Sun —68W 120
Heathlands Clo. Twic —61Ha 122
Heathlands Clo. Wok —86A 156
Heathlands Rise. Dart —58Kd 111
Heathlands Way. Houn —57Aa 99
Heath La. SE3 —54Fc 107
Heath La. (Lower) Dart —60Ld 111
Heath La. (Upper) Dart —61Jd 132
Heathlee Rd. SE3 —56Hc 107
Heathlee Rd. Dart —58Gd 110
Heathley End. Chst —65Sc 130
Heath Lodge. Bush —18Ga 20
Heathmans Rd. SW6 —53Bb 103
Heath Mead. SW19 —62Za 124
Heath Pk. Ct. Romf —29Jd 48
Heath Pk. Dri. Brom —69Nc 130
Heath Pk. Rd. Romf —29Jd 48
Heath Pas. NW3 —32Eb 61
Heath Ridge Grn. Cob —85Ca 159
Heath Rise. SW15 —58Za 102
Heath Rise. Brom —72Hc 149
Heath Rise. Rip —95K 173
Heath Rise. Vir W —10P 117
Heath Rd. SW8 —54Kb 104
Heath Rd. Bex —60Ed 110
Heath Rd. Cat —95Tb 181

Heath Rd.—Higham Pl.

Heath Rd. Dart —58Hd 110
Heath Rd. Grays —6B 92
Heath Rd. Harr —31Ea 58
Heath Rd. Houn —56Da 99
Heath Rd. Oxs —84Ea 160
Heath Rd. Pot B —2Cb 9
Heath Rd. Romf —31Zc 67
Heath Rd. T Hth —69Sb 127
Heath Rd. Twic —60Ha 100
Heath Rd. Uxb —42S 76
Heath Rd. Wat —17Z 19
Heath Rd. Wey —77Q 140
Heath Rd. Wok —87B 156
Heathrow Airport. Houn —54N 97
Heathrow Clo. W Dray —53K 97
Heathrow International Trading Est. Houn —55X 99
Heathrow Summit Cen. W Dray —52M 97
Heaths Clo. Enf —12Ub 25
Heath Side. NW3 —35Fb 61
Heathside. NW11 —32Cb 61
Heathside. SE13 —54Ec 106
Heathside. Esh —76Ga 142
Heathside. Houn —59Ba 99
Heathside. Orp —73Tc 150
Heathside. Wey —78R 140
Heathside Av. Bexh —54Ad 109
Heathside Clo. Esh —76Ga 142
Heathside Clo. N'wd —22T 36
Heathside Clo. Tad —95Ya 178
Heathside Cres. Wok —89B 156
Heathside Gdns. Wok —89C 156
Heathside Pk. Rd. Wok —90B 156
Heathside Rd. N'wd —21T 36
Heathside Rd. Wok —90B 156
Heathstan Rd. W12 —44Wa 80
Heath St. NW3 —34Eb 61
Heath St. Dart —59Md 111
Heath, The. W7 —46Ga 78
Heath, The. Cat —96Tb 181
Heath, The. Rad —5Ja 6
Heathurst Rd. S Croy —81Tb 165
Heath View. N2 —28Eb 41
Heathview. NW5 —35Jb 62
Heath View. E Hor —97V 174
Heathview Av. Dart —58Gd 110
Heath View Clo. N2 —28Eb 41
Heathview Cres. Dart —60Kd 111
Heathview Dri. SE2 —51Zc 109
Heathview Gdns. SW15 —59Ya 102
Heath View Gdns. Grays —47Ee 91
Heath View Rd. Grays —47Ee 91
Heathview Rd. T Hth —70Qb 126
Heath Vs. NW3 —34Fb 61
Heath Vs. SE18 —50Vc 87
Heathville Rd. N19 —31Nb 62
Heathwall St. SW11 —55Hb 103
Heathway. SE3 —52Jc 107
Heathway. Cat —97Sb 181
Heathway. Croy —75Bc 148
Heathway. Dag —34Bd 67
Heathway. E Hor —96V 174
Heath Way. Eri —53Ed 110
Heathway. Iver —40F 54
Heathway. S'hall —49Z 77
Heath Way. Wfd G —22Lc 45
Heathway Ct. NW3 —33Cb 61
Heathwood Gdns. SE7 —49Nc 86
Heathwood Gdns. Swan —68Ed 132
Heathwood Wlk. Bex —60Gd 110
Heaton Av. Romf —24Kd 49
Heaton Clo. E4 —20Ec 26
Heaton Clo. Romf —24Ld 49
Heaton Ct. Chesh —1Zb 12
Heaton Grange Rd. Romf —26Hd 48
Heaton Rd. SE15 —54Xb 105
Heaton Rd. Mitc —66Jb 126
Heaton Way. Romf —24Ld 49
Heaverham Rd. Kems —89Rd 171
Heaver Rd. SW11 —55Fb 103
Heavitree Rd. SE18 —50Tc 86
Hebden Ct. E2 —39Vb 63 (1K 195)
Hebdon Rd. SW17 —62Gb 125
Heber Rd. NW2 —36Za 60
Heber Rd. SE22 —58Vb 105
Hebron Rd. W6 —48Ya 80
Hecham Clo. E17 —26Ac 44
Heckfield Pl. SW6 —52Cb 103
Heckford St. E1 —45Zb 84
Heckford St. Bus. Cen. E1 —45Zb 84 (off Heckford St.)
Hector. NW9 —25Va 40 (off Five Acre)
Hector Peterson Ho. Wemb (off Wilson Dri.) —31Pa 59
Hector St. SE18 —49Uc 86
Heddington Gro. N7 —36Pb 62
Heddon Clo. Iswth —56Ja 100
Heddon Ct. Av. Barn —15Hb 23
Heddon Ct. Pde. Barn —15Jb 24
Heddon Rd. Barn —15Hb 23
Heddon St. W1 —45Lb 82 (4B 198)
Hedgecroft Cotts. Rip —93K 173
Hedge Hill. Enf —11Rb 25
Hedge La. N13 —20Rb 25
Hedgemans Rd. Dag —38Zc 67
Hedgemans Way. Dag —37Ad 67
Hedge Pl. Rd. Grnh —58Vd 112
Hedgerley Ct. Wok —5F 188
Hedgerley Gdns. Gnfd —40Ea 58
Hedgerley Hill. Hedg —4H 53
Hedgerley La. Hedg & Ger X —1J 53
Hedgerow. Ger X —23A 34
Hedgerows, The. Grav —1A 136
Hedgers Clo. Lou —14Qc 28
Hedgers Gro. E9 —37Ac 64
Hedgeside Rd. N'wd —22S 36
Hedge Wlk. SE6 —63Dc 128
Hedgewood Gdns. Ilf —29Qc 46
Hedgley. Ilf —28Pc 46
Hedgley St. SE12 —57Hc 107
Hedingham Clo. N1 —38Sb 63
Hedingham Rd. Dag —36Xc 67
Hedingham Rd. Horn —32Qd 69
Hedley Av. Grays —52Yd 112
Hedley Rd. Twic —59Ca 99
Hedley Row. N5 —36Tb 63
Hedworth Av. Wal X —5Zb 12
Heenan Clo. Bark —37Sc 66
Heene Rd. Enf —11Tb 25
Heideck Gdns. Hut —20De 33
Heigham Rd. E6 —38Mc 65
Heighton Gdns. Croy —78Rb 147
Heights Clo. SW20 —66Xa 124
Heights Clo. Bans —88Ab 162
Heights, The. SE7 —50Mc 85
Heights, The. Beck —66Ec 128
Heights, The. Lou —12Pc 28
Heights, The. N'holt —36Ca 57
Heights, The. Wey —82Q 158
Heiron St. SE17 —51Rb 105
Helby Rd. SW4 —58Mb 104
Heldar Ct. SE1 —47Tb 83 (2G 207) (off Kipling Est.)
Helder Ct. SE1 —47Tb 83
Helder Gro. SE12 —59Hc 107
Helder St. S Croy —79Tb 147
Heldmann Clo. Houn —56Fa 100
Helena Clo. Barn —10Fb 9
Helena Clo. Wall —80Pb 146
Helena Ct. W5 —43Ma 79
Helena Pl. E9 —39Xb 63
Helena Rd. E13 —40Hc 65
Helena Rd. E17 —29Cc 44
Helena Rd. NW10 —36Xa 60
Helena Rd. W5 —43Ma 79
Helena Rd. Wind —4H 95
Helen Av. Felt —59X 99
Helen Clo. N2 —27Eb 41
Helen Clo. Dart —59Kd 111
Helen Clo. W Mol —70Da 121
Helen Rd. Horn —27Md 49
Helensiea Av. NW11 —32Cb 61
Helen's Pl. E2 —41Yb 84
Helen St. SE18 —49Rc 86
Helford Clo. Ruis —33U 56
Helford Ct. S Ock —45Xd 90
Helford Wlk. Wok —6D 188
Helford Way. Upm —30Td 50
Helgiford Gdns. Sun —66U 120
Helix Gdns. SW2 —58Pb 104
Helix Rd. SW2 —58Pb 104
Helleborine. Grays —50Be 91
Hellings St. E1 —46Wb 83
Helme Clo. SW19 —64Bb 125
Helmet Row. EC1 —42Sb 83 (5E 194)
Helmsdale. Wok —6E 188
Helmsdale Clo. Hay —42Aa 77
Helmsdale Clo. Romf —24Gd 48
Helmsdale Rd. SW16 —67Mb 126
Helmsdale Rd. Romf —24Gd 48
Helmsley Pl. E8 —38Xb 63
Helmsley St. E8 —38Xb 63
Helsinki Sq. SE16 —48Ac 84
Helston La. Wind —3F 94
Helston Clo. Pinn —24Ba 37
Helston Ct. N15 —29Ub 43 (off Culvert Rd.)
Helston Ho. SE11 —50Qb 82 (7A 206) (off Kennings Way)
Helston La. Wind —3F 94
Helston Pl. Abb L —4V 4
Helvellyn Clo. Egh —66D 118
Helvetia St. SE6 —61Bc 128
Hemans St. SW8 —52Mb 104
Hemans St. Est. SW8 —52Mb 104
Hemberton Rd. SW9 —55Nb 104
Hemery Rd. Gnfd —36Fa 58
Hemingford Rd. N1 —39Pb 62 (1J 193)
Hemingford Rd. Sutt —77Ya 144
Hemingford Rd. Wat —8U 4
Heming Rd. Edgw —24Ra 39
Hemington Av. N11 —22Hb 41
Hemley Rd. Ors —4F 92
Hemlock Clo. Tad —95Ab 178
Hemlock Rd. W12 —45Va 80
Hemmen La. Hay —44V 76
Hemming Clo. Hamp —67Ca 121
Hemming St. E1 —42Wb 83
Hemming Way. Wat —7W 4
Hemnall St. Epp —3Vc 15
Hempshaw Av. Bans —88Hb 163
Hempson Av. Slou —8N 73
Hempstead Clo. Buck H —19Jc 27
Hempstead Rd. E17 —26Fc 45
Hempstead Rd. K Lan —1Q 4
Hempstead Rd. Wat —8T 4
Hemp Wlk. SE17 —49Tb 83 (5G 207)
Hemsby Rd. Chess —79Pa 143
Hemstal Rd. NW6 —38Cb 61
Hemsted Rd. Eri —52Gd 110
Hemswell Dri. NW9 —25Ua 40
Hemsworth Ct. N1 —40Ub 63 (1H 195)
Hemsworth St. N1 —40Ub 63 (1H 195)
Hemus Pl. SW3 —50Gb 81 (7E 202)
Hemwood Rd. Wind —5B 94
Henbane Path. Romf —24Md 49
Henbit Clo. Eps —91Xa 178
Henbury Way. Wat —20Z 19
Henchman St. W12 —44Va 80
Hencroft St. Slou —8K 73
Hendale Av. NW4 —27Wa 40
Henderson Clo. NW10 —37Sa 59
Henderson Clo. Horn —33Kd 69
Henderson Dri. NW8 —42Fb 81 (5B 190)
Henderson Dri. Dart —56Pd 111
Henderson Ho. Dag —34Cd 68 (off Kershaw Rd.)
Henderson Rd. E7 —37Lc 65
Henderson Rd. N9 —18Xb 25
Henderson Rd. SW18 —59Gb 103
Henderson Rd. Big H —84Lc 167
Henderson Rd. Croy —72Tb 147
Henderson Rd. Hay —41W 76
Hendham Rd. SW17 —61Gb 125
Hendon Av. N3 —25Ab 40
Hendon Gdns. Romf —23Ed 48
Hendon Hall Ct. NW4 —27Za 40
Hendon Ho. NW4 —29Za 40
Hendon La. N3 —27Ab 40
Hendon Lodge. NW4 —27Xa 40
Hendon Pk. Mans. NW4 —29Ya 40
Hendon Pk. Row. NW11 —30Bb 41
Hendon Rd. N9 —19Wb 25
Hendon Urban Motorway. Edgw & NW7 —18Na 21
Hendon Way. NW4 & NW2 —30Xa 40
Hendon Way. Stai —58M 97
Hendon Wood La. NW7 —17Va 22
Hendren Clo. Gnfd —36Fa 58
Hendre Rd. SE1 —49Ub 83 (6J 207)
Hendrick Av. SW12 —59Hb 103
Hendy Ct. Enf —13Tb 25
Heneage Cres. New Ad —82Ec 166
Heneage La. EC3 —44Ub 83 (3J 201)
Heneage Pl. EC3 —44Ub 83 (3J 201)
Heneage St. E1 —43Vb 83
Henfield Clo. N19 —32Lb 62
Henfield Clo. Bex —58Cd 110
Henfield Rd. SW19 —67Bb 125
Hengelo Gdns. Mitc —70Fb 125
Hengist Rd. SE12 —59Kc 107
Hengist Rd. Eri —52Dd 110
Hengist Way. Brom —70Gc 129
Hengrave Rd. SE23 —59Yb 106
Hengrove Ct. Bex —60Ad 109
Hengrove Cres. Ashf —62M 119
Henham Ct. Romf —26Ed 48
Henhurst Rd. Sole S —8G 136
Henley Av. Sutt —76Ab 144
Henley Clo. Gnfd —40Ea 58
Henley Clo. Iswth —53Ha 100
Henley Ct. N14 —17Lb 24
Henley Ct. Sev —95Kd 187
Henley Ct. Wok —92D 172
Henley Deane. Grav —3A 136
Henley Dri. SE1 —49Vb 83 (5K 207)
Henley Dri. King T —66Va 124
Henley Gdns. Pinn —27X 37
Henley Gdns. Romf —29Ad 47
Henley Rd. E16 —47Pc 86
Henley Rd. N18 —21Ub 43
Henley Rd. NW10 —39Ya 60
Henley Rd. Ilf —35Sc 66
Henley Rd. Slou —4C 72
Henley St. SW11 —54Jb 104
Henley Way. Felt —64Z 121
Hennel Clo. SE23 —62Yb 128
Henniker Gdns. E6 —41Mc 85
Henniker M. SW3 —51Fb 103
Henniker Rd. E15 —36Fc 65
Henningham Rd. N17 —25Tb 43
Henning St. SW11 —53Gb 103
Henrietta Ho. N15 —30Ub 43 (off St Ann's Rd.)
Henrietta Ho. W6 —50Ya 80 (off Queen Caroline St.)
Henrietta M. WC1 —42Nb 82 (5G 193)
Henrietta Pl. W1 —44Kb 82 (3K 197)
Henrietta St. E15 —36Ec 64
Henrietta St. WC2 —45Nb 82 (4G 199)
Henriques St. E1 —44Wb 83
Henry Cooper Way. SE9 —62Mc 129
Henry Darlot Dri. NW7 —22Za 40
Henry Dickens Ct. W11 —45Za 80
Henry Hatch Wlk. Sutt —80Eb 145
Henry Jackson Rd. SW15 —55Za 102
Henry Rd. E6 —40Nc 66
Henry Rd. N4 —32Sb 63
Henry Rd. Barn —15Fb 23
Henry Rd. Slou —7H 73
Henrys Av. Wfd G —22Hc 45
Henryson Rd. SE4 —57Cc 106
Henry St. Brom —67Kc 129
Henry St. Grays —51Ee 113
Henry's Wlk. Ilf —24Tc 46
Hensford Gdns. SE26 —63Xb 127
Henshall St. N1 —37Tb 63
Henshawe Rd. Dag —34Zc 67
Henshaw St. SE17 —49Tb 83 (5F 207)
Henslowe Rd. SE22 —57Wb 105
Henslow Way. Wok —86F 156
Henson Av. NW2 —36Ya 60
Henson Clo. Orp —75Rc 150
Henson Path. Harr —27Ma 39
Henson Pl. N'holt —39Y 57
Henstridge Pl. NW8 —40Gb 61 (1D 190)
Hensworth Rd. Ashf —64M 119
Henty Clo. SW11 —52Gb 103
Henty Wlk. SW15 —57Xa 102
Henville Rd. Brom —67Kc 129
Henwick Rd. SE9 —55Mc 107
Henwood Rd. SE16 —48Yb 84
Hepburn Gdns. Brom —74Gc 149
Hepburn M. SW11 —57Hb 103
Hepple Clo. Iswth —54Ka 100
Hepplestone Clo. SW15 —58Xa 102
Hepscott Rd. E9 —37Cc 64
Hepworth Ct. NW3 —36Gb 61
Hepworth Gdns. Bark —36Wc 67
Hepworth Rd. SW16 —66Nb 126
Hepworth Way. W on T —74V 140
Heracles. NW9 —25Va 40 (off Five Acre)
Heracles Clo. Wall —80Nb 146
Herald Gdns. Wall —75Kb 146
Herald's Pl. SE11 —49Rb 83
Herald St. E2 —42Xb 83
Herald Wlk. Dart —57Pd 111
Herbal Hill. EC1 —42Qb 82 (6A 194)
Herbal Pl. EC1 —42Qb 82 (6A 194) (off Herbal Hill)
Herbert Cres. SW1 —48Hb 81 (3G 203)
Herbert Cres. Knap —6B 188
Herbert Gdns. NW10 —40Xa 60
Herbert Gdns. W4 —51Ra 101
Herbert Gdns. Romf —31Zc 67
Herbert Morrison Ho. SW6 (off Clem Attlee Ct.) —51Bb 103
Herbert Pl. SE18 —51Rc 108
Herbert Rd. E12 —35Nc 66
Herbert Rd. E17 —31Bc 64
Herbert Rd. N11 —24Nb 42
Herbert Rd. N15 —29Vb 43
Herbert Rd. NW9 —30Wa 40
Herbert Rd. SE18 —52Qc 108
Herbert Rd. SW19 —66Bb 125 (in two parts)
Herbert Rd. Bexh —54Ad 109
Herbert Rd. Brom —71Mc 149
Herbert Rd. Horn —31Nd 69
Herbert Rd. Ilf —33Uc 66
Herbert Rd. King T —69Pa 123
Herbert Rd. S'hall —46Ba 77
Herbert Rd. Swan —65Kd 133
Herbert Rd. Swans —58Be 113
Herbert St. E13 —40Jc 65
Herbert St. NW5 —37Jb 62
Herbert Ter. SE18 —52Rc 108
Herbrand St. WC1 —42Nb 82 (5F 193)
Hercies Rd. Uxb —38P 55
Hercules Pl. N7 —34Nb 62 (in two parts)
Hercules Rd. SE1 —48Pb 82 (4J 205)
Hercules St. N7 —34Nb 62
Hercules Tower. SE14 —51Ac 106
Hercules Yd. N7 —34Nb 62
Hereford Av. Barn —18Hb 23
Hereford Clo. Eps —85Ta 161
Hereford Clo. Stai —67K 119
Hereford Copse. Wok —7E 188
Hereford Ct. Harr —27Ga 38
Hereford Ct. Sutt —80Cb 145
Hereford Gdns. Ilf —31Nc 66
Hereford Gdns. Pinn —29Aa 37
Hereford Gdns. Twic —60Ea 100
Hereford M. W2 —44Cb 81
Hereford Pl. SE14 —52Bc 106
Hereford Retreat. SE15 —52Wb 105
Hereford Rd. E11 —29Kc 45
Hereford Rd. W2 —44Cb 81
Hereford Rd. W3 —45Ra 79
Hereford Rd. W5 —48La 78
Hereford Rd. Felt —60Y 99
Hereford Sq. SW7 —49Eb 81 (6A 202)
Hereford St. E2 —42Wb 83
Hereford Way. Chess —78La 142
Herent Dri. Ilf —28Nc 46
Hereward Av. Purl —83Qb 164
Hereward Clo. Wal A —4Fc 13
Hereward Gdns. N13 —22Qb 42
Hereward Grn. Lou —11Sc 28
Hereward Rd. SW17 —63Hb 125
Herga Ct. Harr —34Ga 58
Herga Ct. Wat —12W 18
Herga Hyll. Ors —3C 92
Herga Rd. Harr —28Ha 38
Herington Gro. Hut —17Ce 33
Heriot Av. E4 —19Cc 26
Heriot Rd. NW4 —29Ya 40
Heriot Rd. Cher —73J 139
Heriots Clo. Stan —21Ja 38
Heritage Clo. Uxb —42L 75
Heritage Hill. Kes —78Lc 149
Heritage View. Harr —34Ha 58
Herkomer Clo. Bush —16Da 19
Herkomer Rd. Bush —15Ca 19
Herlwyn Av. Ruis —34U 56
Herlwyn Gdns. SW17 —63Hb 125
Hermes Point. W9 —42Cb 81 (off Chippenham Rd.)
Hermes St. N1 —40Qb 62 (2K 193)
Hermes Wlk. N'holt —40Ca 57
Hermes Way. Wall —80Mb 146
Herm Ho. N1 —37Sb 63
Herm Ho. Enf —10Zb 12
Hermiston Av. N8 —29Nb 42
Hermitage Bri. Cotts. Knap —7A 188
Hermitage Clo. E18 —28Hc 45
Hermitage Clo. Clay —79Ja 142
Hermitage Clo. Enf —12Rb 25
Hermitage Clo. Shep —70Q 120
Hermitage Clo. Slou —8N 73
Hermitage Ct. E18 —28Jc 45
Hermitage Ct. NW2 —34Cb 61
Hermitage Ct. Pot B —5Eb 9
Hermitage Gdns. NW2 —34Cb 61
Hermitage Gdns. SE19 —66Sb 127
Hermitage Grn. SW16 —67Nb 126
Hermitage La. N18 —22Tb 43
Hermitage La. NW2 —34Cb 61
Hermitage La. SE25 —72Wb 147 (in two parts)
Hermitage La. SW16 —66Pb 126
Hermitage La. Croy & SE25 —73Wb 147
Hermitage La. Wind —6E 94
Hermitage Path. SW16 —67Nb 126
Hermitage Rd. N4 & N15 —31Sb 63
Hermitage Rd. SE19 —66Sb 127
Hermitage Rd. Kenl —87Sb 165
Hermitage Rd. Wok —8A 188
Hermitage St. W2 —43Fb 81 (1B 196)
Hermitage, The. SE23 —60Yb 106
Hermitage, The. SW13 —53Va 102
Hermitage, The. Felt —62V 120
Hermitage, The. Rich —57Na 101
Hermitage, The. Uxb —38N 55
Hermitage Wlk. E18 —28Hc 45
Hermitage Wall. E1 —46Wb 83
Hermitage Way. Stan —25Ja 38
Hermitage Woods Cres. Wok —8A 188
Hermitage Woods Est. Knap —7B 188
Hermit Pl. NW6 —39Db 61
Hermit Rd. E16 —43Hc 85
Hermit St. EC1 —41Rb 83 (3B 194)
Hermon Gro. Hay —46W 76
Hermon Hill. E11 & E18 —29Jc 45
Herndon Clo. Egh —63C 118
Herndon Rd. SW18 —57Eb 103
Herne Clo. NW10 —36Ta 59
Herne Ct. Bush —17Ea 20
Herne Hill. SE24 —58Sb 105
Herne Hill Ho. SE24 —58Rb 105 (off Railton Rd.)
Herne Hill Rd. SE24 —55Sb 105
Herne M. N18 —21Wb 43
Herne Pl. SE24 —57Rb 105
Herne Rd. Bush —16Da 19
Herne Rd. Surb —75Ma 143
Hernshaw. Heron —24Fe 51
Heron Chase. Heron —24Fe 51
Heron Clo. E17 —26Bc 44
Heron Clo. NW10 —37Ua 60
Heron Clo. Buck H —18Jc 27
Heron Clo. Rick —19M 17
Heron Clo. Uxb —37M 55
Heron Ct. Brom —70Lc 129
Heron Ct. Eps —86Wa 162
Heron Ct. Heron —25Fe 51
Heron Ct. Ruis —33T 56
Heron Cres. Sidc —62Uc 130
Heron Dale. Add —78M 139
Herondale. S Croy —81Zb 166
Herondale Av. SW18 —60Fb 103
Heron Dri. Slou —49D 74
Heronfield. Egh —5M 117
Heronfield. Pot B —2Eb 9
Heron Flight Av. Horn —38Jd 68
Herongate Clo. Enf —12Vb 25
Herongate Rd. E12 —33Lc 65
Herongate Rd. Swan —65Gd 132
Heron Hill. Belv —50Bd 87
Heron Ho. E6 —38Nc 66
Heron Ho. W13 —42Ja 78
Heron Ind. Est. E15 —39Dc 64
Heron M. Ilf —33Rc 66
Heron Pl. SE16 —46Ac 84
Heron Quay. E14 —46Cc 84
Heron Quays Development. E14 —46Dc 84
Heron Rd. SE24 —56Sb 105
Heron Rd. Croy —75Ub 147
Heron Rd. Twic —56Ja 100
Heronry, The. W on T —79W 140
Heronsbrook. Asc —8C 116
Herons Croft. Wey —79S 140
Heronsforde. W13 —44La 78
Herons Ga. Edgw —22Qa 39
Heronsgate Rd. Chor —16D 16
Herons Lea. Wat —8Y 5
Heronslea Dri. Stan —22Na 39
Heron's Pl. Iswth —55Ka 100
Heron Sq. Rich —57Ma 101
Herons Rise. New Bar —14Gb 23
Herons, The. E11 —30Hc 45
Heronswood. Wal A —6Gc 13
Heron Wlk. N'wd —21U 36
Heron Wlk. Wok —86E 156
Heron Way. Grays —50Xd 90
Heronway. Hut —18De 33
Heron Way. Upm —32Ud 70
Heron Way. Wfd G —21Lc 45
Herrick Rd. N5 —34Sb 63
Herrick St. SW1 —49Mb 82 (6E 204)
Herries St. W10 —41Ab 80
Herringham Rd. SE7 —48Lc 85
Herrings La. Cher —72J 139
Herring St. SE5 —51Ub 105
Herron Ct. Short —70Hc 129
Hersant Clo. NW10 —39Wa 60
Herschell Rd. SE23 —59Ac 106
Herschel Pk. Dri. Slou —7K 73
Herschel St. Slou —7K 73
Hersham By-Pass. W on T —78X 141
Hersham Cen., The. W on T —78Z 141
Hersham Clo. SW15 —59Wa 102
Hersham Gdns. W on T —77Y 141
Hersham Rd. W on T —74W 140
Hersham Trading Est. W on T —75Aa 141
Hertford Av. SW14 —57Ta 101
Hertford Clo. Barn —13Eb 23
Hertford Ct. E6 —41Pc 86 (off Vicarage La.)
Hertford Ct. N13 —20Qb 24
Hertford M. Pot B —3Eb 9
Hertford Pl. W1 —42Lb 82 (6B 192)
Hertford Rd. N1 —39Ub 63 (in two parts)
Hertford Rd. N2 —27Gb 41
Hertford Rd. N9 —19Xb 25
Hertford Rd. Bark —38Qc 66
Hertford Rd. Barn —13Eb 23
Hertford Rd. Enf —14Yb 26
Hertford Rd. Ilf —30Uc 46
Hertford Sq. Mitc —70Nb 126
Hertford St. W1 —46Kb 82 (7K 197)
Hertford Wlk. Belv —50Cd 88
Hertford Way. Mitc —70Nb 126
Hertslet Rd. N7 —34Pb 62
Hertsmere Rd. E14 —46Cc 84
Hervey Clo. N3 —25Cb 41
Hervey Pk. Rd. E17 —28Ac 44
Hervey Rd. SE3 —53Kc 107
Hervey Way. N3 —25Cb 41
Hesa Rd. Hay —44W 76
Hesiers Hill. Warl —89Gc 167
Hesiers Rd. Warl —88Gc 167
Hesketh Av. Dart —60Rd 111
Hesketh Pl. W11 —45Ab 80
Hesketh Rd. E7 —34Jc 65
Heslop Rd. SW12 —60Hb 103
Hesper M. SW5 —49Db 81
Hesperus Cres. E14 —49Dc 84
Hessel Rd. W13 —47Ja 78
Hessel St. E1 —44Xb 83
Hesselyn Dri. Rain —38Kd 69
Hessle Gro. Eps —83Va 162
Hestercombe Av. SW6 —54Ab 102
Hester Rd. N18 —22Wb 43
Hester Rd. SW11 —52Gb 103
Heston Av. Houn —51Aa 99
Heston Grange. Houn —51Ba 99
Heston Grange La. Houn —51Ba 99
Heston Ind. Cen. Houn —51Y 99
Heston Ind. Mall. Houn —52Ba 99
Heston Rd. Houn —52Ca 99
Heston St. SE14 —53Cc 106
Heswell Grn. Wat —20W 18
Hetherington Clo. Slou —1D 72
Hetherington Rd. SW4 —56Nb 104
Hetherington Rd. Shep —68S 120
Hetherington Way. Uxb —35N 55
Hetley Gdns. SE19 —66Vb 127
Hetley Ho. W12 —47Xa 80 (off Hetley Rd.)
Hetley Rd. W12 —46Xa 80
Heton Gdns. NW4 —28Xa 40
Heusden Way. Ger X —32B 54
Hevelius Clo. SE10 —50Hc 85
Hever Av. W King —80Ud 154
Hever Cotts. Sole S —10G 136
Hever Ct. Rd. Grav —5E 136
Hever Croft. SE9 —63Qc 130
Hever Gdns. Brom —68Qc 130
Heverham Rd. SE18 —49Uc 86
Hever Rd. W King —79Ud 154
Heversham Rd. Bexh —54Cd 110
Hever Wood Rd. W King —80Ud 154
Hewens Rd. Uxb —42S 76
Hewer St. W10 —43Za 80
Hewers Way. Tad —92Xa 178
Hewett Clo. Stan —21Ka 38
Hewett Pl. Swan —70Fd 132
Hewett Rd. Dag —35Zc 67
Hewett St. EC2 —42Ub 83 (6J 195)
Hewish Rd. N18 —21Ub 43
Hewison St. E3 —40Bc 64
Hewitt Av. N22 —26Rb 43
Hewitt Rd. N8 —29Qb 42
Hewitts Rd. Orp —80Bd 151
Hewlett Rd. E3 —40Ac 64
Hexagon Ho. Romf —29Hd 48 (off Mercury Gdns.)
Hexagon, The. N6 —32Hb 61
Hexal Rd. SE6 —62Gc 129
Hexham Gdns. Iswth —52Ja 100
Hexham Rd. SE27 —61Sb 127
Hexham Rd. Barn —14Db 23
Hexham Rd. Mord —74Db 145
Hextalls La. Blet —100Tb 181
Heybourne Rd. N17 —24Xb 43
Heybridge Av. SW16 —66Nb 126
Heybridge Dri. Ilf —26Tc 46
Heybridge Way. E10 —31Ac 64
Heyford Av. SW8 —52Nb 104
Heyford Av. SW20 —69Bb 125
Heyford Rd. Mitc —68Gb 125
Heyford Rd. Rad —9Ha 6
Heygate St. SE17 —49Sb 83 (6D 206)
Heylyn Sq. E3 —41Bc 84
Heymede. Lea —95La 176
Heynes Rd. Dag —35Yc 67
Heysham Dri. Wat —22Y 37
Heysham La. NW3 —34Db 61
Heysham Rd. N15 —30Tb 43
Heythorpe Clo. Knap —5C 188
Heythorp St. SW18 —60Bb 103
Heywood. Stan —22La 38
Heywood Av. NW9 —25Ua 40
Heyworth Rd. E5 —35Xb 63
Heyworth Rd. E15 —35Hc 65
Hibbert Av. Wat —10Z 5
Hibbert Rd. E17 —31Bc 64
Hibbert Rd. Harr —26Ha 38
Hibbert's All. Wind —3H 95
Hibbert St. SW11 —55Fb 103
Hibberts Way. Ger X —27A 34
Hibernia Dri. Grav —2H 137
Hibernia Gdns. Houn —56Ca 99
Hibernia Point. SE2 —47Zc 87 (off Wolvercote Rd.)
Hibernia Rd. Houn —56Ca 99
Hichisson Rd. SE15 —57Yb 106
Hickey's Almshouses. Rich —56Pa 101
Hickin Clo. SE7 —49Mc 85
Hickin St. E14 —48Ec 84
Hickling Rd. Ilf —36Rc 66
Hickman Av. E4 —23Ec 44
Hickman Clo. E16 —43Mc 85
Hickman Rd. Romf —31Yc 67
Hickmore Wlk. SW4 —55Mb 104
Hickory Clo. N9 —18Wb 25
Hicks Av. Gnfd —41Fa 78
Hicks Clo. SW11 —55Gb 103
Hicks Ct. Dag —34Dd 68
Hicks St. SE8 —50Ac 84
Hidcote Gdns. SW20 —69Xa 124
Hide. E6 —44Qc 86
Hide Pl. SW1 —49Mb 82 (6D 204)
Hide Rd. Harr —28Ea 38
Hides St. N7 —37Pb 62
Higgs Ind. Est. SE24 —55Rb 105
High Acres. Abb L —4T 4
High Acres. Enf —13Rb 25
Higham Hill Rd. E17 —25Ac 44
Higham Pk. Ind. Est. E4 —23Ec 44
Higham Path. E17 —27Ac 44
Higham Pl. E17 —27Ac 44

Higham Rd.—Hillhurst Gdns.

Higham Rd. N17 —27Tb 43
Higham Rd. Wfd G —23Jc 45
Highams Ct. E4 —20Fc 27
Highams Hill. Warl —84Jc 167
Highams Lodge Bus. Cen. E17 —27Zb 44
Higham Sta. Av. E4 —23Cc 44
Higham St. E17 —27Ac 44
High Ash Clo. Linf —8J 93
Highbanks Clo. Well —52Xc 109
Highbanks Rd. Pinn —23Da 37
High Barn Rd. Eff & Ran C —100Z 175
Highbarrow Rd. Croy —74Wb 147
High Beech. N21 —16Pb 24
High Beech. S Croy —80Ub 147
High Beeches. Bans —86Ya 162
High Beeches. Ger X —2P 53
High Beeches. Orp —79Wc 151
High Beeches. Sidc —64Ad 131
High Beeches Clo. Purl —82Mb 164
High Beech Rd. Lou —14Mc 27
High Birch Ct. New Bar —14Gb 23
(off Park Rd.)
High Bri. SE10 —50Fc 85
Highbridge Rd. Bark —39Rc 66
Highbridge St. Wal A —5Dc 12
(in two parts)
Highbrook Rd. SE3 —55Mc 107
High Broom Cres. W Wick —73Dc 148
Highbury Av. T Hth —68Qb 126
Highbury Barn. N5 —35Rb 63
Highbury Clo. N Mald —70Sa 123
Highbury Clo. W Wick —75Dc 148
Highbury Cres. N5 —36Rb 63
Highbury Est. N5 —36Sb 63
Highbury Gdns. Ilf —33Uc 66
Highbury Grange. N5 —35Sb 63
Highbury Gro. N5 —36Rb 63
Highbury Hill. N5 —34Qb 62
Highbury M. N7 —37Qb 62
Highbury New Pk. N5 —36Sb 63
Highbury Pk. N5 —34Rb 63
Highbury Pk. M. N5 —35Sb 63
Highbury Pl. N5 —37Rb 63
Highbury Quadrant. N5 —34Sb 63
Highbury Rd. SW19 —64Ab 124
Highbury Sta. Rd. N1 —37Qb 62
Highbury Ter. N5 —36Rb 63
Highbury Ter. M. N5 —36Rb 63
High Canons. Borwd —9Sa 7
High Cedar Dri. SW20 —66Ya 124
Highclere. Asc —10B 116
Highclere Clo. Kenl —87Sb 165
Highclere Ct. Knap —5A 188
Highclere Gdns. Knap —5A 188
Highclere Rd. Knap —5A 188
Highclere Rd. N Mald —69Ta 123
Highclere St. SE26 —63Ac 128
Highcliffe. W13 —43Ka 78
(off Clivedon Ct.)
Highcliffe Dri. SW15 —58Va 102
Highcliffe Gdns. Ilf —29Nc 46
High Clo. Rick —15L 17
Highcombe. SE7 —51Kc 107
Highcombe Clo. SE9 —60Mc 107
High Coombe Pl. King T —66Ta 123
Highcotts La. Send —97H 173
(in two parts)
High Croft. NW9 —29Ua 40
Highcroft Av. Wemb —38Qa 59
High Croft Cotts. Swan —70Jd 132
Highcroft Ct. Bookh —95Ca 175
Highcroft Est. N19 —31Nb 62
Highcroft Gdns. NW11 —30Bb 41
Highcroft Rd. N19 —31Nb 62
High Cross. Ald —9Fa 6
High Cross Rd. N17 —27Wb 43
Highcross Rd. S'fleet —64Zd 135
Highcross Way. SW15 —60Wa 102
Highdaun Dri. SW16 —70Pb 126
Highdown. Wor Pk —75Ua 144
Highdown La. Sutt —83Db 163
Highdown Rd. SW15 —58Xa 102
High Dri. N Mald —67Sa 123
High Dri. Oxs —86Fa 160
High Dri. Wold —94Cc 182
High Elms. Chig —21Uc 46
High Elms. Upm —32Ud 70
High Elms. Wfd G —22Jc 45
High Elms Clo. N'wd —23T 36
High Elms La. Wat —3X 5
High Elms Rd. Dow —83Qc 168
Higher Dri. Bans —84Za 162
Higher Dri. E Hor —99U 174
Higher Dri. Purl —85Qb 164
Higher Grn. Eps —85Wa 162
Highfield. Bans —89Gb 163
Highfield. Chal G —18A 16
Highfield. Felt —60W 98
Highfield. K Lan —1N 3
Highfield Av. NW9 —29Sa 39
Highfield Av. NW11 —31Za 60
Highfield Av. Eri —51Dd 110
Highfield Av. Gnfd —36Ga 58
Highfield Av. Orp —78Vc 151
Highfield Av. Pinn —29Ba 37
Highfield Av. Wemb —34Pa 59
Highfield Clo. NW9 —29Sa 39
Highfield Clo. Egh —5N 117
Highfield Clo. N'wd —25U 36
Highfield Clo. Oxs —83Fa 160
Highfield Clo. Romf —23Ed 48
Highfield Clo. Surb —74La 142
Highfield Clo. W Byf —85J 157
Highfield Ct. N14 —16Lb 24
Highfield Ct. NW11 —30Ab 40
Highfield Ct. Farn R —9F 52
Highfield Ct. Ger X —22B 34
Highfield Cres. Horn —33Pd 69
Highfield Cres. N'wd —25U 36
Highfield Dri. Brom —70Gc 129
Highfield Dri. Eps —79Va 144
Highfield Dri. Uxb —35N 55
Highfield Dri. W Wick —75Dc 148
Highfield Gdns. NW11 —30Ab 40
Highfield Gdns. Grays —47Fe 91
Highfield Grn. Epp —3Uc 14
Highfield Hill. SE19 —66Tb 127
Highfield Link. Romf —23Ed 48
Highfield Pl. Epp —3Uc 14
Highfield Rd. N21 —19Rb 25
Highfield Rd. NW11 —30Ab 40
Highfield Rd. W3 —43Ra 79
Highfield Rd. Bexh —57Bd 109
Highfield Rd. Big H —89Lc 167
Highfield Rd. Brom —70Pc 130
Highfield Rd. Bush —15Aa 19
Highfield Rd. Cat —94Wb 181
Highfield Rd. Cher —74J 139
Highfield Rd. Chst —69Vc 131
Highfield Rd. Dart —59Md 111
Highfield Rd. Felt —61W 120
Highfield Rd. Horn —33Pd 69
Highfield Rd. Iswth —53Ha 100
Highfield Rd. Kems —88Nd 171
Highfield Rd. N'wd —25U 36
Highfield Rd. Purl —82Pb 164
Highfield Rd. Romf —24Ed 48
Highfield Rd. Sun —71V 140
Highfield Rd. Surb —73Sa 143
Highfield Rd. Sutt —78Gb 145
Highfield Rd. W on T —74W 140
Highfield Rd. W Byf —85J 157
Highfield Rd. Wind —5D 94
Highfield Rd. Wfd G —24Nc 46
Highfield Rd. N. Dart —58Md 111
Highfield Rd. S. Dart —59Md 111
Highfields. Asht —91Ma 177
Highfields. Cuff —1Nb 10
Highfields. E Hor —100V 174
Highfields. Fet —96Fa 176
Highfields. Rad —7Ha 6
Highfields. Sutt —75Cb 145
Highfields Gro. N6 —32Hb 61
Highfield Towers. Romf —22Fd 48
Highfield Way. Horn —33Pd 69
Highfield Way. Pot B —4Db 9
Highfield Way. Rick —16J 17
High Firs. Rad —7Ja 6
High Firs. Swan —70Gd 132
High Foleys. Clay —80Ka 160
High Gables. Brom —68Gc 129
High Gables. Lou —15Mc 27
High Gdns. Wok —7E 188
High Garth. Esh —79Ea 142
Highgate Av. N6 —31Kb 62
Highgate Clo. N6 —31Jb 62
Highgate Edge. N2 —29Gb 41
Highgate Heights. N6 —30Lb 42
Highgate High St. N6 —32Jb 62
Highgate Hill. N6 & N19 —32Kb 62
Highgate Ho. SE26 —62Wb 127
Highgate Rd. NW5 —34Jb 62
Highgate Spinney. N8 —30Mb 42
Highgate Wlk. SE23 —61Yb 128
Highgate W. Hill. N6 —33Jb 62
High Gro. SE18 —52Tc 108
High Gro. Brom —67Mc 129
Highgrove Clo. Chst —67Nc 130
Highgrove Ct. Beck —66Cc 128
Highgrove Ct. Wal X —6Yb 12
Highgrove Ho. Brtwd —19Yd 32
(off Regency Ct.)
Highgrove M. Grays —50Ee 91
Highgrove Rd. Dag —36Yc 67
Highgrove Way. Ruis —30W 36
High Hill Est. E5 —32Xb 63
High Hill Ferry. E5 —32Xb 63
High Hill Rd. Warl —87Ec 166
High Holborn. WC1 —44Nb 82 (2F 199)
High Ho. La. W Til —8F 92
Highland Av. W7 —44Ga 78
Highland Av. Brtwd —18Yd 32
Highland Av. Dag —34Ed 68
Highland Av. Lou —16Nc 28
Highland Cotts. Wall —77Kb 146
Highland Ct. E18 —25Kc 45
Highland Croft. Beck —64Dc 128
Highland Dri. Bush —17Da 19
Highland Pk. Felt —63V 120
Highland Rd. SE19 —65Ub 127
Highland Rd. Badg M —82Dd 170
Highland Rd. Bexh —57Cd 110
Highland Rd. Brom —67Hc 129
Highland Rd. N'wd —26V 36
Highland Rd. Purl —86Qb 164
Highlands. Wat —18Y 19
Highlands Av. W3 —45Sa 79
Highlands Av. Lea —94La 176
Highlands Clo. N4 —31Nb 62
Highlands Clo. Ger X —24B 34
Highlands Clo. Houn —53Da 99
Highlands Clo. Lea —94Ka 176
Highlands Ct. SE19 —65Ub 127
Highlands End. Ger X —24B 34
Highlands Gdns. Ilf —32Pc 66
Highlands Heath. SW15 —59Ya 102
Highlands Hill. Swan —67Jd 132
Highlands La. Ger X —24B 34
Highlands La. Wok —93A 172
Highlands Pk. Lea —95Ma 177
Highlands Pk. Seal —93Nd 187
Highlands Rd. Barn —15Cb 23
Highlands Rd. Lea —94Ka 176
Highlands Rd. Orp —73Xc 151
Highlands, The. E Hor —97U 174
Highlands, The. Edgw —26Ra 39
Highlands, The. Pot B —2Eb 9
Highlands, The. Rick —17K 17
High La. W7 —43Fa 78
High La. Warl —90Bc 166
Highlea Clo. NW9 —24Ua 40
High Level Dri. SE26 —63Wb 127
Highlever Rd. W10 —43Ya 80
Highmead. SE18 —52Uc 108
High Mead. Cars —83Fb 163
(off Pine Cres.)
High Mead. Chig —19Sc 28
High Mead. Harr —29Ga 38
High Mead. W Wick —75Fc 149
Highmead Ct. Brtwd —18Zd 33
Highmead Cres. Wemb —38Pa 59
High Meadow Clo. Pinn —28Y 37
High Meadow Cres. NW9 —29Ta 39
High Meadows. Chig —22Tc 46
High Meads Rd. E16 —44Mc 85
Highmore Rd. SE3 —52Gc 107
High Mt. NW4 —30Wa 40
High Oaks. Enf —10Pb 10
High Pk. Av. E Hor —98V 174
(in two parts)
High Pk. Av. Rich —53Qa 101
High Pk. Rd. Rich —53Qa 101
High Path. SW19 —67Db 125
High Pine Clo. Wey —78S 140
High Pines. Warl —91Yb 182
Highpoint. N6 —31Jb 62
High Point. SE9 —62Rc 130
Highpoint. Wey —78Q 140
Highridge Clo. Eps —86Ua 162
High Ridge Pl. Enf —10Pb 10
High Rd. E18 —25Jc 45
High Rd. N11 —22Kb 42
High Rd. N15 & N17 —29Vb 43
High Rd. N22 —25Pb 42
High Rd. NW10 —37Ua 60
High Rd. Buck H & Lou —19Kc 27
High Rd. Bush —18Fa 20
High Rd. Byfl —84M 157
High Rd. Chig —22Qc 46
High Rd. Dart —62Ld 133
High Rd. Eastc —29X 37
High Rd. Epp —5Rc 14
High Rd. Harr —24Ga 38
High Rd. Hay —43U 76
High Rd. Ick —34R 56
High Rd. Ilf & Romf —34Rc 66
(in five parts)
High Rd. Leav —7V 4
High Rd. N Stif —46Zd 91
High Rd. Ors —4A 92
High Rd. Red & Coul —99Eb 179
High Rd. Stanf —2P 93
High Rd. Uxb —43L 75
High Rd. Wemb —36Ma 59
High Rd. Wfd G —23Hc 45
High Rd. E. Finchley. N2 —25Fb 41
High Rd. Leyton. E10 & E15 —30Dc 44
High Rd. Leytonstone. E11 & E15 —35Gc 65
High Rd. N. Finchley. N12 —20Eb 23
High Rd. Whetstone. N20 —17Eb 23
High Sheldon. N6 —29Hb 41
Highshore Rd. SE15 —54Vb 105
High Silver. Lou —14Mc 27
Highstead Cres. Eri —53Gd 110
Highstone Av. E11 —30Jc 45
Highstone Ct. E11 —30Hc 45
(off New Wanstead)
High St. Bean, Bean —62Xd 134
High St. Cheam, Cheam —79Ab 144
High St. Eton, Eton —1H 95
High St. Iver, Iver —44G 74
High St. Abbots Langley, Abb L —3U 4
High St. Acton, W3 —46Ra 79
High St. Addlestone, Add —77K 139
High St. Aveley, S Ock —46Sd 90
High St. Banstead, Bans —87Cb 163
High St. Barkingside, B'side —27Sc 46
High St. Barnet, Barn —13Ab 22
High St. Beckenham, Beck —68Cc 128
High St. Brasted, Bras —96Xc 185
High St. Brentford, Bren —52La 100
High St. Brentwood, Brtwd —19Yd 32
High St. Bromley, Brom —68Jc 129
High St. Burnham, Burn —1A 72
High St. Bushey, Bush —16Ca 19
High St. Carshalton, Cars —77Jb 146
High St. Caterham, Cat —95Ub 181
High St. Chalfont St Peter, Chal P —25A 34
High St. Chalvey, Chalv —8G 72
High St. Cheshunt, Chesh —1Zb 12
High St. Chipstead, Chip —94Ed 186
High St. Chislehurst, Chst —65Rc 130
High St. Claygate, Clay —79Ha 142
High St. Cobham, Cob —86X 159
High St. Colliers Wood, SW19 —66Fb 125
High St. Colnbrook, Coln —52E 96
High St. Cowley, Cow —42L 75
High St. Cranford, Cran —53W 98
High St. Croydon, Croy —76Sb 147
High St. Dartford, Dart —58Nd 111
High St. Datchet, Dat —3M 95
High St. Downe, Dow —83Qc 168
High St. Ealing, W5 —45Ma 79
High St. East Molesey, E Mol —70Ca 121
High St. Edgware, Edgw —23Qa 39
High St. Egham, Egh —64B 118
High St. Epping, Epp —3Vc 15
High St. Epsom, Eps —85Ta 161
High St. Esher, Esh —77Da 141
High St. Ewell, Eps —81Va 162
High St. Eynsford, Eyns —75Nd 153
High St. Farnborough, F'boro —78Rc 150
High St. Farningham, F'ham —72Pd 153
High St. Feltham, Felt —62V 120
High St. Gravesend, Grav —8D 114
High St. Grays, Grays —51Ce 113
(in two parts)
High St. Great Bookham, Bookh —97Da 175
High St. Greenhithe, Grnh —56Xd 112
High St. Green Street Green, Grn St —80Vc 151
High St. Hampton, Hamp —67Ea 122
High St. Hampton Hill, Hamp H —65Ea 122
High St. Hampton Wick, King T —67La 122
High St. Harefield, Hare —26L 35
High St. Harlesden, NW10 —40Va 60
High St. Harlington, Hay —51T 98
High St. Harmondsworth, Harm —51M 97
High St. Harrow, Harr —32Ga 58
High St. Hornchurch, Horn —32Md 69
High St. Hornsey, N8 —28Nb 42
High St. Horsell, Hors —3E 188
High St. Hounslow, Houn —55Da 99
High St. Kemsing, Kems —89Rd 171
High St. Kings Langley, K Lan —1Q 4
High St. Kingston upon Thames, King T —69Ma 123
High St. Knaphill, Knap —5A 188
High St. Langley, Langl —50B 74
High St. Leatherhead, Lea
(in two parts) —94Ka 176
High St. Limpsfield, Limp —100Jc 183
High St. Merstham, Mers —100Kb 180
High St. M. SW19 —64Ab 124
High St. Mill Hill, NW7 —22Xa 40
High St. New Malden, N Mald —70Ua 124
High St. N. E12 & E6 —36Nc 66
High St. Northfleet, N'fleet —58De 113
High St. Northwood, N'wd —25V 36
High St. Old Woking, Old Wok —93C 172
High St. Orpington, Orp —74Wc 151
High St. Otford, Otf —88Jd 170
High St. Oxshott, Oxs —85Fa 160
High St. Penge, SE20 —65Yb 128
High St. Pinner, Pinn —27Aa 37
High St. Plaistow, E13 —40Jc 65
High St. Ponders End, Enf —15Yb 26
High St. Potters Bar, Pot B —5Db 9
High St. Purfleet, Purf —50Qd 89
High St. Purley, Purl —83Qb 164
High St. Rickmansworth, Rick —18M 17
High St. Ripley, Rip —93L 173
High St. Romford, Romf —29Gd 48
High St. Ruislip, Ruis —31U 56
High St. Seal, Seal —93Pd 187
High St. Sevenoaks, Sev —96Ld 187
High St. Shepperton, Shep —72R 140
High St. Shoreham, Shor —82Hd 170
High St. Slough, Slou —6K 73
High St. S. E6 —40Pc 66
High St. Southall, S'hall —46Ba 77
High St. Southgate, N14 —18Mb 24
High St. South Norwood, SE25 —70Vb 127
High St. Staines, Stai —63H 119
High St. Stanford-le-Hope, Stanf —2L 93
High St. Stanwell, Stanw —58M 97
High St. St Mary Cray, St M —72Yc 151
High St. Stratford, E15 —40Ec 64
High St. Sunningdale, S'dale —10E 116
High St. Sunninghill, S'hill —10B 116
High St. Sutton, Sutt —77Db 145
High St. Swanley, Swan —70Hd 132
High St. Swanscombe, Swans —57Be 113
High St. Tadworth, Tad —95Ya 178
High St. Teddington, Tedd —64Ha 122
High St. Thames Ditton, Th Dit —72Ja 142
High St. Thornton Heath, T Hth —70Sb 127
High St. Uxbridge, Uxb —38L 55
(in two parts)
High St. Waltham Cross, Wal X
(in two parts) —5Ac 12
High St. Walthamstow, E17 —29Ac 44
High St. Walton-on-Thames, W on T —74W 140
High St. Wanstead, E11 —29Jc 45
High St. Watford, Wat —13X 19
High St. Wealdstone, W'stone —26Ga 38
High St. Wembley, Wemb —35Pa 59
High St. W. Slou —7J 73
High St. Westerham, W'ham —99Sc 184
High St. West Wickham, W Wick —74Dc 148
High St. Weybridge, Wey —77Q 140
High St. Whitton, Twic —59Ea 100
High St. Wimbledon, SW19 —64Za 124
High St. Windsor, Wind —3H 95
High St. Woking, Wok —89B 156
High St. Woolwich, SE18 —48Qc 86
High St. Wraysbury, Wray —58A 96
High St. Yiewsley, Yiew —45M 75
High, The. SW16 —62Nb 126
High Timber St. EC4 —45Sb 83 (4D 200)
High Tor Clo. Brom —66Kc 129
High Tree Clo. Add —78J 139
High Trees. SW2 —60Qb 104
High Trees. Barn —15Gb 23
High Trees. Croy —74Ac 148
High Trees Clo. Cat —94Vb 181
Hightrees Ct. War —21Yd 50
Highview. N6 —30Lb 42
Highview. NW7 —20Ta 21
High View. Chor —14J 17
Highview. Knap —5B 188
High View. Pinn —28Y 37
High View. Sutt —83Bb 163
High View. Wat —16V 18
Highview Av. Edgw —21Sa 39
High View Av. Grays —50Ee 91
Highview Av. Wall —78Pb 146
High View Clo. SE19 —68Vb 127
High View Clo. Lou —15Lc 27
Highview Clo. Pot B —5Eb 9
High View Ct. Har W —24Ga 38
Highview Ct. Lou —15Mc 27
Highview Cres. Hut —16Ee 33
Highview Gdns. N3 —27Ab 40
Highview Gdns. N11 —22Lb 42
Highview Gdns. Edgw —21Sa 39
Highview Gdns. Pot B —5Eb 9
Highview Gdns. Upm —33Rd 69
Highview Ho. Romf —28Ad 47
Highview Path. Bans —87Cb 163
High View Rd. E18 —26Hc 45
High View Rd. N2 —25Hb 41
Highview Rd. SE19 —65Tb 127
Highview Rd. W13 —43Ja 78
High View Rd. Dow —82Qc 168
High View Rd. Sidc —63Xc 131
Highway, The. E1 & E14 —45Yb 84
Highway, The. Orp —78Yc 151
Highway, The. Stan —24Ja 38
Highway, The. Sutt —81Eb 163
Highway Trading Cen., The. E1
(off Heckford St.) —45Zb 84
Highwold. Coul —90Jb 164
Highwood. Short —69Gc 129
Highwood Av. N12 —21Eb 41
Highwood Av. Bush —11Ba 19
Highwood Clo. Brtwd —17Xd 32
Highwood Clo. Kenl —88Sb 165
Highwood Clo. Orp —75Sc 150
Highwood Ct. N12 —20Eb 23
Highwood Ct. Barn —15Cb 23
Highwood Dri. Orp —75Sc 150
Highwood Gdns. Ilf —29Pc 46
Highwood Gro. NW7 —22Ta 39
Highwood Hill. NW7 —19Va 22
Highwood La. Lou —15Qc 28
Highwood Rd. N19 —34Nb 62
Highwoods. Cat —97Ub 181
Highwoods. Lea —93La 176
High Worple. Harr —31Ba 57
Highworth Rd. N11 —23Mb 42
Hilary Av. Mitc —69Jb 126
Hilary Clo. E11 —29Jc 45
Hilary Clo. SW6 —52Db 103
Hilary Clo. Eri —53Dd 110
Hilary Clo. Horn —36Md 69
Hilary Rd. W12 —45Va 80
Hilbert Rd. Sutt —76Za 144
Hilborough Ct. E8 —39Vb 63
Hilborough Way. Orp —78Tc 150
Hilda Ct. Surb —73Ma 143
Hilda May Av. Swan —68Gd 132
Hilda Rd. E6 —38Mc 65
Hilda Rd. E16 —42Gc 85
Hilda Ter. SW9 —54Qb 104
Hilda Vale Clo. Orp —77Rc 150
Hilda Vale Rd. Orp —77Qc 150
Hildenborough Gdns. Brom —65Gc 129
Hildenborough Ho. Beck —66Bc 128
(off Bethersden Clo.)
Hilden Dri. Eri —52Kd 111
Hildenlea Pl. Brom —68Gc 129
Hildenley Clo. Red —100Mb 180
Hilders, The. Asht —89Ra 161
Hildreth St. SW12 —60Kb 104
Hildyard Rd. SW6 —51Cb 103
Hiley Rd. NW10 —41Ya 80
Hilgrove Rd. NW6 —38Eb 61
Hiliary Gdns. Stan —26La 38
Hiljon Cres. Ger X —25A 34
Hillars Heath Rd. Coul —87Nb 164
Hillary Av. Grav —2A 136
Hillary Cres. W on T —74Y 141
Hillary Ho. Borwd —13Ra 21
Hillary Rise. Barn —14Cb 23
Hillary Rd. Slou —47A 74
Hillary Rd. S'hall —48Ca 77
Hill Barn. S Croy —83Ub 165
Hillbeck Clo. SE15 —52Yb 106
Hillbeck Way. Gnfd —39Fa 58
Hillboro Ct. E11 —31Fc 65
Hillborough Av. Sev —94Md 187
Hillborough Clo. SW19 —66Eb 125
Hillbourne Clo. Hay —50W 76
Hillbrook Gdns. Wey —80Q 140
Hillbrook Rd. SW17 —62Hb 125
Hill Brow. Brom —67Mc 129
Hill Brow. Dart —58Hd 110
Hillbrow. N Mald —69Va 124
Hill Brow Clo. Bex —63Fd 132
Hillbrow Rd. Brom —66Gc 129
Hillbrow Rd. Esh —77Ea 142
Hillbury Av. Harr —29Ka 38
Hillbury Clo. Warl —90Yb 166
Hillbury Gdns. Warl —90Yb 166
Hillbury Rd. SW17 —62Kb 126
Hillbury Rd. Warl & Warl —89Wb 165
Hill Clo. NW2 —34Xa 60
Hill Clo. NW11 —30Cb 41
Hill Clo. Barn —15Ya 22
Hill Clo. Chst —64Rc 130
Hill Clo. Grav —6A 136
Hill Clo. Harr —34Ga 58
Hill Clo. Purl —85Sb 165
Hill Clo. Stan —21Ka 38
Hill Clo. Wok —4G 188
Hillcote Av. SW16 —66Qb 126
Hill Ct. Barn —14Gb 23
Hill Ct. Romf —28Hd 48
Hillcourt Av. N12 —23Db 41
Hillcourt Est. N16 —32Tb 63
Hillcourt Rd. SE22 —58Xb 105
Hill Cres. N20 —19Db 23
Hill Cres. Bex —60Ed 110
Hill Cres. Harr —29Ja 38
Hill Cres. Horn —30Ld 49
Hill Cres. Pot B —6Eb 9
Hill Cres. Surb —71Pa 143
Hill Cres. Wor Pk —75Ya 144
Hillcrest. N6 —31Jb 62
Hillcrest. N21 —17Qb 24
Hillcrest. SE25 —56Tb 105
Hill Crest. Sev —94Jd 186
Hillcrest. Sidc —59Wc 109
Hillcrest. Wey —77R 140
Hillcrest Av. NW11 —29Ab 40
Hillcrest Av. Cher —76G 138
Hillcrest Av. Edgw —21Ra 39
Hillcrest Av. Grays —51Wd 112
Hillcrest Av. Pinn —28Z 37
Hillcrest Clo. SE26 —63Wb 127
Hillcrest Clo. Beck —72Bc 148
Hillcrest Clo. Eps —87Va 162
Hillcrest Ct. Sutt —79Fb 145
Hillcrest Dri. Grnh —57Wd 112
Hillcrest Gdns. N3 —28Ab 40
Hillcrest Gdns. NW2 —34Wa 60
Hillcrest Gdns. Esh —76Ha 142
Hillcrest Pde. Coul —86Kb 164
Hillcrest Rd. E17 —26Fc 45
Hillcrest Rd. E18 —26Jc 45
Hillcrest Rd. W3 —46Qa 79
Hillcrest Rd. W5 —43Na 79
Hillcrest Rd. Big H —88Mc 167
Hillcrest Rd. Brom —64Jc 129
Hillcrest Rd. Dart —59Gd 110
Hillcrest Rd. Horn —31Jd 68
Hillcrest Rd. Lou —16Mc 27
Hillcrest Rd. Orp —75Wc 151
Hillcrest Rd. Purl —82Pb 164
Hillcrest Rd. Shenl —5Qa 7
Hillcrest Rd. Whyt —89Vb 165
Hillcrest View. Beck —72Bc 148
Hillcrest Way. Epp —3Wc 15
Hillcrest Waye. Ger X —31B 54
Hillcroft. Lou —12Qc 28
Hillcroft Av. Pinn —30Ba 37
Hillcroft Av. Purl —85Lb 164
Hillcroft Cres. W5 —44Na 79
Hillcroft Cres. Ruis —34Z 57
Hillcroft Cres. Wat —18X 19
Hillcroft Cres. Wemb —35Pa 59
Hillcroft Rd. E6 —43Rc 86
Hillcroome Rd. Sutt —79Fb 145
Hillcross Av. Mord —72Za 144
Hilldale Rd. Sutt —77Bb 145
Hilldeane Rd. Purl —81Qb 164
Hilldene Av. Romf —23Ld 49
Hilldene Clo. H Hill —22Md 49
Hilldown Rd. SW16 —66Nb 126
Hilldown Rd. Brom —74Gc 149
Hill Dri. NW9 —32Sa 59
Hill Dri. SW16 —69Pb 126
Hilldrop Cres. N7 —36Mb 62
Hilldrop Est. N7 —35Mb 62
Hilldrop La. N7 —36Mb 62
Hilldrop Rd. N7 —36Mb 62
Hilldrop Rd. Brom —65Kc 129
Hillend. SE18 —53Qc 108
Hill End. Orp —75Vc 151
Hill End Rd. Hare —24L 35
Hillersdon. Slou —3M 73
Hillersdon Av. SW13 —54Wa 102
Hillersdon Av. Edgw —22Pa 39
Hillery Clo. SE17 —49Tb 83 (6G 207)
Hilley Field La. Fet —94Ea 176
Hill Farm Av. Wat —5W 4
Hill Farm Clo. Wat —5W 4
Hill Farm Cotts. Ruis —31S 56
Hill Farm Rd. W10 —43Ya 80
Hill Farm Rd. Ger X —24A 34
Hill Farm Rd. Uxb —35T 56
Hillfield Av. N8 —29Nb 42
Hillfield Av. NW9 —29Ua 40
Hillfield Av. Mord —72Gb 145
Hillfield Av. Wemb —38Na 59
Hillfield Clo. Harr —28Ea 38
Hillfield Ct. NW3 —36Gb 61
Hillfield Ct. Esh —78Da 141
Hillfield Ho. N5 —36Sb 63
Hillfield La. Bush —11Da 19
Hillfield La. S. Bush —16Ha 20
Hillfield Pk. N10 —28Kb 42
Hillfield Pk. N21 —19Qb 24
Hillfield Pk. M. N10 —28Kb 42
Hillfield Rd. NW6 —36Bb 61
Hillfield Rd. Dun G —92Gd 186
Hillfield Rd. Ger X —24A 34
Hill Field Rd. Hamp —66Ba 121
Hillfield Sq. Ger X —24A 34
Hillfoot Av. Romf —25Ed 48
Hillfoot Rd. Romf —25Ed 48
Hillgate Pl. SW12 —59Kb 104
Hillgate Pl. W8 —46Cb 81
Hillgate St. W8 —46Cb 81
Hillgrove. Ger X —25A 34
Hill Gro. Romf —27Gd 48
Hill Ho. E5 —32Xb 63
(off Harrington Hill)
Hillhouse. Wal A —5Hc 13
Hillhouse Av. Stan —24Ha 38
Hill Ho. Clo. N21 —17Qb 24
Hill Ho. Clo. Ger X —24A 34
Hill Ho. Dri. Wey —83Q 158
Hill Ho. Rd. SW16 —64Pb 126
Hill Ho. Rd. Dart —59Sd 112
Hillhurst Gdns. Cat —92Ub 181

Hilliard Rd.—Holmes Av.

Hilliard Rd. N'wd —25V **36**
Hilliards Ct. E1 —46Yb **84**
Hilliards Rd. Uxb —44M **75**
Hillier Clo. Barn —16Db **23**
Hillier Gdns. Croy —78Qb **146**
Hillier Lodge. Tedd —64Fa **122**
Hillier Rd. SW11 —58Hb **103**
Hilliers Av. Uxb —41Q **76**
Hilliers La. Croy —76Nb **146**
Hillingdale. Big H —90Kc **167**
Hillingdon Av. Sev —93Ld **187**
Hillingdon Av. Stai —60N **97**
Hillingdon Hill. Uxb —40N **55**
Hillingdon Rise. Sev —94Md **187**
Hillingdon Rd. Bexh —54Ed **110**
Hillingdon Rd. Grav —1D **136**
Hillingdon Rd. Uxb —39M **55**
Hillingdon Rd. Wat —6W **4**
Hillingdon St. SE5 & SE17
—51Rb **105**
Hillington Gdns. Wfd G —26Mc **45**
Hill La. Ruis —32S **56**
Hill La. Tad —93Ab **178**
Hillman Clo. Horn —27Md **49**
Hillman Clo. Uxb —36N **55**
Hillman St. E8 —37Xb **63**
Hillmarton Rd. N7 —36Nb **62**
Hillmead Dri. SW9 —56Rb **105**
Hillmont Rd. Esh —76Ga **142**
Hillmore Gro. SE26 —64Ac **128**
Hillmount. Wok —90A 156
(off Constitution Hill)
Hill Path. SW16 —64Pb **126**
Hill Pl. Farn C —8F **52**
Hillreach. SE18 —50Pc **86**
Hill Rise. N9 —16Xb **25**
Hill Rise. NW11 —28Db **41**
Hill Rise. SE23 —60Xb **105**
Hill Rise. Cuff —1Nb **10**
Hill Rise. Dart —64Td **134**
Hill Rise. Esh —75Ka **142**
Hill Rise. Ger X —26A **34**
Hill Rise. Gnfd —38Ea **58**
Hill Rise. Pot B —6Eb **9**
Hill Rise. Rich —57Ma **101**
Hill Rise. Rick —16K **17**
Hill Rise. Ruis —32S **56**
Hill Rise. Slou —51C **96**
Hill Rise. Upm —33Qd **69**
Hill Rise. W on T —73V **140**
Hillrise Av. Wat —10Z **5**
Hill Rise Cres. Ger X —26A **34**
Hillrise Mans. N19 —31Nb 62
(off Warltersvill Rd.)
Hillrise Rd. N19 —31Nb **62**
Hillrise Rd. Romf —23Ed **48**
Hill Rd. N10 —25Hb **41**
Hill Rd. NW8 —41Eb **81** (3A **190**)
Hill Rd. Brtwd —20Wd **32**
Hill Rd. Cars —79Gb **145**
Hill Rd. Dart —61Nd **133**
Hill Rd. Fet —94Da **175**
Hill Rd. Harr —29Ja **38**
Hill Rd. Mitc —67Kb **126**
Hill Rd. N'wd —23T **36**
Hill Rd. Pinn —29Aa **37**
Hill Rd. Purl —84Pb **164**
Hill Rd. Sutt —78Db **145**
Hill Rd. They B —10Uc **14**
Hill Rd. Wemb —34Ka **58**
Hillsborough Grn. Wat —20W **18**
Hillsborough Rd. SE22 —57Ub **105**
Hill's Chase. War —21Yd **50**
Hillside. N8 —30Mb **42**
Hillside. NW5 —34Jb **62**
Hillside. NW9 —28Ta **39**
Hillside. NW10 —38Sa **59**
Hillside. SW19 —65Za **124**
Hillside. Bans —87Ab **162**
Hillside. Barn —15Eb **23**
Hillside. Dart —64Ud **134**
Hillside. F'ham —73Pd **153**
Hillside. Grays —49Fe **91**
Hillside. Hare —29Ba **37**
Hillside. H Hill —21Md **49**
Hillside. Slou —7J **73**
Hillside. Wok —8G **188**
Hillside Av. N11 —23Hb **41**
Hillside Av. Borwd —14Ra **21**
Hillside Av. Chesh —3Zb **12**
Hillside Av. Grav —1F **136**
Hillside Av. Purl —85Rb **165**
Hillside Av. Wemb —35Pa **59**
Hillside Av. Wfd G —23Lc **45**
Hillside Clo. NW6 —40Db **61**
Hillside Clo. NW8 —40Db **61**
Hillside Clo. Abb L —4U **4**
Hillside Clo. Bans —88Ab **162**
Hillside Clo. Ger X —23A **34**
Hillside Clo. Knap —5A **188**
Hillside Clo. Mord —70Ab **124**
Hillside Clo. Wfd G —22Lc **45**
Hillside Cres. Chesh —3Zb **12**
Hillside Cres. Enf —10Tb **11**
Hillside Cres. Harr —32Ea **58**
Hillside Cres. N'wd —25W **36**
Hillside Cres. Wat —16Aa **19**
Hillside Dri. Edgw —23Qa **39**
Hillside Dri. Grav —1F **136**
Hillside Est. N15 —30Vb **43**
Hillside Gdns. E17 —27Fc **45**
Hillside Gdns. N6 —30Kb **42**
Hillside Gdns. N11 —23Lb **42**
Hillside Gdns. SW2 —61Qb **126**
Hillside Gdns. Add —78H **139**
Hillside Gdns. Barn —14Ab **22**
Hillside Gdns. Edgw —20Pa **39**
Hillside Gdns. Harr —31Na **59**
Hillside Gdns. N'wd —24W **36**
Hillside Gdns. Wall —80Lb **146**
Hillside Gro. N14 —17Mb **24**
Hillside Gro. NW7 —24Wa **40**
Hillside La. Brom —75Hc **149**
(in two parts)
Hillside Pas. SW16 —61Pb **126**
Hillside Rise. N'wd —24W **36**
Hillside Rd. N15 —31Ub **43**
Hillside Rd. SW2 —61Pb **126**
Hillside Rd. W5 —43Na **79**
Hillside Rd. Asht —89Pa **161**
Hillside Rd. Brom —69Hc **129**
Hillside Rd. Bush —15Aa **19**
Hillside Rd. Chor —15E **16**
Hillside Rd. Coul —90Pb **164**
Hillside Rd. Croy —78Pb **147**
Hillside Rd. Dart —58Jd **110**
Hillside Rd. Eps —82Ya **162**
Hillside Rd. Kems —89Pd **171**
Hillside Rd. N'wd —24W **36**
Hillside Rd. Pinn —24X **37**
Hillside Rd. Rad —7Ka **6**
Hillside Rd. Sev —95Md **187**
Hillside Rd. S'hall —42Ca **77**
Hillside Rd. Surb —70Qa **123**
Hillside Rd. Sutt —80Bb **145**
Hillside Rd. Tats —91Nc **184**
Hillside Rd. Whyt —90Wb **165**
Hillside, The. Orp —81Xc **169**
Hillside Wlk. Brtwd —20Vd **32**
Hills La. Knat —85Rd **171**
Hills La. N'wd —25U **36**
Hillsleigh Rd. W8 —46Bb **81**
Hillsmead Way. S Croy —86Wb **165**
Hills M. W5 —45Na **79**
Hills Pl. W1 —44Lb **82** (3B **198**)
Hills Rd. Buck H —18Kc **27**
Hillstowe St. E5 —34Yb **64**
Hill St. W1 —46Jb **82** (6J **197**)
Hill St. Rich —57Ma **101**
Hill, The. Cat —96Vb **181**
Hill, The. Grav —58Ee **113**
Hilltop. NW11 —28Db **41**
Hill Top. Lou —12Qc **28**
Hill Top. Mord —72Cb **145**
Hill Top. Sutt —73Bb **145**
Hill Top. Wfd G —23Pc **46**
Hilltop Clo. Asc —8C **116**
Hilltop Clo. Lea —95La **176**
Hill Top Clo. Lou —13Qc **28**
Hilltop Gdns. NW4 —26Xa **40**
Hilltop Gdns. Dart —57Pd **111**
Hilltop Gdns. Orp —75Uc **150**
Hilltop La. Red & Cat —98Qb **180**
Hill Top Pl. Lou —13Qc **28**
Hilltop Rise. Bookh —98Ea **176**
Hilltop Rd. NW6 —38Cb **61**
Hilltop Rd. Grays —51Xd **112**
Hilltop Rd. Whyt —89Ub **165**
Hilltop Wlk. Wold —92Ac **182**
Hilltop Way. Stan —20Ja **20**
Hillview. SW20 —66Xa **124**
Hillview. Whyt —90Wb 165
(off Brocklebank Ct.)
Hillview Av. Harr —29Na **39**
Hillview Av. Horn —30Ld **49**
Hillview Clo. Pinn —23Ba **37**
Hillview Clo. Purl —83Rb **165**
Hill View Clo. Tad —93Ya **178**
Hillview Ct. Wok —90B **156**
Hill View Cres. Ilf —30Pc **46**
Hill View Cres. Orp —74Vc **151**
Hill View Dri. Well —54Uc **108**
Hillview Gdns. NW4 —28Za **40**
Hill View Gdns. NW9 —29Ta **39**
Hillview Gdns. Harr —27Ca **37**
Hillview Rd. NW7 —21Za **40**
Hillview Rd. Chst —64Qc **130**
Hill View Rd. Clay —80Ja **142**
Hill View Rd. Long —69De **135**
Hill View Rd. Orp —74Uc **150**
Hillview Rd. Pinn —24Ba **37**
Hillview Rd. Sutt —76Eb **145**
Hill View Rd. Twic —58Ja **100**
Hill View Rd. Wok —90B **156**
Hillview Rd. Wray —8P **95**
Hillway. N6 —33Jb **62**
Hillway. NW9 —32Ua **60**
Hill Waye. Ger X —30B **34**
Hill Way, The. Mount —11Fe **33**
Hillwood Clo. Hut —18De **33**
Hillwood Gro. Hut —18De **33**
Hillworth. Beck —68Dc **128**
Hillworth Rd. SW2 —59Qb **104**
Hillyard Rd. W7 —43Ga **78**
Hillyard St. SW9 —53Qb **104**
Hillydeal Rd. Otf —87Ld **171**
Hillyfield. E17 —26Ac **44**
Hillyfields. Lou —12Qc **28**
Hilly Fields Cres. SE4 —55Cc **106**
Hilperton Rd. Slou —7J **73**
Hilsea St. E5 —35Yb **64**
Hilton Av. N12 —22Fb **41**
Hilton Clo. Uxb —40K **55**
Hilton Way. S Croy —87Xb **165**
Hilversum Cres. SE22 —57Ub **105**
Himley Rd. SW17 —64Gb **125**
Hinchcliffe Clo. Wall —80Pb **146**
Hinchley Clo. Esh —77Ha **142**
Hinchley Dri. Esh —76Ha **142**
Hinchley Way. Esh —76Ja **142**
Hinckley Rd. SE15 —56Wb **105**
Hind Clo. Chig —22Vc **47**
Hind Ct. EC4 —44Qb **82** (3A **200**)
Hind Cres. N Hth —51Fd **110**
Hinde M. W1 —44Jb 82 (2J 197)
(off Marylebone La.)
Hindes Rd. Harr —29Fa **38**
Hinde St. W1 —44Jb **82** (2J **197**)
Hind Gro. E14 —44Cc **84**
Hindhead Clo. N16 —32Ub **63**
Hindhead Clo. Uxb —43R **76**
Hindhead Gdns. N'holt —39Aa **57**
Hindhead Way. Wall —78Nb **146**
Hindlip Ho. SW8 —53Mb **104**
Hindmans Rd. SE22 —57Wb **105**
Hindmans Way. Dag —42Bd **87**
Hindmarsh Clo. E1 —45Wb **83**
Hindrey Rd. E5 —36Xb **63**
Hindsley's Pl. SE23 —61Yb **128**
Hinhead Grn. Wat —22Y **37**
Hinkler Clo. Wall —80Nb **146**
Hinkler Rd. Harr —27Ma **39**
Hinkley Clo. Hare —28L **35**
Hinksey Clo. Slou —48D **74**
Hinksey Path. SE2 —48Zc **87**
Hinstock Rd. SE18 —51Sc **108**
Hinton Av. Houn —56Z **99**
Hinton Clo. SE9 —60Nc **108**
Hinton Rd. N18 —21Ub **43**
Hinton Rd. SE24 —55Rb **105**
Hinton Rd. Slou —5C **72**
Hinton Rd. Uxb —39L **55**
Hinton Rd. Wall —79Lb **146**
Hipley St. Wok —92D **172**
Hippodrome M. W11 —45Ab **80**
Hippodrome Pl. W11 —45Ab **80**
Hiroshima Promenade. SE7
—48Lc **85**
Hisocks Ho. NW10 —38Sa **59**
Hitcham Rd. E17 —31Bc **64**
Hitchcock Clo. Shep —69P **119**
Hitchen Hatch La. Sev —96Jd **186**
Hitchin Clo. Romf —21Ld **49**
Hitchin Sq. E3 —40Ac **64**
Hitherbroom Rd. Hay —46W **76**
Hitherfield Rd. SW16 —62Pb **126**
Hitherfield Rd. Dag —33Ad **67**
Hither Grn. La. SE13 —57Ec **106**
Hither Meadow. Ger X —25A **34**
Hithermoor Rd. Stai —58H **97**
Hitherwell Dri. Harr —25Fa **38**
Hitherwood Clo. Horn —35Md **69**
Hitherwood Dri. SE19 —63Vb **127**
Hive Clo. Bush —19Fa **20**
Hive La. Grav —58De **113**
Hive Rd. Bush —19Fa **20**
Hive, The. Grav —58De **113**
Hoadly Rd. SW16 —62Mb **126**
Hobart Clo. N20 —19Gb **23**
Hobart Clo. Hay —42Z **77**
Hobart Dri. Hay —42Z **77**
Hobart Gdns. T Hth —69Tb **127**
Hobart La. Hay —42Z **77**
Hobart Pl. SW1 —48Kb **82** (4K **203**)
Hobart Pl. Rich —59Pa **101**
Hobart Rd. Dag —35Zc **67**
Hobart Rd. Hay —42Z **77**
Hobart Rd. Ilf —26Sc **46**
Hobart Rd. Til —3C **114**
Hobart Rd. Wor Pk —76Xa **144**
Hobarts Dri. Den —30H **35**
Hobbayne Rd. W7 —44Fa **78**
Hobbes Wlk. SW15 —57Xa **102**
Hobbs Clo. Chesh —1Zb **12**
Hobbs Clo. W Byf —85K **157**
Hobbs Grn. N2 —27Eb **41**
Hobbs M. Ilf —33Vc **67**
Hobbs Pl. N1 —39Ub **63** (1H **195**)
Hobbs Pl. Est. N1
—39Ub 63 (1H 195)
(off Hobbs Pl.)
Hobbs Rd. SE27 —63Sb **127**
Hobday St. E14 —44Dc **84**
Hobill Wlk. Surb —72Pa **143**
Hoblands End. Chst —65Uc **130**
Hobsons Pl. E1 —43Wb **83**
Hobury St. SW10 —51Fb **103**
Hockenden La. Swan —69Cd **132**
Hockering Est. Wok —90D **156**
Hockering Gdns. Wok —90C **156**
Hockering Rd. Wok —90C **156**
Hocker St. E2 —41Vb **83** (4K **195**)
Hockett Clo. SE8 —49Ac **84**
Hockley Av. E6 —40Nc **66**
Hockley Ct. E18 —25Jc **45**
Hockley Dri. Romf —26Kd **49**
Hockley La. Stoke P —8M **53**
Hocroft Av. NW2 —34Bb **61**
Hocroft Ct. NW2 —34Bb **61**
Hocroft Rd. NW2 —34Bb **61**
Hocroft Wlk. NW2 —34Bb **61**
Hodder Dri. Gnfd —40Ha **58**
Hoddesdon Rd. Belv —50Cd **88**
Hodford Rd. NW11 —32Bb **61**
Hodgkin Clo. SE28 —45Zc **87**
Hodister Clo. SE5 —52Sb **105**
Hodnet Gro. SE16 —49Zb **84**
Hodsoll Ct. Orp —71Zc **151**
Hodsoll St. Sev —80Fe **155**
Hodson Clo. Harr —34Ba **57**
Hodson Cres. Orp —71Zc **151**
Hoecroft Ct. Enf —10Yb 12
(off Hoe La.)
Hoe La. Abr —13Xc **29**
Hoe La. Enf —10Wb **11**
Hoe St. E17 —28Cc **44**
Hoe, The. Wat —19Z **19**
Hoever Ho. SE6 —63Ec **128**
Hofland Rd. W14 —48Ab **80**
Hoford Rd. Grays & Stanf —9F **92**
Hogan M. W2 —43Eb **81** (7B **190**)
Hogan Way. E5 —33Wb **63**
Hogarth Av. Ashf —65S **120**
Hogarth Av. Brtwd —20Ae **33**
Hogarth Clo. E16 —43Mc **85**
Hogarth Clo. W5 —43Na **79**
Hogarth Clo. Slou —5C **72**
Hogarth Ct. EC3 —44Ub **83** (3J **201**)
Hogarth Ct. SE19 —63Vb **127**
Hogarth Ct. Bush —17Da **19**
Hogarth Ct. Houn —52Aa **99**
Hogarth Cres. SW19 —67Fb **125**
Hogarth Cres. Croy —73Sb **147**
Hogarth Gdns. Houn —52Ca **99**
Hogarth Hill. NW11 —28Bb **41**
Hogarth Ind. Est. NW10 —42Wa **80**
Hogarth La. W4 —51Ua **102**
Hogarth Pl. SW5 —49Db 81
(off Hogarth Rd.)
Hogarth Reach. Lou —15Pc **28**
Hogarth Rd. SW5 —49Db **81**
Hogarth Rd. Edgw —26Qa **39**
Hogarth Rd. Grays —46Ce **91**
Hogarth Ter. W4 —51Ua **102**
Hogarth Way. Hamp —67Ea **122**
Hogden Clo. Tad —97Bb **179**
Hogfair La. Burn —14Ja **20**
Hogg La. Grays —47Ce **91**
Hog Hill Rd. Romf —24Bd **47**
Hog La. Els —14Ja **20**
Hogscross La. Coul —95Hb **179**
Hogshead Pas. E1 —45Xb 83
(off Pennington St.)
Hogshill La. Cob —86X **159**
Hogs La. Grav —62Fe **135**
Hogsmill Way. Eps —78Sa **143**
Hogtrough Hill. Bras —92Vc **185**
Hogtrough La. God & Oxt
—99Cc **182**
Holbeach Gdns. Sidc —58Vc **109**
Holbeach Rd. SE6 —59Dc **106**
Holbeck Row. SE15 —52Wb **105**
Holbein Ga. N'wd —22U **36**
Holbein M. SW1
—50Jb **82** (7H **203**)
Holbein Pl. SW1
—49Jb **82** (6H **203**)
Holberton Gdns. NW10 —41Xa **80**
Holborn. EC1 —43Qb **82** (1K **199**)
Holborn Cir. EC1
—43Qb **82** (1A **200**)
Holborn Pl. WC1
—43Pb 82 (1H 199)
(off High Holborn)
Holborn Rd. E13 —43Kc **85**
Holborn Viaduct. EC1
—43Rb **83** (1A **200**)
Holborough M. SW12 —60Kb **104**
Holbreck Pl. Wok —90B **156**
Holbroke Ct. N7 —34Nb **62**
Holbrook Clo. N19 —32Kb **62**
Holbrook Clo. Enf —11Vb **25**
Holbrooke Pl. Rich —57Ma **101**
Holbrook Ho. Chst —67Tc **130**
Holbrook La. Chst —66Tc **130**
Holbrook Rd. E15 —40Hc **65**
Holbrook Way. Brom —72Pc **150**
Holburne Clo. SE3 —53Lc **107**
Holburne Gdns. SE3 —53Mc **107**
Holburne Rd. SE3 —53Lc **107**
Holcombe Hill. NW7 —20Wa **22**
Holcombe Ho. SW9 —55Nb 104
(off Landor Rd.)
Holcombe Rd. N17 —27Vb **43**
(in two parts)
Holcombe Rd. Ilf —31Qc **66**
Holcombe St. W6 —49Xa **80**
Holcote Clo. Belv —48Ad **87**
Holcroft Rd. E9 —38Yb **64**
Holdbrook S. Wal X —6Bc **12**
Holdbrook Way. Romf —26Pd **49**
Holden Av. N12 —22Db **41**
Holden Av. NW9 —32Sa **59**
Holdenby Rd. SE4 —57Ac **106**
Holden Clo. Dag —34Xc **67**
Holden Gdns. War —22Zd **51**
Holdenhurst Av. N12 —24Eb **41**
Holden Rd. N12 —22Db **41**
Holden St. SW11 —54Jb **104**
Holden Way. Upm —32Td **70**
Holdernesse Rd. SW17 —62Hb **125**
Holderness Way. SE27 —64Rb **127**
Holder's Hill Av. NW4 —26Za **40**
Holders Hill Cir. NW7 —24Ab **40**
Holders Hill Cres. NW4 —26Za **40**
Holders Hill Dri. NW4 —27Za **40**
Holder's Hill Gdns. NW4 —26Ab **40**
Holders Hill Rd. NW4 & NW7
—26Za **40**
Holecroft. Wal A —6Gc **13**
Hole Farm La. Gt War —26Wd **50**
Holford Pl. WC1 —41Pb **82** (3J **193**)
Holford Rd. NW3 —34Eb **61**
Holford St. WC1
—41Pb **82** (3K **193**)
Holford Yd. WC1
—41Qb **82** (3K **193**)
Holgate Av. SW11 —55Fb **103**
Holgate Gdns. Dag —37Cd **68**
Holgate Rd. Dag —36Cd **68**
Holgate St. SE7 —48Mc **85**
Hollam Ho. N8 —28Pb **42**
Holland Av. SW20 —67Va **124**
Holland Av. Sutt —81Cb **163**
Holland Clo. Barn —17Fb **23**
Holland Clo. Brom —75Hc **149**
Holland Clo. Romf —29Ed **48**
Holland Clo. Stan —22Ka **38**
Holland Ct. E17 —28Ec 44
(off Evelyn Rd.)
Holland Ct. NW7 —23Wa **40**
Holland Dri. SE23 —62Ac **128**
Holland Gdns. W14 —48Ab **80**
Holland Gdns. Egh —68H **119**
Holland Gdns. Wat —7Y **5**
Holland Gro. SW9 —52Qb **104**
Holland Ho. E4 —21Fc **45**
Holland La. W14 —48Bb **81**
Holland Pk. W11 —46Ab **80**
Holland Pk. Av. W11 —47Za **80**
Holland Pk. Av. Ilf —30Uc **46**
Holland Pk. Gdns. W14 —47Ab **80**
Holland Pk. M. W11 —46Ab **80**
Holland Pk. Rd. W14 —48Bb **81**
Holland Pas. N1 —39Sb 63
(off Basire St.)
Holland Pl. W8 —47Db 81
(off Kensington Church St.)
Holland Pl. Chambers. W8 —47Db 81
(off Holland St.)
Holland Rise Ho. SW9 —52Pb 104
(off Clapham Rd.)
Holland Rd. E6 —39Pc **66**
Holland Rd. E15 —41Gc **85**
Holland Rd. NW10 —39Wa **60**
Holland Rd. SE25 —71Wb **147**
Holland Rd. W14 —47Za **80**
Holland Rd. Wemb —37Ma **59**
Hollands Clo. Shorne —4N **137**
(in two parts)
Hollands, The. Felt —63Z **121**
Hollands, The. Wor Pk —74Va **144**
Holland St. SE1 —46Rb **83** (6C **200**)
Holland St. W8 —47Cb **81**
Holland Vs. Rd. W14 —47Ab **80**
Holland Wlk. N19 —32Mb **62**
Holland Wlk. W8 —46Bb **81**
Holland Wlk. Stan —22Ja **38**
Holland Way. Brom —75Hc **149**
Hollar Rd. N16 —34Vb **63**
Hollen St. W1 —44Mb **82** (2D **198**)
Holles Clo. Hamp —65Ca **121**
Holles Ho. SW9 —54Qb **104**
Holles St. W1 —44Kb **82**
Holley Rd. W3 —47Ua **80**
Hollick Wood Av. N12 —23Hb **41**
Holliday Sq. SW11 —55Fb 103
(off Fowler Clo.)
Hollidge Way. Dag —38Dd **68**
Hollies Av. Sidc —61Vc **131**
Hollies Av. W Byf —85H **157**
Hollies Clo. SW16 —65Qb **126**
Hollies Clo. Twic —61Ha **122**
Hollies Ct. Add —78L **139**
Hollies End. NW7 —22Xa **40**
Hollies Rd. W5 —49La **78**
Hollies St. W1 —44Kb **82** (2A **198**)
Hollies, The. N20 —18Fb **23**
Hollies, The. Add —78L 139
(off Crockford Pk. Rd.)
Hollies, The. Bov —1C **2**
Hollies, The. Chor —17E **16**
Hollies, The. Grav —5F **136**
Hollies, The. Harr —28Ja **38**
Hollies, The. Stanf —2M **93**
Hollies Way. SW12 —59Jb **104**
Hollies Way. Pot B —3Eb **9**
Holligrave Rd. Brom —67Jc **129**
Hollingbourne Av. Bexh —53Bd **109**
Hollingbourne Gdns. W13
—43Ka **78**
Hollingbourne Rd. SE24 —57Sb **105**
Hollingsworth Ct. Surb —73Ma **143**
Hollingsworth Rd. Croy —79Xb **147**
Hollington Ct. Chst —65Rc **130**
Hollington Cres. N Mald —72Va **144**
Hollington Rd. E6 —41Pc **86**
Hollington Rd. N17 —26Wb **43**
Hollingworth Rd. Orp —73Rc **150**
Hollingworth Way. W'ham
—98Tc **184**
Hollins Ho. N7 —35Nb **62**
Hollis Pl. Grays —49Ce **91**
Hollman Gdns. SW16 —65Rb **127**
Holloway Clo. W Dray —50N **75**
Holloway Hill. Lyne —76E **138**
Holloway Ho. NW2 —34Ya **60**
Holloway La. Chen —10D **2**
Holloway La. W Dray —51M **97**
Holloway Rd. E6 —41Pc **86**
Holloway Rd. E11 —34Gc **65**
Holloway Rd. N7 —35Pb **62**
Holloway Rd. N19 & N7 —33Mb **62**
Holloway St. Houn —55Da **99**
Hollow Cotts. Purf —50Qd **89**
Hollowfield Av. Grays —49Fe **91**
Hollowfield Wlk. N'holt —38Aa **57**
Hollow Hill La. Iver —45D **74**
Hollow La. Vir W —9N **117**
Hollows, The. Bren —51Pa **101**
Hollow, The. Wfd G —21Hc **45**
Holly Av. New Haw —82J **157**
Holly Av. Stan —26Na **39**
Holly Av. W on T —74Z **141**
Hollybank Clo. Hamp —64Ca **121**
Holly Bank Rd. W Byf —86J **157**
Holly Bank Rd. Wok —9E **188**
Hollyberry La. NW3 —35Eb **61**
Hollybrake Clo. Chst —66Tc **130**
Hollybush Clo. E11 —29Jc **45**
Hollybush Clo. Harr —25Ga **38**
Holly Bush Clo. Sev —96Ld **187**
Hollybush Clo. Wat —17Y **19**
Holly Bush Ct. Sev —96Ld **187**
Hollybush Gdns. E2 —41Xb **83**
Hollybush Hill. E11 —30Hc **45**
Hollybush Hill. NW3 —35Eb **61**
Hollybush Hill. Stoke P —8L **53**
Hollybush Ho. E2 —41Xb **83**
Hollybush La. Den —33E **54**
Holly Bush La. Hamp —66Ba **121**
Hollybush La. Iver —44D **74**
Holly Bush La. Orp —79Cd **152**
Hollybush La. Rip —91M **173**
Holly Bush La. Sev —96Ld **187**
Hollybush Pl. E2 —41Xb **83**
Hollybush Rd. Grav —1E **136**
Hollybush Rd. King T —64Na **123**
Hollybush Steps. NW3 —35Eb 61
(off Holly Mt.)
Hollybush St. E13 —40Kc **65**
Holly Bush Vale. NW3 —35Eb **61**
Hollybush Wlk. SW9 —56Rb **105**
Hollybush Way. Chesh —1Wb **11**
Holly Clo. NW10 —38Ua **60**
Holly Clo. Buck H —20Mc **27**
Holly Clo. Egh —5M **117**
Holly Clo. Farn C —5G **52**
Holly Clo. Felt —64Aa **121**
Holly Clo. Wall —80Kb **146**
Holly Clo. Wok —7E **188**
Hollycombe. Egh —3N **117**
Holly Ct. N15 —28Ub **43**
Holly Ct. Cher —74H 139
(off Eastworth Rd.)
Holly Ct. Sutt —80Cb **145**
Holly Cres. Beck —71Bc **148**
Holly Cres. Wind —4B **94**
Holly Cres. Wfd G —24Fc **45**
Hollycroft Av. NW3 —34Cb **61**
Hollycroft Av. Wemb —33Pa **59**
Hollycroft Clo. W Dray —51Q **98**
Hollycroft Gdns. W Dray —51Q **98**
Hollydale Dri. Brom —76Pc **150**
Hollydale Rd. SE15 —53Yb **106**
Holly Dene. SE15 —53Xb **105**
Hollydown Way. E11 —34Fc **65**
Holly Dri. E4 —17Dc **26**
Holly Dri. Old Win —7J **95**
Holly Dri. Pot B —5Db **9**
Holly Farm Rd. S'hall —50Aa **77**
Hollyfield Av. N11 —22Hb **41**
Hollyfield Rd. Surb —73Pa **143**
Holly Gdns. W Dray —47P **75**
Holly Grn. Wey —77T **140**
Holly Gro. NW9 —31Sa **59**
Holly Gro. SE15 —54Vb **105**
Hollygrove. Bush —17Fa **20**
Holly Gro. Pinn —25Aa **37**
Hollyhead Clo. E3 —41Cc **84**
Hollyhedge Rd. Cob —86X **159**
Holly Hedges La. Bov —2E **2**
Holly Hedge Ter. SE13 —57Fc **107**
Holly Hill. N21 —16Pb **24**
Holly Hill. NW3 —35Eb **61**
Holly Hill Dri. Bans —89Cb **163**
Holly Hill Rd. Belv & Eri —50Dd **88**
Holly Ho. Brtwd —18Zd **33**
Holly Ho. Iswth —51La **100**
Holly Ind. Pk. Wat —11Y **19**
Holly La. Bans —88Cb **163**
Holly La. E. Bans —88Db **163**
Holly La. W. Bans —89Db **163**
Holly Lea. Guild —100A **172**
Holly Lodge. Harr —29Fa **38**
Holly Lodge Gdns. N6 —33Jb **62**
Hollymead. Cars —76Hb **145**
Hollymead Rd. Coul —90Jb **164**
Hollymeoak Rd. Coul —91Kb **180**
Hollymeok Rd. Coul —91Kb **180**
Holly M. SW10 —50Eb 81 (7A 202)
(off Drayton Gdns.)
Hollymoor La. Eps —82Ta **161**
Holly Mt. NW3 —35Eb **61**
Hollymount Clo. SE10 —53Ec **106**
Holly Pk. N3 —27Bb **41**
Holly Pk. N4 —31Nb **62**
(in two parts)
Holly Pk. Est. N4 —31Pb **62**
Holly Pk. Gdns. N3 —27Cb **41**
Holly Pk. Rd. N11 —22Jb **42**
Holly Pk. Rd. W7 —46Ha **78**
Holly Pl. NW3 —35Eb 61
(off Holly Berry La.)
Holly Rd. E11 —31Hc **65**
Holly Rd. W4 —49Ta **79**
Holly Rd. Dart —60Md **111**
Holly Rd. Enf —8Zb **12**
Holly Rd. Hamp —65Ea **122**
Holly Rd. Houn —56Da **99**
Holly Rd. Orp —80Wc **151**
Holly Rd. Twic —60Ha **100**
Holly St. E8 —38Vb **63**
Holly St. Est. E8 —38Vb **63**
Holly Ter. N6 —32Jb **62**
Holly Ter. N20 —19Eb **23**
Hollytree Av. Swan —68Gd **132**
Holly Tree Clo. SW19 —60Za **102**
Holly Tree Clo. Ger X —22A **34**
Hollytree Ho. Wat —8U **4**
Holly Tree Rd. Cat —94Ub **181**
Holly View Clo. NW4 —30Wa **40**
Holly Village. N6 —33Kb **62**
Holly Wlk. NW3 —35Eb **61**
Holly Wlk. Enf —13Sb **25**
Holly Wlk. Wind —3C **116**
Holly Way. Mitc —70Mb **126**
Hollywood Ct. Borwd —14Qa **21**
Hollywood Gdns. Hay —44X **77**
Hollywood M. SW10 —51Eb **103**
Hollywood Rd. E4 —22Ac **44**
Hollywood Rd. SW10 —51Eb **103**
Hollywoods. Croy —81Bc **166**
Hollywood Way. Wfd G —24Fc **45**
Holman Ct. Ewe —81Wa **162**
Holman Hunt Ho. W6 —50Ab 80
(off Field Rd.)
Holman Rd. SW11 —54Fb **103**
Holman Rd. Eps —78Sa **143**
Holmbank Dri. Shep —70U **120**
Holmbridge Gdns. Enf —14Zb **26**
Holmbrook Dri. NW4 —29Za **40**
Holmbury Clo. Bush —19Ga **20**
Holmbury Ct. SW17 —62Hb **125**
Holmbury Ct. S Croy —78Ub **147**
Holmbury Gdns. Hay —46V **76**
Holmbury Gro. Croy —80Bc **148**
Holmbury Ho. SE24 —57Rb **105**
Holmbury Mnr. Sidc —63Wc **131**
Holmbury Pk. Brom —66Nc **130**
Holmbury View. E5 —32Xb **63**
Holmbury Wlk. SW15 —58Ab **102**
Holm Clo. Wdhm —84G **156**
Holmcote Gdns. N5 —36Sb **63**
Holmcroft. Tad —97Xa **178**
Holmcroft Ho. E17 —28Dc **44**
Holmcroft Way. Brom —71Pc **150**
Holmdale Clo. Borwd —12Pa **21**
Holmdale Gdns. NW4 —29Za **40**
Holmdale Rd. NW6 —36Cb **61**
Holmdale Rd. Chst —64Sc **130**
Holmdale Ter. N15 —31Ub **63**
Holmdene. N12 —22Db **41**
Holmdene Av. NW7 —23Wa **40**
Holmdene Av. SE24 —57Sb **105**
Holmdene Av. Harr —27Da **37**
Holmdene Clo. Beck —68Ec **128**
Holmead Rd. SW6 —52Db **103**
Holme Chase. Wey —79S **140**
Holme Clo. Chesh —3Ac **12**
Holmedale. Slou —5N **73**
Holmefield Rd. Bush —14Ca **19**
Holme Lacey Rd. SE12 —58Hc **107**
Holme Lea. Wat —6Y **5**
Holmeleigh Ct. Enf —14Yb **26**
Holme Oak M. SW4 —57Nb **104**
Holme Pk. Borwd —12Pa **21**
Holme Rd. E6 —39Nc **66**
Holme Rd. Horn —32Qd **69**
Holmes Av. E17 —27Bc **44**

Holmes Av. NW7 —22Ab **40**
Holmes Clo. Horn H —1H **93**
Holmesdale. Wal X —7Yb **12**
Holmesdale Av. SW14 —55Ra **101**
Holmesdale Clo. SE25 —69Vb **127**
Holmesdale Clo. Iver —44H **75**
Holmesdale Rd. N6 —31Kb **62**
Holmesdale Rd. Bexh —54Zc **109**
Holmesdale Rd. Croy & SE25
—71Tb **147**
Holmesdale Rd. Rich —53Pa **101**
Holmesdale Rd. Sev —95Md **187**
Holmesdale Rd. S Dar —67Sd **134**
Holmesdale Rd. Tedd —65La **122**
Holmesley Rd. SE23 —58Ac **106**
Holmes Pl. SW10 —51Eb **103**
Holmes Rd. NW5 —36Kb **62**
Holmes Rd. SW19 —66Eb **125**
Holmes Rd. Twic —46Ha **100**
Holmes Ter. SE1 —47Qb **82** (1K 205)
(off Waterloo Rd.)
Holmewood Ct. N22 —26Qb **42**
Holme Way. Stan —23Ha **38**
Holmewood Gdns. SW2 —59Pb **104**
Holmewood Rd. SE25 —69Ub **127**
Holmewood Rd. SW2 —59Pb **104**
Holmfield. NW11 —28Cb **41**
Holmfield Av. NW4 —29Za **40**
Holmfield Ct. NW3 —37Gb **61**
Holm Gro. Uxb —38Q **56**
Holmhurst Rd. Belv —50Dd **88**
Holmlea Rd. Dat —3N **95**
Holmlea Wlk. Dat —3N **95**
Holmleigh Av. Dart —57Ld **111**
Holmleigh Rd. N16 —32Ub **63**
Holmleigh Rd. Est. N16 —32Ub **63**
Holmoak Clo. SW15 —58Bb **103**
Holm Oak Way. Wat —15W **18**
Holmoaks Ho. Beck —68Ec **128**
Holmsdale Gro. Bexh —54Gd **110**
Holmsdale Ho. N11 —21Kb **42**
(off Coppies Gro.)
Holmshaw Clo. SE26 —63Ac **128**
Holmshill La. Borwd —8Ua **8**
Holmside Rise. Wat —20X **19**
Holmside Rd. SW12 —58Jb **104**
Holmsley Clo. N Mald —72Va **144**
Holmstall Av. Edgw —26Sa **39**
Holmstall Pde. Edgw —26Sa **39**
Holm Wlk. SE3 —54Jc **107**
Holmwood Av. Shenf —16Ce **33**
Holmwood Av. S Croy —85Vb **165**
Holmwood Clo. Add —78J **139**
Holmwood Clo. E Hor —100U **174**
Holmwood Clo. Harr —27Ea **38**
Holmwood Clo. N'holt —37Da **57**
Holmwood Clo. Sutt —81Za **162**
Holmwood Gdns. N3 —26Cb **41**
Holmwood Gdns. Wall —79Kb **146**
Holmwood Gro. NW7 —22Ta **39**
Holmwood Rd. Chess —78Ma **143**
Holmwood Rd. Enf —8Zb **12**
Holmwood Rd. Ilf —33Uc **66**
Holmwood Rd. Sutt —81Ya **162**
Holmwood Vs. SE7 —50Jc **85**
Holne Chase. N2 —30Eb **41**
Holne Chase. Mord —72Bb **145**
Holness Rd. E15 —37Hc **65**
Holroyd Clo. Clay —81Ha **160**
Holroyd Rd. SW15 —56Ya **102**
Holroyd Rd. Clay —81Ha **160**
Holst Clo. Stanf —1L **93**
Holstein Av. Wey —77Q **140**
Holstein Way. Eri —48Zc **87**
Holstock Rd. Ilf —33Sc **66**
Holsworth Clo. Harr —29Ea **38**
Holsworthy Ho. H Hill —25Md **49**
Holsworthy Sq. WC1
(off Elm St.) —42Pb **82** (6J 193)
Holsworthy Way. Chess —78La **142**
Holt Clo. N10 —28Jb **42**
Holt Clo. SE28 —45Xc **87**
Holt Clo. Chig —22Vc **47**
Holt Clo. Els —14Pa **21**
Holt Ct. E15 —36Ec **64**
Holt Ho. SW2 —58Qb **104**
Holton St. E1 —42Zb **84**
Holt Rd. E16 —46Nc **86**
Holt Rd. Wemb —34Ka **58**
Holtsmere Clo. Wat —7Y **5**
Holt, The. Ilf —23Sc **46**
Holt, The. Wall —77Lb **146**
Holt Way. Chig —22Vc **47**
Holtwhites Av. Enf —12Sb **25**
Holtwhite's Hill. Enf —11Rb **25**
Holtwood Rd. Oxs —85Ea **160**
Holwell Pl. Pinn —28Aa **37**
Holwood Clo. W on T —75Y **141**
Holwood Pk. Av. Orp —77Pc **150**
Holwood Pl. SW4 —56Mb **104**
Holybourne Av. SW15 —59Wa **102**
Holybush Way. Chesh —1Wb **11**
Holyfield Rd. Wal A —1Ec **12**
Holylake Ct. SE16 —47Bc **84**
Holyoake Av. Wok —5F **188**
Holyoake Cres. Wok —5F **188**
Holyoake Mt. Grav —10F **114**
Holyoake Ter. Sev —96Jd **186**
Holyoake Wlk. N2 —27Eb **41**
Holyoake Wlk. W4 —42La **78**
Holyoak Rd. SE11
—49Rb **83** (5B 206)
Holyport Rd. SW6 —52Za **102**
Holy Rd. Ct. Wat —14X **19**
Holyrood Av. Harr —35Aa **57**
Holyrood Gdns. Edgw —27Ra **39**
Holyrood Gdns. Grays —9E **92**
Holyrood Rd. Barn —16Eb **23**
Holyrood St. SE1
—46Ub **83** (7H 201)
Holywell Clo. SE3 —51Jc **107**
Holywell Clo. Stai —60N **97**
Holywell La. EC2

Holywell Rd. Wat —15W **18**
Holywell Row. EC2
—42Ub **83** (6H 195)
Holywell Way. Stai —60N **97**
Homan Ct. N12 —21Fb **41**
Homebeech Ho. Wok —90A **156**
(off Mt. Hermon Rd.)
Homebush Ho. E4 —17Dc **26**
Homebourne Way. Orp —74Tc **150**
Home Clo. Cars —75Hb **145**
Home Clo. Fet —93Fa **176**
Home Clo. N'holt —41Ba **77**
Home Ct. Felt —60W **98**
Homecroft Gdns. Lou —14Rc **28**
Homecroft Rd. N22 —25Sb **43**
Homecroft Rd. SE26 —64Yb **128**
Homedean Rd. Chip —94Ed **186**
Home Farm Clo. Eps —89Za **162**
Home Farm Clo. Esh —79Da **141**
Home Farm Clo. Ott —80C **138**
Home Farm Clo. Shep —70U **120**
Home Farm Clo. Th Dit —73Ha **142**
Home Farm Gdns. W on T
—75Y **141**
Homefarm Rd. W7 —44Ga **78**
Home Farm Rd. L War —25Ae **51**
Home Farm Rd. Rick —21Q **36**
Home Farm Way. Stoke P —9N **53**
Home Field. Barn —15Bb **23**
Homefield. Wal A —4Jc **13**
Homefield Av. Ilf —29Uc **46**
Homefield Av. W on T —77Z **141**
Homefield Clo. NW10 —38Sa **59**
Homefield Clo. Epp —2Wc **15**
Homefield Clo. Hay —42Z **77**
Homefield Clo. Lea —93La **176**
Homefield Clo. St P —70Xc **131**
Homefield Clo. Swan —69Hd **132**
Homefield Clo. Wdhm —84G **156**
Homefield Ct. SW16 —62Nb **126**
Homefield Gdns. N2 —27Fb **41**
Homefield Gdns. Mitc —68Eb **125**
Homefield Gdns. Tad —92Ya **178**
Homefield Pk. Sutt —79Db **145**
Homefield Rise. Orp —74Wc **151**
Homefield Rd. SW19 —65Ab **124**
Homefield Rd. W4 —49Va **80**
Homefield Rd. Brom —67Lc **129**
Homefield Rd. Chor —14F **16**
Homefield Rd. Coul & Cat
—91Rb **181**
Homefield Rd. Edgw —23Ta **39**
Homefield Rd. Rad —9Ha **6**
Homefield Rd. Sev —94Gd **186**
Homefield Rd. W on T —73Aa **141**
Homefield Rd. Warl —91Yb **182**
Homefield Rd. Wemb —35Ja **58**
Homefield St. N1
—40Ub **63** (2H 195)
Homefirs Ho. Wemb —34Pa **59**
Home Gdns. Dag —34Ed **68**
Home Gdns. Dart —58Nd **111**
Home Hill. Swan —66Hd **132**
Homehurst Ho. Brtwd —18Zd **33**
Homeland Dri. Sutt —81Db **163**
Homelands. Lea —93La **176**
Homelands Dri. SE19 —66Ub **127**
Home Lea. Orp —78Vc **151**
Homeleigh Ct. Chesh —1Xb **11**
Homeleigh Rd. SE15 —57Zb **106**
Homemead. Grav —9D **114**
Home Mead. Stan —25La **38**
Home Meadow. Bans —88Cb **163**
Home Meadow. Farn R —10G **52**
Homemead Rd. Brom —71Pc **150**
Homemead Rd. Croy —72Mb **146**
Home Orchard. Dart —58Nd **111**
Home Pk. Cotts. K Lan —2R **4**
Home Pk. Ind. Est. K Lan —2R **4**
Home Pk. Mill Link Rd. K Lan —2R **4**
Home Pk. Rd. SW19 —63Bb **125**
Home Pk. Wlk. King T —70Ma **123**
Homer Clo. Bexh —53Ed **110**
Homer Dri. E14 —49Cc **84**
Home Rd. SW11 —54Gb **103**
Homer Rd. E9 —37Ac **64**
Homer Rd. Croy —72Zb **148**
Homer Row. W1
—43Gb **81** (1E 196)
Homersham Rd. King T —68Qa **123**
Homers Rd. Wind —3B **94**
Homer St. W1 —43Gb **81** (1E 196)
Homerton Gro. E9 —36Zb **64**
Homerton High St. E9 —36Zb **64**
Homerton Rd. E9 —36Ac **64**
Homerton Row. E9 —36Yb **64**
Homerton Ter. E9 —37Yb **64**
Homesdale Clo. E11 —29Jc **45**
Homesdale Rd. Brom —70Lc **129**
Homesdale Rd. Cat —95Tb **181**
Homesdale Rd. Orp —73Uc **150**
Homestall Rd. SE22 —57Yb **106**
Homestead Ct. Barn —15Cb **23**
Homestead Gdns. Clay —78Ga **142**
Homestead Paddock. N14
—15Kb **24**
Homestead Pk. NW2 —34Va **60**
Homestead Rd. SW6 —52Bb **103**
Homestead Rd. Cat —95Tb **181**
Homestead Rd. Dag —33Bd **67**
Homestead Rd. Orp —80Xc **151**
Homestead Rd. Rick —17M **17**
Homestead Rd. Stai —65K **119**
Homestead, The. N11 —21Kb **42**
Homestead, The. Cray —57Gd **110**
Homestead, The. Dart —58Ld **111**
Homestead Way. New Ad
—83Ec **166**
Homewater Ho. Eps —85Ua **162**
Homewaters Av. Sun —67V **120**
Home Way. Rick —18H **17**
Homeway. Romf —23Rd **49**
Homewillow Clo. N21 —16Rb **25**
Homewood. G Grn —4P **73**
Homewood Clo. Hamp —65Ba **121**
Homewood Cres. Chst —65Uc **130**

Homewoods. SW12 —59Lb **104**
Homeworth Ho. Wok —90A **156**
(off Mt. Hermon Rd.)
Homildon Ho. SE26 —62Wb **127**
Honduras St. EC1
—42Sb **83** (5D 194)
Honeybourne Rd. NW6 —36Db **61**
Honeybourne Way. Orp —74Tc **150**
Honey Brook. Wal A —5Gc **13**
Honeybrook Rd. SW12 —59Lb **104**
Honey Clo. Dag —37Dd **68**
Honeycroft. Lou —14Rc **28**
Honeycroft Hill. Uxb —38N **55**
Honeyden Rd. Sidc —65Ad **131**
Honey Hill. Uxb —38P **55**
Honey La. Ho. Wal A —6Jc **13**
Honey La. EC2 —44Sb **83** (3E 200)
(off Trump St.)
Honeyman Clo. NW6 —38Za **60**
Honeypot Bus. Cen. Stan —25Na **39**
Honeypot Clo. NW9 —28Pa **39**
Honeypot La. Brtwd —20Wd **32**
Honeypot La. Kems —91Rd **187**
Honeypot La. Stan & NW9
—24Ma **39**
Honeypots Rd. Wok —10G **188**
Honeysett Rd. N17 —26Vb **43**
Honeysuckle Clo. Iver —44E **74**
Honeysuckle Clo. Pil H —15Xd **32**
Honeysuckle Clo. Romf —23Ld **49**
Honeysuckle Gdns. Croy —73Zb **148**
Honeysuckle La. N22 —26Sb **43**
Honeywell Rd. SW11 —58Hb **103**
Honeywood Clo. Pot B —5Fb **9**
Honeywood Rd. NW10 —40Va **60**
Honeywood Rd. Iswth —56Ja **100**
Honeywood Wlk. Cars —77Hb **145**
Honister Clo. Stan —25Ka **38**
Honister Gdns. Stan —24Ka **38**
Honister Heights. Purl —86Tb **165**
Honister Pl. Stan —25Ka **38**
Honiton Rd. NW6 —40Bb **61**
Honiton Rd. Romf —30Fd **48**
Honiton Rd. Well —54Vc **109**
Honley Rd. SE6 —59Dc **106**
Honnor Rd. Stai —66M **119**
Honor Oak Pk. SE23 —58Yb **106**
Honor Oak Rise. SE23 —58Yb **106**
Honor Oak Rd. SE23 —60Yb **106**
Hood Av. N14 —16Kb **24**
Hood Av. SW14 —57Sa **101**
Hood Av. Orp —71Xc **151**
Hood Clo. Croy —74Rb **147**
Hoodcote Gdns. N21 —17Rb **25**
Hood Ct. EC4 —44Qb **82** (3A 200)
(off Fleet St.)
Hood Rd. SW20 —66Va **124**
Hood Rd. Rain —40Hd **68**
Hood Wlk. Romf —25Dd **48**
Hooke Rd. E Hor —97V **174**
Hookers Rd. E17 —27Zb **44**
Hook Farm Rd. Brom —71Mc **149**
Hookfield. Eps —85Sa **161**
Hookfields. Grav —2A **136**
Hook Ga. Enf —8Xb **11**
Hook Grn. La. Dart —62Hd **132**
Hook Grn. Rd. S'fleet —66Ae **135**
Hook Heath Av. Wok —7E **188**
Hook Heath Gdns. Wok —9C **188**
Hook Heath Rd. Wok —9C **188**
Hook Hill. S Croy —82Ub **165**
Hook Hill La. Wok —9E **188**
Hook Hill Pk. Wok —9E **188**
Hooking Grn. Harr —29Da **37**
Hook La. N'thaw —4Hb **9**
Hook La. Romf —16Bd **29**
Hook La. Well —57Vc **109**
Hook Rise Bus. Cen. Chess
—76Qa **143**
Hook Rise N. Surb —76Na **143**
Hook Rise S. Surb —76Na **143**
Hook Rd. Chess & Surb —78Ma **143**
Hook Rd. Eps —80Sa **143**
Hooks Clo. SE15 —53Xb **105**
Hookshall Dri. Dag —34Ed **68**
Hookstone Way. Wfd G —24Mc **45**
Hooks Way. SE22 —60Wb **105**
Hooper Rd. E16 —44Jc **85**
Hooper's Ct. SW3
—47Hb **81** (2F 203)
Hooper St. E1 —44Wb **83**
Hoopers Yd. Sev —98Ld **187**
Hoop La. NW11 —31Bb **61**
Hope Clo. N1 —37Sb **63**
Hope Clo. SE12 —62Kc **129**
Hope Clo. Mount —11Fe **33**
Hope Clo. Sutt —78Eb **145**
Hope Clo. Wfd G —23Lc **45**
Hope Ct. SE12 —62Kc **129**
Hopedale Rd. SE7 —51Kc **107**
Hopefield Av. NW6 —40Ab **60**
Hope Grn. Wat —5W **4**
Hope Pk. Brom —66Hc **129**
Hope Rd. Stanf —3M **93**
Hope Rd. Swans —58Be **113**
Hope St. SW11 —55Fb **103**
Hopetown St. E1 —43Vb **83**
Hopewell Dri. Grav —4H **137**
Hopewell St. SE5 —52Tb **105**
Hopfield. Wok —88A **156**
Hopfield Av. Byfl —84N **157**
Hopgarden La. Sev —100Jd **186**
Hop Gdns. WC2 —45Nb **82** (5F 199)
Hopgood St. W12 —47Ya **80**
Hopkins Clo. Romf —27Ld **49**
Hopkins St. W1 —44Lb **82** (3C 198)
Hopkinsons Pl. NW1 —39Jb **62**
Hopper's M. W3 —46Sa **79**
Hoppers Rd. N13 & N21 —19Qb **24**

Hoppett Rd. E4 —19Gc **27**
Hoppety, The. Tad —94Za **178**
Hopping La. N1 —37Rb **63**
Hoppingwood Av. N Mald
—69Ua **124**
Hoppit Rd. Wal A —4Dc **12**
Hoppner Rd. Hay —40T **56**
Hopton Ct. Hayes —74Jc **149**
Hopton Gdns. N Mald —72Wa **144**
Hopton Rd. SW16 —64Pb **126**
Hopton's Gdns. SE1
—46Rb **83** (6C 200)
(off Hopton St.)
Hopton St. SE1 —46Rb **83** (6C 200)
Hopwood Rd. SE17 —51Tb **105**
Hopwood Wlk. E8 —38Wb **63**
Horace Av. Romf —32Ed **68**
Horace Rd. E7 —35Kc **65**
Horace Rd. Ilf —27Sc **46**
Horace Rd. King T —69Pa **123**
Horatio St. E2 —40Wb **63**
Horatius Way. Croy —78Pb **146**
Horbury Cres. W11 —45Cb **81**
Horbury M. W11 —45Bb **81**
Horder Rd. SW6 —53Ab **102**
Hordle Promenade E. SE15
—52Vb **105**
Hordle Promenade N. SE15
—52Ub **105**
Hordle Promenade S. SE15
—52Vb **105**
Hordle Promenade W. SE15
—52Ub **105**
Horizon Ho. Eps —85Ua **162**
Horizon Ho. Swan —70Gd **132**
Horizon Way. SE7 —49Kc **85**
Horksley Gdns. Hut —16Ee **33**
Horle Wlk. SE5 —54Rb **105**
Horley Rd. Bexh —57Cd **110**
Horley Rd. SE9 —63Nc **130**
Hormead Rd. W9 —42Bb **81**
Hornbeam Av. Upm —35Qd **69**
Hornbeam Clo. SE11
—49Qb **82** (5K 205)
Hornbeam Clo. Borwd —11Qa **21**
Hornbeam Clo. Brtwd —20De **33**
Hornbeam Clo. Buck H —20Mc **27**
Hornbeam Clo. N'holt —36Ba **57**
Hornbeam Clo. They B —9Tc **14**
Hornbeam Cres. Bren —52Ka **100**
Hornbeam Gdns. Slou —8L **73**
Hornbeam Ho. E4 —20Gc **27**
Hornbeam La. E4 —15Gc **27**
Hornbeam La. Bexh —54Ed **110**
Hornbeam La. Buck H —20Mc **27**
Hornbeam Rd. Hay —43Y **77**
Hornbeam Rd. They B —9Tc **14**
Hornbeams. Brick —2Ba **5**
Hornbeams Av. Enf —7Yb **12**
Hornbeams Rise. N11 —23Jb **42**
Hornbeam Ter. Cars —74Gb **145**
Hornbeam Wlk. Rich —63Pa **123**
Hornbeam Wlk. W Vill —82U **158**
Hornbeam Way. Brom —72Qc **150**
Hornbeam Way. Wal X —1Vb **11**
Hornbill Clo. Uxb —44M **75**
Hornblower Clo. SE16 —48Ac **84**
Hornbuckle Clo. Harr —33Fa **58**
Hornby Clo. NW3 —38Fb **61**
Hornby Ho. SE11 —51Qb **104**
(off Clayton St.)
Horncastle Clo. SE12 —59Jc **107**
Horncastle Rd. SE12 —59Jc **107**
Hornchurch. N17 —26Tb **43**
(off Gloucester Rd.)
Hornchurch Hill. Whyt —90Vb **165**
Hornchurch Rd. Horn —32Jd **68**
Horndon Clo. SW15 —60Wa **102**
Horndon Clo. Romf —25Ed **48**
Horndon Grn. Romf —25Ed **48**
Horndon Rd. Horn H —2J **93**
Horndon Rd. Romf —25Ed **48**
Horner Ho. N1 —40Ub **63** (1J 195)
(off Whitmore Est.)
Horner La. Mitc —68Fb **125**
Horne Rd. Shep —70Q **120**
Hornets, The. Wat —14X **19**
Horne Way. SW15 —54Ya **102**
Hornfair Rd. SE7 —51Mc **107**
Hornford Way. Romf —31Gd **68**
Horn Hill La. Ger X —22B **34**
Hornhill Rd. Rick —22D **34**
Horniman Dri. SE23 —60Xb **105**
Horning Clo. SE9 —63Nc **130**
Horn La. SE10 —49Jc **85**
Horn La. W3 —46Sa **79**
Horn La. Wfd G —23Jc **45**
Hornminster Glen. Horn —33Qd **69**
Hornpark Clo. SE12 —57Kc **107**
Hornpark La. SE12 —57Kc **107**
Hornsby La. Ors —7C **92**
Horns End Pl. Pinn —28Y **37**
Hornsey La. N6 —32Kb **62**
Hornsey La. Est. N19 —31Mb **62**
Hornsey La. Gdns. N6 —31Lb **62**
Hornsey Pk. Rd. N8 —27Pb **42**
Hornsey Rise. N19 —31Mb **62**
Hornsey Rise Gdns. N19 —31Mb **62**
Hornsey Rd. N19 & N7 —32Nb **62**
Hornsey St. N7 —36Pb **62**
Hornshay St. SE15 —51Yb **106**
Horns Rd. Ilf —29Sc **46**
Hornton Pl. W8 —47Db **81**
Hornton St. W8 —47Cb **81**
Horsa Clo. Wall —80Nb **146**
Horsa Rd. SE12 —59Lc **107**
Horsa Rd. Eri —52Dd **110**
Horsebridge Clo. Dag —39Ad **67**
Horsecroft. Bans —89Bb **163**
Horsecroft Clo. Orp —74Xc **151**
Horsecroft Rd. Edgw —24Ta **39**
Horse & Dolphin Yd. W1
—45Mb **82** (4E 198)
(off Macclesfield St.)

Horse Fair. King T —68Ma **123**
Horseferry Pl. SE10 —51Ec **106**
Horseferry Rd. E14 —45Ac **84**
Horseferry Rd. SW1
—48Mb **82** (4D 204)
Horseguards Av. SW1
—46Nb **82** (7F 199)
Horse Guards Rd. SW1
—46Mb **82** (7E 198)
Horse Hill. Lat —4A **2**
Horse Leaze. E6 —44Qc **86**
Horseleys. W Hyd —22F **34**
Horsell Birch. Wok —2E **188**
Horsell Comn. Rd. Wok —2F **188**
Horsell Ct. Cher —73K **139**
Horsell Moor. Wok —5G **188**
Horsell Pk. Wok —89A **156**
Horsell Pk. Clo. Wok —4G **188**
Horsell Rise. Wok —3G **188**
Horsell Rise Clo. Wok —3G **188**
Horsell Rd. N5 —36Qb **62**
Horsell Rd. Orp —67Xc **131**
Horsell Vale. Wok —88A **156**
Horsell Way. Wok —4F **188**
Horselydown La. SE1
—47Vb **83** (1K 207)
Horseman Side. N'side —17Kd **31**
Horsemoor Clo. Slou —49C **74**
Horsenden Av. Gnfd —36Ga **58**
Horsenden Cres. Gnfd —36Ha **58**
Horsenden La. Gnfd —37Ga **58**
Horsenden La. N. Gnfd —37Ha **58**
Horsenden La. S. Gnfd —39Ja **58**
Horse Ride. SW1
(off Mall, The.) —47Lb **82** (1B 204)
Horse Ride. Cars —82Gb **163**
Horse Ride. Epp —7Rc **14**
Horseshoe Clo. E14 —50Ec **84**
Horseshoe Clo. NW2 —33Xa **60**
Horse Shoe Cres. N'holt —40Ca **57**
Horse Shoe Grn. Sutt —75Db **145**
Horseshoe Hill. Burn —5A **52**
Horseshoe Hill. Wal A —5Lc **13**
Horseshoe La. N20 —18Za **22**
Horseshoe La. Enf —13Sb **25**
Horseshoe La. Wat —4X **5**
Horseshoe, The. Bans —87Cb **163**
Horseshoe, The. Coul —85Mb **164**
Horse Shoe Yd. W1
(off Brook St.) —45Kb **82** (4A 198)
Horse Yd. N1 —39Rb **63**
(off Essex Rd.)
Horsfeld Gdns. SE9 —57Nc **108**
Horsfeld Rd. SE9 —57Mc **108**
Horsfield Clo. Dart —59Sd **112**
Horsford Rd. SW2 —57Pb **104**
Horsham Av. N12 —22Gb **41**
Horsham Ct. N17 —25Wb **43**
(off Lansdowne Rd.)
Horsham Rd. Bexh —57Cd **110**
Horsham Rd. Felt —58S **98**
Horsley Clo. Eps —85Ta **161**
Horsleydown La. SE1 —47Vb **83**
Horsleydown Sq. SE1
—46Vb **83** (7K 201)
Horsley Dri. New Ad —80Ec **148**
Horsley Rd. E4 —19Ec **26**
Horsley Rd. Brom —67Kc **129**
Horsley Rd. D'side —94W **174**
Horsley St. SE17 —51Tb **105**
Horsman St. SE5 —51Sb **105**
Horsmonden Clo. Orp —73Vc **151**
Horsmonden Rd. SE4 —57Bc **106**
Hortensia Rd. SW10 —52Eb **103**
Horticultural Pl. W4 —50Ta **79**
Horton Av. NW2 —35Ab **60**
Horton Bri. Rd. W Dray —46P **75**
Horton Clo. W Dray —46Q **76**
Horton Footpath. Eps —83Sa **161**
Horton Gdns. Eps —83Sa **161**
Horton Gdns. Hort —55Bb **96**
Horton Hill. Eps —83Sa **161**
Horton Ind. Pk. W Dray —46P **75**
Horton Kirby Trading Est. S Dar
—67Sd **134**
Horton La. Eps —83Qa **161**
Horton Pl. W'ham —98Tc **184**
Horton Rd. E8 —37Xb **63**
Horton Rd. Coln —55G **96**
Horton Rd. Dat —3N **95**
Horton Rd. Hort —54C **96**
Horton Rd. Hort K —70Sd **134**
Horton Rd. Stai —56H **97**
Horton Rd. W Dray —46N **75**
Horton St. SE13 —55Dc **106**
Hortons Way. W'ham —98Tc **184**
Horton Way. F'ham —73Pd **153**
Hortus Rd. E4 —19Ec **26**
Hortus Rd. S'hall —47Ba **77**
Horvath Clo. Wey —77T **140**
Horwood Ct. Wat —9Z **5**
Hosack Rd. SW17 —61Jb **126**
Hose Av. SE12 —61Jc **129**
Hosey Comn. Rd. West
—100Uc **184**
Hosey Hill. W'ham —99Uc **184**
Hosier La. EC1 —43Rb **83** (1B 200)
Hoskins Clo. E16 —44Lc **85**
Hoskins Clo. Hay —50V **76**
Hoskins Rd. Oxt —100Gc **183**
Hoskins St. SE10 —50Fc **85**
Hospital Bri. Rd. Twic —59Da **99**
Hospital Rd. E9 —36Zb **64**
Hospital Rd. Houn —56Ca **99**
Hospital Rd. Sev —93Ld **187**
Hospital Way. SE13 —58Fc **107**

Hotham Rd. M. SW19 —66Eb **125**
Hotham St. E15 —39Gc **65**
Hothfield Pl. SE16 —48Yb **84**
Hotspur Ind. Est. N17 —23Xb **43**
Hotspur Rd. N'holt —40Ca **57**
Hotspur St. SE11
—50Qb **82** (7K 205)
Hottsfield. Hart —69Ae **135**
Houblon Rd. Rich —57Na **101**
Houblons Hill. Coop —3Yc **15**
Houghton Clo. E8 —37Vb **63**
Houghton Clo. Hamp —65Aa **121**
Houghton Rd. N15 —28Vb **43**
Houghton St. WC2
—44Pb **82** (3J 199)
Houlder Cres. Croy —79Rb **147**
Houndsditch. EC3
—44Ub **83** (2J 201)
Houndsfield Rd. N9 —17Xb **25**
Hounsden Rd. N21 —16Pb **24**
Hounslow Av. Houn —57Da **99**
Hounslow Bus. Pk. Houn —56Ca **99**
Hounslow Cen. Houn —55Da **99**
Hounslow Gdns. Houn —57Da **99**
Hounslow Rd. Felt —60X **99**
Hounslow Rd. Hanw —63Z **121**
Hounslow Rd. Twic —58Da **99**
Houseman Way. SE5 —52Tb **105**
Houston Bus. Pk. Hay —46Y **77**
Houston Pl. Esh —74Fa **142**
Houston Rd. SE23 —61Ac **128**
Houstoun Ct. Houn —52Ba **99**
Hove Av. E17 —30Bc **44**
Hove Clo. Hut —19Ee **33**
Hoveden Rd. NW2 —36Ab **60**
Hove Gdns. Sutt —74Db **145**
Hoveton St. SE28 —45Yc **87**
Howard Av. Bex —60Yc **109**
Howard Av. Eps —82Wa **162**
Howard Clo. N11 —19Jb **24**
Howard Clo. NW2 —35Ab **60**
Howard Clo. W3 —44Ra **79**
Howard Clo. Asht —90Pa **161**
Howard Clo. Bush —17Ga **20**
Howard Clo. Hamp —66Ea **122**
Howard Clo. Lea —95La **176**
Howard Clo. Sun —65V **120**
Howard Clo. Tad —97Va **178**
Howard Clo. Wal A —6Fc **13**
Howard Clo. Wat —9W **4**
Howard Clo. W Hor —97T **174**
Howard Ct. Bark —39Tc **66**
Howard Ct. E6 —40Pc **66**
Howard Ct. E11 —34Gc **65**
Howard Ct. E17 —27Cc **44**
Howard Ct. N15 —30Ub **43**
Howard Ct. N16 —35Tb **63**
Howard Ct. NW2 —35Za **60**
Howard Ct. SE20 —67Yb **128**
Howard Ct. SE25 —71Wb **147**
Howard Ct. Ashf —63M **119**
Howard Ct. Bark —39Tc **66**
Howard Ct. Bookh —99Da **175**
Howard Ct. Brom —66Jc **129**
Howard Ct. Coul —87Lb **164**
Howard Ct. Dart —58Qd **111**
Howard Ct. Eff J —95W **174**
Howard Ct. Ilf —35Rc **66**
Howard Ct. N Mald —69Ua **124**
Howard Ct. S'hall —44Da **77**
Howard Ct. Surb —72Pa **143**
Howard Ct. Upm —33Sd **70**
Howards Clo. Pinn —26X **37**
Howards Clo. Wok —92C **172**
Howards Crest Clo. Beck —68Ec **128**
Howard's La. SW15 —56Xa **102**
Howards La. Add —79H **139**
Howards Rd. E13 —41Jc **85**
Howards Rd. Wok —92B **172**
Howards Thicket. Ger X —3N **53**
Howard St. Th Dit —73Ka **142**
Howards Wood Dri. Ger X —3P **53**
Howard Wlk. N2 —28Eb **41**
Howard Way. SE22 —60Wb **105**
Howard Way. Barn —15Za **22**
Howarth Rd. SE2 —50Wc **87**
Howberry Clo. Edgw —23Ma **39**
Howberry Rd. Stan & Edgw
—23Ma **39**
Howberry Rd. T Hth —67Tb **127**
Howbury La. Eri —54Jd **110**
Howbury Rd. SE15 —55Yb **106**
Howcroft Cres. N3 —24Cb **41**
Howcroft La. Gnfd —41Fa **78**
Howden Clo. SE28 —45Zc **87**
Howden Ho. Houn —59Aa **99**
Howden Rd. SE25 —68Vb **127**
Howden St. SE15 —55Wb **105**
Howe Clo. Romf —25Cd **48**
Howe Clo. Shenl —4Na **7**
Howe Dri. Cat —94Tb **181**
Howell Clo. Romf —29Zc **47**
Howell Ct. E10 —32Dc **64**
Howell Hill Clo. Eps —83Ya **162**
Howell Hill Gro. Eps —82Ya **162**
Howells Clo. W King —79Ud **154**
Howell Wlk. SE17
—49Rb **83** (6C 206)
Howes Clo. N3 —27Cb **41**
Howfield Pl. N17 —27Vb **43**
Howgate Rd. SW14 —55Ta **101**
Howick Pl. SW1 —48Lb **82** (4C 204)
Howie St. SW11 —52Gb **103**
Howitt Clo. NW3 —37Gb **61**
Howitt Rd. NW3 —37Gb **61**
Howland Est. SE16 —48Yb **84**
Howland M. E. W1
—43Lb **82** (7C 192)
Howland St. W1 —43Lb **82** (7B 192)

Howland Way—Iona Clo.

Howland Way. SE16 —47Ac **84**
How La. Coul —89Jb **164**
Howletts La. Ruis —29S **36**
Howlett's Rd. SE24 —58Sb **105**
Howley Pl. W2 —43Eb **81** (7A **190**)
Howley Rd. Croy —76Rb **147**
Hows Clo. Uxb —39L **55**
Howsman Rd. SW13 —51Wa **102**
Howson Rd. SE4 —56Ac **106**
Howson Ter. Rich —58Na **101**
Hows Rd. Uxb —39L **55**
How's St. E2 —40Vb **63** (1K **195**)
Howton Pl. Bush —18Fa **20**
How Wood. Park —1Da **5**
*Hoxton Mkt. N1 —41Ub **83** (4H **195**)*
(off Boot St.)
Hoxton Sq. N1 —41Ub **83** (4H **195**)
Hoxton St. N1 —39Ub **63** (1H **195**)
Hoylake Cres. Uxb —33Q **56**
Hoylake Gdns. Mitc —69Lb **126**
Hoylake Gdns. Romf —24Qd **49**
Hoylake Gdns. Ruis —32X **57**
Hoylake Gdns. Wat —21Z **37**
Hoylake Rd. W3 —44Ua **80**
Hoyland Clo. SE15 —52Xb **105**
Hoyle Rd. SW17 —64Gb **125**
Hoy St. E16 —44Hc **85**
Hubbard Rd. SE27 —63Sb **127**
Hubbards Chase. Horn —29Qd **49**
Hubbards Clo. Horn —29Qd **49**
Hubbards Rd. Chor —15F **16**
Hubbard St. E15 —39Gc **65**
Hubert Gro. SW9 —55Nb **104**
Hubert Rd. E6 —41Mc **85**
Hubert Rd. Brtwd —20Xd **32**
Hubert Rd. Rain —41Hd **88**
Hubert Rd. Slou —8P **73**
Hucknall Clo. Romf —23Pd **49**
Huddart St. E3 —43Bc **84**
(in two parts)
Huddleston Clo. E2 —40Yb **64**
Huddlestone Cres. Red —100Mb **180**
Huddlestone Rd. E7 —35Hc **65**
Huddlestone Rd. NW2 —37Xa **60**
Huddleston Rd. N7 —34Lb **62**
*Hudson. NW9 —25Va **40***
(off Near Acre)
*Hudson Clo. W12 —45Xa **80***
(off White City Est.)
Hudson Clo. Wat —8V **4**
Hudson Pl. SE18 —50Sc **86**
Hudson Rd. Bexh —54Bd **109**
Hudson Rd. Hay —51T **98**
Hudsons. Tad —93Za **178**
Hudsons Clo. Stanf —1M **93**
Hudson's Pl. SW1
*—49Lb **82** (5B **204**)*
(off Bridge Pl.)
Huggen's College Almshouses. Grav
—57De **113**
*Huggin Ct. EC4 —45Sb **83** (4E **200**)*
(off Huggin Hill)
Huggin Hill. EC4 —45Sb **83** (4E **200**)
Hughan Rd. E15 —36Fc **65**
*Hugh Dalton Ho. SW6 —51Bb **103***
(off Clem Attlee Ct.)
Hughenden Av. Harr —29Ka **38**
Hughenden Gdns. N'holt —41Y **77**
Hughenden Rd. Slou —4H **73**
Hughenden Rd. Wor Pk —73Wa **144**
Hughendon. New Bar —14Db **23**
Hughendon Ter. E15 —35Ec **64**
Hughes Ct. N7 —36Mb **62**
Hughes M. SW11 —57Hb **103**
Hughes Rd. SE20 —66Xb **127**
Hughes Rd. Ashf —65S **120**
Hughes Rd. Grays —8C **92**
Hughes Rd. Hay —45X **77**
*Hughes Ter. E16 —43Hc **85***
(off Clarkson Rd.)
Hughes Wlk. Croy —73Sb **147**
Hugh Gaitskell Ho. N16 —33Vb **63**
*Hugh Gaitskell Ho. SW6 —51Bb **103***
(off Clem Attlee Ct.)
Hugh M. SW1 —49Kb **82** (6A **204**)
Hugh St. SW1 —49Kb **82** (6A **204**)
Hugo Gdns. Rain —37Jd **68**
Hugo Rd. SW6 —55Db **103**
Hugo Rd. N19 —35Lb **62**
Huguenot Pl. E1 —43Vb **83**
Huguenot Pl. SW18 —57Eb **103**
Huguenot Sq. SE15 —55Xb **105**
Hullbridge M. N1 —39Tb **63**
Hull Clo. SE16 —47Zb **84**
Hull Clo. Slou —7G **72**
Hullets Way. Pil H —13Ud **32**
Hull St. EC1 —41Sb **83** (4D **194**)
Hulme Pl. SE1 —47Sb **83** (2E **206**)
Hulse Av. Bark —37Tc **66**
Hulse Av. Romf —25Dd **48**
Hulsewood Clo. Dart —62Kd **133**
Hulton Clo. Lea —95La **176**
Hulverston Clo. Sutt —82Db **163**
Humber Av. S Ock —44Vd **90**
Humber Dri. Upm —30Td **50**
Humber Rd. NW2 —33Xa **60**
Humber Rd. SE3 —51Hc **107**
Humber Rd. Dart —57Md **111**
Humberstone Rd. E13 —41Lc **85**
Humberton Clo. E9 —36Ac **64**
Humber Way. Slou —49C **74**
Humbolt Rd. W6 —51Ab **102**
Hume Av. Til —5D **114**
Hume Point. E16 —43Lc **85**
Humes Av. W7 —48Ga **78**
Hume Ter. E16 —44Kc **85**
Hume Way. Ruis —30W **36**
Hummer Rd. Egh —63C **118**
Humphrey Clo. Fet —94Ea **176**
Humphrey Clo. Ilf —25Pc **46**
Humphrey St. SE1
—50Vb **83** (7K **207**)
Humphries Clo. Dag —35Bd **67**
Hundred Acre. NW9 —26Va **40**
Hungerdown. E4 —18Ec **26**
Hungerford Av. Slou —3J **73**
Hungerford La. WC2
*—46Nb **82** (6F **199**)*
(off Craven St.)
Hungerford Rd. N7 —37Mb **62**
Hungerford Sq. Wey —77T **140**
Hungry Hill La. Send —98L **173**
Hunsdon Clo. Dag —37Ad **67**
Hunsdon Dri. Sev —95Kd **187**
Hunsdon Rd. SE14 —52Zb **106**
Hunslett St. E2 —41Yb **84**
Hunston Rd. Mord —74Db **145**
Hunt Ct. N14 —17Kb **24**
Hunter Av. Shenf —16Ce **33**
Hunter Clo. SE1 —48Tb **83** (4G **207**)
Hunter Clo. Borwd —15Sa **21**
Hunter Clo. Pot B —5Db **9**
Huntercombe Clo. Tap —4A **72**
Huntercombe La. N. Slou & Tap
—3A **72**
Huntercombe La. S. Tap —6A **72**
Huntercombe Spur. Slou —6A **72**
Hunter Ct. Burn —3A **72**
Huntercrombe Gdns. Wat —21Y **37**
Hunter Dri. Horn —35Ld **69**
Hunter Rd. SW20 —67Ya **124**
Hunter Rd. Ilf —36Rc **66**
Hunter Rd. T Hth —69Tb **127**
Hunters Clo. SW12 —60Jb **104**
Hunters Clo. Bov —1C **2**
Hunters Clo. Eps —85Sa **161**
Hunters Ct. Rich —57Ma **101**
Hunters Gro. Harr —28La **38**
Hunters Gro. Hay —46W **76**
Hunters Gro. Orp —77Rc **150**
Hunters Gro. Romf —22Dd **48**
Hunters Hall Rd. Dag —35Cd **68**
Hunters Hill. Ruis —34Y **57**
Hunter's La. Leav —5V **4**
Hunters Meadow. SE19 —63Ub **127**
Hunters Reach. Wal X —1Vb **11**
Hunters Ride. Brick —3Ca **5**
Hunter's Rd. Chess —76Na **143**
Hunters Sq. Dag —35Cd **68**
Hunter St. WC1 —42Nb **82** (5G **193**)
Hunters Wlk. Knock —86Ad **169**
Hunter's Way. Croy —77Ub **147**
Hunters Way. Enf —11Qb **24**
Hunter Wlk. E13 —40Jc **65**
Hunter Wlk. Borwd —15Ta **21**
Hunting Clo. Esh —77Ca **141**
Huntingdon Clo. Mitc —69Nb **126**
Huntingdon Gdns. W4 —52Sa **101**
Huntingdon Gdns. Wor Pk
—76Ya **144**
Huntingdon Rd. N2 —27Gb **41**
Huntingdon Rd. N9 —18Yb **26**
Huntingdon Rd. Wok —5C **188**
Huntingdon St. E16 —44Hc **85**
Huntingdon St. N1 —38Pb **62**
Huntingfield. Croy —80Bc **148**
Huntingfield Rd. SW15 —56Wa **102**
Huntingfield Way. Egh —66F **118**
Hunting Ga. Clo. Enf —13Qb **24**
Hunting Ga. Dri. Chess —80Na **143**
Hunting Ga. M. Sutt —76Db **145**
Hunting Ga. M. Twic —60Ga **100**
Huntings Rd. Dag —37Cd **68**
Huntland Clo. Rain —43Kd **89**
Huntley Av. Grav —58De **113**
Huntley Dri. N3 —23Cb **41**
Huntley St. WC1 —42Lb **82** (6C **192**)
Huntley Way. SW20 —68Wa **124**
Huntly Rd. SE25 —70Ub **127**
Hunton Bri. Hill. K Lan —5S **4**
Hunton St. E1 —43Wb **83**
Hunt Rd. Grav —2A **136**
Hunt Rd. S'hall —48Ca **77**
Hunt's Clo. SE3 —54Jc **107**
Hunt's Ct. WC2 —45Mb **82** (5E **198**)
Hunts La. E15 —40Ec **64**
Huntsman Rd. Ilf —23Wc **47**
Huntsmans Clo. Felt —63X **121**
Huntsmans Clo. Fet —96Fa **176**
Huntsmans Clo. Warl —91Yb **182**
*Huntsmans Ct. Cat —93Sb **181***
(off Coulsdon Rd.)
Huntsmans Dri. Upm —36Sd **70**
Huntsman St. SE17
—49Ub **83** (6H **207**)
Hunts Mead. Enf —13Zb **26**
Huntsmead Clo. Chst —67Pc **130**
Huntsmoor Rd. Eps —78Ta **143**
Huntspill St. SW17 —62Eb **125**
Hunts Slip Rd. SE21 —62Ub **127**
Hunt St. W11 —46Za **80**
Huntsworth M. NW1
—42Hb **81** (5F **191**)
Hunt Way. SE22 —60Wb **105**
Hurdwick Pl. NW1
*—40Lb **62** (1B **192**)*
(off Harrington Sq.)
Hurley Clo. W on T —75X **141**
Hurley Ct. W5 —44La **78**
Hurley Cres. SE16 —47Zb **84**
Hurley Rd. Gnfd —44Da **77**
Hurlfield. Dart —62Ld **133**
Hurlford. Wok —5D **188**
Hurlingham Bus. Pk. SW6
—55Cb **103**
Hurlingham Ct. SW6 —55Bb **103**
Hurlingham Gdns. SW6 —55Bb **103**
Hurlingham Rd. SW6 —54Bb **103**
Hurlingham Rd. Bexh —52Bd **109**
Hurlingham Sq. SW6 —55Cb **103**
Hurlock St. N5 —34Rb **63**
Hurlstone Rd. SE25 —71Ub **147**
Hurn Ct. Houn —54Z **99**
Hurn Ct. Rd. Houn —54Z **99**
Hurnford Clo. S Croy —82Ub **165**
Huron Rd. SW17 —61Jb **126**
Hurren Clo. SE3 —55Gc **107**
Hurry Clo. E15 —38Gc **65**
Hursley Rd. Chig —22Vc **47**
Hurst Av. E4 —21Cc **44**
Hurst Av. N6 —30Lb **42**
Hurstbourne. Clay —79Ha **142**
Hurstbourne Gdns. Bark —37Uc **66**
Hurstbourne Rd. SE23 —60Ac **106**
Hurst Clo. E4 —20Cc **26**
Hurst Clo. NW11 —30Db **41**
Hurst Clo. Brom —74Hc **149**
Hurst Clo. Chess —78Qa **143**
Hurst Clo. H'ley —96Sa **177**
Hurst Clo. N'holt —36Ba **57**
Hurst Clo. Wok —8F **188**
Hurst Ct. Sidc —61Wc **131**
Hurstcourt Rd. Sutt —75Db **145**
Hurstdene Av. Brom —74Hc **149**
Hurstdene Av. Stai —65K **119**
Hurstdene Gdns. N15 —31Ub **63**
Hurst Dri. Tad —98Wa **178**
Hurst Dri. Wal X —6Zb **12**
Hurstfield. Brom —71Jc **149**
Hurstfield Cres. Hay —42U **76**
Hurstfield Dri. Tap —4A **72**
Hurstfield Rd. W Mol —69Ca **121**
Hurst Gro. W on T —74V **140**
Hurstlands Clo. Horn —31Ld **69**
Hurst La. SE2 —50Zc **87**
Hurst La. E Mol —70Ea **122**
Hurst La. Egh —68C **118**
Hurst La. H'ley —96Sa **177**
Hurst La. Est. SE2 —50Zc **87**
Hurstleigh Gdns. Ilf —25Pc **46**
Hurst Lodge. Wey —79T **140**
Hurstmead Ct. Edgw —21Ra **39**
Hurst Pk. Av. Horn —35Nd **69**
Hurst Pl. Dart —58Ld **111**
Hurst Pl. N'wd —25R **36**
Hurst Rise. Barn —13Cb **23**
Hurst Rd. E17 —27Dc **44**
Hurst Rd. N21 —18Qb **24**
Hurst Rd. Buck H —18Mc **27**
Hurst Rd. Croy —77Tb **147**
Hurst Rd. Eps —83Ta **161**
Hurst Rd. Eri —53Ed **110**
Hurst Rd. H'ley & Tad —95Ta **177**
Hurst Rd. Sidc & Bex —61Wc **131**
Hurst Rd. Slou —3B **72**
Hurst Rd. W on T & W Mol
—71Y **141**
Hurst Springs. Bex —60Ad **109**
Hurst St. SE24 —58Rb **105**
Hurstview Grange. S Croy
—80Rb **147**
Hurst View Rd. S Croy —80Ub **147**
Hurstway. Pyr —86G **156**
Hurst Way. Sev —99Ld **187**
Hurst Way. S Croy —79Ub **147**
Hurstway Wlk. W11 —45Za **80**
Hurstwood Av. E18 —28Kc **45**
Hurstwood Av. Bex —60Ad **109**
Hurstwood Av. Eri & Bexh
—53Gd **110**
Hurstwood Av. Pil H —17Xd **32**
Hurstwood Ct. N12 —23Gb **41**
Hurstwood Ct. NW11 —28Bb **41**
Hurstwood Ct. Upm —32Sd **70**
Hurstwood Dri. Brom —69Pc **130**
Hurstwood Rd. NW11 —28Ab **40**
Hurtwood Rd. W on T —73Ba **141**
Hurworth Rd. Slou —8N **73**
Huskards. Upm —33Rd **69**
Huson Clo. NW3 —38Gb **61**
Husseywell Cres. Brom —74Jc **149**
Hutchingsons Rd. New Ad
—83Ec **166**
Hutchings St. E14 —47Cc **84**
Hutchings Wlk. NW11 —28Db **41**
Hutchins Clo. E15 —38Ec **64**
Hutchins Clo. Horn —34Nd **69**
Hutchinson Ct. Romf —28Zc **47**
Hutchinson Ter. Wemb —34Ma **59**
Hutson Ter. Purf —51Td **112**
Hutton Clo. Gnfd —36Fa **58**
Hutton Clo. Wfd G —23Kc **45**
*Hutton Ct. N4 —32Pb **62***
(off Victoria Rd.)
*Hutton Ct. N9 —17Yb **26***
(off Tramway Av.)
Hutton Dri. Hut —17Ee **33**
Hutton Gdns. Harr —24Ea **38**
Hutton Ga. Hut —17De **33**
Hutton Gro. N12 —22Db **41**
Hutton La. Harr —24Ea **38**
Hutton Rd. Shenf —17Be **33**
Hutton Row. Edgw —24Sa **39**
Hutton St. EC4 —44Rb **83** (3B **200**)
Hutton Village. Hut —17Fe **33**
Hutton Wlk. Harr —24Ea **38**
Huxbear St. SE4 —57Bc **106**
Huxley Clo. N'holt —39Aa **57**
Huxley Clo. Uxb —42M **75**
Huxley Dri. Romf —31Xc **67**
Huxley Gdns. NW10 —41Pa **79**
Huxley Pde. N18 —22Tb **43**
Huxley Pl. N13 —20Rb **25**
Huxley Rd. E10 —33Ec **64**
Huxley Rd. N18 —21Tb **43**
Huxley Rd. Well —55Vc **109**
Huxley Sayze. N18 —22Tb **43**
Huxley S. N18 —22Tb **43**
Huxley St. W10 —41Ab **80**
Hyacinth Clo. Hamp —65Ca **121**
Hyacinth Clo. Ilf —37Rc **66**
Hyacinth Dri. Uxb —38Nb **55**
Hyacinth Rd. SW15 —60Wa **102**
Hyburn Clo. Brick —2Ba **5**
Hycliffe Gdns. Chig —21Sc **46**
Hyde Av. Pot B —5Db **9**
Hyde Clo. E13 —40Jc **65**
Hyde Clo. Ashf —65U **120**
Hyde Clo. Barn —13Bb **23**
Hyde Ct. N20 —20Fb **23**
Hyde Cres. NW9 —29Ua **40**
Hyde Dri. St P —69Xc **131**
Hyde Est. Rd. NW9 —29Va **40**
Hydefield Clo. N21 —18Tb **25**
Hydefield Ct. N9 —19Ub **25**
Hyde Ind. Est. NW9 —29Va **40**
Hyde La. SW11 —53Gb **103**
Hyde La. Bov —1C **2**
Hyde La. Frog —1Fa **6**
Hyde La. Ock —92R **174**
Hyde Pk. Av. N21 —19Sb **25**
Hyde Pk. Clo. W2 —45Gb **81**
Hyde Pk. Corner. SW1 —47Jb **82**
Hyde Pk. Corner. W1
—47Jb **82** (1J **203**)
Hyde Pk. Cres. W2
—44Gb **81** (3D **196**)
Hyde Pk. Gdns. N21 —18Sb **25**
Hyde Pk. Gdns. W2
—45Fb **81** (4C **196**)
Hyde Pk. Gdns. M. W2
—45Fb **81** (4C **196**)
Hyde Pk. Ga. SW7
(in two parts) —47Eb **81** (2A **202**)
Hyde Pk. Ga. M. SW7
—47Eb **81** (2A **202**)
Hyde Pk. Pl. W2 —45Gb **81** (4E **196**)
Hyde Pk. Sq. W2
—44Gb **81** (3D **196**)
Hyde Pk. Sq. M. W2
*—44Gb **81** (3D **196**)*
(off Southwick Pl.)
Hyde Pk. St. W2
—44Gb **81** (3D **196**)
Hyde Pk. Towers. W2
*—45Eb **81** (5A **196**)*
(off Porchester Ter.)
Hyde Rd. N1 —39Tb **63** (1G **195**)
Hyde Rd. Bexh —54Bd **109**
Hyde Rd. Rich —57Pa **101**
Hyde Rd. S Croy —85Ub **165**
Hyde Rd. Wat —12W **18**
Hyder Rd. Grays —8E **92**
Hydeside Gdns. N9 —19Vb **25**
Hydes Pl. N1 —38Rb **63**
Hyde St. SE8 —51Cc **106**
Hyde Ter. Ashf —65U **120**
Hyde, The. NW9 —29Va **40**
Hydethorpe Av. N9 —19Vb **25**
Hydethorpe Rd. SW12 —60Lb **104**
Hyde Vale. SE10 —52Ec **106**
Hyde Wlk. Mord —73Cb **145**
Hyde Way. N9 —19Vb **25**
Hyde Way. Hay —49V **76**
Hyland Clo. Horn —31Kd **69**
Hylands Clo. Eps —87Sa **161**
Hylands M. Eps —87Sa **161**
Hylands Rd. E17 —26Fc **45**
Hylands Rd. Eps —87Sa **161**
Hyland Way. Horn —31Kd **69**
Hylle Clo. Wind —3C **94**
Hylton St. SE18 —49Vc **87**
Hyndewood. SE23 —62Zb **128**
*Hyndman Ho. Dag —34Cd **68***
(off Kershaw Rd.)
Hyndman St. SE15 —51Xb **105**
Hynton Rd. Dag —33Yc **67**
Hyperion Ho. SW2 —58Pb **104**
Hyperion Pl. Eps —81Ta **161**
Hyrstdene. S Croy —78Rb **147**
Hyson Rd. SE16 —50Xb **83**
Hythe Av. Bexh —52Ad **109**
Hythe Clo. N18 —21Wb **43**
Hythe Clo. St M —70Yc **131**
Hythe End Rd. Wray —61B **118**
Hythe Field Av. Egh —65F **118**
Hythe Pk. Rd. Egh —64E **118**
Hythe Rd. NW10 —41Va **80**
Hythe Rd. Stai —64F **118**
Hythe Rd. T Hth —68Tb **127**
Hythe Rd. Ind. Est. NW10 —41Wa **80**
Hythe St. Dart —58Nd **111**
(in two parts)
Hythe, The. Stai —64G **118**
Hyver Hill. NW7 —16Ta **21**

Ian Bowater Ct. N1
*(off East Rd.) —41Tb **83** (3G **195**)*
Ian Sq. Enf —11Zb **26**
Ibbetson Path. Lou —13Rc **28**
Ibbotson Av. E16 —44Hc **85**
Ibbott St. E1 —42Yb **84**
Iberia Ho. N19 —31Mb **62**
Iberian Av. Wall —77Mb **146**
Ibis La. W4 —53Sa **101**
Ibis Way. Hay —44Z **77**
Ibscott Clo. Dag —37Ed **68**
Ibsley Gdns. SW15 —60Wa **102**
Ibsley Way. Barn —14Gb **23**
Iceland Rd. E3 —39Cc **64**
Ickburgh Est. E5 —33Xb **63**
Ickburgh Rd. E5 —34Xb **63**
Ickenham Clo. Ruis —33T **56**
Ickenham Grn. Uxb —32R **56**
Ickenham Rd. Ruis —33S **56**
Ickleton Rd. SE9 —63Nc **130**
Icklingham Rd. Cob —84Y **159**
Icknield Dri. Ilf —29Rc **46**
Ickworth Pk. Rd. E17 —28Ac **44**
Ida Rd. N15 —28Tb **43**
Ida St. E14 —44Ec **84**
(in two parts)
Ide Hill Rd. Sev —100Ad **185**
Iden Clo. Brom —69Gc **129**
Idlecombe Rd. SW17 —65Jb **126**
Idleigh Ct. Rd. Meop —75De **155**
Idmiston Rd. E15 —35Hc **65**
Idmiston Rd. SE27 —62Sb **127**
Idmiston Rd. Wor Pk —73Va **144**
Idmiston Sq. Wor Pk —73Va **144**
Idol La. EC3 —45Ub **83** (5H **201**)
Idonia St. SE8 —52Cc **106**
Iffley Clo. Uxb —38M **55**
Iffley Rd. W6 —48Xa **80**
Ifield Rd. SW10 —51Db **103**
Ifield Rd. Meop —78Fe **155**
Ifield Way. Grav —5F **136**
*Ightham Ho. Beck —66Bc **128***
(off Bethersden Clo.)
Ightham Rd. Eri —52Cd **110**
Ikea Way. Croy —74Pb **146**
Ikona Ct. Wey —78S **140**
Ilbert St. W10 —41Za **80**
Ilchester Gdns. W2 —45Db **81**
Ilchester Pl. W14 —48Bb **81**
Ilchester Rd. Dag —36Xc **67**
Ildersey Gro. SE21 —61Tb **127**
Ilderton Rd. SE16 & SE15
—50Yb **84**
Ilex Clo. Egh —6M **117**
Ilex Clo. Sun —68Y **121**
Ilex Ho. Wdhm —82J **157**
Ilex Rd. NW10 —37Va **60**
Ilex Way. SW16 —64Qb **126**
Ilford Hill. Ilf —34Qc **66**
*Ilford Ho. N1 —37Tb **63***
(off Dove Rd.)
Ilford La. Ilf —34Rc **66**
Ilfracombe Cres. Horn —35Ld **69**
Ilfracombe Gdns. Romf —31Xc **67**
Ilfracombe Rd. Brom —62Hc **129**
Iliffe St. SE17 —50Rb **83** (7C **206**)
*Iliffe Yd. SE17 —50Rb **83** (7C **206**)*
(off Crampton St.)
*Ilkeston Ct. E5 —35Zb **64***
(off Overbury St.)
Ilkley Clo. SE19 —65Tb **127**
Ilkley Rd. E16 —43Lc **85**
Ilkley Rd. Wat —22Z **37**
Illiffe St. SE17 —50Rb **83**
Illingworth. Wind —5C **94**
Illingworth Clo. Mitc —69Fb **125**
Illingworth Way. Enf —15Ub **25**
Ilmington Rd. Harr —30Ma **39**
Ilminster Gdns. SW11 —56Gb **103**
Imani Mans. SW11 —54Fb **103**
Imber Clo. N14 —17Lb **24**
Imber Clo. Esh —74Fa **142**
Imber Ct. Trading Est. E Mol
—72Fa **142**
Imber Cross. Th Dit —72Ha **142**
Imber Gro. Esh —73Fa **142**
Imber Pk. Rd. Esh —74Fa **142**
Imber St. N1 —39Tb **63** (1F **195**)
Impact Ct. SE20 —68Xb **127**
Imperial Av. N16 —35Ub **63**
Imperial Bus. Est. Grav —8B **114**
Imperial Clo. Harr —30Ca **37**
Imperial College Rd. SW7
—48Fb **81** (4B **202**)
Imperial Ct. N20 —20Eb **23**
Imperial Ct. S Harr —31Ca **57**
Imperial Ct. Wind —5E **94**
Imperial Dri. Grav —4H **137**
Imperial Dri. Harr —31Ca **57**
Imperial Gdns. Mitc —67Kb **126**
Imperial M. E6 —40Mc **65**
Imperial Pl. Borwd —13Ra **21**
Imperial Rd. N22 —25Nb **42**
Imperial Rd. SW6 —53Db **103**
Imperial Rd. Felt —59U **98**
Imperial Rd. Wind —5E **94**
Imperial Sq. SW6 —53Db **103**
Imperial St. E3 —41Ec **84**
Imperial Way. Chst —63Sc **130**
Imperial Way. Croy —79Pb **146**
Imperial Way. Harr —30Na **39**
Imperial Way. Wat —11Y **19**
Inca Dri. SE9 —59Rc **108**
Ince Rd. W on T —79U **140**
Inchmery Rd. SE6 —61Dc **128**
Inchwood. Croy —77Dc **148**
Independent Pl. E8 —36Vb **63**
Independents Rd. SE3 —55Hc **107**
Inderwick Rd. N8 —29Pb **42**
Indescon Ct. E14 —47Cc **84**
India Rd. Slou —7M **73**
India St. EC3 —44Vb **83** (3K **201**)
India Way. W12 —45Xa **80**
Indus Rd. SE7 —52Lc **107**
Industry Ter. SW9 —55Qb **104**
*Infirmary Ct. SW3 —51Hb **103***
(off West Rd.)
Ingal Rd. E13 —42Jc **85**
Ingate Pl. SW8 —53Kb **104**
Ingatestone Rd. E12 —32Lc **65**
Ingatestone Rd. SE25 —70Xb **127**
Ingatestone Rd. Wfd G —24Kc **45**
Ingelow Rd. SW8 —54Kb **104**
Ingels Mead. Epp —1Vc **15**
Ingersoll Rd. W12 —46Xa **80**
Ingersoll Rd. Enf —10Yb **12**
Ingestre Pl. W1 —44Lb **82** (3C **198**)
Ingestre Rd. E7 —35Jc **65**
Ingestre Rd. NW5 —35Kb **62**
Ingham Clo. SE11 —49Pb **82**
Ingham Clo. S Croy —81Zb **166**
Ingham Rd. NW6 —35Cb **61**
Ingham Rd. S Croy —81Yb **166**
Inglebert St. EC1 —41Qb **82** (3K **193**)
Ingleboro Dri. Purl —85Tb **165**
Ingleborough Ct. N17 —27Vb **43**
Ingleborough St. SW9 —54Qb **104**
Ingleby Dri. Harr —34Fa **58**
Ingleby Gdns. Chig —20Xc **29**
Ingleby Rd. N7 —34Nb **62**
Ingleby Rd. Dag —37Dd **68**
Ingleby Rd. Grays —8D **92**
Ingleby Rd. Ilf —32Rc **66**
Ingleby Way. Chst —64Qc **130**
Ingleby Way. Wall —81Mb **164**
Ingle Clo. Pinn —27Aa **37**
Ingledew Rd. SE18 —50Tc **86**
Inglefield. Pot B —2Cb **9**
Ingleglen. Farn C —6F **52**
Ingleglen. Horn —31Pd **69**
Inglehurst. New Haw —82K **157**
Inglehurst Gdns. Ilf —29Pc **46**
Inglemere Rd. SE23 —62Zb **128**
Inglemere Rd. Mitc —66Hb **125**
Inglenorth Ct. Swan —72Ed **152**
Inglesham Wlk. E9 —37Bc **64**
Ingleside. Coln —53H **97**
Ingleside Clo. Beck —66Cc **128**
Ingleside Gro. SE3 —51Hc **107**
Inglethorpe St. SW6 —53Za **102**
Ingleton Av. Well —57Wc **109**
Ingleton Rd. N18 —23Wb **43**
Ingleton Rd. Cars —81Gb **163**
Ingleton St. SW9 —54Qb **104**
Ingleway. N12 —23Fb **41**
Inglewood. Cher —76H **139**
Inglewood. Croy —81Ac **166**
Inglewood. Swan —68Gd **132**
Inglewood. Wok —6E **188**
Inglewood Clo. E14 —49Cc **84**
Inglewood Clo. Horn —35Md **69**
Inglewood Clo. Ilf —23Vc **47**
Inglewood Copse. Brom —68Nc **130**
Inglewood Rd. NW6 —36Cb **61**
Inglewood Rd. Bexh —56Fd **110**
Inglis Rd. W5 —45Pa **79**
Inglis Rd. Croy —74Vb **147**
Inglis St. SE5 —53Rb **105**
Ingoldsby Rd. Grav —10G **114**
Ingram Av. NW11 —31Eb **61**
Ingram Clo. SE11
—49Pb **82** (5J **205**)
Ingram Clo. Stan —22La **38**
Ingram Rd. N2 —28Gb **41**
Ingram Rd. Dart —60Nd **111**
Ingram Rd. Grays —49Ee **91**
Ingram Rd. T Hth —67Sb **127**
Ingrams Clo. W on T —78Y **141**
Ingram Way. Gnfd —39Fa **58**
Ingrave Rd. Brtwd —19Zd **33**
Ingrave Rd. Romf —28Gd **49**
Ingrave St. SW11 —55Fb **103**
Ingrebourne Gdns. Upm —32Sd **70**
Ingrebourne Rd. Rain —42Kd **89**
Ingresbourne Ct. E4 —20Dc **26**
Ingress Gdns. Grnh —57Zd **113**
Ingress Pk. Grnh —57Yd **112**
Ingress St. W4 —50Ua **80**
Ingress Ter. Grnh —56Xd **112**
Ingress Ter. S'fleet —63Ae **135**
Ingreway. Romf —23Rd **49**
Inigo Jones Rd. SE7 —52Nc **108**
*Inigo Pl. WC2 —45Nb **82** (4G **199**)*
(off Bedford St.)
Inishowen. SE3 —55Gc **107**
Inkerman Rd. NW5 —37Kb **62**
Inkerman Rd. Eton W —9D **72**
Inkerman Rd. Knap —6B **188**
*Inkerman Ter. W8 —48Cb **81***
(off Allen St.)
Inkerman Way. Wok —6B **188**
Inks Grn. E4 —22Dc **44**
Inman Rd. NW10 —39Ua **60**
Inman Rd. SW18 —59Eb **103**
Inmans Row. Wfd G —21Jc **45**
Inner Circ. NW1 —41Jb **82** (4H **191**)
Inner Pk. Rd. SW19 —60Za **102**
Inner Ring E. H'row A —55R **98**
Inner Ring W. Houn —55Q **98**
Inner Staithe. W4 —53Sa **101**
Inner Temple La. EC4
—44Qb **82** (3K **199**)
Innes Clo. SW20 —68Ab **124**
Innes Gdns. SW15 —58Xa **102**
*Innis Ho. SE17 —50Ub **83** (7H **207**)*
(off East St.)
Inniskilling Rd. E13 —40Lc **65**
Innis Yd. Croy —76Sb **147**
Inskip Clo. E10 —33Dc **64**
Inskip Dri. Horn —32Nd **69**
Inskip Rd. Dag —32Zc **67**
Institute Pl. E8 —36Xb **63**
Institute Rd. Coop —1Zc **15**
Instone Clo. Wall —80Nb **146**
Instone Rd. Dart —59Md **111**
Insurance St. WC1
—41Qb **82** (4K **193**)
Integer Gdns. E11 —31Fc **65**
*Interface Ho. Houn —55Ca **99***
(off Staines Rd.)
International Av. Houn —50Y **77**
International Trading Est. S'hall
—48X **77**
Inverary Pl. SE18 —51Tc **108**
Inver Clo. E5 —33Yb **64**
Inverclyde Gdns. Romf —28Yc **47**
(in two parts)
Inver Ct. W2 —44Db **81**
Inveresk Gdns. Wor Pk —76Va **144**
Inverforth Clo. NW3 —33Eb **61**
Inverforth Rd. N11 —22Kb **42**
Inverine Rd. SE7 —50Kc **85**
Invermore Pl. SE18 —49Sc **86**
Inverness Av. Enf —11Ub **25**
Inverness Dri. Ilf —23Uc **46**
Inverness Gdns. W8 —46Db **81**
Inverness M. W2 —45Db **81**
Inverness Pl. W2 —45Db **81**
Inverness Rd. N18 —22Xb **43**
Inverness Rd. Houn —56Ba **99**
Inverness Rd. S'hall —49Aa **77**
Inverness Rd. Wor Pk —74Za **144**
Inverness St. NW1 —39Kb **62**
Inverness Ter. W2 —44Db **81**
Inverton Rd. SE15 —56Zb **106**
Invicta Clo. Chst —64Qc **130**
Invicta Gro. N'holt —41Ba **77**
Invicta Pde. Sidc —63Xc **131**
Invicta Rd. SE3 —52Jc **107**
Invicta Rd. Dart —58Rd **111**
Inville Rd. SE17 —50Tb **83** (7G **207**)
Inville Wlk. SE17 —50Tb **83**
Inwen Ct. SE8 —50Ac **84**
Inwood Av. Coul —92Db **180**
Inwood Av. Houn —55Ea **100**
Inwood Bus. Cen. Houn —56Da **99**
Inwood Clo. Croy —75Ac **148**
Inwood Ct. W on T —75Y **141**
Inwood Rd. Houn —56Da **99**
Inworth St. SW11 —54Gb **103**
*Inworth Wlk. N1 —39Sb **63***
(off Popham St.)
Iona Clo. SE6 —59Cc **106**

Iona Cres.—Juliet Ho.

Iona Cres. Slou —4C 72
Ion Sq. E2 —40Wb 63
Ipsden Bldgs. SE1 —47Qb 82 (1A 206)
(off Windmill Wlk.)
Ipswich Rd. SW17 —65Jb 126
Ipswich Rd. Slou —4D 72
Ireland Pl. N22 —24Nb 42
Ireland Yd. EC4 —44Rb 83 (3C 200)
Irene Rd. SW6 —53Cb 103
Irene Rd. Orp —73Vc 151
Irene Rd. Stoke D —86Da 159
Ireton Av. W on T —75U 140
Ireton Ho. SW9 —54Qb 104
Ireton Pl. Grays —49Ce 91
Ireton Rd. N19 —33Mb 62
Ireton St. E3 —42Cc 84
Iris Av. Bex —58Ad 109
Iris Clo. Croy —74Zb 148
Iris Clo. Pil H —15Xd 32
Iris Clo. Surb —73Pa 143
Iris Cres. Bexh —51Bd 109
Iris Path. Romf —24Ld 49
Iris Rd. Eps —78Ra 143
Iris Way. E4 —23Bc 44
Irkdale Av. Enf —11Vb 25
Iron Bri. Clo. NW10 —36Ua 60
Ironbridge Clo. S'hall —46Ea 78
Iron Bri. Rd. W Dray & Uxb —46Q 76
Iron Mill La. Dart —56Gd 110
Iron Mill Pl. SW18 —58Db 103
Iron Mill Pl. Dart —56Hd 110
Iron Mill Rd. SW18 —58Db 103
Ironmonger La. EC2 —44Sb 83 (3E 200)
Ironmonger Row. EC1 —41Sb 83 (4E 194)
Ironmongers Pl. E14 —49Cc 84
Ironside Clo. SE16 —47Zb 84
Ironside Ho. E9 —35Ac 64
Irons Way. Romf —24Ed 48
Irvine Av. Harr —27Ja 38
Irvine Clo. N20 —19Gb 23
Irvine Gdns. S Ock —44Vd 90
Irvine Ho. N7 —37Pb 62
(off Caledonian Rd.)
Irvine Pl. Vir W —71A 138
Irvine Way. Orp —73Vc 151
Irving Av. N'holt —39Z 57
Irving Gro. SW9 —54Pb 104
Irving Ho. SE17 —50Rb 83
(off Doddington Gro.)
Irving Rd. W14 —48Za 80
Irving St. WC2 —45Mb 82 (5E 198)
Irving Wlk. Swans —59Ae 113
Irving Way. NW9 —30Va 40
Irving Way. Swan —68Fd 132
Irwell Est. SE16 —48Yb 84
Irwin Av. SE18 —52Uc 108
Irwin Gdns. NW10 —39Xa 60
Isabella Clo. N14 —17Lb 24
Isabella Ct. Rich —58Pa 101
Isabella Dri. Orp —77Sc 150
Isabella Ho. SE11 —50Rb 83 (7B 206)
(off Othello Clo.)
Isabella Rd. E9 —36Yb 64
Isabella St. SE1 —46Rb 83 (7B 200)
Isabelle Clo. Wal X —1Sb 11
Isabel St. SW9 —53Pb 104
Isambard Clo. Uxb —42M 75
Isambard M. E14 —48Ec 84
Isambard Pl. SE16 —46Yb 84
Isard Ho. Hayes —74Kc 149
Isbell Gdns. Romf —24Gd 48
Isel Way. SE22 —57Ub 105
Isham Rd. SW16 —68Nb 126
Isis Clo. SW15 —56Ya 102
Isis Clo. Ruis —30S 36
Isis Ct. W4 —52Ra 101
Isis Dri. Upm —30Ud 50
Isis Ho. N18 —23Vb 43
Isis St. SW18 —61Eb 125
Island Clo. Stai —63G 118
Island Farm Av. W Mol —71Ba 141
Island Farm Rd. W Mol —71Ba 141
Island Rd. Mitc —66Hb 125
Island Row. E14 —44Bc 84
Island, The. Th Dit —72Ja 142
Island, The. W Dray —52L 97
Island, The. Wray —62C 118
Isla Rd. SE18 —51Sc 108
Islay Gdns. Houn —57Z 99
Islay Wlk. N1 —37Sb 63
Isledon Rd. N7 —34Qb 62
Islehurst Clo. Chst —67Qc 130
Isleworth Bus. Complex. Iswth —54Ha 100
Isleworth Promenade. Twic —56Ka 100
Islington Grn. N1 —39Rb 63 (1B 194)
Islington High St. N1 —40Qb 62 (2A 194)
Islington Pk. N1 —38Qb 62
Islington Pk. M. N1 —38Rb 63
Islip Gdns. Edgw —24Ta 39
Islip Gdns. N'holt —38Aa 57
Islip Mnr. Rd. N'holt —38Aa 57
Islip St. NW5 —36Lb 62
Ismailia Rd. E7 —38Kc 65
Ismay Ct. Slou —4J 73
Isobel Ho. Harr —29Ha 38
Isom Clo. E13 —41Kc 85
Isopad Ho. Borwd —13Ra 21
Istead Rise. Grav —6B 136
Itaska Cotts. Bush —18Ga 20
Ivanhoe Clo. Uxb —43M 75
Ivanhoe Dri. Harr —27Ja 38
Ivanhoe Rd. SE5 —55Vb 105
Ivanhoe Rd. Houn —55Z 99
Ivatt Pl. W14 —50Bb 81
Ivatt Way. N17 —27Sb 43
Iveagh Av. NW10 —40Qa 59
Iveagh Clo. E9 —39Zb 64
Iveagh Clo. NW10 —40Qa 59
Iveagh Clo. N'wd —25R 36
Iveagh Ct. Beck —69Ec 128
Iveagh Ho. SW9 —54Rb 105
Iveagh Rd. Knap —6C 188
Iveagh Ter. NW10 —40Qa 59
(off Iveagh Av.)
Ivedon Rd. Well —54Yc 109
Ive Farm Clo. E10 —33Cc 64
Ive Farm La. E10 —33Cc 64
Iveley Rd. SW4 —54Lb 104
Iverdale Clo. Iver —45E 74
Ivere Dri. Barn —16Db 23
Iverhurst Clo. Bexh —59Zc 109
Iver La. Iver & Uxb —44J 75
Iverna Gdns. W8 —48Cb 81
Iverna Gdns. Felt —57T 98
Iverson Rd. NW6 —37Bb 61
Ivers Way. New Ad —80Dc 148
Ives Gdns. Romf —28Hd 48
Ives Rd. E16 —43Gc 85
Ives Rd. Slou —48B 74
Ives St. SW3 —49Gb 81 (5E 202)
Ivestor Ter. SE23 —59Yb 106
Ivimey St. E2 —41Wb 83
Ivinghoe Clo. Enf —11Ub 25
Ivinghoe Ho. N7 —36Mb 62
Ivinghoe Rd. Bush —17Fa 20
Ivinghoe Rd. Dag —36Xc 67
Ivinghoe Rd. Rick —17J 17
Ivor Ct. N8 —30Nb 42
Ivor Gro. SE9 —60Rc 108
Ivor Pl. NW1 —42Hb 81 (6F 191)
Ivor Rd. Pil H —16Xd 32
Ivor St. NW1 —38Lb 62
Ivorydown. Brom —63Jc 129
Ivory Ho. E1 —46Vb 83
Ivory Sq. SW11 —55Eb 103
Ivy Bower Clo. Grnh —57Xd 112
Ivybridge Clo. Twic —59Ja 100
Ivybridge Clo. Uxb —41N 75
Ivybridge Ct. Chst —67Qc 130
(off Old Hill)
Ivybridge La. WC2 —45Nb 82 (5G 199)
Ivy Chimneys Rd. Epp —4Uc 14
Ivychurch Clo. SE20 —66Yb 128
Ivychurch La. SE17 —50Vb 83
Ivy Clo. Dart —58Qd 111
Ivy Clo. Grav —2E 136
Ivy Clo. Harr —35Ba 57
Ivy Clo. Pinn —31Y 57
Ivy Clo. Sun —68Y 121
Ivy Cotts. E14 —45Dc 84
Ivy Cres. W4 —49Sa 79
Ivy Cres. Slou —5D 72
Ivydale Rd. SE15 —55Zb 106
Ivydale Rd. Cars —75Hb 145
Ivyday Gro. SW16 —62Pb 126
Ivydene. W Mol —71Ba 141
Ivydene Clo. Sutt —77Eb 145
Ivy Gdns. N8 —30Nb 42
Ivy Gdns. Mitc —69Mb 126
Ivy Ho. Flats. Wat —16Z 19
Ivy Ho. La. Sev —90Fd 170
Ivyhouse Rd. Dag —37Zc 67
Ivyhouse Rd. Uxb —34R 56
Ivy La. Houn —56Ba 99
Ivy La. Knock —88Ad 169
Ivy La. Wok —90D 156
Ivy Lodge La. H Wood —25Rd 49
Ivymount Rd. SE27 —62Qb 126
Ivy Rd. E16 —44Jc 85
Ivy Rd. E17 —30Cc 44
Ivy Rd. N14 —17Lb 24
Ivy Rd. NW2 —35Ya 60
Ivy Rd. SE4 —56Bc 106
Ivy Rd. SW17 —64Gb 125
Ivy Rd. Houn —56Da 99
Ivy Rd. Surb —74Qa 143
Ivy St. N1 —40Ub 63 (1H 195)
Ivy Vs. Grnh —57Wd 112
Ivy Wlk. Dag —37Ad 67
Ivy Wlk. N'wd —25U 36
Ixworth Pl. SW3 —50Gb 81 (7D 202)
Izane Rd. Bexh —56Bd 109

Jackass La. Kes —78Kc 149
Jack Barnett Way. N22 —26Pb 42
Jack Clow Rd. E15 —40Gc 65
Jack Cook Ho. Bark —38Rc 66
Jack Cornwell St. E12 —35Qc 66
Jackets La. Hare & N'wd —24Q 36
Jacketts Field. Abb L —3V 4
Jack Evans Ct. S Ock —44Wd 90
Jacklin Grn. Wfd G —21Jc 45
Jackman M. NW10 —34Ua 60
Jackmans La. Wok —7D 188
Jackman St. E8 —39Xb 63
Jacks La. Hare —25J 35
Jackson Clo. Eps —86Ta 161
Jackson Clo. Uxb —38N 55
Jackson Rd. N7 —35Pb 62
Jackson Rd. Bark —39Tc 66
Jackson Rd. Barn —16Gb 23
Jackson Rd. Brom —75Pc 150
Jackson Rd. Uxb —38N 55
Jacksons La. N6 —31Jb 62
Jacksons Pl. Croy —74Ub 147
Jackson St. SE18 —51Qc 108
Jackson Way. S'hall —47Da 77
Jack Walker Ct. N5 —35Rb 63
Jacob Clo. Wind —3C 94
Jacob Ho. Eri —47Zc 87
Jacobin Lodge. N7 —36Nb 62
Jacobs Av. H Wood —26Nd 49
Jacobs Ho. E13 —41Lc 85
(off New City Rd.)
Jacob's Ladder. Warl —91Wb 181
Jacob St. SE1 —47Wb 83
Jacob's Well M. W1 —44Jb 82 (2J 197)
Jacob's Well Rd. Guild —100A 172
Jacqueline Clo. N'holt —39Aa 57
Jade Clo. E16 —44Mc 85
Jade Clo. Dag —32Yc 67
Jade Ho. Rain —42Jd 88
Jaffe Rd. Ilf —32Tc 66
Jaffray Pl. SE27 —63Rb 127
Jaffray Rd. Brom —70Mc 129
Jaggard Way. SW12 —59Hb 103
Jagger Clo. Dart —59Sd 112
Jago Clo. SE18 —51Sc 108
Jago Wlk. SE5 —52Tb 105
Jail La. Big H —87Mc 167
Jamaica Rd. SE1 & SE16 —47Vb 83 (2K 207)
Jamaica Rd. T Hth —72Rb 147
Jamaica St. E1 —44Yb 84
James Anderson Ct. E2 —40Ub 63 (1J 195)
(off Kingsland Rd.)
James Av. NW2 —36Ya 60
James Av. Dag —32Bd 67
James Bedford Clo. Pinn —26Y 37
James Boswell Clo. SW16 —63Pb 126
James Clo. E13 —40Jc 65
James Clo. NW11 —30Ab 40
James Clo. Bush —15Aa 19
James Clo. Romf —29Jd 48
James Collins Clo. W9 —42Bb 81
James Ct. NW9 —26Ua 40
James Ct. N'wd —25V 36
James Dudson Ct. NW10 —38Sa 59
James Gdns. N22 —24Rb 43
James Joyce Wlk. SE24 —56Rb 105
James La. E10 & E11 —31Ec 64
James Martin Clo. Den —30J 35
Jameson Ho. SE11 —50Pb 82 (7H 205)
(off Glasshouse Wlk.)
Jameson Lodge. N6 —30Lb 42
Jameson St. W8 —46Cb 81
James Pl. N17 —25Vb 43
James Rd. Dart —59Jd 110
James's Cotts. Rich —52Qa 101
James St. W1 —44Jb 82 (2J 197)
James St. WC2 —45Nb 82 (3G 199)
James St. Bark —38Sc 66
James St. Enf —15Vb 25
James St. Epp —1Wc 15
James St. Houn —55Fa 100
James St. Wind —3H 95
Jamestown Rd. NW1 —39Kb 62
James Yd. E4 —23Fc 45
Jamnagar Clo. Stai —65H 119
Jane St. E1 —44Xb 83
Janet St. E14 —48Cc 84
Janeway Pl. SE16 —47Xb 83
Janeway St. SE16 —47Wb 83
Janice M. Ilf —33Rc 66
Janmead. Hut —17De 33
Janoway Hill La. Wok —6F 188
Jansen Wlk. SW11 —55Fb 103
Janson Clo. E15 —36Gc 65
Janson Clo. NW10 —34Ta 59
Janson Rd. E15 —36Gc 65
Jansons Rd. N15 —27Ub 43
Japan Cres. N4 —31Pb 62
Japan Rd. Romf —30Zc 47
Japonica Clo. Wok —6F 188
Jardine Rd. E1 —45Zb 84
Jarrah Cotts. Purf —51Td 112
Jarrett Clo. SW2 —60Rb 105
Jarrow Clo. Mord —71Db 145
Jarrow Rd. N17 —28Xb 43
Jarrow Rd. SE16 —49Yb 84
Jarrow Rd. Romf —30Yc 47
Jarrow Way. E9 —35Bc 64
Jarvis Clo. Barn —15Za 22
Jarvis Rd. SE22 —56Ub 105
Jarvis Rd. S Croy —79Tb 147
Jarvis Way. H Wood —26Nd 49
Jasmin Clo. N'wd —25V 36
Jasmine Clo. Ilf —36Rc 66
Jasmine Clo. Orp —75Rc 150
Jasmine Clo. Wok —4C 188
Jasmine Ct. SW19 —64Cb 125
Jasmine Gdns. Croy —76Dc 148
Jasmine Gdns. Harr —33Ca 57
Jasmine Gro. SE20 —67Xb 127
Jasmine Ter. W Dray —47Q 76
Jasmine Way. E Mol —70Ga 122
Jasmin Rd. Eps —78Ra 143
Jason Clo. Brtwd —21Vd 50
Jason Clo. Ors —5F 92
Jason Clo. Wey —78S 140
Jason Ct. W1 —44Jb 82 (2J 197)
(off Wigmore St.)
Jason Wlk. SE9 —63Qc 130
Jasper Clo. Enf —10Yb 12
Jasper Pas. SE19 —65Vb 127
Jasper Rd. E16 —44Mc 85
Jasper Rd. SE19 —64Vb 127
Jasper Wlk. N1 —41Tb 83 (3F 195)
Javelin Way. N'holt —41Z 77
Jay Av. Add —76N 139
Jaycroft. Enf —11Qb 24
Jay Gdns. Chst —63Pc 130
Jay M. SW7 —47Eb 81 (2A 202)
Jebb Av. SW2 —58Nb 104
Jebb St. E3 —40Cc 64
Jedburgh Rd. E13 —41Lc 85
Jedburgh St. SW11 —56Jb 104
Jeddo Rd. W12 —47Va 80
Jefferson Clo. W13 —48Ka 78
Jefferson Clo. Ilf —29Rc 46
Jefferson Clo. Slou —49C 74
Jeffery. Sidc —64Xc 131
Jeffrey Row. SE12 —57Kc 107
Jeffrey's Pl. NW1 —38Lb 62
Jeffreys Rd. SW4 —54Nb 104
Jeffreys Rd. Enf —14Ac 26
Jeffrey's St. NW1 —38Kb 62
Jeffreys Wlk. SW4 —54Nb 104
Jeffries Way. Stanf —1P 93
Jeffs Clo. Hamp —65Da 121
Jeffs Rd. Sutt —77Bb 145
Jegrove Ct. EC1 —43Qb 82 (1A 200)
(off Hatton Gdn.)
Jeken Rd. SE9 —56Lc 107
Jelf Rd. SW2 —57Qb 104
Jellicoe Av. Grav —2E 136
Jellicoe Av. W. Grav —2E 136
Jellicoe Clo. Slou —7F 72
Jellicoe Gdns. Stan —23Ha 38
(in two parts)
Jellicoe Rd. E13 —42Jc 85
Jellicoe Rd. N17 —24Tb 43
Jem Peterson Ct. Harr —35Ga 58
Jengar Clo. Sutt —77Db 145
Jenkins Av. Brick —2Aa 5
Jenkins La. Bark —40Sc 66
Jenkins Rd. E13 —42Kc 85
Jenner Av. W3 —43Ta 79
Jenner Clo. W3 —43Ta 79
Jenner Pl. SW13 —51Xa 102
Jenner Rd. N16 —34Vb 63
Jennery La. Burn —1A 72
Jennett Rd. Croy —76Qb 146
Jennifer Ho. SE11 —49Qb 82 (6A 206)
(off Reedworth St.)
Jennifer Rd. Brom —62Hc 129
Jenningham Dri. Grays —46Ce 91
Jennings Clo. Wdhm —81L 157
Jennings Rd. SE22 —58Vb 105
Jennings Way. Barn —13Ya 22
Jenningtree Rd. Eri —52Kd 111
Jenningtree Way. Belv —47Ed 88
Jenny Hammond Clo. E11 —34Hc 65
Jenny Path. Romf —24Md 49
Jenson Way. SE19 —66Vb 127
Jenton Av. Bexh —54Ad 109
Jephson Ct. SW4 —54Nb 104
Jephson Ho. SE17 —51Rb 105
(off Doddington Gro.)
Jephson Rd. E7 —38Lc 65
Jephson St. SE5 —53Tb 105
Jeppos La. Mitc —70Hb 125
Jepson Ho. SW6 —53Db 103
(off Pearscroft Rd.)
Jeptha Rd. SW18 —58Cb 103
Jerdan Pl. SW6 —52Cb 103
Jeremiah St. E14 —44Dc 84
Jeremy's Grn. N18 —21Xb 43
Jermyn St. SW1 —46Lb 82 (6B 198)
(in two parts)
Jerningham Av. Ilf —26Rc 46
Jerningham Rd. SE14 —54Ac 106
Jerome Cres. NW8 —42Gb 81 (5D 190)
Jerome St. E1 —43Vb 83 (7K 195)
(off Commercial St.)
Jerome Tower. W3 —48Ra 79
Jerrard St. SE13 —55Dc 106
Jerrold St. N1 —40Ub 63 (2J 195)
Jersey Av. Stan —26Ka 38
Jersey Clo. Cher —76H 139
Jersey Dri. Orp —72Tc 150
Jersey Ho. N1 —37Sb 63
Jersey Ho. Enf —10Zb 12
(off Eastfield Rd.)
Jersey Rd. E11 —32Fc 65
Jersey Rd. E16 —44Lc 85
Jersey Rd. SW17 —65Kb 126
Jersey Rd. W7 —47Ja 78
Jersey Rd. Houn & Iswth —52Da 99
Jersey Rd. Ilf —35Rc 66
Jersey Rd. Rain —38Jd 68
Jersy St. E2 —41Xb 83
Jerusalem Pas. EC1 —42Rb 83 (6B 194)
Jervis Av. Enf —7Ac 12
Jervis Ct. W1 —44Kb 82 (3A 198)
(off Princes St.)
Jervis Ct. Dag —37Dd 68
Jerviston Gdns. SW16 —65Qb 126
Jeskyns Rd. Cobh & Sole S —9E 136
Jesmond Av. Wemb —37Pa 59
Jesmond Clo. Mitc —69Kb 126
Jesmond Dene. They B —8Tc 14
Jesmond Rd. Croy —73Vb 147
Jesmond Rd. Grays —46Fe 91
Jesmond Way. Stan —22Na 39
Jessam Av. E5 —32Xb 63
Jessamine Pl. Dart —59Sd 112
Jessamine Rd. W7 —46Ha 78
Jessamy Rd. Wey —75R 140
Jessel Dri. Lou —11Sc 28
Jesse Rd. E10 —32Ec 64
Jessica Rd. SW18 —58Eb 103
Jessie Blythe La. N19 —31Nb 62
Jessiman Ter. Shep —71Q 140
Jessop Av. S'hall —49Ba 77
Jessop Ct. Wal A —6Hc 13
Jessop Rd. SE24 —56Rb 105
Jessops Way. Croy —72Lb 146
Jessup Clo. SE18 —49Sc 86
Jetstar Way. N'holt —41Aa 77
Jetty Wlk. Grays —51Ce 113
Jevington Way. SE12 —60Kc 107
Jewel Rd. E17 —27Cc 44
Jewels Hill. Big H —84Jc 167
Jewry St. EC3 —44Vb 83 (3K 201)
Jew's Row. SW18 —56Db 103
Jews Wlk. SE26 —63Xb 127
Jeymer Av. NW2 —36Xa 60
Jeymer Dri. Gnfd —39Da 57
Jeypore Pas. SW18 —58Eb 103
Jeypore Rd. SW18 —59Eb 103
Jillian Clo. Hamp —66Ca 121
Jim Bradley Clo. SE18 —49Qc 86
Jim Griffiths Ho. SW6 —51Bb 103
(off Clem Attlee Ct.)
Joan Cres. SE9 —59Mc 107
Joan Gdns. Dag —33Ad 67
Joan Rd. Dag —33Ad 67
Joan St. SE1 —46Rb 83 (7B 200)
Jocelin Ho. N1 —39Pb 62 (1J 193)
(off Barnsbury Est.)
Jocelyn Rd. Rich —55Na 101
Jockey's Fields. WC1 —43Pb 82 (7J 193)
Jodane St. SE8 —49Bc 84
Jodrell Rd. E3 —39Bc 64
Jodrell Way. W Thur —50Vd 90
Joe Hunte Ct. SE27 —64Rb 127
Joel St. N'wd & Pinn —26W 36
Johanna St. SE1 —47Qb 82 (2K 205)
John Adams Ct. N9 —19Vb 25
John Adam St. WC2 —45Nb 82 (5G 199)
John Aird Ct. W2 —43Eb 81 (7A 190)
(off Howley Pl.)
John Ashby Clo. SW2 —58Nb 104
John Baird Ct. SE26 —63Yb 128
John Barnes Wlk. E15 —37Hc 65
John Bradshaw Rd. N14 —18Mb 24
John Brent Ho. SE8 —49Zb 84
(off Haddonfield)
John Burns Dri. Bark —38Uc 66
Johnby Clo. Enf —9Ac 12
John Campbell Rd. N16 —36Ub 63
John Carpenter St. EC4 —45Rb 83 (4B 200)
John Clay Gdns. Grays —45De 91
John Cobb Rd. Wey —80Q 140
John Felton Rd. SE16 —47Wb 83
John Fisher St. E1 —45Wb 83
John Gale Ct. Eps —81Va 162
(off West St.)
John Gooch Dri. Enf —11Rb 25
John Islip St. SW1 —49Mb 82 (7E 204)
John Kennedy Ct. N1 —37Tb 63
(off Newington Grn. Rd.)
John Lamb Ct. Harr —25Ga 38
John Masefield Ho. N15 —30Tb 43
(off Fladbury Rd.)
John Maurice Clo. SE17 —49Tb 83 (5F 207)
John McKenna Wlk. SE16 —48Wb 83
John Newton Ct. Well —55Xc 109
John Parker Clo. Dag —38Dd 68
John Parker Sq. SW11 —55Fb 103
John Parry Ct. N1
(off Hare Wlk.) —40Ub 63 (1J 195)
John Penn St. SE13 —53Dc 106
John Perrin Pl. Harr —31Na 59
John Prince's St. W1 —44Kb 82 (2A 198)
John Rennie Wlk. E1 —45Xb 83
John Roll Way. SE16 —48Wb 83
John Ruskin St. SE5 —52Rb 105
John's Av. NW4 —28Ya 40
John's Clo. Ashf —63S 120
John's Ct. Sutt —79Db 145
Johnsdale. Oxt —100Hc 183
John Silkin La. SE8 —50Zb 84
John's La. Mord —71Eb 145
John's M. WC1 —42Pb 82 (6J 193)
Johnson Clo. E8 —39Wb 63
Johnson Clo. Grav —62Fe 135
Johnson Rd. Brom —71Mc 149
Johnson Rd. Croy —73Tb 147
Johnson Rd. Houn —52Y 99
Johnson's Av. Badg M —82Dd 170
Johnsons Clo. Cars —75Hb 145
Johnson's Ct. EC4 —44Qb 82 (3A 200)
Johnsons Ct. Seal —93Pd 187
Johnsons Dri. Hamp —67Ea 122
Johnson's Pl. SW1 —50Lb 82 (7B 204)
Johnson St. E1 —45Yb 84
Johnson St. S'hall —48Y 77
Johnsons Way. NW10 —42Ra 79
Johnson's Way. Grnh —58Yd 112
Johnson's Yd. Uxb —38L 55
John Spencer Sq. N1 —37Rb 63
John's Pl. E1 —44Yb 84
John's Rd. Meop —10B 136
John's Rd. Tats —92Mc 183
John's Ter. Croy —74Ub 147
John's Ter. Romf —23Rd 49
Johnstone Rd. E6 —41Pc 86
Johnston Rd. Wfd G —22Jc 45
Johnston Ter. NW2 —34Za 60
John St. E15 —39Hc 65
John St. SE25 —70Wb 127
John St. WC1 —42Pb 82 (6J 193)
John St. Enf —15Vb 25
John St. Grays —51Ee 113
John St. Houn —54Aa 99
John Strype Ct. E10 —33Dc 64
Johns Wlk. Whyt —91Wb 181
John Taylor Ct. Slou —6D 72
John Trundle Ct. EC2
(off Barbican) —43Sb 83 (7D 194)
John Trundle Highwalk. EC2
(off Barbican) —43Sb 83 (7D 194)
John Wesley Ct. Twic —60Ja 100
John Wesley Highwalk. EC2
(off Barbican) —43Sb 83 (1D 200)
John Williams Clo. SE14 —51Zb 106
John Wilson St. SE18 —48Qc 86
John Woolley Clo. SE13 —56Fc 107
Joiners Arms Yd. SE5 —53Tb 105
Joiners Clo. Ger X —24B 34
Joiner's La. Ger X —25A 34
Joiner St. SE1 —46Tb 83 (7G 201)
Joiner St. SW1 —46Tb 83
Joiners Way. Ger X —24A 34
Joint Rd. N2 —25Gb 41
Joinville Pl. Add —77M 139
Jolliffe Rd. Mers —98Lb 180
Jollys La. Harr —32Fa 58
Jollys La. Hay —43Z 77
Jonathan St. SE11 —50Pb 82 (7H 205)
Jones Cotts. Barn —15Wa 22
Jones M. SW15 —56Ab 102
Jones Rd. E13 —42Kc 85
Jones Rd. Chesh —2Rb 11
Jones St. W1 —45Kb 82 (5K 197)
Jones Wlk. Rich —58Pa 101
Jones Way. Hedg —3H 53
Jonquil Gdns. Hamp —65Ca 121
Jonson Clo. Hay —43W 76
Jonson Clo. Mitc —70Kb 126
Joram Way. SE16 —50Xb 83
Jordan Clo. Dag —35Dd 68
Jordan Clo. Leav —7V 4
Jordan Clo. S Croy —83Vb 165
Jordan Clo. S Harr —34Ba 57
Jordan Ho. N1 —39Tb 63
(off Colville Est.)
Jordan Rd. Gnfd —39Ka 58
Jordans Clo. Iswth —53Ga 100
Jordans Clo. Stai —59L 97
Jordan's Way. Brick —2Ba 5
Jordans Way. Rain —40Md 69
Joseph Av. W3 —44Ta 79
Joseph Ct. N16 —31Ub 63
(off Amhurst Pk.)
Josephine Av. SW2 —57Pb 104
Josephine Av. Tad —98Bb 179
Josephine Clo. Tad —99Bb 179
Joseph Lister Ct. E7 —38Jc 65
(off Upton La.)
Joseph Locke Way. Esh —75Ca 141
Joseph Powell Clo. SW12 —58Kb 104
Joseph Ray Rd. E11 —33Gc 65
Joseph St. E3 —42Bc 84
Joshua St. E14 —44Ec 84
Joslin Rd. Purf —50Td 90
Joubert St. SW11 —54Hb 103
Journeys End. Stoke P —3J 73
Jowett St. SE15 —52Vb 105
Joyce Av. N18 —22Vb 43
Joyce Butler Ho. N22 —25Pb 42
Joyce Ct. Wal A —6Fc 13
Joyce Dawson Way. SE28 —45Wc 87
Joyce Grn. La. Dart —56Pd 111
Joyce Grn. Wlk. Dart —56Pd 111
Joyce Page Clo. SE7 —51Mc 107
Joyce Wlk. SW2 —58Qb 104
Joydens Wood Rd. Bex —63Fd 132
Joydon Dri. Romf —30Xc 47
Joyes Clo. Romf —21Md 49
Joyners Clo. Dag —35Bd 67
Joy Rd. Grav —10E 114
Joystone Ct. New Bar —14Gb 23
(off Park Rd.)
Jubb Powell Ho. N15 —30Ub 43
Jubilee Av. E4 —23Ec 44
Jubilee Av. Romf —29Dd 48
Jubilee Av. Twic —60Ea 100
Jubilee Clo. NW9 —30Ta 39
Jubilee Clo. Grnh —58Yd 112
Jubilee Clo. King T —67La 122
Jubilee Clo. Pinn —26Y 37
Jubilee Clo. Romf —29Dd 48
Jubilee Clo. Stai —59L 97
Jubilee Cotts. Sev —92Kd 187
Jubilee Ct. Harr —31Na 59
Jubilee Ct. Stai —63J 119
Jubilee Ct. Wal A —5Hc 13
Jubilee Cres. E14 —48Ec 84
Jubilee Cres. N9 —18Wb 25
Jubilee Cres. Add —78M 139
Jubilee Cres. Grav —1G 136
Jubilee Dri. Ruis —35Z 57
Jubilee Gdns. S'hall —43Ca 77
Jubilee Ho. SE11 —49Qb 82 (6A 206)
(off Reedworth St.)
Jubilee Ho. WC1 —42Pb 82 (5H 193)
(off Gray's Inn Rd.)
Jubilee Pl. SW3 —50Gb 81 (7E 202)
Jubilee Rise. Seal —93Pd 187
Jubilee Rd. Grays —51Xd 112
Jubilee Rd. Gnfd —39Ka 58
Jubilee Rd. Orp —79Cd 152
Jubilee Rd. Sutt —80Za 144
Jubilee Rd. Wat —10W 4
Jubilee St. E1 —44Yb 84
Jubilee Ter. N1 —40Tb 63 (1G 195)
Jubilee Way. SW19 —67Db 125
Jubilee Way. Chess —77Qa 143
Jubilee Way. Sidc —61Wc 131
Judd St. WC1 —41Nb 82 (3F 193)
Jude St. E16 —44Hc 85
Judge Heath La. Uxb & Hay —44S 76
Judge's Hill. N'thaw —1Gb 9
Judge St. Wat —10X 5
Judges Wlk. NW3 —34Eb 61
Judge Wlk. Clay —79Ga 142
Judith Anne Ct. Upm —33Ud 70
Judith Av. Romf —23Dd 48
Judith Gdns. Grav —4G 136
Juer St. SW11 —52Gb 103
Jug Hill. Big H —88Mc 167
Juglans Rd. Orp —74Wc 151
Julia Ct. E17 —29Dc 44
Julia Gdns. Bark —40Zc 67
Julian Av. W3 —45Ra 79
Julian Clo. Barn —13Db 23
Julian Clo. Wok —6F 188
Julian Hill. Harr —33Ga 58
Julian Hill. Wey —80Q 140
Julian Pl. E14 —50Dc 84
Julian Rd. Orp —79Wc 151
Julians Clo. Sev —99Jd 186
Julians Way. Sev —99Jd 186
Julian Taylor Path. SE23 —61Xb 127
Julia St. NW5 —35Jb 62
Julien Rd. W5 —49La 78
Julien Rd. Coul —87Mb 164
Juliet Ho. N1 —40Ub 63 (2H 195)
(off Arden Est.)

Juliette Rd.—Keston Rd.

Juliette Rd. E13 —40Jc 65
Juliette Way. S Ock —47Pd 89
Junction App. SE13 —55Ec 106
Junction App. SW11 —55Gb 103
Junction M. W2 —44Gb 81 (2D 196)
Junction Pl. W2 —44Gb 81 (2D 196)
(off Praed St.)
Junction Rd. E13 —40Kc 65
Junction Rd. N9 —18Wb 25
Junction Rd. N17 —27Wb 43
Junction Rd. N19 —35Lb 62
Junction Rd. W5 —49La 78
Junction Rd. Ashf —64S 120
Junction Rd. Dart —58Md 111
Junction Rd. Harr —30Ga 38
Junction Rd. Romf —28Hd 48
Junction Rd. S Croy —78Tb 147
Junction Rd. War —21Yd 50
Junction Rd. E. Romf —31Ad 67
Junction Rd. W. Romf —31Ad 67
Junction Wharf. N1 —40Sb 63 (2D 194)
June Clo. Coul —86Kb 164
Junewood Clo. Wdhm —83H 157
Juniper Av. Brick —3Ca 5
Juniper Clo. Barn —15Za 22
Juniper Clo. Big H —89Nc 168
Juniper Clo. Rick —20M 17
Juniper Clo. Wemb —36Qa 59
Juniper Ct. W8 —48Db 81
(off St. Marys Pl.)
Juniper Ct. Brtwd —20Be 33
(off Beech Av.)
Juniper Ct. Harr —25Ha 38
Juniper Ct. N'wd —25W 36
Juniper Ct. Slou —7L 73
Juniper Gdns. SW16 —67Lb 126
Juniper Gdns. Sun —65V 120
Juniper Ga. Rick —20M 17
Juniper Gro. Wat —10W 4
Juniper La. E6 —43Nc 86
Juniper Rd. Ilf —34Qc 66
Juniper St. E1 —45Yb 84
Juniper Wlk. Swan —68Fd 132
Juniper Way. Hay —45T 76
Juniper Way. Romf —25Nd 49
Juno Way. SE14 —51Zb 106
Jupiter Way. N7 —37Pb 62
Jupp Rd. E15 —38Fc 65
Jupp Rd. W. E15 —39Fc 65
Jurgens Rd. Purf —51Td 112
Jury St. Grav —8D 114
Justice Wlk. SW3 —51Gb 103
(off Lawrence St.)
Justin Clo. Bren —52Ma 101
Justin Rd. E4 —23Bc 44
Jute La. Enf —13Ac 26
Jutland Clo. N19 —32Nb 62
Jutland Gdns. Coul —92Pb 180
Jutland Pl. Egh —64E 118
Jutland Rd. E13 —42Jc 85
Jutland Rd. SE6 —59Ec 106
Jutsums Av. Romf —30Dd 48
Jutsums Ct. Romf —30Dd 48
Jutsums La. Romf —30Dd 48
Juxon Clo. Harr —25Da 37
Juxon St. SE11 —49Pb 82 (5J 205)
JVC Bus. Pk. NW2 —32Wa 60

Kaduna Clo. Pinn —29W 36
Kale Rd. Eri —47Ad 87
Kambala Rd. SW11 —55Fb 103
Kandlewood. Hut —17De 33
Kangley Bri. Rd. SE26 —64Bc 128
Kangley Bus. Cen. SE26 —64Bc 128
Karen Clo. Brtwd —17Yd 32
Karen Clo. Rain —40Gd 68
Karen Clo. Stanf —1L 93
Karen Ct. Brom —67Hc 129
Karen Ter. E11 —33Hc 65
Kashgar Rd. SE18 —49Vc 87
Kashmir Clo. New Haw —81M 157
Kashmir Rd. SE7 —52Mc 107
Kassala Rd. SW11 —53Hb 103
Kates Clo. Barn —15Wa 22
Katharine St. Croy —76Sb 147
Katherine Clo. Add —79J 139
Katherine Gdns. SE9 —56Mc 107
Katherine Gdns. Ilf —24Sc 46
Katherine Rd. E7 & E6 —36Lc 65
Katherine Rd. Twic —59Ja 100
Katherine Sq. W11 —46Ab 80
Kathleen Av. W3 —43Sa 79
Kathleen Av. Wemb —38Na 59
Kathleen Godfree Ct. SW19 —64Cb 125
Kathleen Rd. SW11 —55Hb 103
Kavanaghs Rd. Brtwd —20Wd 32
Kavanaghs Ter. Brtwd —20Xd 32
Kay Av. Add —76N 139
Kaye Don Way. Wey —82Q 158
Kayemoor Rd. Sutt —79Fb 145
Kay Rd. SW9 —54Nb 104
Kaysland Caravan Cen. W King —80Ud 154
Kay St. E2 —40Wb 63
Kay St. E15 —38Fc 65
Kay St. Well —53Xc 109
Kaywood Clo. Slou —8P 73
Kean Ho. SE17 —51Rb 105
Kean St. WC2 —44Pb 82 (3H 199)
Kearton Clo. Kenl —89Sb 165
Keary Rd. Swans —59Ae 113
Keats Av. Romf —24Kd 49
Keats Clo. E11 —29Kc 45
Keat's Clo. NW3 —35Gb 61
Keats Clo. SE1 —49Vb 83 (6K 207)
Keats Clo. SW19 —65Fb 125
Keats Clo. Chig —23Sc 46
Keats Clo. Enf —15Zb 26
Keats Clo. Hay —43W 76
Keats Gdns. Til —4D 114
Keat's Gro. NW3 —35Gb 61
Keats La. Eton —1G 94
Keats Pl. EC2 —43Tb 83 (1F 201)
(off Moorgate)
Keats Rd. Belv —48Ed 88
Keats Rd. Well —53Uc 108
Keats Wlk. Hut —17Fe 33
Keats Way. Croy —72Yb 148
Keats Way. Gnfd —43Da 77
Keats Way. W Dray —49P 75
Kebbell Ter. E7 —36Kc 65
(off Claremont Rd.)
Keble Clo. N'holt —36Ea 58
Keble Clo. Wor Pk —74Va 144
Keble St. SW17 —63Eb 125
Keble Ter. Abb L —4V 4
Kechill Gdns. Brom —73Jc 149
Kedeston Ct. Sutt —74Db 145
Kedleston Dri. Orp —71Vc 151
Kedleston Wlk. E2 —41Xb 83
Kedyngton Ho. Edgw —26Sa 39
(off Burnt Oak B'way.)
Keedonwood Rd. Brom —64Gc 129
Keel Clo. SE16 —46Zb 84
Keel Dri. Slou —7F 72
Keeler Clo. Wind —5C 94
Keeley Rd. Croy —75Sb 147
Keeley St. WC2 —44Pb 82 (3H 199)
Keeling Rd. SE9 —57Mc 107
Keely Clo. Barn —15Gb 23
Keemor Clo. SE18 —52Qc 108
Keensacre. Iver —40F 54
Keens Clo. SW16 —64Mb 126
Keens Rd. Croy —77Sb 147
Keen's Yd. N1 —37Rb 63
Keepers Farm Clo. Wind —4C 94
(in two parts)
Keepers Wlk. Vir W —10P 117
Keep, The. SE3 —54Jc 107
Keep, The. King T —65Pa 123
Keeton's Rd. SE16 —48Xb 83
Keevil Dri. SW19 —59Za 102
Keighley Clo. N7 —36Nb 62
Keighley Rd. Romf —24Nd 49
Keightley Dri. SE9 —60Sc 108
Keilder Clo. Uxb —40Q 56
Keildon Rd. SW11 —56Hb 103
Keir Hardie Est. E5 —32Xb 63
Keir Hardie Ho. N19 —31Mb 62
Keir Hardie Way. Bark —38Wc 67
Keir Hardie Way. Hay —41W 76
Keith Av. S at H —65Rd 133
Keith Connor Clo. SW8 —55Kb 104
Keith Gro. W12 —47Wa 80
Keith Pk. Cres. Big H —84Kc 167
Keith Pk. Rd. Uxb —38P 55
Keith Rd. E17 —25Bc 44
Keith Rd. Bark —40Tc 66
Keith Rd. Hay —48U 76
Keith Way. Horn —31Nd 69
Kelbrook Rd. SE3 —54Nc 108
Kelburn Way. Rain —41Jd 88
Kelby Path. SE9 —62Rc 130
Kelceda Clo. NW2 —33Wa 60
Kelf Gro. Hay —44V 76
Kelfield Ct. W10 —44Za 80
Kelfield Gdns. W10 —44Ya 80
Kelfield M. W10 —44Za 80
Kelland Clo. N8 —29Mb 42
Kelland Rd. E13 —42Jc 85
Kellaway Rd. SE3 —54Mc 107
Kellerton Rd. SE13 —57Gc 107
Kellett Ho. N1 —39Ub 63
(off Colville Est.)
Kellett Rd. SW2 —56Qb 104
Kelling Gdns. Croy —73Rb 147
Kelling Rd. SE9 —57Mc 107
Kellino St. SW17 —63Hb 125
Kellner Rd. SE28 —48Vc 87
Kell St. SE1 —48Rb 83 (3C 206)
Kelly Clo. Shep —68U 120
Kelly Ct. Borwd —12Ta 21
Kelly Rd. NW7 —23Ab 40
Kelly St. NW1 —37Kb 62
Kelly Way. Romf —29Ad 47
Kelman Clo. SW4 —54Mb 104
Kelman Clo. Wal X —3Ac 12
Kelmore Gro. SE22 —56Wb 105
Kelmscott Clo. E17 —25Bc 44
Kelmscott Clo. Wat —15W 18
Kelmscott Cres. Wat —15W 18
Kelmscott Gdns. W12 —48Wa 80
Kelmscott Rd. SW11 —57Gb 103
Kelpatrick Rd. Slou —4B 72
Kelross Pas. N5 —35Sb 63
Kelross Rd. N5 —35Sb 63
Kelsall Clo. SE3 —54Kc 107
Kelsey Ga. Beck —68Dc 128
Kelsey La. Beck —68Cc 128
Kelsey Pk. Av. Beck —68Dc 128
Kelsey Pk. Rd. Beck —68Cc 128
Kelsey Rd. Orp —68Xc 131
Kelsey Sq. Beck —68Cc 128
Kelsey St. E2 —42Wb 83
Kelsey Way. Beck —69Cc 128
Kelshall. Wat —8Aa 5
Kelsie Way. Ilf —23Uc 46
Kelso Dri. Grav —3H 137
Kelso Ho. E14 —48Fc 85
Kelso Pl. W8 —48Db 81
Kelso Rd. Cars —73Eb 145
Kelston Rd. Ilf —26Rc 46
Kelvedon Av. W on T —80U 140
Kelvedon Clo. Hut —16Fe 33
Kelvedon Clo. King T —65Qa 123
Kelvedon Ho. SW8 —53Nb 104
Kelvedon Rd. SW6 —52Bb 103
Kelvedon Wlk. Rain —39Hd 68
Kelvedon Way. Wfd G —23Pc 46
Kelvin Av. N13 —23Pb 42
Kelvin Av. Lea —92Ha 176
Kelvinbrook. W Mol —69Da 121
Kelvin Clo. Eps —79Qa 143
Kelvin Ct. Iswth —54Ga 100
Kelvin Cres. Harr —24Ga 38
Kelvin Dri. Twic —58Ka 100
Kelvin Gdns. Croy —73Pb 146
Kelvin Gdns. S'hall —44Ca 77
Kelvin Gro. SE26 —62Xb 127
Kelvin Gro. Chess —76Ma 143
Kelvington Clo. Croy —73Ac 148
Kelvington Rd. SE15 —57Zb 106
Kelvin Pde. Orp —74Uc 150
Kelvin Rd. N5 —35Sb 63
Kelvin Rd. Til —4C 114
Kelvin Rd. Well —55Wc 109
Kember St. N1 —38Pb 62
Kemble Clo. Pot B —5Fb 9
Kemble Clo. Wey —77T 140
Kemble Cotts. Add —77J 139
Kemble Ct. SE15 —52Ub 105
(off Ludney Clo.)
Kemble Dri. Brom —76Nc 150
Kemble Ho. SW9 —55Rb 105
(off Barrington Rd.)
Kemble Pde. Pot B —4Eb 9
Kemble Rd. N17 —25Wb 43
Kemble Rd. SE23 —60Zb 106
Kemble Rd. Croy —76Rb 147
Kembleside Rd. Big H —90Lc 167
Kemble St. WC2 —44Pb 82 (3H 199)
Kemerton Rd. SE5 —55Sb 105
Kemerton Rd. Beck —68Dc 128
Kemerton Rd. Croy —73Vb 147
Kemeys St. E9 —36Ac 64
Kemnal Rd. Chst —66Sc 130
Kemp. NW9 —25Va 40
(off Concourse, The)
Kemp Ct. SW8 —52Nb 104
(off Hartington Rd.)
Kempe Rd. NW6 —40Za 60
Kempe Rd. Enf —8Xb 11
(in two parts)
Kemp Gdns. Croy —72Sb 147
Kemp Ho. E6 —37Qc 66
Kempis Way. SE22 —57Ub 105
Kemplay Rd. NW3 —35Fb 61
Kempley Ct. Grays —51Fe 113
Kemp Pl. Bush —16Ca 19
Kemp Rd. Dag —32Zc 67
Kemprow. Ald —8Fa 6
Kemps Dri. E14 —45Cc 84
Kemps Dri. N'wd —24V 36
Kempsford Gdns. SW5 —50Cb 81
Kempsford Rd. SE11 —49Qb 82 (6A 206)
Kemps Gdns. SE13 —57Ec 106
Kempshott Rd. SW16 —66Mb 126
Kempson Rd. SW6 —53Cb 103
Kempthorne Rd. SE8 —49Bc 84
Kempthorne St. Grav —8D 114
Kempton Av. Horn —35Pd 69
Kempton Av. N'holt —37Ca 57
Kempton Av. Sun —67X 121
Kempton Clo. Eri —51Ed 110
Kempton Clo. Uxb —35S 56
Kempton Ct. Sun —67X 121
Kempton Rd. E6 —39Pc 66
Kempton Rd. Hamp —68Ba 121
Kempton Wlk. Croy —72Ac 148
Kempt St. SE18 —51Qc 108
Kemsing Clo. Bex —59Ad 109
Kemsing Clo. Brom —75Hc 149
Kemsing Clo. T Hth —70Sb 127
Kemsing Rd. SE10 —50Jc 85
Kemsley Clo. Grav —3B 136
Kemsley Clo. Grnh —58Xd 112
Kemsley Rd. Tats —91Mc 183
Kenbury Clo. Uxb —34Q 56
Kenbury St. SE5 —54Sb 105
Kenchester Clo. SW8 —52Nb 104
Kencot Way. Eri —47Bd 87
Kendal Av. N18 —21Tb 43
Kendal Av. W3 —42Qa 79
(in two parts)
Kendal Av. Bark —39Uc 66
Kendal Av. Epp —2Wc 15
Kendal Clo. SW9 —52Rb 105
Kendal Clo. Felt —60V 98
Kendal Clo. Hay —40W 56
Kendal Clo. Slou —5L 73
Kendal Clo. Wfd G —19Hc 27
Kendal Ct. W3 —43Qa 79
Kendal Ct. Borwd —11Sa 21
Kendal Croft. Horn —36Jd 68
Kendal Dri. Slou —5L 73
Kendale. Grays —8D 92
Kendale Rd. Brom —64Gc 129
Kendal Gdns. N18 —21Tb 43
Kendal Gdns. Sutt —75Eb 145
Kendal Ho. SE20 —68Xb 127
(off Derwent Rd.)
Kendall Av. Beck —68Ac 128
Kendall Av. S Croy —81Tb 165
Kendall Av. S. S Croy —82Sb 165
Kendall Lodge. Epp —2Wc 15
Kendall Pl. W1 —43Jb 82
Kendall Rd. Beck —68Ac 128
Kendall Rd. Iswth —54Ja 100
Kendalmere Clo. N10 —25Kb 42
Kendal Pde. N18 —21Tb 43
Kendal Pl. SW15 —57Bb 103
Kendal Pl. W1 —43Jb 82 (1H 197)
Kendal Rd. NW10 —35Wa 60
Kendals Clo. Rad —8Ga 6
Kendal St. W2 —44Gb 81 (3E 196)
Kender St. SE14 —52Yb 106
Kendoa Rd. SW4 —56Mb 104
Kendon Clo. E11 —29Kc 45
Kendor Av. Eps —83Sa 161
Kendra Hall Rd. S Croy —80Rb 147
Kendrey Gdns. Twic —59Ga 100
Kendrick M. SW7 —49Fb 81 (5B 202)
Kendrick Pl. SW7 —49Fb 81 (6B 202)
Kendrick Rd. Slou —8M 73
Keneally. Wind —4A 94
Keneally Clo. Wind —4A 94
Keneally Wlk. Wind —4A 94
Kenelm Clo. Harr —34Ja 58
Kenerne Dri. Barn —15Ab 22
Kenford Clo. Wat —4X 5
Kenia Wlk. Grav —2H 137
Kenilford Rd. SW12 —59Kb 104
Kenilworth Av. E17 —26Cc 44
Kenilworth Av. SW19 —64Cb 125
Kenilworth Av. Harr —35Ba 57
Kenilworth Av. Romf —23Rd 49
Kenilworth Av. Stoke D —86Da 159
Kenilworth Clo. Bans —88Db 163
Kenilworth Clo. Borwd —13Sa 21
Kenilworth Clo. Slou —8K 73
Kenilworth Ct. Dart —58Rd 111
(off Bow Arrow La.)
Kenilworth Ct. Dart —58Rd 111
(off Grange Cres.)
Kenilworth Ct. Wat —11W 18
Kenilworth Cres. Enf —11Ub 25
Kenilworth Dri. Borwd —13Sa 21
Kenilworth Dri. Crox —14R 18
Kenilworth Dri. W on T —76Z 141
Kenilworth Gdns. SE18 —54Rc 108
Kenilworth Gdns. Hay —43V 76
Kenilworth Gdns. Horn —34Ld 69
Kenilworth Gdns. Ilf —33Vc 67
Kenilworth Gdns. Lou —16Pc 28
Kenilworth Gdns. S'hall —41Ba 77
Kenilworth Gdns. Stai —64L 119
Kenilworth Gdns. Wat —22Y 37
Kenilworth Rd. E3 —40Ac 64
Kenilworth Rd. NW6 —39Bb 61
Kenilworth Rd. SE20 —67Zb 128
Kenilworth Rd. W5 —46Na 79
Kenilworth Rd. Ashf —62M 119
Kenilworth Rd. Edgw —20Sa 21
Kenilworth Rd. Eps —78Wa 144
Kenilworth Rd. Orp —72Sc 150
Kenley Av. NW9 —25Ua 40
Kenley Clo. Barn —14Gb 23
Kenley Clo. Bex —59Cd 110
Kenley Clo. Cat —92Ub 181
Kenley Clo. Chst —69Uc 130
Kenley Ct. Kenl —87Rb 165
Kenley Gdns. Horn —33Pd 69
Kenley Gdns. T Hth —70Rb 127
Kenley La. Kenl —86Sb 165
Kenley Rd. SW19 —68Cb 125
Kenley Rd. King T —68Ra 123
Kenley Rd. Twic —58Ka 100
Kenley Wlk. W11 —45Ab 80
Kenley Wlk. Sutt —77Za 144
Kenlor Rd. SW17 —64Fb 125
Kenmare Dri. Mitc —66Hb 125
Kenmare Gdns. N13 —21Sb 43
Kenmare Rd. T Hth —72Qb 146
Kenmere Gdns. Wemb —39Qa 59
Kenmere Rd. Well —54Yc 109
Kenmont Gdns. NW10 —41Xa 80
Kenmore Av. Harr —28Ja 38
Kenmore Clo. Rich —52Qa 101
Kenmore Cres. Hay —41V 76
Kenmore Gdns. Edgw —26Ra 39
Kenmore Rd. Harr —27Ma 39
Kenmore Rd. Kenl —86Rb 165
Kenmure Rd. E8 —36Xb 63
Kenmure Yd. E8 —36Xb 63
Kennard Rd. E15 —38Fc 65
Kennard Rd. N11 —22Hb 41
Kennard St. E16 —46Pc 86
Kennard St. SW11 —53Jb 104
Kennedy Av. Enf —16Yb 26
Kennedy Clo. E13 —40Jc 65
Kennedy Clo. Chesh —1Ac 12
Kennedy Clo. Farn C —7G 52
Kennedy Clo. Orp —74Tc 150
Kennedy Clo. Pinn —23Ba 37
Kennedy Ct. Beck —72Bc 148
Kennedy Ct. Bush —19Fa 20
Kennedy Ct. Croy —72Bc 148
Kennedy Gdns. Sev —94Md 187
Kennedy Ho. SE11 —50Pb 82 (7H 205)
(off Vauxhall Wlk.)
Kennedy Ho. Grav —2A 136
Kennedy Path. W7 —42Ha 78
Kennedy Rd. W7 —43Ga 78
Kennedy Rd. Bark —39Uc 66
Kennedy Wlk. SE17 —49Tb 83 (6G 207)
(off Tisdall Pl.)
Kennel Clo. Fet —96Ea 176
Kennel La. Fet —94Da 175
(in two parts)
Kennel La. Pil H —11Ud 32
Kennel Wood Cres. New Ad —83Fc 167
Kennet Clo. SW11 —56Fb 103
Kennet Clo. Upm —30Ud 50
Kennet Grn. S Ock —45Xd 90
Kenneth Av. Ilf —35Rc 66
Kenneth Ct. SE11 —49Qb 82 (5A 206)
Kenneth Cres. NW2 —36Xa 60
Kenneth Gdns. Stan —23Ja 38
Kenneth More Rd. Ilf —34Rc 66
Kenneth Rd. Bans —87Fb 163
Kenneth Rd. Romf —31Zc 67
Kenneth Robbins Ho. N17 —24Xb 43
Kennet Rd. W9 —42Bb 81
Kennet Rd. Dart —55Jd 110
Kennet Rd. Iswth —55Ha 100
Kennet Sq. Mitc —67Gb 125
Kennet St. E1 —46Wb 83
Kennett Ct. W4 —52Ra 101
Kennett Dri. Hay —43Aa 77
Kennett Rd. Slou —48D 74
Kenninghall Rd. E5 —34Wb 63
Kenninghall Rd. N18 —22Yb 44
Kenning St. SE16 —47Yb 84
Kennings Way. SE11 —50Qb 82 (7B 206)
Kenning Ter. N1 —39Ub 63
Kennington Grn. SE11 —50Qb 82
Kennington Gro. SE11 —51Pb 104
Kennington La. SE11 —50Pb 82
Kennington Oval. SE11 —51Pb 104
Kennington Pal. Ct. SE11 —50Qb 82 (7K 205)
(off Sancroft St.)
Kennington Pk. Gdns. SE11 —51Rb 105
Kennington Pk. Pl. SE11 —51Qb 104
Kennington Pk. Rd. SE11 —51Qb 104
Kennington Rd. SE1 & SE11 —48Qb 82 (3K 205)
Kennyland Ct. NW4 —30Xa 40
(off Hendon Way)
Kennylands Rd. Ilf —24Wc 47
Kenny Rd. NW7 —23Ab 40
Kenrick Pl. W1 —43Jb 82 (7H 191)
Kensal Rd. W10 —42Ab 80
Kensington Av. E12 —37Nc 66
Kensington Av. T Hth —67Qb 126
Kensington Av. Wat —14V 18
Kensington Chu. Ct. W8 —47Db 81
Kensington Chu. St. W8 —46Cb 81
Kensington Chu. Wlk. W8 —47Db 81
Kensington Ct. W8 —47Db 81
Kensington Ct. Grays —51Ee 113
Kensington Ct. Gdns. W8 —48Db 81
(off Kensington Ct. Pl.)
Kensington Ct. M. W8 —48Db 81
(off Kensington Ct. Pl.)
Kensington Ct. Pl. W8 —48Db 81
Kensington Dri. Wfd G —26Mc 45
Kensington Gdns. Ilf —32Pc 66
Kensington Gdns. Sq. W2 —44Db 81
Kensington Ga. W8 —48Eb 81 (3A 202)
Kensington Gore. SW7 —47Eb 81 (2A 202)
Kensington Hall Gdns. W14 —50Bb 81
Kensington High St. W14 & W8 —48Bb 81
Kensington Mall. W8 —46Cb 81
Kensington Pal. Gdns. W8 —46Db 81
Kensington Pk. Gdns. W11 —45Bb 81
Kensington Pk. M. W11 —44Bb 81
Kensington Pk. Rd. W11 —44Bb 81
Kensington Pl. W8 —46Cb 81
Kensington Rd. W8 & SW7 —47Db 81 (2A 202)
Kensington Rd. N'holt —41Ca 77
Kensington Rd. Pil H —16Wd 32
Kensington Rd. Romf —30Ed 48
Kensington Sq. W8 —48Db 81
Kensington Ter. S Croy —80Tb 147
Kenswick Ct. SE13 —57Dc 106
Kensworth Ho. EC1 —41Tb 83 (4G 195)
(off Cranwood St.)
Kent Av. W13 —43Ka 78
Kent Av. Dag —42Cd 88
Kent Av. Slou —3G 72
Kent Av. Well —57Vc 109
Kent Clo. Borwd —10Ta 7
Kent Clo. Mitc —70Nb 126
Kent Clo. Orp —79Uc 150
Kent Clo. Stai —65M 119
Kent Clo. Uxb —37L 55
Kent Ct. E2 —40Vb 63
Kent Ct. NW9 —26Ua 40
Kent Dri. Barn —14Jb 24
Kent Dri. Horn —35Md 69
Kent Dri. Tedd —64Ga 122
Kentford Way. N'holt —39Aa 57
Kent Gdns. W13 —43Ka 78
Kent Gdns. Ruis —30W 36
Kent Ga. Way. Croy —79Bc 148
Kent Ho. SE1 —50Vb 83 (7K 207)
Kent Ho. W4 —50Ua 80
(off Devonshire Rd.)
Kent Ho. Ger X —22A 34
Kent Ho. La. Beck —64Ac 128
Kent Ho. Rd. SE26 & Beck —64Ac 128
Kentish Bldgs. SE1 —46Tb 83 (7F 201)
(off Borough High St.)
Kentish Rd. Belv —49Cd 88
Kentish Town Ind. Est. NW5 —36Kb 62
Kentish Town Rd. NW1 & NW5 —38Kb 62
Kentish Way. Brom —68Jc 129
Kentmere Mans. W5 —42La 78
Kentmere Rd. SE18 —49Uc 86
Kenton Av. Harr —31Ha 58
Kenton Av. S'hall —45Ca 77
Kenton Av. Sun —68Z 121
Kenton Ct. W14 —48Bb 81
Kenton Ct. Kent —30Ka 38
Kentone Ct. SE25 —70Xb 127
Kenton Gdns. Harr —29La 38
Kenton La. Harr —23Ha 38
Kenton Pk. Av. Harr —28Ma 39
Kenton Pk. Clo. Harr —28La 38
Kenton Pk. Cres. Harr —28Ma 39
Kenton Pk. Mans. Kent —29La 38
(off Kenton Rd.)
Kenton Pk. Pde. Harr —29La 38
Kenton Pk. Rd. Harr —28La 38
Kenton Rd. E9 —37Zb 64
Kenton Rd. Harr —31Ha 58
Kenton Rd. Kent —30Ja 38
Kentons La. Wind —4C 94
Kenton St. WC1 —42Nb 82 (5F 193)
Kenton Way. Wok —5C 188
Kent Pas. NW1 —42Hb 81 (5F 191)
Kent Rd. N21 —18Tb 25
Kent Rd. W4 —48Sa 79
Kent Rd. Dag —36Dd 68
Kent Rd. Dart —58Md 111
Kent Rd. E Mol —70Ea 122
Kent Rd. Grav —10C 114
Kent Rd. Grays —51Ee 113
Kent Rd. King T —69Ma 123
Kent Rd. Long —68Zd 135
Kent Rd. Rich —52Qa 101
Kent Rd. St M —72Yc 151
Kent Rd. W Wick —74Dc 148
Kent Rd. Wok —88D 156
Kent's Pas. Hamp —67Ba 121
Kent St. E2 —40Vb 63 (1K 195)
Kent St. E13 —41Lc 85
Kent Ter. NW1 —41Gb 81 (4E 190)
Kent View. S Ock —47Sd 90
Kent View Gdns. Ilf —33Uc 66
Kent Wlk. SW9 —56Rb 105
Kent Way. SE15 —53Vb 105
Kent Way. Surb —76Na 143
Kentwode Grn. SW13 —52Wa 102
Kent Yd. SW7 —47Gb 81
Kenver Av. N12 —23Fb 41
Kenward Rd. SE9 —57Lc 107
Kenway. Rain —41Md 89
Kenway. Romf —26Ed 48
Kenway Clo. Rain —41Ld 89
Kenway Rd. SW5 —49Db 81
Kenway Wlk. Rain —41Md 89
Kenwood Av. N14 —15Mb 24
Kenwood Av. SE14 —53Zb 106
Kenwood Av. Long —69Ee 135
Kenwood Clo. NW3 —32Fb 61
Kenwood Clo. W Dray —51Q 98
Kenwood Dri. Beck —68Ec 128
Kenwood Dri. Rick —19H 17
Kenwood Dri. W on T —79X 141
Kenwood Gdns. E18 —27Kc 45
Kenwood Gdns. Ilf —28Qc 46
Kenwood Ho. SW9 —56Rb 105
Kenwood Ho. Wat —17T 18
Kenwood Pk. Wey —79T 140
Kenwood Ridge. Kenl —89Rb 165
Kenwood Rd. N6 —30Hb 41
Kenwood Rd. N9 —18Wb 25
Kenworth Clo. Wal X —5Zb 12
Kenworthy Rd. E9 —36Ac 64
Kenwrick Ho. N1 —39Pb 62 (1J 193)
(off Barnsbury Est.)
Kenwyn Dri. NW2 —33Ua 60
Kenwyn Lodge. N2 —28Hb 41
Kenwyn Rd. SW4 —56Mb 104
Kenwyn Rd. SW20 —67Ya 124
Kenwyn Rd. Dart —57Md 111
Kenya Rd. SE7 —52Mc 107
Kenyngton Ct. Sun —64W 120
Kenyngton Dri. Sun —64W 120
Kenyngton Pl. Harr —29La 38
Kenyons. W Hor —100R 174
Kenyon St. SW6 —53Za 102
Keogh Rd. E15 —37Gc 65
Kepler Rd. SW4 —56Nb 104
Keppel Rd. E6 —38Pc 66
Keppel Rd. Dag —35Ad 67
Keppel Row. SE1 —46Sb 83 (7D 200)
Keppel Spur. Old Win —9M 95
Keppel St. WC1 —43Mb 82 (7E 192)
Kepple Row. SE1 —46Sb 83
Kepple St. Wind —4H 95
Kerbela St. E2 —42Wb 83
Kerbey St. E14 —44Dc 84
Kerdistone Clo. Pot B —1Db 9
Kerfield Cres. SE5 —53Tb 105
Kerfield Pl. SE5 —53Tb 105
Kernow Clo. Horn —33Nd 69
Kerri Clo. Barn —14Ya 22
Kerridge Ct. N1 —37Ub 63
(off Balls Pond Rd.)
Kerrill Av. Coul —91Qb 180
Kerrin Point. SE11 —50Qb 82 (7K 205)
(off Hotspur St.)
Kerrison Pl. W5 —46Ma 79
Kerrison Rd. E15 —39Fc 65
Kerrison Rd. SW11 —55Gb 103
Kerrison Rd. W5 —46Ma 79
Kerrison Vs. W5 —46Na 79
Kerry. N7 —37Nb 62
Kerry Av. S Ock —47Qd 89
Kerry Av. Stan —21La 38
Kerry Clo. E16 —44Kc 85
Kerry Clo. Upm —31Vd 70
Kerry Ct. Stan —21Ma 39
Kerry Dri. Upm —31Vd 70
Kerry Path. SE14 —51Bc 106
Kerry Rd. Grays —46Fe 91
Kerry Ter. Wok —88D 156
Kersey Dri. S Croy —84Yb 166
Kersey Gdns. SE9 —63Nc 130
Kersey Gdns. Romf —24Nd 49
Kersfield Rd. SW15 —58Za 102
Kershaw Clo. SW18 —58Fb 103
Kershaw Rd. Dag —34Cd 68
Kerslake Ho. Ger X —22A 34
Kersley M. SW11 —53Hb 103
Kersley Rd. N16 —33Ub 63
Kersley St. SW11 —54Hb 103
Kerstin Clo. Hay —45V 76
Kerswell Clo. N15 —29Ub 43
Kerwick Clo. N7 —38Nb 62
Keslake Mans. NW10 —40Za 60
(off Station Ter.)
Keslake Rd. NW6 —40Za 60
Kessock Clo. N17 —29Xb 43
Kesteven Clo. Ilf —23Vc 47
Kestlake Rd. Bex —58Yc 109
Kestner Ind. Est. Grnh —56Wd 112
Keston Av. Coul —91Qb 180
Keston Av. Kes —78Lc 149
Keston Av. New Haw —83J 157
Keston Clo. N18 —20Tb 25
Keston Clo. Well —52Yc 109
Keston Gdns. Kes —77Lc 149
Keston M. Wat —12X 19
Keston Pk. Clo. Kes —76Pc 150
Keston Rd. N17 —27Tb 43

Keston Rd.—Kingston Av.

Keston Rd. SE15 —55Wb 105
Keston Rd. T Hth —72Qb 146
Kestrel Av. E6 —43Nc 86
Kestrel Av. SE24 —57Rb 105
Kestrel Av. Stai —62H 119
Kestrel Clo. NW9 —26Ua 40
Kestrel Clo. NW10 —36Ta 59
Kestrel Clo. Horn —38Kd 69
Kestrel Clo. Ilf —21Xc 47
Kestrel Clo. Wat —6Aa 5
Kestrel Ct. E17 —26Zb 44
Kestrel Ct. Ruis —33T 57
Kestrel Path. Slou —2C 72
Kestrel Rd. Wal A —6Jc 13
Kestrels, The. Brick —3Ba 5
Kestrel Way. New Ad —81Fc 167
Keswick Av. SW15 —64Ua 124
Keswick Av. SW19 —68Cb 125
Keswick Av. Horn —32Md 69
Keswick Clo. Sutt —77Eb 145
Keswick Ct. Short —70Hc 129
Keswick Ct. Slou —5K 73
Keswick Dri. Enf —8Yb 12
Keswick Gdns. Ilf —28Nc 46
Keswick Gdns. Ruis —30T 36
Keswick Gdns. Wemb —35Na 59
Keswick Ho. SE5 —54Sb 105
Keswick M. W5 —46Na 79
Keswick Rd. SW15 —57Ab 102
Keswick Rd. Bexh —53Cd 110
Keswick Rd. Bookh & Fet —97Ea 176
Keswick Rd. Egh —66D 118
Keswick Rd. Fet —96Ea 176
Keswick Rd. Orp —74Vc 151
Keswick Rd. Twic —58Ea 100
Keswick Rd. W Wick —75Gc 149
Ketley Ho. SE15 —52Wb 105
(off Sumner Est.)
Kettering Rd. Enf —9Zb 12
Kettering Rd. Romf —24Nd 49
Kettering St. SW16 —65Lb 126
Kett Gdns. SW2 —57Pb 104
Kettlebaston Rd. E10 —32Bc 64
Kettleby Ho. SW9 —55Rb 105
(off Barrington Rd.)
Kettlewell Clo. Wok —2G 188
Kettlewell Ct. Swan —68Hd 132
Kettlewell Dri. Wok —86A 156
Kettlewell Hill. Wok —86A 156
Ketton Grn. Red —100Mb 180
Kevan Ct. E17 —28Dc 44
Kevan Dri. Send —97G 172
Kevan Ho. SE5 —52Sb 105
Kevelioc Rd. N17 —25Sb 43
Kevere Ct. N'wd —22R 36
Kevin Clo. Houn —54Z 99
Kevington Clo. Croy —73Ac 148
Kevington Clo. Orp —70Vc 131
Kevington Dri. Chst & St M —70Vc 131
Kew Bri. Bren & Kew —51Pa 101
Kew Bri. Arches. Rich —51Qa 101
Kew Bri. Ct. W4 —50Qa 79
Kew Bri. Rd. Bren —51Pa 101
Kew Cres. Sutt —76Ab 144
Kewferry Dri. N'wd —22R 36
Kewferry Rd. N'wd —23S 36
Kew Foot Rd. Rich —56Na 101
Kew Gdns. Rd. Rich —52Pa 101
Kew Grn. Rich —51Pa 101
Kew Meadow Path. Rich —53Ra 101
Kew Rd. Rich —51Qa 101
Key Clo. E1 —42Yb 84
Keyes Rd. NW2 —36Za 60
Keyes Rd. Dart —56Pd 111
Key Ho. SE11 —51Qb 104
Keymer Clo. Big H —88Lc 167
Keymer Rd. SW2 —61Pb 126
Keynes Clo. N2 —28Hb 41
Keynsham Av. Wfd G —21Gc 45
Keynsham Gdns. SE9 —57Nc 108
Keynsham Rd. SE9 —57Mc 107
Keynsham Rd. Mord —74Db 145
Keynsham Wlk. Mord —74Db 145
Keyse Rd. SE1 —48Vb 83 (4K 207)
Keysham Av. Houn —53W 98
Keystone Cres. N1 —40Nb 62 (2G 193)
Keywood Dri. Sun —65W 120
Keyworth Pl. SE1 —48Rb 83 (3C 206)
(off Keyworth St.)
Keyworth St. SE1 —48Rb 83 (3C 206)
Kezia St. SE8 —50Ac 84
Khama Rd. SW17 —63Gb 125
Khartoum Pl. Grav —8E 114
Khartoum Rd. E13 —41Kc 85
Khartoum Rd. SW17 —63Fb 125
Khartoum Rd. Ilf —36Rc 66
Khyber Rd. SW11 —54Gb 103
Kibworth St. SW8 —52Pb 104
Kidborough Down. Bookh —99Ca 175
Kidbrooke Gdns. SE3 —54Jc 107
Kidbrooke Gro. SE3 —53Jc 107
Kidbrooke La. SE9 —56Nc 108
Kidbrooke Pk. Clo. SE3 —53Kc 107
Kidbrooke Pk. Rd. SE3 —55Lc 107
Kidbrooke Way. SE3 —54Kc 107
Kidderminster Rd. Croy —74Rb 147
Kidderminster Rd. Slou —1E 72
Kidderpore Av. NW3 —35Cb 61
Kidderpore Gdns. NW3 —35Cb 61
Kidd Pl. SE7 —50Nc 86
Kidlington Way. NW9 —26Ta 39
Kidron Way. E9 —39Yb 64
Kielder Clo. Ilf —23Vc 47
Kier Hardie Ct. NW10 —38Va 60
Kier Hardie Ho. Grays —6A 92
Kier Pk. Asc —9A 116
Kiffen St. EC2 —42Tb 83 (5G 195)
Kilberry Clo. Iswth —53Fa 100
Kilburn Bri. NW6 —39Cb 61
Kilburn High Rd. NW6 —38Bb 61
Kilburn La. W10 & W9 —41Za 80
Kilburn Pk. Rd. NW6 —41Cb 81
Kilburn Pl. NW6 —39Cb 61
Kilburn Priory. NW6 —39Db 61
Kilburn Sq. NW6 —39Cb 61
Kilburn Vale. NW6 —39Db 61
Kilburn Vale Est. NW6 —39Db 61
(off Kilburn Vale)
Kilby Clo. Wat —7Z 5
Kilcorral Clo. Eps —86Wa 162
Kildare Clo. Ruis —32Y 57
Kildare Gdns. W2 —44Cb 81
Kildare Rd. E16 —43Jc 85
Kildare Ter. W2 —44Cb 81
Kildare Wlk. E14 —44Cc 84
Kildonan Clo. Wat —11V 18
Kildoran Rd. SW2 —57Nb 104
Kildowan Rd. Ilf —32Wc 67
Kilgour Rd. SE23 —58Ac 106
Kilkie St. SW6 —54Eb 103
Killarney Rd. SW18 —58Eb 103
Killaser Ct. Tad —95Ya 178
Killearn Rd. SE6 —60Fc 107
Killester Gdns. Wor Pk —77Xa 144
Killewarren Way. Orp —72Yc 151
Killick Ho. Sutt —77Db 145
Killick St. N1 —40Pb 62 (1H 193)
Killieser Av. SW2 —61Nb 126
Killigarth Ct. Sidc —63Wc 131
Killip Clo. E16 —44Hc 85
Killowen Av. N'holt —36Ea 58
Killowen Rd. E9 —37Zb 64
Killyon Rd. SW8 —54Lb 104
Killyon Ter. SW8 —54Lb 104
Kilmaine Rd. SW6 —52Ab 102
Kilmarnock Gdns. Dag —34Yc 67
Kilmarnock Rd. Wat —21Z 37
Kilmarsh Rd. W6 —49Ya 80
Kilmartin Av. SW16 —69Qb 126
Kilmartin Rd. Ilf —33Wc 67
Kilmartin Way. Horn —36Kd 69
Kilmington Clo. Hut —19De 33
Kilmington Rd. SW13 —51Wa 102
Kilmington Way. SE15 —52Vb 105
Kilmiston Av. Shep —72S 140
Kilmorey Gdns. Twic —57Ka 100
Kilmorey Rd. Twic —56Ka 100
Kilmorie Rd. SE23 —60Ac 106
Kiln Clo. Hay —51T 98
Kilndown. Grav —5F 136
Kilner Ho. SE11 —51Qb 104
(off Clayton St.)
Kilner St. E14 —43Cc 84
Kilnfields. Orp —79Cd 152
Kiln La. Asc —10E 116
Kiln La. Eps —83Ua 162
Kiln La. Hedg —2G 52
Kiln La. Rip —96J 173
Kiln La. Wink —5A 116
Kiln Pl. NW5 —35Jb 62
Kilnside. Clay —80Ja 142
Kiln Way. Grays —50Be 91
Kiln Way. N'wd —23U 36
Kilnwood. Hals —85Bd 169
Kilpatrick Way. Hay —43Aa 77
Kilravock St. W10 —41Ab 80
Kilross Rd. Felt —60T 98
Kilrue La. W on T —77V 140
Kilrush Ter. Wok —88C 156
Kilsby Wlk. Dag —37Xc 67
Kilsha Rd. W on T —72Y 141
Kilsmore La. Chesh —1Zb 12
Kilvinton Dri. Enf —10Tb 11
Kilworth Av. Shenf —16Ce 33
Kimbell Gdns. SW6 —53Ab 102
Kimber Clo. Wind —5E 94
Kimberely Rd. Beck —68Zb 128
Kimberley Av. E6 —40Nc 66
Kimberley Av. SE15 —54Xb 105
Kimberley Av. Ilf —31Tc 66
Kimberley Av. Romf —30Ed 48
Kimberley Clo. Slou —49B 74
Kimberley Dri. Sidc —61Zc 131
Kimberley Gdns. N4 —29Rb 43
Kimberley Gdns. Enf —13Vb 25
Kimberley Ga. Brom —66Gc 129
Kimberley Ind. Est. E17 —25Bc 44
Kimberley Pl. Purl —83Qb 164
Kimberley Ride. Cob —85Da 159
Kimberley Rd. E4 —18Gc 27
Kimberley Rd. E11 —33Fc 65
Kimberley Rd. E16 —42Hc 85
Kimberley Rd. E17 —25Bc 44
Kimberley Rd. N17 —26Wb 43
Kimberley Rd. N18 —23Xb 43
Kimberley Rd. NW6 —39Ab 60
Kimberley Rd. SW9 —54Nb 104
Kimberley Rd. Beck —68Zb 128
Kimberley Rd. Croy —72Rb 147
Kimberley Wlk. W on T —73X 141
Kimberley Way. E4 —18Gc 27
Kimber Rd. SW18 —59Cb 103
Kimbers Dri. Burn —1B 72
Kimble Clo. Wat —17U 18
Kimble Cres. Bush —17Ea 20
Kimble Rd. SW19 —65Fb 125
Kimbolton Clo. SE12 —58Hc 107
Kimbolton Grn. Borwd —14Sa 21
Kimmeridge Gdns. SE9 —63Nc 130
Kimmeridge Rd. SE9 —63Nc 130
Kimpton Av. Brtwd —17Xd 32
Kimpton Ind. Est. Sutt —75Bb 145
Kimpton Pl. Wat —6Z 5
Kimpton Rd. SE5 —53Tb 105
Kimpton Rd. Sutt —75Bb 145
Kimptons Clo. Pot B —4Za 8
Kimptons Mead. Pot B —5Za 8
Kimburn Dri. Egh —64A 118
Kinburn St. SE16 —47Zb 84
Kincaid Rd. SE15 —52Xb 105
Kincardine Gdns. W9 —42Cb 81
Kinch Gro. Wemb —31Pa 59
Kincraig Dri. Sev —95Jd 186
Kinder Clo. SE28 —45Yc 87
Kinder Ho. N1 —40Tb 63 (1G 195)
(off Cranston Est.)
Kindersley Way. Abb L —3S 4
Kinder St. E1 —44Xb 83
Kinefold Ho. N7 —37Nb 62
Kinfauns Av. Horn —30Ld 49
Kinfauns Rd. SW2 —61Qb 126
Kinfauns Rd. Ilf —32Wc 67
Kingaby Gdns. Rain —38Jd 68
King Acre Ct. Stai —62G 118
King Alfred Av. SE6 —63Cc 128
(in two parts)
King Alfred Rd. Romf —26Pd 49
King and Queen Clo. SE9 —63Nc 130
King and Queen St. SE17 —50Sb 83 (7E 206)
King Arthur Clo. SE15 —52Yb 106
King Arthur Ct. Wal X —2Ac 12
King Charles Cres. Surb —73Pa 143
King Charles Ho. SW6 —52Db 103
(off Wandon Rd.)
King Charles Rd. Shenl —4Na 7
King Charles Rd. Surb —71Pa 143
King Charles St. SW1 —47Mb 82 (1E 204)
King Charles Wlk. SW19 —60Ab 102
King Ct. E10 —31Dc 64
Kingcup Clo. Croy —73Zb 148
King David La. E1 —45Yb 84
Kingdon Rd. NW6 —37Cb 61
King Edward Av. Dart —58Md 111
King Edward Av. Rain —40Md 69
King Edward Dri. Chess —76Na 143
King Edward Dri. Grays —7A 92
King Edward M. SW13 —53Wa 102
King Edward Rd. E10 —32Ec 64
King Edward Rd. E17 —27Ac 44
King Edward Rd. Barn —14Cb 23
King Edward Rd. Brtwd —20Yd 32
King Edward Rd. Grnh —57Wd 112
King Edward Rd. Romf —30Hd 48
King Edward Rd. Shenl —5Pa 7
King Edward Rd. Wal X —5Ac 12
King Edward Rd. Wat —16Aa 19
King Edward VII Av. Wind —2J 95
King Edward's Gdns. W3 —46Qa 79
King Edwards Gro. Tedd —65Ka 122
King Edwards Mans. SW6 —52Cb 103
(off Fulham Rd.)
King Edward's Pl. W3 —46Qa 79
King Edward's Rd. E9 —39Xb 63
King Edward's Rd. N9 —17Xb 25
King Edwards Rd. Bark —39Tc 66
King Edward's Rd. Enf —14Zb 26
King Edward's Rd. Ruis —32T 56
King Edward's Rd. Stanf —3M 93
King Edward St. EC1 —44Sb 83 (2D 200)
King Edward St. Slou —7H 73
King Edward Wlk. SE1 —48Qb 82 (3A 206)
Kingfield Clo. Wok —92B 172
Kingfield Dri. Wok —92B 172
Kingfield Gdns. Wok —92B 172
Kingfield Rd. W5 —42Ma 79
Kingfield Rd. Wok —92B 172
Kingfield St. E14 —49Ec 84
Kingfisher Clo. SE28 —45Yc 87
Kingfisher Clo. Hut —17Ce 33
Kingfisher Clo. N'wd —25R 36
Kingfisher Clo. Orp —70Zc 131
Kingfisher Clo. W on T —78Aa 141
Kingfisher Ct. SW19 —61Za 124
Kingfisher Ct. Enf —10Pb 10
Kingfisher Ct. Slou —2F 72
Kingfisher Ct. Wok —86E 156
Kingfisher Dri. Rich —63Ka 122
Kingfisher Dri. Stai —63H 119
Kingfisher Gdns. S Croy —83Zb 166
Kingfisher Lure. K Lan —1R 4
Kingfisher Lure. Loud —14K 17
Kingfisher Pl. N22 —26Pb 42
Kingfisher Rd. Upm —32Vd 70
Kingfisher St. E6 —43Nc 86
Kingfisher Wlk. NW9 —26Ua 40
Kingfisher Way. NW10 —37Ta 59
Kingfisher Way. Beck —71Zb 148
King Frederick II Tower. SE16 —48Bc 84
King Gdns. Croy —78Rb 147
King George Av. E16 —44Mc 85
King George Av. Bush —16Da 19
King George Av. Ilf —29Tc 46
King George Av. W on T —74Z 141
King George Clo. Romf —27Ed 48
King George Clo. Sun —64U 120
King George Rd. Wal A —6Ec 12
King George's Av. Wat —15U 18
King George's Dri. New Haw —82J 157
King George's Dri. S'hall —43Ba 77
King George VI Av. Big H —88Mc 167
King George VI Av. E Til —9K 93
King George VI Av. Mitc —70Hb 125
King George Sq. Rich —58Pa 101
King Georges Rd. Pil H —16Xd 32
King George's Trading Est. Chess —77Qa 143
King George St. SE10 —52Ec 106
Kingham Clo. SW18 —59Eb 103
Kingham Clo. W11 —47Ab 80
King Harolds Way. Bexh —52Zc 109
King Henry M. Orp —78Vc 151
King Henry's Dri. New Ad —81Dc 166
King Henry's M. Enf —9Cc 12
King Henry's Rd. NW3 —38Hb 61
King Henry's Rd. King T —69Ra 123
King Henry St. N16 —36Ub 63
King Henry's Wlk. N1 —37Ub 63
Kinghorn St. EC1 —43Sb 83 (1D 200)
King James Av. Cuff —1Nb 10
King James St. SE1 —47Rb 83 (2C 206)
King John Ct. EC2 —42Ub 83 (5J 195)
King John's Clo. Stai —8N 95
King John's Wlk. SE9 —60Mc 107
Kinglake Ct. Wok —6B 188
Kinglake Est. SE17 —50Ub 83 (7J 207)
Kinglake St. SE17 —50Ub 83 (7H 207)
Kingly Ct. W1 —45Lb 82 (4C 198)
(off Beak St.)
Kingly St. W1 —44Lb 82 (3B 198)
King & Queen St. SE17 —50Sb 83
Kings Arbour. S'hall —50Aa 77
King's Arms All. Bren —51Ma 101
Kings Arms Yd. EC2 —44Tb 83 (2F 201)
Kings Arms Yd. Romf —29Gd 48
Kingsash Dri. Hay —42Aa 77
King's Av. N10 —27Jb 42
Kings Av. N21 —18Rb 25
King's Av. SW12 & SW4 —60Mb 104
Kings Av. W5 —44Ma 79
Kings Av. Brom —65Hc 129
King's Av. Buck H —19Mc 27
Kings Av. Byfl —84M 157
King's Av. Cars —80Gb 145
King's Av. Gnfd —43Da 77
Kings Av. Houn —53Da 99
Kings Av. N Mald —70Ua 124
Kings Av. Romf —30Bd 47
King's Av. Sun —64V 120
King's Av. Wat —14V 18
King's Av. Wfd G —23Kc 45
King's Bench St. SE1 —47Rb 83 (1C 206)
King's Bench Wlk. EC4 —45Qb 82 (4A 200)
Kingsbridge Av. W3 —47Pa 79
Kingsbridge Cir. Romf —23Nd 49
Kingsbridge Clo. Romf —23Nd 49
Kingsbridge Cres. S'hall —43Ba 77
Kingsbridge Rd. W10 —44Ya 80
Kingsbridge Rd. Bark —40Tc 66
Kingsbridge Rd. Mord —73Za 144
Kingsbridge Rd. Romf —23Nd 49
Kingsbridge Rd. S'hall —49Ba 77
Kingsbridge Rd. W on T —73X 141
Kingsbridge Way. Hay —41U 76
Kingsbrook. Lea —90Ja 160
Kingsbury Circ. NW9 —29Qa 39
Kingsbury Cres. Stai —63F 118
Kingsbury Dri. Old Win —9L 95
Kingsbury Rd. N1 —37Ub 63
Kingsbury Rd. NW9 —29Qa 39
Kingsbury Ter. N1 —37Ub 63
Kingsbury Trading Est. NW9 —30Ta 39
King's Chase. Brtwd —20Yd 32
Kings Chase. E Mol —69Ea 122
Kingsclere Clo. SW15 —59Wa 102
Kingsclere Ct. N12 —22Gb 41
Kingscliffe Gdns. SW19 —60Bb 103
Kings Clo. E10 —31Dc 64
King's Clo. NW4 —28Za 40
King's Clo. Chal G —19A 16
King's Clo. Chfd —3K 3
King's Clo. Dart —56Gd 110
Kings Clo. N'wd —23V 36
Kings Clo. Stai —65M 119
Kings Clo. W on T —74X 141
King's Clo. Wat —14X 19
King's College Rd. NW3 —38Gb 61
Kings College Rd. Ruis —30V 36
Kingscote Rd. W4 —48Ta 79
Kingscote Rd. Croy —73Xb 147
Kingscote Rd. N Mald —69Ta 123
Kingscote St. EC4 —45Rb 83 (4B 200)
King's Ct. E13 —39Kc 65
King's Ct. SE1 —47Rb 83 (1C 206)
Kings Ct. W6 —49Wa 80
(off King St.)
Kings Ct. Byfl —83M 157
King's Ct. Tad —94Xa 178
Kings Ct. N. SW3 —50Gb 81
Kingscourt Rd. SW16 —62Mb 126
Kings Ct. S. SW3 —50Gb 81
(off King's Rd.)
King's Cres. N4 —34Sb 63
Kings Cres. Est. N4 —33Sb 63
Kingscroft. SW4 —58Nb 104
Kingscroft Rd. NW2 —37Bb 61
Kingscroft Rd. Bans —87Fb 163
Kingscroft Rd. Lea —92Ka 176
King's Cross Bri. N1 —41Nb 82 (3G 193)
(off Gray's Inn Rd.)
King's Cross Rd. WC1 —41Pb 82 (3H 193)
Kingsdale Gdns. W11 —46Za 80
Kingsdale Rd. SE18 —52Vc 109
Kingsdale Rd. SE20 —66Zb 128
Kingsdene. Tad —93Xa 178
Kingsdown Av. W3 —45Ua 80
Kingsdown Av. W13 —47Ka 78
Kingsdown Av. S Croy —82Rb 165
Kingsdown Clo. W10 —44Za 80
Kingsdown Clo. Grav —10H 115
Kingsdowne Rd. Surb —73Na 143
Kingsdown Ho. E8 —36Wb 63
Kingsdown Rd. E11 —34Gc 65
Kingsdown Rd. N19 —33Nb 62
Kingsdown Rd. Eps —85Wa 162
Kingsdown Rd. Sutt —78Ab 144
Kingsdown Way. Brom —72Jc 149
King's Dri. Edgw —21Pa 39
King's Dri. Grav —2D 136
King's Dri. Surb —73Qa 143
Kings Dri. Tedd —64Fa 122
Kings Dri. Th Dit —72Ka 142
Kings Dri. W on T —81V 158
Kings Dri. Wemb —33Ra 59
Kingsend. Ruis —32T 56
Kings Farm Av. Rich —56Qa 101
Kings Farm Rd. Chor —16F 16
Kingsfield. Wind —3B 94
Kingsfield Av. Harr —28Da 37
Kingsfield Ct. Wat —17Z 19
Kingsfield Dri. Enf —7Zb 12
Kingsfield Rd. Harr —31Fa 58
Kingsfield Rd. Wat —17Z 19
Kingsfield Ter. Dart —57Md 111
Kingsfield Ter. Harr —32Fa 58
Kingsfield Way. Enf —7Zb 12
Kingsford Av. Wall —80Nb 146
Kingsford St. NW5 —36Hb 61
Kingsford Way. E6 —43Pc 86
King's Gdns. NW6 —38Cb 61
Kings Gdns. Ilf —32Tc 66
Kings Gdns. Upm —31Ud 70
Kings Garth M. SE23 —61Yb 128
Kingsgate. Wemb —34Sa 59
Kingsgate Av. N3 —27Cb 41
Kingsgate Clo. Bexh —53Ad 109
Kingsgate Clo. Orp —68Yc 131
Kingsgate Est. N1 —37Ub 63
Kingsgate Ho. SW9 —53Qb 104
Kingsgate Pde. SW1 —48Lb 82 (4C 204)
(off Victoria St.)
Kingsgate Pl. NW6 —38Cb 61
Kingsgate Rd. NW6 —38Cb 61
Kingsgate Rd. King T —67Na 123
Kings Grange. Ruis —32V 56
Kings Grn. Lou —13Nc 28
Kingsground. SE9 —59Mc 107
King's Gro. SE15 —53Xb 105
(in two parts)
Kings Gro. Romf —29Jd 48
Kings Hall Rd. Beck —66Ac 128
Kings Head Ct. EC3 —45Tb 83 (5G 201)
(off Pudding La.)
Kings Head Hill. E4 —17Dc 26
Kings Head La. Byfl —83M 157
Kings Head Pas. SW4 —56Mb 104
(off Clapham Pk. Rd.)
King's Head Yd. SE1 —46Tb 83 (7F 201)
King's Highway. SE18 —51Uc 108
King's Hill. Lou —12Nc 28
Kingshill Av. Harr —28Ka 38
Kingshill Av. Hay & N'holt —41U 76
Kingshill Av. Romf —23Ed 48
Kingshill Av. Wor Pk —73Wa 144
Kingshill Ct. Barn —14Ab 22
Kingshill Dri. Harr —27Ka 38
Kingshold Rd. E9 —38Yb 64
Kingsholm Gdns. SE9 —56Mc 107
Kings Ho. SW8 —52Nb 104
(off S. Lambeth Rd.)
Kingshurst Rd. SE12 —59Jc 107
Kingsingfield Clo. W King —80Ud 154
Kingsingfield Rd. W King —80Ud 154
Kings Keep. Brom —69Gc 129
Kings Keep. King T —70Na 123
Kingsland Grn. E8 —37Ub 63
Kingsland Gro. N16 —37Ub 63
Kingsland High St. E8 —37Vb 63
Kingsland Pas. E8 —37Ub 63
Kingsland Rd. E2 & E8 —41Ub 83 (4J 195)
Kingsland Rd. E13 —41Lc 85
King's La. Chfd —3J 3
Kings La. Egh —4L 117
Kings La. Sutt —78Fb 145
Kingslawn Clo. SW15 —57Xa 102
Kingslea. Lea —92Ja 176
Kingsleigh Pl. Mitc —69Hb 125
Kingsleigh Wlk. Brom —70Hc 129
Kingsley Av. W13 —44Ja 78
Kingsley Av. Bans —87Cb 163
Kingsley Av. Borwd —12Pa 21
Kingsley Av. Chesh —1Xb 11
Kingsley Av. Dart —57Qd 111
Kingsley Av. Egh —5M 117
Kingsley Av. Houn —54Ea 100
Kingsley Av. S'hall —45Ca 77
Kingsley Av. Sutt —77Fb 145
Kingsley Clo. N2 —29Eb 41
Kingsley Clo. Dag —35Dd 68
Kingsley Ct. Bexh —57Cd 110
Kingsley Ct. Edgw —19Ra 21
Kingsley Ct. Romf —30Kd 49
Kingsley Ct. Sutt —80Db 145
Kingsley Ct. Wor Pk —75Va 144
(off Avenue, The.)
Kingsley Dri. Wor Pk —75Va 144
Kingsley Flats. SE1 —49Ub 83 (5H 207)
Kingsley Gdns. E4 —22Cc 44
Kingsley Gdns. Horn —28Md 49
Kingsley M. E1 —45Xb 83
Kingsley M. W8 —48Db 81
Kingsley Path. Slou —2B 72
Kingsley Pl. N6 —31Jb 62
Kingsley Rd. E7 —38Jc 65
Kingsley Rd. E17 —26Ec 44
Kingsley Rd. N13 —21Qb 42
Kingsley Rd. NW6 —39Bb 61
Kingsley Rd. SW19 —64Db 125
Kingsley Rd. Croy —74Qb 146
Kingsley Rd. Harr —35Ea 58
Kingsley Rd. Houn —53Da 99
Kingsley Rd. Hut —17Ee 33
Kingsley Rd. Ilf —25Sc 46
Kingsley Rd. Lou —13Tc 28
Kingsley Rd. Orp —80Vc 151
Kingsley Rd. Pinn —28Ba 37
Kingsley St. SW11 —55Hb 103
Kingsley Wlk. Grays —9C 92
Kingsley Way. N2 —30Eb 41
Kingsley Wood Dri. SE9 —62Pc 130
Kingslyn Cres. SE19 —68Ub 127
Kings Lynn Clo. H Hill —23Md 49
Kings Lynn Dri. Romf —23Md 49
Kings Lynn Path. H Hill —23Md 49
Kings Mall. W6 —49Ya 80
Kingsman Dri. Grays —45De 91
Kingsman Pde. SE18 —48Pc 86
Kingsman Rd. Stanf —2K 93
Kingsman St. SE18 —48Pc 86
Kingsmead. Barn —14Cb 23
Kingsmead. Big H —88Mc 167
Kingsmead. Cuff —1Nb 10
Kings Mead. Rich —58Pa 101
Kingsmead. Wal X —1Zb 12
Kingsmead. Wok —88C 156
Kingsmead Av. N9 —18Xb 25
Kingsmead Av. NW9 —31Ta 59
Kingsmead Av. Mitc —69Lb 126
Kingsmead Av. Romf —30Hd 48
Kingsmead Av. Sun —68Y 121
Kingsmead Av. Surb —75Qa 143
Kingsmead Av. Wor Pk —75Xa 144
Kingsmead Clo. Eps —80Ta 143
Kingsmead Clo. Sidc —61Wc 131
Kingsmead Clo. Tedd —65Ka 122
Kingsmead Cotts. Brom —74Nc 150
Kingsmead Ct. N6 —31Mb 62
Kingsmead Dri. N'holt —38Ba 57
Kingsmead Ho. E9 —35Ac 64
Kingsmead Mans. Romf —30Hd 48
(off Kingsmead Av.)
Kings Meadow. K Lan —1Q 4
Kingsmeadow. King T —69Ra 123
Kings Meadow Ct. Wal A —6Jc 13
(off Horseshoe Clo.)
Kings Mead Pk. Clay —80Ga 142
Kingsmead Rd. SW2 —61Qb 126
King's Mead Way. E9 —35Ac 64
Kingsmere Clo. SW15 —55Za 102
Kingsmere Pk. NW9 —32Ra 59
Kingsmere Rd. SW19 —61Za 124
King's M. SW4 —57Nb 104
King's M. WC1 —42Pb 82 (6J 193)
Kings M. Chig —19Sc 28
Kingsmill Gdns. Dag —36Bd 67
Kingsmill Rd. Dag —36Bd 67
Kingsmill Ter. NW8 —40Fb 61 (1C 190)
Kingsnorth Ho. W10 —44Za 80
Kingsnympton Pk. King T —65Ra 123
King's Orchard. SE9 —58Nc 108
Kings Paddock. Hamp —67Ea 122
Kings Pde. Stanf —2L 93
(off King St.)
Kingspark Ct. E18 —27Jc 45
Kings Pas. King T —68Ma 123
King's Pl. SE1 —47Sb 83 (2D 206)
King's Pl. W4 —50Sa 79
Kings Pl. Buck H —19Lc 27
King Sq. EC1 —41Sb 83 (4D 194)
King's Quay. SW10 —53Eb 103
(off Chelsea Harbour)
Kings Reach Tower. SE1 —46Rb 83 (6B 200)
(off Stamford St.)
Kings Ride Ga. Rich —56Qa 101
Kingsridge. SW19 —61Ab 124
Kingsridge Gdns. Dart —58Md 111
Kings Rd. E4 —18Fc 27
King's Rd. E6 —39Lc 65
King's Rd. E11 —31Gc 65
King's Rd. N17 —25Vb 43
King's Rd. N18 —22Wb 43
Kings Rd. N22 —25Pb 42
King's Rd. NW10 —38Xa 60
King's Rd. SE25 —69Wb 127
King's Rd. SW3 —51Fb 103
King's Rd. SW6 & SW10 —52Db 103
Kings Rd. SW14 —55Ta 101
Kings Rd. SW19 —65Cb 125
Kings Rd. W5 —43Ma 79
Kings Rd. Bark —38Sc 66
King's Rd. Barn —13Ya 22
Kings Rd. Big H —88Lc 167
King's Rd. Brtwd —19Yd 32
Kings Rd. Chal G —18A 16
King's Rd. Egh —63C 118
Kings Rd. Felt —60Y 99
Kings Rd. Harr —33Ba 57
King's Rd. King T —67Na 123
King's Rd. Mitc —69Jb 126
Kings Rd. New Ham —82K 157
King's Rd. Orp —77Vc 151
King's Rd. Rich —58Pa 101
King's Rd. Romf —29Jd 48
King's Rd. Slou —8J 73
King's Rd. S'hill —10B 116
King's Rd. Surb —74La 142
King's Rd. Sutt —82Cb 163
King's Rd. Tedd —64Fa 122
King's Rd. Twic —58Ka 100
King's Rd. Uxb —40M 55
King's Rd. W on T —75X 141
King's Rd. W Dray —47P 75
King's Rd. Wind —6H 95
Kings Rd. Wok —88C 156
Kings Rd. Bungalows. S Harr —34Ba 57
King's Scholars' Pas. SW1 —48Lb 82 (4B 204)
(off Carlisle Pl.)
King's Shade Wlk. Eps —85Ta 161
Kingstable St. Eton —2H 95
King Stairs Clo. SE16 —47Xb 83
King's Ter. NW1 —39Lb 62 (1B 192)
King's Ter. Iswth —56Ja 100
Kingsthorpe Rd. SE26 —63Zb 128
Kingston Av. E Hor —98U 174
Kingston Av. Felt —58U 98
Kingston Av. Lea —93Ka 176
Kingston Av. Sutt —76Ab 144
Kingston Av. W Dray —45P 75
(in two parts)

Kingston Bri.—Lambeth Rd.

Kingston Bri. King T —68Ma 123
Kingston By-Pass. SW15 & SW20 —64Ua 124
Kingston By-Pass. Surb & N Mald —76Ma 143
Kingston By-Pass Rd. Esh & Surb —75Ga 142
Kingston Clo. N'holt —39Ba 57
Kingston Clo. Romf —27Ad 47
Kingston Clo. Tedd —65Ka 122
Kingston Ct. Grav —57De 113
Kingston Cres. Ashf —64L 119
Kingston Cres. Beck —67Bc 128
Kingston Gdns. Croy —76Nb 146
Kingston Hall Rd. King T —69Ma 123
Kingston Hill. King T —67Qa 123
Kingston Hill Av. Romf —26Ad 47
Kingston Hill Pl. King T —63Ta 123
Kingston Ho. Est. Surb —72La 142
Kingston Ho. Gdns. Lea —93Ka 176
Kingston La. Tedd —64Ja 122
Kingston La. Uxb —41N 75
Kingston La. W Dray —47P 75
Kingston La. W Hor —99Q 174
Kingston Pl. Harr —24Ha 38
Kingston Rise. New Haw —82J 157
Kingston Rd. N9 —19Wb 25
Kingston Rd. SW15 —61Wa 124
Kingston Rd. SW20 & SW19 —68Ya 124
Kingston Rd. Ashf —65N 119
Kingston Rd. Barn —15Fb 23
Kingston Rd. Eps —81Va 162
Kingston Rd. Ilf —35Rc 66
Kingston Rd. King T & N Mald —69Ra 123
Kingston Rd. Lea —93Ja 176
(in two parts)
Kingston Rd. Romf —28Hd 48
Kingston Rd. S'hall —47Ba 77
Kingston Rd. Stai & Ashf —63J 119
Kingston Rd. Surb & Wor Pk —75Ra 143
Kingston Rd. Tedd —64Ka 122
Kingston Sq. SE19 —64Tb 127
Kingston Vale. SW15 —63Ta 123
Kingstown St. NW1 —39Jb 62
King St. E13 —42Jc 85
King St. EC2 —44Sb 83 (3E 200)
King St. N2 —27Fb 41
King St. N17 —25Vb 43
King St. SW1 —46Lb 82 (7C 198)
King St. W3 —46Ra 79
King St. W6 —49Wa 80
King St. WC2 —45Nb 82 (4F 199)
King St. Cher —74J 139
King St. Grav —8D 114
King St. Rich —57Ma 101
King St. S'hall —48Aa 77
King St. Stanf —2L 93
King St. Twic —60Ja 100
King St. Wat —14Y 19
Kingsvale Ct. W Dray —45M 75
Kings Wlk. Grays —51Ce 113
King's Wlk. King T —67Ma 123
Kings Wlk. S Croy —86Xb 165
Kingswater Pl. SW11 —52Gb 103
Kingsway. N12 —23Eb 41
Kingsway. SW14 —55Ra 101
Kingsway. WC2 —44Pb 82 (2H 199)
King's Way. Croy —78Pb 146
Kingsway. Cuff —2Nb 10
Kingsway. Enf —15Xb 25
Kingsway. Farn C —7F 52
Kingsway. Ger X —27A 34
Kings Way. Harr —28Ga 38
Kingsway. Hay —43S 76
Kingsway. Iver —44G 74
Kingsway. N Mald —71Ya 144
Kingsway. Orp —71Tc 150
Kingsway. Stai —60M 97
Kingsway. Wemb —35Na 59
Kingsway. W Wick —76Gc 149
Kingsway. Wok —6G 188
Kings Way. Wfd G —22Lc 45
Kingsway Av. S Croy —81Yb 166
Kingsway Av. Wok —6G 188
Kingsway Bus. Pk. Hamp —67Ba 121
Kingsway Cres. Harr —28Ea 38
Kingsway N. Orbital Rd. Wat —7V 4
Kingsway Rd. Sutt —80Ab 144
Kingsway, The. Eps —82Va 162
Kingswear Rd. NW5 —34Kb 62
Kingswear Rd. Ruis —33W 56
Kingswell Ride. Cuff —2Nb 10
Kingswick Clo. Asc —10B 116
Kingswick Dri. Asc —10B 116
Kingswood Av. NW6 —39Ab 60
Kingswood Av. Belv —49Bd 87
Kingswood Av. Brom —70Gc 129
Kingswood Av. Hamp —65Da 121
Kingswood Av. Houn —54Ba 99
Kingswood Av. S Croy —87Xb 165
Kingswood Av. Swan —70Hd 132
Kingswood Av. T Hth —71Qb 146
Kingswood Clo. N20 —17Eb 23
Kingswood Clo. SW8 —52Nb 104
Kingswood Clo. Dart —58Ld 111
Kingswood Clo. Egh —3P 117
Kingswood Clo. Enf —15Ub 25
Kingswood Clo. N Mald —72Va 144
Kingswood Clo. Orp —73Tc 150
Kingswood Clo. Surb —73Na 143
Kingswood Clo. Wey —80R 140
Kingswood Ct. Hors —88A 156
Kingswood Ct. Tad —96Ab 178
Kingswood Creek. Wray —7P 95
Kingswood Dri. SE19 —63Ub 127
Kingswood Dri. Cars —74Hb 145
Kingswood Dri. Sutt —81Db 163
Kingswood Est. SE21 —63Ub 127
Kingswood Ho. Slou —3G 72
Kingswood La. Warl —87Yb 166
Kingswood Pk. N3 —25Bb 41
Kingswood Pl. SE13 —56Gc 107
Kingswood Rise. Egh —4P 117
Kingswood Rd. SE20 —65Yb 128
Kingswood Rd. SW2 —58Nb 104
Kingswood Rd. SW19 —66Bb 125
Kingswood Rd. W4 —48Sa 79
Kingswood Rd. Brom —70Fc 129
Kingswood Rd. Dun G —92Gd 186
Kingswood Rd. Ilf —32Wc 67
Kingswood Rd. Tad —93Xa 178
Kingswood Rd. Wat —6X 5
Kingswood Rd. Wemb —34Qa 59
Kingswood Way. S Croy —85Yb 166
(in two parts)
Kingswood Way. Wall —78Nb 146
Kingsworth Clo. Beck —71Ac 148
Kingsworthy Clo. King T —69Pa 123
Kingthorpe Rd. NW10 —38Ta 59
Kingthorpe Ter. NW10 —38Ta 59
(off Brentfield Rd.)
Kingwell Rd. Barn —10Fb 9
King William IV Gdns. SE20 —65Yb 128
King William La. SE10 —50Gc 85
King William St. EC4 —44Tb 83 (4G 201)
King William Wlk. SE10 —51Ec 106
(in two parts)
Kingwood Rd. SW6 —53Ab 102
Kinlet Rd. SE18 —53Sc 108
Kinloch Dri. NW9 —31Ta 59
Kinloch St. N7 —34Pb 62
Kinloss Ct. N3 —28Bb 41
Kinloss Gdns. N3 —27Bb 41
Kinloss Rd. Cars —73Eb 145
Kinnaird Av. W4 —52Sa 101
Kinnaird Av. Brom —65Hc 129
Kinnaird Clo. Brom —65Hc 129
Kinnaird Clo. Slou —4A 72
Kinnaird Way. Wfd G —23Pc 46
Kinnear Rd. W12 —47Va 80
Kinnerton Pl. N. SW1 —47Hb 81 (2G 203)
(off Kinnerton St.)
Kinnerton Pl. S. SW1 —47Hb 81 (2G 203)
(off Kinnerton St.)
Kinnerton St. SW1 —47Jb 82 (2H 203)
Kinnerton Yd. SW1 —47Jb 82 (2H 203)
(off Kinnerton St.)
Kinnoul Rd. W6 —51Ab 102
Kinross Av. Wor Pk —75Wa 144
Kinross Clo. Edgw —19Ra 21
Kinross Clo. Harr —29Na 39
Kinross Clo. Sun —64V 120
Kinross Dri. Sun —64V 120
Kinsale Rd. SE15 —55Wb 105
Kintore Way. SE1 —49Vb 83 (5K 207)
Kintyre Clo. SW16 —68Pb 126
Kintyre Ct. SW2 —59Nb 104
Kinveachy Gdns. SE7 —50Nc 86
Kinver Rd. SE26 —63Yb 128
Kipings. Tad —93Za 178
Kipling Av. Til —3D 114
Kipling Ct. W7 —45Ha 78
Kipling Dri. SW19 —65Fb 125
Kipling Est. SE1 —47Tb 83 (2G 207)
(off Kipling St.)
Kipling Est. SW1 —47Tb 83
Kipling Pl. Stan —23Ha 38
Kipling Rd. Bexh —53Ad 109
Kipling Rd. Dart —57Rd 111
Kipling St. SE1 —47Tb 83 (2G 207)
Kipling St. SW1 —47Tb 83
Kipling Ter. N9 —20Tb 25
Kippington Clo. Sev —96Hd 186
Kippington Dri. SE9 —60Mc 107
Kippington Rd. Sev —96Jd 186
Kirby Clo. Eps —78Va 144
Kirby Clo. Ilf —23Uc 46
Kirby Clo. Lou —17Nc 28
Kirby Clo. N'wd —23V 36
Kirby Clo. Romf —22Qd 49
Kirby Est. SE16 —48Xb 83
Kirby Gro. SE1 —47Ub 83 (1H 207)
Kirby Rd. Dart —59Td 112
Kirby Rd. Wok —5F 188
Kirby St. EC1 —43Qb 82 (7A 194)
Kirchen Rd. W13 —45Ka 78
Kirkcaldy Grn. Wat —20Y 19
Kirkcourt. Sev —95Jd 186
Kirkdale. SE26 —61Xb 127
Kirkdale Rd. E11 —32Gc 65
Kirkgate, The. Eps —85Ua 162
Kirkham Rd. E6 —44Nc 86
Kirkham St. SE18 —51Uc 108
Kirkland Av. Ilf —26Qc 46
Kirkland Av. Wok —4B 188
Kirkland Clo. Sidc —58Uc 108
Kirkland Wlk. E8 —37Vb 63
Kirk La. SE18 —51Sc 108
Kirkleas Rd. Surb —74Na 143
Kirklees Rd. Dag —36Yc 67
Kirklees Rd. T Hth —71Qb 146
Kirkley Rd. SW19 —67Cb 125
Kirkly Clo. S Croy —81Ub 165
Kirkman Pl. W1 —43Mb 82 (1D 198)
(off Tottenham Ct. Rd.)
Kirkmichael Rd. E14 —44Ec 84
Kirk Rise. Sutt —76Db 145
Kirk Rd. E17 —30Bc 44
Kirkside Rd. SE3 —51Jc 107
Kirk's Pl. E14 —43Bc 84
Kirkstall Av. N17 —28Tb 43
Kirkstall Gdns. SW2 —60Nb 104
Kirkstall Rd. SW2 —60Mb 104
Kirksted Rd. Mord —74Db 145
Kirkstone Way. Brom —66Gc 129
Kirk St. WC1 —42Pb 82 (6J 193)
(off Northington St.)
Kirkton Rd. N15 —28Ub 43
Kirkwall Pl. E2 —41Yb 84
Kirkwall Spur. Slou —3J 73
Kirkwood La. NW1 —38Jb 62
Kirkwood Rd. SE15 —54Xb 105
Kirtley Rd. SE26 —63Ac 128
Kirtling St. SW8 —52Lb 104
Kirton Clo. W4 —49Ta 79
Kirton Clo. Horn —37Ld 69
Kirton Gdns. E2 —41Vb 83 (4K 195)
Kirton Rd. E13 —40Lc 65
Kirton Wlk. Edgw —24Sa 39
Kirwyn Way. SE5 —52Sb 105
Kitcat Ter. E3 —41Cc 84
Kitchener Av. Grav —3E 136
Kitchener Ho. Ger X —21A 34
Kitchener Rd. E7 —37Kc 65
Kitchener Rd. E17 —25Dc 44
Kitchener Rd. N2 —27Gb 41
Kitchener Rd. N17 —27Ub 43
Kitchener Rd. Dag —37Ed 68
Kitchener Rd. T Hth —69Tb 127
Kite Pl. E2 —41Wb 83
(off Lampern St.)
Kite Yd. SW11 —53Hb 103
Kitley Gdns. SE19 —67Vb 127
Kitsmead La. Longc —75A 138
Kitson Rd. SE5 —52Tb 105
Kitson Rd. SW13 —53Wa 102
Kitswell Way. Rad —5Ha 6
Kitters Grn. Abb L —3U 4
Kittiwake Clo. S Croy —82Ac 166
Kittiwake Rd. N'holt —41Z 77
Kittiwake Way. Hay —43Z 77
Kitto Rd. SE14 —54Zb 106
Kitts End Rd. Barn —8Za 8
Kiver Rd. N19 —33Mb 62
Klea Av. SW4 —58Lb 104
Knaresborough Pl. SW5 —49Db 81
Knapdale Clo. SE23 —61Xb 127
Knapmill Rd. SE6 —61Cc 128
Knapmill Way. SE6 —61Dc 128
Knapp Clo. NW10 —37Ua 60
Knapp Rd. E3 —42Cc 84
Knapp Rd. Ashf —63P 119
Knapton M. SW17 —65Jb 126
Knaresborough Pl. SW5 —49Db 81
Knatchbull Rd. NW10 —39Ta 59
Knatchbull Rd. SE5 —54Rb 105
Knatts Valley Rd. Knat —80Td 154
Knave Wood Rd. Kems —89Nd 171
Knebworth Av. E17 —25Cc 44
Knebworth Ho. SW8 —53Mb 104
Knebworth Path. Borwd —14Ta 21
Knebworth Rd. N16 —35Ub 63
Knee Hill. SE2 —49Yc 87
Kneehill Cres. SE2 —49Yc 87
Kneller Gdns. Iswth —58Fa 100
Kneller Rd. SE4 —56Ac 106
Kneller Rd. N Mald —73Ua 144
Kneller Rd. Twic —58Ea 100
Knighten St. E1 —46Xb 83
Knighthead Point. E14 —47Cc 84
Knightland Rd. NW10 —38Ta 59
Knightland Rd. E5 —33Xb 63
Knighton Clo. Romf —30Fd 48
Knighton Clo. S Croy —81Rb 165
Knighton Clo. Wfd G —21Kc 45
Knighton Dri. Wfd G —21Kc 45
Knighton La. Buck H —19Kc 27
Knighton Pk. Rd. SE26 —64Zb 128
Knighton Rd. E7 —34Jc 65
Knighton Rd. Otf —88Gd 170
Knighton Rd. Romf —30Ed 48
Knighton Way La. Den —37K 55
Knightrider Ct. EC4 —45Sb 83 (4D 200)
(off Knightrider St.)
Knightrider St. EC4 —44Rb 83 (4C 200)
Knight's Arc. SW1 —47Hb 81 (2F 203)
(off Knightsbridge)
Knights Av. W5 —47Na 79
Knightsbridge. SW7 & SW1 —47Gb 81 (2D 202)
Knightsbridge Ct. SW1 —47Hb 81 (2G 203)
(off Sloane St.)
Knightsbridge Cres. Stai —65K 119
Knightsbridge Gdns. Romf —29Fd 48
Knightsbridge Grn. SW1 —47Hb 81 (2F 203)
Knights Clo. E9 —36Yb 64
Knights Clo. Egh —65F 118
Knights Clo. Wind —3B 94
Knights Ct. Brom —62Hc 129
Knights Ct. King T —69Na 123
Knights Croft. New Ash —76Be 155
Knights Hill. SE27 —64Rb 127
Knight's Hill Sq. SE27 —63Rb 127
Knights La. N9 —20Wb 25
Knights Mnr. Way. Dart —57Pd 111
Knight's Pk. King T —69Na 123
Knights Ridge. Orp —78Xc 151
Knight's Rd. E16 —47Jc 85
Knights Rd. Stan —21La 38
Knights Wlk. SE11 —49Rb 83 (6B 206)
Knights Wlk. Abr —13Xc 29
Knights Way. Brtwd —20Ce 33
Knights Way. Ilf —23Sc 46
Knightswood. Wok —6C 188
Knightswood Clo. Edgw —19Sa 21
Knightswood Ct. N6 —31Mb 62
Knightswood Ho. N12 —23Eb 41
Knightwood Cres. N Mald —72Ua 144
Knipp Hill. Cob —85Ba 159
Knivet Rd. SW6 —51Cb 103
Knobs Hill Rd. E15 —39Dc 64
Knockhall Chase. Grnh —57Xd 112
Knockhall Rd. Grnh —58Yd 112
Knockholt Clo. Sutt —82Db 163
Knockholt Main Rd. Knock —91Vc 185
Knockholt Rd. SE9 —57Mc 107
Knockholt Rd. Hals —86Bd 169
Knole Clo. Croy —72Yb 148
Knole Ga. Sidc —62Uc 130
Knole La. Sev —98Ld 187
Knole Rd. Dart —59Jd 110
Knole Rd. Sev —95Md 187
Knole, The. SE9 —63Qc 130
Knole, The. Grav —6A 136
Knole Way. Sev —97Ld 187
Knoll Cres. N'wd —26U 36
(in two parts)
Knoll Dri. N14 —17Jb 24
Knoll Ho. Pinn —26Z 37
Knollmead. Surb —74Sa 143
Knoll Rise. Orp —74Vc 151
Knoll Rd. SW18 —57Eb 103
Knoll Rd. Bex —59Cd 110
Knoll Rd. Sidc —64Xc 131
Knoll Roundabout. Lea —93La 176
Knolls Clo. Wor Pk —76Xa 144
Knolls, The. Eps —88Ya 162
Knoll, The. W5 —43La 78
Knoll, The. Beck —67Dc 128
Knoll, The. Brom —74Jc 149
Knoll, The. Cob —85Ca 159
Knoll, The. Lea —93La 176
Knollys Clo. SW16 —62Qb 126
Knollys Rd. SW16 —62Qb 126
Knolton Way. Slou —4M 73
Knottisford St. E2 —41Yb 84
Knotts Grn. Rd. E10 —30Dc 44
Knotts Pl. Sev —96Jd 186
Knowland Way. Den —30H 35
Knowle Av. Bexh —52Ad 109
Knowle Clo. SW9 —55Qb 104
Knowle Gdns. W Byf —85H 157
Knowle Grn. Stai —64J 119
Knowle Pk. Cob —87Aa 159
Knowle Pk. Av. Stai —65K 119
Knowle Rd. Brom —75Pc 150
Knowle Rd. Twic —60Ga 100
Knowles Clo. W Dray —46N 75
Knowles Ct. Harr —30Ha 38
(off Gayton Rd.)
Knowles Hill Cres. SE13 —57Fc 107
Knowles Wlk. SW4 —55Lb 104
Knowle, The. Tad —93Ya 178
Knowl Hill. Wok —91D 172
Knowl Pk. Els —15Na 21
Knowlton Cotts. S Ock —43Yd 90
Knowlton Grn. Brom —71Hc 149
Knowlton Ho. SW9 —53Rb 105
(off Cowley Rd.)
Knowl Way. Els —15Pa 21
Knowsley Av. S'hall —46Da 77
Knowsley Rd. SW11 —54Hb 103
Knox Ct. SW4 —54Nb 104
Knox Rd. E7 —37Hc 65
Knox St. W1 —43Hb 81 (7F 191)
Knoyle St. SE14 —51Ac 106
Knutsford Av. Wat —10Z 5
Koblenz Ho. N8 —27Nb 42
(off Newland Rd.)
Kohat Rd. SW19 —64Db 125
Koh-I-Noor Av. Bush —16Ca 19
Komeheather Ho. Ilf —29Pc 46
Koonowla Clo. Big H —87Mc 167
Kooringa. Warl —91Xb 181
Korda Clo. Shep —69P 119
Kossuth St. SE10 —50Gc 85
Kotree Way. SE1 —49Wb 83
Koya Ct. Wex —4M 73
Kramer M. SW5 —50Cb 81
Kreisel Wlk. Rich —51Pa 101
Kristina Ct. Sutt —80Cb 145
(off Overton Rd.)
Krupnik Pl. EC2 —42Ub 83 (5J 195)
(off Krupnik Pl.)
Kuala Gdns. SW16 —67Pb 126
Kuhn Way. E7 —36Jc 65
Kydbrook Clo. Orp —73Sc 150
Kylemore Clo. E6 —40Mc 65
Kylemore Rd. NW6 —38Cb 61
Kymberley Rd. Harr —30Ga 38
Kyme Rd. Horn —30Hd 48
Kymes Ct. S Harr —33Fa 58
Kynance Clo. Romf —20Ld 31
Kynance Gdns. Stan —25La 38
Kynance M. SW7 —48Db 81
Kynance Pl. SW7 —48Eb 81 (4A 202)
Kynaston Av. N16 —34Vb 63
Kynaston Av. T Hth —71Sb 147
Kynaston Clo. Harr —24Fa 38
Kynaston Ct. Cat —97Ub 181
Kynaston Cres. T Hth —71Sb 147
Kynaston Rd. N16 —34Ub 63
Kynaston Rd. Brom —64Jc 129
Kynaston Rd. Enf —11Tb 25
Kynaston Rd. Orp —73Xc 151
Kynaston Rd. T Hth —71Sb 147
Kynaston Wood. Harr —24Fa 38
Kynnersley Clo. Cars —76Hb 145
Kynoch Ct. Stanf —2N 93
Kynoch Rd. N18 —21Yb 44
Kyrle Rd. SW11 —58Jb 104
Kytes Dri. Wat —5Z 5
Kytes Est. Wat —5Z 5
Kyverdale Rd. N16 —32Vb 63
Laburnham Clo. Upm —31Wd 70
Laburnham Gdns. Upm —31Vd 70
Laburnum Av. N9 —19Vb 25
Laburnum Av. N17 —24Tb 43
Laburnum Av. Dart —60Ld 111
Laburnum Av. Horn —33Jd 68
Laburnum Av. Sutt —76Gb 145
Laburnum Av. Swan —69Fd 132
Laburnum Av. W Dray —45P 75
Laburnum Clo. E4 —23Bc 44
Laburnum Clo. N11 —23Kb 42
Laburnum Clo. SE15 —52Yb 106
Laburnum Clo. Chesh —3Zb 12
Laburnum Ct. E2 —39Vb 63 (1K 195)
Laburnum Ct. SE16 —47Yb 84
(off Albion St.)
Laburnum Ct. SE19 —67Vb 127
Laburnum Ct. Harr —30Da 37
Laburnum Ct. Stan —21La 38
Laburnum Cres. Sun —67X 121
Laburnum Gdns. N21 —19Sb 25
Laburnum Gdns. Croy —74Zb 148
Laburnum Gro. N21 —19Sb 25
Laburnum Gro. NW9 —31Sa 59
Laburnum Gro. Grav —59Fe 113
Laburnum Gro. Houn —56Ba 99
Laburnum Gro. N Mald —68Ta 123
Laburnum Gro. Ruis —30T 36
Laburnum Gro. Slou —51D 96
Laburnum Gro. S'hall —42Ba 77
Laburnum Ho. Brom —67Gc 129
Laburnum Lodge. N3 —26Bb 41
Laburnum Pl. Egh —5M 117
Laburnum Rd. SW19 —66Eb 125
Laburnum Rd. Cher —74J 139
Laburnum Rd. Coop —1Yc 15
Laburnum Rd. Eps —85Ua 162
Laburnum Rd. Hay —49V 76
Laburnum Rd. Mitc —68Jb 126
Laburnum Rd. Wok —8G 188
Laburnum St. E2 —39Vb 63 (1K 195)
Laburnum Wlk. Horn —36Ld 69
Laburnum Way. Brom —73Qc 150
Laburnum Way. Stai —60P 97
Lacebark Gdns. Sidc —59Vc 109
Lacey Av. Coul —92Qb 180
Lacey Clo. N9 —19Wb 25
Lacey Clo. Egh —66F 118
Lacey Dri. Coul —92Rb 181
Lacey Dri. Edgw —21Pa 39
Lacey Dri. Hamp —67Ba 121
Lacey Grn. Coul —92Qb 180
Lacey Wlk. E3 —40Cc 64
Lackford Rd. Coul —90Hb 163
Lackington St. EC2 —43Tb 83 (7G 195)
Lackmore Rd. Enf —7Yb 12
Lacock Clo. SW19 —65Eb 125
Lacon Rd. SE22 —56Wb 105
Lacy Rd. SW15 —56Za 102
Ladas Rd. SE27 —63Sb 127
Ladbroke Cres. W11 —44Ab 80
Ladbroke Gdns. W11 —45Bb 81
Ladbroke Gro. W10 & W11 —42Za 80
Ladbroke M. W11 —46Ab 80
Ladbroke Rd. W11 —46Bb 81
Ladbroke Rd. Enf —16Vb 25
Ladbroke Rd. Eps —86Ta 161
Ladbroke Sq. W11 —45Bb 81
Ladbroke Ter. W11 —45Bb 81
Ladbroke Wlk. W11 —46Bb 81
Ladbrook Clo. Pinn —29Ba 37
Ladbrook Clo. Pot B —4Cb 9
Ladbrooke Cres. Sidc —62Zc 131
Ladbrooke Dri. Pot B —4Cb 9
Ladbrooke Rd. Slou —8G 72
Ladbrook Rd. SE25 —70Tb 127
Ladderstile Ride. King T —64Ra 123
Ladderswood. N11 —22Lb 42
Ladds Way. Swan —70Fd 132
Lady Booth Rd. King T —68Na 123
Ladycroft Gdns. Orp —78Sc 150
Ladycroft Rd. SE13 —55Dc 106
Ladycroft Wlk. Stan —25Ma 39
Ladycroft Way. Orp —78Sc 150
Ladyday Pl. Slou —6G 72
Lady Dock Wlk. SE16 —47Ac 84
Ladyfields. Grav —3B 136
Ladyfields. Lou —14Sc 28
Ladyfields Clo. Lou —14Sc 28
Ladygate La. Ruis —30R 36
Ladygrove. Croy —81Ac 166
Ladygrove Dri. Guild —100C 172
Lady Hay. Wor Pk —75Va 144
Lady Margaret Rd. NW5 & N19 —36Lb 62
Lady Margaret Rd. S'hall —45Ba 77
Lady's Clo. Wat —14Y 19
Lady Shaw Ct. N13 —19Pb 24
Ladyship Ter. SE22 —59Wb 105
Ladysmith Av. E6 —40Nc 66
Ladysmith Av. Ilf —31Tc 66
Ladysmith Rd. E16 —41Hc 85
Ladysmith Rd. N17 —26Wb 43
Ladysmith Rd. N18 —22Xb 43
Ladysmith Rd. SE9 —58Qc 108
Ladysmith Rd. Enf —13Ub 25
Ladysmith Rd. Harr —26Ga 38
Lady Somerset Rd. NW5 —35Kb 62
Ladythorpe Clo. Add —77K 139
Ladywalk. Rick —22G 34
Ladywell Clo. SE4 —57Cc 106
Ladywell Heights. SE4 —58Bc 106
Ladywell Rd. SE13 —57Cc 106
Ladywell St. E15 —39Hc 65
Ladywood Av. Orp —71Uc 150
Ladywood Clo. Rick —13K 17
Ladywood Rd. Dart —63Rd 134
Ladywood Rd. Surb —75Qa 143
Lafone Av. Felt —61Y 121
Lafone St. SE1 —47Vb 83 (1K 207)
Lagado M. SE16 —46Zb 84
Lagan Ho. SE15 —52Wb 105
(off Sumner Est.)
Lagonda Av. Ilf —23Vc 47
Lagonda Way. Dart —56Ld 111
Lagoon Rd. Orp —71Yc 151
Laing Clo. Ilf —23Tc 46
Laing Dean. N'holt —39Y 57
Laing Ho. SE5 —52Sb 105
Laings Av. Mitc —68Hb 125
Lainlock Pl. Houn —53Da 99
Lainson St. SW18 —59Cb 103
Lairdale Clo. SE21 —60Sb 105
Laird Av. Grays —47Fe 91
Lairs Clo. N7 —36Nb 62
Laitwood Rd. SW12 —60Kb 104
Lake Av. Brom —65Jc 129
Lake Av. Rain —40Md 69
Lake Av. Slou —5H 73
Lake Bus. Cen. N17 —24Wb 43
Lake Clo. Byfl —84M 157
Lakedale Rd. SE18 —51Uc 108
Lake Dri. Bush —19Ea 20
Lake End Rd. Tap —5A 72
Lakefield Rd. N22 —26Rb 43
Lakefields Clo. Rain —40Md 69
Lake Footpath. SE2 —47Zc 87
Lake Gdns. Dag —36Cd 68
Lake Gdns. Rich —61Ka 122
Lake Gdns. Wall —76Kb 146
Lakehall Gdns. T Hth —71Rb 147
Lakehall Rd. T Hth —71Rb 147
Lake Ho. Rd. E11 —34Jc 65
Lakehurst Rd. Eps —78Ua 144
Lakeland Clo. Chig —21Xc 47
Lakeland Clo. Harr —23Fa 38
Lakeman Ho. Ger X —22B 34
Lakenheath. N14 —15Lb 24
Laker Ct. SW4 —53Nb 104
Lake Rise. Romf —26Hd 48
Lake Rise. W Thur —49Wd 90
Lake Rise Trading Est. W Thur —49Wd 90
Lake Rd. SW19 —64Bb 125
Lake Rd. Croy —75Bc 148
Lake Rd. Romf —28Zc 47
Lake Rd. Vir W —10M 117
Laker Pl. SW15 —58Bb 103
Lakers Rise. Bans —88Gb 163
Lakeside. N3 —26Db 41
Lakeside. SE2 —48Zc 87
Lakeside. W13 —44La 78
Lakeside. Beck —69Dc 128
Lakeside. Enf —14Mb 24
Lakeside. Eps —79Ua 144
Lakeside. Rain —40Nd 69
Lakeside. Wall —77Kb 146
Lakeside. Wey —75U 140
Lakeside. Wok —7B 188
Lakeside Av. Ilf —28Mc 45
Lakeside Clo. SE25 —68Wb 127
Lakeside Clo. Ruis —28S 36
Lakeside Clo. Sidc —57Yc 109
Lakeside Clo. Wok —7B 188
Lakeside Ct. N4 —33Sb 63
Lakeside Ct. Els —15Qa 21
Lakeside Cres. Barn —15Hb 23
Lakeside Cres. Brtwd —20Zd 33
Lakeside Dri. Brom —76Nc 150
Lakeside Dri. Esh —79Ea 142
Lakeside Dri. Stoke P —9J 53
Lakeside Grange. Wey —76S 140
Lakeside Retail Pk. Grays —49Wd 90
Lakeside Rd. N13 —21Pb 42
Lakeside Rd. W14 —48Za 80
Lakeside Rd. Chesh —1Yb 12
Lakeside Rd. Coln —52H 97
Lakeside Ter. EC2 —43Sb 83 (7E 194)
(off Barbican)
Lakeside Way. Wemb —35Qa 59
Lakes Rd. Kes —78Lc 149
Lakestreet Grn. Oxt —100Mc 183
Lakeswood Rd. Orp —72Sc 150
Lake, The. Bush —18Fa 20
Lake View. Edgw —22Pa 39
Lake View. Pot B —5Eb 9
Lake View Est. E3 —40Ac 64
Lakeview Rd. SE27 —64Qb 126
Lake View Rd. Sev —95Jd 186
Lakeview Rd. Well —56Xc 109
Lakis Clo. NW3 —35Eb 61
Laleham Av. NW7 —20Ta 21
Laleham Ct. Wok —88A 156
Laleham Rd. SE6 —59Ec 106
Laleham Rd. Shep —70P 119
Laleham Rd. Stai —64H 119
Lalor St. SW6 —54Ab 102
Lambarde Av. SE9 —63Qc 130
Lambarde Dri. Sev —95Jd 186
Lambarde Rd. Sev —94Jd 186
Lambardes. New Ash —76Be 155
Lambardes Clo. Prat B —83Yc 169
Lamb Clo. Til —4E 114
Lamb Clo. Wat —6Y 5
Lamberhurst Clo. Orp —74Zc 151
Lamberhurst Rd. SE27 —63Qb 126
Lamberhurst Rd. Dag —32Bd 67
Lambert Av. Rich —55Qa 101
Lambert Av. Slou —48A 74
Lambert Clo. Big H —88Mc 167
Lambert Ct. Wat —14Z 19
Lambert Jones M. EC2 —43Sb 83 (7D 194)
(off Barbican)
Lambert Lodge. Bren —50Ma 79
(off Layton Rd.)
Lamberton Ct. Borwd —11Pa 21
(off Gateshead Rd.)
Lambert Rd. E16 —44Kc 85
Lambert Rd. N12 —22Fb 41
Lambert Rd. SW2 —57Nb 104
Lambert Rd. Bans —86Cb 163
Lambert's Pl. Croy —74Tb 147
Lamberts Rd. Surb —71Pa 143
Lambert St. N1 —38Qb 62
Lambert Wlk. Wemb —34Ma 59
Lambert Way. N12 —22Eb 41
Lambeth Bri. SW1 & SE1 —49Nb 82 (5G 205)
Lambeth High St. SE1 —49Pb 82 (6H 205)
Lambeth Hill. EC4 —45Sb 83 (4D 200)
Lambeth Pal. Rd. SE1 —48Pb 82 (4H 205)
Lambeth Rd. SE1 —48Pb 82 (5H 205)

Lambeth Rd.—Latymer Way

Lambeth Rd. Croy —74Qb 146
Lambeth Wlk. SE11 —49Pb 82 (5J 205)
Lambfold Ho. N7 —37Nb 62
Lamb La. E8 —38Xb 63
Lamble St. NW5 —36Jb 62
Lambley Rd. Dag —37Xc 67
Lambly Hill. Vir W —69A 118
Lambolle Pl. NW3 —37Gb 61
Lambolle Rd. NW3 —37Gb 61
Lambourn Chase. Rad —8Ha 6
Lambourn Clo. W7 —47Ha 78
Lambourne. E Til —9L 93
Lambourne Av. SW19 —63Bb 125
Lambourne Ct. Uxb —39K 55
Lambourne Cres. Chig —19Xc 29
Lambourne Cres. Wok —85F 156
Lambourne Dri. Cob —87Z 159
Lambourne Dri. Hut —16Fe 33
Lambourne Gdns. E4 —19Cc 26
Lambourne Gdns. Bark —38Vc 67
Lambourne Gdns. Enf —12Vb 25
Lambourne Gdns. Horn —33Md 69
Lambourne Ho. SE16 —49Zb 84
Lambourne Pl. SE3 —53Kc 107
Lambourne Rd. E11 —31Ec 64
Lambourne Rd. Bark —38Uc 66
Lambourne Rd. Chig —21Vc 47
Lambourne Rd. Ilf —33Uc 66
Lambourn Gro. King T —68Ra 123
Lambourn Rd. SW4 —55Kb 104
Lamb Pas. Bren —51Pa 101
Lambrook Ho. SE15 —53Wb 105
Lambrook Ter. SW6 —53Ab 102
Lamb's Bldgs. EC1 —42Tb 83 (6F 195)
Lamb's Clo. N9 —19Wb 25
Lambs Clo. Cuff —1Pb 10
Lamb's Conduit Pas. WC1 —43Pb 82 (7H 193)
Lamb's Conduit St. WC1 —42Pb 82 (6H 193)
(in three parts)
Lambscroft Av. SE9 —62Lc 129
Lambscroft Way. Ger X —26A 34
Lamb's La. Rain —43Kd 89
Lambs Meadow. Wfd G —26Mc 45
Lamb's M. N1 —39Rb 63 (1B 194)
Lamb's Pas. EC1 —42Tb 83 (7F 195)
Lambs Ter. N9 —19Tb 25
Lamb St. E1 —43Vb 83 (7K 195)
Lamb's Wlk. Enf —12Sb 25
Lambton Av. Wal X —4Zb 12
Lambton Pl. W11 —45Bb 81
Lambton Rd. N19 —32Nb 62
Lambton Rd. SW20 —67Ya 124
Lamb Wlk. SE1 —47Ub 83 (2H 207)
Lamerock Rd. Brom —63Hc 129
Lamerton Rd. Ilf —26Rc 46
Lamerton St. SE8 —51Cc 106
Lamford Clo. N17 —24Tb 43
Lamington St. W6 —49Xa 80
Lamlash St. SE11 —49Rb 83 (5B 206)
Lammas Av. Mitc —68Jb 126
Lammas Ct. Stai —61F 118
Lammas Ct. Wind —4G 94
Lammas Dri. Stai —63F 118
Lammas Grn. SE26 —62Xb 127
Lammas Hill. Esh —77Da 141
Lammas La. Esh —78Ca 141
Lammas Pk. Gdns. W5 —46La 78
Lammas Pk. Rd. W5 —47Ma 79
Lammas Rd. E9 —38Zb 64
Lammas Rd. E10 —33Ac 64
Lammas Rd. Rich —63La 122
Lammas Rd. Slou —3B 72
Lammas Rd. Wat —15Y 19
Lammermuir Rd. SW12 —59Kb 104
Lamont Rd. SW10 —51Eb 103
Lamont Rd. Pas. SW10 —51Fb 103
(off Lamont Rd.)
Lamorbey Clo. Sidc —60Vc 109
Lamorna Av. Grav —1F 136
Lamorna Clo. Orp —73Wc 151
Lamorna Clo. Rad —6Ka 6
Lamorna Gro. Stan —25Ma 39
Lampard Gro. N16 —32Vb 63
Lampern Sq. E2 —41Wb 83
Lampeter Clo. Wok —90A 156
Lampeter Sq. W6 —51Ab 102
Lamplighter Clo. E1 —42Yb 84
Lamplighters Clo. Dart —58Pd 111
Lamplighters Clo. Wal A —6Jc 13
Lampmead Rd. SE12 —56Hc 107
Lamp Office Ct. WC1 —42Pb 82 (6H 193)
Lamport Clo. SE18 —49Pc 86
Lamps Ct. SE5 —52Sb 105
Lampton Av. Houn —53Da 99
Lampton Ct. Houn —53Da 99
Lampton Ho. Clo. SW19 —63Za 124
Lampton Pk. Rd. Houn —54Da 99
Lampton Rd. Houn —54Da 99
Lamson Rd. Rain —43Hd 88
Lanacre Av. NW9 —25Ta 39
Lanark Clo. W5 —43La 78
Lanark Ho. SE1 —50Wb 83
(off Old Kent Rd.)
Lanark Pl. W9 —42Eb 81 (5A 190)
Lanark Rd. W9 —40Db 61
Lanark Sq. E14 —48Dc 84
Lanata Wlk. Hay —42Z 77
(off Alba Clo.)
Lanbury Rd. SE15 —56Zb 106
Lancashire Ct. W1 —45Kb 82 (4A 198)
(off New Bond St.)
Lancaster Av. E18 —28Kc 45
Lancaster Av. SE27 —61Rb 127
Lancaster Av. SW19 —64Za 124
Lancaster Av. Bark —38Uc 66
Lancaster Av. Barn —10Eb 9
Lancaster Av. Mitc —71Nb 146
Lancaster Av. Slou —2G 72
Lancaster Clo. N1 —38Ub 63
Lancaster Clo. SE27 —61Rb 127
Lancaster Clo. Brom —70Hc 129
Lancaster Clo. Croy —75Nb 146
Lancaster Clo. King T —64Ma 123
Lancaster Clo. Pil H —15Wd 32
Lancaster Cotts. Rich —58Na 101
Lancaster Ct. SW6 —52Bb 103
Lancaster Ct. Bans —86Bb 163
Lancaster Ct. Sutt —80Cb 145
(off Mulgrave Rd.)
Lancaster Ct. W on T —73W 140
Lancaster Dri. E14 —46Ec 84
Lancaster Dri. NW3 —37Gb 61
Lancaster Dri. Horn —36Kd 69
Lancaster Gdns. SW19 —64Ab 124
Lancaster Gdns. W13 —47Ka 78
Lancaster Gdns. King T —64Ma 123
Lancaster Ga. W2 —45Eb 81 (5A 196)
Lancaster Gro. NW3 —37Fb 61
Lancaster Ho. Enf —11Tb 25
Lancaster M. SW18 —57Db 103
Lancaster M. W2 —45Eb 81 (4A 196)
Lancaster M. Rich —58Na 101
Lancaster Pk. Rich —57Na 101
Lancaster Pl. SW19 —64Za 124
Lancaster Pl. WC2 —45Pb 82 (4H 199)
Lancaster Pl. Houn —54Z 99
Lancaster Pl. Ilf —35Sc 66
Lancaster Pl. Twic —58Ja 100
Lancaster Rd. E7 —38Jc 65
Lancaster Rd. E11 —33Gc 65
Lancaster Rd. E17 —26Zb 44
Lancaster Rd. N4 —31Pb 62
Lancaster Rd. N11 —23Mb 42
Lancaster Rd. N18 —22Vb 43
Lancaster Rd. NW10 —36Wa 60
Lancaster Rd. SE25 —68Vb 127
Lancaster Rd. SW19 —64Za 124
Lancaster Rd. W11 —44Ab 80
Lancaster Rd. Barn —14Fb 23
(in two parts)
Lancaster Rd. Enf —11Tb 25
Lancaster Rd. Harr —29Ca 37
Lancaster Rd. N'holt —37Ea 58
Lancaster Rd. S'hall —45Aa 77
Lancaster Rd. Uxb —37M 55
Lancaster Stables. NW3 —37Gb 61
Lancaster St. SE1 —47Rb 83 (2B 206)
Lancaster St. SE18 —52Uc 108
Lancaster Ter. W2 —45Fb 81 (4B 196)
Lancaster Wlk. W2 —46Eb 81 (5A 196)
Lancaster Wlk. Hay —44S 76
Lancaster Way. Abb L —3V 4
Lance Croft. New Ash —75Be 155
Lancefield Ho. SE15 —55Xb 105
Lancefield St. W10 —40Ab 60
(in two parts)
Lancell St. N16 —33Ub 63
Lancelot Av. Wemb —35Ma 59
Lancelot Clo. Slou —7E 72
Lancelot Cres. Wemb —35Ma 59
Lancelot Gdns. Barn —17Jb 24
Lancelot Pl. SW7 —47Hb 81 (2F 203)
Lancelot Rd. Ilf —23Uc 46
Lancelot Rd. Well —56Wc 109
Lancelot Rd. Wemb —35Ma 59
Lance Rd. Harr —31Ea 58
Lancer Sq. W8 —47Db 81
Lancey Clo. SE7 —49Nc 86
Lanchester Rd. N6 —29Hb 41
Lancing Gdns. N9 —18Vb 25
Lancing Rd. W13 —45Ka 78
Lancing Rd. Croy —73Pb 146
Lancing Rd. Felt —61V 120
Lancing Rd. Ilf —30Tc 46
Lancing Rd. Orp —75Wc 151
Lancing Rd. Romf —24Nd 49
Lancing St. NW1 —41Mb 82 (4D 192)
Lancing Way. Crox —15R 18
Lancresse Clo. Uxb —37M 55
Lancresse Ct. N1 —39Ub 63
(off De Beauvoir Est.)
Landau Way. Eri —50Md 89
Landcroft Rd. SE22 —57Vb 105
Landells Rd. SE22 —58Vb 105
Lander Rd. Grays —50Fe 91
Landford Clo. Rick —19N 17
Landford Rd. SW15 —55Ya 102
Landgrove Rd. SW19 —64Cb 125
Landmann Way. SE14 —50Zb 84
Landmead Rd. Chesh —1Ac 12
Landon Pl. SW1 —48Hb 81 (3F 203)
Landon's Clo. E14 —46Ec 84
Landon Wlk. E14 —45Dc 84
Landon Way. Ashf —65R 120
Landor Rd. SW9 —55Nb 104
Landor Wlk. W12 —47Wa 80
Landport Way. SE15 —52Vb 105
Landra Gdns. N21 —16Rb 25
Landridge Rd. SW6 —54Bb 103
Landrock Rd. N8 —30Nb 42
Landscape Rd. Warl —91Xb 181
Landscape Rd. Wfd G —24Kc 45
Landseer Av. E12 —36Qc 66
Landseer Av. Grav —62Fe 135
Landseer Clo. SW19 —67Eb 125
Landseer Clo. Edgw —26Qa 39
Landseer Clo. Horn —32Kd 69
Landseer Ct. Hay —40T 56
Landseer Rd. N19 —34Nb 62
Landseer Rd. Enf —15Wb 25
Landseer Rd. N Mald —73Ta 143
Landseer Rd. Sutt —79Cb 145
Lands End. Els —16Ma 21
Landstead Rd. SE18 —52Tc 108
Landulph Ho. SE11 —50Qb 82 (7A 206)
(off Kennings Way)
Landway. Seal —92Pd 187
Landway, The. Kems —89Qd 171
Landway, The. Orp —69Yc 131
Lane App. NW7 —22Ab 40
Lane Av. Grnh —58Yd 112
Lane Clo. NW2 —34Xa 60
Lane Clo. Add —78K 139
Lane End. Bexh —55Dd 110
Lane End. Eps —86Ra 161
Lane End Dri. Knap —5A 188
Lane Gdns. Bush —17Ga 20
Lane M. E12 —34Pc 66
Lanercost Clo. SW2 —61Qb 126
Lanercost Gdns. N14 —17Nb 24
Lanercost Rd. SW2 —61Qb 126
Lanes Av. Grav —2B 136
Lanesborough Pl. SW1 —47Jb 82 (1J 203)
(off Grosvenor Pl.)
Laneside. Chst —64Sc 130
Laneside. Edgw —22Sa 39
Laneside Av. Dag —31Bd 67
Lane, The. NW8 —40Eb 61
Lane, The. SE3 —55Jc 107
Lane, The. Cher —69J 119
Lane, The. Vir W —69B 118
Laneway. SW15 —57Xa 102
Lanfrac Ct. Harr —34Ha 58
Lanfranc Rd. E3 —40Ac 64
Lanfrey Pl. W14 —50Bb 81
Langafel Clo. Long —68Ae 135
Langaller La. Fet —94Da 175
Langbourne Av. N6 —33Jb 62
Langbourne Way. Clay —79Ja 142
Langbrook Rd. SE3 —55Mc 107
Lang Clo. Fet —95Da 175
Langcroft Clo. Cars —76Hb 145
Langdale Av. Mitc —69Hb 125
Langdale Clo. SE17 —51Sb 105
Langdale Clo. SW14 —56Ra 101
Langdale Clo. Dag —32Yc 67
Langdale Clo. Orp —76Rc 150
Langdale Clo. Wok —4F 188
Langdale Cres. Bexh —52Cd 110
Langdale Dri. Hay —40U 56
Langdale Gdns. Gnfd —41Ka 78
Langdale Gdns. Horn —36Jd 68
Langdale Gdns. Wal X —7Zb 12
Langdale Pde. Mitc —69Hb 125
Langdale Rd. SE10 —52Ec 106
Langdale Rd. T Hth —70Qb 126
Langdale St. E1 —44Xb 83
Langdale Wlk. Grav —2A 136
Langdon Ct. NW10 —39Ua 60
Langdon Cres. E6 —40Qc 66
Langdon Dri. NW9 —32Sa 59
Langdon Pk. N6 —31Lb 62
Langdon Pl. SW14 —55Sa 101
Langdon Rd. E6 —39Qc 66
Langdon Rd. Brom —69Kc 129
Langdon Rd. Mord —71Eb 145
Langdons Ct. S'hall —48Ca 77
Langdon Shaw. Sidc —64Vc 131
Langdon Wlk. Mord —71Eb 145
Langdon Way. SE1 —49Wb 83
Langford Clo. E8 —36Wb 63
Langford Clo. N15 —30Ub 43
Langford Clo. NW8 —40Eb 61 (1A 190)
Langford Cres. Barn —14Hb 23
Langford Grn. SE5 —55Ub 105
Langford Grn. Hut —15Ee 33
Langford Pl. NW8 —40Eb 61 (1A 190)
Langford Pl. Sidc —62Wc 131
Langford Rd. SW6 —54Db 103
Langford Rd. Barn —14Hb 23
Langford Rd. Wfd G —23Lc 45
Langfords. Buck H —19Mc 27
Langham Clo. N15 —27Rb 43
Langham Ct. NW4 —29Za 40
Langham Ct. Horn —31Md 69
Langham Dene. Kenl —87Rb 165
Langham Dri. Romf —30Xc 47
Langham Gdns. N21 —15Qb 24
Langham Gdns. W13 —45Ka 78
Langham Gdns. Edgw —24Sa 39
Langham Gdns. Rich —63La 122
Langham Gdns. Wemb —33La 58
Langham Ho. Clo. Rich —63Ma 123
Langham Mans. SW5 —50Db 81
(off Earl's Ct. Sq.)
Langham Pl. N15 —27Rb 43
Langham Pl. W1 —43Kb 82 (1A 198)
Langham Pl. W4 —51Ua 102
Langham Pl. Egh —64B 118
Langham Rd. N15 —27Rb 43
Langham Rd. SW20 —67Ya 124
Langham Rd. Edgw —23Sa 39
Langham Rd. Tedd —64Ka 122
Langham St. W1 —43Kb 82 (1A 198)
Langhedge Clo. N18 —23Vb 43
Langhedge La. N18 —23Vb 43
Langhedge La. Ind. Est. N18 —23Vb 43
Langholm Clo. SW12 —59Mb 104
Langholme. Bush —18Ea 20
Langhorne Rd. Dag —38Cd 68
Langland Ct. N'wd —24S 36
Langland Cres. Stan —26Ma 39
Langland Dri. Pinn —24Aa 37
Langland Gdns. NW3 —36Db 61
Langland Gdns. Croy —75Bc 148
Langlands Dri. Dart —64Ud 134
Langlands Rise. Eps —85Sa 161
Langler Rd. NW10 —40Ya 60
Langley Av. Ruis —33X 57
Langley Av. Surb —74Ma 143
Langley Av. Wor Pk —75Za 144
Langley Broom. Slou —50B 74
Langleybury La. Wat & K Lan —9R 4
Langley Bus. Cen. Langl —47C 74
Langley Bus. Pk. Langl —47B 74
Langley Clo. Eps —91Ta 177
Langley Clo. Romf —24Md 49
Langley Clo. Wok —90A 156
Langley Ct. WC2 —45Nb 82 (4F 199)
Langley Ct. Chesh —1Rb 11
Langley Cres. E11 —31Lc 65
Langley Cres. Dag —38Yc 67
Langley Cres. Edgw —20Sa 21
Langley Cres. Hay —52V 98
Langley Cres. K Lan —2Q 4
Langley Dri. E11 —31Kc 65
Langley Dri. W3 —47Ra 79
Langley Dri. Brtwd —20Wd 32
Langley Gdns. Brom —70Lc 129
Langley Gdns. Dag —38Zc 67
Langley Gdns. Orp —72Rc 150
Langley Gro. N Mald —68Ua 124
Langley Hill. K Lan —1P 3
Langley Hill Clo. K Lan —1Q 4
Langley La. SW8 —51Nb 104
Langley La. Abb L —3V 4
Langley La. Dork & Head —97Ra 177
Langley Mans. SW8 —51Pb 104
(off Langley La.)
Langley Meadow. Lou —12Tc 28
Langley Oaks Av. S Croy —82Wb 165
Langley Pk. NW7 —23Ua 40
Langley Pk. Rd. Iver —45D 74
Langley Pk. Rd. Slou & Iver —47C 74
Langley Pk. Rd. Sutt —78Eb 145
Langley Quay. Langl —47C 74
Langley Rd. SW19 —67Bb 125
Langley Rd. Abb L —3U 4
Langley Rd. Beck —70Ac 128
Langley Rd. Chfd —2K 3
Langley Rd. Isw th —54Ha 100
Langley Rd. Slou —7N 73
Langley Rd. S Croy —81Zb 166
Langley Rd. Stai —65H 119
Langley Rd. Surb —73Na 143
Langley Rd. Wat —11V 18
Langley Rd. Well —51Yc 109
Langley St. WC2 —44Nb 82 (3F 199)
Langley Vale Rd. Eps —92Sa 177
Langley Wlk. Wok —91A 172
Langley Way. Wat —12U 18
Langley Way. W Wick —74Fc 149
Langmans La. Wok —6E 188
Langmans Way. Wok —4B 188
Langmead Dri. Bush —18Ga 20
Langmead St. SE27 —63Sb 127
Langmore Ct. Bexh —55Zc 109
Langport Ct. W on T —74Y 141
Langport Ho. SW9 —54Rb 105
Langport Ho. H Hill —24Nd 49
(off Leyburn Rd.)
Langroyd Rd. SW17 —61Hb 125
Langshott Clo. Wdhm —83G 156
Langside Av. SW15 —56Wa 102
Langside Cres. N14 —20Mb 24
Langston Hughes Clo. SE24 —56Rb 105
Langston Rd. Lou —15Sc 28
Lang St. E1 —42Yb 84
Langthorn Ct. EC2 —44Tb 83 (2G 201)
Langthorne Cres. Grays —49Ee 91
Langthorne Ho. Hay —49U 76
Langthorne Rd. E11 —34Ec 64
Langthorne St. SW6 —52Za 102
Langton Av. E6 —41Qc 86
Langton Av. N20 —17Eb 23
Langton Av. Eps —83Va 162
Langton Clo. WC1 —42Pb 82 (5J 193)
Langton Clo. Add —76K 139
Langton Clo. Slou —6B 72
Langton Clo. Wok —5C 188
Langton Gro. N'wd —22S 36
Langton Rise. SE23 —59Xb 105
Langton Rd. NW2 —34Ya 60
Langton Rd. SW9 —52Rb 105
Langton Rd. Harr —24Ea 38
Langton Rd. W Mol —70Ea 122
Langton's Meadow. Farn C —7G 52
Langton St. SW10 —51Eb 103
Langton Way. SE3 —53Hc 107
Langton Way. Croy —77Ub 147
Langton Way. Egh —65E 118
Langton Way. Grays —9E 92
Langtry Rd. NW8 —39Db 61
Langtry Rd. N'holt —40Z 57
Langtry Wlk. NW8 —39Db 61
Langwood Chase. Tedd —65La 122
Langwood Gdns. Wat —11W 18
Langworth Clo. Dart —62Md 133
Langworth Dri. Hay —44W 76
Langworthy. Pinn —23Ca 37
Lanhill Rd. W9 —42Cb 81
Lanier Rd. SE13 —58Fc 107
Lanigan Dri. Houn —57Da 99
Lankaster Gdns. N2 —25Fb 41
Lankers Dri. Harr —30Ba 37
Lankton Clo. Beck —67Ec 128
Lannock Rd. Hay —46V 76
Lannoy Point. SW6 —52Ab 102
(off Pellant Rd.)
Lannoy Rd. SE9 —60Sc 108
Lanrick Rd. E14 —44Fc 85
Lanridge Rd. SE2 —48Zc 87
Lansbury Av. N18 —22Tb 43
Lansbury Av. Bark —38Wc 67
Lansbury Av. Felt —58X 99
Lansbury Av. Romf —29Ad 47
Lansbury Clo. NW10 —36Sa 59
Lansbury Cres. Dart —57Qd 111
Lansbury Dri. Hay —43V 76
Lansbury Est. E14 —44Dc 84
Lansbury Gdns. E14 —44Fc 85
Lansbury Gdns. Til —3C 114
Lansbury Rd. Enf —11Zb 26
Lansbury Way. N18 —22Ub 43
Lanscombe Wlk. SW8 —53Nb 104
Lansdell Ho. SW2 —57Qb 104
(off Tulse Hill)
Lansdell Rd. Mitc —68Jb 126
Lansdown Clo. W on T —74Y 141
Lansdown Clo. Wok —7C 188
Lansdowne Av. Bexh —52Zc 109
Lansdowne Av. Orp —74Rc 150
Lansdowne Av. Slou —6J 73
Lansdowne Clo. SW20 —66Za 124
Lansdowne Clo. Twic —60Ha 100
Lansdowne Clo. Wat —7Z 5
Lansdowne Ct. Purl —82Rb 165
Lansdowne Ct. Slou —6J 73
Lansdowne Ct. Wor Pk —75Wa 144
Lansdowne Cres. W11 —45Ab 80
Lansdowne Dri. E8 —37Wb 63
Lansdowne Gdns. SW8 —53Nb 104
Lansdowne Gro. NW10 —35Ua 60
Lansdowne Hill. SE27 —62Rb 127
Lansdowne La. SE7 —50Mc 85
Lansdowne M. SE7 —50Mc 85
Lansdowne M. W11 —46Bb 81
Lansdowne Pl. SE1 —48Tb 83 (3G 207)
Lansdowne Pl. SE19 —66Vb 127
Lansdowne Rise. W11 —45Ab 80
Lansdowne Rd. E4 —19Cc 26
Lansdowne Rd. E11 —33Hc 65
Lansdowne Rd. E17 —30Cc 44
Lansdowne Rd. E18 —27Jc 45
Lansdowne Rd. N3 —24Cb 41
Lansdowne Rd. N10 —26Lb 42
Lansdowne Rd. N17 —25Wb 43
Lansdowne Rd. SW20 —66Ya 124
Lansdowne Rd. W11 —45Ab 80
Lansdowne Rd. Brom —66Jc 129
Lansdowne Rd. Croy —75Tb 147
Lansdowne Rd. Eps —80Sa 143
Lansdowne Rd. Harr —31Ga 58
Lansdowne Rd. Houn —55Da 99
Lansdowne Rd. Ilf —32Vc 67
Lansdowne Rd. Purl —84Qb 164
Lansdowne Rd. Sev —94Md 187
Lansdowne Rd. Stai —66K 119
Lansdowne Rd. Stan —23La 38
Lansdowne Rd. Til —4B 114
Lansdowne Rd. Uxb —44S 76
Lansdowne Row. W1 —46Kb 82 (6A 198)
Lansdowne Sq. Grav —8B 114
Lansdowne Ter. WC1 —42Nb 82 (6G 193)
Lansdowne Wlk. W11 —46Bb 81
Lansdowne Way. SW8 —53Mb 104
Lansdowne Wood Clo. SE27 —62Rb 127
Lansdown Pl. Grav —10B 114
Lansdown Rd. E7 —38Lc 65
Lansdown Rd. Ger X —25A 34
Lansdown Rd. Grav —10B 114
Lansdown Rd. Sidc —62Xc 131
Lansfield Av. N18 —21Wb 43
Lantern Clo. SW15 —56Wa 102
Lantern Clo. Wemb —36Ma 59
Lanterns Ct. E14 —48Cc 84
Lant St. SE1 —47Sb 83 (1D 206)
Lanvanor Rd. SE15 —54Yb 106
Lanyard Ho. SE8 —49Bc 84
Lapford Clo. W9 —42Bb 81
Lapis Clo. Grav —10K 115
La Plata Gro. Brtwd —20Xd 32
Lapponum Wlk. Hay —42Z 77
Lapse Wood Wlk. SE23 —60Xb 105
Lapstone Gdns. Harr —30La 38
Lapwing Clo. S Croy —82Ac 166
Lapwing Ct. Surb —76Qa 143
Lapwing Pl. Wat —4Y 5
Lapwings. Long —69De 135
Lapwings, The. Grav —1F 136
Lapwing Way. Hay —44Z 77
Lapworth. N11 —21Kb 42
(off Coppies Gro.)
Lapworth Clo. Orp —75Yc 151
Lara Clo. SE13 —58Ec 106
Lara Clo. Chess —80Na 143
Larbert Rd. SW16 —66Lb 126
Larby Pl. Eps —82Ua 162
Larch Av. W3 —46Ua 80
Larch Av. Asc —10C 116
Larch Av. Brick —2Aa 5
Larch Clo. N11 —24Jb 42
Larch Clo. N19 —33Lb 62
Larch Clo. SE8 —51Bc 106
Larch Clo. SW12 —61Kb 126
Larch Clo. Slou —3F 72
Larch Clo. Tad —93Eb 179
Larch Clo. Warl —91Ac 182
Larch Cres. Eps —79Ra 143
Larch Cres. Hay —43Y 77
Larch Dene. Orp —75Qc 150
Larch Dri. W4 —50Qa 79
Larches Av. SW14 —56Ta 101
Larches Av. Enf —7Yb 12
Larches, The. N13 —20Sb 25
Larches, The. Bush —15Z 19
Larches, The. N'wd —23S 36
Larches, The. Uxb —41R 76
Larches, The. Wok —88A 156
Larch Grn. NW9 —25Ua 40
Larch Gro. Sidc —60Vc 109
Larch Ho. Brom —67Gc 129
Larch Ho. Hay —43Y 77
Larchmoor Pk. Stoke P —5L 53
Larch Rd. NW2 —35Ya 60
Larch Rd. Dart —59Md 111
Larch Tree Way. Croy —76Cc 148
Larchvale Ct. Sutt —80Db 145
Larch Wlk. Swan —68Fd 132
Larch Way. Brom —73Qc 150
Larchwood Av. Romf —23Dd 48
Larchwood Clo. Bans —87Ab 162
Larchwood Clo. Romf —23Ed 48
Larchwood Dri. Egh —5M 117
Larchwood Gdns. Pil H —16Wd 32
Larchwood Rd. SE9 —61Rc 130
Larchwood Rd. Wok —8A 188
Larcombe Clo. Croy —77Vb 147
Larcombe Ct. Sutt —80Db 145
(off Worcester Rd.)
Larcom St. SE17 —49Sb 83 (6D 206)
Larden Rd. W3 —46Ua 80
Largewood Av. Surb —75Qa 143
Largo Wlk. Eri —53Gd 110
Larissa St. SE17 —50Tb 83 (7G 207)
Lark Av. Stai —62H 119
Larkbere Rd. SE26 —63Ac 128
Larken Clo. Bush —18Ea 20
Larken Dri. Bush —18Ea 20
Larkfield. Cob —85W 158
Larkfield Av. Harr —27Ka 38
Larkfield Clo. Brom —75Hc 149
Larkfield Rd. Rich —56Na 101
Larkfield Rd. Sev —95Ed 186
Larkfield Rd. Sidc —62Vc 131
Larkfields. Grav —2A 136
Larkhall Clo. W on T —79Y 141
Larkhall La. SW4 —54Mb 104
Larkhall Rise. SW4 —55Lb 104
Larkham Clo. Felt —62U 120
Larkin Clo. Coul —89Pb 164
Larkin Clo. Hut —17Ee 33
Larkings La. Stoke P —9M 53
Lark Row. E2 —39Yb 64
Larksfield. Egh —6N 117
Larks Field. Hart —70Be 135
Larksfield Gro. Enf —11Xb 25
Larks Gro. Bark —38Uc 66
Larkshall Ct. Romf —26Ed 48
Larkshall Cres. E4 —21Ec 44
Larkshall Rd. E4 —22Ec 44
Larkspur Clo. E6 —43Nc 86
Larkspur Clo. N17 —24Tb 43
Larkspur Clo. Orp —75Yc 151
Larkspur Clo. S Ock —41Yd 90
Larkspur Lodge. Sidc —62Xc 131
Larkspur Way. Eps —78Sa 143
Larks Way. Knap —4A 188
Larkswood Clo. Eri —53Jd 110
Larkswood Ct. E4 —22Fc 45
Larkswood Rise. Pinn —28Y 37
Larkswood Rd. E4 —21Cc 44
Larkway Clo. NW9 —28Ta 39
Larmans Rd. Enf —8Yb 12
Larnach Rd. W6 —51Za 102
Larne Rd. Ruis —31V 56
Larner Rd. Eri —52Gd 110
La Roche Clo. Slou —8N 73
Larpent Av. SW15 —57Ya 102
Larsen Dri. Wal A —6Fc 13
Larshall Rd. E4 —20Fc 27
Larwood Clo. Gnfd —36Fa 58
Lascelles Av. Harr —31Fa 58
Lascelles Clo. E11 —33Fc 65
Lascelles Clo. Pil H —15Wd 32
Lascelles Rd. Slou —8M 73
Lascotts Rd. N22 —23Pb 42
Lassa Rd. SE9 —57Nc 108
Lassell St. SE10 —50Fc 85
Lasswade Ct. Cher —73G 138
Lasswade Rd. Cher —73H 139
Latchett Rd. E18 —25Kc 45
Latchford Pl. Chig —21Xc 47
Latching Clo. Romf —21Md 49
Latchingdon Ct. E17 —28Zb 44
Latchingdon Gdns. Wfd G —23Nc 46
Latchmere Clo. Rich —64Na 123
Latchmere La. King T —65Pa 123
Latchmere Pas. SW11 —54Gb 103
Latchmere Rd. SW11 —54Hb 103
Latchmere Rd. King T —66Na 123
Latchmere St. SW11 —54Hb 103
Latchmoor Av. Ger X —28A 34
Latchmoor Gro. Ger X —28A 34
Latchmoor Way. Ger X —28A 34
Lateward Rd. Bren —51Ma 101
Latham Clo. E6 —43Nc 86
Latham Clo. Big H —88Lc 167
Latham Clo. Twic —59Ja 100
Latham Rd. Bexh —57Cd 110
Latham Rd. Twic —59Ha 100
Latham's Way. Croy —74Nb 146
Lathkill Clo. Enf —17Wb 25
Lathkill Ct. Beck —67Bc 128
Lathom Rd. E6 —38Nc 66
Latimer Av. E6 —39Pc 66
Latimer Clo. Pinn —25Y 37
Latimer Clo. Wat —17U 18
Latimer Clo. Wok —88D 156
Latimer Clo. Wor Pk —77Xa 144
Latimer Dri. Horn —34Md 69
Latimer Gdns. Pinn —25Y 37
Latimer Ho. E9 —37Zb 64
Latimer Ind. Est. W10 —44Ya 80
Latimer Pl. W10 —44Ya 80
Latimer Rd. E7 —35Kc 65
Latimer Rd. N15 —30Ub 43
Latimer Rd. SW19 —65Db 125
Latimer Rd. W10 —43Ya 80
Latimer Rd. Barn —13Db 23
Latimer Rd. Che & Chen —10A 2
Latimer Rd. Croy —76Rb 147
Latimer Rd. Tedd —64Ha 122
Latona Dri. Grav —4H 137
Latona Rd. SE15 —51Wb 105
La Tourne Gdns. Orp —76Sc 150
Latton Clo. Esh —77Da 141
Latton Clo. W on T —73Aa 141
Latymer Clo. Wey —77S 140
Latymer Ct. W6 —49Za 80
Latymer Gdns. N3 —26Ab 40
Latymer Rd. N9 —18Vb 25
Latymer Way. N9 —19Ub 25

Lauder Clo.—Leonard Av.

Lauder Clo. N'holt —40Z 57
Lauder Ct. N14 —17Nb 24
Lauderdale Dri. Rich —62Ma 123
Lauderdale Mans. W9 —41Db 81
(off Lauderdale Rd.)
Lauderdale Pl. EC2
(off Barbican) —43Sb 83 (7D 194)
Lauderdale Rd. W9 —41Db 81
Lauderdale Rd. K Lan —5S 4
Lauderdale Tower. EC2
(off Barbican) —43Sb 83 (7D 194)
Laud St. SE11 —50Pb 82 (7H 205)
Laud St. Croy —76Sb 147
Laughton Ct. Borwd —12Sa 21
Laughton Rd. N'holt —39Z 57
Launcelot Rd. Brom —63Jc 129
Launcelot St. SE1
—47Qb 82 (2K 205)
Launceston Clo. Romf —25Ld 49
Launceston Gdns. Gnfd —39La 58
Launceston Pl. W8 —48Eb 81
Launceston Rd. Gnfd —39La 58
Launch St. E14 —48Ec 84
Launder's La. Rain —43Nd 89
Laundry La. N1 —38Sb 63
Laundry La. Mount —11Fe 33
Laundry Rd. W6 —51Ab 102
Laura Clo. E11 —29Lc 45
Laura Clo. Enf —15Ub 25
Lauradale Rd. N2 —28Hb 41
Laura Dri. Swan —66Jd 132
Laura Pl. E5 —35Yb 64
Laurel Av. Egh —4M 117
Laurel Av. Grav —1E 136
Laurel Av. Pot B —4Bb 9
Laurel Av. Slou —47A 74
Laurel Av. Twic —60Ha 100
Laurel Bank Gdns. SW6 —54Bb 103
Laurel Bank Rd. Enf —11Sb 25
Laurel Bank Vs. W7 —46Ga 78
(off Lwr. Boston Rd.)
Laurelbrook. SE6 —62Gc 129
Laurel Clo. N19 —33Lb 62
Laurel Clo. SW17 —64Gb 125
Laurel Clo. Coln —52G 96
Laurel Clo. Dart —60Ld 111
Laurel Clo. Hut —15De 33
Laurel Clo. Ilf —23Sc 46
Laurel Clo. Sidc —62Wc 131
Laurel Ct. E8 —37Vb 63
Laurel Ct. Cuff —1Pb 10
Laurel Ct. Hut —16Ee 33
(off Spinney, The)
Laurel Ct. Wemb —40Na 59
Laurel Cres. Croy —76Cc 148
Laurel Cres. Romf —32Gd 68
Laurel Cres. Wok —85E 156
Laurel Dri. N21 —17Qb 24
Laurel Fields. Pot B —3Bb 9
Laurel Gdns. E4 —17Dc 26
Laurel Gdns. NW7 —20Ta 21
Laurel Gdns. W7 —46Ga 78
Laurel Gdns. Houn —56Aa 99
Laurel Gro. SE20 —66Yb 128
Laurel Gro. SE26 —63Zb 128
Laurel Ho. Brom —67Gc 129
Laurel La. W Dray —49N 75
Laurel Lodge La. Barn —8Ya 8
Laurel Pk. Harr —24Ha 38
Laurel Rd. SW13 —54Wa 102
Laurel Rd. SW20 —67Xa 124
Laurel Rd. Ger X —25A 34
Laurel Rd. Hamp —64Fa 122
Laurels End. Iver —40F 54
Laurels, The. Bans —89Bb 163
Laurels, The. Borwd —11Qa 21
Laurels, The. Brom —69Jc 129
Laurels, The. Cob —87Aa 159
Laurels, The. Long —69Fe 135
Laurels, The. Wey —76T 140
Laurels, The. Wilm —62Ld 133
Laurel St. E8 —37Vb 63
Laurel View. N12 —20Db 23
Laurel Way. E18 —28Hc 45
Laurel Way. N20 —20Cb 23
Laurence Ct. E10 —31Dc 64
Laurence M. W12 —47Wa 80
Laurence Pountney Hill. EC4
—45Tb 83 (4F 201)
Laurence Pountney La. EC4
—45Tb 83 (5F 201)
Laurie Gro. SE14 —53Ac 106
Laurie Rd. W7 —43Ga 78
Laurier Rd. NW5 —34Kb 62
Laurier Rd. Croy —73Vb 147
Laurie Wlk. Romf —29Gd 48
Laurimel Clo. Stan —23Ka 38
Laurino Pl. Bush —19Ea 20
Lauriston Clo. Knap —5A 188
Lauriston Rd. E9 —38Yb 64
Lauriston Rd. SW19 —65Za 124
Lausanne Rd. N8 —28Qb 42
Lausanne Rd. SE15 —53Yb 106
Lauser Rd. Stai —59L 97
Lavell St. N16 —35Tb 63
Lavender Av. NW9 —32Sa 59
Lavender Av. Mitc —67Gb 125
Lavender Av. Pil H —16Xd 32
Lavender Av. Wor Pk —76Ya 144
Lavender Clo. SW3 —51Gb 103
Lavender Clo. Cars —77Kb 146
Lavender Clo. Cat —97Sb 181
Lavender Clo. Coul —91Lb 180
Lavender Clo. Romf —24Md 49
Lavender Ct. Felt —58X 99
Lavender Gdns. SW11 —56Hb 103
Lavender Gdns. Enf —11Rb 25
Lavender Gro. E8 —38Wb 63
Lavender Gro. Mitc —67Gb 125
Lavender Hill. SW11 —56Gb 103
Lavender Hill. Enf —11Qb 24
Lavender Hill. Swan —69Fd 132
Lavender Pk. Rd. W Byf —84J 157
Lavender Pl. Ilf —36Rc 66
Lavender Rise. W Dray —47Q 76
Lavender Rd. SE16 —46Ac 84
Lavender Rd. SW11 —55Fb 103
Lavender Rd. Cars —77Jb 146
Lavender Rd. Croy —72Pb 146
Lavender Rd. Enf —11Tb 25
Lavender Rd. Eps —78Ra 143
Lavender Rd. Sutt —77Fb 145
Lavender Rd. Uxb —43P 75
Lavender Rd. Wok —88D 156
Lavender St. E15 —37Gc 65
Lavender Sweep. SW11 —56Hb 103
Lavender Ter. SW11 —55Gb 103
Lavender Vale. Wall —79Mb 146
Lavender Wlk. SW11 —56Hb 103
Lavender Wlk. Mitc —69Jb 126
Lavender Way. Croy —72Zb 148
Lavengro Rd. SE27 —61Sb 127
Lavenha Ct. Brtwd —18Zd 33
Lavenham Rd. SW18 —61Bb 125
Lavernock Rd. Bexh —54Cd 110
Lavers Rd. N16 —34Ub 63
Laverstoke Gdns. SW15 —59Va 102
Laverton M. SW5 —49Db 81
Laverton Pl. SW5 —49Db 81
Lavidge Rd. SE9 —61Nc 130
Lavina Gro. N1 —40Pb 62 (1H 193)
Lavington Rd. W13 —46Ka 78
Lavington Rd. Croy —76Pb 146
Lavington St. SE1
—46Rb 83 (7C 200)
Lavinia Av. Wat —6Z 5
Lavinia Gro. N1 —40Pb 62
Lavinia Rd. Dart —58Pd 111
Lawdons Gdns. Croy —77Rb 147
Lawford Av. Chor —16E 16
Lawford Clo. Chor —16E 16
Lawford Clo. Horn —35Ld 69
Lawford Clo. Wall —81Nb 164
Lawford Gdns. Dart —57Ld 111
Lawford Gdns. Kenl —88Sb 165
Lawford Rd. N1 —38Ub 63
Lawford Rd. NW5 —37Lb 62
Lawford Rd. W4 —52Sa 101
Law Ho. Bark —40Wc 67
Lawkland. Farn R —1G 72
Lawless St. E14 —45Dc 84
Lawley Rd. N14 —17Kb 24
Lawley St. E5 —35Yb 64
Lawn Av. W Dray —47L 75
Lawn Clo. N9 —17Vb 25
Lawn Clo. Brom —65Kc 129
Lawn Clo. Dat —2N 95
Lawn Clo. Hex —68Ed 132
Lawn Clo. N Mald —68Ua 124
Lawn Clo. Ruis —34V 56
Lawn Cres. Rich —54Qa 101
Lawn Dri. E7 —35Mc 65
Lawn Farm Gro. Romf —28Ad 47
Lawn Gdns. W7 —46Ga 78
Lawn Ho. Clo. E14 —47Ec 84
Lawn La. SW8 —51Nb 104
Lawn Pk. Sev —99Kd 187
Lawn Pl. SE15 —53Vb 105
Lawn Rd. NW3 —36Hb 61
Lawn Rd. Beck —66Bc 128
Lawn Rd. Grav —57Ee 113
Lawn Rd. Uxb —38L 55
Lawns Ct. Wemb —33Pa 59
Lawns Cres. Grays —51Fe 113
Lawnside. SE3 —56Hc 107
Lawns Pl. Grays —51Fe 113
Lawns, The. E4 —22Cc 44
Lawns, The. SE3 —55Hc 107
Lawns, The. SE19 —67Tb 127
Lawns, The. SW19 —64Bb 125
Lawns, The. Coln —53G 96
Lawns, The. Pinn —24Da 37
Lawns, The. Sidc —63Yc 131
Lawns, The. Sutt —80Ab 144
Lawns, The. War —22Ae 51
Lawnsway. Romf —24Ed 48
Lawn Ter. SE3 —55Gc 107
Lawn, The. S'hall —50Ca 77
Lawn Vale. Pinn —26Aa 37
Lawrance Sq. Grav —1B 136
Lawrence Av. E12 —35Qc 66
Lawrence Av. E17 —25Zb 44
Lawrence Av. N13 —21Rb 43
Lawrence Av. NW7 —21Ua 40
Lawrence Av. N Mald —72Ta 143
Lawrence Bldgs. N16 —34Vb 63
Lawrence Campe Clo. N20
—20Fb 23
Lawrence Clo. E3 —41Cc 84
Lawrence Clo. N15 —27Ub 43
Lawrence Clo. W12 —45Xa 80
(off White City Est.)
Lawrence Clo. Guild —100D 172
Lawrence Ct. NW7 —22Ua 40
Lawrence Ct. Wind —4G 94
Lawrence Cres. Dag —34Dd 68
Lawrence Cres. Edgw —26Qa 39
Lawrence Dri. Cobh —10J 137
Lawrence Dri. Uxb —35S 56
Lawrence Gdns. NW7 —20Va 22
Lawrence Gdns. Chesh —1Zb 12
Lawrence Gdns. Til —2D 114
Lawrence Hill. E4 —19Cc 26
Lawrence Hill Gdns. Dart —58Ld 111
Lawrence Hill Rd. Dart —58Ld 111
Lawrence La. EC2
—44Sb 83 (3E 200)
Lawrence Pl. N1 —39Nb 62
(off Brydon Wlk.)
Lawrence Rd. E6 —39Nc 66
Lawrence Rd. E13 —39Kc 65
Lawrence Rd. N15 —28Ub 43
Lawrence Rd. N18 —21Xb 43
Lawrence Rd. SE25 —70Vb 127
Lawrence Rd. W5 —49La 78
Lawrence Rd. Hamp —66Ba 121
Lawrence Rd. Hay —40S 56
Lawrence Rd. Houn —56Y 99
Lawrence Rd. Pinn —30Z 37
Lawrence Rd. Rich —63La 122
Lawrence Rd. Romf —29Kd 49
Lawrence Rd. W Wick —77Jc 149
Lawrence St. E16 —43Hc 85
Lawrence St. NW7 —21Va 40
Lawrence St. SW3 —51Gb 103
Lawrence Way. NW10 —34Ta 59
Lawrence Way. Slou —3B 72
Lawrence Weaver Clo. Mord
—72Cb 145
Lawrence Yd. N15 —28Ub 43
Lawrie Pk. Av. SE26 —64Xb 127
Lawrie Pk. Cres. SE26 —64Xb 127
Lawrie Pk. Gdns. SE26 —63Xb 127
Lawrie Pk. Rd. SE26 —65Xb 127
Lawson Clo. E16 —43Lc 85
Lawson Clo. SW19 —62Za 124
Lawson Ct. N4 —32Pb 62
(off Lorne Rd.)
Lawson Ct. Surb —73Ma 143
Lawson Gdns. Dart —57Md 111
Lawson Gdns. Pinn —27X 37
Lawson Ho. W12 —45Xa 80
(off White City Est.)
Lawson Rd. Dart —56Md 111
Lawson Rd. Enf —11Yb 26
Lawson Rd. S'hall —42Ca 77
Law St. SE1 —48Tb 83 (3G 207)
Lawton Rd. E3 —41Ac 84
(in two parts)
Lawton Rd. E10 —32Ec 64
Lawton Rd. Barn —13Fb 23
Lawton Rd. Lou —12Rc 28
Laxcon Clo. NW10 —36Ta 59
Laxey Rd. Orp —79Vc 151
Laxley Clo. SE5 —52Rb 105
Laxton Gdns. Red —100Mb 180
Laxton Pl. NW1 —42Kb 82 (5A 192)
Layard Rd. SE16 —49Xb 83
Layard Rd. Enf —11Vb 25
Layard Rd. T Hth —68Tb 127
Layard Sq. SE16 —49Xb 83
Laybourne Ho. E14 —47Dc 84
(off Admirals Way)
Laybrook Lodge. E18 —28Hc 45
Layburn Cres. Slou —51D 96
Laycock St. N1 —37Qb 62
Layer Gdns. W3 —45Qa 79
Layfield Clo. NW4 —31Xa 60
Layfield Cres. NW4 —31Xa 60
Layfield Rd. NW4 —31Xa 60
Layhams Rd. W Wick & Kes
—77Gc 149
Laymarsh Clo. Belv —48Bd 87
Laymead Clo. N'holt —37Aa 57
Layrock La. Rick —17P 17
Laystall St. EC1 —42Qb 82 (6K 193)
Layters Way. Ger X —29A 34
Layton Ct. Bren —50Ma 79
Layton Ct. Wey —77R 140
Layton Cres. Croy —78Qb 146
Layton Rd. N1 —40Qb 62 (1A 194)
Layton Rd. Bren —50Ma 79
Layton Rd. Houn —56Da 99
Layton's Bldgs. SE1
—47Tb 83 (1F 207)
Laytons Bldgs. SW1 —47Tb 83
Layton's La. Sun —68V 120
Layzell Wlk. SE9 —60Mc 107
Lazar Wlk. N7 —33Pb 62
Lazenby Ct. WC2 —45Nb 82 (4F 199)
(off Floral St.)
Leabank Clo. Harr —34Ga 58
Leabank Sq. E9 —37Cc 64
Leabank View. N15 —30Wb 43
Leabourne Rd. N16 —31Wb 63
Lea Bri. Rd. E5, E10 & E17
—34Yb 64
Lea Bushes. Wat —7Aa 5
Leach Gro. Lea —94La 176
Lea Clo. Bush —15Da 19
Lea Ct. E4 —19Ec 26
Lea Ct. E13 —41Jc 85
Lea Cres. Ruis —35V 56
Leacroft. Asc —10E 116
Leacroft. Stai —64J 119
Leacroft Av. SW12 —59Hb 103
Leacroft Clo. Kenl —88Sb 165
Leacroft Clo. Stai —63K 119
Leacroft Clo. W Dray —44N 75
Leacroft Rd. Iver —44G 74
Leadale Av. E4 —19Cc 26
Leadale Rd. N15 & N16 —30Wb 43
Leadbetter Ct. NW10 —38Ta 59
(off Melville Rd.)
Leadenhall Mkt. EC3
—44Ub 83 (3H 201)
(off Leadenhall Pl.)
Leadenhall Pl. EC3
—44Ub 83 (3H 201)
Leadenhall St. EC3
—44Ub 83 (3H 201)
Leadenham Ct. E3 —42Cc 84
Leader Av. E12 —36Qc 66
Leadings, The. Wemb —34Sa 59
Leaf Clo. N'wd —24T 36
Leaf Clo. Th Dit —71Ga 142
Leaf Gro. SE27 —64Qb 126
Leafield Clo. SW16 —65Rb 127
Leafield Clo. Wok —6E 188
Leafield La. Sidc —62Bd 131
Leafield Rd. SW20 —69Bb 125
Leafield Rd. Sutt —75Cb 145
Leaford Cres. Wat —9V 4
Leaforis Rd. Chesh —1Wb 11
Leafy Gro. Kes —78Lc 149
Leafy Oak Rd. SE12 —63Lc 129
Leafy Way. Croy —75Vb 147
Leafy Way. Hut —18Fe 33
Lea Gdns. Wemb —36Pa 59
Leagrave St. E5 —34Yb 64
Lea Hall Rd. E10 —32Cc 64
Leaholme Gdns. Slou —3A 72
Leaholme Way. Ruis —30S 36
Leahurst Rd. SE13 —57Fc 107
Leake Clo. SE1 —47Pb 82
Leake Ct. SE1 —47Pb 82 (2J 205)
Leake St. SE1 —47Pb 82 (1J 205)
Lealand Rd. N15 —30Vb 43
Leamington Av. E17 —29Cc 44
Leamington Av. Brom —64Lc 129
Leamington Av. Mord —70Ab 124
Leamington Av. Orp —77Uc 150
Leamington Clo. E12 —36Nc 66
Leamington Clo. Brom —63Lc 129
Leamington Clo. Houn —57Ea 100
Leamington Clo. Romf —23Qd 49
Leamington Cres. Harr —34Aa 57
Leamington Gdns. Ilf —33Vc 67
Leamington Ho. Edgw —22Pa 39
Leamington Pk. W3 —43Ta 79
Leamington Pl. Hay —42V 76
Leamington Rd. Romf —22Qd 49
Leamington Rd. S'hall —49Z 77
Leamington Rd. Vs. W11 —43Bb 81
Leamore St. W6 —49Ya 80
Leamouth Rd. E6 —43Nc 86
Leamouth Rd. E14 —44Fc 85
Leander Ct. SE8 —53Cc 106
Leander Ct. SE16 —46Bc 84
Leander Ct. Surb —73Ma 143
Leander Dri. Grav —3H 137
Leander Gdns. Wat —9Aa 5
Leander Rd. SW2 —58Pb 104
Leander Rd. N'holt —40Ca 57
Leander Rd. T Hth —70Pb 126
Leapold M. E9 —39Yb 64
Lea Rd. Beck —68Cc 128
Lea Rd. Enf —11Tb 25
Lea Rd. Grays —10C 92
Lea Rd. Sev —99Ld 187
Lea Rd. S'hall —49Aa 77
Lea Rd. Wal A —6Cc 12
Lea Rd. Wat —10X 5
Lea Rd. Ind. Pk. Wal A —6Cc 12
Learoyd Gdns. E6 —45Qc 86
Leary Ho. SE11 —50Pb 82 (7J 205)
Leas Clo. Chess —80Pa 143
Leas Dale. SE9 —62Qc 130
Leas Dri. Iver —44G 74
Leas Grn. Chst —65Vc 131
Leaside. Bookh —95Ca 175
Leaside Av. N10 —27Jb 42
Leaside Ct. Uxb —41R 76
Lea Side Ind. Est. Enf —13Bc 26
Leaside Mans. N10 —27Jb 42
(off Fortis Grn.)
Leaside Rd. E5 —32Yb 64
Leas La. Warl —90Zb 166
Leasowes Rd. E10 —32Cc 64
Leas Rd. Warl —90Zb 166
Leas, The. Bush —11Ba 19
Leas, The. Upm —31Td 70
Leasway. Brtwd —20Zd 33
Leasway. Grays —46Ee 91
Leasway. Upm —34Sd 70
Leathart Clo. Horn —38Kd 69
Lea, The. Egh —66E 118
Leatherbottle Grn. Eri —48Bd 87
Leather Bottle La. Belv —49Ad 87
Leather Clo. Mitc —68Jb 126
Leatherdale St. E1 —42Yb 84
(in two parts)
Leather Gdns. E15 —39Gc 65
Leatherhead By-Pass Rd. Lea
—92Ka 176
Leatherhead Clo. N16 —32Vb 63
Leatherhead Ind. Est. Lea —93Ja 176
Leatherhead Rd. Bookh & Oxs
—98Da 175
Leatherhead Rd. Chess —86Ka 160
Leatherhead Rd. Lea & Asht
—93Ma 177
Leatherhead Rd. Oxs —86Fa 160
Leather La. EC1 —43Qb 82 (7K 193)
(in two parts)
Leather La. Horn —32Md 69
Leathermarket St. SE1
—47Ub 83 (2H 207)
Leathersellers Clo. Barn —13Ab 22
Leathsail Rd. Harr —34Da 57
Leathwaite Rd. SW11 —56Hb 103
Leathwell Rd. SE8 —54Dc 106
Lea Valley Rd. Enf & E4 —15Ac 26
Lea Vale. Dart —56Fd 110
Lea Valley Viaduct. N18 & E4
—22Zb 44
Leaveland Clo. Beck —70Cc 128
Leaver Gdns. Gnfd —40Fa 58
Leavesden Rd. Stan —23Ja 38
Leavesden Rd. Wat —10X 5
Leavesden Rd. Wey —78R 140
Leaves Grn. Cres. Kes —83Lc 167
Leaves Grn. Rd. Kes —83Mc 167
Leaview. Wal A —5Dc 12
Lea View Ho. E5 —32Xb 63
Leaway. E10 —32Zb 64
Leazes Av. Cat —96Qb 180
Leazes La. Cat —95Qb 180
Lebanon Av. Felt —64Z 121
Lebanon Clo. Wat —8T 4
Lebanon Dri. Cob —85Ca 159
Lebanon Gdns. SW18 —58Cb 103
Lebanon Gdns. Big H —89Mc 167
Lebanon Pk. Twic —59Ka 100
Lebanon Rd. SW18 —57Cb 103
Lebanon Rd. Croy —74Ub 147
Lebrun Sq. SE3 —56Kc 107
Lechmere App. Wfd G —26Lc 45
Lechmere Av. Chig —21Sc 46
Lechmere Av. Wfd G —26Mc 45
Lechmere Rd. NW2 —37Xa 60
Leckford Rd. SW18 —61Eb 125
Leckwith Av. Bexh —51Ad 109
Lecky St. SW7 —50Fb 81 (7B 202)
Leconfield Av. SW13 —55Va 102
Leconfield Rd. N5 —35Tb 63
Leconfield Wlk. Horn —37Ld 69
Leda Av. Enf —10Zb 12
Leda Rd. SE18 —48Pc 86
Ledbury M. N. W11 —44Cb 81
Ledbury M. W. W11 —45Cb 81
Ledbury Pl. Croy —77Tb 147
Ledbury Rd. W11 —44Bb 81
Ledbury Rd. Croy —77Tb 147
Ledbury St. SE15 —52Wb 105
Ledger Dri. Add —78H 139
Ledgers La. Warl —89Dc 166
Ledgers Rd. Slou —7H 73
Ledgers Rd. Warl —88Cc 166
Ledrington Rd. SE19 —65Wb 127
Ledway Dri. Wemb —31Pa 59
Lee Av. Romf —30Ad 47
Lee Bri. SE13 —55Ec 106
Leechcroft Av. Sidc —57Vc 109
Leechcroft Av. Swan —69Hd 132
Leechcroft Rd. Wall —76Jb 146
Leech La. Dork & Eps —98Ra 177
Lee Chu. St. SE13 —56Gc 107
Lee Clo. E17 —25Zb 44
Lee Conservancy Rd. E9 —36Bc 64
Leecroft Rd. Barn —15Ab 22
Leeds Clo. Orp —75Zc 151
Leeds Pl. N4 —32Pb 62
Leeds Rd. Ilf —32Tc 66
Leeds Rd. Slou —5J 73
Leeds St. N18 —22Wb 43
Leefern Rd. W12 —47Wa 80
Lee Gdns. Av. Horn —32Qd 69
Leegate. SE12 —57Hc 107
Lee Grn. Orp —71Wc 151
Lee Green La. Eps —96Ra 177
Lee Gro. Chig —19Rc 28
Lee High Rd. SE13 & SE12
—55Ec 106
Lee Ho. EC2 —43Sb 83 (1E 200)
(off Monkwell Sq.)
Leeke St. WC1 —41Pb 82
Leeland Rd. W13 —46Ja 78
Leeland Ter. W13 —46Ja 78
Leeland Way. NW10 —35Va 60
Leeming Rd. Borwd —11Pa 21
Leemount Ho. NW4 —28Za 40
Lee Pk. SE3 —56Hc 107
Lee Pk. Way. N18, N9 & E4
—21Zb 44
Leerdam Dri. E14 —48Ec 84
Lee Rd. NW7 —24Za 40
Lee Rd. SE3 —55Hc 107
Lee Rd. SW19 —67Db 125
Lee Rd. Enf —16Wb 25
Lee Rd. Gnfd —39La 58
Lees Av. N'wd —25V 36
Leeside. Barn —15Ab 22
Leeside Cres. NW11 —30Ab 40
Leeside Ind. Est. N17 —24Yb 44
Leeside Rd. N17 —23Xb 43
Leeson Gdns. Eton W —9C 72
Leeson Ho. Twic —59Ka 100
Leeson Rd. SE24 —56Qb 104
Leeson's Hill. Chst & St M
—69Uc 130
Leeson's Way. Orp —68Vc 131
Lees Pl. W1 —45Jb 82 (4H 197)
Lees Rd. Uxb —42R 76
Lees, The. Croy —75Bc 148
Lee St. E8 —39Ub 63
Lee Ter. SE13 & SE3 —55Gc 107
Lee View. Enf —11Rb 25
Leeward Ct. E1 —45Wb 83
Leeward Gdns. SW19 —64Ab 124
Leeway. SE8 —50Bc 84
Leeway Clo. H End —24Ba 37
Leewood Pl. Swan —70Fd 132
Leewood Way. Eff —99Y 175
Lefevre Wlk. E3 —39Bc 64
Lefroy Rd. W12 —47Va 80
Legard Rd. N5 —34Rb 63
Legatt Rd. SE9 —57Mc 107
Leggatt Rd. E15 —40Ec 64
Leggatts Clo. Wat —8V 4
Leggatts Rise. Wat —7W 4
Leggatts Way. Wat —8V 4
Leggatts Wood Av. Wat —8X 5
Legge St. SE13 —57Ec 106
Leghorn Rd. NW10 —40Va 60
Leghorn Rd. SE18 —50Tc 86
Legion Clo. N1 —38Qb 62
Legion Ct. Mord —72Cb 145
Legion Rd. Gnfd —40Ea 58
Legion Way. N12 —24Gb 41
Legon Av. Romf —32Ed 68
Legrace Av. Houn —54Z 99
Leicester Av. Mitc —70Nb 126
Leicester Clo. Wor Pk —77Ya 144
Leicester Ct. WC2
(off Lisle St.) —45Mb 82 (4E 198)
Leicester Gdns. Ilf —31Uc 66
Leicester Ho. SW9 —55Rb 105
(off Loughborough Rd.)
Leicester Pl. WC2
—45Mb 82 (4E 198)
Leicester Rd. E11 —29Kc 45
Leicester Rd. N2 —27Gb 41
Leicester Rd. NW10 —38Ta 59
Leicester Rd. Barn —15Db 23
Leicester Rd. Croy —73Ub 147
Leicester Rd. Til —3B 114
Leicester Sq. WC2
—45Mb 82 (5E 198)
Leicester St. WC2
—45Mb 82 (4E 198)
Leigham Av. SW16 —62Nb 126
Leigham Clo. SW16 —62Pb 126
Leigham Ct. Rd. SW16 —61Nb 126
Leigham Dri. Iswth —52Ga 100
Leigham Vale. SW16 & SW2
—62Pb 126
Leigh Av. Ilf —28Mc 45
Leigh Clo. Add —80H 139
Leigh Clo. N Mald —70Ta 123
Leigh Corner. Cob —87Y 159
Leigh Ct. Borwd —12Ta 21
Leigh Ct. Harr —32Ga 58
Leigh Ct. Clo. Cob —86Y 159
Leigh Cres. New Ad —80Dc 148
Leigh Dri. Romf —21Md 49
Leigh Gdns. NW10 —40Ya 60
Leigh Hill Rd. Cob —87Y 159
Leigh Orchard Clo. SW16
—62Pb 126
Leigh Pk. Dat —2N 95
Leigh Pl. EC1 —43Qb 82 (7K 193)
Leigh Pl. Cob —87Y 159
Leigh Pl. Well —54Wc 109
Leigh Rd. E6 —37Qc 66
Leigh Rd. E10 —31Ec 64
Leigh Rd. N5 —35Rb 63
Leigh Rd. Cob —86X 159
Leigh Rd. Grav —1D 136
Leigh Rd. Houn —56Fa 100
Leigh Rd. Slou —5F 72
Leigh Rd. Wat —20Ba 19
Leigh Sq. Wind —4B 94
Leigh St. WC1 —41Nb 82 (5F 193)
Leigh Ter. Orp —69Xc 131
Leighton Av. E12 —36Qc 66
Leighton Av. Pinn —27Aa 37
Leighton Clo. Edgw —26Qa 39
Leighton Ct. Chesh —1Zb 12
Leighton Cres. NW5 —36Lb 62
Leighton Gdns. NW10 —40Xa 60
Leighton Gdns. S Croy —85Xb 165
Leighton Gdns. Til —2C 114
Leighton Gro. NW5 —36Lb 62
Leighton Pl. NW5 —36Lb 62
Leighton Rd. NW5 —36Lb 62
Leighton Rd. W13 —47Ja 78
Leighton Rd. Enf —15Vb 25
Leighton Rd. Har W —26Fa 38
Leighton St. Croy —74Rb 147
Leighton Way. Eps —86Ta 161
Leila Parnell Pl. SE7 —51Lc 107
Leinester Rd. NW6 —41Cb 81
Leinster Av. SW14 —55Sa 101
Leinster Gdns. W2 —44Eb 81
Leinster M. W2 —45Eb 81 (5A 196)
Leinster Pl. W2 —44Eb 81
Leinster Rd. N10 —28Kb 42
Leinster Sq. W2 —44Cb 81
Leinster Ter. W2
—45Eb 81 (4A 196)
Leiston Spur. Slou —4J 73
Leisure La. W Byf —84K 157
Leith Clo. NW9 —32Ta 59
Leithcote Gdns. SW16 —63Pb 126
Leithcote Path. SW16 —62Pb 126
Leith Hill. Orp —67Wc 131
Leith Hill Grn. Orp —67Wc 131
Leith Mans. W9 —41Db 81
(off Grantully Rd.)
Leith Pk. Rd. Grav —10D 114
Leith Rd. N22 —25Rb 43
Leith Rd. Eps —84Ua 162
Lela Av. Houn —54Y 99
Lelitia Clo. E8 —39Wb 63
Leman St. E1 —44Vb 83
Lemark Clo. Stan —23La 38
Le May Av. SE12 —62Kc 129
Lemmon Rd. SE10 —51Gc 107
Lemna Rd. E11 —31Gc 65
Lemonfield Dri. Wat —4Aa 5
Lemonwell Dri. SE9 —58Sc 108
Lemsford Clo. N15 —30Wb 43
Lemsford Ct. N4 —33Sb 63
Lemsford Ct. Borwd —14Sa 21
Lemuel St. SW18 —58Eb 103
Lena Gdns. W6 —48Ya 80
Lena Kennedy Clo. E4 —23Ec 44
Lendal Ter. SW4 —55Mb 104
Lenelby Rd. Surb —74Qa 143
Len Freeman Pl. SW6 —51Bb 103
Lenham Rd. SE12 —56Hc 107
Lenham Rd. Bexh —51Bd 109
Lenham Rd. Sutt —77Db 145
Lenham Rd. T Hth —68Tb 127
Lenmore Av. Grays —48Ee 91
Lennard Av. W Wick —75Gc 149
Lennard Clo. W Wick —75Gc 149
Lennard Rd. SE20 & Beck
—65Zb 128
Lennard Rd. Brom —74Pc 150
Lennard Rd. Croy —74Sb 147
Lennard Rd. Dun G —92Gd 186
Lennard Row. S Ock —46Td 90
Lennon Rd. NW2 —36Ya 60
Lennox Av. Grav —8C 114
Lennox Clo. Romf —30Hd 48
Lennox Gdns. NW10 —35Va 60
Lennox Gdns. SW1
—48Hb 81 (4F 203)
Lennox Gdns. Croy —77Rb 147
Lennox Gdns. Ilf —32Pc 66
Lennox Gdns. M. SW1
—48Hb 81 (4F 203)
Lennox Ho. Belv —48Cd 88
Lennox Rd. E17 —30Bc 44
Lennox Rd. N4 —33Pb 62
Lennox Rd. Grav —8B 114
Lennox Rd. E. Grav —9C 114
Lenor Clo. Bexh —56Ad 109
Lensbury Clo. Chesh —1Ac 12
Lensbury Way. SE2 —48Yc 87
Lens Rd. E7 —38Lc 65
Lent Grn. Burn —2A 72
Lent Grn. La. Burn —2A 72
Lenthall Av. Grays —47Ce 91
Lenthall Ho. E8 —38Vb 63
Lenthall Rd. E8 —38Wb 63
Lenthall Rd. Lou —14Tc 28
Lenthorp Rd. SE10 —49Hc 85
Lentmead Rd. Brom —62Hc 129
Lenton Rise. Rich —55Na 101
Lenton Rd. SE18 —49Tc 86
Lenville Way. SE16 —50Wb 83
Leo Ct. Bren —52Ma 101
Leof Cres. SE6 —64Dc 128
Leominster Rd. Mord —72Eb 145
Leominster Wlk. Mord —72Eb 145
Leonard Av. Mord —71Eb 145
Leonard Av. Otf —87Kd 171
Leonard Av. Romf —32Fd 68

Leonard Av.—Links Rd.

Leonard Av. Swans —59Ae 113
Leonard Ct. Har W —25Ga 38
Leonard Rd. E4 —23Cc 44
Leonard Rd. E7 —35Jc 65
Leonard Rd. N9 —20Vb 25
Leonard Rd. SW16 —67Lb 126
Leonard Rd. S'hall —48Z 77
Leonard St. E16 —46Nc 86
Leonard St. EC2 —42Tb 83 (5G 195)
Leonard Way. Brtwd —21Ud 50
Leontine Clo. SE15 —52Wb 105
Leopards Ct. EC1
—43Qb 82 (7K 193)
(off Baldwins Gdns.)
Leopold Av. SW19 —64Bb 125
Leopold Rd. E17 —29Cc 44
Leopold Rd. N2 —27Fb 41
Leopold Rd. N18 —22Xb 43
Leopold Rd. NW10 —38Ua 60
Leopold Rd. SW19 —63Bb 125
Leopold Rd. W5 —46Pa 79
Leopold St. E3 —43Bc 84
Leo St. SE15 —52Xb 105
Leo Yd. EC1 —42Rb 83 (6C 194)
(off St John St.)
Le Personne Homes. Cat —94Tb 181
(off Banstead Rd.)
Le Personne Rd. Cat —94Tb 181
Leppoc Rd. SW4 —57Mb 104
Leret Way. Lea —93Ka 176
Leroy St. SE1 —49Ub 83 (5H 207)
Lerwick Ct. Enf —15Ub 25
Lerwick Dri. Slou —3J 73
Lescombe Clo. SE23 —62Ac 128
Lescombe Rd. SE23 —62Ac 128
Lesley Clo. Bex —59Dd 110
Lesley Clo. Grav —7B 136
Lesley Clo. Swan —69Fd 132
Leslie Dunne Ho. Wind —4C 94
Leslie Gdns. Sutt —80Cb 145
Leslie Gro. Croy —74Ub 147
Leslie Pk. Rd. Croy —74Ub 147
Leslie Prince Ct. SE5 —52Tb 105
Leslie Rd. E11 —35Ec 64
Leslie Rd. E16 —44Kc 85
Leslie Rd. N2 —27Fb 41
Leslie Smith Sq. SE18 —51Qc 108
Lesney Farm Est. Eri —52Fd 110
Lesney Pk. Eri —51Fd 110
Lesney Pk. Rd. Eri —51Fd 110
Lessar Av. SW4 —58Lb 104
Lessingham Av. SW17 —63Hb 125
Lessingham Av. Ilf —27Qc 46
Lessing St. SE23 —59Ac 106
Lessington Av. Romf —30Ed 48
Lessness Av. Bexh —52Zc 109
Lessness Pk. Belv —50Bd 87
Lessness Rd. Belv —50Cd 88
Lessness Rd. Mord —72Eb 145
Lester Av. E15 —42Gc 85
Lester Ct. Wat —9Y 5
Leston Clo. Rain —41Kd 89
Leswin Pl. N16 —34Vb 63
Leswin Rd. N16 —34Vb 63
Letchford Gdns. NW10 —41Wa 80
Letchford M. NW10 —41Wa 80
Letchford Ter. Harr —25Da 37
Letchmore Rd. Rad —8Ja 6
Letchworth Clo. Brom —71Jc 149
Letchworth Clo. Wat —22Z 37
Letchworth Dri. Brom —71Jc 149
Letchworth St. SW17 —63Hb 125
Lethbridge Clo. SE13 —53Ec 106
Letter Box La. Sev —100Ld 187
Letterstone Rd. SW6 —52Bb 103
Lettice St. SW6 —53Bb 103
Lett Rd. E15 —38Fc 65
Lettsom St. SE5 —54Ub 105
Lettsom Wlk. E13 —40Jc 65
Leucha Rd. E17 —29Ac 44
Levana Clo. SW19 —60Ab 102
Leven Clo. Wal X —5Zb 12
Leven Clo. Wat —22Z 37
Levendale Rd. SE23 —61Ac 128
Leven Dri. Wal X —5Zb 12
Levenhurst Way. SW4 —54Nb 104
Leven Rd. E14 —43Ec 84
Leven Way. Hay —44U 76
Leveret Clo. New Ad —83Fc 167
Leveret Clo. Wat —6W 4
Leverett St. SW3
—49Gb 81 (5E 202)
Leverholme Gdns. SE9 —63Qc 130
Leverington Pl. N1
—41Ub 83 (4H 195)
(off Charles Sq.)
Leverson St. SW16 —65Lb 126
Lever Sq. Grays —9B 92
Lever St. EC1 —41Rb 83 (4C 194)
Leverton Pl. NW5 —36Lb 62
Leverton St. NW5 —36Lb 62
Leverton Way. Wal A —5Ec 12
Leveson Rd. Grays —8D 92
Levett Gdns. Ilf —35Vc 67
Levett Rd. Bark —37Uc 66
Levett Rd. Lea —92Ka 176
Levett Rd. Stanf —1N 93
Levine Gdns. Bark —40Zc 67
Levison Way. N19 —32Mb 62
Lewen's Ct. EC1 —42Sb 83 (5D 194)
(off Mitchell St.)
Lewes Clo. N'holt —37Ca 57
Lewesdon Clo. SW19 —60Za 102
Lewes Rd. N12 —22Gb 41
Lewes Rd. Brom —68Mc 129
Lewes Rd. Romf —21Md 49
Leweston Pl. N16 —31Vb 63
Lewes Way. Crox —14S 18
Lewgars Av. NW9 —30Sa 39
Lewin Rd. SW14 —55Ta 101
Lewin Rd. SW16 —65Mb 126
Lewin Rd. Bexh —56Ad 109
Lewins Farm Ct. Cipp —5D 72
Lewins Rd. Eps —86Ra 161
Lewins Rd. Ger X —27A 34
Lewins Way. Slou —5D 72
Lewis Av. E17 —25Cc 44
Lewis Clo. N14 —17Lb 24
Lewis Clo. Add —77L 139
Lewis Clo. Hare —26L 35
Lewis Clo. Shenf —17Be 33
Lewis Ct. Grav —1B 136
Lewis Cres. NW10 —36Ta 59
Lewis Gdns. N2 —26Fb 41
Lewis Gro. SE13 —55Ec 106
Lewisham Cen. SE13 —55Ec 106
Lewisham High St. SE13 —58Dc 106
Lewisham Hill. SE13 —54Ec 106
Lewisham Pk. SE13 —58Ec 106
Lewisham Rd. SE13 —53Dc 106
Lewisham St. SW1
—47Mb 82 (2E 204)
Lewisham Way. SE14 & SE4
—53Bc 106
Lewis Hunt Dri. N14 —17Lb 24
Lewis La. Ger X —25A 34
Lewis Rd. Grav —7B 136
Lewis Rd. Horn —30Ld 49
Lewis Rd. Mitc —68Fb 125
Lewis Rd. Rich —57Ma 100
Lewis Rd. Sidc —62Yc 131
Lewis Rd. S'hall —47Aa 77
Lewis Rd. Sutt —77Db 145
Lewis Rd. Swans —58Ae 113
Lewis Rd. Well —55Yc 109
Lewis St. NW1 —38Kb 62
(in two parts)
Lewis Way. Dag —37Dd 68
Lexden Dri. Romf —30Xc 47
Lexden Rd. W3 —45Ra 79
Lexden Rd. Mitc —70Mb 126
Lexham Gdns. W8 —49Cb 81
Lexham Gdns. M. W8 —48Db 81
Lexham Ho. Bark —39Tc 66
(off St Margarets)
Lexham M. W8 —49Cb 81
Lexham Wlk. W8 —48Db 81
Lexington Clo. Borwd —13Pa 21
Lexington Ct. Purl —82Sb 165
Lexington St. W1
—45Lb 82 (3C 198)
Lexington Way. Barn —14Za 22
Lexington Way. Upm —30Vd 50
Lexton Gdns. SW12 —60Mb 104
Leyborne Pk. Rich —53Qa 101
Leybourne Av. W13 —47Ka 78
Leybourne Av. Byfl —85P 157
Leybourne Clo. Brom —72Jc 149
Leybourne Clo. Byfl —85P 157
Leybourne Ho. SE15 —51Yb 106
Leybourne Pk. Rich —53Qa 101
Leybourne Rd. E11 —32Hc 65
Leybourne Rd. NW1 —38Kb 62
Leybourne Rd. NW9 —29Qa 39
Leybourne Rd. Uxb —39S 56
Leybourne St. NW1 —38Kb 62
Leybridge Ct. SE12 —57Jc 107
Leyburn Clo. E17 —28Dc 44
Leyburn Cres. Romf —24Nd 49
Leyburn Gdns. Croy —75Ub 147
Leyburn Gro. N18 —23Wb 43
Leyburn Rd. N18 —23Wb 43
Leyburn Rd. Romf —24Nd 49
Leycroft Clo. Lou —15Qc 28
Leycroft Gdns. Eri —53Kd 111
Leydenhatch La. Swan —67Ed 132
Leyden Mans. N19 —31Nb 62
(off Warltersville Rd.)
Leyden St. E1 —43Vb 83 (1K 201)
Leydon Clo. SE16 —46Zb 84
Leyes Rd. E16 —44Lc 85
Leyfield. Wor Pk —74Ua 144
Leyhill Clo. Swan —70Gd 132
Leyland Av. Enf —12Ac 26
Leyland Clo. Chesh —1Yb 12
Leyland Gdns. Wfd G —22Lc 45
Leyland Rd. SE12 —57Jc 107
Leylands La. Stai —56H 97
(in two parts)
Leylang Rd. SE14 —52Zb 106
Leys Av. Dag —39Ed 68
Leys Clo. Dag —38Fd 68
(in two parts)
Leys Clo. Hare —25M 35
Leys Clo. Harr —29Fa 38
Leys Ct. SW9 —54Qb 104
Leysdown Av. Bexh —56Ed 110
Leysdown Rd. SE9 —61Nc 130
Leysfield Rd. W12 —48Wa 80
Leys Gdns. Barn —15Jb 24
Leyspring Rd. E11 —32Hc 65
Leys Rd. Oxs —84Fa 160
Leys Rd. E. Enf —11Ac 26
Leys Rd. W. Enf —11Ac 26
Leys Sq. N3 —25Db 41
Leys, The. N2 —28Eb 41
Leys, The. Harr —30Pa 39
Ley St. Ilf —33Rc 66
Leyswood Dri. Ilf —29Uc 46
Leythe Rd. W3 —47Sa 79
Leyton Bus. Cen. E10 —33Cc 64
Leyton Ct. SE23 —60Yb 106
Leyton Cross Rd. Dart —62Hd 132
Leyton Grange Est. E10 —33Cc 64
Leyton Grn. Rd. E10 —30Ec 44
Leyton Ind. Village. E10 —31Zb 64
Leyton Pk. Rd. E10 —34Ec 64
Leyton Rd. E15 —36Ec 64
Leyton Rd. SW19 —66Eb 125
Leytonstone Rd. E15 —35Gc 65
Leyton Way. E11 —31Gc 65
Leywick St. E15 —40Gc 65
Lezayre Rd. Orp —79Vc 151
Liardet St. SE14 —51Ac 106
Liberia Rd. N5 —37Rb 63
Liberty Av. SW19 —67Eb 125
Liberty Hall Rd. Add —78J 139
Liberty La. Add —78J 139
Liberty M. SW12 —58Kb 104
Liberty Rise. Add —79J 139
Liberty II Cen. Romf —28Hd 48
Liberty St. SW9 —53Pb 104
Liberty, The. Romf —29Gd 48
Libra Ct. E4 —21Cc 44
Libra Rd. E3 —39Bc 64
Libra Rd. E13 —40Jc 65
Library Hill. Brtwd —19Zd 33
Library Pl. E1 —45Xb 83
Library St. SE1 —47Rb 83 (2B 206)
Library Way. Twic —59Ea 100
Lichfield Gdns. Rich —56Na 101
Lichfield Gro. N3 —25Cb 41
Lichfield M. E3 —41Ac 84
Lichfield Rd. E3 —41Ac 84
Lichfield Rd. E6 —41Mc 85
Lichfield Rd. N9 —19Wb 25
Lichfield Rd. NW2 —35Ab 60
Lichfield Rd. Dag —35Xc 67
Lichfield Rd. Houn —55Y 99
Lichfield Rd. N'wd —27W 36
Lichfield Rd. Rich —53Pa 101
Lichfield Rd. Wfd G —21Gc 45
Lichfield Sq. Rich —56Na 101
Lichfield Ter. Upm —33Ud 70
Lichfield Way. S Croy —82Zb 166
Lichlade Clo. Orp —77Vc 151
Lickey Ho. W14 —51Bb 103
(off N. End Rd.)
Lidbury Rd. NW7 —23Ab 40
Lidcote Gdns. SW9 —54Qb 104
Liddall Way. W Dray —46P 75
Liddell Clo. Harr —27Ma 39
Liddell Gdns. NW10 —40Ya 60
Liddell Pl. Wind —5A 94
Liddell Rd. NW6 —37Cb 61
Liddell Sq. Wind —4A 94
Liddell Way. Wind —5A 94
Lidding Rd. Harr —29Ma 39
Liddington Rd. E15 —39Hc 65
Liddon Rd. E13 —41Kc 85
Liddon Rd. Brom —69Lc 129
Liden Clo. E17 —31Bc 64
Lidfield Rd. N16 —35Tb 63
Lidiard Rd. SW18 —61Eb 125
Lidlington Pl. NW1 —40Lb 62
Lido Sq. N17 —26Tb 43
Lidstone Clo. Wok —5E 188
Lidyard Rd. N19 —32Lb 62
Liffler Rd. SE18 —50Uc 86
Liffords Pl. SW13 —54Va 102
Lifford St. SW15 —56Za 102
Light App. NW9 —26Va 40
Lightcliffe Rd. N13 —21Qb 42
Lightermans Rd. E14 —47Cc 84
Lightfoot Rd. N8 —29Nb 42
Light Horse Ct. SW3
—50Jb 82 (7H 203)
(off Royal Hospital Rd.)
Lightley Clo. Wemb —39Na 59
Ligonier St. E2 —42Vb 83 (5K 195)
Lilac Av. Wok —8G 188
Lilac Clo. E4 —23Bc 44
Lilac Clo. Chesh —3Xb 11
Lilac Clo. Pil H —15Xd 32
Lilac Ct. E13 —39Lc 65
Lilac Ct. Slou —1D 72
Lilac Ct. Tedd —63Ha 122
Lilac Gdns. W5 —48Ma 79
Lilac Gdns. Croy —76Cc 148
Lilac Gdns. Hay —44U 76
Lilac Gdns. Ilf —36Rc 66
Lilac Gdns. Romf —32Gd 68
Lilac Gdns. Swan —69Fd 132
Lilac Pl. SE11 —49Pb 82 (6H 205)
Lilac Pl. W Dray —45P 75
Lilacs Av. Enf —8Yb 12
Lilac St. W12 —45Wa 80
Lila Pl. Swan —70Gd 132
Lilburne Gdns. SE9 —57Nc 108
Lilburne Rd. SE9 —57Nc 108
Lilburne Wlk. NW10 —37Sa 59
Lile Cres. W7 —43Ga 78
Lilestone St. NW8
—42Gb 81 (5D 190)
Lilford Ho. SE5 —54Sb 105
Lilford Rd. SE5 —54Rb 105
Lilian Barker Clo. SE12 —57Jc 107
Lilian Board Way. Gnfd —36Fa 58
Lilian Clo. N16 —34Ub 63
Lilian Cres. Hut —19Ee 33
Lilian Gdns. Wfd G —25Kc 45
Lilian Rd. SW16 —67Lb 126
Lillechurch Rd. Dag —37Xc 67
Lilleshall Rd. Mord —72Fb 145
Lilley Clo. Brtwd —21Vd 50
Lilley Dri. Tad —94Db 179
Lillian Av. W3 —47Qa 79
Lillian Rd. SW13 —51Wa 102
Lillie Rd. SW6 —51Za 102
Lillie Rd. Big H —90Mc 167
Lillieshall Rd. SW4 —55Kb 104
Lillie Yd. SW6 —51Cb 103
Lillington Gdns. Est. SW1
—49Lb 82 (6C 204)
(off Vauxhall Bri. Rd.)
Lilliot's La. Lea —91Ja 176
Lilliput Av. N'holt —39Aa 57
Lilliput Ct. SE12 —57Kc 107
Lilliput Rd. Romf —31Fd 68
Lily Clo. W14 —49Za 80
(in two parts)
Lily Gdns. Wemb —40La 58
Lily Pl. EC1 —43Qb 82 (7A 194)
Lily Rd. E17 —30Cc 44
Lilyville Rd. SW6 —53Bb 103
Limbourne Av. Dag —31Bd 67
Limburg Rd. SW11 —56Gb 103
Lime Av. Brtwd —20Be 33
Lime Av. Grav —59Fe 113
Lime Av. Upm —35Qd 69
Lime Av. W Dray —45P 75
Lime Av. Wind —2D 116
(Windsor Great Park)
Lime Av. Wind —3K 95
(Windsor)
Limeburner La. EC4
—44Rb 83 (3B 200)
Limebush Clo. New Haw —81L 157
Lime Clo. E1 —46Wb 83
Lime Clo. Buck H —19Mc 27
Lime Clo. Cars —75Hb 145
Lime Clo. Harr —26Ja 38
Lime Clo. Pinn —27V 36
Lime Clo. Romf —28Ed 48
Lime Clo. S Ock —41Yd 90
Lime Clo. Wat —17Z 19
Lime Clo. W Cla —100K 173
Lime Ct. E11 —33Gc 65
(off Trinity Clo.)
Lime Ct. E17 —29Ec 44
Lime Ct. SE9 —61Rc 130
Lime Ct. Harr —30Ha 38
Lime Ct. Mitc —68Fb 125
Lime Cres. Sun —68Y 121
Limecroft Clo. Eps —80Ta 143
Limedene Clo. Pinn —25Z 37
Lime Gro. N20 —18Bb 23
Lime Gro. W12 —47Ya 80
Lime Gro. Add —77J 139
Lime Gro. Hay —45T 76
Lime Gro. Ilf —23Vc 47
Lime Gro. N Mald —69Ta 123
Lime Gro. Orp —75Rc 150
Lime Gro. Ruis —30X 37
Lime Gro. Sidc —58Vc 109
Lime Gro. Twic —58Ha 100
Lime Gro. Warl —90Ac 166
Lime Gro. W Cla —100J 173
Lime Gro. Wok —93A 172
Limeharbour. E14 —48Dc 84
Limeharbour Ct. E14 —48Dc 84
Limehouse Causeway. E14
—45Bc 84
Limehouse Fields Est. E14
—43Ac 84
Limehouse Link. E14 —45Bc 84
Lime Meadow Av. S Croy
—85Wb 165
Lime Pit La. Sev —89Ed 170
Limerick Clo. SW12 —59Lb 104
Limerick Gdns. Upm —31Vd 70
Lime Rd. Epp —2Vc 15
Lime Rd. Eri —48Bd 87
Lime Rd. Rich —56Pa 101
Lime Rd. Swan —69Fd 132
Lime Row. Eri —48Bd 87
Limerston St. SW10 —51Eb 103
Limes Av. E11 —28Kc 45
Limes Av. E12 —34Nc 66
Limes Av. N12 —21Eb 41
Limes Av. NW7 —23Ua 40
Limes Av. NW11 —31Ab 60
Limes Av. SE20 —66Xb 127
Limes Av. SW13 —54Va 102
Limes Av. Cars —74Hb 145
Limes Av. Chig —22Sc 46
Limes Av. Croy —76Qb 146
Limes Av., The. N11 —22Kb 42
Limes Clo. N11 —22Lb 42
Limes Clo. Ashf —64Q 120
Limes Ct. Brtwd —18Zd 33
Limesdale Gdns. Edgw —26Sa 39
Limes Field Rd. SW14 —55Ua 102
Limesford Rd. SE15 —56Zb 106
Limes Gdns. SW18 —58Cb 103
Limes Gro. SE13 —56Ec 106
Limes Pl. Croy —73Tb 147
Limes Rd. Beck —68Dc 128
Limes Rd. Chesh —4Ac 12
Limes Rd. Croy —73Tb 147
Limes Rd. Egh —64B 118
Limes Rd. Wey —77Q 140
Limes Row. F'boro —78Rc 150
Limes, The. W2 —45Cb 81
(off Linden Gdns.)
Limes, The. Brtwd —20Be 33
Limes, The. Kes —75Nc 150
Limes, The. W Mol —70Da 121
Limes, The. Wok —3G 188
Limestone Wlk. Eri —47Zc 87
Lime St. E17 —28Ac 44
Lime St. EC3 —45Ub 83 (4H 201)
Lime St. Pas. EC3
—44Ub 83 (4H 201)
Limes Wlk. SE15 —56Yb 106
Limes Wlk. W5 —47Ma 79
Lime Ter. W7 —45Ga 78
Lime Tree Av. Esh & Th Dit
—74Ga 142
Limetree Clo. SW2 —60Pb 104
Lime Tree Clo. Bookh —96Ca 175
Lime Tree Ct. Asht —90Na 161
Lime Tree Gro. Croy —76Bc 148
Lime Tree Pl. Mitc —67Kb 126
Lime Tree Rd. Houn —53Da 99
Lime Tree Ter. SE6 —60Bc 106
Limetree Wlk. SW17 —64Jb 126
Lime Tree Wlk. Bush —18Ga 20
Lime Tree Wlk. Enf —10Sb 11
Lime Tree Wlk. Rick —15K 17
Lime Tree Wlk. Sev —97Kd 187
Lime Tree Wlk. W Wick —77Hc 149
Lime Wlk. E15 —39Gc 65
Lime Wlk. Den —36L 55
Limewood Clo. W13 —44Ka 78
Limewood Clo. Wok —8A 188
Limewood Ct. Ilf —29Pc 46
Limewood Rd. Eri —52Ed 110
Lime Works Rd. Mers —98Lb 180
Limpsfield Av. SW19 —61Za 124
Limpsfield Av. T Hth —71Pb 146
Limpsfield Rd. S Croy & Warl
—84Wb 165
Linacre Rd. NW2 —37Xa 60
Linberry Wlk. SE8 —49Bc 84
Linchfield Rd. Dat —3N 95
Linchmere Rd. SE12 —59Hc 107
Lincoln Av. N14 —20Lb 24
Lincoln Av. SW19 —62Za 124
Lincoln Av. Romf —33Fd 68
Lincoln Av. Twic —61Ea 122
Lincoln Clo. SE25 —72Wb 147
Lincoln Clo. Eri —54Hd 110
Lincoln Clo. Gnfd —39Ea 58
Lincoln Clo. Harr —29Ba 37
Lincoln Clo. Horn —29Qd 49
Lincoln Ct. N16 —31Tb 63
Lincoln Ct. Borwd —15Ta 21
Lincoln Cres. Enf —15Ub 25
Lincoln Dri. Crox —14R 18
Lincoln Dri. Wat —20Y 19
Lincoln Dri. Wok —87G 156
Lincoln Gdns. Ilf —31Nc 66
Lincoln Grn. Rd. Orp —71Vc 151
Lincoln Hatch La. Burn —2A 72
Lincoln Ho. SW9 —52Qb 104
Lincoln M. NW6 —39Bb 61
Lincoln M. SE21 —61Tb 127
Lincoln Rd. E7 —37Mc 65
Lincoln Rd. E13 —42Kc 85
Lincoln Rd. E18 —25Hc 45
Lincoln Rd. N2 —27Gb 41
Lincoln Rd. SE25 —69Xb 127
Lincoln Rd. Enf —14Ub 25
Lincoln Rd. Eri —54Hd 110
(in two parts)
Lincoln Rd. Felt —62Ba 121
Lincoln Rd. Ger X —25A 34
Lincoln Rd. Harr —29Ba 37
Lincoln Rd. Mitc —71Nb 146
Lincoln Rd. N Mald —69Sa 123
Lincoln Rd. N'wd —27V 36
Lincoln Rd. Sidc —64Xc 131
Lincoln Rd. Wemb —37Ma 59
Lincoln Rd. Wor Pk —74Xa 144
Lincolns Field. Epp —2Vc 15
Lincolnshire Ter. Dart —63Td 134
Lincoln's Inn Fields. WC2
—44Pb 82 (2H 199)
Lincolns La. Brtwd —15Sd 32
Lincolns, The. NW7 —20Va 22
Lincoln St. E11 —33Gc 65
Lincoln St. SW3 —49Hb 81 (6F 203)
Lincoln Wlk. Eps —82Ta 161
(in two parts)
Lincoln Way. Crox —14R 18
Lincoln Way. Enf —15Xb 25
Lincoln Way. Slou —5B 72
Lincoln Way. Sun —67U 120
Lincombe Ct. Add —78K 139
Lincombe Rd. Brom —62Hc 129
Lindal Cres. Enf —14Nb 24
Lindale Clo. Vir W —10K 117
Lindal Rd. SE4 —57Bc 106
Lindbergh Rd. Wall —80Nb 146
Linden Av. NW10 —40Za 60
Linden Av. Coul —88Kb 164
Linden Av. Dart —60Ld 111
Linden Av. Enf —11Wb 25
Linden Av. Houn —57Da 99
Linden Av. Ruis —32W 56
Linden Av. T Hth —70Rb 127
Linden Av. Wemb —36Pa 59
Linden Chase Rd. Sev —94Kd 187
Linden Clo. N14 —16Lb 24
Linden Clo. New Haw —83J 157
Linden Clo. Orp —78Wc 151
Linden Clo. Purf —51Sd 112
Linden Clo. Ruis —32W 56
Linden Clo. Stan —22Ka 38
Linden Clo. Tad —92Za 178
Linden Clo. Th Dit —73Ha 142
Linden Clo. Wal X —2Xb 11
Linden Ct. W12 —46Ya 80
Linden Ct. Egh —5M 117
Linden Ct. Lea —93Ka 176
Linden Ct. Sidc —63Uc 130
Linden Cres. Gnfd —37Ha 58
Linden Cres. King T —68Pa 123
Linden Cres. Wfd G —23Kc 45
Linden Dri. Cat —96Sb 181
Linden Dri. Farn R —9G 52
Linden Dri. Ger X —25A 34
Lindenfield. Chst —68Rc 130
Linden Gdns. W2 —45Cb 81
Linden Gdns. W4 —50Ua 80
Linden Gdns. Enf —11Wb 25
Linden Gdns. Lea —93La 176
Linden Gro. SE15 —55Xb 105
Linden Gro. SE26 —65Yb 128
Linden Gro. N Mald —69Ua 124
Linden Gro. Tedd —64Ha 122
Linden Gro. W on T —75V 140
Linden Gro. Warl —90Ac 166
Linden Ho. SE15 —55Xb 105
Linden Ho. Hamp —65Da 121
Linden Ho. Langl —50D 74
Linden Lawns. Wemb —35Pa 59
Linden Lea. N2 —29Eb 41
Linden Lea. Pinn —24Ba 37
Linden Lea. Wat —5W 4
Linden Leas. W Wick —75Fc 149
Linden M. N1 —36Tb 63
Linden M. W2 —45Cb 81
Linden Pit Path. Lea —93Ka 176
(in two parts)
Linden Pl. E Hor —98U 174
Linden Pl. Eps —84Ua 162
Linden Pl. Stai —63J 119
Linden Rise. War —22Zd 51
Linden Rd. N10 —28Kb 42
Linden Rd. N11 —19Hb 23
Linden Rd. N15 —28Sb 43
Linden Rd. Hamp —66Ca 121
Linden Rd. Lea —93Ka 176
Linden Rd. Wey —81S 158
Lindens Clo. Eff —100Aa 175
Linden Sq. Sev —94Gd 186
Lindens, The. N12 —22Fb 41
Lindens, The. W4 —53Sa 101
Lindens, The. Lou —15Qc 28
Lindens, The. New Ad —79Ec 148
Linden St. Romf —28Fd 48
Linden Wlk. N19 —33Lb 62
Linden Way. N14 —16Lb 24
Linden Way. Purl —82Lb 164
Linden Way. Rip —97H 173
Linden Way. Shep —71S 140
Linden Way. Wok —93B 172
Lindeth Clo. Stan —23Ka 38
Lindfield Gdns. NW3 —36Db 61
Lindfield Rd. W4 —42La 78
Lindfield Rd. Croy —72Vb 147
Lindfield Rd. Romf —22Nd 49
Lindfield St. E14 —44Cc 84
Lindholme Ct. NW9 —25Ua 40
(off Pageant Av.)
Lindisfarne Clo. Grav —1G 136
Lindisfarne Rd. SW20 —66Wa 124
Lindisfarne Rd. Dag —34Yc 67
Lindisfarne Way. E9 —35Ac 64
Lindley Ct. King T —67La 122
Lindley Est. SE15 —52Wb 105
Lindley Rd. E10 —33Ec 64
Lindley Rd. W on T —76Z 141
Lindley St. E1 —43Yb 84
Lindore Rd. SW11 —56Hb 103
Lindores Rd. Cars —74Eb 145
Lindo St. SE15 —54Yb 106
Lind Rd. Sutt —78Eb 145
Lindrop St. SW6 —54Eb 103
Lindsay Clo. Chess —80Na 143
Lindsay Clo. Eps —85Sa 161
Lindsay Clo. Stai —57M 97
Lindsay Dri. Harr —30Na 39
Lindsay Dri. Shep —72T 140
Lindsay Pl. Chesh —2Xb 11
Lindsay Rd. Hamp —63Da 121
Lindsay Rd. New Haw —82J 157
Lindsay Rd. Wor Pk —75Xa 144
Lindsay Sq. SW1
—50Mb 82 (7E 204)
Lindsell St. SE10 —53Ec 106
Lindsey Clo. Brtwd —21Wd 50
Lindsey Clo. Brom —69Mc 129
Lindsey Clo. Mitc —70Nb 126
Lindsey Ct. N13 —20Qb 24
(off Green Lanes)
Lindsey Gdns. Felt —59T 98
Lindsey M. N1 —38Sb 63
Lindsey Rd. Dag —35Yc 67
Lindsey Rd. Den —34J 55
Lindsey St. EC1
—43Rb 83 (7C 194)
Lindsey St. Epp —1Vc 15
Lindsey Way. Horn —29Ld 49
Lind St. SE8 —54Cc 106
Lindum Rd. Tedd —66La 122
Lindway. SE27 —64Rb 127
Linfield Clo. W on T —78X 141
Linford Rd. E17 —27Ec 44
Linford Rd. Grays —9D 92
Linford St. SW8 —53Lb 104
Lingards Rd. SE13 —56Ec 106
Lingey Clo. Sidc —61Vc 131
Lingfield Av. Dart —59Rd 111
Lingfield Av. King T —70Na 123
Lingfield Av. Upm —34Pd 69
Lingfield Clo. Enf —16Ub 25
Lingfield Clo. N'wd —24U 36
Lingfield Ct. N'holt —40Ca 57
Lingfield Cres. SE9 —56Tc 108
Lingfield Gdns. N9 —17Xb 25
Lingfield Gdns. Coul —91Rb 181
Lingfield Rd. SW19 —64Za 124
Lingfield Rd. Grav —1D 136
Lingfield Rd. Wor Pk —76Ya 144
Lingham St. SW9 —54Nb 104
Lingholm Way. Barn —15Za 22
Lingmere Clo. Chig —19Sc 28
Ling Rd. E16 —43Jc 85
Ling Rd. Eri —51Ed 110
Lingrove Gdns. Buck H —19Kc 27
Lings Coppice. SE21 —61Tb 127
Lingwell Rd. SW17 —62Gb 125
Lingwood. Bexh —54Dd 110
Lingwood Gdns. Iswth —52Ga 100
Lingwood Rd. E5 —31Wb 63
Linhope St. NW1
—42Hb 81 (5F 191)
Link Av. Wok —87F 156
Linkenholt Mans. W6 —49Va 80
(off Stamford Brook Av.)
Linkfield. Hayes —72Jc 149
Linkfield. W Mol —69Da 121
Linkfield Rd. Iswth —54Ha 100
Link La. Wall —79Mb 146
Linklea Clo. NW9 —24Ua 40
Link Rd. N8 —27Qb 42
Link Rd. N11 —21Jb 42
Link Rd. Add —77N 139
Link Rd. Dag —40Dd 68
Link Rd. Dat —3N 95
Link Rd. Felt —59V 98
Link Rd. Stanf —1M 93
Link Rd. Wall —74Jb 146
Link Rd. Wat —12Z 19
Links Av. Mord —70Cb 125
Links Av. Romf —26Kd 49
Links Brow. Fet —96Ga 176
Links Clo. Asht —89La 160
Linkscroft Av. Ashf —65R 120
Links Dri. N20 —18Cb 23
Links Dri. Els —13Pa 21
Links Dri. Rad —5Ha 6
Links Gdns. SW16 —66Qb 126
Links Grn. Way. Cob —86Ca 159
Linkside. N12 —23Cb 41
Linkside. Chig —22Sc 46
Linkside. N Mald —68Ua 124
Linkside Clo. Enf —13Pb 24
Linkside Gdns. Enf —13Pb 24
Links Pl. Asht —89Ma 161
Links Rd. NW2 —33Va 60
Links Rd. SW17 —65Jb 126
Links Rd. W3 —44Qa 79
Links Rd. Ashf —64N 119
Links Rd. Asht —90La 160
Links Rd. Eps —85Wa 162
Links Rd. W Wick —74Ec 148

Long Elms—Lulworth Clo.

Long Elms. Abb L —5T 4
Long Elms Clo. Abb L —5T 4
Longfellow Dri. Hut —17Ee 33
Longfellow Rd. E3 —41Ac 84
Longfellow Rd. E17 —30Bc 44
Longfellow Rd. Wor Pk —74Wa 144
Longfellow Way. SE1 —49Vb 83 (6K 207)
Long Field. NW9 —24Ua 40
Longfield. Brom —67Hc 129
Longfield. Hedg —4H 53
Longfield. Lou —15Mc 27
Longfield Av. E17 —28Ac 44
Longfield Av. NW7 —24Wa 40
Longfield Av. W5 —45La 78
Longfield Av. Enf —9Yb 12
Longfield Av. Horn —31Hd 68
Longfield Av. Long & Grav —68Ee 135
Longfield Av. Wall —74Jb 146
Longfield Av. Wemb —32Na 59
Longfield Cres. SE26 —62Yb 128
Longfield Cres. Tad —92Ya 178
Longfield Dri. SW14 —57Ra 101
Longfield Dri. Mitc —67Gb 125
Longfield Est. SE1 —49Vb 83 (6K 207)
Longfield Rd. W5 —44La 78
Longfield Rd. Long & Meop —71Fe 155
Longfield St. SW18 —59Cb 103
Longfield Wlk. W5 —44La 78
Longford Av. Felt —58U 98
Longford Av. S'hall —45Da 77
Longford Av. Stai —60N 97
Longford Cir. W Dray —53K 97
Longford Clo. Hamp —63Ca 121
Longford Clo. Hay —45Z 77
Longford Ct. NW4 —28Za 40
Longford Ct. Eps —77Sa 143
Longford Ct. Sev —92Gd 186
Longford Gdns. Hay —45Z 77
Longford Gdns. Sutt —76Eb 145
Longford Ho. Hamp —63Ca 121
Longford Rd. Twic —60Ca 99
Longford St. NW1 —42Kb 82 (5A 192)
Longford Wlk. SW2 —59Qb 104
Longford Way. Stai —60N 97
Long Furlong Dri. Slou —2C 72
Long Grn. Chig —21Uc 46
Long Gro. H Wood —26Nd 49
Long Gro. Rd. Eps —82Ra 161
Longhayes Av. Romf —28Zc 47
Longhayes Ct. Romf —28Zc 47
Longheath Gdns. Croy —71Yb 148
Long Hedges. Houn —54Ca 99
Longhedge St. SW11 —54Jb 104
Long Hill. Wold —93Zb 182
Longhill Rd. SE6 —61Fc 129
Longhook Gdns. N'holt —41X 77
Longhope Clo. SE15 —51Ub 105
Longhouse Rd. Grays —8D 92
Longhurst Rd. SE13 —57Gc 107
Longhurst Rd. Croy —72Xb 147
Longland Ct. SE1 —50Wb 83
Longland Dri. N20 —20Db 23
Longlands Av. Coul —86Jb 164
Longlands Clo. Chesh —4Zb 12
Longlands Ct. Sidc —61Vc 131
Longlands Pk. Cres. Sidc —62Uc 130
Longlands Rd. Sidc —62Uc 130
Long La. EC1 —43Rb 83 (1C 200)
Long La. N3 & N2 —25Db 41
Long La. SE1 —47Tb 83
Long La. Bexh —52Zc 109
Long La. Bov —3B 2
Long La. Chor —16E 16
Long La. Croy —72Yb 148
Long La. Flau —4C 2
Long La. Grays —47Ce 91
Long La. Hil —41Q 76
Long La. Ick —36R 56
Long La. Stai —61P 119
Longleat M. St M —70Yc 131
Longleat Rd. Enf —15Ub 25
Longleat Way. Felt —59T 98
Longlees. Rick —22F 34
Longleigh Ho. SE5 —53Ub 105 (off Peckham Rd.)
Longleigh La. Bexh —51Yc 109
Longley Av. Wemb —39Pa 59
Longley Ct. SW8 —53Nb 104
Longley Rd. SW17 —65Gb 125
Longley Rd. Croy —73Rb 147
Longley Rd. Harr —29Ea 38
Long Leys. E4 —23Dc 44
Longley St. SE1 —49Wb 83
Longley Way. NW2 —34Ya 60
Long Lodge Dri. W on T —76Y 141
Longman Ho. E8 —39Vb 63 (1K 195)
Long Mark Rd. E16 —43Mc 85
Longmarsh View. S at H —67Rd 133
Long Mead. NW9 —25Va 40
Longmead. Chst —68Qc 130
Longmead. Wind —3C 94
Longmead Bus. Cen. Eps —83Ta 161
Longmead Clo. Cat —94Ub 181
Longmead Clo. Shenf —18Ae 33
Longmead Dri. Sidc —61Zc 131
Longmead Ho. SE27 —64Sb 127
Longmead La. Burn —8B 52
Long Meadow. NW5 —36Mb 62
Longmeadow. Bookh —97Ba 175
Long Meadow. Hut —19Ee 33
Long Meadow Clo. W Wick —73Ec 148
Longmeadow Rd. Sidc —60Uc 108
Longmead Rd. SW17 —64Hb 125
Longmead Rd. Eps —83Ta 161
Longmead Rd. Hay —45V 76
Longmead Rd. Th Dit —73Ga 142
Longmere Gdns. Tad —91Ya 178
Long Moor. Chesh —1Ac 12
Longmoore St. SW1 —49Lb 82 (6B 204)
Longmore Av. Barn —16Eb 23
Longmore Clo. Rick —21H 35
Longmore Rd. W on T —77Aa 141
Longmore St. SW1 —49Lb 82
Longnor Est. E1 —41Zb 84
Longnor Rd. E1 —41Zb 84
Long Pond Rd. SE3 —53Gc 107
Longport Clo. Ilf —23Wc 47
Long Reach. Ock & W Hors —95Q 174
Longreach Ct. Bark —40Tc 66
Long Reach Rd. Bark —42Vc 87
Longreach Rd. Eri —52Kd 111
Long Readings La. Slou —1F 72
Longridge Gro. Wok —86H 157
Longridge Ho. SE1 —48Sb 83 (4E 206)
Longridge La. S'hall —44Da 77
Longridge Rd. SW5 —49Cb 81
Long Ridges. N2 —27Jb 42 (off Fortis Grn.)
Long Ridings Av. Hut —15De 33
Long Rd. SW4 —56Kb 104
Longs Clo. Wok —88J 157
Long's Ct. WC2 —45Mb 82 (5E 198) (off Orange St.)
Longs Ct. Rich —56Pa 101
Long Shaw. Lea —92Ja 176
Longshaw Rd. E4 —20Fc 27
Longshore. SE8 —49Bc 84
Longside Clo. Egh —67E 118
Longspring. Wat —10X 5
Longstaff Cres. SW18 —59Cb 103
Longstaff Rd. SW18 —58Cb 103
Longstone Av. NW10 —38Va 60
Longstone Rd. SW17 —64Kb 126
Longstone Rd. Iver —40E 54
Long St. E2 —41Vb 83 (3K 195)
(in two parts)
Long St. Wal A —4Nc 14
Longthornton Rd. SW16 —68Lb 126
Longton Av. SE26 —63Wb 127
Longton Gro. SE26 —63Xb 127
Longtown Clo. Romf —22Ld 49
Longtown Ct. Dart —58Rd 111 (off Clifton Wlk.)
Longtown Ct. Dart —58Rd 111 (off Osborne Rd.)
Longtown Rd. Romf —22Ld 49
Longview Vs. Romf —25Bd 47
Longview Way. Romf —25Fd 48
Longville Rd. SE11 —49Rb 83 (5B 206)
Long Wlk. SE1 —48Ub 83 (3J 207)
Long Wlk. SE18 —51Rc 108
Long Wlk. SW13 —54Va 102
Long Wlk. Chal G —13A 16
Long Wlk. Eps —91Ya 178
Longwalk. Grav —7A 136
Long Wlk. N Mald —69Sa 123
Long Wlk. Wal A —2Cc 12
Long Wlk. W Byf —86L 157
Longwalk Rd. Uxb —46R 76
Long Wlk., The. Wind —7H 95
Long Wall. E15 —41Fc 85
Long Ways. Stai —67G 118
Longwood Clo. Upm —36Sd 70
Longwood Ct. Upm —36Sd 70 (off Corbets Tey Rd.)
Longwood Dri. SW15 —58Wa 102
Longwood Gdns. Ilf —28Pc 46
Longwood Rd. Kenl —88Tb 165
Longworth Clo. SE28 —44Zc 87
Long Yd. WC1 —42Pb 82 (6H 193)
Loning, The. NW9 —28Va 40
Loning, The. Enf —10Yb 12
Lonsdale Av. E6 —41Mc 85
Lonsdale Av. Hut —16Fe 33
Lonsdale Av. Romf —30Ed 48
Lonsdale Av. Wemb —36Na 59
Lonsdale Clo. E6 —42Nc 86
Lonsdale Clo. SE9 —62Mc 129
Lonsdale Clo. Edgw —22Pa 39
Lonsdale Clo. Pinn —24Aa 37
Lonsdale Clo. Uxb —43S 76
Lonsdale Ct. Surb —73Ma 143
Lonsdale Cres. Dart —60Sd 112
Lonsdale Cres. Ilf —30Rc 46
Lonsdale Dri. Enf —14Mb 24
Lonsdale Gdns. T Hth —70Pb 126
Lonsdale M. Rich —53Qa 101
Lonsdale Pl. N1 —38Qb 62
Lonsdale Rd. E11 —31Hc 65
Lonsdale Rd. NW6 —40Bb 61
Lonsdale Rd. SE25 —70Xb 127
Lonsdale Rd. SW13 —53Va 102
Lonsdale Rd. W4 —49Va 80
Lonsdale Rd. W11 —44Bb 81
Lonsdale Rd. Bexh —54Bd 109
Lonsdale Rd. S'hall —48Z 77
Lonsdale Rd. Wey —80Q 140
Lonsdale Sq. N1 —38Qb 62
Lonsdale Yd. W11 —45Cb 81
Loobert Rd. N15 —27Ub 43
Looe Gdns. Ilf —27Rc 46
Loom La. Rad —9Ha 6
Loom Pl. Rad —8Ja 6
Loop Rd. Chst —65Sc 130
Loop Rd. Eps —88Sa 161
Loop Rd. Wal A —4Dc 12
Loop Rd. Wok —92B 172
Lopen Rd. N18 —21Ub 43
Lopez Ho. SW9 —55Nb 104
Lorac Ct. Sutt —80Cb 145
Loraine Clo. Enf —15Yb 26
Loraine Ct. Chst —64Rc 130
Loraine Gdns. Asht —89Na 161
Loraine Ho. Wall —77Kb 146
Loraine Rd. N7 —35Pb 62
Loraine Rd. W4 —51Ra 101
Lorane Ct. Wat —12W 18
Lord Av. Ilf —28Pc 46
Lord Chancellor Wlk. King T —67Ta 123
Lorden Wlk. E2 —41Wb 83
Lord Gdns. Ilf —28Pc 46
Lord Hills Bri. W2 —43Db 81
Lord Hills Rd. W2 —43Db 81
Lord Holland La. SW9 —54Qb 104
Lord Knyvett Clo. Stai —58M 97
Lord Mayor's Dri. Farn C —7D 52
Lord Napier Pl. W6 —50Wa 80
Lord North St. SW1 —48Nb 82 (4F 205)
Lord Roberts M. SW6 —52Db 103
Lord Robert's Ter. SE18 —50Qc 86
Lordsbury Field. Wall —82Lb 164
Lord's Clo. SE21 —61Sb 127
Lords Clo. Felt —61Aa 121
Lords Clo. Shenl —4Na 7
Lordsgrove Clo. Tad —92Xa 178
Lordship Clo. Hut —17Fe 33
Lordship Gro. N16 —33Tb 63
Lordship La. N22 & N17 —26Qb 42
Lordship La. SE22 —56Vb 105
Lordship La. Est. SE22 —59Wb 105
Lordship Pk. N16 —33Sb 63
Lordship Pk. M. N16 —33Sb 63
Lordship Pl. SW3 —51Gb 103
Lordship Rd. N16 —32Tb 63
Lordship Rd. Chesh —2Xb 11
Lordship Rd. N'holt —38Aa 57
Lordship Ter. N16 —33Tb 63
Lordsmead Rd. N17 —25Ub 43
Lord St. E16 —46Nc 86
Lord St. Grav —9D 114
Lord St. Wat —13Y 19
Lords View. NW8 —41Gb 81 (4D 190)
Lordswood Clo. Dart —63Ud 134
Lord Warwick St. SE18 —48Pc 86
Loreburn Ho. N7 —35Pb 62
Lorenzo St. WC1 —41Pb 82 (3H 193)
Loretto Gdns. Harr —28Na 39
Lorian Clo. N12 —21Db 41
Loring Rd. N20 —19Gb 23
Loring Rd. Iswth —54Ha 100
Loring Rd. Wind —3D 94
Loris Rd. W6 —48Ya 80
Lorn Ct. SW9 —53Qb 104
Lorne Av. Croy —73Zb 148
Lorne Clo. NW8 —41Gb 81 (4E 190)
Lorne Clo. Slou —8F 72
Lorne Ct. Chalv —8G 72
Lorne Gdns. E11 —28Lc 45
Lorne Gdns. W11 —47Za 80
Lorne Gdns. Croy —73Zb 148
Lorne Rd. E7 —35Kc 65
Lorne Rd. E17 —29Cc 44
Lorne Rd. N4 —32Pb 62
Lorne Rd. Harr —26Ha 38
Lorne Rd. Rich —57Pa 101
Lorne Rd. War —21Yd 50
Lorne Ter. N3 —26Bb 41
Lorne, The. Bookh —98Ca 175
Lorn Rd. SW9 —54Pb 104
Lorraine Clo. S Ock —48Pd 89
Lorraine Pk. Harr —24Ga 38
Lorrimore Rd. SE17 —51Rb 105
Lorrimore Sq. SE17 —51Rb 105
Lorton Clo. Grav —1G 136
Lorton Rd. Grav —1F 136
Losberne Way. SE16 —50Wb 83
Loseberry Rd. Clay —78Fa 142
Losfield Rd. Wind —3C 94
Lossie Dri. Iver —45D 74
Lothair Rd. W5 —47Ma 79
Lothair Rd. N. N4 —30Rb 43
Lothair Rd. S. N4 —31Qb 62
Lothbury. EC2 —44Tb 83 (2F 201)
Lothian Av. Hay —43X 77
Lothian Clo. Wemb —34Ja 58
Lothian Rd. SW9 —53Rb 105
Lothian Wood. Tad —94Xa 178
Lothrop St. W10 —41Ab 80
Lots Rd. SW10 —52Eb 103
Lotus Clo. SE21 —62Tb 127
Lotus Rd. Big H —90Pc 168
Loubet St. SW17 —65Hb 125
Loudhams Wood La. Chal G —12A 16
Loudon Rd. NW8 —39Eb 61 (1A 190)
Loudoun Av. Ilf —29Rc 46
Loudoun Rd. NW8 —39Eb 61
Loudwater Clo. Sun —70W 120
Loudwater Dri. Loud —14L 17
Loudwater Heights. Loud —13K 17
Loudwater La. Loud —15L 17
Loudwater Ridge. Loud —14L 17
Loudwater Rd. Sun —70W 120
Loughborough Est. SW9 —55Rb 105
Loughborough Pk. SW9 —56Rb 105
Loughborough Rd. SW9 —54Qb 104
Loughborough St. SE11 —50Pb 82 (7J 205)
Lough Rd. NW9 —29Sa 39
Lough Rd. N7 —36Pb 62
Loughton Ct. Wal A —5Kc 13
Loughton La. They B —10Tc 14
Loughton Way. Buck H —18Mc 27
Louisa Ct. Twic —61Ga 122
Louisa Gdns. E1 —42Zb 84
Louisa St. E1 —42Zb 84
Louis Bennet Clo. SE24 —56Rb 105
Louis Clo. N10 —25Kb 42
Louise Ct. N22 —25Qb 42
Louise Gdns. Rain —41Gd 88
Louise Rd. E15 —37Gc 65
Louise Wlk. Bov —1C 2
Louisville Rd. SW17 —62Jb 126
Lousada Lodge. N14 —16Lb 24 (off Avenue Rd.)
Louvaine Rd. SW11 —56Fb 103
Louvain Rd. Grnh —59Ud 112
Louvain Way. Wat —4X 5
Lovage App. E6 —43Nc 86
Lovat Clo. NW2 —34Va 60
Lovat Dri. Ruis —29V 36
Lovat La. EC3 —45Ub 83 (5H 201)
Lovatt Clo. Edgw —23Ra 39
Lovatts. Rick —14Q 18
Lovat Wlk. Houn —52Aa 99
Loveday Rd. W13 —47Ka 78
Love Grn. La. Iver —43F 74
Lovegrove St. SE1 —50Wb 83
Lovegrove Wlk. E14 —46Ec 84
Love Hill La. Slou —45C 74
Lovejoy La. Wind —4B 94
Lovekyn Clo. King T —68Na 123
Lovelace Av. Brom —72Qc 150
Lovelace Clo. Eff J —95W 174
Lovelace Clo. W King —79Ud 154
Lovelace Dri. Wok —88G 156
Lovelace Gdns. Bark —35Wc 67
Lovelace Gdns. Surb —73Ma 143
Lovelace Gdns. W on T —78Y 141
Lovelace Grn. SE9 —55Pc 108
Lovelace Rd. SE21 —61Sb 127
Lovelace Rd. Barn —17Gb 23
Lovelace Rd. Surb —73La 142
Loveland Mans. Bark —38Vc 67 (off Upney La.)
Lovelands La. Chob —1A 188
Lovelands La. Tad —99Db 179
Love La. EC2 —44Sb 83 (2E 200)
Love La. N17 —24Vb 43
Love La. SE18 —49Qc 86
Love La. SE25 —69Xb 127
(in two parts)
Love La. Abb L —2V 4
Love La. Bex —58Bd 109
Love La. Brom —69Kc 129 (off Elmfield Rd.)
Love La. E Til —1K 115
Love La. Grav —9E 114
Love La. Hat —1Xa 8
Love La. Iver —44F 74
Love La. K Lan —1N 3
Love La. Mitc —69Gb 125
(in two parts)
Love La. Mord —73Cb 145
Love La. Pinn —26Z 37
Love La. S Ock —47Sd 90
Love La. Surb —75La 142
Love La. Sutt —79Ab 144
Love La. Tad —98Va 178
Love La. Wfd G —23Pc 46
Lovel Av. Well —54Wc 109
Lovelinch Clo. SE15 —51Yb 106
Lovel La. Wink —3A 116
Lovell Pl. SE16 —48Ac 84
Lovell Rd. Enf —7Xb 11
Lovell Rd. Rich —62La 122
Lovell Rd. S'hall —44Da 77
Lovell Wlk. Rain —37Jd 68
Lovelock Clo. Kenl —89Sb 165
Loveridge M. NW6 —37Bb 61
Loveridge Rd. NW6 —37Bb 61
Lovers La. Grnh —56Yd 112
Lovers Wlk. NW7 & N3 —23Bb 41
Lovers Wlk. SE10 —51Fc 107
Lovers' Wlk. W1 —46Jb 82 (6H 197) (off Broad Wlk.)
Lovers Wlk. Romf —22Fd 48
Lovett Dri. Cars —73Cb 145
Lovett Rd. Hare —27L 35
Lovett Rd. Stai —63E 118
Lovett Way. NW10 —36Sa 59
Love Wlk. SE5 —54Tb 105
Lovibonds Av. Orp —76Rc 150
Lovibonds Av. W Dray —44P 75
Lowbrook Rd. Ilf —35Rc 66
Low Clo. Grnh —57Wd 112
Low Cross Wood La. SE21 —62Vb 127
Lowdell Clo. W Dray —44N 75
Lowden Rd. N9 —18Xb 25
Lowden Rd. SE24 —56Rb 105
Lowden Rd. S'hall —45Aa 77
Lowe Av. E16 —43Jc 85
Lowe Clo. Chig —22Wc 47
Lowell St. E14 —44Ac 84
Lowen Rd. Rain —40Fd 68
Lwr. Addiscombe Rd. Croy —74Ub 147
Lwr. Addison Gdns. W14 —47Ab 80
Lwr. Alderton Hall La. Lou —15Qc 28
Lwr. Barn Rd. Purl —84Sb 165
Lwr. Bedfords Rd. Romf —23Gd 48
Lwr. Belgrave St. SW1 —48Kb 82 (4K 203)
Lwr. Boston Rd. W7 —46Ga 78
Lwr. Britwell Rd. Slou —2B 72
Lwr. Broad St. Dag —39Cd 68
Lwr. Bury La. Epp —3Uc 14
Lwr. Camden. Chst —66Pc 130
Lwr. Church Hill. Grnh —57Ud 112
Lwr. Church St. Croy —75Rb 147
Lwr. Cippenham La. Slou —6C 72
Lwr. Clapton Rd. E5 —34Xb 63
Lwr. Clarendon Wlk. W11 —44Ab 80 (off Clarendon Rd.)
Lwr. Common S. SW15 —55Xa 102
Lwr. Coombe St. Croy —77Sb 147
Lwr. Court Rd. Eps —83Sa 161
Lower Cres. Linf —8J 93
Lwr. Croft. Swan —70Hd 132
Lwr. Downs Rd. SW20 —67Za 124
Lwr. Drayton Pl. Croy —75Rb 147
Lwr. Dunnymans. Bans —86Bb 163
Lwr. Farm Rd. Eff —96X 175
Lwr. Fosters. NW4 —29Ya 40 (off New Brent St.)
Lwr. George St. Rich —57Ma 101
Lwr. Gravel Rd. Brom —74Nc 150
Lwr. Green Rd. Esh —75Da 141
Lwr. Green W. Mitc —69Gb 125
Lwr. Grosvenor Pl. SW1 —48Kb 82 (3A 204)
Lwr. Grove Rd. Rich —58Pa 101
Lwr. Guildford Rd. Knap —5A 188
Lwr. Hall La. E4 —22Ac 44
Lwr. Hampton Rd. Sun —69Y 121
Lwr. Ham Rd. King T —64Ma 123
Lwr. Higham Rd. Grav —10H 115
Lwr. High St. Wat —14Y 19
Lwr. Hill Rd. Eps —84Ra 161
Lwr. Hythe St. Dart —57Nd 111
Lwr. Island Way. Wal A —7Dc 12
Lwr. James St. W1 —45Lb 82 (4C 198)
Lwr. John St. W1 —45Lb 82 (4C 198)
Lwr. Kenwood Av. Enf —15Mb 24
Lwr. Lees Rd. Slou —1E 72
Lwr. Maidstone Rd. N11 —23Lb 42
Lwr. Mall. W6 —50Xa 80
Lwr. Mardyke Av. Rain —40Ed 68
Lwr. Marsh. SE1 —47Qb 82 (2K 205)
Lwr. Marsh La. King T —70Pa 123
Lwr. Mead. Iver —41F 74
Lwr. Merton Rise. NW3 —38Gb 61
Lwr. Morden La. Mord —72Ya 144
Lwr. Mortlake Rd. Rich —56Na 101
Lwr. Noke Clo. Brtwd —19Nd 31
Lwr. Northfield. Bans —86Bb 163
Lwr. Paddock Rd. Wat —16Aa 19
Lwr. Park Rd. N11 —22Lb 42
Lwr. Park Rd. Belv —49Cd 88
Lwr. Park Rd. Coul —90Gb 163
Lwr. Park Rd. Lou —15Mc 27
Lower Pk. Trading Est. W5 —42Sa 79
Lwr. Peryers. E Hor —100U 174
Lwr. Pillory Downs. Cars —85Kb 164
Lwr. Place Bus. Cen. NW10 —40Sa 59
Lwr. Plantation. Loud —13L 17
Lwr. Pyrford Rd. Wok —88K 157
Lwr. Queen's Rd. Buck H —19Mc 27
Lwr. Range Rd. Grav —9G 114
Lwr. Richmond Rd. SW15 & SW15 —55Xa 102
Lwr. Richmond Rd. Rich & SW14 —55Qa 101
Lower Rd. N11 —22Kb 42
Lower Rd. SE16 & SE8 —47Yb 84
(in two parts)
Lower Rd. Belv & Eri —48Dd 88
Lower Rd. Bookh & Fet —97Ca 175
Lower Rd. Chor —14E 16
Lower Rd. Den —31E 54
Lower Rd. Eff —99Z 175
Lower Rd. Ger X —25A 34
Lower Rd. Grav —56Ae 113
Lower Rd. Harr —32Fa 58
Lower Rd. Kenl —85Rb 165
Lower Rd. Lou —11Qc 28
Lower Rd. Mount & Hut —12Fe 33
Lower Rd. Shorne —1N 137
Lower Rd. St M —72Xc 151
Lower Rd. Sutt —77Eb 145
Lower Rd. Swan —66Hd 132
Lower Rd. Til —6C 114
Lwr. Robert St. WC2 —45Nb 82 (5G 199) (off Robert St.)
Lwr. Sandfields. Send —96F 172
Lwr. Sawleywood. Bans —86Bb 163
Lwr. Shott. Bookh —98Ca 175
Lwr. Sloane St. SW1 —49Jb 82 (6H 203)
Lower Sq. Iswth —55Ka 100
Lower Sq., The. Sutt —78Db 145
Lwr. Staithe. W4 —53Sa 101
Lwr. Station Rd. Cray —58Gd 110
Lwr. Strand. NW9 —26Va 40
Lwr. Sunbury Rd. Hamp —68Ba 121
Lwr. Swaines. Epp —2Uc 14
Lwr. Sydenham Ind. Est. SE26 —64Bc 128
Lwr. Tail. Wat —20Aa 19
Lwr. Teddington Rd. King T —67Ma 123
Lower Ter. NW3 —34Eb 61
Lwr. Thames St. EC3 —45Tb 83 (5G 201)
Lower Tub. Bush —17Fa 20
Lwr. Village Rd. Asc —10A 116
Lwr. Wood Rd. Clay —79Ka 142
Lowestoft Clo. E5 —33Yb 64 (off Southwold Rd.)
Lowestoft Dri. Slou —4B 72
Lowestoft Rd. Wat —11X 19
Loweswater Clo. Wemb —33Ma 59
Lowe, The. Chig —22Wc 47
Lowfield Rd. NW6 —38Cb 61
Lowfield Rd. W3 —44Ra 79
Lowfield St. Dart —59Nd 111
Low Hall Clo. E4 —17Dc 26
Lowhall La. E17 —30Ac 44
Lowick Rd. Harr —28Ga 38
Lowlands Dri. Stai —57M 97
Lowlands Gdns. Romf —29Dd 48
Lowlands Rd. Harr —30Ga 38
Lowlands Rd. Pinn —31Y 57
Lowlands Rd. S Ock —46Sd 90
Lowman Rd. N7 —35Pb 62
Lowndes Clo. SW1 —48Jb 82 (4J 203)
Lowndes Ct. SW1 —48Hb 81 (3G 203)
Lowndes Ct. W1 —44Lb 82 (3B 198) (off Kingly St.)
Lowndes Pl. SW1 —48Jb 82 (4H 203)
Lowndes Sq. SW1 —47Hb 81 (2G 203)
Lowndes St. SW1 —48Jb 82 (3G 203)
Lownds Ct. Brom —68Jc 129
Lowood St. E1 —45Xb 83
Lowry Cres. Mitc —68Gb 125
Lowry Ho. N17 —25Vb 43 (off Pembury Rd.)
Lowshoe La. Romf —25Cd 48
Lowson Gro. Wat —17Aa 19
Low St. La. E Til —9H 93
Lowswood Clo. N'wd —26S 36
Lowther Clo. Els —15Pa 21
Lowther Dri. Enf —14Nb 24
Lowther Gdns. SW7 —48Fb 81 (3C 202)
Lowther Hill. SE23 —59Ac 106
Lowther Rd. E17 —26Ac 44
Lowther Rd. N7 —36Qb 62
Lowther Rd. SW13 —53Va 102
Lowther Rd. King T —67Pa 123
Lowther Rd. Stan —27Pa 39
Lowthorpe. St J —6D 188
Lowth Rd. SE5 —53Sb 105
Low Wlk. E17 —29Bc 44
Loxford Av. E6 —40Mc 65
Loxford Ho. Eps —84Ua 162
Loxford La. Ilf —36Sc 66
Loxford Rd. Bark —37Rc 66
Loxford Rd. Cat —97Vb 181
Loxford Ter. Bark —37Sc 66
Loxford Way. Cat —97Vb 181
Loxham Rd. E4 —24Dc 44
Loxham St. WC1 —41Nb 82 (4G 193)
Loxley Clo. SE26 —64Zb 128
Loxley Rd. SW18 —60Fb 103
Loxley Rd. Hamp —63Ba 121
Loxton Rd. SE23 —60Zb 106
Loxwood Clo. Felt —60T 98
Loxwood Clo. Orp —75Zc 151
Loxwood Rd. N17 —27Ub 43
Lubbock Rd. Chst —66Pc 130
Lubbock St. SE14 —52Yb 106
Lucan Dri. Stai —66M 119
Lucan Ho. N1 —39Tb 63 (1G 195) (off Colville Est.)
Lucan Pl. SW3 —49Gb 81 (6D 202)
Lucan Rd. Barn —13Ab 22
Lucas Av. E13 —39Kc 65
Lucas Av. Harr —33Ca 57
Lucas Ct. SE26 —64Ac 128
Lucas Ct. Wal A —5Hc 13
Lucas Rd. SE20 —65Yb 128
Lucas Rd. Grays —48Ce 91
Lucas Sq. NW11 —30Cb 41
Lucas St. SE8 —53Cc 106
Lucerne Clo. N13 —20Nb 24
Lucerne Clo. Wok —91A 172
Lucerne Ct. Eri —48Ad 87
Lucerne Gro. E17 —28Fc 45
Lucerne M. W8 —46Cb 81
Lucerne Rd. N5 —35Rb 63
Lucerne Rd. Orp —74Vc 151
Lucerne Rd. T Hth —70Sb 127
Lucerne Way. Romf —23Md 49
Lucey Rd. SE16 —48Wb 83
Lucey Way. SE16 —48Wb 83
(in two parts)
Lucie Av. Ashf —65R 120
Lucien Rd. SW17 —63Jb 126
Lucien Rd. SW19 —61Db 125
Lucinda Ct. Enf —14Ub 25
Lucknow St. SE18 —52Uc 108
Lucorn Clo. SE12 —58Hc 107
Luctons Av. Buck H —18Lc 27
Lucy Cres. W3 —43Sa 79
Lucy Gdns. Dag —34Ad 67
Luddesdon Rd. Eri —52Cd 110
Luddington Av. Vir W —68B 118
Ludford Clo. NW9 —26Ua 40
Ludford Clo. Croy —76Qb 146
Ludgate B'way. EC4 —44Rb 83 (3B 200)
Ludgate Cir. EC4 —44Rb 83 (3B 200)
Ludgate Hill. EC4 —44Rb 83 (3B 200)
Ludgate Sq. EC4 —44Rb 83 (3C 200)
Ludham Clo. SE28 —44Yc 87
Ludlow Clo. Brom —69Jc 129
Ludlow Clo. Harr —35Ba 57
Ludlow Ct. W3 —47Sa 79
Ludlow Mead. Wat —20X 19
Ludlow Pl. Grays —48De 91
Ludlow Rd. W5 —42La 78
Ludlow Rd. Felt —63W 120
Ludlow St. EC1 —42Sb 83 (5D 194)
Ludlow Way. N2 —28Eb 41
Ludlow Way. Crox —14S 18
Ludovick Wlk. SW15 —56Va 102
Ludwick M. SE14 —52Ac 106
Luff Clo. Wind —5C 94
Luffield Rd. SE2 —48Xc 87
Luffman Rd. SE12 —62Kc 129
Lugard Rd. SE15 —54Xb 105
Lugg App. E12 —34Qc 66
Luke St. EC2 —42Ub 83 (5H 195)
Lukin Cres. E4 —20Fc 27
Lukin St. E1 —44Yb 84
Lukey La. NW7 —22Ta 39
Lullarook Clo. Big H —88Lc 167
Lullingstone Av. Swan —69Hd 132
Lullingstone Clo. Orp —66Xc 131
Lullingstone Cres. Orp —66Wc 131
Lullingstone La. Eyns —75Ld 153
Lullingstone Rd. Belv —51Bd 109
Lullington Garth. N12 —22Bb 41
Lullington Garth. Borwd —15Ra 21
Lullington Garth. Brom —66Gc 129
Lullington Rd. SE20 —66Wb 127
Lullington Rd. Dag —38Ad 67
Lulot Gdns. N19 —33Kb 62
Lulworth Av. Chesh —1Rb 11
Lulworth Av. Houn —53Da 99
Lulworth Av. Wemb —31La 58
Lulworth Clo. Harr —34Ba 57

Lulworth Clo. Stanf —3K 93
Lulworth Cres. Mitc —68Gb 125
Lulworth Dri. Pinn —30Z 37
Lulworth Dri. Romf —22Dd 48
Lulworth Gdns. Harr —33Aa 57
Lulworth Ho. SW8 —52Pb 104
Lulworth Rd. SE9 —61Nc 130
Lulworth Rd. SE15 —54Xb 105
Lulworth Rd. Well —54Vc 109
Lulworth Waye. Hay —44X 77
Lumen Rd. Wemb —33Ma 59
Lumley Clo. Belv —50Cd 88
Lumley Ct. WC2 —45Nb 82 (5G 199)
Lumley Gdns. Sutt —78Ab 144
Lumley Rd. Sutt —78Ab 144
Lumley St. W1 —44Jb 82 (3J 197)
Lunar Clo. Big H —88Mc 167
Luna Rd. T Hth —69Sb 127
Lundin Wlk. Wat —21Z 37
Lund Point. E15 —39Ec 64
Lundy Dri. Hay —49U 76
Lundy Wlk. N1 —37Sb 63
Lunedale Rd. Dart —60Sd 112
Lunghurst Rd. Wold —92Bc 182
Lunham Rd. SE19 —65Ub 127
Lupin Clo. SW2 —61Rb 127
Lupin Clo. Croy —74Zb 148
Lupin Clo. W Dray —50M 75
Lupin Gdns. Ilf —37Rc 66
Luppit Clo. Hut —18Ce 33
Lupton Clo. SE12 —62Kc 129
Lupton St. NW5 —35Lb 62
Lupus St. SW1 —50Kb 82
Luralda Gdns. E14 —50Fc 85
Lurgan Av. W6 —51Za 102
Lurline Gdns. SW11 —53Jb 104
Luscombe Ct. Short —68Gc 129
Luscombe Way. SW8 —52Nb 104
Lushes Rd. Lou —15Rc 28
Lushington Dri. Cob —86X 159
Lushington Ho. W on T —72Y 141
Lushington Rd. NW10 —40Xa 60
Lushington Rd. SE6 —63Dc 128
Lusitania Building. E1 —45Zb 84
(off Jardine Rd.)
Lusted Hall La. Tats —92Kc 183
Lusted Rd. Sev —92Gd 186
Lutea Ho. Sutt —80Eb 145
(off Walnut M.)
Luther Clo. Edgw —19Sa 21
Luther King Clo. E17 —30Ac 44
Luther Rd. Tedd —64Ha 122
Luton Pl. SE10 —52Ec 106
Luton Rd. E13 —42Jc 85
Luton Rd. E17 —27Bc 44
Luton Rd. Sidc —62Yc 131
Luton St. NW8 —42Fb 81 (6C 190)
Lutton Ter. NW3 —35Eb 61
(off Heath St.)
Luttrell Av. SW15 —57Xa 102
Lutwyche Rd. SE6 —61Bc 128
Luxborough La. Chig —20Nc 28
Luxborough St. W1 —43Jb 82 (7H 191)
Luxemburg Gdns. W6 —49Za 80
Luxfield Rd. SE9 —60Nc 108
Luxford St. SE16 —49Zb 84
Luxmore Gdns. SE4 —54Bc 106
Luxmore St. SE4 —53Bc 106
Luxor St. SE5 —55Sb 105
Luxted Rd. Orp —84Qc 168
Lyall Av. SE21 —63Ub 127
Lyall M. SW1 —48Jb 82 (4H 203)
Lyall M. W. SW1 —48Jb 82 (4H 203)
Lyall St. SW1 —48Jb 82 (4H 203)
Lyal Rd. E3 —40Ac 64
Lycett Pl. W12 —47Wa 80
Lych Ga. Wat —5Z 5
Lych Ga. Rd. Orp —74Wc 151
Lych Ga. Wlk. Hay —45V 76
(in two parts)
Lych Way. Wok —4G 188
Lyconby Gdns. Croy —73Ac 148
Lydd Clo. Sidc —62Uc 130
Lydden Gro. SW18 —59Db 103
Lydden Rd. SW18 —59Db 103
Lydd Rd. Bexh —52Bd 109
Lydeard Rd. E6 —38Pc 66
Lydele Clo. Wok —87B 156
Lydford Av. Slou —3H 73
Lydford Clo. N16 —36Ub 63
(off Pellerin Rd.)
Lydford Ct. Dart —58Rd 111
(off Clifton Wlk.)
Lydford Rd. N15 —29Tb 43
Lydford Rd. NW2 —37Ya 60
Lydford Rd. W9 —42Bb 81
Lydhurst Av. SW2 —61Pb 126
Lydia Cotts. Grav —9D 114
Lydia Ct. N12 —23Eb 41
Lydia Rd. Eri —51Hd 110
Lydney Clo. SE15 —52Ub 105
Lydney Clo. SW19 —61Ab 124
Lydon Rd. SW4 —55Lb 104
Lydsell Clo. Slou —1E 72
Lydstep Rd. Chst —63Qc 130
Lye La. Brick —2Ca 5
Lyell. Wind —5A 94
Lyell Pl. E. Wind —5A 94
Lye, The. Tad —95Ya 178
Lyfield. Oxs —86Da 159
Lyford Rd. SW18 —59Fb 103
Lyford St. SE7 —49Nc 86
Lygon Ho. SW6 —53Ab 102
(off Fulham Pal. Rd.)
Lygon Pl. SW1 —48Kb 82 (4K 203)
Lyham Clo. SW2 —58Nb 104
Lyham Rd. SW2 —57Nb 104
Lyle Clo. Mitc —73Jb 146
Lyle Pk. Sev —95Kd 187
Lymbourne Clo. Sutt —82Cb 163
Lyme Farm Rd. SE12 —56Jc 107
Lyme Gro. E9 —38Yb 64
Lymer Av. SE19 —64Vb 127
Lyme Regis Rd. Bans —89Bb 163
Lyme Rd. Well —53Xc 109
Lymescote Gdns. Sutt —75Cb 145
Lyme St. NW1 —38Lb 62
Lyme Ter. NW1 —38Lb 62
Lyminge Clo. Sidc —63Vc 131
Lyminge Gdns. SW18 —60Gb 103
Lymington Av. N22 —26Qb 42
Lymington Clo. SW16 —68Mb 126
Lymington Ct. Sutt —76Db 145
Lymington Dri. Ruis —33T 56
Lymington Gdns. Eps —78Va 144
Lymington Rd. NW6 —37Db 61
Lymington Rd. Dag —32Zc 67
Lympne. N17 —26Tb 43
(off Gloucester Rd.)
Lympstone Gdns. SE15 —52Wb 105
Lynbridge Gdns. N13 —21Rb 43
Lynbrook Clo. SE15 —52Ub 105
Lynbrook Clo. Rain —40Fd 68
Lynbury Ct. Wat —13W 18
Lynceley Grange. Epp —1Wc 15
Lynch Clo. Uxb —38L 55
Lynchen Clo. Houn —53X 99
Lynch Hill La. Slou —2C 72
Lynch, The. Uxb —38L 55
Lynch Wlk. SE8 —51Bc 106
Lynchwood. SE3 —54Hc 107
Lyncott Cres. SW4 —56Kb 104
Lyncroft Av. Pinn —29Aa 37
Lyncroft Gdns. NW6 —36Cb 61
Lyncroft Gdns. W13 —47La 78
Lyncroft Gdns. Eps —81Va 162
Lyncroft Gdns. Houn —57Ea 100
Lyndale. NW2 —35Bb 61
Lyndale Av. NW2 —34Bb 61
Lyndale Clo. SE3 —51Hc 107
Lyndale Ct. W Byf —85J 157
Lyndale Est. W Thur —51Xd 112
Lynde Ho. W on T —72Y 141
Lynden Way. Swan —69Ed 132
Lyndhurst Av. N12 —23Hb 41
Lyndhurst Av. NW7 —23Ua 40
Lyndhurst Av. SW16 —68Mb 126
Lyndhurst Av. Pinn —25X 37
Lyndhurst Av. S'hall —46Da 77
Lyndhurst Av. Sun —69W 120
Lyndhurst Av. Surb —74Ra 143
Lyndhurst Av. Twic —60Ba 99
Lyndhurst Clo. NW10 —34Ta 59
Lyndhurst Clo. Bexh —55Dd 110
Lyndhurst Clo. Croy —76Vb 147
Lyndhurst Clo. Orp —77Rc 150
Lyndhurst Clo. Wok —3G 188
Lyndhurst Ct. E18 —25Jc 45
Lyndhurst Dri. E10 —31Ec 64
Lyndhurst Dri. Horn —32Ld 69
Lyndhurst Dri. N Mald —73Ua 144
Lyndhurst Dri. Sev —96Gd 186
Lyndhurst Gdns. N3 —25Ab 40
Lyndhurst Gdns. NW3 —36Fb 61
Lyndhurst Gdns. Bark —37Uc 66
Lyndhurst Gdns. Enf —14Ub 25
Lyndhurst Gdns. Ilf —30Tc 46
Lyndhurst Gdns. Pinn —25X 37
Lyndhurst Gro. SE15 —54Ub 105
Lyndhurst Rise. Chig —21Qc 46
Lyndhurst Rd. E4 —24Ec 44
Lyndhurst Rd. N18 —21Wb 43
Lyndhurst Rd. N22 —23Qb 42
Lyndhurst Rd. NW3 —36Fb 61
Lyndhurst Rd. Bexh —55Dd 110
Lyndhurst Rd. Coul —88Jb 164
Lyndhurst Rd. Gnfd —42Da 77
Lyndhurst Rd. T Hth —70Qb 126
Lyndhurst Sq. SE15 —53Vb 105
Lyndhurst Ter. NW3 —36Fb 61
Lyndhurst Way. SE15 —53Vb 105
Lyndhurst Way. Cher —76G 138
Lyndhurst Way. Grav —7A 136
Lyndhurst Way. Hut —17Ee 33
Lyndhurst Way. Sutt —81Cb 163
Lyndon Av. Pinn —23Aa 37
Lyndon Av. Sidc —57Vc 109
Lyndon Av. Wall —76Jb 146
Lyndon Rd. Belv —49Cd 88
Lyne Clo. Vir W —72B 138
Lyne Cres. E17 —25Bc 44
Lyne Crossing Rd. Lyne —72C 138
Lynegrove Av. Ashf —64S 120
Lyneham Wlk. E5 —36Ac 64
Lyneham Wlk. Pinn —27V 36
Lyne La. Lyne & Egh —72C 138
Lyne Rd. Vir W —72A 138
Lynette Av. SW4 —58Lb 104
Lynett Rd. Dag —33Zc 67
Lynford Clo. Edgw —25Sa 39
Lynford Gdns. Edgw —20Ra 21
Lynford Gdns. Ilf —33Vc 67
Lynford Ter. N9 —18Vb 25
Lynhurst Cres. Uxb —38S 56
Lynhurst Rd. Uxb —38S 56
Lynmere Rd. Well —54Xc 109
Lynmouth Av. Enf —16Vb 25
Lynmouth Av. Mord —72Za 144
Lynmouth Dri. Ruis —33X 57
Lynmouth Gdns. Gnfd —39Ka 58
Lynmouth Gdns. Houn —53Z 99
Lynmouth Rise. Orp —70Xc 131
Lynmouth Rd. E17 —30Ac 44
Lynmouth Rd. N2 —27Hb 41
Lynmouth Rd. N16 —32Vb 63
Lynmouth Rd. Gnfd —39Ka 58
Lynn Clo. Ashf —64T 120
Lynn Clo. Harr —26Fa 38
Lynn Ct. Whyt —90Vb 165
Lynne Clo. SE23 —59Bc 106
Lynne Clo. Orp —79Vc 151
Lynne Clo. S Croy —83Yb 166
Lynne Wlk. Esh —78Ea 142
Lynne Way. NW10 —37Ua 60
Lynne Way. N'holt —40Z 57
Lynn M. E11 —33Gc 65
Lynn Rd. E11 —33Gc 65
Lynn Rd. SW12 —59Kb 104
Lynn Rd. Ilf —31Tc 66
Lynn St. Enf —11Tb 25
Lynross Clo. Romf —26Pd 49
Lynscott Way. S Croy —81Rb 165
Lynstead Ct. Beck —68Ac 128
Lynsted Clo. Bexh —57Dd 110
Lynsted Clo. Brom —68Lc 129
Lynsted Ct. Beck —68Ac 128
Lynsted Gdns. SE9 —56Mc 107
Lynton Av. N12 —21Fb 41
Lynton Av. NW9 —28Va 40
Lynton Av. W13 —44Ja 78
Lynton Av. Orp —70Xc 131
Lynton Av. Romf —25Cd 48
Lynton Clo. NW10 —36Ua 60
Lynton Clo. Chess —77Na 143
Lynton Clo. Isw th —56Ha 100
Lynton Cres. Ilf —30Rc 46
Lynton Est. SE1 —50Wb 83
Lynton Gdns. N11 —23Mb 42
Lynton Gdns. Enf —17Ub 25
Lynton Grange. N2 —27Hb 41
Lynton Mead. N20 —20Cb 23
Lynton Pde. Chesh —2Ac 12
Lynton Rd. E4 —22Dc 44
Lynton Rd. N8 —29Mb 42
(in two parts)
Lynton Rd. NW6 —40Bb 61
Lynton Rd. SE1 —49Vb 83 (6K 207)
Lynton Rd. W3 —45Qa 79
Lynton Rd. Croy —72Qb 146
Lynton Rd. Grav —10C 114
Lynton Rd. Harr —33Aa 57
Lynton Rd. N Mald —71Ta 143
Lynton Rd. S. Grav —10C 114
Lynton Wlk. Hay —41U 76
Lynwood Av. Coul —87Kb 164
Lynwood Av. Egh —65A 118
Lynwood Av. Eps —86Va 162
Lynwood Av. Slou —8P 73
Lynwood Clo. E18 —25Lc 45
Lynwood Clo. Harr —34Aa 57
Lynwood Clo. Romf —23Dd 48
Lynwood Clo. Wok —85F 156
Lynwood Ct. Eps —85Va 162
Lynwood Ct. King T —68Ra 123
Lynwood Dri. N'wd —25V 36
Lynwood Dri. Old Win —8L 95
Lynwood Dri. Romf —23Dd 48
Lynwood Dri. Wor Pk —75Wa 144
Lynwood Gdns. Croy —77Pb 146
Lynwood Gdns. S'hall —44Ba 77
Lynwood Gro. N21 —18Qb 24
Lynwood Gro. Orp —73Uc 150
Lynwood Heights. Rick —15K 17
Lynwood Rd. SW17 —62Hb 125
Lynwood Rd. W5 —41Na 79
Lynwood Rd. Eps —86Va 162
Lynwood Rd. Th Dit —75Ha 142
Lynx Hill. E Hor —100V 174
Lyon Bus. Pk. Bark —40Uc 66
Lyon Ct. Ruis —32V 56
Lyon Ind. Est. NW2 —33Xa 60
Lyon Meade. Stan —25La 38
Lyon Pk. Av. Wemb —37Na 59
(in two parts)
Lyon Rd. SW19 —67Eb 125
Lyon Rd. Harr —30Ha 38
Lyon Rd. Romf —31Hd 68
Lyon Rd. W on T —75Aa 141
Lyonsdene. Tad —99Bb 179
Lyonsdown Av. Barn —16Eb 23
Lyonsdown Rd. Barn —16Eb 23
Lyons Pl. NW8 —42Fb 81 (6B 190)
Lyon St. N1 —38Pb 62
Lyons Wlk. W14 —49Ab 80
Lyon Way. Gnfd —39Ga 58
Lyoth Rd. Orp —75Sc 150
Lyric Dri. Gnfd —42Da 77
Lyric Rd. SW13 —53Va 102
Lysander Gro. N19 —32Mb 62
Lysander Rd. Croy —79Pb 146
Lysander Rd. Ruis —33T 56
Lysander Way. Orp —76Sc 150
Lysias Rd. SW12 —58Kb 104
Lysia St. SW6 —52Za 102
Lysons Wlk. SW15 —56Wa 102
Lytchet Rd. Brom —66Kc 129
Lytchet Way. Enf —11Yb 26
Lytchgate Clo. S Croy —80Ub 147
Lytcott Dri. W Mol —69Ba 121
Lytcott Gro. SE22 —57Ub 105
Lytham Av. Wat —22Z 37
Lytham Ct. S'hill —10A 116
Lytham Gro. W5 —41Pa 79
Lytham St. SE17 —51Tb 105
Lyttelton Clo. NW3 —38Gb 61
Lyttelton Ct. N2 —29Eb 41
Lyttelton Rd. E10 —34Dc 64
Lyttelton Rd. N2 —29Eb 41
Lyttelton Rd. N8 —27Qb 42
Lytton Av. N13 —19Qb 24
Lytton Av. Enf —10Ac 12
Lytton Clo. N2 —30Fb 41
Lytton Clo. Lou —13Tc 28
Lytton Clo. N'holt —38Ba 57
Lytton Gdns. Wall —77Mb 146
Lytton Gro. SW15 —57Za 102
Lytton Rd. E11 —31Gc 65
Lytton Rd. Barn —14Eb 23
Lytton Rd. Grays —9C 92
Lytton Rd. Pinn —24Aa 37
Lytton Rd. Romf —29Kd 49
Lytton Rd. Wok —88D 156
Lytton Strachey Path. SE28 —45Xc 87
Lyveden Rd. SE3 —52Kc 107
Lyveden Rd. SW17 —65Hb 125
Lywood Clo. Tad —94Ya 178

Mabbotts. Tad —93Za 178
Mabbutt Clo. Brick —2Aa 5
Mabel Rd. Swan —65Jd 132
Mabel St. Wok —5G 188
Maberley Cres. SE19 —66Wb 127
Maberley Rd. SE19 —67Wb 127
Maberley Rd. Beck —69Zb 128
Mabledon Pl. WC1 —41Mb 82 (4E 192)
Mablethorpe Rd. SW6 —52Ab 102
Mabley St. E9 —36Ac 64
Mablin Lodge. Buck H —18Lc 27
Macaret Clo. N20 —17Db 23
Macarthur Clo. E7 —37Jc 65
Macarthur Ter. SE7 —51Mc 107
Macaulay Av. Esh —75Ha 142
Macaulay Ct. SW4 —55Kb 104
(off Macaulay Rd.)
Macaulay Rd. E6 —40Mc 65
Macaulay Rd. SW4 —55Kb 104
Macaulay Rd. Cat —94Ub 181
Macaulay Sq. SW4 —56Kb 104
Macaulay Way. SE28 —46Xc 87
McAuley Clo. SE1 —48Qb 82 (3K 205)
McAuley Clo. SE9 —57Qc 108
Macaulay M. SE13 —53Ec 106
McAuliffe Dri. Farn C —5D 52
Macbean St. SE18 —48Rc 86
Macbeth Ho. N1 —40Ub 63 (1H 195)
Macbeth St. W6 —50Xa 80
McCall Clo. SW4 —54Nb 104
McCall Cres. SE7 —50Nc 86
McCall Ho. N7 —35Nb 62
McCarthy Rd. Felt —64Z 121
Macclesfield Rd. EC1 —41Sb 83 (3D 194)
Macclesfield Rd. SE25 —71Yb 148
Macclesfield St. W1 —45Mb 82 (4E 198)
McCoid Way. SE1 —47Sb 83 (2D 206)
McConnell M. NW1 —41Mb 82 (4D 192)
McCrone M. NW3 —37Fb 61
McCullum Rd. E3 —39Bc 64
McDermott Clo. SW11 —55Gb 103
McDermott Rd. SE15 —55Wb 105
Macdonald Av. Dag —34Dd 68
Macdonald Av. Horn —27Nd 49
Macdonald Rd. E7 —35Jc 65
Macdonald Rd. E17 —26Ec 44
Macdonald Rd. N11 —22Hb 41
Macdonald Rd. N19 —33Lb 62
Macdonald Rd. Dag —34Dd 68
Macdonald Way. Horn —28Nd 49
Macdonnell Gdns. Wat —7V 4
McDonough Clo. Chess —77Na 143
McDowall Clo. E16 —43Hc 85
McDowall Rd. SE5 —53Sb 105
Macduff Rd. SW11 —53Jb 104
Mace Clo. E1 —46Xb 83
Mace Ct. Grays —1A 114
Mace La. Cud —85Tc 168
McEntee Av. E17 —25Ac 44
Mace St. E2 —40Zb 64
Mace St. SE1 —47Vb 83 (1K 207)
McEwen Way. E15 —39Fc 65
Macfarlane La. Isw th —51Ha 100
Macfarlane Rd. W12 —46Ya 80
Macfarren Pl. NW1 —42Jb 82 (6J 191)
McGrath Rd. E15 —36Hc 65
McGredy. Chesh —1Xb 11
McGregor Ct. N1 —41Ub 83 (3J 195)
(off Hoxton St.)
MacGregor Rd. E16 —43Lc 85
McGregor Rd. W11 —43Bb 81
Machell Rd. SE15 —55Yb 106
McIntosh Clo. Romf —27Gd 48
McIntosh Clo. Wall —80Nb 146
McIntosh Rd. Romf —27Gd 48
McIntyre Ct. SE18 —49Nc 86
(off Prospect Vale)
Mackay Ho. W12 —45Xa 80
(off White City Est.)
Mackay Rd. SW4 —55Kb 104
McKay Rd. SW20 —66Xa 124
McKay Trading Est. W10 —42Ab 80
McKay Trading Est. Coln —54G 96
McKellar Clo. Bush —19Ea 20
Mackennal St. NW8 —40Gb 61 (2E 190)
Mackenzie Clo. W12 —45Xa 80
(off White City Est.)
Mackenzie Ho. NW2 —34Wa 60
Mackenzie Mall. Slou —7K 73
Mackenzie Rd. N7 —37Pb 62
Mackenzie Rd. Beck —68Yb 128
Mackenzie Wlk. E14 —46Cc 84
Mackenzie Way. Grav —5F 136
McKerrell Rd. SE15 —53Wb 105
Mackeson Rd. NW3 —35Hb 61
Mackie Rd. SW2 —59Qb 104
Mackintosh La. E9 —36Zb 64
Macklin St. WC2 —44Nb 82 (2G 199)
Mackrow Wlk. E14 —45Ec 84
Mack's Rd. SE16 —49Wb 83
Mackworth St. NW1 —41Lb 82 (3B 192)
Maclaren M. SW15 —56Ya 102
Maclean Rd. SE23 —58Ac 106
Maclennan Av. Rain —41Md 89
Macleod Clo. Grays —49Fe 91
McLeod Rd. SE2 —49Xc 87
McLeod's M. SW7 —49Db 81
Macleod St. SE17 —50Sb 83
Maclise Rd. W14 —48Ab 80
Macmillan Ct. S Harr —32Ca 57
Macmillan Gdns. Dart —56Qd 111
McMillan St. SE8 —51Cc 106
McNeil Rd. SE5 —54Ub 105
Macoma Rd. SE18 —51Tc 108
Macoma Ter. SE18 —51Tc 108
Maconochies Rd. E14 —50Dc 84
Macon Way. Upm —31Ud 70
Macquarie Way. E14 —49Dc 84
Macready Pl. N7 —35Nb 62
Macroom Rd. W9 —41Bb 81
Madan Rd. W'ham —97Tc 184
Madans Wlk. Eps —87Ta 161
Mada Rd. Orp —76Rc 150
Maddams St. E3 —42Dc 84
Madden Clo. Swans —58Zd 113
Maddison Clo. Tedd —65Ha 122
Maddocks Clo. Sidc —64Ad 131
Maddock Way. SE17 —51Rb 105
Maddox La. Bookh —94Aa 175
(in two parts)
Maddox Pk. Bookh —95Aa 175
Maddox St. W1 —45Kb 82 (4A 198)
Madeira Av. Brom —66Gc 129
Madeira Clo. W Byf —85J 157
Madeira Cres. W Byf —85H 157
Madeira Gro. Wfd G —23Lc 45
Madeira Rd. E11 —33Fc 65
Madeira Rd. N13 —21Rb 43
Madeira Rd. SW16 —64Nb 126
Madeira Rd. Mitc —70Hb 125
Madeira Rd. W Byf —85H 157
Madeira Wlk. Brtwd —20Ae 33
Madeira Wlk. Wind —3H 95
Madeley Rd. W5 —44Ma 79
Madeline Rd. SE20 —66Wb 127
Madells. Epp —3Vc 15
Madison Cres. Bexh —52Yc 109
Madison Gdns. Bexh —52Yc 109
Madison Gdns. Brom —69Hc 129
Madison Way. Sev —95Hd 186
Madras Pl. N7 —37Qb 62
Madras Rd. Ilf —35Rc 66
Madrid Rd. SW13 —53Wa 102
Madrigal La. SE5 —52Rb 105
Madron St. SE17 —50Ub 83 (7J 207)
Maes Ho. E17 —27Dc 44
Maesmaur Rd. Tats —93Mc 183
Mafeking Av. E6 —40Nc 66
Mafeking Av. Bren —51Na 101
Mafeking Av. Ilf —31Tc 66
Mafeking Rd. E16 —42Hc 85
Mafeking Rd. N17 —26Wb 43
Mafeking Rd. Enf —13Vb 25
Mafeking Rd. Wray —61D 118
Magazine Pl. Lea —94Ka 176
Magazine Rd. Cat —94Rb 181
Magdala Av. N19 —33Lb 62
Magdala Rd. Isw th —55Ja 100
Magdala Rd. S Croy —80Tb 147
Magdalen Clo. Byfl —86N 157
Magdalen Cres. Byfl —86N 157
Magdalene Clo. SE15 —54Xb 105
Magdalene Gdns. E6 —42Qc 86
Magdalene Rd. Shep —70P 119
Magdalen Gro. Orp —77Xc 151
Magdalen Pas. E1 —45Vb 83
Magdalen Rd. SW18 —60Eb 103
Magdalen St. SE1 —46Ub 83 (7H 201)
Magee St. SE11 —51Qb 104
Magellan Ct. NW10 —38Ta 59
(off Stonebridge Pk.)
Magna Carta La. Wray —10P 95
Magna Rd. Egh —5M 117
Magnaville Rd. Bush —17Ga 20
Magnet Rd. S Stif —51Yd 112
Magnet Rd. Wemb —33Ma 59
Magnin Clo. E8 —39Wb 63
Magnolia Clo. King T —65Ra 123
Magnolia Ct. SW4 —57Nb 104
Magnolia Ct. Sutt —80Db 145
(off Grange Rd.)
Magnolia Ct. Uxb —37R 56
Magnolia Ct. Wall —78Kb 146
Magnolia Dri. Big H —88Mc 167
Magnolia Gdns. Slou —8N 73
Magnolia Lodge. E4 —20Dc 26
Magnolia Pl. W5 —43Ma 79
Magnolia Pl. Harr —31Pa 59
Magnolia Rd. W4 —51Ra 101
Magnolia St. W Dray —50M 75
Magnolia Way. Eps —78Sa 143
Magnolia Way. Pil H —15Xd 32
Magnum Clo. Rain —42Kd 89
Magpie All. EC4 —44Qb 82 (3A 200)
Magpie Av. EC4 —44Qb 82
Magpie Bottom. Shor & Knat —85Md 171
Magpie Clo. E7 —36Hc 65
Magpie Clo. NW9 —26Ua 40
Magpie Clo. Coul —90Lb 164
Magpie Clo. Enf —11Wb 25
Magpie Hall Clo. Brom —72Nc 150
Magpie Hall La. Brom —73Nc 150
Magpie Hall Rd. Bush —19Ga 20
Magpie La. L War —26Zd 51
Magpie Pl. Wat —4Y 5
Magpie Way. Slou —2C 72
Magri Wlk. E1 —43Yb 84
Maguire Dri. Rich —63La 122
Maguire St. SE1 —47Vb 83 (1K 207)
Mahatma Gandhi Ind. Est. SE24 —56Rb 105
Mahatma Gandhi Ho. Wemb —31Pa 59
Mahlon Av. Ruis —36X 57
Mahogany Clo. SE16 —46Ac 84
Mahon Clo. Enf —11Vb 25
Maida Av. E4 —17Dc 26
Maida Av. W2 —43Eb 81 (7A 190)
Maida Rd. Belv —48Cd 88
Maida Vale. W9 —40Db 61
Maida Vale Rd. Dart —57Jd 110
Maida Way. E4 —17Dc 26
Maiden Erlegh Av. Bex —60Ad 109
Maidenhead Rd. Wind —2A 94
Maiden La. NW1 —38Mb 62
Maiden La. SE1 —46Sb 83 (7E 200)
Maiden La. WC2 —45Nb 82 (5G 199)
Maiden La. Dart —56Jd 110
Maiden Rd. E15 —38Gc 65
Maidenshaw Rd. Eps —84Ta 161
Maidenstone Hill. SE10 —53Ec 106
Maids of Honour Row. Rich —57Ma 101
Maidstone Av. Romf —26Ed 48
Maidstone Bldgs. SE1 —46Sb 83 (7E 200)
Maidstone Rd. N11 —23Mb 42
Maidstone Rd. Grays —51Ce 113
Maidstone Rd. Seal —93Qd 187
Maidstone Rd. Sev —94Gd 186
Maidstone Rd. Sidc —65Zc 131
Mail Coach Yd. E2 —41Ub 83 (3J 195)
Main Av. Enf —15Vb 25
Main Av. N'wd —20S 18
Main Dri. Ger X —29A 34
Main Dri. Iver —49G 74
Main Dri. Wemb —34Ma 59
Main Pde. Chor —14E 16
Mainridge Rd. Chst —63Qc 130
Main Rd. Big H —85Lc 167
Main Rd. Crock —72Fd 152
Main Rd. F'ham —72Pd 153
Main Rd. Hex —66Hd 132
Main Rd. Long —68Zd 135
Main Rd. Mount —11Fe 33
Main Rd. Orp —69Yc 131
Main Rd. Romf —28Hd 48
Main Rd. Sidc —62Tc 130
Main Rd. Sund —96Zc 185
Main Rd. S at H —65Rd 133
Main St. Add —76N 139
Main St. Felt —64Z 121
Mais Ho. SE26 —61Xb 127
Maisie Webster Clo. Stai —59L 97
Maismore St. SE15 —51Wb 105
Maisonettes, The. Sutt —78Bb 145
Maitland Clo. Houn —55Ba 99
Maitland Clo. W Byf —85J 157
Maitland Pk. Est. NW3 —37Hb 61
Maitland Pk. Rd. NW3 —37Hb 61
Maitland Pk. Vs. NW3 —37Hb 61
Maitland Pl. E5 —35Xb 63
Maitland Rd. E15 —37Hc 65
Maitland Rd. SE26 —65Zb 128
Maitlands. Lou —13Pc 28
Maizey Ct. Pil H —15Wd 32
Majendie Rd. SE18 —50Tc 86
Majestic Way. Mitc —68Hb 125
Major Rd. E15 —36Fc 65
Major Rd. SE16 —48Wb 83
Majors Farm Rd. Dat —2P 95
Makepeace Av. N6 —33Jb 62
Makepeace Rd. N'holt —40Aa 57
Makinen Ho. Buck H —18Lc 27
Makins St. SW3 —49Gb 81 (6E 202)
Malabar Ct. W12 —45Xa 80
(off White City Est.)
Malabar St. E14 —47Cc 84
Malacca Farm. Guild —100K 173
Malam Ct. SE11 —49Qb 82 (6K 205)
Malam Gdns. E14 —45Dc 84
Malan Clo. Big H —89Nc 168
Malan Sq. Rain —37Kd 69
Malbrook Rd. SW15 —56Xa 102
Malcolm Clo. SE20 —66Yb 128
Malcolm Ct. E7 —37Hc 65
Malcolm Ct. NW4 —30Wa 40
Malcolm Ct. Stan —22La 38
Malcolm Cres. NW4 —30Wa 40
Malcolm Dri. Surb —74Ma 143
Malcolm Ho. N1 —40Ub 63 (2H 195)
(off Arden Est.)
Malcolm Pl. E2 —42Yb 84
Malcolm Rd. E1 —42Yb 84
Malcolm Rd. SE25 —72Wb 147
Malcolm Rd. SW19 —65Ab 124
Malcolm Rd. Coul —87Mb 164
Malcolm Rd. Uxb —35P 55
Malcolm Way. E11 —29Jc 45
Malcom Rd. SE25 —72Wb 147
Malden Av. SE25 —69Xb 127
Malden Av. Gnfd —36Ga 58
Malden Ct. N4 —30Sb 43
Malden Ct. N Mald —69Xa 124
Malden Cres. NW1 —37Jb 62
Malden Grn. Av. Wor Pk —74Va 144
Malden Hill. N Mald —69Va 124
Malden Hill Gdns. N Mald —69Va 124
Malden La. NW1 —38Mb 62
Malden Pk. N Mald —72Va 144
Malden Pl. NW5 —36Jb 62
Malden Rd. NW5 —36Hb 61
Malden Rd. Borwd —13Qa 21
Malden Rd. N Mald & Wor Pk —71Ua 144
Malden Rd. Sutt —77Za 144
Malden Rd. Wat —12X 19
Malden Way. N Mald —72Ua 144
Maldon Clo. E15 —36Gc 65
Maldon Clo. N1 —39Sb 63
Maldon Clo. SE5 —55Ub 105
Maldon Ct. E6 —39Qc 66
(off Langdon Rd.)
Maldon Rd. N9 —20Vb 25
Maldon Rd. W3 —45Sa 79
Maldon Rd. Romf —31Ed 68
Maldon Rd. Wall —78Kb 146
Maldon Wlk. Wfd G —23Lc 45
Malet Clo. Egh —65F 118
Malet Pl. WC1 —42Mb 82 (6D 192)
Malet St. WC1 —42Mb 82 (6D 192)
Maley Av. SE27 —61Rb 127
Malford Ct. E18 —26Jc 45
Malford Gro. E18 —28Hc 45
Malfort Rd. SE5 —55Ub 105
Malham Rd. SE23 —60Zb 106
Malham Ter. N18 —23Xb 43
(off Dysons Rd.)
Malibu Ct. SE26 —62Xb 127

Malins Clo.—Marco Rd.

Malins Clo. Barn —15Xa **22**
Mallams M. SW9 —55Rb **105**
Mallard Clo. E9 —37Bc **64**
Mallard Clo. Barn —16Fb **23**
Mallard Clo. Dart —57Pd **111**
Mallard Clo. Twic —59Ca **99**
Mallard Clo. Upm —31Vd **70**
Mallard Ct. E17 —27Fc **45**
Mallard Dri. Slou —5D **72**
Mallard Path. SE28 —48Tc ***86***
(off Goosander Way)
Mallard Pl. N22 —26Pb **42**
Mallard Pl. Twic —62Ja **122**
Mallard Rd. S Croy —82Zb **166**
Mallards Reach. Wey —75T **140**
Mallards Rd. Wfd G —24Kc **45**
Mallards, The. Stai —68K **119**
Mallard Wlk. Beck —71Zb **148**
Mallard Wlk. Sidc —65Yc **131**
Mallard Way. NW9 —31Sa **59**
Mallard Way. Hut —17De **33**
Mallard Way. N'wd —24S **36**
Mallard Way. Wall —81Lb **164**
Mallard Way. Wat —9Aa **5**
Mall Chambers. W8 —46Cb ***81***
(off Kensington Mall)
Mallet Dri. N'holt —36Ba **57**
Mallet Rd. SE13 —58Fc **107**
Mall Gallery. WC2
—44Nb ***82*** *(3F* ***199****)*
(off Shorts Gdns.)
Malling Clo. Croy —72Yb **148**
Malling Gdns. Mord —72Eb **145**
Malling Way. Brom —73Hc **149**
Mallinson Clo. Horn —36Ld **69**
Mallinson Rd. SW11 —57Gb **103**
Mallinson Rd. Croy —76Mb **146**
Mallion Ct. Wal A —5Hc **13**
Mallon Gdns. E1 —44Vb **83** (2K **201**)
Mallord St. SW3 —51Fb **103**
Mallory Clo. SE4 —56Ac **106**
Mallory Gdns. Barn —17Jb **24**
Mallory St. NW8
—42Gb **81** (5E **190**)
Mallow Clo. Croy —74Zb **148**
Mallow Clo. Grav —3A **136**
Mallow Ct. Grays —51Fe **113**
Mallow Mead. NW7 —24Ab **40**
Mallows, The. Uxb —34R **56**
Mallow St. EC1 —42Tb **83** (5F **195**)
Mall Rd. W6 —50Xa **80**
Mall, The. E15 —38Fc **65**
Mall, The. N14 —19Nb **24**
Mall, The. SW1 —46Mb **82** (7E **198**)
Mall, The. SW14 —57Sa **101**
Mall, The. W5 —45Na **79**
Mall, The. Bexh —56Cd **110**
Mall, The. Bren —51Ma **101**
Mall, The. Brom —69Jc **129**
Mall, The. Croy —75Sb **147**
Mall, The. Dag —37Cd **68**
Mall, The. Harr —30Pa **39**
Mall, The. Surb —72Ma **143**
Mall, The. Swan —69Gd **132**
Mall, The. W on T —78Z **141**
Mallys Pl. S Dar —67Sd **134**
Malmains Clo. Beck —70Fc **129**
Malmains Way. Beck —70Ec **128**
Malm Clo. Rick —19M **17**
Malmesbury Clo. Pinn —28V **36**
Malmesbury Rd. E3 —41Bc **84**
Malmesbury Rd. E16 —43Gc **85**
Malmesbury Rd. E18 —25Hc **45**
Malmesbury Rd. Mord —73Eb **145**
Malmesbury Ter. E16 —43Hc **85**
Malmsey Ho. SE11
—50Pb **82** (7J **205**)
Malmsmead Ho. E9 —36Ac ***64***
(off Homerton Rd.)
Malmstone Av. Red —100Lb **180**
Malpas Dri. Pinn —29Z **37**
Malpas Rd. E8 —36Xb **63**
Malpas Rd. SE4 —54Bc **106**
Malpas Rd. Dag —37Zc **67**
Malpas Rd. Grays —8E **92**
Malpas Rd. Slou —5M **73**
Malta Rd. E10 —32Cc **64**
Malta Rd. Til —4B **114**
Malta St. EC1 —42Rb **83** (5C **194**)
Maltby Clo. Orp —74Wc **151**
Maltby Dri. Enf —10Xb **11**
Maltby Rd. Chess —79Qa **143**
Maltby St. SE1 —47Vb **83** (2K **207**)
Maltese Dri. Felt —64Z **121**
Malt Hill. Egh —64A **118**
Malthouse Clo. Old Win —9M **95**
Malthouse La. Shorne —4N **137**
Malt Ho. Pl. Red —8Ja **6**
Malthouse Rd. Stans —80Be **155**
Malthus Path. SE28 —46Yc **87**
Malting La. Ors —2C **92**
Maltings. W4 —50Qa **79**
Maltings Clo. SW13 —54Va **102**
Maltings Dri. Epp —1Wc **15**
Maltings La. Epp —1Wc **15**
Maltings M. Sidc —62Wc **131**
Maltings Pl. SW6 —53Db **103**
Maltings, The. Byfl —85P **157**
Maltings, The. Grav —8C ***114***
(off Clifton Rd.)
Maltings, The. K Lan —6S **4**
Maltings, The. Orp —74Vc **151**
Maltings, The. Stai —63G **118**
Malt La. Rad —7Ja **6**
Malton Av. Slou —4F **72**
Malton M. SE18 —51Uc **108**
Malton M. W10 —44Ab **80**
Malton Rd. W10 —44Ab **80**
Malton St. SE18 —51Uc **108**
Maltravers St. WC2
—45Pb **82** (4K **199**)
Malt Shovel Cotts. Eyns —76Md **153**
Malt St. SE1 —51Wb **105**
Malus Clo. Add —80H **139**
Malus Dri. Add —80H **139**
Malva Clo. SW18 —57Db **103**
Malvern Av. E4 —24Fc **45**
Malvern Av. Bexh —52Ad **109**
Malvern Av. Harr —34Aa **57**
Malvern Clo. SE20 —68Wb **127**
Malvern Clo. W10 —43Bb **81**
Malvern Clo. Mitc —69Lb **126**
Malvern Clo. Ott —79E **138**
Malvern Clo. Surb —74Na **143**
Malvern Clo. Uxb —33Q **56**
Malvern Ct. W12 —47Wa ***80***
(off Hadyn Pk. Rd.)
Malvern Ct. Coln —51C **96**
Malvern Ct. Eps —86Ta **161**
Malvern Ct. Sutt —80Cb **145**
Malvern Dri. Felt —64Z **121**
Malvern Dri. Ilf —35Vc **67**
Malvern Dri. Wfd G —22Lc **45**
Malvern Gdns. NW2 —33Ab **60**
Malvern Gdns. Harr —28Na **39**
Malvern Gdns. Lou —16Pc **28**
Malvern Ho. N16 —32Vb **63**
Malvern Ho. Grav —58Fe ***113***
(off Laburnum Gro.)
Malvern Ho. Wat —16T **18**
Malvern M. NW6 —41Cb **81**
Malvern Pl. NW6 —41Bb **81**
Malvern Rd. E6 —39Nc **66**
Malvern Rd. E8 —38Wb **63**
Malvern Rd. E11 —33Gc **65**
Malvern Rd. N8 —27Qb **42**
Malvern Rd. N17 —27Wb **43**
Malvern Rd. NW6 —41Cb **81**
Malvern Rd. Enf —9Ac **12**
Malvern Rd. Grays —9A **92**
Malvern Rd. Hamp —66Ca **121**
Malvern Rd. Hay —52U **98**
Malvern Rd. Horn —30Jd **48**
Malvern Rd. Orp —77Xc **151**
Malvern Rd. Surb —75Na **143**
Malvern Rd. T Hth —70Qb **126**
Malvern Ter. N1 —39Qb **62**
Malvern Ter. N9 —18Vb **25**
Malvern Way. W13 —43Ka **78**
Malvern Way. Crox —15R **18**
Malvina Av. Grav —1D **136**
Malwood Rd. SW12 —58Kb **104**
Malyons Rd. SE13 —58Dc **106**
Malyons Rd. Swan —66Hd **132**
Malyons Ter. SE13 —57Dc **106**
Malyons, The. Shep —72T **140**
Managers St. E14 —46Ec **84**
Manaton Clo. SE15 —55Xb **105**
Manaton Cres. S'hall —44Ca **77**
Manbey Gro. E15 —37Gc **65**
Manbey Pk. Rd. E15 —37Gc **65**
Manbey Rd. E15 —37Gc **65**
Manbey St. E15 —38Gc **65**
Manbre Rd. W6 —51Ya **102**
Manbrough Av. E6 —41Oc **86**
Manchester Dri. W10 —42Ab **80**
Manchester Gro. E14 —50Ec **84**
Manchester M. W1
—43Jb ***82*** *(1H* ***197****)*
(off Manchester St.)
Manchester Rd. E14 —50Ec **84**
Manchester Rd. N15 —30Tb **43**
Manchester Rd. T Hth —69Sb **127**
Manchester Sq. W1
—44Jb **82** (2J **197**)
Manchester St. W1
—43Jb **82** (1H **197**)
Manchester Way. Dag —35Dd **68**
Manchuria Rd. SW11 —58Jb **104**
Manciple St. SE1
—47Tb **83** (2F **207**)
Manciple St. SW1 —47Tb **83**
Mandalay Rd. SW4 —57Lb **104**
Mandarin Ct. NW10 —37Ta ***59***
(off Mitchellbrook Way)
Mandarin St. E14 —45Cc **84**
Mandarin Way. Hay —44Z **77**
Mandela Clo. NW10 —38Sa **59**
Mandela Ho. SE5 —54Rb **105**
Mandela Pl. Wat —12Z **19**
Mandela Rd. E16 —44Jc **85**
Mandela St. NW1 —39Lb **62**
Mandela St. SW9 —52Qb **104**
Mandela Way. SE1
—49Ub **83** (5H **207**)
Mandeville Clo. SE3 —52Hc **107**
Mandeville Clo. SW20 —67Ab **124**
Mandeville Clo. Wat —10V **4**
Mandeville Ct. E4 —21Ac **44**
Mandeville Ct. Egh —63C **118**
Mandeville Dri. Surb —74Ma **143**
Mandeville Ho. SW4 —57Lb **104**
Mandeville Pl. W1
—44Jb **82** (2J **197**)
Mandeville Rd. N14 —19Kb **24**
Mandeville Rd. Enf —8Ac **12**
Mandeville Rd. Iswth —54Ja **100**
Mandeville Rd. N'holt —38Ca **57**
Mandeville Rd. Pot B —4Eb **9**
Mandeville Rd. Shep —71Q **140**
Mandeville St. E5 —34Ac **64**
Mandeville Wlk. Hut —16Fe **33**
Mandrake Rd. SW17 —61Hb **125**
Mandrell Rd. SW2 —57Nb **104**
Manesty Ct. N14 —17Mb ***24***
(off Ivy Rd.)
Manette St. W1 —44Mb **82** (3E **198**)
Manfield Clo. Slou —1E **72**
Manford Clo. Chig —21Wc **47**
Manford Cross. Chig —22Wc **47**
Manford Ind. Est. Eri —51Kd **111**
Manford Way. Chig —21Uc **46**
Manfred Rd. SW15 —57Bb **103**
Manger Rd. N7 —37Nb **62**
Mangold Way. Eri —48Zc **87**
Manilla St. E14 —47Cc **84**
Manister Rd. SE2 —48Wc **87**
Manley Ct. N16 —34Vb **63**
Manley Ho. SE11
—50Qb **82** (7K **205**)
Manley St. NW1 —39Jb **62**
Manly Dixon Dri. Enf —9Ac **12**
Manning Ct. Wat —16Z **19**
Manningford Clo. EC1
—41Rb **83** (3B **194**)
Manning Gdns. Harr —31Ma **59**
Manning Rd. E17 —29Ac **44**
Manning Rd. Dag —37Cd **68**
Manning Rd. Orp —71Zc **151**
Manning St. S Ock —46Sd **90**
Manningtree Clo. SW19 —60Ab **102**
Manningtree Rd. Ruis —35X **57**
Manningtree St. E1 —44Wb **83**
Mannin Rd. Romf —31Xc **67**
Mannock Dri. Lou —12Sc **28**
Mannock Rd. N22 —27Rb **43**
Mann's Clo. Iswth —57Ha **100**
Manns Rd. Edgw —23Qa **39**
Manoel Rd. Twic —62Ea **122**
Manor Av. E7 —35Lc **65**
Manor Av. SE4 —54Bc **106**
Manor Av. Cat —96Ub **181**
Manor Av. Horn —29Ld **49**
Manor Av. Houn —55Z **99**
Manor Av. N'holt —38Ba **57**
Manor Brook. SE3 —56Jc **107**
Manor Chase. Wey —78R **140**
Manor Clo. E17 —26Ac **44**
Manor Clo. NW7 —22Ta **39**
Manor Clo. NW9 —29Ra **39**
Manor Clo. SE28 —45Yc **87**
Manor Clo. Barn —14Ab **22**
Manor Clo. Cray —56Fd **110**
Manor Clo. Dag —37Fd **68**
Manor Clo. E Hor —100U **174**
Manor Clo. Grav —1K **137**
Manor Clo. Romf —29Jd **48**
Manor Clo. Ruis —32V **56**
Manor Clo. S Ock —46Sd **90**
Manor Clo. Warl —89Ac **166**
Manor Clo. Wilm —62Jd **132**
Manor Clo. Wok —89H **157**
Manor Clo. Wor Pk —74Ua **144**
Manor Clo. S. S Ock —46Sd **90**
Manor Cotts. N2 —26Eb **41**
Manor Cotts. N'wd —25V **36**
Manor Cotts. App. N2 —26Eb **41**
Manor Ct. E4 —18Gc **27**
Manor Ct. E10 —32Dc **64**
Manor Ct. N2 —29Hb ***41***
(off Aylmer Rd.)
Manor Ct. N20 —20Hb ***23***
(off York Way)
Manor Ct. SW2 —57Pb **104**
Manor Ct. SW16 —62Nb **126**
Manor Ct. W3 —49Qa **79**
Manor Ct. Bark —38Vc **67**
Manor Ct. Bexh —57Dd **110**
Manor Ct. Chesh —3Zb ***12***
(off Hillside Av.)
Manor Ct. Enf —8Xb **11**
Manor Ct. Harr —30Ha **38**
Manor Ct. Pot B —4Bb **9**
Manor Ct. Twic —61Ea **122**
Manor Ct. Wemb —36Na **59**
Manor Ct. W Mol —70Ca **121**
Manor Ct. W Wick —74Dc **148**
Manor Ct. Wey —77R **140**
Manor Ct. Rd. W7 —45Ga **78**
Manor Cres. Byfl —85P **157**
Manor Cres. Horn —29Ld **49**
Manor Cres. Surb —72Qa **143**
Manorcrofts Rd. Egh —65C **118**
Manor Deerfield Cotts. NW9
—29Va **40**
Manor Dene. SE28 —44Yc **87**
Manordene Clo. Th Dit —74Ja **142**
Manordene Rd. SE28 —44Zc **87**
Manor Dri. N14 —18Kb **24**
Manor Dri. N20 —21Gb **41**
Manor Dri. NW7 —22Ta **39**
Manor Dri. Eps —79Ua **144**
Manor Dri. Esh —75Ha **142**
Manor Dri. Felt —64Z **121**
Manor Dri. Hart —72Ce **155**
Manor Dri. New Haw —82J **157**
Manor Dri. Sun —68W **120**
Manor Dri. Surb —72Pa **143**
Manor Dri. Wemb —35Pa **59**
Manor Dri. N. N Mald & Wor Pk
—73Ta **143**
Manor Dri., The. Wor Pk
—74Ua **144**
Manor Est. SE16 —49Xb **83**
Manor Farm. F'ham —72Pd **153**
Manor Farm Av. Shep —72R **140**
Manor Farm Clo. Wind —5D **94**
Manor Farm Ct. E6 —41Pc ***86***
(off Holloway Rd.)
Manor Farm Ct. Egh —64C **118**
Manor Farm Dri. E4 —20Gc **27**
Manor Farm Est. Byfl —86P **157**
Manor Farm La. Egh —64C **118**
Manor Farm Rd. SW16 —68Qb **126**
Manor Farm Rd. Enf —7Xb **11**
Manor Farm Rd. Wemb —40Ma **59**
Manor Field. Shorne —4N **137**
Manorfield Clo. N19 —35Lb ***62***
(off Fulbeck M.)
Manor Fields. SW15 —58Za **102**
Manorfields Clo. Chst —69Vc **131**
Manor Forstal. New Ash —76Be **155**
Manor Gdns. N7 —34Nb **62**
Manor Gdns. SW20 —68Bb **125**
Manor Gdns. W3 —49Qa **79**
Manor Gdns. W4 —50Ua **80**
Manor Gdns. Eff —100Z **175**
Manor Gdns. Hamp —66Da **121**
Manor Gdns. Rich —56Pa **101**
Manor Gdns. Ruis —36Y **57**
Manor Gdns. S Croy —79Vb **147**
Manor Gdns. Sun —67W **120**
Manor Ga. N'holt —38Aa **57**
Manorgate Rd. King T —67Qa **123**
Manor Grn. Rd. Eps —85Ra **161**
Manor Gro. SE15 —51Yb **106**
Manor Gro. Beck —68Dc **128**
Manor Gro. Rich —56Qa **101**
Manor Hall Av. NW4 —26Za **40**
Manor Hall Dri. NW4 —26Za **40**
Manorhall Gdns. E10 —32Cc **64**
Manor Hill. Bans —87Hb **163**
Manor Ho. Fawk —76Td **154**
Manor Ho. Ct. Eps —85Sa **161**
Manor Ho. Ct. Shep —73R **140**
Manor Ho. Dri. NW6 —38Za **60**
Manor Ho. Dri. N'wd —24R **36**
Manor Ho. Est. Stan —22Ka **38**
Manor Ho. Gdns. Abb L —3T **4**
Manorhouse La. Bookh —98Aa **175**
Manor Ho. La. Dat —2M **95**
Manor Ho. Way. Iswth —55Ka **100**
Manor La. SE13 & SE12
—57Gc **107**
Manor La. Fawk & Sev —73Yd **154**
Manor La. Felt —61W **120**
Manor La. Ger X —1P **53**
Manor La. Hart —72Ce **155**
Manor La. Hay —51T **98**
Manor La. Sun —68W **120**
Manor La. Sutt —78Eb **145**
Manor La. Tad —100Cb **179**
Manor La. Ter. SE13 —56Gc **107**
Manor Leaze. Egh —64D **118**
Manor M. SE4 —54Bc **106**
Manor Mt. SE23 —60Yb **106**
Manor Pde. Harr —30Ha **38**
Manor Pk. SE13 —56Fc **107**
Manor Pk. Chst —68Tc **130**
Manor Pk. Rich —56Pa **101**
Manor Pk. Clo. W Wick —74Dc **148**
Manor Pk. Cres. Edgw —23Qa **39**
Manor Pk. Dri. Harr —27Da **37**
Manor Pk. Gdns. Edgw —22Qa **39**
Manor Pk. Rd. E12 —35Mc **65**
Manor Pk. Rd. N2 —27Eb **41**
Manor Pk. Rd. NW10 —39Va **60**
Manor Pk. Rd. Chst —67Sc **130**
Manor Pk. Rd. Sutt —78Eb **145**
Manor Pk. Rd. W Wick —74Dc **148**
Manor Pl. SE17 —50Rb **83** (7C **206**)
Manor Pl. Chst —68Tc **130**
Manor Pl. Dart —60Nd **111**
Manor Pl. Felt —60W **98**
Manor Pl. Mitc —69Lb **126**
Manor Pl. Stai —64K **119**
Manor Pl. Sutt —77Db **145**
Manor Rd. E10 —31Cc **64**
Manor Rd. E15 & E16 —40Gc **65**
Manor Rd. E17 —26Ac **44**
Manor Rd. N16 —33Tb **63**
Manor Rd. N17 —25Wb **43**
Manor Rd. N22 —23Nb **42**
Manor Rd. SE25 —70Wb **127**
Manor Rd. SW20 —68Bb **125**
Manor Rd. W13 —45Ja **78**
Manor Rd. Abr —19Yc **29**
Manor Rd. Ashf —64P **119**
Manor Rd. Bark —38Vc **67**
Manor Rd. Barn —14Ab **22**
Manor Rd. Beck —68Dc **128**
Manor Rd. Bex —60Dd **110**
Manor Rd. Chad —30Zc **47**
Manor Rd. Dag —37Ed **68**
Manor Rd. Dart —56Gd **110**
Manor Rd. E Mol —70Fa **122**
Manor Rd. Enf —12Sb **25**
Manor Rd. Eri —51Hd **110**
Manor Rd. Grav —8D **114**
Manor Rd. Grays —51Ee **113**
Manor Rd. Harr —30Ja **38**
Manor Rd. Hay —44W **76**
Manor Rd. H Bee —11Kc **27**
Manor Rd. Long —71Ee **155**
Manor Rd. Lou —16Kc **27**
Manor Rd. Mitc —70Lb **126**
Manor Rd. Pot B —3Bb **9**
Manor Rd. Red —100Lb **180**
Manor Rd. Rich —56Qa **101**
Manor Rd. Rip —95H **173**
Manor Rd. Romf —29Jd **48**
Manor Rd. Ruis —32T **56**
Manor Rd. Sidc —62Wc **131**
Manor Rd. Sole S & Grav —10E **136**
Manor Rd. Stanf —2M **93**
Manor Rd. Sund —96Zc **185**
Manor Rd. Sutt —80Bb **145**
Manor Rd. Swans —58Zd **113**
Manor Rd. Tats —92Nc **184**
Manor Rd. Tedd —64Ja **122**
Manor Rd. Til —4C **114**
Manor Rd. Twic —61Ea **122**
Manor Rd. Wall —77Kb **146**
Manor Rd. Wal A —5Fc **13**
Manor Rd. W on T —73V **140**
Manor Rd. Wat —11X **19**
Manor Rd. W Thur —51Yd **112**
Manor Rd. W Wick —75Dc **148**
Manor Rd. Wind —4C **94**
Manor Rd. Wok —4F **188**
Manor Rd. Wfd G & Chig —23Pc **46**
Manor Rd. Ho. Harr —30Ja **38**
Manor Rd. N. Hin W & Th Dit
—76Ha **142**
Manor Rd. N. Wall —77Kb **146**
Manor Rd. S. Esh —77Ga **142**
Manorside. Barn —14Ab **22**
Manorside Clo. SE2 —49Yc **87**
Manor Sq. Dag —33Yc **67**
Manor Vale. Bren —50La **78**
Manor View. N3 —26Db **41**
Manor View. Hart —72Ce **155**
Manor Wlk. Wey —78R **140**
Manor Way. E4 —21Fc **45**
Manor Way. NW9 —28Ua **40**
Manor Way. SE3 —56Hc **107**
Manor Way. Bans —88Hb **163**
Manor Way. Beck —68Cc **128**
Manor Way. Bex —60Cd **110**
Manor Way. Bexh —55Fd **110**
Manor Way. Borwd —13Sa **21**
Manor Way. Brtwd —20Wd **32**
Manor Way. Brom —72Nc **150**
Manor Way. Chesh —2Ac **12**
Manor Way. Crox —14Q **18**
Manor Way. Egh —65B **118**
Manorway. Enf —17Ub **25**
Manor Way. Grays —52De **113**
Manor Way. Harr —28Da **37**
Manor Way. Mitc —69Lb **126**
Manor Way. Orp —70Sc **130**
Manor Way. Oxs —87Ea **160**
Manor Way. Pot B —2Cb **9**
Manor Way. Purl —84Nb **164**
Manor Way. Rain —44Gd **88**
(in two parts)
Manor Way. Ruis —31U **56**
Manor Way. S'hall —49Z **77**
Manor Way. S Croy —79Ub **147**
Manor Way. Stanf —1P **93**
Manor Way. Swans —56Zd **113**
Manor Way. Wok —93D **172**
Manor Way. Wfd G —22Lc **45**
Manor Way. Wor Pk —74Ua **144**
Manor Waye. Uxb —39M **55**
Manorway, The. Stanf —1N **93**
Manor Way, The. Wall —77Kb **146**
Manor Wood Rd. Purl —85Nb **164**
Manresa Rd. SW3
—50Gb **81** (7D **202**)
Mansard Beeches. SW17
—64Jb **126**
Mansard Clo. Horn —33Jd **68**
Mansard Clo. Pinn —27Z **37**
Manse Clo. Hay —51T **98**
Mansel Clo. Slou —3M **73**
Mansel Clo. Wind —3C **94**
Mansel Gro. E17 —25Cc **44**
Mansell Rd. W3 —47Ta **79**
Mansell Rd. Gnfd —43Da **77**
Mansell St. E1 —44Vb **83** (3K **201**)
Mansell Way. Cat —94Tb **181**
Mansel Rd. SW19 —65Ab **124**
Mansen Rd. Grav —4F **136**
Manse Pde. Swan —70Jd **132**
Mansergh Clo. SE18 —52Nc **108**
Manse Rd. N16 —34Vb **63**
Manser Rd. Rain —41Gd **88**
Manse Way. Swan —70Jd **132**
Mansfield Av. N15 —28Tb **43**
Mansfield Av. Barn —16Hb **23**
Mansfield Av. Ruis —32X **57**
Mansfield Clo. N9 —16Wb **25**
Mansfield Clo. Orp —73Zc **151**
Mansfield Dri. Hay —42U **76**
Mansfield Dri. Red —100Mb **180**
Mansfield Gdns. Horn —33Md **69**
Mansfield Heights. N2 —29Hb **41**
Mansfield Hill. E4 —17Dc **26**
Mansfield M. W1
—43Kb **82** (1K **197**)
Mansfield Pl. NW3 —35Eb **61**
Mansfield Rd. E11 —30Kc **45**
Mansfield Rd. E17 —28Bc **44**
Mansfield Rd. NW3 —36Hb **61**
Mansfield Rd. W3 —42Ra **79**
Mansfield Rd. Chess —78La **142**
Mansfield Rd. Ilf —33Qc **66**
Mansfield Rd. S Croy —79Tb **147**
Mansfield Rd. Swan —65Gd **132**
Mansfield St. W1
—43Kb **82** (1K **197**)
Mansford St. E2 —40Wb **63**
Manship Rd. Mitc —66Jb **126**
Mansion Gdns. NW3 —34Db **61**
Mansion Ho. Pl. EC4
—44Tb **83** (3F **201**)
Mansion Ho. St. EC2
—44Tb ***83*** *(3F* ***201****)*
(off Victoria St.)
Mansion La. Iver —46E **74**
Mansions, The. SW5 —50Db **81**
Manson M. SW7
—49Eb **81** (6A **202**)
Manson Pl. SW7
—49Fb **81** (6B **202**)
Manstead Gdns. Rain —44Kd **89**
Mansted Gdns. Romf —31Yc **67**
Manston. N17 —26Tb ***43***
(off Adams Rd.)
Manston Av. S'hall —49Ca **77**
Manston Clo. SE20 —67Yb **128**
Manston Clo. Chesh —2Yb **12**
Manstone Rd. NW2 —36Ab **60**
Manston Way. Horn —37Kd **69**
Manthorp Rd. SE18 —50Sc **86**
Mantilla Rd. SW17 —63Jb **126**
Mantle Rd. SE4 —55Ac **106**
Mantlet Clo. SW16 —66Lb **126**
Manton Av. W7 —47Ha **78**
Manton Clo. Hay —45U **76**
Manton Rd. SE2 —49Wc **87**
Mantua Rd. SW11 —55Fb **103**
Mantus Clo. E1 —42Yb **84**
Mantus Rd. E1 —42Yb **84**
Manus Way. N20 —19Eb **23**
Manville Gdns. SW17 —62Kb **126**
Manville Rd. SW17 —61Jb **126**
Manwood Rd. SE4 —57Bc **106**
Manwood St. E16 —46Pc **86**
Manygate La. Shep —73S **140**
Manygates. SW12 —61Kb **126**
Mapesbury Rd. NW2 —38Ab **60**
Mape St. E2 —42Xb **83**
Maple Av. E4 —22Bc **44**
Maple Av. W3 —46Ua **80**
Maple Av. Harr —33Da **57**
Maple Av. Upm —34Rd **69**
Maple Av. W Dray —45N **75**
Maple Clo. N16 —30Wb **43**
Maple Clo. SW4 —58Mb **104**
Maple Clo. Brtwd —20Be **33**
Maple Clo. Buck H —20Mc **27**
Maple Clo. Bush —12Aa **19**
Maple Clo. Hamp —65Ba **121**
Maple Clo. Hay —41Z **77**
Maple Clo. Horn —34Kd **69**
Maple Clo. Ilf —22Uc **46**
Maple Clo. Mitc —67Kb **126**
Maple Clo. Orp —71Tc **150**
Maple Clo. Ruis —30X **37**
Maple Clo. Swan —68Gd **132**
Maple Clo. Whyt —89Vb **165**
Maple Ct. E6 —43Qc **86**
Maple Ct. Borwd —14Qa **21**
Maple Ct. Egh —5M **117**
Maple Ct. Hors —4F **188**
Maple Ct. N Mald —69Ta **123**
Maple Ct. Wat —8Z **5**
Maple Cres. Sidc —58Wc **109**
Maple Cres. Slou —5M **73**
Maplecroft Clo. E6 —44Mc **85**
Mapledale Av. Croy —75Wb **147**
Mapledene. Chst —64Sc **130**
Mapledene Est. E8 —38Wb **63**
Mapledene Rd. E8 —38Wb **63**
Maplefield. Park —1Da **5**
Maple Gdns. Edgw —24Ua **40**
Maple Gdns. Stai —61N **119**
Maple Gro. NW9 —31Sa **59**
Maple Gro. W5 —48Ma **79**
Maple Gro. Bren —52Ka **100**
Maple Gro. S'hall —43Ba **77**
Maple Gro. Wat —11W **18**
Maple Gro. Wok —93A **172**
Maple Ho. E17 —27Dc **44**
Maplehurst. Brom —68Gc **129**
Maplehurst. Lea —95Fa **176**
Maplehurst Clo. King T —70Na **123**
Maple Ind. Est. Felt —62W **120**
Maple Leaf Clo. Big H —88Mc **167**
Maple Leaf Dri. Sidc —60Vc **109**
Mapleleafe Gdns. Ilf —27Rc **46**
Maple Leaf Sq. SE16 —47Zb **84**
Maplelodge Clo. Rick —21G **34**
Maple M. NW6 —40Db **61**
Maple M. SW16 —64Pb **126**
Maple Pl. W1 —42Lb **82** (6C **192**)
Maple Pl. Bans —86Za **162**
Maple Pl. W Dray —46N **75**
Maple Rd. E11 —30Gc **45**
Maple Rd. SE20 —67Xb **127**
Maple Rd. Asht —91Ma **177**
Maple Rd. Dart —61Ld **133**
Maple Rd. Grav —3E **136**
Maple Rd. Grays —51Ee **113**
Maple Rd. Hay —41Y **77**
Maple Rd. Rip —96J **173**
Maple Rd. Surb —72Ka **142**
Maple Rd. Whyt —89Vb **165**
Maples. Stanf —1N **93**
Maplescombe La. F'ham
—76Qd **153**
Maples Pl. E1 —43Xb **83**
Maple Springs. Wal A —5Jc **13**
Maplestead Rd. SW2 —59Pb **104**
Maplestead Rd. Dag —39Xc **67**
Maples, The. Bans —86Db **163**
Maples, The. Borwd —11Qa **21**
Maples, The. Ott —79E **138**
Maple St. W1 —43Lb **82** (7B **192**)
Maple St. Romf —28Ed **48**
Maplethorpe Rd. T Hth —70Rb **127**
Mapleton Clo. Brom —72Jc **149**
Mapleton Cres. SW18 —58Db **103**
Mapleton Cres. Enf —10Yb **12**
Mapleton Rd. E4 —20Ec **26**
Mapleton Rd. SW18 —58Cb **103**
(in two parts)
Mapleton Rd. Enf —12Xb **25**
Maple Wlk. W10 —41Za **80**
Maple Wlk. Sutt —82Db **163**
Maple Way. Coul —93Kb **180**
Maple Way. Felt —62W **120**
Maplin Clo. N21 —16Pb **24**
Maplin Ho. SE2 —47Zc ***87***
(off Wolvercote Rd.)
Maplin Pk. Slou —47D **74**
Maplin Rd. E16 —44Jc **85**
Maplin St. E3 —42Bc **84**
Mapperley Clo. E11 —30Hc **45**
Mapperley Dri. Wfd G —24Gc **45**
Maran Way. Eri —48Zc **87**
Marban Rd. W9 —41Bb **81**
Marbeck Clo. Wind —3B **94**
Marble Arch. W1
—45Hb **81** (4F **197**)
Marble Clo. W3 —46Ra **79**
Marble Hill Clo. Twic —59Ka **100**
Marble Hill Gdns. Twic —59Ka **100**
Marble Quay. E1 —46Wb **83**
Marbles Way. Tad —91Za **178**
Marbrook Ct. SE12 —62Lc **129**
Marcellina Way. Orp —76Vc **151**
Marcet Rd. Dart —57Ld **111**
March. NW9 —25Va ***40***
(off Concourse, The)
Marchant Ct. SE17 —50Ub **83**
Marchant Rd. E11 —33Fc **65**
Marchant St. SE14 —51Ac **106**
Marchbank Rd. W14 —51Bb **103**
Marchmont Clo. Horn —34Ld **69**
Marchmont Rd. Rich —57Pa **101**
Marchmont Rd. Wall —80Lb **146**
Marchmont St. WC1
—42Nb **82** (5F **193**)
March Rd. Twic —62Aa **121**
March Rd. Wey —78Q **140**
Marchside Clo. Houn —53Z **99**
Marchwood Clo. SE5 —52Ub **105**
Marchwood Cres. W5 —44La **78**
Marcia Rd. SE1 —49Ub **83** (6J **207**)
Marcilly Rd. SW18 —57Fb **103**
Marcon Ct. E8 —36Xb ***63***
(off Amhurst Rd.)
Marconi Rd. Grav —62Fe **135**
Marconi Way. S'hall —44Da **77**
Marcon Pl. E8 —36Xb **63**
Marco Rd. W6 —48Ya **80**

Marcourt Lawns—Matlock Way

Marcourt Lawns. W5 —42Na **79**
Marcus Ct. E15 —39Gc **65**
Marcus Garvey Way. SE24 —56Qb **104**
Marcus Rd. Dart —59Jd **110**
Marcus St. E15 —39Gc **65**
Marcus St. SW18 —58Db **103**
Marcus Ter. SW18 —58Db **103**
Mardale Dri. NW9 —29Ta **39**
Mardell Rd. Croy —71Zb **148**
Marden Av. Brom —72Jc **149**
Marden Clo. Chig —19Xc **29**
Marden Ct. SE8 —51Cc **106**
Marden Cres. Bex —57Ed **110**
Marden Cres. Croy —72Pb **146**
Marden Ho. E8 —36Xb **63**
Marden Rd. N17 —26Ub **43**
Marden Rd. Croy —72Pb **146**
Marden Rd. Romf —30Gd **48**
Marden Sq. SE16 —48Xb **83**
Marder Rd. W13 —47Ja **78**
Mardon. Pinn —24Ba **37**
Mardyke Wlk. Grays —46Ce **91**
Marechal Neil Av. Sidc —62Tc **130**
*Marechal Niel Pde. Sidc —62Tc **130***
(off Main Rd.)
Maresby Ho. E4 —19Dc **26**
Marescroft Rd. Slou —2C **72**
Mares Field. Croy —76Ub **147**
Maresfield Gdns. NW3 —36Eb **61**
Mare St. E8 —39Xb **63**
Marfleet Clo. Cars —75Gb **145**
Margaret Av. E4 —16Dc **26**
Margaret Av. Shenf —16Ce **33**
Margaret Bondfield Av. Bark —38Wc **67**
Margaret Bldgs. N16 —32Vb **63**
Margaret Clo. Abb L —4V **4**
Margaret Clo. Pot B —5Eb **9**
Margaret Clo. Romf —29Kd **49**
Margaret Clo. Stai —65M **119**
Margaret Clo. Wal A —5Fc **13**
*Margaret Ct. W1 —44Lb **82** (2B **198**)*
(off Margaret St.)
Margaret Ct. Barn —14Fb **23**
Margaret Dri. Horn —32Pd **69**
Margaret Gardner Dri. SE9 —61Pc **130**
Margaret Rd. N16 —32Vb **63**
Margaret Rd. Barn —14Fb **23**
Margaret Rd. Bex —58Zc **109**
Margaret Rd. Epp —1Wc **15**
Margaret Rd. Romf —29Kd **49**
Margaret Sq. Uxb —39L **55**
Margaret St. W1 —44Kb **82** (2A **198**)
Margaretta Ter. SW3 —51Gb **103**
Margaretting Rd. E12 —32Lc **65**
Margaret Way. Coul —91Rb **181**
Margaret Way. Ilf —30Nc **46**
Margate Rd. SW2 —57Nb **104**
Margeholes. Wat —19Aa **19**
Margery Fry Ct. N7 —34Nb **62**
Margery Gro. Tad —100Ab **178**
Margery La. Tad —100Bb **179**
Margery Pk. Rd. E7 —37Jc **65**
Margery Rd. Dag —34Zc **67**
Margery St. WC1 —41Qb **82** (4K **193**)
Margin Dri. SW19 —64Za **124**
Margravine Gdns. W6 —50Za **80**
Margravine Rd. W6 —50Za **80**
Marham Gdns. SW18 —60Gb **103**
Marham Gdns. Mord —72Eb **145**
Maria Clo. SE1 —49Xb **83**
Mariam Gdns. Horn —33Pd **69**
Marian Clo. Hay —42Z **77**
Marian Clo. N Stif —46Ae **91**
Marian Ct. E9 —37Yb **64**
Marian Ct. Sutt —78Db **145**
Marian Pl. E2 —40Xb **63**
Marian Rd. SW16 —67Lb **126**
Marian St. E2 —40Xb **63**
Marian Way. NW10 —38Va **60**
Maria Ter. E1 —42Zb **84**
Maria Theresa Clo. N Mald —71Ta **143**
Maricas Av. Harr —25Fa **38**
Marie Lloyd Gdns. N19 —31Nb **62**
Marie Lloyd Wlk. E8 —37Vb **63**
Mariette Way. Wall —81Nb **164**
*Marigold All. SE1 —45Rb **83** (5B **200**)*
(off Up. Ground)
Marigold Rd. N17 —24Yb **44**
Marigold St. SE16 —47Xb **83**
Marigold Way. E4 —23Bc **44**
Marigold Way. Croy —74Zb **148**
Marina App. Hay —43Aa **77**
Marina Av. N Mald —71Xa **144**
Marina Clo. Brom —69Jc **129**
Marina Dri. Dart —60Qd **111**
Marina Dri. Grav —9B **114**
Marina Dri. Well —54Uc **108**
Marina Gdns. Chesh —2Yb **12**
Marina Gdns. Romf —30Dd **48**
Marina Way. Iver —45J **75**
Marina Way. Slou —5B **72**
Marina Way. Tedd —66Ma **123**
Marine Ct. Eri —52Hd **110**
Marine Dri. SE18 —49Pc **86**
Marinefield Rd. SW6 —54Db **103**
Marinel Ho. SE5 —52Sb **105**
Mariner Gdns. Rich —62La **122**
Mariner Rd. E12 —35Qc **66**
Mariners Ct. Grnh —56Xd **112**
Mariners M. E14 —49Fc **85**
Mariners Wlk. Eri —51Hd **110**
Marine St. SE16 —48Wb **83**
Marion Av. Shep —71R **140**
Marion Clo. Bush —11Ba **19**
Marion Clo. Ilf —24Tc **46**
Marion Cres. Orp —71Wc **151**
Marion Gro. Wfd G —22Gc **45**
Marion Rd. NW7 —22Wa **40**
Marion Rd. T Hth —71Sb **147**
Marion Sq. E2 —40Xb **63**
Marischal Rd. SE13 —55Fc **107**
Marisco Clo. Grays —9D **92**
Marish Ct. Langl —48C **74**
Marish La. Den —29E **34**
Marish Wharf. Mid —47A **74**
Maritime Clo. Grnh —57Xd **112**
Maritime St. E3 —42Bc **84**
Marius Pas. SW17 —61Jb **126**
Marius Rd. SW17 —61Jb **126**
Marjorams Av. Lou —12Qc **28**
Marjorie Gro. SW11 —56Hb **103**
Marjorie M. E1 —44Zb **84**
Markab Rd. N'wd —22V **36**
Mark Av. E4 —16Dc **26**
Mark Clo. Bexh —53Ad **109**
Mark Dri. Ger X —21A **34**
Marke Clo. Kes —77Nc **150**
Markedge La. Coul & Red —96Hb **179**
Markeston Grn. Wat —21Z **37**
Market All. Grav —8D **114**
Market Cen., The. S'hall —49X **77**
*Market Ct. W1 —44Lb **82** (2B **198**)*
(off Market Pl.)
Market Entrance. SW8 —52Lb **104**
Market Est. N7 —37Nb **62**
Market Hill. SE18 —48Qc **86**
Market La. Edgw —25Sa **39**
Market La. Slou & Iver —48E **74**
Market Link. Romf —28Gd **48**
Market Meadow. Orp —70Yc **131**
Market M. W1 —46Kb **82** (7K **197**)
Market Pde. Sidc —63Xc **131**
Market Pavilion. E10 —34Cc **64**
Market Pl. N2 —27Gb **41**
Market Pl. NW11 —28Db **41**
Market Pl. SE16 —49Wb **83**
Market Pl. W1 —44Lb **82** (2B **198**)
Market Pl. W3 —46Sa **79**
Market Pl. Abr —13Xc **29**
Market Pl. Bexh —56Cd **110**
Market Pl. Bren —52La **100**
Market Pl. Dart —59Nd **111**
Market Pl. Enf —13Tb **25**
Market Pl. Ger X —25A **34**
Market Pl. King T —68Ma **123**
Market Pl. Romf —29Gd **48**
Market Pl. S'hall —46Ba **77**
Market Rd. N7 —37Nb **62**
Market Rd. Rich —55Qa **101**
Market Row. SW9 —56Qb **104**
Market Sq. E14 —44Dc **84**
Market Sq. N9 —19Xb **25**
Market Sq. Brom —68Jc **129**
Market Sq. Stai —63G **118**
Market Sq. Uxb —38L **55**
Market Sq. Wal A —5Ec **12**
Market Sq. W'ham —98Tc **184**
Market Sq. Wok —89A **156**
Market St. E6 —40Pc **66**
Market St. SE18 —49Qc **86**
Market St. Dart —59Nd **111**
Market St. Wat —14X **19**
Market St. Wind —3H **95**
*Market Ter. Bren —51Na **101***
(off Albany Rd.)
Market Way. E14 —44Dc **84**
Market Way. Wemb —36Na **59**
Market Way. W'ham —98Tc **184**
Markfield. Croy —82Bc **166**
(in two parts)
Markfield Gdns. E4 —17Dc **26**
Markfield Rd. N15 —28Wb **43**
Markfield Rd. Cat —93Xb **181**
*Markham Ho. Dag —34Cd **68***
(off Uvedale Rd.)
Markham Pl. SW3 —50Hb **81** (7F **203**)
Markhams. Stanf —1P **93**
Markham Sq. SW3 —50Hb **81** (7F **203**)
Markham St. SW3 —50Gb **81** (7E **202**)
Markhole Clo. Hamp —66Ba **121**
Markhouse Av. E17 —30Ac **44**
*Markhouse Pas. E17 —30Bc **44***
(off Markhouse Rd.)
Markhouse Rd. E17 —30Bc **44**
Mark La. EC3 —45Ub **83** (4J **201**)
Mark La. Grav —9G **114**
(in two parts)
Markmanor Av. E17 —31Ac **64**
Mark Oak La. Fet —94Ca **175**
Mark Rd. N22 —25Rb **43**
Marksbury Av. Rich —55Qa **101**
Marks Lodge. Romf —29Fd **48**
Marks Rd. Romf —29Ed **48**
Marks Rd. Warl —90Ac **166**
Marks Sq. Grav —3B **136**
Mark St. E15 —38Gc **65**
Mark St. EC2 —42Ub **83** (5H **195**)
Markville Gdns. Cat —97Wb **181**
Markway. Sun —68Y **121**
Mark Way. Swan —71Jd **152**
Markwell Clo. SE26 —63Xb **127**
Markyate Rd. Dag —36Xc **67**
Marlands Rd. Ilf —27Nc **46**
Marlborough Av. E8 —39Wb **63**
(in two parts)
Marlborough Av. N14 —20Lb **24**
Marlborough Av. Edgw —20Ra **21**
Marlborough Av. Ruis —30S **36**
*Marlborough Bldgs. SW3 —49Gb **81** (5E **202**)*
(off Walton St.)
Marlborough Clo. N20 —20Hb **23**
Marlborough Clo. SE17 —49Sb **83** (6C **206**)
Marlborough Clo. SW19 —65Gb **125**
Marlborough Clo. Grays —47Ee **91**
Marlborough Clo. Orp —72Vc **151**
Marlborough Clo. Upm —32Ud **70**
Marlborough Clo. W on T —76Z **141**
Marlborough Ct. W1
*(off Kingly St.) —45Lb **82** (4B **198**)*
Marlborough Ct. Enf —15Ub **25**
Marlborough Ct. Harr —28Fa **38**
Marlborough Ct. N'wd —24V **36**
Marlborough Cres. W4 —48Ta **79**
Marlborough Cres. Sev —96Gd **186**
Marlborough Dri. Ilf —27Nc **46**
Marlborough Dri. Wey —76S **140**
Marlborough Gdns. N20 —20Hb **23**
Marlborough Gdns. Surb —73Ma **143**
Marlborough Gdns. Upm —32Td **70**
*Marlborough Ga. Stables. W2 —45Fb **81** (4B **196**)*
(off Elms M.)
Marlborough Gro. SE1 —50Wb **83**
Marlborough Hill. NW8 —40Eb **61**
Marlborough Hill. Harr —28Fa **38**
Marlborough La. SE7 —52Lc **107**
*Marlborough Mans. NW6 —36Db **61***
(off Cannon Hill)
Marlborough Pde. Uxb —42R **76**
Marlborough Pk. Av. Sidc —59Wc **109**
Marlborough Pl. NW8 —40Eb **61**
Marlborough Rd. E4 —23Dc **44**
Marlborough Rd. E7 —38Lc **65**
Marlborough Rd. E15 —35Gc **65**
Marlborough Rd. E18 —26Jc **45**
Marlborough Rd. N9 —18Vb **25**
Marlborough Rd. N19 —33Mb **62**
Marlborough Rd. N22 —24Nb **42**
Marlborough Rd. SW1 —46Lb **82** (7C **198**)
Marlborough Rd. SW19 —65Gb **125**
Marlborough Rd. W4 —50Sa **79**
Marlborough Rd. W5 —47Ma **79**
Marlborough Rd. Ashf —64M **119**
Marlborough Rd. Bexh —55Zc **109**
Marlborough Rd. Brom —70Lc **129**
Marlborough Rd. Dag —35Xc **67**
Marlborough Rd. Dart —58Ld **111**
Marlborough Rd. Felt —61Z **121**
Marlborough Rd. Hamp —65Ca **121**
Marlborough Rd. Iswth —53Ka **100**
Marlborough Rd. Pil H —16Wd **32**
Marlborough Rd. Rich —58Pa **101**
Marlborough Rd. Romf —28Cd **48**
Marlborough Rd. Slou —9P **73**
Marlborough Rd. S'hall —48Y **77**
Marlborough Rd. S Croy —80Sb **147**
Marlborough Rd. Sutt —76Cb **145**
Marlborough Rd. Uxb —42R **76**
Marlborough Rd. Wat —14X **19**
Marlborough Rd. Wok —88C **156**
Marlborough St. SW3 —49Gb **81** (6D **202**)
Marlborough Yd. N19 —33Mb **62**
Marld, The. Asht —90Pa **161**
Marle Gdns. Wal A —4Ec **12**
Marler Rd. SE23 —60Ac **106**
Marlescroft Way. Lou —15Rc **28**
Marley Av. Bexh —51Zc **109**
Marley Clo. Add —79H **139**
Marley Clo. Gnfd —41Ca **77**
Marley Wlk. NW2 —36Ya **60**
Marlingdene Clo. Hamp —65Ca **121**
Marlings Clo. Chst —70Uc **130**
Marlings Clo. Whyt —89Ub **165**
Marlings Pk. Av. Chst —70Uc **130**
Marling Way. Grav —5G **136**
Marlin Ho. Wat —16T **18**
Marlins Clo. Rick —12G **16**
Marlins Clo. Sutt —78Eb **145**
Marlins Meadow. Wat —16T **18**
Marlin Sq. Abb L —3V **4**
Marloes Clo. Wemb —35Ma **59**
Marloes Rd. W8 —48Db **81**
Marlow Av. Purf —49Qd **89**
Marlow Clo. SE20 —69Xb **127**
*Marlow Ct. N14 —17Lb **24***
(off Chase Side)
Marlow Ct. NW9 —27Va **40**
Marlow Cres. Twic —58Ha **100**
Marlow Dri. Sutt —75Za **144**
Marlowe Clo. Chst —65Tc **130**
Marlowe Clo. Ilf —25Sc **46**
Marlowe Gdns. SE9 —58Qc **108**
Marlowe Gdns. Romf —25Ld **49**
Marlowe Rd. E17 —28Ec **44**
Marlowe Sq. Mitc —70Lb **126**
Marlowes, The. NW8 —39Fb **61**
Marlowes, The. Dart —56Fd **110**
Marlow Gdns. Hay —48T **76**
Marlow Rd. E6 —41Pc **86**
Marlow Rd. SE20 —69Xb **127**
Marlow Rd. S'hall —48Ba **77**
Marlow Way. SE16 —47Zb **84**
Marlpit Av. Coul —89Nb **164**
Marlpit La. Coul —88Mb **164**
Marlton St. SE10 —50Hc **85**
Marlyon Rd. Ilf —22Xc **47**
Marmadon Rd. SE18 —49Vc **87**
Marmion App. E4 —21Cc **44**
Marmion Av. E4 —21Bc **44**
Marmion Clo. E4 —21Bc **44**
Marmion M. SW11 —55Jb **104**
Marmion Rd. SW11 —56Jb **104**
Marmont Rd. SE15 —53Wb **105**
Marmora Rd. SE22 —58Yb **106**
Marmot Rd. Houn —55Z **99**
Marne Av. N11 —21Kb **42**
Marne Av. Well —55Wc **109**
*Marne Ho. SE15 —52Wb **105***
(off Sumner Est.)
Marnell Way. Houn —55Z **99**
Marne St. W10 —41Ab **80**
Marney Rd. SW11 —56Jb **104**
Marneys Clo. Eps —87Qa **161**
Marnham Av. NW2 —35Ab **60**
Marnham Ct. Wemb —36La **58**
Marnham Cres. Gnfd —41Da **77**
Marnham Pl. Add —77L **139**
Marnock Rd. SE4 —57Bc **106**
Maroon St. E14 —43Ac **84**
Maroons Way. SE6 —64Cc **128**
Marquess Rd. N1 —37Tb **63**
Marquis Clo. Wemb —38Pa **59**
*Marquis Ct. N4 —31Qb **62***
(off Marquis Rd.)
Marquis Ct. Bark —36Uc **66**
Marquis Rd. N4 —32Pb **62**
Marquis Rd. N22 —23Pb **42**
Marquis Rd. NW1 —37Mb **62**
Marram Ct. Grays —1A **114**
Marrick Clo. SW15 —56Wa **102**
Marriett Ho. SE6 —63Ec **128**
Marrilyne Av. Enf —10Bc **12**
Marriott Clo. Felt —58T **98**
Marriott Lodge Clo. Add —77L **139**
Marriott Rd. E15 —39Gc **65**
Marriott Rd. N4 —32Pb **62**
Marriott Rd. N10 —25Hb **41**
Marriott Rd. Barn —13Za **22**
Marriott Rd. Dart —59Pd **111**
Marriotts Clo. NW9 —30Va **40**
Marriotts Wharf. Grav —7D **114**
Mar Rd. S Ock —42Yd **90**
Marrowells. Wey —76V **140**
Marryat Pl. SW19 —63Ab **124**
Marryat Rd. SW19 —64Za **124**
Marryat Rd. Enf —7Xb **11**
Marsala Rd. SE13 —56Dc **106**
Marsden Rd. N9 —19Xb **25**
Marsden Rd. SE15 —55Vb **105**
Marsden St. NW5 —37Jb **62**
Marsden Way. Orp —76Vc **151**
Marshall Clo. SW18 —58Eb **103**
Marshall Clo. Harr —31Fa **58**
Marshall Clo. Houn —57Ba **99**
Marshall Dri. Hay —43V **76**
Marshall Est. NW7 —21Wa **40**
*Marshall Ho. N1 —40Tb **63** (1G **195**)*
(off Cranston Est.)
Marshall Ho. Eri —47Zc **87**
Marshall Path. SE28 —45Xc **87**
Marshall Rd. N17 —25Tb **43**
Marshalls Clo. N11 —21Kb **42**
Marshalls Clo. Eps —85Sa **161**
Marshalls Dri. Romf —27Gd **48**
Marshalls Gro. SE18 —49Nc **86**
Marshall's Pl. SE16 —48Vb **83** (4K **207**)
Marshalls Rd. Romf —28Fd **48**
Marshall's Rd. Sutt —77Db **145**
Marshall St. W1 —44Lb **82** (3C **198**)
Marshalsea Rd. SE1 —47Sb **83** (1E **206**)
Marsham Clo. Chst —64Rc **130**
Marsham Ct. SW1 —49Mb **82** (5E **204**)
Marsham La. Ger X —30A **34**
Marsham Lodge. Ger X —30A **34**
Marsham St. SW1 —48Mb **82** (4E **204**)
Marsham Way. Ger X —29A **34**
Marsh Av. Eps —82Ua **162**
Marsh Av. Mitc —68Hb **125**
Marshbrook Clo. SE3 —55Mc **107**
Marsh Clo. NW7 —20Va **22**
Marsh Clo. Wal X —5Ac **12**
Marsh Ct. E8 —38Wb **63**
Marshcroft Dri. Chesh —2Ac **12**
Marsh Dri. NW9 —30Va **40**
Marshe Clo. Pot B —4Fb **9**
Marsh Farm Rd. Twic —60Ha **100**
Marshfield. Dat —3P **95**
Marshfield St. E14 —48Ec **84**
Marshfoot Rd. Grays —10A **92**
Marsh Ga. Bus. Cen. E15 —40Ec **64**
Marshgate La. E15 —38Dc **64**
Marshgate Path. SE18 —48Sc **86**
Marshgate Trading Est. E15 —38Dc **64**
Marsh Grn. Rd. Dag —39Cd **68**
Marsh Hall. Wemb —34Pa **59**
Marsh Hill. E9 —36Ac **64**
Marsh La. E10 —33Bc **64**
Marsh La. N17 —25Xb **43**
Marsh La. NW7 —20Ua **22**
Marsh La. Add —77K **139**
Marsh La. Stan —22La **38**
Marsh Rd. Pinn —28Aa **37**
Marsh Rd. Wemb —41Ma **79**
Marsh St. E14 —49Dc **84**
Marsh St. Dart —54Qd **111**
(in two parts)
Marsh Wall. E14 —46Cc **84**
Marsh Way. Rain —44Fd **88**
Marsland Clo. SE17 —50Rb **83** (7C **206**)
*Marsom Ho. N1 —41Tb **83** (3F **195**)*
(off Provost Est.)
Marston. Eps —83Sa **161**
Marston Av. Chess —79Na **143**
Marston Av. Dag —33Cd **68**
Marston Clo. NW6 —38Eb **61**
Marston Clo. Dag —34Cd **68**
Marston Ct. W on T —74Y **141**
Marston Dri. Warl —90Ac **166**
Marston Ho. SW9 —54Qb **104**
Marston Ho. Grays —51Ce **113**
Marston Rd. Ilf —25Nc **46**
Marston Rd. Tedd —64Ka **122**
Marston Rd. Wok —5E **188**
Marston Way. SE19 —66Rb **127**
Marsworth Av. Pinn —25Z **37**
Marsworth Clo. Hay —43Aa **77**
Marsworth Clo. Wat —17U **18**
Martaban Rd. N16 —33Vb **63**
Martello St. E8 —38Xb **63**
Martello Ter. E8 —38Xb **63**
Martell Rd. SE21 —62Tb **127**
Martel Pl. E8 —37Vb **63**
Marten Rd. E17 —26Cc **44**
Martens Av. Bexh —56Dd **110**
Martens Clo. Bexh —56Ed **110**
Martha Ct. E2 —40Xb **63**
Martham Clo. SE28 —45Zc **87**
Martha Rd. E15 —37Gc **65**
Martha St. E1 —44Yb **84**
Marthorne Cres. Harr —26Fa **38**
Martin Bowes Rd. SE9 —55Pc **108**
Martinbridge Trading Est. Enf —15Wb **25**
Martin Clo. N9 —18Zb **26**
Martin Clo. S Croy —83Zb **166**
Martin Clo. Warl —88Xb **165**
Martin Clo. Wind —3A **94**
Martin Cres. Croy —74Qb **146**
Martindale. SW14 —57Sa **101**
Martindale. Iver —42F **74**
Martindale Av. E16 —45Jc **85**
Martindale Av. Orp —78Wc **151**
Martin Dale Ind. Est. Enf —13Xb **25**
Martindale Rd. SW12 —59Kb **104**
Martindale Rd. Houn —55Aa **99**
Martindale Rd. Wok —6D **188**
Martin Dene. Bexh —57Bd **109**
Martin Dri. Dart —58Sd **112**
Martin Dri. N'holt —36Ba **57**
Martin Dri. Rain —42Kd **89**
Martineau Clo. Esh —77Fa **142**
Martineau Est. E1 —44Yb **84**
Martineau Ho. Ger X —22A **34**
Martineau M. N5 —35Rb **63**
Martineau Rd. N5 —35Rb **63**
Martingale Clo. Sun —70W **120**
Martingales Clo. Rich —62Ma **123**
Martin Gdns. Dag —35Yc **67**
Martin Gro. Mord —70Cb **125**
Martin Ho. SE1 —48Sb **83** (4E **206**)
Martin Ho. Grav —2C **136**
Martin La. EC4 —45Tb **83** (4G **201**)
Martin Rise. Bexh —57Bd **109**
Martin Rd. Dag —35Yc **67**
Martin Rd. Dart —62Ld **133**
Martin Rd. Slou —8J **73**
Martin Rd. S Ock —46Td **90**
Martins Clo. Orp —69Zc **131**
Martins Clo. Rad —8Ga **6**
Martins Clo. Stanf —1M **93**
Martins Clo. W Wick —75Fc **149**
Martins Dri. Chesh —1Ac **12**
Martinsfield Clo. Chig —21Uc **46**
*Martinside. NW9 —25Va **40***
(off Concourse, The)
Martins Mt. Barn —14Cb **23**
Martin's Pl. SE14 —53Zb **106**
Martins Plain. Stoke P —1K **73**
Martin's Rd. Brom —68Hc **129**
Martins Shaw. Chip —94Ed **186**
Martins, The. Wemb —34Pa **59**
Martinstown Clo. Horn —30Qd **49**
Martins Wlk. N10 —25Jb **42**
Martins Wlk. Borwd —14Qa **21**
Martin Way. SW20 & Mord —69Ab **124**
Martin Way. Wok —6D **188**
*Martlesham. N17 —26Ub **43***
(off Adams Rd.)
Martlesham Clo. Horn —36Ld **69**
Martlet Gro. N'holt —41Z **77**
Martlett Ct. WC2 —44Nb **82** (3G **199**)
Martley Dri. Ilf —29Rc **46**
Martock Clo. Harr —28Ja **38**
Marton Clo. SE6 —62Cc **128**
Marton Rd. N16 —33Ub **63**
Mart St. WC2 —45Nb **82** (4G **199**)
Martyr's La. Wok —84D **156**
Marunden Grn. Slou —1D **72**
Marvell Av. Hay —43W **76**
Marvels Clo. SE12 —61Kc **129**
Marvels La. SE12 —61Kc **129**
Marville Rd. SW6 —52Bb **103**
Marvin St. E8 —37Xb **63**
Marwell. W'ham —98Rc **184**
Marwell Clo. Romf —29Jd **48**
Marwell Clo. W Wick —75Hc **149**
Marwood Clo. K Lan —1P **3**
Marwood Clo. Well —55Xc **109**
Marwood Way. SE16 —50Xb **83**
Mary Adelaide Clo. SW15 —63Ua **124**
Mary Ann Gdns. SE8 —51Cc **106**
Maryatt Av. Harr —33Da **57**
Mary Bank. SE18 —49Pc **86**
Mary Burrows Gdns. Kems —89Rd **171**
Mary Clo. Stan —28Pa **39**
Mary Datchelor Clo. SE5 —53Tb **105**
Mary Drew Almshouses. Egh —5P **117**
Maryfield Clo. Bex —62Gd **132**
Mary Grn. NW8 —39Db **61**
Maryhill Clo. Kenl —89Sb **165**
*Maryland Ho. E15 —37Gc **65***
(off Manbey Pk. Rd.)
Maryland Pk. E15 —36Gc **65**
Maryland Rd. E15 —36Fc **65**
Maryland Rd. N22 —23Pb **42**
Maryland Rd. T Hth —67Rb **127**
Maryland Sq. E15 —36Gc **65**
Marylands Rd. W9 —42Cb **81**
Maryland St. E15 —36Fc **65**
*Maryland Wlk. N1 —39Sb **63***
(off Popham St.)
Maryland Way. Sun —68W **120**
Mary Lawrenson Pl. SE3 —52Jc **107**
Marylebone Fly-Over. W2 —43Gb **81**
Marylebone High St. W1 —43Jb **82** (7J **191**)
Marylebone La. W1 —43Jb **82** (1J **197**)
Marylebone M. W1 —43Kb **82** (1K **197**)
Marylebone Pas. W1 —44Lb **82** (2C **198**)
Marylebone Rd. NW1 —43Gb **81** (7E **190**)
Marylebone St. W1 —43Jb **82** (1J **197**)
Marylee Way. SE11 —49Pb **82** (6J **205**)
Mary Macarthur Ho. W6 —51Ab **102**
*Mary Macarthur Ho. Dag —34Cd **68***
(off Wythenshawe Rd.)
Mary Morgan Ct. Slou —3H **73**
Maryon Gro. SE7 —49Nc **86**
Maryon M. NW3 —35Gb **61**
Maryon Rd. SE7 —49Nc **86**
Maryon Rd. SE18 —49Nc **86**
Mary Peters Dri. Gnfd —36Fa **58**
Mary Pl. W11 —45Ab **80**
Mary Rose Clo. Hamp —67Ca **121**
Mary Rose Mall. E6 —43Pc **86**
Mary Rose Way. N20 —18Fb **23**
Mary Seacole Clo. E8 —39Vb **63**
Maryside. Slou —47A **74**
Mary's Ter. Twic —59Ja **100**
Mary St. E16 —43Hc **85**
Mary St. N1 —39Sb **63** (1E **194**)
Mary Ter. NW1 —39Kb **62** (1A **192**)
Maryville. Well —54Vc **109**
Marzena Ct. Houn —58Ea **100**
Masbro Rd. W14 —48Za **80**
Mascalls Gdns. Brtwd —21Vd **50**
Mascalls La. Gt War —21Vd **50**
Mascalls Rd. SE7 —51Lc **107**
Mascoll Path. Slou —1D **72**
Mascotte Rd. SW15 —56Za **102**
Mascotts Clo. NW2 —34Xa **60**
Masefield Av. Borwd —15Ra **21**
Masefield Av. S'hall —45Ca **77**
Masefield Av. Stan —22Ha **38**
Masefield Clo. Eri —53Hd **110**
Masefield Clo. Romf —25Ld **49**
Masefield Ct. Brtwd —21Yd **50**
Masefield Ct. New Bar —14Eb **23**
Masefield Ct. Surb —73Ma **143**
Masefield Cres. N14 —16Lb **24**
Masefield Cres. Romf —25Ld **49**
Masefield Dri. Upm —31Sd **70**
Masefield Gdns. E6 —42Qc **86**
Masefield La. Hay —42X **77**
Masefield Rd. Dart —57Rd **111**
Masefield Rd. Grav —62Fe **135**
Masefield Rd. Grays —7A **92**
Masefield Rd. Hamp —63Ba **121**
Masefield View. Orp —76Sc **150**
Masefield Way. Stai —60P **97**
Mashie Rd. W3 —44Ua **80**
Mashiters Hill. Romf —25Fd **48**
Mashiters Wlk. Romf —27Gd **48**
Maskall Clo. SW2 —60Qb **104**
Maskani Wlk. SW16 —66Lb **126**
Maskell Rd. SW17 —62Eb **125**
Maskelyne Clo. SW11 —53Gb **103**
Mason Clo. E16 —45Jc **85**
Mason Clo. SE16 —50Wb **83**
Mason Clo. Bexh —55Dd **110**
Mason Clo. Borwd —12Ta **21**
Mason Clo. Hamp —67Ca **121**
Mason Dri. H Wood —26Nd **49**
*Masonettes. Eps —82Sa **161***
(off Sefton Rd.)
Masonic Hall Rd. Cher —72H **139**
Mason Rd. Wfd G —21Gc **45**
Mason's Arms M. W1 —44Kb **82** (3A **198**)
Mason's Av. EC2 —44Tb **83** (2F **201**)
Masons Av. Croy —76Sb **147**
Masons Av. Harr —28Ha **38**
Masons Ct. Cipp —5C **72**
Masons Grn. La. W3 —42Qa **79**
Masons Hill. SE18 —49Rc **86**
Masons Hill. Brom —69Kc **129**
Mason's Pl. EC1 —41Sb **83** (3D **194**)
Masons Pl. Mitc —67Hb **125**
Masons Rd. Enf —8Xb **11**
Masons Rd. Slou —5C **72**
Mason St. SE17 —49Tb **83** (5G **207**)
Mason's Yd. SW1 —46Lb **82** (6C **198**)
Mason's Yd. SW19 —64Za **124**
Mason Way. Wal A —6Hc **13**
Massey Clo. N11 —22Kb **42**
Massie Rd. E8 —37Wb **63**
Massinger St. SE17 —49Ub **83** (6H **207**)
Massingham St. E1 —42Zb **84**
Masson Av. Ruis —37Y **57**
Master Clo. Oxt —100Gc **183**
Master Gunners Pl. SE18 —52Nc **108**
Masterman Rd. E6 —41Nc **86**
Master's St. E1 —43Zb **84**
Masthead Clo. Dart —56Sd **112**
Masthouse Ter. E14 —49Cc **84**
Mastmaker Ct. E14 —47Cc **84**
Mastmaker Rd. E14 —47Cc **84**
Maswell Pk. Cres. Houn —57Ea **100**
Maswell Pk. Rd. Houn —57Da **99**
Matcham Rd. E11 —34Gc **65**
Matchless Dri. SE18 —52Qc **108**
Matfield Clo. Brom —71Jc **149**
Matfield Rd. Belv —51Cd **110**
Matham Gro. SE22 —56Vb **105**
Matham Rd. E Mol —71Fa **142**
*Matheson Lang Ho. SE1 —47Qb **82** (2K **205**)*
(off Baylis Rd.)
Matheson Rd. W14 —49Bb **81**
Mathews Pk. Av. E15 —37Hc **65**
Mathias Clo. Eps —85Sa **161**
Mathisen Way. Coln —53G **96**
Matilda St. N1 —39Pb **62** (1J **193**)
Matlock Clo. SE24 —56Sb **105**
Matlock Cres. Sutt —77Ab **144**
Matlock Cres. Wat —20Y **19**
Matlock Gdns. Horn —34Nd **69**
Matlock Gdns. Sutt —77Ab **144**
Matlock Pl. Sutt —77Ab **144**
Matlock Rd. E10 —30Ec **44**
Matlock Rd. Cat —93Ub **181**
Matlock St. E14 —44Ac **84**
Matlock Way. N Mald —67Ta **123**

Matrimony Pl.—Melina Pl.

Matrimony Pl. SW4 —54Lb **104**
Matson Ct. E4 —24Gc **45**
Matthew Arnold Clo. Cob
—86W **158**
Matthew Clo. W10 —42Za **80**
Matthew Ct. E17 —27Ec **44**
Matthew Ct. Mitc —71Mb **146**
Matthew Parker St. SW1
—47Mb **82** (2E **204**)
Matthews Av. E6 —40Qc **66**
Matthews Clo. Romf —25Pd **49**
Matthews Gdns. New Ad —83Fc **167**
Matthews La. Stai —63H **119**
Matthews Rd. Gnfd —36Fa **58**
Matthews St. SW11 —54Hb **103**
Matthew St. SW1 —48Mb **82**
Matthews Wlk. E17 —25Cc 44
(off Chingford Rd.)
Matthews Yd. WC2
—44Nb **82** (3F **199**)
Matthias Rd. N16 —36Ub **63**
Mattingley Way. SE15 —52Vb 105
(off Longhope Clo.)
Mattison Rd. N4 —30Qb **42**
Mattock La. W13 & W5 —46Ka **78**
Maud Cashmore Way. SE18
—48Pc **86**
Maude Cres. Wat —10X **5**
Maude Rd. E17 —29Ac **44**
Maude Rd. SE5 —53Ub **105**
Maude Rd. Swan —65Jd **132**
Maude Ter. E17 —29Ac **44**
Maud Gdns. E13 —39Hc **65**
Maud Gdns. Bark —40Vc **67**
Maudlins Grn. E1 —46Wb **83**
Maud Rd. E10 —34Ec **64**
Maud Rd. E13 —40Hc **65**
Maudslay Rd. SE9 —55Pc **108**
Maudsley Ho. Bren —50Na **79**
Maud St. E16 —43Hc **85**
Maudsville Cotts. W7 —46Ga **78**
Mauleverer Rd. SW2 —57Nb **104**
Maundeby Wlk. NW10 —37Ua **60**
Maunder Rd. W7 —46Ha **78**
Maunsell St. SW1 —49Mb **82**
Maunsel St. SW1
—49Mb **82** (5D **204**)
Maureen Ct. Beck —68Yb **128**
Mauretania Building. E1 —45Zb 84
(off Jardine Rd.)
Maurice Av. N22 —26Rb **43**
Maurice Av. Cat —94Tb **181**
Maurice Brown Clo. NW7 —22Za **40**
Maurice Ct. Bren —52Ma **101**
Maurice St. W12 —44Xa **80**
Maurice Wlk. NW11 —28Eb **41**
Maurier Clo. N'holt —39Y **57**
Mauritius Rd. SE10 —49Gc **85**
Maury Rd. N16 —33Wb **63**
Mavelstone Clo. Brom —67Nc **130**
Mavelstone Rd. Brom —67Mc **129**
Maverton Rd. E3 —39Cc **64**
Mavis Av. Eps —78Ua **144**
Mavis Clo. Eps —78Ua **144**
Mavis Gro. Horn —33Nd **69**
Mavis Wlk. E6 —43Nc 86
(off Greenwich Cres.)
Mawbey Ho. SE1 —50Vb **83**
Mawbey Pl. SE1
—50Vb **83** (7K **207**)
Mawbey Rd. SE1
—50Vb **83** (7K **207**)
Mawbey Rd. Ott —79F **138**
Mawbey St. SW8 —52Nb **104**
Mawney Clo. Romf —26Dd **48**
Mawney Rd. Romf —26Dd **48**
Mawson Clo. SW20 —68Ab **124**
Mawson La. W4 —51Va **102**
Maxden Ct. SE15 —55Wb **105**
Maxey Gdns. Dag —35Ad **67**
Maxey Rd. SE18 —49Sc **86**
Maxey Rd. Dag —35Ad **67**
Maxfield Clo. N20 —17Eb **23**
Maxilla Wlk. W10 —44Za **80**
Maximfeldt Rd. Eri —50Gd **88**
Maxim Rd. N21 —16Qb **24**
Maxim Rd. Dart —57Gd **110**
Maxim Rd. Eri —49Fd **88**
Maxted Pk. Harr —31Ga **58**
Maxted Rd. SE15 —55Vb **105**
Maxwell Clo. Rick —19J **17**
Maxwell Ct. SW4 —57Mb **104**
Maxwell Dri. W Byf —83L **157**
Maxwell Gdns. Orp —76Vc **151**
Maxwell Rise. Wat —17Aa **19**
Maxwell Rd. SW6 —52Db **103**
Maxwell Rd. Ashf —65S **120**
Maxwell Rd. Borwd —13Ra **21**
Maxwell Rd. N'wd —24T **36**
Maxwell Rd. Well —55Vc **109**
Maxwell Rd. W Dray —49P **75**
Maxwelton Av. NW7 —22Ta **39**
Maxwelton Clo. NW7 —22Ta **39**
Maya Angelou Ct. E4 —21Ec **44**
Mayall Rd. SE24 —56Rb **105**
Maya Rd. N2 —28Eb **41**
May Av. Grav —10B **114**
May Av. Orp —71Xc **151**
May Av. Ind. Est. Grav —10B 114
(off May Av.)
Maybank Av. E18 —26Kc **45**
Maybank Av. Horn —36Kd **69**
Maybank Av. Wemb —36Ha **58**
Maybank Gdns. Pinn —29W **36**
Maybank Lodge. Horn —36Ld **69**
Maybank Rd. E18 —25Kc **45**
Maybells Commercial Est. Bark
—40Zc **67**
Mayberry Pl. Surb —73Pa **143**
Maybourne Clo. SE26 —65Xb **127**
Maybourne Rise. Wok —96A **172**
Maybrick Rd. Horn —30Ld **49**
Maybury Av. Chesh —1Xb **11**
Maybury Av. Dart —60Sd **112**
Maybury Clo. Orp —71Rc **150**
Maybury Clo. Slou —4B **72**
Maybury Clo. Tad —91Ab **178**
Maybury Ct. Harr —30Fa **38**
Maybury Est. Wok —88E **156**
Maybury Gdns. NW10 —37Xa **60**
Maybury Hill. Wok —88D **156**
Maybury M. N6 —31Lb **62**
Maybury Rd. E13 —42Lc **85**
Maybury Rd. Bark —40Vc **67**
Maybury Rd. Wok —89B **156**
Maybury St. SW17 —64Gb **125**
Maybush Rd. Horn —31Nd **69**
Maychurch Clo. Stan —24Ma **39**
May Clo. Chess —79Pa **143**
Maycock Gro. N'wd —23V **36**
May Ct. Grays —1A **114**
Maycroft. Pinn —26X **37**
Maycroft Av. Grays —50Fe **91**
Maycroft Gdns. Grays —50Fe **91**
Maycross Av. Mord —70Bb **125**
Mayday Gdns. SE3 —54Nc **108**
Mayday Rd. T Hth —72Rb **147**
Maydwell Lodge. Borwd —12Pa **21**
Mayell Clo. Lea —95La **176**
Mayerne Rd. SE9 —57Mc **107**
Mayesbrook Rd. Bark —39Vc **67**
Mayesbrook Rd. Ilf & Dag
—34Wc **67**
Mayes Clo. Swan —70Jd **132**
Mayes Clo. Warl —90Zb **166**
Mayesford Rd. Romf —31Yc **67**
Mayes Rd. N22 —26Pb **42**
Mayeswood Rd. SE12 —63Lc **129**
Mayfair. Crox —15T **18**
Mayfair Av. Bexh —53Zc **109**
Mayfair Av. Ilf —33Pc **66**
Mayfair Av. Romf —30Zc **47**
Mayfair Av. Twic —59Ea **100**
Mayfair Av. Wor Pk —74Wa **144**
Mayfair Clo. Beck —67Dc **128**
Mayfair Clo. Surb —74Na **143**
Mayfair Gdns. N17 —23Sb **43**
Mayfair Gdns. Wfd G —24Jc **45**
Mayfair M. NW1 —38Hb 61
(off Regents Pk. Rd.)
Mayfair Pl. W1 —46Kb **82** (6A **198**)
Mayfair Rd. Dart —57Md **111**
Mayfair Ter. N14 —17Mb **24**
Mayfield. Bexh —55Bd **109**
Mayfield. Wal A —6Fc **13**
Mayfield Av. N12 —21Eb **41**
Mayfield Av. N14 —19Mb **24**
Mayfield Av. W4 —49Ua **80**
Mayfield Av. W13 —48Ka **78**
Mayfield Av. Harr —29Ka **38**
Mayfield Av. New Haw —82K **157**
Mayfield Av. Orp —74Vc **151**
Mayfield Av. Wfd G —23Jc **45**
Mayfield Caravan Pk. W Dray
—48L **75**
Mayfield Clo. E8 —37Vb **63**
Mayfield Clo. SE20 —67Xb **127**
Mayfield Clo. SW4 —57Mb **104**
Mayfield Clo. Ashf —65R **120**
Mayfield Clo. New Haw —82L **157**
Mayfield Clo. Th Dit —74Ka **142**
Mayfield Clo. Uxb —41R **76**
Mayfield Clo. W on T —77W **140**
Mayfield Cres. N9 —16Xb **25**
Mayfield Cres. T Hth —70Pb **126**
Mayfield Dri. Pinn —28Ba **37**
Mayfield Gdns. NW4 —30Za **40**
Mayfield Gdns. W7 —44Fa **78**
Mayfield Gdns. Brtwd —18Xd **32**
Mayfield Gdns. Stai —65H **119**
Mayfield Gdns. W on T —77W **140**
Mayfield Rd. E4 —19Ec **26**
Mayfield Rd. E8 —38Vb **63**
Mayfield Rd. E13 —42Hc **85**
Mayfield Rd. E17 —26Ac **44**
Mayfield Rd. N8 —29Pb **42**
Mayfield Rd. SW19 —67Bb **125**
Mayfield Rd. W3 —45Ra **79**
Mayfield Rd. W12 —47Ua **80**
Mayfield Rd. Belv —49Ed **88**
Mayfield Rd. Brom —71Nc **150**
Mayfield Rd. Dag —32Yc **67**
Mayfield Rd. Enf —12Zb **26**
Mayfield Rd. Grav —9B **114**
Mayfield Rd. S Croy —81Tb **165**
Mayfield Rd. Sutt —79Fb **145**
Mayfield Rd. T Hth —70Pb **126**
Mayfield Rd. W on T —77W **140**
Mayfield Rd. Wey —78P **139**
Mayfield Rd. Flats. N8 —30Pb **42**
Mayfields. Grays —47Ee **91**
Mayfields. Swans —58Ae **113**
Mayfields. Wemb —33Qa **59**
Mayfields Clo. Wemb —33Qa **59**
Mayflower Clo. SE16 —49Zb **84**
Mayflower Clo. Ruis —30S **36**
Mayflower Clo. S Ock —42Yd **90**
Mayflower Ct. SE16 —47Xb **83**
Mayflower Ct. Bark —39Tc **66**
Mayflower Ho. Gt War —23Yd **50**
Mayflower Path. Gt War —23Yd **50**
Mayflower Rd. SW9 —55Nb **104**
Mayflower St. SE16 —47Yb **84**
Mayflower Way. Farn C —6G **52**
Mayfly Clo. Eastc —31Y **57**
Mayfly Gdns. N'holt —41Z **77**
Mayford Clo. SW12 —59Hb **103**
Mayford Clo. Beck —69Zb **128**
Mayford Clo. Wok —10G **188**
Mayford Rd. SW12 —59Hb **103**
May Gdns. Wemb —41La **78**
Maygoods Clo. Uxb —43M **75**
Maygoods Grn. Uxb —43M **75**
Maygoods La. Uxb —43M **75**
Maygood St. N1
—40Qb **62** (1J **193**)
Maygoods View. Cow —43L **75**
Maygreen Cres. Horn —31Jd **68**
Maygrove Rd. NW6 —37Bb **61**
Mayhew Clo. E4 —20Cc **26**
Mayhew Ct. SE5 —56Tb **105**
Mayhill Rd. SE7 —51Kc **107**
Mayhill Rd. Barn —16Ab **22**
Mayhurst Av. Wok —88E **156**
Mayhurst Clo. Wok —88E **156**
Mayhurst Cres. Wok —88E **156**
Mayland Mans. Bark —38Rc 66
(off Whiting Av.)
Maylands Av. Horn —35Kd **69**
Maylands Dri. Sidc —62Zc **131**
Maylands Dri. Uxb —37M **55**
Maylands Rd. Wat —21Y **37**
Maylands Way. Romf —23Sd **50**
Maynard Clo. N15 —29Ub **43**
Maynard Clo. SW6 —52Db **103**
Maynard Clo. Eri —52Hd **110**
Maynard Ct. Stai —63J **119**
Maynard Ct. Wal A —6Hc **13**
Maynard Path. E17 —29Ec **44**
Maynard Pl. Cuff —1Pb **10**
Maynard Rd. E17 —29Ec **44**
Maynards. Horn —31Nd **69**
Maynards Quay. E1 —45Yb **84**
Maynooth Gdns. Cars —73Hb **145**
Mayo Clo. Chesh —1Yb **12**
Mayo Ct. W13 —48Ka **78**
Mayola Rd. E5 —35Yb **64**
Mayor Ho. N1 —39Pb 62 (1J 193)
(off Barnsbury Est.)
Mayo Rd. NW10 —37Ua **60**
Mayo Rd. Croy —71Tb **147**
Mayo Rd. W on T —73V **140**
Mayor's La. Dart —63Ld **133**
Mayow Rd. SE26 & SE23
—63Zb **128**
Mayplace Av. Dart —56Jd **110**
Mayplace Clo. Bexh —55Dd **110**
Mayplace La. SE18 —52Rc **108**
Mayplace Rd. E. Bexh & Dart
—55Dd **110**
Mayplace Rd. W. Bexh —56Cd **110**
Maypole Cres. Eri —51Md **111**
Maypole Cres. Ilf —24Tc **46**
Maypole Dri. Chig —20Wc **29**
Maypole Rd. Grav —10H **115**
Maypole Rd. Orp —78Bd **151**
May Rd. E4 —23Cc **44**
May Rd. E13 —40Jc **65**
May Rd. Dart —63Pd **133**
May Rd. Twic —60Ga **100**
Mayroyd Av. Surb —75Qa **143**
May's Bldgs. M. SE10 —52Fc **107**
May's Ct. SE10 —52Fc **107**
Mays Ct. WC2 —45Nb **82** (5F **199**)
Maysfield Rd. Send —95F **172**
Mays Gro. Send —95F **172**
Mays Hill Rd. Brom —68Gc **129**
Mays La. Barn —17Xa **22**
Maysoule Rd. SW11 —56Fb **103**
Mays Rd. Tedd —64Fa **122**
May St. W14 —50Bb **81**
Mayswood Gdns. Dag —37Ed **68**
Maythorne Clo. Wat —14U **18**
Mayton St. N7 —34Pb **62**
Maytree Clo. Edgw —20Sa **21**
Maytree Clo. Rain —40Gd **68**
Maytree Ct. N'holt —41Aa **77**
Maytree Cres. Wat —7V **4**
Maytree La. Stan —24Ja **38**
Maytrees. Rad —9Ja **6**
Maytree Wlk. SW2 —61Qb **126**
Mayville Est. N16 —36Ub **63**
Mayville Rd. E11 —33Gc **65**
Mayville Rd. Ilf —36Rc **66**
May Wlk. E13 —40Kc **65**
Mayward Ho. SE5 —53Ub 105
(off Peckham Rd.)
Maywater Clo. S Croy —83Tb **165**
Maywin Dri. Horn —32Pd **69**
Maywood Clo. Beck —66Dc **128**
Maze Hill. SE10 & SE3 —51Gc **107**
Mazenod Av. NW6 —38Cb **61**
Maze Rd. Rich —52Qa **101**
Mead Av. Slou —47D **74**
Mead Clo. Den —33J **55**
Mead Clo. Egh —65D **118**
Mead Clo. Grays —47De **91**
Mead Clo. Harr —25Fa **38**
Mead Clo. Romf —26Jd **48**
Mead Clo. Slou —47D **74**
Mead Clo. Swan —71Jd **152**
Mead Ct. NW9 —29Sa **39**
Mead Ct. Knap —4B **188**
Mead Ct. Wal A —6Dc **12**
Mead Cres. E4 —21Ec **44**
Mead Cres. Bookh —97Ca **175**
Mead Cres. Dart —60Md **111**
Mead Cres. Sutt —76Gb **145**
Meadcroft Rd. SE11 —51Rb **105**
(in two parts)
Meade Clo. W4 —51Qa **101**
Mead End. Asht —89Pa **161**
Meader Ct. SE14 —52Zb **106**
Meades, The. Wey —79S **140**
Meadfield. Edgw —19Ra **21**
Mead Field. Harr —34Ba **57**
Meadfield Av. Slou —47C **74**
Meadfield Grn. Edgw —19Ra **21**
Meadfield Rd. Slou —48C **74**
Meadfoot Rd. SW16 —66Lb **126**
Meadgate Av. Wfd G —22Nc **46**
Mead Gro. Romf —27Zc **47**
Mead Ho. La. Hay —42T **76**
Meadhurst Rd. Cher —74K **139**
Meadlands Dri. Rich —61Ma **123**
Mead La. Cher —73K **139**
Mead La. Caravan Pk. Cher
—74L **139**
Mead Lodge. W4 —47Ta **79**
Meadow Av. Croy —72Zb **148**
Meadow Bank. N21 —16Pb **24**
Meadowbank. NW3 —38Hb **61**
Meadow Bank. SE3 —55Hc **107**
Meadow Bank. E Hor —99V **174**
Meadowbank. K Lan —2Q **4**
Meadowbank. Surb —72Pa **143**
Meadowbank. Wat —17Y **19**
Meadowbank Clo. SW6 —52Ya **102**
Meadowbank Clo. Barn —15Wa **22**
Meadow Bank Clo. W King
—80Vd **154**
Meadowbank Gdns. Houn —53X **99**
Meadowbank Rd. NW9 —31Ta **59**
Meadow Brook Clo. Coln —53H **97**
Meadow Clo. E4 —18Dc **26**
Meadow Clo. SE6 —64Cc **128**
Meadow Clo. SW20 —70Ya **124**
Meadow Clo. Barn —16Bb **23**
Meadow Clo. Brick —1Ca **5**
Meadow Clo. Chst —64Rc **130**
Meadow Clo. Enf —10Ac **12**
Meadow Clo. Esh —76Ha **142**
Meadow Clo. Houn —59Ca **99**
Meadow Clo. Linf —8J **93**
Meadow Clo. N'holt —40Ca **57**
Meadow Clo. Old Win —7M **95**
Meadow Clo. Purl —85Mb **164**
Meadow Clo. Rich —60Na **101**
Meadow Clo. Ruis —30V **36**
Meadow Clo. Sev —95Jd **186**
Meadow Clo. Sutt —75Eb **145**
Meadow Clo. W on T —77Ba **141**
Meadow Ct. Eps —85Sa **161**
Meadow Ct. Houn —58Fa **100**
Meadow Ct. Stai —62G **118**
Meadowcourt Rd. SE3 —56Hc **107**
Meadowcroft. W4 —50Qa 79
(off Brooks La.)
Meadowcroft. Brom —69Pc **130**
Meadowcroft. Bush —16Da 19
(off High St. Bushey)
Meadowcroft. Ger X —26A **34**
Meadowcroft Clo. N13 —19Qb **24**
Meadowcroft Rd. N13 —19Qb **24**
Meadow Dri. N10 —27Kb **42**
Meadow Dri. NW4 —26Ya **40**
Meadow Dri. Rip —95H **173**
Meadow Gdns. Edgw —23Ra **39**
Meadow Gdns. Stai —64F **118**
Meadow Garth. NW10 —37Sa **59**
Meadow Hill. N Mald —72Ua **144**
Meadow Hill. Purl —86Lb **164**
Meadowlands. Cob —85W **158**
Meadowlands. Horn —31Nd **69**
Meadowlands. Seal —92Pd **187**
Meadowlands Caravan Pk. Add
—76N **139**
Meadow La. Eton —1F **94**
Meadow La. Fet —94Ea **176**
Meadow La. New Ash —75Be **155**
Meadow La. Stai —63H **119**
Meadow Mead. Rad —5Ha **6**
Meadow M. SW8 —51Pb **104**
Meadow Pl. SW8 —52Nb **104**
Meadow Pl. W4 —52Ua **102**
Meadow Rise. Coul —85Mb **164**
Meadow Rise. Knap —5A **188**
Meadow Rd. SW8 —52Pb **104**
Meadow Rd. SW19 —67Eb **125**
Meadow Rd. Ashf —64T **120**
Meadow Rd. Asht —89Na **161**
Meadow Rd. Bark —38Vc **67**
Meadow Rd. Borwd —12Ra **21**
Meadow Rd. Brom —67Gc **129**
Meadow Rd. Bush —15Da **19**
Meadow Rd. Clay —79Ga **142**
Meadow Rd. Dag —37Bd **67**
Meadow Rd. Epp —1Vc **15**
Meadow Rd. Felt —61Aa **121**
Meadow Rd. Grav —1C **136**
Meadow Rd. Grays —46Ee **91**
Meadow Rd. Lou —15Nc **28**
Meadow Rd. N'fleet —60Ee **113**
Meadow Rd. Pinn —28Z **37**
Meadow Rd. Romf —32Ed **68**
Meadow Rd. Slou —48A **74**
Meadow Rd. S'hall —45Ba **77**
Meadow Rd. Sutt —77Gb **145**
Meadow Rd. Vir W —10J **117**
Meadow Rd. Wat —6W **4**
Meadow Row. SE1
—48Sb **83** (4D **206**)
Meadows Clo. E10 —33Cc **64**
Meadows Ct. Ingve —23Ee **51**
Meadows Ct. Sidc —65Xc **131**
Meadows End. Sun —67W **120**
Meadowside. SE9 —56Lc **107**
Meadowside. Bookh —95Ca **175**
Meadowside. Dart —60Nd **111**
Meadowside. Twic —59Ma **101**
Meadowside. W on T —75Y **141**
Meadowside Rd. Sutt —81Ab **162**
Meadowside Rd. Upm —36Sd **70**
Meadows Leigh Clo. Wey —76S **140**
Meadows, The. Hals —85Bd **169**
Meadows, The. Ingve —23Ee **51**
Meadows, The. Orp —79Yc **151**
Meadows, The. Warl —89Zb **166**
Meadow Stile. Croy —76Sb **147**
Meadowsweet Clo. E16 —43Mc **85**
Meadow, The. N10 —27Kb **42**
Meadow, The. Chst —65Sc **130**
Meadow View. Harr —32Ga **58**
Meadow View. Orp —69Yc **131**
Meadow View. Sev —90Fd **170**
Meadow View. Sidc —59Xc **109**
Meadowview. Stai —57J **97**
Meadowview Rd. SE6 —64Bc **128**
Meadowview Rd. Bex —58Ad **109**
Meadowview Rd. Eps —81Ua **162**
Meadow View Rd. Hay —42T **76**
Meadow View Rd. T Hth
—71Rb **147**
Meadow Wlk. E18 —28Jc **45**
Meadow Wlk. Dag —37Bd **67**
Meadow Wlk. Dart —63Ld **133**
Meadow Wlk. Eps —79Ua **144**
Meadow Wlk. Tad —96Xa **178**
Meadow Wlk. Wall —76Kb **146**
Meadow Way. NW9 —29Ta **39**
Meadow Way. Add —77K **139**
Meadow Way. Bookh —95Da **175**
Meadow Way. Chess —78Na **143**
Meadow Way. Chig —20Sc **28**
Meadow Way. Dart —59Sd **112**
Meadow Way. K Lan —2Q **4**
Meadow Way. Old Win —8M **95**
Meadow Way. Orp —76Qc **150**
Meadow Way. Pot B —6Cb **9**
Meadow Way. Rick —17L **17**
Meadow Way. Ruis —30X **37**
Meadow Way. Tad —89Ab **162**
Meadow Way. Upm —34Sd **70**
Meadow Way. Wemb —35Ma **59**
Meadow Way. W Hor —97T **174**
Meadow Waye. Houn —51Aa **99**
Meadow Way, The. Harr —25Ga **38**
Mead Path. SW17 —63Eb **125**
Mead Pl. E9 —37Yb **64**
Mead Pl. Croy —74Sb **147**
Mead Pl. Rick —18K **17**
Mead Plat. NW10 —37Sa **59**
Mead Rd. Cat —95Vb **181**
Mead Rd. Chst —65Sc **130**
Mead Rd. Dart —60Md **111**
Mead Rd. Edgw —23Qa **39**
Mead Rd. Grav —1D **136**
Mead Rd. Rich —62La **122**
Mead Rd. Shenl —5Qa **7**
Mead Rd. Uxb —38M **55**
Mead Rd. W on T —77Aa **141**
Mead Row. SE1
—48Qb **82** (3K **205**)
Meads Ct. E15 —37Hc **65**
Meads La. Ilf —31Uc **66**
Meads Rd. N22 —26Rb **43**
Meads Rd. Enf —11Ac **26**
Meads, The. Brick —2Ca **5**
Meads, The. Edgw —23Ta **39**
Meads, The. Sutt —76Ab **144**
Meads, The. Upm —33Ud **70**
Meads, The. Uxb —42N **75**
Meadsway. Gt War —23Xd **50**
Mead Ter. Wemb —35Ma **59**
Mead, The. N2 —26Eb **41**
Mead, The. W13 —43Ka **78**
Mead, The. Abr —13Xc **29**
Mead, The. Asht —91Na **177**
Mead, The. Beck —67Ec **128**
Mead, The. Chesh —1Yb **12**
Mead, The. New Ash —75Ae **155**
Mead, The. Uxb —33Q **56**
Mead, The. Wall —79Mb **146**
Mead, The. Wat —20Aa **19**
Mead, The. W Wick —74Fc **149**
Meadvale Rd. W5 —42Ka **78**
Meadvale Rd. Croy —73Vb **147**
Mead Wlk. Slou —51D **96**
Meadway. N14 —19Mb **24**
Meadway. NW11 —30Cb **41**
Mead Way. SW20 —70Ya **124**
Meadway. Ashf —63Q **120**
Meadway. Barn —14Cb **23**
Meadway. Beck —67Ec **128**
Mead Way. Brom —72Hc **149**
Mead Way. Bush —12Aa **19**
Mead Way. Coul —90Nb **164**
Mead Way. Croy —75Ac **148**
Meadway. Eff —100Aa **175**
Meadway. Enf —8Yb **12**
Meadway. Eps —84Sa **161**
Meadway. Esh —81Da **159**
Meadway. Grays —49Fe **91**
Mead Way. Guild —100E **172**
Meadway. Hals —85Bd **169**
Meadway. Ilf —35Uc **66**
Meadway. Oxs —86Ga **160**
Meadway. Romf —26Jd **48**
Mead Way. Ruis —30T **36**
Mead Way. Slou —3B **72**
Meadway. Stai —66J **119**
Meadway. Surb —74Sa **143**
Meadway. Twic —60Fa **100**
Meadway. Warl —88Yb **166**
Mead Way. Wfd G —22Lc **45**
Meadway Clo. NW11 —30Db **41**
Meadway Clo. Barn —13Cb **23**
Meadway Clo. Pinn —23Da **37**
Meadway Clo. Stai —66H **119**
Meadway Ct. NW11 —30Db **41**
Meadway Ct. W5 —42Pa **79**
Meadway Ct. Dag —33Bd **67**
Meadway Ct. Tedd —64La **122**
Meadway Dri. Add —80L **139**
Meadway Dri. Wok —4F **188**
Meadway Gdns. Ruis —30T **36**
Meadway Ga. NW11 —30Cb **41**
Meadway Pk. Ger X —2P **53**
Meadway, The. SE3 —54Fc **107**
Meadway, The. Buck H —18Mc **27**
Meadway, The. Cuff —1Pb **10**
Meadway, The. Lou —16Pc **28**
Meadway, The. Orp —79Xc **151**
Meadway, The. Sev —94Hd **186**
Meaford Way. SE20 —66Xb **127**
Meakin Est. SE1
—48Ub **83** (3H **207**)
Meanley Rd. E12 —35Nc **66**
Meard St. W1 —44Mb **82** (3D **198**)
Meare Clo. Tad —95Ya **178**
Meath Clo. Orp —71Yc **151**
Meath Rd. E15 —40Hc **65**
Meath Rd. Ilf —34Sc **66**
Meath St. SW11 —53Kb **104**
Mechanics Path. SE8 —52Cc **106**
Mecklenburgh Pl. WC1
—42Pb **82** (5H **193**)
Mecklenburgh Sq. WC1
—42Pb **82** (5H **193**)
Mecklenburgh St. WC1
—42Pb **82** (5H **193**)
Medburn St. NW1
—40Mb **62** (1D **192**)
Medbury Rd. Grav —10H **115**
Medcalf Rd. Enf —9Bc **12**
Medcroft Gdns. SW14 —56Sa **101**
Medebourne Clo. SE3 —55Jc **107**
Medebridge Rd. Grays —45Be **91**
Mede Clo. Wray —10P **95**
Mede Ct. Stai —62G **118**
Mede Field. Fet —96Fa **176**
Medesenge Way. N13 —23Rb **43**
Medfield St. SW15 —59Wa **102**
Medhurst Clo. E3 —40Ac **64**
Medhurst Cres. Grav —1H **137**
Medhurst Gdns. Grav —2H **137**
Median Rd. E5 —36Yb **64**
Medlar Ct. Slou —6N **73**
Medick Ct. Grays —1A **114**
Medina Av. Esh —76Ga **142**
Medina Gro. N7 —34Qb **62**
Medina Ho. Eri —52Gd **110**
Medina Rd. N7 —34Qb **62**
Medina Rd. Grays —50Fe **91**
Medlake Rd. Egh —65E **118**
Medland Clo. Wall —74Jb **146**
Medlar Clo. N'holt —40Z **57**
Medlar Ho. Sidc —62Wc **131**
Medlar Rd. Grays —51Fe **113**
Medlar St. SE5 —53Sb **105**
Medley Rd. NW6 —37Cb **61**
Medman Clo. Uxb —40L **55**
Medmenham. Cars —83Fb 163
(off Pine Cres.)
Medora Rd. SW2 —59Pb **104**
Medora Rd. Romf —28Fd **48**
Medusa Rd. SE6 —58Dc **106**
Medway Clo. Croy —72Yb **148**
Medway Clo. Ilf —36Sc **66**
Medway Clo. Wat —6Y **5**
Medway Dri. Gnfd —40Ha **58**
Medway Gdns. Wemb —35Ja **58**
Medway M. E3 —40Ac **64**
Medway Pde. Gnfd —40Ha **58**
Medway Rd. E3 —40Ac **64**
Medway Rd. Dart —55Jd **110**
Medway St. SW1
—48Mb **82** (4D **204**)
Medwin St. SW4 —56Pb **104**
Meek Clo. E8 —39Xb **63**
Meerbrook Rd. SE3 —55Lc **107**
Meeson Rd. E15 —39Hc **65**
Meesons La. Grays —49Be **91**
Meeson St. E5 —35Ac **64**
Meeting All. Wat —14Y **19**
Meeting Field Path. E9 —37Yb **64**
Meetinghouse All. E1 —46Xb **83**
Meeting Ho. La. SE15 —53Xb **105**
Megg La. Chfd —1K **3**
Mehetabel Rd. E9 —37Yb **64**
Meister Clo. Ilf —32Tc **66**
Melancholy Wlk. Rich —61La **122**
Melanda Clo. Chst —64Pc **130**
Melanie Clo. Bexh —53Ad **109**
Melba Gdns. Til —2C **114**
Melba Way. SE13 —53Dc **106**
Melbourne Av. N13 —23Pb **42**
Melbourne Av. W13 —46Ja **78**
Melbourne Av. Pinn —27Da **37**
Melbourne Av. Slou —4G **72**
Melbourne Clo. SE20 —66Wb **127**
Melbourne Clo. Orp —73Uc **150**
Melbourne Clo. Uxb —35Q **56**
Melbourne Clo. Wall —78Lb **146**
Melbourne Ct. N10 —24Kb **42**
Melbourne Ct. Grav —7D **114**
Melbourne Gdns. Romf —29Ad **47**
Melbourne Gro. SE22 —56Ub **105**
Melbourne M. SE6 —59Ec **106**
Melbourne M. SW9 —53Qb **104**
Melbourne Pl. WC2
—44Pb **82** (4J **199**)
Melbourne Rd. E6 —40Pc **66**
Melbourne Rd. E10 —31Dc **64**
Melbourne Rd. E17 —28Ac **44**
Melbourne Rd. SW19 —67Cb **125**
Melbourne Rd. Bush —16Da **19**
Melbourne Rd. Ilf —32Rc **66**
Melbourne Rd. Tedd —65La **122**
Melbourne Rd. Til —3A **114**
Melbourne Rd. Wall —78Kb **146**
Melbourne Sq. SW9 —53Qb **104**
Melbourne Way. Enf —16Vb **25**
Melbury Av. S'hall —48Da **77**
Melbury Clo. Cher —73J **139**
Melbury Clo. Chst —65Pc **130**
Melbury Clo. Clay —79Ka **142**
Melbury Clo. W Byf —86J **157**
Melbury Ct. W8 —48Bb **81**
Melbury Dri. SE5 —52Ub **105**
Melbury Gdns. SW20 —67Wa **124**
Melbury Rd. W14 —48Bb **81**
Melbury Rd. Harr —29Pa **39**
Melbury Ter. NW1
—42Gb **81** (6E **190**)
Melchester Ho. N19 —34Mb 62
(off Wedmore St.)
Melcombe Gdns. Harr —30Pa **39**
Melcombe Pl. NW1
—43Hb **81** (7F **191**)
Melcombe St. NW1
—42Hb **81** (6G **191**)
Meldon Clo. SW6 —53Db **103**
Meldrum Clo. Orp —72Yc **151**
Meldrum Rd. Ilf —33Wc **67**
Melfield Gdns. SE6 —63Ec **128**
Melford Av. Bark —37Uc **66**
Melford Clo. Chess —78Pa **143**
Melford Ct. SE22 —60Wb **105**
Melford Rd. E6 —41Pc **86**
Melford Rd. E11 —33Gc **65**
Melford Rd. E17 —28Ac **44**
Melford Rd. SE22 —59Wb **105**
Melford Rd. Ilf —33Tc **66**
Melfort Av. T Hth —69Rb **127**
Melfort Rd. T Hth —69Rb **127**
Melgund Rd. N5 —36Qb **62**
Melina Clo. Hay —43T **76**
Melina Ct. SW15 —55Wa **102**
Melina Pl. NW8 —41Fb **81** (4B **190**)

Melina Rd.—Mill Grn. Rd.

Melina Rd. W12 —47Xa 80
Melior Ct. N6 —30Lb 42
Melior Pl. SE1 —47Ub 83
Melior St. SE1 —47Ub 83 (1H 207)
Meliot Rd. SE6 —61Fc 129
Melksham Clo. H Hill —24Pd 49
Melksham Dri. Romf —24Pd 49
Melksham Gdns. Romf —24Nd 49
Melksham Grn. Romf —24Pd 49
Meller Clo. Croy —76Nb 146
Melling St. SE18 —51Uc 108
Mellish Clo. Bark —39Vc 67
Mellish Gdns. Wfd G —22Jc 45
Mellish Ind. Est. SE18 —48Mc 85
Mellish St. E14 —48Cc 84
Mellison Rd. SW17 —64Gb 125
Mellitus St. W12 —43Va 80
Mellor Clo. W on T —73Ba 141
Mellor Pl. SE1 —47Ub 83 (1H 207)
Mellow Clo. Bans —86Db 163
Mellow La. E. Hay —42S 76
Mellow La. W. Uxb —41S 76
Mellows Rd. Ilf —27Pc 46
Mellows Rd. Wall —78Mb 146
Mells Cres. SE9 —63Pc 130
Mell St. SE10 —50Gc 85
Melody Rd. SW18 —57Eb 103
Melody Rd. Big H —90Lc 167
Melon Pl. W8 —47Cb 81
Melon Rd. SE15 —53Wb 105
Melrose Av. N22 —25Rb 43
Melrose Av. NW2 —36Xa 60
Melrose Av. SW16 —69Qb 126
Melrose Av. SW19 —61Bb 125
Melrose Av. Borwd —15Ra 21
Melrose Av. Gnfd —40Da 57
Melrose Av. Mitc —66Kb 126
Melrose Av. Pot B —4Cb 9
Melrose Av. Twic —59Da 99
Melrose Clo. SE12 —60Jc 107
Melrose Clo. Gnfd —40Da 57
Melrose Clo. Hay —43W 76
Melrose Ct. Chesh —1Zb 12
(off Hatton Rd.)
Melrose Cres. Orp —77Tc 150
Melrose Dri. S'hall —46Ca 77
Melrose Gdns. W6 —48Ya 80
Melrose Gdns. Edgw —27Ra 39
Melrose Gdns. N Mald —69Ta 123
Melrose Gdns. W on T —78Y 141
Melrose Pl. Wat —10V 4
Melrose Rd. SW13 —54Va 102
Melrose Rd. SW18 —58Bb 103
Melrose Rd. SW19 —67Cb 125
Melrose Rd. W3 —48Sa 79
Melrose Rd. Big H —88Lc 167
Melrose Rd. Coul —87Kb 164
Melrose Rd. Pinn —28Ba 37
Melrose Rd. Wey —78Q 140
Melrose Ter. W6 —48Ya 80
Melrose Tudor. Wall —78Nb 146
(off Plough La.)
Melsa Rd. Mord —72Eb 145
Melstock Av. Upm —35Sd 70
Meltham Way. SE16 —50Xb 83
Melthorne Dri. Ruis —34Y 57
Melthorpe Gdns. SE3 —53Nc 108
Melton Clo. Ruis —32Y 57
Melton Ct. SW7 —49Fb 81 (6C 202)
Melton Ct. Sutt —80Eb 145
Melton Fields. Eps —81Ta 161
Melton Gdns. Romf —31Hd 68
Melton Pl. Eps —81Ta 161
Melton St. NW1 —41Lb 82 (4C 192)
Melville Av. SW20 —66Wa 124
Melville Av. Gnfd —36Ha 58
Melville Av. S Croy —78Vb 147
Melville Clo. Uxb —33T 56
Melville Ct. SE8 —49Ac 84
Melville Ct. W12 —47Xa 80
(off Goldhawk Rd.)
Melville Ct. H Hill —24Nd 49
Melville Ct. N'wd —23T 36
Melville Gdns. N13 —22Rb 43
Melville Ho. SE10 —53Ec 106
Melville Ho. New Bar —15Fb 23
Melville Rd. E17 —27Bc 44
Melville Rd. NW10 —38Ta 59
Melville Rd. SW13 —53Wa 102
Melville Rd. Rain —42Jd 88
Melville Rd. Romf —24Dd 48
Melville Rd. Sidc —61Yc 131
Melville St. N1 —38Sb 63
Melvin Rd. SE20 —67Yb 128
Melvinshaw. Lea —93La 176
Melyn Clo. N7 —35Lb 62
Memel Ct. EC1 —42Sb 83 (6D 194)
(off Memel St.)
Memel St. EC1 —42Sb 83 (6D 194)
Memess Path. SE18 —51Qc 108
Memorial Av. E15 —41Gc 85
Memorial Clo. Houn —51Ba 99
Mendip Clo. SE26 —63Yb 128
Mendip Clo. SW19 —61Ab 124
Mendip Clo. Hay —52T 98
Mendip Clo. Slou —50C 74
Mendip Clo. Wor Pk —75Ya 144
Mendip Dri. NW2 —33Ab 60
Mendip Houses. E2 —41Yb 84
(off Welwyn St.)
Mendip Rd. SW11 —55Eb 103
Mendip Rd. Bexh —53Gd 110
Mendip Rd. Bush —16Ea 20
Mendip Rd. Horn —31Jd 68
Mendip Rd. Ilf —29Uc 46
Mendora Rd. SW6 —52Ab 102
Mendoza Clo. Horn —29Nd 49
Menelik Rd. NW2 —35Ab 60
Menlo Gdns. SE19 —66Tb 127
Menlo Lodge. N13 —20Pb 24
(off Crothall Clo.)
Menotti St. E2 —42Wb 83
Menthone Pl. Horn —31Md 69
Mentmore Clo. Harr —30La 38
Mentmore Ter. E8 —38Xb 63
Meon Clo. Tad —94Xa 178
Meon Ct. Iswth —54Ga 100
Meon Rd. W3 —47Sa 79
Meopham Rd. Mitc —67Lb 126
Mepham Cres. Harr —24Ea 38
Mepham Gdns. Harr —24Ea 38
Mepham St. SE1
—46Pb 82 (7J 199)
Mera Dri. Bexh —56Cd 110
Merantun Way. SW19 —67Db 125
Merbury Clo. SE13 —57Fc 107
Merbury Rd. SE28 —47Uc 86
Mercator Rd. SE13 —56Fc 107
Mercer Clo. Th Dit —73Ja 142
Merceron Houses. E2 —41Yb 84
(off Globe Rd.)
Merceron St. E1 —42Xb 83
Mercer Pl. Pinn —26Y 37
Mercers Clo. SE10 —49Hc 85
Mercers Pl. W6 —49Ya 80
Mercers Rd. N19 —34Mb 62
Mercer St. WC2 —44Nb 82 (3F 199)
Mercer Wlk. Uxb —38L 55
Merchant Ind. Est. NW10 —42Sa 79
Merchant St. E3 —41Bc 84
Merchiston Rd. SE6 —61Fc 129
Merchland Rd. SE9 —60Sc 108
Mercia Gro. SE13 —56Ec 106
Mercian Way. Slou —6B 72
Mercia Wlk. Wok —89B 156
Mercier Rd. SW15 —57Ab 102
Mercury. NW9 —25Va 40
(off Concourse, The)
Mercury Cen. Felt —57W 98
Mercury Gdns. Romf —29Gd 48
Mercury Ho. Bren —51La 100
(off Glenhurst Rd.)
Mercury Rd. Bren —51La 100
Mercury Way. SE14 —51Zb 106
Mercy Ter. SE13 —57Dc 106
Merebank La. Croy —78Pb 146
Mere Clo. SW15 —59Za 102
Mere Clo. Orp —75Qc 150
Meredith Av. NW2 —36Ya 60
Meredith Clo. Pinn —24Z 37
Meredith Ho. N16 —36Ub 63
Meredith Rd. Grays —9C 92
Meredith St. E13 —41Jc 85
Meredith St. EC1
—41Rb 83 (4B 194)
Meredyth Rd. SW13 —54Wa 102
Mere End. Croy —73Zb 148
Merefield Gdns. Tad —91Za 178
Mere Rd. Shep —72R 140
Mere Rd. Slou —8K 73
Mere Rd. Tad —96Xa 178
Mere Rd. Wey —76T 140
Mere Side. Orp —75Qc 150
Mereside Pl. Vir W —71A 138
(Virginia Water)
Meretone Clo. SE4 —56Ac 106
Merevale Cres. Mord —72Eb 145
Mereway Rd. Twic —60Fa 100
Merewood Clo. Brom —68Qc 130
Merewood Rd. Bexh —54Ed 110
Mereworth Clo. Brom —71Hc 149
Mereworth Dri. SE18 —52Rc 108
Mereworth Ho. SE15 —51Yb 106
Merganser Gdns. SE28 —48Tc 86
Meriden Clo. Brom —66Mc 129
Meriden Clo. Ilf —25Sc 46
Meriden Ct. SW3
—50Gb 81 (7D 202)
(off Chelsea Manor St.)
Meriden Way. Wat —8Aa 5
Meridian Ga. E14 —47Ec 84
Meridian Rd. SE7 —52Mc 107
Meridian Wlk. N17 —23Ub 43
Meridian Way. N18 —22Yb 44
Meridian Way. N18, N9 & Enf
—22Yb 44
Merifield Rd. SE9 —56Lc 107
Merino Clo. E11 —28Lc 45
Merino Pl. Sidc —58Wc 109
Merivale Rd. SW15 —56Ab 102
Merivale Rd. Harr —31Ea 58
Merland Clo. Tad —92Ya 178
Merland Grn. Tad —92Ya 178
Merland Rise. Eps & Tad
—91Ya 178
Merle Av. Hare —26K 35
Merlewood. Sev —95Kd 187
Merlewood Clo. Cat —92Tb 181
Merlewood Dri. Chst —67Pc 130
Merlewood Pl. SE9 —58Pc 108
Merley Ct. NW9 —32Sa 59
Merlin. NW9 —25Va 40
(off Concourse, The)
Merlin Clo. Croy —77Ub 147
Merlin Clo. Ilf —22Yc 47
Merlin Clo. N'holt —41Y 77
Merlin Clo. Romf —23Fd 48
Merlin Clo. Slou —51D 96
Merlin Ct. SE8 —51Bc 106
Merlin Ct. Ruis —33T 56
Merlin Ct. Short —69Hc 129
Merlin Ct. Wok —86E 156
Merlin Cres. Edgw —25Pa 39
Merlin Gdns. Brom —62Jc 129
Merlin Gdns. Romf —23Fd 48
Merlin Gro. Beck —70Bc 128
Merlin Gro. Ilf —24Rc 46
Merlin Rd. E12 —33Mc 65
Merlin Rd. Romf —23Fd 48
Merlin Rd. Well —56Wc 109
Merlin Rd. N. Well —56Wc 109
Merlins Av. Harr —34Ba 57
Merlin St. WC1 —41Qb 82 (4K 193)
Mermagen Dri. Rain —38Kd 69
Mermaid Ct. SE1 —47Tb 83 (1F 207)
(off Borough High St.)
Mermaid Ct. SE16 —46Bc 84
Mermaid Ct. SW1 —47Tb 83
Mermerus Gdns. Grav —3H 137
Merredene St. SW2 —58Pb 104
Merrick Ho. SE8 —49Bc 84
Merrick Rd. S'hall —48Ba 77
Merrick Sq. SE1 —48Tb 83 (3F 207)
Merridene. N21 —16Rb 25
Merrielands Cres. Dag —40Bd 67
Merrilands Rd. Wor Pk —74Ya 144
Merrilees Rd. Sidc —59Uc 108
Merrilyn Clo. Clay —79Ja 142
Merriman Rd. SE3 —53Lc 107
Merrington Rd. SW6 —51Cb 103
Merrion Av. Stan —22Ma 39
Merrit Ho. Romf —31Hd 68
(off Frazer Clo.)
Merritt Rd. SE4 —57Bc 106
Merritt's Bldgs. EC2
—42Ub 83 (6H 195)
(off Worship St.)
Merrivale. N14 —16Mb 24
Merrivale Av. Ilf —28Mc 45
Merrivale Gdns. Wok —5F 188
Merrivale M. W Dray —46M 75
Merrow La. Guild —100E 172
Merrow Rd. Sutt —81Za 162
Merrows Clo. N'wd —23S 36
Merrow St. SE17 —50Tb 83
Merrow Wlk. SE17
—50Tb 83 (7G 207)
Merrow Way. New Ad —79Ec 148
Merrydown Way. Chst —67Nc 130
Merryfield. SE3 —54Hc 107
Merryfield Gdns. Stan —22La 38
Merryfields. Uxb —40N 55
(in two parts)
Merryfields Way. SE6 —59Dc 106
Merryhill Clo. E4 —17Dc 26
Merry Hill Mt. Bush —18Da 19
Merry Hill Rd. Bush —16Ba 19
Merryhills Clo. Big H —88Mc 167
Merryhills Ct. N14 —15Lb 24
Merryhills Dri. Enf —14Mb 24
Merrylands. Cher —76G 138
Merrylands Rd. Bookh —96Ba 175
Merrymeet. Bans —86Hb 163
Merryweather Ct. N19 —34Lb 62
Mersey Av. Upm —30Td 50
Mersey Rd. E17 —27Bc 44
Mersey Wlk. N'holt —40Ca 57
Mersham Dri. NW9 —29Qa 39
Mersham Pl. SE20 —67Xb 127
Mersham Rd. T Hth —69Tb 127
Merten Rd. Romf —31Ad 67
Merthyr Ter. SW13 —51Xa 102
Merton Av. W4 —49Va 80
Merton Av. Hart —70Ae 135
Merton Av. N'holt —36Ea 58
Merton Av. Uxb —38R 56
Merton Ct. Ilf —30Nc 46
Merton Ct. Well —54Xc 109
Merton Gdns. Orp —71Rc 150
Merton Gdns. Tad —91Za 178
Merton Hall Gdns. SW20
—67Ab 124
Merton Hall Rd. SW19 —66Ab 124
Merton High St. SW19 —66Db 125
Merton La. N6 —33Hb 61
Merton Lodge. New Bar —15Eb 23
Merton Mans. SW20 —68Za 124
Merton Pk. Ind. Est. SW19
—67Db 125
Merton Pl. Grays —9C 92
Merton Rise. NW3 —38Gb 61
Merton Rd. E17 —29Ec 44
Merton Rd. SE25 —71Wb 147
Merton Rd. SW18 —58Cb 103
Merton Rd. SW19 —66Db 125
Merton Rd. Bark —38Vc 67
Merton Rd. Enf —10Tb 11
Merton Rd. Harr —32Ea 58
Merton Rd. Ilf —31Vc 67
Merton Rd. Slou —8L 73
Merton Rd. Wat —14X 19
Merton Wlk. Lea —90Ja 160
Merton Way. Lea —91Ja 176
Merton Way. Uxb —38R 56
Merton Way. W Mol —70Da 121
Merttins Rd. SE15 & SE4
—57Zb 106
Meru Clo. NW5 —35Jb 62
Mervan Rd. SW2 —56Qb 104
Mervyn Av. SE9 —62Sc 130
Mervyn Rd. W13 —48Ja 78
Mervyn Rd. Shep —73S 140
Merwin Way. Wind —4B 94
Meryfield Clo. Borwd —12Pa 21
Mesne Way. Shor —84Hd 170
Messaline Av. W3 —44Sa 79
Messant Clo. H Wood —26Nd 49
Messent Rd. SE9 —57Lc 107
Messeter Pl. SE9 —58Qc 108
Messina Av. NW6 —38Cb 61
Messiter Ho. N1 —39Pb 62 (1J 193)
(off Barnsbury Est.)
Metcalf Rd. Ashf —64R 120
Metcalf Wlk. Felt —63Aa 121
Meteor St. SW11 —56Jb 104
Meteor Way. Wall —80Nb 146
Metheringham Way. NW9
—25Ua 40
Methley St. SE11
—50Qb 82 (7A 206)
Methuen Clo. Edgw —24Qa 39
Methuen Pk. N10 —27Kb 42
Methuen Rd. Belv —49Dd 88
Methuen Rd. Bexh —56Bd 109
Methuen Rd. Edgw —24Qa 39
Methwold Rd. W10 —43Za 80
Metro Bus. Pk. Wemb —35Ra 59
Metro Cen. Wat —17T 18
Metropolitan Sta. App. Wat
—13V 18
Meux Clo. Chesh —3Wb 11
Mews End. Big H —90Mc 167
Mews Pl. Wfd G —21Jc 45
Mews St. E1 —46Wb 83
Mews, The. N1 —39Sb 63
Mews, The. Grays —49Ee 91
Mews, The. Hart —69Ae 135
Mews, The. Ilf —29Mc 45
Mews, The. Romf —28Gd 48
Mews, The. Sev —96Jd 186
(Sevenoaks)
Mews, The. Sev —95Ld 187
(St John's)
Mews, The. Sidc —63Wc 131
Mews, The. Slou —8J 73
Mews, The. Twic —58Ka 100
Mexfield Rd. SW15 —57Bb 103
Meyer Grn. Enf —10Wb 11
Meyer Rd. Eri —51Fd 110
Meymott St. SE1
—46Rb 83 (7B 200)
Meynell Cres. E9 —38Zb 64
Meynell Gdns. E9 —38Zb 64
Meynell Rd. E9 —38Zb 64
Meynell Rd. Romf —24Kd 49
Meyrick Clo. Knap —4B 188
Meyrick Rd. NW10 —37Wa 60
Meyrick Rd. SW11 —55Fb 103
Mezen Clo. N'wd —22T 36
Miall Wlk. SE26 —63Ac 128
Micawber Av. Uxb —42Q 76
Micawber Ho. SE16 —47Wb 83
(off Llewellyn St.)
Micawber St. N1
—41Sb 83 (3E 194)
Michael Gdns. Grav —4G 136
Michael Gdns. Horn —28Md 49
Michael Gaynor Clo. W7 —46Ha 78
Michael Manley Ind. Est. SW8
—54Mb 104
Michael Rd. E11 —32Gc 65
Michael Rd. SE25 —69Ub 127
Michael Rd. SW6 —53Db 103
Michael's Clo. SE13 —56Gc 107
Michaels La. Fawk & Sev
—75Xd 154
Michael's Row. Rich —56Na 101
Michael Stewart Ho. SW6
—51Bb 103
(off Clem Attlee Ct.)
Micheldever Rd. SE12 —58Hc 107
Michelham Gdns. Tad —92Ya 178
Michelham Gdns. Twic —62Ha 122
Michelle Ct. N12 —22Eb 41
Michel's Row. Rich —56Na 101
Michigan Av. E12 —35Pc 66
Michigan Ho. E14 —49Cc 84
Michleham Down. N12 —21Bb 41
Micholls Av. Ger X —21A 34
Micklefield Way. Borwd —10Na 7
Mickleham By-Pass. Mick
—100Ka 176
Mickleham Clo. Orp —68Vc 131
Mickleham Dri. Mick —98La 176
Mickleham Gdns. Sutt —79Ab 144
Mickleham Rd. Orp —67Vc 131
Mickleham Way. New Ad —80Fc 149
Micklethwaite Rd. SW6 —51Cb 103
Midas Ind. Est. Cow —40K 55
Midas Metropolitan Ind. Est. Mord
—73Ya 144
Midcroft. Ruis —32U 56
Midcroft. Slou —2F 72
Mid Cross La. Ger X —22B 34
Middle Boy. Abr —13Yc 29
Middle Clo. Coul —92Qb 180
Middle Clo. Eps —84Ua 162
Middle Cres. Den —31F 54
Middle Dene. NW7 —20Ta 21
Middle Farm Pl. Eff —99Y 175
Middle Field. NW8 —39Fb 61
Middlefielde. W13 —43Ka 78
Middlefield Gdns. Ilf —30Rc 46
Middlefields. Croy —81Ac 166
Middle Furlong. Bush —14Da 19
Middle Grn. Slou —46A 74
Middle Grn. Stai —66M 119
Middle Grn. Clo. Surb —72Pa 143
Middlegreen Rd. Slou —7P 73
Middleham Ct. Dart —58Rd 111
(off Osborne Rd.)
Middleham Gdns. N18 —23Wb 43
Middleham Rd. N18 —23Wb 43
Middle Hill. Egh —3N 117
Middle La. N8 —29Nb 42
Middle La. Bov —1C 2
Middle La. Eps —84Ua 162
Middle La. Seal —93Pd 187
Middle La. Tedd —65Ha 122
Middle La. M. N8 —29Nb 42
Middlemead Clo. Bookh —97Ca 175
Middlemead Rd. Bookh —97Ba 175
Middle Ope. Wat —9X 5
Middle Pk. Av. SE9 —58Mc 107
Middle Path. Harr —32Fa 58
Middle Rd. E13 —40Jc 65
Middle Rd. SW16 —68Mb 126
Middle Rd. Barn —16Gb 23
Middle Rd. Den —31E 54
Middle Rd. Harr —33Fa 58
Middle Rd. Ingve —22Ee 51
Middle Rd. Lea —93Ka 176
Middle Rd. Wal A —4Dc 12
Middle Row. W10 —42Ab 80
Middlesborough Rd. N18
—23Wb 43
Middlesex Bus. Pk. S'hall —47Ba 77
Middlesex Ct. W4 —50Va 80
Middlesex Ct. Add —78L 139
(off Marnham Pl.)
Middlesex Pas. EC1
—43Rb 83 (1C 200)
(off Bartholomew Clo.)
Middlesex Rd. Mitc —71Nb 146
Middlesex St. E1
—43Ub 83 (1J 201)
Middlesex Wharf. E5 —33Yb 64
Middle St. EC1 —43Sb 83 (7D 194)
Middle St. Croy —76Sb 147
(in two parts)
Middle Temple La. EC4
—44Qb 82 (3K 199)
Middleton Av. E4 —21Bc 44
Middleton Av. Gnfd —40Fa 58
Middleton Av. Sidc —65Xc 131
Middleton Bldgs. W1
—43Lb 82 (1B 198)
(off Langham St.)
Middleton Clo. E4 —20Bc 26
Middleton Dri. SE16 —47Zb 84
Middleton Dri. Pinn —27W 36
Middleton Gdns. Ilf —30Rc 46
Middleton Gro. N7 —36Nb 62
Middleton Hall La. Brtwd —19Ae 33
Middleton M. N7 —36Nb 62
Middleton Rd. E8 —38Vb 63
Middleton Rd. NW11 —31Cb 61
Middleton Rd. D'side —91Y 175
Middleton Rd. Eps —82Ta 161
Middleton Rd. Hay —43T 76
Middleton Rd. Mord & Cars
—72Db 145
Middleton Rd. N Mald —68Sa 123
Middleton Rd. Rick —18J 17
Middleton Rd. Shenf —18Ae 33
Middleton St. E2 —41Xb 83
Middleton Way. SE13 —56Fc 107
Middle Wlk. Burn —1A 72
Middle Wlk. Wok —89A 156
Middleway. NW11 —29Db 41
Middle Way. SW16 —68Mb 126
Middle Way. Hay —42Y 77
Middle Way. Wat —9W 4
Middle Way, The. Harr —26Ha 38
Middle Yd. SE1 —46Ub 83
Middlings Rise. Sev —97Hd 186
Middlings, The. Sev —97Hd 186
Middlings Wood. Sev —97Hd 186
Midfield Av. Bexh —55Ed 110
Midfield Av. Swan —65Jd 132
Midfield Pl. Bexh —55Ed 110
Midfield Way. Orp —67Xc 131
Midford Ho. NW4 —28Za 40
(off Belle Vue Est.)
Midford Pl. W1 —42Lb 82 (6C 192)
Midholm. Wemb —32Qa 59
Midholm Clo. N2 —28Db 41
Midholm Clo. NW11 —28Db 41
Midholm Rd. Croy —75Ac 148
Midhope Clo. Wok —91A 172
Midhope Gdns. Wok —91A 172
Midhope Rd. Wok —91A 172
Midhope St. WC1
—41Nb 82 (4G 193)
Midhurst. SE26 —65Yb 128
Midhurst Av. N10 —27Jb 42
Midhurst Av. Croy —73Qb 146
Midhurst Clo. Horn —35Jd 68
Midhurst Gdns. Uxb —38S 56
Midhurst Hill. Bexh —58Cd 110
Midhurst Pde. N10 —27Jb 42
(off Fortis Grn.)
Midhurst Rd. W13 —47Ja 78
Midland Cres. NW3 —37Eb 61
Midland Pde. NW6 —37Db 61
Midland Pl. E14 —50Ec 84
Midland Rd. E10 —31Ec 64
Midland Rd. NW1
—40Mb 62 (2E 192)
Midland Ter. NW2 —34Za 60
Midland Ter. NW10 —42Ua 80
Midlothian Rd. E3 —43Bc 84
Midmoor Rd. SW12 —60Lb 104
Midmoor Rd. SW19 —67Ab 124
Midship Clo. SE16 —46Zb 84
Midship Point. E14 —47Cc 84
(off Quarterdeck, The)
Midstrath Rd. NW10 —35Ua 60
Midsummer Av. Houn —56Ba 99
Midsummer Wlk. Wok —4G 188
Midway. Sutt —73Bb 145
Midway. W on T —75X 141
Midway Av. Cher —69J 119
Midway Av. Egh —69D 118
Midwood Clo. NW2 —34Xa 60
Mid Yd. SE1 —46Ub 83 (6H 201)
Miena Way. Asht —89Ma 161
Miers Clo. E6 —39Qc 66
Mighell Av. Ilf —29Mc 45
Mike Spring Ct. Grav —3F 136
Milborne Gro. SW10 —50Eb 81
Milborne St. E9 —37Yb 64
Milborough Cres. SE12 —58Gc 107
Milbourne Ct. Wat —12W 18
Milbourne La. Esh —79Ea 142
Milbrook. Esh —79Ea 142
Milburn Dri. W Dray —44N 75
Milburn Wlk. Eps —87Ua 162
Milbury Grn. Warl —90Fc 167
Milby Ct. Borwd —11Pa 21
Milcombe Clo. Wok —6F 188
Milcote St. SE1 —47Rb 83 (2B 206)
Mildenhall Rd. E5 —35Yb 64
Mildenhall Rd. Slou —4J 73
Mildmay Av. N1 —37Tb 63
Mildmay Gro. N1 —36Tb 63
Mildmay Pk. N1 —36Tb 63
Mildmay Pl. N16 —36Ub 63
Mildmay Pl. Shor —83Hd 170
Mildmay Rd. N1 —36Tb 63
Mildmay Rd. Ilf —34Rc 66
Mildmay Rd. Romf —29Ed 48
Mildmay St. N1 —37Tb 63
Mildred Av. Borwd —14Qa 21
Mildred Av. Hay —49T 76
Mildred Av. N'holt —36Da 57
Mildred Av. Wat —14V 18
Mildred Clo. Dart —58Qd 111
Mildred Rd. Eri —50Gd 88
Mildura Ct. N8 —28Pb 42
Mile Clo. Wal A —5Ec 12
Mile End Pl. E1 —42Zb 84
Mile End Rd. E1 & E3 —43Yb 84
Mile End, The. E17 —25Zb 44
Mile Path. Wok —9C 188
Mile Rd. Wall —74Kb 146
Miles La. Cob —85Aa 159
Miles Lodge. Harr —29Fa 38
Milespit Hill. NW7 —22Xa 40
Miles Pl. NW8 —43Gb 81 (7D 190)
(off Broadley St.)
Miles Pl. Surb —70Pa 123
Miles Rd. N8 —27Nb 42
Miles Rd. Eps —84Ta 161
Miles Rd. Mitc —69Gb 125
Miles St. SW8 —51Nb 104
Milestone Clo. Rip —94J 173
Milestone Clo. Sutt —80Fb 145
Mile Stone Ct. Rad —6Ja 6
Milestone Rd. SE19 —65Vb 127
Milestone Rd. Dart —58Rd 111
Miles Way. N20 —19Gb 23
Milfoil St. W12 —45Wa 80
Milford Clo. SE2 —51Ad 109
Milford Ct. Slou —7L 73
Milford Gdns. Edgw —24Qa 39
Milford Gdns. Wemb —35Ma 59
Milford Gro. Sutt —77Eb 145
Milford La. WC2
—45Qb 82 (4K 199)
Milford M. SW16 —62Pb 126
Milford Rd. W13 —46Ka 78
Milford Rd. Grays —46Fe 91
Milford Rd. S'hall —45Ca 77
Milford Towers. SE6 —59Dc 106
Milford Way. SE15 —53Vb 105
Milking La. Kes —83Mc 167
Milking La. Orp —84Nc 168
Milk St. E16 —46Rc 86
Milk St. EC2 —44Sb 83 (3E 200)
Milk St. Brom —65Kc 129
Milkwell Gdns. Wfd G —24Kc 45
Milkwell Yd. SE5 —53Sb 105
Milkwood Rd. SE24 —57Rb 105
Milk Yd. E1 —45Yb 84
Millais Av. E12 —36Qc 66
Millais Gdns. Edgw —26Qa 39
Millais Pl. Til —2C 114
Millais Rd. E11 —35Ec 64
Millais Rd. Enf —15Vb 25
Millais Rd. N Mald —73Ua 144
Millais Way. Eps —77Sa 143
Millan Clo. Wdhm —82K 157
Millard Clo. N16 —36Ub 63
Millard Ter. Dag —37Cd 68
Mill Av. Uxb —40L 55
Millbank. SW1 —48Nb 82 (4F 205)
Millbank Way. SE12 —57Jc 107
Millbourne Rd. Felt —63Aa 121
Mill Bri. Barn —16Bb 23
Millbro. Swan —67Jd 132
Millbrook. Wey —77U 140
Millbrook Av. Well —56Tc 108
Millbrook Gdns. Chad —30Bd 47
Millbrook Gdns. Gid P —26Gd 48
Millbrook Pas. SW9 —55Rb 105
Millbrook Pl. NW1
—40Lb 62 (1B 192)
(off Hampstead Rd.)
Millbrook Rd. N9 —18Xb 25
Millbrook Rd. SW9 —55Rb 105
Millbrook Rd. Bush —11Ba 19
Mill Brook Rd. St M —70Yc 131
Millbrook Way. Coln —54G 96
Mill Clo. Bookh —96Ca 175
Mill Clo. Cars —75Jb 146
Mill Clo. W Dray —48M 75
Mill Corner. Barn —11Bb 23
Mill Ct. E10 —34Ec 64
Mill Ct. Hort K —68Sd 134
Mill Ct. Slou —6K 73
Millcrest Rd. Chesh —1Rb 11
Milledge Corner. SE16 —50Xb 83
Millender Wlk. SE16 —49Yb 84
Millenium Pl. E2 —40Xb 63
Miller Clo. Pinn —26Y 37
Miller Pl. Ger X —29A 34
Miller Rd. SW19 —65Fb 125
Miller Rd. Croy —74Pb 146
Miller Rd. Grav —1J 137
Miller's Av. E8 —36Vb 63
Millers Clo. NW7 —21Wa 40
Millers Clo. Chig —19Xc 29
Millers Clo. Stai —64K 119
Millers Copse. Eps —91Ta 177
Millers Ct. W6 —50Va 80
Millers Ct. Wemb —40Na 59
(off Vicars Bri. Clo.)
Millers Grn. Clo. Enf —13Rb 25
Miller's La. Chig —18Xc 29
Miller's La. Old Win —8K 95
Miller's Ter. E8 —36Vb 63
Miller St. NW1 —40Lb 62 (1B 192)
Millers Way. W6 —47Ya 80
Miller Wlk. SE1 —46Qb 82 (7A 200)
Millet Rd. Gnfd —41Da 77
Mill Farm Av. Sun —66U 120
Mill Farm Clo. Pinn —26Y 37
Mill Farm Cres. Houn —60Aa 99
Millfield. N4 —33Qb 62
Millfield. New Ash —75Ae 155
Millfield. Sun —67T 120
Millfield Av. E17 —25Ac 44
Millfield Cotts. Orp —70Xc 131
Millfield Dri. Grav —1A 136
Millfield Ho. Wat —16S 18
Millfield La. N6 —32Gb 61
Millfield La. New Ash —75Ae 155
Millfield La. Tad —97Bb 179
Millfield Pl. N6 —33Jb 62
Millfield Rd. Edgw —26Sa 39
Millfield Rd. Houn —60Aa 99
Millfield Rd. W King —79Td 154
Millfields Clo. St M —70Xc 131
Millfields Rd. E5 —35Yb 64
Millford. Wok —5E 188
Mill Gdns. SE26 —62Xb 127
Mill Grn. Mitc —73Jb 146
Mill Grn. Bus. Pk. Mitc —73Jb 146
Mill Grn. Rd. Mitc —73Jb 146

Millgrove St.—Montfort Rd.

Millgrove St. SW11 —53Jb 104
Millharbour. E14 —47Dc 84
Millhaven Clo. Romf —30Xc 47
Millhedge Clo. Cob —88Aa 159
Mill Hill. Shenf —17Ae 33
Mill Hill Cir. NW7 —22Va 40
Mill Hill Gro. W3 —46Ra 79
Mill Hill La. Shorne —4M 137
Mill Hill Rd. SW13 —54Wa 102
Mill Hill Rd. W3 —47Ra 79
Mill Hill Ter. W3 —46Ra 79
Mill Hill Yd. W3 —47Qa 79
Mill Ho. Clo. Eyns —74Nd 153
Mill Ho. La. Stai —64F 118
Mill Ho. La. Thorpe —70D 118
Millhouse Pl. SE27 —63Rb 127
Millicent Fawcett Ct. N17 —25Vb 43
Millicent Rd. E10 —32Bc 64
Milligan St. E14 —45Bc 84
Milling Rd. Edgw —24Ta 39
Millington Ho. N16 —34Tb 63
Millington Rd. Hay —48U 76
Mill La. E4 —13Dc 26
Mill La. NW6 —36Bb 61
Mill La. SE18 —50Qc 86
Mill La. Asc —8D 116
Mill La. Byfl —85P 157
Mill La. Cars —77Hb 145
Mill La. Crox —16S 18
Mill La. Croy —76Pb 146
Mill La. Egh —70E 118
Mill La. Eps —87Va 162
Mill La. Eyns —74Nd 153
Mill La. Fet —94Ja 176
Mill La. Ger X —30B 34
Mill La. Grays —49Zd 91
Mill La. Hort —55D 96
Mill La. K Lan —1Q 4
Mill La. Nave —11Kd 31
Mill La. Orp —82Qc 168
Mill La. Ors —3C 92
Mill La. Rip —91M 173
Mill La. Romf —30Ad 47
Mill La. Sev —93Ld 187
Mill La. Shor —82Hd 170
Mill La. W'ham —99Sc 184
Mill La. Wind —2E 94
Mill La. Wfd G —22Hc 45
Millman M. WC1
—42Pb 82 (6H 193)
Millman Pl. WC1
—42Pb 82 (6H 193)
(off Millman St.)
Millman St. WC1
—42Pb 82 (6H 193)
Millmark Gro. SE14 —54Ac 106
Millmarsh La. Enf —12Ac 26
Millmead. Byfl —84P 157
Mill Mead. Stai —63H 119
Millmead Ind. Cen. N17 —27Xb 43
Mill Mead Rd. N17 —27Xb 43
Mill Pk. Av. Horn —33Nd 69
Mill Pl. E14 —44Ac 84
Mill Pl. Chst —67Rc 130
Mill Pl. Dart —56Jd 110
Mill Pl. Dat —4P 95
Mill Pl. King T —69Pa 123
Mill Plat. Iswth —54Ja 100
(in two parts)
Mill Plat Av. Iswth —54Ja 100
Millpond Ct. Add —78N 139
Millpond Est. SE16 —47Xb 83
Mill Pond Rd. Dart —58Nd 111
Mill Ridge. Edgw —22Pa 39
Mill River Trading Est. Enf —14Ac 26
Mill Rd. E16 —46Kc 85
Mill Rd. SE13 —55Ec 106
Mill Rd. SW19 —66Eb 125
Mill Rd. Cob —87Y 159
Mill Rd. Dart —63Pd 133
Mill Rd. Dun G —93Gd 186
Mill Rd. Eps —84Va 162
Mill Rd. Eri —52Ed 110
Mill Rd. Esh —75Ca 141
Mill Rd. Grav —9A 114
Mill Rd. Ilf —34Qc 66
Mill Rd. Purf —51Rd 111
Mill Rd. S Ock —45Sd 90
Mill Rd. Tad —95Za 178
Mill Rd. Twic —61Ea 122
Mill Rd. W Dray —48L 75
Mill Row. N1 —39Ub 63 (1J 195)
Mill Row. Bex —59Dd 110
Mills Clo. Uxb —40Q 56
Mills Ct. EC2 —42Ub 83 (5H 195)
(off Curtain Rd.)
Mills Cres. Seal —91Pd 187
Mills Gro. E14 —44Ec 84
Mills Gro. NW4 —27Za 40
Mill Shot Clo. SW6 —53Ya 102
Millside. Cars —75Hb 145
Millside Pl. Iswth —54Ka 100
Millsmead Way. Lou —12Pc 28
Millson Clo. N20 —19Fb 23
Mills Rd. W on T —78Y 141
Mills Row. W4 —49Ta 79
Mills Spur. Old Win —9M 95
Millstead Clo. Tad —94Xa 178
Mill Stone Clo. S Dar —68Sd 134
Mill Stone M. Hort K —67Sd 134
Millstream Clo. N13 —22Qb 42
Millstream La. Slou —6C 72
Millstream Rd. SE1
—47Vb 83 (2K 207)
Mill St. SE1 —47Vb 83 (2K 207)
Mill St. W1 —45Kb 82 (4B 198)
Mill St. Coln —52F 96
Mill St. King T —69Na 123
Mill St. Slou —6K 73
Mill St. W'ham —99Tc 184
Mills Way. Hut —18Ee 33
Millthorne Clo. Crox —15P 17
Mill Vale. Brom —68Hc 129
Mill View Clo. Ewe —80Va 144
Mill View Gdns. Croy —76Zb 148
Millwall Dock Rd. E14 —48Cc 84
Millway. NW7 —21Ua 40
Mill Way. Bush —12Aa 19
Mill Way. Dork —96Pa 177
Mill Way. Felt —57X 99
Mill Way. Rick —18H 17
Millway Gdns. N'holt —37Ba 57
Millwell Cres. Chig —22Tc 46
Millwood Rd. Houn —57Ea 100
Millwood Rd. Orp —69Yc 131
Millwood St. W10 —43Ab 80
Mill Yd. E1 —45Wb 83
Milman Clo. Pinn —27Z 37
Milman Rd. NW6 —40Za 60
Milman's St. SW10 —51Fb 103
Milne Feild. Pinn —24Ca 37
Milne Gdns. SE9 —57Nc 108
Milne Ho. SE18 —49Pc 86
(off Ogilby St.)
Milne Pk. E. New Ad —83Fc 167
Milne Pk. W. New Ad —83Fc 167
Milner App. Cat —93Wb 181
Milner Clo. Cat —94Vb 181
Milner Clo. Wat —6X 5
Milner Ct. Bush —16Da 19
Milner Dri. Cob —84Ba 159
Milner Dri. Twic —59Fa 100
Milner Pl. N1 —39Qb 62
Milner Pl. Cars —77Jb 146
Milner Rd. E15 —41Gc 85
Milner Rd. SW19 —67Db 125
Milner Rd. Cat —94Wb 181
Milner Rd. Dag —33Yc 67
Milner Rd. King T —69Ma 123
Milner Rd. Mord —71Fb 145
Milner Rd. T Hth —69Tb 127
Milner Sq. N1 —38Rb 63
Milner St. SW3 —49Hb 81 (5F 203)
Milner Wlk. Sidc —61Tc 130
Milne Way. Hare —25K 35
Milnthorpe Rd. W4 —51Ta 101
Milo Gdns. SE22 —58Vb 105
Milo Rd. SE22 —58Vb 105
Milroy Av. Grav —1A 136
Milroy Wlk. SE1 —46Rb 83 (6B 200)
Milson Rd. W14 —48Za 80
Milstead Ho. E5 —36Xb 63
Milton Av. E6 —38Mc 65
Milton Av. N6 —31Lb 62
Milton Av. NW9 —27Sa 39
Milton Av. NW10 —39Sa 59
Milton Av. Badg M —82Dd 170
Milton Av. Barn —15Bb 22
Milton Av. Croy —73Tb 147
Milton Av. Ger X —28A 34
Milton Av. Grav —10E 114
Milton Av. Horn —33Hd 68
Milton Av. Sutt —76Fb 145
Milton Clo. N2 —29Eb 41
Milton Clo. SE1 —49Vb 83 (6K 207)
Milton Clo. Hay —44W 76
Milton Clo. Hort —55C 96
Milton Clo. Sutt —76Fb 145
Milton Ct. EC2 —43Tb 83 (7F 195)
Milton Ct. Grav —10E 114
Milton Ct. Twic —62Ga 122
Milton Ct. Uxb —34R 56
Milton Ct. Wal A —6Ec 12
Milton Ct. Highwalk. EC2
(off Milton Ct.) —43Tb 83 (7F 195)
Milton Ct. Rd. SE14 —51Ac 106
Milton Cres. Ilf —31Rc 66
Milton Dri. Borwd —15Ra 21
Milton Dri. Shep —70N 119
Milton Garden Est. N16 —35Ub 63
Milton Gdns. Eps —86Ua 162
Milton Gdns. Stai —60P 97
Milton Gdns. Til —3D 114
Milton Gro. N11 —22Lb 42
Milton Gro. N16 —35Tb 63
Milton Hall Rd. Grav —10F 114
Milton Ho. E17 —28Cc 44
Milton Ho. Ger X —21A 34
Milton Ho. Sutt —76Cb 145
Milton Lodge. Twic —59Ha 100
Milton Pk. N6 —31Lb 62
Milton Pl. N7 —36Qb 62
Milton Pl. Grav —8E 114
Milton Rd. E17 —28Cc 44
Milton Rd. N6 —31Lb 62
Milton Rd. N15 —28Rb 43
Milton Rd. NW7 —22Wa 40
Milton Rd. NW9 —31Wa 60
Milton Rd. SE24 —57Rb 105
Milton Rd. SW14 —55Ta 101
Milton Rd. SW19 —65Eb 125
Milton Rd. W3 —46Ta 79
Milton Rd. W7 —45Ha 78
Milton Rd. Add —79J 139
Milton Rd. Belv —49Cd 88
Milton Rd. Cat —93Tb 181
Milton Rd. Croy —73Tb 147
Milton Rd. Dun G —93Gd 186
Milton Rd. Egh —64B 118
Milton Rd. Grav —8D 114
(in two parts)
Milton Rd. Grays —50De 91
Milton Rd. Hamp —66Ca 121
Milton Rd. Harr —28Ga 38
Milton Rd. Mitc —66Jb 126
Milton Rd. Romf —30Jd 48
Milton Rd. Slou —2H 73
Milton Rd. Sutt —76Cb 145
Milton Rd. Swans —58Ae 113
Milton Rd. Uxb —35R 56
Milton Rd. Wall —79Lb 146
Milton Rd. W on T —76Z 141
Milton Rd. War —21Yd 50
Milton Rd. Well —53Vc 109
Milton St. EC2 —43Tb 83 (7F 195)
Milton St. Swans —58Zd 113
Milton St. Wal A —6Ec 12
Milton St. Wat —10X 5
Milton, The. Uxb —34R 56
Milton Way. Fet —97Ea 176
Milton Way. W Dray —49P 75
Milverton Dri. Uxb —35S 56
Milverton Gdns. Ilf —33Vc 67
Milverton Rd. NW6 —38Ya 60
Milverton St. SE11
—50Qb 82 (7A 206)
Milverton Way. SE9 —63Qc 130
Milward Wlk. E1 —43Xb 83
Milward Wlk. SE18 —51Qc 108
Mimms Hall Rd. Pot B —3Za 8
Mimms La. Shenl & Pot B —5Qa 7
Mimosa Clo. Orp —75Yc 151
Mimosa Clo. Pil H —15Xd 32
Mimosa Clo. Romf —24Ld 49
Mimosa Ho. Hay —43Y 77
Mimosa Lodge. NW10 —36Va 60
Mimosa Rd. Hay —43Y 77
Mimosa St. SW6 —53Bb 103
Mina Av. Slou —7P 73
Minard Rd. SE6 —59Gc 107
(in two parts)
Mina Rd. SE17 —50Ub 83 (7J 207)
Mina Rd. SW19 —67Cb 125
Minchenden Ct. N14 —19Mb 24
Minchenden Cres. N14 —20Lb 24
Minchin Clo. Lea —94Ja 176
Mincing La. EC3 —45Ub 83 (4H 201)
Minden Rd. SE20 —67Xb 127
Minden Rd. Sutt —75Bb 145
Minehead Rd. SW16 —64Pb 126
Minehead Rd. Harr —34Ca 57
Mineral St. SE18 —49Uc 86
Minera M. SW1 —49Jb 82 (5J 203)
Minerva Clo. SW9 —52Qb 104
Minerva Clo. Sidc —62Uc 130
Minerva Clo. Stai —57J 97
Minerva Dri. Wat —8U 4
Minerva Rd. E4 —24Dc 44
Minerva Rd. NW10 —42Sa 79
Minerva Rd. King T —68Pa 123
Minerva St. E2 —40Xb 63
Minet Av. NW10 —40Ua 60
Minet Dri. Hay —46W 76
Minet Gdns. NW10 —40Ua 60
Minet Gdns. Hay —46X 77
Minet Rd. SW9 —54Rb 105
Minford Gdns. W14 —47Za 80
Mingard Wlk. N7 —33Pb 62
Ming St. E14 —45Cc 84
Ministry Way. SE9 —61Pc 130
Miniver Pl. EC4 —45Sb 83 (4E 200)
(off Garlick Hill)
Miniver St. SE1 —47Rb 83 (2C 206)
(off Boyfield St.)
Mink Ct. Houn —54Y 99
Minniecroft Rd. Burn —1A 72
Minniedale. Surb —71Pa 143
Minnis, The. New Ash —76Be 155
Minnow Wlk. SE17
—49Ub 83 (6J 207)
Minoco Wharf. E16 —47Lc 85
Minorca Rd. Wey —77Q 140
Minories. EC3 —44Vb 83 (3K 201)
Minshaw Ct. Sidc —63Wc 131
Minshill St. SW8 —53Mb 104
Minshull Pl. Beck —66Cc 128
Minson Rd. E9 —39Zb 64
Minstead Gdns. SW15 —59Va 102
Minstead Way. N Mald —72Ua 144
Minster Av. Sutt —75Cb 145
Minster Ct. EC3 —45Ub 83 (4J 201)
(off Mincing La.)
Minster Dri. Croy —77Ub 147
Minster Gdns. W Mol —70Ba 121
Minsterley Av. Shep —70U 120
Minster Pavement. EC3
—45Ub 83 (4J 201)
(off Mincing La.)
Minster Rd. NW2 —36Ab 60
Minster Rd. Brom —66Kc 129
Minster Wlk. N8 —28Nb 42
Minster Way. Horn —32Pd 69
Minster Way. Slou —47B 74
Minstrel Gdns. Surb —70Pa 123
Mintern Clo. N13 —20Rb 25
Minterne Av. S'hall —49Ca 77
Minterne Rd. Harr —29Pa 39
Minterne Waye. Hay —44Y 77
Mintern St. N1 —40Tb 63 (1G 195)
Mint La. Tad —100Cb 179
Minton Ho. SE11
—49Qb 82 (5K 205)
(off Walnut Tree Wlk.)
Minton M. NW6 —37Db 61
Minton Rise. Tap —4A 72
Mint Rd. Bans —88Eb 163
Mint Rd. Wall —77Kb 146
Mint St. SE1 —47Sb 83 (1D 206)
Mint Wlk. Croy —76Sb 147
Mint Wlk. Knap —5B 188
Mint Wlk. Warl —89Zb 166
Minverva Rd. NW10 —42Sa 79
Mirabel Rd. SW6 —52Bb 103
Mirador Cres. Slou —5M 73
Miramar Way. Horn —36Md 69
Miranda Clo. E1 —43Yb 84
Miranda Rd. N19 —32Lb 62
Mirfield St. SE7 —49Mc 85
Miriam Rd. SE18 —50Uc 86
Mirren Clo. Harr —35Ba 57
Mirrie La. Den —29E 34
Mirror Path. SE9 —62Lc 129
Misbourne Av. Ger X —22A 34
Misbourne Clo. Ger X —22A 34
Misbourne Ct. Langl —49C 74
Misbourne Rd. Uxb —39Q 56
Misbourne Vale. Ger X —22A 34
Miskin Rd. Dart —59Ld 111
Miskin Way. Grav —5F 136
Missenden. SE17 —50Tb 83
(off Roland Way)
Missenden Gdns. Burn —4A 72
Missenden Gdns. Mord —72Eb 145
Missenden Ho. Wat —17U 18
(off Chenies Way)
Mission Gro. E17 —29Ac 44
Mission Pl. SE15 —53Wb 105
Mission Sq. Bren —51Na 101
Mistletoe Clo. Croy —74Zb 148
Misty's Field. W on T —74Y 141
Mitcham Garden Village. Mitc
—71Jb 146
Mitcham Ho. SE5 —53Sb 105
Mitcham La. SW16 —65Lb 126
Mitcham Pk. Mitc —70Gb 125
Mitcham Rd. E6 —41Nc 86
Mitcham Rd. SW17 —64Hb 125
Mitcham Rd. Croy —72Nb 146
Mitcham Rd. Ilf —31Vc 67
Mitcheldean Ct. SE15 —52Ub 105
(off Newent Clo.)
Mitchell. NW9 —25Va 40
(off Concourse, The)
Mitchell Av. Grav —61Fe 135
Mitchellbrook Way. NW10
—37Ta 59
Mitchell Clo. SE2 —49Yc 87
Mitchell Clo. Belv —48Ed 88
Mitchell Clo. Dart —61Nd 133
Mitchell Clo. Rain —40Ld 69
Mitchell Clo. Slou —8E 72
Mitchell Ho. W12 —45Xa 80
(off White City Est.)
Mitchell Rd. N13 —22Sb 43
Mitchell Rd. Orp —77Vc 151
Mitchell St. EC1 —42Sb 83 (5D 194)
Mitchell Wlk. E6 —43Mc 85
(off Neats Ct. Rd.)
Mitchell Wlk. Swans —59Ae 113
Mitchell Way. NW10 —37Sa 59
Mitchell Way. Brom —67Jc 129
Mitchem Clo. W King —80Ud 154
Mitchison Rd. N1 —37Tb 63
Mitchley Av. Purl & S Croy
—85Sb 165
Mitchley Gro. S Croy —85Wb 165
Mitchley Hill. S Croy —85Ub 165
Mitchley Rd. N17 —27Wb 43
Mitchley View. S Croy —85Wb 165
Mitford Rd. N19 —33Nb 62
Mitre Bri. Ind. Pk. W10 —42Xa 80
Mitre Clo. Brom —68Hc 129
Mitre Clo. Shep —73T 140
Mitre Clo. Sutt —80Eb 145
Mitre Ct. EC2 —44Sb 83 (2E 200)
(off Wood St.)
Mitre Ct. EC4 —44Qb 82 (3A 200)
Mitre Rd. E15 —40Gc 65
Mitre Rd. SE1 —47Qb 82 (1A 206)
Mitre Sq. EC3 —44Ub 83 (3J 201)
Mitre St. EC3 —44Ub 83 (3J 201)
Mitre, The. E14 —45Bc 84
Mitre Way. NW10 —43Xa 80
Mitre Yd. SW3 —49Gb 81 (5E 202)
Mixbury Gro. Wey —79T 140
Mixnams La. Cher —69J 119
Mizen Clo. Cob —86Z 159
Mizen Way. Cob —87Y 159
Moat Clo. Bush —15Da 19
Moat Clo. Orp —79Vc 151
Moat Ct. Asht —89Na 161
Moat Ct. Sidc —62Vc 131
Moat Cres. N3 —27Db 41
Moat Croft. Well —55Yc 109
Moat Dri. E13 —40Lc 65
Moat Dri. Harr —28Ea 38
Moat Dri. Ruis —31U 56
Moat Dri. Slou —3N 73
Moat Farm Rd. N'holt —37Ba 57
Moatfield. NW6 —38Ab 60
Moatfield Rd. Bush —15Da 19
Moat Gdns. SE28 —45Yc 87
Moat La. Eri —53Jd 110
Moat Pl. SW9 —54Pb 104
Moat Pl. W3 —44Ra 79
Moat Pl. Den —36K 55
Moatside. Enf —14Zb 26
Moatside. Felt —63Y 121
Moat, The. N Mald —67Ua 124
Moat View Ct. Bush —15Da 19
Moberley Rd. SW4 —59Mb 104
Modbury Gdns. NW5 —37Jb 62
Modder Pl. SW15 —56Za 102
Model Bldgs. WC1
(off Cubitt St.) —41Pb 82 (4J 193)
Model Cotts. SW14 —56Sa 101
Model Cotts. W13 —47Ka 78
Model Farm Clo. SE9 —62Nc 130
Modern Ct. EC4 —44Rb 83 (2B 200)
(off Farringdon St.)
Modern Wharf Rd. SE10 —48Gc 85
Moelwyn. N7 —36Mb 62
Moelyn M. Harr —29Ja 38
Moffat Ct. SW19 —64Cb 125
Moffat Gdns. Mitc —69Gb 125
Moffat Ho. SE5 —52Sb 105
Moffat Rd. N13 —23Nb 42
Moffat Rd. SW17 —63Hb 125
Moffat Rd. T Hth —68Sb 127
Mogador Rd. Tad —100Ab 178
Mogden La. Iswth —57Ha 100
Moiety Rd. E14 —47Cc 84
Moineau. NW9 —25Va 40
(off Concourse, The)
Moira Clo. N17 —26Ub 43
Moira Rd. SE9 —56Pc 108
Moir Clo. S Croy —81Wb 165
Mokswell Ct. N10 —25Jb 42
Moland Mead. SE16 —50Zb 84
Molash Rd. Orp —70Zc 131
Mole Abbey Gdns. W Mol
—69Da 121
Mole Bus. Pk. Lea —93Ha 176
Mole Ct. Eps —77Sa 143
Molember Ct. E Mol —70Ga 122
Molember Rd. E Mol —71Ga 142
Mole Rd. Fet —93Fa 176
Mole Rd. W on T —78Z 141
Molescroft. SE9 —62Sc 130
Molesey Av. W Mol —71Ba 141
Molesey Clo. W on T —77Aa 141
Molesey Dri. Sutt —75Ab 144
Molesey Pk. Av. W Mol —71Da 141
Molesey Pk. Clo. E Mol —71Ea 142
Molesey Pk. Rd. W Mol —71Da 141
Molesey Rd. W on T & W Mol
—78Z 141
Molesford Rd. SW6 —53Cb 103
Molesham Clo. W Mol —69Da 121
Molesham Way. W Mol —69Da 121
Moles Hill. Oxs —83Fa 160
Molesworth Rd. Cob —85W 158
Molesworth St. SE13 —55Ec 106
Mole Valley Pl. Asht —91Ma 177
Moliner Ct. Beck —66Cc 128
Mollands Ct. S Ock —42Ae 91
Mollands La. S Ock —42Yd 90
Mollison Av. Enf —7Ac 12
Mollison Dri. Wall —80Mb 146
Mollison Way. Edgw —26Pa 39
Molloy Ct. Wok —88C 156
Molly Huggins Clo. SW12
—59Lb 104
Molteno Rd. Wat —10W 4
Molton Ho. N1 —39Pb 62 (1J 193)
(off Barnsbury Est.)
Molyneux Rd. Wey —78Q 140
Molyneux St. W1
—43Gb 81 (1E 196)
Monahan Av. Purl —84Pb 164
Monarch Clo. Felt —59U 98
Monarch Clo. Til —4D 114
Monarch Clo. W Wick —77Hc 149
Monarch Ct. N2 —29Fb 41
Monarch Dri. E16 —43Mc 85
Monarch M. SW16 —64Qb 126
Monarch Rd. Belv —48Cd 88
Monarchs Way. Ruis —32U 56
Monarchs Way. Wal X —5Ac 12
Mona Rd. SE15 —54Yb 106
Monastery Gdns. Enf —12Tb 25
Mona St. E16 —43Hc 85
Monaveen Gdns. W Mol —69Da 121
Monck St. SW1
—48Mb 82 (4E 204)
Monclar Rd. SE5 —56Tb 105
Moncorvo Clo. SW7
—47Gb 81 (2D 202)
Moncrieff Clo. E6 —44Nc 86
Moncrieff St. SE15 —54Wb 105
(in two parts)
Mondial Way. Hay —52S 98
Monds Cotts. Sund —96Ad 185
Monega Rd. E7 & E12 —37Lc 65
Money Av. Cat —94Ub 181
Moneyer Ho. N1 —41Tb 83 (3F 195)
(off Provost Est.)
Moneyhill Ct. Rick —18K 17
Moneyhill Pde. Rick —18K 17
Money Hill Rd. Rick —18L 17
Money La. W Dray —48M 75
Money Rd. Cat —94Tb 181
Monfitchet. E6 —44Rc 86
Mongers La. Eps —82Va 162
Monica Clo. Wat —12Y 19
Monica Ct. Enf —15Ub 25
Monica James Ho. Sidc —62Wc 131
Monier Rd. E3 —38Cc 64
Monivea Rd. Beck —66Bc 128
Monkchester Clo. Lou —11Pc 28
Monk Dri. E16 —45Jc 85
Monkfrith Av. N14 —16Kb 24
Monkfrith Clo. N14 —17Kb 24
Monkfrith Way. N14 —17Jb 24
Monkham's Av. Wfd G —22Kc 45
Monkham's Dri. Wfd G —22Kc 45
Monkham's La. Buck H —20Kc 27
Monkham's La. Wfd G —21Jc 45
Monkleigh Rd. Mord —69Ab 124
Monk Pas. E16 —45Jc 85
(off Monk Dri.)
Monks Av. Barn —16Eb 23
Monks Av. W Mol —71Ba 141
Monks Chase. Ingve —22Ee 51
Monks Clo. SE2 —49Zc 87
Monks Clo. Enf —12Sb 25
Monks Clo. Harr —33Ca 57
Monks Clo. Ruis —35Z 57
Monks Cres. Add —78K 139
Monks Cres. W on T —74X 141
Monksdene Gdns. Sutt —76Db 145
Monks Dri. W3 —43Qa 79
Monksfield Way. Slou —2E 72
Monks Gdns. Stanf —1N 93
Monks Grn. Fet —93Ea 176
Monksgrove. Lou —15Qc 28
Monks Haven. Stanf —1N 93
Monksmead. Borwd —14Sa 21
Monks Orchard. Dart —61Md 133
Monks Orchard Rd. Beck
—74Cc 148
Monks Pk. Wemb —37Ra 59
Monks Pk. Gdns. Wemb —38Ra 59
Monks Pl. Cat —94Xb 181
Monks Rd. Bans —88Cb 163
Monks Rd. Enf —12Sb 25
Monks Rd. Vir W —10P 117
Monks Rd. Wind —4B 94
Monk St. SE18 —49Qc 86
Monk's Wlk. Egh & Cher —69F 118
Monks Wlk. S'fleet —65Ce 135
Monks Way. NW11 —28Bb 41
Monks Way. Beck —72Cc 148
Monks Way. Orp —74Sc 150
Monks Way. Stai —66M 119
Monks Way. W Dray —51N 97
Monkswell La. Coul —96Db 179
Monkswood Av. Wal A —5Fc 13
Monkswood Gdns. Borwd —15Ta 21
Monkswood Gdns. Ilf —27Qc 46
Monkton Ho. E5 —36Xb 63
Monkton Rd. Well —54Vc 109
Monkton St. SE11
—49Qb 82 (5A 206)
Monkville Av. NW11 —28Bb 41
Monkville Pde. NW11 —28Bb 41
Monkwell St. EC2
—43Sb 83 (1E 200)
Monmouth Av. E18 —27Kc 45
Monmouth Av. King T —66La 122
Monmouth Clo. Mitc —70Nb 126
Monmouth Clo. Well —56Wc 109
Monmouth Gro. Bren —49Na 79
Monmouth Pl. W2 —44Db 81
(off Monmouth Rd.)
Monmouth Rd. E6 —41Pc 86
Monmouth Rd. N9 —19Xb 25
Monmouth Rd. W2 —44Cb 81
Monmouth Rd. Dag —36Bd 67
Monmouth Rd. Hay —49V 76
Monmouth Rd. Wat —13X 19
Monmouth St. WC2
—44Nb 82 (3F 199)
Monnery Rd. N19 —34Lb 62
Monnow Grn. S Ock —45Sd 90
Monnow Rd. SE1 —49Wb 83
Monnow Rd. S Ock —45Sd 90
Mono La. Felt —61X 121
Monoux Almshouses. E17 —28Dc 44
Monoux Gro. E17 —25Cc 44
Monroe Cres. Enf —11Xb 25
Monroe Dri. SW14 —57Ra 101
Monro Gdns. Harr —24Ga 38
Monsell Gdns. Stai —64G 118
Monsell Rd. N4 —34Rb 63
Monson Rd. NW10 —40Wa 60
Monson Rd. SE14 —52Zb 106
Mons Wlk. Egh —64E 118
Mons Way. Brom —72Nc 150
Montacute Rd. SE6 —59Bc 106
Montacute Rd. Bush —17Ga 20
Montacute Rd. Mord —72Fb 145
Montacute Rd. New Ad —81Ec 166
Montagu Cres. N18 —21Xb 43
Montague Av. SE4 —56Bc 106
Montague Av. W7 —46Ha 78
Montague Av. S Croy —84Ub 165
Montague Clo. SE1
—46Tb 83 (6F 201)
Montague Clo. W on T —73X 141
Montague Gdns. W3 —45Qa 79
Montague Pas. Uxb —38M 55
Montague Pl. EC1
—43Sb 83 (1D 200)
Montague Pl. WC1
—43Mb 82 (7E 192)
Montague Rd. E8 —36Wb 63
Montague Rd. E11 —33Hc 65
Montague Rd. N8 —29Pb 42
Montague Rd. N15 —28Wb 43
Montague Rd. SW19 —66Db 125
Montague Rd. W7 —46Ha 78
Montague Rd. W13 —44Ka 78
Montague Rd. Croy —74Rb 147
Montague Rd. Houn —55Da 99
Montague Rd. Rich —58Na 101
Montague Rd. Slou —5K 73
Montague Rd. S'hall —49Aa 77
Montague Rd. Uxb —38M 55
Montague Sq. SE15 —52Yb 106
Montague St. WC1
—43Nb 82 (7F 193)
Montague Ter. Brom —69Hc 129
Montague Waye. S'hall —48Aa 77
Montagu Gdns. N18 —21Xb 43
Montagu Gdns. Wall —77Lb 146
Montagu Mans. W1
—43Hb 81 (7G 191)
Montagu M. W1 —43Hb 81
Montagu M. N. W1
—43Hb 81 (1G 197)
Montagu M. S. W1
—44Hb 81 (2G 197)
Montagu M. W. W1
—44Hb 81 (2G 197)
Montagu Pl. W1 —43Hb 81 (1F 197)
Montagu Rd. N18 & N9 —22Xb 43
Montagu Rd. NW4 —30Wa 40
Montagu Rd. Dat —3M 95
Montagu Rd. Ind. Est. N18
—21Yb 44
Montagu Row. W1
—43Hb 81 (1G 197)
Montagu Sq. W1
—43Hb 81 (1G 197)
Montagu St. W1
—44Hb 81 (2G 197)
Montalt Rd. Wfd G —22Hc 45
Montana Clo. S Croy —82Tb 165
Montana Rd. SW17 —62Jb 126
Montana Rd. SW20 —67Ya 124
Montayne Rd. Chesh —4Zb 12
Montbelle Rd. SE9 —62Rc 130
Montcalm Clo. Brom —72Jc 149
Montcalm Clo. Hay —41X 77
Montcalm Ho. E14 —49Bc 84
Montcalm Rd. SE7 —52Mc 107
Montclare St. E2
—42Vb 83 (4K 195)
Monteagle Av. Bark —37Sc 66
Monteagle Ct. N1
—40Ub 63 (1J 195)
Monteagle Way. E5 —34Wb 63
Monteagle Way. SE15 —55Xb 105
Montefiore St. SW8 —54Kb 104
Monteith Rd. E3 —39Bc 64
Montem La. Slou —6H 73
Montem Rd. SE23 —59Bc 106
Montem Rd. N Mald —70Ua 124
Montem St. N4 —32Pb 62
Montenotte Rd. N8 —29Lb 42
Monterey Clo. Bex —61Ed 132
Montesole Ct. Pinn —26Y 37
Montesquieu Ter. E16 —44Hc 85
(off Clarkson Rd.)
Montford Pl. SE11 —50Qb 82
Montford Rd. Sun —70W 120
Montfort Gdns. Ilf —23Sc 46
Montfort Pl. SW19 —60Za 102
Montfort Rd. Kems —89Nd 171

Montgolfier Wlk. N'holt —41Aa 77
Montgomery Av. Esh —75Ga 142
Montgomery Clo. Grays —47Ee 91
Montgomery Clo. Mitc —70Nb 126
Montgomery Clo. Sidc —58Vc 109
Montgomery Cres. Romf —22Ld 49
Montgomery Dri. Chesh —1Ac 12
Montgomery Pl. Slou —4N 73
Montgomery Rd. W4 —49Sa 79
Montgomery Rd. Edgw —23Pa 39
Montgomery Rd. S Dar —67Td 134
Montgomery Rd. Wok —90A 156
Montholme Rd. SW11 —58Hb 103
Monthope Rd. E1 —43Wb 83
Montolieu Gdns. SW15 —57Xa 102
Montpelier Av. W5 —43La 78
Montpelier Av. Bex —59Zc 109
Montpelier Clo. Uxb —39Q 56
Montpelier Ct. W5 —43Ma 79
Montpelier Ct. Wind —4G 94
Montpelier Gdns. E6 —41Mc 85
Montpelier Gdns. Romf —31Yc 67
Montpelier Gro. NW5 —36Lb 62
Montpelier M. SW7 —48Gb 81 (3E 202)
Montpelier Pl. SW7 —48Gb 81 (3E 202)
Montpelier Rise. NW11 —31Ab 60
Montpelier Rise. Wemb —32Ma 59
Montpelier Rd. N3 —25Eb 41
Montpelier Rd. SE15 —53Xb 105
Montpelier Rd. W5 —43Ma 79
Montpelier Rd. Purl —82Rb 165
Montpelier Rd. Sutt —77Eb 145
Montpelier Row. SE3 —54Hc 107
Montpelier Row. Twic —59La 100
Montpelier Sq. SW7 —47Gb 81 (2E 202)
Montpelier St. SW7 —48Gb 81 (3E 202)
Montpelier Ter. SW7 —47Gb 81 (2E 202)
Montpelier Vale. SE3 —54Hc 107
Montpelier Wlk. SW7 —48Gb 81 (3E 202)
Montpelier Way. NW11 —31Ab 60
Montrave Rd. SE20 —65Yb 128
Montreal Pl. WC2 —45Pb 82 (4H 199)
Montreal Rd. Ilf —31Sc 66
Montreal Rd. Sev —95Gd 186
Montreal Rd. Til —5C 114
Montrell Rd. SW2 —60Nb 104
Montrose Av. NW6 —40Ab 60
Montrose Av. Dat —2N 95
Montrose Av. Edgw —26Sa 39
Montrose Av. Romf —26Ld 49
Montrose Av. Sidc —59Wc 109
Montrose Av. Slou —4F 72
Montrose Av. Twic —59Da 99
Montrose Av. Well —55Tc 108
Montrose Clo. Ashf —65S 120
Montrose Clo. Well —55Vc 109
Montrose Clo. Wfd G —21Jc 45
Montrose Ct. NW9 —26Sa 39
Montrose Ct. NW11 —28Bb 41
Montrose Ct. SW7 —47Fb 81 (2C 202)
Montrose Ct. Harr —29Da 37
Montrose Cres. N12 —23Eb 41
Montrose Cres. Wemb —37Na 59
Montrose Gdns. Mitc —68Hb 125
Montrose Gdns. Oxs —84Fa 160
Montrose Gdns. Sutt —75Db 145
Montrose Ho. E14 —48Cc 84
Montrose Pl. SW1 —47Jb 82 (2J 203)
Montrose Rd. Felt —58T 98
Montrose Rd. Harr —26Ga 38
Montrose Ter. W Dray —45M 75
Montrose Wlk. Stan —23Ka 38
Montrose Wlk. Wey —76R 140
Montrose Way. SE23 —60Zb 106
Montrose Way. Dat —3P 95
Montrouge Cres. Eps —88Ya 162
Montserrat Av. Wfd G —24Fc 45
Montserrat Clo. SE19 —64Tb 127
Montserrat Rd. SW15 —56Ab 102
Monument Bri. Ind. Est. Wok —87C 156
Monument Bri. Ind. Est. E. Wok —87D 156
Monument Gdns. SE13 —57Ec 106
Monument Grn. Wey —76R 140
Monument Hill. Wey —77R 140
Monument La. Ger X —23A 34
Monument Rd. Wey —77R 140
Monument Rd. Wok —86C 156
Monument St. EC3 —45Tb 83 (5G 201)
Monument Way. N17 —27Vb 43
Monument Way E. Wok —87D 156
Monument Way W. Wok —87C 156
Monza St. E1 —45Yb 84
Moodkee St. SE16 —48Yb 84
Moody St. E1 —41Zb 84
Moon Ct. SE12 —56Jc 107
Moon La. Barn —13Bb 23
Moon St. N1 —39Rb 63
Moorcroft Gdns. Brom —71Nc 150
Moorcroft La. Uxb —43Q 76
Moorcroft Rd. SW16 —62Nb 126
Moorcroft Way. Pinn —29Aa 37
Moordown. SE18 —53Qc 108
Moore Av. Grays —50Ae 91
Moore Av. Til —4D 114
Moore Clo. SW14 —55Sa 101
Moore Clo. Add —78K 139
Moore Clo. Mitc —68Kb 126
Moore Clo. Slou —7F 72
Moore Clo. Wall —80Nb 146
Moore Cres. Dag —39Xc 67
Moore Gro. Cres. Egh —65B 118
Moore Ho. N8 —28Nb 42
(off Pembroke Rd.)
Moore Ho. Horn —30Jd 48
(off Globe Rd.)
Mooreland Rd. Brom —66Hc 129
Moore Pk. Rd. SW6 —52Cb 103
Moore Rd. SE19 —65Sb 127
Moore Rd. Swans —58Ae 113
Moores La. Eton W —9D 72
Moore's Pl. Brtwd —19Zd 33
Moore St. SW3 —49Hb 81 (5F 203)
Moore Wlk. E7 —35Jc 65
Moore Way. Sutt —81Cb 163
Moorey Clo. E15 —39Hc 65
Moorfield Av. W5 —42Ma 79
Moorfield Rd. N17 —26Vb 43
Moorfield Rd. Chess —78Na 143
Moorfield Rd. Den —31J 55
Moorfield Rd. Enf —11Yb 26
Moorfield Rd. Orp —73Wc 151
Moorfield Rd. Uxb —44M 75
Moorfields. EC2 —43Tb 83 (1F 201)
Moorfields Clo. Stai —67G 118
Moorfields Highwalk. EC2
(off Fore St.) —43Tb 83 (1F 201)
Moorgate. EC2 —44Tb 83 (2F 201)
Moorgate Pl. EC2 —44Tb 83 (2F 201)
(off Swan All.)
Moorhall Rd. Hare —30K 35
Moorhayes Dri. Stai —69L 119
Moorhead Way. SE3 —55Kc 107
Moorholme. Wok —91A 172
Moorhouse. NW9 —25Va 40
Moorhouse Rd. W2 —44Cb 81
Moorhouse Rd. Harr —27Ma 39
Moorhouse Rd. West —100Qc 184
Moorhurst Av. Chesh —1Qb 10
Moorings, The. E16 —43Lc 85
(off Prince Regent La.)
Moorland Clo. Romf —24Dd 48
Moorland Clo. Twic —59Ca 99
Moorland Rd. SW9 —56Rb 105
Moorland Rd. W Dray —51L 97
Moorlands. N'holt —39Aa 57
Moorlands Av. NW7 —23Xa 40
Moorlands, The. Wok —93B 172
Moor La. EC2 —43Tb 83 (1F 201)
Moor La. Chess —77Na 143
Moor La. Rick —18P 17
Moor La. Sarr —8G 2
Moor La. Stai —60F 96
Moor La. Upm —32Ud 70
Moor La. W Dray —51L 97
Moor La. Wok —94A 172
Moor La. Crossing. Wat —17S 18
Moormead Cres. Stai —63H 119
Moormead Dri. Eps —78Ua 144
Moor Mead Rd. Twic —58Ja 100
Moor Mill La. Col S —1Ga 6
Moor Pk. Gdns. King T —66Ua 124
Moor Pk. Ind. Cen. Wat —17S 18
Moor Pk. Rd. N'wd —22T 36
Moor Pl. EC2 —43Tb 83 (1F 201)
Moor Rd. Sev —92Kd 187
Moor Rd. Stai —58J 97
Moorside Rd. Brom —62Gc 129
Moorsom Way. Coul —89Mb 164
Moorstown Ct. Slou —7J 73
Moor St. W1 —44Mb 82 (3E 198)
Moortown Rd. Wat —21Y 37
Moor View. Wat —17W 18
Moot Ct. NW9 —29Qa 39
Morant Gdns. Romf —22Dd 48
Morant Pl. N22 —25Pb 42
Morant Rd. Grays —8D 92
Morants Ct. Rd. Dun G & Sev —90Ed 170
Morant St. E14 —45Cc 84
Mora Rd. NW2 —35Ya 60
Mora St. EC1 —41Sb 83 (4E 194)
Morat St. SW9 —53Pb 104
Moravian Clo. SW10 —51Fb 103
Moravian Pl. SW10 —51Fb 103
Moravian St. E2 —40Yb 64
Moray Av. Hay —46V 76
Moray Clo. Edgw —19Ra 21
Moray Clo. Romf —24Gd 48
Moray Dri. Slou —4L 73
Moray M. N7 —33Pb 62
Moray Rd. N4 —33Pb 62
Moray Way. Romf —24Fd 48
Mordaunt Gdns. Dag —38Ad 67
Mordaunt Ho. NW10 —39Ta 59
Mordaunt St. SW9 —55Pb 104
Morden Clo. Tad —92Ja 178
Morden Ct. Mord —70Db 125
Morden Ct. Pde. Mord —70Db 125
Morden Gdns. Gnfd —36Ha 58
Morden Gdns. Mitc —70Fb 125
Morden Hall Rd. Mord —69Db 125
Morden Hill. SE13 —54Ec 106
Morden La. SE13 —53Ec 106
Morden Rd. SE3 —54Jc 107
Morden Rd. SW19 —67Db 125
Morden Rd. Mord & Mitc —70Eb 125
Morden Rd. Romf —31Ad 67
Morden Rd. M. SE3 —54Jc 107
Morden St. SE13 —53Dc 106
Morden Way. Sutt —73Cb 145
Morden Wharf Rd. SE10 —48Gc 85
Mordon Rd. Ilf —31Vc 67
Mordred Rd. SE6 —61Gc 129
Moreau Wlk. G Grn —44A 74
Morecambe Clo. E1 —43Zb 84
Morecambe Clo. Horn —36Kd 69
Morecambe Gdns. Stan —21Ma 39
Morecambe St. SE17 —50Sb 83 (6E 206)
Morecambe Ter. N18 —21Tb 43
More Clo. E16 —44Hc 85
More Clo. W14 —49Za 80
More Clo. Purl —83Qb 164
Morecoombe Clo. King T —66Ra 123
Moree Way. N18 —21Wb 43
Moreland Av. Coln —52E 96
Moreland Av. Grays —47Ee 91
Moreland Clo. Coln —52E 96
Moreland Ct. NW2 —34Cb 61
Moreland Dri. Ger X —31B 54
Moreland St. EC1 —41Rb 83 (3C 194)
Moreland Way. E4 —20Dc 26
More La. Esh —76Da 141
Morella Clo. Vir W —10P 117
Morella Rd. SW12 —59Hb 103
Morello Av. Uxb —43R 76
Morello Clo. Swan —70Fd 132
Moremead Rd. SE6 —63Bc 128
Morena St. SE6 —59Dc 106
Moresby Av. Surb —73Ra 143
Moresby Rd. E5 —32Xb 63
Moresby Wlk. SW8 —54Kb 104
More's Gdns. SW3 —51Fb 103
(off Cheyne Wlk.)
Mores La. Pil H —14Sd 32
Moretaine Rd. Ashf —62M 119
Moreton Av. Iswth —53Ga 100
Moreton Clo. E5 —33Xb 63
Moreton Clo. N15 —30Tb 43
Moreton Clo. Swan —68Gd 132
Moreton Ct. Dart —55Hd 110
Moreton Gdns. Wfd G —22Nc 46
Moreton Ind. Est. Swan —70Kd 133
Moreton Pl. SW1 —50Lb 82 (7C 204)
Moreton Rd. N15 —30Tb 43
Moreton Rd. S Croy —78Tb 147
Moreton Rd. Wor Pk —75Wa 144
Moreton St. SW1 —50Lb 82 (7C 204)
Moreton Ter. SW1 —50Lb 82 (7C 204)
Moreton Ter. M. N. SW1 —50Lb 82 (7C 204)
Moreton Ter. M. S. SW1 —50Lb 82 (7C 204)
Moreton Tower. W3 —46Ra 79
Moreton Way. Slou —6B 72
Morewood Clo. Sev —95Hd 186
Morfe Way. N18 —21Wb 43
Morford Clo. Ruis —31X 57
Morford Way. Ruis —31X 57
Morgan Av. E17 —28Fc 45
Morgan Clo. Dag —38Cd 68
Morgan Clo. N'wd —23V 36
Morgan Cres. They B —8Tc 14
Morgan Dri. Grnh —59Ud 112
Morgan Mans. N7 —36Qb 62
(off Morgan Rd.)
Morgan Rd. N7 —36Qb 62
Morgan Rd. W10 —43Bb 81
Morgan Rd. Brom —66Jc 129
Morgan Rd. Tedd —65Ga 122
Morgan's La. SE1 —46Ub 83 (7H 201)
Morgan's La. Hay —43T 76
Morgan St. E3 —41Ac 84
Morgan St. E16 —43Hc 85
Morgan Way. Rain —41Ld 89
Morgan Way. Wfd G —23Nc 46
Moriatry Clo. N7 —35Nb 62
Morie St. SW18 —57Db 103
Morieux Rd. E10 —32Bc 64
Moring Rd. SW17 —63Jb 126
Morkyns Wlk. SE21 —62Ub 127
Morland Av. Croy —74Ub 147
Morland Av. Dart —57Kd 111
Morland Clo. NW11 —32Db 61
Morland Clo. Hamp —64Ba 121
Morland Clo. Mitc —69Gb 125
Morland Est. E8 —38Wb 63
Morland Gdns. NW10 —38Ta 59
Morland Gdns. S'hall —46Da 77
Morland M. N1 —38Qb 62
Morland Rd. E17 —29Zb 44
Morland Rd. SE20 —65Zb 128
Morland Rd. Croy —74Ub 147
Morland Rd. Dag —38Cd 68
Morland Rd. Harr —29Na 39
Morland Rd. Ilf —33Rc 66
Morland Rd. Sutt —78Eb 145
Morland Way. Chesh —1Ac 12
Morley Av. E4 —24Fc 45
Morley Av. N18 —21Wb 43
Morley Av. N22 —26Qb 42
Morley Clo. Orp —75Rc 150
Morley Clo. Slou —47B 74
Morley Ct. E4 —22Bc 44
Morley Ct. Short —70Hc 129
Morley Cres. Edgw —19Sa 21
Morley Cres. Ruis —33Y 57
Morley Cres. E. Stan —26La 38
Morley Cres. W. Stan —27La 38
Morley Hill. Enf —10Tb 11
Morley Ho. N16 —33Wb 63
Morley Rd. E10 —32Ec 64
Morley Rd. E15 —40Hc 65
Morley Rd. SE13 —56Ec 106
Morley Rd. Bark —39Tc 66
Morley Rd. Chst —67Sc 130
Morley Rd. Romf —29Ad 47
Morley Rd. S Croy —82Vb 165
Morley Rd. Sutt —74Bb 145
Morley Rd. Twic —58Ma 101
Morley Sq. Grays —9C 92
Morley St. SE1 —48Qb 82 (3A 206)
Morna Rd. SE5 —54Sb 105
Morning La. E9 —37Yb 64
Morningside Rd. Wor Pk —75Ya 144
Mornington Av. W14 —49Bb 81
Mornington Av. Brom —69Lc 129
Mornington Av. Ilf —31Qc 66
Mornington Clo. Big H —89Mc 167
Mornington Clo. Wfd G —21Jc 45
Mornington Ct. Bex —60Fd 110
Mornington Cres. NW1 —40Lb 62 (1B 192)
Mornington Cres. Houn —53X 99
Mornington Gro. E3 —41Cc 84
Mornington M. SE5 —53Sb 105
Mornington Pl. NW1 —40Kb 62 (1B 192)
Mornington Rd. E4 —17Fc 27
Mornington Rd. E11 —31Hc 65
Mornington Rd. SE8 —52Bc 106
Mornington Rd. Ashf —64S 120
Mornington Rd. Gnfd —43Da 77
Mornington Rd. Lou —13Sc 28
Mornington Rd. Rad —6Ja 6
Mornington Rd. Wfd G —21Hc 45
Mornington St. NW1 —40Kb 62 (1A 192)
Mornington Ter. NW1 —39Kb 62 (1A 192)
Mornington Wlk. Rich —63La 122
Morocco St. SE1 —47Ub 83 (2H 207)
Morpeth Av. Borwd —10Pa 7
Morpeth Gro. E9 —39Zb 64
Morpeth Rd. E9 —39Yb 64
Morpeth St. E2 —41Zb 84
Morpeth Ter. SW1 —48Lb 82 (4B 204)
Morpeth Wlk. N17 —24Xb 43
Morrab Gdns. Ilf —34Vc 67
Morrell Clo. New Bar —13Eb 23
Morrice Clo. Slou —49B 74
Morris Av. E12 —36Pc 66
Morris Blitz Ct. N16 —35Vb 63
Morris Clo. Croy —72Ac 148
Morris Clo. Ger X —25B 34
Morris Clo. Orp —76Uc 150
Morris Ct. E4 —20Dc 26
Morris Ct. Wal A —6Hc 13
Morris Gdns. SW18 —59Cb 103
Morris Gdns. Dart —57Qd 111
Morris Ho. SE16 —47Xb 83
(off Cherry Garden St.)
Morrish Rd. SW2 —59Nb 104
Morrison Av. N17 —27Ub 43
Morrison Ho. Grays —47Fe 91
Morrison Rd. Bark —40Ad 67
Morrison Rd. Hay —41X 77
Morrison St. SW11 —55Jb 104
Morris Pl. N4 —33Qb 62
Morris Rd. E14 —43Dc 84
Morris Rd. E15 —35Gc 65
Morris Rd. Dag —33Bd 67
Morris Rd. Iswth —55Ha 100
Morris Rd. Romf —24Kd 49
Morris St. E1 —44Xb 83
Morriston Clo. Wat —22Y 37
Morse Clo. E13 —41Jc 85
Morse Clo. Hare —26L 35
Morshead Mans. W9 —41Db 81
(off Morshead Rd.)
Morshead Rd. W9 —41Cb 81
Morson Rd. Enf —16Ac 26
Morston Clo. Tad —92Xa 178
Morston Gdns. SE9 —63Pc 130
Morten Clo. SW4 —58Mb 104
Morten Gdns. Den —31J 55
Morteyne Rd. N17 —25Tb 43
Mortgramit Sq. SE18 —48Qc 86
Mortham St. E15 —39Gc 65
Mortimer Clo. NW2 —33Bb 61
Mortimer Clo. SW16 —61Mb 126
Mortimer Clo. Bush —16Da 19
Mortimer Cres. NW6 —39Db 61
Mortimer Cres. Wor Pk —76Ta 143
Mortimer Dri. Enf —15Ub 25
Mortimer Est. NW6 —39Db 61
(off Mortimer Pl.)
Mortimer Ho. W11 —46Za 80
(off Queensdale Cres.)
Mortimer Mkt. WC1 —42Lb 82 (6C 192)
Mortimer Pl. NW6 —39Db 61
Mortimer Rd. E6 —41Pc 86
Mortimer Rd. N1 —38Ub 63
Mortimer Rd. NW10 —41Ya 80
Mortimer Rd. W13 —44La 78
Mortimer Rd. Big H —84Lc 167
Mortimer Rd. Eri —51Fd 110
Mortimer Rd. Mitc —67Hb 125
Mortimer Rd. Orp —74Wc 151
Mortimer Rd. Slou —8H 73
Mortimer Sq. W11 —45Za 80
Mortimer St. W1 —44Lb 82 (2A 198)
Mortimer Ter. NW5 —35Kb 62
Mortlake Clo. Croy —76Nb 146
Mortlake Dri. Mitc —67Gb 125
Mortlake High St. SW14 —55Ta 101
Mortlake Rd. E16 —44Kc 85
Mortlake Rd. Ilf —35Sc 66
Mortlake Rd. Rich —52Qa 101
Mortlock Clo. SE15 —53Xb 105
Mortlock Ct. E12 —35Mc 65
Morton. Tad —93Za 178
Morton Clo. Wok —3F 188
Morton Cres. N14 —21Mb 42
Morton Dri. Farn C —6C 52
Morton Gdns. Wall —78Lb 146
Morton M. SW5 —49Db 81
Morton Pl. SE1 —48Qb 82 (4K 205)
Morton Rd. E15 —38Hc 65
Morton Rd. N1 —38Sb 63
Morton Rd. Mord —71Fb 145
Morton Rd. Wok —3G 188
Morton Way. N14 —20Lb 24
Morvale Clo. Belv —49Bd 87
Morval Rd. SW2 —57Qb 104
Morven Clo. Pot B —3Eb 9
Morven Rd. SW17 —62Hb 125
Morville St. E3 —40Cc 64
Morwell St. WC1 —43Mb 82 (1D 198)
Mosbach Gdns. Hut —19De 33
Moscow Pl. W2 —45Db 81
Moscow Rd. W2 —45Cb 81
Moselle Av. N22 —26Qb 42
Moselle Clo. N8 —27Pb 42
Moselle Ho. N17 —24Vb 43
(off William St.)
Moselle Pl. N17 —24Vb 43
Moselle Rd. Big H —90Nc 168
Moselle St. N17 —24Vb 43
Mospey Cres. Eps —87Va 162
Moss Bank. Grays —50Be 91
Mossborough Clo. N12 —23Db 41
Mossbury Rd. SW11 —55Gb 103
Moss Clo. E1 —43Wb 83
Moss Clo. Pinn —26Ba 37
Moss Clo. Rick —19M 17
Mossdown Clo. Belv —49Cd 88
Mossendew Clo. Hare —25M 35
Mossfield. Cob —85W 158
Mossford Ct. Ilf —26Rc 46
Mossford Grn. Ilf —27Rc 46
Mossford La. Ilf —26Rc 46
Mossford St. E3 —42Bc 84
Moss Gdns. Felt —61W 120
Moss Gdns. S Croy —80Zb 148
Moss Hall Ct. N12 —23Db 41
Moss Hall Cres. N12 —23Db 41
Moss Hall Gro. N12 —23Db 41
Mossington Gdns. SE16 —49Yb 84
Moss La. Pinn —25Aa 37
Moss La. Romf —30Hd 48
Mosslea Rd. SE20 —65Yb 128
(in two parts)
Mosslea Rd. Brom —71Mc 149
Mosslea Rd. Orp —76Sc 150
Mosslea Rd. Whyt —88Vb 165
Mossop St. SW3 —49Gb 81 (5E 202)
Moss Rd. Dag —38Cd 68
Moss Rd. S Ock —43Yd 90
Moss Rd. Wat —6X 5
Moss Side. Brick —2Ba 5
Mossville Gdns. Mord —69Bb 125
Mosswell Ho. N10 —25Jb 42
Moston Clo. Hay —50V 76
Mostyn Av. Wemb —36Pa 59
Mostyn Gdns. NW10 —40Za 60
Mostyn Gro. E3 —40Cc 64
Mostyn Rd. SW9 —53Qb 104
Mostyn Rd. SW19 —67Bb 125
Mostyn Rd. Bush —15Ea 20
Mostyn Rd. Edgw —24Ua 40
Mosul Way. Brom —72Nc 150
Mosyer Dri. Orp —75Zc 151
Motcomb St. SW1 —48Jb 82 (3H 203)
Mote, The. New Ash —75Be 155
Mothers Sq. E5 —35Yb 64
Motherwell Way. Grays —50Wd 90
Motley Av. EC2 —42Ub 83 (5H 195)
(off Christina St.)
Motley St. SW8 —54Lb 104
Motspur Pk. N Mald —72Va 144
Mottingham Gdns. SE9 —60Mc 107
Mottingham La. SE12 & SE9 —60Lc 107
Mottingham Rd. N9 —16Zb 26
Mottingham Rd. SE9 —61Nc 130
Mottisfont Rd. SE2 —48Wc 87
Motts Hill La. Tad —95Wa 178
Mott St. E4 & Lou —10Ec 12
Mouchotte Clo. Big H —86Kc 167
Moules Ct. SE5 —52Sb 105
Moulins Rd. E9 —38Yb 64
Moulsford Ho. N7 —36Mb 62
Moultain Hill. Swan —70Jd 132
Moulton Av. Houn —54Aa 99
Moultrie Way. Upm —31Ud 70
Moundfield Rd. N16 —30Wb 43
Mound, The. SE9 —62Qc 130
Mountacre Clo. SE26 —63Vb 127
Mt. Adon Pk. SE22 —59Wb 105
Mountague Pl. E14 —45Ec 84
Mountain Ho. SE11 —50Pb 82 (7J 205)
Mt. Angelus Rd. SW15 —59Va 102
Mt. Ararat Rd. Rich —57Na 101
Mt. Arlington. Short —68Gc 129
(off Park Hill Rd.)
Mt. Ash Rd. SE26 —62Xb 127
Mount Av. E4 —20Cc 26
Mount Av. W5 —43La 78
Mount Av. Cat —96Sb 181
Mount Av. Romf —23Sd 50
Mount Av. Shenf —17De 33
Mount Av. S'hall —44Ca 77
Mountbatten Clo. SE18 —51Uc 108
Mountbatten Clo. SE19 —64Ub 127
Mountbatten Clo. Slou —8L 73
Mountbatten Ho. N6 —31Jb 62
(off Hillcrest)
Mountbatten Ho. N'wd —23U 36
Mountbatten M. SW18 —59Eb 103
Mountbatten Sq. Wind —3G 94
Mountbel Rd. Stan —25Ja 38
Mount Clo. W5 —43La 78
Mount Clo. Barn —14Jb 24
Mount Clo. Brom —67Nc 130
Mount Clo. Cars —81Jb 164
Mount Clo. Fet —95Ga 176
Mount Clo. Kenl —88Tb 165
Mount Clo. Sev —95Hd 186
Mount Clo. Wok —9E 188
Mount Clo., The. Vir W —72A 138
Mountcombe Clo. Surb —73Na 143
Mount Cotts. Farn C —5G 52
Mount Ct. SW15 —55Ab 102
Mount Ct. W Wick —75Gc 149
Mount Cres. War —21Zd 51
Mt. Culver Av. Sidc —65Zc 131
Mount Dri. Bexh —57Ad 109
Mount Dri. Harr —29Ba 37
Mount Dri. Wemb —33Sa 59
Mountearl Gdns. SW16 —62Pb 126
Mt. Echo Av. E4 —18Dc 26
Mt. Echo Dri. E4 —18Dc 26
Mt. Ephraim La. SW16 —62Mb 126
Mt. Ephraim Rd. SW16 —62Mb 126
Mt. Felix. W on T —73V 140
Mountfield Clo. Stanf —1N 93
Mountfield Rd. E6 —40Qc 66
Mountfield Rd. N3 —27Bb 41
Mountfield Rd. W5 —44Ma 79
Mountfield Way. Orp —70Yc 131
Mountford Rd. E8 —36Wb 63
Mountford St. E1 —44Wb 83
Mountfort Cres. N1 —38Qb 62
Mountfort Ter. N1 —38Qb 62
Mount Gdns. SE26 —62Xb 127
Mt. Grace Rd. Pot B —3Cb 9
Mount Gro. Edgw —20Sa 21
Mountgrove Rd. N5 —34Rb 63
Mt. Harry Rd. Sev —95Jd 186
Mt. Hermon Clo. Wok —7G 188
Mt. Hermon Rd. Wok —7G 188
Mount Hill. Knock —89Wc 169
Mt. Hill La. Ger X —2M 53
Mounthurst Rd. Brom —73Hc 149
Mountington Pk. Clo. Harr —30Ma 39
Mountjoy Clo. EC2 —43Sb 83 (1E 200)
(off Thomas More Highwalk.)
Mountjoy Clo. SE2 —47Xc 87
Mountjoy Ho. EC2
(off Barbican) —43Sb 83 (1E 200)
Mount La. Den —33F 54
Mt. Lee. Egh —64B 118
Mt. Lodge. N6 —31Lb 42
Mount M. Hamp —67Da 121
Mt. Mills. EC1 —41Rb 83 (4C 194)
Mountnessing By-Pass. Mount —13Fe 33
Mountnessing La. Dodd —11Zd 33
Mt. Nod Rd. SW16 —62Pb 126
Mount Pde. Barn —14Gb 23
Mount Pk. Cars —80Jb 146
Mount Pk. Av. Harr —33Fa 58
Mount Pk. Av. S Croy —81Rb 165
Mount Pk. Cres. W5 —44Ma 79
Mount Pk. Rd. W5 —43Ma 79
Mount Pk. Rd. Harr —34Fa 58
Mount Pk. Rd. Pinn —29W 36
Mount Pl. W3 —46Ra 79
Mt. Pleasant. N14 —18Mb 24
(off Wells, The.)
Mt. Pleasant. SE27 —63Sb 127
Mt. Pleasant. WC1 —42Qb 82 (6K 193)
Mt. Pleasant. Barn —14Gb 23
Mt. Pleasant. Big H —89Mc 167
Mt. Pleasant. Eff —100Aa 175
Mt. Pleasant. Eps —82Va 162
Mt. Pleasant. Ger X —22A 34
Mt. Pleasant. Hare —25J 35
Mt. Pleasant. Ruis —33Y 57
Mt. Pleasant. Wemb —39Na 59
Mt. Pleasant. W Hor —100R 174
Mt. Pleasant. Wey —76Q 140
Mt. Pleasant Av. Hut —16Fe 33
Mt. Pleasant Cres. N4 —32Pb 62
Mt. Pleasant Hill. E5 —33Xb 63
Mt. Pleasant La. E5 —33Xb 63
Mt. Pleasant La. Brick —2Aa 5
Mt. Pleasant Rd. E17 —26Ac 44
Mt. Pleasant Rd. N17 —26Ub 43
Mt. Pleasant Rd. NW10 —38Ya 60
Mt. Pleasant Rd. SE13 —58Dc 106
Mt. Pleasant Rd. W5 —42La 78
Mt. Pleasant Rd. Cat —95Wb 181
Mt. Pleasant Rd. Chig —21Tc 46
Mt. Pleasant Rd. Dart —58Pd 111
Mt. Pleasant Rd. N Mald —69Sa 123
Mt. Pleasant Rd. Romf —23Fd 48
Mt. Pleasant Vs. N4 —31Pb 62
Mt. Pleasant Wlk. Bex —57Ed 110
Mount Rd. NW2 —34Xa 60
Mount Rd. NW4 —30Wa 40
Mount Rd. SW19 —61Cb 125
Mount Rd. Barn —15Gb 23
Mount Rd. Bexh —57Zc 109
Mount Rd. Chess —78Pa 143
Mount Rd. Chob —1E 188
Mount Rd. Dag —32Bd 67
Mount Rd. Dart —58Hd 110
Mount Rd. Felt —62Aa 121
Mount Rd. Hay —47W 76
Mount Rd. Ilf —36Rc 66
Mount Rd. Mitc —68Fb 125
Mount Rd. N Mald —69Ta 123
Mount Rd. They G —4Yc 15
Mount Rd. Wok —9E 188
Mount Row. W1 —45Kb 82 (5K 197)
Mountsfield Clo. Stai —58J 97
Mountsfield Ct. SE13 —58Fc 107
Mounts Hill. Wind —1A 116
Mountside. Stan —25Ha 38
Mounts Pond Rd. SE3 —54Fc 107
(in two parts)
Mount Sq., The. NW3 —34Eb 61
Mounts Rd. Grnh —57Xd 112
Mt. Stewart Av. Harr —31Ma 59
Mount St. SE18 —49Rc 86
Mount St. W1 —45Jb 82 (5H 197)
Mount Ter. E1 —43Xb 83
Mount, The. E5 —33Xb 63
Mount, The. N20 —19Eb 23
Mount, The. NW3 —35Eb 61
Mount, The. W3 —46Ra 79
Mount, The. Bexh —57Dd 110
Mount, The. Coul —86Kb 164
Mount, The. Eps —82Va 162
Mount, The. Esh —79Ca 141
Mount, The. Fet —96Ga 176
Mount, The. N Mald —69Va 124
Mount, The. Pot B —2Db 9
Mount, The. Rick —16L 17
Mount, The. Romf —20Ld 31
Mount, The. Stanf —1P 93
Mount, The. Tad —98Bb 179
Mount, The. Vir W —72A 138
Mount, The. Warl —91Wb 181
Mount, The. Wemb —33Sa 59
Mount, The. Wey —75U 140
Mount, The. Wok —6G 188
(Elm Rd.)

Mount, The—Nevin Ho.

Mount, The. Wok —7D 188
(St John's Hill Rd.)
Mount, The. Wor Pk —77Xa 144
Mt. Vernon. NW3 —35Eb 61
Mount View. NW7 —20Ta 21
Mount View. W5 —42Ma 79
Mount View. Enf —10Pb 10
Mount View. N'wd —23V 36
Mount View. Rick —18K 17
Mountview Ct. N15 —28Rb 43
Mt. View Rd. E4 —17Fc 27
Mt. View Rd. N4 —31Nb 62
Mt. View Rd. NW9 —29Ta 39
Mt. View Rd. Clay —80Ka 142
Mountview Rd. Orp —73Wc 151
(in two parts)
Mount Vs. SE27 —62Rb 127
Mount Way. Cars —81Jb 164
Mountway. Pot B —2Cb 9
Mount Wood. W Mol —69Da 121
Mountwood Clo. S Croy —82Xb 165
Movers La. Bark —39Tc 66
Mowat Ct. Wor Pk —75Va 144
(off Avenue, The)
Mowatt Clo. N19 —33Mb 62
Mowbray Av. Byfl —85N 157
Mowbray Ct. N22 —25Qb 42
Mowbray Ct. SE19 —66Vb 127
Mowbray Cres. Egh —64C 118
Mowbray Gdns. N'holt —39Ca 57
Mowbray Ho. N2 —26Fb 41
(off Grange, The)
Mowbray Pde. Edgw —21Qa 39
Mowbray Pde. N'holt —39Ca 57
Mowbray Rd. NW6 —37Ab 60
Mowbray Rd. SE19 —67Vb 127
Mowbray Rd. Barn —14Eb 23
Mowbray Rd. Edgw —21Qa 39
Mowbray Rd. Rich —62La 122
Mowbrays Clo. Romf —25Ed 48
Mowbrays Rd. Romf —26Ed 48
Mowbrey Gdns. Lou —11Sc 28
Mowlem St. E2 —40Xb 63
Mowlem Trading Est. N17 —24Yb 44
Mowll St. SW9 —52Qb 104
Moxon Clo. E13 —40Hc 65
Moxon St. W1 —43Jb 82 (1H 197)
Moxon St. Barn —13Bb 23
Moye Clo. E2 —40Wb 63
Moyers Rd. E10 —31Ec 64
Moylan Rd. W6 —51Ab 102
Moyne Ct. Wok —6C 188
Moyne Ho. SE24 —57Rb 105
Moyne Pl. NW10 —40Qa 59
Moys Clo. Croy —72Nb 146
Moyser Rd. SW16 —64Kb 126
Mozart St. W10 —41Bb 81
Mozart Ter. SW1 —49Jb 82 (6J 203)
Muchelney Rd. Mord —72Eb 145
Muckhatch La. Egh —69D 118
Muckingford Rd. W Til & SS17 —9F 92
Mucking Wharf Rd. Stanf —4L 93
Muddy La. Slou —3J 73
Mudlands Ind. Est. Rain —41Hd 88
Mudlarks Way. SE10 & SE7 —48Hc 85
Muggeridge Rd. Dag —35Dd 68
Muggins La. Shorne —3L 137
Muirdown Av. SW14 —56Ta 101
Muirfield. W3 —44Ua 80
Muirfield Clo. Wat —22Y 37
Muirfield Cres. E14 —48Dc 84
Muirfield Grn. Wat —21X 37
Muirfield Rd. Wat —21X 37
Muirfield Rd. Wok —6D 188
Muirkirk Rd. SE6 —60Ec 106
Muir Rd. E5 —35Wb 63
Muir St. E16 —46Nc 86
Mulberry Av. Stai —60N 97
Mulberry Av. Wind —5K 95
Mulberry Bus. Pk. SE16 —47Zb 84
Mulberry Clo. E4 —19Cc 26
Mulberry Clo. NW3 —35Fb 61
Mulberry Clo. NW4 —27Ya 40
Mulberry Clo. SE22 —57Wb 105
Mulberry Clo. SW3 —51Fb 103
Mulberry Clo. SW16 —63Lb 126
Mulberry Clo. Barn —14Fb 23
Mulberry Clo. N'holt —40Aa 57
Mulberry Clo. Park —1Da 5
Mulberry Clo. Romf —28Ld 49
Mulberry Clo. Wey —76R 140
Mulberry Clo. Wok —86A 156
Mulberry Ct. Bark —38Vc 67
Mulberry Ct. Surb —73Ma 143
Mulberry Ct. Twic —62Ha 122
Mulberry Cres. Bren —52Ka 100
Mulberry Cres. W Dray —47Q 76
Mulberry Dri. Purf —49Pd 89
Mulberry Dri. Slou —50A 74
Mulberry Hill. Shenf —17Be 33
Mulberry Ho. Short —68Gc 129
Mulberry La. Croy —74Vb 147
Mulberry M. Wall —79Lb 146
Mulberry Pde. W Dray —48Q 76
Mulberry Pl. W6 —50Wa 80
Mulberry Rd. Grav —2A 136
Mulberry St. E1 —44Wb 83
Mulberry Trees. Shep —73T 140
Mulberry Wlk. SW3 —51Fb 103
Mulberry Way. E18 —26Kc 45
Mulberry Way. Belv —47Ed 88
Mulberry Way. Ilf —28Sc 46
Mulgrave Ct. Sutt —79Db 145
(off Mulgrave Rd.)
Mulgrave Rd. NW10 —35Va 60
Mulgrave Rd. SW6 —51Bb 103
Mulgrave Rd. W5 —41Ma 79
Mulgrave Rd. Croy —76Tb 147
Mulgrave Rd. Harr —33Ja 58
Mulgrave Rd. Sutt —80Bb 145
Mulgrave Way. Knap —6B 188
Mulhaney Way. SE1 —47Tb 83 (2G 207)
Mulholland Clo. Mitc —68Kb 126
Mulkern Rd. N19 —32Mb 62
Mullein Ct. Grays —51Fe 113
Mullender Ct. Grav —10J 115
Mullens Rd. Egh —64E 118
Muller Rd. SW4 —58Mb 104
Mullet Gdns. E2 —41Wb 83
Mullins Path. SW14 —55Ta 101
Mullion Clo. Harr —25Da 37
Mullion Wlk. Wat —21Z 37
Mull Wlk. N1 —37Sb 63
(off Clephane Rd.)
Mulready St. NW8 —42Gb 81 (6D 190)
Multi Way. W3 —47Ua 80
Multon Rd. SW18 —59Fb 103
Multon Rd. W King —79Ud 154
Mumford Ct. EC2 —44Sb 83 (2E 200)
Mumford Rd. SE24 —57Rb 105
Muncaster Clo. Ashf —63Q 120
Muncaster Rd. SW11 —57Hb 103
Muncaster Rd. Ashf —64R 120
Muncies M. SE6 —61Ec 128
Mundania Rd. SE22 —58Xb 105
Munday Rd. E16 —45Jc 85
Munden Dri. Wat —9Aa 5
Munden Gro. Wat —10Y 5
Munden St. W14 —49Ab 80
Mundesley Clo. Wat —20Y 19
Mundesley Spur. Slou —4J 73
Mundford Rd. E5 —33Yb 64
Mundon Gdns. Ilf —32Tc 66
Mund St. W14 —50Bb 81
Mundy St. N1 —41Ub 83 (3H 195)
Munford Dri. Swans —59Ae 113
Mungo Pk. Clo. Bush —19Ea 20
Mungo Pk. Rd. Grav —4F 136
Mungo Pk. Rd. Rain —36Jd 68
Mungo Pk. Way. Orp —73Yc 151
Munnery Way. Orp —76Qc 150
Munnings Gdns. Iswth —57Fa 100
Munro Dri. N11 —23Lb 42
Munro Ho. SE1 —47Qb 82 (2K 205)
Munro M. W10 —43Ab 80
Munro Rd. Bush —15Da 19
Munro Ter. SW10 —51Fb 103
Munster Av. Houn —57Aa 99
Munster Gdns. N13 —21Rb 43
Munster Rd. SW6 —52Ab 102
Munster Rd. Tedd —65La 122
Munster Sq. NW1 —41Kb 82 (4A 192)
Munton Rd. SE17 —49Sb 83 (5E 206)
Murchison Av. Bex —60Zc 109
Murchison Rd. E10 —33Ec 64
Murdoch Clo. Stai —64J 119
Murdock Clo. E16 —44Hc 85
Murdock St. SE15 —51Xb 105
Murfett Clo. SW19 —61Ab 124
Murfitt Way. Upm —35Qd 69
Muriel Av. Wat —15Y 19
Muriel Ct. E10 —31Dc 64
Muriel St. N1 —40Pb 62 (1J 193)
(in two parts)
Murillo Rd. SE13 —56Fc 107
Murphy St. SE1 —47Qb 82 (2K 205)
Murray Av. Brom —69Kc 129
Murray Av. Houn —57Da 99
Murray Bus. Cen. St M —69Xc 131
Murray Ct. Harr —30Ha 38
Murray Ct. Twic —61Fa 122
Murray Cres. Pinn —25Z 37
Murray Grn. Wok —86E 156
Murray Gro. N1 —40Sb 63 (2E 194)
Murray Ho. SE18 —49Pc 86
(off Rideout St.)
Murray Ho. Ott —79E 138
Murray M. NW1 —38Mb 62
Murray Rd. SW19 —65Za 124
Murray Rd. W5 —49La 78
Murray Rd. N'wd —25U 36
Murray Rd. Orp —69Xc 131
Murray Rd. Ott —79E 138
Murray Rd. Rich —61La 122
Murray's La. W Byf —86M 157
Murray Sq. E16 —44Jc 85
Murray St. NW1 —38Lb 62
Murray Ter. NW3 —35Eb 61
Murrell's Wlk. Bookh —95Ca 175
Murreys Ct. Asht —90Ma 161
Murreys, The. Asht —91Ma 177
Mursell Est. SW8 —53Pb 104
Murthering La. Romf —17Hd 30
Murtwell Dri. Chig —23Sc 46
Musard Rd. W6 —51Ab 102
Musbury St. E1 —44Yb 84
Muscatel Pl. SE5 —52Ub 105
Muschamp Rd. SE15 —55Vb 105
Muschamp Rd. Cars —75Gb 145
Muscovy Ho. Eri —47Ad 87
(off Kale Rd.)
Muscovy St. EC3 —45Ub 83 (5J 201)
Museum Path. E2 —41Yb 84
Museum St. WC1 —43Nb 82 (1F 199)
Musgrave Clo. Barn —11Eb 23
Musgrave Cres. SW6 —52Cb 103
Musgrave Rd. Iswth —53Ha 100
Musgrove Rd. SE14 —53Zb 106
Musjid Rd. SW11 —54Fb 103
Musquash Way. Houn —56Y 99
Mussenden La. Hort K & Fawk —71Sd 154
Mustard Mill Rd. Stai —63G 118
Muston Rd. E5 —33Xb 63
Mustow Pl. SW6 —54Bb 103
Muswell Av. N10 —25Kb 42
Muswell Hill. N10 —27Kb 42
Muswell Hill B'way. N10 —27Kb 42
Muswell Hill Pl. N10 —28Kb 42
Muswell Hill Rd. N6 & N10 —30Jb 42
Muswell M. N10 —27Kb 42
Muswell Rd. N10 —27Kb 42
Mutchetts Clo. Wat —5Aa 5
Mutrix Rd. NW6 —39Cb 61
Mutton La. Pot B —3Ya 8
Mutton Pl. NW1 —37Jb 62
Muybridge Rd. N Mald —68Sa 123
Myatt Rd. SW9 —53Rb 105
Mycenae Rd. SE3 —52Jc 107
Myddelton Clo. Enf —11Vb 25
Myddelton Gdns. N21 —17Sb 25
Myddelton Pk. N20 —20Fb 23
Myddelton Pas. EC1 —41Qb 82 (3A 194)
Myddelton Rd. N8 —27Nb 42
Myddelton Sq. EC1 —41Qb 82 (3A 194)
Myddelton St. EC1 —41Qb 82 (4A 194)
Myddleton Av. Enf —10Ub 11
Myddleton Ho. WC1 —40Qb 62 (2K 193)
(off Pentonville Rd.)
Myddleton M. N22 —24Nb 42
Myddleton Path. Chesh —3Xb 11
Myddleton Rd. N22 —24Nb 42
Myddleton Rd. Uxb —39L 55
Myers Clo. SE14 —51Zb 106
Mygrove Clo. Rain —40Md 69
Mygrove Gdns. Rain —40Md 69
Mygrove Rd. Rain —40Md 69
Myles Ct. Chesh —1Sb 11
Mylis Clo. SE26 —63Xb 127
Mylne Clo. W6 —50Wa 80
Mylne St. EC1 —41Qb 82 (3K 193)
Mylor Clo. Wok —86A 156
Mynn's Clo. Eps —86Ra 161
Myra St. SE2 —49Wc 87
Myrdle St. E1 —43Wb 83
Myrke, The. Dat —9K 73
Myrna Clo. SW19 —66Gb 125
Myron Pl. SE13 —55Ec 106
Myrtle Av. Felt —57U 98
Myrtle Av. Ruis —31W 56
Myrtleberry Clo. E8 —37Vb 63
(off Beechwood Rd.)
Myrtle Clo. Barn —18Hb 23
Myrtle Clo. Coln —53G 96
Myrtle Clo. Eri —52Gd 110
Myrtle Clo. Uxb —43P 75
Myrtle Clo. W Dray —48P 75
Myrtle Cres. Slou —5K 73
Myrtledene Rd. SE2 —50Wc 87
Myrtle Gdns. W7 —46Ga 78
Myrtle Gro. Enf —10Tb 11
Myrtle Gro. N Mald —68Sa 123
Myrtle Gro. S Ock —47Sd 90
Myrtle Pl. Dart —59Pd 112
Myrtle Rd. E6 —39Nc 66
Myrtle Rd. E17 —30Ac 44
Myrtle Rd. N13 —20Sb 25
Myrtle Rd. W3 —46Sa 79
Myrtle Rd. Croy —76Cc 148
Myrtle Rd. Dart —60Md 111
Myrtle Rd. Hamp —65Ea 122
Myrtle Rd. Houn —54Ea 100
Myrtle Rd. Ilf —33Rc 66
Myrtle Rd. Romf —23Ld 49
Myrtle Rd. Sutt —78Eb 145
Myrtle Rd. War —21Yd 50
Myrtleside Clo. N'wd —24T 36
Myrtle Wlk. N1 —40Ub 63 (2H 195)
Mysore Rd. SW11 —56Hb 103
Myton Rd. SE21 —62Tb 127
Nadine Ct. Wall —81Lb 164
Nadine St. SE7 —50Lc 85
Nagasaki Wlk. SE7 —48Kc 85
Nagle Clo. E17 —26Fc 45
Nags Head Ct. EC1 —42Sb 83 (6E 194)
(off Golden La.)
Nags Head La. Upm & Brtwd —26Sd 50
Nags Head La. Well —55Xc 109
Nags Head Rd. Enf —14Yb 26
Nags Head Shopping Cen. N7 —35Pb 62
Nailsworth Ct. SE15 —51Ub 105
(off Birdlip Clo.)
Nailsworth Cres. Red —100Mb 180
Nailzee Clo. Ger X —31A 54
Nainby Ho. SE11 —49Qb 82 (6K 205)
(off Hotspur St.)
Nairn Ct. Til —4B 114
Nairne Gro. SE24 —57Tb 105
Nairn Grn. Wat —20W 18
Nairn Rd. Ruis —37Y 57
Nairn St. E14 —43Ec 84
Naish Ct. N1 —38Nb 62
(in two parts)
Naldera Gdns. SE3 —51Jc 107
Nallhead Rd. Felt —64Y 121
Namton Dri. T Hth —70Pb 126
Nan Clark's La. NW7 —19Ua 22
Nancy Downs. Wat —17Y 19
Nankin St. E14 —44Cc 84
Nansen Ho. NW10 —38Ta 59
(off Stonebridge Pk.)
Nansen Rd. SW11 —55Jb 104
Nansen Rd. Grav —3F 136
Nansen Village. N12 —21Db 41
Nant Ct. NW2 —33Bb 61
Nantes Clo. SW18 —56Eb 103
Nantes Pas. E1 —43Vb 83 (7K 195)
Nant Rd. NW2 —33Bb 61
Nant St. E2 —41Xb 83
Napier. NW9 —25Va 40
Napier Av. E14 —50Cc 84
Napier Av. SW6 —55Bb 103
Napier Clo. SE8 —52Bc 106
Napier Clo. W14 —48Ab 80
Napier Clo. Horn —32Kd 69
Napier Clo. W Dray —48P 75
Napier Ct. SW6 —55Bb 103
(off Ranelagh Gdns.)
Napier Ct. Cat —94Ub 181
Napier Gro. N1 —40Sb 63 (1E 194)
Napier Ho. Rain —41Hd 88
(off Dunedin Rd.)
Napier Pl. W14 —48Bb 81
Napier Rd. E6 —39Qc 66
Napier Rd. E11 —35Gc 65
Napier Rd. E15 —40Gc 65
(in two parts)
Napier Rd. N17 —27Ub 43
Napier Rd. NW10 —41Xa 80
Napier Rd. SE25 —70Xb 127
Napier Rd. W14 —48Ab 80
Napier Rd. Ashf —66T 120
Napier Rd. Belv —49Bd 87
Napier Rd. Brom —70Kc 129
Napier Rd. Enf —15Zb 26
Napier Rd. Grav —10B 114
Napier Rd. Houn —53M 97
Napier Rd. Iswth —56Ja 100
Napier Rd. S Croy —80Tb 147
Napier Rd. Wat —14Aa 19
Napier Rd. Wemb —36Ma 59
Napier Ter. N1 —38Rb 63
Napier Wlk. Ashf —66T 120
Napoleon Rd. E5 —34Xb 63
Napoleon Rd. Twic —59Ka 100
Nap, The. K Lan —1Q 4
Napton Clo. Hay —42Aa 77
Narbonne Av. SW4 —57Lb 104
Narboro Ct. Romf —29Jd 48
Narborough Clo. Uxb —33S 56
Narborough St. SW6 —54Db 103
Narcissus Rd. NW6 —36Cb 61
Nardini. NW9 —25Va 40
(off Concourse, The)
Nare Rd. S Ock —45Sd 90
Naresby Fold. Stan —23La 38
Narford Rd. E5 —34Wb 63
Narrow La. Warl —91Xb 181
Narrow St. E14 —45Ac 84
Narrow St. W3 —46Ra 79
Narrow Way. Brom —72Nc 150
Nascot Pl. Wat —12X 19
Nascot Rd. Wat —12X 19
Nascot St. W12 —44Ya 80
Nascot St. Wat —12X 19
Nascot Wood Rd. Wat —9V 4
Naseby Clo. NW6 —38Eb 61
Naseby Clo. Iswth —53Ga 100
Naseby Ct. Sidc —63Vc 131
Naseby Ct. W on T —75Y 141
Naseby Rd. SE19 —65Tb 127
Naseby Rd. Dag —34Cd 68
Naseby Rd. Ilf —25Pc 46
Nash Bank. Meop —8B 136
Nash Clo. Els —14Pa 21
Nash Croft. Grav —3A 136
Nashdom La. Burn —7A 52
Nash Grn. Brom —65Jc 129
Nash Ho. E17 —28Dc 44
Nash La. Kes —80Jc 149
Nash Pl. E14 —46Dc 84
Nash Rd. N9 —19Yb 26
Nash Rd. SE4 —56Ac 106
Nash Rd. Romf —28Zc 47
Nash Rd. Slou —49B 74
Nash St. NW1 —41Kb 82 (3A 192)
Nash St. Meop —8C 136
Nash's Yd. Uxb —38M 55
Nasmyth St. W6 —48Xa 80
Nassau Path. SE28 —46Yc 87
Nassau Rd. SW13 —53Ua 102
Nassau St. W1 —43Lb 82 (1B 198)
Nassington Rd. NW3 —35Gb 61
Natalie Clo. Felt —59T 98
Natal Rd. N11 —23Nb 42
Natal Rd. SW16 —65Mb 126
Natal Rd. Ilf —35Rc 66
Natal Rd. T Hth —69Tb 127
Nathan Clo. Upm —32Ud 70
Nathan Ct. N9 —17Yb 26
(off Causeyware Rd.)
Nathan Ho. SE11 —49Qb 82 (6A 206)
(off Reedworth St.)
Nathaniel Clo. E1 —43Vb 83 (1K 201)
Nathaniel Ct. E17 —30Ac 44
Nathans Rd. Wemb —32La 58
Nathan Way. SE28 —49Uc 86
National Westminster Ho. Borwd —13Ra 21
Nation Way. E4 —18Ec 26
Naunton Way. Horn —34Md 69
Naval Row. E14 —45Ec 84
Naval Wlk. Brom —68Jc 129
Navarino Gro. E8 —37Wb 63
Navarino Mans. E8 —37Wb 63
Navarino Rd. E8 —37Wb 63
Navarre Gdns. Romf —22Dd 48
Navarre Rd. E6 —40Nc 66
Navarre St. E2 —42Vb 83 (5K 195)
Navenby Wlk. E3 —42Cc 84
Navestock Clo. E4 —20Ec 26
Navestock Cres. Wfd G —24Lc 45
Navestock Ho. Bark —40Xc 67
Navestockside. Brtwd —12Sd 32
Navy St. SW4 —55Mb 104
Naylor Gro. Enf —15Zb 26
Naylor Rd. N20 —19Eb 23
Naylor Rd. SE15 —52Xb 105
Nazeing Wlk. Rain —38Hd 68
Nazrul St. E2 —41Vb 83 (3K 195)
Neagle Clo. E7 —35Jc 65
Neagle Clo. Borwd —11Sa 21
Neagle Ho. NW2 —34Ya 60
(off Stoll Clo.)
Neal Av. S'hall —42Ba 77
Neal Clo. Ger X —32D 54
Neal Clo. N'wd —25W 36
Neal Ct. Wal A —5Hc 13
Nealden St. SW9 —55Pb 104
Neale Clo. N2 —27Eb 41
Neal Rd. W King —79Ud 154
Neal St. WC2 —44Nb 82 (3F 199)
Neal St. Wat —15Y 19
Neal's Yd. WC2 —44Nb 82 (3F 199)
Near Acre. NW9 —25Va 40
Neasden Clo. NW10 —36Ua 60
Neasden La. NW10 —34Ua 60
Neasden La. N. NW10 —34Ta 59
Neasham Rd. Dag —36Xc 67
Neate St. SE5 —51Ub 105
Neath Gdns. Mord —72Eb 145
Neath Ho. SE24 —58Rb 105
(off Dulwich Rd.)
Neathouse Pl. SW1 —49Lb 82 (5B 204)
Neats Acre. Ruis —31T 56
Neatscourt Rd. E6 —43Mc 85
Neave Cres. Romf —25Ld 49
Nebraska St. SE1 —47Tb 83 (2F 207)
Nebraska St. SW1 —47Tb 83
Neckinger. SE16 —48Vb 83 (3K 207)
Neckinger Est. SE1 —48Vb 83 (3K 207)
Neckinger Est. SE16 —48Vb 83
Neckinger St. SE1 —47Vb 83
Nectarine Way. SE13 —54Dc 106
Needham Clo. Wind —3C 94
Needham Ho. SE11 —49Qb 82 (6K 205)
(off Tracey St.)
Needham Rd. W11 —44Cb 81
Needham Ter. NW2 —34Za 60
Needleman St. SE16 —47Zb 84
Needwood Ho. N4 —32Sb 63
Neela Clo. Uxb —35R 56
Neeld Cres. NW4 —29Xa 40
Neeld Cres. Wemb —36Qa 59
Neil Clo. Ashf —64S 120
Neil Wates Cres. SW2 —60Qb 104
Nelgarde Rd. SE6 —59Cc 106
Nella Rd. W6 —51Za 102
Nelldale Rd. SE16 —49Yb 84
Nellgrove Rd. Uxb —42R 76
Nell Gwynn Clo. Shenl —4Na 7
Nell Gwynne Av. Asc —10B 116
Nell Gwynne Av. Shep —72T 140
Nell Gwynne Clo. Asc —10B 116
Nello James Gdns. SE27 —63Tb 127
Nelmes Clo. Horn —29Pd 49
Nelmes Cres. Horn —29Nd 49
Nelmes Rd. Horn —31Nd 69
Nelmes Way. Horn —28Md 49
Nelson Clo. Big H —89Nc 168
Nelson Clo. Croy —74Rb 147
Nelson Clo. Romf —25Dd 48
Nelson Clo. Slou —9P 73
Nelson Clo. Uxb —41R 76
Nelson Clo. W on T —74X 141
Nelson Clo. War —22Zd 51
Nelson Ct. SE1 —47Rb 83 (1C 206)
(off Suffolk St.)
Nelson Ct. Cher —74J 139
Nelson Ct. Eri —52Hd 110
(off Frobisher Rd.)
Nelson Gdns. E2 —41Wb 83
Nelson Gdns. Houn —58Ca 99
Nelson Gro. Rd. SW19 —67Eb 125
Nelson Ho. Grnh —57Zd 113
Nelson Ind. Est. SW19 —67Db 125
Nelson La. Uxb —41R 76
Nelson Mandela Rd. N10 —26Jb 42
Nelson Mandella Rd. SE3 —55Lc 107
Nelson Pas. EC1 —41Sb 83 (4E 194)
Nelson Pl. N1 —40Rb 63 (2C 194)
Nelson Pl. Sidc —63Wc 131
Nelson Rd. E4 —23Dc 44
Nelson Rd. E11 —28Jc 45
Nelson Rd. N8 —29Pb 42
Nelson Rd. N9 —19Xb 25
Nelson Rd. N15 —28Ub 43
Nelson Rd. SE10 —51Ec 106
Nelson Rd. SW19 —66Eb 125
Nelson Rd. Ashf —64N 119
Nelson Rd. Belv —50Bd 87
Nelson Rd. Brom —70Lc 129
Nelson Rd. Cat —95Tb 181
Nelson Rd. Dart —58Ld 111
Nelson Rd. Enf —16Zb 26
Nelson Rd. Harr —32Fa 58
Nelson Rd. Houn —58Ca 99
Nelson Rd. H'row A —53P 97
Nelson Rd. N Mald —71Ta 143
Nelson Rd. Ors —4F 92
Nelson Rd. Rain —40Hd 68
Nelson Rd. Sidc —63Wc 131
Nelson Rd. S Ock —45Vd 70
Nelson Rd. Stan —23La 38
Nelson Rd. Twic —58Ca 99
Nelson Rd. Uxb —41R 76
Nelson Rd. Wind —5D 94
Nelson Sq. SE1 —47Rb 83 (1B 206)
Nelson's Row. SW4 —56Mb 104
Nelson St. E1 —44Xb 83
Nelson St. E6 —40Pc 66
(in two parts)
Nelson St. E16 —45Hc 85
(in two parts)
Nelsons Yd. NW1 —40Lb 62 (1B 192)
(off Mornington Cres.)
Nelson Ter. N1 —40Rb 63 (2C 194)
Nelson Wlk. SE16 —46Ac 84
Nelwyn Av. Horn —29Pd 49
Nemoure Rd. W3 —45Sa 79
Nene Gdns. Felt —61Ba 121
Nene Rd. Houn —53R 98
Nepal Rd. SW11 —55Gb 103
Nepean St. SW15 —58Wa 102
Neptune Ct. Eri —52Hd 110
(off Frobisher Rd.)
Neptune Rd. Harr —30Fa 38
Neptune Rd. Houn —53T 98
Neptune St. SE16 —48Yb 84
Nero Ct. Bren —52Ma 101
Nesbit Rd. SE9 —56Mc 107
Nesbitt Clo. SE3 —55Gc 107
Nesbitts All. Barn —13Bb 23
Nesbitt Sq. SE19 —66Ub 127
Nesham St. E1 —46Wb 83
Ness Rd. Eri —51Md 111
Ness St. SE16 —48Wb 83
Nesta Rd. Wfd G —23Gc 45
Nestles Av. Hay —48V 76
Neston Rd. Wat —9Y 5
Nestor Av. N21 —16Rb 25
Nethan Dri. S Ock —45Sd 90
Netheravon Rd. W7 —46Ha 78
Netheravon Rd. N. W4 —49Va 80
Netheravon Rd. S. W4 —50Va 80
Netherbury Rd. W5 —48Ma 79
Netherby Gdns. SW5 —49Eb 81
Netherby Gdns. Enf —14Nb 24
Netherby Pk. Wey —78U 140
Netherby Rd. SE23 —59Yb 106
Nether Clo. N3 —24Cb 41
Nethercote Av. Wok —5C 188
Nethercourt Av. N3 —23Cb 41
Netherfield Gdns. Bark —38Tc 66
Netherfield Rd. N12 —22Db 41
Netherfield Rd. SW17 —62Jb 126
Netherford Rd. SW4 —54Lb 104
Netherhall Gdns. NW3 —37Eb 61
Netherhall Way. NW3 —36Eb 61
Netherlands Rd. Barn & N20 —16Fb 23
Netherlands, The. Coul —91Lb 180
Netherleigh Clo. N19 —32Kb 62
Nethern Ct. Rd. Wold —95Cc 182
Netherne La. Coul —95Lb 180
Netherpark Dri. Romf —26Hd 48
Nether St. N3 & N12 —25Cb 41
Netherton Gro. SW10 —51Eb 103
Netherton Rd. N15 —30Tb 43
Netherton Rd. Twic —57Ja 100
Netherwood. N2 —26Fb 41
Netherwood Rd. W14 —48Za 80
Netherwood St. NW6 —38Bb 61
Netley Clo. New Ad —80Ec 148
Netley Clo. Sutt —78Za 144
Netley Dri. W on T —73Ba 141
Netley Gdns. Mord —73Eb 145
Netley Rd. E17 —29Ac 44
Netley Rd. Bren —51Na 101
Netley Rd. Houn —53T 98
Netley Rd. Ilf —29Tc 46
Netley Rd. Mord —73Eb 145
Netley Rd. W. Houn —53T 98
Netley St. NW1 —41Lb 82 (4B 192)
Nettlecombe Clo. Sutt —81Db 163
Nettleden Av. Wemb —37Qa 59
Nettlefold Pl. SE27 —62Rb 127
Nettlestead Clo. Beck —66Bc 128
Nettleton Ct. EC2 —43Sb 83 (1D 200)
(off London Wall)
Nettleton Rd. SE14 —53Zb 106
Nettleton Rd. Houn —53R 98
Nettleton Rd. Uxb —35P 55
Nettlewood Rd. SW16 —66Mb 126
Neuchatel Rd. SE6 —61Bc 128
Nevada Clo. N Mald —70Sa 123
Nevada St. SE10 —51Ec 106
Nevada Rd. Grays —8D 92
Nevern Mans. SW5 —49Cb 81
(off Warwick Rd.)
Nevern Pl. SW5 —49Cb 81
Nevern Rd. SW5 —49Cb 81
Nevern Sq. SW5 —49Cb 81
Nevil Ho. SW9 —54Rb 105
(off Rupert Gdns.)
Nevill Clo. W3 —47Sa 79
Neville Av. N Mald —67Ta 123
Neville Clo. E11 —34Hc 65
Neville Clo. NW1 —40Mb 62 (2E 192)
Neville Clo. NW6 —40Bb 61
Neville Clo. SE15 —53Wb 105
Neville Clo. Bans —86Db 163
Neville Clo. Esh —79Ba 141
Neville Clo. Houn —54Da 99
Neville Clo. Pot B —3Bb 9
Neville Clo. Sidc —63Vc 131
Neville Clo. Stoke P —7K 53
Neville Ct. Burn —1A 72
Neville Dri. N2 —30Eb 41
Neville Gdns. Dag —34Zc 67
Neville Gill Clo. SW18 —58Cb 103
Neville Ho. N11 —21Jb 42
Neville Ho. N22 —23Pb 42
(off Neville Pl.)
Neville Pl. N22 —25Pb 42
Neville Rd. E7 —38Jc 65
Neville Rd. NW6 —40Bb 61
Neville Rd. W5 —42Ma 79
Neville Rd. Croy —73Tb 147
Neville Rd. Dag —33Zc 67
Neville Rd. Ilf —25Sc 46
Neville Rd. King T —68Qa 123
Neville Rd. Rich —62La 122
Nevilles Ct. NW2 —34Wa 60
Neville St. SW7 —50Fb 81 (7B 202)
Neville Ter. SW7 —50Fb 81 (7B 202)
Neville Wlk. Cars —73Gb 145
Nevill Gro. Wat —11X 19
Nevill Pl. Meop —10C 136
Nevill Rd. N16 —35Ub 63
Nevill Way. Lou —16Nc 28
Nevin Dri. E4 —18Dc 26
Nevin Ho. Hay —48S 76

Nevis Clo.—Norbury Av.

Nevis Clo. Romf —23Gd 48
Nevis Rd. SW17 —61Jb 126
Nevitt Ho. N1 —40Tb 63 (2G 195)
(off Cranston Est.)
Newall Rd. H'row A —53S 98
Newark Clo. Guild —100D 172
Newark Clo. Rip —93J 173
Newark Cotts. Rip —93J 173
Newark Ct. W on T —74Y 141
Newark Cres. NW10 —41Ta 79
Newarke Ho. SW9 —54Rb 105
Newark Grn. Borwd —13Ta 21
Newark Knok. E6 —44Qc 86
Newark La. Wok & Rip —90H 157
Newark Pde. NW4 —27Wa 40
Newark Rd. S Croy —79Tb 147
Newark St. E1 —43Xb 83
(in two parts)
Newark Way. NW4 —28Wa 40
New Ash Clo. N2 —27Fb 41
New Barn La. W'ham & Cud —90Sc 168
New Barn La. Whyt —88Ub 165
New Barn Rd. Long & S'fleet —69De 135
New Barn Rd. Swan —67Gd 132
New Barns Av. Mitc —70Mb 126
New Barn St. E13 —42Jc 85
New Barns Way. Chig —20Rc 28
Newberries Av. Rad —7Ka 6
New Berry La. W on T —78Z 141
Newbery Rd. Eri —53Hd 110
Newbery Way. Slou —7H 73
Newbiggin Path. Wat —21Y 37
Newbolt Av. Sutt —78Ya 144
Newbolt Ho. SE17 —50Tb 83 (7F 207)
(off Brandon Est.)
Newbolt Rd. Stan —22Ha 38
New Bond St. W1 —44Kb 82 (3K 197)
Newborough Grn. N Mald —70Ta 123
New Brent St. NW4 —29Ya 40
New Bridge St. EC4 —44Rb 83 (3B 200)
New Broad St. EC2 —43Ub 83 (1G 201)
New Broadway. W5 —45Ma 79
New Broadway. Hamp —64Fa 122
New Broadway. Uxb —42R 76
Newburgh Rd. W3 —46Sa 79
Newburgh St. W1 —44Lb 82 (3B 198)
New Burlington M. W1 —45Lb 82 (4B 198)
New Burlington Pl. W1 —45Lb 82 (4B 198)
New Burlington St. W1 —45Lb 82 (4B 198)
Newburn Ho. SE11 —50Pb 82 (7J 205)
(off Newburn St.)
Newburn St. SE11 —50Pb 82 (7J 205)
Newbury Av. Enf —10Bc 12
Newbury Clo. N'holt —37Ba 57
Newbury Clo. Romf —23Ld 49
Newbury Ct. Sidc —63Vc 131
Newbury Cres. Wind —4B 94
Newbury Gdns. Eps —77Va 144
Newbury Gdns. Romf —23Md 49
Newbury Gdns. Upm —34Pd 69
Newbury Ho. N22 —25Nb 42
Newbury Ho. SW9 —54Rb 105
Newbury M. NW5 —37Jb 62
Newbury Rd. E4 —23Ec 44
Newbury Rd. Brom —69Jc 129
Newbury Rd. Houn —53P 97
Newbury Rd. Ilf —30Uc 46
Newbury Rd. Romf —22Md 49
Newbury St. EC1 —43Sb 83 (1D 200)
Newbury Wlk. Romf —22Md 49
Newbury Way. N'holt —37Aa 57
New Business Cen., The. NW10 —41Va 80
New Butt La. SE8 —52Cc 106
New Butt La. N. SE8 —52Cc 106
(off Reginald Rd.)
Newby Clo. Enf —12Ub 25
Newby Pl. E14 —45Ec 84
Newby St. SW8 —55Kb 104
New Caledonian Wharf. SE16 —48Bc 84
Newcastle Av. Ilf —23Wc 47
Newcastle Clo. EC4 —44Rb 83 (2B 200)
Newcastle Ct. EC4 —45Sb 83 (4E 200)
(off College Hill.)
Newcastle Pl. W2 —43Fb 81 (7C 190)
Newcastle Row. EC1 —42Qb 82 (6A 194)
New Cavendish St. W1 —43Jb 82 (1J 197)
New Change. EC4 —44Sb 83 (3D 200)
New Chapel Sq. Felt —60X 99
New Chu. Rd. SE5 —52Sb 105
(in two parts)
Newchurch Rd. Slou —3D 72
New City Rd. E13 —41Lc 85
New Clo. SW19 —69Eb 125
New Clo. Felt —64Aa 121
New Colebrooke Ct. Cars —80Jb 146
(off Stanley Rd.)
New College Ct. NW3 —37Eb 61
(off College Cres.)
New College M. N1 —38Qb 62
New College Pde. NW3 —37Fb 61
(off College Cres.)
Newcombe Gdns. SW16 —63Nb 126
Newcombe Pk. NW7 —22Ua 40
Newcombe Pk. Wemb —39Pa 59
Newcombe Rise. W Dray —44N 75
Newcombe St. W8 —46Cb 81
Newcomen Rd. E11 —34Hc 65
Newcomen Rd. SW11 —55Fb 103
Newcomen St. SE1 —47Tb 83 (1F 207)
Newcomen St. SW1 —47Tb 83
Newcome Path. Shenl —6Qa 7
Newcome Rd. Shenl —6Qa 7
New Compton St. WC2 —44Mb 82 (3E 198)
New Concordia Wharf. SE1 —47Wb 83
New Cotts. Wal X —6Yb 12
New Ct. EC4 —45Qb 82 (4K 199)
(off Temple)
New Ct. Add —76L 139
Newcourt. Uxb —43L 75
Newcourt St. NW8 —40Gb 61 (2D 190)
New Covent Garden Mkt. SW8 —52Mb 104
New Coventry St. W1 —45Mb 82 (5E 198)
New Crane Pl. E1 —46Yb 84
Newcroft Clo. Uxb —43P 75
New Cross Rd. SE15 & SE14 —52Yb 106
Newdales Clo. N9 —19Wb 25
Newdene Av. N'holt —40Z 57
Newdigate Grn. Hare —25M 35
Newdigate Rd. Hare —25L 35
Newdigate Rd. E. Hare —25M 35
Newell St. E14 —44Bc 84
New End. NW3 —34Eb 61
New End Sq. NW3 —35Fb 61
Newenham Rd. Bookh —98Ca 175
Newent Clo. SE15 —52Ub 105
New Era Est. N1 —39Ub 63 (1H 195)
(off Phillipp St.)
New Farm Av. Brom —70Jc 129
New Farm Dri. Abr —13Yc 29
New Farm La. N'wd —25U 36
New Fetter La. EC4 —44Qb 82 (2A 200)
Newfield Clo. Hamp —67Ca 121
Newfield Rise. NW2 —34Xa 60
New Ford Rd. Wal X —6Bc 12
New Forest La. Chig —23Qc 46
Newgale Gdns. Edgw —25Pa 39
New Garden Dri. W Dray —47N 75
Newgate. Croy —74Sb 147
Newgate Clo. Felt —62Aa 121
Newgate St. E4 —20Gc 27
Newgate St. EC1 —44Rb 83 (2C 200)
Newgatestreet Rd. Chesh —1Sb 11
New Globe Wlk. SE1 —46Sb 83 (6D 200)
New Goulston St. E1 —44Vb 83 (2K 201)
New Hall Dri. Romf —25Nd 49
Newham Pl. Grays —9C 92
Newham's Row. SE1 —47Ub 83 (2J 207)
Newham Way. E16 & E6 —43Hc 85
Newhaven Clo. Hay —49V 76
Newhaven Cres. Ashf —64T 120
Newhaven Gdns. SE9 —56Mc 107
Newhaven Rd. SE25 —71Tb 147
Newhaven Spur. Slou —2F 72
New Haw Rd. Add —78L 139
New Heston Rd. Houn —52Ba 99
Newhouse Av. Romf —27Zc 47
Newhouse Clo. N Mald —73Ua 144
Newhouse Cres. Wat —4X 5
New Ho. La. Grav —2B 136
Newhouse Wlk. Mord —73Eb 145
Newick Clo. Bex —58Dd 110
Newick Rd. E5 —35Xb 63
Newing Grn. Brom —66Mc 129
Newington Barrow Way. N7 —34Pb 62
Newington Butts. SE11 & SE1 —49Rb 83 (6C 206)
Newington Causeway. SE1 —48Sb 83 (4C 206)
Newington Grn. N16 & N1 —36Tb 63
Newington Grn. Mans. N16 —36Tb 63
Newington Grn. Rd. N1 —37Tb 63
Newington Ind. Est. SE17 —49Sb 83 (6D 206)
(off Crampton St.)
New Inn B'way. EC2 —42Ub 83 (5J 195)
New Inn Pas. WC2 —44Pb 82 (3J 199)
(off Houghton St.)
New Inn Sq. EC2 —42Ub 83 (5J 195)
(off Bateman's Row)
New Inn St. EC2 —42Ub 83 (5J 195)
New Inn Yd. EC2 —42Ub 83 (5J 195)
New Jubilee Ct. Wfd G —24Jc 45
New Kelvin Av. Tedd —65Ga 122
New Kent Rd. SE1 —48Sb 83 (4D 206)
New Kings Rd. SW6 —54Bb 103
New King St. SE8 —51Cc 106
Newland Clo. Pinn —23Aa 37
Newland Dri. Enf —11Xb 25
Newland Gdns. W13 —47Ja 78
Newland Ho. N8 —27Nb 42
(off Newland Rd.)
Newland Rd. N8 —27Nb 42
Newlands Av. Rad —6Ha 6
Newlands Av. Th Dit —74Ga 142
Newlands Av. Wok —93B 172
Newlands Clo. Edgw —20Na 21
Newlands Clo. Hut —17Fe 33
Newlands Clo. S'hall —50Aa 77
Newlands Clo. W on T —77Aa 141
Newlands Clo. Wemb —37La 58
Newlands Ct. SE9 —58Qc 108
Newlands Ct. Add —78K 139
(off Addlestone Pk.)
Newlands Ct. Cat —93Sb 181
(off Coulsdon Rd.)
Newlands Dri. Coln —55G 96
Newlands Pk. SE26 —65Yb 128
Newlands Pl. Barn —15Za 22
Newlands Quay. E1 —45Yb 84
Newlands Rd. SW16 —68Nb 126
Newlands Rd. Wfd G —19Hc 27
Newlands, The. Wall —80Mb 146
Newland St. E16 —46Nc 86
Newlands Wlk. Wat —5Z 5
Newlands Way. Chess —78La 142
Newlands Way. Pot B —2Db 9
Newlands Wood. New Ad —81Bc 166
New La. Wok & Sut G —94A 172
Newling Clo. E6 —44Pc 86
New Lodge Dri. Oxt —100Hc 183
New London St. EC3 —45Ub 83 (4J 201)
(off Hart St.)
New Lydenburg Commercial Est. SE7 —48Lc 85
New Lydenburg St. SE7 —48Lc 85
Newlyn Clo. Brick —2Aa 5
Newlyn Clo. Uxb —43Q 76
Newlyn Gdns. Harr —31Ba 57
Newlyn Ho. Pinn —24Ba 37
Newlyn Rd. N17 —25Vb 43
Newlyn Rd. Barn —14Bb 23
Newlyn Rd. Well —54Vc 109
New Maltings. S Ock —46Td 90
Newman Clo. Horn —29Nd 49
Newman Pas. W1 —43Lb 82 (1C 198)
Newman Pl. W1 —43Lb 82
Newman Rd. E13 —41Kc 85
Newman Rd. E17 —29Zb 44
Newman Rd. Brom —67Jc 129
Newman Rd. Croy —74Pb 146
Newman Rd. Hay —45X 77
Newman Rd. Ind. Est. Croy —73Pb 146
Newmans Clo. Lou —13Qc 28
Newman's Ct. EC3 —44Tb 83 (3G 201)
(off Cornhill)
Newmans Dri. Hut —17Ee 33
Newmans La. Lou —14Qc 28
Newmans La. Surb —72Ma 143
Newmans Rd. Grav —1B 136
Newman's Row. WC2 —43Pb 82 (1J 199)
Newman St. W1 —43Lb 82 (1C 198)
Newman's Way. Barn —11Eb 23
Newman Yd. W1 —44Mb 82 (2D 198)
Newmarket Av. N'holt —36Ca 57
Newmarket Grn. SE9 —59Mc 107
Newmarket Way. Horn —35Nd 69
New Mile Rd. Asc —8A 116
New Mill Rd. Orp —67Yc 131
Newminster Rd. Mord —72Eb 145
New Mount St. E15 —38Fc 65
Newnes Path. SW15 —56Xa 102
Newnet Clo. Cars —74Hb 145
Newnham Av. Ruis —32Y 57
Newnham Clo. Lou —16Mc 27
Newnham Clo. N'holt —37Ea 58
Newnham Clo. Slou —6L 73
Newnham Clo. T Hth —68Sb 127
Newnham Gdns. N'holt —37Ea 58
Newnham Ho. Lou —16Mc 27
Newnham M. N22 —24Qb 42
Newnham Pde. Chesh —2Zb 12
Newnham Rd. N22 —25Pb 42
Newnhams Clo. Brom —69Pc 130
Newnham Ter. SE1 —48Qb 82 (3K 205)
Newnham Way. Harr —29Na 39
New North Pl. EC2 —42Ub 83 (5H 195)
New North Rd. N1 —38Sb 63
New North Rd. Ilf —24Tc 46
New North St. WC1 —43Pb 82 (7H 193)
Newnton Clo. N4 —31Tb 63
New Oak Rd. N2 —26Eb 41
New Orleans Wlk. N19 —31Mb 62
New Oxford St. WC1 —44Mb 82 (2E 198)
New Pde. Ashf —63P 119
New Pde. Chor —14E 16
New Pk. Av. N13 —20Sb 25
New Pk. Clo. N'holt —37Aa 57
New Park Ho. N13 —21Pb 42
New Pk. Rd. SW2 —60Mb 104
New Pk. Rd. Ashf —64S 120
New Pk. Rd. Hare —25L 35
New Peachey La. Uxb —44M 75
Newpiece. Lou —13Rc 28
New Pl. New Ad —79Cc 148
New Pl. Gdns. Upm —33Td 70
New Place Sq. SE16 —48Xb 83
New Plaistow Rd. E15 —39Gc 65
New Plymouth Ho. Rain —41Hd 88
(off Dunedin Rd.)
Newport Av. E13 —42Kc 85
Newport Clo. Enf —9Ac 12
Newport Ct. WC2 —45Mb 82 (4E 198)
Newport Lodge. Enf —15Ub 25
(off Village Rd.)
Newport Mead. Wat —21Z 37
Newport Pl. WC2 —45Mb 82 (4E 198)
Newport Rd. E10 —33Ec 64
Newport Rd. E17 —28Ac 44
Newport Rd. SW13 —53Wa 102
Newport Rd. Hay —43T 76
Newport Rd. Houn —53Q 98
Newport Rd. Slou —2C 72
Newports. Swan —73Fd 152
Newport St. SE11 —49Pb 82 (6H 205)
Newquay Cres. Harr —33Aa 57
Newquay Gdns. Wat —19X 19
Newquay Ho. SE11 —50Qb 82 (7K 205)
Newquay Rd. SE6 —61Dc 128
New Quebec St. W1 —44Hb 81 (3G 197)
New Ride. SW7 & SW1 —47Fb 81 (2C 202)
New River Ct. N5 —35Sb 63
New River Ct. Chesh —3Xb 11
New River Cres. N13 —21Rb 43
New River Wlk. N1 —37Sb 63
New Rd. E1 —43Xb 83
New Rd. E4 —21Dc 44
New Rd. N8 —29Nb 42
New Rd. N9 —20Wb 25
New Rd. N17 —25Vb 43
New Rd. N22 —25Sb 43
New Rd. NW7 —17Va 22
(Highwood Hill)
New Rd. NW7 —24Ab 40
(Mill Hill)
New Rd. SE2 —49Zc 87
New Rd. Abr —16Zc 29
New Rd. Bedf —58T 98
New Rd. Bren —51Ma 101
New Rd. Brtwd —19Zd 33
New Rd. Chal G —13A 16
New Rd. Cher —73H 139
New Rd. Chfd —2H 3
New Rd. Crox —15Q 18
New Rd. Dag & Rain —40Cd 68
New Rd. Dat —3P 95
New Rd. Els —16Ma 21
New Rd. Esh —76Ea 142
New Rd. Felt —60X 99
New Rd. Grav —8D 114
New Rd. Grays —51Ce 113
(in two parts)
New Rd. Hanw —64Aa 121
New Rd. Harr —35Ha 58
New Rd. Hay —52S 98
New Rd. Hex —66Hd 132
New Rd. Houn —56Da 99
New Rd. Ilf —33Uc 66
New Rd. King T —66Qa 123
New Rd. Langl —48C 74
New Rd. Let H —11Ga 20
New Rd. Meop —10B 136
New Rd. Mitc —74Hb 145
New Rd. Orp —73Wc 151
New Rd. Oxs —83Ha 160
New Rd. Rad —8Ga 6
New Rd. Rich —63La 122
New Rd. Sarr —11H 17
New Rd. Shenl —6Qa 7
New Rd. Shep —69Q 120
New Rd. S Dar —68Sd 134
New Rd. S Mim —5Wa 8
New Rd. Stai —64E 118
New Rd. Sund —96Zc 185
New Rd. Swan —69Hd 132
New Rd. Tad —95Ya 178
New Rd. Uxb —42S 76
New Rd. Wat —14Y 19
New Rd. Well —54Xc 109
New Rd. W Mol —70Ca 121
New Rd. Wey —78S 140
New Rd. Hill. Kes & Orp —81Nc 168
New Rochford St. NW5 —36Hb 61
New Row. WC2 —45Nb 82 (4F 199)
Newry Rd. Twic —57Ja 100
Newsam Av. N15 —29Tb 43
Newsham Rd. Wok —5C 188
New Southgate Ind. Est. N11 —22Lb 42
New Spitalfields Mkt. E10 —34Dc 64
New Spring Gdns. Wlk. SE11 —50Nb 82 (7G 205)
New Sq. WC2 —44Pb 82 (2K 199)
New Sq. Felt —60S 98
New Sq. Slou —7K 73
Newstead Av. Orp —76Tc 150
Newstead Ct. N'holt —41Aa 77
Newstead Ho. Romf —21Md 49
(off Troopers Dri.)
Newstead Rise. Cat —98Xb 181
Newstead Rd. SE12 —59Hc 107
Newstead Wlk. Cars —73Cb 145
Newstead Way. SW19 —63Za 124
New St. EC2 —43Ub 83 (1J 201)
New St. EC4 —44Qb 82 (2A 200)
New St. Stai —63J 119
New St. Wat —14Y 19
New St. W'ham —99Sc 184
New St. Hill. EC4 —44Qb 82 (2A 200)
(off Printer St.)
New St. Hill. Brom —64Kc 129
New St. Rd. Meop & Sev —76Ee 155
New St. Sq. EC4 —44Qb 82 (2A 200)
Newteswell Dri. Wal A —4Fc 13
Newton Abbot Rd. Grav —1B 136
Newton Av. N10 —25Jb 42
Newton Av. W3 —47Sa 79
Newton Clo. Slou —47B 74
Newton Ct. Old Win —8L 95
Newton Cres. Borwd —14Sa 21
Newton Gro. W4 —49Ua 80
Newton Ho. E17 —27Dc 44
(off Prospect Hill)
Newton Ho. SE20 —67Zb 128
Newton Ho. Borwd —13Ta 21
Newton La. Old Win —8M 95
Newton Point. E16 —44Hc 85
(off Clarkson Rd.)
Newton Rd. E15 —36Fc 65
Newton Rd. N15 —29Wb 43
Newton Rd. NW2 —35Ya 60
Newton Rd. SW19 —66Ab 124
Newton Rd. W2 —44Db 81
Newton Rd. Chig —22Xc 47
Newton Rd. Harr —26Ga 38
Newton Rd. Houn —53N 97
Newton Rd. Iswth —54Ha 100
Newton Rd. Purl —84Lb 164
Newton Rd. Til —5C 114
Newton Rd. Well —55Wc 109
Newton Rd. Wemb —38Pa 59
Newtons Clo. Rain —38Hd 68
Newtons Ct. Dart —56Td 112
Newton St. WC2 —44Nb 82 (2G 199)
Newton's Yd. SW18 —57Cb 103
Newton Wlk. Edgw —25Ra 39
Newton Way. N18 —22Sb 43
Newton Wood Rd. Asht —88Pa 161
Newtown Rd. Den —37K 55
Newtown St. SW11 —53Kb 104
(in two parts)
New Trinity Rd. N2 —27Fb 41
New Turnstile. WC1 —43Pb 82 (1H 199)
New Union Clo. E14 —48Ec 84
New Union St. EC2 —43Tb 83 (1F 201)
New Wanstead. E11 —30Hc 45
New Way Rd. NW9 —28Ua 40
New Wharf Rd. N1 —40Nb 62 (1G 193)
New Wickham La. Egh —66C 118
New Windsor St. Uxb —39L 55
Newyears Grn. La. Hare —30N 35
New Years La. Knock —88Vc 169
New Zealand Av. W on T —74V 140
New Zealand Way. W12 —45Xa 80
New Zealand Way. Rain —41Hd 88
Niagara Av. W5 —49La 78
Niagara Clo. Chesh —1Zb 12
Niagra Clo. N1 —40Sb 63 (1E 194)
Nibbs Clo. Swan —68Fd 132
Nibthwaite Rd. Harr —29Ga 38
Nicholas Clo. Gnfd —40Da 57
Nicholas Clo. S Ock —41Yd 90
Nicholas Clo. Wat —9X 5
Nicholas Gdns. W5 —47Ma 79
Nicholas Gdns. Wok —88H 157
Nicholas La. EC4 —45Tb 83 (4G 201)
Nicholas Pas. EC4 —45Tb 83 (4G 201)
(off Nicholas La.)
Nicholas Rd. E1 —42Yb 84
Nicholas Rd. Croy —77Nb 146
Nicholas Rd. Dag —33Bd 67
Nicholas Rd. Els —16Pa 21
Nicholas St. SE8 —53Bc 106
Nicholas Wlk. Grays —7D 92
Nicholas Way. N'wd —26S 36
Nicholay Rd. N19 —32Mb 62
Nichol Clo. N14 —18Mb 24
Nicholes Rd. Houn —56Ca 99
Nichol La. Brom —66Jc 129
Nicholl Ho. N4 —32Sb 63
Nicholl Rd. Epp —3Vc 15
Nicholls. Wind —5A 94
Nicholls Av. Uxb —42Q 76
Nichollsfield Wlk. N7 —36Pb 62
Nicholls Point. E15 —39Jc 65
(off Park Gro.)
Nicholl St. E2 —39Wb 63
Nicholls Wlk. Wind —5A 94
Nichols Clo. N4 —32Qb 62
(off Osborne Rd.)
Nichols Grn. W5 —43Ma 79
Nicholson Ct. E17 —28Ac 44
Nicholson Dri. Bush —18Ea 20
Nicholson Ho. SE17 —50Tb 83 (7F 207)
Nicholson M. Egh —64C 118
(off Nicholson Wlk.)
Nicholson Rd. Croy —74Vb 147
Nicholson St. SE1 —46Rb 83 (7B 200)
Nicholson Wlk. Egh —64C 118
Nichol's Sq. E2 —40Vb 63 (2K 195)
Nickelby Clo. SE28 —44Yc 87
Nickelby Clo. Uxb —44R 76
Nickleby Rd. Grav —10J 115
Nicola Clo. Harr —26Fa 38
Nicola Clo. S Croy —79Sb 147
Nicola M. Ilf —24Rc 46
Nicol Clo. Twic —58Ka 100
Nicoll Ct. N10 —24Kb 42
Nicoll Ct. NW10 —39Ua 60
Nicoll Pl. NW4 —30Xa 40
Nicoll Rd. NW10 —39Ua 60
Nicoll Way. Borwd —15Ta 21
Nicol Rd. Ger X —25A 34
Nicolson. NW9 —25Ua 40
Nicolson Rd. Orp —73Zc 151
Nicolson Way. Sev —94Md 187
Nicosia Rd. SW18 —59Gb 103
Niederwald Rd. SE26 —63Ac 128
Nield Rd. Hay —47V 76
Nigel Clo. N'holt —39Aa 57
Nigel Ct. N3 —24Db 41
Nigel M. Ilf —35Rc 66
Nigel Playfair Av. W6 —50Xa 80
Nigel Rd. E7 —36Lc 65
Nigel Rd. SE15 —55Wb 105
Nigeria Rd. SE7 —52Lc 107
Nighthawk. NW9 —25Va 40
Nightingale Av. E4 —22Gc 45
Nightingale Av. Upm —32Vd 70
Nightingale Av. W Hor —96T 174
Nightingale Clo. E4 —21Fc 45
Nightingale Clo. W4 —51Sa 101
Nightingale Clo. Cars —75Jb 146
Nightingale Clo. Cob —83Z 159
Nightingale Clo. Grav —2A 136
Nightingale Clo. Pinn —29Y 37
Nightingale Clo. Rad —8Ha 6
Nightingale Corner. Orp —70Zc 131
Nightingale Ct. SW6 —53Db 103
(off Maltings Pl.)
Nightingale Ct. Short —68Gc 129
Nightingale Ct. Wok —6B 188
Nightingale Cres. W Hor —97S 174
Nightingale Dri. Eps —79Ra 143
Nightingale Gro. SE13 —57Fc 107
Nightingale Gro. Dart —56Qd 111
Nightingale Ho. E1 —46Wb 83
(off Thomas More St.)
Nightingale Ho. N1 —39Ub 63 (1J 195)
(off Wilmer Gdns.)
Nightingale Ho. Eps —84Ua 162
Nightingale Ho. Ott —79F 138
Nightingale La. E11 —29Jc 45
Nightingale La. N8 —28Nb 42
Nightingale La. SW12 & SW4 —59Hb 103
Nightingale La. Brom —68Lc 129
Nightingale La. Rich —59Na 101
Nightingale Pk. Farn C —8D 52
Nightingale Pl. SE18 —51Qc 108
Nightingale Pl. SW10 —51Eb 103
Nightingale Pl. Rick —17M 17
Nightingale Rd. E5 —34Xb 63
Nightingale Rd. N9 —16Yb 26
Nightingale Rd. N22 —24Nb 42
Nightingale Rd. NW10 —40Va 60
Nightingale Rd. W7 —46Ha 78
Nightingale Rd. Bush —15Ca 19
Nightingale Rd. Cars —76Hb 145
Nightingale Rd. E Hor —97V 174
Nightingale Rd. Esh —78Ba 141
Nightingale Rd. Hamp —64Ca 121
Nightingale Rd. Kems —89Md 171
Nightingale Rd. Orp —72Sc 150
Nightingale Rd. Rick —17L 17
Nightingale Rd. S Croy —83Zb 166
Nightingale Rd. W on T —73Y 141
Nightingale Rd. W Mol —71Da 141
Nightingales. Wal A —6Gc 13
Nightingales La. Chal G —18A 16
Nightingale Sq. SW12 —59Jb 104
Nightingales, The. Stai —60P 97
Nightingale Vale. SE18 —51Qc 108
Nightingale Wlk. SW4 —58Kb 104
Nightingale Way. E6 —43Nc 86
Nightingale Way. Den —31H 55
Nightingale Way. Swan —69Gd 132
Nile Path. SE18 —51Qc 108
Nile Rd. E13 —40Lc 65
Nile St. N1 —41Sb 83 (3E 194)
Nile Ter. SE15 —50Vb 83
Nimbus Rd. Eps —82Ta 161
Nimegen Way. SE22 —57Ub 105
Nimmo Dri. Bush —17Fa 20
Nimrod. NW9 —25Ua 40
Nimrod Clo. N'holt —41Z 77
Nimrod Pas. N1 —37Ub 63
Nimrod Rd. SW16 —65Kb 126
Nine Acres Clo. E12 —36Nc 66
Nineacres Way. Coul —88Nb 164
Nine Elms Av. Uxb —43M 75
Nine Elms Clo. Uxb —43M 75
Nine Elms Gro. Grav —9C 114
Nine Elms La. SW8 —52Lb 104
Ninehams Clo. Cat —92Tb 181
Ninehams Gdns. Cat —92Tb 181
Ninehams Rd. Cat —93Tb 181
Ninehams Rd. Tats —93Lc 183
Nine Stiles Clo. Den —37K 55
Nineteenth Rd. Mitc —70Nb 126
Ninhams Wood. Orp —77Qc 150
Ninnings Rd. Ger X —24B 34
Ninnings Way. Ger X —24B 34
Ninth Av. Hay —45W 76
Nita Rd. War —22Yd 50
Nithdale Rd. SE18 —52Rc 108
Nithsdale Gro. Uxb —34S 56
Niton Clo. Barn —16Za 22
Niton Ct. Stanf —3L 93
(off St Margaret's Av.)
Niton Rd. Rich —55Qa 101
Niton St. SW6 —52Za 102
Niven Clo. Borwd —11Sa 21
Niven Ct. S'hill —10B 116
Nixley Clo. Slou —7L 73
Noah's Ark. Kems —90Qd 171
Noak Hill Rd. H Hill —21Ld 49
Nobel Dri. Hay —52U 98
Nobel Ho. SE5 —54Sb 105
Nobel Rd. N18 —21Yb 44
Noble Corner. Houn —53Ca 99
Noble Ct. Mitc —68Fb 125
Noblefield Heights. N2 —29Gb 41
Noble St. EC2 —44Sb 83 (2D 200)
Nobles Way. Egh —65A 118
Noel. NW9 —25Ua 40
Noel Ct. Houn —55Ba 99
Noel Pk. Rd. N22 —26Qb 42
Noel Rd. E6 —42Nc 86
Noel Rd. N1 —40Rb 63 (1B 194)
Noel Rd. W3 —45Qa 79
Noel Sq. Dag —35Yc 67
Noel St. W1 —44Lb 82 (3C 198)
Noel Ter. SE23 —61Yb 128
Noel Ter. Sidc —63Xc 131
Nolan Way. E5 —35Wb 63
Nolton Pl. Edgw —25Pa 39
Nonsuch Clo. Ilf —23Rc 46
Nonsuch Ct. Av. Eps —82Xa 162
Nonsuch Wlk. Sutt —82Ya 162
(in two parts)
Noorwood Gdns. Hay —42Y 77
Nora Gdns. NW4 —28Za 40
Norbiton Av. King T —67Qa 123
Norbiton Comn. Rd. King T —69Ra 123
Norbiton Rd. E14 —44Bc 84
Norbreck Gdns. NW10 —41Pa 79
Norbreck Pde. NW10 —41Na 79
Norbroke St. W12 —45Va 80
Norburn St. W10 —43Ab 80
Norbury Av. SW16 & T Hth —67Pb 126
Norbury Av. Houn —56Fa 100

Norbury Av.—Nugent Rd.

Norbury Av. Wat —11Y 19
Norbury Clo. SW16 —67Qb 126
Norbury Ct. Rd. SW16 —69Nb 126
Norbury Cres. SW16 —67Pb 126
Norbury Cross. SW16 —69Nb 126
Norbury Gdns. Romf —29Zc 47
Norbury Gro. NW7 —20Ua 22
Norbury Hill. SW16 —66Qb 126
Norbury Rise. SW16 —69Nb 126
Norbury Rd. E4 —22Cc 44
Norbury Rd. T Hth —68Sb 127
Norbury Trading Est. SW16 —68Pb 126
Norbury Way. Bookh —97Ea 176
Norcombe Gdns. Harr —30La 38
Norcombe Ho. N19 —34Mb 62
(off Wedmore St.)
Norcott Clo. Hay —42Y 77
Norcott Rd. N16 —33Wb 63
Norcroft Gdns. SE22 —59Wb 105
Norcutt Rd. Twic —60Ga 100
Nordenfeldt Rd. Eri —50Fd 88
Norelands Dri. Burn —10A 52
Norfield Rd. Dart —63Ed 132
Norfolk Av. N13 —23Rb 43
Norfolk Av. N15 —30Vb 43
Norfolk Av. Slou —3G 72
Norfolk Av. S Croy —82Vb 165
Norfolk Av. Wat —10Y 5
Norfolk Clo. N2 —27Gb 41
Norfolk Clo. N13 —23Rb 43
Norfolk Clo. Barn —14Jb 24
Norfolk Clo. Dart —57Qd 111
Norfolk Clo. Twic —58Ka 100
Norfolk Cres. W2 —44Gb 81 (2D 196)
Norfolk Cres. Sidc —59Uc 108
Norfolk Farm Clo. Wok —88F 156
Norfolk Farm Rd. Wok —87F 156
Norfolk Gdns. Bexh —53Bd 109
Norfolk Gdns. Borwd —14Ta 21
Norfolk Gdns. Houn —57Ba 99
Norfolk Ho. Beck —67Yb 128
Norfolk Ho. Rd. SW16 —62Mb 126
Norfolk Pl. W2 —44Fb 81 (2C 196)
Norfolk Pl. Well —54Wc 109
Norfolk Rd. E6 —39Pc 66
Norfolk Rd. E17 —26Zb 44
Norfolk Rd. NW8 —39Fb 61 (1C 190)
Norfolk Rd. NW10 —38Ua 60
Norfolk Rd. SW19 —66Gb 125
Norfolk Rd. Bark —38Uc 66
Norfolk Rd. Barn —13Cb 23
Norfolk Rd. Clay —78Ga 142
Norfolk Rd. Dag —36Dd 68
Norfolk Rd. Enf —16Xb 25
Norfolk Rd. Felt —60Y 99
Norfolk Rd. Grav —8F 114
(in two parts)
Norfolk Rd. Harr —29Da 37
Norfolk Rd. Ilf —32Uc 66
Norfolk Rd. Rick —18N 17
Norfolk Rd. Romf —30Ed 48
Norfolk Rd. T Hth —69Sb 127
Norfolk Rd. Upm —34Qd 69
Norfolk Rd. Uxb —37M 55
Norfolk Row. SE1 —49Pb 82 (5J 205)
Norfolk Row. SE11
(in two parts) —49Pb 82 (5J 205)
Norfolk Sq. W2 —44Fb 81 (3C 196)
Norfolk Sq. M. W2 —44Fb 81 (3C 196)
(off London St.)
Norfolk St. E7 —36Jc 65
Norfolk Ter. W6 —50Ab 80
Norgrove Pk. Ger X —28A 34
Norgrove St. SW12 —59Jb 104
Norham Ct. Dart —58Rd 111
(off Osborne Rd.)
Norheads La. Warl & Big H —91Jc 183
Norhyrst Av. SE25 —69Vb 127
Nork Gdns. Bans —86Ab 162
Nork Rise. Bans —88Za 162
Nork Way. Bans —88Ya 162
Norland Pl. W11 —46Ab 80
Norland Rd. W11 —46Za 80
Norlands Cres. Chst —67Rc 130
Norlands La. Egh —69G 118
Norland Sq. W11 —46Ab 80
Norley Vale. SW15 —60Wa 102
Norlington Rd. E10 & E11 —32Ec 64
Norman Av. N22 —25Rb 43
Norman Av. Eps —84Va 162
Norman Av. Felt —61Aa 121
Norman Av. S'hall —45Aa 77
Norman Av. S Croy —82Sb 165
Norman Av. Twic —59La 100
Normanby Rd. NW10 —35Va 60
Norman Clo. N22 —25Sb 43
Norman Clo. Kems —89Md 171
Norman Clo. Orp —76Sc 150
Norman Clo. Romf —25Dd 48
Norman Clo. Wal A —5Fc 13
Norman Colyer Ct. Eps —82Ta 161
Norman Ct. N4 —31Qb 62
Norman Ct. NW10 —38Wa 60
Norman Ct. Ilf —31Tc 66
Norman Ct. Pot B —3Eb 9
Norman Cres. Brtwd —20Ce 33
Norman Cres. Houn —52Z 99
Norman Cres. Pinn —25Y 37
Normand M. W14 —51Ab 102
Normand Rd. W14 —51Bb 103
Normandy Av. Barn —15Bb 23
Normandy Clo. SW15 —57Bb 103
Normandy Dri. Hay —44S 76
Normandy Rd. SW9 —53Qb 104
Normandy Ter. E16 —44Kc 85
Normandy Wlk. Egh —64E 118
Normandy Way. Eri —53Gd 110
Norman Gro. E3 —40Ac 64
Norman Ho. Felt —61Ba 121
Normanhurst. Ashf —64Q 120
Normanhurst. Hut —16Ee 33
Normanhurst Av. Bexh —53Zc 109
Normanhurst Dri. Twic —57Ja 100
Normanhurst Rd. SW2 —61Pb 126
Normanhurst Rd. Orp —68Xc 131
Normanhurst Rd. W on T —75Z 141
Norman Rd. E6 —42Pc 86
Norman Rd. E11 —33Fc 65
Norman Rd. N15 —29Vb 43
Norman Rd. SE10 —52Dc 106
Norman Rd. SW19 —66Eb 125
Norman Rd. Ashf —65T 120
Norman Rd. Belv —48Dd 88
Norman Rd. Dart —60Nd 111
Norman Rd. Horn —31Jd 68
Norman Rd. Ilf —36Rc 66
Norman Rd. Sutt —78Cb 145
Norman Rd. T Hth —71Rb 147
Norman's Bldgs. EC1 —41Sb 83 (4D 194)
Norman's Clo. NW10 —37Ta 59
Norman's Clo. Grav —9C 114
Normans Clo. Uxb —42P 75
Normansfield Av. Tedd —66La 122
Normans Field Clo. Bush —17Da 19
Normanshire Av. E4 —21Ec 44
Normanshire Dri. E4 —21Cc 44
Norman's Mead. NW10 —37Ta 59
Normans, The. Slou —4M 73
Norman St. EC1 —41Sb 83 (4D 194)
Normanton Av. SW19 —61Cb 125
Normanton Pk. E4 —19Gc 27
Normanton Rd. S Croy —79Ub 147
Normanton St. SE23 —61Zb 128
Norman Way. N14 —19Nb 24
Norman Way. W3 —43Ra 79
Normington Clo. SW16 —64Qb 126
Norrels Dri. E Hor —98V 174
Norrels Ride. E Hor —97V 174
Norrice Lea. N2 —29Fb 41
Norris. NW9 —25Va 40
(off Concourse, The)
Norris Rd. Stai —63H 119
Norris St. SW1 —45Mb 82 (5D 198)
Norris Way. Dart —55Hd 110
Norroy Rd. SW15 —56Za 102
Norry's Clo. Barn —14Hb 23
Norry's Rd. Barn —14Hb 23
Norseman Clo. Ilf —32Xc 67
Norseman Way. Gnfd —39Da 57
Norstead Pl. SW15 —61Wa 124
Norsted La. Prat B —84Wc 169
N. Access Rd. E17 —30Zb 44
North Acre. NW9 —25Ua 40
North Acre. Bans —88Bb 163
N. Acton Rd. NW10 —40Ta 59
Northallerton Way. Romf —22Md 49
Northall Rd. Bexh —54Ed 110
Northampton Av. Slou —4G 72
Northampton Gro. N1 —36Tb 63
Northampton Pk. N1 —37Sb 63
Northampton Rd. EC1 —42Qb 82 (5A 194)
Northampton Rd. Croy —75Wb 147
Northampton Rd. Enf —14Ac 26
Northampton Row. EC1 —42Qb 82 (5A 194)
(off Rosoman Pl.)
Northampton Sq. EC1 —41Rb 83 (4B 194)
Northampton St. N1 —38Sb 63
Northanger Rd. SW16 —65Nb 126
North App. N'wd —19S 18
North App. Wat —7V 4
N. Ash Rd. New Ash —76Ae 155
N. Audley St. W1 —44Jb 82 (3H 197)
North Av. N18 —21Wb 43
North Av. W13 —43Ka 78
North Av. Cars —80Jb 146
North Av. Harr —30Da 37
North Av. Hay —45W 76
North Av. Rich —53Qa 101
North Av. Shenl —4Na 7
North Av. S'hall —45Ba 77
North Av. W Vill —81U 158
Northaw Rd. E. Cuff —3Mb 10
Northaw Rd. W. N'thaw —2Hb 9
N. Bank. NW8 —41Gb 81 (4D 190)
Northbank Rd. E17 —26Ec 44
N. Birkbeck Rd. E11 —34Fc 65
Northborough Rd. SW16 —69Mb 126
Northborough Rd. Slou —2E 72
Northbourne. Brom —73Jc 149
Northbourne Rd. SW4 —57Mb 104
Northbrook Dri. N'wd —25U 36
Northbrook Rd. N22 —24Nb 42
Northbrook Rd. SE13 —57Gc 107
Northbrook Rd. Barn —16Ab 22
Northbrook Rd. Croy —71Tb 147
Northbrook Rd. Ilf —33Qc 66
Northburgh St. EC1 —42Rb 83 (6C 194)
N. Burnham Clo. Burn —10A 52
N. Carriage Dri. W2 —45Gb 81 (4D 196)
(off Ring, The.)
Northchurch. SE17
(in two parts) —50Tb 83 (7G 207)
Northchurch Rd. N1 —38Tb 63
Northchurch Rd. Wemb —37Qa 59
Northchurch Ter. N1 —38Ub 63
(in two parts)
N. Circular Rd. E18 —26Lc 45
N. Circular Rd. N3 —28Bb 41
N. Circular Rd. N12 —25Fb 41
N. Circular Rd. N13 —22Qb 42
N. Circular Rd. NW2 —34Ua 60
N. Circular Rd. NW4 —32Xa 60
N. Circular Rd. NW10 —41Pa 79
N. Circular Rd. NW11 —30Za 40
Northcliffe Clo. Wor Pk —76Ua 144
Northcliffe Dri. N20 —18Bb 23
North Clo. Barn —15Ya 22
North Clo. Bexh —56Zc 109
North Clo. Chig —22Wc 47
North Clo. Dag —39Cd 68
North Clo. Felt —58T 98
North Clo. Mord —70Ab 124
North Clo. Wind —3D 94
N. Colonnade. E14 —46Cc 84
North Comn. Wey —77S 140
N. Common Rd. W5 —45Na 79
N. Common Rd. Uxb —36M 55
Northcote. Add —77M 139
Northcote. Lea —86Ea 160
Northcote. Pinn —26Y 37
Northcote Av. W5 —45Na 79
Northcote Av. Iswth —57Ja 100
Northcote Av. S'hall —45Aa 77
Northcote Av. Surb —73Ra 143
Northcote Clo. W Hor —97S 174
Northcote Cres. W Hor —97S 174
Northcote M. SW11 —56Gb 103
Northcote Rd. E17 —28Ac 44
Northcote Rd. NW10 —38Ua 60
Northcote Rd. SW11 —57Gb 103
Northcote Rd. Croy —72Tb 147
Northcote Rd. Grav —10B 114
Northcote Rd. N Mald —69Sa 123
Northcote Rd. Sidc —63Uc 130
Northcote Rd. Twic —57Ja 100
Northcote Rd. W Hor —97S 174
Northcott Av. N22 —25Nb 42
N. Countess Rd. E17 —26Bc 44
North Ct. W1 —43Lb 82 (7C 192)
North Ct. Rick —18J 17
N. Cray Rd. Sidc & Bex —65Ad 131
North Cres. E16 —42Fc 85
North Cres. N3 —26Bb 41
North Cres. WC1 —43Mb 82 (7D 192)
Northcroft. Slou —2F 72
Northcroft Clo. Egh —4M 117
Northcroft Gdns. Egh —4M 117
Northcroft Rd. W13 —47Ka 78
Northcroft Rd. Egh —4M 117
Northcroft Rd. Eps —80Ta 143
N. Crofts. SE23 —60Xb 105
Northcroft Vs. Egh —4M 117
N. Cross Rd. SE22 —57Vb 105
N. Cross Rd. Ilf —28Sc 46
North Dene. NW7 —20Ta 21
Northdene. Chig —22Tc 46
North Dene. Houn —53Da 99
Northdene Gdns. N15 —30Vb 43
North Down. S Croy —83Ub 165
Northdown Clo. Ruis —34V 56
Northdown Gdns. Ilf —29Uc 46
N. Down Rd. Ger X —23A 34
Northdown Rd. Horn —31Kd 69
Northdown Rd. Kems —89Nd 171
Northdown Rd. Long —68Zd 135
Northdown Rd. Sutt —82Db 163
Northdown Rd. Well —54Xc 109
Northdown Rd. Wold —96Cc 182
N. Downs Cres. New Ad —81Dc 166
N. Downs Rd. New Ad —81Dc 166
Northdown St. N1 —40Nb 62 (1G 193)
North Dri. SW16 —63Lb 126
North Dri. Houn —54Ea 100
North Dri. Orp —77Uc 150
North Dri. Romf —27Ld 49
North Dri. Ruis —31U 56
North Dri. Slou —1J 73
North Dri. Vir W —10J 117
N. East Pier. E1 —46Xb 83
Northeast Pl. N1 —40Qb 62 (1A 194)
(off Chapel Mkt.)
North End. NW3 —33Eb 61
North End. Buck H —17Lc 27
North End. Croy —75Sb 147
Northend. War —22Yd 50
N. End Av. NW3 —33Eb 61
N. End Cres. W14 —49Bb 81
N. End La. Orp —83Qc 168
N. End Pde. W14 —49Ab 80
(off N. End Rd.)
N. End Rd. NW11 —32Cb 61
N. End Rd. W14 & SW6 —49Ab 80
Northend Rd. Eri —52Hd 110
N. End Rd. Wemb —34Qa 59
N. End Way. NW3 —33Eb 61
Northern Av. N9 —19Ub 25
Northernhay Wlk. Mord —70Ab 124
Northern Perimeter Rd. H'row A —53R 98
Northern Perimeter Rd. W. Houn —53N 97
Northern Precinct. W Thur —49Vd 90
Northern Rd. E13 —40Kc 65
Northern Rd. Slou —2H 73
Northey Av. Sutt —82Za 162
N. Eyot Gdns. W6 —50Va 80
Northey St. E14 —45Ac 84
N. Feltham Trading Est. Felt —57X 99
Northfield. Hart —69Be 135
Northfield Av. W13 & W5 —46Ka 78
Northfield Av. Orp —72Yc 151
Northfield Av. Pinn —28Z 37
Northfield Clo. Brom —67Nc 130
Northfield Clo. Hay —48V 76
Northfield Ct. Stai —67K 119
Northfield Cres. Sutt —77Ab 144
Northfield Gdns. Dag —35Bd 67
Northfield Gdns. Wat —9Y 5
Northfield Ind. Est. NW10 —41Qa 79
Northfield Ind. Est. Wemb —39Qa 59
Northfield Pde. Hay —48U 76
Northfield Pk. Hay —48V 76
Northfield Path. Dag —33Bd 67
Northfield Pl. Wey —80R 140
Northfield Rd. E6 —38Pc 66
Northfield Rd. N16 —31Ub 63
Northfield Rd. W13 —47Ka 78
Northfield Rd. Barn —13Gb 23
Northfield Rd. Borwd —11Ra 21
Northfield Rd. Cob —85W 158
Northfield Rd. Dag —35Bd 67
Northfield Rd. Enf —15Xb 25
Northfield Rd. Eton W —9D 72
Northfield Rd. Houn —51Z 99
Northfield Rd. Stai —67K 119
Northfield Rd. Wal X —4Ac 12
Northfields. SW18 —56Cb 103
Northfields. Asht —90Na 161
Northfields. Eps —83Ua 162
Northfields. Grays —49Ee 91
Northfields Prospect Bus. Cen. SW18 —56Cb 103
Northfields Rd. W3 —43Ra 79
Northfleet Ind. Est. Grav —56Be 113
N. Flockton St. SE16 —47Wb 83
N. Flower Wlk. W2 —45Eb 81 (5A 196)
(off Lancaster Wlk.)
North Gdns. SW19 —66Fb 125
Northgate. N'wd —24S 36
Northgate Bus.Pk. Enf —13Xb 25
Northgate Dri. NW9 —30Ua 40
Northgate Path. Borwd —10Pa 7
N. Glade, The. Bex —60Bd 109
N. Gower St. NW1 —41Lb 82 (4C 192)
North Grn. NW9 —24Ua 40
North Grn. Slou —5J 73
North Gro. N6 —31Jb 62
North Gro. N15 —29Tb 43
North Gro. Cher —72H 139
N. Hatton Rd. Houn —53T 98
North Hill. N6 —30Hb 41
North Hill. Chor —12G 16
N. Hill Av. N6 —30Jb 42
N. Hill Dri. Romf —21Md 49
N. Hill Grn. Romf —21Md 49
North Ho. SE8 —50Bc 84
N. Hyde Gdns. Hay —49W 76
N. Hyde La. S'hall & Houn —50Z 77
N. Hyde Rd. Hay —48U 76
Northiam. N12 —21Cb 41
(in two parts)
Northiam St. E8 —39Xb 63
Northington St. WC1 —42Pb 82 (6J 193)
N. Kent Av. Grav —58Ee 113
N. Kent Gro. SE18 —49Pc 86
Northlands. Pot B —3Fb 9
Northlands Av. Orp —77Uc 150
Northlands St. SE5 —54Sb 105
North La. Tedd —65Ha 122
Northleach Ct. SE15 —51Ub 105
(off Birdlip Clo.)
N. Lodge. New Bar —15Eb 23
N. Lodge Clo. SW15 —57Za 102
North Mall. N9 —19Xb 25
North Mall. Stai —63H 119
Northmead Rd. Slou —3D 72
North M. WC1 —42Pb 82 (6J 193)
North Mt. N20 —19Eb 23
(off High Rd.)
Northolm. Edgw —21Ta 39
Northolme Clo. Grays —48Ee 91
Northolme Gdns. Edgw —25Qa 39
Northolme Rise. Orp —75Uc 150
Northolme Rd. N5 —35Sb 63
Northolt. N17 —26Ub 43
(off Griffin Rd.)
Northolt Av. Ruis —36X 57
Northolt Gdns. Gnfd —36Ha 58
Northolt Rd. Harr —35Da 57
Northolt Rd. Houn —53M 97
Northolt Way. Horn —37Ld 69
N. Orbital Rd. Rick & Den —23G 34
N. Orbital Rd. Wat & St Alb —5Z 5
Northover. Brom —62Hc 129
North Pde. Chess —78Pa 143
North Pde. S'hall —44Ca 77
(off North Rd.)
North Pk. SE9 —58Pc 108
North Pk. Ger X —27A 34
N. Park Rd. Iver —48F 74
North Pl. SW18 —57Cb 103
North Pl. Mitc —66Hb 125
North Pl. Tedd —65Ha 122
North Pl. Wal A —5Dc 12
N. Pole La. Kes —79Hc 149
N. Pole Rd. W10 —43Ya 80
Northport St. N1 —39Tb 63 (1G 195)
N. Quebec St. W1 —44Hb 81
N. Ride. W2 —45Fb 81 (5C 196)
N. Ridge Rd. Grav —2E 136
N. Riding. Brick —2Ca 5
N. Riding. Hart —69Fe 135
North Rd. N2 —26Gb 41
North Rd. N6 —31Jb 62
North Rd. N7 —37Nb 62
North Rd. N9 —18Xb 25
North Rd. SE18 —49Uc 86
North Rd. SW19 —65Eb 125
North Rd. W5 —48Ma 79
North Rd. Belv —48Dd 88
North Rd. Bren —51Na 101
North Rd. Brtwd —18Yd 32
North Rd. Brom —67Kc 129
North Rd. Chad —29Ad 47
North Rd. Chor —15F 16
North Rd. Dart —58Hd 110
North Rd. Edgw —25Ra 39
North Rd. Felt —58T 98
North Rd. Hav —20Gd 30
North Rd. Hay —43T 76
North Rd. Ilf —33Uc 66
North Rd. Purf —49Sd 90
North Rd. Rich —55Qa 101
North Rd. S'hall —45Ca 77
North Rd. S Ock —40Yd 70
North Rd. Surb —72Ma 143
North Rd. Upm & S Ock —38Yd 70
North Rd. Wal X —5Ac 12
North Rd. W on T —78Y 141
North Rd. W Dray —48P 75
North Rd. W Wick —74Dc 148
North Rd. Wok —88C 156
North Rd. Av. Brtwd —18Yd 32
Northrop Rd. H'row A —53U 98
North Row. W1 —45Hb 81 (4G 197)
N. Service Rd. Brtwd —19Yd 32
North Several. SE3 —54Fc 107
Northside Rd. Brom —67Jc 129
North-South Route. N17 —26Xb 43
Northspur Rd. Sutt —76Cb 145
North Sq. N9 —19Xb 25
North Sq. NW11 —29Cb 41
North Sq. New Ash —75Be 155
Northstead Rd. SW2 —61Qb 126
North St. E13 —40Kc 65
North St. NW4 —29Ya 40
North St. SW4 —55Lb 104
North St. Bark —37Rc 66
North St. Bexh —56Cd 110
North St. Brom —67Jc 129
North St. Cars —76Hb 145
North St. Dart —59Md 111
North St. Egh —64B 118
North St. Grav —9D 114
North St. Horn —32Md 69
North St. Iswth —55Ja 100
North St. Lea —93Ja 176
North St. Romf —27Fd 48
North St. Wink —1A 116
North St. Pas. E13 —40Kc 65
N. Tenter St. E1 —44Vb 83
North Ter. SW3 —48Gb 81 (4D 202)
North Ter. Wind —2J 95
Northumberland All. EC3 —44Ub 83 (3J 201)
Northumberland Av. E12 —32Lc 65
Northumberland Av. WC2 —46Nb 82 (6F 199)
Northumberland Av. Enf —11Xb 25
Northumberland Av. Horn —29Ld 49
Northumberland Av. Iswth —53Ha 100
Northumberland Av. Well —55Uc 108
Northumberland Clo. Eri —52Ed 110
Northumberland Clo. Stai —58N 97
Northumberland Cres. Felt —58U 98
Northumberland Gdns. N9 —20Vb 25
Northumberland Gdns. Brom —70Qc 130
Northumberland Gdns. Iswth —52Ja 100
Northumberland Gdns. Mitc —71Mb 146
Northumberland Gro. N17 —24Xb 43
Northumberland Pk. N17 —24Vb 43
Northumberland Pk. Eri —52Ed 110
Northumberland Pl. W2 —44Cb 81
Northumberland Pl. Rich —58Ma 101
Northumberland Rd. E6 —44Nc 86
Northumberland Rd. E17 —31Cc 64
Northumberland Rd. Barn —16Eb 23
Northumberland Rd. Grav —6B 136
Northumberland Rd. Harr —29Ba 37
Northumberland Rd. Linf —7H 93
Northumberland Row. Twic —60Ga 100
Northumberland St. WC2 —46Nb 82 (6F 199)
Northumberland Way. Eri —53Ed 110
Northumbria St. E14 —44Cc 84
N. Verbena Gdns. W6 —50Wa 80
Northview. N7 —34Nb 62
North View. SW19 —64Ya 124
North View. W5 —42La 78
North View. Ilf —24Wc 47
North View. Pinn —31Y 57
Northview. Swan —68Gd 132
N. View Av. Til —3C 114
N. View Cres. NW10 —35Va 60
N. View Cres. Eps —89Ya 162
Northview Dri. Wfd G —26Mc 45
N. View Rd. N8 —28Mb 42
N. View Rd. Sev —93Ld 187
North Vs. NW1 —37Mb 62
North Wlk. W2 —45Db 81 (5A 196)
(off Bayswater Rd.)
North Wlk. New Ad —79Dc 148
(in two parts)
North Way. N9 —19Zb 26
North Way. N11 —23Lb 42
North Way. NW9 —27Ra 39
Northway. NW11 —29Db 41
Northway. Mord —70Ab 124
North Way. Pinn —28Z 37
Northway. Rick —17M 17
North Way. Uxb —38N 55
Northway. Wall —77Lb 146
Northway Cir. NW7 —21Ta 39
Northway Cres. NW7 —21Ta 39
Northway Gdns. NW11 —29Db 41
Northway Rd. SE5 —55Sb 105
Northway Rd. Croy —72Vb 147
Northways Pde. NW3 —38Fb 61
(off College Cres.)
N. Western Av. Wat —7T 4
N. West Pier. E1 —46Xb 83
Northwest Pl. N1 —40Qb 62 (1A 194)
N. Wharf Rd. W2 —43Fb 81 (1B 196)
Northwick Av. Harr —30Ja 38
Northwick Circ. Harr —30La 38
Northwick Clo. NW8 —42Fb 81 (5B 190)
Northwick Pk. Rd. Harr —30Ha 38
Northwick Rd. Wat —21Y 37
Northwick Rd. Wemb —39Ma 59
Northwick Sq. Houn —53S 98
Northwick Ter. NW8 —42Fb 81 (5B 190)
Northwick Wlk. Harr —31Ha 58
Northwold Dri. Pinn —26Y 37
Northwold Est. E5 —33Wb 63
Northwold Rd. N16 & E5 —33Vb 63
Northwood. Grays —7D 92
Northwood Av. Horn —35Jd 68
Northwood Av. Knap —6A 188
Northwood Av. Purl —85Qb 164
N. Wood Ct. SE25 —69Wb 127
Northwood Gdns. N12 —22Fb 41
Northwood Gdns. Gnfd —36Ha 58
Northwood Gdns. Ilf —28Qc 46
Northwood Hills Cir. N'wd —25W 36
Northwood Ho. SE27 —63Tb 127
Northwood Pl. Eri —48Bd 87
Northwood Rd. N6 —31Kb 62
Northwood Rd. SE23 —60Bc 106
Northwood Rd. Cars —79Jb 146
Northwood Rd. Hare —25L 35
Northwood Rd. Houn —53M 97
Northwood Rd. T Hth —68Rb 127
Northwood Way. SE19 —65Tb 127
Northwood Way. Hare —25M 35
Northwood Way. N'wd —24V 36
N. Woolwich Rd. E16 —46Jc 85
N. Worple Way. SW14 —55Ta 101
Norton Av. Ger X —23B 34
Norton Almshouses. Chesh —2Zb 12
(off Turner's Hill)
Norton Av. Surb —73Ra 143
Norton Clo. E4 —22Cc 44
Norton Clo. Borwd —11Qa 21
Norton Clo. Enf —12Xb 25
Norton Folgate. E1 —43Ub 83 (7J 195)
Norton Gdns. SW16 —68Nb 126
Norton Ho. SW9 —54Pb 104
(off Aytoun Rd.)
Norton La. D'side —91V 174
Norton Pk. Asc —10A 116
Norton Rd. E10 —32Bc 64
Norton Rd. Dag —37Fd 68
Norton Rd. Uxb —41M 75
Norton Rd. Wemb —37Ma 59
Norval Rd. Wemb —33Ka 58
Norway Dri. Slou —3M 73
Norway Ga. SE16 —48Ac 84
Norway Pl. E14 —44Bc 84
Norway St. SE10 —51Dc 106
Norway Wlk. Rain —42Ld 89
Norwich Ho. Borwd —12Qa 21
Norwich M. Ilf —32Wc 67
Norwich Pl. Bexh —56Cd 110
Norwich Rd. E7 —36Jc 65
Norwich Rd. Dag —40Cd 68
Norwich Rd. Gnfd —39Da 57
Norwich Rd. N'wd —27V 36
Norwich Rd. T Hth —69Sb 127
Norwich St. EC4 —44Qb 82 (2K 199)
Norwich Wlk. Edgw —24Sa 39
Norwich Way. Crox —13R 18
Norwood Av. Romf —31Gd 68
Norwood Av. Wemb —39Pa 59
Norwood Clo. Eff —100Aa 175
Norwood Clo. S'hall —49Ca 77
Norwood Cres. Houn —53S 98
Norwood Dri. Harr —30Ba 37
Norwood Farm La. Cob —83W 158
Norwood Gdns. Hay —42Y 77
Norwood Gdns. S'hall —49Ba 77
Norwood Grn. Rd. S'hall —49Ca 77
Norwood High St. SE27 —62Rb 127
Norwood La. Iver —42F 74
Norwood Pk. Rd. SE27 —64Sb 127
Norwood Rd. SE24 —60Rb 105
Norwood Rd. SE27 —61Rb 127
Norwood Rd. Eff —100Aa 175
Norwood Rd. S'hall —48Aa 77
Norwood Ter. S'hall —49Da 77
Noss Clo. Sutt —78Gb 145
Notley End. Egh —6N 117
Notley St. SE5 —52Tb 105
Notson Rd. SE25 —70Xb 127
Notting Barn Rd. W10 —42Za 80
Nottingdale Sq. W11 —46Ab 80
Nottingham Av. E16 —43Lc 85
Nottingham Clo. Wat —5W 4
Nottingham Clo. Wok —6C 188
Nottingham Ct. WC2 —44Nb 82 (3F 199)
Nottingham Ct. Wok —6C 188
(off Nottingham Clo.)
Nottingham Pl. W1 —43Jb 82 (6H 191)
Nottingham Rd. E10 —30Ec 44
Nottingham Rd. SW17 —60Hb 103
Nottingham Rd. Herons —17E 16
Nottingham Rd. Iswth —54Ha 100
Nottingham Rd. S Croy —77Sb 147
Nottingham St. W1 —43Jb 82 (7H 191)
Nottingham Ter. NW1 —42Jb 82 (6H 191)
(off York Ter. W.)
Notting Hill Ga. W11 —46Cb 81
Nova M. Sutt —74Ab 144
Novar Clo. Orp —75Vc 151
Nova Rd. Croy —73Rb 147
Novar Rd. SE9 —60Sc 108
Novello St. SW6 —53Cb 103
Novello Way. Borwd —11Sa 21
Nowell Rd. SW13 —51Wa 102
Nower Ct. Pinn —28Ba 37
Nower Hill. Pinn —28Ba 37
Nower, The. Chev —92Vc 185
Noyna Rd. SW17 —62Hb 125
Nuding Clo. SE13 —55Cc 106
Nuffield Lodge. N6 —30Lb 42
Nuffield Rd. Swan —65Jd 132
Nugent Ind. Pk. Orp —70Yc 131
Nugent Rd. N19 —32Nb 62

Nugent Rd.—Ohio Cotts.

Nugent Rd. SE25 —69Vb 127
Nugents Ct. Pinn —25Aa 37
Nugents Pk. Pinn —25Aa 37
Nugent Ter. NW8
—40Eb 61 (2A 190)
Numa Ct. Bren —52Ma 101
Nun Ct. EC2 —44Tb 83 (2F 201)
(off Coleman St.)
Nuneaton Rd. Dag —38Ad 67
Nunfield. Chfd —3K 3
Nunhead Cres. SE15 —55Xb 105
Nunhead Est. SE15 —56Xb 105
Nunhead Grn. SE15 —55Xb 105
Nunhead Gro. SE15 —55Yb 106
Nunhead La. SE15 —55Xb 105
Nunhead Pas. SE15 —56Xb 105
Nunnington Clo. SE9 —62Nc 130
Nunns Rd. Enf —12Sb 25
Nunns Way. Grays —49Fe 91
Nuns Wlk. Vir W —10P 117
Nupton Dri. Barn —16Ya 22
Nursery App. N12 —23Gb 41
Nursery Av. N3 —26Eb 41
Nursery Av. Bexh —55Bd 109
Nursery Av. Croy —75Zb 148
Nursery Clo. SW15 —56Za 102
Nursery Clo. Croy —75Zb 148
Nursery Clo. Dart —59Sd 112
Nursery Clo. Enf —11Zb 26
Nursery Clo. Eps —82Ua 162
Nursery Clo. Felt —59X 99
Nursery Clo. Orp —73Vc 151
Nursery Clo. Romf —30Zc 47
Nursery Clo. Sev —94Ld 187
Nursery Clo. S Ock —42Yd 90
Nursery Clo. Swan —68Ed 132
Nursery Clo. Tad —97Xa 178
Nursery Clo. Wok —4F 188
Nursery Clo. Wfd G —22Kc 45
Nursery Clo. Wdhm —82H 157
Nursery Ct. N17 —24Vb 43
Nursery Gdns. Chst —65Rc 130
Nursery Gdns. Enf —11Zb 26
Nursery Gdns. Stai —65K 119
Nursery Gdns. Sun —68V 120
Nursery La. E7 —37Jc 65
Nursery La. W10 —43Ya 80
Nursery La. Slou —6N 73
Nursery La. Uxb —42M 75
Nursery Pl. Sev —94Fd 186
Nursery Rd. E9 —37Yb 64
Nursery Rd. N2 —25Fb 41
Nursery Rd. N14 —17Lb 24
Nursery Rd. SW9 —56Pb 104
Nursery Rd. SW19 —68Db 125
(Merton)
Nursery Rd. SW19 —66Ab 124
(Wimbledon)
Nursery Rd. H Bee —11Lc 27
Nursery Rd. Knap —5A 188
Nursery Rd. Lou —15Lc 27
Nursery Rd. Meop —10C 136
Nursery Rd. Pinn —27Y 37
Nursery Rd. Stanf —1N 93
Nursery Rd. Sun —68U 120
Nursery Rd. Sutt —77Eb 145
Nursery Rd. Tad —97Wa 178
Nursery Rd. Tap —4A 72
Nursery Rd. T Hth —70Tb 127
Nursery Row. Barn —13Ab 22
Nursery St. N17 —24Vb 43
Nursery, The. Eri —52Hd 110
Nursery Wlk. NW4 —27Xa 40
Nursery Wlk. Romf —31Fd 68
Nursery Way. Wray —8P 95
Nursery Waye. Uxb —39M 55
Nurstead Av. Long —70Fe 135
Nurstead Chu. Rd. Meop —10B 136
Nurstead La. Long —70Fe 135
Nurstead Rd. Eri —52Cd 110
Nutberry Av. Grays —47Ce 91
Nutberry Clo. Grays —47Ce 91
Nutbourne St. W10 —41Ab 80
Nutbrook St. SE15 —55Wb 105
Nutbrowne Rd. Dag —39Bd 67
Nutcroft Gro. Fet —93Ga 176
Nutcroft Rd. SE15 —52Xb 105
Nutfield Clo. N18 —23Vb 43
Nutfield Clo. Cars —76Gb 145
Nutfield Gdns. Ilf —33Vc 67
Nutfield Gdns. N'holt —40Y 57
Nutfield Rd. E15 —35Ec 64
Nutfield Rd. NW2 —34Wa 60
Nutfield Rd. SE22 —56Vb 105
Nutfield Rd. Coul —88Jb 164
Nutfield Rd. Mers —100Lb 180
Nutfield Rd. T Hth —70Rb 127
Nutfield Way. Orp —75Rc 150
Nutford Pl. W1 —44Hb 81 (2E 196)
Nuthatch. Long —69De 135
Nuthatch Clo. Stai —60P 97
Nuthatch Gdns. SE28 —47Tc 86
Nuthurst Av. SW2 —61Pb 126
Nutley Clo. Swan —67Hd 132
Nutley Ter. NW3 —37Eb 61
Nutmead Clo. Bex —60Ed 110
Nutmeg Clo. E16 —42Gc 85
Nutmeg La. E14 —44Fc 85
Nuttall St. N1 —40Ub 63 (1J 195)
Nutter La. E11 —30Lc 45
Nuttfield Clo. Crox —16S 18
Nutt Gro. Edgw —19Ma 21
Nut Tree Clo. Orp —76Zc 151
Nutt St. SE15 —52Vb 105
Nutty La. Shep —69S 120
Nutwell St. SW17 —64Gb 125
Nuxley Rd. Belv —51Bd 109
Nyanza St. SE18 —51Tc 108
Nye Bevan Est. E5 —34Zb 64
Nyefield Pk. Tad —98Wa 178
Nylands Av. Rich —53Qa 101
Nymans Gdns. SW20 —69Xa 124
Nynehead St. SE14 —52Ac 106
Nyon Gro. SE6 —61Bc 128
Nyssa Clo. Wfd G —23Pc 46
Nyssa Ct. E15 —41Gc 85
(off Teasel Way)
Nyth Clo. Upm —30Td 50
Nyton Clo. N19 —32Nb 62

Oakapple Clo. S Croy —86Xb 165
Oak Apple Ct. SE12 —60Jc 107
Oak Av. N8 —28Nb 42
Oak Av. N10 —24Kb 42
Oak Av. N17 —24Tb 43
Oak Av. Brick —2Ca 5
Oak Av. Croy —75Cc 148
Oak Av. Egh —66E 118
Oak Av. Enf —10Pb 10
Oak Av. Hamp —64Aa 121
Oak Av. Houn —52Z 99
Oak Av. Sev —100Kd 187
Oak Av. Upm —34Rd 69
Oak Av. Uxb —33R 56
Oak Av. W Dray —48Q 76
Oakbank. Fet —95Fa 176
Oakbank. Hut —15Fe 33
Oak Bank. New Ad —79Ec 148
Oakbank. Wok —91A 172
Oakbank Av. W on T —73Ba 141
Oakbank Gro. SE24 —56Sb 105
Oakbrook Clo. Brom —63Kc 129
Oakbury Rd. SW6 —54Db 103
Oak Clo. N14 —17Kb 24
Oak Clo. Dart —56Hd 110
Oak Clo. Sutt —75Eb 145
Oakcombe Clo. N Mald —67Ua 124
Oak Cottage Clo. SE6 —60Hc 107
Oak Cotts. W7 —47Ga 78
Oak Ct. SE1 —52Vb 105
(off Sumner Rd.)
Oak Ct. N'wd —23T 36
Oak Cres. E16 —43Gc 85
Oakcroft Bus. Cen. Chess
—77Pa 143
Oakcroft Clo. Pinn —26X 37
Oakcroft Clo. W Byf —86H 157
Oakcroft Rd. SE13 —54Fc 107
Oakcroft Rd. Chess —77Pa 143
Oakcroft Rd. W Byf —86H 157
Oakcroft Vs. Chess —77Pa 143
Oakdale. N14 —18Kb 24
Oakdale Av. Harr —29Na 39
Oakdale Av. N'wd —26W 36
Oakdale Clo. Wat —21Y 37
Oakdale Ct. E4 —22Ec 44
Oakdale Rd. E7 —38Kc 65
Oakdale Rd. E11 —33Fc 65
Oakdale Rd. E18 —26Kc 45
Oakdale Rd. N4 —30Sb 43
Oakdale Rd. SE15 & SE4
—55Yb 106
Oakdale Rd. SW16 —64Nb 126
Oakdale Rd. Eps —81Ta 161
Oakdale Rd. Wat —20Y 19
Oakdale Rd. Wey —76Q 140
Oakdale Way. Mitc —73Jb 146
Oak Dene. SE15 —53Xb 105
Oakdene. W13 —43Ka 78
Oakdene. Chesh —2Ac 12
Oakdene. Tad —92Ab 178
Oakdene Av. Chst —64Qc 130
Oakdene Av. Eri —51Ed 110
Oakdene Av. N'wd —26W 36
Oakdene Av. Th Dit —74Ja 142
Oakdene Clo. Bookh —99Ea 176
Oakdene Clo. Horn —30Kd 49
Oakdene Clo. Pinn —24Ba 37
Oakdene Dri. Surb —73Sa 143
Oakdene M. Sutt —74Bb 145
Oakdene Pde. Cob —86X 159
Oakdene Pk. N3 —24Bb 41
Oakdene Rd. Bookh —96Ba 175
Oakdene Rd. Cob —86X 159
Oakdene Rd. Orp —71Vc 151
Oakdene Rd. Sev —94Jd 186
Oakdene Rd. Uxb —40R 56
Oakdene Rd. Wat —8X 5
Oakden St. SE11
—49Qb 82 (5A 206)
Oake Ct. SW15 —57Ab 102
Oakefield Rd. N14 —19Nb 24
Oaken Coppice. Asht —91Qa 177
Oakend Ho. N4 —31Tb 63
Oaken Dri. Clay —79Ha 142
Oak End Way. Ger X —29A 34
Oak End Way. Iver —40E 54
Oak End Way. Wdhm —84G 156
Oakenholt Ho. SE2 —46Zc 87
Oaken La. Clay —77Ga 142
Oakenshaw Clo. Surb —73Na 143
Oakes Clo. E6 —44Pc 86
Oakeshott Av. N6 —33Jb 62
Oakey La. SE1 —48Qb 82 (3K 205)
Oak Farm. Borwd —15Sa 21
Oakfield. E4 —22Dc 44
Oakfield. Rick —17H 17
Oakfield. Wok —5B 188
Oakfield Av. Harr —27Ka 38
Oakfield Av. Slou —6F 72
Oakfield Clo. N Mald —71Va 144
Oakfield Clo. Pot B —3Bb 9
Oakfield Clo. Ruis —30Y 38
Oakfield Clo. Wey —77S 140
Oakfield Ct. N8 —31Nb 62
Oakfield Ct. NW2 —31Za 60
Oakfield Ct. Borwd —13Ra 21
Oakfield Gdns. N18 —21Ub 43
Oakfield Gdns. SE19 —64Ub 127
(in two parts)
Oakfield Gdns. Beck —71Dc 148
Oakfield Gdns. Cars —74Gb 145
Oakfield Gdns. Gnfd —42Ha 78
Oakfield Glade. Wey —77S 140
Oakfield La. Dart —61Gd 132
Oakfield La. Kes —77Lc 149
Oakfield Lodge. Ilf —34Rc 66
(off Albert Rd.)
Oakfield Pk. Rd. Dart —61Md 133
Oakfield Pl. Dart —61Md 133
Oakfield Rd. E6 —39Nc 66
Oakfield Rd. E17 —26Ac 44
Oakfield Rd. N3 —25Db 41
Oakfield Rd. N4 —30Qb 42
Oakfield Rd. N14 —19Nb 24
Oakfield Rd. SE20 —66Xb 127
Oakfield Rd. SW19 —62Za 124
Oakfield Rd. Ashf —64R 120
Oakfield Rd. Asht —89Ma 161
Oakfield Rd. Cob —86X 159
Oakfield Rd. Croy —74Sb 147
Oakfield Rd. Ilf —34Rc 66
Oakfield Rd. Orp —73Wc 151
Oakfield Rd. Th Dit —71Ha 142
Oakfields. Sev —98Kd 187
Oakfields. W on T —74W 140
Oakfields. W Byf —86K 157
Oakfields Rd. NW11 —30Ab 40
Oakfield St. SW10 —51Eb 103
Oakford Rd. NW5 —35Lb 62
Oak Gdns. Croy —75Cc 148
Oak Gdns. Edgw —26Sa 39
Oak Glade. Coop —1Zc 15
Oak Glade. Eps —84Qa 161
Oak Glade. N'wd —25R 36
Oak Glen. Horn —27Nd 49
Oak Grange Rd. W Cla —100K 173
Oak Grn. Abb L —4U 4
Oak Grn. Way. Abb L —4U 4
Oak Gro. NW2 —35Za 60
Oak Gro. Ruis —31X 57
Oak Gro. Sun —66X 121
Oak Gro. W Wick —74Ec 148
Oak Gro. Rd. SE20 —67Yb 128
Oakhall Ct. E11 —30Kc 45
Oakhall Dri. Sun —64V 120
Oak Hall Rd. E11 —30Kc 45
Oakham Clo. SE6 —61Bc 128
Oakham Dri. Brom —70Hc 129
Oakhampton Rd. NW7 —24Za 40
Oakhill. Clay —79Ja 142
Oak Hill. Eps —88Ta 161
Oak Hill. Sev —96Jd 186
Oakhill. Surb —73Na 143
Oak Hill. Wfd G —24Fc 45
Oakhill Av. NW3 —35Db 61
Oakhill Av. Pinn —26Aa 37
Oakhill Clo. Asht —90La 160
Oak Hill Clo. Wfd G —24Fc 45
Oakhill Ct. SW19 —66Za 124
Oak Hill Ct. Wfd G —24Gc 45
Oakhill Cres. Surb —73Na 143
Oak Hill Cres. Wfd G —24Fc 45
Oakhill Dri. Surb —73Na 143
Oakhill Gdns. Wey —75U 140
Oak Hill Gdns. Wfd G —25Gc 45
Oakhill Gro. Surb —72Na 143
Oak Hill Pk. NW3 —35Db 61
Oak Hill Pk. M. NW3 —35Eb 61
Oakhill Path. Surb —72Na 143
Oakhill Pl. SW15 —57Cb 103
Oakhill Rd. SW15 —57Bb 103
Oakhill Rd. SW16 —67Pb 126
Oakhill Rd. Add —79H 139
Oakhill Rd. Asht —90La 160
Oakhill Rd. Beck —68Ec 128
Oakhill Rd. Orp —74Vc 151
Oakhill Rd. Purf —50Rd 89
Oakhill Rd. Rick —21F 34
Oakhill Rd. Sev —96Jd 186
Oak Hill Rd. Stap A —17Fd 30
Oakhill Rd. Surb —72Na 143
Oakhill Rd. Sutt —76Db 145
Oak Hill Way. NW3 —35Eb 61
Oak Ho. N2 —26Fb 41
Oakhouse Rd. Bexh —57Cd 110
Oakhurst Av. Barn —17Gb 23
Oakhurst Av. Bexh —53Ad 109
Oakhurst Clo. E17 —28Gc 45
Oakhurst Clo. Ilf —25Sc 46
Oakhurst Clo. Tedd —64Ga 122
Oakhurst Gdns. E4 —18Hc 27
Oakhurst Gdns. E17 —28Gc 45
Oakhurst Gdns. Bexh —52Ad 109
Oakhurst Gro. SE22 —56Wb 105
Oakhurst Rise. Cars —82Gb 163
Oakhurst Rd. Enf —8Zb 12
Oakhurst Rd. Eps —79Sa 143
Oakington Av. Amer —11A 16
Oakington Av. Harr —31Ca 57
Oakington Av. Hay —49T 76
Oakington Av. Wemb —34Pa 59
Oakington Dri. Sun —68Y 121
Oakington Mnr. Dri. Wemb
—36Qa 59
Oakington Rd. W9 —42Cb 81
Oakington Way. N8 —31Nb 62
Oakland Ct. Add —76K 139
Oakland Gdns. Hut —15Ee 33
Oaklands. N21 —19Pb 24
Oaklands. Beck —67Dc 128
Oaklands. Fet —96Fa 176
Oaklands. Kenl —86Sb 165
Oaklands Av. N9 —16Xb 25
Oaklands Av. Esh —74Fa 142
Oaklands Av. Iswth —51Ha 100
Oaklands Av. Romf —27Gd 48
Oaklands Av. Sidc —59Vc 109
Oaklands Av. T Hth —70Qb 126
Oaklands Av. Wat —18X 19
Oaklands Av. W Wick —76Dc 148
Oaklands Clo. Bexh —57Bd 109
Oaklands Clo. Chess —77La 142
Oaklands Clo. Orp —72Uc 150
Oaklands Clo. Wemb —36Ma 59
Oaklands Clo. W King —79Ud 154
Oaklands Ct. NW10 —38Ta 59
(off Nicoll Rd.)
Oaklands Ct. Wat —11W 18
Oaklands Ct. Wemb —36Ma 59
Oaklands Dri. S Ock —43Yd 90
Oaklands Dri. Twic —59Ea 100
Oaklands Est. SW4 —58Lb 104
Oaklands Gdns. Kenl —86Sb 165
Oaklands Ga. N'wd —23U 36
Oaklands Gro. W12 —46Wa 80
Oaklands La. Barn —14Xa 22
Oaklands La. Big H —85Kc 167
Oaklands Pk. Av. Ilf —33Sc 66
Oaklands Pl. SW4 —56Mb 104
Oaklands Rd. N20 —17Bb 23
Oaklands Rd. NW2 —35Za 60
Oaklands Rd. SW14 —55Ta 101
Oaklands Rd. W7 —47Ha 78
Oaklands Rd. Bexh —56Bd 109
Oaklands Rd. Brom —66Gc 129
Oaklands Rd. Dart —60Sd 112
Oaklands Rd. Grav —3B 136
Oaklands Way. Tad —94Ya 178
Oaklands Way. Wall —80Mb 146
Oakland Way. Eps —79Ua 144
Oak La. E14 —45Bc 84
Oak La. N2 —26Fb 41
Oak La. N11 —23Mb 42
Oak La. Cuff —1Pb 10
Oak La. Egh —2N 117
Oak La. Iswth —56Ga 100
Oak La. Sev —100Hd 186
Oak La. Twic —59Ja 100
Oak La. Wind —3E 94
Oak La. Wok —88E 156
Oak La. Wfd G —21Hc 45
Oaklawn Rd. Lea —90Ga 160
Oak Leaf Clo. Eps —84Sa 161
Oakleafe Gdns. Ilf —27Rc 46
Oaklea Pas. King T —69Ma 123
Oakleigh Av. N20 —19Fb 23
Oakleigh Av. Edgw —26Ra 39
Oakleigh Av. Surb —74Qa 143
Oakleigh Clo. N20 —20Hb 23
Oakleigh Clo. Swan —69Gd 132
Oakleigh Ct. Edgw —26Sa 39
Oakleigh Ct. S'hall —46Ba 77
Oakleigh Cres. N20 —19Gb 23
Oakleigh Dri. Crox —16S 18
Oakleigh Gdns. N20 —18Eb 23
Oakleigh Gdns. Edgw —22Pa 39
Oakleigh Gdns. Orp —77Uc 150
Oakleigh M. N20 —18Eb 23
Oakleigh Pk. Av. Chst —67Qc 130
Oakleigh Pk. N. N20 —18Fb 23
Oakleigh Pk. S. N20 —19Gb 23
Oakleigh Rise. Epp —4Wc 15
Oakleigh Rd. Pinn —23Ba 37
Oakleigh Rd. Uxb —38S 56
Oakleigh Rd. N. N20 —19Fb 23
Oakleigh Rd. S. N11 —20Jb 24
Oakleigh Way. Mitc —67Kb 126
Oakleigh Way. Surb —74Qa 143
Oakley Av. W5 —45Qa 79
Oakley Av. Bark —38Vc 67
Oakley Av. Croy —77Pb 146
Oakley Clo. E4 —20Ec 26
Oakley Clo. E6 —44Nc 86
Oakley Clo. W7 —45Ga 78
Oakley Clo. Add —77M 139
Oakley Clo. Grays —51Yd 112
Oakley Clo. Iswth —53Fa 100
Oakley Ct. Lou —12Qc 28
Oakley Cres. EC1 —40Rb 63
Oakley Cres. Slou —5J 73
Oakley Dri. SE9 —60Tc 108
Oakley Dri. Brom —76Nc 150
Oakley Dri. Romf —22Qd 49
Oakley Gdns. N8 —29Pb 42
Oakley Gdns. SW3 —51Gb 103
Oakley Gdns. Bans —87Db 163
Oakley Grange. Harr —34Ea 58
Oakley Grn. Rd. Wind —4A 94
Oakley Pk. Bex —59Yc 109
Oakley Pl. SE1 —50Vb 83 (7K 207)
Oakley Rd. N1 —38Tb 63
Oakley Rd. SE25 —71Xb 147
Oakley Rd. Brom —76Nc 150
Oakley Rd. Harr —30Ga 38
Oakley Rd. Warl —90Wb 165
Oakley Sq. NW1 —40Lb 62 (1C 192)
Oakley St. SW3 —51Gb 103
Oakley Wlk. W6 —51Za 102
Oak Lodge. E11 —30Jc 45
Oak Lodge. W8 —48Db 81
(off Chantry Sq.)
Oak Lodge Av. Chig —22Tc 46
Oak Lodge Clo. Stan —22La 38
Oak Lodge Clo. W on T —78Y 141
Oak Lodge Dri. W Wick —73Dc 148
Oak Lodge La. W'ham —97Tc 184
Oaklodge Way. NW7 —23Va 40
Oakmead Av. Brom —72Jc 149
Oakmead Ct. Stan —21La 38
Oak Meade. Pinn —23Ca 37
Oakmead Gdns. Edgw —21Ta 39
Oakmead Grn. Eps —87Sa 161
Oakmead Pl. Mitc —67Gb 125
Oakmead Rd. SW12 —60Jb 104
Oakmead Rd. Croy —72Mb 146
Oakmede. Barn —14Za 22
Oakmere Av. Pot B —5Eb 9
Oakmere Clo. Pot B —3Fb 9
Oakmere La. Pot B —4Eb 9
Oakmere Rd. SE2 —51Wc 109
Oakmont Pl. Orp —74Tc 150
Oakmoor Way. Chig —22Uc 46
Oak Pk. W Byf —85G 156
Oak Pk. Gdns. SW19 —60Za 102
Oak Path. Bush —16Da 19
(off Mortimer Clo.)
Oak Pl. SW18 —57Db 103
Oakridge. Brick —1Ba 5
Oakridge Av. Rad —6Ha 6
Oakridge Dri. N2 —27Fb 41
Oakridge La. Ald & Rad —7Fa 6
Oakridge La. Brom —64Fc 129
Oakridge Rd. Brom —63Fc 129
Oak Rise. Buck H —20Mc 27
Oak Rd. W5 —45Ma 79
Oak Rd. Cat —94Ub 181
Oak Rd. Cob —87Z 159
Oak Rd. Epp —2Vc 15
Oak Rd. Eri —54Jd 110
Oak Rd. Grav —2E 136
Oak Rd. Grays —51Ee 113
Oak Rd. Grnh —58Ud 112
Oak Rd. Lea —90Ja 160
Oak Rd. N Mald —68Ta 123
Oak Rd. N Hth —52Ed 110
Oak Rd. Orp —80Wc 151
Oak Rd. Romf —25Pd 49
Oak Rd. W'ham —97Tc 184
Oak Row. SW16 —68Lb 126
Oakroyd Av. Pot B —5Bb 9
Oakroyd Clo. Pot B —5Bb 9
Oaks Av. SE19 —64Ub 127
Oaks Av. Felt —61Aa 121
Oaks Av. Romf —26Ed 48
Oaks Av. Wor Pk —76Xa 144
Oaks Clo. Lea —93Ja 176
Oaks Clo. Rad —7Ha 6
Oaksford Av. SE26 —62Xb 127
Oaks Gro. E4 —19Gc 27
Oakshade Rd. Brom —63Fc 129
Oakshade Rd. Oxs —86Ea 160
Oakshaw. Oxt —99Fc 183
Oakshaw Rd. SW18 —59Db 103
Oakside. Den —37K 55
Oaks La. Croy —76Yb 148
Oaks La. Ilf —29Uc 46
Oak Sq. Sev —98Ld 187
Oaks Rd. Croy —78Xb 147
Oaks Rd. Kenl —86Rb 165
Oaks Rd. Stai —58M 97
Oaks Rd. Wok —89A 156
Oaks, The. E4 —24Gc 45
Oaks, The. N12 —21Db 41
Oaks, The. NW10 —38Xa 60
Oaks, The. SE18 —50Sc 86
Oaks, The. Borwd —11Qa 21
Oaks, The. Enf —13Rb 25
(off Bycullah Rd.)
Oaks, The. Eps —86Ua 162
Oaks, The. Hay —40S 56
Oaks, The. Ruis —31U 56
Oaks, The. Stai —63H 119
Oaks, The. Swan —68Gd 132
Oaks, The. Wat —18Y 19
Oaks, The. W Byf —86K 157
Oaks Track. Cars & Wall —83Hb 163
Oak St. Romf —29Ed 48
Oaks Way. Cars —80Hb 145
Oaks Way. Eps —91Xa 178
Oaks Way. Kenl —86Sb 165
Oaksway. Surb —74Ma 143
Oakthorpe Ct. N18 —22Sb 43
Oakthorpe Pk. Est. N13 —22Sb 43
Oakthorpe Rd. N13 —22Qb 42
Oaktree Av. N13 —20Rb 25
Oak Tree Clo. W5 —44La 78
Oaktree Clo. Brtwd —20Be 33
Oaktree Clo. Chesh —1Rb 11
Oak Tree Clo. Stan —24La 38
Oak Tree Clo. Vir W —72A 138
Oak Tree Ct. W3 —45Ra 79
Oak Tree Ct. Els —16Ma 21
(off Barnet La.)
Oak Tree Ct. N'holt —40Z 57
Oak Tree Dell. NW9 —29Ta 39
Oak Tree Dri. N20 —18Db 23
Oak Tree Dri. Egh —4N 117
Oak Tree Gdns. Brom —64Kc 129
Oak Tree Rd. NW8
—41Gb 81 (4C 190)
Oakview Clo. Chesh —1Xb 11
Oakview Gdns. N2 —28Fb 41
Oakview Gro. Croy —74Ac 148
Oakview Lodge. NW11 —31Bb 61
(off Beechcroft Av.)
Oakview Rd. SE6 —64Dc 128
Oak Village. NW5 —35Jb 62
Oak Way. N14 —17Kb 24
Oak Way. SW20 —70Ya 124
Oak Way. W3 —46Ua 80
Oak Way. Asht —88Qa 161
Oakway. Brom —68Fc 129
Oak Way. Croy —72Zb 148
Oak Way. Felt —60U 98
Oakway. Grays —46De 91
Oakway. Wok —7B 188
Oakway Clo. Bex —58Ad 109
Oakways. SE9 —58Rc 108
Oakwood. Wall —81Kb 164
Oakwood. Wal A —6Gc 13
Oakwood Av. N14 —17Mb 24
Oakwood Av. Beck —68Ec 128
Oakwood Av. Borwd —14Ra 21
Oakwood Av. Brom —69Kc 129
Oakwood Av. Mitc —68Fb 125
Oakwood Av. Purl —84Rb 165
Oakwood Av. S'hall —45Ca 77
Oakwood Bus. Pk. NW10 —42Ta 79
Oakwood Chase. Horn —30Pd 49
Oakwood Clo. N14 —16Lb 24
Oakwood Clo. Chst —65Pc 130
Oakwood Clo. Dart —60Rd 111
Oakwood Clo. E Hor —99U 174
Oakwood Clo. Wfd G —23Nc 46
Oakwood Ct. E6 —39Nc 66
Oakwood Ct. W14 —48Bb 81
Oakwood Ct. Hart —30Fa 38
Oakwood Ct. Swan —68Ed 132
(off Lawn Clo.)
Oakwood Cres. N21 —16Nb 24
Oakwood Cres. Gnfd —37Ja 58
Oakwood Dri. SE19 —65Tb 127
Oakwood Dri. Bexh —56Fd 110
Oakwood Dri. E Hor —99U 174
Oakwood Dri. Edgw —23Sa 39
Oakwood Dri. Sev —95Kd 187
Oakwood Dri. S'hall —45Ca 77
Oakwood Gdns. Ilf —33Vc 67
Oakwood Gdns. Orp —75Sc 150
Oakwood Gdns. Sutt —75Cb 145
Oakwood Hill. Lou —16Pc 28
Oakwood Hill Ind. Est. Lou
—15Sc 28
Oakwood La. W14 —48Bb 81
Oakwood Lodge. N14 —16Lb 24
(off Avenue Rd.)
Oakwood Pk. Rd. N14 —17Mb 24
Oakwood Pl. Croy —72Qb 146
Oakwood Rise. Long —69Ae 135
Oakwood Rd. NW11 —28Cb 41
Oakwood Rd. SW20 —67Wa 124
Oakwood Rd. Brick —1Ba 5
Oakwood Rd. Croy —72Qb 146
Oakwood Rd. Mers —100Qb 180
Oakwood Rd. Orp —75Sc 150
Oakwood Rd. Pinn —26X 37
Oakwood Rd. Vir W —10N 117
Oakwood Rd. Wok —7B 188
Oakwood View. N14 —16Mb 24
Oakworth Rd. W10 —43Ya 80
Oasis, The. Brom —68Lc 129
Oast Cotts. Sev —94Jd 186
Oast Ho. Clo. Wray —59A 96
Oasthouse Way. Orp —70Xc 131
Oast Way. Hart —72Ae 155
Oates Clo. Brom —69Fc 129
Oates Rd. Romf —22Dd 48
Oatfield Ho. N15 —30Ub 43
(off Perry Ct.)
Oatfield Rd. Orp —74Vc 151
Oatfield Rd. Tad —92Xa 178
Oatland Rise. E17 —26Ac 44
Oatlands Av. Wey —78T 140
Oatlands Chase. Wey —76U 140
Oatlands Clo. Wey —77S 140
Oatlands Dri. Slou —4H 73
Oatlands Dri. Wey —77S 140
Oatlands Grn. Wey —76T 140
Oatlands Mere. Wey —76T 140
Oatlands Rd. Enf —11Yb 26
Oatlands Rd. Tad —91Ab 178
Oat La. EC2 —44Sb 83 (2E 200)
Oban Clo. E13 —42Lc 85
Oban Ct. Chalv —7H 73
Oban Ho. Bark —40Tc 66
Oban Rd. E13 —41Lc 85
Oban Rd. SE25 —70Tb 127
Oban St. E14 —44Fc 85
Oberon Clo. Borwd —11Sa 21
Oberon Ho. N1 —40Ub 63 (1H 195)
(off Arden Est.)
Oberon Way. Shep —69N 119
Oberstein Rd. SW11 —56Fb 103
Oborne Clo. SE24 —57Rb 105
Observatory Gdns. W8 —47Cb 81
Observatory Rd. SW14 —56Sa 101
Observatory Shopping Cen., The. Slou
—7L 73
Occupation La. SE18 —53Rc 108
Occupation La. W5 —49Ma 79
Occupation Rd. SE17
—50Sb 83 (7D 206)
Occupation Rd. W13 —47Ka 78
Occupation Rd. Eps —80Ta 143
Occupation Rd. Wat —15X 19
Ocean Est. E1 —42Zb 84
(in two parts)
Ocean St. E1 —43Zb 84
Ockenden Clo. Wok —90B 156
Ockenden Gdns. Wok —90B 156
Ockenden Rd. Wok —90B 156
Ockendon Rd. N1 —37Tb 63
Ockendon Rd. N Ock —36Sd 70
Ockham Dri. Orp —66Wc 131
Ockham Dri. W Hor —96T 174
Ockham La. Ock & Cob —93Q 174
Ockham Rd. N. Ock & W Hors
—92N 173
Ockham Rd. S. E Hor —98U 174
Ockley Ct. Sidc —62Uc 130
Ockley Ct. Sutt —77Eb 145
Ockley Rd. SW16 —63Nb 126
Ockley Rd. Croy —73Pb 146
Octagon Arc. EC2
—43Ub 83 (1H 201)
Octagon Rd. W Vill —81U 158
Octavia Clo. Mitc —71Gb 145
Octavia Ct. Wat —12Z 19
Octavia Rd. Iswth —55Ga 100
Octavia St. SW11 —53Gb 103
Octavia Way. SE28 —45Xc 87
Octavia Way. Stai —65J 119
Octavius St. SE8 —52Cc 106
Odard Rd. W Mol —70Ca 121
Oddesey Rd. Borwd —11Ra 21
Oddmark Rd. Bark —40Tc 66
Odencroft Rd. Slou —1E 72
Odeon Ct. E16 —43Jc 85
Odeon Ct. NW10 —39Ua 60
Odessa Rd. E7 —34Hc 65
Odessa Rd. NW10 —40Wa 60
Odessa St. SE16 —48Bc 84
Odger St. SW11 —54Hb 103
Odhams Trading Est. Wat —9Y 5
Odhams Wlk. WC2
—44Nb 82 (3G 199)
Odin Ho. SE5 —54Sb 105
O'Donaghue Houses. Stanf —1N 93
O'Donnell Ct. WC1
—42Nb 82 (5G 193)
O'Driscoll Ho. W12 —44Xa 80
Odyssey Bus. Pk. Ruis —36X 57
Offa's Mead. E9 —35Bc 64
Offenham Rd. SE9 —63Pc 130
Offenham Rd. SE12 —63Pc 130
Offerton Rd. SW4 —55Lb 104
Offham Slope. N12 —22Bb 41
Offley Rd. SW9 —52Qb 104
Offord Clo. N17 —23Wb 43
Offord Rd. N1 —38Pb 62
Offord St. N1 —38Pb 62
Ogden Ho. Felt —62Aa 121
Ogilby St. SE18 —49Pc 86
Oglander Rd. SE15 —56Vb 105
Ogle St. W1 —43Lb 82 (7B 192)
Oglethorpe Rd. Dag —34Cd 68
O'Grandy Ho. E17 —27Dc 44
Ohio Cotts. Pinn —26Y 37

Ohio Rd.—Oriel Rd.

Ohio Rd. E13 —42Hc **85**
Oil Mill La. W6 —50Wa **80**
Okeburn Rd. SW17 —64Jb **126**
Okehampton Clo. N12 —22Fb **41**
Okehampton Cres. Well —53Xc **109**
Okehampton Rd. NW10 —39Ya **60**
Okehampton Rd. H Hill —23Ld **49**
Okehampton Sq. Romf —23Ld **49**
Okemore Gdns. Orp —70Yc **131**
Olaf St. W11 —45Za **80**
Old Acre. Wok —86J **157**
Oldacre M. SW12 —59Kb **104**
Old Av. W Byf —85G **156**
Old Av. Wey —80S **140**
Old Av. Clo. W Byf —85G **156**
Old Bailey. EC4 —44Rb **83** (3C **200**)
*Old Barge Ho. All. SE1 —45Qb **82** (5A **200**)*
(off Barge Ho. St.)
Old Barn Clo. Kems —89Qd **171**
Old Barn Clo. Sutt —80Ab **144**
Old Barn La. Crox —15P **17**
Old Barn La. Kenl —88Vb **165**
Old Barn Rd. Eps —89Sa **161**
Old Barn Way. Bexh —56Fd **110**
Old Barrack Yd. SW1 —47Jb **82** (2H **203**)
Old Barrowfield. E15 —39Gc **65**
Old Beechwood Gdns. Slou —7J **73**
Oldberry Rd. Edgw —23Ta **39**
Old Bethnal Grn. Rd. E2 —41Wb **83**
Old Bexley La. Bex & Dart (in two parts) —61Fd **132**
Old Billingsgate Wlk. EC3 —45Ub **83** (5H **201**)
Old Bond St. W1 —45Lb **82** (5B **198**)
Oldborough Rd. Wemb —34La **58**
Old Brewer's Yd. WC2 —44Nb **82** (3F **199**)
Old Brewery M. NW3 —35Fb **61**
Old Bri. Clo. N'holt —40Ca **57**
Old Bri. St. Hamp W —68Ma **123**
Old Broad St. EC2 —44Tb **83** (3G **201**)
Old Bromley Rd. Brom —64Fc **129**
Old Brompton Rd. SW5 & SW7 —50Cb **81**
*Old Bldgs. WC2 —44Qb **82** (2K **199**)*
(off Chancery La.)
Old Burlington St. W1 —45Lb **82** (4B **198**)
Old Burton St. W1 —45Lb **82**
Oldbury Clo. Cher —73G **138**
Oldbury Clo. Orp —70Yc **131**
Oldbury Pl. W1 —43Jb **82** (7J **191**)
Oldbury Rd. Cher —73G **138**
Oldbury Rd. Enf —12Wb **25**
Old Carriageway, The. Sev —94Ed **186**
Old Castle St. E1 —44Vb **83** (2K **201**)
Old Cavendish St. W1 —44Kb **82** (3A **198**)
*Old Change Ct. EC4 (off Carter La.) —44Sb **83** (3D **200**)*
Old Chapel Pl. SW9 —54Qb **104**
Old Chapel Rd. Swan —73Ed **152**
Old Charlton Rd. Shep —71S **140**
Old Chelsea M. SW3 —51Gb **103**
Old Chestnut Av. Clar P —79Ca **141**
Old Chu. Ct. N11 —22Kb **42**
Oldchurch Gdns. Romf —31Fd **68**
Old Chu. La. NW9 —33Sa **59**
Old Chu. La. Gnfd —41Ja **78**
Old Chu. La. Stan —22Ka **38**
Old Chu. Path. Esh —77Ea **142**
Oldchurch Rise. Romf —31Gd **68**
Old Chu. Rd. E1 —44Zb **84**
Old Chu. Rd. E4 —21Cc **44**
Oldchurch Rd. Romf —31Fd **68**
Old Chu. St. SW3 —50Fb **81** (7C **202**)
Old Claygate La. Clay —78Ja **142**
Old Coach Rd. Cher —71F **138**
Old Common Rd. Cob —85X **159**
Old Compton St. W1 —45Mb **82** (4D **198**)
Old Cote Dri. Houn —51Ca **99**
Old Cottages. St Alb —1Na **7**
Old Ct. Asht —91Na **177**
Old Ct. Pl. W8 —47Db **81**
Old Crown Cen. Slou —7K **73**
Old Crown La. Kel H —11Td **32**
Old Dartford Rd. F'ham —72Pd **153**
Old Deer Pk. Gdns. Rich —55Na **101**
Old Devonshire Rd. SW12 —59Kb **104**
Old Dock Clo. Rich —51Qa **101**
Old Dover Rd. SE3 —52Jc **107**
Old Downs. Hart —71Ae **155**
Oldegate Ho. E6 —39Mc **65**
Olden La. Purl —84Qb **164**
Old Esher Clo. W on T —78Z **141**
Old Esher Rd. W on T —78Z **141**
Old Farleigh Rd. S Croy & Warl —82Yb **166**
Old Farm Av. N14 —17Lb **24**
Old Farm Av. Sidc —60Tc **108**
Old Farm Clo. Houn —56Ba **99**
Old Farm Gdns. Swan —69Hd **132**
Old Farm Ho. Dri. Oxs —87Fa **160**
Old Farm Pas. Hamp —67Ea **122**
Old Farm Rd. N2 —25Fb **41**
Old Farm Rd. Hamp —65Ba **121**
Old Farm Rd. W Dray —47M **75**
Old Farm Rd. E. Sidc —61Wc **131**
Old Farm Rd. W. Sidc —61Vc **131**
Old Ferry Dri. Wray —8P **95**
Oldfield Clo. Brom —70Pc **130**
Old Field Clo. Chal G —11A **16**
Oldfield Clo. Chesh —1Ac **12**
Oldfield Clo. Gnfd —36Ga **58**
Oldfield Clo. Stan —22Ja **38**
Oldfield Dri. Chesh —1Ac **12**
Oldfield Farm Gdns. Gnfd —39Fa **58**
Oldfield Gdns. Asht —90Ma **161**
Oldfield Gro. SE16 —49Zb **84**
*Oldfield Ho. W4 —50Ua **80***
(off Devonshire Rd.)
Oldfield La. Gnfd —38Fa **58**
Oldfield La. N. Gnfd —40Fa **58**
Oldfield La. S. Gnfd —42Ea **78**
Oldfield M. N6 —31Lb **62**
Oldfield Rd. N16 —34Ub **63**
Oldfield Rd. NW10 —38Ua **60**
Oldfield Rd. SW19 —65Ab **124**
Oldfield Rd. W3 —47Va **80**
Oldfield Rd. Bexh —54Ad **109**
Oldfield Rd. Brom —70Pc **130**
Oldfield Rd. Hamp —67Ba **121**
Oldfields. War —21Yd **50**
Oldfields Cir. N'holt —37Ea **58**
Oldfields Rd. Sutt —76Bb **145**
Oldfields Trading Est. Sutt —76Cb **145**
Old Files Ct. Burn —1A **72**
*Old Fish St. Hill. EC4 —45Sb **83** (4D **200**)*
(off Victoria St.)
Old Fleet La. EC4 —44Rb **83** (2B **200**)
Old Fold Clo. Barn —11Bb **23**
Old Fold La. Barn —11Bb **23**
Old Fold View. Barn —13Ya **22**
Old Ford Rd. E2 & E3 —41Yb **84**
Old Forge Clo. Stan —21Ja **38**
Old Forge Clo. Wat —5W **4**
Old Forge Cres. Shep —72R **140**
Old Forge M. W12 —47Xa **80**
Old Forge Rd. Enf —10Vb **11**
Old Forge Way. Sidc —63Xc **131**
Old Fox Clo. Cat —93Rb **181**
Old Gannon Clo. N'wd —21S **36**
Old Garden, The. Sev —95Fd **186**
Old Gloucester St. WC1 —43Nb **82** (7G **193**)
Old Hall Clo. Pinn —25Aa **37**
Old Hall Dri. Pinn —25Aa **37**
Oldham Ter. W3 —46Sa **79**
Old Harrow La. W'ham —91Sc **184**
Old Hatch Mnr. Ruis —31V **56**
Old Hill. Chst —67Qc **130**
Old Hill. Orp —79Tc **150**
Old Hill. Wok —8G **188**
Old Hill Est. Wok —8G **188**
Oldhill St. N16 —32Wb **63**
Old Homesdale Rd. Brom —70Lc **129**
Old Hospital Clo. SW17 —60Hb **103**
Old Ho. Clo. SW19 —65Ab **124**
Old Ho. Clo. Eps —82Va **162**
Old House Ct. Wex —3P **73**
Old Ho. Gdns. Twic —58La **100**
Oldhouse La. K Lan —7N **3**
Old Howlett's La. Ruis —30T **36**
Old Jamaica Rd. SE16 —48Wb **83**
Old James St. SE15 —55Xb **105**
Old Jenkins Clo. Stanf —2K **93**
Old Jewry. EC2 —44Tb **83** (3F **201**)
Old Kenton La. NW9 —29Ra **39**
Old Kent Rd. SE1 & SE15 —49Ub **83** (5H **207**)
Old Kingston Rd. Wor Pk —76Sa **143**
Old La. Cob —89R **158**
Old La. Tats —92Mc **183**
Old La. Gdns. Cob —94W **174**
Old Laundry, The. Chst —67Sc **130**
Old Lodge La. Purl —85Pb **164**
Old Lodge Pl. Twic —58Ka **100**
Old Lodge Way. Stan —22Ja **38**
Old London Rd. Badg M —81Bd **169**
Old London Rd. E Hor —98W **174**
Old London Rd. Eps —90Wa **162**
Old London Rd. Knock —87Ad **169**
Old London Rd. Mick —99La **176**
Old London Rd. Sidc —66Dd **132**
Old Maidstone Rd. Sidc —66Bd **131**
Old Malden La. Wor Pk —75Ua **144**
Old Malt Way. Wok —5G **188**
Old Manor Dri. Grav —10E **114**
Old Manor Dri. Iswth —58Ea **100**
Old Manor Way. Bexh —54Fd **110**
Old Manor Way. Chst —64Pc **130**
Old Manor Yd. SW5 —49Db **81**
Old Market Sq. E2 —41Vb **83** (3K **195**)
Old Marylebone Rd. NW1 —43Gb **81** (1E **196**)
Old Mead. Ger X —23A **34**
Oldmead Ho. Dag —37Dd **68**
Old M. Harr —29Ga **38**
Old Mill Clo. E18 —27Lc **45**
Old Mill Clo. Eyns —74Nd **153**
Old Mill La. Red —100Kb **180**
Old Mill La. Uxb —44K **75**
Old Mill Pde. Romf —29Hd **48**
Old Mill Rd. SE18 —51Tc **108**
Old Mill Rd. Den —34J **55**
Old Mill Rd. K Lan —5S **4**
Old Montague St. E1 —43Wb **83**
Old Nichol St. E2 —42Vb **83** (5K **195**)
*Old North St. WC1 —43Pb **82** (7H **193**)*
(off Theobald's Rd.)
Old Nursery Ct. Hedg —3G **52**
Old Oak Av. Coul —91Gb **179**
Old Oak Comn. La. NW10 & W3 —43Ua **80**
Old Oak La. NW10 —41Ua **80**
Old Oak Rd. W3 —45Va **80**
Old Oaks. Wal A —4Gc **13**
Old Orchard. Byfl —84P **157**
Old Orchard. Sun —68Y **121**
Old Orchard Clo. Uxb —44Q **76**
Old Orchard, The. NW3 —35Gb **61**
Old Otford Rd. Sev —90Kd **171**
Old Palace La. Rich —57La **100**
Old Palace Rd. Croy —76Rb **147**
Old Palace Rd. Wey —76R **140**
Old Palace Ter. Rich —57Ma **101**
Old Palace Yd. SW1 —48Nb **82** (3F **205**)
Old Palace Yd. Rich —57La **100**
Old Paradise St. SE11 —49Pb **82** (5H **205**)
Old Pk. Av. SW12 —58Jb **104**
Old Pk. Av. Enf —14Sb **25**
Old Parkbury La. Col S —2Ka **6**
Old Pk. Gro. Enf —14Sb **25**
*Old Park Ho. N13 —21Pb **42***
(off Old Park Rd.)
Old Park La. W1 —46Kb **82** (7J **197**)
Old Pk. M. Houn —52Ba **99**
Oldpark Ride. Wal X —4Rb **11**
Old Pk. Ridings. N21 —16Rb **25**
Old Pk. Rd. N13 —21Pb **42**
Old Pk. Rd. SE2 —50Wc **87**
Old Pk. Rd. Enf —13Rb **25**
Old Pk. Rd. S. Enf —14Rb **25**
Old Pk. View. Enf —13Qb **24**
Old Parsonage Yd., The. Hort K —70Sd **134**
Old Parvis Rd. W Byf —84L **157**
Old Perry St. Chst —65Uc **130**
Old Perry St. Grav —1A **136**
Old Polhill. Sev —86Ed **170**
Old Pye St. SW1 —48Mb **82** (3D **204**)
Old Quebec St. W1 —44Hb **81** (3G **197**)
Old Queen St. SW1 —47Mb **82** (2E **204**)
Old Rectory Clo. Tad —96Wa **178**
Old Rectory Gdns. Edgw —23Qa **39**
Old Rectory La. Den —31G **54**
Old Rectory La. E Hor —98U **174**
Old Redding. Harr —22Da **37**
Oldridge Rd. SW12 —59Jb **104**
Old Rd. SE13 —56Gc **107**
Old Rd. Add —80H **139**
Old Rd. Dart —57Fd **110**
Old Rd. Enf —11Yb **26**
Old Rd. Nave —12Md **31**
Old Rd. E. Grav —10D **114**
Old Rd. W. Grav —10B **114**
*Old Royal Free Pl. N1 —39Qb **62** (1A **194**)*
(off Liverpool Rd.)
*Old Royal Free Sq. N1 —39Qb **62** (1A **194**)*
(off Old Royal Free Pl.)
Old Ruislip Rd. N'holt —40Z **57**
Old Ruslip Rd. N'holt —40Y **57**
Old's App. Wat —18S **18**
Old School Clo. SW19 —68Cb **125**
Old School Clo. Beck —68Ac **128**
Old School Ct. Sev —94Ld **187**
Old School Ct. Wray —59A **96**
Old School M. Wey —77T **140**
Old School Pl. Wok —93A **172**
Old Schools La. Eps —81Va **162**
Old School Sq. Th Dit —72Ha **142**
Old's Clo. Wat —17S **18**
Old Seacoal La. EC4 —44Rb **83** (3B **200**)
Old Shire La. Chor —16C **16**
Old Shire La. Wal A —7Jc **13**
Old Slade La. Iver —48G **74**
Old South Clo. H End —25Z **37**
Old S. Lambeth Rd. SW8 —52Nb **104**
Old Sq. WC2 —44Pb **82** (2K **199**)
Old Stable M. N5 —34Sb **63**
Old Sta. App. Lea —93Ja **176**
Old Sta. Rd. Hay —48V **76**
Old Station Rd. Lou —15Nc **28**
Oldstead Rd. Brom —63Fc **129**
Old Stockley Rd. W Dray —47R **76**
Old St. E13 —40Kc **65**
Old St. EC1 —42Sb **83** (6D **194**)
Old Sungate Cotts. Romf —25Bd **47**
Old Swan Yd. Cars —77Hb **145**
Old Town. SW4 —55Lb **104**
Old Town. Croy —76Rb **147**
Old Tye Av. Big H —88Nc **168**
Old Uxbridge Rd. W Hyd —22G **34**
Old Walk, The. Otf —89Ld **171**
Old Watford Rd. Brick —2Aa **5**
Old Watling St. Grav —4C **136**
Oldway La. Slou —7B **72** (in three parts)
Old Westhall Clo. Warl —91Yb **182**
Old Windsor Lock. Old Win —7N **95**
Old Woking Rd. W Byf —85H **157**
Old Woking Rd. Wok —91D **172**
Old Woolwich Rd. SE10 —51Fc **107**
Old Yews, The. Long —69De **135**
Old York Rd. SW18 —57Db **103**
Oleander Clo. Orp —78Tc **150**
O'Leary Sq. E1 —43Yb **84**
Olga St. E3 —40Ac **64**
Olinda Rd. N16 —30Vb **43**
Oliphant St. W10 —41Za **80**
Oliver Av. SE25 —69Vb **127**
Oliver Clo. E10 —33Dc **64**
Oliver Clo. W4 —51Ra **101**
Oliver Clo. Add —77K **139**
Oliver Clo. Grays —52Vd **112**
Oliver Ct. SE18 —49Sc **86**
Oliver Cres. F'ham —73Pd **153**
Oliver Gdns. E6 —43Nc **86**
Oliver Goldsmith Est. SE15 —53Wb **105**
Oliver Gro. SE25 —70Vb **127**
*Oliver Ho. SE16 —47Wb **83***
(off George Row)
Olive Rd. E13 —41Lc **85**
Olive Rd. NW2 —35Ya **60**
Olive Rd. SW19 —66Eb **125**
Olive Rd. W5 —48Ma **79**
Olive Rd. Dart —60Md **111**
Oliver Rd. E10 —33Dc **64**
Oliver Rd. E17 —29Ec **44**
Oliver Rd. Grays —53Vd **112**
Oliver Rd. N Mald —68Sa **123**
Oliver Rd. Rain —39Hd **68**
Oliver Rd. Shenf —15Ce **33**
Oliver Rd. Sutt —77Fb **145**
Oliver Rd. Swan —69Fd **132**
Olivers Mill. New Ash —75Ae **155**
Olivers Yd. EC1 —42Tb **83** (5G **195**)
Olive St. Romf —29Fd **48**
Olivette St. SW15 —55Za **102**
*Olivia Ct. Enf —11Sb **25***
(off Chase Side)
Olivia Gdns. Hare —25L **35**
Ollard's Ct. Lou —15Nc **28**
Ollard's Gro. Lou —14Mc **27**
Olleberrie La. Sarr —3F **2**
Ollerton Grn. E3 —39Bc **64**
Ollerton Rd. N11 —22Mb **42**
Olley Clo. Wall —80Nb **146**
Ollgar Clo. W12 —46Va **80**
Olliffe St. E14 —48Ec **84**
Olmar St. SE1 —51Wb **105**
Olney Rd. SE17 —51Rb **105** (in two parts)
Olron Cres. Bexh —57Zc **109**
Olven Rd. SE18 —51Sc **108**
Olveston Wlk. Cars —72Fb **145**
Olwen M. Pinn —26Z **37**
Olyffe Av. Well —53Wc **109**
Olyffe Dri. Beck —67Ec **128**
Olympia M. W2 —45Db **81**
Olympia Way. W14 —48Ab **80**
Olympic Way. Gnfd —39Ea **58**
Olympic Way. Wemb —34Qa **59**
Olympic Way Ind. Est. Wemb —35Qa **59**
Olympus Sq. E5 —34Wb **63**
Oman Av. NW2 —35Xa **60**
O'Meara St. SE1 —46Sb **83** (7E **200**)
*Omega Pl. N1 —40Nb **62** (2G **193**)*
(off Caledonian Rd.)
Omega Rd. Wok —87C **156**
Omega St. SE14 —53Cc **106**
Omega Way. Egh —67E **118**
Ommaney Rd. SE14 —53Zb **106**
Ondine Rd. SE15 —56Vb **105**
Onega Ga. SE16 —48Ac **84**
O'Neill Path. SE18 —51Qc **108**
One Pin La. Farn C —5G **52**
One Tree Clo. SE23 —58Yb **106**
Ongar Clo. Add —79H **139**
Ongar Clo. Romf —29Yc **47**
Ongar Hill. Add —79J **139**
Ongar Pde. Add —79J **139**
Ongar Pl. Add —79J **139**
Ongar Pl. Brtwd —19Zd **33**
Ongar Rd. SW6 —51Cb **103**
Ongar Rd. Abr —13Xc **29**
Ongar Rd. Add —78J **139**
Ongar Rd. Brtwd & Kel H —13Td **32**
Ongar Way. Rain —39Gd **68**
Onra Rd. E17 —31Cc **64**
Onslow Av. Rich —57Na **101**
Onslow Av. Sutt —82Bb **163**
Onslow Clo. E4 —19Ec **26**
Onslow Clo. Th Dit —74Ga **142**
Onslow Clo. Wok —89C **156**
Onslow Cres. Chst —67Rc **130**
Onslow Cres. Wok —89C **156**
Onslow Dri. Sidc —61Zc **131**
Onslow Gdns. E18 —27Kc **45**
Onslow Gdns. N10 —29Kb **42**
Onslow Gdns. N21 —15Qb **24**
Onslow Gdns. SW7 —49Fb **81** (6B **202**)
Onslow Gdns. S Croy —84Wb **165**
Onslow Gdns. Th Dit —74Ga **142**
Onslow Gdns. Wall —79Lb **146**
Onslow M. Cher —72J **139**
Onslow M. E. SW7 —49Fb **81** (6B **202**)
Onslow M. W. SW7 —49Fb **81** (6B **202**)
Onslow Pde. N14 —18Kb **24**
Onslow Rd. Croy —73Qb **146**
Onslow Rd. N Mald —70Wa **124**
Onslow Rd. Rich —57Na **101**
Onslow Rd. W on T —77V **140**
Onslow Sq. SW7 —49Fb **81** (5C **202**)
Onslow St. EC1 —42Qb **82** (6A **194**)
Onslow Way. Th Dit —74Ga **142**
Onslow Way. Wok —87H **157**
Ontario St. SE1 —48Rb **83** (3C **206**)
Ontario Way. E14 —46Cc **84**
On the Hill. Wat —19Aa **19**
Opal Clo. E16 —44Mc **85**
Opal M. NW6 —39Bb **61**
Opal M. Ilf —33Rc **66**
Opal St. SE11 —50Rb **83** (7B **206**)
Opendale Rd. Burn —3A **72**
Openshaw Rd. SE2 —49Xc **87**
Openview. SW18 —60Eb **103**
Ophelia Gdns. NW2 —34Ab **60**
Ophir Ter. SE15 —53Wb **105**
Opossum Way. Houn —55Y **99**
Oppenheim Rd. SE13 —54Ec **106**
Oppidans M. NW3 —38Hb **61**
Oppidans Rd. NW3 —38Hb **61**
Orange Ct. E1 —46Wb **83**
Orange Ct. La. Orp —81Qc **168**
Orange Hill Rd. Edgw —24Sa **39**
Orange Pl. SE16 —48Yb **84**
Orangery La. SE9 —57Pc **108**
Orange St. WC2 —45Mb **82** (5E **198**)
Orange Tree Hill. Hav —22Fd **48**
*Orange Yd. W1 —44Mb **82** (3E **198**)*
(off Manette St.)
*Oratory La. SW3 —50Fb **81** (7C **202**)*
(off Stewart's Gro.)
Orbain Rd. SW6 —52Ab **102**
Orbel St. SW11 —53Gb **103**
Orbital Cres. Wat —7V **4**
Orbital One. Dart —61Rd **133**
Orb St. SE17 —49Tb **83** (6F **207**)
Orchard Av. N3 —27Cb **41**
Orchard Av. N14 —16Lb **24**
Orchard Av. N20 —19Fb **23**
Orchard Av. Ashf —65S **120**
Orchard Av. Belv —51Ad **109**
Orchard Av. Brtwd —20Be **33**
Orchard Av. Croy —74Ac **148**
Orchard Av. Dart —59Kd **111**
Orchard Av. Felt —57T **98**
Orchard Av. Grav —4D **136**
Orchard Av. Houn —52Aa **99**
Orchard Av. Mitc —74Jb **146**
Orchard Av. N Mald —69Ua **124**
Orchard Av. Rain —42Ld **89**
Orchard Av. Slou —3B **72**
Orchard Av. S'hall —46Ba **77**
Orchard Av. Th Dit —74Ja **142**
Orchard Av. Wat —4X **5**
Orchard Av. Wind —3E **94**
Orchard Av. Wdhm —83H **157**
Orchard Bus. Cen. SE26 —64Bc **128**
Orchard Clo. E4 —21Cc **44**
Orchard Clo. E11 —28Kc **45**
Orchard Clo. N1 —38Sb **63**
Orchard Clo. NW2 —34Wa **60**
Orchard Clo. SE23 —58Yb **106**
Orchard Clo. SW20 —70Ya **124**
Orchard Clo. W10 —43Bb **81**
Orchard Clo. Ashf —65S **120**
Orchard Clo. Bans —86Db **163**
Orchard Clo. Bexh —53Ad **109**
Orchard Clo. Bush —18Fa **20**
Orchard Clo. Chor —14F **16**
Orchard Clo. Cuff —1Nb **10**
Orchard Clo. Den —37K **55**
Orchard Clo. E Hor —96V **174**
Orchard Clo. Edgw —23Na **39**
Orchard Clo. Egh —63D **118**
Orchard Clo. Els —14Pa **21**
Orchard Clo. Fet —94Fa **176**
Orchard Clo. Long —68De **135**
Orchard Clo. N'holt —37Ea **58**
Orchard Clo. Rad —9Ga **6**
Orchard Clo. Ruis —31S **56**
Orchard Clo. Sev —92Ld **187**
Orchard Clo. S Ock —42Yd **90**
Orchard Clo. Surb —74Ka **142**
Orchard Clo. W on T —73X **141**
Orchard Clo. Wat —12V **18**
Orchard Clo. Wemb —39Na **59**
Orchard Clo. W Ewe —79Ra **143**
Orchard Clo. Wok —88D **156**
Orchard Cotts. Hay —47U **76**
Orchard Ct. E10 —32Dc **64**
Orchard Ct. N14 —16Lb **24**
Orchard Ct. Edgw —22Pa **39**
Orchard Ct. Iswth —52Fa **100**
Orchard Ct. New Bar —13Db **23**
Orchard Ct. Twic —61Fa **122**
Orchard Ct. W Dray —52L **97**
Orchard Ct. Wor Pk —74Wa **144**
Orchard Cres. Edgw —22Sa **39**
Orchard Cres. Enf —11Vb **25**
Orchard Dri. SE3 —54Fc **107**
Orchard Dri. Asht —92Ma **177**
Orchard Dri. Chor —13E **16**
Orchard Dri. Edgw —22Pa **39**
Orchard Dri. Grays —47Ce **91**
Orchard Dri. Meop —10B **136**
Orchard Dri. They B —8Uc **14**
Orchard Dri. Uxb —42M **75**
Orchard Dri. Wat —11V **18**
Orchard Dri. Wok —87A **156**
Orchard End. Cat —94Ub **181**
Orchard End. Fet —96Ea **176**
Orchard End. Wey —75U **140**
Orchard Gdns. Chess —77Na **143**
Orchard Gdns. Eff —100Aa **175**
Orchard Gdns. Eps —86Sa **161**
Orchard Gdns. Sutt —78Cb **145**
Orchard Gdns. Wal A —6Ec **12**
Orchard Ga. NW9 —28Ua **40**
Orchard Ga. Esh —74Fa **142**
Orchard Ga. Farn C —6G **52**
Orchard Ga. Gnfd —40Ka **58**
Orchard Grn. Orp —75Uc **150**
Orchard Gro. SE20 —66Wb **127**
Orchard Gro. Croy —73Ac **148**
Orchard Gro. Edgw —25Qa **39**
Orchard Gro. Harr —29Pa **39**
Orchard Gro. Orp —75Vc **151**
Orchard Hill. SE13 —54Dc **106**
Orchard Hill. Cars —78Hb **145**
Orchard Hill. Dart —57Gd **110**
Orchard Ho. SE16 —48Yb **84**
Orchard Ho. W12 —46Wa **80**
Orchard La. SW20 —67Xa **124**
Orchard La. E Mol —72Fa **142**
Orchard La. Pil H —15Vd **32**
Orchard La. Wfd G —21Lc **45**
Orchard Lea. S'fleet —64Be **135**
Orchard Lea Clo. Wok —87G **156**
Orchard Leigh. Lea —94Ka **176**
Orchardleigh Av. Enf —12Yb **26**
Orchard Mains. Wok —7F **188**
Orchard Mead Ho. NW11 —33Cb **61**
Orchardmede. N21 —16Tb **25**
Orchard M. N1 —38Tb **63**
Orchard Pde. Pot B —3Za **8**
Orchard Pl. E14 —45Gc **85**
Orchard Pl. N17 —24Vb **43**
Orchard Pl. Cow —38M **55**
Orchard Pl. Orp —69Yc **131**
Orchard Pl. Sund —96Ad **185**
Orchard Rise. Croy —74Ac **148**
Orchard Rise. King T —67Sa **123**
Orchard Rise. Pinn —27V **36**
Orchard Rise. Rich —57Ra **101**
Orchard Rise E. Sidc —57Vc **109**
Orchard Rise W. Sidc —57Uc **108**
Orchard Rd. N6 —31Kb **62**
Orchard Rd. SE3 —54Gc **107**
Orchard Rd. SE18 —49Tc **86**
Orchard Rd. Barn —14Bb **23**
Orchard Rd. Belv —49Cd **88**
Orchard Rd. Bren —51La **100**
Orchard Rd. Brom —67Lc **129**
Orchard Rd. Chess —77Na **143**
Orchard Rd. Dag —39Cd **68**
Orchard Rd. Enf —15Yb **26**
Orchard Rd. F'boro —78Rc **150**
Orchard Rd. Grav —61Ee **135**
Orchard Rd. Hamp —66Ba **121**
Orchard Rd. Hay —45W **76**
Orchard Rd. Houn —57Ba **99**
Orchard Rd. King T —68Na **123**
Orchard Rd. Mitc —74Jb **146**
Orchard Rd. Old Win —8M **95**
Orchard Rd. Otf —88Hd **170**
Orchard Rd. Prat B —82Yc **169**
Orchard Rd. Rich —55Qa **101**
Orchard Rd. Romf —25Dd **48**
Orchard Rd. Sev —94Gd **186**
Orchard Rd. Sidc —63Uc **130**
Orchard Rd. S Croy —86Xb **165**
Orchard Rd. S Ock —42Yd **90**
Orchard Rd. Sun —66W **120**
Orchard Rd. Sutt —78Cb **145**
Orchard Rd. Swans —57Ae **113**
Orchard Rd. Twic —58Ja **100**
Orchard Rd. Well —55Xc **109**
Orchards Clo. W Byf —86J **157**
Orchards N., The. Epp —4Wc **15**
Orchardson St. NW8 —42Fb **81** (6B **190**)
Orchards S., The. Epp —4Wc **15**
Orchards, The. Dart —58Nd **111**
Orchard St. E17 —28Ac **44**
Orchard St. W1 —44Jb **82** (3H **197**)
Orchard St. Dart —58Nd **111**
Orchard Ter. Enf —16Wb **25**
Orchard, The. N14 —15Kb **24**
Orchard, The. N21 —16Tb **25**
Orchard, The. NW11 —29Cb **41**
Orchard, The. SE3 —54Fc **107**
Orchard, The. W4 —49Ta **79**
*Orchard, The. W5 —44Ma **79***
(off Helena Rd.)
Orchard, The. Bans —87Cb **163**
Orchard, The. Dun G —93Gd **186**
Orchard, The. Eps —80Va **144** (Meadow Wlk.)
Orchard, The. Eps —82Va **162** (Tayles Hill)
Orchard, The. Houn —54Ea **100**
Orchard, The. K Lan —1Q **4**
Orchard, The. Swan —68Fd **132**
Orchard, The. Vir W —71A **138**
Orchard, The. Wey —77R **140**
Orchard, The. Wok —94A **172**
Orchard View. Uxb —42M **75**
Orchardville. Burn —2A **72**
Orchard Way. Add —78K **139**
Orchard Way. Ashf —61P **119**
Orchard Way. Bov —1C **2**
Orchard Way. Chig —20Wc **29**
Orchard Way. Croy & Beck —73Ac **148**
Orchard Way. Dart —62Md **133**
Orchard Way. Enf —13Ub **25**
Orchard Way. Esh —79Ea **142**
Orchard Way. Kems —89Qd **171**
Orchard Way. Pot B —1Db **9**
Orchard Way. Rick —17J **17**
Orchard Way. Send —97E **172**
Orchard Way. Sutt —77Fb **145**
Orchard Way. Tad —98Bb **179**
Orchard Waye. Uxb —40M **55**
Orchehill Av. Ger X —28A **34**
Orchehill Rise. Ger X —29A **34**
Orchid Clo. E6 —43Nc **86**
Orchid Ct. Egh —63D **118**
Orchid Grange. N14 —17Lb **24**
Orchid Rd. N14 —17Lb **24**
Orchid St. W12 —45Wa **80**
Orchis Gro. Grays —50Be **91**
Orchis Way. Romf —23Pd **49**
Orde. NW9 —25Va **40**
Orde Hall St. WC1 —43Pb **82** (6H **193**)
Ordell Rd. E3 —40Bc **64**
Ordnance Clo. Felt —61W **120**
Ordnance Cres. SE10 —47Gc **85**
Ordnance Hill. NW8 —39Fb **61** (1C **190**)
Ordnance M. NW8 —40Fb **61** (1C **190**)
Ordnance Rd. E16 —43Hc **85**
Ordnance Rd. SE18 —51Qc **108**
Ordnance Rd. Enf —9Zb **12**
Ordnance Rd. Grav —8E **114**
Oregano Dri. E14 —44Fc **85**
Oregon Av. E12 —35Pc **66**
Oregon Clo. N Mald —70Sa **123**
Oregon Sq. Orp —74Tc **150**
Orestan La. Eff —99X **175**
Orestes M. NW6 —36Cb **61**
Oreston Rd. Rain —41Md **89**
Orford Ct. SE27 —61Rb **127**
*Orford Ct. Dart —58Rd **111***
(off Grange Cres.)
*Orford Ct. Dart —58Rd **111***
(off Osborne Rd.)
Orford Ct. Stan —23La **38**
Orford Gdns. Twic —61Ha **122**
Orford Rd. E17 —29Cc **44**
Orford Rd. E18 —27Kc **45**
Orford Rd. SE6 —62Dc **128**
Organ Hall Rd. Borwd —11Na **21**
Organ La. E4 —19Ec **26**
Oriel Clo. Mitc —70Mb **126**
Oriel Ct. NW3 —35Eb **61**
Oriel Ct. Croy —74Tb **147**
Oriel Gdns. Ilf —27Pc **46**
*Oriel Pl. NW3 —35Eb **61***
(off Heath St.)
Oriel Rd. E9 —37Zb **64**

Oriel Way—Palm Ct.

Oriel Way. N'holt —38Da 57
Oriental Clo. Wok —89B 156
Oriental Rd. E16 —46Mc 85
Oriental Rd. Asc —10B 116
Oriental Rd. Wok —89B 156
Orient Ind. Pk. E10 —33Cc 64
Orient St. SE11 —49Rb 83 (5B 206)
Orient Way. E5 —34Zb 64
Oriole Way. SE28 —45Xc 87
Orion Bus. Cen. SE14 —50Zb 84
Orion Way. N'wd —21V 36
Orissa Rd. SE18 —50Uc 86
Orkney Ho. N1 —39Pb 62
(off Bemerton Est.)
Orkney St. SW11 —54Jb 104
Orlando Gdns. Eps —82Ta 161
Orlando Rd. SW4 —55Lb 104
Orleans Clo. Esh —75Fa 142
Orleans Ct. Twic —59Ka 100
Orleans Rd. SE19 —65Tb 127
Orleans Rd. Twic —59Ka 100
Orlestone Gdns. Orp —78Ad 151
Orleston M. N7 —37Qb 62
Orleston Rd. N7 —37Qb 62
Orley Ct. Harr —35Ha 58
Orley Farm Rd. Harr —34Ga 58
Orlick Rd. Grav —10K 115
Orlop St. SE10 —50Gc 85
Ormanton Rd. SE26 —63Wb 127
Orme Ct. W2 —45Db 81
Orme Ct. M. W2 —45Db 81
(off Orme La.)
Orme Ho. E8 —39Vb 63
Orme La. W2 —45Db 81
Ormeley Rd. SW12 —60Kb 104
Orme Rd. King T —68Ra 123
Ormerod Gdns. Mitc —68Jb 126
Ormesby Clo. SE28 —45Zc 87
Ormesby Dri. Pot B —4Za 8
Ormesby Way. Harr —30Pa 39
Orme Sq. W2 —45Db 81
Ormiston Gro. W12 —46Xa 80
Ormiston Rd. SE10 —50Jc 85
Ormond Av. Hamp —67Da 121
Ormond Av. Rich —57Ma 101
Ormond Clo. WC1
—43Nb 82 (7G 193)
Ormond Clo. H Wood —26Md 49
Ormond Cres. Hamp —67Da 121
Ormond Dri. Hamp —66Da 121
Ormonde Av. Eps —82Ta 161
Ormonde Av. Orp —75Sc 150
Ormonde Ct. Horn —31Hd 68
(off Clydesdale Rd.)
Ormonde Ga. SW3 —50Hb 81
Ormonde Pl. SW1
—49Jb 82 (6H 203)
Ormonde Rise. Buck H —18Lc 27
Ormonde Rd. SW14 —55Sa 101
Ormonde Rd. N'wd —21T 36
Ormonde Rd. Wok —4F 188
Ormonde Ter. NW8
—39Hb 61 (1F 191)
Ormond M. WC1
—42Nb 82 (6G 193)
Ormond Rd. N19 —32Nb 62
Ormond Rd. Rich —57Ma 101
Ormond Yd. SW1
—46Lb 82 (6C 198)
Ormsby Gdns. Gnfd —40Ea 58
Ormsby Lodge. W4 —48Ua 80
Ormsby Pl. N16 —34Vb 63
Ormsby St. E2 —40Vb 63 (1K 195)
Ormside St. SE15 —51Yb 106
Ormskirk Rd. Wat —21Z 37
Ornan Rd. NW3 —36Gb 61
Oronsay Wlk. N1 —38Sb 63
Orphanage Rd. Wat —12Y 19
Orphen Wlk. N16 —34Ub 63
Orpheus St. SE5 —53Tb 105
Orpington By-Pass. Orp —75Xc 151
Orpington By-Pass Rd. Orp & Bad M
—81Cd 170
Orpington Gdns. N18 —20Ub 25
Orpington Mans. N21 —18Qb 24
Orpington Rd. N21 —18Rb 25
Orpington Rd. Chst —69Uc 130
Orpwood Clo. Hamp —65Ba 121
Orsett Heath Cres. Grays —8C 92
Orsett Rd. Grays —50Ce 91
Orsett Rd. Ors & Horn H —2E 92
Orsett St. SE11 —50Pb 82 (7J 205)
Orsett Ter. W2 —44Db 81
Orsett Ter. Wfd G —24Lc 45
Orsman Rd. N1 —39Ub 63
Orton St. E1 —46Wb 83
Orville Rd. SW11 —54Fb 103
Orwell. E Til —9L 93
Orwell Clo. Rain —43Fd 88
Orwell Clo. Wind —5H 95
Orwell Ct. N5 —35Sb 63
Orwell Ct. Wat —12Z 19
Orwell Rd. E13 —39Lc 65
Osbaldeston Rd. N16 —33Wb 63
Osberton Rd. SE12 —57Jc 107
Osbert St. SW1
—49Mb 82 (6D 204)
Osborn Clo. E8 —39Wb 63
Osborne Av. Stai —60P 97
Osborne Clo. Beck —70Ac 128
Osborne Clo. Felt —64Z 121
Osborne Clo. Horn —30Kd 49
Osborne Ct. E10 —31Dc 64
Osborne Ct. W5 —43Ma 79
Osborne Ct. Wind —4G 94
Osborne Gdns. Pot B —2Db 9
Osborne Gdns. T Hth —68Sb 127
Osborne Gro. E17 —28Bc 44
Osborne Gro. N4 —32Qb 62
Osborne M. E17 —28Bc 44
Osborne M. Wind —4G 94
Osborne Pl. Sutt —78Fb 145
Osborne Rd. E7 —36Kc 65
Osborne Rd. E9 —37Bc 64
Osborne Rd. E10 —34Dc 64
Osborne Rd. N4 —32Qb 62
Osborne Rd. N13 —20Qb 24
Osborne Rd. NW2 —37Xa 60
Osborne Rd. W3 —48Ra 79
Osborne Rd. Belv —50Bd 87
Osborne Rd. Buck H —18Kc 27
Osborne Rd. Dag —36Bd 67
Osborne Rd. Dart —58Rd 111
Osborne Rd. Egh —65B 118
Osborne Rd. Enf —12Ac 26
Osborne Rd. Horn —30Kd 49
Osborne Rd. Houn —55Ba 99
Osborne Rd. King T —66Na 123
Osborne Rd. Pil H —16Wd 32
Osborne Rd. Pot B —2Db 9
Osborne Rd. S'hall —44Ea 78
Osborne Rd. T Hth —68Sb 127
Osborne Rd. Uxb —38L 55
Osborne Rd. W on T —74W 140
Osborne Rd. Wat —10Y 5
Osborne Rd. Wind —4G 94
Osborne Sq. Dag —35Bd 67
Osborne St. Slou —7K 73
Osborn Gdns. NW7 —24Za 40
Osborn La. SE23 —59Ac 106
Osborn St. E1 —43Vb 83
Osborn Ter. SE3 —56Hc 107
Osbourne Av. K Lan —1P 3
Osbourne Ho. Twic —61Ea 122
Oscar St. SE8 —53Cc 106
Oseney Cres. NW5 —36Lb 62
Osgood Av. Orp —78Vc 151
Osgood Gdns. Orp —78Vc 151
O'Shea Gro. E3 —39Bc 64
Osidge La. N14 —18Jb 24
Osier Ct. Romf —30Fd 48
Osiers Rd. SW18 —56Cb 103
Osier St. E1 —42Yb 84
Osier Way. E10 —34Dc 64
Osier Way. Bans —86Ab 162
Osier Way. Mitc —71Hb 145
Oslac Rd. SE6 —64Dc 128
Oslo Ct. NW8 —40Gb 61 (2D 190)
(off Prince Albert Rd.)
Oslo Sq. SE16 —48Ac 84
Osman Clo. N15 —30Tb 43
Osman Rd. N9 —20Wb 25
Osman Rd. W6 —48Ya 80
Osmond Clo. Harr —33Ea 58
Osmond Gdns. Wall —78Lb 146
Osmund St. W12 —43Va 80
Osnaburgh St. NW1
—42Kb 82 (6A 192)
Osnaburgh Ter. NW1
—42Kb 82 (5A 192)
Osney Ho. SE2 —47Zc 87
Osney Wlk. Cars —72Fb 145
Osney Way. Grav —1H 137
Osprey Clo. E6 —43Nc 86
Osprey Clo. E11 —28Jc 45
Osprey Clo. E17 —24Ac 44
Osprey Clo. Fet —94Ea 176
Osprey Clo. W Dray —47N 75
Osprey Ct. Beck —66Cc 128
Osprey Ct. Brtwd —20Xd 32
Osprey Est. SE16 —49Zb 84
Osprey Gdns. S Croy —82Zb 166
Osprey M. Enf —15Yb 26
Ospringe Clo. SE20 —66Yb 128
Ospringe Rd. NW5 —35Lb 62
Osram Rd. Wemb —34Ma 59
Osric Path. N1 —40Ub 63 (2H 195)
Ossian M. N4 —31Pb 62
Ossian Rd. N4 —31Pb 62
Ossington Bldgs. W1
—43Jb 82 (1H 197)
Ossington Clo. W2 —45Cb 81
Ossington St. W2 —45Db 81
Ossory Rd. SE1 —51Wb 105
Ossulston St. NW1
—40Mb 62 (2D 192)
Ossulton Pl. N2 —27Eb 41
Ossulton Way. N2 —28Eb 41
Ostade Rd. SW2 —59Pb 104
Ostend Pl. SE17
—49Sb 83 (5D 206)
Osten M. SW7 —48Db 81
Osterberg Rd. Dart —56Pd 111
Osterley Av. Iswth —52Fa 100
Osterley Clo. Orp —67Wc 131
Osterley Ct. Iswth —53Fa 100
Osterley Cres. Iswth —53Ga 100
Osterley Gdns. T Hth —68Sb 127
Osterley La. S'hall & Iswth
—50Ca 77
Osterley Lodge. Iswth —52Ga 100
(off Church Rd.)
Osterley Pk. Rd. S'hall —48Ba 77
Osterley Pk. View Rd. W7 —47Ga 78
Osterley Rd. N16 —35Ub 63
Osterley Rd. Iswth —52Ga 100
Ostliffe Rd. N13 —21Rb 43
Oswald Clo. Fet —94Ea 176
Oswald Rd. Fet —94Ea 176
Oswald Rd. S'hall —46Aa 77
Oswald's Mead. E9 —35Ac 64
Oswald St. E5 —34Zb 64
Oswald Ter. NW2 —34Ya 60
Osward. Croy —82Bc 166
(in three parts)
Osward Pl. N9 —19Xb 25
Osward Rd. SW17 —61Hb 125
Osward Vs. N9 —19Xb 25
Oswin St. SE11 —49Rb 83 (5C 206)
Oswyth Rd. SE5 —54Ub 105
Otford Clo. SE20 —67Yb 128
Otford Clo. Bex —58Dd 110
Otford Clo. Brom —69Qc 130
Otford Cres. SE4 —58Bc 106
Otford La. Hals —84Bd 169
Otford Rd. Sev —91Kd 187
Othello Clo. SE11
—50Rb 83 (7B 206)
Otho Ct. Bren —52Ma 101
Otis St. E3 —41Ec 84
Otley App. Ilf —30Rc 46
Otley Dri. Ilf —29Rc 46
Otley Ho. N5 —34Rb 63
Otley Rd. E16 —44Lc 85
Otley Ter. E5 —34Zb 64
Otley Way. Wat —20Y 19
Otlinge Clo. Orp —70Zc 131
Ottawa Gdns. Dag —38Fd 68
Ottawa Rd. Til —4C 114
Ottaway Ct. E5 —34Wb 63
Ottaway St. E5 —34Wb 63
Otterbourne Rd. E4 —20Fc 27
Otterbourne Rd. Croy —75Sb 147
Otterburn Gdns. Iswth —52Ja 100
Otterburn St. SW17 —65Hb 125
Otter Clo. Ott —79D 138
Otterden Clo. Orp —76Uc 150
Otterden St. SE6 —63Cc 128
Otterfield Rd. W Dray —45N 75
Ottermead La. Ott —79E 138
Otter Rd. Gnfd —42Ea 78
Ottershaw Pk. Ott —80C 138
Otterspool La. Wat —10Aa 5
Otterspool Way. Wat —11Ba 19
Otto Clo. SE26 —62Xb 127
Ottoman Ter. Wat —13Y 19
Otto St. SE17 —51Rb 105
Ottway's Av. Asht —91Ma 177
Ottways Clo. Pot B —4Db 9
Ottways La. Asht —92Ma 177
Oulton Clo. E5 —33Yb 64
Oulton Clo. SE28 —44Yc 87
Oulton Cres. Bark —36Vc 67
Oulton Cres. Pot B —3Za 8
Oulton Rd. N15 —29Tb 43
Oulton Way. Wat —21Ba 37
Oundle Av. Bush —16Ea 20
Oundle Ho. H Hill —22Md 49
(off Montgomery Cres.)
Ousden Clo. Chesh —2Ac 12
Ousden Dri. Chesh —2Ac 12
Ouseley Rd. SW12 —60Hb 103
Ouseley Rd. Old Win —9N 95
Ouseley Rd. Wray —9N 95
Outer Circ. NW1
—41Gb 81 (1F 191)
Outgate Rd. NW10 —38Va 60
Outram Pl. N1 —39Nb 62
Outram Pl. Wey —78S 140
Outram Rd. E6 —39Nc 66
Outram Rd. N22 —25Mb 42
Outram Rd. Croy —75Vb 147
Outwich St. EC3 —44Ub 83 (2J 201)
(off Houndsditch)
Outwood Ho. SW2 —59Pb 104
(off Deepdene Gdns.)
Outwood La. Tad & Coul
—94Db 179
Oval Gdns. Grays —48Ee 91
Oval Mans. SE11 —51Pb 104
Oval Pl. SW8 —52Pb 104
Oval Rd. NW1 —39Kb 62
Oval Rd. Croy —75Tb 147
Oval Rd. N. Dag —39Dd 68
Oval Rd. S. Dag —40Dd 68
Oval, The. E2 —40Xb 63
Oval, The. Bans —86Cb 163
Oval, The. Long —69Ee 135
Oval, The. Sidc —59Wc 109
Oval Way. SE11 —50Pb 82
Oval Way. Ger X —28A 34
Ovenden Rd. Sund —92Zc 185
Overbrae. Beck —64Cc 128
Overbrook. W Hor —100R 174
Overbrook Wlk. Edgw —24Qa 39
(in two parts)
Overbury Av. Beck —69Dc 128
Overbury Cres. New Ad —82Ec 166
Overbury Rd. N15 —30Tb 43
Overbury St. E5 —35Zb 64
Overchess Ridge. Chor —13H 17
Overcliffe. Grav —8C 114
Overcliff Rd. SE13 —55Cc 106
Overcliff Rd. Grays —49Fe 91
(in two parts)
Overcourt Clo. Sidc —58Xc 109
Overdale. Asht —88Na 161
Overdale Av. N Mald —68Ta 123
Overdale Rd. W5 —48La 78
Overdown Rd. SE6 —63Cc 128
Overhill. Warl —91Yb 182
Overhill Rd. SE22 —59Wb 105
Overhill Rd. Purl —81Qb 164
Overhill Way. Beck —71Fc 149
Overlea Rd. E5 —31Wb 63
Overmead. Sidc —59Tc 108
Overmead. Swan —71Gd 152
Over Minnis. New Ash —76Be 155
Overstand Clo. Beck —71Cc 148
Overstone Gdns. Croy —73Bc 148
Overstone Rd. W6 —48Ya 80
Overstrand Mans. SW11
—53Hb 103
Overstream. Loud —14K 17
Over the Misbourne. Ger X & Den
(in two parts) —30C 34
Overthorpe Clo. Knap —5B 188
Overton Clo. NW10 —37Sa 59
Overton Clo. Iswth —53Ha 100
Overton Ct. E11 —31Jc 65
Overton Ct. Sutt —80Cb 145
Overton Dri. E11 —31Jc 65
Overton Dri. Chad —31Yc 67
Overton Rd. E10 —32Ac 64
Overton Rd. N14 —15Nb 24
Overton Rd. SE2 —48Yc 87
Overton Rd. SW9 —54Qb 104
Overton Rd. Sutt —79Cb 145
Overton Rd. E. SE2 —48Zc 87
Overtons Yd. Croy —76Sb 147
Overy Ho. SE1 —47Rb 83 (2B 206)
Overy St. Dart —58Nd 111
Ovesdon Av. Harr —32Ba 57
Oveton Way. Bookh —98Da 175
Ovett Clo. SE19 —65Ub 127
Ovex Clo. E14 —47Ec 84
Ovington Ct. Wok —4C 188
Ovington Gdns. SW3
—48Gb 81 (4E 202)
Ovington M. SW3
—48Gb 81 (4E 202)
Ovington Sq. SW3
—48Gb 81 (4E 202)
Ovington St. SW3
—49Gb 81 (5E 202)
Owen Clo. SE28 —46Yc 87
Owen Clo. N'holt —41X 77
Owen Gdns. Wfd G —23Nc 46
Owen Ho. Felt —59W 98
Owen Ho. Twic —59Ka 100
Owenite St. SE2 —49Xc 87
Owen Pl. Lea —94Ka 176
Owen Rd. N13 —22Sb 43
Owen Rd. Hay —41X 77
Owen's Ct. EC1 —41Rb 83 (3B 194)
Owen's Row. EC1
—41Rb 83 (3B 194)
Owen St. EC1 —40Rb 63 (2B 194)
Owens Way. SE23 —59Ac 106
Owens Way. Crox —15Q 18
Owen Wlk. SE20 —66Wb 127
Owen Way. NW10 —36Sa 59
Owgan Clo. SE5 —52Tb 105
Owl Clo. S Croy —82Zb 166
Owletts Hall Clo. Horn —27Pd 49
Ownstead Gdns. S Croy —83Vb 165
Ownsted Hill. New Ad —82Ec 166
Oxberry Av. SW6 —54Ab 102
Oxdowne Clo. Stoke D —86Da 159
Oxenden Wood Rd. Orp —80Yc 151
Oxendon St. SW1
—45Mb 82 (5D 198)
Oxenford St. SE15 —55Vb 105
Oxenhill Rd. Kems —89Nd 171
Oxenpark Av. Wemb —32Na 59
Oxestall's Rd. SE8 —50Ac 84
Oxford Av. NW10 —41Xa 80
Oxford Av. SW20 —68Ab 124
Oxford Av. Burn —10A 52
Oxford Av. Grays —9C 92
Oxford Av. Hay —52Y 98
Oxford Av. Horn —28Qd 49
Oxford Av. Houn —50Ca 77
Oxford Av. Slou —3D 72
Oxford Cir. W1 —44Lb 82 (3B 198)
(off Oxford St.)
Oxford Cir. Av. W1
—44Lb 82 (3B 198)
Oxford Clo. N9 —19Xb 25
Oxford Clo. Ashf —66S 120
Oxford Clo. Chesh —1Zb 12
Oxford Clo. Grav —1H 137
Oxford Clo. Mitc —69Lb 126
Oxford Cotts. Felt —61U 120
Oxford Ct. EC4 —45Tb 83 (4F 201)
(off Salter's Hall Ct.)
Oxford Ct. W3 —44Qa 79
Oxford Ct. W4 —50Ra 79
Oxford Ct. Felt —63Z 121
Oxford Ct. War —21Zd 51
Oxford Cres. N Mald —72Ta 143
Oxford Dri. Ruis —33Y 57
Oxford Gdns. N20 —18Fb 23
Oxford Gdns. N21 —17Sb 25
Oxford Gdns. W4 —50Qa 79
Oxford Gdns. W10 —44Ya 80
Oxford Gdns. Den —34H 55
Oxford Ga. W6 —49Za 80
Oxford Ho. Borwd —12Qa 21
(off Stratfield Rd.)
Oxford M. Bex —59Cd 110
Oxford Pl. NW10 —34Ta 59
(off Neasden La. N.)
Oxford Rd. E15 —37Fc 65
(in two parts)
Oxford Rd. N4 —32Qb 62
Oxford Rd. N9 —19Xb 25
Oxford Rd. NW6 —40Cb 61
Oxford Rd. SE19 —65Tb 127
Oxford Rd. SW15 —56Ab 102
Oxford Rd. W5 —45Ma 79
Oxford Rd. Cars —79Gb 145
Oxford Rd. Den & Uxb —33F 54
Oxford Rd. Enf —15Xb 25
Oxford Rd. Ger X —30A 34
Oxford Rd. Harr —30Ea 38
Oxford Rd. Ilf —36Sc 66
Oxford Rd. Romf —23Pd 49
Oxford Rd. Sidc —64Xc 131
Oxford Rd. Stanf —2K 93
Oxford Rd. Tedd —64Fa 122
Oxford Rd. Wall —78Lb 146
Oxford Rd. W'stone —27Ha 38
Oxford Rd. Wind —3H 95
Oxford Rd. Wfd G —22Mc 45
Oxford Rd. N. W4 —50Ra 79
Oxford Rd. S. W4 —50Qa 79
Oxford Sq. W2 —44Gb 81 (3E 196)
Oxford St. W1 —44Hb 81 (3G 197)
Oxford St. Wat —15X 19
Oxford Wlk. S'hall —46Ba 77
Oxford Way. Felt —63Z 121
Oxgate Cen. NW2 —33Xa 60
Oxgate Ct. NW2 —33Wa 60
Oxgate Gdns. NW2 —34Xa 60
Oxgate La. NW2 —33Xa 60
Oxhawth Cres. Brom —71Qc 150
Oxhey Av. Wat —17Z 19
Oxhey Clo. Shenl —4Na 7
Oxhey Dri. N'wd & Wat —22X 37
Oxhey La. Wat & Harr —18Aa 19
Oxhey Ridge Clo. N'wd —21X 37
Oxhey Rd. Wat —17Y 19
Ox La. Eps —81Wa 162
Oxleas. E6 —44Rc 86
Oxleas Clo. Well —54Tc 108
Oxleay Rd. Harr —32Ca 57
Oxleigh Clo. N Mald —71Ua 144
Oxley Clo. SE1 —50Vb 83 (7K 207)
Oxley Clo. Romf —26Ld 49
Oxleys Rd. NW2 —34Xa 60
Oxleys Rd. Wal A —4Jc 13
Oxlip Clo. Croy —74Zb 148
Oxlow La. Dag —35Bd 67
Oxonian St. SE22 —56Vb 105
Oxshott Rise. Cob —85Z 159
Oxshott Rd. Lea —88Ga 160
Oxshott Way. Cob —87Aa 159
Oxted Clo. Mitc —69Fb 125
Oxtoby Way. SW16 —67Mb 126
Oystercatcher Clo. E16 —44Kc 85
Oystergate Wlk. EC4
(off Swan La.) —45Tb 83 (5F 201)
Oyster La. Byfl —82M 157
Oyster Row. E1 —44Yb 84
Ozolins Way. E16 —44Jc 85

Pablo Neruda Clo. SE24 —55Rb 105
Pace Heath Clo. Romf —23Fd 48
Pace Pl. E1 —44Xb 83
Pachesham Dri. Oxs —88Ha 160
Pachesham Pk. Lea —88Ja 160
Pacific Rd. E16 —44Jc 85
Packet Boat La. Uxb —44K 75
Packham Clo. Orp —75Yc 151
Packham Rd. Grav —2B 136
Packhorse La. Borwd —9Ua 8
Packhorse La. S Mim —2Ta 7
Packhorse Rd. Ger X —30A 34
Packhorse Rd. Sev —95Ed 186
Packington Rd. W3 —48Sa 79
Packington Sq. N1
—39Sb 63 (1D 194)
Packington St. N1 —39Rb 63
Packmores Rd. SE9 —57Tc 108
Padbrook. Oxt —100Jc 183
Padbury. SE5 —50Ub 83
(off Bagshot St.)
Padbury. SE17 —50Ub 83 (7J 207)
(off Bagshot St.)
Padbury Clo. Felt —60T 98
Padbury Ct. E2 —41Vb 83
Padcroft Rd. W Dray —46M 75
Paddenswick Rd. W6 —48Wa 80
Paddington Clo. Hay —42Z 77
Paddington Grn. W2
—43Fb 81 (7C 190)
Paddington St. W1
—43Jb 82 (7H 191)
Paddock Clo. SE3 —55Jc 107
Paddock Clo. SE26 —63Zb 128
Paddock Clo. F'boro —77Rc 150
Paddock Clo. N'holt —40Ca 57
Paddock Clo. Ors —3D 92
Paddock Clo. S Dar —67Sd 134
Paddock Clo. Wor Pk —74Ua 144
Paddock Gdns. SE19 —65Ub 127
Paddock Lodge. Enf —7Ub 11
(off Village Rd.)
Paddock Pas. SE19 —65Ub 127
(off Paddock Gdns.)
Paddock Rd. NW2 —33Wa 60
Paddock Rd. Bexh —56Ad 109
Paddock Rd. Ruis —34Z 57
Paddocks Clo. Asht —90Na 161
Paddocks Clo. Cob —86Y 159
Paddocks Clo. Harr —35Da 57
Paddocks Clo. Orp —75Zc 151
Paddocks Grn. NW9 —32Ra 59
Paddocks Mead. Wok —4B 188
Paddocks, The. Barn —13Hb 23
Paddocks, The. Bookh —98Da 175
Paddocks, The. Chor —14H 17
Paddocks, The. New Ad —78Cc 148
Paddocks, The. New Haw —82K 157
Paddocks, The. Wemb —33Ra 59
Paddocks, The. Wey —76U 140
Paddocks Way. Asht —90Na 161
Paddocks Way. Cher —74K 139
Paddock, The. NW9 —29Ua 40
Paddock, The. Dat —3M 95
Paddock, The. Ger X —23A 34
Paddock, The. Uxb —35R 56
Paddock, The. W'ham —98Sc 184
Paddock, The. Wink —10A 94
Paddock Wlk. Warl —91Xb 181
Paddock Way. Chst —66Tc 130
Paddock Way. Eps —83Ya 162
Paddock Way. Wok —86D 156
Padfield Rd. SE5 —55Sb 105
Padgets, The. Wal A —6Gc 13
Padnall Ct. Romf —27Zc 47
Padnall Rd. Chad —27Zc 47
Padstow Clo. Slou —48A 74
Padstow Rd. Enf —11Rb 25
Padua Rd. SE20 —67Yb 128
Pagden St. SW8 —53Kb 104
Pageant Av. NW9 —25Ua 40
Pageant Clo. Til —3E 114
Pageantmaster Ct. EC4
—44Rb 83 (3B 200)
(off Ludgate Hill.)
Pageant Wlk. Croy —76Ub 147
Page Clo. Bean —62Yd 134
Page Clo. Dag —36Ad 67
Page Clo. Hamp —65Aa 121
Page Clo. Harr —30Pa 39
Page Cres. Croy —78Rb 147
Page Cres. Eri —52Hd 110
Page Croft. Add —75K 139
Page Grn. Rd. N15 —29Wb 43
Page Grn. Ter. N15 —29Vb 43
Page Heath La. Brom —69Mc 129
Page Heath Vs. Brom —69Mc 129
Pagehurst Rd. Croy —73Xb 147
Page Meadow. NW7 —24Xa 40
Page Rd. Felt —58T 98
Pages Hill. N10 —26Jb 42
Pages La. N10 —26Jb 42
Pages La. Romf —26Rd 49
Pages La. Uxb —37L 55
Page St. NW7 —25Wa 40
Page St. SW1 —49Mb 82 (5E 204)
Page's Wlk. SE1 —49Ub 83 (5H 207)
Pages Yd. W4 —51Ua 102
Paget Av. Sutt —76Fb 145
Paget Clo. Hamp —63Fa 122
Paget Gdns. Chst —67Rc 130
Paget Ho. Ger X —21A 34
(off Micholls Av.)
Paget La. Iswth —55Fa 100
Paget Pl. King T —65Sa 123
Paget Pl. Th Dit —74Ja 142
Paget Rise. SE18 —51Qc 108
Paget Rd. N16 —32Tb 63
Paget Rd. Ilf —35Rc 66
Paget Rd. Slou —49B 74
Paget Rd. Uxb —42S 76
Paget St. EC1 —41Rb 83 (3B 194)
Paget Ter. SE18 —51Rc 108
Pagette Way. Grays —50Ce 91
Pagin Ho. N15 —29Ub 43
(off Braemar Rd.)
Pagitts Gro. Barn —11Db 23
Pagles Field. Hut —16Ee 33
Pagnell St. SE14 —52Bc 106
Pagoda Av. Rich —55Pa 101
Pagoda Gdns. SE3 —54Fc 107
Pagoda Vista. Rich —54Pa 101
Paignton Rd. N15 —30Ub 43
Paignton Rd. Ruis —34W 56
Paines Brook Rd. Romf —23Pd 49
Paines Brook Way. Romf —23Pd 49
Paines Clo. Pinn —27Aa 37
Paines La. Pinn —25Aa 37
Pain's Clo. Mitc —68Kb 126
Painsthorpe Rd. N16 —34Ub 63
Painswick Ct. SE15 —52Vb 105
(off Daniel Gdns.)
Painters Ash La. Grav —62Fe 135
Painters La. Enf —7Ac 12
Painters Rd. Ilf —27Vc 47
Paisley Rd. N22 —25Rb 43
Paisley Rd. Cars —74Fb 145
Pakeman St. N7 —34Pb 62
Pakenham Clo. SW12 —60Jb 104
Pakenham St. WC1
—41Pb 82 (4J 193)
Pakes Way. They B —9Uc 14
Pakington Ho. SW9 —54Nb 104
(off Stockwell Gdns. Est.)
Palace Av. W8 —47Db 81
Palace Clo. K Lan —2P 3
Palace Ct. NW3 —36Db 61
Palace Ct. W2 —45Db 81
Palace Ct. Harr —30Na 39
Palace Ct. Gdns. N10 —27Lb 42
Palace Dri. Wey —76R 140
Palace Gdns. Buck H —18Mc 27
Palace Gdns. Enf —14Tb 25
Palace Gdns. M. W8 —46Db 81
Palace Gdns. Shopping Cen. Enf
—14Tb 25
Palace Gdns. Ter. W8 —46Cb 81
Palace Ga. W8 —47Eb 81 (2A 202)
Palace Gates Rd. N22 —25Mb 42
Palace Grn. W8 —46Db 81
Palace Grn. Croy —80Bc 148
Palace Gro. SE19 —66Vb 127
Palace Gro. Brom —67Kc 129
Palace M. E17 —28Bc 44
Palace M. SW1 —49Jb 82 (6J 203)
(off Eaton Ter.)
Palace M. SW6 —52Bb 103
Palace M. Enf —13Tb 25
Palace Pde. E17 —28Bc 44
Palace Pl. SW1 —48Lb 82 (3B 204)
Palace Pl. Mans. W8 —47Db 81
(off Kensington Ct.)
Palace Rd. N8 —29Mb 42
(in two parts)
Palace Rd. N11 —24Nb 42
Palace Rd. SE19 —66Vb 127
Palace Rd. SW2 —60Pb 104
Palace Rd. Brom —67Kc 129
Palace Rd. E Mol —69Fa 122
Palace Rd. King T —70Ma 123
Palace Rd. Ruis —35Aa 57
Palace Rd. W'ham —93Qc 184
Palace Sq. SE19 —66Vb 127
Palace St. SW1 —48Lb 82 (3B 204)
Palace View. SE12 —61Jc 129
Palace View. Brom —69Kc 129
(in two parts)
Palace View. Croy —77Bc 148
Palace View Rd. E4 —22Dc 44
Palace Way. Wey —76R 140
Palamos Rd. E10 —32Cc 64
Palatine Av. N16 —35Ub 63
Palatine Rd. N16 —35Ub 63
Palermo Rd. NW10 —40Wa 60
Palestine Gro. SW19 —67Fb 125
Palewell Clo. Orp —68Xc 131
Palewell Comn. Dri. SW14
—57Ta 101
Palewell Pk. SW14 —57Ta 101
Paley Gdns. Lou —13Rc 28
Palfrey Pl. SW8 —52Pb 104
Palgrave Av. S'hall —45Ca 77
Palgrave Ho. Twic —59Ea 100
Palgrave Rd. W12 —48Va 80
Palins Way. Grays —46Ce 91
Palissy St. E2 —41Vb 83 (4K 195)
Pallant Ho. SE1 —48Tb 83 (4G 207)
(off Tabard St.)
Pallant Way. Orp —76Qc 150
Pallett Way. SE18 —53Nc 108
Palliser Rd. W14 —50Ab 80
Pall Mall. SW1 —46Lb 82 (7C 198)
Pall Mall E. SW1
—46Mb 82 (6E 198)
Pall Mall Pl. SW1
(off Pall Mall) —46Lb 82 (7C 198)
Palmar Cres. Bexh —55Cd 110
Palmar Rd. Bexh —54Cd 110
Palmarsh Clo. Orp —70Zc 131
Palm Av. Sidc —65Zc 131
Palm Ct. SE1 —52Vb 105
(off Garnies Clo.)

Palmeira Rd.—Parkway

Palmeira Rd. Bexh —55Zc 109
Palmer Av. Bush —15Da 19
Palmer Av. Grav —3F 136
Palmer Av. Sutt —77Ya 144
Palmer Clo. Houn —53Ca 99
Palmer Clo. W Wick —75Fc 149
Palmer Cres. King T —69Na 123
Palmer Cres. Ott —79F 138
Palmer Gdns. Barn —15Za 22
Palmer Gdns. Epp —3Wc 15
Palmer Pl. N7 —36Qb 62
Palmer Rd. E13 —42Kc 85
Palmer Rd. Dag —32Zc 67
Palmers. Stanf —1P 93
Palmers Av. Grays —50Ee 91
Palmer's Ct. N11 —22Lb 42
(off Palmer's Rd.)
Palmers Dri. Grays —49Ee 91
Palmersfield Rd. Bans —86Cb 163
Palmers Gro. W Mol —70Ca 121
Palmers Hill. Epp —1Wc 15
Palmers La. Enf —11Xb 25
Palmer's Moor La. Iver —42J 75
Palmers Orchard. Shor —83Hd 170
Palmers Pas. SW14 —55Sa 101
Palmer's Rd. E2 —40Zb 64
Palmer's Rd. N11 —22Lb 42
Palmers Rd. SW14 —55Sa 101
Palmers Rd. SW16 —68Pb 126
Palmers Rd. Borwd —11Ra 21
Palmerston Av. Slou —8M 73
Palmerston Cen. W'stone —27Ha 38
Palmerston Clo. Wok —86C 156
Palmerston Ct. Surb —73Ma 143
Palmerston Cres. N13 —22Pb 42
Palmerston Cres. SE18 —51Sc 108
Palmerston Gdns. Grays —50Zd 91
Palmerston Gro. SW19 —66Cb 125
Palmerston Rd. E7 —37Kc 65
Palmerston Rd. E17 —27Bc 44
Palmerston Rd. N22 —24Pb 42
Palmerston Rd. NW6 —38Bb 61
(in two parts)
Palmerston Rd. SW14 —56Sa 101
Palmerston Rd. SW19 —66Cb 125
Palmerston Rd. W3 —48Sa 79
Palmerston Rd. Buck H —19Kc 27
Palmerston Rd. Cars —77Hb 145
Palmerston Rd. Grays —51Zd 113
Palmerston Rd. Harr —27Ga 38
Palmerston Rd. Orp —78Sc 150
Palmerston Rd. Rain —40Ld 69
Palmerston Rd. Sutt —78Eb 145
Palmerston Rd. T Hth —71Tb 147
Palmerston Rd. Twic —58Ha 100
Palmer St. SW1
—48Mb 82 (3D 204)
Palmers Way. Chesh —1Ac 12
Palm Gro. W5 —48Na 79
Palm Rd. Romf —29Ed 48
Pamela Ct. N12 —23Db 41
Pamela Gdns. Pinn —29X 37
Pamela Wlk. E8 —39Wb 63
Pampisford Rd. Purl & S Croy
—83Qb 164
Pam's Way. Eps —78Ta 143
Pancras La. EC4 —44Sb 83 (3E 200)
Pancras Rd. NW1
—40Mb 62 (1D 192)
Pancroft. Abr —13Xc 29
Pandora Rd. NW6 —37Cb 61
Panfield M. Ilf —30Qc 46
Panfield Rd. SE2 —48Wc 87
Pangbourne Av. W10 —43Ya 80
Pangbourne Dri. Stan —22Ma 39
Panhard Pl. S'hall —45Da 77
Pank Av. Barn —15Eb 23
Pankhurst Clo. SE14 —53Zb 106
Pankhurst Pl. Wat —13Z 19
Pankhurst Rd. W on T —73Y 141
Panmuir Rd. SW20 —67Xa 124
Panmure Clo. N5 —35Rb 63
Panmure Rd. SE26 —62Xb 127
Panorama Ct. N6 —30Lb 42
Pansy Gdns. W12 —45Wa 80
Panter's. Swan —66Hd 132
Pantile Rd. Wey —77T 140
Pantile Row. Slou —49C 74
Pantiles Clo. N13 —22Rb 43
Pantiles Clo. Wok —6E 188
Pantiles, The. NW11 —29Ab 40
Pantiles, The. Bexh —52Bd 109
Pantiles, The. Brom —69Nc 130
Pantiles, The. Bush —18Fa 20
Pantiles Wlk. Uxb —38L 55
Panton St. SW1
—45Mb 82 (5D 198)
Panyer All. EC4 —44Sb 83 (3D 200)
(off Newgate St.)
Paper Bldgs. EC4
(off Temple) —45Qb 82 (4A 200)
Papercourt La. Rip —93H 173
Paper Mill Wharf. E14 —45Ac 84
Papillons Wlk. SE3 —55Jc 107
Papworth Gdns. N7 —36Pb 62
Papworth Way. SW2 —59Qb 104
Parade Mans. NW4 —29Xa 40
Parade M. SE27 —61Rb 127
Parade, The. N4 —33Qb 62
Parade, The. SW11 —52Hb 103
Parade, The. Brtwd —20Yd 32
Parade, The. Clay —79Ga 142
Parade, The. Dart —57Hd 110
Parade, The. Eps —85Ta 161
(in two parts)
Parade, The. Grav —1F 136
Parade, The. Hamp —64Fa 122
Parade, The. Kems —89Nd 171
Parade, The. Romf —23Rd 49
Parade, The. Sun —66V 120
Parade, The. Swan —69Gd 132
Parade, The. Swans —57Be 113
Parade, The. Vir W —72A 138
Parade, The. Wat —13X 19
(High St. Watford)
Parade, The. Wat —20Aa 19
(Prestwick Rd.)
Parade, The. Wind —3B 94
Parade, The. Wor Pk —77Va 144
Paradise Ct. Wemb —34Ra 59
Paradise Pas. N7 —36Qb 62
Paradise Pl. SE18 —49Nc 86
Paradise Rd. SW4 —54Nb 104
Paradise Rd. Rich —57Ma 101
Paradise Rd. Wal A —6Ec 12
Paradise Row. E2 —41Xb 83
Paradise St. SE16 —47Xb 83
Paradise Wlk. SW3 —51Hb 103
Paragon All. SE1
—48Ub 83 (4H 207)
Paragon Clo. E16 —44Jc 85
Paragon Gro. Surb —72Pa 143
Paragon M. SE1 —49Tb 83 (5G 207)
Paragon Pl. SE3 —54Hc 107
Paragon Pl. Surb —72Pa 143
Paragon Rd. E9 —37Yb 64
Paragon Row. SE17
—49Tb 83 (5F 207)
Paragon, The. SE3 —54Jc 107
Paraside Pl. SE18 —49Nc 86
Parbury Rise. Chess —79Na 143
Parbury Rd. SE23 —58Ac 106
Parchmore Rd. T Hth —68Rb 127
Parchmore Way. T Hth —68Rb 127
Pardoner St. SE1
—48Tb 83 (3G 207)
Pardon St. EC1 —42Rb 83 (5C 194)
Pares Clo. Wok —4G 188
Parfett St. E1 —43Wb 83
Parfitt Clo. NW3 —32Eb 61
Parfour Dri. Kenl —88Sb 165
Parfrey St. W6 —51Ya 102
Pargreaves Ct. Wemb —33Qa 59
Parham Dri. Ilf —30Rc 46
Parham Way. N10 —26Lb 42
Paris Garden. SE1
—46Rb 83 (6B 200)
Parish Clo. Horn —33Kd 69
Parish Cotts. Dag —33Cd 68
Parish Ct. Surb —72Na 143
Parish Ga. Dri. Sidc —58Uc 108
Parish La. SE20 —65Zb 128
Parish La. Farn C —3F 52
Parish M. SE20 —66Zb 128
Park App. SE16 —48Xb 83
Park App. Well —56Xc 109
Park Av. E6 —39Qc 66
Park Av. E15 —37Gc 65
Park Av. N3 —25Db 41
Park Av. N13 —20Qb 24
Park Av. N18 —21Wb 43
Park Av. N22 —26Nb 42
Park Av. NW2 —36Xa 60
Park Av. NW10 —40Pa 59
(in two parts)
Park Av. NW11 —32Db 61
Park Av. SW14 —56Ta 101
Park Av. Bark —37Sc 66
Park Av. Brom —65Hc 129
Park Av. Bush —12Z 19
Park Av. Cars —79Jb 146
Park Av. Cat —96Ub 181
Park Av. Chor —15J 17
Park Av. Egh —65E 118
Park Av. Enf —15Tb 25
Park Av. F'boro —76Pc 150
Park Av. Grav —10E 114
Park Av. Grays —51Wd 112
Park Av. Houn —58Da 99
Park Av. Hut —18Ee 33
Park Av. Ilf —32Qc 66
Park Av. Mitc —66Kb 126
Park Av. N'fleet —10A 114
Park Av. Orp —75Wc 151
Park Av. Pot B —6Eb 9
Park Av. Rad —5Ka 6
Park Av. Ruis —30T 36
Park Av. S'hall —47Ba 77
Park Av. Stai —65H 119
Park Av. Upm —31Ud 70
Park Av. Wat —14W 18
Park Av. W Wick —75Ec 148
Park Av. Wfd G —22Kc 45
Park Av. Wray —7P 95
Park Av. E. Eps —79Wa 144
Park Av. M. Mitc —66Kb 126
Park Av. N. N8 —28Mb 42
Park Av. N. NW10 —36Xa 60
Park Av. Rd. N17 —24Xb 43
Park Av. S. N8 —28Mb 42
Park Av. W. Eps —79Wa 144
Park Boulevd. Romf —25Hd 48
Park Bus. Cen. NW6 —41Cb 81
Park Chase. Wemb —35Pa 59
Park Clo. E9 —39Yb 64
Park Clo. N12 —21Fb 41
Park Clo. NW2 —34Xa 60
Park Clo. NW10 —41Pa 79
Park Clo. SE7 —50Nc 86
Park Clo. SW1 —47Hb 81 (2F 203)
Park Clo. W4 —50Ta 79
Park Clo. W14 —48Bb 81
Park Clo. Bush —13Z 19
Park Clo. Cars —79Hb 145
Park Clo. Esh —79Ca 141
Park Clo. Fet —96Fa 176
Park Clo. Hamp —67Ea 122
Park Clo. Harr —25Ga 38
Park Clo. Houn —57Ea 100
Park Clo. New Haw —82K 157
Park Clo. Rick —21R 36
Park Clo. W on T —75V 140
Park Clo. Wind —4H 95
Park Corner. Wind —5C 94
Park Corner Dri. E Hor —100U 174
Park Corner Rd. Grav —62Ce 135
Park Corner Rd. S'fleet —63Be 135
Park Ct. E4 —19Ec 26
Park Ct. E17 —29Dc 44
Park Ct. N11 —24Mb 42
Park Ct. N17 —24Wb 43
Park Ct. SE26 —65Xb 127
Park Ct. Harr —31Na 59
Park Ct. King T —67La 122
Park Ct. N Mald —70Ta 123
Park Ct. Wemb —36Na 59
Park Ct. Wok —90B 156
Park Cres. N3 —24Db 41
Park Cres. W1 —42Kb 82 (6K 191)
Park Cres. Els —13Pa 21
Park Cres. Enf —14Tb 25
Park Cres. Eri —51Ed 110
Park Cres. Harr —25Ga 38
Park Cres. Horn —31Jd 68
Park Cres. Twic —60Fa 100
Park Cres. M. E. W1
—42Kb 82 (6A 192)
Park Cres. M. W. W1
—42Kb 82 (6K 191)
Park Cres. Rd. Eri —51Fd 110
Park Croft. Edgw —25Sa 39
Parkcroft Rd. SE12 —59Hc 107
Parkdale. N11 —23Mb 42
Parkdale Cres. Wor Pk —76Ta 143
Parkdale Rd. SE18 —50Uc 86
Park Dri. N21 —16Sb 25
Park Dri. NW11 —32Db 61
Park Dri. SE7 —51Nc 108
Park Dri. SW14 —57Ta 101
Park Dri. W3 —48Qa 79
Park Dri. Asht —90Qa 161
Park Dri. Dag —34Ed 68
Park Dri. Har W —23Fa 38
Park Dri. Long —69Ae 135
Park Dri. N Har —31Ca 57
Park Dri. Pot B —3Db 9
Park Dri. Romf —28Fd 48
Park Dri. Upm —35Rd 69
Park Dri. Wey —78R 140
Park Dri. Wok —90B 156
Park Dwellings. NW3 —36Hb 61
Park End. NW3 —35Gb 61
Park End. Brom —67Hc 129
Park End Rd. Romf —28Gd 48
Parker Av. Til —3E 114
Parker Clo. E16 —46Nc 86
Parker Ho. E14 —47Cc 84
(off Admirals Way)
Parker M. WC2 —44Nb 82 (2G 199)
Parke Rd. SW13 —53Wa 102
Parke Rd. Sun —70W 120
Parker Rd. Croy —77Sb 147
Parker Rd. Grays —50Be 91
Parker's Clo. Asht —91Na 177
Parker's Hill. Asht —91Na 177
Parker's La. Asht —91Na 177
Parkers Row. SE1 —47Wb 83
Parker St. E16 —46Nc 86
Parker St. WC2 —44Nb 82 (3G 199)
Parker St. Wat —11X 19
Parkes Rd. Chig —22Uc 46
Park Farm Clo. N2 —27Eb 41
Park Farm Clo. Pinn —29X 37
Park Farm Ct. Hay —45U 76
Park Farm Rd. Brom —67Mc 129
Park Farm Rd. King T —66Na 123
Park Farm Rd. Upm —36Pd 69
Parkfield. Chor —14H 17
Parkfield. Hart —70Ae 135
Parkfield. Iswth —53Ga 100
Parkfield. Sev —95Nd 187
Parkfield Av. SW14 —56Ua 102
Parkfield Av. Felt —62W 120
Parkfield Av. Harr —26Ea 38
Parkfield Av. N'holt —40Z 57
Parkfield Av. Uxb —41R 76
Parkfield Clo. Edgw —23Ra 39
Parkfield Clo. N'holt —40Aa 57
Parkfield Cres. Felt —62W 120
Parkfield Cres. Harr —26Ea 38
Parkfield Cres. Ruis —33Aa 57
Parkfield Dri. N'holt —40Z 57
Parkfield Gdns. Harr —27Da 37
Parkfield Ho. N Har —25Da 37
Parkfield Pde. Felt —62W 120
Parkfield Rd. NW10 —38Xa 60
Parkfield Rd. SE14 —53Bc 106
Parkfield Rd. Felt —62W 120
Parkfield Rd. Harr —34Ea 58
Parkfield Rd. N'holt —40Aa 57
Parkfield Rd. Uxb —33R 56
Parkfields. SW15 —56Ya 102
Parkfields. Croy —74Bc 148
Parkfields. Oxs —83Fa 160
Parkfields Av. NW9 —32Ta 59
Parkfields Av. SW20 —67Xa 124
Parkfields Clo. Cars —77Jb 146
Parkfields Rd. King T —64Pa 123
Parkfield St. N1 —40Qb 62 (1A 194)
Parkfield Way. Brom —72Pc 150
Park Gdns. E10 —32Cc 64
Park Gdns. NW9 —27Ra 39
Park Gdns. Eri —49Fd 88
Park Gdns. King T —64Pa 123
Park Ga. N2 —27Fb 41
Park Ga. N21 —17Pb 24
Park Ga. SE3 —55Hc 107
Park Ga. W5 —43Ma 79
Parkgate. Burn —2A 72
Parkgate Av. Barn —11Eb 23
Park Ga. Clo. King T —65Ra 123
Park Ga. Ct. Wok —90A 156
Parkgate Cres. Barn —11Eb 23
Parkgate Gdns. SW14 —57Ta 101
Parkgate Rd. SW11 —52Gb 103
Parkgate Rd. Orp —77Dd 152
Parkgate Rd. Wall —78Jb 146
Parkgate Rd. Wat —9Y 5
Park Gates. Harr —35Ca 57
Park Grange Gdns. Sev —99Ld 187
Park Grn. Bookh —96Ca 175
Park Gro. E15 —39Jc 65
Park Gro. N11 —24Mb 42
Park Gro. Bexh —56Ed 110
Park Gro. Brom —67Kc 129
Park Gro. Chal G —13A 16
Park Gro. Edgw —22Pa 39
Park Gro. Rd. E11 —33Gc 65
Parkhall Rd. N2 —28Gb 41
Park Hall Rd. SE21 —62Tb 127
Park Hall Trading Est. SE21
—62Sb 127
Parkham Ct. Short —68Gc 129
Parkham St. SW11 —53Gb 103
Park Hill. SE23 —61Xb 127
Park Hill. SW4 —57Mb 104
Park Hill. W5 —43Ma 79
Park Hill. Brom —70Nc 130
Park Hill. Cars —79Gb 145
Park Hill. Lou —15Mc 27
Park Hill. Meop —10A 136
Park Hill. Rich —58Pa 101
Park Hill Clo. Cars —78Gb 145
Parkhill Clo. Horn —34Ld 69
Park Hill Ct. SW17 —62Hb 125
Park Hill Rise. Croy —75Ub 147
Parkhill Rd. E4 —18Ec 26
Parkhill Rd. NW3 —36Hb 61
Parkhill Rd. Bex —59Bd 109
Park Hill Rd. Brom —68Gc 129
Park Hill Rd. Croy —77Ub 147
Parkhill Rd. Eps —83Va 162
Park Hill Rd. Otf —89Nd 171
Parkhill Rd. Sidc —62Uc 130
Park Hill Rd. Wall —80Kb 146
Parkhill Wlk. NW3 —36Hb 61
Parkholme Rd. E8 —37Wb 63
Park Ho. N21 —17Pb 24
Park Ho. Sev —94Ld 187
Park Ho. Gdns. Twic —57La 100
Park Ho. Pas. N6 —31Jb 62
Parkhouse St. SE5 —52Tb 105
Parkhurst. Eps —82Sa 161
Parkhurst Gdns. Bex —59Cd 110
Parkhurst Rd. E12 —35Qc 66
Parkhurst Rd. E17 —28Ac 44
Parkhurst Rd. N7 —35Nb 62
Parkhurst Rd. N11 —21Jb 42
Parkhurst Rd. N17 —26Wb 43
Parkhurst Rd. N22 —23Pb 42
Parkhurst Rd. Bex —59Cd 110
Parkhurst Rd. Sutt —77Fb 145
Parkland Av. Romf —26Hd 48
Parkland Av. Slou —9P 73
Parkland Av. Upm —36Rd 69
Parkland Clo. Sev —100Ld 187
Parkland Ct. E15 —36Gc 65
(off Maryland Pk.)
Parkland Gdns. SW19 —60Za 102
Parkland Gro. Ashf —62Q 120
Parkland Rd. N22 —26Pb 42
Parkland Rd. Ashf —63Q 120
Parkland Rd. Wfd G —24Jc 45
Parklands. Add —78L 139
Parklands. Bookh —95Ca 175
Parklands. Chig —20Sc 28
Parklands. Coop —1Zc 15
Parklands. Surb —71Pa 143
Parklands Clo. SW14 —57Sa 101
Parklands Clo. Barn —10Fb 9
Parklands Clo. Chig —20Sc 28
Parklands Ct. Houn —54Z 99
Parklands Dri. N3 —27Ab 40
Parklands Pde. Houn —54Z 99
Parklands Rd. SW16 —64Kb 126
Parklands Way. Wor Pk —75Ua 144
Park La. E15 —39Fc 65
Park La. N9 —20Ub 25
Park La. N17 —24Vb 43
Park La. W1 —45Hb 81 (4G 197)
Park La. Asht —90Pa 161
Park La. Cars & Wall —77Jb 146
Park La. Chad —30Zc 47
Park La. Coul —93Mb 180
Park La. Croy —76Tb 147
Park La. Elm P —37Kd 69
Park La. Farn C —6C 52
Park La. Hare —25J 35
Park La. Harr —34Da 57
Park La. Hay —43U 76
Park La. Heron —24Fe 51
Park La. Horn —30Hd 48
Park La. Houn —52W 98
Park La. Kems —90Qd 171
Park La. Rich —56Ma 101
Park La. Seal —93Qd 187
Park La. Sev —96Ld 187
Park La. Slou —8M 73
Park La. S Ock —46Td 90
(in two parts)
Park La. Stan —20Ja 20
Park La. Sutt —79Ab 144
Park La. Swan —68Ld 133
Park La. Tedd —65Ha 122
Park La. Wal X —5Yb 12
Park La. Wemb —36Na 59
Park La. Wink —10A 94
Park La. Clo. N17 —24Wb 43
Parklawn Av. Eps —85Ra 161
Park Lawn Rd. Wey —77S 140
Park Lawns. Wemb —35Pa 59
Parklea Clo. NW9 —25Ua 40
Park Lee Ct. N16 —31Ub 63
Parkleigh Rd. SW19 —68Db 125
Park Ley Rd. Wold —92Zb 182
Parkleys. Rich —63Ma 123
Park Mnr. Sutt —80Eb 145
(off Christchurch Pk.)
Park Mans. NW4 —29Xa 40
Park Mans. SW8 —51Nb 104
Parkmead. SW15 —58Xa 102
Park Mead. Harr —34Da 57
Parkmead. Lou —15Qc 28
Park Mead. Sidc —57Xc 109
Parkmead Gdns. NW7 —23Va 40
Park Meadow. Dodd —11Zd 33
Park M. SE24 —59Sb 105
Park M. Chst —65Rc 130
Parkmore Clo. Wfd G —21Jc 45
Park Nook Gdns. Enf —9Tb 11
Park Pale. Roch —7P 137
Park Pde. NW10 —40Va 60
Park Pl. E14 —46Cc 84
Park Pl. SW1 —46Lb 82 (7B 198)
Park Pl. W3 —49Qa 79
Park Pl. W5 —46Ma 79
Park Pl. Grav —8E 114
Park Pl. Hamp —65Ea 122
Park Pl. Hare —25L 35
Park Pl. Sev —95Fd 186
Park Pl. Wemb —35Pa 59
Park Pl. Wok —90B 156
(off Hill View Rd.)
Park Pl. Gdns. W2
—43Eb 81 (7A 190)
Park Pl. Vs. W2 —43Eb 81 (7A 190)
Park Ride. Wind —9B 94
Park Ridings. N8 —27Qb 42
Park Rise. SE23 —60Ac 106
Park Rise. Harr —25Ga 38
Park Rise. Lea —93Ka 176
Park Rise Clo. Lea —93Ka 176
Park Rise Rd. SE23 —60Ac 106
Park Rd. E6 —39Lc 65
Park Rd. E10 —32Cc 64
Park Rd. E12 —32Kc 65
Park Rd. E15 —39Jc 65
Park Rd. E17 —29Bc 44
Park Rd. N2 —27Fb 41
Park Rd. N8 —28Lb 42
Park Rd. N11 —24Mb 42
Park Rd. N14 —18Mb 24
Park Rd. N15 —28Rb 43
Park Rd. N18 —21Wb 43
Park Rd. NW4 —31Wa 60
Park Rd. NW8 & NW1
—41Gb 81 (3D 190)
Park Rd. NW9 —31Ta 59
Park Rd. NW10 —39Ua 60
Park Rd. SE25 —70Ub 127
Park Rd. SW19 —65Fb 125
Park Rd. W4 —52Sa 101
Park Rd. W7 —45Ha 78
Park Rd. Ashf —64R 120
Park Rd. Asht —90Na 161
Park Rd. Bans —87Db 163
Park Rd. Beck —66Bc 128
Park Rd. Brtwd —18Xd 32
Park Rd. Brom —67Kc 129
Park Rd. Bush —16Ca 19
Park Rd. Cat —95Ub 181
Park Rd. Chst —65Rc 130
Park Rd. Dart —59Qd 111
Park Rd. E Mol —70Ea 122
Park Rd. Egh —63C 118
Park Rd. Enf —8Ac 12
Park Rd. Esh —77Da 141
Park Rd. Farn R —10G 52
Park Rd. Felt —63Z 121
Park Rd. Grav —10D 114
Park Rd. Grays —50De 91
Park Rd. Hack —75Kb 146
Park Rd. Hamp —63Da 121
Park Rd. Hamp W —67La 122
Park Rd. Hay —43U 76
Park Rd. H Bar —14Bb 23
Park Rd. Houn —57Da 99
Park Rd. Ilf —34Tc 66
Park Rd. Iswth —53Ka 100
Park Rd. Kenl —87Sb 165
Park Rd. King T —64Pa 123
Park Rd. New Bar —14Fb 23
Park Rd. N Mald —70Ta 123
Park Rd. N'thaw —2Jb 10
Park Rd. Orp —71Yc 151
Park Rd. Oxt —100Hc 183
Park Rd. Rad —7Ja 6
Park Rd. Rich —58Pa 101
Park Rd. Rick —17M 17
Park Rd. Shep —74Q 140
Park Rd. Stai —58K 97
Park Rd. Stanf —2K 93
Park Rd. Sun —66X 121
Park Rd. Surb —71Pa 143
Park Rd. Sutt —79Ab 144
Park Rd. Swan —69Hd 132
Park Rd. Swans —58Ae 113
Park Rd. Tedd —65Ha 122
Park Rd. Twic —58La 100
Park Rd. Uxb —38N 55
Park Rd. Wall —78Kb 146
Park Rd. Wal X —5Zb 12
Park Rd. Warl —86Gc 167
Park Rd. Wat —11W 18
Park Rd. Wemb —37Na 59
Park Rd. Wok —89B 156
Park Rd. E. W3 —47Sa 79
Park Rd. E. Uxb —40M 55
Park Rd. Ho. King T —66Qa 123
Park Rd. Ind. Est. Swan —69Ha 122
Park Rd. N. W3 —47Ra 79
Park Rd. N. W4 —50Ta 79
Park Row. SE10 —50Fc 85
Park Royal Metro Cen. NW10
—42Ra 79
Park Royal Rd. NW10 & W3
—41Sa 79
Parkshot. Rich —56Ma 101
Parkside. N3 —25Db 41
Parkside. NW2 —34Wa 60
Parkside. NW7 —23Wa 40
Parkside. SW19 —62Za 124
Parkside. W5 —45Na 79
Parkside. Buck H —19Kc 27
Parkside. Grays —48Fe 91
Parkside. Hals —85Bd 169
Parkside. Hamp —64Fa 122
Parkside. Hay —45U 76
Park Side. New Haw —83K 157
Parkside. Pot B —4Eb 9
Parkside. Sidc —61Xc 131
Parkside. Sutt —79Ab 144
Parkside. Wat —16Y 19
Parkside Av. SW19 —64Za 124
Parkside Av. Bexh —54Fd 110
Parkside Av. Brom —70Nc 130
Parkside Av. Romf —27Fd 48
Parkside Av. Til —4D 114
Parkside Clo. E Hor —97V 174
Parkside Ct. Wey —77Q 140
Parkside Cres. N7 —34Qb 62
Parkside Cres. Surb —72Sa 143
Parkside Cross. Bexh —54Gd 110
Parkside Dri. Edgw —20Qa 21
Parkside Dri. Wat —12U 18
Parkside Est. E9 —39Zb 64
Parkside Gdns. SW19 —63Za 124
Parkside Gdns. Barn —18Hb 23
Parkside Gdns. Coul —89Kb 164
Parkside Ho. Dag —34Ed 68
Parkside Pl. E Hor —97V 174
Parkside Rd. SW11 —53Jb 104
Parkside Rd. Belv —49Dd 88
Parkside Rd. Houn —57Da 99
Parkside Rd. N'wd —22V 36
Parkside Ter. N18 —21Tb 43
Parkside Way. Harr —28Da 37
Parkspring Gro. Iver —37C 54
Park Sq. Esh —77Da 141
Park Sq. Wink —10A 94
Park Sq. E. NW1
—42Kb 82 (5K 191)
Park Sq. M. NW1
—42Kb 82 (6K 191)
(off Up. Harley St.)
Park Sq. W. NW1
—42Kb 82 (5K 191)
Parkstead Rd. SW15 —57Wa 102
Parkstone Av. N18 —23Vb 43
Parkstone Av. Horn —30Nd 49
Parkstone Rd. E17 —27Ec 44
Parkstone Rd. SE15 —54Wb 105
Park St. SE1 —46Sb 83 (6D 200)
Park St. W1 —45Jb 82 (3H 197)
Park St. Coln —53F 96
Park St. Croy —75Sb 147
Park St. Slou —8K 73
Park St. Tedd —65Ga 122
Park St. Wind —3H 95
Park St. La. Park —2Da 5
Park Ter. Enf —10Ac 12
Park Ter. Grnh —57Yd 112
Park Ter. Sund —96Zc 185
Park Ter. Wor Pk —74Wa 144
Park, The. N6 —30Jb 42
Park, The. NW11 —32Db 61
Park, The. SE19 —66Ub 127
Park, The. SE23 —60Yb 106
Park, The. W5 —46Ma 79
Park, The. Bookh —96Ca 175
Park, The. Cars —79Hb 145
Park, The. Sidc —64Wc 131
Parkthorne Clo. Harr —30Da 37
Parkthorne Dri. Harr —30Ca 37
Parkthorne Rd. SW12 —59Mb 104
Park Towers. W2 —45Eb 81
Park Vale Ct. Brtwd —18Yd 32
Park View. N5 —35Sb 63
Park View. N21 —17Pb 24
Park View. W3 —43Sa 79
Park View. Add —78L 139
Park View. Bookh —97Ca 175
Parkview. Eri —48Zc 87
Park View. Hods —80Ee 155
Park View. N Mald —69Va 124
Park View. Pinn —25Ba 37
Park View. Pot B —5Eb 9
Park View. Romf —30Zc 47
Park View. S Ock —46Td 90
Park View. Wemb —36Ra 59
Parkview Chase. Slou —4C 72
Park View Ct. SE20 —67Xb 127
Parkview Ct. SW18 —57Cb 103
Parkview Ct. Har W —24Ga 38
Park View Ct. Wok —91B 172
Park View Cres. N11 —21Kb 42
Park View Est. E2 —40Zb 64
Park View Gdns. N22 —25Qb 42
Park View Gdns. NW4 —29Ya 40
Park View Gdns. Bark —40Uc 66
Park View Gdns. Grays —50De 91
Park View Gdns. Ilf —28Pc 46
Park View Ho. E4 —22Cc 44
Parkview Ho. N9 —17Xb 25
Park View Ho. SE24 —58Rb 105
(off Hurst St.)
Parkview Ho. Wat —16Z 19
Park View Mans. N4 —31Rb 63
Park View Rd. N3 —25Db 41
Park View Rd. N17 —27Wb 43
Park View Rd. NW10 —35Va 60
Parkview Rd. SE9 —60Rc 108
Park View Rd. W5 —43Na 79
Parkview Rd. Croy —74Wb 147
Park View Rd. Pinn —24X 37
Park View Rd. S'hall —46Ca 77
Park View Rd. Uxb —44Q 76
Park View Rd. Well —55Yc 109
Park View Rd. Wold —94Ac 182
Park Village E. NW1
—40Kb 62 (1K 191)
Park Village W. NW1
—40Kb 62 (1K 191)
Park Vs. Romf —30Zc 47
Parkville Rd. SW6 —52Bb 103
Park Vista. SE10 —51Fc 107
Park Wlk. N6 —31Jb 62
Park Wlk. SW10 —51Eb 103
Park Wlk. Asht —91Pa 177
Park Wlk. Barn —13Fb 23
Parkway. N14 —19Nb 24
Park Way. N20 —21Hb 41
Parkway. NW1 —39Kb 62 (1K 191)
Park Way. NW11 —29Ab 40
Parkway. SW20 —70Za 124
Park Way. Bex —62Gd 132
Park Way. Bookh —95Ca 175
Park Way. Edgw —25Ra 39
Park Way. Enf —12Qb 24
Parkway. Eri —48Ad 87

Park Way—Pennyroyal Av.

Park Way. Felt —59X 99
Park Way. Ilf —34Vc 67
Parkway. New Ad —81Dc 166
Parkway. Ors —3C 92
Parkway. Rain —42Jd 88
Park Way. Rick —18L 17
Parkway. Romf —26Hd 48
Park Way. Ruis —32W 56
Park Way. Shenf —18Be 33
Parkway. Uxb —38Q 56
Park Way. W Mol —69Da 121
Park Way. Wey —77T 140
Park Way. Wfd G —22Lc 45
Park Way Ct. Ruis —32V 56
Parkway, The. Hay & N'holt —48X 77
Parkway, The. Houn & S'hall —49W 76
Parkway, The. Iver —39E 54
Parkway Trading Est. Houn —51Y 99
Park W. Pl. W2 —44Gb 81 (2E 196)
Parkwood. N20 —20Hb 23
Parkwood. Beck —66Cc 128
Parkwood Av. Esh —74Ea 142
Park Wood Clo. Bans —87Za 162
Parkwood Gro. Sun —69W 120
Parkwood M. N6 —30Kb 42
Parkwood Rd. SW19 —64Bb 125
Park Wood Rd. Bans —87Za 162
Park Wood Rd. Bex —59Bd 109
Parkwood Rd. Iswth —53Ha 100
Parkwood Rd. Tats —93Nc 184
Park Wood View. Bans —88Za 162
Parlaunt Rd. Slou —49C 74
Parley Dri. St J —5F 188
Parliament Ct. E1 —43Ub 83 (1J 201) (off Artillery La.)
Parliament Hill. NW3 —35Gb 61
Parliament Sq. SW1 —47Nb 82 (2F 205)
Parliament St. SW1 —47Nb 82 (1F 205)
Parluke Clo. SE7 —50Mc 85
Parma Cres. SW11 —56Hb 103
Parmiter St. E2 —40Xb 63
Parndon Ho. Lou —17Nc 28
Parnel Clo. Abb L —2V 4
Parnell Clo. Edgw —21Ra 39
Parnell Ho. WC1 —44Mb 82 (2E 198)
Parnell Rd. E3 —39Bc 64 (in two parts)
Parnham St. E14 —44Ac 84
Parolles Rd. N19 —32Lb 62
Paroma Rd. Belv —48Cd 88
Parr Av. Eps —81Xa 162
Parr Clo. N9 —21Xb 43
Parr Clo. Lea —92Ha 176
Parr Ct. Felt —63Y 121
Parrock Av. Grav —10E 114
Parrock Rd. Grav —10E 114
Parrock St. Grav —8D 114
Parrock, The. Grav —10E 114
Parrots Clo. Crox —14Q 18
Parr Rd. E6 —39Mc 65
Parr Rd. Stan —25Na 39
Parrs Clo. S Croy —81Tb 165
Parrs Pl. Hamp —66Ca 121
Parr St. N1 —40Tb 63 (1F 195)
Parry Av. E6 —44Pc 86
Parry Clo. Eps —80Xa 144
Parry Clo. Stanf —1M 93
Parry Cotts. Ger X —21A 34 (off Chesham La.)
Parry Dri. Wey —82Q 158
Parry Grn. Langl —49B 74
Parry Pl. SE18 —49Rc 86
Parry Rd. SE25 —69Ub 127
Parry Rd. W10 —41Ab 80
Parry St. SW8 —51Nb 104
Parsifal Rd. NW6 —36Cb 61
Parsley Gdns. Croy —74Zb 148
Parsloes Av. Dag —35Zc 67
Parsonage Clo. Abb L —2U 4
Parsonage Clo. Hay —44V 76
Parsonage Clo. Warl —88Ac 166
Parsonage Ct. Lou —13Sc 28 (off Rectory La.)
Parsonage Gdns. Enf —12Sb 25
Parsonage La. Enf —12Sb 25
Parsonage La. Farn C —7G 52
Parsonage La. Sidc —63Bd 131
Parsonage La. S at H —65Rd 133
Parsonage La. Wind —3E 94
Parsonage Manorway. Belv —51Cd 110
Parsonage Rd. Egh —4P 117
Parsonage Rd. Grays —51Yd 112
Parsonage Rd. Rain —40Ld 69
Parsonage Rd. Rick —17M 17
Parsonage St. E14 —49Ec 84
Parson's Cres. Edgw —20Qa 21
Parsonsfield Clo. Bans —87Za 162
Parsonsfield Rd. Bans —88Za 162
Parson's Grn. SW6 —53Cb 103
Parson's Grn. La. SW6 —53Cb 103
Parson's Gro. Edgw —20Qa 21
Parsons La. Dart —62Kd 133
Parsons Mead. Croy —74Rb 147
Parsons Mead. E Mol —69Ea 122
Parson's Rd. E13 —40Lc 65
Parson St. NW4 —28Ya 40
Parthenia Rd. SW6 —53Cb 103
Parthia Clo. Tad —91Xa 178
Partingdale La. NW7 —22Za 40
Partington Clo. N19 —32Mb 62
Partridge Clo. E16 —43Mc 85
Partridge Clo. Bush —18Ea 20
Partridge Ct. EC1 —42Rb 83 (5B 194) (off Cyprus St.)
Partridge Dri. Orp —76Sc 150
Partridge Grn. SE9 —62Qc 130
Partridge Knoll. Purl —85Rb 165
Partridge Mead. Bans —88Ya 162
Partridge Rd. Hamp —65Ba 121
Partridge Rd. Sidc —63Uc 130
Partridge Sq. E6 —43Nc 86
Partridge Way. N22 —25Nb 42
Parvills Rd. Wal A —4Fc 13
Parvin St. SW8 —53Mb 104
Parvis Rd. W Byf —85K 157
Pasadena Clo. Hay —47X 77
Pascal St. SW8 —52Mb 104
Pascoe Rd. SE13 —57Fc 107
Pasefield. Wal A —5Fc 13
Pasley Clo. SE17 —50Sb 83 (7D 206)
Pasquier Rd. E17 —27Ac 44
Passage, The. W6 —48Ya 80
Passage, The. Rich —57Na 101
Passey Pl. SE9 —58Pc 108
Passfield Dri. E14 —43Dc 84
Passfield Path. SE28 —45Xc 87
Passfields. SE6 —62Ec 128
Passing All. EC1 —43Rb 83 (7C 194) (off St. John St.)
Passingham Ho. Houn —51Ca 99
Passmore Edwards Ho. Ger X —22A 34
Passmore Gdns. N11 —23Mb 42
Passmore St. SW1 —50Jb 82 (7H 203)
Pasteur Clo. NW9 —26Ua 40
Pasteur Dri. H Wood —26Md 49
Pasteur Gdns. N18 —22Rb 43
Paston Clo. E5 —34Zb 64
Paston Cres. SE12 —59Kc 107
Pastor Ct. N6 —30Lb 42
Pastor St. SE11 —49Rb 83 (5C 206)
Pasture Clo. Bush —17Ea 20
Pasture Clo. Wemb —34Ka 58
Pasture Rd. SE6 —60Hc 107
Pasture Rd. Dag —35Bd 67
Pasture Rd. Wemb —33Ka 58
Pastures Mead. Uxb —37Q 56
Pastures, The. N20 —18Bb 23
Pastures, The. Wat —17Y 19
Patcham Ter. SW8 —53Kb 104
Patch Clo. Uxb —39P 55
Patch, The. Sev —94Gd 186
Patchway Ct. SE15 —51Ub 105 (off Newent Clo.)
Paternoster Clo. Wal A —5Hc 13
Paternoster Hill. Wal A —4Hc 13
Paternoster Row. EC4 —44Sb 83 (3D 200)
Paternoster Row. Noak H —18Ld 31
Paternoster Sq. EC4 —44Rb 83 (3C 200)
Paterson Rd. Ashf —64M 119
Pater St. W8 —48Cb 81
Pates Mnr. Dri. Felt —59T 98
Pathfield Rd. SW16 —65Mb 126
Path, The. SW19 —67Db 125
Pathway, The. Rad —8Ja 6
Pathway, The. Send —97H 173
Pathway, The. Wat —18Z 19
Patience Rd. SW11 —54Gb 103
Patio Clo. SW4 —58Mb 104
Patmore Est. SW8 —53Lb 104
Patmore Ho. N16 —36Ub 63
Patmore La. W on T —79V 140
Patmore Lodge. N6 —28Hb 41
Patmore Rd. Wal A —6Gc 13
Patmore St. SW8 —53Lb 104
Patmore Way. Romf —22Dd 48
Patmos Rd. SW9 —52Rb 105
Paton Clo. E3 —41Cc 84
Paton Ho. SW9 —54Pb 104 (off Stockwell Rd.)
Paton St. EC1 —41Sb 83 (4D 194)
Patricia Clo. Slou —5C 72
Patricia Ct. Chst —67Tc 130
Patricia Ct. Well —52Xc 109
Patricia Dri. Horn —32Nd 69
Patricia Gdns. Sutt —83Cb 163
Patrick Connolly Gdns. E3 —41Dc 84
Patrick Pas. SW11 —54Gb 103
Patrick Rd. E13 —41Lc 85
Patrington Clo. Uxb —41L 75
Patriot Sq. E2 —40Xb 63
Patrol Pl. SE6 —58Dc 106
Patrons Dri. Den —30H 35
Patshull Pl. NW5 —37Lb 62
Patshull Rd. NW5 —37Lb 62
Patten All. Rich —57Ma 101
Pattenden Rd. SE6 —60Bc 106
Patten Ho. N4 —32Sb 63
Patten Rd. SW18 —59Gb 103
Patterdale Clo. Brom —65Hc 129
Patterdale Rd. SE15 —52Yb 106
Patterdale Rd. Dart —60Td 112
Patterson Ct. SE19 —66Vb 127
Patterson Ct. Dart —57Qd 111
Patterson Rd. SE19 —65Vb 127
Pattinson Point. E16 —43Jc 85 (off Fife Rd.)
Pattison Rd. NW2 —34Cb 61
Pattison Wlk. SE18 —50Sc 86
Paul Byrne Ho. N2 —27Eb 41
Paul Clo. E15 —39Gc 65
Paul Ct. Romf —30Ed 48
Paulet Rd. SE5 —54Rb 105
Paul Gdns. Croy —76Vb 147
Paulhan Rd. Harr —28Ma 39
Paulin Dri. N21 —17Qb 24
Pauline Cres. Twic —60Ea 100
Paulinus Clo. Orp —68Yc 131
Paul Julius Clo. E14 —45Fc 85
Paul Robeson Clo. E6 —41Qc 86
Pauls Grn. Wal X —5Ac 12
Paul's Pl. Asht —91Ra 177
Paul St. E15 —39Gc 65
Paul St. EC2 —42Tb 83 (6H 195)
Paul's Wlk. EC4 —45Sb 83 (4C 200)
Paultons Sq. SW3 —51Fb 103
Paultons St. SW3 —51Fb 103
Pauntley St. N19 —32Lb 62
Paved Ct. Rich —57Ma 101
Paveley Dri. SW11 —52Gb 103
Paveley St. NW8 —41Gb 81 (4E 190)
Pavement M. Romf —31Zc 67
Pavement Sq. Croy —74Wb 147
Pavement, The. SW4 —56Lb 104
Pavement, The. W5 —48Na 79
Pavet Clo. Dag —37Dd 68
Pavilion Gdns. Sev —96Kd 187
Pavilion Gdns. Stai —66K 119
Pavilion Lodge. Harr —32Fa 58
Pavilion M. N3 —26Cb 41
Pavilion Rd. Ilf —31Pc 66
Pavilions, The. Uxb —38L 55
Pavilion St. SW1 —48Hb 81 (4G 203)
Pavilion Way. Edgw —24Ra 39
Pavilion Way. Ruis —33Y 57
Pawleyne Clo. SE20 —66Yb 128
Pawsey Clo. E13 —39Kc 65
Pawsons Rd. Croy —72Sb 147
Paxfold. Stan —23Ma 39
Paxford Rd. Wemb —33Ka 58
Paxton Av. Slou —8G 72
Paxton Clo. Rich —54Pa 101
Paxton Clo. W on T —73Y 141
Paxton Gdns. Wok —84G 156
Paxton Pl. SE27 —63Ub 127
Paxton Rd. N17 —24Wb 43
Paxton Rd. SE23 —62Ac 128
Paxton Rd. W4 —51Ua 102
Paxton Rd. Brom —66Jc 129
Paxton Ter. SW1 —51Kb 104
Payne Ho. N1 —39Pb 62 (1J 193) (off Barnsbury Est.)
Paynell Ct. SE3 —55Gc 107
Payne Rd. E3 —40Dc 64
Paynes Cotts. Sev —90Ed 170
Paynesfield Av. SW14 —55Ta 101
Paynesfield Rd. Bush —17Ha 20
Paynesfield Rd. Tats —93Lc 183
Payne St. SE8 —52Bc 106
Paynes Wlk. W6 —51Ab 102
Payzes Gdns. E4 —22Hc 45
Peabody Av. SW1 —50Kb 82 (7K 203)
Peabody Bldgs. SE1 —46Sb 83 (7D 200) (off Southwark St.)
Peabody Bldgs. SW3 —51Gb 103
Peabody Clo. SE10 —53Dc 106
Peabody Clo. SW1 —51Kb 104
Peabody Cotts. N17 —25Ub 43
Peabody Est. N1 —39Sb 63
Peabody Est. SE1 —47Sb 83 (1E 206) (off Mint St.)
Peabody Est. SE24 —59Sb 105
Peabody Est. SW3 —51Gb 103
Peabody Est. SW6 —51Cb 103 (off Lillie Rd.)
Peabody Est. SW11 —56Gb 103
Peabody Est. W6 —50Ya 80
Peabody Est. W10 —42Ya 80
Peabody Hill. SE21 —60Rb 105
Peabody Sq. SE1 —47Rb 83
Peabody Yd. N1 —39Sb 63
Peace Clo. N14 —15Kb 24
Peace Clo. Chesh —1Xb 11
Peace Prospect. Wat —13W 18
Peace Rd. Slou & Iver —41B 74
Peace St. SE18 —51Qc 108
Peach Croft. Grav —62Fe 135
Peaches Clo. Sutt —80Ab 144
Peachey Clo. Uxb —44M 75
Peachey La. Uxb —43M 75
Peach Gro. Wemb —34Ra 59
Peach Rd. W10 —41Za 80
Peach Tree Av. W Dray —44P 75
Peachum Rd. SE3 —51Hc 107
Peacock Av. Felt —60T 98
Peacock Clo. Horn —28Nd 49
Peacock Gdns. S Croy —82Ac 166
Peacock Ga. Slou —5H 73
Peacocks Shopping Cen., The. Wok —89A 156
Peacock St. SE17 —49Rb 83 (6C 206)
Peacock St. Grav —9E 114
Peacock Wlk. E16 —44Kc 85 (off Mortlake Rd.)
Peacock Wlk. N6 —31Kb 62
Peacock Yd. SE17 —49Rb 83 (6C 206) (off Iliffe St.)
Peaketon Av. Ilf —28Mc 45
Peak Hill. SE26 —63Yb 128
Peak Hill Av. SE26 —63Yb 128
Peak Hill Gdns. SE26 —63Yb 128
Peak Ho. N4 —32Sb 63 (off Woodberry Down Est.)
Peaks Hill. Purl —82Mb 164
Peaks Hill Rise. Purl —82Nb 164
Peak, The. SE26 —62Yb 128
Pea La. Upm —38Wd 70
Peal Gdns. W13 —41Ja 78
Peall Rd. Croy —72Pb 146
Pearcefield Av. SE23 —60Yb 106
Pearce Rd. W Mol —69Da 121
Pear Clo. NW9 —28Ta 39
Pear Clo. SE14 —52Ac 106
Pearcroft Rd. E11 —33Fc 65
Peardon St. SW8 —54Kb 104
Peareswood Gdns. Stan —25Ma 39
Peareswood Rd. Eri —53Hd 110
Pearfield Rd. SE23 —62Ac 128
Pear Gdns. Chalv —6F 72
Pearl Clo. E6 —44Qc 86
Pearl Ct. Wok —4B 188
Pearl Rd. E17 —27Cc 44
Pearl St. E1 —46Xb 83
Pearmain Clo. Shep —71R 140
Pearman St. SE1 —48Qb 82 (3A 206)
Pear Pl. SE1 —47Qb 82 (1K 205)
Pearscroft Ct. SW6 —53Db 103
Pearscroft Rd. SW6 —53Db 103
Pearson's Av. SE14 —53Cc 106
Pearson St. E2 —40Vb 63 (1K 195)
Pears Rd. Houn —55Ea 100
Peartree Av. SW17 —62Eb 125
Pear Tree Av. W Dray —44P 75
Pear Tree Clo. Add —78J 139
Pear Tree Clo. Chess —78Qa 143
Peartree Clo. Dodd —11Zd 33
Peartree Clo. Eri —53Fd 110
Peartree Clo. Mitc —68Gb 125
Peartree Clo. S Croy —86Xb 165
Peartree Clo. S Ock —40Yd 70
Pear Tree Clo. Swan —68Fd 132
Pear Tree Ct. E18 —25Kc 45
Pear Tree Ct. EC1 —42Qb 82 (6A 194)
Peartree Ct. Wat —8Z 5
Peartree Gdns. Dag —35Xc 67
Peartree Gdns. Romf —26Dd 48
Peartree La. E1 —45Yb 84
Peartree La. Shorne —6N 137
Pear Tree Rd. Add —78J 139
Pear Tree Rd. Ashf —64S 120
Peartree Rd. Enf —13Ub 25
Pear Trees. Ingve —23Ee 51
Pear Tree St. EC1 —42Rb 83 (5C 194)
Peary Ho. NW10 —38Ta 59
Peary Pl. E2 —41Yb 84
Peascod Pl. Wind —3H 95
Peascod St. Wind —3G 94
Pease Clo. Horn —38Kd 69
Pease Hill. Ash —79Ae 155
Peas Mead Ter. E4 —21Ec 44
Peatfield Clo. Sidc —62Uc 130
Peatmore Av. Wok —88J 157
Peatmore Clo. Wok —88J 157
Pebble Clo. Tad —100Ua 178
Pebble Hill Rd. Bet —100Ua 178
Pebble La. Lea & Eps —96Pa 177
Pebworth Rd. Harr —33Ja 58
Peckarmans Wood. SE26 —62Wb 127
Peckett Sq. N5 —35Sb 63
Peckford Clo. SW9 —54Qb 104
Peckford Pl. SW9 —54Qb 104
Peckham Gro. SE15 —52Ub 105
Peckham High St. SE15 —53Wb 105
Peckham Hill St. SE15 —52Wb 105
Peckham Pk. Rd. SE15 —52Wb 105
Peckham Rd. SE5 & SE15 —53Ub 105
Peckham Rye. SE15 & SE22 —55Wb 105
Peckham Rye Ind. Est. SE15 —54Vb 105
Peckwater St. NW5 —36Lb 62
Pedham Pl. Est. Swan —72Jd 152
Pedhoulas. N14 —20Nb 24
Pedlar's Wlk. N7 —36Pb 62
Pedley Rd. Dag —32Yc 67
Pedley St. E1 —42Vb 83
Pedro St. E5 —34Zb 64
Pedworth Gdns. SE16 —49Yb 84
Peek Cres. SW19 —64Za 124
Peel Cen. Ind. Est. Eps —83Va 162
Peel Clo. E4 —19Dc 26
Peel Clo. N9 —20Wb 25
Peel Clo. Wind —5F 94
Peel Ct. Slou —3G 72
Peel Dri. NW9 —27Wa 40
Peel Dri. Ilf —27Nc 46
Peel Gro. E2 —40Yb 64 (in two parts)
Peel Pl. Ilf —26Nc 46
Peel Precinct. NW6 —40Cb 61
Peel Rd. E18 —25Hc 45
Peel Rd. NW6 —41Cb 81
Peel Rd. Orp —78Sc 150
Peel Rd. W'stone —27Ha 38 (in two parts)
Peel Rd. Wemb —34Ma 59
Peel St. W8 —46Cb 81
Peel Way. Romf —26Pd 49
Peel Way. Uxb —43N 75
Peerage Way. Horn —31Pd 69
Peerless Dri. Hare —28K 35
Peerless St. EC1 —41Tb 83 (4F 195)
Pegamoid Rd. N18 —20Yb 26
Pegasus Clo. Abb L —4V 4
Pegasus Ct. Grav —2E 136
Pegasus Ct. King T —69Ma 123
Pegasus Pl. SE11 —51Qb 104
Pegelm Gdns. Horn —31Pd 69
Peggotty Way. Uxb —44R 76
Pegg Rd. Houn —52Z 99
Pegley Gdns. SE12 —61Jc 129
Pegmire La. Ald —11Ea 20
Pegwell St. SE18 —52Uc 108
Pekin Clo. Stai —67G 118
Pekin St. E14 —44Cc 84
Peldon Ct. Rich —57Pa 101
Peldon Pas. Rich —56Pa 101
Peldon Wlk. N1 —39Rb 63 (off Popham St.)
Pelham Av. Bark —39Vc 67
Pelham Clo. SE5 —55Ub 105
Pelham Cotts. Bex —60Dd 110
Pelham Ct. Sidc —62Wc 131
Pelham Cres. SW7 —49Gb 81 (6D 202)
Pelham Ho. W14 —49Bb 81 (off Mornington Av.)
Pelham Pl. SW7 —49Gb 81 (6D 202)
Pelham Pl. Est. Swan —71Jd 152
Pelham Rd. E18 —27Kc 45
Pelham Rd. N15 —28Vb 43
Pelham Rd. N22 —26Qb 42
Pelham Rd. SW19 —66Cb 125
Pelham Rd. Beck —68Yb 128
Pelham Rd. Bexh —55Cd 110
Pelham Rd. Grav —10B 114
Pelham Rd. Ilf —33Tc 66
Pelham Rd. S. Grav —10B 114
Pelham's Clo. Esh —77Ca 141
Pelhams, The. Wat —7Z 5
Pelham St. SW7 —49Fb 81 (5C 202)
Pelham's Wlk. Esh —77Ca 141
Pelham Ter. Grav —9B 114
Pelham Way. Bookh —98Ea 176
Pelican Est. SE15 —53Vb 105
Pelican Ho. SE8 —49Bc 84
Pelican Pas. E1 —42Yb 84
Pelican Wlk. SW9 —56Rb 105
Pelier St. SE17 —51Sb 105
Pelinore Rd. SE6 —61Gc 129
Pella Ho. SE11 —50Pb 82 (7J 205)
Pellant Rd. SW6 —52Ab 102
Pellatt Gro. N22 —25Qb 42
Pellatt Rd. SE22 —57Vb 105
Pellatt Rd. Wemb —33Ma 59
Pellerin Rd. N16 —36Ub 63
Pelling Hill. Old Win —9M 95
Pelling St. E14 —44Cc 84
Pellipar Clo. N13 —20Qb 24
Pellipar Gdns. SE18 —50Pc 86
Pelly Ct. Epp —3Vc 15
Pelly Rd. E13 —39Jc 65 (in two parts)
Pelter St. E2 —41Vb 83 (3K 195)
Pelton Av. Sutt —82Db 163
Pelton Rd. SE10 —50Gc 85
Pembar Av. E17 —27Ac 44
Pember Rd. NW10 —41Za 80
Pemberton Av. Romf —27Kd 49
Pemberton Gdns. N19 —34Lb 62
Pemberton Gdns. Romf —29Ad 47
Pemberton Gdns. Swan —69Gd 132
Pemberton Pl. E8 —38Yb 64
Pemberton Pl. Esh —76Ea 142
Pemberton Rd. N4 —29Qb 42
Pemberton Rd. E Mol —70Ea 122
Pemberton Rd. Slou —2C 72
Pemberton Row. EC4 —44Qb 82 (2A 200)
Pemberton Ter. N19 —34Lb 62
Pembrey Way. Horn —37Ld 69
Pembridge Av. Twic —60Ba 99
Pembridge Chase. Bov —1B 2
Pembridge Clo. Bov —1B 2
Pembridge Cres. W11 —45Cb 81
Pembridge Gdns. W2 —45Cb 81
Pembridge M. W11 —45Cb 81
Pembridge Pl. W2 —45Cb 81
Pembridge Rd. W11 —45Cb 81
Pembridge Rd. Bov —1C 2
Pembridge Sq. W2 —45Cb 81
Pembridge Vs. W11 & W2 —45Cb 81
Pembroke Av. Enf —10Xb 11
Pembroke Av. Harr —27Ja 38
Pembroke Av. Surb —71Ra 143
Pembroke Av. W on T —77Z 141
Pembroke Bldgs. NW10 —41Wa 80
Pembroke Cen., The. Ruis —32V 56
Pembroke Clo. SW1 —47Jb 82 (2J 203)
Pembroke Clo. Asc —10B 116
Pembroke Clo. Bans —89Db 163
Pembroke Clo. Horn —28Pd 49
Pembroke Cotts. W8 —48Cb 81 (off Pembroke Sq.)
Pembroke Dri. Chesh —1Rb 11
Pembroke Gdns. W8 —49Bb 81
Pembroke Gdns. Dag —34Dd 68
Pembroke Gdns. Wok —90C 156
Pembroke Gdns. Clo. W8 —48Cb 81
Pembroke Hall. NW4 —27Ya 40 (off Mulberry Clo.)
Pembroke Lodge. Stan —23La 38
Pembroke M. E2 —41Yb 84 (off Wessex St.)
Pembroke M. N10 —25Kb 42
Pembroke M. W8 —48Cb 81
Pembroke M. Sev —97Kd 187
Pembroke Pl. W8 —48Cb 81
Pembroke Pl. Edgw —24Qa 39
Pembroke Pl. Iswth —54Ga 100
Pembroke Pl. S at H —67Rd 133
Pembroke Rd. E6 —43Pc 86
Pembroke Rd. E17 —29Dc 44
Pembroke Rd. N8 —28Nb 42
Pembroke Rd. N10 —25Jb 42
Pembroke Rd. N13 —20Sb 25
Pembroke Rd. N15 —29Vb 43
Pembroke Rd. SE25 —70Ub 127
Pembroke Rd. W8 —49Bb 81
Pembroke Rd. Brom —68Lc 129
Pembroke Rd. Eri —50Ed 88
Pembroke Rd. Gnfd —42Da 77
Pembroke Rd. Ilf —32Vc 67
Pembroke Rd. Mitc —68Jb 126
Pembroke Rd. N'wd —20S 18
Pembroke Rd. Ruis —32U 56
Pembroke Rd. Sev —97Kd 187
Pembroke Rd. Wemb —34Ma 59
Pembroke Rd. Wok —90C 156
Pembroke Sq. W8 —48Cb 81
Pembroke St. N1 —38Nb 62
Pembroke Vs. W8 —49Cb 81
Pembroke Vs. Rich —56Ma 101
Pembroke Wlk. W8 —49Cb 81
Pembroke Way. Hay —48S 76
Pembury Av. Wor Pk —74Wa 144
Pembury Clo. E5 —36Xb 63
Pembury Clo. Brom —73Hc 149
Pembury Clo. Coul —86Jb 164
Pembury Ct. Hay —51T 98
Pembury Cres. Sidc —61Ad 131
Pembury Pl. E5 —36Xb 63
Pembury Rd. E5 —36Xb 63
Pembury Rd. N17 —25Vb 43
Pembury Rd. SE25 —70Wb 127
Pembury Rd. Bexh —52Ad 109
Pemdevon Rd. Croy —73Qb 146
Pemell Clo. E1 —42Yb 84
Pemerich Clo. Hay —50V 76
Pempath Pl. Wemb —33Ma 59
Penally Pl. N1 —39Tb 63
Penalty Pl. N1 —39Tb 63
Penang St. E1 —46Xb 83
Penarth St. SE15 —51Yb 106
Penates. Esh —77Fa 142
Penberth Rd. SE6 —61Ec 128
Penbury Rd. S'hall —49Ba 77
Pencombe M. W11 —45Bb 81
Pencraig Way. SE15 —51Xb 105
Pencroft Dri. Dart —59Ld 111
Pendall Clo. Barn —14Gb 23
Penda Rd. Eri —52Dd 110
Pendarves Rd. SW20 —67Ya 124
Penda's Mead. E9 —35Ac 64
Pendell Av. Hay —52V 98
Pendennis Clo. W Byf —86J 157
Pendennis Ho. SE8 —49Ac 84
Pendennis Rd. N17 —27Tb 43
Pendennis Rd. SW16 —63Nb 126
Pendennis Rd. Orp —75Yc 151
Pendennis Rd. Sev —95Kd 187
Penderel Rd. Houn —57Ca 99
Penderry Rise. SE6 —61Fc 129
Penderyn Way. N7 —35Mb 62
Pendle Ct. Uxb —39R 56
Pendle Ho. SE26 —62Wb 127
Pendle Rd. SW16 —65Kb 126
Pendlestone Rd. E17 —29Dc 44
Pendragon Rd. Brom —62Hc 129
Pendragon Wlk. NW9 —30Ua 40
Pendrell Rd. SE4 —54Ac 106
Pendrell St. SE18 —51Tc 108
Pendula Dri. Hay —42Z 77
Penenden. New Ash —75Be 155
Penerley Rd. SE6 —60Dc 106
Penerley Rd. Rain —43Kd 89
Penfields Ho. N7 —37Nb 62
Penfold Clo. Croy —76Qb 146
Penfold La. Bex —61Zc 131 (in two parts)
Penfold Pl. NW1 —43Gb 81 (7D 190)
Penfold Rd. N9 —18Zb 26
Penfold St. NW8 & NW1 —42Fb 81 (6C 190)
Penford Gdns. SE9 —55Mc 107
Penford St. SE5 —54Rb 105
Pengarth Rd. Bex —57Zc 109
Penge La. SE20 —66Yb 128
Pengelly Clo. Chesh —2Xb 11
Penge Rd. E13 —39Lc 65
Penge Rd. SE25 & SE20 —69Wb 127
Penhall Rd. SE7 —49Mc 85
Penhill Rd. Bex —58Yc 109
Penhurst. Wok —86B 156
Penhurst Rd. Ilf —24Rc 46
Penifather La. Gnfd —41Fa 78
Peninsular Clo. Felt —58T 98
Penistone Rd. SW16 —66Nb 126
Penistone Wlk. Romf —23Ld 49
Penketh Dri. Harr —34Fa 58
Penman's Grn. K Lan —5H 3
Penmayne Ho. SE11 —50Qb 82 (7A 206) (off Kennings Way)
Penmon Rd. SE2 —48Wc 87
Pennack Rd. SE15 —51Vb 105
Pennant M. W8 —49Db 81
Pennant Ter. E17 —26Bc 44
Pennard Rd. W12 —47Ya 80
Pennards, The. Sun —69Y 121
Penn Clo. Chor —16F 16
Penn Clo. Gnfd —40Da 57
Penn Clo. Harr —28La 38
Penn Clo. Ors —2D 92
Penn Clo. Uxb —42M 75
Penn Ct. NW9 —27Ta 39
Penn Dri. Den —30H 35
Penne Clo. Rad —6Ja 6
Penner Clo. SW19 —61Ab 124
Pennethorne Clo. E9 —39Yb 64
Pennethorne Rd. SE15 —52Xb 105
Penney Clo. Dart —59Md 111
Penn Gdns. Chst —68Rc 130
Penn Gdns. Romf —24Cd 48
Penn Gaskell La. Ger X —22B 34
Penn Ho. Ger X —22A 34
Pennine Dri. NW2 —33Za 60
Pennine La. NW2 —33Ab 60
Pennine Pde. NW2 —33Ab 60
Pennine Rd. Slou —3E 72
Pennine Way. Bexh —53Gd 110
Pennine Way. Grav —2A 136
Pennine Way. Hay —52T 98
Pennington Clo. SE27 —63Tb 127
Pennington Clo. Romf —22Cd 48
Pennington Dri. Wey —76U 140
Pennington Rd. Ger X —24A 34
Pennington St. E1 —45Xb 83
Pennis La. Fawk —72Zd 155
Penn La. Bex —57Zc 109
Penn Meadow. Stoke P —9K 53
Penn Pl. Rick —17M 17
Penn Rd. N7 —36Nb 62
Penn Rd. Dat —3P 95
Penn Rd. Ger X —25A 34
Penn Rd. Rick —18H 17
Penn Rd. Slou —2H 73
Penn Rd. Wat —11X 19
Penn St. N1 —39Tb 63 (1G 195)
Penn Way. Chor —16F 16
Penny Clo. Rain —41Kd 89
Pennycroft. Croy —81Ac 166
Pennyfield. Cob —85W 158
Pennyfields. E14 —45Cc 84
Pennyfields. War —21Yd 50
Penny La. Shep —73U 140
Pennylets Grn. Stoke P —8K 53
Pennymead Dri. E Hor —99V 174
Pennymead Rise. E Hor —99V 174
Pennymoor Wlk. W9 —41Bb 81
Penny Royal. Wall —79Mb 146
Pennyroyal Av. E6 —44Qc 86

Penpoll Rd.—Pinewood Av.

Penpoll Rd. E8 —37Xb 63
Penpool La. Well —55Xc 109
Penrhyn Av. E17 —25Bc 44
Penrhyn Cres. E17 —25Cc 44
Penrhyn Cres. SW14 —56Sa 101
Penrhyn Gro. E17 —25Cc 44
Penrhyn Rd. King T —70Na 123
Penrith Clo. SW15 —57Ab 102
Penrith Clo. Beck —67Dc 128
Penrith Clo. Uxb —38M 55
Penrith Cres. Rain —36Jd 68
Penrith Pl. SE27 —61Rb 127
Penrith Rd. N15 —29Tb 43
Penrith Rd. Ilf —23Vc 47
Penrith Rd. N Mald —70Ta 123
Penrith Rd. Romf —23Qd 49
Penrith Rd. T Hth —68Sb 127
Penrith St. SW16 —65Lb 126
Penrose Av. Wat —19Aa 19
Penrose Ct. Egh —5N 117
Penrose Gro. SE17
—50Sb 83 (7D 206)
Penrose Rd. Fet —94Ea 176
Penrose St. SE17
—50Sb 83 (7D 206)
Penryn Ho. SE11
—50Rb 83 (7B 206)
(off Seaton Clo.)
Penryn St. NW1
—40Mb 62 (1D 192)
Penry St. SE1 —49Ub 83 (6J 207)
Pensbury Pl. SW8 —54Lb 104
Pensbury St. SW8 —54Lb 104
Penscroft Gdns. Borwd —14Ta 21
Pensford Av. Rich —54Qa 101
Penshurst Av. Sidc —58Wc 109
Penshurst Clo. Ger X —26A 34
Penshurst Clo. Long —68Fe 135
Penshurst Clo. W King —79Ud 154
Penshurst Gdns. Edgw —22Ra 39
Penshurst Grn. Brom —71Hc 149
Penshurst Pl. SE1
—48Pb 82 (4J 205)
(off Carlisle La.)
Penshurst Rd. E9 —38Zb 64
Penshurst Rd. N17 —24Vb 43
Penshurst Rd. Bexh —53Bd 109
Penshurst Rd. Pot B —3Fb 9
Penshurst Rd. T Hth —71Rb 147
Penshurst Wlk. Brom —71Hc 149
Penshurst Way. Orp —70Yc 131
Penshurst Way. Sutt —81Cb 163
Pensilver Clo. Barn —14Gb 23
Penstemon Clo. N3 —23Cb 41
Penta Ct. Borwd —14Qa 21
Pentagon, The. W13 —45Ja 78
Pentavia Retail Pk. NW7 —24Va 40
Pentelow Gdns. Felt —58W 98
Pentire Clo. Upm —30Ud 50
Pentire Rd. E17 —25Fc 45
Pentland Av. Edgw —19Ra 21
Pentland Av. Shep —71Q 140
Pentland Clo. NW11 —33Ab 60
Pentland Gdns. SW18 —58Eb 103
Pentland Pl. N'holt —38Aa 57
Pentland Rd. Bush —16Ea 20
Pentland Rd. Slou —3E 72
Pentlands Clo. Mitc —69Kb 126
Pentland St. SW18 —58Eb 103
Pentland Way. Uxb —34S 56
Pentlow St. SW15 —55Ya 102
Pentlow Way. Buck H —17Nc 28
Pentney Rd. E4 —18Fc 27
Pentney Rd. SW12 —60Lb 104
Pentney Rd. SW19 —67Ab 124
Penton Av. Stai —66H 119
Penton Dri. Chesh —1Zb 12
Penton Gro. N1 —40Qb 62 (2K 193)
Penton Hall Dri. Stai —67J 119
Penton Hook Rd. Stai —66J 119
Penton Ho. SE2 —46Zc 87
Penton Pl. SE17
—50Rb 83 (6C 206)
Penton Rise. WC1
—41Pb 82 (3J 193)
Penton Rd. Stai —66H 119
Penton St. N1 —40Qb 62 (1K 193)
Pentonville Rd. N1
—40Pb 62 (3G 193)
Pentrich Av. Enf —10Wb 11
Pentridge St. SE15 —52Vb 105
Pentyre Av. N18 —22Tb 43
Penwerris Av. Iswth —52Ea 100
Penwerris Ct. Houn —52Ea 100
Penwith Rd. SW18 —61Cb 125
Penwith Wlk. Wok —7G 188
Penwood Ct. Pinn —28Ba 37
Penwood End. Wok —9E 188
Penwortham Ct. N22 —26Qb 42
Penwortham Rd. SW16 —65Kb 126
Penwortham Rd. S Croy —82Tb 165
Penylan Pl. Edgw —24Qa 39
Penywern Rd. SW5 —50Cb 81
Penzance Clo. Hare —26M 35
Penzance Gdns. Romf —23Qd 49
Penzance Ho. SE11
—50Rb 83 (7B 206)
(off Seaton Clo.)
Penzance Pl. W11 —46Ab 80
Penzance Rd. Romf —23Qd 49
Penzance Spur. Slou —2F 72
Penzance St. W11 —46Ab 80
Peony Clo. Pil H —16Xd 32
Peony Ct. E4 —24Gc 45
Peony Gdns. W12 —45Wa 80
Peploe Rd. NW6 —40Za 60
Peplow Clo. W Dray —46M 75
Pepper All. Lou —12Hc 27
Pepper Clo. E6 —43Pc 86
Pepper Clo. Cat —97Ub 181
Pepperhill. Grav —62Ee 135
Pepperhill La. Grav —61Ee 135
Peppermint Clo. Croy —73Nb 146
Pepper St. E14 —48Dc 84
Pepper St. SE1 —47Sb 83 (1D 206)
Peppie Clo. N16 —33Ub 63
Pepys Clo. Asht —89Qa 161
Pepys Clo. Dart —56Qd 111
Pepys Clo. Grav —62Fe 135
Pepys Clo. Slou —51D 96
Pepys Clo. Til —3E 114
Pepys Clo. Uxb —35R 56
Pepys Ct. SW4 —55Kb 104
Pepys Cres. Barn —15Ya 22
Pepys Rise. Orp —74Vc 151
Pepys Rd. SE14 —53Zb 106
Pepys Rd. SW20 —66Ya 124
Pepys St. EC3 —45Ub 83 (4J 201)
Perceval Av. NW3 —36Gb 61
Perceval Ct. N'holt —36Ca 57
Perceval Ho. W5 —45La 78
Percheron Rd. Borwd —16Ta 21
Perch St. E8 —35Vb 63
Percival Ct. N17 —24Vb 43
Percival Ct. Chesh —2Ac 12
Percival Gdns. Romf —30Yc 47
Percival Rd. SW14 —56Sa 101
Percival Rd. Enf —14Vb 25
Percival Rd. Felt —61V 120
Percival Rd. Horn —30Ld 49
Percival Rd. Orp —75Rc 150
Percival St. EC1 —42Rb 83 (5B 194)
Percival Way. Eps —77Ta 143
Percy Av. Ashf —64Q 120
Percy Bryant Rd. Sun —66U 120
Percy Cir. WC1 —41Pb 82 (3J 193)
Percy Gdns. Enf —15Zb 26
Percy Gdns. Hay —41U 76
Percy Gdns. Iswth —55Ja 100
Percy Gdns. Wor Pk —74Ua 144
Percy Ho. Iswth —54Ja 100
Percy M. W1 —43Mb 82 (1D 198)
(off Rathbone Pl.)
Percy Pas. W1 —43Mb 82 (1D 198)
(off Rathbone St.)
Percy Pl. W12 —47Wa 80
Percy Pl. Dat —3M 95
Percy Rd. E11 —31Gc 65
Percy Rd. E16 —43Gc 85
Percy Rd. N12 —22Eb 41
Percy Rd. N21 —17Sb 25
Percy Rd. NW6 —41Cb 81
Percy Rd. SE20 —67Zb 128
Percy Rd. SE25 —71Wb 147
Percy Rd. W12 —47Wa 80
Percy Rd. Bexh —54Ad 109
Percy Rd. Dag —42Cd 88
Percy Rd. Hamp —66Ca 121
Percy Rd. Ilf —31Wc 67
Percy Rd. Iswth —56Ja 100
Percy Rd. Mitc —73Jb 146
Percy Rd. Romf —27Dd 48
Percy Rd. Twic —60Da 99
Percy Rd. Wat —14X 19
Percy St. W1 —43Mb 82 (1D 198)
Percy St. Grays —51Ee 113
Percy Way. Twic —60Ea 100
Percy Yd. WC1 —41Pb 82 (3J 193)
Peregrine Clo. NW10 —36Ta 59
Peregrine Clo. Wat —6Aa 5
Peregrine Ct. SW16 —63Pb 126
Peregrine Ct. Well —53Vc 109
Peregrine Gdns. Croy —75Ac 148
Peregrine Rd. Ilf —22Xc 47
Peregrine Rd. Sun —68V 120
Peregrine Wlk. Horn —37Kd 69
Peregrine Way. SW19 —66Ya 124
Peregrin Rd. Wal A —6Jc 13
Perham Rd. W14 —50Ab 80
Peridot St. E6 —43Nc 86
Perifield. SE21 —60Sb 105
Perimeade Rd. Gnfd —40La 58
Perimeter Rd. Wind —3H 95
Periton Rd. SE9 —56Mc 107
Perivale Gdns. W13 —42Ka 78
Perivale Gdns. Wat —6X 5
Perivale Grange. Gnfd —41Ja 78
Perivale Ind. Pk. Gnfd —40Ka 58
Perivale La. Gnfd —41Ja 78
Perivale New Bus. Cen. Gnfd
—40La 58
Perkin Clo. Wemb —36Ka 58
Perkins Clo. Grnh —57Vd 112
Perkins Ct. Ashf —64P 119
Perkin's Rents. SW1
—48Mb 82 (4E 204)
Perkins Rd. Ilf —29Tc 46
Perkins Sq. SE1 —46Sb 83 (6E 200)
(off Porter St.)
Perks Clo. SE3 —55Gc 107
Perleybrooke La. Wok —5D 188
Perpins Rd. SE9 —58Uc 108
Perram Clo. Hart —70Be 135
Perran Rd. SW2 —60Rb 105
Perran Wlk. Bren —50Na 79
Perren St. NW5 —37Kb 62
Perrers Rd. W6 —49Xa 80
Perrin Clo. Ashf —64P 119
Perrin Ct. Wok —87D 156
Perrin Rd. Wemb —35Ka 58
Perrin's Ct. NW3 —35Eb 61
Perrin's La. NW3 —35Eb 61
Perrin's Wlk. NW3 —35Eb 61
Perronet Ho. SE1
—48Rb 83 (4C 206)
(off Princess St.)
Perrott St. SE18 —49Sc 86
Perry Av. W3 —44Ta 79
Perry Clo. Rain —40Fd 68
Perry Clo. Uxb —44R 76
Perry Ct. N15 —30Ub 43
Perrycroft. Wind —5C 94
Perryfields. Burn —2A 72
Perryfield Way. NW9 —30Va 40
Perryfield Way. Rich —62Ka 122
Perry Gdns. N9 —20Ub 25
Perry Garth. N'holt —39Y 57
Perry Gro. Dart —56Qd 111
Perry Hall Clo. Orp —73Wc 151
Perry Hall Rd. Orp —72Vc 151
Perry Hill. SE6 —62Bc 128
Perry How. Wor Pk —74Va 144
Perrymans Farm Rd. Ilf —30Tc 46
Perryman Way. Slou —1D 72
Perry Mead. Bush —16Ea 20
Perry Mead. Enf —12Rb 25
Perrymead Gdns. Gnfd —40Da 57
Perrymead St. SW6 —53Cb 103
Perryn Ct. Twic —59Ja 100
Perryn Ho. W3 —45Ua 80
Perryn Rd. SE16 —48Xb 83
Perryn Rd. W3 —46Ta 79
Perry Oaks Dri. W Dray & Houn
—54K 97
Perry Rise. SE23 —62Ac 128
Perrys La. Prat B —85Xc 169
Perry's Pl. W1 —44Mb 82 (2D 198)
Perry St. Chst —66Tc 130
Perry St. Dart —56Gd 110
Perry St. Grav —10B 114
Perry St. Gdns. Chst —65Uc 130
Perry St. Shaw. Chst —66Uc 130
Perry Vale. SE23 —61Yb 128
Perry Way. S Ock —45Sd 90
Persant Rd. SE6 —61Gc 129
Perseverance Cotts. Rip —93L 173
Perseverance Pl. SW9 —52Qb 104
Perseverance Pl. Rich —56Na 101
Perseverence Pl. Rich —56Na 101
Persfield Clo. Eps —82Va 162
Pershore Clo. Ilf —29Rc 46
Pershore Gro. Cars —72Fb 145
Pert Clo. N10 —23Kb 42
Perth Av. NW9 —31Ta 59
Perth Av. Hay —42Y 77
Perth Av. Slou —4F 72
Perth Clo. SW20 —68Wa 124
Perth Ho. Til —4C 114
Perth Rd. E10 —32Ac 64
Perth Rd. E13 —40Kc 65
Perth Rd. N4 —32Qb 62
Perth Rd. N22 —25Rb 43
Perth Rd. Bark —40Tc 66
Perth Rd. Beck —68Ec 128
Perth Rd. Ilf —30Qc 46
Perth Ter. Ilf —31Sc 66
Perth Trading Est. Slou —3F 72
Perwell Av. Harr —32Ba 57
Perystreete. SE23 —61Yb 128
Pescot Av. Long —69Ce 135
Petands Ct. Horn —34Md 69
(off Randall Dri.)
Peter Av. NW10 —38Xa 60
Peterboat Clo. SE10 —49Gc 85
Peterborough Av. Upm —32Ud 70
Peterborough Ct. EC4
—44Qb 82 (3A 200)
Peterborough Gdns. Ilf —31Nc 66
Peterborough Ho. Borwd —12Qa 21
(off Stratfield Rd.)
Peterborough M. SW6 —54Cb 103
Peterborough Rd. E10 —29Ec 44
Peterborough Rd. SW6 —54Cb 103
Peterborough Rd. Cars —72Gb 145
Peterborough Rd. Harr —32Ga 58
Peterborough Vs. SW6 —53Db 103
Peter Butler Ho. SE1 —47Wb 83
(off Wolseley St.)
Petergate. SW11 —56Eb 103
Peterhead M. Langl —50C 74
Peterhill Clo. Ger X —22A 34
Peter James Bus. Cen. Hay
—47W 76
Peter James Enterprise Cen. NW10
—41Sa 79
Peterley Cen. E2 —40Xb 63
Peters Clo. Dag —32Zc 67
Peters Clo. Stan —23Ma 39
Peters Clo. Well —54Uc 108
Petersfield Av. Romf —23Nd 49
Petersfield Av. Slou —6L 73
Petersfield Av. Stai —64L 119
Petersfield Clo. N18 —22Sb 43
Petersfield Clo. Romf —23Qd 49
Petersfield Cres. Coul —87Nb 164
Petersfield Rise. SW15 —60Xa 102
Petersfield Rd. W3 —47Sa 79
Petersfield Rd. Stai —64L 119
Petersfield Way. W Horn —30Ee 51
Petersham Av. Byfl —84N 157
Petersham Clo. Byfl —84N 157
Petersham Clo. Rich —61Ma 123
Petersham Clo. Sutt —78Cb 145
Petersham Dri. Orp —68Vc 131
Petersham Gdns. Orp —68Vc 131
Petersham La. SW7
—48Eb 81 (3A 202)
Petersham M. SW7
—48Eb 81 (4A 202)
Petersham Pl. SW7
—48Eb 81 (4A 202)
Petersham Rd. Rich —58Ma 101
Petersham Ter. Mitc —76Nb 146
(off Richmond Grn.)
Peters Hill. EC4 —45Sb 83 (4D 200)
Peter's La. EC1 —43Rb 83 (7C 194)
Peter's Path. SE26 —63Xb 127
Peterstone Rd. SE2 —48Xc 87
Peterstow Clo. SW19 —61Ab 124
Peter St. W1 —45Mb 82 (4D 198)
Peter St. Grav —9D 114
Petherton Ct. Harr —30Ha 38
(off Gayton Rd.)
Petherton Ho. N4 —32Sb 63
(off Woodberry Down Est.)
Petherton Rd. N5 —36Sb 63
Petley Rd. W6 —51Za 102
Peto Pl. NW1 —42Kb 82 (5A 192)
Peto St. N. E16 —44Hc 85
Peto St. S. E16 —45Hc 85
Petrie Clo. NW2 —37Ab 60
Pett Clo. Horn —33Kd 69
Petten Clo. Orp —74Zc 151
Petten Gro. Orp —74Yc 151
Petters Rd. Asht —88Pa 161
Petticoat La. E1 —43Ub 83 (2K 201)
Petticoat Sq. E1 —44Vb 83 (2K 201)
Petticoat Tower. E1
—44Vb 83 (2K 201)
(off Petticoat Sq.)
Pettits Boulevd. Romf —25Gd 48
Pettits Clo. Romf —26Gd 48
Pettits La. Romf —26Gd 48
Pettits La. N. Romf —25Fd 48
Pettits Pl. Dag —36Cd 68
Pettits Rd. Dag —36Cd 68
Pettiward Clo. SW15 —56Ya 102
Pettley Gdns. Romf —29Fd 48
Pettman Cres. SE28 —48Tc 86
Pettsgrove Av. Wemb —36La 58
Pett's Hill. N'holt —36Da 57
Petts La. Shep —70Q 120
Pett St. SE18 —49Nc 86
Petts Wood Rd. Orp —71Sc 150
Petty France. SW1
—48Lb 82 (3C 204)
Petworth Clo. Coul —91Lb 180
Petworth Clo. N'holt —38Ba 57
Petworth Gdns. SW20 —69Xa 124
Petworth Gdns. Uxb —39S 56
Petworth Rd. N12 —22Gb 41
Petworth Rd. Bexh —57Cd 110
Petworth St. SW11 —53Gb 103
Petworth Way. Horn —35Hd 68
Petyt Pl. SW3 —51Gb 103
Petyward. SW3 —49Gb 81 (6E 202)
Pevensey Av. N11 —22Mb 42
Pevensey Av. Enf —12Ub 25
Pevensey Clo. Iswth —52Ea 100
Pevensey Ct. W3 —47Ra 79
Pevensey Rd. E7 —35Hc 65
Pevensey Rd. SW17 —63Fb 125
Pevensey Rd. Felt —60Aa 99
Pevensey Rd. Slou —3E 72
Peverel. E6 —44Qc 86
Peverel Ho. Dag —33Cd 68
Peveret Clo. N11 —22Kb 42
Peveril Ct. Dart —58Rd 111
(off Clifton Wlk.)
Peveril Dri. Tedd —64Fa 122
Pewsey Clo. E4 —22Cc 44
Peyton Pl. SE10 —52Ec 106
Pharaoh's Island. Shep —75P 139
Pheasant Clo. E16 —44Kc 85
Pheasant Clo. Purl —85Rb 165
Pheasants Way. Rick —17K 17
Pheasant Wlk. Ger X —21A 34
Phelps Clo. W King —79Ud 154
Phelp St. SE17 —51Tb 105
Phelps Way. Hay —49V 76
Phene St. SW3 —51Gb 103
Philan Way. Romf —23Fd 48
Philbeach Gdns. SW5 —50Cb 81
Philchurch Pl. E1 —44Wb 83
Philip Av. Romf —32Fd 68
Philip Av. Swan —70Fd 132
Philip Clo. Pil H —16Xd 32
Philip Clo. Romf —32Fd 68
Philip Gdns. Croy —75Bc 148
Philip La. N15 —28Tb 43
Philipot Path. SE9 —58Pc 108
Philippa Gdns. SE9 —57Mc 107
Philippa Way. Grays —9D 92
Philip Rd. Rain —41Gd 88
Philip Rd. Stai —65M 119
Philip St. E13 —42Jc 85
Philip Wlk. SE15 —55Wb 105
(in three parts)
Phillida Rd. Romf —26Qd 49
Phillimore Ct. Rad —8Ga 6
Phillimore Gdns. NW10 —39Ya 60
Phillimore Gdns. W8 —47Cb 81
Phillimore Gdns. Clo. W8 —48Cb 81
Phillimore Pl. W8 —47Cb 81
Phillimore Pl. Rad —8Ga 6
Phillimore Ter. W8 —48Cb 81
(off Allen St.)
Phillimore Wlk. W8 —48Cb 81
Phillipers. Wat —8Z 5
Phillipp St. N1 —39Ub 63 (1H 195)
Phillips Clo. Dart —58Kd 111
Phillips Ct. Edgw —23Qa 39
Philpot La. EC3 —45Ub 83 (4H 201)
Philpot La. Chob —1E 188
Philpot Path. Ilf —34Sc 66
Philpots Clo. W Dray —45M 75
Philpot Sq. SW6 —55Db 103
Philpot St. E1 —43Xb 83
(in two parts)
Phineas Pett Rd. SE9 —55Nc 108
Phipp Point. W Mol —69Da 121
Phipp's Bri. Rd. SW19 & Mitc
—68Eb 125
Phipps Hatch La. Enf —10Sb 11
Phipps Ho. W12 —45Xa 80
(off White City Est.)
Phipp's M. SW1
—49Kb 82 (4K 203)
Phipps Rd. Slou —3B 72
(in three parts)
Phipp St. EC2 —42Ub 83 (5H 195)
Phoebeth Rd. SE4 —57Cc 106
Phoenix Clo. E8 —39Vb 63
Phoenix Clo. W Wick —75Fc 149
Phoenix Ct. E4 —20Dc 26
Phoenix Ct. E14 —49Cc 84
Phoenix Ct. Houn —57Z 99
Phoenix Ct. Wemb —34Ra 59
Phoenix Dri. Kes —77Mc 149
Phoenix Pl. WC1
—42Pb 82 (5J 193)
Phoenix Pl. Dart —59Md 111
Phoenix Rd. NW1
—41Mb 82 (3D 192)
Phoenix Rd. SE20 —65Yb 128
Phoenix St. WC2
—44Mb 82 (3E 198)
Phoenix Trading Est. Gnfd
—39La 58
Phoenix Trading Pk. Bren
—50Ma 79
Phoenix Way. Houn —51Y 99
Phoenix Way. N'wd —21V 36
Phygtle, The. Ger X —23A 34
Phyllis Av. N Mald —71Xa 144
Physic Pl. SW3 —51Hb 103
Piazza, The. WC2
—45Nb 82 (4G 199)
(off Covent Garden)
Picardy Manorway. Belv —48Dd 88
Picardy Rd. Belv —50Cd 88
Picardy St. Belv —48Cd 88
Piccadilly. W1 —46Kb 82 (1K 203)
Piccadilly Arc. SW1
(off Piccadilly) —46Lb 82 (6B 198)
Piccadilly Cir. W1
—45Mb 82 (5D 198)
Piccadilly Pl. W1 —45Lb 82 (5C 198)
(off Piccadilly)
Pickard St. EC1 —41Rb 83 (3C 194)
Pickering Av. E6 —41Qc 86
Pickering Ct. Dart —58Rd 111
(off Osborne Rd.)
Pickering M. W2 —44Db 81
Pickering Pl. SW1
—46Lb 82 (7C 198)
(off St James's St.)
Pickering St. N1 —39Rb 63
Pickets Clo. Bush —18Fa 20
Pickets St. SW12 —59Kb 104
Pickett Croft. Stan —25Ma 39
Picketts Lock La. N9 —19Yb 26
Picketts Lock La. Ind. Est. N9
—19Ac 26
Pickford Clo. Bexh —54Ad 109
Pickford La. Bexh —54Ad 109
Pickford Rd. Bexh —55Ad 109
Pickfords Wharf. N1
—40Sb 63 (2D 194)
Pickfords Yd. N17 —23Vb 43
Pick Hill. Wal A —4Hc 13
Pickhurst Grn. Brom —73Hc 149
Pickhurst La. W Wick & Brom
—71Gc 149
Pickhurst Mead. Brom —73Hc 149
Pickhurst Pk. Brom —71Gc 149
Pickhurst Rise. W Wick —74Fc 149
Pickins Piece. Hort —54C 96
Pickmoss La. Otf —88Jd 170
Pickwick Clo. Houn —57Aa 99
Pickwick Gdns. Grav —62Fe 135
Pickwick Ho. SE16 —47Wb 83
(off George Row)
Pickwick Ho. Grav —62Fe 135
Pickwick M. N18 —22Ub 43
Pickwick Pl. Harr —31Ga 58
Pickwick Rd. SE21 —59Tb 105
Pickwick St. SE1
—47Sb 83 (2D 206)
Pickwick Way. Chst —65Sc 130
Pickworth Clo. SW8 —52Nb 104
Picquets Way. Bans —89Bb 163
Picton Pl. W1 —44Jb 82 (3J 197)
Picton St. SE5 —52Tb 105
Piedmont Rd. SE18 —50Tc 86
Pield Heath Av. Uxb —42Q 76
Pield Heath Rd. Uxb —42N 75
Piercing Hill. They B —7Tc 14
Pier Head. E1 —46Xb 83
(off Wapping High St.)
Piermont Pl. Brom —68Nc 130
Piermont Rd. SE22 —57Xb 105
Pier Pde. E16 —46Qc 86
(off Pier Rd.)
Pierrepoint Arc. N1
—40Rb 63 (1B 194)
(off Pierrepoint Row)
Pierrepoint Rd. W3 —45Ra 79
Pierrepoint Row. N1
—40Rb 63 (1B 194)
(off Camden Pas.)
Pier Rd. E16 —47Pc 86
Pier Rd. Eri —51Gd 110
(in two parts)
Pier Rd. Felt —57X 99
Pier Rd. Grav —8B 114
Pier Rd. Grnh —56Xd 112
Pierson Rd. Wind —3B 94
Pier St. E14 —49Ec 84
Pier Ter. SW18 —56Db 103
Pier Wlk. Grays —51Ce 113
Pier Way. SE28 —48Tc 86
Pigeon Ho. La. Coul —97Eb 179
Pigeon La. Hamp —63Ca 121
Piggott St. E14 —44Cc 84
Piggs Corner. Grays —48Ee 91
Piggy La. Chor —16D 16
Pike Clo. Brom —64Kc 129
Pike Clo. Uxb —39P 55
Pike La. Upm —36Vd 70
Pike Rd. NW7 —21Ta 39
Pike's End. Pinn —28X 37
Pikes Hill. Eps —85Ua 162
Pikestone Clo. Hay —42Aa 77
Pikethorne. SE23 —61Zb 128
Pilgrimage St. SE1
—47Tb 83 (2F 207)
Pilgrimage St. SW1 —47Tb 83
Pilgrim Clo. Mord —73Db 145
Pilgrim Clo. Wat —5Z 5
Pilgrim Hill. SE27 —63Sb 127
Pilgrims Clo. N13 —21Pb 42
Pilgrims Clo. N'holt —36Ea 58
Pilgrim's Clo. Pil H —15Vd 32
Pilgrim's Ct. Dart —57Qd 111
Pilgrim's La. NW3 —35Fb 61
Pilgrims' La. Cat —98Pb 180
Pilgrims La. N Stif —46Yd 90
Pilgrims La. Pil H —14Td 32
Pilgrims La. T'sey & W'ham
—96Lc 183
Pilgrim's Pl. NW3 —35Fb 61
Pilgrims Rise. Barn —15Gb 23
Pilgrims Rd. Swans —56Ae 113
Pilgrim St. EC4 —44Rb 83 (3B 200)
Pilgrims View. Grnh —58Yd 112
Pilgrims Way. N19 —32Mb 62
Pilgrims Way. Dart —60Qd 111
Pilgrims Way. Otf & Sev
—88Md 171
Pilgrims Way. S Croy —78Vb 147
Pilgrim's Way. Wemb —32Ra 59
Pilgrims Way. W'ham & Sund
—95Qc 184
Pilgrims Way Cotts. Kems
—89Qd 171
Pilgrims Way E. Otf —87Ld 171
Pilgrims Way W. Otf —88Fd 170
Pilkington Rd. SE15 —54Xb 105
Pilkington Rd. Orp —75Sc 150
Pillions La. Hay —42T 76
Pilot Ind. Cen., The. NW10
—42Ta 79
Pilots Pl. Grav —8E 114
Pilsden Clo. SW19 —60Za 102
Piltdown Rd. Wat —21Z 37
Pilton Est., The. Croy —75Rb 147
Pilton Pl. SE17 —50Sb 83 (7E 206)
Pimlico Rd. SW1
—50Jb 82 (7H 203)
Pimlico Wlk. N1
—41Ub 83 (3H 195)
Pimpernel Way. Romf —23Md 49
Pinchbeck Rd. Orp —79Vc 151
Pinchfield. Rick —22F 34
Pinchin St. E1 —45Wb 83
Pincott La. W Hor —100R 174
Pincott Pl. SE4 —56Zb 106
Pincott Rd. SW19 —66Eb 125
Pincott Rd. Bexh —57Cd 110
Pincroft Wood. Long —69Ee 135
Pindar St. EC2 —43Ub 83 (7H 195)
Pindock M. W9 —42Db 81
Pineapple Ct. SW1
—48Lb 82 (3B 204)
(off Wilfred St.)
Pine Av. E15 —36Fc 65
Pine Av. Grav —10F 114
Pine Av. W Wick —74Dc 148
Pine Clo. N14 —17Lb 24
Pine Clo. N19 —33Lb 62
Pine Clo. SE20 —67Yb 128
Pine Clo. Chesh —1Zb 12
Pine Clo. Kenl —89Tb 165
Pine Clo. New Haw —83K 157
Pine Clo. Stan —21Ka 38
Pine Clo. Swan —70Hd 132
Pine Clo. Wok —4F 188
Pine Coombe. Croy —77Zb 148
Pine Ct. E4 —23Bc 44
Pine Ct. N21 —16Pb 24
Pine Ct. N'holt —42Aa 77
Pinecourt. Upm —35Rd 69
Pine Cres. Cars —83Fb 163
Pine Cres. Hut —14Fe 33
Pinecrest Gdns. Orp —77Rc 150
Pinecroft. Gid P —28Ld 49
Pinecroft. Hut —17De 33
Pinecroft Ct. SE18 —52Wc 109
Pinecroft Cres. Barn —14Ab 22
Pine Dean. Bookh —97Da 175
Pine Dene. SE15 —53Xb 105
Pinefield Clo. E14 —45Cc 84
Pinefields. Add —77K 139
(off Church Rd.)
Pine Gdns. Ruis —32X 57
Pine Gdns. Surb —72Qa 143
Pine Glade. Orp —77Pc 150
Pine Gro. N4 —33Nb 62
Pine Gro. N20 —18Bb 23
Pine Gro. SW19 —64Bb 125
Pine Gro. Brick —2Ba 5
Pine Gro. Bush —12Ba 19
Pine Gro. Wey —78R 140
Pine Gro. M. Wey —78S 140
Pine Hill. Eps —87Ta 161
Pinehurst. Sev —93Nd 187
Pinehurst Clo. Abb L —4U 4
Pinehurst Clo. Tad —94Cb 179
Pinehurst Wlk. Orp —74Tc 150
Pine Needle La. Sev —95Kd 187
Pine Pl. Bans —86Za 162
Pine Pl. Hay —42W 76
Pine Ridge. Cars —81Jb 164
Pineridge Ct. Barn —14Za 22
Pine Rd. N11 —19Jb 24
Pine Rd. NW2 —35Ya 60
Pine Rd. Wok —8F 188
Pines Av. Enf —8Yb 12
Pines Clo. N'wd —23U 36
Pines Rd. Brom —68Nc 130
Pines, The. N14 —15Lb 24
Pines, The. SE19 —66Rb 127
Pines, The. Borwd —12Pa 21
Pines, The. Coul —90Kb 164
Pines, The. Grays —46De 91
Pines, The. Purl —85Sb 165
Pines, The. Sun —69W 120
Pines, The. Wfd G —20Jc 27
Pine St. EC1 —42Qb 82 (5K 193)
Pine Tree Clo. Houn —53X 99
Pine Tree Hill. Wok —88F 156
Pinetree Ho. Wat —8Aa 5
Pine Tree Lodge. Short —70Hc 129
Pine Trees Bus. Pk. Stai —64G 118
Pine Trees Dri. Uxb —35N 55
Pine View Mnr. Epp —2Vc 15
Pine Wlk. Bans —89Hb 163
Pine Wlk. Bookh —97Da 175
Pine Wlk. Cars —82Fb 163
Pine Wlk. Cat —94Ub 181
Pine Wlk. Cob —86Z 159
Pine Wlk. E Hor —100V 174
Pine Wlk. Surb —72Qa 143
Pine Wlk. E. Cars —83Fb 163
Pine Wlk. W. Cars —82Fb 163
Pine Way. Egh —5M 117
Pine Wood. Sun —67W 120
Pinewood Av. New Haw —81L 157

Pinewood Av.—Postway M.

Pinewood Av. Pinn —23Da 37
Pinewood Av. Rain —42Kd 89
Pinewood Av. Sev —93Md 187
Pinewood Av. Sidc —60Uc 108
Pinewood Av. Uxb —44P 75
Pinewood Clo. Borwd —11Ta 21
Pinewood Clo. Croy —76Ac 148
Pinewood Clo. Ger X —31A 54
Pinewood Clo. Iver —38E 54
Pinewood Clo. Orp —74Tc 150
Pinewood Clo. Pinn —23Da 37
Pinewood Clo. Stanf —8K 93
Pinewood Clo. Wok —87C 156
Pinewood Ct. SW4 —58Mb 104
Pinewood Ct. Add —77L 139
Pinewood Ct. Enf —14Rb 25
Pinewood Dri. Orp —78Uc 150
Pinewood Dri. Pot B —3Bb 9
Pinewood Dri. Stai —64J 119
Pinewood Grn. Iver —38E 54
Pinewood Gro. W5 —44La 78
Pinewood Gro. New Haw —82K 157
Pinewood Lodge. Bush —18Fa 20
Pinewood M. Stai —58M 97
Pinewood Pk. New Haw —83K 157
Pinewood Rd. SE2 —51Zc 109
Pinewood Rd. Brom —70Jc 129
Pinewood Rd. Felt —62X 121
Pinewood Rd. Hav —21Ed 48
Pinewood Rd. Iver —37D 54
Pinewood Rd. Vir W —10L 117
Pinewood Way. Hut —15Fe 33
Pinfold Rd. SW16 —63Nb 126
Pinfold Rd. Bush —12Ba 19
Pinglestone Clo. W Dray —52N 97
Pinkcoat Clo. Felt —62X 121
Pinkerton Pl. SW16 —63Mb 126
Pinkham Mans. W4 —50Qa 79
Pinkham Way. N11 —24Jb 42
Pink La. Burn —10A 52
Pink's Hill. Swan —71Gd 152
Pinkwell Av. Hay —49T 76
Pinkwell La. Hay —49S 76
Pinley Gdns. Dag —39Xc 67
Pinnacle Hill. Bexh —56Dd 110
Pinnacle Hill N. Bexh —56Dd 110
Pinnacle Pl. Stan —21Ka 38
Pinnacles. Wal A —6Gc 13
Pinn Clo. Uxb —44M 75
Pinnell Rd. SE9 —56Mc 107
Pinner Ct. Pinn —28Ca 37
Pinner Grn. Pinn —26Y 37
Pinner Gro. Pinn —28Aa 37
Pinner Hill. Pinn —24X 37
Pinner Hill Farm. Pinn —25X 37
Pinner Hill Rd. Pinn —24X 37
Pinner Pk. Av. Harr —27Da 37
Pinner Pk. Gdns. Harr —26Ea 38
Pinner Rd. Harr —28Ca 37
Pinner Rd. N'wd & Pinn —25V 36
Pinner Rd. Pinn —28Ba 37
Pinner Rd. Wat —16Z 19
Pinner View. Harr —28Ea 38
Pinnocks Av. Grav —10D 114
Pinn Way. Ruis —31T 56
Pinstone Way. Ger X —33D 54
Pintail Clo. E6 —43Nc 86
Pintail Rd. Wfd G —24Kc 45
Pintail Way. Hay —43Z 77
Pinter Ho. SW9 —54Nb 104
(off Grantham Rd.)
Pinto Clo. Borwd —16Ta 21
Pinto Way. SE3 —56Kc 107
Pioneer Pl. Croy —81Cc 166
Pioneer Way. W12 —44Xa 80
Pioneer Way. Swan —69Gd 132
Piper Clo. N7 —36Pb 62
Piper Rd. King T —69Qa 123
Pipers Clo. Burn —1A 72
Pipers Clo. Cob —87Z 159
Piper's End. Vir W —9P 117
Piper's Gdns. Croy —73Ac 148
Pipers Grn. NW9 —29Sa 39
Pipers Grn. La. Edgw —20Na 21
(in two parts)
Piper's Grn. Rd. Bras —100Wc 185
Pipers La. Bras —99Wc 185
Pipewell Rd. Cars —72Gb 145
Pippin Clo. Croy —74Bc 148
Pippins Clo. W Dray —48M 75
Pippins Ct. Ashf —65R 120
Piquet Rd. SE20 —68Yb 128
Pirbright Cres. New Ad —79Ec 148
Pirbright Rd. SW18 —60Bb 103
Pirie Clo. SE5 —55Tb 105
Pirie St. E16 —46Kc 85
Pirrip Clo. Grav —10H 115
Pitcairn Clo. Romf —28Cd 48
Pitcairn Ho. E9 —38Yb 64
Pitcairn Rd. Mitc —66Hb 125
Pitchford La. Oxt —96Hc 183
Pitchford St. E15 —38Fc 65
Pitfield. Hart —70Be 135
Pitfield Cres. SE28 —46Wc 87
Pitfield Est. N1 —41Ub 83 (3H 195)
Pitfield St. N1 —41Ub 83 (4H 195)
Pitfield Way. NW10 —37Sa 59
Pitfield Way. Enf —11Yb 26
Pitfold Clo. SE12 —58Kc 107
Pitfold Rd. SE12 —58Jc 107
Pitlake. Croy —75Rb 147
Pitman St. SE5 —52Sb 105
Pitsea Pl. E1 —44Zb 84
Pitsea St. E1 —44Zb 84
Pitshanger La. W5 —42Ka 78
Pitson Clo. Add —77M 139
Pitt Cres. SW19 —63Db 125
Pittman Clo. Ingve —22Ee 51
Pittman Gdns. Ilf —36Sc 66
Pitt Pl. Eps —86Ua 162
Pitt Rd. Eps —86Ua 162
Pitt Rd. Harr —33Ea 58
Pitt Rd. Orp —77Sc 150
Pitt Rd. T Hth —71Sb 147
Pitt's Ct. SE1 —46Ub 83
Pitt's Head M. W1
—46Jb 82 (7J 197)
Pitts Ho. M. W1 —46Jb 82
Pittsmead Av. Brom —73Jc 149
Pitts Rd. Slou —6G 72
Pitt St. SE15 —53Vb 105
Pitt St. W8 —47Cb 81
Pittville Gdns. SE25 —69Wb 127
Pittwood. Shenf —18Ce 33
Pitwood Grn. Tad —92Ya 178
Pixley St. E14 —44Bc 84
Pixton Way. Croy —81Ac 166
Place Farm Av. Orp —74Tc 150
Placehouse La. Coul —91Pb 180
Plackett Way. Slou —6B 72
Plain Ride. Wind —10A 94
Plain, The. Epp —1Xc 15
Plaisterers Highwalk. EC2
(off Noble St.) —43Sb 83 (1D 200)
Plaistow Clo. Stanf —1M 93
Plaistow Gro. E15 —39Hc 65
Plaistow Gro. Brom —66Kc 129
Plaistow La. Brom —66Jc 129
(in two parts)
Plaistow Pk. Rd. E13 —40Kc 65
Plaistow Rd. E15 & E13 —39Hc 65
Plaistow Wharf. E16 —46Jc 85
Plaitford Clo. Rick —19N 17
Plane Av. Grav —59Fe 113
Plane Ho. Short —68Gc 129
Planes, The. Cher —73L 139
Plane St. SE26 —62Xb 127
Planetree Ct. W6 —49Za 80
(off Brook Grn.)
Plane Tree Cres. Felt —62X 121
Plane Tree Wlk. SE19 —65Ub 127
Plantagenet Clo. Wor Pk —77Ta 143
Plantagenet Gdns. Romf —31Zc 67
Plantagenet Pl. Romf —31Zc 67
Plantagenet Rd. Barn —14Eb 23
Plantain Pl. SE1 —47Tb 83 (1F 207)
Plantation Dri. Orp —74Zc 151
Plantation Ho. EC3
—45Ub 83 (4H 201)
Plantation La. Warl —91Ac 182
Plantation Pl. SW1 —47Tb 83
Plantation Rd. Eri —53Jd 110
Plantation Rd. Swan —66Jd 132
Plantation, The. SE3 —54Jc 107
Plasel Ct. E13 —39Kc 65
(off Pawsey Clo.)
Plashet Clo. Stanf —1M 93
Plashet Gdns. Brtwd —21Ce 51
Plashet Gro. E6 —39Lc 65
Plashet Rd. E13 —39Jc 65
Plassy Rd. SE6 —59Dc 106
Platford Grn. Horn —28Nd 49
Platina St. EC2 —42Tb 83 (5G 195)
(off Tabernacle St.)
Plato Rd. SW2 —56Nb 104
Platt's La. NW3 —35Cb 61
Platts Rd. Enf —11Yb 26
Platt St. NW1 —40Mb 62 (1D 192)
Plawsfield Rd. Beck —67Zb 128
Plaxtol Clo. Brom —67Lc 129
Plaxtol Rd. Eri —52Cd 110
Plaxton Ct. E11 —34Hc 65
Playfair St. W6 —50Ya 80
Playfield Av. Romf —25Ed 48
Playfield Cres. SE22 —57Vb 105
Playfield Rd. Edgw —26Sa 39
Playford Rd. N4 —33Pb 62
(in two parts)
Playgreen Way. SE6 —62Cc 128
Playground Clo. Beck —68Zb 128
Playhouse Yd. EC4
—44Rb 83 (3B 200)
Plaza, The. W1 —44Lb 82 (2C 198)
Pleasance Rd. SW15 —57Xa 102
Pleasance Rd. Orp —68Xc 131
Pleasance, The. SW15 —56Xa 102
Pleasant Gro. Croy —76Bc 148
Pleasant Pl. N1 —38Rb 63
Pleasant Pl. Rick —24G 34
Pleasant Pl. S Harr —32Fa 58
Pleasant Pl. W on T —79Y 141
Pleasant Row. NW1 —39Kb 62
Pleasant View. Eri —50Gd 88
Pleasant View Pl. Orp —78Rc 150
Pleasant Way. Wemb —40La 58
Pleasure Pit Rd. Asht —90Na 161
Plender Pl. NW1 —39Lb 62 (1C 192)
(off Plender St.)
Plender St. NW1
—39Lb 62 (1B 192)
Pleshey Rd. N7 —35Mb 62
Plesman Way. Wall —81Nb 164
Plevna Cres. N15 —30Ub 43
Plevna Rd. N9 —20Wb 25
Plevna Rd. Hamp —67Da 121
Plevna St. E14 —48Ec 84
Pleydell Av. SE19 —66Vb 127
Pleydell Av. W6 —49Va 80
Pleydell Ct. EC4 —44Qb 82 (3A 200)
(off Mitre Ct.)
Pleydell Est. EC1 —41Sb 83 (4E 194)
(off Lever St.)
Pleydell St. EC4 —44Qb 82 (3A 200)
(off Bouverie St.)
Plimsoll Clo. E14 —44Dc 84
Plimsoll Rd. N4 —34Qb 62
Plough Ct. EC3 —45Tb 83 (4G 201)
Plough Farm Clo. Ruis —30T 36
Plough Hill. Cuff —1Nb 10
Plough Ind. Est. Lea —92Ja 176
Plough La. SE22 —58Vb 105
Plough La. SW19 & SW17
—64Db 125
Plough La. D'side —89W 158
Plough La. Hare —23L 35
Plough La. Purl —81Pb 164
Plough La. Sarr —5H 3
Plough La. Stoke P —9M 53
Plough La. Wall —77Nb 146
Plough La. Clo. Wall —78Nb 146
Plough Lees La. Slou —5J 73
Ploughmans Clo. NW1 —39Mb 62
Ploughmans End. Iswth —57Fa 100
Plough Pl. EC4 —44Qb 82 (2A 200)
Plough Rise. Upm —31Ud 70
Plough Rd. SW11 —55Fb 103
Plough Rd. Eps —81Ta 161
Plough St. E1 —44Wb 83
Plough Ter. SW11 —56Fb 103
Plough Way. SE16 —49Zb 84
Plough Yd. EC2 —42Ub 83 (6J 195)
Plover Clo. Stai —62H 119
Plover Gdns. Upm —32Vd 70
Plover Way. SE16 —48Ac 84
Plover Way. Hay —44Z 77
Plowden Bldgs. EC4
(off Temple) —45Qb 82 (4K 199)
Plowman Clo. N18 —22Tb 43
Plowman Way. Dag —32Yc 67
Plumber's Row. E1 —43Wb 83
Plumbridge St. SE10 —53Ec 106
Plum Garth. Bren —49Ma 79
Plum La. SE18 —52Rc 108
Plummer La. Mitc —68Hb 125
Plummer Rd. SW4 —59Mb 104
Plumpton Av. Horn —35Nd 69
Plumpton Clo. N'holt —37Ca 57
Plumpton Way. Cars —76Gb 145
Plums Clo. E14 —44Dc 84
Plumstead Comn. Rd. SE18
—51Rc 108
Plumstead High St. SE18 —49Tc 86
Plumstead Rd. SE18 —49Rc 86
Plumtree Clo. Dag —37Dd 68
Plumtree Clo. Wall —80Mb 146
Plumtree Ct. EC4 —44Rb 83 (2B 200)
Plumtree Mead. Lou —13Qc 28
Plymouth Dri. Sev —96Ld 187
Plymouth Ho. Bark —38Wc 67
(off Keir Hardie Way)
Plymouth Pk. Sev —96Ld 187
Plymouth Rd. E16 —43Jc 85
Plymouth Rd. Brom —67Kc 129
Plymouth Rd. Slou —3C 72
Plymouth Wharf. E14 —49Fc 85
Plympton Av. NW6 —38Bb 61
Plympton Clo. Belv —48Ad 87
Plympton Pl. NW8
—42Gb 81 (6D 190)
Plympton Rd. NW6 —38Bb 61
Plympton St. NW8
—42Gb 81 (6D 190)
Plymstock Rd. Well —52Yc 109
Pocketsdell La. Bov —1A 2
Pocklington Clo. NW9 —26Ua 40
Pocklington Clo. W12 —48Wa 80
(off Goldhawk Rd.)
Pococks La. Eton —10J 73
Pocock St. SE1 —47Rb 83 (1B 206)
Podmore Rd. SW18 —56Eb 103
Poet's Rd. N5 —36Tb 63
Poets Way. Harr —28Ga 38
Pointalls Clo. N3 —26Eb 41
Point Clo. SE10 —53Ec 106
Pointer Clo. SE28 —44Zc 87
Pointers Clo. E14 —50Dc 84
Pointers Cotts. Rich —61La 122
Pointers Rd. Cob —88S 158
Pointers, The. Asht —92Na 177
Point Hill. SE10 —53Ec 106
Point Pleasant. SW18 —56Cb 103
Point Ter. E7 —36Kc 65
(off Claremont Rd.)
Point, The. Ruis —35W 56
Poland M. W1 —44Lb 82
Poland St. W1 —44Lb 82 (2C 198)
Polebrook Rd. SE3 —55Lc 107
Pole Cat All. Brom —75Hc 149
Polecroft La. SE6 —61Bc 128
Pole Hill Rd. E4 —17Ec 26
Pole Hill Rd. Uxb —42R 76
Polesden Gdns. SW20 —68Xa 124
Polesden La. Send —95H 173
Polesden Rd. Bookh —100Da 175
Polesden View. Bookh —99Da 175
Poles Hill. Sarr —5G 2
Polesteeple Hill. Big H —89Mc 167
Polesworth Rd. Dag —38Zc 67
Poley Rd. Stanf —2L 93
Polhill. Hals —87Ed 170
Police Sta. La. Bush —17Da 19
Police Sta. Rd. W on T —79Y 141
Pollard Av. Den —30H 35
Pollard Clo. E16 —45Jc 85
Pollard Clo. N7 —35Pb 62
Pollard Clo. Chig —22Wc 47
Pollard Clo. Old Win —7M 95
Pollard Rd. N20 —19Gb 23
Pollard Rd. Mord —71Fb 145
Pollard Rd. Wok —88D 156
Pollard Row. E2 —41Wb 83
Pollards. Rick —22F 34
Pollards Clo. Chesh —1Sb 11
Pollards Clo. Lou —15Lc 27
Pollards Cres. SW16 —69Nb 126
Pollards Hill E. SW16 —69Pb 126
Pollards Hill N. SW16 —69Nb 126
Pollards Hill S. SW16 —69Nb 126
Pollards Hill W. SW16 —69Pb 126
Pollard St. E2 —41Wb 83
Pollardswood Grange. Chal G
—14A 16
Pollards Wood Rd. SW16
—69Nb 126
Pollard Wlk. Sidc —65Yc 131
Pollen St. W1 —44Kb 82 (3B 198)
Pollitt Dri. NW8 —42Fb 81 (5C 190)
Pollyhaugh. Eyns —76Nd 153
Polperro Clo. Orp —72Vc 151
Polsted Rd. SE6 —59Bc 106
Polthorne Gro. SE18 —49Tc 86
Polworth Rd. SW16 —64Nb 126
Polygon Bus. Cen. Coln —54H 97
Polygon Rd. NW1
—40Mb 62 (2D 192)
Polygon, The. SW4 —56Lb 104
Polytechnic St. SE18 —49Qc 86
Pomell Way. E1 —44Vb 83 (2K 201)
Pomeroy Cres. Wat —8X 5
Pomeroy St. SE14 —52Yb 106
Pomfret Rd. SE5 —55Sb 105
Pompadour Clo. War —22Yd 50
Pond Clo. SE3 —54Jc 107
Pond Clo. Hare —26L 35
Pond Clo. W on T —79V 140
Pond Cottage La. W Wick
—74Cc 148
Pond Cotts. SE21 —60Ub 105
Ponders End. Ind. Est. Enf
—15Ac 26
Ponder St. N7 —38Pb 62
Pond Farm Est. E5 —34Yb 64
Pondfield Ho. SE27 —64Sb 127
Pondfield La. Brtwd —21Ce 51
Pondfield La. Shorne —6N 137
Pondfield Rd. Brom —74Gc 149
Pondfield Rd. Dag —36Dd 68
Pondfield Rd. Kenl —88Rb 165
Pondfield Rd. Orp —76Rc 150
Pond Grn. Ruis —33U 56
Pond Hill Gdns. Sutt —79Ab 144
Pond Mead. SE22 —58Tb 105
Pond Path. Chst —65Rc 130
Pond Piece. Oxs —85Da 159
Pond Pl. SW3 —49Gb 81 (6D 202)
Pond Pl. Asht —89Na 161
Pond Rd. E15 —40Gc 65
Pond Rd. SE3 —54Hc 107
Pond Rd. Egh —65E 118
Pond Rd. Wok —8D 188
Pondside Clo. Hay —51T 98
Pond Sq. N6 —32Jb 62
Ponds, The. Wey —79U 140
Pond St. NW3 —36Gb 61
Pond Wlk. Upm —33Ud 70
Pond Way. Tedd —65La 122
Pondwood Rise. Orp —73Uc 150
Ponler St. E1 —44Xb 83
Ponsard Rd. NW10 —41Xa 80
Ponsford St. E9 —37Yb 64
Ponside Clo. Hay —51T 98
Ponsonby Pl. SW1
—50Mb 82 (7E 204)
Ponsonby Rd. SW15 —59Xa 102
Ponsonby Ter. SW1
—50Mb 82 (7E 204)
Pontefract Rd. Brom —64Hc 129
Pontoise Clo. Sev —94Hd 186
Ponton Rd. SW8 —52Mb 104
Pont St. SW1 —48Hb 81 (4F 203)
Pont St. M. SW1
—48Hb 81 (4F 203)
Pontypool Pl. SE1
—47Rb 83 (1B 206)
Pontypool Wlk. Romf —23Ld 49
Pony Chase. Cob —85Ba 159
Pool Clo. Beck —64Cc 128
Pool Clo. W Mol —71Ba 141
Pool Ct. SE6 —61Cc 128
Poole Clo. Ruis —33U 56
Poole Ct. Houn —54Aa 99
Poole Ct. Rd. Houn —54Aa 99
Poole Ho. Grays —7E 92
Poole Rd. E9 —37Zb 64
Poole Rd. Eps —79Ta 143
Poole Rd. Horn —31Pd 69
Poole Rd. Wok —90A 156
Pooles Bldgs. WC1
—42Qb 82 (6K 193)
(off Mt. Pleasant)
Pooles Cotts. Rich —61Ma 123
Pooles La. SW10 —52Eb 103
Pooles La. Dag —40Ad 67
Pooles Pk. N4 —33Qb 62
Poole St. N1 —39Tb 63 (1F 195)
Poole Way. Hay —41U 76
Pooley Av. Egh —64D 118
Pooley Grn. Clo. Egh —64E 118
Pooley Grn. Rd. Egh —64D 118
Pool La. Slou —5J 73
Poolmans Rd. Wind —5B 94
Poolmans St. SE16 —47Zb 84
Pool Rd. Harr —31Fa 58
Pool Rd. W Mol —71Ba 141
Poolsford Rd. NW9 —28Ua 40
Poonah St. E1 —44Yb 84
Pope Clo. SW19 —65Fb 125
Pope Clo. Felt —60V 98
Pope Rd. Brom —71Mc 149
Popes Av. Twic —61Ga 122
Popes Clo. Coln —52D 96
Popes Ct. Twic —61Ga 122
Popes Dri. N3 —25Cb 41
Popes Gro. Croy —76Bc 148
Popes Gro. Twic —61Ha 122
Pope's Head All. EC3
—44Tb 83 (3G 201)
Popes La. W5 —48Ma 79
Popes La. Wat —9X 5
Pope's Rd. SW9 —55Qb 104
Pope's Rd. Abb L —3U 4
Pope St. SE1 —47Ub 83 (2J 207)
Popham Clo. Felt —62Ba 121
Popham Gdns. Rich —55Qa 101
Popham Rd. N1 —39Sb 63
Popham St. N1 —39Rb 63
(in two parts)
Pop-In Commercial Cen. Wemb
—36Ra 59
Popinjays Row. Cheam —78Za 144
(off Netley Clo.)
Poplar Av. Grav —3E 136
Poplar Av. Lea —94Ka 176
Poplar Av. Mitc —67Hb 125
Poplar Av. Orp —75Rc 150
Poplar Av. S'hall —48Da 77
Poplar Av. W Dray —45P 75
Poplar Bath St. E14 —44Dc 84
Poplar Bus. Pk. E14 —45Ec 84
Poplar Clo. Coln —53G 96
Poplar Clo. Pinn —25Z 37
Poplar Ct. SW19 —64Cb 125
Poplar Ct. N'holt —40Y 57
Poplar Cres. Eps —79Sa 143
Poplar Dri. Bans —86Za 162
Poplar Dri. Hut —16Ee 33
Poplar Farm Clo. Eps —79Sa 143
Poplar Gdns. SE28 —45Yc 87
Poplar Gdns. N Mald —68Ta 123
Poplar Gro. N11 —23Jb 42
Poplar Gro. W6 —47Ya 80
Poplar Gro. N Mald —68Ta 123
Poplar Gro. Wemb —34Sa 59
Poplar Gro. Wok —91A 172
Poplar High St. E14 —45Dc 84
Poplar Ho. Langl —50B 74
Poplar M. W12 —46Ya 80
(off Uxbridge Rd.)
Poplar Mt. Belv —49Dd 88
Poplar Pl. SE28 —45Yc 87
Poplar Pl. W2 —45Db 81
Poplar Pl. Hay —45W 76
Poplar Rd. SE24 —56Sb 105
Poplar Rd. SW19 —68Cb 125
Poplar Rd. Ashf —64S 120
Poplar Rd. Den —36L 55
Poplar Rd. Lea —94Ka 176
Poplar Rd. Sutt —74Bb 145
Poplar Rd. S. SW19 —69Cb 125
Poplar Row. They B —9Uc 14
Poplars Av. NW2 —37Ya 60
Poplars Clo. Long —69Ee 135
Poplars Clo. Ruis —32U 56
Poplars Clo. Wat —4X 5
Poplar Shaw. Wal A —5Hc 13
Poplars Rd. E17 —30Dc 44
Poplars, The. N14 —15Kb 24
Poplars, The. Abr —13Xc 29
Poplars, The. Borwd —11Qa 21
Poplar St. Romf —28Ed 48
Poplar View. Wemb —33Ma 59
Poplar Wlk. SE24 —56Sb 105
Poplar Wlk. Cat —95Ub 181
Poplar Wlk. Croy —74Sb 147
Poplar Way. Felt —62W 120
Poplar Way. Ilf —28Sc 46
Poppins Ct. EC4
—44Rb 83 (3B 200)
Poppleton Rd. E11 —30Gc 45
Poppy Clo. Pil H —15Xd 32
Poppy Clo. Wall —74Jb 146
Poppy La. Croy —73Yb 148
Porchester Clo. SE5 —56Tb 105
Porchester Clo. Hart —70Be 135
Porchester Clo. Horn —30Nd 49
Porchester Gdns. W2 —45Db 81
Porchester Gdns. M. W2 —44Db 81
Porchester Mead. Beck —65Cc 128
Porchester M. W2 —44Db 81
Porchester Pl. W2
—44Gb 81 (3E 196)
Porchester Rd. W2 —44Db 81
Porchester Rd. King T —68Ra 123
Porchester Sq. W2 —44Db 81
Porchester Ter. W2 —45Eb 81
Porchester Ter. Gdns. M. W2
—44Db 81
Porchester Ter. N. W2 —44Db 81
Porchfield Clo. Grav —1E 136
Porchfield Clo. Sutt —82Db 163
Porch Way. N20 —20Hb 23
Porcupine Clo. SE9 —61Nc 130
Porden Rd. SW2 —56Pb 104
Porlock Av. Harr —32Ea 58
Porlock Ho. SE26 —62Wb 127
Porlock Rd. W10 —42Za 80
Porlock Rd. Enf —17Vb 25
Porlock St. SE1 —47Tb 83 (1G 207)
Porlock St. SW1 —47Tb 83
Porrington Clo. Chst —67Qc 130
Porson Ct. SE13 —55Dc 106
Portal Clo. SE27 —62Qb 126
Portal Clo. Ruis —35X 57
(in two parts)
Portal Clo. Uxb —38N 55
(in two parts)
Port Av. Grnh —58Xd 112
Portbury Clo. SE15 —53Wb 105
Port Cres. E13 —42Kc 85
Portcullis Lodge Rd. Enf —13Tb 25
Portelet Rd. E1 —41Zb 84
Porten Rd. W14 —48Ab 80
Porter Clo. Grays —51Yd 112
Porter Rd. E6 —44Pc 86
Porters Av. Dag —37Xc 67
Porters Clo. Brtwd —18Wd 32
Porters Pk. Dri. Shenl —4Na 7
Porter St. SE1 —46Sb 83 (6E 200)
Porter St. W1 —43Hb 81 (7G 191)
Porters Wlk. E1 —45Xb 83
(off Pennington St.)
Porters & Walters Almshouses. N22
(off Nightingale Rd.) —24Pb 42
Porters Way. W Dray —48P 75
Porteus Rd. W2 —43Eb 81 (7B 190)
Portgate Clo. W9 —42Bb 81
Porthcawe Rd. SE26 —63Ac 128
Port Hill. Prat B —84Xc 169
Porthkerry Av. Well —56Wc 109
Portia Ct. SE11 —50Rb 83 (7B 206)
(off Opal St.)
Portia Ct. Bark —38Wc 67
Portia Way. E3 —42Bc 84
Porticos, The. SW3 —51Fb 103
(off Kings Rd.)
Portinscale Rd. SW15 —57Ab 102
Portland Av. N16 —32Vb 63
Portland Av. Grav —1D 136
Portland Av. N Mald —73Va 144
Portland Av. Sidc —58Wc 109
Portland Clo. Romf —29Ad 47
Portland Clo. Slou —2B 72
Portland Cres. SE9 —61Nc 130
Portland Cres. Felt —63T 120
Portland Cres. Gnfd —42Da 77
Portland Cres. Stan —26Ma 39
Portland Dri. Chesh —3Wb 11
Portland Dri. Enf —10Ub 11
Portland Dri. Red —100Mb 180
Portland Gdns. N4 —30Rb 43
Portland Gdns. Romf —29Zc 47
Portland Gro. SW8 —53Pb 104
Portland Ho. Mers —100Lb 180
Portland M. W1 —44Lb 82 (3C 198)
(off Livonia St.)
Portland Pl. W1 —42Kb 82 (6K 191)
Portland Pl. Eps —84Ua 162
Portland Rise. N4 —32Rb 63
Portland Rise Est. N4 —32Sb 63
Portland Rd. N15 —28Vb 43
Portland Rd. SE9 —61Nc 130
Portland Rd. SE25 —70Wb 127
Portland Rd. W11 —45Ab 80
Portland Rd. Ashf —62N 119
Portland Rd. Brom —63Lc 129
Portland Rd. Grav —10D 114
Portland Rd. Hay —41U 76
Portland Rd. King T —69Na 123
Portland Rd. Mitc —68Gb 125
Portland Rd. N'fleet —58Fe 113
Portland Rd. S'hall —48Ba 77
Portlands. Ger X —30A 34
Portland Sq. E1 —46Xb 83
Portland St. SE17
—50Tb 83 (7F 207)
Portland Ter. Rich —56Ma 101
Portland Wlk. SE17 —51Tb 105
Portley La. Cat —93Ub 181
Portley Wood Rd. Whyt —92Vb 181
Portman Av. SW14 —55Ta 101
Portman Bldgs. NW1
—42Gb 81 (6E 190)
(off Broadley Ter.)
Portman Clo. W1
—44Jb 82 (2G 197)
Portman Clo. Bex —60Gd 110
Portman Clo. Bexh —55Ad 109
Portman Dri. Wfd G —26Mc 45
Portman Gdns. NW9 —26Ta 39
Portman Gdns. Uxb —38Q 56
Portman M. S. W1
—44Jb 82 (3H 197)
Portman Pl. E2 —41Yb 84
Portman Rd. King T —68Pa 123
Portman Sq. W1
—44Jb 82 (2H 197)
Portman St. W1 —44Jb 82 (3H 197)
Portmeadow Wlk. SE2 —47Zc 87
Portmeers Clo. E17 —30Bc 44
Portmore Gdns. Romf —22Cd 48
Portmore Pk. Rd. Wey —77P 139
Portmore Quays. Wey —77P 139
Portmore Way. Wey —76Q 140
Portnall Dri. Vir W —10K 117
Portnall Rise. Vir W —10K 117
Portnall Rd. W9 —40Bb 61
Portnall Rd. Vir W —10K 117
Portnalls Clo. Coul —88Kb 164
Portnalls Rise. Coul —88Lb 164
Portnalls Rd. Coul —90Kb 164
Portnoi Clo. Romf —26Fd 48
Portobello Ct. W11 —44Bb 81
Portobello M. W11 —45Cb 81
Portobello Pde. W King —80Wd 154
Portobello Rd. W10 —43Ab 80
Portobello Rd. W11 —44Bb 81
Portpool La. EC1
—43Qb 82 (7K 193)
Portree Clo. N22 —24Pb 42
Portree St. E14 —44Fc 85
Portsdown. Edgw —22Qa 39
Portsdown Av. NW11 —30Bb 41
Portsdown M. NW11 —30Bb 41
Portsea M. W2 —44Gb 81 (3E 196)
(off Portsea Pl.)
Portsea Pl. W2 —44Gb 81 (3E 196)
Portsea Rd. Til —3E 114
Portslade Rd. SW8 —54Lb 104
Portsmouth Av. Th Dit —73Ja 142
Portsmouth Bldgs. SE1
—48Ub 83 (4H 207)
(off Swan Mead)
Portsmouth Ct. Slou —5J 73
Portsmouth Rd. SW15 —59Xa 102
Portsmouth Rd. Cob —89R 158
Portsmouth Rd. Esh —79Ca 141
Portsmouth Rd. King T —70Ma 123
Portsmouth Rd. Rip —97H 173
Portsmouth Rd. Th Dit & Surb
—75Ga 142
Portsmouth Rd. W End —82Aa 159
Portsmouth St. WC2
—44Pb 82 (3H 199)
Portsoken St. E1
—45Vb 83 (4K 201)
Portswood Pl. SW15 —58Va 102
Portugal Gdns. Twic —61Ea 122
Portugal Rd. Wok —88B 156
Portugal St. WC2
—44Pb 82 (3H 199)
Portway. E15 —39Hc 65
Portway. Eps —81Wa 162
Portway Cres. Eps —81Wa 162
Portway Gdns. SE18 —52Mc 107
Postern Grn. Enf —13Qb 24
Postern, The. EC2
(off Barbican) —43Sb 83 (1E 200)
Post Ho. La. Bookh —97Ca 175
Post La. Sole S —10E 136
Post La. Twic —60Fa 100
Post Meadow. Iver —41F 74
Postmill Clo. Croy —76Yb 148
Post Office All. Hamp —68Da 121
Post Office App. E7 —36Kc 65
Post Office Ct. EC3
(off Barbican) —44Tb 83 (3G 201)
Post Office La. G Grn —4P 73
Post Office Way. SW8 —51Mb 104
Postway M. Ilf —34Rc 66
(in two parts)

Potier St.—Pulman Gdns.

Potier St. SE1 —48Tb 83 (4G 207)
Potter Clo. Mitc —68Kb 126
Potteries, The. Barn —15Cb 23
Potterne Clo. SW19 —59Za 102
Potters Clo. Croy —74Ac 148
Potters Clo. Lou —12Nc 28
Potters Cross. Iver —41G 74
Potters End. Pinn —23X 37
Pottersfield. Enf —14Ub 25
(off Lincoln Rd.)
Potters Fields. SE1
—46Ub 83 (7J 201)
Potters Gro. N Mald —70Sa 123
Potters Heights Clo. Pinn —24X 37
Potter's La. SW16 —65Mb 126
Potters La. Barn —14Cb 23
Potters La. Borwd —11Sa 21
Potters La. Send —95D 172
Potters Rd. SW6 —54Eb 103
Potter's Rd. Barn —14Db 23
Potter St. N'wd —25W 36
Potter St. Pinn —25X 37
Potter St. Hill. Pinn —23X 37
Pottery La. W11 —45Ab 80
Pottery Rd. Bex —61Ed 132
Pottery Rd. Bren —51Na 101
Pottery St. SE16 —47Xb 83
Pott St. E2 —41Xb 83
Poulcott. Wray —58A 96
Poulett Gdns. Twic —60Ja 100
Poulett Rd. E6 —40Pc 66
Poulner Way. SE15 —52Vb 105
Poulters Wood. Kes —78Mc 149
Poultney Clo. Shenl —4Pa 7
Poulton Av. Sutt —76Fb 145
Poulton Clo. E8 —37Xb 63
Poultry. EC2 —44Tb 83 (3F 201)
Pound Bank Clo. W King
—80Vd 154
Pound Clo. Orp —75Tc 150
Pound Clo. Surb —74La 142
Pound Ct. Asht —90Pa 161
Pound Ct. Dri. Orp —75Tc 150
Pound Cres. Fet —93Fa 176
Poundfield. Wat —7V 4
Poundfield Ct. Wok —93E 172
Poundfield Gdns. Wok —92E 172
(in two parts)
Poundfield Rd. Lou —15Qc 28
Poundfield Rd. Wok —92E 172
Pound Grn. Bex —59Cd 110
Pound La. NW10 —37Wa 60
Pound La. Eps —84Sa 161
Pound La. Knock —87Zc 169
Pound La. Ors —2C 92
Pound La. Sev —96Ld 187
Pound La. Shenl —5Pa 7
Pound Pk. Rd. SE7 —49Mc 85
Pound Pl. SE9 —58Qc 108
Pound Rd. Bans —89Cb 163
Pound Rd. Cher —73K 139
Pound St. Cars —78Hb 145
Pound, The. Burn —2B 72
Pounsley Rd. Dun G —93Gd 186
Pountney Rd. SW11 —55Jb 104
Poverest Rd. Orp —71Vc 151
Powderham Ct. Knap —6A 188
Powder Mill La. Dart —61Nd 133
Powder Mill La. Twic —60Ba 99
Powdermill La. Wal A —5Dc 12
Powdermill Way. Wal A —4Dc 12
Powell Clo. Edgw —23Pa 39
Powell Clo. Wall —80Nb 146
Powell Ct. E17 —27Dc 44
Powell Gdns. Dag —35Cd 68
Powell Rd. E5 —34Xb 63
Powell Rd. Buck H —17Lc 27
Powell's Wlk. W4 —51Ua 102
Power. Ind. Est. Eri —53Jd 110
Power Rd. W4 —49Qa 79
Powers Ct. Twic —59Ma 101
Powerscroft Rd. E5 —35Yb 64
Powerscroft Rd. Sidc —65Yc 131
Powis Ct. Pot B —6Eb 9
Powis Gdns. NW11 —31Bb 61
Powis Gdns. W11 —44Bb 81
Powis M. W11 —44Bb 81
Powis Pl. WC1 —42Nb 82 (6G 193)
Powis Rd. E3 —41Dc 84
Powis Sq. W11 —44Bb 81
Powis St. SE18 —48Qc 86
Powis Ter. W11 —44Bb 81
Powlett Pl. NW1 —38Jb 62
Pownall Gdns. Houn —56Da 99
Pownall Rd. E8 —39Wb 63
Pownall Rd. Houn —56Da 99
Powster Rd. Brom —64Jc 129
Powys Clo. Bexh —51Zc 109
Powys Ct. N11 —22Nb 42
Powys La. N14 & N13 —21Nb 42
Poxon Ct. EC4 —44Rb 83 (3C 200)
Poyle Clo. Coln —54G 96
Poyle Ind. Est. Coln —54G 96
Poyle La. Burn —9A 52
Poyle Rd. Coln —55G 96
Poyle Technical Cen. Coln —54G 96
Poyle Trading Est. Coln —55G 96
Poynder Rd. Til —3D 114
Poynders Ct. SW4 —58Lb 104
Poynders Gdns. SW4 —59Lb 104
Poynders Rd. SW4 —58Lb 104
Poynings Clo. Orp —75Yc 151
Poynings Rd. N19 —34Lb 62
Poynings, The. Iver —49H 75
Poynings Way. N12 —22Cb 41
Poynings Way. H Wood —25Nd 49
Poyntell Cres. Chst —67Tc 130
Poynter Ho. W11 —46Za 80
(off Queensdale Cres.)
Poynter Rd. Enf —15Wb 25
Poynton Rd. N17 —26Wb 43
Poyntz Rd. SW11 —54Hb 103
Poyser St. E2 —40Xb 63
Praed M. W2 —44Fb 81 (2C 196)
Praed St. W2 —44Fb 81 (3B 196)
Prae, The. Wok —90H 157
Pragel St. E13 —40Lc 65
Pragnell Rd. SE12 —61Kc 129
Prague Pl. SW2 —57Nb 104
Prah Rd. N4 —33Qb 62
Prairie Clo. Add —76K 139
Prairie Rd. Add —76K 139
Prairie St. SW8 —54Jb 104
Pratt M. NW1 —39Lb 62 (1B 192)
Pratts La. W on T —77Z 141
Pratts Pas. King T —68Na 123
Pratt St. NW1 —39Lb 62
Pratt Wlk. SE11 —49Pb 82 (5J 205)
Prayle Gro. NW2 —32Za 60
Prebend Gdns. W6 & W4 —48Va 80
(in two parts)
Prebend Mans. W4 —49Va 80
(off Chiswick High Rd.)
Prebend St. N1 —39Sb 63 (1D 194)
Precinct Rd. Hay —45W 76
Precincts, The. Burn —2A 72
Precinct, The. Egh —64C 118
Precinct, The. Stanf —2M 93
Premier Av. Grays —47Ee 91
Premier Corner. W9 —40Bb 61
Premier Ct. Enf —10Yb 12
Premier Pl. SW15 —56Ab 102
Prendergast Rd. SE3 —55Gc 107
Prentice Ct. SW19 —64Bb 125
Prentis Rd. SW16 —63Mb 126
Prentiss Ct. SE7 —49Mc 85
Presburg Rd. N Mald —71Ua 144
Presburg St. E5 —34Zb 64
Presbury Ct. St J —6D 188
Prescelly Pl. Edgw —25Pa 39
Prescot St. E1 —45Vb 83 (4K 201)
Prescott Av. Orp —72Rc 150
Prescott Clo. SW16 —66Nb 126
Prescott Clo. Horn —32Kd 69
Prescott Grn. Lou —13Sc 28
Prescott Pl. SW4 —55Mb 104
Prescott Rd. Coln —54G 96
Presentation M. SW2 —60Pb 104
Preshaw Cres. Mitc —69Gb 125
President Dri. E1 —46Xb 83
President St. EC1
—41Sb 83 (3D 194)
(off Central St.)
Press Ho. NW10 —34Ta 59
Press Rd. NW10 —34Ta 59
Press Rd. Uxb —37M 55
Prestbury Cres. Bans —88Hb 163
Prestbury Rd. E7 —38Lc 65
Prestbury Sq. SE9 —63Pc 130
Prestbury Sq. SE12 —63Pc 130
Prested Rd. SW11 —56Gb 103
Preston Av. E4 —23Fc 45
Preston Clo. SE1
—49Ub 83 (5H 207)
Preston Clo. Twic —62Ga 122
Preston Ct. New Bar —14Eb 23
Preston Ct. Sidc —63Vc 131
(off Crescent, The)
Preston Ct. W on T —74Y 141
Preston Dri. E11 —29Lc 45
Preston Dri. Bexh —53Zc 109
Preston Dri. Eps —79Ua 144
Preston Gdns. NW10 —37Va 60
Preston Gdns. Enf —9Ac 12
Preston Gdns. Ilf —30Nc 46
Preston Gro. Asht —89La 160
Preston Hill. Harr —31Na 59
Preston Ho. Dag —34Cd 68
(off Uvedale Rd.)
Preston La. Tad —93Xa 178
Preston Pl. NW2 —37Wa 60
Preston Pl. Rich —57Na 101
Preston Rd. E11 —30Gc 45
Preston Rd. SE19 —65Rb 127
Preston Rd. SW20 —66Va 124
Preston Rd. Grav —10A 114
Preston Rd. Romf —21Md 49
Preston Rd. Shep —71Q 140
Preston Rd. Slou —5N 73
Preston Rd. Wemb & Harr
—32Na 59
Preston's Rd. E14 —45Ec 84
Prestons Rd. Brom —76Jc 149
Preston Waye. Harr —32Na 59
Prestwick Clo. S'hall —50Aa 77
Prestwick Rd. Wat —22X 37
Prestwood. Slou —4M 73
Prestwood Av. Harr —28Ka 38
Prestwood Clo. SE18 —52Wc 109
Prestwood Clo. Harr —28Ka 38
Prestwood Dri. Romf —22Ed 48
Prestwood Gdns. Croy —73Sb 147
Prestwood St. N1
—40Sb 63 (2E 194)
Pretoria Av. E17 —28Ac 44
Pretoria Clo. N17 —24Vb 43
Pretoria Cres. E4 —18Ec 26
Pretoria Ho. Eri —52Gd 110
Pretoria Rd. E4 —18Ec 26
Pretoria Rd. E11 —32Fc 65
Pretoria Rd. E16 —42Hc 85
Pretoria Rd. N17 —24Vb 43
Pretoria Rd. SW16 —65Kb 126
Pretoria Rd. Cher —74H 139
Pretoria Rd. Ilf —36Rc 66
Pretoria Rd. Romf —28Ed 48
Pretoria Rd. Wat —14W 18
Pretoria Rd. N. N18 —23Vb 43
Prevost Rd. N11 —19Jb 24
Price Clo. NW7 —23Ab 40
Price Clo. SW17 —62Hb 125
Price Rd. Croy —78Rb 147
Price's St. SE1 —46Rb 83 (7C 200)
Price's Yd. N1 —39Pb 62
Price Way. Hamp —65Aa 121
Prichard Ct. N7 —36Pb 62
Pricklers Hill. Barn —16Db 23
Prickley Wood. Brom —74Hc 149
Priddy's Yd. Croy —75Sb 147
Prideaux Pl. W3 —45Ta 79
Prideaux Pl. WC1
—41Pb 82 (3J 193)
Prideaux Rd. SW9 —55Nb 104
Pridham Rd. T Hth —70Tb 127
Priestfield Rd. SE23 —62Ac 128
Priest Hill. Egh & Old Win —2N 117
Priest Hill. Oxt —100Kc 183
Priestlands Pk. Rd. Sidc —62Vc 131
Priestley Clo. N16 —31Vb 63
Priestley Ct. Grays —49Ee 91
Priestley Gdns. Romf —30Xc 47
Priestley Gdns. Wok —92C 172
Priestley Ho. Wemb —34Sa 59
(off Barnhill Rd.)
Priestley Rd. Mitc —68Jb 126
Priestley Way. E17 —27Zb 44
Priestley Way. NW2 —32Wa 60
Priest Pk. Av. Harr —33Ca 57
Priests Av. Romf —26Fd 48
Priest's Bri. SW14 & SW15
—55Ua 102
Priest's Ct. EC2 —44Sb 83 (2D 200)
(off Foster La.)
Priest's Field. Ingve —22Ee 51
Priests La. Brtwd —19Ae 33
Priest Wlk. Grav —1J 137
Prima Rd. SW9 —52Qb 104
Primmett Clo. W King —79Ud 154
Primrose Av. Enf —11Tb 25
Primrose Av. Romf —31Xc 67
Primrose Clo. SE6 —64Ec 128
Primrose Clo. Harr —34Ba 57
Primrose Clo. Mitc —73Kb 146
Primrose Gdns. NW3 —37Gb 61
Primrose Gdns. Bush —17Da 19
Primrose Gdns. Ruis —36Y 57
Primrose Glen. Horn —28Nd 49
Primrose Hill. EC4
—44Qb 82 (3A 200)
Primrose Hill. Brtwd —20Yd 32
Primrose Hill. K Lan —1R 4
Primrose Hill Rd. NW3 —38Gb 61
Primrose La. Croy —74Yb 148
Primrose Mans. SW11 —53Jb 104
Primrose M. NW1 —38Hb 61
(off Sharpleshall St.)
Primrose Path. Chesh —3Wb 11
Primrose Rd. E10 —32Dc 64
Primrose Rd. E18 —26Kc 45
Primrose Rd. W on T —78Y 141
Primrose St. EC2
—43Ub 83 (7H 195)
Primrose Ter. Grav —10E 114
Primrose Way. Wemb —40Ma 59
Primula St. W12 —44Wa 80
Prince Albert Rd. NW8 & NW1
—41Gb 81 (3D 190)
Prince Albert's Wlk. Wind —3L 95
Prince Arthur M. NW3 —35Eb 61
Prince Arthur Rd. NW3 —36Eb 61
Prince Charles Av. Ors —2D 92
Prince Charles Av. S Dar
—68Td 134
Prince Charles Dri. NW4 —31Ya 60
Prince Charles Rd. SE3 —54Hc 107
Prince Charles Way. Wall
—76Kb 146
Prince Consort Cotts. Wind —4H 95
Prince Consort Dri. Chst —67Tc 130
Prince Consort Rd. SW7
—48Eb 81 (3A 202)
Prince Consort's Dri. Wind —8D 94
Princedale Rd. W11 —46Ab 80
Prince Edward Rd. E9 —37Bc 64
Prince George Av. N14 —15Mb 24
Prince George Rd. N16 —35Ub 63
Prince George's Av. SW20
—68Ya 124
Prince Georges Rd. SW19
—67Fb 125
Prince Henry Rd. SE7 —52Mc 107
Prince Imperial Rd. SE18
—53Pc 108
Prince Imperial Rd. Chst
—67Rc 130
Prince John Rd. SE9 —57Nc 108
Princelet St. E1 —43Vb 83 (7K 195)
Prince of Orange La. SE10
—52Ec 106
Prince of Wales Clo. NW4 —28Ya 40
Prince of Wales Dri. SW11 & SW8
—53Gb 103
Prince of Wales Footpath. Enf
—10Zb 12
Prince of Wales Mans. SW11
—53Jb 104
Prince of Wales Pas. NW1
—41Lb 82 (4B 192)
(off Hampstead Rd.)
Prince of Wales Rd. E16 —44Lc 85
Prince of Wales Rd. NW5 —37Jb 62
Prince of Wales Rd. SE3 —53Hc 107
Prince of Wales Rd. Sutt —75Fb 145
Prince of Wales Ter. W4 —50Ua 80
Prince of Wales Ter. W8 —47Db 81
Prince Philip Av. Grays —46Ce 91
Prince Regent Ct. NW8
—40Gb 61 (1E 190)
(off Avenue Rd.)
Prince Regent La. E13 & E16
—41Kc 85
Prince Regent M. NW1
—41Lb 82 (4B 192)
(off Hampstead Rd.)
Prince Regent Rd. Houn —55Ea 100
Prince Rd. SE25 —71Ub 147
Prince Rupert Rd. SE9 —56Pc 108
Prince's Arc. SW1
(off Piccadilly) —46Lb 82 (6C 198)
Princes Av. N3 —25Cb 41
Princes Av. N10 —27Kb 42
Princes Av. N13 —22Qb 42
Princes Av. N22 —25Mb 42
Princes Av. NW9 —28Qa 39
Princes Av. W3 —48Qa 79
Princes Av. Cars —80Hb 145
Princes Av. Cob —1P 93
Princes Av. Dart —60Rd 111
Princes Av. Enf —8Ac 12
Prince's Av. Gnfd —44Da 77
Princes Av. Orp —71Uc 150
Princes Av. S Croy —87Xb 165
Princes Av. Surb —74Qa 143
Prince's Av. Wat —15V 18
Princes Av. Wfd G —21Kc 45
Princes Cir. WC2
—44Nb 82 (2F 199)
Princes Clo. NW9 —28Qa 39
Princes Clo. SW4 —55Lb 104
Princes Clo. Edgw —22Qa 39
Princes Clo. Eton W —10D 72
Princes Clo. Sidc —62Zc 131
Princes Clo. S Croy —87Xb 165
Prince's Clo. Tedd —63Fa 122
Princes Ct. Wemb —36Na 59
Princes Ct. Bus. Cen. E1 —45Xb 83
Princes Dri. Harr —27Ga 38
Prince's Dri. Oxs —84Ga 160
Princesfield Rd. Wal A —5Kc 13
Prince's Gdns. SW7
—48Fb 81 (3C 202)
Princes Gdns. W3 —43Qa 79
Princes Gdns. W5 —42La 78
Prince's Ga. SW7
—47Fb 81 (2C 202)
Prince's Ga. Ct. SW7
—47Fb 81 (2C 202)
Prince's Ga. M. SW7
—48Fb 81 (3C 202)
Princes La. N10 —27Kb 42
Prince's M. W2 —45Db 81
Princes Pde. NW11 —30Ab 40
(off Golders Grn. Rd.)
Princes Pde. Pot B —4Db 9
Princes Pk. Rain —38Jd 68
Princes Pk. Av. NW11 —30Ab 40
Princes Pk. Av. Hay —45T 76
Princes Pk. Circ. Hay —45T 76
Princes Pk. Clo. Hay —45T 76
Princes Pk. La. Hay —45T 76
Princes Pk. Pde. Hay —45T 76
Prince's Pl. SW1
—46Lb 82 (6C 198)
(off Duke St. Saint James's)
Princes Pl. W11 —46Ab 80
Prince's Plain. Brom —73Nc 150
Prince's Rise. SE13 —54Ec 106
Princes Rd. N18 —21Yb 44
Princes Rd. SE20 —65Zb 128
Princes Rd. SW14 —55Ta 101
Prince's Rd. SW19 —65Cb 125
Princes Rd. W13 —46Ka 78
Princes Rd. Ashf —64P 119
Prince's Rd. Brtwd —11Nd 31
Princes Rd. Buck H —19Lc 27
Princes Rd. Dart —58Jd 110
Princes Rd. Egh —65B 118
Princes Rd. Felt —61Y 120
Princes Rd. Grav —2E 136
Princes Rd. Ilf —28Tc 46
Princes Rd. Kew —53Pa 101
Princes Rd. King T —66Qa 123
Princes Rd. Rich —57Pa 101
Prince's Rd. Romf —29Jd 48
Princes Rd. Swan —66Jd 132
Prince's Rd. Tedd —63Fa 122
Princes Rd. Wey —78R 140
Princessa Ct. Enf —15Tb 25
Princess Alice Ho. W10 —42Ya 80
Princess Av. E Til —9L 93
Princess Av. Wind —5F 94
Princess Ct. N6 —31Lb 62
Princess Ct. SE16 —48Bc 84
Princess Cres. N4 —33Rb 63
Princesses Pde. Dart —57Gd 110
(off Waterside)
Princess Gdns. Wok —88D 156
Princess La. Ruis —32U 56
Princess Margaret Rd. E Til —8K 93
Princess Marys Rd. Add —77L 139
Princess May Rd. N16 —35Ub 63
Princess M. NW3 —36Fb 61
Princess of Wales Ho. Ger X
—22B 34
Princess Pde. Orp —76Qc 150
Prince's Sq. W2 —45Db 81
Princess Rd. NW1 —39Jb 62
Princess Rd. NW6 —40Cb 61
Princess Rd. Croy —72Sb 147
Princess Rd. Wok —88D 156
Princess St. SE1
—48Rb 83 (4C 206)
Prince's St. EC2 —44Tb 83 (3F 201)
Princes St. N17 —23Ub 43
Princes St. W1 —44Kb 82 (3A 198)
Princes St. Bexh —55Bd 109
Princes St. Grav —8D 114
Princes St. Rich —56Na 101
Princes St. Slou —7M 73
Princes St. Sutt —77Fb 145
Princes Ter. E13 —39Kc 65
Prince St. SE8 —51Bc 106
Prince St. Wat —13Y 19
Princes View. Dart —60Qd 111
Princes Way. SW19 —59Za 102
Princes Way. Buck H —19Lc 27
Princes Way. Croy —78Pb 146
Princes Way. Hut —19Ce 33
Princes Way. Ruis —35Aa 57
Princes Way. W Wick —77Hc 149
Princethorpe Rd. SE26 —63Zb 128
Princeton Ct. SW15 —55Za 102
Princeton M. King T —67Qa 123
Princeton St. WC1
—43Pb 82 (1H 199)
Pringle Gdns. SW16 —63Lb 126
Printer St. EC4 —44Qb 82 (2A 200)
Printinghouse La. Hay —47U 76
Printing Ho. Yd. E2
—41Vb 83 (4J 195)
Priolo Rd. SE7 —50Lc 85
Prior Av. Sutt —80Gb 145
Prior Bolton St. N1 —37Rb 63
Prior Chase. Grays —49Be 91
Prioress Rd. SE27 —62Rb 127
Prioress St. SE1
—48Ub 83 (4G 207)
Prior Rd. Ilf —34Qc 66
Priors Ct. Slou —8L 73
Priors Ct. St J —6D 188
Priors Croft. E17 —26Ac 44
Prior's Croft. Wok —92C 172
Priors Field. N'holt —37Aa 57
Priorsford Av. Orp —70Wc 131
Priors Gdns. Ruis —36Y 57
Priors Mead. Bookh —97Ea 176
Priors Mead. Enf —11Ub 25
Priors Pk. Horn —34Ld 69
Priors Rd. Wind —5B 94
Priors, The. Asht —91Ma 177
Prior St. SE10 —52Ec 106
Priory Av. E4 —20Bc 26
Priory Av. E17 —29Cc 44
Priory Av. N8 —28Mb 42
Priory Av. W4 —49Ua 80
Priory Av. Hare —28L 35
Priory Av. Orp —72Tc 150
Priory Av. Sutt —77Za 144
Priory Av. Wemb —35Ha 58
Priory Cen. Dart —58Md 111
Priory Clo. E4 —20Bc 26
Priory Clo. E18 —25Jc 45
Priory Clo. N3 —25Bb 41
Priory Clo. N14 —15Kb 24
Priory Clo. N20 —17Bb 23
Priory Clo. SW19 —67Db 125
Priory Clo. Beck —69Ac 128
Priory Clo. Chst —67Pc 130
Priory Clo. Dart —57Md 111
Priory Clo. Den —34J 55
Priory Clo. Hamp —67Ba 121
Priory Clo. Hare —28K 35
Priory Clo. Hay —45X 77
Priory Clo. Pil H —15Wd 32
Priory Clo. Ruis —32V 56
Priory Clo. Stan —20Ha 20
Priory Clo. Sun —66W 120
Priory Clo. W on T —76W 140
Priory Clo. Wemb —35Ha 58
Priory Clo. Wok —85F 156
Priory Ct. E6 —39Mc 65
Priory Ct. E9 —36Zb 64
Priory Ct. E17 —26Bc 44
Priory Ct. EC4 —44Rb 83 (3C 200)
(off Pilgrim St.)
Priory Ct. SW8 —53Mb 104
Priory Ct. Bush —18Ea 20
Priory Ct. Dart —58Md 111
Priory Ct. Eps —81Va 162
Priory Ct. Houn —55Da 99
Priory Ct. Sutt —77Ab 144
Priory Ct. Wemb —40Na 59
Priory Ct. Est. E17 —26Bc 44
Priory Cres. SE19 —66Sb 127
Priory Cres. Sutt —77Za 144
Priory Cres. Wemb —34Ja 58
Priory Dri. SE2 —50Zc 87
Priory Dri. Stan —20Ha 20
Prioryfield Dri. Edgw —21Ra 39
Priory Fields. Eyns —75Pd 153
Priory Gdns. N6 —30Kb 42
Priory Gdns. SW13 —55Va 102
Priory Gdns. W4 —49Ua 80
Priory Gdns. W5 —40Na 59
Priory Gdns. Dart —57Md 111
Priory Gdns. Hamp —66Ba 121
Priory Gdns. Hare —28L 35
Priory Gdns. Wemb —35Ja 58
Priory Grange. N2 —27Hb 41
(off Fortis Grn.)
Priory Grn. Stai —64K 119
Priory Grn. Est. N1
—40Pb 62 (1H 193)
Priory Gro. SW8 —53Nb 104
Priory Gro. Barn —15Cb 23
Priory Gro. Romf —20Nd 31
Priory Hill. Dart —58Md 111
Priory Hill. Wemb —35Ja 58
Priory La. SW15 —58Ua 102
Priory La. Eyns —74Pd 153
Priory La. Rich —52Qa 101
Priory La. W Mol —70Da 121
Priory M. SW8 —53Mb 104
Priory M. Stai —64K 119
Priory Pk. SE3 —55Hc 107
Priory Pk. Rd. NW6 —39Bb 61
Priory Pk. Rd. Wemb —35Ja 58
Priory Path. Romf —20Nd 31
Priory Pl. Dart —58Md 111
Priory Pl. W on T —76W 140
Priory Rd. E6 —39Mc 65
Priory Rd. N8 —28Lb 42
Priory Rd. NW6 —39Db 61
Priory Rd. SW19 —66Fb 125
Priory Rd. W4 —48Ta 79
Priory Rd. Bark —38Tc 66
Priory Rd. Chess —76Na 143
Priory Rd. Croy —73Qb 146
Priory Rd. Dart —56Md 111
(in two parts)
Priory Rd. Ger X —26A 34
Priory Rd. Hamp —66Ba 121
Priory Rd. Houn —57Ea 100
Priory Rd. Lou —14Nc 28
Priory Rd. Rich —51Qa 101
Priory Rd. Romf —20Nd 31
Priory Rd. Slou —3A 72
Priory Rd. Stanf —1N 93
Priory Rd. Sutt —77Za 144
Priory St. E3 —41Dc 84
Priory Ter. NW6 —39Db 61
Priory Ter. Sun —66W 120
Priory, The. SE3 —56Hc 107
Priory, The. Croy —77Qb 146
Priory, The. Lea —94Ka 176
Priory View. Bush —17Ga 20
Priory Vs. N11 —23Hb 41
(off Colney Hatch La.)
Priory Wlk. SW10
—50Eb 81 (7A 202)
Priory Way. Dat —2M 95
Priory Way. Harr —28Da 37
Priory Way. S'hall —48Z 77
Priory Way. W Dray —51N 97
Pritchard's Rd. E2 —39Wb 63
Priter Rd. SE16 —48Wb 83
Priter Way. SE16 —48Wb 83
Private Rd. Enf —15Tb 25
Probert Rd. SW2 —57Qb 104
Probyn Rd. SW2 —61Rb 127
Procter St. WC1
—43Pb 82 (1H 199)
Proctor Gdns. Bookh —97Da 175
Proctors Clo. Felt —60W 98
Proffits Cotts. Tad —94Za 178
Profumo Rd. W on T —78Z 141
Progress Bus. Cen. Burn —4B 72
Progress Bus. Pk., The. Croy
—75Pb 146
Progress Way. N22 —25Qb 42
Progress Way. Croy —75Pb 146
Progress Way. Enf —15Wb 25
Project Pk. E16 —42Fc 85
Promenade App. Rd. W4
—52Ua 102
Promenade de Verdun. Purl
—83Mb 164
Promenade Mans. Edgw —22Qa 39
Promenade, The. W4 —53Ua 102
Prospect Av. Stanf —2K 93
Prospect Clo. SE26 —63Xb 127
Prospect Clo. Belv —49Cd 88
Prospect Clo. Houn —54Ba 99
Prospect Clo. Ruis —31Z 57
Prospect Cotts. SW18 —56Cb 103
Prospect Cres. Twic —58Ea 100
Prospect Gro. Grav —9F 114
Prospect Hill. E17 —28Dc 44
Prospect Ho. E17 —27Ec 44
(off Prospect Hill.)
Prospect La. Egh —4L 117
Prospect Pl. E1 —46Yb 84
Prospect Pl. N2 —28Fb 41
Prospect Pl. N17 —24Ub 43
Prospect Pl. NW2 —34Bb 61
Prospect Pl. NW3 —35Eb 61
Prospect Pl. W4 —50Ta 79
Prospect Pl. Brom —69Kc 129
Prospect Pl. Dart —58Nd 111
Prospect Pl. Eps —84Ua 162
Prospect Pl. Grav —9F 114
Prospect Pl. Grays —51De 113
Prospect Pl. Romf —26Ed 48
Prospect Pl. Stai —64H 119
Prospect Ring. N2 —27Fb 41
Prospect Rd. NW2 —34Bb 61
Prospect Rd. Barn —14Cb 23
Prospect Rd. Chesh —1Yb 12
Prospect Rd. Horn —27Pd 49
Prospect Rd. Sev —95Ld 187
Prospect Rd. Surb —72La 142
Prospect Rd. Wfd G —23Lc 45
Prospect St. SE16 —48Xb 83
Prospect Vale. SE18 —49Nc 86
Prospect Way. Hut —14Fe 33
Prospero Rd. N19 —32Mb 62
Prossers. Tad —93Za 178
Protheroe Ho. N17 —27Vb 43
Protheroe Rd. SW6 —52Ab 102
Prothero Gdns. NW4 —29Xa 40
Prout Gro. NW10 —35Ua 60
Prout Rd. E5 —34Xb 63
Provence St. N1 —40Sb 63
Providence Ct. W1
—45Jb 82 (4J 197)
Providence La. Hay —52T 98
Providence Pl. N1 —39Rb 63
Providence Pl. Eps —84Ua 162
Providence Pl. Romf —26Bd 47
Providence Pl. W Byf —86J 157
Providence Rd. W Dray —46N 75
Providence Row. N1
—40Pb 62 (2H 193)
(off Pentonville Rd.)
Providence St. Grnh —57Wd 112
Provident Ind. Est. Hay —47W 76
Province St. N1 —40Sb 63 (1D 194)
Provost Est. N1 —40Tb 63 (3F 195)
Provost Rd. NW3 —38Hb 61
Provost St. N1 —40Tb 63 (2F 195)
Prowse Av. Bush —18Ea 20
Prowse Pl. NW1 —38Lb 62
Pruden Clo. N14 —19Lb 24
Prudent Pas. EC2
(off King St.) —44Sb 83 (3E 200)
Prudhoe Ct. Dart —58Rd 111
(off Osborne Rd.)
Prune Hill. Egh —6P 117
Prusom St. E1 —46Xb 83
Pryor Clo. Abb L —4V 4
Pryors, The. NW3 —34Fb 61
Puck La. Wal A —1Gc 13
Puckshill. Knap —5A 188
Pudding La. EC3
—45Tb 83 (5G 201)
Pudding La. Chig —16Uc 28
Pudding La. Seal —93Pd 187
Pudding Mill La. E15 —39Dc 64
Puddledock. EC4
(in two parts) —45Rb 83 (4C 200)
Puddledock La. Dart —64Qd 132
Puffin Clo. Beck —71Zb 148
Pulborough Rd. SW18 —59Bb 103
Pulborough Way. Houn —56Y 99
Pulford Rd. N15 —30Tb 43
Pulham Av. N2 —28Eb 41
Puller Rd. Barn —12Ab 22
Pulleyns Av. E6 —41Nc 86
Pullman Ct. SW2 —57Nb 104
Pulman Gdns. SW15 —58Ya 102

Pulross Rd.—Radnor Rd.

Pulross Rd. SW9 —55Pb 104
Pulteney Clo. E3 —39Bc 64
Pulteney Rd. E18 —27Kc 45
Pulteney Ter. N1 —39Pb 62 (1J 193)
Pulton Pl. SW6 —52Cb 103
Puma Ct. E1 —43Vb 83 (7K 195)
Pump All. Bren —52Ma 101
Pump Clo. N'holt —40Ca 57
Pump Ct. EC4 —44Qb 82 (3K 199)
Pump Hill. Lou —12Pc 28
Pumping Sta. Rd. W4 —52Ua 102
Pumpkin Hill. Farn C —7C 52
Pump La. SE14 —52Yb 106
Pump La. Asc —7C 116
Pump La. Hay —47W 76
Pump La. Orp —78Dd 152
Pump Pail N. Croy —76Sb 147
Pump Pail S. Croy —76Sb 147
Pump St. Horn H —1J 93
Punch Croft. New Ash —76Ae 155
Punderson's Gdns. E2 —41Xb 83
Purbeck Av. N Mald —72Va 144
Purbeck Clo. Red —100Mb 180
Purbeck Dri. NW2 —33Za 60
Purbeck Dri. Wok —86B 156
Purbeck Rd. Horn —31Jd 68
Purbeck St. SE1 —48Ub 83
Purberry Gro. Eps —82Va 162
Purbrock Av. Wat —8Y 5
Purbrook Est. SE1
—47Ub 83 (2J 207)
Purbrook St. SE1
—48Ub 83 (3J 207)
Purcell Clo. Borwd —11Ma 21
Purcell Clo. Stanf —1L 93
Purcell Cres. SW6 —52Ab 102
Purcell M. NW10 —38Ua 60
Purcell Rd. Gnfd —43Da 77
Purcells Av. Edgw —22Qa 39
Purcell's Clo. Asht —90Pa 161
Purcell St. N1 —40Ub 63 (1H 195)
Purcell Way. Stanf —1L 93
Purchese St. NW1
—40Mb 62 (1E 192)
Purdey Ct. Wor Pk —74Wa 144
Purdon Ho. SE15 —53Wb 105
(off Oliver Goldsmith Est.)
Purdy St. E3 —42Dc 84
Purfleet By-Pass. Purf —49Rd 89
Purfleet Ind. Pk. S Ock —47Pd 89
Purfleet Rd. S Ock —47Qd 89
Purland Clo. Dag —32Bd 67
Purland Rd. SE28 —47Vc 87
Purleigh Av. Wfd G —23Nc 46
Purley Av. NW2 —33Ab 60
Purley Bury Av. Purl —83Sb 165
Purley Bury Clo. Purl —83Sb 165
Purley Clo. Ilf —26Qc 46
Purley Downs Rd. Purl & S Croy
—82Sb 165
Purley Hill. Purl —84Rb 165
Purley Knoll. Purl —83Pb 164
Purley Oaks Rd. S Croy —81Tb 165
Purley Pde. Purl —83Qb 164
Purley Pk. Rd. Purl —82Rb 165
Purley Pl. N1 —38Rb 63
Purley Rise. Purl —84Pb 164
Purley Rd. N9 —20Ub 25
Purley Rd. Purl —83Qb 164
Purley Rd. S Croy —80Tb 147
Purley Vale. Purl —85Rb 165
Purley Way. Croy & Purl —73Pb 146
Purley Way Cen., The. Croy
—75Qb 146
Purley Way Corner. Croy
—73Pb 146
Purley Way Cres. Croy —73Pb 146
Purlieu Way. They B —7Uc 14
Purlings Rd. Bush —15Da 19
Purneys Rd. SE9 —56Mc 107
Purrett Rd. SE18 —50Vc 87
Purser Ho. SW2 —58Qb 104
(off Tulse Hill)
Pursers Cross Rd. SW6 —53Bb 103
Purse Wardens Clo. W13 —46La 78
Pursley Gdns. Borwd —10Qa 7
Pursley Rd. NW7 —24Xa 40
Purton Ct. Farn C —8G 52
Purton La. Farn R —8G 52
Purves Rd. NW10 —40Xa 60
Putney Bri. SW15 & SW6
—55Ab 102
Putney Bri. App. SW6 —55Ab 102
Putney Bri. Rd. SW15 & SW18
—56Ab 102
Putney Comn. SW15 —55Ya 102
Putney Exchange Shopping Cen.
SW15 —56Za 102
Putney Heath. SW15 —59Xa 102
Putney Heath La. SW15 —58Za 102
Putney High St. SW15 —56Za 102
Putney Hill. SW15 —59Za 102
(in two parts)
Putney Pk. Av. SW15 —56Wa 102
Putney Pk. La. SW15 —56Xa 102
Putney Rd. Enf —8Zb 12
Puttenham Clo. Wat —19Y 19
Pycroft Way. N9 —21Vb 43
Pyecombe Corner. N12 —21Bb 41
Pyghtle, The. Den —31J 55
Pylbrook Rd. Sutt —76Cb 145
Pyle Hill. Wok —96A 172
Pylon Trading Est. E16 —42Gc 85
Pylon Way. Croy —74Nb 146
Pym Clo. Barn —15Fb 23
Pymers Mead. SE21 —60Sb 105
Pym Ho. SW9 —54Qb 104
Pymmes Brook Ho. N10 —24Jb 42
Pymmes Clo. N13 —22Pb 42
Pymmes Clo. N17 —25Xb 43
Pymmes Gdns. N. N9 —20Vb 25
Pymmes Gdns. S. N9 —20Vb 25
Pymmes Grn. Rd. N11 —21Kb 42
Pymmes Rd. N13 —23Nb 42
Pymms Brook Dri. Barn —14Gb 23
Pym Orchard. Bras —96Yc 185
Pym Pl. Grays —49Ce 91
Pynchester Clo. Uxb —33Q 56
Pyne Rd. Surb —74Qa 143
Pynest Grn. La. Wal A —10Jc 13
Pynfolds. SE16 —47Xb 83
Pynham Clo. SE2 —48Xc 87
Pynnacles Clo. Stan —22Ka 38
Pynnersmead. SE24 —57Sb 105
Pyramid Ho. Houn —55Aa 99
Pyrcroft La. Wey —78R 140
Pyrcroft Rd. Cher —73G 138
Pyrford Comn. Rd. Wok —88F 156
Pyrford Ct. Wok —89H 157
Pyrford Heath. Wok —88H 157
Pyrford Rd. W Byf & Wok
—85J 157
Pyrford Wood Est. Wok —88E 156
Pyrford Woods Clo. Wok —87H 157
Pyrford Woods Rd. Wok —87G 156
Pyrland Rd. N5 —36Tb 63
Pyrland Rd. Rich —58Pa 101
Pyrles Grn. Lou —11Rc 28
Pyrles La. Lou —12Rc 28
Pyrmont Gro. SE27 —62Rb 127
Pyrmont Rd. W4 —51Qa 101
Pytchley Cres. SE19 —65Sb 127
Pytchley Rd. SE22 —55Ub 105

Quadrangle M. Stan —24La 38
Quadrangle, The. E17 —26Bc 44
Quadrangle, The. SE24 —57Sb 105
Quadrangle, The. SW10 —53Eb 103
Quadrant Arc. W1
—45Lb 82 (5C 198)
(off Regent St.)
Quadrant Arc. Romf —29Gd 48
Quadrant Clo. Wok —90A 156
Quadrant Gro. NW5 —36Hb 61
Quadrant Ho. SE1
—46Rb 83 (6B 200)
(off Burrell St.)
Quadrant Rd. Rich —56Ma 101
Quadrant Rd. T Hth —70Rb 127
Quadrant, The. NW4 —28Ya 40
Quadrant, The. SW20 —67Ab 124
Quadrant, The. W2
—44Gb 81 (2D 196)
(off Southwick St.)
Quadrant, The. W10 —41Za 80
Quadrant, The. Bexh —52Zc 109
Quadrant, The. Harr —27Fa 38
Quadrant, The. Purf —49Sd 90
Quadrant, The. Rich —56Na 101
Quadrant, The. Sutt —79Eb 145
Quadrant, The. Wey —77Q 140
Quad Rd. Wemb —34Ma 59
Quaggy Wlk. SE3 —56Jc 107
Quail Gdns. S Croy —82Ac 166
Quainton St. NW10 —34Ta 59
Quaker Clo. Sev —95Md 187
Quaker La. S'hall —48Ca 77
Quaker La. Wal A —6Ec 12
Quakers Clo. Hart —69Ae 135
Quakers Course. NW9 —25Va 40
Quakers Hall La. Sev —94Ld 187
Quakers La. Iswth —52Ha 100
Quakers La. Pot B —2Db 9
Quaker St. E1 —42Vb 83 (6K 195)
Quakers Wlk. N21 —16Tb 25
Quality Ct. WC2 —44Qb 82 (2K 199)
(off Chancery La.)
Quality St. Red —100Kb 180
Quandrant Gro. NW5 —36Hb 61
Quantock Clo. Hay —52T 98
Quantock Clo. Slou —50C 74
Quantock Dri. Wor Pk —75Ya 144
Quantock Gdns. NW2 —33Za 60
Quantock Ho. N16 —32Vb 63
Quantock Rd. Bexh —54Gd 110
Quarles Clo. Romf —24Cd 48
Quarley Way. SE15 —52Vb 105
Quarrendon St. SW6 —54Cb 103
Quarr Rd. Cars —72Gb 145
Quarry Cotts. Sev —95Jd 186
Quarry Hill. Grays —50Ce 91
Quarry Hill. Sev —95Md 187
Quarry M. Purf —49Qd 89
Quarry Pk. Rd. Sutt —79Bb 145
Quarry Rise. Sutt —79Bb 145
Quarry Rd. SW18 —58Eb 103
Quarry Rd. God —100Yb 182
Quarterdeck, The. E14 —47Cc 84
Quartermaine Av. Wok —94B 172
Quarter Mile La. E10 —35Dc 64
Quaves Rd. Slou —8M 73
Quay La. Grnh —56Xd 112
Quayside Ho. E14 —46Cc 84
Quay S. Ct. Hare —25J 35
Quay W. Ct. Hare —24J 35
Quebec Av. W'ham —98Tc 184
Quebec Cotts. W'ham —99Tc 184
Quebec M. W1 —44Hb 81 (3G 197)
Quebec Rd. Hay —44Y 77
Quebec Rd. Ilf —31Rc 66
Quebec Rd. Til —4C 114
Quebec Sq. W'ham —98Tc 184
Quebec Way. SE16 —47Zb 84
Quedgeley Ct. SE15 —51Vb 105
(off Ebley Clo.)
Queen Adelaide Ct. SE20
—65Yb 128
Queen Adelaide Rd. SE20
—65Yb 128
Queen Adelaide's Ride. Wind
—8B 94
Queen Anne Av. Brom —69Hc 129
Queen Anne Dri. Clay —80Ga 142
Queen Anne M. W1
—43Kb 82 (1A 198)
Queen Anne Rd. E9 —37Zb 64
Queen Anne's Clo. Twic —62Fa 122
Queen Anne's Gdns. W4 —48Ua 80
Queen Anne's Gdns. W5 —47Na 79
Queen Anne's Gdns. Enf —16Ub 25
Queen Anne's Gdns. Lea —93Ka 176
Queen Anne's Gdns. Mitc
—69Hb 125
Queen Anne's Ga. SW1
—47Mb 82 (2D 204)
Queen Anne's Ga. Bexh —55Zc 109
Queen Anne's Gro. W4 —48Ua 80
Queen Anne's Gro. W5 —47Na 79
Queen Anne's Gro. Enf —17Tb 25
Queen Anne's Pl. Enf —16Ub 25
Queen Anne's Ride. Asc & Wind
—5E 116
Queen Anne's Rd. Wind —6G 94
Queen Anne's Ter. Lea —93Ka 176
Queen Anne St. W1
—43Kb 82 (2K 197)
Queen Anne's Wlk. WC1
—42Nb 82 (6G 193)
(off Queen Sq.)
Queenborough Gdns. Chst
—65Tc 130
Queenborough Gdns. Ilf —28Qc 46
Queen Caroline St. W6 —49Ya 80
Queendale Ct. Wok —4C 188
Queen Elizabeth Av. E Til —9K 93
Queen Elizabeth Bldgs. EC4
(off Temple) —45Qb 82 (4K 199)
Queen Elizabeth Gdns. Mord
—70Cb 125
Queen Elizabeth Ho. SW12
—59Jb 104
Queen Elizabeth Pl. Til —6C 114
Queen Elizabeth Rd. E17 —27Ac 44
Queen Elizabeth Rd. King T
—68Pa 123
Queen Elizabeth's Clo. N16
—33Tb 63
Queen Elizabeth's Dri. N14
—18Nb 24
Queen Elizabeth's Dri. New Ad
—81Fc 167
Queen Elizabeth II Bri. Dart & Grays
—55Td 112
Queen Elizabeth's Gdns. New Ad
—82Fc 167
Queen Elizabeth's Wlk. N16
—32Tb 63
Queen Elizabeth's Wlk. Wind —4J 95
Queen Elizabeth Wlk. SW13
—53Wa 102
Queen Elizabeth Wlk. Wall
—77Mb 146
Queen Elizabeth Way. Wok
—91B 172
Queengate Ct. N12 —22Db 41
Queenhill Rd. S Croy —82Xb 165
Queenhithe. EC4
—45Sb 83 (4E 200)
Queenhythe Rd. Guild —100A 172
Queen Margaret's Gro. N1 —36Ub 63
Queen Mary Av. E Til —9L 93
Queen Mary Av. Mord —71Za 144
Queen Mary Clo. Romf —30Hd 48
Queen Mary Clo. Wok —88E 156
Queen Mary Ct. Til —9L 93
Queen Mary Rd. SE19 —65Rb 127
Queen Mary Rd. Shep —68S 120
Queen Mary's Av. Cars —80Hb 145
Queen Mary's Av. Wat —14U 18
Queen Mary's Dri. New Haw
—82H 157
Queen Mothers Dri. Den —30H 35
Queen of Denmark Ct. SE16
—48Bc 84
Queens Acre. Sutt —80Ab 144
Queens Acre. Wind —6H 95
Queens All. Epp —3Vc 15
Queens Av. N3 —24Eb 41
Queens Av. N10 —27Jb 42
Queens Av. N20 —19Fb 23
Queens Av. N21 —18Rb 25
Queen's Av. Byfl —84M 157
Queens Av. Felt —63Y 121
Queen's Av. Gnfd —44Da 77
Queen's Av. Stan —27La 38
Queen's Av. Wat —14V 18
Queen's Av. Wfd G —22Kc 45
Queensberry M. W. SW7
—49Fb 81 (5B 202)
Queensberry Pl. SW7
—49Fb 81 (5B 202)
Queensberry Way. SW7
—49Fb 81 (5B 202)
Queensborough Ct. N3 —28Bb 41
(off N. Circular Rd.)
Queensborough M. W2 —45Eb 81
Queensborough Pas. W2 —45Eb 81
(off Queensborough M.)
Queensborough Studios. W2
(off Queensborough M.) —45Eb 81
Queensborough Ter. W2 —45Db 81
Queensbridge Ct. E2
—39Vb 63 (1K 195)
(off Queensbridge Ct.)
Queensbridge Pk. Iswth —57Ga 100
Queensbridge Rd. E8 & E2
—37Vb 63
Queensbury Circ. Pde. Harr & Stan
—27Na 39
Queensbury Ho. Rich —57Ma 101
Queensbury Rd. NW9 —31Ta 59
Queensbury Rd. Wemb —40Pa 59
Queensbury Sta. Pde. Edgw
—27Pa 39
Queensbury St. N1 —38Sb 63
Queen's Cir. SW8 —52Kb 104
Queen's Clo. Edgw —22Qa 39
Queen's Clo. Esh —77Da 141
Queen's Clo. Old Win —7L 95
Queens Clo. Tad —96Wa 178
Queens Clo. Wall —78Kb 146
Queen's Club Gdns. W14
—51Ab 102
Queens Ct. NW11 —29Bb 41
Queens Ct. SE23 —61Yb 128
Queens Ct. Rich —58Pa 101
Queens Ct. Slou —5K 73
Queen's Ct. W'stone —26La 38
Queenscourt. Wemb —35Na 59
Queens Ct. Wey —79U 140
Queens Ct. Wok —90B 156
Queens Ct. Ride. Cob —85W 158
Queen's Cres. NW5 —37Jb 62
Queen's Cres. Rich —57Pa 101
Queenscroft Rd. SE9 —57Mc 107
Queensdale Cres. W11 —46Za 80
Queensdale Pl. W11 —46Ab 80
Queensdale Rd. W11 —46Za 80
Queensdale Wlk. W11 —46Ab 80
Queensdown Rd. E5 —35Xb 63
Queens Dri. E10 —31Cc 64
Queen's Dri. N4 —33Rb 63
Queens Dri. W5 & W3 —44Pa 79
Queens Dri. Abb L —4V 4
Queen's Dri. Oxs —83Ea 160
Queens Dri. Sev —92Ld 187
Queen's Dri. Slou —40B 54
Queen's Dri. Surb —73Qa 143
Queen's Dri. Th Dit —72Ja 142
Queen's Dri. Wal X —6Cc 12
Queens Dri., The. Rick —16H 17
Queen's Elm Pde. SW3
—50Fb 81 (7C 202)
(off Old Church St.)
Queen's Elm Sq. SW3
—50Fb 81 (7C 202)
Queen's Farm Rd. Shorne —1N 137
Queens Ferry Wlk. N17 —28Xb 43
Queensfield Ct. Sutt —77Ya 144
Queen's Gdns. NW4 —29Ya 40
Queen's Gdns. W2
—45Eb 81 (4A 196)
Queen's Gdns. W5 —42La 78
Queens Gdns. Dart —60Rd 111
Queen's Gdns. Houn —53Aa 99
Queen's Gdns. Rain —40Fd 68
Queens Gdns. Upm —30Vd 50
Queen's Ga. SW7
—47Eb 81 (2A 202)
Queensgate. Wal X —6Bc 12
Queens Ga. Cen. Grays —50De 91
Queen's Ga. Gdns. SW7
—48Eb 81 (4A 202)
Queens Ga. Gdns. SW15
—56Xa 102
Queensgate Gdns. Chst —67Tc 130
Queen's Ga. M. SW7
—48Eb 81 (3A 202)
Queensgate Pl. NW6 —38Cb 61
Queen's Ga. Pl. SW7
—48Eb 81 (4A 202)
Queen's Ga. Pl. M. SW7
—48Eb 81 (4A 202)
Queen's Ga. Ter. SW7
—48Eb 81 (3A 202)
Queen's Gro. NW8
—39Fb 61 (1B 190)
Queens Gro. Rd. E4 —18Fc 27
Queen's Head St. N1
—39Rb 63 (1C 194)
Queen's Head Yd. SE1
—46Tb 83 (7F 201)
(off Borough High St.)
Queens Hill Rise. Asc —9A 116
Queens Ho. Tedd —65Ha 122
Queensland Av. N18 —23Sb 43
Queensland Av. SW19 —67Db 125
Queensland Ho. E16 —46Qc 86
(off Rymill St.)
Queensland Pl. N7 —35Qb 62
Queensland Rd. N7 —35Qb 62
Queens La. N10 —27Kb 42
Queens La. Ashf —63P 119
Queens Mkt. E13 —39Lc 65
Queensmead. NW8 —39Fb 61
Queensmead. Dat —3M 95
Queensmead Av. Eps —82Xa 162
Queens Mead Rd. Brom —68Hc 129
Queensmere. Slou —7K 73
Queensmere Clo. SW19 —61Za 124
Queensmere Ct. SW13 —51Va 102
Queensmere Rd. SW19 —61Za 124
Queensmere Rd. Slou —7L 73
Queen's M. W2 —45Db 81
Queensmill Rd. SW6 —52Za 102
Queens Pde. N8 —28Rb 43
Queens Pde. N11 —22Hb 41
Queens Pde. W5 —44Pa 79
Queen's Pk. Gdns. Felt —62V 120
Queen's Pk. Rd. Cat —95Ub 181
Queen's Pk. Rd. Romf —25Qd 49
Queens Pas. Chst —65Rc 130
Queens Pl. Mord —70Cb 125
Queens Pl. Wat —13Y 19
Queen's Promenade. King T
—70Ma 123
Queen Sq. WC1 —42Nb 82 (6G 193)
Queen Sq. Pl. WC1
—42Nb 82 (6G 193)
(off Queen Sq.)
Queens Reach. E Mol —70Ga 122
Queens Reach. King T —68Ma 123
Queens Ride. SW13 & SW15
—55Wa 102
Queens Rise. Rich —58Pa 101
Queens Rd. E11 —31Fc 65
Queens Rd. E13 —39Kc 65
Queen's Rd. E17 —30Bc 44
Queens Rd. N3 —25Eb 41
Queens Rd. N9 —19Xb 25
Queens Rd. N11 —24Nb 42
Queens Rd. NW4 —29Ya 40
Queen's Rd. SE15 & SE14
—53Xb 105
Queen's Rd. SW14 —55Ta 101
Queens Rd. SW19 —65Bb 125
Queen's Rd. W5 —44Na 79
Queen's Rd. Asc —10B 116
Queens Rd. Bark —37Sc 66
Queens Rd. Barn —13Za 22
Queens Rd. Beck —68Ac 128
Queens Rd. Brtwd —20Yd 32
Queens Rd. Brom —68Jc 129
Queen's Rd. Buck H —19Kc 27
Queens Rd. Chst —65Rc 130
Queens Rd. Croy —72Rb 147
Queens Rd. Dat —2M 95
Queen's Rd. Egh —64B 118
Queen's Rd. Enf —14Ub 25
Queen's Rd. Eri —51Gd 110
Queens Rd. Eton W —10D 72
Queen's Rd. Felt —60X 99
Queens Rd. Grav —2E 136
Queens Rd. Hamp —63Da 121
Queens Rd. Hay —44U 76
Queen's Rd. Houn —55Da 99
Queen's Rd. King T —66Qa 123
Queen's Rd. Knap —6A 188
Queen's Rd. Lou —13Nc 28
Queen's Rd. Mitc —69Fb 125
Queens Rd. Mord —70Cb 125
Queens Rd. N Mald —70Va 124
Queen's Rd. Rich —59Pa 101
Queens Rd. Slou —5K 73
Queens Rd. S'hall —47Z 77
Queen's Rd. Sutt —82Cb 163
Queen's Rd. Tedd —65Ha 122
Queen's Rd. Th Dit —71Ha 142
Queen's Rd. Twic —60Ja 100
Queen's Rd. Uxb —41L 75
Queens Rd. Wall —78Kb 146
Queen's Rd. Wal X —5Ac 12
Queen's Rd. Wat —13Y 19
(in two parts)
Queen's Rd. Well —54Xc 109
Queens Rd. W Dray —47P 75
Queen's Rd. Wey & W on T
—78S 140
Queens Rd. Wind —4G 94
Queens Rd. W. E13 —40Jc 65
Queen's Row. SE17 —51Tb 105
Queen's St. Eri —51Gd 110
Queens Ter. E1 —42Yb 84
Queen's Ter. E13 —39Kc 65
Queen's Ter. NW8
—40Fb 61 (1B 190)
Queens Ter. Iswth —56Ja 100
Queen's Ter. Cotts. W7 —47Ga 78
Queensthorpe Rd. SE26 —63Zb 128
Queenstown Gdns. Rain —41Hd 88
Queenstown M. SW8 —54Kb 104
Queenstown Rd. SW8 —51Kb 104
Queen St. EC4 —45Sb 83 (4E 200)
Queen St. N17 —23Ub 43
Queen St. W1 —46Kb 82 (6K 197)
Queen St. Bexh —55Bd 109
Queen St. Cher —74J 139
Queen St. Chfd —4J 3
Queen St. Croy —77Sb 147
Queen St. Grav —8D 114
Queen St. Romf —30Fd 48
Queen St. War —22Yd 50
Queen St. Pl. EC4
—45Sb 83 (5E 200)
Queensville Rd. SW12 —59Mb 104
Queens Wlk. E4 —18Fc 27
Queens Wlk. NW9 —33Sa 59
Queen's Wlk. SW1
—46Lb 82 (6B 198)
Queen's Wlk. W5 —42La 78
Queen's Wlk. Ashf —63M 119
Queens Wlk. Harr —28Ga 38
Queens Wlk. Ruis —33Y 57
Queens Wlk. Ter. Ruis —34Y 57
Queen's Wlk., The. SE1
—46Pb 82 (6J 199)
(off Waterloo Rd.)
Queen's Way. NW4 —29Ya 40
Queensway. W2 —44Db 81
Queensway. Croy —78Pb 146
Queensway. Enf —14Xb 25
Queens Way. Felt —63Y 121
Queensway. Orp —71Sc 150
Queens Way. Shenl —4Na 7
Queensway. Sun —68X 121
Queens Way. Wal X —6Bc 12
Queensway. W Wick —76Gc 149
Queensway Ind. Est. Enf —14Yb 26
Queensway N. W on T —77Y 141
Queensway S. W on T —78Y 141
Queensway, The. Ger X —28A 34
Queenswell Av. N20 —20Gb 23
Queenswood Av. E17 —25Ec 44
Queenswood Av. Hamp —65Da 121
Queenswood Av. Houn —54Ba 99
Queenswood Av. Hut —15Fe 33
Queenswood Av. T Hth —71Qb 146
Queenswood Av. Wall —77Mb 146
Queenswood Ct. SE27 —63Tb 127
Queenswood Ct. SW4 —57Nb 104
Queenswood Cres. Wat —5W 4
Queenswood Gdns. E11 —32Kc 65
Queenswood Pk. N3 —26Ab 40
Queens Wood Rd. N10 —30Kb 42
Queenswood Rd. SE23 —62Zb 128
Queenswood Rd. Sidc —57Vc 109
Queenswood Rd. Wok —7A 188
Queen's Yd. WC1
—42Lb 82 (6C 192)
Queen Victoria Av. Wemb
—38Ma 59
Queen Victoria St. EC4
—45Rb 83 (4B 200)
Queen Victoria Wlk. Wind —3J 95
Quelmans Head Ride. Wind
—1B 116
Quemerford Rd. N7 —36Pb 62
Quendon Dri. Wal A —5Fc 13
Quenington Ct. SE15 —51Vb 105
(off Ebley Clo.)
Quennell Clo. Asht —91Pa 177
Quennell Way. Hut —17Ee 33
Quentin Pl. SE13 —55Gc 107
Quentin Rd. SE13 —55Gc 107
Quentins Dri. Berr G —88Rc 168
Quentin Way. Vir W —10M 117
Quernmore Clo. Brom —65Jc 129
Quernmore Rd. N4 —30Qb 42
Quernmore Rd. Brom —65Jc 129
Querrin St. SW6 —54Eb 103
Quested Ct. E8 —36Xb 63
(off Brett Rd.)
Quex M. NW6 —39Cb 61
Quex Rd. NW6 —39Cb 61
Quickley La. Chor —16D 16
Quickley Rise. Chor —16E 16
Quickmoor La. K Lan —5K 3
Quick Pl. N1 —39Rb 63
Quick Rd. W4 —50Ua 80
Quicksilver Pl. N22 —26Pb 42
Quicks Rd. SW19 —66Db 125
Quick St. N1 —40Rb 63 (2C 194)
Quick St. M. N1
—40Rb 63 (2B 194)
Quickswood. NW3 —38Gb 61
Quickwood Clo. Rick —16J 17
Quiet Clo. Add —77J 139
Quiet Nook. Brom —76Mc 149
Quill La. SW15 —56Za 102
Quillot, The. W on T —78V 140
Quill St. W5 —41Na 79
Quilp St. SE1 —47Sb 83 (1D 206)
Quilter Gdns. Orp —74Yc 151
Quilter Rd. Orp —74Yc 151
Quilter St. E2 —41Wb 83
Quinbrookes. Wex —4N 73
Quin Bldgs. SE1
—47Qb 82 (2A 206)
Quince Ct. S'hill —10A 116
Quince Tree Clo. S Ock —42Yd 90
Quincy Rd. Egh —64C 118
Quinta Dri. Barn —15Xa 22
Quintin Av. SW20 —67Bb 125
Quintin Clo. Pinn —28X 37
Quinton Clo. Beck —69Ec 128
Quinton Clo. Houn —52X 99
Quinton Clo. Wall —77Kb 146
Quinton Rd. Th Dit —74Ja 142
Quinton St. SW18 —61Eb 125
Quintow Way. Wal A —7Ec 12
Quintrell Clo. Wok —5E 188
Quixley St. E14 —45Fc 85
Quorn Rd. SE22 —56Ub 105

Rabbit La. W on T —80W 140
Rabbit Row. W8 —46Cb 81
Rabbit's Rd. E12 —35Nc 66
Rabbits Rd. S Dar —68Td 134
Rabbs Mill Ho. Uxb —40L 55
Rabournmead Dri. N'holt —36Aa 57
Raby Rd. N Mald —70Ta 123
Raby St. E14 —44Ac 84
Raccoon Way. Houn —54Y 99
Racefield Clo. Shorne —6N 137
Rachel Point. E5 —35Wb 63
Rackham M. SW16 —65Lb 126
Racton Rd. SW6 —51Cb 103
Radbourne Av. W5 —49La 78
Radbourne Clo. E5 —35Zb 64
Radbourne Ct. Harr —30Ka 38
Radbourne Cres. E17 —26Fc 45
Radbourne Rd. SW12 —59Lb 104
Radbroke. Lea —94La 176
Radcliffe Av. NW10 —40Wa 60
Radcliffe Av. Enf —11Sb 25
Radcliffe Gdns. Cars —80Gb 145
Radcliffe M. Hamp —64Ea 122
Radcliffe Rd. N21 —18Rb 25
Radcliffe Rd. Croy —75Vb 147
Radcliffe Rd. Harr —26Ja 38
Radcliffe Sq. SW15 —58Za 102
Radcliffe Way. N'holt —41Z 77
Radcot Av. Langl —48D 74
Radcot St. SE11
—50Qb 82 (7A 206)
Raddington Rd. W10 —43Ab 80
Radett Pk. Rd. Rad —6Ja 6
Radfield Way. Sidc —59Tc 108
Radford Rd. SE13 —58Ec 106
Radford Way. Bark —41Vc 87
Radipole Rd. SW6 —53Bb 103
Radius Pk. Felt —56V 98
Radland Rd. E16 —44Hc 85
Radlet Av. SE26 —61Xb 127
Radlett Clo. E7 —37Hc 65
Radlett La. Shenl —6Ma 7
Radlett Pl. NW8 —39Gb 61
Radlett Rd. Ald —10Da 5
Radlett Rd. Col S —1Ga 6
Radlett Rd. Wat —13Y 19
Radley Av. Ilf —35Wc 67
Radley Ct. SE16 —47Zb 84
Radley Gdns. Harr —28Na 39
Radley Ho. SE2 —47Zc 87
(off Wolvercote Rd.)
Radley M. W8 —48Cb 81
Radley Rd. N17 —26Ub 43
Radley's La. E18 —26Jc 45
Radleys Mead. Dag —37Dd 68
Radley Sq. E5 —33Yb 64
Radley Ter. E16 —43Hc 85
(off Hermit Rd.)
Radlix Rd. E10 —32Cc 64
Radnor Av. Harr —29Ga 38
Radnor Av. Well —57Xc 109
Radnor Clo. Chst —65Uc 130
Radnor Clo. Mitc —70Nb 126
Radnor Ct. Har W —25Ha 38
Radnor Cres. SE18 —52Wc 109
Radnor Cres. Ilf —29Pc 46
Radnor Gdns. Enf —11Ub 25
Radnor Gdns. Twic —61Ha 122
Radnor Gro. Uxb —40Q 56
Radnor M. W2 —44Fb 81 (3C 196)
Radnor Pl. W2 —44Gb 81 (3D 196)
Radnor Rd. NW6 —39Ab 60
Radnor Rd. SE15 —52Wb 105
Radnor Rd. Harr —29Fa 38

Radnor Rd.—Redcross Way

Radnor Rd. Twic —60Ha **100**
Radnor Rd. Wey —76Q **140**
Radnor St. EC1 —41Sb **83** (4E **194**)
Radnor Ter. W14 —49Bb **81**
Radnor Wlk. E14 —49Cc 84
(off Copeland Dri.)
Radnor Wlk. SW3 —50Gb **81** (7E **202**)
Radnor Wlk. Croy —72Bc **148**
Radnor Way. NW10 —42Ra **79**
Radnor Way. Slou —49A **74**
Radolphs. Tad —94Za **178**
Radstock Av. Harr —27Ja **38**
Radstock Ho. H Hill —22Md 49
(off Darlington Gdns.)
Radstock St. SW11 —52Gb **103**
Radstock Way. Red —100Mb **180**
Radstone Ct. Wok —90B **156**
Raeburn Gdns. Barn —15Xa **22**
Raeburn Av. Dart —57Kd **111**
Raeburn Av. Surb —74Ra **143**
Raeburn Clo. NW11 —30Eb **41**
Raeburn Clo. King T —66Ma **123**
Raeburn Gro. St J —7D **188**
Raeburn Rd. Edgw —25Qa **39**
Raeburn Rd. Hay —40T **56**
Raeburn Rd. Sidc —58Uc **108**
Raeburn St. SW2 —56Nb **104**
Rafford Way. Brom —68Kc **129**
Ragge Way. Seal —92Pd **187**
Raggleswood. Chst —67Qc **130**
Rag Hill Clo. Tats —93Nc **184**
Rag Hill Rd. Tats —93Mc **183**
Raglan Av. Wal X —6Zb **12**
Raglan Clo. Houn —57Ba **99**
Raglan Ct. SE12 —57Jc **107**
Raglan Ct. S Croy —78Rb **147**
Raglan Gdns. Wat —18X **19**
Raglan Ho. Slou —6K **73**
Raglan Precinct. Cat —94Ub **181**
Raglan Rd. E17 —29Ec **44**
Raglan Rd. SE18 —50Sc **86**
Raglan Rd. Belv —49Bd **87**
Raglan Rd. Brom —70Lc **129**
Raglan Rd. Enf —17Vb **25**
Raglan Rd. Knap —6B **188**
Raglan St. NW5 —37Kb **62**
Raglan Ter. Gnfd —35Da **57**
Raglan Way. N'holt —37Ea **58**
Ragley Clo. W3 —47Sa **79**
Ragstone Rd. Slou —8H **73**
Rahn Rd. Epp —3Wc **15**
Raider Clo. Romf —25Cd **48**
Railey M. NW5 —35Lb **62**
Railpit La. Warl —87Gc **167**
Railshead Rd. Iswth —56Ka **100**
Railton Rd. SE24 —56Qb **104**
Railway App. N4 —30Qb **42**
Railway App. SE1 —46Tb **83** (7G **201**)
Railway App. Cher —74H **139**
Railway App. Harr —28Ha **38**
Railway App. Twic —59Ja **100**
Railway App. Wall —78Kb **146**
Railway Av. SE16 —47Yb **84**
Railway Cotts. Borwd —14Qa **21**
Railway Cotts. Rad —7Ka **6**
Railway Cotts. Twic —58Ca **99**
Railway Cotts. Wat —11X **19**
Railway M. E3 —41Cc 84
(off Wellington Way)
Railway M. W11 —44Ab **80**
Railway Pde. Shenf —17Ce **33**
Railway Pas. Tedd —65Ja **122**
Railway Pl. Belv —48Cd **88**
Railway Pl. Grav —8D **114**
Railway Rise. SE22 —56Ub **105**
Railway Rd. Tedd —63Ga **122**
Railway Side. SW13 —55Va **102**
Railway Sq. Brtwd —20Yd **32**
Railway St. N1 —40Nb **62** (2G **193**)
Railway St. Grav —57Ce **113**
Railway St. Romf —31Yc **67**
Railway Ter. E17 —25Ec **44**
Railway Ter. SE13 —57Dc **106**
Railway Ter. Coul —87Mb 164
(off Station App.)
Railway Ter. Felt —60W **98**
Railway Ter. Slou —6K **73**
Railway Ter. Stai —64F **118**
Railway Ter. W'ham —97Tc **184**
Rainborough Clo. NW10 —37Sa **59**
Rainbow Av. E14 —50Dc **84**
Rainbow Ct. Wat —16Y **19**
Rainbow Ct. Wok —4B **188**
Rainbow Ind. Est. W Dray —45M **75**
Rainbow La. Stanf —1P **93**
Rainbow St. SE5 —52Ub **105**
Rainer Clo. Chesh —1Zb **12**
Raine St. E1 —46Xb **83**
Rainham Clo. SE9 —58Uc **108**
Rainham Clo. SW11 —58Gb **103**
Rainham Rd. NW10 —41Ya **80**
Rainham Rd. Horn & Rain —36Hd **68**
Rainham Rd. N. Dag —33Cd **68**
Rainham Rd. S. Dag —35Dd **68**
Rainhill Way. E3 —41Cc **84**
Rainsborough Av. SE8 —49Ac **84**
Rainsford Clo. Stan —21La **38**
Rainsford Rd. NW10 —40Ra **59**
Rainsford St. W2 —44Gb **81** (2D **196**)
Rainsford Way. Horn —32Jd **68**
Rainton Rd. SE7 —50Jc **85**
Rainville Rd. W6 —51Ya **102**
Raisins Hill. Pinn —27Y **37**
Raith Av. N14 —20Mb **24**
Raleana Rd. E14 —46Ec **84**
Raleigh Av. Hay —43X **77**
Raleigh Av. Wall —77Mb **146**
Raleigh Clo. NW4 —29Ya **40**
Raleigh Clo. Eri —51Hd **110**
Raleigh Clo. Pinn —31Z **57**
Raleigh Clo. Ruis —33V **56**
Raleigh Clo. Slou —6E **72**
Raleigh Ct. Beck —67Dc **128**
Raleigh Ct. Eri —52Hd **110**
Raleigh Ct. Stai —63J **119**
Raleigh Ct. Wall —79Kb **146**
Raleigh Dri. N20 —20Gb **23**
Raleigh Dri. Clay —78Fa **142**
Raleigh Dri. Surb —74Sa **143**
Raleigh Gdns. SW2 —58Pb **104**
Raleigh Gdns. Mitc —69Hb **125**
(in two parts)
Raleigh Ho. E14 —47Dc 84
(off Admirals Way)
Raleigh M. N1 —39Rb 63
(off Queen's Head St.)
Raleigh M. Orp —78Vc **151**
Raleigh Rd. N2 —26Gb **41**
Raleigh Rd. N8 —28Qb **42**
Raleigh Rd. SE20 —66Zb **128**
Raleigh Rd. Enf —14Tb **25**
Raleigh Rd. Felt —62V **120**
Raleigh Rd. Rich —55Pa **101**
Raleigh Rd. S'hall —50Aa **77**
Raleigh St. N1 —39Rb **63** (1C **194**)
Raleigh Way. N14 —18Mb **24**
Raleigh Way. Felt —64Y **121**
Ralliwood Rd. Asht —91Qa **177**
Ralph Brook Ct. N1 —41Tb 83 (3G 195)
(off Haberdasher Est.)
Ralph Perring Ct. Beck —70Cc **128**
Ralston St. SW3 —50Hb **81**
Ralston Way. Wat —19Z **19**
Rama Clo. SW16 —66Nb **126**
Rama Ct. Harr —33Ga **58**
Ramac Way. SE7 —50Kc **85**
Rambler Clo. SW16 —63Lb **126**
Rambler Clo. Tap —4A **72**
Rambler La. Slou —8N **73**
Ramilles Clo. SW2 —58Nb **104**
Ramillies Pl. W1 —44Lb **82** (3B **198**)
Ramillies Rd. NW7 —19Ua **22**
Ramillies Rd. W4 —49Ta **79**
Ramillies Rd. Sidc —58Xc **109**
Ramillies St. W1 —44Lb **82** (3B **198**)
Ramney Dri. Enf —8Ac **12**
Ramornie Clo. W on T —77Ba **141**
Rampart St. E1 —44Xb **83**
Rampayne St. SW1 —50Mb **82** (7D **204**)
Ram Pl. E9 —37Yb **64**
Ram Pl. King T —68Ma **123**
Rampton Clo. E4 —20Cc **26**
Ramsay Gdns. Romf —25Ld **49**
Ramsay Pl. Harr —32Ga **58**
Ramsay Rd. E7 —35Gc **65**
Ramsay Rd. W3 —48Sa **79**
Ramscroft Clo. N9 —17Ub **25**
Ramsdale Rd. SW17 —64Jb **126**
Ramsden Clo. Orp —74Yc **151**
Ramsden Dri. Romf —24Cd **48**
Ramsden Rd. N11 —22Hb **41**
Ramsden Rd. SW12 —58Jb **104**
Ramsden Rd. Eri —52Fd **110**
Ramsden Rd. Orp —74Xc **151**
Ramsey Clo. NW9 —30Va **40**
Ramsey Clo. Gnfd —36Fa **58**
Ramsey Ct. Slou —2B **72**
Ramsey Rd. T Hth —72Pb **146**
Ramsey St. E2 —42Wb **83**
Ramsey Wlk. N1 —37Tb **63**
Ramsey Way. N14 —17Lb **24**
Ramsgate St. E8 —37Vb **63**
Ramsgill App. Ilf —28Vc **47**
Ramsgill Dri. Ilf —29Vc **47**
Rams Gro. Romf —28Ad **47**
Ram St. SW18 —57Db **103**
Ramulis Dri. Hay —42Aa **77**
Ramuswood Av. Orp —78Uc **150**
Rancliffe Gdns. SE9 —56Nc **108**
Rancliffe Rd. E6 —40Nc **66**
Randall Av. NW2 —33Ua **60**
Randall Clo. SW11 —53Gb **103**
Randall Clo. Eri —51Ed **110**
Randall Clo. Slou —50B **74**
Randall Ct. NW7 —24Wa **40**
Randall Dri. Horn —35Ld **69**
Randall Farm La. Lea —91Ja **176**
Randall Pl. SE10 —52Ec **106**
Randall Rd. SE11 —50Pb **82** (7H **205**)
Randall Row. SE11 —49Pb **82** (6H **205**)
Randalls Cres. Lea —92Ja **176**
Randalls Dri. Hut —16Fe **33**
Randalls Pk. Av. Lea —92Ja **176**
Randalls Pk. Dri. Lea —93Ja **176**
Randalls Research Pk. Lea —92Ja **176**
Randalls Rd. Lea —91Ga **176**
Randalls Way. Lea —93Ja **176**
Randell's Rd. N1 —39Nb **62**
Randisbourne Gdns. SE6 —62Dc **128**
Randle Rd. Rich —63La **122**
Randlesdown Rd. SE6 —63Cc **128**
(in two parts)
Randles La. Knock —86Zc **169**
Randolph App. E16 —44Lc **85**
Randolph Av. W9 —40Db **61**
Randolph Clo. Bexh —55Ed **110**
Randolph Clo. King T —64Sa **123**
Randolph Clo. Knap —5B **188**
Randolph Clo. Stoke D —87Ca **159**
Randolph Ct. Pinn —24Ca 37
(off Avenue, The)
Randolph Cres. W9 —42Eb **81** (6A **190**)
Randolph Gdns. NW6 —40Db **61**
Randolph Gro. Romf —29Yc **47**
Randolph M. W9 —42Eb **81** (6A **190**)
Randolph Rd. E17 —29Dc **44**
Randolph Rd. W9 —42Eb **81** (6A **190**)
Randolph Rd. Eps —86Va **162**
Randolph Rd. Slou —51A **96**
Randolph Rd. S'hall —47Ba **77**
Randolph's La. W'ham —98Rc **184**
Randolph St. NW1 —38Lb **62**
Randon Clo. Harr —26Da **37**
Ranelagh Av. SW6 —55Bb **103**
Ranelagh Av. SW13 —54Wa **102**
Ranelagh Bri. W2 —43Db **81**
Ranelagh Clo. Edgw —21Qa **39**
Ranelagh Dri. Edgw —21Qa **39**
Ranelagh Dri. Twic —57Ka **100**
Ranelagh Gdns. E11 —29Lc **45**
Ranelagh Gdns. SW6 —55Ab **102**
Ranelagh Gdns. W4 —52Sa **101**
Ranelagh Gdns. W6 —48Va **80**
Ranelagh Gdns. Grav —9B **114**
Ranelagh Gdns. Ilf —32Pc **66**
Ranelagh Gdns. Mans. SW6
(off Ranelagh Gdns.) —55Ab 102
Ranelagh Gro. SW1 —50Jb **82** (7J **203**)
Ranelagh M. W5 —47Ma **79**
Ranelagh Pl. N Mald —71Ua **144**
Ranelagh Rd. E6 —39Qc **66**
Ranelagh Rd. E11 —35Gc **65**
Ranelagh Rd. E15 —40Gc **65**
Ranelagh Rd. N17 —27Ub **43**
Ranelagh Rd. N22 —25Pb **42**
Ranelagh Rd. NW10 —40Va **60**
Ranelagh Rd. SW1 —50Lb **82** (7C **204**)
Ranelagh Rd. W5 —47Ma **79**
Ranelagh Rd. S'hall —46Z **77**
Ranelagh Rd. Wemb —37Ma **59**
Ranfurly Rd. Sutt —75Cb **145**
Rangbourne Ho. N7 —36Nb **62**
Rangefield Rd. Brom —64Gc **129**
Rangemoor Rd. N15 —29Vb **43**
Range Rd. Grav —9G **114**
Ranger's Rd. E4 —17Gc **27**
Rangers Sq. SE10 —53Fc **107**
Range Wlk. Add —78K **139**
Range Way. Shep —73Q **140**
Rangeworth Pl. Sidc —62Vc **131**
Rangoon St. EC3 —44Vb 83 (3K 201)
(off Crutched Friars)
Rankin Clo. NW9 —27Ua **40**
Ranleigh Gdns. Bexh —52Bd **109**
Ranmere St. SW12 —60Kb **104**
Ranmoor Clo. Harr —28Fa **38**
Ranmoor Gdns. Harr —28Fa **38**
Ranmore Av. Croy —76Vb **147**
Ranmore Path. Orp —70Wc **131**
Ranmore Rd. Sutt —81Za **162**
Rannoch Clo. Edgw —19Ra **21**
Rannoch Rd. W6 —51Ya **102**
Rannock Av. NW9 —31Ta **59**
Ranskill Ct. Borwd —11Qa **21**
Ranskill Rd. Borwd —11Qa **21**
Ransom Clo. Wat —17Y **19**
Ransom Rd. SE7 —50Lc **85**
Ransom Wlk. SE7 —49Lc **85**
Ranston Clo. Den —30H **35**
Ranston St. NW1 —43Gb **81** (7D **190**)
Ranulf Rd. NW2 —35Bb **61**
Ranwell Clo. E3 —39Bc **64**
Ranworth Clo. Eri —54Gd **110**
Ranworth Rd. N9 —19Yb **26**
Ranyard Clo. Chess —76Pa **143**
Raphael Av. Romf —27Hd **48**
Raphael Av. Til —2C **114**
Raphael Clo. Shenl —4Na **7**
Raphael Dri. Wat —12Z **19**
Raphael Rd. Grav —9F **114**
Raphael St. SW7 —47Hb **81** (2F **203**)
Rapier Clo. Purf —49Pd **89**
Raplace Ho. SE14 —52Ac **106**
Rase Hill Clo. Rick —15L **17**
Rashleigh Ct. SW8 —54Kb **104**
Rashleigh Way. Hort K —70Sd **134**
Rasper Rd. N20 —19Eb **23**
Rastell Av. SW2 —61Mb **126**
Ratcliffe Clo. Uxb —41M **75**
Ratcliffe Cross St. E1 —44Zb **84**
Ratcliffe La. E14 —44Ac **84**
Ratcliffe Orchard. E1 —45Zb **84**
Ratcliff Gro. EC1 —41Sb **83** (4E **194**)
Ratcliff Rd. E7 —36Lc **65**
Rathbone Pl. W1 —43Mb **82** (1D **198**)
Rathbone Point. E5 —35Wb **63**
Rathbone Sq. Croy —77Sb **147**
Rathbone St. E16 —44Hc **85**
Rathbone St. W1 —43Lb **82** (1C **198**)
Rathcoole Av. N8 —29Pb **42**
Rathcoole Gdns. N8 —29Pb **42**
Rathfern Rd. SE6 —60Bc **106**
Rathgar Av. W13 —46Ka **78**
Rathgar Clo. N3 —26Bb **41**
Rathgar Rd. SW9 —55Rb **105**
Rathlin Wlk. N1 —37Sb **63**
Rathmell Dri. SW4 —58Mb **104**
Rathmore Rd. SE7 —50Kc **85**
Rathmore Rd. Grav —9D **114**
Rats La. Lou —10Kc **13**
Rattray Rd. SW2 —56Qb **104**
Raul Rd. SE15 —54Wb **105**
Raveley St. NW5 —35Lb **62**
Ravel Gdns. S Ock —44Sd **90**
Ravel Rd. S Ock —44Sd **90**
Raven Clo. Rick —17L **17**
Ravencroft. Grays —7D **92**
Ravendale Rd. Sun —68V **120**
Ravenet St. SW11 —53Kb **104**
Ravenfield Rd. SW17 —62Hb **125**
Ravenhill Rd. E13 —40Lc **65**
Ravenna Rd. SW15 —57Za **102**
Ravenor Pk. Rd. Gnfd —41Da **77**
Raven Rd. E18 —26Lc **45**
Raven Row. E1 —43Xb **83**
Ravensbourne Av. Beck & Brom —66Fc **129**
Ravensbourne Av. Stai —60N **97**
Ravensbourne Cres. Romf —27Pd **49**
Ravensbourne Gdns. W13 —43Ka **78**
Ravensbourne Gdns. Ilf —25Qc **46**
Ravensbourne Pk. SE6 —59Cc **106**
Ravensbourne Pk. Cres. SE6 —59Bc **106**
Ravensbourne Pl. SE13 —54Dc **106**
Ravensbourne Rd. SE6 —59Bc **106**
Ravensbourne Rd. Brom —69Jc **129**
Ravensbourne Rd. Dart —55Jd **110**
Ravensbourne Rd. Twic —58La **100**
Ravensbury Av. Mord —71Eb **145**
Ravensbury Gro. Mitc —70Fb **125**
Ravensbury La. Mitc —70Fb **125**
Ravensbury Path. Mitc —70Fb **125**
Ravensbury Rd. SW18 —61Db **125**
Ravensbury Rd. Orp —70Vc **131**
Ravensbury Ter. SW18 —61Db **125**
Ravenscar Rd. Brom —63Gc **129**
Ravenscar Rd. Surb —75Pa **143**
Ravens Clo. NW9 —26Ua **40**
Ravens Clo. Brom —68Hc **129**
Ravens Clo. Enf —12Ub **25**
Ravens Clo. Knap —4A **188**
Ravens Ct. Brtwd —18Zd **33**
Ravenscourt. Sun —67V **120**
Ravenscourt Av. W6 —49Wa **80**
Ravenscourt Clo. Horn —34Nd **69**
Ravenscourt Clo. Ruis —31S **56**
Ravenscourt Dri. Horn —34Nd **69**
Ravenscourt Gdns. W6 —49Wa **80**
Ravenscourt Gro. Horn —33Nd **69**
Ravenscourt Pk. W6 —48Wa **80**
Ravenscourt Pk. Barn —14Za **22**
Ravenscourt Pk. Mans. W6
(off Paddenswick Rd.) —48Xa 80
Ravenscourt Pl. W6 —49Xa **80**
Ravenscourt Rd. W6 —49Xa **80**
Ravenscourt Rd. Orp —69Wc **131**
Ravenscourt Sq. W6 —48Wa **80**
Ravenscraig Rd. N11 —21Lb **42**
Ravenscroft. Wat —7Aa **5**
Ravenscroft Av. NW11 —31Bb **61**
Ravenscroft Av. Wemb —32Na **59**
Ravenscroft Clo. E16 —43Jc **85**
Ravenscroft Cotts. Barn —14Cb **23**
Ravenscroft Cres. SE9 —62Pc **130**
Ravenscroft Pk. Barn —13Za **22**
Ravenscroft Rd. E16 —43Jc **85**
Ravenscroft Rd. W4 —49Sa **79**
Ravenscroft Rd. Beck —68Yb **128**
Ravenscroft Rd. Wey —83S **158**
Ravenscroft St. E2 —40Vb **63**
Ravensdale Av. N12 —21Eb **41**
Ravensdale Gdns. SE19 —66Tb **127**
Ravensdale Ho. Stai —65K **119**
Ravensdale Rd. N16 —31Vb **63**
Ravensdale Rd. Houn —55Aa **99**
Ravensdon St. SE11 —50Qb **82** (7A **206**)
Ravensfield. Egh —5N **117**
Ravensfield. Slou —7P **73**
Ravensfield Clo. Dag —35Zc **67**
Ravensfield Gdns. Eps —78Ua **144**
Ravenshaw St. NW6 —36Bb **61**
Ravenshead Clo. S Croy —83Yb **166**
Ravenshill. Chst —67Rc **130**
Ravenshurst Av. NW4 —28Ya **40**
Ravenside Clo. N18 —22Zb **44**
Ravenside Retail Pk. N18 —22Zb **44**
Ravenslea Rd. SW12 —59Hb **103**
Ravensmead. Ger X —22B **34**
Ravensmead Rd. Brom —66Fc **129**
Ravensmede Way. W4 —49Va **80**
Ravensmere. Epp —3Wc **15**
Ravens M. SE12 —57Jc **107**
Ravensquay Bus. Cen. St M —71Xc **151**
Ravenstone. SE17 —50Ub 83 (7J 207)
(off Bagshot St.)
Ravenstone Rd. N8 —27Qb **42**
Ravenstone Rd. NW9 —30Va **40**
Ravenstone St. SW12 —60Jb **104**
Ravens Way. SE12 —57Jc **107**
Ravens Wold. Kenl —87Sb **165**
Ravenswood. Bex —60Ad **109**
Ravenswood Av. Surb —75Pa **143**
Ravenswood Av. W Wick —74Ec **148**
Ravenswood Clo. Cob —87Z **159**
Ravenswood Clo. Romf —22Dd **48**
Ravenswood Ct. King T —65Ra **123**
Ravenswood Ct. Wok —90B **156**
Ravenswood Cres. Harr —33Ba **57**
Ravenswood Cres. W Wick —74Ec **148**
Ravenswood Gdns. Iswth —53Ga **100**
Ravenswood Ind. Est. E17 —28Ec **44**
Ravenswood Pk. N'wd —23W **36**
Ravenswood Rd. E17 —28Ec **44**
Ravenswood Rd. SW12 —59Kb **104**
Ravenswood Rd. Croy —76Rb **147**
Ravensworth Rd. NW10 —41Xa **80**
Ravensworth Rd. SE9 —63Pc **130**
Ravensworth Rd. Slou —1E **72**
Ravent Rd. SE11 —49Pb **82** (6J **205**)
Ravey St. EC2 —42Ub **83** (5H **195**)
Ravine Gro. SE18 —51Uc **108**
Rawalpindi Ho. E16 —42Hc **85**
Rawchester Clo. SW18 —60Bb **103**
Rawlings Clo. Orp —78Vc **151**
Rawlings St. SW3 —49Hb **81** (5F **203**)
Rawlins Clo. N3 —25Ab **40**
Rawlins Clo. S Croy —80Ac **148**
Rawlinson Ct. NW2 —31Ya **60**
Rawlinson Point. E16 —43Hc 85
(off Fox Rd.)
Rawlinson Ter. N17 —27Vb **43**
Rawnsley Av. Mitc —71Fb **145**
Rawreth Wlk. N1 —39Sb 63
(off Basire St.)
Rawson St. SW11 —53Jb **104**
(in two parts)
Rawsthorne Clo. E16 —46Pc **86**
Rawsthorne Ct. Houn —56Ba **99**
Rawstone Wlk. E13 —40Jc **65**
Rawstorne Pl. EC1 —41Rb **83** (3B **194**)
Rawstorne St. EC1 —41Rb **83** (3B **194**)
Rawthorn Av. N13 —22Nb **42**
Raybell Ct. Iswth —54Ja **100**
Rayburne Ct. W14 —48Ab **80**
Rayburne Ct. Buck H —18Lc **27**
Rayburn Rd. Horn —31Qd **69**
Raydean Rd. Barn —15Db **23**
Raydons Gdns. Dag —36Ad **67**
Raydons Rd. Dag —36Ad **67**
Raydon St. N19 —33Kb **62**
Rayfield. Epp —2Vc **15**
Rayfield Clo. Brom —72Nc **150**
Rayford Av. SE12 —59Hc **107**
Rayford Clo. Dart —57Ld **111**
Ray Gdns. Bark —40Wc **67**
Ray Gdns. Stan —22Ka **38**
Ray Ho. N1 —39Ub 63
(off Colville Est.)
Rayleas Clo. SE18 —53Rc **108**
Rayleigh Av. Tedd —65Ga **122**
Rayleigh Clo. N13 —20Tb **25**
Rayleigh Clo. Hut —16Ee **33**
Rayleigh Ct. N22 —25Sb **43**
Rayleigh Ct. King T —68Qa **123**
Rayleigh Rise. S Croy —79Ub **147**
Rayleigh Rd. N13 —20Sb **25**
Rayleigh Rd. SW19 —67Bb **125**
Rayleigh Rd. Hut —16De **33**
Rayleigh Rd. Stanf —2K **93**
Rayleigh Rd. Wfd G —23Lc **45**
Ray Lodge Rd. Wfd G —23Lc **45**
Raymead. NW4 —28Ya **40**
Raymead Av. T Hth —71Qb **146**
Raymead Clo. Fet —94Ga **176**
Raymead Way. Fet —94Ga **176**
Raymere Gdns. SE18 —52Tc **108**
Raymond Av. E18 —27Hc **45**
Raymond Av. W13 —48Ja **78**
Raymond Bldgs. WC1 —43Pb **82** (7J **193**)
Raymond Clo. SE26 —64Yb **128**
Raymond Clo. Abb L —4T **4**
Raymond Clo. Coln —53G **96**
Raymond Ct. N10 —24Kb **42**
Raymond Ct. Sutt —79Db **145**
Raymond Gdns. Chig —20Xc **29**
Raymond Postage Ct. SE28 —45Xc **87**
Raymond Rd. E13 —39Lc **65**
Raymond Rd. SW19 —65Ab **124**
Raymond Rd. Beck —70Ac **128**
Raymond Rd. Ilf —31Tc **66**
Raymond Rd. Slou —48C **74**
Raymond Way. Clay —79Ja **142**
Raymouth Ho. SE16 —49Yb 84
(off Rotherhithe New Rd.)
Raymouth Rd. SE16 —49Xb **83**
Rayne Ct. E18 —28Hc **45**
Rayners Clo. Coln —52E **96**
Rayners Clo. Wemb —36Ma **59**
Rayner's Ct. Grav —58Ee **113**
Rayners Cres. N'holt —41X **77**
Rayners Gdns. N'holt —40X **57**
Rayners La. Pinn & Harr —29Ba **37**
Rayners Rd. SW15 —57Ab **102**
Raynes Av. E11 —31Lc **65**
Raynes Pk. Bri. SW20 —68Ya **124**
Raynham Av. N18 —23Wb **43**
Raynham Rd. N18 —22Wb **43**
Raynham Rd. W6 —49Xa **80**
Raynham Ter. N18 —22Wb **43**
Raynor Clo. S'hall —46Ba **77**
Raynor Pl. N1 —39Sb **63**
Raynton Clo. Harr —32Aa **57**
Raynton Clo. Hay —42V **76**
Raynton Dri. Hay —42V **76**
Raynton Rd. Enf —9Zb **12**
Ray Rd. Romf —22Dd **48**
Ray Rd. W Mol —71Da **141**
Rays Av. N18 —21Yb **44**
Rays Av. Wind —2D **94**
Rays Hill. Hort K —70Sd **134**
Rays Rd. N18 —21Yb **44**
Rays Rd. W Wick —73Ec **148**
Ray St. EC1 —42Qb **82** (6A **194**)
Ray St. Bri. EC1 —42Qb 82 (6A 194)
(off Farringdon Rd.)
Ray Wlk. N7 —33Pb **62**
Raywood Clo. Hay —52S **98**
Reachview Clo. NW1 —38Lb **62**
Read Ct. E17 —30Cc **44**
Read Ct. Wal A —5Jc **13**
Readens, The. Bans —88Gb **163**
Reade Wlk. NW10 —38Ua **60**
Read Ho. SE11 —51Qb 104
(off Clayton Est.)
Reading La. E8 —37Xb **63**
Reading Rd. N'holt —36Da **57**
Reading Rd. Sutt —78Eb **145**
Readings, The. Chor —13H **17**
Reading Way. NW7 —22Za **40**
Read Rd. Asht —89Ma **161**
Reads Clo. Ilf —34Rc **66**
Reads Rest La. Tad —92Cb **179**
Read Way. Grav —4F **136**
Reapers Clo. NW1 —39Mb **62**
Reapers Way. Iswth —57Fa **100**
Reardon Path. E1 —46Xb **83**
Reardon St. E1 —46Xb **83**
Reaston St. SE14 —52Zb **106**
Rebecca Ter. SE16 —48Yb **84**
Reckitt Rd. W4 —50Ua **80**
Record St. SE15 —51Yb **106**
Recovery St. SW17 —64Gb **125**
Recreation Av. H Wood —26Pd **49**
Recreation Av. Romf —29Ed **48**
Recreation Rd. SE26 —63Zb **128**
Recreation Rd. Brom —68Hc **129**
Recreation Rd. Sidc —62Uc **130**
Recreation Rd. S'hall —49Aa **77**
Recreation Way. Mitc —69Nb **126**
Rector St. N1 —39Sb **63** (1D **194**)
Rectory Chase. L War —28Zd **51**
Rectory Clo. E4 —20Cc **26**
Rectory Clo. N3 —25Bb **41**
Rectory Clo. SW20 —69Ya **124**
Rectory Clo. Asht —91Pa **177**
Rectory Clo. Byfl —85N **157**
Rectory Clo. Dart —56Gd **110**
Rectory Clo. Farn R —1G **72**
Rectory Clo. Shep —69Q **120**
Rectory Clo. Sidc —63Xc **131**
Rectory Clo. Stan —22Ka **38**
Rectory Clo. Surb —74La **142**
Rectory Clo. Wind —3E **94**
Rectory Ct. Felt —63Y **121**
Rectory Cres. E11 —30Lc **45**
Rectory Farm Rd. Enf —10Pb **10**
Rectory Field Cres. SE7 —52Lc **107**
Rectory Gdns. N8 —28Nb **42**
Rectory Gdns. SW4 —55Lb **104**
Rectory Gdns. N'holt —39Ba **57**
Rectory Gdns. Upm —33Td **70**
Rectory Grn. Beck —67Bc **128**
Rectory Gro. SW4 —55Lb **104**
Rectory Gro. Croy —75Rb **147**
Rectory Gro. Hamp —63Ba **121**
Rectory La. SW17 —65Jb **126**
Rectory La. Asht —91Pa **177**
Rectory La. Bans —87Hb **163**
Rectory La. Bookh —98Ba **175**
Rectory La. Bras —96Yc **185**
Rectory La. Byfl —86N **157**
Rectory La. Edgw —23Qa **39**
Rectory La. Heron —24Fe **51**
Rectory La. K Lan —1Q **4**
Rectory La. Lou —12Qc **28**
Rectory La. Rick —18M **17**
Rectory La. Sev —98Ld **187**
Rectory La. Shenl —5Pa **7**
Rectory La. Sidc —63Xc **131**
Rectory La. Stan —22Ka **38**
Rectory La. Surb —74Ka **142**
Rectory La. Wall —77Lb **146**
Rectory La. W'ham —95Nc **184**
Rectory Meadow. S'fleet —65Ce **135**
Rectory Orchard. SW19 —63Ab **124**
Rectory Pk. S Croy —85Ub **165**
Rectory Pk. Av. N'holt —41Ba **77**
Rectory Pl. SE18 —49Qc **86**
Rectory Rd. E12 —36Pc **66**
Rectory Rd. E17 —28Dc **44**
Rectory Rd. N16 —33Vb **63**
Rectory Rd. SW13 —54Wa **102**
Rectory Rd. W3 —46Ra **79**
Rectory Rd. Ash —78De **155**
Rectory Rd. Beck —67Cc **128**
Rectory Rd. Coul —87Fb **179**
Rectory Rd. Dag —37Dd **68**
Rectory Rd. Grays —48Fe **91**
Rectory Rd. Hay —44W **76**
Rectory Rd. Houn —54Y **99**
Rectory Rd. Kes —80Mc **149**
Rectory Rd. Ors —3D **92**
Rectory Rd. Rick —18M **17**
Rectory Rd. S'hall —48Ba **77**
Rectory Rd. Stanf —2L **93**
Rectory Rd. Sutt —76Cb **145**
Rectory Rd. Swans —59Ae **113**
Rectory Rd. W Til —1F **114**
Rectory Sq. E1 —43Zb **84**
Rectory Ter. Stanf —2L **93**
Rectory Way. Uxb —33R **56**
Reculver Rd. SE16 —50Zb **84**
Red Anchor Clo. SW3 —51Fb **103**
Redan Pl. W2 —44Db **81**
Redan St. W14 —48Za **80**
Redan Ter. SE5 —54Rb **105**
Redbarn Clo. Purl —83Rb **165**
Red Barracks Rd. SE18 —49Pc **86**
Redberry Gro. SE26 —62Yb **128**
Redbourne Av. N3 —25Cb **41**
Redbridge Gdns. SE5 —52Ub **105**
Redbridge La. E. Ilf —30Mc **45**
Redbridge La. W. E11 —30Kc **45**
Redbrooke Ct. Linf —8J **93**
Redburn Ind. Est. Enf —16Zb **26**
Redburn St. SW3 —51Hb **103**
Redbury Clo. Rain —42Ld **89**
Redcar Clo. N'holt —36Da **57**
Redcar Rd. Romf —22Pd **49**
Redcar St. SE5 —52Sb **105**
Redcastle Clo. E1 —45Yb **84**
Red Cedars Rd. Orp —73Uc **150**
Redchurch St. E2 —42Vb **83** (5K **195**)
Redcliffe Clo. SW5 —50Db **81**
Redcliffe Gdns. SW5 & SW10 —50Db **81**
Redcliffe Gdns. Ilf —32Qc **66**
Redcliffe M. SW10 —50Db **81**
Redcliffe Pl. SW10 —51Eb **103**
Redcliffe Rd. SW10 —50Eb **81** (7A **202**)
Redcliffe Sq. SW10 —50Db **81**
Redcliffe St. SW10 —51Db **103**
Redcliffe Wlk. Wemb —34Ra **59**
Redclose Av. Mord —71Cb **145**
Redclyffe Rd. E6 —39Lc **65**
Red Cottage M. Slou —8N **73**
Redcourt. Croy —76Ub **147**
Red Ct. Slou —6J **73**
Redcourt. Wok —87F **156**
Redcroft Rd. S'hall —45Ea **78**
Redcross Way. SE1 —47Sb **83** (1E **206**)

Redden Ct. Rd. Romf —27Nd 49
Redding. Sidc —65Xc 131
Redding Ho. Wat —16U 18
Reddings Av. Bush —15Da 19
Reddings Clo. NW7 —21Va 40
Reddings Rd. SE15 —52Wb 105
Reddings, The. NW7 —20Va 22
Reddings, The. Borwd —13Pa 21
Reddington Clo. S Croy —81Tb 165
Reddington Dri. Slou —49A 74
Reddons Rd. Beck —66Ac 128
Reddown Rd. Coul —90Mb 164
Reddy Rd. Eri —51Hd 110
Rede Pl. W2 —44Cb 81
Redesdale Gdns. Iswth —52Ja 100
Redesdale St. SW3 —51Gb 103
Redfern Av. Houn —59Ca 99
Redfern Clo. Uxb —39L 55
Red Fern Ct. Wat —15V 18
Redfern Gdns. Romf —26Md 49
Redfern Ho. E13 —39Hc 65
(off Redriffe Rd.)
Redfern Rd. NW10 —38Ua 60
Redfern Rd. SE6 —59Ec 106
Redfield La. SW5 —49Cb 81
Redfield M. SW5 —49Db 81
Redford Av. Coul —87Kb 164
Redford Av. T Hth —70Pb 126
Redford Av. Wall —79Nb 146
Redford Rd. Wind —3B 94
Redford Wlk. N1 —39Sb 63
(off Popham St.)
Redford Way. Uxb —38M 55
Redgate Dri. Brom —75Kc 149
Redgate Ter. SW15 —58Za 102
Redgrave Clo. Croy —72Vb 147
Redgrave Rd. SW15 —55Za 102
Redhall Ct. Cat —95Tb 181
Redhall La. Chan X —11N 17
Redheath Clo. Wat —7V 4
Red Hill. Chst —64Rc 130
Red Hill. Den —33F 54
Redhill Ct. SW2 —61Qb 126
Redhill Dri. Edgw —26Ra 39
Redhill Rd. Cob —85R 158
Redhill Rd. New Ash —77Ae 155
Redhill St. NW1 —40Kb 62 (2A 192)
Redhill Wood. New Ash —76Ce 155
Redholm Vs. N16 —35Tb 63
Red Ho. Cotts. Sev —97Ld 187
Red Ho. La. Bexh —56Zc 109
Red Ho. La. W on T —75W 140
Redhouse Rd. Croy —72Mb 146
Redhouse Rd. Tats —93Lc 183
Redington Gdns. NW3 —35Db 61
Redington Rd. NW3 —34Db 61
Redlands. N15 —28Tb 43
Redlands. Coul —88Nb 164
Redlands. Tedd —65Ja 122
Redlands Ct. Brom —66Hc 129
Redlands Gdns. W Mol —70Ba 121
Redlands Rd. Enf —11Ac 26
Redlands Rd. Sev —96Hd 186
Redlands, The. Beck —68Dc 128
Redlands Way. SW2 —59Pb 104
Red La. Clay —79Ja 142
Redlaw Way. SE16 —50Wb 83
Redleaf Clo. Belv —51Cd 110
Redleaves Av. Ashf —65R 120
Redlees Clo. Iswth —56Ja 100
Red Lion Clo. SE17 —51Tb 105
(off Red Lion Row)
Red Lion Clo. Orp —72Yc 151
Red Lion Ct. EC4
—44Qb 82 (3A 200)
Red Lion Ct. SE1
—46Sb 83 (6E 200)
Red Lion Hill. N2 —26Fb 41
Red Lion La. SE18 —52Qc 108
Red Lion La. Sarr —7J 3
Red Lion Pde. Pinn —27Aa 37
Red Lion Pl. SE18 —53Qc 108
Red Lion Rd. Surb —75Pa 143
Red Lion Row. SE17 —51Sb 105
Red Lion Sq. SW18 —57Cb 103
Red Lion Sq. WC1
—43Pb 82 (1H 199)
Red Lion St. WC1
—43Pb 82 (7H 193)
Red Lion St. Rich —57Ma 101
Red Lion Yd. W1
—46Kb 82 (6K 197)
(off Waverton St.)
Red Lion Yd. Wat —14Y 19
Red Lodge. W Wick —74Ec 148
Red Lodge Cres. Bex —62Fd 132
Red Lodge Rd. Bex —62Fd 132
Red Lodge Rd. W Wick —74Ec 148
Redman Clo. N'holt —40Y 57
Redmans La. Sev —79Ed 152
Redman's Rd. E1 —43Yb 84
Redmead La. E1 —46Wb 83
Redmead Rd. Hay —49U 76
Redmond Ho. N1
—39Pb 62 (1J 193)
(off Barnsbury Est.)
Redmore Rd. W6 —49Xa 80
Redmount Clo. Buck H —19Kc 27
Red Oak Clo. Orp —76Rc 150
Red Oaks Mead. They B —9Tc 14
Red Path. E9 —37Ac 64
Red Pl. W1 —45Jb 82 (4H 197)
Redpoll Way. Eri —48Zc 87
Red Post Hill. SE24 & SE21
—56Tb 105
Red Post Ho. E6 —38Mc 65
Redriffe Rd. E13 —39Hc 65
Redriff Est. SE16 —48Bc 84
Redriff Rd. SE16 —49Zb 84
Redriff Rd. Romf —26Dd 48
Red Rd. Borwd —13Pa 21
Red Rd. War —21Xd 50
Redroofs Clo. Beck —67Dc 128
Red Rose Ind. Est. Barn —15Fb 23
Redruth Clo. N22 —24Pb 42
Redruth Gdns. Romf —22Pd 49
Redruth Ho. Sutt —80Db 145
Redruth Rd. E9 —39Yb 64
Redruth Rd. Romf —22Pd 49
Redruth Wlk. Romf —22Pd 49
Redstart Clo. E6 —43Nc 86
Redstart Clo. SE14 —52Ac 106
Redstart Clo. New Ad —82Fc 167
Redston Rd. N8 —28Mb 42
Red St. S'fleet —64Ce 135
Redvers Rd. N22 —26Qb 42
Redvers Rd. Warl —90Zb 166
Redvers St. N1 —41Ub 83 (3J 195)
Redwald Rd. E5 —35Zb 64
Redway Dri. Twic —59Ea 100
Redwing Clo. S Croy —83Zb 166
Redwing Ct. H Hill —25Md 49
Redwing Path. SE28 —48Tc 86
Redwood. Egh —68G 118
Redwood Clo. N14 —17Mb 24
Redwood Clo. SE16 —46Ac 84
Redwood Clo. Kenl —86Sb 165
Redwood Clo. Sidc —59Wc 109
Redwood Clo. Uxb —40R 56
Redwood Clo. Wat —21Z 37
Redwood Ct. N19 —31Mb 62
Redwood Ct. N'holt —41Aa 77
Redwood Ct. Surb —73Ma 143
Redwood Est. Houn —51X 99
Redwood Gdns. Chig —22Wc 47
Redwood Gdns. Slou —5H 73
Redwood Mans. W8 —48Db 81
(off Chantry Sq.)
Redwood Rise. Borwd —9Ra 7
Redwoods. SW15 —60Wa 102
Redwood Wlk. Surb —74Ma 143
Redwood Way. Barn —15Za 22
Reece M. SW7 —49Fb 81 (5B 202)
Reed Av. Orp —76Uc 150
Reed Clo. E16 —43Jc 85
Reed Clo. SE12 —57Jc 107
Reed Clo. Iver —44G 74
Reede Gdns. Dag —36Dd 68
Reede Rd. Dag —37Cd 68
Reede Way. Dag —37Dd 68
Reedham Clo. N17 —28Xb 43
Reedham Clo. Brick —1Ca 5
Reedham Dri. Purl —85Pb 164
Reedham Pk. Av. Purl —88Qb 164
Reedham St. SE15 —54Wb 105
Reed Pl. W Byf —85G 156
Reed Pond Wlk. Romf —26Hd 48
Reed Rd. N17 —26Vb 43
Reeds Cres. Wat —12Y 19
Reedsfield Rd. Ashf —63R 120
Reed's Pl. NW1 —38Lb 62
Reeds Wlk. Wat —12Y 19
Reedworth St. SE11
—49Qb 82 (6A 206)
Reenglass Rd. Stan —21Ma 39
Rees Gdns. Croy —72Vb 147
Reesland Clo. E12 —36Qc 66
Rees St. N1 —39Sb 63 (1E 194)
Reets Farm Clo. NW9 —30Ua 40
Reeves Av. NW9 —31Ta 59
Reeves Corner. Croy —75Rb 147
Reeves Cres. Swan —69Fd 132
Reeves Ho. SE1 —47Qb 82 (2K 205)
(off Baylis Rd.)
Reeves M. W1 —45Jb 82 (5H 197)
Reeves Path. Hay —49V 76
Reeves Rd. E3 —42Dc 84
Reeves Rd. SE18 —51Rc 108
Reform Row. N17 —26Vb 43
Reform St. SW11 —54Hb 103
Regal Clo. E1 —43Wb 83
Regal Clo. W5 —43Ma 79
Regal Ct. N18 —22Vb 43
Regal Cres. Wall —76Kb 146
Regal La. NW1 —39Jb 62 (1J 191)
Regal Pl. SW6 —52Db 103
(off Maxwell Rd.)
Regal Way. Harr —30Ma 39
Regal Way. Wat —10Y 5
Regan Ho. N18 —23Vb 43
Regan Way. N1 —40Ub 63 (1H 195)
Regarder Rd. Chig —22Wc 47
Regarth Av. Romf —30Gd 48
Regency Clo. W5 —44Na 79
Regency Clo. Chig —22Sc 46
Regency Clo. Hamp —64Ba 121
Regency Clo. W King —79Ud 154
Regency Ct. Brtwd —19Yd 32
Regency Ct. Enf —15Tb 25
Regency Ct. Surb —77Db 145
Regency Ct. Tedd —65Ka 122
Regency Cres. NW4 —26Za 40
Regency Dri. Ruis —32U 56
Regency Dri. W Byf —85H 157
Regency Gdns. Horn —31Ld 69
Regency Gdns. W on T —74Y 141
Regency Lodge. NW3 —38Fb 61
(off Adelaide Rd.)
Regency M. NW10 —37Wa 60
Regency M. Beck —75Ec 148
Regency M. Iswth —57Ga 100
Regency Pl. SW1
—49Mb 82 (5E 204)
Regency St. SW1
—49Mb 82 (5E 204)
Regency Ter. SW7
—50Fb 81 (7B 202)
(off Fulham Rd.)
Regency Wlk. Croy —72Bc 148
Regency Wlk. Rich —57Na 101
(off Grosvenor Av.)
Regency Way. Bexh —55Zc 109
Regent Av. Uxb —38R 56
Regent Clo. N12 —22Eb 41
Regent Clo. Grays —47Ee 91
Regent Clo. Harr —30Na 39
Regent Clo. Houn —53X 99
Regent Clo. New Haw —81M 157
Regent Ct. N3 —24Db 41
Regent Ct. N20 —19Eb 23
Regent Ct. Slou —4J 73
Regent Ct. Wat —21Wc 67
Regent Ga. Wal X —6Ac 12
(off High St. Waltham Cross)
Regent Ho. Brtwd —20Xd 32
Regent Ho. Eps —83Ua 162
Regent Pl. SW19 —64Eb 125
Regent Pl. W1 —45Lb 82 (4C 198)
Regent Pl. Croy —74Vb 147
Regent Rd. SE24 —58Rb 105
Regent Rd. Epp —2Vc 15
Regent Rd. Surb —71Pa 143
Regents Av. N13 —22Qb 42
Regent's Bri. Gdns. SW8 —52Nb 104
Regents Clo. Hay —43V 76
Regents Clo. Rad —6Ja 6
Regents Clo. S Croy —79Ub 147
Regents Clo. Stan —21Na 39
Regents Clo. Whyt —90Ub 165
Regents Ct. Brom —66Hc 129
Regents Ct. Grav —7D 114
Regents Dri. Kes —78Mc 149
Regents M. NW8
—40Eb 61 (1A 190)
Regents Pk. Est. NW1
—41Lb 82 (3B 192)
(off Robert St.)
Regent's Pk. Gdns. M. NW1
—39Hb 61
Regents Pk. Rd. N3 —27Bb 41
Regent's Pk. Rd. NW1 —39Hb 61
Regent's Pk. Ter. NW1 —39Kb 62
Regent's Pl. SE3 —54Jc 107
Regent Sq. E3 —41Dc 84
Regent Sq. WC1
—41Nb 82 (4G 193)
Regent Sq. Belv —49Dd 88
Regent's Row. E8 —39Wb 63
Regent St. NW10 —41Za 80
Regent St. SW1 —45Mb 82
Regent St. W1 —44Kb 82 (2A 198)
Regent St. W4 —50Qa 79
Regent St. Wat —10X 5
Regina Clo. Barn —13Za 22
Regina Ho. SE20 —67Zb 128
Reginald Rd. E7 —37Jc 65
Reginald Rd. SE8 —52Cc 106
Reginald Rd. N'wd —25V 36
Reginald Rd. Romf —25Qd 49
Reginald Sq. SE8 —52Cc 106
Regina Rd. N4 —32Pb 62
Regina Rd. SE25 —69Wb 127
Regina Rd. W13 —46Ja 78
Regina Rd. S'hall —49Aa 77
Regina Ter. W13 —46Ja 78
Regis Rd. NW5 —36Kb 62
Regnart Bldgs. NW1
—42Lb 82 (5C 192)
(off Euston St.)
Reid Av. Cat —93Tb 181
Reid Clo. Pinn —28W 36
Reidhaven Rd. SE18 —49Uc 86
Reigate Av. Sutt —74Cb 145
Reigate Rd. Brom —62Hc 129
Reigate Rd. Eps —82Wa 162
Reigate Rd. Ilf —33Vc 67
Reigate Rd. Lea —95La 176
Reigate Way. Wall —78Nb 146
Reighton Rd. E5 —34Wb 63
Relay Rd. W12 —46Ya 80
Relf Rd. SE15 —55Wb 105
Reliance Arc. SW9 —56Qb 104
Reliance Sq. EC2 —42Ub 83 (5J 195)
(off Anning St.)
Relko Ct. Eps —83Ta 161
Relko Gdns. Sutt —78Fb 145
Relton M. SW7 —48Gb 81 (3E 202)
Rembrandt Clo. E14 —48Fc 85
Rembrandt Clo. SW1
—50Jb 82 (7H 203)
(off Graham Ter.)
Rembrandt Dri. Grav —62Fe 135
Rembrandt Rd. SE13 —56Gc 107
Rembrandt Rd. Edgw —26Qa 39
Rembrandt Way. W on T —75X 141
Rememberance Rd. E7 —35Mc 65
Remington Rd. E6 —44Nc 86
Remington Rd. N15 —30Tb 43
Remington St. N1
—40Rb 63 (2C 194)
Remnant St. WC2
—44Pb 82 (2H 199)
Rempstone M. N1
—40Tb 63 (1G 195)
Remus Rd. E3 —38Cc 64
Rendlesham Av. Rad —9Ha 6
Rendlesham Rd. E5 —35Wb 63
Rendlesham Rd. Enf —11Rb 25
Rendlesham Way. Chor —16E 16
Renforth St. SE16 —47Yb 84
Renfree Way. Shep —73Q 140
Renfrew Clo. E6 —45Qc 86
Renfrew Ct. Houn —54Aa 99
Renfrew Rd. SE11
—49Rb 83 (5B 206)
Renfrew Rd. Houn —54Aa 99
Renfrew Rd. King T —66Ra 123
Renmans, The. Asht —88Pa 161
Renmuir St. SW17 —65Hb 125
Rennell St. SE13 —55Ec 106
Rennels Way. Iswth —54Ga 100
Renness Rd. E17 —27Ac 44
Rennets Clo. SE9 —57Uc 108
Rennets Wood Rd. SE9 —57Tc 108
Rennie Clo. Ashf —62M 119
Rennie Ct. SE1 —46Ub 83
(off Stamford St.)
Rennie Est. SE16 —49Xb 83
Rennie St. SE1 —46Rb 83 (6B 200)
Renown Clo. Croy —74Rb 147
Renown Clo. Romf —25Cd 48
Rensburg Rd. E17 —29Zb 44
Renshaw Clo. Belv —51Bd 109
Renters Av. NW4 —30Ya 40
Renton Clo. SW2 —58Pb 104
Renton Dri. Orp —73Zc 151
Renwick Rd. Bark —42Xc 87
Repens Way. Hay —42Z 77
Rephidim St. SE1
—48Ub 83 (4H 207)
Replingham Rd. SW18 —60Bb 103
Reporton Rd. SW6 —52Ab 102
Repository Rd. SE18 —51Pc 108
Repton Av. Hay —49T 76
Repton Av. Romf —27Jd 48
Repton Av. Wemb —35La 58
Repton Clo. Cars —78Gb 145
Repton Ct. E5 —34Ac 64
Repton Ct. Beck —67Dc 128
Repton Ct. Ilf —25Pc 46
Repton Dri. Romf —28Jd 48
Repton Gdns. Romf —27Jd 48
Repton Gro. Ilf —25Pc 46
Repton Rd. Harr —28Pa 39
Repton Rd. Orp —76Wc 151
Repton St. E14 —44Ac 84
Repton Way. Crox —15Q 18
Repulse Clo. Romf —25Dd 48
Reservoir Rd. N14 —15Lb 24
Reservoir Rd. SE4 —54Ac 106
Reservoir Rd. Lou —11Kc 27
Reservoir Rd. Ruis —28S 36
Resolution Wlk. SE18 —48Pc 86
Restell Clo. SE3 —51Gc 107
Reston Clo. Borwd —10Qa 7
Reston Path. Borwd —10Qa 7
Reston Pl. SW7 —47Eb 81 (2A 202)
Restons Cres. SE9 —58Tc 108
Restormel Clo. Houn —57Ca 99
Retcar Clo. NW5 —33Kb 62
Retcar Pl. N19 —33Kb 62
(off Retcar Clo.)
Retford Clo. Borwd —10Qa 7
Retford Clo. Romf —23Qd 49
Retford Path. Romf —23Qd 49
Retford Rd. Romf —23Pd 49
Retford St. N1 —40Ub 63 (2J 195)
Retingham Way. E4 —19Dc 26
Retles Ct. Harr —31Fa 58
Retreat Clo. Harr —29La 38
Retreat Rd. E9 —37Yb 64
Retreat Pl. E9 —37Yb 64
Retreat Rd. Rich —57Ma 101
Retreat, The. NW9 —29Ta 39
Retreat, The. SW14 —55Ua 102
Retreat, The. Brtwd —18Xd 32
Retreat, The. Chal G —11A 16
Retreat, The. Egh —4P 117
Retreat, The. Grays —51De 113
Retreat, The. Harr —31Ca 57
Retreat, The. Hut —16De 33
Retreat, The. K Lan —3S 4
Retreat, The. Orp —79Xc 151
Retreat, The. Sev —96Kd 187
Retreat, The. Surb —72Pa 143
Retreat, The. T Hth —70Tb 127
Retreat, The. Wor Pk —76Xa 144
Retreat Way. Chig —20Xc 29
Reubens Ct. W4 —50Ra 79
(off Chaseley Dri.)
Reubens Rd. Hut —16De 33
Reunion Row. E1 —45Xb 83
Reveley Sq. SE16 —47Ac 84
Revell Clo. Fet —94Da 175
Revell Dri. Fet —94Da 175
Revell Rise. SE18 —51Vc 109
Revell Rd. King T —68Ra 123
Revell Rd. Sutt —79Bb 145
Revelon Rd. SE4 —56Ac 106
Revelstoke Rd. SW18 —61Bb 125
Reventlow Rd. SE9 —60Sc 108
Reverdy Rd. SE1 —49Wb 83
Reverend Clo. Harr —34Da 57
Revesby Rd. Cars —72Gb 145
Review Rd. NW2 —33Va 60
Review Rd. Dag —40Dd 68
Rewell St. SW6 —52Eb 103
Rewley Rd. Cars —72Fb 145
Rex Av. Ashf —65Q 120
Rex Clo. Romf —24Dd 48
Rex Pl. W1 —45Jb 82 (5J 197)
Reydon Av. E11 —30Lc 45
Reynard Clo. Brom —69Qc 130
Reynard Dri. SE19 —66Vb 127
Reynardson Rd. N17 —24Sb 43
Reynards Way. Brick —1Ba 5
Reynolds Av. E12 —36Qc 66
Reynolds Av. Chad —31Yc 67
Reynolds Av. Chess —80Na 143
Reynolds Clo. NW11 —31Db 61
Reynolds Clo. SW19 —67Fb 125
Reynolds Clo. Cars —74Hb 145
Reynolds Ct. Romf —27Zc 47
Reynolds Dri. Edgw —27Pa 39
Reynolds Pl. SE3 —52Kc 107
Reynolds Pl. Rich —58Pa 101
Reynolds Rd. SE15 —56Yb 106
Reynolds Rd. W4 —48Sa 79
Reynolds Rd. Hay —42Y 77
Reynolds Rd. N Mald —73Ta 143
Reynolds Way. Croy —77Ub 147
Rheidol M. N1 —40Sb 63 (1D 194)
Rheidol Ter. N1 —39Sb 63 (1C 194)
Rheingold Way. Wall —81Nb 164
Rhein Ho. N8 —27Nb 42
(off Campsbourne Rd.)
Rheola Clo. N17 —25Vb 43
Rhoda St. E2 —42Vb 83 (5K 195)
Rhodes Av. N22 —25Lb 42
Rhodes Clo. Egh —64E 118
Rhodes Ct. Egh —64E 118
(off Pooley Grn. Clo.)
Rhodes Ho. N1 —41Tb 83 (3F 195)
(off Provost Est.)
Rhodes Ho. W12 —46Xa 80
(off White City Est.)
Rhodesia Rd. E11 —33Fc 65
Rhodesia Rd. SW9 —54Nb 104
Rhodesmoor Ho. Ct. Mord
—72Cb 145
Rhodes St. N7 —36Pb 62
Rhodes Way. Wat —12Z 19
Rhodeswell Rd. E14 —43Ac 84
Rhododendron Ride. Egh —5K 117
Rhodrons Av. Chess —78Na 143
Rhondda Gro. E3 —41Ac 84
Rhyl Rd. Gnfd —40Ha 58
Rhyl St. NW5 —37Jb 62
Rhys Av. N11 —24Mb 42
Rialto Rd. Mitc —68Jb 126
Ribble Clo. Wfd G —23Lc 45
Ribblesdale Av. N'holt —37Da 57
Ribblesdale Rd. N8 —28Pb 42
Ribblesdale Rd. SW16 —65Kb 126
Ribblesdale Rd. Dart —60Sd 112
Ribchester Av. Gnfd —41Ha 78
Ribston Clo. Brom —74Pc 150
Ricardo Path. SE28 —46Yc 87
Ricardo Rd. Old Win —8M 95
Ricardo St. E14 —44Dc 84
Ricards Rd. SW19 —64Bb 125
Riccall Ct. NW9 —25Ua 40
(off Pageant Av.)
Rice Pde. Orp —71Tc 150
Richard Clo. SE18 —49Nc 86
Richard Fell Ho. E12 —35Qc 66
(off Walton Rd.)
Richard Foster Clo. E17 —31Bc 64
Richards Av. Romf —30Ed 48
Richards Clo. Bush —17Fa 20
Richards Clo. Harr —29Ja 38
Richards Clo. Hay —51T 98
Richards Clo. Uxb —39Q 56
Richardson Clo. E8 —39Vb 63
Richardson Clo. Grnh —57Vd 112
Richardson Ct. SW4 —54Nb 104
(off Studley Rd.)
Richardson Rd. E15 —40Gc 65
Richardson's M. W1
—42Lb 82 (6B 192)
(off Warren St.)
Richards Pl. E17 —27Cc 44
Richard's Pl. SW3
—49Gb 81 (5E 202)
Richards Rd. Stoke D —86Da 159
Richard St. E1 —44Xb 83
Richbell Clo. Asht —90Ma 161
Richbell Pl. WC1
—43Pb 82 (7H 193)
Richborne Ter. SW8 —52Pb 104
Richborough Clo. Orp —70Zc 131
Richborough Rd. NW2 —35Ab 60
Riches Rd. Ilf —33Sc 66
Richfield Rd. Bush —17Ea 20
Richford Rd. E15 —39Hc 65
Richford St. W6 —47Ya 80
Rich Ind. Est. Dart —57Hd 110
Richings Way. Iver —48G 74
Richland Av. Coul —86Jb 164
Richlands Av. Eps —77Wa 144
Rich La. SW5 —50Db 81
Richmer Rd. Eri —52Jd 110
Richmond Av. E4 —22Fc 45
Richmond Av. N1 —39Pb 62
Richmond Av. NW10 —37Ya 60
Richmond Av. SW20 —67Ab 124
Richmond Av. Felt —58U 98
Richmond Av. Uxb —37R 56
Richmond Bri. Twic & Rich
—58Ma 101
Richmond Bldgs. W1
—44Mb 82 (3D 198)
Richmond Clo. E17 —30Bc 44
Richmond Clo. Big H —91Kc 183
Richmond Clo. Chesh —1Yb 12
Richmond Clo. Eps —86Ua 162
Richmond Clo. Fet —96Ea 176
Richmond Cotts. W14 —49Ab 80
(off Hammersmith Rd.)
Richmond Ct. Lou —15Mc 27
Richmond Ct. Pot B —3Eb 9
Richmond Ct. Wemb —34Pa 59
Richmond Cres. E4 —22Fc 45
Richmond Cres. N1 —39Pb 62
Richmond Cres. N9 —18Wb 25
Richmond Cres. Slou —6L 73
Richmond Cres. Stai —64H 119
Richmond Dri. Shep —72T 140
Richmond Dri. Wat —12U 18
Richmond Gdns. NW4 —29Wa 40
Richmond Gdns. Harr —23Ha 38
Richmond Grn. Croy —76Nb 146
Richmond Gro. N1 —38Rb 63
Richmond Gro. Surb —72Pa 143
Richmond Hill. Rich —58Na 101
Richmond Hill Ct. Rich —58Na 101
Richmond Mans. Twic —58Ma 101
Richmond M. W1
—44Mb 82 (3D 198)
Richmond M. Tedd —64Ha 122
Richmond Pk. Rd. SW14
—57Sa 101
Richmond Pk. Rd. King T
—66Na 123
Richmond Pl. SE18 —49Sc 86
Richmond Rd. E4 —18Fc 27
Richmond Rd. E7 —36Kc 65
Richmond Rd. E8 —38Vb 63
Richmond Rd. E11 —33Fc 65
Richmond Rd. N2 —26Eb 41
Richmond Rd. N11 —23Nb 42
Richmond Rd. N15 —30Ub 43
Richmond Rd. SW20 —67Xa 124
Richmond Rd. W5 —47Na 79
Richmond Rd. Barn —15Db 23
Richmond Rd. Coul —87Kb 164
Richmond Rd. Croy —76Nb 146
Richmond Rd. Grays —50Ee 91
Richmond Rd. Ilf —34Sc 66
Richmond Rd. Iswth —55Ja 100
Richmond Rd. King T —64Ma 123
Richmond Rd. Pot B —3Eb 9
Richmond Rd. Romf —30Hd 48
Richmond Rd. Stai —64H 119
Richmond Rd. T Hth —69Rb 127
Richmond Rd. Twic —59Ka 100
Richmond St. E13 —40Jc 65
Richmond Ter. SW1
—47Nb 82 (1F 205)
Richmond Ter. M. SW1
—47Nb 82 (1F 205)
Richmond Way. E11 —33Jc 65
Richmond Way. W12 & W14
—47Za 80
Richmond Way. Crox —14S 18
Richmond Way. Fet —95Da 175
(in two parts)
Richmount Gdns. SE3 —55Jc 107
Rich St. E14 —45Bc 84
Rickard Clo. NW4 —28Xa 40
Rickard Clo. SW2 —60Qb 104
Rickard Clo. W Dray —48M 75
Rickards Clo. Surb —74Na 143
Ricketts Hill Rd. Tats —90Mc 167
Rickett St. SW6 —51Cb 103
Rickman Ct. Add —76K 139
Rickman Cres. Add —76K 139
Rickman Hill. Coul —89Kb 164
Rickman Hill Rd. Coul —90Kb 164
Rickman's La. Stoke P —7J 53
Rickman St. E1 —42Yb 84
Rickmansworth La. Ger X —24A 34
Rickmansworth Rd. Chor —13G 16
Rickmansworth Rd. Hare —25L 35
Rickmansworth Rd. N'wd —22R 36
Rickmansworth Rd. Pinn —26X 37
Rickmansworth Rd. Wat —14U 18
Ricksons La. W Hor —99R 174
Rickthorne Rd. N19 —33Nb 62
Rickyard Path. SE9 —56Nc 108
Ridding La. Gnfd —36Ha 58
Riddings, The. Cat —97Vb 181
Riddlesdown Av. Purl —84Sb 165
Riddlesdown Rd. Purl —82Sb 165
Riddons Rd. SE12 —62Lc 129
Rideout St. SE18 —49Pc 86
Rider Clo. Sidc —58Uc 108
Ride, The. Bren —49La 78
Ride, The. Enf —14Zb 26
Ridgdale St. E3 —40Dc 64
Ridge Av. N21 —17Sb 25
Ridge Av. Dart —58Hd 110
Ridgebank. Slou —5D 72
Ridgebrook Rd. SE3 —55Mc 107
Ridge Clo. NW4 —26Za 40
Ridge Clo. NW9 —28Ta 39
Ridge Clo. Wok —9E 188
Ridge Ct. SE22 —59Wb 105
Ridge Ct. Warl —90Wb 165
Ridge Crest. Enf —11Pb 24
Ridgecroft Clo. Bex —60Ed 110
Ridgefield. Wat —9U 4
Ridge Hill. NW11 —32Ab 60
Ridgehurst Av. Wat —6V 4
Ridgelands. Fet —96Fa 176
Ridge La. Wat —9V 4
Ridge Langley. S Croy —81Wb 165
Ridgemead Rd. Egh —2L 117
Ridgemont End. Ger X —22A 34
Ridgemont Gdns. Edgw —21Sa 39
Ridgemount. Wey —75U 140
Ridgemount Av. Coul —89Kb 164
Ridgemount Av. Croy —74Zb 148
Ridgemount Clo. SE20 —66Xb 127
Ridgemount Gdns. Enf —13Rb 25
Ridge Pk. Purl —82Mb 164
Ridge Rise. Add —78H 139
Ridge Rd. N8 —30Pb 42
Ridge Rd. N21 —18Sb 25
Ridge Rd. NW2 —34Bb 61
Ridge Rd. Mitc —66Kb 126
Ridge Rd. Sutt —74Ab 144
Ridge St. Wat —10X 5
Ridge, The. Barn —15Bb 23
Ridge, The. Bex —59Bd 109
Ridge, The. Coul —86Nb 164
Ridge, The. Eps —90Sa 161
Ridge, The. Fet —96Fa 176
Ridge, The. Orp —75Tc 150
Ridge, The. Purl —82Mb 164
Ridge, The. Surb —71Qa 143
Ridge, The. Twic —59Fa 100
Ridge, The. Wok —89D 156
Ridge, The Wold & Warl
—97Ec 182
Ridgeview Clo. Barn —16Za 22
Ridgeview Rd. N20 —20Db 23
Ridge Way. SE19 —65Ub 127
Ridgeway. Brom —75Jc 149
Ridge Way. Cray —58Hd 110
Ridgeway. Dart —64Ud 134
Ridgeway. Eps —84Sa 161
Ridge Way. Felt —62Aa 121
Ridgeway. Grays —9A 92
Ridgeway. Hors —3G 188
Ridgeway. Hut —18De 33
Ridge Way. Iver —45H 75
Ridge Way. Rick —17K 17
Ridge Way. Wfd G —21Lc 45
Ridgeway Av. Barn —16Hb 23
Ridgeway Av. Grav —2D 136
Ridgeway Bungalows. Shorne
—6P 137
Ridgeway Clo. Oxs —86Ea 160
Ridgeway Clo. Wok —4G 188
Ridgeway Ct. Pinn —24Ca 37
Ridgeway Cres. Orp —76Uc 150
Ridgeway Cres. Gdns. Orp
—76Uc 150
Ridgeway Dri. Brom —63Kc 129
Ridgeway E. Sidc —57Vc 109
Ridgeway Gdns. N6 —31Mb 62
Ridgeway Gdns. Ilf —29Nc 46
Ridgeway Gdns. Wok —3G 188
Ridgeway Rd. Iswth —52Ga 100
Ridgeway Rd. N. Iswth —52Ga 100
Ridgeway, The. E4 —18Ec 26
Ridgeway, The. N3 —24Db 41
Ridgeway, The. N11 —21Hb 41
Ridgeway, The. N14 —19Nb 24

Ridgeway, The—Roffey Clo.

Ridgeway, The. NW7 —21Xa 40
Ridgeway, The. NW9 —28Ta 39
Ridgeway, The. NW11 —32Bb 61
Ridgeway, The. W3 —48Qa 79
Ridgeway, The. Croy —76Pb 146
Ridgeway, The. Cuff —1Mb 10
Ridgeway, The. Fet —96Ga 176
Ridgeway, The. Ger X —27A 34
Ridgeway, The. Gid P —28Jd 48
Ridgeway, The. H Wood —25Pd 49
Ridgeway, The. Kent —30La 38
Ridgeway, The. N Har —29Ba 37
(in two parts)
Ridgeway, The. Oxs —86Ea 160
Ridgeway, The. Pot B & Enf —7Hb 9
Ridgeway, The. Rad —9Ja 6
Ridgeway, The. Ruis —31W 56
Ridgeway, The. Shorne —6N 137
Ridge Way, The. S Croy —82Ub 165
Ridgeway, The. Stan —23La 38
Ridgeway, The. Sutt —79Fb 145
Ridgeway, The. W on T —74V 140
Ridgeway, The. Wat —9U 4
Ridgeway Trading Est. Iver —45H 75
Ridgeway Wlk. N'holt —37Aa 57
(off Arnold Rd.)
Ridgeway W. Sidc —57Uc 108
Ridgewell Av. Ors —2C 92
Ridgewell Clo. N1 —39Sb 63
Ridgewell Clo. Dag —39Dd 68
Ridgmont Pl. Horn —30Md 49
Ridgmount Gdns. WC1
—43Mb 82 (6D 192)
Ridgmount Pl. WC1
—43Mb 82 (7D 192)
Ridgmount Rd. SW18 —57Db 103
Ridgmount St. WC1
—43Mb 82 (7D 192)
Ridgway. SW19 —66Ya 124
Ridgway. Pyr —87J 157
Ridgway Gdns. SW19 —66Za 124
Ridgway Pl. SW19 —65Ab 124
Ridgway Rd. SW9 —55Rb 105
Ridgway Rd. Pyr —87H 157
Ridgwell Rd. E16 —43Lc 85
Riding Ct. Rd. Dat —2N 95
Riding Hill. S Croy —85Wb 165
Riding Ho. St. W1
—43Kb 82 (1A 198)
Ridings Av. N21 —15Sb 25
Ridings Clo. N6 —31Lb 62
Ridings La. Ock —95R 174
Ridings, The. W5 —43Pa 79
Ridings, The. Add —79G 138
Ridings, The. Asht —89Ma 161
Ridings, The. Barn —17Fb 23
Ridings, The. Big H —89Nc 168
Ridings, The. Chig —21Xc 47
Ridings, The. Cob —84Ca 159
Ridings, The. E Hor —97V 174
Ridings, The. Eps —87Va 162
Ridings, The. Ewe —81Va 162
Ridings, The. Iver —49H 75
Ridings, The. Lat —8A 2
Ridings, The. Rip —95J 173
Ridings, The. Sun —67W 120
Ridings, The. Surb —71Qa 143
Ridings, The. Tad —92Bb 179
Riding, The. NW11 —31Bb 61
Riding, The. Wok —86D 156
Ridler Rd. Enf —10Ub 11
Ridley Av. W13 —48Ka 78
Ridley Clo. Romf —25Kd 49
Ridley Ct. SW16 —65Nb 126
Ridley Rd. E7 —35Lc 65
Ridley Rd. E8 —36Vb 63
Ridley Rd. NW10 —40Wa 60
Ridley Rd. SW19 —66Db 125
Ridley Rd. Brom —69Hc 129
Ridley Rd. Warl —90Yb 166
Ridley Rd. Well —53Xc 109
Ridley Several. SE3 —54Jc 107
Ridsdale Rd. SE20 —67Xb 127
Ridsdale Rd. Wok —5E 188
Riefield Rd. SE9 —56Sc 108
(in two parts)
Riesco Dri. Croy —79Yb 148
Riffel Rd. NW2 —36Ya 60
Rifhams. Brtwd —20De 33
Rifle Butts All. Eps —86Va 162
Rifle Ct. SE11 —51Qb 104
Rifle Pl. W11 —46Za 80
Rifle St. E14 —43Dc 84
Rigault Rd. SW6 —54Ab 102
Rigby Clo. Croy —76Qb 146
Rigby Gdns. Grays —9D 92
Rigby La. Hay —47S 76
Rigby M. Ilf —33Qc 66
Rigden St. E14 —44Dc 84
Rigeley Rd. NW10 —41Wa 80
Rigg App. E10 —32Zb 64
Rigge Pl. SW4 —56Mb 104
Riggindale Rd. SW16 —64Mb 126
Riley Rd. SE1 —48Vb 83 (3K 207)
Riley Rd. Enf —10Yb 12
Riley St. SW10 —52Fb 103
Rinaldo Rd. SW12 —59Kb 104
Ring Clo. Brom —66Kc 129
Ringcroft St. N7 —36Qb 62
Ringers Rd. Brom —69Jc 129
Ringford Rd. SW18 —57Bb 103
Ringles Ct. E6 —39Pc 66
Ringmer Av. SW6 —53Ab 102
Ringmer Gdns. N19 —33Nb 62
Ringmer Pl. N21 —15Tb 25
Ringmer Way. Brom —71Nc 150
Ringmore Rise. SE23 —59Xb 105
Ringmore Rd. W on T —76Y 141
Ringshall Rd. Orp —69Wc 131
Ringslade Rd. N22 —26Pb 42
Ringstead Rd. SE6 —59Dc 106
Ringstead Rd. Sutt —77Fb 145
Ring, The. W2 —46Gb 81 (6D 196)
Rington Rd. SW6 —51Cb 103
Ring Way. N11 —23Lb 42
Ringway. S'hall —50Z 77
Ringwold Clo. Beck —66Ac 128
Ringwood Av. N2 —26Hb 41
Ringwood Av. Croy —73Nb 146
Ringwood Av. Horn —33Md 69
Ringwood Av. Orp —82Yc 169
Ringwood Clo. Pinn —27Y 36
Ringwood Gdns. E13 —49Cc 84
Ringwood Gdns. SW15 —60Wa 102
Ringwood Rd. E17 —30Bc 44
Ringwood Way. N21 —18Rb 25
Ringwood Way. Hamp —63Ca 121
Ripley Av. Egh —65A 118
Ripley By-Pass. Rip —95L 173
Ripley Clo. Brom —71Pc 150
Ripley Clo. New Ad —79Ec 148
Ripley Clo. Slou —49A 74
Ripley Ct. Mitc —68Fb 125
Ripley Gdns. SW14 —55Ta 101
Ripley Gdns. Sutt —77Eb 145
Ripley La. Rip & W Hors —95N 173
Ripley M. E11 —30Gc 45
Ripley Rd. E16 —44Lc 85
Ripley Rd. Belv —49Cd 88
Ripley Rd. Enf —11Sb 25
Ripley Rd. Hamp —66Ca 121
Ripley Rd. Ilf —33Vc 67
Ripley Rd. Send —98L 173
Ripley View. Lou —10Rc 14
Ripley Vs. W5 —44La 78
Ripley Way. Chesh —2Xb 11
Ripon Clo. N'holt —36Ca 57
Ripon Gdns. Chess —78Ma 143
Ripon Gdns. Ilf —31Nc 66
Ripon Rd. N9 —17Xb 25
Ripon Rd. N17 —27Tb 43
Ripon Rd. SE18 —51Rc 108
Ripon Way. Borwd —15Ta 21
Rippersley Rd. Well —53Wc 109
Ripple Rd. Bark & Dag —38Sc 66
Rippleside Commercial Cen. Bark
—40Yc 67
Ripplevale Gro. N1 —38Pb 62
Rippolson Rd. SE18 —50Vc 87
Ripston Rd. Ashf —64T 120
Risborough Clo. N10 —27Kb 42
Risborough Dri. Wor Pk
—73Wa 144
Risborough St. SE1
—46Rb 83 (1C 206)
Risdon St. SE16 —47Yb 84
Risebridge Chase. Romf —24Hd 48
Risebridge Rd. Romf —26Hd 48
Risedale Rd. Bexh —55Ed 110
Riseholme St. E9 —37Bc 64
Riseldine Rd. SE23 —58Ac 106
Rise Pk. Boulevd. Romf —25Hd 48
Rise Park Pde. Romf —26Gd 48
Rise, The. E11 —29Jc 45
Rise, The. N13 —21Qb 42
Rise, The. NW7 —23Va 40
Rise, The. NW10 —35Ta 59
Rise, The. Bex —59Yc 109
Rise, The. Buck H —17Mc 27
Rise, The. Dart —56Hd 110
Rise, The. E Hor —98U 174
Rise, The. Edgw —22Ra 39
Rise, The. Els —15Pa 21
Rise, The. Eps —82Va 162
Rise, The. Grav —3G 136
Rise, The. Gnfd —36Ja 58
Rise, The. Sev —100Ld 187
Rise, The. S Croy —81Yb 166
Rise, The. Tad —92Ya 178
Rise, The. Uxb —40P 55
Riseway. Brtwd —20Ae 33
Rising Hill Clo. N'wd —23S 36
Risinghill St. N1 —40Pb 62 (1K 193)
Risingholme Clo. Bush —17Da 19
Risingholme Clo. Harr —25Ga 38
Risingholme Rd. Harr —26Ga 38
Risings Ter. Horn —27Pd 49
(off Prospect Rd.)
Risings, The. E17 —28Fc 45
Rising Sun Ct. EC1
(off Cloth Fair) —43Rb 83 (1C 200)
Risley Av. N17 —25Sb 43
Rita Rd. SW8 —51Nb 104
Ritches Rd. N15 —29Sb 43
Ritchie Ho. N19 —32Mb 62
Ritchie Rd. Croy —72Xb 147
Ritchie St. N1 —40Qb 62 (1A 194)
Ritchings Av. E17 —28Ac 44
Ritherdon Rd. SW17 —61Jb 126
Ritson Ho. N1 —39Pb 62 (1J 193)
(off Barnsbury Est.)
Ritson Rd. E8 —37Wb 63
Ritter St. SE18 —51Qc 108
Ritz Ct. Pot B —3Cb 9
Ritz Pde. W5 —42Pa 79
Rivaz Pl. E9 —37Yb 64
Rivenhall Gdns. E18 —28Hc 45
River Av. N13 —20Rb 25
River Av. Th Dit —73Ja 142
River Bank. N21 —17Sb 25
River Bank. E Mol —69Ga 122
Riverbank. Stai —65H 119
River Bank. Th Dit —71Ha 142
River Bank. W Mol —69Ca 121
Riverbank Way. Bren —51La 100
River Barge Clo. E14 —47Ec 84
River Brent Bus. Pk. W7 —48Ga 78
River Clo. E11 —30Lc 45
River Clo. Rain —43Kd 89
River Clo. Ruis —30V 36
River Clo. Wal X —6Cc 12
River Ct. SE1 —46Rb 83 (6B 200)
River Ct. Sev —94Gd 186
River Ct. Wok —86E 156
Rivercourt Rd. W6 —49Xa 80
Riverdale. SE13 —55Ec 106
Riverdale Ct. N21 —15Tb 25
Riverdale Dri. Wok —93B 172
Riverdale Gdns. Twic —58La 100
Riverdale Rd. SE18 —50Vc 87
Riverdale Rd. Bex —59Bd 109
Riverdale Rd. Eri —50Dd 88
Riverdale Rd. Felt —63Aa 121
Riverdale Rd. Twic —58La 100
Riverdene. Edgw —20Sa 21
Riverdene Ind. Est. W on T
—78Z 141
Riverdene Rd. Ilf —34Qc 66
River Dri. Upm —30Sd 50
Riverfield Rd. Stai —65H 119
River Front. Enf —13Ub 25
River Gdns. Cars —75Jb 146
River Gdns. Felt —57X 99
River Gdns. Bus. Cen. Houn
—56X 99
River Gro. Pk. Beck —67Bc 128
Riverhead Clo. E17 —26Zb 44
Riverhead Dri. Sutt —82Cb 163
River Hill. Cob —87X 159
Riverhill. Wor Pk —75Ta 143
Riverholme Dri. Eps —81Ta 161
River Ho. SE26 —62Xb 127
River Island Clo. Fet —92Fa 176
River La. Fet —93Fa 176
River La. Rich —60Ma 101
River La. Stoke D —88Aa 159
Riverleigh Ct. E4 —22Bc 44
Rivermead. Byfl —85P 157
Rivermead Clo. Add —80L 139
Rivermead Clo. Tedd —64Ka 122
Rivermead Ct. SW6 —55Bb 103
Rivermead Ho. E9 —36Ac 64
River Meads Av. Twic —62Ca 121
River Mt. W on T —73V 140
Rivernook Clo. W on T —71Y 141
River Pde. Riv —94Gd 186
River Pk. N22 —26Pb 42
River Pk. Av. Stai —63F 118
River Pk. Gdns. Brom —66Fc 129
River Pk. Trading Est. E14
—48Cc 84
River Pl. N1 —38Sb 63
River Reach. Tedd —64La 122
River Rd. Bark —40Uc 66
River Rd. Brtwd —21Vd 50
River Rd. Buck H —18Nc 28
River Rd. Stai —67H 119
Riversdale. Grav —2A 136
Riversdale Rd. N5 —34Rb 63
Riversdale Rd. Romf —24Dd 48
Riversdale Rd. Th Dit —71Ja 142
Riversdell Clo. Cher —73H 139
Riversfield Rd. Enf —13Ub 25
Riverside. NW4 —31Xa 60
Riverside. SE7 —48Lc 85
Riverside. Egh —62C 118
Riverside. Eyns —75Md 153
Riverside. Rich —57Ma 101
Riverside. Shep —73U 140
Riverside. Stai —64H 119
Riverside. Twic —60Ka 100
Riverside. Wray —9N 95
Riverside Apartments. N11
—22Pb 42
Riverside Av. E Mol —71Fa 142
Riverside Av. Rich —53Na 101
Riverside Bus. Cen. SW18
—60Db 103
Riverside Bus. Cen. Twic
—56Ka 100
Riverside Clo. E5 —33Yb 64
Riverside Clo. W7 —42Ga 78
Riverside Clo. K Lan —1R 4
Riverside Clo. King T —70Ma 123
Riverside Clo. Orp —68Yc 131
Riverside Clo. Stai —67H 119
Riverside Clo. Wall —76Kb 146
Riverside Cotts. Bark —40Tc 66
Riverside Ct. E4 —16Cc 26
Riverside Ct. SE12 —56Hc 107
Riverside Ct. SW8 —51Mb 104
Riverside Ct. Felt —58U 98
Riverside Ct. Fet —94Ja 176
Riverside Ct. Iswth —54Ha 100
(off Woodlands Rd.)
Riverside Dri. NW11 —30Ab 40
Riverside Dri. W4 —52Ta 101
Riverside Dri. Esh —77Ca 141
Riverside Dri. Mitc —71Gb 145
Riverside Dri. Rich —61Ka 122
Riverside Dri. Rick —18M 17
Riverside Dri. Stai —64G 118
(off Chertsey La.)
Riverside Dri. Stai —66H 119
(off Wheatsheaf La.)
Riverside Gdns. W6 —50Xa 80
Riverside Gdns. Enf —12Sb 25
Riverside Gdns. Wemb —40Na 59
Riverside Gdns. Wok —93D 172
Riverside Ind. Est. Bark —41Wc 87
Riverside Ind. Est. Dart —57Nd 111
Riverside Ind. Est. Enf —16Ac 26
Riverside Pk. Coln —54G 96
Riverside Path. Chesh —1Yb 12
Riverside Pl. Stai —58M 97
Riverside Rd. E15 —40Ec 64
Riverside Rd. N15 —30Wb 43
Riverside Rd. SW17 —63Db 125
Riverside Rd. Sidc —62Ad 131
Riverside Rd. Stai —66H 119
Riverside Rd. Stanw —57M 97
Riverside Rd. W on T —77Aa 141
Riverside Rd. Wat —16X 19
Riverside Wlk. N12 & N20
—20Db 23
Riverside Wlk. SE10 —48Gc 85
Riverside Wlk. SW6 —55Ab 102
Riverside Wlk. Barn —16Za 22
Riverside Wlk. Iswth —55Ga 100
Riverside Wlk. King T —69Ma 123
Riverside Wlk. W Wick —74Dc 148
Riverside Way. Cow —39K 55
Riverside Way. Dart —57Nd 111
River St. EC1 —41Qb 82 (3K 193)
River St. Wind —2H 95
River Ter. W6 —50Ya 80
Riverton Clo. W9 —41Bb 81
River View. Add —78L 139
River View. Enf —13Sb 25
River View. Grays —9C 92
Riverview Gdns. SW13 —51Xa 102
River View Gdns. Twic —61Ha 122
Riverview Gro. W4 —51Ra 101
Riverview Pk. SE6 —61Cc 128
Riverview Rd. W4 —52Ra 101
Riverview Rd. Eps —77Sa 143
Riverview Rd. Grnh —57Wd 112
River Wlk. W6 —52Ya 102
River Wlk. Den —36L 55
River Wlk. W on T —72W 140
Riverway. N13 —21Qb 42
River Way. SE10 —48Hc 85
River Way. Eps —78Ta 143
River Way. Lou —16Pc 28
Riverway. Stai —67K 119
River Way. Twic —61Da 121
Riverwood La. Chst —67Tc 130
Rivey Clo. W Byf —86H 157
Rivington Av. Wfd G —26Mc 45
Rivington Bldgs. EC2
—41Ub 83 (4H 195)
Rivington Ct. NW10 —39Wa 60
Rivington Cres. NW7 —24Va 40
Rivington Pl. EC2
—41Ub 83 (4J 195)
Rivington St. EC2
—41Ub 83 (4H 195)
Rivington Wlk. E8 —39Wb 63
Rivulet Rd. N17 —24Sb 43
Rixon Clo. G Grn —44A 74
Rixon St. N7 —34Qb 62
Rixsen Rd. E12 —36Nc 66
Roach. E Til —9L 93
Roach Rd. E3 —38Cc 64
Road Ho. Est. Old Wok —92C 172
Roads Pl. N19 —33Nb 62
Roakes Av. Add —75K 139
Roan St. SE10 —51Ec 106
Roasthill La. Eton W —1B 94
Robarts Clo. Pinn —30X 37
Robb Rd. Stan —23Ja 38
Robert Adam St. W1
—44Jb 82 (2H 197)
Roberta St. E2 —41Wb 83
Robert Clo. W9 —42Eb 81 (6A 190)
Robert Clo. Chig —22Vc 47
Robert Clo. Pot B —5Ab 8
Robert Clo. W on T —78X 141
Robert Daniels Ct. They B —9Uc 14
Robert Dashwood Way. SE17
—49Sb 83 (6D 206)
Robert Keen Clo. SE15 —53Wb 105
Robert Lowe Clo. SE14 —52Zb 106
Robert M. Orp —74Wc 151
Roberton Dri. Brom —67Lc 129
Robert Owen Ho. SW6 —53Za 102
(off Fulham Pal. Rd.)
Robert Rd. Hedg —3H 53
Roberts All. W5 —47Ma 79
Robertsbridge Rd. Cars —74Eb 145
Roberts Clo. SE9 —60Tc 108
Roberts Clo. Orp —71Yc 151
Roberts Clo. Romf —25Kd 49
Roberts Clo. Stai —58L 97
Roberts Clo. Sutt —80Za 144
Roberts Clo. W Dray —46N 75
Roberts Ct. SE20 —67Yb 128
(off Maple Rd.)
Roberts La. Ger X —22C 34
Roberts M. SW1
—48Jb 82 (4H 203)
Robertson Ct. Grays —49De 91
(off Hathaway Rd.)
Robertson Ct. Wok —6B 188
Robertson Rd. E15 —39Ec 64
Robertson St. SW8 —55Kb 104
Roberts Pl. EC1 —42Qb 82 (5A 194)
Roberts Rd. E17 —25Dc 44
Roberts Rd. NW7 —23Ab 40
Roberts Rd. Belv —50Cd 88
Roberts Rd. Wat —15Y 19
Robert St. E16 —46Rc 86
Robert St. NW1 —41Kb 82 (4A 192)
Robert St. SE18 —50Tc 86
Robert St. WC2 —45Nb 82 (5G 199)
Robert St. Croy —76Sb 147
Roberts Way. Egh —6N 117
Roberts Wood Dri. Ger X —22B 34
Robertswood Lodge. Ger X
—23B 34
Robeson St. E3 —42Bc 84
Robina Av. Grav —59Fe 113
Robina Clo. Bexh —56Zc 109
Robina Clo. N'wd —25V 36
Robina Ct. Swan —70Jd 132
Robin Clo. NW7 —20Ua 22
Robin Clo. Add —78M 139
Robin Clo. Hamp —64Aa 121
Robin Clo. Romf —24Fd 48
Robin Ct. E14 —48Ec 84
Robin Ct. SE16 —49Vb 83
Robin Cres. E6 —43Mc 85
Robin Gro. N6 —33Jb 62
Robin Gro. Bren —51La 100
Robin Gro. Harr —30Pa 39
Robin Hill Dri. Chst —65Nc 130
Robinhood Clo. Mitc —70Lb 126
Robin Hood Clo. Slou —6D 72
Robin Hood Clo. Wok —6C 188
Robin Hood Cres. Knap —5B 188
Robin Hood Dri. Bush —11Ba 19
Robin Hood Dri. Harr —24Ha 38
Robin Hood Gdns. E14 —45Ec 84
(off Robin Hood La.)
Robin Hood Grn. Orp —71Wc 151
Robin Hood La. E14 —45Ec 84
Robin Hood La. SW15 —63Ua 124
Robin Hood La. Bexh —57Ad 109
Robinhood La. Mitc —69Lb 126
Robin Hood La. Sutt —78Cb 145
Robin Hood La. Wok & Sut G
—96B 172
Robin Hood Rd. SW19 & SW15
—64Wa 124
Robin Hood Rd. Brtwd —17Xd 32
Robin Hood Rd. Knap —5A 188
Robin Hood Way. SW15 & SW20
—62Ua 124
Robin Hood Way. Gnfd —37Ha 58
Robinia Clo. Ilf —23Uc 46
Robins Clo. Uxb —43L 75
Robins Ct. SE12 —62Lc 129
Robin's Ct. Beck —68Fc 129
Robinscroft M. SE10 —53Dc 106
Robins Dale. Knap —5A 188
Robins Gro. W Wick —76Jc 149
Robinson Av. Chesh —1Rb 11
Robinson Clo. Horn —38Kd 69
Robinson Cres. Bush —18Ea 20
Robinson Rd. E2 —40Yb 64
Robinson Rd. SW17 & SW19
—65Gb 125
Robinson Rd. Dag —35Cd 68
Robinson's Clo. W13 —43Ja 78
Robinson St. SW3 —51Hb 103
Robins Orchard. Ger X —23A 34
Robinsway. W on T —77Y 141
Robin Way. Cuff —1Nb 10
Robin Way. Orp —69Xc 131
Robin Way. Stai —62H 119
Robinwood Dri. Seal —91Pd 187
Robinwood Gro. Uxb —42P 75
Robinwood Pl. SW15 —63Ta 123
Roborough Wlk. Horn —37Ld 69
Robsart St. SW9 —54Pb 104
Robson Av. NW10 —39Wa 60
Robson Clo. E6 —44Nc 86
Robson Clo. Enf —12Rb 25
Robson Clo. Ger X —22A 34
Robson Rd. SE27 —62Rb 127
Robsons Clo. Chesh —1Yb 12
Robyns Croft. Grav —3A 136
Robyns Way. Sev —94Hd 186
Roch Av. Edgw —26Pa 39
Rochdale Rd. E17 —31Cc 64
Rochdale Rd. SE2 —50Xc 87
Rochdale Way. SE8 —52Cc 106
Rochelle Clo. SW11 —56Fb 103
Rochelle St. E2 —41Vb 83 (4K 195)
Roche Rd. SW16 —67Pb 126
Rochester Av. E13 —39Lc 65
Rochester Av. Brom —68Kc 129
Rochester Av. Felt —61V 120
Rochester Clo. SE3 —55Lc 107
Rochester Clo. SW16 —66Nb 126
Rochester Clo. Enf —11Ub 25
Rochester Clo. Sidc —58Xc 109
Rochester Dri. Bex —58Bd 109
Rochester Dri. Pinn —29Z 37
Rochester Dri. Wat —7Y 5
Rochester Gdns. Cat —94Ub 181
Rochester Gdns. Croy —76Ub 147
Rochester Gdns. Ilf —31Pc 66
Rochester M. NW1 —38Lb 62
Rochester Pde. Felt —61W 120
Rochester Pl. NW1 —37Lb 62
(in two parts)
Rochester Rd. NW1 —37Lb 62
Rochester Rd. Cars —77Hb 145
Rochester Rd. Dart —59Qd 111
Rochester Rd. Grav —9G 114
Rochester Rd. N'wd —27V 36
Rochester Rd. Stai —65F 118
Rochester Row. SW1
—49Lb 82 (5C 204)
Rochester Sq. NW1 —38Lb 62
Rochester St. SW1
—48Mb 82 (4D 204)
Rochester Ter. NW1 —37Lb 62
Rochester Wlk. SE1
(off Stoney St.) —46Tb 83 (7F 201)
Rochester Way. SE3 & SE9
—53Kc 107
Rochester Way. Bex & Dart
—58Ed 110
Rochester Way. Crox —14R 18
Rochester Way Relief Rd. SE3 & SE9
—53Kc 107
Roche Wlk. Cars —72Fb 145
Rochford. N17 —26Ub 43
(off Griffin Rd.)
Rochford Av. Lou —13Sc 28
Rochford Av. Romf —29Yc 47
Rochford Av. Shenf —15Ce 33
Rochford Av. Wal A —5Fc 13
Rochford Clo. E6 —40Mc 65
Rochford Clo. Horn —37Kd 69
Rochford Grn. Lou —13Sc 28
Rochford Ho. SE8 —50Bc 84
Rochfords Gdns. Slou —6N 73
Rochford Wlk. E8 —38Wb 63
Rochford Way. Croy —72Nb 146
Rockall Ct. Slou —48D 74
Rock Av. SW14 —55Ta 101
Rockbourne M. SE23 —60Zb 106
Rockbourne Rd. SE23 —60Zb 106
Rockchase Gdns. Horn —30Nd 49
Rockcliffe Av. K Lan —2Q 4
Rockdale Rd. Sev —97Ld 187
Rockell's Pl. SE22 —58Xb 105
Rockett Clo. SE8 —49Ac 84
Rockfield Ho. NW4 —28Za 40
(off Belle Vue Est.)
Rockford Av. Gnfd —40Ja 58
Rock Gdns. Dag —36Dd 68
Rock Gro. Way. SE16 —49Xb 83
Rockhall Rd. NW2 —35Za 60
Rockhampton Clo. SE27
—63Qb 126
Rockhampton Rd. SE27 —63Qb 126
Rockhampton Rd. S Croy
—79Ub 147
Rock Hill. SE26 —63Vb 127
Rock Hill. Orp —79Dd 152
Rockingham Av. Horn —30Kd 49
Rockingham Clo. SW15 —56Va 102
Rockingham Clo. Uxb —39L 55
Rockingham Pde. Uxb —38L 55
Rockingham Rd. Uxb —39K 55
Rockingham St. SE1
—48Sb 83 (4D 206)
Rockland Rd. SW15 —56Ab 102
Rocklands Dri. Stan —26Ka 38
Rockley Ct. W14 —47Za 80
(off Rockley Rd.)
Rockley Rd. W14 —47Za 80
Rockmount Rd. SE18 —50Vc 87
Rockmount Rd. SE19 —65Tb 127
Rockshaw Rd. Red —99Lb 180
Rocks La. SW13 —53Wa 102
Rock St. N4 —33Qb 62
Rockware Av. Gnfd —39Fa 58
Rockware Av. Bus. Cen. Gnfd
—39Fa 58
Rockways. Barn —16Va 22
Rockwell Gdns. SE19 —64Ub 127
Rockwell Rd. Dag —36Dd 68
Rockwood Pl. W12 —47Ya 80
Rocky La. Mers —100Hb 179
Rocliffe St. N1 —40Rb 63 (2C 194)
Rocombe Cres. SE23 —59Yb 106
Rocque Ho. SW6 —52Bb 103
(off Estcourt Rd.)
Rocque La. SE3 —55Hc 107
Rodborough Rd. NW11 —32Cb 61
Rodborough Wlk. Horn —37Ld 69
Roden Gdns. Croy —72Ub 147
Rodenhurst Rd. SW4 —58Lb 104
Roden St. N7 —34Pb 62
Roden St. Ilf —34Qc 66
Roderick Rd. NW3 —35Hb 61
Rodgers Clo. Els —16Ma 21
Rodgers Ho. SW4 —59Mb 104
(off Clapham Pk. Est.)
Roding. Brtwd —18Xd 32
Roding Av. Wfd G —23Nc 46
Roding Ho. N1 —39Qb 62 (1K 193)
(off Barnsbury Est.)
Roding La. Buck H & Chig
—18Mc 27
Roding La. N. Wfd G —23Nc 46
Roding La. S. Ilf & Wfd G
—28Mc 45
Roding M. E1 —46Wb 83
Roding Rd. E5 —35Zb 64
Roding Rd. E6 —43Rc 86
Roding Rd. Lou —15Nc 28
Rodings, The. Upm —30Ud 50
Rodings, The. Wfd G —23Lc 45
Roding Trading Est. Bark —38Rc 66
Roding View. Buck H —18Mc 27
Roding Way. Rain —40Md 69
Rodmarton St. W1
—43Hb 81 (1G 197)
Rodmell Clo. Hay —42Aa 77
Rodmell Slope. N12 —22Bb 41
Rodmere St. SE10 —50Gc 85
Rodmill La. SW2 —59Nb 104
Rodney Clo. Croy —74Rb 147
Rodney Clo. N Mald —71Ua 144
Rodney Clo. Pinn —31Aa 57
Rodney Clo. W on T —74Y 141
Rodney Ct. W9 —42Eb 81 (5A 190)
(off Maida Vale)
Rodney Ct. Barn —13Bb 23
Rodney Gdns. Pinn —29X 37
Rodney Gdns. W Wick —77Jc 149
Rodney Grn. W on T —75Y 141
Rodney Pl. E17 —26Ac 44
Rodney Pl. SE17
—49Sb 83 (5E 206)
Rodney Pl. SW19 —67Eb 125
Rodney Rd. E11 —28Kc 45
Rodney Rd. SE17 —49Sb 83
Rodney Rd. Mitc —69Gb 125
Rodney Rd. N Mald —71Ua 144
Rodney Rd. Twic —58Ca 99
Rodney Rd. W on T —75Y 141
Rodney St. N1 —40Pb 62 (1J 193)
Rodney Way. Coln —53G 96
Rodney Way. Romf —25Cd 48
Rodona Rd. Wey —83T 158
Rodsley St. SE1 —51Wb 105
Rodway Rd. SW15 —59Wa 102
Rodway Rd. Brom —67Kc 129
Rodwell Clo. Ruis —32Y 57
Rodwell Ct. Add —77L 139
Rodwell Pl. Edgw —23Qa 39
Rodwell Rd. SE22 —58Vb 105
Rodwell Rd. N'holt —39Ca 57
Roe. NW9 —25Va 40
Roebourne Way. E16 —46Qc 86
Roebuck Clo. Asht —92Na 177
Roebuck Clo. Felt —63X 121
Roebuck Grn. Slou —6C 72
Roebuck La. N17 —23Vb 43
Roebuck La. Buck H —17Lc 27
Roebuck Rd. Chess —78Qa 143
Roebuck Rd. Ilf —22Xc 47
Roedean Av. Enf —11Yb 26
Roedean Clo. Enf —11Yb 26
Roedean Clo. Orp —77Xc 151
Roedean Cres. SW15 —58Ua 102
Roe End. NW9 —28Sa 39
Roe Grn. NW9 —29Sa 39
Roehampton Clo. SW15
—56Wa 102
Roehampton Clo. Grav —9G 114
Roehampton Dri. Chst —65Sc 130
Roehampton Ga. SW15 —58Ua 102
Roehampton High St. SW15
—59Wa 102
Roehampton La. SW15 —56Wa 102
Roehampton Vale. SW15
—62Va 124
Roe La. NW9 —28Ra 39
Roe Way. Wall —79Nb 146
Rofant Rd. N'wd —23U 36
Roffe's La. Cat —96Tb 181
Roffey Clo. Purl —88Rb 165

Roffey St.—Rowan Ct.

Roffey St. E14 —47Ec 84
Roffords. Wok —5E 188
Rogate Ho. E5 —34Wb 63
Roger Dowley Ct. E2 —40Yb 64
Roger Reede's Almshouses. Romf —28Gd 48
Rogers Clo. Cat —94Xb 181
Rogers Clo. Coul —90Rb 165
Rogers Ct. Swan —70Jd 132
Rogers Est. E2 —41Yb 84
Rogers Gdns. Dag —36Cd 68
Roger's Ho. Dag —34Cd 68
Roger Simmons Ct. Bookh —96Ba 175
Roger's La. Stoke P —8K 53
Rogers La. Warl —90Bc 166
Rogers Rd. E16 —44Hc 85
Rogers Rd. SW17 —63Fb 125
Rogers Rd. Dag —36Cd 68
Rogers Rd. Grays —49Ee 91
Rogers Ruff. N'wd —25S 36
Roger St. WC1 —42Pb 82 (6J 193)
Rogers Wlk. N12 —20Db 23
Rogers Wood La. Fawk —77Wd 154
Rojack Rd. SE23 —60Zb 106
Rokeby Ct. Wok —5C 188
Rokeby Gdns. Wfd G —25Jc 45
Rokeby Pl. SW20 —66Xa 124
Rokeby Rd. SE4 —54Bc 106
Rokeby Rd. Harr —27Fa 38
Rokeby St. E15 —39Gc 65
Roke Clo. Kenl —86Sb 165
Roke Lodge Rd. Kenl —85Rb 165
Roke Rd. Kenl —87Sb 165
Roker Pk. Av. Uxb —35N 55
Rokesby Clo. Well —54Tc 108
Rokesby Pl. Wemb —36Ma 59
Rokesby Rd. Slou —1D 72
Rokesly Av. N8 —29Nb 42
Roland Gdns. SW7 —50Eb 81 (7A 202)
Roland M. E1 —43Zb 84
Roland Rd. E17 —28Fc 45
Roland Way. SE17 —50Tb 83
Roland Way. SW7 —50Eb 81 (7A 202)
Roland Way. Wor Pk —75Va 144
Roles Gro. Romf —28Zc 47
Rolfe Clo. Barn —14Gb 23
Rolinsden Way. Kes —78Mc 149
Rolland Ho. W7 —43Ga 78
Rollesby Rd. Chess —79Qa 143
Rollesby Way. SE28 —44Yc 87
Rolleston Av. Orp —72Rc 150
Rolleston Clo. Orp —73Rc 150
Rolleston Rd. S Croy —80Tb 147
Roll Gdns. Ilf —29Qc 46
Rollins St. SE15 —51Yb 106
Rollit Cres. Houn —57Ca 99
Rollit St. N7 —36Qb 62
Rollo Rd. Swan —66Hd 132
Rolls Bldgs. EC4 —44Qb 82 (2A 200)
Rollscourt Av. SE24 —57Sb 105
Rolls Pk. Av. E4 —22Cc 44
Rolls Pk. Rd. E4 —22Dc 44
Rolls Pas. EC4 —44Qb 82 (2K 199) (off Chancery La.)
Rolls Rd. SE1 —50Vb 83 (7K 207)
Rolt St. SE8 —51Ac 106
Rolvenden Gdns. Brom —66Mc 129
Rolvenden Pl. N17 —25Wb 43
Romagne Clo. Horn H —1H 93
Roman. E Til —9L 93
Roman Clo. W3 —47Ra 79
Roman Clo. Felt —57Y 99
Roman Clo. Hare —25K 35
Roman Clo. Rain —40Fd 68
Roman Gdns. K Lan —2R 4
Roman Ho. EC2 —43Sb 83 (1E 200) (off Wind St.)
Romanhurst Av. Brom —70Gc 129
Romanhurst Gdns. Brom —70Gc 129
Roman Ind. Est. Croy —73Ub 147
Roman Rise. SE19 —65Tb 127
Roman Rd. E2 & E3 —41Yb 84
Roman Rd. E6 —42Nc 86
Roman Rd. N10 —24Kb 42
Roman Rd. NW2 —34Ya 60
Roman Rd. W4 —49Va 80
Roman Rd. Grav —62Ee 135
Roman Rd. Ilf —37Rc 66
Roman Rd. Mount —13Ee 33
Roman Sq. SE28 —46Wc 87
Romans Way. Wok —87J 157
Roman Villa Rd. Dart —64Sd 134
Roman Way. N7 —37Pb 62
Roman Way. SE15 —52Yb 106
Roman Way. Croy —75Rb 147
Roman Way. Dart —57Gd 110
Roman Way. Enf —15Vb 25
Romany Gdns. E17 —25Ac 44
Romany Gdns. Sutt —73Cb 145
Romany Rise. Orp —74Sc 150
Roma Read Clo. SW15 —59Xa 102
Roma Rd. E17 —27Ac 44
Romberg Rd. SW17 —62Jb 126
Romborough Gdns. SE13 —57Ec 106
Romborough Way. SE13 —57Ec 106
Rom Cres. Romf —31Hd 68
Romeland. Els —16Ma 21
Romeland. Wal A —5Ec 12
Romero Clo. SW9 —55Pb 104
Romero Sq. SE3 —56Lc 107
Romeyn Rd. SW16 —62Pb 126
Romford Rd. E15, E7 & E12 —38Gc 65
Romford Rd. Chig —20Xc 29
Romford Rd. Romf —24Ad 47
Romford Rd. S Ock —45Sd 90
Romford St. E1 —43Xb 83
Romilly Dri. Wat —21Aa 37
Romilly Rd. N4 —33Rb 63
Romilly St. W1 —45Mb 82 (4E 198)
Romily Ct. SW6 —54Ab 102
Rommany Rd. SE27 —63Tb 127 (in two parts)
Romney Chase. Horn —30Qd 49
Romney Clo. NW11 —32Eb 61
Romney Clo. SE14 —52Yb 106
Romney Clo. Ashf —64S 120
Romney Clo. Chess —77Na 143
Romney Clo. Harr —31Ca 57
Romney Ct. W12 —47Ya 80 (off Shepherd's Bush Grn.)
Romney Dri. Brom —66Mc 129
Romney Dri. Harr —31Ca 57
Romney Gdns. Bexh —53Bd 109
Romney Lock Rd. Wind —2H 95
Romney M. W1 —43Jb 82 (7H 191)
Romney Pde. Hay —40T 56
Romney Rd. SE10 —51Fc 107
Romney Rd. Grav —2A 136
Romney Rd. Hay —40T 56
Romney Rd. N Mald —72Ta 143
Romney St. SW1 —48Nb 82 (4E 204)
Romney St. Knat —83Qd 171
Romola Rd. SE24 —60Rb 105
Romsey Clo. Orp —77Rc 150
Romsey Clo. Slou —48B 74
Romsey Clo. Stanf —2K 93
Romsey Dri. Farn C —4H 53
Romsey Gdns. Dag —39Zc 67
Romsey Rd. W13 —45Ja 78
Romsey Rd. Dag —39Zc 67
Romulus Ct. Bren —52Ma 101
Rom Valley Way. Romf —30Gd 48
Ronald Av. E15 —41Gc 85
Ronald Clo. Beck —71Bc 148
Ronald Ct. New Bar —13Db 23
Ronald Rd. Romf —25Qd 49
Ronaldsay Spur. Slou —3J 73
Ronaldshay. N4 —32Qb 62
Ronalds Rd. N5 —36Qb 62
Ronalds Rd. Brom —67Jc 129
Ronaldstone Rd. Sidc —58Uc 108
Ronald St. E1 —44Yb 84
Rona Rd. NW3 —35Jb 62
Ronart St. W'stone —27Ha 38
Rona Wlk. N1 —37Tb 63 (off Ramsey Wlk.)
Rondu Rd. NW2 —36Ab 60
Ronelean Rd. Surb —76Pa 143
Roneo Corner. Horn —32Hd 68
Ronfearn Av. Orp —71Zc 151
Ronley Ct. Sev —93Ld 187 (off Hillingdon Av.)
Ronneby Clo. Wey —76U 140
Ronver Rd. SE12 —60Hc 107
Rood La. EC3 —45Ub 83 (4H 201)
Rookby Ct. N21 —19Rb 25
Rook Clo. Horn —38Jd 68
Rookdean. Chip —94Ed 186
Rookeries Clo. Felt —62Y 121
Rookery Clo. NW9 —29Va 40
Rookery Clo. Fet —96Ga 176
Rookery Clo. Stanf —2K 93
Rookery Ct. Grays —51Wd 112
Rookery Cres. Dag —38Dd 68
Rookery Dri. Chst —67Qc 130
Rookery Gdns. St M —71Yc 151
Rookery Hill. Asht —90Qa 161
Rookery La. Brom —72Mc 149
Rookery La. Grays —50Fe 91
Rookery Rd. SW4 —56Lb 104
Rookery Rd. Orp —82Pc 168
Rookery Rd. Stai —64K 119
Rookery, The. Grays —51Wd 112
Rookery View. Grays —50Fe 91
Rookery Way. NW9 —29Va 40
Rookery Way. Tad —99Bb 179
Rookesley Rd. Orp —73Zc 151
Rooke Way. SE10 —50Hc 85
Rookfield Av. N10 —28Lb 42
Rookfield Clo. N10 —28Lb 42
Rook La. Cat —97Pb 180
Rookley Clo. Sutt —81Db 163
Rooks Hill. Loud —14L 17
Rooksmead Rd. Sun —68W 120
Rookstone Rd. SW17 —64Hb 125
Rook Wlk. E6 —44Mc 85
Rookwood Av. Lou —13Sc 28
Rookwood Av. N Mald —70Wa 124
Rookwood Av. Wall —77Mb 146
Rookwood Clo. Grays —50De 91
Rookwood Clo. Mers —100Kb 180
Rookwood Gdns. E4 —19Hc 27
Rookwood Gdns. Lou —13Sc 28
Rookwood Ho. Bark —41Tc 66
Rookwood Rd. N16 —31Vb 63
Roosevelt Way. Dag —37Fd 68
Ropemaker Rd. SE16 —47Ac 84
Ropemaker's Field. E14 —45Bc 84
Ropemaker St. EC2 —43Tb 83 (7F 195)
Roper La. SE1 —47Ub 83 (2J 207)
Ropers Av. E4 —22Dc 44
Ropers Orchard. SW3 —51Gb 103 (off Danvers St.)
Roper St. SE9 —57Pc 108
Ropers Wlk. SW2 —59Qb 104
Roper Way. Mitc —68Jb 126
Ropery St. E3 —42Bc 84
Rope St. SE16 —49Ac 84
Rope Wlk. Sun —69Y 121
Rope Wlk. Gdns. E1 —44Wb 83
Rope Yd. Rails. SE18 —48Rc 86
Ropley St. E2 —40Wb 63
Rosa Alba M. N5 —35Sb 63
Rosa Av. Ashf —63Q 120
Rosalind Ct. Bark —38Wc 67 (off Meadow Rd.)
Rosalind Ho. N1 —40Ub 63 (2J 195) (off Arden Ho.)
Rosaline Rd. SW6 —52Ab 102
Rosamond St. SE26 —62Xb 127
Rosamund Clo. S Croy —77Tb 147
Rosary Clo. Houn —54Aa 99
Rosary Ct. Pot B —2Db 9
Rosary Gdns. SW7 —49Eb 81 (6A 202)
Rosary Gdns. Ashf —63R 120
Rosaville Rd. SW6 —52Bb 103
Roscoe St. EC1 —42Sb 83 (6E 194)
Roscoe St. Est. EC1 —42Sb 83 (6E 194) (off Roscoe St.)
Roscoff Clo. Edgw —25Sa 39
Roseacre Clo. W13 —43Ka 78
Roseacre Clo. Horn —31Pd 69
Roseacre Clo. Shep —71Q 140
Roseacre Rd. Well —55Xc 109
Rose All. SE1 —45Sb 83
Roseary Clo. W Dray —49M 75
Rose Av. E18 —26Kc 45
Rose Av. Grav —10G 114
Rose Av. Mitc —67Hb 125
Rose Av. Mord —71Eb 145
Rosebank. SE20 —66Xb 127
Rose Bank. Brtwd —20Zd 33
Rosebank. Eps —86Sa 161
Rosebank. Wal A —5Gc 13
Rosebank Av. Horn —36Ld 69
Rosebank Av. Wemb —35Ha 58
Rose Bank Clo. N12 —22Gb 41
Rose Bank Cotts. Wok —94A 172
Rosebank Gdns. E3 —40Bc 64
Rosebank Gro. E17 —27Bc 44
Rosebank Rd. E17 —30Dc 44
Rosebank Rd. W7 —47Ga 78
Rosebank Vs. E17 —28Cc 44
Rosebank Wlk. NW1 —38Mb 62
Rosebank Wlk. SE18 —49Nc 86
Rosebank Way. W3 —44Ta 79
Rose Bates Dri. NW9 —28Qa 39
Roseberry Av. N Mald —68Ua 124
Roseberry Av. T Hth —68Sb 127
Roseberry Clo. Upm —30Vd 50
Roseberry Ct. Wat —11W 18
Roseberry Gdns. N4 —30Rb 43
Roseberry Gdns. N8 —29Nb 42
Roseberry Gdns. Dart —59Ld 111
Roseberry Gdns. Orp —76Uc 150
Roseberry Gdns. Upm —30Ud 50
Roseberry Pl. E8 —37Vb 63
Roseberry St. SE16 —49Xb 83
Rosebery Av. E12 —37Nc 66
Rosebery Av. EC1 —42Qb 82 (6K 193)
Rosebery Av. N17 —26Wb 43
Rosebery Av. Eps —86Ua 162
Rosebery Av. Harr —35Aa 57
Rosebery Av. Sidc —59Uc 108
Rosebery Clo. Mord —72Za 144
Rosebery Ct. EC1 —42Qb 82 (5K 193) (off Rosebery Av.)
Rosebery Cres. Wok —92B 172
Rosebery Gdns. W13 —44Ja 78
Rosebery Gdns. Sutt —77Db 145
Rosebery Ind. Est. N17 —26Xb 43
Rosebery Ind. Pk. N17 —26Xb 43
Rosebery M. N10 —26Lb 42
Rosebery Rd. N9 —20Wb 25
Rosebery Rd. N10 —26Lb 42
Rosebery Rd. SW2 —58Nb 104
Rosebery Rd. Bush —17Da 19
Rosebery Rd. Eps —91Ta 177
Rosebery Rd. Grays —51Ae 113
Rosebery Rd. Houn —57Ea 100
Rosebery Rd. King T —68Ra 123
Rosebery Rd. Sutt —79Bb 145
Rosebery Sq. EC1 —42Qb 82 (6K 193) (off Rosebery Av.)
Rosebery Sq. King T —68Ra 123
Rosebine Av. Twic —59Fa 100
Rosebriar Clo. Wok —88J 157
Rosebriars. Cat —92Ub 181
Rosebriar Wlk. Wat —8V 4
Rosebury Rd. SW6 —54Db 103
Rosebury Vale. Ruis —33W 56
Rosebushes. Eps —88Ya 162
Rose Cotts. Brick —2Da 5
Rose Ct. E1 —43Vb 83 (1K 201) (off Wentworth St.)
Rose Ct. S Harr —33Ea 58
Rose Ct. Wemb —40Na 59 (off Vicars Bri. Clo.)
Rosecourt Rd. Croy —72Pb 146
Rosecroft. N14 —19Mb 24
Rosecroft Av. NW3 —34Cb 61
Rosecroft Clo. Big H —90Pc 168
Rosecroft Clo. Orp —72Yc 151
Rosecroft Ct. N'wd —23S 36
Rosecroft Dri. Wat —8U 4
Rosecroft Gdns. NW2 —34Wa 60
Rosecroft Gdns. Twic —60Fa 100
Rosecroft Rd. S'hall —42Ca 77
Rosecroft Wlk. Pinn —29Z 37
Rosecroft Wlk. Wemb —36Ma 59
Rose & Crown Ct. EC2 —44Sb 83 (2D 200) (off Foster La.)
Rose & Crown Pas. Iswth —53Ja 100
Rose & Crown Yd. SW1 —46Lb 82 (7C 198)
Rosedale. Asht —90La 160
Rosedale. Cat —95Ub 181
Rose Dale. Orp —75Rc 150
Rosedale Av. Chesh —1Vb 11
Rosedale Av. Hay —43T 76
Rosedale Clo. SE2 —48Xc 87
Rosedale Clo. W7 —47Ha 78
Rosedale Clo. Brick —2Aa 5
Rosedale Clo. Dart —59Rd 111
Rosedale Clo. Stan —23Ka 38
Rosedale Ct. N5 —35Rb 63
Rosedale Gdns. Dag —38Xc 67
Rosedale Ho. N16 —32Tb 63
Rosedale Rd. E7 —36Lc 65
Rosedale Rd. SE21 —60Sb 105
Rosedale Rd. Dag —38Xc 67
Rosedale Rd. Eps —78Wa 144
Rosedale Rd. Grays —50Fe 91
Rosedale Rd. Rich —56Na 101
Rosedale Rd. Romf —26Ed 48
Rosedale Ter. W6 —48Xa 80 (off Dalling Rd.)
Rosedale Way. Chesh —1Wb 11
Rosedene. NW6 —39Za 60
Rosedene Av. SW16 —62Pb 126
Rosedene Av. Croy —73Nb 146
Rosedene Av. Gnfd —41Ca 77
Rosedene Av. Mord —71Cb 145
Rosedene Ct. Dart —59Ld 111
Rosedene Ct. Ruis —32U 56
Rosedene Gdns. Ilf —28Qc 46
Rosedene Ter. E10 —33Dc 64
Rosedew Rd. W6 —51Za 102
Rose End. Wor Pk —74Za 144
Rosefield. Sev —96Jd 186
Rosefield Clo. Cars —78Gb 145
Rosefield Gdns. E14 —45Cc 84
Rosefield Gdns. Ott —79F 138
Rosefield Rd. Stai —63J 119
Roseford Ct. W12 —47Za 80 (off Shepherd's Bush Grn.)
Rose Garden Clo. Edgw —23Na 39
Rose Gdns. W5 —48Ma 79
Rose Gdns. Felt —61W 120
Rose Gdns. S'hall —42Ca 77
Rose Gdns. Stai —59M 97
Rose Gdns. Wat —15W 18
Rosegarth. Grav —7A 136
Rose Glen. NW9 —28Ta 39
Rose Glen. Romf —32Gd 68
Rosehart M. W11 —44Cb 81
Rosehatch Av. Romf —27Zc 47
Roseheath Rd. Houn —57Ba 99
Rosehill. Clay —79Ja 142
Rosehill. Hamp —67Ca 121
Rose Hill. Sutt —76Db 145
Rosehill Av. Sutt —74Eb 145
Rosehill Av. Wok —4F 188
Rosehill Ct. Mord —73Eb 145 (off St Helier Av.)
Rosehill Ct. Slou —8L 73
Rosehill Farm Meadow. Bans —87Db 163
Rosehill Gdns. Abb L —4S 4
Rosehill Gdns. Gnfd —36Ha 58
Rosehill Gdns. Sutt —75Db 145
Rose Hill Pk. W. Sutt —74Eb 145
Rosehill Rd. SW18 —58Eb 103
Rosehill Rd. Big H —89Lc 167
Roseland Clo. N17 —24Tb 43
Rose La. Rip —93L 173
Rose La. Romf —27Zc 47
Rose Lawn. Bush —18Ea 20
Roseleigh Av. N5 —35Rb 63
Roseleigh Clo. Twic —58Ma 101
Rosemary Av. N2 —28Db 41
Rosemary Av. N3 —26Db 41
Rosemary Av. N9 —18Xb 25
Rosemary Av. Enf —11Ub 25
Rosemary Av. Houn —54Z 99
Rosemary Av. Romf —27Hd 48
Rosemary Av. W Mol —69Ca 121
Rosemary Clo. S Ock —41Yd 90
Rosemary Clo. Uxb —43Q 76
Rosemary Dri. E14 —44Fc 85
Rosemary Dri. Ilf —29Mc 45
Rosemary Gdns. SW14 —55Sa 101
Rosemary Gdns. Chess —77Na 143
Rosemary Gdns. Dag —32Bd 67
Rosemary Ho. N1 —39Tb 63 (off Colville Est.)
Rosemary La. SW14 —55Sa 101
Rosemary La. Egh —69D 118
Rosemary La. Hods —80Fe 155
Rosemary Rd. SE15 —52Vb 105
Rosemary Rd. SW17 —62Eb 125
Rosemary Rd. Well —53Vc 109
Rosemary St. N1 —39Tb 63
Rosemead. NW9 —31Va 60
Rose Mead. Pot B —2Eb 9
Rosemead Av. Felt —61V 120
Rosemead Av. Mitc —69Lb 126
Rosemead Av. Wemb —36Na 59
Rosemead Gdns. Hut —14Fe 33
Rosemont Av. N12 —23Eb 41
Rosemont Rd. NW3 —37Eb 61
Rosemont Rd. W3 —45Ra 79
Rosemont Rd. N Mald —69Sa 123
Rosemont Rd. Rich —58Na 101
Rosemont Rd. Wemb —39Na 59
Rosemoor St. SW3 —49Hb 81 (6F 203)
Rosemount Av. W Byf —85J 157
Rosemount Clo. Wfd G —23Pc 46
Rosemount Dri. Brom —70Pc 130
Rosemount Rd. W13 —44Ja 78
Rosenau Cres. SW11 —53Hb 103
Rosenau Rd. SW11 —53Gb 103
Rosendale Rd. SE21 —62Tb 127
Rosendale Rd. SE24 & SE21 —59Sb 105
Roseneath Av. N21 —18Rb 25
Roseneath Clo. Orp —80Yc 151
Roseneath Rd. SW11 —58Jb 104
Roseneath Wlk. Enf —14Tb 25
Rosen's Wlk. Edgw —20Ra 21
Rosenthal Rd. SE6 —58Dc 106
Rosenthorpe Rd. SE15 —57Zb 106
Rose Pk. Caravan Site. Wdhm —81G 156
Rosepark Ct. Ilf —26Pc 46
Roserton St. E14 —47Ec 84
Rosery, The. Croy —72Zb 148
Rosery, The. Egh —68G 118
Roses La. Wind —4B 94
Roses, The. Wfd G —24Hc 45
Rose St. WC2 —45Nb 82 (4F 199)
Rose St. Grav —58De 113
Rosethorn Clo. SW12 —59Mb 104
Rosetta Clo. SW8 —52Nb 104
Rose Valley. Brtwd —20Yd 32
Roseveare Rd. SE12 —63Lc 129
Rose View. Add —78L 139
Rose Vs. Dart —59Rd 111
Roseville Av. Houn —57Ca 99
Roseville Rd. Hay —50W 76
Rosevine Rd. SW20 —67Ya 124
Rose Wlk. Purl —83Mb 164
Rose Wlk. Slou —3F 72
Rose Wlk. Surb —71Ra 143
Rose Wlk. W Wick —75Ec 148
Rose Wlk., The. Rad —9Ka 6
Rosewarne Clo. Wok —6D 188
Rose Way. SE12 —57Jc 107
Roseway. SE21 —58Tb 105
Rose Way. Edgw —21Sa 39
Rosewood. Dart —63Gd 132
Rosewood. Sutt —82Eb 163
Rosewood. Wok —91C 172
Rosewood Av. Gnfd —36Ja 58
Rosewood Av. Horn —36Jd 68
Rosewood Clo. Sidc —62Yc 131
Rosewood Ct. E8 —38Vb 63
Rosewood Ct. Brom —67Lc 129
Rosewood Dri. Enf —7Qb 10
Rosewood Dri. Shep —71P 139
Rosewood Gdns. SE13 —54Ec 106
Rosewood Gro. Sutt —75Eb 145
Rosewood Sq. W12 —44Wa 80
Rosewood Way. Farn C —6G 52
Rosher Clo. E15 —38Fc 65
Rosher Ho. Grav —8B 114
Rosherville Way. Grav —9A 114
Roshni Ho. SW17 —65Gb 125
Rosina St. E9 —37Zb 64
Roskell Rd. SW15 —55Za 102
Rosken Gdns. Farn R —10F 52
Roslin Rd. W3 —48Ra 79
Roslin Way. Brom —64Jc 129
Roslyn Clo. Mitc —68Fb 125
Roslyn Ct. Wok —6D 188
Roslyn Gdns. Romf —26Hd 48
Roslyn M. N15 —29Ub 43
Roslyn Rd. N15 —29Tb 43
Rosmead Rd. W11 —45Ab 80
Rosoman Pl. EC1 —42Qb 82 (5A 194)
Rosoman St. EC1 —41Qb 82 (4A 194)
Rossall Clo. Horn —30Jd 48
Rossall Cres. NW10 —41Pa 79
Ross Av. NW7 —22Ab 40
Ross Av. Dag —32Bd 67
Ross Clo. Hare —24Ea 38
Ross Clo. Hay —49T 76
Ross Ct. NW9 —27Ua 40
Ross Cres. Wat —7W 4
Rossdale. Sutt —78Gb 145
Rossdale Dri. N9 —16Yb 26
Rossdale Dri. NW9 —32Sa 59
Rossdale Rd. SW15 —56Ya 102
Rosse M. SE3 —53Kc 107
Rossendale St. E5 —33Xb 63
Rossendale Way. NW1 —38Lb 62
Rossetti Clo. Coul —90Pb 164
Rossignol Gdns. Cars —75Jb 146
Rossindel Rd. Houn —57Ca 99
Rossington Av. Borwd —10Na 7
Rossington St. E5 —33Wb 63
Rossiter Clo. Slou —49A 74
Rossiter Fields. Barn —16Bb 23
Rossiter Rd. SW12 —60Kb 104
Rosslake Clo. W'ham —98Tc 184
Rossland Clo. Bexh —57Dd 110
Rosslyn Av. E4 —19Hc 27
Rosslyn Av. SW13 —55Ua 102
Rosslyn Av. Barn —16Gb 23
Rosslyn Av. Dag —31Bd 67
Rosslyn Av. Felt —58W 98
Rosslyn Av. Romf —26Nd 49
Rosslyn Clo. Hay —43T 76
Rosslyn Clo. Sun —65U 120
Rosslyn Clo. W Wick —76Hc 149
Rosslyn Cres. Harr —28Ha 38
Rosslyn Cres. Wemb —35Na 59
Rosslyn Gdns. Wemb —34Na 59 (off Rosslyn Cres.)
Rosslyn Hill. NW3 —35Fb 61
Rosslyn M. NW3 —35Fb 61
Rosslyn Pk. Wey —77T 140
Rosslyn Pk. M. NW3 —36Fb 61
Rosslyn Rd. E17 —28Ec 44
Rosslyn Rd. Bark —38Tc 66
Rosslyn Rd. Twic —58La 100
Rosslyn Rd. Wat —13X 19
Rossmore Rd. NW1 —42Gb 81 (6E 190)
Ross Pde. Wall —79Kb 146
Ross Rd. SE25 —69Tb 127
Ross Rd. Cob —85Y 159
Ross Rd. Dart —58Jd 110
Ross Rd. Twic —60Da 99
Ross Rd. Wall —78Lb 146
Ross Way. SE9 —55Nc 108
Ross Way. N'wd —21V 36
Rossway Dri. Bush —15Fa 20
Rosswood Gdns. Wall —79Lb 146
Ross Wyld Lodge. E17 —27Cc 44 (off Forest Rd.)
Rostella Rd. SW17 —63Fb 125
Rostrevor Av. N15 —30Vb 43
Rostrevor Gdns. Hay —46U 76
Rostrevor Gdns. Iver —40F 54
Rostrevor Gdns. S'hall —50Aa 77
Rostrevor M. SW6 —53Bb 103
Rostrevor Rd. SW6 —53Bb 103
Rostrevor Rd. SW19 —64Cb 125
Roswell Clo. Chesh —2Ac 12
Rotary St. SE1 —48Rb 83 (3B 206)
Rothbury Av. Rain —43Kd 89
Rothbury Gdns. Iswth —52Ja 100
Rothbury Rd. E9 —38Bc 64
Rothbury Wlk. N17 —24Wb 43
Roth Dri. Hut —19De 33
Rother Clo. Wat —6Y 5
Rotherfield Rd. Cars —77Jb 146
Rotherfield Rd. Enf —9Zb 12
Rotherfield St. N1 —38Sb 63
Rotherham Wlk. SE1 —46Rb 83 (7B 200) (off Nicholson St.)
Rotherhill Av. SW16 —65Mb 126
Rotherhithe New Rd. SE16 —50Wb 83
Rotherhithe Old Rd. SE16 —49Zb 84
Rotherhithe St. SE16 —47Yb 84
Rother Ho. SE15 —56Xb 105
Rothermere Rd. Croy —78Pb 146
Rotherwick Hill. W5 —42Pa 79
Rotherwick Rd. NW11 —31Cb 61
Rotherwood Clo. SW20 —67Ab 124
Rotherwood Rd. SW15 —55Za 102
Rothery St. N1 —39Rb 63 (off St Marys Path)
Rothesay Av. SW20 —68Ab 124
Rothesay Av. Gnfd —37Ea 58
Rothesay Av. Rich —56Ra 101
Rothesay Ct. SE11 —51Qb 104 (off Harleyford St.)
Rothesay Ct. SE12 —62Kc 129
Rothesay Rd. SE25 —70Tb 127
Rothsay Rd. E7 —38Lc 65
Rothsay St. SE1 —48Ub 83 (3H 207)
Rothsay Wlk. E14 —49Cc 84 (off Charnwood Gdns.)
Rothschild Rd. W4 —49Sa 79
Rothschild St. SE27 —63Rb 127
Roth Wlk. N7 —33Pb 62
Rothwell Ct. Harr —29Ha 38
Rothwell Gdns. Dag —38Yc 67
Rothwell Ho. Houn —51Ca 99
Rothwell Rd. Dag —39Yc 67
Rothwell St. NW1 —39Hb 61
Rotten Row. NW3 —32Eb 61
Rotten Row. SW7 & SW1 —47Fb 81 (1C 202)
Rotterdam Dri. E14 —48Ec 84
Rotunda, The. Romf —29Fd 48 (off Yew Tree Gdns.)
Rouel Rd. SE16 —48Wb 83 (in two parts)
Rouge La. Grav —9D 114
Rougemont Av. Mord —72Cb 145
Roughets La. Red —100Ub 181
Roughlands. Wok —87G 156
Rough Rd. Wok —10A 188
Roughs, The. N'wd —20U 18
Roughwood Clo. Wat —10U 4
Roughwood Croft. Chal G —15A 16
Roughwood La. Chal G —17A 16
Roundabout Ho. N'wd —25W 36
Roundacre. SW19 —61Za 124
Round Ash Way. Hart —72Ae 155
Roundaway Rd. Ilf —26Pc 46
Roundel Clo. SE4 —56Bc 106
Round Gro. Croy —73Zb 148
Roundhay Clo. SE23 —61Zb 128
Roundhedge Way. Enf —10Pb 10
Round Hill. SE26 —62Yb 128
Roundhill. Wok —91D 172
Roundhill Dri. Enf —14Pb 24
Roundhill Dri. Wok —90D 156
Roundhills. Wal A —6Gc 13
Roundhill Way. Cob —83Da 159
Roundmead Av. Lou —12Qc 28
Roundmead Clo. Lou —13Qc 28
Roundmoor Dri. Chesh —2Ac 12
Round Oak Rd. Wey —77P 139
Round St. Sole S —9E 136
Roundtable Rd. Brom —62Hc 129
Roundthorn Way. Wok —4C 188
Roundtree Rd. Wemb —36Ka 58
Roundway. Big H —88Lc 167
Roundway. Egh —64E 118
Roundways. Ruis —34V 56
Roundway, The. N17 —25Tb 43
Roundway, The. Clay —79Ha 142
Roundway, The. Wat —16V 18
Roundwood. Chst —68Rc 130
Roundwood Av. Hut —18Ce 33
Roundwood Av. Uxb —46S 76
Roundwood Clo. Ruis —31T 56
Roundwood Gro. Hut —17De 33
Roundwood Rd. NW10 —37Va 60
Roundwood View. Bans —87Za 162
Roundwood Way. Bans —87Za 162
Rounton Dri. Wat —10V 4
Rounton Rd. E3 —42Cc 84
Rounton Rd. Wal A —5Gc 13
Roupel Ho. SE15 —52Wb 105 (off Sumner Est.)
Roupell Rd. SW2 —60Pb 104
Roupell St. SE1 —46Qb 82 (7A 200)
Rousden St. NW1 —38Lb 62
Rousebarn La. Chan X —10P 3
Rouse Gdns. SE21 —63Ub 127
Rous Rd. Buck H —18Nc 28
Routh Ct. Felt —60T 98
Routh Rd. SW18 —59Gb 103
Routh St. E6 —43Pc 86
Routledge Clo. N19 —32Mb 62
Rover Av. Ilf —23Vc 47
Rover Ho. N1 —39Ub 63 (1J 195) (off Whitmore Est.)
Rowallan Rd. SW6 —52Ab 102
Rowan. N10 —26Kb 42
Rowan Av. E4 —23Bc 44
Rowan Av. Egh —64E 118
Rowan Clo. SW16 —67Lb 126
Rowan Clo. W5 —47Na 79
Rowan Clo. Brick —3Ca 5
Rowan Clo. N Mald —68Ua 124
Rowan Clo. Stan —23Ha 38
Rowan Clo. Wemb —34Ja 58
Rowan Ct. E8 —38Vb 63
Rowan Ct. E13 —40Kc 65 (off High St. Plaistow)
Rowan Ct. SE15 —52Vb 105 (off Garnies Clo.)

Rowan Ct. SW11 —58Hb 103
Rowan Cres. SW16 —67Lb 126
Rowan Cres. Dart —60Ld 111
Rowan Dri. NW9 —27Wa 40
Rowan Gdns. Croy —76Vb 147
Rowan Gdns. Iver —40E 54
Rowan Grn. Wey —77T 140
Rowan Grn. E. Brtwd —20Be 33
Rowan Grn. W. Brtwd —20Be 33
Rowan Gro. Coul —93Kb 180
Rowan Ho. W5 —43Ka 78
Rowan Ho. Hayes —68Gc 129
Rowan Ho. Sidc —62Vc 131
Rowan Hurst Dri. Farn C —6G 52
Rowan Pl. Hay —45V 76
Rowan Rd. SW16 —68Lb 126
Rowan Rd. W6 —49Za 80
Rowan Rd. Bexh —55Ad 109
Rowan Rd. Bren —52Ka 100
Rowan Rd. Swan —69Fd 132
Rowan Rd. W Dray —49M 75
Rowans Clo. Long —68Zd 135
Rowans, The. N13 —20Rb 25
Rowans, The. S Ock —46Sd 90
Rowans, The. Sun —64V 120
Rowans, The. Wok —90A 156
Rowan Ter. W6 —49Za 80
(off Rowan Rd.)
Rowantree Clo. N21 —18Tb 25
Rowantree Rd. N21 —18Tb 25
Rowantree Rd. Enf —12Rb 25
Rowan Wlk. N2 —30Eb 41
Rowan Wlk. N19 —33Lb 62
Rowan Wlk. W10 —42Ab 80
Rowan Wlk. Brom —76Pc 150
Rowan Wlk. Horn —28Md 49
Rowan Way. Lou —14Pc 28
Rowan Way. Romf —27Yc 47
Rowan Way. Slou —3F 72
Rowanwood Av. Sidc —60Uc 108
Rowben Clo. N20 —18Db 23
Rowberry Clo. SW6 —52Ya 102
Rowcross Pl. SE1 —50Vb 83 (7K 207)
(off Rowcross St.)
Rowcross St. SE1 —50Vb 83 (7K 207)
Rowdell Rd. N'holt —39Ca 57
Rowden Rd. E4 —23Dc 44
Rowden Rd. Beck —67Ac 128
Rowden Rd. Eps —77Ra 143
Rowditch La. SW11 —54Jb 104
Rowdon Av. NW10 —38Xa 60
Rowdow. Otf —88Md 171
Rowdow La. Sev & Knat —85Md 171
Rowdown Cres. New Ad —81Fc 167
Rowdowns Rd. Dag —39Bd 67
Rowe Gdns. Bark —40Vc 67
Rowe La. E9 —36Yb 64
Rowena Cres. SW11 —54Gb 103
Rowe Wlk. Harr —34Ca 57
Rowfant Rd. SW17 —60Jb 104
Rowhedge. Brtwd —20Ce 33
Row Hill. Add —79H 139
Rowhill Rd. E5 —35Xb 63
Rowhill Rd. Swan & Dart —65Hd 132
Rowhurst Av. Add —79K 139
Rowhurst Av. Lea —89Ha 160
Rowington Clo. W2 —43Db 81
Rowland Av. Harr —27La 38
Rowland Clo. Wind —5B 94
Rowland Ct. E16 —42Hc 85
Rowland Cres. Chig —21Uc 46
Rowland Gro. SE26 —62Xb 127
Rowland Hill Almshouses. Ashf (off Feltham Hill Rd.) —64R 120
Rowland Hill Av. N17 —24Sb 43
Rowland Hill Ho. SE1 —47Rb 83 (1B 206)
Rowland Hill St. NW3 —36Gb 61
Rowland Pl. N'wd —23U 36
Rowlands Av. Pinn —22Ca 37
Rowlands Clo. N6 —30Jb 42
Rowlands Clo. NW7 —24Wa 40
Rowlands Clo. Chesh —2Zb 12
Rowlands Fields. Chesh —1Zb 12
Rowlands Rd. Dag —33Bd 67
Rowland Wlk. Hav —20Gd 30
Rowland Way. SW19 —67Db 125
Rowland Way. Ashf —66S 120
Rowlatt Clo. Dart —63Ld 133
Rowlatt Rd. Dart —63Ld 133
Rowley Av. Sidc —59Xc 109
Rowley Clo. Pyr —88K 157
Rowley Clo. Wat —16Aa 19
Rowley Clo. Wemb —38Pa 59
Rowley Ct. Cat —94Tb 181
Rowley Ct. Enf —15Ub 25
(off Wellington Rd.)
Rowley Gdns. N4 —31Sb 63
Rowley Gdns. Chesh —1Zb 12
Rowley Grn. Rd. Barn —15Va 22
Rowley Ind. Pk. W3 —48Ra 79
Rowley La. Barn —14Ua 22
Rowley La. Borwd —11Ta 21
Rowley La. Wex —9N 53
Rowley Rd. N15 —29Sb 43
Rowley Rd. Ors —3C 92
Rowley Way. NW8 —39Db 61
Rowlheys Pl. W Dray —48N 75
Rowlls Rd. King T —69Pa 123
Rowney Gdns. Dag —37Yc 67
Rowney Rd. Dag —37Xc 67
Rowntree Clifford Clo. E13 —42Kc 85
Rowntree Path. SE28 —46Xc 87
Rowntree Rd. Twic —60Ga 100
Rowse Clo. E15 —39Ec 64
Rowsley Av. NW4 —27Ya 40
Rowstock Gdns. N7 —36Mb 62
Row, The. New Ash —75Be 155
Rowton Rd. SE18 —52Sc 108
Rowtown. Add —80H 139
Rowzil Rd. Swan —65Hd 132
Roxborough Av. Harr —31Fa 58
Roxborough Av. Iswth —52Ha 100
Roxborough Pk. Harr —31Ga 58
Roxborough Rd. Harr —29Fa 38
Roxbourne Clo. N'holt —37Aa 57
Roxburgh Av. Upm —34Sd 70
Roxburgh Rd. SE27 —64Rb 127
Roxburn Way. Ruis —34V 56
Roxby Pl. SW6 —51Cb 103
Roxeth Ct. Ashf —64Q 120
Roxeth Grn. Av. Harr —34Da 57
Roxeth Gro. Harr —35Da 57
Roxeth Hill. Harr —33Fa 58
Roxford Clo. Shep —71U 140
Roxley Rd. SE13 —58Dc 106
Roxton Gdns. Croy —78Cc 148
Roxwell Clo. Slou —6C 72
Roxwell Gdns. Hut —15Ee 33
Roxwell Ho. Lou —17Nc 28
Roxwell Rd. W12 —47Wa 80
Roxwell Rd. Bark —40Wc 67
Roxwell Trading Pk. E10 —31Ac 64
Roxwell Way. Wfd G —24Lc 45
Roxy Av. Romf —31Yc 67
Royal Albert Way. E16 —45Mc 85
Royal Arc. W1 —45Lb 82 (5B 198)
(off Old Bond St.)
Royal Av. SW3 —50Hb 81 (7F 203)
Royal Av. Wal X —5Ac 12
Royal Av. Wor Pk —75Ua 144
Royal Cir. SE27 —62Qb 126
Royal Clo. Ilf —31Wc 67
Royal Clo. Uxb —44P 75
Royal Clo. Wor Pk —75Ua 144
Royal College St. NW1 —38Lb 62
Royal Ct. SE16 —48Bc 84
Royal Cres. W11 —46Za 80
Royal Cres. Ruis —35Aa 57
Royal Cres. M. W11 —46Za 80
Royal Docks Rd. E6 & Bark —43Rc 86
Royal Dri. Eps —90Xa 162
Royal Exchange Av. EC3
(off Finch La.) —44Tb 83 (3G 201)
Royal Exchange Bldgs. EC3 —44Tb 83 (3G 201)
(off Threadneedle St.)
Royal Gdns. W7 —48Ja 78
Royal Hill. SE10 —52Ec 106
Royal Horticultural Society Cotts. Wis —88N 157
Royal Hospital Rd. SW3 —51Hb 103
Royal La. Uxb & W Dray —43P 75
Royal London Est., The. N17 —23Xb 43
Royal London Ind. Est. NW10 —40Ta 59
Royal M. Wind C —3H 95
Royal Mint Ct. EC3 —45Vb 83 (5K 201)
Royal Mint Pl. E1 —45Wb 83
Royal Mint St. E1 —45Vb 83
Royal Naval Pl. SE14 —52Bc 106
Royal Oak Hill. Knock —90Vc 169
Royal Oak Pl. SE22 —58Xb 105
Royal Oak Rd. E8 —37Xb 63
Royal Oak Rd. Bexh —57Bd 109
Royal Oak Rd. Wok —6F 188
Royal Oak Ter. Grav —10E 114
(off Constitution Hill)
Royal Opera Arc. SW1 —46Mb 82 (6D 198)
Royal Orchard Clo. SW18 —59Ab 102
Royal Pde. SE3 —54Hc 107
Royal Pde. SW6 —52Ab 102
Royal Pde. W5 —41Na 79
Royal Pde. Chst —66Sc 130
Royal Pde. Dag —37Dd 68
(off Church St.)
Royal Pde. Rich —53Qa 101
Royal Pde. M. Chst —66Sc 130
(off Royal Pde.)
Royal Pier M. Grav —8D 114
Royal Pier Rd. Grav —8D 114
Royal Pl. SE10 —52Ec 106
Royal Rd. E16 —44Lc 85
Royal Rd. SE17 —51Rb 105
Royal Rd. Dart —64Qd 133
Royal Rd. Sidc —62Zc 131
Royal Rd. Tedd —64Fa 122
Royal Route. Wemb —36Pa 59
Royal St. SE1 —48Pb 82 (3J 205)
Royalty M. W1 —44Mb 82 (3D 198)
(off Dean St.)
Royal Victoria Patriotic Building. SW18 —58Fb 103
Royal Victor Pl. E3 —40Zb 64
Royal Wlk. Wall —75Kb 146
Roycraft Av. Bark —40Vc 67
Roycroft Clo. E18 —25Kc 45
Roycroft Clo. SW2 —60Qb 104
Roydene Rd. SE18 —51Uc 108
Roy Dennison Ho. E13 —41Jc 85
Roydon Clo. Lou —17Nc 28
Roydon Ct. W on T —77X 141
Royds La. Kel H —11Td 32
Roy Gdns. Ilf —28Uc 46
Roy Gro. Hamp —65Da 121
Royle Clo. Ger X —24B 34
Royle Clo. Romf —29Kd 49
Royle Cres. W13 —42Ja 78
Roymount Ct. Twic —62Ga 122
Roy Rd. N'wd —24V 36
Roy Sq. E14 —45Ac 84
Royston Av. E4 —22Cc 44
Royston Av. Byfl —84N 157
Royston Av. Sutt —76Fb 145
Royston Av. Wall —77Mb 146
Royston Clo. Houn —53X 99
Royston Clo. W on T —74W 140
Royston Ct. E13 —39Jc 65
(off Stopford Rd.)
Royston Ct. SE24 —58Sb 105
Royston Ct. Rich —53Pa 101
Royston Gdns. Ilf —30Mc 45
Royston Gro. Pinn —23Ba 37
Royston Ho. N11 —21Hb 41
Royston Pde. Ilf —30Mc 45
Royston Pk. Rd. Pinn —23Ba 37
Royston Rd. SE20 —67Zb 128
Royston Rd. Byfl —84N 157
Royston Rd. Dart —58Hd 110
Royston Rd. Rich —57Na 101
Royston Rd. Romf —24Qd 49
Roystons, The. Surb —71Ra 143
Royston St. E2 —40Yb 64
Royston Way. Slou —3A 72
Rozel Ct. N1 —39Ub 63
Rozel Rd. SW4 —55Lb 104
Rubastic Rd. S'hall —48Y 77
Rubens Rd. N'holt —40Y 57
Rubens St. SE6 —61Bc 128
Ruberoid Rd. Enf —13Bc 26
Ruby Clo. Slou —8E 72
Ruby M. E17 —27Cc 44
Ruby Rd. E17 —27Cc 44
Ruby St. SE15 —51Xb 105
Ruby Triangle. SE15 —51Xb 105
Ruckholt Clo. E10 —34Dc 64
Ruckholt Rd. E10 —35Dc 64
Rucklidge Av. NW10 —40Va 60
Rucklidge Pas. NW10 —40Va 60
(off Rucklidge Av.)
Rudall Cres. NW3 —35Fb 61
Ruddlesway. Wind —3B 94
(in three parts)
Ruddstreet Clo. SE18 —49Rc 86
Ruddy Way. NW7 —23Va 40
Ruden Way. Eps —88Xa 162
Rudge Rise. Add —78H 139
Rudgwick Ct. SE18 —49Nc 86
(off Woodville St.)
Rudland Rd. Bexh —55Dd 110
Rudloe Rd. SW12 —59Lb 104
Rudolf Pl. SW8 —51Nb 104
Rudolph Rd. E13 —40Hc 65
Rudolph Rd. NW6 —40Cb 61
Rudolph Rd. Bush —16Ca 19
Rudsworth Clo. Coln —52F 96
Rudyard Gro. NW7 —23Sa 39
Rue de St Lawrence. Wal A —6Ec 12
Ruffets Wood. Grav —5E 136
Ruffetts Clo. S Croy —80Xb 147
Ruffetts, The. S Croy —80Xb 147
Ruffetts Way. Tad —90Ab 162
Rufford Clo. Harr —30Ja 38
Rufford St. N1 —39Nb 62
Rufford Tower. W3 —46Ra 79
Rufforth Ct. NW9 —25Ua 40
(off Pageant Av.)
Rufus Clo. Ruis —34Aa 57
Rufus St. N1 —41Ub 83 (4H 195)
Rugby Av. N9 —18Vb 25
Rugby Av. Gnfd —37Fa 58
Rugby Av. Wemb —36Ka 58
Rugby Clo. Harr —28Ga 38
Rugby Gdns. Dag —37Yc 67
Rugby La. Sutt —81Za 162
Rugby Rd. NW9 —28Ra 39
Rugby Rd. W4 —47Ua 80
Rugby Rd. Dag —38Xc 67
Rugby Rd. Twic —57Ga 100
Rugby St. WC1 —42Pb 82 (6H 193)
Rugby Way. Crox —15R 18
Rugged La. Wal A —5Mc 13
Ruggles-Brise Rd. Ashf —64M 119
Rugg St. E14 —45Cc 84
Ruislip Clo. Gnfd —42Da 77
Ruislip Ct. Ruis —33V 56
Ruislip Rd. N'holt & Gnfd —39Y 57
Ruislip Rd. E. Gnfd & W13 & W7 —42Fa 78
Ruislip St. SW17 —63Hb 125
Rumania Wlk. Grav —2H 137
Rumbold Rd. SW6 —52Db 103
Rum Clo. E1 —45Yb 84
Rumsey Clo. Hamp —65Ba 121
Rumsey M. N4 —34Rb 63
Rumsey Rd. SW9 —55Pb 104
Runbury Circ. NW9 —33Ta 59
Runciman Clo. Orp —82Yc 169
Runcorn Clo. N17 —28Xb 43
Runcorn Pl. W11 —45Ab 80
Rundell Cres. NW4 —29Xa 40
Rundell Tower. SW8 —53Pb 104
Runnel Field. Harr —34Ga 58
Runnemede Rd. Egh —63C 118
Running Horse Yd. Bren —51Na 101
Running Waters. Brtwd —21Ce 51
Runnymede. SW19 —67Fb 125
Runnymede Clo. Twic —58Da 99
Runnymede Ct. SW15 —60Wa 102
Runnymede Ct. Dart —60Sd 112
Runnymede Ct. Egh —63C 118
Runnymede Ct. Stanf —2L 93
Runnymede Cres. SW16 —67Mb 126
Runnymede Gdns. Gnfd —40Ga 58
Runnymede Gdns. Twic —58Da 99
Runnymede Ho. E9 —35Ac 64
Runnymede Ho. Cher —73J 139
(off Heriot Rd.)
Runnymede Rd. Stanf —2L 93
Runnymede Rd. Twic —58Da 99
Runtley Wood La. Sut G —97B 172
Runway, The. Ruis —36Y 57
Rupack St. SE16 —47Yb 84
Rupert Av. Wemb —36Na 59
Rupert Ct. W1 —45Mb 82 (4D 198)
Rupert Gdns. SW9 —54Rb 105
Rupert Ho. SE11 —49Qb 82 (6A 206)
Rupert Rd. N19 —34Mb 62
(in two parts)
Rupert Rd. NW6 —40Bb 61
Rupert Rd. W4 —48Ua 80
Rupert St. W1 —45Mb 82 (4D 198)
Rural Clo. Horn —32Kd 69
Rural Vale. Grav —9A 114
Rural Way. SW16 —66Kb 126
Ruscoe Dri. Wok —89C 156
Ruscoe Rd. E16 —44Hc 85
Ruscombe Gdns. Dat —1L 95
Ruscombe Way. Felt —59V 98
Rusham Ct. Egh —65C 118
Rusham Pk. Av. Egh —65B 118
Rusham Rd. SW12 —58Hb 103
Rusham Rd. Egh —65B 118
Rushbrook Cres. E17 —25Bc 44
Rushbrook Rd. SE9 —61Sc 130
Rushbury Ct. Hamp —67Ca 121
Rushcroft Rd. E4 —24Dc 44
Rushcroft Rd. SW2 —56Qb 104
Rushden Clo. SE19 —66Tb 127
Rushdene. SE2 —48Zc 87
(in two parts)
Rushdene Av. Barn —17Gb 23
Rushdene Clo. N'holt —40Y 57
Rushdene Cres. N'holt —40X 57
Rushdene Rd. Brtwd —16Yd 32
Rushdene Rd. Pinn —30Z 37
Rushdene Wlk. Big H —89Mc 167
Rushden Gdns. NW7 —23Ya 40
Rushden Gdns. Ilf —26Qc 46
Rushdon Clo. Grays —48Ce 91
Rushdon Clo. Romf —29Jd 48
Rushen Wlk. Cars —74Fb 145
Rushes Mead. Uxb —39L 55
Rushet Rd. Orp —68Xc 131
Rushett Clo. Th Dit —74Ka 142
Rushett La. Chess & Eps —83La 160
Rushett Rd. Th Dit —73Ka 142
Rushetts Rd. W King —80Ud 154
Rushey Clo. N Mald —70Ta 123
Rushey Grn. SE6 —59Dc 106
Rushey Hill. Enf —14Pb 24
Rushey Mead. SE4 —57Cc 106
Rushfield. Pot B —4Za 8
Rushford Rd. SE4 —58Bc 106
Rush Grn. Gdns. Romf —32Ed 68
Rush Grn. Rd. Romf —32Dd 68
Rushgrove Av. NW9 —29Ua 40
Rushgrove Pde. NW9 —29Ua 40
Rushgrove St. SE18 —49Pc 86
Rush Hill Rd. SW11 —55Jb 104
Rushleigh Av. Chesh —3Zb 12
Rushley Clo. Grays —46Fe 91
Rushley Clo. Kes —77Mc 149
Rushmead. E2 —41Xb 83
Rushmead. Rich —62Ka 122
Rushmead Clo. Croy —77Vb 147
Rushmead Clo. Edgw —19Ra 21
Rushmere Av. Upm —34Sd 70
Rushmere Ct. Wor Pk —75Wa 144
Rushmere Pl. SW19 —64Za 124
Rushmon Gdns. W on T —75X 141
Rushmoor Clo. Pinn —28X 37
Rushmoor Clo. Rick —19M 17
Rushmoor Ct. Wat —16S 18
Rushmore Clo. Brom —69Nc 130
Rushmore Hill. Orp & Knock —81Yc 169
Rushmore Rd. E5 —35Yb 64
Rusholme Av. Dag —34Cd 68
Rusholme Gro. SE19 —64Ub 127
Rusholme Rd. SW15 —58Za 102
Rushout Av. Harr —30Ka 38
Rushton Av. Wat —7W 4
Rushton Ct. Chesh —1Zb 12
(off Blindman's La.)
Rushton Ho. SW8 —54Mb 104
Rushton St. N1 —40Tb 63 (1G 195)
Rushworth Av. NW4 —27Wa 40
Rushworth Gdns. NW4 —28Wa 40
Rushworth St. SE1 —47Rb 83 (1C 206)
Rushymead. Kems —90Qd 171
Rushy Meadow La. Cars —76Gb 145
Ruskin Av. E12 —37Nc 66
Ruskin Av. Felt —58V 98
Ruskin Av. Rich —52Qa 101
Ruskin Av. Upm —31Sd 70
Ruskin Av. Wal A —6Gc 13
Ruskin Av. Well —55Wc 109
Ruskin Clo. NW11 —30Db 41
Ruskin Ct. N21 —17Pb 24
Ruskin Ct. SE5 —55Tb 105
(off Champion Hill)
Ruskin Dri. Orp —76Uc 150
Ruskin Dri. Well —55Wc 109
Ruskin Dri. Wor Pk —75Xa 144
Ruskin Gdns. W5 —42Ma 79
Ruskin Gdns. Harr —29Pa 39
Ruskin Gdns. Romf —24Kd 49
Ruskin Gro. Dart —58Qd 111
Ruskin Gro. Well —54Wc 109
Ruskin Pk. Ho. SE5 —55Tb 105
Ruskin Rd. N17 —25Vb 43
Ruskin Rd. Belv —49Cd 88
Ruskin Rd. Cars —78Hb 145
Ruskin Rd. Croy —75Rb 147
Ruskin Rd. Grays —9C 92
Ruskin Rd. Iswth —55Ha 100
Ruskin Rd. S'hall —45Aa 77
Ruskin Rd. Stai —65H 119
Ruskin Rd. Stanf —2L 93
Ruskin Wlk. N9 —19Wb 25
Ruskin Wlk. SE24 —57Sb 105
Ruskin Wlk. Brom —72Pc 150
Ruskin Way. SW19 —67Fb 125
Rusland Av. Orp —76Tc 150
Rusland Heights. Harr —28Ga 38
Rusland Pk. Rd. Harr —28Ga 38
Ruslip Rd. E. W7 —42Ga 78
Rusper Clo. NW2 —34Ya 60
Rusper Clo. Stan —21La 38
Rusper Ct. SW9 —54Nb 104
(off Clapham Rd.)
Rusper Rd. N22 & N17 —26Sb 43
Rusper Rd. Dag —37Yc 67
Russell Av. N22 —26Qb 42
Russell Clo. NW10 —38Sa 59
Russell Clo. SE7 —52Lc 107
Russell Clo. Amer —11A 16
Russell Clo. Bexh —56Cd 110
Russell Clo. Brtwd —17Xd 32
Russell Clo. Dart —58Jd 110
Russell Clo. N'wd —22S 36
Russell Clo. Ruis —33Y 57
Russell Clo. Tad —97Wa 178
Russell Clo. Wok —3F 188
Russell Ct. E10 —31Dc 64
Russell Ct. N14 —16Mb 24
Russell Ct. SE15 —54Xb 105
(off Heaton Rd.)
Russell Ct. SW1 —46Lb 82 (7C 198)
(off Cleveland Row)
Russell Ct. Brick —2Ca 5
Russell Ct. Lea —94Ka 176
Russell Ct. New Bar —14Eb 23
Russell Ct. S Croy —82Qb 164
Russell Ct. Wall —78Lb 146
(off Ross Rd.)
Russell Courtyard. Chst —67Qc 130
Russell Cres. Wat —7V 4
Russell Dri. Stai —58M 97
Russell Gdns. N20 —19Gb 23
Russell Gdns. NW11 —30Ab 40
Russell Gdns. W14 —48Ab 80
Russell Gdns. Ilf —31Tc 66
Russell Gdns. Rich —61La 122
Russell Gdns. W Dray —50Q 76
Russell Gdns. M. W14 —47Ab 80
Russell Grn. Clo. Purl —82Qb 164
Russell Gro. NW7 —22Ua 40
Russell Gro. SW9 —52Qb 104
Russell Hill. Purl —82Pb 164
Russell Hill Pl. Purl —83Qb 164
Russell Hill Rd. Purl —83Qb 164
Russell Kerr Clo. W4 —52Sa 101
Russell La. N20 —19Gb 23
Russell La. Wat —8T 4
Russell Lodge. E4 —19Ec 26
Russell Mead. Har W —25Ha 38
Russell Pde. NW11 —30Ab 40
(off Golders Grn. Rd.)
Russell Pl. NW3 —36Gb 61
Russell Pl. SE16 —48Ac 84
Russell Pl. S at H —67Qd 133
Russell Rd. E4 —21Bc 44
Russell Rd. E10 —30Dc 44
Russell Rd. E16 —44Jc 85
Russell Rd. E17 —27Bc 44
Russell Rd. N8 —30Mb 42
Russell Rd. N13 —23Pb 42
Russell Rd. N15 —29Ub 43
Russell Rd. N20 —19Gb 23
Russell Rd. NW9 —30Va 40
Russell Rd. SW19 —66Cb 125
Russell Rd. W14 —48Ab 80
Russell Rd. Buck H —18Kc 27
Russell Rd. Enf —10Vb 11
Russell Rd. Grav —8F 114
Russell Rd. Mitc —69Gb 125
Russell Rd. N'holt —36Ea 58
Russell Rd. N'wd —22S 36
Russell Rd. Shep —73S 140
Russell Rd. Til —3A 114
Russell Rd. Twic —58Ha 100
Russell Rd. W on T —72W 140
Russell Rd. Wok —3F 188
Russells. Tad —94Za 178
Russell's Footpath. SW16 —64Nb 126
Russell Sq. WC1 —43Nb 82 (6F 193)
Russell Sq. Long —69Zd 135
Russell's Ride. Chesh —3Ac 12
Russell St. WC2 —45Nb 82 (4G 199)
Russell St. Grav —9D 114
Russell St. Wind —3H 95
Russell Ter. Hort K —70Sd 134
Russell Wlk. Rich —58Pa 101
Russell Way. Sutt —78Db 145
Russell Yd. SW15 —56Ab 102
Russel Rd. Grays —49Ce 91
Russet Clo. Stai —58H 97
Russet Clo. Uxb —42S 76
Russet Clo. W on T —76Aa 141
Russet Cres. N7 —36Pb 62
Russet Dri. Croy —74Ac 148
Russet Ho. Grays —52Ee 113
Russets Clo. E4 —21Fc 45
Russett Clo. Orp —78Xc 151
Russett Hill. Cat —97Wb 181
Russett Hill. Ger X —27A 34
Russettings. Pinn —24Ba 37
(off Westfield Pk.)
Russetts. Horn —28Nd 49
Russetts Clo. Wok —87B 156
Russett Way. SE13 —54Dc 106
Russett Way. Swan —67Fd 132
Russia Ct. EC2 —44Sb 83 (3E 200)
(off Russia Row)
Russia Dock Rd. SE16 —46Ac 84
Russia La. E2 —40Yb 64
Russia Row. EC2 —44Sb 83 (3E 200)
Russia Wlk. SE16 —47Ac 84
Russington Rd. Shep —72T 140
Rusthall Av. W4 —49Ta 79
Rusthall Clo. Croy —71Yb 148
Rustic Av. SW16 —66Kb 126
Rustic Clo. Upm —32Ud 70
Rustic Pl. Wemb —35Ma 59
Rustic Wlk. E16 —44Kc 85
(off Lambert Rd.)
Rustington Wlk. Mord —73Bb 145
Ruston Av. Surb —73Ra 143
Ruston Gdns. N14 —16Kb 24
Ruston M. W11 —44Ab 80
Ruston St. E3 —39Bc 64
Rust Sq. SE5 —52Tb 105
Rutford Rd. SW16 —64Nb 126
Ruth Clo. Stan —28Pa 39
Ruth Ct. E3 —40Ac 64
Ruthen Clo. Eps —86Ra 161
Rutherford Clo. Sutt —79Fb 145
Rutherford Clo. Wind —3D 94
Rutherford Ho. Wemb —34Sa 59
(off Barnhill Rd.)
Rutherford St. SW1 —49Mb 82 (5D 204)
Rutherford Way. Bush —18Fa 20
Rutherford Way. Wemb —35Qa 59
Rutherglen Rd. SE2 —51Wc 109
Rutherwick Rise. Coul —89Nb 164
Rutherwyke Clo. Eps —79Wa 144
Ruthin Clo. NW9 —30Ua 40
Ruthin Rd. SE3 —51Jc 107
Ruthven Av. Wal X —5Zb 12
Ruthven St. E9 —39Zb 64
Rutland App. Horn —29Qd 49
Rutland Av. Sidc —59Wc 109
Rutland Av. Slou —3G 72
Rutland Clo. SW14 —55Ra 101
Rutland Clo. SW19 —66Gb 125
Rutland Clo. Bex —61Zc 131
Rutland Clo. Chess —79Pa 143
Rutland Clo. Dart —59Md 111
Rutland Clo. Eps —82Ta 161
Rutland Ct. EC1 —42Sb 83 (6D 194)
(off Goswell Rd.)
Rutland Ct. SE5 —56Tb 105
Rutland Ct. SE9 —61Sc 130
Rutland Ct. W3 —44Qa 79
Rutland Ct. Chst —67Qc 130
Rutland Ct. Enf —15Xb 25
Rutland Dri. Horn —29Qd 49
Rutland Dri. Mord —72Bb 145
Rutland Dri. Rich —60Na 101
Rutland Gdns. N4 —30Rb 43
Rutland Gdns. SW7 —47Gb 81 (2E 202)
Rutland Gdns. W13 —43Ja 78
Rutland Gdns. Croy —77Ub 147
Rutland Gdns. Dag —36Yc 67
Rutland Gdns. M. SW7 —47Gb 81 (2E 202)
Rutland Ga. SW7 —47Gb 81 (2E 202)
Rutland Ga. Belv —50Dd 88
Rutland Ga. Brom —70Hc 129
Rutland Ga. M. SW7 —47Gb 81 (2D 202)
(off Rutland Ga.)
Rutland Gro. W6 —50Xa 80
Rutland Ho. W8 —48Db 81
(off Marloes Rd.)
Rutland M. NW8 —39Db 61
Rutland M. E. SW7 —48Gb 81 (3E 202)
(off Ennismore St.)
Rutland M. S. SW7 —48Gb 81 (3D 202)
(off Ennismore St.)
Rutland Pk. NW2 —37Ya 60
Rutland Pk. SE6 —61Bc 128
Rutland Pk. Mans. NW2 —37Ya 60
Rutland Pl. EC1 —42Rb 83 (7C 194)
Rutland Pl. Bush —18Fa 20
Rutland Rd. E7 —38Mc 65
Rutland Rd. E9 —39Zb 64
Rutland Rd. E11 —29Kc 45
Rutland Rd. E17 —30Cc 44
Rutland Rd. SW19 —66Gb 125
Rutland Rd. Harr —30Ea 38
Rutland Rd. Hay —49T 76
Rutland Rd. Ilf —34Rc 66
Rutland Rd. S'hall —43Ca 77
Rutland Rd. Twic —61Fa 122
Rutland St. SW7 —48Gb 81 (3E 202)
Rutland Wlk. SE6 —61Bc 128
Rutland Way. Orp —72Yc 151
Rutley Clo. SE17 —51Rb 105
Rutley Clo. H Wood —26Md 49
Rutlish Rd. SW19 —67Cb 125
Rutson Rd. Byfl —86P 157
Rutter Gdns. Mitc —70Eb 125
Rutters Clo. W Dray —47Q 76
Rutt's Ter. SE14 —53Zb 106
Rutts, The. Bush —18Fa 20
Ruvigny Gdns. SW15 —55Za 102
Ruxbury Rd. Cher —72E 138
Ruxley Clo. Eps —78Ra 143
Ruxley Clo. Sidc —65Zc 131
Ruxley Corner Ind. Est. Sidc —65Zc 131
Ruxley Ct. Wor Pk —78Sa 143
Ruxley Cres. Clay —79Ka 142
Ruxley La. Eps —79Ra 143
Ruxley M. Eps —78Ra 143
Ruxley Ridge. Clay —80Ja 142
Ruxton Clo. Swan —69Gd 132
Ruxton Ct. Swan —69Gd 132
Ryalls Ct. N20 —20Hb 23
Ryan Clo. SE3 —56Lc 107
Ryan Clo. Ruis —32X 57
Ryan Ct. SW16 —66Nb 126
Ryan Way. Wat —11Y 19
Ryarsh Cres. Orp —77Uc 150
Rycott Path. SE22 —59Wb 105
Rycroft. Wind —5D 94
Rycroft Way. N17 —27Vb 43
Ryculff Sq. SE3 —54Hc 107
Rydal Clo. NW4 —26Za 40
Rydal Clo. Purl —85Tb 165
Rydal Ct. Edgw —22Pa 39
Rydal Ct. Leav —4X 5
Rydal Ct. Wemb —31Pa 59
Rydal Cres. Gnfd —41Ka 78
Rydal Dri. Bexh —53Cd 110
Rydal Dri. W Wick —75Gc 149
Rydal Gdns. NW9 —29Ua 40
Rydal Gdns. SW15 —64Ua 124
Rydal Gdns. Houn —58Da 99
Rydal Gdns. Wemb —32La 58

Rydal Rd. SW16 —63Mb **126**
Rydal Water. NW1 —41Lb **82** (4B **192**)
Rydal Way. Egh —66D **118**
Rydal Way. Enf —16Yb **26**
Rydal Way. Ruis —35Y **57**
Ryde Bldgs. SE1 —48Ub 83 (4H 207)
(off Swan Mead)
Ryde Clo. Rip —93L **173**
Ryde Dri. Stanf —3L **93**
Ryde Heron. Knap —5B **188**
Rydens Av. W on T —75X **141**
Rydens Clo. W on T —75Y **141**
Rydens Gro. W on T —77Z **141**
Rydens Pk. W on T —75Z **141**
Rydens Rd. W on T —76X **141**
Rydens Way. Wok —92C **172**
Ryde Pl. Twic —58Ma **101**
Ryder Clo. Brom —64Kc **129**
Ryder Clo. Bush —16Da **19**
Ryder Ct. E10 —33Dc **64**
Ryder Ct. SW1 —46Lb 82 (6C 198)
(off Ryder St.)
Ryder Gdns. Rain —37Hd **68**
Ryder M. E9 —36Yb **64**
Ryder's Ter. NW8 —40Eb **61**
Ryder St. SW1 —46Lb **82** (6C **198**)
Ryder Yd. SW1 —46Lb **82** (6C **198**)
Rydes Clo. Wok —92E **172**
Ryde, The. Stai —67K **119**
Ryde Vale Rd. SW12 —61Lb **126**
Rydinghurst Rd. Ger X —22A **34**
Rydings. Wind —5D **94**
Rydons Clo. SE9 —55Nc **108**
Rydon's La. Coul —92Sb **181**
Rydon St. N1 —39Sb **63**
Rydon's Wood Clo. Coul —92Sb **181**
Rydston Clo. N7 —38Nb **62**
Ryebridge Clo. Lea —90Ja **160**
Ryebrook. Lea —92Ja **176**
Ryebrook Rd. Lea —90Ja **160**
Rye Clo. Bex —58Dd **110**
Rye Clo. Horn —36Ld **69**
Ryecotes Mead. SE21 —60Ub **105**
Rye Ct. Slou —8L **73**
Rye Cres. Orp —74Yc **151**
Ryecroft Av. Ilf —26Rc **46**
Ryecroft Av. Twic —59Da **99**
Ryecroft Cres. Barn —15Xa **22**
Ryecroft Lodge. SW16 —65Rb **127**
Ryecroft Rd. SE13 —57Ec **106**
Ryecroft Rd. SW16 —65Qb **126**
Ryecroft Rd. Orp —72Tc **150**
Ryecroft Rd. Otf —88Jd **170**
Ryecroft St. SW6 —53Db **103**
Ryedale. SE22 —58Xb **105**
Rye Field. Orp —74Zc **151**
Ryefield Av. Uxb —38R **56**
Ryefield Ct. N'wd —26W **36**
Ryefield Cres. N'wd —26W **36**
Ryefield Path. SW15 —60Wa **102**
Ryefield Rd. SE19 —65Sb **127**
Rye Hill Pk. SE15 —56Yb **106**
Ryeland Clo. W Dray —44N **75**
Ryelands Clo. Cat —93Ub **181**
Ryelands Ct. Lea —90Ja **160**
Ryelands Cres. SE12 —58Lc **107**
Ryelands Pl. Wey —76U **140**
Rye La. SE15 —53Wb **105**
Rye La. Dun G & Otf —92Hd **186**
Rye Pas. SE15 —55Wb **105**
Rye Rd. SE15 —56Zb **106**
Rye, The. N14 —17Mb **24**
Rye Wlk. SW15 —57Za **102**
Rye Way. Edgw —23Pa **39**
Ryfold Rd. SW19 —62Cb **125**
Ryhope Rd. N11 —21Kb **42**
Rykhill. Grays —8D **92**
(in two parts)
Ryland Clo. Felt —63V **120**
Rylandes Rd. NW2 —34Wa **60**
Rylandes Rd. S Croy —81Xb **165**
Ryland Rd. NW5 —37Kb **62**
Rylett Cres. W12 —47Va **80**
Rylett Rd. W12 —47Va **80**
Rylston Rd. N13 —20Tb **25**
Rylston Rd. SW6 —51Bb **103**
Rymer Rd. Croy —73Ub **147**
Rymer St. SE24 —58Rb **105**
Rymill Clo. Bov —1C **2**
Rymill St. E16 —46Qc **86**
Rysbrack St. SW3 —48Hb **81** (3F **203**)
Rysted La. W'ham —98Sc **184**
Rythe Ct. Th Dit —73Ja **142**
Rythe Rd. Clay —78Fa **142**
Ryvers Rd. Slou —48B **74**

Sabah Ct. Ashf —63Q **120**
Sabbarton St. E16 —44Hc **85**
Sabella Ct. E3 —40Bc **64**
Sabina Rd. Grays —9E **92**
Sabine Rd. SW11 —55Hb **103**
Sabine's Rd. Nave & N'side —12Md **31**
Sable Clo. Houn —55Y **99**
Sable St. N1 —38Rb **63**
Sach Rd. E5 —33Xb **63**
Sackville Av. Brom —74Jc **149**
Sackville Clo. Harr —34Fa **58**
Sackville Clo. Sev —94Kd **187**
Sackville Cres. Romf —25Nd **49**
Sackville Gdns. Ilf —32Pc **66**
Sackville Rd. Dart —61Nd **133**
Sackville Rd. Sutt —80Cb **145**
Sackville St. W1 —45Lb **82** (5C **198**)
Sackville Way. SE22 —60Wb **105**
Saddington St. Grav —9D **114**
Saddlers Clo. Borwd —15Ta **21**
Saddlers Clo. Pinn —23Ca **37**
Saddlers M. SW8 —53Nb **104**
Saddlers M. Wemb —35Ha **58**
Saddler's Pk. Eyns —76Md **153**
Saddlers Path. Borwd —15Ta 21
(off Farriers Way)
Saddlers Way. Eps —91Ta **177**
Saddlescombe Way. N12 —22Db **41**
Saddleworth Rd. H Hill —23Ld **49**
Saddleworth Sq. Romf —23Ld **49**
Saddle Yd. W1 —46Kb **82** (6K **197**)
Sadler Clo. Mitc —68Hb **125**
Sadlers Ride. W Mol —69Da **121**
Saffron Av. E14 —45Fc **85**
Saffron Clo. NW11 —30Bb **41**
Saffron Clo. Dat —3M **95**
Saffron Clo. Horn H —1J **93**
Saffron Clo. W Horn —30Fe **51**
Saffron Ct. E15 —36Gc 65
(off Maryland Pk.)
Saffron Ct. Felt —59S **98**
Saffron Hill. EC1 —43Qb **82** (6A **194**)
Saffron Rd. Romf —26Fd **48**
Saffron St. EC1 —43Qb **82** (7A **194**)
Saffron Way. Surb —74Ma **143**
Sage St. E1 —45Yb **84**
Sage Way. WC1 —41Pb 82 (4H 193)
(off Cubitt St.)
Sahara Clo. F'boro —78Tc **150**
Saigasso Clo. E16 —44Mc **85**
Sail St. SE11 —49Pb **82** (5J **205**)
Saimet. NW9 —24Va 40
(off Satchell Mead)
Sainfoin Rd. SW17 —61Jb **126**
Sainsbury Rd. SE19 —64Ub **127**
St Agatha's Dri. King T —65Pa **123**
St Agatha's Gro. Cars —74Hb **145**
St Agnes Clo. E9 —39Yb **64**
St Agnes Pl. SE11 —51Qb **104**
St Agnes Well. EC1 —42Tb **83** (5G **195**)
St Aidan's Rd. SE22 —58Xb **105**
St Aidan's Rd. W13 —47Ka **78**
St Aidan's Way. Grav —2G **136**
St Alban's Av. E6 —41Pc **86**
St Alban's Av. W4 —49Ta **79**
St Albans Av. Felt —64Z **121**
St Albans Av. Upm —33Ud **70**
St Albans Av. Wey —76Q **140**
St Alban's Clo. NW11 —32Cb **61**
St Alban's Clo. Grav —2F **136**
St Albans Ct. EC2 —44Sb 83 (2E 200)
(off Wood St.)
St Alban's Cres. N22 —25Qb **42**
St Alban's Cres. Wfd G —24Jc **45**
St Alban's Gdns. Grav —2F **136**
St Alban's Gdns. Tedd —64Ja **122**
St Alban's Gro. W8 —48Db **81**
St Alban's Gro. Cars —73Gb **145**
St Alban's La. NW11 —32Cb **61**
St Albans Mans. W8 —48Db 81
(off Kensington Ct. Pl.)
St Alban's M. W2 —43Fb **81** (7C **190**)
St Alban's Pl. N1 —39Rb **63** (1B **194**)
St Alban's Rd. NW5 —34Jb **62**
St Alban's Rd. NW10 —39Ua **60**
St Albans Rd. Barn —7Xa **8**
St Alban's Rd. Coop —12Zc **15**
St Alban's Rd. Dart —58Pd **111**
St Albans Rd. Ilf —32Vc **67**
St Alban's Rd. King T —65Na **123**
St Albans Rd. S Mim —3Va **8**
St Alban's Rd. Sutt —77Bb **145**
St Albans Rd. Wat —12X **19**
St Alban's Rd. Wfd G —24Jc **45**
St Alban's St. SW1 —45Mb **82** (5D **198**)
St Alban's St. Wind —3H **95**
St Alban's Ter. W6 —51Ab **102**
St Alban's Vs. NW5 —34Jb **62**
St Alfege Pas. SE10 —51Ec **106**
St Alfege Rd. SE7 —51Mc **107**
St Alphage Garden. EC2 —43Sb **83** (1E **200**)
St Alphage Highwalk. EC2 —43Sb 83 (1E 200)
(off London Wall)
St Alphage Ho. EC2
(off Fore St.) —43Tb 83 (1F 201)
St Alphage Wlk. Edgw —26Sa **39**
St Alphege Rd. N9 —17Yb **26**
St Alphonsus Rd. SW4 —56Lb **104**
St Amunds Clo. SE6 —63Cc **128**
St Andrew's Av. Horn —36Hd **68**
St Andrew's Av. Wemb —35Ja **58**
St Andrews Av. Wind —4D **94**
St Andrew's Clo. N12 —21Eb **41**
St Andrew's Clo. NW2 —34Xa **60**
St Andrew's Clo. Iswth —53Ga **100**
St Andrew's Clo. Old Win —8L **95**
St Andrew's Clo. Ruis —33Z **57**
St Andrew's Clo. Shep —70T **120**
St Andrew's Clo. Stan —26La **38**
St Andrews Clo. Wok —5F **188**
St Andrews Clo. Wray —58A **96**
St Andrew's Ct. SW18 —61Eb **125**
St Andrew's Ct. Grav —8D 114
(off Queen St.)
St Andrews Ct. Sutt —76Gb **145**
St Andrews Ct. Swan —69Gd **132**
St Andrews Ct. Wat —11X **19**
St Andrew's Cres. Wind —4D **94**
St Andrew's Dri. Orp —72Xc **151**
St Andrews Dri. Stan —25La **38**
St Andrew's Gro. N16 —32Tb **63**
St Andrew's Hill. EC4 —45Rb **83** (4C **200**)
St Andrews Mans. W14 —51Ab 102
(off St Andrews Rd.)
St Andrew's M. N16 —32Ub **63**
St Andrew's M. SE3 —52Jc **107**
St Andrew's Pl. NW1 —42Kb **82** (5A **192**)
St Andrew's Pl. Shenf —19Be **33**
St Andrew's Rd. E11 —30Gc **45**
St Andrew's Rd. E13 —41Kc **85**
St Andrew's Rd. E17 —26Zb **44**
St Andrew's Rd. N9 —17Yb **26**
St Andrew's Rd. NW9 —32Ta **59**
St Andrew's Rd. NW10 —37Xa **60**
St Andrew's Rd. NW11 —30Bb **41**
St Andrew's Rd. W3 —45Ua **80**
St Andrews Rd. W7 —47Ga **78**
St Andrew's Rd. W14 —51Ab **102**
St Andrew's Rd. Cars —76Gb **145**
St Andrew's Rd. Coul —88Jb **164**
St Andrew's Rd. Croy —77Sb **147**
St Andrew's Rd. Enf —13Tb **25**
St Andrew's Rd. Grav —9D **114**
St Andrew's Rd. Ilf —31Pc **66**
St Andrew's Rd. Romf —30Fd **48**
St Andrew's Rd. Sidc —62Zc **131**
St Andrew's Rd. Surb —72Ma **143**
St Andrew's Rd. Til —3A **114**
St Andrew's Rd. Uxb —39N **55**
St Andrews Rd. Wat —20Z **19**
St Andrew's Sq. W11 —44Ab **80**
St Andrew's Sq. Surb —72Ma **143**
St Andrew St. EC4 —43Qb **82** (1A **200**)
St Andrew's Wlk. Cob —87X **159**
St Andrews Way. E3 —42Dc **84**
St Andrews Way. Slou —5B **72**
St Andrews Wharf. SE1 —47Vb **83** (1K **207**)
St Anna Rd. Barn —15Za **22**
St Anne's Av. Stai —59M **97**
St Anne's Clo. N6 —34Jb **62**
St Anne's Clo. Chesh —1Wb **11**
St Annes Clo. Grays —46De **91**
St Anne's Clo. Wat —21Y **37**
St Anne's Ct. W1 —44Mb **82** (3D **198**)
St Anne's Ct. W Wick —77Gc **149**
St Anne's Gdns. NW10 —41Pa **79**
St Anne's Pas. SW13 —55Ua **102**
St Anne's Rd. E11 —33Fc **65**
St Anne's Rd. Hare —27L **35**
St Anne's Rd. Mount —11Ee **33**
St Anne's Rd. Wemb —36Ma **59**
St Anne's Row. E14 —44Bc **84**
St Anne's St. E14 —44Bc **84**
St Ann's. Bark —39Sc **66**
St Ann's Clo. Cher —72H **139**
St Ann's Ct. NW4 —27Xa **40**
St Ann's Cres. SW18 —58Eb **103**
St Ann's Gdns. NW5 —37Jb **62**
St Ann's Hill. SW18 —57Db **103**
St Ann's Hill Rd. Cher —72F **138**
St Ann's La. SW1 —48Mb **82** (4E **204**)
St Ann's Pk. Rd. SW18 —58Eb **103**
St Ann's Pas. E14 —44Bc **84**
St Ann's Rd. N9 —19Vb **25**
St Ann's Rd. N15 —29Rb **43**
St Ann's Rd. SW13 —54Va **102**
St Ann's Rd. W11 —45Za **80**
St Ann's Rd. Bark —39Sc **66**
St Ann's Rd. Cher —72G **138**
(in three parts)
St Ann's Rd. Harr —30Ga **38**
St Ann's Shopping Cen. Harr —30Ga **38**
St Ann's St. SW1 —48Mb **82** (3E **204**)
St Ann's Ter. NW8 —40Fb **61** (1C **190**)
St Ann's Vs. W11 —46Za **80**
St Anns Way. Berr G —88Rc **168**
St Ann's Way. S Croy —79Rb **147**
St Anselm's Pl. W1 —45Kb **82** (4K **197**)
St Anselm's Rd. Hay —47V **76**
St Anthony's Av. Wfd G —23Lc **45**
St Anthony's Clo. E1 —46Wb **83**
St Anthony's Clo. SW17 —61Gb **125**
St Anthony's Way. Felt —56V **98**
St Antony's Rd. E7 —38Kc **65**
St Arvan's Clo. Croy —76Ub **147**
St Asaph Rd. SE4 —55Zb **106**
St Aubins Ct. N1 —39Ub **63**
St Aubyn's Av. SW19 —64Bb **125**
St Aubyn's Av. Houn —57Ca **99**
St Aubyn's Clo. Orp —76Vc **151**
St Aubyn's Gdns. Orp —75Vc **151**
St Aubyn's Rd. SE19 —65Vb **127**
St Audrey Av. Bexh —54Cd **110**
St Augustine Rd. Grays —9D **92**
St Augustine's Av. W5 —40Na **59**
St Augustine's Av. Brom —71Nc **150**
St Augustine's Av. S Croy —79Sb **147**
St Augustines Av. Wemb —34Na **59**
St Augustine's Rd. NW1 —38Mb **62**
St Augustine's Rd. Belv —49Bd **87**
St Austell Clo. Edgw —26Pa **39**
St Awdry's Rd. Bark —38Tc **66**
St Awdry's Wlk. Bark —38Sc **66**
St Barnabas Clo. Beck —68Ec **128**
St Barnabas Ct. Har W —25Ea **38**
St Barnabas Rd. E17 —30Cc **44**
St Barnabas Rd. Mitc —66Jb **126**
St Barnabas Rd. Sutt —78Fb **145**
St Barnabas Rd. Wfd G —25Kc **45**
St Barnabas St. SW1 —50Jb **82** (7J **203**)
St Barnabas Ter. E9 —36Zb **64**
St Barnabas Vs. SW8 —53Nb **104**
St Bartholomew Pl. EC1 —43Sb 83 (1D 200)
(off Kinghorn St.)
St Bartholomew's Clo. SE26 —63Xb **127**
St Bartholomew's Ct. E6 —40Nc 66
(off St Bartholomew's Rd.)
St Bartholomew's Rd. E6 —40Pc **66**
St Benedict's Av. Grav —2G **136**
St Benedict's Clo. SW17 —64Jb **126**
St Benet's Clo. SW17 —61Gb **125**
St Benet's Gro. Cars —73Eb **145**
St Benet's Pl. EC3 —45Tb **83** (4G **201**)
St Bernards. Croy —76Ub **147**
St Bernard's Clo. SE27 —63Tb **127**
St Bernard's Rd. E6 —39Mc **65**
St Bernards Rd. Slou —8N **73**
St Blaise Av. Brom —68Kc **129**
St Botolph Rd. Grav —62Fe **135**
St Botolph Row. EC3 —44Vb **83** (3K **201**)
St Botolph's Av. Sev —96Jd **186**
St Botolph's Rd. Sev —96Kd **187**
St Botolph's Row. EC3 —44Vb **83**
St Botolph St. EC3 —44Vb **83** (3K **201**)
St Brelades Ct. N1 —39Ub **63**
St Briavel's Ct. SE15 —52Ub 105
(off Lynbrook Clo.)
St Bride's Av. EC4 —44Rb 83 (3B 200)
(off Bride La.)
St Bride's Av. Edgw —25Pa **39**
St Brides Clo. Eri —47Zc **87**
St Bride's Pas. EC4 —44Rb 83 (3B 200)
(off Dorset Rise)
St Bride St. EC4 —44Rb **83** (2B **200**)
St Catherines. Wey —76R **140**
St Catherines. Wok —7F **188**
St Catherine's Clo. SW17 —61Gb **125**
St Catherine's Ct. W4 —48Ua **80**
St Catherines Ct. Stai —63J **119**
St Catherine's Dri. SE14 —54Zb **106**
St Catherine's Farm Ct. Ruis —30S **36**
St Catherines M. SW3 —49Hb **81** (5F **203**)
St Catherine's Rd. E4 —19Cc **26**
St Catherine's Rd. Ruis —30T **36**
St Catherines Tower. E10 —31Dc **64**
St Cecilia Rd. Grays —9D **92**
St Cedd's Ct. Grays —46De **91**
St Chads Clo. Surb —73La **142**
St Chad's Dri. Grav —2G **136**
St Chad's Gdns. Romf —31Ad **67**
St Chad's Pl. WC1 —41Pb **82** (3G **193**)
St Chad's Rd. Romf —31Ad **67**
St Chads Rd. Til —3C **114**
St Chad's St. WC1 —41Nb **82** (3G **193**)
St Charles Pl. W10 —43Ab **80**
St Charles Pl. Wey —78Q **140**
St Charles Rd. Brtwd —18Xd **32**
St Charles Sq. W10 —43Za **80**
St Christopher Rd. Uxb —44M **75**
St Christopher's Clo. Iswth —53Ga **100**
St Christophers Dri. Hay —45X **77**
St Christopher's Gdns. T Hth —69Qb **126**
St Christopher's M. Wall —78Lb **146**
St Christopher's Pl. W1 —44Jb **82** (2J **197**)
St Clair Clo. Ilf —26Pc **46**
St Clair Dri. Wor Pk —76Xa **144**
St Clair Rd. E13 —40Kc **65**
St Clair's Rd. Croy —75Ub **147**
St Clare Bus. Pk. Hamp —65Ea **122**
St Clare St. EC3 —44Vb **83** (3K **201**)
St Clement Clo. Uxb —44M **75**
St Clement's Av. Grays —51Xd **112**
St Clement's Ct. EC4 —45Tb 83 (4G 201)
(off Clements La.)
St Clement's Ct. N7 —37Pb **62**
St Clements Ct. Grays —51Be **113**
St Clements Ct. Purf —49Qd **89**
St Clement's Heights. SE26 —62Wb **127**
St Clement's La. WC2 —44Pb **82** (3J **199**)
St Clements Mans. SW6 —51Za 102
(off Lillie Rd.)
St Clement's Rd. S Stif —52Yd **112**
St Clement St. N7 —38Qb **62**
St Cloud Rd. SE27 —63Sb **127**
St Columba's Clo. Grav —2G **136**
St Columbas Ho. E17 —28Dc **44**
St Crispin's Clo. NW3 —35Gb **61**
St Crispin's Clo. S'hall —48Ba **77**
St Crispins Way. Ott —81E **156**
St Cross St. EC1 —43Qb **82** (7A **194**)
St Cuthberts Gdns. Pinn —24Ba **37**
St Cuthbert's Rd. NW2 —37Bb **61**
St Cuthberts Wlk. NW6 —37Bb **61**
St Cyprian's St. SW17 —63Hb **125**
St David Clo. Uxb —43M **75**
St David's. Coul —89Pb **164**
St David's Clo. Iver —39F **54**
St David's Clo. Wemb —34Sa **59**
St David's Clo. W Wick —73Dc **148**
St David's Cres. Grav —3F **136**
St David's Dri. Edgw —25Pa **39**
St David's Pl. NW4 —31Xa **60**
St Davids Rd. Swan —65Hd **132**
St Denis Rd. SE27 —63Tb **127**
St Denys Clo. Knap —6A **188**
St Dionis Rd. SW6 —54Bb **103**
St Donatt's Rd. SE14 —53Bc **106**
St Dunstans All. EC3 —45Ub 83 (5H 201)
(off St Dunstans Hill)
St Dunstan's Av. W3 —45Ta **79**
St Dunstan's Clo. Hay —50V **76**
St Dunstans Ct. EC4 —44Qb **82** (3A **200**)
St Dunstan's Dri. Grav —2G **136**
St Dunstan's Gdns. W3 —45Ta **79**
St Dunstans Hill. EC3 —45Ub **83** (5H **201**)
St Dunstan's Hill. Sutt —78Ab **144**
St Dunstans La. EC3 —45Ub **83** (5H **201**)
St Dunstan's La. Beck —72Ec **148**
St Dunstan's Rd. E7 —37Lc **65**
St Dunstan's Rd. SE25 —70Vb **127**
St Dunstan's Rd. W6 —50Za **80**
St Dunstan's Rd. W7 —47Ga **78**
St Dunstan's Rd. Felt —62V **120**
St Dunstan's Rd. Houn —54Y **99**
St Edith's Farm Cotts. Kems —90Rd **171**
St Edith's Rd. Kems —89Qd **171**
St Edmund's Av. Ruis —30T **36**
St Edmund's Clo. NW8 —39Hb **61** (1F **191**)
St Edmund's Clo. SW17 —61Gb **125**
St Edmunds Clo. Eri —47Zc **87**
St Edmund's Ct. W King —80Vd **154**
St Edmund's Dri. Stan —25Ja **38**
St Edmund's La. Twic —59Da **99**
St Edmund's Rd. N9 —17Wb **25**
St Edmund's Rd. Dart —56Qd **111**
St Edmund's Rd. Ilf —30Pc **46**
St Edmund's Ter. NW8 —39Gb **61** (1E **190**)
St Edward's Clo. NW11 —30Cb **41**
St Edward's Clo. New Ad —83Fc **167**
St Edwards Ct. E10 —31Dc **64**
St Edwards Ct. SW8 —51Mb 104
(off Nine Elms La.)
St Edwards Way. Romf —29Fd **48**
St Egberts Way. E4 —18Ec **26**
St Elizabeth Ct. E10 —31Dc **64**
St Elmo Clo. Slou —2H **73**
St Elmo Cres. Slou —2H **73**
St Elmo Rd. W12 —46Va **80**
St Elmos Rd. SE16 —47Ac **84**
St Erkenwald Rd. Bark —39Tc **66**
St Ermin's Hill. SW1 —48Mb 82 (3D 204)
(off Broadway)
St Ervan's Rd. W10 —43Bb **81**
St Faith's Clo. Enf —11Sb **25**
St Faith's Rd. SE21 —60Rb **105**
St Fidelis Rd. Eri —50Fd **88**
St Fillans Rd. SE6 —60Ec **106**
St Francis Av. Grav —3G **136**
St Francis Clo. Orp —72Uc **150**
St Francis Clo. Pot B —6Eb **9**
St Francis Clo. Wat —18X **19**
St Francis Rd. SE22 —56Ub **105**
St Francis Rd. Den —30H **35**
St Francis Rd. Eri —49Fd **88**
St Francis Way. Grays —8E **92**
St Gabriel's Clo. E11 —33Kc **65**
St Gabriels Rd. NW2 —36Za **60**
St George's Av. E7 —38Kc **65**
St George's Av. N7 —35Mb **62**
St George's Av. NW9 —28Ta **39**
St George's Av. W5 —47Ma **79**
St George's Av. Grays —49Ee **91**
St George's Av. Horn —31Pd **69**
St George's Av. S'hall —45Ba **77**
St George's Av. Wey —79R **140**
St George's Bldgs. SE1 —47Sb **83** (1E **206**)
St George's Cen. Grav —8D **114**
St George's Cir. SE1 —48Rb **83** (3B **206**)
St George's Clo. NW11 —30Bb **41**
St George's Clo. Wemb —34Ja **58**
St George's Clo. Wey —78S **140**
St Georges Clo. Wind —3C **94**
St Georges Ct. E6 —42Pc **86**
St Georges Ct. E17 —29Fc **45**
St Georges Ct. EC4 —44Rb **83** (2B **200**)
St George's Ct. SW15 —56Bb **103**
St Georges Ct. Add —77L **139**
St George's Ct. Brtwd —17Xd **32**
St Georges Ct. Harr —30Ja 38
(off Kenton Rd.)
St George's Cres. Grav —3F **136**
St George's Cres. Slou —5B **72**
St George's Dri. SW1 —49Kb **82** (6A **204**)
St George's Dri. Uxb —34P **55**
St George's Dri. Wat —20Aa **19**
St George's Fields. W2 —44Gb **81** (3E **196**)
St George's Gdns. Eps —86Va **162**
St George's Gdns. Surb —75Ra **143**
St George's Gro. SW17 —62Fb **125**
St Georges Ind. Est. N17 —24Rb **43**
St Georges La. EC3 —45Tb 83 (5G 201)
(off Pudding La.)
St George's La. Asc —9A **116**
St George's M. NW1 —38Hb **61**
St George's Pl. Twic —60Ja **100**
St George's Rd. E7 —38Kc **65**
St George's Rd. E10 —34Ec **64**
St George's Rd. N9 —20Wb **25**
St George's Rd. N13 —19Pb **24**
St George's Rd. NW11 —30Bb **41**
St George's Rd. SE1 —48Qb **82** (3A **206**)
St George's Rd. SW19 —65Bb **125**
St George's Rd. W4 —47Ta **79**
St George's Rd. W7 —46Ha **78**
St George's Rd. Add —77L **139**
St George's Rd. Beck —67Dc **128**
St George's Rd. Brom —68Pc **130**
(in two parts)
St George's Rd. Dag —36Ad **67**
St George's Rd. Enf —10Vb **11**
St George's Rd. Felt —63Z **121**
St George's Rd. Ilf —31Pc **66**
St George's Rd. King T —66Qa **123**
St George's Rd. Mitc —69Kb **126**
St George's Rd. Orp —72Tc **150**
St Georges Rd. Rich —55Pa **101**
St George's Rd. Sev —94Kd **187**
St George's Rd. Sidc —65Zc **131**
St Georges Rd. Swan —70Hd **132**
St George's Rd. Twic —57Ka **100**
St George's Rd. Wall —78Kb **146**
St George's Rd. Wat —10X **5**
St George's Rd. Wey —79T **140**
St George's Rd. W. Brom —68Nc **130**
St George's Sq. E7 —38Kc **65**
St Georges Sq. E14 —45Ac **84**
St Georges Sq. SE8 —49Bc **84**
St George's Sq. SW1 —50Mb **82** (7D **204**)
St Georges Sq. Grav —8D **114**
St Georges Sq. Long —69Ae **135**
St George's Sq. N Mald —69Ua **124**
St George's Sq. M. SW1 —50Mb **82** (7D **204**)
St George's Ter. NW1 —38Hb **61**
St George St. W1 —45Kb **82** (3A **198**)
St George's Wlk. Croy —76Sb **147**
St George's Wlk. Wemb —34Ra **59**
St George's Way. SE15 —51Ub **105**
St Gerards Clo. SW4 —57Lb **104**
St German's Pl. SE3 —53Jc **107**
St German's Rd. SE23 —60Ac **106**
St Giles Av. Dag —38Dd **68**
St Giles Av. Pot B —4Xa **8**
St Giles Av. Uxb —35S **56**
St Giles Cir. W1 —44Mb **82**
St Giles Cir. WC2 —44Mb **82** (2E **198**)
St Giles Clo. Dag —38Dd **68**
St Giles Clo. Orp —78Tc **150**
St Giles Clo. Ors —2C **92**
St Giles Ct. WC2 —44Nb 82 (2F 199)
(off St Giles High St.)
St Giles Ct. Enf —7Yb **12**
St Giles High St. WC2 —44Mb **82** (2E **198**)
St Giles Ho. New Bar —14Eb **23**
St Giles Pas. WC2 —44Mb 82 (3E 198)
(off New Compton St.)
St Giles Rd. SE5 —52Ub **105**
St Giles Ter. EC2 —43Sb 83 (1E 200)
(off Barbican)
St Gothard Rd. SE27 —63Tb **127**
St Gregory Clo. Ruis —35Y **57**
St Gregory's Ct. Grav —1G **136**
St Gregory's Cres. Grav —1G **136**
St Helena Rd. SE16 —49Zb **84**
St Helena St. WC1 —41Qb **82** (4K **193**)
St Helen Clo. Uxb —43M **75**
St Helens. Th Dit —73Ha **142**
St Helens Ct. Epp —2Wc **15**
St Helen's Ct. Rain —42Jd **88**
St Helen's Cres. SW16 —67Pb **126**
St Helen's Gdns. W10 —43Za **80**
St Helen's Pl. EC3 —44Ub **83** (2H **201**)
St Helen's Rd. SW16 —67Pb **126**
St Helen's Rd. W13 —46Ka **78**
St Helen's Rd. Eri —47Zc **87**
St Helen's Rd. Ilf —30Pc **46**
St Helier Av. Mord —73Eb **145**
St Helier's Av. Houn —57Ca **99**
St Helier's Rd. E10 —30Ec **44**
St Hilda's Av. Ashf —64N **119**
St Hilda's Clo. NW6 —39Za **60**
St Hilda's Clo. SW17 —61Gb **125**
St Hilda's Clo. Knap —5A **188**
St Hilda's Rd. SW13 —51Xa **102**
St Hilda's Way. Grav —3F **136**
St Hubert's Clo. Ger X —33A **54**
St Hubert's La. Ger X —33B **54**
St Hughes Clo. SW17 —61Gb **125**
St Hugh's Rd. SE20 —67Xb **127**
St Ivian's Dri. Romf —27Jd **48**
St James Apartments. E17 —29Ac 44
(off Pretoria Av.)
St James Av. N20 —20Gb **23**
St James Av. W13 —46Ja **78**
St James Av. Beck —69Ac **128**
St James Av. Eps —83Va **162**
St James Av. Sutt —78Cb **145**
St James Av. E. Stanf —1N **93**
St James Av. W. Stanf —1N **93**
St James Clo. N20 —20Gb **23**
St James Clo. SE18 —50Sc **86**
St James Clo. Eps —86Ua **162**
St James Clo. N Mald —71Va **144**
St James Clo. Ruis —33Y **57**
St James Clo. Wok —6D **188**
St James Ct. SE3 —53Kc **107**
St James' Ct. SW1 —48Lb **82** (3C **204**)
St James Ct. Asht —89Ma **161**
St James' Gdns. Wemb —38Na **59**
St James Ga. NW1 —38Mb **62**
St James Gro. SW11 —54Hb **103**
St James La. Grnh —60Ud **112**
St James M. E14 —48Ec **84**
St James M. Wey —77R **140**
St James Oak. Grav —9C **114**
St James Pl. Dart —58Md **111**
St James Pl. Slou —4A **72**
St James' Rd. E15 —36Hc **65**
St James' Rd. N9 —19Xb **25**
St James Rd. Cars —76Gb **145**
St James Rd. Chesh —1Sb **11**
St James' Rd. King T —68Ma **123**
St James Rd. Mitc —66Jb **126**
St James Rd. Purl —85Rb **165**
St James Rd. Sev —94Kd **187**
St James Rd. Sutt —78Cb **145**
St James Rd. Wat —15X **19**
St James's. SE14 —53Ac **106**
St James's App. EC2 —42Ub **83** (6H **195**)
St James's Av. E2 —40Yb **64**
St James's Av. Beck —69Ac **128**
St James's Av. Grav —9C **114**
St James's Av. Hamp —64Ea **122**
St James's Clo. SW17 —61Hb **125**

St James's Cotts.—St Peter's Vs.

St James's Cotts. Rich —57Ma 101
St James's Ct. N18 —22Wb 43 (off Fore St.)
St James's Ct. Harr —30Ja 38
St James's Cres. SW9 —55Qb 104
St James's Dri. SW17 —60Hb 103
St James's Gdns. W11 —46Ab 80
St James's Ho. Romf —29Hd 48 (off Eastern Rd.)
St James's La. N10 —28Kb 42
St James's Mkt. SW1 —45Mb 82 (5D 198)
St James's Pk. Croy —73Sb 147
St James's Pas. EC3 (off Duke's Pl.) —44Ub 83 (3J 201)
St James's Pl. SW1 —46Lb 82 (7B 198)
St James Sq. Long —69Ae 135
St James's Rd. SE1 —51Wb 105
St James's Rd. SE16 —48Wb 83
St James's Rd. SW1 —46Lb 82
St James's Rd. Brtwd —20Yd 32
St James's Rd. Croy —73Rb 147
St James's Rd. Grav —8C 114
St James's Rd. Hamp —64Da 121
St James's Rd. Surb —72Ma 143
St James's Row. EC1 —42Rb 83 (6B 194)
St James's Sq. SW1 —46Lb 82 (6C 198)
St James's St. SW1 —46Lb 82 (6B 198)
St James's St. Grav —8C 114
St James's Ter. NW8 —40Hb 61 (1F 191) (off Prince Albert Rd.)
St James's Ter. M. NW8 —39Hb 61 (1F 191)
St James St. E17 —29Ac 44
St James St. W6 —50Ya 80
St James's Wlk. EC1 —42Rb 83 (5B 194)
St James Wlk. SE15 —53Vb 105 (off Pitt St.)
St James Wlk. Iver —47G 74
St James Way. Sidc —64Ad 131
St Jeromes Gro. Hay —44S 76
St Joan's Rd. N9 —19Vb 25
St John's Av. N11 —22Hb 41
St John's Av. NW10 —39Va 60
St John's Av. SW15 —57Za 102
St John's Av. Eps —84Wa 162
St John's Av. Lea —93Ka 176
St John's Av. War —21Zd 51
St Johns Chu. Rd. E9 —36Yb 64
St John's Clo. N20 —20Eb 23 (off Rasper Rd.)
St John's Clo. SW6 —52Cb 103
St John's Clo. Hart —71Be 155
St John's Clo. Lea —92La 176
St John's Clo. Pot B —5Eb 9
St John's Clo. Rain —38Jd 68
St Johns Clo. Uxb —39K 55
St John's Clo. Wemb —36Na 59
St John's Cotts. SE20 —66Yb 128
St John's Ct. N4 —33Rb 63
St John's Ct. N5 —35Rb 63
St John's Ct. SE13 —54Ec 106
St John's Ct. W6 —49Xa 80 (off Glenthorne Rd.)
St John's Ct. Buck H —18Kc 27
St John's Ct. Egh —64C 118
St John's Ct. Eri —50Fd 88
St John's Ct. Harr —30Ha 38
St John's Ct. Iswth —54Ha 100
St Johns Ct. N'wd —25U 36
St John's Ct. Sev —94Ld 187
St John's Ct. St J —7D 188
St Johns Cres. SW9 —55Qb 104
St Johns Dri. SW18 —60Db 103
St John's Dri. W on T —74Y 141
St John's Dri. Wind —4E 94
St John's Est. N1 —40Tb 63 (2G 195)
St John's Est. SE1 (off Fair St.) —47Vb 83 (1K 207)
St John's Gdns. W11 —45Ab 80
St John's Gro. N19 —33Lb 62
St John's Gro. SW13 —54Va 102
St John's Gro. Rich —56Na 101
St John's Hill. SW11 —56Fb 103
St John's Hill. Coul —89Qb 164
St John's Hill. Purl —88Qb 164
St John's Hill. Sev —93Ld 187
St John's Hill Gro. SW11 —56Fb 103
St John's Hill Rd. Wok —7D 188
St John's La. EC1 —42Rb 83 (6B 194)
St John's La. Hart —72Be 155
St John's Lye. Wok —7E 188
St John's M. W11 —44Cb 81
St John's M. Wok —6C 188
St Johns Pde. Sidc —63Xc 131 (off Sidcup High St.)
St John's Pk. SE3 —52Hc 107
St John's Pk. Mans. N19 —34Lb 62
St John's Pas. SW19 —65Ab 124
St John's Path. EC1 —42Rb 83 (6B 194) (off Britton St.)
St Johns Pathway. SE23 —60Yb 106
St John's Pl. EC1 —42Rb 83 (6B 194)
St Johns Rise. Berr G —88Rc 168
St John's Rise. Wok —7E 188
St John's Rd. E4 —21Dc 44
St John's Rd. E6 —39Nc 66
St John's Rd. E16 —44Jc 85
St John's Rd. E17 —26Dc 44
St John's Rd. N15 —30Ub 43
St John's Rd. NW11 —30Bb 41
St John's Rd. SE20 —65Yb 128
St John's Rd. SW11 —56Gb 103
St John's Rd. SW19 —66Ab 124
St John's Rd. Bark —39Uc 86
St John's Rd. Cars —76Gb 145
St John's Rd. Croy —76Rb 147
St John's Rd. Dart —59Sd 112
St John's Rd. E Mol —70Fa 122
St John's Rd. Epp —2Vc 15
St John's Rd. Eri —50Fd 88
St John's Rd. Felt —63Aa 121
St John's Rd. Grav —9F 114
St Johns Rd. Grays —10D 92
St John's Rd. Harr —30Ha 38
St John's Rd. Ilf —31Uc 66
St John's Rd. Iswth —54Ga 100
St John's Rd. King T —68La 122
St John's Rd. Lea —93La 176
St John's Rd. Lou —12Pc 28
St John's Rd. N Mald —69Sa 123
St John's Rd. Orp —72Tc 150
St John's Rd. Rich —56Na 101
St Johns Rd. Romf —22Ed 48
St John's Rd. Sev —93Kd 187
St John's Rd. Sidc —63Xc 131
St Johns Rd. Slou —5L 73
St John's Rd. S'hall —48Aa 77
St John's Rd. Sutt —75Db 145
St John's Rd. Uxb —39K 55
St John's Rd. Wat —12X 19
St John's Rd. Well —55Xc 109
St John's Rd. Wemb —35Ma 59
St John's Rd. Wind —4E 94
St John's Rd. Wok —6D 188
St John's Sq. EC1 (in two parts) —42Rb 83 (6B 194)
St John's Ter. E7 —37Kc 65
St John's Ter. SE18 —51Sc 108
St John's Ter. W10 —42Za 80
St John's Ter. Enf —9Tb 11
St John St. EC1 —40Qb 62 (2A 194)
St John's Vale. SE8 —54Cc 106
St John's Vs. N11 —22Hb 41 (off Friern Barnet Rd.)
St John's Vs. N19 —33Mb 62
St John's Vs. W8 —48Db 81
St John's Way. N19 —33Lb 62
St John's Wood Ct. NW8 —41Fb 81 (4C 190) (off St John's Wood Rd.)
St John's Wood High St. NW8 —40Fb 61 (2C 190)
St John's Wood Pk. NW8 —39Fb 61
St John's Wood Rd. NW8 —42Fb 81 (5B 190)
St John's Wood Ter. NW8 —40Fb 61 (1C 190)
St John's Yd. N17 —24Vb 43
St Joseph's Clo. W10 —43Ab 80
St Joseph's Clo. Orp —76Vc 151
St Joseph's Ct. E4 —17Fc 27
St Josephs Ct. SE7 —51Kc 107
St Joseph's Dri. S'hall —46Aa 77
St Joseph's Gro. NW4 —28Xa 40
St Joseph's Rd. N9 —17Xb 25
St Joseph's St. SW8 —53Kb 104
St Joseph's Vale. SE3 —55Fc 107
St Jude's Clo. Egh —4N 117
St Jude's Rd. E2 —40Xb 63
St Jude's Rd. Egh —3N 117
St Jude St. N16 —36Ub 63
St Julian's Clo. SW16 —63Qb 126
St Julian's Farm Rd. SE27 —63Qb 126
St Julian's Rd. NW6 —39Bb 61
St Justin Clo. St P —69Zc 131
St Katharine's Precinct. NW1 —40Kb 62 (1K 191)
St Katharine's Way. E1 —46Vb 83 (6K 201)
St Katherines Rd. Cat —97Wb 181
St Katherine's Rd. Eri —47Zc 87
St Katherine's Row. EC3 —45Ub 83 (4J 201) (off Fenchurch St.)
St Keverne Rd. SE9 —63Nc 130
St Kilda Rd. W13 —46Ja 78
St Kilda Rd. Orp —74Vc 151
St Kilda's Rd. N16 —32Tb 63
St Kilda's Rd. Brtwd —17Xd 32
St Kilda's Rd. Harr —30Ga 38
St Kitts Ter. SE19 —64Ub 127
St Laurence Clo. Orp —69Zc 131
St Laurence Clo. Uxb —43L 75
St Laurence's Clo. NW6 —39Za 60
St Laurence Way. Slou —8L 73
St Lawrence Bus. Cen. Twic —61X 121
St Lawrence Clo. Abb L —2U 4
St Lawrence Clo. Edgw —24Pa 39
St Lawrence Ct. N1 —39Ub 63
St Lawrence Dri. Pinn —29X 37
St Lawrence Rd. Upm —33Sd 70
St Lawrence St. E14 —46Ec 84
St Lawrence Ter. W10 —43Ab 80
St Lawrence Way. SW9 —54Qb 104
St Lawrence Way. Brick —2Ba 5
St Leonard's Av. E4 —23Fc 45
St Leonard's Av. Harr —29La 38
St Leonard's Av. Wind —4G 94
St Leonard's Clo. Bush —14Aa 19
St Leonard's Clo. Well —55Wc 109
St Leonard's Ct. N1 —41Tb 83 (3G 195) (off New North Rd.)
St Leonard's Gdns. Houn —53Aa 99
St Leonard's Gdns. Ilf —36Sc 66
St Leonard's Hill. Wind —6B 94
St Leonard's Rise. Orp —77Uc 150
St Leonard's Rd. E14 —43Ec 84 (in two parts)
St Leonard's Rd. NW10 —42Ta 79
St Leonard's Rd. SW14 —55Ra 101
St Leonard's Rd. W13 —45La 78
St Leonard's Rd. Clay —79Ha 142
St Leonard's Rd. Croy —76Rb 147
St Leonard's Rd. Eps —91Ya 178
St Leonard's Rd. Surb —71Ma 143
St Leonard's Rd. Th Dit —72Ja 142
St Leonard's Rd. Wind —8A 94 (Windsor Safari Park)
St Leonard's Rd. Wind —5E 94 (Windsor)
St Leonards Sq. NW5 —37Jb 62
St Leonards Sq. Surb —71Ma 143
St Leonard's St. E3 —41Dc 84
St Leonard's Ter. SW3 —50Hb 81 (7F 203)
St Leonard's Wlk. SW16 —66Pb 126
St Leonards Wlk. Iver —48H 75
St Leonards Way. Horn —33Kd 69
St Loo Av. SW3 —51Gb 103
St Louis Rd. SE27 —63Tb 127
St Loy's Rd. N17 —26Ub 43
St Luke Clo. Uxb —44M 75
St Luke's Av. SW4 —56Mb 104
St Luke's Av. Enf —10Tb 11
St Luke's Av. Ilf —36Rc 66
St Luke's Clo. SE25 —72Xb 147
St Luke's Clo. Dart —64Ud 134
St Luke's Clo. Swan —68Fd 132
St Lukes Ct. E10 —31Dc 64 (off Capworth St.)
St Luke's Est. EC1 —41Tb 83 (5F 195)
St Luke's M. W11 —44Bb 81
St Luke's Pas. King T —67Pa 123
St Luke's Path. Ilf —36Rc 66
St Luke's Rd. W11 —43Bb 81
St Luke's Rd. Old Win —8L 95
St Luke's Rd. Uxb —38N 55
St Luke's Rd. Whyt —90Vb 165
St Luke's Sq. E16 —44Hc 85
St Luke's St. SW3 —50Gb 81 (7E 202)
St Luke's Yd. W9 —40Bb 61
St Magarets Rd. SE4 —56Bc 106
St Magaret's Ter. SE18 —50Sc 86
St Malo Av. N9 —20Yb 26
St Margaret's. Bark —39Tc 66
St Margaret's Av. N15 —28Rb 43
St Margaret's Av. N20 —18Eb 23
St Margaret's Av. Ashf —64R 120
St Margarets Av. Berr G —88Rc 168
St Margaret's Av. Harr —34Ea 58
St Margaret's Av. Sidc —62Tc 130
St Margaret's Av. Stanf —3L 93
St Margaret's Av. Sutt —76Ab 144
St Margarets Av. Uxb —42Q 76
St Margarets Bus. Cen. Twic —58Ka 100
St Margarets Clo. Iver —40F 54
St Margaret's Clo. Orp —77Xc 151
St Margaret's Ct. N11 —21Jb 42
St Margaret's Ct. SE1 —46Tb 83 (7F 201)
St Margarets Ct. Edgw —22Ra 39
St Margaret's Cres. SW15 —57Xa 102
St Margaret's Cres. Grav —2G 136
St Margaret's Dri. Twic —57Ka 100
St Margarets Ga. Iver —40F 54
St Margaret's Gro. E11 —34Hc 65
St Margaret's Gro. SE18 —51Sc 108
St Margaret's Gro. Twic —58Ja 100
St Margaret's Pas. SE13 —55Gc 107
St Margaret's Rd. E12 —33Lc 65
St Margaret's Rd. N17 —27Ub 43
St Margaret's Rd. NW10 —41Ya 80
St Margaret's Rd. SE4 —56Bc 106
St Margaret's Rd. W7 —47Ga 78
St Margaret's Rd. Beck —70Zb 128
St Margaret's Rd. Coul —93Kb 180
St Margaret's Rd. Edgw —22Ra 39
St Margaret's Rd. Grav —10A 114
St Margarets Rd. Iswth & Twic —56Ka 100
St Margaret's Rd. Ruis —30T 36
St Margarets Rd. S Dar & Grn St —67Td 134
St Margaret's Sq. SE4 —56Bc 106
St Margaret's Ter. SE18 —50Sc 86
St Margaret St. SW1 —47Nb 82 (2F 205)
St Margarets Vicarage. E11 —34Hc 65
St Mark's Av. Grav —9A 114
St Mark's Clo. SE10 —52Ec 106
St Mark's Clo. W11 —44Ab 80
St Mark's Clo. Barn —13Db 23
St Marks Ct. E10 —31Dc 64 (off Capworth St.)
St Mark's Cres. NW1 —39Jb 62
St Mark's Ga. E9 —38Bc 64
St Mark's Gro. SW10 —51Db 103
St Mark's Hill. Surb —72Na 143
St Marks Ind. Est. E16 —46Mc 85
St Mark's Pl. SW19 —65Bb 125
St Mark's Pl. W11 —44Ab 80
St Marks Pl. Wind —4G 94
St Mark's Rise. E8 —36Vb 63
St Mark's Rd. SE25 —70Wb 127
St Mark's Rd. W5 —46Na 79
St Mark's Rd. W7 —47Ga 78
St Mark's Rd. W10 —43Za 80
St Mark's Rd. W11 —44Ab 80
St Mark's Rd. Brom —69Kc 129
St Mark's Rd. Enf —16Vb 25
St Mark's Rd. Eps —90Ya 162
St Marks Rd. Mitc —68Hb 125
St Mark's Rd. Tedd —66Ka 122
St Marks Rd. Wind —4G 94
St Mark's Sq. NW1 —39Jb 62
St Mark St. E1 —44Vb 83
St Martha's Av. Wok —93B 172
St Martin Clo. Uxb —44M 75
St Martin's App. Ruis —31U 56
St Martin's Av. E6 —40Mc 65
St Martin's Av. Eps —86Ua 162
St Martin's Clo. NW1 —39Lb 62
St Martins Clo. E Hor —100U 174
St Martin's Clo. Enf —11Xb 25
St Martins Clo. Eps —85Ua 162
St Martin's Clo. Eri —47Zc 87
St Martin's Clo. Hut —19Ee 33
St Martins Clo. Wat —21Y 37
St Martin's Clo. W Dray —48M 75
St Martins Ct. N1 —39Ub 63 (off De Beauvoir Est.)
St Martin's Ct. WC2 —45Nb 82 (4F 199)
St Martin's Ct. Ashf —64L 119
St Martin's Ct. E Hor —100U 174
St Martin's Dri. Eyns —76Md 153
St Martin's Dri. W on T —76Y 141
St Martins Est. SW2 —60Qb 104
St Martin's La. WC2 —45Nb 82 (4F 199)
St Martin's le Grand. EC1 —44Sb 83 (2D 200)
St Martins Meadow. Bras —95Yc 185
St Martin's Pl. WC2 —45Nb 82 (5F 199)
St Martin's Rd. N9 —19Xb 25
St Martin's Rd. SW9 —54Pb 104
St Martin's Rd. Dart —58Pd 111
St Martin's Rd. W Dray —48M 75
St Martin's St. WC2 —45Mb 82 (5E 198)
St Martin's Wlk. SE1 —46Tb 83 (6G 201) (off Borough High St.)
St Martins Way. SW17 —62Eb 125
St Mary Abbot's Ct. W14 —48Bb 81 (off Warwick Gdns.)
St Mary Abbot's Pl. W8 —48Bb 81
St Mary Abbot's Ter. W14 —48Bb 81
St Mary at Hill. EC3 —45Ub 83 (5H 201)
St Mary Av. Wall —76Kb 146
St Mary Axe. EC3 —44Ub 83 (3J 201)
St Marychurch St. SE16 —47Yb 84
St Mary Graces Ct. E1 —45Vb 83
St Mary Newington Clo. SE17 —50Ub 83 (7J 207) (off Surrey Sq.)
St Mary Rd. E17 —28Cc 44
St Mary's. Bark —39Tc 66
St Marys. Wey —76T 140
St Mary's App. E12 —36Pc 66
St Mary's Av. E11 —31Kc 65
St Mary's Av. N3 —26Ab 40
St Mary's Av. Brom —69Gc 129
St Mary's Av. N'wd —22U 36
St Mary's Av. Shenf —15Ce 33
St Mary's Av. S'hall —49Da 77
St Mary's Av. Stai —59M 97
St Mary's Av. Tedd —65Ha 122
St Mary's Clo. N17 —25Vb 43
St Mary's Clo. Chess —80Pa 143
St Mary's Clo. Eps —80Va 144
St Mary's Clo. Fet —95Fa 176
St Mary's Clo. Grav —1E 136
St Marys Clo. Grays —51Fe 113
St Mary's Clo. Hare —27K 35
St Mary's Clo. Orp —68Xc 131
St Mary's Clo. Oxt —100Gc 183
St Mary's Clo. Stai —59M 97
St Mary's Clo. Sun —70W 120
St Mary's Ct. E6 —42Pc 86
St Mary's Ct. SE7 —52Mc 107
St Mary's Ct. W5 —47Ma 79
St Mary's Ct. W14 —48Va 80
St Mary's Ct. Wall —77Lb 146
St Mary's Cres. NW4 —27Xa 40
St Mary's Cres. Hay —45V 76
St Mary's Cres. Iswth —52Fa 100
St Mary's Cres. Stai —59M 97
St Mary's Dri. Felt —59S 98
St Mary's Dri. Sev —95Gd 186
St Mary's Gdns. SE11 —49Qb 82 (5A 206)
St Mary's Ga. W8 —48Db 81
St Mary's Grn. N2 —26Eb 41
St Mary's Grn. Big H —90Lc 167
St Mary's Gro. N1 —37Rb 63
St Mary's Gro. SW13 —55Xa 102
St Mary's Gro. W4 —51Ra 101
St Mary's Gro. Big H —90Lc 167
St Mary's Gro. Rich —56Pa 101
St Mary's Hill. Asc —10A 116
St Mary's La. W8 —48Db 81
St Mary's La. Upm & W Horn —33Rd 69
St Mary's Mans. W2 —43Fb 81 (7B 190)
St Mary's M. NW6 —38Db 61
St Marys M. Rich —61La 122
St Mary's Path. N1 —39Rb 63
St Mary's Pl. SE9 —58Qc 108
St Mary's Pl. W5 —47Ma 79
St Mary's Pl. W8 —48Db 81
St Mary's Rd. E10 —34Ec 64
St Mary's Rd. E13 —40Kc 65
St Mary's Rd. N8 —28Nb 42
St Mary's Rd. N9 —18Xb 25
St Mary's Rd. NW10 —39Ua 60
St Mary's Rd. NW11 —31Ab 60
St Mary's Rd. SE15 —53Yb 106
St Mary's Rd. SE25 —69Ub 127
St Mary's Rd. SW19 —64Ab 124
St Marys Rd. W5 —47Ma 79
St Mary's Rd. Barn —17Hb 23
St Mary's Rd. Bex —60Ed 110
St Mary's Rd. Chesh —1Yb 12
St Mary's Rd. Den —30H 35
St Mary's Rd. Dit H —73La 142
St Mary's Rd. E Mol —71Fa 142
St Mary's Rd. Grays —9D 92
St Mary's Rd. Grnh —57Ud 112
St Mary's Rd. Hare —27K 35
St Mary's Rd. Hay —45V 76
St Mary's Rd. Ilf —33Sc 66
St Mary's Rd. Langl —46A 74
St Mary's Rd. Lea —94Ka 176
St Mary's Rd. S Croy —82Tb 165
St Mary's Rd. Surb —72Ma 143
St Mary's Rd. Swan —70Fd 132
St Mary's Rd. Wat —14X 19
St Mary's Rd. Wey —77T 140
St Mary's Rd. Wok —5F 188
St Mary's Rd. Wor Pk —75Ua 144
St Mary's Sq. W2 —43Fb 81 (7B 190)
St Mary's Sq. W5 —47Ma 79
St Mary's Ter. W2 —43Fb 81 (7A 190)
St Mary St. SE18 —49Pc 86
St Mary's View. Kent —29La 38
St Mary's Wlk. SE11 —49Qb 82 (5A 206)
St Mary's Wlk. Hay —45V 76
St Mary's Way. Chig —22Qc 46
St Mary's Way. Ger X —26A 34
St Mary's Way. Long —69Ae 135
St Matthew Clo. Uxb —44M 75
St Matthew's Av. Surb —74Na 143
St Matthew's Clo. Rain —38Jd 68
St Matthews Clo. Wat —16Z 19
St Matthews Ct. E10 —31Dc 64 (off Capworth St.)
St Matthews Ct. N10 —26Jb 42
St Matthew's Dri. Brom —69Pc 130
St Matthew's Lodge. NW1 —40Lb 62 (1C 192) (off Oakley Sq.)
St Matthew's Pl. Cat —95Tb 181
St Matthew's Rd. SW2 —56Pb 104
St Matthew's Rd. W5 —46Na 79
St Matthew's Row. E2 —41Wb 83
St Matthew St. SW1 —48Mb 82 (4D 204)
St Matthias Clo. NW9 —29Va 40
St Maur Rd. SW6 —53Bb 103
St Merryn Clo. SE18 —52Tc 108
St Merryn Ct. Beck —66Cc 128
St Michael's All. EC3 —44Tb 83 (3G 201)
St Michael's Av. N9 —17Yb 26
St Michael's Av. Enf —17Yb 26
St Michael's Av. Wemb —37Qa 59
St Michaels Clo. E16 —43Mc 85
St Michael's Clo. N3 —26Bb 41
St Michael's Clo. N12 —22Gb 41
St Michael's Clo. Brom —69Nc 130
St Michael's Clo. Eri —47Zc 87
St Michael's Clo. S Ock —45Sd 90
St Michael's Clo. W on T —75Y 141
St Michael's Clo. Wor Pk —75Va 144
St Michaels Ct. E14 —43Ec 84 (off St Leonards Rd.)
St Michaels Ct. Slou —2B 72
St Michael's Cres. Pinn —30Aa 37
St Michael's Dri. Otf —88Md 171
St Michaels Dri. Wat —5X 5
St Michael's Gdns. W10 —43Ab 80
St Michael's Pde. Wat —10X 5
St Michael's Rise. Well —53Xc 109
St Michael's Rd. NW2 —35Ya 60
St Michael's Rd. SW9 —54Pb 104
St Michaels Rd. Ashf —64Q 120
St Michael's Rd. Cat —94Tb 181
St Michael's Rd. Croy —74Sb 147
St Michael's Rd. Grays —10D 92
St Michael's Rd. Wall —79Lb 146
St Michael's Rd. Well —55Xc 109
St Michael's Rd. Wok —86F 156
St Michael's St. W2 —44Fb 81 (2C 196)
St Michael's Ter. N22 —25Nb 42
St Michaels Way. Pot B —2Db 9
St Michael Tower. E17 —29Bc 44
St Mildred's Ct. EC2 —44Tb 83 (3F 201)
St Mildreds Rd. SE12 —59Hc 107
St Mirren Ct. New Bar —15Eb 23
St Monica's Rd. Tad —93Bb 179
St Nazaire Clo. Egh —64F 118
St Neots Clo. Borwd —10Qa 7
St Neot's Rd. H Hill —24Pd 49
St Neot's Rd. Romf —24Pd 49
St Nicholas Av. Bookh —97Da 175
St Nicholas Av. Horn —34Jd 68
St Nicholas Cen. Sutt —78Db 145
St Nicholas Clo. Els —16Ma 21
St Nicholas Clo. Uxb —44M 75
St Nicholas Dri. Sev —98Kd 187
St Nicholas Dri. Shep —73Q 140
St Nicholas Glebe. SW17 —65Jb 126
St Nicholas Gro. Ingve —22Ee 51
St Nicholas Hill. Lea —94Ka 176
St Nicholas Rd. SE18 —50Vc 87
St Nicholas Rd. Sutt —78Db 145
St Nicholas Rd. Th Dit —72Ha 142
St Nicholas Way. Sutt —77Db 145
St Nicolas La. Chst —67Nc 130
St Ninian's Ct. N20 —20Hb 23
St Norbert Grn. SE4 —56Ac 106
St Norbert Rd. SE4 —57Zb 106
St Normans Way. Eps —82Wa 162
St Olaf Ho. SE1 —46Tb 83 (6G 201) (off Tooley St.)
St Olaf's Rd. SW6 —52Ab 102
St Olaf Stairs. SE1 (off Tooley St.) —46Tb 83 (6G 201)
St Olaves Clo. Stai —66H 119
St Olave's Ct. EC2 —44Tb 83 (3F 201)
St Olave's Est. SE1 —47Ub 83 (1J 207)
St Olave's Gdns. SE11 —49Qb 82 (5K 205)
St Olave's Mans. SE11 —49Qb 82 (5K 205) (off Walnut Tree Wlk.)
St Olave's Rd. E6 —39Qc 66
St Olave's Ter. SE1 (off Fair St.) —47Ub 83 (1J 207)
St Olaves Wlk. SW16 —68Lb 126
St Oswald's Pl. SE11 —50Pb 82 (7H 205)
St Oswald's Rd. SW16 —67Rb 127
St Oswulf St. SW1 —49Mb 82 (6E 204) (off Erasmus St.)
St Pancras Clo. N2 —26Fb 41
St Pancras Way. NW1 —38Lb 62
St Patrick's Ct. E4 —24Gc 45
St Patrick's Ct. SE4 —57Cc 106
St Patrick's Gdns. Grav —2F 136
St Patrick's Pl. Grays —9E 92
St Paul Clo. Uxb —43M 75
St Paulinus Ct. Dart —56Gd 110 (off Manor Rd.)
St Paul's All. EC4 —44Rb 83 (3C 200) (off St Paul's Chu. Yd.)
St Paul's Av. NW2 —37Ya 60
St Paul's Av. SE16 —46Zb 84
St Paul's Av. Harr —28Pa 39
St Pauls Av. Slou —5K 73
St Paul's Chyd. EC4 —44Rb 83 (3C 200)
St Pauls Clo. SE7 —50Mc 85
St Paul's Clo. W5 —47Pa 79
St Paul's Clo. Add —78J 139
St Paul's Clo. Ashf —64S 120
St Paul's Clo. Cars —74Gb 145
St Paul's Clo. Chess —77Ma 143
St Paul's Clo. Hay —50T 76
St Paul's Clo. Houn —54Aa 99
St Paul's Clo. S Ock —45Sd 90
St Paul's Clo. Swans —59Ae 113
St Pauls Ct. Chfd —5M 3
St Paul's Ct. Houn —55Aa 99
St Pauls Courtyard. SE8 —52Cc 106
St Paul's Cray Rd. Chst —67Tc 130
St Paul's Cres. NW1 —38Mb 62 (in two parts)
St Paul's Dri. E15 —36Fc 65
St Paul's M. NW1 —38Mb 62
St Paul's Pl. N1 —37Tb 63
St Pauls Pl. S Ock —45Sd 90
St Paul's Rise. N13 —23Rb 43
St Paul's Rd. N1 —37Rb 63
St Paul's Rd. N11 —22Kb 42
St Paul's Rd. N17 —24Wb 43
St Paul's Rd. Bark —39Sc 66
St Paul's Rd. Bren —51Ma 101
St Paul's Rd. Eri —52Ed 110
St Paul's Rd. Rich —55Pa 101
St Paul's Rd. Stai —64F 118
St Paul's Rd. T Hth —69Sb 127
St Paul's Rd. Wok —89C 156
St Paul's Shrubbery. N1 —37Tb 63
St Paul's Sq. Brom —68Hc 129
St Paul's Studios. W14 —50Ab 80 (off Talgarth Rd.)
St Paul's Ter. SE17 —51Rb 105
St Paul St. N1 —39Sb 63 (1D 194) (in two parts)
St Paul's Vs. Romf —30Hd 48
St Paul's Wlk. King T —66Qa 123
St Paul's Way. E3 —43Bc 84
St Pauls Way. N3 —24Db 41
St Pauls Way. Wal A —5Fc 13
St Paul's Way. Wat —12Y 19
St Paul's Wood Hill. Orp —68Uc 130
St Peter By-Pass. Ger X —27B 34
St Peter's All. EC3 (off Cornhill) —44Tb 83 (3G 201)
St Peter's Av. E2 —40Wb 63
St Peter's Av. E17 —28Gc 45
St Peters Av. N2 —24Gb 41
St Peter's Av. N18 —21Wb 43
St Peters Av. Berr G —88Rc 168
St Petersburgh M. W2 —45Db 81
St Petersburgh Pl. W2 —45Db 81
St Peters Chu. Ct. N1 —40Rb 63 (1C 194) (off Devonia Rd.)
St Peter's Clo. E2 —40Wb 63
St Peter's Clo. SW17 —61Gb 125
St Peter's Clo. Barn —15Xa 22
St Peter's Clo. Burn —2A 72
St Peters Clo. Bush —18Fa 20
St Peter's Clo. Chst —66Tc 130
St Peters Clo. Ger X —25A 34
St Peter's Clo. Ilf —28Vc 47
St Peter's Clo. Old Win —7L 95
St Peters Clo. Rick —18K 17
St Peter's Clo. Ruis —33Z 57
St Peter's Clo. Stai —65H 119
St Peter's Clo. Swans —59Be 113
St Peter's Clo. Wok —92E 172
St Peter's Ct. NW4 —29Ya 40
St Peter's Ct. Ger X —25A 34
St Peters Ct. W Mol —70Ca 121
St Peters Gdns. SE27 —62Qb 126
St Peter's Gro. W6 —49Wa 80
St Peter's La. St P —67Wc 131
St Peters Pl. W9 —42Db 81
St Peter's Rd. N9 —18Xb 25
St Peter's Rd. W6 —50Wa 80
St Peter's Rd. Croy —77Tb 147
St Peter's Rd. Grays —9D 92
St Peter's Rd. King T —68Qa 123
St Peter's Rd. S'hall —43Ca 77
St Peter's Rd. Twic —57Ka 100
St Peters Rd. Uxb —43M 75
St Peter's Rd. War —21Xd 50
St Peter's Rd. W Mol —70Ca 121
St Peter's Rd. Wok —92D 172
St Peter's Sq. E2 —40Wb 63
St Peter's Sq. W6 —49Va 80
St Peter's St. N1 —39Rb 63 (1C 194)
St Peter's St. S Croy —78Tb 147
St Peter's St. M. N1 —40Rb 63 (1C 194) (off St Peters St.)
St Peter's Ter. SW6 —52Bb 103
St Peter's Vs. W6 —49Wa 80

St Peter's Way. N1 —38Ub **63**
St Peter's Way. W5 —43Ma **79**
St Peter's Way. Cher & Add —77F **138**
St Peters Way. Chor —14C **16**
St Peter's Way. Hay —50T **76**
St Philips Av. N2 —24Gb **41**
St Philip's Av. Wor Pk —75Xa **144**
St Philip Sq. SW8 —54Kb **104**
St Philip's Rd. E8 —37Wb **63**
St Philip St. SW8 —54Kb **104**
St Philip's Way. N1 —39Sb **63**
St Phillips Rd. Surb —72Ma **143**
St Pinnock Av. Stai —67J **119**
St Quentin Rd. Well —55Vc **109**
St Quintin Av. W10 —43Ya **80**
St Quintin Gdns. W10 —43Ya **80**
St Quintin Rd. E13 —41Kc **85**
St Raphael's Way. NW10 —36Sa **59**
St Regis Clo. N10 —26Kb **42**
St Regis Heights. NW3 —34Db **61**
St Ronan's Clo. Barn —10Fb **9**
St Ronan's Cres. Wfd G —24Jc **45**
St Rule St. SW8 —54Lb **104**
St Saviors Clo. E17 —31Cc **64**
St Saviour's College. SE27 —63Tb **127**
St Saviours Ct. Harr —29Ga **38**
St Saviour's Est. SE1 —48Vb **83** (3K **207**)
St Saviour's Rd. SW2 —57Pb **104**
St Saviour's Rd. Croy —72Sb **147**
Saints Clo. SE27 —63Rb **127**
Saints Dri. E7 —36Mc **65**
St Silas Pl. NW5 —37Jb **62**
St Simon's Av. SW15 —57Ya **102**
St Stephen's Av. E17 —29Ec **44**
St Stephen's Av. W12 —47Xa **80**
St Stephen's Av. W13 —44Ka **78**
St Stephen's Av. Asht —88Na **161**
St Stephen's Clo. E17 —29Dc **44**
St Stephen's Clo. NW8 —39Gb **61** (1E **190**)
St Stephen's Clo. Purf —50Qd **89**
St Stephen's Clo. S'hall —43Ca **77**
St Stephen's Ct. Enf —16Ub **25**
St Stephen's Cres. W2 —44Cb **81**
St Stephen's Cres. Brtwd —21Ce **51**
St Stephen's Cres. T Hth —69Qb **126**
St Stephen's Gdns. SW15 —57Bb **103**
St Stephen's Gdns. W2 —44Cb **81**
St Stephen's Gdns. Twic —58La **100**
St Stephens Gro. SE13 —55Ec **106**
St Stephen's M. W2 —43Cb **81**
St Stephens Pde. E7 —38Lc **65**
St Stephens Pde. SW1 —47Nb **82** (2G **205**)
St Stephen's Pas. Twic —58La **100**
St Stephen's Rd. E3 —39Ac **64**
St Stephen's Rd. E6 —38Lc **65**
St Stephen's Rd. E17 —29Dc **44**
St Stephen's Rd. W13 —44Ka **78**
St Stephen's Rd. Barn —15Za **22**
St Stephens Rd. Enf —9Zb **12**
St Stephen's Rd. Houn —58Ca **99**
St Stephen's Rd. W Dray —46M **75**
St Stephen's Row. EC4 —44Tb 83 (3F 201)
(off Walbrook)
St Stephens Ter. SW8 —52Pb **104**
St Stephen's Wlk. SW7 —49Eb **81**
St Stephen's Wlk. Purf —50Qd **89**
Saint's Wlk. Grays —9E **92**
St Swithins La. EC4 —45Tb **83** (4F **201**)
St Swithun's Rd. SE13 —58Fc **107**
St Teresa Wlk. Grays —9D **92**
St Theresa Ct. E4 —17Fc **27**
St Theresa's Rd. Felt —56Y **98**
St Thomas Clo. Surb —74Pa **143**
St Thomas Clo. Wok —5F **188**
St Thomas Ct. E10 —31Dc 64
(off Skelton's La.)
St Thomas Ct. Bex —59Cd **110**
St Thomas Ct. Pinn —25Aa **37**
St Thomas Dri. Orp —74Sc **150**
St Thomas Dri. Pinn —25Aa **37**
St Thomas Gdns. Ilf —37Sc **66**
St Thomas Pl. Grays —51De **113**
St Thomas Rd. E16 —44Jc **85**
St Thomas Rd. N14 —17Mb **24**
St Thomas Rd. W4 —51Sa **101**
St Thomas Rd. Belv —47Ed **88**
St Thomas' Rd. Brtwd —19Zd **33**
St Thomas Rd. Grav —1A **136**
St Thomas's Almshouses. Grav —10D **114**
St Thomas's Av. Grav —10D **114**
St Thomas's Clo. Wal A —5Kc **13**
St Thomas's Gdns. NW5 —37Jb **62**
St Thomas's Pl. E9 —38Yb **64**
St Thomas's Rd. N4 —33Qb **62**
St Thomas's Rd. NW10 —39Ua **60**
St Thomas's Sq. E9 —38Yb **64**
St Thomas St. SE1 —46Tb **83** (7F **201**)
St Thomas's Way. SW6 —52Bb **103**
St Thomas Wlk. Coln —52F **96**
St Timothys M. Brom —67Kc **129**
St Ursula Gro. Pinn —29Z **37**
St Ursula Rd. S'hall —44Ca **77**
St Vincent Clo. SE27 —64Rb **127**
St Vincent Rd. Twic —58Ea **100**
St Vincent Rd. W on T —76X **141**
St Vincents Av. Dart —57Qd **111**
St Vincents Rd. Dart —58Qd **111**
St Vincent St. W1 —43Jb **82** (1J **197**)
St Vincents Vs. Dart —58Nd **111**
St Vincents Way. Pot B —6Eb **9**
St Wilfrid's Clo. Barn —15Gb **23**
St Wilfrid's Rd. Barn —15Gb **23**
St Winefride's Av. E12 —36Pc **66**
St Winifreds. Kenl —87Sb **165**
St Winifred's Clo. Chig —22Sc **46**
St Winifred's Rd. Big H —90Pc **168**
St Winifred's Rd. Tedd —65Ka **122**
Saladin Dri. Purf —49Qd **89**
Salamanca Pl. SE1 —49Pb **82** (6H **205**)
Salamanca St. SE1 & SE11 —49Pb **82** (6H **205**)
Salamons Way. Rain —44Gd **88**
Salcombe Dri. Mord —74Za **144**
Salcombe Dri. Romf —30Bd **47**
Salcombe Gdns. NW7 —23Ya **40**
Salcombe Rd. E17 —31Bc **64**
Salcombe Rd. N16 —36Ub **63**
Salcombe Rd. Ashf —63N **119**
Salcombe Way. Hay —41T **76**
Salcombe Way. Ruis —33W **56**
Salcot Cres. New Ad —82Ec **166**
Salcote Rd. Grav —4G **136**
Salcott Rd. SW11 —57Gb **103**
Salcott Rd. Croy —76Nb **146**
Salehurst Clo. Harr —29Na **39**
Salehurst Rd. SE4 —58Bc **106**
Salem Pl. Croy —76Sb **147**
Salem Pl. Grav —59Fe **113**
Salem Rd. W2 —45Db **81**
Sale Pl. W2 —44Gb **81** (1D **196**)
Sale St. E2 —42Wb **83**
Salford Rd. SW2 —60Mb **104**
Salhouse Clo. SE28 —44Yc **87**
Salisbury Av. N3 —27Bb **41**
Salisbury Av. Bark —38Tc **66**
Salisbury Av. Slou —2G **72**
Salisbury Av. Stanf —2M **93**
Salisbury Av. Sutt —79Bb **145**
Salisbury Av. Swan —70Jd **132**
Salisbury Clo. SE17 —49Tb **83** (6F **207**)
Salisbury Clo. Pot B —4Eb **9**
Salisbury Clo. Upm —33Ud **70**
Salisbury Clo. Wor Pk —76Va **144**
Salisbury Ct. EC4 —44Rb **83** (3B **200**)
Salisbury Cres. Chesh —4Zb **12**
Salisbury Gdns. SW19 —66Ab **124**
Salisbury Gdns. Buck H —19Mc **27**
Salisbury Hall Gdns. E4 —23Cc **44**
Salisbury Ho. Stan —23Ja **38**
Salisbury Mans. N15 —29Rb **43**
Salisbury M. SW6 —52Bb **103**
Salisbury Pas. SW6 —52Bb 103
(off Dawes Rd.)
Salisbury Pl. SW9 —52Rb **105**
Salisbury Pl. W1 —43Hb **81** (7G **191**)
Salisbury Pl. W Byf —83L **157**
Salisbury Rd. E4 —20Cc **26**
Salisbury Rd. E7 —37Jc **65**
Salisbury Rd. E10 —33Ec **64**
Salisbury Rd. E12 —36Mc **65**
Salisbury Rd. E17 —29Ec **44**
Salisbury Rd. N4 —29Rb **43**
Salisbury Rd. N9 —20Wb **25**
Salisbury Rd. N22 —25Rb **43**
Salisbury Rd. SE25 —72Wb **147**
Salisbury Rd. SW19 —66Ab **124**
Salisbury Rd. W13 —47Ka **78**
Salisbury Rd. Bans —86Db **163**
Salisbury Rd. Barn —13Ab **22**
Salisbury Rd. Bex —60Cd **110**
Salisbury Rd. Brom —71Nc **150**
Salisbury Rd. Cars —79Hb **145**
Salisbury Rd. Dag —37Dd **68**
Salisbury Rd. Dart —59Sd **112**
Salisbury Rd. Enf —9Bc **12**
Salisbury Rd. Felt —60Y **99**
Salisbury Rd. Grav —10B **114**
Salisbury Rd. Grays —51Ee **113**
Salisbury Rd. Harr —29Fa **38**
Salisbury Rd. Houn —55Y **99**
Salisbury Rd. Ilf —33Uc **66**
Salisbury Rd. H'row A —57S **98**
Salisbury Rd. N Mald —69Ta **123**
Salisbury Rd. Pinn —28W **36**
Salisbury Rd. Rich —56Na **101**
Salisbury Rd. Romf —29Kd **49**
Salisbury Rd. S'hall —49Aa **77**
Salisbury Rd. Uxb —40K **55**
Salisbury Rd. Wat —10X **5**
Salisbury Rd. Wok —91A **172**
Salisbury Rd. Wor Pk —77Ta **143**
Salisbury Sq. EC4 —44Qb **82** (3A **200**)
Salisbury St. NW8 —42Gb **81** (6D **190**)
Salisbury St. W3 —47Sa **79**
Salisbury Ter. SE15 —55Yb **106**
Salisbury Wlk. N19 —33Lb **62**
Salix Clo. Sun —66X **121**
Salix Ct. N3 —23Cb **41**
Salix Rd. Grays —51Fe **113**
Salliesfield. Twic —58Fa **100**
Sallows Shaw. Sole S —10E **136**
Sally Motland Ho. Wemb —31Pa **59**
Salmen Rd. E13 —40Hc **65**
Salmond Clo. Stan —23Ja **38**
Salmonds Gro. Ingve —22Ee **51**
Salmon La. E14 —44Ac **84**
Salmon Rd. Belv —50Cd **88**
Salmons La. Whyt —92Ub **181**
Salmons La. W. Cat —92Ub **181**
Salmons Rd. N9 —18Wb **25**
Salmons Rd. Chess —79Na **143**
Salmons Rd. Eff —100X **175**
Salmon St. E14 —44Bc **84**
Salmon St. NW9 —32Ra **59**
Salomons Rd. E13 —43Lc **85**
Salop Rd. E17 —30Zb **44**
Saltash Clo. Sutt —77Bb **145**
Saltash Ho. SE11 —50Rb 83 (7B 206)
(off Seaton Clo.)
Saltash Rd. Ilf —24Tc **46**
Saltash Rd. Well —53Vc **109**
Saltbox Hill. Big H —85Kc **167**
Saltcoats Rd. W4 —47Ua **80**
Saltcroft Clo. Wemb —32Ra **59**
Salterford Rd. SW17 —65Jb **126**
Salter Rd. SE16 —46Zb **84**
Salters Ct. EC4 —44Sb 83 (3E 200)
(off Bow La.)
Salters Gdns. Wat —11W **18**
Salter's Hall Ct. EC4 —45Tb 83 (4F 201)
(off Cannon St.)
Salter's Hill. SE19 —64Tb **127**
Salters Rd. E17 —28Fc **45**
Salters Rd. W10 —42Za **80**
Salter St. E14 —45Cc **84**
Salter St. NW10 —41Wa **80**
Salterton Rd. N7 —34Pb **62**
Saltford Clo. Eri —50Gd **88**
Salt Hill Av. Slou —6G **72**
Salt Hill Clo. Uxb —36N **55**
Salt Hill Dri. Slou —6G **72**
Salt Hill Mans. Slou —6G **72**
Salt Hill Way. Slou —6G **72**
Saltoun Rd. SW2 —56Qb **104**
Saltram Clo. N15 —28Vb **43**
Saltram Cres. W9 —41Bb **81**
Saltwell St. E14 —45Cc **84**
Saltwood Clo. Orp —77Yc **151**
Saltwood Gro. SE17 —50Tb **83**
Salusbury Rd. NW6 —39Ab **60**
Salvador. SW17 —64Hb **125**
Salva Gdns. Gnfd —40Ja **58**
Salvation Pl. Lea —96Ja **176**
Salvia Gdns. Gnfd —40Ja **58**
Salvin Rd. SW15 —55Za **102**
Salway Clo. Wfd G —24Jc **45**
Salway Pl. E15 —37Fc **65**
Salway Rd. E15 —37Fc **65**
Samantha Clo. E17 —31Bc **64**
Samantha M. Hav —20Gd **30**
Sam Bartram Clo. SE7 —50Lc **85**
Sambrook Ho. SE11 —49Qb 82 (6K 205)
(off Hotspur St.)
Sambruck M. SE6 —60Dc **106**
Samels Ct. W6 —50Wa **80**
Samford Ho. N1 —39Qb 62 (1K 193)
(off Barnsbury Est.)
Samford St. NW8 —42Fb **81** (6D **190**)
Samos Rd. SE20 —68Xb **127**
Samphire Ct. Grays —1A **114**
Sampson Av. Barn —15Za **22**
Sampson Clo. Belv —48Zc **87**
Sampsons Ct. Shep —71S **140**
Sampson's Grn. Slou —1D **72**
Sampson St. E1 —46Wb **83**
Samsbrooke Ct. Enf —15Vb **25**
Samson St. E13 —40Lc **65**
Samuda Est. E14 —48Ec **84**
Samuel Clo. E8 —39Vb **63**
Samuel Clo. SE14 —51Zb **106**
Samuel Clo. SE18 —49Nc **86**
Samuel Johnson Clo. SW16 —63Pb **126**
Samuel Jones Ind. Est. SE15
(off Peckham Gro.) —52Ub 105
Samuel Lewis Bldgs. N1 —37Qb **62**
Samuel Lewis Trust Dwellings. E8
(Amhurst Rd.) —36Wb **63**
Samuel Lewis Trust Dwellings. E8
(Dalston La.) —36Wb **63**
Samuel Lewis Trust Dwellings. N16 —30Ub **43**
Samuel Lewis Trust Dwellings. SE5
(off Warner Rd.) —53Sb 105
Samuel Lewis Trust Dwellings. SW3 —49Gb 81 (6D 202)
(off Ixworth Pl.)
Samuel Lewis Trust Dwellings. SW6
(off Vanston Pl.) —52Cb 103
Samuel Lewis Trust Dwellings. W14
(off Lisgar Ter.) —49Bb 81
Samuel Palmer Ct. Orp —73Wc 151
(off Chislehurst Rd.)
Samuel St. SE18 —49Pc **86**
Sancroft Clo. NW2 —34Xa **60**
Sancroft Ho. SE11 —50Pb 82 (7J 205)
(off Sancroft St.)
Sancroft Rd. Harr —26Ha **38**
Sancroft St. SE11 —50Pb **82** (7J **205**)
Sanctuary Clo. Dart —58Ld **111**
Sanctuary Clo. Hare —24L **35**
Sanctuary Garden. Stanf —1N **93**
Sanctuary Rd. H'row A —58Q **98**
Sanctuary St. SE1 —47Sb **83** (1E **206**)
Sanctuary, The. SW1 —48Mb 82 (3E 204)
(off Broad Sanctuary)
Sanctuary, The. Bex —58Zc **109**
Sanctuary, The. Mord —72Cb **145**
Sandale Clo. N16 —34Tb **63**
Sandall Clo. W5 —42Na **79**
Sandall Rd. NW5 —37Lb **62**
Sandall Rd. W5 —42Na **79**
Sandal Rd. N18 —22Wb **43**
Sandal Rd. N Mald —71Ta **143**
Sandal St. E15 —39Gc **65**
Sandalwood Av. Cher —76G **138**
Sandalwood Clo. E1 —42Ac **84**
Sandalwood Ho. Sidc —62Vc **131**
Sandalwood Rd. Felt —62X **121**
Sandbach Pl. SE18 —49Sc **86**
Sandbanks Hill. Bean —65Xd **134**
Sandbourne Av. SW19 —68Db **125**
Sandbourne Rd. SE4 —54Ac **106**
Sandbrook Clo. NW7 —23Ta **39**
Sandbrook Rd. N16 —34Ub **63**
Sandby Grn. SE9 —55Nc **108**
Sandcliff Rd. Eri —49Fd **88**
Sandcroft Clo. N13 —23Rb **43**
Sandell's Av. Ashf —63S **120**
Sandell St. SE1 —47Qb **82** (1K **205**)
Sanderling Ct. SE28 —45Yc **87**
Sanders Clo. Hamp —64Ea **122**
Sandersfield Gdns. Bans —87Cb **163**
Sandersfield Rd. Bans —87Db **163**
Sanders La. NW7 —24Ya **40**
(in three parts)
Sanderson Clo. NW5 —35Kb **62**
Sanderson Clo. W Horn —30Ee **51**
Sanderson Gdns. Wfd G —25Lc **45**
Sandersons Av. Badg M —82Cd **170**
Sanderson Shaw. SE28 —45Zc **87**
Sanderstead Av. NW2 —33Ab **60**
Sanderstead Clo. SW12 —59Lb **104**
Sanderstead Ct. Av. S Croy —85Wb **165**
Sanderstead Hill. S Croy —83Ub **165**
Sanderstead Rd. E10 —32Ac **64**
Sanderstead Rd. Orp —72Xc **151**
Sanderstead Rd. S Croy —80Tb **147**
Sanders Way. N19 —32Mb **62**
Sandes Pl. Lea —90Ja **160**
Sandfield Gdns. T Hth —69Rb **127**
Sandfield Rd. T Hth —69Rb **127**
Sandfields. Send —96F **172**
Sandford Av. N22 —25Sb **43**
Sandford Av. Lou —13Sc **28**
Sandford Clo. E6 —42Pc **86**
Sandford Ct. N16 —32Ub **63**
Sandford Ct. New Bar —13Db **23**
Sandford Rd. E6 —41Nc **86**
Sandford Rd. Bexh —56Ad **109**
Sandford Rd. Brom —70Jc **129**
Sandford St. SW6 —52Db **103**
Sandgate Clo. Romf —31Fd **68**
Sandgate Ho. E5 —35Xb **63**
Sandgate La. SW18 —60Gb **103**
Sandgate Rd. Well —52Yc **109**
Sandgate St. SE15 —51Xb **105**
Sandham Ct. SW4 —53Nb **104**
Sandhills. Wall —77Mb **146**
Sandhills Ct. Vir W —71A **138**
Sandhills La. Vir W —71A **138**
Sandhills Meadow. Shep —73S **140**
Sandhills, The. SW10 —51Eb 103
(off Limerston St.)
Sandhurst Av. Harr —30Da **37**
Sandhurst Av. Surb —73Ra **143**
Sandhurst Cen. Wat —11Y **19**
Sandhurst Clo. NW9 —27Qa **39**
Sandhurst Clo. S Croy —81Ub **165**
Sandhurst Ct. SW2 —56Nb **104**
Sandhurst Dri. Ilf —35Vc **67**
Sandhurst Rd. N9 —16Yb **26**
Sandhurst Rd. NW9 —27Qa **39**
Sandhurst Rd. SE6 —60Fc **107**
Sandhurst Rd. Bex —57Zc **109**
Sandhurst Rd. Orp —76Wc **151**
Sandhurst Rd. Sidc —62Vc **131**
Sandhurst Rd. Til —4E **114**
Sandhurst Way. S Croy —80Ub **147**
Sandiford Rd. Sutt —75Bb **145**
Sandiland Cres. Brom —75Hc **149**
Sandilands. Croy —75Wb **147**
Sandilands. Sev —94Fd **186**
Sandilands Rd. SW6 —53Db **103**
Sandison St. SE15 —55Wb **105**
Sandlands Gro. Tad —95Wa **178**
Sandlands Rd. Tad —95Wa **178**
Sandland St. WC1 —43Pb **82** (1J **199**)
Sandlers End. Slou —2F **72**
Sandling Rise. SE9 —62Qc **130**
Sandlings, The. N22 —27Rb **43**
Sandmere Rd. SW4 —56Nb **104**
Sandon Clo. Esh —73Fa **142**
Sandon Rd. Chesh —2Yb **12**
Sandow Cres. Hay —48V **76**
Sandown Av. Dag —37Ed **68**
Sandown Av. Esh —78Ea **142**
Sandown Av. Horn —33Md **69**
Sandown Clo. Houn —53W **98**
Sandown Ct. Stan —22La **38**
Sandown Ct. Sutt —80Db **145**
Sandown Dri. Cars —81Jb **164**
Sandown Ga. Esh —75Fa **142**
Sandown Ind. Pk. Esh —75Ca **141**
Sandown Lodge. Eps —86Ta **161**
Sandown Rd. SE25 —71Xb **147**
Sandown Rd. Coul —88Jb **164**
Sandown Rd. Esh —77Ea **142**
Sandown Rd. Grav —5E **136**
Sandown Rd. Ors —3G **92**
Sandown Rd. Slou —3D **72**
Sandown Rd. Wat —10Y **5**
Sandown Way. N'holt —37Aa **57**
Sandpiper Clo. E17 —24Yb **44**
Sandpiper Rd. S Croy —83Zb **166**
Sandpipers, The. Grav —1F **136**
Sandpiper Way. Orp —70Zc **131**
Sandpit Hall Rd. Chob —1D **188**
Sandpit La. Brtwd & Pil H —18Vd **32**
Sandpit La. Knap —3A **188**
Sandpit Rd. SE7 —50Nc **86**
Sandpit Rd. Brom —64Gc **129**
Sandpit Rd. Dart —56Ld **111**
Sandpits Rd. Croy —77Zb **148**
Sandpits Rd. Rich —61Ma **123**
Sandra Clo. N22 —25Sb **43**
Sandra Clo. Houn —57Da **99**
Sandridge Clo. Harr —28Ga **38**
Sandridge Ct. N4 —33Sb **63**
Sandridge St. N19 —33Lb **62**
Sandringham Av. SW20 —67Ab **124**
Sandringham Clo. Enf —12Ub **25**
Sandringham Clo. Ilf —27Sc **46**
Sandringham Clo. Wok —88J **157**
Sandringham Ct. W9 —41Eb 81 (4A 190)
(off Maida Vale)
Sandringham Ct. Sidc —58Vc **109**
Sandringham Ct. Slou —4B **72**
Sandringham Ct. Sutt —81Cb **163**
Sandringham Ct. Uxb —42S **76**
Sandringham Cres. Harr —33Ca **57**
Sandringham Dri. Ashf —63M **119**
Sandringham Dri. Well —54Uc **108**
Sandringham Gdns. N8 —30Nb **42**
Sandringham Gdns. N12 —23Fb **41**
Sandringham Gdns. Houn —53W **98**
Sandringham Gdns. Ilf —27Sc **46**
Sandringham M. W5 —45Ma **79**
Sandringham Rd. E7 —36Lc **65**
Sandringham Rd. E8 —36Vb **63**
Sandringham Rd. E10 —30Fc **45**
Sandringham Rd. N22 —27Sb **43**
Sandringham Rd. NW2 —37Xa **60**
Sandringham Rd. NW11 —31Ab **60**
Sandringham Rd. Bark —37Vc **67**
Sandringham Rd. Brom —64Jc **129**
Sandringham Rd. H'row A —57N **97**
Sandringham Rd. N'holt —38Ca **57**
Sandringham Rd. Pil H —16Xd **32**
Sandringham Rd. Pot B —2Db **9**
Sandringham Rd. T Hth —71Sb **147**
Sandringham Rd. Wat —9Y **5**
Sandringham Rd. Wor Pk —76Wa **144**
Sandringham Way. Wal X —6Yb **12**
Sandrock Pl. Croy —77Zb **148**
Sandrock Rd. SE13 —55Cc **106**
Sandroyd Way. Cob —85Ca **159**
Sand's End La. SW6 —53Db **103**
Sands Farm Dri. Burn —2A **72**
Sandstone Pl. N19 —33Kb **62**
Sandstone Rd. SE12 —61Kc **129**
Sands Way. Wfd G —23Pc **46**
Sandtoft Rd. SE7 —51Kc **107**
Sandway Path. St M —70Yc 131
(off Okemore Gdns.)
Sandway Rd. St M —70Yc **131**
Sandwell Cres. NW6 —37Cb **61**
Sandwich St. WC1 —41Nb **82** (4F **193**)
Sandy Bank Rd. Grav —10D **114**
Sandy Bury. Orp —76Tc **150**
Sandy Clo. Wok —89E **156**
Sandycombe Rd. Felt —60W **98**
Sandycombe Rd. Rich —55Pa **101**
Sandycoombe Rd. Twic —58La **100**
Sandycroft. SE2 —51Wc **109**
Sandy Croft. Eps —82Ya **162**
Sandy Dri. Cob —83Ca **159**
Sandy Dri. Felt —60U **98**
Sandy Hill Av. SE18 —50Rc **86**
Sandy Hill Rd. SE18 —49Qc **86**
Sandyhill Rd. Ilf —35Rc **66**
Sandy Hill Rd. Wall —81Lb **164**
Sandy La. Bean —61Yd **134**
Sandy La. Bush —13Ea **20**
Sandy La. Cob & Oxs —84Ba **159**
Sandy La. Grays —1D **114**
Sandy La. Harr —30Pa **39**
Sandy La. Limp —99Kc **183**
Sandy La. Mitc —67Jb **126**
Sandy La. N'wd —19V **18**
Sandy La. Orp —73Wc **151**
Sandy La. Oxt —100Ec **182**
Sandy La. Pyr —89J **157**
Sandy La. Rich —61La **122**
Sandy La. Send —95E **172**
Sandy La. Sev —95Ld **187**
Sandy La. S Ock —45Pd **89**
Sandy La. St P & Sidc —68Zc **131**
Sandy La. S'dale —10E **116**
Sandy La. Sutt —80Ab **144**
Sandy La. Tad —96Bb **179**
Sandy La. Tedd & King T —66Ja **122**
Sandy La. Vir W —70A **118**
Sandy La. W on T —72X **141**
Sandy La. W'ham —97Tc **184**
Sandy La. W Thur —51Xd **112**
Sandy La. Wok —89D **156**
Sandy La. N. Wall —78Mb **146**
Sandy La. S. Wall —81Lb **164**
Sandy Lodge La. N'wd —19T **18**
Sandy Lodge Rd. Rick —19R **18**
Sandy Lodge Way. N'wd —22T **36**
Sandymount Av. Stan —22La **38**
Sandy Ride. S'hill —10C **116**
Sandy Ridge. Chst —65Qc **130**
Sandy Rise. Ger X —25A **34**
Sandy Rd. NW3 —33Db **61**
Sandy Rd. Add —79J **139**
Sandys Row. E1 —43Ub **83** (1J **201**)
Sandy Way. Cob —84Ca **159**
Sandy Way. Croy —76Bc **148**
Sandy Way. W on T —74V **140**
Sandy Way. Wok —89E **156**
Sanford La. N16 —33Vb **63**
(in two parts)
Sanford St. SE14 —51Ac **106**
Sanford Ter. N16 —34Vb **63**
Sanford Wlk. N16 —33Vb **63**
Sanford Wlk. SE14 —51Ac **106**
Sanger Av. Chess —78Na **143**
Sanger Dri. Send —95E **172**
Sangley Rd. SE6 —59Dc **106**
Sangley Rd. SE25 —70Ub **127**
Sangora Rd. SW11 —56Fb **103**
Sansom Rd. E11 —33Hc **65**
Sansom St. SE5 —53Tb **105**
Sans Wlk. EC1 —42Qb **82** (5A **194**)
Santers La. Pot B —5Ab **8**
Santley Ho. SE1 —47Qb **82** (2A **206**)
Santley St. SW4 —56Nb **104**
Santos Rd. SW18 —57Cb **103**
Santway, The. Stan —22Ga **38**
Sanway Clo. Byfl —86N **157**
Sanway Rd. Byfl —86N **157**
Sapcote Trading Est. NW10 —37Va **60**
Saperton Wlk. SE11
(off Juxon St.) —49Pb 82 (5J 205)
Sapho Pk. Grav —3H **137**
Saphora Clo. Orp —78Tc **150**
Sapphire Clo. E6 —44Qc **86**
Sapphire Clo. Dag —32Yc **67**
Sapphire Rd. SE8 —49Ac **84**
Sappho Ct. Wok —4B **188**
Saracen Clo. Croy —72Tb **147**
Saracens Head Yd. EC3
(off Jewry St.) —44Vb 83 (3K 201)
Saracen St. E14 —44Cc **84**
Sara Ho. Eri —52Gd **110**
Sarah St. N1 —41Ub **83** (3J **195**)
Sara Pk. Grav —3G **136**
Saratoga Rd. E5 —35Yb **64**
Sardinia St. WC2 —44Pb **82** (3H **199**)
Sargeants Clo. Uxb —41M **75**
Sarita Clo. Harr —26Fa **38**
Sarjant Path. SW19 —61Za 124
(off Blincoe Clo.)
Sark Clo. Houn —52Ca **99**
Sark Ho. Enf —10Zb **12**
Sark Wlk. E16 —44Kc **85**
Sarnes Ct. N11 —21Kb 42
(off Oakleigh Rd. S.)
Sarnesfield Ho. SE15 —51Xb 105
(off Pencraig Way)
Sarnesfield Rd. Enf —14Tb **25**
Sarratt La. Loud —12K **17**
Sarratt Rd. Sarr —9K **3**
Sarre Av. Horn —37Ld **69**
Sarre Rd. NW2 —36Bb **61**
Sarre Rd. St M —71Yc **151**
Sarsby Dri. Stai —61C **118**
Sarsen Av. Houn —54Ca **99**
Sarsens Clo. Cobh —9H **137**
Sarsfeld Rd. SW12 —60Hb **103**
Sarsfield Rd. Gnfd —40Ka **58**
Sartor Rd. SE15 —56Zb **106**
Sarum Complex. Uxb —41K **75**
Sarum Grn. Wey —76U **140**
Sassoon. NW9 —25Va **40**
Satanita Clo. E16 —44Mc **85**
Satchell Mead. NW9 —25Va **40**
Satchwell Rd. E2 —41Wb **83**
Satis Ct. Eps —83Va **162**
Saul Ct. SE15 —51Vb 105
(off Daniel Gdns.)
Sauls Grn. E11 —34Gc **65**
Saunders Clo. Grav —1A **136**
Saunders Copse. Wok —10E **188**
Saunders Ho. W11 —46Za **80**
Saunders La. Wok —10B **188**
Saunders Ness Rd. E14 —50Ec **84**
Saunders Rd. SE18 —50Vc **87**
Saunders Rd. Uxb —38P **55**
Saunders St. SE11 —49Qb **82** (5J **205**)
Saunders Way. SE28 —45Xc **87**
Saunderton Rd. Wemb —36Ka **58**
Saunton Av. Hay —52Y **98**
Saunton Rd. Horn —33Jd **68**
Savage Gdns. E6 —44Pc **86**
Savage Gdns. EC3 —45Ub **83** (4J **201**)
Savay Clo. Den —31J **55**
Savay La. Den —30J **35**
Savernake Ho. N4 —31Sb **63**
Savernake Rd. N9 —16Wb **25**
Savernake Rd. NW3 —35Hb **61**
Savile Clo. N Mald —71Ua **144**
Savile Gdns. Croy —75Vb **147**
Savile Row. W1 —45Lb **82** (4B **198**)
Saville Cres. Ashf —65T **120**
Saville Gdns. Croy —75Vb **147**
Saville Rd. E16 —46Nc **86**
Saville Rd. W4 —48Ta **79**
Saville Rd. Romf —30Bd **47**
Saville Rd. Twic —60Ha **100**
Saville Row. Brom —74Hc **149**
Saville Row. Enf —12Zb **26**
Savill Gdns. SW20 —69Wa **124**
Savill Ho. E16 —46Rc 86
(off Robert St.)
Savill Row. Wfd G —23Hc **45**
Savin Lodge. Sutt —80Eb 145
(off Walnut M.)
Savona Clo. SW19 —66Za **124**
Savona St. SW8 —52Lb **104**
Savoy Av. Hay —50U **76**
Savoy Bldgs. WC2
(off Strand) —45Pb 82 (5H 199)
Savoy Clo. E15 —39Gc **65**
Savoy Clo. Edgw —22Qa **39**
Savoy Clo. Hare —26M **35**
Savoy Ct. NW3 —34Eb **61**
Savoy Ct. WC2 —45Pb **82** (5H **199**)
Savoy Hill. WC2 —45Pb **82** (5H **199**)
Savoy Pde. Enf —13Ub **25**
Savoy Pl. WC2 —45Nb **82** (5G **199**)
Savoy Rd. Dart —57Md **111**
Savoy Row. WC2
(off Savoy St.) —45Pb 82 (4H 199)
Savoy Steps. WC2 —45Pb 82 (5H 199)
(off Savoy Row)
Savoy St. WC2 —45Pb **82** (4H **199**)
Savoy Way. WC2 —45Pb 82 (5H 199)
(off Savoy Hill)
Sawbill Clo. Hay —43Z **77**
Sawkins Clo. SW19 —61Ab **124**
Sawley Rd. W12 —46Va **80**
Sawtry Clo. Cars —73Gb **145**
Sawtry Way. Borwd —10Qa **7**
Sawyer Clo. N9 —19Wb **25**
Sawyer Ct. NW10 —38Ta **59**
Sawyers Chase. Abr —13Xc **29**
Sawyers Clo. Dag —37Ed **68**
Sawyers Clo. Wind —2C **94**
Sawyers Ct. Shenf —17Ae **33**
Sawyers Hall La. Brtwd —17Yd **32**
Sawyers Hill. Rich —59Pa **101**
Sawyers La. Els —11Ka **20**
Sawyers La. S Mim —5Za **8**
Sawyers Lawn. W13 —44Ja **78**
Sawyer St. SE1 —47Sb **83** (1D **206**)
Saxby Rd. SW2 —59Nb **104**

Saxham Rd.—Shaftesbury Av.

Saxham Rd. Bark —39Uc 66
Saxlingham Rd. E4 —20Fc 27
Saxon Av. Felt —61Aa 121
Saxonbury Av. Sun —69X 121
Saxonbury Clo. Mitc —69Fb 125
Saxonbury Ct. N7 —36Nb 62
Saxonbury Gdns. Surb —74La 142
Saxon Bus. Cen. SW19 —68Eb 125
Saxon Clo. Brtwd —20Ce 33
Saxon Clo. Grav —62Ee 135
Saxon Clo. Romf —26Pd 49
Saxon Clo. Slou —47B 74
Saxon Clo. Surb —72Ma 143
Saxon Clo. Uxb —43P 75
Saxon Ct. Borwd —11Na 21
Saxon Dri. W3 —44Qa 79
Saxon Gdns. S'hall —45Aa 77
Saxon Ho. Felt —61Ba 121
Saxon Pl. Hort K —71Sd 154
Saxon Rd. E3 —40Bc 64
Saxon Rd. E6 —42Pc 86
Saxon Rd. N22 —25Rb 43
Saxon Rd. SE25 —71Tb 147
Saxon Rd. Ashf —65T 120
Saxon Rd. Brom —66Hc 129
Saxon Rd. Dart —63Nd 133
Saxon Rd. Ilf —37Rc 66
Saxon Rd. S'hall —45Aa 77
Saxon Rd. W on T —75Z 141
Saxon Rd. Wemb —34Sa 59
Saxons. Tad —93Za 178
Saxon Wlk. Sidc —65Yc 131
Saxon Way. N14 —16Mb 24
Saxon Way. Old Win —8M 95
Saxon Way. Wal A —5Ec 12
Saxon Way. W Dray —51L 97
Saxony Pde. Hay —43S 76
Saxton Clo. SE13 —55Fc 107
Saxville Rd. Orp —69Xc 131
Sayer Clo. Grnh —57Wd 112
Sayers Clo. Fet —95Ea 176
Sayers Ho. N2 —26Fb 41
(off Grange, The)
Sayer St. SE17 —49Sb 83 (5D 206)
Sayer's Wlk. Rich —59Pa 101
Sayes Ct. SE8 —50Bc 84
Sayes Ct. Add —78L 139
Sayes Ct. Farm Dri. Add —78K 139
Sayes Ct. Rd. Orp —70Wc 131
Sayes Ct. St. SE8 —51Bc 106
Scads Hill Clo. Orp —72Vc 151
Scafell Rd. Slou —2D 72
Scala St. W1 —43Lb 82 (7C 192)
Scales Rd. N17 —27Vb 43
Scampston M. W10 —44Za 80
Scampton Rd. Houn —58P 97
Scandrett St. E1 —46Xb 83
Scantlebury Av. Grav —59Fe 113
Scarba Wlk. N1 —37Tb 63
(off Marquess Rd.)
Scarborough Clo. Big H —90Lc 167
Scarborough Clo. Sutt —83Bb 163
Scarborough Rd. E11 —32Fc 65
Scarborough Rd. N4 —32Qb 62
Scarborough Rd. N9 —17Yb 26
Scarborough Rd. Houn —58S 98
Scarborough St. E1 —44Vb 83
Scarborough Way. Slou —8F 72
Scarbrook Rd. Croy —76Sb 147
Scarle Rd. Wemb —37Ma 59
Scarlet Clo. St P —70Xc 131
Scarlet Rd. SE6 —62Gc 129
Scarlett Clo. Wok —6C 188
Scarlette Mnr. Way. SW2 —59Qb 104
Scarsbrook Rd. SE3 —55Mc 107
Scarsdale Pl. W8 —48Db 81
Scarsdale Rd. Harr —34Ea 58
Scarsdale Vs. W8 —48Cb 81
Scarth Rd. SW13 —55Va 102
Scatterdells La. Chfd —2H 139
Scawen Rd. SE8 —50Ac 84
Scawfell St. E2 —40Vb 63
Sceaux Gdns. SE5 —53Ub 105
Sceptre Rd. E2 —41Yb 84
Sceynes Link. N12 —21Cb 41
Schofield Wlk. SE3 —52Kc 107
Scholars Rd. E4 —18Fc 27
Scholars Rd. SW12 —60Lb 104
Scholars Wlk. Ger X —23A 34
Scholefield Rd. N19 —32Mb 62
School All. Twic —60Ja 100
School Allotment Ride. Wind —9A 94
School App. E2 —41Ub 83 (3J 195)
Schoolbell M. E3 —40Ac 64
School Cotts. Wok —10F 188
Schoolfield Rd. Grays —51Wd 112
School Hill. Red —100Lb 180
School Ho. La. E1 —45Zb 84
School Ho. La. Tedd —66Ka 122
School La. SE23 —61Xb 127
School La. Add —78J 139
School La. Bean —63Yd 134
School La. Brick —6Ba 5
School La. Bush —17Da 19
School La. Cat —98Vb 181
School La. Egh —64C 118
School La. Fet —94Fa 176
School La. Ger X —26A 34
School La. Hort K —70Sd 134
School La. Ingve —23Ee 51
School La. King T —67La 122
School La. Mick —95Ja 176
School La. Ock —94R 174
School La. Ors —3C 92
School La. Pinn —28Aa 37
School La. Seal —93Pd 187
School La. Shep —72R 140
School La. Stoke P —8M 53
School La. Surb —74Qa 143
School La. Swan —67Kd 133
School La. Tad —97Wa 178
School La. Well —55Xc 109
School La. W Hor —100R 174
School Mead. Abb L —4U 4
School Pas. King T —68Pa 123
School Pas. S'hall —45Ba 77
School Rd. E12 —35Pc 66
School Rd. NW10 —42Ta 79
School Rd. Asc —10B 116
School Rd. Ashf —65R 120
School Rd. Chst —67Sc 130
School Rd. Dag —39Cd 68
School Rd. E Mol —70Fa 122
School Rd. Grav —2E 136
School Rd. Hamp —65Ea 122
School Rd. Houn —55Ea 100
School Rd. King T —67La 122
School Rd. Pot B —2Eb 9
School Rd. W on T —78V 140
School Rd. W Dray —51M 97
School Rd. Av. Hamp —65Ea 122
School Wlk. Slou —5M 73
School Wlk. Sun —70V 120
School Way. N12 —23Fb 41
School Way. Dag —34Yc 67
Schooner Clo. SE16 —47Zb 84
Schooner Ct. Dart —56Sd 112
Schopwick Pl. Els —16Ma 21
(off St Nicholas Clo.)
Schroder Ct. Egh —4M 117
Schubert Rd. SW15 —57Bb 103
Schubert Rd. Els —16Ma 21
Scilla Ct. Grays —51Fe 113
Sclater St. E1 —42Vb 83 (5K 195)
Scoble Pl. N16 —35Vb 63
Scoles Cres. SW2 —60Qb 104
Scoresby St. SE1 —46Rb 83 (7B 200)
Scorton Av. Gnfd —40Ja 58
Scotch Comn. W13 —43Ja 78
Scoter Clo. Wfd G —24Kc 45
Scot Gro. Pinn —24Z 37
Scotia Building. E1 —45Zb 84
(off Jardine Rd.)
Scotland Bri. Rd. New Haw —83J 157
Scotland Grn. N17 —26Vb 43
Scotland Grn. Rd. Enf —15Zb 26
Scotland Grn. Rd. N. Enf —14Zb 26
Scotland La. Cobh —9H 137
Scotland Pl. SW1 —46Nb 82 (7F 199)
Scotland Rd. Buck H —18Lc 27
Scotlands Dri. Farn C —7F 52
Scotney Ho. E9 —37Yb 64
Scotney Wlk. Horn —36Ld 69
Scots Clo. Stanw —60M 97
Scotscraig. Rad —7Ha 6
Scotsdale Clo. Orp —70Uc 130
Scotsdale Clo. Sutt —80Ab 144
Scotsdale Rd. SE12 —57Kc 107
Scotshall La. Warl —87Ec 166
Scots Hill. Rick —16P 17
Scots Hill Clo. Rick —16P 17
Scotsmill La. Rick —16N 17
Scotson Ho. SE11 —49Qb 82 (6K 205)
(off Marylee Way)
Scotswood St. EC1 —42Qb 82 (5A 194)
Scotswood Wlk. N17 —24Wb 43
Scott Clo. SW16 —67Pb 126
Scott Clo. Eps —78Sa 143
Scott Clo. Farn C —6G 52
Scott Clo. W Dray —49P 75
Scott Ct. W3 —47Ta 79
Scott Cres. Eri —53Hd 110
Scott Cres. Harr —32Da 57
Scott Ellis Gdns. NW8 —41Fb 81 (4B 190)
Scottes La. Dag —32Zc 67
Scott Farm Clo. Th Dit —74Ka 142
Scott Gdns. Houn —52Z 99
Scott Ho. E13 —40Jc 65
(off Queens Rd. W.)
Scott Ho. E14 —47Cc 84
(off Admirals Way)
Scott Ho. NW10 —38Ta 59
(off Stonebridge Pk.)
Scott Ho. Horn —30Jd 48
(off Benjamin Clo.)
Scott Lidgett Cres. SE16 —47Wb 83
Scott Rd. Grav —4F 136
Scott Rd. Grays —9C 92
Scott Russell Pl. E14 —50Dc 84
Scotts Av. Brom —68Fc 129
Scotts Av. Sun —66U 120
Scotts Clo. Horn —36Ld 69
Scotts Dri. Hamp —66Da 121
Scotts Farm Rd. Eps —79Sa 143
Scott's Gro. Clo. Chob —1A 188
Scott's La. Brom —69Fc 129
Scotts La. W on T —77Z 141
Scotts Pas. SE18 —49Rc 86
Scott's Rd. E10 —32Ec 64
Scott's Rd. W12 —47Xa 80
Scotts Rd. Brom —66Jc 129
Scott's Rd. S'hall —48Y 77
Scott St. E1 —42Xb 83
Scotts Way. Sev —94Gd 186
Scotts Way. Sun —66U 120
Scottswood Clo. Bush —12Aa 19
Scottswood Rd. Bush —12Aa 19
Scott's Yd. EC4 —45Tb 83 (4F 201)
(off Gophir La.)
Scottwell Dri. NW9 —29Va 40
Scoulding Rd. E16 —44Jc 85
Scouler St. E14 —45Fc 85
Scout App. NW10 —35Ua 60
Scout La. SW4 —55Lb 104
Scout Way. NW7 —21Ta 39
Scovell Cres. SE1 —47Sb 83 (2D 206)
(off McCoid Way)
Scovell Rd. SE1 —47Sb 83 (2D 206)
Scratchers La. Fawk —75Td 154
Scratton Fields. Sole S —10F 136
Scratton Rd. Stanf —1M 93
Scrattons Ter. Bark —39Zc 67
Scriven Ct. E8 —39Vb 63
Scriven St. E8 —39Vb 63
Scrooby St. SE6 —58Dc 106
Scrubbitts Pk. Rd. Rad —7Ja 6
Scrubbitts Sq. Rad —7Ja 6
Scrubs La. NW10 —41Wa 80
Scrutton Clo. SW12 —59Mb 104
Scrutton St. EC2 —42Ub 83 (6H 195)
Scudamore La. NW9 —28Sa 39
Scudders Hill. Fawk —72Xd 154
Scutari Rd. SE22 —57Yb 106
Scylla Cres. Houn —58R 98
Scylla Pl. St J —7D 188
Scylla Rd. SE15 —55Wb 105
(in two parts)
Scylla Rd. H'row A —58R 98
Seaborough Rd. Grays —8E 92
Seabright Pas. E2 —40Wb 63
Seabright St. E2 —41Xb 83
Seabrook Dri. W Wick —75Gc 149
Seabrooke Rise. Grays —51De 113
Seabrook Gdns. Romf —31Cd 68
Seabrook Rd. Dag —34Zc 67
Seaburn Clo. Rain —41Gd 88
Seacole Clo. W3 —43Ta 79
Seacourt Rd. SE2 —47Zc 87
Seacourt Rd. Slou —49D 74
Seacroft Gdns. Wat —20Z 19
Seafield Rd. N11 —21Mb 42
Seaford Clo. Ruis —33T 56
Seaford Rd. E17 —27Dc 44
Seaford Rd. N15 —29Tb 43
Seaford Rd. W13 —46Ka 78
Seaford Rd. Enf —14Ub 25
Seaford Rd. Houn —57M 97
Seaford St. WC1 —41Nb 82 (4G 193)
Seaforth Av. N Mald —71Xa 144
Seaforth Clo. Romf —24Gd 48
Seaforth Cres. N5 —36Sb 63
Seaforth Dri. Wal X —6Zb 12
Seaforth Gdns. N21 —17Pb 24
Seaforth Gdns. Eps —77Va 144
Seaforth Gdns. Wfd G —22Lc 45
Seaforth Pl. SW1 —48Lb 82 (3C 204)
(off Buckingham Ga.)
Seager Pl. E3 —43Bc 84
Seagrave Clo. E1 —43Zb 84
Seagrave Rd. SW6 —51Cb 103
Seagry Rd. E11 —30Jc 45
Sealand Rd. Houn —58Q 98
Sealand Wlk. N'holt —41Z 77
Seal Dri. Seal —93Pd 187
Seal Hollow Rd. Sev —96Ld 187
Seal Rd. Sev —93Ld 187
Seal St. E8 —35Vb 63
Searchwood Rd. Warl —90Xb 165
Searle Pl. N4 —32Pb 62
Searles Clo. SW11 —52Gb 103
Searles Rd. SE1 —49Tb 83 (5G 207)
Sears St. SE5 —52Tb 105
Seasprite Clo. N'holt —41Z 77
Seaton Av. Ilf —36Uc 66
Seaton Clo. E13 —42Jc 85
Seaton Clo. SE11 —50Rb 83 (7A 206)
Seaton Clo. SW15 —60Xa 102
Seaton Clo. Twic —58Fa 100
Seaton Dri. Ashf —61N 119
Seaton Gdns. Ruis —34V 56
Seaton Pl. NW1 —42Lb 82 (5B 192)
(off Triton Sq.)
Seaton Point. E5 —35Wb 63
Seaton Rd. Dart —59Jd 110
Seaton Rd. Hay —49T 76
Seaton Rd. Mitc —68Gb 125
Seaton Rd. Twic —58Ea 100
Seaton Rd. Well —52Yc 109
Seaton Rd. Wemb —40Na 59
Seaton St. N18 —22Wb 43
Sebastian Av. Shenf —16Ce 33
Sebastian St. EC1 —41Rb 83 (4C 194)
Sebastopol Rd. N9 —21Wb 43
Sebbon St. N1 —38Rb 63
Sebert Rd. E7 —36Kc 65
Sebright Rd. Barn —12Za 22
Secker Cres. Harr —25Ea 38
Secker Ho. SW9 —54Rb 105
(off Rupert Gdns.)
Secker St. SE1 —46Qb 82 (7K 199)
Second Av. E12 —35Nc 66
Second Av. E13 —41Jc 85
Second Av. E17 —29Cc 44
Second Av. N18 —21Yb 44
Second Av. NW4 —28Za 40
Second Av. SW14 —55Ua 102
Second Av. W3 —46Va 80
Second Av. W10 —42Ab 80
Second Av. Dag —40Dd 68
Second Av. Enf —15Vb 25
Second Av. Grays —51Wd 112
Second Av. Hay —46V 76
Second Av. Romf —29Yc 47
Second Av. Stanf —1M 93
Second Av. W on T —72X 141
Second Av. Wat —7Z 5
Second Av. Wemb —33Ma 59
Second Clo. W Mol —70Ea 122
Second Cres. Slou —3G 72
Second Cross Rd. Twic —61Ga 122
Second Way. Wemb —35Ra 59
Sedan Way. SE17 —50Ub 83 (7H 207)
Sedcombe Clo. Sidc —63Xc 131
Sedcote Rd. Enf —15Yb 26
Sedding St. SW1 —49Jb 82 (5H 203)
Seddon Highwalk. EC2
(off Barbican) —43Sb 83 (7D 194)
Seddon Ho. EC2 —43Sb 83 (1D 200)
(off Barbican)
Seddon Rd. Mord —71Fb 145
Seddon St. WC1 —41Pb 82 (4J 193)
Sedgebrook Rd. SE3 —55Mc 107
Sedgecombe Av. Harr —29La 38
Sedge Ct. Grays —52Fe 113
Sedgefield Clo. Romf —21Pd 49
Sedgefield Cres. Romf —21Pd 49
Sedgeford Rd. W12 —46Va 80
Sedgehill Rd. SE6 —63Cc 128
Sedgemere Av. N2 —27Eb 41
Sedgemere Rd. SE2 —48Yc 87
Sedgemoor Dri. Dag —35Cd 68
Sedge Rd. N17 —24Yb 44
Sedgeway. SE6 —60Hc 107
Sedgewick Av. Uxb —38R 56
Sedgewood Clo. Brom —73Hc 149
Sedgmoor Pl. SE5 —52Ub 105
Sedgwick Rd. E10 —33Ec 64
Sedgwick St. E9 —36Zb 64
Sedleigh Rd. SW18 —58Bb 103
Sedlescombe Rd. SW6 —51Cb 103
Sedley. S'fleet —65Ce 135
Sedley Ct. SE26 —61Xb 127
Sedley Gro. Hare —28L 35
Sedley Ho. SE11 —50Pb 82 (7J 205)
(off Newburn St.)
Sedley Pl. W1 —44Kb 82 (3K 197)
Sedley Rise. Lou —12Pc 28
Seeley Dri. SE21 —63Ub 127
Seelig Av. NW9 —31Wa 60
Seely Rd. SW17 —65Jb 126
Seething La. EC3 —45Ub 83 (4J 201)
Seething Wells La. Surb —72La 142
Sefton Av. NW7 —22Ta 39
Sefton Av. Harr —26Fa 38
Sefton Clo. Orp —70Vc 131
Sefton Clo. Stoke P —9K 53
Sefton Ct. Houn —53Da 99
Sefton Paddock. Stoke P —8L 53
Sefton Rd. Croy —74Wb 147
Sefton Rd. Eps —82Ta 161
Sefton Rd. Orp —70Vc 131
Sefton St. SW15 —55Ya 102
Sefton Way. Uxb —44L 75
Sega Ho. SW5 —49Cb 81
(off Cromwell Rd.)
Segal Clo. SE23 —59Ac 106
Segrave Clo. Wey —80Q 140
Sejant Ho. Grays —51De 113
(off Bridge Rd.)
Sekforde St. EC1 —42Rb 83 (6B 194)
Sekhon Ter. Felt —62Ca 121
Selah Dri. Swan —67Ed 132
Selan Gdns. Hay —43X 77
Selbie Av. NW10 —36Va 60
Selborne Av. E12 —35Qc 66
Selborne Av. Bex —60Ad 109
Selborne Gdns. NW4 —28Wa 40
Selborne Gdns. Gnfd —40Ja 58
Selborne Rd. E17 —29Bc 44
Selborne Rd. N14 —20Nb 24
Selborne Rd. N22 —25Pb 42
Selborne Rd. SE5 —54Tb 105
Selborne Rd. Croy —76Ub 147
Selborne Rd. Ilf —33Qc 66
Selborne Rd. N Mald —68Ua 124
Selborne Rd. Sidc —63Xc 131
Selborne Wlk. E17 —28Bc 44
Selbourne Av. New Haw —82K 157
Selbourne Av. Surb —75Pa 143
Selbourne Clo. Long —69Fe 135
Selbourne Clo. New Haw —82K 157
Selbourne Ho. SE1 —47Tb 83 (2F 207)
(off Gt. Dover St.)
Selby Chase. Ruis —33X 57
Selby Clo. E6 —43Nc 86
Selby Clo. Chess —80Na 143
Selby Clo. Chst —65Qc 130
Selby Gdns. S'hall —42Ca 77
Selby Grn. Cars —73Gb 145
Selby Rd. E11 —34Gc 65
Selby Rd. E13 —43Kc 85
Selby Rd. N17 —24Ub 43
Selby Rd. SE20 —68Wb 127
Selby Rd. W5 —42Ka 78
Selby Rd. Ashf —65S 120
Selby Rd. Cars —73Gb 145
Selby St. E1 —42Wb 83
Selby Wlk. Wok —6E 188
Selcroft Rd. Purl —84Rb 165
Selden Rd. SE15 —54Yb 106
Selden Wlk. N7 —33Pb 62
Selhurst Clo. SW19 —60Za 102
Selhurst Clo. Wok —87B 156
Selhurst New Rd. SE25 —72Ub 147
Selhurst Pl. SE25 —72Ub 147
Selhurst Rd. N9 —20Tb 25
Selhurst Rd. SE25 —72Ub 147
Selinas La. Dag —31Ad 67
Selkirk Dri. Eri —53Gd 110
Selkirk Rd. SW17 —63Gb 125
Selkirk Rd. Twic —61Ea 122
Sellers Clo. Borwd —11Sa 21
Sellers Hall Clo. N3 —24Cb 41
Sellincourt Rd. SW17 —64Gb 125
Sellindge Clo. Beck —66Bc 128
Sellon M. SE11 —49Pb 82 (6H 205)
Sellons Av. NW10 —39Va 60
Selsdon Av. S Croy —79Tb 147
Selsdon Clo. Romf —25Ed 48
Selsdon Clo. Surb —71Na 143
Selsdon Cres. S Croy —82Yb 166
Selsdon Pk. Rd. S Croy —81Zb 166
Selsdon Rd. E11 —31Jc 65
Selsdon Rd. E13 —39Lc 65
Selsdon Rd. NW2 —33Va 60
Selsdon Rd. SE27 —62Rb 127
Selsdon Rd. New Haw —83J 157
Selsdon Rd. S Croy —78Tb 147
Selsdon Way. E14 —48Dc 84
Selsea Pl. N16 —36Ub 63
Selsey Cres. Well —53Zc 109
Selsey St. E14 —43Cc 84
Selvage La. NW7 —22Ta 39
Selway Clo. Pinn —27X 37
Selwood Clo. Stai —58L 97
Selwood Dri. Barn —15Za 22
Selwood Gdns. Stai —58L 97
Selwood Pl. SW7 —50Fb 81 (7B 202)
Selwood Rd. Brtwd —20Vd 32
Selwood Rd. Chess —77Ma 143
Selwood Rd. Croy —75Xb 147
Selwood Rd. Sutt —74Bb 145
Selwood Rd. Wok —92D 172
Selwood Ter. SW7 —50Fb 81 (7B 202)
Selworthy Clo. E11 —29Jc 45
Selworthy Rd. SE6 —62Bc 128
Selwyn Av. E4 —23Ec 44
Selwyn Av. Ilf —30Vc 47
Selwyn Av. Rich —55Na 101
Selwyn Clo. Houn —56Aa 99
Selwyn Ct. E17 —29Cc 44
(off Yunus Khan Clo.)
Selwyn Ct. Edgw —24Ra 39
Selwyn Cres. Well —55Xc 109
Selwyn Pl. Cipp —5D 72
Selwyn Pl. Orp —69Xc 131
Selwyn Rd. E3 —40Bc 64
Selwyn Rd. E13 —39Kc 65
Selwyn Rd. NW10 —38Ta 59
Selwyn Rd. N Mald —71Ta 143
Selwyn Rd. Til —4B 114
Semley Ga. E9 —37Bc 64
Semley Pl. SW1 —49Jb 82 (6J 203)
Semley Rd. SW16 —68Nb 126
Semper Clo. Knap —5B 188
Semper Rd. Grays —7E 92
Semples. Stanf —1P 93
Senate St. SE15 —54Yb 106
Senator Wlk. SE28 —48Tc 86
Send Barns La. Send —96F 172
Send Clo. Send —95E 172
Send Hill. Send —97E 172
Send Marsh Rd. Send —96F 172
Send Pde. Clo. Send —95E 172
Send Rd. Send —94D 172
Seneca Rd. T Hth —70Sb 127
Senga Rd. Wall —74Jb 146
Senhouse Rd. Sutt —76Za 144
Senior St. W2 —43Db 81
Senlac Rd. SE12 —60Kc 107
Sennen Rd. Enf —17Vb 25
Sennen Wlk. SE9 —62Nc 130
Sennocke Ct. Sev —97Kd 187
Senrab St. E1 —44Zb 84
Sentinel Clo. N'holt —42Aa 77
Sentinel Sq. NW4 —28Ya 40
Sentis Ct. N'wd —23V 36
September Ct. Uxb —40M 55
September Way. Stan —23Ka 38
Septimus Pl. Enf —15Wb 25
Sequoia Clo. Bush —18Fa 20
Sequoia Gdns. Orp —73Vc 151
Sequoia Pk. Pinn —23Da 37
Serbin Clo. E10 —31Ec 64
Sergeant Ind. Est. SW18 —58Db 103
Sergeantsgreen La. Wal A —5Lc 13
Serica Ct. SE10 —52Ec 106
Serjeant's Inn. EC4 —44Qb 82 (3A 200)
Serle St. WC2 —44Pb 82 (2J 199)
Sermed Ct. Slou —6N 73
Sermon Dri. Swan —69Ed 132
Sermon La. EC4 —44Sb 83 (3D 200)
(off Carter La.)
Serpentine Ct. Sev —94Md 187
Serpentine Grn. Red —100Mb 180
Serpentine Rd. W2 —46Gb 81 (7D 196)
Serpentine Rd. Sev —95Ld 187
Service Rd., The. Pot B —4Cb 9
Servien Dri. Brom —67Mc 129
Servite Houses. Wor Pk —75Va 144
(off Avenue, The.)
Servius Ct. Bren —52Ma 101
Setchell Rd. SE1 —49Vb 83 (5K 207)
Setchell Way. SE1 —49Vb 83 (5K 207)
Seth St. SE16 —47Yb 84
Seton Gdns. Dag —38Yc 67
Settle Rd. E13 —40Jc 65
Settle Rd. Romf —21Qd 49
Settles St. E1 —43Wb 83
Settrington Rd. SW6 —54Db 103
Seven Acres. Cars —75Gb 145
Seven Acres. New Ash —76Ae 155
Seven Acres. N'wd —23X 37
Seven Acres. Swan —72Fd 152
Seven Arches Rd. Brtwd —20Zd 33
Seven Dials. WC2 —44Nb 82 (3F 199)
Seven Dials Ct. WC2 —44Nb 82 (3F 199)
(off Short Gdns.)
Seven Hills Clo. W on T —81U 158
Seven Hills Rd. Iver H —36D 54
Seven Hills Rd. W on T & Cob —81U 158
Seven Kings Rd. Ilf —33Vc 67
Sevenoaks Bus. Cen. Sev —93Ld 187
Sevenoaks By-Pass. Sev —95Ed 186
Sevenoaks Clo. Bexh —56Dd 110
Sevenoaks Clo. Romf —21Ld 49
Sevenoaks Clo. Sutt —82Cb 163
Sevenoaks Ct. N'wd —24S 36
Sevenoaks Rd. SE4 —58Ac 106
Sevenoaks Rd. Grn St & Hals —78Vc 151
Sevenoaks Rd. Sev —81Ad 169
Sevenoaks Way. Sidc & Orp —66Yc 131
Sevenoaks Way Ind. Est. St P —69Yc 131
Seven Sisters Rd. N7, N4 & N15 —34Pb 62
Seven Stars Corner. W12 —48Wa 80
Seventh Av. E12 —35Pc 66
Seventh Av. Hay —46W 76
Severn. E Til —8K 93
Severnake Clo. E14 —49Cc 84
Severn Av. Romf —27Kd 49
Severn Cres. Slou —50D 74
Severn Dri. Enf —10Wb 11
Severn Dri. Esh —75Ja 142
Severn Dri. Upm —30Td 50
Severn Dri. W on T —75Z 141
Severn Rd. S Ock —44Sd 90
Severns Field. Epp —1Wc 15
Severn Way. NW10 —36Va 60
Severn Way. Wat —6Y 5
Severus Rd. SW11 —56Gb 103
Seville St. SW1 —47Hb 81 (2G 203)
Sevington Rd. NW4 —30Xa 40
Sevington St. W9 —42Db 81
Seward Rd. W7 —47Ja 78
Seward Rd. Beck —68Zb 128
Sewardstone Gdns. E4 —15Dc 26
Sewardstone Rd. E2 —40Yb 64
Sewardstone Rd. E4 —17Dc 26
Sewardstone Rd. Wal A & E4 —6Ec 12
Sewardstone St. Wal A —6Ec 12
Seward St. EC1 —41Rb 83 (5C 194)
Sewdley St. E5 —35Zb 64
Sewell Rd. SE2 —48Wc 87
Sewell St. E13 —41Jc 85
Sextant Av. E14 —49Fc 85
Sexton Clo. Rain —39Hd 68
Sexton Rd. Til —3B 114
Seymer Rd. Romf —27Fd 48
Seymour Av. N17 —26Wb 43
Seymour Av. Eps —81Xa 162
Seymour Av. Mord —73Za 144
Seymour Clo. EC1 —42Rb 83 (6B 194)
Seymour Clo. E Mol —71Ea 142
Seymour Clo. Pinn —25Ba 37
Seymour Ct. E4 —19Ec 27
Seymour Ct. N10 —26Jb 42
Seymour Ct. N21 —16Pb 24
(off Eversley Pk. Rd.)
Seymour Ct. NW2 —33Xa 60
Seymour Dri. Brom —74Pc 150
Seymour Gdns. SE4 —55Ac 106
Seymour Gdns. Felt —63Y 121
Seymour Gdns. Ilf —32Pc 66
Seymour Gdns. Ruis —32Z 57
Seymour Gdns. Surb —71Pa 143
Seymour Gdns. Twic —59Ka 100
Seymour M. W1 —44Jb 82 (2H 197)
Seymour Pl. SE25 —70Xb 127
Seymour Pl. W1 —43Hb 81 (7E 190)
Seymour Rd. E4 —18Dc 26
Seymour Rd. E6 —40Mc 65
Seymour Rd. E10 —32Bc 64
Seymour Rd. N3 —24Db 41
Seymour Rd. N8 —29Qb 42
Seymour Rd. N9 —19Xb 25
Seymour Rd. SW18 —59Bb 103
Seymour Rd. SW19 —62Za 124
Seymour Rd. W4 —49Sa 79
Seymour Rd. Cars —78Jb 146
Seymour Rd. Chaf H —48Yd 90
Seymour Rd. E Mol —71Ea 142
Seymour Rd. Grav —10B 114
Seymour Rd. Hamp —64Ea 122
Seymour Rd. King T —67Ma 123
Seymour Rd. Mitc —73Jb 146
Seymour Rd. Slou —7H 73
Seymour Rd. Til —3B 114
Seymours, The. Lou —11Qc 28
Seymour St. W2 & W1 —44Hb 81 (3F 197)
Seymour Ter. SE20 —67Xb 127
Seymour Vs. SE20 —67Xb 127
Seymour Wlk. SW10 —51Eb 103
Seymour Wlk. Swans —59Ae 113
Seymour Way. Sun —66U 120
Seyssel St. E14 —49Ec 84
Shaa Rd. W3 —45Ta 79
Shab Hall Cotts. Sev —90Ed 170
Shacklands Rd. Badg M —83Dd 170
Shackleford Rd. Wok —92C 172
Shacklegate La. Tedd —63Ga 122
Shackleton Clo. SE23 —61Xb 127
Shackleton Ho. NW10 —38Ta 59
Shackleton Rd. Slou —5K 73
Shackleton Rd. S'hall —45Ba 77
Shacklewell Grn. E8 —35Vb 63
Shacklewell Ho. E8 —35Vb 63
Shacklewell La. E8 —36Vb 63
Shacklewell Rd. N16 —35Vb 63
Shacklewell Row. E8 —35Vb 63
Shacklewell St. E2 —41Vb 83
Shadbolt Clo. Wor Pk —75Va 144
Shad Thames. SE1 —46Vb 83 (7K 201)
Shadwell Ct. N'holt —40Ba 57
Shadwell Dri. N'holt —41Ba 77
Shadwell Pier Head. E1 —45Yb 84
Shadwell Pl. E1 —45Yb 84
Shadybush Clo. Bush —17Ea 20
Shady La. Wat —12X 19
Shaef Way. Tedd —66Ja 122
Shafter Rd. Dag —37Ed 68
Shaftesbury. Lou —13Mc 27
Shaftesbury Av. W1 & WC2 —45Mb 82 (4D 198)
Shaftesbury Av. Barn —14Eb 23
Shaftesbury Av. Enf —12Zb 26
Shaftesbury Av. Felt —58W 98
Shaftesbury Av. Kent —29Ma 39
Shaftesbury Av. S'hall —49Ca 77

Shaftesbury Av.—Shorts Croft

Shaftesbury Av. S Harr —32Da 57
Shaftesbury Circ. S Harr —32Ea 58
Shaftesbury Ct. E6 —44Qc 86
(off Sapphire Clo.)
Shaftesbury Ct. SE5 —56Tb 105
Shaftesbury Ct. SW6 —53Db 103
(off Maltings Pl.)
Shaftesbury Ct. SW16 —62Mb 126
Shaftesbury Ct. Slou —7J 73
Shaftesbury Cres. Stai —66M 119
Shaftesbury La. Dart —56Rd 111
Shaftesbury Pde. S Harr —32Ea 58
Shaftesbury Pl. EC2
(off Barbican) —43Sb 83 (1D 200)
Shaftesbury Point. E13 —40Jc 65
(off High St. Plaistow)
Shaftesbury Rd. E4 —18Fc 27
Shaftesbury Rd. E7 —38Lc 65
Shaftesbury Rd. E10 —32Cc 64
Shaftesbury Rd. E17 —30Dc 44
Shaftesbury Rd. N18 —23Ub 43
Shaftesbury Rd. N19 —32Nb 62
Shaftesbury Rd. Beck —68Bc 128
Shaftesbury Rd. Cars —73Fb 145
Shaftesbury Rd. Epp —1Vc 15
Shaftesbury Rd. Rich —55Na 101
Shaftesbury Rd. Romf —30Hd 48
Shaftesbury Rd. Wat —13Y 19
Shaftesbury Rd. Wok —89D 156
Shaftesburys, The. Bark —40Sc 66
Shaftesbury St. N1
(in two parts) —40Sb 63 (2E 194)
Shaftesbury Way. K Lan —1S 4
Shaftesbury Way. Twic —62Fa 122
Shaftesbury Waye. Hay —43Y 77
Shafto M. SW1 —48Hb 81 (4G 203)
Shafton Rd. E9 —39Zb 64
Shaftsbury Ct. Eri —53Hd 110
(off Selkirk Dri.)
Shafts Ct. EC3 —44Ub 83 (3H 201)
Shaggy Calf La. Slou —5L 73
Shakespeare Av. N11 —22Lb 42
Shakespeare Av. NW10 —39Ta 59
Shakespeare Av. Felt —58W 98
Shakespeare Av. Hay —44W 76
(in two parts)
Shakespeare Av. Til —4D 114
Shakespeare Ct. New Bar —13Db 23
Shakespeare Cres. E12 —37Pc 66
Shakespeare Cres. NW10 —39Ta 59
Shakespeare Dri. Harr —30Pa 39
Shakespeare Gdns. N2 —28Hb 41
Shakespeare Ho. N14 —19Mb 24
Shakespeare Ind. Est. Wat —10X 5
Shakespeare Rd. E17 —26Zb 44
Shakespeare Rd. N3 —25Cb 41
Shakespeare Rd. NW7 —21Va 40
Shakespeare Rd. SE24 —57Rb 105
Shakespeare Rd. W3 —46Sa 79
Shakespeare Rd. W7 —45Ha 78
Shakespeare Rd. Add —77M 139
Shakespeare Rd. Bexh —53Ad 109
Shakespeare Rd. Dart —56Qd 111
Shakespeare Rd. Romf —30Hd 48
Shakespeare Sq. Ilf —23Sc 46
Shakespeare St. Wat —10X 5
Shakespeare Tower. EC2
(off Barbican) —43Sb 83 (7E 194)
Shakespeare Way. Felt —63Y 121
Shakspeare M. N16 —35Ub 63
Shakspeare Wlk. N16 —35Ub 63
Shalcomb St. SW10 —51Eb 103
Shalcross Dri. Chesh —2Bc 12
Shaldon Dri. Mord —71Ab 144
Shaldon Dri. Ruis —34Y 57
Shaldon Rd. Edgw —26Pa 39
Shaldon Way. W on T —76Y 141
Shale Grn. Red —100Mb 180
Shalfleet Dri. W10 —45Za 80
Shalford Clo. Orp —77Sc 150
Shalford Ct. N1 —40Rb 63 (1B 194)
(off Charlton Pl.)
Shalford Ho. SE1
—48Tb 83 (3G 207)
Shalimar Gdns. W3 —45Sa 79
Shalimar Rd. W3 —45Sa 79
Shallons Rd. SE9 —63Rc 130
Shalstone Rd. SW14 —55Ra 101
Shalston Vs. Surb —72Pa 143
Shambles, The. Sev —97Ld 187
Shamrock Clo. Fet —93Fa 176
Shamrock Rd. Croy —72Pb 146
Shamrock Rd. Grav —9G 114
Shamrock St. SW4 —55Mb 104
Shamrock Way. N14 —18Kb 24
Shandon Rd. SW4 —58Lb 104
Shand St. SE1 —47Ub 83 (1H 207)
Shandy St. E1 —43Zb 84
Shanklin Clo. Chesh —1Vb 11
Shanklin Gdns. Wat —21Y 37
Shanklin Rd. N8 —29Mb 42
Shanklin Way. SE15 —52Vb 105
Shannon Clo. NW2 —34Za 60
Shannon Clo. S'hall —50Z 77
Shannon Ct. N16 —34Ub 63
Shannon Gro. SW9 —56Pb 104
Shannon Pl. NW8
—40Gb 61 (1E 190)
Shannon Way. Beck —65Dc 128
Shannon Way. S Ock —44Sd 90
Shanti Ct. SW18 —60Cb 103
Shantock Hall La. Bov —1A 2
Shantock La. Bov —2A 2
Shap Cres. Cars —74Hb 145
Shapland Way. N13 —22Pb 42
Shap St. E2 —40Vb 63 (1K 195)
Shardcroft Av. SE24 —57Rb 105
Shardeloes Rd. SE14 —54Bc 106
Shard's Sq. SE15 —51Wb 105
Sharland Rd. Grav —1E 136
Sharman Ct. Sidc —63Wc 131
Sharnbrooke Clo. Well —55Yc 109
Sharney Av. Slou —48D 74
Sharon Clo. Bookh —96Ca 175
Sharon Clo. Eps —85Sa 161
Sharon Clo. Surb —74Ma 143
Sharon Gdns. E9 —39Yb 64
Sharon Rd. W4 —50Ta 79
Sharon Rd. Enf —12Ac 26
Sharpe Clo. W7 —43Ha 78
Sharp Ho. SW8 —55Kb 104
Sharpleshall St. NW1 —38Hb 61
Sharpness Clo. Hay —43Aa 77
Sharpness Ct. SE15 —52Vb 105
(off Daniel Gdns.)
Sharp's La. Ruis —31T 56
Sharp Way. Dart —55Pd 111
Sharratt St. SE15 —51Yb 106
Sharsted St. SE17
—50Rb 83 (7B 206)
Sharvel La. N'holt —39X 57
Shaver's Pl. SW1
—45Mb 82 (5D 198)
(off Coventry St.)
Shaw Av. Bark —40Ad 67
Shawbrooke Rd. SE9 —57Lc 107
Shawbury Rd. SE22 —57Vb 105
Shaw Clo. SE28 —46Xc 87
Shaw Clo. Bush —19Ga 20
Shaw Clo. Chesh —1Yb 12
Shaw Clo. Eps —83Va 162
Shaw Clo. Horn —32Kd 69
Shaw Clo. Ott —79E 138
Shaw Clo. S Croy —84Vb 165
Shaw Ct. Old Win —7L 95
Shaw Cres. Hut —14Fe 33
Shaw Cres. S Croy —84Vb 165
Shaw Cres. Til —3D 114
Shaw Dri. W on T —73Y 141
Shawfield Ct. W Dray —48N 75
Shawfield Pk. Brom —68Mc 129
Shawfield St. SW3
—50Gb 81 (7E 202)
Shawford Ct. SW15 —59Wa 102
Shawford Rd. Eps —79Ta 143
Shaw Gdns. Bark —40Ad 67
Shaw Ho. E16 —46Qc 86
(off Claremont St.)
Shawley Cres. Eps —90Ya 162
Shawley Way. Eps —90Xa 162
Shaw Rd. Brom —62Hc 129
Shaw Rd. Enf —11Zb 26
Shaw Rd. Tats —92Lc 183
Shaws Path. King T —67La 122
(off High St. Hampton Wick)
Shaw Sq. E17 —25Ac 44
Shaw Way. Wall —80Nb 146
Shaxton Cres. New Ad —81Ec 166
Shearing Dri. Cars —73Cb 145
Shearling Way. N7 —37Nb 62
Shearman Rd. SE3 —56Hc 107
Shears Ct. Sun —66V 120
Shears Grn. Ct. Grav —1C 136
Shearwater Way. Long —69De 135
Shearwater Way. Hay —44Z 77
Shearwood Cres. Dart —55Hd 110
Sheath's La. Oxs —85Da 159
Sheaveshill Av. NW9 —28Ua 40
Sheaveshill Ct. NW9 —28Ta 39
Sheaveshill Pde. NW9 —28Ua 40
(off Sheaveshill Av.)
Sheba St. E1 —42Vb 83 (6K 195)
Sheehy Way. Slou —5M 73
Sheen Comn. Dri. Rich —56Qa 101
Sheen Ct. Rd. Rich —56Qa 101
Sheendale Rd. Rich —56Pa 101
Sheenewood. SE26 —63Xb 127
Sheen Ga. Gdns. SW14 —56Sa 101
Sheen Gro. N1 —39Qb 62
Sheen La. SW14 —57Sa 101
Sheen Pk. Rich —56Na 101
Sheen Rd. Orp —70Vc 131
Sheen Rd. Rich —57Na 101
Sheen Way. Wall —78Pb 146
Sheen Wood. SW14 —57Sa 101
Sheepbarn La. Warl —84Hc 167
Sheepcot Dri. Wat —6Y 5
Sheepcote Clo. Houn —52W 98
Sheepcote Gdns. Den —30J 35
Sheepcote La. SW11 —54Hb 103
Sheepcote La. Orp & Swan
—71Bd 151
Sheepcote Rd. Eton W —10E 72
Sheepcote Rd. Harr —30Ha 38
Sheepcote Rd. Wind —4C 94
Sheepcotes Rd. Romf —28Ad 47
Sheepcot La. Wat —5W 4
Sheephouse Way. N Mald
—74Ta 143
Sheep La. E8 —39Xb 63
Sheep Wlk. Eps —93Ta 177
Sheep Wlk. Shep —73P 139
Sheep Wlk. M. SW19 —65Za 124
Sheep Wlk., The. Wok —90G 156
Sheerwater Av. Wdhm —84G 156
Sheerwater Rd. E16 —43Mc 85
Sheerwater Rd. Wok & Wdhm
—84G 156
Sheet St. Wind —4H 95
Sheet St. Rd. Wind —3B 116
Sheffield Dri. Romf —22Qd 49
Sheffield Gdns. Romf —22Qd 49
Sheffield Rd. Houn —58S 98
Sheffield Rd. Slou —4G 72
Sheffield Sq. E3 —41Bc 84
Sheffield St. WC2
—44Pb 82 (3H 199)
Sheffield Ter. W8 —46Cb 81
Shefton Rise. N'wd —24W 36
Sheila Clo. Romf —24Dd 48
Sheila Rd. Romf —24Dd 48
Sheilings, The. Horn —29Pd 49
Sheilings, The. Seal —92Pd 187
Shelbourne Clo. Pinn —27Ba 37
Shelbourne Pl. Beck —66Cc 128
Shelbourne Rd. N17 —26Xb 43
Shelburne Rd. N7 —35Pb 62
Shelbury Clo. Sidc —63Wc 131
Shelbury Rd. SE22 —57Xb 105
Sheldon Av. N6 —31Gb 61
Sheldon Av. Ilf —26Rc 46
Sheldon Clo. SE12 —57Kc 107
Sheldon Clo. SE20 —67Xb 127
Sheldon Ct. Barn —14Db 23
Sheldon Rd. N18 —21Ub 43
Sheldon Rd. NW2 —35Za 60
Sheldon Rd. Bexh —53Bd 109
Sheldon Rd. Dag —38Ad 67
Sheldon St. Croy —76Sb 147
Sheldrake Ct. E6 —40Nc 66
(off St Bartholomew's Rd.)
Sheldrake Pl. W8 —47Cb 81
Sheldrick Clo. SW19 —68Fb 125
Sheldwich Ter. Brom —72Nc 150
Shelford Pl. N16 —34Tb 63
Shelford Rise. SE19 —66Vb 127
Shelford Rd. Barn —16Ya 22
Shelgate Rd. SW11 —57Gb 103
Shellbank La. Grn St —65Wd 134
Shell Clo. Brom —72Nc 150
Shellduck Clo. NW9 —26Ua 40
Shelley. N8 —27Nb 42
(off Boyton Rd.)
Shelley Av. E12 —37Nc 66
Shelley Av. Gnfd —41Fa 78
Shelley Av. Horn —33Hd 68
Shelley Clo. Bans —87Za 162
Shelley Clo. Coul —89Pb 164
Shelley Clo. Edgw —21Qa 39
Shelley Clo. Gnfd —41Fa 78
Shelley Clo. Hay —43W 76
Shelley Clo. N'wd —22V 36
Shelley Clo. Orp —76Uc 150
Shelley Clo. Slou —50C 74
Shelley Ct. N4 —32Pb 62
Shelley Ct. Wal A —5Hc 13
(off Ninefields)
Shelley Cres. Houn —53Z 99
Shelley Cres. S'hall —44Ba 77
Shelley Dri. Well —53Uc 108
Shelley Gdns. Wemb —33La 58
Shelley Gro. Lou —14Pc 28
Shelley Pl. Til —3D 114
Shelley Rd. SW19 —65Fb 125
Shelley Rd. Hut —17Fe 33
Shelleys La. Knock —88Vc 169
Shellness Rd. E5 —36Xb 63
Shell Rd. SE13 —55Dc 106
Shellwood Rd. SW11 —54Hb 103
Shelly Clo. SE15 —54Xb 105
Shelmerdine Clo. E3 —43Cc 84
Shelson Av. Felt —62V 120
Shelton Av. Warl —89Yb 166
Shelton Clo. Warl —89Yb 166
Shelton Ct. Slou —8N 73
Shelton Rd. SW19 —67Cb 125
Shelton St. WC2 —44Nb 82 (3F 199)
(in two parts)
Shelvers Grn. Tad —93Ya 178
Shelvers Hill. Tad —93Xa 178
Shelvers Spur. Tad —93Ya 178
Shelvers Way. Tad —93Ya 178
Shenden Clo. Sev —99Ld 187
Shenden Way. Sev —100Ld 187
Shenfield Clo. Coul —91Lb 180
Shenfield Cres. Brtwd —19Ae 33
Shenfield Gdns. Hut —16De 33
Shenfield Grn. Shenf —17Ce 33
Shenfield Pl. Shenf —17Ae 33
Shenfield Rd. Brtwd —19Zd 33
Shenfield Rd. Wfd G —24Kc 45
Shenfield St. N1 —40Ub 63 (2J 195)
Shenley Av. Ruis —33V 56
Shenleybury Cotts. Shenl —3Na 7
Shenley Hill. Rad —7Ka 6
Shenley La. Lon C & Rad —1Ma 7
Shenley La. Shenl —4Na 7
Shenley Rd. SE5 —53Ub 105
Shenley Rd. Borwd —14Qa 21
Shenley Rd. Dart —58Qd 111
Shenley Rd. Houn —53Aa 99
Shenley Rd. Rad —6Ka 6
Shenstone Clo. Dart —56Fd 110
Shenstone Dri. Burn —2B 72
Shenstone Gdns. Romf —25Ld 49
Shenstone Pk. S'hill —10C 116
Shenwood Ct. Borwd —9Qa 7
Shepherdess Pl. N1
—41Sb 83 (3F 195)
Shepherdess Wlk. N1
—40Sb 63 (1E 194)
Shepherd Mkt. W1
—46Kb 82 (7K 197)
Shepherds Bush Cen. W12
—47Za 80
Shepherd's Bush Grn. W12
—47Ya 80
Shepherd's Bush Mkt. W12
—47Ya 80
Shepherd's Bush Pl. W12 —47Za 80
Shepherd's Bush Rd. W6 —49Ya 80
Shepherd's Clo. N6 —30Kb 42
Shepherd's Clo. Orp —76Vc 151
Shepherds Clo. Romf —29Zc 47
Shepherds Clo. Shep —72R 140
Shepherds Clo. Uxb —42L 75
Shepherds Ct. W12 —47Za 80
(off Shepherd's Bush Grn.)
Shepherds Grn. Chst —66Tc 130
Shepherd's Hill. N6 —30Kb 42
Shepherd's Hill. Red —98Lb 180
Shepherds Hill. Romf —26Qd 49
Shepherds La. E9 —37Zb 64
Shepherd's La. Chor —16F 16
Shepherd's La. Dart —60Jd 110
Shepherd's Path. NW3 —36Fb 61
(off Lyndhurst Rd.)
Shepherd's Path. Brtwd —17Ud 32
Shepherds Path. N'holt —37Aa 57
(off Arnold Rd.)
Shepherds Pl. W1
—45Jb 82 (4H 197)
Shepherd's Rd. Wat —13V 18
Shepherd St. W1
—46Kb 82 (7K 197)
Shepherd St. Grav —59Fe 113
Shepherds Wlk. N1 —40Sb 63
Shepherds Wlk. NW2 —33Wa 60
Shepherd's Wlk. NW3 —36Fb 61
Shepherds Wlk. Bush —19Fa 20
Shepherd's Wlk. Eps —92Ra 177
Shepherds Way. Rick —17K 17
Shepherds Way. S Croy —80Zb 148
Shepiston La. W Dray & Hay
—49R 76
Shepley Clo. Cars —76Jb 146
Shepley Clo. Horn —36Md 69
Shepley M. Enf —9Cc 12
Sheppard Clo. Enf —10Xb 11
Sheppard Clo. King T —70Na 123
Sheppard Ho. SW2 —60Qb 104
Sheppard St. E16 —42Hc 85
Shepperton Clo. Borwd —11Ta 21
Shepperton Ct. Shep —72R 140
Shepperton Ct. Dri. Shep —71R 140
Shepperton Rd. N1 —39Sb 63
Shepperton Rd. Orp —72Sc 150
Shepperton Rd. Stai & Shep
—69L 119
Sheppey Clo. Eri —52Kd 111
Sheppey Gdns. Dag —38Yc 67
Sheppey Rd. Dag —38Xc 67
Sheppeys La. K Lan & Abb L —1S 4
Sheppey Wlk. N1 —37Sb 63
Sheppy Pl. Grav —9D 114
Shepton Houses. E2 —41Yb 84
(off Welwyn St.)
Sherard Rd. SE9 —57Nc 108
Sheraton Bus. Cen. Gnfd —40La 58
Sheraton Clo. Els —15Pa 21
Sheraton Dri. Eps —85Sa 161
Sheraton M. Wat —14U 18
Sheraton St. W1
—44Mb 82 (3D 198)
Sherborne Av. Enf —12Yb 26
Sherborne Av. S'hall —49Ca 77
Sherborne Clo. Coln —53G 96
Sherborne Clo. Eps —89Ya 162
Sherborne Clo. Hay —44Y 77
Sherborne Cres. Cars —73Gb 145
Sherborne Gdns. NW9 —27Qa 39
Sherborne Gdns. W13 —43Ka 78
Sherborne Gdns. Romf —22Cd 48
Sherborne La. EC4
—45Tb 83 (4F 201)
Sherborne Rd. Chess —78Na 143
Sherborne Rd. Felt —60T 98
(in two parts)
Sherborne Rd. Orp —71Vc 151
Sherborne Rd. Sutt —75Cb 145
Sherborne St. N1 —39Tb 63
Sherborne Wlk. Lea —93La 176
Sherborne Way. Crox —15R 18
Sherboro Rd. N15 —30Vb 43
Sherbourne Clo. W King —79Ud 154
Sherbourne Dri. Wind —6D 94
Sherbourne Ho. Wat —16T 18
Sherbourne Pl. Stan —23Ja 38
Sherbourne Wlk. Farn C —5G 52
Sherbrooke Clo. Bexh —56Cd 110
Sherbrooke Rd. SW6 —52Ab 102
Sherbrook Gdns. N21 —17Rb 25
Shere Av. Sutt —82Ya 162
Shere Clo. Chess —78Ma 143
Sheredan Rd. E4 —22Fc 45
Shere Ho. SE1 —47Tb 83 (2F 207)
(off Gt. Dover St.)
Shere Rd. Ilf —29Qc 46
Sherfield Av. Rick —20M 17
Sherfield Gdns. SW15 —58Va 102
Sherfield Rd. Grays —51De 113
Sheridan Clo. Romf —24Ld 49
Sheridan Clo. Swan —70Hd 132
Sheridan Clo. Uxb —42S 76
Sheridan Ct. Cipp —5C 72
Sheridan Ct. Dart —56Qd 111
Sheridan Ct. Harr —30Fa 38
Sheridan Ct. Houn —57Aa 99
Sheridan Cres. Chst —68Rc 130
Sheridan Gdns. Harr —30Ma 39
Sheridan Ho. SE11
—49Qb 82 (6A 206)
(off Wincott St.)
Sheridan Lodge. Brom —70Lc 129
(off Homesdale Rd.)
Sheridan Pl. SW13 —55Va 102
Sheridan Pl. Hamp —67Da 121
Sheridan Rd. E7 —34Hc 65
Sheridan Rd. E12 —36Nc 66
Sheridan Rd. SW19 —67Bb 125
Sheridan Rd. Belv —49Cd 88
Sheridan Rd. Bexh —55Ad 109
Sheridan Rd. Rich —62La 122
Sheridan Rd. Wat —17Z 19
Sheridans Rd. Bookh —98Ea 176
Sheridan St. E1 —44Xb 83
Sheridan Ter. N'holt —36Da 57
Sheridan Wlk. NW11 —30Cb 41
Sheridan Wlk. Cars —78Hb 145
Sheridan Way. Beck —67Bc 128
Sheriden Pl. Harr —31Ga 58
Sheriff Way. Wat —5W 4
Sheringham. NW8 —38Fb 61
Sheringham Av. E12 —35Pc 66
Sheringham Av. N14 —15Mb 24
Sheringham Av. Felt —62W 120
Sheringham Av. Romf —30Ed 48
Sheringham Av. Twic —60Ba 99
Sheringham Ct. Enf —13Rb 25
Sheringham Ct. Felt —62W 120
(off Sheringham Av.)
Sheringham Dri. Bark —36Vc 67
Sheringham Rd. N7 —37Pb 62
Sheringham Rd. SE20 —69Yb 128
Sheringham Tower. S'hall
—45Da 77
Sherington Av. Pinn —24Ca 37
Sherington Rd. SE7 —51Kc 107
Sherland Ct. Rad —8Ja 6
(off Dell, The)
Sherland Rd. Twic —60Ha 100
Sherlies Av. Orp —75Uc 150
Sherlock M. W1
—43Jb 82 (7H 191)
Shermanbury Pl. Eri —52Hd 110
Sherman Rd. Brom —67Jc 129
Sherman Rd. Slou —3J 73
Shernbroke Rd. Wal A —6Hc 13
Shernhall St. E17 —27Ec 44
Sherrard Rd. E7 & E12 —37Lc 65
Sherrards Way. Barn —15Cb 23
Sherrick Grn. Rd. NW10 —36Xa 60
Sherriff Rd. NW6 —37Cb 61
Sherringham Av. N17 —26Wb 43
Sherrin Rd. E10 —35Dc 64
Sherrock Gdns. NW4 —28Wa 40
Sherston Ct. SE1
—49Rb 83 (5C 206)
(off Newington Butts)
Sherston Ct. WC1
—41Qb 82 (4K 193)
(off Attneave St.)
Sherwin Ho. SE11 —51Qb 104
(off Kennington Rd.)
Sherwin Rd. SE14 —53Zb 106
Sherwood. N Stif —46Ae 91
Sherwood Av. E18 —27Kc 45
Sherwood Av. SW16 —66Mb 126
Sherwood Av. Gnfd —37Ga 58
Sherwood Av. Hay —42X 77
Sherwood Av. Pot B —4Ab 8
Sherwood Av. Ruis —30U 36
Sherwood Clo. SW13 —55Xa 102
Sherwood Clo. W13 —46Ka 78
Sherwood Clo. Bex —58Zc 109
Sherwood Clo. Fet —95Ea 176
Sherwood Clo. Knap —5B 188
Sherwood Clo. Slou —48A 74
Sherwood Ct. Coln —50B 74
Sherwood Ct. S Harr —33Ea 58
Sherwood Gdns. E14 —49Cc 84
Sherwood Gdns. Bark —38Tc 66
Sherwood Pk. Av. Sidc —59Wc 109
Sherwood Pk. Rd. Mitc —70Lb 126
Sherwood Pk. Rd. Sutt —78Cb 145
Sherwood Rd. NW4 —27Ya 40
Sherwood Rd. SW19 —66Bb 125
Sherwood Rd. Coul —88Lb 164
Sherwood Rd. Croy —73Xb 147
Sherwood Rd. Hamp —64Ea 122
Sherwood Rd. Harr —33Ea 58
Sherwood Rd. Ilf —28Tc 46
Sherwood Rd. Well —54Uc 108
Sherwoods Rd. Wat —17Aa 19
Sherwood St. N20 —20Fb 23
Sherwood St. W1
—45Lb 82 (4C 198)
Sherwood Ter. N20 —20Fb 23
Sherwood Way. W Wick —75Ec 148
Shetland Clo. Borwd —16Ta 21
Shetland Clo. Guild —100D 172
Shetland Rd. E3 —40Bc 64
Shevon Way. Brtwd —21Vd 50
Shewens Rd. Wey —77T 140
Shey Copse. Wok —89E 156
Shield Dri. Bren —51Ja 100
Shieldhall St. SE2 —49Yc 87
Shield Rd. Ashf —63S 120
Shields Ct. Til —9L 93
(off Coronation Av.)
Shifford Path. SE23 —62Zb 128
Shilburn Way. Wok —6D 188
Shillibeer Pl. W1 —43Gb 81 (1E 196)
(off York St.)
Shillibeer Wlk. Chig —20Vc 29
Shillingford St. N1 —38Rb 63
Shilltoe Av. Pot B —4Za 8
Shinecroft. Otf —88Jd 170
(off Rye La.)
Shinfield St. W12 —44Ya 80
Shingle Ct. Wal A —5Jc 13
Shingle End. Bren —52La 100
Shinglewell Rd. Eri —52Cd 110
Shinners Clo. SE25 —71Wb 147
Ship All. W4 —51Qa 101
Shipfield Clo. Tats —93Lc 183
Ship & Half Moon Pas. SE18
—48Rc 86
Ship Hill. Farn C & High W —2C 52
Ship Hill. Tats —93Lc 183
Shipka Rd. SW12 —60Kb 104
Ship La. SW14 —55Sa 101
Ship La. S Ock & Grays —46Td 90
Ship La. Swan & S at H —67Md 133
Shipley Hills Rd. Meop —75Fe 155
Shipman Rd. E16 —44Kc 85
Shipman Rd. SE23 —61Zb 128
Ship & Mermaid Row. SE1
—47Tb 83 (1G 207)
(off Snowsfields)
Ship & Mermaid Row. SW1
—47Tb 83
Ship St. SE8 —53Cc 106
Ship Tavern Pas. EC3
—45Ub 83 (4H 201)
Shipton Clo. Dag —34Zc 67
Shipton Pl. NW5 —37Jb 62
Shipton Rd. Uxb —35P 55
Shipton St. E2 —41Vb 83
Shipway Ter. N16 —34Vb 63
Shipwright Rd. SE16 —47Ac 84
Shipwright Yd. SE1
—46Ub 83 (7H 201)
(off Tooley St.)
Ship Yd. E14 —50Dc 84
Ship Yd. Wey —76R 140
Shirburn Clo. SE23 —59Yb 106
Shirbutt St. E14 —45Dc 84
Shirebrook Rd. SE3 —55Mc 107
Shire Ct. Eri —48Zc 87
Shirehall Clo. NW4 —30Za 40
Shirehall Gdns. NW4 —30Za 40
Shirehall La. NW4 —30Za 40
Shirehall Pk. NW4 —29Za 40
Shirehall Rd. Dart —64Ld 133
Shire La. Chal G & Ger X —18C 16
Shire La. Chor —15D 16
Shire La. Kes & Orp —80Pc 150
(in two parts)
Shire La. Orp —78Uc 150
Shiremeade. Borwd —15Pa 21
Shires Clo. Asht —91Ma 177
Shires Ho. Byfl —85N 157
Shires, The. Ham —63Na 123
Shirland M. W9 —41Bb 81
Shirland Rd. W9 —41Bb 81
Shirley Av. Bex —59Zc 109
Shirley Av. Cheam —81Bb 163
Shirley Av. Coul —91Rb 181
Shirley Av. Croy —74Yb 148
Shirley Av. Sutt —77Fb 145
Shirley Av. Wind —3D 94
Shirley Chu. Rd. Croy —76Zb 148
Shirley Clo. E17 —29Dc 44
Shirley Clo. Chesh —1Yb 12
Shirley Clo. Dart —56Ld 111
Shirley Clo. Grav —10K 115
Shirley Clo. Houn —57Ea 100
Shirley Ct. Lou —12Pc 28
Shirley Cres. Beck —70Ac 128
Shirley Dri. Houn —57Ea 100
Shirley Gdns. W7 —46Ha 78
Shirley Gdns. Bark —37Uc 66
Shirley Gdns. Horn —33Ld 69
Shirley Gro. N9 —17Yb 26
Shirley Gro. SW11 —55Jb 104
Shirley Heights. Wall —81Lb 164
Shirley Hills Rd. Croy —78Yb 148
Shirley Ho. Dri. SE7 —52Lc 107
Shirley Oaks Rd. Croy —74Zb 148
Shirley Pk. Rd. Croy —74Xb 147
Shirley Pl. Knap —5A 188
Shirley Rd. E15 —38Gc 65
Shirley Rd. W4 —47Ta 79
Shirley Rd. Abb L —4V 4
Shirley Rd. Croy —73Xb 147
Shirley Rd. Enf —13Sb 25
Shirley Rd. Sidc —62Uc 130
Shirley Rd. Wall —81Lb 164
Shirley St. E16 —44Hc 85
Shirley Way. Croy —76Ac 148
Shirlock Rd. NW3 —35Hb 61
Shobden Rd. N17 —25Tb 43
Shobroke Rd. E6 —38Pc 66
Shoelands Ct. NW9 —27Ta 39
Shoe La. EC4 —44Qb 82 (2A 200)
Sholden Gdns. Orp —71Yc 151
Shonks Mill Rd. Nave —11Kd 31
Shooters Av. Harr —28La 38
Shooter's Hill. SE18 & Well
—53Qc 108
Shooters Hill Rd. SE3 & SE18
—53Fc 107
Shooters Rd. Enf —11Rb 25
Shoot Up Hill. NW2 —36Ab 60
Shord Hill. Kenl —88Tb 165
Shore Clo. Felt —59W 98
Shore Clo. Hamp —65Aa 121
Shorediche Clo. Uxb —34P 55
Shoreditch Ct. E8 —39Vb 63
(off Queensbridge Rd.)
Shoreditch High St. E1
—42Ub 83 (4J 195)
Shore Gro. Felt —61Ca 121
Shoreham Clo. SW18 —57Db 103
Shoreham Clo. Bex —60Zc 109
Shoreham Clo. Croy —71Yb 148
Shoreham La. Hals —84Bd 169
Shoreham La. Orp —79Cd 152
Shoreham La. Sev —94Hd 186
Shoreham Pl. Shor —84Jd 170
Shoreham Rise. Slou —2B 72
Shoreham Rd. Eyns —79Ld 153
Shoreham Rd. Orp —67Xc 131
Shoreham Rd. Shor —83Kd 171
Shoreham Rd. E. H'row A —57N 97
Shoreham Rd. W. H'row A —57N 97
Shoreham Way. Brom —72Jc 149
Shorehill La. Knat —88Pd 171
Shore Ho. SW8 —55Kb 104
Shore Pl. E9 —38Yb 64
Shore Rd. E9 —38Yb 64
Shores Rd. Wok —86A 156
Shore, The. Grav —57Fe 113
(in two parts)
Shorncliffe Rd. SE1
—50Vb 83 (7K 207)
Shorndean St. SE6 —60Ec 106
Shorne Clo. Orp —70Zc 131
Shorne Clo. Sidc —58Xc 109
Shornefield Clo. Brom —69Qc 130
Shorne Ifield Rd. Shorne —5J 137
Shornells Way. SE2 —50Yc 87
Shorrold's Rd. SW6 —52Bb 103
Shortcroft Rd. Eps —80Va 144
Shortcrofts Rd. Dag —37Bd 67
Shorter Av. Shenf —17Be 33
Shorter St. E1 —45Vb 83 (5K 201)
Shortfern. Slou —4N 73
Short Ga. N12 —21Bb 41
Short Hedges. Houn —53Ca 99
Short Hill. Harr —32Ga 58
Shortlands. W6 —49Za 80
Shortlands. Hay —51T 98
Shortlands Clo. N18 —20Tb 25
Shortlands Gdns. Brom —68Gc 129
Shortlands Gro. Brom —69Fc 129
Shortlands Ho. E17 —29Bc 44
Shortlands Rd. E10 —31Dc 64
Shortlands Rd. Brom —69Fc 129
Shortlands Rd. King T —66Pa 123
Short La. Brick —1Aa 5
Short La. Stai —59P 97
Shortmead Dri. Chesh —3Ac 12
Short Path. SE18 —51Rc 108
Short Rd. E11 —33Gc 65
Short Rd. E15 —39Fc 65
Short Rd. W4 —51Ua 102
Short Rd. Houn —58N 97
Shorts Croft. NW9 —28Ra 39

Shorts Gdns.—Sorrells, The

Shorts Gdns. WC2 —44Nb 82 (3F 199)
Shorts Rd. Cars —77Gb 145
Short St. NW4 —28Ya 40
Short St. SE1 —47Qb 82 (1A 206)
Short Wall. E15 —41Ec 84
Short Way. N12 —23Gb 41
Short Way. SE9 —55Nc 108
Short Way. Twic —59Ea 100
Shortwood Av. Stai —62K 119
Shorwell Ct. Purf —50Rd 89
Shotfield. Wall —79Kb 146
Shotfield Av. SW14 —56Ua 102
Shott Clo. Sutt —78Eb 145
Shottendane Rd. SW6 —53Cb 103
Shottery Clo. SE9 —62Nc 130
Shoulder of Mutton All. E14 —45Ac 84
Shouldham St. W1 —43Gb 81 (1E 196)
Showers Way. Hay —46W 76
Shrapnel Clo. SE18 —52Nc 108
Shrapnel Rd. SE9 —55Pc 108
Shrewsbury Av. SW14 —56Ta 101
Shrewsbury Av. Harr —28Na 39
Shrewsbury Clo. Surb —75Na 143
Shrewsbury Cres. NW10 —39Ta 59
Shrewsbury Ho. SW8 —51Pb 104 (off Meadow Rd.)
Shrewsbury La. SE18 —53Rc 108
Shrewsbury Rd. E7 —36Mc 65
Shrewsbury Rd. N11 —23Mb 42
Shrewsbury Rd. W2 —44Cb 81
Shrewsbury Rd. Beck —69Ac 128
Shrewsbury Rd. Cars —73Gb 145
Shrewsbury Rd. Houn —58S 98
Shrewsbury Wlk. Iswth —55Ja 100
Shrewton Rd. SW17 —66Hb 125
Shrimp Brand Cotts. Grav —4C 136
Shroffold Rd. Brom —63Gc 129
Shropshire Clo. Mitc —70Nb 126
Shropshire Pl. WC1 —42Lb 82 (6C 192)
Shropshire Rd. N22 —24Pb 42
Shroton St. NW1 —43Gb 81 (7D 190)
Shrubberies, The. E18 —26Jc 45
Shrubberies, The. Chig —22Sc 46
Shrubbery Gdns. N21 —17Rb 25
Shrubbery Rd. N9 —20Wb 25
Shrubbery Rd. SW16 —63Nb 126
Shrubbery Rd. Grav —10D 114
Shrubbery Rd. S'hall —46Ca 77
Shrubbery Rd. S Dar —67Td 134
Shrubbery, The. Upm —34Sd 70
Shrubland Gro. Wor Pk —76Ya 144
Shrubland Rd. E8 —39Wb 63
Shrubland Rd. E10 —31Cc 64
Shrubland Rd. E17 —29Cc 44
Shrubland Rd. Bans —88Bb 163
Shrublands Av. Croy —76Cc 148
Shrublands Clo. N20 —18Fb 23
Shrublands Clo. SE26 —62Yb 128
Shrublands Clo. Chig —23Sc 46
Shrublands, The. Pot B —5Ab 8
Shrubsall Clo. SE9 —60Nc 108
Shrubs Rd. B Hth —23P 35
Shuna Wlk. N1 —37Tb 63
Shurland Av. Barn —16Fb 23
Shurland Gdns. SE15 —52Vb 105
Shurlock Av. Swan —68Fd 132
Shurlock Dri. Orp —77Sc 150
Shuttle Clo. Sidc —59Vc 109
Shuttlemead. Bex —59Bd 110
Shuttle Rd. Dart —55Jd 110
Shuttle St. E1 —42Wb 83
Shuttleworth Rd. SW11 —54Gb 103
Sibella Rd. SW4 —54Mb 104
Sibley Clo. Bexh —57Ad 109
Sibley Ct. Uxb —43S 76
Sibley Gro. E12 —38Nc 66
Sibthorpe Rd. SE12 —58Kc 107
Sibton Rd. Cars —73Gb 145
Sicilian Av. WC1 —43Nb 82 (1G 199) (off Vernon Pl.)
Sickle Corner. Dag —41Dd 88
Sidbury Clo. Asc —10E 116
Sidbury St. SW6 —53Ab 102
Sidcup By-Pass. Chst & Sidc —62Tc 130
Sidcup High St. Sidc —63Wc 131
Sidcup Hill. Sidc —63Xc 131
Sidcup Hill Gdns. Sidc —64Yc 131
Sidcup Rd. SE12 & SE9 —58Lc 107
Siddons Clo. Linf —8J 93
Siddons La. NW1 —42Hb 81 (6G 191)
Siddons Rd. N17 —25Wb 43
Siddons Rd. SE23 —61Ac 128
Siddons Rd. Croy —76Qb 146
Side Rd. E17 —29Bc 44
Side Rd. Den —31F 54
Sidewood Rd. SE9 —60Tc 108
Sidford Ho. SE1 —48Pb 82 (4J 205) (off Cosser St.)
Sidford Pl. SE1 —48Qb 82 (4J 205)
Sidgwick Ho. SW9 —54Pb 104 (off Stockwell Rd.)
Sidings M. N7 —34Qb 62
Sidings, The. E11 —32Fc 65
Sidlaw Ho. N16 —32Vb 63
Sidmouth Av. Iswth —54Ga 100
Sidmouth Clo. Wat —19X 19
Sidmouth Dri. Ruis —34W 56
Sidmouth Pde. NW10 —38Ya 60
Sidmouth Rd. E10 —34Ec 64
Sidmouth Rd. NW2 —38Ya 60
Sidmouth Rd. SE15 —53Vb 105
Sidmouth Rd. Orp —71Xc 151 (in two parts)
Sidmouth Rd. Well —52Yc 109
Sidmouth St. WC1 —41Pb 82 (4G 193)
Sidney. Sidc —65Xc 131
Sidney Av. N13 —22Pb 42
Sidney Est. E1 —43Yb 84 (in two parts)
Sidney Gdns. Bren —51Ma 101
Sidney Gdns. Otf —89Ld 171
Sidney Gro. EC1 —40Rb 63 (3B 194)
Sidney Miller Ct. W3 —46Ra 79 (off Crown St.)
Sidney Rd. E7 —34Jc 65
Sidney Rd. N22 —24Pb 42
Sidney Rd. SE25 —71Wb 147
Sidney Rd. SW9 —54Pb 104
Sidney Rd. Beck —68Ac 128
Sidney Rd. Harr —27Ea 38
Sidney Rd. Stai —63J 119
Sidney Rd. They B —8Tc 14
Sidney Rd. Twic —58Ja 100
Sidney Rd. W on T —73W 140
Sidney Sq. E1 —43Yb 84
Sidney St. E1 —43Xb 83
Sidworth St. E8 —38Xb 63
Siebert Rd. SE3 —51Jc 107
Siemens Rd. SE18 —48Mc 85
Sigdon Pas. E8 —36Wb 63
Sigdon Rd. E8 —36Wb 63
Sigers, The. Pinn —30X 37
Silbury Av. Mitc —67Gb 125
Silbury Ho. SE26 —62Wb 127
Silbury St. N1 —41Tb 83 (3F 195)
Silchester Rd. W10 —44Za 80
Silecroft Rd. Bexh —53Cd 110
Silesia Bldgs. E8 —38Xb 63
Silex St. SE1 —47Rb 83 (2C 206)
Silicone Bus. Cen. Gnfd —40La 58
Silk Clo. SE12 —57Jc 107
Silkfield Rd. NW9 —29Ua 40
Silkham Rd. Oxt —99Fc 183
Silk Ho. NW9 —27Ta 39
Silk Mill Ct. Wat —16X 19
Silk Mill Rd. Wat —16X 19
Silk Mills Path. SE13 —54Ec 106
Silkmoor La. W Hor —97Q 174
Silks Ct. E11 —32Hc 65
Silkstream Pde. Edgw —25Sa 39
Silkstream Rd. Edgw —25Sa 39
Silk St. EC2 —43Sb 83 (7E 194)
Sillitoe Ho. N1 —39Tb 63 (1G 195) (off Colville Est.)
Silsoe Rd. N22 —26Pb 42
Silver Birch Av. E4 —23Bc 44
Silverbirch Clo. N11 —23Jb 42
Silver Birch Clo. Dart —63Gd 132
Silver Birch Clo. Uxb —35N 55
Silver Birch Clo. Wdhm —84G 156
Silverbirch Ct. E8 —38Vb 63
Silver Birches. Hut —18Ce 33
Silverburn Ho. SW9 —53Rb 105 (off Lothian Rd.)
Silver Chase Ct. Enf —11Rb 25
Silvercliffe Gdns. Barn —14Gb 23
Silver Clo. SE14 —52Ac 106
Silver Clo. Harr —24Fa 38
Silver Clo. Tad —96Ab 178
Silver Cres. W4 —49Ra 79
Silverdale. SE26 —63Yb 128
Silverdale. Enf —14Nb 24
Silverdale. Hart —70Be 135
Silverdale Av. Ilf —29Vc 47
Silverdale Av. Oxs —86Ea 160
Silverdale Av. W on T —75V 140
Silverdale Clo. W7 —46Ga 78
Silverdale Clo. N'holt —36Ba 57
Silverdale Clo. Sutt —77Bb 145
Silverdale Ct. Stai —63K 119
Silverdale Dri. SE9 —61Nc 130
Silverdale Dri. Horn —36Kd 69
Silverdale Dri. Sun —68X 121
Silverdale Gdns. Hay —47W 76
Silverdale Rd. E4 —23Fc 45
Silverdale Rd. Bexh —54Dd 110
Silverdale Rd. Bush —15Aa 19
Silverdale Rd. Hay —47V 76
Silverdale Rd. Pet W —70Sc 130
Silverdale Rd. St P —69Wc 131
Silver Dell. Wat —8V 4
Silverglade Bus. Pk. Chess —84La 160
Silverhall St. Iswth —55Ja 100
Silver Hill. Well E —8Sa 7
Silverholme Clo. Harr —31Na 59
Silver Jubilee Way. Houn —54X 99
Silverland St. E16 —46Pc 86
Silver La. Purl —84Mb 164
Silver La. W Wick —75Fc 149
Silverleigh Rd. T Hth —70Pb 126
Silverlocke Rd. Grays —51Fe 113
Silvermere Av. Romf —23Db 48
Silvermere Ct. Purl —84Qb 164
Silvermere Rd. SE6 —59Dc 106
Silver Pl. W1 —44Lb 82 (4C 198)
Silver Rd. W12 —45Za 80
Silver Rd. Grav —1G 136
Silversmiths Way. Wok —6F 188
Silver Spring Clo. Eri —51Dd 110
Silverstead La. W'ham —93Tc 184
Silverston Way. Stan —23La 38
Silver St. N18 —21Tb 43
Silver St. Chesh —2Rb 11
Silver St. Enf —13Tb 25
Silver St. Wal A —6Ec 12
Silverthorne Gdns. E4 —19Cc 26
Silverthorne Rd. SW8 —54Kb 104
Silverton Rd. W6 —51Za 102
Silvertown Av. Stanf —1M 93
Silvertown Way. E16 —44Hc 85
Silver Tree Clo. W on T —76W 140
Silvertree La. Gnfd —41Fa 78
Silver Trees. Brick —2Ba 5
Silver Wlk. SE16 —46Bc 84
Silver Way. Romf —27Dd 48
Silverwood Clo. Beck —66Cc 128
Silverwood Clo. Croy —81Bc 166
Silverwood Clo. Grays —45Ce 91
Silverwood Clo. N'wd —25S 36
Silvester Rd. SE22 —57Vb 105
Silvester St. SE1 —47Tb 83 (2F 207)
Silvester St. SW1 —47Tb 83
Silwood Clo. Asc —8B 116
Silwood Est. SE16 —49Yb 84
Silwood Rd. Asc —10D 116
Silwood St. SE16 —49Yb 84
Simla Clo. SE14 —51Ac 106
Simmil Rd. Clay —78Ga 142
Simmons Clo. N20 —19Gb 23
Simmons Clo. Slou —49C 74
Simmons La. E4 —19Fc 27
Simmons Pl. Grays —46Ce 91
Simmons Rd. SE18 —50Rc 86
Simmons Way. N20 —19Gb 23
Simmott Rd. E17 —25Zb 44
Simms Clo. Cars —75Gb 145
Simms Rd. SE1 —49Wb 83
Simnel Rd. SE12 —59Kc 107
Simon Clo. W11 —45Bb 81
Simon Ct. Bush —16Ca 19
Simonds Rd. E10 —33Cc 64
Simone Clo. Brom —67Nc 130
Simone Ct. SE26 —62Yb 128
Simone Dri. Kenl —88Sb 165
Simon Peter Ct. Enf —12Rb 25
Simons Clo. Ott —79E 138
Simons Ct. N16 —33Vb 63
Simons Wlk. E15 —36Fc 65
Simons Wlk. Egh —6N 117
Simplemarsh Ct. Add —77K 139
Simplemarsh Rd. Add —77J 139
Simpson Dri. W3 —44Ta 79
Simpson Ho. SE11 —50Pb 82 (7J 205)
Simpson Rd. Houn —58Ba 99
Simpson Rd. Rain —37Hd 68
Simpson Rd. Rich —63La 122
Simpson's Rd. E14 —45Dc 84
Simpsons Rd. Brom —69Jc 129
Simpson St. SW11 —54Gb 103
Simrose Ct. SW18 —57Cb 103
Sims Clo. Romf —28Hd 48
Sims Wlk. SE3 —56Hc 107
Sinclair Ct. Croy —75Ub 147
Sinclair Dri. Sutt —81Db 163
Sinclair Gdns. W14 —47Za 80
Sinclair Gro. NW11 —30Za 40
Sinclair Mans. W12 —47Za 80 (off Richmond Way)
Sinclair Rd. E4 —22Bc 44
Sinclair Rd. W14 —47Za 80
Sinclair Way. Dart —63Td 134
Sinclare Clo. Enf —11Vb 25
Sinderby Clo. Borwd —11Pa 21
Singapore Rd. W13 —46Ja 78
Singer St. EC2 —41Tb 83
Singles Cross La. Knock —86Yc 169
Single St. Berr G —87Rc 168
Singleton Clo. SW17 —66Hb 125
Singleton Clo. Croy —73Sb 147
Singleton Clo. Horn —35Hd 68
Singleton Rd. Dag —36Bd 67
Singleton Scarp. N12 —22Cb 41
Singlewell Rd. Grav —1D 136
Singret Pl. Cow —42L 75
Sinkins Ho. Chalv —6G 72
Sinnott Rd. E17 —25Zb 44
Sion Ct. Twic —60Ka 100
Sion Rd. Twic —60Ka 100
Sippets Ct. Ilf —32Tc 66
Sipson Clo. W Dray —51Q 98
Sipson La. W Dray & Hay —51Q 98
Sipson Rd. W Dray —48P 75
Sipson Way. W Dray —52Q 98
Sir Alexander Clo. W3 —46Va 80
Sir Alexander Rd. W3 —46Va 80
Sir Cyril Black Way. SW19 —66Cb 125
Sirdar Rd. N22 —27Rb 43
Sirdar Rd. W11 —45Za 80
Sirdar Rd. Mitc —65Jb 126
Sirdar Strand. Grav —4H 137
Sir Francis Way. Brtwd —19Xd 32
Sir Henry Floyd Ct. Stan —19Ka 20
Sir Henry Peekes Dri. Farn C —7E 52
Sirinham Point. SW8 —51Pb 104 (off Meadow Rd.)
Sirius Building. E1 —45Zb 84 (off Jardine Rd.)
Sir Oswald Stoll Foundation, The. (off Fulham Rd.) SW6 —52Db 103
Sirus Rd. N'wd —22W 36
Sir William Atkins Ho. Eps —86Ta 161
Sir William Powell's Almshouses. SW6 —54Ab 102
Sise La. EC4 —44Tb 83 (3F 201) (off Victoria St.)
Siskin Clo. Borwd —14Qa 21
Siskin Clo. Bush —14Aa 19
Siskin Ho. Wat —16T 18
Sisley Rd. Bark —39Uc 66
Sispara Gdns. SW18 —58Bb 103
Sissinghurst Rd. Croy —73Wb 147
Sister Mabel's Way. SE15 —52Wb 105
Sisters Av. SW11 —55Hb 103
Sistova Rd. SW12 —60Kb 104
Sisulu Pl. SW9 —55Qb 104
Sittingbourne Av. Enf —16Tb 25
Sitwell Gro. Stan —22Ha 38
Siverst Clo. N'holt —37Da 57
Siviter Way. Dag —38Dd 68
Siward Rd. N17 —25Tb 43
Siward Rd. SW17 —62Eb 125
Siward Rd. Brom —69Kc 129
Six Acres Est. N4 —33Qb 62
Six Bells La. Sev —98Ld 187
Sixth Av. E12 —35Pc 66
Sixth Av. W10 —41Ab 80
Sixth Av. Hay —46V 76
Sixth Av. Wat —7Z 5
Sixth Cross Rd. Twic —62Ea 122
Skardu Rd. NW2 —36Ab 60
Skarnings Ct. Wal A —5Jc 13
Skeena Hill. SW18 —59Ab 102
Skeet Hill La. Orp —75Ad 151
Skeffington Rd. E6 —39Pc 66
Skelbrook St. SW18 —61Eb 125
Skelgill Rd. SW15 —56Bb 103
Skelley Rd. E15 —38Hc 65
Skelton Clo. E8 —37Vb 63
Skelton Rd. E7 —37Jc 65
Skelton's La. E10 —31Dc 64
Skelwith Rd. W6 —51Ya 102
Skerne Rd. King T —67Ma 123
Skerries Ct. Langl —49C 74
Sketchley Gdns. SE16 —50Zb 84
Sketty Rd. Enf —13Vb 25
Skibbs La. Orp —78Ad 151
Skid Hill La. Warl —84Hc 167
Skidmore Way. Rick —18N 17
Skiers St. E15 —39Gc 65
Skiffington Clo. SW2 —60Qb 104
Skinner Ct. E2 —40Xb 63
Skinner Pl. SW1 —49Jb 82 (6H 203) (off Bourne St.)
Skinners La. EC4 —45Sb 83 (4E 200)
Skinners La. Asht —90Ma 161
Skinners La. Houn —53Da 99
Skinner's Row. SE10 —53Dc 106
Skinner St. EC1 —42Qb 82 (5A 194)
Skip La. Uxb —32N 55
Skippers Clo. Grnh —57Xd 112
Skipsey Av. E6 —41Pc 86
Skipton Dri. Hay —48S 76
Skipworth Rd. E9 —39Yb 64
Skomer Wlk. N1 —37Sb 63
Sky Bus. Cen. Egh —68E 118
Skydmore Path. Slou —1D 72
Skye Lodge. Slou —6J 73
Skylark Rd. Den —32E 54
Skylines. E14 —47Ec 84
Sky Peals Rd. Wfd G —24Fc 45
Skyport Dri. Harm —52M 97
Skyway Trading Est. Coln —55H 97
Sladebrook Rd. SE3 —55Mc 107
Slade Ct. New Bar —13Db 23
Slade Ct. Ott —79F 138
Slade Ct. Rad —7Ja 6
Sladedale Rd. SE18 —50Uc 86
Slade End. They B —8Uc 14
Slade Gdns. Eri —53Hd 110
Slade Grn. Rd. Eri —52Jd 110
Sladen Pl. E5 —35Xb 63
Slade Oak La. Ger X & Den —27D 34
Slade Rd. Ott —79F 138
Slades Clo. Enf —13Qb 24
Slades Dri. Chst —63Sc 130
Slades Gdns. Enf —12Qb 24
Slades Hill. Enf —13Qb 24
Slades Rise. Enf —13Qb 24
Slade, The. SE18 —51Uc 108
Slade Wlk. SE17 —51Sb 105
Slagrove Pl. SE13 —57Dc 106
Slaidburn St. SW10 —51Eb 103
Slaithwaite Rd. SE13 —56Ec 106
Slamanca St. SE1 & SE11 —49Pb 82
Slaney Pl. N7 —36Qb 62
Slaney Rd. Romf —29Gd 48
Slapleys. Wok —92A 172
Slatter. NW9 —24Va 40
Sleaford Clo. SE18 —50Qc 86
Sleaford Grn. Wat —20Z 19
Sleaford Ind. Est. SW8 —52Lb 104
Sleaford St. SW8 —52Lb 104
Sledmere Ct. Felt —60U 98
Sleepers Farm Rd. Grays —7D 92
Slewins Clo. Horn —29Ld 49
Slewins La. Horn —29Ld 49
Slewyn Ct. Wemb —34Sa 59
Slievemore Clo. SW4 —55Mb 104
Slindon Ct. N16 —34Vb 63
Slines New Rd. Wold —92Zb 182
Slines Oak Rd. Warl & Wold —91Cc 182
Slingsby Pl. WC2 —45Nb 82 (4F 199)
Slippers Pl. SE16 —48Xb 83
Slip, The. W'ham —98Sc 184
Sloane Av. SW3 —49Gb 81 (6D 202)
Sloane Ct. E. SW3 —50Jb 82 (7H 203)
Sloane Ct. W. SW3 —50Jb 82 (7H 203)
Sloane Gdns. SW1 —49Jb 82 (6H 203)
Sloane Gdns. Orp —76Sc 150
Sloane Sq. SW1 —49Hb 81 (6G 203)
Sloane Sq. Long —69Ae 135
Sloane St. SW1 —47Hb 81 (2G 203)
Sloane Ter. SW1 —49Jb 82 (5H 203)
Sloane Wlk. Croy —72Bc 148
Slocock Hill. St J —5F 188
Slocum Clo. SE28 —45Yc 87
Slough By-Pass. Slou —9H 73
Slough Ind. Est. Slou —4E 72
Slough La. NW9 —29Sa 39
Slough La. H'ley —97Sa 177
Slough Rd. Dat —10L 73
Slough Rd. Eton C & Slou —1H 95
Slough Rd. Iver —41E 74
Slough Trading Est. Slou —3D 72
Sly St. E1 —44Xb 83
Smallberry Av. Iswth —54Ha 100
Smallbrook M. W2 —44Fb 81 (3B 196)
Smalley Clo. N16 —34Vb 63
Smalley Rd. Est. N16 —34Vb 63 (off Smalley Clo.)
Small Grains. Fawk —76Xd 154
Smallholdings Rd. Eps —86Ya 162 (in two parts)
Smallwood Rd. SW17 —63Fb 125
Smarden Clo. Belv —50Cd 88
Smarden Gro. SE9 —63Pc 130
Smart Clo. Romf —25Kd 49
Smart's Heath La. Wok —10D 188
Smart's Heath Rd. Wok —10C 188
Smart's La. Lou —14Mc 27
Smart's Pl. WC2 —44Nb 82 (2G 199)
Smarts Rd. Grav —1E 136
Smart St. E2 —41Zb 84
Smeaton Clo. Wal A —4Gc 13
Smeaton Ct. SE1 —48Sb 83 (4D 206)
Smeaton Rd. SW18 —59Cb 103
Smeaton Rd. Wfd G —22Pc 46
Smeaton St. E1 —46Xb 83
Smedley St. SW8 & SW4 —54Mb 104
Smeed Rd. E3 —38Cc 64
Smiles Pl. SE13 —54Ec 106
Smitham Bottom La. Purl —83Lb 164
Smitham Downs Rd. Purl —85Mb 164
Smith Clo. SE16 —46Zb 84
Smith Ct. Sheer —85F 156
Smithfield St. EC1 —43Rb 83 (1B 200)
Smith Hill. Bren —51Na 101
Smithies Ct. E15 —36Ec 64
Smithies Rd. SE2 —49Xc 87
Smith's Ct. W1 —45Mb 82 (4D 198) (off Gt. Windmill St.)
Smith's La. Wind —4C 94
Smithson Rd. N17 —25Tb 43
Smiths Point. E13 —39Jc 65 (off Brooks Rd.)
Smith Sq. SW1 —48Nb 82 (4F 205)
Smith St. SW3 —50Hb 81 (7F 203)
Smith St. Surb —72Pa 143
Smith St. Wat —14Y 19
Smith's Yd. SW18 —61Eb 125
Smith Ter. SW3 —50Hb 81 (7F 203)
Smithwood Clo. SW19 —60Ab 102
Smithy Clo. Tad —98Bb 179
Smithy La. Tad —99Bb 179
Smithy St. E1 —43Yb 84
Smock Wlk. Croy —72Sb 147
Smoothfield. Houn —56Ca 99
Smugglers Wlk. Grnh —57Xd 112
Smugglers Way. SW18 —56Db 103
Smug Oak Grn. Bus. Cen. Brick —2Da 5
Smug Oak La. Brick —2Da 5
Smyrk's Rd. SE17 —50Ub 83 (7J 207)
Smyrna Rd. NW6 —38Cb 61
Smythe Rd. S at H —67Qd 133
Smythe St. E14 —45Dc 84
Snag La. Cud —83Tc 168
Snakes Hill. N'side —12Sd 32
Snakes La. Barn —13Kb 24
Snakes La. E. Wfd G —23Lc 45
Snakes La. W. Wfd G —22Jc 45
Snape Spur. Slou —4J 73
Snaresbrook Dri. Stan —21Ma 39
Snaresbrook Hall. E18 —28Jc 45
Snaresbrook Rd. E11 —28Gc 45
Snarsgate St. W10 —43Ya 80
Snatts Hill. Oxt —100Hc 183
Sneath Av. NW11 —31Bb 61
Snelgar Rd. Wok —90A 156
Snelling Av. N'fleet —1A 136
Snellings Rd. W on T —78Y 141
Snells Pk. N18 —23Vb 43
Sneyd Rd. NW2 —35Ya 60
Snodland Clo. Orp —82Qc 168
Snowbury Rd. SW6 —54Db 103
Snowden Av. Uxb —40R 56
Snowden Dri. NW9 —30Ua 40
Snowden St. EC2 —43Ub 83 (7H 195)
Snowdon Clo. Wind —6B 94
Snowdon Cres. Hay —48S 76
Snowdon Rd. Houn —58S 98
Snowdon St. EC2 —42Ub 83
Snowdown Clo. SE20 —67Zb 128
Snowdrop Clo. Hamp —65Ca 121
Snowdrop Path. Romf —24Md 49
Snow Hill. EC1 —43Rb 83 (1B 200)
Snow Hill Ct. EC1 —44Rb 83 (2C 200)
Snowsfields. SE1 —47Tb 83 (1G 207)
Snowshill Rd. E12 —36Nc 66
Snowy Fielder Waye. Iswth —54Ka 100
Soames St. SE15 —55Vb 105
Soames Wlk. N Mald —67Ua 124
Socket La. Hayes —72Kc 149
Soham Rd. Enf —9Bc 12
Soho Sq. W1 —44Mb 82 (2D 198)
Soho St. W1 —44Mb 82 (2D 198)
Solar Ct. N3 —24Db 41
Solar Ct. Wat —15V 18
Soldene Ct. N7 —37Pb 62 (off Georges Rd.)
Solebay St. E1 —42Ac 84
Solecote. Bookh —97Ca 175
Sole Farm Av. Bookh —97Ba 175
Sole Farm Clo. Bookh —96Ba 175
Sole Farm Rd. Bookh —97Ba 175
Solefields. Sev —99Ld 187 (off Solefields Rd.)
Solefields Rd. Sev —100Kd 187
Solent Rd. NW6 —36Cb 61
Solent Rd. Houn —58P 97
Soleoak Dri. Sev —99Kd 187
Solesbridge Clo. Chor —13H 17
Solesbridge La. Rick —13H 17
Sole St. Grav —10F 136
Soley M. WC1 —41Qb 82 (3K 193)
Solid La. Dodd —11Vd 32
Solna Av. SW15 —57Ya 102
Solna Rd. N21 —18Tb 25
Solomon's Hill. Rick —17M 17
Solomon's Pas. SE15 —56Xb 105
Soloms Ct. Rd. Bans —89Fb 163
Solon New Rd. SW4 —56Nb 104
Solon New Rd. Est. SW4 —56Nb 104
Solon Rd. SW2 —56Nb 104
Solway. E Til —8L 93
Solway Clo. E8 —37Vb 63 (off Queensbridge Rd.)
Solway Clo. Houn —55Aa 99
Solway Rd. N22 —25Rb 43
Solway Rd. SE22 —56Wb 105
Somaford Gro. Barn —16Fb 23
Somali Rd. NW2 —36Bb 61
Somerby Rd. Bark —38Tc 66
Somercoates Clo. Barn —13Gb 23
Somer Ct. SW6 —51Cb 103 (off Anselm Rd.)
Somerden Rd. Orp —73Zc 151
Somerfield Clo. Tad —91Ab 178
Somerfield Ho. SE8 —50Zb 84
Somerfield Rd. N4 —33Rb 63
Somerford Clo. Pinn —28W 36
Somerford Gro. N16 —35Vb 63
Somerford Gro. N17 —24Wb 43 (in two parts)
Somerford Gro. Est. N16 —35Vb 63
Somerford St. E1 —42Xb 83
Somerford Way. SE16 —47Ac 84
Somerhill Av. Sidc —59Xc 109
Somerhill Rd. Well —54Xc 109
Somerhill Way. Rick —67Jb 126
Somerleyton Pas. SW9 —56Rb 105
Somerleyton Rd. SW9 —56Qb 104
Somersby Gdns. Ilf —29Pc 46
Somers Clo. NW1 —40Mb 62 (1D 192)
Somers Cres. W2 —44Gb 81 (3D 196)
Somerset Av. SW20 —68Xa 124
Somerset Av. Chess —77Ma 143
Somerset Av. Well —56Vc 109
Somerset Clo. N17 —26Tb 43
Somerset Clo. Eps —81Ta 161
Somerset Clo. N Mald —72Ua 144
Somerset Clo. W on T —78X 141
Somerset Clo. Wfd G —25Jc 45
Somerset Est. SW11 —53Fb 103
Somerset Gdns. N6 —31Jb 62
Somerset Gdns. N17 —24Ub 43
Somerset Gdns. SE13 —54Dc 106
Somerset Gdns. SW16 —69Pb 126
Somerset Gdns. Horn —32Qd 69
Somerset Gdns. Tedd —64Ga 122
Somerset Lodge. Bren —51Ma 101
Somerset Rd. E17 —30Cc 44
Somerset Rd. N17 —27Vb 43
Somerset Rd. N18 —22Vb 43
Somerset Rd. NW4 —28Ya 40
Somerset Rd. SW19 —62Za 124
Somerset Rd. W4 —48Ta 79
Somerset Rd. W13 —46Ka 78
Somerset Rd. Barn —15Db 23
Somerset Rd. Bren —51La 100
Somerset Rd. Dart —58Kd 111
Somerset Rd. Enf —10Cc 12
Somerset Rd. Harr —30Ea 38
Somerset Rd. King T —68Pa 123
Somerset Rd. Linf —7J 93
Somerset Rd. Orp —73Wc 151
Somerset Rd. S'hall —43Ba 77
Somerset Rd. Tedd —64Ga 122
Somerset Sq. W14 —47Ab 80
Somerset Way. Iver —47H 75
Somerset Waye. Houn —51Aa 99
Somersham Rd. Bexh —54Ad 109
Somers M. W2 —44Gb 81 (3D 196)
Somers Pl. SW2 —59Pb 104
Somers Rd. E17 —28Bc 44
Somers Rd. SW2 —58Pb 104
Somers Way. Bush —17Ea 20
Somerton Av. Rich —55Ra 101
Somerton Clo. Purl —88Qb 164
Somerton Rd. NW2 —34Ab 60
Somerton Rd. SE15 —56Xb 105
Somertrees Av. SE12 —61Kc 129
Somervell Rd. Harr —36Ba 57
Somerville Rd. SE20 —66Zb 128
Somerville Rd. Cob —86Ca 159
Somerville Rd. Dart —58Pd 111
Somerville Rd. Eton —10G 72
Somerville Rd. Romf —30Yc 47
Sonderburg Rd. N7 —33Pb 62
Sondes St. SE17 —51Tb 105
Sonia Clo. Wat —17Y 19
Sonia Ct. Edgw —24Pa 39
Sonia Ct. Harr —30Ha 38
Sonia Gdns. N12 —21Eb 41
Sonia Gdns. NW10 —35Va 60
Sonia Gdns. Houn —52Ca 99
Sonnet Wlk. Big H —90Kc 167
Sonning Gdns. Hamp —65Aa 121
Sonning Rd. SE25 —72Wb 147
Sontan Ct. Twic —60Fa 100
Soper Clo. E4 —22Bc 44
Sophia Clo. N7 —37Pb 62
Sophia Rd. E10 —32Dc 64
Sophia Rd. E16 —44Kc 85
Sopwith. NW9 —24Va 40
Sopwith Av. Chess —78Na 143
Sopwith Clo. Big H —88Mc 167
Sopwith Clo. King T —64Pa 123
Sopwith Dri. Wey —83N 157
Sopwith Rd. Houn —52Y 99
Sopwith Way. King T —67Na 123
Sorbie Clo. Wey —79T 140
Sorrel Bank. Croy —81Ac 166
Sorrel Clo. SE28 —46Wc 87
Sorrel Ct. Grays —51Fe 113
Sorrel Gdns. E6 —43Nc 86
Sorrel La. E14 —44Fc 85
Sorrell Clo. SE14 —52Ac 106
Sorrell Clo. SW9 —54Qb 104
Sorrells, The. Stanf —1P 93

Sorrel Wlk.—Spire Clo.

Sorrel Wlk. Romf —27Hd 48
Sorrel Way. Grav —3A 136
Sorrento Rd. Sutt —76Db 145
Sospel Ct. Farn R —10G 52
Sotheby Rd. N5 —34Sb 63
Sotheran Clo. E8 —39Wb 63
Sotheron Rd. SW6 —52Db 103
Sotheron Rd. Wat —13Y 19
Soudan Rd. SW11 —53Hb 103
Souldern Rd. W14 —48Za 80
Souldern St. Wat —15X 19
Sounds Lodge. Swan —72Ed 152
S. Access Rd. E17 —31Ac 64
South Acre. NW9 —26Va 40
Southacre Way. Pinn —25Y 37
S. Africa Rd. W12 —46Xa 80
Southall Ct. S'hall —45Ba 77
Southall Enterprise Cen. S'hall —47Ca 77
Southall La. Houn & S'hall —51X 99
Southall Pl. SE1 —47Tb 83 (2F 207)
Southall Way. Brtwd —21Vd 50
Southam Ho. Add —78K 139
(off Addlestone Pk.)
Southampton Bldgs. WC2 —43Qb 82 (1K 199)
Southampton Gdns. Mitc —71Nb 146
Southampton Pl. WC1 —43Nb 82 (1G 199)
Southampton Rd. NW5 —36Hb 61
Southampton Rd. H'row A —58N 97
Southampton Row. WC1 —43Nb 82 (7G 193)
Southampton St. WC2 —45Nb 82 (4G 199)
Southampton Way. SE5 —52Tb 105
Southam St. W10 —42Ab 80
South App. N'wd —20T 18
S. Ash Rd. Ash —80Zd 155
S. Audley St. W1 —45Jb 82 (5J 197)
South Av. E4 —17Dc 26
South Av. N2 —28Db 41
South Av. Cars —80Jb 146
South Av. Egh —65E 118
South Av. Rich —54Qa 101
South Av. S'hall —45Ba 77
South Av. Wey —82Q 158
South Av. W Vill —82U 158
South Av. Gdns. S'hall —45Ba 77
South Bank. Chst —63Sc 130
South Bank. Surb —72Na 143
Southbank. Th Dit —73Ka 142
South Bank. W'ham —98Tc 184
S. Bank Ter. Surb —72Na 143
S. Birkbeck Rd. E11 —34Fc 65
S. Black Lion La. W6 —50Wa 80
S. Bolton Gdns. SW5 —50Eb 81
S. Border, The. Purl —83Mb 164
Southborough Clo. Surb —74Ma 143
Southborough La. Brom —71Nc 150
Southborough Rd. E9 —39Zb 64
Southborough Rd. Brom —69Nc 130
Southborough Rd. Surb —74Na 143
S. Boundary Rd. E12 —34Pc 66
Southbourne. Brom —73Jc 149
Southbourne Av. NW9 —26Sa 39
Southbourne Clo. Pinn —31Aa 57
Southbourne Ct. NW9 —26Sa 39
Southbourne Cres. NW4 —28Ab 40
Southbourne Gdns. SE12 —57Kc 107
Southbourne Gdns. Ilf —36Sc 66
Southbourne Gdns. Ruis —32X 57
Southbridge Pl. Croy —77Sb 147
Southbridge Rd. Croy —77Sb 147
Southbridge Way. S'hall —47Aa 77
Southbrook M. SE12 —58Hc 107
Southbrook Rd. SE12 —58Hc 107
Southbrook Rd. SW16 —67Nb 126
Southbury Av. Enf —14Wb 25
Southbury Clo. Horn —36Md 69
Southbury Rd. Enf —13Ub 25
S. Carriage Dri. SW7 & SW1 —47Fb 81 (2C 202)
Southchurch Ct. E6 —40Pc 66
(off High St. S.)
Southchurch Rd. E6 —40Pc 66
Southcliffe Dri. Ger X —22A 34
South Clo. N6 —30Kb 42
South Clo. Barn —13Bb 23
South Clo. Bexh —56Zc 109
South Clo. Dag —39Cd 68
South Clo. Mord —72Cb 145
South Clo. Pinn —31Ba 57
South Clo. Slou —5B 72
South Clo. Twic —62Ca 121
South Clo. W Dray —48P 75
South Clo. Wok —4F 188
South Clo. Grn. Red —100Kb 180
S. Colonnade. E14 —46Cc 84
Southcombe St. W14 —49Ab 80
S. Common Rd. Uxb —37N 55
Southcote. Wok —3G 188
Southcote Av. Felt —61W 120
Southcote Av. Surb —73Ra 143
Southcote Rise. Ruis —31T 56
Southcote Rd. E17 —29Zb 44
Southcote Rd. N19 —35Lb 62
Southcote Rd. SE25 —71Xb 147
Southcote Rd. S Croy —82Ub 165
S. Cottage Dri. Chor —15H 17
S. Cottage Gdns. Chor —15H 17
S. Countess Rd. E17 —27Bc 44
South Cres. E16 —42Fc 85
(in two parts)
South Cres. WC1 —43Mb 82 (1D 198)
Southcroft. Slou —2F 72
Southcroft Av. Well —55Uc 108
Southcroft Av. W Wick —75Ec 148
Southcroft Rd. SW17 & SW16 —65Jb 126
Southcroft Rd. Orp —76Uc 150
S. Cross Rd. Ilf —29Sc 46
S. Croxted Rd. SE21 —62Tb 127
Southdale. Chig —23Tc 46
Southdean Gdns. SW19 —61Bb 125
South Dene. NW7 —20Ta 21
Southdene. Hals —85Bd 169
Southdene Ct. N11 —20Kb 24
Southdown. N7 —37Nb 62
Southdown Av. W7 —48Ja 78
Southdown Cres. Harr —32Ea 58
Southdown Cres. Ilf —29Uc 46
Southdown Dri. SW20 —66Za 124
Southdown Rd. SW20 —67Za 124
Southdown Rd. Cars —81Jb 164
Southdown Rd. Horn —31Kd 69
Southdown Rd. W on T —77Aa 141
Southdown Rd. Wold —94Bc 182
South Dri. E12 —34Nc 66
South Dri. Bans —85Gb 163
South Dri. Coul —87Mb 164
South Dri. Cuff —2Nb 10
South Dri. Orp —78Uc 150
South Dri. Romf —27Ld 49
South Dri. Ruis —32U 56
South Dri. Sutt —82Ab 162
South Dri. War —21Zd 51
S. Ealing Rd. W5 —47Ma 79
S. Eastern Av. N9 —20Vb 25
S. Eaton Pl. SW1 —49Jb 82 (5J 203)
S. Eden Pk. Rd. Beck —72Dc 148
S. Edwardes Sq. W8 —48Bb 81
South End. W8 —48Db 81
South End. Bookh —98Da 175
South End. Croy —77Sb 147
Southend Arterial Rd. Romf & L War —26Md 49
S. End Clo. NW3 —35Gb 61
Southend Clo. SE9 —58Rc 108
Southend Clo. Uxb —42Q 76
Southend Cres. SE9 —58Rc 108
S. End Grn. NW3 —35Gb 61
Southend La. SE26 & SE6 —63Bc 128
Southend La. Wal A —6Kc 13
Southend Rd. E6 —38Pc 66
Southend Rd. E17 & E18 —25Fc 45
S. End Rd. NW3 —35Gb 61
Southend Rd. Beck —67Cc 128
Southend Rd. Grays —49Ee 91
S. End Rd. Rain & Horn —39Jd 68
Southend Rd. Stanf —1M 93
Southend Rd. Wfd G —26Lc 45
S. End Row. W8 —48Db 81
Southerby Av. Enf —14Wb 25
Southerland Clo. Wey —77S 140
Southern Av. SE25 —69Vb 127
Southern Av. Felt —60W 98
Southern Cotts. Stai —57J 97
Southern Dri. Lou —16Pc 28
Southerngate Way. SE14 —52Ac 106
Southern Gro. E3 —41Bc 84
Southernhay. Lou —14Mc 27
Southern Perimeter Rd. H'row A —57K 97
Southern Pl. Swan —70Fd 132
Southern Rd. E13 —40Kc 65
Southern Rd. N2 —28Hb 41
Southern Row. W10 —42Ab 80
Southerns La. Coul —97Fb 179
Southern St. N1 —40Pb 62 (1H 193)
Southern Way. Romf —30Cd 48
Southerton Rd. W6 —49Ya 80
S. Esk Rd. E7 —37Lc 65
Southey Ct. Bookh —96Da 175
Southey Rd. N15 —29Ub 43
Southey Rd. SW9 —53Qb 104
Southey Rd. SW19 —66Cb 125
Southey St. SE20 —66Zb 128
Southey Wlk. Til —3D 114
Southfield. Barn —16Za 22
Southfield Av. Wat —10Y 5
Southfield Clo. Dor —8A 72
Southfield Clo. Uxb —42Q 76
Southfield Cotts. W7 —47Ha 78
Southfield Gdns. Burn —3A 72
Southfield Gdns. Twic —63Ha 122
Southfield Pk. Harr —28Da 37
Southfield Pl. Wey —80R 140
Southfield Rd. N17 —26Ub 43
Southfield Rd. W4 —47Ta 79
Southfield Rd. Chst —69Wc 131
Southfield Rd. Enf —16Xb 25
Southfield Rd. Wal X —4Ac 12
Southfields. NW4 —27Xa 40
Southfields. E Mol —72Ga 142
Southfields. Swan —66Gd 132
Southfields Av. Ashf —65R 120
Southfields Ct. Sutt —75Cb 145
Southfields Pas. SW18 —58Cb 103
Southfields Rd. SW18 —58Cb 103
Southfields Rd. W King —80Vd 154
Southfields Rd. Wold —94Dc 182
Southfleet Av. Long —68De 135
Southfleet Rd. Bean —63Yd 134
Southfleet Rd. Grav —10B 114
Southfleet Rd. Orp —76Uc 150
Southfleet Rd. Swans —59Be 113
South Gdns. SW19 —66Fb 125
South Gdns. Wemb —33Qa 59
Southgate. Purf —49Sd 90
Southgate Av. Felt —63T 120
Southgate Cir. N14 —18Mb 24
Southgate Gro. N1 —38Tb 63
Southgate Ind. Est. N14 —17Lb 24
Southgate Rd. N1 —39Tb 63
Southgate Rd. Pot B —5Eb 9
S. Gipsy Rd. Well —55Zc 109
S. Glade, The. Bex —60Bd 109
South Grn. NW9 —25Ua 40
South Grn. Slou —5J 73
South Gro. E17 —29Ac 44
South Gro. N6 —32Jb 62
South Gro. N15 —29Tb 43
South Gro. Cher —72H 139
S. Hall Clo. F'ham —73Pd 153
S. Hall Dri. Rain —43Kd 89
S. Harrow Ind. Est. S Harr —33Ea 58
South Hill. Chst —65Pc 130
South Hill. Horn H —1J 93
(off Orsett Rd.)
S. Hill Av. S Harr & Harr —34Ea 58
S. Hill Cres. Horn H —1J 93
S. Hill Gro. Harr —35Ga 58
S. Hill Pk. NW3 —35Gb 61
S. Hill Pk. Gdns. NW3 —35Gb 61
(off S. Hill Pk.)
S. Hill Rd. Brom —69Gc 129
S. Hill Rd. Grav —10E 114
Southholme Clo. SE19 —67Ub 127
Southhill Ct. Hayes —71Hc 149
Southill La. Pinn —28X 37
Southill Rd. Chst —66Nc 130
Southill St. E14 —44Dc 84
S. Island Pl. SW9 —52Pb 104
S. Kensington Sta. Arc. SW7 —49Fb 81 (5C 202)
(off Pelham St.)
S. Kent Av. Grav —58Ee 113
S. Lambeth Pl. SW8 —51Nb 104
S. Lambeth Rd. SW8 —51Nb 104
Southland Rd. SE18 —52Vc 109
Southlands Av. Orp —77Tc 150
Southlands Clo. Coul —89Pb 164
Southlands Gro. Brom —69Nc 130
Southlands Rd. Brom —70Mc 129
Southlands Rd. Den —36H 55
Southland Way. Houn —57Fa 100
South La. King T —69Ma 123
South La. N Mald —70Ta 123
South La. W. N Mald —70Ta 123
Southlea Rd. Dat & Old Win —3M 95
S. Lodge. Twic —59Ea 100
S. Lodge Av. Mitc —70Nb 126
S. Lodge Cres. Enf —14Mb 24
(in two parts)
S. Lodge Dri. N14 —14Mb 24
S. Lodge Rd. W on T —81W 158
Southly Clo. Sutt —76Cb 145
South Mall. N9 —20Wb 25
South Mall. Stai —63H 119
South Mead. NW9 —25Va 40
South Mead. Eps —80Va 144
Southmead Cres. Chesh —2Ac 12
Southmead Dri. SW19 —60Ab 102
S. Meadow La. Eton —1G 94
S. Meadows. Wemb —36Pa 59
S. Molton La. W1 —44Kb 82 (3K 197)
S. Molton Rd. E16 —44Jc 85
S. Molton St. W1 —44Kb 82 (3K 197)
Southmont Rd. Esh —75Ga 142
Southmoor Way. E9 —37Bc 64
South Mt. N20 —19Eb 23
(off High Rd.)
S. Norwood Hill. SE19 & SE25 —68Ub 127
S. Oak Rd. SW16 —63Pb 126
Southold Rise. SE9 —62Pc 130
Southolme Clo. SE19 —67Ub 127
Southolm St. SW11 —53Kb 104
Southover. N12 —20Cb 23
Southover. Brom —64Jc 129
South Pde. SW3 —50Fb 81 (7C 202)
South Pde. W4 —49Ta 79
South Pde. Red —100Lb 180
South Pde. Wal A —5Ec 12
South Pk. Ger X —29B 34
South Pk. Sev —97Kd 187
S. Park Av. Chor —15H 17
South Pk. Ct. Beck —66Cc 128
S. Park Cres. SE6 —60Hc 107
South Pk. Cres. Ger X —28A 34
South Pk. Cres. Ilf —34Tc 66
South Pk. Dri. Bark & Ilf —36Uc 66
South Pk. Dri. Ger X —28A 34
South Pk. Gro. N Mald —70Sa 123
S. Park Hill Rd. S Croy —78Tb 147
S. Park M. SW6 —55Db 103
South Pk. Rd. SW19 —65Cb 125
South Pk. Rd. Ilf —34Tc 66
South Pk. Ter. Ilf —34Tc 66
S. Park View. Ger X —28B 34
S. Park Way. Ruis —37Y 57
S. Path. Wind —3G 94
South Pl. EC2 —43Tb 83 (1G 201)
South Pl. Enf —15Yb 26
South Pl. Surb —73Pa 143
South Pl. M. EC2 —43Tb 83 (1G 201)
Southport Rd. SE18 —49Tc 86
S. Quay Plaza. E14 —47Dc 84
South Ridge. Wey —82R 158
Southridge Pl. SW20 —66Za 124
S. Riding. Brick —2Ba 5
S. Rise. Cars —81Gb 163
South Rd. N9 —18Wb 25
South Rd. SE23 —61Zb 128
South Rd. SW19 —65Eb 125
South Rd. W5 —49Ma 79
South Rd. Chad —30Ad 47
South Rd. Chor —15E 16
South Rd. Edgw —25Ra 39
South Rd. Egh —5N 117
South Rd. Eri —52Hd 110
South Rd. Felt —64Z 121
South Rd. Hamp —65Aa 121
South Rd. L Hth —29Yc 47
South Rd. S'hall —47Ba 77
South Rd. S Ock —43Yd 90
South Rd. St G —81R 158
South Rd. Twic —62Fa 122
South Rd. W Dray —48Q 76
South Rd. Wey —78S 140
South Rd. Wok —3F 188
South Row. SE3 —54Hc 107
Southsea Av. Wat —14W 18
Southsea Ho. H Hill —22Md 49
(off Darlington Gdns.)
Southsea Rd. King T —70Na 123
S. Sea St. SE16 —48Bc 84
South Side. N15 —28Vb 43
South Side. W6 —48Va 80
Southside. Cher —69J 119
South Side. Ger X —27A 34
Southside Comn. SW19 —65Ya 124
Southspring. Sidc —59Tc 108
South Sq. NW11 —30Db 41
South Sq. WC1 —43Qb 82 (1K 199)
South St. W1 —46Jb 82 (6J 197)
South St. Brtwd —19Yd 32
South St. Brom —68Jc 129
South St. Enf —15Yb 26
South St. Eps —85Ta 161
South St. Grav —9D 114
South St. Iswth —55Ja 100
South St. Rain —40Ed 68
South St. Romf —29Gd 48
South St. Stai —64H 119
S. Tenter St. E1 —45Vb 83
South Ter. SW7 —49Gb 81 (5D 202)
South Ter. Surb —72Na 143
Southvale. SE19 —65Ub 127
South Vale. Harr —35Ga 58
Southvale Rd. SE3 —54Gc 107
Southview. Brom —68Lc 129
South View. Ors —3D 92
Southview Av. NW10 —36Va 60
S. View Av. Til —3C 114
S. View Clo. Bex —58Bd 109
S. View Clo. Swan —70Jd 132
S. View Ct. SE19 —66Sb 127
S. View Ct. Wok —90A 156
Southview Cres. Ilf —30Rc 46
S. View Dri. E18 —27Kc 45
S. View Dri. Upm —34Qd 69
Southview Gdns. Wall —80Lb 146
S. View Rd. N8 —27Mb 42
S. View Rd. Asht —91Ma 177
Southview Rd. Brom —63Fc 129
S. View Rd. Dart —62Md 133
S. View Rd. Grays —51Yd 112
S. View Rd. Lou —16Pc 28
S. View Rd. Pinn —23X 37
Southview Rd. Warl —91Wb 181
Southview Rd. Wold —96Dc 182
Southviews. S Croy —81Zb 166
South Vs. NW1 —37Mb 62
Southville. SW8 —53Mb 104
Southville Clo. Eps —81Ta 161
Southville Clo. Felt —60U 98
Southville Cres. Felt —60U 98
Southville Rd. Felt —60U 98
Southville Rd. Th Dit —73Ka 142
South Wlk. Hay —43T 76
South Wlk. W Wick —76Gc 149
Southwark Bri. SE1 & EC4 —45Sb 83 (5E 200)
Southwark Bri. Office Village. SE1 —46Sb 83 (7E 200)
Southwark Bri. Rd. SE1 —48Rb 83 (3C 206)
Southwark Gro. SE1 —46Sb 83 (7D 200)
Southwark Ho. Borwd —12Qa 21
(off Stratfield Rd.)
Southwark Pk. Rd. SE16 —49Vb 83 (5K 207)
Southwark Pk. Rd. Est. SE15 —49Vb 83
Southwark Pk. Rd. Est. SE16 —49Vb 83 (5K 207)
Southwark Pl. Brom —69Pc 130
Southwark St. SE1 —46Rb 83 (6B 200)
Southwater Clo. E14 —44Bc 84
Southwater Clo. Beck —66Dc 128
South Way. N9 —19Yb 26
South Way. N11 —23Lb 42
Southway. N20 —19Cb 23
Southway. NW11 —30Db 41
Southway. SW20 —70Ya 124
South Way. Brom —73Jc 149
South Way. Cars —82Fb 163
South Way. Croy —76Ac 148
South Way. Harr —28Ca 37
South Way. K Lan & Abb L —5T 4
Southway. Wall —77Lb 146
South Way. Wal A —9Dc 12
South Way. Wemb —36Pa 59
S. Weald Dri. Wal A —5Fc 13
S. Weald Rd. Brtwd —20Wd 32
Southwell Av. N'holt —37Ca 57
Southwell Gdns. SW7 —48Eb 81 (5A 202)
Southwell Gro. Rd. E11 —33Gc 65
Southwell Rd. SE5 —55Sb 105
Southwell Rd. Croy —72Qb 146
Southwell Rd. Kent —30Ma 39
S. Western Rd. Twic —58Ja 100
S. W. India Dock Entrance. E14 —47Ec 84
Southwest Rd. E11 —32Fc 65
S. Wharf Rd. W2 —44Fb 81 (2B 196)
Southwick M. W2 —44Fb 81 (2C 196)
Southwick Pl. W2 —44Gb 81 (3D 196)
Southwick St. W2 —44Gb 81 (2D 196)
Southwold Dri. Bark —36Wc 67
Southwold Rd. E5 —33Xb 63
Southwold Rd. Bex —58Dd 110
Southwold Rd. Wat —9Y 5
Southwold Spur. Slou —47E 74
Southwood Av. N6 —31Kb 62
Southwood Av. Coul —87Lb 164
Southwood Av. King T —67Sa 123
Southwood Av. Knap —6A 188
Southwood Av. Ott —80E 138
Southwood Clo. Brom —70Pc 130
Southwood Clo. Wor Pk —74Za 144
Southwood Ct. NW11 —29Db 41
Southwood Dri. Surb —73Sa 143
S. Woodford to Barking Relief Rd. E11 & E12 —29Mc 45
Southwood Gdns. Esh —76Ja 142
Southwood Gdns. Ilf —28Rc 46
Southwood Hall. N6 —30Kb 42
Southwood Heights. N6 —31Kb 62
Southwood La. N6 —32Jb 62
Southwood Lawn Rd. N6 —31Jb 62
Southwood Mans. N6 —30Jb 42
(off Southwood La.)
Southwood Pk. N6 —31Jb 62
Southwood Rd. SE9 —61Rc 130
Southwood Rd. SE28 —46Xc 87
Southwood Smith St. N1 —39Rb 63 (1B 194)
(off Old Royal Free Sq.)
S. Worple Av. SW14 —55Ua 102
S. Worple Way. SW14 —55Ta 101
Southwyck Ho. SW9 —56Rb 105
Sovereign Bus. Cen. Enf —13Bc 26
Sovereign Clo. E1 —45Xb 83
Sovereign Clo. W5 —43La 78
Sovereign Clo. Ruis —32U 56
Sovereign Ct. Houn —55Ca 99
Sovereign Ct. S at H —67Qd 133
(off Barton Rd.)
Sovereign Ct. Wat —14W 18
Sovereign Ct. W Mol —70Ba 121
Sovereign Gro. Wemb —34Ma 59
Sovereign M. E2 —40Vb 63 (1K 195)
Sovereign Pk. NW10 —42Ra 79
Sovereign Pk. Trading Est. NW10 —42Ra 79
Sowerby Clo. SE9 —57Pc 108
Sowrey Av. Rain —37Hd 68
Soyer Ct. Wok —6B 188
Space Waye. Felt —57W 98
Spackmans Way. Slou —8G 72
Spa Clo. SE19 —67Ub 127
Spa Ct. SW16 —63Pb 126
Spa Dri. Eps —86Qa 161
Spafield St. EC1 —42Qb 82 (5K 193)
Spa Grn. Est. EC1 —41Rb 83 (3B 194)
(off St John St.)
Spa Hill. SE19 —67Tb 127
Spalding Rd. NW4 —31Ya 60
Spalding Rd. SW17 —64Kb 126
Spalt Clo. Hut —19De 33
Spanby Rd. E3 —42Cc 84
Spaniards Clo. NW11 —32Fb 61
Spaniards End. NW3 —32Eb 61
Spaniards Rd. NW3 —33Eb 61
Spanish Pl. W1 —44Jb 82 (2J 197)
Spanish Rd. SW18 —57Fb 103
Spanswick Lodge. N15 —28Rb 43
Spareleaze Hill. Lou —14Pc 28
Sparepenny La. Eyns —75Md 153
Sparkbridge Rd. Harr —28Ga 38
Sparkes. Sidc —64Xc 131
Sparke Ter. E16 —44Hc 85
(off Clarkson Rd.)
Sparks Clo. W3 —44Ta 79
Sparks Clo. Hamp —65Aa 121
Spa Rd. SE16 —48Vb 83 (4K 207)
Sparrick's Row. SE1 —47Tb 83 (1G 207)
Sparrow Clo. Hamp —65Aa 121
Sparrow Dri. Orp —74Sc 150
Sparrow Farm Dri. Felt —59Y 99
Sparrow Farm Rd. Eps —77Wa 144
Sparrow Grn. Dag —34Dd 68
Sparrows Herne. Bush —17Da 19
Sparrows La. SE9 —59Sc 108
Sparrows Way. Bush —17Ea 20
Sparsholt Clo. Bark —39Uc 66
(off Sparsholt Rd.)
Sparsholt Rd. N19 —32Nb 62
Sparsholt Rd. Bark —39Uc 66
Sparta St. SE10 —53Ec 106
Speaker's Corner. W2 —45Hb 81 (4G 197)
Speakers Ct. Croy —74Tb 147
Spearman St. SE18 —51Qc 108
Spear M. SW5 —49Cb 81
Spearpoint Gdns. Ilf —29Vc 47
Spears Rd. N19 —32Nb 62
Speart La. Houn —52Aa 99
Spedan Clo. NW3 —34Eb 61
Speedgate Hill. Fawk —75Wd 154
Speed Highwalk. EC2 —43Sb 83 (7E 194)
(off Barbican)
Speed Ho. EC2 —43Tb 83 (7F 195)
(off Barbican)
Speedwell Ct. Grays —2A 114
Speedwell Ho. N12 —15Db 23
Speedwell St. SE8 —52Cc 106
Speedy Pl. WC1 —41Nb 82 (4F 193)
(off Cromer St.)
Speer Rd. Th Dit —72Ha 142
Speirs Clo. N Mald —72Va 144
Speke Hill. SE9 —62Pc 130
Speke Rd. T Hth —68Tb 127
Speldhurst Clo. Brom —71Jc 149
Speldhurst Rd. E9 —38Zb 64
Speldhurst Rd. W4 —48Ta 79
Spellbrook Wlk. N1 —39Sb 63
Spelman St. E1 —43Wb 83
Spelthorne Gro. Sun —66V 120
Spelthorne La. Ashf —67S 120
Spenbrook. Chig —20Rc 28
Spence Av. Byfl —86P 157
Spence Clo. SE16 —47Bc 84
Spencer Av. N13 —23Pb 42
Spencer Av. Hay —43W 76
Spencer Clo. N3 —26Cb 41
Spencer Clo. NW10 —41Pa 79
Spencer Clo. Epp —1Xc 15
Spencer Clo. Eps —91Ua 178
Spencer Clo. Orp —75Uc 150
Spencer Clo. Uxb —41L 75
Spencer Clo. Wok —85F 156
Spencer Clo. Wfd G —22Lc 45
Spencer Dri. N2 —30Eb 41
Spencer Gdns. SE9 —57Pc 108
Spencer Gdns. SW14 —57Sa 101
Spencer Gdns. Egh —4P 117
Spencer Hill. SW19 —65Ab 124
Spencer Ho. NW4 —29Xa 40
Spencer M. W6 —51Ab 102
Spencer Pk. SW18 —57Fb 103
Spencer Pk. E Mol —71Ea 142
Spencer Pas. E2 —40Xb 63
(off Coate St.)
Spencer Pl. Croy —73Tb 147
Spencer Rise. NW5 —35Kb 62
Spencer Rd. E6 —39Mc 65
Spencer Rd. E17 —26Ec 44
Spencer Rd. N8 —29Pb 42
(in two parts)
Spencer Rd. N11 —21Kb 42
Spencer Rd. N17 —25Wb 43
Spencer Rd. SW18 —56Fb 103
Spencer Rd. SW20 —67Xa 124
Spencer Rd. W3 —46Sa 79
Spencer Rd. W4 —52Sa 101
Spencer Rd. Brom —66Hc 129
Spencer Rd. Cat —93Tb 181
Spencer Rd. Cob —87X 159
Spencer Rd. E Mol —70Ea 122
Spencer Rd. Harr —26Ga 38
Spencer Rd. Ilf —32Vc 67
Spencer Rd. Iswth —53Ea 100
Spencer Rd. Mitc —69Jb 126
Spencer Rd. Mit J —73Jb 146
Spencer Rd. Rain —41Fd 88
Spencer Rd. Slou —48B 74
Spencer Rd. S Croy —78Ub 147
Spencer Rd. Twic —62Ga 122
Spencer Rd. Wemb —33La 58
Spencer St. EC1 —41Rb 83 (4B 194)
Spencer St. Grav —9C 114
Spencer St. S'hall —47Z 77
Spencer Wlk. NW3 —35Eb 61
(off Hampstead High St.)
Spencer Wlk. SW15 —56Za 102
Spencer Wlk. Rick —15L 17
Spencer Wlk. Til —4D 114
Spenser Av. Wey —80Q 140
Spenser Cres. Upm —31Sd 70
Spenser Gro. N16 —36Ub 63
Spenser M. SE21 —61Tb 127
Spenser Rd. SE24 —57Rb 105
Spenser St. SW1 —48Lb 82 (3C 204)
Spensley Wlk. N16 —34Tb 63
Speranza St. SE18 —50Vc 87
Sperling Rd. N17 —26Ub 43
Spert St. E14 —45Ac 84
Spey Side. N14 —16Lb 24
Spey St. E14 —43Ec 84
Spey Way. Romf —24Gd 48
Spezia Rd. NW10 —40Wa 60
Spice Ct. E1 —45Wb 83
Spicer Clo. SW9 —54Rb 105
Spicer Clo. W on T —72Y 141
Spicer Ct. Enf —13Ub 25
Spicers Field. Oxs —85Fa 160
Spice's Yd. Croy —77Sb 147
Spielman Rd. Dart —56Pd 111
Spigurnell Rd. N17 —25Tb 43
Spikes Bri. Rd. S'hall —44Aa 77
Spilsby Clo. NW9 —25Ua 40
Spilsby Rd. Romf —24Md 49
Spindles. Til —2C 114
Spindlewood Gdns. Croy —77Ub 147
Spindlewoods. Tad —94Xa 178
Spindrift Av. E14 —49Cc 84
Spinel Clo. SE18 —50Vc 87
Spingate Clo. Horn —36Md 69
Spinnells Rd. Harr —32Ba 57
Spinners Wlk. Wind —3G 94
Spinney. Slou —6F 72
Spinney Clo. Cob —83Ca 159
Spinney Clo. N Mald —71Ua 144
Spinney Clo. Rain —40Gd 68
Spinney Clo. W Dray —45N 75
Spinney Croft. Oxs —87Fa 160
Spinney Dri. Felt —59S 98
Spinney Gdns. SE19 —64Vb 127
Spinney Gdns. Dag —36Ad 67
Spinney Hill. Add —78G 138
Spinney La. Wink —10A 94
Spinney Oak. Brom —68Nc 130
Spinneys, The. Brom —67Pc 130
Spinney, The. N21 —17Qb 24
Spinney, The. SW13 —51Xa 102
Spinney, The. SW16 —62Lb 126
Spinney, The. Asc —10C 116
Spinney, The. Barn —12Db 23
Spinney, The. Bookh —96Da 175
Spinney, The. Chesh —2Xb 11
Spinney, The. Eps —85Ua 162
(Epsom)
Spinney, The. Eps —91Xa 178
(Tattenham Corner)
Spinney, The. Esh —84Ea 160
Spinney, The. Hut —16Ee 33
Spinney, The. Lou —14Rc 28
Spinney, The. Ors —2C 92
Spinney, The. Pot B —3Fb 9
Spinney, The. Purl —83Rb 165
Spinney, The. Send —99L 173
Spinney, The. Sidc —64Ad 131
Spinney, The. Stan —21Na 39
Spinney, The. Sun —67W 120
Spinney, The. Sutt —77Ya 144
Spinney, The. Swan —68Gd 132
Spinney, The. Wat —11W 18
Spinney, The. Wemb —34Ja 58
Spinney Way. Cud —83Tc 168
Spire Clo. Grav —10D 114

Spires Shopping Cen., The—Staplefield Clo.

Spires Shopping Cen., The. Barn —13Ab 22
Spires, The. Dart —61Md 133
Spirit Quay. E1 —46Wb 83
Spital La. Brtwd —20Vd 32
Spital Sq. E1 —43Ub 83 (7J 195)
Spital St. E1 —43Wb 83
Spital St. Dart —58Md 111
Spital Yd. E1 —43Ub 83 (7J 195)
Spitfire Rd. Houn —58S 98
Spitfire Way. Houn —50Y 77
Spode Wlk. NW6 —36Db 61
Spondon Rd. N15 —28Wb 43
Spoonbill Way. Hay —43Z 77
Spooner Ho. Houn —51Ca 99
Spooners M. W3 —46Ta 79
Spooner Wlk. Wall —78Nb 146
Spores Rd. Cuff —1Pb 10
Sportsbank St. SE6 —59Ec 106
Spottons Gro. N17 —25Sb 43
Spout Hill. Croy —78Cc 148
Spout La. Stai —56J 97
Spout La. N. Stai —56K 97
Spratt Hall Rd. E11 —30Jc 45
Spratts All. Ott —79G 138
Spratts La. Ott —79G 138
Spray La. Twic —58Ga 100
Spray St. SE18 —49Rc 86
Spreighton Rd. W Mol —70Da 121
Spriggs Ct. Epp —1Wc 15
(off Palmers Hill)
Sprimont Pl. SW3 —49Hb 81 (7F 203)
Springall St. SE15 —52Xb 105
Springate Field. Slou —47A 74
Spring Av. Egh —65A 118
Spring Bank. N21 —16Pb 24
Springbank Av. Horn —36Ld 69
Springbank Rd. SE13 —58Fc 107
Springbank Wlk. NW1 —38Mb 62
Spring Bottom La. Blet —99Db 180
Springbourne Ct. Beck —67Ec 128
Spring Bri. M. W5 —45Ma 79
Springbridge Rd. W5 —45Ma 79
Spring Clo. Barn —15Za 22
Spring Clo. Borwd —11Qa 21
Spring Clo. Dag —32Zc 67
Spring Clo. Hare —25M 35
Spring Clo. Lat —8A 2
Spring Clo. La. Sutt —79Ab 144
Spring Corner. Felt —62W 120
Spring Cotts. Surb —71Ma 143
Spring Ct. NW6 —37Bb 61
Spring Ct. Eps —81Va 162
Spring Ct. Rd. Enf —10Qb 10
Springcroft. Hart —72Ce 155
Spring Croft. New Ash —76Be 155
Springcroft Av. N2 —28Hb 41
Spring Crofts. Bush —15Ca 19
Spring Cross. New Ash —76Ce 155
Springdale M. N16 —35Tb 63
Springdale Rd. N16 —35Tb 63
Spring Dri. Pinn —30W 36
Springfarm Clo. Rain —41Md 89
Springfield. E5 —32Xb 63
Springfield. Bush —18Fa 20
Springfield. Epp —4Vc 15
Springfield Av. N10 —27Lb 42
Springfield Av. SW20 —69Bb 125
Springfield Av. Hamp —65Da 121
Springfield Av. Hut —17Fe 33
Springfield Av. Swan —70Hd 132
Springfield Clo. N12 —22Db 41
Springfield Clo. Crox —15R 18
Springfield Clo. Knap —6B 188
Springfield Clo. Pot B —3Gb 9
Springfield Clo. Stan —20Ja 20
Springfield Clo. Wind —4F 94
Springfield Ct. Wall —78Kb 146
Springfield Dri. Ilf —29Sc 46
Springfield Gdns. E5 —32Xb 63
Springfield Gdns. NW9 —29Ta 39
Springfield Gdns. Brom —70Pc 130
Springfield Gdns. Ruis —32X 57
Springfield Gdns. Upm —34Rd 69
Springfield Gdns. W Wick —75Dc 148
Springfield Gdns. Wfd G —24Lc 45
Springfield Gro. SE7 —51Lc 107
Springfield Gro. Sun —67W 120
Springfield La. NW6 —39Db 61
Springfield La. Wey —77R 140
Springfield Meadows. Wey —77R 140
Springfield Mt. NW9 —29Ua 40
Springfield Pde. M. N13 —21Qb 42
Springfield Pl. N Mald —70Sa 123
Springfield Rise. SE26 —62Xb 127
(in two parts)
Springfield Rd. E4 —18Gc 27
Springfield Rd. E6 —38Pc 66
Springfield Rd. E15 —41Gc 85
Springfield Rd. E17 —30Bc 44
Springfield Rd. N11 —22Kb 42
Springfield Rd. N15 —28Wb 43
Springfield Rd. NW8 —39Eb 61
Springfield Rd. SE26 —64Xb 127
Springfield Rd. SW19 —64Bb 125
Springfield Rd. W7 —46Ga 78
Springfield Rd. Ashf —64P 119
Springfield Rd. Bexh —56Dd 110
Springfield Rd. Brom —70Pc 130
Springfield Rd. Chesh —4Ac 12
Springfield Rd. Eps —82Ya 162
Springfield Rd. Grays —7A 92
Springfield Rd. Harr —30Ga 38
Springfield Rd. Hay —46Y 77
Springfield Rd. King T —69Na 123
Springfield Rd. Slou —52D 96
Springfield Rd. Tedd —64Ja 122
Springfield Rd. T Hth —67Sb 127
Springfield Rd. Twic —60Ca 99
Springfield Rd. Wall —78Kb 146
Springfield Rd. Wat —5X 5
Springfield Rd. Well —55Xc 109
Springfield Rd. Wind —4F 94
Springfields. New Bar —15Db 23
(off Somerset Rd.)
Springfields. Wal A —6Gc 13
Springfield Wlk. NW6 —39Db 61
Springfield Wlk. Orp —74Uc 150
(off Andover Rd.)
Spring Gdns. N5 —35Sb 63
Spring Gdns. SW1 —46Mb 82 (6E 198)
Spring Gdns. Big H —90Lc 167
Spring Gdns. Horn —35Kd 69
Spring Gdns. Orp —79Xc 151
Spring Gdns. Romf —29Ed 48
Spring Gdns. Wall —78Lb 146
Spring Gdns. Wat —7Y 5
Spring Gdns. W Mol —71Da 141
Spring Gdns. Wfd G —24Lc 45
Spring Gro. SE19 —66Vb 127
Spring Gro. W4 —50Qa 79
Spring Gro. Fet —95Da 175
Spring Gro. Grav —10D 114
Spring Gro. Hamp —67Da 121
Spring Gro. Lou —16Mc 27
Spring Gro. Mitc —67Jb 126
Spring Gro. Cres. Houn —53Ea 100
Spring Gro. Rd. Houn & Iswth —53Da 99
Spring Gro. Rd. Rich —57Pa 101
Springhead Enterprise Pk. Grav —60De 113
Springhead Rd. Eri —51Hd 110
Springhead Rd. Grav —61Ee 135
Spring Head Rd. Kems —89Pd 171
Spring Hill. E5 —31Wb 63
Spring Hill. SE26 —63Yb 128
Springhill Clo. SE5 —55Tb 105
Springholm Clo. Big H —90Lc 167
Springhouse La. Corr —1P 93
Springhouse Rd. Stanf —1P 93
Springhurst Clo. Croy —77Bc 148
Spring Lake. Stan —21Ka 38
Spring La. E5 —31Xb 63
Spring La. SE25 —72Xb 147
Spring La. Farn R —8F 52
Spring La. Slou —6D 72
Spring M. W1 —43Hb 81 (7G 191)
Spring M. Eps —81Va 162
Spring Pk. Av. Croy —75Zb 148
Spring Pk. Dri. N4 —32Sb 63
Springpark Dri. Beck —69Ec 128
Spring Pk. Rd. Croy —75Zb 148
Spring Path. NW3 —36Fb 61
Spring Pl. NW5 —36Jb 62
Springpond Rd. Dag —36Ad 67
Springrice Rd. SE13 —58Ec 106
Spring Rise. Egh —65A 118
Spring Rd. Felt —62V 120
Springshaw Clo. Sev —95Fd 186
Spring St. W2 —44Fb 81 (3B 196)
Spring St. Eps —81Va 162
Spring Ter. Rich —57Na 101
Spring Vale. Bexh —56Dd 110
Spring Vale. Grnh —58Yd 112
Springvale Av. Bren —50Na 79
Spring Vale Clo. Swan —67Hd 132
Springvale Ct. Grav —61Ee 135
Spring Vale N. Dart —59Md 111
Spring Vale S. Dart —59Md 111
Spring Vale Ter. W14 —48Za 80
Springvale Way. St P —69Yc 131
Spring Villa Rd. Edgw —24Qa 39
Spring Wlk. E1 —43Wb 83
Springwater Clo. SE18 —53Qc 108
Springway. Harr —31Fa 58
Springwell Av. NW10 —39Va 60
Springwell Av. Rick —19J 17
Springwell Clo. SW16 —63Pb 126
Springwell Ct. Houn —54Z 99
Springwell La. Rick & Hare —20J 17
Springwell Rd. SW16 —63Qb 126
Springwell Rd. Houn —53Z 99
Springwood Clo. Hare —25M 35
Springwood Ct. S Croy —77Ub 147
Springwood Cres. Edgw —19Ra 21
Spring Woods. Vir W —10M 117
Springwood Way. Romf —29Jd 48
Sprowston M. E7 —37Jc 65
Sprowston Rd. E7 —36Jc 65
Spruce Ct. E4 —23Bc 44
Spruce Ct. E8 —38Vb 63
Spruce Ct. W5 —48Na 79
Spruce Ct. Slou —8K 73
Sprucedale Clo. Swan —68Gd 132
Sprucedale Gdns. Croy —77Zb 148
Sprucedale Gdns. Wall —81Nb 164
Spruce Hills Rd. E17 —26Ec 44
Spruce Pk. Short —70Hc 129
Spruce Rd. Big H —88Mc 167
Sprules Rd. SE4 —54Ac 106
Spur Clo. Abb L —5T 4
Spur Clo. Abr —13Xc 29
Spurfield. W Mol —69Da 121
Spurgate. Hut —19Ce 33
Spurgeon Av. SE19 —67Tb 127
Spurgeon Rd. SE19 —67Tb 127
Spurgeon St. SE1 —48Tb 83 (4F 207)
Spurling Rd. SE22 —56Vb 105
Spurling Rd. Dag —37Bd 67
Spurrell Av. Bex —63Fd 132
Spur Rd. N15 —28Tb 43
Spur Rd. SW1 —47Lb 82 (2B 204)
Spur Rd. Edgw —21Na 39
Spur Rd. Felt —56X 99
Spur Rd. Iswth —52Ja 100
Spur Rd. Orp —75Wc 151
Spurstowe Rd. E8 —37Xb 63
Spurstowe Ter. E8 —36Xb 63
Spur, The. Chesh —1Zb 12
Spur, The. Slou —3B 72
Squadrons App. Horn —37Ld 69
Square Rigger Row. SW11 —55Eb 103
Square, The. W6 —50Ya 80
Square, The. Cars —78Jb 146
Square, The. Cat —96Wb 181
Square, The. Horn H —1H 93
Square, The. Ilf —31Qc 66
Square, The. Rich —57Ma 101
Square, The. Sev —94Gd 186
Square, The. Swan —69Fd 132
Square, The. Tats —92Lc 183
Square, The. Wat —9X 5
Square, The. W Dray —53K 97
Square, The. Wey —78S 140
Square, The. Wis —88N 157
Square, The. Wfd G —22Jc 45
Squarey St. SW17 —62Eb 125
Squerryes Mede. W'ham —99Sc 184
Squire's Bri. Rd. Shep —70P 119
Squires Ct. SW4 —53Nb 104
Squires Ct. SW19 —63Cb 125
Squires La. N3 —26Db 41
Squires Mt. NW3 —34Fb 61
Squire's Rd. Shep —70Q 120
Squires Wlk. Ashf —66T 120
Squires Way. Dart —63Fd 132
Squires Wood Dri. Chst —66Nc 130
Squirrel Clo. Houn —55Y 99
Squirrel Dri. Wink —10A 94
Squirrel La. Wink —10A 94
Squirrel M. W13 —45Ha 78
Squirrels Chase. Grays —7C 92
Squirrels Clo. N12 —21Eb 41
Squirrels Clo. Uxb —38Q 56
Squirrels Ct. Wor Pk —75Va 144
(off Avenue, The)
Squirrels Drey. Short —68Gc 129
(off Park Hill Rd.)
Squirrels Grn. Bookh —95Ca 175
Squirrels Grn. Wor Pk —75Va 144
Squirrels Heath Av. Romf —27Kd 49
Squirrels Heath La. Romf & Horn —28Ld 49
Squirrels Heath Rd. Romf —27Nd 49
Squirrel's La. Buck H —20Mc 27
Squirrels, The. SE13 —55Fc 107
Squirrels, The. Bush —16Fa 20
Squirrels, The. Pinn —27Ba 37
Squirrels Trading Est., The. Hay —48V 76
Squirrels Way. Eps —86Ta 161
Squirrel Wood. W Byf —84K 157
Squirries St. E2 —41Wb 83
Stable Clo. N'holt —40Ca 57
Stable Ct. Sev —98Ld 187
Stable M. SE27 —64Sb 127
Stables End. Orp —76Sc 150
Stables, The. W10 —44Za 80
(off Bassett Rd.)
Stables, The. Buck H —17Lc 27
Stables, The. Cob —86Ba 159
Stables Way. SE11 —50Qb 82 (7K 205)
Stable Wlk. N2 —25Fb 41
Stable Way. W10 —44Ya 80
Stable Yd. SW1 —47Lb 82 (1B 204)
(off St James Pal.)
Stable Yd. SW9 —54Pb 104
Stable Yd. SW15 —55Ya 102
Stable Yd. Rd. SW1 —47Lb 82 (7B 198)
Stacey Av. N18 —21Yb 44
Stacey Clo. E10 —29Fc 45
Stacey Clo. Grav —4G 136
Stacey Ct. Mers —100Lb 180
Stacey St. N7 —34Qb 62
Stacey St. WC2 —44Mb 82 (3E 198)
Stackhouse St. SW3 —48Hb 81 (3F 203)
(off Pavilion Rd.)
Stacklands Clo. W King —79Ud 154
Stack La. Hart —71Be 155
Stack Rd. Hort K —69Sd 134
Stack Rd. Hort K —70Td 134
Stacy Path. SE5 —52Ub 105
Stadbrook Clo. S Harr —34Ba 57
Stadium Rd. NW4 —31Ya 60
Stadium Rd. SE18 —52Pc 108
Stadium St. SW10 —52Eb 103
Stadium Way. Dart —57Gd 110
Stadium Way. Wemb —35Pa 59
Staffa Rd. E10 —32Ac 64
Stafford Av. Horn —27Md 49
Stafford Av. Slou —2G 72
Stafford Clo. N14 —15Lb 24
Stafford Clo. NW6 —41Cb 81
Stafford Clo. Cat —95Vb 181
Stafford Clo. Chesh —1Xb 11
Stafford Clo. Linf —8J 93
Stafford Clo. Sutt —79Ab 144
Stafford Clo. Tap —4A 72
Stafford Ct. SW8 —52Nb 104
Stafford Cripps Ho. SW6 —51Bb 103
(off Clem Attlee Ct.)
Stafford Gdns. Croy —78Pb 146
Stafford Pl. SW1 —48Lb 82 (3B 204)
Stafford Pl. Rich —59Pa 101
Stafford Rd. E3 —40Bc 64
Stafford Rd. E7 —38Lc 65
Stafford Rd. NW6 —41Cb 81
Stafford Rd. Cat —95Vb 181
Stafford Rd. Harr —24Ea 38
Stafford Rd. H Bar —13Ab 22
Stafford Rd. N Mald —69Sa 123
Stafford Rd. Ruis —35V 56
Stafford Rd. Sidc —63Uc 130
Stafford Rd. Wall & Croy —79Lb 146
Staffordshire St. SE15 —53Wb 105
Stafford Sq. Wey —77T 140
Stafford St. W1 —46Lb 82 (6B 198)
Stafford Ter. W8 —48Cb 81
Stafford Way. Sev —99Ld 187
Staff St. EC1 —41Tb 83 (4G 195)
Stagbury Av. Coul —90Gb 163
Stagbury Clo. Coul —91Gb 179
Stagbury Ho. Coul —91Gb 179
Stag Clo. Edgw —26Ra 39
Staggart Grn. Chig —23Vc 47
Stagg Hill. Barn —9Gb 9
Stag La. SW15 —62Va 124
Stag La. Buck H —19Kc 27
Stag La. Chor —16E 16
Stag La. Edgw & NW9 —26Ra 39
Stag Leys. Asht —92Na 177
Stag Pl. SW1 —48Lb 82 (3B 204)
Stags Way. Iswth —52Ha 100
Stainash Cres. Stai —64K 119
Stainash Pde. Stai —64K 119
(off Kingston Rd.)
Stainbank Rd. Mitc —69Kb 126
Stainby Clo. W Dray —48N 75
Stainby Rd. N15 —28Vb 43
Stainer Rd. Borwd —11Ma 21
Stainer St. SE1 —46Tb 83 (7G 201)
Staines Av. Sutt —75Za 144
Staines Bri. Stai —64G 118
Staines By-Pass. Stai —61E 118
Staines Central Trading Est. Stai —63G 118
Staines La. Cher —72H 139
Staines La. Clo. Cher —72H 139
Staines Rd. Cher —68H 119
Staines Rd. Felt & Houn —60Q 98
Staines Rd. Ilf —35Sc 66
Staines Rd. Stai —66J 119
Staines Rd. Twic —62Ca 121
Staines Rd. Wray —59A 96
Staines Rd. E. Sun —66W 120
Staines Rd. W. Ashf & Sun —65R 120
Staines Wlk. Sidc —65Yc 131
Stainford Clo. Ashf —64T 120
Stainforth Rd. E17 —28Cc 44
Stainforth Rd. Ilf —31Tc 66
Staining La. EC2 —44Sb 83 (2E 200)
Stainmore Clo. Chst —67Tc 130
Stainsbury St. E2 —40Yb 64
Stainsby Pl. E14 —44Cc 84
Stainsby Rd. E14 —44Cc 84
Stains Clo. Chesh —1Ac 12
Stainton Rd. SE6 —58Fc 107
Stainton Rd. Enf —11Yb 26
Stainton Wlk. Wok —6F 188
Stairfoot La. Chip —94Ed 186
Staithes Way. Tad —92Xa 178
Stalbridge St. NW1 —43Gb 81 (7E 190)
Stalham St. SE16 —48Xb 83
Stalisfield Pl. Dow —82Qc 168
Stambourne Way. SE19 —66Ub 127
Stambourne Way. W Wick —75Ec 148
Stamford Brook Av. W6 —48Va 80
Stamford Brook Gdns. W6 —48Va 80
Stamford Brook Mans. W6
(off Goldhawk Rd.) —49Va 80
Stamford Brook Rd. W6 —48Va 80
Stamford Clo. N15 —29Wb 43
Stamford Clo. NW3 —34Eb 61
(off Heath St.)
Stamford Clo. Harr —24Ga 38
Stamford Clo. Pot B —4Fb 9
Stamford Clo. S'hall —45Ca 77
Stamford Ct. W6 —49Wa 80
Stamford Dri. Brom —70Hc 129
Stamford Gdns. Dag —38Yc 67
Stamford Grn. Rd. Eps —85Ra 161
Stamford Gro. E. N16 —32Wb 63
Stamford Gro. W. N16 —32Wb 63
Stamford Hill. N16 —33Vb 63
Stamford Lodge. N16 —31Vb 63
Stamford Rd. E6 —39Nc 66
Stamford Rd. N1 —38Ub 63
Stamford Rd. N15 —29Wb 43
Stamford Rd. Dag —39Xc 67
Stamford Rd. W on T —76Z 141
Stamford Rd. Wat —12X 19
Stamford St. SE1 —46Qb 82 (7K 199)
Stamford Wharf. SE1 —45Qb 82 (5A 200)
Stamp Pl. E2 —40Vb 63 (3K 195)
Stanard Clo. N16 —31Ub 63
Stanborough Av. Borwd —9Qa 7
Stanborough Clo. Borwd —10Qa 7
Stanborough Clo. Hamp —65Ba 121
Stanborough Pk. Wat —7X 5
Stanborough Pas. E8 —37Vb 63
Stanborough Rd. Houn —55Fa 100
Stanbridge Pl. N21 —20Rb 25
Stanbridge Rd. SW15 —55Ya 102
Stanbrook Rd. SE2 —47Xc 87
Stanbrook Rd. Grav —10B 114
Stanbury Av. Wat —9U 4
Stanbury Rd. SE15 —54Xb 105
(in two parts)
Stancroft. NW9 —29Ua 40
Standale Gro. Ruis —29S 36
Standard Ind. Est. E16 —47Pc 86
Standard Pl. EC2 —41Ub 83 (4J 195)
(off Rivington St.)
Standard Rd. NW10 —42Sa 79
Standard Rd. Belv —50Cd 88
Standard Rd. Bexh —56Ad 109
Standard Rd. Enf —9Ac 12
Standard Rd. Houn —55Aa 99
Standard Rd. Orp —82Qc 168
Standen Av. Horn —34Md 69
Standen Rd. SW18 —59Bb 103
Standfield. Abb L —3U 4
Standfield Gdns. Dag —37Cd 68
Standfield Rd. Dag —36Cd 68
Standish Ho. W6 —49Wa 80
(off St Peter's Gro.)
Standish Rd. W6 —49Wa 80
Stane Clo. SW19 —66Db 125
Stane Pas. SW16 —64Nb 126
Stane Way. SE18 —52Mc 107
Stane Way. Eps —82Wa 162
Stanfield Rd. E3 —40Ac 64
Stanford Clo. Hamp —65Ba 121
Stanford Clo. Romf —30Dd 48
Stanford Clo. Ruis —30S 36
Stanford Clo. Wfd G —22Nc 46
Stanford Ct. SW6 —53Db 103
Stanford Ct. Wal A —5Jc 13
Stanford Gdns. S Ock —46Ud 90
Stanford Hall. Corr —1P 93
Stanford Ho. Bark —40Xc 67
Stanford Pl. SE17 —49Ub 83 (6H 207)
Stanford Rd. N11 —22Hb 41
Stanford Rd. SW16 —68Mb 126
Stanford Rd. W8 —48Db 81
Stanford Rd. Grays —48Fe 91
Stanford Rd. Stanf —3H 93
Stanfords, The. Eps —84Va 162
(off East St.)
Stanford St. SW1 —49Mb 82 (6D 204)
Stanford Way. SW16 —68Mb 126
Stangate. SE1 —48Pb 82 (3J 205)
(off Royal St.)
Stangate Cres. Borwd —15Ta 21
Stangate Gdns. Stan —21Ka 38
Stangate Lodge. N21 —17Pb 24
Stanger Rd. SE25 —70Wb 127
Stanham Pl. Dart —56Jd 110
Stanham Rd. Dart —57Ld 111
Stanhill Cotts. Dart —66Fd 132
Stanhope Av. N3 —27Bb 41
Stanhope Av. Brom —74Hc 149
Stanhope Av. Harr —25Fa 38
Stanhope Clo. SE16 —47Zb 84
Stanhope Gdns. N4 —30Rb 43
Stanhope Gdns. N6 —30Kb 42
Stanhope Gdns. NW7 —22Va 40
Stanhope Gdns. SW7 —49Eb 81 (5A 202)
Stanhope Gdns. Dag —34Bd 67
Stanhope Gdns. Ilf —32Pc 66
Stanhope Ga. W1 —46Jb 82 (7J 197)
Stanhope Gro. Beck —71Bc 148
Stanhope Heath. Stai —58L 97
Stanhope Ho. N11 —21Kb 42
(off Coppies Gro.)
Stanhope M. E. SW7 —49Eb 81 (5A 202)
Stanhope M. S. SW7 —49Eb 81 (6A 202)
Stanhope M. W. SW7 —49Eb 81 (5A 202)
Stanhope Pde. NW1 —41Lb 82 (3B 192)
Stanhope Pk. Rd. Gnfd —42Ea 78
Stanhope Pl. W2 —45Hb 81 (3F 197)
Stanhope Rd. E17 —29Dc 44
Stanhope Rd. N6 —30Lb 42
Stanhope Rd. N12 —22Eb 41
Stanhope Rd. Barn —16Ya 22
Stanhope Rd. Bexh —54Ad 109
Stanhope Rd. Cars —80Jb 146
Stanhope Rd. Croy —76Ub 147
Stanhope Rd. Dag —33Bd 67
Stanhope Rd. Gnfd —43Ea 78
Stanhope Rd. Rain —40Jd 68
Stanhope Rd. Sidc —63Wc 131
Stanhope Rd. Slou —4B 72
Stanhope Rd. Swans —58Be 113
Stanhope Rd. Wal X —5Ac 12
Stanhope Row. W1 —46Kb 82 (7K 197)
Stanhopes. Oxt —100Kc 183
Stanhope St. NW1 —41Lb 82 (2B 192)
Stanhope Ter. W2 —45Fb 81 (4C 196)
Stanhope Way. Sev —94Fd 186
Stanhope Way. Stai —58L 97
Stanier Clo. W14 —50Bb 81
Stanlake M. W12 —46Ya 80
Stanlake Rd. W12 —46Ya 80
Stanlake Vs. W12 —46Ya 80
Stanley Av. Bark —40Vc 67
Stanley Av. Beck —69Ec 128
Stanley Av. Dag —32Bd 67
Stanley Av. Gnfd —39Ea 58
Stanley Av. N Mald —71Wa 144
Stanley Av. Romf —28Jd 48
Stanley Av. Wemb —38Na 59
Stanley Clo. SW8 —51Pb 104
Stanley Clo. Coul —90Pb 164
Stanley Clo. Grnh —57Ud 112
Stanley Clo. Horn —33Ld 69
Stanley Clo. Romf —28Jd 48
Stanley Clo. Uxb —39M 55
Stanley Clo. Wemb —38Na 59
Stanley Cotts. Grn St —64Ud 134
Stanley Cotts. Slou —6K 73
Stanley Ct. Cars —80Jb 146
Stanley Ct. Sutt —80Db 145
Stanley Cres. W11 —45Bb 81
Stanley Cres. Grav —4F 136
Stanleycroft Clo. Iswth —53Ga 100
Stanley Gdns. NW2 —36Ya 60
Stanley Gdns. W3 —47Ua 80
Stanley Gdns. W11 —45Bb 81
Stanley Gdns. Borwd —11Na 21
Stanley Gdns. Mitc —65Jb 126
Stanley Gdns. S Croy —84Wb 165
Stanley Gdns. Wall —79Lb 146
Stanley Gdns. W on T —79Y 141
Stanley Gdns. Rd. Tedd —64Ga 122
Stanley Grn. Langl —49B 74
Stanley Gro. N17 —24Vb 43
Stanley Gro. SW8 —54Jb 104
Stanley Gro. Croy —72Qb 146
Stanley Horstead Tower. E10 —33Dc 64
Stanley Maude Ho. Ger X —21A 34
(off Micholls Av.)
Stanley Pk. Dri. Wemb —39Pa 59
Stanley Pk. Rd. Cars & Wall —80Hb 145
Stanley Pas. NW1 —40Nb 62 (2F 193)
Stanley Rd. E4 —18Fc 27
Stanley Rd. E10 —30Dc 44
Stanley Rd. E12 —36Nc 66
Stanley Rd. E15 —39Fc 65
Stanley Rd. E18 —25Hc 45
Stanley Rd. N2 —27Fb 41
Stanley Rd. N9 —18Vb 25
Stanley Rd. N10 —24Kb 42
Stanley Rd. N11 —23Mb 42
Stanley Rd. N15 —28Rb 43
Stanley Rd. NW9 —31Wa 60
Stanley Rd. SW14 —56Ra 101
Stanley Rd. SW19 —65Cb 125
Stanley Rd. W3 —48Sa 79
Stanley Rd. Ashf —64N 119
Stanley Rd. Brom —70Lc 129
Stanley Rd. Cars —80Jb 146
Stanley Rd. Croy —73Qb 146
Stanley Rd. Enf —13Ub 25
Stanley Rd. Grav —10A 114
Stanley Rd. Grays —50De 91
Stanley Rd. Harr —33Ea 58
Stanley Rd. Horn —33Ld 69
Stanley Rd. Houn —56Ea 100
Stanley Rd. Ilf —33Tc 66
Stanley Rd. Mitc —66Jb 126
Stanley Rd. Mord —70Cb 125
Stanley Rd. N'wd —25W 36
Stanley Rd. Orp —74Wc 151
Stanley Rd. Sidc —62Wc 131
Stanley Rd. S'hall —45Aa 77
Stanley Rd. Sutt —79Db 145
Stanley Rd. Swans —58Be 113
Stanley Rd. Twic & Tedd —63Fa 122
Stanley Rd. Wat —14Y 19
Stanley Rd. Wemb —37Pa 59
Stanley Rd. Wok —88B 156
Stanley Rd. N. Rain —39Gd 68
Stanley Rd. S. Rain —40Hd 68
Stanley Sidings. NW5 —38Kb 62
Stanley Sq. Cars —81Hb 163
Stanley St. SE8 —52Bc 106
Stanley St. Cat —94Sb 181
Stanley Ter. N19 —33Nb 62
Stanley Way. Orp —71Xc 151
Stanmere St. SW11 —54Gb 103
Stanmore Gdns. Rich —55Pa 101
Stanmore Gdns. Sutt —76Eb 145
Stanmore Hill. Stan —20Ja 20
Stanmore Lodge. Stan —21Ka 38
Stanmore Pl. NW1 —39Kb 62
Stanmore Rd. E11 —32Hc 65
Stanmore Rd. N15 —28Rb 43
Stanmore Rd. Belv —49Ed 88
Stanmore Rd. Rich —55Pa 101
Stanmore Rd. Wat —11X 19
Stanmore St. N1 —39Pb 62
Stanmore Ter. Beck —68Cc 128
Stanmore Way. Lou —11Qc 28
Stannard Rd. E8 —37Wb 63
Stannary Pl. SE11 —50Qb 82
(off Stannary St.)
Stannary St. SE11 —51Qb 104
Stanning La. EC2 —44Sb 83
Stannington Path. Borwd —11Qa 21
Stansfeld Rd. E16 & E6 —43Mc 85
Stansfield Rd. SW9 —55Pb 104
Stansfield Rd. Houn —54X 99
Stansgate Rd. Dag —33Cd 68
Stanstead Clo. Brom —72Hc 149
Stanstead Cres. Bex —60Zc 109
Stanstead Gro. SE6 —60Bc 106
Stanstead Mnr. Sutt —79Cb 145
Stanstead Rd. E11 —29Kc 45
Stanstead Rd. SE23 & SE6 —60Zb 106
Stanstead Rd. Cat —99Tb 181
Stanstead Rd. Houn —58P 97
Stansted Clo. Horn —37Kd 69
Stanswood Gdns. SE5 —52Ub 105
Stanthorpe Clo. SW16 —64Nb 126
Stanthorpe Rd. SW16 —64Nb 126
Stanton Av. Tedd —65Ga 122
Stanton Clo. Eps —78Ra 143
Stanton Clo. Orp —73Yc 151
Stanton Clo. Wor Pk —74Za 144
Stanton Rd. SE26 —63Bc 128
Stanton Rd. SW13 —54Va 102
Stanton Rd. SW20 —67Za 124
Stanton Rd. Croy —73Sb 147
Stanton Sq. SE26 —63Bc 128
Stanton St. SE15 —53Wb 105
Stanton Way. SE26 —63Bc 128
Stanton Way. Slou —49A 74
Stanway Clo. Chig —22Uc 46
Stanway Ct. N1 —40Ub 63 (2J 195)
Stanway Gdns. W3 —46Qa 79
Stanway Gdns. Edgw —22Sa 39
Stanway Rd. Wal A —5Jc 13
Stanway St. N1 —40Ub 63 (1J 195)
Stanwell Clo. Stai —58M 97
Stanwell Gdns. Stai —58M 97
Stanwell Moor Rd. Stai & W Dray —62J 119
Stanwell New Rd. Stai —62J 119
Stanwell Rd. Ashf —63N 119
Stanwell Rd. Felt —59R 98
Stanwell Rd. Hort —55C 96
Stanwick Dri. Chig —22Sc 46
Stanwick Rd. W14 —49Bb 81
Stanworth Ct. Houn —52Ca 99
Stanworth St. SE1 —48Vb 83 (2K 207)
Stanwyck Gdns. H Hill —22Kd 49
Stapenhill Rd. Wemb —34Ka 58
Staple Clo. Bex —62Fd 132
Staplefield Clo. SW2 —60Nb 104

Staplefield Clo.—Stonehouse La.

Staplefield Clo. Pinn —24Aa 37
Stapleford. N17 —26Ub 43
(off Willan Rd.)
Stapleford Av. Ilf —29Uc 46
Stapleford Clo. E4 —20Ec 26
Stapleford Clo. SW19 —59Ab 102
Stapleford Clo. King T —68Qa 123
Stapleford Ct. Sev —96Hd 186
Stapleford Gdns. Romf —23Cd 48
Stapleford Rd. Stap A —14Dd 30
Stapleford Rd. Wemb —38Ma 59
Stapleford Way. Bark —41Xc 87
Staplehurst Rd. SE13 —57Gc 107
Staplehurst Rd. Cars —80Gb 145
Staple Inn. WC1 —43Qb 82 (1K 199)
(off Staple Inn Bldgs.)
Staple Inn Bldgs. WC1
—43Qb 82 (1K 199)
Staples Clo. SE16 —46Ac 84
Staples Ho. E6 —44Qc 86
(off Savage Gdns.)
Staple's Rd. Lou —13Mc 27
Staple St. SE1 —47Tb 83 (2G 207)
Staple St. SW1 —47Tb 83
Stapleton Cres. Rain —37Jd 68
Stapleton Gdns. Croy —78Qb 146
Stapleton Hall Rd. N4 —32Pb 62
Stapleton Rd. SW17 —62Jb 126
Stapleton Rd. Bexh —52Bd 109
Stapleton Rd. Borwd —10Qa 7
Stapleton Rd. Orp —76Vc 151
Stapley Rd. Belv —50Cd 88
Stapylton Rd. Barn —13Ab 22
Star All. EC3 —45Ub 83 (4J 201)
(off Fenchurch St.)
Starboard Av. Grnh —58Xd 112
Starboard Way. E14 —48Cc 84
Starch Ho. La. Ilf —26Tc 46
Starcross St. NW1
—41Lb 82 (4C 192)
Starfield Rd. W12 —47Wa 80
Star & Garter Hill. Rich —60Na 101
Star Hill. Dart —57Qd 110
Star Hill. Wok —7F 188
Star Hill Rd. Dun G —88Bd 169
Starkleigh Way. SE16 —50Xb 83
Star La. E16 —42Gc 85
Star La. Coul —93Jb 180
Star La. Epp —2Wc 15
Star La. Orp —70Yc 131
Starling Clo. Buck H —18Jc 27
Starling Clo. Long —69De 135
Starling Clo. Pinn —27Y 37
Starling La. Cuff —1Pb 10
Starling M. SE28 —47Tc 86
Starling Pl. Wat —4Y 5
Starlings, The. Oxs —85Ea 160
Starling Wlk. Hamp —64Aa 121
Star Path. N'holt —40Ca 57
(off Brabazon Rd.)
Star Rd. W14 —51Bb 103
Star Rd. Iswth —54Fa 100
Star Rd. Uxb —42S 76
Starrock La. Coul —92Hb 179
Starrock Rd. Coul —91Kb 180
Star St. E16 —43Hc 85
Star St. W2 —44Gb 81 (2C 196)
Starts Clo. Orp —76Qc 150
Starts Hill Av. F'boro —77Rc 150
Starts Hill Rd. Orp —76Qc 150
Starwood Clo. W Byf —83L 157
Starwood Ct. Slou —8N 73
Star Yd. WC2 —44Qb 82 (2K 199)
State Farm Av. Orp —77Rc 150
Staten Gdns. Twic —60Ha 100
Statham Gro. N16 —35Tb 63
Statham Gro. N18 —22Ub 43
Stathers, The. Sole S —10F 136
Station App. E7 —35Kc 65
Station App. E11 —29Jc 45
Station App. N11 —22Kb 42
Station App. N12 —21Db 41
Station App. NW10 —41Va 80
Station App. SE3 —55Kc 107
Station App. SE26 —64Bc 128
(Lower Sydenham)
Station App. SE26 —63Yb 128
(Sydenham)
Station App. SW6 —55Ab 102
Station App. SW16 —64Mb 126
Station App. W7 —46Ga 78
Station App. Ashf —62P 119
Station App. B'hurst —54Ed 110
Station App. Beck —67Cc 128
Station App. Belm —82Db 163
Station App. Bex —59Cd 110
Station App. Bexh —54Ad 109
Station App. Buck H —21Mc 45
Station App. Cheam —80Ab 144
Station App. Chels —78Xc 151
Station App. Chips —90Hb 163
Station App. Chst —67Qc 130
(Chislehurst)
Station App. Chst —65Nc 130
(Elmstead Woods)
Station App. Chor —14F 16
Station App. Coul N —88Mb 164
Station App. Cray —58Hd 110
Station App. Croy —75Tb 147
Station App. Dart —58Nd 111
Station App. Den —31F 54
Station App. E Hor —98U 174
Station App. Eps —85Ta 161
Station App. Ewe —82Xa 162
(Ewell East)
Station App. Ewe —81Va 162
(Ewell West)
Station App. Ger X —29A 34
Station App. Grays —51Ce 113
Station App. Gnfd —38Fa 58
Station App. Hamp —67Ca 121
Station App. Harr —31Ga 58
Station App. Hayes —74Jc 149
Station App. Hay —48V 76
Station App. Hin W —76Ha 142
Station App. King T —68Qa 123
Station App. Lea —93Ja 176
Station App. Lou —14Sc 28
(Debden)
Station App. Lou —15Nc 28
(Loughton)
Station App. Meop —10C 136
Station App. New Bar —14Eb 23
Station App. N'wd —24U 36
Station App. Orp —75Vc 151
Station App. Oxs —85Ea 160
Station App. Oxt —100Gc 183
Station App. Pinn —27Aa 37
Station App. Purl —83Qb 164
Station App. Rad —7Ja 6
Station App. Rich —53Qa 101
Station App. Ruis —32U 56
Station App. Shep —71S 140
Station App. S Croy —81Tb 165
Station App. S Ruis —36X 57
Station App. St M —70Xc 131
Station App. S'leigh —78Wa 144
Station App. Sun —67W 120
Station App. Swan —70Gd 132
Station App. They B —8Vc 15
Station App. Vir W —10P 117
Station App. Wal X —6Ac 12
Station App. Wat —20Z 19
Station App. Well —54Wc 109
(in two parts)
Station App. Wemb —37Ka 58
Station App. W Byf —84J 157
Station App. W Dray —46N 75
Station App. W Wick —73Ec 148
Station App. Wey —79Q 140
Station App. Whyt —89Wb 165
Station App. Wind —3H 95
Station App. Wok —90B 156
Station App. Wor Pk —74Wa 144
Station App. N. Sidc —61Wc 131
Station App. Rd. W4 —52Sa 101
Station App. Rd. Coul —87Mb 164
Station App. Rd. Tad —94Ya 178
Station App. Rd. Til —6C 114
Station Av. SW9 —55Rb 105
Station Av. Cat —96Wb 181
Station Av. Eps —81Ua 162
Station Av. N Mald —69Ua 124
Station Av. Rich —53Qa 101
Station Av. W on T —77W 140
Station Clo. N3 —25Cb 41
Station Clo. N12 —21Db 41
Station Clo. Hamp —67Da 121
Station Clo. Pot B —3Bb 9
Station Cotts. Orp —75Vc 151
Station Ct. E10 —31Dc 64
(off Kings Clo.)
Station Cres. N15 —28Tb 43
Station Cres. SE3 —50Jc 85
Station Cres. Ashf —62M 119
Station Cres. Wemb —37Ka 58
Stationers' Hall Ct. EC4
—44Rb 83 (3C 200)
Station Est. Beck —69Zb 128
Station Est. Rd. Felt —60X 99
Station Garage M. SW16
—65Mb 126
Station Gdns. W4 —52Sa 101
Station Gro. Wemb —37Na 59
Station Hill. Brom —75Jc 149
Station Ho. M. N9 —21Wb 43
Station La. Horn —34Md 69
Station Pde. E11 —29Jc 45
Station Pde. N14 —18Mb 24
Station Pde. NW2 —37Ya 60
Station Pde. W3 —44Qa 79
Station Pde. W5 —46Pa 79
Station Pde. Ashf —63P 119
Station Pde. Bark —38Sc 66
Station Pde. Barn —14Jb 24
Station Pde. Chips —90Hb 163
Station Pde. Dag —37Cd 68
Station Pde. Den —31J 55
Station Pde. E Hor —98U 174
(in two parts)
Station Pde. Edgw —24Na 39
Station Pde. Eri —54Gd 110
Station Pde. Felt —60X 99
Station Pde. Harr —35Da 57
Station Pde. Horn —35Kd 69
Station Pde. N'holt —38Ca 57
Station Pde. N'wd —24U 36
Station Pde. Rich —53Qa 101
Station Pde. Sev —96Jd 186
Station Pde. Vir W —10P 117
Station Pde. W'stone —26Ja 38
Station Pas. E18 —26Kc 45
Station Pas. SE15 —53Yb 106
Station Path. Stai —63H 119
Station Pl. N4 —33Qb 62
Station Rise. SE27 —61Rb 127
Station Rd. E4 —18Fc 27
Station Rd. E7 —35Jc 65
Station Rd. E12 —35Nc 66
Station Rd. E17 —30Ac 44
Station Rd. N3 —25Cb 41
Station Rd. N11 —22Kb 42
Station Rd. N17 —27Wb 43
Station Rd. N18 —22Vb 43
Station Rd. N19 —34Lb 62
Station Rd. N21 —18Rb 25
Station Rd. N22 —26Nb 42
Station Rd. NW4 —30Wa 40
Station Rd. NW7 —23Ua 40
Station Rd. NW10 —40Va 60
Station Rd. SE20 —65Yb 128
Station Rd. SE25 —70Vb 127
Station Rd. SW13 —54Va 102
Station Rd. SW19 —67Eb 125
Station Rd. W5 —44Pa 79
Station Rd. W7 —46Ga 78
Station Rd. Add —77L 139
Station Rd. Ashf —63P 119
Station Rd. B'side —27Tc 46
Station Rd. Belv —48Cd 88
Station Rd. Bexh —55Ad 109
Station Rd. Borwd —14Qa 21
Station Rd. Bras —95Xc 185
Station Rd. Brick —3Ca 5
Station Rd. Brom —67Jc 129
Station Rd. Cars —77Hb 145
Station Rd. Cher —74H 139
Station Rd. Chess —78Na 143
Station Rd. Chig —20Rc 28
Station Rd. Chob —1D 188
Station Rd. Cipp —4C 72
Station Rd. Clay —79Ga 142
Station Rd. Cray —59Hd 110
Station Rd. Croy —75Tb 147
Station Rd. Cuff —1Pb 10
Station Rd. Dag & Chad —31Zc 67
Station Rd. Dun G —92Gd 186
Station Rd. E Til —1H 115
Station Rd. Edgw —23Qa 39
Station Rd. Egh —64C 118
Station Rd. Epp —3Vc 15
Station Rd. Eri —50Gd 88
Station Rd. Esh —75Fa 142
Station Rd. Eyns —76Md 153
Station Rd. Ger X —29A 34
Station Rd. Gid P —28Kd 49
Station Rd. Grav —58De 113
Station Rd. Grnh —57Wd 112
Station Rd. Hals —83Bd 169
Station Rd. Hamp —67Ca 121
Station Rd. Hamp W —67Ma 123
Station Rd. H Wood —25Pd 49
Station Rd. Harr —28Ha 38
Station Rd. Hay —49U 76
Station Rd. Houn —56Da 99
Station Rd. Ilf —34Rc 66
Station Rd. Kenl —86Sb 165
Station Rd. K Lan —1R 4
Station Rd. King T —67Qa 123
Station Rd. Langl —48C 74
Station Rd. Lea —93Ja 176
Station Rd. Long —69Ae 135
Station Rd. Lou —14Nc 28
Station Rd. Meop —10C 136
Station Rd. Mers —100Lb 180
Station Rd. New Bar —15Db 23
Station Rd. N Mald —71Xa 144
Station Rd. N Har —29Da 37
Station Rd. Orp —75Vc 151
Station Rd. Otf —88Kd 171
Station Rd. Rad —7Ja 6
Station Rd. Rick —17M 17
Station Rd. Shep —71S 140
Station Rd. Shor —84Jd 170
Station Rd. Short —68Gc 129
Station Rd. Sidc —61Wc 131
Station Rd. S'fleet —63Be 135
Station Rd. Stoke D —88Aa 159
Station Rd. St P —70Yc 131
Station Rd. Sun —66W 120
Station Rd. S'dale —10E 116
Station Rd. Sutt —82Cb 163
Station Rd. S at H —68Rd 133
Station Rd. Swan —70Gd 132
Station Rd. Tedd —64Ha 122
Station Rd. Th Dit —73Ha 142
Station Rd. Twic —60Ha 100
Station Rd. Upm —33Sd 70
Station Rd. Uxb —42L 75
Station Rd. Wal A —6Cc 12
Station Rd. Wat —12X 19
Station Rd. W Byf —84J 157
Station Rd. W Dray —47N 75
Station Rd. W Horn —30Ee 51
Station Rd. W Wick —74Ec 148
Station Rd. Whyt —90Vb 165
Station Rd. Wold —94Ac 182
Station Rd. Wray —58B 96
Station Rd. E. Oxt —100Gc 183
Station Rd. N. Belv —48Dd 88
Station Rd. N. Egh —64C 118
Station Rd. N. Mers —100Lb 180
Station Rd. S. Mers —100Lb 180
Station Rd. W. Oxt —100Gc 183
Station Sq. Gid P —28Kd 49
Station Sq. Pet W —71Sc 150
Station Sq. St M —70Xc 131
Station St. E15 —38Fc 65
Station St. E16 —46Rc 86
Station Ter. NW10 —40Ya 60
Station Ter. SE5 —53Sb 105
Station Ter. Purf —50Qd 89
Station Ter. M. SE3 —50Jc 85
Station View. Gnfd —39Fa 58
Station Way. SE15 —54Wb 105
Station Way. Buck H —21Lc 45
Station Way. Clay —79Ga 142
Station Way. Eps —85Ta 161
Station Way. Sutt —79Ab 144
Station Yd. Sev —96Jd 186
Station Yd. S Croy —84Qb 164
Station Yd. Twic —59Ja 100
Staunton Rd. King T —65Na 123
Staunton Rd. Slou —3H 73
Staunton St. SE8 —51Bc 106
Staveley Clo. E9 —36Yb 64
Staveley Clo. N7 —35Nb 62
Staveley Clo. SE15 —53Yb 106
Staveley Gdns. W4 —53Ta 101
Staveley Rd. W4 —51Sa 101
Staveley Rd. Ashf —65T 120
Staveley Way. Knap —5B 188
Staverton Rd. NW2 —38Ya 60
Staverton Rd. Horn —30Md 49
Stave Yd. Rd. SE16 —46Ac 84
Stavordale Rd. N5 —35Rb 63
Stavordale Rd. Cars —73Eb 145
Stayne End. Vir W —10L 117
Stayner's Rd. E1 —42Zb 84
Stayton Rd. Sutt —76Cb 145
Steadfast Rd. King T —67Ma 123
Steadman Ct. EC1
(off Old St.) —42Sb 83 (5E 194)
Steadman Ho. Dag —34Cd 68
(off Uvedale Rd.)
Stead St. SE17 —49Tb 83 (6F 207)
Steam Farm La. Felt —56V 98
Stean St. E8 —39Vb 63
Stebbing Ho. W11 —46Za 80
(off Queensdale Cres.)
Stebbing Way. Bark —40Wc 67
Stebondale St. E14 —49Ec 84
Stedham Pl. WC1
—44Nb 82 (2F 199)
(off New Oxford St.)
Stedman Clo. Bex —62Gd 132
Stedman Clo. Uxb —34Q 56
Steed Clo. Horn —33Kd 69
Steedman St. SE17
—49Sb 83 (6D 206)
Steeds Rd. N10 —25Hb 41
Steeds Way. Lou —13Nc 28
Steele Av. Grnh —57Vd 112
Steele Gdns. Add —78K 139
Steele Ho. E15 —40Gc 65
(off Eve Rd.)
Steele Rd. E11 —35Gc 65
Steele Rd. N17 —27Ub 43
Steele Rd. NW10 —40Sa 59
Steele Rd. W4 —48Sa 79
Steele Rd. Iswth —56Ja 100
Steele's M. N. NW3 —37Hb 61
Steele's M. S. NW3 —37Hb 61
Steele's Rd. NW3 —37Hb 61
Steel's La. E1 —44Yb 84
Steel's La. Oxs —86Da 159
Steen Way. SE22 —57Ub 105
Steep Clo. Orp —79Vc 151
Steep Hill. SW16 —62Mb 126
Steep Hill. Croy —77Ub 147
Steeplands. Bush —17Da 19
Steeple Clo. SW6 —54Ab 102
Steeple Clo. SW19 —64Ab 124
Steeple Ct. E1 —42Xb 83
Steeple Gdns. Add —78K 139
Steeple Heights Dri. Big H
—89Mc 167
Steeplestone Clo. N18 —22Sb 43
Steerforth St. SW18 —61Eb 125
Steers Mead. Mitc —67Hb 125
Steers Way. SE16 —47Ac 84
Stella Rd. SW17 —65Hb 125
Stelling Rd. Eri —52Fd 110
Stellman Clo. E5 —34Wb 63
Stembridge Rd. SE20 —68Xb 127
Stenning Av. Lfld —9J 93
Stents La. Cob —92Ba 175
Stepbridge Path. Wok —5G 188
Stepgates. Cher —73K 139
Stephan Clo. E8 —39Wb 63
Stephen Av. Rain —37Jd 68
Stephen Clo. Egh —65E 118
Stephen Clo. Orp —76Vc 151
Stephendale Rd. SW6 —55Db 103
Stephen M. W1
—43Mb 82 (1D 198)
Stephen Rd. Bexh —55Ed 110
Stephens Clo. Romf —22Ld 49
Stephens Ct. E16 —42Hc 85
Stephenson Av. Til —3C 114
Stephenson Ct. Slou —7K 73
Stephenson Ho. SE1
—48Sb 83 (4D 206)
Stephenson Rd. W7 —44Ha 78
Stephenson Rd. Twic —59Ca 99
Stephenson St. E16 —42Gc 85
Stephenson St. NW10 —41Ua 80
Stephenson Way. NW1
—42Lb 82 (5C 192)
Stephenson Way. Wat —14Z 19
Stephen's Rd. E3 —40Bc 64
Stephen's Rd. E15 —39Gc 65
Stephen St. W1
—43Mb 82 (1D 198)
Stepney Causeway. E1 —44Zb 84
Stepney Grn. E1 —43Yb 84
Stepney High St. E1 —43Zb 84
Stepney Way. E1 —43Xb 83
Sterling Av. Edgw —21Pa 39
Sterling Av. Wal X —6Zb 12
Sterling Pl. W5 —49Na 79
Sterling Rd. Eri —11Tb 25
Sterling St. SW7
—48Gb 81 (3E 202)
Sterling Way. N18 —22Tb 43
Sterndale Rd. W14 —48Za 80
Sterndale Rd. Dart —59Pd 111
Sterne St. W12 —47Za 80
Sternhall La. SE15 —55Wb 105
Sternhold Av. SW2 —61Mb 126
Sterry Cres. Dag —36Cd 68
Sterry Dri. Eps —77Ua 144
Sterry Dri. Th Dit —72Ga 142
Sterry Gdns. Dag —37Cd 68
Sterry Rd. Bark —39Vc 67
Sterry Rd. Dag —35Cd 68
Sterry St. SE1 —47Tb 83 (2F 207)
Sterry St. SW1 —47Tb 83
Steucers La. SE23 —60Ac 106
Steve Biko Ho. Wemb —31Pa 59
Steve Biko La. SE6 —63Cc 128
Steve Biko Rd. N7 —34Qb 62
Steve Biko Way. Houn —55Ca 99
Stevedale Rd. Well —54Yc 109
Stevedore St. E1 —46Xb 83
Stevenage Cres. Borwd —11Na 21
Stevenage Rd. E6 —37Qc 66
Stevenage Rd. SW6 —52Za 102
Stevens Av. E9 —37Yb 64
Stevens Clo. Beck —65Cc 128
Stevens Clo. Bex —63Fd 132
Stevens Clo. Dart —64Ud 134
Stevens Clo. Eps —85Ua 162
Stevens Clo. Hamp —64Aa 121
Stevens Clo. Pinn —29Y 37
Stevens Grn. Bush —18Ea 20
Stevens La. Clay —80Ja 142
Stevenson Clo. Eri —52Kd 111
Stevenson Cres. SE16 —50Xb 83
Stevenson Dri. Wind —2F 94
Stevenson Rd. Hedg —3H 53
Stevens Rd. Dag —34Xc 67
Stevens Strait. Cher —72J 139
Stevens St. SE1 —48Ub 83 (3J 207)
Stevens Way. Chig —21Uc 46
Steventon Rd. W12 —45Va 80
Steward Clo. Chesh —2Ac 12
Stewards Clo. Epp —5Wc 15
Stewards Grn. La. Epp —4Xc 15
Stewards Grn. Rd. Epp —5Wc 15
Stewards Holte Wlk. N11 —21Kb 42
Steward St. E1 —43Ub 83 (1J 201)
Stewart. Tad —93Za 178
Stewart Av. Shep —70Q 120
Stewart Av. Slou —3K 73
Stewart Av. Upm —34Rd 69
Stewart Clo. NW9 —30Sa 39
Stewart Clo. Abb L —4V 4
Stewart Clo. Chst —64Rc 130
Stewart Clo. Hamp —65Aa 121
Stewart Clo. Wok —5C 188
Stewart Rainbird Ho. E12 —36Qc 66
(off Parkhurst Rd.)
Stewart Rd. E15 —35Fc 65
Stewartsby Clo. N18 —22Sb 43
Stewart's Dri. Farn C —5F 52
Stewart's Gro. SW3
—50Fb 81 (7C 202)
Stewart's Rd. SW8 —52Lb 104
Stewart St. E14 —47Ec 84
Stew La. EC4 —45Sb 83 (4D 200)
Steyne Rd. W3 —46Ra 79
Steyning Clo. Kenl —88Rb 165
Steyning Gro. SE9 —63Pc 130
Steynings Way. N12 —22Cb 41
Steyning Way. Houn —56Y 99
Steynton Av. Bex —61Zc 131
Stickland Rd. Belv —49Cd 88
Stickleton Clo. Gnfd —41Da 77
Stifford Clays Rd. N Stif —46Be 91
(in three parts)
Stifford Hill. S Ock & N Stif
—45Yd 90
Stifford Rd. S Ock —46Ud 90
Stilecroft Gdns. Wemb —34Ka 58
Stile Hall Gdns. W4 —50Qa 79
Stile Hall Pde. W4 —50Qa 79
Stile Path. Sun —69W 120
Stile Rd. Slou —8P 73
Stiles Clo. Brom —72Pc 150
Stillingfleet Rd. SW13 —51Wa 102
Stillington St. SW1
—49Lb 82 (5C 204)
Stillness Rd. SE23 —58Ac 106
Stilton Cres. NW10 —38Ta 59
Stilton Path. Borwd —10Qa 7
Stipularis Dri. Hay —42Z 77
Stirling Clo. SW16 —67Lb 126
Stirling Clo. Bans —89Bb 163
Stirling Clo. Rain —41Kd 89
Stirling Clo. Uxb —41L 75
Stirling Clo. Wind —4B 94
Stirling Corner. Borwd & Barn
—16Ta 21
Stirling Dri. Orp —78Xc 151
Stirling Gro. Houn —54Ea 100
Stirling Ho. Borwd —14Sa 21
Stirling Rd. E13 —40Kc 65
Stirling Rd. E17 —27Ac 44
Stirling Rd. N17 —25Wb 43
Stirling Rd. N22 —25Rb 43
Stirling Rd. SW9 —54Nb 104
Stirling Rd. W3 —48Ra 79
Stirling Rd. Harr —27Ha 38
Stirling Rd. Hay —45X 77
Stirling Rd. Houn —58P 97
Stirling Rd. Slou —3E 72
Stirling Rd. Twic —60Ca 99
Stirling Rd. Path. E17 —27Ac 44
Stirling Wlk. Surb —72Ra 143
Stirling Way. Borwd —16Ta 21
Stirling Way. Croy —73Nb 146
Stites Hill Rd. Coul —92Rb 181
Stiven Cres. Harr —34Ba 57
Stoats Nest Rd. Coul —86Nb 164
Stoats Nest Village. Coul
—87Nb 164
Stockdove Way. Gnfd —41Ha 78
Stockbury Rd. Croy —72Yb 148
Stockdale Rd. Dag —33Bd 67
Stockdales Rd. Eton W —9D 72
Stockdove Way. Gnfd —41Ha 78
Stockers Farm Rd. Rick —20M 17
Stockers La. Wok —92B 172
Stockfield Rd. SW16 —62Pb 126
Stockfield Rd. Clay —78Ga 142
Stockham's Clo. S Croy —83Tb 165
Stock Hill. Big H —88Mc 167
Stockholm Rd. SE16 —50Yb 84
Stockholm Way. E1 —46Wb 83
Stockhurst Clo. SW15 —54Za 102
Stockingswater La. Enf —13Bc 26
Stockland Rd. Romf —30Fd 48
Stock La. Dart —62Ld 133
Stockley Clo. W Dray —47R 76
Stockley Farm Rd. W Dray —48R 76
Stockley Pk. Uxb —46R 76
Stockley Rd. Uxb & W Dray
—44Q 76
Stockley Rd. W Dray —49R 76
Stock Orchard Cres. N7 —36Pb 62
Stock Orchard St. N7 —36Pb 62
Stockport Rd. SW16 —67Mb 126
Stockport Rd. Herons —17E 16
Stocksfield Rd. E17 —27Ec 44
Stocks Pl. E14 —45Bc 84
Stock St. E13 —40Jc 65
Stockton Gdns. N17 —24Sb 43
Stockton Gdns. NW7 —20Ua 22
Stockton Ho. S Harr —32Ca 57
Stockton Rd. N17 —24Sb 43
Stockton Rd. N18 —23Wb 43
Stockton Sq. Brom —69Jc 129
Stockwell Av. SW9 —55Pb 104
Stockwell Clo. Brom —68Kc 129
Stockwell Gdns. SW9 —53Pb 104
Stockwell Gdns. Est. SW9
—54Nb 104
Stockwell Grn. SW9 —54Pb 104
Stockwell Grn. Ct. SW9 —54Pb 104
Stockwell La. SW9 —54Pb 104
Stockwell La. Chesh —1Wb 11
Stockwell M. SW9 —54Pb 104
Stockwell Pk. Cres. SW9
—54Pb 104
Stockwell Pk. Est. SW9 —54Pb 104
Stockwell Pk. Rd. SW9 —53Pb 104
Stockwell Pk. Wlk. SW9 —55Pb 104
Stockwell Rd. SW9 —54Pb 104
Stockwell St. SE10 —51Ec 106
Stockwell Ter. SW9 —53Pb 104
Stodart Rd. SE20 —67Yb 128
Stoddart Ho. SW8 —51Pb 104
Stofield Gdns. SE9 —62Mc 129
Stoke Av. Ilf —23Wc 47
Stoke Clo. Stoke D —88Ba 159
Stoke Comn. Rd. Ful —5L 53
Stoke Cotts. Slou —6K 73
Stoke Ct. Dri. Stoke P —9J 53
Stoke Gdns. Slou —6J 73
Stoke Grn. Stoke P —2L 73
Stokenchurch St. SW6 —53Db 103
Stoke Newington Chu. St. N16
—34Tb 63
Stoke Newington Comn. N16
—33Vb 63
Stoke Newington High St. N16
—34Vb 63
Stoke Newington Rd. N16
—36Vb 63
Stoke Pk. Av. Farn R —1G 72
Stoke Pl. NW10 —41Va 80
Stoke Poges La. Slou —6J 73
Stoke Rd. Cob —87Y 159
Stoke Rd. King T —66Sa 123
Stoke Rd. Rain —40Md 69
Stoke Rd. Slou —6K 73
Stoke Rd. W on T —76Y 141
Stokesay. Slou —5K 73
Stokesay Ct. Dart —58Rd 111
(off Grange Cres.)
Stokesay Ct. Dart —58Rd 111
(off Osborne Rd.)
Stokesby Rd. Chess —79Pa 143
Stokes Cotts. Ilf —25Sc 46
Stokes Ct. N2 —28Gb 41
Stokesheath Rd. Oxs —83Ea 160
Stokesley St. W12 —44Va 80
Stokes Ridings. Tad —95Za 178
Stokes Rd. E6 —42Nc 86
Stokes Rd. Croy —72Zb 148
Stoke Wood. Stoke P —5K 53
Stokley Ct. N8 —28Nb 42
Stoll Clo. NW2 —34Ya 60
Stompond La. W on T —75W 140
Stomp Rd. Burn —3A 72
Stoms Path. SE6 —64Cc 128
Stonard Rd. N13 —20Qb 24
Stonard Rd. Dag —36Xc 67
Stonards Hill. Epp —1Wc 15
Stonards Hill. Lou —16Pc 28
Stondon Ho. E15 —39Hc 65
(off John St.)
Stondon Pk. SE23 —58Ac 106
Stondon Wlk. E6 —40Mc 65
Stonebanks. W on T —73W 140
Stonebridge Clo. S Harr —32Ca 57
Stonebridge Comn. E8 —38Vb 63
Stonebridge Field. Eton —10F 72
Stonebridge Pk. NW10 —38Ta 59
Stonebridge Rd. N15 —29Vb 43
Stonebridge Rd. N'fleet —57Ce 113
Stonebridge Way. Wemb —37Ra 59
Stone Bldgs. WC2
—43Pb 82 (1J 199)
(off Chancery La.)
Stonechat Sq. E6 —43Nc 86
Stone Clo. SW4 —54Lb 104
Stone Clo. Dag —33Bd 67
Stone Clo. W Dray —46P 75
Stonecot Clo. Sutt —74Ab 144
Stonecot Hill. Sutt —74Ab 144
Stone Ct. Eri —50Hd 88
Stone Cres. Felt —59V 98
Stonecroft Av. Iver —44G 74
Stonecroft Rd. Eri —52Ed 110
Stonecroft Way. Croy —73Nb 146
Stonecutter St. EC4
—44Rb 83 (2B 200)
Stonefield. N4 —33Pb 62
Stonefield Clo. Bexh —55Cd 110
Stonefield Clo. Ruis —36Aa 57
Stonefield St. N1 —39Qb 62
Stonefield Way. SE7 —52Mc 107
Stonefield Way. Ruis —36Aa 57
Stonegate Clo. Orp —69Yc 131
Stonegrove. Edgw —21Na 39
Stone Gro. Ct. Edgw —22Pa 39
Stonegrove Gdns. Edgw —22Pa 39
Stonehall Av. Ilf —30Nc 46
Stone Hall Pl. W8 —48Db 81
Stone Hall Rd. N21 —17Pb 24
Stoneham Rd. N11 —22Lb 42
Stonehill Clo. SW14 —57Ta 101
Stonehill Clo. Bookh —97Ca 175
Stonehill Ct. E4 —17Dc 26
Stonehill Cres. Ott —79A 138
Stonehill Rd. SW14 —57Ta 101
Stone Hill Rd. W4 —50Qa 79
Stonehill Rd. Ott —80A 138
Stonehills Ct. SE21 —62Ub 127
Stonehill Woods Pk. Sidc
—65Dd 132
Stonehorse Rd. Enf —15Yb 26
Stone Ho. Ct. EC3
—44Ub 83 (2J 201)
(off Houndsditch)
Stonehouse Gdns. Cat —97Ub 181
Stonehouse La. Grays —51Ud 112

Stonehouse La.—Sunnyfield

Stonehouse La. Hals —81Zc 169
Stonehouse Rd. Hals —82Yc 169
Stoneings La. Knock —90Vc 169
Stoneleigh Av. Enf —10Xb 11
Stoneleigh Av. Wor Pk —77Wa 144
Stoneleigh B'way. Eps —78Wa 144
Stoneleigh Clo. Wal X —5Zb 12
Stoneleigh Cres. Eps —78Va 144
Stoneleigh Pk. Wey —79S 140
Stoneleigh Pk. Av. Croy —72Zb 148
Stoneleigh Pk. Rd. Eps —79Va 144
Stoneleigh Pl. W11 —45Za 80
Stoneleigh Rd. N17 —27Vb 43
Stoneleigh Rd. Cars —73Gb 145
Stoneleigh Rd. Ilf —27Nc 46
Stoneleigh St. W11 —45Za 80
Stoneleigh Ter. N19 —33Kb 62
Stonell's Rd. SW11 —58Hb 103
Stone Ness. W Thur —52Xd 112
Stoneness Rd. W Thur —51Xd 112
Stonenest St. N4 —32Pb 62
Stone Pk. Av. Beck —70Cc 128
Stone Pl. Wor Pk —75Wa 144
Stone Pl. Rd. Grnh —57Ud 112
Stone Rd. Brom —71Hc 149
Stones All. Wat —14X 19
Stones Cross Rd. Swan —72Ed 152
Stones End St. SE1
—47Sb 83 (2D 206)
Stone's Rd. Eps —84Ua 162
Stone St. Croy —78Qb 146
Stone St. Grav —8D 114
Stone St. Ivy H —96Rd 187
Stonewold Ct. W5 —44Ma 79
Stonewood. Bean —62Yd 134
Stonewood Rd. Eri —50Gd 88
Stoney All. SE18 —54Qc 108
Stoneyard La. E14 —45Dc 84
Stoney Corner. Meop —10A 136
Stoneycroft Clo. SE12 —59Hc 107
Stoneycroft Rd. Wfd G —23Nc 46
Stoneydeep. Tedd —63Ja 122
Stoneydown. E17 —28Ac 44
Stoneydown Av. E17 —28Ac 44
Stoneydown Ho. E17 —28Ac 44
(off Blackhorse Rd.)
Stoneyfield Rd. Coul —89Pb 164
Stoneyfields Gdns. Edgw —21Sa 39
Stoneyfields La. Edgw —22Sa 39
Stoneylands Ct. Egh —64B 118
Stoneylands Rd. Egh —64B 118
Stoney La. E1 —44Ub 83 (2J 201)
Stoney La. SE19 —65Vb 127
Stoney La. Chfd —2G 2
Stoney La. Farn C —9E 52
Stoney Meade. Slou —6F 72
Stoney St. SE1 —46Tb 83 (6F 201)
Stonhouse St. SW4 —56Mb 104
Stonny Croft. Asht —89Pa 161
Stonor Rd. W14 —49Bb 81
Stony Hill. W End —80Ba 141
Stony La. Lat —10A 2
Stony Path. Lou —11Pc 28
Stonyshotts. Wal A —5Gc 13
Stoop Ct. W Byf —84K 157
Stopford Clo. SW19 —59Ab 102
Stopford Rd. E13 —39Jc 65
Stopford Rd. SE17
—50Rb 83 (7C 206)
Store Rd. E16 —47Qc 86
Storers Quay. E14 —49Fc 85
Store St. E15 —36Fc 65
Store St. WC1 —43Mb 82 (1D 198)
Storey Rd. E17 —28Bc 44
Storey Rd. N6 —30Hb 41
Storey's Ga. SW1
—47Mb 82 (2E 204)
Storey St. E16 —46Qc 86
Stories M. SE5 —54Ub 105
Stories Rd. SE5 —55Ub 105
Stork Rd. E7 —37Jc 65
Storksmead Rd. Edgw —24Ua 40
Stork's Rd. SE16 —48Wb 83
Stormont Rd. N6 —31Hb 61
Stormont Rd. SW11 —55Jb 104
Stormont Way. Chess —78La 142
Stormount Dri. Hay —47S 76
Stornaway Strand. Grav —2H 137
Storr Gdns. Hut —15Fe 33
Storrington Rd. Croy —74Vb 147
Story St. N1 —38Pb 62
Stothard Pl. EC2
—43Ub 83 (7J 195)
Stothard St. E1 —42Yb 84
Stoughton Av. Sutt —78Za 144
Stoughton Clo. SE11
—49Pb 82 (6J 205)
Stoughton Clo. SW15 —60Wa 102
Stour Av. S'hall —48Ca 77
Stourcliffe St. W1
—44Hb 81 (3F 197)
Stour Clo. Kes —77Lc 149
Stour Clo. Slou —8F 72
Stourhead Clo. SW19 —59Za 102
Stourhead Gdns. SW20 —69Wa 124
Stour Rd. E3 —38Cc 64
Stour Rd. Dag —33Cd 68
Stour Rd. Dart —55Jd 110
Stour Rd. Grays —10C 92
Stourton Av. Felt —63Ba 121
Stour Way. Upm —30Ud 50
Stovell Rd. Wind —2F 94
Stowage. SE8 —51Cc 106
Stow Ct. Dart —59Sd 112
Stow Cres. E17 —24Ac 44
Stowe Cres. Ruis —30R 36
Stowe Gdns. N9 —18Vb 25
Stowe Ho. NW11 —30Eb 41
Stowell Av. New Ad —82Fc 167
Stowe Pl. N15 —27Ub 43
Stowe Rd. W12 —47Xa 80
Stowe Rd. Orp —77Xc 151
Stowe Rd. Slou —5C 72
Stowting Rd. Orp —77Uc 150
Stoxmead. Harr —25Fa 38
Stracey Rd. E7 —35Jc 65
Stracey Rd. NW10 —39Ta 59
Strachan Pl. SW19 —65Ya 124
Stradbroke Dri. Chig —23Qc 46
Stradbroke Gro. Buck H —18Mc 27
Stradbroke Gro. Ilf —27Nc 46
Stradbroke Pk. Chig —23Rc 46
Stradbroke Rd. N5 —35Sb 63
Stradbrook Clo. Harr —34Ba 57
Stradella Rd. SE24 —58Sb 105
Strafford Av. Ilf —26Qc 46
Strafford Clo. Pot B —4Cb 9
Strafford Ga. Pot B —4Cb 9
Strafford Rd. W3 —47Sa 79
Strafford Rd. Barn —13Ab 22
Strafford Rd. Houn —55Ba 99
Strafford Rd. Twic —59Ja 100
Strafford St. E14 —47Cc 84
Strahan Rd. E3 —41Ac 84
Straight Rd. Old Win —7L 95
Straight Rd. Romf —22Kd 49
Straightsmouth. SE10 —52Ec 106
Straight, The. S'hall —47Aa 77
Strait Rd. E6 —45Nc 86
Straits, The. Wal A —4Dc 12
Strakers Rd. SE15 —56Xb 105
Strale Ho. N1 —39Ub 63 (1H 195)
(off Whitmore Est.)
Strand. WC2 —45Nb 82 (6F 199)
Strand Clo. Eps —91Ta 177
Strand Ct. SE18 —50Uc 86
Strandfield Clo. SE18 —50Uc 86
Strand La. WC2 —45Pb 82 (4J 199)
Strand on the Grn. W4 —51Qa 101
Strand Pl. N18 —21Ub 43
Strand School App. W4 —51Qa 101
Strangeways. Wat —8U 4
Strangways Ter. W14 —48Bb 81
Stranraer Rd. Houn —58N 97
Stranraer Way. N1 —38Pb 62
Strasburg Rd. SW11 —53Jb 104
Stratfield Rd. Borwd —13Qa 21
Stratfield Rd. Slou —7L 73
Stratford Av. W8 —48Cb 81
Stratford Av. Uxb —40P 55
Stratford Cen. E15 —38Fc 65
Stratford Clo. Bark —38Wc 67
Stratford Clo. Dag —38Ed 68
Stratford Clo. Slou —2B 72
Stratford Ct. N Mald —70Ta 123
Stratford Ct. Wat —11X 19
Stratford Gdns. Stanf —1M 93
Stratford Gro. SW15 —56Za 102
Stratford Mkt. E15 —39Fc 65
Stratford Pk. Clo. N21 —17Rb 25
Stratford Pl. W1 —44Jb 82 (3K 197)
Stratford Rd. E13 —39Hc 65
Stratford Rd. NW4 —28Za 40
Stratford Rd. W3 —47Sa 79
Stratford Rd. W8 —48Cb 81
Stratford Rd. Hay —42X 77
Stratford Rd. Houn —58R 98
Stratford Rd. S'hall —49Aa 77
Stratford Rd. T Hth —70Qb 126
Stratford Rd. Wat —12W 18
Stratford Vs. NW1 —38Mb 62
Stratford Way. Wat —12V 18
Strathan Clo. SW18 —58Bb 103
Strathaven Rd. SE12 —58Kc 107
Strathblane Rd. SW11 —56Fb 103
Strathbrook Rd. SW16 —66Pb 126
Strathcona Av. Bookh —100Aa 175
Strathcona Rd. Wemb —33Ma 59
Strathdale. SW16 —64Pb 126
Strathdon Dri. SW17 —62Fb 125
Strathearn Av. Hay —52V 98
Strathearn Av. Twic —60Da 99
Strathearn Pl. W2
—44Gb 81 (4D 196)
Strathearn Rd. SW19 —64Cb 125
Strathearn Rd. Sutt —78Cb 145
Stratheden Rd. SE3 —52Jc 107
Strathfield Gdns. Bark —37Tc 66
Strathleven Rd. SW2 —57Nb 104
Strathmore. E Til —9L 93
Strathmore Clo. Cat —93Ub 181
Strathmore Gdns. N3 —25Db 41
Strathmore Gdns. W8 —46Cb 81
Strathmore Gdns. Edgw —26Ra 39
Strathmore Gdns. Horn —32Hd 68
Strathmore Rd. SW19 —62Cb 125
Strathmore Rd. Croy —73Tb 147
Strathmore Rd. Tedd —63Ga 122
Strathnairn St. SE1 —49Wb 83
Strathray Gdns. NW3 —37Gb 61
Strath Ter. SW11 —56Gb 103
Strathville Rd. SW18 —61Cb 125
Strathyre Av. SW16 —69Qb 126
Stratton Av. Enf —9Tb 11
Stratton Av. Wall —81Mb 164
Stratton Clo. SW19 —68Cb 125
Stratton Clo. Bexh —55Ad 109
Stratton Clo. Edgw —23Pa 39
Stratton Clo. Houn —53Ca 99
Stratton Clo. W on T —74Y 141
Stratton Ct. Pinn —24Ba 37
(off Devonshire Rd.)
Strattondale St. E14 —48Ec 84
Stratton Dri. Bark —36Uc 66
Stratton Gdns. S'hall —44Ba 77
Stratton Rd. SW19 —68Cb 125
Stratton Rd. Bexh —55Ad 109
Stratton Rd. Romf —22Qd 49
Stratton Rd. Sun —68V 120
Stratton St. W1 —46Kb 82 (6A 198)
Stratton Ter. W'ham —99Sc 184
Stratton Wlk. Romf —22Qd 49
Strauss Rd. W4 —47Ta 79
Strawberry Fields. Swan —67Gd 132
Strawberry Hill. Twic —62Ha 122
Strawberry Hill Clo. Twic
—62Ha 122
Strawberry Hill Rd. Twic —62Ha 122
Strawberry La. Cars —76Jb 146
Strawberry Vale. N2 —25Fb 41
Strawberry Vale. Twic —62Ja 122
Strayfield Rd. Enf —8Qb 10
Streakes Field Rd. NW2 —33Wa 60
Stream Clo. Byfl —84M 157
Streamdale. SE2 —51Xc 109
Stream La. Edgw —22Ra 39
Streamside Clo. N9 —18Vb 25
Streamside Clo. Brom —70Jc 129
Stream Way. Belv —51Bd 109
Streatfield Av. E6 —39Pc 66
Streatfield Rd. Harr —27La 38
Streatham Clo. SW16 —61Nb 126
Streatham Comn. N. SW16
—64Nb 126
Streatham Comn. S. SW16
—65Nb 126
Streatham Ct. SW16 —62Nb 126
Streatham High Rd. SW16
—63Nb 126
Streatham Hill. SW2 —61Nb 126
Streatham Pl. SW2 —59Nb 104
Streatham Rd. Mitc & SW16
—67Jb 126
Streatham St. WC1
—44Nb 82 (2F 199)
Streatham Vale. SW16 —67Lb 126
Streathbourne Rd. SW17
—61Jb 126
Streatley Pl. NW3 —35Eb 61
Streatley Rd. NW6 —38Bb 61
Streeters La. Wall —76Mb 146
Streetfield M. SE3 —55Jc 107
Street, The. Ash —78Ae 155
Street, The. Asht —90Pa 161
Street, The. Chfd —3J 3
Street, The. Cobh —10J 137
Street, The. Eff —100Z 175
Street, The. Fet —95Fa 176
Street, The. Hort K —70Rd 133
Street, The. Shorne —4N 137
Street, The. W Cla —100J 173
Street, The. W Hor —100R 174
Streimer Rd. E15 —40Ec 64
Strelley Way. W3 —45Ua 80
Stretton Rd. Croy —73Ub 147
Stretton Rd. Rich —61La 122
Stretton Way. Borwd —10Na 7
Strickland Av. Dart —55Pd 111
(in two parts)
Strickland Ct. SE15 —55Wb 105
Strickland Row. SW18 —59Fb 103
Strickland St. SE8 —53Cc 106
Strickland Way. Orp —77Vc 151
Stride Rd. E13 —40Hc 65
Stringer Ho. N1 —39Ub 63 (1J 195)
(off Whitmore Est.)
Stringer's Av. Guild —100A 172
Stringhams Copse. Rip —96J 173
Strode Clo. N10 —24Jb 42
Strode Rd. E7 —35Jc 65
Strode Rd. N17 —26Ub 43
Strode Rd. NW10 —37Wa 60
Strode Rd. SW6 —52Ab 102
Strode's Cres. Stai —64L 119
Strode St. Egh —63C 118
Stroma Ct. Cipp —5B 72
Strone Rd. E7 & E12 —37Lc 65
Strone Way. Hay —42Aa 77
Strongbow Cres. SE9 —57Pc 108
Strongbow Rd. SE9 —57Pc 108
Strongbridge Clo. Harr —32Ca 57
Stronsa Rd. W12 —47Va 80
Strood Av. Romf —32Fd 68
Strood La. Asc —5A 116
Stroud Clo. Wind —5B 94
Stroud Cres. SW15 —62Wa 124
Stroude Rd. Egh & Vir W —65C 118
Stroudes Clo. Wor Pk —73Ua 144
Stroud Field. N'holt —37Aa 57
Stroud Ga. Harr —35Da 57
Stroud Grn. Gdns. Croy —72Yb 148
Stroud Grn. Rd. N4 —32Pb 62
Stroud Grn. Way. Croy —73Xb 147
Stroudley Wlk. E3 —41Dc 84
Stroud Rd. SE25 —72Wb 147
Stroud Rd. SW19 —62Cb 125
Stroudwater Pk. Wey —79R 140
Stroud Way. Ashf —65R 120
Strouts Pl. E2 —41Vb 83 (3K 195)
Strudwick Ct. SW4 —53Nb 104
(off Binfield Rd.)
Strutton Ground. SW1
—48Mb 82 (3D 204)
Struttons Av. Grav —1B 136
Strype St. E1 —43Vb 83 (1K 201)
Stuart Av. NW9 —31Wa 60
Stuart Av. W5 —46Pa 79
Stuart Av. Brom —74Jc 149
Stuart Av. Harr —34Ba 57
Stuart Av. W on T —74X 141
Stuart Clo. Pil H —15Xd 32
Stuart Clo. Swan —66Hd 132
Stuart Clo. Uxb —37Q 56
Stuart Clo. Wind —4D 94
Stuart Ct. Els —16Ma 21
Stuart Cres. N22 —25Pb 42
Stuart Cres. Croy —76Bc 148
Stuart Cres. Hay —44S 76
Stuart Evans Clo. Well —55Yc 109
Stuart Gro. Tedd —64Ga 122
Stuart Mantle Way. Eri —52Gd 110
Stuart Pl. Mitc —67Hb 125
Stuart Rd. NW6 —41Cb 81
Stuart Rd. SE15 —56Yb 106
Stuart Rd. SW19 —62Cb 125
Stuart Rd. W3 —46Sa 79
Stuart Rd. Bark —38Vc 67
Stuart Rd. Barn —17Gb 23
Stuart Rd. Grav —8C 114
Stuart Rd. Grays —50De 91
Stuart Rd. Harr —27Ha 38
Stuart Rd. Rich —61Ka 122
Stuart Rd. T Hth —70Sb 127
Stuart Rd. Warl —92Xb 181
Stuart Rd. Well —53Xc 109
Stuart Way. Chesh —3Xb 11
Stuart Way. Stai —65K 119
Stuart Way. Vir W —10L 117
Stuart Way. Wind —4C 94
Stubbers La. Upm —37Td 70
Stubbs Ct. W4 —50Ra 79
(off Chaseley Dri.)
Stubbs Hill. Orp —85Yc 169
Stubbs La. Tad —100Bb 179
Stubbs Point. E13 —42Kc 85
Stubbs Way. SW19 —67Fb 125
Stucley Pl. NW1 —38Kb 62
Stucley Rd. Houn —52Ea 100
Studdridge St. SW6 —54Cb 103
Studd St. N1 —39Rb 63
Stud Grn. Wat —4W 4
Studholme Ct. NW3 —35Cb 61
Studholme St. SE15 —52Xb 105
Studio Pl. SW1 —47Hb 81 (2G 203)
(off Kinnerton St.)
Studios Rd. Shep —69P 119
Studios, The. Bush —16Ca 19
Studios, The. New Ash —75Be 155
(off Row, The)
Studio Way. Borwd —12Sa 21
Studland Clo. Sidc —62Vc 131
Studland Rd. SE26 —64Zb 128
Studland Rd. W7 —44Fa 78
Studland Rd. Byfl —85P 157
Studland Rd. King T —65Na 123
Studland St. W6 —49Xa 80
Studley Av. E4 —24Fc 45
Studley Clo. E5 —36Ac 64
Studley Ct. Sidc —64Xc 131
Studley Cres. Long —68Ee 135
Studley Dri. Ilf —30Mc 45
Studley Est. SW4 —53Nb 104
Studley Grange Rd. W7 —47Ga 78
Studley Rd. E7 —37Kc 65
Studley Rd. SW4 —53Nb 104
Studley Rd. Dag —38Zc 67
Stukeley Rd. E7 —38Kc 65
Stukeley St. WC2
—44Nb 82 (2G 199)
Stumps Hill La. Beck —65Cc 128
Stumps La. Whyt —89Ub 165
Sturdy Rd. SE15 —54Xb 105
Sturge Av. E17 —26Dc 44
Sturgeon Rd. SE17
—50Sb 83 (7D 206)
Sturges Field. Chst —65Tc 130
Sturgess Av. NW4 —31Xa 60
Sturge St. SE1 —47Sb 83 (1D 206)
Sturlas Way. Wal X —5Zb 12
Sturmer Way. N7 —36Pb 62
Sturminster Clo. Hay —44Y 77
Sturrock Clo. N15 —28Tb 43
Sturry St. E14 —44Dc 84
Sturt's La. Tad —99Ya 178
Sturt St. N1 —40Sb 63 (2E 194)
Stutfield St. E1 —44Wb 83
Stylecroft Rd. Chal G —19A 16
Styles End. Bookh —99Da 175
Styles Gdns. SW9 —55Rb 105
Styles Ho. SE1 —46Rb 83 (7B 200)
(off Eccles Pl.)
Styles Way. Beck —70Ec 128
Styventon Pl. Cher —73H 139
Succombs Hill. Warl —92Xb 181
Succombs Pl. Warl —91Xb 181
Sudbourne Rd. SW2 —57Nb 104
Sudbrooke Rd. SW12 —58Hb 103
Sudbrook Gdns. Rich —62Na 123
Sudbrook La. Rich —60Na 101
Sudbury. E6 —44Qc 86
Sudbury Av. Wemb —34Ma 59
Sudbury Ct. E5 —35Ac 64
Sudbury Ct. SW8 —53Nb 104
Sudbury Ct. Dri. Harr —34Ha 58
Sudbury Ct. Rd. Harr —34Ha 58
Sudbury Cres. Brom —65Jc 129
Sudbury Cres. Wemb —36Ka 58
Sudbury Croft. Wemb —35Ha 58
Sudbury Gdns. Croy —77Ub 147
Sudbury Heights Av. Gnfd
—36Ha 58
Sudbury Hill. Harr —33Ga 58
Sudbury Hill Clo. Wemb —34Ha 58
Sudbury Rd. Bark —36Vc 67
Sudbury Towers. Gnfd —36Ga 58
Sudeley St. N1 —40Rb 63 (2C 194)
Sudicamps Ct. Wal A —5Jc 13
Sudlow Rd. SW18 —57Cb 103
Sudrey St. SE1 —47Sb 83 (2D 206)
Suez Av. Gnfd —40Ha 58
Suez Rd. Enf —14Ac 26
Suffield Clo. S Croy —84Zb 166
Suffield Rd. E4 —21Dc 44
Suffield Rd. N15 —29Vb 43
Suffield Rd. SE20 —68Yb 128
Suffolk Clo. Borwd —15Ta 21
Suffolk Clo. Slou —4C 72
Suffolk Ct. E10 —31Cc 64
Suffolk Ho. SE20 —66Zb 128
(off Croydon Rd.)
Suffolk La. EC4 —45Tb 83 (4F 201)
Suffolk Pk. Rd. E17 —28Ac 44
Suffolk Pl. SW1
—46Mb 82 (6E 198)
Suffolk Rd. E13 —41Jc 85
Suffolk Rd. N15 —29Tb 43
Suffolk Rd. NW10 —38Ua 60
Suffolk Rd. SE25 —70Vb 127
Suffolk Rd. SW13 —52Va 102
Suffolk Rd. Bark —38Tc 66
Suffolk Rd. Dag —36Ed 68
Suffolk Rd. Dart —58Nd 111
Suffolk Rd. Enf —15Xb 25
Suffolk Rd. Grav —8F 114
Suffolk Rd. Harr —30Ba 37
Suffolk Rd. Ilf —30Uc 46
Suffolk Rd. Pot B —4Ab 8
Suffolk Rd. Sidc —65Yc 131
Suffolk Rd. Wor Pk —75Va 144
Suffolk St. E7 —35Jc 65
Suffolk St. SW1
—45Mb 82 (5E 198)
Suffolk Way. Horn —28Qd 49
Suffolk Way. Sev —97Ld 187
Sugar Bakers Ct. EC3
—44Ub 83 (3J 201)
(off Creechurch La.)
Sugar Ho. La. E15 —40Ec 64
Sugar Loaf Wlk. E2 —41Yb 84
Sugar Quay. EC3
—45Ub 83 (5J 201)
(off Lwr. Thames St.)
Sugar Quay Wlk. EC3
—45Ub 83 (5J 201)
Sugden Rd. SW11 —55Jb 104
Sugden Rd. Th Dit —74Ka 142
Sugden Way. Bark —40Vc 67
Sulgrave Gdns. W6 —47Ya 80
Sulgrave Rd. W6 —48Ya 80
Sulina Rd. SW2 —59Nb 104
Sulivan Ct. SW6 —54Cb 103
Sulivan Enterprise Cen. SW6
—55Cb 103
Sulivan Rd. SW6 —55Cb 103
Sullivan Av. E16 —43Mc 85
Sullivan Clo. SW11 —55Gb 103
Sullivan Clo. Dart —58Kd 111
Sullivan Clo. W Mol —69Da 121
Sullivan Ct. N16 —31Vb 63
Sullivan Cres. Hare —26M 35
Sullivan Rd. SE11
—49Rb 83 (5B 206)
Sullivan Rd. Til —3C 114
Sullivans Reach. W on T —73V 140
Sullivan Way. Els —16La 20
Sultan Rd. E11 —28Kc 45
Sultan St. SE5 —52Sb 105
Sultan St. Beck —68Zb 128
Sumatra Rd. NW6 —36Cb 61
Sumburgh Way. Slou —3J 73
Sumburg Rd. SW12 —58Jb 104
Summer Av. E Mol —71Ga 142
Summercourt Rd. E1 —44Yb 84
Summerdene Clo. SW16
—66Lb 126
Summerfield. Asht —91Ma 177
Summerfield Av. NW6 —40Ab 60
Summerfield Clo. Add —78H 139
Summerfield La. Surb —75Ma 143
Summerfield Pl. Ott —79F 138
Summerfield Rd. W5 —42Ka 78
Summerfield Rd. Lou —16Mc 27
Summerfield Rd. Wat —7W 4
Summerfield St. SE12 —59Hc 107
Summer Gdns. E Mol —71Ga 142
Summer Gro. Els —16Ma 21
Summerhayes Clo. Wok —86A 156
Summerhays. Cob —85Z 159
Summer Hill. Chst —68Qc 130
Summer Hill. Els —15Qa 21
Summerhill Clo. Orp —76Uc 150
Summerhill Gro. Enf —16Ub 25
Summerhill Rd. N15 —28Tb 43
Summerhill Rd. Dart —59Md 111
Summerhill Vs. Chst —67Qc 130
Summerhouse Av. Houn —53Aa 99
Summerhouse Dri. Bex & Dart
—63Fd 132
Summerhouse La. Ald —12Ea 20
Summerhouse La. Hare —24J 35
Summerhouse La. W Dray —51M 97
Summerhouse Rd. N16 —33Ub 63
Summerhouse Way. Abb L —2V 4
Summerland Gdns. N10 —27Kb 42
Summerland Grange. N10
—27Kb 42
Summerlands Av. W3 —45Sa 79
Summerlands Lodge. Orp
—77Qc 150
Summerlay Clo. Tad —92Ab 178
Summerlea. Slou —6F 72
Summerlee Av. N2 —28Hb 41
Summerlee Gdns. N2 —28Hb 41
Summerley St. SW18 —61Db 125
Summer Pl. Wat —16V 18
Summer Rd. E Mol & Th Dit
—71Ga 142
Summersby Rd. N6 —30Kb 42
Summers Clo. Sutt —80Cb 145
Summers Clo. Wemb —32Ra 59
Summers Clo. Wey —83Q 158
Summers La. N12 —24Fb 41
Summers Rd. Burn —1A 72
Summers Row. N12 —23Gb 41
Summers St. EC1
—42Qb 82 (6K 193)
Summerstown. SW17 —62Eb 125
Summerswood Clo. Kenl
—88Tb 165
Summerswood La. Borwd —6Ua 8
Summerton Way. SE28 —44Zc 87
Summer Trees. Sun —67X 121
Summerville Gdns. Sutt —79Bb 145
Summerwood Rd. Iswth —57Ha 100
Summit Av. NW9 —29Ta 39
Summit Clo. N14 —19Lb 24
Summit Clo. NW2 —37Ab 60
Summit Clo. NW9 —28Ta 39
Summit Clo. Edgw —24Qa 39
Summit Dri. Wfd G —26Mc 45
Summit Est. N16 —31Wb 63
Summit Rd. E17 —28Dc 44
Summit Rd. N'holt —38Ca 57
Summit Rd. Pot B —2Ab 8
Summit, The. Lou —11Pc 28
Summit Way. N14 —19Kb 24
Summit Way. SE19 —66Ub 127
Sumner Av. SE15 —53Vb 105
Sumner Bldgs. SE1
—46Sb 83 (6D 200)
(off Sumner St.)
Sumner Clo. Fet —96Fa 176
Sumner Clo. Orp —77Sc 150
Sumner Ct. SW8 —53Nb 104
Sumner Est. SE15 —52Vb 105
Sumner Gdns. Croy —74Rb 147
Sumner Pl. SW7
—49Fb 81 (6C 202)
Sumner Pl. M. SW7
—49Fb 81 (6C 202)
Sumner Rd. SE15 —51Vb 105
(in two parts)
Sumner Rd. Croy —74Qb 146
Sumner Rd. Harr —31Ea 58
Sumner Rd. S. Croy —74Qb 146
Sumner St. SE1
—46Rb 83 (6C 200)
Sumpter Clo. NW3 —37Eb 61
Sun All. Rich —56Na 101
Sunbeam Rd. NW10 —42Sa 79
Sunbury Av. NW7 —22Ta 39
Sunbury Av. SW14 —56Ta 101
Sunbury Ct. Barn —14Ab 22
(off Manor Rd.)
Sunbury Ct. M. Sun —68Z 121
Sunbury Ct. Rd. Sun —68Y 121
Sunbury Cres. Felt —63V 120
Sunbury Cross Shopping Cen. Sun
—66V 120
Sunbury Gdns. NW7 —22Ta 39
Sunbury La. SW11 —53Fb 103
Sunbury La. W on T —72W 140
Sunbury Rd. Eton —1H 95
Sunbury Rd. Felt —62V 120
Sunbury Rd. Sutt —76Ab 144
Sunbury St. SE18 —48Pc 86
Sunbury Way. Felt —64Y 121
Sun Clo. Eton —1H 95
Sun Ct. EC3 —44Tb 83 (3G 201)
(off Cornhill)
Suncourt. Eri —54Hd 110
Suncroft Pl. SE26 —62Yb 128
Sundale Av. S Croy —82Yb 166
Sunderland Ct. Stanw —58N 97
Sunderland Rd. SE23 —60Zb 106
Sunderland Rd. W5 —48Ma 79
Sunderland Rd. Houn —58N 97
Sunderland Ter. W2 —44Db 81
Sunderland Way. E12 —33Mc 65
Sundew Av. W12 —45Wa 80
Sundew Ct. Grays —51Fe 113
Sundew Ct. Wemb —40Na 59
(off Elmore Clo.)
Sundial Av. SE25 —69Vb 127
Sundorne Rd. SE7 —50Lc 85
Sundown Av. S Croy —83Vb 165
Sundown Rd. Ashf —64S 120
Sundra Wlk. E1 —42Zb 84
Sundridge Av. Brom & Chst
—67Mc 129
Sundridge Av. Well —54Tc 108
Sundridge Clo. Dart —58Qd 111
Sundridge Hill. Knock —90Yc 169
Sundridge La. Knock —89Xc 169
Sundridge Pde. Brom —66Kc 129
Sundridge Pl. Croy —74Wb 147
Sundridge Rd. Chev —92Cd 186
Sundridge Rd. Croy —73Vb 147
Sundridge Rd. Wok —91C 172
Sunfields Pl. SE3 —52Kc 107
Sunflower Way. Romf —25Md 49
Sungate Cotts. Romf —25Bd 47
Sun Hill. Fawk —76Wd 154
Sun Hill. Wok —9D 188
Sunkist Way. Wall —81Nb 164
Sunland Av. Bexh —56Ad 109
Sun La. SE3 —52Kc 107
Sun La. Grav —1E 136
Sunleigh Rd. Wemb —39Na 59
Sunley Gdns. Gnfd —39Ja 58
Sunmead Clo. Fet —94Ha 176
Sunmead Rd. Sun —68W 120
Sunna Gdns. Sun —68X 121
Sunnindale Av. Felt —61Aa 121
Sunningdale. N14 —22Mb 42
Sunningdale Av. W3 —45Ua 80
Sunningdale Av. Bark —39Tc 66
Sunningdale Av. Rain —42Kd 89
Sunningdale Av. Ruis —32Y 57
Sunningdale Clo. Stan —23Ja 38
Sunningdale Clo. Surb —75Na 143
Sunningdale Ct. Houn —58Fa 100
(off Whitton Dene)
Sunningdale Gdns. NW9 —29Sa 39
Sunningdale Rd. Brom —70Nc 130
Sunningdale Rd. Rain —38Jd 68
Sunningdale Rd. Sutt —77Bb 145
Sunningfields Cres. NW4 —26Xa 40
Sunningfields Rd. NW4 —26Xa 40
Sunning Hill. Grav —1A 136
Sunninghill Clo. Asc —10B 116
Sunninghill Ct. W3 —47Sa 79
Sunninghill Ct. Asc —10B 116
Sunninghill Rd. SE13 —54Dc 106
Sunninghill Rd. Asc —7D 116
Sunninghill Rd. S'hill —10B 116
Sunninghill Rd. Wind & Asc
—4B 116
Sunnings La. Upm —36Sd 70
Sunningvale Av. Big H —87Lc 167
Sunningvale Clo. Big H —87Mc 167
Sunny Bank. SE25 —69Wb 127
Sunnybank. Eps —88Sa 161
Sunnybank. Warl —89Ac 165
Sunnybank Rd. Pot B —5Cb 9
Sunny Cres. NW10 —38Sa 59
Sunnycroft Gdns. Upm —31Ud 70
Sunnycroft Rd. SE25 —70Wb 127
Sunnycroft Rd. Houn —54Da 99
Sunnycroft Rd. S'hall —43Ca 77
Sunnydale. Orp —75Qc 150
Sunnydale Gdns. NW7 —23Ta 39
Sunnydale Rd. SE12 —57Kc 107
Sunnydene Av. E4 —22Fc 45
Sunnydene Av. Ruis —32W 56
Sunnydene Clo. Romf —24Pd 49
Sunnydene Gdns. Wemb —37La 58
Sunnydene Rd. Purl —85Rb 165
Sunnydene St. SE26 —63Ac 128
Sunnyfield. NW7 —21Va 40

Sunnyfield Rd. Chst —69Wc 131
Sunny Gdns. Pde. NW4 —26Xa 40
Sunny Gdns. Rd. NW4 —26Xa 40
Sunny Hill. NW4 —27Xa 40
Sunnyhill Rd. SW16 —63Nb 126
Sunnyhill Rd. W Hyd —23F 34
Sunnyhurst Clo. Sutt —76Cb 145
Sunnymead Av. Mitc —69Mb 126
Sunnymead Rd. NW9 —31Ta 59
Sunnymead Rd. SW15 —57Xa 102
Sunnymede. Chig —20Xc 29
Sunnymede Av. Cars —83Fb 163
Sunnymede Av. Eps —81Ua 162
Sunnymede Dri. Ilf —29Rc 46
Sunny Nook Gdns. S Croy —79Tb 147
Sunny Rise. Cat —96Tb 181
Sunny Rd., The. Enf —11Zb 26
Sunnyside. NW2 —34Bb 61
Sunnyside. SW19 —65Ab 124
Sunnyside. W on T —71Y 141
Sunnyside Dri. E4 —17Ec 26
Sunnyside Gdns. Upm —34Sd 70
Sunnyside Houses. NW2 —34Bb 61
(off Sunnyside)
Sunnyside Pas. SW19 —65Ab 124
Sunnyside Rd. E10 —32Cc 64
Sunnyside Rd. N19 —31Mb 62
Sunnyside Rd. W5 —46Ma 79
Sunnyside Rd. Epp —5Vc 15
Sunnyside Rd. Ilf —34Sc 66
Sunnyside Rd. Tedd —63Fa 122
Sunnyside Rd. E. N9 —20Wb 25
Sunnyside Rd. N. N9 —20Vb 25
Sunnyside Rd. S. N9 —20Vb 25
Sunnyside Ter. NW9 —27Ta 39
Sunny View. NW9 —29Ta 39
Sunny Way. N12 —24Gb 41
Sun Pas. Wind —3H 95
Sunray Av. SE24 —56Tb 105
Sunray Av. Brom —72Nc 150
Sun Ray Av. Hut —16Fe 33
Sunray Av. Surb —75Ra 143
Sunray Av. W Dray —47M 75
Sunrise Av. Horn —34Ld 69
Sunrise Clo. Felt —62Ba 121
Sunrise Cotts. Sev —94Hd 186
Sunrise View. NW7 —23Va 40
Sun Rd. W14 —50Bb 81
Sun Rd. Swans —58Be 113
Sunset Av. E4 —18Dc 26
Sunset Av. Wfd G —21Hc 45
Sunset Dri. Hav —22Kd 49
Sunset Gdns. SE25 —68Vb 127
Sunset Rd. SE5 —56Sb 105
Sunset View. Barn —12Ab 22
Sunshine Way. Mitc —68Hb 125
Sunstone Gro. Red —100Mb 180
Sun St. EC2 —43Tb 83 (7G 195)
Sun St. Wal A —5Ec 12
Sun St. Pas. EC2 —43Ub 83 (1H 201)
Sunwell Clo. SE15 —53Xb 105
Surbiton Ct. Surb —72La 142
Surbiton Cres. King T —70Na 123
Surbiton Hall Clo. King T —70Na 123
Surbiton Hill Pk. Surb —71Pa 143
Surbiton Hill Rd. Surb —71Na 143
Surbiton Pde. Surb —72Na 143
Surbiton Rd. King T —70Ma 123
Surley Hall Wlk. Wind —3D 94
Surlingham Clo. SE28 —45Zc 87
Surma Clo. E1 —42Xb 83
Surman Cres. Hut —17Ee 33
Surrendale Pl. W9 —42Cb 81
Surrey Av. Slou —3G 72
Surrey Canal Rd. SE15 & SE14 —51Yb 106
Surrey Ct. N3 —27Ab 40
Surrey Cres. W4 —50Qa 79
Surrey Dri. Horn —28Qd 49
Surrey Gdns. N4 —30Sb 43
Surrey Gdns. Eff J —94W 174
Surrey Gro. SE17 —50Ub 83
Surrey Gro. Sutt —76Fb 145
Surrey La. SW11 —53Gb 103
Surrey La. Est. SW11 —53Gb 103
Surrey M. SE27 —63Ub 127
Surrey Mt. SE23 —60Xb 105
Surrey Quays Rd. SE16 —48Yb 84
Surrey Quays Shopping Cen. SE16 —48Zb 84
Surrey Rd. SE15 —57Zb 106
Surrey Rd. Bark —38Uc 66
Surrey Rd. Dag —36Dd 68
Surrey Rd. Harr —29Ea 38
Surrey Rd. W Wick —74Dc 148
Surrey Row. SE1 —47Rb 83 (1B 206)
Surrey Sq. SE17 —50Ub 83 (7H 207)
Surrey St. E13 —41Kc 85
Surrey St. SE17 —50Ub 83
Surrey St. WC2 —45Pb 82 (4J 199)
Surrey St. Croy —76Sb 147
Surrey Ter. SE17 —50Ub 83 (7J 207)
Surrey Water Rd. SE16 —46Zb 84
Surridge Clo. Rain —41Ld 89
Surridge Ct. SW9 —54Nb 104
(off Clapham Rd.)
Surridge Gdns. SE19 —65Tb 127
Surr St. N7 —36Nb 62
Susan Clo. Romf —27Ed 48
Susan Edwards Ho. Ger X —21A 34
(off Micholls Av.)
Susan Lawrence Ho. E12 —35Qc 66
(off Walton Rd.)
Susannah St. E14 —44Dc 84
Susan Rd. SE3 —54Kc 107
Susan Wood. Chst —67Qc 130
Sussex Av. Iswth —55Ga 100
Sussex Av. Romf —24Pd 49
Sussex Clo. N19 —33Nb 62
Sussex Clo. Ilf —29Pc 46
Sussex Clo. Knap —6A 188
Sussex Clo. N Mald —70Ua 124
Sussex Clo. Slou —7M 73
Sussex Clo. Twic —58Ka 100
Sussex Ct. Add —78L 139
Sussex Cres. N'holt —37Ca 57
Sussex Gdns. N4 —29Sb 43
Sussex Gdns. N6 —29Hb 41
Sussex Gdns. W2 —45Fb 81 (4B 196)
Sussex Gdns. Chess —79Ma 143
Sussex Ga. N6 —29Hb 41
Sussex Keep. Slou —7M 73
Sussex M. E. W2
(off Clifton Pl.) —44Fb 81 (3C 196)
Sussex M. W. W2 —45Fb 81 (4C 196)
Sussex Pl. NW1 —42Hb 81 (5F 191)
Sussex Pl. W2 —44Fb 81 (3C 196)
Sussex Pl. W6 —50Ya 80
Sussex Pl. Eri —52Dd 110
Sussex Pl. N Mald —70Ua 124
Sussex Pl. Slou —7L 73
Sussex Ring. N12 —22Cb 41
Sussex Rd. E6 —39Qc 66
Sussex Rd. Cars —80Hb 145
Sussex Rd. Dart —59Qd 111
Sussex Rd. Eri —52Dd 110
Sussex Rd. Harr —29Ea 38
Sussex Rd. Knap —6A 188
Sussex Rd. Mitc —71Nb 146
Sussex Rd. N Mald —70Ua 124
Sussex Rd. Orp —72Yc 151
Sussex Rd. Sidc —64Xc 131
Sussex Rd. S'hall —48Z 77
Sussex Rd. S Croy —79Tb 147
Sussex Rd. Uxb —35S 56
Sussex Rd. War —21Xd 50
Sussex Rd. Wat —9W 4
Sussex Rd. W Wick —74Dc 148
Sussex Sq. W2 —45Fb 81 (4C 196)
Sussex St. E13 —41Kc 85
Sussex St. SW1 —50Kb 82 (7A 204)
Sussex Wlk. SW9 —56Rb 105
Sussex Way. N19 & N7 —32Nb 62
Sussex Way. Barn —15Kb 24
Sussex Way. Den —29H 35
Sutcliffe Clo. NW11 —29Db 41
Sutcliffe Clo. Bush —14Ea 20
Sutcliffe Rd. SE18 —51Uc 108
Sutcliffe Rd. Well —54Yc 109
Sutherland Av. W9 —42Cb 81
Sutherland Av. W13 —44Ka 78
Sutherland Av. Big H —89Mc 167
Sutherland Av. Cuff —1Mb 10
Sutherland Av. Hay —49W 76
Sutherland Av. Jac —100A 172
Sutherland Av. Orp —72Vc 151
Sutherland Av. Sun —68V 120
Sutherland Av. Well —56Uc 108
Sutherland Clo. Barn —14Ab 22
Sutherland Clo. Grav —1K 137
Sutherland Ct. NW9 —29Ra 39
Sutherland Dri. SW19 —67Fb 125
Sutherland Gdns. SW14 —55Ua 102
Sutherland Gdns. Sun —68V 120
Sutherland Gdns. Wor Pk —74Xa 144
Sutherland Gro. SW18 —58Ab 102
Sutherland Gro. Tedd —64Ga 122
Sutherland Ho. W8 —48Db 81
Sutherland Pl. W2 —44Cb 81
Sutherland Point. E5 —35Xb 63
(off Tiger Way)
Sutherland Rd. E17 —27Zb 44
Sutherland Rd. N9 —18Xb 25
Sutherland Rd. N17 —25Wb 43
Sutherland Rd. SW1 —50Kb 82
Sutherland Rd. W4 —51Ua 102
Sutherland Rd. W13 —44Ja 78
Sutherland Rd. Belv —48Cd 88
Sutherland Rd. Croy —73Qb 146
Sutherland Rd. Enf —16Zb 26
Sutherland Rd. S'hall —44Ba 77
Sutherland Rd. Path. E17 —27Zb 44
Sutherland Row. SW1 —50Kb 82 (7A 204)
Sutherland Sq. SE17 —50Sb 83
Sutherland St. SW1 —50Kb 82 (7K 203)
Sutherland Wlk. SE17 —50Sb 83 (7E 206)
Sutherland Way. Cuff —1Mb 10
Sutlej Rd. SE7 —52Lc 107
Sutterton St. N7 —37Pb 62
Sutton Arc. Sutt —78Db 145
Sutton Av. Slou —7N 73
Sutton Av. Wok —7B 188
Sutton Clo. Beck —67Dc 128
Sutton Clo. Lou —17Nc 28
Sutton Clo. Pinn —29W 36
Sutton Comn. Rd. Sutt —73Bb 145
Sutton Ct. W4 —51Sa 101
Sutton Ct. Sutt —79Eb 145
Sutton Ct. Rd. E13 —41Lc 85
Sutton Ct. Rd. W4 —52Sa 101
Sutton Ct. Rd. Sutt —79Eb 145
Sutton Ct. Rd. Uxb —39R 56
Sutton Cres. Barn —15Za 22
Sutton Dene. Houn —53Da 99
Sutton Est. EC1 —41Tb 83 (4G 195)
(off City Rd.)
Sutton Est. W10 —43Ya 80
Sutton Est., The. N1 —38Rb 63
Sutton Est., The. SW3 —50Gb 81 (7E 202)
Sutton Gdns. SE25 —71Vb 147
Sutton Gdns. Bark —39Uc 66
Sutton Gdns. Croy —71Vb 147
Sutton Gdns. Red —100Mb 180
Sutton Grn. Bark —39Vc 67
Sutton Grn. Rd. Guild —98A 172
Sutton Gro. Sutt —77Fb 145
Sutton Hall Rd. Houn —52Ca 99
Sutton La. Coln —51D 96
Sutton La. Houn —55Ba 99
Sutton La. Sutt & Bans —83Db 163
Sutton La. N. W4 —50Sa 79
Sutton La. S. W4 —51Sa 101
Sutton Pde. NW4 —28Ya 40
(off Church Rd.)
Sutton Pk. Rd. Sutt —79Db 145
Sutton Path. Borwd —13Qa 21
Sutton Pl. E9 —36Yb 64
Sutton Pl. Slou —51D 96
Sutton Rd. E13 —42Hc 85
Sutton Rd. E17 —25Zb 44
Sutton Rd. N10 —25Jb 42
Sutton Rd. Bark —39Uc 66
Sutton Rd. Houn —53Ca 99
Sutton Rd. Wat —13Y 19
Sutton Row. W1 —44Mb 82 (2E 198)
Suttons Av. Horn —34Ld 69
Suttons Gdns. Horn —34Md 69
Suttons La. Horn —36Md 69
Sutton Sq. E9 —36Yb 64
Sutton Sq. Houn —53Ba 99
Sutton St. E1 —45Yb 84
Sutton's Way. EC1 —42Sb 83 (6E 194)
Sutton Way. W10 —42Ya 80
Sutton Way. Houn —53Ba 99
Swabey Rd. Slou —49C 74
Swaby Rd. SW18 —60Eb 103
Swaffham Way. N17 —24Rb 43
Swaffield Rd. SW18 —59Db 103
Swaffield Rd. Sev —94Ld 187
Swain Clo. SW16 —65Kb 126
Swain Rd. T Hth —71Sb 147
Swains Clo. W Dray —47N 75
Swains La. N6 —32Jb 62
Swainson Rd. W3 —47Va 80
Swains Rd. SW17 —66Hb 125
Swaisland Dri. Dart —57Hd 110
Swaisland Rd. Dart —58Kd 111
Swakeleys Dri. Uxb —35Q 56
Swakeleys Rd. Uxb —35N 55
Swalecliffe Rd. Belv —50Dd 88
Swale Clo. S Ock —44Sd 90
Swaledale Rd. Dart —60Sd 112
Swale Rd. Dart —56Jd 110
Swallands Rd. SE6 —62Cc 128
(in two parts)
Swallowbrook Bus. Cen. Hay —46Z 77
Swallow Clo. SE14 —53Zb 106
Swallow Clo. Bush —18Da 19
Swallow Clo. Grnh —57Vd 112
Swallow Clo. Rick —17L 17
Swallow Clo. Stai —63H 119
Swallow Ct. SE12 —59Jc 107
Swallow Ct. Enf —10Yb 12
Swallow Ct. Ilf —29Rc 46
Swallow Ct. Ruis —32Y 57
Swallowdale. Iver —41F 74
Swallowdale. S Croy —81Zb 166
Swallow Dri. NW10 —37Ta 59
Swallow Dri. N'holt —40Ca 57
Swallowfield. Egh —5M 117
Swallowfield Rd. SE7 —50Kc 85
Swallowfields. Grav —2A 136
Swallowfield Way. Hay —47T 76
Swallow Oaks. Abb L —3V 4
Swallow Pk. Surb —76Qa 143
Swallow Pas. W1 —44Kb 82 (3A 198)
(off Swallow Pl.)
Swallow Pl. W1 —44Kb 82 (3A 198)
Swallow Rise. Knap —5A 188
Swallows Cross Rd. Mount —11Ee 33
Swallow St. E6 —43Nc 86
Swallow St. W1 —45Lb 82 (5C 198)
Swallow St. Iver —41F 74
Swallow Wlk. Horn —37Kd 69
Swanage Rd. E4 —24Ec 44
Swanage Rd. SW18 —58Eb 103
Swanage Waye. Hay —44Y 77
Swan App. E6 —43Nc 86
Swan Av. Upm —32Vd 70
Swanbourne Dri. Horn —36Ld 69
Swanbridge Rd. Bexh —53Cd 110
Swan Bus. Pk. Dart —56Md 111
Swan Cen., The. Lea —93Ka 176
Swan Clo. E17 —25Ac 44
Swan Clo. Croy —73Ub 147
Swan Clo. Felt —63Aa 121
Swan Clo. Orp —69Wc 131
Swan Ct. SW3 —50Gb 81
Swan Ct. Iswth —55Ka 100
(off Swan St.)
Swan Ct. Lea —94Ka 176
Swandon Way. SW18 —57Db 103
Swan Dri. NW9 —26Ua 40
Swanfield Rd. Wal X —5Ac 12
Swanfield St. E2 —41Vb 83 (4K 195)
Swanland Rd. S Mim & Hat —5Xa 8
Swan La. EC4 —45Tb 83 (5G 201)
Swan La. N20 —20Eb 23
Swan La. Dart —59Hd 110
Swanley Bar La. Pot B —1Db 9
Swanley By-Pass. Swan —67Dd 132
Swanley Cen. Swan —69Gd 132
Swanley Cres. Pot B —1Db 9
Swanley La. Swan —69Hd 132
Swanley Rd. Well —53Yc 109
Swanley Village Rd. Swan —67Kd 133
Swan Mead. SE1 —48Ub 83 (4H 207)
Swan M. SW9 —53Pb 104
Swann Ct. Chalv —8J 73
Swanns Meadow. Bookh —98Ca 175
Swan Paddock. Brtwd —19Yd 32
Swan Pas. E1 —45Wb 83
(off Royal Mint St.)
Swan & Pike Rd. Enf —10Cc 12
Swan Pl. SW13 —54Va 102
Swan Rd. SE16 —47Yb 84
Swan Rd. SE18 —48Mc 85
Swan Rd. Felt —64Aa 121
Swan Rd. Iver —44H 75
Swan Rd. S'hall —44Da 77
Swan Rd. W Dray —47M 75
Swanscombe Bus. Cen. Swans —57Ae 113
Swanscombe Ho. W11 —46Za 80
(off St Ann's Rd.)
Swanscombe Point. E16 —43Hc 85
(off Clarkson Rd.)
Swanscombe Rd. W4 —50Ua 80
Swanscombe Rd. W11 —46Za 80
Swanscombe St. Swans —59Ae 113
Swans Ct. Wal X —6Ac 12
Swansea Rd. Enf —14Yb 26
Swansea Rd. Houn —58S 98
Swanshope. Lou —12Rc 28
Swansland Gdns. E17 —25Ac 44
Swanston Path. Wat —20Y 19
Swan St. SE1 —48Sb 83 (3E 206)
Swan St. Iswth —55Ka 100
Swan Ter. Wind —2F 94
Swanton Gdns. SW19 —60Za 102
Swanton Rd. Eri —52Dd 110
Swan Wlk. SW3 —51Hb 103
Swan Wlk. Romf —29Gd 48
Swan Way. Enf —12Zb 26
Swanworth La. Mick —100Ja 176
Swan Yd. N1 —37Rb 63
Swan Yd. Grav —8D 114
Swanzy Rd. Sev —92Ld 187
Sward Rd. Orp —72Wc 151
Swaton Rd. E3 —42Cc 84
Swaylands Rd. Belv —51Cd 110
Swaythling Clo. N18 —21Xb 43
Swedenborg Gdns. E1 —45Xb 83
Sweden Ga. SE16 —48Ac 84
Swedish Quays Development. SE16 —48Ac 84
Sweeney Cres. SE1 —47Vb 83 (2K 207)
Sweeps La. Egh —64B 118
Sweeps La. Orp —71Zc 151
Sweet Briar Grn. N9 —20Vb 25
Sweet Briar Gro. N9 —20Vb 25
Sweet Briar La. Eps —86Ta 161
Sweet Briar Wlk. N18 —21Vb 43
Sweetcroft La. Uxb —38P 55
Sweetland Ct. Dag —37Xc 67
Sweetmans Av. Pinn —27Z 37
Sweets Way. N20 —19Fb 23
Swell Ct. E17 —30Dc 44
Swetenham Wlk. SE18 —50Sc 86
Swete St. E13 —40Jc 65
Sweyne Rd. Swans —58Ae 113
Sweyn Pl. SE3 —54Jc 107
Sweyn Rd. Grnh —57Yd 112
Swievelands Rd. Big H —91Kc 183
Swift Clo. E17 —24Ac 44
Swift Clo. Harr —33Da 57
Swift Clo. Hay —44W 76
Swift Clo. Upm —32Ud 70
Swift Ct. Seal —93Qd 187
Swift Ct. Sutt —80Db 145
Swift Rd. Felt —63Z 121
Swift Rd. S'hall —48Ca 77
Swiftsden Way. Brom —65Gc 129
Swift St. SW6 —53Bb 103
Swiller's La. Shorne —4N 137
Swinbrook Rd. W10 —43Ab 80
Swinburne Ct. SE5 —56Tb 105
(off Basingdon Way)
Swinburne Cres. Croy —72Yb 148
Swinburne Gdns. Til —4D 114
Swinburne Rd. SW15 —56Wa 102
Swinderby Rd. Wemb —37Na 59
Swindon Clo. Ilf —33Uc 66
Swindon Clo. Romf —22Pd 49
Swindon Gdns. Romf —22Pd 49
Swindon La. Romf —22Pd 49
Swindon St. W12 —46Xa 80
Swinfield Clo. Felt —62Aa 121
Swinford Gdns. SW9 —55Rb 105
Swingate La. SE18 —51Uc 108
Swinnerton St. E9 —36Ac 64
Swinton Clo. Wemb —32Ra 59
Swinton Pl. WC1 —41Pb 82 (3H 193)
Swinton St. WC1 —41Pb 82 (3H 193)
Swires Shaw. Kes —77Mc 149
Swiss Av. Wat —14U 18
Swiss Clo. Wat —13U 18
Swiss Ct. WC2 —45Mb 82 (5E 198)
(off Panton St.)
Swiss Ter. NW6 —38Fb 61
Swithland Gdns. SE9 —63Qc 130
Swyncombe Av. W5 —49Ka 78
Swynford Gdns. NW4 —28Wa 40
Sybil M. N4 —30Rb 43
Sybil Phoenix Clo. SE8 —50Zb 84
Sybourn St. E17 —31Bc 64
Sycamore App. Crox —15S 18
Sycamore Av. W5 —48Ma 79
Sycamore Av. Hay —45U 76
Sycamore Av. Sidc —58Vc 109
Sycamore Av. Upm —34Qd 69
Sycamore Clo. E16 —42Gc 85
Sycamore Clo. N9 —21Wb 43
Sycamore Clo. SE9 —61Nc 130
Sycamore Clo. W3 —46Ua 80
Sycamore Clo. Barn —16Fb 23
Sycamore Clo. Bush —12Aa 19
Sycamore Clo. Cars —77Hb 145
Sycamore Clo. Felt —62W 120
Sycamore Clo. Fet —95Ha 176
Sycamore Clo. Grav —9F 114
Sycamore Clo. N'holt —39Aa 57
Sycamore Clo. Wat —7X 5
Sycamore Clo. W Dray —45P 75
Sycamore Ct. E4 —23Bc 44
Sycamore Ct. E7 —37Jc 65
Sycamore Ct. Eri —50Fd 88
Sycamore Ct. Houn —56Aa 99
Sycamore Ct. N Mald —69Ua 124
Sycamore Dri. Brtwd —18Yd 32
Sycamore Dri. Swan —69Gd 132
Sycamore Gdns. W6 —47Xa 80
Sycamore Gdns. Mitc —68Fb 125
Sycamore Gro. NW9 —31Sa 59
Sycamore Gro. SE6 —58Ec 106
Sycamore Gro. SE20 —67Wb 127
Sycamore Gro. N Mald —69Ta 123
Sycamore Hill. N11 —23Kb 42
Sycamore Ho. W6 —47Xa 80
Sycamore Ho. Brom —68Gc 129
Sycamore Lodge. Orp —75Vc 151
Sycamore M. Eri —50Fd 88
Sycamore Rise. Bans —86Za 162
Sycamore Rd. SW19 —65Ya 124
Sycamore Rd. Crox —15S 18
Sycamore Rd. Dart —60Md 111
Sycamores, The. Rad —6Ka 6
Sycamores, The. S Ock —46Td 90
Sycamore St. EC1 —42Sb 83 (6D 194)
Sycamore Wlk. W10 —42Ab 80
Sycamore Wlk. Egh —5M 117
Sycamore Wlk. G Grn —44A 74
Sycamore Wlk. Ilf —28Sc 46
Sycamore Way. Tedd —65La 122
Sycamore Way. T Hth —71Qb 146
Sydcote. SE21 —60Sb 105
Sydenham Av. SE26 —64Xb 127
Sydenham Clo. Romf —28Hd 48
Sydenham Cotts. SE12 —61Lc 129
Sydenham Hill. SE26 & SE23 —63Vb 127
Sydenham Pk. SE26 —62Yb 128
Sydenham Pk. Rd. SE26 —62Yb 128
Sydenham Pl. SE27 —62Rb 127
Sydenham Rise. SE23 —61Xb 127
Sydenham Rd. SE26 —63Yb 128
Sydenham Rd. Croy —74Sb 147
Sydmons Ct. SE23 —59Yb 106
Sydner M. N16 —35Vb 63
Sydner Rd. N16 —35Vb 63
Sydney Av. Purl —84Pb 164
Sydney Clo. SW3 —49Fb 81 (6C 202)
Sydney Cres. Ashf —65R 120
Sydney Elson Way. E6 —40Qc 66
Sydney Gro. NW4 —29Ya 40
Sydney Gro. Slou —4G 72
Sydney M. SW3 —49Fb 81 (6C 202)
Sydney Pl. SW7 —49Fb 81 (6C 202)
Sydney Rd. E11 —30Kc 45
Sydney Rd. N8 —28Qb 42
Sydney Rd. N10 —25Kb 42
Sydney Rd. SE2 —48Yc 87
Sydney Rd. SW20 —68Za 124
Sydney Rd. W13 —46Ja 78
Sydney Rd. Bexh —56Zc 109
Sydney Rd. Enf —14Tb 25
(in two parts)
Sydney Rd. Felt —60W 98
Sydney Rd. Ilf —26Sc 46
Sydney Rd. Rich —56Na 101
Sydney Rd. Sidc —63Uc 130
Sydney Rd. Sutt —77Cb 145
Sydney Rd. Tedd —64Ha 122
Sydney Rd. Til —4C 114
Sydney Rd. Wat —15U 18
Sydney Rd. Wfd G —21Jc 45
Sydney St. SW3 —50Gb 81 (6D 202)
Sykecluan. Iver —47G 74
Sykeings. Iver —48G 74
Sykes Dri. Stai —64K 119
Sykes Rd. Slou —4F 72
Sylvana Clo. Uxb —39P 55
Sylvan Av. N3 —26Cb 41
Sylvan Av. N22 —24Pb 42
Sylvan Av. NW7 —23Ua 40
Sylvan Av. Horn —30Nd 49
Sylvan Av. Romf —30Bd 47
Sylvan Clo. Chaf H —49Ae 91
Sylvan Clo. Oxt —100Kc 183
Sylvan Clo. S Croy —82Xb 165
Sylvan Clo. Wok —89D 156
Sylvan Ct. N12 —20Db 23
Sylvan Est. SE19 —67Vb 127
Sylvan Gdns. Surb —73Ma 143
Sylvan Gro. SE15 —51Xb 105
Sylvan Hill. SE19 —67Ub 127
Sylvan Rd. E7 —37Jc 65
Sylvan Rd. E11 —29Jc 45
Sylvan Rd. E17 —29Cc 44
Sylvan Rd. SE19 —67Vb 127
Sylvan Wlk. Brom —69Nc 130
Sylvan Way. Chig —20Xc 29
Sylvan Way. Dag —35Xc 67
Sylvan Way. W Wick —77Gc 149
Sylverdale Rd. Croy —76Rb 147
Sylverdale Rd. Purl —85Rb 165
Sylvester Av. Chst —65Pc 130
Sylvester Gdns. Ilf —22Xc 47
Sylvester Path. E8 —37Xb 63
Sylvester Rd. E8 —37Xb 63
Sylvester Rd. E17 —31Bc 64
Sylvester Rd. N2 —26Fb 41
Sylvester Rd. Wemb —36La 58
Sylvestrus Clo. King T —67Qa 123
Sylvia Av. Hut —19Ee 33
Sylvia Av. Pinn —23Aa 37
Sylvia Ct. Wemb —38Ra 59
Sylvia Gdns. Wemb —38Ra 59
Sylvia Pankhurst Ho. Dag —34Cd 68
(off Wythenshawe Rd.)
Symes M. NW1 —40Lb 62 (1B 192)
Symonds Clo. W King —78Ud 154
Symons St. SW3 —49Hb 81 (6G 203)
Syndey Pl. SW7 —49Fb 81
Syon Ga. Way. Bren —52Ja 100
Syon La. Iswth —51Ga 100
Syon Pk. Gdns. Iswth —52Ha 100
Syracuse Av. Rain —41Nd 89
Syrett M. Cob —86X 159
Syringa Ct. Grays —52Fe 113
Sythwood. Wok —4E 188

Tabard Garden Est. SE1 —48Tb 83 (2F 207)
Tabard St. SE1 —47Tb 83 (1F 207)
Tabard St. SW1 —47Tb 83
Tabarin Way. Eps —88Ya 162
Tabernacle Av. E13 —42Jc 85
Tabernacle St. EC2 —42Tb 83 (6G 195)
Tableer Av. SW4 —57Mb 104
Tabley Rd. N7 —35Nb 62
Tabor Ct. Sutt —79Ab 144
Tabor Gdns. Sutt —80Bb 145
Tabor Gro. SW19 —66Ab 124
Tabor Rd. W6 —48Xa 80
Tabrums Way. Upm —31Ud 70
Tachbrook Est. SW1 —50Mb 82 (7D 204)
Tachbrook M. SW1 —49Lb 82 (5B 204)
Tachbrook Rd. Felt —59V 98
Tachbrook Rd. S'hall —49Z 77
Tachbrook Rd. Uxb —40L 55
Tachbrook Rd. W Dray —46N 75
Tachbrook St. SW1 —49Lb 82 (6C 204)
Tack M. SE4 —55Cc 106
Tadema Rd. SW10 —52Eb 103
Tadlows Clo. Upm —36Rd 69
Tadmor Clo. Sun —70V 120
Tadmor St. W12 —46Za 80
Tadorne Rd. Tad —93Ya 178
Tadworth Av. N Mald —71Va 144
Tadworth Clo. Tad —94Za 178
Tadworth Ho. SE1 —47Rb 83 (2B 206)
(off Webber St.)
Tadworth Pde. Horn —35Kd 69
Tadworth Rd. NW2 —33Wa 60
Tadworth St. Tad —95Ya 178
Taeping St. E14 —49Dc 84
Taffy's Row. Mitc —69Gb 125
Taft Way. E3 —41Ec 84
Tailworth St. E1 —43Wb 83
(off Chicksand St.)
Tait Ct. SW8 —53Nb 104
(off Allen Edwards Dri.)
Tait Rd. Croy —73Ub 147
Taits. Stanf —1P 93
Takeley Clo. Romf —26Fd 48
Takeley Clo. Wal A —5Fc 13
Talacre Rd. NW5 —37Jb 62
Talbot Av. N2 —27Fb 41
Talbot Av. Slou —47B 74
Talbot Av. Wat —17Aa 19
Talbot Clo. N15 —28Vb 43
Talbot Ct. EC3 —45Tb 83 (4G 201)
(off Gracechurch St.)
Talbot Ct. NW9 —34Ta 59
Talbot Cres. NW4 —29Wa 40
Talbot Gdns. Ilf —33Wc 67
Talbot Pl. SE3 —54Gc 107
Talbot Pl. Dat —3N 95
Talbot Rd. E6 —40Qc 66
Talbot Rd. E7 —35Jc 65
Talbot Rd. N6 —30Jb 42
Talbot Rd. N15 —28Vb 43
Talbot Rd. N22 —26Lb 42
Talbot Rd. SE22 —56Ub 105
Talbot Rd. W11 & W2 —44Bb 81
(in two parts)
Talbot Rd. W13 —46Ja 78
Talbot Rd. Ashf —64N 119
Talbot Rd. Brom —69Kc 129
Talbot Rd. Cars —78Jb 146
Talbot Rd. Dag —37Bd 67
Talbot Rd. Harr —26Ha 38
Talbot Rd. Iswth —56Ja 100
Talbot Rd. Rick —18N 17
Talbot Rd. S'hall —49Aa 77
Talbot Rd. T Hth —70Tb 127
Talbot Rd. Twic —60Ga 100
Talbot Rd. Wemb —37Ma 59
Talbot Sq. W2 —44Fb 81 (3C 196)
Talbot Wlk. NW10 —37Ua 60
Talbot Way. NW10 —37Ua 60
Talbot Yd. SE1 —46Tb 83 (7F 201)
(off Borough High St.)
Talbot Yd. SW1 —46Tb 83
Talbrook. Brtwd —20Vd 32
Talcott Path. SW2 —60Qb 104
Taleworth Clo. Asht —92Ma 177
Taleworth Pk. Asht —92Ma 177
Taleworth Rd. Asht —91Ma 177
Talfourd Pl. SE15 —53Vb 105
Talfourd Rd. SE15 —53Vb 105
Talgarth Mans. W14 —50Ab 80
(off Talgarth Rd.)
Talgarth Rd. W6 & W14 —50Za 80
Talgarth Wlk. NW9 —29Ua 40
Talisman Clo. Ilf —32Xc 67
Talisman Sq. SE26 —63Wb 127
Talisman Way. Eps —88Ya 162
Talisman Way. Wemb —34Pa 59
Tallack Clo. Harr —24Ga 38
Tallack Rd. E10 —32Bc 64
Tall Elms Clo. Brom —71Hc 149
Tallents Clo. S at H —66Rd 133
Tallis Clo. Stanf —1L 93
Tallis Gro. SE7 —51Kc 107
Tallis St. EC4 —45Qb 82 (4A 200)
Tallis View. NW10 —37Ta 59
Tallis Way. Borwd —11Ma 21
Tallon Rd. Hut —15Fe 33
Tall Pines. Eps —83Va 162
Tall Trees. SW16 —70Pb 126
Tall Trees. Coln —53F 96
Tall Trees Clo. Horn —29Nd 49
Talma Gdns. Twic —58Ga 100
Talmage Clo. SE23 —59Yb 106
Talman Gro. Stan —23Ma 39

Talma Rd.—Thavies Inn

Talma Rd. SW2 —56Qb **104**
Talus Clo. Purf —49Td **90**
Talwin St. E3 —41Dc **84**
Tamar Clo. Upm —30Ud **50**
Tamar Dri. S Ock —44Sd **90**
*Tamar Ho. SE11 —50Qb **82** (7A **206**)*
(off Kennington La.)
Tamarind Yd. E1 —46Wb **83**
Tamarisk Rd. S Ock —41Yd **90**
Tamarisk Sq. W12 —45Va **80**
Tamarisk Way. Slou —7F **72**
Tamar Sq. Wfd G —23Kc **45**
Tamar St. SE7 —49Nc **86**
Tamar Way. N17 —27Wb **43**
Tamar Way. Slou —50D **74**
Tamerton Sq. Wok —90A **156**
Tamesis Gdns. Wor Pk —75Ua **144**
Tamesis Strand. Grav —4G **136**
Tamian Way. Houn —56Y **99**
Tamsy Clo. H Hill —23Nd **49**
Tamworth. N7 —37Nb **62**
Tamworth Av. Wfd G —23Gc **45**
Tamworth La. Mitc —68Kb **126**
Tamworth Pk. Mitc —69Kb **126**
Tamworth Pl. Croy —75Sb **147**
Tamworth Rd. Croy —75Rb **147**
Tamworth St. SW6 —51Cb **103**
Tamworth Vs. Mitc —70Lb **126**
Tancred Rd. N4 —31Rb **63**
Tandridge Dri. Orp —74Tc **150**
Tandridge Gdns. S Croy —85Vb **165**
Tandridge Hill La. God —100Bc **182**
Tandridge Pl. Orp —74Tc **150**
Tandridge Rd. Warl —91Zb **182**
Tanfield Av. NW2 —35Va **60**
Tanfield Rd. Croy —77Sb **147**
Tangent Rd. Romf —25Md **49**
Tangier Ct. Eton —1H **95**
Tangier La. Eton —1H **95**
Tangier Rd. Rich —56Qa **101**
Tangier Way. Tad —89Ab **162**
Tangier Wood. Tad —90Ab **162**
Tangleberry Clo. Brom —70Pc **130**
Tanglewood Clo. Croy —76Yb **148**
Tanglewood Clo. Stan —19Ga **20**
Tanglewood Clo. Uxb —42Q **76**
Tanglewood Clo. Wok —88F **156**
Tanglewood Ct. St M —69Yc **131**
Tanglewood Way. Felt —62X **121**
Tangley Gro. SW15 —58Va **102**
Tangley Pk. Rd. Hamp —64Ba **121**
Tanglyn Av. Shep —71Q **140**
*Tangmere. N17 —26Tb **43***
(off Willan Rd.)
Tangmere Cres. Horn —37Kd **69**
Tangmere Gdns. N'holt —40Y **57**
Tangmere Way. NW9 —26Ua **40**
Tan Ho. La. N'side —14Pd **31**
*Tanhurst Ho. SW2 —59Nb **104***
(off Redlands Way)
Tanhurst Wlk. SE2 —48Zc **87**
Tankerton Rd. Surb —75Pa **143**
Tankerton St. WC1
—41Nb **82** (4G **193**)
Tankerton Ter. Croy —72Pb **146**
Tankerville Rd. SW16 —66Mb **126**
Tank Hill Rd. Purf —49Qd **89**
Tank La. Purf —49Qd **89**
Tankridge Rd. NW2 —33Xa **60**
*Tanner Point. E13 —39Jc **65***
(off Brooks Rd.)
Tanners Clo. W on T —72X **141**
Tanners Dean. Lea —94La **176**
Tanners End La. N18 —21Ub **43**
Tanner's Hill. SE8 —53Bc **106**
Tanners Hill. Abb L —3V **4**
Tanners La. Ilf —27Sc **46**
Tanner St. SE1 —47Ub **83** (2J **207**)
Tanner St. Bark —37Sc **66**
Tanners Wood Clo. Abb L —4U **4**
Tanners Wood Ct. Abb L —4U **4**
Tanners Wood La. Abb L —4U **4**
Tannery Clo. Beck —70Zb **128**
Tannery Clo. Dag —34Dd **68**
Tannery La. Send —95F **172**
Tannington Ter. N5 —34Qb **62**
Tannsfeld Rd. SE26 —64Zb **128**
Tansley Clo. N7 —36Mb **62**
Tanswell St. SE1
—47Qb **82** (2K **205**)
Tansy Clo. E6 —44Qc **86**
Tantallon Rd. SW12 —60Jb **104**
Tant Av. E16 —44Hc **85**
Tantony Gro. Romf —27Zc **47**
Tanworth Clo. N'wd —23S **36**
Tanworth Gdns. Pinn —26X **37**
Tanyard Cotts. Shorne —6N **137**
Tanyard Hill. Shorne —5N **137**
Tanyard La. Bex —59Cd **110**
Tanza Rd. NW3 —35Hb **61**
Tapestry Clo. Sutt —80Db **145**
Tapling Trading Est. W Dray
—45M **75**
Taplow Rd. N13 —21Rb **43**
Taplow St. N1 —40Sb **63** (2E **194**)
Tappesfield Rd. SE15 —55Yb **106**
Tapp St. E1 —42Xb **83**
Tapster St. Barn —13Bb **23**
Tara Ct. Beck —68Dc **128**
Tarbay La. Oak G —5A **94**
Tarbert Rd. SE22 —57Ub **105**
Tarbert Wlk. E1 —45Yb **84**
Target Clo. Felt —58U **98**
Tariff Cres. SE8 —49Bc **84**
Tariff Rd. N17 —23Wb **43**
Tarleton Ct. N22 —26Qb **42**
Tarleton Gdns. SE23 —61Xb **127**
Tarling Clo. Sidc —62Xc **131**
Tarling Rd. E16 —44Hc **85**
Tarling Rd. N2 —26Eb **41**
Tarling St. E1 —44Yb **84**
Tarling St. Est. E1 —44Yb **84**
Tarmac Way. W Dray —52K **97**
Tarn Bank. Enf —15Nb **24**
Tarn St. SE1 —48Sb **83** (4D **206**)
Tarnwood Pk. SE9 —60Pc **108**
Tarnworth Rd. Romf —23Qd **49**
Tarragon Clo. SE14 —52Ac **106**
Tarragon Gro. SE26 —65Zb **128**
Tarrant Pl. W1 —43Hb **81** (1F **197**)
Tarrington Clo. SW16 —62Mb **126**
Tarry La. SE8 —49Ac **84**
Tartar Hill. Cob —85Y **159**
Tartar Rd. Cob —85Y **159**
Tarver Rd. SE17
—50Rb **83** (7C **206**)
Tarves Way. SE10 —52Dc **106**
Tash Pl. N11 —22Kb **42**
Tasker Clo. Hay —52S **98**
Tasker Ho. Bark —40Tc **66**
Tasker Rd. NW3 —36Hb **61**
Tasker Rd. Grays —8D **92**
Tasman Ct. Ashf —66U **120**
Tasmania Ter. N18 —23Sb **43**
Tasman Rd. SW9 —55Nb **104**
Tasman Wlk. E16 —44Mc **85**
Tasso Rd. W6 —51Ab **102**
*Tasso Yd. W6 —51Ab **102***
(off Tasso Rd.)
Tatam Rd. NW10 —38Ta **59**
Tate Clo. Lea —95La **176**
Tate Ho. Ger X —22B **34**
Tate Rd. E16 —46Pc **86**
(in two parts)
Tate Rd. Ger X —22B **34**
Tate Rd. Sutt —78Cb **145**
Tates Orchard. Long —72Be **155**
Tatnell Rd. SE23 —58Ac **106**
Tatsfield La. Tats —93Pc **184**
Tattenham Corner Rd. Eps
—89Va **162**
Tattenham Cres. Eps —90Xa **162**
Tattenham Gro. Eps —90Xa **162**
Tattenham Way. Tad —90Za **162**
Tattersall Clo. SE9 —57Nc **108**
Tatton Cres. N16 —31Vb **63**
Tatum St. SE17 —49Tb **83** (6G **207**)
Taunton Av. SW20 —68Xa **124**
Taunton Av. Cat —95Vb **181**
Taunton Av. Houn —54Ea **100**
Taunton Clo. Bexh —54Fd **110**
Taunton Clo. Ilf —23Vc **47**
Taunton Clo. Sutt —74Cb **145**
Taunton Dri. Enf —13Qb **24**
Taunton La. Coul —91Qb **180**
Taunton M. NW1
—42Hb **81** (6F **191**)
Taunton Pl. NW1
—42Hb **81** (5F **191**)
Taunton Rd. SE12 —57Gc **107**
Taunton Rd. Grav —57Ce **113**
Taunton Rd. Gnfd —39Da **57**
Taunton Rd. Romf —21Ld **49**
Taunton Vale. Grav —2F **136**
Taunton Way. Stan —26Na **39**
Taverners Clo. W11 —46Ab **80**
Taverner Sq. N5 —35Sb **63**
Taverners Way. E4 —18Gc **27**
Tavern La. SW9 —54Qb **104**
Tavistock Av. E17 —27Zb **44**
Tavistock Av. Gnfd —40Ja **58**
Tavistock Clo. N16 —36Ub **63**
Tavistock Clo. Pot B —3Fb **9**
Tavistock Clo. Romf —25Md **49**
Tavistock Clo. Stai —66M **119**
Tavistock Cres. W11 —43Bb **81**
Tavistock Cres. Mitc —70Nb **126**
Tavistock Gdns. Ilf —35Uc **66**
Tavistock Ga. Croy —74Tb **147**
Tavistock Gro. Croy —73Tb **147**
Tavistock Ho. WC1 —42Mb **82**
Tavistock Ho. Croy —74Tb **147**
Tavistock M. E18 —28Jc **45**
Tavistock M. W11 —44Bb **81**
Tavistock Pl. E18 —27Jc **45**
Tavistock Pl. N14 —16Kb **24**
Tavistock Pl. WC1
—42Nb **82** (5F **193**)
Tavistock Rd. E7 —35Hc **65**
Tavistock Rd. E15 —37Hc **65**
Tavistock Rd. E18 —27Jc **45**
Tavistock Rd. N4 —30Tb **43**
Tavistock Rd. NW10 —40Va **60**
Tavistock Rd. W11 —44Bb **81**
Tavistock Rd. Brom —70Hc **129**
Tavistock Rd. Cars —74Fb **145**
Tavistock Rd. Croy —74Tb **147**
Tavistock Rd. Edgw —25Qa **39**
Tavistock Rd. Uxb —36T **56**
Tavistock Rd. Wat —11Z **19**
Tavistock Rd. Well —53Yc **109**
Tavistock Rd. W Dray —46M **75**
Tavistock Sq. WC1
—42Mb **82** (5E **192**)
Tavistock St. WC2
(in two parts) —45Nb **82** (4G **199**)
Tavistock Ter. N19 —34Mb **62**
Tavistock Tower. SE16 —48Ac **84**
Tavistock Wlk. Cars —74Fb **145**
Taviton St. WC1
—42Mb **82** (5D **192**)
Tavy Bri. SE2 —47Yc **87**
Tavy Bri. Cen. SE2 —47Yc **87**
*Tavy Clo. SE11 —50Qb **82** (7A **206**)*
(off White Hart St.)
Tawney Comn. They M —4Bd **15**
Tawney Rd. SE28 —45Xc **87**
Tawny Av. Upm —36Rd **69**
Tawny Clo. Felt —62W **120**
Tawny Way. SE16 —49Zb **84**
Tayben Av. Twic —58Ga **100**
Taybridge Rd. SW11 —55Jb **104**
*Tay Bldgs. SE1 —48Ub **83** (3H **207**)*
(off Long La.)
Tayburn Clo. E14 —44Ec **84**
Tayfield Clo. Uxb —34T **56**
Tayles Hill. Eps —82Va **162**
Taylor Av. Rich —54Ra **101**
Taylor Clo. N17 —24Wb **43**
Taylor Clo. Hamp —64Ea **122**
Taylor Clo. Orp —77Vc **151**
Taylor Clo. Romf —24Gd **48**
Taylor Ct. E15 —36Ec **64**
*Taylor Ct. SE20 —68Yb **128***
(off Elmers End Rd.)
Taylormead. NW7 —22Wa **40**
Taylor Rd. Asht —89Ma **161**
Taylor Rd. Mitc —66Gb **125**
Taylor Rd. Wall —78Kb **146**
Taylors Bldgs. SE18 —49Rc **86**
Taylor's Bushes Ride. Wind
—1A **116**
Taylors Clo. Sidc —62Vc **131**
Taylors Grn. W3 —44Ua **80**
Taylors La. NW10 —38Ua **60**
Taylor's La. SE26 —63Xb **127**
Taylors La. Barn —11Bb **23**
Taymount Grange. SE23 —61Yb **128**
Taymount Rise. SE23 —61Yb **128**
Taynton Dri. Red —100Mb **180**
Tayport Clo. N1 —38Nb **62**
Tayside Ct. SE5 —56Tb **105**
Tayside Dri. Edgw —20Ra **21**
Tay Way. Romf —25Hd **48**
Taywood Rd. N'holt —41Ba **77**
Teak Clo. SE16 —46Ac **84**
*Tealby Ct. N7 —37Pb **62***
(off Georges Rd.)
Teal Clo. E16 —43Mc **85**
Teal Clo. S Croy —83Zb **166**
Teal Ct. NW10 —37Ta **59**
Teal Dri. N'wd —24T **36**
Teale St. E2 —40Wb **63**
Teal Ho. Wat —8Aa **5**
Tealing Dri. Eps —77Ta **143**
Teardrop Ind. Est. Swan —71Kd **153**
Teasel Clo. Croy —74Zb **148**
Teasel Way. E15 —41Gc **85**
Teazlewood Pk. Lea —89Ja **160**
Tebworth Rd. N17 —24Vb **43**
Tedder Clo. Chess —78La **142**
Tedder Clo. Ruis —36W **56**
Tedder Clo. Uxb —38P **55**
Tedder Rd. S Croy —80Yb **148**
Teddington Clo. Eps —82Ta **161**
Teddington Pk. Tedd —64Ha **122**
Teddington Pk. Rd. Tedd
—63Ha **122**
*Ted Roberts Ho. E2 —40Yb **64***
(off Parmiter St.)
Tedworth Gdns. SW3 —50Hb **81**
Tedworth Sq. SW3 —50Hb **81**
Tees Av. Gnfd —40Ga **58**
Tees Clo. Upm —31Td **70**
Teesdale Av. Iswth —53Ja **100**
Teesdale Clo. E2 —40Xb **63**
Teesdale Gdns. SE19 —68Ub **127**
Teesdale Gdns. Iswth —53Ja **100**
Teesdale Rd. E11 —31Hc **65**
Teesdale Rd. Dart —60Sd **112**
Teesdale Rd. Slou —3D **72**
Teesdale St. E2 —40Xb **63**
*Teesdale Yd. E2 —40Xb **63***
(off Teesdale St.)
Tees Dri. Romf —20Md **31**
Teeswater Ct. Eri —48Zc **87**
Tee, The. W3 —44Ua **80**
Teevan Clo. Croy —73Wb **147**
Teevan Rd. Croy —74Wb **147**
Tegg's La. Wok —88H **157**
Teignmouth Clo. SW4 —56Mb **104**
Teignmouth Clo. Edgw —26Pa **39**
Teignmouth Gdns. Gnfd —40Ja **58**
Teignmouth Pde. Gnfd —40Ka **58**
Teignmouth Rd. NW2 —36Za **60**
Teignmouth Rd. Well —54Yc **109**
Telcote Way. Ruis —31Y **57**
Telegraph Hill. NW3 —34Db **61**
Telegraph La. Clay —78Ha **142**
Telegraph M. Ilf —32Wc **67**
Telegraph Pas. SW2 —59Nb **104**
Telegraph Rd. SW15 —59Xa **102**
Telegraph St. EC2
—44Tb **83** (2F **201**)
Telegraph Track. Cars —83Jb **164**
Teleman Sq. SE3 —56Kc **107**
Telephone Pl. SW6 —51Bb **103**
Telfer Clo. W3 —47Sa **79**
Telferscot Rd. SW12 —60Mb **104**
Telford Av. SW2 —60Mb **104**
Telford Clo. SE19 —65Vb **127**
Telford Clo. Wat —7Z **5**
Telford Dri. Slou —7E **72**
Telford Dri. W on T —73Y **141**
Telford Rd. N11 —22Lb **42**
Telford Rd. NW9 —30Wa **40**
Telford Rd. SE9 —61Tc **130**
Telford Rd. W10 —43Ab **80**
Telford Rd. S'hall —45Da **77**
Telford Rd. Twic —59Ca **99**
Telfords Yd. E1 —45Wb **83**
Telford Ter. SW1 —51Lb **104**
Telford Way. W3 —43Ua **80**
Telford Way. Hay —43Aa **77**
Telham Rd. E6 —40Qc **66**
Tell Gro. SE22 —56Vb **105**
Tellisford. Esh —77Da **141**
Tellson Av. SE18 —53Mc **107**
Telscombe Clo. Orp —75Uc **150**
Telston La. Otf —89Gd **170**
(in two parts)
Temeraire St. SE16 —47Yb **84**
Temperley Rd. SW12 —59Jb **104**
Tempest Av. Pot B —4Fb **9**
Tempest Rd. Egh —65E **118**
Tempest Way. Rain —37Jd **68**
Templar Dri. SE28 —44Zc **87**
Templar Ho. NW2 —37Bb **61**
Templar Pl. Hamp —66Ca **121**
Templars Av. NW11 —30Bb **41**
Templars Ct. Dart —57Qd **111**
Templars Cres. N3 —26Cb **41**
Templars Dri. Harr —23Fa **38**
Templars Ho. E15 —36Dc **64**
Templar St. SE5 —54Rb **105**
*Temple. EC4 —45Qb **82** (4K **199**)*
(off Middle Temple La.)
Temple Av. EC4 —45Qb **82** (4A **200**)
Temple Av. N20 —17Fb **23**
Temple Av. Croy —75Bc **148**
Temple Av. Dag —32Cd **68**
Temple Bar Rd. Wok —7C **188**
Temple Chambers. EC4
*—45Qb **82** (4A **200**)*
(off Temple Av.)
Temple Clo. E11 —31Gc **65**
Temple Clo. N3 —26Bb **41**
Temple Clo. SE28 —48Sc **86**
Temple Clo. Chesh —3Wb **11**
Temple Clo. Eps —84Ta **161**
Temple Clo. Wat —12V **18**
Templecombe M. Wok —88D **156**
Templecombe Rd. E9 —39Yb **64**
Templecombe Way. Mord
—71Ab **144**
*Temple Ct. SW8 —52Nb **104***
(off Thorncroft St.)
Temple Ct. Pot B —3Ab **8**
Templecroft. Ashf —65T **120**
Templedene Av. Stai —66K **119**
*Temple Dwellings. E2 —40Xb **63***
(off Temple St.)
Templefield Clo. Add —79K **139**
Temple Fortune Hill. NW11
—29Cb **41**
Temple Fortune La. NW11
—30Bb **41**
Temple Fortune Pde. NW11
—29Bb **41**
Temple Gdns. N21 —19Rb **25**
Temple Gdns. NW11 —30Bb **41**
Temple Gdns. Dag —34Zc **67**
Temple Gdns. Moor P —21R **36**
Temple Gdns. Stai —67H **119**
Temple Gro. NW11 —30Cb **41**
Temple Gro. Enf —13Rb **25**
Temple Hall Ct. E4 —19Fc **27**
Temple Hill. Dart —58Pd **111**
Temple Hill Sq. Dart —57Pd **111**
Templehof Av. NW4 —31Ya **60**
Temple La. EC4 —44Qb **82** (3A **200**)
Templeman Clo. Purl —88Rb **165**
Templeman Rd. W7 —43Ha **78**
Templemead Clo. W3 —44Ua **80**
Temple Mead Clo. Stan —23Ka **38**
Templemead Ho. E9 —35Ac **64**
Templemere. Wey —76T **140**
Temple Mill La. E15 —35Dc **64**
Temple Mills Rd. E15 —35Cc **64**
Templepan La. Chan X —9N **3**
Temple Pk. Uxb —41Q **76**
Temple Pl. WC2 —45Pb **82** (4J **199**)
Templar Av. Grays —9C **92**
Templer Dri. Grav —4C **136**
Temple Rd. E6 —39Nc **66**
Temple Rd. N8 —28Pb **42**
Temple Rd. NW2 —35Ya **60**
Temple Rd. W4 —48Sa **79**
Temple Rd. W5 —48Ma **79**
Temple Rd. Big H —89Mc **167**
Temple Rd. Croy —77Tb **147**
Temple Rd. Eps —84Ta **161**
Temple Rd. Houn —56Ea **100**
Temple Rd. Rich —54Pa **101**
Temple Rd. Wind —4G **94**
Temple Sheen. SW14 —57Sa **101**
Temple Sheen Rd. SW14
—56Ra **101**
Temple St. E2 —40Xb **63**
Templeton Av. E4 —21Cc **44**
Templeton Clo. N15 —30Tb **43**
Templeton Clo. N16 —36Ub **63**
Templeton Clo. SE19 —67Tb **127**
Templeton Pl. SW5 —49Cb **81**
Templeton Rd. N15 —30Tb **43**
Temple Way. Farn C —6G **52**
Temple Way. Sutt —76Fb **145**
Temple W. M. SE11
*(off West Sq.) —48Rb **83** (4B **206**)*
Templewood. W13 —43Ka **78**
Templewood Av. NW3 —34Db **61**
Templewood Gdns. NW3 —34Db **61**
Templewood La. Farn C —6G **52**
*Templewood Point. NW2 —33Bb **61***
(off Granville Rd.)
Tempsford Av. Borwd —14Ta **21**
Tempsford Clo. Enf —13Sb **25**
Tempsford Ct. Harr —30Ha **38**
Temsford Clo. Harr —26Ea **38**
Ten Acre. St J —6D **188**
Ten Acre La. Egh —68E **118**
Ten Acres. Fet —96Fa **176**
Ten Acres Clo. Fet —96Fa **176**
Tenbury Clo. E7 —36Mc **65**
Tenbury Ct. SW12 —60Mb **104**
Tenby Av. Harr —26Ka **38**
Tenby Clo. N15 —28Vb **43**
Tenby Clo. Romf —30Ad **47**
Tenby Ct. E17 —29Zb **44**
Tenby Dri. Asc —10B **116**
Tenby Gdns. N'holt —37Ca **57**
Tenby Ho. Hay —48S **76**
Tenby Rd. E17 —29Ac **44**
Tenby Rd. Edgw —25Pa **39**
Tenby Rd. Enf —14Yb **26**
Tenby Rd. Romf —30Ad **47**
Tenby Rd. Well —53Zc **109**
Tench St. E1 —46Xb **83**
Tenda Rd. SE16 —49Xb **83**
Tendring Ct. Hut —15Fe **33**
Tendring Way. Romf —29Yc **47**
Tenham Av. SW2 —61Mb **126**
Tenison Ct. W1 —45Lb **82** (4B **198**)
Tenison Way. SE1
—46Qb **82** (7J **199**)
Tennants Row. Til —4A **114**
Tenniel Clo. W2 —45Eb **81**
Tennis Ct. La. E Mol —69Ha **122**
Tennison Av. Borwd —15Ra **21**
Tennison Clo. Coul —92Rb **181**
Tennison Rd. SE25 —70Vb **127**
Tennis St. SE1 —47Tb **83** (1F **207**)
Tennis St. SW1 —47Tb **83**
Tenniswood Rd. Enf —11Fb **25**
Tenny Ho. Grays —52De **113**
Tennyson Av. E11 —31Jc **65**
Tennyson Av. E12 —38Nc **66**
Tennyson Av. NW9 —27Sa **39**
Tennyson Av. Grays —48De **91**
Tennyson Av. N Mald —71Xa **144**
Tennyson Av. Twic —60Ha **100**
Tennyson Av. Wal A —6Gc **13**
Tennyson Clo. SW19 —65Eb **125**
Tennyson Clo. Enf —16Zb **26**
Tennyson Clo. Felt —58V **98**
Tennyson Clo. Well —53Uc **108**
*Tennyson Ct. SW6 —53Db **103***
(off Maltings Pl.)
Tennyson Ho. SE17
*—50Sb **83** (7E **206**)*
(off Browning St.)
Tennyson Rd. E10 —32Dc **64**
Tennyson Rd. E15 —38Gc **65**
Tennyson Rd. E17 —30Bc **44**
Tennyson Rd. NW6 —39Bb **61**
Tennyson Rd. NW7 —22Wa **40**
Tennyson Rd. SE20 —66Zb **128**
Tennyson Rd. W7 —45Ha **78**
Tennyson Rd. Add —77N **139**
Tennyson Rd. Ashf —64N **119**
Tennyson Rd. Dart —57Qd **111**
Tennyson Rd. Houn —54Ea **100**
Tennyson Rd. Hut —17Ee **33**
Tennyson Rd. Romf —24Ld **49**
Tennyson St. SW8 —54Kb **104**
Tennyson Wlk. Grav —62Fe **135**
Tennyson Wlk. Til —4D **114**
Tennyson Way. Horn —32Hd **68**
Tennyson Way. Slou —2C **72**
Tensing Av. Grav —2A **136**
Tensing Rd. S'hall —48Ca **77**
Tentelow La. S'hall —50Ca **77**
Tenterden Clo. NW4 —27Za **40**
Tenterden Clo. SE9 —63Pc **130**
Tenterden Clo. SE12 —63Nc **130**
Tenterden Dri. NW4 —27Za **40**
Tenterden Gdns. NW4 —27Za **40**
Tenterden Gdns. Croy —73Wb **147**
Tenterden Gro. NW4 —27Za **40**
Tenterden Rd. N17 —24Vb **43**
Tenterden Rd. Croy —73Wb **147**
Tenterden Rd. Dag —33Bd **67**
Tenterden St. W1
—44Kb **82** (3A **198**)
Tenter Ground. E1
—43Vb **83** (1K **201**)
Tenter Pas. E1 —44Vb **83** (3K **201**)
Tent Peg La. Pet W —71Sc **150**
Tent St. E1 —42Xb **83**
Terborch Way. SE22 —57Ub **105**
Tercel Path. Chig —21Xc **47**
Terence Clo. Grav —10H **115**
Teresa Gdns. Wal X —6Yb **12**
Teresa M. E17 —28Cc **44**
Teresa Wlk. N10 —29Kb **42**
Terling Clo. E11 —34Hc **65**
Terling Rd. Dag —33Cd **68**
Terlings, The. Brtwd —20Wd **32**
*Terling Wlk. N1 —39Sb **63***
(off Popham St.)
Terminal Ho. Stan —22Ma **39**
Terminus Pl. SW1
—48Kb **82** (4A **204**)
Tern Gdns. Upm —32Ud **70**
Tern Way. Brtwd —21Ud **50**
Terrace Gdns. SW13 —54Va **102**
Terrace Gdns. Wat —12X **19**
Terrace La. Rich —58Na **101**
Terrace Rd. E9 —38Zb **64**
Terrace Rd. E13 —40Jc **65**
Terrace Rd. W on T —73W **140**
Terraces, The. Dart —59Sd **112**
Terrace St. Grav —8D **114**
(in two parts)
Terrace, The. EC4
*—44Qb **82** (3A **200**)*
(off Crown Office Row)
Terrace, The. N3 —26Bb **41**
Terrace, The. NW6 —39Cb **61**
Terrace, The. SW1 —47Nb **82**
Terrace, The. SW13 —54Ua **102**
Terrace, The. Add —78N **139**
Terrace, The. Asc —10B **116**
Terrace, The. Grav —8D **114**
(in three parts)
Terrace, The. Harr —31Ka **58**
Terrace, The. Sev —94Fd **186**
Terrace, The. Wfd G —23Jc **45**
*Terrace Wlk. SW11 —52Hb **103***
(off Albert Bri. Rd.)
Terrace Wlk. Dag —36Ad **67**
Terrapin Rd. SW17 —62Kb **126**
*Terrence Ct. Belv —51Bd **109***
(off Charton Clo.)
Terretts Pl. N1 —38Rb **63**
Terrick Rd. N22 —25Nb **42**
Terrick St. W12 —44Xa **80**
Terrilands. Pinn —27Ba **37**
Territorial Ho. SE11
*—49Qb **82** (6A **206**)*
(off Reedworth St.)
Terront Rd. N15 —28Sb **43**
Terry Pl. Cow —43L **75**
Tessa Sanderson Pl. SW8
*—55Kb **104***
(off Daley Thompson Way)
Tessa Sanderson Way. Gnfd
—36Fa **58**
Testerton Wlk. W11 —45Za **80**
Testwood Ct. W7 —45Ga **78**
Testwood Rd. Wind —3B **94**
Tetbury Pl. N1 —39Rb **63** (1B **194**)
Tetcott Rd. SW10 —52Eb **103**
Tetherdown. N10 —27Jb **42**
Tetterby Way. SE16 —50Wb **83**
Tetty Way. Brom —68Jc **129**
Teversham La. SW8 —53Nb **104**
Teviot Av. S Ock —44Sd **90**
Teviot Clo. Well —53Xc **109**
Teviot St. E14 —43Ec **84**
Tewkesbury Av. SE23 —59Xb **105**
Tewkesbury Av. Pinn —29Aa **37**
Tewkesbury Clo. N15 —30Tb **43**
Tewkesbury Clo. Byfl —83M **157**
Tewkesbury Gdns. NW9 —27Ra **39**
Tewkesbury Rd. N15 —30Tb **43**
Tewkesbury Rd. W13 —46Ja **78**
Tewkesbury Rd. Cars —74Fb **145**
Tewkesbury Ter. N11 —23Lb **42**
Tewson Rd. SE18 —50Uc **86**
Teynham Av. Enf —16Tb **25**
Teynham Grn. Brom —71Jc **149**
Teynton Ter. N17 —25Sb **43**
Thackeray Av. N17 —26Wb **43**
Thackeray Av. Til —3D **114**
Thackeray Clo. SW19 —66Za **124**
Thackeray Clo. Harr —32Ca **57**
Thackeray Clo. Uxb —44R **76**
*Thackeray Ct. W14 —48Ab **80***
(off Blythe Rd.)
Thackeray Dri. Romf —31Wc **67**
Thackeray Lodge. Felt —58T **98**
Thackeray Rd. E6 —40Mc **65**
Thackeray Rd. SW8 —54Kb **104**
Thackeray St. W8 —48Db **81**
Thackerey M. E8 —37Wb **63**
Thackrah Clo. N2 —26Eb **41**
Thakeham Clo. SE26 —63Xb **127**
Thalia Clo. SE10 —51Fc **107**
Thal Massing Clo. Hut —19De **33**
Thame Rd. SE16 —47Zb **84**
Thames Av. SW10 —53Eb **103**
Thames Av. Cher —69J **119**
Thames Av. Dag —42Dd **88**
Thames Av. Gnfd —40Ha **58**
Thames Av. Wind —2H **95**
Thames Bank. SW14 —54Sa **101**
Thamesbank Pl. SE28 —44Yc **87**
Thames Barrier Ind. Area. SE1
*(off Faraday Way) —48Mc **85***
Thames Clo. Cher —73K **139**
Thames Clo. Corr —1P **93**
Thames Clo. Hamp —68Da **121**
Thames Clo. Rain —44Kd **89**
Thames Dri. Grays —10C **92**
Thames Dri. Ruis —30S **36**
Thames Exchange Building. EC4
*—45Sb **83** (5E **200**)*
(off Up. Thames St.)
Thamesfield Ct. Shep —73S **140**
Thamesfield M. Shep —73S **140**
Thames Ga. Dart —57Qd **111**
Thamesgate Clo. Rich —63Ka **122**
Thameshill Av. Romf —26Ed **48**
*Thames Ho. EC4 —45Sb **83** (5E **200**)*
(off Up. Thames St.)
Thameside. Tedd —66Ma **123**
Thameside Cen. Bren —51Pa **101**
Thameside Ind. Est. E16 —47Mc **85**
Thameside Wlk. SE28 —44Wc **86**
Thames Mead. W on T —72W **140**
Thames Mead. Wind —3C **94**
Thames Meadow. Shep —74T **140**
Thames Meadow. W Mol
—68Ca **121**
Thamesmere Dri. SE28 —45Wc **87**
Thames Pl. SW15 —55Za **102**
(in two parts)
Thames Quay. E14 —47Dc **84**
*Thames Quay. SW10 —53Eb **103***
(off Chelsea Harbour)
Thames Rd. E16 —46Mc **85**
Thames Rd. W4 —51Qa **101**
Thames Rd. Bark —41Vc **87**
Thames Rd. Dart —54Hd **110**
Thames Rd. Grays —52De **113**
Thames Rd. Rich —51Qa **101**
Thames Rd. Slou —49C **74**
Thames Rd. Ind. Est. E16
—47Mc **85**
Thames Side. King T —67Ma **123**
Thames Side. Stai —68K **119**
Thames Side. Wind —2H **95**
Thames St. SE10 —51Dc **106**
Thames St. Hamp —67Da **121**
Thames St. King T —68Ma **123**
Thames St. Stai —64H **119**
Thames St. Sun —70X **121**
Thames St. W on T —73V **140**
Thames St. Wey —75R **140**
Thames St. Wind —3H **95**
Thames Vale Clo. Houn —54Ca **99**
Thames View. Grays —10C **92**
Thamesview Houses. W on T
—72W **140**
Thames Village. W4 —53Sa **101**
Thames Way. Grav —60Fe **113**
(in two parts)
Thamley. Purf —49Qd **89**
Thanescroft Gdns. Croy —76Ub **147**
Thanet Ct. W3 —44Qa **79**
Thanet Dri. Kes —76Mc **149**
Thanet Ho. Grav —10B **114**
Thanet Pl. Croy —75Sb **147**
Thanet Rd. Bex —59Cd **110**
Thanet Rd. Eri —52Gd **110**
Thanet St. WC1 —41Nb **82** (4F **193**)
Thane Vs. N7 —34Pb **62**
Thane Works. N7 —34Pb **62**
Thant Clo. E10 —34Dc **64**
Tharp Rd. Wall —78Mb **146**
Thatcham Ct. N20 —17Eb **23**
Thatcham Gdns. N20 —17Eb **23**
Thatcher Clo. W Dray —47N **75**
Thatcher Ct. Dart —59Md **111**
Thatchers Clo. Lou —12Sc **28**
Thatchers Way. Iswth —57Fa **100**
Thatches Gro. Romf —28Ad **47**
Thavies Inn. EC1
—44Qb **82** (2A **200**)

Thaxted Bold—Tobacco Quay

Thaxted Bold. Hut —15Fe 33
Thaxted Ct. N1 —40Tb 63 (2G 195)
(off Fairbank Est.)
Thaxted Grn. Hut —15Ee 33
Thaxted Ho. Dag —38Dd 68
Thaxted Pl. SW20 —66Za 124
Thaxted Rd. SE9 —61Sc 130
Thaxted Rd. Buck H —17Nc 28
Thaxted Wlk. Rain —38Gd 68
Thaxted Way. Wal A —5Fc 13
Thaxton Rd. W14 —51Bb 103
Thayers Farm Rd. Beck —67Ac 128
Thayer St. W1 —44Jb 82 (1J 197)
Thaynesfield. Pot B —3Fb 9
Theatre St. SW11 —55Hb 103
Theberton St. N1 —39Qb 62
Theed St. SE1 —46Qb 82 (7K 199)
Thelma Clo. Grav —4H 137
Thelma Gdns. SE3 —53Mc 107
Thelma Gro. Tedd —65Ja 122
Thelusson Ct. Rad —7Ja 6
Theobald Cres. Harr —25Ea 38
Theobald Rd. E17 —31Cc 64
Theobald Rd. Croy —75Rb 147
Theobalds Av. N12 —21Eb 41
Theobalds Av. Grays —50Ee 91
Theobalds Clo. Cuff —2Pb 10
Theobalds Clo. Kems —90Qd 171
Theobalds Ct. N4 —34Sb 63
Theobalds La. Chesh & Wal X —4Wb 11
Theobalds Pk. Rd. Enf —7Rb 11
Theobald's Rd. WC1 —43Pb 82 (1G 199)
Theobalds Rd. Cuff —2Nb 10
Theobald St. SE1 —48Tb 83 (4F 207)
(off New Kent Rd.)
Theobald St. Rad & Borwd —8Ka 6
Theodore Ct. SE13 —58Fc 107
Theodore Rd. SE13 —58Fc 107
Therapia La. Croy —73Mb 146
(in two parts)
Therapia Rd. SE22 —58Yb 106
Theresa Rd. W6 —49Wa 80
Theresa's Wlk. S Croy —82Tb 165
Therfield Ct. N4 —33Sb 63
Thermopylae Ga. E14 —49Dc 84
Theseus Wlk. N1 —40Rb 63 (2C 194)
(off City Garden Row)
Thesiger Rd. SE20 —66Zb 128
Thessaly Rd. SW8 —52Lb 104
Thetford Clo. N13 —23Rb 43
Thetford Gdns. Dag —38Ad 67
Thetford Rd. Ashf —63N 119
Thetford Rd. Dag —38Zc 67
Thetford Rd. N Mald —72Ta 143
Thetis Ter. Rich —51Qa 101
Theydon Ct. Wal A —5Jc 13
Theydon Gdns. Rain —38Gd 68
Theydon Gro. Epp —2Wc 15
Theydon Gro. Wfd G —23Lc 45
Theydon Mt. They M —6Bd 15
Theydon Pk. Rd. They B —9Uc 14
Theydon Pl. Epp —3Vc 15
Theydon Rd. E5 —33Yb 64
Theydon Rd. Epp —4Tc 14
Theydon St. E17 —31Bc 64
Thicket Cres. Sutt —77Eb 145
Thicket Gro. SE20 —66Wb 127
Thicket Gro. Dag —37Yc 67
Thicket Rd. SE20 —66Wb 127
Thicket Rd. Sutt —77Eb 145
Thickett Gro. Dag —37Yc 67
Thicket, The. W Dray —44N 75
Thicketts. Sev —95Ld 187
Thickthorne La. Stai —66L 119
Third Av. E12 —35Nc 66
Third Av. E13 —41Jc 85
Third Av. E17 —29Cc 44
Third Av. W3 —46Va 80
Third Av. W10 —41Ab 80
Third Av. Dag —39Dd 68
Third Av. Enf —15Vb 25
Third Av. Grav —10A 114
Third Av. Grays —51Wd 112
Third Av. Hay —46V 76
Third Av. Romf —30Yc 47
Third Av. Wat —7Z 5
Third Av. Wemb —33Ma 59
Third Clo. W Mol —70Ea 122
Third Cres. Slou —3G 72
Third Cross Rd. Twic —61Fa 122
Third Way. Wemb —35Ra 59
Thirkleby Clo. Slou —6G 72
Thirleby Rd. SW1 —48Lb 82 (4C 204)
Thirleby Rd. Edgw —25Ta 39
Thirlmere Av. Gnfd —41La 78
Thirlestane Ct. N10 —26Jb 42
Thirlmere Av. Slou —3A 72
Thirlmere Clo. Egh —66D 118
Thirlmere Gdns. N'wd —22R 36
Thirlmere Gdns. Wemb —32La 58
Thirlmere Rise. Brom —65Hc 129
Thirlmere Rd. N10 —25Kb 42
Thirlmere Rd. SW16 —63Mb 126
Thirlmere Rd. Bexh —53Ed 110
Thirsk Clo. N'holt —37Ca 57
Thirsk Rd. SE25 —70Tb 127
Thirsk Rd. SW11 —55Jb 104
Thirsk Rd. Borwd —9Qa 7
Thirsk Rd. Mitc —66Jb 126
Thirston Path. Borwd —12Qa 21
Thirza Rd. Dart —58Pd 111
Thistlebrook. SE2 —47Yc 87
Thistlecroft Gdns. Stan —25Ma 39
Thistlecroft Rd. W on T —77Y 141
Thistledene. Th Dit —72Ga 142
Thistledene. W Byf —85H 157
Thistledene Av. Harr —34Aa 57
Thistledene Av. Romf —22Dd 48
Thistledown. Grav —5F 136
Thistle Gro. SW10 —50Eb 81 (7A 202)
Thistlemead. Chst —68Rc 130
Thistle Mead. Lou —13Qc 28
Thistle Rd. Grav —9G 114
Thistlewaite Rd. E5 —34Xb 63
Thistlewood Clo. N7 —33Pb 62
Thistlewood Cres. New Ad —84Fc 167
Thistleworth Clo. Iswth —52Fa 100
Thoby La. Mount —11Ee 33
Thomas a' Beckett Clo. Wemb —35Ha 58
Thomas Av. Cat —93Sb 181
Thomas Baines Rd. SW11 —55Fb 103
Thomas Bata Av. E Til —9K 93
Thomas Clo. Brtwd —19Ae 33
Thomas Ct. E17 —29Dc 44
Thomas Doyle St. SE1 —48Rb 83 (3C 206)
Thomas Dri. Grav —1F 136
Thomas England Ho. Romf
(off Waterloo Gdns.) —30Fd 48
Thomas Hewlett Ho. Harr —35Ga 58
Thomas La. SE6 —59Cc 106
Thomas More Highwalk. EC2
(off Barbican) —43Sb 83 (1D 200)
Thomas More Ho. EC2
(off Barbican) —43Sb 83 (1D 200)
Thomas More St. E1 —45Wb 83
Thomas More Way. N2 —27Eb 41
Thomas Neals Shopping Mall. WC2 —44Nb 82 (3F 199)
Thomas North Ter. E16 —43Hc 85
(off Barking Rd.)
Thomas Pl. W8 —48Db 81
Thomas Rd. E14 —44Bc 84
Thomas Rd. Ind. Est. E14 —43Cc 84
Thomas's Av. Grav —10D 114
Thomas Sims Ct. Horn —37Kd 69
Thomas St. SE18 —49Rc 86
Thomas Wall Clo. Sutt —78Db 145
Thompkins La. Farn R —8D 52
Thompson Av. Rich —55Qa 101
Thompson Clo. Ilf —33Sc 66
Thompson Clo. Slou —49B 74
Thompson Rd. SE22 —58Vb 105
Thompson Rd. Dag —34Bd 67
Thompson Rd. Uxb —39N 55
Thompson's Av. SE5 —52Sb 105
Thompson's La. Lou —10Jc 13
Thomson Cres. Croy —74Qb 146
Thomson Ho. SW1 —50Mb 82 (7E 204)
(off Bessborough Pl.)
Thomson Rd. Harr —27Ga 38
Thong La. Grav —3H 137
Thorburn Sq. SE1 —49Wb 83
Thorburn Way. SW19 —67Fb 125
Thoresby St. N1 —41Sb 83 (3E 194)
Thorkhill Gdns. Th Dit —74Ja 142
Thorkhill Rd. Th Dit —74Ja 142
Thorley Clo. W Byf —86J 157
Thorley Gdns. Wok —87J 157
Thorley Rd. Grays —46Ce 91
Thornaby Gdns. N18 —23Wb 43
Thornash Clo. Wok —3F 188
Thornash Rd. Wok —3F 188
Thornash Way. Wok —3F 188
Thorn Av. Bush —18Ea 20
Thorn Bank. Edgw —23Qa 39
Thornbank Clo. Stai —57J 97
Thornbridge Rd. Iver —39E 54
Thornbury. NW4 —28Ya 40
(off Prince Of Wales Clo.)
Thornbury Av. Iswth —52Fa 100
Thornbury Clo. N16 —36Ub 63
Thornbury Ct. Iswth —52Ga 100
Thornbury Gdns. Borwd —14Sa 21
Thornbury Rd. SW2 —58Nb 104
Thornbury Rd. Iswth —52Fa 100
Thornbury Sq. N6 —32Lb 62
Thornby Rd. E5 —34Yb 64
Thorncliffe Rd. SW2 —58Nb 104
Thorncliffe Rd. S'hall —50Ba 77
Thorn Clo. Brom —72Qc 150
Thorn Clo. N'holt —41Ba 77
Thorncombe Rd. SE22 —57Ub 105
Thorncroft. Egh —6N 117
Thorncroft. Horn —30Kd 49
Thorncroft Clo. Coul —91Qb 180
Thorncroft Dri. Lea —95Ka 176
Thorncroft Rd. Sutt —77Db 145
Thorncroft St. SW8 —52Nb 104
Thorndales. War —21Zd 51
Thorndean St. SW18 —61Eb 125
Thorndene. SE28 —45Xc 87
Thorndene Av. N11 —18Jb 24
Thorndike. Slou —3E 72
Thorndike Av. N'holt —39Z 57
Thorndike Clo. SW10 —52Eb 103
Thorndike St. SW1 —49Mb 82 (6D 204)
Thorndon App. Heron —24Fe 51
Thorndon Av. W Horn —28Ee 51
Thorndon Clo. Orp —68Vc 131
Thorndon Gdns. Eps —78Ua 144
Thorndon Ga. Ingve —22Ee 51
Thorndon Rd. Orp —68Vc 131
Thorn Dri. G Grn —44A 74
Thorndyke Ct. Pinn —23Ba 37
Thorne Clo. E11 —35Gc 65
Thorne Clo. E16 —44Jc 85
Thorne Clo. Ashf —66S 120
Thorne Clo. Eri —51Dd 110
Thorne Pas. SW13 —54Ua 102
Thorne Rd. SW8 —52Nb 104
Thornes Clo. Beck —69Ec 128
Thorne St. SW13 —55Ua 102
Thornet Wood Rd. Brom —69Qc 130
Thorney Cres. SW11 —52Fb 103
Thorneycroft Clo. W on T —72Y 141
Thorney Hedge Rd. W4 —49Ra 79
Thorney La. N. Iver —44H 75
Thorney La. S. Iver —47H 75
Thorney Mill Rd. Iver & W Dray —48J 75
Thorney St. SW1 —49Nb 82 (5F 205)
Thornfield Av. NW7 —25Ab 40
Thornfield Ct. NW7 —25Ab 40
Thornfield Rd. W12 —47Xa 80
Thornfield Rd. Bans —89Cb 163
Thornford Rd. SE13 —57Ec 106
Thorngate Rd. W9 —42Cb 81
Thorngrove Rd. E13 —39Kc 65
Thornham Gro. E15 —36Fc 65
Thornham St. SE10 —51Dc 106
Thornhaugh M. WC1 —42Mb 82 (6E 192)
Thornhaugh St. WC1 —42Mb 82 (6E 192)
Thornhill Av. SE18 —52Uc 108
Thornhill Av. Surb —75Na 143
Thornhill Cres. N1 —38Pb 62
Thornhill Gdns. E10 —33Dc 64
Thornhill Gdns. Bark —38Uc 66
Thornhill Gro. N1 —38Pb 62
Thornhill Ho. N1 —38Qb 62
Thornhill Ho. W4 —50Ua 80
(off Wood St.)
Thornhill Point. E9 —38Yb 64
Thornhill Rd. E10 —33Dc 64
Thornhill Rd. N1 —38Qb 62
Thornhill Rd. Croy —73Sb 147
Thornhill Rd. N'wd —21S 36
Thornhill Rd. Surb —75Na 143
Thornhill Rd. Uxb —35P 55
Thornhill Sq. N1 —38Pb 62
Thornhill Way. Shep —71Q 140
Thorn Ho. Borwd —12Sa 21
Thornicroft Ho. SW9 —54Pb 104
(off Stockwell Rd.)
Thorn La. Rain —40Md 69
Thornlaw Rd. SE27 —63Qb 126
Thornley Clo. N17 —24Wb 43
Thornley Dri. Harr —33Da 57
Thornley Pl. SE10 —50Gc 85
Thornloe Gdns. Croy —78Qb 146
Thornridge. Brtwd —18Xd 32
Thornsbeach Rd. SE6 —60Ec 106
Thornsett Pl. SE20 —68Xb 127
Thornsett Rd. SE20 —68Xb 127
Thornsett Rd. SW18 —60Db 103
Thornsett Ter. SE20 —68Xb 127
(off Croydon Rd.)
Thorns Meadow. Bras —95Yc 185
Thorns, The. Kel H —11Ud 32
Thornton Av. SW2 —60Mb 104
Thornton Av. W4 —49Ua 80
Thornton Av. Croy —72Pb 146
Thornton Av. W Dray —48P 75
Thornton Clo. W Dray —48P 75
Thornton Cres. Coul —91Qb 180
Thornton Dene. Beck —68Cc 128
Thornton Gdns. SW12 —60Mb 104
Thornton Gro. Pinn —23Ca 37
Thornton Hill. SW19 —66Ab 124
Thornton Pl. W1 —43Hb 81 (7G 191)
Thornton Rd. E11 —33Fc 65
Thornton Rd. N18 —21Yb 44
Thornton Rd. SW12 —59Mb 104
Thornton Rd. SW14 —56Ta 101
Thornton Rd. SW19 —65Za 124
Thornton Rd. Barn —13Ab 22
Thornton Rd. Belv —49Dd 88
Thornton Rd. Brom —64Jc 129
Thornton Rd. Cars —74Fb 145
Thornton Rd. Croy & T Hth —73Pb 146
Thornton Rd. Ilf —35Rc 66
Thornton Rd. Pot B —2Eb 9
Thornton Rd. E. SW19 —65Za 124
Thornton Row. T Hth —71Qb 146
Thorntons. Ingve —23Ee 51
Thorntons Farm Av. Romf —32Ed 68
Thornton St. SW9 —54Qb 104
Thornton Way. NW11 —29Db 41
Thorntree Ct. W5 —43Na 79
Thorntree Rd. SE7 —50Mc 85
Thornville St. SE8 —53Cc 106
Thornwood Clo. E18 —26Kc 45
Thornwood Rd. SE13 —57Gc 107
Thornwood Rd. Epp —1Xc 15
Thornycroft Ho. W4 —50Ua 80
(off Fraser St.)
Thorogood Gdns. E15 —36Gc 65
Thorogood Way. Rain —39Gd 68
Thorold Clo. S Croy —82Zb 166
Thorold Rd. N22 —24Nb 42
Thorold Rd. Ilf —33Rc 66
Thoroughfare, The. Tad —96Wa 178
Thorparch Rd. SW8 —53Mb 104
Thorpebank Rd. W12 —46Wa 80
Thorpe By-Pass. Egh —68D 118
Thorpe Clo. W10 —44Ab 80
Thorpe Clo. New Ad —83Ec 166
Thorpe Clo. Orp —75Uc 150
Thorpe Ct. Enf —13Rb 25
Thorpe Cres. E17 —26Bc 44
Thorpe Cres. Wat —17Y 19
Thorpedale Gdns. Ilf —28Qc 46
Thorpedale Rd. N4 —33Nb 62
Thorpe Hall Rd. E17 —25Ec 44
Thorpe Ho. N1 —39Pb 62 (1J 193)
(off Barnsbury Est.)
Thorpe Ind. Est. Egh —68E 118
Thorpe Lea Rd. Egh —65D 118
Thorpe Lodge. Horn —30Nd 49
Thorpe Rd. E6 —39Pc 66
Thorpe Rd. E7 —35Hc 65
Thorpe Rd. E17 —26Ec 44
Thorpe Rd. N15 —30Ub 43
Thorpe Rd. Bark —38Tc 66
Thorpe Rd. Cher —71F 138
Thorpe Rd. King T —66Na 123
Thorpe Rd. Stai —65F 118
Thorpewood Av. SE26 —61Xb 127
Thorpland Av. Uxb —34S 56
Thorrington Bold. Hut —15Fe 33
Thorsden Clo. Wok —90A 156
Thorsden Ct. Wok —90A 156
Thorsden Way. SE19 —64Ub 127
Thors Oak. Stanf —1N 93
Thorverton Rd. NW2 —34Ab 60
Thoydon Rd. E3 —40Ac 64
Thrale Rd. SW16 —64Lb 126
Thrale St. SE1 —46Sb 83 (7E 200)
Thrasher Clo. E8 —39Vb 63
Thrawl St. E1 —43Vb 83 (1K 201)
Thrayle Ho. SW9 —55Pb 104
(off Benedict Rd.)
Threadgold Ho. N1 —37Tb 63
(off Dovercourt Est.)
Threadneedle St. EC2 —44Tb 83 (3G 201)
Three Colts La. E2 —42Xb 83
Three Colt St. E14 —44Bc 84
Three Corners. Bexh —54Dd 110
Three Cranes Wlk. EC4 —45Sb 83 (5E 200)
(off Bell Wharf La.)
Three Cups Yd. WC1 —43Pb 82 (1J 199)
(off Sandland St.)
Three Gates Rd. Fawk —74Wd 154
Three Kings Yd. W1 —45Kb 82 (4K 197)
Three Mill La. E3 —41Ec 84
Three Oak La. SE1 —47Vb 83 (1K 207)
Three Oaks Clo. Uxb —34P 55
Three Quays. EC3 —45Ub 83 (5J 201)
(off Tower Hill)
Three Quays Wlk. EC3 —45Ub 83 (5J 201)
Threshers Pl. W11 —45Ab 80
Thriffwood. SE26 —62Yb 128
Thrift Farm La. Borwd —12Sa 21
Thrift Grn. Brtwd —20Ce 33
Thrift La. Cud —89Uc 168
Thrifts Mead. They B —9Uc 14
Thrift, The. Bean —62Yd 134
Thrigby Rd. Chess —79Pa 143
Thring Ho. SW9 —54Pb 104
(off Stockwell Rd.)
Throckmorten Rd. E16 —44Kc 85
Throgmorton Av. EC2 —44Tb 83 (2G 201)
Throgmorton St. EC2 —44Tb 83 (2G 201)
Throstle Pl. Wat —4Y 5
Throwley Clo. SE2 —48Yc 87
Throwley Rd. Sutt —78Db 145
Throwley Way. Sutt —77Db 145
Thrums. Wat —9X 5
Thrupp Clo. Mitc —68Kb 126
Thrupp's Av. W on T —78Z 141
Thrupp's La. W on T —78Z 141
Thrush Grn. Harr —28Ca 37
Thrush Grn. Rick —17L 17
Thrush La. Cuff —1Nb 10
Thrush St. SE17 —50Sb 83 (7D 206)
Thruxton Way. SE15 —52Vb 105
Thurbarn Rd. SE6 —64Dc 128
Thurland Rd. SE16 —48Wb 83
Thurlby Clo. Harr —30Ja 38
Thurlby Clo. Wfd G —22Pc 46
Thurlby Croft. NW4 —27Ya 40
(off Mulberry Clo.)
Thurlby Rd. SE27 —63Qb 126
Thurlby Rd. Wemb —37Ma 59
Thurleigh Av. SW12 —58Jb 104
Thurleigh Rd. SW12 —59Hb 103
Thurleston Av. Mord —71Ab 144
Thurlestone Av. N12 —23Hb 41
Thurlestone Av. Ilf —35Vc 67
Thurlestone Clo. Shep —72S 140
Thurlestone Pde. Shep —72S 140
(off High St. Shepperton)
Thurlestone Rd. SE27 —62Qb 126
Thurloe Clo. SW7 —49Gb 81 (5D 202)
Thurloe Gdns. Romf —30Hd 48
Thurloe Pl. SW7 —49Fb 81 (5C 202)
Thurloe Pl. M. SW7 —49Fb 81 (5C 202)
(off Thurloe Pl.)
Thurloe Sq. SW7 —49Gb 81 (5C 202)
Thurloe St. SW7 —49Fb 81 (5C 202)
Thurloe Wlk. Grays —48Ce 91
Thurlow Clo. E4 —23Ec 44
Thurlow Gdns. Ilf —23Tc 46
Thurlow Gdns. Wemb —36Ma 59
Thurlow Hill. SE21 —60Sb 105
Thurlow Pk. Rd. SE21 —61Rb 127
Thurlow Rd. NW3 —36Fb 61
Thurlow Rd. W7 —47Ja 78
Thurlow St. SE17 —50Tb 83 (7G 207)
Thurlow Ter. NW5 —36Jb 62
Thurlow Wlk. SE17 —50Ub 83 (7H 207)
Thurlston Rd. Ruis —34W 56
Thurlton Ct. Wok —88A 156
Thurnby Ct. Twic —62Ga 122
Thurnham Way. Tad —92Ya 178
Thurrock Bus. Pk. W Thur —51Vd 112
Thurrock Enterprise Cen. Grays —51Ce 113
Thurrock Lakeside Shopping Cen. W Thur —48Xd 90
Thurrock Pk. Way. Til —52Fe 113
Thursby Rd. Wok —6D 188
Thursland Rd. Sidc —64Ad 131
Thursley Cres. New Ad —80Fc 149
Thursley Gdns. SW19 —61Za 124
Thursley Ho. SW2 —59Pb 104
(off Holmewood Gdns.)
Thursley Rd. SE9 —62Pc 130
Thurso Clo. Romf —23Rd 49
Thurso St. SW17 —63Fb 125
Thurston Rd. SE13 —54Dc 106
Thurston Rd. SW20 —66Xa 124
Thurston Rd. Slou —4J 73
Thurston Rd. S'hall —44Ba 77
Thurston Rd. Ind. Est. SE13 —55Dc 106
Thurtle Rd. E2 —40Vb 63 (1K 195)
Thwaite Clo. Eri —51Ed 110
Thyer Clo. Orp —77Sc 150
Thyra Gro. N12 —23Db 41
Tibbatts Rd. E3 —42Dc 84
Tibbenham Wlk. E13 —40Hc 65
Tibberton Sq. N1 —38Sb 63
Tibbet's Clo. SW19 —60Za 102
Tibbet's Ride. SW15 —59Za 102
Tibbles Clo. Wat —7Aa 5
Tibbs Hill Rd. Abb L —2V 4
Tiber Gdns. N1 —39Nb 62 (1G 193)
Ticehurst Clo. Orp —66Wc 131
Ticehurst Rd. SE23 —61Ac 128
Tichmarsh. Eps —83Sa 161
Tickford Clo. SE2 —47Yc 87
Tidal Basin Rd. E16 —45Hc 85
Tidenham Gdns. Croy —76Ub 147
Tideswell Rd. SW15 —56Ya 102
Tideswell Rd. Croy —76Cc 148
Tideway Clo. Rich —63Ka 122
Tideway Ind. Est. SW8 —51Lb 104
(off Tideway Wlk.)
Tideway Wlk. SW8 —51Lb 104
Tidey St. E3 —43Cc 84
Tidford Rd. Well —54Vc 109
Tidworth Rd. E3 —42Cc 84
Tidy's La. Epp —1Xc 15
Tiepigs La. W Wick & Brom —75Gc 149
Tierney Ct. Croy —75Vb 147
Tierney Rd. SW2 —60Nb 104
Tiger La. Brom —70Kc 129
Tiger Way. E5 —35Xb 63
Tilbrook Rd. SE3 —55Lc 107
Tilbury Clo. SE15 —52Vb 105
Tilbury Clo. Orp —68Xc 131
Tilbury Gdns. Til —6C 114
Tilbury Hotel Rd. Til —6C 114
Tilbury Rd. E6 —40Pc 66
Tilbury Rd. E10 —31Ec 64
Tildesley Rd. SW15 —58Ya 102
Tile Farm Rd. Orp —76Tc 150
Tilehouse Clo. Borwd —13Pa 21
Tilehouse La. Den —27G 34
Tilehouse La. W Hyd —26G 34
Tilehouse Way. Den —31H 55
Tilehurst Point. SE2 —47Zc 87
Tilehurst Rd. SW18 —60Fb 103
Tilehurst Rd. Sutt —78Ab 144
Tile Kiln La. N6 —32Kb 62
Tile Kiln La. N13 —22Sb 43
Tile Kiln La. Bex —61Ed 132
(in two parts)
Tile Kiln La. Hare —31R 56
Tile Kiln Studios. N6 —32Lb 62
Tile Yd. E14 —44Bc 84
Tileyard Rd. N7 —38Nb 62
Tilford Av. New Ad —81Ec 166
Tilford Gdns. SW19 —60Za 102
Tilford Ho. SW2 —59Pb 104
(off Holmewood Gdns.)
Tilia Rd. E5 —35Xb 63
Till Av. F'ham —73Pd 153
Tiller Rd. E14 —48Cc 84
Tillet Pl. Til —3D 114
Tillett Clo. NW10 —37Sa 59
Tillett Sq. SE16 —47Ac 84
Tillet Way. E2 —41Wb 83
Tilley La. H'ley —94Sa 177
Tillingbourne Gdns. N3 —27Bb 41
Tillingbourne Grn. Orp —70Wc 131
Tillingbourne Way. N3 —28Bb 41
Tillingdown Hill. Cat —94Wb 181
Tillingdown La. Cat —96Xb 181
(in two parts)
Tillingham Ct. Wal A —5Jc 13
Tillingham Way. N12 —21Cb 41
Tilling Rd. NW2 —32Ya 60
Tilling Way. Wemb —34Ma 59
Tillman St. E1 —44Xb 83
Tilloch St. N1 —38Pb 62
Tillotson Ct. SW8 —52Mb 104
(off Wandsworth Rd.)
Tillotson Rd. N9 —19Vb 25
Tillotson Rd. Harr —24Da 37
Tillotson Rd. Ilf —31Qc 66
Tillys La. Stai —63H 119
Tilmans Mead. F'ham —73Qd 153
Tilney Ct. EC1 —42Sb 83 (5E 194)
Tilney Dri. Buck H —19Jc 27
Tilney Gdns. N1 —37Tb 63
Tilney Rd. Dag —37Bd 67
Tilney Rd. S'hall —49Y 77
Tilney St. W1 —46Jb 82 (6J 197)
Tilson Gdns. SW2 —59Nb 104
Tilson Ho. SW2 —59Nb 104
Tilson Rd. N17 —25Wb 43
Tilston Clo. E11 —34Hc 65
Tilstone Av. Eton W —10C 72
Tilstone Clo. Eton W —10C 72
Tilt Clo. Cob —88Aa 159
Tilt Meadow. Cob —88Aa 159
Tilton St. SW6 —51Ab 102
Tilt Rd. Cob —87Y 159
Tiltwood, The. W3 —45Sa 79
Tilt Yd. App. SE9 —58Pc 108
Timber Clo. Bookh —99Ea 176
Timber Clo. Chst —68Qc 130
Timber Clo. Wok —86H 157
Timber Ct. Grays —51Ce 113
Timbercroft. Eps —77Ua 144
Timbercroft La. SE18 —51Uc 108
Timberdene. NW4 —26Za 40
Timberdene Av. Ilf —25Rc 46
Timberhill. Asht —91Na 177
Timber Hill Rd. Cat —96Wb 181
Timberland Rd. E1 —44Xb 83
Timber La. Cat —96Wb 181
Timberling Gdns. S Croy —81Tb 165
Timber Mill Way. SW4 —55Mb 104
Timber Pond Rd. SE16 —46Zb 84
Timber Ridge. Loud —14M 17
Timberslip Dri. Wall —81Mb 164
Timber St. EC1 —42Sb 83 (5D 194)
Timbertop Rd. Big H —90Lc 167
Timberwharf Rd. N16 —30Wb 43
Times Sq. Sutt —78Db 145
Timothy Clo. SW4 —57Lb 104
Timothy Clo. Bexh —57Ad 109
Timothy Ho. Eri —47Ad 87
(off Kale Rd.)
Timothy Rd. E3 —43Bc 84
Timsbury Wlk. SW15 —60Wa 102
Timsway. Stai —64H 119
Tindale Clo. S Croy —83Tb 165
Tindall Clo. Romf —26Pd 49
Tindal St. SW9 —53Rb 105
Tinderbox All. SW14 —55Ta 101
Tinefields. Tad —91Ab 178
Tine Rd. Chig —22Uc 46
Tingeys Top La. Enf —8Qb 10
Tinkerpot La. W King —86Rd 171
Tinkerpot Rise. W King —86Rd 171
Tinkers La. Wind —4B 94
Tinniswood Clo. N5 —36Qb 62
Tinsey Clo. Egh —64C 118
Tinsley Rd. E1 —43Yb 84
Tintage Ct. Horn —32Kd 69
Tintagel Clo. Eps —86Va 162
Tintagel Cres. SE22 —56Vb 105
Tintagel Dri. Stan —21Ma 39
Tintagel Gdns. SE22 —56Vb 105
Tintagel Rd. Orp —75Yc 151
Tintagel Way. Wok —88C 156
Tintells La. W Hor —100R 174
Tintern Av. NW9 —27Ra 39
Tintern Clo. SW15 —57Ab 102
Tintern Clo. SW19 —65Eb 125
Tintern Clo. Slou —8G 72
Tintern Gdns. N14 —17Nb 24
Tintern Rd. N22 —25Sb 43
Tintern Rd. Cars —74Fb 145
Tintern St. SW4 —56Nb 104
Tintern Way. Harr —32Da 57
Tinto Rd. E16 —42Jc 85
Tinwell M. Borwd —15Ta 21
Tinworth St. SE11 —50Pb 82 (7H 205)
Tippett Ct. E6 —40Pc 66
Tippetts Clo. Enf —11Sb 25
Tipthorpe Rd. SW11 —55Jb 104
Tipton Dri. Croy —77Ub 147
Tiptree Clo. E4 —20Ec 26
Tiptree Clo. Horn —32Qd 69
Tiptree Cres. Ilf —27Qc 46
Tiptree Dri. Enf —14Tb 25
Tiptree Rd. Ruis —35X 57
Tiree Clo. Rich —60Ma 101
Tiree Ho. Slou —2F 72
Tirlemont Rd. S Croy —80Sb 147
Tirrell Rd. Croy —72Sb 147
Tisbury Ct. W1 —45Mb 82 (4D 198)
(off Wardour St.)
Tisbury Rd. SW16 —68Nb 126
Tisdall Pl. SE17 —49Tb 83 (6G 207)
Titan Av. Bush —17Ga 20
Titan Rd. Grays —50Ce 91
Titan Way. Grays —50Ce 91
Titchborne. Hay —22F 34
Titchborne Row. W2 —44Gb 81 (3D 196)
Titchfield Rd. NW8 —40Hb 61 (1F 191)
Titchfield Rd. Cars —74Fb 145
Titchfield Rd. Enf —9Ac 12
Titchfield Wlk. Cars —73Fb 145
Titchwell Rd. SW18 —60Fb 103
Tite Hill. Egh —4P 117
Tite St. SW3 —50Hb 81
Tithe Barn Clo. King T —67Pa 123
Tithebarns La. Send —98J 173
Tithe Barn Way. N'holt —40X 57
Tithe Clo. NW7 —25Wa 40
Tithe Ct. Slou —49C 74
Tithe Farm Av. Harr —34Ca 57
Tithe Farm Clo. Harr —34Ca 57
Tithe La. Wray —58C 96
Tithepit Shaw La. Warl —89Xb 165
Tithe Wlk. NW7 —25Wa 40
Titley Clo. E4 —22Cc 44
Titmus Clo. Uxb —44S 76
Titmuss Av. SE28 —45Xc 87
Titmuss St. W12 —47Xa 80
Titness Pk. S'hill —9E 116
Titsey Hill. T'sey —95Jc 183
Titsey Rd. Oxt —97Kc 183
Tivendale. N8 —27Nb 42
Tiverton Av. Ilf —27Qc 46
Tiverton Dri. SE9 —60Sc 108
Tiverton Gro. Romf —22Qd 49
Tiverton Rd. N15 —30Tb 43
Tiverton Rd. N18 —22Ub 43
Tiverton Rd. NW10 —39Za 60
Tiverton Rd. Edgw —26Pa 39
Tiverton Rd. Houn —54Ea 100
Tiverton Rd. Pot B —3Fb 9
Tiverton Rd. Ruis —34W 56
Tiverton Rd. T Hth —71Qb 146
Tiverton Rd. Wemb —40Na 59
Tiverton St. SE1 —48Sb 83 (4D 206)
Tiverton Way. Chess —78Ma 143
Tivoli Gdns. SE16 —46Bc 84
Tivoli Gdns. SE18 —49Nc 86
Tivoli Gdns. Grav —10D 114
Tivoli Rd. N8 —29Mb 42
Tivoli Rd. SE27 —64Sb 127
Tivoli Rd. Houn —56Aa 99
Tobacco Dock. E1 —45Xb 83
Tobacco Quay. E1 —45Xb 83

Tobago St.—Trinity Way

Tobago St. E14 —47Cc 84
Tobin Clo. NW3 —38Gb 61
Toby Ct. N9 —17Yb 26
(off Tramway Av.)
Toby La. E1 —42Ac 84
Tockley Rd. Burn —1A 72
Tockwith Ct. Sev —95Md 187
Todd Clo. Rain —42Md 89
Todd Ho. N2 —26Fb 41
(off Grange, The)
Todds Wlk. N7 —33Pb 62
Toft Av. Grays —49Fe 91
Tokenhouse Yd. EC2 —44Tb 83 (2F 201)
Token Yd. SW15 —56Ab 102
Tokyngton Av. Wemb —37Qa 59
Toland Sq. SW15 —57Wa 102
Tolbut Ct. Romf —30Hd 48
Tolcarne Dri. Pinn —26W 36
Toley Av. Wemb —31Na 59
Tolhurst Sq. SE4 —55Ac 106
Toll Bar Ct. Sutt —81Db 163
Tollbridge Clo. W10 —42Ab 80
Tolldene Clo. Knap —5B 188
Tollers La. Coul —90Pb 164
Tollesbury Ct. Hut —15Fe 33
Tollesbury Gdns. Ilf —27Tc 46
Tollet St. E1 —42Zb 84
Tollgate Clo. Chor —13H 17
Tollgate Dri. SE21 —61Ub 127
Tollgate Gdns. NW6 —40Db 61
Tollgate Rd. E16 & E6 —43Lc 85
Tollgate Rd. Dart —59Td 112
Tollgate Rd. Wal X —7Zb 12
Tollgate Sq. E6 —43Pc 86
Tollhouse La. Wall —81Lb 164
Tollhouse Way. N19 —33Lb 62
Tollington Pk. N4 —33Pb 62
Tollington Pl. N4 —33Pb 62
Tollington Rd. N7 —35Pb 62
Tollington Way. N7 —34Nb 62
Tolmers Av. Cuff —1Nb 10
Tolmers Gdns. Cuff —1Pb 10
Tolmers Rd. Cuff —1Nb 10
Tolmers Sq. NW1 —42Lb 82 (5B 192)
Tolpaide Ho. SE11 —50Qb 82 (7K 205)
(off Marylee Way)
Tolpits Clo. Wat —15V 18
Tolpits La. Wat —18S 18
Tolpuddle St. N1 —40Qb 62 (1K 193)
Tolsford Rd. E5 —36Xb 63
Tolson Rd. Iswth —55Ja 100
Tolvaddon. St J —5D 188
Tolverne Rd. SW20 —67Ya 124
Tolworth Clo. Surb —74Ra 143
Tolworth Gdns. Romf —29Zc 47
Tolworth Pde. Chad —29Ad 47
Tolworth Pk. Rd. Surb —75Pa 143
Tolworth Rise N. Surb —74Ra 143
Tolworth Rise S. Surb —74Ra 143
Tolworth Rd. Surb —75Na 143
Tolworth Tower. Surb —75Ra 143
Tomahawk Gdns. N'holt —41Z 77
Tom Coombs Clo. SE9 —56Nc 108
Tom Cribb Rd. SE28 —48Sc 86
Tom Hood Clo. E15 —36Fc 65
Tomkins Clo. Borwd —11Na 21
Tomkins Clo. Stanf —1L 93
Tomkyns Ho. SE11
(off Distin St.) —49Qb 82 (6K 205)
Tomkyns La. Upm —26Td 50
Tomlin Ct. Eps —83Ta 161
Tomlin Rd. Slou —2C 72
Tomlins All. Twic —60Ja 100
Tomlin's Gro. E3 —41Cc 84
Tomlinson Clo. E2 —41Vb 83
Tomlinson Clo. W4 —50Ra 79
Tomlins Orchard. Bark —39Sc 66
Tomlins Ter. E14 —44Ac 84
Tomlins Wlk. N7 —33Pb 62
Tomlyns Clo. Hut —16Fe 33
Tom Mann Clo. Bark —39Uc 66
Tom Nolan Clo. E15 —40Gc 65
Tom Oakman Cen. E4 —20Fc 27
Tompion St. EC1 —41Rb 83
Tompton St. EC1 —41Rb 83 (4C 194)
Tom's Hill. Chan X —8N 3
Tom's La. K Lan —1R 4
Tom Smith Clo. SE10 —51Gc 107
Tomswood Ct. Ilf —25Sc 46
Tomswood Hill. Ilf —23Rc 46
Tomswood Rd. Chig —23Qc 46
Tom Williams Ho. SW6 —51Bb 103
(off Clem Attlee Ct.)
Tonbridge Clo. Bans —86Hb 163
Tonbridge Cres. Harr —28Na 39
Tonbridge Rd. Romf —24Md 49
Tonbridge Rd. Sev —99Ld 187
Tonbridge Rd. W Mol —70Ba 121
Tonbridge St. WC1 —41Nb 82 (3F 193)
Tonbridge Wlk. WC1 —41Nb 82 (3F 193)
(off Tonbridge St.)
Tonfield Rd. Sutt —74Bb 145
Tonge Clo. Beck —71Cc 148
Tonge Vs. Beck —71Cc 148
Tonsley Hill. SW18 —57Db 103
Tonsley Pl. SW18 —57Db 103
Tonsley Rd. SW18 —57Db 103
Tonsley St. SW18 —57Db 103
Tonstall Rd. Eps —82Ta 161
Tonstall Rd. Mitc —68Jb 126
Tons Way. SW11 —55Eb 103
Tony Cannell M. E3 —41Bc 84
Tony Law Ho. SE20 —67Xb 127
Tooke Clo. Pinn —25Aa 37
Took's Ct. EC4 —44Qb 82 (2K 199)
Tooley St. SE1 —46Tb 83 (6G 201)
Tooley St. Grav —59Fe 113
Toorack Rd. Harr —26Fa 38
Tooting Bec Gdns. SW16
(in two parts) —63Mb 126
Tooting Bec Rd. SW17 & SW16 —62Jb 126
Tooting B'way. SW17 —64Gb 125
Tooting Gro. SW17 —64Gb 125
Tooting High St. SW17 —64Gb 125
Tootswood Rd. Brom —71Gc 149
Tooveys Mill Clo. K Lan —1Q 4
Topaz Clo. Slou —6F 72
Topcliffe Dri. F'boro —77Tc 150
Top Dartford Rd. Swan & Dart —66Hd 132
Topham Sq. N17 —25Sb 43
Topham St. EC1 —42Qb 82 (5K 193)
Top Ho. Rise. E4 —17Ec 26
Topiary Sq. Rich —55Pa 101
Topiary, The. Asht —92Na 177
Toplands Av. S Ock —46Sd 90
Topley St. SE9 —56Lc 107
Topmast Point. E14 —47Cc 84
Top Pk. Beck —71Gc 149
Top Pk. Ger X —1N 53
Topping La. Uxb —41M 75
Topp Wlk. NW2 —33Ya 60
Topsfield Clo. N8 —29Mb 42
Topsfield Pde. N8 —29Nb 42
Topsfield Rd. N8 —29Nb 42
Topsham Rd. SW17 —62Hb 125
Torbay Rd. NW6 —38Bb 61
Torbay Rd. Harr —33Aa 57
Torbay St. NW1 —38Kb 62
Torbitt Way. Ilf —29Vc 47
Torbridge Clo. Edgw —24Na 39
Torbrook Clo. Bex —58Ad 109
Torcross Dri. SE23 —61Yb 128
Torcross Rd. Ruis —34X 57
Tor Gdns. W8 —47Cb 81
Tor Ho. N6 —30Kb 42
Torin Ct. Egh —4N 117
Torland Dri. Oxs —85Fa 160
Tor La. Wey —83T 158
Tormead Clo. Sutt —79Cb 145
Tormount Rd. SE18 —51Uc 108
Torney Ho. E9 —38Yb 64
Toronto Av. E12 —35Pc 66
Toronto Rd. E11 —35Fc 65
Toronto Rd. Ilf —32Rc 66
Toronto Rd. Til —4C 114
Torquay Gdns. Ilf —28Mc 45
Torquay Spur. Slou —1F 72
Torquay St. W2 —43Db 81
Torrance Clo. Horn —32Kd 69
Torrens Ct. SE5 —55Tb 105
Torrens Rd. E15 —37Hc 65
Torrens Rd. SW2 —57Pb 104
Torrens Sq. E15 —37Hc 65
Torrens St. EC1 —40Qb 62
Torrens Wlk. Grav —4G 136
Torre Wlk. Cars —74Gb 145
Torriano Av. NW5 —36Mb 62
Torriano Cotts. NW5 —36Mb 62
Torriano M. NW5 —36Lb 62
Torridge. E Til —9L 93
Torridge Gdns. SE15 —56Yb 106
Torridge Rd. Slou —51D 96
Torridge Rd. T Hth —71Rb 147
Torridon Clo. St J —5E 188
Torridon Rd. SE6 & SE13 —59Fc 107
Torrington Av. N12 —22Fb 41
Torrington Clo. N12 —21Fb 41
Torrington Clo. Clay —79Ga 142
Torrington Dri. Harr —34Da 57
Torrington Dri. Lou —14Sc 28
Torrington Dri. Pot B —3Fb 9
Torrington Gdns. N11 —23Mb 42
Torrington Gdns. Gnfd —39La 58
Torrington Gdns. Lou —14Sc 28
Torrington Gro. N12 —22Gb 41
Torrington Pk. N12 —22Eb 41
Torrington Pl. E1 —46Wb 83
Torrington Pl. WC1 —43Mb 82 (7D 192)
Torrington Rd. E18 —27Jc 45
Torrington Rd. Clay —79Ga 142
Torrington Rd. Dag —32Bd 67
Torrington Rd. Gnfd —39La 58
Torrington Rd. Ruis —34V 56
Torrington Sq. WC1 —42Mb 82 (6E 192)
Torrington Sq. Croy —73Tb 147
Torrington Way. Mord —72Cb 145
Tor Rd. Well —53Yc 109
Torr Rd. SE20 —66Zb 128
Torver Rd. Harr —28Ga 38
Torver Way. Orp —75Tc 150
Torwood La. Whyt —92Vb 181
Torwood Rd. SW15 —57Wa 102
Torworth Rd. Borwd —11Pa 21
Tot Hill. H'ley —98Sa 177
Tothill St. SW1 —47Mb 82 (2D 204)
Totnes Rd. Well —52Xc 109
Totnes Wlk. N2 —28Fb 41
Tottenhall Rd. N13 —23Qb 42
Tottenham Ct. Rd. W1 —42Lb 82 (6C 192)
Tottenham Grn. E. N15 —28Vb 43
Tottenham Hale Retail Pk. N17 —28Wb 43
Tottenham La. N8 —30Nb 42
Tottenham M. W1 —43Lb 82 (7C 192)
Tottenham Rd. N1 —37Ub 63
Tottenham St. W1 —43Lb 82 (1C 198)
Totterdown St. SW17 —63Hb 125
Totteridge Comn. N20 —19Wa 22
Totteridge Grn. N20 —19Cb 23
Totteridge La. N20 —19Cb 23
Totteridge Rd. Enf —9Zb 12
Totteridge Village. N20 —18Ab 22
Totternhoe Clo. Harr —29La 38
Totton Rd. T Hth —69Qb 126
Toulmin St. SE1 —47Sb 83 (2D 206)
Toulon St. SE5 —52Sb 105
Tournay Rd. SW6 —52Bb 103
Toussaint Wlk. SE16 —48Wb 83
Tovil Clo. SE20 —68Xb 127
Towcester Rd. E3 —42Dc 84
Tower Bri. SE1 & E1 —46Vb 83 (7K 201)
Tower Bri. App. E1 —45Vb 83 (6K 201)
Tower Bri. Rd. SE1 —48Ub 83
Tower Bri. Sq. SE1 —47Vb 83 (1K 207)
(off Queen Elizabeth St.)
Tower Bri. Wharf. E1 —46Wb 83
Tower Bldgs. E1 —46Xb 83
Tower Clo. NW3 —36Fb 61
Tower Clo. SE20 —66Xb 127
Tower Clo. Grav —4G 136
Tower Clo. Ilf —23Rc 46
Tower Clo. Orp —75Vc 151
Tower Clo. Wok —5G 188
Tower Ct. E5 —31Vb 63
Tower Ct. WC2 —44Nb 82 (3F 199)
(off Tower St.)
Tower Ct. Brtwd —19Yd 32
Tower Croft. Eyns —75Nd 153
Tower Gdns. Rd. N17 —25Sb 43
Tower Gro. Wey —75U 140
Tower Hamlets Rd. E7 —35Hc 65
Tower Hamlets Rd. E17 —27Cc 44
Tower Hill. EC3 —45Ub 83 (5J 201)
Tower Hill. Brtwd —19Yd 32
Tower Hill. Chfd —1G 2
Tower Hill Ter. EC3 —45Ub 83 (5J 201)
Tower Ho. Chalv —8J 73
Tower Ho. Iver —44G 74
Tower La. Wemb —34Ma 59
Tower M. E17 —28Cc 44
Tower Pl. EC3 —45Ub 83 (5J 201)
(off Lwr. Thames St.)
Tower Ride. Wind —2C 116
Tower Rise. Rich —55Na 101
Tower Rd. NW10 —38Wa 60
Tower Rd. Belv —49Ed 88
Tower Rd. Bexh —56Cd 110
Tower Rd. Dart —58Ld 111
Tower Rd. Epp —2Uc 14
Tower Rd. Orp —75Vc 151
Tower Rd. Tad —95Ya 178
Tower Rd. Twic —62Ha 122
Tower Royal. EC4 —45Tb 83 (4F 201)
Towers Av. Uxb —41S 76
Towers Bus. Pk. Wemb —35Ra 59
(off Carey Way)
Towers Pl. Rich —57Na 101
Towers Rd. Pinn —25Aa 37
Towers Rd. S'hall —42Ca 77
Towers Rd. Ind. Est. Grays —50Ee 91
Towers, The. Kenl —87Sb 165
Tower St. WC2 —44Nb 82 (3E 198)
Towers Wlk. Wey —79R 140
Towers Wood. S Dar —67Td 134
Tower Ter. N22 —26Pb 42
Tower View. Croy —73Ac 148
Tower Yd. Rich —57Pa 101
Towfield Ct. Felt —61Ba 121
Towfield Rd. Felt —61Ba 121
Towgar Ct. N20 —17Eb 23
Towncourt Cres. Orp —71Sc 150
Towncourt La. Orp —72Tc 150
Towncourt Path. N4 —32Sb 63
Townend. Cat —94Ub 181
Townend Clo. Cat —94Ub 181
Towney Mead. N'holt —40Ba 57
Towney Mead Ct. N'holt —40Ba 57
Town Farm Way. Stanw —59M 97
Town Field. Rick —18L 17
Townfield Corner. Grav —10E 114
Townfield Rd. Hay —46V 76
Townfield Sq. Hay —45V 76
Towngate. Cob —87Aa 159
Town Hall App. N16 —35Tb 63
(off Albion Rd.)
Town Hall App. Rd. N15 —28Vb 43
Town Hall Av. W4 —50Ta 79
Town Hall Rd. SW11 —55Hb 103
Townholm Cres. W7 —48Ha 78
Town La. Stai —58M 97
(in two parts)
Townley Ct. E15 —37Hc 65
Townley Rd. SE22 —57Ub 105
Townley Rd. Bexh —57Bd 109
Townley St. SE17
(in two parts) —50Tb 83 (7F 207)
Town Mead Bus. Cen. SW6 —55Eb 103
Town Meadow. Bren —51Ma 101
Town Meadow Rd. Bren —52Ma 101
Townmead Rd. SW6 —55Db 103
Townmead Rd. Rich —54Ra 101
Townmead Rd. Wal A —6Ec 12
Town Quay. Bark —39Rc 66
Town Rd. N9 —19Xb 25
Townsend. Sidc —65Xc 131
Townsend Av. N14 —21Mb 42
Townsend Ind. Est. NW10 —40Sa 59
Townsend La. NW9 —31Ta 59
Townsend La. Wok —93D 172
Townsend M. SW18 —61Eb 125
Townsend Rd. N15 —29Vb 43
Townsend Rd. Ashf —64N 119
Townsend Rd. S'hall —46Aa 77
Townsend St. SE17 —49Ub 83 (6G 207)
Townsend Way. N'wd —24V 36
Townsend Yd. N6 —32Kb 62
Townshend Clo. Sidc —65Xc 131
Townshend Est. NW8 —40Gb 61 (1D 190)
Townshend Rd. NW8 —39Gb 61 (1D 190)
Townshend Rd. Chst —64Rc 130
Townshend Rd. Rich —56Pa 101
Townshend Ter. Rich —56Pa 101
Townshott Clo. Bookh —98Ca 175
Townslow La. Wis —88L 157
Townson Av. N'holt —40W 56
Townson Way. N'holt —40X 57
Town Sq. Eri —51Gd 110
Town Sq. Iswth —55Ka 100
(off Swan St.)
Town Sq. Wok —89A 156
Town, The. Enf —13Tb 25
Town Tree Rd. Ashf —64Q 120
Town Wharf. Iswth —55Ka 100
Towpath. Shep —74P 139
Towpath, The. SW10 —53Fb 103
Towpath Way. Croy —72Vb 147
Towton Rd. SE27 —61Sb 127
Toynbec Clo. Chst —63Rc 130
Toynbee Rd. SW20 —67Ab 124
Toynbee St. E1 —43Vb 83 (1K 201)
Toyne Way. N6 —30Hb 41
Tozer Wlk. Wind —5B 94
Tracery, The. Bans —87Db 163
Tracey Av. NW2 —36Ya 60
Tracey St. SE11 —50Qb 82 (7K 205)
Tracious Clo. Wok —4E 188
Tracious La. St J —4E 188
Tracy Ct. Stan —24La 38
Trade Clo. N13 —21Qb 42
Tradescant Rd. SW8 —52Nb 104
Tradewinds Ct. E1 —45Wb 83
Trading Est. Rd. NW10 —42Sa 79
Trafalgar Av. N17 —23Ub 43
Trafalgar Av. SE15 —50Vb 83 (7K 207)
Trafalgar Av. Wor Pk —74Za 144
Trafalgar Clo. SE16 —49Ac 84
Trafalgar Ct. Eri —52Hd 110
(off Frobisher Rd.)
Trafalgar Dri. W on T —76X 141
Trafalgar Gdns. E1 —43Zb 84
Trafalgar Gro. SE10 —51Fc 107
Trafalgar Pl. E11 —28Jc 45
Trafalgar Pl. N18 —22Wb 43
Trafalgar Rd. SE10 —51Fc 107
Trafalgar Rd. SW19 —66Db 125
Trafalgar Rd. Dart —61Nd 133
Trafalgar Rd. Grav —9C 114
Trafalgar Rd. Rain —40Hd 68
Trafalgar Rd. Twic —61Fa 122
Trafalgar Sq. WC2 —46Mb 82 (6E 198)
Trafalgar St. SE17 —50Tb 83 (7F 207)
Trafalgar Ter. Harr —32Ga 58
Trafalgar Trading Est. Enf —14Ac 26
Trafalgar Way. E14 —46Ec 84
Trafalgar Way. Croy —75Qb 146
Trafford Clo. E15 —36Dc 64
Trafford Clo. Ilf —23Vc 47
Trafford Clo. Shenl —4Na 7
Trafford Ho. N1 —40Tb 63 (2G 195)
(off Cranston Est.)
Trafford Rd. T Hth —71Pb 146
Tramway Av. E15 —38Gc 65
Tramway Av. N9 —17Xb 25
Tramway Path. Mitc —70Gb 125
(in two parts)
Tranley M. NW3 —35Gb 61
Tranmere Rd. N9 —17Vb 25
Tranmere Rd. SW18 —61Eb 125
Tranmere Rd. Twic —59Da 99
Tranquil Pas. SE3 —54Hc 107
Tranquil Rise. Eri —50Gd 88
Tranquil Vale. SE3 —54Gc 107
Transay Wlk. N1 —37Tb 63
Transept St. NW1 —43Gb 81 (1E 196)
Transmere Clo. Orp —72Sc 150
Transmere Rd. Orp —72Sc 150
Transom Sq. E14 —50Dc 84
Transport Av. Bren —50Ja 78
Tranton Rd. SE16 —48Wb 83
Trap's Hill. Lou —14Pc 28
Traps La. N Mald —67Ua 124
Trash Pl. N11 —22Kb 42
Travellers Way. Houn —54Y 99
Travers Clo. E17 —25Zb 44
Travers Rd. N7 —34Qb 62
Travic Rd. Slou —1D 72
Travis Ct. Farn R —1F 72
Travis Ho. SE10 —53Ec 106
Treacy Clo. Bush —19Ea 20
Treadgold St. W11 —45Za 80
Treadway St. E2 —40Xb 63
Treadwell Rd. Eps —88Ua 162
Treasury Pas. SW1 —47Nb 82 (1F 205)
(off Downing St.)
Treaty Cen. Houn —55Da 99
Treaty St. N1 —39Pb 62 (1H 193)
Trebble Rd. Swans —58Ae 113
Trebeck St. W1 —46Kb 82 (6K 197)
Trebovir Rd. SW5 —50Cb 81
Treby St. E3 —42Bc 84
Trecastle Way. N7 —35Mb 62
Tredegar M. E3 —41Bc 84
Tredegar Rd. E3 —40Bc 64
Tredegar Rd. N11 —24Mb 42
Tredegar Rd. Dart —61Jd 132
Tredegar Sq. E3 —41Bc 84
Tredegar Ter. E3 —41Bc 84
Trederwen Rd. E8 —39Wb 63
Tredown Rd. SE26 —64Yb 128
Tredwell Clo. Brom —70Nc 130
Tredwell Rd. SE27 —63Rb 127
Treebourne Rd. Big H —90Lc 167
Treebys Av. Guild —100A 172
Tree Clo. Rich —60Ma 101
Treemount Ct. Eps —85Ua 162
Treen Av. SW13 —55Va 102
Tree Rd. E16 —44Lc 85
Treeside Clo. W Dray —49M 75
Tree Tops. Brtwd —18Yd 32
Tree Tops. Ger X —22A 34
Treetops. Grav —4D 136
Treetops. Whyt —90Wb 165
Treetops Clo. SE2 —50Ad 87
Treetops Clo. N'wd —22T 36
Treeview Clo. SE19 —67Ub 127
Treewall Gdns. Brom —63Kc 129
Trefgarne Rd. Dag —33Cd 68
Trefil Wlk. N7 —35Nb 62
Trefoil Ho. Eri —47Ad 87
(off Kale Rd.)
Trefoil Ho. Grays —52De 113
Trefoil Rd. SW18 —57Eb 103
Trefusis Ct. Houn —53X 99
Trefusis Wlk. Wat —11U 18
Tregaron Av. N8 —30Nb 42
Tregaron Gdns. N Mald —70Ua 124
Tregarthen Pl. Lea —93La 176
Tregarth Pl. Wok —5C 188
Tregarvon Rd. SW11 —56Jb 104
Tregenna Av. Harr —35Ca 57
Tregenna Clo. N14 —15Lb 24
Tregenna Ct. S Harr —35Ca 57
Trego Rd. E9 —38Cc 64
Tregothnan Rd. SW9 —55Nb 104
Tregunter Rd. SW10 —51Eb 103
Trehearn Rd. Ilf —24Tc 46
Treherne Ct. SW9 —53Rb 105
Treherne Ct. SW17 —63Jb 126
Trehern Rd. SW14 —55Ta 101
Trehurst St. E5 —36Ac 64
Trelawn Clo. Ott —80E 138
Trelawney Av. Slou —8P 73
Trelawney Est. E9 —37Yb 64
Trelawney Gro. Wey —79Q 140
Trelawney Rd. Ilf —24Tc 46
Trelawn Rd. E10 —34Ec 64
Trelawn Rd. SW2 —57Qb 104
Trellis Sq. E3 —41Bc 84
Treloar Gdns. SE19 —65Tb 127
Tremadoc Rd. SW4 —56Mb 104
Tremaine Clo. SE4 —54Cc 106
Tremaine Rd. SE20 —68Xb 127
Trematon Ho. SE11 —50Qb 82 (7A 206)
(off Kennings Way)
Trematon Pl. Tedd —66La 122
Tremlett Gro. N19 —34Lb 62
Tremlett M. N19 —34Lb 62
Trenance. Wok —5D 188
Trenance Gdns. Ilf —34Wc 67
Trenchard Av. Ruis —35X 57
Trenchard Clo. Stan —23Ja 38
Trenchard Clo. W on T —78Y 141
Trenchard Ct. NW4 —29Wa 40
Trenchard Ct. Mord —72Cb 145
Trenchard St. SE10 —50Fc 85
Trenches La. Slou —45C 74
Trenchold St. SW8 —51Nb 104
Trenham Dri. Warl —88Yb 166
Trenholme Clo. SE20 —66Xb 127
Trenholme Ct. Cat —94Wb 181
Trenholme Rd. SE20 —66Xb 127
Trenholme Ter. SE20 —66Xb 127
Trenmar Gdns. NW10 —41Xa 80
Trent. E Til —9L 93
Trent Av. W5 —48La 78
Trent Av. Upm —30Td 50
Trentbridge Clo. Ilf —23Vc 47
Trent Clo. Shenl —4Na 7
Trent Gdns. N14 —16Kb 24
Trentham Cres. Wok —93C 172
Trentham Dri. Orp —70Wc 131
Trentham St. SW18 —60Cb 103
Trent Ho. SE15 —56Yb 106
Trent Rd. SW2 —57Pb 104
Trent Rd. Buck H —18Kc 27
Trent Way. Hay —40U 56
Trent Way. Wor Pk —76Ya 144
Trentwood Side. Enf —13Pb 24
Treport St. SW18 —59Db 103
Tresco Clo. Brom —65Gc 129
Trescoe Gdns. Harr —31Aa 57
Trescoe Gdns. Romf —22Ed 48
Tresco Gdns. Ilf —33Wc 67
Tresco Rd. SE15 —56Xb 105
Tresham Cres. NW8 —42Gb 81 (5D 190)
Tresham Rd. Bark —38Vc 67
Tresham Wlk. E9 —36Yb 64
Tresillian Way. Wok —4D 188
Tressell Clo. N1 —38Rb 63
Tressider Ho. SW4 —59Mb 104
Tressillian Cres. SE4 —55Cc 106
Tressillian Rd. SE4 —56Bc 106
Tresta Wlk. Wok —4D 188
Trestis Clo. Hay —42Z 77
Treswell Rd. Dag —39Ad 67
Tretawn Gdns. NW7 —21Ua 40
Tretawn Pk. NW7 —21Ua 40
Trevanion Rd. W14 —50Ab 80
Treve Av. Harr —31Ea 58
Trevellance Way. Wat —5Z 5
Trevelyan Av. E12 —35Pc 66
Trevelyan Clo. Dart —56Pd 111
Trevelyan Cres. Harr —31Ma 59
Trevelyan Gdns. NW10 —39Ya 60
Trevelyan Rd. E15 —35Hc 65
Trevelyan Rd. SW17 —64Gb 125
Trevera Ct. Enf —15Ac 26
Trevera Ct. Wal X —5Ac 12
(off Eleanor Rd.)
Treveris St. SE1 —46Rb 83 (7C 200)
Treverton St. W10 —42Za 80
Treville St. SW15 —59Xa 102
Treviso Rd. SE23 —61Zb 128
Trevithick Dri. Dart —56Pd 111
Trevithick St. SE8 —51Cc 106
Trevone Ct. SW2 —59Nb 104
(off Doverfield Rd.)
Trevone Gdns. Pinn —30Aa 37
Trevor Clo. Barn —16Fb 23
Trevor Clo. Brom —73Hc 149
Trevor Clo. Harr —24Ha 38
Trevor Clo. Iswth —57Ha 100
Trevor Clo. N'holt —40Y 57
Trevor Cres. Ruis —35V 56
Trevor Gdns. Edgw —25Ta 39
Trevor Gdns. N'holt —40Y 57
Trevor Gdns. Ruis —35W 56
Trevor Pl. SW7 —47Gb 81 (2E 202)
Trevor Rd. SW19 —66Ab 124
Trevor Rd. Edgw —25Ta 39
Trevor Rd. Hay —47U 76
Trevor Rd. Wfd G —24Jc 45
Trevor Sq. SW7 —47Hb 81 (3E 202)
Trevor St. SW7 —47Gb 81 (2E 202)
Trevose Av. W Byf —86H 157
Trevose Ho. SE11
(off Orsett St.) —50Pb 82 (7J 205)
Trevose Rd. E17 —25Fc 45
Trevose Way. Wat —20Y 19
Trewarden Av. Iver —40F 54
Trewenna Dri. Chess —78Ma 143
Trewenna Dri. Pot B —4Fb 9
Trewince Rd. SW20 —67Ya 124
Trewint St. SW18 —61Eb 125
Trewsbury Ho. SE2 —46Zc 87
Trewsbury Rd. SE26 —64Zb 128
Triandra Way. Hay —43Z 77
Triangle Ct. E16 —43Mc 85
Triangle Pas. New Bar —14Eb 23
Triangle Pl. SW4 —56Mb 104
Triangle Rd. E8 —39Xb 63
Triangle, The. E8 —39Xb 63
Triangle, The. EC1 —42Rb 83 (5C 194)
Triangle, The. N13 —21Qb 42
Triangle, The. Bark —37Sc 66
Triangle, The. King T —68Sa 123
Triangle, The. Wok —6F 188
Trickett Ho. Sutt —81Db 163
Trident Gdns. N'holt —41Z 77
Trident Ind. Est. Coln —55G 96
Trident Rd. Wat —6V 4
Trident St. SE16 —49Zb 84
Trident Way. S'hall —48X 77
Trigg's Clo. Wok —7G 188
Trigg's La. Wok —7F 188
Trig La. EC4 —45Sb 83 (4D 200)
Trigo Ct. Eps —83Ta 161
Trigon Rd. SW8 —52Pb 104
Trilby Rd. SE23 —61Zb 128
Trillo Ct. Ilf —31Uc 66
Trimmer Wlk. Bren —51Na 101
Trinder Gdns. N19 —32Nb 62
Trinder Rd. N19 —32Nb 62
Trinder Rd. Barn —15Ya 22
Tring Av. W5 —46Pa 79
Tring Av. S'hall —44Ba 77
Tring Av. Wemb —37Qa 59
Tring Clo. Ilf —29Tc 46
Tring Clo. Romf —21Pd 49
Tring Ct. Twic —63Ja 122
Tring Gdns. Romf —21Nd 49
Tring Grn. Romf —21Nd 49
Tringham Clo. Ott —78E 138
Tring Ho. Wat —17U 18
Tring Wlk. Romf —21Nd 49
Trinidad Gdns. Dag —38Fd 68
Trinidad St. E14 —45Bc 84
Trinity Av. N2 —27Fb 41
Trinity Av. Enf —16Vb 25
Trinity Bus. Cen. SE16 —47Bc 84
Trinity Bus. Pk. E4 —23Bc 44
Trinity Chu. Pas. EC4
(off Fetter La.) —44Qb 82 (2A 200)
Trinity Chu. Pas. SW13 —51Xa 102
Trinity Chu. Rd. SW13 —51Xa 102
Trinity Chu. Sq. SE1 —48Sb 83 (2E 206)
Trinity Clo. E11 —33Gc 65
Trinity Clo. NW3 —35Fb 61
Trinity Clo. SE13 —56Fc 107
Trinity Clo. SW4 —56Lb 104
Trinity Clo. Brom —74Nc 150
Trinity Clo. Houn —56Aa 99
Trinity Clo. N'wd —23U 36
Trinity Clo. S Croy —81Ub 165
Trinity Clo. Stai —58L 97
Trinity Cotts. Rich —55Pa 101
Trinity Ct. N1 —39Ub 63
Trinity Ct. SE7 —49Mc 85
Trinity Ct. SE25 —72Ub 147
Trinity Ct. Croy —75Sb 147
Trinity Cres. SW17 —61Hb 125
Trinity Gdns. E16 —43Hc 85
Trinity Gdns. SW9 —56Pb 104
Trinity Gro. SE10 —53Ec 106
Trinity Hall Clo. Wat —13Y 19
Trinity La. Wal X —4Ac 12
Trinity M. SE20 —67Xb 127
Trinity M. W10 —44Za 80
Trinity Path. SE26 —62Yb 128
(in two parts)
Trinity Pier. E14 —45Gc 85
Trinity Pl. EC3 —45Vb 83 (5K 201)
Trinity Pl. Bexh —56Bd 109
Trinity Pl. Wind —4G 94
Trinity Rise. SW2 —60Qb 104
Trinity Rd. N2 —27Fb 41
Trinity Rd. N22 —24Nb 42
Trinity Rd. SW18 & SW17 —56Eb 103
Trinity Rd. SW19 —65Cb 125
Trinity Rd. Grav —9E 114
Trinity Rd. Ilf —27Sc 46
Trinity Rd. Rich —55Pa 101
Trinity Rd. S'hall —46Aa 77
Trinity Sq. EC3 —45Ub 83 (5J 201)
Trinity St. E16 —43Hc 85
Trinity St. SE1 —47Sb 83 (2E 206)
Trinity St. Enf —12Sb 25
Trinity Wlk. NW3 —37Eb 61
Trinity Way. E4 —23Bc 44
Trinity Way. W3 —45Ub 80

Trio Pl.—Up. Harley St.

Trio Pl. SE1 —47Sb 83 (2E 206)
Tristan Sq. SE3 —55Gc 107
Tristram Clo. E17 —27Fc 45
Tristram Rd. Brom —63Hc 129
Triton Sq. NW1 —42Lb 82 (5B 192)
Tritton Av. Croy —77Nb 146
Tritton Rd. SE21 —62Tb 127
Trittons. Tad —93Za 178
Triumph Clo. Hay —53S 98
Triumph Ho. Bark —41Wc 87
Triumph Rd. E6 —44Pc 86
Trivett Clo. Grnh —57Wd 112
Trojan Way. Croy —76Pb 146
Troon Ct. S'hill —10A 116
Troon St. E1 —44Ac 84
Troopers Dri. Romf —21Md 49
Trosley Av. Grav —1D 136
Trosley Rd. Belv —51Cd 110
Trossachs Rd. SE22 —57Ub 105
Trothy Rd. SE1 —49Wb 83
Trotsworth Av. Vir W —70A 118
Trotsworth Ct. Vir W —10P 117
Trotters Bottom. Barn —9Wa 8
Trott Rd. N10 —24Hb 41
Trotts La. W'ham —99Sc 184
Trotts St. SW11 —53Gb 103
Trotwood. Chig —22Tc 46
Trotwood Clo. Shenf —18Ae 33
Troughton Rd. SE7 —50Kc 85
Troutbeck Clo. Slou —5K 73
Troutbeck Ho. NW1 —41Kb 82 (4A 192) (off Albany St.)
Troutbeck Rd. SE14 —53Ac 106
Trout La. Uxb —41K 75
Trout Rise. Loud —13K 17
Trout Rd. W Dray —46M 75
Troutstream Way. Loud —14J 17
Trouville Rd. SW4 —58Lb 104
Trowbridge Rd. E9 —37Bc 64
Trowbridge Rd. Romf —23Md 49
Trowley Rise. Abb L —3U 4
Trowlock Av. Tedd —65La 122
Trowlock Way. Tedd —65Ma 123
Troy Ct. SE18 —49Rc 86
Troy Rd. SE19 —65Tb 127
Troy St. SE18 —49Rc 86
Troy Town. SE15 —55Wb 105
Truesdale Dri. Hare —28L 35
Truesdale Rd. E6 —44Pc 86
Trulock Ct. N17 —24Wb 43
Trulock Rd. N17 —24Wb 43
Truman Clo. Edgw —24Sa 39
Trumans Rd. N16 —36Vb 63
Trumble Gdns. T Hth —70Rb 127
Trumpers Way. W7 —48Ga 78
Trumper Way. Uxb —38L 55
Trumpington Rd. E7 —35Hc 65
Trumpsgreen Av. Vir W —72A 138
Trumpsgreen Clo. Vir W —71A 138
Trumps Mill La. Vir W —72B 138
Trump St. EC2 —44Sb 83 (3E 200)
Trundlers Way. Bush —18Ga 20
Trundle St. SE1 —47Sb 83 (1D 206) (off Weller St.)
Trundley's M. SE8 —50Zb 84
Trundley's Rd. SE8 —50Zb 84
Trundley's Ter. SE8 —49Zb 84
Trunks All. Swan —68Dd 132
Truro Gdns. Ilf —31Nc 66
Truro Ho. Pinn —24Ba 37
Truro Rd. E17 —28Bc 44
Truro Rd. N22 —24Nb 42
Truro Rd. Grav —2F 136
Truro St. NW5 —37Jb 62
Truro Wlk. Romf —23Ld 49
Truro Way. N'holt —41U 76
Truslove Rd. SE27 —64Qb 126
Truss Hill Rd. Asc —10A 116
Trussley Rd. W6 —48Ya 80
Trustees Way. Den —29H 35
Truston's Gdns. Horn —31Jd 68
Trust Rd. Wal X —6Ac 12
Trust Wlk. SE21 —60Rb 105
Tryfan Clo. Ilf —29Mc 45
Tryon. Sidc —65Xc 131
Tryon St. SW3 —50Hb 81 (7F 203)
Trystings Clo. Clay —79Ja 142
Tuam Rd. SE18 —51Tc 108
Tubbenden Clo. Orp —76Uc 150
Tubbenden Dri. Orp —77Tc 150
Tubbenden La. Orp —77Tc 150
Tubbenden La. S. Orp —78Tc 150
Tubbs Rd. NW10 —40Va 60
Tubs Hill. Sev —96Kd 187
Tubs Hill Ho. Sev —96Jd 186
Tubs Hill Pde. Sev —96Jd 186
Tubwell Rd. Stoke P —9M 53
Tucker Rd. Ott —79F 138
Tucker St. Wat —15Y 19
Tuckey Gro. Rip —95H 173
Tucklow Wlk. SW15 —59Va 102
Tuck Rd. Rain —37Jd 68
Tudor Av. Chesh —3Wb 11
Tudor Av. Hamp —66Ca 121
Tudor Av. Romf —27Jd 48
Tudor Av. Wat —10Z 5
Tudor Av. Wor Pk —76Xa 144
Tudor Clo. N6 —31Lb 62
Tudor Clo. NW3 —36Gb 61
Tudor Clo. NW7 —23Wa 40
Tudor Clo. NW9 —33Sa 59
Tudor Clo. SW2 —58Pb 104
Tudor Clo. Ashf —63N 119
Tudor Clo. Bans —87Ab 162
Tudor Clo. Bookh —96Ca 175 (in two parts)
Tudor Clo. Chesh —3Xb 11
Tudor Clo. Chess —78Na 143
Tudor Clo. Chig —21Qc 46
Tudor Clo. Chst —67Pc 130
Tudor Clo. Cob —85Ba 159
Tudor Clo. Coul —90Qb 164
Tudor Clo. Dart —58Kd 111
Tudor Clo. N'fleet —10A 114
Tudor Clo. Pinn —29W 36
Tudor Clo. Shenf —16Ce 33
Tudor Clo. S Croy —87Xb 165
Tudor Clo. Sutt —79Ab 144
Tudor Clo. Wall —80Lb 146
Tudor Clo. Wok —89C 156
Tudor Clo. Wfd G —22Kc 45
Tudor Ct. E17 —31Bc 64
Tudor Ct. N1 —37Ub 63
Tudor Ct. N22 —24Nb 42
Tudor Ct. W3 —47Qa 79
Tudor Ct. Big H —89Nc 168
Tudor Ct. Borwd —12Na 21
Tudor Ct. Felt —63Y 121
Tudor Ct. Mill E —18J 17
Tudor Ct. Romf —23Rd 49
Tudor Ct. Sidc —62Wc 131
Tudor Ct. Stanw —58N 97
Tudor Ct. Tedd —65Ha 122
Tudor Ct. N. Wemb —36Qa 59
Tudor Ct. S. Wemb —36Qa 59
Tudor Cres. Enf —11Sb 25
Tudor Cres. Ilf —23Rc 46
Tudor Cres. Ott —88Ld 171
Tudor Dri. King T —64Ma 123
Tudor Dri. Mord —72Za 144
Tudor Dri. Ott —88Ld 171
Tudor Dri. Romf —28Jd 48
Tudor Dri. W on T —74Z 141
Tudor Dri. Wat —10Z 5
Tudor Enterprise Pk. Harr —27Fa 38
Tudor Est. NW10 —40Ra 59
Tudor Gdns. NW9 —33Sa 59
Tudor Gdns. SW13 —55Ua 102
Tudor Gdns. W3 —43Qa 79
Tudor Gdns. Harr —26Fa 38
Tudor Gdns. Romf —28Jd 48
Tudor Gdns. Slou —4A 72
Tudor Gdns. Twic —60Ha 100
Tudor Gdns. Upm —33Sd 70
Tudor Gdns. W Wick —76Ec 148
Tudor Gro. E9 —38Yb 64
Tudor Ho. Pinn —26Y 37 (off Pinner Hill Rd.)
Tudor Leys. Old Win —9N 95
Tudor Mnr. Gdns. Wat —4Z 5
Tudor Pde. Rick —17J 17
Tudor Pde. Romf —31Zc 67
Tudor Pl. Mitc —66Gb 125
Tudor Rd. E4 —23Dc 44
Tudor Rd. E6 —39Lc 65
Tudor Rd. E9 —39Xb 63
Tudor Rd. N9 —17Xb 25
Tudor Rd. SE19 —66Vb 127
Tudor Rd. SE25 —71Xb 147
Tudor Rd. Ashf —65T 120
Tudor Rd. Bark —39Vc 67
Tudor Rd. Barn —13Cb 23
Tudor Rd. Beck —69Ec 128
Tudor Rd. Hamp —66Ca 121
Tudor Rd. Harr —26Fa 38
Tudor Rd. Hay —44T 76
Tudor Rd. Houn —56Fa 100
Tudor Rd. King T —66Qa 123
Tudor Rd. Pinn —26Y 37
Tudor Rd. S'hall —45Aa 77
Tudor Sq. Hay —43T 76
Tudor Stacks. SE24 —56Sb 105
Tudor St. EC4 —45Qb 82 (4A 200)
Tudor Vs. Chesh —1Ub 11
Tudor Wlk. Bex —58Ad 109
Tudor Wlk. Lea —92Ha 176
Tudor Wlk. Wat —9Z 5
Tudor Wlk. Wey —76R 140
Tudor Way. N14 —18Mb 24
Tudor Way. W3 —47Qa 79
Tudor Way. Orp —72Tc 150
Tudor Way. Rick —18J 17
Tudor Way. Uxb —37Q 56
Tudor Way. Wal A —5Fc 13
Tudor Way. Wind —3C 94
Tudor Well Clo. Stan —22Ka 38
Tudway Rd. SE3 —55Kc 107
Tufnail Rd. Dart —58Pd 111
Tufnell Pk. Rd. N19 & N7 —35Lb 62
Tufter Rd. Chig —22Vc 47
Tufton Gdns. W Mol —68Da 121
Tufton Rd. E4 —21Cc 44
Tufton St. SW1 —48Nb 82 (3F 205)
Tugela Rd. Croy —72Tb 147
Tugela St. SE6 —61Bc 128
Tugmutton Clo. Orp —77Rc 150
Tulip Clo. Croy —74Zb 148
Tulip Clo. Hamp —65Ba 121
Tulip Clo. Pil H —15Xd 32
Tulip Clo. Romf —23Ld 49
Tulip Dri. Ilf —36Rc 66
Tulip Gdns. E4 —20Fc 27
Tulse Clo. Beck —69Ec 128
Tulse Hill. SW2 —58Qb 104
Tulse Hill Est. SW2 —58Qb 104
Tulse Ho. SW2 —58Qb 104
Tulsemere Rd. SE27 —61Sb 127
Tulyar Clo. Tad —92Xa 178
Tumber St. H'ley —97Sa 177
Tumblewood Rd. Bans —88Ab 162
Tumbling Bay. W on T —72W 140
Tummons Gdns. SE25 —68Ub 127
Tuncombe Rd. N18 —21Ub 43
Tunis Rd. W12 —46Ya 80
Tunley Grn. E14 —43Bc 84
Tunley Rd. NW10 —39Ua 60
Tunley Rd. SW17 —60Jb 104
Tunmarsh La. E13 —41Lc 85
Tunnanleys. E6 —44Qc 86
Tunnel App. E14 —45Ac 84
Tunnel App. SE10 —48Gc 85
Tunnel App. SE16 —47Yb 84
Tunnel Av. SE10 —47Fc 85 (in two parts)
Tunnel Est. Grays —49Vd 90
Tunnel Gdns. N11 —24Lb 42
Tunnel Rd. SE16 —47Yb 84
Tunnel Wood Clo. Wat —9V 4
Tunnel Wood Rd. Wat —9V 4
Tuns La. Slou —8G 72
Tunstall Av. Ilf —23Wc 47
Tunstall Clo. Orp —77Uc 150
Tunstall Rd. SW9 —56Pb 104
Tunstall Rd. Croy —74Ub 147
Tunstall Wlk. Bren —51Na 101
Tunstock Way. Belv —48Bd 87
Tunworth Clo. NW9 —30Sa 39
Tunworth Cres. SW15 —58Va 102
Tupwood La. Cat —97Wb 181
Tupwood Scrubs Rd. Cat —100Wb 181
Turchapel M. SW4 —55Kb 104
Turenne Clo. SW18 —56Eb 103
Turin Rd. N9 —17Yb 26
Turin St. E2 —41Wb 83
Turkey Oak Clo. SE19 —67Ub 127
Turkey St. Enf —8Wb 11
Turks Clo. Uxb —41Q 76
Turk's Head Yd. EC1 —43Rb 83 (7B 194)
Turks Row. SW3 —50Hb 81 (7G 203)
Turle Rd. N4 —33Pb 62
Turle Rd. SW16 —68Nb 126
Turlewray Clo. N4 —32Pb 62
Turley Clo. E15 —39Gc 65
Turnagain La. EC4 —44Rb 83 (2B 200) (off Farringdon St.)
Turnage Rd. Dag —32Ad 67
Turnberry Quay. E14 —48Dc 84
Turnberry Way. Orp —74Tc 150
Turnbull Clo. Grnh —59Ud 112
Turner Av. N15 —28Ub 43
Turner Av. Mitc —67Hb 125
Turner Av. Twic —62Ea 122
Turner Clo. NW11 —30Db 41
Turner Clo. Hay —40S 56
Turner Ct. Dart —57Ld 111
Turner Dri. NW11 —30Db 41
Turner Rd. E17 —27Ec 44
Turner Rd. Bean —62Xd 134
Turner Rd. Big H —84Lc 167
Turner Rd. Bush —14Ea 20
Turner Rd. Edgw —26Na 39
Turner Rd. N Mald —73Ta 143
Turner Rd. Slou —7N 73
Turner's All. EC3 —45Ub 83 (4H 201)
Turners Clo. Stai —64K 119
Turners Gdns. Sev —100Ld 187
Turner's Hill. Chesh —1Zb 12
Turners La. W on T —79X 141
Turners Meadow Way. Beck —67Bc 128
Turners Oak. New Ash —76Ae 155
Turner's Rd. E14 & E3 —43Bc 84
Turners Rd. N1 —40Ub 63 (2H 195)
Turner St. E1 —43Xb 83
Turner St. E16 —44Hc 85
Turner's Way. Croy —75Qb 146
Turners Wood. NW11 —32Eb 61
Turneville Rd. W14 —51Bb 103
Turney Rd. SE21 —59Sb 105
Turneys Orchard. Chor —15F 16
Turnham Grn. Ter. W4 —49Ua 80
Turnham Grn. Ter. M. W4 —49Ua 80
Turnham Rd. SE4 —57Ac 106
Turnmill St. EC1 —42Rb 83 (6B 194)
Turnoak Av. Wok —92A 172
Turnoak La. Wok —92A 172
Turnoak Pk. Wind —6C 94
Turnpike Clo. SE8 —52Bc 106
Turnpike Ct. Bexh —56Zc 109
Turnpike Dri. Orp —81Yc 169
Turnpike La. N8 —28Pb 42
Turnpike La. Sutt —78Eb 145
Turnpike La. Uxb —41N 75
Turnpike La. W Til —9F 92
Turnpike Link. Croy —75Ub 147
Turnpike Pde. N15 —27Rb 43 (off Green Lanes)
Turnpin La. SE10 —51Ec 106
Turnstone. Long —69Ce 135
Turnstone Clo. E13 —41Jc 85
Turnstone Clo. NW9 —26Ua 40
Turnstone Clo. S Croy —82Ac 166
Turnstone Ct. SE8 —51Bc 106
Turnstones, The. Grav —1F 136
Turnstones, The. Wat —8Aa 5
Turp Av. Grays —47Ee 91
Turpentine La. SW1 —50Kb 82 (7A 204)
Turpin Av. Romf —24Cd 48
Turpington Clo. Brom —72Nc 150
Turpington La. Brom —73Nc 150
Turpin La. Eri —51Jd 110
Turpin Rd. Felt —58Y 98
Turpin's La. Wfd G —22Pc 46
Turpin Way. N19 —33Mb 62
Turpin Way. Wall —80Kb 146
Turquand St. SE17 —49Sb 83 (6E 206)
Turret Gro. SW4 —55Lb 104
Turtle Rd. SW16 —68Nb 126
Turton Rd. Wemb —36Na 59
Turton Way. Slou —8H 73
Turville St. E2 —42Vb 83 (5K 195)
Tuscan Rd. SE18 —50Tc 86
Tuskar St. SE10 —51Gc 107
Tustin Est. SE15 —51Yb 106
Tutshill Ct. SE15 —52Ub 105 (off Lynbrook Clo.)
Tuttlebee La. Buck H —19Jc 27
Tuxford Clo. Borwd —10Na 7
Tweed. E Til —9L 93
Tweedale Ct. E15 —36Ec 64
Tweeddale Gro. Uxb —34S 56
Tweeddale Rd. Cars —74Fb 145
Tweed Glen. Romf —24Fd 48
Tweed Grn. Romf —24Fd 48
Tweedmouth Rd. E13 —40Kc 65
Tweed Rd. Slou —51D 96
Tweed Way. Romf —24Fd 48
Tweedy Rd. Brom —67Jc 129
Tweezer's All. WC2 —45Qb 82 (4K 199) (off Milford La.)
Twelve Acre Clo. Bookh —96Ba 175
Twelvetrees Cres. E3 & E16 —42Ec 84
Twentyman Clo. Wfd G —22Jc 45
Twickenham Bri. Twic & Rich —57La 100
Twickenham Clo. Croy —76Pb 146
Twickenham Gdns. Gnfd —36Ja 58
Twickenham Gdns. Harr —24Ga 38
Twickenham Rd. E11 —33Fc 65
Twickenham Rd. Felt —62Ba 121
Twickenham Rd. Iswth —57Ja 100
Twickenham Rd. Rich —56La 100
Twickenham Rd. Tedd —63Ja 122
Twickenham Trading Est. Iswth —58Ha 100
Twigg Clo. Eri —52Gd 110
Twilley St. SW18 —59Db 103
Twin Bridges Bus. Pk. S Croy —79Tb 147
Twinches La. Slou —6F 72
Twine Ct. E1 —45Yb 84
Twineham Grn. N12 —21Cb 41
Twining Av. Twic —62Ea 122
Twinn Rd. NW7 —23Ab 40
Twinoaks. Cob —85Ca 159
Twisden Rd. NW5 —35Kb 62
Twitton La. Ott —87Fd 170
Twitton Meadows. Ott —88Gd 170
Twitton Stream Cotts. Ott —88Gd 170
Twybridge Way. NW10 —38Sa 59
Twyford Abbey Rd. NW10 —41Pa 79
Twyford Av. N2 —27Hb 41
Twyford Av. W3 —45Qa 79
Twyford Ct. N10 —27Jb 42
Twyford Ct. Wemb —40Na 59 (off Vicars Bri. Clo.)
Twyford Cres. W3 —46Qa 79
Twyford Ho. N5 —34Rb 63
Twyford Ho. N15 —30Ub 43 (off Chisley Rd.)
Twyford Pl. WC2 —44Pb 82 (2H 199)
Twyford Rd. Cars —74Fb 145
Twyford Rd. Harr —32Da 57
Twyford Rd. Ilf —36Sc 66
Twyford St. N1 —39Pb 62
Tyas Rd. E16 —42Hc 85
Tybenham Rd. SW19 —69Cb 125
Tyberry Rd. Enf —13Xb 25
Tyburn La. Harr —31Ha 58
Tyburns, The. Hut —19Ee 33
Tyburn Way. W1 —45Hb 81 (4G 197)
Tycehurst Hill. Lou —14Pc 28
Tydcombe Rd. Warl —91Yb 182
Tye La. Orp —78Sc 150
Tye La. Tad —99Ua 178
Tyers Est. SE1 —47Ub 83 (1H 207) (off Bermondsey St.)
Tyers Ga. SE1 —47Ub 83 (2H 207)
Tyers St. SE11 —50Pb 82 (7H 205)
Tyers Ter. SE11 —50Pb 82 (7H 205)
Tyeshurst Clo. SE2 —50Ad 87
Tyfield Clo. Chesh —2Yb 12
Tykeswater La. Els —12La 20
Tylecroft Rd. SW16 —68Nb 126
Tyle Grn. Horn —28Md 49
Tylehurst Gdns. Ilf —36Sc 66
Tyle Pl. Old Win —7L 95
Tyler Clo. E2 —40Vb 63 (1K 195)
Tyler Gdns. Add —77L 139
Tyler Gro. Dart —56Pd 111
Tylers Clo. K Lan —1N 3
Tylers Clo. Lou —17Nc 28
Tyler's Ct. W1 —44Mb 82 (3D 198) (off Wardour St.)
Tylers Ct. Wemb —40Na 59
Tylers Cres. Horn —36Ld 69
Tylersfield. Abb L —3V 4
Tylers Ga. Harr —30Na 39
Tylers Grn. Rd. Swan —72Ed 152
Tylers Path. Cars —77Hb 145
Tyler St. SE10 —50Gc 85 (in two parts)
Tylers Way. Wat —14Fa 20
Tylney Av. SE19 —64Vb 127
Tylney Rd. E7 —35Lc 65
Tylney Rd. Brom —68Mc 129
Tynan Clo. Felt —60W 98
Tyndale Ct. E14 —50Dc 84
Tyndale La. N1 —38Rb 63
Tyndale Mans. N1 —38Rb 63 (off Upper St.)
Tyndale Ter. N1 —38Rb 63
Tyndall Gdns. E10 —33Ec 64
Tyndall Rd. E10 —33Ec 64
Tyndall Rd. Well —55Vc 109
Tyne. E Til —9L 93
Tyne Clo. Upm —30Td 50
Tynedale Clo. Dart —60Td 112
Tyne Gdns. S Ock —45Sd 90
Tyneham Clo. SW11 —55Jb 104
Tyneham Rd. SW11 —54Jb 104
Tynemouth Dri. Enf —10Wb 11
Tynemouth Rd. N15 —28Vb 43
Tynemouth Rd. Mitc —66Jb 126
Tynemouth St. SW6 —54Eb 103
Tyne St. E1 —44Vb 83 (2K 201)
Tynley Av. SE19 —64Vb 127
Tynwald Ho. SE26 —62Wb 127
Type St. E2 —40Zb 64
Tyrawley Rd. SW6 —53Db 103
Tyrell Clo. Harr —35Ga 58
Tyrell Ct. Cars —77Hb 145
Tyrell Gdns. Wind —5D 94
Tyrell Rise. War —22Yd 50
Tyrells Clo. Upm —33Rd 69
Tyrone Rd. E6 —40Pc 66
Tyron Way. Sidc —63Uc 130
Tyrrell Av. Well —57Wc 109
Tyrrell Rd. SE22 —56Wb 105
Tyrrells Hall Clo. Grays —51Fe 113
Tyrrell Sq. Mitc —67Gb 125
Tyrrel Way. NW9 —31Va 60
Tyrwhitt Rd. SE4 —55Cc 106
Tysea Hill. Stap A —18Hd 30
Tysoe Av. Enf —8Bc 12
Tysoe St. EC1 —41Qb 82 (4A 194)
Tyson Gdns. SE23 —59Yb 106
Tyson Rd. SE23 —59Yb 106
Tyssen Pas. E8 —37Vb 63
Tyssen Pl. S Ock —40Yd 70
Tyssen Rd. N16 —34Vb 63
Tyssen St. E8 —37Vb 63
Tythebarn Clo. Guild —100D 172
Tytherton Rd. N19 —34Mb 62
Uamvar St. E14 —43Dc 84
Uckfield Gro. Mitc —67Jb 126
Uckfield Rd. Enf —9Zb 12
Udall Gdns. Romf —23Cd 48
Udall St. SW1 —49Lb 82 (6C 204)
Udney Pk. Rd. Tedd —65Ja 122
Uffington Rd. NW10 —39Wa 60
Uffington Rd. SE27 —63Qb 126
Ufford Clo. Harr —24Da 37
Ufford Rd. Harr —24Da 37
Ufford St. SE1 —47Qb 82 (1A 206)
Ufton Gro. N1 —38Tb 63
Ufton Rd. N1 —38Tb 63
Ujima Ct. SW16 —63Nb 126
Ullathorne Rd. SW16 —63Lb 126
Ulleswater Rd. N14 —20Nb 24
Ullin St. E14 —43Ec 84
Ullswater Clo. SW15 —63Ta 123
Ullswater Clo. Brom —66Gc 129
Ullswater Clo. Hay —40U 56
Ullswater Clo. Slou —3A 72
Ullswater Cres. SW15 —63Ta 123
Ullswater Cres. Coul —88Nb 164
Ullswater Rd. SE27 —61Rb 127
Ullswater Rd. SW13 —52Wa 102
Ullswater Way. Horn —36Jd 68
Ulstan Clo. Wold —95Cc 182
Ulster Gdns. N13 —21Sb 43
Ulster Pl. NW1 —42Kb 82 (6K 191)
Ulster Ter. NW1 —42Jb 82 (6K 191)
Ulundi Rd. SE3 —51Gc 107
Ulva Rd. SW15 —57Za 102
Ulverscroft Rd. SE22 —57Vb 105
Ulverstone Rd. SE27 —61Rb 127
Ulverston Rd. E17 —26Fc 45
Ulwin Av. Byfl —85N 157
Ulysses Rd. NW6 —36Bb 61
Umberston St. E1 —44Wb 83
Umberville Way. Slou —1D 72
Umbria St. SW15 —58Wa 102
Umfreville Rd. N4 —30Rb 43
Underbridge Way. Enf —13Ac 26
Undercliff Rd. SE13 —55Cc 106
Underhill. Barn —15Cb 23
Underhill Ct. Barn —15Cb 23
Underhill Pas. NW1 —39Kb 62 (off Camden High St.)
Underhill Rd. SE22 —57Wb 105
Underhill St. NW1 —39Kb 62
Underne Av. N14 —19Kb 24
Undershaft. EC3 —44Ub 83 (3H 201)
Undershaw Rd. Brom —62Hc 129
Underwood. New Ad —78Ec 148
Underwood Ct. Cat —97Vb 181
Underwood Rd. E1 —42Wb 83
Underwood Rd. E4 —22Dc 44
Underwood Rd. Cat —98Ub 181
Underwood Rd. Wfd G —24Lc 45
Underwood Row. N1 —41Sb 83 (3E 194)
Underwood St. N1 —41Sb 83 (3E 194)
Underwood, The. SE9 —62Pc 130
Undine Rd. E14 —49Dc 84
Undine St. SW17 —64Hb 125
Uneeda Dri. Gnfd —39Fa 58
Unicorn Building. E1 —45Zb 84 (off Jardine Rd.)
Unicorn Pas. SE1 —46Ub 83 (7J 201)
Unicorn Wlk. Grnh —57Vd 112
Union Cotts. E15 —38Gc 65
Union Ct. EC2 —44Ub 83 (2H 201) (off Old Broad St.)
Union Ct. Rich —57Na 101
Union Dri. E1 —42Ac 84
Union Gro. SW8 —54Mb 104
Union Rd. N11 —23Mb 42
Union Rd. SW8 & SW4 —54Mb 104
Union Rd. Brom —71Mc 149
Union Rd. Croy —73Sb 147
Union Rd. N'holt —40Ca 57
Union Rd. Wemb —37Na 59
Union Sq. N1 —39Sb 63 (1E 194)
Union St. E15 —39Ec 64
Union St. SE1 —46Rb 83 (6B 206)
Union St. Barn —13Ab 22
Union St. King T —68Ma 123
Union Wlk. E2 —41Ub 83 (3J 195)
Union Yd. W1 —44Kb 82 (3A 198)
Unity Clo. NW10 —38Wa 60
Unity Clo. SE27 —64Sb 127
Unity Clo. New Ad —81Dc 166
Unity Rd. Enf —9Yb 12
Unity Way. SE18 —48Mc 85
University Clo. NW7 —24Va 40
University Pl. Eri —52Ed 110
University Rd. SW19 —65Fb 125
University St. WC1 —42Lb 82 (6C 192)
University Way. E16 —45Pc 86
Unwin Av. Felt —57T 98
Unwin Clo. SE15 —51Wb 105
Unwin Rd. SW7 —48Fb 81 (3B 202)
Unwin Rd. Iswth —55Ga 100
Upbrook M. W2 —44Eb 81 (3A 196)
Upcerne Rd. SW10 —53Eb 103
Upchurch Clo. SE20 —66Xb 127
Upcroft. Wind —5F 94
Upcroft Av. Edgw —22Sa 39
Updale Clo. Pot B —5Ab 8
Updale Rd. Sidc —63Vc 131
Upfield. Croy —76Xb 147
Upfield Rd. W7 —41Ha 78
Upgrove Mnr. Way. SW2 —59Qb 104
Uphall Rd. Ilf —36Rc 66
Upham Pk. Rd. W4 —49Ua 80
Uphill Dri. NW7 —22Ua 40
Uphill Dri. NW9 —29Sa 39
Uphill Gro. NW7 —21Ua 40
Uphill Rd. NW7 —21Ua 40
Upland Ct. Rd. Romf —26Pd 49
Upland Rd. E13 —42Jc 85
Upland Rd. SE22 —57Wb 105
Upland Rd. Bexh —55Bd 109
Upland Rd. S Croy —78Tb 147
Upland Rd. Sutt —80Fb 145
Upland Rd. Wold —92Cc 182
Uplands. Asht —92Ma 177
Uplands. Beck —68Cc 128
Uplands. Crox —16P 17
Uplands Av. E17 —26Zb 44
Uplands Clo. SW14 —57Ra 101
Uplands Clo. Ger X —32A 54
Uplands Clo. Sev —95Hd 186
Uplands Ct. N21 —17Qb 24 (off Church Hill)
Uplands Dri. Oxs —86Fa 160
Uplands End. Wfd G —24Nc 46
Uplands Pk. Rd. Enf —12Qb 24
Uplands Rd. N8 —29Pb 42
Uplands Rd. Barn —18Jb 24
Uplands Rd. Kenl —88Sb 165
Uplands Rd. Orp —74Xc 151
Uplands Rd. Romf —27Zc 47
Uplands Rd. War —22Ae 51
Uplands Rd. Wfd G —24Nc 46
Uplands, The. Brick —2Aa 5
Uplands, The. Ger X —33A 54
Uplands, The. Lou —13Pc 28
Uplands, The. Ruis —32W 56
Uplands Trading Est. E17 —27Zb 44
Uplands Way. N21 —15Qb 24
Uplands Way. Sev —95Hd 186
Upland Way. Eps —90Ya 162
Upminster Rd. Horn —33Pd 69
Upminster Rd. N. Rain —41Ld 89
Upminster Rd. S. Rain —42Jd 88
Upminster Trading Pk. Upm —31Zd 71
Upnall Ho. SE15 —51Yb 106
Upney Clo. Horn —36Md 69
Upney La. Bark —37Uc 66
Upnor Way. SE17 —50Ub 83 (7J 207)
Uppark Dri. Ilf —30Sc 46
Up. Abbey Rd. Belv —49Bd 87
Up. Addison Gdns. W14 —47Ab 80
Up. Austin Lodge Rd. Eyns —77Md 153
Upper Av. Grav —7A 136
Up. Bardsey Wlk. N1 —37Sb 63 (off Bardsey Wlk.)
Up. Belgrave St. SW1 —48Jb 82 (3J 203)
Up. Berkeley St. W1 —44Hb 81 (3F 197)
Up. Beulah Hill. SE19 —67Ub 127
Up. Brentwood Rd. Romf —28Ld 49
Up. Brighton Rd. Surb —72Ma 143
Up. Brockley Rd. SE4 —55Bc 106
Up. Brook St. W1 —45Jb 82 (5H 197)
Up. Butts. Bren —51La 100
Up. Caldy Wlk. N1 —37Sb 63 (off Caldy Wlk.)
Up. Camelford Wlk. W11 —44Ab 80 (off St Mark's Rd.)
Up. Cavendish Av. N3 —27Cb 41
Up. Cheyne Row. SW3 —51Gb 103
Up. Church Hill. Grnh —57Ud 112
Up. Clapton Rd. E5 —33Xb 63
Up. Clarendon Wlk. W11 —44Ab 80 (off Clarendon Rd.)
Up. Cornsland. Brtwd —20Zd 33
Up. Court Rd. Eps —83Sa 161
Up. Court Rd. Wold —95Cc 182
Up. Dengie Wlk. N1 —39Sb 63 (off Basire St.)
Upper Dri. Big H —90Lc 167
Up. Dunnymans. Bans —86Bb 163
Up. Elmers End Rd. Beck —70Ac 128
Up. Fairfield Rd. Lea —93Ka 176
Up. Farm Rd. W Mol —70Ba 121
Up. Fosters. NW4 —29Ya 40 (off New Brent St.)
Up. Green E. Mitc —69Hb 125
Up. Green W. Mitc —68Hb 125
Up. Grosvenor St. W1 —45Jb 82 (5H 197)
Up. Grotto Rd. Twic —61Ha 122
Up. Ground. SE1 —46Qb 82 (6A 200)
Upper Gro. SE25 —70Vb 127
Up. Grove Rd. Belv —51Bd 109
Up. Gulland Wlk. N1 —37Sb 63 (off Oronsay Wlk.)
Up. Halliford By-Pass. Shep —71U 140
Up. Halliford Grn. Shep —70U 120
Up. Halliford Rd. Shep —69U 120
Up. Ham Rd. Rich —63Ma 123
Up. Handa Wlk. N1 —37Tb 63 (off Handa Wlk.)
Up. Harestone. Cat —99Wb 181
Up. Harley St. NW1 —42Jb 82 (6J 191)

Up. Hawkwell Wlk.—Victoria Ho.

Up. Hawkwell Wlk. N1 —39Sb 63
(off Maldon Clo.)
Up. High St. Eps —85Ua 162
Up. Highway. Abb L —5T 4
Up. Highway. K Lan —4S 4
Up. Hill Rise. Rick —16K 17
Up. Hitch. Wat —18Aa 19
Up. Holly Hill Rd. Belv —50Dd 88
Up. James St. W1 —45Lb 82 (4C 198)
Up. John St. W1 —45Lb 82 (4C 198)
Up. Lees Rd. Slou —1F 72
Up. Lismore Wlk. N1 —37Sb 63
(off Clephane St.)
Up. Mall. W6 —50Wa 80
(in two parts)
Up. Marsh. SE1 —48Pb 82 (3J 205)
Up. Montagu St. W1 —43Hb 81 (7F 191)
Up. Mulgrave Rd. Sutt —80Ab 144
Up. North St. E14 —43Cc 84
Up. Nursery. S'dale —10E 116
Up. Paddock Rd. Wat —16Aa 19
Up. Palace Rd. E Mol —69Fa 122
Upper Pk. N11 —22Kb 42
Upper Pk. Lou —14Mc 27
Up. Park Rd. NW3 —36Hb 61
Up. Park Rd. Belv —49Dd 88
Up. Park Rd. Brom —67Kc 129
Up. Park Rd. King T —65Qa 123
Up. Phillimore Gdns. W8 —47Cb 81
Up. Pillory Downs. Cars —85Jb 164
Up. Pines. Bans —89Hb 163
Up. Rainham Rd. Horn —32Hd 68
Up. Ramsey Wlk. N1 —37Tb 63
(off Ramsey Wlk.)
Up. Rawreth Wlk. N1 —39Sb 63
(off Basire St.)
Up. Richmond Rd. SW15 —56Va 102
Up. Richmond Rd. W. Rich & SW14 —56Qa 101
Upper Rd. E13 —41Jc 85
Upper Rd. Den —31F 54
Upper Rd. Wall —78Mb 146
Up. Ryle. Brtwd —17Xd 32
Up. St Martin's La. WC2 —45Nb 82 (4F 199)
Up. Sawleywood. Bans —86Bb 163
Up. Selsdon Rd. S Croy —80Ub 147
Up. Sheppey Wlk. N1 —37Sb 63
(off Skomer Wlk.)
Up. Sheridan Rd. Belv —49Cd 88
Up. Shirley Rd. Croy —76Yb 148
Upper Sq. Iswth —55Ja 100
Up. Staithe. W4 —53Sa 101
Up. Station Rd. Rad —7Ja 6
Upper St. N1 —40Qb 62 (1A 194)
Upper St. N. New Ash —75Be 155
(off Row, The)
Upper St. S. New Ash —75Be 155
(off Row, The)
Up. Sunbury Rd. Hamp —67Aa 121
Up. Sutton La. Houn —52Ca 99
Up. Swaines. Epp —2Vc 15
Up. Tachbrook St. SW1 —49Lb 82 (5B 204)
Up. Tail. Wat —20Aa 19
Up. Teddington Rd. King T —66La 122
Upper Ter. NW3 —34Eb 61
Up. Thames St. EC4 —45Rb 83 (4C 200)
Up. Tollington Pk. N4 —32Qb 62
(in two parts)
Upperton Rd. Sidc —64Vc 131
Upperton Rd. E. E13 —41Lc 85
Upperton Rd. W. E13 —41Lc 85
Up. Tooting Pk. SW17 —61Hb 125
Up. Tooting Rd. SW17 —63Hb 125
Up. Town Rd. Gnfd —42Da 77
Up. Tulse Hill. SW2 —59Pb 104
Up. Vernon Rd. Sutt —78Fb 145
Up. Village Rd. Asc —10A 116
Up. Walthamstow Rd. E17 —28Ec 44
Up. Wickham La. Well —55Xc 109
Up. Wimpole St. W1 —43Jb 82 (7J 191)
Up. Woburn Pl. WC1 —41Mb 82 (4E 192)
Up. Woodcote Village. Purl —84Mb 164
Uppingham Av. Stan —25Ka 38
Upsdell Av. N13 —23Qb 42
Upshire Rd. Wal A —4Hc 13
Upshott La. Wok —89H 157
Upstall St. SE5 —53Rb 105
Upton. Wok —5E 188
Upton Av. E7 —38Jc 65
Upton Clo. Bex —58Bd 109
Upton Clo. Slou —8K 73
Upton Clo. Stanf —1M 93
Upton Ct. SE20 —66Yb 128
Upton Ct. Rd. Slou —8L 73
Upton Dene. Sutt —80Db 145
Upton Gdns. Harr —29Ka 38
Upton Ho. H Hill —22Md 49
(off Barnstaple Rd.)
Upton La. E7 —38Jc 65
Upton Lea Pde. Slou —5M 73
Upton Lodge. E7 —37Jc 65
Upton Lodge Clo. Bush —17Ea 20
Upton Pk. Slou —8J 73
Upton Pk. Rd. E7 —38Kc 65
Upton Rd. N18 —22Wb 43
Upton Rd. SE18 —51Sc 108
Upton Rd. Bexh —56Ad 109
Upton Rd. Houn —55Ca 99
Upton Rd. Slou —8L 73
Upton Rd. T Hth —68Tb 127
Upton Rd. Wat —14X 19
Upton Rd. S. Bex —58Bd 109
Upton Vs. Bexh —56Ad 109
Upway. N12 —23Gb 41
Upway. Ger X —25B 34
Upwood Rd. SE12 —58Jc 107
Upwood Rd. SW16 —67Nb 126
Urban Av. Horn —34Ld 69
Urlwin St. SE5 —51Sb 105
Urlwin Wlk. SW9 —53Qb 104
Urmston Dri. SW19 —60Ab 102
Urquhart Ct. Beck —66Bc 128
Ursula Lodges. Sidc —64Xc 131
Ursula St. SW11 —53Gb 103
Urswick Gdns. Dag —38Ad 67
Urswick Rd. E9 —36Yb 64
Urswick Rd. Dag —38Zc 67
Usborne M. SW8 —52Pb 104
Usher Rd. E3 —39Bc 64
Usk Rd. SW11 —56Eb 103
Usk Rd. S Ock —44Sd 90
Usk St. E2 —41Zb 84
Utility Cotts. Seal —92Pd 187
Uvedale Clo. New Ad —83Fc 167
Uvedale Cres. New Ad —83Fc 167
Uvedale Rd. Dag —34Cd 68
Uvedale Rd. Enf —15Tb 25
Uverdale Rd. SW10 —52Eb 103
Uxbridge Ind. Est. Uxb —40K 55
Uxbridge Rd. W12 —46Va 80
Uxbridge Rd. W13, W5 & W3 —46Ka 78
Uxbridge Rd. Felt —61Y 121
Uxbridge Rd. Hamp —63Ca 121
Uxbridge Rd. Harr & Stan —24Ea 38
Uxbridge Rd. King T —70Ma 123
Uxbridge Rd. Pinn —26Y 37
Uxbridge Rd. Rick —20H 17
Uxbridge Rd. Slou —7L 73
Uxbridge Rd. S'hall & W7 —46Ca 77
Uxbridge Rd. Uxb & Hay —41Q 76
Uxbridge St. W8 —46Cb 81
Uxendon Cres. Wemb —32Na 59
Uxendon Hill. Wemb —32Pa 59

Vaillant Rd. Wey —77S 140
Valance Av. E4 —18Gc 27
Valan Leas. Brom —69Gc 129
Vale Av. Borwd —15Ra 21
Vale Border. S Croy —83Zb 166
Vale Clo. N2 —27Hb 41
Vale Clo. NW8 —41Eb 81
Vale Clo. W9 —41Eb 81
Vale Clo. Coul —86Nb 164
Vale Clo. Ger X —25A 34
Vale Clo. Orp —77Qc 150
Vale Clo. Pil H —15Vd 32
Vale Clo. Wey —76T 140
Vale Clo. Wok —88A 156
Vale Ct. W3 —46Va 80
Vale Ct. W9 —41Eb 81 (4A 190)
(off Maida Vale)
Vale Ct. New Bar —14Db 23
Vale Ct. Wey —76T 140
Vale Cres. SW15 —63Ua 124
Vale Croft. Clay —81Ha 160
Vale Croft. Pinn —29Aa 37
Vale Dri. Barn —14Bb 23
Vale End. SE22 —56Vb 105
Vale Est., The. W3 —46Ua 80
Vale Farm Rd. Wok —89A 156
Vale Gro. N4 —31Sb 63
Vale Gro. W3 —47Ta 79
Vale Gro. Slou —8J 73
Vale Ind. Pk. Wat —17R 18
Vale La. W3 —43Qa 79
Vale Lodge. SE23 —61Yb 128
Valence Av. Dag —32Zc 67
Valence Cir. Dag —34Zc 67
Valence Dri. Chesh —1Wb 11
Valence Rd. Eri —52Fd 110
Valence Wood Rd. Dag —34Zc 67
Valencia Rd. Stan —21La 38
Valency Clo. N'wd —21V 36
Valentia Pl. SW9 —56Qb 104
Valentine Av. Bex —61Ad 131
Valentine Ct. SE23 —61Zb 128
Valentine Pl. SE1 —47Rb 83 (2B 206)
Valentine Rd. E9 —37Zb 64
Valentine Rd. Harr —34Ea 58
Valentine Row. SE1 —47Rb 83 (2B 206)
Valentines Rd. Ilf —32Rc 66
Valentine's Way. Romf —33Gd 68
Valentine Vs. S Ock —43Yd 90
Valentine Way. Chal G —19A 16
Valentyne Clo. New Ad —83Gc 167
Vale of Health. NW3 —34Eb 61
Valerian Way. E15 —41Gc 85
Valerie Ct. Sutt —80Db 145
Vale Rise. NW11 —32Bb 61
Vale Rd. E7 —37Kc 65
Vale Rd. N4 —31Sb 63
Vale Rd. Brom —67Qc 130
Vale Rd. Bush —15Aa 19
Vale Rd. Clay —81Ga 160
Vale Rd. Dart —60Kd 111
Vale Rd. Eps —77Va 144
Vale Rd. Mitc —70Mb 126
Vale Rd. N'fleet —59Fe 113
Vale Rd. Sutt —77Db 145
Vale Rd. Wey —76T 140
Vale Rd. Wind —2D 94
Vale Rd. Wor Pk —76Va 144
Vale Rd. N. Surb —75Na 143
Vale Rd. S. Surb —75Na 143
Vale Row. N5 —34Rb 63
Vale Royal. N7 —38Nb 62
Vale St. SE27 —62Tb 127
Valeswood Rd. Brom —64Hc 129
Vale Ter. N4 —30Sb 43
Vale, The. N10 —25Jb 42
Vale, The. N14 —16Pb 24
Vale, The. NW11 —33Ab 60
Vale, The. SW3 —51Fb 103
Vale, The. W3 —46Va 80
Vale, The. Brtwd —18Yd 32
Vale, The. Coul —86Nb 164
Vale, The. Croy —75Zb 148
Vale, The. Felt —58X 99
Vale, The. Ger X —25A 34
Vale, The. Houn —51Aa 99
Vale, The. Ruis —35Y 57
Vale, The. Sun —65W 120
Vale, The. Wfd G —24Jc 45
Valetta Gro. E13 —40Jc 65
Valetta Rd. W3 —47Ua 80
Valette Ct. N10 —28Kb 42
(off St James's La.)
Valette St. E9 —37Yb 64
Valiant Clo. N'holt —41Z 77
Valiant Clo. Romf —26Dd 48
Valiant Way. E6 —43Pc 86
Vallance Rd. E2 & E1 —41Wb 83
Vallance Rd. N22 —26Lb 42
Vallentin Rd. E17 —28Ec 44
Valley Av. N12 —21Fb 41
Valley Clo. Dart —58Hd 110
Valley Clo. Lou —16Pc 28
Valley Clo. Pinn —26X 37
Valley Ct. Cat —94Wb 181
Valley Dri. NW9 —30Qa 39
Valley Dri. Grav —3F 136
Valley Dri. Sev —98Kd 187
Valleyfield Rd. SW16 —64Pb 126
Valley Fields Cres. Enf —12Qb 24
Valley Gdns. SW19 —66Fb 125
Valley Gdns. Wemb —38Pa 59
Valley Gro. SE7 —50Lc 85
Valley Hill. Lou —17Nc 28
Valley M. Twic —61Ha 122
Valley Rise. Wat —5X 5
Valley Rd. SW16 —64Pb 126
Valley Rd. Belv —49Dd 88
Valley Rd. Dart —58Hd 110
Valley Rd. Eri —49Fd 88
Valley Rd. Fawk —74Wd 154
Valley Rd. Kenl —87Tb 165
Valley Rd. Orp —67Xc 131
Valley Rd. Rick —15J 17
Valley Rd. Short —68Gc 129
Valley Rd. Uxb —40N 55
Valley Side. E4 —19Cc 26
Valley Side Pde. E4 —19Cc 26
Valley View. Barn —16Ab 22
Valley View. Big H —90Lc 167
Valley View. Chesh —1Sb 11
Valley View. Grnh —58Xd 112
Valley View Gdns. Kenl —87Ub 165
Valley View. Ter. F'ham —74Pd 153
Valley Wlk. Crox —15S 18
Valley Wlk. Croy —75Yb 148
Valley Way. Ger X —1N 53
Valliere Rd. NW10 —41Wa 80
Valliers Wood Rd. Sidc —60Tc 108
Vallis Way. W13 —43Ja 78
Vallis Way. Chess —77Ma 143
Valmar Av. Stanf —2K 93
Valmar Rd. SE5 —53Sb 105
Valmar Trading Est. SE5 —53Sb 105
Valnay St. SW17 —64Hb 125
Valognes Av. E17 —25Ac 44
Valonia Gdns. SW18 —58Bb 103
Vambery Rd. SE18 —51Sc 108
Vanbrough Cres. N'holt —39Y 57
Vanbrugh Clo. E16 —43Mc 85
Vanbrugh Ct. SE11 —49Qb 82 (6A 206)
(off Wincott St.)
Vanbrugh Dri. W on T —72Y 141
Vanbrugh Fields. SE3 —51Hc 107
Vanbrugh Hill. SE10 & SE3 —50Hc 85
Vanbrugh Pk. SE3 —52Hc 107
Vanbrugh Pk. Rd. SE3 —52Hc 107
Vanbrugh Pk. Rd. W. SE3 —52Hc 107
Vanbrugh Rd. W4 —48Ta 79
Vanbrugh Ter. SE3 —53Hc 107
Vanburgh Clo. Orp —74Uc 150
Vanburgh Ct. H Bar —13Ab 22
Vancouver Clo. Eps —83Sa 161
Vancouver Rd. SE23 —61Ac 128
Vancouver Rd. Edgw —25Ra 39
Vancouver Rd. Hay —42X 77
Vancouver Rd. Rich —63La 122
Vanderbilt Rd. SW18 —60Db 103
Vandome Clo. E16 —44Kc 85
Vandon Pas. SW1 —48Lb 82 (3C 204)
Vandon Pl. SW1 —48Lb 82
Vandon St. SW1 —48Lb 82 (3C 204)
Van Dyck Av. N Mald —73Ta 143
Vandyke Clo. SW15 —59Za 102
Vandyke Cross. SE9 —57Nc 108
Vandy St. EC2 —42Ub 83 (6H 195)
Vane Clo. NW3 —36Fb 61
Vane Clo. Harr —30Pa 39
Vanessa Clo. Belv —50Cd 88
Vanessa Wlk. Grav —4H 137
Vanessa Way. Bex —62Fd 132
Vane St. SW1 —49Lb 82 (5C 204)
Van Gogh Ct. E14 —48Fc 85
Vanguard Clo. Croy —74Rb 147
Vanguard Clo. Romf —26Cd 48
Vanguard St. SE8 —53Cc 106
Vanguard Way. Wall —80Nb 146
Vanners Pde. Byfl —85N 157
Vanoc Gdns. Brom —63Jc 129
Vanquisher Wlk. Grav —2H 137
Vanryne Ho. Lou —13Nc 28
Vansittart Est. Wind —2G 94
Vansittart Rd. E7 —35Hc 65
Vansittart Rd. Wind —3F 94
Vansittart St. SE14 —51Ac 106
Vanston Pl. SW6 —52Cb 103
Vantage Rd. Slou —6F 72
Vantage W. W3 —49Pa 79
Vantrey Ho. SE11 —49Qb 82 (6K 205)
(off Marylee Way)
Vant Rd. SW17 —64Hb 125
Varcoe Rd. SE16 —50Xb 83
Vardens Rd. SW11 —56Fb 103
Varden St. E1 —44Xb 83
Vardon Clo. N3 —25Ab 40
Vardon Clo. W3 —44Ta 79
Vardon Ho. SE10 —53Ec 106
Varley Pde. NW9 —28Ua 40
Varley Rd. E16 —44Kc 85
Varley Way. Mitc —68Fb 125
Varna Rd. SW6 —52Ab 102
Varna Rd. Hamp —67Da 121
Varndell St. NW1 —41Lb 82 (3B 192)
Varsity Dri. Twic —57Ga 100
Vartry Rd. N15 —30Tb 43
Vassall Rd. SW9 —52Qb 104
Vauban Est. SE16 —48Vb 83 (4K 207)
Vauban St. SE16 —48Vb 83 (4K 207)
Vaughan Av. NW4 —29Wa 40
Vaughan Av. W6 —49Va 80
Vaughan Av. Horn —35Md 69
Vaughan Clo. Hamp —65Aa 121
Vaughan Est. E2 —41Vb 83 (3K 195)
(off Diss St.)
Vaughan Gdns. Eton W —9D 72
Vaughan Gdns. Ilf —31Pc 66
Vaughan Ho. SW4 —59Lb 104
Vaughan Rd. E15 —37Hc 65
Vaughan Rd. SE5 —54Sb 105
Vaughan Rd. Harr —31Ea 58
Vaughan Rd. Th Dit —73Ka 142
Vaughan Rd. Well —54Vc 109
Vaughan St. SE16 —47Bc 84
Vaughan Way. E1 —45Wb 83
Vaughan Way. Slou —2C 72
Vaughan Williams Clo. SE8 —52Cc 106
Vaux Cres. W on T —79X 141
Vauxhall Bri. SW1 & SE1 —50Nb 82 (7F 205)
Vauxhall Bri. Rd. SW1 —48Lb 82 (4B 204)
Vauxhall Clo. Grav —9B 114
Vauxhall Cross. SE1 —50Nb 82
Vauxhall Gdns. S Croy —79Sb 147
Vauxhall Gro. SW8 —51Pb 104
Vauxhall Pl. Dart —59Nd 111
Vauxhall St. SE11 —50Pb 82 (7J 205)
Vauxhall Wlk. SE11 —50Pb 82 (7H 205)
Vawdrey Clo. E1 —42Yb 84
Veals Mead. Mitc —67Gb 125
Vectis Gdns. SW17 —65Kb 126
Vectis Rd. SW17 —65Kb 126
Veda Rd. SE13 —56Cc 106
Vega Cres. N'wd —22V 36
Vegal Cres. Egh —4N 117
Vega Rd. Bush —17Ea 20
Veitch Gro. W'ham —98Tc 184
Veldene Way. Harr —34Ba 57
Velde Way. SE22 —57Ub 105
Vellum Dri. Cars —76Jb 146
Venables Clo. Dag —35Dd 68
Venables St. NW8 —43Fb 81 (6C 190)
Vencourt Pl. W6 —49Wa 80
Venetian Rd. SE5 —54Sb 105
Venetia Rd. N4 —30Rb 43
Venetia Rd. W5 —47Ma 79
Venette Clo. Rain —43Kd 89
Venner Rd. SE26 —65Yb 128
Venners Clo. Bexh —54Gd 110
Venn Ho. N1 —39Pb 62 (1J 193)
(off Barnsbury Est.)
Venn St. SW4 —56Lb 104
Ventnor Av. Stan —25Ka 38
Ventnor Dri. N20 —20Db 23
Ventnor Gdns. Bark —37Uc 66
Ventnor Rd. SE14 —52Zb 106
Ventnor Rd. Sutt —80Db 145
Venton Clo. Wok —5E 188
Venture Clo. Bex —59Ad 109
Venue St. E14 —43Ec 84
Venus Hill. Bov —3C 2
Venus Rd. SE18 —48Pc 86
Veny Cres. Horn —36Md 69
Vera Av. N21 —15Qb 24
Vera Ct. Wat —17Z 19
Vera Lynn Clo. E7 —35Jc 65
Vera Rd. SW6 —53Ab 102
Verbena Clo. E16 —42Hc 85
Verbena Clo. S Ock —44Yd 90
Verbena Clo. W Dray —50M 75
Verbena Gdns. W6 —50Wa 80
Verdant La. SE6 —59Gc 107
Verdayne Av. Croy —75Zb 148
Verdayne Gdns. Warl —88Yb 166
Verderers Rd. Chig —22Wc 47
Verdun Rd. SE18 —51Wc 109
Verdun Rd. SW13 —51Wa 102
Vereker Dri. Sun —69W 120
Vereker Rd. W14 —50Ab 80
Vere Rd. Lou —14Sc 28
Vere St. W1 —44Kb 82 (3K 197)
Verity Clo. W11 —45Ab 80
Ver Meer Ct. E14 —48Fc 85
Vermont Rd. SE19 —65Ub 127
Vermont Rd. SW18 —58Db 103
Vermont Rd. Slou —2D 72
Vermont Rd. Sutt —76Db 145
Verney Gdns. Dag —35Ad 67
Verney Rd. SE16 —51Wb 105
Verney Rd. Dag —35Ad 67
(in two parts)
Verney Rd. Slou —49C 74
Verney St. NW10 —34Ta 59
Verney Way. SE16 —50Xb 83
Vernham Rd. SE18 —51Sc 108
Vernon Av. E12 —35Pc 66
Vernon Av. SW20 —68Za 124
Vernon Av. Enf —8Ac 12
Vernon Av. Wfd G —24Kc 45
Vernon Clo. Eps —79Sa 143
Vernon Clo. Orp —69Xc 131
Vernon Clo. Ott —79F 138
Vernon Clo. W King —80Vd 154
Vernon Ct. NW2 —34Bb 61
Vernon Ct. W5 —45La 78
Vernon Ct. Stan —25Ka 38
Vernon Cres. Barn —16Jb 24
Vernon Cres. Brtwd —20Ce 33
Vernon Dri. Cat —94Sb 181
Vernon Dri. Hare —25L 35
Vernon Dri. Stan —25Ja 38
Vernon Ho. SE11 —50Pb 82 (7J 205)
(off Vauxhall St.)
Vernon M. E17 —29Bc 44
Vernon Pl. WC1 —43Nb 82 (1G 199)
Vernon Rise. WC1 —41Pb 82 (3J 193)
Vernon Rise. Gnfd —36Fa 58
Vernon Rd. E3 —40Bc 64
Vernon Rd. E11 —32Gc 65
Vernon Rd. E15 —38Gc 65
Vernon Rd. E17 —29Bc 44
Vernon Rd. N8 —27Qb 42
Vernon Rd. SW14 —55Ta 101
Vernon Rd. WC1 —41Pb 82
Vernon Rd. Bush —15Aa 19
Vernon Rd. Felt —61V 120
Vernon Rd. Ilf —32Vc 67
Vernon Rd. Romf —22Ed 48
Vernon Rd. Sutt —78Eb 145
Vernon Rd. Swans —58Be 113
Vernon Sq. WC1 —41Pb 82 (3J 193)
Vernon St. W14 —49Ab 80
Vernon Wlk. Tad —92Za 178
Vernon Yd. W11 —45Bb 81
Veroan Rd. Bexh —54Ad 109
Verona Clo. Uxb —43L 75
Verona Dri. Surb —75Na 143
Verona Gdns. Grav —3G 136
Verona Rd. E7 —38Jc 65
Veronica Clo. Romf —24Ld 49
Veronica Gdns. SW16 —67Lb 126
Veronica Rd. SW17 —61Kb 126
Veronique Gdns. Ilf —29Sc 46
Verralls. Wok —89D 156
Verran Rd. SW12 —59Kb 104
Versailles Rd. SE20 —66Wb 127
Vert Ho. Grays —52Ee 113
Verulam Av. E17 —30Bc 44
Verulam Av. Purl —84Lb 164
Verulam Bldgs. WC1
(off Grays Inn) —43Pb 82 (7J 193)
Verulam Ct. NW9 —31Wa 60
Verulam Pas. Wat —12X 19
Verulam Rd. Gnfd —42Ca 77
Verulam St. WC1 —43Qb 82 (7K 193)
Verwood Rd. Harr —26Ea 38
Veryan. Wok —5D 188
Veryan Ct. N8 —29Mb 42
Vesage Ct. EC1 —43Qb 82 (1A 200)
(off Leather La.)
Vesey Path. E14 —44Dc 84
Vespan Rd. W12 —47Wa 80
Vesta Rd. SE4 —54Ac 106
Vestris Rd. SE23 —61Zb 128
Vestry Cotts. Sev —91Ld 187
Vestry Ind. Est. Sev —91Ld 187
Vestry M. SE5 —53Ub 105
Vestry Rd. E17 —28Dc 44
Vestry Rd. SE5 —53Ub 105
Vestry Rd. Sev —91Kd 187
Vestry St. N1 —41Tb 83 (3F 195)
Vevey St. SE6 —61Bc 128
Vexil Clo. Purf —49Td 90
Veysey Gdns. Dag —34Cd 68
Viaduct Bldgs. EC1 —43Qb 82 (1A 200)
Viaduct Pl. E2 —41Xb 83
Viaduct Rd. N2 —26Fb 41
Viaduct St. E2 —41Xb 83
Viaduct Ter. S Dar —68Sd 134
Viaduct, The. E18 —26Kc 45
Viaduct, The. Wemb —39Na 59
Vian Av. Enf —7Ac 12
Vian St. SE13 —55Dc 106
Viant Ho. NW10 —38Ta 59
Via Romana. Grav —10K 115
Vibart Gdns. SW2 —59Pb 104
Vibart Wlk. N1 —39Nb 62
(off Outram Pl.)
Vicarage Av. SE3 —52Jc 107
Vicarage Av. Egh —64D 118
Vicarage Clo. Bookh —97Ca 175
Vicarage Clo. Brtwd —21Ud 50
Vicarage Clo. Eri —51Ed 110
Vicarage Clo. N'thaw —2Hb 9
Vicarage Clo. N'holt —38Ba 57
Vicarage Clo. Ruis —31T 56
Vicarage Clo. Tad —96Ab 178
Vicarage Ct. W8 —47Db 81
Vicarage Ct. Beck —69Ac 128
Vicarage Ct. Egh —65D 118
Vicarage Ct. Felt —59S 98
Vicarage Ct. Grav —10J 115
Vicarage Ct. Ilf —36Rc 66
Vicarage Ct. Wal A —6Jc 13
(off Horseshoe Clo.)
Vicarage Cres. SW11 —53Fb 103
Vicarage Cres. Egh —64D 118
Vicarage Dri. SW14 —57Ta 101
Vicarage Dri. Bark —38Sc 66
Vicarage Dri. Beck —67Cc 128
Vicarage Dri. Grav —58Ee 113
Vicarage Farm Ct. Houn —52Ba 99
Vicarage Farm Rd. Houn —54Aa 99
Vicarage Fields. W on T —72Y 141
Vicarage Field Shopping Cen. Bark —38Sc 66
Vicarage Gdns. W8 —46Cb 81
Vicarage Gdns. Mitc —69Gb 125
Vicarage Ga. W8 —46Db 81
Vicarage Gro. SE5 —53Tb 105
Vicarage Hill. W'ham —98Tc 184
Vicarage La. E6 —41Pc 86
Vicarage La. E15 —38Gc 65
Vicarage La. Chig —19Sc 28
Vicarage La. Dun G —91Fd 186
Vicarage La. Eps —81Wa 162
Vicarage La. Grav —1J 137
Vicarage La. Ilf —32Tc 66
Vicarage La. K Lan —1P 3
Vicarage La. Lea —94Ka 176
Vicarage La. Send —98E 172
Vicarage La. Stai —69L 119
Vicarage La. Wray —60A 96
Vicarage M. NW9 —33Ta 59
Vicarage Pde. N15 —28Sb 43
Vicarage Pk. SE18 —50Sc 86
Vicarage Pl. Slou —8L 73
Vicarage Rd. E10 —31Cc 64
Vicarage Rd. E15 —38Hc 65
Vicarage Rd. N17 —25Wb 43
Vicarage Rd. NW4 —30Wa 40
Vicarage Rd. SE18 —50Sc 86
Vicarage Rd. SW14 —57Ta 101
Vicarage Rd. Bex —60Dd 110
Vicarage Rd. Coop —1Yc 15
Vicarage Rd. Croy —76Qb 146
Vicarage Rd. Dag —38Dd 68
Vicarage Rd. Egh —64C 118
Vicarage Rd. Hamp W —67La 122
Vicarage Rd. Horn —32Jd 68
Vicarage Rd. King T —68Ma 123
Vicarage Rd. Stai —62G 118
Vicarage Rd. Sun —64V 120
Vicarage Rd. Sutt —76Db 145
Vicarage Rd. Tedd —64Ja 122
Vicarage Rd. Twic —61Ga 122
Vicarage Rd. Wat —17W 18
Vicarage Rd. Whit —58Ea 100
Vicarage Rd. Wok —93B 172
Vicarage Rd. Wfd G —24Nc 46
Vicarage Sq. Grays —51Ce 113
Vicarage Wlk. SW11 —53Fb 103
Vicarage Wlk. W on T —73W 140
Vicarage Way. NW10 —34Ta 59
Vicarage Way. Coln —52E 96
Vicarage Way. Ger X —30B 34
Vicarage Way. Harr —31Ca 57
Vicars Bri. Clo. Wemb —40Na 59
Vicar's Clo. E9 —39Yb 64
Vicars Clo. E15 —39Jc 65
Vicars Clo. Enf —12Ub 25
Vicar's Hill. SE13 —56Dc 106
Vicars Moor La. N21 —17Qb 24
Vicars Oak Rd. SE19 —65Ub 127
Vicar's Rd. NW5 —36Jb 62
Vicars Wlk. Dag —34Xc 67
Viceroy Clo. N2 —28Gb 41
Viceroy Ct. Croy —75Tb 147
Viceroy Pde. N2 —28Gb 41
(off High Rd.)
Viceroy Rd. SW8 —53Nb 104
Vicery Ct. EC1 —42Sb 83 (5E 194)
(off Bartholomew Sq.)
Vickers Dri. N. Wey —82N 157
Vickers Dri. S. Wey —83N 157
Vickers La. Houn —57Aa 99
Vickers Rd. Eri —50Fd 88
Vickers Way. Houn —57Aa 99
Victor App. Horn —32Md 69
Victor Clo. Horn —32Md 69
Victor Ct. Horn —32Md 69
(off Victor Wlk.)
Victor Gdns. Horn —32Md 69
Victor Gro. Wemb —38Na 59
Victoria Arc. SW1 —48Kb 82 (4A 204)
(off Victoria St.)
Victoria Av. E6 —39Mc 65
Victoria Av. EC2 —43Ub 83 (1J 201)
Victoria Av. N3 —25Bb 41
Victoria Av. Barn —14Fb 23
Victoria Av. Grav —9D 114
Victoria Av. Grays —47Ee 91
Victoria Av. Houn —57Ca 99
Victoria Av. Romf —23Dd 48
Victoria Av. S Croy —82Sb 165
Victoria Av. Surb —72Ma 143
Victoria Av. Uxb —37R 56
Victoria Av. Wall —76Jb 146
Victoria Av. Wemb —37Ra 59
Victoria Av. W Mol —69Da 121
Victoria Clo. Barn —14Fb 23
Victoria Clo. Grays —47Ee 91
Victoria Clo. Hay —44T 76
Victoria Clo. Rick —17M 17
Victoria Clo. W Mol —69Ca 121
Victoria Clo. Wey —76T 140
Victoria Cotts. N10 —26Jb 42
Victoria Cotts. Rich —53Pa 101
Victoria Ct. E18 —27Kc 45
Victoria Ct. SE26 —65Yb 128
Victoria Ct. W3 —47Qa 79
Victoria Ct. Brtwd —21Yd 50
Victoria Ct. Romf —29Jd 48
Victoria Ct. Wat —13Y 19
Victoria Ct. Wemb —37Qa 59
Victoria Cres. N15 —29Ub 43
Victoria Cres. SE19 —65Ub 127
Victoria Cres. SW19 —66Bb 125
Victoria Cres. Iver —45H 75
Victoria Dock Rd. E16 —44Gc 85
Victoria Dri. SW19 —59Za 102
Victoria Dri. S Dar —68Td 134
Victoria Embkmt. SW1, WC2 & EC4 —47Nb 82 (1G 205)
Victoria Gdns. W11 —46Cb 81
Victoria Gdns. Big H —87Lc 167
Victoria Gdns. Houn —53Aa 99
Victoria Gro. N12 —22Fb 41
Victoria Gro. W8 —48Eb 81
Victoria Gro. M. W2 —45Cb 81
Victoria Hill Rd. Swan —67Hd 132
Victoria Ho. N1 —39Pb 62 (1J 193)
(off Charlotte Ter.)

Victoria Ho.—Walpole Rd.

Victoria Ho. Edgw —23Ra **39**
Victoria Ho. Ger X —21A ***34***
(off Micholls Av.)
Victoria Ind. Est., The. NW10 & W3 —42Ua **80**
Victoria La. Barn —14Bb **23**
Victoria La. Hay —50S **76**
Victoria Mans. NW10 —38Xa **60**
Victoria M. NW6 —39Cb **61**
Victoria M. SW4 —56Kb **104**
Victorian Gro. N16 —35Ub **63**
Victorian Rd. N16 —34Vb **63**
Victoria Pk. Ind. Cen. E9 —38Cc ***64***
(off Rothbury Rd.)
Victoria Pk. Ind. Est. Dart —57Nd **111**
Victoria Pk. Rd. E2 & E9 —39Yb **64**
Victoria Pk. Sq. E2 —41Yb **84**
Victoria Pas. NW8 —42Fb ***81*** *(5B* ***190****)*
(off Fisherton St.)
Victoria Pas. Wat —14X **19**
Victoria Pl. SW1 —49Kb **82** (5A **204**)
Victoria Pl. Eps —84Ua **162**
Victoria Pl. Esh —77Da **141**
Victoria Pl. Rich —57Ma **101**
Victoria Point. E13 —40Jc ***65***
(off Victoria Rd.)
Victoria Rise. SW4 —55Kb **104**
Victoria Rd. E4 —18Gc **27**
Victoria Rd. E11 —35Gc **65**
Victoria Rd. E13 —40Jc **65**
Victoria Rd. E17 —26Ec **44**
Victoria Rd. E18 —26Kc **45**
Victoria Rd. N4 —31Pb **62**
Victoria Rd. N15 —28Wb **43**
Victoria Rd. N18 & N9 —21Vb **43**
Victoria Rd. N22 —25Lb **42**
Victoria Rd. NW4 —28Ya **40**
Victoria Rd. NW6 —40Bb **61**
Victoria Rd. NW7 —22Va **40**
Victoria Rd. NW10 —43Ta **79**
Victoria Rd. SW14 —55Ta **101**
Victoria Rd. W3 —43Ta **79**
Victoria Rd. W5 —43Ka **78**
Victoria Rd. W8 —48Eb **81**
Victoria Rd. Add —77M **139**
Victoria Rd. Asc —10A **116**
Victoria Rd. Bark —37Rc **66**
Victoria Rd. Barn —14Fb **23**
Victoria Rd. Bexh —56Cd **110**
Victoria Rd. Brom —71Mc **149**
Victoria Rd. Buck H —19Mc **27**
Victoria Rd. Bush —18Da **19**
Victoria Rd. Chst —64Qc **130**
Victoria Rd. Coul —87Mb **164**
Victoria Rd. Dag —36Dd **68**
Victoria Rd. Dart —57Md **111**
Victoria Rd. Eri —51Gd **110**
(in two parts)
Victoria Rd. Eton W —9C **72**
Victoria Rd. Farn C —7G **52**
Victoria Rd. Felt —60X **99**
Victoria Rd. Grav —10B **114**
Victoria Rd. Gnfd —43Ka **78**
Victoria Rd. Horn H —1H **93**
Victoria Rd. King T —68Pa **123**
Victoria Rd. Knap —5A **188**
Victoria Rd. Mitc —66Gb **125**
Victoria Rd. Romf —30Hd **48**
Victoria Rd. Ruis —32W **56**
Victoria Rd. Sev —97Kd **187**
Victoria Rd. Sidc —62Vc **131**
Victoria Rd. Slou —6M **73**
Victoria Rd. S'hall —48Ba **77**
Victoria Rd. Stai —62G **118**
Victoria Rd. Stanf —2L **93**
Victoria Rd. Surb —72Ma **143**
Victoria Rd. Sutt —78Fb **145**
Victoria Rd. Tedd —65Ja **122**
Victoria Rd. Twic —59Ka **100**
Victoria Rd. Uxb —38L **55**
Victoria Rd. Wal A —6Ec **12**
Victoria Rd. War —21Yd **50**
Victoria Rd. Wat —10X **5**
Victoria Rd. Wey —76T **140**
Victoria Rd. Wok —89A **156**
Victoria Scott Ct. Dart —55Gd **110**
Victoria Sq. SW1 —48Kb **82** (3A **204**)
Victoria St. E15 —38Gc **65**
Victoria St. SW1 —48Lb **82** (4A **204**)
Victoria St. Belv —50Bd **87**
Victoria St. Egh —5N **117**
Victoria St. Slou —7K **73**
Victoria St. Wind —3H **95**
Victoria Ter. N4 —32Qb **62**
Victoria Ter. W5 —42Va **80**
Victoria Ter. Harr —32Fa **58**
Victoria Vs. Rich —56Pa **101**
Victoria Way. SE7 —50Kc **85**
Victoria Way. Wey —76T **140**
Victoria Way. Wok —89A **156**
Victor Rd. NW10 —41Xa **80**
Victor Rd. SE20 —66Zb **128**
Victor Rd. Harr —27Ea **38**
Victor Rd. Tedd —63Ga **122**
Victor Rd. Wind —5G **94**
Victor's Cres. Hut —19De **33**
Victors Dri. Hamp —65Aa **121**
Victor Smith Ct. Brick —3Ca **5**
Victors Way. Barn —13Bb **23**
Victor Vs. N9 —20Tb **25**
Victor Wlk. Horn —32Md **69**
Victory Av. Mord —71Eb **145**
Victory Bus. Cen. Iswth —56Ha **100**
Victory Cotts. Eff —100Aa **175**
Victory Ct. Eri —52Hd ***110***
(off Frobisher Rd.)
Victory Pk. Rd. Add —76L **139**
Victory Pl. SE17 —49Tb **83** (5E **206**)
Victory Pl. SE19 —66Vb **127**
Victory Rd. SW19 —66Eb **125**
Victory Rd. Cher —74J **139**
Victory Rd. Rain —40Jd **68**
Victory Rd. M. SW19 —66Eb **125**
Victory Sq. SE5 —52Tb **105**
Victory Wlk. SE8 —53Cc **106**
Victory Way. SE16 —47Ac **84**
Victory Way. Houn —50Y **77**
Victory Way. Romf —26Dd **48**
Vienna Clo. Ilf —26Mc **45**
View Clo. N6 —31Hb **61**
View Clo. Big H —88Lc **167**
View Clo. Chig —22Tc **46**
View Clo. Harr —28Fa **38**
View Cres. N8 —29Mb **42**
Viewfield Clo. Harr —31Na **59**
Viewfield Rd. SW18 —58Bb **103**
Viewfield Rd. Bex —60Yc **109**
Viewland Rd. SE18 —50Vc **87**
Viewlands Av. W'ham —92Uc **184**
View Rd. N6 —31Hb **61**
View Rd. Pot B —4Eb **9**
View, The. SE2 —50Ad **87**
Viga Rd. N21 —16Qb **24**
Vigerons Way. Grays —9D **92**
Viggory La. Wok —3F **188**
Vigilant Clo. SE26 —63Wb **127**
Vigilant Way. Grav —4H **137**
Vignoles Rd. Romf —31Cd **68**
Vigo St. W1 —45Lb **82** (5B **198**)
Viking Clo. E3 —40Ac **64**
Viking Ct. SW6 —51Cb **103**
Viking Pl. E10 —32Bc **64**
Viking Rd. Grav —62Ee **135**
Viking Rd. S'hall —45Aa **77**
Viking Way. Eri —48Ed **88**
Viking Way. Pil H —16Xd **32**
Viking Way. Rain —42Jd **88**
Viking Way. W King —78Ud **154**
Villa Clo. Grav —1K **137**
Villa Ct. Dart —61Nd **133**
Villacourt Rd. SE18 —52Wc **109**
Village Clo. E4 —22Ec **44**
Village Clo. Wey —76T **140**
Village Gdns. Eps —81Va **162**
Village Grn. Av. Big H —89Nc **168**
Village Grn. Rd. Dart —56Jd **110**
Village Grn. Way. Big H —89Nc **168**
Village La. Hedg —2H **53**
Village M. NW9 —33Ta **59**
Village Rd. N3 —26Ab **40**
Village Rd. Den —33H **55**
Village Rd. Dor —8A **72**
Village Rd. Egh —70D **118**
Village Rd. Enf —17Tb **25**
Village Row. Sutt —80Cb **145**
Village, The. SE7 —51Mc **107**
Village Way. NW10 —35Ta **59**
Village Way. SE21 —58Tb **105**
Village Way. Amer —12A **16**
Village Way. Ashf —63Q **120**
Village Way. Beck —68Cc **128**
Village Way. Pinn —31Aa **57**
Village Way. S Croy —85Wb **165**
Village Way E. Harr —31Ca **57**
Villa Rd. SW9 —55Qb **104**
Villas on the Heath. NW3 —34Eb **61**
Villas Rd. SE18 —50Sc **86**
(in two parts)
Villa St. SE17 —50Tb **83** (7G **207**)
Villa Wlk. SE17 —50Tb **83**
Villiers Av. Surb —71Pa **143**
Villiers Av. Twic —60Ba **99**
Villiers Clo. E10 —33Cc **64**
Villiers Clo. Surb —70Pa **123**
Villiers Gro. Sutt —81Za **162**
Villiers Path. Surb —71Na **143**
Villiers Rd. NW2 —37Wa **60**
Villiers Rd. Beck —68Zb **128**
Villiers Rd. Iswth —54Ga **100**
Villiers Rd. King T —70Pa **123**
Villiers Rd. Slou —3H **73**
Villiers Rd. S'hall —46Ba **77**
Villiers Rd. Wat —16Aa **19**
Villiers St. WC2 —46Nb **82** (5F **199**)
Villiers, The. Wey —79T **140**
Villier St. Uxb —41M **75**
Vincam Clo. Twic —59Ca **99**
Vincent Av. Cars —83Fb **163**
Vincent Av. Surb —75Sa **143**
Vincent Clo. SE16 —47Ac **84**
Vincent Clo. Barn —13Db **23**
Vincent Clo. Brom —70Kc **129**
Vincent Clo. Cher —73G **138**
Vincent Clo. Chesh —1Ac **12**
Vincent Clo. Coul —92Hb **179**
Vincent Clo. Esh —76Da **141**
Vincent Clo. Fet —96Da **175**
Vincent Clo. Ilf —23Sc **46**
Vincent Clo. Sidc —60Uc **108**
Vincent Clo. W Dray —51Q **98**
Vincent Ct. N4 —32Nb **62**
Vincent Ct. N'wd —25V **36**
Vincent Dri. Shep —69U **120**
Vincent Dri. Uxb —39P **55**
Vincent Gdns. NW2 —34Va **60**
Vincent Grn. Coul —92Hb **179**
Vincent M. E3 —40Cc **64**
Vincent Rd. E4 —23Fc **45**
Vincent Rd. N15 —28Sb **43**
Vincent Rd. N22 —26Qb **42**
Vincent Rd. SE18 —49Rc **86**
Vincent Rd. W3 —48Sa **79**
Vincent Rd. Cher —73G **138**
Vincent Rd. Coul —88Lb **164**
Vincent Rd. Croy —73Ub **147**
Vincent Rd. Dag —38Ad **67**
Vincent Rd. Houn —55Z **99**
Vincent Rd. Iswth —53Fa **100**
Vincent Rd. King T —69Qa **123**
Vincent Rd. Rain —42Ld **89**
Vincent Rd. Stoke D —88Aa **159**
Vincent Rd. Wemb —38Pa **59**
Vincent Row. Hamp —65Ea **122**
Vincents Path. N'holt —37Aa ***57***
(off Arnold Rd.)
Vincent Sq. N22 —26Qb **42**
Vincent Sq. SW1 —49Mb **82** (5C **204**)
Vincent Sq. Big H —85Lc **167**
Vincent St. E16 —43Hc **85**
Vincent St. SW1 —49Mb **82** (5D **204**)
Vincent Ter. N1 —40Rb **63** (1B **194**)
Vince St. EC1 —41Tb **83** (4G **195**)
Vine Av. Sev —96Kd **187**
Vine Clo. Stai —57J **97**
Vine Clo. Surb —72Pa **143**
Vine Clo. Sutt —76Eb **145**
Vine Clo. W Dray —49Q **76**
Vine Ct. E1 —43Wb **83**
Vine Ct. Harr —30Na **39**
Vine Ct. Rd. Sev —96Ld **187**
Vinegar All. E17 —28Dc **44**
Vine Gdns. Ilf —36Sc **66**
Vinegar St. E1 —46Xb **83**
Vinegar Yd. SE1 —47Ub ***83*** *(1H* ***207****)*
(off St Thomas St.)
Vine Gro. Uxb —38Q **56**
Vine Hill. EC1 —42Qb **82** (6K **193**)
Vine La. SE1 —46Ub **83** (7J **201**)
Vine La. Hil —39P **55**
Vine Lodge. Sev —96Ld **187**
Vine Lodge Ct. Sev —96Ld **187**
Vine Pl. W5 —46Na ***79***
(off Grange Pk.)
Vine Pl. Houn —56Da **99**
Viner Clo. W on T —72Y **141**
Vineries Bank. NW7 —22Xa **40**
Vineries Clo. Dag —37Bd **67**
Vineries Clo. W Dray —51Q **98**
Vineries, The. N14 —16Lb **24**
Vineries, The. SE6 —60Cc **106**
Vineries, The. Enf —13Ub **25**
Vine Rd. E15 —38Hc **65**
Vine Rd. SW13 —55Va **102**
Vine Rd. E Mol —70Ea **122**
Vine Rd. Orp —79Vc **151**
Vine Rd. Stoke P —7K **53**
Vinery Way. W6 —48Xa **80**
Vines Av. N3 —25Db **41**
Vine St. EC3 —44Vb **83** (3K **201**)
Vine St. W1 —45Lb **82** (5C **198**)
Vine St. Romf —28Ed **48**
Vine St. Uxb —39M **55**
Vine St. Bri. EC1 —42Qb **82** (6A **194**)
Vine, The. Sev —96Kd **187**
Vine Way. Brtwd —18Yd **32**
Vine Yd. SE1 —47Sb ***83*** *(1E* ***206****)*
(off Sanctuary St.)
Vineyard Av. NW7 —24Ab **40**
Vineyard Clo. SE6 —60Cc **106**
Vineyard Hill. N'thaw —1Jb **10**
Vineyard Hill Rd. SW19 —63Cb **125**
Vineyard M. EC1 —42Qb ***82*** *(5K* ***193****)*
(off Vineyard Wlk.)
Vineyard Pas. Rich —57Na **101**
Vineyard Path. SW14 —55Ta **101**
Vineyard Rd. Felt —62W **120**
Vineyard Row. King T —67La **122**
Vineyards Rd. N'thaw —2Hb **9**
Vineyards, The. Felt —62W ***120***
(off High St. Feltham)
Vineyard, The. Rich —57Na **101**
Vineyard Wlk. EC1 —42Qb **82** (5K **193**)
Viney Bank. Croy —81Bc **166**
Viney Rd. SE13 —55Dc **106**
Vining St. SW9 —56Qb **104**
Vinlake Av. Uxb —34P **55**
Vinson Clo. Orp —74Wc **151**
Vintners Ct. EC4 —45Sb **83** (5E **200**)
Vintners Hall. EC4 —45Sb ***83*** *(5E* ***200****)*
(off Up. Thames St.)
Vintner's Pl. EC4 —45Sb **83** (5E **200**)
Viola Av. SE2 —49Xc **87**
Viola Av. Felt —58Y **99**
Viola Av. Stai —60N **97**
Viola Clo. S Ock —41Yd **90**
Viola Sq. W12 —45Va **80**
Violet Av. Enf —10Tb **11**
Violet Av. Uxb —43P **75**
Violet Clo. Wall —74Jb **146**
Violet Gdns. Croy —78Rb **147**
Violet Hill. NW8 —40Eb **61** (2A **190**)
Violet La. Croy —79Rb **147**
Violet Rd. E3 —42Dc **84**
Violet Rd. E17 —30Cc **44**
Violet Rd. E18 —26Kc **45**
Violet St. E2 —41Xb **83**
Violet Way. Loud —14L **17**
Virgil Pl. W1 —43Hb **81** (1F **197**)
Virgil St. SE1 —48Pb **82** (3J **205**)
Virginia Av. Vir W —10N **117**
Virginia Beeches. Vir W —9N **117**
Virginia Clo. Asht —90Ma **161**
Virginia Clo. N Mald —70Sa **123**
Virginia Clo. Stai —69L **119**
Virginia Clo. Wey —79S **140**
Virginia Dri. Vir W —10N **117**
Virginia Gdns. Ilf —25Sc **46**
Virginia Rd. E2 —41Vb **83** (4K **195**)
Virginia Rd. T Hth —67Rb **127**
Virginia St. E1 —45Wb **83**
Virginia Wlk. SW2 —58Pb **104**
Virginia Wlk. Grav —5F **136**
Viscount Dri. E6 —43Pc **86**
Viscount Gdns. W Byf —84N **157**
Viscount Gro. N'holt —41Z **77**
Viscount Rd. Stai —60N **97**
Viscount St. EC1 —42Sb **83** (6D **194**)
Viscount Way. Houn —56U **98**
Vista Av. Enf —12Zb **26**
Vista Dri. Ilf —29Mc **45**
Vista, The. SE9 —59Nc **108**
Vista, The. Sidc —64Vc **131**
Vista Way. Harr —30Na **39**
Viveash Clo. Hay —48V **76**
Vivian Av. NW4 —29Xa **40**
Vivian Av. Wemb —36Qa **59**
Vivian Clo. Wat —18W **18**
Vivian Ct. N12 —22Db **41**
Vivian Gdns. Wat —18W **18**
Vivian Gdns. Wemb —36Qa **59**
Vivian Mans. NW4 —29Xa ***40***
(off Vivian Av.)
Vivian Rd. E3 —40Ac **64**
Vivian Sq. SE15 —55Xb **105**
Vivian Way. N2 —29Fb **41**
Vivien Clo. Chess —80Na **143**
Vivienne Clo. Twic —58Ma **101**
Voce Rd. SE18 —52Tc **108**
Voewood Clo. N Mald —72Va **144**
Vogans Wharf. SE1 —47Vb **83** (1K **207**)
Voltaire Rd. SW4 —55Mb **104**
Voltaire Way. Hay —45U **76**
Voluntary Pl. E11 —30Jc **45**
Vorley Rd. N19 —33Lb **62**
Voss Ct. SW16 —65Nb **126**
Voss St. E2 —41Wb **83**
Vulcan Clo. Wall —80Pb **146**
Vulcan Ga. Enf —12Qb **24**
Vulcan Rd. SE4 —54Bc **106**
Vulcan Sq. E14 —49Cc **84**
Vulcan Ter. SE4 —54Bc **106**
Vulcan Way. N7 —37Pb **62**
Vulcan Way. New Ad —82Gc **167**
Vyner Rd. W3 —45Ta **79**
Vyner St. E2 —39Xb **63**
Vyner's Way. Uxb —36Q **56**
Vyne, The. Bexh —55Dd **110**
Vyse Clo. Barn —14Ya **22**

Wadard Ter. Swan —71Ld **153**
Wadding St. SE17 —49Tb **83** (6F **207**)
Waddington Av. Coul —92Qb **180**
Waddington Clo. Coul —91Rb **181**
Waddington Clo. Enf —14Ub **25**
Waddington Rd. E15 —36Fc **65**
Waddington St. E15 —37Fc **65**
Waddington Way. SE19 —66Sb **127**
Waddon Clo. Croy —76Qb **146**
Waddon Ct. Rd. Croy —77Qb **146**
Waddon New Rd. Croy —76Rb **147**
Waddon Pk. Av. Croy —77Qb **146**
Waddon Rd. Croy —76Qb **146**
Waddon Way. Croy —79Qb **146**
Wade Av. Orp —73Zc **151**
Wade Ct. N10 —24Kb **42**
Wade Dri. Slou —6E **72**
Wade Ho. Enf —15Tb **25**
Wade Rd. E16 —44Lc **85**
Wades Gro. N21 —17Qb **24**
Wades Hill. N21 —16Qb **24**
Wades La. Tedd —64Ja **122**
Wadeson St. E2 —40Xb **63**
Wade's Pl. E14 —45Dc **84**
Wadeville Av. Romf —30Ad **47**
Wadeville Clo. Belv —51Cd **110**
Wadham Av. E17 —24Dc **44**
Wadham Clo. Shep —73S **140**
Wadham Gdns. NW3 —39Gb **61**
Wadham Gdns. Gnfd —37Fa **58**
Wadham Rd. E17 —25Dc **44**
Wadham Rd. SW15 —56Ab **102**
Wadham Rd. Abb L —3V **4**
Wadhurst Clo. SE20 —68Xb **127**
Wadhurst Rd. SW8 —53Lb **104**
Wadhurst Rd. W4 —48Ta **79**
Wadley Rd. E11 —31Gc **65**
Wadsworth Bus. Cen. Gnfd —40La **58**
Wadsworth Clo. Enf —15Zb **26**
Wadsworth Clo. Gnfd —40La **58**
Wadsworth Rd. Gnfd —40Ka **58**
Wager St. E3 —42Bc **84**
Waggon M. N14 —18Lb **24**
Waggon Rd. Barn —9Eb **9**
Waghorn Rd. E13 —39Lc **65**
Waghorn Rd. Harr —27Ma **39**
Waghorn St. SE15 —55Wb **105**
Wagner St. SE15 —52Yb **106**
Wagon Rd. Barn —8Db **9**
Wagon Way. Loud —13L **17**
Wagtail Clo. NW9 —26Ua **40**
Wagtail Gdns. S Croy —82Zb **166**
Waid Clo. Dart —58Pd **111**
Waight's Ct. King T —67Na **123**
Wain Clo. Pot B —1Db **9**
Wainfleet Av. Romf —26Ed **48**
Wainford Clo. SW19 —59Za **102**
Wainwright Av. Hut —16Fe **33**
Wainwright Gro. Iswth —56Fa **100**
Waite Davies Rd. SE12 —59Hc **107**
Waite St. SE15 —51Vb **105**
Wakefield Clo. Byfl —84N **157**
Wakefield Ct. SE26 —65Yb **128**
Wakefield Cres. Stoke P —7K **53**
Wakefield Gdns. SE19 —66Ub **127**
Wakefield Gdns. Ilf —30Nc **46**
Wakefield M. WC1 —41Nb **82** (4G **193**)
Wakefield Rd. N11 —22Mb **42**
Wakefield Rd. N15 —29Vb **43**
Wakefield Rd. Rich —57Ma **101**
Wakefield St. E6 —39Mc **65**
Wakefield St. N18 —22Wb **43**
Wakefield St. WC1 —42Nb **82** (4G **193**)
Wakefield St. Grav —8D **114**
Wakefields Wlk. Chesh —3Ac **12**
Wakehams Hill. Pinn —27Ba **37**
Wakeham St. N1 —37Tb **63**
Wakehurst Path. Wok —86E **156**
Wakehurst Rd. SW11 —57Gb **103**
Wakeling Rd. W7 —43Ha **78**
Wakeling St. E14 —44Ac **84**
Wakelin Rd. E15 —40Gc **65**
Wakely Clo. Big H —90Lc **167**
Wakeman Rd. NW10 —41Ya **80**
Wakemans Hill Av. NW9 —29Ta **39**
Wakerfield Clo. Horn —29Pd **49**
Wakering Rd. Bark —37Sc **66**
Wakerings, The. Bark —37Sc **66**
Wakerley Clo. E6 —44Pc **86**
Wake Rd. Lou —10Lc **13**
Wakley St. EC1 —41Rb **83** (3B **194**)
Walberswick St. SW8 —52Nb **104**
Walbrook. EC4 —45Tb **83** (4F **201**)
Walbrook Ho. N9 —19Yb ***26***
(off Huntingdon Rd.)
Walburgh St. E1 —44Xb **83**
Walburton Rd. Purl —85Lb **164**
Walcorde Av. SE17 —49Sb **83** (6E **206**)
Walcot Gdns. SE11 —49Qb ***82*** *(5K* ***205****)*
(off Kennington Rd.)
Walcot Rd. Enf —12Bc **26**
Walcot Sq. SE11 —49Qb **82** (5A **206**)
Walcott St. SW1 —49Lb **82** (5C **204**)
Waldair Ct. E16 —47Rc **86**
Waldeck Gro. SE27 —62Rb **127**
Waldeck Rd. N15 —28Rb **43**
Waldeck Rd. SW14 —55Sa **101**
Waldeck Rd. W4 —51Qa **101**
Waldeck Rd. W13 —44Ka **78**
Waldeck Rd. Dart —59Pd **111**
Waldegrave Av. Tedd —64Ha **122**
Waldegrave Ct. Bark —39Tc **66**
Waldegrave Ct. Upm —32Rd **69**
Waldegrave Gdns. Twic —61Ha **122**
Waldegrave Gdns. Upm —32Rd **69**
Waldegrave Pk. Twic —63Ha **122**
Waldegrave Rd. N8 —27Qb **42**
Waldegrave Rd. SE19 —66Vb **127**
Waldegrave Rd. W5 —45Pa **79**
Waldegrave Rd. Brom —70Nc **130**
Waldegrave Rd. Dag —33Yc **67**
Waldegrave Rd. Twic & Tedd —63Ha **122**
Waldegrove. Croy —77Vb **147**
Waldemar Av. SW6 —53Ab **102**
Waldemar Av. W13 —46La **78**
Waldemar Rd. SW19 —64Cb **125**
Walden Av. N13 —21Sb **43**
Walden Av. Chst —63Pc **130**
Walden Av. Rain —40Fd **68**
Walden Clo. Belv —50Bd **87**
Walden Ct. SW8 —53Mb **104**
Walden Gdns. T Hth —69Pb **126**
Waldenhurst Rd. Orp —73Zc **151**
Walden Pde. Chst —65Pc **130**
(in two parts)
Walden Rd. N17 —25Tb **43**
Walden Rd. Chst —65Pc **130**
Walden Rd. Horn —30Md **49**
Waldens Clo. Orp —73Zc **151**
Waldenshaw Rd. SE23 —60Yb **106**
Waldens Pk. Rd. Wok —4F **188**
Waldens Rd. Orp —73Ad **151**
Waldens Rd. Wok —5G **188**
Walden St. E1 —44Xb **83**
Walden Way. NW7 —23Za **40**
Walden Way. Horn —30Md **49**
Walden Way. Ilf —24Uc **46**
Waldo Clo. SW4 —57Lb **104**
Waldo. E Til —8K **93**
Waldo Pl. Mitc —66Gb **125**
Waldorf Clo. S Croy —81Rb **165**
Waldo Rd. NW10 —41Wa **80**
Waldo Rd. Brom —69Mc **129**
Waldram Cres. SE23 —60Yb **106**
Waldram Pk. Rd. SE23 —60Zb **106**
Waldram Pl. SE23 —60Yb **106**
Waldrist Way. Eri —47Bd **87**
Waldron Gdns. Brom —69Fc **129**
Waldronhyrst. S Croy —77Rb **147**
Waldron M. SW3 —51Fb **103**
Waldron Rd. SW18 —62Eb **125**
Waldron Rd. Harr —32Ga **58**
Waldron's Path. S Croy —77Sb **147**
Waldrons, The. Croy —77Rb **147**
Waldrons Yd. S Harr —33Fa **58**
Waleran Clo. Stan —22Ha **38**
Walerand Rd. SE13 —54Ec **106**
Waleran Flats. SE1 —49Ub **83** (5H **207**)
Wales Av. Cars —78Gb **145**
Wales Farm Rd. W3 —43Ta **79**
Waleton Acres. Wall —79Mb **146**
Waley St. E1 —43Ac **84**
Walfield Av. N20 —17Db **23**
Walford Rd. N16 —35Ub **63**
Walford Rd. Uxb —40L **55**
Walfrey Gdns. Dag —38Ad **67**
Walham Grn. Ct. SW6 —52Db ***103***
(off Waterford Rd.)
Walham Gro. SW6 —52Cb **103**
Walham Rise. SW19 —65Ab **124**
Walham Yd. SW6 —52Cb **103**
Walkden Rd. Chst —64Qc **130**
Walker Clo. N11 —21Lb **42**
Walker Clo. SE18 —49Sc **86**
Walker Clo. W7 —46Ga **78**
Walker Clo. Dart —55Hd **110**
Walker Clo. Hamp —65Ba **121**
Walker's Ct. W1 —45Mb ***82*** *(4D* ***198****)*
(off Brewer St.)
Walkerscroft Mead. SE21 —60Sb **105**
Walkers Pl. SW15 —56Ab **102**
Walkfield Dri. Eps —89Xa **162**
Walkford Way. SE15 —52Vb **105**
Walkley Rd. Dart —57Kd **111**
Walks, The. N2 —27Fb **41**
Walk, The. Eton W —10E **72**
Walk, The. Horn —33Pd **69**
Walk, The. Pot B —4Db **9**
Walk, The. Sun —66V **120**
Wallace Clo. SE28 —45Zc **87**
Wallace Clo. Shep —70T **120**
Wallace Cres. Cars —78Hb **145**
Wallace Fields. Eps —85Wa **162**
Wallace Gdns. Swans —58Ae **113**
Wallace Ho. N7 —37Pb ***62***
(off Caledonian Rd.)
Wallace Rd. N1 —37Sb **63**
Wallace Rd. Grays —48Ce **91**
Wallace Wlk. Add —77L **139**
Wallasey Cres. Uxb —33Q **56**
Wallbutton Rd. SE4 —54Ac **106**
Wall Clo. Uxb —40N **55**
Wallcote Av. NW2 —32Za **60**
Wall Ct. N4 —32Pb ***62***
(off Stroud Grn. Rd.)
Walled Garden, The. Tad —94Za **178**
Wall End Ct. E6 —39Qc ***66***
(off Wall End Rd.)
Wall End Rd. E6 —38Pc **66**
Wallenger Av. Romf —27Kd **49**
Waller Dri. N'wd —26W **36**
Waller La. Cat —95Vb **181**
Waller Rd. SE14 —53Zb **106**
Wallers. New Ash —76Be **155**
Wallers Clo. Dag —39Ad **67**
Wallers Clo. Wfd G —23Pc **46**
Waller's Hoppet. Lou —12Pc **28**
Wallflower St. W12 —45Va **80**
Wallgrave Rd. SW5 —49Db **81**
Wallhouse Rd. Eri —52Kd **111**
Wallingford Av. W10 —44Za **80**
Wallingford Rd. Uxb —40K **55**
Wallington Clo. Ruis —30S **36**
Wallington Ct. Wall —79Kb ***146***
(off Stanley Pk. Rd.)
Wallington Rd. Ilf —31Vc **67**
Wallington Sq. Wall —79Kb **146**
Wallis All. SE1 —47Sb ***83*** *(1E* ***206****)*
(off Marshalsea Rd.)
Wallis Clo. SW11 —55Fb **103**
Wallis Clo. Dart —62Hd **132**
Wallis Clo. Horn —32Kd **69**
Wallis Ct. Slou —7L **73**
Wallis Pk. Grav —57De **113**
Wallis Rd. E9 —37Bc **64**
Wallis Rd. S'hall —44Da **77**
Wallis's Cotts. SW2 —59Nb **104**
Wallorton Gdns. SW14 —56Ta **101**
Wallside. EC2 —43Sb ***83*** *(1E* ***200****)*
(off Barbican)
Wall St. N1 —37Tb **63**
Wallwood Rd. E11 —31Fc **65**
Wallwood St. E14 —43Bc **84**
Walmar Clo. Barn —11Fb **23**
Walmer Clo. E4 —19Dc **26**
Walmer Clo. F'boro —77Tc **150**
Walmer Clo. Romf —26Dd **48**
Walmer Gdns. W13 —47Ja **78**
Walmer Pl. W1 —43Hb ***81*** *(7F* ***191****)*
(off Walmer St.)
Walmer Rd. W10 & W11 —45Ab **80**
Walmer St. W1 —43Hb **81** (7F **191**)
Walmer Ter. SE18 —49Sc **86**
Walmgate Rd. Gnfd —39Ka **58**
Walmington Fold. N12 —23Cb **41**
Walm La. NW2 —37Ya **60**
Walney Wlk. N1 —37Sb **63**
Walnut Av. W Dray —48Q **76**
Walnut Clo. SE8 —51Bc **106**
Walnut Clo. Cars —78Hb **145**
Walnut Clo. Eps —87Va **162**
Walnut Clo. Hay —45U **76**
Walnut Clo. Ilf —28Sc **46**
Walnut Ct. E17 —28Ec **44**
Walnut Ct. W5 —47Na **79**
Walnut Ct. W8 —48Db ***81***
(off St Marys Gate)
Walnut Dri. Tad —96Ab **178**
Walnut Fields. Eps —81Va **162**
Walnut Gdns. E15 —35Gc **65**
Walnut Grn. Bush —12Ba **19**
Walnut Gro. Enf —15Tb **25**
Walnut Hill Rd. Grav —9A **136**
Walnut Lodge. Chalv —8H **73**
Walnut M. Sutt —80Eb **145**
Walnut Rd. E10 —33Cc **64**
Walnuts Rd. Orp —74Wc **151**
Walnuts, The. Orp —74Wc **151**
Walnut Tree Av. Dart —61Nd **133**
Walnut Tree Av. Mitc —69Gb **125**
Walnut Tree Clo. SW13 —53Va **102**
Walnut Tree Clo. Bans —84Ab **162**
Walnut Tree Clo. Chesh —3Zb **12**
Walnut Tree Clo. Chst —67Tc **130**
Walnut Tree Clo. Shep —69S **120**
Walnut Tree Cotts. SW19 —64Ab **124**
Walnut Tree La. Byfl —84M **157**
Walnut Tree Rd. SE10 —50Gc **85**
(in two parts)
Walnut Tree Rd. Bren —51Na **101**
Walnut Tree Rd. Dag —33Zc **67**
Walnut Tree Rd. Eri —50Gd **88**
Walnut Tree Rd. Houn —51Ba **99**
Walnut Tree Rd. Shep —68S **120**
Walnut Tree Wlk. SE11 —49Qb **82** (5K **205**)
Walnut Way. Buck H —20Mc **27**
Walnut Way. Ruis —37Y **57**
Walnut Way. Swan —68Fd **132**
Walpole Av. Coul —91Hb **179**
Walpole Av. Rich —54Pa **101**
Walpole Bus. Cen. Slou —4B **72**
Walpole Clo. W13 —47La **78**
Walpole Clo. Grays —49Ee **91**
Walpole Clo. Pinn —23Ca **37**
Walpole Ct. Twic —61Ga **122**
Walpole Cres. Tedd —64Ha **122**
Walpole Gdns. W4 —50Sa **79**
Walpole Gdns. Twic —61Ga **122**
Walpole M. NW8 —39Fb **61** (1B **190**)
Walpole Pk. Wey —80Q **140**
Walpole Pl. SE18 —49Rc **86**
Walpole Pl. Tedd —64Ha **122**
Walpole Rd. E6 —38Lc **65**

Walpole Rd. E17 —28Ac 44
Walpole Rd. E18 —25Hc 45
Walpole Rd. N17 —26Sb 43
(in two parts)
Walpole Rd. SE14 —52Bc 106
Walpole Rd. SW19 —65Fb 125
Walpole Rd. Brom —71Mc 149
Walpole Rd. Croy —75Tb 147
Walpole Rd. Old Win —9M 95
Walpole Rd. Slou —4B 72
Walpole Rd. Surb —73Na 143
Walpole Rd. Tedd —64Ha 122
Walpole Rd. Twic —61Ga 122
Walpole St. SW3 —50Hb 81 (7F 203)
Walpole Way. Barn —15Ya 22
Walrond Av. Wemb —36Na 59
Walsham Clo. N16 —32Wb 63
Walsham Clo. SE28 —45Zc 87
Walsham Rd. SE14 —54Zb 106
Walsham Rd. Felt —59X 99
Walsh Cres. New Ad —84Gc 167
Walshford Way. Borwd —10Qa 7
Walsingham Gdns. Eps —77Ua 144
Walsingham Pk. Chst —68Tc 130
Walsingham Rd. E5 —34Wb 63
Walsingham Rd. W13 —46Ja 78
Walsingham Rd. Enf —14Tb 25
Walsingham Rd. Mitc —71Hb 145
Walsingham Rd. New Ad —82Ec 166
Walsingham Rd. Orp —67Xc 131
Walsingham Wlk. Belv —51Cd 110
Walter Hurford Pde. E12 —35Qc 66
Walters Clo. SE17 —49Sb 83 (6E 206)
(off Brandon St.)
Walter Sisulu Ho. Wemb —31Pa 59
Walters Mead. Asht —89Na 161
Walters Rd. SE25 —70Ub 127
Walters Rd. Enf —14Yb 26
Walter St. E2 —41Zb 84
Walter St. King T —67Na 123
Walters Way. SE23 —58Zb 106
Walters Yd. Brom —68Jc 129
Walter Ter. E1 —44Zb 84
Walterton Rd. W9 —42Bb 81
Walter Wlk. Edgw —23Sa 39
Waltham Av. NW9 —30Qa 39
Waltham Av. Hay —48S 76
Waltham Clo. Dart —58Jd 110
Waltham Clo. Hut —16Ee 33
Waltham Clo. Orp —74Zc 151
Waltham Dri. Edgw —26Qa 39
Waltham Gdns. Enf —8Yb 12
Waltham Pk. Way. E17 —25Cc 44
Waltham Rd. Cars —73Fb 145
Waltham Rd. Cat —94Xb 181
Waltham Rd. S'hall —48Aa 77
Waltham Rd. Wfd G —23Nc 46
Walthamstow Av. E4 —23Ac 44
Walthamstow Bus. Cen. E17 —26Ec 44
Waltham Way. E4 —20Bc 26
Waltheof Av. N17 —25Tb 43
Waltheof Gdns. N17 —25Tb 43
Walton Av. Harr —36Ba 57
Walton Av. N Mald —70Va 124
Walton Av. Sutt —76Bb 145
Walton Bri. Shep & W on T —73U 140
Walton Bri. Rd. Shep —73U 140
Walton Clo. E5 —34Zb 64
Walton Clo. NW2 —33Xa 60
Walton Clo. SW8 —52Nb 104
Walton Clo. Harr —28Fa 38
Walton Ct. New Bar —15Eb 23
Walton Ct. Wok —87C 156
Walton Croft. Harr —35Ga 58
Walton Dri. NW10 —37Ta 59
Walton Dri. Harr —28Fa 38
Walton Gdns. W3 —43Ra 79
Walton Gdns. Felt —63V 120
Walton Gdns. Hut —15Ee 33
Walton Gdns. Wal A —5Dc 12
Walton Gdns. Wemb —33Na 59
Walton Grn. New Ad —81Dc 166
Walton Ho. E4 —22Cc 44
Walton Ho. E17 —27Dc 44
(off Chingford Mt.)
Walton La. Shep —73T 140
Walton La. Slou —10D 52
Walton La. Wey & W on T —75R 140
Walton Pk. W on T —75Z 141
Walton Pk. La. W on T —75Z 141
Walton Pl. SW3 —48Hb 81 (3F 203)
Walton Rd. E12 —35Qc 66
(in two parts)
Walton Rd. E13 —40Lc 65
Walton Rd. N15 —28Vb 43
Walton Rd. Bush —14Z 19
Walton Rd. Eps —90Va 162
(Epsom Downs)
Walton Rd. Eps —93Sa 177
(Epsom)
Walton Rd. Harr —28Fa 38
Walton Rd. Romf —24Bd 47
Walton Rd. Sidc —62Xc 131
Walton Rd. W on T & W Mol —71Y 141
Walton Rd. Wok —88B 156
Walton's Hall Rd. Stanf —7J 93
Walton St. SW3 —49Gb 81 (5E 202)
Walton St. Enf —11Tb 25
Walton St. Tad —96Wa 178
Walton Ter. Wok —87D 156
Walton Way. W3 —43Ra 79
Walton Way. Mitc —70Lb 126
Walt Whitman Clo. SE24 —56Rb 105
Walverns Clo. Wat —16Y 19
Walworth Pl. SE17 —50Sb 83 (7E 206)
Walworth Rd. SE1 & SE17 —49Rb 83 (5C 206)
Walworth Rd. SE17 —49Sb 83
Walwyn Av. Brom —69Mc 129
Wambrook Clo. Hut —18Ee 33
Wanborough Dri. SW15 —60Xa 102
Wandle Bank. SW19 —65Eb 125
Wandle Bank. Croy —76Nb 146
Wandle Ct. Eps —77Sa 143
Wandle Ct. Gdns. Croy —76Nb 146
Wandle Pk. Trading Est., The. Croy —74Qb 146
Wandle Rd. SW17 —61Gb 125
Wandle Rd. Bedd —76Nb 146
Wandle Rd. Croy —76Sb 147
Wandle Rd. Mord —70Eb 125
Wandle Rd. Wall —76Kb 146
Wandle Side. Croy —76Pb 146
Wandle Side. Wall —76Kb 146
Wandle Way. SW18 —60Db 103
Wandle Way. Mitc —71Hb 145
Wandon Rd. SW6 —52Db 103
Wandsworth Bri. SW6 & SW18 —55Db 103
Wandsworth Bri. Rd. SW6 —53Db 103
Wandsworth Comn. N. Side. SW18 —57Fb 103
Wandsworth Comn. W. Side. SW18 —57Eb 103
Wandsworth High St. SW18 —57Cb 103
Wandsworth Plain. SW18 —57Db 103
Wandsworth Rd. SW8 —55Kb 104
Wangey Rd. Romf —31Zc 67
Wanless Rd. SE24 —55Sb 105
Wanley Rd. SE5 —56Tb 105
Wanlip Rd. E13 —42Kc 85
Wannock Gdns. Ilf —24Rc 46
Wansbeck Ct. Enf —13Rb 25
(off Waverley Rd.)
Wansbeck Rd. E9 & E3 —38Bc 64
Wansbury Way. Swan —71Jd 152
Wansdown Pl. SW6 —52Db 103
Wansey St. SE17 —49Sb 83 (6D 206)
Wansford Clo. Brtwd —20Vd 32
Wansford Grn. Wok —5C 188
Wansford Pk. Borwd —14Ta 21
Wansford Rd. Wfd G —25Lc 45
Wanstead Clo. Brom —68Lc 129
Wanstead Gdns. Ilf —30Mc 45
Wanstead La. Ilf —30Mc 45
Wanstead Pk. Av. E12 —32Mc 65
Wanstead Pk. Rd. Ilf —30Mc 45
Wanstead Pl. E11 —30Jc 45
Wanstead Rd. Brom —68Lc 129
Wansunt Rd. Bex —60Ed 110
Wantage Rd. SE12 —57Hc 107
Wantz La. Rain —42Kd 89
(in two parts)
Wantz Rd. Dag —35Dd 68
Waplings, The. Tad —96Xa 178
Wapping Dock St. E1 —46Xb 83
Wapping High St. E1 —46Wb 83
Wapping La. E1 —45Xb 83
Wapping Wall. E1 —46Yb 84
Wapseys La. Hedg —1J 53
Wapshott Rd. Stai —65G 118
Warbank Clo. New Ad —82Gc 167
Warbank Cres. New Ad —82Gc 167
Warbank La. King T —66Va 124
Warbeck Rd. W12 —47Xa 80
Warberry Rd. N22 —26Pb 42
Warbler's Grn. Cob —86Ba 159
Warboys App. King T —65Ra 123
Warboys Cres. E4 —22Ec 44
Warboys Rd. King T —65Ra 123
Warburton Clo. Harr —23Fa 38
Warburton Ct. Ruis —33W 56
Warburton Rd. E8 —39Xb 63
Warburton Rd. Twic —60Da 99
Warburtons. Stanf —1P 93
Warburton St. E8 —39Xb 63
Warburton Ter. E17 —26Dc 44
War Coppice Rd. Cat —99Tb 181
Wardale Clo. SE16 —48Xb 83
Wardalls Clo. SE14 —52Yb 106
Ward Av. Grays —49Ce 91
Ward Clo. Eri —51Fd 110
Ward Clo. Iver —45H 75
Wardell Clo. NW7 —24Ua 40
Wardell Field. NW9 —25Ua 40
Warden Av. Harr —32Ba 57
Warden Av. Romf —22Ed 48
Warden Rd. NW5 —37Kb 62
Wardens Field Clo. Grn St —79Vc 151
Wardens Gro. SE1 —46Sb 83 (7D 200)
Ward Gdns. H Wood —26Nd 49
Ward Gdns. Slou —5C 72
Ward La. Warl —88Yb 166
Wardle St. E9 —36Zb 64
Wardley St. SW18 —59Db 103
Wardo Av. SW6 —53Ab 102
Wardona Ho. Swans —58Be 113
Wardour Ct. Dart —58Rd 111
(off Bow Arrow La.)
Wardour Ct. Dart —58Rd 111
(off Grange Cres.)
Wardour M. W1 —44Lb 82 (3C 198)
(off D'Arblay St.)
Wardour St. W1 —44Lb 82 (2C 198)
Ward Point. SE11 —49Qb 82 (6K 205)
Ward Rd. E15 —39Fc 65
Ward Rd. N19 —34Lb 62
Ward Rd. SW19 —67Eb 125
Wardrobe Pl. EC4
(off Carter La.) —44Rb 83 (3C 200)
Wardrobe Ter. EC4
(off Addle Hill) —45Rb 83 (4C 200)
Wards La. Els —12Ha 20
Wards Rd. Ilf —31Tc 66
Ware Ct. Sutt —77Bb 145
Wareham Clo. Houn —56Da 99
Wareham Ho. SW8 —52Pb 104
Waremead Rd. Ilf —29Rc 46
Warenford Way. Borwd —11Qa 21
Warenne Rd. Fet —94Ea 176
Warepoint Dri. SE28 —47Tc 86
Warescott Clo. Brtwd —17Xd 32
Warescott Rd. Brtwd —17Xd 32
Warfield Rd. NW10 —41Za 80
Warfield Rd. Felt —59U 98
Warfield Rd. Hamp —67Da 121
Wargrave Av. N15 —30Vb 43
Wargrave Rd. Harr —34Ea 58
Warham Rd. N4 —29Qb 42
Warham Rd. Harr —26Ha 38
Warham Rd. Otf —88Kd 171
Warham Rd. S Croy —78Rb 147
Warham St. SE5 —52Rb 105
(in two parts)
Waring Clo. Orp —79Vc 151
Waring Dri. Orp —79Vc 151
Waring & Gillow Est. W3 —42Qa 79
Waring Rd. Sidc —65Yc 131
Waring St. SE27 —63Sb 127
Warkworth Gdns. Iswth —52Ja 100
Warkworth Rd. N17 —24Tb 43
Warland Rd. SE18 —52Tc 108
Warland Rd. W King —80Vd 154
Warley Av. Dag —31Bd 67
Warley Av. Hay —44W 76
Warley Clo. E10 —32Bc 64
Warley Gap. L War —24Xd 50
Warley Hall La. Upm —31Be 71
Warley Hill. Gt War & War —23Xd 50
Warley Hill Bus. Pk., The. Gt War —23Yd 50
Warley Mt. War —21Yd 50
Warley Rd. N9 —19Yb 26
Warley Rd. Gt War & Upm —26Sd 50
Warley Rd. Hay —44W 76
Warley Rd. Ilf —25Qc 46
Warley Rd. Wfd G —24Kc 45
Warley St. E2 —41Zb 84
Warley St. Gt War & Upm —28Yd 50
Warlingham Rd. T Hth —70Rb 127
Warlock Rd. W9 —42Bb 81
Warlters Clo. N7 —35Nb 62
Warlters Rd. N7 —35Nb 62
Warltersville Mans. N19 —31Nb 62
Warltersville Rd. N19 —31Nb 62
Warmington Clo. E5 —34Zb 64
Warmington Rd. SE24 —58Sb 105
Warmington St. E13 —42Jc 85
Warminster Gdns. SE25 —68Wb 127
Warminster Rd. SE25 —68Vb 127
Warminster Sq. SE25 —68Wb 127
Warminster Way. Mitc —67Kb 126
Warmley Ct. SE15 —51Ub 105
(off Newent Clo.)
Warndon St. SE16 —49Zb 84
Warneford Pl. Wat —16Aa 19
Warneford Rd. Harr —27Ma 39
Warneford St. E9 —39Xb 63
Warne Pl. Sidc —58Xc 109
Warner Av. Sutt —75Ab 144
Warner Clo. E15 —36Gc 65
Warner Clo. NW9 —31Va 60
Warner Clo. Hay —52T 98
Warner Clo. Slou —6C 72
Warner Pde. Hay —52T 98
Warner Pl. E2 —40Wb 63
Warner Rd. E17 —28Ac 44
Warner Rd. N8 —28Mb 42
Warner Rd. SE5 —53Sb 105
Warner Rd. Brom —66Hc 129
Warners Clo. Wfd G —22Jc 45
Warners La. Rich —63Ma 123
Warners Path. Wfd G —22Jc 45
Warner St. EC1 —42Qb 82 (6K 193)
Warner Yd. EC1 —42Qb 82 (6K 193)
(off Warner St.)
Warnford Rd. Orp —78Vc 151
Warnham Ct. Rd. Cars —80Hb 145
Warnham Ho. SW2 —59Pb 104
(off Up. Tulse Hill)
Warnham Rd. N12 —22Gb 41
Warple Way. W3 —47Ua 80
Warren Av. E10 —34Ec 64
Warren Av. Brom —66Gc 129
Warren Av. Orp —78Vc 151
Warren Av. Rich —56Ra 101
Warren Av. S Croy —80Zb 148
Warren Av. Sutt —82Bb 163
Warren Clo. N9 —17Zb 26
Warren Clo. SE21 —59Sb 105
Warren Clo. Bexh —57Cd 110
Warren Clo. Esh —77Da 141
Warren Clo. Hay —43Y 77
Warren Clo. Slou —48A 74
Warren Clo. Stanf —2M 93
Warren Clo. Wemb —33Ma 59
Warren Ct. N17 —27Wb 43
(off High Cross Rd.)
Warren Ct. Beck —66Cc 128
Warren Ct. Chig —21Tc 46
Warren Ct. Croy —74Ub 147
Warren Ct. Sev —96Ld 187
Warren Ct. Wey —78Q 140
Warren Cres. N9 —17Vb 25
Warren Cutting. King T —66Ta 123
Warrender Rd. N19 —35Lb 62
Warrender Way. Ruis —31W 56
Warren Dri. Gnfd —42Da 77
Warren Dri. Horn —35Jd 68
Warren Dri. Orp —78Xc 151
Warren Dri. Ruis —31Z 57
Warren Dri. Tad —94Bb 179
Warren Dri. N. Surb —74Ra 143
Warren Dri. S. Surb —74Sa 143
Warren Dri., The. E11 —31Lc 65
Warreners La. Wey —80T 140
Warren Farm Cotts. Romf —28Bd 47
Warren Farm Mobile Home Pk. Wok —91K 173
Warren Field. Epp —4Wc 15
Warren Field. Iver —40E 54
Warrenfield Clo. Chesh —3Wb 11
Warren Fields. Stan —21Ma 39
Warren Footpath. Twic —60La 100
Warren Gdns. E15 —36Fc 65
Warren Gdns. Orp —78Wc 151
Warrengate La. Pot B —3Ya 8
Warrengate Rd. N Mym —1Ya 8
Warren Gro. Borwd —14Ta 21
Warren Hastings Ct. Grav —8B 114
(off Pier Rd.)
Warren Heights. Chaf H —49Ae 91
Warren Hill. Eps —88Ta 161
Warren Hill. Lou —15Lc 27
Warren La. SE18 —48Rc 86
Warren La. Dodd —11Vd 32
Warren La. Grays —49Zd 91
Warren La. Oxs —83Ea 160
Warren La. Stan —19Ja 20
Warren La. Wok —90J 157
Warren Lodge Dri. Tad —96Ab 178
Warren Mead. Bans —87Ya 162
Warren M. W1 —42Lb 82 (6B 192)
Warren Pde. Slou —6N 73
Warren Pk. King T —65Sa 123
Warren Pk. Warl —90Zb 166
Warren Pk. Rd. Sutt —79Gb 145
Warren Pl. E1 —44Zb 84
(off Caroline St.)
Warren Pond Rd. E4 —18Hc 27
Warren Rise. N Mald —67Ta 123
Warren Rd. E4 —19Ec 26
Warren Rd. E10 —34Ec 64
Warren Rd. E11 —30Lc 45
Warren Rd. NW2 —33Va 60
Warren Rd. SW19 —65Gb 125
Warren Rd. Ashf —66U 120
Warren Rd. Bans —86Ya 162
Warren Rd. Bexh —57Cd 110
Warren Rd. Brom —75Jc 149
Warren Rd. Bush —18Ea 20
Warren Rd. Chels —78Vc 151
Warren Rd. Croy —74Vb 147
Warren Rd. Dart —62Nd 133
Warren Rd. Ilf —29Tc 46
Warren Rd. King T —65Sa 123
Warren Rd. New Haw —82J 157
Warren Rd. Purl —84Rb 165
Warren Rd. Sidc —62Yc 131
Warren Rd. S'fleet —64De 135
Warren Rd. Twic —58Ea 100
Warren Rd. Uxb —35N 55
Warrens Shawe La. Edgw —19Ra 21
Warrens, The. Hart —72Be 155
Warren St. W1 —42Kb 82 (6B 192)
Warren Ter. Grays —47Zd 91
Warren Ter. Romf —28Zc 47
(in two parts)
Warren, The. E12 —35Nc 66
Warren, The. Asht —92Pa 177
Warren, The. Cars —82Gb 163
Warren, The. Ger X —24B 34
Warren, The. Grav —3G 136
Warren, The. Hay —44W 76
Warren, The. Houn —52Ba 99
Warren, The. Oxs —84Ea 160
Warren, The. Rad —6Ka 6
Warren, The. Stanf —4N 93
Warren, The. Tad —95Ab 178
Warren, The. Wor Pk —76Ta 143
Warren View. Shorne —4N 137
Warren Wlk. SE7 —51Lc 107
Warren Way. NW7 —23Ab 40
Warren Way. Knap —6A 188
Warren Way. Wey —78S 140
Warren Wood Clo. Brom —75Hc 149
Warriner Av. Horn —33Md 69
Warriner Gdns. SW11 —53Hb 103
Warrington Av. Slou —4G 72
Warrington Cres. W9 —42Eb 81
Warrington Gdns. W9 —42Eb 81
Warrington Gdns. Horn —30Ld 49
Warrington Rd. Croy —76Rb 147
Warrington Rd. Dag —33Zc 67
Warrington Rd. Harr —29Ga 38
Warrington Rd. Rich —57Ma 101
Warrington Spur. Old Win —9M 95
Warrington Sq. Dag —33Zc 67
Warrior Av. Grav —3E 136
Warrior Sq. E12 —35Qc 66
Warsaw Clo. Ruis —37X 57
Warspite Rd. SE18 —48Nc 86
Warton Rd. E15 —38Ec 64
Warwall. E6 —44Rc 86
Warwick. Sidc —64Xc 131
Warwick Av. W9 & W2 —42Db 81
Warwick Av. Edgw —20Ra 21
Warwick Av. Egh —67E 118
Warwick Av. Harr —35Ba 57
Warwick Av. Slou —2G 72
Warwick Av. Stai —65L 119
Warwick Chambers. W8 —48Cb 81
(off Pater St.)
Warwick Clo. SW15 —59Xa 102
Warwick Clo. Barn —15Fb 23
Warwick Clo. Bex —59Ad 109
Warwick Clo. Bush —17Ga 20
Warwick Clo. Hamp —66Ea 122
Warwick Clo. Orp —76Wc 151
Warwick Ct. WC1 —43Pb 82 (1J 199)
Warwick Ct. Brom —68Gc 129
Warwick Ct. Eri —52Hd 110
Warwick Ct. Harr —27Ga 38
Warwick Ct. New Bar —15Db 23
(off Station Rd.)
Warwick Ct. Sev —97Kd 187
Warwick Cres. W2 —43Eb 81
Warwick Cres. Hay —42V 76
Warwick Deeping. Ott —78E 138
Warwick Dene. W5 —46Na 79
Warwick Dri. SW15 —55Xa 102
Warwick Dri. Chesh —1Zb 12
Warwick Est. W2 —43Db 81
Warwick Gdns. N4 —29Sb 43
Warwick Gdns. W14 —48Bb 81
Warwick Gdns. Asht —89La 160
Warwick Gdns. Barn —10Bb 9
Warwick Gdns. Ilf —32Rc 66
Warwick Gdns. Romf —27Ld 49
Warwick Gdns. Th Dit —71Ha 142
Warwick Gdns. T Hth —69Qb 126
Warwick Gro. E5 —33Xb 63
Warwick Gro. Surb —73Pa 143
Warwick Ho. Swan —70Gd 132
Warwick Ho. St. SW1 —46Mb 82 (6E 198)
Warwick La. EC4 —44Rb 83 (2C 200)
Warwick La. Rain & Upm —40Pd 69
Warwick La. Wok —7D 188
Warwick Lodge. Twic —62Da 121
Warwick Pde. Harr —26Ka 38
Warwick Pl. SW1 —49Lb 82
Warwick Pl. W5 —47Ma 79
Warwick Pl. W9 —43Eb 81
Warwick Pl. Grav —57De 113
Warwick Pl. Pil H —14Sd 32
Warwick Pl. Uxb —38L 55
Warwick Pl. N. SW1 —49Lb 82 (6B 204)
Warwick Rd. E4 —22Cc 44
Warwick Rd. E11 —29Kc 45
Warwick Rd. E12 —36Nc 66
Warwick Rd. E15 —37Hc 65
Warwick Rd. E17 —25Bc 44
Warwick Rd. N11 —23Mb 42
Warwick Rd. N18 —21Ub 43
Warwick Rd. SE20 —69Xb 127
Warwick Rd. W5 —47Ma 79
Warwick Rd. W14 & SW5 —49Bb 81
Warwick Rd. Ashf —64N 119
Warwick Rd. Barn —14Db 23
Warwick Rd. Borwd —13Ta 21
Warwick Rd. Coul —86Lb 164
Warwick Rd. Enf —9Bc 12
Warwick Rd. Houn —55X 99
Warwick Rd. King T —67La 122
Warwick Rd. N Mald —69Sa 123
Warwick Rd. Rain —42Ld 89
Warwick Rd. Sidc —64Xc 131
Warwick Rd. S'hall —48Ba 77
Warwick Rd. Sutt —77Eb 145
Warwick Rd. Th Dit —71Ha 142
Warwick Rd. T Hth —69Qb 126
Warwick Rd. Twic —60Ga 100
Warwick Rd. Well —55Yc 109
Warwick Rd. W Dray —46N 75
Warwick Row. SW1 —48Lb 82 (4A 204)
Warwickshire Path. SE8 —52Bc 106
Warwickshire Rd. N16 —35Ub 63
Warwick Sq. EC4 —44Rb 83 (2C 200)
Warwick Sq. SW1 —50Lb 82 (7B 204)
Warwick Sq. M. SW1 —49Lb 82 (6B 204)
Warwick St. W1 —45Lb 82 (4C 198)
Warwick Ter. SE18 —51Tc 108
Warwick Way. SW1 —50Kb 82 (7K 203)
Warwick Way. Crox —14S 18
Warwick Wold Rd. Red —100Qb 180
Warwick Yd. EC1 —42Sb 83 (6E 194)
Washington Av. E12 —35Nc 66
Washington Dri. Slou —5B 72
Washington Dri. Wind —5C 94
Washington Rd. E6 —38Lc 65
Washington Rd. E18 —26Hc 45
Washington Rd. SW13 —52Wa 102
Washington Rd. King T —68Qa 123
Washington Rd. Wor Pk —75Xa 144
Wash La. Pot B —5Xa 8
Washneys Rd. Orp —86Wc 169
Washpond La. Warl —90Ec 166
Wash Rd. Hut —16Fe 33
Wastdale Rd. SE23 —60Zb 106
Watchfield Ct. W4 —50Sa 79
Watchgate. Dart —64Td 134
Watcombe Cotts. Rich —51Qa 101
Watcombe Pl. SE25 —70Xb 127
Watcombe Rd. SE25 —71Xb 147
Wategate, The. Wat —19Z 19
Waterbank Rd. SE6 —62Dc 128
Waterbeach Rd. Dag —37Yc 67
Waterbeach Rd. Slou —4H 73
Water Brook La. NW4 —29Ya 40
Watercress Clo. Sev —92Ld 187
Watercress Dri. Sev —92Ld 187
Watercress Way. Wok —5E 188
Watercroft Rd. Hals —82Bd 169
Waterdale. Brick —2Aa 5
Waterdale Rd. SE2 —51Wc 109
Waterdales. Grav —60Fe 113
Waterden Rd. E15 —36Cc 64
Water Dri. Rick —18N 17
Waterer Gdns. Tad —90Za 162
Waterer Ho. SE6 —63Ec 128
Waterer Rise. Wall —79Mb 146
Waterers Rise. Knap —5A 188
Waterfall Clo. N14 —20Lb 24
Waterfall Clo. Vir W —9L 117
Waterfall Cotts. SW19 —65Fb 125
Waterfall Rd. N11 & N14 —21Kb 42
Waterfall Rd. SW19 —65Fb 125
Waterfall Ter. SW17 —65Gb 125
Waterfield. Tad —91Xa 178
Waterfield Clo. SE28 —46Xc 87
Waterfield Clo. Belv —48Dd 88
Waterfield Dri. Warl —91Yb 182
Waterfield Gdns. SE25 —70Ub 127
Waterfield Gdns. SE28 —46Xc 87
Waterfield Grn. Tad —92Ya 178
Waterfields. Lea —91Ka 176
Waterfields Way. Wat —15Z 19
Waterford Rd. SW6 —52Db 103
Water Gdns. Stan —23Ka 38
Watergardens, The. King T —65Sa 123
Watergate. EC4 —45Rb 83 (4B 200)
Watergate St. SE8 —51Cc 106
Watergate Wlk. WC2 —46Nb 82 (6G 199)
Water Glade Cen., The. W5 —45Ma 79
Waterglade Ind. Pk. W Thur —51Vd 112
Waterhall Av. E4 —21Gc 45
Waterhall Clo. E17 —25Zb 44
Waterhead Clo. Eri —52Gd 110
Waterhouse Clo. E16 —43Mc 85
Waterhouse Clo. NW3 —36Fb 61
Waterhouse Clo. W6 —49Za 80
Waterhouse La. Kenl —91Sb 181
Waterhouse La. Tad —93Ab 178
Wateringbury Clo. Orp —69Xc 131
Water La. E15 —37Gc 65
Water La. NW1 —38Kb 62
Water La. SE14 —52Yb 106
Water La. Bookh —97Z 175
(in two parts)
Water La. Bov —1C 2
Water La. Cob —87Aa 159
Water La. Ilf —34Uc 66
Water La. K Lan —1R 4
Water La. King T —67Ma 123
Water La. Lon C —1Ma 7
Water La. Purf —49Qd 89
Water La. Rich —57Ma 101
Water La. Shor —84Hd 170
Water La. Sidc —62Bd 131
(in two parts)
Water La. T'sey —98Jc 183
Water La. Twic —60Ja 100
Water La. Wat —14Y 19
Water La. W'ham —99Tc 184
Waterloo Bri. WC2 & SE1 —45Pb 82 (5H 199)
Waterloo Clo. E9 —36Yb 64
Waterloo Gdns. E2 —40Yb 64
Waterloo Gdns. Romf —30Fd 48
Waterloo Pas. NW6 —38Bb 61
Waterloo Pl. SW1 —46Mb 82 (6D 198)
Waterloo Pl. Rich —56Na 101
Waterloo Rd. E6 —38Lc 65
Waterloo Rd. E7 —36Hc 65
Waterloo Rd. E10 —31Cc 64
Waterloo Rd. NW2 —32Wa 60
Waterloo Rd. SE1 —47Qb 82 (6J 199)
Waterloo Rd. Brtwd —18Yd 32
Waterloo Rd. Eps —84Ta 161
Waterloo Rd. Ilf —26Sc 46
Waterloo Rd. Romf —29Gd 48
Waterloo Rd. Sutt —78Fb 145
Waterloo Rd. Uxb —39L 55
Waterloo St. Grav —9E 114
Waterloo Ter. N1 —38Rb 63
Waterlow Ct. NW11 —31Db 61
Waterlow Rd. N19 —32Lb 62
Waterman Clo. Wat —16X 19
Watermans. Romf —29Hd 48
Watermans Bus. Pk. Stai —63F 118
Watermans Clo. King T —66Na 123
Watermans Ct. Bren —51Na 101
Waterman's Sq. SE20 —66Yb 128
Waterman St. SW15 —55Za 102
Waterman's Wlk. EC4 —45Tb 83 (5F 201)
(off Allhallows La.)
Watermans Wlk. SE16 —47Ac 84
Waterman Way. E1 —46Xb 83
Watermead. Felt —60U 98
Watermead. Tad —93Xa 178
Watermead. Wok —4C 188
Watermead Ho. E9 —36Ac 64
Watermead La. Cars —73Hb 145
Watermeadow La. SW6 —54Eb 103
Watermead Rd. SE6 —63Ec 128
Watermead Way. N17 —27Wb 43
Watermen's Sq. SE20 —66Yb 128
Watermill Bus. Cen. Enf —12Bc 26
Watermill Clo. Rich —62La 122
Water Mill Ho. Felt —61Ca 121
Watermill La. N18 —22Ub 43
Watermill Way. SW19 —67Fb 125
Watermill Way. Felt —61Ba 121
Water Mill Way. S Dar —68Rd 133
Watermint Quay. N16 —31Wb 63
Water Rd. Wemb —39Pa 59
Waters Dri. Stai —62H 119
Watersedge. Eps —77Sa 143
Watersfield Way. Edgw —24Ma 39
Waters Gdns. Dag —36Cd 68
Waterside. Beck —67Bc 128
Waterside. Dart —57Gd 110
Waterside. K Lan —1Q 4
Water Side. Uxb —43L 75
Waterside Clo. Bark —35Wc 67
Waterside Clo. N'holt —41Ba 77
Waterside Clo. Surb —75Na 143
Waterside Ct. K Lan —1R 4
Waterside Dri. Langl —47B 74
Waterside Dri. W on T —71W 140
Waterside Pl. NW1 —39Jb 62
Waterside Point. SW11 —52Gb 103
Waterside Rd. S'hall —48Ca 77
Waterside Trading Cen. W7 —48Ga 78
Waterside Trading Est. Add —77N 139
Waterside Way. SW17 —63Eb 125
Waterside Way. Wok —6E 188

Watersmeet Way—Wessex Ct.

Watersmeet Way. SE28 —44Yc 87
Waterson Rd. Grays —9D 92
Waterson St. E2 —41Ub 83 (3J 195)
Watersplash Clo. King T —69Na 123
Watersplash La. Asc —7B 116
Watersplash La. Hay —49W 76
(in two parts)
Watersplash Rd. Shep —70Q 120
Waters Rd. SE6 —62Gc 129
Waters Rd. King T —68Ra 123
Waters Sq. King T —69Ra 123
Water St. WC2 —45Qb 82 (4K 199)
(off Maltravers St.)
Waterton Av. Grav —9G 114
Water Tower Clo. Uxb —36N 55
Water Tower Hill. Croy —77Tb 147
Water Tower Pl. N1 —39Rb 63
Waterway Rd. Fet —94Ja 176
Waterworks La. E5 —33Zb 64
Waterworks Rd. SW2 —58Pb 104
Waterworks Vs. Sev —98Kd 187
Waterworks Yd. Croy —76Sb 147
Watery La. SW20 —68Bb 125
Watery La. Hay —50U 76
Watery La. Lyne —73F 138
Watery La. N'holt —40Y 57
Watery La. Sidc —65Xc 131
Wates Way. Brtwd —18Zd 33
Wates Way. Mitc —72Hb 145
Wateville Rd. N17 —25Sb 43
Watford By-Pass. Stan & Edgw —17Ja 20
Watford Clo. SW11 —53Gb 103
Watford Enterprise Cen. Wat —17U 18
Watford Field Rd. Wat —15Y 19
Watford Heath. Wat —17Z 19
Watford Rd. E16 —43Jc 85
Watford Rd. Crox —16Q 18
Watford Rd. Els —16Ka 20
Watford Rd. Harr & Wemb —31Ja 58
Watford Rd. K Lan —2Q 4
Watford Rd. N'wd —24V 36
Watford Rd. Rad —8Ga 6
Watford Way. NW7 & NW4 —21Ua 40
Watkin Rd. Wemb —34Ra 59
Watkins. Sidc —64Xc 131
Watkinson Rd. N7 —37Pb 62
Watling Av. Edgw —25Sa 39
Watling Ct. EC4 —44Sb 83 (3E 200)
(off Watling St.)
Watling Ct. Els —16Ma 21
Watling Farm Clo. Stan —18La 20
Watling Gdns. NW2 —37Ab 60
Watling Ga. NW9 —28Ta 39
Watling Knoll. Rad —5Ha 6
Watlings Clo. Croy —72Ac 148
Watling St. EC4 —44Sb 83 (3D 200)
Watling St. Bexh —56Dd 110
Watling St. Dart & Grav —59Qd 111
Watling St. Els —12La 20
Watling St. Rad & Els —3Ha 6
Watlington Gro. SE26 —64Ac 128
Watney Mkt. E1 —44Xb 83
Watney Rd. SW14 —55Sa 101
Watney's Rd. Mitc —71Mb 146
Watson Av. E6 —38Qc 66
Watson Av. Sutt —75Ab 144
Watson Clo. N16 —36Tb 63
Watson Clo. SW19 —65Gb 125
Watson Clo. Grays —53Wd 112
Watson Gdns. H Wood —26Nd 49
Watson's M. W1 —43Gb 81 (1E 196)
Watsons Rd. N22 —25Pb 42
Watson's St. SE8 —52Cc 106
Watson St. E13 —40Kc 65
Watsons Yd. NW2 —33Wa 60
Wattendon Rd. Kenl —88Rb 165
Wattisfield Rd. E5 —34Yb 64
Watts Bri. Rd. Eri —51Hd 110
Watts Clo. N15 —29Ub 43
Watts Cres. Purf —49Sd 90
Watts Gro. E3 —43Dc 84
Watts La. Chst —67Rc 130
Watts La. Tad —94Za 178
Watts La. Tedd —64Ja 122
Watt's Mead. Tad —94Za 178
Watts Point. E13 —39Jc 65
(off Brooks Rd.)
Watts Rd. Th Dit —73Ja 142
Watts St. E1 —46Xb 83
Wat Tyler Ho. N8 —27Nb 42
(off Boyton Rd.)
Wat Tyler Rd. SE3 & SE10 —54Ec 106
Wauthier Clo. N13 —22Rb 43
Wavell Dri. Sidc —58Uc 108
Wavell Gdns. Slou —1D 72
Wavel M. N8 —28Mb 42
Wavel M. NW6 —38Db 61
Wavel Pl. SE26 —63Vb 127
Wavendene Av. Egh —66D 118
Wavendon Av. W4 —50Ta 79
Waveney Av. SE15 —56Xb 105
Waveney Clo. E1 —46Wb 83
Waveney Ho. SE15 —56Xb 105
Waverley Av. E4 —21Bc 44
Waverley Av. E17 —27Fc 45
Waverley Av. Kenl —88Ub 165
Waverley Av. Surb —72Ra 143
Waverley Av. Sutt —75Db 145
Waverley Av. Twic —60Ba 99
Waverley Av. Wemb —36Pa 59
Waverley Clo. E18 —25Lc 45
Waverley Clo. Brom —71Mc 149
Waverley Clo. Hay —49T 76
Waverley Ct. SE26 —64Yb 128
Waverley Ct. Enf —13Sb 25
Waverley Ct. Wok —90A 156
Waverley Cres. SE18 —50Tc 86
Waverley Cres. Rom —24Ld 49
Waverley Dri. Cher —76F 138
Waverley Dri. Vir W —9L 117
Waverley Gdns. E6 —43Nc 86
Waverley Gdns. NW10 —40Pa 59
Waverley Gdns. Bark —40Uc 66
Waverley Gdns. Grays —47Ge 91
Waverley Gdns. Ilf —26Sc 46
Waverley Gdns. N'wd —25W 36
Waverley Gro. N3 —27Ab 40
Waverley Ind. Est. Harr —27Fa 38
Waverley Pl. N4 —33Rb 63
Waverley Pl. NW8 —40Fb 61 (1B 190)
Waverley Pl. Lea —94Ka 176
Waverley Rd. E17 —27Ec 44
Waverley Rd. E18 —25Lc 45
Waverley Rd. N8 —30Nb 42
Waverley Rd. N17 —24Xb 43
Waverley Rd. SE18 —50Tc 86
Waverley Rd. SE25 —70Xb 127
Waverley Rd. Enf —13Rb 25
Waverley Rd. Eps —78Xa 144
Waverley Rd. Harr —33Aa 57
Waverley Rd. Rain —42Kd 89
Waverley Rd. Slou —3G 72
Waverley Rd. S'hall —45Ca 77
Waverley Rd. Stoke D & Oxs —86Da 159
Waverley Rd. Wey —78Q 140
Waverley Vs. N17 —26Vb 43
Waverley Way. Cars —79Gb 145
Waverton Rd. SW18 —59Eb 103
Waverton St. W1 —46Jb 82 (6J 197)
Wavertree Ct. SW2 —60Nb 104
Wavertree Rd. E18 —26Jc 45
Wavertree Rd. SW2 —60Pb 104
Waxlow Cres. S'hall —44Ca 77
Waxlow Ho. Hay —43Z 77
Waxlow Rd. NW10 —40Sa 59
Waxwell Clo. Pinn —26Z 37
Waxwell Farm Ho. Pinn —26Z 37
Waxwell La. Pinn —26Z 37
Waxwell Ter. SE1 —47Pb 82 (2J 205)
Wayborne Gro. Ruis —30S 36
Waycross Rd. Upm —31Ud 70
Waye Av. Houn —53W 98
Wayfarer Rd. N'holt —41Z 77
Wayfaring Grn. Grays —50Be 91
Wayfield Link. SE9 —58Tc 108
Wayford St. SW11 —54Gb 103
Wayland Av. E8 —36Wb 63
Wayland Clo. E8 —36Wb 63
Wayland Ho. SW9 —54Qb 104
(off Robsart St.)
Waylands. Hay —43T 76
Waylands. Swan —70Hd 132
Waylands Clo. Knock —87Ad 169
Waylands Mead. Beck —67Dc 128
Waylett Ho. SE11 —50Pb 82 (7J 205)
(off Loughbrough St.)
Waylett Pl. SE27 —62Rb 127
Waylett Pl. Wemb —35Ma 59
Wayne Clo. Orp —76Vc 151
Wayneflete Tower Av. Esh —76Ca 141
Waynflete Av. Croy —76Rb 147
Waynflete Sq. W10 —45Za 80
Waynflete St. SW18 —61Eb 125
Wayside. NW11 —32Ab 60
Wayside. SW14 —57Sa 101
Wayside. Chfd —2K 3
Wayside. New Ad —79Dc 148
Wayside. Pot B —5Fb 9
Wayside Av. Bush —16Fa 20
Wayside Av. Horn —33Md 69
Wayside Clo. N14 —16Lb 24
Wayside Clo. Romf —27Hd 48
Wayside Ct. Twic —58La 100
Wayside Ct. Wemb —34Qa 59
Wayside Ct. Wok —4B 188
Wayside Gdns. SE9 —63Pc 130
Wayside Gdns. Dag —36Cd 68
Wayside Gdns. Ger X —1P 53
Wayside Gro. SE9 —63Pc 130
Wayside M. Ilf —29Qc 46
Wayville Rd. Dart —59Rd 111
Way Volante. Grav —3G 136
Weald Clo. SE16 —50Xb 83
Weald Clo. Brtwd —20Wd 32
Weald Clo. Brom —75Nc 150
Weald Clo. Grav —6A 136
Wealden Pl. Sev —93Kd 187
Weald La. Harr —26Fa 38
Weald Pk. Way. S Wea —20Ud 32
Weald Rise. Harr —24Ha 38
Weald Rd. Brtwd —18Qd 31
Weald Rd. Sev —100Kd 187
Weald Rd. Uxb —40Q 56
Weald Sq. E5 —33Wb 63
Wealdstone Rd. Sutt —75Bb 145
Weald, The. Chst —65Pc 130
Weald Way. Cat —100Ub 181
Weald Way. Hay —41U 76
Weald Way. Romf —30Dd 48
Wealdwood Gdns. Pinn —23Da 37
Weale Rd. E4 —20Fc 27
Weall Ct. Pinn —28Aa 37
Weall Grn. Wat —4X 5
Weardale Av. Dart —61Sd 134
Weardale Gdns. Enf —11Tb 25
Weardale Rd. SE13 —56Fc 107
Wear Pl. E2 —41Xb 83
Wearside Rd. SE13 —56Dc 106
Weasdale Ct. Wok —4C 188
Weatherall Clo. Add —78K 139
Weatherbury Ho. N19 —34Mb 62
(off Wedmore St.)
Weatherley Clo. E3 —43Bc 84
Weavers Clo. Grav —10C 114
Weavers Clo. Iswth —56Ga 100
Weavers La. SE1 —46Ub 83 (7J 201)
Weavers La. Sev —93Ld 187
Weavers Orchard. S'fleet —65Ce 135
Weaver St. E1 —42Wb 83
Weavers Wlk. NW1 —39Mb 62
Weaver Wlk. SE27 —63Sb 127
Webber Clo. Slou —9P 73
Webber Clo. Els —16Ma 21
Webber Clo. Eri —52Kd 111
Webber Row. SE1 —47Rb 83 (2A 206)
Webber St. SE1 —47Qb 82 (1A 206)
Webb Est. E5 —31Wb 63
Webb Gdns. E13 —42Jc 85
Webb Ho. SW8 —52Mb 104
Webb Ho. Dag —34Cd 68
(off Kershaw Rd.)
Webb Ho. Felt —62Aa 121
Webb Pl. NW10 —41Va 80
Webb Rd. SE3 —51Hc 107
Webb's All. Sev —97Ld 187
Webbscroft Rd. Dag —35Dd 68
Webbs Meadow. Sev —97Ld 187
Webb's Rd. SW11 —56Hb 103
Webbs Rd. Hay —41X 77
Webb St. SE1 —48Ub 83 (4H 207)
Webster Clo. Horn —34Md 69
Webster Clo. Oxs —86Da 159
Webster Clo. Wal A —5Hc 13
Webster Gdns. W5 —46Ma 79
Webster Rd. E11 —34Ec 64
Webster Rd. SE16 —48Wb 83
Webster Rd. Stanf —1N 93
Websters Clo. Wok —8E 188
Wedderburn Rd. NW3 —36Fb 61
Wedderburn Rd. Bark —39Uc 66
Wedgewood Clo. Epp —2Wc 15
Wedgewood Clo. N'wd —23S 36
Wedgewood Way. SE19 —66Sb 127
Wedgwood M. W1 —44Mb 82 (3E 198)
Wedgwoods. Tats —93Lc 183
Wedgwood Wlk. NW6 —36Db 61
(off Lymington Rd.)
Wedlake Clo. Horn —32Nd 69
Wedlake St. W10 —42Ab 80
Wedmore Av. Ilf —25Qc 46
Wedmore Gdns. N19 —33Mb 62
Wedmore M. N19 —34Mb 62
Wedmore Rd. Gnfd —41Fa 78
Wedmore St. N19 —34Mb 62
Wednesbury Gdns. Romf —24Pd 49
Wednesbury Grn. Romf —24Pd 49
Wednesbury Rd. Romf —24Pd 49
Weech Rd. NW6 —35Cb 61
Weedan Ho. W12 —44Wa 80
Weedington Rd. NW5 —36Jb 62
Weekes Dri. Slou —6F 72
Weekley Sq. SW11 —55Fb 103
Weelkes Clo. Stanf —1L 93
Weigall Rd. SE12 —57Jc 107
Weighhouse St. W1 —44Jb 82 (4J 197)
Weighton M. SE20 —68Xb 127
Weighton Rd. SE20 —68Xb 127
Weighton Rd. Harr —25Fa 38
Weihurst Ct. Sutt —78Gb 145
Weihurst Gdns. Sutt —78Fb 145
Weimar St. SW15 —55Ab 102
Weind, The. They B —8Uc 14
Weirdale Av. N20 —19Hb 23
Weird Wood. Long —69Ee 135
Weir Hall Av. N18 —23Tb 43
Weir Hall Gdns. N18 —22Tb 43
Weir Hall Rd. N18 & N17 —22Tb 43
Weir Pl. Stai —67G 118
Weir Rd. SW12 —60Lb 104
Weir Rd. SW19 —62Db 125
Weir Rd. Bex —59Dd 110
Weir Rd. Cher —73K 139
Weir Rd. W on T —72W 140
Weir's Pas. NW1 —41Mb 82 (3E 192)
Weiss Rd. SW15 —55Za 102
Welbeck Av. Brom —63Jc 129
Welbeck Av. Hay —42X 77
Welbeck Av. Sidc —60Wc 109
Welbeck Clo. N12 —22Fb 41
Welbeck Clo. Borwd —13Qa 21
Welbeck Clo. Eps —80Wa 144
Welbeck Clo. N Mald —71Va 144
Welbeck Rd. E6 —41Mc 85
Welbeck Rd. Barn —16Gb 23
Welbeck Rd. Harr —32Da 57
Welbeck Rd. Sutt & Cars —75Fb 145
Welbeck St. W1 —43Jb 82 (1J 197)
Welbeck Wlk. Cars —74Gb 145
Welbeck Way. W1 —44Kb 82 (2K 197)
Welbourne Rd. N17 —27Vb 43
Welby Ho. N19 —31Mb 62
Welby St. SE5 —53Rb 105
Welch Pl. Pinn —25X 37
Welcome Ct. Stanf —2L 93
Welcomes Rd. Kenl —89Tb 165
Welcome Ter. Whyt —88Vb 165
Welcote Dri. N'wd —23T 36
Welden. Slou —4N 73
Weldon Clo. Ruis —37X 57
Weldon Ct. N21 —15Pb 24
Weldon Dri. W Mol —70Ba 121
Weldon Way. Red —100Mb 180
Weld Pl. N11 —22Kb 42
Welfare Rd. E15 —38Gc 65
Welford Clo. E5 —34Zb 64
Welford Pl. SW19 —63Ab 124
Welham Rd. SW17 & SW16 —64Jb 126
Welhouse Rd. Cars —74Gb 145
Wellacre Rd. Harr —30Ka 38
Wellan Clo. Sidc —57Xc 109
Welland. E Til —9L 93
Welland Clo. Slou —51D 96
Welland Gdns. Gnfd —40Ha 58
Welland Ho. SE15 —56Yb 106
Welland M. E1 —46Wb 83
Wellands Clo. Brom —68Pc 130
Welland St. SE10 —51Ec 106
Well App. Barn —15Ya 22
Wellbrook Rd. Orp —77Qc 150
Wellby Ct. E13 —39Lc 65
Well Clo. SW16 —63Pb 126
Well Clo. Ruis —34Aa 57
Well Clo. Wok —5F 188
Wellclose Sq. E1 —45Wb 83
Wellcome Av. Dart —56Nd 111
Well Cottage Clo. E11 —30Lc 45
Well Ct. EC4 —44Sb 83 (3E 200)
Wellcroft Rd. Slou —6F 72
Welldon Ct. Harr —29Ga 38
Welldon Cres. Harr —29Ga 38
Well End Rd. Borwd —9Sa 7
Weller Ho. SE16 —47Wb 83
(off George Row)
Weller Pl. Orp —83Qc 168
Wellers Clo. W'ham —99Sc 184
Wellers Ct. NW1 —40Nb 62 (2F 193)
Wellers Gro. Chesh —1Wb 11
Weller St. SE1 —47Sb 83 (1D 206)
Wellesford Clo. Bans —89Bb 163
Wellesley Av. W6 —48Xa 80
Wellesley Av. Iver —48H 75
Wellesley Av. N'wd —22V 36
Wellesley Ct. NW2 —33Wa 60
Wellesley Ct. W9 —41Eb 81
(off Maida Vale)
Wellesley Ct. Sutt —74Ab 144
Wellesley Ct. Rd. Croy —75Tb 147
Wellesley Cres. Pot B —5Ab 8
Wellesley Cres. Twic —61Ga 122
Wellesley Gro. Croy —75Tb 147
Wellesley Lodge. Sutt —80Db 145
(off Worcester Rd.)
Wellesley Pde. Twic —62Ha 122
Wellesley Pk. M. Enf —12Rb 25
Wellesley Pl. NW1 —41Mb 82 (4D 192)
Wellesley Pl. NW5 —36Jb 62
Wellesley Rd. E11 —29Jc 45
Wellesley Rd. E17 —30Cc 44
Wellesley Rd. N22 —26Qb 42
Wellesley Rd. NW5 —36Jb 62
Wellesley Rd. W4 —50Qa 79
Wellesley Rd. Brtwd —18Yd 32
Wellesley Rd. Croy —74Sb 147
Wellesley Rd. Harr —29Ga 38
Wellesley Rd. Ilf —33Rc 66
Wellesley Rd. Slou —6L 73
Wellesley Rd. Sutt —79Eb 145
Wellesley Rd. Twic —62Fa 122
Wellesley St. E1 —43Zb 84
Wellesley Ter. N1 —41Sb 83 (3E 194)
Welley Av. Wray —56A 96
Welley Rd. Wray & Hort —58A 96
Well Farm Rd. Warl —91Wb 181
Well Field. Hart —70Be 135
Wellfield Av. N10 —27Kb 42
Wellfield Rd. SW16 —63Nb 126
Wellfields Rd. Lou —13Qc 28
Wellfield Wlk. SW16 —64Pb 126
Wellfit St. SE24 —55Rb 105
Wellgarth. Gnfd —37Ka 58
Wellgarth Rd. NW11 —32Db 61
Well Gro. N20 —18Eb 23
Well Hall Rd. SE9 —55Nc 108
Well Hill. Orp —79Dd 152
Well Hill La. Orp —79Dd 152
Wellhouse La. Barn —14Ya 22
Wellhouse Rd. Beck —70Cc 128
Welling High St. Well —55Xc 109
Wellings Ho. Hay —43Z 77
Welling Rd. Ors —4E 92
Wellington. N8 —28Nb 42
Wellington Av. E4 —19Cc 26
Wellington Av. N9 —20Xb 25
Wellington Av. N15 —30Vb 43
Wellington Av. Houn —57Ca 99
Wellington Av. Pinn —25Ba 37
Wellington Av. Sidc —58Wc 109
Wellington Av. Vir W —10M 117
Wellington Av. Wor Pk —76Ya 144
Wellington Bldgs. SW1 —50Kb 82
Wellington Clo. SE14 —53Zb 106
Wellington Clo. W11 —44Cb 81
Wellington Clo. Dag —38Ed 68
Wellington Clo. W on T —74V 140
Wellington Ct. NW8 —40Fb 61 (2B 190)
(off Wellington Rd.)
Wellington Ct. SW6 —53Db 103
(off Maltings Pl.)
Wellington Ct. Grays —46De 91
Wellington Ct. Hamp —64Fa 122
Wellington Ct. Pinn —25Ba 37
(off Wellington Rd.)
Wellington Ct. Stanw —59N 97
Wellington Cres. N Mald —69Sa 123
Wellington Dri. Dag —38Ed 68
Wellington Dri. Purl —81Pb 164
Wellington Est. E2 —40Yb 64
Wellington Gdns. SE7 —51Lc 107
Wellington Gdns. Twic —63Fa 122
Wellington Gro. SE10 —52Ec 107
Wellington Hill. Lou —9Jc 13
Wellington Ho. W5 —41Na 79
Wellingtonia Av. Hav —21Ed 48
Wellington Mans. E11 —32Cc 64
Wellington M. SE7 —51Lc 107
Wellington M. SE22 —56Wb 105
Wellington Pde. Sidc —57Wc 109
Wellington Pk. Est. NW2 —33Wa 60
Wellington Pl. N2 —30Gb 41
Wellington Pl. NW8 —41Fb 81 (3C 190)
Wellington Pl. War —22Yd 50
Wellington Rd. E6 —39Pc 66
Wellington Rd. E7 —35Hc 65
Wellington Rd. E10 —32Ac 64
Wellington Rd. E11 —29Jc 45
Wellington Rd. E17 —28Ac 44
Wellington Rd. NW8 —40Fb 61 (2C 190)
Wellington Rd. NW10 —41Za 80
Wellington Rd. SW19 —61Cb 125
Wellington Rd. W5 —48La 78
Wellington Rd. Ashf —60Ma 119
Wellington Rd. Belv —50Bd 87
Wellington Rd. Bex —57Zc 109
Wellington Rd. Brom —70Lc 129
Wellington Rd. Cat —94Sb 181
Wellington Rd. Croy —73Rb 147
Wellington Rd. Dart —58Ld 111
Wellington Rd. Enf —15Ub 25
Wellington Rd. Felt —57U 98
Wellington Rd. Hamp & Twic —64Fa 122
Wellington Rd. Harr —27Ga 38
Wellington Rd. Orp —72Xc 151
Wellington Rd. Pinn —25Ba 37
Wellington Rd. Til —4C 114
Wellington Rd. Uxb —39L 55
Wellington Rd. Wat —12X 19
Wellington Rd. N. Houn —55Ba 99
Wellington Rd. S. Houn —56Ba 99
Wellington Row. E2 —41Vb 83
Wellington Sq. SW3 —50Hb 81 (7F 203)
Wellington St. SE18 —49Qc 86
Wellington St. WC2 —45Nb 82 (4G 199)
Wellington St. Bark —39Sc 66
Wellington St. Grav —9E 114
Wellington St. Slou —7K 73
Wellington Ter. E1 —46Xb 83
Wellington Ter. W2 —45Cb 81
Wellington Ter. Harr —32Fa 58
Wellington Ter. Knap —6B 188
Wellington Way. E3 —41Cc 84
Wellington Way. Wey —82P 157
Welling Way. SE9 & Well —55Sc 108
Well La. SW14 —57Sa 101
Well La. N Stif —46Ae 91
Well La. Pil H —13Vd 32
Well La. Wok —5F 188
Wellmeade Dri. Sev —99Kd 187
Wellmeadow Rd. SE13 & SE6 (in two parts) —58Gc 107
Wellmeadow Rd. W7 —49Ja 78
Wellow Wlk. Cars —74Fb 145
Wellpath. Wok —5F 188
Well Pl. NW3 —34Fb 61
Well Rd. NW3 —34Fb 61
Well Rd. Barn —15Ya 22
Well Rd. N'thaw —1Gb 9
Well Rd. Otf —88Ld 171
Wells Clo. Bookh —96Ea 176
Wells Clo. N'holt —41Y 77
Wells Clo. Wind —3E 94
Wells Dri. NW9 —32Ta 59
Wells Gdns. Dag —36Dd 68
Wells Gdns. Ilf —31Nc 66
Wells Gdns. Rain —37Hd 68
Wells Ho. Bark —38Wc 67
(off Margaret Bondfield Av.)
Wells Ho. Eps —86Qa 161
Wells Ho. Rd. NW10 —43Ua 80
Wellside Clo. Barn —14Ya 22
Wellside Gdns. SW14 —56Sa 101
Wells La. Asc —10A 116
Wells M. W1 —43Lb 82 (1C 198)
Wellsmoor Gdns. Brom —69Qc 130
Wells Pk. Rd. SE26 —62Wb 127
Wells Path. N'holt —41U 76
Wellsprings Cres. Wemb —34Ra 59
Wells Rise. NW8 —39Hb 61 (1F 191)
Wells Rd. W12 —47Ya 80
Wells Rd. Brom —68Pc 130
Wells Rd. Eps —86Qa 161
Wells Sq. WC1 —41Pb 82 (4H 193)
Wells St. W1 —43Lb 82 (1B 198)
Wellstead Av. N9 —17Zb 26
Wellstead Rd. E6 —40Qc 66
Wells Ter. N4 —33Qb 62
Wells, The. N14 —18Mb 24
Wellstones. Wat —14X 19
Well St. E9 —38Yb 64
Well St. E15 —37Gc 65
Wells Way. SE5 —51Tb 105
Wells Way. SW7 —48Fb 81 (3B 202)
Wells Yd. N7 —36Qb 62
Wells Yd. Wat —13X 19
Well Wlk. NW3 —35Fb 61
Well Way. Eps —87Qa 161
Wellwood Clo. Coul —86Nb 164
Wellwood Rd. Ilf —32Wc 67
Welsford St. SE1 —50Wb 83
Welsh Clo. E13 —41Jc 85
Welshpool St. E8 —39Wb 63
Welshside. NW9 —29Ua 40
(off Goldsmith Av.)
Welsingham Lodge. SW13 —53Wa 102
Welsummer Way. Chesh —1Zb 12
Weltje Rd. W6 —49Wa 80
Welton Ct. SE5 —53Ub 105
Welton Rd. SE18 —52Uc 108
Welwyn Av. Felt —58V 98
Welwyn St. E2 —41Yb 84
Welwyn Way. Hay —42U 76
Wembley Commercial Cen. Wemb —33Ma 59
Wembley Hill Rd. Wemb —36Pa 59
Wembley Pk. Bus. Cen. Wemb —34Ra 59
Wembley Pk. Dri. Wemb —35Pa 59
Wembley Rd. Hamp —67Ca 121
Wembley Stadium Ind. Est. Wemb —35Ra 59
Wembley Way. Wemb —37Ra 59
Wemborough Rd. Stan —25Ka 38
Wembury Rd. N6 —31Kb 62
Wemyss Rd. SE3 —54Hc 107
Wendela Clo. Wok —90B 156
Wendela Ct. Harr —33Ga 58
Wendell Rd. W12 —48Va 80
Wendle Ct. SW8 —51Nb 104
Wendley Dri. New Haw —82H 157
Wendling Rd. Sutt —74Fb 145
Wendon St. E3 —39Bc 64
Wendover. SE17 (in two parts) —50Ub 83 (7H 207)
Wendover Clo. Hay —42Aa 77
Wendover Ct. NW2 —34Cb 61
Wendover Dri. N Mald —72Va 144
Wendover Gdns. Brtwd —20De 33
Wendover Ho. Wat —17U 18
(off Chenies Way)
Wendover Pl. Stai —64F 118
Wendover Rd. NW10 —40Va 60
Wendover Rd. SE9 —55Mc 107
Wendover Rd. Brom —69Kc 129
Wendover Rd. Burn —3A 72
Wendover Rd. Stai —64E 118
Wendover Way. Bush —16Ea 20
Wendover Way. Horn —36Ld 69
Wendover Way. St M —72Wc 151
Wendover Way. Well —57Wc 109
Wendron Clo. Wok —6D 188
Wend, The. Coul —86Mb 164
Wendy Clo. Enf —16Vb 25
Wendy Way. Wemb —39Na 59
Wenham Gdns. Hut —16Ee 33
Wenlack Clo. Den —34K 55
Wenlock Barn St. N1 —40Tb 63 (2F 195)
(off Wenlock St.)
Wenlock Ct. N1 —40Tb 63 (2F 195)
Wenlock Gdns. NW4 —28Wa 40
Wenlock Rd. N1 —40Sb 63 (2D 194)
Wenlock Rd. Edgw —24Ra 39
Wenlock St. N1 —40Sb 63 (2E 194)
Wennington Rd. E3 —40Zb 64
Wennington Rd. Rain —42Jd 88
Wensdale Ho. E5 —33Wb 63
Wensley Av. Wfd G —24Hc 45
Wensley Clo. SE9 —58Pc 108
Wensley Clo. Romf —22Cd 48
Wensleydale Av. Ilf —26Nc 46
Wensleydale Gdns. Hamp —66Da 121
Wensleydale Pas. Hamp —66Ca 121
Wensleydale Rd. Hamp —66Ca 121
Wensley Rd. N18 —23Xb 43
Wensum Way. Rick —18M 17
Wentbridge Path. Borwd —10Qa 7
Wentland Clo. SE6 —61Fc 129
Wentland Rd. SE6 —61Fc 129
Wentworth Av. N3 —24Cb 41
Wentworth Av. Els —15Pa 21
Wentworth Av. Slou —1E 72
Wentworth Clo. N3 —24Db 41
Wentworth Clo. Ashf —63R 120
Wentworth Clo. Grav —4C 136
Wentworth Clo. Hayes —75Jc 149
Wentworth Clo. Mord —73Cb 145
Wentworth Clo. Orp —78Uc 150
Wentworth Clo. Pot B —3Cb 9
Wentworth Clo. Rip —93K 173
Wentworth Clo. Surb —75Ma 143
Wentworth Clo. Wat —10V 4
Wentworth Ct. Twic —62Ga 122
Wentworth Cres. SE15 —52Wb 105
Wentworth Cres. Hay —48T 76
Wentworth Dri. Dart —58Jd 110
Wentworth Dri. Pinn —29W 36
Wentworth Dri. Vir W —10K 117
Wentworth Fields. Hay —40T 56
Wentworth Gdns. N13 —20Rb 25
Wentworth Hill. Wemb —32Pa 59
Wentworth Ho. Add —77K 139
Wentworth M. E3 —42Ac 84
Wentworth Pk. N3 —24Cb 41
Wentworth Pl. Grays —48Fe 91
Wentworth Pl. Stan —23Ka 38
Wentworth Rd. E12 —35Mc 65
Wentworth Rd. NW11 —30Bb 41
Wentworth Rd. Barn —13Za 22
Wentworth Rd. Croy —73Qb 146
Wentworth Rd. S'hall —49Y 77
Wentworth St. E1 —44Vb 83 (2K 201)
Wentworth Way. Pinn —28Aa 37
Wentworth Way. Rain —41Kd 89
Wentworth Way. S Croy —86Wb 165
Wenvoe Av. Bexh —54Dd 110
Wernbrook St. SE18 —51Sc 108
Werndee Rd. SE25 —70Wb 127
Wernett Hall Rd. Ilf —27Pc 46
Werrington St. NW1 —40Lb 62 (2C 192)
Werter Rd. SW15 —56Ab 102
Wesco Ct. Wok —88C 156
Wescott Way. Uxb —40L 55
Wesleyan Pl. NW5 —35Kb 62
Wesley Av. NW10 —41Ta 79
Wesley Av. Houn —54Aa 99
Wesley Clo. N7 —33Pb 62
Wesley Clo. SE17 —49Rb 83 (6C 206)
Wesley Clo. Chesh —1Sb 11
Wesley Clo. Harr —33Ea 58
Wesley Clo. Orp —69Yc 131
Wesley Dri. Egh —65C 118
Wesley Rd. E10 —31Ec 64
Wesley Rd. N2 —25Gb 41
Wesley Rd. NW10 —39Sa 59
Wesley Rd. Hay —45W 76
Wesley Sq. W11 —44Ab 80
Wesley St. W1 —43Jb 82 (1J 197)
Wessels. Tad —93Za 178
Wessex Av. SW19 —69Cb 125
Wessex Clo. Ilf —30Uc 46
Wessex Clo. King T —67Ra 123
Wessex Ct. Barn —14Za 22

Wessex Ct. Beck —67Ac 128
Wessex Ct. Stanw —58N 97
Wessex Dri. Eri —54Gd 110
Wessex Dri. Pinn —24Aa 37
Wessex Gdns. NW11 —32Ab 60
Wessex Ho. SE1 —50Vb 83 (7K 207)
Wessex La. Gnfd —40Fa 58
Wessex Rd. H'row A —56L 97
Wessex St. E2 —41Yb 84
Wessex Way. NW11 —32Ab 60
Westacott. Hay —43U 76
Westacott Clo. N19 —32Mb 62
W. Acres. Esh —80Ba 141
Westall Rd. Lou —13Rc 28
West App. Orp —71Sc 150
W. Arbour St. E1 —44Zb 84
West Av. E17 —28Dc 44
West Av. N2 —28Db 41
West Av. N3 —23Cb 41
West Av. NW4 —29Za 40
West Av. Hay —45V 76
West Av. Pinn —30Ba 37
West Av. S'hall —45Ba 77
West Av. Wall —78Nb 146
West Av. W Vill —81U 158
West Av. Rd. E17 —28Cc 44
West Bank. N16 —31Ub 63
West Bank. Bark —39Rc 66
West Bank. Enf —12Sb 25
Westbank Rd. Hamp —65Ea 122
W. Barnes La. N Mald & SW20 —71Xa 144
Westbeech Rd. N22 —27Qb 42
Westbere Dri. Stan —22Ma 39
Westbere Rd. NW2 —35Ab 60
Westbourne Av. W3 —44Ta 79
Westbourne Av. Sutt —75Ab 144
Westbourne Bri. W2 —43Eb 81
Westbourne Clo. Hay —42Y 77
Westbourne Cres. W2 —45Fb 81 (4B 196)
Westbourne Cres. M. W2 —45Fb 81 (4B 196)
(off Westbourne Cres.)
Westbourne Dri. SE23 —61Zb 128
Westbourne Dri. Brtwd —21Vd 50
Westbourne Gdns. W2 —44Db 81
Westbourne Gro. W11 & W2 —45Bb 81
Westbourne Gro. M. W11 —44Cb 81
Westbourne Gro. Ter. W2 —44Db 81
Westbourne Ho. Houn —51Ca 99
Westbourne Pde. Hil —42R 76
Westbourne Pk. M. W2 —44Db 81
Westbourne Pk. Pas. W2 —43Cb 81
Westbourne Pk. Rd. W11 & W2 —44Ab 80
Westbourne Pk. Vs. W2 —43Cb 81
Westbourne Pl. N9 —20Xb 25
Westbourne Rd. N7 —37Pb 62
Westbourne Rd. SE26 —65Zb 128
Westbourne Rd. Bexh —52Ad 109
Westbourne Rd. Croy —72Vb 147
Westbourne Rd. Felt —62V 120
Westbourne Rd. Stai —66K 119
Westbourne Rd. Uxb —42R 76
Westbourne St. W2 —45Fb 81 (4B 196)
Westbourne Ter. W2 —44Eb 81 (2A 196)
Westbourne Ter. M. W2 —44Eb 81 (2A 196)
Westbourne Ter. Rd. W2 —43Db 81
Westbridge Rd. SW11 —53Fb 103
Westbrook Av. Hamp —66Ba 121
Westbrook Clo. Barn —13Fb 23
Westbrook Cres. Barn —13Fb 23
Westbrook Dri. Orp —74Zc 151
Westbrooke Cres. Well —55Yc 109
Westbrooke Rd. Sidc —61Tc 130
Westbrooke Rd. Well —55Xc 109
Westbrook Rd. SE3 —53Kc 107
Westbrook Rd. Houn —52Ba 99
Westbrook Rd. Stai —64H 119
Westbrook Rd. T Hth —67Tb 127
Westbrook Sq. Barn —13Fb 23
Westbury Av. N22 —27Rb 43
Westbury Av. Clay —79Ha 142
Westbury Av. S'hall —42Ca 77
Westbury Av. Wemb —38Na 59
Westbury Clo. Ruis —31W 56
Westbury Clo. Shep —72R 140
Westbury Clo. Whyt —90Vb 165
Westbury Ct. Bark —39Tc 66
(off Westbury Rd.)
Westbury Dri. Brtwd —19Yd 32
Westbury Gro. N12 —23Cb 41
Westbury Ho. E17 —28Bc 44
Westbury La. Buck H —19Lc 27
Westbury Lodge Clo. Pinn —27Z 37
Westbury Pl. Bren —51Ma 101
Westbury Rd. E7 —37Kc 65
Westbury Rd. E17 —28Cc 44
Westbury Rd. N11 —23Nb 42
Westbury Rd. N12 —23Cb 41
Westbury Rd. SE20 —67Zb 128
Westbury Rd. W5 —44Na 79
Westbury Rd. Bark —39Tc 66
Westbury Rd. Beck —69Ac 128
Westbury Rd. Brtwd —19Yd 32
Westbury Rd. Brom —67Mc 129
Westbury Rd. Buck H —19Lc 27
Westbury Rd. Croy —72Tb 147
Westbury Rd. Felt —60Z 99
Westbury Rd. Ilf —33Qc 66
Westbury Rd. N Mald —70Ta 123
Westbury Rd. N'wd —21U 36
Westbury Rd. Wat —15X 19
Westbury Rd. Wemb —38Na 59
Westbury St. SW8 —54Lb 104
Westbury Ter. E7 —37Kc 65
Westbury Ter. Upm —33Ud 70
Westbury Ter. W'ham —99Sc 184
Westcar La. W on T —79X 141
W. Carriage Dri. W2 —45Gb 81 (5D 196)
W. Central St. WC1 —44Nb 82 (2F 199)
W. Centre Av. NW10 —42Xa 80
W. Chantry. Harr —25Da 37
Westchester Dri. NW4 —27Za 40
West Clo. N9 —20Vb 25
West Clo. Ashf —63N 119
West Clo. Barn —15Xa 22
West Clo. Cockf —14Jb 24
West Clo. Gnfd —40Ea 58
West Clo. Hamp —65Aa 121
West Clo. Rain —42Kd 89
West Clo. Wemb —32Pa 59
Westcombe Av. Croy —73Nb 146
Westcombe Dri. Barn —15Cb 23
Westcombe Hill. SE3 —52Jc 107
Westcombe Lodge Dri. Hay —43T 76
Westcombe Pk. Rd. SE3 —51Gc 107
West Comn. Ger X —29A 34
West Comn. Clo. Ger X —29A 34
West Comn. Rd. Hayes —75Jc 149
West Comn. Rd. Uxb —37M 55
Westcoombe Av. SW20 —67Va 124
Westcote Rise. Ruis —31S 56
Westcote Rd. SW16 —64Lb 126
West Cotts. NW6 —36Cb 61
Westcott Av. Grav —2C 136
Westcott Clo. N15 —30Vb 43
Westcott Clo. Brom —71Nc 150
Westcott Clo. New Ad —81Dc 166
Westcott Cres. W7 —44Ga 78
Westcott Ho. E14 —45Cc 84
Westcott Rd. SE17 —51Rb 105
Westcott Way. Sutt —82Ya 162
West Ct. E17 —28Dc 44
West Ct. Houn —52Ea 100
West Ct. Wemb —33La 58
Westcourt La. Grav —10H 115
Westcourt Pde. Grav —2H 137
West Cres. Wind —3D 94
West Cres. Rd. Grav —8D 114
Westcroft. Slou —2F 72
Westcroft Clo. NW2 —35Ab 60
Westcroft Clo. Enf —10Yb 12
Westcroft Gdns. Mord —70Bb 125
Westcroft Rd. Cars & Wall —77Jb 146
Westcroft Sq. W6 —49Wa 80
Westcroft Way. NW2 —35Ab 60
W. Cromwell Rd. W14 & SW5 —50Bb 81
W. Cross Cen. Bren —51Ja 100
W. Cross Route. W10, W11 & W12 —45Za 80
W. Cross Way. Bren —51Ka 100
Westdale Pas. SE18 —51Rc 108
Westdale Rd. SE18 —51Rc 108
Westdean Av. SE12 —60Kc 107
W. Dean Clo. SW18 —58Db 103
West Dene. Sutt —79Ab 144
W. Dene Dri. H Hill —22Md 49
W. Dene Way. Wey —76U 140
West Down. Bookh —99Da 175
Westdown Rd. E15 —35Ec 64
Westdown Rd. SE6 —59Cc 106
W. Drayton Pk. Av. W Dray —48N 75
W. Drayton Rd. Uxb —44R 76
West Dri. SW16 —63Lb 126
West Dri. Cars —82Fb 163
West Dri. Harr —23Fa 38
West Dri. Sutt —81Za 162
West Dri. Tad —90Za 162
West Dri. Wat —8X 5
West Dri. Gdns. Harr —23Fa 38
W. Eaton Pl. SW1 —49Jb 82 (5H 203)
W. Eaton Pl. M. SW1 —49Jb 82 (5H 203)
(off W. Eaton Pl.)
W. Ella Rd. NW10 —38Ua 60
West End. Bras —97Xc 185
West End. Kems —89Pd 171
W. End Av. E10 —29Fc 45
W. End Av. Pinn —28Z 37
W. End Ct. Hedg —9K 53
W. End Ct. Pinn —28Z 37
W. End Gdns. Esh —78Ba 141
W. End Gdns. N'holt —40Y 57
W. End La. NW6 —36Cb 61
W. End La. Barn —14Za 22
W. End La. Esh —80Ba 141
W. End La. Hay —52S 98
W. End La. Pinn —27Z 37
W. End La. Stoke P —9J 53
W. End Rd. Ruis & N'holt —33U 56
W. End Rd. S'hall —46Aa 77
Westerdale Rd. SE10 —50Jc 85
Westerfield Rd. N15 —29Vb 43
Westerfolds Clo. Wok —89E 156
Westergate Rd. SE2 —51Ad 109
Westerham Av. N9 —20Tb 25
Westerham Clo. Add —79L 139
Westerham Clo. Sutt —82Cb 163
Westerham Dri. Sidc —58Xc 109
Westerham Hill. W'ham —93Rc 184
Westerham Ho. SE1
(off Law St.) —48Tb 83 (3G 207)
Westerham Lodge. Beck —66Cc 128
(off Park Rd.)
Westerham Rd. E10 —31Dc 64
Westerham Rd. Kes —80Mc 149
Westerham Rd. Oxt —100Hc 183
Westerham Rd. Sev —95Dd 186
Westerham Rd. W'ham —97Vc 185
Westerley Cres. SE26 —64Bc 128
Western Av. NW11 —30Za 40
Western Av. Brtwd —18Yd 32
Western Av. Cher —69J 119
Western Av. Dag —37Ed 68
Western Av. Egh —69D 118
Western Av. Epp —4Vc 15
Western Av. Gnfd & W5 & W3 —39Da 57
Western Av. Romf —26Ld 49
Western Av. Ruis & N'holt —37T 56
Western Av. Uxb —35K 55
Western Clo. Cher —69J 119
Western Ct. N3 —23Cb 41
Western Ct. Romf —29Gd 48
(off Chandlers Way)
Western Cross Clo. Grnh —58Yd 112
Western Dri. Shep —72T 140
Western Gdns. W5 —45Qa 79
Western Gdns. Brtwd —19Yd 32
Western Gateway. E16 —45Jc 85
Western International Mkt. S'hall —49X 77
Western La. SW12 —59Jb 104
Western M. W9 —42Bb 81
Western Pde. New Bar —15Cb 23
Western Pathway. Horn —38Kd 69
Western Perimeter Rd. W Dray & H'row A —54K 97
Western Pl. SE16 —47Yb 84
Western Rd. E13 —40Lc 65
Western Rd. E17 —29Ec 44
Western Rd. N2 —28Hb 41
Western Rd. N22 —26Pb 42
Western Rd. NW10 —42Sa 79
Western Rd. SW9 —55Qb 104
Western Rd. SW19 & Mitc —67Fb 125
Western Rd. W5 —45Ma 79
Western Rd. Brtwd —19Yd 32
Western Rd. Epp —4Vc 15
Western Rd. Romf —29Gd 48
Western Rd. S'hall —49Y 77
Western Rd. Sutt —78Cb 145
Western View. Hay —47V 76
Westernville Gdns. Ilf —31Sc 66
Western Way. SE28 —47Uc 86
Western Way. Barn —16Cb 23
W. Farm Av. Asht —90La 160
W. Farm Clo. Asht —91La 176
W. Farm Dri. Asht —91Ma 177
Westferry Cir. E14 —46Bc 84
Westferry Rd. E14 —45Cc 84
Westfield. Asht —90Pa 161
Westfield. Lou —15Mc 27
Westfield. New Ash —76Be 155
Westfield. Sev —94Ld 187
Westfield Av. S Croy —85Tb 165
Westfield Av. Wat —10Z 5
Westfield Av. Wok —93A 172
Westfield Clo. Enf —13Ac 26
Westfield Clo. Grav —4E 136
Westfield Clo. Sutt —77Bb 145
Westfield Clo. Wal X —3Bc 12
Westfield Comn. Wok —94A 172
Westfield Dri. Bookh —94Da 175
Westfield Dri. Harr —28Ma 39
Westfield Gdns. Harr —28Ma 39
Westfield Gro. Wok —92A 172
Westfield La. Harr —28Ma 39
(in two parts)
Westfield La. Wex —4P 73
Westfield Pde. New Haw —82M 157
Westfield Pk. Pinn —24Ba 37
Westfield Rd. NW7 —20Ta 21
Westfield Rd. W13 —46Ja 78
Westfield Rd. Beck —68Bc 128
Westfield Rd. Bexh —55Ed 110
Westfield Rd. Croy —75Rb 147
Westfield Rd. Dag —35Ad 67
Westfield Rd. Mitc —68Hb 125
Westfield Rd. Slou —2F 72
Westfield Rd. Surb —71Ma 143
Westfield Rd. Sutt —77Bb 145
Westfield Rd. W on T —73Aa 141
Westfield Rd. Wok —10G 188
Westfields. SW13 —55Va 102
Westfields Av. SW13 —55Ua 102
Westfield Sq. Wok —94A 172
Westfields Rd. W3 —43Ra 79
Westfield St. SE18 —48Mc 85
Westfield Wlk. Wal X —3Bc 12
Westfield Way. E1 —41Ac 84
Westfield Way. Ruis —34U 56
Westfield Way. Wok —94A 172
W. Garden Pl. W2 —44Gb 81 (3E 196)
West Gdns. E1 —45Xb 83
West Gdns. SW17 —65Gb 125
West Gdns. Eps —82Ua 162
Westgate. W5 —41Na 79
Westgate Clo. Eps —87Ta 161
Westgate Ct. SW9 —55Qb 104
(off Canterbury Cres.)
Westgate Ct. Wal X —7Zb 12
Westgate Cres. Slou —5D 72
Westgate Rd. SE25 —70Xb 127
Westgate Rd. Beck —67Ec 128
Westgate Rd. Dart —58Md 111
(in two parts)
Westgate St. E8 —39Xb 63
Westgate Ter. SW10 —50Db 81
Westglade Ct. Kent —29Ma 39
West Grn. Pl. Gnfd —39Fa 58
West Grn. Rd. N15 —28Rb 43
West Gro. SE10 —53Ec 106
West Gro. W on T —78X 141
West Gro. Wfd G —23Lc 45
Westgrove La. SE10 —53Ec 106
W. Halkin St. SW1 —48Jb 82 (3H 203)
W. Hallowes. SE9 —60Mc 107
Westhall Pk. Warl —91Yb 182
W. Hall Rd. Rich —53Ra 101
Westhall Rd. Warl —90Wb 165
W. Ham La. E15 —38Fc 65
W. Hampstead M. NW6 —37Db 61
W. Harding St. EC4 —44Qb 82 (2A 200)
Westharold. Swan —69Fd 132
W. Hatch Mnr. Ruis —32V 56
Westhay Gdns. SW14 —57Ra 101
W. Heath Av. NW11 —32Cb 61
W. Heath Clo. NW3 —34Cb 61
W. Heath Clo. Dart —58Hd 110
W. Heath Cotts. Sev —100Kd 187
W. Heath Ct. NW11 —32Cb 61
W. Heath Dri. NW11 —32Cb 61
W. Heath Gdns. NW3 —34Cb 61
W. Heath La. Sev —100Kd 187
W. Heath Rd. NW3 —33Cb 61
W. Heath Rd. SE2 —51Zc 109
W. Heath Rd. Dart —58Hd 110
West Hill. SW15 & SW18 —59Za 102
West Hill. Dart —58Ld 111
West Hill. Eps —85Ra 161
West Hill. Harr —33Ga 58
West Hill. Orp —84Pc 168
West Hill. S Croy —82Ub 165
West Hill. Wemb —32Pa 59
W. Hill Av. Eps —85Ra 161
Westhill Clo. Grav —10D 114
W. Hill Ct. N6 —34Jb 62
W. Hill Ct. Eps —85Ra 161
(off Court La.)
W. Hill Dri. Dart —58Ld 111
Westhill Pk. N6 —33Hb 61
(in two parts)
W. Hill Rise. Dart —58Md 111
W. Hill Rd. SW18 —58Bb 103
W. Hill Rd. Wok —7G 188
W. Hill Way. N20 —18Db 23
Westholm. NW11 —28Db 41
W. Holme. Eri —53Ed 110
Westholme. Orp —73Uc 150
Westholme Gdns. Ruis —32W 56
W. Horndon Ind. Pk. W Horn —30Ee 51
Westhorne Av. SE12 & SE9 —59Jc 107
Westhorpe Gdns. NW4 —27Ya 40
Westhorpe Rd. SW15 —55Ya 102
West Ho. Clo. SW19 —60Ab 102
West Ho. Cotts. Pinn —28Z 37
Westhurst Dri. Chst —64Rc 130
W. Hyde La. Ger X —24B 34
W. India Av. E14 —46Cc 84
W. India Dock Rd. E14 —45Bc 84
W. Kensington Ct. W14 —50Bb 81
(off Edith Vs.)
W. Kensington Mans. W14
(off Beaumont Cres.) —50Bb 81
W. Kent Av. Grav —58Ee 113
W. Kingsdown Ind. Est. W King —80Ud 154
Westlake Clo. N13 —20Qb 24
Westlake Clo. Hay —42Aa 77
Westlake Rd. Wemb —33Ma 59
Westland Av. Horn —32Nd 69
Westland Clo. Stai —58N 97
Westland Dri. Brom —75Hc 149
Westland Ho. E16 —46Qc 86
(off Rymill St.)
Westland Pl. N1 —41Tb 83 (3F 195)
Westland Rd. Wat —12X 19
Westlands Av. Slou —4A 72
Westlands Clo. Hay —49W 76
Westlands Clo. Slou —4A 72
Westlands Ct. Eps —87Sa 161
Westlands Ter. SW12 —58Lb 104
Westlands Way. Oxt —99Fc 183
Westland View. Grays —46Ce 91
West La. SE16 —47Xb 83
Westlea Av. Wat —9Aa 5
Westlea Rd. W7 —48Ja 78
Westleigh Av. SW15 —57Xa 102
Westleigh Av. Coul —88Kb 164
Westleigh Ct. E11 —29Jc 45
Westleigh Dri. Brom —67Nc 130
Westleigh Gdns. Edgw —25Qa 39
W. Lodge Av. W3 —46Qa 79
Westlyn Clo. Rain —42Ld 89
Westmacott Dri. Felt —60V 98
W. Malling Way. Horn —36Ld 69
Westmead. SW15 —58Xa 102
West Mead. Eps —79Ua 144
West Mead. Ruis —35Y 57
Westmead. Wind —5F 94
Westmead. Wok —5E 188
Westmead Corner. Cars —77Gb 145
Westmead Clo. Chesh —1Xb 11
Westmead Rd. Sutt —77Fb 145
Westmede. Chig —23Sc 46
Westmere Dri. NW7 —20Ta 21
West M. N17 —23Xb 43
West M. SW1 —49Lb 82 (6B 204)
(off W. Warwick Pl.)
West Mill. Grav —8B 114
Westmill Ct. N4 —33Sb 63
(off Brownswood Rd.)
Westminster Av. T Hth —68Rb 127
Westminster Bri. SW1 & SE1 —47Nb 82 (2G 205)
Westminster Bri. Rd. SE1 —47Pb 82 (2H 205)
Westminster Bus. Sq. SE11 —50Pb 82
Westminster Clo. Ilf —26Tc 46
Westminster Clo. Tedd —64Ja 122
Westminster Ct. E11 —30Jc 45
(off Cambridge Pk.)
Westminster Ct. Chesh —5Bc 12
Westminster Ct. Wok —93C 172
Westminster Dri. N13 —22Nb 42
Westminster Gdns. E4 —18Gc 27
Westminster Gdns. Bark —40Uc 66
Westminster Gdns. Ilf —26Sc 46
Westminster Ho. Har W —24Ha 38
Westminster Ind. Est. SE18 —48Mc 85
Westminster Rd. N9 —18Xb 25
Westminster Rd. W7 —46Ga 78
Westminster Rd. Sutt —75Fb 145
Westmoat Clo. Beck —66Ec 128
Westmont Rd. Esh —75Ga 142
Westmoor Gdns. Enf —12Zb 26
Westmoor Rd. Enf —12Zb 26
Westmoor St. SE7 —48Lc 85
Westmore Grn. Tats —92Lc 183
Westmoreland Av. Horn —29Ld 49
Westmoreland Av. Well —56Uc 108
Westmoreland Pl. SW1 —50Kb 82 (7A 204)
Westmoreland Pl. W5 —43Ma 79
Westmoreland Pl. Brom —69Jc 129
Westmoreland Rd. NW9 —27Pa 39
Westmoreland Rd. SE17 —51Tb 105
Westmoreland Rd. SW13 —53Va 102
Westmoreland Rd. Brom —71Gc 149
Westmoreland St. W1 —43Jb 82 (1J 197)
Westmoreland Ter. SW1 —50Kb 82 (7A 204)
Westmoreland Wlk. SE17 —51Tb 105
Westmore Rd. Tats —93Lc 183
Westmorland Clo. E12 —33Mc 65
Westmorland Clo. Eps —82Ua 162
Westmorland Clo. Twic —58Ka 100
Westmorland Ct. Surb —73Ma 143
Westmorland Dri. Sutt —80Db 145
Westmorland Rd. E17 —30Cc 44
Westmorland Rd. Harr —29Da 37
Westmorland St. W1 —43Jb 82
Westmorland Ter. SE20 —66Xb 127
Westmorland Way. Mitc —71Mb 146
Westmount Rd. SE9 —54Pc 108
West Oak. Beck —67Fc 129
Westoe Rd. N9 —19Xb 25
Weston Av. Add —77K 139
Weston Av. Th Dit —73Ga 142
Weston Av. W Mol —70Aa 121
Weston Av. W Thur —51Vd 112
Westonbirt Ct. SE15 —51Vb 105
(off Ebley Clo.)
Weston Clo. Coul —92Pb 180
Weston Clo. Hut —17Ee 33
Weston Ct. N4 —34Sb 63
Weston Dri. Stan —25Ka 38
Westone Mans. Bark —38Vc 67
(off Upney La.)
Weston Gdns. Iswth —53Ga 100
Weston Gdns. Wok —88G 156
Weston Grn. Dag —35Ad 67
Weston Grn. Th Dit —74Ga 142
(in two parts)
Weston Grn. Rd. Esh & Th Dit —74Fa 142
Weston Gro. Brom —67Hc 129
Weston Ho. E9 —39Yb 64
(off King Edwards Rd.)
Westonia Ct. Enf —8Zb 12
Weston Lea. Ock —97T 174
Weston Pk. N8 —30Nb 42
Weston Pk. King T —68Na 123
Weston Pk. Th Dit —74Ga 142
Weston Pk. Clo. Th Dit —74Ga 142
Weston Rise. WC1 —41Pb 82 (3J 193)
Weston Rd. W4 —48Sa 79
Weston Rd. Brom —66Hc 129
Weston Rd. Dag —35Ad 67
Weston Rd. Enf —11Tb 25
Weston Rd. Eps —83Ua 162
Weston Rd. Slou —3D 72
Weston Rd. Th Dit —74Ga 142
Weston St. SE1 —47Ub 83 (3G 207)
(in three parts)
Weston Wlk. E8 —38Xb 63
Weston Way. Wok —88G 156
Westover Clo. Sutt —81Db 163
Westover Hill. NW3 —33Cb 61
Westover Rd. SW18 —59Eb 103
Westow Hill. SE19 —65Ub 127
Westow St. SE19 —65Ub 127
West Pal. Gdns. Wey —76R 140
West Pk. SE9 —61Nc 130
West Pk. Av. Rich —53Ra 101
West Pk. Clo. Houn —51Ba 99
West Pk. Clo. Romf —29Zc 47
West Pk. Hill. Brtwd —20Wd 32
West Pk. Rd. Eps —84Pa 161
West Pk. Rd. Rich —53Qa 101
West Pk. Rd. S'hall —46Ea 78
West Pier. E1 —46Xb 83
West Pl. SW19 —64Ya 124
W. Point. Slou —6B 72
Westpoint Trading Est. W3 —43Qa 79
Westpole Av. Barn —14Jb 24
Westport Rd. E13 —42Kc 85
Westport St. E1 —44Zb 84
W. Poultry Av. EC1 —43Rb 83 (1B 200)
W. Quarters. W12 —44Wa 80
West Quay. SW10 —53Eb 103
W. Quay Dri. Hay —43Aa 77
West Ramp. Houn —53Q 98
W. Ridge Gdns. Gnfd —40Ea 58
W. Riding. Brick —2Ba 5
West Rd. E15 —39Hc 65
West Rd. N2 —26Fb 41
West Rd. N17 —23Xb 43
West Rd. SW3 —50Hb 81
West Rd. SW4 —57Mb 104
West Rd. W5 —43Na 79
West Rd. Barn —18Jb 24
West Rd. Chad —30Zc 47
West Rd. Chess —84La 160
West Rd. Felt —58T 98
West Rd. King T —67Sa 123
West Rd. Rush —31Fd 68
West Rd. S Ock —41Wd 90
West Rd. W Dray —48P 75
West Rd. Wey —81R 158
Westrow. SW15 —58Ya 102
West Row. W10 —42Ab 80
Westrow Dri. Bark —37Vc 67
Westrow Gdns. Ilf —33Vc 67
W. Shaw. Long —68Zd 135
W. Sheen Vale. Rich —56Pa 101
Westside. N2 —27Hb 41
West Side. NW4 —26Xa 40
W. Side Comn. SW19 —64Ya 124
W. Smithfield. EC1 —43Rb 83 (1B 200)
West Sq. SE11 —48Rb 83 (4B 206)
West Sq. Iver —44H 75
West St. E2 —40Xb 63
West St. E11 —34Gc 65
West St. WC2 —44Mb 82 (3E 198)
West St. Bexh —55Bd 109
West St. Bren —51La 100
West St. Brom —67Jc 129
West St. Cars —76Hb 145
West St. Croy —77Sb 147
West St. Eps —85Sa 161
West St. Eri —49Fd 88
West St. Ewe —82Ua 162
West St. Grav —8C 114
West St. Grays —51Ce 113
West St. Harr —32Fa 58
West St. Sutt —78Db 145
West St. Wat —12X 19
West St. La. Cars —77Hb 145
W. Temple Sheen. SW14 —57Ra 101
W. Tenter St. E1 —44Vb 83
West Ter. Sidc —60Uc 108
W. Thurrock Way. W Thur —49Vd 90
W. Towers. Pinn —30Z 37
West View. NW4 —28Ya 40
West View. Felt —59S 98
West View. Lou —14Pc 28
W. View Av. Whyt —90Vb 165
W. View Clo. NW10 —36Va 60
Westview Clo. W7 —44Ga 78
Westview Clo. W10 —44Ya 80
Westview Clo. Rain —41Ld 89
W. View Ct. Els —16Ma 21
Westview Cres. N9 —17Ub 25
Westview Dri. Wfd G —26Mc 45
W. View Gdns. Els —16Ma 21
W. View Rd. Crock —72Fd 152
W. View Rd. Dart —58Pd 111
W. View Rd. Swan —70Jd 132
W. View Rd. Warl —91Xb 181
Westville Rd. W12 —47Wa 80
Westville Rd. Th Dit —74Ja 142
West Wlk. Barn —17Jb 24
West Wlk. Hay —46W 76
Westward Rd. E4 —22Bc 44
Westward Way. Harr —30Na 39
W. Warwick Pl. SW1 —49Lb 82 (6B 204)
Westway. N18 —21Tb 43
West Way. NW10 —34Ta 59
Westway. SW20 —70Xa 124
Westway. W2 —43Db 81 (1A 196)
Westway. W12, W10 & W2 —45Va 80
West Way. Brtwd —20Wd 32
West Way. Cars —82Fb 163
Westway. Cat —94Tb 181
West Way. Croy —75Ac 148
West Way. Edgw —23Ra 39
West Way. Houn —53Ba 99
Westway. Orp —71Tc 150
West Way. Pinn —28Z 37
West Way. Rick —18K 17
West Way. Ruis —32V 56
West Way. Shep —72T 140
West Way. Wal A —8Dc 12
West Way. W Wick —72Fc 149
Westway Clo. SW20 —69Xa 124
Westway Ct. N'holt —39Ca 57
W. Way Gdns. Croy —75Zb 148
Westways. Eps —77Va 144
Westways. N'wd —26W 36
Westways. W'ham —98Sc 184
Westwell Clo. Orp —74Zc 151
Westwell M. SW16 —65Nb 126
Westwell Rd. SW16 —65Nb 126
Westwell Rd. App. SW16 —65Nb 126
Westwick Gdns. W14 —47Za 80
Westwick Gdns. Houn —54X 99
Westwick Pl. Wat —6Y 5
Westwood Av. SE19 —67Tb 127
Westwood Av. Brtwd —21Wd 50
Westwood Av. Harr —35Da 57
Westwood Av. Wdhm —84H 157
Westwood Clo. Amer —11A 16
Westwood Clo. Brom —69Mc 129
Westwood Clo. Esh —76Fa 142
Westwood Clo. Pot B —2Cb 9
Westwood Clo. Ruis —30R 36
Westwood Ct. Gnfd —36Fa 58
Westwood Ct. Wemb —35Ka 58
Westwood Dri. Amer —11A 16
Westwood Gdns. SW13 —55Va 102
Westwood Hill. SE26 —64Wb 127
Westwood La. Sidc —57Wc 109
Westwood La. Well —55Vc 109
Westwood Pk. SE23 —59Xb 105
Westwood Pk. Trading Est. W3 —43Ra 79
Westwood Rd. E16 —46Kc 85
Westwood Rd. SW13 —55Va 102
Westwood Rd. Coul —90Mb 164
Westwood Rd. Ilf —32Vc 67
Westwood Rd. S'fleet —66Ae 135
W. Woodside. Bex —60Ad 109
Westwood Way. Sev —94Hd 186
W. Yoke Rd. New Ash —76Ae 155
Wetheral Dri. Stan —25Ka 38
Wetherby Clo. N'holt —37Da 57
Wetherby Gdns. SW5 —49Eb 81
Wetherby Mans. SW5 —50Db 81
(off Earl's Ct. Sq.)

Wetherby M.—Wildmarsh Ct.

Wetherby M. SW5 —50Db 81
Wetherby Pl. SW7 —49Eb 81 (6A 202)
Wetherby Rd. Borwd —11Na 21
Wetherby Rd. Enf —11Sb 25
Wetherby Way. Chess —80Na 143
Wetherden St. E17 —31Bc 64
Wethered Dri. Burn —3A 72
Wetherell Rd. E9 —39Zb 64
Wetherill Rd. N10 —25Jb 42
Wetsted La. Swan —73Jd 152
Wettern Clo. S Croy —82Ub 165
Wevell Ho. N6 —31Jb 62
(off Hillcrest)
Wexfenne Gdns. Wok —88K 157
Wexford Rd. SW12 —59Hb 103
Wexham Ct. Wex —4N 73
Wexham Pk. La. Wex —2N 73
Wexham Rd. Slou & Wex —7L 73
Wexham St. Wex —2M 73
Wexham Woods. Wex —3N 73
Weybank. Wis —88N 157
Weybarton. Byfl —85P 157
Weybourne Pl. S Croy —82Tb 165
Weybourne St. SW18 —61Eb 125
Weybridge Bus. Pk. Add —77N 139
Weybridge Pk. Wey —78Q 140
Weybridge Rd. Add —77M 139
Weybridge Rd. T Hth —70Qb 126
Weybridge Trading Est. Add —77N 139
Weybrook Dri. Guild —100D 172
Wey Clo. W Byf —85K 157
Wey Ct. Eps —77Sa 143
Wey Ct. New Haw —81M 157
Weydown Clo. SW19 —60Ab 102
Weylands Clo. W on T —74Ba 141
Weylands Pk. Wey —79T 140
Weylond Rd. Dag —34Bd 67
Wey Mnr. Rd. New Haw —81M 157
Weyman Rd. SE3 —53Lc 107
Weymarks, The. N17 —23Tb 43
Weymead Clo. Cher —74L 139
Wey Meadows. Add —78N 139
Weymede. Byfl —84P 157
Weymouth Av. NW7 —22Ua 40
Weymouth Av. W5 —48La 78
Weymouth Ct. Sutt —80Cb 145
Weymouth M. W1 —43Kb 82 (7K 191)
Weymouth Rd. Hay —41U 76
Weymouth St. W1 —43Jb 82 (1J 197)
Weymouth Ter. E2 —40Vb 63 (1K 195)
Weymouth Wlk. Stan —23Ja 38
Wey Rd. Wey —76P 139
Weyside Clo. Byfl —84P 157
Weystone Rd. Add —77P 139
Whadcoat St. N4 —33Qb 62
Whalebone Av. Romf —30Bd 47
Whalebone Ct. EC2 —44Tb 83 (2F 201)
(off Telegraph St.)
Whalebone Gro. Romf —30Bd 47
Whalebone La. E15 —38Gc 65
Whalebone La. N. Romf —24Ad 47
Whalebone La. S. Romf & Dag —31Bd 67
Whales Yd. E15 —38Gc 65
(off W. Ham La.)
Whaley Rd. Pot B —5Eb 9
Wharf Clo. Stanf —2M 93
Wharfdale Rd. N1 —40Nb 62 (1G 193)
Wharfedale Ct. E5 —35Ac 64
Wharfedale Gdns. T Hth —70Pb 126
Wharfedale Rd. Dart —60Sd 112
Wharfedale St. SW10 —50Db 81
Wharf La. Rick —18N 17
Wharf La. Send —95E 172
Wharf La. Twic —60Ja 100
Wharf La. Wis —90M 157
Wharf Pl. E2 —39Xb 63
Wharf Rd. E15 —39Fc 65
Wharf Rd. N1 —40Sb 63 (2D 194)
Wharf Rd. Brtwd —20Yd 32
Wharf Rd. Enf —16Ac 26
Wharf Rd. Grav —8G 114
Wharf Rd. Grays —51Be 113
Wharf Rd. Stanf —2M 93
Wharf Rd. Wray —9N 95
Wharf Rd. Ind. Est. Enf —16Ac 26
Wharf Rd. S. Grays —51Be 113
Wharfside Rd. E16 —43Gc 85
Wharf St. E16 —43Gc 85
Wharncliffe Dri. S'hall —46Fa 78
Wharncliffe Gdns. SE25 —68Ub 127
Wharncliffe Rd. SE25 —68Ub 127
Wharton Clo. NW10 —37Ua 60
Wharton Cotts. WC1 —41Qb 82 (4K 193)
Wharton Rd. Brom —67Kc 129
Wharton St. WC1 —41Pb 82 (4J 193)
Whateley Rd. SE20 —66Zb 128
Whateley Rd. SE22 —57Vb 105
Whatley Av. SW20 —69Za 124
Whatman Rd. SE23 —59Zb 106
Whatmore Clo. Stai —58J 97
Wheatash Rd. Add —75K 139
Wheatcroft. Chesh —1Xb 11
Wheatfield Ct. Wal A —6Jc 13
(off Farthingale La.)
Wheatfields. E6 —44Rc 86
Wheatfields. Enf —11Ac 26
Wheatfield Way. King T —68Na 123
Wheathill Rd. SE20 —68Xb 127
Wheat Knoll. Kenl —88Sb 165
Wheatland Rd. Stan —23Ha 38
Wheatlands. Houn —51Ca 99
Wheatlands Rd. SW17 —62Jb 126
Wheatley Clo. NW4 —26Wa 40
Wheatley Clo. Grnh —57Wd 112
Wheatley Cres. Hay —45W 76
Wheatley Gdns. N9 —19Ub 25
Wheatley Mans. Bark —38Wc 67
(off Bevan Av.)
Wheatley Rd. Iswth —55Ha 100
Wheatley St. W1 —43Jb 82 (1J 197)
Wheatley Ter. Rd. Eri —51Hd 110
Wheatley Way. Ger X —23A 34
Wheatsheaf. Romf —30Hd 48
Wheatsheaf Clo. N'holt —36Aa 57
Wheatsheaf Clo. Ott —79F 138
Wheatsheaf Clo. Wok —88A 156
Wheatsheaf Hill. Hals —81Bd 169
Wheatsheaf La. SW6 —52Ya 102
Wheatsheaf La. SW8 —52Nb 104
Wheatsheaf La. Stai —66H 119
Wheatsheaf Ter. SW6 —52Bb 103
Wheatstone Clo. Mitc —67Gb 125
Wheatstone Rd. W10 —43Ab 80
Wheeler Av. Oxt —100Fc 183
Wheeler Gdns. N1 —39Nb 62
(off Outram Pl.)
Wheelers. Epp —1Vc 15
Wheelers Cross. Bark —40Tc 66
Wheelers Dri. Ruis —30S 36
Wheelers La. Eps —86Ra 161
Wheelers La. Pil H —14Rd 31
Wheelers Orchard. Ger X —23A 34
Wheel Farm Dri. Dag —34Ed 68
Wheelwright Clo. Bush —16Da 19
Wheelwrights Pl. Coln —52E 96
Wheelwright St. N7 —38Pb 62
Whelan Way. Wall —76Mb 146
Wheler St. E1 —42Vb 83 (6K 195)
Whellock Rd. W4 —48Ua 80
Whenman Av. Bex —61Ed 132
Whernside Clo. SE28 —45Yc 87
Whetstone Clo. N20 —19Fb 23
Whetstone Pk. WC2 —44Pb 82 (2H 199)
Whetstone Rd. SE3 —54Lc 107
Whewell Rd. N19 —33Nb 62
Whichcote St. SE1 —46Qb 82 (7K 199)
(off Mepham St.)
Whidborne Clo. SE8 —54Cc 106
Whidborne St. WC1 —41Nb 82 (4G 193)
Whimbrel Clo. SE28 —45Yc 87
Whimbrel Clo. S Croy —83Tb 165
Whimbrel Way. Hay —43Z 77
Whinchat Rd. SE28 —48Tc 86
Whinfell Clo. SW16 —64Mb 126
Whinfell Way. Grav —3H 137
Whinyates Rd. SE9 —55Nc 108
Whippendell Clo. Orp —67Xc 131
Whippendell Hill. Abb L —2L 3
Whippendell Rd. Wat —15U 18
Whippendell Way. Orp —67Xc 131
Whipps Cross. E17 —29Fc 45
Whipps Cross Ho. E17 —28Fc 45
(off Wood St.)
Whipps Cross Rd. E11 —29Fc 45
Whiskin St. EC1 —41Rb 83 (4B 194)
Whisper Wood. Loud —13K 17
Whisperwood Clo. Har W —25Ga 38
Whistler Gdns. Edgw —26Pa 39
Whistlers Av. SW11 —52Fb 103
Whistler St. N5 —36Rb 63
Whistler Tower. SW10 —52Eb 103
(off Worlds End Est.)
Whistler Wlk. SW10 —52Fb 103
Whiston Rd. E2 —40Vb 63 (1K 195)
Whitakers Way. Lou —11Pc 28
Whitbread Clo. N17 —25Wb 43
Whitbread Rd. SE4 —56Ac 106
Whitburn Rd. SE13 —56Dc 106
Whitby Av. NW10 —41Ra 79
Whitby Av. Ingve —23Fe 51
Whitby Clo. Big H —91Kc 183
Whitby Clo. Grnh —57Wd 112
Whitby Ct. N7 —35Nb 62
Whitby Gdns. NW9 —27Qa 39
Whitby Gdns. Sutt —75Fb 145
Whitby Rd. SE18 —49Pc 86
Whitby Rd. Harr —34Ea 58
Whitby Rd. Ruis —34X 57
Whitby Rd. Slou —5G 72
Whitby Rd. Sutt —75Fb 145
Whitby St. E1 —42Vb 83 (5K 195)
Whitcher Clo. SE14 —51Ac 106
Whitcher Pl. NW1 —37Lb 62
Whitchurch Av. Edgw —24Pa 39
Whitchurch Clo. Edgw —23Pa 39
Whitchurch Gdns. Edgw —23Pa 39
Whitchurch La. Edgw —24Ma 39
Whitchurch Pde. Edgw —24Qa 39
Whitchurch Rd. W11 —45Za 80
Whitchurch Rd. Romf —21Md 49
Whitcomb Ct. WC2 —45Mb 82 (5E 198)
(off Whitcomb St.)
Whitcomb St. WC2 —45Mb 82 (5E 198)
White Acre. NW9 —26Ua 40
Whiteacre. Whyt —92Xb 181
Whiteadder Way. E14 —49Dc 84
Whitear Wlk. E15 —37Fc 65
White Av. Grav —2B 136
Whitebarn La. Dag —39Cd 68
Whitebeam Av. Brom —73Qc 150
Whitebeam Clo. SW9 —52Pb 104
White Beams. Park —1Da 5
White Beam Way. Tad —93Wa 178
White Bear Pl. NW3 —35Fb 61
Whitebridge Clo. Felt —58V 98
White Butts Rd. Ruis —34Z 57
Whitechapel High St. E1 —44Vb 83 (2K 201)
Whitechapel Rd. E1 —43Wb 83
Whitechurch La. E1 —44Wb 83
White City Clo. W12 —45Xa 80
White City Est. W12 —45Xa 80
White City Rd. W12 —45Xa 80
White Clo. Slou —6H 73
White Conduit St. N1 —40Qb 62 (1A 194)
Whitecote Rd. S'hall —44Ea 78
White Craig Clo. Pinn —22Ca 37
Whitecroft. Swan —68Gd 132
Whitecroft Clo. Beck —70Ec 129
Whitecroft Way. Beck —71Ec 148
Whitecross Pl. EC2 —43Tb 83 (7G 195)
Whitecross St. EC1 —42Sb 83 (5E 194)
Whitecross St. EC2 —43Sb 83 (7E 194)
Whitefield Av. NW2 —32Ya 60
Whitefield Av. Purl —88Qb 164
Whitefield Clo. SW15 —58Ab 102
Whitefield Clo. Orp —69Yc 131
Whitefields Rd. Chesh —1Yb 12
Whitefoot La. Brom —63Ec 128
Whitefoot Ter. Brom —62Hc 129
Whiteford Rd. Slou —3J 73
White Friars. Sev —99Jd 186
Whitefriars Av. Harr —26Ga 38
Whitefriars Ct. N12 —22Fb 41
Whitefriars Dri. Harr —26Fa 38
Whitefriars St. EC4 —44Qb 82 (3A 200)
Whitefriars Trading Est. Harr —27Fa 38
White Gdns. Dag —37Cd 68
Whitegate Gdns. Harr —24Ha 38
Whitegates. Whyt —91Wb 181
Whitegates. Wok —92B 172
Whitegates Av. W King —79Ud 154
Whitegates Clo. Crox —14Q 18
Whitegate Way. Tad —92Xa 178
Whitehall. SW1 —46Nb 82 (6F 199)
Whitehall Clo. Chig —20Wc 29
Whitehall Clo. Uxb —39L 55
Whitehall Ct. SW1 —46Nb 82 (7F 199)
Whitehall Cres. Chess —78Ma 143
Whitehall Farm La. Vir W —68A 118
Whitehall Gdns. E4 —18Gc 27
Whitehall Gdns. SW1 —46Nb 82 (7F 199)
(off Horseguards Av.)
Whitehall Gdns. W3 —46Qa 79
Whitehall Gdns. W4 —51Ra 101
Whitehall La. Buck H —19Jc 27
Whitehall La. Egh —66B 118
Whitehall La. Eri —54Hd 110
Whitehall La. Grays —50Ee 91
Whitehall La. Wray —58C 96
Whitehall Pde. Grav —2F 136
Whitehall Pk. N19 —32Lb 62
Whitehall Pk. Rd. W4 —51Ra 101
Whitehall Pl. E7 —36Jc 65
Whitehall Pl. SW1 —46Nb 82 (7F 199)
Whitehall Pl. Wall —77Kb 146
Whitehall Rd. E4 & Wfd G —19Gc 27
Whitehall Rd. W7 —47Ja 78
Whitehall Rd. Brom —71Mc 149
Whitehall Rd. Grays —49Ee 91
Whitehall Rd. Harr —31Ga 58
Whitehall Rd. T Hth —71Qb 146
Whitehall Rd. Uxb —39M 55
Whitehall St. N17 —24Vb 43
White Hart Clo. Hay —51T 98
White Hart Clo. Sev —100Ld 187
White Hart Ct. EC2 —43Ub 83 (1H 201)
(off Bishopsgate)
White Hart Ct. Rip —93L 173
White Hart La. N22 & N17 —25Pb 42
White Hart La. NW10 —37Va 60
White Hart La. SW13 —54Ua 102
White Hart La. Brtwd —19Yd 32
White Hart La. Romf —25Cd 48
White Hart Meadows. Rip —93L 173
White Hart Pde. Riv —94Gd 186
White Hart Rd. SE18 —49Uc 86
White Hart Rd. Orp —73Wc 151
White Hart Rd. Slou —8H 73
White Hart Row. Cher —73J 139
White Hart Slip. Brom —68Jc 129
White Hart St. SE11 —50Qb 82 (7A 206)
White Hart Wood. Sev —100Ld 187
White Hart Yd. SE1 —46Tb 83 (7F 201)
Whitehaven. Slou —5K 73
Whitehaven Clo. Brom —70Jc 129
Whitehaven St. NW8 —42Gb 81 (6D 190)
Whitehead Clo. N18 —22Tb 43
Whitehead Clo. SW18 —59Eb 103
Whitehead Clo. Dart —62Ld 133
Whitehead's Gro. SW3 —50Gb 81 (7E 202)
White Heart Av. Uxb —43S 76
Whiteheath Av. Ruis —31S 56
White Heron M. Tedd —65Ha 122
White Hill. B Hth —23Q 36
White Hill. Chips —95Gb 179
White Hill. S Croy —82Tb 165
Whitehill La. Blet —99Tb 181
Whitehill La. Cob —95S 174
Whitehill La. Grav —2E 136
Whitehill Pl. Vir W —71A 138
Whitehill Rd. Dart —57Jd 110
Whitehill Rd. Grav —1E 136
Whitehill Rd. Long —68Zd 135
Whitehills Rd. Lou —13Qc 28
Whitehorn Av. W Dray —45N 75
Whitehorn Gdns. Croy —75Xb 147
Whitehorn St. E3 —43Cc 84
White Horse. Add —77L 139
White Horse All. EC1 —43Rb 83 (7B 194)
(off Cowcross St.)
White Horse Dri. Eps —86Sa 161
White Horse Hill. Chst —63Qc 130
White Horse La. E1 —43Zb 84
Whitehorse La. SE25 —70Tb 127
White Horse La. Rip —93L 173
Whitehorse M. SE1 —48Qb 82 (3A 206)
White Horse Rd. E1 —44Ac 84
White Horse Rd. E6 —41Pc 86
Whitehorse Rd. Croy & T Hth —73Sb 147
White Horse Rd. Wind —5B 94
White Horse St. W1 —46Kb 82 (7A 198)
White Horse Yd. EC2 —44Tb 83 (2F 201)
White Ho. SW4 —59Mb 104
(off Clapham Pk. Est.)
Whitehouse Av. Borwd —13Ra 21
White Ho. Clo. Ger X —24A 34
White Ho. Dri. Stan —21La 38
White Ho. Dri. Wfd G —23Hc 45
Whitehouse Est. E10 —30Ec 44
Whitehouse La. Enf —11Sb 25
White Ho. La. Guild —100A 172
Whitehouse Way. N14 —19Kb 24
Whitehouse Way. Iver —41F 74
White Kennett St. E1 —44Ub 83 (2J 201)
Whiteknights. Cars —83Fb 163
White Knights Rd. Wey —80S 140
White Knobs Way. Cat —97Wb 181
Whitelands Av. Chor —13D 16
Whitelands Way. Romf —25Md 49
White La. Oxt —95Kc 183
Whiteledges. W13 —44La 78
Whitelegg Rd. E13 —40Hc 65
Whiteley. Wind —2C 94
Whiteley Rd. SE19 —64Tb 127
Whiteleys. W2 —44Db 81
Whiteley's Cotts. W14 —49Bb 81
Whiteley's Way. Felt —62Ca 121
White Lion Ct. EC3 —44Ub 83 (3H 201)
(off Cornhill)
White Lion Ct. SE15 —51Yb 106
White Lion Ct. Iswth —55Ka 100
White Lion Hill. EC4 —45Rb 83 (4C 200)
White Lion St. N1 —40Qb 62 (2K 193)
White Lodge. SE19 —66Rb 127
White Lodge. Sev —100Jd 186
White Lodge Clo. N2 —30Fb 41
White Lodge Clo. Sev —95Kd 187
White Lodge Clo. Sutt —80Eb 145
White Lyon Ct. EC2 —43Sb 83 (7D 194)
(off Fann St.)
White Lyons Rd. Brtwd —19Yd 32
Whiteoak Ct. Chst —65Qc 130
White Oak Ct. Swan —69Gd 132
White Oak Dri. Beck —68Ec 128
White Oak Gdns. Sidc —59Vc 109
Whiteoaks. Bans —85Db 163
Whiteoaks La. Gnfd —41Fa 78
White Orchards. N20 —17Bb 23
White Orchards. Stan —22Ja 38
White Post Hill. F'ham —73Qd 153
White Post La. E9 —37Cc 64
Whitepost La. SE13 —55Cc 106
White Post La. Meop —10D 136
White Post St. SE15 —52Vb 106
White Rd. E15 —38Gc 65
White Rose La. Wok —90B 156
Whites Av. Ilf —30Uc 46
Whites Clo. Grnh —57Yd 112
Whites Dri. Brom —72Hc 149
White's Grounds. SE1 —47Ub 83 (2J 207)
White's Grounds Est. SE1 —47Ub 83 (1J 207)
(off White's Gronds)
White Shack La. Chan X —9P 3
Whites La. Dat —1M 95
White's Meadow. Brom —70Qc 130
White's Row. E1 —43Vb 83 (1K 201)
Whites Sq. SW4 —56Mb 104
Whitestile Rd. Bren —50La 78
Whitestone La. NW3 —34Eb 61
Whitestone Wlk. NW3 —34Eb 61
White St. S'hall —47Z 77
Whiteswan M. W4 —50Ua 80
Whitethorn Av. Coul —87Jb 164
Whitethorn Av. W Dray —46P 75
Whitethorn Gdns. Croy —75Xb 147
Whitethorn Gdns. Enf —15Tb 25
Whitethorn Gdns. Horn —30Ld 49
Whitethorn Pl. W Dray —45P 75
White Way. Bookh —98Da 175
Whitewebbs La. Enf —7Ub 11
Whitewebbs Rd. Enf —7Rb 11
Whitewebbs Way. Orp —67Vc 131
Whitewood Cotts. Tats —92Lc 183
Whitfield Pl. W1 —42Lb 82 (6B 192)
(off Whitfield St.)
Whitfield Rd. E6 —38Lc 65
Whitfield Rd. SE3 —54Fc 107
Whitfield Rd. Bexh —52Bd 109
Whitfields. Stanf —1P 93
Whitfield St. W1 —42Lb 82 (6B 192)
Whitfield Way. Rick —18H 17
Whitford Gdns. Mitc —69Hb 125
Whitgift Av. S Croy —78Sb 147
Whitgift Cen. Croy —75Sb 147
Whitgift Sq. Croy —75Sb 147
Whitgift St. SE11 —49Pb 82 (5H 205)
Whitgift St. Croy —76Sb 147
Whiting Av. Bark —38Rc 66
Whitings Rd. Barn —15Ya 22
Whitings Way. E6 —43Qc 86
Whitland Rd. Cars —74Fb 145
Whitlars Dri. K Lan —1P 3
Whitley Clo. Stai —58N 97
Whitley Rd. N17 —26Ub 43
Whitlock Dri. SW19 —60Ab 102
Whitman Rd. E3 —42Ac 84
Whitmead Clo. S Croy —79Ub 147
Whitminster Ct. SE15 —51Ub 105
(off Brockworth Clo.)
Whitmoor Av. H Wood —26Nd 49
Whitmoor La. Guild —98A 172
Whitmore Av. Grays —46De 91
Whitmore Clo. N11 —22Kb 42
Whitmore Est. N1 —39Ub 63 (1J 195)
Whitmore Gdns. NW10 —40Ya 60
Whitmore Ho. N1 —40Ub 63 (1J 195)
(off Whitmore Est.)
Whitmore Rd. N1 —39Ub 63 (1H 195)
Whitmore Rd. Beck —69Bc 128
Whitmore Rd. Harr —31Ea 58
Whitmore Rd. S'dale —10E 116
Whitmores Clo. Eps —87Sa 161
Whitnell Way. SW15 —57Ya 102
Whitney Av. Ilf —28Mc 45
Whitney Rd. E10 —31Dc 64
Whitney Wlk. Sidc —65Ad 131
Whitstable Clo. Beck —67Bc 128
Whitstable Clo. Ruis —33U 56
Whitstable Ho. W10 —44Za 80
(off Walmer Rd.)
Whittaker Av. Rich —57Ma 101
Whittaker Ct. Asht —89Ma 161
Whittaker Pl. Rich —57Ma 101
(off Whittaker Av.)
Whittaker Rd. E6 —38Lc 65
Whittaker Rd. Slou —2B 72
Whittaker Rd. Sutt —76Bb 145
Whittaker St. SW1 —49Jb 82 (6H 203)
Whittaker Way. SE1 —49Wb 83
Whitta Rd. E12 —35Mc 65
Whittell Gdns. SE26 —62Yb 128
Whittenham Clo. Slou —6L 73
Whittingham. N17 —24Xb 43
Whittingham Ct. W4 —52Ua 102
Whittingstall Rd. SW6 —53Bb 103
Whittington Av. EC3 —44Ub 83 (3H 201)
Whittington Av. Hay —43V 76
Whittington Ct. N2 —29Hb 41
Whittington Rd. N22 —24Nb 42
Whittington Rd. Hut —16Ee 33
Whittington Way. Pinn —29Aa 37
Whittlebury Clo. Cars —80Hb 145
Whittle Clo. S'hall —44Da 77
Whittle Parkway. Slou —4B 72
Whittle Rd. Houn —52Y 99
Whittlesea Clo. Harr —24Ea 38
Whittlesea Path. Harr —25Ea 38
Whittlesea Rd. Harr —24Ea 38
Whittlesey St. SE1 —46Qb 82 (7A 200)
Whitton Av. E. Gnfd —36Ga 58
Whitton Av. W. N'holt & Gnfd —36Da 57
Whitton Clo. Gnfd —37Ka 58
Whitton Dene. Houn & Iswth —57Ea 100
Whitton Dri. Gnfd —37Ja 58
Whitton Mnr. Rd. Iswth —58Ea 100
Whitton Rd. Houn —56Da 99
Whitton Rd. Twic —58Ga 100
Whitton Wlk. E3 —41Cc 84
Whitton Waye. Houn —58Ca 99
Whitwell Clo. Stanf —3L 93
Whitwell Rd. E13 —41Jc 85
Whitwell Rd. Wat —7Z 5
Whitworth Ho. SE1 —48Sb 83 (4E 206)
Whitworth Rd. SE18 —52Qc 108
Whitworth Rd. SE25 —69Ub 127
Whitworth St. SE10 —50Gc 85
Whopshott Av. Wok —4F 188
Whopshott Clo. Wok —4F 188
Whopshott Dri. Wok —4F 188
Whorlton Rd. SE15 —55Xb 105
Whybrews. Stanf —1P 93
Whybridge Clo. Rain —39Gd 68
Whymark Av. N22 —27Qb 42
Whytebeam View. Whyt —90Vb 165
Whytecliffe Rd. N. Purl —83Rb 165
Whytecliffe Rd. S. Purl —83Qb 164
Whytecroft. Houn —52Z 99
Whyteleafe Bus. Village. Whyt —89Vb 165
Whyteleafe Hill. Whyt —92Ub 181
Whyteleafe Rd. Cat —92Ub 181
Whyteville Rd. E7 —37Kc 65
Wichling Clo. Orp —74Zc 151
Wickenden Rd. Sev —94Ld 187
Wickens Caravan Site. Dun G —91Jd 186
Wickersley Rd. SW11 —54Jb 104
Wickers Oake. SE19 —63Vb 127
Wicker St. E1 —44Xb 83
Wicket Rd. Gnfd —41Ja 78
Wickets Way. Ilf —23Vc 47
Wicket, The. Croy —78Cc 148
Wickett, The. Chalv —8J 73
Wickford Clo. Romf —22Pd 49
Wickford Dri. Romf —22Pd 49
Wickford St. E1 —42Yb 84
Wickford Way. E17 —28Zb 44
Wickham Av. Croy —75Ac 148
Wickham Av. Sutt —78Ya 144
Wickham Chase. W Wick —74Fc 149
Wickham Clo. Enf —13Xb 25
Wickham Clo. Hare —25M 35
Wickham Clo. N Mald —72Va 144
Wickham Ct. Rd. W Wick —75Ec 148
Wickham Cres. W Wick —75Ec 148
Wickham Field. Otf —88Hd 170
Wickham Gdns. SE4 —55Bc 106
Wickham La. SE2 & Well —50Wc 87
Wickham La. Egh —66C 118
Wickham M. SE4 —54Bc 106
Wickham Rd. E4 —24Ec 44
Wickham Rd. SE4 —56Bc 106
Wickham Rd. Beck —68Dc 128
Wickham Rd. Croy —75Zb 148
Wickham Rd. Grays —7E 92
Wickham Rd. Harr —26Fa 38
Wickham St. SE11 —50Pb 82
Wickham St. Well —54Uc 108
Wickhams Way. Hart —71Be 155
Wickham Way. Beck —70Ec 128
Wick La. E3 —39Cc 64
(in two parts)
Wick La. Egh —5K 117
Wickliffe Av. N3 —26Ab 40
Wickliffe Gdns. Wemb —33Ra 59
Wicklow Ho. N16 —32Vb 63
Wicklow St. WC1 —41Pb 82 (3H 193)
Wick M. E9 —37Ac 64
Wick Rd. E9 —37Zb 64
Wick Rd. Egh —7L 117
Wick Rd. Tedd —66Ka 122
Wicks Clo. SE9 —63Mc 129
Wick Sq. E9 —37Bc 64
Wickstead Ho. SE1 —48Sb 83
Wicksteed Clo. Bex —62Fd 132
Wicksteed Ho. SE1 —48Sb 83 (4E 206)
Wicksteed Ho. Bren —50Pa 79
Wickway Ct. SE15 —51Vb 105
(off Cator St.)
Wickwood St. SE5 —54Rb 105
Wid Clo. Hut —15Fe 33
Widdecombe Av. S Harr —33Aa 57
Widdenham Rd. N7 —35Pb 62
Widdin St. E15 —38Fc 65
Widecombe Clo. Romf —25Md 49
Widecombe Gdns. Ilf —28Nc 46
Widecombe Rd. SE9 —62Nc 130
Widecombe Way. N2 —29Fb 41
Widecroft Rd. Iver —44G 74
Widegate St. E1 —43Ub 83 (1J 201)
Widenham Clo. Pinn —29Y 37
Widewater Bus. Cen. Uxb —29L 35
Wide Way. Mitc —69Mb 126
Widgeon Clo. E16 —44Kc 85
Widgeon Way. Wat —9Aa 5
Widley Rd. W9 —41Cb 81
Widmore Lodge Rd. Brom —68Mc 129
Widmore Rd. Brom —68Jc 129
Widmore Rd. Uxb —42R 76
Widworthy Hayes. Hut —18De 33
Wieland Rd. N'wd —24W 36
Wient, The. Coln —52E 96
Wigan Ho. E5 —32Xb 63
Wigan Pl. SE11 —50Qb 82
Wigeon Path. SE28 —48Tc 86
Wigeon Way. Hay —44Aa 77
Wiggenhall Rd. Wat —15X 19
Wiggins Mead. NW9 —24Va 40
Wigginton Av. Wemb —37Ra 59
Wightman Rd. N8 & N4 —28Qb 42
Wigley Bush La. S Wea —19Ud 32
Wigley Rd. Felt —61Z 121
Wigmore Pl. W1 —44Kb 82 (2K 197)
Wigmore Rd. Cars —75Fb 145
Wigmore St. W1 —44Jb 82 (3H 197)
Wigmore Wlk. Cars —75Fb 145
Wigram Rd. E11 —30Lc 45
Wigram Sq. E17 —27Ec 44
Wigston Clo. N18 —22Ub 43
Wigston Rd. E13 —42Kc 85
Wigton Gdns. Stan —25Na 39
Wigton Pl. SE11 —50Qb 82 (7A 206)
(off Cator St.)
Wigton Rd. E17 —25Bc 44
Wigton Rd. Romf —21Nd 49
Wigton Way. Romf —21Nd 49
Wilberforce Rd. N4 —33Rb 63
Wilberforce Rd. NW9 —30Wa 40
Wilberforce Way. SW19 —65Za 124
Wilberforce Way. Grav —4F 136
Wilbraham Pl. SW1 —49Hb 81 (5G 203)
Wilbury Av. Sutt —82Bb 163
Wilbury Rd. Wok —5G 188
Wilbury Way. N18 —22Tb 43
Wilby M. W11 —46Bb 81
Wilcot Av. Wat —17Aa 19
Wilcox Clo. SW8 —52Nb 104
Wilcox Clo. Borwd —11Sa 21
Wilcox Gdns. Shep —69N 119
Wilcox Pl. SW1 —48Lb 82 (4C 204)
Wilcox Rd. SW8 —52Nb 104
Wilcox Rd. Sutt —77Db 145
Wilcox Rd. Tedd —63Fa 122
Wild Acres. W Byf —83L 157
Wildbank Ct. Wok —90B 156
Wild Ct. WC2 —44Pb 82 (2H 199)
Wildcroft Gdns. Edgw —23Ma 39
Wildcroft Mnr. SW15 —59Ya 102
Wildcroft Rd. SW15 —59Ya 102
Wilde Clo. E8 —39Wb 63
Wilde Clo. Til —4E 114
Wilde Pl. N13 —23Rb 43
Wilde Pl. SW18 —60Fb 103
Wilder Clo. Ruis —32X 57
Wildernesse Av. Sev —94Nd 187
Wildernesse Mt. Sev —94Md 187
Wilderness Rd. Chst —66Rc 130
Wilderness, The. Hamp —63Da 121
Wilders Clo. Wok —6F 188
Wilderton Rd. N16 —31Ub 63
Wildfell Rd. SE6 —59Dc 106
Wild Goose Dri. SE14 —53Yb 106
Wildgreen N. Slou —49C 74
Wildgreen S. Slou —49C 74
Wild Hatch. NW11 —30Cb 41
Wildmarsh Ct. Enf —9Ac 12
(off Manly Dixon Dri.)

Wild Oaks Clo.—Windsor Rd.

Wild Oaks Clo. N'wd —24V 36
Wilds Rents. SE1 —48Ub 83 (3H 207)
Wild St. WC2 —44Nb 82 (3G 199)
Wildwood. N'wd —23T 36
Wildwood Av. Brick —2Ba 5
Wildwood Clo. SE12 —59Hc 107
Wildwood Clo. E Hor —97V 174
Wildwood Clo. Wok —87H 157
Wildwood Ct. Kenl —87Tb 165
Wildwood Gro. NW3 —32Eb 61
Wildwood Rise. NW11 —32Eb 61
Wildwood Rd. NW11 —30Db 41
Wildwood Ter. NW3 —32Eb 61
Wilford Clo. Enf —13Tb 25
Wilford Clo. N'wd —24T 36
Wilford Rd. Slou —49A 74
Wilfred Av. Rain —43Jd 88
Wilfred Owen Clo. SW19 —65Eb 125
Wilfred St. SW1 —48Lb 82 (3B 204)
Wilfred St. Grav —8D 114
Wilfred St. Wok —6G 188
Wilfrid Gdns. W3 —43Sa 79
Wilhelmina Av. Coul —91Lb 180
Wilkes Rd. Hut —15Fe 33
Wilkes St. E1 —43Vb 83 (7K 195)
Wilkie Way. SE22 —60Wb 105
Wilkins Clo. Hay —50V 76
Wilkins Clo. Mitc —67Gb 125
Wilkinson Clo. Dart —56Pd 111
Wilkinson Ct. SW17 —63Fb 125
Wilkinson Ho. N1 —40Tb 63 (2G 195) (off Cranston Est.)
Wilkinson Rd. E16 —44Lc 85
Wilkinson St. SW8 —52Pb 104
Wilkinson Way. W4 —47Ta 79
Wilkin St. NW5 —37Jb 62
Wilkin St. M. NW5 —37Kb 62
Wilkins Way. Bras —96Xc 185
Wilks Gdns. Croy —74Ac 148
Wilks Pl. N1 —40Ub 63 (2J 195)
Willan Rd. N17 —26Tb 43
Willan Wall. E16 —45Hc 85
Willard St. SW8 —55Kb 104
Willats Clo. Cher —72H 139
Willcocks Clo. Chess —76Na 143
Willcott Rd. W3 —46Ra 79
Will Crooks Gdns. SE9 —56Mc 107
Willenhall Av. Barn —16Eb 23
Willenhall Ct. New Bar —16Eb 23
Willenhall Dri. Hay —45U 76
Willenhall Rd. SE18 —50Rc 86
Willersley Av. Orp —76Tc 150
Willersley Av. Sidc —60Vc 109
Willersley Clo. Sidc —60Vc 109
Willesden La. NW2 & NW6 —37Ya 60
Willes Rd. NW5 —37Kb 62
Willett Clo. N'holt —41Y 77
Willett Clo. Orp —72Uc 150
Willett Ho. E13 —40Kc 65 (off Queens Rd. W.)
Willett Pl. T Hth —71Qb 146
Willett Rd. T Hth —71Qb 146
Willetts La. Uxb —35H 55
Willett Way. Orp —71Tc 150
Willet Way. SE16 —50Xb 83
Willey Broom La. Cat —97Qb 180
Willey Farm La. Cat —98Sb 181
Willey La. Cat —97Tb 181
William Allen Ho. Edgw —24Pa 39
William Banfield Ho. SW6 —54Bb 103 (off Munster Rd.)
William Barefoot Dri. SE9 —63Qc 130
William Bonney Est. SW4 —56Mb 104
William Booth Rd. SE20 —67Wb 127
William Carey Way. Harr —30Ga 38
William Clo. Add —78K 139
William Clo. Romf —25Ed 48
William Cobbett Ho. W8 —48Db 81 (off Scarsdale Pl.)
William Cory Promenade. Eri —50Gd 88
William Ct. Gnfd —43La 78
William Covell Clo. Enf —10Pb 10
William Ellis Clo. Old Win —7L 95
William Ellis Way. SE16 —48Wb 83
William Evans Ho. SE8 —49Zb 84 (off Haddonfield)
William IV St. WC2 —45Nb 82 (5F 199)
William Gdns. SW15 —57Xa 102
William Gunn Ho. NW3 —36Gb 61
William Guy Gdns. E3 —41Dc 84
William Henry Wlk. SW8 —51Mb 104
William Ho. Grav —9D 114
William Margrie Clo. SE15 —54Wb 105
William M. SW1 —47Hb 81 (2G 203)
William Morley Clo. E6 —39Mc 65
William Morris Clo. E17 —27Bc 44
William Morris Ho. W6 —51Za 102 (off Margravine Rd.)
William Morris Way. SW6 —55Eb 103
William Nash Ct. St M —69Yc 131
William Paton Ho. E16 —44Kc 85
William Pike Ho. Romf —30Fd 48 (off Waterloo Gdns.)
William Pl. E3 —40Bc 64
William Pl. St M —70Yc 131
William Rd. NW1 —41Kb 82 (4A 192)
William Rd. SW19 —66Ab 124
William Rd. Cat —94Tb 181
William Rd. Sutt —78Eb 145
William Russell Ct. Wok —6B 188
Williams Av. E17 —25Bc 44
Williams Clo. N8 —30Mb 42
Williams Gro. N22 —25Qb 42
Williams Ho. NW2 —34Ya 60 (off Stoll Clo.)
William's La. SW14 —55Sa 101
Williams La. Mord —71Eb 145
William Smith Ho. Belv —48Cd 88
Williamson Clo. SE10 —50Hc 85
Williamson Ct. SE17 —50Sb 83 (7D 206)
Williamson Rd. N4 —30Rb 43
Williamson St. N7 —35Nb 62
Williamson Way. NW7 —23Ab 40
Williams Rd. W13 —46Ja 78
Williams Rd. S'hall —49Aa 77
Williams Ter. Croy —79Qb 146
William St. E10 —30Dc 44
William St. N17 —24Vb 43
William St. SW1 —47Hb 81 (2G 203)
William St. Bark —38Sc 66
William St. Bush —13Z 19
William St. Cars —76Gb 145
William St. Grav —9D 114
William St. Grays —51De 113 (in two parts)
William St. Slou —7K 73
William St. Wind —3H 95
Williams Way. Rad —7Ka 6
William White Ct. E13 —39Lc 65 (off Green St.)
Willifield Way. NW11 —28Bb 41
Willingale Clo. Hut —16Fe 33
Willingale Clo. Lou —12Sc 28
Willingale Clo. Wfd G —23Lc 45
Willingale Rd. Lou —13Sc 28
Willingdon Rd. N22 —26Rb 43
Willinghall Clo. Wal A —4Fc 13
Willingham Clo. NW5 —36Lb 62
Willingham Ter. NW5 —36Lb 62
Willingham Way. King T —69Qa 123
Willington Rd. SW9 —55Nb 104
Willis Av. Sutt —79Gb 145
Willis Clo. Eps —86Ra 161
Willis Rd. E15 —40Hc 65
Willis Rd. Croy —73Sb 147
Willis Rd. Eri —49Fd 88
Willis St. E14 —44Dc 84
Will Miles Ct. SW19 —66Eb 125
Willmore End. SW19 —67Db 125
Willoners. Slou —2E 72
Willoughby Av. Croy —77Pb 146
Willoughby Dri. Rain —38Gd 68
Willoughby Gro. N17 —24Xb 43
Willoughby Highwalk. EC2 (off Barbican) —43Tb 83 (1F 201)
Willoughby Ho. EC2 (off Barbican) —43Tb 83 (1F 201)
Willoughby La. N17 —23Xb 43
Willoughby Pk. Rd. N17 —24Xb 43 (in two parts)
Willoughby Rd. N8 —27Qb 42
Willoughby Rd. NW3 —35Fb 61
Willoughby Rd. King T —67Pa 123
Willoughby Rd. Slou —48C 74
Willoughby Rd. Twic —57La 100
Willoughbys, The. SW14 —55Ua 102
Willoughby St. WC1 —43Nb 82 (1F 199) (off Gt. Russell St.)
Willoughby Way. SE7 —49Kc 85
Willow Av. SW13 —54Va 102
Willow Av. Den —37L 55
Willow Av. Sidc —58Wc 109
Willow Av. Swan —70Hd 132
Willow Av. W Dray —45P 75
Willow Bank. SW6 —55Ab 102
Willowbank. Coul —86Nb 164
Willow Bank. Rich —62Ka 122
Willow Bri. Rd. N1 —37Sb 63
Willowbrook. Eton —9H 73
Willow Brook Rd. SE15 —52Vb 105
Willowbrook Rd. S'hall —48Ca 77
Willowbrook Rd. Stai —61N 119
Willow Bus. Pk. SE26 —62Yb 128
Willow Clo. Bex —58Bd 109
Willow Clo. Bren —51La 100
Willow Clo. Brom —71Pc 150
Willow Clo. Buck H —20Mc 27
Willow Clo. Coln —52E 96
Willow Clo. Horn —34Kd 69
Willow Clo. Hut —16De 33
Willow Clo. Orp —73Xc 151
Willow Clo. Wdhm —83H 157
Willow Cotts. Rich —51Qa 101
Willow Ct. E11 —33Gc 65 (off Trinity Clo.)
Willow Ct. EC2 —42Ub 83 (5H 195) (off Willow St.)
Willow Ct. Edgw —21Na 39
Willowcourt Av. Harr —29Ka 38
Willow Cres. E. Den —36L 55
Willow Cres. W. Den —36L 55
Willowdene. N6 —31Hb 61
Willowdene. SE15 —53Xb 105
Willow Dene. Bush —17Ga 20
Willowdene. Pil H —15Vd 32
Willow Dene. Pinn —26Z 37
Willowdene Clo. Twic —59Ea 100
Willowdene Ct. N20 —17Eb 23 (off High Rd.)
Willowdene Ct. War —21Yd 50
Willow Dri. Barn —14Ab 22
Willow Dri. Rip —96J 173
Willow Edge. K Lan —1Q 4
Willow End. N20 —19Cb 23
Willow End. N'wd —23W 36
Willow End. Surb —74Na 143
Willow Farm La. SW15 —55Xa 102
Willow Gdns. Houn —53Ca 99
Willow Gdns. Ruis —33V 56
Willow Grange. Sidc —62Xc 131
Willow Grn. NW9 —25Ua 40
Willow Grn. Borwd —15Ta 21
Willow Gro. E13 —40Jc 65
Willow Gro. Chst —65Qc 130
Willow Gro. Ruis —33V 56
Willowhayne Dri. W on T —73X 141
Willowhayne Gdns. Wor Pk —76Ya 144
Willowherb Wlk. Romf —24Ld 49
Willow Ho. Brom —68Gc 129
Willow La. Mitc —71Hb 145
Willow La. Wat —15W 18
Willow La. Ind. Est. Mitc —72Hb 145
Willow Lodge. SW6 —53Ya 102
Willow Mead. Chig —20Wc 29
Willowmead. Stai —67M 119
Willowmead Clo. W5 —43Ma 79
Willowmead Clo. Wok —4D 188
Willowmere. Esh —77Ea 142
Willow Mt. Croy —76Ub 147
Willow Pde. Slou —48C 74
Willow Pk. Otf —89Hd 170
Willow Pk. Stoke P —8L 53
Willow Path. Wal A —6Gc 13
Willow Pl. SW1 —49Lb 82 (5C 204)
Willow Pl. Eton —1G 94
Willow Rd. E12 —34Pc 66
Willow Rd. NW3 —35Fb 61
Willow Rd. W5 —47Na 79
Willow Rd. Coln —54G 96
Willow Rd. Dart —60Ld 111
Willow Rd. Enf —13Ub 25
Willow Rd. Eri —53Jd 110
Willow Rd. N Mald —70Sa 123
Willow Rd. Romf —30Ad 47
Willow Rd. Wall —80Kb 146
Willows Av. Mord —71Db 145
Willows Clo. Pinn —26Y 37
Willowside Ct. Enf —13Rb 25
Willows Lodge. Wind —2B 94
Willows Path. Eps —86Ra 161
Willows Riverside Pk. Wind —2A 94 (off Maidenhead Rd.)
Willows, The. E6 —38Qc 66
Willows, The. Borwd —11Qa 21
Willows, The. Byfl —85N 157
Willows, The. Clay —79Ga 142
Willows, The. Grays —51Fe 113
Willows, The. Lou —16Mc 27
Willows, The. Rick —19J 17
Willows, The. Wat —17X 19
Willows, The. Wey —76Q 140
Willow St. E4 —17Fc 27
Willow St. EC2 —42Ub 83 (5H 195)
Willow St. Romf —28Ed 48
Willow Ter. Eyns —75Nd 153
Willow Tree Clo. E3 —39Bc 64
Willow Tree Clo. SW18 —60Db 103
Willow Tree Clo. Hay —42Y 77
Willowtree Clo. Uxb —34S 56
Willow Tree Ct. Sidc —64Vc 131
Willow Tree La. Hay —42Y 77
Willow Tree Wlk. Brom —67Kc 129
Willow Vale. W12 —46Wa 80
Willow Vale. Chst —65Rc 130
Willow Vale. Fet —95Da 175 (in two parts)
Willow View. SW19 —67Fb 125
Willow Wlk. N2 —26Fb 41
Willow Wlk. N15 —28Rb 43
Willow Wlk. N21 —16Pb 24
Willow Wlk. SE1 —49Ub 83 (5J 207)
Willow Wlk. Cher —73J 139
Willow Wlk. Dart —56Ld 111
Willow Wlk. Egh —4N 117
Willow Wlk. Ilf —33Rc 66
Willow Wlk. Orp —76Rc 150
Willow Wlk. Sutt —76Bb 145
Willow Wlk. Upm —32Ud 70
Willow Way. N3 —24Db 41
Willow Way. SE26 —62Yb 128
Willow Way. W11 —45Za 80
Willow Way. Eps —79Ta 143
Willow Way. Pot B —5Db 9
Willow Way. Rad —8Ga 6
Willow Way. Romf —23Rd 49
Willow Way. Sun —70W 120
Willow Way. Twic —61Da 121
Willow Way. Wemb —34Ja 58
Willow Way. W Byf —83L 157
Willow Way. Wok —93A 172
Willow Wood Cres. SE25 —72Ub 147
Will Perrin Ct. Rain —39Jd 68
Willrose Cres. SE2 —50Xc 87
Willsbridge Ct. SE15 —51Vb 105 (off Bibury Clo.)
Wills Cres. Houn —58Da 99
Wills Gro. NW7 —22Wa 40
Wills Hill. Stanf —1M 93
Willson Rd. Egh —4M 117
Wilman Gro. E8 —38Wb 63
Wilmar Clo. Hay —42T 76
Wilmar Clo. Uxb —38M 55
Wilmar Gdns. W Wick —74Dc 148
Wilmar Way. Seal —92Pd 187
Wilmer Clo. King T —64Pa 123
Wilmer Cres. King T —64Pa 123
Wilmer Gdns. N1 —39Ub 63 (1H 195)
Wilmerhatch La. Eps —90Ra 161
Wilmer Lea Clo. E15 —38Fc 65
Wilmer Pl. N16 —33Vb 63
Wilmer Way. N14 —22Mb 42
Wilmington Av. W4 —52Ta 101
Wilmington Av. Orp —75Yc 151
Wilmington Ct. Rd. Dart —62Jd 132
Wilmington Gdns. Bark —37Tc 66
Wilmington Sq. WC1 —41Qb 82 (4K 193)
Wilmington St. WC1 —41Qb 82 (4K 193)
Wilmot Clo. N2 —26Eb 41
Wilmot Clo. SE15 —52Wb 105
Wilmot Cotts. Bans —87Db 163
Wilmot Grn. Gt War —23Yd 50
Wilmot Pl. NW1 —38Lb 62
Wilmot Pl. W7 —46Ga 78
Wilmot Rd. E10 —33Dc 64
Wilmot Rd. N17 —27Tb 43
Wilmot Rd. Burn —1A 72
Wilmot Rd. Cars —78Hb 145
Wilmot Rd. Dart —57Jd 110
Wilmot Rd. Purl —84Qb 164
Wilmot St. E2 —42Xb 83
Wilmot Way. Bans —86Cb 163
Wilmount St. SE18 —49Qc 86
Wilna Rd. SW18 —59Eb 103
Wilsham St. W11 —46Za 80
Wilshaw St. SE14 —53Cc 106
Wilsman Rd. S Ock —40Yd 70
Wilsmere Dri. Har W —24Ga 38
Wilsmere Dri. N'holt —37Aa 57
Wilson Av. Mitc —66Gb 125
Wilson Clo. Stanf —3L 93
Wilson Clo. Wemb —31Pa 59
Wilson Clo. W Dray —51M 97
Wilson Dri. Ott —78D 138
Wilson Dri. Wemb —31Pa 59
Wilson Gdns. Harr —31Ea 58
Wilson Gro. SE16 —47Xb 83
Wilson La. S Dar —68Vd 134
Wilson Rd. E6 —41Mc 85
Wilson Rd. SE5 —53Ub 105
Wilson Rd. Chess —79Pa 143
Wilson Rd. Ilf —31Pc 66
Wilsons. Tad —93Za 178
Wilson's Av. N17 —26Vb 43
Wilson's Pl. E14 —44Bc 84
Wilson's Rd. W6 —50Za 80
Wilson St. E17 —29Ec 44
Wilson St. EC2 —43Tb 83 (1G 201)
Wilson St. N21 —17Qb 24
Wilson Wlk. W4 —49Va 80 (off Prebend Gdns.)
Wilson Way. Wok —4G 188
Wilstone Clo. Hay —42Aa 77
Wilthorne Gdns. Dag —38Dd 68
Wilton Av. W4 —50Ua 80
Wilton Clo. W Dray —51M 97
Wilton Cres. SW1 —47Jb 82 (2H 203)
Wilton Cres. SW19 —66Bb 125
Wilton Cres. Wind —6B 94
Wilton Dri. Romf —24Ed 48
Wilton Est. E8 —37Wb 63
Wilton Gdns. W on T —74Z 141
Wilton Gdns. W Mol —69Ca 121
Wilton Gro. SW19 —66Bb 125
Wilton Gro. N Mald —72Va 144
Wilton M. SW1 —48Jb 82 (3J 203)
Wilton Pde. Felt —61X 121
Wilton Pl. SW1 —47Jb 82 (2H 203)
Wilton Pl. Harr —30Ha 38
Wilton Pl. New Haw —81M 157
Wilton Rd. N10 —26Jb 42
Wilton Rd. SE2 —49Yc 87
Wilton Rd. SW1 —48Lb 82 (4B 204)
Wilton Rd. SW19 —66Db 125
Wilton Rd. Barn —14Hb 23
Wilton Rd. Houn —55Z 99
Wilton Row. SW1 —47Jb 82 (2H 203)
Wilton Row. SW6 —52Ab 102
Wilton Sq. N1 —39Tb 63
Wilton St. SW1 —48Kb 82 (3K 203)
Wilton Ter. SW1 —48Jb 82 (3H 203)
Wilton Vs. N1 —39Tb 63 (off Wilton Sq.)
Wilton Way. E8 —37Wb 63
Wiltshire Av. Horn —28Pd 49
Wiltshire Av. Slou —2G 72
Wiltshire Clo. NW7 —22Va 40
Wiltshire Clo. SW3 —49Hb 81 (6F 203)
Wiltshire Clo. Dart —59Td 112
Wiltshire Ct. N4 —32Pb 62 (off Marquis Rd.)
Wiltshire Ct. Ilf —37Sc 66
Wiltshire Gdns. N4 —30Sb 43
Wiltshire Gdns. Twic —60Ea 100
Wiltshire La. Pinn —27V 36
Wiltshire Rd. N1 —39Tb 63
Wiltshire Rd. SW9 —55Qb 104
Wiltshire Rd. Orp —73Wc 151
Wiltshire Rd. T Hth —69Qb 126
Wiltshire Row. N1 —39Tb 63 (1F 195) (off Bridport Pl.)
Wilverley Cres. N Mald —72Ua 144
Wimbart Rd. SW2 —59Pb 104
Wimbledon Bri. SW19 —65Bb 125
Wimbledon Hill Rd. SW19 —65Ab 124
Wimbledon Pk. Rd. SW19 & SW18 —61Ab 124
Wimbledon Pk. Side. SW19 —62Za 124
Wimbledon Rd. SW17 —63Eb 125
Wimbledon Stadium Bus. Cen. SW17 —62Db 125
Wimbolt St. E2 —41Wb 83
Wimborne Av. Hay —44X 77
Wimborne Av. Orp & Chst —70Vc 131
Wimborne Av. S'hall —49Ca 77
Wimborne Clo. SE12 —57Hc 107
Wimborne Clo. Buck H —19Kc 27
Wimborne Clo. Eps —85Ua 162
Wimborne Clo. Wor Pk —74Ya 144
Wimborne Dri. NW9 —27Qa 39
Wimborne Dri. Pinn —31Z 57
Wimborne Gdns. W13 —43Ka 78
Wimborne Gro. Wat —9U 4
Wimborne Ho. SW8 —52Pb 104 (off Dorset Rd.)
Wimborne Ho. SW12 —62Lb 126
Wimborne Rd. N9 —19Wb 25
Wimborne Rd. N17 —26Ub 43
Wimborne Way. Beck —69Zb 128
Wimbourne Ct. SW12 —62Lb 126
Wimbourne St. N1 —40Tb 63 (1F 195)
Wimpole Clo. Brom —70Lc 129
Wimpole Clo. King T —68Pa 123
Wimpole M. W1 —43Kb 82 (7K 191)
Wimpole Rd. W Dray —46M 75
Wimpole St. W1 —43Kb 82 (7K 191)
Winans Wlk. SW9 —54Qb 104
Wincanton Cres. N'holt —36Ca 57
Wincanton Gdns. Ilf —27Rc 46
Wincanton Rd. SW18 —59Bb 103
Wincanton Rd. Romf —20Md 31
Winchcombe Ct. SE15 —51Ub 105 (off Lydney Clo.)
Winchcombe Rd. Cars —73Fb 145
Winchcomb Gdns. SE9 —55Mc 107
Winchelsea Av. Bexh —52Bd 109
Winchelsea Clo. SW15 —57Za 102
Winchelsea Rd. E7 —34Jc 65
Winchelsea Rd. N17 —27Ub 43
Winchelsea Rd. NW10 —39Ta 59
Winchelsey Rise. S Croy —79Vb 147
Winchendon Rd. SW6 —53Bb 103
Winchendon Rd. Tedd —63Fa 122
Winchester Av. NW6 —39Ab 60
Winchester Av. NW9 —27Qa 39
Winchester Av. Houn —51Ba 99
Winchester Av. Upm —32Vd 70
Winchester Clo. E6 —44Pc 86
Winchester Clo. SE17 —49Rb 83 (6C 206)
Winchester Clo. Brom —69Hc 129
Winchester Clo. Coln —53G 96
Winchester Clo. Enf —15Ub 25
Winchester Clo. Esh —77Ca 141
Winchester Clo. King T —66Ra 123
Winchester Cres. Grav —2F 136
Winchester Dri. Pinn —29Z 37
Winchester Gro. Sev —95Kd 187
Winchester Ho. SW9 —52Qb 104
Winchester Ho. Bark —38Wc 67 (off Keir Hardie Way)
Winchester Pk. Brom —69Hc 129
Winchester Pl. E8 —36Vb 63
Winchester Pl. N6 —32Kb 62
Winchester Rd. E4 —24Ec 44
Winchester Rd. N6 —31Kb 62
Winchester Rd. N9 —18Vb 25
Winchester Rd. NW3 —38Fb 61
Winchester Rd. Bexh —54Zc 109
Winchester Rd. Brom —69Hc 129
Winchester Rd. Felt —62Ba 121
Winchester Rd. Harr —28Na 39
Winchester Rd. Hay —52U 98
Winchester Rd. Ilf —34Tc 66
Winchester Rd. N'wd —27V 36
Winchester Rd. Orp —77Yc 151
Winchester Rd. Twic —58Ka 100
Winchester Rd. W on T —74W 140
Winchester Sq. SE1 —46Tb 83 (6F 201) (off Winchester Wlk.)
Winchester St. SW1 —50Kb 82 (7A 204)
Winchester St. W3 —46Sa 79
Winchester Wlk. SE1 —46Tb 83 (6F 201)
Winchester Way. Crox —15R 18
Winchet Wlk. Croy —72Yb 148
Winchfield Clo. Harr —30La 38
Winchfield Rd. SE26 —64Ac 128
Winchfield Way. Rick —17L 17
Winchilsea Cres. E Mol —68Ea 122
Winchmore Hill Rd. N14 & N21 —18Mb 24
Winchstone Clo. Shep —70P 119
Winckley Clo. Harr —29Pa 39
Wincott St. SE11 —49Qb 82 (5A 206)
Wincrofts Dri. SE9 —56Tc 108
Windborough Rd. Cars —80Jb 146
Windermere Av. N3 —27Cb 41
Windermere Av. NW6 —39Ab 60
Windermere Av. SW19 —69Db 125
Windermere Av. Horn —36Jd 68
Windermere Av. Ruis —31Y 57
Windermere Av. Wemb —31La 58
Windermere Clo. Chor —15F 16
Windermere Clo. Dart —60Kd 111
Windermere Clo. Egh —66C 118
Windermere Clo. Felt —60V 98
Windermere Clo. Orp —76Rc 150
Windermere Clo. Stai —60N 97
Windermere Ct. SW13 —51Va 102
Windermere Ct. Kenl —87Rb 165
Windermere Ct. Wat —12W 18
Windermere Ct. Wemb —31La 58
Windermere Gdns. Ilf —29Nc 46
Windermere Gro. Wemb —32La 58
Windermere Hall. Edgw —22Pa 39
Windermere Ho. New Bar —14Db 23
Windermere Point. SE15 —52Yb 106 (off Old Kent Rd.)
Windermere Rd. N10 —25Kb 42
Windermere Rd. N19 —33Lb 62
Windermere Rd. SW15 —63Ua 124
Windermere Rd. SW16 —67Lb 126
Windermere Rd. W5 —48La 78
Windermere Rd. Bexh —54Ed 110
Windermere Rd. Coul —87Nb 164
Windermere Rd. Croy —74Vb 147
Windermere Rd. S'hall —43Ba 77
Windermere Rd. W Wick —75Gc 149
Windermere Way. Slou —3A 72
Windermere Way. W Dray —46N 75
Winders Rd. SW11 —54Gb 103
Windfield. Lea —93Ka 176
Windfield Clo. SE26 —63Zb 128
Windham Av. New Ad —82Fc 167
Windham Rd. Rich —55Pa 101
Windhover Way. Grav —3G 136
Windings, The. S Croy —83Vb 165
Winding Way. Dag —34Yc 67
Winding Way. Harr —35Ga 58
Windlass Pl. SE8 —49Ac 84
Windlesham Gro. SW19 —60Za 102
Windley Clo. SE23 —61Yb 128
Windmill Av. Eps —83Va 162
Windmill Av. S'hall —47Ea 78
Windmill Cen. S'hall —47Ea 78
Windmill Clo. SE1 —49Wb 83
Windmill Clo. SE13 —54Ec 106
Windmill Clo. Cat —93Sb 181
Windmill Clo. Eps —84Va 162
Windmill Clo. Sun —66U 120
Windmill Clo. Surb —74La 142
Windmill Clo. Upm —33Qd 69
Windmill Clo. Wal A —6Gc 13
Windmill Clo. Wind —4F 94
Windmill Ct. NW2 —37Ab 60
Windmill Dri. SW4 —57Kb 104
Windmill Dri. Crox —16P 17
Windmill Dri. Kes —77Lc 149
Windmill Dri. Lea —95La 176
Windmill End. Eps —84Va 162
Windmill Gdns. Enf —13Qb 24
Windmill Gro. Croy —72Sb 147
Windmill Hill. NW3 —34Eb 61
Windmill Hill. Enf —13Rb 25
Windmill Hill. K Lan —4H 3
Windmill Hill. Ruis —31V 56
Windmill La. E15 —37Fc 65
Windmill La. Barn —16Va 22
Windmill La. Bush —18Ga 20
Windmill La. Chesh —2Ac 12
Windmill La. Eps —84Va 162
Windmill La. Gnfd —43Ea 78
Windmill La. S'hall & Isswth —46Ea 78
Windmill La. Surb —72Ka 142
Windmill M. W4 —49Ua 80
Windmill Pas. W4 —49Ua 80
Windmill Rise. King T —66Ra 123
Windmill Rd. N18 —21Tb 43
Windmill Rd. SW18 —58Fb 103
Windmill Rd. SW19 —63Xa 124
Windmill Rd. W4 —49Ua 80
Windmill Rd. W5 & Bren —49La 78
Windmill Rd. Croy —73Sb 147
Windmill Rd. Ful —6P 53
Windmill Rd. Hamp —64Da 121
Windmill Rd. Mitc —71Lb 146
Windmill Rd. Slou —6H 73
Windmill Rd. Sun —68U 120
Windmill Rd. W. Sun —68U 120
Windmill Row. SE11 —50Qb 82 (7K 205)
Windmill St. W1 —43Mb 82 (1D 198)
Windmill St. Bush —18Ga 20
Windmill St. Grav —8D 114 (in two parts)
Windmill Wlk. SE1 —46Qb 82 (7A 200)
Windmill Way. Ruis —32V 56
Windmore Av. Pot B —3Ya 8
Windover Av. NW9 —28Ta 39
Windrose Clo. SE16 —47Zb 84
Windrush. SE28 —46Xc 87
Windrush Av. Slou —48D 74
Windrush Clo. SW11 —56Fb 103
Windrush Clo. W4 —53Sa 101
Windrush Clo. Uxb —35P 55
Windrush La. SE23 —62Zb 128
Windsor Av. E17 —26Ac 44
Windsor Av. SW19 —67Eb 125
Windsor Av. Edgw —21Ra 39
Windsor Av. Grays —47De 91
Windsor Av. N Mald —71Sa 143
Windsor Av. Sutt —76Ab 144
Windsor Av. Uxb —39R 56
Windsor Av. W Mol —69Ca 121
Windsor Cen., The. N1 —39Rb 63 (off Windsor St.)
Windsor Clo. N3 —26Ab 40
Windsor Clo. SE27 —63Sb 127
Windsor Clo. Borwd —11Qa 21
Windsor Clo. Bov —1C 2
Windsor Clo. Bren —51Ka 100
Windsor Clo. Chesh —2Wb 11
Windsor Clo. Chst —64Rc 130
Windsor Clo. Harr —34Ca 57
Windsor Clo. N'wd —26W 36
Windsor Ct. N14 —17Lb 24
Windsor Ct. NW11 —30Ab 40 (off Golders Grn. Rd.)
Windsor Ct. SW11 —54Fb 103
Windsor Ct. W10 —44Za 80 (off Darfield Way)
Windsor Ct. K Lan —1R 4
Windsor Ct. Pinn —27Z 37
Windsor Ct. Sun —66W 120
Windsor Ct. Whyt —90Vb 165
Windsor Cres. Harr —34Ca 57
Windsor Cres. Wemb —34Ra 59
Windsor Dri. Ashf —63M 119
Windsor Dri. Barn —16Hb 23
Windsor Dri. Dart —58Jd 110
Windsor Dri. Orp —79Wc 151
Windsor & Eton Relief Rd. Wind —3F 94
Windsor Gdns. W9 —43Cb 81
Windsor Gdns. Croy —76Nb 146
Windsor Gdns. Hay —48T 76
Windsor Gro. SE27 —63Sb 127
Windsor Ho. N1 —40Sb 63 (1E 194)
Windsor La. Burn —2A 72
Windsor M. SW18 —59Eb 103 (off Wilna Rd.)
Windsor Pk. Rd. Hay —52V 98
Windsor Pl. SW1 —49Lb 82 (5C 204)
Windsor Pl. Cher —72J 139
Windsor Rd. E4 —21Dc 44

Woodlands Pde.—Wymers Clo.

Woodlands Pde. Ashf —65S **120**
Woodlands Pk. Add —78H **139**
Woodlands Pk. Bex —63Fd **132**
Woodlands Pk. Rd. N15 —29Rb **43**
Woodlands Pk. Rd. SE10 —51Gc **107**
Woodlands Rise. Swan —68Hd **132**
Woodlands Rd. E11 —33Gc **65**
Woodlands Rd. E17 —27Ec **44**
Woodlands Rd. N9 —18Yb **26**
Woodlands Rd. SW13 —55Va **102**
Woodlands Rd. Bexh —55Ad **109**
Woodlands Rd. Bookh —100Ba **175**
Woodlands Rd. Brom —68Nc **130**
Woodlands Rd. Bush —15Aa **19**
Woodlands Rd. Enf —10Tb **11**
Woodlands Rd. Eps —87Qa **161**
Woodlands Rd. H Wood —25Qd **49**
Woodlands Rd. Harr —29Ha **38**
Woodlands Rd. Ilf —34Sc **66**
Woodlands Rd. Iswth —55Fa **100**
Woodlands Rd. Lea —89Fa **160**
Woodlands Rd. Orp —79Wc **151**
Woodlands Rd. Romf —27Hd **48**
Woodlands Rd. S'hall —46Z **77**
Woodlands Rd. Surb —73Ma **143**
Woodlands Rd. Vir W —10N **117**
Woodlands Rd. W Byf —86H **157**
Woodlands Rd. E. Vir W —10N **117**
Woodlands Rd. W. Vir W —10N **117**
Woodlands St. SE13 —59Fc **107**
Woodlands Ter. Swan —72Dd **152**
Woodlands, The. N12 —23Eb **41**
Woodlands, The. N14 —18Kb **24**
Woodlands, The. SE13 —59Fc **107**
Woodlands, The. SE19 —66Sb **127**
Woodlands, The. Esh —74Ea **142**
Woodlands, The. Ger X —30B **34**
Woodlands, The. Harr —33Ga **58**
Woodlands, The. Iswth —54Ha **100**
Woodlands, The. Orp —79Xc **151**
Woodlands, The. Stan —22Ka **38**
Woodlands, The. Wall —81Kb **164**
Woodland St. E8 —37Vb **84**
Woodlands View. Badg M —82Dd **170**
Woodlands Way. SW15 —57Bb **103**
Woodlands Way. Asht —88Qa **161**
Woodland Ter. SE7 —49Nc **86**
Woodland Wlk. NW3 —36Gb **61**
Woodland Wlk. SE10 —50Gc **85**
Woodland Wlk. Brom —63Gc **129**
(in two parts)
Woodland Way. N21 —19Qb **24**
Woodland Way. NW7 —23Ua **40**
Woodland Way. SE2 —49Zc **87**
Woodland Way. Cat —100Ub **181**
Woodland Way. Chesh —1Rb **11**
Woodland Way. Croy —74Ac **148**
Woodland Way. Grnh —57Xd **112**
Woodland Way. Mitc —66Jb **126**
Woodland Way. Mord —70Bb **125**
Woodland Way. Orp —70Sc **130**
Woodland Way. Purl —85Qb **164**
Woodland Way. Surb —75Ra **143**
Woodland Way. Tad —94Ab **178**
Woodland Way. They B —8Tc **14**
Woodland Way. W Wick —77Dc **148**
Woodland Way. Wey —78T **140**
Woodland Way. Wfd G —20Kc **27**
Wood La. N6 —30Kb **42**
Wood La. NW9 —31Ta **59**
Wood La. W12 —44Ya **80**
Wood La. Cat —96Tb **181**
Wood La. Dag —35Zc **67**
Wood La. Dart —63Td **134**
Wood La. Horn —36Jd **68**
Wood La. Iswth —51Ga **100**
Wood La. Iver —41E **74**
Wood La. Knap —6A **188**
Wood La. Ruis —32T **56**
Wood La. Slou —8D **72**
Wood La. Stan —20Ja **20**
Wood La. Tad —89Bb **163**
Wood La. Wey —81S **158**
Wood La. Wfd G —21Hc **45**
Wood La. Clo. Iver —41D **74**
Woodlawn Clo. SW15 —57Bb **103**
Woodlawn Cres. Twic —61Da **121**
Woodlawn Gro. Wok —87B **156**
Woodlawn Rd. SW6 —52Za **102**
Woodlawns. Eps —80Ta **143**
Woodlea Dri. Brom —71Gc **149**
Woodlea Gro. N'wd —23T **36**
Woodlea Rd. N16 —34Ub **63**
Woodlee Clo. Vir W —8N **117**
Woodleigh. E18 —25Jc **45**
Woodleigh Av. N12 —23Gb **41**
Woodleigh Gdns. SW16 —62Nb **126**
Woodley Clo. SW17 —66Hb **125**
Woodley La. Cars —76Gb **145**
Woodley Rd. Orp —75Yc **151**
Wood Lodge Gdns. Brom —66Nc **130**
Wood Lodge Grange. Sev —94Ld **187**
Wood Lodge La. W Wick —76Ec **148**
Woodmancote Gdns. W Byf —85J **157**
Woodman La. E4 —15Gc **27**
Woodman Pde. E16 —46Qc 86
(off Woodman St.)
Woodman Path. Ilf —23Uc **46**
Woodman Rd. Coul —87Lb **164**
Woodman Rd. War —22Yd **50**
Woodmans Gro. NW10 —36Va **60**
Woodman's M. W12 —43Xa **80**
Woodmansterne La. Bans —87Db **163**
Woodmansterne La. Cars & Wall —84Hb **163**
Woodmansterne Rd. SW16 —66Lb **126**
Woodmansterne Rd. Cars —84Hb **163**
Woodmansterne Rd. Coul —87Lb **164**
Woodmansterne St. Bans —87Gb **163**
Woodman St. E16 —46Qc **86**
(in two parts)
Woodmans Yd. Wat —14Z **19**
Woodman Vs. Fawk —76Xd **154**
Wood Mead. N17 —23Wb **43**
Wood Meads. Epp —1Wc **15**
Woodmere. SE9 —60Pc **108**
Woodmere Av. Croy —73Yb **148**
Woodmere Av. Wat —10Z **5**
Woodmere Clo. SW11 —55Jb **104**
Woodmere Clo. Croy —73Zb **148**
Woodmere Ct. N14 —17Kb **24**
Woodmere Gdns. Croy —73Zb **148**
Woodmere Way. Beck —71Fc **149**
Woodmount. Swan —73Fd **152**
Woodnook Rd. SW16 —64Kb **126**
Woodpecker Clo. N9 —16Xb **25**
Woodpecker Clo. Bush —18Ea **20**
Woodpecker Clo. Cob —84Aa **159**
Woodpecker Mt. Croy —81Ac **166**
Woodpecker Rd. SE14 —51Ac **106**
Woodpecker Rd. SE28 —45Yc **87**
Woodpecker Way. Wok —96A **172**
Woodplace Clo. Coul —91Lb **180**
Woodplace La. Coul —90Lb **164**
Woodquest Av. SE24 —57Sb **105**
Woodredon Rd. Wal A —7Mc **13**
Wood Retreat. SE18 —52Tc **108**
Woodridden Hill. Wal A & Epp —7Lc **13**
Wood Ride. Barn —11Fb **23**
Wood Ride. Orp —70Tc **130**
Woodridge Clo. NW2 —34Xa **60**
Woodridge Clo. Enf —12Qb **24**
Woodridge Way. N'wd —23U **36**
Wood Riding. Wok —87G **156**
Woodridings Av. Pinn —25Ba **37**
Woodridings Clo. Pinn —24Aa **37**
Woodridings Ct. N22 —25Mb **42**
Woodriffe Rd. E11 —31Fc **65**
Wood Rise. Pinn —29W **36**
Wood Rd. Big H —90Lc **167**
Wood Rd. Shep —70Q **120**
Woodrow. SE18 —49Pc **86**
Woodrow Av. Hay —43V **76**
Woodrow Clo. Gnfd —38Ka **58**
Woodrow Ct. N17 —24Xb **43**
Woodrush Clo. SE14 —52Ac **106**
Woodrush Way. Romf —28Zc **47**
Woods Dri. Farn C —6D **52**
Woodseer St. E1 —43Vb **83**
Woodsford Sq. W14 —47Ab **80**
Woodshire Rd. Dag —34Dd **68**
Woodshots Meadow. Wat —15T **18**
Woodside. N10 —27Jb **42**
Wood Side. NW11 —29Cb **41**
Woodside. SW19 —65Bb **125**
Woodside. Buck H —19Lc **27**
Woodside. Chesh —3Wb **11**
Woodside. Els —14Na **21**
Woodside. Fet —94Da **175**
Woodside. Orp —78Xc **151**
Woodside. Tad —100Bb **179**
Woodside. W on T —74W **140**
Woodside. Wat —8W **4**
Woodside. W Hor —98S **174**
Woodside Av. N6 & N10 —29Hb **41**
Woodside Av. N12 —21Eb **41**
Woodside Av. SE25 —72Xb **147**
Woodside Av. Chst —64Sc **130**
Woodside Av. Esh —73Ga **142**
Woodside Av. W on T —77X **141**
Woodside Av. Wemb —39Na **59**
Woodside Clo. Bexh —56Fd **110**
Woodside Clo. Cat —96Ub **181**
Woodside Clo. Ger X —26A **34**
Woodside Clo. Hut —15Fe **33**
Woodside Clo. Knap —5A **188**
Woodside Clo. Rain —42Ld **89**
Woodside Clo. Stan —22Ka **38**
Woodside Clo. Surb —73Sa **143**
Woodside Clo. Wemb —39Na **59**
Woodside Ct. E12 —32Lc **65**
Woodside Ct. N12 —21Db **41**
Woodside Ct. W5 —46Na **79**
Woodside Ct. Rd. Croy —73Wb **147**
Woodside Cres. Sidc —62Uc **130**
Woodside Dri. Dart —63Gd **132**
Woodside End. Wemb —39Na **59**
Woodside Gdns. E4 —22Dc **44**
Woodside Gdns. N17 —26Ub **43**
Woodside Grange Rd. N12 —21Db **41**
Woodside Grn. SE25 —72Wb **147**
(in two parts)
Woodside Gro. N12 —20Eb **23**
Woodside Hill. Ger X —26A **34**
Woodside La. N12 —20Eb **23**
Woodside La. Bex —58Zc **109**
Woodside La. Wink —4A **116**
Woodside Pk. SE25 —72Xb **147**
Woodside Pk. Av. E17 —28Fc **45**
Woodside Pk. Rd. N12 —21Db **41**
Woodside Pl. Wemb —39Na **59**
Woodside Rd. E13 —42Lc **85**
Woodside Rd. N22 —24Pb **42**
Woodside Rd. SE25 —72Xb **147**
Woodside Rd. Bexh —56Fd **110**
Woodside Rd. Brick —2Ba **5**
Woodside Rd. Brom —71Nc **150**
Woodside Rd. Cob —85Ca **159**
Woodside Rd. King T —66Na **123**
Woodside Rd. N Mald —68Ta **123**
Woodside Rd. N'wd —24V **36**
Woodside Rd. Purl —85Mb **164**
Woodside Rd. Sev —95Jd **186**
Woodside Rd. Sidc —62Uc **130**
Woodside Rd. Sund —96Ad **185**
Woodside Rd. Sutt —76Eb **145**
Woodside Rd. Wat —3W **4**
Woodside Rd. Wink —5A **116**
Woodside Rd. Wfd G —21Jc **45**
Woodside Way. Croy —72Yb **148**
Woodside Way. Mitc —67Kb **126**
Woodside Way. Vir W —9M **117**
Woods M. W1 —45Jb **82** (4G **197**)
Woodsome Lodge. Wey —79S **140**
Woodsome Rd. NW5 —34Jb **62**
Wood's Pl. SE1 —48Ub **83** (4J **207**)
Woodspring Rd. SW19 —61Ab **124**
Woods Rd. SE15 —53Xb **105**
Woodstead Gro. Edgw —23Na **39**
Woods, The. N'wd —22W **36**
Woods, The. Rad —6Ka **6**
Woods, The. Uxb —35R **56**
Woodstock. W Cla —100K **173**
Woodstock Av. NW11 —31Ab **60**
Woodstock Av. W13 —48Ja **78**
Woodstock Av. Iswth —57Ja **100**
Woodstock Av. Romf —23Rd **49**
Woodstock Av. Slou —9P **73**
Woodstock Av. S'hall —41Ba **77**
Woodstock Av. Sutt —73Bb **145**
Woodstock Clo. Bex —59Bd **109**
Woodstock Clo. Stan —26Na **39**
Woodstock Clo. Wok —88A **156**
Woodstock Ct. SE11 —50Pb **82** (7J **205**)
Woodstock Ct. SE12 —58Jc **107**
Woodstock Cres. N9 —16Xb **25**
Woodstock Dri. Uxb —35N **55**
Woodstock Gdns. Beck —67Dc **128**
Woodstock Gdns. Hay —43V **76**
Woodstock Gdns. Ilf —33Wc **67**
Woodstock Gro. W12 —47Za **80**
Woodstock La. N. Surb —75La **142**
Woodstock La. S. Clay & Chess —79Ka **142**
Woodstock M. W1 —43Jb 82 (1J 197)
(off Westmoreland St.)
Woodstock Rise. Sutt —73Bb **145**
Woodstock Rd. E7 —38Lc **65**
Woodstock Rd. E17 —26Fc **45**
Woodstock Rd. N4 —32Qb **62**
Woodstock Rd. NW11 —31Bb **61**
Woodstock Rd. W4 —49Ua **80**
Woodstock Rd. Bush —17Ga **20**
Woodstock Rd. Cars —78Jb **146**
Woodstock Rd. Coul —87Pb **164**
Woodstock Rd. Croy —76Tb **147**
Woodstock Rd. Wemb —39Pa **59**
Woodstock St. E16 —44Gc **85**
Woodstock St. W1 —44Kb **82** (3K **197**)
Woodstock Ter. E14 —45Dc **84**
Woodstock Way. Mitc —67Kb **126**
Woodstone Av. Eps —78Wa **144**
Wood St. E16 —45Kc **85**
Wood St. E17 —27Ec **44**
Wood St. EC2 —44Sb **83** (3E **200**)
Wood St. W4 —50Ua **80**
Wood St. Barn —14Ya **22**
Wood St. Grays —51Ee **113**
Wood St. King T —68Ma **123**
Wood St. Mitc —73Jb **146**
Wood St. Red —100Lb **180**
Wood St. Swan —68Ld **133**
Woodsway. Oxs —86Ga **160**
Woodsyre. SE26 —63Vb **127**
Woodthorpe Rd. SW15 —56Xa **102**
Woodthorpe Rd. Ashf —65M **119**
Woodtree Clo. NW4 —26Za **40**
Wood Vale. N10 —29Lb **42**
Wood Vale. SE23 —60Xb **105**
Woodvale Av. SE25 —69Vb **127**
Wood Vale Est. SE23 —59Xb **105**
Woodvale Wlk. SE27 —64Sb **127**
Woodvale Way. NW11 —34Za **60**
Woodview. Chess —83La **160**
Wood View. Grays —48Fe **91**
Woodview Av. E4 —21Ec **44**
Woodview Clo. N4 —31Rb **63**
Woodview Clo. SW15 —63Ta **123**
Woodview Clo. Orp —75Sc **150**
Woodview Clo. S Croy —86Xb **165**
Woodview Clo. W King —79Ud **154**
Woodview Rd. Swan —68Ed **132**
Woodville. SE3 —53Kc **107**
Woodville Clo. SE12 —57Jc **107**
Woodville Clo. Tedd —63Ja **122**
Woodville Ct. SE19 —67Vb **127**
Woodville Ct. Wat —12W **18**
Woodville Gdns. NW11 —31Za **60**
Woodville Gdns. W5 —44Na **79**
Woodville Gdns. Ilf —27Rc **46**
Woodville Gdns. Ruis —31S **56**
Woodville Gro. Well —55Wc **109**
Woodville Pl. Cat —93Sb **181**
Woodville Pl. Grav —9D **114**
Woodville Rd. E11 —32Hc **65**
Woodville Rd. E17 —28Bc **44**
Woodville Rd. E18 —26Kc **45**
Woodville Rd. N16 —36Ub **63**
Woodville Rd. NW6 —40Bb **61**
Woodville Rd. NW11 —31Za **60**
Woodville Rd. W5 —44Ma **79**
Woodville Rd. Barn —13Db **23**
Woodville Rd. Mord —70Cb **125**
Woodville Rd. Rich —62Ka **122**
Woodville Rd. T Hth —70Sb **127**
Woodville St. SE18 —49Nc **86**
Woodvill Rd. Lea —92Ka **176**
Wood Wlk. Rick —12G **16**
Woodward Av. NW4 —29Wa **40**
Woodward Clo. Grays —49De **91**
Woodwarde Rd. SE22 —58Ub **105**
Woodward Gdns. Dag —38Yc **67**
Woodward Gdns. Stan —24Ha **38**
Woodward Heights. Grays —49De **91**
Woodward Rd. Dag —38Xc **67**
Woodward's Footpath. Twic —58Fa **100**
Woodward Ter. Grnh —58Ud **112**
Wood Way. Orp —75Qc **150**
Woodway. Shenf & Hut —18Ce **33**
Woodway Cres. Harr —30Ja **38**
Woodwaye. Wat —17Y **19**
Woodwell St. SW18 —57Eb **103**
Wood Wharf Bus. Pk. E14 —46Dc **84**
Woodwicks. Rick —22F **34**
Woodyard Clo. NW5 —36Jb **62**
Woodyard La. SE21 —59Ub **105**
Woodyates Rd. SE12 —58Jc **107**
Woolacombe Rd. SE3 —54Lc **107**
Woolacombe Way. Hay —49U **76**
Wooler St. SE17 —50Tb **83** (7F **207**)
Woolf Clo. SE28 —46Xc **87**
Woolf Wlk. Til —4E **114**
Woolgar M. N16 —36Ub 63
(off Gillett St.)
Woolhampton Way. Chig —20Xc **29**
Woollard St. Wal A —6Ec **12**
Woollaston Rd. N4 —30Rb **43**
Woolley Ho. SW9 —55Rb 105
(off Loughborough Rd.)
Woolmead Av. NW9 —31Wa **60**
Woolmer Clo. Borwd —10Qa **7**
Woolmer Gdns. N18 —22Wb **43**
Woolmer Rd. N18 —22Wb **43**
Woolmore St. E14 —45Ec **84**
Woolneigh St. SW6 —55Db **103**
Woolridge Way. E9 —38Yb **64**
Wool Rd. SW20 —65Xa **124**
Woolstaplers Way. SE16 —48Wb **83**
Woolston Clo. E17 —26Zb **44**
Woolstone Rd. SE23 —61Ac **128**
Woolwich Chu. St. SE18 —48Nc **86**
Woolwich Comn. SE18 —51Qc **108**
Woolwich Dockyard Ind. Est. SE18 —48Nc **86**
Woolwich Ind. Est. SE28 —48Uc **86**
(in two parts)
Woolwich Mnr. Way. E6 & E16 —42Pc **86**
Woolwich New Rd. SE18 —50Qc **86**
Woolwich Rd. SE2 & Belv —51Zc **109**
Woolwich Rd. SE10 & SE7 —50Hc **85**
Woolwich Rd. Bexh —55Cd **110**
Wooster Gdns. E14 —44Fc **85**
Wooster M. Harr —27Ea **38**
Woostock Dri. Uxb —35N **55**
Wootton Clo. Horn —29Md **49**
Wootton Gro. N3 —25Cb **41**
Wootton St. SE1 —46Qb **82** (1A **206**)
Worbeck Rd. SE20 —68Xb **127**
Worcester Av. N17 —24Wb **43**
Worcester Av. Upm —33Vd **70**
Worcester Clo. Croy —75Cc **148**
Worcester Clo. Grav —6B **136**
Worcester Clo. Grnh —56Xd **112**
Worcester Clo. Mitc —69Kb **126**
Worcester Clo. Stanf —1M **93**
Worcester Ct. N12 —22Db **41**
Worcester Ct. Harr —27Ga **38**
Worcester Ct. W on T —74Y **141**
Worcester Ct. Wor Pk —76Ua **144**
Worcester Cres. NW7 —20Ua **22**
Worcester Cres. Wfd G —22Kc **45**
Worcester Dri. W4 —47Ua **80**
Worcester Dri. Ashf —64R **120**
Worcester Gdns. Gnfd —37Fa **58**
Worcester Gdns. Ilf —31Nc **66**
Worcester Gdns. Slou —7H **73**
Worcester Gdns. Wor Pk —76Ua **144**
Worcester Ho. Borwd —12Qa 21
(off Stratfield Rd.)
Worcester M. NW6 —37Db **61**
Worcester Pk. Rd. Wor Pk —76Ta **143**
Worcester Rd. E12 —34Pc **66**
Worcester Rd. E17 —26Zb **44**
Worcester Rd. SW19 —64Bb **125**
Worcester Rd. Sutt —80Cb **145**
Worcester Rd. Uxb —43L **75**
Worcesters Av. Enf —10Wb **11**
Wordsworth Av. E12 —38Nc **66**
Wordsworth Av. E18 —27Hc **45**
Wordsworth Av. Gnfd —41Fa **78**
Wordsworth Av. Kenl —87Tb **165**
Wordsworth Clo. Romf —25Ld **49**
Wordsworth Clo. Til —4E **114**
Wordsworth Ct. Harr —31Ga **58**
Wordsworth Dri. Sutt —77Ya **144**
Wordsworth Pde. N8 —28Rb **43**
Wordsworth Rd. N16 —35Ub **63**
Wordsworth Rd. SE1 —49Vb **83** (6K **207**)
Wordsworth Rd. SE20 —66Zb **128**
Wordsworth Rd. Add —77M **139**
Wordsworth Rd. Hamp —63Ba **121**
Wordsworth Rd. Slou —2B **72**
Wordsworth Rd. Wall —79Lb **146**
Wordsworth Rd. Well —53Uc **108**
Wordsworth Wlk. NW11 —28Cb **41**
Wordsworth Way. Dart —56Qd **111**
Wordsworth Way. W Dray —49N **75**
Worfield St. SW11 —52Gb **103**
Worgan St. SE11 —50Pb **82** (7H **205**)
Worland Rd. E15 —38Gc **65**
World's End. Cob —86W **158**
Worlds End Est. SW10 —52Fb **103**
World's End La. N21 & Enf —15Pb **24**
Worlds End La. Orp —79Vc **151**
World's End Pas. SW10 —52Fb **103**
World's End Pl. SW10 —52Fb **103**
World Trade Cen. E1 —45Vb 83 (5K 201)
(off E. Smithfield)
Worlidge St. W6 —50Ya **80**
Worlingham Rd. SE22 —56Vb **105**
Wormholt Rd. W12 —45Wa **80**
Wormley Ct. Wal A —5Jc **13**
Wormwood St. EC2 —44Ub **83** (2H **201**)
Wormyngford Ct. Wal A —5Jc **13**
Wornington Rd. W10 —42Ab **80**
Woronzow Rd. NW8 —39Fb **61**
Worpin Rd. Shenf —19Be **33**
Worple Av. SW19 —66Za **124**
Worple Av. Iswth —57Ja **100**
Worple Av. Stai —65K **119**
Worple Clo. Harr —32Ba **57**
Worple Rd. SW20 & SW19 —68Ya **124**
Worple Rd. Eps —87Ta **161**
Worple Rd. Iswth —56Ja **100**
Worple Rd. Lea —94Ka **176**
Worple Rd. Stai —65K **119**
Worple Rd. M. SW19 —65Bb **125**
Worplesdon Hill. Wok —10A **188**
Worple St. SW14 —55Ta **101**
Worple, The. Wray —58B **96**
Worple Way. Harr —32Ba **57**
Worple Way. Rich —57Na **101**
Worrin Clo. Shenf —18Be **33**
Worrin Rd. Shenf —19Be **33**
Worships Hill. Sev —95Gd **186**
Worship St. EC2 —42Tb **83** (6G **195**)
Worslade Rd. SW17 —63Fb **125**
Worsley Bri. Rd. SE26 & Beck —63Bc **128**
Worsley Ho. SE23 —61Xb **127**
Worsley Rd. E11 —35Gc **65**
Worsopp Dri. SW4 —57Lb **104**
Worsted Grn. Red —100Lb **180**
Worth Clo. Orp —77Uc **150**
Worthfield Clo. Eps —80Ta **143**
Worth Gro. SE17 —50Tb 83 (7F 207)
(off Liverpool Gro.)
Worthing Clo. E15 —39Gc **65**
Worthing Rd. Houn —51Ba **99**
Worthington Clo. Mitc —69Kb **126**
Worthington Rd. Surb —74Pa **143**
Wortley Rd. E6 —38Mc **65**
Wortley Rd. Croy —73Qb **146**
Worton Ct. Iswth —56Ga **100**
Worton Gdns. Iswth —54Fa **100**
Worton Hall Ind. Est. Iswth —56Ga **100**
Worton Rd. Iswth —56Ga **100**
Worton Way. Houn & Iswth —54Fa **100**
Wotton Grn. Orp —70Zc **131**
Wotton Rd. NW2 —34Ya **60**
Wotton Rd. SE8 —51Bc **106**
Wotton Way. Sutt —82Ya **162**
Wouldham Rd. E16 —44Hc **85**
Wouldham Rd. Grays —51Ae **113**
Wrabness Way. Stai —67K **119**
Wragby Rd. E11 —34Gc **65**
Wrampling Pl. N9 —18Wb **25**
Wrangley Ct. Wal A —5Jc **13**
Wrangthorn Wlk. Croy —77Qb **146**
Wray Av. Ilf —27Qc **46**
Wrayburn Ho. SE16 —47Wb 83
(off Llewellyn St.)
Wray Clo. Horn —30Md **49**
Wray Cres. N4 —33Nb **62**
Wrayfield Rd. Sutt —76Za **144**
Wray Rd. Sutt —81Bb **163**
Wraysbury Clo. Houn —57Aa **99**
Wraysbury Rd. Stai —61D **118**
Wrays Way. Hay —42U **76**
Wrekin Rd. SE18 —52Sc **108**
Wren Av. NW2 —35Ya **60**
Wren Av. S'hall —49Ba **77**
Wren Clo. E16 —44Hc **85**
Wren Clo. N9 —18Zb **26**
Wren Clo. Orp —69Zc **131**
Wren Clo. S Croy —81Zb **166**
Wren Ct. Langl —48C **74**
Wren Cres. Add —78M **139**
Wren Cres. Bush —18Ea **20**
Wren Dri. W Dray —48M **75**
Wren Gdns. Dag —36Zc **67**
Wren Gdns. Horn —32Hd **68**
Wren Landing. E14 —46Cc **84**
Wren Path. SE28 —48Tc **86**
Wren Pl. Brtwd —20Zd **33**
Wren Rd. SE5 —53Tb **105**
Wren Rd. Dag —36Zc **67**
Wren Rd. Sidc —63Yc **131**
Wren's Av. Ashf —63S **120**
Wrens Croft. Grav —3A **136**
Wrens Hill. Oxs —87Ea **160**
Wren's Pk. Ho. E5 —33Xb **63**
Wren St. WC1 —42Pb **82** (5J **193**)
Wrentham Av. NW10 —40Za **60**
Wrenthorpe Rd. Brom —63Gc **129**
Wren Wlk. Til —2D **114**
Wrenwood Way. Pinn —28X **37**
Wrestlers Ct. EC3 —44Ub 83 (2H 201)
(off Clark's Pl.)
Wrexham Rd. E3 —40Cc **64**
Wrexham Rd. Romf —20Md **31**
Wricklemarsh Rd. SE3 —53Kc **107**
(in two parts)
Wrigglesworth St. SE14 —52Zb **106**
Wright. Wind —5A **94**
Wright Clo. Swans —58Zd **113**
Wright Rd. N1 —37Ub **63**
Wright Rd. Houn —52Y **99**
Wrights All. SW19 —65Ya **124**
Wrightsbridge Rd. S Wea —18Pd **31**
Wrights Clo. SE13 —56Fc **107**
Wrights Clo. Dag —35Dd **68**
Wrights Gro. SW4 —56Mb **104**
Wrights La. W8 —48Db **81**
Wrights Pl. NW10 —37Sa **59**
Wright's Rd. E3 —40Bc **64**
Wrights Rd. SE25 —69Ub **127**
Wrights Row. Wall —77Kb **146**
Wrights Wlk. SW14 —55Ta **101**
Wright Way. Wind —5A **94**
Wrigley Clo. E4 —22Fc **45**
Writtle Wlk. Rain —39Gd **68**
Wrotham Ho. Beck —66Bc 128
(off Sellindge Clo.)
Wrotham Rd. NW1 —38Lb **62**
Wrotham Rd. W13 —46La **78**
Wrotham Rd. Barn —12Ab **22**
Wrotham Rd. Meop & Grav —9B **136**
Wrotham Rd. Well —53Yc **109**
Wroth's Path. Lou —11Pc **28**
Wrottesley Rd. NW10 —40Wa **60**
Wrottesley Rd. SE18 —51Sc **108**
Wroughton Rd. SW11 —58Hb **103**
Wroughton Ter. NW4 —28Xa **40**
Wroxall Rd. Dag —37Yc **67**
Wroxham Gdns. N11 —24Mb **42**
Wroxham Gdns. Enf —7Rb **11**
Wroxham Gdns. Pot B —3Za **8**
Wroxham Rd. SE28 —45Zc **87**
Wroxton Rd. SE15 —54Yb **106**
Wrythe Grn. Cars —76Hb **145**
Wrythe Grn. Rd. Cars —76Hb **145**
Wrythe La. Cars —74Eb **145**
Wulfred Way. Kems —90Rd **171**
Wulfstan St. W12 —43Va **80**
Wyatt Clo. SE16 —47Bc **84**
Wyatt Clo. Bush —17Ga **20**
Wyatt Clo. Hay —43W **76**
Wyatt Pk. Rd. SW2 —61Nb **126**
Wyatt Rd. E7 —37Jc **65**
Wyatt Rd. N5 —34Sb **63**
Wyatt Rd. Dart —55Hd **110**
Wyatt Rd. Stai —64J **119**
Wyatt Rd. Wind —5B **94**
Wyatt's Clo. Chor —13J **17**
Wyatt's Covert Caravan Site. Uxb —28H **35**
Wyatts La. E17 —27Ec **44**
Wyatt's Rd. Chor —14H **17**
Wybert St. NW1 —42Lb **82** (5A **192**)
Wyborne Ho. NW10 —38Sa **59**
Wyborne Way. NW10 —38Sa **59**
Wyburn Av. Barn —13Bb **23**
Wyche Gro. S Croy —80Sb **147**
Wych Elm Clo. Horn —31Qd **69**
Wych Elm Lodge. Brom —66Hc **129**
Wych Elm Pas. King T —66Pa **123**
Wych Elm Rd. Horn —30Qd **49**
Wychelms. Park —1Da **5**
Wycherley Clo. SE3 —52Hc **107**
Wycherley Cres. Barn —16Db **23**
Wych Hill. Wok —7F **188**
Wych Hill La. Wok —7G **188**
Wych Hill Pk. Wok —7G **188**
Wych Hill Rise. Wok —7F **188**
Wych Hill Way. Wok —8G **188**
Wychwood Av. Edgw —23Ma **39**
Wychwood Av. T Hth —69Sb **127**
Wychwood Clo. Edgw —23Ma **39**
Wychwood Clo. Sun —65W **120**
Wychwood End. N6 —31Lb **62**
Wychwood Gdns. Ilf —28Pc **46**
Wychwood Way. SE19 —65Tb **127**
Wychwood Way. N'wd —24V **36**
Wycliffe Clo. Well —53Vc **109**
Wycliffe Ct. Abb L —4U **4**
Wycliffe Ho. Grav —10B 114
(off Wycliffe Row)
Wycliffe Houses. Grav —1D **136**
Wycliffe Rd. SW11 —54Jb **104**
Wycliffe Rd. SW19 —65Db **125**
Wycliffe Row. Grav —10B **114**
(in two parts)
Wyclif St. EC1 —41Rb **83** (4B **194**)
Wycombe Gdns. NW11 —33Cb **61**
Wycombe Pl. SW18 —58Eb **103**
Wycombe Rd. N17 —25Wb **43**
Wycombe Rd. Ilf —29Pc **46**
Wycombe Rd. Wemb —39Qa **59**
Wydehurst Rd. Croy —73Wb **147**
Wydell Clo. Mord —72Za **144**
Wydenhurst Rd. Croy —73Wb **147**
Wydeville Mnr. Rd. SE12 —63Kc **129**
Wye Clo. Ashf —63R **120**
Wye Clo. Orp —73Vc **151**
Wye Clo. Ruis —30S **36**
Wyemead Cres. E4 —19Gc **27**
Wye Rd. Grav —1F **136**
Wye St. SW11 —54Fb **103**
Wyeth's Rd. Eps —85Va **162**
Wyevale Clo. Pinn —27W **36**
Wyfields. Ilf —25Rc **46**
Wyfold Ho. SE2 —47Zc 87
(off Wolvercote Rd.)
Wyfold Rd. SW6 —52Ab **102**
Wyhill Wlk. Dag —38Ed **68**
Wyke Clo. Iswth —51Ha **100**
Wyke Gdns. W7 —48Ja **78**
Wykeham Av. Dag —37Yc **67**
Wykeham Av. Horn —30Md **49**
Wykeham Clo. W Dray —50Q **76**
Wykeham Grn. Dag —37Yc **67**
Wykeham Hill. Wemb —32Pa **59**
Wykeham Rise. N20 —18Ab **22**
Wykeham Rd. NW4 —28Ya **40**
Wykeham Rd. Harr —28Ka **38**
Wyke Rd. E3 —38Cc **64**
Wyke Rd. SW20 —68Ya **124**
Wylands Rd. Slou —49C **74**
Wylchin Clo. Pinn —27V **36**
Wyldes Clo. NW11 —32Eb **61**
Wyldfield Gdns. N9 —19Vb **25**
Wyld Way. Wemb —37Ra **59**
Wyleu St. SE23 —59Ac **106**
Wylie Rd. S'hall —48Ca **77**
Wyllen Clo. E1 —42Yb **84**
Wyllyotts Clo. Pot B —4Bb **9**
Wyllyotts La. Pot B —4Bb **9**
Wylo Dri. Barn —16Wa **22**
Wymans Way. E7 —35Lc **65**
Wymering Rd. W9 —41Cb **81**
Wymers Clo. Burn —10A **52**

Wymond St. SW15 —55Ya **102**
Wynan Rd. E14 —50Dc **84**
Wynash Gdns. Cars —78Gb **145**
Wynaud St. N22 —23Pb **42**
Wyncham Av. Sidc —60Uc **108**
Wynchgate. N14 & N21 —18Mb **24**
Wynchgate. Harr —24Ga **38**
Wynchgate. N'holt —36Ba **57**
Wyncombe Av. W5 —49Ka **78**
Wyncote Way. S Croy —81Zb **166**
Wyncroft Clo. Brom —69Pc **130**
Wyndale Av. NW9 —30Qa **39**
Wyndcliffe Rd. SE7 —51Kc **107**
Wyndcroft Clo. Enf —13Rb **25**
Wyndham Av. Cob —85W **158**
Wyndham Clo. Orp —74Sc **150**
Wyndham Clo. Sutt —80Cb **145**
Wyndham Cres. N19 —34Lb **62**
Wyndham Cres. Burn —10A **52**
Wyndham Cres. Houn —58Ca **99**
Wyndham Est. SE5 —52Sb **105**
Wyndham M. W1
     —43Hb **81** (1F **197**)
Wyndham Pl. W1
     —43Hb **81** (1F **197**)
Wyndham Rd. E6 —38Mc **65**
Wyndham Rd. SE5 —52Sb **105**
Wyndham Rd. W13 —48Ka **78**
Wyndham Rd. Barn —18Hb **23**
Wyndham Rd. King T —66Pa **123**
Wyndham Rd. Wok —6E **188**
Wyndham St. W1
     —43Hb **81** (7F **191**)
Wyndham Yd. W1
     —43Hb **81** (1F **197**)
Wyneham Rd. SE24 —57Tb **105**
Wynell Rd. SE23 —62Zb **128**
Wynford Gro. Orp —69Xc **131**
Wynford Pl. Belv —51Cd **110**
Wynford Rd. N1
     —40Pb **62** (1H **193**)
Wynford Way. SE9 —62Pc **130**
Wynlie Gdns. Pinn —26X **37**
Wynndale Rd. E18 —25Kc **45**
Wynne Rd. SW9 —54Qb **104**
Wynnstay Gdns. W8 —48Cb **81**
Wynter St. SW11 —56Eb **103**
Wynton Gdns. SE25 —71Vb **147**
Wynton Gro. W on T —76W **140**
Wynton Pl. W3 —44Ra **79**
Wynyard Clo. Sarr —8J **3**
Wynyard Ho. SE11
     —50Pb **82** (7J **205**)
     (off Newburn St.)
Wynyard Ter. SE11
     —50Pb **82** (7J **205**)
Wynyatt St. EC1
     —41Rb **83** (4B **194**)
Wyre Gro. Edgw —20Ra **21**
Wyre Gro. Hay —49W **76**

Wyresdale Cres. Gnfd —41Ha **78**
Wyteleaf Clo. Ruis —30S **36**
Wythburn Pl. W1
     —44Hb **81** (3F **197**)
Wythenshawe Rd. Dag —34Cd **68**
Wythens Wlk. SE9 —58Rc **108**
Wythes Clo. Brom —68Pc **130**
Wythes Rd. E16 —46Nc **86**
Wythfield Rd. SE9 —58Pc **108**
Wyvenhoe Rd. Harr —34Ea **58**
Wyvern Clo. Dart —59Ld **111**
Wyvern Clo. Orp —76Xc **151**
Wyvern Ho. Grays —51De **113**
     (off Bridge Rd.)
Wyvern Pl. Add —77K **139**
Wyvern Rd. Purl —82Rb **165**
Wyvern Way. Uxb —38K **55**
Wyvil Rd. SW8 —51Nb **104**
Wyvis St. E14 —43Dc **84**

Xylon Ho. Wor Pk —75Xa **144**

Yabsley St. E14 —46Ec **84**
Yaffle Rd. Wey —82S **158**
Yalding Clo. Orp —70Zc **131**
Yalding Rd. SE16 —48Wb **83**
Yale Clo. Brick —2Ba **5**
Yale Clo. Houn —57Ba **99**
Yale Ct. NW6 —36Db **61**
Yale Way. Horn —35Jd **68**
Yaohan Plaza. NW9 —27Ta **39**
Yarborough Rd. SW19 —67Fb **125**
Yarbridge Clo. Sutt —82Db **163**
Yardley Clo. E4 —15Dc **26**
Yardley Ct. Sutt —77Ya **144**
Yardley La. E4 —15Dc **26**
Yardley St. WC1
     —41Qb **82** (4K **193**)
Yard Mead. Egh —62C **118**
Yarm Clo. Lea —95La **176**
Yarm Ct. Rd. Lea —95La **176**
Yarmouth Cres. N17 —29Xb **43**
Yarmouth Pl. W1
     —46Kb **82** (7K **197**)
Yarmouth Rd. Slou —4G **72**
Yarmouth Rd. Wat —10Y **5**
Yarm Way. Lea —95Ma **177**
Yarnfield Sq. SE15 —53Wb **105**
Yarnton Way. SE2 & Eri —47Yc **87**
Yarrow Cres. E6 —43Nc **86**
Yarrowfield. Wok —95A **172**
Yateley Ct. S Croy —86Sb **165**
Yateley Rd. SE18 —48Mc **85**
Yeading Av. Harr —33Aa **57**
Yeading Fork. Hay —43Y **77**
Yeading Gdns. Hay —43X **77**
Yeading Ho. Hay —43Z **77**
Yeading La. Hay & N'holt —44X **77**

Yeading Wlk. N Har —29Ba **37**
Yeames Clo. W13 —44Ja **78**
Yeate St. N1 —38Tb **63**
Yeatman Ho. Wat —8W **4**
Yeatman Rd. N6 —30Hb **41**
Yeats Clo. SE13 —54Fc **107**
Yeldham Rd. W6 —50Za **80**
Yellowpine Way. Chig —21Xc **47**
Yelverton Clo. Romf —25Md **49**
Yelverton Lodge. Twic —59La **100**
Yelverton Rd. SW11 —54Fb **103**
Yenston Clo. Mord —72Cb **145**
Yeoman Clo. SE27 —62Rb **127**
Yeoman Ct. Houn —52Ba **99**
Yeoman Rd. N'holt —38Aa **57**
Yeomanry Clo. Eps —84Va **162**
Yeomans Acre. Ruis —30W **36**
Yeomans Meadow. Sev —98Jd **186**
Yeomans M. Iswth —58Fa **100**
Yeoman's Row. SW3
     —48Gb **81** (4E **202**)
Yeoman St. SE8 —49Ac **84**
Yeomans Way. Enf —12Yb **26**
Yeoman Way. Ilf —23Sc **46**
Yeo St. E3 —43Dc **84**
Yeoveney Clo. Stai —61F **118**
Yeovil Clo. Orp —75Uc **150**
Yeovil Rd. Slou —4C **72**
Yerbury Rd. N19 —34Mb **62**
Yester Dri. Chst —66Nc **130**
Yester Pk. Chst —66Pc **130**
Yester Rd. Chst —66Nc **130**
Yevele Way. Horn —31Nd **69**
Yew Av. W Dray —45N **75**
Yewbank Clo. Kenl —87Tb **165**
Yew Clo. Buck H —19Mc **27**
Yew Ct. E4 —23Bc **44**
Yewdale Clo. Brom —65Gc **129**
Yewfield Rd. NW10 —37Va **60**
Yew Gro. NW2 —35Za **60**
Yewlands Clo. Bans —87Eb **163**
Yew Pl. Wey —77V **140**
Yews Av. Enf —8Xb **11**
Yews, The. Grav —10F **114**
Yewstone Ct. Wat —13W **18**
Yew Tree Bottom Rd. Eps
     —88Xa **162**
Yew Tree Clo. N21 —17Qb **24**
Yewtree Clo. N22 —25Lb **42**
Yew Tree Clo. Coul —91Hb **179**
Yew Tree Clo. Hut —16De **33**
Yew Tree Clo. Long —68Fe **135**
Yewtree Clo. N Har —28Da **37**
Yew Tree Clo. Sev —95Fd **186**
Yewtree Clo. Well —53Wc **109**
Yew Tree Clo. Wor Pk —74Ua **144**
Yew Tree Cotts. Hals —84Bd **169**
Yew Tree Ct. NW11 —29Bb **41**
     (off Bridge La.)
Yew Tree Ct. Els —16Ma **21**

Yew Tree Ct. Sutt —80Eb **145**
     (off Walnut M.)
Yew Tree Dri. Cat —97Vb **181**
Yew Tree Gdns. Chad —29Ad **47**
Yew Tree Gdns. Eps —87Sa **161**
Yew Tree Gdns. Romf —29Fd **48**
Yew Tree Lodge. SW16 —63Lb **126**
Yew Tree Lodge. Romf —29Fd **48**
     (off Yew Tree Gdns.)
Yew Tree Rd. W12 —45Va **80**
Yewtree Rd. Beck —69Bc **128**
Yew Tree Rd. Slou —8L **73**
Yew Tree Rd. Uxb —39P **55**
Yew Trees. Egh —69E **118**
Yew Trees. Shep —70P **119**
Yew Tree Wlk. Eff —99Z **175**
Yew Tree Wlk. Houn —57Ba **99**
Yew Tree Wlk. Purl —82Sb **165**
Yew Tree Way. Croy —82Ac **166**
Yew Wlk. Harr —32Ga **58**
Yiewsley Ct. W Dray —46N **75**
Yoakley Rd. N16 —33Ub **63**
Yoke Clo. N7 —37Nb **62**
Yolande Gdns. SE9 —57Nc **108**
Yonge Pk. N4 —34Qb **62**
York Av. SE17 —50Sb **83** (7E **206**)
York Av. SW14 —57Sa **101**
York Av. W7 —46Ga **78**
York Av. Hay —43S **76**
York Av. Sidc —61Uc **130**
York Av. Slou —4H **73**
York Av. Stan —25Ka **38**
York Av. Wind —4F **94**
York Bri. NW1 —42Jb **82** (5H **191**)
York Bldgs. WC2
     —45Nb **82** (5G **199**)
York Clo. E6 —45Pc **86**
York Clo. W7 —46Ga **78**
York Clo. Byfl —84N **157**
York Clo. K Lan —1Q **4**
York Clo. Mord —70Db **125**
York Clo. Shenf —17Be **33**
York Ct. N13 —20Nb **24**
York Cres. Borwd —12Ta **21**
York Cres. Lou —13Nc **28**
York Ga. Cat —94Tb **181**
Yorke Rd. Crox —16Q **18**
York Gdns. W on T —75Z **141**
York Ga. N14 —17Nb **24**
York Ga. NW1 —42Jb **82** (6H **191**)
York Gro. SE15 —53Yb **106**
York Hill. SE27 —62Rb **127**
York Hill. Lou —13Nc **28**
York Ho. SE1 —48Pb **82** (4J **205**)
York Ho. Borwd —12Qa **21**
     (off Canterbury Rd.)
York Ho. Enf —11Tb **25**
York Ho. Wemb —61Uo **59**
York Ho. Pl. W8 —47Db **81**
Yorkland Av. Well —55Vc **109**

York Mans. SW5 —50Db **81**
     (off Earl's Ct. Rd.)
York Mans. SW11 —53Jb **104**
     (off Prince Of Wales Dri.)
York M. NW5 —36Kb **62**
York M. Ilf —34Qc **66**
York Pde. Bren —50Ma **79**
York Pl. SW11 —55Fb **103**
York Pl. Grays —51Ce **113**
York Pl. Ilf —33Rc **66**
York Pl. WC2 —45Nb **82** (5G **199**)
     (off Villiers St.)
York Pl. Dag —37Ed **68**
York Pl. Grays —51Ce **113**
York Pl. Ilf —33Rc **66**
York Rise. NW5 —34Kb **62**
York Rise. Orp —75Uc **150**
York Rd. E4 —21Cc **44**
York Rd. E7 —37Jc **65**
York Rd. E10 —34Ec **64**
York Rd. E17 —29Zb **44**
York Rd. N11 —23Mb **42**
York Rd. N18 —23Xb **43**
York Rd. N21 —17Tb **25**
York Rd. SE1 —47Pb **82** (2J **205**)
York Rd. SW18 & SW11
     —56Eb **103**
York Rd. SW19 —65Eb **125**
York Rd. W3 —44Sa **79**
York Rd. W5 —48La **78**
York Rd. Barn —15Eb **23**
York Rd. Big H —91Kc **183**
York Rd. Bren —50Ma **79**
York Rd. Byfl —84M **157**
York Rd. Croy —73Qb **146**
York Rd. Dart —59Pd **111**
York Rd. Grav —2E **136**
York Rd. Houn —55Da **99**
York Rd. Ilf —34Qc **66**
York Rd. King T —66Pa **123**
York Rd. N'fleet —59Fe **113**
York Rd. N'wd —26W **36**
York Rd. Rain —38Fd **68**
York Rd. Rich —57Pa **101**
York Rd. Shenf —17Be **33**
York Rd. S Croy —82Zb **166**
York Rd. Sutt —79Cb **145**
York Rd. Tedd —63Ga **122**
York Rd. Uxb —38M **55**
York Rd. Wal X —5Ac **12**
York Rd. Wat —15Y **19**
York Rd. Wey —78S **140**
York Rd. Wind —4F **94**
York Rd. Wok —7G **188**
Yorkshire Clo. N16 —34Ub **63**
Yorkshire Gdns. N18 —22Xb **43**
Yorkshire Grey Pl. NW3 —35Eb **61**
Yorkshire Grey Yd. WC1
     (off Eagle St.) —43Pb **82** (1H **199**)
Yorkshire Pl. E14 —44Ac **84**
Yorkshire Rd. E14 —44Ac **84**
Yorkshire Rd. Mitc —71Nb **146**

York Sq. E14 —44Ac **84**
York St. W1 —43Hb **81** (1F **197**)
York St. Bark —39Sc **66**
York St. Mitc —73Jb **146**
York St. Twic —60Ja **100**
York Ter. Enf —10Sb **11**
York Ter. Eri —53Ed **110**
York Ter. E. NW1
     —42Jb **82** (6J **191**)
York Ter. W. NW1
     —42Jb **82** (6H **191**)
Yorkton St. E2 —40Wb **63**
York Way. N7 & N1 —37Mb **62**
York Way. N20 —20Hb **23**
York Way. Borwd —12Ta **21**
York Way. Chess —80Na **143**
York Way. Felt —62Ba **121**
     (in two parts)
York Way. Wat —8Z **5**
York Way Est. N7 —37Nb **62**
Young Ct. NW6 —38Ab **60**
Youngmans Clo. Enf —11Sb **25**
Young Rd. E16 —44Lc **85**
Youngs Bldgs. EC1
     (off Old St.) —42Sb **83** (5E **194**)
Youngs Rd. Ilf —29Tc **46**
Young St. W8 —47Db **81**
Young St. Fet —97Ga **176**
Youngstroat La. Wok —82A **156**
Yoxley App. Ilf —30Sc **46**
Yoxley Dri. Ilf —30Sc **46**
Yukon Rd. SW12 —59Kb **104**
Yuletide Clo. NW10 —37Ua **60**
Yunus Khan Clo. E17 —29Cc **44**

Zambra Way. Seal —92Pd **187**
Zampa Rd. SE16 —50Yb **84**
Zander Ct. E2 —41Wb **83**
Zangwill Rd. SE3 —53Mc **107**
Zealand Av. W Dray —52M **97**
Zealand Rd. E3 —40Ac **64**
Zelah Rd. Orp —73Yc **151**
Zenith Lodge. N3 —24Db **41**
Zennor Rd. SW12 —60Lb **104**
Zenoria St. SE22 —56Vb **105**
Zermatt Rd. T Hth —70Sb **127**
Zetland Ho. W8 —48Db **81**
     (off Marloes Rd.)
Zetland St. E14 —43Dc **84**
Zig Zag Rd. Kenl —88Sb **165**
Zion Pl. Grav —9D **114**
Zion Pl. T Hth —70Tb **127**
Zion Rd. T Hth —70Tb **127**
Zion St. Seal —93Pd **187**
Zoar St. SE1 —46Sb **83** (6D **200**)
Zoffany St. N19 —33Mb **62**

registered trade marks of
Geographers' A-Z Map Company Ltd

Printed and bound in Great Britain by
BPC Hazell Books Ltd
A member of
The British Printing Company Ltd

AREAS COVERED BY THIS ATLAS

with their map square reference

Names in this index shown in CAPITAL LETTERS, followed by their Postcode District(s), are Postal addresses (Postal Districts in London)

ABBEY WOOD. (SE2) —49Yc 87
ABBOTS LANGLEY. (WD5) —2U 4
ABRIDGE. (RM4) —13Xc 29
Acton Green. —49Ta 79
ACTON. (W3) —46Sa 79
ADDINGTON. (CR0) —78Cc 148
ADDISCOMBE. (CR0) —74Wb 147
ADDLESTONE. (KT15) —77L 139
Addlestone Moor. —75K 139
Aimes Green. —1Hc 13
Aldborough Hatch. —28Vc 47
ALDENHAM. (WD2) —10Da 5
Aldersbrook. —33Kc 65
Alperton. —39Na 59
ANERLEY. (SE20) —68Xb 127
Angell Town. —53Qb 104
Anthonys. —84D 156
Aperfield. —89Nc 168
Ardleigh Green. —28Md 49
ARKLEY. (EN5) —15Wa 22
ASCOT. (SL5) —9A 116
Ashford Common. —66T 120
Ashford Park. —62L 119
ASHFORD. (TW15) —63P 119
Ashley Park. —76W 140
ASHTEAD. (KT21) —90Pa 161
Ashtead Park. —91Qa 177
ASH. (TN15) —78Zd 155
Austenwood. —28A 34
Aveley. —46Sd 90
Avery Hill. —58Tc 108

BADGER'S MOUNT. (TN14) —82Cd 170
Baker Street. —4A 92
BALHAM. (SW12) —60Kb 104
Balstonia. —1N 93
Bandonhill. —77Mb 146
BANSTEAD. (SM7) —87Cb 163
BARKING. (IG11) —38Sc 66
BARKINGSIDE. (IG6) —27Sc 46
BARNEHURST. (DA7) —55Ed 110
Barnes Cray. —56Jd 110
BARNES. (SW13) —54Va 102
BARNET. (EN4 & EN5) —14Ab 22
Barnet Gate. —16Va 22
Barnet Vale. —15Db 23
Barnsbury. —38Pb 62
Barons Court. —50Ab 80
Basted. —95Be
Bat & Ball. —93Ld 187
Batchworth. —19N 17
Batlers Green. —9Ha 6
BATTERSEA. (SW11) —53Fb 103
Battle Street. —9H 137
Bayswater. —45Eb 81 (4A 196)
Beacon Hill. —9Rd
Beacontree Heath. —33Cd 68
BEAN. (DA2) —62Xd 134
BECKENHAM. (BR3) —67Cc 128
Beckton. —43Pc 86
Beckton Park. —44Pc 86
Becontree. —33Ad 67
Beddington Corner. —73Jb 146
BEDDINGTON. (CR0 & SM6) —76Nb 146
Bedford Park. —48Ta 79
Beggar Hill. —4Fe
Beggar's Bush. —10D 116
Belgravia. —48Jb 82 (4J 203)
Bell Common. —4Uc 14
Bell Green. —63Bc 128
Bellingham. —62Dc 128
Belmont. —25Ka 38
(Harrow)
BELMONT. (SM2) —82Cb 163
(Sutton)
Belsize. —4H 3
BELVEDERE. (DA17) —48Cd 88
Benhilton. —75Db 145
Bentley. —13Td 32
Bentley Heath. —7Bb 9
BERMONDSEY. (SE1 & SE16) —47Vb 83
BERRYLANDS. (KT5) —72Qa 143
BERRY'S GREEN. (TN16) —88Rc 168
BETHNAL GREEN. (E2) —41Xb 83
Betsham. —63Be 135
BEXLEY. (DA5) —59Dd 110
BEXLEYHEATH. (DA4 & DA7) —56Cd 110
BICKLEY. (BR1) —69Nc 130
Biggin. —1E 114
BIGGIN HILL. (TN16) —89Mc 167
Bignell's Corner. —5Xa 8
Birch Green. —63J 119
Bishops Gate. —2L 117
Blackfen. —58Wc 109
Blackheath Park. —56Hc 107
BLACKHEATH. (SE3) —54Hc 107
Blackheath Vale. —54Hc 107
Blacknest. —9F 116
Blackwall. —45Ec 84
Blakes Green. —96Td
Blendon. —58Zc 109
Bloomsbury. —43Nb 82 (7F 193)
Blythe Hill. —59Bc 106
BOREHAMWOOD. (WD6) —13Qa 21
BOROUGH GREEN. (TN15) —92Be
Borough, The. —47Tb 83 (1F 207)
Boston Manor. —50Ka 78
Botany Bay. —8Mb 10
Bounds Green. —23Mb 42
Bournebridge. —17Dd 30
Boveney. —1B 94
BOVINGDON. (HP3) —1C 2
Bow Common. —43Cc 84
BOW. (E3) —41Cc 84
Bowes Park. —24Nb 42
Bowmans. —59Hd 110
Brands Hatch, Motor Racing Circuit. —77Ud 154
BRANDS HILL. (SL3) —51D 96
Brasted Chart. —100Xc 185
BRASTED. (TN16) —96Yc 185
Brent Cross. —31Ya 60
Brentford End. —52Ka 100
BRENTFORD. (TW8) —51Ma 101
BRENTWOOD. (CM13 to CM15) —19Zd 33
BRICKET WOOD. (AL2) —2Ba 5
Bridge End. —93R 174
BRIMSDOWN. (EN3) —12Ac 26
BRITWELL. (SL2) —1E 72
BRIXTON. (SW2) —56Pb 104
Broad Colney. —1Ma 7
Broadgate. —43Ub 83 (7H 195)
Broad Green. —73Rb 147
BROCKLEY. (SE4) —56Bc 106
Bromley. —41Dc 84
(Bow)
BROMLEY. (BR1 & BR2) —68Jc 129
(Kent)
Bromley Common. —74Nc 150
Bromley Park. —67Gc 129
Brompton. —47Hb 81 (4E 202)
Brondesbury. —38Bb 61
Brondesbury Park. —39Ab 60
Brook Green. —49Za 80
Brooklands. —82P 157
Brook Street. —21Ud 50
Broom Hill. —73Vc 151
Brownswood Park. —33Rb 63
Brox. —80E 138
Brunswick Park. —20Jb 24
BUCKHURST HILL. (IG9) —19Mc 27
Buckingham Palace. —47Lb 82 (2B 204)
BUCKS HILL. (WD4) —7M 3
Bull's Cross. —7Wb 11
Bullsmoor. —8Yb 12
BURGH HEATH. (KT20) —91Ab 178
Burlings. —89Vc 169
Burnham Beeches. —6F 52
BURNHAM. (SL1) —2A 72
Burntcommon. —97H 173
Burnt Oak. —25Sa 39
Burwood Park. —78V 140
Bury Green. —3Wb 11
Bushey Heath. —18Fa 20
Bushey Mead. —69Za 124
BUSHEY. (WD2) —17Da 19
Bush Hill Park. —16Vb 25
BYFLEET. (KT14) —85P 157

CAMBERWELL. (SE5) —53Tb 105
CAMDEN TOWN. (NW1) —39Kb 62
Cann Hall. —35Gc 65
Canning Town. —44Hc 85
Canonbury. —37Sb 63
Canons Park. —24Na 39
Carpenders Park. —20Aa 19
Carshalton Beeches. —81Gb 163
Carshalton on the Hill. —80Jb 146
CARSHALTON. (SM5) —77Jb 146
Cartbridge. —94D 172
Carter's Hill. —100Rd 187
Castelnau. —51Xa 102
CATERHAM. (CR3) —96Wb 181
Caterham-on-the-Hill. —94Ub 181
CATFORD. (SE6) —59Dc 106
Cattlegate. —5Nb 10
CHADWELL HEATH. (RM6) —31Zc 67
Chadwell St Mary. —9C 92
CHAFFORD HUNDRED. (RM16) —48Be 91
Chaldon. —96Qb 180
CHALFONT COMMON. (SL9) —22B 34
CHALFONT ST PETER. (SL9) —25A 34
Chalk. —1K 137
Chalk Farm. —38Jb 62
CHALVEY. (SL1) —7H 73
CHANDLER'S CROSS. (WD3) —10P 3
Chapel Croft. —3J 3
Chapel End. —25Cc 44
Charlton. —68S 120
(Shepperton)
CHARLTON. (SE7) —51Mc 107
Chase Cross. —25Dd 48
Chase Side. —11Tb 25
Chattern Hill. —63R 120
CHEAM. (SM2 & SM3) —79Ab 144
CHEAPSIDE. (SL5) —7C 116
CHELSEA. (SW3) —50Gb 81 (7D 202)
CHELSFIELD. (BR6) —78Xc 151
Chelsfield Village. —78Ad 151
CHELSHAM. (CR3) —89Cc 166
Chenies Bottom. —9C 2
CHENIES. (WD3) —10D 2
CHERTSEY. (KT16) —73J 139
Chertsey Lock. —73L 139
Chertsey South. —76G 138
CHESHUNT. (EN7 & EN8) —1Zb 12
CHESSINGTON. (KT9) —78Pa 143
CHEVENING. (TN14) —91Bd 185
Cheverells. —87Dc 166
CHIGWELL. (IG7) —20Rc 28
Chigwell Row. —20Xc 29
Childerditch. —27Ce 51
Child's Hill. —34Cb 61
CHINGFORD. (E4) —18Ec 26
Chingford Green. —18Fc 27
Chingford Hatch. —21Fc 45
Chingford Mount. —21Cc 44
Chipperfield Common. —4K 3
CHIPPERFIELD. (WD4) —3J 3
Chipping Barnet. —14Ab 22
Chipstead Bottom. —92Fb 179
CHIPSTEAD. (CR3) —90Hb 163
(Coulsdon)
CHIPSTEAD. (TN13) —94Ed 186
(Sevenoaks)
CHISLEHURST. (BR7) —66Sc 130
Chislehurst West. —64Qc 130
CHISWICK. (W4) —51Ta 101
Chorleywood Bottom. —15F 16
CHORLEYWOOD. (WD3) —15F 16
Chorleywood West. —14D 16
Christian Fields. —3F 136
Church End. —93P 173
(Ockham)
Church End. —10H 3
(Sarratt)
Church End. —37Ua 60
(Willesden)
CHURCH END. (N3) —25Bb 41
(Finchley)
Churchgate. —2Wb 11
Church Lammas. —62F 118
CIPPENHAM. (SL1) —5C 72
CITY OF LONDON. (EC1 to EC4) —44Tb 83 (3F 201)
Clapgate. —6Ud
Clapham Common. —57Kb 104
Clapham Junction. —56Gb 103
Clapham Park. —58Mb 104
CLAPHAM. (SW4) —56Lb 104
Clapton Park. —35Zb 64
CLAREMONT PARK. (KT10) —80Da 141
Claygate Cross. —96Ce
CLAYGATE. (KT10) —79Ha 142
Clayhall. —26Pc 46
Clay Hill. —9Sb 11
Clement Street. —65Md 133
Clerkenwell. —42Qb 82 (6B 194)
Clewer Green. —4D 94
Clewer Hill. —5C 94
Clewer New Town. —4F 94
Clewer St Andrew. —2E 94
Clewer St Stephen. —2F 94
Clewer Village. —2E 94
Clewer Within. —4G 94
Clock House. —86Kb 164
COBHAM. (DA12) —10J 137
(Kent)
COBHAM. (KT11) —86X 159
(Surrey)
COCKFOSTERS. (EN4) —14Jb 24
Coldblow. —60Ed 110
Cole Park. —58Ja 100
Colham Green. —43Q 76
Colindale. —27Ua 40
College Park. —41Xa 80
COLLIER ROW. (RM5) —24Dd 48
Collier's Wood. —66Fb 125
COLNBROOK. (SL3) —52F 96
Colney Hatch. —23Hb 41
COLNEY STREET. (AL2) —2Ha 6
Commonwood. —6K 3
Coney Hall. —76Gc 149
Coombe. —66Ta 123
Coopersale Common. —1Zc 15
Coopersale Street. —3Yc 15
Copse Hill. —66Xa 124
Copthall Green. —5Nc 14
Corbets Tey. —36Sd 70
Cotman's Ash. —87Td
Cottenham Park. —67Xa 124
COULSDON. (CR3) —87Mb 164
Covent Garden. —45Nb 82 (4G 199)
Cowley Peachey. —44M 75
COWLEY. (UB8) —42L 75
Coxtie Green. —15Td 32
Cranbourne. —1A 116
Cranbrook. —32Pc 66
CRANFORD. (TW5) —53W 98
Cranham. —32Ud 70
Cranley Gardens. —28Kb 42
CRAYFORD. (DA1) —57Gd 110
Creekmouth. —42Wc 87
Crews Hill. —7Qb 10
Crickets Hill. —97D 172
CRICKLEWOOD. (NW2) —35Za 60
CROCKENHILL. (BR8) —72Fd 152
Crofton. —75Tc 150
Crofton Park. —57Bc 106
Cross Keys. —99Jd 186
Crouch End. —31Mb 62
CROUCH. (TN15) —94De
Crowdleham. —89Td
Crow Green. —13Wd 32
CROXLEY GREEN. (WD3) —14Q 18
CROYDON. (CR0) —75Sb 147
Crystal Palace. —65Vb 127
Crystal Palace National Recreation Cen. —65Wb 127
Cubitt Town. —49Ec 84
CUDHAM. (TN14) —87Tc 168
CUFFLEY. (EN6) —1Nb 10
Curtismill Green. —14Hd 30
Custom House. —44Lc 85
Cyprus. —45Qc 86

DAGENHAM. (RM8 to RM10) —37Cd 68
Dalston. —37Vb 63
Dancers Hill. —8Za 8
Darenth. —64Sd 134
DARTFORD. (DA1 to DA4) —58Nd 111
Dartmouth Park. —34Kb 62
Dartnell Park. —84L 157
Datchet Common. —3P 95
DATCHET. (SL3) —2M 95
Dean Bottom. —69Xd 134
Debden. —14Sc 28
Debden Green. —10Rc 14
De Beauvoir Town. —38Ub 63
DEDWORTH. (SL4) —4C 94
Denham Garden Village. —29H 35
Denham Green. —30H 35
DENHAM. (UB9) —34J 55
Denton. —9G 114
DEPTFORD. (SE8) —52Cc 106
Derry Downs. —72Yc 151
Dibden. —99Gd 186
DODDINGHURST. (CM15) —8Yd
Dollis Hill. —34Wa 60
Dormer's Wells. —45Da 77
DORNEY. (SL4) —8A 72
DOWNE. (BR6) —83Qc 168
Downham. —64Fc 129
DOWNSIDE. (KT11) —90X 159
Dryhill. —96Dd 186
Ducks Island. —16Za 22
Dudden Hill. —36Xa 60
Dugdale Hill. —5Ab 8
DULWICH. (SE21) —61Ub 127
Dulwich Village. —59Ub 105
DUNTON GREEN. (TN13) —92Gd 186

EALING. (W5) —45Ma 79
EARL'S COURT. (SW5) —50Cb 81
Earlsfield. —60Eb 103
East Acton. —45Ua 80
East Barnet. —16Gb 23
East Bedfont. —59T 98
East Burnham. —8E 52
Eastbury. —21V 36
Eastcote. —31X 57
EAST DULWICH. (SE22) —56Vb 105
East Ewell. —82Ya 162
EAST FINCHLEY. (N2) —28Gb 41
EAST HAM. (E6) —39Pc 66
East Hill. —82Rd 171
EAST HORSLEY. (KT24) —100V 174
Eastly End. —69F 118
EAST MOLESEY. (KT8) —70Fa 122
East Sheen. —56Sa 101
EAST TILBURY. (RM18) —2M 115
East Village. —29X 37
East Wickham. —53Yc 109
Eastworth. —74K 139
EDEN PARK. (BR3) —71Cc 148
Edgware Bury. —18Pa 21
EDGWARE. (HA8) —23Qa 39
Edmonton. —21Wb 43
EFFINGHAM JUNCTION. (KT24) —95W 174
EFFINGHAM. (KT24) —99Z 175
Egham Hythe. —64F 118
EGHAM. (TW20) —64C 118
Egham Wick. —6L 117
Egypt. —5F 52
Elm Corner. —91Q 174
ELMERS END. (BR3) —70Zb 128
ELM PARK. (RM12) —36Kd 69
ELMSTEAD. (BR7) —65Pc 130
ELSTREE. (WD6) —16Ma 21
Eltham Park. —56Qc 108
ELTHAM. (SE9) —58Pc 108
Elthorne Heights. —43Fa 78
Emerson Park. —30Nd 49
ENFIELD. (EN1 to EN3) —13Tb 25
Enfield Highway. —12Zb 26
Enfield Lock. —9Bc 12
Enfield Town. —13Tb 25
Enfield Wash. —9Zb 12
Englefield Green. —5N 117
EPPING. (CM16) —2Wc 15
Epping Forest. —9Nc 14
Epsom Downs. —91Ua 178
EPSOM. (KT17 to KT19) —85Ta 161
Epsom Race Course. —90Va 162
ERITH. (DA8 & DA18) —50Gd 88
ESHER. (KT10) —77Da 141
ETON. (SL4) —1H 95
ETON WICK. (SL4) —10D 72
EWELL. (KT17) —81Va 162
EYNSFORD. (DA4) —75Nd 153

Fair Cross. —36Uc 66
Fairfield. —93Ka 176
Fairlop. —25Vc 47
Fairmile. —84Ba 159
FAIRSEAT. (TN15) —84Ee
Falconwood. —56Uc 108
Fallow Corner. —24Eb 41
Farleigh. —86Bc 166
FARNBOROUGH. (BR6) —78Sc 150
FARNHAM COMMON. (SL2) —7G 52
FARNHAM ROYAL. (SL2) —10G 52
FARNINGHAM. (DA4) —73Pd 153
Farthing Street. —81Pc 168
Fawke Common. —99Rd 187
FAWKHAM. (DA3) —73Xd 154
Fawkham Green. —75Xd 154
Felthamhill. —64V 120
FELTHAM. (TW13 & TW14) —60X 99
FETCHAM. (KT22) —95Fa 176
Fickleshole. —86Fc 167
FIDDLERS HAMLET. (CM16) —4Yc 15
Fieldcommon. —73Ba 141
Fig Street. —100Jd 188
FINCHLEY. (N3) —25Cb 41
Finsbury. —41Qb 82 (4A 194)
FINSBURY PARK. (N4) —33Qb 62
Fishers Green. —1Dc 12
Fitzrovia. —43Lb 82 (7B 192)
FLAUNDEN. (HP3) —5D 2
Fleet Downs. —60Sd 112
Foots Cray. —65Yc 131
Force Green. —96Tc 184
Forestdale. —81Ac 166
FOREST GATE. (E7) —36Kc 65
FOREST HILL. (SE23) —61Yb 128
Fortis Green. —27Jb 42
Fortune Green. —35Cb 61
Forty Hill. —10Vb 11
Fox Hatch. —10Ud
Freezy Water. —8Ac 12
French Street. —100Vc 185
Friary Island. —8N 95
Friday Hill. —19Gc 27
Friern Barnet. —22Hb 41
Frogmore. —5K 95
(Windsor)
FROGMORE. (AL2) —1Ga 6
(St Albans)
FULHAM. (SW6) —54Ab 102
FULMER. (SL3) —5P 53
Fulwell. —63Fa 122
Fulwell Cross. —26Sc 46
Furzedown. —64Kb 126

Gallows Corner. —26Ld 49
Gants Hill. —30Qc 46
Ganwick Corner. —8Db 9
Garston. —7Y 5
Gatton. —100Hb 179
GEORGE GREEN. (SL3) —4P 73
GERRARDS CROSS. (SL9) —29A 34
GIDEA PARK. (RM2) —27Kd 49
Giggshill. —73Ja 142
Givons Grove. —98La 176
Glanty. —63D 118
Globe Town. —41Zb 84
GODDEN GREEN. (TN15) —96Qd 187
Goddington. —76Yc 151
Goff's Oak. —1Sb 11
GOLDERS GREEN. (NW11) —30Ab 40
Gold Street. —10G 136
Goldsworth. —6G 188
Goldsworth Park. —5D 188
Goodmayes. —32Wc 67
Gospel Oak. —35Jb 62
Goulds Green. —44R 76
Grahame Park. —25Va 40
Grange Hill. —22Tc 46
Grange Park. —16Rb 25
GRAVESEND. (DA11 to DA13) —8D 114
GRAYS. (RM16 to RM18) —50Ce 91
GREAT BOOKHAM. (KT23) —97Da 175
Great Burgh. —89Ya 162
Greatness. —93Md 187
GREAT WARLEY. (CM13 & CM14) —25Wd 50
Greenford Green. —37Ga 58
GREENFORD. (UB6) —41Ea 78
Greenhill. —29Ha 38
GREENHITHE. (DA9) —56Xd 112
Green Street Green. —65Wd 134
(Dartford)
GREEN STREET GREEN. (BR6) —76Vc 151
(Orpington)
GREENWICH. (SE10) —52Ec 106
Grove Park. —53Sa 101
(Chiswick)
Grove Park. —62Kc 129
(Lee)
Grubb Street. —67Xd 134
Gunnersbury. —49Ra 79

HACKBRIDGE. (SM6) —74Jb 146
HACKNEY. (E8) —37Xb 63
Hackney Wick. —37Cc 64
Hacton. —36Pd 69
Hadley. —13Bb 23
Hadley Wood. —10Eb 9
Haggerston. —40Vb 63 (1K 195)
Hainault. —22Wc 47
Hale End. —23Fc 45
Hale, The. —22Ta 39
HALSTEAD. (TN14) —84Bd 169
Ham Island. —6P 95
HAMMERSMITH. (W6) —49Ya 80
Ham Moor. —77N 139
Hampstead Garden Suburb. —29Eb 41
HAMPSTEAD. (NW3) —35Eb 61
Hampton Court. —69Ha 122
HAMPTON HILL. (TW12) —64Ea 122
HAMPTON. (TW12) —67Da 121
HAMPTON WICK. (KT1) —67La 122
Hamsey Green. —88Yb 166
HAM. (TW10) —62La 122
Hanger Hill. —42Pa 79
HANWELL. (W7) —46Ha 78
HANWORTH. (TW13) —63Z 121
HAREFIELD. (UB9) —25L 35
Hare Street. —6Md
Harlesden. —40Va 60
Harlington. —51T 98
HARMONDSWORTH. (UB7) —51M 97
HAROLD HILL. (RM3) —22Nd 49
Harold Park. —23Rd 49
HAROLD WOOD. (RM3) —25Pd 49
Harringay. —29Rb 43
HARROW. (HA1 to HA3) —30Ga 38
Harrow on the Hill. —32Ga 58
HARROW WEALD. (HA3) —24Ga 38
HARTLEY. (DA3) —71Be 155
Hartley Green. —71Ae 155
Hartley Hill. —74Ce 155
HATCH END. (HA5) —24Ba 37
Hatchford. —91U 174
HATCHFORD END. (KT11) —91S 174
Hatton. —56V 98
HAVERING-ATTE-BOWER. (RM4) —20Gd 30
Havering Park. —22Dd 48
HAWLEY. (DA2) —63Pd 133
Hawley's Corner. —93Rc 184
HAYES. (BR2) —74Kc 149
(Kent)
Hayes End. —43T 76
Hayes Town. —47V 76
HAYES. (UB3 & UB4) —44U 76
(Middlesex)
Hay Green. —7Be
Hazelwood. —83Tc 168
HEADLEY. (KT18) —98Ta 177
Headstone. —28Ea 38
Heath Park. —30Jd 48
HEATHROW AIRPORT (LONDON) —55R 98
Heath Side. —62Hd 132
Heaverham. —89Ud
Hedgerley Green. —1J 53
Hedgerley Hill. —3H 53
HEDGERLEY. (SL2) —2H 53
HENDON. (NW4) —29Xa 40
Henhurst. —7G 136
HERNE HILL. (SE24) —58Sb 105
HERONGATE. (CM13) —24Fe 51
HERONSGATE. (WD3) —17E 16
HERSHAM. (KT12) —78Z 141
Heston. —52Ca 99
HEXTABLE. (BR8) —66Hd 132
Higham Hill. —26Ac 44
Highams Park. —23Fc 45
HIGH BARNET. (EN5) —13Ab 22
HIGH BEECH. (IG10) —10Kc 13
HIGHBURY. (N5) —35Rb 63
High Cross. —9Fa 6
Higher Denham. —31E 54
HIGHGATE. (N6) —32Kb 62
Highwood Hill. —20Va 22
Hill End. —23K 35
Hillingdon Heath. —42R 76
HILLINGDON. (UB10) —41Q 76
Hill Park. —95Rc 184
HINCHLEY WOOD. (KT10) —76Ha 142
Hither Green. —58Gc 107
Hobbs Cross. —8Zc 15
Hockenden. —68Cd 132
Hockley Hole. —9M 53
HODSOLL STREET. (TN15) —81Fe
Hogpits Bottom. —4D 2
Holborn. —43Qb 82 (1K 199)
Holdbrook. —6Bc 12
Holders Hill. —26Za 40
Holland Park. —46Bb 81
HOLLOWAY. (N7) —34Nb 62
Holyfield. —1Fc 13
Holywell. —16V 18
HOMERTON. (E9) —36Ac 64
Honor Oak. —58Zb 106
Honor Oak Park. —59Ac 106
Hook. —77Ma 143
HOOK END. (CM15) —7Yd
Hook Green. —63Jd 132
(Dartford)
Hook Green. —65Ce 135
(Gravesend)
Hook Heath. —7F 188
HOOLEY. (CR5) —93Kb 180
HORNCHURCH. (RM11 & RM12) —32Nd 69
HORNDON ON THE HILL. (SS17) —1H 93
Horn Hill. —22C 34
Horn Park. —57Kc 107
Horns Cross. —58Ud 112
HORNSEY. (N8) —28Nb 42
Hornsey Vale. —29Pb 42
Horns Green. —89Uc 168
HORSELL. (GU21) —4F 188
Horseman Side. —14Nd 31
Horton. —82Sa 161
(Epsom)
HORTON KIRBY. (DA4) —70Sd 134
HORTON. (SL3) —55C 96
(Slough)
Hosey Hill. —100Uc 184
HOUNSLOW. (TW3 to TW6) —55Da 99
Hounslow West. —54Aa 99
Houses of Parliament. —47Nb 82 (2G 205)
Hoxton. —40Ub 63 (1H 195)
Hulberry. —75Jd 152
Hunton Bridge. —5S 4
Hurlingham. —55Db 103
Hurst Park. —68Ea 122
HUTTON. (CM13) —16Fe 33
Hutton Mount. —18De 33
Hyde Park. —46Hb 81 (6F 197)
HYDE, THE. (NW9) —29Va 40
Hythe End. —61D 118

ICKENHAM. (UB10) —34R 56
Ightham Common. —95Xd
IGHTHAM. (TN15) —93Yd
ILFORD. (IG1 to IG6) —34Rc 66
INGRAVE. (CM13) —23Ee 51
Ingrave Common. —21Ce 51
ISLEWORTH. (TW7) —55Ja 100
ISLINGTON. (N1) —38Rb 63 (1B 194)
Istead Rise. —7B 136
IVER HEATH. (SL0) —40F 54
IVER. (SL0) —44H 75
Ivy Chimneys. —4Vc 15

Jacobswell. —100A 172
John's Hole. —59Td 112
Joyce Green. —56Pd 111
Joydens Wood. —63Fd 132

KELVEDON COMMON. (CM14) —11Td 32
KELVEDON HATCH. (CM14 & CM15) —9Ud
Kemprow. —8Fa 6
Kempton Park Race Course. —66Y 121
KEMSING. (TN15) —89Rd 171
KENLEY. (CR2) —86Sb 165
KENNINGTON. (SE11) —51Qb 104
Kensal Green. —41Ya 80
Kensal Rise. —40Ya 60
Kensal Town. —42Ab 80
KENSINGTON. (W8) —47Db 81
KENTISH TOWN. (NW5) —36Kb 62
KENTON. (HA3) —29La 38
KESTON. (BR2) —78Lc 149
Keston Mark. —76Mc 149
Kevingtown. —72Ad 151
Kew Gardens. —52Pa 101
KEW. (TW9) —52Qa 101
Kidbrooke. —54Kc 107
KILBURN. (NW6) —39Cb 61
KINGFIELD. (GU22) —92C 172
Kingsbury. —30Sa 39
Kingsbury Green. —29Sa 39
King's Cross. —40Nb 62 (2G 193)
Kings Farm. —2E 136
Kingsland. —37Ub 63
KINGS LANGLEY. (WD4) —1Q 4
KINGSTON UPON THAMES. (KT1 & KT2) —68Na 123
Kingston Vale. —63Ua 124
Kingswood. —93Bb 179
(Tadworth)
Kingswood. —6X 5
(Watford)
Kippington. —98Jd 186
Kitt's End. —9Ab 8
KNAPHILL. (GU21) —5A 188
KNATTS VALLEY. (TN15) —82Td
Knightsbridge. —47Hb 81 (2F 203)
Knockhall. —57Yd 112
Knockholt Pound. —87Ad 169
KNOCKHOLT. (TN14) —89Xc 169
Knockmill. —84Ud
Knowle Green. —64K 119

Ladywell. —57Dc 106
Lake End. —7A 72
LALEHAM. (TW18) —69L 119
LAMBETH. (SE1 & SE11) —48Pb 82 (4H 205)
Lambourne. —14Zc 29
Lambourne End. —17Ad 29
Lamorbey. —60Vc 109
Lampton. —53Da 99
Lane End. —63Td 134
Langley Bottom. —91Ta 177
Langleybury. —6R 4
LANGLEY. (SL3) —48C 74

HOSPITALS AND MAJOR CLINICS

Where the Publishers have been unable to actually indicate the hospital or clinic
on the atlas map pages the reference given is to the road in which it is situated.

ABRAHAM COWLEY UNIT —76E **138**
Holloway Hill, Lyne, Chertsey, Surrey. KT16 0AE
Tel: (01932) 872010

ACTON HOSPITAL —47Ra **79**
Gunnersbury La., London. W3 8EG
Tel: (0181) 992 2277

AINSLIE REHABILITATION UNIT —20Ec **26**
1 Friars Clo., Chingford, London. E4 6UW
Tel: (0181) 529 3706

ALEXANDER KORDA HOUSE —30H **35**
Ranston Clo., Nightingale Way, Denham,
Uxbridge, Middx. UB9 5JX
Tel: (01895) 832358

ARCHERY HOUSE —58Rd **111**
Bow Arrow La., Dartford, Kent. DA2 6PB
Tel: (01322) 227211

ARNOLD HOUSE —52Lc **107**
154 Shooters Hill Rd., London. SE3 8RP
Tel: (0181) 319 4099

ASHFORD HOSPITAL —61N **119**
London Rd., Ashford, Middx. TW15 3AA
Tel: (01784) 884488

ASHTEAD HOSPITAL —91Na **177**
The Warren, Ashtead, Surrey. KT21 2SB
Tel: (01372) 276161

ATHLONE HOUSE —32Hb **61**
Hampstead La., Highgate, London. N6 4RX
Tel: (0181) 348 5231

ATKINSON MORLEY'S HOSPITAL —66Xa **124**
31 Copse Hill, Wimbledon, London. SW20 0NE
Tel: (0181) 946 7711

BANCROFT, THE —42Zb **84**
Bancroft Rd., London. E1 4DG
Tel: (0171) 377 7831

BARKING HOSPITAL —38Vc **67**
Upney La., Barking, Essex. IG11 9LX
Tel: (0181) 594 3898

BARNES HOSPITAL —55Ua **102**
South Worple Way, London. SW14 8SU
Tel: (0181) 878 4981

BARNET GENERAL HOSPITAL —14Za **22**
Wellhouse La., Barnet, Herts. EN5 3DJ
Tel: (0181) 440 5111

BECKENHAM HOSPITAL —68Bc **128**
379 Croydon Rd., Beckenham, Kent. BR3 3QL
Tel: (0181) 650 0125

BECONTREE DAY HOSPITAL —33Ad **67**
Becontree Av., Dagenham, Essex. RM8 3HR
Tel: (0181) 984 1234

BEECHLAWN DAY HOSPITAL —59Lb **104**
Belthorn Cres., Weir Road, London. SW12 0NS
Tel: (0181) 675 3415

BELVEDERE PRIVATE CLINIC —50Yc **87**
Knee Hill, Abbey Wood, London. SE2 0AT
Tel: (0181) 311 4464/518 0437

BETHLEM ROYAL HOSPITAL, THE —73Cc **148**
Monks Orchard Rd., Eden Park, Beckenham, Kent.
BR3 3BX Tel: (0181) 777 6611

BEXLEY HOSPITAL —61Gd **132**
Old Bexley La., Bexley, Kent. DA5 2BW
Tel: (01322) 526282 ·

BISHOPSWOOD PRIVATE HOSPITAL —22R **36**
Rickmansworth Rd., Northwood, Middx. HA6 2JW
Tel: (01923) 835814

BLACKHEATH HOSPITAL —55Hc **107**
40-42 Lee Ter., London. SE3 9UD
Tel: (0181) 318 7722

BOLINGBROKE HOSPITAL —57Gb **103**
Bolingbroke Gro., Wandsworth Common, London.
SW11 6HN Tel: (0171) 223 7411

BRENTWOOD COMMUNITY HOSPITAL —18Ae **33**
Crescent Dri., Shenfield, Brentwood, Essex.
CM15 8DR Tel: (01277) 212244

BRITISH HOME AND HOSPITAL FOR INCURABLES
—64Rb **127**
Crown La., Streatham, London. SW16 3JB
Tel: (0181) 670 8261

BROMLEY HOSPITAL —70Kc **129**
Cromwell Av., Bromley, Kent. BR2 9AJ
Tel: (0181) 460 9933

BROOK GENERAL HOSPITAL —53Nc **108**
Shooters Hill Rd., Woolwich, London. SE18 4LW
Tel: (0181) 856 5555

BROOKWOOD DAY HOSPITAL —6A **188**
Knaphill, Woking, Surrey. GU21 3YP
Tel: (01486) 74545

BROOKWOOD HOSPITAL —6A **188**
Knaphill, Woking, Surrey. GU21 2RQ
Tel: (01486) 74545

BUSHEY HOSPITAL (BUPA) —17Ha **20**
Heathbourne Rd., Bushey, Watford. WD2 1RD
Tel: (0181) 950 9090

CARSHALTON WAR MEMORIAL HOSPITAL —79Hb **145**
The Park, Carshalton, Surrey. SM5 3DB
Tel: (0181) 647 5534

CASSEL HOSPITAL —63Ma **123**
1 Ham Comn., Richmond, Surrey. TW10 7JF
Tel: (0181) 940 8181

CASTLEWOOD DAY HOSPITAL —53Qc **108**
25 Shooter's Hill, Woolwich, London. SE18 4LG
Tel: (0181) 856 4970

CATERHAM DENE HOSPITAL —95Vb **181**
Church Rd., Caterham-on-the-Hill, Surrey. CR3 5RA
Tel: (01883) 349324

CENTRAL MIDDLESEX HOSPITAL —41Sa **79**
Acton La., Park Royal, London. NW10 7NS
Tel: (0181) 965 5733

CHADWELL HEATH HOSPITAL —29Xc **47**
Grove Rd., Chadwell Heath, Romford, Essex. RM6 4XH
Tel: (0181) 599 3007

CHALFONTS AND GERRARDS CROSS HOSPITAL, THE
—25A **34**
Hampden Rd., Chalfont St Peter, Gerrards Cross,
Bucks. SL9 9DR Tel: (01753) 883821

CHARING CROSS HOSPITAL —51Za **102**
Fulham Palace Rd., London. W6 8RF
Tel: (0181) 846 1234

CHARTER CLINIC —50Gb **81** (7E **202**)
1-5 Radnor Wlk., London. SW3 4PB
Tel: (0171) 351 1272

CHARTER NIGHTINGALE HOSPITAL —43Gb **81** (7E **190**)
11-19 Lisson Gro., London. NW1 6SH
Tel: (0171) 258 3828

CHASE FARM HOSPITAL —10Qb **10**
127 The Ridgeway, Enfield, Middx. EN2 8JL
Tel: (0181) 366 6600

CHELSEA AND WESTMINSTER HOSPITAL —51Eb **103**
369 Fulham Rd., London. SW10 9NH
Tel: (0181) 746 8000

CHELSFIELD PARK HOSPITAL —78Bd **151**
Bucks Cross Rd., Chelsfield, Orpington, Kent. BR6 7RG
Tel: (01689) 877855

CHESHUNT COTTAGE HOSPITAL —1Zb **12**
Church La., Cheshunt, Waltham Cross, Herts. EN8 0DR
Tel: (01992) 22157

CHEYNE CENTRE FOR CHILDREN WITH CEREBRAL PALSY
—51Gb **103**
61 Cheyne Wlk., London. SW3 5LT
Tel: (0181) 846 6488

CHILD GUIDANCE TRAINING CENTRE DAY UNIT, THE
—37Fb **61**
33 Daleham Gdns., London. NW3 5BU
Tel: (0171) 794 3553

CHILDREN'S TRUST, THE —93Za **178**
Tadworth St., Tadworth, Surrey. KT20 5RU
Tel: (01737) 357171

CHISWICK LODGE —50Va **80**
Netheravon Rd. S., London. W4 2PZ
Tel: (0181) 746 5566

CHURCHILL CLINIC —48Qb **82** (3A **206**)
80 Lambeth Rd., London. SE1 7PP
Tel: (0171) 928 5633

CLAYBURY HOSPITAL —24Qc **46**
Manor Rd., Woodford Bridge, Essex. IG8 8BY
Tel: (0181) 504 7171

CLAYPONDS HOSPITAL —49Na **79**
Occupation La., South Ealing, London. W5 4RN
Tel: (0181) 560 4011

CLEMENTINE CHURCHILL HOSPITAL —34Ha **58**
Sudbury Hill, Harrow, Middx. HA1 3RX
Tel: (0181) 422 3464

COBHAM HOSPITAL —85X **159**
168 Portsmouth Rd., Cobham, Surrey. KT11 1HT
Tel: (01932) 862751

COLINDALE HOSPITAL —26Ua **40**
Colindale Av., London. NW9 5HG
Tel: (0181) 200 1555

COPPETTS WOOD HOSPITAL —25Hb **41**
Coppetts Rd., Muswell Hill, London. N10 1JN
Tel: (0181) 883 9792

CROMWELL HOSPITAL, THE —49Db **81**
162-174 Cromwell Rd., London. SW5 0TU
Tel: (0171) 370 4233

CROYDON GENERAL HOSPITAL —74Sb **147**
London Rd., Croydon, Surrey. CR9 2RH
Tel: (0181) 684 6999

DEBENHAM HOUSE —21A **34**
Chesham La., Chalfont St Peter, Gerrards Cross, Bucks.
SL9 0RN Tel: (01494) 871588

DEVONSHIRE HOSPITAL —43Jb **82** (7J **191**)
29-31 Devonshire St., London. W1N 1RF
Tel: (0171) 486 7131

DONALD WINNICOTT PAEDIATRIC ASSESSMENT CENTRE
—40Wb **63**
Hackney Rd., London. E2 8PS
Tel: (0171) 729 2333

EALING HOSPITAL —46Fa **78**
Uxbridge Rd., Southall, Middx. UB1 3HW
Tel: (0181) 574 2444

EAST HAM MEMORIAL HOSPITAL —38Mc **65**
Shrewsbury Rd., Forest Gate, London. E7 8QR
Tel: (0181) 472 4661

EASTMAN DENTAL HOSPITAL AND EASTMAN DENTAL
INSTITUTE, THE —42Pb **82** (5H **193**)
256 Gray's Inn Rd., London. WC1X 8LD
Tel: (0171) 915 1000

EDENHALL MARIE CURIE CENTRE —36Fb **61**
11 Lyndhurst Gdns., London. NW3 5NS
Tel: (0171) 794 0066

EDGWARE GENERAL HOSPITAL —24Ra **39**
Burnt Oak B'way, Edgware, Middx. HA8 0AD
Tel: (0181) 952 2381

ELLESMERE DAY HOSPITAL —78U **140**
Queens Rd., Walton-on-Thames, Surrey. KT12 5AA
Tel: (01932) 241481

ELMBRIDGE LODGE —73Ha **142**
Weston Green Rd., Thames Ditton, Surrey. KT7 0HY
Tel: (0181) 398 8019

ELM HOUSE DAY HOSPITAL —65Mb **126**
57 Lewin Rd., London. SW16 6JZ
Tel: (0181) 664 6406

EPSOM AND EWELL HOSPITAL —84Na **161**
Horton La., Epsom, Surrey. KT19 8PB
Tel: (01372) 724022

EPSOM GENERAL HOSPITAL —87Sa **161**
Dorking Rd., Epsom, Surrey. KT18 7EG
Tel: (01372) 726100

ERITH AND DISTRICT HOSPITAL —51Fd **110**
Park Cres., Erith, Kent. DA8 3EE
Tel: (0181) 302 2678

ESSEX NUFFIELD HOSPITAL —18Ae **33**
Shenfield Rd., Shenfield, Brentwood, Essex.
CM15 8EH Tel:(01277) 263263

FARNBOROUGH HOSPITAL —77Qc **150**
Farnborough Comn., Locksbottom, Orpington, Kent.
BR6 8ND Tel: (016898) 53333

FAWKHAM MANOR HOSPITAL —74Yd **154**
Manor La., Fawkham, Longfield, Kent. DA3 8ND
Tel: (01474) 879900

FINCHLEY MEMORIAL HOSPITAL —24Eb **41**
Granville Rd., North Finchley, London. N12 0JE
Tel: (0181) 349 3121

FITZROY NUFFIELD HOSPITAL —44Hb **81** (2F **197**)
10-12 Bryanston Sq., London. W1H 8BB
Tel: (0171) 723 1288

GABLES, THE —55Hc **107**
2 Blackheath Pk., Blackheath, London. SE3 9RR
Tel: (0181) 852 8799

GARDEN HOSPITAL, THE —27Ya **40**
46-50 Sunny Gdns. Rd., Hendon, London.
NW4 1RX Tel: (0181) 203 0111

GARDINER HILL UNIT —62Gb **125**
61 Glenburnie Rd., London. SW17 7DJ
Tel: (0181) 767 4626

GARSTON MANOR MEDICAL REHABILITATION CENTRE
—3Y **5**
High Elms La., Garston, Watford, Herts. WD2 7JX
Tel: (01923) 673061

GOLDIE LEIGH —51Yc **109**
Lodge Hill, Abbey Wood, London. SE2 0AY
Tel: (0181) 311 9161

GOODMAYES HOSPITAL —29Wc **47**
157 Barley La., Goodmayes, Ilford, Essex. IG3 8XJ
Tel: (0181) 590 6060

GORDON HOSPITAL —49Mb **82** (6D **204**)
126 Vauxhall Bri. Rd., London. SW1V 2RM
Tel: (0171) 746 8733

GRAVESEND AND NORTH KENT HOSPITAL —8C **114**
Bath St., Gravesend, Kent. DA11 0DG
Tel: (01474) 564333

GREAT WEST HATCH —22Qc **46**
High Rd., Chigwell, Essex. IG7 5BS
Tel: (0181) 504 2855

GREENWICH DISTRICT HOSPITAL —50Hc **85**
Vanbrugh Hill, Greenwich, London. SE10 9HE
Tel: (0181) 858 8141

GROVELANDS PRIORY HOSPITAL —18Nb **24**
The Bourne, Southgate, London. N14 6RA
Tel: (0181) 882 8191

GUY'S HOSPITAL —46Tb **83** (7G **201**)
St Thomas St., London. SE1 9RT
Tel: (0171) 955 5000

GUY'S NUFFIELD HOUSE —47Tb **83** (1F **207**)
Newcomen St., London. SE1 1YR
Tel: (0171) 955 4953

HACKNEY HOSPITAL —36Ac **64**
Homerton High St., London. E9 6BE
Tel: (0181) 985 5555

HAMMERSMITH HOSPITAL —44Wa **80**
Du Cane Rd., London. W12 0HS
Tel: (0181) 743 2030

HAREFIELD HOSPITAL —25L **35**
Hill End Rd., Harefield, Uxbridge, Middx. UB9 6JH
Tel: (01895) 823737

HARESTONE MARIE CURIE CENTRE —97Vb **181**
Harestone Dri., Caterham, Surrey. CR3 6YQ
Tel: (01883) 342226

HARLEY STREET CLINIC, THE —43Kb **82** (7K **191**)
35 Weymouth St., London. W1N 4BJ
Tel: (0171) 935 7700

HAROLD WOOD HOSPITAL —25Nd **49**
Gubbins La., Harold Wood, Romford, Essex.
RM3 0BE Tel: (01708) 345533

HARPERBURY HOSPITAL —3La **6**
Harper La., Shenley, Radlett, Herts. WD7 9HQ
Tel: (01923) 854861/6

HARROW HOSPITAL —33Ga **58**
Roxeth Hill, Harrow, Middx. HA2 0JX
Tel: (0181) 864 5432

HARTSWOOD HOSPITAL (BUPA) —23Xd **50**
Eagle Way, Warley, Brentwood, Essex. CM13 3LF
Tel: (01277) 232525

HAYES COTTAGE NURSING HOME —44U **76**
Grange Rd., Hayes, Middx. UB3 2RR
Tel: (0181) 573 2052

HAYES GROVE PRIORY HOSPITAL —75Jc **149**
Prestons Rd., Hayes, Bromley, Kent. BR2 7AS
Tel: (0181) 462 7722

HENDERSON HOSPITAL —81Db **163**
2 Homeland Dri., Sutton, Surrey. SM2 5LY
Tel: (0181) 661 1611

HRH PRINCESS CHRISTIAN'S HOSPITAL —3G **94**
12 Clarence Rd., Windsor, Berks. SL4 5AG
Tel: (01753) 853121

HIGHGATE PRIVATE HOSPITAL —30Hb **41**
17-19 View Rd., Highgate, London. N6 4DJ
Tel: (0181) 341 4182

HIGHLANDS HOSPITAL —15Pb **24**
Worlds End La., Winchmore Hill, London.
N21 1PN Tel: (0181) 366 6600

HIGHWOOD HOSPITAL —18Yd **32**
Geary Dri., Ongar Rd., Brentwood, Essex.
CM15 9DY Tel: (01277) 219262

HILLINGDON HOSPITAL —43P **75**
Pield Heath Rd., Uxbridge, Middx. UB8 3NN
Tel: (01895) 238282

HILLSIDE HOSPITAL —43Na **79**
22 Corfton Rd., Ealing, London. W5 2HT
Tel: (0181) 998 0045

HITHER GREEN HOSPITAL —58Fc **107**
234-244 Hither Grn. La., London. SE13 6RU
Tel: (0181) 698 4611

HOLLY HOUSE HOSPITAL —19Kc **27**
High Rd., Buckhurst Hill, Essex. IG9 5HX
Tel: (0181) 505 3311

HOMEWOOD RESOURCE CENTRE —77F **138**
Homewood Ho., Guildford Rd., Chertsey, Surrey.
KT16 0QA Tel: (01932) 872010

HORNSEY CENTRAL HOSPITAL —29Mb **42**
Park Rd., Crouch End, London. N8 8JL
Tel: (0181) 340 6244

HORTON HOSPITAL —83Ra **161**
Long Gro. Rd., Epsom, Surrey. KT19 8PZ
Tel: (01372) 729696

HOSPITAL FOR SICK CHILDREN (ITALIAN WING), THE
—43Nb **82** (7G **193**)
Queen Sq., London. WC1N 3AN
Tel: (0171) 405 9200

HOSPITAL FOR SICK CHILDREN, THE —42Nb **82** (6G **193**)
Gt. Ormond St., London. WC1N 3JH
Tel: (0171) 405 9200

HOSPITAL OF SAINT JOHN AND SAINT ELIZABETH
—40Fb **61** (2B **190**)
60 Grove End Rd., St John's Wood, London.
NW8 9NH Tel: (0171) 286 5126

INGREBOURNE CENTRE (PSYCHOTHERAPY) —36Md **69**
St George's Hospital, Suttons La., Hornchurch,
Essex. RM12 6RS Tel: (01708) 443531

JAMES PRINGLE HOUSE —43Lb **82** (7C **192**)
Department Of Genito-Urinary, Medicine,
Charlotte St., London. W1P 1LA
Tel: (0171) 380 9141

JEWISH HOME AND HOSPITAL AT TOTTENHAM, THE
—28Vb **43**
295 High Rd., South Tottenham, London. N15 4RT
Tel: (0181) 800 5138

JOYCE GREEN HOSPITAL —54Pd **111**
Joyce Green La., Dartford, Kent. DA1 5PL
Tel: (01322) 227242

KING EDWARD VII HOSPITAL —5G **94**
St Leonard's Rd., Windsor, Berks. SL4 3DP
Tel: (01753) 860441

KING EDWARD VII'S HOSPITAL —43Jb **82** (7J **191**)
Beaumont Ho., 5-10 Beaumont St., London.
W1N 2AA Tel: (0171) 486 4411

KING GEORGE HOSPITAL —29Wc **47**
Barley La., Goodmayes, Ilford, Essex. IG3 8YB
Tel: (0181) 554 8811

KINGSBURY COMMUNITY HOSPITAL —28Qa **39**
Honeypot La., Kingsbury, London. NW9 9QY
Tel: (0181) 903 1323

KING'S COLLEGE DENTAL HOSPITAL AND SCHOOL
—54Tb **105**
Caldecot Rd., London. SE5 9RS
Tel: (0171) 274 6222

KING'S COLLEGE HOSPITAL —54Tb **105**
Denmark Hill, London. SE5 9RS
Tel: (0171) 274 6222

KING'S COLLEGE HOSPITAL, DULWICH —56Ub **105**
East Dulwich Gro., London. SE22 8PT
Tel: (0171) 737 4000

Hospitals and Major Clinics

KING'S COLLEGE HOSPITAL (PRIVATE WING) —54Tb **105**
Denmark Hill, London. SE5 9RS
Tel: (0171) 326 3193

KINGS OAK PRIVATE HOSPITAL —10Qb **10**
Chase Farm (North Side), The Ridgeway, Enfield, Middx. EN2 8SD Tel: (0181) 364 5520

KINGSTON HOSPITAL —67Ra **123**
Galsworthy Rd., Kingston-upon-Thames, Surrey. KT2 7QB Tel: (0181) 546 7711

LANGTHORNE HOSPITAL —35Gc **65**
1 Langthorne Rd., London. E11 4HJ
Tel: (0181) 539 5511

LEATHERHEAD HOSPITAL —94La **176**
Poplar Rd., Leatherhead, Surrey. KT22 8SD
Tel: (01372) 373466

LEAVESDEN HOSPITAL —3W **4**
College Rd., Abbots Langley, Nr. Watford, Herts. WD5 0NU Tel: (01923) 674090)

LEWISHAM HOSPITAL —57Dc **106**
370-396 High St., Lewisham, London. SE13 6LH
Tel: (0181) 690 4311

LEYTONSTONE HOUSE HOSPITAL —31Hc **65**
High Rd., Leytonstone, London. E11 1HS
Tel: (0181) 989 7701

LIONS HOSPICE, THE —3B **136**
Coldharbour Rd., Northfleet, Gravesend, Kent. DA11 7HQ Tel: (01474) 320007

LISTER HOSPITAL, THE —50Kb **82**
Chelsea Bridge Rd., London. SW1W 8RH
Tel: (0171) 730 3417

LITTLE HIGH WOOD —17Xd **32**
Ongar Rd., Brentwood, Essex. CM15 9DY
Tel: (01277) 219262

LIVINGSTONE HOSPITAL —59Pd **111**
East Hill, Dartford, Kent. DA1 1SA
Tel: (01322) 292233

LONDON BRIDGE HOSPITAL —46Tb **83** (6G **201**)
27 Tooley St., London. SE1 2PR
Tel: (0171) 407 3100

LONDON CHEST HOSPITAL —40Yb **64**
Bonner Rd., London. E2 9JX
Tel: (0181) 980 4433

LONDON CLINIC OF PSYCHO-ANALYSIS —43Kb **82** (1K **197**)
63 New Cavendish St., London. W1M 7RD
Tel: (0171) 580 4952

LONDON CLINIC, THE —42Jb **82** (6J **191**)
20 Devonshire Pl., London. W1N 2DH
Tel: (0171) 935 4444

LONDON FOOT HOSPITAL —42Lb **82** (6B **192**)
33 Fitzroy Sq., London. W1P 6AY
Tel: (0171) 636 0602

LONDON INDEPENDENT HOSPITAL —43Zb **84**
1 Beaumont Sq., Stepney Green, London. E1 4NL
Tel: (0171) 790 0990

LONDON LIGHTHOUSE —44Ab **80**
111-117 Lancaster Rd., London. W11 1QT
Tel: (0171) 792 1200

MANOR HOSPITAL, THE —83Qa **161**
Horton La., Epsom, Surrey. KT19 8NL
Tel: (01372) 722212

MANOR HOUSE HOSPITAL —32Db **61**
North End Rd., Golders Green, London. NW11 7HX
Tel: (0181) 455 6601

MARGARET SCOTT CENTRE —44Jc **85**
63 Appleby Rd., London. E16 1LQ
Tel: (0171) 474 5666

MARIE FOSTER HOME —14Za **22**
Wood St., Barnet, Herts. EN5 4BS
Tel: (0181) 440 5111

MARILLAC, THE —23Zd **51**
Eagle Way, Warley, Brentwood, Essex. CM13 3BL
Tel: (01277) 220276

MARLBOROUGH FAMILY SERVICE —40Eb **61** (1A **190**)
38 Marlborough Pl., London. NW8 0PJ
Tel: (0171) 624 8605

MAUDSLEY HOSPITAL, THE —54Tb **105**
Denmark Hill, London. SE5 8AZ
Tel: (0171) 703 6333

MAYDAY UNIVERSITY HOSPITAL —72Rb **147**
Mayday Rd., Thornton Heath, Surrey. CR7 7YE
Tel: (0181) 684 6999

MEADOW HOUSE HOSPICE —47Fa **78**
Uxbridge Rd., Southall, Middx. UB1 3HW
Tel: (0181) 566 3799

MEMORIAL HOSPITAL —54Qc **108**
Shooters Hill, Woolwich, London. SE18 3RZ
Tel: (0181) 856 5511

MIDDLESEX HOSPITAL —43Lb **82** (1C **198**)
Mortimer St., London. W1N 8AA
Tel: (0171) 636 8333

MILDMAY MISSION HOSPITAL —41Vb **83** (4K **195**)
Hackney Rd., London. E2 7NA
Tel: (0171) 739 2331

MOLESEY HOSPITAL —71Ca **141**
High St., West Molesey, Surrey. KT8 2LU
Tel: (0181) 941 4481

MOORFIELDS EYE HOSPITAL —41Tb **83** (4F **195**)
162 City Rd., London. EC1V 2PD
Tel: (0171) 253 3411

MORLAND ROAD DAY HOSPITAL —38Cd **68**
Morland Rd., Dagenham, Essex. RM10
Tel: (0181) 593 2343

MOUNT VERNON HOSPITAL —23R **36**
Rickmansworth Rd., Northwood, Middx. HA6 2RN
Tel: (01923) 826111

NATIONAL HOSPITAL FOR NEUROLOGY AND NEUROSURGERY (CHALFONT), THE —21A **34**
Chalfont Centre For Epilepsy, Micholls Av., Chalfont St Peter, Gerrards Cross, Bucks. SL9 0RJ Tel: (01240) 73991

NATIONAL HOSPITAL FOR NEUROLOGY AND NEUROSURGERY (FINCHLEY), THE —28Gb **41**
Great North Rd., East Finchley, London. N2 0NW
Tel: (0171) 837 3611

NATIONAL HOSPITAL FOR NEUROLOGY AND NEUROSURGERY, THE —42Nb **82** (6G **193**)
Queen Sq., London. WC1N 3BG
Tel: (0171) 837 3611

NATIONAL TEMPERANCE HOSPITAL —41Lb **82** (4C **192**)
108-110 Hampstead Rd., London. NW1 2LT
Tel: (0171) 387 9300

NELSON HOSPITAL —68Bb **125**
Kingston Rd., Merton, London. SW20 8DB
Tel: (0181) 644 4343

NETHERNE HOSPITAL —94Mb **180**
Netherne La., Coulsdon, Surrey. CR5 1YE
Tel: (01737) 556700

NEWHAM GENERAL HOSPITAL —42Lc **85**
Glen Rd., Plaistow, London. E13 8SL
Tel: (0171) 476 1400

NEW VICTORIA HOSPITAL —67Ua **124**
184 Coombe La. W., Kingston-upon-Thames, Surrey. KT2 7EG Tel: (0181) 949 1661

NORMANSFIELD —66La **122**
Kingston Rd., Teddington, Middx. TW11 9JH
Tel: (0181) 977 7583

NORTHGATE CLINIC —30Ua **40**
Snowdon Dri., off Goldsmith Av., Hendon, London. NW9 7HR
Tel: (0181) 205 8012

NORTH LONDON HOSPICE —20Eb **23**
Woodside Av., London. N12 8TF
Tel: (0181) 343 8841

NORTH LONDON NUFFIELD HOSPITAL —12Qb **24**
Cavell Dri., Uplands Pk. Rd., Enfield, Middx. EN2 7PR Tel: (0181) 366 2122

NORTH MIDDLESEX HOSPITAL, THE —22Ub **43**
Sterling Way, London. N18 1QX
Tel: (0181) 887 2000

NORTHWICK PARK HOSPITAL —31Ja **58**
Watford Rd., Harrow, Middx. HA1 3UJ
Tel: (0181) 864 3232

NORTHWOOD, PINNER AND DISTRICT HOSPITAL —25W **36**
Pinner Rd., Northwood, Middx. HA6 1DE
Tel: (01923) 824182

OLDCHURCH HOSPITAL —30Gd **48**
Oldchurch Rd., Romford, Essex. RM7 0BE
Tel: (01708) 46090

OLD COURT HOSPITAL —43Na **79**
19 Montpelier Rd., Ealing, London. W5 2QT
Tel: (0181) 998 2848

ORCHARD HILL HOSPITAL —82Hb **163**
Fountain Drive, Cashalton, Surrey. SM5 4NR
Tel: (0181) 770 8000

ORPINGTON HOSPITAL —77Wc **151**
Sevenoaks Rd., Orpington, Kent. BR6 9JU
Tel: (016898) 27050

ORSETT HOSPITAL —3C **92**
Rowley Rd., Orsett, Grays, Essex. RM16 3EU
Tel: (01375) 891100

OTTERSHAW HOSPITAL —79F **138**
Murray Rd., Ottershaw, Chertsey, Surrey. KT16 0HW Tel: (01932) 872010

OXTED AND LIMPSFIELD HOSPITAL —100Fc **183**
Eastlands Way, Oxted, Surrey. RH8 0LR
Tel: (01883) 714344

PADDINGTON COMMUNITY HOSPITAL —43Cb **81**
7a Woodfield Rd., London. W9 2BB
Tel: (0171) 286 6669

PARKLANDS DAY HOSPITAL FOR THE ELDERLY MENTALLY INFIRM —84Na **161**
West Park Hospital, Horton La., Epsom, Surrey. KT19 8PB Tel: (01372) 727811 ext 4328

PARKSIDE CENTRE —44Ab **80**
63-65 Lancaster Rd., London. W11 1QG
Tel: (0171) 221 4656

PARKSIDE HOSPITAL —62Za **124**
53 Parkside, Wimbledon, London. SW19 5NX
Tel: (0181) 946 4202

PLAISTOW HOSPITAL —40Lc **65**
Samson St., Plaistow, London. E13 9EH
Tel: (0181) 472 7001

POPLARS DAY HOSPITAL FOR THE ELDERLY —84Na **161**
West Park Hospital, Horton La., Epsom, Surrey. KT19 8PB Tel: (01372) 727811

POPLARS ELDERLY CARE UNIT —84Na **161**
West Park Hospital, Horton La., Epsom, Surrey. KT19 8PB Tel: (01372) 727811

PORTLAND HOSPITAL FOR WOMEN AND CHILDREN, THE —42Kb **82** (6A **192**)
209 Gt. Portland St., London. W1N 6AH
Tel: (0171) 580 4400

PORTMAN CLINIC —37Fb **61**
8 Fitzjohn's Av., London. NW3 5NA
Tel: (0171) 794 8262

POTTERS BAR HOSPITAL —4Db **9**
Mutton La., Potters Bar, Herts. EN6 2PB
Tel: (01707) 53286

PRINCESS GRACE HOSPITAL —42Jb **82** (6H **191**)
42-52 Nottingham Pl., London. W1M 3FD
Tel: (0171) 486 1234

PRINCESS LOUISE HOSPITAL —43Za **80**
St Quintin Av., London. W10 6DL
Tel: (0181) 969 0133

PRINCESS MARGARET HOSPITAL —4H **95**
Osborne Rd., Windsor, Berks. SL4 3SJ
Tel: (01753) 868292

PRIORY HOSPITAL —56Va **102**
Priory La., Roehampton, London. SW15 5JJ
Tel: (0181) 876 8261

PSYCHIATRIC DAY HOSPITAL —56Ad **109**
14 Upton Rd., Bexleyheath, Kent. DA6 8LQ
Tel: (0181) 303 3577

PSYCHIATRIC UNIT BARNET GENERAL HOSPITAL —14Za **22**
Wellhouse La., Barnet, Herts. EN5 3DJ
Tel: (0181) 440 5111

PURLEY HOSPITAL —83Qb **164**
Brighton Rd., Purley, Surrey. CR8 2YL
Tel: (0181) 660 0177

PUTNEY HOSPITAL —55Ya **102**
Commondale, London. SW15 1HW
Tel: (0181) 789 6633

QUEEN CHARLOTTE'S AND CHELSEA HOSPITAL —49Wa **80**
Goldhawk Rd., London. W6 0XG
Tel: (0181) 748 4666

QUEEN ELIZABETH HOSPITAL —90Eb **163**
Holly La., Banstead, Surrey. SM7 2BT
Tel: (01737) 358925

QUEEN ELIZABETH HOSPITAL FOR CHILDREN —40Wb **63**
Hackney Rd., London. E2 8PS
Tel: (0171) 739 8422

QUEEN ELIZABETH HOUSE —4N **117**
Nursing Care Unit, Torin Ct., Englefield Green, Egham, Surrey, TW20 0PJ
Tel: (01784) 471452

QUEEN ELIZABETH MILITARY HOSPITAL, THE —52Nc **108**
Stadium Rd., Woolwich, London. SE18 4QH
Tel: (0181) 856 5533

QUEEN MARY'S HOSPITAL —65Wc **131**
Frognal Av., Sidcup, Kent. DA14 6LT
Tel: (0181) 302 2678

QUEEN MARY'S HOSPITAL FOR CHILDREN —74Eb **145**
St Helier Hospital, Wrythe La., Carshalton, Surrey. SM5 1AA Tel: (0181) 644 4343

QUEEN MARY'S UNIVERSITY HOSPITAL —58Wa **102**
Roehampton La., London. SW15 5PN
Tel: (0181) 789 6611

QUEENS HOSPITAL —72Sb **147**
66a Queens Rd., Croydon, Surrey. CR9 2PQ Tel: (0181) 401 3000

RAINBOW LODGE —58Rd **111**
87 Invicta Rd., Stone, Dartford, Kent. DA2 6AY Tel: (01322) 227211

RODING HOSPITAL (BUPA) —27Mc **45**
Roding La. S., Redbridge, Ilford, Essex. IG4 5PZ Tel: (0181) 551 1100

ROSSLYN —58La **100**
15 Rosslyn Rd., East Twickenham, Middx. TW1 2AR Tel: (0181) 891 3173

ROXBOURNE HOSPITAL —33Da **57**
Rayners La., South Harrow, Middx. HA2 0UE
Tel: (0181) 422 1450

ROYAL BROMPTON NATIONAL HEART AND LUNG HOSPITAL —50Gb **81** (7D **202**)
Sydney St., London. SW3 6PY
Tel: (0171) 352 8121

ROYAL BROMPTON NATIONAL HEART AND LUNG HOSPITAL (ANNEXE) —50Fb **81** (7C **202**)
Fulham Rd., London. SW3 6HP
Tel: (0171) 352 8121

ROYAL FREE HOSPITAL, THE —36Gb **61**
Pond St., London. NW3 2QG
Tel: (0171) 794 0500

ROYAL HOSPITAL AND HOME, PUTNEY —58Ab **102**
West Hill, Putney, London. SW15 3SW
Tel: (0181) 788 4511

ROYAL HOSPITAL RICHMOND —55Na **101**
Mental Health Resource Centre, Kew Foot Rd., Richmond, Surrey. TW9 2TE
Tel: (0181) 940 3331

ROYAL LONDON HOMOEOPATHIC HOSPITAL, THE —43Nb **82** (7G **193**)
Gt. Ormond St., London. WC1N 3HR
Tel: (0171) 837 8833

ROYAL LONDON HOSPITAL MILE END —41Zb **84**
Bancroft Rd., London. E1 4DG
Tel: (0171) 377 7801

ROYAL LONDON HOSPITAL SAINT CLEMENT'S —41Bc **84**
3a Bow Rd., London. E3 4LL
Tel: (0171) 377 7953

ROYAL LONDON HOSPITAL WHITECHAPEL —43Xb **83**
Whitechapel Rd., London. E1 1BB
Tel: (0171) 377 7000

ROYAL MARSDEN HOSPITAL, THE —82Eb **163**
Downs Rd., Sutton, Surrey. SM2 5PT
Tel: (0181) 642 6011

ROYAL MARSDEN HOSPITAL, THE —50Fb **81** (7C **202**)
Fulham Rd., London. SW3 6JJ
Tel: (0171) 352 8171

ROYAL MASONIC HOSPITAL —49Wa **80**
Ravenscourt Pk., London. W6 0TN
Tel: (0181) 748 4611

ROYAL NATIONAL ORTHOPAEDIC HOSPITAL —19Ka **20**
Brockley Hill, Stanmore, Middx. HA7 4LP
Tel: (0181) 954 2300

ROYAL NATIONAL ORTHOPAEDIC HOSPITAL (OUTPATIENTS) —42Kb **82** (6A **192**)
45-51 Bolsover St., London. W1P 8AQ
Tel: (0171) 387 5070

ROYAL NATIONAL THROAT, NOSE & EAR HOSPITAL —41Pb **82** (3H **193**)
330 Gray's Inn Rd., London. WC1X 8DA
Tel: (0171) 915 1300

ROYAL NATIONAL THROAT, NOSE & EAR HOSPITAL- SPEECH & LANGUAGE UNIT —43La **78**
6 Castlebar Hill, Ealing, London. W5 1TD
Tel: (0181) 997 8480

RUSH GREEN HOSPITAL —33Gd **68**
Dagenham Rd., Romford, Essex. RM7 0YA
Tel: (01708) 46066

SAINT ANDREW'S AT HARROW —33Ga **58**
Bowden House Clinic, London Rd., Harrow-on-the-Hill, Middx. HA1 3JL
Tel: (0181) 864 0221

SAINT ANDREW'S HOSPITAL —42Dc **84**
Devons Rd., Bow, London. E3 3NT
Tel: (0171) 987 2030/6

SAINT ANN'S —29Sb **43**
Ward K2, St Ann's Hospital, Centre For Community Care, St Ann's Rd., South Tottenham, London. N15 3T
Tel: (0181) 809 6600

SAINT ANN'S HOSPITAL —29Sb **43**
St Ann's Rd., South Tottenham, London. N15 3TH Tel: (0181) 442 6000

SAINT ANTHONY'S HOSPITAL —75Za **144**
London Rd., North Cheam, Surrey. SM3 9DW
Tel: (0181) 337 6691

SAINT BARTHOLOMEW'S AT HOMERTON —36Zb **64**
Homerton Row, London. E9 6SR
Tel: (0181) 985 5555

SAINT BARTHOLOMEW'S AT SMITHFIELD —43Rb **83** (1C **200**)
W. Smithfield, London. EC1A 7BE
Tel: (0171) 601 8888

SAINT BERNARD'S HOSPITAL —47Fa **78**
Uxbridge Rd., Southall, Middx. UB1 3EU
Tel: (0181) 574 2444

SAINT CHARLES HOSPITAL —43Za **80**
Exmoor St., London. W10 6DZ
Tel: (0181) 969 2488

SAINT CHRISTOPHERS HOSPICE —64Yb **128**
Lawrie Pk. Rd., Sydenham, London. SE26 6DZ
Tel: (0181) 778 9252

SAINT CLEMENTS DAY HOSPITAL —41Bc **84**
Bow Rd., London. E3 4LL
Tel: (0171) 377 7000

SAINT EBBA'S —81Sa **161**
Hook Rd., Epsom, Surrey. KT19 8QJ
Tel: (01372) 722212

SAINT GEORGE'S HOSPITAL —64Fb **125**
Blackshaw Rd., London. SW17 0QT
Tel: (0181) 672 1255

SAINT GEORGE'S HOSPITAL —36Md **69**
117 Suttons La., Hornchurch, Essex. RM12 6RS
Tel: (01708) 443531

SAINT HELIER HOSPITAL —74Eb **145**
Wrythe La., Carshalton, Surrey. SM5 1AA
Tel: (0181) 644 4343

SAINT JAMES'S HOUSE —41Lb **82** (4B **192**)
108 Hampstead Rd., London. NW1 2LS
Tel: (0171) 380 9810

SAINT JOHN'S HEALTH CARE UNIT —56Fb **103**
St John's Hill, London. SW11 1SP
Tel: (0181) 874 1022

SAINT JOSEPH'S HOSPICE —39Xb **63**
Mare St., Hackney, London. E8 4SA
Tel: (0181) 985 0861

SAINT JOSEPH'S HOSPITAL FOR ELDERLY AND HANDICAPPED WOMEN —51Ua **102**
Burlington La., Chiswick, London. W4 2QF
Tel: (0181) 994 4641

SAINT LUKE'S HOSPITAL FOR THE CLERGY —42Lb **82** (6B **192**)
14 Fitzroy Sq., London. W1P 6AH
Tel: (0171) 388 4954

SAINT LUKE'S WOODSIDE HOSPITAL —28Jb **42**
Woodside Av., London. N10 3HU
Tel: (0181) 883 8311

SAINT MARGARET'S HOSPITAL —1Xc **15**
The Plain, Epping, Essex. CM16 6TN
Tel: (01279) 444455

SAINT MARK'S HOSPITAL —41Rb **83** (3C **194**)
City Rd., London. EC1V 2PS
Tel: (0171) 601 7792

SAINT MARY'S HOSPITAL —44Fb **81** (2C **196**)
Praed St., London. W2 1NY
Tel: (0171) 725 6666

SAINT MARY'S LODGE HOSPITAL —67Ba **121**
Up. Sunbury Rd., Hampton, Middx. TW12 2DW
Tel: (0181) 941 7463

SAINT MICHAEL'S HOSPITAL —11Tb **25**
19 Chase Side Cres., Enfield, Middx. EN2 0JB
Tel: (0181) 366 6600

SAINT PANCRAS HOSPITAL AND HOSPITAL FOR TROPICAL DISEASES —39Mb **62** (1D **192**)
4 St Pancras Way, London. NW1 0PE
Tel: (0171) 387 4411

SAINT PETER'S HOSPITAL —43Lb **82** (1C **198**)
Middlesex Hospital, Mortimer St., London.
W1N 8AA Tel: (0171) 636 8333

SAINT PETER'S HOSPITAL —76F **138**
Guildford Rd., Ottershaw, Chertsey, Surrey.
KT16 0PZ Tel: (01932) 872000

SAINT RAPHAELS HOSPICE —74Za **144**
London Rd., North Cheam, Surrey. SM3 9DX
Tel: (0181) 337 4156

SAINT THOMAS' HOSPITAL —48Pb **82** (3H **205**)
Lambeth Palace Rd., London. SE1 7EH
Tel: (0171) 928 9292

SAINT VINCENT'S ORTHOPAEDIC HOSPITAL —27V **36**
Wiltshire La., Eastcote, Pinner,
Middx. HA5 2NB
Tel: (0181) 866 0151

SAMARITAN HOSPITAL FOR WOMEN —43Hb **81** (7F **191**)
153-173 Marylebone Rd., London. NW1 5QH
Tel: (0171) 402 4211

SEVENOAKS HOSPITAL —93Ld **187**
Hospital Rd., Sevenoaks, Kent. TN13 3PG
Tel: (01732) 455155

SHENLEY HOSPITAL —5Na **7**
Black Lion Hill, Shenley, Radlett,
Herts. WD7 9HB
Tel: (01923) 855631

SHIRLEY OAKS HOSPITAL —73Yb **148**
Poppy La., Shirley Oaks Village, Croydon,
CR9 8AB Tel: (0181) 655 2255

SLOANE HOSPITAL, THE —67Fc **129**
125-133 Albemarle Rd., Beckenham, Kent.
BR3 2HS Tel: (0181) 466 6911

SOUTHALL NORWOOD MENTAL HEALTH RESOURCE CENTRE —48Ba **77**
The Green, Southall, Middx. UB2 4BH
Tel: (0181) 571 6110

SOUTH WESTERN HOSPITAL —55Pb **104**
Pulross Rd., Brixton, London. SW9 9NU
Tel: (0171) 346 5400

SOUTHWOOD HOSPITAL —31Jb **62**
Southwood La., Highgate, London. N6 5SP
Tel: (0181) 340 8778

SPENCER CLOSE —1Xc **15**
Spencer Clo., The Plain, Epping, Essex.
CM16 6TU Tel: (01992) 578755

SPRINGFIELD HOSPITAL —62Gb **125**
Hq Mental Health Unit, 61 Glenburnie Rd.,
London. SW17 7DJ Tel: (0181) 672 9911

STEPNEY DAY HOSPITAL —44Yb **84**
Ronald St., Off Commercial Rd., London.
E1 0DT Tel: (0171) 790 1442

STONE HOUSE HOSPITAL —58Sd **112**
Cotton La., Dartford, Kent. DA2 6AU
Tel: (01322) 227211

SUNDRIDGE HOSPITAL —99Ad **185**
Church Rd., Sundridge, Sevenoaks, Kent.
TN14 6AU Tel: (01959) 562841

SURBITON HOSPITAL —72Na **143**
Ewell Rd., Surbiton, Surrey. KT6 6EZ
Tel: (0181) 399 7111

SUTTON HOSPITAL —82Db **163**
Cotswold Rd., Sutton, Surrey. SM2 5NF
Tel: (0181) 644 4343

TANDRIDGE PSYCHIATRIC DAY UNIT —95Vb **181**
Caterham Dene Hospital, Church Rd.,
Caterham-on-the-Hill, Surrey. CR3 5RA
Tel: (01883) 347373

TAVISTOCK CLINIC AND CHILD GUIDANCE TRAINING CENTRE —37Fb **61**
120 Belsize La., London. NW3 5BA
Tel: (0171) 435 7111

TEDDINGTON MEMORIAL HOSPITAL —65Ga **122**
Hampton Rd., Teddington, Middx. TW11 0JL
Tel: (0181) 977 2212

THAMES VALLEY HOSPITAL —9N **53**
Wexham St., Wexham, Slough, Bucks. SL3 6NH
Tel: (01753) 662241

THORPE COOMBE HOSPITAL —27Ec **44**
714 Forest Rd., Walthamstow, London. E17 3HP
Tel: (0181) 520 8971

THURROCK COMMUNITY HOSPITAL —46Ee **91**
Long La., Grays, Essex. RM16 2PX
Tel: (01375) 891100

TOLWORTH HOSPITAL —75Qa **143**
Red Lion Rd., Surbiton, Surrey. KT6 7QU
Tel: (0181) 390 0102

TRINITY HOSPICE —56Kb **104**
30 Clapham Comn. N. Side, London. SW4 0RN
Tel: (0171) 622 9481

UNITED ELIZABETH GARRETT ANDERSON & SOHO HOSPITALS FOR WOMEN, THE —41Mb **82** (4E **192**)
144 Euston Rd., London. NW1 2AP
Tel: (0171) 387 2501

UNIVERSITY COLLEGE HOSPITAL —42Lb **82** (5C **192**)
Gower St., London. WC1E 6AU
Tel: (0171) 387 9300

UPTON HOSPITAL —8K **73**
Albert St., Slough, Berks. SL1 2BJ
Tel: (01753) 821441

VICTORIA CENTRE —27Hd **48**
Pettits La., Romford, Essex. RM1 4HP
Tel: (01708) 766412

WALTON COMMUNITY HOSPITAL —75X **141**
Rodney Rd., Walton-on-Thames, Surrey.
KT12 3LD Tel: (01932) 220060

WARLEY HOSPITAL —22Xd **50**
Warley Hill, Warley, Brentwood, Essex.
CM14 5HQ Tel: (01277) 213241

WARLINGHAM PARK HOSPITAL —87Cc **166**
Warlingham, Surrey. CR6 9YR
Tel: (01883) 22101

WATFORD GENERAL HOSPITAL —15X **19**
60 Vicarage Rd., Watford, Herts. WD1 8HB
Tel: (01923) 244366

WELLINGTON HOSPITAL, THE —41Fb **81** (2C **190**)
Wellington Pl., London. NW8 9LE
Tel: (0171) 586 5959

WEMBLEY COMMUNITY HOSPITAL —37Ma **59**
Fairview Av., Wembley, Middx. HA0 4UH
Tel: (0181) 903 1323

WENSLEY CLOSE —58Pc **108**
Wensley Clo., Court Rd., Eltham, London.
SE9 5AD Tel: (0181) 294 1883

WESTERN EYE HOSPITAL —43Hb **81** (7F **191**)
Marylebone Rd., London. NW1 5QH
Tel: (0171) 402 4211

WEST HILL HOSPITAL —58Md **111**
West Hill, Dartford, Kent. DA1 2HF
Tel: (01322) 223223

WEST MIDDLESEX UNIVERSITY HOSPITAL —54Ja **100**
Twickenham Rd., Isleworth, Middx.
TW7 6AF Tel: (0181) 560 2121

WEST PARK HOSPITAL —84Na **161**
Horton La., Epsom, Surrey. KT19 8PB
Tel: (01372) 727811

WEXHAM PARK HOSPITAL —2M **73**
Wexham St., Wexham, Slough, Berks.
SL2 4HL Tel: (01753) 673000

WEYBRIDGE COMMUNITY HOSPITAL —77Q **140**
22 Church St., Weybridge, Surrey.
KT13 8DY Tel: (01932) 852931

WHIPPS CROSS HOSPITAL —30Fc **45**
Whipps Cross Rd., Leytonstone, London.
E11 1NR Tel: (0181) 539 5522

WHITTINGTON HOSPITAL (ARCHWAY WING) —32Lb **62**
Archway Rd., London. N19 3UA
Tel: (0171) 272 3070

WHITTINGTON HOSPITAL (HIGHGATE WING) —33Kb **62**
Dartmouth Park Hill, London. N19 5JG
Tel: (0171) 272 3070

WHITTINGTON HOSPITAL (ST MARY'S WING) —33Lb **62**
Highgate Hill, London. N19 5NF
Tel: (0171) 272 3070

WILLESDEN COMMUNITY HOSPITAL —38Wa **60**
Harlesden Rd., Willesden, London. NW10 3RY
Tel: (0181) 459 1292

WILSON CLINIC —70Hb **125**
Cranmer Rd., Mitcham, Surrey. CR4 4TP
Tel: (0181) 648 3021

WINIFRED HOUSE —16Va **22**
Barnet Gate, Arkley, Herts. EN5 3HY
Tel: (0181) 449 3343

WOKING COMMUNITY HOSPITAL —90B **156**
Heathside Rd., Woking, Surrey. GU22 7HS
Tel: (01483) 715911

WOKING NUFFIELD HOSPITAL —86A **156**
Shores Rd., Woking, Surrey. GU21 4BY
Tel: (01483) 763511

WOLFSON ASSESSMENT CENTRE, THE —42Pb **82** (5H **193**)
Mecklenburgh Sq., London. WC1N 2AP
Tel: (0171) 837 7618

WOLFSON MEDICAL REHABILITATION CENTRE —66Xa **124**
Copse Hill, Wimbledon, London. SW20 0NQ
Tel: (0181) 946 7711

BRITISH RAIL, DOCKLANDS LIGHT RAILWAY AND LONDON UNDERGROUND STATIONS

with their map square reference

ABBEY WOOD, British Rail —49Yc **87**
ACTON CENTRAL, British Rail —46Ta **79**
ACTON MAIN LINE, British Rail —44Sa **79**
ACTON TOWN, District & Piccadilly —47Qa **79**
ADDISCOMBE, British Rail —74Vb **147**
ADDLESTONE, British Rail —77M **139**
ALBANY PARK, British Rail —61Zc **131**
ALDGATE, Circle & Metropolitan —44Vb **83** (3K **201**)
ALDGATE EAST, District & Hammersmith & City —44Vb **83** (2K **201**)
ALEXANDRA PALACE, British Rail —26Nb **42**
ALL SAINTS, Dockland Light Railway —45Dc **84**
ALPERTON, Piccadilly —39Ma **59**
ANERLEY, British Rail —67Xb **127**
ANGEL, Northern —40Qb **62** (1A **194**)
ANGEL ROAD, British Rail —22Yb **44**
ARCHWAY, Northern —33Lb **62**
ARNOS GROVE, Piccadilly —22Lb **42**
ARSENAL, Piccadilly —34Qb **62**
ASHFORD, British Rail —63P **119**
ASHTEAD, British Rail —89Na **161**

BAKER STREET, Bakerloo, Circle, Hammersmith & City, Jubilee & Metropolitan —42Hb **81** (6G **191**)
BALHAM, British Rail & Northern —60Kb **104**
BANK, Central, Docklands Light Railway, Northern & Waterloo & City —44Tb **83** (3F **201**)
BANSTEAD, British Rail —86Bb **163**
BARBICAN, British Rail, Circle, Hammersmith & City & Metropolitan —43Sb **83** (7D **194**)
BARKING, British Rail, District & Hammersmith & City —38Sc **66**
BARKINGSIDE, Central —27Tc **46**
BARNEHURST, British Rail —54Ed **110**
BARNES BRIDGE, British Rail —54Va **102**
BARNES, British Rail —55Wa **102**
BARONS COURT, District & Piccadilly —50Ab **80**
BAT & BALL, British Rail —93Ld **187**
BATTERSEA PARK, British Rail —52Kb **104**
BAYSWATER, Circle & District —45Db **81**
BECKENHAM HILL, British Rail —64Ec **128**
BECKENHAM JUNCTION, British Rail —67Cc **128**
BECKTON, Docklands Light Railway —43Qc **86**
BECKTON PARK, Docklands Light Railway —45Pc **86**
BECONTREE, District —37Zc **67**
BEDDINGTON LANE, British Rail —72Lb **146**
BELLINGHAM, British Rail —62Dc **128**
BELMONT, British Rail —82Db **163**
BELSIZE PARK, Northern —36Gb **61**
BELVEDERE, British Rail —48Dd **88**
BERMONDSEY, Jubilee —48Wb **83**
(Open 1998)
BERRYLANDS, British Rail —70Ra **123**
BETHNAL GREEN, British Rail —42Xb **83**
BETHNAL GREEN, Central —41Yb **84**
BEXLEY, British Rail —60Cd **110**
BEXLEYHEATH, British Rail —54Ad **109**
BICKLEY, British Rail —69Nc **130**
BIRKBECK, British Rail —69Yb **128**
BLACKFRIARS, British Rail, Circle & District —45Rb **83** (4B **200**)
BLACKHEATH, British Rail —55Hc **107**
BLACKHORSE ROAD, British Rail & Victoria —28Zb **44**

BOND STREET, Central & Jubilee —44Kb **82** (3K **197**)
BOOKHAM, British Rail —95Ba **175**
BOROUGH, Northern —47Sb **83** (2E **206**)
BOSTON MANOR, Piccadilly —49Ja **78**
BOUNDS GREEN, Piccadilly —23Mb **42**
BOW CHURCH, Docklands Light Railway —41Cc **84**
BOWES PARK, British Rail —24Nb **42**
BOW ROAD, District & Hammersmith & City —41Cc **84**
BRENT CROSS, Northern —31Za **60**
BRENTFORD, British Rail —51La **100**
BRENTWOOD, British Rail —20Yd **32**
BRICKET WOOD, British Rail —2Ca **5**
BRIMSDOWN, British Rail —12Ac **26**
BRIXTON, British Rail & Victoria —56Qb **104**
BROCKLEY, British Rail —55Ac **106**
BROMLEY-BY-BOW, District & Hammersmith & City —41Ec **84**
BROMLEY NORTH, British Rail —67Jc **129**
BROMLEY SOUTH, British Rail —69Jc **129**
BRONDESBURY, British Rail —38Bb **61**
BRONDESBURY PARK, British Rail —39Ab **60**
BRUCE GROVE, British Rail —26Vb **43**
BUCKHURST HILL, Central —19Mc **27**
BURNHAM, British Rail —4B **72**
BURNT OAK, Northern —25Sa **39**
BUSHEY, British Rail —16Z **19**
BUSH HILL PARK, British Rail —16Vb **25**
BYFLEET & NEW HAW, British Rail —82M **157**

CALEDONIAN ROAD & BARNSBURY, British Rail —38Pb **62**
CALEDONIAN ROAD, Piccadilly —37Pb **62**
CAMBRIDGE HEATH, British Rail —40Xb **63**
CAMDEN ROAD, British Rail —38Lb **62**
CAMDEN TOWN, Northern —39Kb **62**
CANADA WATER, East London & Jubilee —47Yb **84**
(Open 1998)
CANARY WHARF, Docklands Light Railway —46Cc **84**
CANARY WHARF, Jubilee —46Cc **84**
(Open 1998)
CANNING TOWN, British Rail & Docklands Light Railway —43Gc **85**
CANNING TOWN, Jubilee —44Gc **85**
(Open 1998)
CANNON STREET, British Rail, Circle & District —45Tb **83** (4F **201**)
CANONBURY, British Rail —36Sb **63**
CANONS PARK, Jubilee —24Na **39**
CARPENDERS PARK, British Rail —20Z **19**
CARSHALTON BEECHES, British Rail —79Hb **145**
CARSHALTON, British Rail —77Hb **145**
CASTLE BAR PARK, British Rail —43Ha **78**
CATERHAM, British Rail —96Wb **181**
CATFORD BRIDGE, British Rail —59Cc **106**
CATFORD, British Rail —59Cc **106**
CHADWELL HEATH, British Rail —31Zc **67**
CHALFONT & LATIMER, British Rail & Metropolitan —11A **16**
CHALK FARM, Northern —38Jb **62**
CHANCERY LANE, Central —43Qb **82** (1K **199**)
CHARING CROSS, British Rail, Bakerloo, Jubilee & Northern —46Nb **82** (6F **199**)
CHARLTON, British Rail —50Lc **85**
CHEAM, British Rail —80Ab **144**
CHELSFIELD, British Rail —78Xc **151**

CHERTSEY, British Rail —74H **139**
CHESHUNT, British Rail —2Bc **12**
CHESSINGTON NORTH, British Rail —78Na **143**
CHESSINGTON SOUTH, British Rail —80Ma **143**
CHIGWELL, Central —20Rc **28**
CHINGFORD, British Rail —17Gc **27**
CHIPSTEAD, British Rail —90Hb **163**
CHISLEHURST, British Rail —68Qc **130**
CHISWICK, British Rail —52Sa **101**
CHISWICK PARK, District —49Sa **79**
CHORLEYWOOD, British Rail & Metropolitan —14F **16**
CITY THAMESLINK, British Rail —44Rb **83** (2B **200**)
CLANDON, British Rail —100K **173**
CLAPHAM COMMON, Northern —56Lb **104**
CLAPHAM HIGH ST., British Rail —55Mb **104**
CLAPHAM JUNCTION, British Rail —55Gb **103**
CLAPHAM NORTH, Northern —55Nb **104**
CLAPHAM SOUTH, Northern —58Kb **104**
CLAPTON, British Rail —33Xb **63**
CLAYGATE, British Rail —79Ga **142**
CLOCK HOUSE, British Rail —67Ac **128**
COBHAM & STOKE D'ABERNON, British Rail —89Aa **159**
COCKFOSTERS, Piccadilly —14Jb **24**
COLINDALE, Northern —27Ua **40**
COLLIERS WOOD, Northern —66Fb **125**
COULSDON SOUTH, British Rail —88Mb **164**
COVENT GARDEN, Piccadilly —45Nb **82** (3G **199**)
CRAYFORD, British Rail —58Hd **110**
CREWS HILL, British Rail —6Pb **10**
CRICKLEWOOD, British Rail —35Za **60**
CROFTON PARK, British Rail —57Bc **106**
CROSSHARBOUR, Docklands Light Railway —48Dc **84**
CROUCH HILL, British Rail —31Pb **62**
CROXLEY GREEN, British Rail —15T **18**
CROXLEY, Metropolitan —16R **18**
CRYSTAL PALACE, British Rail —65Wb **127**
CUFFLEY, British Rail —1Pb **10**
CUSTOM HOUSE, British Rail & Docklands Light Railway —45Kc **85**
CYPRUS, Docklands Light Railway —45Qc **86**

DAGENHAM DOCK, British Rail —41Bd **87**
DAGENHAM EAST, District —36Ed **68**
DAGENHAM HEATHWAY, District —37Bd **67**
DALSTON KINGSLAND, British Rail —36Ub **63**
DARTFORD, British Rail —58Nd **111**
DATCHET, British Rail —3M **95**
DEBDEN, Central —14Sc **28**
DENHAM, British Rail —31J **55**
DENHAM GOLF CLUB, British Rail —31F **54**
DENMARK HILL, British Rail —54Tb **105**
DEPTFORD, British Rail —52Cc **106**
DEVONS ROAD, Docklands Light Railway —42Dc **84**
DOLLIS HILL, Jubilee —36Wa **60**
DRAYTON GREEN, British Rail —44Ha **78**
DRAYTON PARK, British Rail —35Qb **62**
DUNTON GREEN, British Rail —91Gd **186**

EALING BROADWAY, British Rail, Central & District —45Ma **79**
EALING COMMON, District & Piccadilly —46Pa **79**
EARL'S COURT, District & Piccadilly —49Db **81**

EARLSFIELD, British Rail —60Eb **103**
EAST ACTON, Central —44Va **80**
EASTCOTE, Metropolitan & Piccadilly —31Y **57**
EAST CROYDON, British Rail —75Tb **147**
EAST DULWICH, British Rail —56Ub **105**
EAST FINCHLEY, Northern —28Gb **41**
EAST HAM, District & Hammersmith & City —38Nc **66**
EAST PUTNEY, District —57Ab **102**
EAST TILBURY, British Rail —9K **93**
EDEN PARK, British Rail —71Cc **148**
EDGWARE, Northern —23Ra **39**
EDGWARE ROAD, Bakerloo —43Gb **81** (7D **190**)
EDGWARE ROAD, Circle, District & Hammersmith & City —43Gb **81** (1D **196**)
EDMONTON GREEN, British Rail. —19Wb **25**
EFFINGHAM JUNCTION, British Rail —95W **174**
EGHAM, British Rail —64C **118**
ELEPHANT & CASTLE, British Rail, Bakerloo & Northern —49Sb **83** (5D **206**)
ELMERS END, British Rail —70Zb **128**
ELM PARK, District —35Kd **69**
ELMSTEAD WOODS, British Rail —65Nc **130**
ELSTREE & BOREHAMWOOD, British Rail —14Qa **21**
ELTHAM, British Rail —57Pc **108**
EMBANKMENT, Bakerloo, Circle, District & Northern —46Nb **82** (6G **199**)
EMERSON PARK, British Rail —31Nd **69**
ENFIELD CHASE, British Rail —13Sb **25**
ENFIELD LOCK, British Rail —9Ac **12**
ENFIELD TOWN, British Rail —13Ub **25**
EPPING, Central —3Wc **15**
EPSOM, British Rail —85Ta **161**
EPSOM DOWNS, British Rail —88Xa **162**
ERITH, British Rail —50Gd **88**
ESHER, British Rail —75Fa **142**
ESSEX ROAD, British Rail —38Sb **63**
EUSTON, British Rail, Northern & Victoria —41Mb **82** (4D **192**)
EUSTON SQUARE, Circle, Hammersmith & City & Metropolitan —42Lb **82** (5C **192**)
EWELL EAST, British Rail —82Xa **162**
EWELL WEST, British Rail —81Ua **162**
EYNSFORD, British Rail —77Md **153**

FAIRLOP, Central —25Tc **46**
FALCONWOOD, British Rail —56Tc **108**
FARNINGHAM ROAD, British Rail —68Rd **133**
FARRINGDON, British Rail, Circle, Hammersmith & City & Metropolitan —43Rb **83** (7B **194**)
FELTHAM, British Rail —60X **99**
FENCHURCH STREET, British Rail —45Ub **83** (4K **201**)
FINCHLEY CENTRAL, Northern —25Cb **41**
FINCHLEY ROAD & FROGNAL, British Rail —36Eb **61**
FINCHLEY ROAD, Jubilee & Metropolitan —37Eb **61**
FINSBURY PARK, British Rail, Piccadilly & Victoria —33Qb **62**
FOREST GATE, British Rail —36Jc **65**
FOREST HILL, British Rail —61Yb **128**
FULHAM BROADWAY, District —52Cb **103**
FULWELL, British Rail —63Fa **122**

GALLIONS REACH, Docklands Light Railway —45Rc **86**

British Rail, Docklands Light Railway and London Underground Stations

GANTS HILL, Central —30Qc 46
GARSTON, British Rail —7Aa 5
GERRARDS CROSS, British Rail —29A 34
GIDEA PARK, British Rail —28Kd 49
GIPSY HILL, British Rail —64Ub 127
GLOUCESTER ROAD, Circle, District & Piccadilly —49Eb 81 (5A 202)
GOLDERS GREEN, Northern —32Cb 61
GOLDHAWK ROAD, Hammersmith & City —47Ya 80
GOODGE STREET, Northern —43Mb 82 (7D 192)
GOODMAYES, British Rail —32Wc 67
GORDON HILL, British Rail —11Rb 25
GOSPEL OAK, British Rail —35Jb 62
GRANGE HILL, Central —21Tc 46
GRANGE PARK, British Rail —15Rb 25
GRAVESEND, British Rail —8D 114
GRAYS, British Rail —51Ce 113
GREAT PORTLAND STREET, Circle, Hammersmith & City & Metropolitan —42Kb 82 (6A 192)
GREENFORD, British Rail & Central —39Fa 58
GREENHITHE, British Rail —57Wd 112
GREEN PARK, Jubilee, Piccadilly & Victoria —46Lb 82 (6A 198)
GREENWICH, British Rail —52Dc 106
GROVE PARK, British Rail —62Kc 129
GUNNERSBURY, British Rail & District —50Ra 79

HACKBRIDGE, British Rail —75Kb 146
HACKNEY CENTRAL, British Rail —37Xb 63
HACKNEY DOWNS, British Rail —36Xb 63
HACKNEY WICK, British Rail —37Cc 64
HADLEY WOOD, British Rail —10Eb 9
HAINAULT, Central —24Uc 46
HAMMERSMITH, District, Hammersmith & City & Piccadilly —49Ya 80
HAMPSTEAD HEATH, British Rail —35Gb 61
HAMPSTEAD, Northern —35Eb 61
HAMPTON, British Rail —67Ca 121
HAMPTON COURT, British Rail —70Ga 122
HAMPTON WICK, British Rail —67La 122
HANGER LANE, Central —41Na 79
HANWELL, British Rail —45Ga 78
HARLESDEN, British Rail & Bakerloo —40Ta 59
HAROLD WOOD, British Rail —25Pd 49
HARRINGAY, British Rail —30Qb 42
HARRINGAY STADIUM, British Rail —30Rb 43
HARROW-ON-THE-HILL, British Rail & Metropolitan —30Ga 38
HARROW & WEALDSTONE, British Rail & Bakerloo —28Ga 38
HATCH END, British Rail —24Ca 37
HATTON CROSS, Piccadilly —56V 98
HAYDONS ROAD, British Rail —64Eb 125
HAYES, British Rail —74Jc 149
HAYES & HARLINGTON, British Rail —48V 76
HEADSTONE LANE, British Rail —25Da 37
HEATHROW TERMINAL 4, Piccadilly —57S 98
HEATHROW TERMINALS 1,2,3, Piccadilly —55R 98
HENDON, British Rail —30Wa 40
HENDON CENTRAL, Northern —29Xa 40
HERNE HILL, British Rail —58Rb 105
HERON QUAYS, Docklands Light Railway —46Cc 84
HERSHAM, British Rail —76Aa 141
HIGHAMS PARK, British Rail —23Fc 45
HIGH BARNET, Northern —14Cb 23
HIGHBURY & ISLINGTON, British Rail & Victoria —37Rb 63
HIGHGATE, Northern —30Kb 42
HIGH STREET, KENSINGTON, Circle & District —47Db 81
HILLINGDON, Metropolitan & Piccadilly —36R 56
HINCHLEY WOOD, British Rail —76Ha 142
HITHER GREEN, British Rail —58Gc 107
HOLBORN, Central & Piccadilly —44Pb 82 (1H 199)
HOLLAND PARK, Central —46Bb 81
HOLLOWAY ROAD, Piccadilly —36Pb 62
HOMERTON, British Rail —37Zb 64
HONOR OAK PARK, British Rail —58Zb 106
HORNCHURCH, District —34Md 69
HORNSEY, British Rail —28Pb 42
HORSLEY, British Rail —97U 174
HOUNSLOW, British Rail —57Da 99
HOUNSLOW CENTRAL, Piccadilly —55Da 99
HOUNSLOW EAST, Piccadilly —54Ea 100
HOUNSLOW WEST, Piccadilly —54Aa 99
HYDE PARK CORNER, Piccadilly —47Jb 82 (1J 203)

ICKENHAM, Metropolitan & Piccadilly —35S 56
ILFORD, British Rail —34Rc 66
ISLAND GARDENS, Docklands Light Railway —50Ec 84
ISLEWORTH, British Rail —54Ha 100
IVER, British Rail —47H 75

KENLEY, British Rail —86Sb 165
KENNINGTON, Northern —50Rb 83 (7B 206)
KENSAL GREEN, British Rail & Bakerloo —41Ya 80
KENSAL RISE, British Rail —40Za 60
KENSINGTON (OLYMPIA), British Rail & District —48Ab 80
KENT HOUSE, British Rail —67Ac 128
KENTISH TOWN, British Rail & Northern —36Lb 62
KENTISH TOWN WEST, British Rail —37Kb 62
KENTON, British Rail & Bakerloo —30Ka 38
KEW BRIDGE, British Rail —50Pa 79
KEW GARDENS, British Rail & District —53Qa 101
KIDBROOKE, British Rail —55Kc 107
KILBURN HIGH ROAD, British Rail —39Db 61
KILBURN, Jubilee —37Bb 61
KILBURN PARK, Bakerloo —40Cb 61
KINGSBURY, Jubilee —29Qa 39
KING'S CROSS, British Rail, Circle, Hammersmith & City, Northern, Metropolitan, Piccadilly & Victoria —40Nb 62 (2G 193)
KING'S CROSS THAMESLINK, British Rail —41Pb 82 (3H 193)
KINGS LANGLEY, British Rail —2S 4
KINGSTON, British Rail —67Na 123
KINGSWOOD, British Rail —93Bb 179
KNIGHTSBRIDGE, Piccadilly —47Hb 81 (2G 203)
KNOCKHOLT, British Rail —81Ad 169

LADBROKE GROVE, Hammersmith & City —44Ab 80
LADYWELL, British Rail —57Dc 106
LAMBETH NORTH, Bakerloo —48Qb 82 (3K 205)
LANCASTER GATE, Central —45Fb 81 (4B 196)
LANGLEY, British Rail —47C 74
LATIMER ROAD, Hammersmith & City —45Za 80
LEATHERHEAD, British Rail —93Ja 176
LEE, British Rail —58Jc 107
LEICESTER SQUARE, Northern & Piccadilly —45Nb 82 (4F 199)
LEWISHAM, British Rail —55Ec 106
LEYTON, Central —34Ec 64
LEYTON MIDLAND ROAD, British Rail —32Ec 64
LEYTONSTONE, Central —32Gc 65
LEYTONSTONE HIGH ROAD, British Rail —33Gc 65
LIMEHOUSE, British Rail & Docklands Light Railway —44Ac 84
LIVERPOOL STREET, British Rail, Central, Circle, Hammersmith & City & Metropolitan —43Ub 83 (1H 201)
LONDON BRIDGE, British Rail & Northern —46Tb 83 (7G 201)
LONDON BRIDGE, Jubilee —46Tb 83 (7G 201) (Open 1998)
LONDON FIELDS, British Rail —38Xb 63
LONGFIELD, British Rail —69Ae 135
LOUGHBOROUGH JUNCTION, British Rail —55Rb 105
LOUGHTON, Central —15Nc 28
LOWER SYDENHAM, British Rail —64Bc 128

MAIDA VALE, Bakerloo —41Db 81
MALDEN MANOR, British Rail —73Ua 144
MANOR HOUSE, Piccadilly —31Sb 63
MANOR PARK, British Rail —35Mc 65
MANSION HOUSE, Circle & District —45Sb 83 (4E 200)
MARBLE ARCH, Central —44Hb 81 (3G 197)
MARYLAND, British Rail —37Gc 65
MARYLEBONE, British Rail & Bakerloo —43Hb 81 (7F 191)
MAZE HILL, British Rail —51Gc 107
MEOPHAM, British Rail —10C 136
MERSTHAM, British Rail —100Lb 180
MERTON PARK, British Rail —67Cb 125
MILE END, Central, District & Hammersmith & City —41Bc 84
MILL HILL BROADWAY, British Rail —23Ua 40
MILL HILL EAST, Northern —24Ab 40
MITCHAM, British Rail —70Gb 125
MITCHAM JUNCTION, British Rail —71Jb 146
MONUMENT, Circle & District —45Tb 83 (4G 201)
MOORGATE, British Rail, Circle, Hammersmith & City, Northern & Metropolitan —43Tb 83 (1F 201)
MOOR PARK, Metropolitan —20T 18
MORDEN, Northern —69Db 125
MORDEN ROAD, British Rail —68Db 125
MORDEN SOUTH, British Rail —71Cb 145
MORNINGTON CRESCENT, Northern —40Lb 62 (1B 192)
MORTLAKE, British Rail —55Sa 101
MOTSPUR PARK, British Rail —71Xa 144
MOTTINGHAM, British Rail —60Pc 108
MUDCHUTE, Dockslands Light Railway —49Dc 84

NEASDEN, Jubilee —36Ua 60
NEW BARNET, British Rail —15Fb 23
NEW BECKENHAM, British Rail —66Bc 128
NEWBURY PARK, Central —30Tc 46
NEW CROSS, British Rail & East London —52Bc 106
NEW CROSS GATE, British Rail & East London —52Ac 106
NEW ELTHAM, British Rail —60Sc 108
NEW MALDEN, British Rail —69Ua 124
NEW SOUTHGATE, British Rail —22Kb 42
NORBITON, British Rail —67Qa 123
NORBURY, British Rail —67Pb 126
NORTH ACTON, Central —43Ta 79
NORTH DULWICH, British Rail —57Tb 105
NORTH EALING, Piccadilly —44Pa 79
NORTHFIELDS, Piccadilly —48La 78
NORTHFLEET, British Rail —58De 113
NORTH GREENWICH, Jubilee —47Gc 85 (Open 1998)
NORTH HARROW, Metropolitan —29Da 37
NORTHOLT, Central —37Ca 57
NORTHOLT PARK, British Rail —35Da 57
NORTH SHEEN, British Rail —56Qa 101
NORTHUMBERLAND PARK, British Rail —24Xb 43
NORTH WEMBLEY, British Rail & Bakerloo —34Ma 59
NORTHWICK PARK, Metropolitan —31Ka 58
NORTHWOOD HILLS, Metropolitan —26W 36
NORTHWOOD, Metropolitan —24U 36
NORTH WOOLWICH, British Rail —47Qc 86
NORWOOD JUNCTION, British Rail —70Wb 127
NOTTING HILL GATE, Central, Circle & District —46Cb 81
NUNHEAD, British Rail —54Yb 106

OAKLEIGH PARK, British Rail —17Fb 23
OAKWOOD, Piccadilly —15Lb 24
OCKENDON, British Rail —41Xd 90
OLD STREET, British Rail & Northern —42Tb 83 (5G 195)
ORPINGTON, British Rail —75Uc 150
OSTERLEY, Piccadilly —52Fa 100
OTFORD, British Rail —88Ld 171
OVAL, Northern —51Qb 104
OXFORD CIRCUS, Bakerloo, Central & Victoria —44Lb 82 (3B 198)
OXSHOTT, British Rail —85Ea 160
OXTED, British Rail —100Gc 183

PADDINGTON, Bakerloo, British Rail, Circle, District & Hammersmith & City —44Fb 81 (3B 196)
PALMERS GREEN, British Rail —21Pb 42
PARK ROYAL, Piccadilly —42Qa 79
PARSONS GREEN, District —53Cb 103
PECKHAM RYE, British Rail —54Wb 105
PENGE EAST, British Rail —65Yb 128
PENGE WEST, British Rail —65Xb 127
PERIVALE, Central —40Ja 58
PETTS WOOD, British Rail —71Sc 150
PICCADILLY CIRCUS, Bakerloo & Piccadilly —45Mb 82 (5D 198)
PIMLICO, Victoria —50Mb 82 (7D 204)
PINNER, Metropolitan —28Aa 37
PLAISTOW, District & Hammersmith & City —40Hc 65
PLUMSTEAD, British Rail —49Tc 86
PONDERS END, British Rail —15Ac 26
POPLAR, Docksland Light Railway —45Dc 84
POTTERS BAR, British Rail —4Bb 9
PRESTON ROAD, Metropolitan —32Na 59
PRIMROSE HILL, British Rail —38Jb 62
PRINCE REGENT, Docklands Light Railway —45Lc 85
PURFLEET, British Rail —50Qd 89
PURLEY, British Rail —83Qb 164
PURLEY OAKS, British Rail —81Tb 165
PUTNEY BRIDGE, District —55Bb 103
PUTNEY, British Rail —56Ab 102

QUEENSBURY, Jubilee —27Pa 39
QUEENS PARK, British Rail & Bakerloo —40Bb 61
QUEEN'S ROAD (PECKHAM), British Rail —53Yb 106
QUEENSTOWN ROAD (BATTERSEA), British Rail —53Kb 104
QUEENSWAY, Central —45Db 81

RADLETT, British Rail —7Ja 6
RAINHAM, British Rail —42Jd 88
RAVENSBOURNE, British Rail —66Fc 129
RAVENSCOURT PARK, District —49Xa 80
RAYNERS LANE, Metropolitan & Piccadilly —31Ba 57
RAYNES PARK, British Rail —68Ya 124
RECTORY ROAD, British Rail —34Vb 63
REDBRIDGE, Central —30Mc 45
REEDHAM, British Rail —85Pb 164
REGENT'S PARK, Bakerloo —42Kb 82 (6K 191)
RICHMOND, British Rail & District —56Na 101
RICKMANSWORTH, British Rail & Metropolitan —17M 17
RIDDLESDOWN, British Rail —85Sb 165
RODING VALLEY, Central —21Mc 45
ROMFORD, British Rail —30Gd 48
ROTHERHITHE, East London —47Yb 84
ROYAL ALBERT, Docklands Light Railway —45Nc 86
ROYAL OAK, Hammersmith & City —43Db 81
ROYAL VICTORIA, Docklands Light Railway —45Jc 85
RUISLIP GARDENS, Central —35W 56
RUISLIP MANOR, Metropolitan & Piccadilly —32W 56
RUISLIP, Metropolitan & Piccadilly —32U 56
RUSSELL SQUARE, Piccadilly —42Nb 82 (6F 193)

SAINT HELIER, British Rail —72Cb 145
SAINT JAMES'S PARK, Circle & District —48Mb 82 (3D 204)
SAINT JAMES STREET, WALTHAMSTOW, British Rail —29Ac 44
SAINT JOHNS, British Rail —54Cc 106
SAINT JOHN'S WOOD, Jubilee —40Fb 61 (1B 190)
SAINT MARGARETS, British Rail —58Ka 100
SAINT MARY CRAY, British Rail —70Xc 131
SAINT PANCRAS, British Rail, Circle, Hammersmith & City, Northern, Metropolitan, Piccadilly & Victoria —41Nb 82 (3F 193)
SAINT PAUL'S, Central —44Sb 83 (2D 200)
SANDERSTEAD, British Rail —81Tb 165
SELHURST, British Rail —71Ub 147
SEVEN KINGS, British Rail —32Uc 66
SEVENOAKS, British Rail —96Jd 186
SEVEN SISTERS, British Rail & Victoria —29Ub 43
SHADWELL, Docklands Light Railway & East London —45Xb 83
SHENFIELD, British Rail —17Ce 33
SHEPHERD'S BUSH, Central —47Za 80
SHEPHERD'S BUSH, Hammersmith & City —46Ya 80
SHEPPERTON, British Rail —71S 140
SHOREDITCH, East London —42Vb 83
SHOREHAM, British Rail —83Kd 171
SHORTLANDS, British Rail —68Gc 129
SIDCUP, British Rail —61Wc 131
SILVER STREET, British Rail —21Vb 43
SILVERTOWN & CITY AIRPORT, British Rail —46Mc 85
SLADE GREEN, British Rail —53Jd 110
SLOANE SQUARE, Circle & District —49Jb 82 (6H 203)
SLOUGH, British Rail —6K 73
SMITHAM, British Rail —87Nb 164
SNARESBROOK, Central —29Jc 45
SOUTH ACTON, British Rail —48Sa 79
SOUTHALL, British Rail —47Ba 77
SOUTH BERMONDSEY, British Rail —50Yb 84
SOUTHBURY, British Rail —14Xb 25
SOUTH CROYDON, British Rail —78Tb 147
SOUTH EALING, Piccadilly —48Ma 79
SOUTHFIELDS, District —60Bb 103
SOUTHGATE, Piccadilly —18Mb 24
SOUTH GREENFORD, British Rail —41Ga 78
SOUTH HAMPSTEAD, British Rail —38Eb 61
SOUTH HARROW, Piccadilly —34Ea 58
SOUTH KENSINGTON, Circle, District & Piccadilly —49Fb 81 (5C 202)
SOUTH KENTON, British Rail & Bakerloo —32La 58
SOUTH MERTON, British Rail —69Bb 125
SOUTH QUAY, Docklands Light Railway —47Dc 84
SOUTH RUISLIP, British Rail & Central —36Y 57
SOUTH TOTTENHAM, British Rail —29Vb 43
SOUTHWARK, British Rail & Jubilee —46Rb 83 (7B 200) (Open 1998)
SOUTH WIMBLEDON, Northern —66Db 125
SOUTH WOODFORD, Central —26Kc 45
STAINES, British Rail —64J 119
STAMFORD BROOK, District —49Va 80
STAMFORD HILL, British Rail —31Ub 63
STANFORD-LE-HOPE, British Rail —2L 93
STANMORE, Jubilee —21Ma 39
STEPNEY GREEN, District & Hammersmith & City —42Zb 84
STOCKWELL, Northern & Victoria —54Nb 104
STOKE NEWINGTON, British Rail —33Vb 63
STONEBRIDGE PARK, British Rail & Bakerloo —38Ra 59
STONE CROSSING, British Rail —57Ud 112
STONELEIGH, British Rail —78Wa 144
STRATFORD, British Rail, Central & Docklands Light Railway —38Fc 65
STRATFORD, Jubilee —38Fc 65 (Open 1998)
STRATFORD (LOW LEVEL), British Rail —38Fc 65
STRAWBERRY HILL, British Rail —62Ha 122
STREATHAM, British Rail —64Mb 126
STREATHAM COMMON, British Rail —66Mb 126
STREATHAM HILL, British Rail —61Nb 126
SUDBURY & HARROW ROAD, British Rail —36Ka 58
SUDBURY HILL, HARROW, British Rail —35Ga 58
SUDBURY HILL, Piccadilly —35Ga 58
SUDBURY TOWN, Piccadilly —37Ka 58
SUNBURY, British Rail —67W 120
SUNDRIDGE PARK, British Rail —66Kc 129
SUNNYMEADS, British Rail —55A 96
SURBITON, British Rail —72Na 143
SURREY QUAYS, East London —49Zb 84
SUTTON, British Rail —79Eb 145
SUTTON COMMON, British Rail —75Db 145
SWANLEY, British Rail —70Fd 132
SWANSCOMBE, British Rail —57Be 113
SWISS COTTAGE, Jubilee —38Fb 61
SYDENHAM, British Rail —63Yb 128
SYDENHAM HILL, British Rail —62Vb 127
SYON LANE, British Rail —52Ja 100

TADWORTH, British Rail —94Ya 178
TATTENHAM CORNER, British Rail —90Xa 162
TEDDINGTON, British Rail —65Ja 122
TEMPLE, Circle & District —45Pb 82 (4J 199)
THAMES DITTON, British Rail —73Ha 142
THEOBALDS GROVE, British Rail —4Zb 12
THEYDON BOIS, Central —8Vc 15
THORNTON HEATH, British Rail —70Sb 127
TILBURY RIVERSIDE, British Rail —6C 114
TILBURY TOWN, British Rail —4B 114
TOLWORTH, British Rail —75Ra 143
TOOTING BEC, Northern —62Jb 126
TOOTING, British Rail —65Hb 125
TOOTING BROADWAY, Northern —64Gb 125
TOTTENHAM COURT ROAD, Central & Northern —44Mb 82 (2E 198)
TOTTENHAM HALE, British Rail & Victoria —27Xb 43
TOTTERIDGE & WHETSTONE, Northern —19Eb 23
TOWER GATEWAY, Docklands Light Railway —45Vb 83 (4K 201)
TOWER HILL, Circle & District —45Vb 83 (4K 201)
TUFNELL PARK, Northern —35Lb 62
TULSE HILL, British Rail —61Rb 127
TURKEY STREET, British Rail —9Yb 12
TURNHAM GREEN, District —49Ua 80
TURNPIKE LANE, Piccadilly —27Rb 43
TWICKENHAM, British Rail —59Ja 100

UPMINSTER BRIDGE, District —33Qd 69
UPMINSTER, British Rail & District —33Sd 70
UPNEY, District —38Vc 67
UPPER HALLIFORD, British Rail —68U 120
UPPER HOLLOWAY, British Rail —33Mb 62
UPPER WARLINGHAM, British Rail —90Wb 165
UPTON PARK, District & Hammersmith & City —39Lc 65
UXBRIDGE, Metropolitan & Piccadilly —38M 55

VAUXHALL, British Rail & Victoria —50Nb 82
VICTORIA, British Rail, Circle, District & Victoria —49Kb 82 (5A 204)
VICTORIA, Coach Station —49Kb 82 (6K 203)
VIRGINIA WATER, British Rail —71A 138

WADDON, British Rail —77Qb 146
WADDON MARSH, British Rail —74Pb 146
WALLINGTON, British Rail —79Kb 146
WALTHAM CROSS, British Rail —6Bc 12
WALTHAMSTOW CENTRAL, British Rail & Victoria —29Cc 44
WALTHAMSTOW QUEENS ROAD, British Rail —29Cc 44
WALTON-ON-THAMES, British Rail —77W 140
WANDSWORTH COMMON, British Rail —60Hb 103
WANDSWORTH ROAD, British Rail —54Lb 104
WANDSWORTH TOWN, British Rail —56Db 103
WANSTEAD, Central —30Kc 45
WANSTEAD PARK, British Rail —35Kc 65
WAPPING, East London —46Yb 84
WARREN STREET, Northern & Victoria —42Lb 82 (5B 192)
WARWICK AVENUE, Bakerloo —42Eb 81 (6A 190)
WATERLOO, British Rail, Bakerloo, Northern & Waterloo & City —47Qb 82 (1K 205)
WATERLOO (EAST), British Rail —46Qb 82 (7A 200)
WATERLOO INTERNATIONAL, British Rail —47Pb 82 (1J 205)
WATERLOO, Jubilee —47Qb 82 (1K 205) (Open 1998)
WATFORD HIGH STREET, British Rail —14Y 19
WATFORD JUNCTION, British Rail —12Y 19
WATFORD, Metropolitan —13V 18
WATFORD NORTH, British Rail —9Y 5
WATFORD STADIUM HALT —16W 18
WATFORD WEST, British Rail —15V 18
WELLING, British Rail —54Wc 109
WEMBLEY CENTRAL, British Rail & Bakerloo —36Na 59
WEMBLEY PARK, Jubilee & Metropolitan —34Qa 59
WEMBLEY STADIUM, British Rail —36Pa 59
WEST ACTON, Central —44Qa 79
WESTBOURNE PARK, Hammersmith & City —43Bb 81
WEST BROMPTON, District —51Cb 103
WEST BYFLEET, British Rail —84J 157
WESTCOMBE PARK, British Rail —50Jc 85
WEST CROYDON, British Rail —74Sb 147
WEST DRAYTON, British Rail —46N 75
WEST DULWICH, British Rail —61Tb 127
WEST EALING, British Rail —45Ka 78
WESTFERRY, Docklands Light Railway —45Cc 84
WEST FINCHLEY, Northern —23Db 41
WEST HAM, British Rail —41Gc 85
WEST HAM, District & Hammersmith & City —41Gc 85
WEST HAM, Jubilee —41Gc 85 (Open 1998)
WEST HAMPSTEAD, British Rail —37Cb 61
WEST HAMPSTEAD, Jubilee —37Db 61
WEST HAMPSTEAD THAMESLINK, British Rail —37Cb 61
WEST HARROW, Metropolitan —30Ea 38
WEST HORNDON, British Rail —30Ee 51
WEST INDIA QUAY, Docklands Light Railway —45Cc 84
WEST KENSINGTON, District —50Bb 81
WESTMINSTER, Circle & District —47Nb 82 (2G 205)
WESTMINSTER, Jubilee —47Nb 82 (2G 205) (Open 1998)
WEST NORWOOD, British Rail —63Rb 127
WEST RUISLIP, British Rail & Central —33S 56
WEST SUTTON, British Rail —77Cb 145
WEST WICKHAM, British Rail —73Ec 148
WEYBRIDGE, British Rail —79Q 140
WHITECHAPEL, District, Hammersmith & City & East London —43Xb 83
WHITE CITY, Central —45Ya 80
WHITE HART LANE, British Rail —24Vb 43
WHITTON, British Rail —59Ea 100
WHYTELEAFE, British Rail —89Vb 165
WHYTELEAFE SOUTH, British Rail —91Wb 181
WILLESDEN GREEN, Jubilee —37Ya 60
WILLESDEN JUNCTION, British Rail & Bakerloo—41Va 80
WIMBLEDON, British Rail & District —65Bb 125
WIMBLEDON CHASE, British Rail —68Ab 124
WIMBLEDON PARK, District —62Cb 125
WINCHMORE HILL, British Rail —17Rb 25
WINDSOR & ETON CENTRAL, British Rail —3H 95
WINDSOR & ETON RIVERSIDE, British Rail —2H 95
WOKING, British Rail —89B 156
WOLDINGHAM, British Rail —94Zb 182
WOODFORD, Central —23Kc 45
WOODGRANGE PARK, British Rail —36Mc 65
WOOD GREEN, Piccadilly —26Qb 42
WOODMANSTERNE, British Rail —88Kb 164
WOODSIDE, British Rail —72Xb 147
WOODSIDE PARK, Northern —21Db 41
WOOD STREET, WALTHAMSTOW, British Rail —28Fc 45
WOOLWICH ARSENAL, British Rail —49Rc 86
WOOLWICH DOCKYARD, British Rail —49Pc 86
WORCESTER PARK, British Rail —74Wa 144
WRAYSBURY, British Rail —58C 96